English Renaissance Drama

A Norton Anthology

English Renaissance Drama

A Norton Anthology

David Bevington, *General Editor*
University of Chicago

Lars Engle
University of Tulsa

Katharine Eisaman Maus
University of Virginia

Eric Rasmussen
University of Nevada, Reno

W · W · Norton & Company · New York · London

Printed in the United States of America.
First Edition.

Editor: Julia Reidhead
Associate Managing Editor: Marian Johnson
Manuscript Editor: Ann Tappert
Assistant Editor/Art Research: Brian Baker
Production Manager: Diane O'Connor
Book Design: Antonina Krass
Cover Design: Debra Morton Hoyt

The text of this book is composed in Fairfield Medium
with the display set in Bernhard Modern.
Composition by Binghamton Valley Composition.
Manufacturing by R. R. Donnelley & Sons.

Library of Congress Cataloging-in-Publication Data

English Renaissance drama : a Norton anthology / David Bevington, general editor; Lars Engle,
Katharine Eisaman Maus, Eric Rasmussen, [editors].
p. cm.
Includes bibliographical references.

ISBN 0-393-97655-6

1. English drama—Early modern and Elizabethan, 1500–1600. 2. English drama—17th
century. I. Bevington, David M. II. Engle, Lars. III. Maus, Katharine Eisaman, 1955–
IV. Rasmussen, Eric, 1960–

PR1263 .E56 2003
822'.308—dc21 2002025074

W. W. Norton & Company, Inc., 500 Fifth Avenue, New York, NY 10110
www.wwnorton.com

W. W. Norton & Company Ltd., Castle House, 75/76 Wells Street, London W1T 3QT

6 7 8 9 0

Contents

Illustrations

Preface

In his prologue to *The Alchemist*, Ben Jonson expresses his hope that "when the wholesome remedies are sweet, / And in their working gain and profit meet," his spectators will both benefit from and thoroughly enjoy his play. Our hope is that you will find both "gain and profit" in this collection of plays from the English Renaissance. We have included the best plays of the era, with generous representations from Marlowe, Jonson, Beaumont, Fletcher, Middleton, and Webster especially, along with important single plays of their contemporaries. (Thomas Dekker is a minor exception in that he is represented by one play that he wrote on his own and one on which he collaborated.)

We have edited every play afresh, basing each text on the most authoritative quarto or folio original. Textual notes record significant departures from that original and indicate the source of the emendation, often some modern editor (marked as "ed."). When the original spelling of a word differs significantly from the modernized spelling in our text, we indicate that fact by a textual note, e.g., "**97 turquoise** [Q1: Turkis]." In other words, we regard "turquoise" in line 97 as a modernization of the first quarto reading, not an emendation, but a modernization that nevertheless is of more than routine interest. The textual notes do not record corrections of simple typographical errors or changes in punctuation that bear only questionably on meaning. Most normalizations of the names of speaking characters receive no comment in the textual notes. Nor, ordinarily, do added stage directions, which are in square brackets in the text.

The square brackets, then, indicate when a stage direction, or part of one, has been editorially inserted. Original stage directions are printed without brackets in most cases, or, if occurring in the middle of a speech, are enclosed in round brackets, or parentheses. We believe that it is important that the reader know when a stage direction belongs to the original. On the other hand, we have not bracketed emended words or single letters inserted in the speakers' names or in the dialogue, as brackets here would be too defacing. These changes are recorded in the textual notes.

Latin phrases indicating speakers and in the stage directions, such as "OMNES" for "All" or "*manent*" for "they remain," are retained in the original language and are translated in a gloss or footnote.

Act and scene divisions follow those in the original text but are rendered in arabic numbers, e.g., "Act five, scene 3" and "*Actus quintus, scena tertia*" both become "5.3." Whenever a scene break is added to the original, square brackets indicate the emendation: "[5.3]." When the original text numbers a scene but does so erroneously, the emendation is indicated as follows: "5.[3]." So-called massed entries in some plays, mostly those by Lyly and Jonson, begin each scene with a stage direction naming all the characters who are to appear in that scene; in these cases, we print at the head of the scene only those characters who do in fact enter at first; we then insert at a later point any subsequent entries, adding "[*Enter*]" and other needed words in brackets but retaining the characters' names without brackets for the first such entry, since they appeared in the original massed entry. Throughout, our intention has been to minimize the visual impact of scene breaks, since performances of these plays on the Elizabethan or Jacobean stage did not stop for changes of scenery. We indicate in a footnote where the action of a given scene appears to take place. This information is most emphatically not meant to imply any provision of scenery onstage; instead, it is meant to help the reader understand the plot.

We have tried to be judicious about emendation, preferring the original reading when it makes sense and considering possible emendations from a textual point of view; that is, we have asked ourselves how the seeming error might have occurred in the process through which the dramatist's manuscript was copied, edited, revised, and set in type. We have consulted subsequent quartos and folios where relevant, along with the work of modern editors. We have repeatedly read proofs of this volume against the originals, not simply against the copy that we sent to the printers. David Bevington and Eric Rasmussen have done most of this verification of the texts, but important parts of the task have also been shared with the other editors.

Our goal has been to make these plays as accessible to the modern reader as possible. Spellings are modernized throughout. When a resonance of meaning is lost or compromised by this process (as, for example, by modernizing the words "trauel" or "trauaile," which can mean both a journey and a labor, to "travel"), a gloss or note explains. Punctuation too is modernized. Our intent has been to use modern conventions of punctuation to clarify for today's readers the language that early modern writers would have punctuated somewhat differently. Speech in dialect, on the other hand, often cannot and should not be modernized. Passages in foreign languages—French, German, and Italian especially—are sometimes discreetly normalized in accord with the modern forms of those languages, but with a sensitivity to dialect use or English misperceptions of the way foreigners speak.

We have glossed and footnoted carefully with undergraduate readers in mind. As in other Norton anthologies, this volume glosses words or short phrases in the right-hand column when a brief explanation is possible. Lines and passages requiring fuller explanation or paraphrase are footnoted. These annotations provide source and background information and help students unpack obscure or puzzling lines.

Along with a general introduction, setting the plays and their authors in historical and cultural context, an introduction precedes each play. A title footnote for each play indicates the individual editors' contributions. A chronology of major events in the English Renaissance, including birth and death dates of the dramatists, follows the general introduction. A general bibliography at the back of the volume, with sections on intellectual and cultural backgrounds, Elizabethan and Jacobean drama generally, the early modern theater, and individual plays and dramatists, can serve as a guide to further study.

Among many others to whom we are indebted, we should like to thank Fred Maus (University of Virginia) and Everett Maus; Donald L. Bailey; Arthur Evenchik; Jennifer Forsyth, Dave Golz, and Dee Anna Phares-Matthews (all at the University of Nevada, Reno); Gordon McMullan (King's College, London); Jesus Tronch (University of Valencia); Holly Laird, Laura Stevens, and Sue Hosterman (all at the University of Tulsa); Sheila Murnaghan (University of Pennsylvania); Michiel Heyns (University of Stellenbosch); Paul A. Taylor; Victoria Hines; and Peggy Bevington. Katharine Eisaman Maus wishes to thank the John Simon Guggenheim Memorial Foundation and the American Council of Learned Societies. At W. W. Norton & Company, we have been assisted remarkably in our task as editors by Julia Reidhead and Marian Johnson and by Ann Tappert as manuscript editor. The degree of enlightened interrogation that these friends have provided us has been extraordinary at every turn, in the recasting of introductions, in finding more felicitous and precise phrasing for the glosses and footnotes, in verifying matters of textual accuracy, and in the checking of the multitudinous pieces of historical information that a project like this one necessarily entails. We owe to them a great debt. This volume is a collaborative project in the best sense.

David Bevington, *University of Chicago*
Lars Engle, *University of Tulsa*
Katharine Eisaman Maus, *University of Virginia*
Eric Rasmussen, *University of Nevada, Reno*

General Introduction

KATHARINE EISAMAN MAUS and DAVID BEVINGTON

Real Estate

In 1576, the prostitutes, pickpockets, and alehouse-keepers who frequented the seedy suburb of Shoreditch, just northeast of London, would have noticed a new building under construction. We no longer know exactly what it looked like, since it was dismantled twenty-two years later and the plans for it have long since vanished. But we do know that it was strikingly big. At probably three stories high and about one hundred feet across, it could accommodate between two and three thousand people. The central area was left roofless, both to take advantage of the natural light pouring in from above and because so large a building would have been prohibitively expensive to cover with beams and thatch. A tall, polygonal enclosure, it hardly resembled an ordinary house or business establishment. The shallow angles of its timber framing required a team of unusually skillful carpenters.

The residents of Shoreditch, as they passed this ambitious construction site, might have assumed that James Burbage and John Brayne, the proprietors, were building an arena for the popular sport of bearbaiting, in which ferocious dogs attacked chained bears. Indeed, such arenas may have been the model for the new edifice. In fact, however, Burbage and Brayne were constructing a purpose-built theater, one of the first in England since the Roman occupation more than a millennium before. Their enterprise was not entirely a novel one: nine years earlier, in 1567, Brayne had erected a smaller theater, the Red Lion, in the London district of Whitechapel. Even so, "The Theatre," as the new building would be called, was unprecedented in its scale, visibility, and expense. It inaugurated a boomlet in theater construction. Over the next three decades or so, more large, well-equipped amphitheaters were built on roughly similar lines—the Curtain, the Rose, the Swan, the Hope, the Fortune, the Boar's Head, the Red Bull. At the end of the sixteenth century, when Burbage's lease on the site of The Theatre expired, the building was carefully dismantled and its valuable timbers recycled in the construction of another large amphitheater, the Globe, located on the south bank of the Thames, where several of the new theaters were already located. In the 1580s, and again after the turn of the century, a number of intimate indoor theaters flourished as well.

These thriving enterprises would have been inconceivable even a few decades earlier. England had long enjoyed a lively tradition of dramatic performance, but in medieval England no single population center was large enough to support a professional acting company on an ongoing basis. Until the sixteenth century, the national government was relatively weak, and the important centers of trade and government were regional: York, Coventry, Lincoln, and so on. In consequence, English intellectual and artistic life tended to be dispersed. Actors traveled from town to town performing in the halls of great houses, in inns, or on temporary platforms set up in town squares. In some instances, their nomadic existence made them liable to arrest for vagrancy. In the sixteenth century, things began to change. The Tudor monarchs—Henry VII, Henry VIII, and later his daughter Elizabeth—consolidated power in the hands of the central government, at the expense of local or regional authorities. The effect of this alteration in England's political structure was to concentrate power and wealth in London, England's commercial and shipping hub, and in Westminster, the seat of the national government, which adjoined London to the west. During the later sixteenth and early seventeenth centuries, huge numbers of people migrated from the provinces to the London area seeking economic opportunity. The theater companies still went on tour as they always had, but their activities focused more and more on London, because increasingly that was where the paying audiences were. When Burbage and Brayne built The Theatre, they could thus count on recouping their investment, and they may have realized too the symbolic importance of their new edifice. The association of actors with a building immediately made the performance of plays seem more socially consequential and less haphazard. The effect was especially marked in early modern England, a society that believed that true wealth inhered in land and buildings—in what people still tellingly call "*real* estate."

The theater historian Andrew Gurr estimates that altogether up to twenty-five thousand people per week attended performances at the various public and private theaters, for a total of about fifty million visits between 1580 and 1640.[1] Obviously the demand for entertainment constituted a significant business opportunity. Playing in the new theaters were repertory companies organized along collaborative lines. Typically about ten adult men in the company would share the financial risks and profits of the enterprise; these actor-sharers took on boy apprentices capable of assuming women's roles until their voices changed with adolescence. Some companies, such as the Lord Chamberlain's Men (the King's Men after 1603), became very wealthy; others came and went in rapid succession. In the 1580s and again between 1600 and 1613, there were also entire companies of boys, supervised by an adult theater manager.

Londoners of the period considered their theaters to be one of the most distinctive features of the city, and foreign tourists were encouraged to visit them. One of our few surviving contemporary depictions of an early modern theater building is a drawing of the Swan by a Dutch visitor (see page li). In about the year 1620, the travel writer Fynes Moryson boasted: "The City of London . . . hath four or five companies of players with their peculiar theatres capable of many thousands, wherein they all play every day in the week except Sunday . . . there be in my opinion more plays in London than in all the world I have seen."[2] Stephen Gosson, who believed that playgoing was sinful, took a less sanguine view, complaining in *Plays Confuted in Five Actions* about the multitudes who "flock to the theaters to gaze upon plays."[3] What Gosson shared with Moryson was the conviction that a very large number of Londoners attended plays. The cheapest price of admission to the amphitheaters, which allowed the theatergoer to stand in the space in front of the raised stage, was one penny—a price that would have excluded the indigent poor but would have put theatergoing financially within the reach of most others.

For the student of literary history, the importance of the early modern theater is a matter not merely of its extraordinary popularity at the time but of the extraordinary and enduring quality of the work produced there. The preeminent examples of this quality are, of course, the plays of William Shakespeare. The emphasis on

1. Andrew Gurr, *Playgoing in Shakespeare's England* (Cambridge: Cambridge University Press, 1996), p. 4.
2. *Fynes Moryson's Itinerary: Being a Survey of the Conditions of Europe at the End of the Sixteenth Century*, ed. Charles Hughes (London: Sherratt and Hughes, 1903), p. 476.
3. Stephen Gosson, *Plays Confuted in Five Actions* (London, 1582), B7r.

This composite scene, from *Scarron's Comical Romance of a Company of Stage Players* (1676), shows two events in the lives of itinerant actors: in the foreground, they are arriving at an inn, with their cartful of props and instruments; in the background, they are performing in the town square on a bare platform stage, with a curtain for a backdrop.

Shakespeare in today's world of higher education and criticism is understandable: his corpus is a sublime achievement, and people everywhere know his plays or at least know of them. Acting companies and festival theaters that put on *Hamlet, Macbeth, Twelfth Night,* or *A Midsummer Night's Dream* know that audiences will come to see Shakespeare's plays if they come to see "classical" theater at all. Yet to the extent that the current canonization of Shakespeare has eclipsed his fellow Renaissance dramatists, an opportunity is being neglected. For if Shakespeare was incomparable, he also had the great good fortune to write in an age and for a theater that fostered astonishing, and astonishingly varied, dramatic work. Tragedy flourished not simply in *Hamlet* and *King Lear* but in Christopher Marlowe's *Doctor Faustus,* John Webster's *The Duchess of Malfi,* and Thomas Middleton and William Rowley's *The Changeling.* Marlowe's *Edward II* ranks alongside a play it clearly influenced deeply, Shakespeare's *Richard II.*

More often, the drama of Shakespeare's contemporaries is simply incommensurable with his work, because it is original along different lines. *The Revenger's Tragedy*, probably by Middleton, and his *Women Beware Women* each push the possibilities of revenge drama in fascinating directions quite unlike those explored by Shakespeare in *Hamlet.* Ben Jonson's *Volpone, Epicene, The Alchemist,* and *Bartholomew Fair* are satiric comedies unsurpassed in a genre Shakespeare left virtually unexplored. Shakespeare tended to portray the pressing issues of his own day at some imaginative remove. He displaced the issue of usury to Venice in *The Merchant of Venice,* the issues of sex legislation and morality to Vienna in *Measure for Measure,* and the issues of class antagonism and political entitlement to ancient Rome in *Coriolanus.* By contrast, Jonson, as well as Thomas Dekker in *The Shoemaker's Holiday,* Middleton in *A Chaste Maid in Cheapside,* Middleton and Dekker in *The Roaring Girl,* and Francis Beaumont in *The Knight of the Burning Pestle,* put directly onstage the street names, local landmarks, slang, and urban folkways of contemporary London.

English Renaissance Drama: A Norton Anthology is dedicated to the proposition that the plays of Marlowe, Jonson, Webster, Middleton, and their contemporaries deserve to be read, taught, and performed. We hope that this volume of plays will reaffirm what many readers have long known, that the greatness of English Renaissance drama was a collaborative and collective phenomenon. It may also help clarify the profound and varied ways English Renaissance drama influenced the literary practices and forms of later ages.

Many of the theater's most important innovations were economic. The willingness of the new theater companies to pay for plays created, for the first time in England, a paying market for literature. The London theaters made possible the advent of the professional writer: a person who writes not as a sideline or for a small coterie of friends and patrons, but as a full-time employment, hoping to address a large, heterogeneous audience. Other innovations were more technical or literary. Playwrights quickly discovered, for instance, that unrhymed iambic pentameter was the most flexible English verse form for oral performance. "Marlowe's mighty line" established a high standard further refined by Shakespeare, Jonson, Webster, and Middleton; their accomplishment helped blank verse become a metrical norm for much English nondramatic poetry as well. City comedy, as written by Dekker, Jonson, Middleton, and their contemporaries, fed the later development of the novel, journalism, and other literary forms that concern themselves with quotidian life.

Playwrights and the Conditions of Production

At first blush, the Renaissance theater might seem an odd place for genius to flourish. In the 1580s and 1590s, public theater was a popular, even "low" form of amusement, as alluring and as condescended to as television often is today. Critics accused the theater of distracting people from work, depleting their intellects, and exciting them to lust and violence. In an age with few resources against disease, the large crowds that assembled at plays could be a public health menace; and indeed, when deaths from plague rose too high the theaters were forced to close until the epidemic died down. The location of the big public theaters in the suburbs of London, such as Shoreditch to the northeast and Southwark across the Thames to the south, was no accident; the London aldermen banned theaters from the city limits. When the professional acting companies did move into areas more convenient for their most affluent customers, they still had to locate their theaters on pockets of land that the municipal authorities did not control. From 1609 on, the King's Men performed not only at the Globe but at an indoor theater in Blackfriars, which was not legally considered part of the city; the land had belonged to a monastery before England broke with the Catholic Church in the 1530s. The Cockpit in Drury Lane, renamed the Phoenix, was outside the old city and thus relatively free of its restrictions.

This panorama shows two theaters near the Thames in Southwark, across from the city of London. Saint Paul's Cathedral appears prominently to the left and London Bridge at the extreme right. The playhouses are flying flags to advertise that a performance is in progress. The Globe is at the bottom; the Beargarden or Hope is to its left, closer to the river.

The national government was somewhat more tolerant of the theaters than the local one. The reigning monarchs of the period—Queen Elizabeth I until 1603, King James I until 1625, and King Charles I thereafter—routinely invited the best companies to perform at court. The rulers also believed that the pleasures of theatrical entertainments and other "innocent sports" distracted their subjects from thoughts of rebellion. Instead of trying to ban the theater entirely, therefore, the Privy Council, an advisory body to the Crown, chose merely to regulate it. Ever alert to the possibility that the theaters might foment sedition, the Council set up a system of censorship to ensure that no play criticized prominent people, commented explicitly on government policies, or encouraged impiety. The Master of the Revels, an officer of the Crown, had to approve each play before performance and often mandated changes or prohibited performance altogether. As years went by, such regulation became increasingly strict. For example, the Act to Restrain Abuses of Players, enacted in 1606, forbade actors to "jestingly or profanely" use God's name onstage.

Over the course of the period, slowly, the prestige of playwriting and acting did begin to rise, partly, no doubt, because of the extraordinary quality of the works themselves and also because some professional playwrights, especially Ben Jonson, were beginning to make strong claims for the significance of their poetic achievement. By the turn of the century, plays were more and more likely to be taken seriously by people who considered themselves literary or intellectual. The affluent, well-educated young men who attended the Inns of Court, or law schools, in London were avid theatergoers, and a few of them—John Marston, Francis Beaumont, and John Ford, for instance—turned to playwriting themselves. In 1598, Francis Meres published *Palladis Tamia, Wit's Treasury,* an annotated anthology of passages from classical literature in which he praised Lyly, Marlowe, Kyd, Shakespeare, Jonson, and other contemporaries as the equals of the great classical authors. In 1603, when King James I came to the throne, he brought London's major theater companies under the direct patronage of the royal family.

Still, the improvement in status was modest. When Thomas Bodley founded his great library at Oxford in 1602, he arranged for printers to deposit therein two copies of every book they produced. He excluded the texts of plays, however, on the grounds that they were irredeemably trivial. "Were it so," he wrote, "that some little profit might be reaped (which God knows is very little) out of some of our playbooks, the benefit thereof will nothing near countervail the harm that the scandal will bring into the library, when it shall be given out, that we stuff it full of baggage [worthless] books."[4]

4. *Letters of Sir Thomas Bodley to Thomas James, First Keeper of the Bodleian Library,* ed. G. W. Wheeler (Clarendon: Oxford, 1926), p. 222.

Artistic merit, however, is not the same thing as high social prestige. The theater of early modern England occupied an interestingly contradictory place in the imaginations of contemporaries. It was a source simultaneously of pride and disquiet, an institution regarded as socially central but at the same time potentially subversive of an orderly society. Those very contradictions arguably put the theatrical life of the time in touch with the contradictions of the age itself, in which religious reform, skepticism, scientific inquiry, overseas exploration, and changing views of moral behavior did battle at every turn with conservative opposition. Moreover, in a society that could be, in some respects, rigidly bound to form and precedent, the very marginality of the theater gave it the freedom to improvise and innovate.

We have already briefly mentioned one of the most important innovations: the theaters provided, for the first time, a literary market. While the traveling companies of old could perform the same play over and over again, as they moved from one provincial town to another, the London companies needed to offer variety to secure repeat business from their customers. They needed plays, lots of plays. The records of Philip Henslowe, landlord of the Rose Theater in the 1590s, indicate that a new play was introduced there about every three weeks. Demand was especially high in the first few decades of the theaters, because the companies had no suitable inherited repertory to fall back on. Later in the period, companies of longer standing, which also tended to be the best financed, had plenty of inventory. In the 1630s, the King's Men, for instance, were commissioning only four new plays a year; it was more profitable to put on one of Shakespeare's, Jonson's, or John Fletcher's reliable and already paid-for hits than to go to the expense of obtaining a risky new work. This financial calculation may account for the unequal distribution of great plays in the period. The theaters began to establish themselves, as we have seen, in the late 1560s and 1570s, and remained open until 1642, at the outset of the English civil war. Yet most of the greatest plays were written between 1585 and 1625, after the theater had become a fairly well-established institution but before the availability of so many fine scripts from the immediate past began to oppress the present.

The willingness of theaters to pay for plays meant that for the first time people from rather ordinary backgrounds could pursue literary careers. In prior generations, literary endeavors had been largely restricted to the clergy or to courtly circles. In rather striking contrast, Marlowe's father was a shoemaker, Shakespeare's a glover, Kyd's a scrivener. Jonson's stepfather was a bricklayer, and Jonson briefly worked as one himself. While leather workers and bricklayers were not necessarily poor—Marlowe's father owned a fine house in Canterbury, and Shakespeare's father, during Shakespeare's childhood, was a substantial Stratford citizen—neither were they members of England's tiny elite class.

What equipped these artisans' sons with the skills they needed to write brilliant drama? Important educational innovations earlier in the sixteenth century helped prepare the cadre of great writers who burst onto the English scene in the 1580s and 1590s. The medieval school curriculum, designed for future clergymen, was heavily weighted toward theology, logic, and metaphysics. It began to change in the 1520s and 1530s after several important Continental humanist thinkers visited England and brought with them a radical idea: a grammar-school curriculum based on Latin classics read in the original language and taught not merely by private tutors to the children of the nobility but to as many boys as possible. (In this patriarchal society, in which women had few political rights, the grammar schools were open to boys only.) This kind of education provided, in the view of the humanist pedagogues, an appropriate background for any kind of public or private endeavor whatever. The claims they made for their new educational plans are the same ones that underlie defenses of a broad liberal education today, with the important difference that Renaissance humanists began their educational pro-

A schoolroom. From *Orbis Sensualium Pictus* (The Visible World in Pictures), by Johann Amos Comenius (1592–1670). Comenius' book (1658; English trans. 1659) is credited with being the first illustrated textbook. The pupil standing before the master is reciting his lesson, presumably in Latin.

gram much earlier in the lives of their students. Beginning in the 1530s and 1540s, schools were set up all over England to teach the new curriculum to boys between the ages of seven and fourteen. In these grammar schools, students read, and often memorized, classical Roman literature: poetry by Ovid, Horace, and Virgil; oratory by Cicero; history by Livy and Tacitus; plays by Plautus and Terence.

In many ways the humanist educational program was a restricted one, lacking any attention to math, science, or the visual arts. Moreover, since the lessons were typically enforced with harsh corporal punishment, school must have been torture for the slow learner. For a verbally gifted child, however, this curriculum had many advantages. It gave him a firm grounding in another language and naturally heightened his awareness of the distinctive structure and character of his own. It introduced him to major literary genres: epic, comedy, tragedy, and lyric. It gave him an understanding of Greek and Roman history. It fostered an awareness of a sophisticated non-Christian culture, with unfamiliar attitudes toward such matters as suicide and sexual passion between men. It acquainted him with pagan myths. Since one very common school exercise required students to compose orations for debates—first on one side of the proposition in question, then on the other—the curriculum also encouraged students to elaborate hypothetical or fictional standpoints, rather as a playwright must. And it did all this at relatively small expense, without requiring university attendance or displacing the apprenticeship system that provided practical training for future artisans in their teenage years.

Not surprisingly, then, even though England continued to lag behind the Continent in painting, architecture, and music, the latter half of the sixteenth century saw a tremendous flowering of literary activity, as the children of this educational revolution came to maturity. The year 1579 saw the publication of Edmund Spenser's *The Shepherd's Calendar*, a set of twelve monthly eclogues in the Virgilian style; it was followed in 1590 by the first three books of his great epic, *The Faerie Queene*. John Lyly, who is represented in this present volume by his 1588 play *Endymion*, scored a huge success in 1579 and 1580 with *Euphues*, a work of prose fiction written in a highly mannered "euphuistic" style. Philip Sidney wrote a version of his epic prose romance, the *Arcadia*, in about 1581, immediately placing him in the ranks of such famous Continental writers of romance as Jacopo Sannazaro, Torquato Tasso, and Ludovico Ariosto. Sidney's sonnet sequence, *Astrophel and Stella* (1591), established a vogue for the lyric form to which the fourteenth-century Italian poet Petrarch had given impetus. Over the next thirty years, many English Renaissance writers composed sonnet sequences: Spenser, Shakespeare, Samuel Daniel, Michael Drayton, and Mary Wroth among them.

For individuals of humble origin, this surplus of talent was actually a problem. The first young men to experience the humanist educational program typically got good jobs in the increasingly complex Tudor bureaucracy, just as their teachers had anticipated. By the 1580s and 1590s, however, the numbers of educated young men far exceeded the available professional opportunities. The result was a cohort of brilliant but impecunious individuals, apparently overeducated for their station. They were unable to return happily to the bricklaying or tanning at which their fathers had toiled, while at the same time they lacked an entrée into the highly rank-conscious world of the elite, in which birth was crucial and connections were indispensable. To such men, the willingness of the theater companies to pay them for their "wit" must have seemed one of very few options available. Thomas Dekker marvels at the novelty of this commercial arrangement: "The theater is your poet's Royal Exchange upon which their Muses—that are now turned to merchants—meeting, barter away that light commodity of words."[5]

Philip Henslowe's records give us insight into how this "Royal Exchange" worked—how the acting companies went about obtaining the plays they needed. Theater companies typically commissioned plays on the basis of an idea or an outline, which might be the theater company's or the playwright's. The writer was paid a small advance and then was subsequently paid in installments or with the full amount when he had delivered the play. In the 1590s, this payment seems to have been about five pounds; by the 1630s it had risen to ten or more. He (professional playwrights were all male) also typically received the profits from either the third or the fourth performance of his play.

Once the play was finished, it was considered the property of the theater company that had commissioned it. The company's ownership rights had important consequences for the printed versions of the play—the ones on which this edition, and all others, must rely—a point to which we will return later. Those ownership rights also had important consequences for the compositional process. Some playwrights were exclusively affiliated with a single theater company. Beginning in 1594, Shakespeare was a shareholder in the Lord Chamberlain's Men (retitled the King's Men in 1603); Fletcher and Philip Massinger were contractually bound to the King's Men. Others, like Jonson, sold their talents to a variety of companies. Either way, a dramatist generally knew, at the time he was writing a play, for whom he was writing it: how many actors he could count on, what their strengths and weaknesses might be, what kinds of audiences normally attended their performances. In such circumstances, the relationship between high-quality plays and high-quality performance was doubtless symbiotic. The existence of professional repertory companies, with stable rosters of actors who committed their entire lives to learning the art, meant that the playwrights could count on having actors good enough to perform anything they wrote. In turn, the actors could count on getting good material specially designed to exhibit their talents to the best effect.

The alliance between writers and theater companies had to be a practical one. The theaters were businesses, and profitability was all-important. The number of people who made their living as playwrights in Renaissance England was small. A mere twenty-two men wrote over half of the twelve hundred plays of which we

5. Thomas Dekker, *The Gull's Hornbook*, ed. R. B. McKerrow (London: De la More Press, 1934), p. 49. Dekker's metaphor refers to a large merchandise mart built between Cornhill and Threadneedle Streets in 1566–68 by Thomas Gresham.

have any records from the period. Probably relatively few people had the talent and stamina to succeed as professional playwrights. Doubtless, too, the typically close collaboration between acting companies and playwrights led the companies to prefer the same dramatists over and over again, because they were confident that those writers knew how to provide them with appropriate material.

The Grafton portrait of Christopher Marlowe.

The small size of the theater community and its geographical concentration meant that everyone knew everyone else. Kyd and Marlowe shared a room. Beaumont and Fletcher were rumored to have once been so poor that they owned a single cloak between them. The relations among playwrights were not always idyllic. Robert Greene attacked Shakespeare in print; Jonson wrote dramatic satires with thinly veiled derogatory portraits of Dekker and Marston, to which they responded in kind. Still, whether or not they liked one another, they learned from one another. We hear echoes of Marlowe's characters Tamburlaine and Faustus in Jonson's Epicure Mammon, in Webster's Duchess of Malfi, and in Ford's Giovanni. In *The Knight of the Burning Pestle*, Beaumont parodies the kind of "resurrection scene" exemplified a few years later in Middleton's *A Chaste Maid in Cheapside*. The author of *The Revenger's Tragedy* (probably Middleton) was clearly familiar with Shakespeare's *Hamlet*, which is itself indebted to Kyd's *The Spanish Tragedy* and may have borrowed materials as well from a lost *Hamlet* by Kyd.

Often, indeed, the playwrights worked together. Many plays of the period were planned and written jointly from the outset. Of the plays in this volume, *The Maid's Tragedy, The Roaring Girl*, and *The Changeling* are collaborations of this type, between two dramatists both of whom are known to us. Eric Rasmussen cogently argues that the A-text *Doctor Faustus*, the text reproduced in this volume, is a similar joint undertaking between Marlowe and an unknown collaborator.[6] Other plays, especially those that found their way into print long after their first performance, often include work added later by a second or third hand, since it was routine to compose new scenes for revivals. Later editions of *The Spanish Tragedy* and *Doctor Faustus*, for instance, include scenes added after the deaths of the original authors. The frequency of collaboration is understandable given the financial exigencies of the early modern theater business. The companies who bought the plays naturally wanted workable scripts composed in relatively short periods of time. Most early modern playgoers were much more aware of the actors onstage than they were of the dramatists behind the scenes, just as modern moviegoers are far more aware of star performers than they are of screenwriters.

Theatrical Language and Vernacular Form

The language of a Renaissance play was extremely important to its successful dramatic performance. The Renaissance stage lacked many of the technological resources on which the modern theater depends. The theaters had neither move-

6. Eric Rasmussen, *A Textual Companion to "Doctor Faustus"* (Manchester, Eng.: Manchester University Press, 1994).

able sets nor sophisticated lighting. Especially in the large amphitheaters, the actors' main tool for riveting the attention of a crowd was beautiful and evocative language.

In modern productions, Renaissance dramatists, Shakespeare included, can seem long-winded. Of course, the language is more difficult for us than it would have been for the original audience. But the unfamiliarity of the words is not the only problem, for an aesthetic gap separates typical modern playgoers from their Elizabethan and Jacobean counterparts. Visually impressive modern staging techniques and the extraordinary technological resources of filmmaking encourage us to attend more closely to visual clues than to auditory ones. For Renaissance audiences, on the other hand, language must have constituted a primary pleasure. In Marlowe's *Tamburlaine,* the Scythian bandit-hero helps the Persian prince Cosroe overthrow his brother and presents him with the crown. "I long to sit upon my brother's throne," Cosroe admits, and a courtier tells him: "Your Majesty shall shortly have your wish / And ride in triumph through Persepolis" (2.5.47–49). The king and his entourage sweep off, leaving the stage to Tamburlaine and his followers. Tamburlaine exclaims:

> And ride in triumph through Persepolis?
> Is it not brave to be a king, Techelles?
> Usumcasane and Theridamas,
> Is it not passing brave to be a king
> And ride in triumph through Persepolis?
> (2.5.50–54)

By the end of the scene, Tamburlaine has resolved to overthrow Cosroe—the first step in what will become a campaign for world domination—seemingly simply because he is intoxicated by the sound of a blank-verse line.

Less exalted characters, too, display the same susceptibility to poetry. In *The Shoemaker's Holiday*, the hero, Simon Eyre, quotes dramatic tags and appropriates from the theater a vivid pseudo-classical bombast. When one of the workers in his shop is conscripted as a soldier, Eyre orates: "See you this man? . . . Hector of Troy was an hackney to him, Hercules and Termagant scoundrels" (1.166–70). Dekker presents Eyre's stagy posturing as both ridiculous and appealing. Similarly, in *The Knight of the Burning Pestle*, a grocer's apprentice recites a few lines, a little inaccurately, from a speech by the nobly born rebel Hotspur, in Shakespeare's *1 Henry IV:*

> "By heaven, methinks it were an easy leap
> To pluck bright honor from the pale-faced moon,
> Or dive into the bottom of the sea,
> Where never fathom line touched any ground,
> And pluck up drownèd honor from the lake of hell."
> (Induction 79–83)

Rafe, the grocer's apprentice, evidently enjoys imagining himself as the bravest of warriors, a delusion of grandeur laughably incommensurate with his lowly status. At the same time, the moment is also charming, because it suggests how ordinary people incorporate the vocabulary of theatrical heroism into their own lives.

In other plays, the power of language is potentially more sinister. In the first scene of *Doctor Faustus*, the hero peruses and then discards works by Aristotle, Galen, Justinian, and Jerome, representing the disciplines of philosophy, medicine, law, and divinity, respectively. Instead, Faustus turns to magic, "ravished" by the prospect of making things happen merely by uttering the right words. Yet the devils he conjures rarely deliver exactly what he demands, and he goes to his damnation twenty-four years later with the great ambitions of the first scene still unrealized. In Jonson's *The Alchemist,* impressive language is a vehicle for a more cynical kind of fraud. Three crooks astonish and mystify their victims with arcane vocabulary drawn from books of alchemy, treatises of obscure biblical exegesis, and manuals on the etiquette of quarreling. In Jonson's *Bartholomew Fair,* language is virtually emptied of content in the drunken "game of vapors," in which each participant furiously contradicts the man who spoke just before him.

Despite their differences, all these plays assume that the audience shares the characters' intense susceptibility to and delight in impressive language. The aim is not necessarily simple, straightforward comprehension, but a poetic effect elicited by strangeness and imagined as pleasurable even in, or perhaps especially in, the absence of total comprehension. The many foreign-language speeches and scenes testify to the potency of this appeal for Renaissance audiences: the Latin invocations in *Doctor Faustus*, the French scenes in Shakespeare's *Henry V,* Lacy's Dutch in *The Shoemaker's Holiday,* Surly's Spanish in *The Alchemist*, the Welsh and Latin in *A Chaste Maid in Cheapside*. Linguistic heterogeneity is part of the Renaissance theater's colorful portrayal of life's diversity.

The playwrights drew heavily on their classical education for these linguistic effects. The Latin dramatist Seneca was an important model for tragic writers, especially in the 1580s, when more recent precedents were wanting. Senecan tragedy is a drama of violent extremes; the Senecan tragic hero is typically a spectacular rule-breaker, prone to long, impressive speeches and showy mad scenes. Senecan rhetorical extravagance attracted the dramatists of the 1580s and early 1590s, who were searching for ways to rivet the attention of large audiences. Yet the influence was not merely stylistic, because Seneca's tragic sensibility attracted them as well. First tutor, and later victim, of the notorious first-century Roman emperor Nero, Seneca wrote about the political and psychological costs of absolutism to those who had to live under it. The topic was a resonant one in the late sixteenth century, as enhanced royal authority across Western Europe came perilously close, in some minds, to tyranny. Many Renaissance tragedies, and revenge tragedies in particular, come to imaginative grips with the problem of bad kings—of what to do when there is no institutionally sanctioned way of getting rid of a powerful but destructive ruler who seems to be above the law.

The Latin training of most Renaissance playwrights shows itself as well in their comedies. The colloquial wit of the Roman comic writers Plautus and Terence, whose works were standard grammar-school texts, transferred nicely to the London playhouses. Again the imitation was not purely a matter of linguistic style. Like the classical comic writers, English dramatists typically organized a comic plot around an initially thwarted but eventually rewarded love affair. They learned from Plautus and Terence an interest in depicting the contemporary urban scene with a mixture of satire and affection, and shared the classical playwrights' delight in trickster characters whose schemes often provide much of the play's momentum.

While Renaissance humanism was grounded in the study of classical texts, it gave a powerful impetus to vernacular literatures in all the European languages. English Renaissance dramatists drew not only on classical prototypes but on the newly vigorous vernacular literatures of Italy, France, Germany, and Spain. Moreover, they absorbed a great deal from the native dramatic tradition and from the English they heard spoken all around them. If, as Dekker and Beaumont suggest in their plays, sumptuous playhouse language could seep into the everyday speech of London citizens, even more so do the rhythms of colloquial English permeate the language of the theater. The colloquialism is especially marked, of course, in comedy set in London, which is particularly concerned with capturing contemporary speech patterns. The irrepressibly talkative Simon Eyre again provides a colorful example. "Away, you Islington whitepot!" he exclaims to his wife. "Hence, you hopper-arse, you barley pudding full of maggots, you broiled carbonado, avaunt, avaunt!" (*The Shoemaker's Holiday,* 20.51–53). This is the invective of the

London streets and alehouses, artistically elaborated on and served up for the pleasure of an audience that recognizes the origins of this kind of ridicule outside the playhouse.

Like the theater itself, the English language was, in these years, a freewheeling, rapidly evolving phenomenon open to heterogeneous influences. Neither grammar nor spelling was fixed, and the rules of punctuation were much less rigid than they are today. Many roughly equivalent grammatical forms coexisted, and the variety provided an unusual range of nuance. For instance, both "thou" and "you" were still current, permitting a distinction between familiar and formal usage that would become unavailable within fifty years. The use of the auxiliary "do" in negative statements was optional: "do not go" and "go not" were both idiomatic, the latter used often with a slightly more emphatic or imperative implication. Double negatives were grammatical and often suggested special emphasis. Newly invented words, many of them made by adding prefixes or suffixes to existing words, or by changing nouns into verbs or vice versa, gave great elasticity to spoken and written English. Imported words also much enriched the vocabulary—taken from humanist scholarship, from theological disputation, from New World exploration, from scientific discourse, from commercial contact with Africa and the East.

English Renaissance playwrights did not merely use what they found but contributed to this creativity. Jonson ridiculed his colleague Marston's fondness for coinages such as "obstupefact" and "lubrical." Yet Jonson, as his plays attest, was as alive to the pleasures of verbal inventiveness as anybody else. The frisson of excitement that attended new words in the period arose not merely from their intrinsic unfamiliarity. It came also from the previously unimagined marvels that they designated and the contexts of voyage, discovery, and new enterprise with which those marvels were associated. For early modern Europeans, the world was turning out to be bigger and more various than anyone had expected, and their languages needed to expand to accommodate that variety.

Just as the classical influence on Renaissance drama can be traced in both the language and the sensibility of the plays, so too do native elements affect not only linguistic style but matters of form and dramatic design as well. Before the 1530s, when England broke with the Roman Catholic Church, most drama was religious. Many plays dramatized tales from the Bible: the Nativity, the story of Noah and his ark. Others were allegorical "morality plays" meant to illustrate an ethical or spiritual principle. In the wake of the Protestant Reformation, however, religion and religious policy became highly controversial matters. Authorities prohibited the performance of overtly religious plays on the grounds that they might foment disorder. Still, the allegorical techniques of medieval morality drama persisted. In Marlowe's *Doctor Faustus*, the outlines of what had originally been an allegorical scene of temptation are visible in the no longer explicitly allegorical relationship between Faustus, the errant human being, and Mephistopheles, the devil who enables his damnation. Yet the very similarity to the medieval prototype helps clarify the nature of Marlowe's innovations. Mephistopheles is not a single-minded representative of an allegorical essence; in the first scenes, especially, he apparently suffers considerable hesitation and regret. Moreover, Faustus is seduced not merely, or even mainly, by a personified agent of darkness, but by exciting new intellectual prospects that challenged traditional ideas. In this sense *Doctor Faustus* typifies something essential to much English Renaissance drama, especially tragic drama. It occupies a cultural moment in which received notions are in sharp conflict with newer ideas.

Even more pervasive than the technique of allegory in Renaissance drama is what might be called the sensibility behind the allegorical form: the sense that particular individuals and events have a larger, even cosmic, significance and are part of a pattern or network that extends beyond the world of the play. The worst moments in Renaissance plays are not, generally, simply those in which bad things happen. The inhabitants of early modern England lived risky lives by our standards and seem to have taken a certain amount of misfortune in stride. Instead, the terrible moments more often involve suffering that is no longer morally intelligible, so that the characters feel adrift without consolation or hope of reprieve in a world that appears determined to reward villainy. In these circumstances, characters often "run mad," lose their sense of connection to a universal order, as Hieronimo and Isabella do in *The Spanish Tragedy,* Zabina does in *Tamburlaine,* or supporting casts of madmen do in *The Duchess of Malfi* and *The Changeling.* Webster's *The Duchess of Malfi* is a particularly interesting example because the villains in the play deliberately, but unsuccessfully, set out to induce despair and madness in its heroine:

DUCHESS I could curse the stars—
BOSOLA Oh, fearful!
DUCHESS And those three smiling seasons of the year
Into a Russian winter, nay, the world
To its first chaos.
BOSOLA Look you, the stars shine still. (4.1.96–101)

Atlas bearing the weight of the heavens ("Coelifer Atlas," as the scroll informs us). The universe depicted is Ptolemaic, with the earth at the center, immediately surrounded by regions of air and fire (the two lighter of the four elements); then by numbered orbits representing the moon, Mercury, Venus, the sun, Mars, Jupiter, and Saturn; then by three outer orbits representing the firmament of the fixed stars, the crystalline sphere, and the primum mobile, which imparts motion to the whole.

After the Duchess beholds the supposed corpses of her murdered husband and children, she wants her curse to ruin the world so that it will adequately reflect her own desolation. When Bosola points out to her that the stars "shine still," he turns the permanence of the heavenly bodies, normally a source of theological consolation, into evidence of cosmic indifference in the face of injustice. In a scene that distantly recalls the temptation scenes of medieval morality plays, in which a devil tries to persuade a victim to despair, Bosola suggests to the Duchess not that she is damned, but that she is impotent and that the world does not respond to her suffering. The Duchess's heroism, in these circumstances, consists in a stubborn refusal to lose her mind. *The Duchess of Malfi,* like *The Spanish Tragedy,* is skeptical, to say the least, that a beneficent cosmic order actually exists. Nonetheless, both plays seem convinced that believing in such an order, however illusory, is a linchpin of sanity.

Another holdover from earlier English drama is the combination of multiple plots and genres in the same play. The dramatists of the English Renaissance preferred to orchestrate a multiplicity of elements rather than to emphasize a single overwhelming effect. With important exceptions (notably Ben Jonson), they generally regarded as optional the classical "unities" of time, place, and action, which were supposed to help a dramatist discipline the flow of experience and create a coherent artistic effect. An English play might happen anywhere, might move anywhere, might treat of any duration of time. It very often, as Philip Sidney remarked disapprovingly, "mingles kings and clowns" to delineate a socially heterogeneous dramatic world. The less successful plays in this mode can seem simply overstuffed with irrelevant detail, like the shapeless tales of derring-do Beaumont parodies in *The Knight of the Burning Pestle*. But in the best of them—in such plays as *The Spanish Tragedy, Volpone, Bartholomew Fair, A Chaste Maid in Cheapside, Women Beware Women, The Changeling,* and *A New Way to Pay Old Debts*—the combination of various plot strands in the same work, all resonating against one another, produces a powerful impression of comprehensiveness and complexity.

In many ways, then, the drama of the English Renaissance is a vital hybrid. It recalls allegorical modes of expressing character while transforming allegory into social and even satiric types. It remembers and invokes the gods of old, but with a deep uncertainty as to whether those gods really exist. In formal terms, the drama of the Renaissance draws on classical prototypes while at the same time combining plot lines, and mixing comic and tragic elements, in a way reminiscent of native English drama. Neoclassical critics did not welcome this hybridity, but it proved enduringly popular on the English stage.

Major Themes

The preoccupations of English Renaissance drama are richly varied, as one might expect of an era of exciting transition. In what follows we explore some of those preoccupations: an interest in self-assertion and its implications for the social structure, a concern with economic disruption, an engagement with new attitudes toward sexuality, and a consideration of the social and emotional consequences of religious change.

Pushy People

Stubborn, self-aggrandizing characters, brazenly pursuing their interests with scant regard for morality or compromise, make for great drama. The Greeks knew this in the fifth century B.C.E.; so do the producers of modern soap operas. Renaissance playwrights, too, were fully aware of the theatrical attractions of self-assertion. Medieval allegorical drama provided them with a useful prototype in the character of the "Vice": part clown, part tempter, part sinister aggressor, capable of being inflected in either a tragic or comic direction depending on the context, but in either case crucial for sustaining dramatic momentum. Such widely varied opportunists as Marlowe's Mephistopheles in *Doctor Faustus* and Barabas in *The Jew of Malta,* Jonson's Mosca in *Volpone,* and Webster's Bosola in *The Duchess of Malfi* all trace their ancestry to the medieval Vice. Both medieval and classical drama provide another paradigm: a protagonist with a surplus of what would, in smaller doses or in different circumstances, be considered a form of excellence. This virtue, in such extraordinary measure, or so divorced from normal inhibitions, veers out of social bounds, creating disaster for the hero, the people around him, or both. Marlowe's characters Tamburlaine and Faustus, Vittoria Corombona in Webster's *The White Devil,* and Giovanni in Ford's *'Tis Pity She's a Whore* exemplify this kind of excess. For instance, Giovanni is described as "a miracle of wit" (1.1.47), an extraordinary success as a student, and yet his restless intelligence inclines him to question conventional moral restrictions and leads him into a disastrous affair with his sister. Marlowe's Edward II displays traits that might well be attractive in a private citizen: loyalty to his friends, a marked artistic sensibility, a yearning for pastoral retirement, an aversion to military aggression. In a king, these characteristics prove disastrous. This tragic pattern encourages a certain relativism about virtue, or at least a sense that virtue must be understood in terms of its context.

While a few characters pursue their agendas openly, more commonly they are masters of conspiracy. In many English Renaissance plays, the protagonist is a person distant from the formal structures of power, who has no way of imposing his or her will over others except by subterfuge. Revenge tragedies, a popular genre in the period, routinely dramatize an underling cleverly achieving mastery over his "betters" by means invisible to the victims until the final bloody scenes of triumph and revelation. Thus in Kyd's *The Spanish Tragedy,* the magistrate Hieronimo secretly collects evidence implicating a prince and a king's nephew in the murder of his son. Once convinced of their guilt, he tricks the malefactors into performing as actors in a tragic play, during the course of which they are actually killed. In *The Revenger's Tragedy,* the hero, Vindice, thwarted in his marriage and excluded from his hereditary privileges by a corrupt ruling family, patiently devises elaborate plans to bring about the death of the Duke and the Duke's son.

Many plays not usually classified as revenge plays likewise set conspirators in a covertly adversarial relationship to the rest of the people in their world. In Marlowe's *The Jew of Malta,* Jonson's *Volpone,* and Massinger's *A New Way to Pay Old Debts,* the villain-heroes' stated aims are not vengeance but the accumulation of wealth. Nonetheless, their motives are often blurry and mutable. Thus in *The Jew of Malta,* the energetically murderous Barabas initially claims that self-enrichment is his aim; what he eventually wants, however, is revenge on Christian society for its unjust treatment of him. In *Volpone,* the title character pretends to be deathly ill in order to attract those who hope to be named his heir. Although he profits enormously from the rich gifts they shower on him, he values "the cunning purchase of my wealth"—the clever process by which he defrauds others—as highly as "the glad possession" (1.1.31–32). Likewise in *A New Way to Pay Old Debts,* Giles Overreach is an urban social climber who hopes to marry his daughter to a highborn member of the provincial gentry; but he wants not so much to improve his social station as to dispossess and humiliate members of a traditionally privileged class. Such characters share with the revengers the pleasures of hoodwinking other people and of enlarging their own sense of agency at the expense of their dupes.

The same pattern of trickery and self-advancement is discernible even when the tone is lighter, the reward less tangible, and the protagonists less rapacious. In Jonson's *Epicene,* the ingenious Truewit hatches a plot that effectively strips two egregiously self-promoting yet foolish acquaintances, Jack Daw and Sir Amorous La Foole, of their pretentions to literary skill and knightly valor—and in front of the leading women of their social circle. He gets nothing himself from this elaborate scheme other than the admiration of his friends and the satisfaction of defending the norms of gentility against unworthy pretenders. In Middleton's *A Chaste Maid in Cheapside,* the oversexed Touchwood Senior, pretending to be a fertility doctor, impregnates the wife of an impotent acquaintance for a large fee. His reward is partly the money, and partly the joy of figuring out a clever way to cuckold his client and indulge himself sexually without having to cope with the inconvenience of a bastard child. It is as if, in the dramatic worlds of these plays, the total amount of human agency were imagined as fixed, so that if one character successfully seizes more than his share, whether by force or by trickery, he becomes the "winner" while the others are correspondingly deprived.

Often, though not always, the acts of fraud or conquest by which one character profits at the expense of others are explicitly condemned at some point in the play. For instance, *Volpone* ends in a courtroom, in which the hero and his associates are sentenced to severe punishment for their knavery. One of the magistrates enunciates a predictably sententious moral: "Let all that see these vices thus rewarded / Take heart, and love to study 'em. Mischiefs feed / Like beasts, till they be fat, and then they bleed" (5.12.149–51). In other words, crime never pays, and its supposed rewards are always fleeting. The truth of this axiom, however, seems dubious, given the highly contingent, almost accidental quality of the play's resolution. Truth has come to light not because of the inevitable triumph of goodness and virtue, but because in the end, Volpone deliberately confesses his wrongdoing to the befuddled authorities. *A New Way to Pay Old Debts* ends on a similarly "edifying" note, with the punishment of the upstart Overreach and the vindication of his erstwhile victims. But for the playgoers, the moral point is qualified by the realization that without the plotter, the play would have no plot. Our entertainment depends on sinful presumption, on more or less ruthless attempts to gain mastery. The spectators are, perhaps, in the same position as the master Lovewit is at the end of *The Alchemist,* when he returns to his London home after an absence of some months and finds his butler involved in a lucrative criminal scheme. Since Lovewit himself profits handsomely from his servant's iniquities, he refrains from punishing him at the play's end. He recognizes his own complicity and knows where his self-interest lies.

Perhaps the precarious social position of so many Renaissance playwrights made them especially alert to the triumphs and transgressions that attend social mobility. Although traditionally one's status and occupation in life depended on one's family background, early modern dramatists very often created characters for whom that criterion was inadequate. With typical forthrightness, the daringly presumptuous Tamburlaine simply seizes what he thinks of as rightfully his: "I am a lord, for so my deeds shall prove, / And yet a shepherd by my parentage" (1.2.34–35); he takes a princess for his wife and embarks on a campaign of conquest. In the finale of *Friar Bacon and Friar Bungay*, the Earl of Lincoln pledges to marry Margaret, a milkmaid of Fressingfield; the nobility of England witness Margaret's trothplight in the same ceremony that unites the future Edward I with Princess Elinor of Castile. *The Shoemaker's Holiday* invites shopkeepers and guild members in the audience to rejoice in the social elevation of one of their own. Eyre clings proudly to his bourgeois heritage even while demonstrating that he is a match for earl or duke, or even the king himself. "Prince am I none, yet bear a princely mind," he declares (17.21). Significantly, his blank-verse line, inserted in the midst of his highly colloquial prose, sounds like, and probably was, a tag from a play.

The portrayal of social mobility is not always so positive. Doctor Faustus, whose parents were "base of stock" (Prologue 11), dreams of outfitting poor university students in the silk ordinarily reserved for the gentry. In order to realize his overweening ambitions, he sells his soul to the devil. *Volpone*'s Mosca, servant to the trickster Volpone and a "parasite," or professional sycophant, rejoices at the physical and moral mobility his role affords him; he can, he claims:

> rise
> And stoop almost together, like an arrow,
> Shoot through the air as nimbly as a star,
> Turn short as doth a swallow, and be here
> And there and here and yonder all at once.
> (3.1.23–27)

Jonson depicts Mosca with some sympathy but also punishes him severely at the play's end.

The representation of social mobility on the Renaissance stage routinely deploys the symbolism of costume. In early modern England, "sumptuary codes," or laws of clothing, assigned different garments to different professions and social ranks. Although such rules were widely flouted, the connection between class and clothing remained much tighter than it is today. When a lowborn character makes a claim to higher status in a Renaissance play, he typically does so by donning the attire typical of the rank to which he aspires. When Marlowe's Tamburlaine proclaims his lordliness, he casts aside his shepherd's "weeds" (1.2.41) and girds himself for war. When Simon Eyre is elected sheriff in Dekker's *The Shoemaker's Holiday,* he enters *"wearing a gold chain"* (10.142.1) as befits his office and bestows on his wife a fashionable French hood. In Jonson's *Volpone,* the servant Mosca dresses as a *clarissimo,* or Venetian aristocrat; at the end of the play, this bit of social presumption seems to incense the magistrates more than the fraud, perjury, and other crimes he has committed. When they sentence Mosca to a life term at hard labor, they publicly strip him of his robe, visibly reducing him to the naked galley-slave he will henceforth be. Conversely, in Massinger's *A New Way to Pay Old Debts,* the impoverished gentleman Wellborn begins to reclaim his birthright when he tricks his enemy, Overreach, into outfitting him in the elegant garments to which his family background entitles him.

A citizen of London. His robes identify him as a holder of civic office.

What makes these moments seem dramatic—both satisfying and unsettling—is not only their intrinsic appropriateness, but the background of theatrical practices from which they acquire meaning. The entire institution of the Renaissance theater depended on such reattiring. Lowborn actors dressed magnificently for their roles as monarchs and aristocrats; often they wore the actual garments of the nobility, bought secondhand but still extremely valuable in an age before the mass production of textiles. Acting companies frequently paid more for a new costume than for a new play. And the actors were joined, in the playhouse, by spectators dressed as splendidly as they could afford. Playgoers could even buy seats over the stage, where their view of the action was limited but where they and their gorgeous outfits were especially visible to the rest of the audience throughout the performance. For authorities who disapproved of plays, the theater seemed a place where both the actors and their audiences engaged in a vast conspiracy to impersonate their betters. If an actor could don a costume and persuasively impersonate a king or an aristocrat, what distinguished the one from the other? The very enterprise of acting embodied a potential subversion of the class structure.

Whether such dramatic renditions of social climbing provided a mechanism for letting off steam so that social pressures outside of the theater would not build to dangerous levels, or whether they constituted instead a force of genuine if gradual subversion, is a matter of critical debate. Most Renaissance plays, despite their dramatizations of social mobility, convey the impression that social organizations are basically hierarchical and that traits conventionally imagined as "noble" do in fact inhere in at least some members of the aristocracy. A very common pattern juxtaposes brave, generous, self-disciplined members of the upper classes with lecherous, power-hungry individuals from the same class. The courtiers of Beaumont and Fletcher's *The Maid's Tragedy* behave according to the most exalted ideals of honor and place an extraordinary premium on the obedience that they owe to the throne; when the King behaves tyrannically by keeping Evadne, Amintor's newly wedded wife, as his mistress, the members of his court behave in a high-minded way and are deeply torn by their eventual need to plot against their monarch. Even in plays with a much more troubled or ambivalent view of the relationship between birth and merit, certain traits are consistently associated with "good nobility." *The Duchess of Malfi* opens, for instance, with a comparison between the virtuous French court and its corrupt Italian counterpart. Later in the play, the imperious but virtuous Duchess is contrasted not only with the principled, timid commoner she chooses for her husband but also with her appalling brothers. The mental resolution and physical courage she displays throughout the play were characteristics identified as "noble"—not merely good or virtuous traits, but ones associated specifically with the best members of the governing class. In *A New Way to Pay Old Debts,* the gentleman Wellborn's generosity and flair distinguish him, despite his many faults, from Overreach's corrupt sidekicks, Marall and Greedy. In *The Knight of the Burning Pestle,* Beaumont wittily makes fun of the way even the relatively lowborn admire "elite" values and traits. When his grocers come to see a play, they want it to be about grocers, but not about grocers going about their ordinary business. Instead, they consider worthwhile and exciting the warlike activities of those far above them on the social scale; so they want to see grocers posing as knights, fighting in far-off lands, rescuing ladies in distress, and dying glamorously on the battlefield.

This kind of social mobility, or fantasy of mobility, does not necessarily demand overhauling the entire status system. It merely requires that a few exceptionally virtuous or decadent individuals be able to move up or down the social ladder. The Earl of Lincoln marries Margaret of Fressingfield in *Friar Bacon and Friar Bungay* but remains still the Earl of Lincoln; he raises her up, rather than descending to her lowly station. Simon Eyre's rapid ascent to become Lord Mayor of London reifies that city's system of hierarchical elections, and does so under the beaming approval of the King, who is glad to have such enterprising and jovial subjects. Even the iconoclastic Marlowe shows traces of this reluctance to abandon class structure entirely. Tamburlaine, for instance, may be an erstwhile shepherd, but he shows his innate kingliness by excelling on the battlefield and taking a princess as his wife. Tamburlaine aims not to do away with kingship but to attain "The sweet fruition of an earthly crown" himself in spite of all obstacles (2.7.29), and he does so at the expense of kings who are individually weak or corrupt, not at the expense of the system itself. Still, English Renaissance drama so often puts such misfits at center stage—shepherds and servants who aspire to be masters, scholars who want magical power, outcasts who desire infinite wealth or social prestige—that the conventional demurrers eventually ring a little hollow. The real, though at the same time frequently disavowed, subject of many Renaissance plays seems to be the more widespread social dislocations of early modern England and the new attitudes and ways of life those dislocations brought into existence. It is to that larger social context that we now turn.

Class, Commerce, and Consumption

Early modern England was a nation newly alive to the pleasures of affluence and newly aware of opportunities for acquiring it. In the late sixteenth century, England vastly expanded its power over the seas. With new trade came a new cosmopolitanism, and with that new cosmopolitanism came a sharply increased desire for new goods. England began to cast envious eyes abroad at the wealth of great mercantile powers such as Venice and Turkey and at the opulence of Spain and Portugal, enriched by their colonies in the New World and their trading outposts in Africa and India. Wealthy travelers to Mediterranean lands brought back unheard-of luxuries. The Earl of Oxford, in the 1570s, came home from Italy laden with embroidered gloves, "sweet bags," scented jerkins, and costly perfumes. In 1592, an English naval squadron captured a Portuguese carrack, or treasure ship, off the Azores, as it attempted to make its way home from a trading voyage to the East Indies. The *Madre de Deus* ("Mother of God") was three times the size of any English ship. It was laden with chests of pearls, jewels, coins, amber, bolts of cloth, tapestries, ebony, and spices: 425 tons of pepper, 45 tons of cloves, 35 tons of cinnamon, as well as huge quantities of mace, nutmeg, and cochineal, the last a precious red dyestuff made from the dried wings of a tropical beetle. The value of its cargo was estimated to be half a million pounds, at a time when the English queen's exchequer held only a bit over a million.[7] This vast capture, and others like it, whetted the English appetite for exploration and colonization. By the beginning of the seventeenth century, England's long adventure as a colonial power was under way.

Desiring something, of course, is not the same as possessing it; for ordinary English people of the period, the kinds of precious things carried by the *Madre de Deus* were far out of reach. Indeed, the very unfamiliarity of such goods was the source of their imaginative appeal. Their novelty and their outrageous expense hinted at alluring, heretofore undiscovered vistas of experience. The most obvious literary consequence of the new alertness to luxury goods is what might be called a "poetics of magnificence," a rapturous list of almost unimaginable plenty that often invokes as well the glamour of exotic locales. Barabas' opening speech in *The Jew of Malta* provides a good example:

> Give me the merchants of the Indian mines,
> That trade in metal of the purest mold;
> The wealthy Moor, that in the Eastern rocks
> Without control can pick his riches up,
> And in his house heap pearl like pebble-stones.
> (1.1.19–23)

In *Volpone*, Volpone's attempt to seduce the beautiful, virtuous Celia strikes a similar note when he promises her endless changes of clothing, gorgeous jewelry,

7. David Landes, *The Wealth and Poverty of Nations: Why Some Are So Rich and Some So Poor* (New York: W. W. Norton & Company, 1998), p. 151, citing contemporary accounts collected by C. C. Kingsford in *Naval Miscellany*, vol. 2 (1912), pp. 89–121.

exquisite delicacies. So does Epicure Mammon, in *The Alchemist*, with his breathless description of the sensuous delights he imagines will be his once he possesses the philosophers' stone. In *The Shoemaker's Holiday*, part of the action turns on Simon Eyre's unlikely good fortune in acquiring at a rock-bottom price the cargo of a ship from Crete, a sort of poor man's *Madre de Deus*: "*dis skip dat comen from Candy is al fol, by Got's sacrament, van sugar, civet, almonds, cambric, end alle dingen—towsand towsand ding,*" exclaims the Dutch skipper in his broken English (7.1–3).

The theater's engagement with the pleasures of consumption was profound. As we have already seen, luxury textiles especially had a strong symbolic charge on the Renaissance stage, and the spectacle of beautiful clothing, worn by both actors and spectators, was widely asserted to be one of the main lures of the playhouse. And this was not the theater's only evocation of magnificence. The interiors of the playhouses were richly decorated to suggest sumptuous materials. The wooden columns in the Swan, for instance, were "painted in such excellent imitation of marble that it might deceive the most prying observer." The custom of playgoing itself, of course, was one of the new tastes of an age newly aware of the pleasures of sensuous indulgence and variety, and of the creative use of leisure time.

Yet the attitude to luxury on the Renaissance stage was hardly one of mere celebration. The English Renaissance inherited the strong antimaterialist bias of medieval Christianity, which identified a desire for wealth with several deadly sins—covetousness, gluttony, and pride. In *The Jew of Malta*, Marlowe puts his most beautifully sensuous lines in the mouth of Barabas, a self-proclaimed villain and atheist. In *Volpone*, too, the hero's pursuit of wealth is patently blasphemous, especially in the first scene, where Volpone worships at the altar of his treasure. In some plays, the sin of greed is a little softened by its apparent triviality, for the rich and stupid cut a large swath in many Renaissance plays. Epicure Mammon may be undone by his own greed in *The Alchemist*, but his raptures appear more ridiculous than dangerous. Likewise in *Epicene*, when Sir Amorous La Foole keeps drawing attention to his "delicate fine black horse" (2.4.102), his lodging in the Strand, his costly embroidered jerkin, his sword with the "gold handle" (4.6.97), he seems almost childishly silly.

Still, the line between foolishness and vice is a fine one. In even these cases, the desire for luxury goods and a penchant for self-display are linked with an almost casual willingness to ruin other people's lives. La Foole's boasting about his wealth is the prelude to his boasting about his sexual conquests. He pretends to have had a liaison with the bride Epicene, a lie that has the potential to destroy her marriage and her reputation. In *The Revenger's Tragedy*, similarly, the court's predilection for splendid clothing might seem the least of its failings; after all, this is a place where rape and murder are commonplace, lethal betrayal routine. Yet for Vindice, the play's satirically minded protagonist, expensive textiles are hardly innocent indulgences. They are the visible sign of a whole decadent system of prodigality, moral bankruptcy, and preference for flashy surface over substantial virtue.

In fact, Vindice argues, conspicuous consumption threatens to disrupt the entire social hierarchy. The gentry and nobility, yearning for luxuries they cannot afford, mortgage and sell the very lands on which their income and status depend in order to raise cash in the short term:

> Lands that were mete by the rod, that labor's spared;
> Tailors ride down and measure 'em by the yard.
> Fair trees, those comely foretops of the field,
> Are cut to maintain head-tires . . . (2.1.225–28)

History offers a real-life basis for Vindice's claims. During the first decades of the seventeenth century, the wealthy, and particularly the members of King James's court, plunged deeply in debt in order to sustain a magnificent style of life. This was not, the dramatists insist, merely a calamity for those bankrupted by their inordinate expenditures. Just as initiative and agency, as we have seen, seem to many Renaissance dramatists to exist in a fixed quantity across the social world, so does wealth. If one person gets rich, cuts an unduly glorious figure in the world, or otherwise seems to accumulate too many visible marks of status, the dark assumption in many Renaissance plays is that somebody else must be being exploited.

This assumption was not entirely unwarranted. While England's increased trade was, in aggregate, enriching the nation, not everyone benefited equally. Some found themselves much worse off. As the mercantile English nation-state formed from a collection of smaller local entities and then English commercial influence began to expand beyond the borders of the realm, new opportunities arose, but so did new possibilities for disaster. Many of the dislocations that attended this socioeconomic revolution will seem uncannily familiar to students of twenty-first century "globalization." The newly powerful nations of Renaissance Europe annihilated boundaries between smaller local economies that, by impeding the movement of people and capital, had limited profits and the ability to create wealth. At the same time, since those boundaries had protected vulnerable populations of workers from unfair economic competition, their elimination caused considerable suffering.

Throughout the early modern period, workers poured into London seeking the higher salaries available in the capital city. The population influx caused serious overcrowding and disease, especially in slum areas. Not all the newcomers hailed from the British countryside. Refugees from religious persecution in France and the Low Countries (modern Belgium, Luxembourg, and the Netherlands) settled in London in large numbers. Like immigrants in any age, they often crowded into tenements and worked for lower wages than did English artisans. We see dramatic representations of the ethnic rivalries growing out of such conflicts in the joking about Dutch shoemakers in Dekker's *The Shoemaker's Holiday*.

In the countryside, the poor fared even less well. In the sixteenth and early seventeenth centuries, as exports became an increasingly important part of the economy, many landowners shifted from growing grain to producing wool, which was easier to store, transport, and sell. They asserted their property rights over acreage traditionally used by the peasantry for food crops or animal pasture, fencing, or "enclosing," the lands for sheep. For lower-class rural residents, the loss of access to what had been considered "common land" was disastrous. With less land devoted to food production, the countryside became more susceptible to famine. To make things worse, since sheepherding was much less labor-intensive than grain cultivation, many peasants were forced off land their families had worked for generations.

The result was a large class of vagrant poor, some of whom suffered severe privations in the countryside, some of whom attempted to find work in London, and some of whom turned to a life of petty crime. The "canting scene" of Middleton and Dekker's *The Roaring Girl*, in which Moll teaches the language of criminals to some gentlemen, romanticizes as carefree the vagrants' nomadic, semilegal life, but in fact their situation was dire. What had always been wide disparities between rich and poor now seemed, to contemporary observers, to gape even wider. At one court banquet, the entire first course was merely to be looked at, then thrown away: "dishes as high as a tall man could well reach," one commentator wrote, "filled with the choicest and dearest viands land or sea could afford."[8] Meanwhile, in Warwickshire, starving peasants rioted and were brutally subdued.

8. Francis Osborne, *Historical Memoirs of the Reigns of Queen Elizabeth and King James* (London, 1658).

The gap between rich and poor was wide during the late sixteenth and early seventeenth centuries in England.

The new economic order reorganized the lives of the upper classes as well. Traditionally, the richest, most powerful people in England had been large landowners, but now the newly wealthy London merchants challenged their social and political preeminence. The reciprocal snobbery of the two groups is on display in the opening scene of Dekker's *The Shoemaker's Holiday*. The Lord Mayor of London, a member of the new urban elite, and the Earl of Lincoln, a scion of the old aristocracy, conspire to prevent a marriage between Lincoln's nephew, Lacy, and the Lord Mayor's daughter, Rose. Lincoln despises Rose, "a gay, wanton, painted citizen" (1.77), for her low birth and presumably vulgar ways, while the Lord Mayor suspects that Lacy is a lazy spendthrift. In *The Shoemaker's Holiday*, the opposition of this older generation to the love match is eventually swept away, but only after Rose proves herself ladylike in manners if not in birth, while Lacy aligns himself with the urban artisan class, abandoning his military commission in order to labor as a shoemaker. The aristocratic shoemaker is of course a fantasy, but the marriage of Rose to Lacy is anchored in historical reality. Down-at-heels aristocrats frequently recouped their fortunes by marrying women from wealthy London families; the brides, for their part, acquired their husbands' social prestige.

As *The Shoemaker's Holiday* suggests, the new commercial class differed, or was thought to differ, from the old nobility in its assumptions about money and power and in the kinds of behavior it valued. On the one hand, the profit-making ventures of the newly rich encouraged imagination, diligence, risk-taking, time consciousness, a keen sense of the bottom line, and other socially useful traits. On the other hand, by emphasizing the success of individuals over the harmony of the group, these competitive ventures threatened the social network. To many Renaissance dramatists, the protocapitalist sensibility appeared to imagine human beings as fundamentally locked in struggle with one another rather than joined in cooperation. Though certainly no businessman, Marlowe's Tamburlaine gives eloquent voice to the assumptions that seemed to lie behind the new attitude: "Nature, that framed us of four elements, / Warring within our breasts for regiment, / Doth teach us all to have aspiring minds" (2.7.18–20). At issue was not merely the question of how people behave, but of what "human nature" entails. The rationale for a traditional social order was rooted in a notion of a natural hierarchy in which each individual, high or low, is required to play his or her assigned role in order to keep social relationships intact. Tamburlaine, by contrast, assumes that everybody "aspires"—some more successfully than others—and that war, not peace, is the state of nature.

In actuality, historians tell us, the new urban rich and the old landed aristocracy were more alike than they seemed to contemporaries. Aristocrats were increasingly entrepreneurial in the way they managed their estates and enterprises, and although they derived much of their income from their land, they were increasingly drawn to life in London. Meanwhile, members of the urban upper classes often bought titles and land in order to set themselves up as country gentry. In fact, businessmen could not afford to operate as amoral individualists; they typically worked and invested collaboratively, in joint-stock companies that were the ancestors of the modern corporation. Still, the dramatists do capture a shift in values that must have seemed both momentous and disturbing to many of them. In Massinger's *A New Way to Pay Old Debts*, the clash between new and old elites is less happily resolved than it is in *The Shoemaker's Holiday*. Sir Giles Overreach, the unprincipled, competitive, enormously wealthy urban upstart of Massinger's play, violates the terms along which provincial English society has, Massinger claims, traditionally been organized. As a result, Overreach presents a powerful threat that must be neutralized by his ruin at the end of this profoundly conservative play.

In the domestic tragedy *Arden of Faversham*, new and traditional mores likewise coexist uneasily. The title character occupies an economic position in his community apparently incompatible with his domestic role. At home, Arden is the much put-upon victim of Alice, his adulterous and eventually murderous wife, who conspires with her lover, two of her servants, and several hired assassins to kill him and abandon his body in a nearby field. We regard Arden the husband with sympathy. Arden is also, however, a grasping landlord who inspires intense resentment. He seizes the land of a poor man, Dick Reede, and undermines the rights of another, Richard Greene, to a different parcel of land. In the Epilogue, Arden's friend Franklin remarks on the murder's uncanny aftermath:

> But this above the rest is to be noted:
> Arden lay murdered in that plot of ground
> Which he by force and violence held from Reede,
> And in the grass his body's print was seen
> Two years and more after the deed was done.
> (Epilogue 9–13)

The indelible print in the grass suggests that Arden's gory end, though apparently unrelated to his treatment of Reede, is in fact a divine retribution for his sharp business practices. Yet the connection between Arden's ferocity toward his neighbors and Alice's ferocity toward Arden remains unclear.

Bosola in Webster's *The Duchess of Malfi*, Flamineo in *The White Devil*, Vindice in *The Revenger's Tragedy*, and De Flores in Middleton and Rowley's *The Changeling* are even more ambivalent depictions. All three are "fallen" or "decayed" gentlemen, born into formerly elite families but bereft of resources. They are the casualties of a system with new possibilities for social mobility. The disparity between their birth and their fortune, between their strong sense of entitlement and their shabby circumstances, makes them extremely dangerous. Even when they are not revengers in the strict sense, as Vindice is, they share the revenger's conviction that they have been treated unfairly, and they are willing to resort to subterfuge and violence to redress their perceived grievances. Yet even if these characters are the "villains," they are also often the shrewdest commentators on the social worlds their plays depict. Their humiliations have distanced them from their society's norms and stripped those norms of much of their sentimental gloss. With distance comes the bitter perspective of the satirist, who is often a powerful truth-teller, despite being a little unhinged.

Sex, Marriage, and Gender

In almost every English Renaissance play, there are fewer female roles than male roles. In *Tamburlaine,* for instance, Zenocrate, Zabina, Anippe, Ebea, and the four virgins of Damascus are the only female characters in a cast of over thirty, and of those female characters, only two are major parts. *Arden of Faversham,* which centers on the character of Arden's wife, Alice, likewise has only two female roles, as does Jonson's *The Alchemist.* This lopsided gender ratio is usually ascribed to the all-male composition of the theater companies. In the adult troupes, most women's roles were played by cross-dressed boys whose voices had not yet changed, and even though, historians tell us, poor nutrition generally delayed puberty until the late teens, presumably the adult companies only had a few boys at any one time who were capable of handling ambitious female roles. Yet in the "children's companies," where all the actors were boys, the usual excuse no longer holds: these players would presumably have been able to impersonate adult women as convincingly as they could impersonate adult men. In fact, a number of plays written for the children's companies, such as Lyly's *Endymion* and Jonson's *Epicene,* include a number of significant female roles. In Lyly's allegorical play, Queen Cynthia, the godlike queen Endymion worships from afar, is a substantial role for a boy actor. It is buttressed by roles for her waiting-women, other court ladies, and a sorceress or two. *Epicene* features the Collegiate Ladies, who spend their time gossiping, shopping, playing cards, and attempting to seduce men. Still, even in this subset of plays, most of the characters are male.

Early modern England was a patriarchal society that severely circumscribed women's legal rights, access to education, and professional opportunities. Many argued that women's inferiority was mandated by God. They pointed to biblical evidence: the story of Adam and Eve in Genesis, and Saint Paul's insistence in 1 Corinthians and Galatians that women submit to male authority both at church and in the family. Many women accepted the supposed moral necessity of their subordination. Thus in Elizabeth Cary's *The Tragedy of Mariam,* the sign of Mariam's virtue is her refusal to resist or disobey her tyrannical husband, King Herod, even when his behavior toward her is violently suspicious and eventually murderous. Moreover, *Mariam,* centered as it is on a woman's experience of a marriage gone wrong, was a closet drama, not written for performance. In the all-male milieu of the professional theaters, perhaps it is not surprising that even the most powerful women characters function most importantly as figures of male sexual interest, as potentially marriageable or beddable partners. When they no longer command such interest, they typically receive only contempt, like the Old Lady in *The Duchess of Malfi* or Putana in *'Tis Pity She's a Whore*.

Many plays are shot through with a sexual double standard. Male licentiousness is, if not approved of, not very strongly proscribed either. Thus in Middleton's *A Chaste Maid in Cheapside,* Touchwood Senior praises his "unmatchèd treasure" (2.1.48) of a wife not only for remaining faithful to him but for restraining her desire for sexual pleasure even within the bonds of marriage. In the same breath, he ruefully admits that when he goes "on progress" through the countryside, he seeds the English provinces with bastards:

> I have such a fatal finger in such business
> I must forth with't, chiefly for country wenches.
> For every harvest I shall hinder haymaking;
> I had no less than seven lay in last progress
> Within three weeks of one another's time.
> (2.1.59–63)

Touchwood is a rake, but he is hardly a villain, and the play represents his helplessly lustful behavior as humorous, not threatening. The blatant but unremarkedon difference between Touchwood's requirements for his wife's behavior and his requirements for his own was entirely ordinary in the period. The opprobrious epithet "whore" was used for any woman who had sex outside the bounds of marriage, whether she was a professional prostitute or a woman who committed adultery on a single occasion. In Middleton and Rowley's *The Changeling,* the cynical but often insightful De Flores succinctly states the reason for this conflation of categories:

for if a woman
Fly from one point, from him she makes a husband,
She spreads and mounts then like arithmetic—
One, ten, a hundred, a thousand, ten thousand—
Proves in time sutler to an army royal.
(2.2.60–64)

In De Flores' account, once released from tight restraint, female appetite expands uncontrollably. The woman's agency, her moral choices, are simply irrelevant. Given this logic, even a woman who does not consent to extramarital sex is still contaminated by it. In *The Revenger's Tragedy,* after Antonio's wife is raped, she realizes that she herself is henceforth tainted and commits suicide.

At the same time, much to the chagrin of their male partners, women in plays throughout the period seem continually to be evading what is expected of them. Married shopkeepers flirt with gentlemen customers; young wives take up with dukes; unmarried ladies escape the control of husbands, brothers, and fathers. Some, such as Alice Arden in *Arden of Faversham,* Beatrice-Joanna in *The Changeling,* and Vittoria Corombona in *The White Devil,* do not shrink from murder if the wrong man stands in their way. Renaissance plays are full of complaints about the hypocrisy and unreliability of women and of suspicion of their "wiles." The trickery and opportunism so often celebrated, however ambivalently, when men are the agents, typically are presented as much more threatening when women betray their men. Clerimont's song, in Jonson's *Epicene,* expresses some of this sense of peril:

Still to be neat, still to be dressed
As you were going to a feast,
Still to be powdered, still perfumed—
Lady, it is to be presumed,
Though art's hid causes are not found,
All is not sweet, all is not sound.
(1.1.87–92)

In other words, the lady's exquisitely soigné appearance, her flawless surface, arouses suspicion even when "art's hid causes are not found"—even when the male observer has no way of knowing how the seductive illusion of beauty has been created. The assumption here seems to be that beauty is required of women, but that when they have it, it probably conceals a rottenness within. In *The Revenger's Tragedy,* Vindice makes a similar point more graphically. Holding the skull of his late betrothed up to the view of the audience, he exclaims: "See, ladies, with false forms / You deceive men, but cannot deceive worms" (3.5.96–97). Of course, these are the sentiments of dramatic characters, not necessarily the playwrights' own opinions. Some characters who are especially brutal to women are clearly meant to be seen as pathological: Corvino in Jonson's *Volpone,* for instance, who is both obsessively jealous of his wife and also eager to prostitute her for personal gain, or Ferdinand in Webster's *The Duchess of Malfi,* who is bizarrely preoccupied with his twin sister's sex life. Even so, their ferocity flourishes in an atmosphere of casual misogyny that circulates widely in many Renaissance plays.

This is not, however, the whole story. For although women's roles are relatively few and their dramatic opportunities circumscribed, nevertheless play after play contains unforgettable portraits of strong-minded, articulate, intelligent women. Their very transgressiveness makes them dramatically interesting. In Kyd's *The Spanish Tragedy,* Bel-imperia takes Don Andrea as her lover from a class below her own; after Andrea's death, she accepts his friend Horatio as her sexual partner, in defiance of her male relatives. Forcibly betrothed to the Prince of Portugal, whom she justifiably considers responsible for her lovers' deaths, she slays him at the wedding ceremony and then takes her own life. In Middleton and Dekker's *The Roaring Girl,* Moll Cutpurse behaves like a swashbuckling urban knight-errant, outdoing the men in the play in strength and valor. The prostitute Doll Common in Jonson's *The Alchemist* helps operate an elaborate and ingenious con game, and Ursula the pig-woman in his *Bartholomew Fair* likewise plays a principal role in a wide array of petty crimes. Annabella in *'Tis Pity She's a Whore* has an affair with her brother. Middleton's *Women Beware Women* features a dazzling display of transgressive women: Isabella, who finds brief happiness as the incestuous lover of her uncle; Bianca, newly married but quickly transformed into an embittered courtesan once her beauty attracts the attention of the libidinous Duke of Florence; and most of all Livia, unable to control her own lusts and repeatedly involved in arranging the seduction of younger women. Beaumont and Fletcher's *The Maid's Tragedy* centers on Evadne, forced by the King to marry Amintor so that the King can enjoy her as his mistress under the cover of her seemingly respectable marriage. Evadne's determination to preserve what is left of her honor by killing the King poses many problems about regicide and the supposedly unquestionable authority of the monarch.

Although these women—hardly shrinking violets—pose powerful moral dilemmas for themselves, for the other characters, and for the audience, many of them are also depicted with considerable sympathy. Very often even an apparently unassertive, "virtuous" woman, such as Celia in *Volpone* or Moll in *A Chaste Maid in Cheapside,* will prove surprisingly steely under pressure and will play an unexpectedly decisive role in the resolution of the plot. The apparently paradoxical combination of women's marginalization and prominence in English Renaissance drama has drawn many feminist critics to this body of work.

One important innovation in the drama of the period took place late in the sixteenth century, when John Lyly and Robert Greene began to develop the potentialities of romantic comedy—a genre that Shakespeare was to explore to rich effect. Romantic comedy organizes many typical features of a comic plot, such as clowning and social commentary, by connecting them to an idealized love story. In such plays, the ancient boy-meets-girl plot of classical Latin comedy is enhanced by a strain of Neoplatonism that links sexual love with universal forces of natural regeneration. Neoplatonic idealism, as embodied, for example, in Baldassare Castiglione's *The Book of the Courtier* (ably translated by Sir Thomas Hoby in 1561), envisaged a continuous ladder of existence connecting animate physical beings with an invisible, divine idea of heavenly harmony. In this system, soul and body were mutually interdependent in a way that could dignify physical love provided it was subordinated to, and subsumed by, a rarified heavenly truth. Neoplatonism idealized romantic pursuit as integral to the union of two souls.

The new comic mode that grew out of this romantic idealism captured some important changes in the theory, and probably also the practice, of marriage in early modern England. After the Protestant Reformation in the mid sixteenth century, marriage acquired an increased spiritual prestige. While the Roman Catholic clergy had taken vows of celibacy, ministers in the new church of England were encouraged to marry. Single-sex religious communities—convents and monasteries—were disbanded. Reformers argued that sexuality in marriage was fully consonant with godliness. Whereas same-sex friendships still were considered essential for both women and men, it was slowly becoming common to think of the marriage relationship as transcending these, as demanding a higher degree of loyalty and offering potentially greater emotional rewards. At the same time, the official atmosphere was hardly one of liberated sexuality. Sexual intercourse was supposed to take place only in marriage, and its main purpose was assumed to be procreation.

How closely practice reflected theory is debatable, and there is certainly evidence of some disparity between the social realities and their representation onstage. Although virginity until marriage, for women at least, is the norm in romantic comedies, sexual intimacy after betrothal was tacitly accepted in early modern England. Birth records indicate that many brides were already pregnant on their wedding day. Likewise, marriages based solely on romantic attraction were far rarer in real life than on stage. Among the propertied classes, parents often arranged the marriages of their children with a view to augmenting the fortunes of the family as a whole; romantic attraction between bride and groom was dispensable. Nonetheless, it can hardly be an accident that romantic comedy emerges in a world that is just beginning to believe that the achievement of a happy, permanent, monogamous relationship is life's supreme good, the quintessential "happy ending."

Most Renaissance drama evinces considerable sympathy for lovers, at least if the lovers are headed toward wedlock. Even Middleton's *A Chaste Maid in Cheapside,* which dramatizes a wide range of unconventional sexual arrangements, includes the marriage of two true lovers as its virtually obligatory climax. That romantic love is usually depicted in the plays as a prerogative of the well-to-do suggests its prestige. Lovers in the plays almost always address one another in "high-status" blank verse rather than in prose, and again and again playwrights associate a desire for a love marriage with the better sort of people. Thus even so unorthodox a figure as Tamburlaine evinces his noble nature by falling in love with, courting, and eventually marrying the captive princess Zenocrate rather than resorting to the quicker expedient of raping her. In the London comedies, too, the romantic plot usually involves relatively high-status characters, the children of aristocrats, gentlemen, and prosperous merchants—Lacy and Rose in *The Shoemaker's Holiday,* Sebastian Wengrave and Mary Fitzallard in *The Roaring Girl,* Touchwood Junior and Moll in *A Chaste Maid in Cheapside.*

One reason, in fact, that class barriers may seem so easy to overcome in some comedies is that romantic heroes and heroines possess "gentle" characteristics even if they are not really members of the gentry class. Thus in Greene's *Friar Bacon and Friar Bungay,* Prince Edward complains that the Keeper's daughter with whom he is infatuated has unexpectedly resisted his advances: "our country Margaret is so coy, / And stands so much upon her honest points, / That marriage or no market with the maid" (1.119–21). In other words, Margaret flatly refuses to become a royal mistress. By the end of the play, her incorruptibility is rewarded in a love marriage to the Earl of Lincoln.

In actuality, since property concerns and family pride mattered little to those who had none of either, in early modern England, love marriages may well have been more common among the humbler sort than among the aristocracy. Traces of this social difference show up not in the way courtship is presented onstage but in the way stage couples behave after marriage. In Middleton and Dekker's *The Roaring Girl,* the citizen husbands are represented as affectionate but overly trusting of their wives, and the play seems faintly contemptuous of their uxoriousness. In Beaumont's *The Knight of the Burning Pestle,* the Citizen and his Wife likewise seem déclassé as they sit incongruously cuddling among a crowd of sophisticated gentlemen.

In cases where, for some reason, the love relationship cannot lead to a marriage, the situation becomes more complex. In these plays, the dramatists' appreciation for the intensity of the lovers' feelings for one another conflicts with the strongly felt imperative to contain that intensity in a socially acceptable form. Such conflicts routinely became the material for tragedy. On the Renaissance stage, lovers who cannot marry one another are doomed: in *Edward II,* the King and his male friend Gaveston; in *'Tis Pity She's a Whore,* the siblings Annabella and Giovanni. In *The Duchess of Malfi,* Webster imagines a variant on this tragic situation: a happy relationship that cannot be publicly disclosed. The Duchess marries Antonio, her steward, in a private exchange of vows, despite their difference in class and in defiance of her brothers' opposition to her marrying anyone at all. Although these promises constitute a legally binding marriage, the impossibility of a public wedding puts the couple in a difficult position, since the public ceremony does not merely bind husband and wife to one another but also affirms their new status as a couple in the eyes of the community. Sin in this play attaches not to the loving couple but to the corrupt environment in which their love cannot be acknowledged. While in a typical romantic comedy the lovers' enthusiasm renews the larger society in which the marriage takes place, in *The Duchess of Malfi* love and virtue avail the protagonists little against the hostile forces ranged against them.

If love outside of marriage in these plays creates one kind of problem, marriage without love created another, for marriage was a virtually indissoluble union in early modern England. In Jonson's *Volpone,* the marriage between Celia and Corvino is irretrievably flawed: not only is Corvino pathologically jealous and domineering, but he also attempts to prostitute his virtuous wife to Volpone in hopes of inheriting Volpone's wealth. The sentence of legal separation, pronounced by the judges at the end of the play, protects the long-suffering Celia from further violence at the hands of her husband but stands in the way of a routine comic ending. The failed unions between Arden and Alice in *Arden of Faversham* and between Camillo and Vittoria in Webster's *The White Devil* precipitate tragedy: unable to be rid of their hated husbands in any other way, both women conspire to murder them. Even the "precontract," or engagement to marry, created a legal obligation that was difficult to break. In Middleton and Rowley's *The Changeling*, Beatrice-Joanna is obviously overhasty when she jumps to the conclusion that the only way to get rid of an unwanted fiancé is to murder him, but it is true that in Renaissance England breaking off a betrothal involved significant social humiliation and sometimes legal complications as well. The play never allows that the cancellation of a betrothal is a possibility.

As these disasters tend to remind us, marriage is not merely an emotional or sexual connection but a social institution with economic consequences. In early modern England, these consequences weighed particularly heavily on women. A single woman was legally under her father's supervision, and a married woman's political and legal rights were strictly subordinated to those of her husband. A married woman who insisted on her own authority or sexual autonomy thus seemed to be usurping the male role. In Fletcher's *The Woman's Prize,* the women refuse their husbands the sexual rights of marriage, barricading themselves in their quarters and forcing the men to conduct what becomes a kind of seige warfare. Faced with this rebellion, Petronius, father of the rebellious Maria, wonders whether the women will soon take to urinating standing up.

In this male-dominated system, widows were the only women with legal independence from male control. Widows, especially wealthy ones, become powerful sites of fantasy in the drama of the period because they could run households as they pleased and dispose of property as they liked. They could also choose new spouses, if they wanted to, without consulting family members and with the ben-

This woodcut from *Roxburghe Ballads* (an antiquarian project published in 1871 to reprint rare examples of earlier literature and popular culture) shows an Elizabethan family having a meal. The parents and older children are sitting, while the younger children are standing. All are eating with spoons; forks were only just starting to be used.

efit of the sexual experience gained during their first marriage. The Duchess of Malfi is a threat to her brothers because her financial independence enables her to choose a partner as she wishes; and indeed, her choice of the steward Antonio confirms their worst fears. In Jonson's *Bartholomew Fair,* the wily, self-willed, well-off Dame Purecraft similarly exemplifies the "widow stereotype": both the impecunious Winwife and the sanctimonious Zeal-of-the-land Busy court her, but she arranges to marry Quarlous instead. Lady Allworth in Massinger's *A New Way to Pay Old Debts* is still another rich widow, virtuously able to use her wealth to advance the fortunes of her stepson Tom and to recover Frank Wellborn from his prodigal ways, thus foiling the machinations of the grasping Sir Giles Overreach. In Jonson's *The Alchemist,* one telling sign of the young widow Dame Pliant's mental vacuity is that she utterly fails to recognize her own potential independence, and simply continues to follow male directions with cowlike placidity.

The economic changes that, as we have seen, so profoundly affected the relationships among the social classes, affected gender roles as well. Middleton's *A Chaste Maid in Cheapside* depicts a world in which marriage and childbearing are subordinated to the same profit motive that drives all other human interactions in the commercial heart of London. While in the countryside children can labor at a young age, so that a large family is economically more successful than a small one, urban children are unproductive and expensive. That expense severs the ordinary relationship, in comedy, between sex and "thriving," since the happily married couple's procreative success runs directly counter to the couple's economic interests. Touchwood Senior and his loving wife thus must resolve to live apart:

> our desires
> Are both too fruitful for our barren fortunes.
> . . . .
> Then 'tis the prudent'st part to check our wills
> And, till our state rise, make our bloods lie still.
> (2.1.8–14)

Compounding their difficulties is the unequal distribution of sexual prowess. While Touchwood Senior has too much, others, like Sir Oliver Kix, have too little, but the institution of monogamy provides no socially acceptable way of redistributing the surplus. Middleton's characters ingeniously work around these constraints, in a series of improvised solutions that are simultaneously funny, scandalous, and economically rational.

Sexually unconventional relationships were easier to undertake in London not merely because, as Middleton suggests, they made financial sense, but because in a large city individuals inevitably feel more anonymous and thus less constrained. In London, the traditional village system of sexual discipline, which had depended on the mutual surveillance of ever-watchful neighbors, no longer served as an effective curb on behavior. City comedies are full of jokes about Brentford and Ware, tavern districts near London where adulterous couples might pursue their pleasure without fear of observation. The very title *A Chaste Maid in Cheapside* is a similar sly joke, implying that in Cheapside, chastity is something remarkable.

Among the urban elite, the availability of leisure, privacy, and like-minded companions combined to give some women the prospect of and a taste for new sexual freedoms. In *Epicene*, Jonson represents female assertiveness as a distinctive feature of the modern age: Morose's desire for a silent, submissive wife is ridiculed as an impossible anachronism. This play depicts a class of women who set up a single-sex "college," a sort of women's social club, modeled on educational institutions that in Jonson's day were restricted to males. These women have the resources to maintain their own living accommodations, travel about London in their own coaches and at their own initiative, make their own purchases, and pursue their own friendships with men or with other women with apparently complete independence from husbands, fathers, or other male guardians.

Some critics believe that the Ladies' College in *Epicene* was inspired by a group of powerful, artistically inclined women associated with the court of Queen Anne, who maintained a household separate from her husband. If so, *Epicene* is only one of numerous plays to attend to the "decadent" court morals of the first decades of the seventeenth century. In *The Maid's Tragedy, Women Beware Women, The White Devil, The Duchess of Malfi,* and *The Revenger's Tragedy*, the court is conveniently displaced to Italy in order to keep the criticism from seeming too pointed and thus running afoul of the censor. But to an early-seventeenth-century audience, its pertinence to England would likely have been obvious. Elizabeth I, who reigned until 1603, had insisted on a strict, even prudish, standard of behavior for both men and women at her court. Her successor, James I, was much more tolerant, perhaps because his own marriage was unsatisfying and his most passionate relationships were with men. James's favorite, Robert Carr, Earl of Somerset, fell in love with the Earl of Essex's wife, Frances Howard, who then, scandalously, sued for divorce from her husband; a few years later, the couple was convicted of murdering Thomas Overbury, an erstwhile friend of Somerset's who had opposed the match. (*The Changeling* may allude topically to this scandal.) The Earl of Pembroke, another prominent courtier, had an affair with his cousin Lady Mary Wroth that resulted in two illegitimate children. Many contemporaries were deeply scandalized by the behavior of James and his courtiers and inclined as well to associate sexual irregularity with all kinds of other corrupt court practices.

The transvestite practices of the Renaissance theater—boys playing female roles—complicated the ways many plays treat the problem of female insubordination. Supposedly the smaller, softer female body "naturally" indicated her inferiority, as did women's more splendid but more confining clothing. But just as the ability of a lowborn actor to play kings and nobles called into question the naturalness of class difference, so, when boys played women, was the inevitability of gender difference called into question. Many plays foreground cross-dressing—a plot device that, by suggesting women and men can successfully impersonate one another, distinguishes "masculine" and "feminine" behavior from male and female bodies. The most successfully "feminine" individual in Jonson's *Epicene* is a cross-dressed boy; the most virile character in Middleton and Dekker's *The Roaring Girl* is Moll Cutpurse, a cross-dressed woman.

It is not surprising, then, that the same critics of the theater who objected to humble actors impersonating kings should focus their attention on cross-

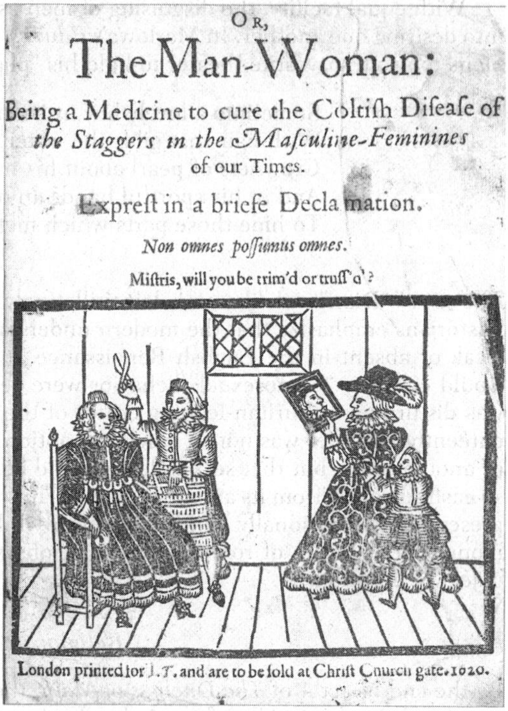

The title page of *Hic Mulier; or, The Man-Woman* (1620), a pamphlet denouncing the "unnatural" practice of women wearing men's clothing and adopting masculine styles (the women in this image are at a men's barber). *Hic Mulier* was answered by *Haec Vir; or, The Womanish Man* (also 1620).

dressing. In the view of these critics, actors routinely violated God's biblical prohibition against men dressing as women or women dressing as men. Some playwrights, such as Jonson in *Bartholomew Fair,* responded to such critiques by ridiculing them. Others attempted to put a positive spin on gender ambiguity: in Lyly's *Endymion*, the frustrated longing of the shepherd Endymion for Queen Cynthia, emblematic of the moon and hence of the divine love to which unworthy mortals can only aspire, is enriched and complicated in the theater by the fact that both Endymion and Cynthia are played by boy actors. The nonsexual resolution of their mutual but impossible attraction for each other fits nicely with the gender ambiguity of their theatrical status.

One reason the moral critiques were so shrill was that actors were not the only offenders. In the early seventeenth century, preachers thundered against men who decked themselves in elaborate ruffs and fancy embroidery and deplored as well the fashion of women wearing such male garments as broad-brimmed hats and doublets, a kind of men's jacket. Just as Tamburlaine makes his claim for ruling-class status by putting on armor, so women who donned doublets seemed to lay claim not merely to the garments themselves but to the privileges of maleness. The theater, where fashion-forward members of the audience vied with the actors for the attention of spectators, seemed to encourage cross-dressing not merely among the few boys who impersonated women onstage but more widely among those who came to see the play as well.

Those who deplored this blurring of the gender boundary feared more than the prospect of gender reversal; they feared the subversion of power relationships—the prospect that women might aspire to escape their subjection to men or that men might abdicate their authority over the household. They also found disquieting the way cross-dressing paradoxically draws attention to sexuality even while obscuring it, in ways that both arouse the spectator and divert his or her desire in unexpected directions. In Middleton and Dekker's *The Roaring Girl*, Moll Cutpurse dresses as a man precisely to avoid arousing male lust; but many of the men respond all the more avidly. When Mary Fitzallard, the romantic heroine, disguises herself as a page in order to visit her betrothed, she likewise finds a warm reception: "Methinks a woman's lip tastes well in a doublet," exclaims her lover (4.1.50).

With equal facility, the disguising of men as women can be used to lure men into desiring one another. In Marlowe's *Edward II*, the King's male lover Gaveston plans to use transvestite theater to hold his "pliant king" in thrall:

> Sometime a lovely boy in Dian's shape,
> With hair that gilds the water as it glides,
> Crownets of pearl about his naked arms,
> And in his sportful hands an olive tree
> To hide those parts which men delight to see.
> (1.1.60–64)

The sex of "Dian" is deliberately left titillatingly unclear, hidden and yet revealed. Historians emphasize that the modern understanding of "sexual orientation" was weak or absent in the English Renaissance and that attitudes toward what we would consider "homosexual" behavior were very different from our own. What was disturbing to Puritan-leaning critics of the theater in the sixteenth and seventeenth centuries was not so much the notion that a man might lust after a boy or another man, but that sexual desire could be so labile and easy to manipulate, so easily diverted from its apparent object. This mobile, novelty-seeking desire was presented as emotionally continuous even while inherently in conflict with the monogamous desire of romantic comedy, obsessively settled as it is on a single object of devotion.

Religion

By the end of act 4 of *The Duchess of Malfi,* the title character has already been murdered. In the middle of act 5, her husband Antonio, as yet unaware of her death, eerily hears her voice echoing his as he walks in an "ancient abbey" with his friend Delio. Immediately prior to these literally haunting moments, Antonio indulges in a little philosophical reflection on his surroundings:

> I do love these ancient ruins.
> We never tread upon them but we set
> Our foot upon some reverend history;
> And questionless, here in this open court,
> Which now lies naked to the injuries
> Of stormy weather, some men lie interred
> Loved the church so well, and gave so largely to't,
> They thought it should have canopied their bones
> Till doomsday. But all things have their end;
> Churches and cities, which have diseases like to men,
> Must have like death that we have. (5.3.9–19)

Antonio mourns the loss of an illusion. An apparently permanent building and institution has proven fragile and contingent. In *The Duchess of Malfi,* the ruined abbey has obvious symbolic resonance; it is adjacent to the corrupt Cardinal's palace and suggests his misappropriation of religious resources. Yet surely the setting evokes not merely Catholic Italy, where ruined abbeys were presumably rare, but England, where after the Protestant Reformation, what Shakespeare called the "bare ruined choirs" of despoiled former monasteries and convents were a familiar sight. Indeed, one of the theaters where *The Duchess of Malfi* was first performed occupied land on which such a monastery had once stood.

Religious changes in early modern England were far-reaching, complex, and unavoidable. While the medieval church was hardly a static institution, its alterations were slow, and when it did change, ecclesiastical authorities emphasized continuity and precedent. Consequently, within a single lifespan, prayers, holiday observances, and religious rites of passage did not change radically. The church could easily seem an enduring institution, its permanence reflecting its origins in and sponsorship by an unchanging God. Moreover, since all of medieval Western Europe accepted the authority of the Roman Catholic Church, from the perspective of a fifteenth-century Englishman the Catholic Church's geographical extent would have seemed, for practical purposes, universal.

All this changed in the 1530s, when King Henry VIII broke with the Catholic Church and reorganized the ecclesiastical hierarchy under his own leadership. During the reign of Henry's short-lived son Edward, the Reformation took an aggressively Protestant turn. When Edward's sister Mary succeeded him in 1553, she forcibly returned England to Catholicism. At Mary's death in 1558, a Protestant monarch, Elizabeth I, was once more supreme governor of the English church. The monarch's religion was not merely a personal matter, since state and church were deeply intertwined. Thus each of these whipsawing changes of direction involved, for even the humblest subjects, disorienting changes in ritual practices and in systems of belief. Under these circumstances, no one, whatever his or her confessional allegiance, could help but notice the ways in which the church was a human institution. The church was evidently not ordained by direct divine decree but mediated by the complex, often conflicting demands of kings, clerics, and worshipers.

As far as can be ascertained, Renaissance dramatists occupied just about every point on the confessional spectrum. Shakespeare was most likely brought up as a Catholic but seems to have made his peace with the established Church of England in early adulthood. Jonson and Cary converted to Catholicism as adults; after about a decade as a Catholic, Jonson returned to the Church of England. Middleton, Dekker, and Fletcher were staunch Protestants. Marlowe was widely rumored to be an atheist, and Kyd was also accused of unorthodox beliefs. What they all inescapably shared, living in a period of religious upheaval, was the sense that ultimate questions were unsettled and the answers to those questions not obvious.

Censorship laws, as already mentioned, prevented the playhouses from staging plays with overtly religious themes. Still it is hardly surprising that the most ambitious art form of the period should address religious issues, though often in oblique ways. The disquiet that attended religious change permeated deep into the mentality of most thoughtful people in Renaissance England. Moreover, the high-stakes spiritual dilemmas opened up by the Reformation offered irresistible dramatic opportunities.

In Marlowe's *Doctor Faustus*, Faustus unsettles orthodoxy at every turn, dismissing ancient authorities and questioning the very existence of hell. In the upshot, he proves disastrously wrong, but his quest for knowledge strikes a resonant chord in an age that saw new scientific discovery challenging older notions of universal order. Faustus's questions about the irregular movements of the planets, for instance, indicate an awareness of Copernicus' revolutionary ideas about a sun-centered universe. Greene's *Friar Bacon and Friar Bungay* deals more playfully with the troubled boundaries between religion and science, religion and black magic. Jonson's *The Alchemist,* though deeply skeptical of the claims of alchemy, suggests at the same time the way quasi-scientific systems of thought might provide a seductive alternative to mainstream religious thinking.

Again and again, the dramatists' hunger for new materials led them into ancient and foreign cultures with religious institutions and beliefs strikingly unlike those of Renaissance England. Lyly's dramatized account of the love between his titular hero, Endymion, and Queen Cynthia is based on an ancient pagan legend in which the Moon falls in love with a mortal shepherd; no matter how Lyly adapts his source material to the court of Queen Elizabeth, the mores of an antique culture manifest themselves in a narrative of witchcraft and a prolonged, magical sleep. Presiding over Kyd's *The Spanish Tragedy* is the pagan spirit of Revenge; and vengeance indeed overwhelms the efforts of the Spanish Christians to find a just solution to their quarrels.

Clearly, the phenomenon of religious heterogeneity, by forcing people to ask, "Who's right?" could lead to skeptical or even nihilist musings. Yet the treatment of religion in Renaissance drama was not limited to metaphysically daring speculation about the ultimate design of the universe or the place of humans within it. Since religion was so closely entwined with political and social institutions, plays could treat religious issues by seeming to focus on their social consequences, in a way that did not necessarily threaten the authority of the established church. In many Renaissance plays, the variety of competing belief systems, considered merely as a social phenomenon, is presented as dramatically interesting.

The theater was not simply a neutral medium for the depiction of religious issues and differences. It was itself an institution fraught with quasi-religious significance. To many strict Protestants, the theater seemed to reproduce, indeed openly to market, what they most hated about the Catholic Church: its impressive but, to the reformed mind, "empty" or merely superficial displays. More moderate Protestants, like Philip Sidney and Thomas Heywood, considered theaters socially desirable because the ritual element was thoroughly desacralized: theater retained its power to "new-mold the heart of the spectator"[9] even while the connection had been severed between that appeal to the heart and actual godly worship. Following these hints, some modern critics have theorized that one social function of the Renaissance theater was to satisfy ritual impulses that had been the prerogative of the church in a Catholic regime but that after the Reformation no longer found a home there and therefore sought an alternative outlet.

Under Elizabeth, the main practical and ideological threats to the English nation came from Catholic sources. In 1570, the Pope declared the Queen an illegitimate ruler and absolved Catholics from allegiance to her. In the mid-1580s and indeed earlier, the Catholic Mary, Queen of Scots, conspired with several prominent English nobles to seize Elizabeth's throne. In 1588, Catholic Spain sent a vast armada to invade England and regain it for the true church; when a storm at sea destroyed almost the entire fleet, it was easy for English Protestants to believe that the hand of God had manifested itself directly. Elizabeth's regime responded to these emergencies with heightened surveillance and persecution of Catholics. The regime was particularly nervous about "missionary priests," Jesuits who were recruited from English Catholic families, trained on the Continent, and then secretly sent back to their homeland. When they were caught, the Jesuits claimed that their aims were purely spiritual, but the government believed that they had worldly aims as well and executed them as traitors.

Marlowe, who during his short, obscure career may have served as a spy at a Jesuit seminary, incorporated raw anti-Catholic humor into a number of his plays. In *The Jew of Malta,* the Catholic clergy are entirely venal: purportedly, the nuns and friars are sleeping together, and one friar attempts to use the sacrament of confession as a means of blackmail. In *Doctor Faustus,* Faustus's visit to Rome provides the occasion for him to humiliate the Pope in a scene of knockabout humor and anticlerical lampooning. In both plays, Marlowe uses anti-Catholicism to unsettle his audience: although Faustus and Barabas are capable of deplorable, even damnable behavior, many English Protestants would have shared their contempt for the Catholic Church.

While most of the English in the late sixteenth century had some knowledge of Catholicism, Judaism was far more exotic. Observant Jews had been expelled from England in the Middle Ages, so that the few Jews in England in the Renaissance period were from immigrant families that had, at least to all appearances,

9. Thomas Heywood, *An Apology for Actors* (London, 1612), B4r.

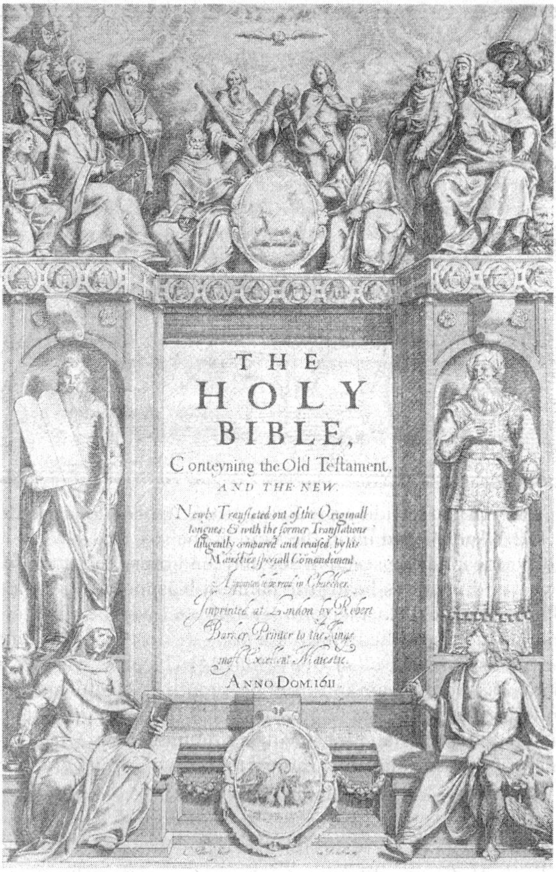

Frontispiece to the King James Version of the Bible, published in 1611.

converted to Christianity. Marlowe exaggerates the "foreignness" of the Jew into an absolute alienation from other human beings. Barabas in *The Jew of Malta* is cut loose from national allegiance and from all sense of obligation to the people around him—even, ultimately, his own daughter. With no foothold in the political hierarchy, he aims merely to enrich himself at the expense of others. Indeed, Marlowe imagines his Jew as the quintessentially successful merchant-capitalist, with no compunction about what becomes, in Barabas' case, literally cutthroat competition. *The Jew of Malta* conveys little sense of Judaism as a religious system or a community of believers. To the contrary, Barabas sets himself against both community and religious belief of any kind.

Yet a strain of pro-Jewish sentiment in England construed Judaism rather differently, as a deeply traditional system of belief and behavior founded on the direct commandment of God. In this view, the Jews are not the enemies of Christians but their forebears. Some of the reformed churches put particular emphasis on the Old Testament—especially the books of Exodus, Deuteronomy, Leviticus, and the prophetic books. Jonson satirizes the Puritans' mixed attitude toward Jews in *Bartholomew Fair;* the gluttonous Puritan preacher titles himself "Rabbi" Zeal-of-the-land Busy, but at the same time proclaims himself eager to eat roast pork "to profess our hate and loathing of Judaism, whereof the brethren stand taxed"

The Pope as Antichrist riding the Beast of the Apocalypse. See Revelation 13.1–2: "And I stood upon the sand of the sea, and saw a beast rise up out of the sea, having seven heads and ten horns, and upon his horns ten crowns, and upon his heads the name of blasphemy. And the beast which I saw was like unto a leopard, and his feet were as the feet of a bear, and his mouth as the mouth of a lion . . ." In this illustration, from the anonymous *Fierie Tryall of God's Saints* (1611), the Pope wears the papal tiara. His words beam out from his mouth as baleful spells seducing men to turn traitors ("proditores") and kill their prince. The papacy was much hated in England for having excommunicated Queen Elizabeth and for promising spiritual reward to any who would end her life.

(1.6.97–98). Elizabeth Cary's decision to dramatize a story from ancient Palestinian history in *The Tragedy of Mariam* is a more serious representation of this philo-Semitism. Cary's Palestine, like Shakespeare's Rome, offers the dramatic advantages of historical distance: her characters must struggle with political and ideological issues similar, but not simply identical, to those of early modern England.

By the 1590s and after, the drama increasingly reflected the contemporary conflict between the established Church of England and the movement for more extreme reform. At times, the depiction of Puritanism can be genial, as in *The Shoemaker's Holiday*, where Simon Eyre's wife, Margery, amuses her husband and his workers (and us) with her pious mannerisms and her namby-pamby oaths. Oftener the portrait is more satiric. In *A Chaste Maid in Cheapside*, the pious sisters and brethren who gather for the baptism of Mrs. Allwit's latest bastard vie with one other in sanctimoniousness and hypocrisy. In *The Alchemist*, Jonson characterizes Tribulation Wholesome and Ananias as inveterate hypocrites: they claim that pious motives to gather wealth justify their illegal alchemical schemes, but in fact they are merely hungry for power. Zeal-of-the-land Busy in Jonson's *Bartholomew Fair* is a reforming zealot who secretly longs for the forbidden pleasures of the fair. His comeuppance takes the form of his being bested by a puppet in a debate. Busy's bigoted attempt to close down the puppet theater, or at least to shout it down by his denunciation of the puppets as profane idols, is manifestly a parable in which Jonson defends the London theaters against their Puritan detractors. Jonson, all too aware of the reformers' hostility to the saturnalian, festive spirit of theater, is willing to declare open war.

Performance and Print

In 1614, Jonson, in the Induction to *Bartholomew Fair,* made gentle fun of a playgoer with deeply conservative tastes: "He that will swear *Jeronimo* or *Andronicus* are the best plays yet shall pass unexcepted at [unobjected to] here as a man whose judgment shows it is constant and hath stood still these five-and-twenty or thirty years" (Induction 105–9). *Jeronimo* is another name for Kyd's *The Spanish Tragedy,* written in the late 1580s, and *Titus Andronicus* is Shakespeare's first tragedy, written perhaps as early as 1589. As Jonson's comment indicates, by the middle of King James's reign the great plays of the 1580s seemed hopelessly outdated. Anyone who sets Kyd's *The Spanish Tragedy,* Lyly's *Endymion,* or Marlowe's *Tamburlaine* beside such Jacobean plays as Webster's *The Duchess of Malfi,* Jonson's *The Alchemist,* or Middleton's *A Chaste Maid in Cheapside* will notice the difference between the formal, declamatory style of the former and the much more interactive, conversational mode of the latter. *The Spanish Tragedy,* for instance, opens with a very long speech by the ghost of Don Andrea that provides the audience with a great deal of necessary background information. This static, "undramatic" opening would be inconceivable in a Jacobean play. Very long speeches do occur, but their function changes. In the 1610 play *The Alchemist,* for instance, when Epicure Mammon launches into an interminable monologue, he is not merely conveying information to the audience, but also suggesting his self-absorption and near total lack of contact with reality. Likewise, in the same play, the "alchemist" Subtle's long speeches are meant not primarily to instruct but to baffle and astonish the victims of his fraudulent schemes.

Between 1570 and 1642, the commercial theater evolved rapidly. In order to keep attracting customers, it needed (especially in the early decades) to offer a constant parade of novelty, and its profit imperatives made it extremely responsive to new market conditions. Moreover, the playwrights' constant collaboration with one another and their keen awareness of one another's work provided the conditions for the swift evolution of dramatic style. As satire became a fashionable literary form in the 1590s, it was almost immediately translated to a theatrical setting. But the evolution was not entirely the consequence of a changing literary environment and the theaters' profit motive. Given the close relationship between the playwrights and the acting companies, these changes doubtless also indicated an evolution in performance conditions and in acting styles.

Looking back after more than four hundred years, we cannot recapture many features of a necessarily ephemeral theatrical practice. We do know, however, that the plays in this volume were written for different acting companies and playing spaces; many of them reflect those differences. One such playing space was the large outdoor amphitheater. In these "public theaters," audiences could have seen *The Spanish Tragedy, Friar Bacon and Friar Bungay, Tamburlaine, The Jew of Malta, Edward II, The Shoemaker's Holiday, Volpone, The Maid's Tragedy,* and *The Revenger's Tragedy,* among others. The amphitheaters were not all alike, of course, and we do not know as much as we could wish about many of them. Our most important evidence comes from two sources: a sketch of the polygonal Swan Theater from the late 1590s, made originally by a Dutch visitor and preserved in a copy by his friend Arend van Buchell (see page li), and a building contract for the Fortune Theater, which was built on a square plan but otherwise seems to have been similar to the Swan in the way it arranged its interior spaces. The stage, a large rectangular platform four or five feet above ground level, thrust out from one wall; behind it was space for the actors to change costumes or wait for their entrance cues. At least two doors led from this so-called tiring room (attiring room) onto the main stage. The back of the stage probably featured an alcove or "discovery space"; such a space could have served as Doctor Faustus's study in the opening scene of that play. Above the back wall stood a gallery in which brief scenes were sometimes acted "above"; characters could appear on the walls of a besieged town (as in *Tamburlaine*) or they could look down, as if from a window, upon action on the main stage (as in *The Spanish Tragedy, Women Beware Women,* and *The Woman's Prize*). Two pillars, arising from the stage platform, supported a roof that provided some shelter for the actors and, especially in later productions, machinery for ascents and descents from the symbolically decorated "heavens." Actors could use the bases of these pillars as means of concealing themselves in eavesdropping scenes and the like. A trapdoor was needed to give access to the space under the stage platform, from which ghosts and otherworldly creatures might emerge (as, perhaps, in the first appearance of the devil Mephistopheles in *Doctor Faustus,* or of a tree and a dragon spouting fire in *Friar Bacon and Friar Bungay*).

In an age before strict fire laws and occupancy limits, a large number of people could be packed into a theater during performances. Playgoers could stand in the open space in front of the stage—the actors' feet would be at approximately their eye level—or they could sit in somewhat greater comfort and expense in the tiers of galleries against the back and side walls. In *The Roaring Girl,* Sir Alexander Wengrave, who is purportedly describing the tapestries in his house, actually describes what the crowd at the Fortune Theater looked like from the actors' point of view, with its crowded ranks of seated spectators and an ocean of humanity in front of them:

> Nay, when you look into my galleries,
> How bravely they are trimmed up, you all shall swear
> You're highly pleased to see what's set down there:
> Stories of men and women, mixed together
> Fair ones with foul, like sunshine in wet weather.
> Within one square a thousand heads are laid
> So close that all of heads the room seems made;
> . . . .
> . . . . Then, sir, below,
> The very floor, as 'twere, waves to and fro,
> And like a floating island seems to move
> Upon a sea bound in with shores above.
> (1.2.14–32)

All told, a theater could accommodate between two and three thousand playgoers at a time. The sheer concentration of bodies must have much amplified the emotional impact of an effective performance. Playgoers surrounded the actors on three sides, a factor that presumably encouraged the direct address from performers to audience so common in the plays of the period.

The theaters lacked movable scenery or elaborate sets. To be sure, the building itself, with its handsome back facade, lent itself to the physical impression of a castle under siege, a house facing out on a garden or street, or a great house in the country, but visual changes to that facade were not practical. One consequence of this relatively unmarked playing space was the heightened importance of props, which the companies possessed in abundance. Thrones were thrust onstage for throne scenes, beds for any scene in which a bed was needed (as in *The Revenger's Tragedy* and *A Chaste Maid in Cheapside*), and so on. In 1598, Philip Henslowe inventoried the property room at the Rose Theater and listed the following items:

> One rock, one cage, one tomb, one hell mouth. One tomb of Guido, one tomb of Dido, one bedstead, eight lances, one pair of stairs for Phaëthon. Two steeples, and one chime of bells, and one beacon. One heifer for the play of Phaëthon, the

This sketch of the Swan Theater, copied by Arend van Buchell from a sketch c. 1596 by Johannes de Witt (a Dutch visitor to London), is the only surviving contemporary representation of the inside of an Elizabethan theater building. The following areas are identified in Latin, from top to bottom and left to right: *tectum* (roof), *porticus* (covered gallery), *sedilia* (seats), *orchestra* (seats for distinguished spectators), *mimorum aedes* (dressing room for the actors), *ingressus* (entry into the galleries), *proscaenium* (the flat open stage), and *planities sive arena* (the "yard" in which spectators stood). The actors onstage seem to be two boy actors in women's roles being greeted by a chamberlain.

> limbs dead. One globe, and one golden scepter, three clubs. Two marchpanes, and the City of Rome. One golden fleece; two rackets, one bay tree. One wooden hatchet; one leather hatchet. One wooden canopy; old Mahomet's head. One lion skin; one bear's skin, and Phaëthon's limbs and Phaëthon's chariot; and Argus's head. Neptune's fork and garland. One crozier's staff; Kent's wooden leg. Iris's head, and rainbow; one little altar. Eight vizards; Tamburlaine's bridle; one wooden mattock. Cupid's bow and quiver; the cloth of the Sun and Moon. One boar's head and Cerberus' three heads. One caduceus; two moss banks, and one snake. Two fans of feathers; Bellendon stable; one tree of golden apples; Tantalus' tree; nine iron targets. One copper target and seventeen foils. Four wooden targets and one grieve armor. One sign for Mother Redcap; one buckler. Mercury's wings, Tasso's picture; one helmet with a dragon; one shield, with three lions; one elm bowl. One chain of dragons; one gilt spear. Two coffins; one bull's head, and one 'vylter.' Three timbrels; one dragon in *Faustus*. One lion, two lions' heads; one great horse with his legs; one sackbut. One wheel and frame in *The Siege of London,* one pair of wrought gloves. One Pope's miter. Three imperial crowns; one plain crown. One ghost's crown; one crown with a sun. One frame for the heading in *Black Joan*. One black dog. One cauldron for the Jew.[10]

Each one of these wildly various items could be pushed, worn, or carried onstage to enhance a performance. Henslowe's list suggests that he associated certain props with particular plays. The cauldron was presumably for boiling Barabas in *The Jew of Malta;* the bridle for the conquered kings in Part 2 of *Tamburlaine*; the "frame for the heading" for a play called *Black Joan.* This last device enabled the illusion of a decapitated head on a platter for spectators who knew what the real thing looked like (see p. liii).

Props frequently provide the playgoers with important information about times of day or offstage events. When Mendoza enters in *The Malcontent* with a "*sconce,*" or lantern, in a scene understood to be located before the Duchess's bedchamber (2.1.0.1), the lantern signifies that the action takes place at night, in a world of dark chicanery and adultery, even though the theater itself is fully illuminated (especially in the King's Men's production at the Globe Theater). The fact that the gentlemen enter in the first scene of *The Woman's Prize* "*with rosemary*" immediately signifies to the audience what the stage direction goes on to clarify: they are are arriving "*as from a wedding.*"

Occasionally, a portable prop will reappear numerous times, eventually accruing great symbolic significance. A handkerchief in *The Spanish Tragedy,* for instance, passes from Don Andrea to Bel-imperia to Horatio to Hieronimo, eventually serving as an exquisitely potent memorial of lost love. In the same play, Horatio is hanged onstage in "an arbor" that possibly doubles as the gallows on which Pedringano is later executed; Isabella, despairing of justice, finally cuts the arbor down just before she commits suicide. Just as the arbor, normally associated with peaceful leisure and agricultural bounty, becomes an instrument of violence in *The Spanish Tragedy*, so originally wholesome relationships between lovers, between parents and children, between masters and servants, and between rulers and subjects are perverted by hatred and injustice. In *The Revenger's Tragedy,* a highly self-conscious play that refers often to its own theatrical conventions, the revenger Vindice uses the skull of his mistress as a similar memorial emblem; he waylays the Duke by so thoroughly seducing him with "*the skull of his love dressed up in tires*" that the Duke mistakes it for one of his sexual victims (3.5.42.1–2). Later in the play, Vindice restages the Duke's death using the Duke's body itself as a prop.

10. Slightly abridged from *Henslowe's Diary, Edited with Supplementary Material Introduction and Notes,* ed. R. A. Foakes and R. T Rickert (Cambridge: Cambridge University Press, 1961), pp. 319–21.

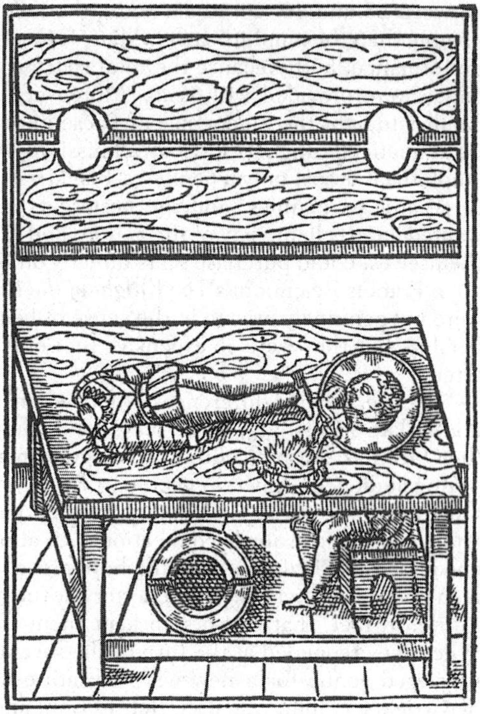

This staging device, called a "frame for the heading," might be used by an Elizabethan acting company to create the illusion of a beheading. An actor is concealed within the structure in such a way that only his head is visible through a hole, thus giving the impression of a head on a platter. Another actor lies in full view except that his head is concealed through another hole, giving the impression of a decapitated body. From Reginald Scot, *The Discoverie of Witchcraft* (1584).

Another effect of the lack of scenery was to minimize the importance of "unity of place," the classical dramatic convention that the action of a play be set in a single location. With important exceptions, many English Renaissance plays pay little heed to this rule and instead move freely and rapidly from location to location. The first part of *Tamburlaine* shifts its scene from Persia to Scythia, then to the vicinity of Constantinople, and finally to Egypt over a period of some years without interruption in the swift-moving action. *Edward II,* though confining its scene for the most part to England, moves from the royal court in London and Westminster to Gloucester, to Tynemouth on England's far northeast coast, to Yorkshire, to Bristol, and, at intervals, to Belgium and France; the audience is made aware of these locations by the dialogue. Often the verbal indication of location occurs at the start of a scene. "This is the marketplace; here let 'em stand," says an officer helpfully at the beginning of a scene set in a slave market in *The Jew of Malta* (2.3). Dialogue can similarly indicate time of day and weather conditions. In *Arden of Faversham*, the three killers Alice has hired to murder her husband approach his house while he sleeps:

> Black night hath hid the pleasures of the day,
> And sheeting darkness overhangs the earth
> And with the black fold of her cloudy robe
> Obscures us from the eyesight of the world.
> (5.1–4)

Shakebag, one of the killers, has to explain to the spectators that the scene is taking place after dark, since there is no way of changing the lighting.

Coexisting for much of the period with the big outdoor amphitheaters were smaller, indoor "private theaters"—Whitefriars, Blackfriars, the Phoenix. The first of these opened in 1575; in the early years, some acting companies also presented indoor performances at inns, though after 1595 this was no longer permitted. At between 25 and 40 feet in diameter, the indoor theaters were more expensive to operate than the amphitheaters. Many fewer spectators could be admitted to each performance, both because the total space was smaller and because all in attendance were provided with seats. Moreover, the acting company had to pay for candles to light the indoor space. These increased operating costs were reflected in dramatically higher costs of admission. Whereas the cheapest places in an amphitheater cost only a penny, at Blackfriars the cost of admission was between three and six pennies, and the best seats cost considerably more. Those who wanted an excellent view of the action, and at the same time hoped to be noticed themselves, could purchase seats directly on the stage, as the "several gentlemen" do in Francis Beaumont's *The Knight of the Burning Pestle*. The "private theaters" were not genuinely private in the sense of being open only to a preselected membership, but they were so expensive that only a wealthy clientele could afford to attend.

These economic differences produced, in turn, differences in repertory. In the mid-to-late 1580s, Lyly wrote plays for a company of boys who performed before the Queen. In advance of their court performances, they "rehearsed" the plays for paying audiences drawn in good part from the intellectual smart set: lawyers and law students at the Inns of Court, ambassadors and visitors from other countries, and persons with courtly connections. An atmosphere of sophistication tended to encourage satiric drama, and the boys proved especially adept at lampooning old men and witty servants. The repertory at the private theaters of the 1580s was so satiric, in fact, that censorship kept them closed for the decade of the 1590s. When they reopened at the turn of the seventeenth century, they soon became a privileged venue for a new wave of satiric drama, the specialty of such young playwrights as John Marston, Ben Jonson, and Thomas Middleton.

In the first decades of the seventeenth century, private theaters become an increasingly important performance venue for some of the best dramatists of the time. Plays written for private theaters include Beaumont's *The Knight of the Burning Pestle,* Jonson's *Epicene*, Massinger's *A New Way to Pay Old Debts,* Middleton and Rowley's *The Changeling,* and Ford's *'Tis Pity She's a Whore*. As these last two plays illustrate especially, the private theater could reveal a fascination with abnormal psychology and the grotesque. Perhaps the closed, candlelit space of the private theaters, which made it possible to darken the auditorium, was especially conducive to such explorations.

At first, just as they had been in Lyly's day, the reopened private theaters were associated with boys' companies. In 1609, however, the King's Men, the dominant company of the day, inaugurated a novel arrangement. During the wintertime, they performed in their indoor Blackfriars Theater, and during the summer season, they moved to the Globe, an outdoor amphitheater. This system had a number of advantages. The Blackfriars Theater permitted performances even in inclement weather, and it was located close to the law courts and to upscale neighborhoods with the kind of inhabitants who could pay for its expensive seats. In the summer, when the law courts were not in session and the King and his courtiers were on progress in the countryside, this select clientele largely left town, and the King's Men moved across the Thames to perform for the large, mixed audiences that attended the amphitheaters. The example of the King's Men was influential, combining for audiences the advantages of an intimate, socially exclusive venue with the experienced professionalism of an adult acting troupe. The boys' companies went into decline; the last of them was absorbed into an adult company in 1613. Thereafter, the acting companies associated with the private theaters, the Lady Elizabeth's Servants and Queen Anne's Men, for example, were comprised mainly of adults.

The increasing importance of the private theaters suggests that as the theatrical marketplace matured, it tended to diversify and specialize, so that different theater companies increasingly occupied different market niches and catered to rather different audience demographics. This theory is consistent with what historians describe as the gradual widening, in the early seventeenth century, of the cultural gap between elite and popular tastes. Still, it would be a mistake to stress too greatly the differences between public-theater plays and private-theater plays. A number of playwrights, including Jonson, Middleton, and Beaumont, wrote successfully for both public and private theaters. The King's Men performed much of the same repertory at their two theaters. Webster's *The Duchess of Malfi* and Jonson's *The Alchemist,* for instance, both of which were probably first performed in the private Blackfriars Theater, also received performances at the Globe amphitheater. Fletcher's and Shakespeare's plays were also popular in both venues. Courtly and bourgeois dramas drew on each other, and English drama was richer for the interchange.

Another, very significant change over the course of the period was in attitudes toward the printing of plays. As we have already mentioned, when an acting company commissioned and paid for a play, it owned the rights to it. Normally, printing plays, especially successful ones, was hardly in the company's interest, since by printing a play, the company would lose its exclusive control over the script. Many plays came into print only when they were considered too old to be revived successfully. Others were sold to the printers by theater companies in financial distress. When deaths from plague in the city of London got too high and the theaters were forced to close, theater companies saw their sources of revenue drastically reduced. They would sometimes resort to selling their play scripts in order to raise funds. In the course of the early seventeenth century, however, the reluctance to print plays eroded somewhat. Relatively more plays began to make their way into print, and the time lag between first performance and printing was no longer so great. As a result, the massive textual problems that attend a play like *Doctor Faustus* do not plague, for example, *A New Way to Pay Old Debts* or *'Tis Pity She's a Whore* to nearly the same extent.

The watershed event in the printing of plays was Jonson's unprecedented supervision of the publication of his works in an expensive folio (large-format) edition in 1616. While most playwrights measured their fame in terms of their contemporary reception, Jonson also wanted to maintain his reputation in the future, after his own death. An avid classical scholar, Jonson could see for himself how important printing had been in making available for Renaissance readers the works of such long-dead authors as Cicero, Horace, and Virgil. He bought back rights to some of his own works from the theater companies, carefully selecting those he wanted to represent him to posterity. The theater manager Philip Henslowe and others record many early and collaborative plays by "Benjamen Johnson" that do not appear in *The Works of Benjamin Jonson.* When Jonson did include an originally collaborative play, his tragedy *Sejanus,* he purged it of the other author's work and rewrote the missing sections anew in order to make the published version entirely his.

Jonson's project, though greeted with some ridicule, did spawn imitators. Shakespeare's colleagues Heminges and Condell published a folio edition of his works in 1623 and asked Jonson to write a prefatory poem. In 1640, after Jonson's death, his friend Sir Kenelm Digby oversaw the publication of a second folio edition of *The Works of Benjamin Jonson.* This volume reprinted earlier work and contained plays, poems, and masques that Jonson had written after about 1612, including *Bartholomew Fair.* In 1647, *The Works of Beaumont and Fletcher* was issued in folio, also posthumously.

One effect of these folio collections was to normalize what had been, for Jonson, a boldly polemical claim: that plays are the creations not primarily of acting

The title page from *The Works of Benjamin Jonson* (1616) shows the title surrounded by architectural motifs that underscore the monumental nature of a work destined for the ages. Jonson was ridiculed for his pretensions in publishing such a sumptuous volume; his writings were not "works," jeered his critics, but "plays."

companies but of playwrights. All four folios use authorship as their principle of selection—they collect works by Shakespeare, by Jonson, by Beaumont and Fletcher rather than by, say, date of performance, or genre, or acting troupe. There is no folio collection called *Greatest Plays of the 1620s* or *The King's Men's Biggest Hits.* In other words, while the theater companies' system of acquiring plays scanted the importance of authorship, folio publication, by contrast, amplified the prestige of the individual playwright. The folio volume, by collecting a playwright's works in a single volume, suggests that those works are best read in conjunction with one another and encourages our attention to the development of his maturing talent. As such—and this was also one of Jonson's hopes—the folio collections also tend to minimize the collaborative aspects of dramatic composition in the interests of suggesting a coherent authorial career. Even in the case of the Beaumont and Fletcher folio, where the facts of collaboration are inescapable, the collection obscures the fluidity and variability of the actual collaborative practice. In fact, Beaumont did not contribute anything to most of the plays in the folio, and the volume includes work by Massinger, Rowley, Nathan Field, and probably others as well.

Most printed plays never appeared in a folio volume. They appeared in single-play quarto (small-format) editions, which have proved more perishable in subsequent centuries than the expensive, carefully produced folios. Our necessary reliance on the surviving printed texts skews our sense of what was actually being performed in the English theaters of the period. Some plays were much more likely to be printed than others. Since the people who bought playbooks were those with disposable income—law students, courtiers, and the like—plays aimed at an elite audience had a better chance of making it into print than did the ones aimed at the low end of the market. And even these plays typically traveled a circuitous route to the printing house, so that by the time they were printed, the original author generally had nothing to do with approving or proofreading the text. In consequence, our sense of the oeuvres of many playwrights of the period is seriously incomplete. Kyd was a highly respected playwright in his own time, but only one surviving play, *The Spanish Tragedy,* is definitely his. Some of Middleton's plays were never printed and the attribution to him is doubtful in other cases, as it is, for instance, in *The Revenger's Tragedy.* Massinger, affiliated with the King's Men in the late 1620s and early 1630s, spent much of his career writing new scenes for the revivals of old plays. It is difficult, however, to retrieve this important aspect of his writing practice, since if the plays were printed at all, authorship was ascribed to the original playwright.

What remains available to the modern reader, then, is a set of remarkable texts that only begins to suggest the richness of the English Renaissance theatrical world. From the wealth of what has survived, the editors of this anthology have selected plays that are compelling as individual achievements and at the same time representative of the greatness of the English Renaissance, in its profound awareness both of human grandeur and of human limitation.

TIMELINE

AUTHORS AND TEXTS	CONTEXTS
1554 (?) Birth of John Lyly	
1557 (?) Birth of Thomas Kyd	
	1558 Accession of Queen Elizabeth I
1560 (?) Birth of Robert Greene	
1564 Births of William Shakespeare and Christopher Marlowe	
1570 (?) Birth of Thomas Middleton	
1572 (?) Birth of Thomas Dekker	
1573 (?) Birth of Ben Jonson	
1575 (?) Birth of John Marston	
	1576 James Burbage's playhouse, The Theater, built in London
	1577–80 Sir Francis Drake's circumnavigation of the globe
1579 Edmund Spenser, *The Shepherd's Calendar* • Lyly, *Euphues* • Thomas North's translation of Plutarch's *Lives* • Birth of John Fletcher	
1580 Lyly, *Euphues His England* • Birth of Thomas Middleton	
1580 (?) Birth of John Webster	
1580–83 Sir Philip Sidney writes *Arcadia*	
1583 Birth of Philip Massinger	
1584 Birth of Francis Beaumont	
1585 (?) Births of William Rowley and Elizabeth Tanfield, later, by marriage, Elizabeth Cary	
1585–87 (?) Kyd, ***The Spanish Tragedy***	
1586 Death of Sidney	
1586 (?) Birth of John Ford	
1587–88 Marlowe, ***Tamburlaine,* Part 1** and Part 2	**1587** Execution of Mary, Queen of Scots
1588 Lyly, ***Endymion***	**1588** The Spanish Armada
1588–89 Marlowe, ***Doctor Faustus***	
1588–92 (?) Anonymous, ***Arden of Faversham***	

Dates of plays record the first performance, as well as is known. Other works in prose and poetry are recorded by date of first publication unless otherwise indicated. Boldface titles indicate works in the anthology.

AUTHORS AND TEXTS	CONTEXTS
1589 (?) Greene, ***Friar Bacon and Friar Bungay***	
1589–90 Marlowe, ***The Jew of Malta***	
1590 Sidney, *The Defense of Poesie*	
1590–96 Spenser, *The Fairie Queene*	
1591–93 Marlowe, ***Edward II***	
1592 Death of Greene	
1592–94 Shakespeare, *Richard III*	
1593 Death of Marlowe	
1594–96 Shakespeare, *Romeo and Juliet*	
1595 (?) Shakespeare, *A Midsummer Night's Dream* • Death of Kyd	
1596–97 Shakespeare, *The Merchant of Venice*	
1596–98 Shakespeare, *1* and *2 Henry IV*	
1598 Jonson, *Every Man in His Humor* • George Chapman's translation of part of Homer's *Iliad*	
1599 Dekker, ***The Shoemaker's Holiday***	**1599** The Globe Theater opens
1599–1601 Shakespeare, *Hamlet*	
1600–1602 Shakespeare, *Twelfth Night*	
1602–4 Marston, ***The Malcontent***	
1603 Thomas Heywood, *A Woman Killed with Kindness* • John Florio's translation of Montaigne's *Essays*	**1603** Death of Queen Elizabeth; accession of James I
1603–4 Shakespeare, *Othello*	
1603–8 Elizabeth Cary writes ***The Tragedy of Mariam***	
1605–6 Shakespeare, *King Lear*	**1605** The Gunpowder Plot to blow up the Houses of Parliament
1606 Jonson, ***Volpone*** • Death of Lyly	
1606–7 Shakespeare, *Macbeth* and *Antony and Cleopatra* • Middleton (?), ***The Revenger's Tragedy***	
1607 Beaumont, ***The Knight of the Burning Pestle***	**1607** Founding of the Jamestown colony in Virginia
1609 Jonson, ***Epicene***	**1609** Galileo uses his telescope to observe Jupiter's moons circling that planet, thus providing evidence for the Copernican theory of a solar system
1610 Jonson, ***The Alchemist***	

AUTHORS AND TEXTS	CONTEXTS
1610–11 Beaumont and Fletcher, ***The Maid's Tragedy***	
1611 Middleton and Dekker, ***The Roaring Girl*** • Shakespeare, *The Tempest*	
1611 (?) Fletcher, ***The Woman's Prize***	
1612 Webster, ***The White Devil***	
1613 Middleton, ***A Chaste Maid in Cheapside***	
1613–14 Webster, ***The Duchess of Malfi***	
1614 Jonson, ***Bartholomew Fair***	
1616 Deaths of Shakespeare and Beaumont	
1620–24 (?) Middleton, ***Women Beware Women***	**1620** Arrival of the Pilgrims in the New World aboard the *Mayflower*
1622 Middleton and Rowley, ***The Changeling***	
	1623 Charles, Prince of Wales, and the Duke of Buckingham go to Spain to negotiate a marriage treaty with the Infanta
1625 Massinger, ***A New Way to Pay Old Debts*** • Death of Fletcher	**1625** Death of James I; accession of Charles I
1625 (?) Death of Webster	
1627 Death of Middleton	
1629–33 Ford, ***'Tis Pity She's a Whore***	**1629** Charles I dissolves Parliament
1632 (?) Death of Dekker	
	1633 Galileo forced by the Inquisition to recant the Copernican theory
1634 Death of Marston	
1637 Death of Jonson	
1638 (or afterward) Death of Ford	
1639 Death of Cary	
1640 Death of Massinger	
1642 (?) Death of Rowley	**1642** Closing of the theaters
	1649 Execution of Charles I

THE PLAYS

The Spanish Tragedy

To be known for only one play is not an ignoble fate when that play is *The Spanish Tragedy.*[1] Virtually no tragedy in this collection of plays is untouched by the tradition of the revenge play that Thomas Kyd initiated on the English stage. *The Spanish Tragedy,* written sometime in the late 1580s, was destined to become the grandfather of all revenge tragedies, including Shakespeare's *Hamlet, The Revenger's Tragedy,* probably by Thomas Middleton, and John Marston's *The Malcontent.* Other plays in the present collection, though not revenge plays in the fullest sense, contain pronounced indebtednesses to the revenge tradition: Elizabeth Cary's *The Tragedy of Mariam,* John Webster's *The White Devil* and *The Duchess of Malfi,* Thomas Middleton and William Rowley's *The Changeling,* and John Ford's *'Tis Pity She's a Whore.* Kyd's play was often quoted by his successors, sometimes in parody, but never without an awareness of its towering influence. Indeed, *The Spanish Tragedy* was so often revived that it was justly viewed as a classic of the London theater.

How did Kyd achieve such canonical success? His great idea was to adapt Seneca to the English popular stage. Lucius Annaeus Seneca (c. 4 B.C.E.–65 C.E.), Stoic philosopher and tutor to Nero, wrote at least nine closet tragedies—i.e., works written to be read, not acted—in imitation of the ancient Greek tragedians, including *Hercules Furens, Medea, Phaedra, Oedipus,* and *Thyestes.* Some are based directly on Aeschylus, Sophocles, and Euripides. They contain long, declamatory, highly rhetorical speeches and soliloquies; they banish violence from the stage, though telling stories of incest, parricide, and the devouring of one's own children; they moralize their tragic stories along philosophical lines; and they observe the classical unities of time, place, and action. Often taught in the Middle Ages, they strongly influenced neoclassical playwrights on the Continent, such as Robert Garnier, whom Kyd translated. In England, especially at the universities, they were widely known and imitated.

Kyd's genius is in bringing to rough-and-tumble life on the popular stage the major elements of the Senecan closet drama. Excitement, intrigue, betrayal, and above all violence pervade *The Spanish Tragedy.* Horatio, son of Hieronimo, Knight Marshal of Spain, is hanged and stabbed to death in an arbor by his enemies, in the presence of the young woman he loves, Bel-imperia (2.4). This gruesome death comes as the climax of a scene in which Horatio and Bel-imperia have declared their passion for one another using the metaphors of war—Mars and Venus in amorous combat, playfully defending themselves against the kisses they fire at one another. The final act of the play is a bloodbath; the stage is littered with the corpses of nearly all the major char-

Introduction, glosses, footnotes, and textual notes by David Bevington; text edited by David Bevington and checked by Eric Rasmussen.

1. Kyd was also responsible for *Cornelia* (1594), a translation of Robert Garnier's French neoclassical tragedy *Cornélie. Soliman and Perseda* (c. 1589–92) is often attributed to Kyd because of its plot resemblance to the play within the play in act 4 of *The Spanish Tragedy.* Kyd may also have done a lost translation of Garnier's *Porcie* (i.e., *Portia*) in 1594. Lost too is an early *Hamlet* (c. 1587–90) that is sometimes attributed to Kyd because of *The Spanish Tragedy*'s resemblances to Shakespeare's *Hamlet.* A fragmentary play called *The First Part of Hieronimo,* featuring many of the characters who appear in *The Spanish Tragedy,* appears to have been written after 1600 and thus cannot be the work of Kyd, who died in 1594.

acters as revenge takes its ominous toll. Gallows humor enlivens the scenes, in act 3, in which Pedringano, the disloyal servant of Bel-imperia, is misled into believing that he will be protected from the law for his part in butchering Horatio when in fact the villainous Lorenzo, who commissioned Pedringano to do the deed (and then to murder his partner in crime, Serberine), is fully resolved to let the law exact the full penalty. *The Spanish Tragedy* is suspenseful, action-packed, and theatrically shocking in a way that Seneca's closet plays could never hope to be.

Part of *The Spanish Tragedy*'s excitement and intrigue arises from the sense of mystery with which the play begins. This puzzlement is essential to our understanding of the tragic structure of the play, as it moves like detective fiction from identification of the crime to the means by which that crime is to be avenged. In a battle between Spain and Portugal, the Portuguese heir to the throne, Prince Balthazar, has been captured and a Spanish gentleman named Andrea has been slain. Andrea, the erstwhile lover of Bel-imperia, appears onstage as a ghost, chorically accompanied by the spirit of Revenge. These two chorus figures introduce the play and then witness the action as an onstage audience. They, and we as the audience, are curious to know the circumstances of Don Andrea's death.

At first, those circumstances appear to have been honorable, so much so that in the richly atmospheric prologue to the play (1.1), Andrea relates how honorably he has been welcomed into the classical underworld of Pluto and Proserpine (king and queen of the underworld) and has been adjudged worthy to dwell through eternity with those who have died nobly in battle. In the court of Spain as well, the first accounts of Andrea's death suggest that he fought bravely but was overcome by the superior might of Prince Balthazar (1.2.63–72). All seems decorous according to the highest standards of chivalric conduct. When, however, we and the onstage chorus are permitted to hear private conversations between Horatio and Bel-imperia and between her brother Lorenzo and the newly captured Balthazar (1.4ff.), a different and more disturbing picture begins to emerge. Horatio did indeed attempt to rescue Andrea as his friend, but it now appears that Andrea was not vanquished in a fair fight. Instead, he was ganged up on unfairly (1.4.9–26). Even more alarming, Balthazar and Lorenzo are in league, and for sinister reasons. Lorenzo and his father, Don Cyprian, have not

Illustration from the title page of the 1615 quarto of *The Spanish Tragedy* showing Horatio hanging in the arbor on the left; Hieronimo with a torch, center, discovering his dead son and preparing to cut him down (saying "Alas it is my son Horatio"); Bel-imperia saying "Murder, helpe Hieronimo"; and Lorenzo, on the right, saying "Stop her mouth" (see 2.4.62–63, 2.5.14).

been happy about Bel-imperia's liaison with Andrea, since they plan for her to marry Balthazar, a future head of state. The death of Andrea in battle begins to look like the result of a conspiracy to do him in, under cover of military action. When Bel-imperia responds to the death of her lover by defiantly turning to Andrea's best friend, Horatio, and inviting him to become her lover in Andrea's stead, Lorenzo's hostility toward Horatio is fully awakened.

Bel-imperia is an astonishing character for the English stage. She is not a wholesome English beauty, like Margaret in Robert Greene's *Friar Bacon and Friar Bungay,* or an innocent virgin, like Lavinia in Shakespeare's *Titus Andronicus;* she is sexually experienced, cool, self-assured. Is she in love with Horatio, or does she take up with him to flout the intent of the domineering men in her family? We cannot be sure, but we surely find her resolution both daunting and admirable. Her frosty put-downs of Balthazar's amorous advances are no less impressive than the calm and poise with which she thrusts and parries in her love conversation with Horatio (2.4.14–49). She is a woman to be reckoned with, ready and able to play her part in the play's revenge-filled denouement.

The shape of Kyd's tragic drama as it moves from exposition to plot complication and finally to denouement is motivated and controlled by the two chorus figures. This tragic form is expressed chiefly in terms of Don Andrea's awakening understanding, his growing frustration, and finally his satisfaction; it is a movement toward closure that we the audience share. Don Andrea, accompanied by Revenge, is increasingly dismayed by the turn of events that leads to the murder of Horatio. Thinking that he has been brought back to earth to see the rewards of justice, Andrea sees instead that his death was dishonorable; that his lover, Bel-imperia, is seemingly being forced on Balthazar by her villainous brother; and that his best friend, Horatio, is about to be murdered by Lorenzo and his henchmen. "Come we for this from depth of underground / To see him feast that gave me my death's wound?" he complains to Revenge (1.5.1–2). Why is Revenge not doing something about this? Revenge's answer is that Andrea must wait. Revenge will come, turning his enemies' "hope into despair, their peace to war, / Their joys to pain, their bliss to misery" (1.5.8–9). Revenge thus anticipates the play's violently tragic outcome, but only after a period of frustration and delay for those Revenge favors. Revenge thus gives the play its tragic structure—one that is visibly Senecan and neoclassical. It provides excitement for the audience accompanied by choric reassurance that all will turn out as Revenge wishes.

Nowhere is this structure of frustrated delay and eventual vindication more evident than in the saga of Hieronimo, Horatio's father and the play's chief avenger. He is, like Shakespeare's Hamlet, a man of moral probity charged with avenging the death of a near relative. Like Hamlet, he faces a canny and dangerous enemy; accordingly, he must use deceptive tactics and even the appearance of madness to throw off his adversary. The play within the play becomes a device of cunning to entrap his antagonist. Like Hamlet, Hieronimo must be sure of his grounds for proceeding as he does, since Lorenzo is clever at covering his tracks. The letter that Hieronimo finds, which Bel-imperia drops from her window during her house arrest, is just the kind of incriminating evidence that Hamlet obtains by staging *The Murder of Gonzago.* Uncertainties nonetheless persist as to the validity of that evidence and as to how the avenger is to pursue his objective. Both Hamlet and Hieronimo have to deal with the huge difficulty that they are aiming at a member of the royal family and thus cannot proceed through normal channels of legal indictment. Hieronimo, Knight Marshal of Spain and his country's chief legal officer, cannot obtain justice for himself, just as Hamlet, crown prince of Denmark, cannot bring his enemy into court.

Hieronimo is an immensely attractive character as he struggles to know what course he must follow and as he laments the inaccessibility of a legal remedy. His anguished cries (see, e.g., 3.7) invoke ideals of cosmic order in ways that anticipate the agony of Titus Andronicus or even of King Lear. He is surely "a man more sinned against than sinning." His loyal wife, Isabella, is another victim of their son's murder; the wrongs done to her cry out for redress. The enormity of Lorenzo's villainy invites us to side with the choric figures, Andrea and Revenge, in calling for some kind of justice. Yet as the play moves toward its violent denouement, we begin to question our endorsement of what it is that Hieronimo seemingly must do. Yes, he has no other means of achieving his end, yet as he proceeds he becomes a person of cunning and violence. The deaths at the end of *The Spanish Tragedy* are garish and wanton, claiming not only the villainous Lorenzo and the morally compromised Balthazar but Hieronimo, Bel-imperia, and Don Cyprian, the Duke of Castile, who has done his best to uncover and discourage his son Lorenzo's villainies. What is more, the peace between Spain and Portugal, which seemed so near at hand, is sacrificed to the ends of revenge. Thus the King of Spain grieves for the end of "My brother and the whole succeeding hope / That Spain expected after my decease!" (4.4.204–5).

The figures most happy with this wholesale slaughter are the chorus of Andrea and Revenge. Andrea, frustrated for so long by the seeming misdirection of the justice he seeks, becomes at last maniacally hungry for carnage and is not disappointed. His enemies are to be haled "down to deepest hell, / Where none but Furies, bugs, and tortures dwell" (4.5.27–28). The play ends as Andrea, able now to exact total revenge, dooms even the relatively well-meaning Don Cyprian to endless torment, along with Lorenzo, Balthazar, Pedringano, and Serberine. The revenge ethic, with its demand of violence in repayment for violence, dominates the structure and conclusion of this play to the exclusion of any softer virtues, including the love of true justice to which Hieronimo had earlier clung. The ending of *The Spanish Tragedy* is genuinely savage; its uncompromising commitment to revenge has swept away everything before it. This is one source of what makes the play so remarkably powerful and also disturbing. (Shakespeare, virtually alone among writers of revenge tragedy, was to seek in *Hamlet* a dramatic resolution that would allow the revenger in his final moments onstage to be something less disturbing than a cold-blooded killer.)

The Spanish Tragedy's ultimate commitment to the revenge ethic is highlighted by the contrasting ethic of the play's secondary plot. Sequestered in alternating scenes, this plot relates the nearly tragic fortunes of a Portuguese nobleman named Alexandro, who is wrongly accused by the self-serving Villuppo of having covertly slain Prince Balthazar in the Spanish-Portuguese battle with which the play begins. We as the audience know this accusation to be a lie, since Balthazar is in fact alive as a royal prisoner at the Spanish court. The Portuguese king has no way of knowing this, however, and he is accordingly disposed to believe the worst. He puts Alexandro under arrest and orders a hasty execution that is barely averted by the arrival of the news that Balthazar is actually alive and well. The Portuguese king then orders the execution of Villuppo, who confesses that he did what he did out of envy and desire for advantage at the court.

The subplot offers itself to a number of interpretive readings, among which is an object lesson to kings not to believe too readily accusations tossed up by possibly envious courtiers. More substantively, the subplot demonstrates justice finding its way to a happy resolution in accord with the dictates of an ethic that is visibly moral. Truth is ultimately discovered, even if at the last moment. Virtue is rewarded and vice is punished. In the context of the play as a whole, this comforting saga of providential certitude serves mainly as a foil to offset the wantonness of vengeful destruction in the main plot. The ethical conflict between the two plots of *The Spanish Tragedy*, however, is left unresolved—another source of dramatic energy in this amazing play.

The Spanish Tragedy was much noted in its time for its fine rhetorical displays. Composed in the prevailing Senecan and florid style of the late 1580s, these stylistic traits came eventually to be laughed at, but were also much imitated, not least by Shakespeare in *Richard III*. One tour de force that Shakespeare may have studied in Kyd's play is Balthazar's response to his friend Lorenzo, who urges Balthazar to be attentive to Bel-imperia in winning her away from Horatio, to be violent if necessary, and to be ready to bribe her with gold when all else fails. "How likes Prince Balthazar this stratagem?" Lorenzo asks (2.1.110). And Balthazar replies:

> Both well and ill. It makes me glad and sad:
> Glad, that I know the hinderer of my love,
> Sad, that I fear she hates me whom I love;
> Glad, that I know on whom to be revenged,
> Sad, that she'll fly me if I take revenge.
> Yet must I take revenge or die myself,
> For love resisted grows impatient.
> I think Horatio be my destined plague!
> First in his hand he brandishèd a sword,
> And with that sword he fiercely wagèd war,
> And in that war he gave me dangerous wounds,
> And by those wounds he forcèd me to yield,
> And by my yielding I became his slave.
> Now in his mouth he carries pleasing words,
> Which pleasing words do harbor sweet conceits,
> Which sweet conceits are limed with sly deceits,
> Which sly deceits smooth Bel-imperia's ears.
> (2.1.111–27)

The passage continues in its highly contrived bringing-together of so many of the rhetorical conceits that the ambitious writers of this era learned in order to practice their skills: anaphora (beginning a series of lines with the same word), antithesis (as in the balanced alternation between "Sad" and "Glad"), parison (the symmetrical repetition of words and phrases in grammatically parallel phrases, as in "Glad, that I know" and "Sad, that I fear"), isocolon (the symmetrical repetition of sounds and words in phrases of equal length), ladder or climax (in which the passage repeatedly mounts, for example, from "sword" to "war" to "wounds" to "yield" and "yielding," and then from "mouth" to "words" to "conceits" to "deceits"), and still more. The effect is pyrotechnic and easily abused, but it breathes a new sense of power into the English language to create a literature capable of rivaling that of the ancient classical world.

THOMAS KYD
The Spanish Tragedy

[The Persons in the Play

The ghost of Don° ANDREA } figures in the frame — *Spanish noble title*
REVENGE } figures in the frame

The KING of Spain
Don Cyprian, Duke of CASTILE, the King's brother
Don LORENZO, the Duke's son and Bel-imperia's brother
BEL-IMPERIA, the Duke's daughter and Lorenzo's sister
GENERAL of the Spanish army

The VICEROY of Portugal
Prince BALTHAZAR, his son
Don PEDRO, the Viceroy's brother
ALEXANDRO } Portuguese noblemen
VILLUPPO } Portuguese noblemen
AMBASSADOR of Portugal to the court of Spain

Don HIERONIMO, Knight Marshal° of Spain — *(see 1.1.25 n)*
ISABELLA, his wife
Don HORATIO, their son

PEDRINGANO, servant to Bel-imperia
SERBERINE, servant to Balthazar
CHRISTOPHIL, servant to Lorenzo
Don BAZULTO, an old man
PAGE ("boy") to Lorenzo
Three WATCHMEN
A MESSENGER
A DEPUTY
A HANGMAN
A MAID to Isabella
Two PORTUGUESE (Portingales)
A SERVANT to Hieronimo
Three CITIZENS
Two NOBLEMEN of Portugal

The 1592 title page reads "*The Spanish Tragedy.* Containing the lamentable end of Don Horatio and Bel-imperia, with the pitiful death of old Hieronimo. Newly corrected and amended of such gross faults as passed in the first impression. At London: Printed by Edward Allde for Edward White."

Soldiers of the Spanish army, officers, trumpeters,
attendants, halberdiers° — *soldiers with pikes*
Three knights, three kings, and a drummer in the first
dumb show
Hymen and two torchbearers in the second dumb show

In Hieronimo's play:
Soliman, Sultan of Turkey (played by Balthazar)
Erasto ("Erastus"), Knight of Rhodes (played by Lorenzo)
Bashaw (played by Hieronimo)
Perseda (played by Bel-imperia)

THE SCENE: The courts of Spain and Portugal.]

1.1

Enter the ghost of Andrea, and with him Revenge.

ANDREA When this eternal substance of my soul
Did live imprisoned in my wanton° flesh, — *sinful, licentious*
Each in their function serving other's need,
I was a courtier in the Spanish court.
My name was Don Andrea; my descent,
Though not ignoble, yet inferior far
To gracious fortunes of my tender youth.[1]
For there, in prime and pride° of all my years, — *springtime; lust*
By duteous service° and deserving love — *as "servant" to a woman*
In secret I possessed a worthy dame
Which hight° sweet Bel-imperia by name. — *Who was called*
But in the harvest of my summer joys
Death's winter nipped the blossoms of my bliss,
Forcing divorce° betwixt my love and me. — *separation*
For in the late° conflict with Portingale° — *recent / Portugal*
My valor drew me into danger's mouth,
Till life to death made passage through my wounds.[2]
When I was slain, my soul descended straight° — *immediately*
To pass the flowing stream of Acheron;° — *a river of the underworld*
But churlish Charon,[3] only boatman there,
Said that my rites of burial not° performed, — *not having been*
I might not sit amongst his passengers.
Ere Sol had slept three nights in Thetis' lap,[4]
And slaked his smoking° chariot in her flood,° — *fiery / ocean*
By Don Horatio, our knight marshal's[5] son,
My funerals and obsequies° were done. — *burial rites*
Then was the ferryman of hell content
To pass me over to the slimy strand° — *shore*
That leads to fell° Avernus'[6] ugly waves. — *fierce, terrible*

1.1. The opening chorus.
1. I.e., To my great good fortune as a young man (in being the lover of the highborn Bel-imperia).
2. At death, the soul was thought to leave the body by the mouth or through wounds.
3. Ferryman for the souls of the dead across the river Styx to the underworld.
4. I.e., Before the sun had set three times into the sea in the west, marking the passage of three days. (Thetis is a sea nymph with whom the god of the sun is imagined to be sleeping.)
5. A knight marshal was both a military officer and magistrate belonging to the royal household and acting for the Crown.
6. A lake near the cave through which Aeneas descended to the underworld (Virgil, *Aeneid*, Book 6).

There pleasing° Cerberus[7] with honeyed speech, *when I had pleased*
I passed the perils of the foremost porch.
Not far from hence, amidst ten thousand souls,
Sat Minos, Aeacus, and Rhadamanth,[8]
To whom no sooner 'gan I make approach
To crave a passport for my wandr'ing ghost,
But Minos, in graven leaves of lottery,
Drew forth the manner of my life and death.[9]
"This knight," quoth he, "both lived and died in love,
And for his love tried fortune of the wars,
And by war's fortune lost both love and life."
"Why, then," said Aeacus, "convey him hence
To walk with lovers in our fields of love,
And spend the course of everlasting time
Under green myrtle trees and cypress shades."
"No, no," said Rhadamanth, "it were not well° *would not be right*
With loving souls to place a martialist;° *warrior*
He died in war, and must to martial fields,
Where wounded Hector lives in lasting pain,
And Achilles' Myrmidons do scour° the plain."[1] *range across*
Then Minos, mildest censor° of the three, *judge*
Made this device to end the difference:
"Send him," quoth he, "to our infernal king,° *king of the underworld*
To doom° him as best seems His Majesty." *sentence*
To this effect my passport straight was drawn.
In keeping on my way to Pluto's° court, *King of Hades*
Through dreadful shades of ever-glooming night,
I saw more sights than thousand tongues can tell,
Or pens can write, or mortal hearts can think.
Three ways there were. That on the right-hand side
Was ready way unto the foresaid fields
Where lovers live, and bloody martialists,
But either sort contained within his° bounds. *its*
The left-hand path, declining fearfully,
Was ready downfall° to the deepest hell, *a sudden descent*
Where bloody Furies° shakes their whips of steel, *avenging primeval deities*
And poor Ixion turns an endless wheel;[2]
Where usurers are choked with melting gold,
And wantons° are embraced with ugly snakes, *lechers*
And murderers groan with never-killing wounds,
And perjured wights° scalded in boiling lead, *persons*
And all foul sins with torments overwhelmed.
'Twixt these two ways, I trod the middle path,
Which brought me to the fair Elysian green,° *abode of the blessed*
In midst whereof there stands a stately tower,
The walls of brass, the gates of adamant.° *diamond*
Here finding Pluto with his Proserpine,° *Queen of Hades*
I showed my passport, humbled on my knee,

7. The many-headed dog guarding the gate to Hades.
8. Judges of the underworld, who assigned to the dead their proper places in the underworld. Rhadamanth's full name is Rhadamanthus.
9. Minos drew forth from an urn the manner of my fate engraved on a lottery slip.
1. Achilles' followers, known as Myrmidons because Zeus had created them out of ants (*murmekes* in Greek), assisted him in killing the Trojan Hector and desecrating his body in vengeance for the death of his beloved friend Patroclus (Homer, *Iliad*, Book 22).
2. For attempting to win the love of Hera, Ixion was punished in Hades by being perpetually bound to a turning wheel.

Whereat fair Proserpine began to smile,
And begged that only she might give my doom.° *sentence*
Pluto was pleased and sealed it with a kiss.
Forthwith, Revenge, she rounded° thee in th'ear, *whispered to*
And bade thee lead me through the gates of horn,
Where dreams have passage in the silent night.[3]
No sooner had she spoke but we were here—
I wot° not how—in twinkling of an eye. *know*
REVENGE Then know, Andrea, that thou art arrived
Where thou shalt see the author of thy death,
Don Balthazar, the Prince of Portingale,
Deprived of life by Bel-imperia.
Here sit we down to see the mystery,° *secret truth; play*
And serve for chorus in this tragedy.
[*They sit and watch the play.*]

[1.2]

Enter Spanish king, General, Castile, [*and*] *Hieronimo.*

KING Now say, Lord General, how fares our camp?° *army*
GENERAL All well, my sovereign liege, except some few
That are deceased by fortune of the war.
KING But what portends thy cheerful countenance,
And posting° to our presence thus in haste? *hastening*
Speak, man, hath fortune given us victory?
GENERAL Victory, my liege, and that with little loss.
KING Our Portingals° will pay us tribute, then? *Portuguese prisoners*
GENERAL Tribute and wonted° homage therewithal. *customary*
KING Then blest be heaven, and guider of the heavens,
From whose fair influence° such justice flows! *celestial emanations*
CASTILE *O multum dilecte Deo, tibi militat aether,*
Et conjuratae curvato poplite gentes
Succumbunt; recti soror est victoria juris.[1]
KING Thanks to my loving brother of Castile.
But, General, unfold in brief discourse
Your form of battle and your war's success,
That, adding all the pleasure of thy news
Unto the height of former happiness,
With deeper wage° and greater dignity *greater reward*
We may reward thy blissful chivalry.° *happy might in arms*
GENERAL Where Spain and Portingale do jointly knit
Their frontiers, leaning on each other's bound,° *boundaries*
There met our armies in their proud array,
Both furnished well, both full of hope and fear,
Both menacing alike with daring shows,
Both vaunting sundry colors of device,° *heraldic displays*
Both cheerly sounding trumpets, drums, and fifes,
Both raising dreadful clamors to the sky,
That° valleys, hills, and rivers made rebound, *So that*
And heaven itself was frighted with the sound.

3. At the end of Aeneas' visit to the underworld in Book 6 of the *Aeneid*, the hero encounters twin gates of sleep, of horn and of ivory. From the first, true dreams and visions emerge; from the second, false dreams.

1.2. The court of Spain.
1. O man much loved of God, for you the heavens fight, and the conspiring peoples fall on bended knee; victory is the sister of just right. (Claudian, c. 400 C.E.)

Our battles both were pitched in squadron form,
Each corner strongly fenced with wings of shot.[2]
But ere we joined and came to push of pike,° *close-order combat*
I brought a squadron of our readiest shot
From out our rearward to begin the fight;
They° brought another wing to encounter us. *(The Portuguese)*
Meanwhile our ordnance played° on either side, *volleyed*
And captains strove to have their valors tried.° *tested*
Don Pedro, their chief horsemen's colonel,
Did with his cornet° bravely make attempt *cavalry company*
To break the order of our battle ranks.
But Don Rogero, worthy man of war,
Marched forth against him with our musketeers,
And stopped the malice of his fell° approach. *fierce*
While they maintain hot skirmish to and fro,
Both battles° join and fall to handy° blows, *armies / hand-to-hand*
Their violent shot resembling th'ocean's rage,
When, roaring loud and with a swelling tide,
It beats upon the rampiers° of huge rocks, *ramparts*
And gapes to swallow neighbor-bounding° lands. *sea-bordering*
Now while Bellona° rageth here and there, *goddess of war*
Thick storms of bullets rain like winter's hail,
And shivered lances dark° the troubled air. *darken*
Pede pes et cuspide cuspis;
Arma sonant armis, vir petiturque viro.[3]
On every side drop captains to the ground,
And soldiers, some ill maimed,° some slain outright; *seriously wounded*
Here falls a body scindered° from his head, *sundered*
There legs and arms lie bleeding on the grass,
Mingled with weapons and unboweled steeds,
That scattering overspread the purple° plain. *bloodred*
In all this turmoil, three long hours and more,
The victory to neither part inclined,
Till Don Andrea with his brave lanciers° *cavalry with lances*
In their° main battle° made so great a breach *(the Portuguese's) / army*
That, half dismayed, the multitude retired;
But Balthazar, the Portingales' young prince,
Brought rescue and encouraged them to stay.° *stand firm*
Herehence° the fight was eagerly renewed, *Accordingly*
And in that conflict was Andrea slain—
Brave man-at-arms, but weak to° Balthazar. *compared with*
Yet while the Prince, insulting° over him, *exulting, vaunting*
Breathed out proud vaunts, sounding to° our reproach, *expressing, intimating*
Friendship and hardy valor, joined in one,
Pricked° forth Horatio, our knight marshal's son, *Spurred*
To challenge forth that prince in single fight.
Not long between these twain the fight endured,
But straight the Prince was beaten from his horse
And forced to yield him° prisoner to his foe. *himself*
When he was taken, all the rest they fled,

2. Both our armies were deployed in a square formation, each corner flanked by armed troops.
3. Foot against foot and lance against lance; arms clash with arms, and man is assailed by man. (No single source is known, though the sentiment is commonplace.)

And our carbines° pursued them to the death, *armed soldiers*
Till, Phoebus° waning to the western deep,° *the sun / ocean*
Our trumpeters were charged to sound retreat.° *withdrawal from battle*
KING Thanks, good Lord General, for these good news,
And, for some argument° of more to come, *token, sign*
Take this and wear it for thy sovereign's sake.
Give him his chain.
But tell me now, hast thou confirmed a peace?
GENERAL No peace, my liege, but° peace conditional, *except*
That if with homage tribute be well paid
The fury of your forces will be stayed;° *restrained*
And to this peace their viceroy hath subscribed,
Give the King a paper.
And made a solemn vow that during life
His tribute shall be truly paid to Spain.
KING These words, these deeds become thy person well.—
But now, Knight Marshal, frolic° with thy king, *celebrate*
For 'tis thy son that wins this battle's prize.
HIERONIMO Long may he live to serve my sovereign liege,
And soon decay° unless he serve my liege! *decline in fortune*
A tucket° afar off. *trumpet flourish*
KING Nor° thou nor he shall die without reward. *Neither*
What means the warning° of this trumpet's sound? *giving notice*
GENERAL This tells me that Your Grace's men of war—
Such as war's fortune hath reserved° from death— *preserved*
Come marching on towards your royal seat
To show themselves before Your Majesty,
For so I gave in charge° at my depart;° *ordered / departure*
Whereby by demonstration shall appear,
That all (except three hundred or few more)
Are safe returned and by their foes enriched.° *(with ransom fees)*

The army enters; Balthazar, between Lorenzo and Horatio, captive.

KING A gladsome sight! I long to see them here.

They enter and pass by.

Was that the warlike prince of Portingale
That by our nephew was in triumph led?
GENERAL It was, my liege, the Prince of Portingale.
KING But what was he that on the other side
Held him by th'arm as partner of the prize?
HIERONIMO That was my son, my gracious sovereign,
Of whom, though from his tender infancy
My loving thoughts did never hope but well,
He never pleased his father's eyes till now,
Nor filled my heart with overcloying° joys. *surfeiting, overabundant*
KING Go let them march once more about these walls,
That, staying° them, we may confer and talk *stopping*
With our brave prisoner and his double guard.—
Hieronimo, it greatly pleaseth us
That in our victory thou have a share,
By virtue of thy worthy son's exploit.

Enter [the army] again.

Bring hither the young prince of Portingale.
The rest march on; but ere they be dismissed,
We will bestow on every soldier
Two ducats,° and on every leader ten, *gold coins*
That they may know our largesse° welcomes them. *bountifulness*

Exeunt all [the army] but Balthazar, Lorenzo, [and] Horatio. [The King, Castile, and the General remain onstage.]

Welcome, Don Balthazar! Welcome, nephew!
And thou, Horatio, thou art welcome too.
Young prince, although thy father's hard misdeeds,
In keeping back the tribute that he owes,
Deserve but evil measure at our hands,
Yet shalt thou know that Spain is honorable.

BALTHAZAR The trespass that my father made in peace
Is now controlled° by fortune of the wars, *checked, canceled*
And, cards once dealt, it boots not° ask why so. *does no good to*
His men are slain—a weakening to his realm;
His colors° seized—a blot unto his name; *military ensigns*
His son distressed—a corsive° to his heart: *corrosive*
These punishments may clear° his late offense. *atone for*

KING Ay, Balthazar, if he observe this truce
Our peace will grow the stronger for these wars.
Meanwhile live thou, though not in liberty,
Yet free from bearing any servile yoke,
For in our hearing thy deserts were great,
And in our sight thyself art gracious.

BALTHAZAR And I shall study° to deserve this grace. *strive*

KING But tell me—for their holding° makes me doubt— *the way they hold you*
To which of these twain art thou prisoner.

LORENZO To me, my liege.

HORATIO To me, my sovereign.

LORENZO This hand first took his courser° by the reins. *stallion*

HORATIO But first my lance did put him from his horse.

LORENZO I seized his weapon and enjoyed° it first. *possessed*

HORATIO But first I forced him lay his weapons down.

KING Let go his arm, upon our privilege.° *Let him go.* *royal prerogative*
Say, worthy Prince, to whether° didst thou yield? *which of the two*

BALTHAZAR To him° in courtesy, to this° perforce. *(Lorenzo) / (Horatio)*
He spake me fair,° this other gave me strokes; *Lorenzo spoke gently*
He promised life, this other threatened death;
He wan° my love, this other conquered me; *won*
And truth to say I yield myself to both.

HIERONIMO But that° I know Your Grace for° just and wise, *Were it not that / to be*
And° might seem partial in this difference,° *And that I / dispute*
Enforced by nature° and by law of arms, *blood ties*
My tongue should plead for young Horatio's right.
He hunted well that was a lion's death,
Not he that in a garment wore his skin;[4]
So hares may pull dead lions by the beard.

4. I.e., The real hero is the man who has actually killed a lion, not the one who (like the ass in Aesopian fable) has made a garment of a lion's skin as hollow proof of his prowess.

KING Content thee, Marshal, thou shalt have no wrong,
And for thy sake thy son shall want° no right.— *lack*
Will both abide the censure of my doom?° *my judgment*
LORENZO I crave no better than Your Grace awards.
HORATIO Nor I, although I sit beside my right.[5]
KING Then by my judgment thus your strife shall end:
You both deserve and both shall have reward.
Nephew, thou took'st his weapon and his horse;
His weapons and his horse are thy reward.
Horatio, thou didst force him first to yield;
His ransom therefore is thy valor's fee.
Appoint the sum as you shall both agree.
But, nephew, thou shalt have the Prince in guard,° *custody*
For thine estate° best fitteth such a guest; *social rank*
Horatio's house were small for all his train.° *retinue*
Yet in regard thy substance° passeth his, *because your wealth*
And that just guerdon may befall desert,[6]
To him° we yield the armor of the Prince. *(Horatio)*
How likes Don Balthazar of this device?
BALTHAZAR Right well, my liege, if this proviso were,
That Don Horatio bear us company,
Whom I admire and love for chivalry.
KING Horatio, leave him not that loves thee so.
Now let us hence to see our soldiers paid,
And feast our prisoner as our friendly guest. *Exeunt.*

[1.3]

Enter Viceroy, Alexandro, Villuppo [*and attendants*].

VICEROY Is our ambassador dispatched for Spain?
ALEXANDRO Two days, my liege, are passed since his depart.
VICEROY And tribute payment gone along with him?
ALEXANDRO Ay, my good lord.
VICEROY Then rest we here awhile in our unrest,
And feed our sorrows with some inward sighs,
For deepest cares break never into tears.
But wherefore sit I in a regal throne?
This better fits a wretch's endless moan.
Falls to the ground.
Yet this is higher than my fortunes reach,[1]
And therefore better than my state° deserves. *state of affairs*
Ay, ay, this earth, image of melancholy,[2]
Seeks him whom fates adjudge to misery.
Here let me lie, now am I at the lowest.
Qui jacet in terra non habet unde cadat.
In me consumpsit vires fortuna nocendo,
Nil superest ut iam possit obesse magis.[3]

5. Nor I, even if I were to lose what is rightfully mine.
6. And in order that merit may be justly rewarded.
1.3. The Portuguese court.
1. Yet even being thus low cannot fully indicate how miserable are my fortunes.
2. In the theory of the four bodily humors—blood (hot and moist, like air), choler (hot and dry, like fire), phlegm (cold and moist, like water), and black bile or melancholy (cold and dry, like earth)—the earth is associated with melancholy.
3. He who lies on the ground can fall no farther. In me, Fortune has exhausted her power of hurting; nothing remains that can harm me anymore. (Kyd's own medley of sentiments taken out of Seneca and other classical writers.)

Yes, Fortune may bereave me of my crown.
Here, take it now! Let Fortune do her worst.
[*He takes off his crown.*]
She will not rob me of this sable weed;° *black mourning garment*
Oh, no, she envies° none but pleasant things. *feels ill will toward*
Such is the folly of despiteful° chance! *spiteful*
Fortune is blind and sees not my deserts;
So is she deaf and hears not my laments;
And could she hear, yet is she willful mad,
And therefore will not pity my distress.
Suppose that she could pity me, what then?
What help can be expected at her hands,
Whose foot is standing on a rolling stone,
And mind more mutable than fickle winds?
Why wail I, then, where's hope of no redress?
Oh, yes, complaining makes my grief seem less.
My late ambition hath distained my faith;[4]
My breach of faith occasioned bloody wars;
Those bloody wars have spent my treasure,
And with my treasure my people's blood,
And with their blood, my joy and best beloved,
My best beloved, my sweet and only son.
Oh, wherefore went I not to war myself?
The cause was mine; I might have died for both.° *(myself and my son)*
My years were mellow, his but young and green;
My death were° natural, but his was forced. *would have been*

ALEXANDRO No° doubt, my liege, but° still the Prince survives. *There's no / but that*

VICEROY Survives? Ay, where?

ALEXANDRO In Spain, a prisoner by mischance of war.

VICEROY Then they have slain him for his father's fault.

ALEXANDRO That were a breach to common law of arms.

VICEROY They reck° no laws that° meditate revenge. *heed / they who*

ALEXANDRO His ransom's worth will stay° from foul revenge. *preserve (him)*

VICEROY No, if he lived the news would soon be here.

ALEXANDRO Nay, evil news fly faster still° than good. *always*

VICEROY Tell me no more of news, for he is dead.

VILLUPPO [*kneeling*] My sovereign, pardon the author of ill news,
And I'll bewray° the fortune of thy son. *reveal*

VICEROY Speak on; I'll guerdon° thee whate'er it be. *reward*
Mine ear is ready to receive ill news,
My heart grown hard 'gainst mischief's battery.° *assault*
Stand up, I say, and tell thy tale at large.° *at length*

VILLUPPO [*standing*] Then hear that truth which these mine eyes have seen.
When both the armies were in battle joined,
Don Balthazar, amidst the thickest troops,
To win renown did wondrous feats of arms.
Amongst the rest I saw him hand to hand
In single fight with their lord general;
Till Alexandro, that here counterfeits
Under the color° of a duteous friend, *pretext*

4. My recent ambition (to conquer Spain) has sullied and stained my faith and honor.

Discharged his pistol at the Prince's back,
As though he would have slain their general;
But therewithal Don Balthazar fell down,
And when he fell then we began to fly;
But had he lived the day had sure been ours.
ALEXANDRO Oh, wicked forgery!° O traitorous miscreant! — *falsehood, invention*
VICEROY Hold thou thy peace!—But now, Villuppo, say,
Where then became° the carcass of my son? — *What then became of*
VILLUPPO I saw them drag it to the Spanish tents.
VICEROY Ay, ay, my nightly dreams have told me this.—
Thou false, unkind,° unthankful traitorous beast, — *unnatural*
Wherein had Balthazar offended thee,
That thou shouldst thus betray him to our foes?
Was't Spanish gold that bleared° so thine eyes — *dazzled*
That thou couldst see no part of our deserts?
Perchance because thou art Terceira's° lord, — *an island in the Azores*
Thou hadst some hope to wear this diadem
If first my son and then myself were slain;
But thy ambitious thought shall break thy neck.
Ay, this was it that made thee spill his blood,
Take the crown and put it on again.
But I'll now wear it till thy blood be spilt.
ALEXANDRO Vouchsafe, dread sovereign, to hear me speak.
VICEROY Away with him! His sight is second hell.
Keep him till we determine of his death.
[*Exeunt attendants, guarding Alexandro.*]
If Balthazar be dead, he° shall not live. — *(Alexandro)*
Villuppo, follow us for thy reward. *Exit Viceroy.*
VILLUPPO Thus have I with an envious forgèd° tale — *malicious fabricated*
Deceived the King, betrayed mine enemy,
And hope for guerdon of my villainy. *Exit.*

[1.4]

Enter Horatio and Bel-imperia.

BEL-IMPERIA Signor Horatio, this is the place and hour
Wherein I must entreat thee to relate
The circumstance of Don Andrea's death,
Who, living, was my garland's sweetest flower,
And in his death hath buried my delights.
HORATIO For love of him and service to yourself,
I nill° refuse this heavy, doleful charge. — *will not*
Yet tears and sighs, I fear, will hinder me.
When both our armies were enjoined° in fight, — *joined*
Your worthy chevalier amidst the thick'st,
For glorious cause still aiming at the fairest,[1]
Was at the last by young Don Balthazar
Encountered hand to hand. Their fight was long,
Their hearts were great, their clamors menacing,
Their strength alike, their strokes both dangerous.
But wrathful Nemesis,° that wicked power, — *goddess of retribution*

1.4. The court of Spain.
1. Striving continually to excel in the glorious cause and thus to be worthy of your beauty.

Envying at Andrea's praise and worth,
Cut short his life to end his praise and worth.
She, she herself, disguised in armor's mask
(As Pallas was before proud Pergamus),[2]
Brought in a fresh supply of halberdiers,° *soldiers with pikes*
Which paunched° his horse and dinged° him to the ground. *stabbed / hurled*
Then young Don Balthazar, with ruthless° rage, *pitiless*
Taking advantage of his foe's distress,
Did finish what his halberdiers begun,
And left° not till Andrea's life was done. *ceased*
Then, though too late, incensed with just remorse,° *indignation; pity*
I with my band set forth against the Prince,
And brought him prisoner from his halberdiers.

BEL-IMPERIA Would thou hadst slain him that so slew my love!
But then was Don Andrea's carcass lost?

HORATIO No, that was it for which I chiefly strove,
Nor stepped I back till I recovered him.
I took him up and wound him in mine arms,
And, wielding° him unto my private tent, *carrying*
There laid him down and dewed him with my tears,
And sighed and sorrowed as became a friend.
But neither friendly sorrow, sighs, nor tears
Could win pale Death from his° usurpèd right. *(Death's)*
Yet this I did, and less I could not do:
I saw him honored with due funeral.
This scarf I plucked from off his lifeless arm,
And wear it in remembrance of my friend.

BEL-IMPERIA I know the scarf; would he had kept it still!
For had he lived he would have kept it still,
And worn it for his Bel-imperia's sake,
For 'twas my favor° at his last depart. *love token*
But now wear thou it both for him and me,
For after him thou hast deserved it best.
But, for thy kindness in his life and death,
Be sure, while Bel-imperia's life endures,
She will be Don Horatio's thankful friend.

HORATIO And, madam, Don Horatio will not slack° *fail in duty; be slow*
Humbly to serve fair Bel-imperia.
But now if your good liking stand thereto,° *if you approve*
I'll crave your pardon to go seek the Prince,
For so the Duke your father gave me charge. *Exit.*

BEL-IMPERIA Ay, go, Horatio, leave me here alone,
For solitude best fits my cheerless mood.
Yet what avails to wail Andrea's death,
From whence Horatio proves my second love?
Had he not loved Andrea as he did,
He could not sit in Bel-imperia's thoughts.
But how can love find harbor in my breast
Till I revenge the death of my beloved?
Yes, second love shall further my revenge.
I'll love Horatio, my Andrea's friend,

2. Homer's *Iliad* describes Pallas Athene appearing armed, taking the Greek side against the Trojans. Pergamus, or Pergamum, a hill fortress in the northwest of Asia Minor, is a poetic name for Troy.

The more to spite the Prince that wrought his end;
And where Don Balthazar, that slew my love,
Himself now pleads for favor at my hands,
He shall, in rigor of my just disdain,
Reap long repentance for his murderous deed.
For what was't else but murderous cowardice,
So many to oppress one valiant knight
Without respect of honor in the fight?
And here he comes that murdered my delight.

Enter Lorenzo and Balthazar.

LORENZO Sister, what means this melancholy walk?
BEL-IMPERIA That for awhile I wish no company.
LORENZO But here the Prince is come to visit you.
BEL-IMPERIA That argues that he lives in liberty.
BALTHAZAR No, madam, but in pleasing servitude.° *service to a lady*
BEL-IMPERIA Your prison then belike is your conceit.[3]
BALTHAZAR Ay, by conceit my freedom is enthralled.[4]
BEL-IMPERIA Then with conceit enlarge yourself again.[5]
BALTHAZAR What if conceit have laid my heart to gage?[6]
BEL-IMPERIA Pay that° you borrowed and recover it.° *that which / (your heart)*
BALTHAZAR I die if it return from whence it lies.
BEL-IMPERIA A heartless man and live? A miracle!
BALTHAZAR Ay, lady, love can work such miracles.
LORENZO Tush, tush, my lord, let go these ambages,° *circuitous windings*
And in plain terms acquaint her with your love.
BEL-IMPERIA What boots° complaint, when there's no remedy? *avails*
BALTHAZAR Yes, to your gracious self must I complain,
In whose fair answer lies my remedy,
On whose perfection all my thoughts attend,
On whose aspect° mine eyes find beauty's bower, *countenance*
In whose translucent breast my heart is lodged.
BEL-IMPERIA Alas, my lord, these are but words of course,° *formulaic expressions*
And but device° to drive me from this place. *merely a way*

She, in going in, lets fall her glove, which Horatio, coming out,° takes up. *entering onstage*

HORATIO Madam, your glove.
BEL-IMPERIA Thanks, good Horatio. Take it for thy pains.
[*Exit, leaving the glove with him.*]
BALTHAZAR Signor Horatio stooped in happy time.° *most opportunely*
HORATIO I reaped more grace than I deserved or hoped.
LORENZO [*to Balthazar*] My lord, be not dismayed for what is passed.
You know that women oft are humorous.° *whimsical*
These clouds will overblow with little wind;
Let me alone,° I'll scatter them myself. *Leave it to me*
Meanwhile let us devise to spend the time
In some delightful sports and reveling.
HORATIO The King, my lords, is coming hither straight,° *immediately*

3. Your prison, then, is perhaps only a figment of your imagination.
4. Yes, a fancy of being enthralled and imprisoned by your beauty.
5. Then you can use your fancy to free yourself from that enthrallment.
6. But what if, in my fancy, I have pledged my heart?

To feast the Portingale ambassador;
Things were in readiness before I came.
BALTHAZAR Then here it fits° us to attend the King, *befits*
To welcome hither our ambassador,
And learn my father° and my country's health. *father's*

Enter the banquet,° trumpets,° the King, [*Castile,*] *and Ambassador.* *tables and food / trumpeters*

KING See, Lord Ambassador, how Spain entreats° *treats*
Their prisoner Balthazar, thy viceroy's son.
We pleasure° more in kindness than in wars. *take pleasure*
AMBASSADOR Sad is our king, and Portingale laments,
Supposing that Don Balthazar is slain.
BALTHAZAR So am I slain, by beauty's tyranny.
You see, my lord, how Balthazar is slain:
I frolic with the Duke of Castile's son,
Wrapped every hour in pleasures of the court,
And graced with favors of His Majesty.
KING Put off your greetings till our feast be done.
Now come and sit with us and taste our cheer.
Sit to the banquet.
Sit down, young Prince, you are our second guest.
Brother, sit down, and, nephew, take your place.
Signor Horatio, wait thou upon our cup,° *serve as cupbearer*
For well thou hast deservèd to be honored.
Now, lordings,° fall to. Spain is Portugal, *lords*
And Portugal is Spain; we both are friends,
Tribute is paid, and we enjoy our right.
But where is old Hieronimo, our marshal?
He promised us, in honor of our guest,
To grace our banquet with some pompous jest.° *ceremonious show*

Enter Hieronimo with a drum,° three knights, each his scutcheon.° Then he fetches three kings; they take their crowns and them captive.[7] *drummer / heraldic shield*

Hieronimo, this masque contents mine eye,
Although I sound° not well the mystery. *fathom*
HIERONIMO The first armed knight that hung his scutcheon up
He takes the scutcheon and gives it to the King.
Was English Robert, Earl of Gloucester,
Who, when King Stephen bore sway in Albion,° *England (in 1135–54)*
Arrived with five-and-twenty thousand men
In Portingale, and by success of war
Enforced the King, then but a Saracen,° *pagan, non-Christian*
To bear the yoke of English monarchy.
KING My lord of Portingale, by this you see
That which may comfort both your king and you,
And make your late discomfort seem the less.—

7. The three knights, representing England, capture and dethrone the three Iberian kings. (The following quasi-historical account of English victories in Spain and Portugal is fancifully and unabashedly pro-English.)

But say, Hieronimo, what was the next?
HIERONIMO The second knight that hung his scutcheon up
He doth as he did before.
Was Edmund, Earl of Kent in Albion,
When English Richard° wore the diadem. *Richard II (r. 1377–99)*
He came likewise and razèd Lisbon walls,
And took the King of Portingale in fight,
For which, and other suchlike service done,
He after was created Duke of York.
KING This is another special° argument *compelling, pertinent*
That Portingale may deign to bear our yoke,
When it by little England hath been yoked.
But now, Hieronimo, what were the last?
HIERONIMO The third and last, not least in our account,
Doing as before.
Was, as the rest, a valiant Englishman,
Brave John of Gaunt, the Duke of Lancaster,
As by his scutcheon plainly may appear.
He with a puissant° army came to Spain, *powerful*
And took our King of Castile prisoner.
AMBASSADOR This is an argument for our viceroy
That Spain may not insult° for her success, *proudly exult*
Since English warriors likewise conquered Spain
And made them bow their knees to Albion.
KING Hieronimo, I drink to thee for this device,° *show, masque*
Which hath pleased both the ambassador and me.
Pledge me,° Hieronimo, if thou love thy king. *Drink to me*
Takes the cup of° Horatio. *from*
[*To the Ambassador*] My lord, I fear we sit but overlong,
Unless our dainties were more delicate;[8]
But welcome are you to the best we have.
Now let us in, that you may be dispatched;
I think our council is already set.[9] *Exeunt omnes.*

[1.5]

ANDREA Come we for this from depth of underground
To see him feast that gave me my death's wound?
These pleasant sights are sorrow to my soul—
Nothing but league, and love, and banqueting!
REVENGE Be still, Andrea. Ere we go from hence
I'll turn their friendship into fell° despite, *fierce, cruel*
Their love to mortal° hate, their day to night, *deadly*
Their hope into despair, their peace to war,
Their joys to pain, their bliss to misery.

8. Unless we were able to provide you with more delicate fare.
9. Our council is already in session to determine or negotiate terms of peace.
1.5. The chorus figures remain onstage.

2.1

Enter Lorenzo and Balthazar.

LORENZO My lord, though Bel-imperia seem thus coy,
Let reason hold you in your wonted° joy. *accustomed*
In time the savage bull sustains° the yoke, *undergoes, submits to*
In time all haggard° hawks will stoop to lure, *wild*
In time small wedges cleave the hardest oak,
In time the flint is pierced with softest shower,
And she in time will fall from her disdain
And rue the sufferance of your friendly pain.[1]
BALTHAZAR No, she is wilder and more hard withal
Than beast, or bird, or tree, or stony wall.
But wherefore blot° I Bel-imperia's name? *tarnish, stigmatize*
It is my fault, not she, that merits blame.
My feature° is not° to content her sight; *appearance / not able*
My words are rude° and work her no delight. *unpolished*
The lines I send her are but harsh and ill,
Such as do drop from Pan and Marsyas' quill.[2]
My presents are not of sufficient cost,
And, being worthless, all my labor's lost.
Yet might she love me for my valiancy;
Ay, but that's slandered° by captivity. *discredited*
Yet might she love me to content her sire;
Ay, but her reason masters his desire.
Yet might she love me as her brother's friend;
Ay, but her hopes aim at some other end.
Yet might she love me to uprear her state;° *social status*
Ay, but perhaps she hopes some nobler mate.
Yet might she love me as her beauty's thrall;[3]
Ay, but I fear she cannot love at all.
LORENZO My lord, for my sake leave these ecstasies,° *raptures*
And doubt not but we'll find some remedy.
Some cause there is that lets you not be loved;° *hinders your being loved*
First that must needs be known and then removed.
What if my sister love some other knight?
BALTHAZAR My summer's day will turn to winter's night.
LORENZO I have already found a stratagem
To sound° the bottom of this doubtful theme. *(as in maritime sounding)*
My lord, for once° you shall be ruled by me; *on this occasion*
Hinder me not, whate'er you hear or see.
By force or fair means will I cast about
To find the truth of all this question out.—
Ho, Pedringano!
PEDRINGANO [*from offstage*] Signor?
LORENZO *Vien qui presto.*° *Come here quickly*

Enter Pedringano.

2.1. Castile's house; Lorenzo's apartments.
1. And feel compassion for the pain you suffer in loving her.
2. The rustic god Pan foolhardily challenged Apollo to a musical contest and lost. The satyr Marsyas was flayed alive for losing a similar challenge to Apollo. The quill is used both for writing and for plucking a musical instrument.
3. As one enthralled by her beauty.

PEDRINGANO Hath Your Lordship any service to command me?
LORENZO Ay, Pedringano, service of import.
And, not to spend the time in trifling words,
Thus stands the case: it is not long, thou know'st,
Since I did shield thee from my father's wrath
For thy conveyance° in Andrea's love, — *furtive management*
For which thou wert adjudged to punishment.
I stood betwixt thee and thy punishment;
And since,° thou knowest how I have favored thee. — *since then*
Now to these favors will I add reward,
Not with fair words, but store° of golden coin, — *abundance*
And lands and living° joined with dignities,° — *property / offices*
If thou but satisfy° my just demand.° — *answer / question*
Tell truth and have me for thy lasting friend.
PEDRINGANO Whate'er it be Your Lordship shall demand,
My bounden° duty bids me tell the truth, — *obligated*
If case it lie in me° to tell the truth. — *Supposing I'm able*
LORENZO Then, Pedringano, this is my demand:
Whom loves my sister Bel-imperia?
For she reposeth all her trust in thee.
Speak, man, and gain both friendship and reward.
I mean, whom loves she in Andrea's place?
PEDRINGANO Alas, my lord, since Don Andrea's death
I have no credit with° her as before, — *am not being trusted by*
And therefore know not if she love or no.
LORENZO [*drawing his sword*] Nay, if thou dally, then I am thy foe,
And fear shall force what friendship cannot win.
Thy death shall bury what thy life conceals.
Thou diest for more esteeming her than me.
PEDRINGANO Oh, stay,° my lord! — *wait, hold off*
LORENZO Yet speak the truth and I will guerdon° thee, — *reward*
And shield thee from whatever can ensue,
And will conceal whate'er proceeds from thee;
But if thou dally once again, thou diest.
PEDRINGANO If Madam Bel-imperia be in love—
LORENZO What, villain, ifs and ands?
[*He threatens Pedringano.*]
PEDRINGANO Oh, stay, my lord! She loves Horatio.
Balthazar starts back.
LORENZO What, Don Horatio, our knight marshal's son?
PEDRINGANO Even him, my lord.
LORENZO Now say but how° knowest thou he is her love, — *only say how*
And thou shalt find me kind and liberal.° — *generous*
Stand up, I say, and fearless tell the truth.
PEDRINGANO She sent him letters which myself perused,
Full fraught° with lines and arguments of love, — *Fully laden*
Preferring him before Prince Balthazar.
LORENZO Swear on this cross° that what thou sayest is true, — *i.e., sword hilt*
And that thou wilt conceal what thou hast told.
PEDRINGANO I swear to both, by Him that made us all.
LORENZO In hope thine oath is true, here's thy reward;
[*He gives money.*]
But if I prove thee perjured and unjust,° — *dishonest, disloyal*
This very sword whereon thou took'st thine oath

Shall be the worker of thy tragedy.
PEDRINGANO What I have said is true, and shall for me° *for my part*
Be still° concealed from Bel-imperia. *always*
Besides, Your Honor's liberality
Deserves my duteous service, even till death.
LORENZO Let this be all that thou shalt do for me:
Be watchful when, and where, these lovers meet,
And give me notice in some secret sort.° *manner*
PEDRINGANO I will, my lord.
LORENZO Then shalt thou find that I am liberal.
Thou know'st that I can more advance thy state
Than she; be therefore wise and fail me not.
Go and attend her as thy custom is,
Lest absence make her think thou dost amiss.
Exit Pedringano.
Why so: *Tam armis quam ingenio;*[4]
Where words prevail not, violence prevails,
But gold doth more than either of them both.
How likes Prince Balthazar this stratagem?
BALTHAZAR Both well and ill. It makes me glad and sad:
Glad, that I know the hinderer of my love,
Sad, that I fear she hates me whom I love;
Glad, that I know on whom to be revenged,
Sad, that she'll fly me if I take revenge.
Yet must I take revenge or die myself,
For love resisted grows impatient.
I think Horatio be my destined plague!
First in his hand he brandishèd a sword,
And with that sword he fiercely wagèd war,
And in that war he gave me dangerous wounds,
And by those wounds he forcèd me to yield,
And by my yielding I became his slave.
Now in his mouth he carries pleasing words,
Which pleasing words do harbor sweet conceits,° *figures of speech*
Which sweet conceits are limed[5] with sly deceits,
Which sly deceits smooth° Bel-imperia's ears, *flatter*
And through her ears dive down into her heart,
And in her heart set him where I should stand.
Thus hath he ta'en my body by his force,
And now by sleight° would captivate my soul; *cunning*
But in his fall I'll tempt the Destinies,[6]
And either lose my life or win my love.
LORENZO Let's go, my lord; your staying stays° revenge. *hinders*
Do you but follow me and gain your love;
Her favor must be won by his remove.° *Exeunt.* *removal (by death)*

4. As much by force as by guile. (A well-known Latin motto.)
5. Branches were "limed," i.e., coated with sticky lime, to snare birds.
6. To bring about his downfall, I'll tempt the Fates themselves.

[2.2]

Enter Horatio and Bel-imperia.

HORATIO Now, madam, since by favor of your love
Our hidden smoke is turned to open flame,
And that° with looks and words we feed our thoughts *now that, since*
(Two chief contents,° where more cannot be had), *sources of contentment*
Thus in the midst of love's fair blandishments
Why show you sign of inward languishments?

[*Entering above,*]° *Pedringano showeth all to the Prince and Lorenzo, placing them in secret.* *onto upper acting area*

BEL-IMPERIA My heart, sweet friend, is like a ship at sea:
She wisheth port, where, riding all at ease,
She may repair what stormy times have worn,
And, leaning on° the shore, may sing with joy *i.e., sheltered by*
That pleasure follows pain, and bliss annoy.° *bliss follows sorrow*
Possession of thy love is th'only port
Wherein my heart, with fears and hopes long tossed,
Each hour doth wish and long to make resort,
There to repair° the joys that it hath lost, *restore*
And, sitting safe, to sing in Cupid's quire° *choir*
That sweetest bliss is° crown of love's desire. *which is*
BALTHAZAR (*above*) Oh, sleep,° mine eyes! See not my love profaned. *stay shut*
Be deaf, my ears! Hear not my discontent.
Die, heart! Another joys° what thou deservest. *enjoys*
LORENZO [*aside*] Watch° still, mine eyes, to see this love disjoined; *Be vigilant*
Hear still, mine ears, to hear them both lament;
Live, heart, to joy at fond° Horatio's fall. *besotted; guileless*
BEL-IMPERIA Why stands Horatio speechless all this while?
HORATIO The less I speak, the more I meditate.
BEL-IMPERIA But whereon dost thou chiefly meditate?
HORATIO On dangers past and pleasures to ensue.
BALTHAZAR [*aside*] On pleasures past and dangers to ensue.
BEL-IMPERIA What dangers and what pleasures dost thou mean?
HORATIO Dangers of war, and pleasures of our love.
LORENZO [*aside*] Dangers of death, but pleasures none at all.
BEL-IMPERIA Let dangers go. Thy war shall be with me,
But such a war as breaks no bond of peace.
Speak thou fair words, I'll cross them with fair words;
Send thou sweet looks, I'll meet them with sweet looks;
Write loving lines, I'll answer loving lines;
Give me a kiss, I'll countercheck thy kiss.
Be this our warring peace, or peaceful war.
HORATIO But, gracious madam, then appoint the field
Where trial of this war shall first be made.
BALTHAZAR [*aside*] Ambitious villain, how his boldness grows!

2.2. The court of Spain, perhaps at Castile's house.

BEL-IMPERIA Then be thy father's pleasant bower the field,
Where first we vowed a mutual amity;
The court were° dangerous, that place is safe. *would be*
Our hour shall be when Vesper° 'gins to rise, *the evening star*
That summons home distressful travelers.° *weary laborers*
There none shall hear us but the harmless birds;
Happily° the gentle nightingale *Haply, perchance*
Shall carol us asleep ere we be ware,° *aware*
And, singing with the prickle at her breast,[1]
Tell° our delight and mirthful dalliance. *Sing of*
Till then each hour will seem a year and more.
HORATIO But, honey-sweet and honorable love,
Return we now into your father's sight;
Dangerous suspicion waits on° our delight. *attends, follows*
LORENZO [*aside*] Ay, danger mixed with jealous° despite *(spoken in three syllables)*
Shall send thy soul into eternal night. *Exeunt.*

[2.3]

Enter King of Spain, Portingale Ambassador, Don Cyprian [Duke of Castile, attendants], etc.

KING Brother of Castile, to the Prince's love
What says your daughter Bel-imperia?
CASTILE Although she coy it° as becomes her kind,° *is bashful / sex*
And yet° dissemble that she loves the Prince, *still*
I doubt not, I, but she will stoop in time.[1]
And were she froward,° which she will not be, *stubborn, perverse*
Yet herein shall she follow my advice,
Which is to love him or forgo my love.
KING Then, Lord Ambassador of Portingale,
Advise thy king to make this marriage up,
For strengthening of our late-confirmèd league;
I know no better means to make us friends.
Her dowry shall be large and liberal:
Besides that she is daughter and half heir
Unto our brother here, Don Cyprian,
And shall enjoy the moiety° of his land, *half*
I'll grace her marriage with an uncle's gift,
And this it is: in case the match go forward,
The tribute which you pay shall be released,
And if by Balthazar she have a son,
He shall enjoy the kingdom after us.
AMBASSADOR I'll make the motion° to my sovereign liege, *proposal*
And work it if my counsel may prevail.
KING Do so, my lord, and, if he give consent,
I hope his presence here will honor us
In celebration of the nuptial day;
And let himself determine of° the time. *decide*
AMBASSADOR Will't please Your Grace command me aught beside?

1. The nightingale was said to lean its breast against a thorn in memory of the sad fate of Philomela, who was raped by her brother-in-law, King Tereus.

2.3. The court of Spain.
1. Like a hawk, Bel-imperia must be trained to "stoop," or fly down, to the lure. (See 2.1.4.)

KING Commend me to the King, and so farewell.
But where's Prince Balthazar, to take his leave?
AMBASSADOR That is performed already, my good lord.
KING Amongst the rest of what you have in charge,
The Prince's ransom must not be forgot;
That's none of mine, but his that took him prisoner,
And well his forwardness° deserves reward. *zeal*
It was Horatio, our knight marshal's son.
AMBASSADOR Between us there's a price already pitched,° *settled on*
And shall be sent with all convenient speed.
KING Then once again farewell, my lord.
AMBASSADOR Farewell, my lord of Castile and the rest. *Exit.*
KING Now, brother, you must take some little pains
To win fair Bel-imperia from her will;° *willfulness*
Young virgins must be rulèd by their friends.° *kinfolk*
The Prince is amiable and loves her well;
If she neglect him and forgo his love
She both will wrong her own estate and ours.
Therefore, whiles I do entertain the Prince
With greatest pleasure that our court affords,
Endeavor you to win your daughter's thought;
If she give back,° all this will come to naught. *Exeunt.* *back off, turn away*

[2.4]

Enter Horatio, Bel-imperia, and Pedringano.

HORATIO Now that the night begins with sable wings
To overcloud the brightness of the sun,
And that in darkness pleasures may be done,
Come, Bel-imperia, let us to the bower,
And there in safety pass a pleasant hour.
BEL-IMPERIA I follow thee, my love, and will not back,
Although my fainting heart controls° my soul. *overmasters*
HORATIO Why, make you doubt of Pedringano's faith?
BEL-IMPERIA No, he is as trusty as my second self.—
Go, Pedringano, watch without° the gate, *outside*
And let us know if any make approach.
PEDRINGANO [*aside*] Instead of watching I'll deserve more gold
By fetching Don Lorenzo to this match. *Exit Pedringano.*
HORATIO What means my love?
BEL-IMPERIA I know not what, myself;
And yet my heart foretells me some mischance.
HORATIO Sweet, say not so; fair Fortune is our friend,
And heavens have shut up day to pleasure us.
The stars, thou see'st, hold back their twinkling shine,
And Luna° hides herself to pleasure us. *the moon*
BEL-IMPERIA Thou hast prevailed; I'll conquer my misdoubt,
And in thy love and counsel drown my fear.
I fear no more; love now is all my thoughts.
Why sit we not? For pleasure asketh ease.

2.4. The bower in Hieronimo's garden.

HORATIO The more thou sit'st within these leafy bowers,
The more will Flora° deck it with her flowers. *goddess of flowers*
BEL-IMPERIA Ay, but if Flora spy Horatio here,
Her jealous eye will think I sit too near.
HORATIO Hark, madam, how the birds record° by night, *sing*
For joy that Bel-imperia sits in sight.
BEL-IMPERIA No, Cupid counterfeits the nightingale,
To frame° sweet music to Horatio's tale. *devise*
HORATIO If Cupid sing, then Venus° is not far. *goddess of love*
Ay, thou art Venus, or some fairer star.
BEL-IMPERIA If I be Venus, thou must needs be Mars,° *god of war, Venus's lover*
And where Mars reigneth there must needs be wars.
HORATIO Then thus begin our wars: put forth thy hand,
That it may combat with my ruder° hand. *rougher*
BEL-IMPERIA Set forth thy foot to try the push of mine.
HORATIO But first my looks shall combat against thine.
BEL-IMPERIA Then ward° thyself. I dart this kiss at thee. *guard*
HORATIO Thus I retort the dart thou threw'st at me.
[*They kiss.*]
BEL-IMPERIA Nay, then, to gain the glory of the field,
My twining arms shall yoke and make thee yield.
HORATIO Nay, then, my arms are large and strong withal;° *likewise*
Thus elms by vines are compassed° till they fall. *encircled*
BEL-IMPERIA Oh, let me go! For in my troubled eyes
Now mayst thou read that life in passion dies.
HORATIO Oh, stay awhile and I will die with thee;[1]
So shalt thou yield, and yet have conquered me.
BEL-IMPERIA Who's there? Pedringano? We are betrayed!

Enter Lorenzo, Balthazar, Serberine, [and] Pedringano, disguised.

LORENZO [*to Balthazar*] My lord, away with her! Take her aside.
[*To Horatio*] Oh, sir, forbear, your valor is already tried.° *tested*
[*To Serberine and Pedringano*] Quickly dispatch, my
masters.° *They hang him in the arbor.* *my good sirs*
HORATIO What, will you murder me?
LORENZO Ay, thus, and thus! These are the fruits of love.
They stab him.
BEL-IMPERIA Oh, save his life and let me die for him!
Oh, save him, brother, save him, Balthazar!
I loved Horatio, but he loved not me.
BALTHAZAR But Balthazar loves Bel-imperia.
LORENZO Although his life were still ambitious proud,
Yet is he at the highest° now he is dead. *i.e., hanging*
BEL-IMPERIA Murder, murder! Help, Hieronimo, help!
LORENZO Come, stop her mouth. Away with her!
Exeunt [forcibly taking off Bel-imperia. Horatio's body remains hanging in the arbor].

1. The "dying" the lovers speak of has the connotation of sexual surrender and orgasm; it also ironically anticipates Horatio's imminent fate.

[2.5]

Enter Hieronimo in his shirt,° etc. — *nightshirt*

HIERONIMO What outcries pluck me from my naked bed,
And chill my throbbing heart with trembling fear,
Which never danger yet could daunt before?
Who calls Hieronimo? Speak, here I am.
I did not slumber, therefore 'twas no dream.
No, no, it was some woman cried for help,
And here within this garden did she cry,
And in this garden must I rescue her.—
But stay, what murd'rous spectacle is this?
A man hanged up and all the murderers gone,
And in my bower, to lay the guilt on me?
This place was made for pleasure, not for death.
He cuts him down.
Those garments that he wears I oft have seen—
Alas, it is Horatio, my sweet son!
Oh, no, but he that whilom° was my son. — *formerly*
Oh, was it thou that called'st me from my bed?
Oh, speak if any spark of life remain.
I am thy father. Who hath slain my son?
What savage monster, not of human kind,
Hath here been glutted with thy harmless blood,
And left thy bloody corpse dishonored here,
For me amidst this° dark and deathful shades — *these*
To drown thee with an ocean of my tears?
O heavens, why made you night to cover sin?
By day this deed of darkness had not been.
O earth, why didst thou not in time° devour — *at the due moment*
The vile profaner of this sacred bower?
O poor Horatio, what hadst thou misdone,
To leese° thy life ere life was new begun?° — *lose / in your youth*
O wicked butcher whatsoe'er thou wert,
How could thou strangle virtue and desert?° — *worth*
Ay me, most wretched, that have lost my joy,
In leesing my Horatio, my sweet boy!

Enter Isabella.

ISABELLA My husband's absence makes my heart to throb.—
Hieronimo!
HIERONIMO Here, Isabella, help me to lament,
For sighs are stopped,° and all my tears are spent. — *stopped up*
ISABELLA What world of grief—My son Horatio!
Oh, where's the author of this endless woe?
HIERONIMO To know the author were° some ease of grief, — *would be*
For in revenge my heart would find relief.
ISABELLA Then is he gone? And is my son gone too?
Oh, gush out, tears, fountains and floods of tears!
Blow, sighs, and raise an everlasting storm!
For outrage° fits our cursèd wretchedness. — *passionate outburst*
HIERONIMO Sweet lovely rose, ill-plucked before thy time,

2.5. The scene continues.

Fair worthy son, not conquered but betrayed,
I'll kiss thee now, for words with° tears are stayed.° *by / stopped*
ISABELLA And I'll close up the glasses of his sight,
For once these eyes were only my° delight, *my only*
HIERONIMO See'st thou this handkercher besmeared with blood?
It shall not from me till I take revenge.
See'st thou those wounds that yet are bleeding fresh?
I'll not entomb them till I have revenged.
Then will I joy amidst my discontent;
Till then my sorrow never shall be spent.° *exhausted*
ISABELLA The heavens are just; murder cannot be hid;
Time is the author both of truth and right,
And time will bring this treachery to light.
HIERONIMO Meanwhile, good Isabella, cease thy plaints,° *laments*
Or at the least dissemble them awhile;
So shall we sooner find the practice° out, *plot, conspiracy*
And learn by whom all this was brought about.
Come, Isabel, now let us take him up,
They take him up.
And bear him in from out this cursèd place.
I'll say his dirge; singing fits not this case.
O aliquis mihi quas pulchrum ver educat herbas
(Hieronimo sets his breast unto his sword.)
Misceat, et nostro detur medicina dolori;
Aut, si qui faciunt animis oblivia, succos
Praebeat. Ipse metam magnum quaecunque per orbem
Gramina Sol pulchras effert in luminis oras.
Ipse bibam quicquid meditatur saga veneni,
Quicquid et herbarum vi caeca nenia nectit.
Omnia perpetiar, lethum quoque, dum semel omnis
Noster in extincto moriatur pectore sensus.
Ergo tuos oculos nunquam, mea vita, videbo,
Et tua perpetuus sepelivit lumina somnus?
Emoriar tecum, sic, sic juvat ire sub umbras.
At tamen absistam properato cedere letho,
Ne mortem vindicta tuam tum nulla sequatur.[1]
Here he throws it° from him and bears the body away. [*Exeunt.*] (*his sword; see 67.1*)

[2.6]

ANDREA Brought'st thou me hither to increase my pain?
I looked° that Balthazar should have been slain, *expected, hoped*
But 'tis my friend Horatio that is slain,
And they abuse fair Bel-imperia,
On whom I doted more than all the world,

1. Let someone mix me herbs that the beautiful spring brings forth, and let a medicine be given for our sorrows; or, if there are any juices that will induce oblivion in our minds, let that person offer them. I, for my part, will gather whatever herbs the sun brings forth, throughout all the world, into the fair realms of light. I will drink whatever poison the sorceress contrives, and also whatever herbs the goddess of spells weaves together by her secret power. I will attempt all things, even death, until all feeling dies at once in my dead heart. Shall I never again see your face, you who are my life, and has perpetual sleep entombed your light? I will die with you; thus, thus, will I rejoicingly go to the shades below. Nonetheless, I will hold back from a hasty death, lest your death should be followed by no revenge.

2.6. The chorus figures have been onstage from the start and remain so after this interlude.

Because she loved me more than all the world.
REVENGE Thou talkest of harvest when the corn is green.
The end is crown of every work well done;
The sickle comes not till the corn be ripe.
Be still, and ere I lead thee from this place
I'll show thee Balthazar in heavy case.° *sorrowful plight*

3.1

Enter Viceroy of Portingale, Nobles, [and] Villuppo.

VICEROY Infortunate condition of kings,
Seated amidst so many helpless doubts!° *fears beyond help*
First we are placed upon extremest height,
And oft supplanted with exceeding heat,° *passion, fury*
But ever subject to the wheel of chance;° *wheel of Fortune*
And at our highest never joy we so
As° we both doubt° and dread our overthrow. *But that / fear*
So striveth not the waves with sundry winds
As Fortune toileth in the affairs of kings,[1]
That would° be feared, yet fear to be beloved, *Who wish to be*
Sith° fear or love to kings is flattery.[2] *Since*
For instance, lordings,° look upon your king, *lords*
By hate deprivèd of his dearest son,
The only hope of our successive line.° *line of succession*
FIRST NOBLEMAN I had not thought that Alexandro's heart
Had been envenomed with such extreme hate;
But now I see that words have several works,° *lead to various results*
And there's no credit° in the countenance.° *trustworthiness / face*
VILLUPPO No; for, my lord, had you beheld the train° *deceiving look*
That feignèd love had colored° in his looks *falsely depicted*
When he in camp consorted° Balthazar, *accompanied*
Far more inconstant had you thought the sun,
That hourly coasts° the center of the earth, *circles about*
Than Alexandro's purpose to the Prince.
VICEROY No more, Villuppo. Thou hast said enough,
And with thy words thou slayest our wounded thoughts.
Nor shall I longer dally with the world,
Procrastinating Alexandro's death.—
Go, some of you, and fetch the traitor forth,
That, as he is condemnèd, he may die.
[*One goes to the door.*]

Enter Alexandro with a Nobleman and halberds.° *halberdiers (see 1.4.21)*
[Alexandro and the Noblemen converse among themselves.]

SECOND NOBLEMAN In such extremes, will naught but patience serve.
ALEXANDRO But in extremes, what patience shall I use?[3]
Nor discontents it me to leave the world,
With whom° there nothing can prevail but wrong. *In which world*

3.1. The Portuguese court.
1. The battle of waves and winds is as nothing compared with kings' tribulations at the hands of Fortune.
2. Lines 1–11 are based on Seneca's *Agamemnon*, lines 57–73.
3. Alexandro asks rhetorically if he should hope patiently for deliverance or renounce the world entirely.

SECOND NOBLEMAN Yet hope the best.
ALEXANDRO 'Tis heaven is my hope.
As for the earth, it is too much infect° *diseased, corrupt*
To yield me hope of any of her mold.° *any composed of her dust*
VICEROY Why linger ye? Bring forth that daring° fiend, *audacious*
And let him die for his accursèd deed.
ALEXANDRO Not that I fear the extremity of death,
For nobles cannot stoop to servile fear,
Do I, O King, thus discontented live.
But this, oh, this torments my laboring soul:
That thus I die suspected of a sin
Whereof, as heavens have known my secret thoughts,
So am I free from this suggestion.° *insinuation*
VICEROY No more, I say! To the tortures! When!° *Get on with it!*
Bind him, and burn his body in those flames

They bind him to the stake.

That shall prefigure those unquenchèd fires
Of Phlegethon[4] preparèd for his soul.
ALEXANDRO My guiltless death will be avenged on thee,
On thee, Villuppo, that hath maliced° thus, *slandered, shown malice*
Or for thy meed° hast falsely me accused. *reward*
VILLUPPO Nay, Alexandro, if thou menace me,
I'll lend a hand to send thee to the lake[5]
Where those thy words shall perish with thy works,
Injurious° traitor, monstrous homicide! *Calumnious*

Enter Ambassador [attended].

AMBASSADOR Stay! Hold awhile,
And here, with pardon of His Majesty,° *if His Majesty permits*
Lay hands upon Villuppo.
VICEROY Ambassador,
What news hath urged this sudden entrance?
AMBASSADOR Know, sovereign lord, that Balthazar doth live.
VICEROY What sayest thou? Liveth Balthazar, our son?
AMBASSADOR Your Highness' son, Lord Balthazar, doth live,
And, well entreated° in the court of Spain, *treated*
Humbly commends him° to Your Majesty. *sends greetings*
These eyes beheld, and these my followers,
With these, the letters of the King's commends,° *greetings*

Gives him letters.

Are happy witnesses of His Highness'° health. *(Balthazar's)*

The King° looks on the letters, and proceeds.° *Viceroy / reads*

VICEROY "Thy son doth live, your tribute is received,
Thy peace is made, and we are satisfied.
The rest resolve upon[6] as things proposed
For both our honors and thy benefit."
AMBASSADOR These are His Highness'° farther articles. *(the Spanish king's)*

He gives him more letters.

VICEROY [*to Villuppo*] Accursèd wretch, to intimate these ills
Against the life and reputation
Of noble Alexandro! [*To Alexandro*] Come, my lord,

4. The river of fire in the underworld.
5. Acheron, a river in the underworld.
6. Examine and decide upon the articles that follow in this letter.

Let him unbind thee that is bound to death,
To make a quital for thy discontent.[7] *They unbind him.*
ALEXANDRO Dread lord, in kindness° you could do no less, *by your (kingly) nature*
Upon report of such a damnèd fact;° *deed*
But thus we see our° innocence hath saved *my*
The hopeless life which thou, Villuppo, sought
By thy suggestions° to have massacred. *malicious charges*
VICEROY Say, false Villuppo, wherefore didst thou thus
Falsely betray Lord Alexandro's life,
Him whom thou knowest that no unkindness° else, *unnatural deed*
But even the slaughter of our dearest son,
Could once have moved us to have misconceived?° *misjudged*
ALEXANDRO Say, treacherous Villuppo, tell the King,
Wherein hath Alexandro used thee ill?
VILLUPPO Rent° with remembrance of so foul a deed, *Torn*
My guilty soul submits me to thy doom;° *sentence*
For, not for Alexandro's injuries,[8]
But for reward, and hope to be preferred,° *advanced*
Thus have I shamelessly hazarded his life.
VICEROY Which, villain, shall be ransomed° with thy death, *paid for*
And not so mean° a torment as we here *moderate*
Devised for him, who thou said'st slew our son,
But with the bitterest torments and extremes
That may be yet invented for thine end.
Alexandro seems to° entreat. *is seen to*
Entreat me not.—Go, take the traitor hence.
Exit Villuppo [guarded].
And, Alexandro, let us honor thee
With public notice of thy loyalty.
To end those things articulated° here *written in articles*
By our great lord the mighty king of Spain,
We with our council will deliberate.
Come, Alexandro, keep us company. *Exeunt.*

[3.2]

Enter Hieronimo.

HIERONIMO O eyes, no eyes, but fountains fraught with tears!
O life, no life, but lively° form of death! *lifelike*
O world, no world, but mass of public wrongs,
Confused and filled with murder and misdeeds!
O sacred heavens, if this unhallowed deed,
If this inhuman and barbarous attempt,
If this incomparable murder thus
Of mine—but now no more—my son
Shall unrevealed and unrevengèd pass,
How should we term your dealings to be just,
If you unjustly deal with those that in your justice trust?
The night, sad secretary° to my moans, *confidant*
With direful visions wake° my vexèd soul, *wakes*

7. Let Villuppo's being bound and sentenced to death unbind you and serve as requital for the wrongs done to you.

8. (1) Not to harm Alexandro; (2) not because of any harm that Alexandro might have done to me.

3.2. Near Castile's house.

And with the wounds of my distressful son
Solicit me for notice of° his death. — *to cry out against*
The ugly fiends do sally forth of hell,
And frame° my steps to unfrequented paths, — *direct*
And fear° my heart with fierce inflamèd thoughts. — *terrify*
The cloudy day my discontents records,
Early begins to register my dreams
And drive me forth to seek the murderer.
Eyes, life, world, heavens, hell, night, and day,
See, search, show, send, some man, some mean,° that may— — *means*
A letter falleth.
What's here? A letter? Tush, it is not so.
A letter written to Hieronimo! *Red ink.*° — *(representing blood)*
"For want of ink, receive this bloody writ.
Me hath my hapless° brother hid from thee; — *deserving of bad luck*
Revenge thyself on Balthazar and him,
For these were they that murderèd thy son.
Hieronimo, revenge Horatio's death,
And better fare than Bel-imperia doth."
What means this unexpected miracle?° — *revelation*
My son slain by Lorenzo and the Prince?
What cause had they Horatio to malign?° — *hate*
Or what might move thee, Bel-imperia,
To accuse thy brother, had° he been the mean?° — *even had / means*
Hieronimo, beware, thou art betrayed,
And to entrap thy life this train° is laid. — *trap*
Advise thee, therefore; be not credulous;
This is devisèd to endanger thee,
That thou by this Lorenzo shouldst accuse,
And he, for thy dishonor done, should draw
Thy life in question and thy name in hate.
Dear was the life of my belovèd son,
And of his death behooves me be revenged;
Then hazard not thine own,° Hieronimo, — *your own life*
But live t'effect thy resolution.
I therefore will by circumstances° try — *circumstantial evidence*
What I can gather to confirm this writ,
And, heark'ning near the Duke of Castile's house,
Close° if I can with Bel-imperia, — *Make contact*
To listen more, but nothing to bewray.° — *reveal*

Enter Pedringano.

Now, Pedringano!
PEDRINGANO Now, Hieronimo!
HIERONIMO Where's thy lady?
PEDRINGANO I know not. Here's my lord.

Enter Lorenzo.

LORENZO How now, who's this? Hieronimo?
HIERONIMO My lord.
PEDRINGANO [*to Lorenzo*] He asketh for my lady Bel-imperia.
LORENZO What to do, Hieronimo? The Duke, my father, hath
Upon some disgrace awhile removed her hence,
But if it be aught I may inform her of,
Tell me, Hieronimo, and I'll let her know it.

HIERONIMO Nay, nay, my lord, I thank you, it shall not need;° *isn't necessary*
I had a suit unto her, but too late,
And her disgrace makes me unfortunate.
LORENZO Why so, Hieronimo? Use me.° *Put your suit to me*
HIERONIMO Oh, no, my lord, I dare not, it must not be.
I humbly thank Your Lordship.
LORENZO Why, then, farewell.
HIERONIMO [*aside*] My grief no heart, my thoughts no tongue can tell. *Exit.*
LORENZO Come hither, Pedringano. See'st thou this?° *this snooping around*
PEDRINGANO My lord, I see it, and suspect it too.
LORENZO This is that damnèd villain Serberine,° *(see 2.4.50.1)*
That hath, I fear, revealed Horatio's death.
PEDRINGANO My lord, he could not, 'twas so lately done,
And since° he hath not left my company. *since then*
LORENZO Admit° he have not, his condition's° such *Even if / nature is*
As fear or flattering words may make him false.
I know his humor,° and therewith repent *temperament*
That e'er I used him in this enterprise.
But, Pedringano, to prevent the worst,
And 'cause I know thee secret as my soul,
Here for thy further satisfaction take thou this,
Gives him more gold.
And hearken to me. Thus it is devised:
This night thou must—and prithee so resolve—
Meet Serberine at Saint Luigi's Park;
Thou knowest 'tis here hard by behind the house.
There take thy stand, and see thou strike him sure,
For die he must, if we do mean to live.
PEDRINGANO But how shall Serberine be there, my lord?
LORENZO Let me alone.° I'll send to him to meet *Leave it to me*
The Prince and me, where thou must do this deed.
PEDRINGANO It shall be done, my lord, it shall be done,
And I'll go arm myself to meet him there.
LORENZO When things shall alter, as I hope they will,
Then shalt thou mount[1] for this. Thou knowest my mind.
Exit Pedringano.
Che le, Ieron![2]

Enter Page.

PAGE My lord?
LORENZO Go, sirrah,° to Serberine, *(said to social inferiors)*
And bid him forthwith meet the Prince and me
At Saint Luigi's Park, behind the house,
This evening, boy.
PAGE I go, my lord.
LORENZO But, sirrah, let the hour be eight o'clock.
Bid him not fail.
PAGE I fly, my lord. *Exit.*
LORENZO Now, to confirm the complot thou hast cast° *plot I've devised*
Of all these practices,° I'll spread° the watch, *schemes / station*
Upon° precise commandment from the King, *As if upon*

1. (1) Be advanced; (2) be hanged. (Pedringano is not intended to hear this latter meaning.)
2. Hello there, little thief!

Strongly to guard the place where Pedringano
This night shall murder hapless Serberine.
Thus must we° work that will avoid distrust;° *we schemers / suspicion*
Thus must we practice to prevent mishap,
And thus one ill another must expulse.[3]
This sly inquiry of Hieronimo
For Bel-imperia breeds suspicion,
And this suspicion bodes a further ill.
As for myself, I know my secret fault,° *crime*
And so do they,[4] but I have dealt for them.
They that for coin their souls endangerèd,
To save my life, for coin shall venture theirs,[5]
And better 'tis that base companions° die *lowbred fellows*
Than by their life to hazard our good haps.° *fortunes*
Nor shall they live for me to fear their faith.[6]
I'll trust myself; myself shall be my friend;
For die they shall. Slaves° are ordained to no other end. *Wretches, servants*
Exit.

[3.3]

Enter Pedringano with a pistol.

PEDRINGANO Now, Pedringano, bid thy pistol hold,° *not misfire*
And hold on,° Fortune! Once more favor me; *hold steady, press on*
Give but success to mine attempting spirit,
And let me shift for taking of mine aim.[1]
Here is the gold, this is the gold proposed;° *(as my reward)*
It is no dream° that I adventure for, *mere dream*
But Pedringano is possessed thereof.
And he° that would not strain his conscience *(anyone)*
For him° that thus his liberal purse hath stretched, *(one like Lorenzo)*
Unworthy such a favor may he fail,
And, wishing, want,° when such as I prevail. *be in want*
As for the fear of apprehension,
I know, if need should be, my noble lord
Will stand between me and ensuing harms.
Besides, this place is free from all suspect.° *suspicion*
Here therefore will I stay and take my stand.

Enter the Watch.

FIRST WATCHMAN I wonder much to what intent it is
That we are thus expressly charged to watch?
SECOND WATCHMAN 'Tis by commandment in the King's own name.
THIRD WATCHMAN But we were never wont to watch and ward° *i.e., keep guard*
So near the Duke his brother's house before.
SECOND WATCHMAN Content yourself. Stand close; there's somewhat in't.° *something brewing*

3. One evil deed must drive out another.
4. Pedringano and Serberine.
5. Those two who, in return for money, risked their very souls on my behalf (by committing the sin of murder) will now have to pay their lives in order to save mine.
6. Nor shall they live to have me continually worrying about their keeping my secret.
3.3. Saint Luigi's Park, behind Castile's house.
1. Leave the aiming of the pistol to me.

Enter Serberine.

SERBERINE [*to himself*] Here, Serberine, attend and stay thy pace,° — *halt your steps*
For here did Don Lorenzo's page appoint
That thou by his command shouldst meet with him.
How fit a place, if one were so disposed,
Methinks this corner is to close with one!° — *to assault someone*
PEDRINGANO [*aside*] Here comes the bird that I must seize upon.
Now, Pedringano, or never play the man!° — *or renounce manhood*
SERBERINE [*to himself*] I wonder that His Lordship° stays so long, — *(Lorenzo; see 3.2.88–89)*
Or wherefore should he send for me so late?
PEDRINGANO For this, Serberine, and thou shalt ha't.° — *have it*
Shoots the dag.° [*Serberine falls.*] — *pistol*
So, there he lies. My promise is performed.

The Watch [*come forward*].

FIRST WATCHMAN Hark, gentlemen, this is a pistol shot.
SECOND WATCHMAN And here's one slain. Stay° the murderer. — *Detain, arrest*
PEDRINGANO Now by the sorrows of the souls in hell,
He strives with the Watch.
Who° first lays hand on me, I'll be his priest.[2] — *Whoever*
THIRD WATCHMAN Sirrah, confess, and therein play the priest.[3]
Why hast thou thus unkindly° killed the man? — *unnaturally; brutally*
PEDRINGANO Why, because he walked abroad° so late. — *out of doors*
THIRD WATCHMAN Come, sir, you had been better kept your bed
Than have committed this misdeed so late.° — *recently; at night*
SECOND WATCHMAN Come to the Marshal's with the murderer!
FIRST WATCHMAN On to Hieronimo's! Help me here
To bring the murdered body with us too.
PEDRINGANO Hieronimo? Carry me before whom you will.
Whate'er he be, I'll answer him and you;
And do your worst, for I defy you all.
Exeunt [*with Serberine's body*].

[3.4]

Enter Lorenzo and Balthazar.

BALTHAZAR How now, my lord, what makes you rise so soon?
LORENZO Fear of preventing our mishaps too late.[1]
BALTHAZAR What mischief is it that we not mistrust?° — *are not aware of*
LORENZO Our greatest ills we least mistrust, my lord,
And inexpected harms do hurt us most.
BALTHAZAR Why, tell me, Don Lorenzo, tell me, man,
If aught concerns our honor and your own?
LORENZO Nor you nor me,° my lord, but both in one. — *Neither of us singly*
For I suspect—and the presumption's great—
That by those base confederates in our fault,° — *crime*
Touching° the death of Don Horatio, — *Relating to*
We are betrayed to old Hieronimo.

2. I'll give him his deathbed confession.
3. Be your own confessor by confessing the crime.
3.4. Castile's house.
1. Fear of not anticipating our troubles in time.

BALTHAZAR Betrayed, Lorenzo! Tush, it cannot be.
LORENZO A guilty conscience, urgèd with the thought
Of former evils,° easily cannot err.   *crimes*
I am persuaded—and dissuade me not—
That all's revealèd to Hieronimo.
And therefore know that I have cast° it thus—   *devised*

[*Enter the Page.*]

But here's the page.—How now, what news with thee?
PAGE My lord, Serberine is slain.
BALTHAZAR Who? Serberine, my man?°   *servant*
PAGE Your Highness' man, my lord.
LORENZO Speak, page, who murdered him?
PAGE He that is apprehended for the fact.°   *deed*
LORENZO Who?
PAGE Pedringano.
BALTHAZAR Is Serberine slain, that loved his lord so well?
Injurious villain, murderer of his friend!
LORENZO Hath Pedringano murdered Serberine?
My lord, let me entreat you to take the pains
To exasperate° and hasten his° revenge   *intensify / on him*
With your complaints unto my lord the King.
This their dissension breeds a greater doubt.[2]
BALTHAZAR Assure thee, Don Lorenzo, he shall die,
Or else His Highness hardly° shall deny.   *unjustly, harshly*
Meanwhile, I'll haste the marshal sessions,[3]
For die he shall for this his damnèd deed.
Exit Balthazar.
LORENZO [*to himself*] Why so, this fits our former policy,°   *my earlier stratagem*
And thus experience bids the wise to deal.
I lay the plot, he prosecutes the point;°   *carries it out*
I set the trap, he breaks the worthless twigs,[4]
And sees not that wherewith the bird was limed.[5]
Thus hopeful men that mean to hold their own°   *prosper, stay ahead*
Must look like fowlers° to their dearest friends.   *innocent bird-catchers*
He runs to kill whom° I have holp° to catch,   *the one whom / helped*
And no man knows it was my reaching fetch.°   *farseeing plan*
'Tis hard to trust unto a multitude,
Or anyone, in mine opinion,
When men themselves their secrets will reveal.

Enter a Messenger with a letter.

Boy!
PAGE My lord?
LORENZO What's he?
MESSENGER I have a letter to Your Lordship.
LORENZO From whence?

2. This dissension between Pedringano and Serberine is further cause for worry about our being betrayed.
3. Meantime, I'll hasten on the process of bringing this matter to trial before the Knight Marshal (Hieronimo).
4. Balthazar closes the trap I have set for Pedringano, like a bird-trapper smearing sticky lime on twigs. (Cf. 2.1.126.)
5. And doesn't see what the trap was really about. (On birdlime, see note 5 in 2.1 above.)

MESSENGER From Pedringano that's imprisoned.
[*He hands Lorenzo the letter.*]
LORENZO So, he is in prison, then?
MESSENGER Ay, my good lord.
LORENZO What would he with us? [*He reads.*] He writes us here
To stand good lord° and help him in distress.— *act as patron*
Tell him I have his letters, know his mind,
And what we° may, let him assure him° of. *I / himself*
Fellow, begone. My boy shall follow thee.
Exit Messenger.
This works like wax;° yet once more try thy wits.— *is easily shaped*
Boy, go convey this purse to Pedringano.
[*Lorenzo gives a purse.*]
Thou knowest the prison. Closely° give it him, *Secretly*
And be advised° that none be thereabout. *be sure, take care*
Bid him be merry still, but secret;
And though the marshal sessions be today,
Bid him not doubt of his delivery.
Tell him his pardon is already signed,
And thereon bid him boldly be resolved;° *resolute, assured*
For, were he ready to be turnèd off[6]—
As 'tis my will the uttermost be tried°— *be tried to save him*
Thou with his pardon shalt attend him still.
Show him this box, tell him his pardon's in't,
[*He gives a box.*]
But open't not, an if° thou lovest thy life, *an if = if*
But let him wisely keep his hopes unknown;
He shall not want while Don Lorenzo lives.
Away!
PAGE I go, my lord, I run.
LORENZO But, sirrah, see that this be cleanly° done. *neatly*
Exit Page.
Now stands our fortune on a tickle° point, *ticklish, critical*
And now or never ends Lorenzo's doubts.° *fears*
One only thing is uneffected yet,
And that's to see the executioner.
But to what end? I list not° trust the air *am unwilling to*
With utterance of our pretense° therein, *my intentions*
For fear the privy° whisp'ring of the wind *secret*
Convey our words amongst unfriendly ears,
That lie too open to advantages.° *opportunities*
E quel che voglio io, nessun lo sa;
Intendo io, quel mi basterà.[7] *Exit.*

[3.5]

Enter boy [Page], with the box.

PAGE My master hath forbidden me to look in this box; and by my troth, 'tis likely, if he had not warned me, I should not have had so much idle time,[1] for we men's-kind in our

6. Turned off the gallows ladder and thus hanged. (See also 3.6.107 and note.)
7. And what I want, no one knows; I understand, and that suffices for me. (Italian; no source is known.)

3.5. On the way to the Knight Marshal's courtroom.
1. If he hadn't warned me not to, I wouldn't have bothered to look.

minority[2] are like women in their uncertainty:° that° they are most forbidden, they will soonest attempt. So I now. [*He opens the box.*] By my bare° honesty, here's nothing but the bare empty box! Were it not sin against secrecy, I would say it were a piece of gentlemanlike knavery. I must go to Pedringano, and tell him his pardon is in this box; nay, I would have sworn it, had I not seen the contrary. I cannot choose but smile to think how the villain will flout° the gallows, scorn the audience, and descant on° the hangman, and all presuming of his pardon from hence. Will't not be an odd jest for me to stand and grace every jest he makes, pointing my finger at this box, as who would say,° "Mock on, here's thy warrant"? Is't not a scurvy° jest, that a man should jest himself to death? Alas, poor Pedringano, I am in a sort° sorry for thee, but if I should be hanged[3] with thee, I cannot weep. *Exit.*

perverseness / that which · *simple; threadbare* · *scoff at* · *warble about, mock* · *as if to say* · *shabby, contemptible* · *way, sense*

[3.6]

Enter Hieronimo and the Deputy. [*A gallows is provided onstage.*]

HIERONIMO Thus must we toil in other men's extremes,° — *hardships*
That know not how to remedy our own,
And do them justice, when unjustly we,
For all our wrongs, can compass° no redress. — *encompass; find*
But shall I never live to see the day
That I may come, by justice of the heavens,
To know the cause that may my cares allay?
This toils° my body, this consumeth age,° — *burdens / wears me out*
That only I to all men just must be,
And neither gods nor men be just to me.

DEPUTY Worthy Hieronimo, your office asks
A care° to punish such as do transgress. — *commitment, concern*

HIERONIMO So is't my duty to regard his° death — *care about Horatio's*
Who, when he lived, deserved° my dearest blood. — *merited my spilling*
But come, for that° we came for, let's begin, — *that which*
For here lies that[1] which bids me to be gone.

Enter officers [*one of them the Hangman*], *boy* [*Page, with the box*], *and Pedringano, with a letter in his hand, bound.*

DEPUTY Bring forth the prisoner, for the court is set.

PEDRINGANO [*aside to the Page*] Gramercy,° boy, but it was time to come, — *Many thanks*
For I had written to my lord anew
A nearer° matter that concerneth him, — *more intimate, serious*
For fear His Lordship had forgotten me;
But sith° he hath remembered me so well— — *since*
[*Aloud*] Come, come, come on, when shall we to this gear?° — *business*

HIERONIMO Stand forth, thou monster, murderer of men,

2. For we underage males.
3. The Page plays on the proverbial sense of this phrase—"if my life depended on it"—and the literal meaning.

3.6. The Knight Marshal's courtroom.
1. Here (worn next to my heart) is the bloody handkerchief. (See 2.5.51–52.)

And here, for satisfaction of the world,
Confess thy folly and repent thy fault,
For [*indicating the gallows*] there's thy place of execution.

PEDRINGANO This is short work. Well, to Your Marshalship
First I confess—nor fear I death therefore—
I am the man; 'twas I slew Serberine.
But, sir, then you think this shall be the place
Where we shall satisfy you for this gear?

DEPUTY Ay, Pedringano.

PEDRINGANO Now I think not so.

HIERONIMO Peace,° impudent! For thou shalt find it so. *Shut up*
For blood with blood shall, while I sit as judge,
Be satisfied, and the law discharged.° *fulfilled, satisfied*
And though myself cannot receive the like,° *can't obtain justice*
Yet will I see that others have their right.
Dispatch! The fault's approvèd° and confessed, *proved*
And by our law he is condemned to die.

HANGMAN Come on, sir, are you ready?

PEDRINGANO To do what, my fine officious knave?

HANGMAN To go to this gear.

PEDRINGANO Oh, sir, you are too forward. Thou wouldst fain° furnish me with a halter,° to disfurnish me of my habit;[2] so I should go out of this gear, my raiment, into that gear, the rope. But, hangman, now° I spy your knavery, I'll not change without boot,[3] that's flat.° *You wish to / noose / now that / that's for certain*

HANGMAN Come, sir.

PEDRINGANO So, then I must up?

HANGMAN No remedy.

PEDRINGANO Yes, but there shall be for my coming down.

HANGMAN Indeed, here's a remedy for that.[4]

PEDRINGANO How? Be turned off?° *hanged (see 3.4.72 n)*

HANGMAN Ay, truly. Come, are you ready? I pray, sir, dispatch; the day goes away.

PEDRINGANO What, do you hang by the hour? If you do, I may chance to break your old custom.

HANGMAN Faith, you have reason,° for I am like° to break your young neck. *you're right / likely*

PEDRINGANO Dost thou mock me, hangman? Pray God I be not preserved to break your knave's pate° for this. *hit your knavish head*

HANGMAN Alas, sir, you are a foot too low to reach it, and I hope you will never grow so high while I am in the office.[5]

PEDRINGANO Sirrah,° dost see yonder boy with the box in his hand? *(see 3.2.96)*

HANGMAN What, he that points to it with his finger?

PEDRINGANO Ay, that companion.° *fellow*

HANGMAN I know him not, but what of him?

PEDRINGANO Dost thou think to live till his old doublet° will make thee a new truss?° *waistcoat, jacket / garment (see n. 2)*

HANGMAN Ay, and many a fair year after, to truss up° many an honester man than either thou or he. *string up*

2. Hangmen customarily received the clothing of the hanged criminal.
3. Without benefit or compensation. (Punning also on boots for the feet.)
4. Pedringano insists that a remedy is at hand to save him, but the Hangman has another view of how Pedringano will come down.
5. The Hangman is evidently a foot taller than Pedringano (who is perhaps played by a boy actor).

PEDRINGANO What hath he in his box, as thou think'st?
HANGMAN Faith,° I cannot tell, nor I care not greatly. *In good faith*
Methinks you should rather hearken to your soul's health.
PEDRINGANO Why, sirrah hangman? I take it that that° is good *that which*
for the body is likewise good for the soul; and, it may be, in
that box is balm for both.
HANGMAN Well, thou art even the merriest piece of man's
flesh° that e'er groaned at my office door. *human specimen*
PEDRINGANO Is your roguery become an office, with a knave's
name?[6]
HANGMAN Ay, and that shall all they witness that see you seal° *authenticate*
it with a thief's name.
PEDRINGANO I prithee request this good company° to pray *the audience*
with me.
HANGMAN Ay, marry,° sir, this is a good motion.°—My mas- *by Mary / proposal*
ters,° you see here's a good fellow. *good sirs*
PEDRINGANO Nay, nay, now I remember me, let them alone
till some other time, for now I have no great need.
HIERONIMO I have not seen a wretch so impudent.
Oh, monstrous times, where murder's set so light,
And where the soul, that should be shrined° in heaven, *enshrined*
Solely delights in interdicted° things, *forbidden*
Still wand'ring in the thorny passages
That intercepts itself of° happiness! *cuts itself off from*
Murder, oh, bloody monster! God forbid
A fault so foul should scape unpunishèd.—
Dispatch, and see this execution done.
This makes me to remember thee, my son. *Exit Hieronimo.*
[*Pedringano is readied for the hanging.*]
PEDRINGANO Nay, soft,° no haste. *wait a minute*
DEPUTY Why, wherefore stay you? Have you hope of life?
PEDRINGANO Why, ay.
HANGMAN As how?
PEDRINGANO Why, rascal, by my pardon from the King.
HANGMAN Stand° you on that? Then you shall off with this.[7] *Rely*
He turns him off.
DEPUTY So, executioner, convey him hence,
But let his body be unburièd.
Let not the earth be chokèd or infect
With that which heaven contemns° and men neglect.° *scorns / shun*
Exeunt.

[3.7]

Enter Hieronimo.

HIERONIMO Where shall I run to breathe abroad° my woes— *cry aloud*
My woes, whose weight hath wearièd the earth—
Or mine exclaims,° that have surcharged the air *exclamations, outcries*
With ceaseless plaints° for my deceasèd son? *laments*

6. Do you mean to dignify the degrading thing you do by calling it an "office," or official function, in the name of knavery?

7. I.e., you'll not be "standing" on anything when I turn you off the gallows ladder and hang you.

3.7. The scene continues.

The blust'ring winds, conspiring with my words,
At my lament have moved the leafless trees,[1]
Disrobed the meadows of their flowered green,
Made mountains marsh with spring tides of my tears,
And broken through the brazen gates of hell.
Yet still tormented is my tortured soul
With broken sighs and restless passions,
That, wingèd, mount, and, hovering in the air,
Beat at the windows of the brightest heavens,
Soliciting for justice and revenge.
But they° are placed in those empyreal° heights *(the gods) / heavenly*
Where, countermured° with walls of diamond, *doubly walled*
I find the place impregnable, and they
Resist my woes, and give my words no way.

Enter Hangman with a letter.

HANGMAN Oh, lord, sir, God bless you, sir, the man, sir, Petergade,° sir, he that was so full of merry conceits°— *Pedringano / jests*

HIERONIMO Well, what of him?

HANGMAN Oh, lord, sir, he went the wrong way; the fellow had a fair° commission to the contrary. Sir, here is his passport.° I pray you, sir, we have done him wrong. *valid* / *discharge permit*

HIERONIMO I warrant thee, give it me. [*He takes the letter.*]

HANGMAN You will stand between the gallows and me?

HIERONIMO Ay, ay.

HANGMAN I thank Your Lord Worship. *Exit Hangman.*

HIERONIMO And yet, though somewhat nearer me concerns,[2]
I will, to ease the grief that I sustain,
Take truce with sorrow while I read on this. [*He reads.*]
"My lord, I writ as mine extremes required,
That you would labor my delivery.° *work to free me*
If you neglect, my life is desperate,
And in my death I shall reveal the troth.° *truth*
You know, my lord, I slew him° for your sake, *(Serberine)*
And was confederate with the Prince and you,
Won by rewards and hopeful promises;
I holp° to murder Don Horatio, too." *helped*
Holp he to murder mine Horatio?
An actor in th'accursèd tragedy
Wast thou, Lorenzo—Balthazar, and thou—
Of whom my son, my son, deserved so well?
What have I heard? What have mine eyes beheld?
O sacred heavens, may it come to pass
That such a monstrous and detested deed,
So closely smothered° and so long concealed, *stifled, suppressed*
Shall thus by this° be vengèd° or revealed? *this letter / avenged*
Now see I what I durst° not then suspect: *dared*
That Bel-imperia's letter was not feigned,
Nor feignèd she, though falsely they° have wronged *(Lorenzo and Balthazar)*
Both her, myself, Horatio, and themselves.
Now may I make compare, 'twixt hers and this,° *this letter*
Of every accident.° I ne'er could find° *circumstance / understand*

1. Have stripped the trees of their leaves.
2. Though something more urgently personal concerns me most.

Till now, and now I feelingly perceive,
They did what heaven unpunished would not leave.[3]
O false Lorenzo, are these thy flattering looks?
Is this the honor that thou didst my son?
And Balthazar, bane° to thy soul and me, — *ruin; poison*
Was this the ransom he reserved thee° for? — *spared you from death*
Woe to the cause of these constrainèd° wars, — *violent; unnatural*
Woe to thy baseness° and captivity, — *cowardice in battle*
Woe to thy birth, thy body and thy soul,
Thy cursèd father, and thy conquered self!
And banned° with bitter execrations be — *accursed*
The day and place where he° did pity° thee! — *(Horatio) / spare*
But wherefore waste I mine unfruitful words,
When naught but blood will satisfy my woes?
I will go plain me° to my lord the King, — *complain*
And cry aloud for justice through the court,
Wearing the flints with these my withered feet,[4]
And either purchase° justice by entreats — *obtain*
Or tire° them all with my revenging threats. *Exit.* — *weary; tear apart*

[3.8]

Enter Isabella and her Maid.

ISABELLA So that you say this herb will purge° the eye, — *cleanse, heal*
And this the head?
Ah, but none of them will purge the heart.
No, there's no medicine left for my disease,
Nor any physic° to recure° the dead. *She runs lunatic.* — *medicine / resuscitate*
Horatio, oh, where's Horatio?

MAID Good madam, affright not thus yourself
With outrage° for your son Horatio. — *intemperate grief*
He sleeps in quiet in the Elysian fields.° — *abode of the blessed*

ISABELLA Why, did I not give you gowns and goodly things,
Bought you a whistle and a whip-stalk° too, — *whipstock, whip handle*
To be revengèd on their villainies?

MAID Madam, these humors° do torment my soul. — *mad fancies*

ISABELLA "My soul"? Poor soul, thou talks° of things — *talk'st*
Thou know'st not what. My soul hath silver wings,
That mounts me up unto the highest heavens,
To heaven; ay, there sits my Horatio,
Backed with° a troop of fiery cherubins[1] — *Surrounded by*
Dancing about his newly healèd wounds,
Singing sweet hymns and chanting heavenly notes—
Rare harmony to greet° his innocence, — *greet with acclaim*
That died, ay, died, a mirror° in our days. — *paragon*
But say, where shall I find the men, the murderers,
That slew Horatio? Whither shall I run
To find them out that murderèd my son? *Exeunt.*

3. What heaven would not leave unpunished.
4. Wearing down the very flagstones by passing back and forth on aged feet with my petition.
3.8. Hieronimo's house.
1. The cherubins (or cherubim, the plural of "cherub") dwell in the highest heaven, or empyrean; see 3.7.15. The cherubins are "fiery" because, in some cosmologies, that highest region was also the region of fire, fire being a purifying element that ascends, since (according to the humors theory—see 1.3, note 2) it is hot and dry.

[3.9]

Bel-imperia at a window.° *(on upper acting level)*

BEL-IMPERIA What means this outrage that is offered° me? *done to*
Why am I thus sequestered from the court?
No notice?° Shall I not know the cause *news*
Of this my secret and suspicious ills?
Accursèd brother, unkind° murderer, *cruel; unnatural*
Why bends thou° thus thy mind to martyr me? *do you apply*
Hieronimo, why writ I of thy wrongs,[1]
Or why art thou so slack in thy revenge?
Andrea, O Andrea, that thou sawest[2]
Me for thy friend Horatio handled thus,
And him for me thus causeless murderèd!
Well, force perforce,° I must constrain myself *willy-nilly*
To patience, and apply me to the time,° *bow to circumstances*
Till heaven, as I have hoped, shall set me free.

Enter Christophil.

CHRISTOPHIL Come, Madam Bel-imperia, this may not be.
Exeunt.

[3.10]

Enter Lorenzo, Balthazar, and the Page.

LORENZO Boy, talk no further; thus far things go well.
Thou art assurèd that thou sawest him° dead? *(Pedringano)*
PAGE Or else, my lord, I live not.
LORENZO That's enough.
As for his resolution in his end,[1]
Leave that to him° with whom he sojourns now. *i.e., the devil*
Here, take my ring,° and give it Christophil, *(as proof of authority)*
And bid him let my sister be enlarged,° *freed*
And bring her hither straight. *Exit Page.*
This that I did was for a policy° *stratagem*
To smooth and keep the murder secret,[2]
Which as a nine days' wonder being o'erblown,[3]
My gentle° sister will I now enlarge. *wellborn*
BALTHAZAR And time,° Lorenzo, for my lord the Duke, *in good time*
You heard, inquirèd for her yesternight.
LORENZO Why, and, my lord, I hope you heard me say
Sufficient reason why she kept away.
But that's all one.° My lord, you love her? *i.e., let that go*
BALTHAZAR Ay.
LORENZO Then in your love beware; deal cunningly;
Salve° all suspicions; only soothe me up;[4] *Smooth over*
And if she hap to stand on terms° with us, *make conditions*
As for her sweetheart, and concealment so,

3.9. A window in Castile's house, represented onstage on the upper acting level.
1. (1) What avails it that I wrote you of the wrongs you suffered? (2) Why do you think I wrote?
2. Would that you could see. (A stage irony, since the ghost of Andrea is silently witnessing all that occurs.)

3.10. Castile's house.
1. As for the state of his soul, his readiness for death.
2. To hush things up about the murder.
3. Which, since it is a transient event now having blown over.
4. Corroborate what I say.

Jest with her gently; under feignèd jest
Are things concealed that else would breed unrest.
But here she comes.

Enter Bel-imperia.

Now, sister—

BEL-IMPERIA Sister? No,
Thou art no brother, but an enemy!
Else wouldst thou not have used thy sister so,
First, to affright me with thy weapons drawn,
And with extremes abuse my company,° *companion*
And then to hurry me, like whirlwind's rage,
Amidst a crew of thy confederates,
And clap° me up where none might come at me, *shut*
Nor I at any to reveal my wrongs.
What madding fury did possess thy wits?
Or wherein is't that I offended thee?

LORENZO Advise you better,° Bel-imperia, *Be more careful*
For I have done you no disparagement,
Unless,° by more discretion than deserved, *Unless in that*
I sought to save your honor and mine own.

BEL-IMPERIA Mine honor? Why, Lorenzo, wherein is't
That I neglect my reputation so
As you, or any, need to rescue it?

LORENZO His Highness and my father were resolved
To come confer with old Hieronimo
Concerning certain matters of estate
That by the Viceroy was determinèd.[5]

BEL-IMPERIA And wherein was mine honor touched in that?

BALTHAZAR Have patience, Bel-imperia, hear the rest.

LORENZO Me next in sight° as messenger they sent, *standing nearby*
To give him° notice that they were so nigh. *(Hieronimo)*
Now, when I came, consorted with° the Prince, *accompanied by*
And unexpected in an arbor there
Found Bel-imperia with Horatio—

BEL-IMPERIA How then?

LORENZO Why, then, remembʼring that old disgrace° *secret love affair*
Which you for Don Andrea had endured,
And now were likely longer to sustain,° *i.e., by loving Horatio*
By being found so meanly° accompanied, *unworthily in rank*
Thought rather—for I knew no readier mean°— *means*
To thrust Horatio forth° my father's way. *out of*

BALTHAZAR And carry you obscurely somewhere else,
Lest that His Highness should have found you there.

BEL-IMPERIA Even so, my lord? And you are witness
That this is true which he entreateth of?° *which Lorenzo relates*
You, gentle brother, forged this for my sake,
And you, my lord,° were made his instrument— *(Balthazar)*
A work of worth, worthy the noting too!° *(said sarcastically)*
But what's the cause that you concealed me since?

LORENZO Your melancholy, sister, since the news

5. I.e., Concerning a certain dowry that the Viceroy of Portugal was proposing to settle on his son Balthazar in the event of his marrying Bel-imperia. ("Estate" means both "state" and "property," or "wealth," since this would be a state marriage. See 3.12.32–50.)

Of your first favorite Don Andrea's death
My father's old wrath hath exasperate.° *exacerbated*
BALTHAZAR And better was't for you, being in disgrace,
To absent yourself and give his fury place.° *respectful distance*
BEL-IMPERIA But why had I no notice of his ire?
LORENZO That were to add more fuel to your fire,
Who burnt like Etna° for Andrea's loss. *a volcano in Sicily*
BEL-IMPERIA Hath not my father then inquired for me?
LORENZO Sister, he hath, and thus excused I thee.
He whispereth in her ear.
But, Bel-imperia, see the gentle prince;
Look on thy love, behold young Balthazar,
Whose passions by thy presence are increased,
And in whose melancholy thou mayest see
Thy hate, his love; thy flight, his following thee.[6]
BEL-IMPERIA Brother, you are become an orator—
I know not, I, by what experience—
Too politic° for me, past all compare, *cunning, slick*
Since last I saw you. But content yourself;° *rest assured*
The Prince is meditating higher things.
BALTHAZAR 'Tis of thy beauty, then, that conquers kings;
Of those thy tresses, Ariadne's twines,[7]
Wherewith my liberty thou hast surprised;° *captured*
Of that thine ivory front,° my sorrow's map, *forehead*
Wherein I see no haven to rest my hope.
BEL-IMPERIA To love, and fear, and both at once, my lord,
In my conceit, are things of more import
Than women's wits are to be busied with.[8]
BALTHAZAR 'Tis I that love.
BEL-IMPERIA Whom?
BALTHAZAR Bel-imperia.
BEL-IMPERIA But I that fear.
BALTHAZAR Whom?
BEL-IMPERIA Bel-imperia.
LORENZO Fear yourself?
BEL-IMPERIA Ay, brother.
LORENZO How?
BEL-IMPERIA As those
That what they love are loath and fear to lose.[9]
BALTHAZAR Then, fair, let Balthazar your keeper be.
BEL-IMPERIA No, Balthazar doth fear as well as we.
Et tremulo metui pavidum junxere timorem,
Et vanum stolidae proditionis opus.[1] *Exit.*
LORENZO Nay, an° you argue things so cunningly, *if*
We'll go continue this discourse at court.

6. You may see how his melancholy is brought on by your hatred in return for his love and by your fleeing from his pursuit.

7. Balthazar compares Bel-imperia's hair to the skein of thread given by Ariadne to Theseus to enable him to make his way out of King Minos's labyrinth by unwinding it as he went so that by its guidance he could retrace his steps; or perhaps Balthazar means Arachne, who challenged Athene to a weaving contest and was punished for her presumption by being turned into a spider.

8. Bel-imperia pretends that, as a mere woman, she has only an imperfect understanding of how one might love and fear all at the same time.

9. Bel-imperia's fear is of losing what she cherishes most—her independence, perhaps. ("Fear" means "fearful, afraid.")

1. And they joined timorousness to quaking fear, a futile work and a sottish betrayal. (Bel-imperia sees little hope in a union where the potential partners fear loss and rejection. As at 1.3.15–17, Kyd writes his own Latin saying, based on various possible sources.)

BALTHAZAR Led by the lodestar° of her heavenly looks — *guiding star*
Wends poor oppressèd Balthazar
As o'er the mountains walks the wanderer,
Incertain to effect° his pilgrimage. *Exeunt.* — *achieve*

[3.11]

Enter two Portingales [Portuguese], and Hieronimo meets them.

FIRST PORTUGUESE By your leave, sir.
HIERONIMO Good leave have you. Nay, I pray you, go,[1]
For I'll leave you, if you can leave me so.
SECOND PORTUGUESE Pray you,
Which is the next° way to my lord the Duke's? — *nearest*
HIERONIMO The next way° from me. — *By getting far away*
FIRST PORTUGUESE To his house, we mean.
HIERONIMO Oh, hard by; 'tis yon house that you see.
SECOND PORTUGUESE You could not tell us if his son were there?
HIERONIMO Who, my lord Lorenzo?
FIRST PORTUGUESE Ay, sir.
He goeth in at one door and comes out at another.[2]
HIERONIMO Oh, forbear,
For other talk for us far fitter were.° — *would be much fitter*
But if you be importunate to know
The way to him, and where to find him out,
Then list° to me, and I'll resolve your doubt. — *listen*
There is a path upon your left-hand side° — *a path to hell*
That leadeth from a guilty conscience
Unto a forest of distrust and fear—
A darksome place and dangerous to pass.
There shall you meet with melancholy thoughts,
Whose baleful humors if you but uphold,° — *sustain, continue in*
It will conduct you to despair and death,
Whose rocky cliffs when you have once beheld,
Within a hugy° dale of lasting° night — *huge / everlasting*
That, kindled with the world's iniquities,
Doth cast up filthy and detested fumes.
Not far from thence, where murderers have built
A habitation for their cursèd souls,
There in a brazen caldron fixed by Jove
In his fell° wrath upon a sulfur flame, — *fierce*
Yourselves shall find Lorenzo bathing him° — *himself*
In boiling lead and blood of innocents.
FIRST PORTUGUESE Ha, ha, ha!
HIERONIMO Ha, ha, ha!
Why, ha, ha, ha! Farewell, good, ha, ha, ha! *Exit.*
SECOND PORTUGUESE Doubtless this man is passing° lunatic, — *exceedingly*
Or imperfection of his age doth make him dote.
Come, let's away to seek my lord the Duke. *[Exeunt.]*

3.11. Near Castile's house.
1. Hieronimo pretends madness by seeming to interpret the First Portuguese's "By your leave"—i.e., "Excuse me, may I ask a question?"—as meaning a polite "Good-bye."
2. The First Portuguese enters Castile's house to look for Lorenzo and returns unsuccessful.

[3.12]

Enter Hieronimo with a poniard in one hand and a rope in the other.[1]

HIERONIMO Now, sir,° perhaps I come and see the King; *(an imagined listener)*
The King sees me, and fain would hear my suit.
Why, is not this a strange and seld-seen° thing, *seldom-seen*
That standers-by with toys° should strike me mute? *trifles, inanities*
Go to, I see their shifts,° and say no more. *tricks*
Hieronimo, 'tis time for thee to trudge.° *be on your way*
Down by the dale that flows with purple° gore *bloodred*
Standeth a fiery tower; there sits a judge
Upon a seat of steel and molten brass,
And 'twixt his teeth he holds a firebrand
That leads unto the lake where hell doth stand.
Away, Hieronimo! To him° be gone! *(Pluto, king of hell)*
He'll do thee justice for Horatio's death.
Turn down this path, thou shalt be with him straight,
Or this, and then thou need'st not take thy breath.[2]
This way, or that way? Soft and fair,° not so; *Wait a minute*
For if I hang or kill myself, let's know° *let's consider*
Who will revenge Horatio's murder then?
No, no, fie, no! Pardon me; I'll none of that.
He flings away the dagger and halter.° *noose*
This way I'll take, and this way comes the King,
He takes them up again.
And here I'll have a fling at him, that's flat.° *that's for certain*
And, Balthazar, I'll be with thee to bring,° *I'll be even with you*
And thee, Lorenzo! Here's the King; nay, stay,
And here, ay, here, there goes the hare away.° *the quarry escapes*

Enter King, Ambassador, Castile, and Lorenzo.

KING Now show, Ambassador, what our viceroy° saith. *the Viceroy of Portugal*
Hath he received the articles° we sent? *terms*
HIERONIMO Justice, oh, justice to Hieronimo!
LORENZO Back! See'st thou not the King is busy?
HIERONIMO Oh, is he so?
KING Who is he that interrupts our business?
HIERONIMO Not I. [*Aside*] Hieronimo, beware! Go by,° go by. *Go aside; be wary*
AMBASSADOR Renownèd King, he hath received and read
Thy kingly proffers and thy promised league,
And, as a man extremely overjoyed
To hear his son so princely entertained,
Whose death he had so solemnly bewailed,
This, for thy further satisfaction
And kingly love, he kindly lets thee know:
First, for° the marriage of his princely son *as for*
With Bel-imperia, thy belovèd niece,
The news are more delightful to his soul

3.12. The Spanish royal court.
1. The poniard (dagger) and rope (noose) offer Hieronimo means of suicide, but also (at lines 20–24) of revenge.
2. The two paths, of poniard and rope, both offer a quick means of ending life and proceeding to Hades. ("Needst not take thy breath" means "need not live any longer.")

Than myrrh or incense to the offended heavens.
In person therefore will he come himself
To see the marriage rites solemnizèd;
And, in the presence of the court of Spain,
To knit a sure inexplicable band° *indissoluble bond*
Of kingly love and everlasting league
Betwixt the crowns of Spain and Portingale,
There will he give his crown to Balthazar
And make a queen of Bel-imperia.
KING Brother, how like you this our Viceroy's love?
CASTILE No doubt, my lord, it is an argument° *a proof*
Of honorable care to keep° his friend, *keep you as*
And wondrous zeal to Balthazar, his son;
Nor am I least indebted to His Grace,
That bends° his liking to my daughter thus. *directs*
AMBASSADOR Now last, dread lord, here hath His Highness sent—
Although he send not that his son return[3]—
His ransom due to Don Horatio.
[*The ransom is brought forward.*]
HIERONIMO Horatio? Who calls Horatio?
KING And well remembered; thank His Majesty.—
Here, see it given to Horatio.
HIERONIMO Justice, oh, justice, justice, gentle King!
KING Who is that? Hieronimo?
HIERONIMO Justice, oh, justice! Oh, my son, my son,
My son whom naught can ransom or redeem!
LORENZO Hieronimo, you are not well advised.° *i.e., take care*
HIERONIMO Away, Lorenzo, hinder me no more,
For thou hast made me bankrupt of my bliss.
Give me my son! You shall not ransom him.
Away! I'll rip the bowels of the earth
He diggeth with his dagger.
And ferry over to th'Elysian plains,° *(see 3.8.9)*
And bring my son to show his deadly wounds.
Stand from about me!° *Stand away from me!*
I'll make a pickax of my poniard,
And here surrender up my marshalship;
For I'll go marshal up the fiends in hell
To be avengèd on you all for this.
KING What means this outrage?° *outburst*
Will none of you restrain his fury?
HIERONIMO Nay, soft and fair;° you shall not need to strive. *gently*
Needs must he go that the devils drive.[4] *Exit.*
KING What accident hath happed° Hieronimo? *What has happened to*
I have not seen him to demean him° so. *behave himself*
LORENZO My gracious lord, he is with extreme pride—
Conceived of young Horatio, his son,
And covetous of having to himself
The ransom of the young Prince Balthazar—
Distract and in a manner lunatic.

3. The Viceroy need not now request the return of his son, since Balthazar is to marry Bel-imperia. ("That" means "in order that.")
4. I.e., When the devil is chasing you, you have to keep moving. (A proverb, here changed to plural "devils" in reference to Lorenzo, Balthazar, and their accomplices.)

KING Believe me, nephew, we are sorry for't.
This is the love that fathers bear their sons.
[*To Castile*] But, gentle brother, go give to him this gold,
The Prince's ransom; let him have his due;
For what he hath, Horatio shall not want.
Happily° Hieronimo hath need thereof.[5] *Haply, perchance*
LORENZO But if he be thus helplessly distract,
'Tis requisite his office be resigned
And given to one of more discretion.
KING We shall increase his melancholy so.
'Tis best that we see° further in it first, *inquire*
Till when, ourself will not exempt the place.[6]
And, brother, now bring in° the ambassador, *escort*
That he may be a witness of the match
'Twixt Balthazar and Bel-imperia,
And that we may prefix° a certain time *determine in advance*
Wherein the marriage shall be solemnized,
That we may have thy lord the Viceroy here.
AMBASSADOR Therein Your Highness highly shall content
His Majesty, that longs to hear from hence.
KING On, then, and hear you,[7] Lord Ambassador. *Exeunt.*

[3.13]

Enter Hieronimo with a book° in his hand. *(of Seneca's plays)*

HIERONIMO *Vindicta mihi!°* *Vengeance is mine!*
Ay, heaven will be revenged of ° every ill, *on*
Nor will they° suffer murder unrepaid. *(the heavens)*
Then stay, Hieronimo, attend their will,
For mortal men may not appoint their° time. *(the heavens')*
Per scelus semper tutum est sceleribus iter.[1]
Strike, and strike home,° where wrong is offered thee, *all the way*
For evils unto ills conductors be,
And death's the worst of resolution.[2]
For he that thinks with patience to contend° *strive to attain*
To quiet life, his life shall easily° end. *contentedly*
Fata si miseros juvant, habes salutem;
Fata si vitam negant, habes sepulchrum.[3]
If destiny thy miseries do ease,
Then hast thou health, and happy shalt thou be;
If destiny deny thee life, Hieronimo,
Yet shalt thou be assurèd of a tomb.
If neither,° yet let this thy comfort be: *If no happiness or tomb*
Heaven covereth him that hath no burial.[4]
And to conclude, I will revenge his death!
But how? Not as the vulgar wits of men,

5. Hieronimo can share the ransom with his son.
6. Till which time, I will not vacate the office.
7. Come and hear what you will, then report to the Viceroy.
3.13. The Knight Marshal's courtroom.
1. The safe way for crime is always through crime. (Adapted from Seneca, *Agamemnon,* line 115, and freely translated here in line 8.)
2. For evil deeds lead to further violence, and death is the worst thing that a resolute man will have to pay.
3. From Seneca, *Troades,* lines 510–12, freely translated in lines 14–17. Seneca is an authority for both stoical patience and revenge.
4. The heavens cover the dead who have no burial urn; i.e., burial in a tomb is not necessary to assure heaven's blessing for the person who dies virtuously. (From Lucan, *Pharsalia,* 8.118.)

With open, but inevitable ills,
As by a secret, yet a certain, mean,
Which under kindship will be cloakèd best.[5]
Wise men will take their opportunity,
Closely and safely fitting things to time;° — *picking the right time*
But in extremes advantage hath no time,[6]
And therefore all times fit not for revenge.
Thus therefore will I rest me in unrest,
Dissembling quiet in unquietness,
Not seeming that I know their villainies,
That my simplicity° may make them think — *apparent naïveté*
That ignorantly I will let all slip;
For ignorance, I wot,° and well they know, — *know*
Remedium malorum iners est.[7]
Nor aught avails it me to menace them,
Who, as a wintry storm upon a plain,
Will bear me down with their nobility.° — *seniority in rank*
No, no, Hieronimo, thou must enjoin
Thine eyes to observation,° and thy tongue — *be observant*
To milder speeches than thy spirit affords,
Thy heart to patience, and thy hands to rest,° — *inactivity*
Thy cap to curtsey,° and thy knee to bow, — *doffing*
Till to revenge thou know when, where, and how.

A noise within.

How now, what noise? What coil is that you keep?° — *What fuss is this?*

Enter a Servant.

SERVANT Here are a sort° of poor petitioners, — *group*
That are importunate, an° it shall please you, sir, — *if*
That you should plead their cases to the King.

HIERONIMO That I should plead their several actions?° — *various petitions*
Why, let them enter, and let me see them.

Enter three Citizens and an old man [Don Bazulto].

FIRST CITIZEN [*to his companions*] So I tell you this: for learning and for law,
There's not any advocate in Spain
That can prevail, or will take half the pain,° — *pains*
That he will in pursuit of equity.

HIERONIMO Come near, you men that thus importune me.
[*Aside*] Now must I bear a face of gravity,
For thus I used, before my marshalship,
To plead in causes as corregidor.°— — *i.e., advocate*
Come on, sirs, what's the matter?

SECOND CITIZEN Sir, an action.

HIERONIMO Of battery?

FIRST CITIZEN Mine of debt.

HIERONIMO Give place.° — *Stand back*

SECOND CITIZEN No, sir, mine is an action of the case.° — *a special appeal*

THIRD CITIZEN Mine an *ejectione firmae*° by a lease. — *ejection notice*

5. Hieronimo will not employ the open violence used by men of ordinary intelligence ("vulgar wits") with inevitable bad consequences, but will instead use a safer and more certain course of action, hidden beneath the cloak of pretended kindness.

6. But in extreme situations, there is no such thing as a perfect time to act.

7. Is a futile remedy for evils. (From Seneca, *Oedipus*, line 515.)

HIERONIMO Content you, sirs. Are you determinèd
That I should plead your several actions?
FIRST CITIZEN Ay, sir, and here's my declaration.
SECOND CITIZEN And here is my band.° *bond*
THIRD CITIZEN And here is my lease.
They give him papers.
HIERONIMO But wherefore stands yon silly° man so mute, *pitiful*
With mournful eyes and hands to heaven upreared?
Come hither, father,° let me know thy cause. *old man*
BAZULTO O worthy sir, my cause but° slightly known *even but*
May move the hearts of warlike Myrmidons,° *(see 1.1.49 n)*
And melt the Corsic° rocks with ruthful° tears. *Corsican / pitying*
HIERONIMO Say, father, tell me, what's thy suit?
BAZULTO No, sir, could my woes
Give way unto my most distressful words,
Then should I not in paper, as you see,
With ink bewray what blood began in me.[8]
HIERONIMO [*reading*] What's here? "The humble supplication
Of Don Bazulto for his murdered son."
BAZULTO Ay, sir.
HIERONIMO No, sir, it was my murdered son,
Oh, my son, my son, oh, my son Horatio!
But mine, or thine, Bazulto, be content.
Here, take my handkercher and wipe thine eyes,
Whiles wretched I in thy mishaps may see
The lively° portrait of my dying self. *lifelike*
He draweth out a bloody napkin.
Oh, no, not this! Horatio, this was thine,
And when I dyed it in thy dearest blood,
This was a token 'twixt thy soul and me
That of thy death revengèd I should be.
[*He draws out more objects.*]
But here, take this, and this—what, my purse?—
Ay, this and that, and all of them are thine,
For all as one° are our extremities.° *all alike / sufferings*
FIRST CITIZEN Oh, see the kindness of Hieronimo!
SECOND CITIZEN This gentleness shows him a gentleman.
HIERONIMO See, see, oh, see thy shame, Hieronimo!
See here a loving father to his son!
Behold the sorrows and the sad laments
That he delivereth for his son's decease!
If love's effects so strives in lesser things,
If love enforce such moods in meaner wits,° *lesser intelligences*
If love express such power in poor estates,° *lower classes*
Hieronimo, whenas° a raging sea, *when*
Tossed with the wind and tide, o'erturneth then
The upper billows, course of waves to keep,
Whilest lesser waters labor in the deep,[9]
Then shamest thou not, Hieronimo, to neglect
The sweet revenge of thy Horatio?
Though on this earth justice will not be found,

8. Reveal in writing what blood and passion have stirred up in me.

9. Hieronimo exhorts himself to action by contrasting the blustering surface of the sea with a more forceful if unseen movement in the waters of the deep, as seen in the mute grief of a "lesser" man such as Don Bazulto.

I'll down to hell, and in this passion
Knock at the dismal gates of Pluto's court,
Getting by force, as once Alcides° did, *Hercules*
A troop of Furies and tormenting hags
To torture Don Lorenzo and the rest.
Yet lest the triple-headed porter[1] should
Deny my passage to the slimy strand,° *shore (of Hades)*
The Thracian poet[2] thou shalt counterfeit:
Come on, old father, be my Orpheus,
And if thou canst no notes° upon the harp, *cannot play*
Then sound the burden° of thy sore heart's grief, *refrain; heavy load*
Till we do gain° that Proserpine may grant *obtain*
Revenge on them that murderèd my son.
Then will I rend and tear them thus and thus,
Shivering their limbs in pieces with my teeth.
Tear the papers.

FIRST CITIZEN Oh, sir, my declaration!
Exit Hieronimo, and they after.

SECOND CITIZEN Save my bond!

Enter Hieronimo [followed still by the Citizens].

Save my bond!
THIRD CITIZEN Alas, my lease! It cost me ten pound,
And you, my lord, have torn the same.
HIERONIMO That cannot be; I gave it never a wound.
Show me one drop of blood fall from the same.
How is it possible I should slay it, then?
Tush, no. Run after; catch me if you can.
Exeunt all but the old man [Bazulto].

Bazulto remains till Hieronimo enters again, who, staring him in the face, speaks.

And art thou come, Horatio, from the depth,
To ask for justice in this upper earth?
To tell thy father thou art unrevenged?
To wring more tears from Isabella's eyes,
Whose lights are dimmed with overlong laments?
Go back, my son; complain to Aeacus,° *(see 1.1.33 n)*
For here's no justice. Gentle boy, begone,
For justice is exilèd from the earth.
Hieronimo will bear thee company.
Thy mother cries on righteous Rhadamanth° *(see 1.1.33 n)*
For just revenge against the murderers.
BAZULTO Alas, my lord, whence springs this troubled speech?
HIERONIMO But° let me look on my Horatio. *Only*
Sweet boy, how art thou changed in death's black shade!
Had Proserpine no pity on thy youth,
But suffered thy fair crimson-colored spring
With withered winter to be blasted° thus? *nipped with frost*
Horatio, thou art older than thy father.
Ah, ruthless fate, that favor thus transforms!° *alters the face*

1. Cerberus, the many-headed watchdog of Hades, overcome by Hercules (the "Alcides" of line 111).
2. The "Thracian poet" Orpheus played so well on the harp that he won from Proserpine (line 120), Queen of Hades, the right to bring back his wife, Eurydice, to earth.

BAZULTO Ah, my good lord, I am not your young son.
HIERONIMO What, not my son? Thou, then, a Fury° art, *avenging deity*
Sent from the empty kingdom of black night
To summon me to make appearance
Before grim Minos and just Rhadamanth,
To plague Hieronimo, that° is remiss *who*
And seeks not vengeance for Horatio's death.
BAZULTO I am a grievèd man, and not a ghost,
That came for justice for my murdered son.
HIERONIMO Ay, now I know thee, now thou namest my son:[3]
Thou art the lively image of my grief.
Within thy face, my sorrows I may see.
Thy eyes are gummed with tears, thy cheeks are wan,
Thy forehead troubled, and thy mutt'ring lips
Murmur sad words abruptly broken off;
By force of windy sighs thy spirit breathes,
And all this sorrow riseth for thy son;
And selfsame sorrow feel I for my son.
Come in, old man; thou shalt to Isabel.
Lean on my arm; I thee, thou me shalt stay,° *support*
And thou, and I, and she will sing a song,
Three parts in one, but all of discords framed.° *composed*
Talk not of cords,° but let us now be gone, *chords; ropes*
For with a cord Horatio was slain. *Exeunt.*

[3.14]

Enter King of Spain, the Duke [*of Castile*], *Viceroy, and Lorenzo, Balthazar, Don Pedro, and Bel-imperia* [*attended by servants. The Spanish and Portuguese parties, entering from opposite sides, meet and formally greet one another*].

KING Go, brother, it is the Duke of Castile's cause;[1]
Salute the Viceroy in our name.
CASTILE I go.
[*He embraces the Viceroy.*]
VICEROY Go forth, Don Pedro, for thy nephew's° sake, *(Balthazar's)*
And greet the Duke of Castile.
PEDRO It shall be so.
[*He embraces Castile.*]
KING And now to meet these Portuguese,
For as we now are, so sometimes° were these, *formerly*
Kings and commanders of the western Indies.
[*The King embraces the Viceroy.*]
Welcome, brave Viceroy, to the court of Spain,
And welcome, all his honorable train.° *entourage*
'Tis not unknown to us forwhy° you come, *why*
Or have so kingly° crossed the seas. *in royal splendor*
Sufficeth it in this we note the troth° *fealty*
And more than common love you lend° to us. *give*
So is it that mine honorable niece

3. Hieronimo, in his distraction, confuses "my son" with "thy son."
3.14. The royal court.
1. Castile, as father of the bride-to-be, is vitally involved in this marriage treaty.

(For it beseems° us now that it be known) *suits*
Already is betrothed to Balthazar,
And by appointment and our condescent° *consent*
Tomorrow are they to be married.
To this intent we entertain thyself,
Thy followers, their pleasure, and our peace.[2]
Speak, men of Portingale, shall it be so?
If ay, say so; if not, say flatly no.
VICEROY Renownèd King, I come not as thou think'st,
With doubtful followers, unresolvèd men,
But such as have upon thine articles
Confirmed thy motion° and contented me. *proposal*
Know, sovereign, I come to solemnize
The marriage of thy belovèd niece,
Fair Bel-imperia, with my Balthazar—
With thee, my son, whom, sith I live to see,
Here, take my crown; I give it her and thee—
And let me live a solitary life,
In ceaseless prayers,
To think how strangely° heaven hath thee preserved. *miraculously*
[*He weeps.*]
KING [*to Castile*] See, brother, see, how nature° strives in him!— *natural feeling*
Come, worthy Viceroy, and accompany
Thy friend° with thine extremities;° *(Me) / strong feelings*
A place more private fits this princely mood.
VICEROY Or° here or where Your Highness thinks it good. *Either*
Exeunt all but Castile and Lorenzo [*and servants*].
CASTILE Nay, stay, Lorenzo, let me talk with you.
See'st thou this entertainment° of these kings? *hospitable reception*
LORENZO I do, my lord, and joy to see the same.
CASTILE And knowest thou why this meeting is?
LORENZO For her, my lord, whom Balthazar doth love,
And to confirm their promised marriage.
CASTILE She is thy sister.
LORENZO Who, Bel-imperia?
Ay, my gracious lord, and this is the day
That I have longed so happily to see.
CASTILE Thou wouldst be loath that any fault of thine
Should intercept° her in her happiness. *obstruct*
LORENZO Heavens will not let Lorenzo err so much.
CASTILE Why, then, Lorenzo, listen to my words:
It is suspected, and reported too,
That thou, Lorenzo, wrong'st Hieronimo,
And in his suits towards His Majesty
Still keep'st him back, and seeks to cross° his suit. *thwart*
LORENZO That I, my lord?
CASTILE I tell thee, son, myself have heard it said,
When to my sorrow I have been ashamed
To answer for thee, though thou art my son.
Lorenzo, knowest thou not the common° love *universal*
And kindness that Hieronimo hath won
By his deserts° within the court of Spain? *deservings*

2. The young couple's happiness and peace between our countries.

Or see'st thou not the King my brother's care
In his behalf, and to procure his health?° *well-being*
Lorenzo, shouldst thou thwart his passions,° *laments, complaints*
And he exclaim against° thee to the King, *denounce*
What honor were't in this assembly,
Or what a scandal were't among the kings
To hear Hieronimo exclaim on° thee! *denounce*
Tell me—and look° thou tell me truly too— *see to it*
Whence grows the ground° of this report in court? *basis*
LORENZO My lord, it lies not in Lorenzo's power
To stop the vulgar,° liberal° of their tongues. *commoners / too free*
A small advantage makes a water-breach,[3]
And no man lives that long contenteth all.
CASTILE Myself have seen thee busy to keep back
Him and his supplications from the King.
LORENZO Yourself, my lord, hath seen his passions,
That ill beseemed the presence of a king,
And, for° I pitied him in his distress, *because*
I held him thence with kind and courteous words,
As free from malice to Hieronimo
As to my soul, my lord.
CASTILE Hieronimo, my son, mistakes thee then.
LORENZO My gracious father, believe me, so he doth.
But what's a silly man, distract in mind,
To think upon the murder of his son?
Alas, how easy is it for him to err!
But, for his satisfaction and the world's,
'Twere good, my lord, that Hieronimo and I
Were reconciled, if he misconster° me. *misconstrue*
CASTILE Lorenzo, thou hast said;° it shall be so.— *spoken wisely*
Go, one of you, and call Hieronimo. [*Exit a Servant.*]

Enter Balthazar and Bel-imperia.

BALTHAZAR Come, Bel-imperia, Balthazar's content,
My sorrow's ease and sovereign of my bliss,
Sith heaven hath ordained thee to be mine:
Disperse those clouds and melancholy looks,
And clear them up with those thy sun-bright eyes
Wherein my hope and heaven's fair beauty lies.
BEL-IMPERIA My looks, my lord, are fitting for my love,
Which, new begun, can show° no brighter yet. *look, shine*
BALTHAZAR New-kindled flames should burn as morning sun.
BEL-IMPERIA But not too fast, lest heat and all be done.° *consumed*
I see my lord my father.
BALTHAZAR Truce,[4] my love.
I will go salute him.
CASTILE Welcome, Balthazar,
Welcome, brave Prince, the pledge of Castile's peace![5]
And welcome, Bel-imperia. How now, girl?
Why comest thou sadly to salute us° thus? *greet me*
Content thyelf, for I am satisfied.

3. A small leak, if unchecked, grows into a flood.
4. Let's call a truce to our contest of words.
5. The guarantee of peace between Spain and Portugal, and of my own happiness!

It is not now as when Andrea lived;
We have forgotten and forgiven that,
And thou art gracèd with a happier love.—
But, Balthazar, here comes Hieronimo.
I'll have a word with him.

Enter Hieronimo and a Servant.

HIERONIMO And where's the Duke?
SERVANT Yonder.
HIERONIMO [*aside*] Even so.
What new device have they devisèd, trow?° *do you suppose?*
Pocas palabras,° mild as the lamb. *Few words*
Is't I will be revenged? No, I am not the man.[6]
CASTILE Welcome, Hieronimo.
LORENZO Welcome, Hieronimo.
BALTHAZAR Welcome, Hieronimo.
HIERONIMO My lords, I thank you for Horatio.
CASTILE Hieronimo, the reason that I sent
To speak with you is this.
HIERONIMO What, so short?
Then I'll be gone, I thank you for't.[7] [*He starts to leave.*]
CASTILE Nay, stay, Hieronimo.—Go call him, son.
LORENZO Hieronimo, my father craves a word with you.
HIERONIMO With me, sir? Why, my lord, I thought you had done.
LORENZO [*aside*] No, would he had.
CASTILE Hieronimo, I hear
You find yourself aggrievèd at my son,
Because you have not access unto the King,
And say 'tis he that intercepts your suits.
HIERONIMO Why, is not this a miserable thing, my lord?
CASTILE Hieronimo, I hope you have no cause,
And would° be loath that one of your deserts *I would*
Should once have reason to suspect my son,
Considering how I think of you myself.
HIERONIMO Your son Lorenzo? Whom,° my noble lord? *I suspect whom*
The hope of Spain, mine honorable friend?
Grant me the combat of them,° if they dare. *to challenge them*
Draws out his sword.
I'll meet him face to face to tell me so.
These be the scandalous reports of such
As loves° not me, and hate my lord° too much. *love / you, my lord*
Should I suspect Lorenzo would prevent
Or cross my suit, that loved my son so well?
My lord, I am ashamed it should be said.
LORENZO Hieronimo, I never gave you cause.
HIERONIMO My good lord, I know you did not.
CASTILE There then pause,
And for the satisfaction of the world,
Hieronimo, frequent my homely° house, *humble; hospitable*
The Duke of Castile, Cyprian's ancient seat,

6. Hieronimo assumes the disguise of patient forbearance to deceive his enemies. (See 3.13.39–44.)

7. Hieronimo pretends to suppose, madly, that the conversation is over.

And when thou wilt, use° me, my son, and it; *make use of*
But here, before Prince Balthazar and me,
Embrace each other, and be perfect friends.
HIERONIMO Ay, marry,° my lord, and shall. *by Mary (an oath)*
Friends, quoth he? See, I'll be friends with you all,
[*To Balthazar*] Specially with you, my lovely lord.
For divers causes it is fit for us
That we be friends; the world is suspicious,
And men may think what we imagine not.
BALTHAZAR Why, this is friendly done, Hieronimo.
LORENZO And thus, I hope, old grudges are forgot.
HIERONIMO What else?° It were a shame it should not be so. *i.e., But of course*
CASTILE Come on, Hieronimo, at my request,
Let us entreat your company today.
HIERONIMO Your Lordship's to command.
Exeunt [*all but Hieronimo*].
Pha! Keep your way.
Chi mi fa più carezze che non suole,
Tradito mi ha, o tradir mi voule.[8] *Exit.*

[3.15]

Ghost [*of Andrea*] *and Revenge* [*remain onstage*].

ANDREA Awake, Erictho!° Cerberus, awake! *a sorceress*
Solicit Pluto, gentle Proserpine!
To combat, Acheron and Erebus!° *Hades*
For ne'er by Styx and Phlegethon° in hell *underworld rivers*
. . . .[1]
Nor ferried Charon to the fiery lakes
Such fearful sights as poor Andrea sees!
Revenge, awake!
REVENGE Awake? Forwhy?° *Why?*
ANDREA Awake, Revenge, for thou art ill-advised
To sleep away what thou art warned° to watch. *urged*
REVENGE Content thyself, and do not trouble me.
ANDREA Awake, Revenge, if love,° as love hath had, *my cause of love*
Have yet the power or prevalence in hell!
Hieronimo with Lorenzo is joined in league
And intercepts° our passage to revenge. *cuts off*
Awake, Revenge, or we are woebegone!
REVENGE Thus worldlings ground what they have dreamed upon.[2]
Content thyself, Andrea. Though I sleep,
Yet is my mood soliciting° their souls. *Revenge is demanding*
Sufficeth° thee that poor Hieronimo *Let it suffice*
Cannot forget his son Horatio.
Nor dies Revenge, although he sleep awhile;
For in unquiet, quietness is feigned,[3]
And slumb'ring is a common worldly wile.

8. He who shows an unaccustomed fondness for me either has betrayed me or intends to do so.
3.15. The chorus to act 3.
1. The grammatical lacuna suggests that a line is missing here, saying, "Was I distressed with outrage sore as this," or words to that effect.
2. Thus worldlings take their nightmares for reality.
3. For in a state of unrest, quietness is a ruse designed to mislead while the revenger awaits the perfect opportunity.

Behold, Andrea, for an instance how
Revenge hath slept, and then imagine thou
What 'tis to be subject to destiny.

Enter a dumb show [of two torchbearers and Hymen].° — *god of marriage*

ANDREA Awake, Revenge! Reveal this mystery.[4]
REVENGE The two first the nuptial torches bore
As brightly burning as the midday's sun;
But after them doth Hymen hie° as fast, — *hasten*
Clothèd in sable° and a saffron robe, — *black*
And blows them out and quencheth them with blood,
As° discontent that things continue so. — *As if*
ANDREA Sufficeth me thy meaning's understood,
And thanks to thee and those infernal powers
That will not tolerate a lover's woe.
Rest thee, for I will sit to see the rest.
REVENGE Then argue not, for thou hast thy request.
Exeunt [dumb show].

4.1

Enter Bel-imperia and Hieronimo.

BEL-IMPERIA Is this the love thou bear'st Horatio?
Is this the kindness that thou counterfeits?
Are these the fruits of thine incessant tears?
Hieronimo, are these thy passions,° — *passionate outcries*
Thy protestations, and thy deep laments
That thou wert wont to weary men withal?
O unkind° father! O deceitful world! — *unnatural; unloving*
With what excuses canst thou show thyself?
With what devices seek thyself to save
From this dishonor and the hate of men,
Thus to neglect the loss and life of him
Whom both my letters and thine own belief
Assures thee to be causeless slaughterèd?
Hieronimo, for shame, Hieronimo,
Be not a history° to aftertimes — *object lesson*
Of such ingratitude unto thy son.
Unhappy mothers of such children then,
But monstrous fathers, to forget so soon
The death of those whom they with care and cost
Have tendered° so, thus careless should be lost! — *cherished*
Myself, a stranger in respect of thee,[1]
So loved his life as still° I wish their° deaths, — *constantly / (his enemies')*
Nor shall his death be unrevenged by me,
Although I bear it out° for fashion's sake. — *put up appearances*
For here I swear, in sight of heaven and earth,
Shouldst thou neglect the love thou shouldst retain,
And give it over° and devise° no more, — *give up / plot*
Myself should send their hateful souls to hell
That wrought his downfall with extremest death.

4. Explicate (1) this dramatic spectacle; (2) this enigma.
4.1. Hieronimo's house.

1. I who have only a distant relationship with Horatio compared with you.

HIERONIMO But may it be that Bel-imperia
Vows such revenge as she hath deigned to say?
Why, then, I see that heaven applies our drift,° *aids our intents*
And all the saints do sit soliciting
For vengeance on those cursèd murderers.
Madam, 'tis true, and now I find it so,° *confirmed*
I found a letter, written in your name,
And in that letter how Horatio died.
Pardon, oh, pardon, Bel-imperia,
My fear and care° in not believing it, *caution*
Nor think I thoughtless think upon a mean
To let his death be unrevenged at full![2]
And here I vow, so° you but give consent *provided that*
And will conceal my resolution,
I will ere long determine of° their deaths, *bring about*
That causeless thus have murderèd my son.
BEL-IMPERIA Hieronimo, I will consent, conceal,
And aught that may effect for thine avail° *that can help you*
Join with thee to revenge Horatio's death.
HIERONIMO On, then. Whatsoever I devise,
Let me entreat you grace° my practices, *support*
Forwhy° the plot's already in mine head.— *Because*
Here they are.

Enter Balthazar and Lorenzo.

BALTHAZAR How now, Hieronimo,
What, courting Bel-imperia?
HIERONIMO Ay, my lord,
Such courting as, I promise you,
She hath my heart;° but you, my lord, have hers. *affection; secret*
LORENZO But now, Hieronimo, or never,
We are to entreat your help.
HIERONIMO My help?
Why, my good lords, assure yourselves of me,
For you have given me cause,
Ay, by my faith have you.
BALTHAZAR It pleased you
At the entertainment of the ambassador
To grace the King so much as with a show.° *honor him with a show*
Now, were your study° so well furnished *learning; library*
As, for the passing° of the first night's sport,° *conducting / revels*
To entertain my father with the like,
Or any suchlike pleasing motion,° *show*
Assure yourself it would content them well.
HIERONIMO Is this all?
BALTHAZAR Ay, this is all.
HIERONIMO Why, then, I'll fit you;[3] say no more.
When I was young, I gave my mind
And plied myself to fruitless° poetry, *impractical*
Which, though it profit the professor° naught, *practitioner, poet*
Yet is it passing° pleasing to the world. *exceedingly*

2. And do not suppose me so unconcerned as not to be contemplating a means of avenging Horatio's death to the utmost!

3. (1) I'll suit, accommodate you; (2) I'll "fix," settle your hash. (The latter meaning is for the audience.)

LORENZO And how for that?° *What then, what of it?*
HIERONIMO Marry, my good lord, thus—
And yet methinks you are too quick with us—
When in Toledo there I studied,
It was my chance to write a tragedy—
See here, my lords— *He shows them a book.*
Which, long forgot, I found this° other day. *the*
Now, would Your Lordships favor me so much
As but to grace me with your acting it—
I mean, each one of you to play a part—
Assure you it will prove most passing strange,° *sensational*
And wondrous plausible° to that assembly. *worthy of applause*
BALTHAZAR What, would you have us play a tragedy?
HIERONIMO Why, Nero thought it no disparagement,[4]
And kings and emperors have ta'en delight
To make experience° of their wits in plays! *trial*
LORENZO Nay, be not angry, good Hieronimo;
The Prince but asked a question.
BALTHAZAR In faith, Hieronimo, an you be in earnest,
I'll make one.° *take a part*
LORENZO And I another.
HIERONIMO Now, my good lord, could you entreat
Your sister Bel-imperia to make one—
For what's a play without a woman in it?
BEL-IMPERIA Little entreaty shall serve° me, Hieronimo, *serve to persuade*
For I must needs be employed in your play.
HIERONIMO Why, this is well. I tell you, lordings,
It was determinèd° to have been acted *intended; written*
By gentlemen and scholars too,
Such as could tell° what to speak. *would have the skill*
BALTHAZAR And now it shall be played by princes and courtiers
Such as can tell how to speak,
If, as it is our country manner,° *custom*
You will but let us know the argument.° *plot*
HIERONIMO That shall I roundly.° The chronicles of Spain *without further ado*
Record this written of a knight of Rhodes:
He was betrothed and wedded at the length
To one Perseda, an Italian dame,
Whose beauty ravished all that her beheld,
Especially the soul of Suleiman,° *Turkish emperor*
Who at the marriage was the chiefest guest.
By sundry means sought Suleiman to win
Perseda's love, and could not gain the same.
Then 'gan he break° his passions to a friend, *disclose*
One of his bashaws° whom he held full dear. *pashas, nobles*
Her had this bashaw long solicited,
And saw she was not otherwise to be won
But by her husband's death, this knight of Rhodes,
Whom presently by treachery he slew.
She, stirred with an exceeding hate therefor,
As cause° of this slew Suleiman, *Because*
And, to escape the bashaw's tyranny,
Did stab herself; and this the tragedy.

4. The Roman emperor Nero (r. 54–68 C.E.) delighted in acting (and was scorned for it).

LORENZO Oh, excellent!
BEL-IMPERIA But say, Hieronimo,
What then became of him that was the bashaw?
HIERONIMO Marry, thus: moved with remorse of his misdeeds,
Ran to a mountaintop and hung himself.
BALTHAZAR But which of us is to perform that part?
HIERONIMO Oh, that will I, my lords, make no doubt of it;
I'll play the murderer, I warrant you,
For I already have conceited° that. *formed a conception of*
BALTHAZAR And what shall I?
HIERONIMO Great Suleiman, the Turkish emperor.
LORENZO And I?
HIERONIMO Erastus, the Knight of Rhodes.
BEL-IMPERIA And I?
HIERONIMO Perseda, chaste and resolute.
And here, my lords, are several abstracts° drawn, *individual parts*
For each of you to note° your parts *memorize*
And act it as occasion's offered you.
You must provide a Turkish cap,
A black mustachio, and a fauchion;° *falchion, curved sword*
Gives a paper to Balthazar.
You with a cross like to a knight of Rhodes;
Gives another to Lorenzo.
And, madam, you must attire yourself
He giveth Bel-imperia another.
Like Phoebe, Flora, or the Huntress,[5]
Which to your discretion shall seem best.
And as for me, my lords, I'll look to one,° *prepare my role*
And, with the ransom that the Viceroy sent,
So furnish and perform this tragedy
As all the world shall say Hieronimo
Was liberal° in gracing of it so. *bountiful*
BALTHAZAR Hieronimo, methinks a comedy were better.
HIERONIMO A comedy?
Fie, comedies are fit for common wits;
But to present a kingly troop withal,° *to royal spectators*
Give me a stately written tragedy,
Tragedia cothernata,[6] fitting kings,
Containing matter,° and not common things. *weighty matter*
My lords, all this must be performed
As fitting for the first night's reveling.
The Italian tragedians were so sharp of wit
That in one hour's meditation° *i.e., rehearsal*
They would perform anything in action.[7]
LORENZO And well it may,° for I have seen the like *may be so*
In Paris, 'mongst the French tragedians.
HIERONIMO In Paris? Mass,° and well remembered! *By the Mass (an oath)*
There's one thing more that rests° for us to do. *remains*
BALTHAZAR What's that, Hieronimo? Forget not anything.

5. Phoebe was a Titaness often associated with the moon and Artemis; Flora was a deity of fertility and flowers; the Huntress is Artemis, goddess of the hunt and associated with the moon (her Roman counterpart is Diana).
6. Tragedy wearing the buskin, the boot betokening tragedy.
7. Hieronimo describes the extemporaneous style of commedia dell'arte, a form of Italian comedy of the sixteenth to eighteenth centuries improvised from standardized situations and stock characters, here applied (unhistorically) to tragedy.

HIERONIMO Each one of us must act his part
In unknown languages,
That it may breed the more variety,
As you, my lord, in Latin, I in Greek,
You° in Italian; and forbecause° I know *(Lorenzo) / because*
That Bel-imperia hath practicèd the French,
In courtly French shall all her phrases be.
BEL-IMPERIA You mean to try my cunning° then, Hieronimo. *learning; deceit*
BALTHAZAR But this will be a mere° confusion, *total*
And hardly shall we all be understood.
HIERONIMO It must be so, for the conclusion
Shall prove the invention° and all was good; *fiction; device*
And I myself, in an oration,
And with a strange and wondrous show besides
That I will have there behind a curtain,
Assure yourself, shall make the matter known.° *expound the play*
And all shall be concluded in one scene,
For there's no pleasure ta'en in tediousness.
BALTHAZAR [*aside to Lorenzo*] How like you this?
LORENZO [*aside to Balthazar*] Why, thus, my lord:
We must resolve to soothe his humors up.° *humor him*
BALTHAZAR On, then, Hieronimo. Farewell till soon.
HIERONIMO You'll ply this gear?° *undertake it*
LORENZO I warrant you.
Exeunt all but Hieronimo.
HIERONIMO Why, so.
Now shall I see the fall of Babylon,
Wrought by the heavens in this confusion.[8]
And if the world like not this tragedy,
Hard is the hap of old Hieronimo. *Exit.*

[4.2]

Enter Isabella with a weapon.

ISABELLA Tell me no more! Oh, monstrous homicides!
Since neither piety nor pity moves
The King to justice or compassion,
I will revenge myself upon this place
Where thus they murdered my belovèd son.
She cuts down the arbor.
Down with these branches and these loathsome boughs
Of this unfortunate and fatal pine!
Down with them, Isabella, rend them up,
And burn the roots from whence the rest is sprung!
I will not leave a root, a stalk, a tree,
A bough, a branch, a blossom, nor a leaf,
No, not an herb within this garden plot.
Accursèd complot of my misery![1]

8. The fall of Babylon in Revelation 18 is a major event in the apocalyptic ending of the world. These lines recall also the Tower of Babel, where the building of the tower was thought to have been stopped by God's confounding of the world's one language into many (see Genesis 11.1–9). "Confusion" here can mean both this chaotic mingling of tongues and a complete destruction.

4.2. The garden of Hieronimo's house.

1. (1) Accursed conspiracy, source of my misery; (2) accursed garden plot, in which I am miserable.

Fruitless forever may this garden be,
Barren the earth, and blissless whosoever
Imagines not to keep it unmanured![2]
An eastern wind, commixed with noisome° airs, *noxious*
Shall blast° the plants and the young saplings; *blight*
The earth with serpents shall be pesterèd,
And passengers,° for fear to be infect, *passersby*
Shall stand aloof, and, looking at it, tell,
"There murdered died the son of Isabel."
Ay, here he died, and here I him embrace.
See where his ghost solicits with his wounds
Revenge on her that should revenge his death![3]
Hieronimo, make haste to see thy son,
For sorrow and despair hath cited° me *summoned*
To hear Horatio plead with Rhadamanth.
Make haste, Hieronimo, to hold excused° *offer excuses for*
Thy negligence in pursuit of their deaths
Whose hateful wrath bereaved him of his breath.
Ah, nay, thou dost delay their deaths,
Forgives° the murderers of thy noble son, *Thou forgivest*
And none but I bestir me—to no end.
And as I curse this tree from further fruit,
So shall my womb be cursèd for his sake,
And with this weapon will I wound the breast,
She stabs herself.
The hapless breast that gave Horatio suck. [*Exit.*][4]

[4.3]

Enter Hieronimo; he knocks up° the curtain. Enter the Duke of Castile. *fastens up*

CASTILE How now, Hieronimo, where's your fellows,
That you take all this pain?° *these pains*
HIERONIMO Oh, sir, it is for the author's credit
To look° that all things may go well. *see to it*
But, good my lord, let me entreat Your Grace
To give the King the copy of the play.
This is the argument° of what we show. *plot*
[*He hands Castile a book.*]
CASTILE I will, Hieronimo.
HIERONIMO One thing more, my good lord.
CASTILE What's that?
HIERONIMO Let me entreat Your Grace
That when the train° are passed into the gallery,° *retinue / hall*
You would vouchsafe to throw me down the key.
CASTILE I will, Hieronimo. *Exit Castile.*
HIERONIMO [*calling*] What, are you ready, Balthazar?
Bring a chair and a cushion for the King.

2. May that person be forever damned who would conceive of any plan other than to keep it forever uncultivated.
3. Horatio's ghost calls down vengeance on any woman (especially myself) who fails to revenge his death. ("Should" means "should but does not.")
4. Either Isabella staggers offstage as she stabs herself or her body is concealed at the start of the next scene by Hieronimo's fastening up of the curtain for his play.
4.3. The royal court.

Enter Balthazar with a chair.

Well done, Balthazar. Hang up the title;[1]
Our scene is Rhodes. What, is your beard on?
BALTHAZAR Half on; the other is in my hand.
HIERONIMO Dispatch, for shame! Are you so long?° *slow*
Exit Balthazar.
Bethink thyself, Hieronimo;
Recall thy wits, recount thy former wrongs
Thou hast received by murder of thy son,
And lastly, not least, how Isabel,
Once his mother and thy dearest wife,
All woebegone for him, hath slain herself.
Behooves thee, then, Hieronimo, to be revenged!
The plot is laid of dire revenge.
On, then, Hieronimo, pursue revenge,
For nothing wants° but acting of revenge. *is lacking*
Exit Hieronimo.

[4.4]

Enter Spanish king, Viceroy, the Duke of Castile, and their train [including Don Pedro].

KING Now, Viceroy, shall we see the tragedy
Of Suleiman, the Turkish emperor,
Performed of pleasure° by your son the Prince, *with gracious consent*
My nephew Don Lorenzo, and my niece.
VICEROY Who, Bel-imperia?
KING Ay, and Hieronimo, our marshal,
At whose request they deign to do't themselves.
These be our pastimes in the court of Spain.—
Here, brother, you shall be the bookkeeper.° *prompter*
This is the argument of that they show.
He giveth him° a book. *(Castile)*

(Gentlemen, this play of Hieronimo in sundry languages was thought good to be set down in English more largely for the easier understanding to every public reader.)[1]

Enter Balthazar [as Suleiman], Bel-imperia [as Perseda], and Hieronimo [as the Bashaw].

BALTHAZAR *Bashaw, that Rhodes is ours, yield heavens the honor,*[2]
And holy Mahomet,° our sacred prophet; *Muhammad*
And be thou graced with every excellence
That Suleiman can give or thou desire.
But thy desert in conquering Rhodes is less
Than in reserving° this fair Christian nymph, *sparing the life of*
Perseda, blissful lamp of excellence,

1. A board or other device hung up to inform the audience of the name of the drama or the location of a scene. The practice appears not to have been common, though it seems called for in several boys' plays that were performed in private indoor theaters.
4.4. The scene continues.
1. A publisher's note to the reader, although conceivably Castile could be reading from the playbook.
2. The speeches of the masque are here set in italic type to make clear when Balthazar, Hieronimo, Lorenzo, and Bel-imperia are speaking their lines, as distinguished from the dialogue of the surrounding play of *The Spanish Tragedy.* See the unnumbered text following 4.4.10.1 on the fiction that the characters are supposed to be speaking in foreign languages.

Whose eyes compel, like powerful adamant,° — a powerful magnet
The warlike heart of Suleiman to wait.° — attend on her
KING See, Viceroy, that is Balthazar, your son,
That represents the Emperor Suleiman.
How well he acts his amorous passion!
VICEROY Ay, Bel-imperia hath taught him that.
CASTILE That's because his mind runs all on Bel-imperia.
HIERONIMO *Whatever° joy earth yields betide° Your Majesty!* — May whatever / befall
BALTHAZAR *Earth yields no joy without Perseda's love.*
HIERONIMO *Let then Perseda on Your Grace attend.*
BALTHAZAR *She shall not wait on me, but I on her;*
Drawn by the influence of° her lights,° I yield. — emanation from / eyes
But let my friend the Rhodian knight come forth,
Erasto,° dearer than my life to me, — Erastus (see 4.1.138)
That he may see Perseda, my beloved.

Enter [Lorenzo as] Erasto.

KING Here comes Lorenzo. Look upon the plot° — synopsis
And tell me, brother: what part plays he?
BEL-IMPERIA *Ah, my Erasto, welcome to Perseda!*
LORENZO *Thrice happy is Erasto that thou livest.*
Rhodes' loss is nothing to° Erasto's joy; — compared with
Sith° his Perseda lives, his life survives. — Since
[Suleiman confers privately with the Bashaw.]
BALTHAZAR *Ah, Bashaw, here is love between Erasto*
And fair Perseda, sovereign of my soul!
HIERONIMO *Remove Erasto, mighty Suleiman,*
And then Perseda will be quickly won.
BALTHAZAR *Erasto is my friend, and while he lives*
Perseda never will remove her love.
HIERONIMO *Let not Erasto live to grieve great Suleiman.*
BALTHAZAR *Dear is Erasto in our princely eye.*
HIERONIMO *But if he be your rival, let him die.*
BALTHAZAR *Why, let him die; so love commandeth me.*
Yet grieve I that Erasto should so die.
[The Bashaw approaches Erasto.]
HIERONIMO *Erasto, Suleiman saluteth thee,*
And lets thee wit° by me His Highness' will, — know
Which is, thou shouldst be thus employed. *(Stab him.)*
BEL-IMPERIA *Ay me!*
Erasto! See, Suleiman, Erasto's slain!
BALTHAZAR *Yet liveth Suleiman to comfort thee.*
Fair queen of beauty, let not favor die,[3]
But with a gracious eye behold his grief° — my lovesickness
That with Perseda's beauty is increased,
If by Perseda his grief be not released.
BEL-IMPERIA *Tyrant, desist soliciting vain suits!*
Relentless° are mine ears to thy laments — As unyielding
As thy butcher° is pitiless and base — (the Bashaw)
Which seized on my Erasto, harmless knight.
Yet by thy power thou thinkest to command,
And to thy power Perseda doth obey;
But were she able, thus she would revenge

3. Do not let love go unrequited.

Thy treacheries on thee, ignoble prince, *(Stab him.)*
And on herself she would be thus revenged. *(Stab herself.)*
KING Well said!° Old Marshal, this was bravely° done! *done / excellently*
HIERONIMO But Bel-imperia plays Perseda well.
VICEROY Were this in earnest, Bel-imperia,
You would be better to my son than so.° *than in this play*
KING But now what follows for Hieronimo?
HIERONIMO Marry, this follows for Hieronimo:
Here break we off our sundry languages,
And thus conclude I in our vulgar° tongue. *vernacular*
Haply° you think—but bootless° are your thoughts— *Perhaps / unavailing*
That this is fabulously° counterfeit, *fictionally*
And that we do as all tragedians do:
To die today, for fashioning our scene°— *as part of our fiction*
The death of Ajax,[4] or some Roman peer—
And in a minute, starting up again,
Revive to please tomorrow's audience.
No, princes, know I am Hieronimo,
The hopeless father of a hapless son,
Whose tongue is tuned to tell his latest° tale, *final*
Not to excuse gross errors in the play.° *to speak the epilogue*
I see your looks urge instance° of these words. *proof*
Behold the reason urging me to this.
[*He draws back the curtain and*] *shows his dead son.*° *(see 4.1.184–87)*
See here my show. Look on this spectacle!
Here lay my hope, and here my hope hath end;
Here lay my heart, and here my heart was slain;
Here lay my treasure, here my treasure lost;
Here lay my bliss, and here my bliss bereft;
But hope, heart, treasure, joy, and bliss
All fled, failed, died, yea, all decayed with this.
From forth these wounds came breath that gave me life;[5]
They murdered me that made these fatal marks.
The cause° was love, whence grew this mortal hate: *cause of the murder*
The hate, Lorenzo and young Balthazar,
The love, my son to Bel-imperia.
But night, the coverer of accursèd crimes,
With pitchy° silence hushed these traitors' harms,° *pitch-dark / evil deeds*
And lent them leave,° for they had sorted leisure,[6] *opportunity*
To take advantage in my garden plot
Upon my son, my dear Horatio.
There, merciless, they butchered up my boy,
In black dark night, to pale, dim, cruel death.
He shrieks;° I heard—and yet methinks I hear— *shrieked*
His dismal outcry echo in the air.
With soonest° speed I hasted to the noise, *quickest*
Where, hanging on a tree, I found my son,
Through-girt° with wounds, and slaughtered as you see. *Pierced*
And grieved I, think you, at this spectacle?
Speak, Portuguese, whose loss resembles mine;

4. Sophocles' tragedy of *Ajax* (fifth century B.C.E.) tells of the hero's going mad with resentment for a neglected honor, his venting of his wrath on a flock of sheep that he takes to be his enemies, and his committing suicide in shame and guilt. A Latin version of the story was played before Queen Elizabeth at Cambridge in 1564.
5. Out of these wounds departed the spirit on which my very life depended. (See 1.1.17 and note.)
6. For they had found an opportunity.

If thou canst weep upon thy Balthazar,
'Tis like° I wailed for my Horatio. *likely*
[*To Castile*] And you, my lord, whose reconcilèd° son *(see 3.14.130–64)*
Marched in a net,° and thought himself unseen, *i.e., as if invisible*
And rated° me for brainsick lunacy, *berated*
With "God amend that mad Hieronimo!"
How can you brook° our play's catastrophe? *tolerate*
And here behold this bloody handkercher,
[*He draws forth the handkerchief from his breast.*]
Which at Horatio's death I weeping dipped
Within the river of his bleeding wounds.
It, as propitious,° see, I have reserved,° *as an omen / kept*
And never hath it left my bloody heart,
Soliciting remembrance of my vow
With these,° oh, these accursèd murderers, *To be revenged on these*
Which, now performed, my heart is satisfied.
And to this end the Bashaw I became,
That might revenge me on Lorenzo's life,
Who therefore was appointed to the part
And was to represent the Knight of Rhodes,
That I might kill him more conveniently.
So, Viceroy, was this Balthazar, thy son,
That Suleiman which Bel-imperia,
In person of Perseda, murderèd,
Solely appointed to that tragic part
That she might slay him that offended her.
Poor Bel-imperia missed° her part in this, *deviated from*
For, though the story saith she should have died,
Yet I of kindness and of care to her
Did otherwise determine of her end;
But love of him° whom they did hate too much *(Horatio)*
Did urge her resolution to be such.
And, princes, now behold Hieronimo,
Author and actor in this tragedy,
Bearing his latest fortune in his fist,
And will as resolute conclude his part
As any of the actors gone before.
And, gentles,° thus I end my play. *gentlemen and ladies*
Urge no more words; I have no more to say.
He runs to hang himself.

KING Oh, hearken, Viceroy!—Hold, Hieronimo!—
Brother, my nephew and thy son are slain.

VICEROY We are betrayed! My Balthazar is slain.
Break ope the doors![7] Run, save Hieronimo!
[*Attendants break in and restrain Hieronimo.*]
Hieronimo, do but inform the King of these events.
Upon mine honor, thou shalt have no harm.

HIERONIMO Viceroy, I will not trust thee with my life,
Which I this day have offered° to my son. *offered as a sacrifice*
[*To an attendant*] Accursèd wretch,
Why stayest thou him that was resolved to die?

KING Speak, traitor! Damnèd, bloody murderer, speak!
For, now I have thee, I will make thee speak.

7. At 4.3.11–13, Hieronimo arranged to lock the doors so that no one might escape.

Why hast thou done this undeserving° deed? *undeserved*
VICEROY Why hast thou murderèd my Balthazar?
CASTILE Why hast thou butchered both my children thus?
HIERONIMO Oh, good words!° *appropriately said!*
As dear to me was my Horatio
As yours, or yours, or yours, my lord, to you.
My guiltless son was by Lorenzo slain,
And by° Lorenzo and that Balthazar *by the deaths of*
Am I at last revengèd thoroughly,
Upon whose souls may heavens be yet avenged
With greater far than these afflictions!
CASTILE But who were thy confederates in this?
VICEROY That was thy daughter Bel-imperia,
For by her hand my Balthazar was slain.
I saw her stab him.
KING [*to Hieronimo*] Why speakest thou not?
HIERONIMO What lesser liberty can kings afford
Than harmless silence? Then afford it me.
Sufficeth I may not, nor I will not, tell thee.
KING Fetch forth the tortures!—
Traitor as thou art, I'll make thee tell.
HIERONIMO Indeed,
Thou mayest torment me, as his wretched son
Hath done in murd'ring my Horatio,
But never shalt thou force me to reveal
The thing which I have vowed inviolate;[8]
And therefore, in despite of all thy threats,
Pleased with their deaths and eased with their revenge,
First take my tongue and afterwards my heart.
[*He bites out his tongue.*]
KING Oh, monstrous resolution of a wretch!
See, Viceroy, he hath bitten forth his tongue
Rather than to reveal what we required.
CASTILE Yet can he write.
KING And if in this he satisfy us not,
We will devise th'extremest kind of death
That ever was invented for a wretch.
Then he° makes signs for a knife to mend his pen. (*Hieronimo*)
CASTILE Oh, he would have a knife to mend his pen.
VICEROY Here, and advise thee° that thou write the troth.° *see to it / truth*
He° with a knife stabs the Duke and himself. (*Hieronimo*)
KING Look to my brother! Save Hieronimo!
What age hath ever heard such monstrous deeds?
My brother and the whole succeeding hope
That Spain expected after my decease!
Go bear his° body hence, that we may mourn (*Castile's*)
The loss of our belovèd brother's death,
That he may be entombed whate'er befall.
I am the next, the nearest,° last of all. *nearest in blood*
VICEROY And thou, Don Pedro, do the like for us.
Take up our hapless son, untimely slain;

8. Since Hieronimo has seemingly revealed all, it is hard to guess what secret the King now wants to know about, but as a stage business in the play's catastrophe, this moment affords Hieronimo one last heroic gesture of defiance before his final deeds of vengeance and self-destruction.

Set me with him, and he with woeful me,
Upon the mainmast of a ship unmanned,
And let the wind and tide haul me along
To Scylla's barking and untamèd gulf,[9]
Or to the loathsome pool of Acheron,° *(see 1.1.19)*
To weep my want for° my sweet Balthazar. *my loss of*
Spain hath no refuge for a Portingale.
The trumpets sound a dead march, the King of Spain mourning after his brother's body, and the King° of Portingale bearing the body of his son. [*Exeunt.*] *Viceroy*

[4.5]

Ghost [*of Andrea*] *and Revenge* [*remain onstage*].

ANDREA Ay, now my hopes have end in their effects,
When blood and sorrow finish my desires:
Horatio murdered in his father's bower,
Vile Serberine by Pedringano slain,
False Pedringano hanged by quaint° device, *ingenious*
Fair Isabella by herself misdone,° *done in*
Prince Balthazar by Bel-imperia stabbed,
The Duke of Castile and his wicked son
Both done to death by old Hieronimo,
My Bel-imperia fall'n as Dido fell,[1]
And good Hieronimo slain by himself—
Ay, these were spectacles to please my soul.
Now will I beg at lovely Proserpine,° *(see 1.1.76)*
That by the virtue of her princely doom° *judgment*
I may consort° my friends in pleasing sort, *accompany*
And on my foes work just and sharp revenge.
I'll lead my friend Horatio through those fields
Where never-dying wars are still inured;° *carried on*
I'll lead fair Isabella to that train° *company; way of life*
Where pity weeps but never feeleth pain;
I'll lead my Bel-imperia to those joys
That vestal virgins and fair queens possess;
I'll lead Hieronimo where Orpheus plays,° *(see 3.13.116–17 and n)*
Adding sweet pleasure to eternal days.
But say, Revenge, for thou must help or none,
Against the rest how shall my hate be shown?
REVENGE This hand shall hale them down to deepest hell,
Where none but Furies, bugs,° and tortures dwell. *bugbears, demons*
ANDREA Then, sweet Revenge, do this at my request:
Let me be judge and doom them to unrest.
Let loose poor Tityus[2] from the vulture's gripe,° *grip*
And let Don Cyprian supply his room;° *take his place*
Place Don Lorenzo on Ixion's wheel,
And let the lover's[3] endless pains surcease° *cease*

9. To the terrifying narrow sea passage, described in Homer's *Odyssey*, between the whirlpool of Charybdis and the sea monster Scylla.
4.5. The final chorus.
1. Virgil's *Aeneid*, Book 4, describes how Dido, Queen of Carthage, takes her own life in despair at being deserted by Aeneas.
2. A giant condemned to be confined perpetually in Hades and to have his liver eaten constantly by vultures.
3. Ixion is sardonically called "the lover" here because he had tried to seduce Hera (Roman Juno). See 1.1.66 and note.

(Juno forgets old wrath and grants him° ease); *(Ixion)*
Hang Balthazar about Chimera's[4] neck,
And let him there bewail his bloody love,° *deadly passion*
Repining at our joys that are above;
Let Serberine go roll the fatal stone,
And take from Sisyphus his endless moan;[5]
False Pedringano, for his treachery,
Let him be dragged through boiling Acheron,
And there live, dying still° in endless flames, *endlessly*
Blaspheming gods and all their holy names.

REVENGE Then haste we down to meet thy friends and foes,
To place thy friends in ease, the rest in woes.
For here, though death hath end° their misery, *ended*
I'll there begin their endless tragedy. *Exeunt.*

FINIS.

4. Chimera was a monster, part lion, part goat, and part snake.

5. Take from Sisyphus his endless torment of rolling a huge stone up a hill only to have it roll down again.

TEXTUAL NOTES

The Spanish Tragedy was entered in the Stationers' Register on October 6, 1592, to Abel Jeffes, who apparently published a first edition of the play in that year, though this edition is no longer extant. Later that same year, Edward White published the earliest extant edition, in a format known as "octavo-in-fours," that is, on extra large sheets torn in half to give the normal working size of a quarto. It claims to have corrected "the first impression." Nonetheless, White was fined by the Stationers' Company in December of 1592 for having "offended" by "having printed *The Spanish Tragedy* belonging to Abel Jeffes." Reprints of the 1592 edition followed in 1594 and 1599. In 1602, Thomas Pavier published an edition "Newly corrected, amended, and enlarged with new additions of the Painter's part, and others, as it hath of late been divers times acted." These additions are not by Kyd and, although interesting in terms of the play's history on the stage, are not included in the present edition, which is based on the 1592 edition. Substantive departures from the 1592 edition are noted here, using the following abbreviations, which employ "Q" for the octavo-in-four format of the first two editions since they were printed in such a way as to resemble the quarto format:

Q1: Octavo-in-fours [of 1592] (London: Edward Allde for Edward White)
Q2: Octavo-in-fours of 1594 (London: Abel Jeffes for Edward White)
Q3: Quarto of 1599 (London: William White)
Q4: Quarto of 1602 (London: William White for Thomas Pavier)
Q5: Quarto of 1603 (London: William White for Thomas Pavier)
Q7: Quarto of 1615 (London: William White for William White and Thomas Langley)
Q9: Quarto of 1623 (London: A. Mathewes for J. Grismand)
ed.: A modern editor's emendation, subsequent to Q10 of 1633

1.1.82 horn [ed.] Hor [Q1]
1.2.13 *poplite* [Q2] *poplito* [Q1] **38 ordnance** [Q1: ordinance] **40 colonel** [Q1: Corlonell] **53 rain** [ed.] ran [Q1] **56 *Arma . . . armis*** [ed.] *Anni . . . annis* [Q1] **83 waning** [Q5] wauing [Q1] **101 the** [ed.] this [Q1] **142, 157 seized** [Q1: ceaz'd]

1.3.9.1 [placement, ed.; after 11 in Q1] **29 foot is** [ed.] foot [Q1] **82 Terceira's** [Q1: *Terseraes*] **83 diadem** [Q2] Diadome [Q1]

1.4.35 wielding [Q1: welding] **42 lifeless** [Q1: liueles] **98 but [ed.]** hut [Q1] **146 of English** [this edition] of the English [Q1] **174 thy** [ed.] the [Q1]

2.1.14 words [Q2: wordes] wodres [Q1] **27 beauty's** [Q7] beauteous [Q1] **41** ***qui*** [ed.] *que* [Q1] **106** [and elsewhere] **Lest** [Q1: Least] **133 lose** [Q1: loose]

2.2.3 thoughts [ed.] though [Q1] **9 may** [Q4] mad [Q1] **33 war** [ed.] warring [Q1]

2.3.49 thought [Q7] thoughts [Q1]

2.4.35 wars [ed.] warre [Q1] **44 withal** [ed.] with [Q1] **50 Who's** [ed.] Whose [Q1] **50.1** ***Serberine*** [Q1: *Cerberin*]

2.5.27 vile [Q1: vilde] **48 stayed** [Q5: staide] stainde [Q1] **67** ***ver*** [Q2] *var* [Q1] **67** ***educat*** [Q7] *educet* [Q1] **69** ***animis oblivia*** [ed.] *annum oblimia* [Q1] **70** ***metam*** [ed.] *metum* [Q1] **70** ***magnum*** [Q2] *magnam* [Q1] **70** ***quaecunque*** [ed.] *quicunque* [Q1] **71** ***effert*** [ed.] *effecit* [Q1] **72** ***veneni*** [Q2] *veneri* [Q1] **73** ***herbarum vi caeca nenia*** [ed.] *irraui euecaeca menia* [Q1] **75** ***pectore*** [ed.] *pectora* [Q1] **80** ***tum*** [ed.] *tam* [Q1]

2.6.5 On [ed.] Or [Q1]

3.1.0.1 ***Nobles*** [ed.] *Nobles, Alexandro* [Q1] **58 AMBASSADOR** [ed.; not in Q1] **77 lord,** [ed.] Lord vnbinde him. [Q1] **91 Wherein** [ed.] Or wherein [Q1]

3.2.55 who's [ed.] whose [Q1] **83, 98 Luigi's** [ed.] *Liugis* [Q1] **101 LORENZO** [Q4; not in Q1] **119 'tis** [Q3] its [Q1]

3.4.5 inexpected [ed.] in expected [Q1] **91** ***E . . . che . . . io . . . lo*** [ed.] *Et . . . que . . . Ii . . . le* [Q1] **92** ***basterà*** [ed.] *bassara* [Q1]

3.5.1 PAGE [ed.; not in Q1] **13 Will't** [Q1: Wilt]

3.6.40 And [Q2] Hnd [Q1] **41 sir** [ed.] sit [Q1] **44 too** [Q1: to] **81 groaned** [Q1: gronde] **111 heaven** [Q2] heauens [Q1]

3.7.15 empyreal [Q1: imperiall] **32 writ** [ed.] *write* [Q1] **41 An actor** [ed.] And actors [Q1] **65 banned** [Q1: band]

3.8.0.1 ***Isabella*** [ed.] *Isabell* [Q1] **24 Whither** [ed.] whether [Q1]

3.10.102 ***Et*** [ed.] *Est* [Q1]

3.12.46 inexplicable [ed.] inexecrable [Q1] **101 not exempt** [ed.] exempt [Q1]

3.13.43 curtsey [Q1: cuttesie] **44.1** [placement, Q4; after 45 in Q1] **62** ***firmae*** [ed.] firma [Q1] **70, 74, 80, 144 BAZULTO** [ed.] *Senex* [Q1] **103 o'erturneth** [ed.] ore turnest [Q1] **122 rend** [ed.] rent [Q1] **151 fate** [ed.] Father [Q1]

3.14.23 Renownèd [Q1: Renowmed] **68, 69 were't** [Q1: wert] **102 show no** [Q2] shew [Q1] **117 trow** [Q1: tro] **128 LORENZO** [Q2; not in Q1] **159 fit** [Q2] sit [Q1] **163 thus** [ed.] that [Q1] **167 SD** [placement, ed.; after 166 in Q1] **167 Pha!** [as SH in Q1] **168–69** [ed.] *Mi. Chi mi fa? Pui Correzza Che non sule / Traditio viha otrade vule* [Q1]

3.15.0.1 ***Ghost*** [ed.] Enter *Ghoast* [Q1] **1** ***Erictho*** [ed.] *Erictha* [Q1] **3–6 Acheron . . . lakes** [ed.] *Achinon* and *Ericus* in hell. / For neere by *Stix* and *Phlegeton*: / Nor ferried *Caron* to the fierie lakes [Q1] **7 sees!** [ed.] see? [Q1] **11 To sleep** [ed.] Thsleepe [Q1] **17 woebegone** [ed.] woe degone [Q1]

4.1.9–10 [ed.] With what dishonour, and the hate of men, / From this dishonour and the hate of men: [Q1] **45 murderèd** [ed.] murderd [Q1] **113** [and elsewhere] **Suleiman** [Q1: *Soliman* or *Solyman*] **158 troop** [Q1: troupe] **160** ***cothernata*** [ed.] *cother nato* [Q1] **185–86** [Q4; lines transposed in Q1]

4.2.8 rend [ed.] rent [Q1] **27 cited** [Q1: scited]

4.3.22 recount [Q1: recompt]

4.4.58 ***Perseda his*** [ed.] *Persedaes* [Q1] **76 Haply** [Q1: Happely] **108 shrieks** [Q1: shrikes] **201.1** [placement, ed.; after 202 in Q1] **202 KING** [ed.; at 203 in Q1] **214 haul** [Q1: hall] **215 gulf** [Q9] greefe [Q1]

4.5.0.1 ***Ghost*** [ed.] Enter *Ghoast* [Q1] **4 Vile** [Q1: Vilde] **36 Chimera's** Q1: *Chineras*]

Endymion

Nobody stages John Lyly's plays today, but in the 1580s, when Shakespeare was just getting started in the London theater, Lyly was all the rage. Part of his remarkable success was as a stylist. His major work in prose, *Euphues,* with its elegant figures of speech and mannered comparisons, was the literary sensation of 1579 and 1580. Lyly showed his readers that English could be fashioned into a self-consciously literary vehicle. His early plays, *Campaspe* and *Sappho and Phao* in 1584, were the talk of the town. *Galatea,* staged probably in early 1589, is a play that Shakespeare must have seen and loved: its plot of two young women, drawn to each other when both are obliged to disguise themselves as young men, is a captivating study for *As You Like It, Twelfth Night,* and other Shakespearean comedies making use of young women similarly disguised. All of these comedies by Lyly were acted by boys, in so-called private or indoor theater spaces close by Saint Paul's Cathedral, for well-to-do spectators and then before Queen Elizabeth at court. Lyly was the boys' master, under the patronage of the Earl of Oxford.

Endymion, acted in early 1588, demonstrates Lyly's somewhat precious accomplishment at its very best. As in his other plays, Lyly dramatizes a classical fable in *Endymion* and turns it to contemporary use. The fable of a shepherd beloved by the moon is of ancient origin, having been told in various guises by Apollodorus, Apollonius of Rhodes, Ovid, and Lucian, among others. The story was quickly allegorized, since it offered such a stirring account of a coming together of the divine and the human. The moon's kiss, bestowed on the sleeping shepherd Endymion, came to signify the gods' favor toward a mortal whose worship of the divine takes the form of a deathless and ageless sleep. Endymion's sleep thus took on Neoplatonic resonances of the human soul's longing for contemplative union with the divine. It also suggested a human fascination with scientific and metaphysical discoveries concerning the heavenly bodies that move ceaselessly and mysteriously about the earth.

Lyly's play similarly invites allegorical interpretation, and on multiple levels that make for theatrical complexity. The name of the play's royal figure, Cynthia, signifies that she is very like the moon, even if she is also a mortal queen. ("Cynthia" is a name often given to Artemis or Diana, and hence the moon, derived from "Cynthus," the name of a mountain in Artemis's native Delos.) Endymion prays to her as one who is constant even in her "ebbing and flowing" and who, "being in her fullness, decayeth" (1.1.42, 51–52), just as the moon ceaselessly waxes and wanes, growing old only to grow young again. The moon is, for Lyly as for countless beholders of the heavens in ancient times, a signifier of the boundary between timelessness and flux, eternity and mortality. Located seemingly between the fixed stars of the firmament and the transient "sublunary" world of human endeavor, the moon partakes uniquely of permanence and mutability. Endymion is a philosopher-poet in love with this image of the divine that is also humanly comprehensible.

Lyly introduces many changes in his rendition of the myth of the moon and her

Introduction, glosses, footnotes, and textual notes by David Bevington; text edited by David Bevington and checked by Eric Rasmussen.

lover. Importantly, he represents Endymion as infatuated with a distant and regal celestial figure, whereas in the ancient myth the moon is the one who pursues the man. Lyly also provides Cynthia with a rival for Endymion's affection, in the person of Tellus.

Tellus plainly represents the earthly and ephemeral. ("Tellus" is Latin for "earth.") She is Cynthia's opposite in every respect: vengeful, possessive, spiteful. In her refusal to give Endymion up, Tellus reveals her motives to be those of a goddess determined to exercise authority within her mortal sphere: her "body is decked with fair flowers"; her "veins are vines, yielding sweet liquor to the dullest spirits"; her "ears are corn to bring strength"; her "hairs are grass to bring abundance" (1.2.21–24). She entangles Endymion in a "sweet net" of desire during "the prime of his youth" (1.2.43, 62–63), yet she senses that her hold over Endymion is temporal and that her great rival is the eternal goddess whom Endymion venerates.

Endymion is thus caught in a struggle between fleshly temptation and heavenly contemplation. He longs to be lifted spiritually upward toward Cynthia, and yet, feeling the pull of desire, he has become compromised by his guilty relationship with Tellus. That Tellus is fully prepared to use black magic in her attempts to enslave him further underscores the cosmic dimensions of this struggle for his soul. Cynthia is not only divine and perfect; she represents the good toward which Endymion must imperfectly strive. Yet he cannot deserve her, guilty creature that he is. Endymion's sleep may represent, ambivalently, the conflicted state of his soul: the sleep is inflicted on him by black magic, and yet it puts him in a state of prolonged suspended animation that is conducive to heavenly contemplation. Cynthia's kiss may then represent a kind of rescue of Endymion from the trammels of worldly entanglement and the forgiveness of a well-meaning but deeply flawed worshiper.

At the same time, Lyly's play hints at a more political interpretation. "Cynthia" was a name often bestowed on Queen Elizabeth in her mythic role as Diana, the huntress. The play, performed in her presence in early 1588, is manifestly a hyperbolic tribute to one who triumphs over her enemies and wins the loyal affections of an erring courtier who wishes to learn how to serve her as she deserves. Lyly's Cynthia is a portrait of Elizabeth as the virgin queen, graciously willing to return the affection of her loyal courtier, yet doing so with a conquering of erotic affection. In his earlier plays as well, Lyly had repeatedly praised Elizabeth (by implication) as a female monarch who had overcome erotic desire in order to bestow a more Platonic love on those who best served her. Lyly's audience, composed largely of persons with connections at court, knew well enough the episodes in Elizabeth's early reign to which this flattery pointed, for she had entertained a series of suitors (the Earl of Leicester, the Duc d'Alençon, even her dead sister Mary's husband, Philip II of Spain) only to opt finally for the unmarried state.

Who, then, might Endymion represent in this pattern of contemporary historical allegory? Lyly's audience must have asked the question, since the identification of Cynthia as Elizabeth was so plain. Several candidates have been proposed by scholars, including Leicester, whose secret marriage in 1578 had greatly displeased Elizabeth and who had been proposed at one point as a husband for Mary, Queen of Scots (the "Tellus" of this hypothesis). Yet the story was old news in 1588, whereas the Earl of Oxford's troubled relationship with Elizabeth was much more current. This difficult man, who was Lyly's patron throughout the 1580s and the sponsor of Lyly's dramatic activities, secretly became a Catholic after his return from Italy in 1576. The fact was well known and troublesome to Elizabeth's ministers, chief of whom was Lord Burghley, Oxford's father-in-law. In early 1588, the English court was aware that Philip of Spain was preparing his great Armada for an invasion intended to bring England back into the Catholic fold. It was plain that Philip would have to rely on English Catholics coming over to his side once the invasion began. Therefore, English Catholics—Oxford prominently among them—were under intense suspicion. Would they jump to Philip's side or remain loyal? Theater audiences, in the hysterical atmosphere of early 1588, could hardly think of anything else. These circumstances may suggest an allegory in which Endymion's guilty involvement with Tellus points to the continuing fascination that England's Catholics had had with Mary, Queen of Scots, until her execution in the year before the play was produced. Endymion's long sleep is one of testing and probation; the kiss betokens the Queen's acceptance of his confession and renewed loyalty.

Alternatively, one can read the contemporary allegory on a more general level as portraying the mutual but chaste affection between the virgin queen and an archetypal courtier who must learn to conquer his amorous desire for Cynthia in order to serve her best. Yet a more particular reading of the allegory does seem called for by Endymion's dream. As dramatized first in dumb show (2.3.63.1 ff.) and then in Endymion's narrative recollection of it (5.1.84–142), the dream is filled with topical suggestions of court rivalry. Wolves bark at Cynthia, and drones or beetles attack a princely eagle, endeavoring to suck her nourishment and kill her. The language precisely mirrors a passage of praise and thanksgiving that Lyly had written earlier to celebrate Elizabeth's triumph over her Catholic enemies in the so-called Northern Rebellion of 1569 on behalf of Mary, Queen of Scots (*Euphues*, 2.206 ff.).

However we are to read the contemporary allegory—and the possibilities are many—we are left with a remarkable impression of this play: its highly wrought euphuistic style and its Neoplatonic allegory about contemplation of the divine seem also to have been an elaborate facade for a highly politicized intent to praise Elizabeth, celebrate her victory over her Catholic foes, and promote the cause of an interest group in her court. Mythology is harnessed and transformed into a weapon of political commentary and argument. The stakes are very high.

Endymion's involvement with Cynthia and Tellus is the main plot of this play. At the same time, Lyly calls upon traditions of native English drama, with its delight in multiplicity of episodes, to furnish the story with plots of parallel interest. Endymion's dearest friend is Eumenides (Greek for "the well-wishing one"), who is in love with the sharp-tongued Semele (a name suggestive of ruinous passion: the mythological Semele was consumed by flames when she saw her lover, Jupiter, in his divine form after her passion drove her to ask to see him that way). Eumenides must choose between friendship and love: in order to help his friend wake from his prolonged sleep, he must renounce or at least subordinate his erotic desire. Once he does so, though, he is rewarded with the lady as well, illustrating the commonplace about love and

The moon kisses Endymion. Giovanni Piero Valeriano Bolzani, *Hieroglyphica* (Lyons, 1586).

friendship that friendship must take precedence lest one succumb entirely to enervating passion. In the play's exploration of love in all its permutations, Eumenides and Semele are commendably faithful and true, and yet the strife of their relationship shows them to be set somewhat lower than the idealized Endymion and Cynthia in the play's depiction of love in its varied shapes. They are resolutely human, lacking the metaphysical dimensions of Cynthia and Endymion.

Corsites and Tellus occupy the next lower rung on this same ladder or chain of love's manifestations. Corsites, as his name (meaning "passionate at heart" in Latin) suggests, is strongly under the control of his erotic desires. His infatuation with Tellus leads him into morally compromising situations, especially when, at her behest, he attempts to move the sleeping Endymion from the lunary bank where he reposes. Endymion is protected by a charm against such interference; Corsites learns that his great strength is of no avail. He is a thoroughly worldly male, bound emotionally to the woman who, as we have seen, embodies all that is earthly, sensuous, and therefore dangerous. Tellus, no fit mate for Endymion, is well suited to Corsites.

Occupying the lowest rung on this hierarchical ladder of love's various guises, and in ludicrously comic fashion, is Sir Tophas, a comic braggart indebted to Chaucer's Sir Thopas and to the braggart soldier or miles gloriosus of classical tradition. Tophas is the amusing opposite of Endymion in every way. His bravery is pure sham. He falls in love, but with an aged and ugly sorceress (Dipsas). He falls asleep thinking of her and imagines things that appear to be prognosticatory but turn out to be absurd and meaningless. His visions are earthbound, foolish, self-concerned. Tophas is a parody, intended to display by opposite signs the dramatic significance of Endymion's exalted quest for the ethereal.

Appropriately, Tophas occupies a subplot of the play that is peopled by diminutive pages and maids-in-waiting whose pert dialogue and witty ripostes accentuate Tophas's ungainly size and ridiculousness as a wooer. Multiple plotting of this sort did much to establish the comic subplot routines we see in Shakespeare's comedies, from Bottom, the weaver, in *A Midsummer Night's Dream* to Sir Toby Belch and Sir Andrew in *Twelfth Night*. Quite possibly, in Lyly's play the part of Tophas was played by an adult chorister-actor, surrounded by pint-sized pages and ladies-in-waiting. Perhaps, being the dramatist and master of the boy actors, Lyly took the part himself. (See, however, 5.2.17–20.)

Lyly's famous, or infamous, euphuistic style (from Lyly's prose fictional narrative *Euphues*) fills the play at every point. All the characters, whether high or low, dignified or absurd, speak in Lyly's highly decorated language, employing rhetorical tropes, metaphors usually drawn from an entirely fanciful natural history, and antitheses. By dwelling so formally on oppositions, Lyly manages with remarkable skill to convey a sense of courtly debate: love versus friendship, worldly desire versus heavenly contemplation, factionalism versus loyal duty, and the like. The characters seem at times like mouthpieces for their author in their unceasing wordplay, and yet the delineations of human emotions are often quite subtle. Endymion's longing for Cynthia is marred by his erotic attachment to Tellus, and the result is a genuine rendition of psychological conflict. In terms of gender and power, the play gives a remarkable portrait of an anxious male subjected to the authority of a virgin queen. As a result, Cynthia is both maternal and domineering, tender and awesome, generous and voracious. Being associated with the moon, she is both a positive image of divinity and a supernatural power associated with witchcraft. Endymion is, in the words of the critic and scholar Philippa Berry, a "baffled male courtier" torn between desires for autonomy and dependency, considering uneasily what role he can occupy "in a court so gynocentrially defined."[1]

In stagecraft, *Endymion* is no less innovative. Lyly shows himself to be a masterful classicist, adept at interpreting ancient myths and at quoting in Latin, making use of

1. Philippa Berry, *Of Chastity and Power: Elizabethan Literature and the Unmarried Queen* (London: Routledge, 1989), pp. 111–33.

classical models such as the braggart soldier of the Roman playwrights Plautus and Terence. Yet he deliberately chooses to sidestep classical dramatic structure in favor of the kind of comedy that Shakespeare, among others, would find so inviting. The story occupies many years, since Endymion must alter from youth to old age during his sleep (see, e.g., 2.3.31–39, 5.1.50–52). The action takes the characters on far-flung adventures, as when Eumenides encounters an old man (Geron) at a magical well (3.4). Lyly deliberately transgresses the unities of time and place, and his multiple structure of the theme of transcendent love and variations on that theme is no less natively English than classical. The combination of classical learning (worn lightly) and good, old-fashioned English horseplay was something Shakespeare must have found very attractive.

In its use of stage structures as well, Lyly's play adventurously juxtaposes fixed locations (Cynthia's court, Endymion's lunary bank) with a fluid sense of space, as the actors move from one imagined location to another. Little scenery is called for, yet the play also makes use of striking theatrical effects such as Cynthia's restoration of youth to Endymion and the transformation of Dipsas into a tree and back again. Lyly was a great experimenter and man of the theater. Shakespeare repeatedly paid tribute to his stagecraft in plays such as *The Two Gentlemen of Verona* and *Love's Labor's Lost*.

JOHN LYLY
Endymion

[THE PERSONS OF THE PLAY,[1] IN ORDER OF APPEARANCE

The PROLOGUE
ENDYMION, a young man
EUMENIDES,° his friend — *"the well-wishing one"*
TELLUS,° a lady-in-waiting — *"earth"*
FLOSCULA,° her servant — *"little flower"*
DARES, Endymion's page
SAMIAS, Eumenides' page
Sir TOPHAS, a braggart
EPITON,° his page — *"follower"; "abridgement"*
DIPSAS, an aged sorceress
SCINTILLA° } maids-in-waiting — *"spark"*
FAVILLA° } — *"cinders"*
BAGOA, a sorceress, assistant to Dipsas
Three ladies and an ancient man, in a dumb show
CYNTHIA,° the Queen — *Diana; the moon*
CORSITES, a captain
ZONTES } lords at Cynthia's court
PANELION }
SEMELE,[2] a lady-in-waiting
GERON,° a wise old man, the estranged husband of Dipsas — *"old man"*
Two WATCHMEN
A CONSTABLE
Four FAIRIES
PYTHAGORAS,[3] a Greek philosopher
GYPTES, an Egyptian soothsayer
The EPILOGUE

THE SCENE: At and near the court of Cynthia.]

The original 1591 title page reads "*Endymion, The Man in the Moon.* Played before the Queen's Majesty at Greenwich, on Candlemas Day at night, by the Children of Paul's. At London, printed by J. Charlewood for the widow Broome, 1591."

The Persons of the Play.

1. The names of the characters derive their meanings (see glosses) from Latin and Greek; so too do other foreign-language phrases in the play, most of them from Latin.
2. When Semele, having been tricked by the jealous Juno into making the request, asked that her lover, Jupiter, appear to her in his full splendor, she was consumed in a flash of lightning.
3. A Greek philosopher and mathematician of the sixth century B.C.E.

The Prologue

[*Enter the Prologue.*]

PROLOGUE Most high and happy princess,° we must tell you a tale of the Man in the Moon, which, if it seem ridiculous for the method, or superfluous for the matter, or for the means° incredible, for three faults we can make but one excuse: it is a tale of the Man in the Moon.°

It was forbidden in old time to dispute of Chimera,[1] because it was a fiction. We hope in our times none will apply pastimes, because they are fancies;[2] for there liveth none under the sun that knows what to make of the Man in the Moon. We present neither comedy, nor tragedy, nor story,° nor anything, but that whosoever heareth may say this: "Why, here is a tale of the Man in the Moon." [*Exit.*]

fortunate queen / *i.e., staging* / *i.e., a fairy tale* / *history*

1.1

[*Enter*] *Endymion* [*and*] *Eumenides.*

ENDYMION I find, Eumenides, in all things both variety to content and satiety to glut, saving° only in my affections,° which are so stayed° and withal so stately[1] that I can neither satisfy my heart with love nor mine eyes with wonder. My thoughts, Eumenides, are stitched to the stars, which, being as high as I can see, thou mayst imagine how much higher they are than I can reach.

excepting / desires — *fixed; frustrated*

EUMENIDES If you be enamored of anything above the moon, your thoughts are ridiculous, for that° things immortal are not subject to affections; if allured or enchanted with these transitory things under the moon, you show yourself senseless to attribute such lofty titles to such low trifles.

in that, since

ENDYMION My love is placed neither under the moon nor above.

EUMENIDES I hope you be not sotted° upon the Man in the Moon.

besotted

ENDYMION No, but settled° either to die or possess the moon herself.

resolved

EUMENIDES Is Endymion mad, or do I mistake? Do you love the moon, Endymion?

ENDYMION Eumenides, the moon.

EUMENIDES There was never any so peevish° to imagine the moon either capable of affection or shape of a mistress; for as impossible it is to make love fit to her humor,° which no man knoweth, as a coat to her form, which continueth not in one bigness whilst she is measuring.° Cease off,° Endymion, to feed so much upon fancies. That melancholy blood must be purged° which draweth you to a dotage° no less miserable than monstrous.

foolish; perverse / *disposition* / *being measured / Cease* / *bled medically* / *infatuation*

The Prologue. For a performance at court before Queen Elizabeth.
1. A three-headed monster of Greek mythology, part lion, part goat, and part dragon.
2. We hope none will read this play as a topical allegory of court intrigue, since it is purely imaginary.

1.1. At or near the court of Cynthia.
1. (1) Dignified; (2) concerned with matters of state.

ENDYMION My thoughts have no veins, and yet, unless they be let blood,° I shall perish.

bled for melancholy

EUMENIDES But they have vanities,° which, being reformed, you may be restored.

useless fancies

ENDYMION O fair Cynthia, why do others term thee unconstant whom I have ever found unmovable? Injurious time,° corrupt manners, unkind men, who, finding a constancy not to be matched in my sweet mistress, have christened her with the name of wavering, waxing, and waning! Is she inconstant that keepeth a settled course, which since her first creation altereth not one minute in her moving? There is nothing thought more admirable or commendable in the sea than the ebbing and flowing; and shall the moon, from whom the sea taketh this virtue,° be accounted fickle for increasing and decreasing? Flowers in their buds are nothing worth till they be blown,° nor blossoms accounted till they be ripe fruit; and shall we then say they be changeable for that° they grow from seeds to leaves, from leaves to buds, from buds to their perfection? Then why be not twigs that become trees, children that become men, and mornings that grow to evenings termed wavering, for that they continue not at one stay?° Ay, but Cynthia, being in her fullness, decayeth, as not delighting in her greatest beauty, or withering when she should be most honored. When malice cannot object° anything, folly will, making that a vice which is the greatest virtue. What thing, my mistress excepted, being in the pride of her beauty and latter minute of her age, that waxeth young again?[2] Tell me, Eumenides, what is he that, having a mistress of ripe years and infinite virtues, great honors and unspeakable beauty, but would° wish that she might grow tender again, getting youth by years and never-decaying beauty by time, whose fair face neither the summer's blaze can scorch nor winter's blast chap, nor the numbering of years breed altering of colors? Such is my sweet Cynthia, whom time cannot touch because she is divine, nor will offend because she is delicate. O Cynthia, if thou shouldst always continue at thy fullness, both gods and men would conspire to ravish thee. But thou, to abate the pride of our affections, dost detract from thy perfections, thinking it sufficient if once in a month we enjoy a glimpse of thy majesty; and then, to increase our griefs, thou dost decrease thy gleams, coming out of thy royal robes, wherewith thou dazzlest our eyes, down into thy swath clouts,° beguiling our eyes. And then—

Calumnious generation / *power, essence* / *ripe to overripe* / *because* / *fixed state* / *object to* / *would not* / *swaddling clothes*

EUMENIDES Stay there, Endymion. Thou that committest idolatry wilt straight° blaspheme if thou be suffered.° Sleep would do thee more good than speech. The moon heareth thee not, or, if she do, regardeth thee not.

straightway / allowed

ENDYMION Vain° Eumenides, whose thoughts never grow higher than the crown of thy head! Why troublest thou me, having neither head to conceive the cause of my love or a heart to receive the impressions? Follow thou thine own for-

Foolish

2. What thing, other than the moon, is able to grow young again after having reached fully mature beauty and old age?

tunes, which creep on the earth, and suffer me to fly to mine, whose fall, though it be desperate, yet shall it come by daring.[3] Farewell. [*Exit.*]

EUMENIDES Without doubt Endymion is bewitched; otherwise in a man of such rare° virtues there could not harbor a mind of such extreme madness. I will follow him, lest in this fancy of the moon he deprive himself of the sight of the sun.° *Exit.*

excellent; uncommon / *take his own life*

1.2

[*Enter*] *Tellus* [*and*] *Floscula.*

TELLUS Treacherous and most perjured Endymion, is Cynthia the sweetness of thy life and the bitterness of my death? What revenge may be devised so full of shame as my thoughts are replenished with malice? Tell me, Floscula, if falseness in love can possibly be punished° with extremity of hate. As long as sword, fire, or poison may be hired, no traitor to my love shall live unrevenged. Were thy[1] oaths without number, thy kisses without measure,° thy sighs without end, forged to deceive a poor credulous virgin, whose simplicity had been° worth thy favor and better fortune? If the gods sit unequal° beholders of injuries, or laughers at lovers' deceits, then let mischief° be as well forgiven in women as perjury winked at in men.

be sufficiently punished / *innumerable; wanton* / *might have seemed* / *inequitable* / *vengefulness*

FLOSCULA Madam, if you would compare the state of Cynthia with your own, and the height of Endymion his° thoughts with the meanness° of your fortune, you would rather yield than contend, being between you and her no comparison, and rather wonder than rage at the greatness of his mind, being affected with a thing more than mortal.

Endymion's / *lowliness*

TELLUS No comparison, Floscula? And why so? Is not my beauty divine, whose body is decked with fair flowers, and veins° are vines, yielding sweet liquor to the dullest spirits, whose ears are corn° to bring strength, and whose hairs are grass to bring abundance? Doth not frankincense and myrrh breathe out of my nostrils, and all the sacrifice of° the gods breed in my bowels? Infinite are my creatures,[2] without which neither thou nor Endymion nor any could love or live.

and whose veins / *grain* / *to*

FLOSCULA But know you not, fair lady, that Cynthia governeth all things? Your grapes would be but dry husks, your corn but chaff, and all your virtues° vain, were it not Cynthia that preserveth the one in the bud and nourisheth the other in the blade,° and by her influence° both comforteth all things and by her authority commandeth all creatures. Suffer then Endymion to follow his affections, though to obtain her be impossible, and let him flatter himself in his own imaginations, because they are immortal.

powers / *in harvest* / *(see 3.4.179)*

3. Endymion compares himself to Phaëthon, who (as described in Ovid's *Metamorphoses*, 2.328) fell from the heavens when he unwisely attempted to steer the chariot of his sun-god father. Compare also Icarus, who suffered a similar fate when he attempted to fly with man-made wings.

1.2. As in the previous scene.

1. Tellus addresses the absent Endymion.

2. I.e., The living things that flourish under my divine sustenance are infinite in number.

TELLUS Loath I am, Endymion, thou shouldst die, because I love thee well, and that thou shouldst live it grieveth me, because thou lovest Cynthia too well. In these extremities what shall I do? Floscula, no more words. I am resolved: he shall neither live nor die.

FLOSCULA A strange practice,° if it be possible.

stratagem

TELLUS Yes, I will entangle him in such a sweet net that he shall neither find the means to come out, nor desire it. All allurements of pleasure will I cast before his eyes, insomuch that he shall slake° that love which he now voweth to Cynthia, and burn in mine, of which he seemeth careless.° In this languishing between my amorous devices and his own loose desires, there shall such dissolute thoughts take root in his head, and over his heart grow so thick a skin, that neither hope of preferment,° nor fear of punishment, nor counsel of the wisest, nor company of the worthiest shall alter his humor° nor make him once to think of his honor.

slacken
unaware, inattentive
advancement
disposition

FLOSCULA A revenge incredible and, if it may be, unnatural.

TELLUS He shall know the malice of a woman to have neither mean° nor end, and of a woman deluded in love to have neither rule nor reason. I can do it, I must, I will. All his virtues will I shadow° with vices. His person—ah, sweet person!—shall he deck with such rich robes as he shall forget it is his own person; his sharp wit—ah, wit too sharp, that hath cut off all my joys!—shall he use in flattering of my face and devising sonnets in my favor. The prime of his youth and pride of his time° shall be spent in melancholy passions, careless behavior, untamed thoughts, and unbridled affections.

moderation
pair; obscure
flower of his youth

FLOSCULA When this is done, what then? Shall it continue till his death, or shall he dote forever in this delight?

TELLUS Ah, Floscula, thou rendest my heart in sunder,° in putting me in remembrance of the end.°

in pieces
death and judgment

FLOSCULA Why, if this° be not the end, all the rest is to no end.°

this present life
purpose

TELLUS Yet suffer me to imitate Juno, who would turn Jupiter's lovers to beasts on the earth, though she knew afterwards they should be stars in heaven.[3]

FLOSCULA Affection that is bred by enchantment is like a flower that is wrought° in silk: in color and form most like, but nothing at all in substance or savor.

embroidered

TELLUS It shall suffice me, if° the world talk, that I am favored of° Endymion.

even if
loved by

FLOSCULA Well, use your own will, but you shall find that love gotten with witchcraft is as unpleasant as fish taken with medicines unwholesome.°

poisoned bait

TELLUS Floscula, they that be so poor that they have neither net nor hook will rather poison dough° than pine with hunger; and she that is so oppressed with love that she is neither able with beauty nor wit to obtain her friend° will

fish bait
lover

3. Ovid, in his *Metamorphoses,* 1.568 ff., relates how Juno's jealousy of her husband's philanderings prompted Jupiter to change his beautiful mistress Io into a heifer in a vain attempt at concealment. She was restored to her human shape and eventually died. Subsequently, the Egyptians worshiped her as Isis.

rather use unlawful means than try° untolerable pains. I will do it. *Exit.*

experience

FLOSCULA Then about it.—Poor Endymion, what traps are laid for thee because thou honorest one that all the world wondereth at! And what plots are cast to make thee unfortunate that studiest° of all men to be the faithfullest! *Exit.*

you who strive

1.3

[Enter] Dares [and] Samias.

DARES Now° our masters are in love up to the ears, what have we to do but to be in knavery up to the crowns?°

Now that / *tops of our heads*

SAMIAS Oh, that we had Sir Tophas, that brave squire, in the midst of our mirth! And *ecce autem,*° will you see the devil?

lo and behold

Enter Sir Tophas [ridiculously armed and accoutered, and] Epiton. [Dares and Samias stand aside.]

TOPHAS Epi!

EPITON Here, sir.

TOPHAS I brook not° this idle humor of love.[1] It tickleth not my liver, from whence the lovemongers in former age seemed to infer they° should proceed.

cannot tolerate / *(feelings of love)*

EPITON Love, sir, may lie in your lungs, and I think it doth, and that is the cause you blow° and are so pursy.°

pant / short-winded

TOPHAS Tush, boy, I think it but some device of the poet to get money.

EPITON A poet? What's that?

TOPHAS Dost thou not know what a poet is?

EPITON No.

TOPHAS Why, fool, a poet is as much as one should say, a poet. [*Discovering Dares and Samias*] But soft,° yonder be two wrens. Shall I shoot at them?

gently, wait a minute

EPITON They are two lads.

TOPHAS Larks or wrens, I will kill them.

EPITON Larks? Are you blind? They are two little boys.

TOPHAS Birds or boys, they are both but a pittance for my breakfast. Therefore have at them,° for their brains must, as it were, embroider my bolts.°

here I shoot / *besmear my arrows*

[He takes aim at Samias and Dares.]

SAMIAS [*to Sir Tophas*] Stay° your courage, valiant knight, for your wisdom is so weary that it stayeth itself.

Hold, restrain

DARES Why, Sir Tophas, have you forgotten your old friends?

TOPHAS Friends? *Nego argumentum.*°

I deny your argument

SAMIAS And why not friends?

TOPHAS Because *amicitia,*° as in old annuals° we find, is *inter pares.*° Now, my pretty companions, you shall see how unequal° you be to me. But I will not cut you quite off; you shall be my half friends, for, reaching to my middle, so far as from the ground to the waist I will be your friend.

friendship / almanacs / *among equals* / *(in size)*

1.3. As in the previous scene.

1. According to the theory of the four "humors," or bodily fluids (blood, phlegm, choler or bile, and melancholy or black choler), that were thought to determine by their relative proportions a person's health and temperament, love was an effect of such humors originating primarily in the liver (see lines 8–9).

DARES Learnedly.° But what shall become of the rest of your body, from the waist to the crown? *Wisely said (ironic)*

TOPHAS My children, *quod supra vos nihil ad vos*,[2] you must think the rest immortal because you cannot reach it.

EPITON [*to Samias and Dares*] Nay, I tell ye, my master is more than a man.

DARES [*to Epiton*] And thou less than a mouse.

TOPHAS But what be you two?

SAMIAS I am Samias, page to Eumenides.

DARES And I Dares, page to Endymion.

TOPHAS Of what occupation° are your masters? *trade*

DARES Occupation, you clown? Why, they are honorable, and warriors.

TOPHAS Then are they my prentices.

DARES Thine? And why so?

TOPHAS I was the first that ever devised war, and therefore by Mars° himself given me for my arms a whole armory, and thus I go as you see, clothed with artillery. It is not silks (milksops), nor tissues,° nor the fine wool of Seres,[3] but iron, steel, swords, flame, shot, terror, clamor, blood, and ruin that rocks asleep my thoughts, which never had any other cradle but cruelty. Let me see, do you not bleed? *god of war* / *fine cloth*

DARES Why so?

TOPHAS Commonly my words wound.

SAMIAS What then do your blows?

TOPHAS Not only wound, but also confound.

SAMIAS [*to Epiton*] How dar'st thou come so near thy master, Epi?—Sir Tophas, spare us.

TOPHAS You shall live. You, Samias, because you are little; you, Dares, because you are no bigger; and both of you, because you are but two; for commonly I kill by the dozen, and have for every particular adversary a peculiar° weapon. *unique; ill-suited*
[*He displays his weaponry.*]

SAMIAS May we know the use, for our better skill in war?

TOPHAS You shall. Here is a birdbolt° for the ugly beast, the blackbird. *arrow for bird-shooting*

DARES A cruel sight!

TOPHAS Here is the musket for the untamed, or, as the vulgar sort° term it, the wild mallard. *boorish commoners*
[*He demonstrates, not heeding their talk.*]

SAMIAS Oh, desperate attempt!

EPITON Nay, my master will match° them. *be a match for*

DARES Ay, if he catch them.

TOPHAS Here is spear and shield, and both necessary, the one to conquer, the other to subdue or overcome the terrible trout, which, although he be under the water, yet, tying a string to the top of my spear and an engine of iron° to the end of my line, I overthrow him, and then herein I put him. *i.e., fishhook*
[*He shows his gear and struts about, oblivious to their talk.*]

SAMIAS Oh, wonderful war! Dares, didst thou ever hear such a dolt?

2. That which is above you is nothing to you.
3. Name given by the ancient Greeks and Romans to the inhabitants of eastern Asia (probably China), believed to be the original home of silk.

DARES All the better. We shall have good sport hereafter if we can get leisure.

SAMIAS Leisure? I will rather lose my master's service than his company. Look how he struts. [*To Tophas, pointing to his weapon*] But what is this? Call you it your sword?

TOPHAS No, it is my scimitar, which I, by construction° often studying to be compendious,° call my smiter.

construing

comprehensively brief

DARES What, are you also learned, sir?

TOPHAS Learned? I am all Mars and *Ars*.[4]

SAMIAS Nay, you are all mass and ass.

TOPHAS Mock you me? You shall both suffer, yet with such weapons as you shall make choice of the weapon wherewith you shall perish. Am I all a mass or lump? Is there no proportion in me? Am I all ass? Is there no wit in me?—Epi, prepare them to the slaughter.

SAMIAS I pray, sir, hear us speak. We call you "mass," which your learning doth well understand is all "man," for *mas, maris*° is a man. Then "as," as you know, is a weight,[5] and we for your virtues account you a weight.[6]

a male (Latin)

TOPHAS The Latin hath saved your lives,[7] the which a world of silver could not have ransomed. I understand you and pardon you.

DARES Well, Sir Tophas, we bid you farewell, and at our next meeting we will be ready to do you service.

TOPHAS Samias, I thank you. Dares, I thank you. But especially I thank you both.

SAMIAS [*aside to Dares*] Wisely! Come, next time we'll have some pretty gentlewomen with us to walk, for without doubt with them he will be very dainty.°

debonair

DARES [*to Samias*] Come, let us see what our masters do. It is high time. *Exeunt* [*Dares and Samias*].

TOPHAS Now will I march into the field, where, if I cannot encounter with my foul enemies, I will withdraw myself to the river and there fortify° for fish; for there resteth° no minute free from fight. *Exit* [*with Epiton*].

arm myself / remains

1.4

[*Enter*] *Tellus* [*and*] *Floscula* [*at one door and*] *Dipsas* [*at another*].

TELLUS Behold, Floscula, we have met with the woman by chance that we sought for by travail.° I will break my mind to her without ceremony or circumstance,° lest we lose that time in advice that should be spent in execution.°

labor; travel

beating around the bush

carrying out my plan

FLOSCULA Use your discretion.° I will in this case neither give counsel nor consent, for there cannot be a thing more monstrous than to force affection by sorcery, neither do I imagine anything more impossible.

Do as you wish

TELLUS Tush, Floscula, in obtaining of love what impossibilities will I not try? And for the winning of Endymion what

4. I am the perfect embodiment of warfare and the learned arts.

5. "As" in Latin is a unit of weight, coinage, measure, etc.

6. (1) Valiant; (2) a wight, person; (3) something heavy.

7. The ability to speak Latin could save an accused from hanging.

1.4. As in the previous scene.

impieties will I not practice?—Dipsas, whom as many honor for age as wonder at for cunning,° listen in few words to my tale and answer in one word to the purpose, for that° neither my burning desire can afford long speech nor the short time I have to stay many delays. Is it possible by herbs, stones,° spells, incantation, enchantment, exorcisms, fire, metals, planets, or any practice° to plant affection where it is not and to supplant it where it is?

learning, skill; deceit / *since* / *minerals* / *tricks*

DIPSAS Fair lady, you may imagine that these hoary hairs are not void of experience, nor the great name that goeth of my cunning to be without cause. I can darken the sun by my skill and remove the moon out of her course; I can restore youth to the aged and make hills without bottoms.° There is nothing that I cannot do but that only which you would have me do, and therein I differ from the gods, that I am not able to rule hearts; for, were it in my power to place affection by appointment, I would make such evil appetites, such inordinate lusts, such cursed desires, as all the world should be filled both with superstitious heats° and extreme love.

valleys / *irrational passions*

TELLUS Unhappy Tellus, whose desires are so desperate that they are neither to be conceived of any creature° nor to be cured by any art!

imagined by anyone

DIPSAS This I can: breed slackness in love, though never root it out. What is he whom you love, and what she that he honoreth?

TELLUS Endymion, sweet Endymion, is he that hath my heart; and Cynthia, too too fair Cynthia, the miracle of nature, of time, of fortune, is the lady that he delights in, and dotes on every day, and dies for ten thousand times a day.

DIPSAS Would you have his love, either by absence or sickness, aslaked?° Would you that Cynthia should mistrust him, or be jealous of him without color?°

diminished / *justification*

TELLUS It is the only thing I crave, that, seeing my love to Endymion, unspotted, cannot be accepted, his truth° to Cynthia, though it be unspeakable,° may be suspected.°

loyalty / *inexpressible / doubted*

DIPSAS I will undertake it and overtake him, that all his love shall be doubted of and therefore become desperate. But this will wear out with time, that treadeth all things down but truth.

TELLUS Let us go.

DIPSAS I follow. *Exeunt.*

2.1

[*Enter*] *Endymion.*

ENDYMION O fair Cynthia, O unfortunate Endymion! Why was not thy birth as high as thy thoughts, or her beauty less than heavenly? Or why are not thine honors as rare° as her beauty? Or thy fortunes as great as thy deserts? Sweet Cynthia, how wouldst thou be pleased, how possessed? Will labors, patient of° all extremities, obtain thy love? There is

excellent / *willing to endure*

2.1. Endymion's solitary cell (see lines 44–45).

no mountain so steep that I will not climb, no monster so cruel that I will not tame, no action so desperate that I will not attempt. Desirest thou the passions of love, the sad and melancholy moods of perplexed minds, the not-to-be-expressed torments of racked° thoughts? Behold my sad tears, my deep sighs, my hollow eyes, my broken sleeps, my heavy° countenance. Wouldst thou have me vowed° only to thy beauty and consume every minute of time in thy service? Remember my solitary life, almost these seven years. Whom have I entertained but mine own thoughts and thy virtues? What company have I used but contemplation? Whom have I wondered at but thee? Nay, whom have I not contemned° for thee? Have I not crept° to those on whom I might have trodden, only because thou didst shine upon them? Have not injuries been sweet to me if thou vouchsafed'st I should bear them? Have I not spent my golden years° in hopes, waxing old with wishing, yet wishing nothing but thy love? With Tellus, fair Tellus, have I dissembled, using her but as a cloak for mine affections, that others, seeing my mangled and disordered mind, might think it were for one that loveth me, not for Cynthia, whose perfection alloweth no companion nor comparison.

tormented
sad / committed by vow
disdained
abased myself
prime of youth

In the midst of these distempered thoughts of mine, thou art not only jealous of my truth, but careless, suspicious, and secure,[1] which strange humor° maketh my mind as desperate as thy conceits° are doubtful.° I am none of those wolves that bark most when thou shinest brightest, but that fish—thy fish, Cynthia, in the flood° Araris—which at thy waxing is as white as the driven snow and at thy waning as black as deepest darkness.[2] I am that Endymion, sweet Cynthia, that have carried my thoughts in equal balance with my actions, being always as free from imagining ill as enterprising;[3] that Endymion whose eyes never esteemed anything fair but thy face, whose tongue termed nothing rare° but thy virtues, and whose heart imagined nothing miraculous but thy government;° yea, that Endymion who, divorcing himself from the amiableness of all ladies, the bravery° of all courts, the company of all men, hath chosen in a solitary cell to live only by feeding on thy favor, accounting in the world (but° thyself) nothing excellent, nothing immortal. Thus mayst thou see every vein, sinew, muscle, and artery of my love, in which there is no flattery nor deceit, error nor art.° But soft,° here cometh Tellus. I must turn my other face to her like Janus, lest she be as suspicious as Juno.[4]

disposition
fancies / hard to fathom
river
excellent
conduct; rule
splendor
other than
artfulness / gently

Enter Tellus [with Floscula and Dipsas].

TELLUS Yonder I espy Endymion. I will seem to suspect nothing, but soothe° him, that, seeing I cannot obtain the depth

cajole, deceive

1. You are not only mistrustful of my steadfastness, but negligent, suspecting the worst, and complacent.
2. Plutarch reports a fish that is supposed to have varied in size and fertility with the waxing and waning of the moon. The Araris River may be the Aare in Switzerland or the Arar (modern-day Saône) in eastern France. Endymion sees himself as like the fish in responding deeply to Cynthia's changes, in harmony with her.
3. As free from imagining as from actually undertaking evil deeds.
4. The two faces of the Roman god Janus pointed to the past and the future. Jupiter's queen, Juno, was notoriously jealous, with good cause.

of his love, I may learn the height of his dissembling. Floscula and Dipsas, withdraw yourselves out of our sight, yet be within the hearing of our saluting.° *hailing*

[*Floscula and Dipsas withdraw.*]

How now, Endymion, always solitary? No company but your own thoughts? No friend but melancholy fancies?

ENDYMION You know, fair Tellus, that the sweet remembrance of your love is the only companion of my life, and thy presence my paradise, so that I am not alone when nobody is with me, and in heaven itself when thou art with me.

TELLUS Then you love me, Endymion?

ENDYMION Or else I live not, Tellus.

TELLUS Is it not possible for you, Endymion, to dissemble?

ENDYMION Not, Tellus, unless I could make me° a woman. *turn myself into*

TELLUS Why, is dissembling joined to their sex inseparable,° *inseparably* as heat to fire, heaviness to earth, moisture to water, thinness to air?° *(the four elements)*

ENDYMION No, but found in their sex as common as spots upon doves, moles upon faces, caterpillars upon sweet apples, cobwebs upon fair windows.

TELLUS Do they all dissemble?

ENDYMION All but one.

TELLUS Who is that?

ENDYMION I dare not tell. For if I should say you,° *name you* then would you imagine my flattery to be extreme; if another, then would you think my love to be but indifferent.

TELLUS You will be sure I shall take no vantage of your words.[5] But in sooth,° *in truth* Endymion, without more ceremonies,° *ado* is it not Cynthia?

ENDYMION You know, Tellus, that of the gods we are forbidden to dispute, because their deities come not within the compass of our reasons; and of Cynthia we are allowed not to talk but to wonder, because her virtues are not within the reach of our capacities.

TELLUS Why, she is but a woman.

ENDYMION No more was Venus.° *goddess of love*

TELLUS She is but a virgin.

ENDYMION No more was Vesta.° *goddess of the hearth*

TELLUS She shall have an end.

ENDYMION So shall the world.

TELLUS Is not her beauty subject to time?

ENDYMION No more than time is to standing still.[6]

TELLUS Wilt thou make her immortal?

ENDYMION No, but incomparable.

TELLUS Take heed, Endymion, lest, like the wrestler in Olympia° *site of Olympic games* that, striving to lift an impossible weight, catched an incurable strain, thou, by fixing thy thoughts above thy reach, fall into a disease without all recure.° *recovery, cure* But I see thou art now in love with Cynthia.

ENDYMION No, Tellus. Thou knowest that the stately cedar, whose top reacheth unto the clouds, never boweth his head

5. (1) You are picking your words carefully to fend off my questions; (2) I won't repeat what you say.

6. Time moves constantly and yet is eternal; similarly, Cynthia's beauty changes only to be renewed.

to the shrubs that grow in the valley; nor ivy that climbeth up by the elm can ever get hold of the beams of the sun. Cynthia I honor in all humility, whom none ought or dare adventure to love, whose affections are immortal and virtues infinite. Suffer me therefore to gaze on the moon, at whom, were it not for thyself, I would die with wondering.

Exeunt.

2.2

[*Enter*] *Dares, Samias, Scintilla,* [*and*] *Favilla.*

DARES Come, Samias, didst thou ever hear such a sighing, the one° for Cynthia, the other° for Semele, and both for moonshine in the water?°

(Endymion) / (Eumenides) — *(something illusory)*

SAMIAS Let them sigh, and let us sing.—How say you, gentlewomen, are not our masters too far in love?

SCINTILLA Their tongues haply° are dipped to the root in amorous words and sweet discourses, but I think their hearts are scarce tipped on the side° with constant desires.

perchance — *hardly touched*

DARES How say you, Favilla, is not love a lurcher,° that taketh men's stomachs away that they cannot eat, their spleen° that they cannot laugh, their hearts that they cannot fight, their eyes that they cannot sleep, and leaveth nothing but livers to make nothing but lovers?°

thief — *(organ of laughter)* — *(see 1.3.7–9 and n)*

FAVILLA Away, peevish boy! A rod were better under thy girdle° than love in thy mouth. It will be a forward° cock that croweth in the shell.

striking your bottom — *presumptuous*

DARES Alas, good old gentlewoman,° how it becometh you to be grave!

(said sardonically)

SCINTILLA Favilla, though she be but a spark, yet is she fire.

FAVILLA And you, Scintilla, be not much more than a spark, though you would be esteemed a flame.[1]

SAMIAS [*aside to Dares*] It were good sport to see the fight between two sparks.

DARES [*aside to Samias*] Let them to it, and we will warm us by their words.

SCINTILLA You are not angry, Favilla?

FAVILLA That is, Scintilla, as you list° to take it.

care, wish

SAMIAS That, that!°

(egging them on)

SCINTILLA This it is to be matched with girls, who, coming but yesterday from making of babies,° would before tomorrow be accounted matrons.[2]

dolls

FAVILLA I cry Your Matronship mercy.[3] Because your pantables° be higher with cork, therefore your feet must needs be higher in the insteps. You will be° mine elder because you stand upon a stool and I on the floor.

embroidered slippers — *insist on being*

SAMIAS Good, good.

DARES [*aside to Samias*] Let them alone, and see with what countenance° they will become friends.

show of feeling

2.2. At or near the court.

1. In Latin, "favilla" means "cinders"; "scintilla" means "spark." "Spark" also means "wit"; "fire" and "flame" connote desired beauty and passion.

2. Scintilla replies to Favilla's barbed answer in line 27 by complaining that it is vexing to be partnered with girls (like Favilla) who, though barely out of their infancy, put on the airs of older women.

3. I beg your pardon. (Said sardonically, with a title mockingly like "Your Honor.")

SCINTILLA [*to Favilla*] Nay, you think to be the wiser, because you mean to have the last word.

[*The women threaten each other.*]

SAMIAS Step between them, lest they scratch.—In faith, gentlewomen, seeing we came out to be merry, let not your jarring mar our jests. Be friends. How say you?

SCINTILLA I am not angry, but it spited° me to see how short° she was.

angered / petite; curt

FAVILLA I meant nothing, till she would needs cross° me.

insisted on opposing

DARES Then so let it rest.

SCINTILLA I am agreed.

FAVILLA [*weeping*] And I, yet I never took anything so unkindly in my life.

SCINTILLA [*weeping*] 'Tis I have the cause, that never offered the occasion.°

gave offense

DARES Excellent, and right° like a woman.

just

SAMIAS A strange sight, to see water come out of fire.

DARES It is their property to carry in their eyes fire and water, tears and torches, and in their mouths honey and gall.

SCINTILLA You will be a good one if you live.° But what is yonder formal° fellow?

escape hanging

stately, self-important

Enter Sir Tophas [and Epiton].

DARES [*aside to his friends*] Sir Tophas, Sir Tophas of whom we told you. If you be good wenches, make as though you love him, and wonder at him.

FAVILLA We will do our parts.

DARES But first let us stand aside and let him use his garb,° for all consisteth in his gracing.[4] [*They stand aside.*]

display his bearing

TOPHAS Epi!

EPITON At hand, sir.

TOPHAS How likest thou this martial life, where nothing but blood besprinkleth our bosoms? Let me see, be our enemies fat?°

fattened for the kill

EPITON Passing° fat. And I would not change this life to be a lord; and yourself passeth all comparison, for other captains kill and beat, and there is nothing you kill but you also eat.

Surpassingly

TOPHAS I will draw out their guts out of their bellies and tear the flesh with my teeth, so mortal is my hate and so eager my unstanched stomach.[5]

EPITON [*aside*] My master thinks himself the valiantest man in the world if he kill a wren, so warlike a thing he accounteth to take away life, though it be from a lark.

TOPHAS Epi, I find my thoughts to swell and my spirit to take wings, insomuch that I cannot continue within the compass of so slender combats.°

i.e., I need more action

FAVILLA [*aside*] This passeth!°

I can't believe this!

SCINTILLA [*aside*] Why, is he not mad?

SAMIAS [*aside*] No, but a little vainglorious.

TOPHAS Epi!

EPITON Sir?

TOPHAS I will encounter that black and cruel enemy that

4. The joke depends on his outlandish appearance and absurd attempts at graceful behavior, which we will humor.

5. (1) Ravenous appetite; (2) unstoppable courage.

beareth rough and untewed° locks upon his body, whose sire throweth down the strongest walls,[6] whose legs are as many as both ours,° on whose head are placed most horrible horns by nature as a defense from all harms. *uncombed* / *i.e., four-legged*

EPITON What mean you, master, to be so desperate?° *recklessly brave*

TOPHAS Honor inciteth me, and very hunger compelleth me.

EPITON What is that monster?

TOPHAS The monster *ovis*.° I have said;° let thy wits work. *sheep (Latin) / spoken*

EPITON I cannot imagine it. Yet let me see. A black enemy with rough locks; it may be a sheep, and *ovis* is a sheep. His sire so strong; a ram is a sheep's sire, that being also an engine° of war. Horns he hath, and four legs; so hath a sheep. Without doubt this monster is a black sheep. Is it not a sheep that you mean? *instrument*

TOPHAS Thou hast hit it. That monster will I kill and sup with.° *feed upon*

SAMIAS [*to his friends*] Come, let us take him off.° *divert him*

[*The pages and maids come forward.*]

Sir Tophas, all hail!

TOPHAS Welcome, children. I seldom cast mine eyes so low as to the crowns of your heads, and therefore pardon me that I spake not all this while.

DARES No harm done. Here be fair ladies come to wonder at your person, your valor, your wit, the report whereof hath made them careless of their own honors,[7] to glut their eyes and hearts upon yours.

TOPHAS Report cannot but° injure me, for that,° not knowing fully what I am, I fear she° hath been a niggard in her praises. *can only / since* / *(Report, Fame)*

SCINTILLA No, gentle° knight. Report hath been prodigal, for she hath left you no equal, nor herself credit.[8] So much hath she told, yet no more than we now see. *wellborn; generous*

DARES [*aside*] A good wench!° *(applauding her wit)*

FAVILLA If there remain as much pity toward women as there is in you courage against your enemies, then shall we be happy, who, hearing of your person, came to see it, and, seeing it, are now in love with it.

TOPHAS Love me, ladies? I easily believe it, but my tough heart receiveth no impression with sweet words. Mars may pierce it; Venus shall not paint on it.

FAVILLA A cruel saying.

SAMIAS [*aside*] There's a girl.

DARES [*to Sir Tophas*] Will you cast these ladies away, and all for° a little love? Do but speak kindly. *when all they ask is for*

TOPHAS There cometh no soft syllable within° my lips. Custom hath made my words bloody and my heart barbarous. That pelting° word "love," how waterish it is in my mouth! It carrieth no sound. Hate, horror, death are speeches that nourish my spirits. I like honey, but I care not for the bees; I delight in music, but I love not to play on the bagpipes; I can vouchsafe to hear the voice of women, but to touch their *from within* / *paltry*

6. I.e., whose sire was a ram—a battering ram.

7. Has made them unconcerned with the harm that might be done to their reputations (by being seen in male company without a chaperone).

8. Fame has hyperbolically described you as such a nonpareil that there's no believing her report.

bodies I disdain it as a thing childish and fit for such men as can disgest° nothing but milk. *digest*

SCINTILLA A hard heart. Shall we die for your love and find no remedy?

TOPHAS I have already taken a surfeit.° *had an overdose*

EPITON Good master, pity them.

TOPHAS Pity them, Epi? No, I do not think that this breast shall be pestered with such a foolish passion. What is that the gentlewoman carrieth in° a chain? *on*

EPITON Why, it is a squirrel.[9]

TOPHAS A squirrel? O gods, what things are made for money!

[*The pages and maids speak privately amongst themselves.*]

DARES Is not this gentleman overwise?

FAVILLA I could stay all day with him if I feared not to be shent.° *disgraced, scolded*

SCINTILLA Is it not possible to meet again?

DARES Yes, at any time.

FAVILLA Then let us hasten home.

SCINTILLA [*aloud*] Sir Tophas, the god of war° deal better with you than you do with the god of love.° *may Mars* *Venus*

FAVILLA Our love we may dissemble, disgest we cannot;[1] but I doubt not but time will hamper you and help us.

TOPHAS I defy time, who hath no interest in° my heart.— Come, Epi, let me to the battle with that hideous beast.° Love is pap,° and hath no relish in my taste because it is not terrible.° [*Exeunt Sir Tophas and Epiton.*] *claim upon* *(the sheep)* *baby food* *terrifying*

DARES Indeed, a black sheep is a perilous beast. But let us in till another time.

FAVILLA I shall long for that time. *Exeunt.*

2.3

[*Enter*] *Endymion* [*near the lunary*[1] *bank; and, unseen by him*], *Dipsas* [*and*] *Bagoa.*

ENDYMION No rest, Endymion? Still uncertain how to settle thy steps by day or thy thoughts by night? Thy truth° is measured by thy fortune,° and thou art judged unfaithful because thou art unhappy.° I will see if I can beguile myself with sleep; and, if no slumber will take hold in my eyes, yet will I embrace the golden thoughts in my head and wish to melt by musing, that as ebony, which no fire can scorch, is yet consumed with sweet savors,[2] so my heart, which cannot be bent by the hardness of fortune, may be bruised by amorous desires. On yonder bank never grew anything but lunary, and hereafter I will never have any bed but that bank. O Endymion, Tellus was fair! But what availeth beauty without wisdom? Nay, Endymion, she was wise. But what avail- *loyalty* *misfortune* *unfortunate*

9. Perhaps one of the young ladies present has a squirrel on a chain leash or a squirrel-shaped medallion on a chain—seen by Sir Tophas as a courtly affectation.

1. But we cannot reconcile ourselves to this indifference in love.

2.3. Endymion's fern bank.

1. Lunary ("of or having to do with the moon") is moonwort or some such fern, popularly supposed to embody magical properties. Here it symbolizes Endymion's constancy toward Cynthia.

2. Ebony was thought to burn (and thus consume itself) without a flame but giving off an agreeable perfumed scent.

eth wisdom without honor? She was honorable, Endymion, belie her not. Ay, but how obscure is honor without fortune? Was she not fortunate, whom so many followed? Yes, yes, but base is fortune without majesty. Thy majesty, Cynthia, all the world knoweth and wondereth at, but not one° in the world that can imitate it or comprehend it. No more, Endymion! Sleep or die. Nay, die, for to sleep it is impossible; and yet, I know not how it cometh to pass, I feel such a heaviness both in mine eyes and heart that I am suddenly benumbed, yea, in every joint. It may be weariness, for when did I rest? It may be deep melancholy, for when did I not sigh? Cynthia, ay so, I say, Cynthia! *He falls asleep.*

there is no one

DIPSAS [*advancing*] Little dost thou know, Endymion, when thou shalt wake; for, hadst thou placed thy heart as low in love as thy head lieth now in sleep, thou mightest have commanded Tellus, whom now instead of a mistress thou shalt find a tomb.° These eyes must I seal up by art, not nature, which are to be opened neither by art nor nature. Thou that layest down with golden locks shalt not awake until they be turned to silver hairs; and that chin, on which scarcely appeareth soft down, shall be filled with bristles as hard as broom. Thou shalt sleep out thy youth and flowering time and become dry hay before thou knewest thyself green grass, and ready by age to step into the grave when thou wakest, that was youthful in the court when thou laid'st thee down to sleep. The malice of Tellus hath brought this to pass, which, if she could not have entreated of me by fair means, she would have commanded by menacing; for from her gather we all our simples° to maintain our sorceries. [*To Bagoa*] Fan with this hemlock over his face, and sing the enchantment for sleep, whilst I go in and finish those ceremonies that are required in our art. Take heed ye touch not his face, for the fan is so seasoned° that whoso it toucheth with a leaf shall presently° die, and over whom the wind of it breatheth, he shall sleep forever. *Exit.*

a deathlike sleep

medicinal herbs

anointed with herbs

immediately

BAGOA Let me alone,° I will be careful. [*She fans Endymion as she sings.*] What hap° hadst thou, Endymion, to come under the hands of Dipsas? O fair Endymion, how it grieveth me that that fair face must be turned to a withered skin and taste the pains of death before it feel the reward of love! I fear Tellus will repent that which the heavens themselves seemed to rue.—But I hear Dipsas coming. I dare not repine, lest she make me pine, and rock me into such a deep sleep that I shall not awake to my marriage.

Leave it to me

(mis)fortune

Enter Dipsas.

DIPSAS How now, have you finished?

BAGOA Yea.

DIPSAS Well, then, let us in, and see that you do not so much as whisper that I did this; for if you do, I will turn thy hairs to adders and all thy teeth in thy head to tongues. Come away, come away. *Exeunt [leaving Endymion asleep].*

A DUMB SHOW

Music sounds. Three ladies enter, one with a knife and a looking glass, who, by the procurement° of one of the other two, offers° to stab Endymion as he sleeps, but the third wrings her hands, lamenteth, offering still to prevent it, but dares not. At last, the first lady, looking in the glass, casts down the knife. Exeunt [the ladies]. Enters an ancient man with books with three leaves, offers the same twice. Endymion refuseth. He° rendeth two and offers the third, where he stands awhile, and then Endymion offers to take it. Exit [the old man. Endymion remains sleeping on the lunary bank, curtained off from view].

instigation · *undertakes* · *(The old man)*

3.1

[Enter] *Cynthia, three lords* [*Corsites, Zontes, and Panelion*], *Tellus,* [*Semele, and Eumenides*].

CYNTHIA Is the report true that Endymion is stricken into such a dead sleep that nothing can either wake him or move him?

EUMENIDES Too true, madam, and as much to be pitied as wondered at.

TELLUS As good° sleep and do no harm as wake and do no good.

One might as well

CYNTHIA What maketh you, Tellus, to be so short?° The time was, Endymion only was.°

curt · *was your one and only*

EUMENIDES It is an old saying, madam, that a waking dog doth afar off bark at a sleeping lion.

SEMELE It were° good, Eumenides, that you took a nap with your friend, for your speech beginneth to be heavy.°

would be · *sententious; sarcastic*

EUMENIDES Contrary to your nature, Semele, which hath been always accounted light.°

cheerful; wanton

CYNTHIA What, have we here before my face these unseemly and malapert overthwarts?° I will tame your tongues and your thoughts, and make your speeches answerable° to your duties and your conceits° fit for my dignity; else will I banish you both° my person and the world.

impudent quarrelers · *conformable* · *thoughts* · *both from*

EUMENIDES Pardon, I humbly ask; but such is my unspotted faith to Endymion that whatsoever seemeth a needle to prick his finger is a dagger to wound my heart.

CYNTHIA If you be so dear to him, how happeneth it you neither go to see him nor search for remedy for him?

EUMENIDES I have seen him, to my grief, and sought recure° with despair, for that° I cannot imagine who should restore him that is the wonder to all men. Your Highness, on° whose hands the compass of the earth° is at command (though not in possession), may show yourself both worthy your sex, your nature, and your favor,° if you redeem that honorable Endymion, whose ripe years foretell rare virtues and whose unmellowed conceits promise ripe counsel.[1]

succor · *since* · *in* · *all the earth* · *beauty*

3.1. Cynthia's court.

1. Whose ripening years anticipate remarkable virtues and whose as-yet-immature ideas give promise of wise counsel.

CYNTHIA I have had trial° (made trial) of Endymion, and conceive greater assurance of his age than I could hope of his youth.

TELLUS But timely, madam, crooks that tree that will be a cammock, and young it pricks that will be a thorn;[2] and therefore he that began without care to settle his life, it is a sign without amendment he will end it.° (that he's incorrigible)

CYNTHIA Presumptuous girl, I will make thy tongue an example of unrecoverable displeasure.—Corsites, carry her to the castle in the desert, there to remain and weave.

CORSITES Shall she work stories or poetries?° (truths or fictions)

CYNTHIA It skilleth° (matters) not which. Go to,[3] in both; for she shall find examples infinite in either, what punishment long tongues have.° (deserve, receive) *[Exeunt Corsites and Tellus.]* Eumenides, if either the soothsayers in Egypt, or the enchanters in Thessaly, or the philosophers in Greece, or all the sages of the world can find remedy, I will procure it. Therefore dispatch with all speed: you, Eumenides, into Thessaly; you, Zontes, into Greece (because you are acquainted in Athens); you, Panelion, to Egypt, saying that Cynthia sendeth and, if you will, commandeth.

EUMENIDES On bowed knee I give thanks, and with wings on my legs I fly for remedy.

ZONTES We are ready at Your Highness's command, and hope to return to your full content.

CYNTHIA It shall never be said that Cynthia, whose mercy and goodness filleth the heavens with joys and the world with marvels, will suffer either Endymion or any to perish if he may be protected.

EUMENIDES Your Majesty's words have been always deeds,° (fulfilled in deeds) and your deeds virtues. *Exeunt.*

3.2

[Enter] Corsites [and] Tellus.

CORSITES Here is the castle, fair Tellus, in which you must weave, till either time end your days or Cynthia her displeasure. I am sorry so fair a face should be subject to so hard a fortune, and that the flower of beauty, which is honored in courts, should here wither in prison.

TELLUS Corsites, Cynthia may restrain the liberty of my body; of my thoughts she cannot. And therefore do I esteem myself most free, though I am in greatest bondage.

CORSITES Can you then feed on fancy, and subdue the malice of envy by the sweetness of imagination?

TELLUS Corsites, there is no sweeter music to the miserable than despair; and therefore the more bitterness I feel, the more sweetness I find. For so vain were liberty, and so unwelcome the following of higher fortune, that I choose rather to pine in this castle than to be a prince in any other court.

CORSITES A humor contrary to your years and nothing° (not at all) agree-

2. Crooked trees begin as crooked seedlings, and thorn trees have prickles when they are young.

3. Expressing impatience.

3.2. The castle in the desert (see 3.1.41–42).

able to your sex, the one° commonly allured with delights, the other° always with sovereignty.° *(your youth)* *(your sex) / control*

TELLUS I marvel, Corsites, that you, being a captain, who should sound nothing but terror and suck nothing but blood, can find in your heart to talk such smooth° words, for that it agreeth not with your calling to use words so soft as that of love. *slick, syrupy*

CORSITES Lady, it were unfit of wars to discourse° with women, into whose minds nothing can sink but smoothness. Besides, you must not think that soldiers be so rough-hewn or of such knotty metal° that beauty cannot allure, and you, being beyond perfection, enchant. *to discourse of wars* *metallic hardness; mettle*

TELLUS Good Corsites, talk not of love, but let me to my labor. The little beauty I have shall be bestowed on my loom, which I now mean to make my lover.

CORSITES Let us in,° and what favor Corsites can show, Tellus shall command. *go in*

TELLUS The only favor I desire is now and then to walk.

Exeunt.

3.3

[*Enter*] *Sir Tophas* [*armed as before*] *and Epiton* [*with a gown and other paraphernalia*].

TOPHAS Epi!

EPITON Here, sir.

TOPHAS Unrig me. Heigh-ho!

EPITON What's that?

TOPHAS An interjection, whereof some are of mourning, as *eho, vah.*° *oh, alas (Latin)*

EPITON I understand you not.

TOPHAS Thou see'st me.

EPITON Ay.

TOPHAS Thou hear'st me.

EPITON Ay.

TOPHAS Thou feelest me.

EPITON Ay.

TOPHAS And not understand'st me?

EPITON No.

TOPHAS Then am I but three-quarters of a noun substantive.[1] But alas, Epi, to tell thee the troth° I am a noun adjective. *truth*

EPITON Why?

TOPHAS Because I cannot stand without another.[2]

EPITON Who is that?

TOPHAS Dipsas.

EPITON Are you in love?

TOPHAS No, but love hath, as it were, milked my thoughts and drained from my heart the very substance of my accustomed courage. It worketh in my head like new wine, so as I must

3.3. At or near the court.

1. A noun substantive was defined in William Lily's Latin grammar as "a thing that may be seen, felt, heard, or understood." Sir Tophas complains of lacking the last of these. (This Lily, or Lilly, was John Lyly's grandfather.)

2. A noun adjective was defined as a noun used adjectivally to modify another noun, as in "fruit tree." "Stand" hints at male erection.

hoop my sconce° with iron, lest my head break and so I bewray° my brains. But I pray thee, first discover° me in all parts, that I may be like a lover, and then will I sigh and die. Take my gun, and give me a gown. *Cedant arma togae.*[3]

head / *expose / reveal*

EPITON [*helping Sir Tophas to disarm*] Here.

TOPHAS Take my sword and shield, and give me beard-brush and scissors. *Bella gerant alii; tu, Pari, semper ama.*[4]

EPITON Will you be trimmed, sir?

TOPHAS Not yet, for I feel a contention within me whether I shall frame° the bodkin° beard or the bush. But take my pike and give me pen. *Dicere quae puduit, scribere jussit amor.*[5]

fashion / dagger-shaped

EPITON I will furnish you, sir.

TOPHAS Now for my bow and bolts, give me ink and paper; for my smiter,° a penknife. For *scalpellum, calami, atramentum, charta, libelli, sint semper studiis arma parata meis.*[6]

weapon; scimitar

EPITON Sir, will you give over wars and play with that bauble° called love?

plaything

TOPHAS Give over wars? No, Epi. *Militat omnis amans, et habet sua castra Cupido.*[7]

EPITON Love hath made you very eloquent, but your face is nothing fair.

TOPHAS *Non formosus erat, sed erat facundus Ulysses.*[8]

EPITON Nay, I must seek a new master if you can speak nothing but verses.

TOPHAS *Quicquid conabar dicere versus erat.*[9] Epi, I feel all Ovid *de Arte Amandi*° lie as heavy at my heart as a load of logs. Oh, what a fine thin hair hath Dipsas! What a pretty low forehead! What a tall and stately nose! What little hollow eyes! What great and goodly lips! How harmless she is, being toothless! Her fingers fat and short, adorned with long nails like a bittern!° In how sweet a proportion her cheeks hang down to her breasts like dugs, and her paps to her waist like bags! What a low stature she is, and yet what a great foot she carrieth! How thrifty must she be in whom there is no waste!° How virtuous is she like° to be, over whom no man can be jealous!

On the Art of Love / *heronlike bird* / *(also "waist") / likely*

EPITON Stay, master, you forget yourself.°

you're getting carried away

TOPHAS Oh, Epi, even as a dish melteth by the fire, so doth my wit increase by love.

EPITON Pithily, and to the purpose.° But what, begin you to nod?

(said ironically)

TOPHAS Good Epi, let me take a nap. For as some man may better steal a horse than another look over the hedge, so divers shall be sleepy when they would fainest° take rest.[1]

most willingly

He sleeps.

EPITON Whoever saw such a woodcock?° Love Dipsas? Without doubt all the world will now account him valiant, that

proverbially stupid bird

3. Let the soldier's life give way to a life of wearing a wooer's toga. (From Cicero.)
4. Let others fight; love always, Paris. (From Ovid.)
5. Love bids one write what one is ashamed to speak. (From Ovid.)
6. May penknife, quills, black ink, paper, and notebooks be always at hand as my weapons in writing.
7. Every lover goes to war, and Cupid has his own camp. (From Ovid.)
8. Ulysses was not handsome, but he sure knew how to talk. (From Ovid.)
9. Whatever I tried to say came out as verse. (From Ovid.)
1. Tophas proposes to seize the occasion to sleep, like a thief stealing a horse while another person is napping.

ventureth on her whom none durst° undertake. But here cometh two wags.° — *dare*; *youths; jokers*

Enter Dares and Samias.

SAMIAS [*to Dares*] Thy master hath slept his share.

DARES [*to Samias*] I think he doth it because he would not pay me my board wages.° — *my food allowance*

SAMIAS It is a thing most strange, and I think mine° will never return; so that we must both seek new masters, for we shall never live by our manners. — *(Eumenides)*

EPITON [*to Samias and Dares*] If you want masters, join with me and serve Sir Tophas, who must needs keep more men because he is toward marriage.° — *planning to marry*

SAMIAS What, Epi, where's thy master?

EPITON Yonder sleeping in love.

DARES Is it possible?

EPITON He hath taken his thoughts a hole lower,° and saith, seeing it is the fashion of the world, he will vail bonnet° to beauty. — *down a peg*; *take off his hat*

SAMIAS How is he attired?

EPITON Lovely.° — *As a lover*

DARES Whom loveth this amorous knight?

EPITON Dipsas.

SAMIAS That ugly creature? Why, she is a fool, a scold, fat, without fashion, and quite without favor.° — *quite ugly*

EPITON Tush, you be simple.° My master hath a good marriage. — *simpleminded*

DARES Good? As how?

EPITON Why, in marrying Dipsas, he shall have every day twelve dishes of meat to his dinner, though there be none but Dipsas with him. Four of flesh, four of fish, four of fruit.

SAMIAS As how, Epi?

EPITON For flesh, these: woodcock, goose, bittern, and rail.[2]

DARES Indeed, he shall not miss if Dipsas be there.

EPITON For fish, these: crab, carp, lump,° and pouting. — *a spiny, bulky fish*

SAMIAS Excellent! For, of° my word, she is both crabbish, lumpish, and carping. — *on*

EPITON For fruit, these: fretters, medlers, hart-i-chockes, and lady-longings.[3] Thus you see he shall fare like a king, though he be but a beggar.

DARES Well, Epi, dine thou with him, for I had rather fast than see her face. But see, thy master is asleep. Let us have a song to wake this amorous knight.

EPITON Agreed.

SAMIAS Content.

SONG

EPITON
Here snores Tophas,
That amorous ass,
Who loves Dipsas,
With face so sweet,

2. These birds suggest foolishness and railing, or scolding.

3. These fruits have erotic associations. "Hart-i-chockes" are artichokes.

Nose and chin meet.
ALL THREE At sight of her each Fury° skips *avenging Greek deity*
And flings into her lap their whips.
DARES Holla, holla in his ear.
SAMIAS The witch sure thrust her fingers there.
EPITON Cramp him, or wring the fool by th'nose.
DARES Or clap some burning flax to his toes.
SAMIAS What music's best to wake him?
EPITON Bowwow! Let bandogs° shake him. *chained watchdogs*
DARES Let adders hiss in 's ear.
SAMIAS Else° earwigs wriggle there. *Or else let*
EPITON No, let him batten;° when his tongue *grow fat*
Once goes, a cat is not worse strung.[4]
ALL THREE But if he ope nor° mouth nor eyes, *open neither*
He may in time sleep himself wise.

TOPHAS [*to himself, as he wakens*] Sleep is a binding of the senses, love a loosing.

EPITON [*aside to Samias and Dares*] Let us hear him awhile.

TOPHAS There appeared in my sleep a goodly owl, who, sitting upon my shoulder, cried "Twit, twit," and before mine eyes presented herself the express° image of Dipsas. I marveled what the owl said, till at the last I perceived "Twit, twit," "To it, to it," only by contraction admonished by this vision to make account of my sweet Venus.[5] *exact, living*

SAMIAS [*loudly*] Sir Tophas, you have overslept yourself.

TOPHAS No, youth, I have but slept over° my love. *dreamed about*

DARES Love? Why, it is impossible that into so noble and unconquered a courage,° love should creep, having first a head as hard to pierce as steel, then to pass to a heart armed with a shirt of mail.° *spirited youth* *armor*

EPITON [*aside to Samias and Dares*] Ay, but my master yawning one day in the sun, love crept into his mouth before he could close it, and there kept such a tumbling in his body that he was glad to untruss the points° of his heart and entertain° Love as a stranger. *the fasteners* *welcome*

TOPHAS If there remain any pity in you, plead for me to Dipsas.

DARES Plead? Nay, we will press her to it. [*Aside to Samias*] Let us go with him to Dipsas, and there shall we have good sport.—But, Sir Tophas, when shall we go? For I find my tongue voluble, and my heart venturous, and all myself like myself.° *like my truest self*

SAMIAS [*aside to Dares*] Come, Dares, let us not lose him till we find our masters, for as long as he liveth, we shall lack neither mirth nor meat.

EPITON We will traverse.°—Will you go, sir? *proceed*

TOPHAS *I prae, sequar.*° *Exeunt.* *Go ahead, I'll follow*

4. Once he starts talking, it's as bad as a fiddle strung with catgut.
5. I was admonished, in this vision, by the contracted form of "To it, to it" to be attentive to my mistress, my "Venus" (i.e., Dipsas). An absurd wordplay on the owl's cry: "Too-whit."

3.4

[*Enter*] *Eumenides* [*and*] *Geron* [*near the fountain. Geron sings*].

EUMENIDES Father,° your sad music, being tuned on the same key that my hard fortune is, hath so melted my mind that I wish to hang at your mouth's end° till my life end. *Old man* / *on your lips*

GERON These tunes, gentleman, have I been accustomed with° these fifty winters, having no other house to shroud myself but the broad heavens; and so familiar with me hath use° made misery that I esteem sorrow my chiefest solace. And welcomest is that guest to me that can rehearse° the saddest tale or the bloodiest tragedy. *to* / *custom, habit* / *relate*

EUMENIDES A strange humor. Might I inquire the cause?

GERON You must pardon me if I deny to tell it, for, knowing that the revealing of griefs is, as it were, a renewing of sorrow, I have vowed therefore to conceal them, that I might not only feel the depth of everlasting discontentment, but despair of remedy. But whence are you? What fortune hath thrust you to this distress?

EUMENIDES I am going to Thessaly to seek remedy for Endymion, my dearest friend, who hath been cast into a dead sleep almost these twenty years, waxing old and ready for the grave, being almost but newly come forth of the cradle.

GERON You need not for recure° travel far, for whoso can clearly see the bottom of this fountain shall have remedy for anything. *remedy*

EUMENIDES That, methinketh, is unpossible. Why, what virtue can there be in water?

GERON Yes, whosoever can shed the tears of a faithful lover shall obtain anything he would. Read these words engraven about the brim.

EUMENIDES [*reading*] Have you known this by experience, or is it placed here of purpose to delude men?

GERON I only would have experience of it, and then should there be an end of my misery. And then would I tell the strangest discourse that ever yet was heard.

EUMENIDES [*to himself*] Ah, Eumenides!

GERON What lack you, gentleman? Are you not well?

EUMENIDES Yes, father, but a qualm that often cometh over my heart doth now take hold of me. But did never any lovers come hither?

GERON Lusters, but not lovers. For often have I seen them weep, but never could I hear they saw the bottom.

EUMENIDES Came there women also?

GERON Some.

EUMENIDES What did they see?

GERON They all wept, that the fountain overflowed with tears, but so thick became the water with their tears that I could scarce discern the brim, much less behold the bottom.

EUMENIDES Be faithful lovers so scant?

GERON It seemeth so, for yet heard I never of any.

3.4. Geron's fountain.

EUMENIDES Ah, Eumenides, how art thou perplexed! Call to mind the beauty of thy sweet mistress and the depth of thy never-dying affections. How oft hast thou honored her, not only without spot, but suspicion of falsehood! And how hardly hath she rewarded thee without cause or color of despite!° How secret hast thou been these seven years, that hast not, nor once darest not, to name her for° discontenting her! How faithful, that hast offered to die for her to please her! Unhappy Eumenides!

pretext for her scorn
for fear of

GERON Why, gentleman, did you once love?

EUMENIDES Once? Ay, father, and ever shall.

GERON Was she unkind, and you faithful?

EUMENIDES She of all women the most froward,° and I of all creatures the most fond.°

perverse
foolish, doting

GERON You doted, then, not loved. For affection is grounded on virtue, and virtue is never peevish; or on beauty, and beauty loveth to be praised.

EUMENIDES Ay, but if all virtuous ladies should yield to all that be loving, or all amiable gentlewomen entertain all that be amorous, their virtues would be accounted vices and their beauties deformities, for that love can be but between two, and that not proceeding of him that is most faithful, but most fortunate.[1]

GERON I would you were so faithful that your tears might make you fortunate.

EUMENIDES Yea, father, if that° my tears clear not this fountain, then may you swear it° is but a mere mockery.

if
(my professed true love)

GERON So, faith,° everyone yet that wept.[2]

in faith

EUMENIDES [*looking into the fountain*] Ah, I faint, I die! Ah, sweet Semele, let me alone, and dissolve° by weeping into water!

let me dissolve

GERON [*aside*] This affection seemeth strange. If he see nothing, without doubt this dissembling passeth,° for nothing shall draw me from the belief.[3]

goes beyond belief

EUMENIDES Father, I plainly see the bottom, and there in white marble engraven these words: "Ask one for all, and but one thing at all."

GERON O fortunate Eumenides (for so have I heard thee call thyself), let me see. [*He looks into the fountain.*] I cannot discern any such thing. I think thou dreamest.

EUMENIDES Ah, father, thou art not a faithful lover and therefore canst not behold it.

GERON Then ask, that I may be satisfied by the event, and thyself blessed.

EUMENIDES Ask? So I will. And what shall I do but ask, and whom should I ask° but Semele, the possessing of whose person is a pleasure that cannot come within the compass of comparison, whose golden locks seem most curious° when they seem most careless, whose sweet looks seem most alluring when they are most chaste, and whose words, the

ask for
artfully arranged

1. Since true love can exist only between one man and one woman, whereas the kind of love in which ladies yield to whoever is most amorous has the effect of rewarding not the most faithful male lover but the most importunately successful. ("And that" in line 70 points to faithless, promiscuous love.)

2. Every lover that has come here and wept has sworn the same thing.

3. From my belief in the magical properties of the fountain.

more virtuous they are, the more amorous they be accounted. I pray thee, Fortune, when I shall first meet with fair Semele, dash my delight with some light disgrace, lest, embracing sweetness beyond measure, I take a surfeit without recure.[4] Let her practice her accustomed coyness, that I may diet myself upon my desires. Otherwise the fullness of my joys will diminish the sweetness, and I shall perish by them before I possess them.

Why do I trifle the time in words? The least minute being spent in the getting of Semele is more worth than the whole world; therefore let me ask.°—What now, Eumenides? Whither art thou drawn? Hast thou forgotten both friendship and duty, care of Endymion and the commandment of Cynthia? Shall he die in a leaden sleep because thou sleepest in a golden dream?—Ay, let him sleep ever, so° I slumber but one minute with Semele. Love knoweth° neither friendship nor kindred.

ask for her
provided that
acknowledges

Shall I not hazard the loss of a friend for the obtaining of her for whom I would often lose myself?—Fond° Eumenides, shall the enticing beauty of a most disdainful lady be of more force than the rare fidelity of a tried friend? The love of men to women is a thing common, and of course;° the friendship of man to man infinite, and immortal.—Tush, Semele doth possess my love.—Ay, but Endymion hath deserved it. I will help Endymion; I found Endymion unspotted in his truth.—Ay, but I shall find Semele constant in her love. I will have Semele.—What shall I do? Father, thy gray hairs are ambassadors of experience. Which shall I ask?

Foolish
natural; mortal

GERON Eumenides, release Endymion; for all things, friendship excepted, are subject to fortune. Love is but an eyeworm,° which only tickleth the head with hopes and wishes; friendship the image of eternity, in which there is nothing movable,° nothing mischievous. As much difference as there is between beauty and virtue, bodies and shadows, colors° and life, so great odds is there between love and friendship. Love is a chameleon, which draweth nothing into the mouth but air, and nourisheth nothing in the body but lungs. Believe me, Eumenides, desire dies in the same moment that beauty sickens, and beauty fadeth in the same instant that it flourisheth. When adversities flow, then love ebbs, but friendship standeth stiffly in storms. Time draweth wrinkles in a fair face but addeth fresh colors to a fast friend, which neither heat, nor cold, nor misery, nor place, nor destiny can alter or diminish. O friendship, of all things the most rare, and therefore most rare because most excellent, whose comforts in misery is always sweet and whose counsels in prosperity are ever fortunate! Vain love, that only coming near to friendship in name, would seem to be the same, or better, in nature![5]

worm in the eye
mutable, transitory
outward appearances

EUMENIDES Father, I allow your reasons and will therefore

4. Eumenides recalls the mythical account of Semele, who was consumed by Jupiter's lightning after she asked to see him in all his majesty.

5. How frivolous of love, to claim to be essentially equal to or greater than friendship, when the resemblance between the two is merely specious!

conquer mine own. Virtue shall subdue affections, wisdom lust, friendship beauty. Mistresses are in every place, and as common as hares in Athos, bees in Hybla,[6] fowls in the air; but friends to be found are like the phoenix in Arabia, but one, or the philadelphi in Arays, never above two.[7] I will have Endymion. [*He looks into the fountain again.*] Sacred fountain, in whose bowels are hidden divine secrets, I have increased your waters with the tears of unspotted thoughts, and therefore let me receive the reward you promise. Endymion, the truest friend to me, and faithfullest lover to Cynthia, is in such a dead sleep that nothing can wake or move him.

GERON Dost thou see anything?

EUMENIDES I see in the same pillar° these words: "When she, whose figure of all is the perfectest and never to be measured, always one yet never the same, still inconstant yet never wavering, shall come and kiss Endymion in his sleep, he shall then rise; else, never." This is strange. *(see 83–85 above)*

GERON What see you else?

EUMENIDES There cometh over mine eyes either a dark mist, or upon the fountain a deep thickness, for I can perceive nothing. But how am I deluded? Or what difficult, nay, impossible, thing is this?

GERON Methinketh it easy.

EUMENIDES Good father, and how?

GERON Is not a circle of all figures the perfectest?

EUMENIDES Yes.

GERON And is not Cynthia of all circles the most absolute?

EUMENIDES Yes.

GERON Is it not impossible to measure her, who still° worketh by her influence,° never standing at one stay? *continually* / *celestial emanations*

EUMENIDES Yes.

GERON Is she not always Cynthia, yet seldom in the same bigness, always wavering in her waxing or waning, that our bodies might the better be governed, our seasons the dailier give their increase,° yet never to be removed from her course as long as the heavens continue theirs? *fruitfulness*

EUMENIDES Yes.

GERON Then who can it be but Cynthia, whose virtues, being all divine, must needs bring things to pass that be miraculous? Go humble thyself to Cynthia; tell her the success, of which myself shall be a witness. And this° assure thyself: that she that sent to find means for his safety will now work her cunning.° *of this* / *skill, artistry*

EUMENIDES How fortunate am I, if Cynthia be she that may do it!

GERON How fond° art thou, if thou do not believe it! *foolish*

EUMENIDES I will hasten thither, that I may entreat on my knees for succor, and embrace in mine arms my friend.

GERON I will go with thee, for unto Cynthia must I discover° *reveal*

6. Mount Athos in northeast Greece was noted for its hares, Hybla in Sicily for its bees. (From Ovid.)

7. The phoenix was a unique mythical bird and symbol of reincarnation. The philadelphi may be of Lyly's invention; the name suggests "loving brothers." Eumenides plays on a favorite paradox of two loving friends being but one.

all my sorrows, who also must work in me a contentment.

EUMENIDES May I now know the cause?

GERON That shall be as we walk, and I doubt not but the strangeness of my tale will take away the tediousness of our journey.

EUMENIDES Let us go.

GERON I follow. *Exeunt.*

4.1

[*Enter*] *Tellus.*

TELLUS I marvel Corsites giveth me so much liberty—all the world knowing his charge to be so high[1] and his nature to be most strange,° who hath so ill entreated° ladies of great honor that he hath not suffered° them to look out of windows, much less to walk abroad.° It may be he is in love with me, for, Endymion, hard-hearted Endymion, excepted, what is he that is not enamored of my beauty? But what respectest thou° the love of all the world? Endymion hates thee. Alas, poor Endymion, my malice hath exceeded my love, and thy faith to Cynthia quenched my affections. Quenched, Tellus? Nay, kindled them afresh, insomuch that I find scorching flames for° dead embers, and cruel encounters of war in my thoughts instead of sweet parleys. Ah, that I might once again see Endymion! Accursed girl, what hope hast thou to see Endymion, on whose head already are grown gray hairs, and whose life must yield to nature° before Cynthia end her displeasure? Wicked Dipsas, and most devilish Tellus, the one for cunning too exquisite, the other for hate too intolerable! Thou° wast commanded to weave the stories and poetries wherein were showed both examples and punishments of tattling tongues, and thou hast only embroidered the sweet face of Endymion, devices of love, melancholy imaginations,° and what not out of thy work, that thou shouldst study° to pick out of° thy mind. But here cometh Corsites. I must seem yielding and stout,° full of mildness yet tempered with a majesty. For if I be too flexible I shall give him more hope than I mean; if too froward,° enjoy less liberty than I would. Love him I cannot, and therefore will practice that which is most contrary to our sex, to dissemble.[2]

distant / treated; permitted; out of doors; i.e., Tellus herself; in place of; mortality; (Tellus herself); fancies; endeavor / remove from; unyielding; hard to please

Enter Corsites.

CORSITES Fair Tellus, I perceive you rise with the lark, and to yourself sing with the nightingale.

TELLUS My lord, I have no playfellow but fancy. Being barred of all company, I must question° with myself and make my thoughts my friends.

debate

CORSITES I would° you would account my thoughts also your friends, for they be such as are only busied in wondering at your beauty and wisdom, and some such° as have esteemed

wish; such thoughts

4.1. The castle in the desert.

1. Knowing his commission (as my keeper) to be such a heavy responsibility.

2. Said sardonically as a way of acknowledging that women like to dissemble.

your fortune too hard, and divers of that kind that offer to set you free if you will set them free.[3]

TELLUS There are no colors so contrary as white and black, nor elements so disagreeing as fire and water, nor anything so opposite as men's thoughts and their words.

CORSITES He that gave Cassandra the gift of prophesying, with the curse that, spake she never so true, she should never be believed,[4] hath, I think, poisoned the fortune of men, that, uttering the extremities of their inward passions, are always suspected of outward perjuries.

TELLUS Well, Corsites, I will flatter° myself and believe you. What would you do to enjoy my love? *deceive*

CORSITES Set all the ladies of the castle free and make you the pleasure of my life. More I cannot do; less I will not.

TELLUS These be great words, and fit° your calling, for captains must promise things impossible. But will you do one thing for all? *fit for*

CORSITES Anything, sweet Tellus, that am° ready for all. *I who am*

TELLUS You know that on the lunary bank sleepeth Endymion.

CORSITES I know it.

TELLUS If you will remove him from that place by force and convey him into some obscure cave by policy,° I give you here the faith of an unspotted virgin that you only shall possess me as a lover and, in spite of malice,° have me for a wife. *stratagem* *malicious gossip*

CORSITES Remove him, Tellus? Yes, Tellus, he shall be removed, and that so soon as thou shalt as much commend my diligence as my force. I go. [*He starts to leave.*]

TELLUS Stay. Will yourself attempt it?

CORSITES Ay, Tellus. As I would have none° partaker of my sweet love, so shall none be partners of my labors. But I pray thee go at your best leisure, for Cynthia beginneth to rise, and if she discover our love we both perish, for nothing pleaseth her but the fairness of virginity. All things must be not only without lust but without suspicion of lightness.° *none be* *wantonness*

TELLUS I will depart, and go you to Endymion.

CORSITES I fly, Tellus, being of all men the most fortunate.

Exit.

TELLUS Simple Corsites! I have set thee about a task, being but a man, that the gods themselves cannot perform. For little dost thou know how heavy his head lies, how hard his fortune. But such shifts° must women have to deceive men, and, under color° of things easy, entreat that which is impossible. Otherwise we should be cumbered with importunities, oaths, sighs, letters, and all implements of love, which, to one resolved to the contrary, are most loathsome. I will in and laugh with the other ladies at Corsites' sweating. *stratagems* *pretext*

Exit.

3. I.e., if you will gratify my desire for you. ("Them" refers to Corsites' thoughts of Tellus.)

4. When Cassandra refused Apollo's love, he gave her the gift of prophecy but without the power to be believed.

4.2

[Enter] Samias [and] Dares.

SAMIAS Will thy master never awake?

DARES No, I think he sleeps for a wager. But how shall we spend the time? Sir Tophas is so far in love that he pineth in his bed and cometh not abroad.° *away from home*

SAMIAS But here cometh Epi, in a pelting chafe.° *a childish rage*

[Enter] Epiton.

EPITON A pox of° all false proverbs! And, were a proverb a page, I would have him by the ears. *A plague on*

SAMIAS Why art thou angry?

EPITON Why? You know it is said, the tide tarrieth no man.

SAMIAS True.

EPITON A monstrous lie; for I was tied two hours, and tarried for one to unloose me.

DARES Alas, poor Epi!

EPITON Poor? No, no, you base-conceited slaves,° I am a most complete° gentlemen, although I be in disgrace with Sir Tophas. *base-minded wretches* *accomplished*

DARES Art thou out° with him? *out of favor*

EPITON Ay, because I cannot get him a lodging with Endymion. He would fain take a nap for forty or fifty years.

DARES A short sleep, considering our long life.° *(said ironically)*

SAMIAS Is he still in love?

EPITON In love? Why, he doth nothing but make sonnets.

SAMIAS Canst thou remember any one of his poems?

EPITON Ay, this is one:

> The beggar Love that knows not where to lodge,
> At last within my heart when I slept,
> He crept.
> I waked, and so my fancies began to fodge.° *fit together*

SAMIAS That's a very long verse.

EPITON Why, the other was short. The first is called from the thumb to the little finger, the second from the little finger to the elbow, and some he hath made to reach to the crown of his head and down again to the sole of his foot. It is set to the tune of the Black Saunce,[1] *ratio est,*° because Dipsas is a black saint. *the reason is*

DARES Very wisely. But pray thee, Epi, how, art thou complete? And, being from° thy master, what occupation wilt thou take? *absent from*

EPITON Know, my hearts, I am an absolute microcosmos, a petty world of° myself. My library is my head, for I have no other books but my brains; my wardrobe on my back, for I have no more apparel than is on my body; my armory at my fingers' ends, for I use no other artillery than my nails; my treasure in my purse. *Sic omnia mea mecum porto.*[2] *unto*

DARES Good.

4.2. Near Endymion's fern bank.
1. The Black Saunce, or Sanctus, was a parodic hymn to Satan.
2. Thus I carry all that I have with me—the motto of the snail. (From Cicero.)

EPITON Now, sirs, my palace is paved with grass and tiled° with stars; for *caelo tegitur qui non habet urnam,*[3] he that hath no house must lie in the yard.

roofed

SAMIAS A brave resolution. But how wilt thou spend thy time?

EPITON Not in any melancholy sort. For mine exercise I will walk horses.

DARES Too bad.°

Not very funny

EPITON Why, is it not said, "It is good walking when one hath his horse in his hand"?[4]

SAMIAS Worse and worse. But how wilt thou live?

EPITON By angling.° Oh, 'tis a stately occupation to stand four hours in a cold morning and to have his nose bitten with frost before his bait be mumbled with° a fish.

fishing; finagling / *bitten by*

DARES A rare attempt. But wilt thou never travel?

EPITON Yes, in a western° barge, when, with a good wind and lusty pugs,° one may go ten miles in two days.

westward-traveling / *strong bargemen*

SAMIAS Thou art excellent at thy choice. But what pastime wilt thou use? None?

EPITON Yes, the quickest of all.

SAMIAS What, dice?

EPITON No. When I am in haste, one-and-twenty games at chess to pass a few minutes.

DARES A life for a little lord, and full of quickness.

EPITON Tush, let me alone.° But I must needs see if I can find where Endymion lieth, and then go to a certain fountain hard by,° where they say faithful lovers shall have all things they will ask. If I can find out any of these, *ego et magister meus erimus in tuto,*[5] I and my master shall be friends. He is resolved to weep some three or four pailfuls to avoid the rheum° of love that wambleth° in his stomach.

leave it to me / *nearby* / *runny discharge / rumbles*

Enter the Watch [*two Watchmen and the Constable*].

SAMIAS Shall we never see thy master, Dares?

DARES Yes, let us go now, for tomorrow Cynthia will be there.

EPITON I will go with you. But how shall we see for the watch?[6]

SAMIAS Tush, let me alone. I'll begin to them.—Masters,° God speed you.

Good sirs

FIRST WATCHMAN Sir boy, we are all sped° already.

done for

EPITON [*aside to Samias and Dares*] So methinks, for they smell all of drink like a beggar's beard.

DARES But I pray, sirs, may we see Endymion?

SECOND WATCHMAN No, we are commanded in Cynthia's name that no man shall see him.

SAMIAS No man? Why, we are but boys.°

only boys, not men

FIRST WATCHMAN [*to his fellow Watchmen*] Mass,° neighbors, he says true. For if I swear I will never drink my liquor by the quart, and yet call for two pints, I think with a safe conscience I may carouse° both.[7]

By the Mass (an oath) / *drink down*

3. He who has no burial urn lies under the heavens. (From Lucan.)
4. Epiton deliberately misapplies a proverb, the gist of which is that it is safer walking alone when one has a horse by the bridle. Epiton jestingly speaks as though he were earning a little income as a horse groom.
5. My master and I will be in a safe place.
6. Epiton asks how they can hope to see Endymion, since a "watch" has been posted to guard him.
7. I.e., true, half-pint lads are not men, just as one can drink two pints and pretend it isn't a quart.

DARES [*aside to Samias and Epiton*] Pithily, and to the purpose.° *(said ironically)*

SECOND WATCHMAN [*to his fellow Watchmen*] Tush, tush, neighbors, take me with you.° *explain your meaning*

SAMIAS [*aside to Dares and Epiton*] This will grow hot.

DARES [*aside to Samias and Epiton*] Let them alone.

SECOND WATCHMAN [*to his fellow Watchmen*] If I say to my wife, "Wife, I will have no raisins in my pudding," she puts in currants. Small raisins are raisins, and boys are men.[8] Even as my wife should have put no raisins in my pudding, so shall there no boys see Endymion.

DARES [*aside*] Learnedly.° *(said ironically)*

EPITON Let Master Constable speak; I think he is the wisest among you.

CONSTABLE You know, neighbors, 'tis an old said saw,° "Children and fools speak true." *common proverb*

ALL THE WATCH True.

CONSTABLE Well, there you see the men be the fools, because it is provided from the children.[9]

DARES Good.

CONSTABLE Then say I, neighbors, that children must not see Endymion, because children and fools speak true.[1]

EPITON Oh, wicked application!

SAMIAS Scurvily brought about.

FIRST WATCHMAN Nay, he says true; and therefore till Cynthia have been here he shall not be uncovered. Therefore, away.

DARES [*aside to Samias and Epiton*] A watch, quoth you?° A man may watch seven years for a wise word and yet go without it. Their wits are all as rusty as their bills.°—But come on, Master Constable, shall we have a song before we go? *forsooth* / *long-handled weapons*

CONSTABLE With all my heart.

SONG

WATCH Stand. Who goes there?
We charge you appear
'Fore our constable here.
In the name of the Man in the Moon,
To us billmen° relate *armed night watchmen*
Why you stagger so late,
And how you come drunk so soon.

PAGES What are ye, scabs?° *"scurvy" fellows*

WATCH The watch;
This is the constable.

PAGES A patch.° *fool*

CONSTABLE Knock 'em down unless they all stand.
If any run away,
'Tis the old watchman's play° *ploy*
To reach him a bill of his hand.° *detain him by force*

PAGES Oh, gentlemen, hold.

8. Currants are small raisins, and similarly we'll allow no quibble that boys aren't men.

9. Well, by saying "True" as you just did, you proclaim yourselves fools, according to the specious argumentation of the children.

1. Since I've proved that children and men are alike, these children fall under the category of "men" that must not see Endymion.

Your gowns freeze with cold,
And your rotten teeth dance in your head.

EPITON Wine nothing shall cost ye,

SAMIAS Nor huge fires to roast ye.

DARES Then soberly let us be led.

CONSTABLE Come, my brown bills,[2] we'll roar,
Bounce loud° at tavern door, *Knock loudly*

OMNES° And i'th'morning steal all to bed. *Exeunt.* *All*

4.3

[*Enter*] *Corsites solus.*° [*Endymion lies asleep on the lunary bank.*] *alone*

CORSITES I am come in sight of the lunary bank. Without doubt Tellus doteth upon me; and cunningly, that I might not perceive her love, she hath set me to a task that is done before it is begun.° Endymion, you must change your pillow, and, if you be not weary of sleep, I will carry you where at ease you shall sleep your fill. It were good that without more ceremonies I took him, lest, being espied, I be entrapped and so incur the displeasure of Cynthia, who commonly setteth watch that Endymion have no wrong. *(He lifts.)* What now, is Your Mastership° so heavy? Or are you nailed to the ground? Not stir one whit?—Then use all thy° force, though he feel it and wake.—What, stone still? Turned, I think, to earth, with lying so long on the earth. Didst not thou, Corsites, before Cynthia pull up a tree that forty years was fastened with roots and wreathed in knots to the ground? Didst not thou with main° force pull open the iron gates which no ram or engine could move? Have my weak thoughts made brawn-fallen° my strong arms? Or is it the nature of love or the quintessence of the mind to breed numbness, or litherness,° or I know not what languishing in my joints and sinews, being but the base strings of my body? Or doth the remembrance of Tellus so refine my spirits into a matter so subtle and divine that the other fleshy parts cannot work whilst they° muse? Rest thyself, rest thyself; nay, rend thyself in pieces, Corsites, and strive, in spite of love, fortune, and nature, to lift up this dulled body, heavier than dead and more senseless° than death.

is easily done · *are you (honorific)* · *(said to himself)* · *sheer, brute* · *shrunken* · *lassitude* · *(my spirits, my mind)* · *deprived of sensation*

Enter Fairies.

But what are these so fair fiends that cause my hairs to stand upright and spirits to fall down? Hags—out, alas! Nymphs, I crave pardon. Ay me, out! What do I here?

The Fairies dance, and with a song pinch him, and he falleth asleep.

2. Officers of the watch with bronzed (hence brownish) weapons.

4.3. Endymion's fern bank.

[SONG]

OMNES° Pinch him, pinch him, black and blue. *All (Fairies)*
Saucy mortals must not view
What the Queen of Stars is doing,
Nor pry into our fairy wooing.
FIRST FAIRY Pinch him blue
SECOND FAIRY And pinch him black.
THIRD FAIRY Let him not lack
Sharp nails to pinch him blue and red,
Till sleep has rocked his addle° head. *empty, muddled*
FOURTH FAIRY For the trespass he hath done,
Spots o'er all his flesh shall run.
Kiss Endymion, kiss his eyes;
Then to our midnight hay-de-guise.° *country-dance*

They kiss Endymion and depart. [*Endymion and the spotted Corsites remain asleep.*]

[*Enter*] *Cynthia, Floscula, Semele, Panelion, Zontes, Pythagoras,* [*and*] *Gyptes.*

CYNTHIA You see, Pythagoras, what ridiculous opinions you hold, and I doubt not but you are now of another mind.

PYTHAGORAS Madam, I plainly perceive that the perfection of your brightness hath pierced through the thickness that covered my mind, insomuch that I am no less glad to be reformed than ashamed to remember my grossness.

GYPTES They are thrice fortunate that live in your palace, where truth is not in colors° but life, virtues not in imagination but execution. *specious appearances*

CYNTHIA I have always studied° to have rather living virtues than painted gods, the body of truth than the tomb. But let us walk to Endymion; it may be it lieth in your arts to deliver° him. As for Eumenides, I fear he is dead. *striven / release*

PYTHAGORAS I have alleged° all the natural reasons I can for such a long sleep. *cited, proffered*

GYPTES I can do nothing till I see him.

CYNTHIA Come, Floscula, I am sure you are glad that you shall behold Endymion.

FLOSCULA I were blessed if I might have him recovered.

CYNTHIA Are you in love with his person?

FLOSCULA No, but with his virtue.

CYNTHIA What say you, Semele?

SEMELE Madam, I dare say nothing for fear I offend.

CYNTHIA Belike° you cannot speak except° you be spiteful. But as good be silent as saucy. Panelion, what punishment were fit for Semele, in whose speech and thoughts is only contempt and sourness? *Perchance / unless*

PANELION I love not, madam, to give any judgment. Yet sith° Your Highness commandeth: I think, to commit her tongue close prisoner to her mouth. *since*

CYNTHIA Agreed. Semele, if thou speak this twelvemonth, thou shalt forfeit thy tongue.—Behold Endymion. Alas, poor gentleman, hast thou spent thy youth in sleep, that once vowed all to my service? Hollow eyes? Gray hairs? Wrinkled cheeks? And decayed limbs? Is it destiny or deceit that hath brought this to pass? If the first, who could prevent thy wretched stars?° If the latter, I would I might know thy cruel enemy. I favored thee, Endymion, for thy honor, thy virtues, thy affections; but to bring thy thoughts within the compass of thy fortunes, I have seemed strange,° that I might have thee stayed.° And now are thy days ended before my favor begin. But whom have we here? Is it not Corsites?

destiny / *distant* / *restrained*

ZONTES It is, but more like a leopard than a man.

CYNTHIA Awake him. [*Corsites is awakened.*]
How now, Corsites, what make° you here? How came you deformed? Look on thy hands, and then thou see'st the picture of thy face.

do

CORSITES Miserable wretch, and accursed! How am I deluded? Madam, I ask pardon for my offense, and you see my fortune deserveth pity.

CYNTHIA Speak on. Thy offense cannot deserve greater punishment; but see thou rehearse° the truth, else shalt thou not find me as thou wishest me.

tell

CORSITES Madam, as it is no offense to be in love, being a man mortal, so I hope can it be no shame to tell with whom, my lady being heavenly. Your Majesty committed to my charge fair Tellus, whose beauty in the same moment took my heart captive that I undertook to carry her body prisoner. Since that time have I found such combats in my thoughts between love and duty, reverence and affection,[1] that I could neither endure the conflict nor hope for the conquest.

CYNTHIA In love? A thing far unfitting the name of a captain, and, as I thought, the tough and unsmoothed nature of Corsites. But forth.°

continue

CORSITES Feeling this continual war, I thought rather by parley° to yield than by certain danger to perish. I unfolded to Tellus the depth of my affections, and framed° my tongue to utter a sweet tale of love, that was wont° to sound nothing but threats of war. She, too fair to be true and too false for one so fair, after a nice° denial practiced a notable deceit, commanding me to remove Endymion from this cabin and carry him to some dark cave, which I, seeking to accomplish, found impossible, and so by fairies or fiends have been thus handled.

negotiation / *shaped* / *I who was accustomed* / *coy*

CYNTHIA How say you, my lords, is not Tellus always practicing of some deceits?—In sooth,° Corsites, thy face is now too foul for a lover and thine heart too fond for a soldier. You may see, when warriors become wantons, how their manners alter with their faces. Is it not a shame, Corsites, that, having lived so long in Mars his° camp, thou shouldst now be rocked in Venus's cradle? Dost thou wear Cupid's quiver at thy girdle, and make lances of looks?° Well, Corsites, rouse thyself and be as thou hast been, and let Tellus, who is made all of love, melt herself in her own looseness.

truth / *Mars's* / *amorous gazes*

CORSITES Madam, I doubt not but to recover my former state,

1. Reverence for Cynthia and desire for Tellus.

for Tellus's beauty never wrought such love in my mind as now her deceit hath despite;[2] and yet to be revenged of° a *on* woman were a thing than love itself more womanish.[3]

GYPTES These spots, gentleman, are to be worn° *rubbed* out if you rub them over with this lunary, so that in place where you received this maim° *injury* you shall find a medicine.

CORSITES I thank you for that. The gods bless° *shield* me from love and these pretty ladies° *fairies* that haunt this green!

FLOSCULA Corsites, I would° *wish that* Tellus saw your amiable face.

[*Corsites rubs out his spots with lunary from the bank. Semele laughs.*]

ZONTES How spitefully Semele laugheth, that dare not speak!

CYNTHIA Could you not stir Endymion with that doubled strength of yours?

CORSITES Not so much as his finger with all my force.

CYNTHIA Pythagoras and Gyptes, what think you of Endymion? What reason is to be given, what remedy?

PYTHAGORAS Madam, it is impossible to yield reason for things that happen not in compass of nature. It is most certain that some strange enchantment hath bound all his senses.

CYNTHIA What say you, Gyptes?

GYPTES With Pythagoras, that it is enchantment, and that so strange that no art can undo it, for that heaviness argueth a malice unremovable in the enchantress, and that no power can end it till she die that did it or the heavens show some means more than miraculous.

FLOSCULA O Endymion, could spite itself devise a mischief so monstrous as to make thee dead with life, and living being altogether dead? Where others number their years, their hours, their minutes, and step to age by stairs, thou only hast thy years and times in a cluster, being old before thou rememberest thou wast young.

CYNTHIA No more, Floscula; pity doth him no good. I would anything else might, and I vow by the unspotted honor of a lady he should not miss it. But is this all, Gyptes, that is to be done?

GYPTES All as yet. It may be that either the enchantress shall die or else be discovered. If either happen I will then practice the utmost of my art. In the mean season,° *meantime* about this grove would I have a watch, and the first living thing that toucheth Endymion to be taken.

CYNTHIA Corsites, what say you, will you undertake this?

CORSITES Good madam, pardon me; I was overtaken too late.[4] I should rather break into the midst of a main battle than again fall into the hands of those fair babies.° *i.e., fairies*

CYNTHIA Well, I will provide others. Pythagoras and Gyptes, you shall yet remain in my court till I hear what may be done in this matter.

2. As now her deceit has prompted an angry response from me.

3. A thing even more womanish than being in love.

4. I was overwhelmed (by fairies) too recently.

PYTHAGORAS We attend.
CYNTHIA Let us go in.

Exeunt. [*Endymion continues asleep on his lunary bed, near a tree, but perhaps curtained off during the entr'acte music.*]

5.1

[*Enter*] *Samias* [*and*] *Dares.*

SAMIAS Eumenides hath told such strange tales as I may well wonder at them but never believe them.

DARES The other old man,° what a sad speech used he, that caused us almost all to weep! Cynthia is so desirous to know the experiment of her own virtue,° and so willing to ease Endymion's hard fortune, that she no sooner heard the discourse but she made herself in a readiness to try the event.

(Geron) / *try her own strength*

SAMIAS We will also see the event.° But whist!° Here cometh Cynthia with all her train. Let us sneak in amongst them.

outcome / be silent

Enter Cynthia, Floscula, Semele, Panelion, etc. [*Eumenides, Zontes, Gyptes, and Pythagoras. Samias and Dares join the throng.*]

CYNTHIA Eumenides, it cannot sink into my head that I should be signified by that sacred fountain, for many things are there in the world to which those words may be applied.

EUMENIDES Good madam, vouchsafe but to try, else shall I think myself most unhappy that I asked not my sweet mistress.[1]

CYNTHIA Will you not yet tell me her name?

EUMENIDES Pardon me, good madam, for if Endymion awake he shall. Myself have sworn never to reveal it.

CYNTHIA Well, let us to Endymion. [*They approach the sleeping Endymion.*] I will not be so stately, good Endymion, not to stoop to do thee good; and if thy liberty consist in a kiss from me, thou shalt have it. And although my mouth hath been heretofore as untouched as my thoughts, yet now to recover thy life (though to restore thy youth it be impossible) I will do that to Endymion which yet never mortal man could boast of heretofore, nor shall ever hope for hereafter.

She kisseth him.

EUMENIDES Madam, he beginneth to stir.

CYNTHIA Soft, Eumenides. Stand still.

EUMENIDES Ah, I see his eyes almost open.

CYNTHIA I command thee once again, stir not. I will stand behind him.

[*She stands where Endymion cannot see her at first.*]

PANELION What do I see, Endymion almost awake?

EUMENIDES Endymion, Endymion, art thou deaf or dumb? Or hath this long sleep taken away thy memory? Ah, my sweet Endymion, see'st thou not Eumenides, thy faithful friend, thy faithful Eumenides, who for thy safety hath been care-

5.1. The scene continues.

1. That I did not ask for Semele instead of Endymion.

less of his own content? Speak, Endymion, Endymion, Endymion!

ENDYMION Endymion? I call to mind such a name.

EUMENIDES Hast thou forgotten thyself, Endymion? Then do I not marvel thou rememberest not thy friend. I tell thee thou art Endymion and I Eumenides. Behold also Cynthia, by whose favor thou art awaked, and by whose virtue thou shalt continue thy natural course.° *normal life*

CYNTHIA Endymion, speak, sweet Endymion. Knowest thou not Cynthia?

ENDYMION Oh, heavens, whom do I behold? Fair Cynthia, divine Cynthia?

CYNTHIA I am Cynthia, and thou Endymion.

ENDYMION Endymion? What do I hear? What, a gray beard? Hollow eyes? Withered body? Decayed limbs? And all in one night?

EUMENIDES One night? Thou hast here slept forty years, by what enchantress as yet it is not known. And behold, the twig to which thou laid'st thy head is now become a tree. Callest thou not Eumenides to remembrance?

ENDYMION Thy name I do remember by the sound, but thy favor° I do not yet call to mind. Only divine Cynthia, to whom time, fortune, destiny, and death are subject, I see and remember, and in all humility I regard and reverence. *face*

CYNTHIA You have good cause to remember Eumenides, who hath for thy safety forsaken his own solace.

ENDYMION Am I that Endymion who was wont in court to lead my life, and in jousts, tourneys,° and arms to exercise my youth? Am I that Endymion? *tournaments*

EUMENIDES Thou art that Endymion and I Eumenides. Wilt thou not yet call me to remembrance?

ENDYMION Ah, sweet Eumenides, I now perceive thou art he, and that myself have the name of Endymion. But that this should be my body I doubt; for how could my curled locks be turned to gray hairs and my strong body to a dying weakness, having waxed old and not knowing it?

CYNTHIA Well, Endymion, arise. Awhile sit down, for that° thy limbs are stiff and not able to stay° thee, and tell what hast thou seen in thy sleep all this while? What dreams, visions, thoughts, and fortunes? For it is impossible but in so long time thou shouldst see things strange. *because* *support*

ENDYMION Fair Cynthia, I will rehearse° what I have seen, humbly desiring that when I exceed in length, you give me warning, that I may end. For to utter all I have to speak would be troublesome, although haply the strangeness may somewhat abate the tediousness. *relate*

CYNTHIA Well, Endymion, begin.

ENDYMION Methought I saw a lady passing° fair but very mischievous, who in the one hand carried a knife with which she offered° to cut my throat, and in the other a looking glass, wherein, seeing how ill anger became ladies, she refrained from intended violence. She was accompanied with other damsels, one of which, with a stern countenance, and as it were with a settled malice engraven in her eyes, provoked her to execute mischief. Another with visage sad, *surpassingly* *made as if* and constant only in sorrow, with her arms crossed, and watery eyes, seemed to lament my fortune, but durst not offer° to prevent the force. I started in my sleep, feeling my very veins to swell and my sinews to stretch with fear, and such a cold sweat bedewed all my body that death itself could not be so terrible as the vision.

attempt

CYNTHIA A strange sight! Gyptes at our better leisure shall expound it.

ENDYMION After long debating with herself, mercy overcame anger, and there appeared in her heavenly face such a divine majesty, mingled with a sweet mildness, that I was ravished with the sight above measure, and wished that I might have enjoyed the sight without end. And so she departed with the other ladies, of which the one retained still an unmovable cruelty, the other a constant pity.

CYNTHIA Poor Endymion, how wast thou affrighted! What else?

ENDYMION After her immediately appeared an aged man with a beard as white as snow, carrying in his hand a book with three leaves, and speaking, as I remember, these words: "Endymion, receive this book with three leaves, in which are contained counsels, policies,° and pictures." And with that, he offered me the book, which I rejected; wherewith moved with a disdainful pity, he rent the first leaf in a thousand shivers.° The second time he offered it, which I refused also; at which, bending his brows° and pitching° his eyes fast to the ground as though they were fixed to the earth and not again to be removed, then suddenly casting them up to the heavens, he tore in a rage the second leaf and offered the book only with one leaf. I know not whether fear to offend or desire to know some strange thing moved me; I took the book, and so the old man vanished.

stratagems, statecraft

fragments

frowning / casting

CYNTHIA What didst thou imagine was in the last leaf?

ENDYMION There—ay, portrayed to life—with a cold quaking in every joint, I beheld many wolves barking at thee, Cynthia, who, having ground their teeth to bite, did with striving bleed themselves to death. There might I see Ingratitude with an hundred eyes, gazing for benefits,° and with a thousand teeth gnawing on the bowels wherein she was bred. Treachery stood all clothed in white, with a smiling countenance but both her hands bathed in blood. Envy, with a pale and meager face, whose body was so lean that one might tell° all her bones, and whose garment was so tattered that it was easy to number every thread, stood shooting at stars, whose darts fell down again on her own face. There might I behold drones, or beetles, I know not how to term them, creeping under the wings of a princely eagle, who, being carried into her nest, sought there to suck that vein that would have killed the eagle. I mused that things so base should attempt a fact° so barbarous or durst imagine a thing so bloody. And many other things, madam, the repetition whereof may at your better leisure seem more pleasing; for bees surfeit° sometimes with honey, and the gods are glutted with harmony, and Your Highness may be dulled with delight.

looking for rewards

count

deed

overindulge

CYNTHIA I am content to be dieted; therefore let us in. Eumenides, see that Endymion be well tended, lest, either eating immoderately or sleeping again too long, he fall into a deadly surfeit° or into his former sleep. See this also be proclaimed: that whosoever will discover this practice° shall have of Cynthia infinite thanks and no small rewards.

overindulgence
uncover this plot

Exit [attended by her courtly entourage. Floscula, Endymion, and Eumenides remain].

FLOSCULA Ah, Endymion, none so joyful as Floscula of thy restoring!

EUMENIDES Yes, Floscula, let Eumenides be somewhat gladder, and do not that wrong to the settled friendship of a man as to compare it with the light affection of a woman.—Ah, my dear friend Endymion, suffer me to die with gazing at thee!

ENDYMION Eumenides, thy friendship is immortal and not to be conceived, and thy good will, Floscula, better than I have deserved. But let us all wait on° Cynthia. I marvel Semele speaketh not a word.

attend

EUMENIDES Because if she do she loseth her tongue.

ENDYMION But how prospereth your love?

EUMENIDES I never yet spake word° since your sleep.

i.e., spoke of love

ENDYMION I doubt not but your affection is old and your appetite cold.

EUMENIDES No, Endymion, thine° hath made it stronger, and now are my sparks grown to flames and my fancies° almost to frenzies. But let us follow, and within we will debate all this matter at large. *Exeunt.*

my affection for you
amorous inclinations

5.2

[Enter] Sir Tophas [and] Epiton.

TOPHAS Epi, love hath jostled my liberty from the wall° and taken the upper hand of my reason.

out into the gutter

EPITON Let me then trip up the heels of your affection and thrust your good will° into the gutter.

desire

TOPHAS No, Epi, love is a lord of misrule,[1] and keepeth Christmas in my corpse.°

body

EPITON No doubt there is good cheer. What dishes of delight doth His Lordship feast you withal?

TOPHAS First, with a great platter of plum porridge of pleasure, wherein is stewed the mutton of mistrust.

EPITON Excellent love-lap!°

love-portion

TOPHAS Then cometh a pie of patience, a hen of honey, a goose of gall, a capon of care, and many other viands, some sweet and some sour, which proveth love to be as it was said of in old years: *dulce venenum.*°

sweet poison

EPITON A brave° banquet!

splendid

TOPHAS But, Epi, I pray thee feel on my chin; something pricketh me. What dost thou feel or see?

5.2. At or near the court.

1. In fifteenth- and sixteenth-century England, the Lord of Misrule was elected by revelers to preside over mock ceremonials and festive events during the long Christmas season.

EPITON [*examining Tophas's chin*] There are three or four little hairs.

TOPHAS I pray thee call it my beard. How shall I be troubled when this young spring° shall grow to a great wood! *grove of saplings*

EPITON Oh, sir, your chin is but a quiller° yet. You will be most majestical when it is full fledge.° But I marvel that you love Dipsas, that old crone. *bird not fully feathered* / *fully feathered*

TOPHAS *Agnosco veteris vestigia flammæ*,[2] I love the smoke of an old fire.

EPITON Why, she is so cold that no fire can thaw her thoughts.

TOPHAS It is an old goose, Epi, that will eat no oats; old kine° will kick, old rats gnaw cheese, and old sacks will have much patching. I prefer an old cony° before a rabbit-sucker,° and an ancient hen before a young chicken peeper. *cattle* / *rabbit / baby rabbit*

EPITON *Argumentum ab antiquitate*.[3] [*Aside*] My master loveth antique work.

TOPHAS Give me a pippin° that is withered like an old wife. *species of apple*

EPITON Good, sir.

TOPHAS Then *a contrario sequitur argumentum*.[4] Give me a wife that looks like an old pippin.

EPITON [*aside*] Nothing hath made my master a fool but flat scholarship.° *plain disputation*

TOPHAS Knowest thou not that old wine is best?

EPITON Yes.

TOPHAS And thou knowest that like will to like?[5]

EPITON Ay.

TOPHAS And thou knowest that Venus loved the best wine?

EPITON So.

TOPHAS Then I conclude that Venus was an old woman in an old cup of wine. For, *est Venus in vinis, ignis in igne fuit*.[6]

EPITON *O lepidum caput*,° O madcap master! You were worthy to win Dipsas, were she as old again,° for in your love you have worn the nap of your wit quite off and made it threadbare. But soft, who comes here? *fine head* / *twice as old*

[*Enter Samias and Dares.*]

TOPHAS My solicitors.° *(see 3.3.154–55)*

SAMIAS All hail, Sir Tophas! How feel you yourself?

TOPHAS Stately in every joint, which the common people term stiffness. Doth Dipsas stoop? Will she yield? Will she bend?

DARES Oh, sir, as much as you would wish, for her chin almost toucheth her knees.

EPITON Master, she is bent, I warrant you.

TOPHAS What conditions doth she ask?

SAMIAS She hath vowed she will never love any that hath not a tooth in his head less than she.

TOPHAS How many hath she?

DARES One.

2. I acknowledge the vestiges of an old fire.
3. An argument from ancient authorities.
4. The converse holds true as well.
5. And you know that things or persons that are alike are attracted to one another? (Proverbial.)
6. Venus (i.e., Love) in the wine is like fire in fire. (From Ovid.)

EPITON That goeth hard, master, for then you must have none.

TOPHAS A small request, and agreeable to the gravity of her years. What should a wise man do with his mouth full of bones like a charnel house?° The turtle° true hath ne'er a tooth.

bone vault / turtledove

SAMIAS [*aside to Epiton*] Thy master is in a notable vein, that will lose his teeth to be like a turtle.

EPITON [*aside to Samias*] Let him lose his tongue too, I care not.

DARES Nay, you must also have no nails, for she long since hath cast° hers.

shed

TOPHAS That I yield to. What a quiet life shall Dipsas and I lead, when we can neither bite nor scratch! You may see, youths, how age provides for peace.

SAMIAS [*aside to Epiton and Dares*] How shall we do to make him leave his love? For we never spake to her.

DARES [*aside to Samias*] Let me alone.° [*To Sir Tophas*] She is a notable witch, and hath turned her maid Bagoa to an aspen tree for bewraying° her secrets.

Leave it to me / divulging

TOPHAS I honor her for her cunning, for now, when I am weary of walking on two legs, what a pleasure may she do me to turn me to some goodly ass and help me to four!

DARES Nay, then, I must tell you the truth: her husband Geron is come home, who this fifty years hath had her to wife.°

as his wife

TOPHAS What do I hear? Hath she an husband? Go to the sexton and tell him Desire is dead, and will him to dig his grave. Oh, heavens, an husband? What death is agreeable° to my fortune?

suitable

SAMIAS Be not desperate, and we will help you to find a young lady.

TOPHAS I love no Grissels;[7] they are so brittle they will crack like glass, or so dainty that if they be touched they are straight of the fashion of wax.° *Animus maioribus instat;*[8] I desire old matrons. What a sight would it be to embrace one whose hair were as orient° as the pearl, whose teeth shall be so pure a watchet° that they shall stain° the truest turquoise, whose nose shall throw more beams from it than the fiery carbuncle, whose eyes shall be environed about with redness exceeding the deepest coral, and whose lips might compare with silver for the paleness! Such a one if you can help me to, I will by piecemeal curtail my affections towards Dipsas and walk my swelling thoughts till they be cold.

impressionable / lustrous / light blue / dim

EPITON Wisely provided.° How say you, my friends, will you angle° for my master's cause?

said as a proviso / devise stratagems

SAMIAS Most willingly.

DARES If we speed° him not shortly, I will burn my cap. We will serve him of the spades,° and dig an old wife out of the grave that shall be answerable° to his gravity.

aid, prosper / serve him right / well suited

7. Tophas curtly dismisses all young ladies as too apt to be like many a patient and long-suffering heroine of medieval and Renaissance fictional accounts, including Chaucer's *Clerk's Tale* and Thomas Dekker's *Patient Grissel* (1600); whatever her virtues, she is not to Tophas's taste. Perhaps also a reference to "gristle," as in the still-unformed bones and joints of infancy.

8. My spirit ventures greater themes. (From Ovid.)

TOPHAS Youths, adieu. He that bringeth me first news shall possess mine inheritance. [*Exit.*]

DARES [*to Epiton*] What, is thy master landed?° — *possessing land; hooked*

EPITON Know you not that my master is *liber tenens*?° — *a freeholder*

SAMIAS What's that?

EPITON A freeholder. But I will after him.

SAMIAS And we, to hear what news of Endymion for the conclusion. *Exeunt.*

5.3

[*Enter*] *Panelion* [*and*] *Zontes.*

PANELION Who would have thought that Tellus, being so fair by nature, so honorable by birth, so wise by education, would have entered into a mischief to the gods so odious, to men so detestable, and to her friend° so malicious? — *(Endymion)*

ZONTES If Bagoa had not bewrayed it, how then should it have come to light? But we see that gold and fair words are of force to corrupt the strongest men, and therefore able to work silly women like wax.

PANELION I marvel° what Cynthia will determine° in this cause.° — *wonder / decide; case*

ZONTES I fear as in all causes: hear of it in justice and then judge of it in mercy. For how can it be that she that is unwilling to punish her deadliest foes with disgrace will revenge injuries of her train° with death? — *retinue*

PANELION That old witch Dipsas, in a rage, having understood her practice° to be discovered, turned poor Bagoa to an aspen tree. But let us make haste and bring Tellus before Cynthia, for she was coming out after us. — *sorcery*

ZONTES Let us go. *Exeunt.*

[5.4]

[*Enter*] *Cynthia, Semele, Floscula, Dipsas, Endymion, Eumenides,* [*Geron, Pythagoras, Gyptes, and Sir Tophas. A tree stands by the lunary bank*].

CYNTHIA Dipsas, thy years are not so many as thy vices, yet more in number than commonly nature doth afford or justice should permit. Hast thou almost these fifty years practiced that detested wickedness of witchcraft? Wast thou so simple° as for to know the nature of simples,° of all creatures to be most sinful? Thou hast threatened to turn my course awry and alter by thy damnable art the government that I now possess by the eternal gods. But know thou, Dipsas, and let all the enchanters know, that Cynthia, being placed for light on earth, is also protected by the powers of heaven. Breathe out thou mayst words, gather thou mayst herbs, find out thou mayst stones° agreeable to thine art, yet of no force to appall my heart, in which courage is so rooted, and constant persuasion of the mercy of the gods so grounded, that all thy witchcraft I esteem as weak as the world doth thy — *foolish / magical drugs; special minerals*

5.3. Cynthia's court. **5.4.** Endymion's fern bank.

case wretched. This noble gentleman Geron, once thy husband but now thy mortal° hate, didst thou procure° to live in a desert, almost desperate. Endymion, the flower of my court and the hope of succeeding time,° hast thou bewitched by art before thou wouldst suffer him to flourish by nature.

deadly / cause; of time to come

DIPSAS Madam, things past may be repented, not recalled. There is nothing so wicked that I have not done, nor anything so wished for as death. Yet among all the things that I committed, there is nothing so much tormenteth my rented° and ransacked thoughts as that in the prime of my husband's youth I divorced him by my devilish art, for which, if to die might be amends, I would not live till tomorrow. If to live and still be more miserable would better content him, I would wish of all creatures to be oldest and ugliest.

torn

GERON Dipsas, thou hast made this difference between me and Endymion, that, being both young,° thou hast caused me to wake° in melancholy, losing the joys of my youth, and him to sleep, not remembering youth.

when we were young; remain awake

CYNTHIA Stay, here cometh Tellus. We shall now know all.

Enter Corsites [*and*] *Tellus,* [*escorted by*] *Panelion, etc.* [*and Zontes.*]

CORSITES [*to Tellus*] I would to Cynthia thou couldst make as good an excuse in truth as to me thou hast done by wit.

TELLUS Truth shall be mine answer, and therefore I will not study° for an excuse.

look around

CYNTHIA Is it possible, Tellus, that so few years should harbor so many mischiefs? Thy swelling pride have I borne because it is a thing that beauty maketh blameless,° which, the more it exceedeth fairness in measure,° the more it stretcheth° itself in disdain. Thy devices° against Corsites I smile at, for that° wits the sharper they are, the shrewder° they are. But this unacquainted° and most unnatural practice with a vile enchantress against so noble a gentleman as Endymion I abhor as a thing most malicious, and will revenge as a deed most monstrous. And as for you, Dipsas, I will send you into the desert amongst wild beasts, and try whether you can cast lions, tigers, boars, and bears into as dead a sleep as you did Endymion, or turn them to trees as you have done Bagoa. But tell me, Tellus, what was the cause of this cruel part,° far unfitting thy sex, in which nothing should be but simpleness,° and much disagreeing from thy face, in which nothing seemed to be but softness?

excuses, mitigates; normal beauty / raises; plots; since / more abusive; unprecedented; conduct; innocence, honesty

TELLUS Divine Cynthia, by whom I receive my life and am content to end it, I can neither excuse my fault without lying nor confess it without shame. Yet were it possible that in so heavenly thoughts as yours there could fall such earthly motions° as mine, I would then hope, if not to be pardoned without extreme punishment, yet to be heard without great marvel.

promptings

CYNTHIA Say on, Tellus. I cannot imagine anything that can color° such a cruelty.

excuse

TELLUS Endymion, that Endymion, in the prime of his youth so ravished my heart with love that to obtain my desires I could not find means, nor to resist them reason. What was she that favored not Endymion, being young, wise, honorable, and virtuous?[1] Besides, what metal° was she made of, be she mortal, that is not affected with the spice, nay, infected with the poison, of that not-to-be-expressed yet always-to-be-felt love, which breaketh the brains and never bruiseth the brow, consumeth the heart and never toucheth the skin, and maketh a deep wound to be felt before any scar at all be seen? My heart, too tender to withstand such a divine fury, yielded to love—madam, I not without blushing confess, yielded to love.

substance; temperament

CYNTHIA A strange effect of love, to work such an extreme hate. How say you, Endymion, all this was for love?

ENDYMION I say, madam, then the gods send me a woman's hate.[2]

CYNTHIA That were as bad, for then by contrary you should never sleep.[3] But on, Tellus, let us hear the end.

TELLUS Feeling a continual burning in all my bowels and a bursting almost in every vein, I could not smother the inward fire, but it must needs be perceived by the outward smoke; and, by the flying abroad of divers sparks, divers judged of my scalding flames.[4] Endymion, as full of art as wit, marking mine eyes (in which he might see almost his own), my sighs (by which he might ever hear his name sounded), aimed at my heart (in which he was assured his person was imprinted), and by questions wrung out that which was ready to burst out. When he saw the depth of my affections, he sware that mine in respect of his were as fumes to Etna,° valleys to Alps, ants to eagles, and nothing could be compared to my beauty but his love and eternity. Thus drawing a smooth shoe upon a crooked foot, he made me believe that (which all of our sex willingly acknowledge) I was beautiful, and to wonder (which indeed is a thing miraculous) that any of his sex should be faithful.

famous Sicilian volcano

CYNTHIA Endymion, how will you clear yourself?

ENDYMION Madam, by mine own accuser.[5]

CYNTHIA Well, Tellus, proceed, but briefly, lest, taking delight in uttering thy love, thou offend us with the length of it.

TELLUS I will, madam, quickly make an end of my love and my tale. Finding continual increase of my tormenting thoughts, and that the enjoying° of my love made deeper wounds than the entering into it, I could find no means to ease my grief but to follow Endymion, and continually to have him in the object of mine eyes,° who had me slave and subject to his love. But in the moment that I feared his falsehood, and fried° myself most in mine affections, I found (ah, grief! even then I lost myself), I found him in most melancholy and desperate terms, cursing his stars, his state, the earth, the heavens, the world, and all for the love of—

experiencing

always before my eyes

overheated

CYNTHIA Of whom? Tellus, speak boldly.

1. What woman was there who did not fall in love with Endymion, he being young, wise, honorable, and virtuous?
2. I.e., If Tellus did what she did to me out of love, then I would prefer to be hated.
3. That would be as bad, for then, to the contrary, you would never have a moment's peace (since the woman would plague you ceaselessly).
4. Tellus (whose name means "earth") speaks of her emotional distress as though of a volcanic eruption.
5. I.e., I will allow Tellus to tell my story.

TELLUS Madam, I dare not utter for fear to offend.

CYNTHIA Speak, I say. Who dare take offense if thou be commanded by Cynthia?

TELLUS For the love of Cynthia.

CYNTHIA For my love, Tellus? That were strange. Endymion, is it true?

ENDYMION In all things, madam. Tellus doth not speak false.

CYNTHIA What will this breed to° in the end? Well, Endymion, we shall hear all.

come to

TELLUS I, seeing my hopes turned to mishaps, and a settled dissembling towards me, and an unmovable desire to Cynthia, forgetting both myself and my sex, fell unto° this unnatural hate. For knowing your virtues, Cynthia, to be immortal, I could not have an imagination to° withdraw him; and finding mine own affections unquenchable, I could not carry the mind° that any else should possess what I had pursued. For though in majesty, beauty, virtue, and dignity I always humbled and yielded myself to Cynthia, yet in affections I esteemed myself equal with the goddesses, and all other creatures, according to their states, with myself. For stars to° their bigness have their lights, and the sun hath no more. And little pitchers, when they can hold no more, are as full as great vessels that run over. Thus, madam, in all truth have I uttered the unhappiness of my love and the cause of my hate, yielding wholly to that divine judgment which never erred for want of wisdom or envied for too much partiality.

into
imagine how to
bear the thought
in proportion to

CYNTHIA How say you, my lords, to this matter? But what say you, Endymion, hath Tellus told truth?

ENDYMION Madam, in all things but in that she said I loved her and swore to honor her.

CYNTHIA Was there such a time whenas for my love thou didst vow thyself to death, and in respect of it loathed thy life? Speak, Endymion. I will not revenge it with hate.

ENDYMION The time was, madam, and is, and ever shall be, that I honored Your Highness above all the world; but to stretch it so far as to call it love, I never durst.° There hath none pleased mine eye but Cynthia, none delighted mine ears but Cynthia, none possessed my heart but Cynthia. I have forsaken all other fortunes to follow Cynthia, and here I stand ready to die if it please Cynthia. Such a difference hath the gods set between our states that all must be duty, loyalty, and reverence; nothing, without it vouchsafe Your Highness,° be termed love. My unspotted thoughts, my languishing body, my discontented life, let them obtain by princely favor that which to challenge° they must not presume, only wishing of impossibilities;[6] with imagination of which I will spend my spirits,° and to myself, that no creature may hear, softly call it love. And if any urge° to utter what I whisper, then will I name it honor.° From this sweet contemplation if I be not driven, I shall live of all men the most content, taking more pleasure in mine aged thoughts than ever I did in my youthful actions.

would have dared
unless you allow it
assert a right to
expend my breath
urge me
unspotted devotion

6. Even though in my thoughts I may secretly wish for something impossible.

CYNTHIA Endymion, this honorable respect of thine shall be christened "love" in thee, and my reward for it "favor." Persevere, Endymion, in loving me, and I account more strength in a true heart than in a walled city. I have labored to win all, and study° [endeavor] to keep such as I have won; but those that neither my favor can move to continue constant, nor my offered benefits get to be faithful, the gods shall either reduce to truth° [bring into obedience] or revenge their treacheries with justice. Endymion, continue as thou hast begun, and thou shalt find that Cynthia shineth not on thee in vain.

[*Endymion's youthful looks are restored to him.*]

ENDYMION Your Highness hath blessed me, and your words have again restored my youth. Methinks I feel my joints strong, and these moldy hairs to molt, and all by your virtue, Cynthia, into whose hands the balance° [scales of Justice] that weigheth° [weighs] time and fortune are committed.

CYNTHIA What, young again? Then it is pity to punish Tellus.

TELLUS Ah, Endymion, now I know° [recognize] thee and ask pardon of thee. Suffer me still° [Allow me always] to wish thee well.

ENDYMION Tellus, Cynthia must command what she will.

FLOSCULA Endymion, I rejoice to see thee in thy former estate.

ENDYMION Good Floscula, to thee also am I in my former affections.

EUMENIDES Endymion, the comfort of my life, how am I ravished with a joy matchless, saving only the enjoying of my mistress!

CYNTHIA Endymion, you must now tell who Eumenides shrineth° [worships] for his saint.

ENDYMION Semele, madam.

CYNTHIA Semele, Eumenides? Is it Semele? The very wasp of all women, whose tongue stingeth as much as an adder's tooth?

EUMENIDES It is Semele, Cynthia, the possessing of whose love must only° [can alone] prolong my life.

CYNTHIA Nay, sith Endymion is restored, we will have all parties pleased. Semele, are you content after so long trial of his faith, such rare secrecy, such unspotted love, to take Eumenides?—Why speak you not? Not a word?

ENDYMION Silence, madam, consents. That is most true.

CYNTHIA It is true, Endymion. Eumenides, take Semele. Take her, I say.

EUMENIDES Humble thanks, madam. Now only do I begin to live.

SEMELE A hard choice, madam, either to be married if I say nothing or to lose my tongue if I speak a word. Yet do I rather choose to have my tongue cut out than my heart distempered. I will not have him.

CYNTHIA Speaks the parrot? She shall nod hereafter with signs. Cut off her tongue, nay, her head, that, having a servant° [wooer] of honorable birth, honest manners, and true love, will not be persuaded!

SEMELE He is no faithful lover, madam, for then would he have asked his mistress.° [asked for Semele]

GERON Had he not been faithful, he had never seen into the

fountain, and so lost his friend and mistress.

EUMENIDES Thine own thoughts, sweet Semele, witness against thy words, for what hast thou found in my life but love? And as yet what have I found in my love but bitterness? Madam, pardon Semele, and let my tongue ransom hers.° *take my tongue instead*

CYNTHIA Thy tongue, Eumenides? What° shouldst thou live, *How* wanting° a tongue to blaze° the beauty of Semele?—Well, *lacking / proclaim* Semele, I will not command love, for it cannot be enforced. Let me entreat it.

SEMELE I am content Your Highness shall command, for now only do I think Eumenides faithful, that is willing to lose his tongue for my sake; yet loath, because it should do me better service.[7] Madam, I accept of° Eumenides. *I accept*

CYNTHIA I thank you, Semele.

EUMENIDES Ah, happy Eumenides, that hast a friend so faithful and a mistress so fair! With what sudden mischief will the gods daunt° this excess of joy? Sweet Semele, I live or *subdue* die as thou wilt.

CYNTHIA What shall become of Tellus? Tellus, you know Endymion is vowed to a service[8] from which death cannot remove him. Corsites casteth still a lovely° look towards you. *loving* How say you, will you have your Corsites and so receive pardon for all that is past?

TELLUS Madam, most willingly.

CYNTHIA But I cannot tell whether Corsites be agreed.

CORSITES Ay, madam, more happy to enjoy Tellus than the monarchy of the world.

EUMENIDES Why, she caused you to be pinched with fairies.

CORSITES Ay, but her fairness hath pinched my heart more deeply.

CYNTHIA Well, enjoy thy love. But what have you wrought° in *embroidered* the castle, Tellus?

TELLUS Only the picture of Endymion.

CYNTHIA Then so much of Endymion as his picture cometh to, possess and play withal.[9]

CORSITES Ah, my sweet Tellus, my love shall be as thy beauty is: matchless.

CYNTHIA Now it resteth,° Dipsas, that if thou wilt forswear *remains* that vile art of enchanting, Geron hath promised again to receive thee; otherwise, if thou be wedded to that wickedness, I must and will see it punished to the uttermost.

DIPSAS Madam, I renounce both substance and shadow of that most horrible and hateful trade, vowing to the gods continual penance and to Your Highness obedience.

CYNTHIA How say you, Geron, will you admit her to° your *accept her as* wife?

GERON Ay, with more joy than I did the first day, for nothing could happen to make me happy but only her forsaking that lewd° and detestable course. Dipsas, I embrace thee. *wicked*

7. Even though I am reluctant to obey your royal command, feeling as I do that Eumenides should have used his tongue in such a way as to serve me better (by putting me ahead of Endymion).

8. To the service of Cynthia (which necessarily excludes his being the servant in love of Tellus).

9. Cynthia will allow Tellus to keep only the physical resemblance of Endymion, as a chaste reminder of a past erotic attachment, while Cynthia will possess the eternal spirit of her platonic admirer.

DIPSAS And I thee, Geron, to whom I will hereafter recite° *recount* the cause of these my first follies. [*They embrace.*]

CYNTHIA Well, Endymion, nothing resteth now but that we depart. Thou hast my favor, Tellus her friend, Eumenides in paradise with his Semele, Geron contented with Dipsas.

TOPHAS Nay, soft. I cannot handsomely go to bed without Bagoa.

CYNTHIA Well, Sir Tophas, it may be there are more virtues in me than myself knoweth of, for Endymion I awaked, and at my words he waxed young. I will try whether I can turn this tree again to thy true love.

TOPHAS Turn her to a true love or false, so° she be a wench° *provided / female* I care not.

CYNTHIA Bagoa, Cynthia putteth an end to thy hard fortunes, for, being turned to a tree for revealing a truth, I will recover thee again if in my power be the effect of truth.

[*Bagoa regains her human shape.*]

TOPHAS Bagoa? A bots upon thee![1]

CYNTHIA Come, my lords, let us in. You, Gyptes and Pythagoras, if you cannot content yourselves in our court to fall from vain follies of philosophers to such virtues as are here practiced, you shall be entertained° *employed* according to your deserts, for Cynthia is no stepmother to strangers.[2]

PYTHAGORAS I had rather in Cynthia's court spend ten years than in Greece one hour.

GYPTES And I choose rather to live by the sight of Cynthia than by the possessing of all Egypt.

CYNTHIA Then follow.

EUMENIDES We all attend. *Exeunt.*

FINIS.

The Epilogue

[*Enter the Epilogue, with the cast.*]

EPILOGUE A man walking abroad, the wind and sun strove for sovereignty; the one with his blast, the other with his beams. The wind blew hard; the man wrapped his garment about him harder. It blustered more strongly; he then girt it fast to him. "I cannot prevail," said the wind. The sun, casting her crystal beams, began to warm the man; he unloosed his gown. Yet° *Still* it shined brighter; he then put it off. "I yield," said the wind, "for if thou continue shining he will also put off his coat."

Dread sovereign, the malicious that seek to overthrow us with threats do but stiffen our thoughts and make them sturdier in storms. But if Your Highness vouchsafe with your favorable beams to glance upon us, we shall not only stoop, but with all humility lay both our hands and hearts at Your Majesty's feet.

[*All kneel before the Queen, and then exeunt.*]

1. Tophas curses Bagoa, presumably because she's so old and ugly.
2. Cynthia intends to nurture the learned men who gather to her court from afar, not to deny them coldly as a stepmother would.

TEXTUAL NOTES

Endymion was entered in the Stationers' Register on October 4, 1591, and was published in the same year. The play was not published subsequently during Lyly's lifetime. The quarto was printed with care and provides a reliable basis for the present edition, other than for the songs, which first appeared in Edward Blount's *Six Court Comedies* (1632). Substantive departures from Q1 are noted here, using the following abbreviations:

Q1: *Endimion, The Man in the Moon*. Printed by J. Charlewood for the widow Broome (London, 1591)
Blount: *Six Court Comedies*, often presented and acted before Queen Elizabeth by the Children of Her Majesty's Chapel and the Children of Paul's, written by the only rare poet of that time, the witty, comical, facetiously quick and unparalleled John Lyly, Master of Arts. . . . London: printed by William Stansby for Edward Blount (London, 1632)
ed.: An emendation by an editor subsequent to Edward Blount's 1632 edition

Prologue 1 PROLOGUE [ed.; not in Q1]
1.1.0.1 [and throughout] ***Endymion*** [Q1: *Endimion*] **12 low** [ed.] loue [Q1] **26 off** [ed.] of [Q1] **87** [and elsewhere] **lest** [Q1: least]
1.2.23 hairs [Q1: heares] **84 dough** [Q1: dowe]
1.3.0.1 [ed.; all the names of characters within a scene are given in massed entries at the heads of scenes throughout] **44 Eumenides** [ed.] *Endimion* [Q1] **45 Endymion** [ed.] *Eumenides* [Q1] **54 Seres** [ed.] *Ceres* [Q1] **61 wound** [ed.] confound [Q1] **69 birdbolt** [Q1: burbolt] **86** [and elsewhere] **lose** [Q1: loose] **87 struts** [Q1: stroutes]
1.4.2 travail [Q1: trauell] **16 incantation** [ed.] incantantation [Q1] **19 hairs** [Q1: heares]
2.1.21 vouchsafed'st [ed.] vouchsafest [Q1] **34 Araris** [ed.] *Aranis* [Q1]
2.2.6 haply [Q1: happily] **35 floor** [ed.] flowre [Q1] **77–78 accounteth** [Q1: accompteth]
2.3.7 ebony [Q1: Ebone] **23 joint** [Q1: iont] **57 awake** [ed.] awakd [Q1] **63.1–12** [Blount; not in Q1] **63.8 *rendeth*** [ed.] *readeth* [Blount]
3.1.28 wonder [Q1: wounder] **52 Panelion** [ed.] *Pantlion* [Q1]
3.2.28 metal [Q1: mettle]
3.3.31 beard-brush [ed.] beard, brush [Q1] **32 scissors** [Q1: Cyssers] **44 *castra*** [Blount] *castea* [Q1] **53 tall** [Blount] tale [Q1] **56 bittern** [Q1: Bytter] **57 waist** [Q1: waste] **102 bittern** [Q1: bitter] **115–33** [Blount; not in Q1] **148 mail** [Q1: male] **164 traverse** [ed.] trauice [Q1]
3.4.3 till [Q1: tell] **110 Whither** [Q: Whether] **151 Athos** [ed.] *Atho* [Q1]
4.2.12 unloose [Q1: vnlose] **39 Know,** [ed.] No [Q1] **41 wardrobe** [Q1: wardrope] **100, 101, 102 raisins** [Q1: Reysons] **101 currants** [Q1: Corance] **107 an** [ed.] an an [Q1] **109 ALL THE WATCH** [ed.] *All say.* [Q1] **124–45** [Blount; not in Q1]
4.3.25 rend [Q1: rent] **31–43** [Blount; not in Q1] **43.4 *Gyptes*** [ed.] *Gyptes, Corsites* [Q1] **134 maim** [Blount] maine [Q1] **171 midst** [Q1: middest]
5.1.50 hear [Q1: heere] **64 jousts** [Q1: Iustes] **81 haply** [Q1: happilie] **125 There—ay** [ed.] There I [Q1] **134 tattered** [Q1: totterd]
5.2.70 charnel [Blount] channel [Q1] **89 truth** [Q1: troth] **93 sexton** [Blount] Sexteene [Q1] **103 turquoise** [Q1: Turkis] **108 curtail** [Q1: curtoll]
5.4.32 losing [Q1: loosing] **67 resist** [ed.] resite [Q1] **74 wound . . . felt** [ed.] skarre . . . seene [Q1] **74–75 scar . . . seen** [ed.] wounde . . . felt [Q1] **144 truth** [Q1: troth] **243 look** [Blount] lookes [Q1]
Epilogue 1 EPILOGUE [ed.; not in Q1]

Friar Bacon and Friar Bungay

Robert Greene was fairly typical of the young men of his day known as "university wits": those who graduated from Oxford or Cambridge (he graduated from St. John's, Cambridge, in 1578) only to discover that few careers were open to them other than in the church or writing. Greene tried his hand at everything. His thirty-eight or so publications include confessional pamphlets with titles such as *Never Too Late* (1590), *Farewell to Folly* (1591), and *Greene's Groatsworth of Wit Bought with a Million of Repentance* (1592), the last with its famous jibe at Shakespeare as an "upstart crow." His coney-catching pamphlets purported to expose the shenanigans of London's underworld population of swindlers and con men. His prose romances, exploiting the vogue made popular by Philip Sidney (*Arcadia*) and others, included *Pandosto, or Dorastus and Fawnia* (1588), from which Shakespeare was to draw his source material for *The Winter's Tale*.

Greene tried his hand at a number of plays, virtually all of them attempts to capitalize on some theatrical vogue. *Alphonsus, King of Aragon* (1587–88), for example, features such an exaggeratedly Marlovian superman in the style of Tamburlaine as to make one wonder if Greene is emulating Marlowe or lampooning him. *Selimus* (1591–92) is filled with Senecan sensationalism in the style of Kyd and Marlowe. *Orlando Furioso* (1588–92) revels in an unstable mix of titillation and moral denunciation of Marlowe's realpolitik. *George a Greene, The Pinner of Wakefield* (1587–93) capitalizes on the newly emerging English history play, with its mix of historical and fictional figures. So does *The Scottish History of James the Fourth* (1590–91), in which James IV's marriage to the daughter of an English queen and his unfaithful pursuit of a Scottish beauty named Ida are framed by a plot presided over by Oberon, King of Fairies.

Surrounded as he was by men of towering genius in the theater, aware at the last of the emergence of a new star in Shakespeare, Greene appears to have been an envious and disappointed man. He led a dissolute life, eventually becoming a drifter. Rumor had it that he died (in 1592) of a surfeit of pickled herrings and Rhenish wine.

Friar Bacon and Friar Bungay (c. 1589), his most successful play, resembles *George a Greene* in its mix of bogus history and cheerful romantic nonsense. It does so with such panache as to suggest a formula for native English romantic comedy that proved invaluable to Shakespeare. Greene's play centers in part on Edward, Prince of Wales,[1] son of King Henry III, who is to marry Elinor, daughter of the King of Castile. Thus far, we are in the realm of historical fact: the Edward who was to become Edward I of England from 1272 until his death in 1307 did marry Elinor (or Eleanor) of Castile in 1254. Edward was only fifteen at the time, however. Greene suggests that he is several years older and is, moreover, smitten with the charms of a country maid named Margaret, daughter of the Keeper of Fressingfield, in Suffolk. Edward has happened upon her while hunting with his gentlemanly companions, and he can scarcely think or talk of anything else—least of all his forthcoming marriage to Elinor.

Introduction, glosses, footnotes, and textual notes by David Bevington; text edited by David Bevington and Eric Rasmussen.

1. Historically, Edward I was not Prince of Wales; his son, who became Edward II, was the first heir to the throne to be so designated.

At this point, clearly, history goes out the window. In its place, Greene cheekily substitutes pure romance, and of a sort calculated to explore all sorts of social differences and tensions. Edward's choice is between Elinor and Margaret: that is to say, between court and countryside, Spain and England, artifice and natural beauty, courtly mannerisms and spontaneity, aristocratic hauteur and yeomanlike sincerity, arranged marriage and falling in love at first sight. Elinor doesn't stand a chance.

Greene shamelessly idealizes his heroine. He invokes the classical gods and goddesses to invest Margaret with dignity; at the same time, she is wholesome and English to the core. Edward describes his first encounter with her as follows:

> Whenas she swept like Venus through the house,
> And in her shape fast folded up my thoughts,
> Into the milk house went I with the maid,
> And there amongst the cream bowls she did shine
> As Pallas 'mongst her princely huswifery.
> (1.72–76)

As Margaret does her innocent and productive farmwork, plunging her arms into the milk to run her cheese, her skin is whiter than the milk, and her beauty outshines that of Lucrece who, in classical legend, tempted Tarquin's son to "hazard Rome and all" to win her (1.77–86).

The story of Tarquin's son and Lucrece (or Lucretia) hints at a darker side of this relationship, of course: Tarquin's son raped Lucrece, whereupon she took her own life. Edward, as Prince of Wales, cannot expect or want to marry Margaret, and so it appears that his interest is largely one of sexual conquest. Yet Greene assiduously protects Margaret against these insinuations and dangers. Edward is accompanied by a court fool, Rafe, whose wry observations help to undercut the pretenses of Edward's romantic claims. Even Edward understands fully that with Margaret, it is "marriage or no market" (1.121), i.e., no sex. She is wittily self-possessed and in charge of her destiny. Among her fellow milkmaids she is entirely at ease and enjoys chaffing with the rustic young farmers who pay her court. As her friend Joan puts the matter, "Margaret, a farmer's daughter for a farmer's son! / I warrant you the meanest of us both / Shall have a mate to lead us from the church" (3.27–29). Such a destiny contents Margaret: she is of yeoman stock and is proud of her heritage.

Social ambition does not interest her. She is attracted to the young aristocrat Lacy, Earl of Lincoln, who comes courting her in disguise when he is supposed to be wooing her as a deputy on behalf of Prince Edward; and indeed she eventually marries the Earl, thus becoming a countess, but for purely romantic reasons, it would seem. Conversely, we are to believe that the Earl of Lincoln counts himself lucky to woo and marry a milkmaid of Suffolk because she is fair and virtuous. Love can conquer all ranks, or nearly all.

This is a pipe dream, one that no doubt appealed to the fantasies of Londoners imagining a world of social equality. The political and social implications are clear: a good-hearted girl of yeoman stock is worthy of marriage into the aristocracy because she embodies hearty English values of sturdy independence, honesty, moral probity, and patriotic loyalty to her country and her way of life. She need offer no apologies for who she is. She is worth ten of any princesses from Spain. Her marriage is elevated to one of central importance in English national politics: she and Lacy are joined in a double wedding, alongside the state marriage of Prince Edward to Elinor. England's yeomen are not to be discounted henceforth.

As for Prince Edward, his petticoat-chasing and ruthlessness toward his rival are no doubt to be excused in one who, like Prince Hal, experiences youthful indiscretions but will one day become the mighty ruler of England. He accedes to an arranged marriage with the daughter of a foreign king in the interests of his nation's foreign policy; Elinor is the right wife for Edward after all. Quasi-historical drama of this sort flirts with criticism of the monarchy only to plump at last for affirmations of loyalty to the Crown.

The play's imagined political and social alignments are further demonstrated in Greene's presentation of two Suffolk gentlemen, Lambert and Serlsby, who seek the hand of Margaret in marriage. They exercise economic power over Margaret's father, the "Keeper of our liege's game" (10.1). Serlsby is the landlord of Margaret's father and the keeper of his holds: "By copy [i.e., copyhold] all thy living lies in me," he says pointedly (10.12). This is a naked threat: if Serlsby can have Margaret, the Keeper need not worry about losing his lands and living. Lambert attempts to bribe the Keeper with the promise of a large jointure of land (10.8–9). The Keeper has to be circumspect in this, and Margaret too temporizes with them, but she will have nothing to do with arranged matches under these conditions. Greene's play is thus at pains to forge imagined alliances between the yeoman class and the country's ruling elite at the expense of the gentlemanly class lying socially in between. England's destiny lies importantly in the hands of her yeomen, now afforded new recognition and centrality that has been won at the expense of the gentry by yeomanly virtue and common sense.

Greene's play is resolutely English and Protestant in these alliances. When, as part of the turnings of the romantic plot, Margaret learns that her beloved Lacy has apparently been forced by royal command to give her up for a Spanish lady, chief waiting-woman to the Princess Elinor, her response is to renounce all earthly happiness for the life of a nun: "The world shall be to her as vanity; / Wealth, trash; love, hate; pleasure, despair" (10.157–58). She appears onstage in nun's apparel, her soul wedded to the harmony of heaven, persuaded that "all love is lust but love of heavens": "Farewell to friends and father! Welcome, Christ! / Adieu to dainty robes!" (14.17, 30–31). Yet when she learns that Lacy is true to her after all, and that the story of his being obliged to marry was only a ruse to try her constancy, her renunciation of a nun's life is as sudden as was her adoption of it. "The flesh is frail," she concludes; "all the show of holy nuns, farewell!" (14.87, 92).

Like Isabella in Shakespeare's *Measure for Measure*, the heroine of this romantic comedy concludes that the pleasures of this world are to be embraced. Marriage, sexual consummation, emotional fulfillment, harmony of the sexes in resolving a romantic plot of sexual conflict—these are the hallmarks of the romantic comedy that would prove to be such a compellingly successful theatrical genre during the first decade of Shakespeare's professional career.

In his writing of romantic comedies, such as *The Two Gentlemen of Verona*, *A Midsummer Night's Dream*, *The Merchant of Venice*, and others, Shakespeare could also have learned a lot from Greene about double plotting. The story of Margaret's eventual marriage to the Earl of Lincoln is paired with a dramatic account of two learned men, Friar Bacon and Friar Bungay, whose presence underscores still another political and social realignment, in which England's men of learning gain an extraordinary prominence in national affairs. The Margaret plot is a fantasy of crossing social distinctions through love and marriage; the Bacon-Bungay plot imagines how those same boundaries might be transcended through the power of books and ideas.

Bungay is a Greene invention, added perhaps for the euphony and alliteration of the names Bacon and Bungay. Bacon is named for the famous Roger Bacon (c. 1220–1292), a philosopher at Oxford who wrote on chemistry and alchemy and was confined for long periods for his heretical ideas. He had acquired a legendary reputation as a magician, as many learned men had done. Greene also presumably had his eye on Doctor Faustus, the protagonist of Marlowe's tragedy of that name that had probably been acted in 1588–89; the dating of both plays is uncertain, but the probability is that Greene knew Marlowe's work.[2] Greene was never loath to exploit a line that Marlowe had made notorious.

2. See Christopher Marlowe, *Doctor Faustus, A- and B-texts (1604, 1616)*, ed. David Bevington and Eric Rasmussen (Manchester: Manchester University Press, 1993), pp. 1–3.

In his gloved left hand, the fashionably dressed gentleman on the left controls a falcon fitted out with hood, bells, and a leash. At his heels are spaniels, ready to retrieve the game hunted by the falcon. From George Turberville, *The Book of Falconry or Hawking* (London, 1575).

Once again, Greene shows no interest in historical accuracy, not even in the recorded legends about Bacon. The chief magician in this play is an Oxford scholar of such admired skill that the rulers of England consult him about their affairs. Europe too knows of his reputation (2.40). Among his other accomplishments, he has devised a brazen head that can speak and predict the future—a tribute paid by Greene to Brasenose College in Oxford, where legends of such a talking head are part of college tradition. Like Doctor Faustus, Bacon has an ambition to "compass England with a wall of brass" (2.30), and he has a comic servant, named Miles.

He also has a "glass prospective," a kind of crystal ball or magic mirror (5.105). Prince Edward comes to Bacon in order to witness, by means of the magic glass, a consultation between Margaret and Bungay, Bacon's rival in magic. Bungay is assisting Lacy in his wooing of Margaret; in the magic glass, Edward perceives the perfidy of his friend in taking Margaret away from him. Bacon frustrates the match, striking Bungay dumb and conveying him on a devil's back to Oxford. In this way, the rivalry of the two magicians is woven into the play's romantic love plot.

Bacon demonstrates his greatness internationally when the English king arrives at Oxford in order to entertain the King of Castile, the German emperor, and Castile's daughter Elinor. Here is a dream of academic glory not unlike that of Marlowe's *Doctor Faustus*, in which Faustus amazes with his magical stunts Charles V of the Holy Roman Empire and the Duke and Duchess of Vanholt (i.e., Anhalt, in Germany). Greene supposes that England can afford its royal visitors no greater spectacle than that of Oxford University and its leading scholars. The Emperor is impressed by Oxford's verdant rural setting, its "high-built colleges," its scholars "seemly in their grave attire" (9.5–6).

The contest between Bungay and the Emperor's champion magician, Jaques Vandermast, turns on the relative merits of pyromancy and geomancy, and produces amazing theatrical devices such as a tree that "*appears with the dragon shooting fire*" and "*Hercules . . . in his lion's skin*" (9.83.2, 92.1). Bungay proves no match for Vandermast, but Bacon puts down his German rival effortlessly. The English king is impressed: "Bacon, thou hast honored England with thy skill, / And made fair Oxford famous by thine art" (9.165–66). At the same time, Greene cannot resist a joke about the legendarily poor fare in England's colleges. He serves up to his royal visitors a "*mess of pottage and broth*," bidding them enjoy this "academic fare" and "frugal cates" with a proper awareness that "No riot" is to be found "where philosophy doth reign" (9.222.1, 230–33). Having wittily made his point, Bacon then proceeds to order a royal banquet of Rabelaisian proportions (9.251–72). Greene has it both ways: he jokes that scholars lead a spare, abstemious life and at the same time gives to Bacon the power of providing hospitality that the rulers of Europe cannot match.

All of this foolery reminds us of Doctor Faustus, frittering away his gift of magic with splendid shows and practical jokes. Greene accordingly pursues the issue of damnation that Marlowe had explored so devastatingly. Is Bacon's magic white or black? Is it capable of doing good or harm, and will it damn Bacon's soul? The harmful effects are not hard to discover. Bacon uses his magic to frustrate the virtuous love of Margaret and Lacy that will eventually triumph. His seven years' labor to produce a brazen head that will speak through diabolical inspiration is frustrated by his need for sleep and by the inability of his comic servant, Miles, to understand that the long-awaited moment of revelation has arrived (scene 11). When Bacon uses his magic glass to reveal to the two sons of Lambert and Serlsby the story of their fathers' rivalry over Margaret, the sons are horrified to see the fathers fight and kill each other, at which point the sons too turn on one another with fatal stabbings. Bacon sees too well that "This glass prospective worketh many woes," and thereupon resolves to "End all thy magic and thine art at once" (13.77, 80). In his sermon of repentance to Bungay, Bacon speaks of having abused "the holy name of God," for which he fully realizes that he "must be damned" (13.93, 97). He has indeed conjured "*Per omnes deos infernales*" ("By all the infernal gods") (2.117).

Yet in this play the magician is able to repent and find forgiveness, as Faustus is not. Bacon's comic servant, Miles, is intrigued by what he hears about hell and agrees to be carried there on the devil's back, in scene 15; it is as though Miles serves as a scapegoat for the damnable aspect of Bacon's personality. Once again, Greene has it both ways. In a romantic comedy such as this, the threat of damnation is only one of the perils that must be encountered on the way to resolution and a happy ending.

Margaret and Bacon are thus emblematic heroes in this double-plotted play. Margaret represents yeomanly integrity and feminine virtue, unassailably loyal to her social class and yet worthy of marriage into the highest reaches of the aristocracy. Bacon is, like Greene himself in part, a university scholar accustomed to a life of severe plainness and yet dreaming of unprecedented power and notoriety. The unstable dream is one that seems to have fascinated Greene's audience, perhaps because the elements of escapism in it are linked to social issues of conflict and aspiration that Elizabethans could find wholly familiar and plausible. Greene's theater is a place of dreaming.

ROBERT GREENE

The Honorable History of Friar Bacon and Friar Bungay

[THE PERSONS IN THE PLAY

KING HENRY the Third of England
EDWARD, Prince of Wales, his son
Edward LACY, Earl of Lincoln } Edward's friends
John WARREN, Earl of Sussex } Edward's friends
Will ERMSBY, a gentleman } Edward's friends
RAFE Simnell, the King's fool

MARGARET, daughter of the Keeper of Fressingfield
The KEEPER of Fressingfield
Their FRIEND

King of CASTILE
ELINOR, his daughter
EMPEROR (Frederick) of Germany
The Duke of Saxony

Friar BACON of Brazennose (Brasenose) College, Oxford
MILES, his poor scholar
Friar BUNGAY
Jaques VANDERMAST, a German magician
BURDEN } learned scholars of Oxford
MASON } learned scholars of Oxford
CLEMENT } learned scholars of Oxford

LAMBERT } gentlemen
SERLSBY } gentlemen
FIRST SCHOLAR } their sons
SECOND SCHOLAR } their sons

THOMAS } country-folk from Fressingfield
RICHARD } country-folk from Fressingfield
JOAN } country-folk from Fressingfield
HOSTESS of the Bell Tavern at Henley
CONSTABLE

The original 1594 title page reads "*The Honorable History of Friar Bacon and Friar Bungay*. As it was played by Her Majesty's Servants. Made by Robert Greene, Master of Arts. London, printed for Edward White, and are to be sold at his shop, at the little north door of Paul's, at the sign of the Gun. 1594."

A POST boy
A DEVIL
A speaker for the Brazen HEAD
A spirit in the shape of HERCULES

Lords, country clowns, attendants

THE SCENE: England, at court, at Oxford, and at Fressingfield in Suffolk.]

[Scene 1]

Enter Edward the First,° malcontented, with Lacy, Earl of Lincoln; John Warren, Earl of Sussex; and Ermsby, gentleman; Rafe° Simnell, the King's fool. — *the future Edward I* / *(a variant of "Ralph")*

LACY Why looks my lord like to a troubled sky
When heaven's bright shine is shadowed with a fog?
Alate° we ran the deer, and through the launds° — *Of late / glades*
Stripped° with our nags the lofty frolic bucks — *Outstripped*
That scudded 'fore the teasers° like the wind. — *hunting hounds*
Ne'er was the deer of merry Fressingfield
So lustily° pulled down by jolly mates,° — *vigorously / companions*
Nor shared the farmers such fat venison,
So frankly dealt,° this hundred years before; — *generously dealt out*
Nor have I seen my lord more frolic in the chase—
And now changed to a melancholy dump.° — *fit of musing*
WARREN After the Prince got to the Keeper's lodge
And had been jocund° in the house awhile, — *merry*
Tossing of ale and milk in country cans,
Whether it was the country's sweet content,
Or else the bonny° damsel filled° us drink, — *pretty / who filled*
That seemed so stately° in her stammel° red, — *majestic / woolen cloth*
Or that a qualm did cross his stomach then,
But straight° he fell into his passions. — *at once*
ERMSBY Sirrah° Rafe, what say you to your master? — *(said to inferiors)*
Shall he thus all amort° live malcontent? — *dejected*
RAFE Hearest thou, Ned?°—Nay, look if he will speak to me! — *i.e., Edward*
EDWARD What say'st thou to me, fool?
RAFE I prithee tell me, Ned, art thou in love with the Keeper's daughter?
EDWARD How if I be, what then?
RAFE Why, then, sirrah, I'll teach thee how to deceive Love.
EDWARD How, Rafe?
RAFE Marry,° sirrah Ned, thou shalt put on my cap and my coat and my dagger, and I will put on thy clothes and thy sword, and so thou shalt be my fool. — *By Mary (an oath)*
EDWARD And what of this?
RAFE Why, so thou shalt beguile Love, for Love is such a proud scab° that he will never meddle with fools nor children. Is not Rafe's counsel good, Ned? — *scoundrel*
EDWARD Tell me, Ned Lacy, didst thou mark the maid,
How lively in her country weeds she looked?

Scene 1. Near Fressingfield in Suffolk.

A bonnier wench all Suffolk cannot yield.
All Suffolk? Nay, all England holds none such.
RAFE Sirrah Will Ermsby, Ned is deceived.
ERMSBY Why, Rafe?
RAFE He says all England hath no such, and I say—and I'll stand to it—there is one better in Warwickshire.
WARREN How provest thou that, Rafe?
RAFE Why, is not the abbot a learned man, and hath read many books, and thinkest thou he hath not more learning than thou to choose a bonny wench? Yes, I warrant thee, by his whole grammar.[1]
ERMSBY A good reason, Rafe.
EDWARD I tell thee, Lacy, that her sparkling eyes
Do lighten forth sweet Love's alluring fire,
And in her tresses she doth fold° the looks *enfold, capture*
Of such as gaze upon her golden hair.
Her bashful white, mixed with the morning's red,
Luna doth boast upon her lovely cheeks;[2]
Her front° is Beauty's table, where she° paints *forehead / (Beauty)*
The glories of her° gorgeous excellence; *(Margaret's)*
Her teeth are shelves of precious margarites,° *pearls*
Richly enclosed with ruddy coral cliffs.° *i.e., red lips*
Tush, Lacy, she is Beauty's overmatch,
If thou survey'st her curious imagery.° *fine, delicate beauty*
LACY I grant, my lord, the damsel is as fair
As simple Suffolk's homely° towns can yield; *rustic*
But in the court be quainter° dames than she, *more fashionable*
Whose faces are enriched with honor's taint,° *tincture*
Whose beauties stand upon the stage of fame
And vaunt their trophies in the courts of love.
EDWARD Ah, Ned, but hadst thou watched her as myself,
And seen the secret° beauties of the maid, *not widely known*
Their° courtly coyness were but foolery. *(Such courtly ladies')*
ERMSBY Why, how watched you her, my lord?
EDWARD Whenas° she swept like Venus through the house, *When*
And in her shape fast folded up my thoughts,
Into the milk house went I with the maid,
And there amongst the cream bowls she did shine
As Pallas[3] 'mongst her princely huswifery.° *housekeeping*
She turned her smock over her lily arms
And dived them into milk to run° her cheese; *form a curd in*
But, whiter than the milk, her crystal skin,
Checked with lines of azure,[4] made her° blush *(any other woman)*
That art or nature durst bring for compare.
Ermsby, if thou hadst seen—as I did note it well—
How Beauty played the huswife,[5] how this girl
Like Lucrece[6] laid her fingers to the work,
Thou wouldest with Tarquin hazard Rome and all

1. A man that learned would certainly know how to find a handsome woman. (An anticlerical dig; the clergy were supposed to lead celibate lives.)
2. The pale moon triumphs in the chaste whiteness of her cheeks, mixed with the red of the morning sun. (This image begins Edward's blazon, a poetically conventional catalogue of a woman's charms. Luna is the moon.)
3. Pallas Athene, patroness of arts and handicrafts.
4. Variegated by the azure blue of her veins.
5. How Beauty was personified in her at her household work.
6. The rape of the virtuous Roman matron Lucrece, or Lucretia, by the son of the tyrant Tarquin the Proud was the subject of a long poem by Shakespeare in 1593. This son is referred to as "Tarquin" in line 85.

To win the lovely maid of Fressingfield.
RAFE Sirrah Ned, wouldst fain° have her? *gladly*
EDWARD Ay, Rafe.
RAFE Why, Ned, I have laid the plot in my head thou° shalt *how thou*
have her already.
EDWARD I'll give thee a new coat an learn° me that. *if you teach*
RAFE Why, sirrah Ned, we'll ride to Oxford to Friar Bacon.
Oh, he is a brave° scholar, sirrah. They say he is a brave *splendid*
necromancer,° that he can make women of devils, and he *magician, conjurer*
can juggle cats° into costermongers.° *spirits / fruit-sellers*
EDWARD And how then, Rafe?
RAFE Marry, sirrah, thou shalt go to him, and because° thy *in order that*
father Harry shall not miss thee, he shall turn me into thee;
and I'll to the court, and I'll prince it out, and he° shall make *(Bacon)*
thee either a silken purse full of gold or else a fine wrought
smock.° *embroidered petticoat*
EDWARD But how shall I have the maid?
RAFE Marry, sirrah, if thou be'st a silken purse full of gold,
then on Sundays she'll hang thee by her side, and you must
not say a word. Now, sir, when she comes into a great press° *crowd*
of people, for fear of the cutpurse on a sudden she'll swap
thee into her plackerd;° then, sirrah, being there you may *placket, petticoat*
plead for yourself.
ERMSBY Excellent policy!° *stratagem*
EDWARD But how if I be a wrought smock?
RAFE Then she'll put thee into her chest and lay thee into
lavender, and upon some good day she'll put thee on, and at
night when you go to bed, then being turned from a smock
to a man, you may make up the match.° *close the deal*
LACY Wonderfully wisely counseled, Rafe.
EDWARD Rafe shall have a new coat.
RAFE God thank you—when I have it on my back, Ned.
EDWARD Lacy, the fool hath laid a perfect plot,
Forwhy° our country Margaret is so coy, *Because*
And stands so much upon her honest points,° *is so resolutely chaste*
That marriage or no market° with the maid. *no deal, no sex*
Ermsby, it must be necromantic spells
And charms of art that must enchain her love,
Or else shall Edward never win the girl.
Therefore, my wags,° we'll horse us in the morn, *jolly companions*
And post° to Oxford to this jolly friar. *hasten*
Bacon shall by his magic do this deed.
WARREN Content, my lord; and that's a speedy way
To wean these headstrong puppies from the teat.° *To break their will*
EDWARD I am unknown, not taken for° the prince; *recognized as*
They only deem us frolic courtiers
That revel thus among our liege's game.° *royal hunting rights*
Therefore I have devised a policy.° *stratagem*
Lacy, thou know'st next Friday is Saint James',° *July 25*
And then the country flocks to Harleston° Fair; *(near Fressingfield)*
Then will the Keeper's daughter frolic there
And overshine the troop of all the maids
That come to see and to be seen that day.
Haunt thee° disguised among the country swains. *Make frequent visit*
Feign thou'rt a farmer's son, not far from thence;

Espy her loves, and who she liketh best;
Cote° him, and court her to control the clown.[7] *Surpass, outstrip*
Say that the courtier tirèd° all in green, *attired*
That helped her handsomly to run her cheese
And filled her father's lodge with venison,
Commends him, and sends fairings,° to herself. *gifts bought at a fair*
Buy something worthy of her parentage,
Not worth her beauty—for, Lacy, then the fair
Affords no jewel fitting for the maid.
And when thou talkest of me, note if she blush.
Oh, then she loves! But if her cheeks wax pale,
Disdain it is. Lacy, send° how she fares, *send word*
And spare no time nor cost to win her loves.

LACY I will, my lord, so execute this charge
As if that° Lacy were in love with her. *As if*

EDWARD Send letters speedily to Oxford of the news.

RAFE And, sirrah Lacy, buy me a thousand thousand million of fine bells.

LACY What wilt thou do with them, Rafe?

RAFE Marry, every time that Ned sighs for the Keeper's daughter, I'll tie a bell about him, and so within three or four days I will send word to his father Harry that his son and my master Ned is become Love's morris dance.[8]

EDWARD Well, Lacy, look with care unto thy charge,
And I will haste to Oxford to the friar,
That he by art, and thou by secret gifts,
Mayst make me lord of merry Fressingfield.

LACY God send Your Honor your heart's desire! *Exeunt.*

[Scene 2]

Enter Friar Bacon, with Miles, his poor scholar, with books under his arm; with them Burden, Mason, Clement, three doctors.° *scholars*

BACON Miles, where are you?

MILES *Hic sum, doctissime et reverendissime doctor.*[1]

BACON *Attulisti nos libros meos de necromantia?*[2]

MILES *Ecce quam bonum et quam jocundum, habitares libros in unum!*[3]

BACON Now, masters of our academic state,
That rule in Oxford, viceroys in your place,[4]
Whose heads contain maps of the liberal arts,
Spending your time in depth of learnèd skill,
Why flock you thus to Bacon's secret cell,
A friar newly stalled° in Brazennose?° *installed / Brasenose*
Say what's your mind, that I may make reply.

BURDEN Bacon, we hear that° long we have suspect,° *that which / suspected*
That thou art read° in magic's mystery: *deeply learned*
In pyromancy, to divine° by flames; *prophesy*

7. Court her in such a way as to put the bumpkin in his place.
8. A country-dance in which the dancers wore bells at their wrists and ankles. Ned has become a rustic lover.
Scene 2. Brasenose College, Oxford.
1. Here I am, most learned and venerable scholar.
2. Have you brought us my books of magic?
3. Lo, how good and how pleasant it is to live together among books!
4. Governors of this institution by virtue of your academic eminence.

To tell, by hydromancy, ebbs and tides;
By aeromancy, to discover doubts,° *resolve uncertainties*
To plain out° questions, as Apollo did. *elucidate*
BACON Well, Master Burden, what of all this?
MILES Marry, sir, he doth but fulfill, by rehearsing° of these names, the fable of the Fox and the Grapes:[5] that which is above us pertains nothing° to us. *reciting* / *not at all*
BURDEN I tell thee, Bacon, Oxford makes report—
Nay, England, and the court of Henry says—
Thou'rt making of a brazen head by art
Which shall unfold strange doubts and aphorisms[6]
And read° a lecture in philosophy; *deliver*
And, by the help of devils and ghastly fiends,
Thou mean'st, ere many years or days be past,
To compass° England with a wall of brass. *encompass, surround*
BACON And what of this?
MILES What of this, master? Why, he doth speak mystically, for he knows, if your skill fail to make a brazen head, yet Mother Waters'° strong ale will fit his turn° to make him have a copper nose.[7] *an innkeeper's / purposes*
CLEMENT Bacon, we come not grieving at thy skill,
But joying that our academy yields
A man supposed the wonder of the world;
For, if thy cunning work these miracles,
England and Europe shall admire thy fame,
And Oxford shall, in characters of brass,
And statues such as were built up in Rome,
Eternize Friar Bacon for his art.
MASON Then, gentle Friar, tell us thy intent.
BACON Seeing you come as friends unto the friar,
Resolve you,° doctors, Bacon can by books *Understand*
Make storming Boreas° thunder from his cave, *the north wind*
And dim fair Luna to a dark eclipse.
The great archruler, potentate of hell,
Trembles when Bacon bids him or his fiends
Bow to the force of his pentageron.[8]
What art can work, the frolic° friar knows, *merry*
And therefore will I turn° my magic books, *turn the pages of*
And strain out necromancy to the deep.[9]
I have contrived and framed° a head of brass *devised*
(I made Belcephon° hammer out the stuff), *(the name of a devil)*
And that by art shall read° philosophy. *teach*
And I will strengthen England by my skill,
That, if ° ten Caesars lived and reigned in Rome, *even if*
With all the legions Europe doth contain,
They should not touch a grass of English ground.
The work that Ninus reared at Babylon,[1]
The brazen walls framed by Semiramis,[2]

5. Aesop's fable of the fox who lost the grapes he had in his greediness to obtain more applies here as a moral against unwarranted aspiration.
6. Concise statements of principles in any science.
7. A nose red from excessive drinking. Miles sardonically contrasts Bacon's aspirations to be a magician with Burden's penchant for drinking and womanizing; see line 92 ff. below.
8. Pentagonon, or pentagram, a five-pointed star serving as an occult symbol.
9. And exert magical powers to the fullest extent possible.
1. According to legend, Ninus was the husband of Semiramis; see next note.
2. Wife of Ninus and reputed builder of the walls of Babylon, ninth century B.C.E.

Carved out like to the portal of the sun,
Shall not be such as rings the English strand
From Dover to the marketplace of Rye.[3]

BURDEN Is this possible?

MILES I'll bring ye two or three witnesses.

BURDEN What be those?

MILES Marry, sir, three or four as honest devils and good companions as any be in hell.

MASON No doubt but magic may do much in this,
For he that reads but° mathematic rules *only; simple*
Shall find conclusions that avail to work
Wonders that pass the common sense of men.

BURDEN But Bacon roves a bow beyond his reach,[4]
And tells of more than magic can perform,
Thinking to get a fame by fooleries.
Have I not passed as far in state of schools,° *in academic learning*
And read of many secrets? Yet to think
That heads of brass can utter any voice,
Or, more,° to tell of deep philosophy— *even more*
This is a fable Aesop had forgot.[5]

BACON Burden, thou wrong'st me in detracting thus;
Bacon loves not to stuff himself with lies.
But tell me 'fore these doctors, if thou dare,
Of certain questions I shall move° to thee. *propound*

BURDEN I will. Ask what thou can.

MILES Marry, sir, he'll straight be on your pickpack[6] to know whether the feminine or the masculine gender be most worthy.[7]

BACON Were you not yesterday, Master Burden, at Henley-upon-the-Thames?° *(southeast of Oxford)*

BURDEN I was. What then?

BACON What book studied you thereon all night?

BURDEN I? None at all; I read not there a line.

BACON Then, doctors, Friar Bacon's art knows naught.

CLEMENT What say you to this, Master Burden? Doth he not touch you?

BURDEN I pass not of° his frivolous speeches. *care not about*

MILES Nay, Master Burden, my master, ere he hath done with you, will turn you from a doctor to a dunce, and shake you so small that he will leave no more learning in you than is in Balaam's ass.[8]

BACON Masters,° *Good sirs*
For that° learnèd Burden's skill is deep, *Since*
And sore° he doubts of Bacon's cabalism,° *sorely / occultism*
I'll show you why he haunts to Henley oft:
Not, doctors, for° to taste the fragrant air, *in order*
But there to spend the night in alchemy,
To multiply° with secret spells of art. *do alchemy; have sex*
Thus private° steals he learning from us all. *in private*

3. Dover and Rye are both on the extreme southeast coast of England, at the narrow point of the English Channel, about twenty miles apart.
4. I.e., But Bacon boasts more than he can in fact accomplish.
5. This is a whopper too outlandish even for Aesop.
6. He'll be on you pickaback (piggyback), be "riding" you, pressing his argument.
7. A common academic debating topic.
8. The famous speaking animal of Numbers 22, which refused to obey Balaam's order to go forward when it saw an angel of the Lord standing in their way.

To prove my sayings true, I'll show you straight
The book he keeps at Henley for himself.

MILES Nay, now° my master goes to conjuration, take heed! *now that*

BACON Masters, stand still. Fear not; I'll show you but his book.
(*Here he conjures.*) *Per omnes deos infernales, Belcephon!*[9]

Enter a woman [*the Hostess of the Bell Tavern*] *with a shoulder of mutton on a spit, and a devil.*

MILES Oh, master, cease your conjuration, or you spoil all, for here's a she-devil come with a shoulder of mutton on a spit. You have marred the devil's supper; but no doubt he thinks our college fare is slender, and so hath sent you his cook with a shoulder of mutton to make it exceed.° *become better*

HOSTESS Oh, where am I, or what's become of me?

BACON What art thou?

HOSTESS Hostess at Henley, mistress of the Bell.° *Bell Tavern*

BACON How camest thou here?

HOSTESS As I was in the kitchen 'mongst the maids,
Spitting° the meat against[1] supper for my guests, *Putting on a spit*
A motion° moved me to look forth of door.° *impulse / out the door*
No sooner had I pried° into the yard, *peered*
But straight a whirlwind hoisted me from thence
And mounted me aloft unto the clouds.
As in a trance, I thought nor fearèd naught,
Nor know I where or whither I was ta'en,
Nor where I am, nor what these persons be.

BACON No? Know you not Master Burden?

HOSTESS Oh, yes, good sir, he is my daily guest.—
What, Master Burden? 'Twas but yesternight
That you and I at Henley played at cards.

BURDEN I know not what we did. A pox of ° all conjuring friars! *i.e., A curse on*

CLEMENT Now, jolly Friar, tell us, is this the book
That Burden is so careful to look on?

BACON It is.—But, Burden, tell me now,
Thinkest thou that Bacon's necromantic skill
Cannot perform his head and wall of brass,
When he can fetch thine hostess in such post?° *haste*

MILES I'll warrant you, master, if Master Burden could conjure as well as you, he would have his book every night from Henley to study on at Oxford.

MASON Burden, what, are you mated° by this frolic friar?— *checkmated*
Look how he droops! His guilty conscience
Drives him to bash,° and makes his hostess blush. *Makes him abashed*

BACON Well, mistress, for° I will not have you missed, *because*
You shall to Henley to cheer up your guests
'Fore supper 'gin.—Burden, bid her adieu;
Say farewell to your hostess 'fore she goes.
[*To the devil*] Sirrah, away, and set her safe at home.

HOSTESS Master Burden, when shall we see you at Henley?

Exeunt Hostess and the devil.

BURDEN The devil take thee, and Henley too!

MILES Master, shall I make a good motion?° *proposal*

BACON What's that?

9. By all the infernal gods, Belcephon!

1. In preparation for.

MILES Marry, sir, now that my hostess is gone to provide supper, conjure up another spirit, and send Doctor Burden flying after.

BACON Thus, rulers of our academic state,
You have seen the friar frame° his art by° proof. *devise / by way of*
And, as the college callèd Brazennose
Is under him° and he the master there, *(Bacon)*
So surely shall this head of brass be framed,° *fashioned*
And yield forth strange and uncouth° aphorisms; *strange, unknown*
And hell and Hecate° shall fail the friar *goddess of witchcraft*
But I will circle[2] England round with brass.

MILES So be it *et nunc et semper*,° amen. *Exeunt omnes.* *now and forever more*

[Scene 3]

Enter Margaret, the fair maid of Fressingfield, with Thomas, [Richard,] and Joan, and other clowns;° Lacy disguised in country apparel. *rustics*

THOMAS By my troth, Margaret, here's a weather is able to make a man call his father whoreson.[1] If this weather hold, we shall have hay good cheap,° and butter and cheese at Harleston will bear no price.° *at a good price* / *be almost priceless*

MARGARET Thomas, maids, when they come to see the fair,
Count not to make a cope° for dearth of hay. *bargain*
When we have turned our butter to the salt,° *salted our butter*
And set our cheese safely upon the racks,
Then let our fathers prise° it as they please. *prize; price*
We country sluts° of merry Fressingfield *girls, wenches*
Come to buy needless naughts° to make us fine,° *trifles / handsome*
And look that young men should be frank° this day, *generous*
And court us with such fairings° as they can. *fair gifts*
Phoebus is blithe, and frolic looks from heaven,
As when he courted lovely Semele,[2]
Swearing the peddlers shall have empty packs,
If that fair weather may make chapmen° buy. *merchants*

LACY But, lovely Peggy,° Semele is dead, *i.e., Margaret*
And therefore Phoebus from his palace pries,° *gazes from heaven*
And, seeing such a sweet and seemly saint,
Shows all his glories for to° court yourself. *in order to*

MARGARET This is a fairing,° gentle sir, indeed, *complimentary gift*
To soothe me up with such smooth flattery.
But, learn of me, your scoff's too broad before.°— *too obvious*
Well, Joan, our beauties must abide their jests;
We serve the turn° in jolly Fressingfield. *the purpose*

JOAN Margaret, a farmer's daughter for a farmer's son!
I warrant you the meanest° of us both *lowliest born*
Shall have a mate to lead us from the church.—
But, Thomas, what's the news? What, in a dump?° *reverie*
Give me your hand; we are near a peddler's shop.
Out with your purse; we must have fairings now.

2. Unless hell and Hecate fail me, I will encircle.
Scene 3. Harleston Fair, near Fressingfield.
1. I.e., weather so favorable that a farmer can thumb his nose at his poor father.
2. Beloved of Zeus (not Phoebus Apollo); destroyed by Zeus's lightning when she insisted on seeing her lover in all the splendor of the god.

THOMAS Faith, Joan, and shall. I'll bestow a fairing on you, and then we will to the tavern, and snap off a pint of wine or two.

All this while Lacy whispers [to] Margaret in the ear.

MARGARET Whence are you, sir? Of Suffolk? For your terms° *choice of words*
Are finer than the common sort of men.
LACY Faith, lovely girl, I am of Beccles by,° *from near Beccles*
Your neighbor, not above six miles from hence,
A farmer's son, that never was so quaint° *proud*
But that he could do courtesy to such dames.
But trust me, Margaret, I am sent in charge
From him that reveled in your father's house,
And filled his lodge with cheer and venison,
Tirèd° in green. [*Offering money*] He sent you this rich purse, *Attired*
His token, that he helped you run your cheese,
And in the milk house chatted with yourself.
MARGARET To me? You forget yourself.° *Surely you mistake*
LACY Women are often weak in memory.
MARGARET Oh, pardon, sir, I call to mind the man.
'Twere little manners to refuse his gift,
And yet I hope he sends it not for love;
For we have little leisure to debate of that.
JOAN What, Margaret, blush not. Maids must have their loves.
THOMAS Nay, by the mass,° she looks pale as if she were angry. *(an oath)*

RICHARD [*to Lacy*] Sirrah, are you of Beccles? I pray, how doth goodman° Cob? My father bought a horse of him.—I'll tell you, Margaret, 'a° were good to be a gentleman's jade,° for of all things the foul hilding° could not abide a dung-cart. *farmer* / *he / worthless horse* / *worthless beast*

MARGARET [*aside*] How different is this farmer from the rest
That erst as yet° hath pleased my wand'ring sight! *up until now*
His words are witty, quickened with a smile,
His courtesy gentle,° smelling of the court; *well-bred*
Facile° and debonair in all his deeds, *Affable, courteous*
Proportioned as was Paris, when, in gray,
He courted Oenone in the vale by Troy.[3]
Great lords have come and pleaded for my love—
Who but the Keeper's lass of Fressingfield?—
And yet methinks this farmer's jolly son
Passeth the proudest that hath pleased mine eye.
But, Peg, disclose not that thou art in love,
And show as yet no sign of love to him,
Although thou well wouldst wish him for thy love.
Keep that to thee till time doth serve thy turn
To show the grief wherein thy heart doth burn.—
Come, Joan and Thomas, shall we to the fair?
You, Beccles man, will not forsake us now?
LACY Not whilst I may have such quaint° girls as you. *pretty*
MARGARET Well, if you chance to come by Fressingfield,
Make but a step into the Keeper's lodge,
And such poor fare as woodmen° can afford— *keepers of forests*
Butter and cheese, cream, and fat venison—

3. Paris, dressed in the traditional gray of shepherds, fell in love with Oenone on Mount Ida but deserted her when offered the chance to be Helen's lover.

You shall have store,° and welcome therewithal. *plenty*
LACY Gramercies,° Peggy. Look for me ere long. *Many thanks*
Exeunt omnes.

[Scene 4]

Enter Henry the Third, the Emperor, the King of Castile, Elinor his daughter, [and] Jaques Vandermast, a German.

KING HENRY Great men of Europe, monarchs of the West,
Ringed with the walls of old Oceanus,
Whose lofty surge is like the battlements
That compassed high-built Babel° in with towers, *(see Genesis 11)*
Welcome, my lords, welcome, brave Western kings,
To England's shore, whose promontory cliffs
Shows Albion° is another little world. *England*
Welcome, says English Henry to you all—
Chiefly unto the lovely Elinor,
Who dared for Edward's sake cut° through the seas, *to cut*
And venture as Agenor's damsel through the deep,[1]
To get the love of Henry's wanton° son. *amorous*
CASTILE England's rich monarch, brave Plantagenet,[2]
The Pyren Mounts,° swelling above the clouds, *Pyrenees Mountains*
That ward the wealthy Castile in with walls,
Could not detain the beauteous Elinor;
But, hearing of the fame of Edward's youth,
She dared to brook Neptunus'° haughty pride, *endure the seas'*
And bide the brunt of froward Aeolus.° *god of adverse winds*
Then may fair England welcome her the more.
ELINOR After that° English Henry, by° his lords, *After / by means of*
Had sent Prince Edward's lovely counterfeit° *picture*
A present to the Castile Elinor,
The comely portrait of so brave° a man, *handsome, splendid*
The virtuous fame discoursèd of his deeds,
Edward's courageous resolution
Done at the Holy Land° 'fore Damas'° walls, *(on crusade) / Damascus'*
Led both mine eye and thoughts in equal links° *in equal parts united*
To like so of the English monarch's son
That I attempted perils for his sake.
EMPEROR Where is the Prince, my lord?
KING HENRY He posted° down, not long since, from the court, *hastened*
To Suffolk side, to merry Framlingham,[3]
To sport himself amongst my fallow deer.
From thence, by packets° sent to Hampton House, *mail dispatches*
We hear the Prince is ridden with his lords
To Oxford, in the academy there
To hear dispute amongst the learnèd men.
But we will send forth letters for my son
To will him come from Oxford to the court.

Scene 4. The royal court of England.
1. Europa, daughter of Agenor, King of Tyre, was carried off by her lover Zeus in the shape of a bull, through the Aegean to Crete.
2. Henry III was of the family of Plantagenet, which ruled England from the twelfth to the fifteenth centuries.
3. In Suffolk, near Fressingfield.

EMPEROR Nay, rather, Henry, let us, as we be,
Ride for to visit Oxford with our train.° *retinue*
Fain would I see your universities
And what learned men your academy yields.
From Hapsburg have I brought a learnèd clerk° *scholar*
To hold dispute with English orators.
This doctor, surnamed Jaques Vandermast,
A German born, passed° into Padua, *journeyed*
To Florence, and to fair Bologna,
To Paris, Rheims, and stately Orleans,
And, talking there with men of art,° put down *learning*
The chiefest of them all in aphorisms,
In magic, and the mathematic rules.
Now let us, Henry, try° him in your schools. *test*
KING HENRY He shall, my lord; this motion likes° me well. *proposal pleases*
We'll progress straight to Oxford with our trains,
And see what men our academy brings.°— *brings forth*
And, wonder° Vandermast, welcome to me. *wondrous*
In Oxford shalt thou find a jolly friar
Called Friar Bacon, England's only flower.° *chief ornament*
Set him but nonplus° in his magic spells, *Confound him*
And make him yield in mathematic rules,
And for thy glory I will bind thy brows—
Not with a poet's garland made of bays,
But with a coronet of choicest gold.
Whilst then° we flit to Oxford with our troops, *Until the time that*
Let's in and banquet in our English court. *Exeunt.*

[Scene 5]

Enter Rafe Simnell in Edward's apparel, Edward [disguised as Rafe],° Warren [and] Ermsby disguised [as the Prince's followers]. *(see 1.98–99)*

RAFE [*posing as Prince Edward*] Where be these vagabond knaves, that they attend no better on their master?

EDWARD [*as Rafe*] If it please Your Honor, we are all ready at an inch.° *at an instant*

RAFE Sirrah Ned, I'll have no more post-horse to ride on. I'll have another fetch.° *trick, device*

ERMSBY I pray you, how is that, my lord?

RAFE Marry, sir, I'll send to the Isle of Ely° *(in Norfolk)* for four or five dozen of geese, and I'll have them tied six and six together with whipcord. Now upon their backs will I have a fair field bed,° *portable military bed* with a canopy, and so when it is my pleasure I'll flee° *fly* into what place I please. This will be easy.

WARREN Your Honor hath said well. But shall we to Brazennose College before we pull off our boots?

ERMSBY Warren, well motioned.° *urged* We will to the friar
Before we revel it within the town.—
Rafe, see you keep your countenance like a prince.

RAFE Wherefore have I such a company of cutting° *swaggering* knaves to

Scene 5. Oxford.

wait upon me but to keep and defend my countenance° [reputation] against all mine enemies? Have you not good swords and bucklers?° [shields]

Enter Bacon and Miles [not at first noticing Edward, Ermsby, Warren, and Rafe].

ERMSBY Stay, who comes here?

WARREN Some scholar; and we'll ask him where Friar Bacon is.

[They stand aside for a moment and watch.]

BACON Why, thou arrant dunce, shall I never make thee good scholar? Doth not all the town cry out and say, "Friar Bacon's subsizar[1] is the greatest blockhead in all Oxford"? Why, thou canst not speak one word of true Latin.

MILES No, sir? Yes. What is this else: *Ego sum tuus homo*, "I am your man"? I warrant you, sir, as good Tully's° [Cicero's] phrase as any is in Oxford.

BACON Come on, sirrah: what part of speech is *Ego*?

MILES *Ego*, that is "I"; marry, *nomen substantivo*.° [noun substantive]

BACON How prove you that?

MILES Why, sir, let him prove himself an 'a will;° [if he wishes] "I" can be heard, felt, and understood.[2]

BACON Oh, gross dunce! *Here beat him.*

EDWARD Come, let us break off this dispute between these two. [*To Miles*] Sirrah, where is Brazennose College?

MILES Not far from Coppersmiths' Hall.[3]

EDWARD What, dost thou mock me?

MILES Not I, sir, but what would you at Brazennose?

ERMSBY Marry, we would speak with Friar Bacon.

MILES Whose men be you?

ERMSBY Marry, scholar, here's our master.

[He indicates Rafe.]

RAFE Sirrah, I am the master of these good fellows. Mayst thou not know me to be a lord by my reparel?° [apparel]

MILES Then here's good game° [quarry] for the hawk, for here's the master fool and a covey of coxcombs. One wise man, I think, would springe° [ensnare] you all.

EDWARD Gog's wounds!° [God's wounds (an oath)] Warren, kill him.

[Bacon charms them by magic, so that they are powerless to draw their swords.]

WARREN Why, Ned, I think the devil be in my sheath! I cannot get out my dagger.

ERMSBY Nor I mine. 'Swounds,° [By God's wounds] Ned, I think I am bewitched.

MILES A company of scabs!° [scoundrels] The proudest of you all draw your weapon, if he can. [*Aside*] See how boldly I speak, now my master is by!° [at hand]

EDWARD I strive in vain; but if my sword be shut
And conjured fast by magic in my sheath,
Villain, here is my fist. *Strike him a box on the ear.*

MILES [*to Bacon*] Oh, I beseech you, conjure his hands too,

1. An undergraduate earning his keep and tuition doing menial chores.
2. The traditional pedagogical definition of a noun, as in William Lily's much-used Latin grammar.
3. Miles's saucy answer plays on the literal meaning of "Brazennose" (i.e., Brasenose), "having a brass nose"; as such, it is akin to the "copper" of Coppersmith.

that he may not lift his arms to his head, for he is light-fingered.

RAFE Ned, strike him. I'll warrant thee,° by mine honor. *I'll back you up*
BACON What means the English prince to wrong my man?° *servant*
EDWARD To whom speakest thou?
BACON To thee.
EDWARD Who art thou?
BACON Could you not judge, when all your swords grew fast,° *stuck fast*
That Friar Bacon was not far from hence?
Edward, King Henry's son and Prince of Wales,
Thy fool disguised cannot conceal thyself.
I know both Ermsby and the Sussex earl,
Else Friar Bacon had but little skill.
Thou comest in post from merry Fressingfield,
Fast fancied° to the Keeper's bonny lass, *Bound by love*
To crave some succor of the jolly friar;
And Lacy, Earl of Lincoln, hast thou left
To treat° fair Margaret to allow° thy loves. *entreat / receive*
But friends are men,[4] and love can baffle lords;
The Earl both woos and courts her for himself.
WARREN Ned, this is strange! The friar knoweth all.
ERMSBY Apollo[5] could not utter more than this.
EDWARD I stand amazed to hear this jolly friar
Tell even the very secrets of my thoughts.—
But, learnèd Bacon, since thou knowest the cause
Why I did post so fast from Fressingfield,
Help, Friar, at a pinch, that I may have
The love of lovely Margaret to myself;
And, as I am true Prince of Wales, I'll give
Living and lands to strength° thy college state.° *strengthen / estate*
WARREN Good Friar, help the Prince in this.

RAFE Why, servant Ned, will not the friar do it? Were not my sword glued to my scabbard by conjuration, I would cut off his head and make him do it by force.

MILES In faith, my lord,[6] your manhood and your sword is all alike; they are so fast conjured that we shall never see them.

ERMSBY What, Doctor, in a dump?° Tush, help the Prince, *reverie*
And thou shalt see how liberal° he will prove. *generous*
BACON Crave not such actions greater dumps than these?
I will, my lord, strain out° my magic spells, *employ to the utmost*
For this day comes the Earl° to Fressingfield, *(Lacy)*
And, 'fore that° night shuts in the day with dark, *before*
They'll be betrothèd each to other fast.
But come with me; we'll to my study straight,
And in a glass prospective° I will show *magic mirror*
What's done this day in merry Fressingfield.
EDWARD Gramercies, Bacon. I will quite thy pain.° *requite your efforts*
BACON But send your train,° my lord, into the town. *retinue*
My scholar shall go bring them to their inn.

4. But even friends, being mortal males, are subject to love (and hence likely to sacrifice friendship to love).
5. The greatest oracle in ancient Greece was that of Apollo.
6. Miles addresses the disguised Rafe as though he were the real Prince of Wales.

Meanwhile we'll see the knavery of the Earl.
EDWARD Warren, leave me, and Ermsby, take the fool;
Let him be master and go revel it° *have fun*
Till I and Friar Bacon talk awhile.
WARREN We will, my lord.
RAFE Faith, Ned, and I'll lord it out° till thou comest. I'll be Prince of Wales over all the black pots° in Oxford. *playact the Prince* / *leather wine jugs*
Exeunt.

[Scene 6]

Bacon and Edward goes° into the study. *go*

BACON Now, frolic Edward, welcome to my cell.
Here tempers° Friar Bacon many toys,° *mixes / trifles*
And holds this place his consistory court,° *ecclesiastical tribunal*
Wherein the devils plead homage to his words.° *obey his commands*
Within this glass prospective thou shalt see
This day what's done in merry Fressingfield
'Twixt lovely Peggy and the Lincoln earl.
EDWARD Friar, thou glad'st me. Now shall Edward try° *test*
How Lacy meaneth to° his sovereign lord. *is disposed toward*
BACON Stand there and look directly in the glass.

Enter Margaret and Friar Bungay [as if in the magic glass. They are visible to Edward but cannot be heard by him].

BACON What sees my lord?
EDWARD I see the Keeper's lovely lass appear,
As brightsome as the paramour of Mars,° *As beautiful as Venus*
Only attended by a jolly friar.
BACON Sit still and keep the crystal in your eye.° *sight*
MARGARET *But tell me, Friar Bungay, is it true*
That this fair courteous country swain,
Who says his father is a farmer nigh,
Can be Lord Lacy, Earl of Lincolnshire?[1]
BUNGAY *Peggy, 'tis true. 'Tis Lacy, for° my life—* *on*
Or else mine art and cunning both doth fail—
Left by Prince Edward to procure his loves;° *woo for him*
For he in green that holp° you run your cheese *helped*
Is son to Henry, and the Prince of Wales.
MARGARET *Be what he will, his lure° is but for lust.* *pursuing the lure*
But did Lord Lacy like° poor Margaret, *But if Lord Lacy loves*
Or would he deign to wed a country lass,
Friar, I would his humble handmaid be,
And for° great wealth quite° him with courtesy. *in return for / requite*
BUNGAY *Why, Margaret, dost thou love him?*
MARGARET *His personage, like the pride of vaunting Troy,*
Might well avouch to shadow° Helen's scape.° *excuse / transgression*
His wit is quick and ready in conceit° *as quick-witted*
As Greece afforded in her chiefest prime;° *golden age*
Courteous—ah, Friar!—full of pleasing smiles.

Scene 6. Oxford. Bacon's study.
1. All speech that occurs within the magic mirror appears here in italics.

Trust me, I love too much to tell thee more.
Suffice° to me he is England's paramour.° — *Suffice it that / darling*
BUNGAY *Hath not each eye that viewed thy pleasing face*
Surnamèd thee fair maid of Fressingfield?
MARGARET *Yes, Bungay, and would God the lovely earl*
Had that in esse° *that so many sought!* — *in actuality*
BUNGAY *Fear not; the Friar° will not be behind°* — *(Bungay) / left behind*
To show his cunning to entangle love.
EDWARD [*to Bacon*] I think the Friar courts the bonny wench!
Bacon, methinks he is a lusty churl.° — *lustful peasant*
BACON Now look, my lord.

Enter Lacy [*disguised in country garb, as before*].

EDWARD Gog's wounds, Bacon, here comes Lacy!
BACON Sit still, my lord, and mark the comedy.
BUNGAY *Here's Lacy. Margaret, step aside awhile.*
[*They step aside and overhear Lacy in soliloquy.*]
LACY [*to himself*] *Daphne, the damsel that caught Phoebus fast,*[2]
And locked him in the brightness of her looks,
Was not so beauteous in Apollo's eyes
As is fair Margaret to the Lincoln earl.
Recant thee, Lacy! Thou art put in trust.
Edward thy sovereign's son hath chosen thee
A secret friend to court her for himself,
And darest thou wrong thy prince with treachery?
Lacy, love makes no exception of° a friend, — *for*
Nor deems it of a prince but as a man.[3]
Honor bids thee control him in his lust.
His wooing is not for to wed the girl,
But to entrap her and beguile the lass.
Lacy, thou lovest; then brook not° such abuse, — *do not tolerate*
But wed her, and abide thy prince's frown;
For better die than see her live disgraced.
MARGARET *Come, Friar, I will shake him from his dumps.*
[*She approaches Lacy.*]
How cheer you, sir? A penny for your thought.
You're early up; pray God it be the near.° — *nearer for your purpose*
What, come from Beccles in a morn so soon?
LACY *Thus watchful are such men as live in love,*
Whose eyes brook° broken slumbers for their sleep. — *endure, undergo*
I tell thee, Peggy, since last Harleston Fair,
My mind hath felt a heap of passions.
MARGARET *A trusty man, that court it for your friend!*
Woo you still for the courtier all in green?
I marvel that he sues° not for himself. — *woos*
LACY *Peggy, I pleaded first to get your grace for him,*
But when mine eyes surveyed your beauteous looks,
Love, like a wag,° straight dived into my heart, — *mischievous boy*
And there did shrine the idea° of yourself. — *enshrine the image*
Pity me, though I be a farmer's son,
And measure not my riches, but my love.

2. Ardently pursued by Phoebus Apollo, the river nymph Daphne chose to be metamorphosed into a bay tree or laurel.
3. Love treats a prince as any other man.

MARGARET *You are very hasty; for, to garden well,*
Seeds must have time to sprout before they spring.
Love ought to creep as doth the dial's° shade, sundial's
For timely° ripe is rotten too too soon. prematurely
BUNGAY [*coming forward*] Deus hic!° *Room for a merry friar!* May God be here!
What, youth of Beccles, with the Keeper's lass?
'Tis well. But tell me, hear you any news?
MARGARET *No, Friar. What news?*
BUNGAY *Hear you not how the pursuivants° do post* royal messengers
With proclamations through each country town?
LACY *For what, gentle Friar? Tell the news.*
BUNGAY *Dwell'st thou in Beccles and hear'st not of these news?*
Lacy, the Earl of Lincoln, is late fled
From Windsor court, disguisèd like a swain,° rustic
And lurks about the country here unknown.
Henry suspects him of some treachery,
And therefore doth proclaim in every way
That who° can take the Lincoln earl shall have whoever
Paid in the Exchequer twenty thousand crowns.
LACY *The Earl of Lincoln! Friar, thou art mad.*
It was some other; thou mistakest the man.
The Earl of Lincoln? Why, it cannot be.
MARGARET *Yes, very well, my lord, for you are he.*
The Keeper's daughter took you prisoner.
Lord Lacy, yield. I'll be your jailer once.° for this once
EDWARD How familiar they be, Bacon!
BACON Sit still and mark the sequel of their loves.
LACY *Then am I double prisoner to thyself.*
Peggy, I yield. But are these news in jest?
MARGARET *In jest with you, but earnest unto me,*
Forwhy° these wrongs do wring me at the heart. Because
Ah, how these earls and noble men of birth
Flatter and feign to forge° poor women's ill! bend, fashion
LACY *Believe me, lass, I am the Lincoln earl.*
I not deny but, tirèd° thus in rags, attired
I lived disguised to win fair Peggy's love.
MARGARET *What love is there where wedding ends° not love?* completes
LACY *I meant, fair girl, to make thee Lacy's wife.*
MARGARET *I little think that earls will stoop so low.*
LACY *Say, shall I make thee countess ere I sleep?*
MARGARET *Handmaid unto the Earl, so please himself;*
A wife in name, but servant in obedience.
LACY *The Lincoln countess, for it shall be so!*
I'll plight the bands° and seal it with a kiss. [*They kiss.*] confirm our union
EDWARD Gog's wounds, Bacon, they kiss! I'll stab them.
[*He threatens the magic glass with his sword.*]
BACON Oh, hold your hands, my lord! It is the glass.
EDWARD Choler° to see the traitors 'gree° so well Wrath / agree
Made me think the shadows substances.
BACON 'Twere a long poniard,° my lord, to reach between dagger
Oxford and Fressingfield. But sit still and see more.
BUNGAY *Well, Lord of Lincoln, if your loves be knit,*
And that your tongues and thoughts do both agree,
To avoid ensuing jars,° I'll hamper up° the match. quarrels / make secure

I'll take my portace° forth, and wed you here; service book
Then go to bed and seal up your desires.

LACY *Friar, content.—Peggy, how like you this?*

MARGARET *What likes° my lord is pleasing unto me.* pleases

BUNGAY *Then hand-fast° hand, and I will to my book.* join

BACON What sees my lord now?

EDWARD Bacon, I see the lovers hand in hand,
The Friar ready with his portace there
To wed them both. Then am I quite undone.
Bacon, help now, if e'er thy magic served!
Help, Bacon, stop the marriage now,
If devils or necromancy may suffice,
And I will give thee forty thousand crowns.° gold coins

BACON Fear not, my lord, I'll stop the jolly friar
For° mumbling up his orisons° this day. From / prayers

[*Bacon puts a spell on Bungay.*]

LACY *Why speak'st not, Bungay? Friar, to thy book.*

(*Bungay is mute, crying "Hud hud!"*)

MARGARET *How lookest thou, Friar, as a man distraught!*
Reft° of thy senses? Bungay, show by signs, Bereft
If thou be dumb, what passions holdeth thee.

LACY *He's dumb indeed. Bacon hath with his devils*
Enchanted him, or else some strange disease
Or apoplexy hath possessed his lungs.
But, Peggy, what he cannot with his book
We'll 'twixt us both unite it up in heart.

MARGARET *Else let me die, my lord, a miscreant.°* heretic, unbeliever

EDWARD Why stands Friar Bungay so amazed?° stunned

BACON I have struck him dumb, my lord, and if Your Honor please
I'll fetch this Bungay straightway from Fressingfield,
And he shall dine with us in Oxford here.

EDWARD Bacon, do that, and thou contentest me.

LACY *Of° courtesy, Margaret, let us lead the Friar* As a matter of
Unto thy father's lodge, to comfort him
With broths to bring him from this hapless trance.

MARGARET *Or else, my lord, we were passing° unkind* exceedingly
To leave the Friar so in his distress.

Enter a devil, and carry Bungay on his back [*and so exeunt*].

Oh, help, my lord! A devil, a devil, my lord!
Look how he carries Bungay on his back!
Let's hence, for Bacon's spirits be abroad!

Exeunt [*Margaret and Lacy*].

EDWARD Bacon, I laugh to see the jolly friar
Mounted upon the devil, and how the Earl
Flees with his bonny lass for fear!
As soon as Bungay is at Brazennose,
And I have chatted with the merry friar,
I will in post hie me° to Fressingfield, hasten
And quite° these wrongs on Lacy ere it be long. requite

BACON So be it, my lord. But let us to our dinner,
For, ere we have taken our repast awhile,
We shall have Bungay brought to Brazennose. *Exeunt.*

[Scene 7]

Enter three doctors: Burden, Mason, [and] Clement.

MASON Now that we are gathered in the Regent House,[1]
It fits° us talk about the King's repair,° — *befits / coming hither*
For he, trooped with° all the Western kings — *accompanied by*
That lie alongst the Danzig° seas by east, — *i.e., Baltic*
North by the clime of frosty Germany,
The Almain° monarch, and the Saxon duke,[2] — *German*
Castile, and lovely Elinor with him,
Have in their jests° resolved for Oxford town. — *exploits*
BURDEN We must lay° plots of stately tragedies, — *set out, devise*
Strange comic shows, such as proud Roscius[3]
Vaunted before the Roman emperors—
CLEMENT To welcome all the Western potentates.
But more: the King by letters hath foretold
That Frederick, the Almain emperor,
Hath brought with him a German of esteem,
Whose surname is Don Jaques Vandermast,
Skillful in magic and those secret arts.
MASON Then must we all make suit unto the friar,
To Friar Bacon, that he vouch° this task, — *vouchsafe, undertake*
And undertake to countervail in skill
The German, else there's none in Oxford can° — *who can*
Match and dispute with learnèd Vandermast.
BURDEN Bacon, if he will hold° the German play,° — *engage / in play*
We'll teach him what an English friar can do.
The devil, I think, dare not dispute with him.
CLEMENT Indeed, Mas' Doctor, he pleasured you,
In that he brought your hostess with her spit
From Henley, posting unto Brazennose.
BURDEN A vengeance on the Friar for his pains!
But, leaving that, let's hie° to Bacon straight, — *hasten*
To see if he will take this task in hand.
CLEMENT Stay, what rumor° is this? The town is up in a mutiny. What hurly-burly is this? — *noise*

Enter a Constable, with Rafe [disguised as Prince Edward], Warren, Ermsby, and Miles.

CONSTABLE Nay, masters,° if you were ne'er so good, you shall before the doctors to answer your misdemeanor. — *good sirs*
BURDEN What's the matter, fellow?
CONSTABLE Marry, sir, here's a company of rufflers° that, drinking in the tavern, have made a great brawl, and almost killed the vintner.° — *swaggerers / tavern-keeper*
MILES *Salve*,° Doctor Burden! This lubberly lurdane,° — *Hail / blockhead*
Ill-shaped and ill-faced, disdained and disgraced,
What he tells unto *vobis, mentitur de nobis*.[4]
BURDEN Who is the master and chief of this crew?

Scene 7. Oxford. The Regent House.
1. A building housing the university senate.
2. A silent character who does not actually speak in the play.
3. The most famous comic actor of his day in Rome (died 62 B.C.E.).
4. Whatever he tells you, he lies about us.

MILES [*indicating Rafe*] *Ecce asinum mundi, fugura rotundi,*[5]
Neat, sheat,° and fine, as brisk as a cup of wine. *trim, neat*
BURDEN What are you?
RAFE I am, Father Doctor, as a man would say, the bell-wether° of this company; these are my lords, and I the Prince of Wales. *i.e., leader*
CLEMENT Are you Edward, the King's son?
RAFE Sirrah Miles, bring hither the tapster that drew° the wine, and I warrant when they see how soundly I have broke° his head, they'll say 'twas done by no less man than a prince. *drew from the barrel* / *banged*
MASON I cannot believe that this is the Prince of Wales.
WARREN And why so, sir?
MASON For they say the Prince is a brave and a wise gentleman.
WARREN Why, and thinkest thou, Doctor, that he is not so?
Dar'st thou detract and derogate from him,
Being so lovely and so brave° a youth? *fine, handsome*
ERMSBY Whose face, shining with many a sugared smile,
Bewrays° that he is bred of princely race. *Reveals*
MILES And yet, Master Doctor, to speak like a proctor,° *university official*
And tell unto you what is veriment° and true, *veritable*
To cease of this quarrel, look but on his apparel;
Then mark but my talis,° he is great Prince of Walis, *tale (comic rhyme)*
The chief of our *gregis,*° and *filius regis.*° *company / king's son*
Then ware° what is done, for he is Henry's white° son. *beware / white-haired*
RAFE Doctors, whose doting nightcaps are not capable of° my ingenious° dignity, know that I am Edward Plantagenet, whom if you displease will make a ship that shall hold all your colleges, and so carry away the Niniversity with a fair wind to the Bankside in Southwark.[6]—How say'st thou, Ned Warren, shall I not do it? *able to comprehend* / *high-minded, noble*
WARREN Yes, my good lord, and, if it please Your Lordship, I will gather up all your old pantofles,° and with the cork make you a pinnace° of five hundred ton that shall serve the turn marvelous well, my lord. *cork-heeled slippers* / *small sailing vessel*
ERMSBY And I, my lord, will have pioneers° to undermine the town, that the very gardens and orchards be carried away for your summer walks. *diggers*
MILES And I with *scientia,*° and great *diligentia,*° *learning / diligence*
Will conjure and charm, to keep you from harm,
That *utrum horum mavis,*[7] your very great *navis,*° *ship*
Like Bartlet's ship,[8] from Oxford do skip
With colleges and schools, full loaden with fools.
Quid dices ad hoc, worshipful *Domine* Dawcock?[9]
CLEMENT Why, harebrained courtiers, are you drunk or mad,
To taunt us up with such scurrility?
Deem you us men of base and light esteem,
To bring us such a fop for Henry's son?—

5. Behold the jackass of the round-shaped world.
6. The location of many of London's playhouses.
7. Whichever of these you prefer.
8. Sebastian Brandt's *Ship of Fools,* a late medieval satire of folly, translated by Alexander Barclay (whom Miles calls "Bartlet"). The conversation in this passage burlesques the madcap style of *Ship of Fools.*
9. What do you say to this, most distinguished Master Jackdaw? (The jackdaw, a large blackbird, was a byword for stupidity.)

Call out the beadles° and convey them hence, *minor officials*
Straight to Bocardo!° Let the roisters lie *an Oxford prison*
Close clapped° in bolts, until their wits be tame. *Securely confined*

ERMSBY [*to Rafe*] Why, shall we to prison, my lord?

RAFE What say'st, Miles, shall I honor the prison with my presence?

MILES No, no! Out with your blades, and hamper these
jades.° *i.e., worthless wretches*
Have a flirt° and a crash! Now play revel-dash,° *blow / a rowdy game*
And teach these *sacerdos*° that the Bocardos,° *priests / prisons*
Like peasants and elves,[1] are meet° for themselves. *suitable*

MASON To the prison with them, Constable!

WARREN Well, doctors, seeing I have sported me° *amused myself*
With laughing at these mad and merry wags,
Know that Prince Edward is at Brazennose,
And this, attirèd like the Prince of Wales,
Is Rafe, King Henry's only lovèd fool,
I, Earl of Sussex, and this Ermsby,
One of the privy chamber to the King,
Who, while the Prince with Friar Bacon stays,
Have reveled it in Oxford as you see.

MASON My lord, pardon us, we knew not what you were.
But courtiers may make greater scapes° than these. *pranks*
Will't please Your Honor dine with me today?

WARREN I will, Master Doctor, and satisfy° the vintner for his hurt; only I must desire you to imagine him° all this forenoon the Prince of Wales. *compensate* *(Rafe)*

MASON I will, sir.

RAFE And upon that I will lead the way, only I will have Miles go before me, because I have heard Henry say that wisdom must go before majesty. *Exeunt omnes.*

[Scene 8]

Enter Prince Edward with his poniard° in his hand, Lacy, and Margaret. *dagger*

EDWARD Lacy, thou canst not shroud thy trait'rous thoughts,
Nor cover, as did Cassius,[1] all his wiles,
For Edward hath an eye that looks as far
As Lynceus[2] from the shores of Grecia.° *Greece*
Did not I sit in Oxford by the Friar
And see thee court the maid of Fressingfield,
Sealing thy flattering fancies with a kiss?
Did not proud Bungay draw his portace° forth, *service book*
And, joining hand in hand, had° married you *would have*
If Friar Bacon had not struck him dumb,
And mounted him upon a spirit's back
That we might chat at Oxford with the Friar?
Traitor, what answer'st? Is not all this true?

1. They being the peasants and malignant imps that they are.

Scene 8. Fressingfield.

1. One of the chief conspirators in the assassination of Julius Caesar in 44 B.C.E.

2. One of the Argonauts, the band of heroes who sailed with Jason in quest of the Golden Fleece, reputedly of such keen eyesight that he could see through the earth.

LACY Truth all, my lord, and thus I make reply:
At Harleston Fair, there courting for Your Grace,
Whenas° mine eye surveyed her curious° shape, *When / dainty*
And drew the beauteous glory of her looks
To dive into the center of my heart,
Love taught me that Your Honor did but jest,° *dally*
That princes were in fancy° but as men; *in affairs of the heart*
How that the lovely maid of Fressingfield
Was fitter to be Lacy's wedded wife
Than concubine unto the Prince of Wales.
EDWARD Injurious Lacy! Did I love thee more
Than Alexander his Hephestion?[3]
Did I unfold° the passion of my love, *disclose*
And lock them in the closet of thy thoughts?
Wert thou to Edward second to himself,
Sole friend, and partner of his secret loves?
And could a glance of fading beauty[4] break
The enchainèd fetters of such private friends?
Base coward, false, and too effeminate° *weak, self-indulgent*
To be corrival° with a prince in thoughts! *partner*
From Oxford have I posted since I dined,
To quite° a traitor 'fore that° Edward sleep. *requite / before*
MARGARET 'Twas I, my lord, not Lacy, stepped awry;
For oft he sued and courted for yourself,
And still wooed for the courtier all in green.
But I, whom fancy° made but overfond, *love*
Pleaded myself with looks as if I loved;
I fed mine eye with gazing on his face,
And, still bewitched, loved Lacy with my looks.
My heart with sighs, mine eyes pleaded with tears,
My face held pity and content° at once, *contentment, happiness*
And more I could not cipher out° by signs *concealingly express*
But that I loved Lord Lacy with my heart.
Then, worthy Edward, measure with thy mind
If women's favors will not force men fall,
If beauty and if darts of piercing love
Is° not of force° to bury thoughts of friends. *Are / strong enough*
EDWARD I tell thee, Peggy, I will have thy loves!
Edward or none shall conquer Margaret.
In frigates° bottomed with rich Shittim° planks, *ships / acacia wood*
Topped with the lofty firs of Lebanon,
Stemmed and encased with burnished ivory
And overlaid with plates of Persian wealth,
Like Thetis° shalt thou wanton on the waves *a Nereid, sea nymph*
And draw the dolphins to thy lovely eyes,
To dance lavoltas° in the purple streams; *lively dances*
Sirens with harps and silver psalteries° *harplike instruments*
Shall wait° with music at thy frigate's stem,° *attend / bow*
And entertain fair Margaret with their lays.° *songs*
England and England's wealth shall wait on thee;
Britain shall bend unto her prince's love,
And do due homage to thine excellence,

3. One of Alexander the Great's captains and his intimate friend, who died in 324 B.C.E.

4. Beauty that will fade in time.

If thou wilt be but Edward's Margaret.
MARGARET Pardon, my lord. If Jove's great royalty
Sent me such presents as to Danaë,[5]
If Phoebus, tirèd° in Latona's webs,[6] *attired*
Come° courting from the beauty of his lodge,° *Came / (the sky)*
The dulcet tunes of frolic Mercury
Nor all the wealth heaven's treasury affords
Should make me leave Lord Lacy or his love.
EDWARD I have learned at Oxford, then, this point of schools:° *of scholastic debate*
Ablata causa, tollitur effectus.[7]
Lacy—the cause that Margaret cannot love
Nor fix her liking on the English prince—
Take him away, and then the effects will fail.
Villain, prepare thyself, for I will bathe
My poniard in the bosom of an earl.
LACY [*kneeling*] Rather than live and miss fair Margaret's love,
Prince Edward, stop not at the fatal doom,° *sentence*
But stab it home;° end both my loves and life. *all the way*
MARGARET [*kneeling*] Brave Prince of Wales, honored for royal deeds,
'Twere sin to stain fair Venus' courts with blood!
Love's conquests ends, my lord, in courtesy.
Spare Lacy, gentle Edward; let me die,
For so° both you and he do cease your loves. *in that way*
EDWARD Lacy shall die as traitor to his lord.
LACY I have deserved it, Edward. Act it well.
MARGARET What hopes the Prince to gain by Lacy's death?
EDWARD To end the loves 'twixt him and Margaret.
MARGARET Why, thinks King Henry's son that Margaret's love
Hangs in the uncertain balance of proud Time?
That death shall make a discord of our thoughts?
No! Stab the Earl, and, 'fore the morning sun
Shall vaunt him° thrice over the lofty east, *display himself*
Margaret will meet her Lacy in the heavens.
LACY If aught betides to lovely Margaret
That wrongs or wrings° her honor from content, *wrests, twists*
Europe's rich wealth nor England's monarchy
Should not allure Lacy to overlive.° *outlive (her)*
Then Edward, short my life and end her loves.
MARGARET Rid° me, and keep a friend worth many loves. *Get rid of*
LACY Nay, Edward, keep a love worth many friends.
MARGARET And if thy mind be such as fame hath blazed,° *rumor has reported*
Then, princely Edward, let us both abide
The fatal resolution of thy rage.
Banish thou fancy° and embrace revenge, *love*
And in one tomb knit both our carcasses,
Whose hearts were linkèd in one perfect love.

5. Zeus came as a lover to Danaë in a shower of gold, since she was confined to a brazen tower.
6. Latona, or Leto, was the mother of Phoebus Apollo and Artemis; Zeus was the father. Greene implies that she was an expert weaver.
7. When the cause is removed, the effect disappears.

EDWARD [*aside*] Edward, art thou that famous Prince of
 Wales
Who at Damasco° beat the Saracens,° *Damascus / (see 4.26–27)*
And brought'st home triumph on thy lance's point,
And shall thy plumes be pulled by Venus down?
Is it princely to dissever lovers' leagues,
To part such friends as glory in their loves?
Leave,° Ned, and make a virtue of this fault, *Cease*
And further Peg and Lacy in their loves.
So in subduing fancy's passion,
Conquering thyself, thou get'st the richest spoil.° *booty*
[*To them*] Lacy, rise up! Fair Peggy, here's my hand.
[*He raises them up.*]
The Prince of Wales hath conquered all his thoughts,
And all his loves he yields unto the Earl.
Lacy, enjoy the maid of Fressingfield;
Make her thy Lincoln countess at the church,
And Ned, as he is true Plantagenet,
Will give her to thee frankly for thy wife.
LACY Humbly I take her of my sovereign,
As if that Edward gave me England's right,
And riched me with the Albion diadem.° *English crown*
MARGARET And doth the English prince mean true?
Will he vouchsafe to cease his former loves
And yield the title of a country maid
Unto Lord Lacy?
EDWARD I will, fair Peggy, as I am true lord.
MARGARET Then, lordly sir, whose conquest is as great
In conquering love as Caesar's victories,
Margaret, as mild and humble in her thoughts
As was Aspasia[8] unto Cyrus' self,
Yields thanks, and, next Lord Lacy, doth enshrine
Edward the second° secret in her heart. *second (next to Lacy)*
EDWARD Gramercy,° Peggy. Now that vows are passed, *Many thanks*
And that your loves are not to be revolt,° *withdrawn, overturned*
Once, Lacy, friends again, come, we will post
To Oxford; for this day the King is there,
And brings for Edward Castile Elinor.
Peggy, I must go see and view my wife;
I pray God I like her as I loved thee.
Beside, Lord Lincoln, we shall hear dispute
'Twixt Friar Bacon and learned Vandermast.
Peggy, we'll leave you for a week or two.
MARGARET As it please Lord Lacy; but love's foolish looks
Think footsteps miles and minutes to be hours.
LACY I'll hasten, Peggy, to make short return.—
But, please Your Honor, go unto the lodge.
We shall have butter, cheese, and venison,
And yesterday I brought for Margaret
A lusty bottle of neat claret wine;
Thus can we feast and entertain Your Grace.
EDWARD 'Tis cheer, Lord Lacy, for an emperor,

8. This celebrated courtesan was a longtime companion to Pericles of Athens (fifth century B.C.E.). She came from Miletus, near the coast of what was then Persia under King Cyrus, and was an accomplished woman.

If he respect the person and the place.
Come, let us in, for I will all this night
Ride post until I come to Bacon's cell. *Exeunt.*

[Scene 9]

Enter [King] Henry, Emperor, Castile, [the Duke of Saxony,] Elinor, Vandermast, Bungay [and other lords and attendants].

EMPEROR [*to King Henry*] Trust me, Plantagenet, these Oxford schools
Are richly seated near the riverside,
The mountains full of fat and fallow deer,
The battling pastures laid with kine[1] and flocks,
The town gorgeous with high-built colleges,
And scholars seemly in their grave attire,
Learnèd in searching principles of art.—
What is thy judgment, Jaques Vandermast?
VANDERMAST That lordly are the buildings of the town,
Spacious the rooms, and full of pleasant walks.
But for° the doctors, how that they be learnèd, *as for*
It may be meanly,° for aught I can hear. *slenderly*
BUNGAY I tell thee, German, Hapsburg holds none such,
None read so deep° as Oxenford contains. *deeply, widely*
There are within our academic state
Men that may lecture it in Germany
To all the doctors of your Belgic schools.
KING HENRY Stand to him, Bungay. Charm° this Vandermast, *Overcome*
And I will use thee as a royal king.° *as a king should do*
VANDERMAST [*to Bungay*] Wherein darest thou dispute with me?
BUNGAY In what a doctor and a friar can.
VANDERMAST Before rich Europe's worthies,° put thou forth *aristocrats*
The doubtful question° unto Vandermast. *question for debate*
BUNGAY Let it be this: whether the spirits of pyromancy° *divination by fire*
Or geomancy° be most predominant in magic. *divination by earth*
VANDERMAST I say, of pyromancy.
BUNGAY And I, of geomancy.
VANDERMAST The cabalists that write of magic spells,
As Hermes, Melchie, and Pythagoras,[2]
Affirm that 'mongst the quadruplicity
Of elemental essence,° *terra*° is but thought *the four elements / earth*
To be a *punctum* squarèd to° the rest, *an atom compared with*
And that the compass° of ascending elements *proportionate size*
Exceed in bigness as they do in height—
Judging the concave circle of the sun
To hold the rest in his° circumference. *its*
If then, as Hermes says, the fire be great'st,
Purest, and only° giveth shapes to spirits, *alone*
Then must these demons° that haunt that place *supernatural beings*
Be every way superior to the rest.

Scene 9. Oxford.
1. The nourishing pastures laden with cattle.
2. Hermes Trismagistrus was a famous medieval occultist; Malchus Porphyry was a Neoplatonic philosopher; Pythagoras practiced his mystical numerology in the sixth century B.C.E.

BUNGAY I reason not of elemental shapes,
Nor tell I of the concave latitudes,
Noting their essence nor their quality,
But of the spirits that pyromancy calls,
And of the vigor of the geomantic fiends.
I tell thee, German, magic haunts the grounds,° *earth*
And those strange necromantic spells
That work such shows and wondering in the world
Are acted by those geomantic spirits
That Hermes calleth *terrae filii*.° *sons of the earth*
The fiery spirits are but transparant shades,° *specters, ghosts*
That lightly pass as heralds to bear news;
But earthly fiends, closed in the lowest deep,
Dissever mountains, if they be but charged,° *commanded*
Being more gross and massy° in their power. *massive and mighty*
VANDERMAST Rather, these earthly geomantic spirits
Are dull and like the place where they remain;
For when proud Lucifer fell from the heavens,
The spirits and angels that did sin with him
Retained their local essence° as their faults, *defining character*
All subject under Luna's continent.[3]
They which offended less[4] hang in the fire,
And second° faults did rest within the air; *lesser*
But Lucifer and his proudhearted fiends
Were thrown into the center of the earth,
Having less understanding than the rest,
As having greater sin and lesser grace.
Therefore such gross and earthly spirits do serve
For jugglers, witches, and vile sorcerers,
Whereas the pyromantic genii
Are mighty, swift, and of far-reaching power.
But, grant° that geomancy hath most force, *supposing*
Bungay, to please these mighty potentates,
Prove by some instance what thy art can do.
BUNGAY I will.
EMPEROR Now, English Harry, here begins the game;
We shall see sport between these learnèd men.
VANDERMAST What wilt thou do?
BUNGAY Show thee the tree, leaved with refinèd gold,
Whereon the fearful dragon held his seat
That watched the garden called Hesperides,
Subdued and won by conquering Hercules.[5]
VANDERMAST Well done!

Here Bungay conjures, and the tree appears with the dragon shooting fire.

KING HENRY What say you, royal lordings, to my friar?
Hath he not done a point of cunning skill?
VANDERMAST Each scholar in the necromantic spells
Can do as much as Bungay hath performed.
But as Alcmena's bastard° razed this tree, *i.e., Hercules*

3. All confined to the sublunary sphere, subject to mutability.
4. I.e., Those angels who did not revolt.
5. The last of Hercules' twelve labors was to carry off the golden apples in the garden of the Hesperides, after having slain the guarding dragon.

So will I raise him up as when he lived,
And cause him pull the dragon from his seat,
And tear the branches piecemeal from the root.—
Hercules, *prodi!*° *Prodi,* Hercules! *come forth!*

Hercules appears in his lion's skin.

HERCULES *Quis me vult?*° *Who asks for me?*
VANDERMAST Jove's bastard son, thou Libyan Hercules,
Pull off the sprigs from off the Hesperian tree,
As once thou didst to win the golden fruit.
HERCULES *Fiat.*° *Here he begins to break the branches.* *Let it be done*
VANDERMAST Now, Bungay, if thou canst by magic charm° *bind, prevent*
The fiend appearing like great Hercules
From pulling down the branches of the tree,
Then art thou worthy to be counted learnèd.
BUNGAY [*trying with no success*] I cannot.
VANDERMAST Cease, Hercules, until I give thee charge.° *an order*
[*Hercules obeys.*]
[*To King Henry*] Mighty commander of this English isle,
Henry, come from the stout° Plantagenets, *brave*
Bungay is learned enough to be a friar,
But, to compare with Jaques Vandermast,
Oxford and Cambridge must go seek their cells
To find a man to match him in his art.
I have given nonplus° to the Paduans, *utter bafflement*
To them of Sien,° Florence, and Bologna, *Siena (Italy)*
Rheims, Louvain, and fair Rotterdam,
Frankfort, Utrecht, and Orleans.
And now must Henry, if he do me right,
Crown me with laurel, as they all have done.

Enter Bacon.

BACON All hail to this royal company
That sit to hear and see this strange dispute!—
Bungay, how stand'st thou as a man amazed!° *perplexed, stunned*
What, hath the German acted more than thou?
VANDERMAST What art thou that questions thus?
BACON Men call me Bacon.
VANDERMAST Lordly thou lookest, as if that thou wert learned;
Thy countenance, as if science° held her seat *learning*
Between the circled arches of thy brows.
KING HENRY Now, monarchs, hath the German found his match.
EMPEROR Bestir thee, Jaques. Take not now the foil,° *Don't get thrown*
Lest thou dost lose what foretime° thou didst gain. *previously*
VANDERMAST Bacon, wilt thou dispute?
BACON No, unless he° were more learned than Vandermast. *(the one I'm to confront)*
For yet, tell me, what hast thou done?
VANDERMAST Raised Hercules to ruinate that tree
That Bungay mounted° by his magic spells. *raised up*
BACON Set Hercules to work.
VANDERMAST Now, Hercules, I charge thee to thy task:
Pull off the golden branches from the root.
HERCULES I dare not. See'st thou not great Bacon here,

Whose frown doth act more than thy magic can?
VANDERMAST By all the thrones and dominations,° *orders of spirits*
Virtues, powers, and mighty hierarchies,
I charge thee to obey to° Vandermast. *give obedience to*
HERCULES Bacon, that bridles headstrong Belcephon,° *(see 2.56 and 117)*
And rules Asmenoth,° guider of the north, *another devil*
Binds me from yielding unto° Vandermast. *obeying*
KING HENRY How now, Vandermast, have you met with your match?
VANDERMAST Never before was't known to Vandermast
That men held devils in such obedient awe.
Bacon doth more than art,° or else I fail. *magical skill*
EMPEROR Why, Vandermast, art thou overcome?—
Bacon, dispute with him and try his skill.
BACON I come not, monarchs, for to hold dispute
With such a novice as is Vandermast;
I come to have your royalties to dine
With Friar Bacon here in Brazennose.
And, for° this German troubles but° the place, *because / merely troubles*
And holds this audience with a long suspense,
I'll send him to his academy hence.—
Thou Hercules, whom Vandermast did raise,
Transport the German unto Hapsburg straight,
That he may learn by travail, 'gainst the spring,° *in time for spring*
More secret dooms° and aphorisms of art. *judgments*
Vanish° the tree, and thou away with him! *Cause to vanish*
Exit the spirit° with Vandermast and the tree. *(Hercules)*
EMPEROR Why, Bacon, whither dost thou send him?
BACON To Hapsburg; there Your Highness, at return,
Shall find the German in his study safe.
KING HENRY Bacon, thou hast honored England with thy skill,
And made fair Oxford famous by thine art;
I will be English Henry to thyself.[6]
But tell me, shall we dine with thee today?
BACON With me, my lord. And, while I fit my cheer,° *prepare my feast*
See where Prince Edward comes to welcome you,
Gracious as the morning star of heaven. *Exit.*

Enter Edward, Lacy, Warren, [and] Ermsby.

EMPEROR Is this Prince Edward, Henry's royal son?
How martial is the figure of his face,
Yet lovely and beset with amorets!° *looks inspiring love*
KING HENRY Ned, where hast thou been?
EDWARD At Framlingham, my lord, to try your bucks,
If they could scape the teasers° or the toil.° *hunting hounds / net*
But hearing of these lordly potentates
Landed and progressed° up to Oxford town, *coming in a royal tour*
I posted to give entertain° to them— *welcome*
Chief to the Almain monarch. Next to him,
And joint with him, Castile and Saxony° *(see scene 7, n. 2)*
Are welcome as they may be to the English court.
Thus for the men. But see! Venus appears,
Or one that overmatcheth Venus in her shape.—

6. I.e., As King of England, I will acknowledge and proclaim your greatness.

Sweet Elinor, beauty's high-swelling pride,
Rich nature's glory and her wealth at once,
Fair of all fairs, welcome to Albion!
Welcome to me, and welcome to thine own,
If that thou deign'st the welcome from myself.

ELINOR Martial Plantagenet, Henry's high-minded son,
The mark that Elinor did count her aim,[7]
I liked thee 'fore I saw thee. Now I love,
And so° as in so short a time I may; *even so*
Yet so as° time shall never break that "so," *in such a way as*
And therefore so accept of Elinor.

CASTILE [*to King Henry*] Fear not, my lord, this couple will agree,
If love may creep into their wanton eyes.—
And therefore, Edward, I accept thee here,
Without suspense, as my adopted son.

KING HENRY Let me, that joy in these consorting greets,° *greetings at joining*
And glory in these honors done to Ned,
Yield° thanks for all these favors to my son, *Give*
And rest° a true Plantagenet to all. *remain*

Enter Miles with a cloth and trenchers° and salt. *wooden plates*

MILES *Salvete, omnes reges,°* *Hail, all you kings*
That govern your *greges°* *subjects*
In Saxony and Spain,
In England and in Almain!
For all this frolic rabble
Must I cover the table,
With trenchers, salt, and cloth;
And then look for your broth.

EMPEROR What pleasant° fellow is this? *jocular*

KING HENRY 'Tis, my lord, Doctor Bacon's poor scholar.

MILES [*aside*] My master hath made me sewer° of these great lords; and, God knows, I am as serviceable at a table as a sow is under an apple tree. 'Tis no matter; their cheer° shall not be great, and therefore what skills where the salt stand, before or behind?[8] [*Exit.*]
butler / *repast, entertainment*

CASTILE These scholars knows° more skill in axioms, *know*
How to use quips and sleights° of sophistry, *tricks*
Than for to cover° courtly for a king. *lay the table*

Enter Miles with a mess° of pottage° and broth, and, after him, Bacon. *helping / thick soup*

MILES Spill, sir? Why, do you think I never carried twopenny
chop° before in my life?— *cut of meat*
By your leave, *nobile decus,°* *Your worshipful Honor*
For here comes Doctor Bacon's *pecus,°* *beast of burden*
Being in his full age,
To carry a mess of pottage.

BACON Lordings, admire not° if your cheer be this, *do not wonder*
For we must keep° our academic fare; *keep to*
No riot° where philosophy doth reign. *extravagance*

7. The person at whom Elinor has aimed her intent.
8. What does it matter who sits above or below the salt, marking the division between the most honored guests and the rest?

And therefore, Henry, place° these potentates, *assign places to*
And bid them fall unto their frugal cates.° *provisions*
EMPEROR Presumptuous friar! What, scoff'st thou at a king?
What, dost thou taunt us with thy peasants' fare,
And give us cates fit for country swains?—
Henry, proceeds this jest of° thy consent, *with*
To twit us with a pittance of such price?
Tell me, and Frederick will not grieve thee long.° *i.e., won't stay long*
KING HENRY By Henry's honor, and the royal faith
The English monarch beareth to his friend,
I knew not of the Friar's feeble fare,
Nor am I pleased he entertains you thus.
BACON Content thee, Frederick, for I showed the cates
To let thee see how scholars use° to feed, *are accustomed*
How little meat° refines our English wits.— *food*
Miles, take away, and let it be thy dinner.
MILES Marry, sir, I will.
This day shall be a festival day with me,
For I shall exceed in the highest degree. *Exit Miles.*
BACON [*to the Emperor*] I tell thee, monarch, all the German peers
Could not afford thy entertainment, such—
So royal and so full of majesty—
As Bacon will present to Frederick.
The basest waiter that attends thy cups
Shall be in honors greater than thyself;
[*To Henry*] And for thy cates, rich Alexandria drugs,° *spices*
Fetched by carvels° from Egypt's richest straits, *caravels, ships*
Found in the wealthy strand° of Africa, *shore*
Shall royalize the table of my king.
Wines, richer than the 'Gyptian courtesan° *Cleopatra*
Quaffed to Augustus' kingly countermatch,° *rival, i.e., Antony*
Shall be caroused° in English Henry's feasts; *drunk abundantly*
Candy° shall yield the richest of her canes;° *Crete / sugarcanes*
Persia, down her Volga° by canoes, *(in Russia, not Persia)*
Send° down the secrets of her spicery; *Will send*
The Afric dates, mirabiles° of Spain, *myrobalans, dried plums*
Conserves, and suckets° from Tiberias,° *sweetmeats / (in Galilee)*
Cates from Judaea choicer than the lamp[9]
That fired Rome with sparks of gluttony,
Shall beautify the board for Frederick;
And therefore grudge° not at a friar's feast. [*Exeunt.*] *complain*

[Scene 10]

Enter two gentlemen, Lambert and Serlsby, with the Keeper.

LAMBERT Come, frolic Keeper of our liege's game,
Whose table spread hath ever venison
And jacks° of wine to welcome passengers,° *pitchers / travelers*
Know I am in love with jolly Margaret,

9. Perhaps the lamprey eel, a delicacy in some of the more decadant Roman meals.

Scene 10. Fressingfield.

That overshines our damsels as the moon
Dark'neth the brightest sparkles° of the night. *stars*
In Laxfield° here my land and living lies. *(near Framlingham)*
I'll make thy daughter jointure° of it all, *joint possession*
So° thou consent to give her to° my wife; *Provided / for, to be*
And I can spend° five hundreth° marks a year. *My income is / hundred*
SERLSBY I am the landslord, Keeper, of thy holds;° *holdings, property*
By copy° all thy living lies in me. *copyhold tenure*
Laxfield did never see me raise my due.° *the rent due to me*
I will enfeoff° fair Margaret in all, *give possession to*
So she will take° her to a lusty squire. *betake*
KEEPER Now, courteous gentles,° if the Keeper's girl *gentlemen*
Hath pleased the liking fancy of you both,
And with her beauty hath subdued your thoughts,
'Tis doubtful° to decide the question. *difficult*
It joys me that such men of great esteem
Should lay their liking on this base estate,
And that her state should grow so fortunate
To be a wife to meaner° men than you. *even to humbler*
But sith° such squires will stoop to keeper's fee,° *since / income, status*
I will, to avoid displeasure of you both,
Call Margaret forth, and she shall make her choice.
LAMBERT Content, Keeper. Send her unto us. *Exit [Keeper].*
Why, Serlsby, is thy wife so lately dead?
Are all thy loves° so lightly passèd over *loyalty to her memory*
As thou canst wed before the year be out?
SERLSBY I live not, Lambert, to content the dead,
Nor was I wedded but for life to her.
The grave ends and begins a married state.[1]

Enter Margaret.

LAMBERT Peggy, the lovely flower of all towns,
Suffolk's fair Helen,° and rich England's star, *Helen of Troy*
Whose beauty, tempered° with her huswif'ry, *mixed, accompanied*
Makes England talk of merry Fressingfield!
SERLSBY I cannot trick it up with poesies,[2]
Nor paint my passions with comparisons,° *poetic metaphors*
Nor tell a tale of Phoebus° and his loves, *Apollo, god of light*
But this believe me: Laxfield here is mine,
Of ancient° rent seven hundred pounds a year, *long-standing*
And if thou canst but love a country squire
I will enfeoff thee, Margaret, in all.
I cannot flatter; try me, if thou please.
MARGARET Brave neighboring squires, the stay° of Suffolk's *mainstay*
clime,° *region*
A keeper's daughter is too base in 'gree° *degree*
To match with men accounted of such worth.
But might I not displease, I would reply.
LAMBERT Say, Peggy. Naught shall make us discontent.
MARGARET Then, gentles, note that love hath little stay,° *staying power*
Nor can the flames that Venus sets on fire
Be kindled but by fancy's motion.° *urging*

1. Death ends one marriage and provides opportunity for another.
2. I cannot decorate my speech with flowery conceits.

Then pardon, gentles, if a maid's reply
Be doubtful, while° I have debated with myself, *until*
Who, or of whom, love shall constrain me like.

SERLSBY Let it be me; and trust me, Margaret,
The meads° environed with the silver streams, *meadows*
Whose battling° pastures fatt'neth all my flocks, *nourishing*
Yielding forth fleeces stapled° with such wool *fibered*
As Lempster° cannot yield more finer stuff, *Leominster*
And forty kine° with fair and burnished heads, *cattle*
With strouting° dugs that paggle° to the ground, *swelling / hang down*
Shall serve thy dairy, if thou wed with me.

LAMBERT Let pass° the country wealth, as flocks and kine, *Forget about*
And lands that wave with Ceres'° golden sheaves, *goddess of the harvest*
Filling my barns with plenty of the fields.
But, Peggy, if thou wed thyself to me,
Thou shalt have garments of embroidered silk,
Lawns,° and rich networks for thy head-attire. *Fine linen*
Costly shall be thy fair habiliments,° *garments*
If thou wilt be but Lambert's loving wife.

MARGARET Content you, gentles. You have proffered fair,
And more than fits a country maid's degree;
But give me leave to counsel me° a time, *consider by myself*
For fancy blooms not at the first assault.
Give me but ten days' respite and I will reply,
Which or to whom myself affectionates.° *I feel affection*

SERLSBY Lambert, I tell thee, thou art importunate.
Such beauty fits not such a base esquire.
It is for Serlsby to have Margaret.

LAMBERT Think'st thou with wealth to overreach me?
Serlsby, I scorn to brook° thy country braves.° *put up with / boasts*
I dare thee, coward, to maintain this wrong,
At dint of rapier,° single in the field. *By means of sword*

SERLSBY I'll answer, Lambert, what I have avouched.—
Margaret, farewell. Another time shall serve. *Exit Serlsby.*

LAMBERT I'll follow.—Peggy, farewell to thyself.
Listen how well I'll answer for thy love. *Exit Lambert.*

MARGARET How Fortune tempers lucky haps° with frowns, *happenings*
And wrongs me with the sweets of my delight!
Love is my bliss, and love is now my bale.° *woe*
Shall I be Helen in my forward° fates, *froward, perverse*
As I am Helen in my matchless hue,
And set rich Suffolk with my face afire?
If lovely Lacy were but with his Peggy,
The cloudy darkness of his bitter frown
Would check the pride of these aspiring squires.
Before the term of ten days be expired,
Whenas they look for answer of their loves,
My lord will come to merry Fressingfield
And end their fancies and their follies both;
Till when, Peggy, be blithe and of good cheer.

Enter a Post with a letter and a bag of gold.

POST Fair lovely damsel, which way leads this path?
How might I post me° unto Fressingfield? *hasten*
Which footpath leadeth to the Keeper's lodge?

MARGARET Your way is ready° and this path is right. — *close at hand*
Myself do dwell hereby in Fressingfield,
And if the Keeper be the man you seek,
I am his daughter. May I know the cause?
POST Lovely and once belovèd of my lord—
No marvel if his eye was lodged so low,
When brighter beauty is not in the heavens—
The Lincoln earl hath sent you letters here,
And with them, just° an hundred pounds in gold. — *exactly*
[*He delivers the money and the letter.*]
Sweet bonny wench, read them and make reply.
MARGARET The scrolls that Jove sent Danaë,° — *(see 8.68 n)*
Wrapped in rich closures° of fine burnished gold, — *coverings*
Were not° more welcome than these lines to me. — *Would not be*
Tell me, whilst that I do unrip the seals,
Lives Lacy well? How fares my lovely lord?
POST Well, if that° wealth may make men to live well. — *if*
The letter, and Margaret reads it.
MARGARET "The blooms of the almond tree grow in a night and vanish in a morn; the flies hemerae,[3] fair Peggy, take life with the sun and die with the dew; fancy, that slippeth in with a gaze, goeth out with a wink; and too timely loves° (*overhasty passions*) have ever the shortest length. I write this as thy grief and my folly, who at Fressingfield loved that which time hath taught me to be but mean° (*lowly, unworthy*) dainties. Eyes are dissemblers, and fancy is but queasy.° (*nothing if not fickle*) Therefore know, Margaret, I have chosen a Spanish lady to be my wife, chief waiting-woman to the Princess Elinor—a lady fair, and no less fair than thyself, honorable, and wealthy. In that I forsake thee, I leave thee to thine own liking;° (*inclination*) and for thy dowry I have sent thee an hundred pounds, and ever assure thee of my favor, which shall avail° (*benefit*) thee and thine much.
Farewell. Not thine nor his own,
Edward Lacy."
Fond Até,° doomer° of bad-boding fates, — *Blind Folly / judge*
That wraps proud Fortune in thy snaky locks,
Didst thou enchant° my birthday with such stars — *lay under a spell*
As lightened° mischief from their infancy? — *beamed down*
If heavens had vowed, if stars had made decree
To show on me their froward° influence, — *malign*
If° Lacy had but loved, heavens, hell, and all — *So long as*
Could not have wronged the patience of my mind.
POST It grieves me, damsel, but the Earl is forced
To love the lady, by the King's command.
MARGARET The wealth combined within the English shelves,° — *cliffs*
Europe's commander,° nor the English king — *emperor*
Should not have moved the love of Peggy from her lord.
POST What answer shall I return to my lord?
MARGARET First, for° thou cam'st from Lacy, whom I loved— — *because*
Ah, give me leave to sigh at every thought!—
Take thou, my friend, the hundred pound he sent,

3. Ephemerae, insects that live for only a day. The letter is in the euphuistic style, after John Lyly's *Euphues* (1578–80), with fanciful natural history, antithetical sentence structures, etc.

For Margaret's resolution craves no dower.
[*She returns the gold.*]
The world shall be to her as vanity;
Wealth, trash; love, hate; pleasure, despair.
For I will straight to stately Framlingham,
And in the abbey there be shorn° a nun, *have my hair cut short as*
And yield my loves and liberty to God.
Fellow, I give thee this, not for the news—
For those be hateful unto Margaret—
But for° thou'rt Lacy's man, once Margaret's love. *because*
POST What I have heard, what passions I have seen,
I'll make report of them unto the Earl. *Exit Post.*
MARGARET Say that she joys his fancies be at rest,
And prays that his misfortune may be hers.[4] *Exit.*

[Scene 11]

Enter Friar Bacon, drawing the curtains with a white stick,° a book in his hand, and a lamp lighted by him; and the Brazen Head, and Miles, with weapons by him. *conjuring wand*

BACON Miles, where are you?
MILES Here, sir.
BACON How chance you tarry so long?
MILES Think you that the watching of the Brazen Head craves no furniture?° I warrant you, sir, I have so armed myself that, if all your devils come, I will not fear them an inch. *requires no weapons*
BACON Miles, thou knowest that I have dived into hell,
And sought the darkest palaces of fiends,
That with my magic spells great Belcephon
Hath left his lodge and kneelèd at my cell;
The rafters of the earth rent° from the poles, *were torn*
And three-formed Luna[1] hid her silver looks,
Trembling upon her concave continent,° *sphere, orbit*
When Bacon[2] read upon his magic book.
With seven years' tossing necromantic charms,
Poring upon dark Hecate's° principles, *goddess of witchcraft*
I have framed out° a monstrous head of brass, *fashioned*
That, by the enchanting forces of the devil,
Shall tell out strange and uncouth° aphorisms, *remarkable*
And girt fair England with a wall of brass.
Bungay and I have watched these threescore days,
And now our vital spirits crave some rest.
If Argus[3] lived and had his hundred eyes,
They could not overwatch Phobeter's[4] night.
Now, Miles, in thee rests Friar Bacon's weal;° *welfare*
The honor and renown of all his life
Hangs in the watching of this Brazen Head.
Therefore I charge thee by the immortal God,

4. And prays that any misfortune falls on me, leaving him entirely fortunate.
Scene 11. Oxford. Bacon's cell.
1. Comprising simultaneously Luna (the moon), Diana, and Hecate, forming a triple deity.
2. Recalling also Roger Bacon, a thirteenth-century English philosopher, scientist, and reputed magician.
3. The watchman with eyes all over his body, sent by Hera to watch over Io (a princess of Argos) when Hera's husband, Zeus, fell in love with Io and transformed her into a heifer in an ineffectual attempt to conceal her from Hera's eyes.
4. I.e., Morpheus' (the god of sleep). Literally, "the terrifier."

That holds the souls of men within his fist,
This night thou watch, for, ere the morning star
Sends out his glorious glister on the north,
The Head will speak. Then, Miles, upon thy life,
Wake me; for then by magic art I'll work
To end my seven years' task with excellence.
If that a wink but shut thy watchful eye,
Then farewell Bacon's glory and his fame!
Draw close the curtains. Miles, now for thy life,
Be watchful and— *Here he falleth asleep.*

MILES So, I thought you would talk yourself asleep anon; and
'tis no marvel, for Bungay on the days, and he on the nights,
have watched just these ten-and-fifty days. Now this is the
night, and 'tis my task, and no more. [*He examines the Brazen Head.*] Now Jesus bless me! What a goodly head it is,
and a nose! You talk of *nos autem glorificare*,° but here's a *yet glorify us*
nose that, I warrant, may be called *nos autem popelare*[5] for
the people of the parish. Well, I am furnished with weapons.
Now, sir, I will set me down by a post, and make it° as good *(the Brazen Head)*
as a watchman to wake me if I chance to slumber. I thought,
goodman° Head, I would call you out of your *memento*.° (*Sit* *(cf. 3.56) / reverie*
down, and knock your head.) Passion o' God! I have almost
broke my pate. Up, Miles, to your task! Take your brown
bill° in your hand. Here's some of your master's hobgoblins *a pike, halberd*
abroad. *With this, a great noise. The Head speaks.*

HEAD Time is.

MILES Time is? Why, Master Brazen Head, have you such a
capital nose, and answer you with syllables, "Time is"? Is
this all my master's cunning, to spend seven years' study
about "Time is"? Well, sir, it may be we shall have some
better orations of it anon. Well, I'll watch you as narrowly
as ever you were watched, and I'll play with you as the nightingale with the slowworm;° I'll set a prick against my breast.[6] *a small lizard*
[*He leans a halberd against his breast.*] Now rest there, Miles.
[*He falls over.*] Lord have mercy upon me! I have almost
killed myself. Up, Miles! [*A loud noise again.*] List° how they *Listen*
rumble!

HEAD Time was.

MILES Well, Friar Bacon, you spent your seven years' study
well, that can make your Head speak but two words at once.
"Time was." Yea, marry, time was when my master was a
wise man, but that was before he began to make the Brazen
Head. You shall lie° while your arse ache an° your Head *lie abed / if*
speak no better. Well, I will watch and walk up and down,
and be a peripatetian and a philosopher of Aristotle's stamp.[7]
[*A loud noise again.*] What, a fresh noise? Take thy pistols
in hand, Miles.

5. An overly ingenious and untranslatable Latin pun on the liturgical phrase in line 44. *Popa* in Latin means "parish priest"; hence, perhaps, "the parish" in line 46.

6. The nightingale traditionally leaned its breast against a thorn to keep itself in pain and thus awake in order to render its sad song. This image is combined with that of a bird seeming to play with its prey, a small wormlike lizard.

7. Aristotle founded the school of philosophy that came to be known as the Peripatetic school, owing to his habit of walking up and down in the paths of the Lyceum while conversing with his pupils.

Here the Head speaks, and a lightning flasheth forth, and a hand appears that breaketh down the Head with a hammer.

HEAD Time is past.

MILES Master, master, up! Hell's broken loose! Your Head speaks, and there's such a thunder and lightning that, I warrant, all Oxford is up in arms. Out of your bed and take a brown bill in your hand! The latter day° is come. — *Judgment Day*

BACON [*awaking*] Miles, I come. Oh, passing° warily watched! — *exceedingly*
Bacon will make thee next himself in love.[8]
When spake the Head?

MILES When spake the Head? Did not you say that he should tell strange principles of philosophy? Why, sir, it speaks but two words at a time.

BACON Why, villain, hath it spoken oft?

MILES Oft? Ay, marry, hath it, thrice: but in all those three times it hath uttered but seven words.

BACON As how?

MILES Marry, sir, the first time he said, "Time is," as if Fabius Cumentator[9] should have pronounced a sentence. He said, "Time was," and the third time, with thunder and lightning, as in great choler,° he said, "Time is past." — *anger*

BACON 'Tis past indeed. Ah, villain! Time is past:
My life, my fame, my glory, all are past!
Bacon, the turrets of thy hope are ruined down.
Thy seven years' study lieth in the dust;
Thy Brazen Head lies broken through a slave° — *wretch, menial*
That watched, and would not when the Head did will.[1]—
What said the Head first?

MILES Even, sir, "Time is."

BACON Villain, if thou hadst called to Bacon then,
If thou hadst watched and waked the sleepy friar,
The Brazen Head had uttered aphorisms,
And England had been circled round with brass.
But proud Astmeroth,° ruler of the north, — *i.e., Asmenoth (9.142)*
And Demogorgon, master of the Fates,
Grudge that a mortal man should work° so much. — *achieve*
Hell trembled at my deep commanding spells;
Fiends frowned to see a man their overmatch.
Bacon might boast more than a man might boast,
But now the braves° of Bacon hath an end; — *boasts*
Europe's conceit° of Bacon hath an end. — *opinion*
His seven years' practice sorteth° to ill end; — *comes*
And, villain, sith° my glory hath an end, — *since*
I will appoint thee fatal to some end.° — *doomed to a fatal end*
Villain, avoid!° Get thee from Bacon's sight. — *get away, begone!*
Vagrant, go roam and range about the world,
And perish as a vagabond on earth.

MILES Why then, sir, you forbid me your service?

8. You will be famous and revered second only to myself.
9. Presumably Miles means the ancient Roman general Fabius Maximus, surnamed "Cunctator," Latin for "the delayer," for his canny reluctance to engage in battle with Hannibal after the latter's victory over the Romans at Lake Trasimene, in 217 B.C.E.
1. And who failed to keep watch properly when the Head wished to speak.

BACON My service, villain, with a fatal curse
That direful plagues and mischief fall on thee!

MILES 'Tis no matter. I am against you° with the old proverb "The more the fox is cursed, the better he fares."[2] God be with you, sir. I'll take but a book in my hand, a wide-sleeved gown on my back, and a crowned cap on my head, and see if I can want° promotion. *beforehand with you* / *lack*

BACON Some fiend or ghost haunt on thy weary steps,
Until they do transport thee quick° to hell! [*Exit Miles.*] *alive*
For Bacon shall have never merry day
To lose the fame and honor of his Head. *Exit.*

[Scene 12]

Enter Emperor, Castile, [*King*] *Henry, Elinor, Edward, Lacy,* [*and*] *Rafe.*

EMPEROR [*to Edward*] Now, lovely prince, the prince of Albion's wealth,
How fares the Lady Elinor and you?
What, have you courted and found Castile fit
To answer England in equivalence?
Will't be a match 'twixt bonny Nell and thee?

EDWARD Should Paris enter in the courts of Greece
And not lie fettered in fair Helen's looks?
Or Phoebus scape those piercing amorets° *looks of love*
That Daphne glancèd at his deity?° *(see 6.50)*
Can Edward then sit by a flame and freeze,
Whose heat puts Helen and fair Daphne down?° *in the shade*
Now, monarchs, ask the lady if we 'gree.

KING HENRY [*to Elinor*] What, madam, hath my son found grace or no?

ELINOR Seeing, my lord, his lovely counterfeit,° *portrait*
And hearing how his mind and shape agreed,
I come not, trooped° with all this warlike train,° *accompanied / retinue*
Doubting of love, but so affectionate
As° Edward hath in England what he won in Spain. *That*

CASTILE [*to King Henry*] A match, my lord! These wantons needs must love.
Men must have wives, and women will be wed.
Let's haste the day to honor up the rites.

RAFE Sirrah Harry, shall Ned marry Nell?

KING HENRY Ay, Rafe. How then?

RAFE Marry, Harry, follow my counsel: send for Friar Bacon to marry them, for he'll so conjure him and her with his necromancy that they shall love together like pig and lamb whilst they live.

CASTILE But hear'st thou, Rafe: art thou content to have Elinor to thy lady?

RAFE Ay, so she will promise me two things.

2. With puns: "cursed": (1) sworn at; (2) coursed, pursued; "fares": (1) succeeds; (2) goes.

Scene 12. The royal court.

CASTILE What's that, Rafe?
RAFE That she will never scold with Ned nor fight with me.
[Castile and Lacy converse privately apart.]
[*To King Henry*] Sirrah Harry, I have put her down with a thing unpossible.
KING HENRY What's that, Rafe?
RAFE Why, Harry, didst thou ever see that a woman could both hold her tongue and her hands? No. But when egg pies grows° on apple trees, then will thy gray mare prove a bagpiper.° — *grow* / *(impossibilities)*
EMPEROR What says the Lord of Castile and the Earl of Lincoln, that they are in such earnest and secret talk?
CASTILE I stand, my lord, amazèd at his talk,
How he discourseth of the constancy
Of one surnamed, for beauty's excellence,
The fair maid of merry Fressingfield.
KING HENRY 'Tis true, my lord, 'tis wondrous for to hear;
Her beauty passing Mars's paramour,° — *Venus*
Her virgin's right as rich as Vesta's° was. — *goddess of the hearth*
Lacy and Ned hath told me miracles.
CASTILE What says Lord Lacy? Shall she be his wife?
LACY Or else Lord Lacy is unfit to live.—
May it please Your Highness give me leave to post
To Fressingfield, I'll fetch the bonny girl,
And prove in true appearance at the court
What I have vouchèd often with my tongue.
KING HENRY Lacy, go to the querry° of my stable, — *equerry, groom*
And take such coursers° as shall fit thy turn. — *spirited horses*
Hie thee to Fressingfield and bring home the lass,
And, for° her fame flies through the English coast,° — *because / land*
If it may please the Lady Elinor,
One day shall match Your Excellence and her.[1]
ELINOR We Castile ladies are not very coy.° — *distant, aloof*
Your Highness may command a greater boon,
And glad were I to grace the Lincoln earl
With being partner of his marriage day.
EDWARD Gramercy, Nell, for I do love the lord
As he that's second to myself in love.[2]
RAFE You love her?—Madam Nell, never believe him you, though he swears he loves you.
ELINOR Why, Rafe?
RAFE Why, his love is like unto a tapster's° glass that is broken with every touch, for he loved the fair maid of Fressingfield once out of all ho.°—Nay, Ned, never wink upon me. I care not, I. — *bartender's* / *out of all bounds*
KING HENRY Rafe tells all; you shall have a good secretary of him.—
But, Lacy, haste thee post to Fressingfield;
For, ere thou hast fitted all things for her state,
The solemn° marriage day will be at hand. — *ceremonial*
LACY I go, my lord. *Exit Lacy.*

1. One day will serve for both weddings.
2. I love Lacy as the closest to my heart after my first attachment to you (Elinor).

EMPEROR How shall we pass this day, my lord?
KING HENRY To horse, my lord. The day is passing fair.
We'll fly° the partridge or go rouse the deer.— *flush from cover*
Follow, my lords; you shall not want for sport. *Exeunt.*

[Scene 13]

Enter Friar Bacon with Friar Bungay to his cell.

BUNGAY What means the friar, that frolicked it of late,
To sit as melancholy in his cell
As if he had neither lost nor won today?° *As if at a loss*
BACON Ah, Bungay, my Brazen Head is spoiled,
My glory gone, my seven years' study lost!
The fame of Bacon, bruited° through the world, *reported*
Shall end and perish with this deep disgrace.
BUNGAY Bacon hath built foundation of his fame
So surely on the wings of true report,
With acting strange and uncouth° miracles, *remarkable*
As this cannot infringe what he deserves.
BACON Bungay, sit down, for by prospective skill
I find this day shall fall out ominous.
Some deadly act shall 'tide° me ere I sleep; *betide, happen to*
But what and wherein, little can I guess.
BUNGAY My mind is heavy, whatsoe'er shall hap. *Knock.*
BACON Who's that knocks?
BUNGAY [*going to the door*] Two scholars that desires° to speak with you. *desire*
BACON Bid them come in.

Enter two Scholars, sons to Lambert and Serlsby.

Now, my youths, what would you have?
FIRST SCHOLAR Sir, we are Suffolk men and neighboring friends;
Our fathers in their countries lusty° squires. *vigorous*
Their lands adjoin: in Crackfield° mine doth dwell, *Cratfield*
And his in Laxfield. We are college mates,
Sworn brothers, as our fathers lives° as friends. *live*
BACON To what end is all this?
SECOND SCHOLAR Hearing Your Worship kept within your cell
A glass prospective wherein men might see
Whatso their thoughts or hearts' desire could wish,
We come to know how that our fathers fare.
BACON My glass is free for every honest man.
Sit down, and you shall see ere long
How or in what state your friendly fathers lives.° *live*
Meanwhile, tell me your names.
FIRST SCHOLAR Mine, Lambert.
SECOND SCHOLAR And mine, Serlsby.
BACON [*aside to Bungay*] Bungay, I smell there will be a tragedy.

Enter [as in the magic glass] Lambert and Serlsby, with rapiers and daggers.

Scene 13. Oxford. Bacon's cell.

LAMBERT *Serlsby, thou hast kept thine hour° like a man.* *appointment*
Thou'rt worthy of the title of a squire,
That durst, for proof of thy affection,
And for thy mistress' favor, prize° thy blood. *risk*
Thou know'st what words did pass at Fressingfield,
Such shameless braves° as manhood cannot brook°— *taunts / tolerate*
Ay, for I scorn to bear such piercing taunts.
Prepare thee, Serlsby; one of us will die.
SERLSBY *Thou see'st I single meet thee in the field,*
And what I spake I'll maintain with my sword.
Stand on thy guard; I cannot scold it out.
And if thou kill me, think I have a son,
That lives in Oxford in the Broadgates Hall,
Who will revenge his father's blood with blood.
LAMBERT *And, Serlsby, I have there a lusty boy,*
That dares at weapon buckle° with thy son, *encounter*
And lives in Broadgates too, as well as thine.
But draw thy rapier, for we'll have a bout.
BACON Now, lusty younkers,° look within the glass, *youths*
And tell me if you can discern your sires.
FIRST SCHOLAR Serlsby, 'tis hard; thy father offers wrong
To combat with my father in the field.
SECOND SCHOLAR Lambert, thou liest! My father's is the abuse,° *My father is wronged*
And thou shalt find it, if my father harm.° *comes to harm*
BUNGAY How goes it, sirs?
FIRST SCHOLAR Our fathers are in combat hard by Fressingfield.
BACON Sit still, my friends, and see the event.° *outcome*
LAMBERT *Why stand'st thou, Serlsby? Doubt'st thou of° thy life?* *Do you fear for*
A veney,° man! Fair Margaret craves so much. *A bout*
SERLSBY *Then this for her!* [*They fight.*]
FIRST SCHOLAR Ah, well thrust!
SECOND SCHOLAR But mark the ward.° *guard, parry*
They° fight and kill each other. *(The fathers)*
LAMBERT *Oh, I am slain!*
SERLSBY *And I. Lord have mercy on me!*
FIRST SCHOLAR My father slain!—Serlsby, ward° that! *guard, parry*
SECOND SCHOLAR And so is mine! Lambert, I'll quite° thee well. *requite*
The two scholars stab one another.
BUNGAY Oh, strange stratagem!° *violent outcome*
BACON See, Friar, where the fathers° both lie dead!— *(and the sons)*
Bacon, thy magic doth effect this massacre.
This glass prospective worketh many woes,
And therefore, seeing these brave lusty brutes,° *Britons; bruisers*
These friendly youths, did perish by thine art,
End all thy magic and thine art at once.
The poniard that did end the fatal° lives *doomed, fated*
Shall break the cause efficient° of their woes. *effective cause*
So fade the glass! And end with it the shows
That necromancy did infuse the crystal with.
He breaks the glass.
BUNGAY What means learned Bacon thus to break his glass?
BACON I tell thee, Bungay, it repents me sore

That ever Bacon meddled in this art.
The hours I have spent in pyromantic spells,
The fearful tossing in the latest night° *deep of night*
Of papers full of necromantic charms,
Conjuring and adjuring devils and fiends,
With stole and alb° and strange pentagonon,° *vestments / (see 2.51 n)*
The wresting° of the holy name of God, *misusing*
As Sother, Eloim, and Adonai,
Alpha, Manoth, and Tetragrammaton,[1]
With praying to the fivefold powers of heaven,
Are instances that Bacon must be damned
For using devils to countervail his God.
Yet, Bacon, cheer thee; drown not in despair!
Sins have their salves; repentance can do much.
Think Mercy sits where Justice holds her seat;
And from those wounds those° bloody Jews did pierce— *which those*
Which by thy magic oft did bleed afresh—
From thence for thee the dew of mercy drops
To wash the wrath of high Jehovah's ire,
And make thee as a newborn babe from sin.—
Bungay, I'll spend the remnant of my life
In pure devotion, praying to my God
That he would save what Bacon vainly lost.
Exit [*with Bungay*].

[Scene 14]

Enter Margaret in nun's apparel, Keeper (her father), and their Friend.

KEEPER Margaret, be not so headstrong in these vows.
Oh, bury not such beauty in a cell
That England hath held famous for the hue!
Thy father's hair, like to the silver blooms
That beautify the shrubs of Africa,
Shall fall before the dated° time of death, *destined*
Thus to forgo his lovely Margaret.
MARGARET Ah, father, when the harmony of heaven
Soundeth the measures of a lively faith,[1]
The vain illusions of this flattering world
Seems° odious to the thoughts of Margaret. *Seem*
I lovèd once—Lord Lacy was my love—
And now I hate myself for that I loved,
And doted more on him than on my God.
For this I scourge myself with sharp repents.° *penances*
But now the touch of such aspiring sins
Tells me all love is lust but love of heavens,
That° beauty used for love is vanity. *And tells me that*
The world contains naught but alluring baits:
Pride, flattery, and inconstant thoughts.
To shun the pricks of death I leave the world,
And vow to meditate on heavenly bliss,

1. Various emblematic and cabalistic ways of translating the Hebrew for "our Lord"—words thought to have occult power in themselves.

Scene 14. Fressingfield.
1. Sounds the celestial harmony of eternal, living faith.

To live in Framlingham a holy nun,
Holy and pure in conscience and in deed;
And for to wish all maids to learn of me
To seek heaven's joy before earth's vanity.

FRIEND And will you then, Margaret, be shorn a nun,° and so leave us all? *(see 10.160)*

MARGARET Now farewell, world, the engine° of all woe! *instrument*
Farewell to friends and father! Welcome, Christ!
Adieu to dainty robes! This base attire
Better befits an humble mind to God
Than all the show of rich habiliments.
Love, O love, and, with fond° love, farewell! *foolish*
Sweet Lacy, whom I lovèd once so dear,
Ever be well, but never in my thoughts,
Lest I offend to think on Lacy's love;
But even to that, as to the rest, farewell!

Enter Lacy, Warren, [and] Ermsby, booted and spurred.° [They do not see Margaret, the Keeper, and the Friend at first. Margaret stands to one side.] *dressed for travel*

LACY Come on, my wags. We're near the Keeper's lodge.
Here have I oft walked in the wat'ry meads,
And chatted with my lovely Margaret.

WARREN [*seeing the Keeper*] Sirrah Ned, is not this the Keeper?

LACY 'Tis the same.

ERMSBY The old lecher hath gotten holy mutton° to him: a nun, my lord! *i.e., a prostitute*

LACY [*approaching the Keeper*] Keeper, how farest thou?
Holla, man, what cheer?
How doth Peggy, thy daughter and my love?

KEEPER Ah, good my lord, oh, woe is me for Peg!
See where she stands clad in her nun's attire,
Ready for to be shorn in Framlingham.
She leaves the world because she left° your love. *i.e., lost*
Oh, good my lord, persuade her if you can.

LACY Why, how now, Margaret, what, a malcontent?
A nun? What holy father taught you this,
To task yourself to such a tedious life
As die a maid? 'Twere injury to me
To smother up such beauty in a cell.

MARGARET Lord Lacy, thinking of my former miss,° *error*
How fond° the prime of wanton years were spent *foolishly*
In love—oh, fie upon that fond conceit,° *foolish notion*
Whose hap and essence hangeth in the eye!°— *is only superficial*
I leave both love and love's content at once,
Betaking me to Him that is true Love,
And leaving all the world for love of Him.

LACY Whence, Peggy, comes this metamorphosis?
What, shorn a nun, and I have from the court
Posted with coursers to convey thee hence
To Windsor, where our marriage shall be kept?° *celebrated*
Thy wedding robes are in the tailors' hands.
Come, Peggy, leave these peremptory° vows. *obstinate*

MARGARET Did not my lord resign his interest,

And make divorce 'twixt Margaret and him?
LACY 'Twas but to try sweet Peggy's constancy.
But will fair Margaret leave her love and lord?
MARGARET Is not heaven's joy before earth's fading bliss,
And life above sweeter than life in love?
LACY Why, then, will Margaret be shorn a nun?
MARGARET Margaret hath made a vow which may not be
revoked.
WARREN We cannot stay, my lord. An if she be so strict,
Our leisure grants us not to woo afresh.
ERMSBY Choose you, fair damsel. Yet the choice is yours:
Either a solemn nunnery or the court,
God or Lord Lacy. Which contents you best,
To be a nun, or else Lord Lacy's wife?
LACY A good motion.°—Peggy, your answer must be short. *good way of putting it*
MARGARET The flesh is frail. My lord doth know it well,
That when he comes with his enchanting face,
Whatsoe'er betide, I cannot say him nay.
[*Removing her nun's apparel*] Off goes the habit of a
maiden's heart,
And, seeing Fortune will, fair Framlingham,
And all the show of holy nuns, farewell!
Lacy for me, if he will be my lord.
LACY Peggy, thy lord, thy love, thy husband!
Trust me, by truth° of knighthood, that the King *solemn covenant*
Stays for to marry matchless Elinor
Until I bring thee richly to the court,
That one day may both marry her and thee.—
How say'st thou, Keeper? Art thou glad of this?
KEEPER As if the English king had given
The park and deer of Fressingfield to me.
ERMSBY [*to Warren*] I pray thee, my lord of Sussex, why art
thou in a brown study?° *in a reverie*
WARREN To see the nature of women, that, be they never so
near God, yet they love to die° in a man's arms. *(with pun on "have sex")*
LACY What have you fit for breakfast? We have hied
And posted all this night to Fressingfield.
MARGARET Butter and cheese and humbles° of a deer, *heart, kidneys, liver*
Such as poor keepers have within their lodge.
LACY And not a bottle of wine?
MARGARET We'll find one for my lord.
LACY Come, Sussex, let's in. We shall have more,
For she speaks least, to hold her promise sure.[2] *Exeunt.*

[Scene 15]

Enter a Devil to seek Miles.

DEVIL How restless are the ghosts of hellish spirits,
When every charmer° with his magic spells *magician, conjurer*
Calls us from ninefold-trenchèd Phlegethon,° *river of fire in Hades*
To scud and overscour the earth in post

2. Margaret understates her promises, to make sure she can deliver.

Scene 15. Oxford.

Upon the speedy wings of swiftest winds!
Now Bacon hath raised me from the darkest deep
To search about the world for Miles his man,
For Miles, and to torment his lazy bones
For careless watching of his Brazen Head.
See where he comes. Oh, he is mine!

Enter Miles with a gown and a corner cap.° — *academic garb*

MILES A scholar, quoth you!° Marry, sir, I would I had been made a bottle-maker when I was made a scholar, for I can get neither° to be a deacon, reader, nor schoolmaster, no, not the clerk of a parish. Some call me dunce; another saith my head is as full of Latin as an egg's full of oatmeal. Thus I am tormented, that the devil and Friar Bacon haunts me.—Good Lord, here's one of my master's devils. I'll go speak to him.—What, Master Plutus![1] How cheer you?°

forsooth, indeed! / can't manage either / How are you?

DEVIL Dost thou know me?

MILES Know you, sir? Why, are not you one of my master's devils, that were wont° to come to my master, Doctor Bacon, at Brazennose?

accustomed

DEVIL Yes, marry, am I.

MILES Good Lord, Master Plutus, I have seen you a thousand times at my master's, and yet I had never the manners to make you° drink. But, sir, I am glad to see how conformable you are to the statute.° [*To the audience*] I warrant you he's as yeomanly a man as you shall see. Mark you, masters, here's a plain honest man, without welt or guard.° [*To the Devil*] But I pray you, sir, do you come lately from hell?

offer you / laws governing dress / facing or trimming

DEVIL Ay, marry. How then?

MILES Faith, 'tis a place I have desired long to see. Have you not good tippling houses there? May not a man have a lusty fire there, a pot of good ale, a pair° of cards, a swingeing° piece of chalk,[2] and a brown toast that will clap a white waistcoat° on a cup of good drink?

deck / nifty; huge / i.e., head of foam

DEVIL All this you may have there.

MILES You are for me, friend, and I am for you. But I pray you, may I not have an office° there?

position

DEVIL Yes, a thousand. What wouldst thou be?

MILES By my troth, sir, in a place° where I may profit myself. I know hell is a hot place, and men are marvelous dry, and much drink is spent° there. I would be a tapster.

position, situation / consumed

DEVIL Thou shalt.

MILES There's nothing lets° me from going with you but that 'tis a long journey, and I have never a horse.°

hinders / no horse at all

DEVIL Thou shalt ride on my back.

MILES Now surely here's a courteous devil, that for to pleasure his friend will not stick° to make a jade° of himself.—But I pray you, goodman° friend, let me move° a question to you.

scruple / worthless horse / worthy / propose

DEVIL What's that?

MILES I pray you, whether is your pace a trot or an amble?

DEVIL An amble.

1. Probably a comic confusion of Plutus, god of wealth, with Pluto, king of the underworld.

2. Used to mark up alehouse accounts.

MILES 'Tis well, but take heed it be not a trot. But 'tis no matter; I'll prevent it. [*He puts on spurs.*]

DEVIL What dost?

MILES Marry, friend, I put on my spurs, for if I find your pace either a trot or else uneasy, I'll put you to a false gallop; I'll make you feel the benefit of my spurs.

DEVIL Get up upon my back.

MILES Oh, Lord, here's even a goodly marvel, when a man rides to hell on the devil's back! *Exeunt roaring.*

[Scene 16]

Enter the Emperor with a pointless sword,[1] *next the King of Castile carrying a sword with a point, Lacy carrying the globe,°* *Edward, Warren carrying a rod of gold with a dove on it, Ermsby with a crown and scepter, the Queen* [*Elinor*] *with* [*Margaret*] *the fair maid of Fressingfield on her left hand,* [*King*] *Henry,* [*and*] *Bacon, with other lords attending.* — *orb*

EDWARD [*kneeling*] Great potentates, earth's miracles for state,° — *stately authority*
Think that Prince Edward humbles° at your feet, — *humbles himself*
And for these favors, on his martial sword
He vows perpetual homage to yourselves,
Yielding these honors unto Elinor. [*He rises.*]

KING HENRY Gramercies, lordlings. Old Plantagenet,° — *(King Henry himself)*
That rules and sways the Albion diadem,
With tears discovers° these conceivèd joys, — *manifests*
And vows requital, if his men-at-arms,
The wealth of England, or due honors done
To Elinor, may quite his favorites.[2]
But all this while what say you to the dames,
That shine like to the crystal lamps of heaven?

EMPEROR If but a third were added to these two,° — *(Elinor and Margaret)*
They did surpass those gorgeous images
That gloried Ida with rich beauty's wealth.[3]

MARGARET [*kneeling*] 'Tis I, my lords, who humbly on my knee
Must yield her orisons° to mighty Jove — *offer up her prayers*
For lifting up his handmaid to this state,
Brought from her homely° cottage to the court, — *humble*
And graced with kings, princes, and emperors,
To whom (next to the noble Lincoln earl)
I vow obedience and such humble love
As may a handmaid to such mighty men. [*She rises.*]

ELINOR Thou martial man that wears the Almain crown,
And you the Western potentates of might,
The Albion princess, English Edward's wife,

Scene 16. The royal court.
1. The blunted sword of Edward the Confessor symbolized mercy.
2. Can repay all the favors you have shown me.
3. They would outshine the three goddesses Juno, Pallas Athene, and Venus, who, on Mount Ida, vied for first place in the famous judgment of Paris.

Proud that the lovely star of Fressingfield,
Fair Margaret, countess to the Lincoln earl,
Attends on Elinor—gramercies, lord, for her—
'Tis I give thanks for Margaret to you all,
And rest, for her,° due bounden to yourselves. *remain on her behalf*
KING HENRY Seeing the marriage is solemnized,
Let's march in triumph to the royal feast.—
But why stands Friar Bacon here so mute?
BACON Repentant for the follies of my youth,
That magic's secret mysteries misled,
And joyful that this royal marriage
Portends such bliss unto this matchless realm.
KING HENRY Why, Bacon,
What strange event shall happen to this land,
Or what shall grow from Edward and his queen?
BACON I find by deep prescience of mine art,
Which once I tempered° in my secret cell, *mixed, concocted*
That here where Brut did build his Troynovant,[4]
From forth the royal garden of a king
Shall flourish out so rich and fair a bud° *i.e., Elizabeth I*
Whose brightness shall deface proud Phoebus' flower° *sunflower*
And overshadow Albion with her leaves.
Till then, Mars shall be master of the field,
But then the stormy threats of wars shall cease.
The horse shall stamp as careless° of the pike; *as if fearless*
Drums shall be turned to timbrels° of delight. *tambourines*
With wealthy favors, plenty shall enrich
The strand° that gladded° wand'ring Brut to see, *shore / gladdened*
And peace from heaven shall harbor in these leaves
That gorgeous beautifies this matchless flower.
Apollo's hellitropian° then shall stoop, *heliotrope, sunflower*
And Venus' hyacinth shall vail her top;° *lower her topsail*
Juno shall shut her gillyflowers up,
And Pallas' bay° shall bash° her brightest green; *laurel / humbly doff*
Ceres' carnation, in consort° with those, *harmony*
Shall stoop and wonder at Diana's rose.[5]
KING HENRY This prophecy is mystical.°— *allegorical*
But, glorious commanders of Europa's love,° *well-disposed Europe*
That makes° fair England like that wealthy isle *You who make*
Circled with Gihon and swift Euphrates[6]
In royalizing Henry's Albion
With presence of your princely mightiness,
Let's march. The tables all are spread,
And viands° such as England's wealth affords *food*
Are ready set to furnish out the boards.
You shall have welcome, mighty potentates.
It rests° to furnish up this royal feast; *only remains*
Only your hearts° be frolic, for the time *let your hearts*

4. Legend held that Brut, great-grandson of Aeneas, came to England and founded Troynovant, or the New Troy, where London now stands.

5. The Tudor rose, here associated (as was Queen Elizabeth) with Diana, the virgin huntress. Pallas is Athene; Ceres is a harvest deity.

6. The Gihon flowed out of Eden (Genesis 2.13). England is compared here with Eden and with ancient Mesopotamia, surrounded by the Tigris and Euphrates Rivers.

Craves that we taste of naught but jouissance.° *joy, pleasure*
Thus glories England over all the West. *Exeunt omnes.*

FINIS *Friar Bacon,*
made by Robert Greene, Master of Arts.

[*Omne tulit punctum qui miscuit utile dulci.*[7]]

7. He will gain everyone's approval who blends the instructive with the delightful. (Horace, *Ars Poetica*, line 343.)

TEXTUAL NOTES

Friar Bacon and Friar Bungay exists in three early quarto editions. The first of these, printed in 1594, is the authoritative edition on which this present text is based. The quarto of 1630 was reprinted from the first, and that of 1655 was mainly or entirely reprinted from the 1630 quarto. Substantive departures from Q1 are noted here, using the following abbreviations:

Q1: The first quarto (London, 1594)
Q1 corr.: The corrected first quarto
Q1 uncorr.: The uncorrected first quarto
Q2: The second quarto (London, 1630)
Q3: The third quarto (London, 1655)
ed.: A modern editor's emendation
subst.: the substantive (not exact) reading

1.0.3 [and elsewhere] ***Rafe*** [Q1: *Raph* or *Raphe*] **50 thee** [Q1: the] **59 cliffs** [Q1: cleues] **94** [and elsewhere] **necromancer** [Q1: Nigromancer] **142 Cote** [Q1: Coat]

2.2 ***doctissime*** [ed.] *dostissime* [Q1] **16 hydromancy** [ed.] Hadromaticke [Q1] **68 two** [ed.] to [Q1]

3.24 too [ed.] to [Q1] **57 Margaret** [ed.] Marget [Q1] **65 Oenone** [Q1: Aenon]

4.3 surge is [ed.] surges [Q1] **9** [and elsewhere] **Elinor** [Q1: Eleanour, Ellinor] **33** [and elsewhere] **Framlingham** [Q1: Fremingham] **45** [and elsewhere] **Hapsburg** [ed.] Haspurg [Q1] **66 flit** [ed.] fit [Q1] sit [Q2, Q3] **67** ***Exeunt*** [ed.] *Exit* [Q1]

5.9 tied [Q1: tide] **35 heard** [Q1: hard] **80 woos** [Q2, Q3] woes [Q1] **95 is all** [Q1 corr.] all [Q1 uncorr.]

6.4 plead [Q2] pleads [Q1] **13 brightsome** [ed.] bright-sunne [Q1] **32** ***scape*** [ed.] cape [Q1] **58** ***exception*** [ed.] acception [Q1] **111, 112** ***in jest*** [Q1: iniest] **161 Bungay** [ed.] Bacon [Q1]

7.6 Saxon [ed.] Scocon [Q1] **12 CLEMENT** [Q1; omitted by some eds.] **16** [and elsewhere] **Jaques** [Q1: Iaquesse, Iaquis] **77 pinnace** [Q1: Pinnis] **101 peasants** [Q1: pezzants] **108 Sussex** [ed.] Essex [Q1]

8.10 struck [ed.] stroke [Q1] strook [Q2, Q3] **49 piercing** [Q1: persing] **53 Shittim** [ed.] Sethin [Q1, Q2] Stething [Q3] **61 wait** [Q1: waight] **61 frigate's** [Q1: frigots] **62 their** [ed.] her [Q1] **69 tirèd** [ed.] tied [Q1, Q2] try [Q3] **69 webs** [Q1] weeds [some eds.] **72 Nor** [ed.] Not [Q1] **75** ***Ablata*** [ed.] *Abbata* [Q1] **80 earl** [ed.] eatle [Q1] **143 passed** [Q1: past] **144 not to be** [Q2] not be [Q1]

9.69 vile [Q1: vild] **70 genii** [ed.] gemij [Q1] **113 Utrecht** [ed.] Lutrech [Q1] **127** [and elsewhere] **Lest** [Q1: Least] **127** [and elsewhere] **lose** [Q1: loose] **159 spring** [ed.] springs [Q1] **162 whither** [Q1: whether] **177 the teasers** [Q2] they teisers [Q1] **210 the** [ed.] thee [Q1] **220 axioms** [Q2] actiomes

[Q1] **231 reign** [Q1: raine] **238 with a** [Q2] with such a [Q1] **239 thee** [ed.] the [Q1]

10.27 SD [placement, ed.; after 26 in Q1] **33 grave** [Q2] graues [Q1] **40 tale** [ed.] tall [Q1] **47 daughter** [Q2] daughters [Q1] **48 accounted** [Q1: accoumpted]

11.23 Argus [ed.] Argos [Q1] **71 arse ache** [Q1: arce ake]

12.5 Will't [ed.] Wilt [Q1] **56 querry** [Q1: quirie] **78 For, ere** [ed.] Eor ere [Q1]

13.2 [line repeated in Q1] **8 of** [ed.] on [Q1] **19.1** [placement, ed.; after 16 in Q1] **33 fathers** [Q2] father [Q1] **46 *meet thee in*** [ed.] thee [Q1] **55 *a bout*** [ed.] about [Q1] **73.1** [placement, ed.; after 72 in Q1] **82 efficient** [ed.] efficiat [Q1] **94 Eloim** [Q1: Elaim]

14.59 my [ed.] thy [Q1] **78 will Margaret** [ed.] Margret will [Q1]

15.3 Phlegethon [Q2, subst.] Blegiton [Q1] **48 here's a courteous** [ed.] hers acourteous [Q1]

16.67 swift [ed.] first [Q1]

Tamburlaine the Great, Part 1

The first of Christopher Marlowe's *Tamburlaine the Great* plays, Marlowe's debut as a playwright for the public theater, took London by storm in 1587–88. So did Part 2, written in response to the first play's popular success and appearing shortly after it. Together, these two plays dramatize the career of the last great Central Asian conqueror, Timur the Lame, "Timer Lenk" in Persian, and thence known as Tamerlane or Tamburlaine. Born a member of a Turkic clan in 1336 near Samarkand, he ruled at his death in 1405 an enormous empire stretching from Asia Minor through the Middle East to northern India and from southern Russia to Mongolia, and received tribute from Egypt, Byzantium, and Turkey. Many of the particular events in the two parts of *Tamburlaine the Great* (which stop only with the completion of Timur's westward conquests and his eventual death) are historical. Bajazeth's Turks were indeed besieging Constantinople when Timur conquered them in 1402; this conquest did, as Bajazeth laments in the play (3.3.238), occasion celebratory bonfires throughout Christian Europe, because in ending the siege Timur thwarted Muslim conquest of the capital of Eastern Christianity, delaying it for fifty years.

Part 1 of *Tamburlaine* treats this career as a relentless series of willed successes. The Scythian brigand Tamburlaine captures the Egyptian princess Zenocrate; persuades the Persian lord Theridamas (sent to capture him) to become his lieutenant; joins Cosroe in overthrowing Cosroe's weak brother, Mycetes, the Emperor of Persia; turns on Cosroe and defeats him, becoming Persian emperor himself; defeats and captures Bajazeth, the Emperor of Turkey (thus joining the Persian and Ottoman Empires); and then finally defeats and pardons Zenocrate's father, the Sultan of Egypt, on the condition that the Sultan accept him as his son-in-law. As he prepares to marry Zenocrate, Tamburlaine at last declares a peace, though he calls it a "truce" (5.1.529), and Part 2 begins with a resumption of hostilities. Marlowe and his audience knew that Tamburlaine's career was no fantasy and that this humbly born alien had achieved an empire greater than that of any Christian. Thus Tamburlaine, like Barabas in *The Jew of Malta*, Mephistopheles in *Doctor Faustus*, and Gaveston in *Edward II*, is given a strong position from which to express skepticism about the centrality of Christian civilization; to test the moral and social conventions of Marlowe's audiences; and to cast doubt on their claims to know the truth, whether about history, politics, religious doctrine, or what individual men and women really want and need.

Tamburlaine also responds to English interests and fears concerning the world beyond England's national boundaries. The Persian Meander comments that Tamburlaine the thief has been disrupting merchant caravans that trade by land "unto the Western Isles" (1.1.38), and at a later point, Tamburlaine plans to send a fleet around the world to "the British shore" (3.3.259). Without much direct discussion, the play evokes and reflects England's emergence as an international commercial power with imperial ambitions. Tamburlaine marches through what would be the trading territories of the English Muscovy and Levant Companies, associations set up to conduct

Introduction, glosses, and footnotes by Lars Engle; text edited by Lars Engle; textual notes and checking of text and footnotes by David Bevington.

Edward Alleyn (1566–1626) was famous in the roles of Tamburlaine the Great and Doctor Faustus. (Artist unknown.)

foreign trade, exploration, and colonization; and the play's wonderful catalogues of exotic place-names—a kind of poetry in which *Tamburlaine* rivals John Milton's later *Paradise Lost*—bespeak an imaginative capacity to appropriate the exotic for the projection of power.

Marlowe's fascination with geography is integral to his dramatic portrayal of a world in constant turmoil. The national and religious conflicts he portrays, such as that between Bajazeth's Muslim Turks and the Greek Christians of Byzantium in Part 1 of *Tamburlaine*, parallel the national and religious conflicts racking Europe and threatening the English as Marlowe wrote. The Turks had taken over Cyprus in 1571 and seemed to be winning their long war with Christian Venice for control of the eastern Mediterranean; France was embroiled in a religious civil war; and, as the London acting company known as the Admiral's Men prepared the first performance of *Tamburlaine* in 1587–88, the Spanish were preparing the invasion fleet that was intended to return England to Catholicism and make it part of Spain's world-spanning empire. The Spaniards Cortés and Pizarro, in fact, offered late-sixteenth-century audiences recent analogues to Tamburlaine's extraordinary imposition of his individual will on history. With their small bands of followers, their guns, their belief that they were doing God's work, and their unscrupulous cruelty, the conquistadores had conquered the huge empires of the Aztecs in Mexico and the Incas in Peru. Perhaps in recognition of this, Marlowe has Tamburlaine plan to send a fleet to Mexico (3.3.255), even though the historical Timur died almost a century before Columbus opened the New World.

Above all, *Tamburlaine the Great* presents modern readers with the same problem that faced its first auditors: How are we to evaluate its protagonist? Do we applaud his fortunes, or should we deplore them? The play raises questions about whether ordinary moral principles apply to extremely successful people. Tamburlaine makes readers and viewers suspect that the most powerful and most interesting people get that way by ignoring normal rules. Could it be that if you are sufficiently successful you do not need to be good? Indeed, must you ignore moral limits in order to be supremely powerful and effective?

Suspicions of this kind got a mighty boost from Niccolò Machiavelli's 1513 treatise, *The Prince*, which by Marlowe's time was widely known, even though proscribed in Catholic Europe as immoral, and difficult to obtain in England. Machiavelli shocked Europe (and seems to have fascinated Marlowe) by arguing that deceit and intimidation help rulers achieve success and that a prince, while striving to appear as good and as godly as possible, should reserve the option to circumvent conventional morality when circumstances demand it. His book was taken by many to suggest that religion serves mainly to keep people submissive to authority—an opinion attributed to Marlowe himself by Richard Baines in a note to the Privy Council accusing Marlowe of atheism. Machiavelli also pointed out, in passages directly relevant to *Tamburlaine*, that acts of spectacular cruelty can be beneficial to princes, while humane moderation in punishment can lead to political failure.

In its attention to these and similar precepts, *Tamburlaine* focuses on the political process that most fascinated Machiavelli: the combination of luck and skill that permits an obscure person to establish himself as a new prince and found a new political institution around himself. In act 1, scene 2, Tamburlaine, at this point the leader of a small troop of bandits, boldly seizes the opportunity Fortune sends him in the person and goods of the Egyptian princess Zenocrate, whom he has captured. Rather than holding her for ransom, he announces that he will keep her and make her his empress. Their conversation marks a social transition: though initially addressing him as "shepherd" (1.2.7), she now calls him "my lord" (1.2.33). At this he casts off his shepherd's garments and puts on a suit of armor (probably taken from her baggage) that shows his lordliness. When, moments later, the Persian general Theridamas arrives with a thousand horsemen to arrest him, Tamburlaine promptly turns his new acquisitions to account by using them to persuade the Persian to become his follower. Bidding his soldiers to "Lay out our golden wedges to the view, / That their reflections may amaze the Persians" (1.2.139–40), and placing the beautiful Zenocrate near him, Tamburlaine addresses Theridamas on his arrival as follows:

> Forsake thy king and do but join with me,
> And we will triumph over all the world.
> I hold the Fates bound fast in iron chains,
> And with my hand turn Fortune's wheel about,
> And sooner shall the sun fall from his sphere
> Than Tamburlaine be slain or overcome.
> (1.2.172–77)

Impressed at the outset by Tamburlaine's appearance and bearing in his newly stolen armor, Theridamas now encounters both Tamburlaine's startling audacity and the possibility offered by Tamburlaine of an enormously exciting future. Persian soldiers have been rioting for lack of pay (1.1.140–49). Tamburlaine, by contrast, displays in his glittering gold the sinews of war and, in Zenocrate, a token of royal legitimacy. These reinforce Tamburlaine's claim to control fate, as he points out:

> See how [Jove] rains down heaps of gold in showers
> As if he meant to give my soldiers pay,
> And, as a sure and grounded argument
> That I shall be the monarch of the East,
> He sends this sultan's daughter, rich and brave,
> To be my queen and portly emperess. (1.2.182–87)

Tamburlaine's rhetoric conveys not only boundless self-confidence but also strong political sense. Theridamas recognizes both and commits himself to Tamburlaine.

So, in time, does Zenocrate, the play's central female character. As a beautiful captive princess in the control of a hypermasculine barbarian, she might be expected to be the victim in a plot of subjugation in which both her social prejudices and her moral conventions are overwhelmed by Tamburlaine's aggressive sexuality. This plot of ravishment is, to be sure, a hardy perennial, but it is not exactly what we get in *Tamburlaine*. Like a respectful suitor, Tamburlaine defers sexual relations with her until he has won her father's permission to marry her. For her part, Zenocrate, like Theridamas but more slowly and with more pain, comes to love Tamburlaine and to acquiesce in his projects, even when they involve the destruction of her own people. In doing this, she assumes a role typical of female characters in Marlowe's plays: helplessly enmeshed in male rivalries, she offers a viewpoint from which their risks and excesses are described and even criticized. She not only suffers from her future husband's actions, she fears for the stability of his accomplishments, commenting on the hazards of fighting "for scepters and for slippery crowns" (5.1.356). Her point of view on power and worldly achievements thus differs radically from that of Tamburlaine, who, for example, justifies his betrayal of Cosroe by saying that nature, in forming us of warring elements, "Doth teach us all to have aspiring minds" and thus moves men to work without ceasing until they achieve "The sweet fruition of an earthly crown" (2.7.20, 29). Tamburlaine's taste for this sweet fruit is not easily satisfied: at least five crowns pass into his hands, and many more kingdoms come under his political control. Conversely, Zenocrate's anxious warnings about the notorious slipperiness of political fortune offer a significant critique of the male protagonist's insatiable drive for power.

Tamburlaine's boast that he is heaven's "scourge and terror" (4.2.32) and his comment that he is "termed the scourge and wrath of God" (3.3.44), a claim echoed by his opponents (4.3.9), present a calculated challenge by Marlowe to the habits of ethical and religious interpretation of many of his English contemporaries. This phrase, "the scourge and wrath of God," which also appears in shortened form on the title page of the 1590 edition of *Tamburlaine*, was widely interpreted in providential terms. To a culture that insisted on seeing the world as a theater of God's judgments, the phrase offered a way of explaining the huge success of a powerful, transgressive, and balefully violent figure such as Tamburlaine: he was put on earth to punish others for their wickedness and thus, despite his personal evil, could be seen as a part of God's plan for humankind. (Richard III provides another well-known example.) Yet Marlowe's Tamburlaine has no patience with this Christian interpretation of "the scourge of God." Tamburlaine sees himself as God's rival, a mortal before whom the heavens themselves stagger in fear:

> Jove, viewing me in arms, looks pale and wan,
> Fearing my power should pull him from his throne.
> Where'er I come, the Fatal Sisters sweat,
> And grisly Death, by running to and fro,
> To do their ceaseless homage to my sword.
> (5.1.452–56)

Such a claim by one who is mortal seems, on its surface, outrageous and hubristic. Moreover, such claims by dramatic characters have in the history of drama almost invariably been punished. Yet by the end of Part 1 of *Tamburlaine*, the protagonist's continued success obliges us to wonder whether the gods do not indeed serve him. In many ways, Tamburlaine's astonishing career illustrates Theridamas' comment that "A god is not so glorious as a king" (2.5.57). When Zenocrate's Median follower Agydas is overheard attempting to persuade Zenocrate that Tamburlaine does not love her, Tamburlaine needs no more than a wordless frown and the gift of a dagger to persuade Agydas to commit suicide (3.2). Tamburlaine assumes the role of the Fates themselves, determining whether Agydas shall live or die.

During his invasion of Egypt, now in command of an army that has grown from five hundred to eight hundred thousand, Tamburlaine reveals a military system that similarly illustrates his godlike power over others and the dangers of thwarting his will. On the first day of a siege, his tents and clothing are white, to indicate to the besieged that if they surrender he will not harm them but will be "satiate with spoil" (4.1.53)—that is, he will satisfy himself by merely taking all their possessions. On the second day, when his tents and clothing are red, a surrendering city will suffer the execution of all men that bear arms, while the rest of its inhabitants will be spared. On the third day, Tamburlaine wears black, signifying that everyone within the besieged city must die in a general sack. Acts 4 and 5 of the play are set before the walls of Damascus; at the beginning of act 4, Tamburlaine wears white; in the final scene, red. Then, in act 5, he enters *"all in black, and very melancholy"* to meet a delegation of virgins sent by the Governor of Damascus to offer to surrender and to plead with him for mercy

(5.1.63.3–4). These are Zenocrate's countrywomen, and Zenocrate herself has been pleading for Damascus throughout act 4. Tamburlaine may be melancholy, but he is also terrifyingly firm:

> TAMBURLAINE Virgins, in vain ye labor to prevent
> That which mine honor swears shall be performed.
> Behold my sword. What see you at the point?
> VIRGINS Nothing but fear and fatal steel, my lord.
> TAMBURLAINE Your fearful minds are thick and misty, then,
> For there sits Death, there sits imperious Death,
> Keeping his circuit by the slicing edge. (5.1.106–12)

Choosing not to kill them himself, Tamburlaine has Techelles lead a cavalry charge in which the virgins are spitted on lances in full view of the Damascenes. Their bodies are then hung on the walls of the city in preparation for the general sack that Tamburlaine's black clothing has promised.

In part, the play contrasts Tamburlaine's remorseless cruelty and inflexible will with Zenocrate's softer mercifulness and her skepticism about the value of worldly conquest. At the same time, Tamburlaine exhibits some contrasts himself. Marlowe chooses to juxtapose Tamburlaine's most brutal manifestation of outwardness with his most revealing exposure of inwardness. We see this especially when, in act 5, Tamburlaine turns immediately from ordering the slaughter of the innocent virgins to a loving soliloquy evoking Zenocrate and expressing concern over the inner disturbance and pain she is suffering at the loss of her fellow Egyptians: "But go, my lords, put the rest [of Damascus] to the sword. / Ah, fair Zenocrate, divine Zenocrate, / Fair is too foul an epithet for thee . . ." (5.1.134–36). The point is not, or not only, to reassure us that Tamburlaine has a heart after all. Marlowe forces us to recognize that what we gravitate toward in attractive leaders is bound up with their power to kill, while asking us to recognize also that we must value any glimpses we get of the inner life of someone who might destroy us. The plot goes a fair way toward underwriting Tamburlaine's evident belief that he is in a special relation to the gods and to people other than himself, a relation that allows him to invoke the gods as allies or rivals and to treat other people exactly as he likes. Tamburlaine's charisma derives from this conviction. Like Cleopatra or Falstaff, Tamburlaine considers himself to be exempt from the rules that constrain ordinary people. Unlike Cleopatra and Falstaff, however, Tamburlaine becomes more rather than less exempt from most of these rules as his play unfolds, since Tamburlaine masters and restructures the world he surveys. By the end of Part 1 of *Tamburlaine*, even his opponents believe that Tamburlaine is probably invincible; he and his followers are sure of it. Invincibility combined with a taste for rule-breaking seems a good recipe for insane manifestations of cruelty, yet on the whole we find instead in Tamburlaine a very sane cruelty. Indeed, his conduct might be said to offer an approximation of godlike fairness, particularly if one starts from the Calvinist concept of God that was a major feature of an Anglican upbringing in Marlowe's time. Accept him and be saved if in his unknowable will he chooses you; reject him and be utterly destroyed. Tamburlaine's will may be less unknowable than God's, but Tamburlaine's displeasure is equally decisive. One can see why this version of Machiavellianism, in which a ruler's arbitrary power to kill is a truth underlying both politics and religion, might make orthodox defenders of Christian monarchy uneasy with Marlowe.

Tamburlaine both knows what he wants to do from the start and improvises brilliantly when opportunity presents itself, as we have seen in his capture of Zenocrate. One could argue that he chooses to transform himself from a shepherd to a lord because Zenocrate, herself unimpeachably noble, takes seriously Tamburlaine's claims to nobility: she is the first person in the play to address him as "my lord" (1.2.33). Similarly, Tamburlaine learns how to torment a fallen rival from the Turkish emperor Bajazeth, who announces on the eve of battle how he will deal with Tamburlaine after defeating him:

> by the holy Alcoran, I swear
> He shall be made a chaste and lustless eunuch
> And in my sarell tend my concubines,
> And all his captains that thus stoutly stand
> Shall draw the chariot of my empress.
> (3.3.76–80)

Tamburlaine is, for once, threateningly vague in his reply: "I will not tell thee how I'll handle thee, / But every common soldier of my camp / Shall smile to see thy miserable state" (3.3.84–86). Despite the momentary obscurity of his intent, Tamburlaine later seems to remember this moment, and he fulfills his vague threat. After his victory, he starves Zabina and Bajazeth, the latter confined to a cage, taunting them with offers of table scraps from his sword point. In act 5, accepting the inevitability of Tamburlaine's victory over the Sultan, they brain themselves on the bars of the cage. In Part 2, Tamburlaine, evidently still remembering Bajazeth's threats, drives a chariot pulled by captive kings with bits in their mouths and burns the Koran. If Zenocrate's willingness to credit Tamburlaine as a lord in act 1 is a key point in his development toward being a leader others can love, Bajazeth's intention to emasculate and humiliate him educates him in practices that will make him a leader others must fear. Again, this evolution seems indebted to *The Prince,* where Machiavelli argues that although ideally a prince should be both feared and loved, he should be aware that if only one of these responses is attainable, he must choose to be feared.

As readers, to be sure, we need not fear Tamburlaine directly, and that leaves us open to a variety of other responses to him. He alternately thrills and horrifies, and sometimes amuses us, while remaining to an extraordinary degree consistent in attitude and approach. He incarnates charisma, he scorns limitation, he revels in killing, and yet he is an object of devotion for the most thoughtful and temperate observers in the play, namely, Theridamas and Zenocrate. To the extent that the play contains a normative viewpoint, it is theirs. Both abandon previous allegiances to join with Tamburlaine, experience some dismay (in Zenocrate's case, deep suffering) at Tamburlaine's rigid pursuit of his purposes, and are in the end rewarded not only with excitement and increased power, but also with something like a return to normalcy. Zenocrate, reconciled with her father, marries Tamburlaine, who in celebration "takes truce with all the world" (5.1.529) and orders Theridamas, Techelles, and Usumcasane to

> Cast off your armor, put on scarlet robes,
> Mount up your royal places of estate,
> Environèd with troops of noble men,
> And there make laws to rule your provinces.
> (5.1.524–27)

In a play structured as a series of victories and thus unremittingly devoted to conflict, this ending offers a glimpse of a world of peace in which leadership might consist not of dominating others but rather of making laws and delegating authority to worthy followers, thereby shaping a productive world for others to inhabit or inherit. Perhaps this is why the Tamburlaine of Part 1 (unlike the Tamburlaine of the sequel, who shows tendencies toward tyrannical madness) has little in common with the unhinged tyrants of later Renaissance drama or with those of both Renaissance and modern history. Unlike Macbeth or the Tiberius of Ben Jonson's *Sejanus*, Tamburlaine is on the whole cheerful, rational, and rewarding to be close to. When we see him sad (as he is before Damascus), it is because he finds that the logic of his warfare—"reason of state," in Machiavellian terms—makes him cruel to people who have not individually chosen to oppose him, including obvious innocents such as the tear-stained, white-clad virgins. And though the play celebrates Tamburlaine's war-making, war gets more hellish and less exhilarating as the play proceeds, until even Tamburlaine needs a break from it.

CHRISTOPHER MARLOWE

Tamburlaine the Great, Part 1

To the Gentlemen Readers and Others That Take Pleasure in Reading Histories[1]

Gentlemen and courteous readers whosoever: I have here published in print, for your sakes, the two tragical discourses of the Scythian shepherd Tamburlaine, that became so great a conqueror and so mighty a monarch. My hope is that they will be now no less acceptable unto you to read after your serious affairs and studies[2] than they have been lately delightful for many of you to see when the same were showed in London upon stages. I have purposely omitted and left out some fond° and frivolous gestures, digressing and, in my poor opinion, far unmeet° for the matter, which I thought might seem more tedious unto the wise than any way else to be regarded, though haply° they have been of some vain conceited fondlings° greatly gaped at,[3] what times° they were showed upon the stage in their graced deformities. Nevertheless, now, to be mixtured° in print with such matter of worth, it would prove a great disgrace to so honorable and stately a history.° Great folly were it in me to commend unto your wisdoms either the eloquence of the author that writ them[4] or the worthiness of the matter itself. I therefore leave unto your learned censures° both the one and the other, and myself, the poor printer of them, unto your most courteous and favorable protection, which, if you vouchsafe to accept, you shall evermore bind me to employ what travail° and service I can to the advancing and pleasuring of your excellent degree.°

foolish
unfitting
perchance
fools
when
mixed
chronicle
judgments
labor
high social station

Yours, most humble at commandment,
R. J., Printer

The original title page reads "*Tamburlaine the Great,* who, from a Scythian shepherd, by his rare and wonderful conquests became a most puissant and mighty monarch, and, for his tyranny and terror in war, was termed the scourge of God. Divided into two tragical discourses, as they were sundry times showed upon stages in the city of London by the right honorable the Lord Admiral his servants. Now first and newly published. London: printed by Richard Jones. At the sign of the Rose and Crown near Holborn Bridge. 1590."

To the Gentleman Readers.
1. This letter from the printer Richard Jones was included in the 1590 edition, in which were published both *Tamburlaine* plays.
2. After work and heavier reading.
3. I have omitted inappropriate comical material that would bore wise readers, even though some fools in the audience found it funny.
4. *Tamburlaine the Great* was published without naming the author, but Jones either expects that his readers will know the author is Marlowe or is encouraging them to guess who wrote the plays.

[THE PERSONS OF THE PLAY, IN ORDER OF APPEARANCE

The PROLOGUE
MYCETES, King of Persia
COSROE, his brother
MEANDER, counselor to Mycetes
THERIDAMAS, Persian commander, later follower of Tamburlaine
ORTYGIUS, CENEUS, MENAPHON } followers of Cosroe
TAMBURLAINE, a Scythian shepherd and brigand
ZENOCRATE, daughter of the Sultan of Egypt
TECHELLES, USUMCASANE } followers of Tamburlaine
MAGNETES, AGYDAS } Median lords accompanying Zenocrate
A SOLDIER in Tamburlaine's army
A SPY or scout in Tamburlaine's army
A MESSENGER in Tamburlaine's army
BAJAZETH, Emperor of Turkey
King of FEZ, King of MOROCCO, King of ARGIER } followers and allies of Bajazeth
A BASSO° serving Bajazeth — *pasha, Turkish general*
ANIPPE, lady-in-waiting to Zenocrate
ZABINA, wife to Bajazeth
EBEA, lady-in-waiting to Zabina
SULTAN of Egypt
CAPOLIN, follower of the Sultan
A MESSENGER serving the Sultan of Egypt
Alcidamus, King of ARABIA, formerly betrothed to Zenocrate
GOVERNOR of Damascus
Four VIRGINS
PHILEMUS, a messenger to Zenocrate
Bassos, lords, two Moors, soldiers, citizens of Damascus, attendants

THE SCENE: Persia, Scythia, Turkey, Asia Minor, and Egypt.]

Prologue

[*Enter*] *the Prologue.*

PROLOGUE From jigging veins of rhyming mother wits,[1]
And such conceits as clownage keeps in pay,[2]
We'll lead you to the stately tent of war,
Where you shall hear the Scythian Tamburlaine
Threat'ning the world with high astounding terms
And scourging kingdoms with his conquering sword.
View but his picture in this tragic glass,° — *mirror*
And then applaud his fortunes as you please. [*Exit.*]

Prologue.
1. From the rhymed doggerel of uneducated poets.
2. (1) Such tricks as keep stage clowns employed; (2) such conceptions of theater as ignorant rustic audiences pay to see.

1.1

[Enter] Mycetes, Cosroe, Meander, Theridamas, Ortygius, Ceneus, [and Menaphon,] with others.

MYCETES Brother Cosroe, I find myself aggrieved,
Yet insufficient to express the same,
For it requires a great and thund'ring speech.
Good brother, tell the cause unto my lords;
I know you have a better wit° than I. *more intelligence*
COSROE Unhappy° Persia, that in former age *Unfortunate*
Hast been the seat of mighty conquerors,
That in their prowess and their policies
Have triumphed over Afric and the bounds
Of Europe where the sun dares scarce appear
For freezing meteors and congealèd cold°— *Because of sleet and snow*
Now to be ruled and governed by a man
At whose birthday Cynthia with Saturn joined,
And Jove, the sun, and Mercury denied
To shed their influence in his fickle brain![1]
Now Turks and Tartars shake their swords at thee,
Meaning to mangle all thy provinces.
MYCETES Brother, I see your meaning well enough,
And through your planets° I perceive you think *your astrological talk*
I am not wise enough to be a king.
But I refer me to my noblemen
That know my wit and can be witnesses.
I might command you to be slain for this.—
Meander, might I not?
MEANDER Not for so small a fault, my sovereign lord.
MYCETES I mean it not,° but yet I know I might.— *I do not intend it*
Yet live, yea, live; Mycetes wills it so.—
Meander, thou my faithful counselor,
Declare the cause of my conceivèd grief,° *the grief I feel*
Which is, God knows, about that Tamburlaine,
That like a fox in midst of harvest time
Doth prey upon my flocks of passengers,° *travelers*
And, as I hear, doth mean to pull my plumes.° *humiliate me; challenge me*
Therefore 'tis good and meet° for to be wise. *appropriate*
MEANDER Oft have I heard Your Majesty complain
Of Tamburlaine, that sturdy° Scythian thief, *violent, fierce*
That robs your merchants of Persepolis
Trading by land unto the Western Isles,° *Britain (?); Aegean isles (?)*
And in your confines with his lawless train° *retinue*
Daily commits incivil outrages,
Hoping, misled by dreaming prophecies,
To reign in Asia and with barbarous arms
To make himself the monarch of the East.
But ere he march in Asia, or display
His vagrant ensign° in the Persian fields, *roving banner*
Your Grace hath taken order by° Theridamas, *given order to*
Charged with° a thousand horse,° to apprehend *Given command of / cavalry*

1.1. The Persian court, Persepolis.
1. The moon (Cynthia) and Saturn combined at his birth (to make him effeminate, vacillating, and cold), while Jupiter (Jove), the sun, and Mercury denied him their influences (which would have made him confident, warm, brave, and witty).

And bring him captive to Your Highness' throne.
MYCETES Full true thou speak'st, and like thyself,° my lord, *as is worthy of you*
Whom I may term a Damon for thy love.[2]
Therefore 'tis best, if so it like° you all, *please*
To send my thousand horse incontinent° *immediately*
To apprehend that paltry Scythian.
How like you this, my honorable lords?
Is it not a kingly resolution?
COSROE It cannot choose, because it comes from you.[3]
MYCETES Then hear thy charge, valiant Theridamas,
The chiefest captain of Mycetes' host,° *army*
The hope of Persia, and the very legs
Whereon our state doth lean as on a staff
That holds us up and foils° our neighbor foes. *defeats, frustrates*
Thou shalt be leader of this thousand horse,
Whose foaming gall° with rage and high disdain *overflowing spite*
Have sworn the death of wicked Tamburlaine.
Go frowning forth, but come thou smiling home
As did Sir Paris with the Grecian dame.° *Helen of Troy*
Return with speed! Time passeth swift away;
Our life is frail, and we may die today.
THERIDAMAS Before the moon renew her borrowed light,
Doubt not, my lord and gracious sovereign,
But Tamburlaine and that Tartarian rout° *mob of Tartars*
Shall either perish by our warlike hands
Or plead for mercy at Your Highness' feet.
MYCETES Go, stout° Theridamas. Thy words are swords, *brave*
And with thy looks thou conquerest all thy foes.
I long to see thee back return from thence,
That I may view these milk-white steeds of mine
All loaden with the heads of killèd men,
And from their knees even to their hoofs below
Besmeared with blood, that makes a dainty show.
THERIDAMAS Then now, my lord, I humbly take my leave.
Exit.
MYCETES Theridamas, farewell ten thousand times!—
Ah, Menaphon, why stayest thou thus behind
When other men press forward for renown?
Go, Menaphon, go into Scythia
And foot by foot follow Theridamas.
COSROE Nay, pray you, let him stay. A greater task
Fits Menaphon than warring with a thief:
Create him Prorex° of Africa *Viceroy*
That he may win the Babylonians' hearts,[4]
Which will revolt from Persian government
Unless they have a wiser king than you.
MYCETES "Unless they have a wiser king than you"?
These are his words, Meander; set° them down. *write*
COSROE And add this to them: that all Asia
Lament to see the folly of their king.

2. Damon and Pythias, Pythagoreans of Syracuse, were cited by Cicero as models of faithful male friendship.
3. It cannot help being kingly, since you say it. (Cosroe speaks sarcastically.)
4. "Africa" in *Tamburlaine* includes what we would call Asia Minor and the Arabian Peninsula and hence contains Babylon.

MYCETES Well, here I swear by this my royal seat°— *throne; backside*
COSROE You may do well to kiss it, then.
MYCETES Embossed° with silk, as best beseems my state,° *Covered / rank*
To be revenged for these contemptuous words.
Oh, where is duty and allegiance now?
Fled to the Caspian or the ocean main?° *high seas*
What, shall I call thee brother? No, a foe,
Monster of nature, shame unto thy stock,
That dar'st presume thy sovereign for to mock.—
Meander, come; I am abused,° Meander. *wronged*
Exit [Mycetes with Meander and his entourage].
Manent Cosroe and Menaphon.[5]
MENAPHON How now, my lord? What, mated° and amazed° *daunted / stunned*
To hear the King thus threaten like himself?° *threaten as a king should*
COSROE Ah, Menaphon, I pass° not for his threats. *care*
The plot is laid° by Persian noblemen *There is a plot*
And captains of the Median garrisons
To crown me emperor of Asia.
But this it is that doth excruciate° *torment*
The very substance of my vexèd soul:
To see our neighbors, that were wont° to quake *accustomed*
And tremble at the Persian monarch's name,
Now sits and laughs our regiment° to scorn; *royal authority*
And that which might resolve° me into tears, *dissolve*
Men from the farthest equinoctial line° *most distant tropics*
Have swarmed in troops into the eastern India
Lading° their ships with gold and precious stones, *Loading*
And made° their spoils° from all our provinces. *taken / war booty*
MENAPHON This should entreat° Your Highness to rejoice, *persuade*
Since Fortune gives you opportunity
To gain the title of a conqueror
By curing of this maimèd empery.° *empire*
Afric and Europe bordering on your land
And continent to° your dominions, *contiguous with*
How easily may you with a mighty host° *army*
Pass into Graecia, as did Cyrus once,[6]
And cause them to withdraw their forces home,
Lest you subdue the pride of Christendom!
[*A trumpet sounds.*]
COSROE But, Menaphon, what means this trumpet's sound?
MENAPHON Behold, my lord, Ortygius and the rest,
Bringing the crown to make you emperor.

Enter Ortygius and Ceneus, bearing a crown, with others.

ORTYGIUS Magnificent and mighty prince Cosroe,
We in the name of other Persian states° *aristocrats*
And commons of this mighty monarchy
Present thee with th'imperial diadem.° *crown*

5. Cosroe and Menaphon remain on stage. Standard stage directions appear in Latin in most Renaissance play texts: *exit* has passed into modern English, but *exeunt* ("they exit"), *manet* ("s/he remains"), and *manent* ("they remain") have not.

6. Cyrus was King of Persia in the sixth century B.C.E. It was his successors Darius I (r. 521–486 B.C.E.) and Xerxes (r. 486–465 B.C.E.) who invaded Greece.

CENEUS The warlike soldiers and the gentlemen
That heretofore have filled Persepolis
With Afric captains taken in the field,
Whose ransom made them march in coats of gold
With costly jewels hanging at their ears
And shining stones upon their lofty crests,
Now living idle in the wallèd towns,
Wanting° both pay and martial discipline, *Lacking*
Begin in troops to threaten civil war
And openly exclaim against the King.
Therefore, to stay° all sudden mutinies, *prevent*
We will invest° Your Highness emperor, *install*
Whereat the soldiers will conceive more joy
Than did the Macedonians at the spoil° *rack, ruin*
Of great Darius and his wealthy host.[7]

COSROE Well, since I see the state of Persia droop
And languish in my brother's government,
I willingly receive th'imperial crown,
And vow to wear it for my country's good,
In spite of them shall malice° my estate. *who will resent*

ORTYGIUS [*crowning Cosroe*] And in assurance of desired success
We here do crown thee monarch of the East,
Emperor of Asia and of Persia,
Great lord of Media and Armenia,
Duke of Africa and Albania,
Mesopotamia and of Parthia,
East India and the late-discovered isles,
Chief lord of all the wide vast Euxine Sea,° *Black Sea*
And of the ever-raging Caspian Lake.
Long live Cosroe, mighty emperor!

COSROE And may Jove never let me longer live
Than I may seek to gratify your love
And cause the soldiers that thus honor me
To triumph over many provinces!
By whose desires of discipline in arms[8]
I doubt not shortly but to reign sole king,
And with the army of Theridamas,
Whither we presently will fly, my lords,
To rest secure against my brother's force.

ORTYGIUS We knew, my lord, before we brought the crown,
Intending your investion° so near *investiture*
The residence of your despisèd brother,
The lords would not be too exasperate° *so exasperated as*
To injure or suppress your worthy title;
Or if they would, there are in readiness
Ten thousand horse to carry you from hence,
In spite of all suspected enemies.

COSROE I know it well, my lord, and thank you all.

ORTYGIUS Sound up the trumpets, then. God save the King!
[*Trumpets sound.*] *Exeunt.*

7. The soldiers of Alexander the Great, who conquered the Persian army under Darius III in 333 B.C.E.

8. By fulfilling their desire for disciplined military leadership.

1.2

[Enter] Tamburlaine [dressed as a shepherd] leading Zenocrate, [accompanied by] Techelles, Usumcasane, other lords [among them Magnetes and Agydas], and soldiers loaden with treasure.

TAMBURLAINE Come, lady, let not this appall your thoughts.
The jewels and the treasure we have ta'en° *taken*
Shall be reserved,° and you in better state *safely kept*
Than if you were arrived in Syria,
Even in the circle of your father's arms,
The mighty Sultan of Egyptia.
ZENOCRATE Ah, shepherd, pity my distressèd plight,
If, as thou seem'st, thou art so mean° a man, *lower-class*
And seek not to enrich thy followers
By lawless rapine° from a silly° maid, *seizure / helpless*
Who, traveling with these Median lords
To Memphis, from my uncle's country of Media,[1]
Where all my youth I have been governèd,° *educated, raised*
Have passed the army of the mighty Turk,
Bearing his privy signet and his hand[2]
To safe conduct us thorough Africa.[3]
MAGNETES And since we have arrived in Scythia,
Besides rich presents from the puissant Cham,° *powerful ruler of Tartary*
We have His Highness' letters to command
Aid and assistance if we stand in need.
TAMBURLAINE But now you see these letters and commands
Are countermanded by a greater man,
And through my provinces you must expect
Letters of conduct° from my mightiness *safe-conduct*
If you intend to keep your treasure safe.
But since I love to live at liberty,
As easily may you get the Sultan's crown
As any prizes out of my precinct,
For they are friends that help to wean my state[4]
Till men and kingdoms help to strengthen it,
And must maintain my life exempt from servitude.
But tell me, madam, is Your Grace betrothed?
ZENOCRATE I am, my lord—for so you do import.[5]
TAMBURLAINE I am a lord, for so my deeds shall prove,
And yet a shepherd by my parentage.
But, lady, this fair face and heavenly hue
Must grace his bed that conquers Asia
And means to be a terror to the world,
Measuring the limits of his empery
By east and west, as Phoebus° doth his course. *god of the sun*

1.2. Tamburlaine's camp in Scythia, near the Caspian Sea.
1. Memphis was in Egypt, on the Nile River near its delta; Media lay between modern-day Turkey and Iran (Persia) in what today is northern Persia and Syria; Scythia (line 17) is usually thought of as east of the Caspian Sea, but is spoken of here as lying between Memphis and Media. The boundaries of these territories were fluid, since they were named after the warlike nomadic tribes that occupied them.
2. A letter of safe-conduct, signed by the Emperor of Turkey (or possibly the King of Media) and bearing the impression of his seal ring.
3. Through Asia Minor. (See 1.1.90 and note.)
4. For the prizes are friends that assist my power in growing out of its infancy toward adulthood.
5. For you appear to be and speak of yourself as a lord.

Lie here, ye weeds° that I disdain to wear; *you clothes*
[*He takes off his shepherd's garments.*]
This complete armor and this curtal ax° *cutlass, short sword*
Are adjuncts more beseeming Tamburlaine.
[*He puts on armor.*]
And, madam, whatsoever you esteem
Of this success and loss unvaluèd,[6]
Both may invest you empress of the East,
And these,[7] that seem but silly country swains,° *ignorant bumpkins*
May have the leading of so great an host° *army*
As with their weight shall make the mountains quake,
Even as when windy exhalations,
Fighting for passage, tilt within the earth.[8]
TECHELLES As princely lions when they rouse themselves,
Stretching their paws, and threat'ning herds of beasts,
So in his armor looketh Tamburlaine.
Methinks I see kings kneeling at his feet,
And he, with frowning brows and fiery looks,
Spurning° their crowns from off their captive heads. *Striking*
USUMCASANE And making thee and me, Techelles, kings,
That even to death will follow Tamburlaine.
TAMBURLAINE Nobly resolved, sweet friends and followers.
These lords, perhaps, do scorn our estimates° *predictions; reputations*
And think we prattle with distempered° spirits, *unbalanced*
But since they measure our deserts so mean,° *think so ill of us*
That° in conceit° bear empires on our spears, *Who / imagination*
Affecting thoughts coequal with the clouds,° *Daring to think sky-high*
They shall be kept our forcèd followers
Till with their eyes they view us emperors.
ZENOCRATE The gods, defenders of the innocent,
Will never prosper your intended drifts,° *plans*
That thus oppress poor friendless passengers.° *travelers*
Therefore at least admit us liberty
Even as thou hop'st to be eternized
By living° Asia's mighty emperor. *living as*
AGYDAS I hope our lady's treasure and our own
May serve for ransom to our liberties.
Return our mules and empty camels back,
That we may travel into Syria,
Where her betrothèd, Lord Alcidamus,
Expects th'arrival of Her Highness' person.
MAGNETES And wheresoever we repose ourselves
We will report but well of Tamburlaine.
TAMBURLAINE Disdains Zenocrate to live with me?
Or you, my lords, to be my followers?
Think you I weigh° this treasure more than you? *value*
Not all the gold in India's wealthy arms
Shall buy the meanest° soldier in my train.° *lowliest / retinue*
Zenocrate, lovelier than the love of Jove,[9]

6. (1) Of my transformation and the loss of these worthless clothes; (2) of this event and your loss of this invaluable treasure.
7. Techelles and Usumcasane.
8. Earthquakes were understood in the Renaissance as attempts by underground gases to break free from containment.
9. (1) Lovelier than Juno, Jove's wife, or than Jove's human lovers, such as Leda or Europa; (2) more desirable than being loved and favored by Jove.

Brighter than is the silver Rhodope,[1]
Fairer than whitest snow on Scythian hills,
Thy person is more worth to Tamburlaine
Than the possession of the Persian crown,
Which gracious stars have promised at my birth.
A hundred Tartars shall attend on thee,
Mounted on steeds swifter than Pegasus.° *a mythical winged horse*
Thy garments shall be made of Median silk,
Enchased° with precious jewels of mine own *Set*
More rich and valurous° than Zenocrate's. *valuable*
With milk-white harts° upon an ivory sled *deer*
Thou shalt be drawn amidst the frozen pools
And scale the icy mountains' lofty tops,
Which with thy beauty will be soon resolved.° *melted*
My martial prizes with five hundred men,
Won on the fifty-headed° Volga's waves, *having fifty sources*
Shall all we offer to Zenocrate,
And then myself to fair Zenocrate.

TECHELLES [*to Tamburlaine*] What now? In love?
TAMBURLAINE Techelles, women must be flatterèd.
But this is she with whom I am in love.

Enter a Soldier.

SOLDIER News, news!
TAMBURLAINE How now, what's the matter?
SOLDIER A thousand Persian horsemen are at hand,
Sent from the King to overcome us all.
TAMBURLAINE How now, my lords of Egypt and Zenocrate?
Now must your jewels be restored again
And I that triumphed so be overcome.
How say you, lordings?° Is not this your hope? *little lords*
AGYDAS We hope yourself will willingly restore them.
TAMBURLAINE Such hope, such fortune have the thousand horse.[2]
Soft ye,° my lords and sweet Zenocrate. *Take it easy*
You must be forcèd from me ere you go.
A thousand horsemen? We, five hundred foot?
An odds too great for us to stand against.[3]
But are they rich? And is their armor good?
SOLDIER Their plumèd helms are wrought with beaten gold,
Their swords enameled, and about their necks
Hangs massy° chains of gold down to the waist,[4] *massive*
In every part exceeding brave° and rich. *very splendid*
TAMBURLAINE Then shall we fight courageously with them.
Or look you° I should play the orator? *do you think*
TECHELLES No. Cowards and fainthearted runaways
Look for orations when the foe is near.
Our swords shall play the orators for us.
USUMCASANE Come, let us meet them at the mountaintop,
And with a sudden and an hot alarm° *foray*

1. A snowy, silver-bearing mountain in the ancient country of Thrace (located on the border of modern-day Bulgaria), named after a queen who challenged Juno over her beauty.
2. I.e., The thousand Persian horsemen should hope so too. (Said sardonically.)
3. Said ironically, perhaps again suggesting the thoughts of his captives.
4. The disagreement in number between verb and subject ("chains hangs") is not uncommon in early modern English.

Drive all their horses headlong down the hill.
TECHELLES Come, let us march.
TAMBURLAINE Stay, Techelles, ask° a parley first. *ask for*

The soldiers [of Tamburlaine] enter.

Open the mails,° yet guard the treasure sure. *saddlebags*
Lay out our golden wedges to the view,
That° their reflections may amaze the Persians. *So that*
[*The soldiers set up a dazzling display.*]
And look we friendly on them when they come;
But if they offer word or violence,
We'll fight five hundred men-at-arms to one
Before we part with our possession,
And 'gainst the general we will lift our swords
And either lanch° his greedy thirsting throat, *lance, pierce*
Or take him prisoner, and his chain shall serve
For manacles till he be ransomed home.
TECHELLES I hear them come. Shall we encounter them?
TAMBURLAINE Keep all your standings° and not stir a foot. *Stay where you are*
Myself will bide° the danger of the brunt.° *abide / assault*

Enter Theridamas with others.

THERIDAMAS Where is this Scythian Tamburlaine?
TAMBURLAINE Whom seek'st thou, Persian? I am Tamburlaine.
THERIDAMAS [*aside*] Tamburlaine?
A Scythian shepherd, so embellishèd
With nature's pride and richest furniture?[5]
His looks do menace heaven and dare the gods;
His fiery eyes are fixed upon the earth
As if he now devised some stratagem,
Or meant to pierce Avernus' darksome vaults
To pull the triple-headed dog from hell.[6]
TAMBURLAINE [*to Techelles*] Noble and mild this Persian seems to be,
If outward habit judge the inward man.
TECHELLES [*to Tamburlaine*] His deep affections make him passionate.
TAMBURLAINE [*to Techelles*] With what a majesty he rears his looks!
[*To Theridamas*] In thee, thou valiant man of Persia,
I see the folly of thy emperor.
Art thou but captain of a thousand horse,
That by characters[7] graven in thy brows,
And by thy martial face and stout° aspect *brave*
Deserv'st to have the leading of an host?
Forsake thy king and do but join with me,
And we will triumph over all the world.
I hold the Fates bound fast in iron chains,
And with my hand turn Fortune's wheel about,[8]
And sooner shall the sun fall from his° sphere *its*

5. (1) With natural personal beauty; (2) with natural self-assurance, combined with (a) richest personal attributes; (b) richest outfit.

6. Cerberus, the three-headed watchdog of Hades in classical myth, dwelt in dark subterranean Avernus. Theridamas implicitly compares Tamburlaine to Hercules, who captured Cerberus and brought him to the earth's surface.

7. Pronounced "charácters." Tamburlaine reads the signs of Theridamas' superiority on his forehead; there is also perhaps a suggestion that astrological influences have left visible traces there.

8. Tamburlaine claims to control the three Fates, who spin, measure, and cut (at death) the thread of each person's life, and thus to be in the position of Fortune, who turns the wheel that takes people suddenly from failure to prosperity or vice versa.

Than Tamburlaine be slain or overcome.
Draw forth thy sword, thou mighty man-at-arms,
Intending but to raze° my charmèd skin, *graze*
And Jove himself will stretch his hand from heaven
To ward° the blow and shield me safe from harm. *deflect*
See how he rains down heaps of gold in showers
As if he meant to give my soldiers pay,
And, as a sure and grounded argument
That I shall be the monarch of the East,
He sends this sultan's daughter, rich and brave,° *good-looking*
To be my queen and portly° emperess. *stately*
If thou wilt stay with me, renownèd man,
And lead thy thousand horse with my conduct,° *at my command*
Besides thy share of this Egyptian prize,
Those thousand horse shall sweat with martial spoil
Of conquered kingdoms and of cities sacked.
Both° we will walk upon the lofty cliffs, *Together*
And Christian merchants, that with Russian stems° *prows (of ships)*
Plow up huge furrows in the Caspian Sea,
Shall vail to us,[9] as lords of all the lake.
Both we will reign as consuls[1] of the earth,
And mighty kings shall be our senators.° *statesmen, counselors*
Jove sometime maskèd° in a shepherd's weed,° *disguised / clothes*
And by those steps that he hath scaled the heavens
May we become immortal like the gods.[2]
Join with me now in this my mean° estate *lowly*
(I call it mean because, being yet obscure,
The nations far removed admire me not),
And when my name and honor shall be spread
As far as Boreas° claps his brazen wings, *the north wind*
Or fair Boötes[3] sends his cheerful light,
Then shalt thou be competitor° with me, *partner*
And sit with Tamburlaine in all his majesty.

THERIDAMAS Not Hermes, prolocutor° to the gods, *herald*
Could use persuasions more pathetical.° *moving*

TAMBURLAINE Nor are Apollo's oracles more true
Than thou shalt find my vaunts substantial.

TECHELLES We are his friends, and if the Persian king
Should offer present dukedoms to our state,
We think° it loss to make exchange for that° *would think / that which*
We are assured of by our friend's success.

USUMCASANE And kingdoms at the least we all expect,
Besides the honor in assurèd conquests
Where kings shall crouch unto our conquering swords
And hosts of soldiers stand amazed at us,
When with their fearful tongues they shall confess,
"These are the men that all the world admires."

THERIDAMAS What strong enchantments 'tice° my yielding soul? *entice*

9. Will lower their topsails out of respect for us.
1. Joint rulers in the Roman republic who presided over the senate.
2. By the same methods that Jove used to gain control of heaven (which included overthrowing his king-father Saturn), we may ourselves become immortal. Jove (or Jupiter, the Greek Zeus) disguised himself as an ordinary mortal (see line 199) when he and Mercury, also in disguise, visited the humble cottage of Philemon and Baucis (Ovid, *Metamorphoses*, Book 8).
3. A northern constellation, the Ploughman, or Wagoner, following behind the Big Dipper, or Great Bear. Boötes is visible throughout the Northern Hemisphere and in much of the Southern Hemisphere as well.

Are these resolvèd noble Scythians?[4]
But shall I prove a traitor to my king?
TAMBURLAINE No, but the trusty friend of Tamburlaine.
THERIDAMAS Won with thy words and conquered with thy looks,
I yield myself, my men, and horse to thee,
To be partaker of thy good or ill
As long as life maintains Theridamas.
TAMBURLAINE Theridamas, my friend, take here my hand,
Which is as much as if I swore by heaven
And called the gods to witness of my vow:
Thus shall my heart be still combined with thine
Until our bodies turn to elements
And both our souls aspire° celestial thrones. *fly up to*
Techelles and Casane,° welcome him. *Usumcasane*
TECHELLES Welcome, renownèd Persian, to us all!
USUMCASANE Long may Theridamas remain with us!
TAMBURLAINE These are my friends, in whom I more rejoice
Than doth the King of Persia in his crown,
And by the love of Pylades and Orestes,[5]
Whose statues we adore in Scythia,
Thyself and them shall never part from me
Before I crown you kings in Asia.
Make much of them, gentle Theridamas,
And they will never leave thee till the death.
THERIDAMAS Nor thee, nor them, thrice noble Tamburlaine,
Shall want my heart to be with gladness pierced
To do you honor and security.[6]
TAMBURLAINE A thousand thanks, worthy Theridamas.
And now, fair madam, and my noble lords,
If you will willingly remain with me,
You shall have honors as your merits be°— *as you deserve*
Or else you shall be forced with slavery.
AGYDAS We yield unto thee, happy Tamburlaine.
TAMBURLAINE For you then, madam, I am out of doubt.[7]
ZENOCRATE I must be pleased perforce.° Wretched *of necessity*
Zenocrate! *Exeunt.*

2.1

[*Enter*] *Cosroe, Menaphon, Ortygius,* [*and*] *Ceneus, with other soldiers.*

COSROE Thus far are we° towards Theridamas *have we come*
And valiant Tamburlaine, the man of fame,
The man that in the forehead of his fortune
Bears figures of renown and miracle.[1]
But tell me, that hast seen him,° Menaphon, *you who have seen him*
What stature wields he, and what personage?° *appearance*
MENAPHON Of stature tall, and straightly fashionèd,

4. Can Scythians be this resolute and noble?
5. Pylades, Orestes' faithful friend, stood by Orestes in exile and on his return to take vengeance on Clytemnestra for the murder of Orestes' father, Agamemnon.
6. Shall find me wanting in glad desire to honor and defend you.
7. As far as you are concerned, madam, I consider things settled.
2.1. Near the Araris River in Parthia, near the Caspian Sea.
1. (1) Bears signs of success on his forehead; (2) succeeds so brilliantly that his fortune presents itself as blessed.

Like his desire, lift° upwards and divine, *lifted*
So large of limbs, his joints so strongly knit,
Such breadth of shoulders as might mainly° bear *entirely*
Old Atlas' burden;[2] 'twixt his manly pitch° *i.e., shoulders*
A pearl° more worth° than all the world is placed *i.e., a head / worth more*
Wherein, by curious sovereignty° of art, *intricate craft*
Are fixed his piercing instruments of sight,
Whose fiery circles bear encompassèd
A heaven of heavenly bodies in their spheres[3]
That guides his steps and actions to the throne
Where honor sits invested royally.
Pale of complexion, wrought in him with passion,
Thirsting with sovereignty, with love of arms,
His lofty brows in folds do figure death,
And in their smoothness, amity and life.[4]
About them hangs a knot of amber hair
Wrappèd in curls, as fierce Achilles' was,[5]
On which the breath of heaven delights to play,
Making it dance with wanton majesty.
His arms and fingers long and sinewy,
Betokening valor and excess of strength;
In every part proportioned like the man
Should make the world subdued to Tamburlaine.[6]

COSROE Well hast thou portrayed in thy terms of life° *lively terms*
The face and personage of a wondrous man.
Nature doth strive with Fortune and his stars
To make him famous in accomplished worth,
And well his merits show him to be made
His fortune's master and the king of men
That could persuade at such a sudden pinch,° *crisis*
With reasons of his valor and his life,
A thousand sworn and overmatching foes.[7]
Then when our powers in points of swords are joined
And closed° in compass of the killing bullet, *enclosed*
Though strait° the passage and the port° be made *narrow / gateway*
That leads to palace of my brother's life,
Proud is his fortune if we pierce it not.[8]
And when the princely Persian diadem° *crown*
Shall overweigh his weary witless head
And fall like mellowed fruit with shakes of death,
In fair Persia noble Tamburlaine
Shall be my regent, and remain as king.

ORTYGIUS In happy hour we have set the crown
Upon your kingly head, that seeks our honor
In joining with the man ordained by heaven

2. In Greek myth, Atlas was condemned to bear the sky on his shoulders.
3. (1) His eyes take in the heavenly signs that he will conquer; (2) his eyes appear to others to contain a heaven of stars that signifies conquest.
4. His frowns signify death, and in their absence, his smooth brow signifies friendship and life.
5. Achilles, the foremost Greek warrior in Homer's *Iliad,* was preeminent in beauty as well as prowess.
6. In every part he seems a man capable of subduing the world.
7. Who, at such a critical moment, could persuade, through his own courage and excellence, a thousand men who were sworn to defeat Tamburlaine, and who greatly outnumbered his forces, to become instead his followers. (Cosroe refers to Tamburlaine's success in persuading Theridamas and his soldiers to switch to Tamburlaine's side.)
8. Then when Tamburlaine's new and augmented army is joined with ours against Mycetes, sword against sword and within bullet range, no matter how well guarded Mycetes may be from an assault aimed at his very heart, he'll be fortunate indeed if we do not succeed in killing him.

To further every action to the best.
CENEUS He that with shepherds and a little spoil° *captured treasure*
Durst° in disdain of wrong and tyranny *Dared*
Defend his freedom 'gainst a monarchy,
What will he do supported by a king,
Leading a troop of gentlemen and lords,
And stuffed with treasure for his highest thoughts?[9]
COSROE And such shall wait on° worthy Tamburlaine. *attend, serve*
Our army will be forty thousand strong
When Tamburlaine and brave Theridamas
Have met us by the river Araris,
And all conjoined to meet the witless king° *(Mycetes)*
That now is marching near to Parthia,
And with unwilling soldiers faintly armed,
To seek revenge on me and Tamburlaine.—
To whom, sweet Menaphon, direct me straight.° *immediately*
MENAPHON I will, my lord. *Exeunt.*

2.2

[*Enter*] *Mycetes* [*and*] *Meander, with other lords and soldiers.*

MYCETES Come, my Meander, let us to this gear.° *this business*
I tell you true, my heart is swoll'n with wrath
On this same thievish villain Tamburlaine,
And of that false Cosroe, my traitorous brother.
Would it not grieve a king to be so abused
And have a thousand horsemen ta'en away?
And, which is worst, to have his diadem
Sought for by such scald° knaves as love him not? *scurvy, contemptible*
I think it would. Well, then, by heavens I swear,
Aurora° shall not peep out of her doors *goddess of dawn*
But I will have Cosroë by the head
And kill proud Tamburlaine with point of sword.
Tell you the rest, Meander; I have said.° *finished*
MEANDER Then having passed Armenian deserts now,
And pitched our tents under the Georgian hills
Whose tops are covered with Tartarian thieves
That lie in ambush waiting for a prey,
What should we do but bid them battle straight,° *immediately*
And rid the world of those detested troops,
Lest, if we let them linger here awhile
They gather strength by power of fresh supplies?
This country swarms with vile outrageous men
That live by rapine and by lawless spoil,° *plunder*
Fit soldiers for the wicked Tamburlaine.
And he that could with gifts and promises
Inveigle° him that led a thousand horse, *Beguile*
And make him false° his faith unto his king, *Theridamas falsify*
Will quickly win such as are like himself.
Therefore cheer up your minds; prepare to fight.

9. And richly rewarded for his most ambitious thoughts and actions.

2.2. Parthia still.

He that can take or slaughter Tamburlaine
Shall rule the province of Albania.
Who brings that traitor's head° Theridamas *the head of that traitor*
Shall have a government in Media
Beside° the spoil° of him and all his train. *As well as / booty*
But if Cosroë (as our spials° say, *spies*
And as we know) remains with Tamburlaine,
His Highness' pleasure is that he should live
And be reclaimed with princely lenity.° *lenience*

[*Enter a Spy, or scout.*]

SPY An hundred horsemen of my company,
Scouting abroad upon these champaign° plains, *level, open*
Have viewed the army of the Scythians,
Which make reports it far exceeds the King's.

MEANDER Suppose they be in number infinite,
Yet, being void of martial discipline,
All running headlong after greedy spoils
And more regarding gain than victory,
Like to the cruel brothers of the earth
Sprung of the teeth of dragons venomous,[1]
Their careless swords shall lanch° their fellows' throats *lance, pierce*
And make us triumph in their overthrow.

MYCETES Was there such brethren, sweet Meander, say,
That sprung of teeth of dragons venomous?

MEANDER So poets say, my lord.[2]

MYCETES And 'tis a pretty toy° to be a poet. *neat trick*
Well, well, Meander, thou art deeply read,
And having thee I have a jewel sure.
Go on, my lord, and give your charge,° I say; *orders*
Thy wit will make us conquerors today.

MEANDER Then, noble soldiers, to entrap these thieves,
That live confounded° in disordered troops, *confusedly*
If wealth or riches may prevail with them,
We have our camels laden all with gold,
Which you that be but common soldiers
Shall fling in every corner of the field,
And while the baseborn Tartars take it up,
You, fighting more for honor than for gold,
Shall massacre those greedy-minded slaves;° *wretches*
And when their scattered army is subdued° *defeated*
And you march on their slaughtered carcasses,
Share equally the gold that bought their lives
And live like gentlemen in Persia.
Strike up the drum and march courageously!
Fortune herself doth sit upon our crests.

MYCETES He tells you true, my masters,° so he does. *my good sirs*
Drums, why sound ye not when Meander speaks? *Exeunt.*

1. Alluding to the myth of Cadmus, who sowed a dragon's teeth (though plural "dragons" in this text; see line 48) and reaped an immediate crop of angry earth-born warriors who promptly attacked each other.

2. Meander may have Ovid's *Metamorphoses*, Book 3, in mind, where the Cadmus story appears. Since Ovid was standard reading for the educated, the exchange illustrates Mycetes' ignorance.

2.3

[Enter] Cosroe, Tamburlaine, Theridamas, Techelles, Usumcasane, [and] Ortygius, with others.

COSROE Now, worthy Tamburlaine, have I reposed
In thy approvèd fortunes° all my hope. *past successes; prospects*
What think'st thou, man, shall come of our attempts?
For even as from assurèd oracle
I take thy doom° for satisfaction. *prediction*
TAMBURLAINE And so mistake you not a whit,° my lord, *not at all*
For fates and oracles of heaven have sworn
To royalize the deeds of Tamburlaine
And make them° blest that share in his attempts. *(those persons)*
And doubt you not but if you favor me,
And let my fortunes and my valor sway
To some direction in your martial deeds,[1]
The world will strive with hosts of men-at-arms
To swarm unto the ensign° I support. *banner*
The host of Xerxes, which by fame is said
To drink the mighty Parthian Araris,[2]
Was but a handful to that° we will have. *that which*
Our quivering lances shaking in the air
And bullets like Jove's dreadful thunderbolts
Enrolled in° flames and fiery smoldering mists *Surrounded by*
Shall threat° the gods more than Cyclopian wars,[3] *threaten*
And with our sun-bright armor as we march
We'll chase the stars from heaven and dim their eyes
That stand and muse at our admirèd arms.
THERIDAMAS [*to Cosroe*] You see, my lord, what working words he hath.
But when you see his actions top his speech
Your speech will stay,° or so extol his worth *pause (in wonder)*
As I shall be commended and excused
For turning my poor charge to his direction.[4]
And these his two renownèd friends, my lord,
Would make one thrust and strive to be retained
In such a great degree of amity.[5]
TECHELLES With duty and with amity we yield
Our utmost service to the fair Cosroe.
COSROE Which I esteem as portion of my crown.
Usumcasane and Techelles both,
When she that rules in Rhamnus' golden gates[6]
And makes a passage for° all prosperous arms *assists the progress of*
Shall make me solely emperor of Asia,
Then shall your meeds° and valors be advancèd *merited rewards*

2.3. The field of battle.
1. And let me direct the course of battle.
2. In accounts by the Greek historian Herodotus, the Persian army of Xerxes caused the river Araxes, or Araris, to be diverted from its course.
3. The Cyclops, one-eyed giants, are being identified here with the Titans, who attacked Olympus, the mountain home of the gods.
4. That I will be praised and excused for giving my small command over to him.
5. And these two famous friends of his (Techelles and Usumcasane) are such that one is inspired to press forward and wish to be joined in such admirable comradeship in arms.
6. The goddess Nemesis, to whom a temple stood at Rhamnus in ancient Greece. This invocation, like many in *Tamburlaine*, is dangerous, since Nemesis punishes mortal presumption, and it is presumptuous to assume, as Cosroe does, that Nemesis will grant Cosroe victory.

To rooms of honor and nobility.
TAMBURLAINE Then haste, Cosroë, to be king alone,° *sole monarch*
That I with these my friends and all my men
May triumph in our long-expected fate.
The King your brother is now hard° at hand; *near*
Meet with the fool, and rid your royal shoulders
Of such a burden as outweighs the sands
And all the craggy rocks of Caspia.

[*Enter a Messenger.*]

MESSENGER My lord, we have discoverèd the enemy
Ready to charge you with a mighty army.
COSROE Come, Tamburlaine, now whet thy wingèd sword
And lift thy lofty arm into the clouds,
That it may reach the King of Persia's crown
And set it safe on my victorious head.
TAMBURLAINE [*drawing his sword*] See where it is, the keenest curtal ax° *cutlass*
That e'er made passage thorough° Persian arms. *through*
These are the wings shall make it fly as swift
As doth the lightning or the breath of heaven
And kill as sure as it swiftly flies.
COSROE Thy words assure me of kind° success. *fitting*
Go, valiant soldier, go before and charge
The fainting army of that foolish king.
TAMBURLAINE Usumcasane and Techelles, come;
We are enough to scare the enemy
And more than needs to make an emperor. [*Exeunt.*]

[2.4]

[*Enter armies*] *to the battle* [*and exeunt*], *and Mycetes comes out alone with his crown in his hand, offering° to hide it.* *attempting*

MYCETES Accurst be he that first invented war!
They knew not, ah, they knew not, simple° men, *foolish*
How those were° hit by pelting cannon shot *who have been*
Stand staggering like a quivering aspen leaf
Fearing the force of Boreas'° boist'rous blasts. *the north wind's*
In what a lamentable case were I
If nature had not given me wisdom's lore?
For kings are clouts° that every man shoots at, *targets*
Our crown the pin° that thousands seek to cleave. *center, bull's-eye*
Therefore in policy° I think it good *craftiness*
To hide it° close; a goodly stratagem, *(the crown)*
And far from any man that is a fool.° *And far from foolish*
So shall not I be known, or if I be,
They cannot take away my crown from me.
Here will I hide it in this simple° hole. *plain*
[*Mycetes hides the crown.*]

Enter Tamburlaine.

2.4. The field of battle.

TAMBURLAINE What, fearful coward, straggling from the camp,
When kings themselves are present in the field?
MYCETES Thou liest.
TAMBURLAINE Base villain, dar'st thou give the lie?[1]
MYCETES Away! I am the King. Go, touch me not.
Thou break'st the law of arms unless thou kneel
And cry me° "mercy, noble King." *beg from me*
TAMBURLAINE Are you the witty king of Persia?
MYCETES Ay, marry,° am I. Have you any suit to me? *by Mary (an oath)*
TAMBURLAINE I would entreat you to speak but three wise words.
MYCETES So I can, when I see my time.
TAMBURLAINE [*picking up the crown*] Is this your crown?
MYCETES Ay. Didst thou ever see a fairer?
TAMBURLAINE You will not sell it, will ye?
MYCETES Such another word and I will have thee executed.
Come, give it me.
TAMBURLAINE No, I took it prisoner.
MYCETES You lie; I gave it you.
TAMBURLAINE Then 'tis mine.
MYCETES No, I mean, I let you keep it.
TAMBURLAINE Well, I mean you shall have it again.
Here, take it for a while. [*He gives Mycetes the crown.*] I lend it thee
Till I may see thee hemmed with armèd men;
Then shalt thou see me pull it from thy head.
Thou art no match for mighty Tamburlaine.
[*Exit Tamburlaine.*]
MYCETES O gods, is this Tamburlaine the thief?
I marvel much he stole it not away.
Sound trumpets to the battle, and he runs in.° *leaves the stage*

[2.5]

[*Enter*] *Cosroe* [*wearing a crown*], *Tamburlaine, Theridamas, Menaphon, Meander, Ortygius, Techelles,* [*and*] *Usumcasane, with others.*

TAMBURLAINE [*giving Cosroe the crown taken from Mycetes*]
Hold thee, Cosroe, wear two imperial crowns.
Think thee invested° now as royally, *established in office*
Even by the mighty hand of Tamburlaine,
As if as many kings as could encompass° thee *surround*
With greatest pomp had crowned thee emperor.
COSROE So do I, thrice-renownèd man-at-arms,
And none shall keep° the crown but Tamburlaine. *protect*
Thee do I make my regent of Persia
And general lieutenant° of my armies. *lieutenant general*
Meander, you that were our brother's guide
And chiefest counselor in all his acts,

1. To call someone a liar to his face justified a deadly response. Mycetes' informal "thou" (used to address friends and social inferiors) also places Tamburlaine in a lower class by addressing him as a social inferior (since Tamburlaine is not a friend), and Tamburlaine responds in kind.
2.5. The field of battle.

Since he is yielded to the stroke of war,
On your submission we with thanks excuse,
And give you equal place in our affairs.[1]
MEANDER [*kneels*] Most happy Emperor, in humblest terms
I vow my service to Your Majesty
With utmost virtue of my faith and duty.
COSROE Thanks, good Meander. [*Meander rises.*] Then, Cosroe, reign
And govern Persia in her former pomp.
Now send embassage° to thy neighbor kings, *diplomatic missions*
And let them know the Persian king is changed
From one that knew not what a king should do
To one that can command what 'longs thereto.[2]
And now we will to fair Persepolis
With twenty thousand expert soldiers.
The lords and captains of my brother's camp
With little slaughter take Meander's course
And gladly yield them to my gracious rule.
Ortygius and Menaphon, my trusty friends,
Now will I gratify° your former good, *reward*
And grace your calling with a greater sway.° *leadership positions*
ORTYGIUS And as we ever aimed at your behoof,° *your best interests*
And sought° your state° all honor it deserved, *sought for / authority*
So will we with our powers and our lives
Endeavor to preserve and prosper it.
COSROE I will not thank thee,° sweet Ortygius; *merely thank you*
Better replies shall prove my purposes.
And now, Lord Tamburlaine, my brother's camp
I leave to thee and to Theridamas,
To follow me to fair Persepolis.
Then will we march to all those Indian mines
My witless brother to the Christians lost° *(see 1.1.118–22)*
And ransom° them with fame and usury;° *recover / profit*
And till thou overtake me, Tamburlaine,
Staying to order all the scattered troops,
Farewell, Lord Regent, and his happy friends!
I long to sit upon my brother's throne.
MENAPHON Your Majesty shall shortly have your wish
And ride in triumph through Persepolis.
Exeunt. Manent Tamburlaine, Techelles,
Theridamas, [*and*] *Usumcasane.*
TAMBURLAINE And ride in triumph through Persepolis!
Is it not brave° to be a king, Techelles? *splendid*
Usumcasane and Theridamas,
Is it not passing° brave to be a king *surpassingly*
And ride in triumph through Persepolis?
TECHELLES O my lord, 'tis sweet and full of pomp.
USUMCASANE To be a king is half to be a god.
THERIDAMAS A god is not so glorious as a king.
I think the pleasure they enjoy in heaven

1. After your submission to us we will, with thanks, excuse you your past actions and give you the same position under us you held under Mycetes. (Cosroe uses the royal "we.")
2. To one that can command in the way that belongs to kingship.

Cannot compare with kingly joys in earth.
To wear a crown enchased° with pearl and gold, *adorned*
Whose virtues carry with it life and death;
To ask, and have; command, and be obeyed;
When looks breed love, with looks to gain the prize—
Such power attractive shines in princes' eyes.

TAMBURLAINE Why, say, Theridamas, wilt thou be a king?

THERIDAMAS Nay, though I praise it, I can live without it.

TAMBURLAINE What says my other friends? Will you be kings?

TECHELLES Ay, if I could, with all my heart, my lord.

TAMBURLAINE Why, that's well said, Techelles. So would I,
And so would you, my masters,° would you not? *good sirs*

USUMCASANE What then, my lord?

TAMBURLAINE Why, then, Casane, shall we wish for aught
The world affords in greatest novelty
And rest attemptless,° faint, and destitute? *without trying*
Methinks we should not. I am strongly moved° *inclined to believe*
That if I should desire the Persian crown
I could attain it with a wondrous ease;
And would not all our soldiers soon consent
If we should aim at such a dignity?

THERIDAMAS I know they would, with our persuasions.

TAMBURLAINE Why, then, Theridamas, I'll first assay° *attempt*
To get the Persian kingdom to myself,
Then thou for Parthia, they for Scythia and Media.[3]
And if I prosper, all shall be as sure
As if the Turk, the Pope, Afric, and Greece
Came creeping to us with their crowns apace.

TECHELLES Then shall we send to this triumphing king
And bid him battle for his novel° crown? *newly acquired*

USUMCASANE Nay, quickly, then, before his room be hot.[4]

TAMBURLAINE 'Twill prove a pretty° jest, in faith, my friends. *clever*

THERIDAMAS A jest to charge on twenty thousand men?
I judge the purchase° more important far. *final result*

TAMBURLAINE Judge by thyself, Theridamas, not me,
For presently Techelles here shall haste
To bid him battle ere he pass too far
And lose more labor than the gain will quite.[5]
Then shalt thou see the Scythian Tamburlaine
Make but a jest to win the Persian crown.
Techelles, take a thousand horse with thee,
And bid him turn him back to war with us,
That° only made him king to make us sport. *Who*
We will not steal upon him cowardly,
But give him warning and more warriors.[6]
Haste thee, Techelles; we will follow thee.
What saith Theridamas?

THERIDAMAS Go on, for me.° *Exeunt.* *for my part*

3. Then the crown of Parthia will go to you, and the crowns of Scythia and Media will go to Usumcasane and Theridamas.

4. Before he has warmed up to being king.

5. And cause us to lose more labor than the reward of victory will be worth. (Said facetiously.)

6. (1) Numerical superiority; (2) the chance to assemble yet more troops.

2.6

[Enter] Cosroe, Meander, Ortygius, [and] Menaphon, with other soldiers.

COSROE What means this devilish shepherd to aspire
With such a giantly presumption,
To cast up hills against the face of heaven
And dare the force of angry Jupiter?° *king of the gods*
But as he thrust them underneath the hills
And pressed out fire from their burning jaws,[1]
So will I send this monstrous slave to hell,
Where flames shall ever feed upon his soul.

MEANDER Some powers divine, or else infernal, mixed
Their angry seeds at his conception,
For he was never sprung of human race,
Since with the spirit of his fearful pride
He dares so doubtlessly resolve of rule[2]
And by profession° be ambitious. *by explicit declaration*

ORTYGIUS What god, or fiend, or spirit of the earth,
Or monster turnèd to a manly shape,
Or of what mold or mettle° he be made, *form or substance*
What star or state soever govern him,
Let us put on our meet encount'ring minds,[3]
And, in detesting such a devilish thief,
In love of honor and defense of right,
Be armed against the hate of such a foe,
Whether from earth, or hell, or heaven he grow.

COSROE Nobly resolved, my good Ortygius.
And since we all have sucked one wholesome air,
And with the same proportion of elements
Resolve, I hope we are resembled,
Vowing our loves to equal death and life.[4]
Let's cheer our soldiers to encounter him,
That grievous image of ingratitude,
That fiery thirster after sovereignty,
And burn him in the fury of that flame° *i.e., his ambition*
That none° can quench but blood and empery.° *nothing / dominion*
Resolve, my lords and loving soldiers, now
To save your king and country from decay.
Then strike up drum! And all the stars that make
The loathsome circle of my dated life[5]
Direct my weapon to his barbarous heart
That thus opposeth him against the gods
And scorns the powers that govern Persia!

[Exeunt, to sound of drums.]

2.6. The Persian camp.
1. When Jupiter, or Zeus, defeated the rebellion of the giants, he cast them down under the mountains, where their wrath fueled volcanoes such as Mount Etna.
2. He dares so unhesitatingly to resolve to become king.
3. Let our minds be appropriate for the encounter, i.e., firm and fierce.
4. (1) Since we all breathe the same wholesome air (as Ortygius), and are composed of and will decompose into the same four elements, I hope we resemble him and one another in vowing mutual love whether for death or (victorious) life; (2) since we make resolutions with the same breath and the same bodily elements (as Ortygius), let us resemble him in vowing to meet death or life resolutely together.
5. All the stars and planets that determine the detestable way in which my life shall end.

[2.7]

Enter [the armies of Tamburlaine and Cosroe] to the battle, and, after the battle, enter Cosroe wounded, Theridamas, Tamburlaine, Techelles, [and] Usumcasane, with others.

COSROE Barbarous and bloody Tamburlaine,
Thus to deprive me of my crown and life!
Treacherous and false Theridamas,
Even at the morning of my happy state,
Scarce being seated in my royal throne,
To work my downfall and untimely end!
An uncouth° pain torments my grievèd soul, *strange; unpleasant*
And death arrests the organ of my voice,
Who, ent'ring at the breach thy sword hath made,
Sacks° every vein and artier° of my heart. *Lays waste / artery*
Bloody and insatiate Tamburlaine!

TAMBURLAINE The thirst of reign and sweetness of a crown,
That caused the eldest son of heavenly Ops
To thrust his doting father from his chair
And place himself in the empyreal heaven,[1]
Moved me to manage arms° against thy state. *make war*
What better precedent than mighty Jove?
Nature, that framed° us of four elements, *composed*
Warring within our breasts for regiment,° *dominance*
Doth teach us all to have aspiring minds.
Our souls, whose faculties can comprehend
The wondrous architecture of the world
And measure every wand'ring° planet's course, *(through the fixed stars)*
Still° climbing after knowledge infinite, *Ceaselessly*
And always moving as the restless spheres,
Wills us to wear° ourselves and never rest *weary*
Until we reach the ripest fruit of all:
That perfect bliss and sole felicity,
The sweet fruition of an earthly crown.

THERIDAMAS And that made me to join with Tamburlaine,
For he° is gross and like the massy earth *(anyone)*
That moves not upwards, nor by princely deeds
Doth mean to soar above the highest sort.

TECHELLES And that made us, the friends of Tamburlaine,
To lift our swords against the Persian king.

USUMCASANE For as when Jove did thrust old Saturn down
Neptune and Dis gained each of them a crown,[2]
So do we hope to reign in Asia
If Tamburlaine be placed in Persia.

COSROE The strangest men that ever nature made!
I know not how to take their tyrannies.
My bloodless body waxeth chill and cold,

2.7. The field of battle.
1. Jove, or Zeus, son of Saturn, or Cronus, and his wife, Ops, or Rhea (who preserved Jove at birth from his father's attempts to eat him), overthrew his father and became king of the gods, reigning through "the empyreal heaven," the outermost fixed sphere of fire and light beyond the stars. "Empyreal" also suggests "imperial" here.
2. After overthrowing his father, Jove created his brothers Neptune, or Poseidon, and Dis, or Hades, who had been regurgitated by their father undigested, as kings of the ocean and the underworld, respectively.

And with my blood my life slides through my wound.
My soul begins to take her flight to hell
And summons all my senses to depart;
The heat and moisture which did feed each other,
For want of nourishment to feed them both
Is dry and cold, and now doth ghastly death
With greedy talons grip my bleeding heart,
And like a harpy[3] tires° on my life. *preys, tears with a beak*
Theridamas and Tamburlaine, I die,
And fearful vengeance light upon you both!

[*Cosroe dies.*] *He* [*Tamburlaine*] *takes the crown and puts it on.*

TAMBURLAINE Not all the curses which the Furies breathe
Shall make me leave so rich a prize as this.
Theridamas, Techelles, and the rest,
Who think you now is king of Persia?
ALL Tamburlaine! Tamburlaine!
TAMBURLAINE Though Mars himself, the angry god of arms,
And all the earthly potentates conspire
To dispossess me of this diadem,
Yet will I wear it in despite of them
As great commander of this Eastern world,
If you but say that Tamburlaine shall reign.
ALL Long live Tamburlaine, and reign in Asia!
TAMBURLAINE So, now it is more surer on my head
Than if the gods had held a parliament
And all pronounced me king of Persia. [*Exeunt.*]

3.1

[*Enter*] *Bajazeth* [*Emperor of Turkey*]; *the Kings of Fez, Morocco, and Argier;* [*and a Basso,*]° *with others, in great pomp.* *pasha, Turkish general*

BAJAZETH Great kings of Barbary,° and my portly° bassos, *northwest Africa / stately*
We hear the Tartars and the Eastern thieves,
Under the conduct of one Tamburlaine,
Presume a bickering with your emperor
And thinks to rouse us from our dreadful siege
Of the famous Grecian Constantinople.
You know our army is invincible:
As many circumcisèd Turks we have
And warlike bands of Christians renièd[1]
As hath the ocean or the Terrene° Sea *Mediterranean*
Small drops of water when the moon begins
To join in one her semicircled horns.[2]
Yet would we not be braved° with foreign power, *challenged*
Nor raise our siege before the Grecians yield
Or breathless° lie before the city walls. *dead*
FEZ Renownèd Emperor and mighty general,

3. Harpies are mythological creatures with the wings and claws of a bird of prey and the face and upper body of a woman.

3.1. At the siege of Constantinople.
1. Apostatized, converted to Islam.
2. I.e., at the full moon, when tides are highest.

What if you sent the bassos of your guard
To charge him° to remain in Asia, — *order Tamburlaine*
Or else to threaten death and deadly arms
As from the mouth of mighty Bajazeth?

BAJAZETH Hie thee,° my basso, fast to Persia. — *Betake yourself, go*
Tell him° thy lord the Turkish emperor, — *(Tamburlaine)*
Dread lord of Afric, Europe, and Asia,
Great king and conqueror of Graecia,
The ocean Terrene, and the coal-black sea,° — *the Black Sea*
The high and highest monarch of the world,
Wills and commands (for say not I entreat)
Not once to set° his foot in Africa, — *That he should not set*
Or spread his colors° in Graecia, — *banners*
Lest he incur the fury of my wrath.
Tell him I am content to take a truce
Because I hear he bears a valiant mind.
But if, presuming on his silly° power, — *feeble*
He be so mad to manage arms° with me, — *to fight*
Then stay thou with him; say I bid thee so.
And if before the sun have measured heaven
With triple circuit thou regreet° us not, — *return to*
We mean to take his morning's next arise
For messenger he will not be reclaimed,[3]
And mean to fetch thee in despite of him.

BASSO Most great and puissant monarch of the earth,
Your basso will accomplish your behest
And show your pleasure to the Persian
As fits the legate° of the stately Turk. *Exit Basso.* — *emissary*

ARGIER They say he° is the king of Persia, — *(Tamburlaine)*
But if he dare attempt to stir° your siege — *disturb*
'Twere requisite he should be ten times more,
For all flesh quakes at your magnificence.

BAJAZETH True, Argier, and tremble at my looks.

MOROCCO The spring is hindered by your smothering host,° — *army*
For neither rain can fall upon the earth
Nor sun reflex° his virtuous beams thereon, — *shine*
The ground is mantled° with such multitudes. — *clothed, covered*

BAJAZETH All this is true as holy Mahomet,° — *Muhammad*
And all the trees are blasted° with our breaths. — *withered*

FEZ What thinks Your Greatness best to be achieved
In pursuit of the city's overthrow?

BAJAZETH I will the captive pioners° of Argier — *military miners*
Cut off° the water that by leaden pipes — *To cut off*
Runs to the city from the mountain Carnon;
Two thousand horse shall forage up and down
That no relief or succor come by land,
And all the sea my galleys countermand.° — *command and patrol*
Then shall our footmen lie within the trench,
And, with their cannons mouthed like Orcus' gulf,° — *hell's entry*
Batter the walls, and we will enter in,
And thus the Grecians shall be conquerèd. *Exeunt.*

3. We intend to take the fourth morning's sunrise as a sign that Tamburlaine will not be reclaimed to his duty to us, or to his senses as a military leader.

3.2

[Enter] Agydas, Zenocrate, [and] Anippe, with others.

AGYDAS Madam Zenocrate, may I presume
To know the cause of these unquiet fits
That work such trouble to your wonted° rest? *accustomed*
'Tis more than pity such a heavenly face
Should by heart's sorrow wax so wan and pale,
When your offensive rape° by Tamburlaine *seizure*
(Which of your whole displeasures should be most)[1]
Hath seemed to be digested° long ago. *accepted by you*
ZENOCRATE Although it be digested long ago,
As his exceeding favors have deserved,
And might content the Queen of Heaven as well
As it hath changed my first-conceived° disdain, *my initial*
Yet, since,° a farther passion feeds my thoughts *since then*
With ceaseless and disconsolate conceits,° *worries*
Which dyes my looks so lifeless as they are,
And might, if my extremes had full events,[2]
Make me the ghastly counterfeit of death.
AGYDAS Eternal heaven sooner be dissolved
And all that pierceth Phoebe's silver eye,[3]
Before such hap° fall to Zenocrate! *chance*
ZENOCRATE Ah, life and soul, still hover in his breast
And leave my body senseless as the earth,
Or else unite you to his life and soul,[4]
That I may live and die with Tamburlaine!

Enter Tamburlaine with Techelles and others [unseen by Agydas and Zenocrate].

AGYDAS With Tamburlaine? Ah, fair Zenocrate,
Let not a man so vile and barbarous,
That holds you from your father in despite
And keeps you from the honors of a queen
(Being supposed his worthless concubine)
Be honored with your love but for necessity.
So now° the mighty Sultan hears of you *As soon as*
Your Highness needs not doubt but in short time
He will with Tamburlaine's destruction
Redeem you from this deadly servitude.
ZENOCRATE Agydas, leave to° wound me with these words, *cease to*
And speak of Tamburlaine as he deserves.
The entertainment° we have had of him *reception*
Is far from villainy or servitude,
And might in noble minds be counted° princely. *accounted*
AGYDAS How can you fancy one that looks so fierce,
Only disposed to martial stratagems?
Who, when he shall embrace you in his arms,
Will tell how many thousand men he slew,
And when you look for amorous discourse

3.2. Somewhere in Asia Minor.
1. Which should be your greatest grievance. ("Rape," in line 6 above, can mean abduction as well as sexual assault, and here means the former; see lines 37–39 below and 5.1.486–87.)
2. (1) If my extremes of feeling had full expression; (2) if my extreme fears were to come to pass as events.
3. All that the moon shines upon.
4. Zenocrate here addresses her life and soul as "you," urging them to unite with Tamburlaine's life and soul.

Will rattle forth his facts° of war and blood, *acts*
Too harsh a subject for your dainty ears.
ZENOCRATE As looks the sun through Nilus'° flowing stream, *the Nile's*
Or when the morning° holds him° in her arms, *the Dawn / (the Sun)*
So looks my lordly love, fair Tamburlaine;
His talk much sweeter than the Muses' song
They sung for honor 'gainst Pierides,[5]
Or when Minerva did with Neptune strive,[6]
And higher would I rear my estimate
Than Juno, sister to the highest god,[7]
If I were matched with mighty Tamburlaine.
AGYDAS Yet be not so inconstant in your love,
But let the young Arabian° live in hope *the Arabian king*
After your rescue to enjoy his choice.° *i.e., by marrying you*
You see, though first the king of Persia,
Being a shepherd, seemed to love you much,
Now in his majesty he leaves those looks,
Those words of favor, and those comfortings,
And gives no more than common courtesies.
ZENOCRATE Thence rise the tears that so distain° my cheeks, *stain*
Fearing his love° through my unworthiness. *the loss of his love*

Tamburlaine goes to her, and takes her away lovingly by the hand, looking wrathfully on Agydas, and says nothing. [*Exeunt all but Agydas.*]

AGYDAS Betrayed by fortune and suspicious love,
Threatened with frowning wrath and jealousy,
Surprised with fear of hideous revenge,
I stand aghast, but most astonièd° *astonished*
To see his choler° shut in secret thoughts *anger*
And wrapped in silence of his angry soul.
Upon his brows was portrayed ugly Death,
And in his eyes the fury of his heart,
That shine as comets, menacing revenge,
And casts a pale complexion on his cheeks.
As when the seaman sees the Hyades
Gather an army of Cimmerian clouds—
Auster and Aquilon, with wingèd steeds
All sweating, tilt about the watery heavens
With shivering spears enforcing thunderclaps
And from their shields strike flames of lightning[8]—
All fearful folds his sails, and sounds the main,[9]
Lifting his prayers to the heavens for aid
Against the terror of the winds and waves,
So fares Agydas for the late-felt frowns
That sent a tempest to my daunted thoughts
And makes my soul divine° her overthrow. *foresee*

Enter Techelles with a naked dagger.

5. The nine daughters of King Pierus, called "the Pierides," challenged the Muses to a singing contest; defeated, they were turned into magpies.
6. Minerva, or Athena, and Neptune, or Poseidon, engaged in a competition of gifts to become the patron deity of Athens; Athena's gift of the olive tree won over Poseidon's gift of the horse.
7. Juno is of course not only Jove's, or Jupiter's, sister but also his wife.
8. The Hyades are a constellation in Taurus, associated with water; Cimmerian clouds are black, named after those who dwell in perpetual night; Auster is the south wind and Aquilon the north or north-northeast wind. Thus the seaman sees a major storm brewing.
9. Fearfully stows his sails to lessen the force of the wind, and takes soundings to avoid striking a shoal.

TECHELLES [*giving the dagger*] See you, Agydas, how the
King salutes° you. *greets*
He bids you prophesy what it imports. *Exit.*
AGYDAS I prophesied before, and now I prove° *experience*
The killing frowns of jealousy and love.
He needed not with words confirm my fear,
For words are vain where working tools present
The naked action of my threatened end.
It° says, Agydas, thou shalt surely die, *(The dagger)*
And of extremities elect the least;
More honor and less pain it may procure
To die by this resolvèd hand of thine
Than stay° the torments he and heaven have sworn. *await*
Then haste, Agydas, and prevent the plagues
Which thy prolongèd fates may draw on thee.
Go wander free from fear of tyrant's rage,
Removèd from the torments and the hell
Wherewith he may excruciate° thy soul, *torment*
And let Agydas by Agydas die,
And with this stab slumber eternally. [*Agydas stabs himself.*]

[*Enter Techelles and Usumcasane.*]

TECHELLES Usumcasane, see how right the man
Hath hit the meaning of my lord the King.
USUMCASANE Faith,° and, Techelles, it was manly done; *In faith*
And since he was so wise and honorable,
Let us afford him now the bearing hence
And crave° his triple-worthy burial. *ask permission for*
TECHELLES Agreed, Casane. We will honor him.
[*Exeunt, bearing Agydas' body.*]

3.3

[*Enter*] *Tamburlaine, Techelles, Usumcasane, Theridamas, Basso, Zenocrate,* [*and Anippe,*] *with others* [*with a throne*].

TAMBURLAINE Basso, by this° thy lord and master knows *by this time*
I mean to meet him in Bithynia.[1]
See how he comes!° Tush, Turks are full of brags *(said sarcastically)*
And menace more than they can well perform.
He meet me in the field and fetch thee hence?[2]
Alas, poor Turk, his fortune is too weak
T'encounter with the strength of Tamburlaine.
View well my camp, and speak indifferently:° *objectively*
Do not my captains and my soldiers look
As if they meant to conquer Africa?
BASSO Your men are valiant, but their number few
And cannot terrify his mighty host.
My lord, the great commander of the world,
Besides fifteen contributory kings,[3]

3.3. Asia Minor still, near Constantinople.
1. A region near Constantinople.
2. Bajazeth had promised to come get his basso if Tamburlaine did not promptly send him back with an agreement. Tamburlaine has kept the basso and points out sarcastically that Bajazeth, now overdue, has not arrived.
3. And commander also of fifteen tribute-paying kings who acknowledge Bajazeth's sovereignty as emperor.

Hath now in arms ten thousand janizaries,[4]
Mounted on lusty° Mauritanian steeds *fierce*
Brought to the war by men of Tripoli;
Two hundred thousand footmen that have served
In two set battles fought in Graecia,
And for the expedition of° this war, *to speed up*
If he think good, can from his garrisons
Withdraw as many more to follow him.

TECHELLES The more he brings, the greater is the spoil,° *plunder; overthrow*
For, when they perish by our warlike hands,
We mean to seat our footmen on their steeds
And rifle° all those stately janizars. *plunder*

TAMBURLAINE But will those kings accompany your lord?

BASSO Such as His Highness please, but some must stay
To rule the provinces he late° subdued. *lately*

TAMBURLAINE [*to Techelles, Theridamas, and Usumcasane*]
Then fight courageously! Their crowns are yours.
This hand shall set them on your conquering heads
That made me emperor of Asia.

USUMCASANE Let him bring millions infinite of men,
Unpeopling western Africa and Greece,
Yet we assure us of the victory.

THERIDAMAS Even he° that in a trice vanquished two kings *(Tamburlaine)*
More mighty than the Turkish emperor
Shall rouse him° out of Europe, and pursue *(Bajazeth)*
His scattered army till they yield or die.

TAMBURLAINE Well said, Theridamas! Speak in that mood,
For "will" and "shall" best fitteth Tamburlaine,
Whose smiling stars gives him assurèd hope
Of martial triumph ere he meet his foes.
I that am termed the scourge and wrath of God,
The only fear and terror of the world,
Will first subdue the Turk and then enlarge° *free*
Those Christian captives which you keep as slaves,
Burdening their bodies with your heavy chains
And feeding them with thin and slender fare,
That naked row about the Terrene° Sea, *Mediterranean*
And when they chance to breathe and rest a space
Are punished with bastones° so grievously *batons, cudgels*
That they lie panting on the galley's side
And strive for life at every stroke they° give. *(the Turks)*
These are the cruel pirates of Argier,
That damnèd train,° the scum of Africa, *crew*
Inhabited with straggling runagates,° *vagabonds; renegades*
That make quick havoc of the Christian blood.[5]
But, as I live, that town shall curse the time
That Tamburlaine set foot in Africa.

Enter Bajazeth with his bassos and contributory kings [*of Fez, Morocco, and Argier; Zabina; and Ebea. A throne is brought on*].

4. Special Turkish soldiers, in this case cavalry (see next line), often ex-Christians obtained as children by capture or tribute and intensively trained after their forced conversion.

5. This extended passage refers to the way Algerian pirates hunted and captured Christians and chained them as slaves to row their galleys, beating them in order to make them row in time.

BAJAZETH Bassos and janizaries of my guard,
Attend upon the person of your lord,
The greatest potentate of Africa.
TAMBURLAINE Techelles and the rest, prepare your swords.
I mean t'encounter with that Bajazeth.
BAJAZETH Kings of Fez, Moroccus, and Argier,
He calls me Bajazeth, whom you call lord.
Note the presumption of this Scythian slave.—
I tell thee, villain, those that lead my horse
Have to their names titles of dignity;
And dar'st thou bluntly call me Bajazeth?
TAMBURLAINE And know thou, Turk, that those which lead my horse
Shall lead thee captive thorough° Africa; *through*
And dar'st thou bluntly call me Tamburlaine?
BAJAZETH By Mahomet my kinsman's sepulcher,
And by the holy Alcoran,° I swear *Koran*
He shall be made a chaste and lustless eunuch
And in my sarell tend my concubines,[6]
And all his captains that thus stoutly° stand *bravely*
Shall draw the chariot of my emperess,
Whom I have brought to see their overthrow.
TAMBURLAINE By this my sword that conquered Persia,
Thy fall shall make me famous through the world.
I will not tell thee how I'll handle thee,
But every common soldier of my camp
Shall smile to see thy miserable state.
FEZ [*to Bajazeth*] What means the mighty Turkish emperor
To talk with one so base as Tamburlaine?
MOROCCO Ye Moors and valiant men of Barbary,
How can ye suffer° these indignities? *put up with*
ARGIER Leave words, and let them feel your lances' points,
Which glided through the bowels of the Greeks.
BAJAZETH Well said, my stout contributory kings!
Your threefold army and my hugy° host *huge*
Shall swallow up these baseborn Persians.
TECHELLES Puissant,° renowned, and mighty Tamburlaine, *Powerful*
Why stay we thus prolonging all their lives?
THERIDAMAS I long to see those crowns won by our swords,
That we may reign as kings of Africa.
USUMCASANE What coward would not fight for such a prize?
TAMBURLAINE Fight all courageously, and be you kings!
I speak it, and my words are oracles.
BAJAZETH Zabina, mother of three braver boys
Than Hercules, that in his infancy
Did pash° the jaws of serpents venomous,[7] *bash, smite*
Whose hands are made to grip a warlike lance,
Their shoulders broad, for complete armor fit,
Their limbs more large and of a bigger size
Than all the brats ysprung from Typhon's loins,[8]
Who, when they come unto their father's age,

6. The concubines in the Grand Turk's seraglio ("sarell") were tended by castrated eunuchs to preserve them for the Turk's sole use.
7. As an infant, Hercules strangled two poisonous serpents set in his cradle by Juno.
8. Typhon, a large monster, sired numerous other large monsters, including Cerberus, Chimera, the Nemean lion, and the Theban Sphinx. "Ysprung" ("ysprong" in the 1590 octavo; see Textual Notes, 3.3.109) is an archaic participial form meaning "having sprung."

Will batter turrets with their manly fists:
Sit here upon this royal chair of state
And on thy head wear my imperial crown
Until I bring this sturdy° Tamburlaine *unruly*
And all his captains bound in captive chains.

ZABINA [*putting on the Turkish crown and sitting on the Turkish throne*] Such good success happen to Bajazeth!

TAMBURLAINE Zenocrate, the loveliest maid alive,
Fairer than rocks of pearl and precious stone,
The only paragon° of Tamburlaine, *consort*
Whose° eyes are brighter than the lamps of heaven *You whose*
And speech more pleasant than sweet harmony,
That with thy looks canst clear the darkened sky
And calm the rage of thund'ring Jupiter:
Sit down by her, adornèd with my crown,
As if thou wert the empress of the world.
Stir not, Zenocrate, until thou see
Me march victoriously with all my men
Triumphing over him and these his kings,
Which I will bring as vassals to thy feet.
Till then, take thou my crown, vaunt of° my worth, *praise*
And manage words° with her as we will arms. *fight in words*

ZENOCRATE [*putting on the Persian crown and sitting on the Persian throne*] And may my love, the King of Persia,
Return with victory and free from wound!

BAJAZETH [*to Tamburlaine*] Now shalt thou feel the force of Turkish arms,
Which lately made all Europe quake for fear.
I have of Turks, Arabians, Moors, and Jews
Enough to cover all Bithynia.
Let thousands die! Their slaughtered carcasses
Shall serve for walls and bulwarks to the rest,
And as the heads of Hydra, so my power,
Subdued, shall stand as mighty as before.[9]
If they° should yield their necks unto the sword, *Even if my soldiers*
Thy soldiers' arms could not endure to strike
So many blows as I have heads for thee.
Thou knowest not, foolish-hardy° Tamburlaine, *foolhardy*
What 'tis to meet me in the open field,
That leave no ground for thee to march upon.

TAMBURLAINE Our conquering swords shall marshal us the way
We use to march upon the slaughtered foe,
Trampling their bowels with our horses' hooves—
Brave horses, bred on the white Tartarian hills.
My camp is like to° Julius Caesar's host, *My army is like*
That never fought but had the victory;
Nor in Pharsalia was there such hot war
As these my followers willingly would have.[1]
Legions of spirits fleeting in the air
Direct our bullets and our weapons' points

9. The Hydra, another of Typhon's brood (see note 8 above), had many heads and grew new ones whenever one of them was cut off.
1. Though heavily outnumbered, Julius Caesar defeated his rival Pompey the Great at the battle of Pharsalus in 48 B.C.E., thus establishing control over the Roman world.

And make your strokes to wound the senseless air,[2]
And when she sees our bloody colors spread,
Then Victory begins to take her flight,
Resting herself upon my milk-white tent.
But come, my lords, to weapons let us fall!
The field is ours, the Turk, his wife, and all.

Exit, with his followers.

BAJAZETH Come, kings and bassos, let us glut our swords
That thirst to drink the feeble Persians' blood.

Exit, with his followers.

ZABINA Base concubine, must thou be placed by me
That am the empress of the mighty Turk?
ZENOCRATE Disdainful Turkess and unreverend boss,° — *disrespectful fat woman*
Call'st thou me concubine, that am betrothed
Unto the great and mighty Tamburlaine?
ZABINA To Tamburlaine the great Tartarian thief?
ZENOCRATE Thou wilt repent these lavish° words of thine — *excessive*
When thy great basso-master and thyself
Must plead for mercy at his kingly feet
And sue to me° to be your advocates. — *beg me*
ZABINA And sue to thee? I tell thee, shameless girl,
Thou shalt be laundress to my waiting-maid.—
How lik'st thou her, Ebea? Will she serve?
EBEA Madam, she thinks perhaps she is too fine,
But I shall turn her into other weeds° — *change her clothes*
And make her dainty fingers fall to work.
ZENOCRATE Hear'st thou, Anippe, how thy drudge doth talk,
And how my slave, her mistress, menaceth?
Both, for their sauciness, shall be employed
To dress° the common soldiers' meat and drink, — *prepare*
For we will scorn they should come near ourselves.
ANIPPE Yet sometimes let Your Highness send for them
To do the work my chambermaid disdains.

They sound [trumpets to] the battle within, and stay.[3]

ZENOCRATE Ye gods and powers that govern Persia
And made my lordly love her worthy king,
Now strengthen him against the Turkish Bajazeth
And let his foes, like flocks of fearful roes° — *deer*
Pursued by hunters, fly his angry looks,
That I may see him issue° conqueror! — *return from battle*
ZABINA Now, Mahomet, solicit God Himself
And make Him rain down murdering shot from heaven
To dash the Scythians' brains and strike them dead
That dare to manage arms° with him — *engage in combat*
That offered jewels to thy sacred shrine
When first he warred against the Christians!

[Trumpets sound within] to the battle again.

ZENOCRATE By this° the Turks lie welt'ring in their blood, — *this time*
And Tamburlaine is lord of Africa.
ZABINA Thou art deceived; I heard the trumpets sound

2. This is an editorial emendation that gives Tamburlaine's spirit legions something to do. The 1590 octavo reads "And make our strokes to wound the sencelesse lure," which could conceivably mean "Make our blows, like well-trained falcons striking a lure, hit the target."
3. Trumpets sound backstage ("*within*"), then cease ("*stay*").

As when my emperor overthrew the Greeks
And led them captive into Africa.
Straight° will I use thee as thy pride deserves; *Straightaway*
Prepare thyself to live and die my slave.

ZENOCRATE If Mahomet should come from heaven and swear
My royal lord is slain or conquerèd,
Yet should he not persuade me otherwise
But that he lives and will be conqueror.

[Enter Bajazeth and Tamburlaine.] Bajazeth flies, and he [Tamburlaine] pursues him. [Both exeunt.] The battle short, and they enter; Bajazeth is overcome.

TAMBURLAINE Now, king of bassos, who is conqueror?

BAJAZETH Thou, by the fortune of this damnèd foil.° *defeat*

TAMBURLAINE Where are your stout° contributory kings? *brave*

Enter Techelles, Theridamas, [and] Usumcasane [carrying crowns].

TECHELLES We have their crowns; their bodies strew the field.

TAMBURLAINE Each man a crown? Why, kingly fought, i'faith!
Deliver them into my treasury.

ZENOCRATE Now let me offer to my gracious lord
His royal crown again, so highly won.

TAMBURLAINE Nay, take the Turkish crown from her, Zenocrate,
And crown me emperor of Africa.

ZABINA No, Tamburlaine, though now thou gat the best,° *just now you won*
Thou shalt not yet be lord of Africa.

THERIDAMAS Give her the crown, Turkess, you were best.[4]

He takes it from her and gives it [to] Zenocrate.

ZABINA Injurious villains, thieves, runagates!° *vagabonds*
How dare you thus abuse my majesty?

THERIDAMAS *[to Zenocrate]* Here, madam. You are empress; she is none.

TAMBURLAINE *[as Zenocrate crowns him]* Not now, Theridamas, her time is past.
The pillars that have bolstered up those terms
Are fall'n in clusters at my conquering feet.

ZABINA Though he be prisoner, he may be ransomed.

TAMBURLAINE Not all the world shall ransom Bajazeth.

BAJAZETH Ah, fair Zabina, we have lost the field,
And never had the Turkish emperor
So great a foil by any foreign foe.
Now will the Christian miscreants° be glad, *misbelievers*
Ringing with joy their superstitious bells
And making bonfires for my overthrow.
But ere I die, those foul idolaters
Shall make me bonfires with their filthy bones,
For though the glory of this day be lost,
Afric and Greece have garrisons enough
To make me sovereign of the earth again.

TAMBURLAINE Those wallèd garrisons will I subdue,
And write myself great lord of Africa;
So from the east unto the furthest west

4. If you know what's good for you.

Shall Tamburlaine extend his puissant arm.
The galleys and those pilling brigantines,[5]
That yearly sail to the Venetian gulf
And hover in the straits for Christians' wrack,[6]
Shall lie at anchor in the Isle Asant° *Zante (in Greece)*
Until the Persian fleet and men-of-war,
Sailing along the Oriental sea,° *Indian and Pacific Oceans*
Have fetched about the Indian continent
Even from Persepolis to Mexico,
And thence unto the straits of Jubalter,° *Gibraltar*
Where they shall meet and join their force in one,
Keeping in awe the Bay of Portingale° *Portugal*
And all the ocean by the British shore;[7]
And by this means I'll win the world at last.

BAJAZETH Yet set a ransom on me, Tamburlaine.

TAMBURLAINE What, think'st thou Tamburlaine esteems thy gold?
I'll make the kings of India, ere I die,
Offer their mines, to sue for peace, to me,
And dig for treasure to appease my wrath.—
Come, bind them both, and one lead in the Turk.
The Turkess let my love's maid lead away.

They bind them [*Bajazeth and Zabina*].

BAJAZETH Ah, villains, dare ye touch my sacred arms?
O Mahomet, O sleepy Mahomet!

ZABINA O cursèd Mahomet, that makest us thus
The slaves to Scythians rude and barbarous!

TAMBURLAINE Come, bring them in, and for this happy conquest
Triumph and solemnize° a martial feast. *celebrate*

Exeunt [*with Bajazeth and Zabina led, Zabina by Anippe*].

4.1

[*Enter the*] *Sultan of Egypt with three or four lords, Capolin* [*and a Messenger*].

SULTAN Awake, ye men of Memphis! Hear the clang
Of Scythian trumpets, hear the basilisks,[1]
That, roaring, shake Damascus' turrets down.[2]
The rogue of Volga holds Zenocrate,
The Sultan's daughter, for his concubine,
And with a troop of thieves and vagabonds
Hath spread his colors° to our high disgrace, *banners*
While you fainthearted base Egyptians
Lie slumbering on the flow'ry banks of Nile

5. Small pillaging pirate ships.
6. That wait in the straits giving entry to the Adriatic to prey on Christian vessels.
7. Tamburlaine will send the existing Persian navy eastward around India, across the Indian and Pacific Oceans ("the Oriental sea") and by Mexico across the Atlantic to rendezvous at Gibraltar (Jubalter) with the existing Muslim navies in the Mediterranean (which will await the circumnavigating Persians at Zante, or Zacynthus ["Asant"], on the western side of Greece); then the joint navy of Tamburlaine will take control of the Atlantic coast of Europe from Portugal ("Portingale") northward to Britain.
4.1. Memphis, on the Nile River near its delta.
1. Basilisks are siege cannon, also mythical reptiles that could kill or petrify with their gaze.
2. Cannon in Syrian Damascus would in fact be inaudible in Egyptian Memphis. The Sultan could be exhorting the men of Memphis to think about the outrage Tamburlaine commits by besieging Damascus. But Marlowe evidently thinks that Damascus and Memphis are near each other; see, e.g., 4.2.48, 4.4.69 ff., and 5.1.123 and note.

As° crocodiles that unaffrighted rest — *Like*
While thund'ring cannons rattle on their skins.

MESSENGER Nay, mighty Sultan, did Your Greatness see
The frowning looks of fiery Tamburlaine,
That with his terror and imperious eyes
Commands the hearts of his associates,
It might amaze Your royal Majesty.

SULTAN Villain, I tell thee, were that Tamburlaine
As monstrous as Gorgon, prince of hell,[3]
The Sultan would not start° a foot from him. — *step back*
But speak, what power hath he?

MESSENGER Mighty lord,
Three hundred thousand men in armor clad
Upon their prancing steeds, disdainfully
With wanton paces trampling on the ground;
Five hundred thousand footmen threat'ning shot,
Shaking their swords, their spears, and iron bills,° — *halberds*
Environing their standard round,° that stood — *Surrounding their banner*
As bristle-pointed as a thorny wood.
Their warlike engines and munition
Exceed the forces of their martial men.

SULTAN Nay, could their numbers countervail° the stars — *equal*
Or ever-drizzling drops of April showers
Or withered leaves that autumn shaketh down,
Yet would the Sultan by his conquering power
So scatter and consume them in his rage
That not a man should live to rue their fall.

CAPOLIN So might Your Highness, had you time to sort° — *put in order*
Your fighting men and raise your royal host.
But Tamburlaine by expedition° — *speed*
Advantage takes of your unreadiness.

SULTAN Let him take all th'advantages he can.
Were all the world conspired to fight for him,
Nay, were he devil, as he is no man,
Yet in revenge of fair Zenocrate,
Whom he detaineth in despite of us,
This arm should send him down to Erebus° — *hell*
To shroud his shame in darkness of the night.

MESSENGER Pleaseth° Your Mightiness to understand, — *May it please*
His resolution far exceedeth all.
The first day when he pitcheth down° his tents, — *sets up*
White is their hue, and on his silver crest
A snowy feather spangled white he bears,
To signify the mildness of his mind
That, satiate with spoil, refuseth blood.
But when Aurora° mounts the second time, — *Dawn*
As red as scarlet is his furniture;° — *tents, armor, etc.*
Then must his kindled wrath be quenched with blood,
Not sparing any that can manage arms.° — *wield weapons*
But if these threats move not submission,
Black are his colors, black pavilion,

3. Demogorgon, with a suggestion of the petrifying power of Gorgons, such as Medusa, mythological snake-haired monsters whose appearance turned beholders to stone. "Monstrous" is pronounced here with three syllables.

His spear, his shield, his horse, his armor, plumes,
And jetty° feathers menace death and hell. *jet-black*
Without respect of sex, degree, or age
He razeth all his foes with fire and sword.
SULTAN Merciless villain, peasant ignorant
Of lawful arms or martial discipline!
Pillage and murder are his usual trades;
The slave usurps the glorious name of war.
See,° Capolin, the fair Arabian king, *See to it that*
That hath been disappointed by this slave° *i.e., Tamburlaine*
Of my fair daughter and his princely love,
May have fresh warning to go war with us[4]
And be revenged for her disparagement.° [*Exeunt.*] *degrading misalliance*

4.2

[*Enter*] *Tamburlaine* [*clothed in white*], *Techelles, Theridamas, Usumcasane, Zenocrate, Anippe, two Moors drawing Bajazeth in his cage, and his wife* [*Zabina*] *following him* [*with others bringing a throne*].

TAMBURLAINE Bring out my footstool.
They [*the Moors*] *take him* [*Bajazeth*] *out of the cage.*
BAJAZETH Ye holy priests of heavenly Mahomet,
That, sacrificing, slice and cut your flesh,
Staining his altars with your purple blood,
Make heaven to frown and every fixèd star
To suck up poison from the Moorish fens
And pour it in this glorious° tyrant's throat! *vainglorious*
TAMBURLAINE The chiefest God, first mover of that sphere
Enchased° with thousands ever-shining lamps,[1] *Adorned (with stars)*
Will sooner burn the glorious frame of heaven
Than it should so conspire my overthrow.
But, villain, thou that wishest this to me,
Fall prostrate on the low disdainful earth
And be the footstool of great Tamburlaine,
That I may rise into my royal throne.
BAJAZETH First shalt thou rip my bowels with thy sword
And sacrifice my heart to death and hell
Before I yield to such a slavery.° *slavish action*
TAMBURLAINE Base villain, vassal, slave to Tamburlaine,
Unworthy to embrace or touch the ground
That bears the honor of my royal weight!
Stoop, villain! Stoop! Stoop! For so he bids
That may command thee piecemeal to be torn
Or scattered like the lofty cedar trees
Struck with the voice of thund'ring Jupiter.
BAJAZETH [*stooping on hands and knees in front of the throne*] Then as I look down to the damnèd fiends,
Fiends, look on me, and thou, dread god of hell,

4. May have a fresh notification to go to war alongside us against Tamburlaine.
4.2. The siege of Damascus.
1. God is described in medieval and Renaissance cosmology as the unmoved mover who imparts energy to the universe by rotating the outermost sphere of the fixed stars.

With ebon° scepter strike this hateful earth *ebony, black*
And make it swallow both of us at once!
He [Tamburlaine] gets up upon him to his chair.

TAMBURLAINE Now clear the triple region of the air,[2]
And let the majesty of heaven behold
Their scourge and terror tread on emperors.
Smile, stars that reigned at my nativity,
And dim the brightness of their neighbor lamps!
Disdain to borrow light of Cynthia,° *the moon*
For I, the chiefest lamp of all the earth,
First rising in the east with mild aspect
But fixèd now in the meridian line,° *zenith*
Will send up fire to your turning spheres
And cause the sun to borrow light of you.[3]
My sword struck fire from his coat of steel
Even in Bithynia, when I took this Turk,
As when a fiery exhalation
Wrapped in the bowels of a freezing cloud,
Fighting for passage, makes the welkin° crack, *heavens*
And casts a flash of lightning to the earth.
But ere I march to wealthy Persia,
Or leave Damascus and th'Egyptian fields,
As was the fame of Clymene's brainsick son
That almost brent the axletree of heaven,[4]
So shall our swords, our lances, and our shot
Fill all the air with fiery meteors.
Then, when the sky shall wax as red as blood,
It shall be said I made it red myself,
To make me think of naught but blood and war.

ZABINA Unworthy king, that by thy cruelty
Unlawfully usurpest the Persian seat,
Dar'st thou, that never saw an emperor
Before thou met my husband in the field,
Being thy captive, thus abuse his state,
Keeping his kingly body in a cage,
That roofs of gold and sun-bright palaces
Should have prepared to entertain His Grace,
And treading him beneath thy loathsome feet
Whose feet the kings of Africa have kissed?

TECHELLES [*to Tamburlaine*] You must devise some torment worse, my lord,
To make these captives rein their lavish° tongues. *insolent*

TAMBURLAINE Zenocrate, look better to° your slave.° *govern better / (Zabina)*

ZENOCRATE She is my handmaid's slave, and she° shall look *(Anippe)*
That these abuses flow not from her° tongue.— *(Zabina's)*
Chide her, Anippe.

ANIPPE [*to Zabina*] Let these be warnings for you then, my slave,
How you abuse the person of the King,

2. The air was thought to be divided into three zones: a region of sun-warmed air closest to the earth, a region of cold above that, and a region of fire above that and under the moon's sphere.
3. The stars were sometimes thought to borrow their light from the moon (Cynthia) and the sun. Tamburlaine, now risen from his mild beginnings in the east to his zenith in midsky ("the meridian line"), will impart so much light to his birth stars that the sun will be compelled to borrow light from them.
4. Phaëthon, son of the nymph Clymene and Apollo Helios, god of the sun, begged leave to drive his father's sun-chariot and then did so recklessly, nearly burning up the world and thus the axle on which the heavens turn. Zeus was forced to destroy him.

Or else I swear to have you whipped stark naked.
BAJAZETH Great Tamburlaine, great in my overthrow,
Ambitious pride shall make thee fall as low
For treading on the back of Bajazeth,
That should be horsèd on four mighty kings.
TAMBURLAINE Thy names and titles and thy dignities
Are fled from Bajazeth and remain with me,
That will maintain it 'gainst a world of kings.—
Put him in again. [*The Moors recage Bajazeth.*]
BAJAZETH Is this a place for mighty Bajazeth?
Confusion° light on him that helps thee thus! *Destruction*
TAMBURLAINE There whiles° he lives shall Bajazeth be kept, *while*
And where I go be thus in triumph drawn,[5]
And thou his wife shalt feed him with the scraps
My servitures° shall bring thee from my board,° *servants / table*
For he that gives him other food than this
Shall sit by him and starve to death himself.
This is my mind, and I will have it so.
Not all the kings and emperors of the earth,
If they would lay their crowns before my feet,
Shall ransom him or take him from his cage.
The ages that shall talk of Tamburlaine,
Even from this day to Plato's wondrous year,[6]
Shall talk how I have handled Bajazeth.
These Moors that drew him from Bithynia
To fair Damascus, where we now remain,
Shall lead him with us wheresoe'er we go.
Techelles and my loving followers,
Now may we see Damascus' lofty towers,
Like to the shadows of pyramides,[7]
That with their beauties graced the Memphian fields.
The golden statue of their feathered bird[8]
That spreads her wings upon the city walls
Shall not defend it from our battering shot.
The townsmen mask° in silk and cloth of gold, *dress up*
And every house is as a treasury.
The men, the treasure, and the town is ours.
THERIDAMAS Your tents of white now pitched before the gates,
And gentle flags of amity displayed,
I doubt not but the Governor will yield,
Offering Damascus to Your Majesty.
TAMBURLAINE So shall he have his life, and all the rest.
But if he stay until the bloody flag
Be once advanced° on my vermilion tent, *raised aloft*
He dies, and those that kept us out so long.
And when they see me march in black array,
With mournful streamers hanging down their heads,° *drooping*
Were in that city all the world contained,
Not one should scape,° but perish by our swords. *escape, survive*

5. Tamburlaine will have Bajazeth drawn caged behind him as part of triumphal processions.
6. The Platonic year, around thirty thousand ordinary years, is the time taken for the sun, the moon, and the five visible planets to return to any particular apparent position relative to one another. Plato suggests in *Timaeus*, 38b–39e, that the world will end when the planets, the sun, and the moon return to their original positions.
7. Like copies or imitations of pyramids.
8. The sacred ibis, which was worshiped as a god by the Egyptians. See 4.3.37.

ZENOCRATE Yet would you have some pity for my sake,
Because it is my country's, and my father's.
TAMBURLAINE Not for the world, Zenocrate, if I have sworn.—
Come, bring in the Turk.
Exeunt [the Moors drawing Bajazeth in his cage].

4.3

[Enter the] Sultan, [the King of] Arabia, [and] Capolin, with streaming colors, and soldiers.

SULTAN *[to the King of Arabia]* Methinks we march as Meleager did,
Environèd° with brave Argolian knights, *Surrounded*
To chase the savage Calydonian boar,
Or Cephalus with lusty Theban youths
Against the wolf that angry Themis sent
To waste and spoil° the sweet Aonian fields.[1] *despoil*
A monster of five hundred thousand heads,
Compact of° rapine, piracy, and spoil, *Made up of*
The scum of men, the hate and scourge of God,
Raves° in Egyptia and annoyeth us. *Roves; ravens, plunders*
My lord, it is the bloody Tamburlaine,
A sturdy felon and a base-bred thief,
By murder raisèd to the Persian crown,
That dares control° us in our territories. *challenge*
To tame the pride of this presumptuous beast,
Join your Arabians with the Sultan's power;
Let us unite our royal bands in one
And hasten to remove° Damascus' siege. *relieve, raise*
It is a blemish to the majesty
And high estate of mighty emperors
That such a base usurping vagabond
Should brave° a king or wear a princely crown. *challenge*
ARABIA Renownèd Sultan, have ye lately heard
The overthrow of mighty Bajazeth
About the confines° of Bithynia, *Near the borders*
The slavery wherewith he° persecutes *(Tamburlaine)*
The noble Turk and his great emperess?
SULTAN I have, and sorrow for his bad success.
But, noble lord of great Arabia,
Be so persuaded that the Sultan is
No more dismayed with tidings of his fall
Than in the haven° when the pilot stands *harbor*
And views a stranger's ship rent in the winds
And shiverèd against a craggy rock.
Yet in compassion of his° wretched state, *(Bajazeth's)*
A sacred vow to heaven and him I make,
Confirming it with Ibis'° holy name, *Egyptian bird-god*
That Tamburlaine shall rue the day, the hour,
Wherein he wrought such ignominious wrong

4.3. Near Damascus.
1. Meleager, in company with the warriors of Argolis in the Greek Peloponnese, hunted and killed a wild boar sent by Artemis to ravage Calydon. Cephalus hunted a fox (here a wolf) sent by Themis (a Titaness) that was devastating the Theban countryside (here called the Aonian fields) and was uncatchable until Zeus turned both it and Cephalus' marvelous hound into stone.

Unto the hallowed person of a prince,
Or kept the fair Zenocrate so long
As concubine, I fear, to feed his lust.

ARABIA Let grief and fury hasten on revenge!
Let Tamburlaine for his offenses feel
Such plagues as heaven and we can pour on him.
I long to break my spear upon his crest
And prove° the weight of his victorious arm, *test*
For fame, I fear, hath been too prodigal
In sounding through the world his partial praise.[2]

SULTAN Capolin, hast thou surveyed our powers?

CAPOLIN Great emperors of Egypt and Arabia,
The number of your hosts united is
A hundred and fifty thousand horse,
Two hundred thousand foot, brave men-at-arms,
Courageous and full of hardiness,
As frolic° as the hunters in the chase *merry*
Of savage beasts amid the desert° woods. *wild*

ARABIA My mind presageth fortunate success,
And, Tamburlaine, my spirit doth foresee
The utter ruin of thy men and thee.

SULTAN Then rear your standards! Let your sounding drums
Direct our soldiers to Damascus' walls.
Now, Tamburlaine, the mighty Sultan comes
And leads with him the great Arabian King
To dim thy baseness and obscurity,
Famous for nothing but for theft and spoil,
To raze and scatter thy inglorious crew
Of Scythians and slavish Persians.

Exeunt [to sound of drums].

4.[4]

[Enter servants to set up] the banquet, and to it cometh Tamburlaine all in scarlet, [Zenocrate,] Theridamas, Techelles, Usumcasane, the Turk [Bajazeth, drawn in his cage by two Moors, and Zabina], with others.

TAMBURLAINE Now hang our bloody° colors by Damascus, *bloodred*
Reflexing° hues of blood upon their heads *Reflecting*
While they walk quivering on their city walls,
Half-dead for fear before° they feel my wrath. *even before*
Then let us freely banquet and carouse° *drink heartily*
Full bowls of wine unto the god of war,
That means to fill your helmets full of gold
And make Damascus' spoils as rich to you
As was to Jason Colchos' Golden Fleece.[1]
And now, Bajazeth, hast thou any stomach?° *appetite*

BAJAZETH Ay, such a stomach, cruel Tamburlaine, as I could willingly feed upon thy blood-raw heart.

TAMBURLAINE Nay, thine own is easier to come by; pluck out

2. Fame has been reckless ("prodigal") and biased ("partial") in sounding Tamburlaine's praises through the world.

4.4. The siege of Damascus.

1. Jason led the Argonauts to Colchis on the Black Sea in search of the Golden Fleece.

that, and 'twill serve thee and thy wife. Well, Zenocrate,
Techelles, and the rest, fall to your victuals.

BAJAZETH Fall to, and never may your meat digest!
Ye Furies that can mask° invisible, *disguise yourselves as*
Dive to the bottom of Avernus' pool,° *lake of hell*
And in your hands bring hellish poison up
And squeeze it in the cup of Tamburlaine!
Or, wingèd snakes of Lerna, cast your stings
And leave your venoms in this tyrant's dish![2]

ZABINA And may this banquet prove as ominous
As Procne's to th'adulterous Thracian king
That fed upon the substance of his child![3]

ZENOCRATE My lord, how can you suffer° these outrageous curses by these slaves of yours? *put up with*

TAMBURLAINE To let them see, divine Zenocrate,
I glory in the curses of my foes,
Having the power from the empyreal heaven
To turn them all upon their proper° heads. *their own*

TECHELLES I pray you give them leave, madam. This speech is a goodly refreshing to them.

THERIDAMAS But if His Highness would let them be fed, it would do them more good.

TAMBURLAINE [*to Bajazeth*] Sirrah, why fall you not to?[4] Are you so daintily brought up you cannot eat your own flesh?

BAJAZETH First, legions of devils shall tear thee in pieces.

USUMCASANE Villain, knowest thou to whom thou speakest?

TAMBURLAINE [*offering food to Bajazeth with his sword*] Oh, let him alone.—Here, eat, sir; take it from my sword's point, or I'll thrust it to thy heart.

He [*Bajazeth*] *takes it and stamps upon it.*

THERIDAMAS He stamps it under his feet, my lord.

TAMBURLAINE Take it up, villain, and eat it, or I will make thee slice the brawns° of thy arms into carbonados[5] and eat them. *muscles*

USUMCASANE Nay, 'twere better he killed his wife, and then she shall be sure not to be starved, and he be provided for a month's victual beforehand.

TAMBURLAINE [*to Bajazeth*] Here is my dagger. Dispatch her while she is fat, for if she live but a while longer, she will fall into a consumption with fretting, and then she will not be worth the eating.

THERIDAMAS Dost thou think that Mahomet will suffer this?

TECHELLES 'Tis like° he will, when he cannot let° it. *likely / prevent*

TAMBURLAINE [*to Bajazeth*] Go to, fall to your meat. What, not a bit? Belike° he hath not been watered today.[6]—Give him some drink. *Probably*

They [*the Moors*] *give him* [*Bajazeth*] *water to drink, and he flings it on the ground.*

2. The Lernaean Hydra had many snakelike heads whose poison was deadly. The Furies (line 17) pursued sacrilegious criminals in classical myth.

3. After her husband, King Tereus of Thrace, raped and mutilated her sister Philomela, Procne served Tereus their son in a stew.

4. To "fall to" a meal is to dig in. "Sirrah" is a mode of address used in speaking to a social inferior, usually used to address servants.

5. Pieces of meat that are scored with a knife in order to be grilled more effectively.

6. Animals are "watered," i.e., given water to drink.

Fast, and welcome, sir, while° hunger make you eat. How now, Zenocrate, doth not the Turk and his wife make a goodly show at a banquet? — *until*

ZENOCRATE Yes, my lord.

THERIDAMAS Methinks 'tis a great deal better than a consort° of music. — *instrumental group*

TAMBURLAINE Yet music would do well to cheer up Zenocrate. [*To Zenocrate*] Pray thee, tell: why art thou so sad? If thou wilt have a song, the Turk shall strain his voice. But why is it?

ZENOCRATE My lord, to see my father's town besieged,
The country wasted where myself was born—
How can it but° afflict my very soul? — *do anything but*
If any love remain in you, my lord,
Or if my love unto Your Majesty
May merit favor at Your Highness' hands,
Then raise your siege from fair Damascus' walls
And with my father take° a friendly truce. — *make, accept*

TAMBURLAINE Zenocrate, were Egypt Jove's own land,
Yet would I with my sword make Jove to stoop.
I will confute those blind geographers
That make a triple region in the world,[7]
Excluding regions which I mean to trace,[8]
And with this pen° reduce them to a map, — *i.e., sword*
Calling the provinces, cities, and towns
After my name and thine, Zenocrate.
Here at Damascus will I make the point
That shall begin the perpendicular.[9]
And wouldst thou have me buy thy father's love
With such a loss? Tell me, Zenocrate.

ZENOCRATE Honor still wait on happy Tamburlaine!
Yet give me leave to plead for him, my lord.

TAMBURLAINE Content thyself, his person shall be safe,
And all the friends of fair Zenocrate,
If with their lives they will be pleased to yield
Or may be forced to make me emperor,
For Egypt and Arabia must be mine.
[*To Bajazeth*] Feed, you slave. Thou mayst think thyself happy to be fed from my trencher.

BAJAZETH My empty stomach, full of idle heat,
Draws bloody humors from my feeble parts,
Preserving life by hasting cruel death.[1]
My veins are pale, my sinews hard and dry,
My joints benumbed. Unless I eat, I die.

ZABINA Eat, Bajazeth. Let us live in spite of them, looking° some happy power will pity and enlarge° us. — *hoping that*; *free*

7. Who divide the world into Europe, Asia, and Africa. (Tamburlaine objects to the geographers' division of areas he intends to unite by conquest.)
8. (1) To travel; (2) to chart or draw.
9. Tamburlaine may have in mind a "T in O" map, in which a capital T is inscribed in a circle to symbolically divide the world in three. In this case his conquest of Damascus, by opening the continent of Africa to him (and perhaps that of Europe as well), will be a key moment in his making that T his own initial, with a point at Damascus serving as the beginning of the downstroke (Damascus being just the first of many conquests Tamburlaine imagines for himself; see lines 140–46 below).
1. Bajazeth's stomach, full of digestive energy without anything to work on ("idle heat"), draws blood from the rest of his body, thus attempting to preserve the stomach's life but hastening his death.

TAMBURLAINE [*offering a clean plate*] Here, Turk, wilt thou have a clean trencher?

BAJAZETH Ay, tyrant, and more meat.

TAMBURLAINE Soft, sir, you must be dieted; too much eating will make you surfeit.° *sick from overindulgence*

THERIDAMAS So it would, my lord, specially having so small a walk and so little exercise.

Enter a second course of crowns.[2]

TAMBURLAINE Theridamas, Techelles, and Casane, here are the cates° you desire to finger, are they not? *dainty dishes*

THERIDAMAS Ay, my lord, but none save kings must feed with these.

TECHELLES 'Tis enough for us to see them, and for Tamburlaine only to enjoy them.

TAMBURLAINE [*offering a toast*] Well, here is now to the Sultan of Egypt, the King of Arabia, and the Governor of Damascus. Now take these three crowns, and pledge me, my contributory kings. [*He presents the crowns in turn.*] I crown you here, Theridamas, King of Argier; Techelles, King of Fez; and Usumcasane, King of Moroccus.—How say you to this, Turk? These are not your contributory kings.

BAJAZETH Nor shall they long be thine, I warrant them.

TAMBURLAINE Kings of Argier, Moroccus, and of Fez,
You that have marched with happy° Tamburlaine *fortunate*
As far as from the frozen plage of heaven
Unto the wat'ry morning's ruddy bower
And thence by land unto the torrid zone,[3]
Deserve these titles I endow you with
By valor and by magnanimity.
Your births shall be no blemish to your fame,
For Virtue is the fount whence honor springs,
And they are worthy she investeth kings.[4]

THERIDAMAS And since Your Highness hath so well vouchsafed,° *granted*
If we deserve them not with higher meeds° *deserts*
Than erst° our states and actions have retained,° *hitherto / maintained*
Take them away again and make us slaves.

TAMBURLAINE Well said, Theridamas. When holy Fates
Shall 'stablish me in strong Egyptia,
We mean to travel to th'Antarctic pole,
Conquering the people underneath our feet,
And be renowned as never emperors were.—
Zenocrate, I will not crown thee yet
Until with greater honors I be graced.

[*Exeunt, two Moors dragging Bajazeth in his cage.*]

2. The second course, in that the first course of the banquet has already come in, and in that Techelles, Usumcasane, and Theridamas have already been promised kingdoms in Asia in act 2. The crowns brought in are those Tamburlaine sent to his treasury after the defeat of Bajazeth in Bithynia (see 3.3.216–17).

3. From the frozen highlands (of Scythia) that are the boundary ("plage") between earth and the cold middle air of heaven, to the ruddy bower of the dawn in the eastern oceans (presumably at Persepolis), to the edge of the Sahara (the torrid zone of desert separating the Northern from the Southern Hemisphere).

4. And those whom Virtue makes kings are worthy.

5.1

[Enter] the Governor of Damascus, with three or four citizens, and four Virgins with branches of laurel in their hands.

GOVERNOR Still doth this man, or rather god of war,
Batter our walls and beat our turrets down,
And to resist with longer stubbornness
Or hope of rescue from the Sultan's power
Were but to bring our willful overthrow
And make us desperate of our threatened lives.[1]
We see his tents have now been alterèd
With terrors to the last and cruelest hue.
His coal-black colors, everywhere advanced,° *raised aloft*
Threaten our city with a general spoil;° *sack*
And if we should, with common rites of arms,
Offer° our safeties to his clemency, *Entrust*
I fear the custom proper to his sword,[2]
Which he observes as parcel of° his fame, *an integral part of*
Intending so to terrify the world,
By any innovation or remorse
Will never be dispensed with till our deaths.[3]
Therefore, for these our harmless virgins' sakes,
Whose honors and whose lives rely on him,
Let us have hope that their unspotted prayers,
Their blubbered° cheeks, and hearty humble moans *tear-stained*
Will melt his fury into some remorse,
And use us° like a loving conqueror. *get him to treat us*
FIRST VIRGIN If humble suits or imprecations° *prayers*
Uttered with tears of wretchedness and blood
Shed from the heads and hearts of all our sex
(Some made your wives, and some your children)
Might have entreated your obdurate breasts
To entertain some care of our securities
Whiles only danger° beat upon our walls, *threat of force*
These more-than-dangerous warrants of our death° *i.e., the black colors*
Had never been erected as they be,
Nor you depend on such weak helps as we.
GOVERNOR Well, lovely virgins, think our country's care,
Our love of honor, loath to be enthralled
To foreign powers and rough imperious yokes,
Would not with too much cowardice or fear,
Before all hope of rescue were denied,
Submit yourselves and us to servitude.
Therefore, in that your safeties and our own,
Your honors, liberties, and lives were weighed
In equal care and balance with our own,
Endure as we the malice of our stars,
The wrath of Tamburlaine, and power of wars,
Or be the means the overweighing° heavens *all-controlling*

5.1. The siege of Damascus.
1. Would only be to destroy ourselves deliberately and make us hopeless about our threatened lives.
2. The particular custom associated with Tamburlaine's sword (that black means no mercy).
3. Will not, by either innovation or remorse, be set aside until we are all dead.

Have kept to qualify these hot extremes,
And bring us pardon in your cheerful looks.
SECOND VIRGIN Then here before the majesty of heaven
And holy patrons° of Egyptia, *guardian gods*
With knees and hearts submissive we entreat
Grace to our words and pity to our looks,
That this device may prove propitious,
And through the eyes and ears of Tamburlaine
Convey events of mercy to his heart.[4]
Grant that these signs of victory we yield
May bind the temples of his conquering head
To hide the folded furrows of his brows° *his frowns*
And shadow° his displeasèd countenance *overshadow*
With happy looks of ruth and lenity.[5]
Leave us, my lord, and loving countrymen;
What simple° virgins may persuade, we will. *innocent*
GOVERNOR Farewell, sweet virgins, on whose safe return
Depends our city, liberty, and lives!
Exeunt [*Governor and citizens*].

[*Enter*] *Tamburlaine, Techelles, Theridamas, Usumcasane, with others; Tamburlaine all in black, and very melancholy.* [*The Virgins kneel.*]

TAMBURLAINE What, are the turtles frayed° out of their nests? *turtledoves frightened*
Alas, poor fools, must you be first° shall feel *the first that*
The sworn destruction of Damascus?
They know my custom. Could they not as well
Have sent ye out when first my milk-white flags
Through which sweet mercy threw her gentle beams,
Reflexing° them on your disdainful eyes, *Reflecting*
As now when fury and incensèd hate
Flings slaughtering terror from my coal-black tents
And tells for truth submissions° comes too late? *acts of submission*
FIRST VIRGIN Most happy king and emperor of the earth,
Image of honor and nobility,
For whom the powers divine have made the world
And on whose throne the holy Graces° sit, *goddesses of beauty*
In whose sweet person is comprised the sum
Of nature's skill and heavenly majesty:
Pity our plights, O, pity poor Damascus!
Pity old age, within whose silver hairs
Honor and reverence evermore have reigned!
Pity the marriage-bed, where many a lord
In prime and glory of his loving joy
Embraceth now with tears of ruth° and blood *pity*
The jealous° body of his fearful wife, *anxious*
Whose cheeks and hearts—so punished with conceit° *worry*
To think thy puissant never-stayèd° arm *never yet stopped*
Will part their bodies and prevent° their souls *deprive*
From° heavens of comfort yet their age° might bear— *Of / old age*

4. May convey the desirability of a merciful outcome to his heart. (The heart is here considered the seat of deliberation as well as of emotion.)

5. Pity and mercy. (The Virgins hope that Tamburlaine will accept the laurel boughs they bear as signs of Damascus' capitulation, wear the boughs as a victor's garland, and thus cover over his threatening expression with a merciful one.)

Now wax all pale and withered to the death,[6]
As well for° grief our ruthless governor *Both for*
Have thus refused the mercy of thy hand
(Whose scepter angels kiss and Furies° dread) *avenging spirits*
As for° their liberties, their loves, or lives. *And also for*
Oh, then, for these, and such as we ourselves,
For us, for infants, and for all our bloods,° *i.e., lives*
That never nourished thought against thy rule,
Pity, oh, pity, sacred emperor,
The prostrate service° of this wretched town! *abject submission*
And take in sign thereof this gilded wreath,
Whereto each man of rule° hath given his hand *each political leader*
And wished, as worthy subjects, happy means
To be investors of thy royal brows
Even with the true Egyptian diadem.[7] [*She offers a wreath.*]
TAMBURLAINE Virgins, in vain ye labor to prevent
That which mine honor swears shall be performed.
Behold my sword. What see you at the point?
VIRGINS Nothing but fear° and fatal steel, my lord. *fearfulness*
TAMBURLAINE Your fearful minds are thick and misty, then,
For there sits Death, there sits imperious Death,
Keeping his circuit° by the slicing edge. *Holding court*
But I am pleased you shall not see him there.
He now is seated on my horsemen's spears,
And on their points his fleshless body feeds.—
Techelles, straight go charge° a few of them *command*
To charge° these dames, and show my servant Death *charge upon*
Sitting in scarlet on their armèd spears.
OMNES° Oh, pity us! *All Virgins*
TAMBURLAINE Away with them, I say, and show them Death!
They [Techelles and others] take them away.
I will not spare these proud Egyptians
Nor change my martial observations° *system of making war*
For all the wealth of Gihon's golden waves,[8]
Or for the love of Venus,° would she leave *goddess of love*
The angry god of arms° and lie with me. *Mars*
They have refused the offer of their lives,° *to spare their lives*
And know my customs are as peremptory° *final*
As wrathful planets, death, or destiny.

Enter Techelles.

What, have your horsemen shown the virgins Death?
TECHELLES They have, my lord, and on Damascus' walls
Have hoisted up their slaughtered carcasses.
TAMBURLAINE A sight as baneful° to their souls, I think, *poisonous*
As are Thessalian drugs or mithridate.[9]
But go, my lords, put the rest to the sword.
Exeunt [except Tamburlaine].

6. The cheeks and hearts of the husband and wife wither at the fear that Tamburlaine's strong, undefeated arm will part them physically and thus keep their spirits from knowing the heavens of comfort they might have enjoyed in the future.
7. To be those who put the Egyptian crown on Tamburlaine's royal brow. (The golden wreath has been designated as a symbol of this intention.)
8. Gihon, one of the four rivers flowing out of Paradise through Eden, was sometimes identified with the Nile, thus collapsing the geographical distinction between Egypt and Syria, where Eden was often located.
9. Thessaly, in Greece, was famous for poisons. Mithridate is a mixture of drugs believed to be a universal antidote to poisons; perhaps the term is misused here to mean a poison.

Ah, fair Zenocrate, divine Zenocrate,
Fair is too foul an epithet for thee,
That, in thy passion for thy country's love
And fear to see thy kingly father's harm,
With hair disheveled wip'st thy watery cheeks,
And, like to Flora° in her morning's pride, *goddess of flowers*
Shaking her silver tresses in the air,
Rain'st on the earth resolvèd° pearl in showers *dissolved*
And sprinklest sapphires on thy shining face
Where Beauty, mother to the Muses, sits
And comments volumes with her ivory pen,[1]
Taking instructions from thy flowing eyes—
Eyes, when that Ebena° steps to heaven *Night*
In silence of thy solemn evening's walk,
Making the mantle of the richest night,
The moon, the planets, and the meteors, light.[2]
There° angels in their crystal armors fight *i.e., in Zenocrate's eyes*
A doubtful° battle with my tempted thoughts *uncertain of outcome*
For Egypt's freedom and the Sultan's life—
His life that so consumes Zenocrate,
Whose sorrows lay more siege unto my soul
Than all my army to Damascus' walls;
And neither Persia's sovereign nor the Turk
Troubled my senses with conceit of foil° *fear of defeat*
So much by much as doth Zenocrate.
What is beauty, saith my sufferings, then?
If all the pens that ever poets held
Had fed the feeling of their masters' thoughts
And every sweetness that inspired their hearts,
Their minds, and muses on admirèd themes,
If all the heavenly quintessence they still° *distill*
From their immortal flowers of poesy,
Wherein as in a mirror we perceive
The highest reaches of a human wit—
If these had made one poem's period° *complete accomplishment*
And all combined in beauty's worthiness,
Yet should there hover in their restless heads
One thought, one grace, one wonder at the least,
Which into words no virtue° can digest. *poetic power*
But how unseemly is it for my sex,
My discipline of arms and chivalry,
My nature and the terror of my name,
To harbor thoughts effeminate[3] and faint!
Save only that in beauty's just applause,
With whose instinct the soul of man is touched—
And every warrior that is rapt with love
Of fame, of valor, and of victory
Must needs have beauty beat on his conceits[4]—

1. Memory is usually the mother of the Muses; Tamburlaine often revises myth for his purposes. Here Beauty is imagined sitting on Zenocrate's face writing a commentary on her grief or perhaps on the situation that causes her grief. The idea is that Zenocrate's beauty, even when affected by her misery, remains an important factor in the situation.

2. Zenocrate's eyes are imagined as "making" the light of the stars, moon, planets, and meteors.

3. Overly loving (and hence female).

4. Every warrior that loves fame, valor, and victory must by the same faculty of conception be susceptible to the influence of beauty.

I, thus conceiving and subduing both,
That which hath stopped the tempest of the gods,
Even from the fiery spangled veil of heaven,
To feel the lovely warmth of shepherds' flames
And march in cottages of strewèd weeds,° *rush-strewn floors (?)*
Shall give the world to note, for all my birth,
That virtue solely is the sum of glory,
And fashions men with true nobility.[5]—
Who's within there?

Enter two or three [attendants].

Hath Bajazeth been fed today?
ATTENDANT Ay, my lord.
TAMBURLAINE Bring him forth, and let us know if the town be ransacked. *[Exeunt attendants.]*

Enter Techelles, Theridamas, Usumcasane, and others.

TECHELLES The town is ours, my lord, and fresh supply
Of conquest and of spoil is offered us.
TAMBURLAINE That's well, Techelles. What's the news?
TECHELLES The Sultan and the Arabian king together
March on us with such eager violence
As if there were no way but one with us.° *As if battle were inevitable*
TAMBURLAINE No more there is not, I warrant thee, Techelles.

They [attendants] bring in the Turk [Bajazeth, caged, and Zabina].

THERIDAMAS We know the victory is ours, my lord,
But let us save the reverend Sultan's life
For fair Zenocrate, that so laments his state.
TAMBURLAINE That will we chiefly see unto, Theridamas,
For sweet Zenocrate, whose worthiness
Deserves a conquest over every heart.—
And now, my footstool, if I lose the field,
You hope of liberty and restitution.—
Here let him stay, my masters, from° the tents, *outside*
Till we have made us ready for the field.—
Pray for us, Bajazeth! We are going.
Exeunt [all except Bajazeth and Zabina].
BAJAZETH Go, never to return with victory!
Millions of men encompass thee about
And gore thy body with as many wounds!
Sharp forkèd arrows light upon thy horse!
Furies from the black Cocytus° lake *a river in Hades*
Break up the earth, and with their firebrands
Enforce thee run° upon the baneful° pikes! *Force you to run / fatal*
Volleys of shot pierce through thy charmèd skin,
And every bullet dipped in poisoned drugs,
Or roaring cannons sever all thy joints,
Making thee mount° as high as eagles soar! *i.e., Blowing you up*
ZABINA Let all the swords and lances in the field

5. I, both feeling and conquering the love of beauty, which has drawn the gods down from the starry heavens to lovemaking like shepherds in humble cottages, will make the world see, despite my humble birth, that glory comes from virtuous action and internal excellence, which alone make true nobility.

Stick in his breast as in their proper rooms!° — *natural resting places*
At every pore let blood come dropping forth,
That ling'ring pains may massacre his heart
And madness send his damnèd soul to hell!

BAJAZETH Ah, fair Zabina, we may curse his power,
The heavens may frown, the earth for anger quake,
But such a star hath influence in his sword
As rules the skies and countermands the gods
More than Cimmerian Styx or Destiny.[6]
And then shall we in this detested guise,° — *appearance; situation*
With shame, with hunger, and with horror aye° — *always*
Griping our bowels with retorquèd° thoughts, — *obsessive, recurrent*
And have no hope to end our ecstasies.° — *frenzies*

ZABINA Then is there left no Mahomet, no god,
No fiend, no fortune, nor no hope of end
To our infamous, monstrous slaveries?
Gape, earth, and let the fiends infernal view
A hell as hopeless and as full of fear
As are the blasted banks of Erebus,
Where shaking ghosts with ever-howling groans
Hover about the ugly ferryman[7]
To get a passage to Elysium!
Why should we live, oh, wretches, beggars, slaves?
Why live we, Bajazeth, and build up nests° — *i.e., hopes*
So high within the region of the air,
By living long in this oppression,
That all the world will see and laugh to scorn
The former triumphs of our mightiness
In this obscure infernal servitude?

BAJAZETH O life more loathsome to my vexèd thoughts
Than noisome parbreak° of the Stygian snakes — *stinking vomit*
Which fills the nooks of hell with standing° air, — *stagnant*
Infecting all the ghosts with cureless griefs!
O dreary engines of my loathèd sight° — *my eyes*
That sees my crown, my honor, and my name
Thrust under yoke and thralldom of a thief!
Why feed ye still on day's accursèd beams
And sink not quite into my tortured soul?
You see my wife, my queen and emperess,
Brought up andproppèd by the hand of fame,
Queen of fifteen contributory queens,
Now thrown to rooms of black abjection,° — *degradation*
Smeared with blots of basest drudgery,
And villeiness° to shame, disdain, and misery! — *bondslave*
Accursèd Bajazeth, whose words of ruth° — *compassion*
That would with pity cheer Zabina's heart
And make our souls resolve° in ceaseless tears, — *dissolve*
Sharp hunger bites upon and gripes the root
From whence the issues of my thoughts do break.[8]
O poor Zabina, O my queen, my queen,

6. Both Styx (by which the Olympian gods swore unbreakable oaths) and Destiny are forces that can constrain the Olympian gods. Cimmeria is the land of darkness, and the river Styx flows out of Hades there.

7. Charon, who ferries the dead across the river Styx to the pagan afterworld, sometimes conceived pleasantly as Elysium, sometimes hellishly as Erebus.

8. Hunger grips and causes pangs at the root of Bajazeth's sympathy, so that even his loving thoughts for Zabina are tormented.

Fetch me some water for my burning breast,
To cool and comfort me with longer date,[9]
That in the shortened sequel of my life
I may pour forth my soul into thine arms
With words of love, whose moaning intercourse
Hath hitherto been stayed with° wrath and hate — *impeded by*
Of our expressless banned° inflictions. — *inexpressible cursed*

ZABINA Sweet Bajazeth, I will prolong thy life
As long as any blood or spark of breath
Can quench or cool the torments of my grief.

She goes out.

BAJAZETH Now, Bajazeth, abridge thy baneful° days — *pernicious*
And beat thy brains out of thy conquered head,
Since other means are all forbidden me
That may be ministers° of my decay. — *instruments*
O highest lamp of ever-living Jove,
Accursèd Day, infected with my griefs,
Hide now thy stainèd face in endless night
And shut the windows of the lightsome° heavens! — *radiant*
Let ugly Darkness with her rusty coach,° — *chariot*
Engirt° with tempests wrapped in pitchy clouds, — *Encircled*
Smother the earth with never-fading mists,
And let her horses from their nostrils breathe
Rebellious winds and dreadful thunderclaps,
That in this terror Tamburlaine may live,
And my pined° soul, resolved° in liquid air, — *tortured / dissolved*
May still excruciate° his tormented thoughts! — *torture*
Then let the stony dart of senseless cold
Pierce through the center of my withered heart
And make a passage for my loathèd life.

He brains himself against the cage.

Enter Zabina [with water in a drinking vessel].

ZABINA What do mine eyes behold? My husband dead!
His skull all riven in twain, his brains dashed out!
The brains of Bajazeth, my lord and sovereign!
O Bajazeth, my husband and my lord,
O Bajazeth, O Turk, O Emperor! Give him his liquor? Not I! Bring milk and fire, and my blood I bring him again; tear me in pieces, give me the sword with a ball of wildfire upon it. Down with him, down with him! Go to my child, away, away, away! Ah, save that infant! Save him! Save him! I, even I, speak to her. The sun was down. Streamers white, red, black, here, here, here. Fling the meat in his face. Tamburlaine, Tamburlaine! Let the soldiers be buried. Hell, death, Tamburlaine, hell! Make ready my coach, my chair, my jewels. I come, I come, I come!

She runs against the cage and brains herself.

[Enter] Zenocrate with Anippe.

ZENOCRATE Wretched Zenocrate, that livest to see
Damascus' walls dyed with Egyptian blood,
Thy father's subjects and thy countrymen,

9. To cool me, comfort me, and make my life last longer.

Thy streets strewed with dissevered joints of men
And wounded bodies gasping yet for life,
But most accurst to see the sun-bright troop
Of heavenly virgins and unspotted maids,
Whose looks might make the angry god of arms° *Mars*
To break his sword and mildly treat of° love, *speak of*
On horsemen's lances to be hoisted up
And guiltlessly endure a cruel death!
For every fell° and stout° Tartarian steed, *fierce / brave*
That stamped on others with their thund'ring hooves,
When all their riders charged their quivering spears,
Began to check the ground and rein themselves,
Gazing upon the beauty of their looks.[1]
Ah, Tamburlaine, wert thou the cause of this,
That term'st Zenocrate thy dearest love—
Whose° lives were dearer to Zenocrate *i.e., The virgins'*
Than her own life, or aught save thine own love?
[*Zenocrate sees the bodies of Bajazeth and Zabina.*]
But see, another bloody spectacle!
Ah, wretched eyes, the enemies of my heart,
How are ye glutted with these grievous objects,
And tell my soul more tales of bleeding ruth!° *pity*
See, see, Anippe, if they breathe or no.

ANIPPE No breath, nor sense, nor motion in them both.
Ah, madam, this their slavery hath enforced,
And ruthless cruelty of Tamburlaine.

ZENOCRATE Earth, cast up fountains from thy entrails
And wet thy cheeks for their untimely deaths;
Shake with their weight in sign of fear and grief!
Blush, heaven, that gave them honor at their birth,
And let them die a death so barbarous!
Those that are proud of fickle empery,
And place their chiefest good in earthly pomp,
Behold the Turk and his great emperess!
Ah, Tamburlaine, my love, sweet Tamburlaine,
That fights for scepters and for slippery crowns,
Behold the Turk and his great emperess!
Thou that in conduct of thy happy stars
Sleep'st every night with conquest on thy brows
And yet wouldst shun the wavering turns° of war, *reversals of fortune*
In fear and feeling of the like distress
Behold the Turk and his great emperess!
Ah, mighty Jove and holy Mahomet,
Pardon my love, oh, pardon his contempt
Of earthly fortune and respect of pity,
And let not conquest ruthlessly pursued
Be equally against his life incensed
In this great Turk and hapless emperess!
And pardon me that was not moved with ruth
To see them live so long in misery.
Ah, what may chance to thee, Zenocrate?

ANIPPE Madam, content yourself and be resolved.

1. The very warhorses, which trample enemies, checked their charge and reined themselves in when they saw the virgins' beauty.

Your love° hath Fortune so at his command *(Tamburlaine)*
That she shall stay and turn her wheel no more
As long as life maintains his mighty arm,
That fights for honor to adorn your head.

Enter a messenger [Philemus].

ZENOCRATE What other heavy news now brings Philemus?
PHILEMUS Madam, your father and th'Arabian king,
The first affecter of your excellence,° *i.e., Your first suitor*
Comes now as Turnus 'gainst Aeneas did,[2]
Armèd with lance into the Egyptian fields,
Ready for battle 'gainst my lord the King.
ZENOCRATE Now shame and duty, love and fear, presents
A thousand sorrows to my martyred soul.
Whom should I wish° the fatal victory, *wish to have*
When my poor pleasures are divided thus
And racked° by duty from my cursèd heart? *tortured*
My father and my first betrothèd love
Must fight against my life and present love,
Wherein the change I use condemns my faith
And makes my deeds infamous[3] through the world.
But as the gods, to end the Troyans'° toil, *Trojans'*
Prevented° Turnus of Lavinia *Deprived*
And fatally enriched Aeneas' love,
So for a final issue to my griefs,
To pacify my country and my love,
Must Tamburlaine by their resistless powers,
With virtue of a gentle victory,
Conclude a league of honor to my hope;
Then, as the powers divine have preordained
With happy safety of my father's life,
Send like defense of fair Arabia.[4]

They sound to the battle [with offstage trumpets], and Tamburlaine enjoys the victory.

After, [the King of] Arabia enters, wounded.

ARABIA What cursèd power guides the murdering hands
Of this infamous tyrant's soldiers,
That no escape may save their enemies
Nor fortune keep themselves from victory?
Lie down, Arabia, wounded to the death,
And let Zenocrate's fair eyes behold
That, as for her thou bear'st these wretched arms,° *defeated weapons*
Even so for her thou diest in these arms,
Leaving thy blood for witness of thy love.
ZENOCRATE Too dear a witness for such love, my lord.
Behold Zenocrate, the cursèd object
Whose fortunes never masterèd her griefs![5]

2. In Virgil's *Aeneid*, Turnus is killed making war on Aeneas. Turnus fights because Lavinia, first engaged to him, has been betrothed to Aeneas.
3. My change (in affection, from the King of Arabia to my present love, Tamburlaine) condemns my faithfulness and makes me infamous.
4. To conclude my griefs and bring my country and my love to peace, Tamburlaine must, in the name of the irresistible powers of heaven, achieve a gentle victory and an honorable settlement, sparing, if the gods permit, both my father and the King of Arabia.
5. Whose fortune (which gave her to Tamburlaine) never overcame her grief and regret at leaving the King of Arabia behind.

Behold her wounded in conceit° for thee *thought, sympathy*
As much as thy fair body is for me.
ARABIA Then shall I die with full contented heart,
Having beheld divine Zenocrate,
Whose sight with joy would take away my life—
As now it bringeth sweetness to my wound—
If I had not been wounded as I am.
Ah, that the deadly pangs I suffer now
Would lend an hour's license to my tongue
To make discourse of some sweet accidents° *happenings*
Have° chanced thy merits in this worthless bondage, *That have*
And that I might be privy to the state
Of thy deservèd contentment and thy love![6]
But, making now a virtue of thy sight
To drive all sorrow from my fainting soul,
Since death denies me further cause of joy,
Deprived of care, my heart with comfort dies,
Since thy desirèd hand shall close mine eyes. [*He dies.*]

Enter Tamburlaine leading the Sultan, Techelles, Theridamas, [*and*] *Usumcasane* [*bearing a crown*], *with others.*

TAMBURLAINE Come, happy father of Zenocrate,
A title higher than thy sultan's name.
Though my right hand have thus enthrallèd thee,
Thy princely daughter here shall set thee free—
She that hath calmed the fury of my sword
Which had ere this been bathed in streams of blood
As vast and deep as Euphrates or Nile.
ZENOCRATE O sight thrice welcome to my joyful soul,
To see the King, my father, issue safe
From dangerous battle of° my conquering love! *with*
SULTAN Well met, my only dear Zenocrate,
Though with the loss of Egypt and my crown.
TAMBURLAINE 'Twas I, my lord, that gat the victory,
And therefore grieve not at your overthrow,
Since I shall render all into your hands
And add more strength to your dominions
Than ever yet confirmed° th'Egyptian crown. *supported; established*
The god of war resigns his room to me,
Meaning to make me general of the world.
Jove, viewing me in arms, looks pale and wan,
Fearing my power should pull him from his throne.
Where'er I come, the Fatal Sisters[7] sweat,
And grisly Death, by running to and fro,
To do their ceaseless homage to my sword;
And here in Afric, where it seldom rains,
Since I arrived with my triumphant host
Have swelling clouds, drawn from wide gasping wounds,
Been oft resolved° in bloody purple showers— *distilled*

6. The dying King of Arabia wishes he had time to hear of good things that have happened to Zenocrate during her bondage, and to learn of her contentment with and love for Tamburlaine.

7. The three Fates; see 1.2.174–75 and note.

A meteor° that might terrify the earth *weather event*
And make it quake at every drop it drinks.
Millions of souls sit on the banks of Styx,
Waiting the back return of Charon's boat.° *(see 5.1.246 n)*
Hell and Elysium swarm with ghosts of men
That I have sent from sundry foughten fields° *battlegrounds*
To spread my fame through hell and up to heaven.
And see, my lord, a sight of strange import:
[*Tamburlaine indicates the bodies of Bajazeth, Zabina, and Arabia.*]
Emperors and kings lie breathless° at my feet. *dead*
The Turk and his great emperess, as it seems,
Left to themselves while we were at the fight,
Have desperately dispatched their slavish lives.
With them Arabia too hath left his life—
All sights of power to grace my victory.
And such are objects fit for Tamburlaine,
Wherein, as in a mirror, may be seen
His honor, that consists in shedding blood
When men presume to manage arms° with him. *to combat*

SULTAN Mighty hath God and Mahomet made thy hand,
Renownèd Tamburlaine, to whom all kings
Of force° must yield their crowns and emperies,° *Of necessity / empires*
And I am pleased with this my overthrow
If, as beseems a person of thy state,
Thou hast with honor used Zenocrate.

TAMBURLAINE Her state and person wants° no pomp, you see, *lack*
And, for° all blot of foul inchastity, *as for*
I record° heaven, her heavenly self is clear. *call as a witness*
Then let me find no further time° to grace *let me not delay*
Her princely temples with the Persian crown;
But here these kings, that on my fortunes wait
And have been crowned for provèd worthiness
Even by this hand that shall establish them,
Shall now, adjoining all their hands with mine,
Invest her here my queen of Persia.
What saith the noble Sultan and Zenocrate?

SULTAN I yield with thanks and protestations
Of endless honor to thee for her love.

TAMBURLAINE Then doubt I not but fair Zenocrate
Will soon consent to satisfy us both.

ZENOCRATE Else should I much forget myself, my lord.

THERIDAMAS Then let us set the crown upon her head
That long hath lingered for so high a seat.

TECHELLES My hand is ready to perform the deed,
For now her marriage time shall work us rest.° *create a rest for us*

USUMCASANE And here's the crown, my lord. Help set it on.

TAMBURLAINE Then sit thou down, divine Zenocrate,
And here we crown thee Queen of Persia [*She is crowned.*]
And all the kingdoms and dominions
That late° the power of Tamburlaine subdued. *of late*
As Juno, when the giants were suppressed
That darted mountains at her brother Jove,
So looks my love, shadowing in her brows
Triumphs and trophies for my victories,

Or as Latona's daughter° bent to arms, *the goddess Diana*
Adding more courage to my conquering mind.[8]
To gratify thee, sweet Zenocrate,
Egyptians, Moors, and men of Asia,
From Barbary unto the Western Indie,° *India*
Shall pay a yearly tribute to thy sire,
And from the bounds of Afric to the banks
Of Ganges shall his mighty arm extend.
And now, my lords and loving followers,
That purchased kingdoms by your martial deeds,
Cast off your armor, put on scarlet robes,
Mount up your royal places of estate,[9]
Environèd° with troops of noble men, *Surrounded*
And there make laws to rule your provinces.
Hang up your weapons on Alcides' post,[1]
For Tamburlaine takes truce with all the world.
[*To Zenocrate*] Thy first betrothèd love, Arabia,
Shall we with honor, as beseems,° entomb, *is appropriate*
With this great Turk and his fair emperess.
Then after all these solemn exequies° *funerals*
We will our celebrated rites of marriage solemnize.
[*Exeunt, bearing the dead bodies in a procession.*]

8. Zenocrate's relieved and loving looks, prefiguring in her smiling brows a series of loving rewards for Tamburlaine's victories, resemble those of Juno when her brother Jove (Jupiter) overcame the mountain-throwing Titans; or those same looks may also be compared to the looks of the goddess Diana, ready for conflict, bringing still more courage to Tamburlaine's invincible spirit.

9. Mount thrones in your royal palaces.

1. The doorpost of the temple of Hercules (Alcides is another name for Hercules), or, metaphorically, the Pillars of Hercules that bound the Strait of Gibraltar, indicating the extent of Tamburlaine's African conquest.

TEXTUAL NOTES

Part 1 of *Tamburlaine the Great* was entered in the Stationers' Register, along with Part 2, by Richard Jones in 1590 as "The twooe commicall discourses of Tomberlein the Cithian shepparde." Together they were published by Jones in octavo form that same year. The printer evidently chose to excise the "commicall" elements of the play, as he explains in his note "To the Gentlemen Readers." Other early editions of these plays, appearing in 1592 or 1593 (the date on the title page of the British Library's unique copy of O2 has been tampered with and reads either "1592" or "1593"), 1597, and 1605–6, have no authority. The present text is based on the octavo of 1590. Substantive departures from it are noted here, using the following abbreviations:

O1: The octavo of 1590 (London: Richard Jones)
O2: The octavo of 1592 or 1593 (London: Richard Jones)
O3: The octavo of 1597 (London: Richard Jones)
Q: The quarto of 1605–6 (London: Richard Jones)
ed.: A modern editor's emendation

To the Gentlemen Readers 24 [and elsewhere] **travail** [O1: trauell]
Prologue 1 PROLOGUE [ed.; not in O1]
1.1.15 their [ed.] his [O1] **19 through** [O3] thorough [O1] **38 Trading** [O2] Treading [O1] **87 task** [ed.; not in O1] **132** [and elsewhere] **Lest** [O1:

Least] **135.1** ***Ceneus*** [O3] *Conerus* [O1] **170 may Jove** [ed.] Ioue may [O1] **177 Whither** [O1: Whether] **182 lords** [O3] Lord [O1]

1.2.6 [and elsewhere] **Sultan** [O1: Souldan] **12** [and elsewhere] **Media** [O1: *Medea*] **67 they** [O3] thee [O1] **84** [and elsewhere] **weigh** [O1: way] **88 Rhodope** [ed.] Rhodolfe [O1] **93 hundred** [O1: hundreth] **126 waist** [O1: waste] **133 mountaintop** [Q] mountain foot [O1] **138 mails** [O1: Males] **188** [and elsewhere] **renownèd** [O1: renowmed] **193 cliffs** [O1: clifts] **207 Boötes** [O1: Botëes] **244 statues** [O3] statutes [O1]

2.1.27 sinewy [ed.] snowy [O1] **42 strait** [O1: straight] **46 overweigh** [O1: ouerway]

2.2.15 pitched [O2] pitch [O1] **26 led** [O1: lead] **40 champaign** [O1: champion] **48, 52** [and elsewhere] **Sprung** [O1: Sprong]

2.3.7 oracles of heaven [ed.] Oracles, heauen [O1] **26 top** [ed.] stop [O1] **33 and** [Q] not [O1] **64 scare** [O1: scarre]

2.5.32 aimed [O3] and [O1] **96 quite** [O1: quight] **100 him back** [ed.] his back [O1] **104 thee** [ed.] the [O1]

2.6.30 ingratitude [O2] ingratude [O1] **33 quench** [O1: quence]

2.7.17 precedent [O1: president] **49 talons** [O1: tallents] **49** [and elsewhere] **grip** [O1: gripe] **67 SD** [O1 follows with "*Finis Actus 2.*"]

3.1.0.2 [and elsewhere] ***Fez*** [O1: *Fess* or *Fesse*]

3.2.1 AGYDAS [ed.; not in O1] **15 dyes** [O1: dies] **35 Agydas** [ed.; not in O1] **58 enjoy** [O1: eioy] **81 lightning** [O1: lightening]

3.3.6 too [O1: to] **51 breathe** [O1: breath] **73 thorough** [O1: thorow] **76 Alcoran** [ed.] *Alcaron* [O1] **109 ysprung** [O1: ysprong] **158 your** [ed.] our [O1] **158 air** [ed.] lure [O1] **213 foil** [ed.] soile [O1] **215** [and elsewhere] **strew** [O1: strowe] **248 galleys** [O1: Galles] **248 brigantines** [O1: Briggandines] **250 straits** [O1: straightes] **273.1–2** [O1 follows with "*Finis Actus tertii*"]

4.1.63 razeth [O1: raceth]

4.2.25 Struck [O1: Strocke] **41 struck** [O1: stroke] **45 makes** [ed.] make [O1] **49 Clymene's** [O2: *Clymenes*] *Clymeus* [O1] **81 'gainst** [O1: against] **105 statue** [O3] stature [O1]

4.3.0.2 ***streaming colors*** [O3] *steaming collors* [O1] **3 Calydonian** [O2] Caldonian [O1] **67 raze** [O1: race]

4.4.0 [ed.] *Actus.4. Scaena.5* [O1] **1 Damascus** [O1: *Damascns*] **24 Procne's** [O1: *Prognes*] **36 to** [O1: too] **89 wait** [O1: waight] **128 plage** [ed.] place [O1] **129 bower** [O3] hower [O1] **132 valor** [ed.] value [O1] **142 travel** [O1: traueile] **142 Antarctic** [O2] Antatique [O1] **146.1** [O1 follows with "*Finis Actus quarti*"]

5.1.0.1 ***Damascus*** [O1: *Damasco*] **24** FIRST VIRGIN [ed.] *Virg.* [O1] **63.1** [O1 follows with "*Actus 5. Scaena.2.*"] **141 tresses** [O2] treshes [O1] **157 Persia's** [ed.] Perseans [O1] **168 human** [O1: humaine] **185 veil** [O1: vaile] **193** ATTENDANT [O1: *An.*] **209 lose** [O1: loose] **229 damnèd** [O2: damned] danmed [O1] **243 A hell** [ed.] As hell [O1] **282 banned inflictions** [O1: band inflictious] **300 air** [O3] ay [O1] **319** ZENOCRATE [ed.; not in O1] **320 dyed** [O1: di'd] **330 steed** [O1: Stead] **458 triumphant** [O2] triumphat [O1] **459 drawn** [O1: drawen] **516 thee** [ed.] the [O1] **523 martial** [O2] matiall [O1] **534.1** [O1 follows with "*Finis Actus quinti & vltimi huius primae partis*"] fount] 185.1 *Usumcasane* [O2]; *Casanes* [O1] 170 may [*om.* O2] doing my [O1] 177 Whether [O1 Whether] 182 lords [O2]; lord [O1]

1.2.6 [and elsewhere] Sultan [O1 Souldan] 12 [and elsewhere] Medea [O1 Madea] 30 thee] of thee [O1] 34 [and elsewhere] weigh [O1 waie] 38 Rhodope [O1 Rhodolfe] 75 hundreds [O1 hundreth] 126 waste [O1 wasted] 134 mountain top] mountain foot [O1] 155 mails [O1 Males] 158 [and elsewhere] renowned [O1 renowmed] 178 cliffs [O1 clifts] 207 Boötes [O1 Botes] 244 augury [O1 ...] stables [O1]

2.1.27 sinewy ed.; sinowy [O1] 48 'gainst [O1 gainst] 46 overweigh [O1 ouer-wey]

2.2.15 pitched [O2]; pitch [O1] 28 led [O1 lead] 40 champaign [O1 champion] 48, 52 [and elsewhere] spring [O1 spreng]

2.3 7 oracles of heaven [ed.]; Oracles, heaven [O1] 26 stay [ed.]; stop [O1] 33 and [O2]; nor [O1] 64 scare [O1 scarce]

2.5.42 united [O2]; and [O1] 86 gotte [O1 ...] 100 him back [ed.]; his back [O1] 104 the [ed.]; cat [O1]

2.6.30 ingratitude [O2]; ingratitude [O1] 33 quench [O1 quence]

2.7.17 of [ed.]; [O1 ...] 49 talons [O1 tallents] 49 [and elsewhere] gripe [O1 grape] 67.SD [O1 follows with "*Finis Actus 2.*"]

3.1.2 and elsewhere] Bey [O1 Bassoe]

3.2 32 aye ... [ed.]; and in [O1] 38 dies [O1 dyes] 35 Wyclas [ed.]; not in [O1] 58 envy [O1 enuy] 81 lightning [O1 lightning]

3.3.0 to [O1 ...] 51 Trench [O1 French] 73 thorough [O1 thorow] 78 Afric [ed.]; Africa [O1] 109 yapping [O1 yawping] 158 vaunt [ed.]; and [O1] 185 uttermost [O1] 218 fail [ed.]; sole [O1] 275 [and elsewhere] arrow [O1 ...] 246 valley [O1 ...] 248 brigandines [O1 Brigandines] 250 spoils [O] ... [O1 follows with "*Finis Actus tertii*"]

4.1.63 earth [O1 earth]

4.2.25 shrink [O1 shrincke] 41 stick [O1 stricke] 48 snakes [O1 snaikes] 59 Zenocrate's [O2 Zenocrates] [O1] 81 'gainst [O1 against] 105 stake [O2; stakes [O1]]

4.3.12 streaming colours [O2]; streaming colors [O1] 23 Caledonian [O1 Calidonian] 67 rose [O1 rosse]

4.4.0 feast [O1 ...] 3 Damascus [O1 Damascus] 24 French [O1 Fraunce] 36 for [O1 ...] 99 walk [O1 ...] 128 place [ed.]; place [O1] 129 power [O1 ...] 132 value [ed.]; value [O1] 142 travel [O1 travell] 142 Antarctic [O1 Antartique] 146.1 [O1 follows with "*Finis Actus quarti*"]

5.1.3 Damascus [O1 Damascus] 24 sires [O1 ...] 63 [O1 follows with "*Exeunt*"] 142 kisses [O2]; ... [O1] 157 Roses [ed.]; Rosses [O1] ... human [O2 humane] 185 vail [O1 vaile] 195 *Tamburlaine* [O1 ...] 209 lose [O1 loose] 228 damned [O2 damned]; damned [O1] 246 [and elsewhere] Arabia [O1 ...] 262 humanity [O1 ... humanitie] 300 [O1 ...] 319 *Zenocrate* [ed.]; not in [O1] 320 dead [O1 ...] 330 [O1 ...] 458 triumph [O2 triumph [O1]] 459 draw [O1 ...] 476 ... [O1 ...] 524 ... [O2] [O1] 534 [O1 follows with "*Finis Actus quinti & vltimi huius primæ partis.*"]

Doctor Faustus

The era of greatness in Elizabethan tragedy begins with Thomas Kyd's *The Spanish Tragedy* and Christopher Marlowe's *Doctor Faustus*. Both plays are from the late 1580s, just about the time Shakespeare moved to London and began his work in the theater. Kyd and Marlowe were well acquainted; they shared rooms for a time. Both were obliged to rely on their wits in order to survive and prosper. They were well educated (Kyd at the Merchant Taylors' School in London, Marlowe at Cambridge), but as persons of no social distinction, they found few career opportunities open to them other than writing. Kyd served as a scrivener for a time; Marlowe, coming from a family of shoemakers in Canterbury, was sent up to Cambridge on scholarship in 1580, where he seems to have become radicalized. And after Cambridge, London was the place for such young men of literary ambition.

Whether fairly or not, Marlowe was known in his time as a freethinker and a debauchee. He spent time in jail for his participation in a fatal duel. In May of 1593, he was arrested on order of the Privy Council as part of an investigation into matters of religious heterodoxy and disloyalty to the Crown. A man named Baines accused Marlowe of having said, among other things, that John the Evangelist and Christ were lovers, that anyone who loved not boys and tobacco was a fool, and that Moses had led the Israelites out of Egypt into the wilderness for forty years, "which journey might have been done in less than one year." When Marlowe died violently in a private house (perhaps a tavern) in Deptford in 1593, the Puritan Thomas Beard saw in that event the avenging hand of God: this young playwright and "poet of scurrility," having given "too large a swinge to his own wit" and having permitted his lusts "to have the full reins," fell, "not without just desert, to that outrage and extremity that he denied God and his son Christ." His death, to Beard, was "not only a manifest sign of God's judgment but also an horrible and fearful terror to all that beheld him."[1]

Such a towering reputation for blasphemy is bound to seem relevant to the author of *Doctor Faustus*, for that tragedy presents to us a learned scholar who blasphemes, sells his soul to the devil, and, at the conclusion of the four-and-twenty years of hedonistic pleasure and power for which he has bargained, is carried off to hell by devils. To point out this striking biographical resonance (more so than in any play yet written in the English Renaissance) is, however, to raise an unending set of questions. Was Marlowe in fact an atheist and sybarite? Even if he was, does the play sympathize with Doctor Faustus or condemn him as a reprobate? Is the play subversive or orthodox? Whether designedly or not, the play has become a kind of Rorschach test for readers, revealing in all of us an inclination toward skepticism or faith. Critics simply do not agree, and show no signs of ever being ready to do so. A beauty of the play may well be that it is so magnificently ambiguous about such precious matters as salvation, faith, doubt, and despair.

The case for orthodoxy in *Doctor Faustus* can be simply stated, even though the issue is far from simple. This is a play in which a man succumbs to pride, the most

Introduction, glosses, footnotes, and textual notes by David Bevington; text edited by David Bevington and Eric Rasmussen.

1. Thomas Beard, *The Theatre of God's Judgments* (London, 1597), pp. 147–48.

deadly of the Seven Deadly Sins, sells his soul to the devil for knowledge and power and pleasure, and is horribly punished for his presumption. Faustus's sin is that of Lucifer himself, when that great angel rose in arrogance against the seat of God and was thrown into eternal torment. Marlowe begins and ends his tragedy with choruses that warn didactically of Faustus's sin and its fearful consequences. The opening Chorus speaks of Faustus as one who, though baseborn, was brilliantly educated and successful as a doctor of divinity: "Till, swoll'n with cunning of a self-conceit, / His waxen wings did mount above his reach, / And, melting, heavens conspired his overthrow" (Prologue 20–22). Having fallen "to a devilish exercise," Faustus "surfeits upon cursèd necromancy" (Prologue 23, 25). The final Chorus, no less plainly, urges us as spectators to "Regard his hellish fall, / Whose fiendful fortune may exhort the wise / Only to wonder at unlawful things." The language here is filled with moralistic absolutes: "swoll 'n," "cunning," "self-conceit," "devilish," "hellish," "fiendful," "unlawful." The condemnation seems total and devastating.

In the course of the play, as well, Faustus's reckless course of self-damnation can be seen as an orthodox demonstration of the wages of sin. He is given plentiful warning of the terrors of hell. Mephistopheles himself cannot deny that he is in hell perpetually. Although God never appears as a character in the play, Faustus invokes God and Christ often (see, for example, 5.2.28–117), plentifully acknowledging God's existence. Faustus is intensely aware of his guilt and his deserving of punishment, as when he confesses to his companion scholars, "But Faustus' offense can ne'er be pardoned. The serpent that tempted Eve may be saved, but not Faustus" (5.2.15–16). The Good and Evil Angels are manifestations of a clear choice. Almost to the last minute, the Old Man attempts to save Faustus through the teachings of penitence and faith.

Viewed in this context, Faustus's choices are foolish. Audiences and readers become increasingly aware that the power for which Faustus has sold his soul is rapidly dissipated in frivolities: interviewing the Seven Deadly Sins, touring the sights of Europe (Trier, Naples, Venice, Rome) in a dragon-drawn chariot, invisibly snatching food and drink from the table of the Pope in Rome, conjuring up spirits in the form of Alexander the Great and his paramour for the delectation of Emperor Charles V, causing horns to be placed on the brow of a knight who has dared to challenge his authority, tricking a horse-courser (a horse-dealer) in the purchase of a horse, deceiving this same man with a false leg when the horse-courser attempts to pull Faustus by the leg to awaken him, causing grapes to be fetched from India at the behest of the pregnant Duchess of Vanholt, and the like. Perhaps even more deplorable, he commands that the devil provide him with a fair wife to feed his lasciviousness (2.1.141–43) and later takes up with Helen of Troy (5.1.83–109). Since these apparitions are diabolical spirits summoned for Faustus by Mephistopheles, the good doctor is guilty of sexual congress with succubi—an unforgivably damnable act, according to some medieval theologians.

Even at the start of the play, Faustus's impatience with the standard learning of his time spills rapidly over into a blasphemy that is manifestly damnable. His dismissal of Aristotle, Galen, and Justinian in act 1, scene 1 may be understandable, but his flippancy about Jerome's Bible (the standard Vulgate translation) is quite another matter. When Faustus quotes the Bible against itself as though by way of refuting nonsense, quoting first the dictum of Saint Paul in Romans 6 that "The reward of sin is death" and then Paul's observation (1 John 1) that "If we say that we have no sin, / We deceive ourselves, and there's no truth in us," Faustus appears superficially to have identified a problem that his own clever syllogism can resolve: "Why then belike we must sin, / And so consequently die" (1.1.39–47). Any good Christian in Marlowe's audience would presumably know, however, that Faustus is quoting selectively and unfairly, playing games with the profundities of Christian faith that concede the inevitable sinfulness of humankind only to insist that God's great mercies are open to those who truly repent. From the start, Faustus betrays himself as a fool and an unrepentant sinner.

The title page of the so-called B-text of *Doctor Faustus*, the quarto of 1616.

Yet the case for an orthodox reading of *Doctor Faustus* is far from simple or assured. Counterbalancing the image of the damned fool is that of the inquisitive thinker, impatient with the state of learning in late medieval Europe because it is so mindlessly bound to ancient authorities. The books he so scornfully casts aside—those of Aristotle, Galen, and Justinian—are the very authorities that new thinkers in the Renaissance were also eager to cast aside. Ramus in rhetoric, Paracelsus in medicine, Machiavelli in matters of statecraft and law—these were the new names to conjure with. Not surprisingly, then, Faustus is associated in this play with figures of aspiration, such as Icarus, who had dared, with fatal results, to mount on waxen wings. Icarus could of course be read as a cautionary figure, warning against such arrogance, but even in the opening Chorus's invocation of this story, there is also a note of cosmic conspiracy against such an attempt: "And, melting, heavens conspired his overthrow" (Prologue 22).

The final Chorus, too, if we read it again carefully, invokes the memory of one who aspired to learning and greatness: "Cut is the branch that might have grown full straight, / And burnèd is Apollo's laurel bough / That sometime grew within this learnèd man" (Epilogue 1–3). The tone here is of admiring regret for a tragic fall, not moral denunciation. The final Chorus acknowledges also a divine conspiracy intent on suppressing human rebellion: Faustus must not be allowed "To practice more than heavenly power permits" (Epilogue 8). The image here is of Faustus as a kind of Prometheus, daring to steal fire from the gods and suffering torment on behalf of the human race.

Much of Faustus's use of magical powers is indeed frivolous, but his aspirations are not uniformly demeaning. His longing to "wall all Germany with brass" and "chase the Prince of Parma from our land" identifies him as a German Protestant patriot defying the haughty Spanish Catholic powers serving Philip II (1.1.90, 95). His intent to "fill the public schools with silk, / Wherewith the students shall be bravely clad" bespeaks his sympathy for intellectuals who are oppressed by restrictive sumptuary laws (1.1.92–93). Even his trompe l'oeil tricks for the emperors of Europe evince a desire to show these rulers that academics, through the power of books and intellect, can cut a powerful figure in the courts of the mighty. His travels bespeak a genuine curiosity to know what Venice and Rome are like. If his tricks in the dining chamber of the Pope are sophomoric, they are at least directed against the hated pontiff of the Catholic Church. When he longs to see the wonders of the ancient world—Alexander and his paramour, blind Homer, Paris and Oenone—he speaks as the poet Marlowe might speak, intoxicated by the beauty of long-ago adventures (2.3.26–27). Faustus is evidently so much loved in his university that the scholars with whom he spends part of his last night on earth are desperate with sorrow at losing him.

No passage in the play better illustrates Faustus's genuine passion for learning, and his frustration at not being able to know more, than his interrogation of Mephistopheles about the universe. "Are there many heavens above the moon?" he wishes to know. "Are all celestial bodies but one globe, / As is the substance of this centric earth?" (2.3.35–37). To this and other eager questions Mephistopheles provides answers that are the stuff of the old Ptolemaic earth-centered cosmos. Mars, Jupiter, Saturn, etc. are "erring stars," that is, planets (the word *planetes* in Greek and Latin means "wandering"), revolving around the earth in varied yet predictable orbits. All this Faustus knows already, of course, and he is dismissive of such "freshmen's suppositions." Can we come to the hard question? he insists. "Why have we not conjunctions, oppositions, aspects, eclipses all at one time, but in some years we have more, in some less?" These are the questions that perplexed and fascinated Europe of the late sixteenth and early seventeenth centuries. What can one make of the irregular and at times visibly retrograde motion of a planet such as Mars or Jupiter? Why are such orbits not regular? Ptolemy had explained this by means of epicycles built on the cyclical orbits, in such a way as to satisfy the mathematics of visual observation; and as observation became more accurate, more and more epicycles had been needed to make the scheme work. Mephistopheles' answer to Faustus's question gets nowhere further than this: he says merely that there are irregularities "Because of their uneven motion in relation to the whole." The transparent circularity and emptiness of such a formulaic answer prompts Faustus to realize that he has been told all that he is going to be told: "Well, I am answered" (2.3.35–66).

Some, at least, of Marlowe's audience must have known that Copernicus had provided a better or at least mathematically simpler answer some decades earlier. The solar-centered hypothesis took away the necessity of epicycles, substituting instead a set of neat orbits around the sun, including that of the earth. Copernicus' theories, as yet unconfirmed by Galileo's observations of the moons of Jupiter, were nonetheless much talked about in London. They raised the possibility of human explanation of the movement of the heavenly bodies. Marlowe does not mention Copernicus, but he does present us with a Faustus who is sure that better answers than Ptolemy's might be found, if the human mind could only inquire in the right way. Faustus's profound disappointment and his turning back to trivial pursuits suggest once again the tragic picture of a Promethean figure struggling imperfectly for human knowledge against the "conspiracy" of the gods to deny this knowledge.

Caught between the polarities of faith and reason, Faustus struggles to understand, and damns himself by doing so. His other great curiosity is about hell. Does it exist? Mephistopheles gives him a clear answer. When Faustus asks, "Where are you damned?" Mephistopheles replies, "In hell," and when Faustus persists in asking how Mephistopheles can now be out of hell, the devil corrects his misunderstanding: "Why, this is hell, nor am I out of it" (1.3.75–78). Yet Faustus persists in regarding talk of hell as "mere old wives' tales" (2.1.136). If Mephistopheles is in hell even as the two of them are talking, what can be so bad about hell? "Nay, an this be hell, / I'll willingly be damned here. What? Walking, disputing, etc.?" (2.1.136–41). We are allowed to see that Faustus is indeed terribly misled: hell is a state of being, an eternal absence from God, not something that the childish imaginations of artists render as a place of physical torment inflicted by grotesque devils with pitchforks and instruments of torture. Yet we see too that Faustus has been led into his questioning by a genuine skepticism. What proof is there of torment after death? If such tales are indeed old wives' tales, ought not the enlightened person cast off superstition and deal with the tangible realities of this world?

This humanistic reading of *Doctor Faustus* can offer us a protagonist of truly tragic conflict, and one that is potentially autobiographical as well. Is the play the study of a man who, through the "magic" of books, enters into a love affair with forbidden learning—of astronomy, of the ancient pagan world of Greece and Rome, of poetry—only to discover at last that he has lost his faith in the process and cannot get it back? One cannot will oneself to believe. In Faustus, we encounter a man who comes to see that he ought to believe but cannot. He acknowledges the reality of Christ and the devil but cannot will himself to believe himself worthy of forgiveness. He cannot repent.

Calvinist theology provides a ready enough answer for such a condition: Faustus is a reprobate sinner. For reasons we can never understand, God chooses those who are to be saved and those who are to be damned. The gift of salvation is His alone; we cannot deserve anything on our own merits. The choice is therefore His, not to be quarreled with. Faustus's very questionings are, in this theological scheme, manifestations of his loss of faith, his being reprobate. Yet the play pulls us also in the direction of sympathizing with Faustus's aspirations, if for no other reason than that they are quintessentially human. To be human is to question everything, to look for new answers. If the wages of such inquisitiveness is damnation at the hands of God, there is no way that a human like Faustus can simply will himself to be uninquisitive.

Dramatically, this unceasing paradox takes the form in *Doctor Faustus* of a genuine uncertainty about whether Faustus is damned or is not damned at any given point. Whenever the Good and Evil Angels appear to him, their answers are theologically incommensurate. When the Good Angel says, "Faustus, repent yet, God will pity thee," the Evil Angel has his answer: "Thou art a spirit. God cannot pity thee" (2.3.12–13). "Too late," insists the Evil Angel at his next entrance. "Never too late, if Faustus can repent," contradicts the Good Angel (2.3.78–79). But can Faustus repent? God will pity him if he repents, but much hangs upon that "if." "Faustus never shall repent," insists the Evil Angel (2.3.17). At every moment in the play until the very end, two things are contradictorily true: God offers forgiveness to all who penitently turn to Him, no matter what sins they have committed, so that in this crucial sense it is not too late, and yet somehow it is too late and always has been too late for Faustus. In this terrible paradox hangs the tragedy of a man at once so wise and so foolish.

Doctor Faustus exists in two very different texts: one published in 1604, long after Marlowe had died, in a short version that seems to combine Marlowe's seriously tragic scenes with the farcical contributions of a collaborator, and a longer version published in 1616 that seems to incorporate a number of extensive enlargements paid for by the theatrical entrepreneur Philip Henslowe, who, over the years, had made a great deal of money from this play. At Henslowe's behest, the revisers went back to Marlowe's source, *The History of the Damnable Life and Deserved Death of Doctor John Faustus* (translated from a German original), for more episodes of the sort that Elizabethan audiences had learned to love. These were chiefly the comic episodes that had been written in the first instance by some dramatist other than Marlowe. In the earlier version, which is the one presented here, these comic scenes serve well to parody the main tragic action: the clowns quarrel with each other for precedence, try their hands at conjuring with alarming results (since the devil will come to anyone who abjures the Trinity), steal things, play practical jokes, etc. The resemblance of their antics to Faustus's own increasingly debased practice of magic reinforces, through lampooning, the essentially comic nature of evil. If the comic scenes appear to attenuate the taut drama of damnation in the main plot, they do provide an essential dramatic function of undercutting the seriousness of Faustus's claims to intellectual eminence. In the later version of 1616, the antics are at times unnecessarily prolonged, but even here we have a theatrical version that is fascinating, if only as a demonstration of what it was that Elizabethan audiences wanted to see.

The play clearly fascinated those audiences; it was revived over a succession of years. It collected legends. According to one account, the actors in a performance of *Doctor Faustus* looked around onstage and suddenly realized that they had been joined by one more devil than could be accounted for in their company's roster. Old Nick himself had come to take part in the performance! The hope of such an event was possibly one fascination that drew audiences to the play, in somewhat the same fashion as spectators flock to the circus wondering if the high-wire artist will fall and be killed. The sensation of "there but for the grace of God go I" must have made for special excitement in the persons who saw this play. A similar sense of tragic identification can work even today.

CHRISTOPHER MARLOWE

The Tragical History of Doctor Faustus

[CHARACTERS IN THE PLAY, IN ORDER OF APPEARANCE

The CHORUS
Doctor John FAUSTUS
WAGNER, his servant
The GOOD ANGEL
The EVIL ANGEL
VALDES } famous magicians
CORNELIUS } famous magicians
Three SCHOLARS
MEPHISTOPHELES
ROBIN, the clown, a stableman
Devils
RAFE, a stableman, another clown
LUCIFER
Beelzebub
PRIDE } the Seven Deadly Sins
COVETOUSNESS
WRATH
ENVY
GLUTTONY
SLOTH
LECHERY
The POPE
The Cardinal of LORRAINE
FRIARS
A VINTNER
The EMPEROR of Germany, Charles V
A KNIGHT
Attendants
Alexander the Great } spirits
His paramour } spirits
A HORSE-COURSER° *horse-dealer*
The DUKE of Vanholt
The DUCHESS of Vanholt
Helen of Troy, a spirit
An OLD MAN

THE SCENE: Doctor Faustus's study at Wittenberg, and on his travels.]

The original 1604 title page reads "*The Tragical History of D. Faustus.* As it hath been acted by the right Honorable the Earl of Nottingham his servants. Written by Ch. Marl. London. Printed by V. S. for Thomas Bushell. 1604."

[Prologue]

Enter Chorus.

CHORUS Not marching now in fields of Trasimene,° *(in Italy)*
Where Mars did mate° the Carthaginians, *the god of war overcame*
Nor sporting in the dalliance of love
In courts of kings where state° is overturned, *government; ceremony*
Nor in the pomp of proud audacious deeds,
Intends our muse to vaunt his heavenly verse.
Only this, gentlemen: we must perform
The form° of Faustus' fortunes, good or bad. *course*
To patient judgments we appeal our plaud,° *seek approval, applause*
And speak for Faustus in his infancy.
Now is he born, his parents base of stock,
In Germany, within a town called Rhode.
Of riper years to Wittenberg he went,
Whereas° his kinsmen chiefly brought him up. *Where*
So soon he profits in divinity,
The fruitful plot of scholarism graced,[1]
That shortly he was graced with doctor's name,
Excelling all whose sweet delight disputes
In heavenly matters of theology;
Till, swoll'n with cunning° of a self-conceit, *learning; craftiness*
His waxen wings did mount above his reach,
And, melting, heavens conspired his overthrow.[2]
For, falling to a devilish exercise,
And glutted more with learning's golden gifts,
He surfeits upon cursèd necromancy;
Nothing so sweet as magic is to him,
Which he prefers before his chiefest bliss.° *hope of salvation*
And this the man that in his study sits. *Exit.*

[1.1]

Enter Faustus in his study.

FAUSTUS Settle thy studies, Faustus, and begin
To sound the depth of that° thou wilt profess.° *what / be expert in*
Having commenced, be a divine in show,
Yet level° at the end° of every art, *aim / intent*
And live and die in Aristotle's works.
Sweet *Analytics,*° 'tis thou hast ravished me! *analytical logic*
[*He reads.*] *"Bene disserere est finis logices."*[1]
Is to dispute well logic's chiefest end?
Affords this art no greater miracle?
Then read no more; thou hast attained the end.
A greater subject fitteth Faustus' wit.° *intellect*
Bid *On kai me on*° farewell. Galen,[2] come! *Being and not being*
Seeing *ubi desinit philosophus, ibi incipit medicus,*[3]

Prologue.
1. That scholarly field enriched by learning.
2. Faustus is compared to Icarus, who dared to fly on man-made wings and fell to his death (Ovid, *Metamorphoses,* Book 8).

1.1. Faustus's study.
1. Translated in the next line.
2. The standard ancient authority (129–c. 199 C.E.) on medicine.
3. Where the philosopher leaves off, there the physician begins.

Be a physician, Faustus. Heap up gold,
And be eternized° for some wondrous cure. — *immortalized*
[*He reads.*] "*Summum bonum medicinae sanitas*":
"The end of physic° is our body's health." — *medicine*
Why, Faustus, hast thou not attained that end?
Is not thy common talk sound aphorisms?° — *(medical) maxims*
Are not thy bills° hung up as monuments, — *prescriptions*
Whereby whole cities have escaped the plague
And thousand desp'rate maladies been eased?
Yet art thou still but Faustus, and a man.
Wouldst thou make man to live eternally,
Or, being dead, raise them to life again,
Then this profession were to be esteemed.
Physic, farewell. Where is Justinian?[4]
[*He reads.*] "*Si una eademque res legatur duobus,*
Alter rem, alter valorem rei,"[5] etc.
A pretty° case of paltry legacies! — *petty*
[*He reads.*] "*Exhaereditare filium non potest pater nisi—*"[6]
Such is the subject of the Institute° — *Justinian's* Institutes
And universal body of the church.° — *canon law*
His study° fits a mercenary drudge — *The study of Justinian*
Who aims at nothing but external trash—
Too servile and illiberal° for me. — *nonliberal (arts)*
When all is done,° divinity is best. — *said and done*
Jerome's Bible,[7] Faustus, view it well.
[*He reads.*] "*Stipendium peccati mors est.*" Ha!
"*Stipendium,*" etc.
"The reward of sin is death." That's hard.
[*He reads.*] "*Si peccasse negamus, fallimur,*
Et nulla est in nobis veritas."
"If we say that we have no sin,
We deceive ourselves, and there's no truth in us."
Why then belike° we must sin, — *in all likelihood*
And so consequently die.
Ay, we must die an everlasting death.
What doctrine call you this? *Che serà, serà,*
"What will be, shall be"? Divinity, adieu!
[*He picks up a book of magic.*]
These metaphysics° of magicians — *This occult lore*
And necromantic books are heavenly,
Lines, circles, signs, letters, and characters°— — *astrological signs*
Ay, these are those that Faustus most desires.
Oh, what a world of profit and delight,
Of power, of honor, of omnipotence
Is promised to the studious artisan!° — *student of liberal arts*
All things that move between the quiet° poles — *motionless*
Shall be at my command. Emperors and kings
Are but obeyed in their several° provinces, — *various; respective*
Nor can they raise the wind or rend the clouds;
But his° dominion that exceeds° in this — *(a person's) / excels*

4. Roman emperor from 527 to 565 C.E., the great codifier of Roman law.
5. "If one and the same thing is willed to two persons, one of them gets the thing, and the other gets the value of the thing."
6. "A father cannot disinherit his son unless—"
7. Saint Jerome was the fourth-century C.E. translator of what became the canonical "Vulgate," or Latin, text of the Bible.

Stretcheth as far as doth the mind of man.
A sound magician is a mighty god.
Here, Faustus, try° thy brains to gain a deity.° [test / godlike power]
[*Calling*] Wagner!

Enter Wagner.

Commend me to my dearest friends,
The German Valdes and Cornelius.
Request them earnestly to visit me.

WAGNER I will, sir. *Exit.*

FAUSTUS Their conference will be a greater help to me
Than all my labors, plod I ne'er so fast.

Enter the Good Angel and the Evil Angel.

GOOD ANGEL O Faustus, lay that damnèd book aside
And gaze not on it, lest it tempt thy soul
And heap God's heavy wrath upon thy head!
Read, read the Scriptures. That° is blasphemy. [*That damnèd book*]

EVIL ANGEL Go forward, Faustus, in that famous art
Wherein all nature's treasury° is contained. [*treasure*]
Be thou on earth as Jove° is in the sky, [*i.e., God*]
Lord and commander of these elements. *Exeunt* [*Angels*].

FAUSTUS How am I glutted with conceit° of this! [*contemplation*]
Shall I make spirits fetch me what I please,
Resolve me of° all ambiguities, [*Clear up for me*]
Perform what desperate° enterprise I will? [*extravagant*]
I'll have them fly to India° for gold, [*East and West Indies*]
Ransack the ocean for orient pearl,
And search all corners of the newfound world
For pleasant fruits and princely delicates.° [*delicacies*]
I'll have them read me° strange philosophy [*tutor me in*]
And tell the secrets of all foreign kings.
I'll have them wall all Germany with brass
And make swift Rhine circle fair Wittenberg.
I'll have them fill the public schools° with silk, [*university lecture rooms*]
Wherewith the students shall be bravely° clad.[8] [*splendidly*]
I'll levy soldiers with the coin they° bring [*(the spirits; see 81)*]
And chase the Prince of Parma[9] from our land,
And reign sole king of all our provinces;
Yea, stranger engines° for the brunt° of war [*machines / assault*]
Than was the fiery keel at Antwerp's bridge[1]
I'll make my servile spirits to invent.
Come, German Valdes and Cornelius,
And make me blest with your sage conference!

Enter Valdes and Cornelius.

Valdes, sweet Valdes, and Cornelius,
Know that your words have won me at the last
To practice magic and concealèd° arts. [*occult*]

8. Rigorous dress codes forbade students and others below the ranks of the privileged classes to wear silk.
9. Spanish governor-general in the Netherlands from 1579 to 1592 and commander of the Spanish Armada in 1588, during Spain's failed invasion of England.
1. The defense of Antwerp against the Spanish in 1585 used a fire ship to destroy Parma's bridge over the Scheldt River.

Yet not your words only, but mine own fantasy,
That will receive no object,° for my head — *other idea; objection*
But ruminates° on necromantic skill. — *Ruminates solely*
Philosophy is odious and obscure;
Both law and physic° are for petty wits; — *medicine*
Divinity is basest of the three,
Unpleasant, harsh, contemptible, and vile.
'Tis magic, magic that hath ravished me.
Then, gentle° friends, aid me in this attempt, — *wellborn; kind*
And I, that have with concise syllogisms
Graveled° the pastors of the German church — *Floored, confounded*
And made the flow'ring pride° of Wittenberg — *the leading thinkers*
Swarm to my problems° as the infernal spirits — *disputations, lectures*
On sweet Musaeus when he came to hell,[2]
Will be as cunning° as Agrippa[3] was, — *learned; crafty*
Whose shadows° made all Europe honor him. — *spirits*

VALDES Faustus, these books, thy wit, and our experience
Shall make all nations to canonize us.
As Indian Moors° obey their Spanish lords, — *natives*
So shall the subjects° of every element — *servant-spirits*
Be always serviceable to us three.
Like lions shall they guard us when we please,
Like Almaine rutters° with their horsemen's staves,° — *German cavalry / lances*
Or Lapland giants, trotting by our sides;
Sometimes like women, or unwedded maids,
Shadowing° more beauty in their airy° brows — *Harboring / ethereal*
Than in the white breasts of the Queen of Love.° — *Venus*
From Venice shall they drag huge argosies,° — *large merchant ships*
And from America the golden fleece
That yearly stuffs old Philip's° treasury, — *Philip II's (of Spain)*
If learnèd Faustus will be resolute.

FAUSTUS Valdes, as resolute am I in this
As thou to live. Therefore object it not.° — *raise no objection*

CORNELIUS The miracles that magic will perform
Will make thee vow to study nothing else.
He that is grounded in astrology,
Enriched with tongues,° well seen° in minerals, — *languages / versed*
Hath all the principles magic doth require.
Then doubt not, Faustus, but to be renowned
And more frequented° for this mystery° — *resorted to / art*
Than heretofore the Delphian° oracle. — *at Delphi (in Greece)*
The spirits tell me they can dry the sea
And fetch the treasure of all foreign wrecks—
Ay, all the wealth that our forefathers hid
Within the massy° entrails of the earth. — *solid, weighty*
Then tell me, Faustus, what shall we three want?° — *lack*

FAUSTUS Nothing, Cornelius. Oh, this cheers my soul!
Come, show me some demonstrations magical,
That I may conjure in some lusty° grove — *delightful*
And have these joys in full possession.

2. The poet Musaeus visits the underworld in Virgil's *Aeneid,* Book 6. Cf. also the descent to the underworld of the poet and musician Orpheus to bring back his wife Eurydice.

3. Henry Cornelius Agrippa (1486–1535) was famed as a magician.

VALDES Then haste thee to some solitary grove,
And bear wise Bacon's and Albanus' works,[4]
The Hebrew Psalter, and New Testament;
And whatsoever else is requisite
We will inform thee ere our conference cease.

CORNELIUS Valdes, first let him know the words of art,° — *of incantation*
And then, all other ceremonies learned,° — *having been learned*
Faustus may try his cunning by himself.

VALDES First I'll instruct thee in the rudiments,
And then wilt thou be perfecter than I.

FAUSTUS Then come and dine with me, and after meat° — *food*
We'll canvass° every quiddity° thereof, — *scrutinize / nicety*
For ere I sleep I'll try what I can do.
This night I'll conjure, though I die therefore. *Exeunt.*

[1.2]

Enter two Scholars.

FIRST SCHOLAR I wonder what's become of Faustus, that was wont to make our schools ring with "*sic probo*."° — *"I prove it thus"*

SECOND SCHOLAR That shall we know, for see, here comes his boy.° — *servant*

Enter Wagner [carrying wine].

FIRST SCHOLAR How now, sirrah,° where's thy master? — *(said to social inferiors)*

WAGNER God in heaven knows.

SECOND SCHOLAR Why, dost not thou know?

WAGNER Yes, I know, but that follows not.

FIRST SCHOLAR Go to, sirrah! Leave your jesting, and tell us where he is.

WAGNER That follows not necessary by force of argument that you, being licentiate,° should stand upon't. Therefore, acknowledge your error, and be attentive. — *advanced scholars*

SECOND SCHOLAR Why, didst thou not say thou knew'st?

WAGNER Have you any witness on't?

FIRST SCHOLAR Yes, sirrah, I heard you.

WAGNER Ask my fellow if I be a thief.[1]

SECOND SCHOLAR Well, you will not tell us.

WAGNER Yes, sir, I will tell you. Yet if you were not dunces, you would never ask me such a question. For is not he *corpus naturale?*° And is not that *mobile?* Then, wherefore should you ask me such a question? But that° I am by nature phlegmatic, slow to wrath, and prone to lechery—to love, I would say—it were not for you to come within forty foot of the place of execution,° although I do not doubt to see you both hanged the next sessions.° Thus, having triumphed over you, I will set my countenance like a precisian° and begin to speak thus: Truly, my dear brethren, my master is within at dinner with Valdes and Cornelius, as this wine, if it could speak, it would inform Your Worships. And so the Lord bless you, — *a natural body* / *Were it not that* / *dining room; gallows* / *law-court sessions* / *Puritan*

4. Roger Bacon (c. 1220–1292) and Pietro d'Abano (c. 1250–1316) were philosophers renowned for magic.
1.2. Faustus's chambers.
1. Thieves proverbially cannot be expected to tell the truth about one another.

preserve you, and keep you, my dear brethren, my dear brethren. *Exit.*

FIRST SCHOLAR Nay, then, I fear he is fall'n into that damned art for which they two are infamous through the world.

SECOND SCHOLAR Were he a stranger, and not allied° to me, yet should I grieve for him. But come, let us go and inform the rector,° and see if he, by his grave counsel, can reclaim him. *bound in friendship* / *university head*

FIRST SCHOLAR Oh, but I fear me° nothing can reclaim him. *fear*

SECOND SCHOLAR Yet let us try what we can do. *Exeunt.*

[1.3]

Enter Faustus to conjure.

FAUSTUS Now that the gloomy shadow of the earth,
Longing to view Orion's drizzling look,[1]
Leaps from th'Antarctic world unto the sky
And dims the welkin° with her pitchy breath, *sky*
Faustus, begin thine incantations,
And try if devils will obey thy hest,° *behest*
Seeing thou hast prayed and sacrificed to them.
Within this circle is Jehovah's name,
Forward and backward anagrammatized,
The breviated names of holy saints,
Figures of every adjunct to the heavens,
And characters of signs° and erring stars° *the zodiac / planets*
By which the spirits are enforced to rise.
Then fear not, Faustus, but be resolute,
And try the uttermost magic can perform.
Sint mihi dei Acherontis propitii! Valeat numen triplex Jehovae! Ignei, aerii, aquatici, terreni, spiritus, salvete! Orientis princeps Lucifer, Beelzebub, inferni ardentis monarcha, et Demogorgon, propitiamus vos, ut appareat et surgat Mephistopheles. Quid tu moraris? Per Jehovam, Gehennam, et consecratam aquam quam nunc spargo, signumque crucis quod nunc facio, et per vota nostra, ipse nunc surgat nobis dicatus Mephistopheles![2]
[*Faustus sprinkles holy water and makes a sign of the cross.*]

Enter a devil [*Mephistopheles*].

I charge thee to return and change thy shape.
Thou art too ugly to attend on me.
Go, and return an old Franciscan friar;
That holy shape becomes a devil best.
Exit devil [*Mephistopheles*].
I see there's virtue° in my heavenly words. *efficacy*
Who would not be proficient in this art?

1.3. A solitary grove (see 1.1.153–55).

1. Perhaps Orion is a "drizzling" constellation because it is visible in winter.

2. May the gods of Acheron be propitious to me! Away with the threefold godhead of Jehovah! Spirits of fire, air, water, and earth, all hail! Lucifer, Prince of the East, Beelzebub, monarch of burning hell, and Demogorgon, we propitiate you, that Mephistopheles may appear and rise. Why do you delay? By Jehovah, Gehenna, and the holy water that I now sprinkle, and the sign of the cross that I now make, and by our prayers, may Mephistopheles himself, invoked by us, now rise! (Acheron is a river of the underworld; Jehovah is God; Gehenna is hell; Beelzebub and the others are devils.)

How plaint is this Mephistopheles,
Full of obedience and humility!
Such is the force of magic and my spells.
Now, Faustus, thou art conjurer laureate,
That canst command great Mephistopheles.
Quin redis, Mephistopheles, fratris imagine![3]

Enter Mephistopheles [dressed as a friar].

MEPHISTOPHELES Now, Faustus, what wouldst thou have me do?
FAUSTUS I charge thee wait upon me whilst I live,
To do whatever Faustus shall command,
Be it to make the moon drop from her sphere
Or the ocean to overwhelm the world.
MEPHISTOPHELES I am a servant to great Lucifer
And may not follow thee without his leave.
No more than he commands must we perform.
FAUSTUS Did not he charge thee to appear to me?
MEPHISTOPHELES No, I came now hither of mine own accord.
FAUSTUS Did not my conjuring speeches raise thee? Speak.
MEPHISTOPHELES That was the cause, but yet *per accidens.*° *incidentally*
For when we hear one rack° the name of God, *torture, tear*
Abjure the Scriptures and his Savior Christ,
We fly in hope to get his glorious soul,
Nor will we come unless he use such means
Whereby he is in danger to be damned.
Therefore, the shortest cut for conjuring
Is stoutly° to abjure the Trinity *manfully, stubbornly*
And pray devoutly to the prince of hell.
FAUSTUS So Faustus hath
Already done, and holds this principle:
There is no chief but only Beelzebub,
To whom Faustus doth dedicate himself.
This word "damnation" terrifies not him,
For he confounds hell in Elysium.[4]
His ghost be with the old philosophers![5]
But leaving these vain trifles of men's souls,
Tell me what is that Lucifer thy lord?
MEPHISTOPHELES Archregent and commander of all spirits.
FAUSTUS Was not that Lucifer an angel once?
MEPHISTOPHELES Yes, Faustus, and most dearly loved of God.
FAUSTUS How comes it then that he is prince of devils?
MEPHISTOPHELES Oh, by aspiring pride and insolence,
For which God threw him from the face of heaven.
FAUSTUS And what are you that live with Lucifer?
MEPHISTOPHELES Unhappy spirits that fell with Lucifer,
Conspired against our God with Lucifer,
And are forever damned with Lucifer.
FAUSTUS Where are you damned?
MEPHISTOPHELES In hell.
FAUSTUS How comes it then that thou art out of hell?
MEPHISTOPHELES Why, this is hell, nor am I out of it.

3. Truly, you rule in the image of a friar, Mephistopheles!
4. He sees no important distinction between the Christian hell and the pagan Elysian Fields.
5. May his spirit rest with the pre-Christian philosophers!

Think'st thou that I, who saw the face of God
And tasted the eternal joys of heaven,
Am not tormented with ten thousand hells
In being deprived of everlasting bliss?
O Faustus, leave these frivolous demands,
Which strike a terror to my fainting soul!

FAUSTUS What, is great Mephistopheles so passionate
For being deprived of the joys of heaven?
Learn thou of Faustus manly fortitude,
And scorn those joys thou never shalt possess.
Go bear these tidings to great Lucifer:
Seeing Faustus hath incurred eternal death
By desp'rate thoughts against Jove's deity,
Say he surrenders up to him his soul,
So° he will spare him four-and-twenty years, *Provided*
Letting him live in all voluptuousness,
Having thee ever to attend on me,
To give me whatsoever I shall ask,
To tell me whatsoever I demand,
To slay mine enemies and aid my friends,
And always be obedient to my will.
Go and return to mighty Lucifer,
And meet me in my study at midnight,
And then resolve° me of thy master's mind. *inform*

MEPHISTOPHELES I will, Faustus. *Exit.*

FAUSTUS Had I as many souls as there be stars,
I'd give them all for Mephistopheles.
By him I'll be great emperor of the world
And make a bridge through the moving air
To pass the ocean with a band of men;
I'll join the hills that bind° the Afric shore *gird*
And make that land continent° to Spain, *connected, contiguous*
And both contributory to my crown.
The emp'ror shall not live but by my leave,
Nor any potentate of Germany.
Now that I have obtained what I desire,
I'll live in speculation° of this art *contemplation*
Till Mephistopheles return again. *Exit.*

[1.4]

Enter Wagner and [Robin] the clown.

WAGNER Sirrah boy, come hither.

ROBIN How, "boy"? 'Swounds,° "boy"! I hope you have seen many boys with such pickedevants° as I have. "Boy," quotha?° *By God's wounds* / *pointed beards / forsooth*

WAGNER Tell me, sirrah, hast thou any comings in?° *income*

ROBIN Ay, and goings out° too, you may see else. *expenses; poverty*

WAGNER Alas, poor slave,° see how poverty jesteth in his nakedness! The villain° is bare and out of service,° and so hungry that I know he would give his soul to the devil for a shoulder of mutton, though it were blood raw. *rogue* / *wretch / unemployed*

ROBIN How? My soul to the devil for a shoulder of mutton,

1.4. An unspecified location.

though 'twere blood raw? Not so, good friend. By'r Lady,° I had need have it well roasted, and good sauce to it, if I pay so dear.

By the Virgin Mary

WAGNER Well, wilt thou serve me, and I'll make thee go like *Qui mihi discipulus?*°

You who are my pupil

ROBIN How, in verse?

WAGNER No, sirrah, in beaten° silk and stavesacre.[1]

stamped and embroidered

ROBIN How, how, knave's acre?[2] [*Aside*] Ay, I thought that was all the land his father left him. [*To Wagner*] Do ye hear? I would be sorry to rob you of your living.

WAGNER Sirrah, I say in stavesacre.

ROBIN Oho, oho, "stavesacre"! Why then, belike,° if I were your man,° I should be full of vermin.

probably / *servant*

WAGNER So thou shalt, whether thou be'st with me or no. But, sirrah, leave your jesting, and bind° yourself presently° unto me for seven years, or I'll turn all the lice about thee into familiars,[3] and they shall tear thee in pieces.

apprentice / *now*

ROBIN Do you hear, sir? You may save that labor. They are too familiar with me already. 'Swounds, they are as bold with my flesh as if they had paid for my meat and drink.

WAGNER Well, do you hear, sirrah? [*Offering money*] Hold, take these guilders.°

coins

ROBIN Gridirons? What be they?

WAGNER Why, French crowns.

ROBIN Mass, but for° the name of French crowns a man were as good have as many English counters.[4] And what should I do with these?

were it not for

WAGNER Why now, sirrah, thou art at an hour's warning° whensoever or wheresoever the devil shall fetch thee.

notice

ROBIN No, no, here, take your gridirons again.

[*He attempts to return the money.*]

WAGNER Truly, I'll none of them.

ROBIN Truly, but you shall.

WAGNER [*to the audience*] Bear witness I gave them him.

ROBIN Bear witness I gave them you again.

WAGNER Well, I will cause two devils presently to fetch thee away. [*Calling*] Balioll° and Belcher!°

Belial / *a devil's name*

ROBIN Let your Balio and your Belcher come here and I'll knock them. They were never so knocked since they were devils. Say I should kill one of them, what would folks say? "Do ye see yonder tall° fellow in the round slop?° He has killed the devil." So I should be called "Kill devil" all the parish over.

brave / *baggy breeches*

Enter two devils, and [*Robin*] *the clown runs up and down crying.*

WAGNER Balioll and Belcher! Spirits, away! *Exeunt* [*devils*].

ROBIN What, are they gone? A vengeance on them! They have vile long nails. There was a he-devil and a she-devil. I'll tell you how you shall know them:° all he-devils has horns,[5] and

tell them apart

1. An herbal delousing medicine made from larkspur; with wordplay on the idea of being beaten with "staves," resulting in aches or achers ("acres"). Jokes about beating servants were common.
2. The clown's punning reply hints at financial ruin by invoking the name of a street in a run-down area of London.
3. Attendant evil spirits in animal shapes.
4. Tokens used in computation and exchange, but without intrinsic value.
5. (1) Devils' horns; (2) cuckolds' horns.

all she-devils has clefts° and cloven feet. *cleft hooves; vulvas*
WAGNER Well, sirrah, follow me.
ROBIN But do you hear? If I should serve you, would you teach me to raise up Banios and Belcheos?
WAGNER I will teach thee to turn thyself to anything, to a dog, or a cat, or a mouse, or a rat, or anything.
ROBIN How? A Christian fellow to a dog or a cat, a mouse or a rat? No, no, sir. If you turn me into anything, let it be in the likeness of a little, pretty, frisking flea, that I may be here and there and everywhere. Oh, I'll tickle the pretty wenches' plackets!° I'll be amongst them, i'faith! *slits in petticoats*
WAGNER Well, sirrah, come.
ROBIN But do you hear, Wagner?
WAGNER How? [*Calling*] Balioll and Belcher!
ROBIN Oh, Lord, I pray sir, let Banio and Belcher go sleep.
WAGNER Villain, call me Master Wagner, and let thy left eye be diametarily° fixed upon my right heel, with *quasi vestigiis nostris insistere.*[6] *Exit.* *diametrically*
ROBIN God forgive me, he speaks Dutch fustian.° Well, I'll follow him, I'll serve him, that's flat.° *Exit.* *bombast; that's for sure*

[2.1]

Enter Faustus in his study.

FAUSTUS Now, Faustus, must thou needs be damned,
And canst thou not be saved.
What boots° it then to think of God or heaven? *avails*
Away with such vain fancies, and despair!
Despair in God and trust in Beelzebub.
Now go not backward. No, Faustus, be resolute.
Why waverest thou? Oh, something soundeth in mine ears:
"Abjure this magic, turn to God again!"
Ay, and Faustus will turn to God again.
To God? He loves thee not.
The god thou servest is thine own appetite,
Wherein is fixed the love of Beelzebub.
To him I'll build an altar and a church,
And offer lukewarm blood of newborn babes.

Enter Good Angel and Evil [Angel].

GOOD ANGEL Sweet Faustus, leave that execrable art.
FAUSTUS Contrition, prayer, repentance—what of them?
GOOD ANGEL Oh, they are means to bring thee unto heaven.
EVIL ANGEL Rather illusions, fruits of lunacy,
That makes men foolish that do trust them most.
GOOD ANGEL Sweet Faustus, think of heaven and heavenly things!
EVIL ANGEL No, Faustus, think of honor and wealth.
Exeunt [Angels].
FAUSTUS Of wealth?
Why, the seigniory of Emden° shall be mine. *(a north German port)*
When Mephistopheles shall stand by me,
What god can hurt thee, Faustus? Thou art safe;

6. As if to walk in our (my) footsteps.

2.1. Faustus's study.

Cast° no more doubts. Come, Mephistopheles, — *Ponder, consider*
And bring glad tidings from great Lucifer.
Is't not midnight? Come, Mephistopheles!
Veni, veni,° Mephistophile! — *O come, O come*

Enter Mephistopheles.

Now tell, what says Lucifer, thy lord?
MEPHISTOPHELES That I shall wait on Faustus whilst he lives,
So° he will buy my service with his soul. — *Provided*
FAUSTUS Already Faustus hath hazarded that for thee.
MEPHISTOPHELES But, Faustus, thou must bequeath it solemnly
And write a deed of gift with thine own blood,
For that security craves great Lucifer.[1]
If thou deny it, I will back to hell.
FAUSTUS Stay, Mephistopheles, and tell me, what good
Will my soul do thy lord?
MEPHISTOPHELES Enlarge his kingdom.
FAUSTUS Is that the reason he tempts us thus?
MEPHISTOPHELES *Solamen miseris socios habuisse doloris.*[2]
FAUSTUS Have you any pain, that tortures others?° — *you who torture others*
MEPHISTOPHELES As great as have the human souls of men.
But tell me, Faustus, shall I have thy soul?
And I will be thy slave, and wait on thee,
And give thee more than thou hast wit to ask.
FAUSTUS Ay, Mephistopheles, I give it thee.
MEPHISTOPHELES Then stab thine arm courageously,
And bind thy soul that at some certain day
Great Lucifer may claim it as his own,
And then be thou as great as Lucifer.
FAUSTUS [*cutting his arm*] Lo, Mephistopheles, for love of thee
I cut mine arm, and with my proper° blood — *own*
Assure my soul to be great Lucifer's,
Chief lord and regent of perpetual night.
View here the blood that trickles from mine arm,
And let it be propitious for my wish.
MEPHISTOPHELES But, Faustus, thou must
Write it in manner of a deed of gift.
FAUSTUS Ay, so I will. [*He writes.*] But Mephistopheles,
My blood congeals, and I can write no more.
MEPHISTOPHELES I'll fetch thee fire to dissolve it straight.° — *immediately*
Exit.
FAUSTUS What might the staying of my blood portend?
Is it unwilling I should write this bill?° — *deed*
Why streams it not, that I may write afresh?
"Faustus gives to thee his soul"—ah, there it stayed!
Why shouldst thou not? Is not thy soul thine own?
Then write again: "Faustus gives to thee his soul."

Enter Mephistopheles with a chafer° of coals. — *portable grate*

MEPHISTOPHELES Here's fire. Come, Faustus, set it on.
FAUSTUS So. Now the blood begins to clear again.
Now will I make an end immediately. [*He writes.*]

1. For Lucifer demands that guarantee.
2. I.e., Misery loves company.

MEPHISTOPHELES [*aside*] Oh, what will not I do to obtain his soul?

FAUSTUS *Consummatum est.*[3] This bill is ended,
And Faustus hath bequeathed his soul to Lucifer.
But what is this inscription on mine arm?
"Homo, fuge!"° Whither should I fly? ["Fly, O man!"]
If unto God, he'll throw thee down to hell.—
My senses are deceived; here's nothing writ.—
I see it plain. Here in this place is writ
"Homo, fuge!" Yet shall not Faustus fly.

MEPHISTOPHELES [*aside*] I'll fetch him somewhat° [something] to delight his mind. *Exit.*

Enter [Mephistopheles] with devils, giving crowns and rich apparel to Faustus, and dance and then depart.

FAUSTUS Speak, Mephistopheles. What means this show?

MEPHISTOPHELES Nothing, Faustus, but to delight thy mind withal° [with]
And to show thee what magic can perform.

FAUSTUS But may I raise up spirits when I please?

MEPHISTOPHELES Ay, Faustus, and do greater things than these.

FAUSTUS Then there's enough for° [to pay for] a thousand souls.
Here, Mephistopheles, receive this scroll,
A deed of gift of body and of soul—
But yet conditionally that thou perform
All articles prescribed between us both.

MEPHISTOPHELES Faustus, I swear by hell and Lucifer
To effect all promises between us made.

FAUSTUS Then hear me read them.
"On these conditions following:

First, that Faustus may be a spirit in form and substance.

Secondly, that Mephistopheles shall be his servant, and at his command.

Thirdly, that Mephistopheles shall do for him and bring him whatsoever.° [whatsoever it be]

Fourthly, that he shall be in his chamber or house invisible.

Lastly, that he shall appear to the said John Faustus at all times in what form or shape soever he please.

I, John Faustus of Wittenberg, Doctor, by these presents° [this deed] do give both body and soul to Lucifer, Prince of the East, and his minister Mephistopheles; and furthermore grant unto them that, four-and-twenty years being expired, the articles above written inviolate,° [not violated] full power to fetch or carry the said John Faustus, body and soul, flesh, blood, or goods, into their habitation wheresoever.

By me, John Faustus."

MEPHISTOPHELES Speak, Faustus. Do you deliver this as your deed?

FAUSTUS [*giving the deed*] Ay. Take it, and the devil give thee good on't.

MEPHISTOPHELES Now, Faustus, ask what thou wilt.

FAUSTUS First will I question with thee about hell.

3. It is finished—Christ's last words on the cross (John 19.30).

Tell me, where is the place that men call hell?
MEPHISTOPHELES Under the heavens.
FAUSTUS Ay, but whereabout?
MEPHISTOPHELES Within the bowels of these elements,
Where we are tortured and remain forever.
Hell hath no limits, nor is circumscribed
In one self place,° for where we are is hell, *one and the same place*
And where hell is must we ever be.
And, to conclude, when all the world dissolves,
And every creature shall be purified,
All places shall be hell that is not heaven.
FAUSTUS Come, I think hell's a fable.
MEPHISTOPHELES Ay, think so still, till experience change thy mind.
FAUSTUS Why, think'st thou then that Faustus shall be damned?
MEPHISTOPHELES Ay, of necessity, for here's the scroll
Wherein thou hast given thy soul to Lucifer.
FAUSTUS Ay, and body too. But what of that?
Think'st thou that Faustus is so fond° *foolish*
To imagine that after this life there is any pain?
Tush, these are trifles and mere old wives' tales.
MEPHISTOPHELES But, Faustus, I am an instance to prove the contrary,
For I am damned and am now in hell.
FAUSTUS How? Now in hell? Nay, an° this be hell, *if*
I'll willingly be damned here. What? Walking, disputing, etc.? But leaving off this, let me have a wife, the fairest maid in Germany, for I am wanton and lascivious and cannot live without a wife.
MEPHISTOPHELES How, a wife? I prithee, Faustus, talk not of a wife.
FAUSTUS Nay, sweet Mephistopheles, fetch me one, for I will have one.
MEPHISTOPHELES Well, thou wilt have one. Sit there till I come. I'll fetch thee a wife, in the devil's name. [*Exit.*]

Enter [*Mephistopheles*] *with a devil dressed like a woman, with fireworks.*

MEPHISTOPHELES Tell, Faustus, how dost thou like thy wife?
FAUSTUS A plague on her for a hot whore!
MEPHISTOPHELES Tut, Faustus, marriage is but a ceremonial toy.
If thou lovest me, think no more of it. [*Exit devil*].
I'll cull° thee out the fairest courtesans *pick*
And bring them ev'ry morning to thy bed.
She whom thine eye shall like thy heart shall have,
Be she as chaste as was Penelope,° *Odysseus' wife*
As wise as Saba,° or as beautiful *the Queen of Sheba*
As was bright Lucifer before his fall.
[*Presenting a book*] Hold, take this book. Peruse it thoroughly.
The iterating° of these lines brings gold; *repeating, reciting*
The framing° of this circle on the ground *inscribing*
Brings whirlwinds, tempests, thunder, and lightning.
Pronounce this thrice devoutly to thyself,
And men in armor shall appear to thee,

Ready to execute what thou desir'st.

FAUSTUS Thanks, Mephistopheles. Yet fain° would I have a book wherein I might behold all spells and incantations, that I might raise up spirits when I please. *gladly*

MEPHISTOPHELES Here they are in this book.

There turn to them.

FAUSTUS Now would I have a book where I might see all characters° and planets of the heavens, that I might know their motions and dispositions. *astrological symbols*

MEPHISTOPHELES Here they are too. *Turn to them.*

FAUSTUS Nay, let me have one book more—and then I have done—wherein I might see all plants, herbs, and trees that grow upon the earth.

MEPHISTOPHELES Here they be. *Turn to them.*

FAUSTUS Oh, thou art deceived.[4]

MEPHISTOPHELES Tut, I warrant thee. [*Exeunt.*]

[2.2]

Enter Robin the ostler° with a book in his hand. *stable groom*

ROBIN Oh, this is admirable! Here I ha' stol'n one of Doctor Faustus' conjuring books, and, i'faith, I mean to search some circles[1] for my own use. Now will I make all the maidens in our parish dance at my pleasure stark naked before me, and so by that means I shall see more than e'er I felt or saw yet.

Enter Rafe, calling Robin.

RAFE Robin, prithee, come away.° There's a gentleman tarries to have his horse, and he would have his things[2] rubbed and made clean; he keeps such a chafing with my mistress about it, and she has sent me to look thee out.° Prithee, come away. *come along* / *look for you*

ROBIN Keep out, keep out, or else you are blown up, you are dismembered, Rafe! Keep out, for I am about a roaring piece of work.

RAFE Come, what dost thou with that same book?° Thou canst not read? *that book there*

ROBIN Yes, my master and mistress shall find that I can read—he for his forehead, she for her private study.[3] She's born to bear with me,[4] or else my art fails.

RAFE Why, Robin, what book is that?

ROBIN What book? Why the most intolerable[5] book for conjuring that e'er was invented by any brimstone devil.

RAFE Canst thou conjure with it?

ROBIN I can do all these things easily with it: first, I can make thee drunk with hippocras° at any tavern in Europe for nothing. That's one of my conjuring works. *spiced wine*

RAFE Our Master Parson says that's nothing.° *worthless; easy*

ROBIN True, Rafe; and more, Rafe, if thou hast any mind to Nan Spit,[6] our kitchen maid, then turn her and wind her to

4. Faustus is skeptical still, as in his repeated inquiries about hell.
2.2. A hostelry.
1. (1) Conjuring circles; (2) vaginas.
2. His leather riding gear. (With erotic suggestion.)
3. Robin plans to put cuckold's horns on his master's forehead by means of "private study" with the mistress.
4. She is destined to (1) put up with me; (2) support my body in sex; (3) bear my child.
5. Robin may mean "incomparable."
6. Nan Spit is named for a device on which cooking meat is turned and wound about—as Rafe is urged to do with her.

thy own use as often as thou wilt, and at midnight.
RAFE Oh, brave,° Robin! Shall I have Nan Spit, and to mine own use? On that condition I'll feed thy devil with horse-bread° as long as he lives, of free cost. *splendid* / *horse-feed, fodder*
ROBIN No more, sweet Rafe. Let's go and make clean our boots, which lie foul° upon our hands, and then to our conjuring, in the devil's name. *Exeunt.* *muddy, filthy*

[2.3]

[*Enter Faustus in his study, and Mephistopheles.*]

FAUSTUS When I behold the heavens, then I repent
And curse thee, wicked Mephistopheles,
Because thou hast deprived me of those joys.
MEPHISTOPHELES Why, Faustus,
Think'st thou heaven is such a glorious thing?
I tell thee, 'tis not half so fair as thou
Or any man that breathes on earth.
FAUSTUS How provest thou that?
MEPHISTOPHELES It was made for man; therefore is man more excellent.
FAUSTUS If it were made for man, 'twas made for me.
I will renounce this magic and repent.

Enter Good Angel and Evil Angel.

GOOD ANGEL Faustus, repent yet, God will pity thee.
EVIL ANGEL Thou art a spirit. God cannot pity thee.
FAUSTUS Who buzzeth in mine ears I am a spirit?
Be I a devil,[1] yet God may pity me;
Ay, God will pity me if I repent.
EVIL ANGEL Ay, but Faustus never shall repent.
Exeunt [*Angels*].
FAUSTUS My heart's so hardened I cannot repent.
Scarce can I name salvation, faith, or heaven
But fearful echoes thunders in mine ears:
"Faustus, thou art damned!" Then swords and knives,
Poison, guns, halters,° and envenomed steel° *nooses / swords*
Are laid before me to dispatch myself;
And long ere this I should have slain myself
Had not sweet pleasure conquered deep despair.
Have not I made blind Homer sing to me
Of Alexander's love and Oenone's death?[2]
And hath not he that built the walls of Thebes
With ravishing sound of his melodious harp[3]
Made music with my Mephistopheles?
Why should I die, then, or basely despair?
I am resolved Faustus shall ne'er repent.
Come, Mephistopheles, let us dispute again
And argue of divine astrology.

2.3. Faustus's study.
1. (1) Even though I am a devil; (2) Even if I were a devil.
2. The story of Paris's (Alexander's) desertion of the nymph Oenone for Helen and of Oenone's eventual suicide is partly post-Homeric.
3. Amphion, ruler of Thebes, moved stones by his powerful music and thereby built the city walls. (Another post-Homeric legend.)

Tell me, are there many heavens above the moon?
Are all celestial bodies but one globe,
As is the substance of this centric earth?[4]
MEPHISTOPHELES As are the elements, such are the spheres,
Mutually folded in each others' orb;
And, Faustus, all jointly move upon one axletree,° *axle, pole*
Whose terminine° is termed the world's wide pole.[5] *limit*
Nor are the names of Saturn, Mars, or Jupiter
Feigned, but are erring stars.° *(wandering) planets*
FAUSTUS But tell me, have they all one motion, both *situ et tempore?*° *in space and time*
MEPHISTOPHELES All jointly move from east to west in four-and-twenty hours upon the poles of the world, but differ in their motion upon the poles of the zodiac.° *along the zodiac*
FAUSTUS Tush, these slender trifles Wagner can decide.
Hath Mephistopheles no greater skill?
Who knows not the double motion of the planets?
The first is finished in a natural day,
The second thus, as Saturn in thirty years, Jupiter in twelve, Mars in four,° the Sun, Venus, and Mercury in a year, the moon in twenty-eight days. Tush, these are freshmen's suppositions.° But tell me, hath every sphere a dominion or intelligentia?° *(actually, more like two)* *arguing points* *controlling spirit*
MEPHISTOPHELES Ay.
FAUSTUS How many heavens or spheres are there?
MEPHISTOPHELES Nine: the seven planets, the firmament, and the empyreal heaven.° *highest heaven*
FAUSTUS Well, resolve me in this question: why have we not conjunctions, oppositions,[6] aspects, eclipses all at one time,° but in some years we have more, in some less? *at regular intervals*
MEPHISTOPHELES *Per inaequalem motum respectu totius.*[7]
FAUSTUS Well, I am answered. Tell me who made the world.
MEPHISTOPHELES I will not.
FAUSTUS Sweet Mephistopheles, tell me.
MEPHISTOPHELES Move° me not, for I will not tell thee. *Anger; urge*
FAUSTUS Villain, have I not bound thee to tell me anything?
MEPHISTOPHELES Ay, that is not against our kingdom, but this is. Think thou on hell, Faustus, for thou art damned.
FAUSTUS Think, Faustus, upon God, that made the world.
MEPHISTOPHELES Remember this.° *Exit.* *You'll pay for this*
FAUSTUS Ay, go, accursèd spirit, to ugly hell!
'Tis thou hast damned distressèd Faustus' soul.
Is't not too late?

Enter Good Angel and Evil [Angel].

EVIL ANGEL Too late.
GOOD ANGEL Never too late, if Faustus can repent.

4. Faustus asks about the Ptolemaic universe, with the earth at its center.
5. The axis of the heavenly spheres is the same as the earth's.
6. Heavenly bodies are in "conjunction" when they appear near to each other from an earthbound point of view and in "opposition" when they appear opposite each other.
7. Because of their uneven motion in relation to the whole.

EVIL ANGEL If thou repent, devils shall tear thee in pieces.
GOOD ANGEL Repent, and they shall never raze thy skin.
Exeunt [*Angels*].
FAUSTUS Ah, Christ, my Savior,
Seek to save distressèd Faustus' soul!

Enter Lucifer, Beelzebub, and Mephistopheles.

LUCIFER Christ cannot save thy soul, for he is just.
There's none but I have int'rest in the same.
FAUSTUS Oh, who art thou that look'st so terrible?
LUCIFER I am Lucifer,
And this is my companion prince in hell.
FAUSTUS O Faustus, they are come to fetch away thy soul!
LUCIFER We come to tell thee thou dost injure us.
Thou talk'st of Christ, contrary to thy promise.
Thou shouldst not think of God. Think of the devil,
And of his dame,° too. *dam; wife*
FAUSTUS Nor will I henceforth. Pardon me in this,
And Faustus vows never to look to heaven,
Never to name God or to pray to him,
To burn his Scriptures, slay his ministers,
And make my spirits pull his churches down.
LUCIFER Do so, and we will highly gratify° thee. *reward*
Faustus, we are come from hell to show thee some pastime.
Sit down, and thou shalt see all the Seven Deadly Sins appear in their proper° shapes. *own*

FAUSTUS That sight will be as pleasing unto me as Paradise was to Adam the first day of his creation.

LUCIFER Talk not of Paradise nor creation, but mark this show. Talk of the devil, and nothing else.—Come away!
[*Faustus sits.*]

Enter the Seven Deadly Sins.

Now, Faustus, examine them of their several° names and dispositions. *various*

FAUSTUS What art thou, the first?

PRIDE I am Pride. I disdain to have any parents. I am like to Ovid's flea:[8] I can creep into every corner of a wench. Sometimes like a periwig° I sit upon her brow, or like a fan of feathers I kiss her lips. Indeed I do. What do I not? But fie, what a scent is here! I'll not speak another word except° the ground were perfumed and covered with cloth of arras.° *wig* / *unless* / *rich tapestry*

FAUSTUS What art thou, the second?

COVETOUSNESS I am Covetousness, begotten of an old churl in an old leathern bag;° and might I have my wish, I would desire that this house and all the people in it were turned to gold, that I might lock you up in my good chest. O my sweet gold! *money bag*

FAUSTUS What art thou, the third?

WRATH I am Wrath. I had neither father nor mother. I leaped out of a lion's mouth when I was scarce half an hour old, and ever since I have run up and down the world with this case° of rapiers,° wounding myself when I had nobody to *pair / swords*

8. A medieval "Elegy of a Flea" was falsely attributed to Ovid.

fight withal. I was born in hell, and look to it,° for some of *look sharp*
you shall be my father.

FAUSTUS What art thou, the fourth?

ENVY I am Envy, begotten of a chimney sweeper and an
oyster-wife.° I cannot read, and therefore wish all books were *oyster-seller*
burnt. I am lean with seeing others eat. Oh, that there would
come a famine through all the world, that all might die, and
I live alone! Then thou shouldst see how fat I would be. But
must thou sit and I stand? Come down, with a vengeance!° *with a curse on you!*

FAUSTUS Away, envious rascal!—What are thou, the fifth?

GLUTTONY Who, I, sir? I am Gluttony. My parents are all dead,
and the devil a penny° they have left me but a bare pension, *not so much as a penny*
and that is thirty meals a day, and ten bevers°—a small trifle *snacks*
to suffice nature.° Oh, I come of a royal parentage. My *bodily needs*
grandfather was a gammon of bacon,° my grandmother a *ham*
hogshead° of claret wine. My godfathers were these: Peter *large cask*
Pickle-herring° and Martin Martlemas-beef.[9] Oh, but my *pickled herring*
godmother, she was a jolly gentlewoman, and well beloved in
every good town and city; her name was Mistress Margery
March-beer.° Now, Faustus, thou hast heard all my progeny, *strong beer*
wilt thou bid me to supper?

FAUSTUS No, I'll see thee hanged. Thou wilt eat up all my victuals.

GLUTTONY Then the devil choke thee!

FAUSTUS Choke thyself, glutton!—What art thou, the sixth?

SLOTH I am Sloth. I was begotten on a sunny bank, where I have lain ever since, and you have done me great injury to bring me from thence. Let me be carried thither again by Gluttony and Lechery. I'll not speak another word for a king's ransom.

FAUSTUS What are you, Mistress Minx, the seventh and last?

LECHERY Who, I, sir? I am one that loves an inch of raw mutton better than an ell of fried stockfish,[1] and the first letter of my name begins with lechery.

LUCIFER Away, to hell, to hell! *Exeunt the Sins.*
Now, Faustus, how dost thou like this?

FAUSTUS Oh, this feeds my soul!

LUCIFER Tut, Faustus, in hell is all manner of delight.

FAUSTUS Oh, might I see hell and return again, how happy were I then!

LUCIFER Thou shalt. I will send for thee at midnight. [*He presents a book.*] In meantime, take this book. Peruse it
throughly,° and thou shalt turn thyself into what shape thou *thoroughly*
wilt.

FAUSTUS [*taking the book*] Great thanks, mighty Lucifer. This
will I keep as chary° as my life. *carefully*

LUCIFER Farewell, Faustus, and think on the devil.

FAUSTUS Farewell, great Lucifer. Come, Mephistopheles.

Exeunt omnes [*Faustus and Mephistopheles by one way, Lucifer and Beelzebub by another*].

9. Beef slaughtered at the Feast of Saint Martin, November 11.

1. I.e., I am one who prefers even a small amount of raw pleasure to a great deal of insufficiency. (Mutton is red-blooded meat; stockfish is dried cod.)

[3. Chorus]

Enter Wagner solus.° *alone*

WAGNER Learnèd Faustus,
To know the secrets of astronomy
Graven° in the book of Jove's high firmament, *Engraved*
Did mount himself to scale Olympus' top,
Being seated in a chariot burning bright
Drawn by the strength of yoky° dragons' necks. *yoked*
He now is gone to prove° cosmography, *make trial of*
And, as I guess, will first arrive at Rome
To see the Pope and manner of his court
And take some part of° holy Peter's feast° *in / festival worship*
That to this day is highly solemnized. *Exit Wagner.*

[3.1]

Enter Faustus and Mephistopheles.

FAUSTUS Having now, my good Mephistopheles,
Passed with delight the stately town of Trier,° *(in western Germany)*
Environed round with airy mountaintops,
With walls of flint and deep intrenchèd lakes,° *moats*
Not to be won by any conquering prince;
From Paris next, coasting° the realm of France, *skirting*
We saw the river Maine fall into Rhine,
Whose banks are set with groves of fruitful vines.
Then up to Naples, rich Campania,
Whose buildings, fair and gorgeous to the eye,
The streets straight forth° and paved with finest brick, *perfectly straight*
Quarters the town in four equivalents.
There saw we learnèd Maro's° golden tomb, *Virgil's*
The way he cut an English mile in length
Thorough° a rock of stone in one night's space.[1] *Through*
From thence to Venice, Padua, and the rest,
In midst of which a sumptuous temple° stands *(St. Mark's in Venice)*
That threats° the stars with her aspiring top. *threatens*
Thus hitherto hath Faustus spent his time.
But tell me now, what resting place is this?
Hast thou, as erst° I did command, *earlier*
Conducted me within the walls of Rome?

MEPHISTOPHELES Faustus, I have. And because° we will not be unprovided, I have taken up His Holiness's privy° chamber for our use. *so that* / *private*

FAUSTUS I hope His Holiness will bid us welcome.

MEPHISTOPHELES Tut, 'tis no matter, man. We'll be bold with his good cheer.
And now, my Faustus, that thou mayst perceive
What Rome containeth to delight thee with,
Know that this city stands upon seven hills
That underprops the groundwork of the same.

3.1. Rome.
1. Virgil was fabled to have fashioned a tunnel through rock in one night by magic.

Just° through the midst runs flowing Tiber's stream, *Right*
With winding banks that cut it in two parts,
Over the which four stately bridges lean,
That makes safe passage to each part of Rome.
Upon the bridge called Ponte Angelo
Erected is a castle passing° strong, *surpassingly*
Within whose walls such store of ordnance are,
And double cannons, framed° of carvèd brass, *devised*
As match the days within one complete year°— *(365 in number)*
Besides the gates and high pyramides° *obelisks*
Which Julius Caesar brought from Africa.

FAUSTUS Now, by the kingdoms of infernal rule,
Of Styx, Acheron, and the fiery lake
Of ever-burning Phlegethon,[2] I swear
That I do long to see the monuments
And situation of bright splendent° Rome. *shining, resplendent*
Come, therefore, let's away!

MEPHISTOPHELES Nay, Faustus, stay. I know you'd fain see the Pope
And take some part of° holy Peter's feast, *partake of*
Where thou shalt see a troupe° of bald-pate friars *(or troop)*
Whose *summum bonum*° is in belly cheer. *highest good*

FAUSTUS Well, I am content to compass° then some sport, *devise*
And by their folly make us merriment.
Then charm° me, that I may be invisible, to do what I please unseen of any whilst I stay in Rome. *endow with magic*

MEPHISTOPHELES [*placing a robe on Faustus*] So, Faustus, now do what thou wilt, thou shalt not be discerned.

Sound a sennet.° *Enter the Pope and the Cardinal of Lorraine to the banquet, with Friars attending.* *trumpet signal*

POPE My lord of Lorraine, will't please you draw near?

FAUSTUS Fall to, and the devil choke you an you spare.° *if you hold back*

POPE How now, who's that which spake?—Friars, look about.
[*Some Friars attempt to search.*]

FRIAR Here's nobody, if it like° Your Holiness. *please*

POPE [*presenting a dish*] My lord, here is a dainty dish was° sent me from the Bishop of Milan. *that was*

FAUSTUS (*snatch*[*ing*] *it*) I thank you, sir.

POPE How now, who's that which snatched the meat from me? Will no man look? [*Some Friars search about.*] My lord, this dish was sent me from the Cardinal of Florence.

FAUSTUS [*snatching the dish*] You say true. I'll ha't.

POPE What, again?—My lord, I'll drink to Your Grace.

FAUSTUS [*snatching the cup*] I'll pledge Your Grace.

LORRAINE My lord, it may be some ghost, newly crept out of purgatory, come to beg a pardon of Your Holiness.

POPE It may be so.—Friars, prepare a dirge to lay the fury of this ghost.—Once again, my lord, fall to.° *partake of the feast*
The Pope crosseth himself.

2. Faustus names three of the four rivers of the underworld.

FAUSTUS What, are you crossing of yourself?
Well, use that trick no more, I would advise you.
[The Pope] cross[es himself] again.
Well, there's a second time. Aware° the third, *Beware*
I give you fair warning.
[The Pope] cross[es himself] again, and Faustus hits him a box of the ear, and they all [except Faustus and Mephistopheles] run away.
Come on, Mephistopheles. What shall we do?

MEPHISTOPHELES Nay, I know not. We shall be cursed with bell, book, and candle.

FAUSTUS How? Bell, book, and candle, candle, book, and bell,
Forward and backward, to curse Faustus to hell.
Anon you shall hear a hog grunt, a calf bleat, and an ass bray,
Because it is Saint Peter's holy day.

Enter all the Friars to sing the dirge.

FRIAR Come, brethren, let's about our business with good devotion. *[The Friars] sing this.*
Cursèd be he that stole away His Holiness's meat from the table.
Maledicat Dominus!° *The Lord curse him!*
Cursèd be he that struck His Holiness a blow on the face.
Maledicat Dominus!
Cursèd be he that took° Friar Sandelo a blow on the pate. *gave*
Maledicat Dominus!
Cursèd be he that disturbeth our holy dirge.
Maledicat Dominus!
Cursèd be he that took away His Holiness's wine.
Maledicat Dominus!
Et omnes sancti.[3] Amen.
[Faustus and Mephistopheles] beat the Friars, and fling fireworks among them, and so exeunt.

[3.2]

Enter Robin [with a conjuring book] and Rafe with a silver goblet.

ROBIN Come, Rafe, did not I tell thee we were forever made by this Doctor Faustus' book? *Ecce signum!*° Here's a simple purchase° for horse-keepers! Our horses shall eat no hay[1] as long as this lasts. *Behold the sign!* / *plunder*

Enter the Vintner.° *an innkeeper*

RAFE But, Robin, here comes the Vintner.

ROBIN Hush, I'll gull° him supernaturally.—Drawer,° I hope all is paid. God be with you. Come, Rafe. [*They start to go.*] *trick* / *Bartender*

VINTNER [*to Robin*] Soft,° sir, a word with you. I must yet have a goblet paid from you ere you go. *Take it easy*

3. And may all the saints (curse him).
3.2. A tavern or hostelry.
1. I.e., eat like kings.

ROBIN I, a goblet? Rafe, I, a goblet? I scorn you, and you are but a etc.[2] I, a goblet? Search me.

VINTNER I mean so, sir, with your favor.° *by your leave*

[*The Vintner searches Robin.*]

ROBIN How say you now?

VINTNER I must say somewhat° to your fellow.—You, sir. *something*

RAFE Me, sir? Me, sir? Search your fill.

[*He tosses the goblet to Robin; then the Vintner searches Rafe.*]

Now, sir, you may be ashamed to burden honest men with a matter of truth.° *question of honesty*

VINTNER Well, t'one of you hath this goblet about you.

ROBIN You lie, drawer, 'tis afore me.[3] Sirrah, you, I'll teach ye to impeach° honest men. Stand by. I'll scour° you for a goblet. Stand aside, you had best,° I charge you in the name of Beelzebub. [*He tosses the goblet to Rafe.*] *accuse / beat* *you'd better*

[*Aside to Rafe*] Look to the goblet, Rafe.

VINTNER What mean you, sirrah?

ROBIN I'll tell you what I mean. (*He reads.*) *"Sanctobulorum Periphrasticon!"*°—Nay, I'll tickle you, Vintner. [*Aside to Rafe*] Look to the goblet, Rafe.—*"Polypragmos Belseborams framanto pacostiphos tostu Mephistopheles!"* etc.° *(Latin gibberish)* *(Latin gibberish)*

Enter to them Mephistopheles.

[*Exit the Vintner, running.*]

MEPHISTOPHELES Monarch of hell, under whose black survey
Great potentates do kneel with awful° fear, *terrified*
Upon whose altars thousand souls do lie,
How am I vexèd with these villains' charms!° *incantations*
From Constantinople am I hither come
Only for pleasure of these damnèd slaves.

ROBIN How, from Constantinople? You have had a great journey. Will you take sixpence in your purse to pay for your supper and be gone?

MEPHISTOPHELES Well, villains, for your presumption I transform thee [*to Robin*] into an ape, and thee [*to Rafe*] into a dog. And so, begone! [*They are transformed in shape.*]

Exit [Mephistopheles].

ROBIN How, into an ape? That's brave.° I'll have fine sport with the boys; I'll get nuts and apples enough. *excellent*

RAFE And I must be a dog.

ROBIN I'faith, thy head will never be out of the pottage° pot. *porridge*

Exeunt.

[4. Chorus]

Enter Chorus.

CHORUS When Faustus had with pleasure ta'en the view
Of rarest° things and royal courts of kings, *most remarkable*
He stayed his course° and so returnèd home, *ceased his travels*
Where such as bear his absence but with grief—

2. Here the actor playing Robin improvises an insult.
3. Robin quibbles: "the goblet isn't *about* me, i.e., on my person, but *afore* me, right in front of me."

I mean his friends and nearest companions—
Did gratulate° his safety with kind words. *rejoice at*
And in their conference of what befell,
Touching° his journey through the world and air, *Regarding*
They put forth questions of astrology,
Which Faustus answered with such learnèd skill
As° they admired and wondered at his wit. *That*
Now is his fame spread forth in every land.
Amongst the rest the Emperor° is one, *Holy Roman Emperor*
Carolus the Fifth,° at whose palace now *Charles V of Spain*
Faustus is feasted 'mongst his noblemen.
What there he did in trial° of his art° *demonstration / skill*
I leave untold, your eyes shall see performed. *Exit.*

[4.1]

Enter Emperor, Faustus, [Mephistopheles,] and a Knight, with attendants.

EMPEROR Master Doctor Faustus, I have heard strange° report of thy knowledge in the black art—how that none in my empire, nor in the whole world, can compare with thee for the rare° effects of magic. They say thou hast a familiar spirit[1] by whom thou canst accomplish what thou list.° This, therefore, is my request: that thou let me see some proof of thy skill, that mine eyes may be witnesses to confirm what mine ears have heard reported. And here I swear to thee, by the honor of mine imperial crown, that whatever thou dost, thou shalt be no ways prejudiced or endamaged. *wondrous / extraordinary / desire*

KNIGHT (*aside*) I'faith, he looks much like a conjurer.° *(said ironically)*

FAUSTUS My gracious sovereign, though I must confess myself far inferior to the report men have published,° and nothing answerable° to the honor of Your Imperial Majesty, yet, for that° love and duty binds me thereunto, I am content to do whatsoever Your Majesty shall command me. *spread abroad / not at all suited / because*

EMPEROR Then, Doctor Faustus, mark what I shall say.
As I was sometime° solitary set *recently*
Within my closet,° sundry thoughts arose *private room, study*
About the honor of mine ancestors—
How they had won by prowess such exploits,
Got such riches, subdued so many kingdoms
As we that do succeed° or they that shall *follow, inherit*
Hereafter possess our throne shall,
I fear me, never attain to that degree
Of high renown and great authority.
Amongst which kings is Alexander the Great,
Chief spectacle of the world's preeminence,
The bright shining of whose glorious acts
Lightens the world with his reflecting beams—
As° when I hear but motion° made of him, *So that / mention*
It grieves my soul I never saw the man.
If, therefore, thou by cunning of thine art

4.1. The court of the Emperor Charles V, and, at 103ff., on the return to Wittenberg.

1. Demon or evil spirit, usually in the form of an animal, attending a mortal in return for his soul. Cf. 1.4.25–26 and note.

Canst raise this man from hollow vaults below
Where lies entombed this famous conqueror,
And bring with him his beauteous paramour,
Both in their right shapes, gesture, and attire
They used to wear during their time of life,
Thou shalt both satisfy my just desire
And give me cause to praise thee whilst I live.

FAUSTUS My gracious lord, I am ready to accomplish your request, so far forth as by art and power of my spirit I am able to perform.

KNIGHT (*aside*) I'faith, that's just nothing at all.

FAUSTUS But if it like° Your Grace, it is not in my ability to present before your eyes the true substantial bodies of those two deceased princes, which long since are consumed to dust. *please*

KNIGHT (*aside*) Ay, marry,° Master Doctor, now there's a sign of grace in you, when you will confess the truth. *by Mary (an oath)*

FAUSTUS But such spirits as can lively° resemble Alexander and his paramour shall appear before Your Grace in that manner that they best lived in, in their most flourishing estate—which I doubt not shall sufficiently content Your Imperial Majesty. *in lifelike manner*

EMPEROR Go to,° Master Doctor. Let me see them presently. *i.e., Get on with it*

KNIGHT Do you hear, Master Doctor? You bring Alexander and his paramour before the Emperor?

FAUSTUS How then, sir?

KNIGHT I'faith, that's as true as° Diana turned me to a stag. *as true as if*

FAUSTUS No, sir, but when Actaeon died,[2] he left the horns for you. [*Aside to Mephistopheles*] Mephistopheles, begone!

Exit Mephistopheles.

KNIGHT Nay, an you go to conjuring, I'll be gone.

Exit Knight.

FAUSTUS [*aside*] I'll meet with° you anon for interrupting me so.—Here they are, my gracious lord. *get even with*

Enter Mephistopheles with Alexander and his paramour.

EMPEROR Master Doctor, I heard this lady while she lived had a wart or mole in her neck. How shall I know whether it be so or no?

FAUSTUS Your Highness may boldly go and see.

[*The Emperor makes an inspection, and then*] *exit Alexander* [*with his paramour*].

EMPEROR Sure these are no spirits, but the true substantial bodies of those two deceased princes.

FAUSTUS Will't please Your Highness now to send for the knight that was so pleasant° with me here of late? *jocular*

EMPEROR One of you call him forth.

[*An attendant goes to summon the Knight.*]

Enter the Knight with a pair of horns on his head.

How now, Sir Knight? Why, I had thought thou hadst been a bachelor,° but now I see thou hast a wife, that not only gives thee horns but makes thee wear them. Feel on thy head. *knight; unmarried man*

KNIGHT [*to Faustus*] Thou damnèd wretch and execrable dog,

2. Because Actaeon offended Diana, he was turned into a stag and hunted to death by his own hounds.

Bred in the concave° of some monstrous rock, *hollow*
How dar'st thou thus abuse a gentleman?
Villain, I say, undo what thou hast done.

FAUSTUS Oh, not so fast, sir. There's no haste but good.° *Don't be too hasty*
Are you remembered° how you crossed me in my conference *Do you remember*
with the Emperor? I think I have met° with you for it. *am even*

EMPEROR Good Master Doctor, at my entreaty release him.
He hath done penance sufficient.

FAUSTUS My gracious lord, not so much for the injury° he *insult*
offered me here in your presence as to delight you with some
mirth hath Faustus worthily° requited this injurious knight; *deservedly*
which being all I desire, I am content to release him of his
horns.—And, Sir Knight, hereafter speak well of scholars.
[*Aside to Mephistopheles*] Mephistopheles, transform him
straight.° [*The horns are removed.*] Now, my good lord, *at once*
having done my duty, I humbly take my leave.

EMPEROR Farewell, Master Doctor. Yet, ere you go,
Expect from me a bounteous reward.

Exeunt Emperor, [*Knight, and attendants*].

FAUSTUS Now, Mephistopheles, the restless course
That time doth run with calm and silent foot,
Short'ning my days and thread of vital life,
Calls for the payment of my latest° years. *last, final*
Therefore, sweet Mephistopheles, let us make haste
To Wittenberg.

MEPHISTOPHELES What, will you go on horseback or on foot?

FAUSTUS Nay, till I am past this fair and pleasant green,
I'll walk on foot.

Enter a Horse-courser.° *Horse-dealer*

HORSE-COURSER I have been all this day seeking one Master
Fustian.° Mass,° see where he is.—God save you, Master *Bombast / By the Mass*
Doctor.

FAUSTUS What, Horse-courser! You are well met.° *I am happy to see you*

HORSE-COURSER [*offering money*] Do you hear, sir? I have
brought you forty dollars for your horse.

FAUSTUS I cannot sell him so. If thou lik'st him for fifty, take
him.

HORSE-COURSER Alas, sir, I have no more. [*To Mephistopheles*] I pray you, speak for me.

MEPHISTOPHELES [*to Faustus*] I pray you, let him have him.
He is an honest fellow, and he has a great charge,° neither *expense*
wife nor child.

FAUSTUS Well, come, give me your money. [*He takes the
money.*] My boy° will deliver him to you. But I must tell you *servant*
one thing before you have him: ride him not into the water,[3] at
any hand.° *on any account*

HORSE-COURSER Why, sir, will he not drink of all waters?° *be ready for anything*

FAUSTUS Oh, yes, he will drink of all waters. But ride him not
into the water. Ride him over hedge, or ditch, or where thou
wilt, but not into the water.

HORSE-COURSER Well, sir. [*Aside*] Now am I made man for-

3. Superstition held that a witch's horse, if ridden into the water, would turn into a bundle of hay.

ever! I'll not leave my horse for forty. If he had but the quality of hey, ding, ding, hey, ding, ding, I'd make a brave living on him; he has a buttock as slick as an eel.[4] [*To Faustus*] Well, good-bye, sir. Your boy will deliver him me? But hark ye, sir: if my horse be sick or ill at ease, if I bring his water° to you, you'll tell me what it is? *urine (for diagnosis)*

FAUSTUS Away, you villain! What, dost think I am a horse doctor? *Exit Horse-courser.*

What art thou, Faustus, but a man condemned to die?
Thy fatal time doth draw to final end.
Despair doth drive distrust unto my thoughts.
Confound° these passions with a quiet sleep. *Allay*
Tush! Christ did call the thief upon the cross;
Then rest thee, Faustus, quiet in conceit.° *in thought*

[*Faustus*] *sleep*[*s*] *in his chair.*

Enter Horse-courser all wet, crying.

HORSE-COURSER Alas, alas! "Doctor" Fustian, quotha!° Mass, Doctor Lopus[5] was never such a doctor. He's given me a purgation, he's purged me of forty dollars. I shall never see them more. But yet, like an ass as I was, I would not be ruled by him, for he bade me I should ride him into no water. Now I, thinking my horse had had some rare quality that he would not have had me known of,° I, like a venturous youth, rid° him into the deep pond at the town's end. I was no sooner in the middle of the pond but my horse vanished away and I sat upon a bottle° of hay, never so near drowning in my life. But I'll seek out my doctor and have my forty dollars again, or I'll make it the dearest horse! Oh, yonder is his snippersnapper.°—Do you hear? You, hey-pass,° where's your master? *forsooth* / *aware of / rode* / *bundle* / *saucy servant / trickster*

MEPHISTOPHELES Why, sir, what would you? You cannot speak with him.

HORSE-COURSER But I will speak with him.

MEPHISTOPHELES Why, he's fast asleep. Come some other time.

HORSE-COURSER I'll speak with him now, or I'll break his glass windows° about his ears. *spectacles*

MEPHISTOPHELES I tell thee he has not slept this eight nights.

HORSE-COURSER An he have not slept this eight weeks, I'll speak with him.

MEPHISTOPHELES See where he is, fast asleep.

HORSE-COURSER Ay, this is he.—God save ye, Master Doctor. Master Doctor, Master Doctor Fustian! Forty dollars, forty dollars for a bottle of hay!

MEPHISTOPHELES Why, thou see'st he hears thee not.

HORSE-COURSER (*holler*[*s*] *in his ear*) So-ho, ho! So-ho, ho! No? Will you not wake? I'll make you wake ere I go.

[*The Horse-courser*] *pull*[*s*] *him by the leg, and pull*[*s*] *it away.*

Alas, I am undone! What shall I do?

4. The Horse-courser dreams of charging stud fees for his virile new animal.

5. Dr. Lopez, a Portuguese Jew, was Queen Elizabeth's physician.

FAUSTUS Oh, my leg, my leg! Help, Mephistopheles! Call the officers! My leg, my leg!

MEPHISTOPHELES [*seizing the Horse-courser*] Come, villain, to the constable.

HORSE-COURSER Oh, Lord, sir, let me go, and I'll give you forty dollars more.

MEPHISTOPHELES Where be they?

HORSE-COURSER I have none about me. Come to my hostry° and I'll give them you. *hostelry, inn*

MEPHISTOPHELES Begone, quickly. *Horse-courser runs away.*

FAUSTUS What, is he gone? Farewell, he!° Faustus has his leg again, and the Horse-courser, I take it, a bottle of hay for his labor. Well, this trick shall cost him forty dollars more. *Good riddance to him!*

Enter Wagner.

How now, Wagner, what's the news with thee?

WAGNER Sir, the Duke of Vanholt° doth earnestly entreat your company. *Anhalt (in Germany)*

FAUSTUS The Duke of Vanholt! An honorable gentleman, to whom I must be no niggard of my cunning.° Come, Mephistopheles, let's away to him. *Exeunt.* *skill, artistry*

[4.2]

[*Enter Faustus with Mephistopheles.*] *Enter to them the Duke* [*of Vanholt*] *and the* [*pregnant*] *Duchess. The Duke speaks.*

DUKE Believe me, Master Doctor, this merriment hath much pleased me.

FAUSTUS My gracious lord, I am glad it contents you so well.—But it may be, madam, you take no delight in this. I have heard that great-bellied° women do long for some dainties or other. What is it, madam? Tell me, and you shall have it. *pregnant*

DUCHESS Thanks, good Master Doctor. And, for° I see your courteous intent to pleasure me, I will not hide from you the thing my heart desires. And were it now summer, as it is January and the dead time of the winter, I would desire no better meat° than a dish of ripe grapes. *since* *food*

FAUSTUS Alas, madam, that's nothing. [*Aside to Mephistopheles*] Mephistopheles, begone! *Exit Mephistopheles.* Were it a greater thing than this, so° it would content you, you should have it. *provided*

Enter Mephistopheles with the grapes.

Here they be, madam. Will't please you taste on them? [*The Duchess tastes the grapes.*]

DUKE Believe me, Master Doctor, this makes me wonder above the rest, that, being in the dead time of winter and in the month of January, how you should come by these grapes.

FAUSTUS If it like Your Grace, the year is divided into two circles over the whole world, that when it is here winter with

4.2. The court of the Duke of Vanholt.

us, in the contrary circle it is summer with them, as in India, Saba, and farther countries in the East;[1] and by means of a swift spirit that I have, I had them brought hither, as ye see.—How do you like them, madam? Be they good?

DUCHESS Believe me, Master Doctor, they be the best grapes that e'er I tasted in my life before.

FAUSTUS I am glad they content you so, madam.

DUKE Come, madam, let us in,
Where you must well reward this learnèd man
For the great kindness he hath showed to you.

DUCHESS And so I will, my lord, and whilst I live
Rest beholding° for this courtesy. *Remain beholden*

FAUSTUS I humbly thank Your Grace.

DUKE Come, Master Doctor, follow us and receive your reward.

Exeunt.

[5.1]

Enter Wagner solus.

WAGNER I think my master means to die shortly,
For he hath given to me all his goods.
And yet methinks if that° death were near *if*
He would not banquet and carouse and swill
Amongst the students, as even now he doth,
Who are at supper with such belly-cheer
As Wagner ne'er beheld in all his life.
See where they come. Belike° the feast is ended. [*Exit.*] *Probably*

Enter Faustus with two or three Scholars [and Mephistopheles].

FIRST SCHOLAR Master Doctor Faustus, since our conference about fair ladies—which was the beautifull'st in all the world—we have determined with° ourselves that Helen of Greece was the admirablest lady that ever lived. Therefore, Master Doctor, if you will do us that favor as to let us see that peerless dame of Greece, whom all the world admires for majesty, we should think ourselves much beholding° unto you. *among* / *beholden*

FAUSTUS Gentlemen,
For that° I know your friendship is unfeigned, *Because*
And Faustus' custom is not to deny
The just requests of those that wish him well,
You shall behold that peerless dame of Greece,
No otherways° for pomp and majesty *otherwise*
Than when Sir Paris crossed the seas with her
And brought the spoils° to rich Dardania.° *booty / Troy*
Be silent then, for danger is in words.

Music sounds and Helen [led in by Mephistopheles] passeth over the stage.

1. Faustus's observations would be more geographically correct if India and Saba, or Sheba (in the Middle East), were in the Southern Hemisphere, but they do at least have warm climates year-round.

5.1. Faustus's study.

SECOND SCHOLAR Too simple is my wit to tell her praise,
Whom all the world admires for majesty.
THIRD SCHOLAR No marvel though the angry Greeks pursued° *sought to avenge*
With ten years' war the rape° of such a queen, *abduction*
Whose heavenly beauty passeth all compare.° *comparison*
FIRST SCHOLAR Since we have seen the pride of nature's works
And only paragon of excellence,

Enter an Old Man.

Let us depart; and for this glorious deed
Happy and blest be Faustus evermore!
FAUSTUS Gentlemen, farewell. The same I wish to you.
Exeunt Scholars.
OLD MAN Ah, Doctor Faustus, that I might prevail
To guide thy steps unto the way of life,
By which sweet path thou mayst attain the goal
That shall conduct thee to celestial rest!
Break heart, drop blood, and mingle it with tears—
Tears falling from repentant heaviness
Of thy most vile and loathsome filthiness,
The stench whereof corrupts the inward soul
With such flagitious° crimes of heinous sins *horrendous*
As no commiseration may expel
But mercy, Faustus, of thy Savior sweet,
Whose blood alone must wash away thy guilt.
FAUSTUS Where art thou, Faustus? Wretch, what hast thou done?
Damned art thou, Faustus, damned! Despair and die!
Hell calls for right, and with a roaring voice
Says, "Faustus, come! Thine hour is come."
Mephistopheles gives him a dagger.
And Faustus will come to do thee right.
[*Faustus prepares to stab himself.*]
OLD MAN Ah, stay, good Faustus, stay thy desperate steps!
I see an angel hovers o'er thy head,
And with a vial full of precious grace
Offers to pour the same into thy soul.
Then call for mercy and avoid despair.
FAUSTUS Ah, my sweet friend, I feel thy words
To comfort my distressèd soul.
Leave me awhile to ponder on my sins.
OLD MAN I go, sweet Faustus, but with heavy cheer,° *mood, countenance*
Fearing the ruin of thy hopeless soul. [*Exit.*]
FAUSTUS Accursèd Faustus, where is mercy now?
I do repent, and yet I do despair.
Hell strives with grace for conquest in my breast.
What shall I do to shun the snares of death?
MEPHISTOPHELES Thou traitor, Faustus, I arrest thy soul
For disobedience to my sovereign lord.
Revolt,° or I'll in piecemeal tear thy flesh. *Draw back, return*
FAUSTUS Sweet Mephistopheles, entreat thy lord
To pardon my unjust presumption,
And with my blood again I will confirm
My former vow I made to Lucifer.

MEPHISTOPHELES Do it then quickly, with unfeignèd heart,
Lest greater danger do attend thy drift.° (*the way you're going*)
[*Faustus cuts his arm and writes with his blood.*]
FAUSTUS Torment, sweet friend, that base and crooked age° (*old man*)
That durst dissuade me from thy Lucifer,
With greatest torments that our hell affords.
MEPHISTOPHELES His faith is great. I cannot touch his soul.
But what I may afflict his body with
I will attempt, which is but little worth.
FAUSTUS One thing, good servant, let me crave of thee
To glut the longing of my heart's desire:
That I might have unto° my paramour (*as*)
That heavenly Helen which I saw of late,
Whose sweet embracings may extinguish clean° (*wholly*)
These thoughts that do dissuade me from my vow,
And keep mine oath I made to Lucifer.
MEPHISTOPHELES Faustus, this, or what else thou shalt desire,
Shall be performed in twinkling of an eye.

Enter Helen [*brought in by Mephistopheles*].

FAUSTUS Was this the face that launched a thousand ships
And burnt the topless[1] towers of Ilium?° (*Troy*)
Sweet Helen, make me immortal with a kiss. [*They kiss.*]
Her lips sucks forth my soul. See where it flies!
Come, Helen, come, give me my soul again.
[*They kiss again.*]
Here will I dwell, for heaven be in these lips,
And all is dross° that is not Helena. (*impurity, inferior*)

Enter Old Man.

I will be Paris, and for love of thee
Instead of Troy shall Wittenberg be sacked,
And I will combat with weak Menelaus,° (*Helen's cuckolded husband*)
And wear thy colors° on my plumèd crest. (*emblems, escutcheon*)
Yea, I will wound Achilles in the heel[2]
And then return to Helen for a kiss.
Oh, thou art fairer than the evening air,
Clad in the beauty of a thousand stars.
Brighter art thou than flaming Jupiter
When he appeared to hapless Semele,[3]
More lovely than the monarch of the sky
In wanton Arethusa's azured° arms;[4] (*reflecting blue water*)
And none but thou shalt be my paramour.
Exeunt [*Faustus and Helen, with Mephistopheles*].
OLD MAN Accursèd Faustus, miserable man,
That from thy soul exclud'st the grace of heaven
And fliest the throne of His tribunal seat!

1. Extending upwards out of sight.
2. According to legend, Achilles was invulnerable except for the heel by which his mother held him when she immersed him as an infant in the river Styx.
3. Semele begged her lover, Zeus (or Jupiter), to appear to her in his full splendor. When he reluctantly complied, she was consumed by lightning.
4. The nymph Arethusa fled from the lust of the river god Alpheus (not from Jupiter or Apollo, both monarchs of the sky) and was transformed by the goddess Artemis into a fountain, where the river god was finally united with her.

Enter the devils [with Mephistopheles. They menace the Old Man].

Satan begins to sift me with his pride.
As in this furnace God shall try my faith,
My faith, vile hell, shall triumph over thee.
Ambitious fiends, see how the heavens smiles
At your repulse and laughs your state to scorn!
Hence, hell! For hence I fly unto my God. *Exeunt.*

[5.2]

Enter Faustus with the Scholars.

FAUSTUS Ah, gentlemen!

FIRST SCHOLAR What ails Faustus?

FAUSTUS Ah, my sweet chamber-fellow! Had I lived with thee, then had I lived still, but now I die eternally. Look, comes he not? Comes he not?

[*The Scholars speak among themselves.*]

SECOND SCHOLAR What means Faustus?

THIRD SCHOLAR Belike he is grown into some sickness by being oversolitary.

FIRST SCHOLAR If it be so, we'll have physicians to cure him. [*To Faustus*] 'Tis but a surfeit.° Never fear, man. *intemperate indulgence*

FAUSTUS A surfeit of deadly sin that hath damned both body and soul.

SECOND SCHOLAR Yet, Faustus, look up to heaven. Remember God's mercies are infinite.

FAUSTUS But Faustus' offense can ne'er be pardoned. The serpent that tempted Eve may be saved, but not Faustus. Ah, gentlemen, hear me with patience, and tremble not at my speeches. Though my heart pants and quivers to remember that I have been a student here these thirty years, oh, would I had never seen Wittenberg, never read book! And what wonders I have done, all Germany can witness, yea, all the world, for which Faustus hath lost both Germany and the world, yea, heaven itself—heaven, the seat of God, the throne of the blessed, the kingdom of joy—and must remain in hell forever. Hell, ah, hell forever! Sweet friends, what shall become of Faustus, being in hell forever?

THIRD SCHOLAR Yet, Faustus, call on God.

FAUSTUS On God, whom Faustus hath abjured? On God, whom Faustus hath blasphemed? Ah, my God, I would weep, but the devil draws in my tears. Gush forth blood instead of tears! Yea, life and soul! Oh, he stays my tongue! I would lift up my hands, but see, they hold them, they hold them!

ALL [THE SCHOLARS] Who, Faustus?

FAUSTUS Lucifer and Mephistopheles. Ah, gentlemen! I gave them my soul for my cunning.

ALL [THE SCHOLARS] God forbid!

5.2. Faustus's study.

FAUSTUS God forbade it indeed, but Faustus hath done it. For vain pleasure of four-and-twenty years hath Faustus lost eternal joy and felicity. I writ them a bill with mine own blood. The date is expired, the time will come, and he will fetch me.

FIRST SCHOLAR Why did not Faustus tell us of this before, that divines might have prayed for thee?

FAUSTUS Oft have I thought to have done so, but the devil threatened to tear me in pieces if I named God, to fetch both body and soul if I once gave ear to divinity. And now 'tis too late. Gentlemen, away, lest you perish with me.

SECOND SCHOLAR Oh, what shall we do to save Faustus?

FAUSTUS Talk not of me, but save yourselves and depart.

THIRD SCHOLAR God will strengthen me. I will stay with Faustus.

FIRST SCHOLAR [*to the Third Scholar*] Tempt not° God, sweet friend, but let us into the next room and there pray for him. *Presume not on*

FAUSTUS Ay, pray for me, pray for me! And what noise soever ye hear, come not unto me, for nothing can rescue me.

SECOND SCHOLAR Pray thou, and we will pray that God may have mercy upon thee.

FAUSTUS Gentlemen, farewell. If I live till morning, I'll visit you; if not, Faustus is gone to hell.

ALL [THE SCHOLARS] Faustus, farewell!

Exeunt Scholars. The clock strikes eleven.

FAUSTUS Ah, Faustus,
Now hast thou but one bare hour to live,
And then thou must be damned perpetually.
Stand still, you ever-moving spheres of heaven,
That time may cease and midnight never come!
Fair Nature's eye,° rise, rise again, and make *The sun*
Perpetual day; or let this hour be but
A year, a month, a week, a natural day,
That Faustus may repent and save his soul!
O lente, lente currite noctis equi![1]
The stars move still; time runs; the clock will strike;
The devil will come, and Faustus must be damned.
Oh, I'll leap up to my God! Who pulls me down?
See, see where Christ's blood streams in the firmament!
One drop would save my soul, half a drop. Ah, my Christ!
Ah, rend not my heart for naming of my Christ!
Yet will I call on him. Oh, spare me, Lucifer!
Where is it now? 'Tis gone; and see where God
Stretcheth out his arm and bends his ireful brows!
Mountains and hills, come, come and fall on me,
And hide me from the heavy wrath of God!
No, no!
Then will I headlong run into the earth.
Earth, gape! Oh, no, it will not harbor me.
You stars that reigned at my nativity,
Whose influence° hath allotted death and hell, *celestial emanation*

1. Oh, run slowly, slowly, horses of the night! (Ovid, *Amores*, 1.13.40, here taken ironically out of the context of that erotic poem and its plea that night last forever for the lovers).

Now draw up Faustus like a foggy mist
Into the entrails of yon laboring cloud,
That when you vomit forth into the air,° *hurl a thunderbolt*
My limbs may issue from your smoky° mouths, *i.e., fiery*
So that my soul may but ascend to heaven.

The watch strikes.

Ah, half the hour is past!
'Twill all be past anon.
O God,
If thou wilt not have mercy on my soul,
Yet for Christ's sake, whose blood hath ransomed me,
Impose some end to my incessant pain.
Let Faustus live in hell a thousand years,
A hundred thousand, and at last be saved!
Oh, no end is limited to damnèd souls.
Why wert thou not a creature wanting soul?
Or why is this immortal that thou hast?
Ah, Pythagoras' metempsychosis,[2] were that true,
This soul should fly from me and I be changed
Unto some brutish beast.
All beasts are happy, for, when they die,
Their souls are soon dissolved in elements;
But mine must live still° to be plagued in hell. *forever*
Curst be the parents that engendered me!
No, Faustus, curse thyself. Curse Lucifer,
That hath deprived thee of the joys of heaven.

The clock striketh twelve.

Oh, it strikes, it strikes! Now, body, turn to air,
Or Lucifer will bear thee quick° to hell. *alive*

Thunder and lightning.

O soul, be changed into little waterdrops,
And fall into the ocean, ne'er be found!
My God, my God, look not so fierce on me!

Enter [Lucifer, Mephistopheles, and other] devils.

Adders and serpents, let me breathe awhile!
Ugly hell, gape not. Come not, Lucifer!
I'll burn my books. Ah, Mephistopheles!

[The devils] exeunt with him.

[Epilogue]

Enter Chorus.

CHORUS Cut is the branch that might have grown full straight,
And burnèd is Apollo's laurel bough[1]
That sometime° grew within this learnèd man. *formerly*
Faustus is gone. Regard his hellish fall,
Whose fiendful fortune may exhort the wise
Only to wonder at unlawful things,

2. Pythagoras of Samos (sixth century B.C.E.) espoused the theory of the transmigration of souls.
Epilogue.
1. The laurel, sacred to Apollo, was regarded as an emblem of poetic inspiration.

Whose deepness doth entice such forward° wits *presumptuous*
To practice more than heavenly power permits. [*Exit.*]

Terminat hora diem; terminat author opus.[2]

2. The hour (midnight) ends the day; the author ends his work.

TEXTUAL NOTES

Doctor Faustus was printed in two considerably different versions: one, the so-called A-text, in 1604, and the other, the so-called B-text, in 1616. As the introduction indicates, the second of these is almost certainly an expanded version put together long after Marlowe's death in response to popular demand for more clowning, so that its textual authority is minimal as regards Marlowe and his collaborator on the original version. We regard the A-text as closer to what Marlowe and his collaborator wrote; it has distinctly authorial characteristics, including the misordering of scenes owing perhaps to the shuffling of papers by the two collaborating authors. This present text follows the A-text of 1604 and is indebted to the ordering and numbering of scenes in the Revels Plays edition of 1993, edited by David Bevington and Eric Rasmussen; see their discussion on the nature of the copy-text and the rationale for scenic rearrangement. Substantive departures from the A-text are noted here, using the following abbreviations:

A1: Quarto of 1604 (London: Thomas Bushell)
A2: Quarto of 1609 (London: John Wright)
A3: Quarto of 1611 (London: John Wright)
B1: Quarto of 1616 (London: John Wright)
B3: Quarto of 1620 (London: John Wright)
B4: Quarto of 1624 (London: John Wright)
ed.: A modern editor's emendation

Prologue 1 CHORUS [ed.; not in A1] **12 Rhode** [ed.] *Rhodes* [A1] **13** [and elsewhere] **Wittenberg** [A3] *Wertenberg* or *Wertenberge* [A1] **25** [and elsewhere] **necromancy** [ed.] Negromancy [A1]

1.1.6 ***Analytics*** [A1: *Anulatikes*] **7** ***logices*** [B4] *logicis* [A1] **12** ***On kai me on*** [A1: *Oncaymaeon*] **28** ***legatur*** [ed.] *legatus* [A1] **31** ***Exhaereditare*** [A1: *Ex haered tari*] **36 Too servile** [B1] The deuill [A1] **53 signs** [ed.] sceanes [A1] **66 SD** *Enter Wagner* [placement, ed.; after 65 in A1] **92 silk** [ed.] skill [A1] **101.1** [placement, B1; after 102 in A1] **111** [and elsewhere] **vile** [A1: vilde] **114 concise syllogisms** [A1: Consissylogismes] **131 in the** [ed.] in their [A1] **132 From** [B1] For [A1] **132 drag** [A2] dregge [A1] **141 seen in** [A2] seene [A1] **143 renowned** [A1: renowmd] **145 Delphian** [A2] Dolphian [A1] **147 wrecks** [A1: wrackes]

1.3.9 anagrammatized [B1: Anagrammatis'd] and Agramithist [A1] **17** ***aquatici*** [ed.] *Aquatani* [A1] **17** ***terreni*** [ed.; not in A1] **18** ***Lucifer*** [ed.; not in A1] **19** ***appereat*** [B1] *apariat* [A1] **19–20** ***Mephistopheles*** [variously spelled throughout as *Mephastophilis, Mephostophilis, Mephastophilus* in A1] **22** ***dicatus*** [B3] *dicatis* [A1] **33 Now** [ed.] No [A1] **35** ***redis*** [ed.] *regis* [A1] **47** ***accidens*** [B4] accident [A1] **89 these** [B1] those [A1]

1.4.2 [and throughout scene] **ROBIN** [ed.] *Clo.* or *Clow.* [A1] **2** [and elsewhere] **'Swounds** [A1: swowns] **11 By'r Lady** [A1: burladie] **72–73** ***vestigiis nostris*** [ed.] *vestigias nostras* [A1]

2.1.2 saved. [ed.] saued? [A1] **18 illusions, fruits** [A1: illusious fruites] **21.1**

[placement, B1; after 22 in A1] **31 he lives** [B1] I liue [A1] **43 human** [A1: humane] **139 an** [A1: and] **153 no more** [B1] more [A1] **178 SD** [placement, ed.; after 180 in A1]

2.2 [placement of scene, ed.; after 3.1 and a misplaced Chorus to act 4 in A1]

2.3.57 intelligentia [B1] *Intelligentij* [A1] **61 empyreal** [A1: imperiall] **63 eclipses** [A1: eclipsis] **81 raze** [A1: race] **109 FAUSTUS** [A1: Eau:] **160 LUCIFER** [B1; at 161 in A1]

3.1.12 equivalents [ed.] equiuolence [A1] **33–34** [B1; not in A1] **37 Ponte** [ed.] *Ponto* [A1] **39 ordnance** [A1: ordonance] **59.1 *sennet*** [A1: *Sonnet*] **59.2 *banquet*** [A1: *banket*] **60** [and elsewhere] **will't** [A1: wilt] **62, 67 who's** [A1: whose] **70 ha't** [A1: hate] **101.1–2** [A1 follows with the Chorus to act 4]

3.2.28.1 [A1 here prints a first-shot ending to the scene, presumably meant to be canceled] **42 enough** [A1: enow] **44.1** [placement, ed.; opposite 43 in A1]

4. Chorus [placement, ed.; after 3.1 in A1]

4.1.27 Amongst [A1: amongest] **94.1 *Exeunt*** [A1: *exit*] **129 good-bye** [A1: god buy] **133 SD** [placement, ed.; after 131 in A1] **141–42 He's . . . he's** [ed.] has . . . has [A1] **152 hey-pass** [A1: hey, passe] **169 SD *holler*** [A1: *Hallow*] **179 hostry** [A1: Oastrie]

5.1.18 deny [A1: deuie] **54 vial** [A1: violl]

5.2.49 to save [B1] to [A1] **92.1** [placement, B1; after 93 in A1]

Epilogue 1 CHORUS [ed.; not in A1]

The Jew of Malta

Competition, vengeance, and categorical hatreds fill *The Jew of Malta.* The play focuses relentlessly on relations among people who regard one another as alien and accursed. At the geopolitical level, Spanish Christians and Turkish Muslims vie for control of the island of Malta as part of an ongoing struggle in the Mediterranean between these powers. The Knights of Malta, caught in the middle, play one side against the other with the canniness that is demanded by their minor economic and military status as a Christian monastic order that rules only one small island. Ferneze, their governor, has become a formal tributary to the Turks as a matter of necessity, though his ideological allegiances are to Spain and the Catholic Church. Possibly because of this, Malta has fallen a decade behind on its tribute payments. When the Spanish vice admiral, Martin del Bosco, arrives and offers protection if the Knights of Malta will stop paying tribute to the Turks and align themselves with Spain instead, Ferneze readily accepts. His Knights eagerly encourage him to do so, and del Bosco shames them with the memory of their loss of Rhodes to the Turks (2.2.30–33). Their cause is religious as well as economic and military. High political and religious motives coincide with a low commercial one: Martin del Bosco wishes to sell captured Turks in Malta's slave market, and Ferneze cannot permit this profitable transaction unless the Spanish admiral will back him in breaking his treaty with the Turks. With del Bosco's military support and the money being raised to pay the demanded tribute, Ferneze can thumb his nose at Selim Calymath, the Turkish emperor's son, and all his bashaws and janizaries. Betrayal is natural when the parties to political transactions demonize one another.

Before the Spanish arrive, the tribute money demanded by the Turks sparks another religious, ethnic, and economic conflict on Malta. Ferneze has been given a month's respite by Calymath, whose fleet lies ready to invade if the money is not forthcoming. A calculating statesman, Ferneze does not ask his own Christian subjects for the burdensome one hundred thousand crowns demanded by the Turks. Instead, Ferneze demands half the estate of each of the Jews. They have grown rich through trade, they are aliens, and they are, from the viewpoint of the Christian Maltese, the hated descendants of those Jews who crucified Christ. Lacking any legal or social standing, and lacking military force of their own, they are in no position to resist.

This is power politics, and Ferneze's ruthless exercise of power marks him as a close student of Niccolò Machiavelli's political realism. A caricature of that writer calling himself Machiavel speaks the play's prologue, introducing the Jewish merchant Barabas to us as one who practices the Machiavellian techniques of climbing to power, including secret poisonings and the dismissal of religion as "a childish toy" (Prologue 14). Though this prologue digests some important Machiavellian ideas, the speaker's confrontational and sensational self-presentation marks him as the stage Machiavel, the bogeyman of England and indeed of Christian Europe, whose name was synonymous with atheism and ruthlessness. The real Machiavelli—the Florentine diplomat,

Introduction by Lars Engle and David Bevington; glosses, footnotes, and textual notes by David Bevington; text edited by David Bevington and checked by Eric Rasmussen and Lars Engle.

political philosopher, historian, and dramatist—was rarely read in England because his books were banned.

One could find out what he wrote, however, and Marlowe, polyglot, curious, and attracted to the scandalous, evidently did. The Machiavelli of *The Prince,* preoccupied with what history could teach us about how to be politically effective, was an optimist in that he believed gifted leaders can alter history for the betterment of their people as well as themselves. Such leaders, he argued, need above all to hold on to power, for themselves and their state, and while doing so they need to maintain both the freedom to act immorally and, if possible, the public image of a moral man. The ruler's religious conviction is his own affair as long as it does not restrict his ability to lie and kill where appropriate, but a leader needs to know how to appeal to religion as a way of inspiring his subjects to follow his lead. Thus he must be a pragmatist, free from the constraints of religious and moral tradition. This pragmatism explains why Machiavelli's was such a feared name: though he did not espouse confrontation, he preached a subtle gospel of iconoclasm and skeptical thought as a kind of humanist realism, a liberation of the individual and society from the dead hand of the past.

Though no liberator, Ferneze follows Machiavellian dicta for princely success, and through Ferneze, Marlowe gives serious dramatic attention to the idea that the ruler's first responsibility is to ensure his own survival and that of his domain. Moreover, though *The Jew of Malta* is not primarily an exercise in Machiavellian political philosophy, in it Marlowe subverts established patterns of thought in a somewhat Machiavellian way: upending his audience's comfortable assumptions about race, religion, politics, and public morality. If he makes us uncomfortable, he may have achieved what he most wanted.

Marlowe's chief agent of discomfort is not Ferneze but the play's protagonist, Barabas, named after the thief whom the Jews asked Pontius Pilate to release instead of Jesus. The wealthiest of the Maltese Jews, Barabas seeks to survive in a hostile environment through cunning, deceit, and exploitation of the greed, lust, and hypocrisy of his opponents. As an idiosyncratic, resourceful character, Barabas arouses particular responses, and as a stage Jew produced for an early modern Christian audience he also stands categorically as an outsider with complex and provocative dimensions. Throughout Renaissance Europe, Jews refused to convert to Christianity, even given such threats as the expulsion of nonconverting Jews from Spain in 1492; many of those who did convert were strongly suspected of practicing Judaism in secret. In remaining loyal to their faith despite persecution, the Jews offered a contrast to many of the English: most members of Marlowe's original audience who were older than thirty-five had converted from Catholicism to Protestantism after the accession of Elizabeth I in 1558, and many of those over fifty had switched faiths thrice—born Catholic, they became Protestant under Henry VIII and his short-lived son Edward VI, Catholic again under Mary, and finally Protestant again under Elizabeth. In their refusal to intermarry, Jews also exemplified ethnic antiquity and purity in ways that English Christians, members of a new nation with a mixed heritage, could not rival. In these

A marble bust of the Italian political philosopher Niccolò Machiavelli (1469–1527).

senses, Jews stood for tradition and identity, focusing English anxieties about what it meant to be a nation or a people. At the same time, because of laws limiting their ownership of land and their participation in particular trades, Jews tended to occupy urban professions that were, economically speaking, progressive in their concentration and use of liquid assets (being jewelers, merchants, goldsmiths, moneylenders, bankers), thus focusing English anxieties about the dissolution of stable identities in a new urban marketplace in which money in hand trumped social status. Finally, especially for reformers who felt that changes in religion heralded the Second Coming, the Jews were a weather vane, since according to a prominent interpretation of Saint Paul's Epistle to the Romans and of Revelation, their mass conversion would signal the imminence of Christ's return.

In many ways, then, Europeans generally, and the English in particular, regarded Jews with suspicion and ambivalence, and such feelings also cling to the character Barabas in *The Jew of Malta*. At the opening of the play, he is a striking figure with whom we are invited to sympathize and even identify. His almost unimaginable wealth—"Infinite riches in a little room" (1.1.37)—inspires awe; he has reached that plutocratic level at which money, whether amassed by mere cleverness or some more exalted faculty, represents the potential to realize almost any dream. His resolve to be content with amassing wealth and not to seek direct political power—a resolve he never entirely abandons, despite his political involvement at the play's end—shows that he has reflected on the special historical role of the Jews, as expressed in soliloquy at 1.1.102–34. Most important, he immediately suffers an open and apparent injustice at the hands of Ferneze. The Governor taxes the Jews explicitly because they cannot defend themselves against him. The tax of half of a person's entire wealth is confiscatory. Still worse, when Barabas refuses at first to comply, Ferneze simply takes all that Barabas has and refuses to allow him to accept the terms as first offered:

FERNEZE Sir, half is the penalty of our decree.
Either pay that, or we will seize on all.
BARABAS *Corpe di dio!* Stay, you shall have half.
Let me be used but as my brethren are.
FERNEZE No, Jew, thou hast denied the articles,
And now it cannot be recalled. (1.2.89–94)

This exercise of arbitrary power establishes, early in the play, a case for Barabas as persecuted victim. Moreover, Ferneze and one of the Knights justify the confiscation with self-righteous anti-Jewish sentiments: "If your first curse fall heavy on thy head, / And make thee poor and scorned of all the world, / 'Tis not our fault, but thy inherent sin" (1.2.108–10). In words that would be echoed some five years later by Shylock in Shakespeare's *The Merchant of Venice*, Barabas demands justice against this terrible and obvious wrong:

What, bring you Scripture to confirm your wrongs?
Preach me not out of my possessions.
. . . .
The man that dealeth righteously shall live;
And which of you can charge me otherwise?
(1.2.111–18)

When Barabas goes on to compare his sufferings with those of Job (1.2.182–99), the comparison does not seem unjust.

Twenty-first-century readers, remembering Nazism, are likely to take anti-Semitism linked to power politics as a sign of the worst sort of evil and corruption. Ferneze is, after all, reinforcing Christian solidarity against the Muslim Turks by stigmatizing Jews and expropriating their property; his actions as well as his remarks brand him for modern readers as an opportunistic racist. It seems virtually certain, however, that

Elizabethan audiences would not, perhaps could not, have thought in these terms. They had no systematic distaste for ethnic stereotyping, and their views of Jews were colored by widely circulated medieval European legends of Jewish hatred of Christians, of Jews kidnapping and murdering Christian children in order to use their blood in the preparation of matzos for Passover, and so on. Yet the manifest unfairness of Ferneze's treatment of the Jews on his island, and especially of Barabas, complicates the audience's emotional response, precisely by showing how a ruthless dominant group exploits an economically successful but politically powerless minority. Up to this point, Marlowe, always the iconoclast, seems intent on disrupting his audience's basic beliefs and allegiances by inviting sympathy for his Jewish protagonist.

Even when Barabas resorts to villainy as a way of getting back at Ferneze, Marlowe allows his audience some room to sympathize with, or at least understand, the motive of revenge. Nevertheless, once launched on this path, Barabas' hatred grows excessive and ranges far beyond its original target. It is one thing for him to plot against Ferneze; it is less excusable when he arranges to kill Ferneze's son, Lodowick, and Lodowick's friend Mathias. The two have become rivals for the love of Abigail, Barabas' beautiful daughter; she loves Mathias. Barabas sets the two against each other, using Abigail to inflame their rivalry, and sends a feigned challenge from Lodowick to Mathias, with the result that the young men meet and kill each other. Abigail, heartbroken, says in soliloquy:

> Hard-hearted father, unkind Barabas,
> Was this the pursuit of thy policy,
> To make me show them favor severally,
> That by my favor they should both be slain?
> Admit thou loved'st not Lodowick for his sire,
> Yet Don Mathias ne'er offended thee.
> (3.3.41–46)

Abigail's lament points out what seems so excessive in this business: Mathias was not the son of any offending prince, and he was the person Abigail loved. Barabas' earlier protestations of caring only for himself and his daughter against all the world (1.1.151–52) now seem hollow, or conditional to a terrifying degree on Abigail's constancy to Barabas and to Judaism, a constancy she compromises by intending to marry outside the faith.

It is when Barabas teams up with Ithamore that Barabas' inventive viciousness becomes most fully revealed. They are an interesting pair. Barabas is a Jew; Ithamore, "a poor Turk of tenpence" (4.2.42), is one of the "Grecians, Turks, and Afric Moors" Martin del Bosco has captured and put up for sale in Malta (2.2.9), where Barabas buys him in the slave market. Barabas senses a kinship at once: "We are villains both," he says in welcoming Ithamore to his service; "Both circumcisèd, we hate Christians both" (2.3.218–19). Ithamore's circumcision suggests that he comes from a non-Christian community, but the faith he professes is "what you please" (2.3.170), and Barabas employs him as villain's assistant.

In summarizing his own career in villainy for Ithamore, Barabas rather implausibly transforms himself from the proto-Rothschild at the center of Mediterranean commerce presented in act 1 into a virtuoso murderer in the style of Lightborn, the stealth assassin in *Edward II*. Barabas regales Ithamore with stories of poisoning wells and of night walks to "kill sick people groaning under walls" (2.3.179). He so delights in causing suffering that he lays out money as an enticement in his premises just to see the would-be thieves wriggling when they are trapped. Barabas notes that he has studied medicine in Italy and that his practice has kept the sexton constantly busy digging graves for the victims. As a military engineer, he has practiced his trade for both opposing armies. As a usurer, he has filled the jails with bankrupts through his extortions and forfeitures; his tricks have caused madness and suicide on such a scale that new orphanages have been built to house the resultant orphans. When, we begin to wonder, has Barabas the respectable merchant had the time and opportunity to do all this? There are two possible answers. Perhaps Barabas embroiders his past to seduce Ithamore into becoming his accomplice—that is, in keeping with his transformation from merchant to covert vengeful activist, Barabas makes up a past to fit his present. Perhaps instead, however, we should not at this point look for consistency in character, but should rather see Barabas as a theatrical phenomenon, a genius of every kind of evil who has been released by the plot from his nominal identity as an entrepreneurial Maltese Jew to become the dramatic embodiment of gleeful, malicious revenge. Ithamore, for his part, makes no attempt to hide his admiration for his phenomenal new master: "Oh, brave, master! I worship your nose for this" (2.3.177). He himself boasts of setting Christian churches on fire; capturing eunuchs and galley-slaves; cutting the throats of travelers in their beds; and sprinkling a powder on the stones of Jerusalem that cripples pilgrims as they kneel, sending them hobbling home on crutches. These recitals pulse with competitive excitement. The acts are gruesome, but the manic excess invites our amazement at bravura performances rather than any measured ethical response.

Barabas' schemes against the Christian nuns and friars, in which Ithamore willingly assists, complicate the picture of religious conflict in *The Jew of Malta*. Since Barabas is a Jew and his assistant is also a non-Christian of some kind, one might suppose that the deadly tricks they perpetrate at Christians' expense would merit stern disapprobation from an Elizabethan audience. Both villains confess to hating Christians, mainly just because they hate Christians; while plausible local motives for this hatred exist, those motives seem largely subordinated to an extravagantly gleeful animus toward everybody. Yet many of Barabas' victims are Catholic nuns or friars. For Elizabethan audiences in 1589 or 1590, recently spared invasion by the Spanish Armada, Catholics, especially Spanish Catholics, were hated as much as and feared more than Jews or Muslims. The representatives of the Catholic Church in this play are openly ridiculed. Barabas and Ithamore deliver the standard defamations of raw anti-Catholic propaganda, and the play suggests that these stereotypes are just, hinting for instance that nuns and priests sleep together. Friar Bernardine laments, when he hears that Abigail has died, and died a good Christian, that she has also died a virgin: "That grieves me most," he confesses (3.6.41). The friars are eager to make money and quarrel openly among themselves in competition for patronage. Barabas has a splendid time setting Friar Jacomo and Friar Bernardine against each other in a bidding war for his presumed wealth; they offer him the church's absolution for whatever crimes he may have committed and promise to spare him any inconveniences of monastic life if he will come live in a religious house as its benefactor. Using deliberately crude humor, Barabas points out for the audience the alleged hypocrisies of monastic life. We must assume that English audiences were delighted.

Barabas' plot to destroy the inmates of a convent darkens Marlowe's comic exploitation of anti-Catholic humor. As he prepares the fatal bowl of rice porridge that Ithamore will carry to the alms door, Barabas chants a curse as bloodcurdling as that of the weird sisters in Shakespeare's *Macbeth* over "a drench to poison a whole stable of Flanders mares" (3.4.96–114). Barabas intends revenge on his daughter, Abigail, for deserting him, for becoming a Christian, and for entering the convent into which Barabas' own house has been converted—a convent she had entered earlier in the play as a ruse to recover a hidden treasure. The sequence of confiscations and conversions associated with Barabas' house and treasure alludes with Marlowe's usual sharpness to some aspects of recent English history, since the English Crown had massively reendowed itself, and the English gentry and aristocracy rehoused themselves, through Henry VIII's dissolution, confiscation, and sale of English Catholic monasteries earlier in Marlowe's century. Moreover, Marlowe heightens the horror of Barabas' vengeance by having him poison his own daughter in the house that had been theirs.

Abigail's second conversion, after the killing of her beloved Mathias, seems genuinely religious, and her indictment of worldly corruption is amply justified by her experience. Indeed, she is a kind of vanishing heroine for the play, offering a temporary moral ground in its amoral quicksands: she seems the center of her father's genuine feelings at the outset, and her own love for Mathias and his for her seem sincere as well. When she dies, any spirit of intergroup conciliation in the play dies with her.

The rest of the play underlines and makes explicit the parallels between local self-protective trickery and high geopolitics that were implied in act 1. Barabas' poison, though it kills Abigail along with the other nuns, works sufficiently slowly that Abigail has time to confess her father's role in the deaths of Lodowick and Mathias to Friar Bernardine, who then tries to blackmail Barabas. In ingeniously doing away with him and with Friar Jacomo, Barabas uses Ithamore as an accomplice, and Ithamore, seduced by the prostitute Bellamira and her grotesque pimp Pilia-Borza, turns on his master and attempts to blackmail him too, so that Barabas has to get rid of the three of them. The pattern of schemes whose imperfect execution creates the necessity for further rapidly improvised schemes—a central feature of Ben Jonson's comedies—fills *The Jew of Malta* with manic energy, giving it some of the characteristics of a comedy. But Barabas' schemes kill, and they are surrounded and given wider significance by the play's realistic representation of how politics seizes on racial and religious difference to justify domination and betrayal. The Governor's shakedown of the island's Jews, for instance, serves as a high-level model for Pilia-Borza's and Friar Bernardine's separate attempts to blackmail Barabas. And while Barabas' Jewishness allows any act against him by a Christian to be justified for an Elizabethan audience as appropriate recompense for the rejection of Christ, these actions are also presented as an everyday taking of advantage where advantage offers, all in the spirit of a power politics overseen by the ghost of Machiavelli and driven by what a Turkish bashaw describes as "The wind that bloweth all the world besides: / Desire of gold" (3.5.3–4).

In the play's furious finale, Barabas by sheer virtuosity transforms himself as one unarmed Jew into a major though transient political force. And at the very end, tricked by Ferneze into being boiled alive in his own cauldron after betraying the Christians and the Turks in rapid succession, Barabas exemplifies a kind of poetic justice. Yet what are we to make of the moral morass in which Barabas also turns out to be the scapegoat, the man who takes the fall? Ferneze seems little better than his Jewish antagonist; the elaborate plotting and counterplotting by which the Turkish Calymath is delivered finally into the hands of Ferneze hardly seems a vindication of moral justice. Ferneze simply emerges as the winner of a bewilderingly fast competition in gamesmanship. Ferneze's last words in the play drip with religious hypocrisy: "So, march away, and let due praise be given / Neither to fate or fortune, but to heaven" (5.5.122–23). Perhaps nowhere does Ferneze show himself more astutely a practitioner of Machiavellianism than in the way he caps his final political success with this bland appropriation of Providence's blessing.

The play's ironic ending also leaves us with a question. If we are not to moralize over Barabas' career, what exactly are we to do with it? At his most powerful, Marlowe challenges readers to second-guess their attempts to sum him up and make sense of the dramatic experience he provides. He pushes us to examine the complacencies of our own culture, to demystify its hypocritical rationalizations of human aggression and rapacity, and then to ask ourselves whether we have other, better rationalizations to offer. Marlowe keeps us continually off balance. It is hard to judge Barabas without feeling a bit like Ferneze.

CHRISTOPHER MARLOWE

The Jew of Malta

[The Persons in the Play

MACHIAVEL, speaker of the Prologue
BARABAS,[1] a rich Jewish merchant of Malta
ABIGAIL, his daughter
ITHAMORE, his slave
FERNEZE, Governor of Malta
Don LODOWICK, his son
Don MATHIAS, Lodowick's friend
KATHARINE, Mathias' mother
Friar JACOMO
Friar BERNARDINE
ABBESS
Selim CALYMATH, son of the Emperor of Turkey
CALLAPINE, a bashaw° *Turkish officer*
Martin del BOSCO, Vice Admiral of Spain
BELLAMIRA, a courtesan
PILIA-BORSA, her pimp
Two MERCHANTS
Three JEWS
A MESSENGER
A SLAVE
KNIGHTS of Malta
OFFICERS of Malta
Bashaws serving the Turkish emperor
Carpenters
A nun
Citizens of Malta, Turkish janizaries,° guards, attendants, slaves. *elite troops*

THE SCENE: Malta.]

The original 1633 title page reads "*The Famous Tragedy of the Rich Jew of Malta.* As it was played before the King and Queen in His Majesty's Theatre at Whitehall, by His Majesty's Servants at the Cockpit. Written by Christopher Marlowe. London; printed by J[ohn] B[eale] for Nicholas Vavasour, and are to be sold at his shop in the Inner Temple, near the church. 1633."

The Persons in the Play.
1. As related in John 18.39–40, when Pontius Pilate, in response to the custom of releasing a prisoner in honor of a feast day, asked the Jews if they wished him to release Jesus or a robber named Barabas (also spelled Barabbas), they cried out, "Not this man, but Barabbas." The account appears in all four Gospels.

[Prologue]

[Enter] Machiavel.

MACHIAVEL Albeit the world think Machiavel is dead,
Yet was his soul but flown beyond the Alps,° — *to France*
And, now the Guise is dead,[1] is come from France
To view this land° and frolic with his friends. — *(England)*
To some, perhaps, my name is odious,
But such as love me guard me from their tongues,[2]
And let them know that I am Machiavel,
And weigh not° men, and therefore not men's words. — *care nothing for*
Admired I am of those that hate me most.
Though some speak openly against my books,
Yet will they read me, and thereby attain
To Peter's chair,° and, when they cast me off, — *the papacy*
Are poisoned by my climbing followers.
I count religion but a childish toy,
And hold there is no sin but ignorance.
Birds of the air will tell of murders past.
I am ashamed to hear such fooleries!
Many will talk of title to a crown.
What right had Caesar to the empire?
Might first made kings, and laws were then most sure
When, like the Draco's, they were writ in blood.[3]
Hence comes it that a strong-built citadel
Commands much more than letters° can import; — *learning*
Which maxima° had Phalaris observed, — *maxim*
He'd never bellowed in a brazen bull
Of° great ones' envy.[4] O'th'poor petty wits° — *Because of / commoners*
Let me be envied and not pitied!
But whither am I bound? I come not, I,
To read° a lecture here in Britany, — *give*
But to present the tragedy of a Jew,
Who smiles to see how full his bags are crammed,
Which money was not got without my means.
I crave but this: grace° him as he deserves, — *show favor to*
And let him not be entertained° the worse — *welcomed*
Because he favors° me. [*Exit.*] — *resembles; follows*

[1.1]

Enter Barabas in his countinghouse,[1] with heaps of gold before him.

BARABAS So that of thus much° that return° was made; — *much investment / profit*
And of the third part of the Persian ships,

Prologue.
1. Henry, third Duke of Guise, was responsible for the slaughter of the Huguenots at the Saint Bartholomew's Day massacre in 1572. He was assassinated on December 23, 1588.
2. Those who admire me (1) protect me from the slander of my detractors; (2) never allow my name to cross their lips, admiring me in secret.
3. Draco was an Athenian legislator who prepared the first written code of laws for Athens (c. 621 B.C.E.), a code of "draconian" severity—thus, "writ in blood."
4. Phalaris was a tyrant (sixth century B.C.E.) known both for his cruelty and for his love of letters; according to one account, he died at the hands of his envious people by being roasted in a brazen bull he had used to conduct human sacrifices.

1.1. Barabas' countinghouse.
1. Perhaps Barabas is "discovered" backstage by the opening of a curtain at a stage door or alcove.

There was the venture summed and satisfied.° *totaled and paid off*
As for those Samnites° and the men of Uz[2] *an Italian tribe*
That bought my Spanish oils and wines of Greece,
Here have I pursed° their paltry silverlings.° *pocketed / coins*
Fie, what a trouble 'tis to count this trash!
Well fare the Arabians, who so richly pay
The things they traffic for with wedge° of gold, *ingot*
Whereof a man may easily in a day
Tell° that which may maintain him all his life. *Count*
The needy groom° that never fingered groat° *wretch / a small coin*
Would make a miracle of° thus much coin; *be astonished at*
But he whose steel-barred coffers are crammed full,
And all his lifetime hath been tired,
Wearying his fingers' ends with telling° it, *counting*
Would in his age be loath to labor so,
And for a pound to sweat himself to death.
Give me the merchants of the Indian mines,
That trade in metal of the purest mold;° *form, type*
The wealthy Moor, that in the Eastern° rocks *i.e., Arabian, Indian*
Without control° can pick his riches up, *restraint*
And in his house heap pearl like pebble-stones,
Receive them free and sell them by the weight:° *i.e., in bulk*
Bags of fiery opals, sapphires, amethysts,
Jacinths, hard topaz, grass-green emeralds,
Beauteous rubies, sparkling diamonds,
And seld-seen° costly stones of so great price *seldom-seen*
As° one of them, indifferently° rated *That / impartially*
And of a carat of this quantity,
May serve, in peril of calamity,° *in times of peril*
To ransom great kings from captivity.
This is the ware wherein consists my wealth;
And thus, methinks, should men of judgment frame° *shape, adapt*
Their means of traffic from° the vulgar° trade, *apart from / common*
And, as their wealth increaseth, so enclose
Infinite riches in a little room.
But now, how stands the wind?
Into what corner peers my halcyon's bill?[3]
Ha! To the east? Yes. See, how stands° the vanes?° *points / weather vane*
East and by south. Why, then, I hope my ships
I sent for Egypt and the bordering isles° *(Cyprus and Crete)*
Are gotten up by Nilus'° winding banks. *Have reached the Nile's*
Mine argosy° from Alexandria, *large merchant ships*
Loaden with spice and silks, now under sail,
Are smoothly gliding down by Candy° shore *Crete's*
To Malta, through our Mediterranean Sea.
But who comes here?

Enter a [First] Merchant.

How now?

FIRST MERCHANT Barabas, thy ships are safe,
Riding in Malta road;° and all the merchants *roadstead, harbor*
With other merchandise are safe arrived,

2. The land where Job resided, in the Syrian desert.
3. The body of a halcyon, or kingfisher, could be used as a weather vane.

And have sent me to know whether yourself
Will come and custom° them. / *pay customs duties on*

BARABAS The ships are safe, thou say'st, and richly fraught?° / *freighted*

FIRST MERCHANT They are.

BARABAS Why, then, go bid them come ashore,
And bring with them their bills of entry.
I hope our credit in the customhouse
Will serve as well as° I were present there. / *as if*
Go send 'em threescore camels, thirty mules,
And twenty wagons to bring up the ware.
But art thou master in a ship of mine,
And is thy credit not enough for that?

FIRST MERCHANT The very custom barely° comes to more / *The customs duties alone*
Than many merchants of the town are worth,
And therefore far exceeds my credit, sir.

BARABAS Go tell 'em the Jew of Malta sent thee, man.
Tush, who amongst 'em knows not Barabas?

FIRST MERCHANT I go. [*He starts to leave.*]

BARABAS So, then, there's somewhat° come.— / *something*
Sirrah,° which of my ships art thou master of? / *(said to inferiors)*

FIRST MERCHANT Of the *Speranza*, sir.

BARABAS And saw'st thou not
Mine argosy at Alexandria?
Thou couldst not come from Egypt, or by Caire,° / *Cairo*
But at the entry there into the sea
Where Nilus pays his tribute to the main° / *the Mediterranean*
Thou needs must sail by Alexandria.

FIRST MERCHANT I neither saw them nor inquired of them.
But this we heard some of our seamen say:
They wondered how you durst° with so much wealth / *dare*
Trust such a crazèd° vessel, and so far. / *cracked, unseaworthy*

BARABAS Tush, they are wise! I know her and her strength.
But go, go thou thy ways; discharge thy ship,
And bid my factor° bring his loading° in. / *agent / bill of lading*
[*Exit First Merchant.*]
And yet I wonder at° this argosy. / *about*

Enter a Second Merchant.

SECOND MERCHANT Thine argosy from Alexandria,
Know, Barabas, doth ride in Malta road,
Laden with riches and exceeding store
Of Persian silks, of gold, and orient pearl.

BARABAS How chance you came not with those other ships
That sailed by Egypt?

SECOND MERCHANT Sir, we saw 'em not.

BARABAS Belike° they coasted round by Candy shore / *Perhaps*
About their oils or other businesses.
But 'twas ill done of you to come so far
Without the aid or conduct° of their ships. / *escort*

SECOND MERCHANT Sir, we were wafted° by a Spanish fleet / *convoyed*
That never left us till within a league,° / *about three miles*
That had the galleys of the Turk in chase.° / *were chasing the Turks*

BARABAS Oh, they were going up to Sicily. Well, go,
And bid the merchants and my men dispatch
And come ashore, and see the freight discharged.

SECOND MERCHANT I go. *Exit.*
BARABAS Thus trolls° our fortune in by land and sea, *comes abundantly*
And thus are we on every side enriched.
These are the blessings promised to the Jews,
And herein was old Abram's happiness.° *(see Genesis 15, 17)*
What more may heaven do for earthly man
Than thus to pour out plenty in their laps,
Ripping the bowels of the earth for them,
Making the sea their servants, and the winds
To drive their substance° with successful blasts?° *wealthy ships / winds*
Who hateth me but for my happiness?
Or who is honored now but for his wealth?
Rather had I, a Jew, be hated thus
Than pitied in a Christian poverty;
For I can see no fruits in all their faith
But malice, falsehood, and excessive pride,
Which methinks fits not their profession.° *professing charity*
Haply° some hapless man hath conscience, *Perchance*
And for his conscience lives in beggary.
They say we are a scattered nation;
I cannot tell, but we have scambled up° *accumulated*
More wealth by far than those that brag of faith.
There's Kirriah Jairim, the great Jew of Greece,
Obed in Bairseth, Nones in Portugal,
Myself in Malta, some in Italy,
Many in France, and wealthy every one—
Ay, wealthier far than any Christian.
I must confess we come not to be° kings. *don't manage to become*
That's not our fault. Alas, our number's few,
And crowns come either by succession
Or urged° by force; and nothing violent, *compelled*
Oft have I heard tell, can be permanent.
Give us a peaceful rule; make Christians kings,
That thirst so much for principality.° *sovereignty*
I have no charge,° nor many children, *financial burden*
But one sole daughter, whom I hold as dear
As Agamemnon did his Iphigen;[4]
And all I have is hers.—But who comes here?

Enter three Jews [*speaking among themselves*].

FIRST JEW Tush, tell not me; 'twas done of policy.° *statecraft*
SECOND JEW Come, therefore let us go to Barabas,
For he can counsel best in these affairs;
And here he comes.
BARABAS Why, how now, countrymen?
Why flock you thus to me in multitudes?
What accident's betided to the Jews?
FIRST JEW A fleet of warlike galleys, Barabas,
Are come from Turkey, and lie in our road;
And they° this day sit in the council house *(the Knights of Malta)*
To entertain them° and their embassy. *receive the Turks*
BARABAS Why, let 'em come, so° they come not to war; *provided*
Or let 'em war, so we be conquerors.

4. Agamemnon had to sacrifice his daughter Iphigenia to obtain favorable winds for the expedition to Troy.

(*Aside*) Nay, let 'em combat, conquer, and kill all,
So they spare me, my daughter, and my wealth.
FIRST JEW Were it for confirmation of a league,° *treaty*
They would not come in warlike manner thus.
SECOND JEW I fear their coming will afflict us all.
BARABAS Fond° men, what dream you of their multitudes? *Foolish*
What need they treat of peace that are in league?° *bound by treaty*
The Turks and those of Malta are in league.
Tut, tut, there is some other matter in't.
FIRST JEW Why, Barabas, they come for peace or war.
BARABAS Haply for neither, but to pass along
Towards Venice by the Adriatic Sea,
With° whom they have attempted° many times, *Against / fought*
But never could effect their stratagem.
THIRD JEW And very wisely said; it may be so.
SECOND JEW But there's a meeting in the senate house,
And all the Jews in Malta must be there.
BARABAS Umph. All the Jews in Malta must be there?
Ay, like° enough. Why, then, let every man *likely*
Provide him,° and be there for fashion sake. *Ready himself*
If anything shall there concern our state,° *well-being*
Assure yourselves I'll look (*aside*) unto myself.
FIRST JEW I know you will.—Well, brethren, let us go.
SECOND JEW Let's take our leaves. Farewell, good Barabas.
BARABAS Do so. Farewell, Zaareth, farewell, Temainte.
[*Exeunt the Jews.*]
And, Barabas, now search this secret out.
Summon thy senses; call thy wits together.
These silly° men mistake the matter clean.° *foolish / entirely*
Long to the Turk° did Malta contribute; *the Turkish emperor*
Which tribute—all in policy, I fear—
The Turks have let increase to such a sum
As all the wealth of Malta cannot pay,
And now, by that advantage, thinks, belike,
To seize upon the town. Ay, that he seeks.
Howe'er the world go, I'll make sure for one,° *look out for myself*
And seek in time to intercept° the worst, *anticipate*
Warily guarding that which I ha' got.
Ego mihimet sum semper proximus.[5]
Why, let 'em enter; let 'em take the town! [*Exit.*]

[1.2]

Enter Governors of Malta[1] [*presided over by Ferneze, Chief Governor*]. [*The Officers and*] *Knights* [*of Malta are*] *met by* [*Callapine and other*] *bashaws*° *of the Turk;* *Turkish officers*
Calymath [*is their head*].

FERNEZE Now, Bashaws, what demand you at our hands?
CALLAPINE Know, Knights of Malta, that we came from Rhodes,
From Cyprus, Candy,° and those other isles *Crete*
That lie betwixt the Mediterranean seas—

5. My own affairs are my chief concern. (Terence, *Andria*, 4.1.12.)

1.2. Malta's senate house, and then the vicinity of Barabas' house.

1. The so-called Knights of Malta, stationed there as of 1530.

FERNEZE What's Cyprus, Candy, and those other isles
To us, or Malta? What at our hands demand ye?
CALYMATH The ten years' tribute that remains unpaid.
FERNEZE Alas, my lord, the sum is overgreat.
I hope Your Highness will consider us.° *consider our needs*
CALYMATH I wish, grave° governors, 'twere in my power *honored, noble*
To favor you, but 'tis my father's° cause, *(the Turkish emperor's)*
Wherein I may not—nay, I dare not—dally.
FERNEZE Then give us leave,° great Selim Calymath. *allow us to consult*
[*Ferneze consults privately with his Knights.*]
CALYMATH [*to his Bashaws*] Stand all aside, and let the Knights determine;
And send° to keep our galleys under sail, *send word*
For happily° we shall not tarry here. *with luck; perchance*
[*Ferneze and his Knights conclude their conference.*]
Now, governors, how are you resolved?
FERNEZE Thus: since your hard conditions are such
That you will needs have ten years' tribute past,
We° may have time to make collection *We ask that we*
Amongst the inhabitants of Malta for't.
CALLAPINE That's more than is in our commission.
CALYMATH What, Callapine, a little courtesy!
Let's know their time.° Perhaps it is not long; *what time they ask*
And 'tis more kingly to obtain by peace
Than to enforce conditions by constraint.—
What respite ask you, governors?
FERNEZE But a month.
CALYMATH We grant a month. But see you keep your promise.
Now, launch our galleys back again to sea,
Where we'll attend° the respite you have ta'en, *wait out*
And for the money send our messenger.
Farewell, great governors and brave Knights of Malta!
FERNEZE And all good fortune wait on Calymath!
Exeunt [*Calymath and Bashaws*].
Go, one, and call those Jews of Malta hither.
Were they not summoned to appear today?
FIRST OFFICER They were, my lord, and here they come.

Enter Barabas and three Jews.

FIRST KNIGHT Have you determined what to say to them?
FERNEZE Yes. Give me leave°—and Hebrews, now come near. *Allow me*
From the Emperor of Turkey is arrived
Great Selim Calymath, His Highness' son,
To levy of us ten years' tribute past.
Now, then, here know that it concerneth us—
BARABAS Then, good my lord, to keep your quiet° still, *peaceful state*
Your Lordship shall do well to let them have it.
FERNEZE Soft, Barabas, there's more 'longs to't than so.° *more to it than that*
To what this ten years' tribute will amount,
That we have cast,° but cannot compass° it *reckoned / achieve*
By reason of the wars, that robbed our store;
And therefore are we to request your aid.
BARABAS Alas, my lord, we are no soldiers.
And what's our aid against so great a prince?
FIRST KNIGHT Tut, Jew, we know thou art no soldier;

Thou art a merchant, and a moneyed man,
And 'tis thy money, Barabas, we seek.
BARABAS How, my lord, my money?
FERNEZE Thine and the rest;
For, to be short, amongst you 't must be had.
FIRST JEW Alas, my lord, the most of us are poor!
FERNEZE Then let the rich increase your portions.° *their share*
BARABAS Are strangers° with your tribute to be taxed? *aliens*
SECOND KNIGHT Have strangers leave° with us to get their wealth? *permission*
Then let them with us contribute.
BARABAS How, equally?
FERNEZE No, Jew, like infidels.
For, through our sufferance° of your hateful lives, *allowance*
Who stand accursèd in the sight of heaven,
These taxes and afflictions are befall'n,
And therefore thus we are determinèd.
[*To an Officer*] Read there the articles of our decrees.
OFFICER (*reads*) "First, the tribute money of the Turks shall all be levied amongst the Jews, and each of them to pay one half of his estate."
BARABAS How, half his estate? [*Aside*] I hope you mean not mine.
FERNEZE Read on.
OFFICER (*reads*) "Secondly, he that denies to pay shall straight become a Christian."
BARABAS How, a Christian? [*Aside*] Hum, what's here to do?
OFFICER (*reads*) "Lastly, he that denies this shall absolutely lose all he has."
ALL THREE JEWS Oh, my lord, we will give half!
BARABAS O earth-mettled villains,° and no Hebrews born! *dull wretches*
And will you basely thus submit yourselves
To leave your goods to their arbitrament?° *control*
FERNEZE Why, Barabas, wilt thou be christened?
BARABAS No, Governor, I will be no convertite.
FERNEZE Then pay thy half.
BARABAS Why, know you what you did by this device?
Half of my substance is a city's wealth.
Governor, it was not got so easily;
Nor will I part so slightly therewithal.
FERNEZE Sir, half is the penalty of our decree.
Either pay that, or we will seize on all.
BARABAS *Corpe di dio!*° Stay, you shall have half. *By God's body!*
Let me be used but as my brethren are.
FERNEZE No, Jew, thou hast denied the articles,
And now it cannot be recalled.
[*Ferneze signals to Officers, who exeunt.*]
BARABAS Will you then steal my goods?
Is theft the ground of your religion?
FERNEZE No, Jew, we take particularly thine
To save the ruin of a multitude;
And better one want° for a common good *that someone do without*
Than many perish for a private man.
Yet, Barabas, we will not banish thee,
But here in Malta, where thou got'st thy wealth,

Live still; and, if thou canst, get more.
BARABAS Christians, what or how can I multiply?
Of naught is nothing made.
FIRST KNIGHT From naught at first thou cam'st to little wealth,
From little unto more, from more to most.
If your first curse fall heavy on thy head,[2]
And make thee poor and scorned of all the world,
'Tis not our fault, but thy inherent sin.
BARABAS What, bring you Scripture to confirm your wrongs?
Preach me not out of my possessions.
Some Jews are wicked, as all Christians are;
But say the tribe that I descended of
Were all in general cast away° for sin, *rejected by God*
Shall I be tried by their transgression?
The man that dealeth righteously shall live;
And which of you can charge me otherwise?
FERNEZE Out,° wretched Barabas! *(expressing indignation)*
Sham'st thou not thus to justify thyself,
As if we knew not thy profession?° *professed creed*
If thou rely upon thy righteousness,
Be patient, and thy riches will increase.
Excess of wealth is cause of covetousness,
And covetousness, oh, 'tis a monstrous sin!
BARABAS Ay, but theft is worse. Tush, take not from me, then,
For that is theft; and if you rob me thus,
I must be forced to steal and compass° more. *attain, amass*
FIRST KNIGHT Grave governors, list° not to his exclaims. *listen*
Convert his mansion to a nunnery;
His house will harbor many holy nuns.

Enter Officers.

FERNEZE It shall be so.—Now, officers, have you done?
FIRST OFFICER Ay, my lord, we have seized upon the goods
And wares of Barabas, which, being valued,
Amount to more than all the wealth in Malta;
And of the other° we have seizèd half. *other Jews*
Then we'll take order for the residue.
BARABAS Well, then, my lord, say, are you satisfied?
You have my goods, my money, and my wealth,
My ships, my store, and all that I enjoyed;
And, having all, you can request no more—
Unless your unrelenting, flinty hearts
Suppress all pity in your stony breasts,
And now shall move you to bereave my life.
FERNEZE No, Barabas, to stain our hands with blood
Is far from us and our profession.
BARABAS Why, I esteem the injury far less
To take the lives of miserable men
Than be the causers of their misery.
You have my wealth, the labor of my life,

2. The Jews took on themselves a "first curse," in the Knight's view, by, according to Christian theology, demanding Christ's crucifixion (see Matthew 27.25 and "The Persons in the Play," note 1).

The comfort of mine age, my children's hope;
And therefore ne'er distinguish of the wrong.[3]
FERNEZE Content thee, Barabas, thou hast naught but right.° *justice*
BARABAS Your extreme right does me exceeding wrong.
But take it to you, i'th'devil's name!
FERNEZE [*to his Knights*] Come, let us in, and gather of these goods
The money for this tribute of the Turk.
FIRST KNIGHT 'Tis necessary that be looked unto;
For if we break our day,° we break the league, *miss our deadline*
And that will prove but simple policy.° *foolish statecraft*
Exeunt [*Ferneze, Knights, and Officers*].
BARABAS Ay, policy,° that's their profession, *cunning*
And not simplicity,° as they suggest. [*He kneels.*] *lack of guile*
The plagues of Egypt and the curse of heaven,
Earth's barrenness, and all men's hatred
Inflict upon them, thou great Primus Motor!° *First Mover, God*
And here upon my knees, striking the earth,
I ban° their souls to everlasting pains *curse*
And extreme tortures of the fiery deep
That thus have dealt with me in my distress!
FIRST JEW Oh, yet be patient, gentle Barabas.
BARABAS Oh, silly brethren, born° to see this day! *i.e., destined*
Why stand you thus unmoved with my laments?
Why weep you not to think upon my wrongs?
Why pine not I and die in this distress?
FIRST JEW Why, Barabas, as hardly° can we brook° *scarcely / tolerate*
The cruel handling of ourselves in this.
Thou see'st they have taken half our goods.
BARABAS Why did you yield to their extortion?
You were a multitude, and I but one,
And of me only have they taken all.
FIRST JEW Yet, brother Barabas, remember Job.[4]
BARABAS What tell you me of Job? I wot° his wealth *know*
Was written thus: he had seven thousand sheep,
Three thousand camels, and two hundred yoke
Of laboring oxen, and five hundred
She-asses; but for every one of those,
Had they been valued at indifferent° rate, *impartial*
I had at home, and in mine argosy
And other ships that came from Egypt last,° *just now*
As much as would have bought his beasts and him,
And yet have kept enough to live upon;
So that not he, but I, may curse the day,
Thy fatal birthday, forlorn Barabas,
And henceforth wish for an eternal night,
That clouds of darkness may enclose my flesh
And hide these extreme sorrows from mine eyes.
For only I have toiled to inherit here
The months of vanity° and loss of time, *vain striving*
And painful nights have been appointed me.
SECOND JEW Good Barabas, be patient.
BARABAS Ay, ay.

3. Do not try to distinguish your deed from wrongdoing.

4. The biblical man of Uz whose sufferings are a trial of his constancy of faith in God (see the Book of Job).

Pray leave me in my patience.° You that *suffering*
Were ne'er possessed of wealth are pleased with want.° *content with little*
But give him liberty at least to mourn
That in a field amidst his enemies
Doth see his soldiers slain, himself disarmed,
And knows no means of° his recovery. *for*
Ay, let me sorrow for this sudden chance.
'Tis in the trouble of my spirit I speak;
Great injuries are not so soon forgot.

FIRST JEW Come, let us leave him in his ireful mood.
Our words will but increase his ecstasy.° *passion, frenzy*

SECOND JEW On, then. But trust me, 'tis a misery
To see a man in such affliction.
Farewell, Barabas. *Exeunt* [*the three Jews*].

BARABAS [*getting up*] Ay, fare you well.
See the simplicity of these base slaves,
Who, for° the villains have no wit themselves, *because*
Think me to be a senseless lump of clay
That will with every water wash to dirt!
No, Barabas is born to better chance,° *fortune*
And framed° of finer mold° than common men *fashioned / pattern*
That measure naught but by the present time.
A reaching thought° will search his deepest wits *A foresighted person*
And cast° with cunning for the time to come; *reckon, deliberate*
For evils are apt to happen every day.

Enter Abigail, the Jew's daughter.

But whither wends my beauteous Abigail?
Oh, what has made my lovely daughter sad?
What, woman, moan not for a little loss.
Thy father has enough in store for thee.

ABIGAIL Not for myself, but agèd Barabas,
Father, for thee lamenteth Abigail.
But I will learn to leave these fruitless tears,
And, urged thereto with° my afflictions, *by*
With fierce exclaims run to the senate house,
And in the senate reprehend them all,
And rend their hearts with tearing of my hair,
Till they reduce° the wrongs done to my father. *restore*

BARABAS No, Abigail, things past recovery
Are hardly cured with exclamations.
Be silent, daughter; sufferance° breeds ease, *patient endurance*
And time may yield us an occasion
Which on the sudden cannot serve the turn.
Besides, my girl, think me not all so fond° *foolish*
As negligently to forgo so much
Without provision for thyself and me.
Ten thousand portagues,° besides great pearls, *Portuguese gold coins*
Rich costly jewels, and stones infinite,
Fearing the worst of this before it fell,
I closely hid.

ABIGAIL Where, father?

BARABAS In my house, my girl.

ABIGAIL Then shall they ne'er be seen of Barabas;
For they have seized upon thy house and wares.

BARABAS But they will give me leave once more, I trow,° *trust*
To go into my house.
ABIGAIL That may they not,
For there I left the Governor placing nuns,
Displacing me; and of thy house they mean
To make a nunnery, where none but their own sect° *sex; religion*
Must enter in—men generally° barred. *totally*
BARABAS My gold! My gold and all my wealth is gone!
You partial° heavens, have I deserved this plague? *biased*
What, will you thus oppose me, luckless° stars, *unlucky*
To make me desperate in my poverty,
And, knowing me impatient in distress,
Think me so mad as° I will hang myself, *that*
That I may vanish o'er° the earth in air *from*
And leave no memory that e'er I was?
No! I will live, nor loathe I this my life.
And since you leave me in the ocean thus
To sink or swim, and put me to my shifts,[5]
I'll rouse my senses and awake myself.
Daughter, I have it! Thou perceiv'st the plight
Wherein these Christians have oppressèd me.
Be ruled° by me, for in extremity *guided*
We ought to make bar of no policy.[6]
ABIGAIL Father, whate'er it be to injure them
That have so manifestly wrongèd us,
What will not Abigail attempt?
BARABAS Why, so.
Then thus: thou told'st me they have turned my house
Into a nunnery, and some nuns are there.
ABIGAIL I did.
BARABAS Then, Abigail, there must my girl
Entreat the abbess to be entertained.° *admitted*
ABIGAIL How, as a nun?
BARABAS Ay, daughter, for religion
Hides many mischiefs from suspicion.
ABIGAIL Ay, but father, they will suspect me there.
BARABAS Let 'em suspect, but be thou so precise° *religiously austere*
As they may think it done of holiness.
Entreat 'em fair,° and give them friendly speech, *Be courteous*
And seem to them as if thy sins were great,
Till thou hast gotten to be entertained.
ABIGAIL Thus, father, shall I much dissemble.
BARABAS Tush!
As good dissemble that° thou never mean'st *that which*
As first mean truth and then dissemble it;
A counterfeit profession is better
Than unseen hypocrisy.[7]
ABIGAIL Well, father, say I be entertained,
What then shall follow?
BARABAS This shall follow, then:
There have I hid, close underneath the plank

5. Oblige me to fend for myself.
6. We should not rule out any cunning device.
7. It's better to deceive deliberately than to be guilty of unconscious hypocrisy.

That runs along the upper chamber floor,
The gold and jewels which I kept for thee.—
But here they come! Be cunning, Abigail.

ABIGAIL Then, father, go with me.

BARABAS No, Abigail, in this
It is not necessary I° be seen, *It's necessary I not*
For I will seem° offended with thee for't. *pretend to be*
Be close,° my girl, for this must fetch my gold. *secret*
[*He stands aside.*]

Enter two friars [*Jacomo and Bernardine*] *and two nuns* [*one of them the Abbess*].

JACOMO Sisters, we now
Are almost at the new-made nunnery.

ABBESS The better; for we love not to be seen.
'Tis thirty winters long since some of us
Did stray so far amongst the multitude.

JACOMO But, madam, this house
And waters° of this new-made nunnery *water source*
Will much delight you.

ABBESS It may be so. [*Abigail approaches them.*]
But who comes here?

ABIGAIL Grave Abbess, and you happy virgins' guide,[8]
Pity the state of a distressèd maid!

ABBESS What art thou, daughter?

ABIGAIL The hopeless daughter of a hapless Jew,
The Jew of Malta, wretched Barabas,
Sometimes° the owner of a goodly house *Formerly*
Which they have now turned to a nunnery.

ABBESS Well, daughter, say, what is thy suit with us?

ABIGAIL Fearing the afflictions which my father feels
Proceed from sin, or want of faith in us,° *Jewish faithlessness*
I'd pass away my life in penitence,
And be a novice in your nunnery,
To make atonement for my laboring soul.

JACOMO [*to Bernardine*] No doubt, brother, but this proceedeth of the spirit.

BERNARDINE [*to Jacomo*] Ay, and of a moving spirit,[9] too, brother. But come,
Let us entreat she may be entertained.

ABBESS Well, daughter, we admit you for a nun.

ABIGAIL First, let me as a novice learn to frame° *fashion*
My solitary life to your strait° laws, *strict*
And let me lodge where I was wont to lie;
I do not doubt, by your divine precepts
And mine own industry, but to profit much.

BARABAS (*aside*) As much, I hope, as all I hid is worth.

ABBESS Come, daughter, follow us. [*They start to leave.*]

BARABAS [*coming forward*] Why, how now, Abigail, what mak'st thou° *what are you doing*
Amongst these hateful Christians?

8. You friars who serve as confessors to these blessed virgins.

9. Suggestive of sexual arousal.

JACOMO Hinder her not, thou man of little faith!
For she has mortified herself.[1]
BARABAS How, mortified?
JACOMO And is admitted to the sisterhood.
BARABAS Child of perdition and thy father's shame,
What wilt thou do among these hateful fiends?
I charge° thee on my blessing that thou leave *command*
These devils and their damnèd heresy.
ABIGAIL Father, give me—
BARABAS Nay, back, Abigail!
(*Whispers to her.*) And think upon the jewels and the gold;
The board is markèd thus [*making a sign*] that covers it.
[*Aloud*] Away, accursèd, from thy father's sight!
JACOMO Barabas, although thou art in misbelief,
And wilt not see thine own afflictions,
Yet let thy daughter be no longer blind.° *spiritually blind*
BARABAS Blind, friar? I reck not° thy persuasions. *do not heed*
(*Aside to Abigail*) The board is markèd thus (*making a sign*) that covers it.
[*Aloud*] For I had rather die than see her thus.
[*To her*] Wilt thou forsake me too in my distress,
Seducèd daughter? (*Aside to her*) Go! Forget not.
[*Aloud to her*] Becomes it Jews to be so credulous?
(*Aside to her*) Tomorrow early I'll be at the door.
[*Aloud*] No, come not at me! If thou wilt be damned,
Forget me, see me not, and so be gone.
(*Aside*) Farewell! Remember tomorrow morning.
[*Aloud*] Out,° out, thou wretch! *(exclamation of anger)*
[*Exeunt the friars and nuns with Abigail. Exit Barabas another way.*]

Enter Mathias [*as they are leaving*].

MATHIAS [*to himself*] Who's this? Fair Abigail, the rich Jew's daughter,
Become a nun? Her father's sudden fall
Has humbled her and brought her down to this.
Tut, she were fitter for a tale of love
Than to be tirèd out with orisons;° *prayers*
And better would she far become a bed,
Embracèd in a friendly lover's arms,
Than rise at midnight to a solemn mass.

Enter Lodowick.

LODOWICK Why, how now, Don Mathias, in a dump?° *in the dumps*
MATHIAS Believe me, noble Lodowick, I have seen
The strangest sight, in my opinion,
That ever I beheld.
LODOWICK What was't, I prithee?
MATHIAS A fair young maid, scarce fourteen years of age,
The sweetest flower in Cytherea's° field, *Venus's*
Cropped from the pleasures of the fruitful earth
And strangely metamorphosed nun.
LODOWICK But say, what was she?

1. She has become as one who is dead to this world.

MATHIAS Why, the rich Jew's daughter.
LODOWICK What, Barabas, whose goods were lately seized?
Is she so fair?
MATHIAS And matchless beautiful;
As, had you seen her, 'twould have moved your heart,
Though countermured° with walls of brass, to love, *double-walled*
Or at the least to pity.
LODOWICK And if she be so fair as you report,
'Twere time well spent to go and visit her.
How say you, shall we?
MATHIAS I must and will, sir; there's no remedy.
LODOWICK And so will I too, or it shall go hard.[2]
Farewell, Mathias.
MATHIAS Farewell, Lodowick. *Exeunt.*

2.1

Enter Barabas with a light.

BARABAS Thus, like the sad presaging raven that tolls° *sounds the bell for*
The sick man's passport° in her hollow beak, *(to the underworld)*
And in the shadow of the silent night
Doth shake contagion from her sable wings,
Vexed and tormented runs poor Barabas
With fatal curses towards these Christians.
The incertain pleasures of swift-footed time
Have ta'en their flight and left me in despair;
And of my former riches rests° no more *remains*
But bare remembrance, like a soldier's scar,
That has no further comfort for his maim.
O Thou that with a fiery pillar led'st
The sons of Israel through the dismal shades,° *(see Exodus 13.18–22)*
Light° Abraham's offspring, and direct the hand *Give light to*
Of Abigail this night! Or let the day
Turn to eternal darkness after this!
No sleep can fasten on my watchful eyes,
Nor quiet enter my distempered thoughts
Till I have answer of my Abigail.

Enter Abigail above.

ABIGAIL [*to herself*] Now have I happily° espied a time *haply; fortunately*
To search the plank my father did appoint.
[*Finding riches*] And here, behold, unseen, where I have found
The gold, the pearls, and jewels which he hid!
BARABAS [*to himself*] Now I remember those old women's words,
Who in my wealth° would tell me winter's tales *days of wealth*
And speak of spirits and ghosts that glide by night
About the place where treasure hath been hid;
And now methinks that I am one of those.
For whilst I live, here lives my soul's sole hope,
And when I die, here shall my spirit walk.
ABIGAIL Now that° my father's fortune were so good *would that*

2. Or there will be trouble. (With a suggestion of sexual arousal.)

2.1. Barabas' house.

As but to be about this happy place!
'Tis not so happy; yet when we parted last,
He said he would attend me in the morn.
Then, gentle sleep, where'er his body rests,
Give charge to Morpheus° that he may dream — *god of dreams*
A golden dream, and of° the sudden wake, — *on*
Come, and receive the treasure I have found.

BARABAS *Bueno para todos mi ganado no era.*[1]
As good go on as sit so sadly thus. [*He sees Abigail.*]
But stay! What star shines yonder in the east?
The lodestar° of my life, if Abigail! — *guiding star*
[*He calls*] Who's there?

ABIGAIL Who's that?

BARABAS Peace, Abigail. 'Tis I.

ABIGAIL Then, father, here receive thy happiness.

BARABAS Hast thou 't?

ABIGAIL Here. (*Throws down bags.*) Hast thou 't?
There's more, and more, and more.

BARABAS O my girl,
My gold, my fortune, my felicity,
Strength to my soul, death to mine enemy!
Welcome, the first beginner of my bliss!
Oh, Abigail, Abigail, that I had thee here too!
Then my desires were fully satisfied.
But I will practice° thy enlargement° thence. — *plot, devise / release*
Oh, girl, oh, gold, oh, beauty, oh, my bliss!
(*Hugs his bags.*)

ABIGAIL Father, it draweth towards midnight now,
And 'bout this time the nuns begin to wake;[2]
To shun suspicion, therefore, let us part.

BARABAS Farewell, my joy, and by my fingers take
A kiss from him that sends it from his soul.
[*He blows her a kiss. Exit Abigail.*]
Now, Phoebus,° ope the eyelids of the day, — *god of the sun*
And for° the raven wake the morning lark, — *in place of*
That I may hover with her in the air,
Singing o'er these,° as she does o'er her young: — *(the money-bags)*
Hermoso placer de los dineros.[3] *Exit.*

[2.2]

Enter Governor [*Ferneze*], *Martin del Bosco* [*Vice Admiral of Spain*], *the Knights* [*and Officers*].

FERNEZE Now, Captain, tell us whither thou art bound,
Whence is thy ship that anchors in our road,
And why thou cam'st ashore without our leave.

BOSCO Governor of Malta, hither am I bound;
My ship, the *Flying Dragon*, is of Spain,
And so am I. Del Bosco is my name,
Vice Admiral unto the Catholic king.

FIRST KNIGHT 'Tis true, my lord; therefore entreat° him well. — *treat*

1. My flock, good for everyone else, was of no benefit to me.
2. The nuns wake at midnight to sing matins. (See 1.2.371.)
3. Beautiful pleasure of money.
2.2. The senate house.

BOSCO Our freight is Grecians, Turks, and Afric Moors.
For late° upon the coast of Corsica, *lately*
Because we vailed not[1] to the Turkish fleet
Their creeping° galleys had us in the chase; *slow-moving*
But suddenly the wind began to rise,
And then we luffed, and tacked,° and fought at ease. *maneuvered for position*
Some have we fired,° and many have we sunk, *set on fire*
But one amongst the rest became our prize.
The captain's slain; the rest remain our slaves,
Of whom we would make sale in Malta here.
FERNEZE Martin del Bosco, I have heard of thee.
Welcome to Malta, and to all of us!
But to admit a sale of these thy Turks
We may not—nay, we dare not—give consent,
By reason of a tributary° league. *tribute-paying*
FIRST KNIGHT Del Bosco, as thou lovest and honor'st us,
Persuade our governor against the Turk!
This truce we have is but in hope of gold,
And with that sum he° craves might we wage war. *(the Turkish emperor)*
BOSCO Will Knights of Malta be in league with Turks,
And buy it basely, too, for sums of gold?
My lord, remember that to Europe's shame
The Christian isle of Rhodes, from whence you came,
Was lately lost, and you were stated° here *installed (in 1530)*
To be at deadly enmity with Turks.[2]
FERNEZE Captain, we know it, but our force is small.
BOSCO What is the sum that Calymath requires?
FERNEZE A hundred thousand crowns.° *gold coins*
BOSCO My lord and king hath title to this isle,
And he means quickly to expel them hence;
Therefore be ruled° by me and keep the gold. *counseled*
I'll write unto His Majesty for aid,
And not depart until I see you free.
FERNEZE On this condition shall thy Turks be sold.—
Go, officers, and set them straight in show.° *at once on display*
[*Exeunt Officers.*]
Bosco, thou shalt be Malta's general;
We and our warlike knights will follow thee
Against these barbarous, misbelieving Turks.
BOSCO So shall you imitate those you succeed;[3]
For when their° hideous force environed Rhodes, *(the Turks')*
Small though the number was that kept the town,
They fought it out, and not a man survived
To bring the hapless news to Christendom.
FERNEZE So will we fight it out. Come, let's away!
Proud-daring Calymath,[4] instead of gold
We'll send thee bullets wrapped in smoke and fire.

1. Because we did not lower our flag in a salute of respect.
2. The Spanish vice admiral recounts how those who became the Knights of Malta had once patrolled the Mediterranean, fighting battles against the Muslims in the name of Christianity until they were driven from Rhodes in 1522. They were reestablished on Malta in 1530, where they withstood a Turkish siege in 1565. The island was taken by Napoleon (in 1798) and then restored to the Order of the Knights of Malta in 1802.
3. In that way will you emulate the Knights of Rhodes (who lost to the Turks in 1522, but, according to lines 48–51, fought bravely). See previous note.
4. Ferneze apostrophizes, at a large distance, the Turkish emperor's son.

Claim tribute where thou wilt; we are resolved.
Honor is bought with blood and not with gold. *Exeunt.*

[2.3]

Enter Officers with slaves [*among whom is Ithamore*].

FIRST OFFICER This is the marketplace; here let 'em stand.
Fear not their sale,° for they'll be quickly bought. *not being sold*
SECOND OFFICER Every one's price is written on his back,
And so much must they yield or not be sold.

Enter Barabas.

FIRST OFFICER Here comes the Jew. Had not his goods been seized,
He'd give us present money° for them all. *ready cash*
BARABAS [*aside*] In spite of these swine-eating Christians—
Unchosen nation,° never circumcised, *Not chosen of God*
Such as, poor villains, were ne'er thought upon° *were poorly regarded*
Till Titus and Vespasian conquered us[1]—
Am I become as wealthy as I was.
They hoped my daughter would ha' been a nun;
But she's at home, and I have bought a house
As great and fair as is the Governor's;
And there, in spite of Malta, will I dwell,
Having Ferneze's hand,° whose heart I'll have— *authorization*
Ay, and his son's too, or it shall go hard.[2]
I am not of the tribe of Levi, I,
That can so soon forget an injury.[3]
We Jews can fawn like spaniels when we please,
And when we grin, we bite; yet are our looks
As innocent and harmless as a lamb's.
I learned in Florence how to kiss my hand,
Heave up my shoulders when they call me dog,
And duck as low as any barefoot friar,
Hoping to see them starve upon a stall,° *shop bench or table*
Or else be gathered for[4] in our synagogue,
That when the offering basin comes to me,
Even for charity I may spit into't.
Here comes Don Lodowick, the Governor's son,
One that I love for his good father's sake.° *(said ironically)*

Enter Lodowick.

LODOWICK [*to himself*] I hear the wealthy Jew walked this way;
I'll seek him out, and so insinuate° *ingratiate myself*
That I may have a sight of Abigail,
For Don Mathias tells me she is fair.
BARABAS [*aside*] Now will I show myself to have more of the

2.3. The marketplace, then near Barabas' new house (line 222 ff.).
1. Vespasian, Roman commander in Palestine and later Emperor of Rome, and his son Titus suppressed the revolt of the Jews and then captured Jerusalem in 66–70 C.E.
2. I.e., or I'll know the reason why.
3. The Levites were the descendants of Levi, the third son of Jacob and Leah, who took part with his brother Simeon in a massacre of revenge for a wrong done to their sister Dinah (Genesis 34.25–31). Perhaps Barabas is being ironic in speaking of the Levites as though they were inclined to shrug off insults, saying in essence, "Compared to me, the Levites were positively peace-loving. I am no temple functionary committed to being merciful."
4. Or else have a collection taken up.

serpent than the dove—that is, more knave than fool.
LODOWICK Yond walks the Jew. Now for fair Abigail.
BARABAS [*aside*] Ay, ay, no doubt but she's at your command.
LODOWICK Barabas, thou know'st I am the Governor's son.
BARABAS I would you were his father too, sir, that's all the
harm I wish you.[5] [*Aside*] The slave looks like a hog's cheek
new singed.° [*He turns away.*] *scorched*
LODOWICK Whither walk'st thou, Barabas?
BARABAS No further. 'Tis a custom held with us
That when we speak with Gentiles like to you
We turn into the air to purge° ourselves; *cleanse from defilement*
For unto us the promise° doth belong. *God's covenant*
LODOWICK Well, Barabas, canst help me to a diamond?
BARABAS Oh, sir, your father had my diamonds.
Yet I have one left that will serve your turn.
(*Aside*) I mean my daughter; but ere he shall have her
I'll sacrifice her on a pile of wood.[6]
I ha' the poison of the city[7] for him,
And the white leprosy.[8]
LODOWICK What sparkle does it give without a foil?[9]
BARABAS The diamond that I talk of ne'er was foiled.° *set against metal foil*
[*Aside*] But when he touches it, it will be foiled.° *defiled*
[*Aloud*] Lord Lodowick, it sparkles bright and fair.
LODOWICK Is it square or pointed? Pray let me know.
BARABAS Pointed° it is, good sir—(*aside*) but not for you. *Sharp; appointed*
LODOWICK I like it much the better.
BARABAS So do I too.
LODOWICK How shows it by night?
BARABAS Outshines Cynthia's° rays. *the moon's*
(*Aside*) You'll like it better far o'nights than days.
LODOWICK And what's the price?
BARABAS [*aside*] Your life, an if you have it.[1]—Oh, my lord,
We will not jar° about the price. Come to my house, *quarrel*
And I will give't Your Honor—(*aside*) with a vengeance.
LODOWICK No, Barabas, I will deserve it first.
BARABAS Good sir,
Your father has deserved it at my hands,
Who—of mere° charity and Christian ruth,° *utter / compassion*
To bring me to religious purity,
And as it were in catechizing° sort, *question and answer*
To make me mindful of my mortal sins—
Against my will, and whether I would or no,
Seized all I had and thrust me out o'doors,
And made my house a place for nuns most chaste.
LODOWICK No doubt your soul shall reap the fruit of it.
BARABAS Ay, but, my lord, the harvest is far off.
And yet I know the prayers of those nuns
And holy friars, having money for their pains,

5. Barabas seems to say that he means no more harm to Lodowick than he does to his father, who, as governor, deserves warm respect. Since, however, he has just sworn to have Ferneze's heart and his son's as well (lines 16–17 above), the speech here is equally ominous for both.
6. As Abraham was on the verge of doing with his son Isaac in response to God's commandment that he offer Isaac as a burnt offering (see Genesis 22).
7. I.e., I have a poison of the sort for which the Italian city-states are infamous.
8. Leprosy can produce shiny white scales on the skin.
9. Without a metallic background used to show off the gem.
1. It will cost you your life if you take my diamond (Abigail).

Are wondrous, (*aside*) and indeed do no man good.
[*Aloud*] And, seeing they are not idle, but still doing,[2]
'Tis likely they in time may reap some fruit[3]—
I mean, in fullness of perfection.
LODOWICK Good Barabas, glance not at° our holy nuns. *do not impugn*
BARABAS No, but I do it through a burning° zeal, *fervent; incendiary*
(*Aside*) Hoping ere long to set the house afire!
For, though they do awhile increase and multiply,
I'll have a saying to that nunnery.[4]
[*Aloud*] As for the diamond, sir, I told you of,
Come home, and there's no price shall make us part,[5]
Even for your honorable father's sake.
(*Aside*) It shall go hard° but I will see your death. *(see 17 n above)*
[*Aloud*] But now I must be gone to buy a slave.
LODOWICK And, Barabas, I'll bear thee company.
BARABAS Come, then; here's the marketplace. [*To the First Officer*] What's the price of this slave? Two hundred crowns?° Do the Turks weigh so much? *gold coins*
FIRST OFFICER Sir, that's his price.
BARABAS What, can he steal, that you demand so much?
Belike he has some new trick for a purse;° *for purse snatching*
And if he has, he is worth three hundred plates,° *Spanish silver coins*
So that, being bought, the town seal might be got
To keep him for his lifetime from the gallows.[6]
The sessions° day is critical to thieves, *court sessions*
And few or none scape but by being purged.° *punished*
LODOWICK [*to the First Officer*] Ratest thou this Moor but at two hundred plates?
FIRST OFFICER No more, my lord.
BARABAS [*indicating another slave*] Why should this Turk be dearer than that Moor?
FIRST OFFICER Because he is young and has more qualities.° *abilities*
BARABAS [*to the Slave*] What, hast the philosophers' stone?[7]
An thou hast, break my head with it, I'll forgive thee.[8]
SLAVE No, sir. I can cut and shave.
BARABAS Let me see, sirrah. Are you not an old shaver?° *barber; rascal*
SLAVE Alas, sir, I am a very youth.
BARABAS A youth? I'll buy you, and marry you to Lady Vanity[9] if you do well.
SLAVE I will serve you, sir—
BARABAS Some wicked trick or other.[1] It may be, under color° of shaving, thou'lt cut my throat for my goods. Tell me, hast thou thy health well? *pretext*
SLAVE Ay, passing° well. *very*
BARABAS So much the worse. I must have one that's sickly,

2. They are continually doing good works. (With a suggestion too of being sexually active.)
3. "Fruit" suggests both spiritual harvest and child-bearing.
4. I'll have something to say to that nunnery—something they won't like hearing.
5. The matter of price won't come between us. (With a suggestion that Lodowick will not leave alive.)
6. Barabas sardonically suggests that a pickpocket would be worth buying only if he came with a warranty that he would not be subject to criminal prosecution.
7. A presumed quintessential substance thought capable of turning all metals into gold.
8. Barabas would be glad to have the philosophers' stone at any price or inconvenience.
9. A generic name for the temptress of youth in a morality play.
1. Barabas playfully turns the Slave's "serve you" into "do some trick."

an't be but for sparing victuals;° 'tis not a stone of beef a day will maintain you in these chops.[2] [*To the First Officer*] Let me see one that's somewhat leaner. *if only to save on food*

FIRST OFFICER [*indicating Ithamore*] Here's a leaner. How like you him?

BARABAS [*to Ithamore*] Where was thou born?

ITHAMORE In Thrace; brought up in Arabia.

BARABAS So much the better; thou art for my turn.° *suited for my purposes*
[*To the First Officer*] An hundred crowns? I'll have him; there's the coin. [*He pays the First Officer.*]

FIRST OFFICER Then mark° him, sir, and take him hence. *brand*

BARABAS [*aside*] Ay, mark° him, you were best, for this is he *take notice of*
That by my help shall do much villainy.
[*To Lodowick*] My lord, farewell. [*To Ithamore*] Come, sirrah, you are mine.
[*To Lodowick*] As for the diamond, it shall be yours.
I pray, sir, be no stranger at my house;
All that I have shall be at your command.

Enter Mathias [and Katharine, his] mater.° *mother*

MATHIAS [*to himself*] What makes the Jew and Lodowick so private?
I fear me 'tis about fair Abigail. [*Exit Lodowick.*]

BARABAS [*aside to Ithamore*] Yonder comes Don Mathias; let us stay.° *stay and watch*
He loves my daughter, and she holds him dear;
But I have sworn to frustrate both their hopes,
And be revenged upon the—Governor.

KATHARINE [*to Mathias, as they inspect the slaves*] This Moor is comeliest, is he not? Speak, son.

MATHIAS No, this is the better, mother. View this well.

BARABAS [*aside to Mathias*] Seem not to know me here before your mother,
Lest she mistrust° the match that is in hand. *suspect*
When you have brought her home, come to my house.
Think of me as thy father. Son, farewell.

MATHIAS [*aside to Barabas*] But wherefore talked Don Lodowick with you?

BARABAS Tush, man, we talked of diamonds, not of Abigail.

KATHARINE Tell me, Mathias, is not that the Jew?

BARABAS [*aloud to Mathias*] As for the comment on the Maccabees,
I have it, sir, and 'tis at your command.[3]

MATHIAS [*to Katharine*] Yes, madam, and my talk with him was but
About the borrowing of a book or two.

KATHARINE Converse not with him; he is cast off from heaven.
[*To the First Officer*] Thou hast thy crowns, fellow. [*To Mathias*] Come, let's away.

2. Even fourteen pounds ("a stone") of beef a day wouldn't satisfy your huge appetite. ("Chops" means "jaws.")

3. Speaking aloud to hoodwink Katharine, Barabas talks as though he and Mathias have been discussing some commentary on apocryphal books of the Bible that tell how the Maccabees, a Jewish family of the second and first century B.C.E., delivered the Jews from persecution by Antiochus IV of Syria in 175–165 B.C.E.

MATHIAS [*to Barabas*] Sirrah Jew, remember the book.
BARABAS Marry,° will I, sir. *By Mary (an oath)*
Exeunt [*Katharine, Mathias, and a slave*].
FIRST OFFICER Come, I have made a reasonable market. Let's away. [*Exeunt First Officer with the remaining slaves.*]
BARABAS [*to Ithamore*] Now, let me know thy name, and therewithal
Thy birth, condition,° and profession. *social status*
ITHAMORE Faith, sir, my birth is but mean,° my name's Ithamore, my profession what you please. *lowly*
BARABAS Hast thou no trade? Then listen to my words,
And I will teach thee that° shall stick by thee. *that which*
First, be thou void of these affections:
Compassion, love, vain hope, and heartless° fear. *craven*
Be moved at nothing; see thou pity none,
But to thyself smile when the Christians moan.
ITHAMORE Oh, brave,° master! I worship your nose for this.[4] *excellent*
BARABAS As for myself, I walk abroad a-nights
And kill sick people groaning under walls.
Sometimes I go about and poison wells;
And now and then, to cherish Christian thieves,
I am content to lose some of my crowns,
That I may, walking in my gallery,
See 'em go pinioned along by my door.[5]
Being young, I studied physic,° and began *medicine*
To practice first upon the Italian;[6]
There I enriched the priests with burials,
And always kept the sexton's arms in ure° *tools in use*
With digging graves and ringing dead men's knells.
And after that was I an engineer,
And in the wars 'twixt France and Germany,
Under pretense of helping Charles the Fifth,° *Hapsburg emperor 1519–56*
Slew friend and enemy with my stratagems.
Then after that was I an usurer,
And with extorting, cozening,° forfeiting, *cheating*
And tricks belonging unto brokery,° *usury, rascally dealing*
I filled the jails with bankrupts in a year,
And with young orphans planted hospitals,[7]
And every moon[8] made some° or other mad, *someone*
And now and then one hang° himself for grief, *drove someone to hang*
Pinning° upon his breast a long great scroll *He pinning*
How I with interest° tormented him. *interest payments*
But mark how I am blest for plaguing them:
I have as much coin as will buy the town!
But tell me now, how hast thou spent thy time?
ITHAMORE Faith,° master, *In faith*
In setting Christian villages on fire,
Chaining of eunuchs, binding galley-slaves.

4. A prominent nose is a common feature in medieval and early modern caricatures of Jews—a prejudicial insult not unknown in anti-Semitism today. Here, apparently, it is intended to be taken by Barabas as the sort of joshing insult that one swaggerer might offer to another.
5. Barabas evidently leaves some of his wealth lying around to entrap Christian thieves and then gloats as, watching from his balcony, he sees them led off under arrest.
6. "To practice upon" means "to practice medicine on," but with a suggestion also of "to practice deception on." "Italian" means "Italians."
7. And created the need for more orphanages.
8. "Moon" means "change of the moon, month." The moon, *luna* in Latin, was associated with lunacy.

One time I was an ostler° in an inn, *innkeeper, stable groom*
And in the nighttime secretly would I steal
To travelers' chambers and there cut their throats.
Once at Jerusalem, where the pilgrims kneeled,
I strewèd powder on the marble stones,
And therewithal their knees would rankle° so *fester*
That I have laughed a-good° to see the cripples *heartily*
Go limping home to Christendom on stilts.° *crutches*

BARABAS Why, this is something! Make account of me
As of thy fellow.° We are villains both; *Count me as a partner*
Both circumcisèd, we hate Christians both.
Be true and secret, thou shalt want no gold.—
But stand aside! Here comes Don Lodowick.

Enter Lodowick.

LODOWICK Oh, Barabas, well met. Where is the diamond
You told me of?

BARABAS I have it for you, sir.
Please you walk in with me.[9]
[*He calls*] What ho, Abigail! Open the door, I say.

Enter Abigail [with letters].

ABIGAIL In good time,° father. Here are letters come *Just at the right time*
From Ormuz, and the post stays° here within. *messenger waits*

BARABAS Give me the letters. [*She gives them.*] Daughter, do you hear?
Entertain Lodowick, the Governor's son,
With all the courtesy you can afford,
Provided that you keep your maidenhead.
Use him as if he were a—(*aside*) Philistine.° *ancient enemy of the Jews*
Dissemble, swear, protest,° vow to love him; *utter vows*
He is not of the seed of Abraham.
[*To him*] I am a little busy, sir, pray pardon me.—
Abigail, bid him welcome for my sake.

ABIGAIL For your sake and his own he's welcome hither.

BARABAS Daughter, a word more. [*Aside to her*] Kiss him, speak him fair,° *sweet-talk him*
And like a cunning Jew so cast about° *contrive, see to it*
That ye be both made sure° ere you come out. *engaged*

ABIGAIL [*aside to Barabas*] Oh, father, Don Mathias is my love!

BARABAS [*aside to her*] I know it. Yet, I say, make love to him.
Do! It is requisite it should be so.
[*Aloud, looking at the letters*] Nay, on my life it is my factor's hand.° *agent's handwriting*
But go you in; I'll think upon the account.° *business account*

[*Exeunt Lodowick and Abigail.*]

The account° is made, for Lodowick dies. *fatal reckoning*
My factor sends me word a merchant's fled
That owes me for a hundred tun° of wine. *barrels*
I weigh it thus much;° I have wealth enough. *i.e., as insignificant*

9. The flexible, presentational Elizabethan stage allowed the audience to understand that Barabas and Ithamore, formerly at the slave market, are now at the door of Barabas' house, signified by a stage door. A few steps, and the audience's understanding of stage convention, are all that is required to provide an imaginative relocation of the scene.

For now by this° has he kissed Abigail, *this time*
And she vows love to him, and he to her.
As sure as heaven rained manna for the Jews,[1]
So sure shall he and Don Mathias die.
His father was my chiefest enemy.

Enter Mathias.

Whither goes Don Mathias? Stay awhile.
MATHIAS Whither but to my fair love Abigail?
BARABAS Thou know'st, and heaven can witness it is true,
That I intend my daughter shall be thine.
MATHIAS Ay, Barabas, or else thou wrong'st me much.
BARABAS Oh, heaven forbid I should have such a thought!
Pardon me though I weep. The Governor's son
Will, whether I will or no, have Abigail.
He sends her letters, bracelets, jewels, rings.
MATHIAS Does she receive them?
BARABAS She? No, Mathias, no, but sends them back,
And when he comes she locks herself up fast.° *securely*
Yet through the keyhole will he talk to her,
While she runs to the window, looking out
When° you should come and hale° him from the door. *To see when / drag*
MATHIAS Oh, treacherous Lodowick!
BARABAS Even now, as I came home, he slipped me in,° *slipped in past me*
And I am sure he is with Abigail.
MATHIAS I'll rouse him thence!° [*He draws his sword.*] *I'll rout him out!*
BARABAS Not for all Malta! Therefore sheathe your sword.
If you love me, no quarrels in my house.
But steal you in, and seem to see him not.
I'll give him such a warning ere he goes
As° he shall have small hopes of Abigail.— *That*
Away! For here they come.

Enter Lodowick [and] Abigail.

MATHIAS [*to Barabas*] What, hand in hand? I cannot suffer° this. *allow; endure*
BARABAS Mathias, as thou lov'st me, not a word.
MATHIAS Well, let it pass. Another time shall serve. *Exit.*
LODOWICK Barabas, is not that the widow's son?
BARABAS Ay, and take heed, for he hath sworn your death.
LODOWICK My death? What, is the baseborn peasant mad?
BARABAS No, no, but happily° he stands in fear *haply, perhaps*
Of° that which you, I think, ne'er dream upon: *Of losing*
My daughter here, a paltry, silly girl.
LODOWICK Why, loves she Don Mathias?
BARABAS Doth she not with her smiling answer you?° *that she loves you*
ABIGAIL [*aside*] He° has my heart; I smile against my will. *(Mathias)*
LODOWICK Barabas, thou know'st I have loved thy daughter long.
BARABAS And so has she done you, even from a child.
LODOWICK And now I can no longer hold my mind.° *hold back my feelings*

1. Manna is the food described in Exodus as descending from heaven to sustain the Israelites during their forty years' sojourn in the wilderness.

BARABAS Nor I the affection that I bear to you.
LODOWICK This is thy diamond. Tell me, shall I have it?
BARABAS Win it and wear it; it is yet unsoiled.° *unsullied; unfoiled*
Oh, but I know Your Lordship would disdain
To marry with the daughter of a Jew;
And yet I'll give her many a golden cross,° *gold coin (with pun)*
With Christian posies° round about the ring. *engraved mottoes*
LODOWICK 'Tis not thy wealth, but her, that I esteem.
Yet crave I thy consent.
BARABAS And mine you have. Yet let me talk to her.
(*Aside* [*to Abigail*]) This offspring of Cain, this Jebusite,° *ancient Palestinian*
That never tasted of the Passover,
Nor e'er shall see the land of Canaan,
Nor our Messias that is yet to come,[2]
This gentle° maggot, Lodowick, I mean, *wellborn; gentile*
Must be deluded. Let him have thy hand,
But keep thy heart till Don Mathias comes.
ABIGAIL [*aside to Barabas*] What, shall I be betrothed to Lodowick?
BARABAS [*aside to her*] It's no sin to deceive a Christian,
For they themselves hold it a principle
Faith is not to be held with heretics;
But all are heretics that are not Jews.[3]
This follows well,° and therefore, daughter, fear not. *follows logically*
[*Aloud*] I have entreated her, and she will grant.
LODOWICK Then, gentle Abigail, plight thy faith° to me. *vow your engagement*
ABIGAIL [*aside*] I cannot choose, seeing my father bids.
[*Aloud*] Nothing but death shall part my love and me.[4]
LODOWICK Now have I that for which my soul hath longed.
BARABAS (*aside*) So have not I! But yet I hope I shall.
ABIGAIL [*aside*] Oh, wretched Abigail, what hast thou done?
LODOWICK Why on the sudden is your color changed?
ABIGAIL I know not; but farewell, I must be gone.
[*She starts to leave.*]
BARABAS [*aside to Ithamore*] Stay her! But let her not speak one word more.
LODOWICK Mute o'the sudden? Here's a sudden change.
BARABAS Oh, muse not at it. 'Tis the Hebrews' guise,° *custom*
That maidens new betrothed should weep awhile.
Trouble her not. Sweet Lodowick, depart.
She is thy wife, and thou shalt be mine heir.
LODOWICK Oh, is't the custom? Then I am resolved.° *answered, satisfied*
But rather let the brightsome heavens be dim,
And nature's beauty choke with stifling clouds,
Than my fair Abigail should frown on me.

Enter Mathias.

There comes the villain! Now I'll be revenged.

2. The Jews expected a Messiah, but did not accept Christ as having fulfilled Old Testament prophecy. The spelling "Messias" is found in early modern Bibles; see, for example, John 1.41 and 4.25 in the King James Version.
3. Barabas argues that since Christians do not feel obliged to honor any vows they make to non-Christians, Jews should do the same with non-Jews.
4. Nothing but death shall part you and me. (But with a hidden and contrary meaning: Nothing but death shall part Mathias and me.)

BARABAS Be quiet, Lodowick. It is enough
That I have made thee sure to Abigail.
LODOWICK Well, let him go. *Exit.*
BARABAS [*to Mathias*] Well, but for me, as you went in at doors
You had been stabbed; but not a word on't now.
Here must no speeches pass, nor swords be drawn.
MATHIAS Suffer° me, Barabas, but to follow him. *Allow*
BARABAS No. So shall I, if any hurt be done,
Be made an accessory of your deeds.
Revenge it on him when you meet him next.
MATHIAS For this I'll have his heart.
BARABAS Do so. Lo, here I give thee Abigail.
MATHIAS What greater gift can poor Mathias have?
Shall Lodowick rob me of so fair a love?
My life is not so dear as Abigail.
BARABAS My heart misgives me that, to cross° your love, *thwart*
He's with your mother. Therefore, after him.
MATHIAS What, is he gone unto my mother?
BARABAS Nay, if you will,° stay till she comes herself. *if you don't believe me*
MATHIAS I cannot stay; for if my mother come,
She'll die with grief.[5] *Exit.*
ABIGAIL I cannot take my leave of him for tears.[6]
Father, why have you thus incensed them both?
BARABAS What's that to thee?
ABIGAIL I'll make 'em friends again.
BARABAS You'll make 'em friends?
Are there not Jews enough in Malta
But thou must dote upon a Christian?
ABIGAIL I will have Don Mathias; he is my love.
BARABAS Yes, you shall have him. [*To Ithamore*] Go put her in.
ITHAMORE Ay, I'll put her in. [*He puts Abigail in the house.*]
BARABAS Now tell me, Ithamore, how lik'st thou this?
ITHAMORE Faith, master, I think by this
You purchase both their lives.° Is it not so? *plot their deaths*
BARABAS True; and it shall be cunningly performed.
ITHAMORE Oh, master, that I might have a hand in this!
BARABAS Ay, so thou shalt; 'tis thou must do the deed.
[*Giving him a letter*] Take this and bear it to Mathias straight,
And tell him that it comes from Lodowick.
ITHAMORE 'Tis poisoned, is it not?
BARABAS No, no; and yet it might be done that way.
It is a challenge feigned from Lodowick.
ITHAMORE Fear not; I'll so set his heart afire that he shall
verily think it comes from him.
BARABAS I cannot choose but like thy readiness.
Yet be not rash, but do it cunningly.
ITHAMORE As I behave myself in this, employ me hereafter.
BARABAS Away, then! *Exit* [*Ithamore*].
So, now will I go in to Lodowick,
And like a cunning spirit° feign some lie *devil*
Till I have set 'em both at enmity. *Exit.*

5. I.e., She'll die of grief at my marrying a Jewess.
6. I couldn't even bid him good-bye, I was weeping so.

3.1

Enter a courtesan [*Bellamira*].

BELLAMIRA Since° this town was besieged, my gain° grows cold. *Ever since / profit*
The time has been that but° for one bare° night *only / sole; naked*
A hundred ducats° have been freely given; *gold coins*
But now against my will I must be chaste.
And yet I know my beauty doth not fail.
From Venice merchants, and from Padua,
Were wont to come rare-witted gentlemen,
Scholars, I mean, learned and liberal;[1]
And now, save Pilia-Borza, comes there none,
And he is very seldom from° my house. *absent from*
And here he comes.

Enter Pilia-Borza.

PILIA-BORZA Hold thee, wench. There's something for thee to spend. [*He shows her money in a sack.*]
BELLAMIRA 'Tis silver. I disdain it.
PILIA-BORZA Ay, but the Jew has gold,
And I will have it, or it shall go hard.° *I'll know the reason why*
BELLAMIRA Tell me, how cam'st thou by this?
PILIA-BORZA Faith, walking the back lanes through the gardens I chanced to cast mine eye up to the Jew's counting-house, where I saw some bags of money, and in the night I clambered up with my hooks,° and, as I was taking my choice, I heard a rumbling in the house; so I took only this, and run my way.°—But here's the Jew's man.° *climbing hooks* *ran away / servant*

Enter Ithamore.

BELLAMIRA [*to Pilia-Borza*] Hide the bag!
PILIA-BORZA Look not towards him. Let's away. Zounds,° what a looking thou keep'st![2] Thou'lt betray 's anon.° *By God's wounds* *immediately*
[*Exeunt Bellamira and Pilia-Borza.*]
ITHAMORE Oh, the sweetest face that ever I beheld! I know she is a courtesan by her attire. Now would I give a hundred of the Jew's crowns that I had such a concubine.
Well, I have delivered the challenge[3] in such sort° *manner*
As meet they will, and fighting die. Brave sport! *Exit.*

[3.2]

Enter Mathias.

MATHIAS This is the place.° Now Abigail shall see *place for the duel*
Whether Mathias holds her dear or no.

Enter Lodowick, reading.[1]

3.1. Outside Bellamira's house.
1. (1) Well-educated; (2) free spending.
2. What a guilty look you have!
3. The forged challenge sent in Lodowick's name to Mathias.

3.2. The place appointed for the duel.
1. Lodowick is reading Mathias' reply to Lodowick's supposed challenge, which Ithamore has deceitfully given to Mathias; see 2.3.374–82.

LODOWICK [*to himself*] What, dares the villain write in such base terms?

MATHIAS [*coming forward*] I did it, and revenge it if thou dar'st! [*They*] *fight.*

Enter Barabas above.

BARABAS Oh, bravely fought! And yet they thrust not home.°— *all the way*
Now, Lodowick! Now, Mathias! [*Both fall, slain.*] So.
So, now they have showed themselves to be tall° fellows. *brave*

[VOICES] WITHIN Part 'em! Part 'em!

BARABAS Ay, part 'em now they are dead. Farewell, farewell! *Exit* [*above*].

Enter Governor [*Ferneze*], *mater*° [*Katharine, and citizens of Malta*]. *mother*

FERNEZE What sight is this? My Lodowick slain!
These arms of mine shall be thy sepulchre.

KATHARINE Who is this? My son Mathias slain!

FERNEZE Oh, Lodowick, hadst thou perished by the Turk,
Wretched Ferneze might have venged thy death.[2]

KATHARINE Thy son slew mine, and I'll revenge his death.

FERNEZE Look, Katharine, look, thy son gave mine these wounds.

KATHARINE Oh, leave° to grieve me! I am grieved enough. *cease*

FERNEZE Oh, that my sighs could turn to lively° breath, *life-giving, vital*
And these my tears to blood, that he might live!

KATHARINE Who made them enemies?

FERNEZE I know not, and that grieves me most of all.

KATHARINE My son loved thine.

FERNEZE And so did Lodowick him.

KATHARINE Lend me that weapon that did kill my son,
And it shall murder me.

FERNEZE Nay, madam, stay. That weapon was my son's,
And on that rather should Ferneze die.

KATHARINE Hold. Let's inquire the causers of their deaths,
That we may venge their blood upon their heads.[3]

FERNEZE Then take them up, and let them be interred
Within one sacred monument of stone,
Upon which altar I will offer up
My daily sacrifice of sighs and tears,
And with my prayers pierce impartial° heavens, *unmoved; just; partial*
Till they reveal the causers of our smarts,° *sorrows, hurts*
Which forced their hands divide° united hearts. *to divide*
Come, Katharine. Our losses equal are;
Then of true grief let us take equal share.
Exeunt [*with the bodies*].

2. Ferneze says that since Mathias killed Lodowick, and since Mathias is dead and was a member of the Christian community, Ferneze cannot resort to violent revenge and must wretchedly grieve. Katharine answers in line 15 by declaring herself bound by no such convention; she will be governed by her grief alone.

3. That we may venge our sons' blood upon the instigators' heads.

[3.3]

Enter Ithamore.

ITHAMORE [*laughing*] Why, was there ever seen such villainy,
So neatly plotted and so well performed?
Both held in hand,° and flatly° both beguiled! *Both men led on / utterly*

Enter Abigail.

ABIGAIL Why, how now, Ithamore, why laugh'st thou so?
ITHAMORE Oh, mistress, ha, ha, ha!
ABIGAIL Why, what ail'st thou?
ITHAMORE Oh, my master!
ABIGAIL Ha!
ITHAMORE Oh, mistress, I have the bravest,° gravest, secret, subtle bottle-nosed° knave to° my master that ever gentleman had. *finest* *(see 2.3.177 and n) / as*
ABIGAIL Say, knave, why rail'st upon° my father thus? *why do you mock*
ITHAMORE Oh, my master has the bravest policy!° *cleverest plot*
ABIGAIL Wherein?
ITHAMORE Why, know you not?
ABIGAIL Why, no.
ITHAMORE Know you not of Mathias' and Don Lodowick's disaster?
ABIGAIL No, what was it?
ITHAMORE Why, the devil invented a challenge, my master writ it, and I carried it, first[1] to Lodowick and *imprimis*° to Mathias. *first*
And then they met, and, as the story says,
In doleful wise they ended both their days.
ABIGAIL And was my father furtherer of their deaths?
ITHAMORE Am I Ithamore?
ABIGAIL Yes.
ITHAMORE So sure did your father write, and I carry, the challenge.
ABIGAIL Well, Ithamore, let me request thee this:
Go to the new-made nunnery, and inquire
For any of the friars of Saint Jacques,° *Dominicans*
And say, I pray them come and speak with me.
ITHAMORE I pray, mistress, will you answer me to one question?
ABIGAIL Well, sirrah, what is't?
ITHAMORE A very feeling one: have not the nuns fine sport with the friars now and then?
ABIGAIL Go to, sirrah sauce,° is this your question? Get ye gone. *impudent fellow*
ITHAMORE I will, forsooth, mistress. *Exit.*
ABIGAIL Hard-hearted father, unkind Barabas,
Was this the pursuit° of thy policy, *aim*
To make me show them favor severally,° *to both separately*
That by my favor° they should both be slain? *through love of me*
Admit° thou loved'st not Lodowick for his sire, *Admittedly*
Yet Don Mathias ne'er offended thee.

3.3. Barabas' house.
1. "First" is perhaps Ithamore's error for "second"; see 3.2.2.1 and note.

But thou wert set upon extreme revenge,
Because the prior° dispossessed thee once, *i.e., Ferneze*
And couldst not venge it but upon his son,
Nor on his son but by Mathias' means,
Nor on Mathias but by murdering me.
But I perceive there is no love on earth,
Pity in Jews, nor piety in Turks.—
But here comes cursèd Ithamore with the friar.

Enter Ithamore [*and*] *Friar* [*Jacomo*].

JACOMO *Virgo, salve!*° *Hail, maiden!*
ITHAMORE When, duck you?[2]
ABIGAIL Welcome, grave friar.—Ithamore, begone.
Exit [*Ithamore*].
Know, holy sir, I am bold to solicit thee.
JACOMO Wherein?
ABIGAIL To get me be admitted for° a nun. *as*
JACOMO Why, Abigail, it is not yet long since
That I did labor° thy admission, *strive for*
And then thou didst not like that holy life.
ABIGAIL Then were my thoughts so frail and unconfirmed,
And I was chained to follies of the world.
But now experience, purchasèd with grief,
Has made me see the difference of things.
My sinful soul, alas, hath paced too long
The fatal labyrinth of misbelief,
Far from the Son that gives eternal life.
JACOMO Who taught thee this?
ABIGAIL The abbess of the house,
Whose zealous admonition I embrace.
Oh, therefore, Jacomo, let me be one,
Although unworthy, of that sisterhood.
JACOMO Abigail, I will, but see thou change no more,
For that will be most heavy to thy soul.
ABIGAIL That was my father's fault.
JACOMO Thy father's? How?
ABIGAIL Nay, you shall pardon me.[3] [*Aside*] Oh, Barabas,
Though thou deservest hardly° at my hands, *to be treated harshly*
Yet never shall these lips bewray thy life.[4]
JACOMO Come, shall we go?
ABIGAIL My duty waits on° you. *Exeunt.* *attends*

[3.4]

Enter Barabas, reading a letter.

BARABAS What, Abigail become a nun again?
False and unkind!° What, hast thou lost thy father, *unnatural; disloyal*
And, all unknown and unconstrained of me,
Art thou again got to the nunnery?

2. Ithamore heaps scorn on the friars for their genuflecting and bowing. "When" expresses impatience.
3. Please excuse my not answering that.
4. These lips will never endanger your life by revealing the truth about you.
3.4. Barabas' house.

Now here she writes, and wills° me to repent. *urges*
Repentance? *Spurca!*[1] What pretendeth this?° *What does this portend?*
I fear she knows—'tis so!—of my device
In Don Mathias' and Lodovico's deaths.
If so, 'tis time that it be seen° into, *looked*
For she that varies from me in belief
Gives great presumption that she loves me not,
Or, loving, doth dislike of something done.

[*Enter Ithamore.*]

But who comes here? Oh, Ithamore, come near!
Come near, my love; come near, thy master's life—
My trusty servant, nay, my second self!
For I have now no hope but even in thee,
And on that hope my happiness is built.
When saw'st thou Abigail?

ITHAMORE Today.

BARABAS With whom?

ITHAMORE A friar.

BARABAS A friar? False villain! He hath done the deed.

ITHAMORE How, sir?

BARABAS Why, made mine Abigail a nun.

ITHAMORE That's no lie, for she sent me for him.

BARABAS Oh, unhappy day!
False, credulous,° inconstant Abigail! *easily misled*
But let 'em go. And, Ithamore, from hence° *henceforth*
Ne'er shall she grieve me more with her disgrace;
Ne'er shall she live to inherit aught of mine,
Be blest of me, nor come within my gates,
But perish underneath my bitter curse
Like Cain by Adam, for his brother's death.[2]

ITHAMORE Oh, master!

BARABAS Ithamore, entreat not for her. I am moved,° *angry*
And she is hateful to my soul and me;
And, 'less thou yield to this that I entreat,
I cannot think but that thou hat'st my life.

ITHAMORE Who, I, master? Why, I'll run to some rock and throw myself headlong into the sea. Why, I'll do anything for your sweet sake.

BARABAS Oh, trusty Ithamore! No servant, but my friend!
I here adopt thee for mine only heir.
All that I have is thine when I am dead,
And, whilst I live, use half. Spend as myself.
Here, take my keys. [*He starts to give keys, then hesitates.*]
I'll give 'em thee anon.
Go buy thee garments— [*He starts to offer money, then hesitates again.*] But thou shalt not want.
Only know this, that thus thou art° to do. *can expect*
But first go fetch me in the pot of rice
That for our supper stands upon the fire.

ITHAMORE [*to the audience*] I hold my head° my master's hungry. [*To Barabas*] I go, sir. *Exit.* *i.e., I bet my life*

1. An Italian imprecation, from *sporco*, meaning "dirty."

2. In Genesis 4, God (not Adam) curses Cain for having slain his brother, Abel.

BARABAS Thus every villain ambles after wealth,
Although he ne'er be richer than in hope.—
But husht!° *hush*

Enter Ithamore with the pot.

ITHAMORE Here 'tis, master.
BARABAS Well said,° Ithamore! *Well done*
What, hast thou brought the ladle with thee too?
ITHAMORE Yes, sir. The proverb says, he that eats with the devil had need of a long spoon. I have brought you a ladle.
BARABAS Very well, Ithamore. Then, now be secret.
And for for thy sake, whom I so dearly love,
Now shalt thou see the death of Abigail,
That thou mayst freely live to be my heir.
ITHAMORE Why, master, will you poison her with a mess° of rice porridge, that will preserve life, make her round and plump, and batten° more than you are aware? *serving, portion* *fatten up*
BARABAS Ay, but Ithamore, see'st thou this?
[*He shows a poison.*]
It is a precious powder that I bought
Of an Italian in Ancona once,
Whose operation is to bind,° infect, *constipate, constrict*
And poison deeply, yet not appear
In forty hours after it is ta'en.
ITHAMORE How, master?
BARABAS Thus, Ithamore:
This even, they use° in Malta here ('tis called *make it a practice*
Saint Jacques' even),° and then, I say, they use *eve*
To send their alms unto the nunneries.
Among the rest° bear this, and set it there. *the other almsgivers*
There's a dark entry where they take it in,
Where they must neither see the messenger
Nor make inquiry who hath sent it them.
ITHAMORE How so?
BARABAS Belike there is some ceremony in't.
There, Ithamore, must thou go place this pot.
[*Ithamore starts to go.*]
Stay, let me spice it first.
ITHAMORE Pray do, and let me help you, master. Pray let me taste first.
BARABAS Prithee do. [*Ithamore tastes.*] What say'st thou now?
ITHAMORE Troth, master, I'm loath such a pot of pottage should be spoiled.
BARABAS [*adding poison*] Peace, Ithamore. 'Tis better so than spared.[3]
Assure thyself thou shalt have broth by the eye.° *all you want*
My purse, my coffer, and myself is thine.
ITHAMORE Well, master, I go. [*He starts to leave again.*]
BARABAS Stay! First let me stir it, Ithamore.
[*He chants a curse as he stirs the poisoned pottage.*]
As fatal be it to her as the draft
Of which great Alexander drunk and died!
And with her let it work like Borgia's wine,

3. Better to use it thus than save it for eating.

Whereof his sire, the Pope, was poisonèd![4]
In few,° the blood of Hydra, Lerna's bane, *In short*
The juice of hebon, and Cocytus' breath,
And all the poisons of the Stygian pool[5]
Break from the fiery kingdom, and in this° *this porridge*
Vomit your venom, and envenom her
That like a fiend hath left her father thus!

ITHAMORE [*aside*] What a blessing has he giv'n 't! Was ever pot of rice porridge so sauced?° [*Aloud*] What shall I do with it? *seasoned*

BARABAS Oh, my sweet Ithamore, go set it down,
And come again so soon as thou hast done,
For I have other business for thee.

ITHAMORE Here's a drench° to poison a whole stable of Flanders mares![6] I'll carry't to the nuns with a powder.[7] *dose*

BARABAS And the horse pestilence to boot.° Away! *in addition*

ITHAMORE I am gone.
Pay me my wages, for my work is done. *Exit* [*with the pot*].

BARABAS I'll pay thee with a vengeance, Ithamore. *Exit.*

[3.5]

Enter Governor [*Ferneze*], *Bosco, Knights,* [*Callapine, the*] *bashaw,* [*and janizaries*].

FERNEZE Welcome, great bashaw. How fares Calymath?
What wind drives you thus into Malta road?

CALLAPINE The wind that bloweth all the world besides:
Desire of gold.

FERNEZE Desire of gold, great sir?
That's to be gotten in the Western Ind;° *West Indies*
In Malta are no golden minerals.

CALLAPINE To you of Malta thus saith Calymath:
The time you took for respite is at hand
For the performance of your promise passed,° *duly given*
And for the tribute money I am sent.

FERNEZE Bashaw, in brief, shalt° have no tribute here, *thou shalt*
Nor shall the heathens live upon our spoil.° *plundering of us*
First will we raze the city walls ourselves,
Lay waste the island, hew the temples down,
And, shipping off our goods to Sicily,
Open an entrance for the wasteful° sea, *destructive*
Whose billows, beating the resistless banks,
Shall overflow it with their refluence.° *flowing back*

CALLAPINE Well, Governor, since thou hast broke the league
By flat denial of the promised tribute,
Talk not of razing down your city walls;
You shall not need trouble yourselves so far.
For Selim Calymath shall come himself,
And with brass bullets batter down your towers,

4. Barabas gives popular but inaccurate accounts of the deaths of Alexander the Great in 323 B.C.E. and Pope Alexander VI in 1503.

5. As one of his twelve labors, Hercules had to slay the Lernaean Hydra, a huge water snake; hebon is a poison; Cocytus is the river of lamentation in Hades; the river Styx ("Stygian pool") is the chief river in Hades.

6. (1) Temperamental horses; (2) wanton women. Henry VIII described his fourth wife, Anne of Cleves, as a "Flanders mare" in 1539.

7. (1) With poisoned powder; (2) in haste.

3.5. The senate house.

And turn proud Malta to a wilderness
For these intolerable wrongs of yours.
And so farewell.
FERNEZE Farewell! [*Exeunt Bashaw and his janizaries.*]
And now, you men of Malta, look about,
And let's provide to welcome Calymath.
Close your portcullis,° charge your basilisks,° *grated gate / cannons*
And as you profitably° take up arms, *in a worthy cause*
So now courageously encounter them;
For by this answer, broken is the league,
And naught is to be looked for now but wars,
And naught to us more welcome is than wars. *Exeunt.*

[3.6]

Enter [*the*] *two friars* [*Jacomo and Bernardine*].

JACOMO Oh, brother, brother, all the nuns are sick,
And physic° will not help them! They must die. *medicine*
BERNARDINE The abbess sent for me to be confessed.
Oh, what a sad confession will there be!
JACOMO And so did fair Maria send for me.
I'll to her lodging; hereabouts she lies.° *Exit.* *lodges*
Enter Abigail.
BERNARDINE What, all dead save only Abigail?
ABIGAIL And I shall die too, for I feel death coming.
Where is the friar that conversed with me?° *(see 3.3.55–82)*
BERNARDINE Oh, he is gone to see the other nuns.
ABIGAIL I sent for him, but, seeing you are come,
Be you my ghostly father;° and first know *confessor*
That in this house I lived religiously,
Chaste, and devout, much sorrowing for my sins.
But ere I came—
BERNARDINE What then?
ABIGAIL I did offend high heaven so grievously
As I am almost desperate for my sins;
And one offense torments me more than all.
You knew Mathias and Don Lodowick?
BERNARDINE Yes. What of them?
ABIGAIL My father did contract me to 'em both:
First to Don Lodowick; him I never loved.
Mathias was the man that I held dear,
And for his sake did I become a nun.
BERNARDINE So. Say, how was their end?
ABIGAIL Both, jealous of my love, envied each other;
And by my father's practice,° which is there *cunning*
Set down at large° [*giving a paper*], the gallants were both slain. *at length*
BERNARDINE Oh, monstrous villainy!
ABIGAIL To work my peace,° this I confess to thee. *spiritual peace*
Reveal it not, for then my father dies.
BERNARDINE Know that confession must not be revealed;
The canon law forbids it, and the priest

3.6. The convent.

That makes it known, being degraded° first, *defrocked*
Shall be condemned and then sent to the fire.
ABIGAIL So I have heard. Pray therefore keep it close.° *secret*
Death seizeth on my heart. Ah, gentle friar!
Convert my father that he may be saved,
And witness that I die a Christian! [*She dies.*]
BERNARDINE Ay, and a virgin, too. That grieves me most.[1]
But I must to the Jew and exclaim on° him, *cry out against*
And make him stand in fear of me.

Enter the first friar [Jacomo].

JACOMO Oh, brother, all the nuns are dead! Let's bury them.
BERNARDINE First help to bury this;° then go with me *(Abigail)*
And help me to exclaim against the Jew.
JACOMO Why, what has he done?
BERNARDINE A thing that makes me tremble to unfold.
JACOMO What, has he crucified a child?[2]
BERNARDINE No, but a worse thing. 'Twas told me in shrift.° *confession*
Thou know'st 'tis death an if° it be revealed. *an if = if*
Come, let's away. *Exeunt [carrying the dead Abigail].*

4.1

Enter Barabas [and] Ithamore. Bells within.

BARABAS There is no music to° a Christian's knell. *comparable to*
How sweet the bells ring, now the nuns are dead,
That sound at other times like tinkers' pans!
I was afraid the poison had not wrought,° *taken effect*
Or, though it wrought, it would have done no good,
For every year they swell, and yet they live.[1]
Now all are dead; not one remains alive.
ITHAMORE That's brave, master! But think you it will not be known?
BARABAS How can it, if we two be secret?
ITHAMORE For my part, fear you not.
BARABAS I'd cut thy throat if I did.
ITHAMORE And reason,° too. *with reason*
But here's a royal° monastery hard by. *royally sponsored*
Good master, let me poison all the monks.
BARABAS Thou shalt not need, for, now the nuns are dead,
They'll die with grief.
ITHAMORE Do you not sorrow for your daughter's death?
BARABAS No, but I grieve because she lived so long.
An Hebrew born, and would become a Christian!
Cazzo, diavola!° *(a vulgar Italian oath)*

Enter the two friars [Jacomo and Bernardine].

1. Even more than for Abigail's death, Bernardine grieves because Abigail died without having enjoyed sexual experience. (Ironic, since chastity is a Christian virtue. Presumably Bernardine would have liked to have enjoyed sex with her during her "confession" to him. The idea was a standard anti-Catholic smear.)
2. Jews were unjustly accused of such crimes.

4.1. Barabas' house.
1. Barabas jests that he thought his poison might have no discernible effect on the nuns, since they swell with pregnancy every year and manage to live through that; therefore, a midriff swollen with poison would hardly be noticed. This is more anti-Catholic slander.

ITHAMORE Look, look, master, here come two religious caterpillars.° *wool-clad parasites*

BARABAS I smelt 'em ere they came.

ITHAMORE God-a-mercy, nose![2] Come, let's be gone.

[*Barabas and Ithamore start to leave.*]

BERNARDINE Stay, wicked Jew! Repent, I say, and stay!

JACOMO Thou hast offended, therefore must be damned.

BARABAS [*aside to Ithamore*] I fear they know we sent the poisoned broth.

ITHAMORE [*aside to Barabas*] And so do I, master. Therefore, speak 'em fair.° *flatter them*

BERNARDINE Barabas, thou hast—

JACOMO Ay, that thou hast—

BARABAS True, I have money; what though I have?

BERNARDINE Thou art a—

JACOMO Ay, that thou art a—

BARABAS What needs all this? I know I am a Jew.

BERNARDINE Thy daughter—

JACOMO Ay, thy daughter—

BARABAS Oh, speak not of her! Then I die with grief.

BERNARDINE Remember that—

JACOMO Ay, remember that—

BARABAS I must needs say that I have been a great usurer.

BERNARDINE Thou hast committed—

BARABAS Fornication?
But that was in another country,
And besides, the wench is dead.

BERNARDINE Ay, but Barabas, remember Mathias and Don Lodowick.

BARABAS Why, what of them?

BERNARDINE I will not say that by a forged challenge they met.

BARABAS [*aside to Ithamore*] She has confessed, and we are both undone.
[*Aloud*] My bosom inmates!° (*Aside*) But I must dissemble. *dearest companions*
[*Aloud*] Oh, holy friars, the burden of my sins
Lie heavy on my soul. Then, pray you, tell me:
Is't not too late now to turn Christian?
I have been zealous in the Jewish faith,
Hard-hearted to the poor, a covetous wretch,
That would for lucre's sake have sold my soul.
A hundred for a hundred° I have ta'en, *100% interest*
And now for store of wealth may I compare
With all the Jews in Malta. But what is wealth?
I am a Jew, and therefore am I lost.° *damned*
Would penance serve for this my sin,
I could afford to whip myself to death—

ITHAMORE [*aside*] And so could I; but penance will not serve.

BARABAS To fast, to pray, and wear a shirt of hair,
And on my knees creep to Jerusalem.
Cellars of wine and sollars° full of wheat, *lofts, granaries*

2. I.e., Thank God for a nose of such wonderful sensitivity! (A sardonic use of a defamatory stereotype about Jewish noses; see 2.3.177 and note. Ithamore could be speaking in an aside here, but his similar remark at 2.3.177 is said directly to Barabas.)

Warehouses stuffed with spices and with drugs,
Whole chests of gold, in bullion and in coin,
Besides I know not how much weight in pearl,
Orient° and round, have I within my house; *Lustrous*
At Alexandria, merchandise unsold.° *not yet sold*
But° yesterday two ships went from this town; *Only*
Their voyage will be worth ten thousand crowns.
In Florence, Venice, Antwerp, London, Seville,
Frankfurt, Lübeck, Moscow, and where not,
Have I debts owing, and, in most of these,
Great sums of money lying in the banco.° *bank*
All this I'll give to some religious house,
So I may be baptized and live therein.

JACOMO Oh, good Barabas, come to our house!

BERNARDINE Oh, no, good Barabas, come to our house!
And, Barabas, you know—

BARABAS [*to Barnardine*] I know that I have highly sinned.
You shall convert me; you shall have all my wealth.

JACOMO Oh, Barabas, their laws are strict.

BARABAS [*to Jacomo*] I know they are, and I will be with you.

JACOMO They wear no shirts, and they go barefoot too.

BARABAS Then 'tis not for me; and I am resolved
You shall confess me, and have all my goods.

BERNARDINE Good Barabas, come to me!

BARABAS [*to Jacomo*] You see I answer him, and yet he stays.
Rid him away, and go you home with me.

JACOMO [*to Barabas*] I'll be with you tonight.

BARABAS [*to Jacomo*] Come to my house at one o'clock this night.

JACOMO [*to Bernardine*] You hear your answer, and you may be gone.

BERNARDINE Why, go get you away.

JACOMO I will not go for thee.° *at your bidding*

BERNARDINE Not? Then I'll make thee, rogue.

JACOMO How, dost call me rogue? [*They*] *fight.*

ITHAMORE Part 'em, master, part 'em!

BARABAS This is mere frailty. Brethren, be content.
Friar Bernardine, go you with Ithamore.
[*Aside to Bernardine*] You know my mind; let me alone with him.° *let me deal with him*

JACOMO Why does he go to thy house? Let him be gone.

BARABAS [*aside to Bernardine*] I'll give him something, and so stop his mouth. *Exit* [*Ithamore with Bernardine*].
I never heard of any man but he° *(Bernardine)*
Maligned the order of the Jacobins.° *Dominican friars*
But do you think that I believe his words?
Why, brother, you converted Abigail,
And I am bound in charity to requite° it; *repay; revenge*
And so I will. Oh, Jacomo, fail not, but come!

JACOMO But, Barabas, who shall be your godfathers?
For presently you shall be shrived.° *given absolution*

BARABAS Marry, the Turk° shall be one of my godfathers; *(Ithamore)*
But not a word to any of your convent.

JACOMO I warrant° thee, Barabas. *Exit.* *assure*

BARABAS So, now the fear is past, and I am safe,

For he that shrived her° is within my house. *(Bernardine)*
What if I murdered him ere Jacomo comes?
Now I have such a plot for both their lives
As never Jew or Christian knew the like.
One turned° my daughter; therefore he shall die. *Jacomo converted*
The other° knows enough to have my life; *(Bernardine)*
Therefore 'tis not requisite he should° live. *it's needful that he not*
But are not both these wise men to suppose
That I will leave my house, my goods, and all,
To fast and be well whipped? I'll none of that.
Now, Friar Bernardine, I come to you.
I'll feast you, lodge you, give you fair words,
And after that, I and my trusty Turk—
No more but so:° it must and shall be done. *Without further ado*

Enter Ithamore.

Ithamore, tell me, is the friar asleep?

ITHAMORE Yes; and I know not what the reason is,
Do what I can, he will not strip himself,
Nor go to bed, but sleeps in his own clothes.
I fear me he mistrusts what we intend.

BARABAS No, 'tis an order° which the friars use. *religious rule*
Yet if° he knew our meanings,° could he scape? *even if / intent*

ITHAMORE No, none can hear him, cry he ne'er so loud.

BARABAS Why, true. Therefore did I place him there.
The other chambers open towards the street.

ITHAMORE You loiter, master. Wherefore stay° we thus? *hesitate, delay*
Oh, how I long to see him shake his heels!° *dangle from a rope*

[*Bernardine is discovered asleep by the drawing apart of curtains.*]

BARABAS Come on, sirrah,
Off with your girdle, make a handsome noose.
Friar, awake! [*They put Bernardine's rope belt around his neck as a noose.*]

BERNARDINE What, do you mean to strangle me?

ITHAMORE Yes, 'cause you use to confess.° *practice confession*

BARABAS Blame not us, but the proverb "Confess and be hanged." [*To Ithamore*] Pull hard.

BERNARDINE What, will you have my life?

BARABAS [*to Ithamore*] Pull hard, I say! [*To Bernardine*] You would have had my goods.

ITHAMORE Ay, and our lives too. Therefore, pull amain.° *with all your might*
'Tis neatly done, sir. Here's no print° at all. *mark on the neck*

BARABAS Then is it as it should be. Take him up.

ITHAMORE Nay, master, be ruled by me a little. [*He stands up the body.*] So. Let him lean upon his staff. [*He adjusts the body.*] Excellent! He stands as if he were begging of bacon.

BARABAS Who would not think but that this friar lived?
What time o'night is't now, sweet Ithamore?

ITHAMORE Towards one.

BARABAS Then will not Jacomo be long from hence.

[*They conceal themselves.*]

Enter Jacomo.

JACOMO This is the hour wherein I shall proceed.° *prosper*
Oh, happy hour, wherein I shall convert
An infidel, and bring his gold into our treasury!
But soft,° is not this Bernardine? It is; *wait a minute*
And, understanding I should come this way,
Stands here o'purpose, meaning me some wrong,
And intercept° my going to the Jew.— *meaning to cut off*
Bernardine!
Wilt thou not speak? Thou think'st I see thee not.
Away, I'd wish thee, and let me go by.
No? Wilt thou not? Nay, then, I'll force my way.
And see, a staff stands ready for the purpose.
Strike him; he falls.
As thou lik'st that, stop me another time.

Enter Barabas [and Ithamore from concealment].

BARABAS Why, how now, Jacomo, what hast thou done?
JACOMO Why, stricken him that would have struck at me.
BARABAS Who is it? Bernardine? Now out,° alas, he is slain! *(expression of dismay)*
ITHAMORE Ay, master, he's slain. Look how his brains drop out on's° nose. *of his*
JACOMO Good sirs, I have done't, but nobody knows it but you two, I may escape.
BARABAS So might my man and I hang with you for company.° *as accomplices*
ITHAMORE No, let us bear him to the magistrates.
JACOMO Good Barabas, let me go.
BARABAS No, pardon me, the law must have his° course. *its*
I must be forced to give in evidence° *to testify*
That, being importuned by this Bernardine
To be a Christian, I shut him out,
And there he sat. Now I, to keep my word
And give my goods and substance to your house,
Was up thus early with intent to go
Unto your friary, because you stayed.° *waited; delayed*
ITHAMORE Fie upon 'em, master. Will you turn Christian, when holy friars turn devils and murder one another?
BARABAS No. For° this example I'll remain a Jew. *Taught by*
Heaven bless me! What, a friar a murderer?
When shall you see a Jew commit the like?
ITHAMORE Why, a Turk could ha' done no more.
BARABAS Tomorrow is the sessions; you shall to it.—
Come, Ithamore, let's help to take him hence.
JACOMO Villains, I am a sacred person. Touch me not.
BARABAS The law shall touch you. We'll but lead you, we.
'Las, I could weep at your calamity!
[*To Ithamore*] Take in the staff too, for that must be shown.
Law wills° that each particular be known. *Exeunt.* *requires*

[4.2]

Enter courtesan [Bellamira] and Pilia-Borza.

BELLAMIRA Pilia-Borza, didst thou meet with Ithamore?

PILIA-BORZA I did.

BELLAMIRA And didst thou deliver my letter?

PILIA-BORZA I did.

BELLAMIRA And what think'st thou, will he come?

PILIA-BORZA I think so, and yet I cannot tell, for at the reading of the letter he looked like a man of another world.° [*like a ghost*]

BELLAMIRA Why so?

PILIA-BORZA That such a base slave as he should be saluted° [*greeted*] by such a tall° [*brave*] man as I am, from such a beautiful dame as you.

BELLAMIRA And what said he?

PILIA-BORZA Not a wise word; only gave me a nod, as who should° [*as if one were to*] say, "Is it even so?"; and so I left him, being driven to a nonplus° [*state of confusion*] at the critical aspect[1] of my terrible countenance.

BELLAMIRA And where didst meet him?

PILIA-BORZA Upon mine own freehold,° [*i.e., territory, turf*] within forty foot of the gallows, conning his neck-verse,[2] I take it, looking of a friar's° [*witnessing Jacomo's*] execution, whom I saluted with an old hempen[3] proverb, "*Hodie tibi, cras mihi,*"[4] and so I left him to the mercy of the hangman; but the exercise° [*ceremony*] being done, see where he comes.

Enter Ithamore.

ITHAMORE [*to himself*] I never knew a man take his death so patiently as this friar. He was ready to leap off ere the halter was about his neck, and when the hangman had put on his hempen tippet,° [*neck-band, i.e., noose*] he made such haste to his prayers as if he had had another cure° [*parish*] to serve. Well, go whither he will, I'll be none of his followers in haste. And now I think on't, going to the execution, a fellow met me with a muschatoes° [*mustache*] like a raven's wing and a dagger with a hilt like a warming pan,° [*bed warming pan*] and he gave me a letter from one Madam Bellamira, saluting me in such sort° [*fashion*] as if he had meant to make clean my boots with his lips; the effect° [*purport*] was that I should come to her house. I wonder what the reason is. It may be she sees more in me than I can find in myself, for she writes further that she loves me ever since she saw me; and who would not requite such love? Here's her house, and here she comes, and now would I were gone! I am not worthy to look upon her.

PILIA-BORZA [*to Bellamira*] This is the gentleman you writ to.

ITHAMORE [*aside*] "Gentleman"! He flouts° me. What gentry° [*mocks / gentlemanliness*] can be in a poor Turk of tenpence? I'll be gone.

BELLAMIRA Is't not a sweet-faced youth, Pilia?

4.2. Bellamira's house.

1. Look, expression. (Also with a suggestion of malign planetary influence.)
2. Ithamore was trying to memorize the fifty-first psalm (*Miserere mei*) in order to be able to recite it in Latin, to enable him to escape hanging by virtue of being learned.
3. (1) Homespun; (2) made of rope, like a noose.
4. "Today your turn, tomorrow mine."

ITHAMORE [*aside*] Again, "sweet youth"! [*To Pilia-Borza*] Did not you, sir, bring the "sweet youth" a letter?

PILIA-BORZA I did, sir, and from this gentlewoman, who, as myself and the rest of the family,° stand or fall[5] at your service. *household*

BELLAMIRA Though woman's modesty should hale° me back, *hold*
I can withhold no longer.—Welcome, sweet love!

ITHAMORE [*aside*] Now am I clean,° or rather foully, out of the way.° [*He starts to leave.*] *wholly* *going wrong*

BELLAMIRA Whither so soon?

ITHAMORE [*aside*] I'll go steal some money from my master to make me handsome. [*To her*] Pray pardon me. I must go see a ship discharged.° *unloaded*

BELLAMIRA Canst thou be so unkind to leave me thus?

PILIA-BORZA An° ye did but know how she loves you, sir! *If only*

ITHAMORE [*aside*] Nay, I care not how much she loves me. [*To her*] Sweet Bellamira, would I had my master's wealth for thy sake!

PILIA-BORZA And you can have it, sir, an if you please.

ITHAMORE If 'twere above ground I could and would have it, but he hides and buries it up as partridges do their eggs, under the earth.

PILIA-BORZA And is't not possible to find it out?

ITHAMORE By no means possible.

BELLAMIRA [*aside to Pilia-Borza*] What shall we do with this base villain, then?

PILIA-BORZA [*aside to her*] Let me alone.° Do you but speak him fair. *Leave it to me*
[*To Ithamore*] But you know some secrets of the Jew,
Which, if they were revealed, would do him harm.

ITHAMORE Ay, and such as—
Go to, no more. I'll make him send me
Half he has, and glad he scapes so, too.
Pen and ink!
I'll write unto him; we'll have money straight.

PILIA-BORZA Send for a hundred crowns at least.

ITHAMORE Ten hundred thousand crowns. (*He writes.*) "Master Barabas—"

PILIA-BORZA Write not so submissively, but threat'ning him.

ITHAMORE "Sirrah Barabas, send me a hundred crowns."

PILIA-BORZA Put in two hundred at least.

ITHAMORE "I charge thee send me three hundred by this bearer, and this shall be your warrant. If you do not, no more but so."[6]

PILIA-BORZA Tell him you will confess.

ITHAMORE "Otherwise I'll confess all." [*To Pilia-Borza*] Vanish, and return in a twinkle.

PILIA-BORZA Let me alone. I'll use him in his kind.° [*Exit.*] *as his kind deserves*

ITHAMORE Hang him, Jew!

BELLAMIRA Now, gentle Ithamore, lie in my lap.
[*Calling*] Where are my maids? Provide a running banquet.° *light repast*
Send to the merchant; bid him bring me silks.

5. Prosper or do poorly. (Also with a sexual suggestion of erection and detumescence.)

6. Ithamore hints darkly at some dire reprisal.

Shall Ithamore my love go° in such rags? *go about*

ITHAMORE And bid the jeweler come hither, too.

BELLAMIRA I have no husband, sweet; I'll marry thee.

ITHAMORE Content.° But we will leave this paltry land *Agreed*
And sail from hence to Greece, to lovely Greece.
I'll be thy Jason, thou my Golden Fleece.[7]
Where painted carpets o'er the meads are hurled[8]
And Bacchus'° vineyards overspread the world, *god of wine*
Where woods and forests go in goodly green,
I'll be Adonis, thou shalt be Love's queen.[9]
The meads, the orchards, and the primrose lanes,
Instead of sedge and reed, bear sugarcanes.
Thou in those groves, by Dis above,[1]
Shalt live with me and be my love.

BELLAMIRA Whither will I not go with gentle Ithamore?

Enter Pilia-Borza.

ITHAMORE How now? Hast thou the gold?

PILIA-BORZA Yes.

ITHAMORE But came it freely? Did the cow give down her milk freely?

PILIA-BORZA At reading of the letter, he stared and stamped, and turned aside. I took him by the beard, and looked upon him thus,[2] told him he were best to° send it. Then he hugged and embraced me. *he had better*

ITHAMORE Rather for fear than love.

PILIA-BORZA Then like a Jew he laughed and jeered, and told me he loved me for your sake, and said what a faithful servant you had been.

ITHAMORE The more villain he to keep me thus. Here's goodly 'parel, is there not?[3]

PILIA-BORZA To conclude, he gave me ten crowns.° *(as a tip)*

ITHAMORE But ten? I'll not leave him worth a gray groat.° Give me a ream° of paper. We'll have a kingdom of gold for't. *small coin* *(punning on "realm")*

PILIA-BORZA Write for five hundred crowns.

ITHAMORE [*writing*] "Sirrah Jew, as you love your life, send me five hundred crowns, and give the bearer one hundred."° Tell him I must have't. *(as a tip)*

PILIA-BORZA I warrant Your Worship shall have't.

ITHAMORE And if he ask why I demand so much, tell him I scorn to write a line under° a hundred crowns. *for anything less than*

PILIA-BORZA You'd make a rich poet, sir. I am gone. *Exit.*

ITHAMORE [*to Bellamira*] Take thou the money. Spend it for my sake.

BELLAMIRA 'Tis not thy money, but thyself I weigh.° *hold worthy*
[*Throwing the money aside*] Thus Bellamira esteems of gold!
But thus of thee. *Kiss him.*

ITHAMORE [*aside*] That kiss again! She runs division of my lips.[4]

7. Jason sailed with the Argonauts in quest of the Golden Fleece.

8. Where meadows are carpeted with flowers.

9. Venus ("Love's queen") fell in love with Adonis, a handsome young mortal—with tragic consequences.

1. Ithamore seemingly invokes Dis, or Pluto (Hades), as an Olympian god, though in fact he ruled the underworld. Lines 97–107 parody Marlowe's well-known lyric "The Passionate Shepherd to His Love," which begins, "Come live with me and be my love."

2. At "thus," Pilia-Borza presumably makes a fierce face.

3. Ithamore complains that Barabas affords him only wretched clothing.

4. She executes musical flourishes on my lips.

What an eye she casts on me! It twinkles like a star.
BELLAMIRA Come, my dear love, let's in and sleep together.
ITHAMORE Oh, that ten thousand nights were put in one,
That we might sleep seven years together afore we wake!
BELLAMIRA Come, amorous wag.° First banquet and then sleep. [*Exeunt.*] — *scalawag*

[4.3]

Enter Barabas reading a letter.[1]

BARABAS "Barabas, send me three hundred crowns."
Plain "Barabas." Oh, that wicked courtesan!
He was not wont° to call me "Barabas." — *accustomed*
"Or else I will confess." Ay, there it goes!
But if I get him, *coupe de gorge*° for that. — *cut the throat*
He sent a shaggy, tattered, staring slave,° — *lunatic ruffian*
That when he speaks draws out his grisly beard
And winds it twice or thrice about his ear;
Whose face has been a grindstone for men's swords;
His hands are hacked, some fingers cut quite off;
Who, when he speaks, grunts like a hog, and looks
Like one that is employed in catzerie° — *swindling*
And crossbiting;° such a rogue — *con artistry*
As is the husband° to a hundred whores— — *pimp*
And I by him must send three hundred crowns!
Well, my hope is he° will not stay there still;° — *(Ithamore) / forever*
And when he comes—Oh, that he were but here!

Enter Pilia-Borza.

PILIA-BORZA Jew, I must ha' more gold.
BARABAS Why, want'st thou any of thy tale?[2]
PILIA-BORZA No; but three hundred will not serve his turn.
BARABAS Not serve his turn, sir?
PILIA-BORZA No, sir; and therefore I must have five hundred more.
BARABAS I'll rather—
PILIA-BORZA Oh, good words,° sir; and send it, you were best. — *i.e., take it easy*
See, there's his letter. [*He presents another letter.*]
BARABAS Might he not as well come as send? Pray bid him come and fetch it. What he writes for you,° ye shall have straight. — *for your tip*
PILIA-BORZA Ay, and the rest too, or else—
BARABAS [*aside*] I must make this villain away.° [*Aloud*] Please you dine with me, sir, and you shall be most heartily—(*aside*) poisoned. — *do away with him*
PILIA-BORZA No, God-a-mercy.° Shall I have these crowns? — *thanks*
BARABAS I cannot do it. I have lost my keys.
PILIA-BORZA Oh, if that be all, I can pick ope your locks.
BARABAS Or climb up to my countinghouse window? You know my meaning.[3]

4.3. Barabas' house.
1. Ithamore's first letter; see 4.2.78–87.
2. Are you lacking any part of what you asked for?
3. I.e., You know I'm onto your tricks and am aware that you climbed up to the room where I count my money in order to rob me. (See 3.1.15–23.)

PILIA-BORZA I know enough, and therefore talk not to me of your countinghouse. The gold,° or know, Jew, it is in my power to hang thee. *Give me the gold*

BARABAS [*aside*] I am betrayed.
[*To him*] 'Tis not five hundred crowns that I esteem;
I am not moved° at that. This angers me: *angered*
That he who knows I love him as myself
Should write in this imperious vein. Why, sir,
You know I have no child, and unto whom
Should I leave all but unto Ithamore?

PILIA-BORZA Here's many words, but no crowns. The crowns!

BARABAS Commend me to him, sir, most humbly,
And unto your good mistress, as unknown.° *not yet known to me*

PILIA-BORZA Speak, shall I have 'em, sir?

BARABAS Sir, here they are. [*He gives money.*]
[*Aside*] Oh, that I should part with so much gold!
[*To him*] Here, take 'em, fellow, with as good a will—
(*Aside*) As I would see thee hanged. [*To him*] Oh, love stops my breath!
Never loved man servant as I do Ithamore.

PILIA-BORZA I know it, sir.

BARABAS Pray when, sir, shall I see you at my house?

PILIA-BORZA Soon enough, to your cost, sir. Fare you well.
Exit.

BARABAS Nay, to thine own cost, villain, if thou com'st.
Was ever Jew tormented as I am?
To have a shag-rag knave to come demand
Three hundred crowns, and then five hundred crowns!
Well, I must seek a means to rid 'em all,
And presently, for in his villainy
He will tell all he knows, and I shall die for't.
I have it!
I will in some disguise go see the slave,
And how the villain revels with my gold. *Exit.*

[4.4]

Enter courtesan [Bellamira], Ithamore, [and] Pilia-Borza.

BELLAMIRA I'll pledge° thee, love, and therefore drink it off. *drink to*

ITHAMORE Say'st thou me so? Have at it!° And, do you hear? *Here goes!*
[*He whispers.*][1]

BELLAMIRA Go to, it shall be so.

ITHAMORE Of° that condition I will drink it up. *On*
Here's to thee! [*He drinks.*]

BELLAMIRA Nay, I'll have all or none.[2]

ITHAMORE [*finishing off*] There. If thou lov'st me, do not leave a drop.

BELLAMIRA Love thee?—Fill me three glasses!

ITHAMORE Three-and-fifty dozen I'll pledge thee.

4.4. Bellamira's house.
1. Probably Ithamore suggests that they make love.
2. Bellamira (who wants to get Ithamore drunk) insists that Ithamore drain his cup. He replies by bidding her to finish in her turn.

PILIA-BORZA Knavely spoke, and like a knight-at-arms.

ITHAMORE Hey! *Rivo Castiliano!*° A man's a man. *Let the drink flow!*

BELLAMIRA Now to the Jew.[3]

ITHAMORE Ha, to the Jew! "And send me money, you were best."

PILIA-BORZA What wouldst thou do if he should send thee none?

ITHAMORE Do nothing; but I know what I know. He's a murderer.

BELLAMIRA I had not thought he had been so brave a man.

ITHAMORE You knew Mathias and the Governor's son? He and I killed 'em both, and yet never touched 'em.

PILIA-BORZA Oh, bravely done!

ITHAMORE I carried the broth that poisoned the nuns, and he and I—snickle, hand to! Fast![4]—strangled a friar.

BELLAMIRA You two alone?

ITHAMORE We two, and 'twas never known, nor never shall be, for me.° *for my part*

PILIA-BORZA [*aside to Bellamira*] This shall with me unto the Governor.

BELLAMIRA [*aside to Pilia-Borza*] And fit it should; but first let's ha' more gold.

[*To Ithamore*] Come, gentle Ithamore, lie in my lap.

ITHAMORE "Love me little, love me long."° Let music rumble, *(probably a song)*
Whilst I in thy incony[5] lap do tumble.

Enter Barabas with a lute, disguised.

BELLAMIRA A French musician! Come, let's hear your skill.

BARABAS Must tuna my lute for sound—twang, twang!—first.

ITHAMORE Wilt drink, Frenchman? Here's to thee with a—[*He hiccups.*] Pox on this drunken hiccup!

BARABAS Gramercy,° monsieur. *Many thanks*

BELLAMIRA Prithee, Pilia-Borza, bid the fiddler give me the posy° in his hat there. *nosegay, bouquet*

PILIA-BORZA [*to Barabas*] Sirrah, you must give my mistress your posy.

BARABAS *À votre commandement,° madame.* *As you wish*
[*He gives her his bouquet.*]

BELLAMIRA How sweet, my Ithamore, the flowers smell!

ITHAMORE Like thy breath, sweetheart; no violet like 'em.

PILIA-BORZA Foh! Methinks they stink like a hollyhock.

BARABAS [*aside*] So, now I am revenged upon 'em all.
The scent thereof was death; I poisoned it.

ITHAMORE Play, fiddler, or I'll cut your cat's guts into chitterlings.[6]

BARABAS *Pardonnez-moi*, be no in tune yet. [*He tunes.*] So, now, now all be in.

ITHAMORE [*to Pilia-Borza*] Give him a crown, and fill° me out more wine. *pour*

PILIA-BORZA [*giving money*] There's two crowns for thee. Play!

3. (1) Now let's drink to Barabas; (2) now let's write him a letter.
4. Strangle him, hold tight! Hold fast!
5. Fine, delicate. (With a suggestion of "in cunny," meaning "inside her sex.")
6. Ithamore threatens to cut Barabas' guts until they look like pig's intestines. (With verbal play on the fact that cat guts were used to string instruments.)

BARABAS (*aside*) How liberally the villain gives me mine own gold!

PILIA-BORZA Methinks he fingers very well.

BARABAS (*aside*) So did you when you stole my gold.[7]

PILIA-BORZA How swift he runs!° *plays passages*

BARABAS (*aside*) You run° swifter when you threw my gold out of my window. *ran*

BELLAMIRA Musician, hast been in Malta long?

BARABAS Two, three, four month, madam.

ITHAMORE Dost not know a Jew, one Barabas?

BARABAS Very mush, monsieur. You no be his man?

PILIA-BORZA His man?

ITHAMORE I scorn the peasant. Tell him so.

BARABAS [*aside*] He knows it already.

ITHAMORE 'Tis a strange thing of that Jew: he lives upon pickled grasshoppers and sauced mushrooms.

BARABAS (*aside*) What a slave's this! The Governor feeds not as I do.

ITHAMORE He never put on clean shirt since he was circumcised.

BARABAS (*aside*) Oh, rascal! I change myself twice a day.

ITHAMORE The hat he wears Judas left under the elder when he hanged himself.[8]

BARABAS (*aside*) 'Twas sent me for a present from the Great Cham.° *Khan*

PILIA-BORZA A masty° slave he is! [*Barabas prepares to leave.*] Whither now, fiddler? *hoglike, gross*

BARABAS *Pardonnez-moi*, monsieur, me be no well.

PILIA-BORZA Farewell, fiddler. *Exit* [*Barabas*].
One letter more to the Jew.

BELLAMIRA [*to Ithamore*] Prithee, sweet love, one more, and write it sharp.

ITHAMORE No, I'll send by word of mouth now. [*To Pilia-Borza*] Bid him deliver thee a thousand crowns, by the same token that the nuns loved rice, that Friar Bernardine slept in his own clothes—any of 'em will do it.

PILIA-BORZA Let me alone to urge it, now I know the meaning.

ITHAMORE The meaning has a meaning.[9]—Come, let's in.
To undo a Jew is charity and not sin. *Exeunt.*

5.1

Enter Governor [*Ferneze*], *Knights, Martin del Bosco* [*and Officers*].

FERNEZE Now, gentlemen, betake you to your arms
And see that Malta be well fortified.
And it behooves you to be resolute;
For Calymath, having hovered here so long,

7. Playing on "fingers" in line 55, meaning "fingers the strings," Barabas wryly comments that Pilia-Borza "fingered" (with his thief's fingers) Barabas' gold.
8. According to one tradition, Judas hanged himself from an elder tree after betraying Christ.
9. Ithamore hints at dark secrets.
5.1. Malta, near the town walls, and then (at line 61 ff.) outside the walls.

Will win the town or die before the walls.
FIRST KNIGHT And die he shall, for we will never yield.

Enter courtesan [Bellamira and] Pilia-Borza.

BELLAMIRA Oh, bring us to the Governor!
FERNEZE Away with her! She is a courtesan.
BELLAMIRA Whate'er I am, yet, Governor, hear me speak.
I bring thee news by whom thy son was slain:
Mathias did it not, it was the Jew.
PILIA-BORZA Who, besides the slaughter of these gentlemen, poisoned his own daughter and the nuns, strangled a friar, and I know not what mischief beside.
FERNEZE Had we but proof of this!
BELLAMIRA Strong proof, my lord. His man's now at my lodging, that was his agent. He'll confess it all.
FERNEZE [*to the Officers*] Go fetch him straight.
[*Exeunt Officers.*]
I always feared° that Jew. *mistrusted*

Enter [Officers with Barabas the] Jew [and] Ithamore.

BARABAS I'll go alone. Dogs, do not hale me this.
ITHAMORE Nor me neither. I cannot outrun you, Constable.
Oh, my belly![1]
BARABAS [*aside*] One dram of powder more had made all sure.
What a damned slave was I!
FERNEZE Make fires, heat irons, let the rack° be fetched! *torture rack*
FIRST KNIGHT Nay, stay, my lord, 't may be he will confess.
BARABAS Confess? What mean you, lords? Who should confess?
FERNEZE Thou and thy Turk. 'Twas you that slew my son.
ITHAMORE Guilty, my lord! I confess. Your son and Mathias were both contracted unto Abigail; he° forged a counterfeit challenge. *(Barabas)*
BARABAS Who carried that challenge?
ITHAMORE I carried it, I confess, but who writ it? Marry, even he that strangled Bernardine, poisoned the nuns and his own daughter.
FERNEZE Away with him!° His sight is death to me. *(Barabas)*
BARABAS For what? You men of Malta, hear me speak.
She is a courtesan and he a thief,
And he my bondman.° Let me have law,° *slave / justice*
For none of this can prejudice my life.
FERNEZE Once more, away with him! [*To Barabas*] You shall have law.° *the full penalty*
BARABAS Devils, do your worst! I'll live in spite of you.
As these have spoke, so be it to their souls![2]
[*Aside*] I hope the poisoned flowers will work anon.
Exit [Barabas, taken away by the Officers, along with Ithamore, Bellamira, and Pilia-Borza].

Enter mater [Katharine].

1. Ithamore begins to suffer the effects of the poisoned flowers.

2. May their souls get what they deserve for speaking thus!

KATHARINE Was my Mathias murdered by the Jew?
Ferneze, 'twas thy son that murdered him.
FERNEZE Be patient, gentle madam, it was he.
He forged the daring challenge made them fight.[3]
KATHARINE Where is the Jew? Where is that murderer?
FERNEZE In prison, till the law has passed° on him. — *passed sentence*

Enter [the First] Officer.

FIRST OFFICER My lord, the courtesan and her man are dead;
So is the Turk, and Barabas the Jew.
FERNEZE Dead?
FIRST OFFICER Dead, my lord, and here they bring his body.

[Enter Officers and attendants, carrying Barabas as dead.]

BOSCO This sudden death of his is very strange.
FERNEZE Wonder not at it, sir; the heavens are just.
Their deaths were like their lives. Then think not of 'em.
Since they are dead, let them be buried.
For° the Jew's body, throw that o'er the walls — *As for*
To be a prey for vultures and wild beasts.
[Barabas is thrown to one side.]
So, now away and fortify the town.
Exeunt [all but Barabas].
BARABAS [*rising*] What, all alone? Well fare, sleepy drink![4]
I'll be revenged on this accursèd town,
For by my means Calymath shall enter in.
I'll help to slay their children and their wives,
To fire° their churches, pull their houses down, — *set fire to*
Take° my goods too, and seize upon my lands. — *Take back*
I hope to see the Governor a slave,
And, rowing in a galley, whipped to death.

Enter Calymath, Bashaws, [and] Turks.

CALYMATH Whom have we there, a spy?
BARABAS Yes, my good lord, one that can spy a place
Where you may enter and surprise° the town. — *take by surprise*
My name is Barabas; I am a Jew.
CALYMATH Art thou that Jew whose goods we heard were sold
For tribute money?
BARABAS The very same, my lord.
And since that time they have hired° a slave, my man, — *bribed*
To accuse me of a thousand villainies.
I was imprisonèd, but scaped their hands.
CALYMATH Didst break prison?
BARABAS No, no.
I drank of poppy and cold mandrake juice,
And, being asleep, belike° they thought me dead, — *probably, evidently*
And threw me o'er the walls. So, or how else,° — *Thus, or in any case*
The Jew is here, and rests° at your command. — *remains*
CALYMATH 'Twas bravely done. But tell me, Barabas,

3. Barabas forged the dare, in the form of a challenge, that made them fight.

4. Thanks to the soporific drink for saving me! (Barabas drank it to feign death.)

Canst thou, as thou reportest, make Malta ours?
BARABAS Fear not, my lord; for here, against the sluice,[5]
The rock is hollow, and of purpose° digged *on purpose*
To make a passage for the running streams
And common channels° of the city. *sewer drains*
Now whilst you give assault unto the walls,
I'll lead five hundred soldiers through the vault° *manhole*
And rise with them i'th'middle of the town,
Open the gates for you to enter in,
And by this means the city is your own.
CALYMATH If this be true, I'll make thee governor.
BARABAS And if it be not true, then let me die.
CALYMATH Thou'st doomed° thyself. Assault it presently. *You've sentenced*
Exeunt.

[5.2]

Alarms. Enter [*Calymath,*] *Turks,* [*and*] *Barabas* [*as victors*]; *Governor* [*Ferneze*] *and Knights* [*as*] *prisoners.*

CALYMATH Now vail° your pride, you captive Christians, *humble, lower*
And kneel for mercy to your conquering foe.
Now where's the hope you had of haughty Spain?
Ferneze, speak. Had it not been much better
To keep thy promise than be thus surprised?° *taken by surprise*
FERNEZE What should I say? We are captives and must yield.
CALYMATH Ay, villains, you must yield, and under Turkish yokes
Shall groaning bear the burden of our ire;
And Barabas, as erst° we promised thee, *just now*
For thy desert we make thee governor.
Use them° at thy discretion. *(the captive Maltese)*
BARABAS Thanks, my lord.
FERNEZE Oh, fatal day, to fall into the hands
Of such a traitor and unhallowed° Jew! *unholy, wicked*
What greater misery could heaven inflict?
CALYMATH 'Tis our command. And, Barabas, we give,
To guard thy person, these our janizaries.° *elite troops*
Entreat° them well, as we have usèd thee.— *Treat*
And now, brave bashaws, come, we'll walk about
The ruined town and see the wrack° we made. *destruction*
Farewell, brave Jew! Farewell, great Barabas!
BARABAS May all good fortune follow Calymath!
Exeunt [*Calymath and Bashaws*].
And now, as entrance° to our safety, *first step*
To prison with the Governor and these
Captains, his consorts° and confederates. *companions*
FERNEZE Oh, villain! Heaven will be revenged on thee.
BARABAS Away! No more!—Let him not trouble me.
Exeunt [*Ferneze and Knights, under Turkish guard*].
Thus hast thou° gotten, by thy policy, *(said to himself)*
No simple place, no small authority.
I now am Governor of Malta. True,

5. Right next to the main outlet for the town sewer.

5.2. Malta, at the citadel.

But Malta hates me, and, in hating me,
My life's in danger; and what boots° it thee, *avails*
Poor Barabas, to be the governor,
Whenas° thy life shall be at their command? *When, seeing that*
No, Barabas, this must be looked into;
And since by wrong thou got'st authority,
Maintain it bravely by firm policy—
At least unprofitably lose it not.
For he that liveth in authority,
And neither gets him friends nor fills his bags,
Lives like the ass that Aesop speaketh of,° *(in Aesop's fables)*
That labors with a load of bread and wine
And leaves it off° to snap° on thistle tops. *passes it up / graze*
But Barabas will be more circumspect.
Begin betimes;° Occasion's bald behind;[1] *quickly*
Slip not thine opportunity, for fear too late
Thou seek'st for much, but canst not compass° it. *encompass*
[*He calls*] Within there!

Enter Governor [*Ferneze*] *with a guard.*° *under guard*

FERNEZE My lord?
BARABAS [*aside*] Ay, "lord." Thus slaves will learn.
[*To him*] Now, Governor, stand by there. [*To the guard*]
Wait within. [*The guard retires.*]
This is the reason that I sent for thee:
Thou see'st thy life, and Malta's happiness,
Are at my arbitrament,° and Barabas *power to decide*
At his discretion may dispose of both.
Now tell me, Governor, and plainly too,
What think'st thou shall become of it and thee?
FERNEZE This, Barabas: since things are in thy power,
I see no reason but of Malta's wrack,[2]
Nor hope of thee but extreme cruelty;
Nor fear I death, nor will I flatter thee.
BARABAS Governor, good words!° Be not so furious; *speak calmly!*
'Tis not thy life which can avail me aught.
Yet you do live, and live for me° you shall; *for all I care*
And, as for Malta's ruin, think you not
'Twere slender° policy for Barabas *weak, senseless*
To dispossess himself of such a place?
For sith,° as once you said, within this isle, *since*
In Malta here, that I have got° my goods, *acquired*
And in this city still° have had success, *always*
And now at length am grown your governor,
Yourselves shall see it shall not be forgot;
For as a friend not known but in distress[3]
I'll rear up Malta, now remediless.
FERNEZE Will Barabas recover Malta's loss?
Will Barabas be good to Christians?

1. Occasion is traditionally portrayed as bald on the back of the head and with a forelock that a person must seize quickly in order to be successful.
2. I see no reason to expect anything other than the destruction of Malta.
3. For as one not known to be a friend to Malta until distress creates the need for such friendship.

BARABAS What wilt thou give me, Governor, to procure
A dissolution of the slavish bands° *bonds of slavery*
Wherein the Turk hath yoked your land and you?
What will you give me if I render you° *hand over to you*
The life of Calymath, surprise his men,
And in an outhouse of the city° shut *building outside the city*
His soldiers till I have consumed 'em all with fire?
What will you give him that procureth° this? *accomplishes*
FERNEZE Do but bring this to pass which thou pretendest,° *propose*
Deal truly with us as thou intimatest,
And I will send amongst the citizens
And by my letters privately procure
Great sums of money for thy recompense.
Nay, more: do this, and live thou Governor still.
BARABAS Nay, do thou this, Ferneze, and be free.
Governor, I enlarge° thee. Live with me,[4] *set free*
Go walk about the city, see thy friends.
Tush, send not letters to 'em. Go thyself,
And let me see what money thou canst make.° *raise*
Here is my hand that I'll set Malta free.
And thus we cast° it: to a solemn° feast *devise / ceremonial*
I will invite young Selim Calymath,
Where be thou present only to perform
One stratagem that I'll impart to thee,
Wherein no danger shall betide° thy life, *befall*
And I will warrant Malta free forever.
FERNEZE Here is my hand. Believe me, Barabas,
I will be there and do as thou desirest.
When is the time?
BARABAS Governor, presently.
For Calymath, when he hath viewed the town,
Will take his leave and sail toward Ottoman.° *Turkey*
FERNEZE Then will I, Barabas, about this coin,° *set to work raising money*
And bring it with me to thee in the evening.
BARABAS Do so, but fail not. Now farewell, Ferneze.
[*Exit Ferneze.*]
And thus far roundly° goes the business. *briskly*
Thus, loving neither, will I live with both,
Making a profit of my policy;
And he from whom my most advantage comes
Shall be my friend.
This is the life we Jews are used to lead,
And reason,° too, for Christians do the like. *with good reason*
Well, now about effecting this device:
First, to surprise great Selim's soldiers,
And then to make provision for the feast,
That at one instant all things may be done.
My policy detests prevention.[5]
To what event my secret purpose drives,
I know;° and they shall witness with their lives. *Exit.* *I alone know*

4. Live freely as my fellow resident in Malta.
5. My stratagems do everything to avoid being outguessed.

[5.3]

Enter Calymath [and] Bashaws.

CALYMATH Thus have we viewed the city, seen the sack,° *plundering*
And caused the ruins to be new repaired,
Which with our bombards' shot and basilisks'° *types of cannon*
We rent in sunder at our entry.
And now I see the situation—
Two lofty turrets that command the town,
And how secure this conquered island stands
Environed with the Mediterranean Sea,
Strong countermured° with other petty isles, *double-walled*
And toward Calabria backed by Sicily,
Where Syracusian Dionysius reigned[1]—
I wonder how it could be conquered thus.° *given these defenses*

Enter a Messenger.

MESSENGER From Barabas, Malta's governor, I bring
A message unto mighty Calymath:
Hearing his sovereign was bound for sea,
To sail to Turkey, to great Ottoman,
He humbly would entreat Your Majesty
To come and see his homely citadel,
And banquet with him ere thou leav'st the isle.
CALYMATH To banquet with him in his citadel?
I fear me,° messenger, to feast my train° *fear / troops*
Within a town of war so lately pillaged
Will be too costly and too troublesome.
Yet would I gladly visit Barabas,
For well has Barabas deserved of us.
MESSENGER Selim, for° that, thus saith the Governor: *as for*
That he hath in store a pearl so big,
So precious, and withal so orient,° *lustrous*
As, be it valued but indifferently,° *at its least value*
The price thereof will serve to entertain
Selim and all his soldiers for a month.
Therefore he humbly would entreat Your Highness
Not to depart till he has feasted you.
CALYMATH I cannot feast my men in Malta walls,
Except° he place his tables in the streets. *Unless*
MESSENGER Know, Selim, that there is a monastery
Which standeth as an outhouse to the town;
There will he banquet them, but thee at home,
With all thy bashaws and brave followers.
CALYMATH Well, tell the Governor we grant his suit.
We'll in this summer evening feast with him.
MESSENGER I shall, my lord. *Exit.*
CALYMATH And now, bold bashaws, let us to our tents,
And meditate how we may grace us° best *adorn ourselves*
To solemnize our governor's great feast. *Exeunt.*

5.3. Calymath's encampment.
1. Dionysius of Syracuse was renowned as a tyrant (r. 405–367 B.C.E.).

[5.4]

Enter Governor [*Ferneze*], *Knights,* [*and*] *del Bosco.*

FERNEZE In this, my countrymen, be ruled by me:
Have special care that no man sally forth
Till you shall hear a culverin° discharged — *a cannon*
By him that bears the linstock,[1] kindled thus;
Then issue out and come to rescue me,
For happily° I shall be in distress, — *haply, perchance*
Or you releasèd of this servitude.
FIRST KNIGHT Rather than thus to live as Turkish thralls,° — *slaves, captives*
What will we not adventure?
FERNEZE On, then, begone.
KNIGHTS Farewell, grave° Governor. — *honored, noble*
[*Exeunt.*]

[5.5]

Enter [*Barabas*] *with a hammer, above, very busy* [*assisted by carpenters*].[1]

BARABAS How stand the cords? How hang these hinges, fast?
Are all the cranes and pulleys sure?
A CARPENTER All fast.
BARABAS Leave nothing loose, all leveled to my mind.° — *done as I wish it*
Why, now I see that you have art° indeed! — *skill*
There, carpenters, divide that gold amongst you.
[*He gives them money.*]
Go swill in bowls of sack° and muscadine. — *white Spanish wine*
Down to the cellar, taste of all my wines.
CARPENTERS We shall, my lord, and thank you.
Exeunt [*carpenters*].
BARABAS And if you like them, drink your fill—and die;
For, so° I live, perish may all the world. — *so long as*
Now, Selim Calymath, return me word
That thou wilt come, and I am satisfied.

Enter Messenger.

Now, sirrah, what, will he come?
MESSENGER He will; and has commanded all his men
To come ashore and march through Malta streets,
That thou mayst feast them in thy citadel. [*Exit.*]
BARABAS Then now are all things as my wish would have 'em.
There wanteth nothing but the Governor's pelf°— — *Ferneze's money*

Enter Governor [*Ferneze, with a bag of money*].

And see, he brings it!—Now, Governor, the sum?
FERNEZE With free consent, a hundred thousand pounds.

5.4. Ferneze's place of assembling his allies.
1. A forked staff holding the lighted material used to fire a cannon.

5.5. Barabas' citadel.
1. The acting area *"above"* represents Barabas' gallery, fitted out with a trapdoor.

BARABAS Pounds, say'st thou, Governor? Well, since it is no more,
I'll satisfy myself with that. [*Ferneze offers the money.*]
Nay, keep it still,
For if I keep not promise, trust not me.
And, Governor, now partake° my policy.° *be acquainted with / plan*
First, for his army: they are sent before,
Entered the monastery, and underneath
In several places are fieldpieces° pitched, *light cannons*
Bombards,° whole barrels full of gunpowder, *Cannons*
That on the sudden shall dissever it° *blow up the monastery*
And batter all the stones about their ears,
Whence none can possibly escape alive.
Now, as for Calymath and his consorts,° *companions*
Here have I made a dainty° gallery, *ingeniously designed*
The floor whereof, this cable being cut,
Doth fall asunder, so that it doth sink
Into a deep pit past recovery. [*He throws down a knife.*]
Here, hold that knife, and when thou see'st he comes,
And with his bashaws shall be blithely set,° *seated at table*
A warning-piece° shall be shot off from the tower *signal shot*
To give thee knowledge when to cut the cord
And fire° the house. Say, will not this be brave? *set afire*

FERNEZE Oh, excellent! Here, hold thee, Barabas.
[*He offers the money again.*]
I trust thy word; take what I promised thee.

BARABAS No, Governor, I'll satisfy thee first.
Thou shalt not live in doubt of anything.—
Stand close,° for here they come! [*Ferneze retires.*] *concealed*
Why, is not this
A kingly kind of trade, to purchase towns
By treachery and sell 'em by deceit?
Now tell me, worldlings,° underneath the sun *(the audience)*
If greater falsehood ever has been done?

Enter Calymath and Bashaws.

CALYMATH Come, my companion bashaws, see, I pray,
How busy Barabas is there above
To entertain us in his gallery.
Let us salute him.—Save thee, Barabas!

BARABAS Welcome, great Calymath.

FERNEZE [*aside*] How the slave jeers at him![2]

BARABAS Will't please thee, mighty Selim Calymath,
To ascend our homely stairs?

CALYMATH Ay, Barabas.—
Come, bashaws, attend.

FERNEZE [*coming forward*] Stay, Calymath!
For I will show thee greater courtesy
Than Barabas would have afforded thee.

KNIGHT [*within*] Sound a charge° there! *Sound the attack*

A [*trumpet*] *charge* [*sounds*]. *The cable cut, a caldron* [*is*] *discovered°* [*into which Barabas has fallen*]. *(by drawing a curtain)*

[*Enter Martin del Bosco and Knights.*]

2. Ferneze wonders, aside, at Barabas' brazen self-assurance in greeting the Turkish commander he plans to massacre.

CALYMATH How now, what means this?
BARABAS Help! Help me, Christians, help!
FERNEZE See, Calymath, this was devised for thee.
CALYMATH Treason! Treason! Bashaws, fly!
FERNEZE No, Selim, do not fly.
See his end first, and fly then if thou canst.
BARABAS Oh, help me, Selim! Help me, Christians!
Governor, why stand you all so pitiless?
FERNEZE Should I, in pity of thy plaints or thee,
Accursèd Barabas, base Jew, relent?
No! Thus I'll see thy treachery repaid,
But wish thou hadst behaved thee otherwise.
BARABAS You will not help me, then?
FERNEZE No, villain, no.
BARABAS And, villains, know you cannot help me now.
Then Barabas, breathe forth thy latest fate,° *breathe your last*
And in the fury of thy torments strive
To end thy life with resolution.
Know, Governor, 'twas I that slew thy son;
I framed° the challenge that did make them meet. *devised*
Know, Calymath, I aimed° thy overthrow, *aimed at*
And, had I but escaped this stratagem,
I would have brought confusion° on you all, *destruction*
Damned Christian dogs and Turkish infidels!
But now begins the extremity of heat
To pinch me with intolerable pangs.
Die, life! Fly, soul! Tongue, curse thy fill and die!
[*He dies.*]
CALYMATH Tell me, you Christians, what doth this portend?
FERNEZE This train° he laid to have entrapped thy life. *trap, plot*
Now, Selim, note the unhallowed deeds of Jews.
Thus he determined to have handled thee;
But I have rather chose to save thy life.
CALYMATH Was this the banquet he prepared for us?
Let's hence, lest further mischief be pretended.° *intended, offered*
FERNEZE Nay, Selim, stay, for since we have thee here,
We will not let thee part so suddenly.
Besides, if we should let thee go, all's one,° *it wouldn't matter*
For with thy galleys couldst thou not get hence
Without fresh men to rig and furnish them.
CALYMATH Tush, Governor, take thou no care for° that. *don't worry about*
My men are all aboard,
And do attend my coming there by this.° *by this time*
FERNEZE Why, heard'st thou not the trumpet sound a charge?
CALYMATH Yes. What of that?
FERNEZE Why, then the house was fired,
Blown up, and all thy soldiers massacred.
CALYMATH Oh, monstrous treason!
FERNEZE A Jew's courtesy;
For he that did by treason work our fall
By treason hath delivered thee to us.
Know, therefore, till thy father hath made good
The ruins done to Malta and to us,
Thou canst not part; for Malta shall be freed,
Or Selim ne'er return to Ottoman.

CALYMATH Nay, rather, Christians, let me go to Turkey,
In person there to mediate° your peace. *negotiate*
To keep me here will naught advantage you.
FERNEZE Content thee, Calymath, here thou must stay
And live in Malta prisoner; for come all the world
To rescue thee, so will we guard us now
As sooner shall they drink the ocean dry
Than conquer Malta or endanger us.
[*To his followers*] So, march away, and let due praise be given
Neither to fate or fortune, but to heaven. [*Exeunt.*]

FINIS.

TEXTUAL NOTES

The Jew of Malta was entered in the Stationers' Register on May 17, 1594, but the earliest printed edition of the play to survive is the quarto of 1633. Although the quarto contains a number of misprints, few of them pose a serious editorial problem, and at all events this quarto necessarily stands as the authoritative version on which the present edition is based. Some scholars have argued that the 1633 quarto incorporates a revision, perhaps by Thomas Heywood, but the evidence is inconclusive and in any case there is no reliable way to sort out what might arguably be the Marlovian original and what is not. The quarto probably gives us a reasonably reliable text of what Marlowe wrote. The following textual notes, indicating the departures of the present edition from the 1633 quarto, employ these abbreviations:

Q1: Quarto of 1633 (London: Nicholas Vavasour)
ed.: A modern editor's emendation

Prologue 0.1 ***Machiavel*** [Q1: *Macheuil*] **1 MACHIAVEL** [ed.; not in Q1] **1, 7 Machiavel** [Q1: Machevill] **21 Draco's** [ed.] *Drancus* [Q1] **24 maxima** [Q1: maxime] **25 He'd** [Q1: H'had] **26 wits** [ed.] wites [Q1] **29 Britany** [Q1: *Britaine*]

1.1.1 [and elsewhere] **BARABAS** [ed.] *Iew* [Q1] **4 Samnites** [ed.] *Samintes* [Q1] **6 silverlings** [ed.] siluerbings [Q1] **30 carat** [Q1: Carrect] **48 SD** [placement, ed.; after 48 in Q1] **50** [and elsewhere] **road** [Q1: Rhode] **70 master of** [Q1: Master off] **82 But** [ed.] By [Q1] **100** [and elsewhere] **freight** [Q1: fraught] **102 trolls** [Q1: trowles] **103 every** [Q1: enery] **118, 161** [and elsewhere] **Haply** [Q1: Happily] **188** ***proximus*** [Q1: *proximas*]

1.2.0.3 [and elsewhere] ***Bashaws*** [Q1: *Bassoes*] **1** [and elsewhere] **FERNEZE** [ed.] *Gouer., Gov.* [Q1] **2, 22 CALLAPINE** [Q1: *Bass.*] **33.1** [placement, ed.; after 32 in Q1] **36 FIRST OFFICER** [Q1: *Officer*] **57 FIRST JEW** [ed.] *Iew.* [Q1] **68 OFFICER (*reads*)** [ed.] *Reader.* [Q1] **73, 76 OFFICER (*reads*)** [ed.] *Read.* [Q1] **91** ***Corpe*** [ed.] *Corpo* [Q1] **131.1** [placement, ed.; opposite 130 in Q1] **165 Primus** [ed.] *Primas* [Q1] **200–201 patient. / BARABAS Ay, ay. / Pray** [Q1: patient. / *Bar.* I, I pray] **216 slaves** [Q: ssaues] **225.1** [placement, ed.; after 226 in Q1] **236 rend** [Q1: rent] **303.2** ***two friars*** [ed.] *three Fryars* [Q1] **304** [and elsewhere] **JACOMO** [Q1: *I. Fry.*] **306 ABBESS** [ed.] *I Nun.* [Q1] **312 ABBESS** [ed.] *Nun.* [Q1] **327** [and elsewhere] **BERNARDINE** [ed.] 2 *Fry.* [Q1] **331 strait** [Q1: streight] **353 reck** [Q1: wrecke] **354** [and elsewhere] [asides indicated by italics in Q1] **354 SD** ***making a sign*** [indicated by a † in Q1] **357 not** [ed.] *net* [Q1] **364 Who's** [Q1: Whose] **384 countermured** [ed.] countermin'd [Q1]

2.1.37 wake [ed.] walke [Q1] **39** ***Bueno*** [ed.] *Birn* [Q1] **39** ***mi ganado no era*** [ed.] *my ganada no er* [Q1] **45 SD** [placement, ed.; after the first "Hast thou 't?"

in Q1] **50 Abigail, Abigail** [Q1: *Aigal, Abigal*] **63 *placer*** [ed.] *Piarer* [Q1] **63 *los dineros*** [ed.] *les Denirch* [Q1] **63 SD *Exit*** [ed.] *Exeunt* [Q1]

2.2.7 Vice Admiral [Q1: Vizadmirall] **11 Turkish** [ed.] *Spanish* [Q1] **14 luffed, and tacked** [ed.] left, and tooke [Q1] **38 them** [ed.] you [Q1] **54 thee** [ed.] the [Q1]

2.3.6 [Q1 repeats the SD at 2.3.4.1 following this line] **28 offering basin** [Q1: offering-Bason] **100 Turks** [ed.] *Turke* [Q1] **101, 112, 165** FIRST OFFICER [ed.] *Off.* [Q1] **113 stone** [ed.] stoue [Q1] **115** SLAVE [ed.] *Itha.* [Q1] **117, 120, 124** SLAVE [ed.] *Ith.* [Q1] **126 an't** [Q1: And] **126 victuals** [Q1: vittles] **132 Thrace** [ed.] *Trace* [Q1] **148** [and elsewhere] KATHARINE [ed.] *Mater* [Q1] **159 was but** [ed.] was [Q1] **164.1** [placement, ed.; after 162 in Q1] **169–70 Ithamore** [Q1: *Ithimer;* usually spelled *Ithimore* but also occasionally *Ithamore*] **172 teach thee** [ed.] teach [Q1] **197 bankrupts** [Q1: Bankrouts] **213 strewèd** [Q1: strowed] **254.1** [placement, ed.; after 255 in Q1] **298 would** [Q1: wud] **300 yet** [ed.] yer [Q1] **324 thou** [ed.] thee [Q1] **336.1** [placement, ed.; after 337 in Q1] **363 enough** [Q1: Enow]

3.1.14 [and elsewhere] BELLAMIRA [ed.] *Curt.* [Q1] **25 Zounds** [Q1: Zoon's]

3.2.3 LODOWICK [ed.] *Math.* [Q1] 4 MATHIAS [ed.] *Lod.* [Q1] **34 reveal** [ed.; not in Q1]

3.3.17 Mathias' [ed.] *Mathia* [Q1] 17 **Lodowick's** [ed.] *Lodowick* [Q1] **23 and** [ed.; not in Q1] **32 Jacques** [ed.] Iaynes [Q1] **45 sire** [ed.] sinne [Q1] **55** [and throughout scene] JACOMO [ed.] *Fry.* [Q1]

3.4.15 self [ed.] life [Q1] **37 'less** [ed.] least [Q1] **45 half** [ed.] helfe [Q1] **77 Jacques'** [Q1: *Iagues*] **85 pot** [ed.] plot [Q1] **102 juice** [Q1: iouyce]

3.5.1 bashaw [ed.] *Bashaws* [Q1] **3, 7, 19** CALLAPINE [ed.] *Bash.* [Q1] **9 passed** [ed.] past [Q1] **13 raze** [Q1: race] **15 off** [ed.] of [Q1] **21 razing** [Q1: racing]

3.6.0.1 *friars* [ed.] *Fryars and Abigall* [Q1] **1** [and elsewhere] JACOMO [Q1: *1 Fry.*] 3 [and elsewhere] BERNARDINE [Q1: 2 *Fry.*] **49 has** [Q1: haa]

4.1.21 *Cazzo, diavola* [ed.] *Catho diabola* [Q1] **69 bullion** [Q1: *Bulloine*] **75 Seville** [ed.] *Ciuill* [Q1] **76 Frankfurt** [Q1: *Frankeford*] **78 banco** [Q1: bancho] **91** BERNARDINE [ed.] 1. [Q1] **94** JACOMO [ed.] 2. [Q1] **99 thee, rogue** [ed.] thee goe [Q1] **104** [ed.; assigned to *Ith.* in Q1] **105** JACOMO [ed.; not in Q1] **113, 117** JACOMO [ed.] *Fry.* [Q1] **120** [and elsewhere] **Jacomo** [Q1: *Iocoma*] **132.1** [placement, ed.; after 133 in Q1] **148, 152** BERNARDINE [ed.] *Fry.* [Q1] **152 have** [ed.] saue [Q1] **163.2** [placement, ed.; after 162 in Q1] **175.1** [placement, ed.; after 176 in Q1] **178 struck** [Q1: stroke]

4.2.60 Bellamira [ed.] *Allamira* [Q1] **76 straight** [Q1: strait] **78 SD** [placement, ed.; after 77 in Q1] **101 overspread** [ed.] ore-spread [Q1] **114 beard** [ed.] sterd [Q1]

4.3.6 tattered [Q1: totter'd] **56** [aside indicated by italics in Q1] **63 demand** [ed.; not in Q1]

4.4.5 BELLAMIRA [ed.] *Pil.* [Q1] **23 I—snickle, hand to! Fast!** [Q1: I snicle hand too fast,] **31 incony** [ed.] *incoomy* [Q1] **41 *votre*** [Q1: *voustre*] **49, 80 *Pardonnez-moi*** [Q1: Pardona moy] **58 you** [ed.] yon [Q1] **79 Whither** [Q1: Whether] **80 me** [ed.] we [Q1] **81 SD** [placement, ed.; after 80 in Q1]

5.1.6, 25 FIRST KNIGHT [Q1: *Kni.*] **29 he** [ed.; not in Q1] **41 I'll** [ed.] I [Q1] **49 passed** [Q1: past] **50, 53** FIRST OFFICER [Q1: *Offi.*] **86 sluice** [ed.] Truce [Q1]

5.2.5 keep [ed.] kept [Q1] **10 thee** [Q1: the] **21.1** [placement, ed.; after 20 in Q1] **26.1** [placement, ed.; after 25 in Q1] **47 there** [ed.] here [Q1]

5.3.3 basilisks' [ed.] Basiliske **6** [placement, ed.; after 10 in Q1] **9 countermured** [ed.] contermin'd [Q1] **11 Where** [ed.] When [Q1]

5.5.2 A CARPENTER [ed.] *Serv.* [Q1] **8** CARPENTERS [ed.] *Carp.* [Q1] **12.1** [placement, ed.; after 13 in Q1] **18.1** [placement, ed.; after 19 in Q1] **49 sun** [ed.] summe [Q1] **85 Christian dogs** [ed.] Christians, dogges [Q1] **115 mediate** [ed.] meditate [Q1] **118 all** [ed.] call [Q1]

Edward II

Written and staged around 1592, Christopher Marlowe's *Edward II* participates in a vogue for English history plays about weak kings that includes Shakespeare's *King John; 1, 2,* and 3 *Henry VI;* and *Richard II*. Weak kings have troubled reigns, troubled reigns breed conflict, conflict makes for drama, and so one can see why dramatists looked into Holinshed's *Chronicles* and other such sources to discover stories of royal failure as well as stories of royal success. Weak kings also suffer, sometimes tragically, and through their limitations and failures they map and recast the contours of political authority. English Renaissance drama worked through history to develop a new kind of tragic writing, and the theater was also a kind of laboratory in which thought experiments about politics could be conducted. Marlowe, Shakespeare, and their contemporaries developed the history play in order to pursue such experiments as the substance of dramatic entertainment.

Marlowe's *Edward II* traces Edward's long reign from its first moments to its tragic end, showing cool evenhandedness in the representation of political behavior and considerable dramatic skill in condensing the struggles of twenty-three historical years (from Edward's accession in 1307 to Mortimer Junior's death in 1330) into a thematically unified and fast-moving drama. Audience sympathies are pulled in several directions and, at least until act 5, never settle firmly on any one character. No one is utterly wrong, not even the usurper, Mortimer Junior, whose early claims to be defending England's welfare by ridding Edward of corrupting favorites seem public-spirited, though such claims also serve the ends of Mortimer and his cohort of barons. If audiences have trouble deciding with whom to side, so do several characters, notably Edward's brother, Edmund, who allies himself with the King at the beginning, goes over to the barons in exasperation, then returns to die for Edward at the play's end. Edward's French queen, Isabella, at first garners our sympathy as a loving wife who is puzzled and resentful when her husband ignores her in favor of Gaveston. She expresses love for Edward in soliloquies—speeches delivered by a character alone onstage that, by dramatic convention, offer true thoughts and feelings—and in the first three acts she refuses to take part actively in the revolts against him. She retains some sympathy even at the play's end, when she connives with her lover Mortimer to order the murder of her husband, since she shows consistent loyalty to what she takes to be the best interests of her son, the prince who becomes Edward III and who in a final turn of the screw sends her in the last lines of the play to the Tower to await trial.

The political struggle between Edward and his barons involves issues important in Renaissance monarchy, since Edward in effect tests his royal prerogative against their feudal rights and tries to convert a military monarchy, in which he leads through the personal loyalty of magnates with their own private armies, into a court-centered monarchy, in which politics consists of a competition for royal favor. Yet the play also affects readers and viewers more viscerally as a study in passion and cruelty. It is the one play in which Marlowe, not usually a compassionate playwright, looks at cruelty

Introduction by Lars Engle; glosses, footnotes, and textual notes by David Bevington and checked by Lars Engle; text edited by David Bevington and checked by Eric Rasmussen.

from the victim's viewpoint. Audience sympathy fixes itself on Edward by the play's end, and the play's focus on his suffering contributes to its claim to be the most intense, nuanced, and realistic of Marlowe's many studies of strong male bonding and of the attempts of outsiders to find a place at the center of a resistant social order.

Edward II begins in a brilliant burst of erotic excitement. Gaveston, exiled by Edward I, reads aloud a letter from the newly crowned king Edward II requesting his return in terms that immediately show that for Edward personal bonds outweigh political prudence: " 'My father is deceased. Come, Gaveston, / And share the kingdom with thy dearest friend' " (1.1.1–2). To the ears of Elizabethans, this invitation would sound alarm bells not necessarily audible to us. The idea that any person would "share the kingdom" with a legitimate monarch on the basis of dear friendship raises much-discussed political issues having to do with monarchical authority and favoritism. Gaveston's eagerness to share the kingdom on these terms and his awareness that he can mold Edward to his will mark him as a potentially destructive favorite, one who will divert the King from a proper focus on the kingdom's good by misleading him into extravagance, neglect of duty, and obsession with private pleasures.

Though Queen Elizabeth I, as England's successful ruler in the second half of the sixteenth century, had no favorite who succeeded in misleading her so entirely, Edward II's fourteenth-century reign was notorious for a number of the things Elizabethans feared and to some degree experienced in their own time: civil wars, factional struggles between royal favorites and feudal magnates, church-state conflicts, papal encouragement of resistance to monarchical authority, and issues over succession. The full title of the play's first publication in 1594, a year after Marlowe's death, records some of the political meanings attached to the play's topic: *The Troublesome Reign and Lamentable Death of Edward the Second, King of England, with the Tragical Fall of Proud Mortimer*. This title suggests that Edward's life is full of troubles, that his death is full of pathos, and that the career of his overmighty subject Mortimer will exhibit the hubris-nemesis pattern of tragedy. A second edition in 1598 adds to the end of the original title *"and Also the Life and Death of Piers Gaveston, the Great Earl of Cornwall, and Mighty Favorite of King Edward the Second,"* thus highlighting the play's third male protagonist.

Gaveston is immediately cast into focus as Edward's lover by the following lines of his opening speech:

> Ah, words that make me surfeit with delight!
> What greater bliss can hap to Gaveston
> Than live and be the favorite of a king?
> Sweet prince, I come. These, these thy amorous lines
> Might have enforced me to have swum from France,
> And, like Leander, gasped upon the sand,
> So thou wouldst smile and take me in thy arms.
> (1.1.3–9)

Though he has employed more prosaic modes of transport, Gaveston has eagerly made his way to London, a place like Elysium, the abode of the blessed, to him because "it harbors him I hold so dear, / The King, upon whose bosom let me die" (1.1.13–14). Gaveston's return to Edward involves a mixture of eros and ambition characteristic of courtiers seeking to become favorites of monarchs.

Such a mixture was familiar to Elizabethans in the relations between male courtiers and their queen, and recent gender criticism has emphasized the continued importance of such combinations of the erotic and the professional as the core of the homosocial bonds that link younger and older men in all-male or male-dominated organizations. A conversation between the upwardly mobile courtiers Spencer and Baldock, as they decide to attach themselves to Gaveston rather than to Mortimer and the barons, explores this mingling of professional ambition with personal affection:

SPENCER JR. The liberal Earl of Cornwall [i.e., Gaveston] is the man
On whose good fortune Spencer's hope depends.
BALDOCK What, mean you then to be his follower?
SPENCER JR. No, his companion, for he loves me well,
And would have once preferred me to the King.
(2.1.10–14)

Marlowe chooses, then, to emphasize from the play's opening lines a confrontation between the political and the erotic, which will also, to some extent, shape itself as a confrontation between what we today would call the homosexual and the heterosexual, or gay and straight, as broad orientations including sexual expression but not confined to it.

Gaveston concludes his rapture, however, on a politically, rather than erotically, provocative note: "Farewell, base stooping to the lordly peers! / My knee shall bow to none but to the King"; later in the scene, he also mocks three commoners who seek his patronage and dismisses "the multitude" as not worth fawning on (1.1.18–19, 20–49). Thus in the first speech of the play, Marlowe introduces three of the four great forces in the kingdom—the monarch, the peers, and the common people—through the words of a man who evidently will not hesitate to set those social powers at odds with one another. And when at the end of this scene the Bishop of Coventry (who had called for Gaveston's exile in the previous reign) is first assaulted by Gaveston and then imprisoned by order of King Edward (who also proceeds to bestow on his favorite the Bishop's lands and office), the conflict is significantly enlarged to embrace the fourth great power, the church.

Amid this reckless alienation of estates of the realm, Gaveston gives a remarkable picture of how he intends to retain an exclusive hold on Edward's affection and attention:

I must have wanton poets, pleasant wits,
Musicians that with touching of a string
May draw the pliant king which way I please.
Music and poetry is his delight;
Therefore I'll have Italian masques by night,
Sweet speeches, comedies, and pleasing shows;
And in the day, when he shall walk abroad,
Like sylvan nymphs my pages shall be clad;
My men, like Satyrs grazing on the lawns,
Shall with their goat feet dance an antic hay.
Sometime a lovely boy in Dian's shape,
With hair that gilds the water as it glides,
Crownets of pearl about his naked arms,
And in his sportful hands an olive tree
To hide those parts which men delight to see,
Shall bathe him in a spring . . . (1.1.50–65)

Almost all critics see this as a scene of male-male desire in which the imagined boy is meant to arouse male spectators sexually and delight a homosexual monarch. Surely they are right. Simultaneously, Marlowe reflects brilliantly here on the generally ambiguous erotics of a cross-dressed theater in which all female characters are represented by boys, chosen for their androgynous beauty as well as histrionic gifts. The olive tree hides the boy's genitals, but at a further level of representation it also hides the imaginary female genitals of the goddess Diana and, probably, her breasts. The passage asks spectators to reflect on how exactly "those parts which men delight to see" are constituted, particularly when they are both hidden and hinted at by costume or prop.

Moreover, this scene of male arousal of the male turns out also to be admonitory and problematic:

and there hard by
One like Actaeon peeping through the grove
Shall by the angry goddess be transformed,
And running in the likeness of an hart
By yelping hounds pulled down and seem to die.
(1.1.65–69)

Marlowe reminds us that Actaeon was killed by his own hounds after gazing lustfully on naked Diana. In this play, Edward will, largely because of his passion for Gaveston, be destroyed by his own noblemen, that is, by men feudally committed, like loyal dogs, to hunting down his foes. The scene therefore depicts misdirected desire as having the power to render one vulnerable to one's social inferiors. Much depends on whether one does or does not respect a social screen that hides "those parts which men delight to see." In a play in which men make reckless emotional commitments with full awareness of their dangers, it is appropriate that Marlowe sets this fairly obvious emblematic warning in the mouth of Gaveston himself. The peers, for their part, underline the warning with their own blunt demand: Mortimer Senior comments, "If you love us, my lord, hate Gaveston" (1.1.79).

From the outset, then, *Edward II* links the political troubles of a weak king to the erotic behavior of a homosexual king and portrays the opposition to Edward as united by hatred of Gaveston. This hatred is partly homophobic, partly patriotic, and partly a political defense of traditional baronial prerogatives. Readers today tend to think more about sexuality than about kingship, and to us the most obvious interest in *Edward II* lies in its treatment of homosexuality, or what we would today identify by that term. The Renaissance had no such word and probably no such concept: that is, early modern thinkers did not divide humanity into groups of people with differing sexual behaviors and draw the most significant line between those who primarily exhibit same-sex desires and those who show desire primarily for the opposite sex. Edward favors Gaveston by marrying Gaveston to his niece, for instance, and though Isabella bemoans Edward's sexual coldness toward her, everyone who discusses her situation assumes that it is a result of Edward's specific preference for Gaveston, not a categorical preference for males over females. Let us get rid of Gaveston, they tell her, and Edward will love you again.

"Let these their heads / Preach upon poles for trespass of their tongues" (*Edward II*, 1.1.116–17; see also 3.1.20). London Bridge adorned with the heads of traitors. From Claes Jansz Vischer, *Londinum florentissima Britanniae urbs* (1625).

Early modern discourse did include the legal and religious category of "sodomy" (the word derived from the city of Sodom in the Bible, a place associated with vice), and such discourse sometimes alluded to sodomy in a revealing paraphrase as "the horrible sin not to be named among Christians." Although the category of sodomy designated a set of behaviors as criminal, in England at least the laws against it were not often officially invoked. Very few people were prosecuted for it, and according to historians, only one person was convicted and executed for sodomy during the reigns of Elizabeth I and

James I together—and this act of sodomy was also one of rape.[1] Moreover, the laws were almost never invoked except in conjunction with a number of other categories of what was considered immoral, irreligious, and antihierarchical behavior. Thus those accused of being "sodomites" ("sodomites" is the collective word for those given to acts of sodomy) were usually also assumed to be atheists and disturbers of the peace. The term is never used in Marlowe's works (nor in Shakespeare's). In a note to the Privy Council denouncing Marlowe as a seditious atheist, however, Richard Baines did claim that Marlowe said "that St. John the Evangelist was bedfellow to Christ, and . . . that he used him as the sinners of Sodoma."[2]

Edward and Gaveston presumably use each other as did the sinners of Sodom. Yet the play, though stressing loving gestures between them, is far from showing the sexual act, and male-male sex is evoked only implicitly in its horrible parody in the murder of Edward at the play's end, long after Gaveston has been killed. As noted, the barons' enmity toward Gaveston combines moral disapproval of male-male love, patriotic dismay at the distraction of the King's attention (hearing about French assaults on English territories, Edward dismisses them as "A trifle" in comparison to his interest in Gaveston [2.2.10]), and, perhaps most important, class sentiment. The peers bitterly resent Edward's elevation of the upstart Gaveston to a rank either equal or superior to their own:

MORTIMER SR. How now, why droops the Earl of Lancaster?
MORTIMER JR. Wherefore is Guy of Warwick discontent?
LANCASTER That villain Gaveston is made an earl.
MORTIMER SR. An earl!
WARWICK Ay, and besides, Lord Chamberlain of the realm,
And Secretary too, and Lord of Man.
MORTIMER SR. We may not nor we will not suffer this.
(1.2.9–15)

Later in the play, at the end of a scene of short-lived reconciliation between Edward and the barons negotiated by Queen Isabella (who has pointed out to Mortimer Junior that the best solution to their problem is not to outrage Edward by exiling Gaveston but to have Gaveston murdered by some untraceable assassin), Mortimer Senior, seeing in Edward a disposition to leave the barons in charge of policy, tells his nephew to let Edward and Gaveston alone. The elder Mortimer goes on to say that Edward's passionate love for Gaveston has many distinguished precedents:

The mightiest kings have had their minions:
Great Alexander loved Hephaestion,
The conquering Hercules for Hylas wept,
And for Patroclus stern Achilles drooped.
(1.4.390–93)

Mortimer Junior replies at first by suggesting that Gaveston misleads Edward into realm-ruining extravagance and goes on to point out that he also finds Gaveston and Edward personally humiliating: "Whiles other walk below, the King and he / From out a window laugh at such as we, / And flout our train, and jest at our attire" (1.4.415–17). Edward and Gaveston outdress the barons and laugh at their clothing, respecting them neither as men nor as powers in the realm, and it is this dismissive arrogance above all that the barons find unacceptable.

Marlowe compresses a narrative of a twenty-year reign followed by a three-year protectorate into a play with a fairly clear structure: the first half is devoted to Edward's conflict with the barons over Gaveston, whose murder by the Earl of Warwick takes place at the beginning of act 3, and the second half is devoted to Edward's conflict

1. See Bruce Smith, *Homosexual Desire in Shakespeare's England: A Cultural Poetics* (Chicago: University of Chicago Press, 1994), p. 48.

2. Millar MacLure, *Marlowe, The Critical Heritage, 1588–1896* (London: Routledge and Kegan Paul, 1979), p. 37.

with the same set of barons over his alliance with his new political and emotional favorites (though not in any evident way sexual ones), the Spencers and Baldock. Though Gaveston's death robs Edward of a lover, the play's second half focuses on the personal aspects of power politics with undiminished intensity. Isabella, after Gaveston's death, joins with Mortimer Junior to force Edward to abdicate in favor of his son, Edward III, under Mortimer's guardianship. Marlowe writes a scene of extraordinary political pathos in Edward's deposition, many elements of which reappear in the similar scene in Shakespeare's *Richard II*, written a few years later. Marlowe depicts with great power and horror the cruelty with which Mortimer's agents hound Edward from one prison to another, degrade him physically, house him in a castle sewer where he must live drenched in urine and excrement, and, finally, murder him. Marlowe ends the play by compressing the historical three years of Mortimer's guardianship into one dramatic scene in which the boy Edward III turns on Mortimer, has him tortured and executed, and witnesses (as do we as the audience) the severed head of Mortimer brought in to him during the final solemn moments of the play.

Marlowe leaves crucial details of the murder of Edward up to the imaginations of readers and stage directors. Lightborn, Mortimer's hired assassin, a specialist in deniable homicides, mentions untraceable poisons and inconspicuous modes of asphyxiation, then tells the Protector that "yet I have a braver way than these" (5.4.37). But he will not say what that "braver way" is, and when he commits the murder, the stage directions are vague, perhaps deliberately so, since the play script had to pass under the eyes of the censor. Nonetheless, in having Lightborn order his accomplices to prepare a red-hot spit, a table, and a featherbed, and in mentioning Edward's loud cry as he is murdered (which rules out suffocation) (5.5.30–32, 113), the text gestures clearly enough at the murder clinically described in Holinshed, in which Edward is held down on a bed under a table and has a red-hot poker thrust into his intestines through a horn inserted in his anus—partly, no doubt, so that no physical mark of his death will be evident (Renaissance kings were usually not autopsied), but partly also, it would seem, as a Dantesque *contrapasso*: a form of punishment that reenacts the sin it punishes. Marlowe thus ends his most realistic play with a scene that modern audiences can take as a brutal reminder of something that seems to be more true now than it was in Marlowe's time: homosexuals sometimes get murdered in horrible ways merely for being what they are.

The play begins when a strong king dies, freeing his son to summon his lover. At the play's end, a weak king's death frees his son to clear both the audience and the English kingdom of discomfort, as Edward III begins what promises to be a strong reign by ordering the execution of his father's persecutors and imprisoning his mother. In Marlowe's political world, emotional dependency is a vulnerability a king must either shed or suffer for. Ordinary people in Marlowe's early modern audiences, reliant for their well-being on a political order over which they exercised little control, could note with interest and dismay Marlowe's presentation of political stability as frail and transient, dependent not on divine intent or human progress, but on the strengths and weaknesses of the person who happens at any given historical moment to rule.

CHRISTOPHER MARLOWE

Edward II

[THE PERSONS IN THE PLAY

KING EDWARD II
QUEEN Isabella, his wife
PRINCE EDWARD, their son, later EDWARD III
Edmund, Earl of KENT, Edward's brother
NIECE to King Edward and daughter of the Duke of Gloucester

Piers GAVESTON
Hugh SPENCER SENIOR
Hugh SPENCER JUNIOR, his son
BALDOCK, a tutor and cleric
LEVUNE, a Frenchman
Earl of ARUNDEL
} royal favorites and supporters

Bishop of WINCHESTER

MORTIMER SENIOR
MORTIMER JUNIOR, his nephew
Guy, Earl of WARWICK
Earl of LANCASTER
Earl of PEMBROKE
Archbishop of CANTERBURY
Bishop of COVENTRY
Earl of LEICESTER
} opposing King Edward

MATREVIS
GURNEY
} followers of Mortimer Junior

LIGHTBORN, a murderer

BEAUMONT, Clerk of the Crown
Sir William TRUSSEL, Proctor of Parliament
SIR JOHN of Hainault° — *Hainaut, Belgium*
RICE ap Howell
Sir Thomas BERKELEY
JAMES, one of the Earl of Pembroke's men
A HORSEBOY
A HERALD

The 1594 quarto-form octavo title page reads "*The Troublesome Reign and Lamentable Death of Edward the Second, King of England, with the tragical fall of proud Mortimer.* As it was sundry times publicly acted in the honorable city of London, by the Right Honorable the Earl of Pembroke his Servants. Written by Christopher Marlowe, Gent. Imprinted at London for William Jones, dwelling near Holborn Conduit at the sign of the Gun. 1594."

An ABBOT
A MOWER
The King's CHAMPION
Three POOR MEN petitioning Gaveston
Monks
Lords and ladies
Messengers
Guards
Soldiers
The Mayor of Bristol
Attendants

THE SCENE: England and Paris.]

[1.1]

Enter Gaveston reading on a letter that was brought him from the King.

GAVESTON [*reads*] "My father is deceased. Come, Gaveston,
And share the kingdom with thy dearest friend."
Ah, words that make me surfeit with delight!
What greater bliss can hap to° Gaveston — *happen to, befall*
Than live and be the favorite of a king?
Sweet prince, I come. These, these thy amorous lines
Might have enforced me to have swum from France,
And, like Leander,[1] gasped upon the sand,
So° thou wouldst smile and take me in thy arms. — *Provided that*
The sight of London to my exiled eyes
Is as Elysium° to a new-come soul— — *abode of the blessed*
Not that I love the city or the men,
But that it harbors him I hold so dear,
The King, upon whose bosom let me die° — *swoon; climax*
And with the world be still° at enmity. — *continually*
What need the Arctic people love starlight,
To whom the sun shines both by day and night?[2]
Farewell, base stooping to the lordly peers!
My knee shall bow to none but to the King.
As for the multitude, that are but sparks
Raked up in embers of their poverty,
Tanti!° I'll fawn first on the wind — *So much for that!*
That glanceth at my lips and flieth away.
But how now, what are these?

Enter three Poor Men.

POOR MEN Such as desire Your Worship's service.° — *to serve you*
GAVESTON [*to the first*] What canst thou do?
FIRST POOR MAN I can ride.
GAVESTON But I have no horses.—What art thou?

1.1. Near the royal English court, London.
1. A legendary youth of the ancient town Abydos, on the Hellespont (modern-day Dardanelles), whose love for the beautiful Hero, priestess of Aphrodite at Sestos, on the opposite shore, drove him to swim the Hellespont, in which he was drowned one stormy night. Marlowe's unfinished amorous poem on the subject was published in 1598.
2. Just as those who dwell in the land of the midnight sun have no need for starlight during their brief summer, Gaveston has no need for the favor of lesser persons since he basks in royal sunlike favor.

SECOND POOR MAN A traveler.
GAVESTON Let me see: thou wouldst do well to wait° at my trencher° and tell me lies° at dinnertime, and, as I like your discoursing, I'll have you.—And what art thou? *serve* *plate / travelers' tales*
THIRD POOR MAN A soldier, that hath served against the Scot.
GAVESTON Why, there are hospitals for such as you.
I have no war, and therefore, sir, begone.
THIRD POOR MAN Farewell, and perish by a soldier's hand,
That wouldst reward them with an hospital!
[*They start to go.*]
GAVESTON [*aside*] Ay, ay, these words of his move me as much
As if a goose should play the porcupine° *(thought to shoot quills)*
And dart her plumes, thinking to pierce my breast.
But yet it is no pain to speak men fair;° *to flatter*
I'll flatter these, and make them live in hope.
[*To them*] You know that I came lately out of France,
And yet I have not viewed my lord the King;
If I speed° well, I'll entertain° you all. *succeed / employ*
OMNES° We thank Your Worship. *All*
GAVESTON I have some business. Leave me to myself.
OMNES We will wait here about the court.
GAVESTON Do. *Exeunt* [*Poor Men*].
These are not men for me.
I must have wanton poets, pleasant wits,
Musicians that with touching of a string
May draw the pliant king which way I please.
Music and poetry is his delight;
Therefore I'll have Italian masques° by night, *masked entertainments*
Sweet speeches, comedies, and pleasing shows;
And in the day, when he shall walk abroad,° *outdoors*
Like sylvan nymphs my pages shall be clad;
My men, like Satyrs grazing on the lawns,
Shall with their goat feet dance an antic hay.° *country-dance*
Sometime a lovely boy in Dian's° shape, *Diana, goddess of the hunt*
With hair that gilds the water as it glides,
Crownets° of pearl about his naked arms, *Coronets, garlands*
And in his sportful hands an olive tree° *branch*
To hide those parts which men delight to see,
Shall bathe him in a spring, and there hard by
One like Actaeon[3] peeping through the grove
Shall by the angry goddess be transformed,
And running in the likeness of an hart° *deer*
By yelping hounds pulled down and seem to die.
Such things as these best please His Majesty,
My lord.—Here comes the King and the nobles
From the Parliament. I'll stand aside.
[*He stands aside, unseen.*]

Enter the King [*Edward*]; *Lancaster; Mortimer Senior; Mortimer Junior; Edmund, Earl of Kent; Guy, Earl of Warwick; etc.* [*and attendants*].

3. A young man who, because he boasted that he was a better hunter than Artemis or because he looked upon her while she was bathing, was changed into a stag and torn apart by his own hounds.

KING EDWARD Lancaster!
LANCASTER My lord?
GAVESTON [*aside*] That Earl of Lancaster do I abhor.
KING EDWARD Will you not grant me this? [*Aside*] In spite of them
I'll have my will, and these two Mortimers
That cross me thus shall know I am displeased.
MORTIMER SR. If you love us, my lord, hate Gaveston.
GAVESTON [*aside*] That villain Mortimer! I'll be his death.
MORTIMER JR. Mine uncle here, this earl,° and I myself *(Lancaster)*
Were sworn to your father at his death
That he° should ne'er return into the realm; *(Gaveston)*
And know, my lord, ere I will break my oath,
This sword of mine that should offend your foes
Shall sleep within the scabbard at thy need;° *when you need help*
And underneath thy banners march who will,° *whoever wishes to*
For Mortimer will hang his armor up.
GAVESTON [*aside*] *Mort Dieu!*° *God's death!*
KING EDWARD Well, Mortimer, I'll make thee rue these words.
Beseems° it thee to contradict thy king? *Suits*
Frown'st thou thereat, aspiring Lancaster?
The sword shall plane the furrows of thy brows,
And hew these knees that now are grown so stiff.° *unbending*
I will have Gaveston, and you shall know
What danger 'tis to stand against your king.
GAVESTON [*aside*] Well done, Ned!° *(nickname for "Edward")*
LANCASTER My lord, why do you thus incense your peers,
That naturally would love and honor you
But for that base and obscure° Gaveston? *lowborn*
Four earldoms have I besides Lancaster—
Derby, Salisbury, Lincoln, Leicester.
These will I sell to give my soldiers pay
Ere Gaveston shall stay within the realm.
Therefore, if he be come, expel him straight.° *at once*
KENT Barons and earls, your pride hath made me mute,
But now I'll speak, and to the proof,° I hope. *irrefutably*
I do remember in my father's° days *(Edward I's)*
Lord Percy of the north, being highly moved,° *angered*
Braved° Mowbray in presence of the King, *Defied*
For which, had not His Highness loved him well,
He should have lost his head; but with his° look *(the King's)*
The undaunted spirit of Percy was appeased,
And Mowbray and he were reconciled.
Yet dare you brave the King unto his face!
[*To the King*] Brother, revenge it, and let these their heads
Preach upon poles for trespass of their tongues.[4]
WARWICK Oh, our heads?
KING EDWARD Ay, yours; and therefore I would wish you grant.° *grant my request*
WARWICK Bridle thy anger, gentle Mortimer.
MORTIMER JR. I cannot, nor I will not; I must speak.
[*To the King*] Cousin,° our hands, I hope, shall fence° our heads, *Kinsman / guard*

4. The heads of beheaded criminals, especially traitors, were put up on poles (often on London Bridge) to be viewed as object lessons. See introduction, p. 354, for an illustration of this.

And strike off his° that makes you threaten us. *(Gaveston's)*
[*To Mortimer Senior*] Come, uncle, let us leave the brain-
sick king,
And henceforth parley with our naked swords.
MORTIMER SR. Wilshire° hath men enough to save our heads. *in Wales (?)*
WARWICK All Warwickshire will love him for my sake.° *(said ironically)*
LANCASTER And, northward, Gaveston hath many friends.° *(said ironically)*
[*To the King*] Adieu, my lord, and either change your mind
Or look to see the throne where you should sit
To float in blood, and at thy wanton° head *ungovernable*
The glozing° head of thy base minion thrown. *flattering*
Exeunt nobles [*the Mortimers,*
Lancaster, and Warwick].
KING EDWARD I cannot brook° these haughty menaces! *tolerate*
Am I a king, and must be overruled?
[*To Kent*] Brother, display my ensigns° in the field! *banners, standards*
I'll bandy° with the barons and the earls, *exchange blows*
And either die or live with Gaveston.
GAVESTON [*coming forward*] I can no longer keep me from
my lord. [*He kneels and offers to kiss the King's hand.*]
KING EDWARD [*raising him*] What, Gaveston, welcome! Kiss
not my hand;
Embrace me, Gaveston, as I do thee. [*They embrace.*]
Why shouldst thou kneel? Knowest thou not who I am?
Thy friend, thyself, another Gaveston.
Not Hylas was more mourned of Hercules[5]
Than thou hast been of me since thy exile.
GAVESTON And, since I went from hence, no soul in hell
Hath felt more torment than poor Gaveston.
KING EDWARD I know it. [*To Kent*] Brother, welcome home my friend.
[*To Gaveston*] Now let the treacherous Mortimers conspire,
And that high-minded° Earl of Lancaster! *haughty*
I have my wish, in that I joy° thy sight; *enjoy*
And sooner shall the sea o'erwhelm my land
Than bear the ship that shall transport thee hence.
I here create thee Lord High Chamberlain,
Chief Secretary to the state and me,
Earl of Cornwall, King and Lord of Man.° *the Isle of Man*
GAVESTON My lord, these titles far exceed my worth.
KENT Brother, the least of these may well suffice
For one of greater birth than Gaveston.
KING EDWARD Cease, brother, for I cannot brook these words.
[*To Gaveston*] Thy worth, sweet friend, is far above my gifts;
Therefore, to equal it, receive my heart.
If for these dignities thou be envied,
I'll give thee more, for but to honor thee
Is Edward pleased with kingly regiment.[6]
Fear'st thou° thy person? Thou shalt have a guard. *Do you fear for*
Wants thou° gold? Go to my treasury. *Do you need*

5. When Hylas, a favorite page of Hercules, was sent for water during the expedition of the Argonauts at the island of Lemnos, the water nymphs became so enamored of his beauty that they drew him into the spring, where he was drowned. Hercules would not leave the island without him and stayed behind to search for him while the rest of the Argonauts continued on their voyage.

6. My only solace in possessing royal authority is to be able to honor you with titles.

Wouldst thou be loved and feared? Receive my seal;° *the great seal*
Save or condemn, and in our name command
Whatso thy mind affects° or fancy likes. *desires*
GAVESTON It shall suffice me to enjoy your love,
Which whiles I have, I think myself as great
As Caesar riding in the Roman street
With captive kings at his triumphant car.° *chariot*

Enter the Bishop of Coventry.

KING EDWARD Whither goes my lord of Coventry so fast?
COVENTRY To celebrate your father's exequies.° *funeral rites*
But is that wicked Gaveston returned?
KING EDWARD Ay, priest, and lives to be revenged on thee
That wert the only cause of his exile.
GAVESTON 'Tis true, and, but for reverence of these robes,
Thou shouldst not plod one foot beyond this place.
COVENTRY I did no more than I was bound to do;
And, Gaveston, unless thou be reclaimed,° *tamed, restrained*
As then I did incense the Parliament
So will I now, and thou shalt back to France.
GAVESTON Saving your reverence,° you must pardon me. *With all due respect*
[*Gaveston manhandles the Bishop.*]
KING EDWARD Throw off his golden miter! Rend his stole,° *ecclesiastical garb*
And in the channel° christen him anew! *gutter*
KENT Ah, brother, lay not violent hands on him,
For he'll complain unto the see of Rome.° *the papacy*
GAVESTON Let him complain unto the see of hell!
I'll be revenged on him for my exile.
KING EDWARD No, spare his life, but seize upon his goods.
Be thou Lord Bishop, and receive his rents,° *incomes*
And make him serve thee as thy chaplain.
I give him thee. Here, use him as thou wilt.
GAVESTON He shall to prison, and there die in bolts.° *fetters*
KING EDWARD Ay, to the Tower, the Fleet,° or where thou wilt. *a London prison*
COVENTRY For this offense be thou accurst of God!
KING EDWARD [*calling to attendants*] Who's there? Convey this priest to the Tower.
COVENTRY True, true.[7]
[*Exit the Bishop of Coventry, under guard.*]
KING EDWARD But in the meantime, Gaveston, away,
And take possession of his house and goods.
Come, follow me, and thou shalt have my guard° *royal guard*
To see it done, and bring thee safe again.° *back again*
GAVESTON What should a priest do with so fair a house?
A prison may beseem His Holiness. [*Exeunt.*]

7. The Bishop of Coventry responds bitterly to King Edward's "Convey" (line 199), which can mean "steal, remove furtively or feloniously." Edward presumably meant "Escort under guard."

[1.2]

Enter both the Mortimers, Warwick, and Lancaster.

WARWICK 'Tis true, the Bishop is in the Tower,
And goods and body° given to Gaveston. — *custody of his person*
LANCASTER What, will they tyrannize upon the church?
Ah, wicked king! Accursèd Gaveston!
This ground, which is corrupted with their steps,
Shall be their timeless° sepulchre or mine. — *untimely*
MORTIMER JR. Well, let that peevish° Frenchman guard him sure. — *wretched, malignant*
Unless his breast be swordproof, he shall die.
MORTIMER SR. How now, why droops the Earl of Lancaster?
MORTIMER JR. Wherefore is Guy of Warwick discontent?
LANCASTER That villain Gaveston is made an earl.
MORTIMER SR. An earl!
WARWICK Ay, and besides, Lord Chamberlain of the realm,
And Secretary too, and Lord of Man.
MORTIMER SR. We may not nor we will not suffer this.
MORTIMER JR. Why post° we not from hence to levy men? — *hasten*
LANCASTER "My lord of Cornwall" now at every word!
And happy is the man whom he vouchsafes,
For vailing° of his bonnet, one good look. — *doffing*
Thus, arm in arm, the King and he doth march.
Nay, more, the guard° upon His Lordship waits,° — *royal guard / attends*
And all the court begins to flatter him.
WARWICK Thus leaning on the shoulder of the King,
He nods, and scorns, and smiles at those that pass.
MORTIMER SR. Doth no man take exceptions at the slave?° — *object to the wretch*
LANCASTER All stomach° him, but none dare speak a word. — *resent*
MORTIMER JR. Ah, that bewrays° their baseness, Lancaster. — *reveals*
Were all the earls and barons of my mind,
We'll° hale him from the bosom of the King — *We'd*
And at the court gate hang the peasant up,
Who, swoll'n with venom of ambitious pride,
Will be the ruin of the realm and us.

Enter the [Arch]bishop of Canterbury [and an attendant].

WARWICK Here comes my lord of Canterbury's Grace.° — *His Grace the Archbishop*
LANCASTER His countenance bewrays he is displeased.
CANTERBURY [*to an attendant*] First were his° sacred garments rent and torn, — *(the Bishop of Coventry's)*
Then laid they violent hands upon him, next
Himself imprisoned and his goods asseized.° — *seized upon*
This certify° the Pope. Away, take horse! [*Exit attendant.*] — *inform, assure*
LANCASTER [*to Canterbury*] My lord, will you take arms against the King?
CANTERBURY What need I? God himself is up in arms
When violence is offered to the church.
MORTIMER JR. Then will you join with us that be his peers° — *the King's nobles*
To banish or behead that Gaveston?

1.2. Historically, set at Westminster.

CANTERBURY What else, my lords? For it concerns me near:
The bishopric of Coventry is his.

Enter the Queen.

MORTIMER JR. Madam, whither walks Your Majesty so fast?
QUEEN Unto the forest, gentle Mortimer,
To live in grief and baleful° discontent; *sorrowful*
For now my lord the King regards me not,
But dotes upon the love of Gaveston.
He claps° his cheeks and hangs about his neck, *pats*
Smiles in his face and whispers in his ears,
And when I come he frowns, as who should say,° *as if to say*
"Go whither thou wilt, seeing I have Gaveston."
MORTIMER SR. Is it not strange that he is thus bewitched?
MORTIMER JR. Madam, return unto the court again.
That sly, inveigling Frenchman we'll exile
Or lose our lives; and yet ere that day come,
The King shall lose his crown, for we have power,
And courage too, to be revenged at full.
CANTERBURY But yet lift not your swords against the King.
LANCASTER No, but we'll lift° Gaveston from hence. *remove, steal*
WARWICK And war must be the means, or he'll stay still.
QUEEN Then let him stay, for, rather than my lord
Shall be oppressed by civil mutinies,
I will endure a melancholy life,
And let him frolic with his minion.° *male lover; favorite*
CANTERBURY My lords, to ease all this, but° hear me speak. *only*
We and the rest that are his° counselors *(the King's)*
Will meet and with a general consent
Confirm his° banishment with our hands and seals. *(Gaveston's)*
LANCASTER What we confirm the King will frustrate.
MORTIMER JR. Then may we lawfully revolt from him.
WARWICK But say, my lord, where shall this meeting be?
CANTERBURY At the New Temple.° *(in London)*
MORTIMER JR. Content.
CANTERBURY And in the meantime I'll entreat you all
To cross to Lambeth[1] and there stay with me.
LANCASTER Come, then, let's away.
MORTIMER JR. Madam, farewell.
QUEEN Farewell, sweet Mortimer, and for my sake
Forbear to levy arms against the King.
MORTIMER JR. Ay, if words will serve; if not, I must.
[*Exeunt.*]

[1.3]

Enter Gaveston and the Earl of Kent.

GAVESTON Edmund, the mighty prince of Lancaster,
That hath more earldoms than an ass can bear,
And both the Mortimers, two goodly men,

1. The site of the Archbishop's palace on the south bank of the Thames, opposite Westminster.

1.3. London.

With Guy of Warwick, that redoubted° knight, *dreaded, formidable*
Are gone towards Lambeth. There let them remain!
Exeunt.

[1.4]

Enter nobles [Lancaster, Warwick, the Mortimers, Pembroke, and the Archbishop of Canterbury, attended by guards. A throne and chair are brought on].

LANCASTER [*presenting Canterbury with a document*] Here is the form° of Gaveston's exile. *document*
May it please Your Lordship to subscribe your name.
CANTERBURY Give me the paper.
[*He signs; the others do so after him.*]
LANCASTER Quick, quick, my lord, I long to write my name.
WARWICK But I long more to see him banished hence.
MORTIMER JR. The name of Mortimer shall fright the King,
Unless he be declined° from that base peasant. *disengaged*

Enter the King, [Kent,] and Gaveston. [The King takes his throne, with Gaveston at his side.]

KING EDWARD What, are you moved° that Gaveston sits here? *angered*
It is our pleasure; we will have it so.
LANCASTER Your Grace doth well to place him by your side,
For nowhere else the new earl is so safe.
MORTIMER SR. What man of noble birth can brook this sight?
Quam male conveniunt!° *How ill they agree!*
See what a scornful look the peasant casts!
PEMBROKE Can kingly lions fawn on creeping ants?
WARWICK Ignoble vassal, that like Phaëthon
Aspir'st unto the guidance of the sun![1]
MORTIMER JR. Their downfall° is at hand, their forces down; *The downfall of such*
We will not thus be faced and overpeered.° *outfaced and scorned*
KING EDWARD Lay hands on that traitor Mortimer!
MORTIMER SR. Lay hands on that traitor Gaveston!
[*Gaveston is seized.*]
KENT Is this the duty that you owe your king?
WARWICK We know our duties. Let him know his peers.
KING EDWARD Whither will you bear him? Stay, or ye shall die.
MORTIMER SR. We are no traitors; therefore threaten not.
GAVESTON [*to the King*] No, threaten not, my lord, but pay them home.° *strike decisively*
Were I a king—
MORTIMER JR. Thou villain, wherefore talks thou of a king,
That hardly art a gentleman by birth?
KING EDWARD Were he a peasant, being my minion,
I'll make the proudest of you stoop to him.
LANCASTER My lord, you may not thus disparage us.—
Away, I say, with hateful Gaveston!
MORTIMER SR. And with the Earl of Kent that favors him!
[*Kent is seized. Exeunt Kent and Gaveston, guarded.*]
KING EDWARD Nay, then lay violent hands upon your king.

1.4. The New Temple.
1. Phaëthon mismanaged the horses of his sun-god father's chariot and had to be thrown down to earth by Zeus's thunderbolt.

Here, Mortimer, sit thou in Edward's throne;
Warwick and Lancaster, wear you my crown.
Was ever king thus overruled as I?
LANCASTER Learn then to rule us better, and the realm.
MORTIMER JR. What we have done, our heart-blood° shall maintain. *lifeblood*
WARWICK Think you that we can brook this upstart pride?
KING EDWARD Anger and wrathful fury stops my speech.
CANTERBURY Why are you moved? Be patient, my lord,
And see what we your counselors have done.
MORTIMER JR. My lords, now let us all be resolute,
And either have our wills or lose our lives.
KING EDWARD Meet you for this, proud overdaring peers?
Ere my sweet Gaveston shall part from me,
This isle shall fleet° upon the ocean *float*
And wander to the unfrequented Inde.° *East (or West) Indies*
CANTERBURY You know that I am legate to the Pope.
On your allegiance to the see of Rome,
Subscribe as we have done to his exile.
[*The King is presented with the document.*]
MORTIMER JR. [*to Canterbury*] Curse° him if he refuse, and then may we *Excommunicate*
Depose him and elect another king.
KING EDWARD Ay, there it goes! But yet I will not yield.
Curse me, depose me, do the worst you can.
LANCASTER Then linger not, my lord, but do it straight.° *at once*
CANTERBURY Remember how the Bishop° was abused. *Bishop of Coventry*
Either banish him that was the cause thereof,
Or I will presently° discharge these lords *immediately*
Of duty and allegiance due to thee.
KING EDWARD [*aside*] It boots° me not to threat; I must speak fair. *avails*
The legate of the Pope will be obeyed.
[*To Canterbury*] My lord, you shall be chancellor of the realm,
Thou, Lancaster, high admiral of our fleet,
Young Mortimer and his uncle shall be earls,
And you, Lord Warwick, President of the North,
[*To Pembroke*] And thou of Wales. If this content you not,
Make several kingdoms of this monarchy
And share it equally amongst you all,
So° I may have some nook or corner left *Provided that*
To frolic with my dearest Gaveston.
CANTERBURY Nothing shall alter us. We are resolved.
LANCASTER Come, come, subscribe.
MORTIMER JR. Why should you love him whom the world hates so?
KING EDWARD Because he loves me more than all the world.
Ah, none but rude° and savage-minded men *uncivilized*
Would seek the ruin of my Gaveston.
You that be noble born should pity him.
WARWICK You that are princely born should shake him off.
For shame, subscribe, and let the loon° depart. *worthless wretch*
MORTIMER SR. [*to Canterbury*] Urge him, my lord.
CANTERBURY Are you content to banish him the realm?
KING EDWARD I see I must, and therefore am content.
Instead of ink, I'll write it with my tears. [*He signs.*]
MORTIMER JR. The King is lovesick for his minion.

KING EDWARD 'Tis done, and now, accursèd hand, fall off!
LANCASTER [*taking the document*] Give it me. I'll have it
published in the streets.
MORTIMER JR. I'll see him presently dispatched away.
CANTERBURY Now is my heart at ease.
WARWICK And so is mine.
PEMBROKE This will be good news to the common sort.° *citizens*
MORTIMER SR. Be it or no, he shall not linger here.
Exeunt nobles. [*King Edward remains.*]
KING EDWARD How fast they run to banish him I love!
They would not stir, were it to do me good.
Why should a king be subject to a priest?
Proud Rome, that hatchest such imperial grooms,° *imperious underlings*
For these thy superstitious taper lights,
Wherewith thy anti-Christian° churches blaze, *Antichrist-serving*
I'll fire thy crazèd° buildings, and enforce *cracked, flawed*
The papal towers to kiss the lowly ground.
With slaughtered priests may Tiber's channel° swell, *the Tiber River*
And banks raised higher with their sepulchres!
As for the peers that back the clergy thus,
If I be king, not one of them shall live.

Enter Gaveston.

GAVESTON My lord, I hear it whispered everywhere
That I am banished and must fly the land.
KING EDWARD 'Tis true, sweet Gaveston. Oh, were it° false! *would it were*
The legate of the Pope will have it so,
And thou must hence or I shall be deposed.
But I will reign to be revenged of° them; *on*
And therefore, sweet friend, take it patiently.
Live where thou wilt, I'll send thee gold enough;
And long thou shalt not stay, or, if thou dost,
I'll come to thee. My love shall ne'er decline.
GAVESTON Is all my hope turned to this hell of grief?
KING EDWARD Rend not my heart with thy too-piercing words.
Thou from this land, I from myself am banished.
GAVESTON To go from hence grieves not poor Gaveston,
But to forsake you, in whose gracious looks
The blessedness of Gaveston remains,
For nowhere else seeks he felicity.
KING EDWARD And only this torments my wretched soul,
That, whether I will or no, thou must depart.
Be governor of Ireland in my stead,
And there abide till fortune call thee home.
Here, take my picture and let me wear thine.
[*They exchange lockets.*]
Oh, might I keep thee here as I do this,
Happy were I, but now most miserable!
GAVESTON 'Tis something to be pitied of a king.
KING EDWARD Thou shalt not hence; I'll hide thee, Gaveston.
GAVESTON I shall be found, and then 'twill grieve me more.
KING EDWARD Kind words and mutual talk makes our grief greater;
Therefore with dumb° embracement let us part. *mute*
[*They embrace. Gaveston starts to leave.*]
Stay, Gaveston! I cannot leave thee thus.

GAVESTON For every look, my lord, drops down a tear;
Seeing I must go, do not renew my sorrow.
KING EDWARD The time is little that thou hast to stay,
And therefore give me leave to look my fill.
But come, sweet friend, I'll bear thee on thy way.° *I'll see you off*
GAVESTON The peers will frown.
KING EDWARD I pass° not for their anger. Come, let's go. *care*
Oh, that we might as well° return as go! *as easily*

Enter Queen Isabel.

QUEEN Whither goes my lord?
KING EDWARD Fawn not on me, French strumpet! Get thee gone.
QUEEN On whom but on my husband should I fawn?
GAVESTON On Mortimer, with whom, ungentle Queen—
I say no more. Judge you the rest, my lord.
QUEEN In saying this, thou wrong'st me, Gaveston.
Is't not enough that thou corrupts my lord,
And art a bawd to his affections,° *pander to his desires*
But thou must call mine honor thus in question?
GAVESTON I mean not so; Your Grace must pardon me.
KING EDWARD [*to the Queen*] Thou art too familiar with that Mortimer,
And by thy means is Gaveston exiled;
But I would wish thee reconcile the lords,
Or thou shalt ne'er be reconciled to me.
QUEEN Your Highness knows it lies not in my power.
KING EDWARD Away, then! Touch me not.—Come, Gaveston.
QUEEN [*to Gaveston*] Villain, 'tis thou that rob'st me of my lord.
GAVESTON Madam, 'tis you that rob me of my lord.
KING EDWARD Speak not unto her; let her droop and pine.
QUEEN Wherein, my lord, have I deserved these words?
Witness the tears that Isabella sheds,
Witness this heart that, sighing for thee, breaks,
How dear my lord is to poor Isabel.
KING EDWARD [*pushing her away*] And witness heaven how dear thou art to me!
There weep, for, till my Gaveston be repealed,° *recalled from exile*
Assure thyself thou com'st not in my sight.
Exeunt Edward and Gaveston.
QUEEN Oh, miserable and distressèd queen!
Would, when I left sweet France and was embarked,
That charming Circes,° walking on the waves, *Circe (see* Odyssey*, Bk. 10)*
Had changed my shape, or at the marriage day
The cup of Hymen° had been full of poison, *god of marriage*
Or with those arms that twined about my neck
I had been stifled, and not lived to see
The King my lord thus to abandon me.
Like frantic Juno[2] will I fill the earth
With ghastly murmur of my sighs and cries,
For never doted Jove on Ganymede° *Jove's cupbearer*
So much as he on cursèd Gaveston.
But that will more exasperate his wrath.
I must entreat him, I must speak him fair,
And be a means to call home Gaveston.

2. Juno was often driven into a jealous rage by her husband Jove's amours.

And yet he'll ever dote on Gaveston,
And so am I forever miserable.

Enter the nobles [Lancaster, Warwick, Pembroke, and the Mortimers] to the Queen.

LANCASTER Look where the sister of the King of France
Sits wringing of her hands and beats her breast.
WARWICK The King, I fear, hath ill entreated° her. *treated*
PEMBROKE Hard is the heart that injures such a saint.
MORTIMER JR. I know 'tis long of° Gaveston she weeps. *because of*
MORTIMER SR. Why? He is gone.
MORTIMER JR. [*to the Queen*] Madam, how fares Your Grace?
QUEEN Ah, Mortimer! Now breaks the King's hate forth,
And he confesseth that he loves me not.
MORTIMER JR. Cry quittance,° madam, then, and love not him. *Get even; quit him*
QUEEN No, rather will I die a thousand deaths.
And yet I love in vain; he'll ne'er love me.
LANCASTER Fear ye not, madam. Now his minion's gone,
His wanton humor° will be quickly left. *amorous disposition*
QUEEN Oh, never, Lancaster! I am enjoined
To sue° unto you all for his° repeal. *plead / (Gaveston's)*
This wills my lord, and this must I perform,
Or else be banished from His Highness' presence.
LANCASTER For his repeal? Madam, he comes not back
Unless the sea cast up his shipwrack° body. *shipwrecked*
WARWICK And to behold so sweet a sight as that
There's none here but would° run his horse to death. *none here who wouldn't*
MORTIMER JR. But, madam, would you have us call him home?
QUEEN Ay, Mortimer, for till he be restored
The angry king hath banished me the court;
And therefore, as thou lovest and tend'rest° me, *care for*
Be thou my advocate unto these peers.
MORTIMER JR. What, would ye have me plead for Gaveston?
MORTIMER SR. Plead for him he that will,° I am resolved. *No matter who pleads*
LANCASTER And so am I, my lord. Dissuade the Queen.
QUEEN Oh, Lancaster, let him dissuade the King,
For 'tis against my will he should return.
WARWICK Then speak not for him. Let the peasant go.
QUEEN 'Tis for myself I speak, and not for him.
PEMBROKE No speaking will prevail,° and therefore cease. *avail*
MORTIMER JR. Fair Queen, forbear to angle° for the fish *go fishing*
Which, being caught, strikes him that takes it dead—
I mean that vile torpedo,° Gaveston, *electric ray*
That now, I hope, floats° on the Irish Seas. *sails; floats as a corpse*
QUEEN Sweet Mortimer, sit down by me awhile,
And I will tell thee reasons of such weight
As thou wilt soon subscribe to his repeal.
MORTIMER JR. It is impossible; but speak your mind.
QUEEN Then thus—but none shall hear it but ourselves.
[*They sit and talk apart.*]
LANCASTER My lords, albeit the Queen win Mortimer,
Will you be resolute and hold with me?
MORTIMER SR. Not I against my nephew.

PEMBROKE Fear not, the Queen's words cannot alter him.
WARWICK No? Do but mark how earnestly she pleads.
LANCASTER And see how coldly his looks make denial.
WARWICK She smiles. Now, for my life, his mind is changed.
LANCASTER I'll rather lose his friendship, I, than grant.° *assent*
MORTIMER JR. [*returning to the lords*] Well, of necessity it
 must be so.—
My lords, that I abhor base Gaveston
I hope your honors° make no question, *you men of honor*
And therefore, though I plead for his repeal,
'Tis not for his sake but for our avail°— *benefit*
Nay, for the realm's behoof° and for the King's. *welfare*
LANCASTER Fie, Mortimer, dishonor not thyself.
Can this be true, 'twas good to banish him,
And is this true,° to call him home again? *right*
Such reasons make white black and dark night day.
MORTIMER JR. My lord of Lancaster, mark the respect.° *consider the reason*
LANCASTER In no respect° can contraries be true. *way*
QUEEN Yet, good my lord, hear what he can allege.
WARWICK All that he speaks is nothing; we are resolved.
MORTIMER JR. Do you not wish that Gaveston were dead?
PEMBROKE I would he were!
MORTIMER JR. Why, then, my lord, give me but leave to speak.
MORTIMER SR. But, nephew, do not play the sophister.° *unscrupulous arguer*
MORTIMER JR. This which I urge is of a burning zeal
To mend the King and do our country good.
Know you not Gaveston hath store of gold
Which may in Ireland purchase him such friends
As he will front° the mightiest of us all? *confront*
And whereas° he shall live and be beloved, *while*
'Tis hard for us to work his overthrow.
WARWICK Mark you but that, my lord of Lancaster.
MORTIMER JR. But were he here, detested as he is,
How easily might some base slave be suborned° *secretly hired*
To greet His Lordship with a poniard,° *dagger*
And none so much as blame the murderer,
But rather praise him for that brave attempt,° *undertaking*
And in the chronicle enroll his name
For purging of the realm of such a plague.
PEMBROKE He saith true.
LANCASTER Ay, but how chance° this was not done before? *how does it happen*
MORTIMER JR. Because, my lords, it was not thought upon.
Nay, more, when he shall know it lies in us
To banish him and then to call him home,
'Twill make him vail the top-flag° of his pride *lower the topsail*
And fear to offend the meanest° nobleman. *lowest-ranked*
MORTIMER SR. But how if he do not, nephew?
MORTIMER JR. Then may we with some color° rise in arms; *excuse, pretext*
For, howsoever we have borne it out,° *made it seem*
'Tis treason to be up° against the King. *up in arms*
So shall we have the people of° our side, *on*
Which for his father's sake lean to the King
But cannot brook° a night-grown mushroom, *tolerate (it that)*
Such a one as my lord of Cornwall° is, *i.e., Gaveston*
Should bear us down° of the nobility. *triumph over us*

And when the commons and the nobles join,
'Tis not° the King can buckler° Gaveston; *Not even / shield*
We'll pull him from the strongest hold° he hath. *stronghold*
My lords, if to perform this I be slack,
Think me as base a groom° as Gaveston. *slave, wretch*
LANCASTER On that condition, Lancaster will grant.
PEMBROKE And so will Pembroke.
WARWICK And I.
MORTIMER SR. And I.
MORTIMER JR. In this I count me highly gratified,
And Mortimer will rest° at your command. *remain*
QUEEN And when this favor Isabel forgets,
Then let her live abandoned and forlorn.
But see, in happy time,° my lord the King, *by fortunate chance*
Having brought the Earl of Cornwall on his way,
Is new returned. This news will glad him much,
Yet not so much as me. I love him more
Than he can Gaveston. Would he loved me
But half so much, then were I treble blest.

Enter King Edward, mourning° [and attendants, including Beaumont, Clerk of the Crown]. *dressed in mourning*

KING EDWARD He's gone, and for his absence thus I mourn.
Did never sorrow go so near my heart
As doth the want of my sweet Gaveston,
And, could my crown's revenue bring him back,
I would freely give it to his enemies,
And think I gained, having bought so dear a friend.
QUEEN [*to the lords*] Hark, how he harps upon his minion.
KING EDWARD [*to himself*] My heart is as an anvil unto sorrow,
Which beats upon it like the Cyclops' hammers,[3]
And with the noise turns up° my giddy brain *upside down*
And makes me frantic for my Gaveston.
Ah, had some bloodless Fury rose from hell[4]
And with my kingly scepter struck me dead,
When I was forced to leave my Gaveston!
LANCASTER *Diablo!*° What passions call you these? *The devil!*
QUEEN [*to the King*] My gracious lord, I come to bring you news—
KING EDWARD That you have parlèd° with your Mortimer? *parleyed, conferred*
QUEEN That Gaveston, my lord, shall be repealed.
KING EDWARD Repealed! The news is too sweet to be true.
QUEEN But will you love me if you find it so?
KING EDWARD If it be so, what will not Edward do?
QUEEN For Gaveston, but not for Isabel.
KING EDWARD For thee, fair Queen, if thou lovest Gaveston;
I'll hang a golden tongue° about thy neck, *(as a jewel, a token)*
Seeing thou hast pleaded with so good success.
QUEEN [*holding his arms around her*] No other jewels hang about my neck
Than these, my lord, nor let me have more wealth
Than I may fetch from this rich treasury. [*She kisses him.*]
Oh, how a kiss revives poor Isabel!

3. The one-eyed giants of Homer's *Odyssey* were sometimes portrayed as smiths with hammers.

4. Ah, would that some deathly-pale avenging goddess had risen up from hell.

KING EDWARD Once more receive my hand, and let this be
A second marriage 'twixt thyself and me.
QUEEN And may it prove more happy than the first!
[*The lords kneel.*]
My gentle lord, bespeak° these nobles fair,° *speak to / courteously*
That wait attendance for a gracious look,
And on their knees salute Your Majesty.
KING EDWARD [*raising and embracing them*] Courageous
Lancaster, embrace thy king,
And, as gross vapors° perish by the sun, *thick mists*
Even so let hatred with thy sovereign's smile.
Live thou with me as my companion.
LANCASTER This salutation overjoys my heart.
KING EDWARD Warwick shall be my chiefest counselor;
These silver hairs will more adorn my court
Than gaudy silks or rich embroidery.
Chide me, sweet Warwick, if I go astray.
WARWICK Slay me, my lord, when I offend Your Grace.
KING EDWARD In solemn° triumphs and in public shows *ceremonious*
Pembroke shall bear the sword before the King.
PEMBROKE And with this sword Pembroke will fight for you.
KING EDWARD But wherefore walks young Mortimer aside?
Be thou commander of our royal fleet,
Or, if that lofty office like° thee not, *please*
I make thee here Lord Marshal of the realm.
MORTIMER JR. My lord, I'll marshal° so your enemies *dispose of*
As England shall be quiet and you safe.
KING EDWARD And as for you, Lord Mortimer of Chirke,° *Welsh-Shropshire border*
Whose great achievements in our foreign war
Deserves no commonplace nor mean° reward, *lowly; small*
Be you the general of the levied troops
That now are ready to assail the Scots.
MORTIMER SR. In this Your Grace hath highly honored me,
For with my nature war doth best agree.
QUEEN Now is the King of England rich and strong,
Having the love of his renownèd peers.
KING EDWARD Ay, Isabel, ne'er was my heart so light.—
Clerk of the Crown, direct our warrant forth
For Gaveston to Ireland! Beaumont, fly
As fast as Iris or Jove's Mercury.[5]
BEAUMONT It shall be done, my gracious lord. [*Exit.*]
KING EDWARD Lord Mortimer, we leave you to your charge.
Now let us in and feast it royally.
Against our friend the Earl of Cornwall comes,[6]
We'll have a general tilt° and tournament, *joust*
And then his marriage shall be solemnized,
For wot° you not that I have made him sure° *know / betrothed him*
Unto our cousin,° the Earl of Gloucester's heir? *i.e., niece*
LANCASTER Such news we hear, my lord.
KING EDWARD That day, if not for him, yet for my sake,
Who° in the triumph° will be challenger, *Whoever / tournament*
Spare for no cost; we will requite your love.

5. In addition to being goddess of the rainbow, Iris was also a messenger of the gods, as was Mercury.

6. In preparation for Gaveston's arrival.

WARWICK In this, or aught, Your Highness shall command us.
KING EDWARD Thanks, gentle Warwick. Come, let's in and revel. *Exeunt. Manent° Mortimers.* *Remain onstage*
MORTIMER SR. Nephew, I must to Scotland; thou stayest here.
Leave° now to oppose thyself against the King. *Cease*
Thou see'st by nature he is mild and calm,
And, seeing his mind so dotes on Gaveston,
Let him without controlment have his will.
The mightiest kings have had their minions:
Great Alexander loved Hephaestion,
The conquering Hercules for Hylas wept,
And for Patroclus stern Achilles drooped.[7]
And not kings only, but the wisest men:
The Roman Tully loved Octavius,
Grave Socrates, wild Alcibiades.[8]
Then let His Grace, whose youth is flexible,
And promiseth as much as we can wish,
Freely enjoy that vain, light-headed earl,
For riper years will wean him from such toys.° *amorous trifling*
MORTIMER JR. Uncle, his wanton humor grieves not me,
But this I scorn, that one so basely born
Should by his sovereign's favor grow so pert
And riot it° with the treasure of the realm *revel in dissipation*
While soldiers mutiny for want of pay.
He wears a lord's revenue on his back,[9]
And Midas-like[1] he jets it° in the court, *struts about*
With base outlandish cullions° at his heels, *rogues (lit., "testicles")*
Whose proud, fantastic liveries make such show
As if that Proteus,[2] god of shapes, appeared.
I have not seen a dapper jack° so brisk. *knave*
He wears a short Italian hooded cloak,
Larded° with pearl, and in his Tuscan cap *Festooned*
A jewel of more value than the crown.
Whiles other° walk below, the King and he *While others*
From out a window laugh at such as we,
And flout our train,° and jest at our attire. *retinue, followers*
Uncle, 'tis this that makes me impatient.
MORTIMER SR. But, nephew, now you see the King is changed.
MORTIMER JR. Then so am I, and live to do him service.
But whiles I have a sword, a hand, a heart,
I will not yield to any such upstart.
You know my mind. Come, uncle, let's away. *Exeunt.*

7. Hephaestion was one of Alexander the Great's captains and his lover; he died in 324 B.C.E. On Hylas, see note 5 to 1.1 above. Patroclus, a Greek general at Troy, was the favorite companion of Achilles in the *Iliad*.
8. The Roman Tully is Cicero, the great Roman orator and statesman, whose death in 43 B.C.E., ordered by Marc Antony, was reluctantly consented to by Octavius (or Octavianus, later Emperor Augustus), who admired Cicero despite his republican opposition to Julius Caesar's tyranny and later to Antony. The idea of a love relationship between Cicero and Octavius has no historical basis. Socrates' erotic relationship with Alcibiades, the arrogant Athenian political leader, is suggested in Plato's *Symposium*.
9. He spends a lord's revenue for the rich clothes he wears.
1. King Midas of Phrygia obtained his wish that all he touched would turn to gold.
2. An "ancient one" of the sea capable of assuming different shapes in order to escape being questioned.

[2.1]

Enter Spencer [Junior] and Baldock.

BALDOCK Spencer,
Seeing that our lord th'Earl of Gloucester's dead,
Which of the nobles dost thou mean to serve?
SPENCER JR. Not Mortimer, nor any of his side,
Because the King and he are enemies.
Baldock, learn this of me: a factious lord
Shall hardly do himself good, much less us,
But he that hath the favor of a king
May with one word advance us while we live.
The liberal° Earl of Cornwall is the man — *free-spending*
On whose good fortune Spencer's hope depends.
BALDOCK What, mean you then to be his follower?
SPENCER JR. No, his companion, for he loves me well,
And would have once preferred° me to the King. — *recommended*
BALDOCK But he is banished; there's small hope of him.
SPENCER JR. Ay, for a while. But, Baldock, mark the end:
A friend of mine told me in secrecy
That he's repealed and sent for back again,
And even now a post° came from the court — *messenger*
With letters to our lady° from the King, — *(the King's niece; 2.1.56.2)*
And as she read, she smiled, which makes me think
It is about her lover Gaveston.
BALDOCK 'Tis like° enough, for since he was exiled — *likely*
She neither walks abroad nor comes in sight.
But I had thought the match had been broke off
And that his banishment had changed her mind.
SPENCER JR. Our lady's first love is not wavering.
My life for° thine, she will have Gaveston. — *I bet my life against*
BALDOCK Then hope I by her means to be preferred,
Having read unto° her since she was a child. — *tutored*
SPENCER JR. Then, Baldock, you must cast the scholar off
And learn to court it° like a gentleman. — *be courtly*
'Tis not a black coat and a little band,° — *neck-band; cuff or ruff*
A velvet-caped cloak faced before° with serge, — *trimmed in front*
And smelling to a nosegay° all the day, — *sniffing a bouquet*
Or holding of a napkin in your hand,
Or saying a long grace at a table's end,
Or making low legs° to a nobleman, — *bows*
Or looking downward with your eyelids close,° — *shut*
And saying, "Truly, an't° may please Your Honor," — *if it*
Can get you any favor with great men;
You must be proud, bold, pleasant,° resolute, — *jocular*
And now and then stab as occasion serves.
BALDOCK Spencer, thou knowest I hate such formal toys,° — *mannered trifles*
And use them but of° mere hypocrisy. — *out of*
Mine old lord, while he lived, was so precise° — *puritanical*
That he would take exceptions at my buttons,
And, being° like pins' heads, blame me for the bigness, — *they being*
Which made me curatelike in mine attire,

2.1. The Earl of Gloucester's castle.

Though inwardly licentious enough
And apt for any kind of villainy.
I am none of these common pedants,° I, *pedagogues*
That cannot speak without "*propterea quod*."° *"on account of which"*
SPENCER JR. But one of those that saith "*quandoquidem*"° *"seeing that"*
And hath a special gift to form a verb.° *has a rhetorical flair*
BALDOCK Leave off this jesting; here my lady comes.
[*They stand aside.*]

Enter the lady [*Niece to the King, with letters*].

NIECE [*to herself*] The grief for his exile was not so much
As is the joy of his returning home.
This letter came from my sweet Gaveston.
[*She reads silently.*]
What need'st thou, love, thus to excuse thyself?
I know thou couldst not come and visit me.
[*Reading aloud*] "I will not long be from thee, though I die."
This argues the entire love of my lord.
[*Reading*] "When I forsake thee, death seize on my heart!"
But rest thee here where Gaveston shall sleep.
[*She places the letter in her bosom.*]
Now to the letter of my lord the King.
[*She examines another letter.*]
He wills me to repair° unto the court *betake myself*
And meet my Gaveston. Why do I stay,
Seeing that he talks thus of my marriage day?
[*Calling*] Who's there? Baldock?
See that my coach be ready; I must hence.
BALDOCK It shall be done, madam.
NIECE And meet me at the park pale° presently. *fence enclosing estate*
Exit [*Baldock*].
Spencer, stay you and bear° me company, *keep*
For I have joyful news to tell thee of:
My lord of Cornwall is a-coming over,
And will be at the court as soon as we.
SPENCER JR. I knew the King would have him home again.
NIECE If all things sort out as I hope they will,
Thy service, Spencer, shall be thought upon.° *i.e., rewarded*
SPENCER JR. I humbly thank Your Ladyship.
NIECE Come, lead the way. I long till I am there. [*Exeunt.*]

[2.2]

Enter [*King*] *Edward, the Queen, Lancaster, Mortimer* [*Junior*], *Warwick, Pembroke, Kent,* [*and*] *attendants.* [*The lords bear heraldic devices° on their shields.*] *emblems, mottoes*

KING EDWARD The wind is good. I wonder why he stays;
I fear me he is wracked° upon the sea. *shipwrecked*
QUEEN [*aside to Lancaster*] Look, Lancaster, how passionate he is,
And still his mind runs on his minion.
LANCASTER [*to the King*] My lord—
KING EDWARD How now, what news? Is Gaveston arrived?

2.2. Located historically at Tynemouth, on England's northeast coast (see line 51).

MORTIMER JR. Nothing but Gaveston! What means Your Grace?
You have matters of more weight to think upon;
The King of France sets foot in Normandy.
KING EDWARD A trifle. We'll expel him when we please.
But tell me, Mortimer, what's thy device
Against° the stately triumph we decreed? *In preparation for*
MORTIMER JR. A homely one, my lord, not worth the telling.
KING EDWARD Prithee let me know it.
MORTIMER JR. But seeing you are so desirous, thus it is:
A lofty cedar tree, fair flourishing,
On whose top branches kingly eagles perch,
And by the bark a canker creeps me up° *cankerworm creeps up*
And gets unto the highest bough of all.
The motto: *Aeque tandem*.° *Equally at length*
KING EDWARD And what is yours, my lord of Lancaster?
LANCASTER My lord, mine's more obscure than Mortimer's.
Pliny[1] reports there is a flying fish
Which all the other fishes deadly hate,
And therefore, being pursued, it takes the air;
No sooner is it up, but there's a fowl
That seizeth it. This fish, my lord, I bear;
The motto this: *Undique mors est*.° *Death is on all sides*
KING EDWARD Proud Mortimer! Ungentle Lancaster!
Is this the love you bear your sovereign?
Is this the fruit your reconcilement bears?
Can you in words make show of amity,
And in your shields display your rancorous minds?
What call you this but private libeling
Against the Earl of Cornwall and my brother?° *my friend (Gaveston)*
QUEEN Sweet husband, be content. They all love you.
KING EDWARD They love me not that hate my Gaveston.
I am that cedar; shake me not too much.
And you the eagles, soar ye ne'er so high,
I have the jesses[2] that will pull you down,
And *Aeque tandem* shall that canker° cry *i.e., Gaveston*
Unto the proudest peer of Britainy.° *Great Britain*
[*To Lancaster*] Though thou compar'st him° to a flying fish, *(Gaveston)*
And threatenest death whether he rise or fall,
'Tis not the hugest monster of the sea
Nor foulest harpy that shall swallow him.[3]
MORTIMER JR. [*to the lords*] If in his absence thus he favors him,
What will he do whenas° he shall be present? *when*
LANCASTER That shall we see. Look where His Lordship comes.

Enter Gaveston.

KING EDWARD My Gaveston!
Welcome to Tynemouth, welcome to thy friend!
Thy absence made me droop and pine away;
For, as the lovers of fair Danaë,
When she was locked up in a brazen tower,[4]

1. Author of an extensive natural history published in 77 C.E.
2. Short straps fastened on the leg of a hawk, usually with a ring to which a leash might be attached.
3. Not even a whale or a harpy would be able to swallow this flying fish (Gaveston); he'll prove too much for his enemies. (Harpies were violent mythological creatures, part woman, part bird, who were descended from Pontus and Oceanus, both sea gods.)
4. Danaë was confined to a tower of brass by her father in a vain attempt to avoid an oracle's prophecy that he would be killed by her son. Zeus came to her as a lover

Desired her more and waxed outrageous,° — *became unruly*
So did it sure with me; and now thy sight
Is sweeter far than was thy parting hence
Bitter and irksome to my sobbing heart.

GAVESTON Sweet lord and king, your speech preventeth° mine; — *anticipates*
Yet have I words left to express my joy.
The shepherd, nipped with biting winter's rage,
Frolics not more to see the painted° spring — *gaily colored*
Than I do to behold Your Majesty.

KING EDWARD Will none of you salute my Gaveston?

LANCASTER Salute him? Yes. Welcome, Lord Chamberlain.

MORTIMER JR. Welcome is the good Earl of Cornwall.

WARWICK Welcome, Lord Governor of the Isle of Man.

PEMBROKE Welcome, Master Secretary.

KENT Brother, do you hear them?

KING EDWARD Still will these earls and barons use° me thus? — *treat*

GAVESTON My lord, I cannot brook these injuries.

QUEEN [*aside*] Ay me, poor soul, when these begin to jar.° — *quarrel*

KING EDWARD [*to Gaveston*] Return it to their throats;° I'll be thy warrant. — *Make them eat their words*

GAVESTON Base-leaden° earls, that glory in your birth, — *Base-mettled*
Go sit at home and eat your tenants' beef,[5]
And come not here to scoff at Gaveston,
Whose mounting thoughts did never creep so low
As to bestow a look on such as you.

LANCASTER Yet I disdain not to do this for you.

[*He draws his sword. In the scuffle, Mortimer Junior and Gaveston draw also.*]

KING EDWARD Treason, treason! Where's the traitor?

PEMBROKE [*pointing to Gaveston*] Here, here![6]

KING EDWARD Convey hence Gaveston! They'll murder him.

GAVESTON [*to Lancaster or Mortimer Junior*] The life of thee shall salve° this foul disgrace. — *heal, remedy*

MORTIMER JR. Villain, thy life, unless I miss mine aim.

[*He wounds Gaveston.*]

QUEEN Ah, furious Mortimer, what hast thou done?

MORTIMER JR. No more than I would answer,° were he slain. — *answer for*

[*Exit Gaveston, attended.*]

KING EDWARD Yes, more than thou canst answer,° though he live. — *pay for judicially*
Dear shall you both aby° this riotous deed. — *pay for*
Out of my presence! Come not near the court!

MORTIMER JR. I'll not be barred the court for Gaveston.

LANCASTER We'll hale him by the ears unto the block.° — *executioner's block*

KING EDWARD Look to your own heads; his is sure° enough. — *secure*

WARWICK Look to your own crown, if you back him thus.

KENT Warwick, these words do ill beseem thy years.

KING EDWARD Nay, all of them conspire to cross me thus;
But if I live, I'll tread upon their heads
That think with high looks thus to tread me down.

---

in a shower of gold. Their son was Perseus, who later accidentally killed Danaë's father.

5. Live off the income you derive from the tenants on your land.

6. To draw a sword in the King's presence was a treasonable offense. Pembroke here suggests that though technically Lancaster is guilty of this, Gaveston is the real traitor.

Come, Edmund, let's away and levy men.
'Tis war that must abate these barons' pride.
Exeunt the King [*and the Queen and Kent, attended*].

WARWICK Let's to our castles, for the King is moved.° *angered*
MORTIMER JR. Moved may he be, and perish in his wrath!
LANCASTER Cousin,° it is° no dealing with him now. *Friend / there is*
He means to make us stoop by force of arms;
And therefore let us jointly here protest° *swear, vow*
To prosecute that Gaveston to the death.
MORTIMER JR. By heaven, the abject villain shall not live.
WARWICK I'll have his blood or die in seeking it.
PEMBROKE The like oath Pembroke takes.
LANCASTER And so doth Lancaster.
Now send our heralds to defy the King,
And make the people swear to put him down.

Enter a post [*Messenger*].

MORTIMER JR. Letters? From whence?
MESSENGER From Scotland, my lord.
[*Mortimer Junior takes and reads a letter.*]
LANCASTER Why, how now, cousin, how fares all our friends?
MORTIMER JR. My uncle's taken prisoner by the Scots.
LANCASTER We'll have him ransomed, man; be of good cheer.
MORTIMER JR. They rate his ransom at five thousand pound.
Who should defray the money but the King,
Seeing he is taken prisoner in his wars?
I'll to the King.
LANCASTER Do, cousin, and I'll bear thee company.
WARWICK Meantime, my lord of Pembroke and myself
Will to Newcastle here and gather head.° *assemble troops*
MORTIMER JR. About it, then, and we will follow you.
LANCASTER Be resolute and full of secrecy.
WARWICK I warrant you.
[*Exeunt all but Mortimer Junior and Lancaster.*]
MORTIMER JR. Cousin, an if° he will not ransom him, *an if = if*
I'll thunder such a peal into his ears
As never subject did unto his king.
LANCASTER Content. I'll bear my part. [*Calling*] Holla! Who's there?

[*Enter Guard.*]

MORTIMER JR. Ay, marry, such a guard as this doth well.° *(said sarcastically)*
LANCASTER Lead on the way.
A GUARD Whither will Your Lordships?
MORTIMER JR. Whither else but to the King?
A GUARD His Highness is disposed to be alone.
LANCASTER Why, so he may, but we will speak to him.
A GUARD You may not in, my lord.
MORTIMER JR. May we not?

[*Enter the King and Kent.*]

KING EDWARD How now, what noise is this?
Who have we there? Is't you? [*He starts to go back.*]
MORTIMER JR. Nay, stay, my lord. I come to bring you news:
Mine uncle's taken prisoner by the Scots.

KING EDWARD Then ransom him.
LANCASTER 'Twas in your wars; you should ransom him.
MORTIMER JR. And you shall ransom him, or else.
KENT What, Mortimer, you will not threaten him?
KING EDWARD Quiet yourself. You shall have the broad seal° *i.e., taxing authority*
To gather for him thoroughout the realm.
LANCASTER Your minion Gaveston hath taught you this.
MORTIMER JR. My lord, the family of the Mortimers
Are not so poor but, would they° sell their land, *if they chose to*
Would levy men enough to anger you.
We never beg, but use such prayers as these.
[*He puts his hand on his sword.*]
KING EDWARD Shall I still be haunted thus?
MORTIMER JR. Nay, now you are here alone, I'll speak my mind.
LANCASTER And so will I; and then, my lord, farewell.
MORTIMER JR. The idle triumphs, masques, lascivious shows,
And prodigal gifts bestowed on Gaveston
Have drawn thy treasure° dry and made thee weak; *treasury*
The murmuring commons overstretchèd hath.[7]
LANCASTER Look for rebellion; look to be deposed.
Thy garrisons are beaten out of France,
And lame and poor lie groaning at the gates.[8]
The wild O'Neill, with swarms of Irish kerns,° *foot soldiers*
Lives uncontrolled within the English pale.[9]
Unto the walls of York the Scots made road,° *raid; inroad*
And, unresisted, drave° away rich spoils.° *carted / booty*
MORTIMER JR. The haughty Dane commands the narrow seas,° *English Channel*
While in the harbor ride thy ships unrigged.
LANCASTER What foreign prince sends thee ambassadors?
MORTIMER JR. Who loves thee but a sort° of flatters? *company, gang*
LANCASTER Thy gentle queen, sole sister to Valois,° *the King of France*
Complains that thou hast left her all forlorn.
MORTIMER JR. Thy court is naked, being bereft of those
That makes a king seem glorious to the world—
I mean the peers, whom thou shouldst dearly love.
Libels are cast again thee° in the street; *Pamphlets defame you*
Ballads and rhymes made of thy overthrow.
LANCASTER The northern borderers, seeing their houses burnt,
Their wives and children slain, run up and down,
Cursing the name of thee and Gaveston.
MORTIMER JR. When wert thou in the field with banner spread
But once? And then thy soldiers marched like players,° *actors*
With garish robes, not armor; and thyself,
Bedaubed with gold, rode laughing at the rest,[1]
Nodding and shaking of thy spangled crest,° *plumed helmet*
Where women's favors hung like labels down.[2]

7. Expenditures on masques and idle entertainments have overstretched the endurance of the restive commoners.
8. The lame and unemployed customarily gathered at the city gates to beg.
9. The "pale" was the area around Dublin in which English settlers enjoyed relative safety against the depradations of O'Neill, the Irish guerilla leader.
1. You egged on the soldiers with your foolish laughter as you rode among them.
2. And love tokens (such as ribbons, scarves, or gloves) hung down from your helmet like the strips of parchment with which official seals are attached to documents.

LANCASTER And thereof came it that the fleering° Scots, *jeering*
To England's high disgrace, have made this jig:° *jingle*
"Maids of England, sore may you mourn,
For your lemans° you have lost at Bannocksbourn,[3] *lovers*
With a heave and a ho!
What, weeneth° the King of England *expects, hopes*
So soon to have won Scotland?
With a rumbelow!"° *(a nonsense refrain)*
MORTIMER JR. Wigmore shall fly,[4] to set my uncle free.
LANCASTER And when 'tis gone, our swords shall purchase° more. *win militarily*
If ye be moved, revenge it as you can.
Look next to see us with our ensigns° spread. *banners*
Exeunt nobles [*Mortimer Junior and Lancaster*].
KING EDWARD My swelling heart for very anger breaks.
How oft have I been baited° by these peers, *harassed, attacked*
And dare not be revenged, for their power is great!
Yet shall the crowing of these cockerels° *young roosters*
Affright a lion? Edward, unfold thy paws,
And let their lives' blood slake thy fury's hunger.
If I be cruel and grow tyrannous,
Now let them thank themselves, and rue too late.
KENT My lord, I see your love to Gaveston
Will be the ruin of the realm and you,
For now the wrathful nobles threaten wars,
And therefore, brother, banish him forever.
KING EDWARD Art thou an enemy to my Gaveston?
KENT Ay, and it grieves me that I favored him.
KING EDWARD Traitor, begone! Whine thou with Mortimer.
KENT So will I, rather than with° Gaveston. *than put up with*
KING EDWARD Out of my sight, and trouble me no more!
KENT No marvel though thou scorn thy noble peers,
When I thy brother am rejected thus.
KING EDWARD Away! *Exit* [*Kent*].
Poor Gaveston, that hast no friend but me.
Do what they can, we'll live in Tynemouth here,
And, so° I walk with him about the walls, *so long as*
What care I though the earls begirt us round?
Here comes she that's cause of all these jars.° *quarrels*

Enter the Queen, ladies three [*the King's Niece and two ladies-in-waiting*], *Baldock and Spencer* [*Junior, and Gaveston*].

QUEEN My lord, 'tis thought the earls are up in arms.
KING EDWARD Ay, and 'tis likewise thought you favor 'em.
QUEEN Thus do you still suspect me without cause.
NIECE Sweet uncle, speak more kindly to the Queen.
GAVESTON [*aside to the King*] My lord, dissemble with her, speak her fair.
KING EDWARD [*to the Queen*] Pardon me, sweet, I forgot myself.
QUEEN Your pardon is quickly got of Isabel.

3. At the Battle of Bannockburn, in 1314, Robert Bruce soundly defeated the English forces under the command of Edward II and established himself on the Scottish throne, thus postponing for centuries the union of Scotland with England.
4. My estate of Wigmore Castle will have to be sold.

KING EDWARD The younger Mortimer is grown so brave° *insolent, defiant*
That to my face he threatens civil wars.
GAVESTON Why do you not commit him to the Tower?
KING EDWARD I dare not, for the people love him well.
GAVESTON Why, then, we'll have him privily made away.° *secretly done away with*
KING EDWARD Would Lancaster and he had both caroused° *drunk*
A bowl of poison to each other's health!
But let them go,° and tell me what° are these. *forget them / who*
[*He indicates Baldock and Spencer Junior.*]
NIECE Two of my father's servants° whilst he lived. *followers*
May't please Your Grace to entertain° them now? *take into service*
KING EDWARD [*to Baldock*] Tell me, where wast thou born?
What is thine arms?° *heraldry*
BALDOCK My name is Baldock, and my gentry° *rank as gentleman*
I fetched from Oxford, not from heraldry.
KING EDWARD The fitter art thou, Baldock, for my turn.° *my purposes*
Wait on° me, and I'll see thou shalt not want. *Attend*
BALDOCK I humbly thank Your Majesty.
KING EDWARD [*indicating Spencer Junior*] Knowest thou him, Gaveston?
GAVESTON Ay, my lord,
His name is Spencer; he is well allied.° *connected by family*
For my sake, let him wait upon Your Grace;
Scarce shall you find a man of more desert.° *deserving*
KING EDWARD Then, Spencer, wait upon me. For his sake
I'll grace thee with a higher style° ere long. *title*
SPENCER JR. No greater titles happen unto me
Than to be favored of Your Majesty.
KING EDWARD [*to his Niece*] Cousin, this day shall be your marriage feast.
And, Gaveston, think that I love thee well
To wed thee to our niece, the only heir
Unto the Earl of Gloucester late deceased.
GAVESTON I know, my lord, many will stomach° me, *resent*
But I respect neither their love nor hate.
KING EDWARD The headstrong barons shall not limit me;
He that I list° to favor shall be great. *wish, choose*
Come, let's away, and, when the marriage ends,
Have at the rebels and their complices!° *Exeunt omnes.* *accomplices, allies*

[2.3]

Enter Lancaster, Mortimer [*Junior*], *Warwick, Pembroke,* [*their followers, and*] *Kent.*

KENT My lords, of° love to this our native land *out of*
I come to join with you and leave the King,
And in your quarrel and the realm's behoof° *benefit, behalf*
Will be the first that shall adventure life.° *risk death*
LANCASTER I fear me you are sent of policy,° *out of cunning*
To undermine us with a show of love.
WARWICK He is your brother; therefore have we cause
To cast° the worst, and doubt of° your revolt. *forecast / suspect*

2.3. The battle sequence in the ensuing scenes historically took place in the vicinity of Tynemouth.

KENT Mine honor shall be hostage of my truth.
If that will not suffice, farewell, my lords.
MORTIMER JR. Stay, Edmund. Never was Plantagenet[1]
False of his word, and therefore trust we thee.
PEMBROKE But what's the reason you should leave him now?
KENT I have informed the Earl of Lancaster.
LANCASTER And it sufficeth. Now, my lords, know this,
That Gaveston is secretly arrived
And here in Tynemouth frolics with the King.
Let us with these our followers scale the walls
And suddenly surprise them unawares.
MORTIMER JR. I'll give the onset.° *lead the attack*
WARWICK And I'll follow thee.
MORTIMER JR. This tattered ensign of my ancestors,
Which swept the desert shore of that Dead Sea
Whereof we got the name of Mortimer,[2]
Will I advance upon this castle walls.—
Drums, strike alarum!° Raise them from their sport, *the call to arms*
And ring aloud the knell of Gaveston!
LANCASTER None be so hardy as to touch the King,
But neither spare you Gaveston nor his friends. *Exeunt.*

[2.4]

[*Alarums.*][1] *Enter the King and Spencer* [*Junior, meeting*].

KING EDWARD Oh, tell me, Spencer, where is Gaveston?
SPENCER JR. I fear me he is slain, my gracious lord.
KING EDWARD No, here he comes. Now let them spoil° and kill. *plunder*

[*Enter*] *to them Gaveston, etc.* [*the Queen, the Niece, and lords*].

Fly, fly, my lords! The earls have got the hold.° *captured the stronghold*
Take shipping and away to Scarborough!
Spencer and I will post away by land.
GAVESTON Oh, stay, my lord. They will not injure you.
KING EDWARD I will not trust them, Gaveston. Away!
GAVESTON Farewell, my lord.
KING EDWARD [*to his Niece*] Lady, farewell.
NIECE Farewell, sweet uncle, till we meet again.
KING EDWARD Farewell, sweet Gaveston, and farewell, niece.
QUEEN No farewell to poor Isabel, thy queen?
KING EDWARD Yes, yes, for Mortimer, your lover's sake.
Exeunt omnes; manet° [*Queen*] *Isabella.* *remains*
QUEEN Heavens can witness I love none but you!
From my embracements thus he breaks away.

1. Roger (IV) de Mortimer (Mortimer Junior) was the eighth Baron of Wigmore and the first Earl of March. The name of Plantagenet was adopted as a surname by Richard, Duke of York, around 1460 as a title claiming superiority of descent over the Lancastrians (Henry IV, V, and VI). The earls of March in the fifteenth century were connected by marriage with this so-called Yorkist claim.

2. According to a false etymology, "Mortimer" was thought to come from "*de Mortuo Mari,*" meaning "from the Dead Sea," in memory of their involvement in the Crusades.

2.4. The battle of Tynemouth continues.

1. Alarms, signals (by means of trumpet and drum) calling men to arms (see 2.3.25). Used in the theater as a shorthand to indicate fighting.

Oh, that mine arms could close this isle about,
That I might pull him to me where I would,
Or that these tears that drizzle from mine eyes
Had power to mollify his stony heart,
That when I had him we might never part!

Enter the barons [Lancaster, Warwick, Mortimer Junior, and others]. Alarums.

LANCASTER I wonder how he scaped.° — *escaped*
MORTIMER JR. Who's this, the Queen?
QUEEN Ay, Mortimer, the miserable Queen,
Whose pining heart her inward sighs have blasted
And body with continual mourning wasted.
These hands are tired with haling° of my lord — *dragging*
From Gaveston, from wicked Gaveston,
And all in vain, for when I speak him fair
He turns away and smiles upon his minion.
MORTIMER JR. Cease to lament, and tell us where's the King?
QUEEN What would you with the King? Is't him you seek?
LANCASTER No, madam, but that cursèd Gaveston.
Far be it from the thought of Lancaster
To offer violence to his sovereign;
We would but rid the realm of Gaveston.
Tell us where he remains, and he shall die.
QUEEN He's gone by water unto Scarborough;
Pursue him quickly, and he cannot scape.
The King hath left him, and his train is small.
WARWICK Forslow° no time, sweet Lancaster; let's march. — *Lose, delay*
MORTIMER JR. How comes it that the King and he is parted?
QUEEN That this your army, going several ways,° — *being divided in two*
Might be of lesser force, and with the power
That he intendeth presently to raise
Be easily suppressed; and therefore begone.
MORTIMER JR. Here in the river rides a Flemish hoy.° — *small sailing vessel*
Let's all aboard and follow him amain.° — *with all our might*
LANCASTER The wind that bears him hence will fill our sails.
Come, come, aboard. 'Tis but an hour's sailing.
MORTIMER JR. Madam, stay you within this castle here.
QUEEN No, Mortimer, I'll to my lord the King.
MORTIMER JR. Nay, rather sail with us to Scarborough.
QUEEN You know the King is so suspicious
As, if he hear I have but talked with you,
Mine honor will be called in question;
And therefore, gentle Mortimer, begone.
MORTIMER JR. Madam, I cannot stay to answer you;
But think of Mortimer as he deserves.

[*Exeunt all but the Queen.*]

QUEEN So well hast thou deserved, sweet Mortimer,
As Isabel could live with thee forever.
In vain I look for love at Edward's hand,
Whose eyes are fixed on none but Gaveston.
Yet once more I'll importune him with prayers.
If he be strange° and not regard my words, — *distant, unresponsive*
My son and I will over into France,
And to the King, my brother, there complain

How Gaveston hath robbed me of his love;
But yet I hope my sorrows will have end,
And Gaveston this blessèd day be slain. *Exit.*

[2.5]

Enter Gaveston, pursued.

GAVESTON Yet, lusty° lords, I have escaped your hands, *insolent*
Your threats, your 'larums, and your hot pursuits;
And, though divorcèd from King Edward's eyes,
Yet liveth Piers of Gaveston unsurprised,° *uncaptured*
Breathing, in hope—*malgrado* all your beards,[1]
That muster rebels thus against your king—
To see his royal sovereign once again.

Enter the nobles [Warwick, Lancaster, Pembroke, Mortimer Junior, with soldiers and attendants].

WARWICK Upon him, soldiers! Take away his weapons.
MORTIMER JR. [*as the soldiers attack Gaveston*] Thou proud disturber of thy country's peace,
Corrupter of thy king, cause of these broils,° *quarrels*
Base flatterer, yield! And were it not for shame,
Shame and dishonor to a soldier's name,
Upon my weapon's point here shouldst thou fall,
And welter in thy gore. [*Gaveston is taken.*]
LANCASTER Monster of men,
That, like the Greekish strumpet,° trained° to arms *Helen of Troy / lured*
And bloody wars so many valiant knights,
Look for no other fortune, wretch, than death.
King Edward is not here to buckler° thee. *shield*
WARWICK Lancaster, why talk'st thou to the slave?
Go, soldiers, take him hence, for, by my sword,
His head shall off.—Gaveston, short warning
Shall serve thy turn;[2] it is our country's cause
That here severely we will execute
Upon thy person.—Hang him at a bough.
GAVESTON My lord!
WARWICK Soldiers, have him away!—
But, for° thou wert the favorite of a king, *because*
Thou shalt have so much honor at our hands.[3]
GAVESTON I thank you all, my lords. Then I perceive
That heading° is one, and hanging is the other, *beheading*
And death is all.

Enter Earl of Arundel.

LANCASTER How now, my lord of Arundel?
ARUNDEL My lords, King Edward greets you all by me.
WARWICK Arundel, say your message.
ARUNDEL His Majesty,

2.5. Near Pembroke's castle; historically, in the vicinity of Scarborough.
1. In spite of all your beards. (Gaveston heaps scorn on the beards worn in the English style by his baronial opponents. To insult a man's beard was a quick way to start a violent quarrel.)
2. A brief respite is all you'll get before you're executed.
3. I.e., You'll be beheaded, then, like a gentleman (instead of being hanged, as threatened in line 24).

Hearing that you had taken Gaveston,
Entreateth you by me yet but he may
See him[4] before he dies. Forwhy,° he says, *Because*
And sends you word, he knows that die he shall;
And if you gratify His Grace so far,
He will be mindful of the courtesy.

WARWICK How now?

GAVESTON [*aside*] Renownèd Edward, how thy name
Revives poor Gaveston!

WARWICK No, it needeth not.° *it is inadvisable*
Arundel, we will gratify the King
In other matters; he must pardon us in this.—
Soldiers, away with him!

GAVESTON Why, my lord of Warwick,
Will not these delays beget my hopes?° *give me some hope*
I know it, lords, it is this life you aim at;
Yet grant King Edward this.

MORTIMER JR. Shalt thou appoint° *specify, dictate*
What we shall grant?—Soldiers, away with him!—
[*To Arundel*] Thus we'll gratify the King:
We'll send his head by thee. Let him bestow
His tears on that, for that is all he gets
Of Gaveston, or else his senseless trunk.

LANCASTER Not so,[5] my lord, lest he bestow more cost
In burying him than he° hath ever earned. *(Gaveston)*

ARUNDEL My lords, it is His Majesty's request,
And, in the honor of a king, he swears
He will but talk with him and send him back.

WARWICK When, can you tell?[6] Arundel, no.
We wot° he that the care of realm remits,° *know / abandons*
And drives his nobles to these exigents° *extremities*
For Gaveston, will, if he seize him once,
Violate any promise to possess him.

ARUNDEL Then if you will not trust His Grace in keep,° *to have custody*
My lords, I will be pledge° for his° return. *hostage / (Gaveston's)*

MORTIMER JR. It is honorable in thee to offer this,
But, for° we know thou art a noble gentleman, *because*
We will not wrong thee so
To make away a true man for a thief.

GAVESTON How mean'st thou, Mortimer? That is overbase.° *too insulting*

MORTIMER JR. Away, base groom, robber of kings' renown!
Question° with thy companions and thy mates. *Argue, wrangle*

PEMBROKE My Lord Mortimer, and you my lords each one,
To gratify the King's request therein
Touching° the sending of this Gaveston, *Regarding*
Because His Majesty so earnestly
Desires to see the man before his death,
I will upon mine honor undertake
To carry him and bring him back again,
Provided this: that you, my lord of Arundel,
Will join with me.

4. Entreats you through me as ambassador that he may be allowed to see Gaveston.

5. I.e., Let's not even send Gaveston's corpse to the King.

6. A colloquial expression of scornful incredulity.

WARWICK Pembroke, what wilt thou do?
Cause yet more bloodshed? Is it not enough
That we have taken him, but must we now
Leave him on "had-I-wist"[7] and let him go?
PEMBROKE My lords, I will not overwoo your honors,
But, if you dare trust Pembroke with the prisoner,
Upon mine oath, I will return him back.
ARUNDEL My lord of Lancaster, what say you in this?
LANCASTER Why, I say, let him go on Pembroke's word.
PEMBROKE And you, Lord Mortimer?
MORTIMER JR. How say you, my lord of Warwick?
WARWICK Nay, do your pleasures. I know how 'twill prove.° *turn out*
PEMBROKE Then give him me.
GAVESTON Sweet sovereign, yet I come
To see thee ere I die.
WARWICK [*aside*] Yet not, perhaps,
If Warwick's wit and policy° prevail. *cleverness and cunning*
MORTIMER JR. My lord of Pembroke, we deliver him you;
Return him on your honor.—Sound! Away!

[*Gaveston is delivered into Pembroke's custody. Trumpets sound.*] *Exeunt. Manent Pembroke, Arundel, Gaveston, and Pembroke's men, four soldiers* [*among them James and a Horseboy*].

PEMBROKE [*to Arundel*] My lord, you shall go with me.
My house is not far hence, out of the way
A little, but our men shall go along.
We that have pretty wenches to° our wives, *as*
Sir, must not come so near and balk° their lips. *refuse, pass by*
ARUNDEL 'Tis very kindly spoke, my lord of Pembroke.
Your Honor hath an adamant° of power *magnet*
To draw a prince.
PEMBROKE So, my lord.—Come hither, James.
I do commit this Gaveston to thee.
Be thou this night his keeper; in the morning
We will discharge thee of thy charge. Begone.
GAVESTON Unhappy Gaveston, whither goest thou now?

Exit [*Gaveston*] *cum servis Pembroke*° [*under James's command*]. *with Pembroke's servants*

HORSEBOY [*to Arundel*] My lord, we'll quickly be at Cobham.[8]

Exeunt ambo° [*Pembroke and Arundel, the Horseboy leading*]. *both*

[2.6]

Enter Gaveston mourning, and the Earl of Pembroke's men [*James and other soldiers. They see the approach of Warwick and his men*].

GAVESTON Oh, treacherous Warwick, thus to wrong thy friend![1]
JAMES I see it is your life these arms pursue.

7. Must we now return Gaveston to the King only to say to ourselves afterwards, "If only we'd known"?
8. Probably the wrong name; there are two Cobhams near London, whereas this scene takes place historically in the north of England.
2.6. In the vicinity of the previous scene; historically, near Boroughbridge, Yorkshire.
1. The "friend" is Pembroke, who has pledged his honor to take Gaveston to the King and return with him (see 2.5.71–79 and lines 8–9 in this scene).

GAVESTON Weaponless must I fall, and die in bands?° *bonds, shackles*
Oh, must this day be period of my life,
Center of all my bliss?[2] [*To James and soldiers*] An° ye be men, *If*
Speed to the King!

Enter Warwick and his company.

WARWICK My lord of Pembroke's men,
Strive you no longer; I will have that Gaveston.
JAMES Your Lordship doth dishonor to yourself
And wrong our lord,° your honorable friend. *(Pembroke)*
WARWICK No, James, it is my country's cause I follow.—
Go, take the villain. [*Gaveston is taken.*]
Soldiers, come away.
We'll make quick work. [*To James*] Commend me to your master,
My friend, and tell him that I watched it well.° *kept vigilant watch*
[*To Gaveston*] Come, let thy shadow° parley with King Edward. *shade, ghost*
GAVESTON Treacherous earl, shall I not see the King?
WARWICK The King of Heaven, perhaps, no other king.—
Away! *Exeunt Warwick and his men, with Gaveston.*
Manet James cum ceteris.° *with the others*
JAMES Come, fellows, it booted° not for us to strive. *availed*
We will in haste go certify° our lord. *Exeunt.* *inform*

[3.1]

Enter King Edward and Spencer [Junior and Baldock], with drums and fifes.

KING EDWARD I long to hear an answer from the barons
Touching my friend, my dearest Gaveston.
Ah, Spencer, not the riches of my realm
Can ransom him! Ah, he is marked to die.
I know the malice of the younger Mortimer;
Warwick, I know, is rough, and Lancaster
Inexorable; and I shall never see
My lovely Piers, my Gaveston again.
The barons overbear me with their pride.
SPENCER JR. Were I King Edward, England's sovereign,
Son to the lovely Eleanor of Spain,° *Eleanor of Castile*
Great Edward Longshanks' issue,° would I bear *Edward I's son*
These braves,° this rage, and suffer uncontrolled *insults*
These barons thus to beard° me in my land, *defy*
In mine own realm? My lord, pardon my speech.
Did you° retain your father's magnanimity, *If you did*
Did you regard the honor of your name,
You would not suffer° thus Your Majesty *allow*
Be counterbuffed of° your nobility. *To be rebuffed by*
Strike off their heads, and let them preach on poles!° *(see 1.1.116–17 n)*
No doubt such lessons they will teach the rest

2. Must this day, which was to have been the center of my bliss in reuniting me with Edward, turn out instead to mark the end of my life?

3.1. Historically, in part near Boroughbridge, Yorkshire, though the scene compresses action occurring over a period of thirteen years.

As, by their preachments, they° will profit much *(the rebels)*
And learn obedience to their lawful king.

KING EDWARD Yea, gentle Spencer, we have been too mild,
Too kind to them, but now have drawn our sword,
And if they send me not my Gaveston
We'll steel it° on their crest and poll° their tops. *strike / lop off*

BALDOCK This haught° resolve becomes Your Majesty, *lofty, bold*
Not to be tied to their affection,° *inclination*
As though Your Highness were a schoolboy still
And must be awed and governed like a child.

Enter Hugh Spencer (an old man, father to the young Spencer), with his truncheon,° and soldiers. *officer's baton*

SPENCER SR. Long live my sovereign, the noble Edward,
In peace triumphant, fortunate in wars!

KING EDWARD Welcome, old man. Com'st thou in Edward's aid?
Then tell thy prince of whence and what thou art.

SPENCER SR. Lo, with a band of bowmen and of pikes,
Brown bills and targeteers,[1] four hundred strong,
Sworn to defend King Edward's royal right,
I come in person to Your Majesty—
Spencer, the father of Hugh Spencer there,
Bound to Your Highness everlastingly
For favors done in him unto us all.° *through him to us all*

KING EDWARD Thy father, Spencer?

SPENCER JR. True, an it like° Your Grace, *if it please*
That pours, in lieu of° all your goodness shown, *in repayment of*
His life, my lord, before your princely feet.

KING EDWARD Welcome ten thousand times, old man, again.
[*To Spencer Junior*] Spencer, this love, this kindness to thy king
Argues° thy noble mind and disposition. *Gives evidence of*
Spencer, I here create thee Earl of Wiltshire,
And daily will enrich thee with our favor,
That, as the sunshine, shall reflect o'er thee.
Beside, the more to manifest our love,
Because we hear Lord Bruce doth sell his land,
And that the Mortimers are in hand withal,[2]
Thou shalt have crowns° of us t'outbid the barons; *gold coins*
And, Spencer, spare them not, but lay it on.—
Soldiers, a largesse,° and thrice welcome all! *a bonus payment*

SPENCER JR. My lord, here comes the Queen.

Enter [with a letter] the Queen and her son [Prince Edward], and Levune, a Frenchman.

KING EDWARD Madam, what news?

QUEEN News of dishonor, lord, and discontent.
Our friend Levune, faithful and full of trust,
Informeth us, by letters and by words,
That Lord Valois, our brother, King of France,
Because Your Highness hath been slack in homage,
Hath seizèd Normandy into his hands.

1. Soldiers with bronzed pikes and shields.
2. The Mortimers are negotiating about the sale of the land. Lord Bruce, known to history as William de Braose, is not mentioned otherwise in this play.

These be the letters, this the messenger.
[*She shows the letter to Edward.*]
KING EDWARD Welcome, Levune.—Tush, Sib,° if this be all, *kinswoman, Isabella*
Valois and I will soon be friends again.
But to my Gaveston: shall I never see,
Never behold thee now? Madam, in this matter
We will employ you and your little son;
You shall go parley° with the King of France.— *negotiate*
Boy, see you bear you bravely° to the King *bear yourself nobly*
And do your message with a majesty.
PRINCE EDWARD Commit not to my youth things of more weight
Than fits a prince so young as I to bear;
And fear not, lord and father, heaven's great beams
On Atlas'° shoulder shall not lie more safe *bearer of the heavens*
Than shall your charge committed to my trust.
QUEEN Ah, boy, this towardness° makes thy mother fear *aptness, precocity*
Thou art not marked to many days on earth.
KING EDWARD Madam, we will that you with speed be shipped,
And this our son; Levune shall follow you
With all the haste we can dispatch him hence.
Choose of our lords to bear you company,
And go in peace; leave us in wars at home.
QUEEN Unnatural wars, where subjects brave their king;
God end them once!° My lord, I take my leave *once and for all*
To make my preparation for France.
[*Exeunt Queen and Prince Edward.*]

Enter Lord Arundel.

KING EDWARD What, Lord Arundel, dost thou come alone?
ARUNDEL Yea, my good lord, for Gaveston is dead.
KING EDWARD Ah, traitors! Have they put my friend to death?
Tell me, Arundel, died he ere thou cam'st,
Or didst thou see my friend to take his death?° *be slain*
ARUNDEL Neither, my lord, for, as he was surprised,° *captured suddenly*
Begirt with weapons and with enemies round,
I did Your Highness' message to them all,
Demanding him of them—entreating rather—
And said, upon the honor of my name,
That I would undertake to carry him
Unto Your Highness and to bring him back.
KING EDWARD And tell me, would the rebels deny me that?
SPENCER JR. Proud recreants!° *betrayers*
KING EDWARD Yea, Spencer, traitors all.
ARUNDEL I found them at the first inexorable.
The Earl of Warwick would not bide the hearing;
Mortimer hardly; Pembroke and Lancaster
Spake least. And, when they flatly° had denied, *unconditionally*
Refusing to receive me pledge° for him, *me as hostage*
The Earl of Pembroke mildly thus bespake:° *spoke*
"My lords, because our sovereign sends for him,
And promiseth he shall be safe returned,
I will this undertake: to have him hence
And see him redelivered to your hands."
KING EDWARD Well, and how fortunes° that he came not? *does it happen*
SPENCER JR. Some treason or some villainy was cause.

ARUNDEL The Earl of Warwick seized him on his way;
For, being delivered unto Pembroke's men,
Their lord rode home, thinking his prisoner safe;
But ere he came, Warwick in ambush lay
And bare° him to his death, and in a trench *bore*
Strake° off his head, and marched unto the camp. *Struck*
SPENCER JR. A bloody part,° flatly against law of arms! *deed*
KING EDWARD Oh, shall I speak, or shall I sigh and die?
SPENCER JR. My lord, refer° your vengeance to the sword *commit, assign*
Upon these barons! Hearten up your men;
Let them° not unrevenged murder your friends. *(the rebel barons)*
Advance° your standard,° Edward, in the field, *Lift high / banner*
And march to fire them from their starting-holes!° *lairs, hiding places*
KING EDWARD (*kneels and saith*) By earth, the common
mother of us all,
By heaven, and all the moving orbs° thereof, *orbiting planets, etc.*
By this right hand, and by my father's sword,
And all the honors 'longing° to my crown, *belonging*
I will have heads and lives for him, as many
As I have manors, castles, towns, and towers.
Treacherous Warwick, traitorous Mortimer!
If I be England's king, in lakes of gore
Your headless trunks, your bodies will I trail,
That you may drink your fill and quaff in blood,
And stain my royal standard with the same,
That so my bloody colors may suggest
Remembrance of revenge immortally
On your accursèd traitorous progeny,
You villains that have slain my Gaveston! [*He rises.*]
And in this place of honor and of trust,
Spencer, sweet Spencer, I adopt thee here,
And merely° of our love we do create thee *entirely*
Earl of Gloucester and Lord Chamberlain,
Despite of times, despite of enemies.

[*Enter an attendant and whispers to Spencer Junior.*]

SPENCER JR. My lord, here is a messenger from the barons
Desires access unto Your Majesty.
KING EDWARD Admit him near.

Enter the Herald from the barons, with his coat of arms.

HERALD Long live King Edward, England's lawful lord!
KING EDWARD So wish not they, iwis,° that sent thee hither. *certainly*
Thou com'st from Mortimer and his complices.
A ranker° rout of rebels never was. *more flagrant*
Well, say thy message.
HERALD The barons, up in arms, by me salute
Your Highness with long life and happiness,
And bid me say, as plainer° to Your Grace, *complainant, petitioner*
That if without effusion of blood
You will this grief have ease and remedy,[3]
That from your princely person you remove
This Spencer, as a putrefying branch

3. Your wish is to find ease and remedy for this grievance.

That deads° the royal vine whose golden leaves — *deadens, kills*
Impale° your princely head, your diadem, — *Encircle*
Whose brightness such pernicious upstarts dim,[4]
Say they—and lovingly advise Your Grace
To cherish virtue and nobility,
And have old servitors° in high esteem, — *i.e., nobles, barons*
And shake off smooth° dissembling flatterers. — *insinuating*
This granted, they, their honors, and their lives
Are to Your Highness vowed and consecrate.

SPENCER JR. Ah, traitors, will they still display their pride?

KING EDWARD Away! Tarry no answer, but begone.
Rebels, will they appoint° their sovereign — *prescribe for*
His sports, his pleasures, and his company?
Yet ere thou go, see how I do divorce
Spencer from me. (*Embrace Spencer.*) Now get thee to thy lords,
And tell them I will come to chastise them
For murdering Gaveston. Hie thee, get thee gone.
Edward with fire and sword follows at thy heels.
[*Exit the Herald.*]
My lords, perceive you how these rebels swell?° — *are swollen with pride*
Soldiers, good hearts, defend your sovereign's right,
For now, even now, we march to make them stoop.
Away! *Exeunt.*

[3.2]

Alarums, excursions,° a great fight, and a retreat. Enter the King, Spencer the father, Spencer the son, and the noblemen of the King's side. — *military sorties*

KING EDWARD Why do we sound retreat? Upon them, lords!
This day I shall pour vengeance with my sword
On those proud rebels that are up in arms
And do confront and countermand° their king. — *oppose*

SPENCER JR. I doubt it not, my lord; right will prevail.

SPENCER SR. 'Tis not amiss, my liege, for either part° — *side, army*
To breathe° awhile. Our men, with sweat and dust — *pause*
All choked well near, begin to faint for heat,
And this retire° refresheth horse and man. — *strategic retreat*

SPENCER JR. Here come the rebels.

Enter the barons: Mortimer [Junior], Lancaster, Warwick, Pembroke, cum ceteris.° — *with others*

MORTIMER JR. Look, Lancaster,
Yonder is Edward among his flatterers.

LANCASTER And there let him be,
Till he pay dearly for their company.

WARWICK And shall, or Warwick's sword shall smite in vain.

KING EDWARD What, rebels, do you shrink and sound retreat?

MORTIMER JR. No, Edward, no. Thy flatterers faint and fly.

LANCASTER Thou'd best betimes° forsake them and their trains,° — *quickly / intrigues*
For they'll betray thee, traitors as they are.

4. The brightness of which is dimmed by such pernicious upstarts.

3.2. The battle continues.

SPENCER JR. Traitor in thy face, rebellious Lancaster!
PEMBROKE Away, base upstart! Brav'st° thou nobles thus? *Defy*
SPENCER SR. A noble attempt and honorable deed
Is it not, trow ye,° to assemble aid *think you*
And levy arms against your lawful king?
KING EDWARD For which ere long their heads shall satisfy,° *make reparation*
T'appease the wrath of their offended king.
MORTIMER JR. Then, Edward, thou wilt fight it to the last,
And rather bathe thy sword in subjects' blood
Than banish that pernicious company?
KING EDWARD Ay, traitors all! Rather than thus be braved,
Make England's civil towns huge heaps of stones,
And plows to go about our palace gates.
WARWICK A desperate and unnatural resolution.
Alarum!° To the fight! *Sound the alarm!*
Saint George° for England and the barons' right! *England's patron saint*
KING EDWARD Saint George for England and King Edward's right!
[*Alarums. Exeunt on two sides.*]

[3.3]

Enter [*King*] *Edward* [*and his followers, including the Spencers, Levune, and Baldock*], *with the barons* [*including Warwick, Lancaster, and Mortimer Junior*] *captives* [*along with Kent*].

KING EDWARD Now, lusty° lords, now, not by chance of war, *mighty (ironic)*
But justice of the quarrel and the cause,
Vailed° is your pride. Methinks you hang the heads, *Humbled, lowered*
But we'll advance° them, traitors. Now 'tis time *raise up (on poles)*
To be avenged on you for all your braves° *boasts*
And for the murder of my dearest friend,
To whom right well you knew our° soul was knit: *(the royal "we")*
Good Piers of Gaveston, my sweet favorite.
Ah, rebels, recreants,° you made him away!° *betrayers / killed him*
KENT Brother, in regard of thee and of thy land
Did they remove that flatterer from thy throne.
KING EDWARD So, sir, you have spoke. Away, avoid our presence!
[*Exit Kent.*]
Accursèd wretches, was't in regard of us,° *(the royal "we")*
When we had sent our messenger to request
He might be spared to come to speak with us,
And Pembroke undertook for his return,
That thou, proud Warwick, watched° the prisoner, *kept watch over*
Poor Piers, and headed° him against law of arms? *beheaded*
For which thy head shall overlook° the rest *be higher than*
As much as thou in rage outwent'st the rest.
WARWICK Tyrant, I scorn thy threats and menaces.
'Tis but temporal° that thou canst inflict. *physical, of this world*
LANCASTER The worst is death, and better die to live° *live in eternal honor*
Than live in infamy under such a king.
KING EDWARD [*to Spencer Senior*] Away with them, my lord of Winchester!

3.3. The battle continues.

These lusty leaders, Warwick and Lancaster,
I charge you roundly: off with both their heads.
Away!

WARWICK Farewell, vain world!

LANCASTER Sweet Mortimer, farewell!

[Exeunt Warwick and Lancaster, guarded, led off by Spencer Senior.]

MORTIMER JR. England, unkind to thy nobility,
Groan for this grief! Behold how thou art maimed.

KING EDWARD Go take that haughty Mortimer to the Tower;
There see him safe bestowed. And, for the rest,
Do speedy execution on them all.
Begone!

MORTIMER JR. What, Mortimer, can ragged° stony walls — *rugged, rough*
Immure thy virtue° that aspires to heaven?° — *strength / upward*
No, Edward, England's scourge, it may not be;
Mortimer's hope surmounts his fortune far.

[Exit Mortimer Junior, guarded.]

KING EDWARD Sound drums and trumpets! March with me, my friends.
Edward this day hath crowned him° king anew. — *himself*

[Drums and trumpets sound.] Exeunt. Manent Spencer filius,° Levune, and Baldock. — *son*

SPENCER JR. Levune, the trust° that we repose in thee — *commission*
Begets° the quiet of King Edward's land. — *Is essential to*
Therefore begone in haste, and with advice° — *judiciously*
Bestow that treasure on° the lords of France — *Give enough bribes to*
That, therewithal enchanted, like the guard
That suffered° Jove to pass in showers of gold — *permitted*
To Danaë,° all aid may be denied — *(see 2.2.54 n)*
To Isabel the Queen—that now in France
Makes friends—to cross the seas with her young son
And step into his father's regiment.° — *authority, throne*

LEVUNE That's it these barons and the subtle queen
Long leveled° at. — *aimed*

BALDOCK Yea, but, Levune, thou see'st
These barons lay their heads on blocks together.[1]
What they intend, the hangman frustrates clean.° — *entirely*

LEVUNE Have you no doubts, my lords. I'll clap so close° — *deal so secretly*
Among the lords of France with England's gold
That Isabel shall make her plaints in vain,
And France shall be obdurate with° her tears. — *in response to*

SPENCER JR. Then make for France amain.° Levune, away! — *without delay*
Proclaim King Edward's wars and victories.

Exeunt omnes.

[4.1]

Enter Edmund [Earl of Kent].

KENT Fair blows the wind for France. Blow, gentle gale,
Till Edmund be arrived for England's good!

1. I.e., These barons lay down their heads in a row on the chopping blocks—thus being "leveled" (line 53) in another, grisly sense.

4.1. The vicinity of the Tower of London.

Nature, yield to my country's cause in this.
A brother? No, a butcher of thy friends.
Proud Edward, dost thou banish me thy presence?
But I'll to France, and cheer the wrongèd queen,
And certify what Edward's looseness is.
Unnatural king, to slaughter noblemen
And cherish flatterers! Mortimer, I stay° *wait for*
Thy sweet escape. Stand gracious,° gloomy night, *Be favorable*
To his device!° *escape plot*

Enter Mortimer [Junior] disguised.

MORTIMER JR. Holla! Who walketh there?
Is't you, my lord?
KENT Mortimer, 'tis I.
But hath thy potion° wrought so happily?° *sleeping potion / luckily*
MORTIMER JR. It hath, my lord. The warders all asleep,
I thank them, gave me leave to pass in peace.
But hath Your Grace got shipping unto France?
KENT Fear it not. *Exeunt.*

[4.2]

Enter the Queen and her son [Prince Edward].

QUEEN Ah, boy, our friends do fail us all in France.
The lords are cruel, and the King unkind.
What shall we do?
PRINCE EDWARD Madam, return to England,
And please my father well, and then a fig° *(expressing scorn)*
For all my uncle's° friendship here in France. *(Kent's)*
I warrant you, I'll win His Highness quickly;
'A° loves me better than a thousand Spencers. *He*
QUEEN Ah, boy, thou art deceived, at least in this,
To think that we° can yet be tuned together. *(Edward and I)*
No, no, we jar° too far. Unkind Valois,° *quarrel / French king*
Unhappy Isabel! When France rejects,
Whither, oh, whither dost thou bend° thy steps? *direct*

Enter Sir John of Hainault.[1]

SIR JOHN Madam, what cheer?
QUEEN Ah, good Sir John of Hainault,
Never so cheerless nor so far distressed.
SIR JOHN I hear, sweet lady, of the King's° unkindness. *King of France's*
But droop not, madam; noble minds contemn° *scorn*
Despair. Will Your Grace with me to Hainault
And there stay time's advantage° with your son?— *await good opportunity*
How say you, my lord, will you go with your friends
And shake off° all our fortunes equally? *leave behind*
PRINCE EDWARD So° pleaseth the Queen my mother, me it likes.° *Provided it pleases*
The King° of England nor the court of France *Neither the King*
Shall have me from my gracious mother's side
Till I be strong enough to break a staff,° *fight with a lance*

4.2. The French court.

1. Hainaut, Belgium, bordering France.

And then have at° the proudest Spencer's head! *have a go at*
SIR JOHN Well said, my lord.
QUEEN Oh, my sweet heart, how do I moan thy wrongs,
Yet triumph in the hope of thee, my joy!—
Ah, sweet Sir John, even to the utmost verge
Of Europe, or the shore of Tanais,° *the river Don*
Will we with thee; to Hainault, so we will.
The Marquis° is a noble gentleman; *The Count of Hainault*
His Grace, I dare presume, will welcome me.—
But who are these?

Enter Edmund [Earl of Kent] and Mortimer [Junior].

KENT Madam, long may you live,
Much happier than your friends in England do.
QUEEN Lord Edmund, and Lord Mortimer alive!
Welcome to France. [*To Mortimer Junior*] The news was here, my lord,
That you were dead, or very near your death.
MORTIMER JR. Lady, the last was truest of the twain,
But Mortimer, reserved° for better hap,° *set apart / fortune*
Hath shaken off the thraldom of the Tower,
[*To the Prince*] And lives t'advance your standard, good my lord.
PRINCE EDWARD How mean you, an the King, my father, lives?[2]
No, my Lord Mortimer, not I, I trow.° *indeed, surely*
QUEEN Not, son? Why not? I would it were no worse.[3]
But, gentle° lords, friendless we are in France. *noble*
MORTIMER JR. Monsieur le Grand, a noble friend of yours,
Told us at our arrival all the news:
How hard the nobles, how unkind the King° *King of France*
Hath showed himself. But, madam, right makes room° *makes way*
Where weapons want;° and, though a many friends *are insufficient*
Are made away—as Warwick, Lancaster,
And others of our party and faction—
Yet have we friends, assure Your Grace, in England
Would° cast up caps and clap their hands for joy *Who would*
To see us there, appointed for° our foes. *outfitted to encounter*
KENT Would all were well, and Edward well reclaimed
For England's honor, peace, and quietness!
MORTIMER JR. But by the sword, my lord, it must be deserved.° *earned*
The King will ne'er forsake his flatterers.
SIR JOHN My lords of England, sith° the ungentle King *since*
Of France refuseth to give aid of arms
To this distressèd queen, his sister here,
Go you with her to Hainault. Doubt ye not
We will find comfort, money, men, and friends
Ere long to bid the English king a base.[4]
How say,° young prince, what think you of the match? *How say you*
PRINCE EDWARD I think King Edward will outrun us all.
QUEEN Nay, son, not so, and you must not discourage

2. How can you propose to raise high *my* standard in battle, my father being the true king? ("An" ambiguously means both "if" and "since.")
3. I.e., We could have worse luck than to be befriended by Mortimer Junior in support of your claim.
4. To challenge the English king to a game of prisoner's base, or tag.

Your friends that are so forward in your aid.
KENT Sir John of Hainault, pardon us, I pray.
These comforts that you give our woeful queen
Bind us in kindness all at your command.
QUEEN Yea, gentle brother,° and the God of heaven — *brother-in-law*
Prosper your happy motion,° good Sir John! — *proposal*
MORTIMER JR. This noble gentleman, forward° in arms, — *eager*
Was born, I see, to be our anchor-hold.—
Sir John of Hainault, be it thy renown
That England's queen and nobles in distress
Have been by thee restored and comforted.
SIR JOHN Madam, along,° and you, my lord, with me, — *come along*
That England's peers may Hainault's welcome see.[5]
[*Exeunt.*]

[4.3]

Enter the King, Arundel, the two Spencers, with others.

KING EDWARD Thus after many threats of wrathful war
Triumpheth England's Edward with his friends;
And triumph Edward° with his friends, uncontrolled! — *May Edward triumph*
[*To Spencer Junior*] My lord of Gloucester, do you hear the news?
SPENCER JR. What news, my lord?
KING EDWARD Why, man, they say there is great execution
Done through the realm.—My lord of Arundel,
You have the note,° have you not? — *official report*
ARUNDEL [*producing a paper*] From the Lieutenant of the Tower, my lord.
KING EDWARD I pray let us see it. What have we there?
Read it, Spencer.
Spencer [*Junior*] *reads their names* [*of those executed*].° — *(not given in the text)*
Why, so. They barked° apace a month ago; — *embarked (on treason)*
Now, on my life, they'll neither bark nor bite.
Now, sirs, the news from France. Gloucester, I trow
The lords of France love England's gold so well
As Isabella gets no aid from thence.
What now remains? Have you proclaimed, my lord,
Reward for them can° bring in Mortimer? — *who can*
SPENCER JR. My lord, we have, and if he be in England,
'A will be had° ere long, I doubt it not. — *He'll be captured*
KING EDWARD "If," dost thou say? Spencer, as true° as death, — *sure*
He is in England's ground. Our port-masters
Are not so careless of their king's command.

Enter a post [*Messenger, with a letter*].

How now, what news with thee? From whence come these?
MESSENGER Letters, my lord, and tidings forth of France,
To you, my lord of Gloucester, from Levune.
KING EDWARD Read.
SPENCER JR. (*reads the letter*) "My duty to your honor prem-

5. May see how Hainault welcomes guests.

4.3. The royal palace, London.

ised,° etc., I have, according to instructions in that behalf, dealt with the King of France his° lords, and effected that the Queen, all discontented and discomforted, is gone—whither, if you ask, with Sir John of Hainault, brother to the Marquis, into Flanders. With them are gone Lord Edmund and the Lord Mortimer, having in their company divers of your nation and others; and, as constant° report goeth, they intend to give King Edward battle in England sooner than he can look for them. This is all the news of import.
Your honor's in all service, Levune."

axiomatically assumed / *King of France's* / *consistent, reliable*

KING EDWARD Ah, villains, hath that Mortimer escaped?
With him is Edmund gone associate?
And will Sir John of Hainault lead the round?° *dance*
Welcome, i'God's name, madam, and your son;
England shall welcome you and all your rout.° *mob, crowd*
Gallop apace, bright Phoebus,° through the sky, *god of the sun*
And dusky Night, in rusty iron car!° *chariot*
Between you both, shorten the time, I pray,
That I may see that most desirèd day
When we may meet these traitors in the field.
Ah, nothing grieves me but° my little boy *but that*
Is thus misled to countenance° their ills. *sanction*
Come, friends, to Bristol, there to make us strong;
And, winds, as equal° be to bring them in *impartial*
As you injurious were to bear them forth! [*Exeunt.*]

[4.4]

Enter the Queen, her son [Prince Edward], Edmund [Earl of Kent], Mortimer [Junior], and Sir John [of Hainault].

QUEEN Now, lords, our loving friends and countrymen,
Welcome to England all, with prosperous winds!
Our kindest friends in Belgia° have we left, *Hainaut, Belgium*
To cope with friends at home—a heavy case,° *sad state of affairs*
When force to force is knit, and sword and glaive° *lance*
In civil broils makes kin and countrymen
Slaughter themselves in others, and their sides
With their own weapons gored.[1] But what's the help?
Misgoverned kings are cause of all this wrack;° *destruction*
And, Edward, thou art one among them all
Whose looseness hath betrayed thy land to spoil° *plundering*
And made the channels° overflow with blood. *gutters*
Of thine own people patron shouldst thou be,
But thou—
MORTIMER JR. Nay, madam, if you be a warrior,
Ye must not grow so passionate in speeches.—
Lords, sith that° we are by sufferance° of heaven *since / permission*
Arrived and armèd in this prince's right,
Here for our country's cause swear we to him

4.4. Historically, this landing took place near Harwich, in Essex, on the English coast facing toward the Netherlands. The ensuing fighting, on the other hand, occurred near Bristol, to the west. The play's language shows awareness of this setting.

1. Slaughter others so like themselves, and inflict wounds as though upon themselves.

All homage, fealty, and forwardness;° *alacrity*
And, for the open wrongs and injuries
Edward hath done to us, his queen, and land,
We come in arms to wreak° it with the sword, *avenge*
That England's queen in peace may repossess
Her dignities and honors, and withal
We may remove these flatterers from the King
That havocs° England's wealth and treasury. *That lay waste*

SIR JOHN Sound trumpets, my lord, and forward let us march.
Edward will think we come to flatter him.[2]

KENT I would he never had been flattered more!
[*Trumpets sound. Exeunt.*]

[4.5]

Enter the King, Baldock, and Spencer the son, flying about the stage.

SPENCER JR. Fly, fly, my lord! The Queen is overstrong;
Her friends do multiply, and yours do fail.
Shape we our course to Ireland, there to breathe.° *catch our breath*

KING EDWARD What, was I born to fly and run away,
And leave the Mortimers conquerors behind?
Give me my horse, and let's reinforce our troops,
And in this bed of honor die with fame.

BALDOCK Oh no, my lord, this princely resolution
Fits not the time. Away! We are pursued. [*Exeunt.*]

[4.6]

[*Enter*] *Edmund* [*Earl of Kent*] *alone, with a sword and target.*° *shield*

KENT This way he fled, but I am come too late.
Edward, alas, my heart relents for thee!
Proud traitor Mortimer, why dost thou chase
Thy lawful king, thy sovereign, with thy sword?
[*To himself*] Vile wretch, and why hast thou, of all unkind,° *most unnatural of all*
Borne arms against thy brother and thy king?
Rain showers of vengeance on my cursèd head,
Thou God, to whom in justice it belongs
To punish this unnatural revolt!
Edward, this Mortimer aims at thy life;
Oh, fly him, then!—But, Edmund, calm this rage.
Dissemble or thou diest, for Mortimer
And Isabel do kiss while they conspire;
And yet she bears a face of love, forsooth.
Fie on that love that hatcheth death and hate!
Edmund, away! Bristol to Longshanks' blood
Is false. Be not found single for suspect;[1]
Proud Mortimer pries near into thy walks.

2. I.e., If we don't move decisively, Edward won't take us seriously as a military threat.
4.5. Near Bristol.
4.6. The battle continues.
1. Bristol has let down the royal lineage of Edward I and his son. Don't be found alone, for fear of suspicion.

Enter the Queen, Mortimer [*Junior*], *the young prince* [*Edward*], *and Sir John of Hainault* [*with soldiers*].

QUEEN Successful battles gives the God of kings° *God gives success*
To them that fight in right and fear His wrath.
Since then successfully we have prevailed,
Thanks be heaven's great Architect, and you.
Ere farther we proceed, my noble lords,
We here create our well-belovèd son,
Of° love and care unto his royal person, *Out of*
Lord Warden of the realm; and sith the Fates° *controllers of destiny*
Have made his father so infortunate,
Deal you, my lords, in this, my loving lords,
As to your wisdoms fittest seems in all.
KENT Madam, without offense if I may ask,
How will you deal with Edward in his fall?
PRINCE EDWARD Tell me, good uncle, what Edward do you mean?
KENT Nephew, your father; I dare not call him king.
MORTIMER JR. My lord of Kent, what needs these questions?
'Tis not in her controlment, nor in ours,
But as the realm and Parliament shall please,
So shall your brother be disposèd of.
[*Aside to the Queen*] I like not this relenting mood in Edmund.
Madam, 'tis good to look to him betimes.° *expeditiously*
QUEEN [*to Mortimer Junior*] My lord, the Mayor of Bristol knows our mind?[2]
MORTIMER JR. [*aside to her*] Yea, madam, and they scape not easily
That fled the field.
QUEEN Baldock is with the King;
A goodly chancellor, is he not, my lord?° *(said sarcastically)*
SIR JOHN So are the Spencers, the father and the son.
KENT [*aside*] This, Edward, is the ruin of the realm.

Enter Rice ap Howell and the Mayor of Bristol, with Spencer the father [*prisoner, and guards*].

RICE God save Queen Isabel and her princely son!
Madam, the Mayor and citizens of Bristol,
In sign of love and duty to this presence,° *royal presence*
Present by me this traitor to the state,
Spencer, the father to that wanton Spencer
That, like the lawless Catiline of Rome,[3]
Reveled in England's wealth and treasury.
QUEEN We thank you all.
MORTIMER JR. Your loving care in this
Deserveth princely favors and rewards.
But where's the King and the other Spencer fled?
RICE Spencer the son, created Earl of Gloucester,
Is with that smooth-tongued scholar Baldock gone
And shipped but late° for Ireland with the King. *just now*
MORTIMER JR. Some whirlwind fetch them back or sink them all!
They shall be started° thence, I doubt it not. *routed out of a lair*

2. I.e., understands that we wish Edward's favorites to be apprehended? (See lines 47–58.)

3. A dissolute Roman politician who led an unsuccessful attempt at a coup in 63 B.C.E.

PRINCE EDWARD Shall I not see the King, my father, yet?
KENT [*aside*] Unhappy Edward, chased from England's bounds!
SIR JOHN Madam, what resteth?° Why stand ye in a muse? *remains to be done*
QUEEN I rue my lord's ill fortune; but alas,
Care of my country called me to this war.
MORTIMER JR. Madam, have done with care and sad complaint.
Your king hath wronged your country and himself,
And we must seek to right it as we may.
Meanwhile, have hence this rebel to the block.
[*To Spencer Senior*] Your Lordship cannot privilege° your head. *exempt, save*
SPENCER SR. "Rebel" is he that fights against his prince;° *king*
So fought not they that fought in Edward's right.
MORTIMER JR. Take him away! He prates.
[*Spencer Senior is led off.*]
You, Rice ap Howell,
Shall do good service to Her Majesty,
Being of countenance° in your country here, *of good reputation*
To follow these rebellious runagates.° *renegades, runaways*
We in meanwhile, madam, must take advice
How Baldock, Spencer, and their complices
May in their fall be followed to their end. *Exeunt omnes.*

[4.7]

Enter the Abbot, monks; [*King*] *Edward, Spencer* [*Junior*], *and Baldock* [*disguised in religious garb*].

ABBOT Have you no doubt, my lord; have you no fear.
As silent and as careful will we be
To keep your royal person safe with us,
Free from suspect° and fell° invasion *apprehensiveness / cruel*
Of such as have Your Majesty in chase—
Yourself, and those your chosen company—
As danger of this stormy time requires.
KING EDWARD Father, thy face should° harbor no deceit. *would appear to*
Oh, hadst thou ever been a king, thy heart,
Pierced deeply with sense of my distress,
Could not but take compassion of° my state. *on*
Stately and proud, in riches and in train,° *retinue*
Whilom° I was, powerful and full of pomp; *Formerly*
But what is he° whom rule and empery *what ruler is there*
Have not in life or death made miserable?
Come, Spencer, come, Baldock, come sit down by me;
Make trial now of that philosophy
That in our famous nurseries of arts° *universities*
Thou sucked'st from Plato and from Aristotle.
Father, this life contemplative is heaven.
Oh, that I might this life in quiet lead!
But we, alas, are chased; and you, my friends,
Your lives, and my dishonor they pursue.
Yet, gentle monks, for° treasure, gold, nor fee *neither for*
Do you° betray us and our company. *Do not*

4.7. Historically, the abbey is identified as Neath, in southern Wales, near Bristol.

A MONK Your Grace may sit secure, if none but we
Do wot° of your abode. *know*
SPENCER JR. Not one alive but,° shrewdly I suspect, *No one so much as*
A gloomy fellow in a mead° below. *meadow*
'A gave a long° look after us, my lord; *scrutinizing*
And all the land, I know, is up in arms—
Arms that pursue our lives with deadly hate.
BALDOCK We were embarked for Ireland, wretched we,
With awkward winds and sore tempests driven,
To fall on shore° and here to pine in fear *run aground*
Of Mortimer and his confederates.
KING EDWARD Mortimer! Who talks of Mortimer?
Who wounds me with the name of Mortimer,
That bloody man? Good father, on thy lap
Lay I this head, laden with mickle° care. *much*
[*The King sits with his head in the Abbot's lap.*]
Oh, might I never open these eyes again,
Never again lift up this drooping head,
Oh, never more lift up this dying heart!
SPENCER JR. Look up, my lord.—Baldock, this drowsiness
Betides° no good; here, even, we are betrayed. *Portends*

Enter, with Welsh hooks,° [soldiers,] Rice ap Howell, a Mower, and the Earl of Leicester. *hook-shaped weapons*

MOWER Upon my life, those be the men ye seek.
RICE Fellow, enough. [*To the King*] My lord, I pray be short.° *come along quickly*
A fair commission warrants what we do.
LEICESTER [*aside*] The Queen's commission, urged by Mortimer.
What cannot gallant Mortimer with the Queen?
Alas, see where he° sits and hopes unseen *(Edward)*
T'escape their hands that seek to reave° his life! *take away*
Too true it is, *Quem dies vidit veniens superbum,*
Hunc dies vidit fugiens iacentem.[1]
But, Leicester, leave° to grow so passionate.— *cease*
[*Aloud*] Spencer and Baldock, by no other names° *without your titles*
I arrest you of high treason here.
Stand not on titles, but obey th'arrest;
'Tis in the name of Isabel the Queen.
[*To the King*] My lord, why droop you thus?
KING EDWARD O day, the last of all my bliss on earth,
Center of all misfortune! O my stars!
Why do you lour° unkindly on a king? *frown*
Comes Leicester, then, in Isabella's name
To take my life, my company from me?
Here, man, rip up this panting breast of mine
And take my heart in rescue of° my friends. *in return for releasing*
RICE Away with them!
SPENCER JR. It may become thee yet
To let us take our farewell of His Grace.
ABBOT My heart with pity earns° to see this sight— *grieves, sorrows*
A king to bear these words and proud commands!
KING EDWARD Spencer, ah, sweet Spencer, thus then must we part?

1. He whom the dawning day sees proud, the departing day sees put to flight. (Seneca, *Thyestes*, line 613.)

SPENCER JR. We must, my lord; so will° the angry heavens. *decree*
KING EDWARD Nay, so will hell and cruel Mortimer.
The gentle heavens have not to do in this.
BALDOCK My lord, it is in vain to grieve or storm.
Here humbly of Your Grace we take our leaves.
Our lots are cast; I fear me, so is thine.
KING EDWARD In heaven we may, in earth never shall we meet.
And, Leicester, say, what shall become of us?
LEICESTER Your Majesty must go to Killingworth.[2]
KING EDWARD "Must"! 'Tis somewhat hard when kings "must" go.
LEICESTER Here is a litter ready for Your Grace
That waits your pleasure, and the day grows old.
RICE As good be gone as stay and be benighted.
KING EDWARD A litter hast thou? Lay me in a hearse,
And to the gates of hell convey me hence!
Let Pluto's bells ring out my fatal knell,
And hags howl for my death at Charon's shore,[3]
For friends hath Edward none but these and these,° *(Spencer, Baldock, monks)*
And these° must die under a tyrant's sword. *(Spencer and Baldock)*
RICE My lord, be going. Care not for these,
For we shall see them shorter by the heads.
KING EDWARD Well, that shall be,° shall be. Part we must, *whatever must be*
Sweet Spencer; gentle Baldock, part we must.
[*He throws aside his disguise.*]
Hence, feignèd weeds! Unfeignèd are my woes.
Father, farewell! Leicester, thou stay'st for me,
And go I must. Life, farewell, with my friends.[4]
Exeunt Edward [guarded] and Leicester.
SPENCER JR. Oh, is he gone? Is noble Edward gone,
Parted from hence, never to see us more?
Rend,° sphere of heaven, and fire, forsake thy orb;[5] *Split apart*
Earth, melt to air! Gone is my sovereign,
Gone, gone, alas, never to make return.
BALDOCK Spencer, I see our souls are fleeted hence;° *have flown away*
We are deprived the sunshine of our life.
Make for a new life, man; throw up thy eyes
And heart and hand to heaven's immortal throne;
Pay nature's debt with cheerful countenance.
Reduce we all our lessons unto this:
To die, sweet Spencer, therefore live we all;
Spencer, all live to die, and rise to fall.
RICE Come, come, keep these preachments till you come to the place appointed.° You, and such as you are, have made wise work in England. Will Your Lordships° away? *(gallows or scaffold)* *(with mock politeness)*
MOWER [*to Rice*] Your Worship, I trust, will remember me?° *reward my services*
RICE Remember thee, fellow? What else?° Follow me to the town. *Of course, rest assured*
[*Exeunt, with Spencer Junior and Baldock under guard.*]

2. Killingworth (Kenilworth) Castle.
3. Charon ferried the dead across the river Styx to Pluto's kingdom of Hades.
4. Farewell to life itself when I must part with such dear friends.
5. May the sphere of fire be torn asunder and may the sun be deprived of its fire!

[5.1]

Enter the King [wearing the crown], Leicester, with a bishop [of Winchester, and Trussel] for the crown[1] *[with attendants].*

LEICESTER Be patient, good my lord; cease to lament.
Imagine Killingworth Castle were your court,
And that you lay° for pleasure here a space,° *reside / time*
Not of compulsion or necessity.
KING EDWARD Leicester, if gentle words might comfort me,
Thy speeches long ago had eased my sorrows,
For kind and loving hast thou always been.
The griefs of private men are soon allayed,
But not of kings. The forest deer, being struck,
Runs to an herb that closeth up the wounds;
But when the imperial lion's flesh is gored,
He rends and tears it with his wrathful paw,
And, highly scorning that the lowly earth
Should drink his blood, mounts up into the air.° *rears aloft*
And so it fares with me, whose dauntless mind
The ambitious Mortimer would seek to curb,
And that unnatural queen, false Isabel,
That thus hath pent and mewed° me in a prison. *penned and caged*
For such outrageous passions cloy° my soul *fill to overflowing*
As° with the wings of rancor and disdain *That*
Full often am I soaring up to heaven,
To plain me° to the gods against them both; *make my complaint*
But when I call to mind I am a king,
Methinks I should revenge me of the wrongs
That Mortimer and Isabel have done.
But what are kings, when regiment° is gone, *authority*
But perfect° shadows in a sunshine day? *mere*
My nobles rule; I bear the name of king.
I wear the crown but am controlled by them,
By Mortimer and my unconstant queen,
Who spots my nuptial bed with infamy,
Whilst I am lodged within this cave of care,
Where sorrow at my elbow still attends
To company° my heart with sad laments *accompany*
That bleeds within me for this strange exchange.° *change of fortune*
But tell me, must I now resign my crown
To make usurping Mortimer a king?
WINCHESTER Your Grace mistakes; it is for England's good
And princely Edward's right we crave the crown.
KING EDWARD No, 'tis for Mortimer, not Edward's head,
For he's a lamb encompassèd by wolves
Which in a moment will abridge his life.
But if proud Mortimer do wear this crown,
Heavens, turn it to a blaze of quenchless fire,
Or, like the snaky wreath of Tisiphon,[2]

5.1. Killingworth (Kenilworth) Castle.
1. For purposes of transporting the crown to the royal palace in London. (See next scene.)
2. One of the Furies, primeval goddesses dedicated to avenging crimes committed against ties of kinship; sometimes represented with snakes, like the Gorgons, mythological snake-haired sisters.

Engirt° the temples of his hateful head! — *Encircle*
So shall not England's vine be perishèd,
But Edward's name survive, though Edward dies.
LEICESTER My lord, why waste you thus the time away?
They stay° your answer. Will you yield your crown? — *await*
KING EDWARD Ah, Leicester, weigh how hardly° I can brook° — *scarcely / tolerate*
To lose my crown and kingdom without cause,
To give ambitious Mortimer my right,
That,° like a mountain, overwhelms my bliss, — *Who*
In which extreme my mind here murdered is!
But what the heavens appoint, I must obey.
[*He takes off the crown.*]
Here, take my crown—the life of Edward too!
Two kings in England cannot reign at once.
But stay awhile. Let me be king till night,
That I may gaze upon this glittering crown;
So shall my eyes receive their last content,
My head, the latest° honor due to it, — *last*
And jointly both yield up their wishèd° right. — *sought after, coveted*
Continue ever, thou celestial sun;
Let never silent night possess this clime;
Stand still, you watches of the element;° — *celestial bodies*
All times and seasons, rest you at a stay,° — *remain motionless*
That Edward may be still fair England's king.
But day's bright beams doth vanish fast away,
And needs I must resign my wishèd crown.
Inhuman creatures, nursed with tiger's milk,
Why gape you for your sovereign's overthrow?
My diadem, I mean, and guiltless life.
[*He puts the crown back on.*]
See, monsters, see, I'll wear my crown again.
What, fear you not the fury of your king?
But, hapless Edward, thou art fondly led;° — *foolishly misled*
They pass not° for thy frowns as late° they did, — *do not care / lately*
But seek to make a new-elected king—
Which fills my mind with strange, despairing thoughts,
Which thoughts are martyrèd with endless torments,
And in this torment comfort find I none
But that I feel the crown upon my head;
And therefore let me wear it yet awhile.
TRUSSEL My lord, the Parliament must have present news,
And therefore say: will you resign or no?
The King rageth.
KING EDWARD I'll not resign, but whilst I live°— — *I'll reign till I die*
Traitors, begone, and join you with Mortimer!
Elect, conspire, install, do what you will;
Their blood and yours shall seal° these treacheries. — *attest to; complete*
WINCHESTER This answer we'll return, and so farewell.
[*Winchester and Trussel start to go.*]
LEICESTER [*to the King*] Call them again, my lord, and speak them fair,° — *flatter them*
For if they go, the Prince shall lose his right.
KING EDWARD Call thou them back. I have no power to speak.
LEICESTER [*to Winchester*] My lord, the King is willing to resign.
WINCHESTER If he be not, let him choose.

KING EDWARD Oh, would I might! But heavens and earth conspire
To make me miserable. Here, receive my crown.
[He starts to give them the crown.]
Receive it? No, these innocent hands of mine
Shall not be guilty of so foul a crime.
He of you all that most desires my blood,
And will be called the murderer of a king,
Take it. What, are you moved? Pity you me?
Then send for unrelenting Mortimer,
And Isabel, whose eyes, being turned to steel,
Will sooner sparkle fire than shed a tear.
Yet stay, for rather than I will look on them—
Here, here! [*He resigns the crown.*] Now, sweet God of heaven,
Make me despise this transitory pomp,
And sit for aye° enthronizèd in heaven! — *forever*
Come, Death, and with thy fingers close my eyes,
Or if I live, let me forget myself.
WINCHESTER My lord—
KING EDWARD Call me not lord. Away, out of my sight!
Ah, pardon me. Grief makes me lunatic.
Let not that Mortimer protect° my son; — *act as Protector for*
More safety is there in a tiger's jaws
Than his embracements. [*Giving a handkerchief*] Bear this to the Queen,
Wet with my tears and dried again with sighs;
If with the sight thereof she be not moved,
Return it back and dip it in my blood.
Commend me to my son, and bid him rule
Better than I. Yet how have I transgressed,
Unless it be with too much clemency?
TRUSSEL And thus most humbly do we take our leave.
KING EDWARD Farewell.
[Exeunt Bishop of Winchester and Trussel with the crown.]
I know the next news that they bring
Will be my death, and welcome shall it be;
To wretched men death is felicity.

Enter Berkeley [*with a letter*].

LEICESTER Another post.° What news bring he? — *news-bearer*
[He reads the letter.]
KING EDWARD Such news as I expect. Come, Berkeley, come,
And tell thy message to my naked breast.
BERKELEY My lord, think not a thought so villainous
Can harbor in a man of noble birth.
To do Your Highness service and devoir,° — *duty*
And save you from your foes, Berkeley would die.
LEICESTER My lord, the Council of the Queen commands
That I resign my charge.
KING EDWARD And who must keep me now? [*To Berkeley*] Must you, my lord?
BERKELEY Ay, my most gracious lord, so 'tis decreed.
[He shows the letter to Edward.]
KING EDWARD By Mortimer, whose name is written here.
Well may I rend his name that rends my heart!
[He tears the letter.]

This poor revenge hath something° eased my mind. *somewhat*
So may his limbs be torn, as is this paper!
Hear me, immortal Jove, and grant it too.
BERKELEY Your Grace must hence with me to Berkeley straight.
KING EDWARD Whither you will; all places are alike,
And every earth is fit for burial.
LEICESTER [*to Berkeley*] Favor him, my lord, as much as lieth in you.° *as you can*
BERKELEY Even so betide° my soul as I use him. *happen to*
KING EDWARD Mine enemy° hath pitied my estate,° *(Leicester) / condition*
And that's the cause that I am now removed.
BERKELEY And thinks Your Grace that Berkeley will be cruel?
KING EDWARD I know not, but of this am I assured:
That death ends all, and I can die but once.
Leicester, farewell.
LEICESTER Not yet, my lord. I'll bear you on your way.
Exeunt omnes.

[5.2]

Enter Mortimer [*Junior*] *and Queen Isabel.*

MORTIMER JR. Fair Isabel, now have we our desire:
The proud corrupters of the light-brained king
Have done their homage to the lofty gallows,
And he himself lies in captivity.
Be ruled by me and we will rule the realm.
In any case, take heed of childish fear,
For now we hold an old wolf by the ears,
That, if he slip, will seize upon us both
And grip the sorer, being gripped himself.
Think therefore, madam, that imports us much° *behooves us*
To erect° your son with all the speed we may, *set upon the throne*
And that I be Protector over him,
For our behoof° will bear the greater sway *the advantage we enjoy*
Whenas° a king's name shall be underwrit. *When*
QUEEN Sweet Mortimer, the life of Isabel,
Be thou persuaded that I love thee well;
And therefore, so° the Prince, my son, be safe, *provided that*
Whom I esteem as dear as these mine eyes,
Conclude against his father what thou wilt,
And I myself will willingly subscribe.
MORTIMER JR. First would I hear news that he were deposed,
And then let me alone° to handle him. *leave it to me*

Enter Messenger [*with a letter, and then the Bishop of Winchester with the crown*].

Letters? From whence?
MESSENGER [*presenting the letter*] From Killingworth, my lord.
QUEEN How fares my lord the King?
MESSENGER In health, madam, but full of pensiveness.
QUEEN Alas, poor soul, would I could ease his grief!—

5.2. The royal palace, London.

Thanks, gentle Winchester. [*To the Messenger*] Sirrah,° *(said to social inferiors)*
begone. [*Exit Messenger.*]

WINCHESTER The King hath willingly resigned his crown.

QUEEN Oh, happy news! Send for the Prince, my son.

WINCHESTER Further,° ere this letter was sealed, Lord *Furthermore*
Berkeley came,
So that he now is gone° from Killingworth; *the King is removed*
And we have heard that Edmund laid a plot
To set his brother free; no more but so.° *that's where things are*
The Lord of Berkeley is so° pitiful *as*
As Leicester, that had charge of him before.

QUEEN Then let some other be his guardian.

MORTIMER JR. Let me alone. Here is the privy seal.° *official royal seal*
[*Exit the Bishop of Winchester.*]
[*Calling*] Who's there? Call hither Gurney and Matrevis.—
To dash° the heavy-headed Edmund's drift,° *frustrate / scheme*
Berkeley shall be discharged, the King removed,
And none but we shall know where he lieth.° *is being kept*

QUEEN But, Mortimer, as long as he survives,
What safety rests° for us or for my son? *is there*

MORTIMER JR. Speak, shall he presently be dispatched and die?

QUEEN I would he were, so it were not by my means.

Enter Matrevis and Gurney.

MORTIMER JR. Enough.
[*He speaks out of the Queen's hearing.*]
Matrevis, write a letter presently
Unto the Lord of Berkeley from ourself° *(the royal "we")*
That he resign the King to thee and Gurney,
And when 'tis done we will subscribe our name.

MATREVIS It shall be done, my lord.
[*Matrevis writes the letter.*]

MORTIMER JR. Gurney!

GURNEY My lord?

MORTIMER JR. As thou intendest to rise by Mortimer,
Who now makes Fortune's wheel turn as he please,
Seek all the means thou canst to make him° droop, *(King Edward)*
And neither give him kind word nor good look.

GURNEY I warrant you, my lord.

MORTIMER JR. And this above the rest: because we hear
That Edmund casts° to work his° liberty, *plots / (the King's)*
Remove him still° from place to place by night *repeatedly*
Till at the last he come to Killingworth
And then from thence to Berkeley back again;
And by the way,° to make him fret the more, *along the way*
Speak curstly° to him, and in any case *harshly*
Let no man comfort him if he chance to weep,
But amplify his grief with bitter words.

MATREVIS Fear not, my lord, we'll do as you command.

MORTIMER JR. So now, away. Post thitherwards amain.° *Go there quickly*

QUEEN [*joining the conversation*] Whither goes this letter?
To my lord the King?
Commend me humbly to His Majesty,
And tell him that I labor all in vain

To ease his grief and work his liberty;
And bear him this as witness of my love.
[*She gives Matrevis a jewel or ring.*]

MATREVIS I will, madam. *Exeunt Matrevis and Gurney. Manent Isabel and Mortimer.*

Enter the young Prince [*Edward*], *and the Earl of Kent talking with him.* [*Mortimer and the Queen speak apart.*]

MORTIMER JR. Finely dissembled. Do so still, sweet Queen.
Here comes the young Prince with the Earl of Kent.

QUEEN Something he whispers in his childish ears.

MORTIMER JR. If he have such access unto the Prince,
Our plots and stratagems will soon be dashed.

QUEEN Use Edmund friendly, as if all were well.

MORTIMER JR. [*aloud to Kent*] How fares my honorable lord of Kent?

KENT In health, sweet Mortimer. [*To the Queen*] How fares Your Grace?

QUEEN Well, if my lord your brother were enlarged.° *freed*

KENT I hear of late he hath deposed himself.

QUEEN The more my grief.

MORTIMER JR. And mine.

KENT [*aside*] Ah, they do dissemble!

QUEEN Sweet son, come hither. I must talk with thee.
[*She takes Prince Edward aside.*]

MORTIMER JR. [*to Kent*] Thou, being his uncle and the next of blood,
Do look to be Protector over the Prince.

KENT Not I, my lord. Who should protect the son
But she that gave him life, I mean the Queen?

PRINCE EDWARD Mother, persuade me not to wear the crown.
Let him° be king; I am too young to reign. *(Edward II)*

QUEEN But be content, seeing 'tis His Highness' pleasure.

PRINCE EDWARD Let me but see him first, and then I will.

KENT Ay, do, sweet nephew.

QUEEN Brother, you know it is impossible.

PRINCE EDWARD Why, is he dead?

QUEEN No. God forbid!

KENT I would those words proceeded from your heart.

MORTIMER JR. Inconstant Edmund, dost thou favor him,
That wast° a cause of his imprisonment? *You who were*

KENT The more cause have I now to make amends.

MORTIMER JR. [*to the Queen*] I tell thee, 'tis not meet that one so false
Should come about the person of a prince.
[*To Prince Edward*] My lord, he° hath betrayed the King, his brother, *(Kent)*
And therefore trust him not.

PRINCE EDWARD But he repents and sorrows for it now.

QUEEN Come, son, and go with this gentle lord and me.

PRINCE EDWARD With you I will, but not with Mortimer.

MORTIMER JR. Why, youngling, 'sdain'st thou so° of Mortimer? *are you so disdainful*
[*Seizing him*] Then I will carry thee by force away.

PRINCE EDWARD Help, Uncle Kent! Mortimer will wrong me.
[*Exit Mortimer Junior with the Prince.*]

QUEEN Brother Edmund, strive not; we are his friends.
Isabel is nearer° than the Earl of Kent. *closer by blood tie*

KENT Sister, Edward is my charge. Redeem him.° *Give him back to me*
QUEEN Edward is my son, and I will keep him. [*Exit.*]
KENT Mortimer shall know that he hath wronged me!
Hence will I haste to Killingworth Castle
And rescue agèd Edward from his foes,
To be revenged on Mortimer and thee.° *Exit.* *(the Queen)*

[5.3]

Enter Matrevis and Gurney with the King [*and soldiers, with torches*].

MATREVIS My lord, be not pensive; we are your friends.
Men are ordained to live in misery;
Therefore come. Dalliance dangereth° our lives. *Delay endangers*
KING EDWARD Friends, whither must unhappy° Edward go? *wretched; unlucky*
Will hateful Mortimer appoint no rest?
Must I be vexèd like the nightly bird,° *moved about like an owl*
Whose sight is loathsome to all wingèd fowls?
When will the fury of his mind assuage?° *be assuaged*
When will his heart be satisfied with blood?
If mine will serve, unbowel straight this breast
And give my heart to Isabel and him;
It is the chiefest mark they level° at. *aim*
GURNEY Not so, my liege. The Queen hath given this charge° *order*
To keep Your Grace in safety.
Your passions make your dolors to increase.
KING EDWARD This usage makes my misery increase.
But can my air of life° continue long *breath*
When all my senses are annoyed with stench?
Within a dungeon England's king is kept,
Where I am starved for want of sustenance;
My daily diet is heartbreaking sobs
That almost rends° the closet° of my heart. *tear apart / chamber*
Thus lives old Edward, not relieved by any,
And so must die, though pitièd by many.
Oh, water, gentle friends, to cool my thirst
And clear my body from foul excrements!
[*Sewer water is brought.*]
MATREVIS Here's channel water, as our charge is given.° *as we are commanded*
Sit down, for we'll be barbers to Your Grace.
KING EDWARD Traitors, away! What, will you murder me,
Or choke your sovereign with puddle water?
GURNEY No, but wash your face and shave away your beard,
Lest you be known and so be rescuèd.
MATREVIS Why strive you thus? Your labor is in vain.
KING EDWARD The wren may strive against the lion's strength,
But all in vain; so vainly do I strive
To seek for mercy at a tyrant's hand.
They wash him with puddle water and shave his beard away.
Immortal powers, that knows the painful cares
That waits upon my poor distressèd soul,

5.3. At Killingworth (Kenilworth) Castle, as in 5.1.

O, level all your looks upon these daring men
That wrongs their liege and sovereign, England's king!
O Gaveston, it is for thee that I am wronged!
For me, both thou and both the Spencers died,
And for your sakes a thousand wrongs I'll take.
The Spencers' ghosts, wherever they remain,
Wish well to mine. Then, tush! For them I'll die.

MATREVIS 'Twixt theirs and yours shall be no enmity.[1]
Come, come, away. Now put the torches out;
We'll enter in by darkness to Killingworth.
[*They put out their torches.*]

Enter Edmund [*Earl of Kent*].

GURNEY How now, who comes there?
[*They draw their weapons.*]

MATREVIS Guard the King sure! It is the Earl of Kent.

KING EDWARD O gentle brother, help to rescue me!

MATREVIS Keep them asunder! Thrust in the King!

KENT Soldiers, let me but talk to him one word.

GURNEY Lay hands upon the earl for this assault.

KENT Lay down your weapons; traitors, yield the King!

MATREVIS Edmund, yield thou thyself, or thou shalt die.
[*Kent is seized.*]

KENT Base villains, wherefore do you grip me thus?

GURNEY [*to the soldiers*] Bind him and so convey him to the court.

KENT Where is the court but here? Here is the King,
And I will visit him. Why stay° you me? *stop, hinder*

MATREVIS The court is where Lord Mortimer remains.
Thither shall Your Honor go, and so farewell.
Exeunt Matrevis and Gurney with the King. Manent Edmund [*Earl of Kent*] *and the soldiers.*

KENT Oh, miserable is that commonweal° *body politic*
Where lords keep courts and kings are locked in prison!

A SOLDIER Wherefore stay we? On, sirs, to the court.

KENT Ay, lead me whither you will, even to my death,
Seeing that my brother cannot be released.
Exeunt omnes [*Kent under guard*].

[5.4]

Enter Mortimer [*Junior*] *alone* [*with a letter*].

MORTIMER JR. The King must die, or Mortimer goes down.
The commons now begin to pity him;
Yet he that is the cause of Edward's death
Is sure to pay for it when his son is of age,
And therefore will I do it cunningly.
This letter, written by a friend of ours,
Contains his death, yet bids them save his life.
"Edwardum occidere nolite timere, bonum est,"
"Fear not to kill the king, 'tis good he die."
But read it thus, and that's another sense:
"Edwardum occidere nolite, timere bonum est,"

1. I.e., Your spirit will soon join theirs in death.

5.4. The royal palace, London.

"Kill not the king, 'tis good to fear the worst."
Unpointed° as it is, thus shall it go, *Unpunctuated*
That, being dead,° if it chance to be found, *when Edward is dead*
Matrevis and the rest may bear the blame
And we be quit° that caused it to be done. *free of suspicion*
Within this room is locked the messenger
That shall convey it and perform the rest,
And by a secret token that he bears
Shall he be murdered when the deed is done.
[*He unlocks and opens a door.*]
Lightborn,
Come forth.

[*Enter Lightborn.*]

Art thou as resolute as thou wast?
LIGHTBORN What else, my lord? And far more resolute.
MORTIMER JR. And hast thou cast° how to accomplish it? *devised*
LIGHTBORN Ay, ay, and none shall know which way he died.
MORTIMER JR. But at his looks, Lightborn, thou wilt relent.
LIGHTBORN Relent? Ha, ha! I use much° to relent. *It's my habit (ironic)*
MORTIMER JR. Well, do it bravely,° and be secret. *handsomely*
LIGHTBORN You shall not need to give instructions;
'Tis not the first time I have killed a man.
I learned in Naples how to poison° flowers, *poison the fragrance of*
To strangle with a lawn° thrust through° the throat, *linen thread / down*
To pierce the windpipe with a needle's point,
Or, whilst one is asleep, to take a quill
And blow a little powder in his ears,
Or open his mouth and pour quicksilver down;
But yet I have a braver way than these.
MORTIMER JR. What's that?
LIGHTBORN Nay, you shall pardon me; none shall know my tricks.
MORTIMER JR. I care not how it is, so it be not spied.
[*Giving the letter*] Deliver this to Gurney and Matrevis.
At every ten miles' end thou hast a horse.
[*Giving money and a token*] Take this. Away, and never see me more.
LIGHTBORN No?
MORTIMER JR. No,
Unless thou bring me news of Edward's death.
LIGHTBORN That will I quickly do. Farewell, my lord. [*Exit.*]
MORTIMER JR. The Prince I rule, the Queen I do command,
And with a lowly congé° to the ground *bow*
The proudest lords salute me as I pass.
I seal,° I cancel, I do what I will. *authorize*
Feared am I more than loved. Let me be feared,
And when I frown make all the court look pale.
I view the Prince with Aristarchus' eyes,[1]
Whose looks were as a breeching° to a boy. *spanking, flogging*
They thrust upon me the protectorship
And sue to me for° that that I desire. *beg me to take*
While at the council table, grave enough,
And not unlike a bashful Puritan,

1. Aristarchus was perhaps the most famous of all schoolmasters of antiquity (second century B.C.E.). His name had become a byword for severity.

First I complain of imbecility,° *debility*
Saying it is *onus quam gravissimum*,° *a very heavy burden*
Till, being interrupted by my friends,
Suscepi° that *provinciam*,° as they term it, *I've taken on / office*
And, to conclude, I am Protector now.
Now is all sure. The Queen and Mortimer
Shall rule the realm, the King, and none rule us.
Mine enemies will I plague, my friends advance,
And what I list° command who dare control? *wish to*
Maior sum quam cui possit fortuna nocere.[2]
And that this be the Coronation Day
It pleaseth me and Isabel the Queen.
[*Trumpets are sounded offstage.*]
The trumpets sound. I must go take my place.

Enter the young King [*Edward III*], [*Arch*]*bishop* [*of Canterbury*], *Champion,*[3] *nobles, Queen* [*and attendants*].

CANTERBURY Long live King Edward, by the grace of God
King of England and Lord of Ireland!
CHAMPION If any Christian, Heathen, Turk, or Jew
Dares but affirm that Edward's not true king,
And will avouch° his saying with the sword, *confirm, vouch for*
I am the champion that will combat him.
MORTIMER JR. None comes.—Sound, trumpets!
[*The trumpets sound.*]
EDWARD III Champion, here's to thee.
[*He drinks a toast and gives the goblet to the Champion.*]
QUEEN Lord Mortimer, now take him to your charge.

Enter soldiers with the Earl of Kent prisoner.

MORTIMER JR. What traitor have we there, with blades and bills?° *swords and pikes*
A SOLDIER Edmund, the Earl of Kent.
EDWARD III What hath he done?
A SOLDIER 'A would have taken the King away perforce
As we were bringing him to Killingworth.
MORTIMER JR. Did you attempt his rescue, Edmund? Speak.
KENT Mortimer, I did; he is our king,
And thou compell'st this prince to wear the crown.
MORTIMER JR. Strike off his head! He shall have martial law.
KENT Strike off my head? Base traitor, I defy thee.
EDWARD III [*to Mortimer Junior*] My lord, he is my uncle and shall live.
MORTIMER JR. My lord, he is your enemy and shall die.
[*The soldiers start to remove Kent.*]
KENT Stay, villains!
EDWARD III Sweet mother, if I cannot pardon him,
Entreat my Lord Protector for his life.
QUEEN Son, be content. I dare not speak a word.
EDWARD III Nor I, and yet methinks I should command;

2. I am too mighty for Fortune to be able to harm me. (Ovid, *Metamorphoses*, 6.195.)
3. A warrior who, on Coronation Day, stood ready to challenge any person who might question the King's right to rule.

But seeing I cannot, I'll entreat for him.—
My lord, if you will let my uncle live,
I will requite it when I come of age.

MORTIMER JR. 'Tis for Your Highness' good, and for the realm's.
[*To soldiers*] How often shall I bid you bear him hence?

KENT Art thou king? Must I die at thy command?

MORTIMER JR. At our command.—Once more, away with him!

KENT Let me but stay and speak. I will not go.
Either my brother or his son is king,
And none of both them° thirst for Edmund's blood. *neither of them*
And therefore, soldiers, whither will you hale me?

They hale Edmund [Earl of Kent] away and carry him to be beheaded. [The Queen and her son speak privately as the others leave the stage.]

EDWARD III What safety may I look for at his° hands *(Mortimer's)*
If that my uncle shall be murdered thus?

QUEEN Fear not, sweet boy, I'll guard thee from thy foes.
Had Edmund lived, he would have sought thy death.
Come, son, we'll ride a-hunting in the park.

EDWARD III And shall my uncle Edmund ride with us?

QUEEN He is a traitor. Think not on him. Come.

Exeunt omnes.

[5.5]

Enter Matrevis and Gurney [with lights. A bed is thrust onstage].

MATREVIS Gurney, I wonder the King dies not,
Being in a vault up to the knees in water
To which the channels° of the castle run, *sewer pipes*
From whence a damp continually ariseth
That were enough to poison any man—
Much more a king brought up so tenderly.

GURNEY And so do I, Matrevis. Yesternight
I opened but the door to throw him meat,° *food*
And I was almost stifled with the savor.

MATREVIS He hath a body able to endure
More than we can inflict; and therefore now
Let us assail his mind another while.

GURNEY Send for him out thence, and I will anger him.

MATREVIS But stay, who's this?

Enter Lightborn.

LIGHTBORN [*giving them the letter*] My Lord Protector greets you. [*Matrevis and Gurney read the letter.*]

GURNEY [*aside to Matrevis*] What's here? I know not how to conster° it. *construe*

MATREVIS [*aside to Gurney*] Gurney, it was left unpointed for the nonce.° *for this purpose*
"*Edwardum occidere nolite timere,*"° *(see 5.4.6–16)*
That's his meaning.

5.5. Berkeley Castle.

LIGHTBORN [*showing them the token*] Know you this token?
I must have the King.
MATREVIS Ay. Stay awhile; thou shalt have answer straight.
[*Aside to Gurney*] This villain's sent to make away the King.
GURNEY [*aside to Matrevis*] I thought as much.
MATREVIS [*aside to Gurney*] And when the murder's done,
See how he must be handled for his labor:
"*Pereat iste.*"° Let him have the King. *"Let this man die"*
[*To Lightborn*] What else? Here is the keys; this is the
lake.° [*He indicates the door of Edward's dungeon.*] *sewer, now a dungeon*
Do as you are commanded by my lord.
LIGHTBORN I know what I must do. Get you away.
Yet be not far off; I shall need your help.
See that in the next room I have a fire,
And get me a spit, and let it be red-hot.
MATREVIS Very well.
GURNEY Need you anything besides?
LIGHTBORN What else? A table and a featherbed.
GURNEY That's all?
LIGHTBORN Ay, ay; so, when I call you, bring it° in. *it all*
MATREVIS Fear not you that.° *Don't worry about us*
GURNEY [*giving a light*] Here's a light to go into the dungeon.
LIGHTBORN So. [*Exeunt Matrevis and Gurney.*]
Now must I about this gear.° Ne'er was there any *business*
So finely handled as this king shall be.
[*Lightborn opens the door or trapdoor of Edward's dungeon.*]
Foh! Here's a place indeed, with all my heart.° *truly*

[*Enter Edward.*]

KING EDWARD Who's there? What light is that? Wherefore
comes thou?
LIGHTBORN To comfort you and bring you joyful news.
KING EDWARD Small comfort finds poor Edward in thy looks.
Villain, I know thou com'st to murder me.
LIGHTBORN To murder you, my most gracious lord?
Far is it from my heart to do you harm.
The Queen sent me to see how you were used,
For she relents at this your misery.
And what eyes can refrain from shedding tears
To see a king in this most piteous state?
KING EDWARD Weep'st thou already? List° awhile to me, *Listen*
And then thy heart, were it as Gurney's is,
Or as Matrevis', hewn from the Caucasus,° *mountains near Black Sea*
Yet will it melt ere I have done my tale.
The dungeon where they keep me is the sink
Wherein the filth of all the castle falls.
LIGHTBORN Oh, villains!
KING EDWARD And there in mire and puddle have I stood
This ten days' space, and, lest that I should sleep,
One plays continually upon a drum.
They give me bread and water, being a king,° *albeit I am a king*
So that for want of sleep and sustenance
My mind's distempered and my body's numbed,

And whether I have limbs or no I know not.
Oh, would my blood dropped out from every vein
As doth this water from my tattered robes!
Tell Isabel the Queen I looked not thus
When for her sake I ran at tilt° in France — *jousted in a tournament*
And there unhorsed the Duke of Cleremont.

LIGHTBORN Oh, speak no more, my lord! This breaks my heart.
Lie on this bed and rest yourself awhile.

KING EDWARD These looks of thine can harbor naught but death;
I see my tragedy written in thy brows.
Yet stay awhile; forbear thy bloody hand,
And let me see the stroke before it comes,
That, even then when I shall lose my life,
My mind may be more steadfast on my God.

LIGHTBORN What means Your Highness to mistrust me thus?

KING EDWARD What means thou to dissemble with me thus?

LIGHTBORN These hands were never stained with innocent blood,
Nor shall they now be tainted with a king's.

KING EDWARD Forgive my thought for having such a thought.
One jewel have I left; receive thou this.
[*He gives a jewel.*]
Still fear I, and I know not what's the cause,
But every joint shakes as I give it thee.
Oh, if thou harbor'st murder in thy heart,
Let this gift change thy mind, and save thy soul!
Know that I am a king. Oh, at that name
I feel a hell of grief. Where is my crown?
Gone, gone! And do I remain alive?

LIGHTBORN You're overwatched,° my lord. Lie down and rest. — *exhausted, sleepless*
[*The King lies down.*]

KING EDWARD But° that grief keeps me waking, I should sleep, — *Were it not*
For not these ten days have these eyes' lids closed.
Now as I speak, they fall, and yet with fear
Open again. [*Lightborn sits on the bed.*] Oh, wherefore sits thou here?

LIGHTBORN If you mistrust me, I'll be gone, my lord.

KING EDWARD No, no, for if thou mean'st to murder me
Thou wilt return again, and therefore stay. [*Edward dozes.*]

LIGHTBORN He sleeps.

KING EDWARD [*starting*] Oh, let me not die yet! Stay, oh, stay awhile!

LIGHTBORN How now, my lord?

KING EDWARD Something still buzzeth in mine ears
And tells me if I sleep I never° wake; — *never shall*
This fear is that which makes me tremble thus.
And therefore tell me: wherefore art thou come?

LIGHTBORN To rid thee of thy life. [*Calling*] Matrevis, come!

[*Enter Matrevis and Gurney.*]

KING EDWARD I am too weak and feeble to resist.—
Assist me, sweet God, and receive my soul!

LIGHTBORN [*to Matrevis and Gurney*] Run for the table.

KING EDWARD Oh, spare me, or dispatch me in a trice!
[Matrevis and Gurney bring in a table and a red-hot spit.]
LIGHTBORN So, lay the table down, and stamp on it,
But not too hard, lest that you bruise his body.
[The King is murdered.]
MATREVIS I fear me that this cry will raise the town,
And therefore let us take horse and away.
LIGHTBORN Tell me, sirs, was it not bravely done?
GURNEY Excellent well. Take this for thy reward.
Then Gurney stabs Lightborn.
Come, let us cast the body in the moat,
And bear the King's to Mortimer, our lord.
Away! *Exeunt omnes [with the bodies].*

[5.6]

Enter Mortimer [Junior] and Matrevis.

MORTIMER JR. Is't done, Matrevis, and the murderer dead?
MATREVIS Ay, my good lord. I would it were undone.
MORTIMER JR. Matrevis, if thou now growest penitent,
I'll be thy ghostly father.° Therefore choose — *priest, confessor*
Whether thou wilt be secret in this
Or else die by the hand of Mortimer.
MATREVIS Gurney, my lord, is fled, and will, I fear,
Betray us both; therefore let me fly.
MORTIMER JR. Fly to the savages!° — *beyond civilization*
MATREVIS I humbly thank Your Honor. *[Exit.]*
MORTIMER JR. As for myself, I stand as Jove's huge tree,° — *the oak*
And others are but shrubs compared to me;
All tremble at my name, and I fear none.
Let's see who dare impeach me for his death!

Enter the Queen.

QUEEN Ah, Mortimer, the King, my son, hath news
His father's dead, and we have murdered him!
MORTIMER JR. What if he have? The King is yet a child.
QUEEN Ay, ay, but he tears his hair, and wrings his hands,
And vows to be revenged upon us both.
Into the council chamber he is gone
To crave the aid and succor of his peers.
Ay me! See where he comes, and they with him.
Now, Mortimer, begins our tragedy.

Enter the King, with the Lords [and attendants].

A LORD Fear not, my lord. Know that you are a king.
EDWARD III [*to Mortimer Junior*] Villain!
MORTIMER JR. How now, my lord?
EDWARD III Think not that I am frighted with thy words.
My father's murdered through thy treachery,
And thou shalt die, and on his mournful hearse
Thy hateful and accursèd head shall lie,

5.6. The royal palace, London.

To witness to the world that by thy means
His kingly body was too soon interred.
QUEEN Weep not, sweet son.
EDWARD III Forbid not me to weep. He was my father,
And, had you loved him half so well as I,
You could not bear his death thus patiently.
But you, I fear, conspired with Mortimer.
A LORD [*to Mortimer Junior*] Why speak you not unto my lord the King?
MORTIMER JR. Because I think scorn° to be accused. *I scorn*
Who is the man dare say I murdered him?
EDWARD III Traitor, in me my loving father speaks,
And plainly saith 'twas thou that murd'red'st him.
MORTIMER JR. But hath Your Grace no other proof than this?
EDWARD III Yes, if this be the hand of Mortimer.
[*He shows the letter.*]
MORTIMER JR. [*aside*] False Gurney hath betrayed me and himself.
QUEEN [*aside*] I feared as much. Murder cannot be hid.
MORTIMER JR. 'Tis my hand. What gather you by this?
EDWARD III That thither thou didst send a murderer.
MORTIMER JR. What murderer? Bring forth the man I sent.
EDWARD III Ah, Mortimer, thou knowest that he is slain,
And so shalt thou be too. [*To attendants*] Why stays he here?° *i.e., Take him away!*
Bring him unto a hurdle![1] Drag him forth;
Hang him, I say, and set his quarters up,[2]
But bring his head back presently to me.
QUEEN For my sake, sweet son, pity Mortimer.
MORTIMER JR. Madam, entreat not. I will rather die
Than sue for life unto a paltry boy.
EDWARD III Hence with the traitor, with the murderer!
MORTIMER JR. Base Fortune, now I see that in thy wheel
There is a point to which when men aspire
They tumble headlong down. That point I touched,
And, seeing there was no place to mount up higher,
Why should I grieve at my declining fall?—
Farewell, fair Queen. Weep not for Mortimer,
That scorns the world, and as a traveler
Goes to discover countries yet unknown.
EDWARD III [*to his Lords and attendants*] What, suffer you the traitor to delay? [*Exit Mortimer Junior, guarded.*]
QUEEN As thou received'st thy life from me,
Spill not the blood of gentle Mortimer.
EDWARD III This argues that you spilt my father's blood,
Else would you not entreat for Mortimer.
QUEEN I spill his blood? No!
EDWARD III Ay, madam, you, for so the rumor runs.
QUEEN That rumor is untrue; for loving thee
Is this report raised on poor Isabel.

1. A sled or frame upon which the condemned criminal was dragged to his execution.
2. Hang and quarter him. (To "quarter" is to tear the body of a condemned traitor or other heinous criminal into parts by pulling on the arms and legs—usually done after hanging until not quite dead and "drawing," or disembowelling, the offender.)

EDWARD III [*to his Lords*] I do not think her so unnatural.
A LORD My lord, I fear me it will prove too true.
EDWARD III Mother, you are suspected for his death,
And therefore we commit you to the Tower
Till further trial may be made thereof.
If you be guilty, though I be your son,
Think not to find me slack or pitiful.
QUEEN Nay, to my death, for too long have I lived
Whenas my son thinks to abridge my days.
EDWARD III [*weeping*] Away with her! Her words enforce these tears,
And I shall pity her if she speak again.
QUEEN Shall I not mourn for my belovèd lord,
And with the rest accompany him to his grave?
A LORD Thus, madam: 'tis the King's will you shall hence.
QUEEN He hath forgotten me. Stay, I am his mother.
A LORD That boots° not. Therefore, gentle madam, go. *avails*
QUEEN Then come, sweet death, and rid me of this grief.
[*Exit Queen, attended.*]

[*Enter a Lord with Mortimer's head.*]

A LORD My lord, here is the head of Mortimer.
EDWARD III Go fetch my father's hearse, where it shall lie,° *(see 5.6.29–30)*
And bring my funeral robes. [*Exeunt attendants.*]
Accursèd head,
Could I have ruled thee then as I do now,
Thou hadst not hatched this monstrous treachery!

[*Enter attendants with Edward II's hearse and funeral robes.*]

Here comes the hearse. Help me to mourn, my lords.
Sweet father, here unto thy murdered ghost
I offer up this wicked traitor's head;
And let these tears distilling from mine eyes
Be witness of my grief and innocency!
[*Exeunt, bearing in the hearse.*]

FINIS.

TEXTUAL NOTES

Edward II was entered in the Stationers' Register on July 6, 1593, and was printed for the bookseller William Jones in 1594 as a quarto-form octavo, that is, printed on double-sized sheets folded thrice (and hence yielding eight leaves or sixteen pages to a sheet, in the manner of an octavo, but in quarto dimensions because of the double-sized sheets; *The Spanish Tragedy* was similarly printed). This edition is the only authoritative text for the play; Marlowe died in 1593. Later quartos provide some helpful emendations but have no intrinsic authority. The present edition is based on the 1594 edition. Substantive departures from it are noted here, using the following abbreviations, with "Q1" referring to the first edition even though technically it is an octavo:

Q1: Quarto-form octavo of 1594 (London: William Jones)
Q2: Quarto of 1598 (London: William Jones)
Q3: Quarto of 1612 (London: Roger Barnes)
Q4: Quarto of 1622 (London: Henry Bell)
ed.: A modern editor's emendation
subst.: The substantive (not exact) reading

1.1.1 GAVESTON [ed.; not in Q1] **22 fawn** [ed.] fanne [Q1] **36** THIRD POOR MAN [ed.] *Sold.* [Q1] **39 porcupine** [Q1: Porpintine] **49 SD** [placement, ed.; after 48 in Q1] **57 sylvan** [Q2, subst.] *Siluian* [Q1] **110, 114 Mowbray** [Q1: *Mowberie*] **125 parley** [ed.] parle [Q1] **174** [and elsewhere] **Whither** [Q4] Whether [Q1] **189, 190** [and elsewhere] **see** [Q1: sea] **199** [and elsewhere] **Who's** [Q1: Whose]

1.2.77 CANTERBURY [ed.; not in Q1]

1.4.82 loon [Q1: lowne] **143.1** ***Enter Queen Isabel*** [ed.] *Enter Edmund and Queen Isabell* [Q1] **237 lose** [Q1: loose] **284 mushroom** [Q1: mushrump] **293** PEMBROKE **And . . . Pembroke.** / WARWICK **And I** [ed.] *War.* And so will *Penbrooke* and I [Q1] **316 struck** [ed.] stroke [Q1] **341 sovereign's** [Q3: soueraignes] soueraigne [Q1] **346 embroidery** [Q1: imbrotherie] **383 aught** [Q1: ought] **392 Hercules** [ed.] *Hector* [Q1] **395 Octavius** [Q1: *Octauis*]

2.1.52 I am [Q1: I'am] **52 pedants** [Q2] pendants [Q1] **73.1** [placement, ed.; after 72 in Q1]

2.2.39 soar [Q1: sore] **40 jesses** [ed.] gresses [Q1] **51 Tynemouth** [Q1: *Tinmouth*] **81–82 Here, here!** / KING EDWARD **Convey** [ed.] Heere here King: conuey [on one line in Q1] **88 aby** [Q1: abie] **99.1** ***Exeunt*** [ed.] *Exit* [Q1] **163 O'Neill** [Q1: *Oneyle*] **178 northern** [Q1: Northren] **178 their** [Q2] the [Q1] **190 lemans** [Q1: lemmons] **218 SD** [placement, ed.; after 217 in Q1] **220 Tynemouth** [Q1: *Tinmoth*] **225 'em** [ed.] him [Q1]

2.3.21 tattered [Q1: tottered]

2.4.3.1 ***to them Gaveston, etc.*** [placement, ed.; after 0.1–2 in Q1] **69 SD** ***Exit*** [ed.] *Exeunt* [Q1]

2.5.4 [and elsewhere] **Piers** [Q1: *Pierce*] **18 King** [Q2] Kind [Q1] **39 Renownèd** [Q1: Renowmed] **60 seize** [Q1: zease] **69 renown** [Q1: renowme] **95.3** ***Arundel*** [ed.] *Mat.* [Q1] **101** ARUNDEL [ed.] *Mat.* [Q1] **103 hither** [Q1: hether]

2.6.18 JAMES [ed.; not in Q1]

3.1.27 poll [Q1: powle] **57 largesse** [Q1: largis] **58.2, 60** [and elsewhere] ***Levune,*** **Levune** [Q1: *Lewne*] **88.2, 89, 90, 92, 94, 103, 115** ***Arundel,*** **Arundel,** ARUNDEL [ed.] *Matre., Mat., Matr.* [Q1] **148 here is** [ed.] heres is [Q1] **151, 156** HERALD [ed.] *Messen.* [Q1] **154 rout** [Q1: route] **181 lords** [ed.] lord [Q1]

3.2.17 Thou'd [Q1: Th'ad] **17 them** [ed.] thee [Q1] **19 in** [ed.] on [Q1]

3.3.41.1 ***Exeunt*** [ed.] *Exit* [Q1] **46 therewithal** [Q1: therewith all] **53 leveled** [ed.] leuied [Q1] **56 clap so** [ed.] claps [Q1]

4.2.12.1, 13 [and elsewhere] ***Hainault*, Hainault** [Q1: *Henolt*]
4.3.0.1, 9 *Arundel*, ARUNDEL [ed.] *Matr.* [Q1] **16 Isabella** [ed.] *Isabell* [Q1] **25 MESSENGER** [ed.] *Post* [Q1] **28–29 premised** [Q2: *praemised*] promised [Q1] **42 i'God's** [Q1: a Gods] **43 rout** [Q1: route] **51** [and elsewhere] **Bristol** [Q1: Bristow]
4.4.17 armèd [Q2: armed] armde [Q1] **22 wreak** [ed.] wrecke [Q1] **22 sword** [Q2] swords [Q1]
4.5.6 reinforce [Q1: r'enforce]
4.6.5 Vile [Q1: Vilde] **45 This, Edward, is** [Q2: This *Edward*, is] This *Edward* is [Q1] **62 Unhappy** [ed.] Vnhappies [Q1]
4.7.26 A MONK [ed.] *Monks* [Q1] **101 Rend** [Q1: Rent]
5.1.13 And, highly [ed.] Highly [Q1] **21 soaring** [Q1: sowring] **47 vine** [ed.] Vines [Q1] **48 survive** [ed.] suruiues [Q1] **52 lose** [Q1: loose] **78 seek** [Q4] seekes [Q1] **84, 124 TRUSSEL** [Q1: *Tru.*] **84 Parliament** [Q1: parlement] **104 being** [Q2] beene [Q1] **112 WINCHESTER** [ed.] *Enter Bartley.* / *Bartley.* [Q1] **117 Than** [Q2: Then] This [Q1] **127.1 *Enter Berkeley*** [ed.] *Enter Bartley* [after 111 in Q1] **129, 134, 144, 151 Berkeley** [ed.] *Bartley* [Q1] **131, 138, 144, 148 BERKELEY** [ed.] *Bart.* [Q1] **140 rend** [Q1: rent] **151 BERKELEY** [ed.] *Bartley* [Q1]
5.2.9 grip [Q1: gripe] **9 gripped** [Q1: gript] **10 us** [Q3] as [Q1] **11 with all** [Q4] withall [Q1] **30 ere** [ed.] or [Q1] **30, 34, 40, 48, 61 Berkeley** [ed.] *Bartley* [Q1] **60 Till** [Q2] And [Q1] **92 'tis** [ed.] it [Q1] **118 SD *Exit*** [ed.] *Exeunt omnes* [Q1]
5.3.22 rends [Q1: rents] **32** [and elsewhere] **Lest** [Q1: Least] **57 grip** [Q1: gripe]
5.4.59 Puritan [Q1: paretaine] **106 both them** [Q2] both, then [Q1]
5.6.24, 38, 77, 89, 91, 93 A LORD [ed.] *Lords* [Q1]

Arden of Faversham

Tragedy, in Aristotle's view, deals best with figures of royal and heroic stature, so that their falls into misfortune are momentous and terrifying. We are invited to look up to tragic protagonists such as Oedipus and Agamemnon—literally so, since historically they were staged in such a way as to make them appear as tall and magisterial as possible. Such figures are drawn usually from the mythic past, when men were demigods. Classical comedy, on the other hand, deals with persons like ourselves, on whom we can look down; they are our contemporaries, ordinary citizens, whose foibles are like our own.

Arden of Faversham, written sometime around 1588–92, proposes that ordinary citizens also can be the subject of tragedy. The anonymous author, drawing his materials from a real-life murder committed in 1551 that was notorious enough to have been recorded in Raphael Holinshed's *Chronicles*, tautly narrates a tempestuous adulterous affair that leads to the murder of the cuckolded husband by his wife and her lover. They and their accomplices are caught and executed for their crime; in fact, Alice Arden is burnt at the stake. The story is straightforward and sensational, a police-blotter account of the sort that would be given prime coverage in today's news media.

The author shows himself to be utterly indifferent to the Aristotelian and neo-Aristotelian tradition, if he even knows about it. He takes pride in plainness. The murdered husband's friend Franklin, speaking as an epilogue, puts the case as follows:

> Gentlemen, we hope you'll pardon this naked tragedy,
> Wherein no filèd points are foisted in
> To make it gracious to the ear or eye;
> For simple truth is gracious enough
> And needs no other points of glozing stuff.
>
> (Epilogue 14–18)

"Naked tragedy," indeed. The play is episodic, chronologically sequential, utilitarian. The author arranges it in eighteen scenes, with no pretense of classical five-act structure. Characters from the *Chronicles* account are brought forth as they are needed in the story and are dropped once their function has been completed. Inconsistencies that are inherent in the source persist quite fascinatingly in the dramatized version. The play's main effort of interpretation is to gain insight into the mental conflicts of the chief participants; it does so with extraordinary vigor and powerful ambiguities. The result is a remarkable glimpse into domestic life in sixteenth-century England, in terms both of sexual rivalry and of economic quarreling over land rights in the wake of the Reformation.

The main figures are ordinary citizens, but this is not to say that they are London shopkeepers and their wives, or courtiers, as in a Jacobean city comedy. Arden of Faversham is a member of the landed gentry. Alice, his wife, speaks of herself as having

Introduction, glosses, footnotes, and textual notes by David Bevington; text edited by David Bevington and checked by Eric Rasmussen.

been "descended of a noble house" and married to "a gentleman" (1.203–4). Arden lives the life of a country squire in Kent whose affairs call him to London from time to time. Franklin, his dearest friend and companion on the trip to London portrayed in this play, is also a gentleman.

Alice's lover, Mosby, on the other hand, is of a lower social station. Alice bitterly upbraids him, when they quarrel, as one who might be an ordinary servant to her husband (1.204–5). Arden contemptuously describes Mosby as a mere "botcher," or tailor, who, by creeping into the service of a certain Lord Clifford through "servile flattery and fawning," has managed to become the steward of that nobleman's house, so that he is now entitled to strut about in a silken gown (1.25–30). To Franklin, Mosby is no better than a "peasant" (1.31). Both Arden and Franklin are deeply affronted, not merely by Alice's entertainment of Mosby, but by the distasteful and indeed "monstrous" spectacle of her doing so with a social inferior (1.23), and by Mosby's offensive social climbing. Conflicts arising out of social difference are thus at the heart of what rapidly becomes an unhappy situation.

The liaison across social barriers of Alice and Mosby brings in other characters of modest means, for the conspiring lovers need assistance in their plan to do away with the husband. Since Mosby's sister, Susan, is the object of Michael's infatuation, and since Michael is Arden's servant, the lovers perceive at once that they can parlay this circumstance into a bid for Michael's active cooperation. Moreover, Michael has a rival in the person of Clarke, a painter. Alice and Mosby put Michael and Clarke in competition with each other, with Susan as the presumed prize and the murder of Arden as the price that the aspiring wooers must pay. Clarke knows how to "temper poison with his oil / That whoso looks upon the work he draws / Shall, with the beams that issue from his [its] sight, / Suck venom to his breast and slay himself" (1.230–33). The lovers choose instead to have Clarke put a dram of poison into Arden's drink or broth, but the intent is still the same.

Mosby's desire for Alice appears to be both sexually and economically inspired. Arden, we learn, enjoys his prosperity and social rank in good part as a reward from his noble patron, the Duke of Somerset, who has bestowed on Arden the lands of the Abbey of Faversham. The date of 1551, the year in which the murder of Arden historically took place, locates the play in the reign of Edward VI, a time of strong Protestant action against the Roman Catholic Church and especially the monasteries. Somerset, the Lord Protector during Edward's minority, vigorously confiscated church lands, continuing a policy begun by Henry VIII when he broke with Rome. The action furthered the Reformation of the Church of England, while at the same time greatly enriching the King's chief ministers and those lucky enough to enjoy the patronage of such powerful men. When we learn that those very abbey lands now enjoyed by Arden were offered at one time to Mosby by Greene, one of Sir Antony Ager's men (1.294–96), we begin to see an economic basis for Mosby's animus toward Arden. When Mosby confronts Arden with this rival claim, Arden does not deny that claim, but simply insists that the lands are his "By letters patents from His Majesty" (1.302). In other words, Arden has the official paperwork to prove his entitlement.

Moreover, this same Greene who tried to help Mosby to the abbey lands has his own deep grudge against Arden. Those letters patents that Arden has managed to obtain in the King's name have had the legal effect of cutting off all former grants, not only of the Catholic Church but of Greene himself. He owned such a grant, "But now my interest by that is void" (1.464). To Greene, Arden is a "crabbèd churl," a miser who is "greedy-gaping still for gain" and who is wholly indifferent to the impoverishment of rival claimants (1.476–78, 89). As one who is himself a gentleman, Greene is further outraged that such a man as Arden should use his wife so badly, refusing to acknowledge her noble birth, her "honorable friends" (i.e., relatives), her "parentage," and all that she has brought him in her dowry (1.490–92). Alice feeds Greene's anger by alleging that her husband has not been faithful to her: he keeps "trulls" or "trugs" in every corner of Kent, she insists, and, when bored with them, rides off to London to revel "among such filthy ones / As counsels him to make away his wife" (1.493–502). The play does not substantiate this claim; Alice may be fabricating an accusation to whet Greene's animus toward Arden. Greene's fury is great enough in any case that he is easily inveigled by Alice and Mosby into joining a growing conspiracy to do away with Arden. We never can be sure if all the allegations against Arden are just, but Greene is reputed to be "religious" and "of great devotion" (1.587–88), and the stories of Arden's sharp dealing simply will not go away.

Still another victim of Arden's grasping ways, it seems, is Dick Reede, a sailor, who confronts Arden about "the plot of ground / Which wrongfully you detain from me" (13.12–13). A property of very small rent, it is nonetheless all that Reede has to enable him to feed his wife and children. When Arden counters these allegations with nothing more generous than a threat to impose a lengthy incarceration on Reede, the latter movingly begs of God that the plot of ground in question may prove ruinous and fatal to Arden at the last (13.21–38). And so it proves. Even Arden's best friend, Franklin, is willing to admit in his epilogue to the play, after Arden's murder, that Arden withheld this plot of land from Reede "by force and violence" (Epilogue 11). The evidence of divine fulfillment of God's curse on Arden is plain for all to see: Arden's body is taken out into the fields and deposited, as it happens, in that very plot of land, in the grass of which "his body's print was seen / Two years and more after the deed was done" (Epilogue 12–13).

Arden is an unusual doomed figure in this homely tragedy—not, perhaps, wholly unlike Agamemnon, who, in Aeschylus' great play, also has lovers and has given his wife, Clytemnestra, occasion for hating him. Still, the mix of sympathy for and disapproval of Arden is remarkable. He is a man of warm friendships and moral concerns about his marriage; his grief over Alice's behavior and especially his intermittent willingness to forgive her and believe that he can trust her bespeak a generous (or perhaps gullible) nature (see, e.g., 1.351). Most of all, he is the victim, the cuckolded husband murdered by his scheming wife and her dangerous lover. At the same time, the dramatist makes no attempt to hide Arden's more grasping nature. That these contradictions are never reconciled is a source of poignant conflict in this jarringly candid dramatic representation. The implied analogy between Arden as husband and Arden as landowner, clinging possessively to "properties" that bring him ever-increasing unhappiness, underscores and heightens the inner tensions of personality. The play argues

Frontispiece to the 1633 quarto of *Arden of Faversham*, illustrating the murder of Arden at a "game at tables," or backgammon (scene 14, lines 100, 165, 224–33).

persuasively that people are often complex, unknowable, a mix of good and bad.

If the portrait of Arden is thus intriguingly ambiguous, the same is even truer of Alice. We understand that she is driven by sexual desire for Mosby and by resentment of her husband's behavior toward her. Yet her mood swings are colossal, and her passionate energy so alarming that we often have trouble sorting out when she is revealing her truest self and when she is acting the role of deceiver. In her first appearance, she speaks as one who wishes to be liberated from conventionalities: tied to Arden in a loveless marriage, resentful of his jealousies, she has given her heart to Mosby so totally that she has no compunctions about the murder of her husband. Or so it seems; for when Mosby announces his intention of backing out of their dangerous liaison, she launches into a tirade against him for having enticed her through "witchcraft and mere sorcery" into cheating on one who "was dearer than my soul" (1.195–201). Mosby, she fears, is using her as a stepping-stone to his own social advancement (1.199–205). Yet when Mosby insists that he spoke of leaving her only to test her constancy, she veers back into a mood of reconcilement. When her husband warily refuses to eat the poisoned porridge she has set out for him, Alice throws a magnificent tantrum of accusation at him that is sheer acting and is displayed to us as consummate feminine wiliness. Her skill in tricking her husband into leaving her alone with Mosby earns Mosby's open admiration for a role that "was cunningly performed" (1.420). Oaths to her mean nothing. Murder is of little consequence other than as a way of getting what one wants. To her despairing husband, she seems "rooted in her wickedness, / Perverse and stubborn, not to be reclaimed" (4.9–10). Alice's is a big part dramatically; she is a woman of towering and complex emotions, not perhaps unworthy of comparison with Clytemnestra or Medea or Lady Macbeth.

Mosby, for all his lower-class background and manifest guilt as an adulterer and murderer, is presented at times with sympathy and insight. His own ambition appalls him. In soliloquy, as he wonders how he can have ventured into a situation from which there is no safe return and nothing for him to do but go on, "although to danger's gate" (8.22), Mosby confesses to being tormented by guilt and worry. A woman who has supplanted her husband with Mosby cannot be trusted; she will "extirpen me to plant another" (8.41). Mosby finds that " 'Tis fearful sleeping in a serpent's bed" (8.42). His only explanation for his plight is that he has been "enchanted" and "bewitched" by Alice's "spells and exorcisms" (8.93–95). He goes on with their desperate plan of murder, partnered with one who is no less unhappy to have earned the title of "an odious strumpet's name" and who is certain that she too has been "bewitched" (8.72–78).

The servants and lower-class characters who play roles in the attempts and eventual success at murdering Arden are studied with condescension and some humor that bespeak an ever-present awareness of social distinctions. Michael, the servant of Arden who is in love with Susan, writes her a love letter filled with absurd details about how he fell asleep one day in St. Paul's Cathedral and lost his master's pantofles, or slippers; and he compares his fixity in loving her to a "plaster of pitch" affixed to the back of a galled horse (3.6–13). Michael feels pangs of conscience about conspiring against Arden (3.191–209), but still agrees to leave open the house door to those who have been commissioned to commit the murder. Black Will and Shakebag, the hired assassins, are comically inept in what they are supposed to do, allowing Arden to escape again and again: an apprentice in a London street lets down the shutters to his stall on Black Will's head just as Arden comes within range (3.50.1–2), the door through which they are to enter Arden's house is shut against them because Arden has tried the doors (4.101–2, 5.34–36), an aristocrat named Lord Cheyne interrupts their plans on Rainham Down as Arden is making his way back to Faversham (9.91–136), a sudden fog confounds them in another location on the coast and then clears the moment that their victim has passed by (12.1–43), and so on. Their talk of the London underworld is pithily laden with colorful narratives of coney catching and with the vocabulary of thieves (14.6–28, 17.1–14). Bradshaw, a former soldier, a goldsmith, and a receiver of stolen goods, is also part of the play's pageantry of lower-class London.

The role of divine Providence in the unfolding saga of Arden's murder suggests the same sort of ambivalence that marks the presentation of the main characters. Arden is rescued from his would-be attackers again and again in a series of what might be interpreted as miraculous escapes, if they were not so ludicrously comic in effect. One potential implication is that Arden is being protected by Almighty Providence, since he is the wronged husband. "The Lord of heaven hath preservèd him," concludes Greene when Lord Cheyne's arrival has frustrated the villains once again (9.142). Yet Black Will is skeptically of the opinion that the Lord of heaven has nothing to do with the matter: "Preserved a fig! / The Lord Cheyne hath preservèd him" (9.143–44). Shakebag has still another view: Arden enjoys "wondrous holy luck" (9.133). Is human agency or divine agency to be credited with the rescue, or just Lady Luck?

At any rate, when the murder does go ahead at last, it appears that Providence, if responsible, has decided not to spare Arden any longer. What is one to make of this? Observers are aware only that the terrible event is accompanied by repeated signs of divine displeasure at the deed itself. Susan, ordered to clean up the spilled blood of the murdered man before guests arrive, notes distractedly that "The blood cleaveth to the ground and will not out" (14.256). Alice can do no better at cleaning up, even by scraping at the blood with her nails; the mores she strives, the more the blood appears, as though in retaliation for the fact that "I blush not at my husband's death" (14.260). The attempt to carry away the corpse in secret is foiled by a sudden storm that plainly reveals the murderers' footprints in the snow. Arden's body, laid out for the funeral, bleeds in Alice's presence, especially when she sounds his name: "This blood condemns me" (16.5). Her confession is prompted by a divine witness that has lent its support to the legal processes of arrest and execution. Heaven's hand is evident, especially in the discovery and condemnation of murder: as Isabella says in Marlowe's *Edward II*, "Murder cannot be hid" (5.6.46). At the same time, heaven's judgment of Arden is far from clear. Franklin's epilogue, as we have seen, speaks of the two-year-long retention of the impression of Arden's body on Reede's little plot of land as if that miracle were divine retaliation for Arden's "force and violence" in his dealings with Reede. Whether Arden deserved death for his own crimes is not for us to judge, it would seem.

Arden of Faversham is of special interest because of its presentation of domestic strife, of the relationships of men and woman, and especially of men's attitudes toward women. Alice is a dominant presence in the play. The ambivalence in her presentation, as a villainous schemer but also as a wronged wife with strongly conflicted feelings about her husband and her lover, bespeaks a male anxiety about women as both betrayers and the source of emotional sustenance. She is dependent, in need of male support, vulnerable; she is also aggressive, wanton, untruthful, calculating. The play invites strong responses from its audience that are hard to reconcile: disapproval of wifely infidelity, but also understanding and sympathy. The ambivalence helps us to perceive why the play sees Arden too in contradictory terms, as a grasping landlord and an upstanding family man. Spectators are being asked to think about their own domestic lives in an era of changing cultural mores about marriage; contemporary manuals on the subject regularly stressed the importance of wifely obedience to the husband, but also generally reflected a trend in the English church toward the encouragement of companionate marriage in which husbands and wives would move closer to some kind of equitable mutuality. Attitudes toward sexuality were changing as well. Seen previously in the later Middle Ages as a sinful appetite that could be narrowly sanctioned only under the rigid control of the marriage contract, and even then prohibited on many days of the calendar, sexual desire was becoming more accepted as a positive pleasure and bond in a good marriage, part of a healthy balance between soul and body.[1]

1. See Mary Beth Rose, *The Expense of Spirit: Love and Sexuality in English Renaissance Drama* (Ithaca: Cornell University Press, 1988).

Such issues of domesticity and personal morals were the subjects of vigorous debate in the late sixteenth century. Nowhere could a better forum for such a debate be found than in the popular drama of urban London. *Arden of Faversham* is but one example. It is followed by such plays as Robert Yarington's *Two Lamentable Tragedies* (1594–98), the anonymous *A Warning for Fair Women* (1598–99), Thomas Heywood's *A Woman Killed with Kindness* (1603), and the anonymous *A Yorkshire Tragedy* (1605–8). Sometimes grouped together as domestic or homiletic tragedy,[2] these bourgeois plays are often derived from actual case histories, as is *Arden of Faversham*. They address their urban audiences in a plain style well suited to moral seriousness and exhortation combined with a fascination with lurid news accounts. As quintessentially London dramas, these plays proclaim the view that the lives of ordinary citizens can be treated with tragic seriousness.

2. See Henry H. Adams, *English Domestic or Homiletic Tragedy, 1575 to 1642* (New York: Columbia University Press, 1943), and Frances E. Dolan, *Dangerous Familiars: Representations of Domestic Crime in England, 1550–1700* (Ithaca: Cornell University Press, 1994).

ANONYMOUS

Arden of Faversham

[PERSONS IN THE PLAY, IN ORDER OF APPEARANCE

Thomas ARDEN of Faversham, a gentleman
FRANKLIN, his friend
ALICE, Arden's wife
ADAM Fowle, landlord of the Flower-de-Luce, an inn
MICHAEL, Arden's servant
MOSBY, Alice's lover
CLARKE, a painter, a suitor of Susan's
Richard GREENE, a tenant of Arden's
SUSAN, Mosby's sister and Alice's waiting-maid
BRADSHAW, a goldsmith and receiver of stolen goods
BLACK WILL } ruffians and hired murderers
SHAKEBAG }
A PRENTICE of a shop in London
LORD CHEYNE
His men
A FERRYMAN
Dick REEDE, a sailor living in Faversham
A SAILOR, his friend
The MAYOR of Faversham
The watch

THE SCENE: Faversham (in Kent), London, and the vicinity.]

[Scene 1]

Enter Arden and Franklin.

FRANKLIN Arden, cheer up thy spirits and droop no more.
My gracious lord, the Duke of Somerset,[1]
Hath freely given to thee and to thy heirs,
By letters patents° from His Majesty, *official documents*
All the lands of the Abbey of Faversham.
Here are the deeds, [*He hands them over.*]

The original 1592 title page reads "*The Lamentable and True Tragedy of Master Arden of Faversham in Kent*, who was most wickedly murdered by the means of his disloyal and wanton wife, who, for the love she bare to one Mosby, hired two desperate ruffians, Black Will and Shakebag, to kill him. Wherein is showed the great malice and dissimulation of a wicked woman, the unsatiable desire of filthy lust, and the shameful end of all murderers. Imprinted at London for Edward White, dwelling at the little north door of Paul's Church at the sign of the Gun, 1592."

Scene 1. Faversham, Kent. Arden's house and, at lines 244–90, Clarke the painter's.

1. The Lord Protector until 1550 in the reign of Edward VI (1547–53); he was responsible for much confiscation of church property in the name of the Reformation.

Sealed and subscribed° with his name and the King's. — *signed*
Read them, and leave this melancholy mood.
ARDEN Franklin, thy love prolongs my weary life,
And, but for thee, how odious were this life,
That shows° me nothing but torments my soul, — *yields, profits*
And those foul objects° that offend mine eyes, — *(see 15–18)*
Which makes me wish that for° this vale of heaven — *in place of*
The earth hung over my head and covered me.
Love letters passed 'twixt Mosby and my wife,
And they have privy° meetings in the town. — *secret*
Nay, on his finger did I spy the ring
Which at our marriage day the priest put on.
Can any grief be half so great as this?
FRANKLIN Comfort thyself, sweet friend. It is not strange
That women will be false and wavering.
ARDEN Ay, but to dote on such a one as he
Is monstrous, Franklin, and intolerable.
FRANKLIN Why, what is he?
ARDEN A botcher° and no better at the first,° — *tailor / at birth*
Who, by base brokage° getting some small stock, — *petty commerce*
Crept into service of a nobleman,
And by his servile flattery and fawning
Is now become the steward[2] of his house,
And bravely jets it° in his silken gown. — *boldly struts about*
FRANKLIN No nobleman will countenance such a peasant.
ARDEN Yes, the Lord Clifford, he that loves not me.
But through his favor° let not him° grow proud, — *sponsorship / (Mosby)*
For, were he° by the Lord Protector backed, — *even if he were*
He should not make me to be pointed at.
I am by birth a gentleman of blood;
And that injurious ribald° that attempts — *insolent knave*
To violate my dear wife's chastity—
For dear I hold her love, as dear as heaven—
Shall on the bed which he thinks to defile
See his dissevered joints and sinews torn,
Whilst on the planchers° pants his weary body, — *floor planks*
Smeared in the channels° of his lustful blood. — *rivulets*
FRANKLIN Be patient, gentle friend, and learn of me
To ease thy grief and save her chastity.
Entreat her fair;° sweet words are fittest engines° — *gently / devices*
To raze° the flint walls of a woman's breast. — *reduce to rubble*
In any case be not too jealous,
Nor make no question of her love to thee,
But as securely,° presently take horse — *as if confidently*
And lie° with me at London all this term;° — *reside / law term*
For women, when° they may,° will not, — *even when / could behave*
But, being kept back, straight grow outrageous.
ARDEN Though this abhors from° reason, yet I'll try it, — *is repugnant to*
And call her forth and presently take leave.—
Ho, Alice!

Here enters Alice.

2. Officer in charge of finances and household management.

ALICE Husband, what mean you to get up so early?
Summer nights are short, and yet you rise ere day.
Had I been wake,° you had not rise° so soon. *awake / risen*
ARDEN Sweet love, thou know'st that we two, Ovid-like,° *(see* Amores, *13.9–40)*
Have often chid the morning when it gan° to peep, *began*
And often wished that dark Night's purblind° steeds *partly or wholly blind*
Would pull her by the purple mantle back
And cast her in the ocean to her love.
But this night, sweet Alice, thou hast killed my heart:
I heard thee call on Mosby in thy sleep.
ALICE 'Tis like° I was asleep when I named him, *likely*
For being awake he comes not in my thoughts.
ARDEN Ay, but you started up, and suddenly,
Instead of him, caught me about the neck.
ALICE Instead of him? Why, who was there but you?
And where but one° is, how can I mistake? *only one person*
FRANKLIN Arden, leave° to urge her overfar. *cease*
ARDEN Nay, love, there is no credit° in a dream. *believability*
Let it suffice I know thou lovest me well.
ALICE Now I remember whereupon it came:° *how it came about*
Had we no talk of Mosby yesternight?
FRANKLIN Mistress Alice, I heard you name him once or twice.
ALICE And thereof came it, and therefore blame not me.
ARDEN I know it did, and therefore let it pass.
I must to London, sweet Alice, presently.
ALICE But tell me, do you mean to stay there long?
ARDEN No longer than till my affairs be done.
FRANKLIN He will not stay above a month at most.
ALICE A month! Ay me! Sweet Arden, come again
Within a day or two, or else I die!
ARDEN I cannot long be from thee, gentle Alice.
Whilst Michael fetch our horses from the field,
Franklin and I will down unto the quay,
For I have certain goods there to unload.
Meanwhile, prepare our breakfast, gentle Alice,
For yet ere noon we'll take horse and away.
Exeunt Arden and Franklin.
ALICE Ere noon he means to take horse and away:
Sweet news is this. Oh, that some airy spirit
Would in the shape and likeness of a horse
Gallop with Arden 'cross the ocean
And throw him from his° back into the waves! *its*
Sweet Mosby is the man that hath my heart,
And he° usurps it, having naught but this: *(Arden)*
That I am tied to him by marriage.
Love is a god, and marriage is but words,
And therefore Mosby's title is the best.
Tush, whether it be or no, he shall be mine,
In spite of him,° of Hymen,° and of rites. *(Arden) / god of marriage*

Here enters Adam of the Flower-de-Luce.° *Fleur-de-lis (lily), an inn*

And here comes Adam of the Flower-de-Luce.
I hope he brings me tidings of my love.—
How now, Adam, what is the news with you?

Be not afraid; my husband is now from home.
ADAM He whom you wot° of, Mosby, Mistress Alice, *know*
Is come to town, and sends you word by me
In any case you may not visit him.
ALICE Not visit him?
ADAM No, nor take no knowledge of his being here.
ALICE But tell me, is he angry or displeased?
ADAM Should seem so,° for he is wondrous sad. *It would appear so*
ALICE Were he as mad as raving Hercules,[3]
I'll see him; ay, and were thy house of force,° *fortified*
These hands of mine should raze it to the ground
Unless that° thou wouldst bring me to my love. *Unless*
ADAM Nay, an° you be so impatient, I'll be gone. *if*
ALICE Stay, Adam, stay! Thou wert wont to be my friend.
Ask Mosby how I have incurred his wrath;
Bear him from me these pair of silver dice
[*Giving him the dice*]
With which we played for kisses many a time,
And when I lost, I won, and so did he—
Such winning and such losing Jove° send me! *may Jove*
And bid him, if his love do not decline,
To come this morning but along° my door *past*
And as a stranger but salute° me there. *simply greet*
This may he do without suspect° or fear. *suspicion*
ADAM I'll tell him what you say, and so farewell.
ALICE Do, and one day I'll make amends for all. *Exit Adam.*
I know he loves me well, but dares not come
Because my husband is so jealous;
And these my narrow-prying neighbors blab,
Hinder our meetings when we would confer.
But, if I live, that block shall be removed,
And Mosby, thou that comes to me by stealth
Shalt neither fear the biting speech of men
Nor Arden's looks. As surely shall he die
As I abhor him and love only thee.

Here enters Michael.

How now, Michael, whither are you going?
MICHAEL To fetch my master's nag.
I hope you'll think on me.
ALICE Ay, but Michael, see you keep your oath,
And be as secret as you are resolute.
MICHAEL I'll see he shall not live above a week.
ALICE On that condition, Michael, here is my hand
None shall have Mosby's sister but thyself.
MICHAEL I understand the painter here hard by° *nearby*
Hath made report that he and Sue is sure.° *are engaged*
ALICE There's no such matter, Michael; believe it not.
MICHAEL But he hath sent a dagger sticking in a heart,
With a verse or two stolen from a painted cloth,° *tapestry*
The which I hear the wench° keeps in her chest. *young woman (Susan)*
Well, let her keep it! I shall find a fellow
That can both write and read, and make rhyme too,

3. Hercules was driven mad by a poisoned shirt mistakenly given him by his second wife, Deianira.

And if I do—well, I say no more.
I'll send from London such a taunting letter
As she shall eat the heart he sent with salt
And fling the dagger at the painter's head.

ALICE What needs all this? I say that Susan's thine.

MICHAEL Why, then, I say that I will kill my master
Or anything that you will have me do.

ALICE But, Michael, see you do it cunningly.

MICHAEL Why, say I should be took,° I'll ne'er confess — *taken, arrested*
That you know anything; and Susan, being a maid,
May beg me from the gallows of the sheriff.[4]

ALICE Trust not to that, Michael.

MICHAEL You cannot tell me; I have seen it, I.
But, mistress, tell her, whether I live or die
I'll make her more worth° than twenty painters can; — *wealthy*
For I will rid mine elder brother away,
And then the farm of Bolton is mine own.
Who would not venture upon house and land
When he may have it for a right-down° blow? — *downright*

Here enters Mosby.

ALICE Yonder comes Mosby. Michael, get thee gone,
And let not him nor any know thy drifts.° *Exit Michael.* — *schemes*
Mosby, my love!

MOSBY Away, I say, and talk not to me now.

ALICE A word or two, sweetheart, and then I will.
'Tis yet but early days;° thou needest not fear. — *early in the day*

MOSBY Where is your husband?

ALICE 'Tis now high water, and he is at the quay.

MOSBY There let him be! Henceforward know me not.

ALICE Is this the end of all thy solemn oaths?
Is this the fruit thy reconcilement buds?° — *causes to bud*
Have I for this given thee so many favors,
Incurred my husband's hate, and—out,° alas!— — *(exclamation of dismay)*
Made shipwreck of mine honor for thy sake?
And dost thou say, "Henceforward know me not"?
Remember, when I locked thee in my closet,° — *private room*
What were thy words and mine? Did we not both
Decree to murder Arden in the night?
The heavens can witness, and the world can tell,
Before I saw that falsehood look of thine,
'Fore I was tangled with thy 'ticing° speech, — *enticing*
Arden to me was dearer than my soul—
And shall be still. Base peasant, get thee gone,
And boast not of thy conquest over me,
Gotten by witchcraft and mere sorcery.
For what hast thou to countenance° my love, — *be in keeping with*
Being° descended of a noble house, — *I being*
And matched already with a gentleman
Whose servant thou mayst be? And so farewell.

MOSBY Ungentle and unkind Alice, now I see
That which I ever feared, and find too true:
A woman's love is as the lightning flame,

4. According to popular belief, a virgin could save a condemned man from execution by offering to marry him.

Which even in bursting forth consumes itself.
To try thy constancy have I been strange.° *distant, reserved*
Would I had never tried, but lived in hope!

ALICE What needs thou try me, whom thou never found false?

MOSBY Yet pardon me, for love is jealous.

ALICE So lists° the sailor to the mermaids' song; *listens*
So looks the traveler to the basilisk.[5]
I am content for to be reconciled,
And that, I know, will be mine overthrow.

MOSBY Thine overthrow? First let the world dissolve!

ALICE Nay, Mosby, let me still enjoy thy love,
And, happen what will, I am resolute.
My saving husband hoards up bags of gold
To make our children rich, and now is he
Gone to unload the goods that shall be thine,
And he and Franklin will to London straight.° *at once*

MOSBY To London, Alice? If thou'lt be ruled by me,
We'll make him sure enough for° coming there. *to prevent him from*

ALICE Ah, would we could!

MOSBY I happened on a painter yesternight,
The only° cunning man of Christendom, *uniquely*
For he can temper° poison with his oil *mix*
That° whoso looks upon the work he draws *So that*
Shall, with the beams that issue from his sight,
Suck venom to his breast and slay himself.
Sweet Alice, he shall draw thy counterfeit,° *portrait, likeness*
That Arden may by gazing on it perish.

ALICE Ay, but Mosby, that is dangerous,
For thou or I, or any other else,
Coming into the chamber where it hangs, may die.

MOSBY Ay, but we'll have it covered with a cloth
And hung up in the study for himself.

ALICE It may not be, for when the picture's drawn,
Arden, I know, will come and show it me.

MOSBY Fear not. We'll have that shall serve the turn.° *a thing that'll work*
[*They cross the stage.*]
This is the painter's house. I'll call him forth.

ALICE But, Mosby, I'll have no such picture, I.

MOSBY I pray thee leave it to my discretion.—
Ho, Clarke!

Here enters Clarke.

Oh, you are an honest man of your word; you served me well.

CLARKE Why, sir, I'll do it for you at any time,
Provided, as you have given your word,
I may have Susan Mosby to my wife.
For, as sharp-witted poets—whose sweet verse
Make heavenly gods break off their nectar drafts
And lay their ears down to the lowly earth—

5. The gaze of the basilisk, a fabulous serpent, was fabled to be fatal. The mermaids are Sirens, mythical creatures that lured sailors to their death by making their boats crash on the rocks; no sailor could navigate while listening to the Sirens' song. (The song of the Sirens tempts Odysseus in Book 12 of Homer's *Odyssey*.)

Use humble promise to their sacred Muse,
So we that are the poets' favorites
Must have a love. Ay, Love is the painter's Muse
That makes him frame° a speaking countenance, *fashion*
A weeping eye that witnesses heart's grief.
Then tell me, Master Mosby, shall I have her?
ALICE [*to Mosby*] 'Tis pity but° he should; he'll use her well. *but that, unless*
MOSBY Clarke, here's my hand my sister shall be thine.
CLARKE Then, brother, to requite this courtesy,
You shall command my life, my skill, and all.
ALICE Ah, that° thou couldst be secret! *would that*
MOSBY Fear him not. Leave;° I have talked sufficient. *Cease*
CLARKE You know not me that ask such questions.
Let it suffice I know you love him well
And fain° would have your husband made away— *willingly*
Wherein, trust me, you show a noble mind,
That, rather than you'll live with him you hate,
You'll venture life and die with him you love.
The like will I do for my Susan's sake.
ALICE Yet nothing could enforce me to the deed
But Mosby's love. Might I without control° *hindrance*
Enjoy thee still, then Arden should not die;
But seeing I cannot, therefore let him die.
MOSBY Enough, sweet Alice; thy kind words makes me melt.
[*To Clarke*] Your trick of poisoned pictures we dislike;
Some other poison would do better far.
ALICE Ay, such as might be put into his broth,
And yet in taste not to be found at all.
CLARKE I know your mind, and here I have it for you.
[*He produces a vial of poison.*]
Put but a dram of this into his drink
Or any kind of broth that he shall eat,
And he shall die within an hour after.
ALICE As I am a gentlewoman, Clarke, next day
Thou and Susan shall be marrièd.
MOSBY And I'll make her dowry more than I'll talk of,
Clarke.
CLARKE Yonder's your husband. Mosby, I'll be gone.
Exit Clarke.

Here enters Arden and Franklin [*and Michael*].

ALICE In good time, see where my husband comes.
Master Mosby, ask him the question yourself.
MOSBY Master Arden, being at London yesternight,
The abbey lands whereof you are now possessed
Were offered me on some occasion
By Greene, one of Sir Antony Ager's men.
I pray you, sir, tell me, are not the lands yours?
Hath any other interest herein?
ARDEN Mosby, that question we'll decide anon.—
Alice, make ready my breakfast; I must hence. *Exit Alice.*
As for the lands, Mosby, they are mine,
By letters patents from His Majesty.
But I must have a mandate° for my wife; *injunction*
They say you seek to rob me of her love.

Villain, what makes thou° in her company? *are you doing*
She's no companion for so base a groom.° *man of inferior status*
MOSBY Arden, I thought not on her; I came to thee,
But rather than I pocket up° this wrong— *meekly submit to*
FRANKLIN What will you do, sir?
MOSBY Revenge it on the proudest of you both.
Then Arden draws forth Mosby's sword.
ARDEN So, sirrah, you may not wear a sword;
The statute makes against artificers.° *denies this to craftsmen*
I warrant that° I do. Now use your bodkin,° *that which / needle*
Your Spanish needle, and your pressing iron,° *tailor's iron*
For this shall go with me. And mark my words—
You, goodman botcher,° 'tis to you I speak— *tailor*
The next time that I take° thee near my house, *find, come upon*
Instead of legs I'll make thee crawl on stumps.
MOSBY Ah, Master Arden, you have injured° me! *insulted*
I do appeal to God and to the world.
FRANKLIN Why, canst thou deny thou wert a botcher once?
MOSBY Measure me what I am, not what I was.
ARDEN Why, what art thou now but a velvet drudge,° *menial in velvet livery*
A cheating steward, and base-minded peasant?
MOSBY Arden, now thou hast belched and vomited
The rancorous venom of thy misswoll'n heart,
Hear me but speak: as I intend to live
With God and His elected saints in heaven,
I never meant more to solicit her,
And that she knows, and all the world shall see.
I loved her once—sweet Arden, pardon me;
I could not choose, her beauty fired my heart.
But time hath quenched these overraging coals,
And, Arden, though I now frequent thy house,
'Tis for my sister's sake, her waiting-maid,
And not for hers. Mayest thou enjoy her long!
Hellfire and wrathful vengeance light on me
If I dishonor her or injure thee!
ARDEN Mosby, with these thy protestations
The deadly hatred of my heart is appeased,
And thou and I'll be friends, if this prove true.
As for the base terms I gave thee late,° *just now*
Forget them, Mosby; I had cause to speak,
When all the knights and gentlemen of Kent
Make common table talk of her and thee.
MOSBY Who lives that is not touched with slanderous tongues?
FRANKLIN Then, Mosby, to eschew the speech of men,
Upon whose general bruit° all honor hangs, *rumor, report*
Forbear his house.
ARDEN Forbear it? Nay, rather frequent it more!
The world shall see that I distrust her not.
To warn° him on the sudden from my house *order to stay away*
Were to confirm the rumor that is grown.
MOSBY By my faith, sir, you say true.
And therefore will I sojourn here awhile
Until our enemies have talked their fill;
And then I hope they'll cease and at last confess

How causeless they have injured her and me.
ARDEN And I will lie° at London all this term — *reside*
To let them see how light I weigh their words.

Here enters Alice.

ALICE Husband, sit down. Your breakfast will be cold.
ARDEN Come, Master Mosby, will you sit with us?
MOSBY I cannot eat, but I'll sit for company. [*They sit.*]
ARDEN Sirrah° Michael, see our horse be ready. — *(said to social inferiors)*
[*Exit Michael, and then reenter shortly.*]
ALICE Husband, why pause ye? Why eat you not?
ARDEN I am not well. There's something in this broth
That is not wholesome. Didst thou make it, Alice?
ALICE I did, and that's the cause it likes not° you. — *displeases; makes ill*
Then she throws down the broth on the ground.
There's nothing that I do can please your taste.
You were best to say I would have poisoned you!—
I cannot speak or cast aside my eye
But he imagines I have stepped awry.—
Here's he that you cast in my teeth° so oft; — *accused me with*
Now will I be convinced° or purge° myself. — *convicted / clear*
[*To Mosby*] I charge thee speak to this mistrustful man—
Thou that wouldst see me hang, thou, Mosby, thou.
What favor hast thou had more than a kiss
At coming or departing from the town?
MOSBY You wrong yourself and me to cast° these doubts. — *utter*
Your loving husband is not jealous.
ARDEN Why, gentle mistress Alice, cannot I be ill
But you'll accuse yourself?—
Franklin, thou hast a box of mithridate;° — *a poison antidote*
I'll take a little to prevent the worst.
FRANKLIN [*offering medicine*] Do so, and let us presently take horse.
My life for yours,° ye shall do well enough. — *i.e., On my life*
ALICE Give me a spoon. I'll eat of it myself.
Would it were full of poison to the brim!
Then should my cares and troubles have an end.
Was ever silly° woman so tormented? — *innocent*
ARDEN Be patient, sweet love; I mistrust not thee.
ALICE God will revenge it, Arden, if thou dost,
For never woman loved her husband better
Than I do thee.
ARDEN I know it, sweet Alice. Cease to complain,
Lest that in tears I answer thee again.
FRANKLIN Come, leave this dallying, and let us away.
ALICE Forbear to wound me with that bitter word!
Arden shall go to London in my arms.° — *i.e., will stay here*
ARDEN Loath am I to depart, yet I must go.
ALICE Wilt thou to London, then, and leave me here?
Ah, if thou love me, gentle Arden, stay.
Yet if thy business be of great import,
Go, if thou wilt; I'll bear it as I may.
But write from London to me every week,
Nay, every day, and stay no longer there
Than thou must needs, lest that I die for sorrow.

ARDEN I'll write unto thee every other tide,° *turning of the tide*
And so farewell, sweet Alice, till we meet next.
ALICE Farewell, husband, seeing you'll have it so.
And, Master Franklin, seeing you take him hence,
In hope you'll hasten him home I'll give you this.
And then she kisseth him.
FRANKLIN And if he stay the fault shall not be mine.—
Mosby, farewell, and see you keep your oath.
MOSBY I hope he is not jealous of me now.
ARDEN No, Mosby, no. Hereafter think of me
As of your dearest friend, and so farewell.
Exeunt Arden, Franklin, and Michael.
ALICE I am glad he is gone. He was about to stay.
But did you mark me then how I brake off?
MOSBY Ay, Alice, and it was cunningly performed.
But what a villain is this painter Clarke!
ALICE Was it not a goodly poison that he gave!
Why, he's° as well now as he was before. *(Arden is)*
It should have been some fine confection
That might have given the broth some dainty taste.
This powder was too gross and populous.° *obvious*
MOSBY But had he eaten but three spoonfuls more,
Then had he died and our love continued.
ALICE Why so it shall, Mosby, albeit he live.
MOSBY It is unpossible, for I have sworn
Never hereafter to solicit thee
Or, whilst he lives, once more importune thee.
ALICE Thou shalt not need; I will importune thee.
What, shall an oath make thee forsake my love?
As if I have not sworn as much myself,
And given my hand unto him in the church!
Tush, Mosby, oaths are words, and words is wind,
And wind is mutable. Then I conclude
'Tis childishness to stand upon an oath.
MOSBY Well proved, Mistress Alice. Yet, by your leave,
I'll keep mine unbroken whilst he lives.
ALICE Ay, do, and spare not. His time is but short,
For if thou be'st as resolute as I
We'll have him murdered as he walks the streets.
In London many alehouse ruffians keep,° *dwell*
Which, as I hear, will murder men for gold.
They shall be soundly fee'd to pay him home.° *fully, to the death*

Here enters Greene.

MOSBY Alice, what's he that comes yonder? Knowest thou him?
ALICE Mosby, begone. I hope 'tis one that comes
To put in practice our intended drifts.° *Exit Mosby.* *schemes*
GREENE Mistress Arden, you are well met.
I am sorry that your husband is from home,
Whenas° my purposed journey was to him. *When, since*
Yet all my labor is not spent in vain,
For I suppose that you can full° discourse *fully*
And flat resolve me° of the thing I seek. *fully satisfy me*
ALICE What is it, Master Greene? If that I may

Or can, with safety, I will answer you.
GREENE I heard your husband hath the grant of late,
Confirmed by letters patents from the King,
Of all the lands of the Abbey of Faversham,
Generally intitled,° so that all former grants *Given absolute title*
Are cut off, whereof I myself had one,
But now my interest by that is void.
This is all, Mistress Arden. Is it true nor no?° *or not*
ALICE True, Master Greene. The lands are his in state,° *by legal right*
And whatsoever leases were before
Are void for term of Master Arden's life;
He hath the grant under the Chancery° seal. *(of the Lord Chancellor)*
GREENE Pardon me, Mistress Arden. I must speak,
For I am touched;° your husband doth me wrong *affected*
To wring me from° the little land I have. *wrest from me*
My living° is my life; only that *land*
Resteth° remainder of my portion.° *Remains / inheritance*
Desire of wealth is endless in his mind,
And he is greedy-gaping still for gain;
Nor cares he though young gentlemen do beg,
So° he may scrape and hoard up in his pouch. *So long as*
But, seeing he hath taken my lands, I'll value life
As careless as he is careful for to get.° *shrewd in acquiring*
And tell him this from me: I'll be revenged,
And so as he shall wish the abbey lands
Had rested still within their former state.
ALICE Alas, poor gentleman, I pity you,
And woe is me that any man should want.° *be in need*
God knows, 'tis not my fault. But wonder not
Though he be hard to others, when to me—
Ah, Master Greene, God knows how I am used!
GREENE Why, Mistress Arden, can the crabbèd° churl *ill-tempered*
Use you unkindly? Respects he not your birth,
Your honorable friends,° nor what you brought?° *kin / brought as dowry*
Why, all Kent knows your parentage, and what you are.
ALICE Ah, Master Greene, be it spoken in secret here,
I never live good day with him alone.
When he is at home, then have I froward° looks, *bad-tempered*
Hard words, and blows to mend the match withal.° *to match*
And, though I might content as good a man,
Yet doth he keep in every corner trulls;° *loose women*
And, weary with his trugs° at home, *whores*
Then rides he straight to London. There, forsooth,
He revels it among such filthy ones
As counsels him to make away° his wife. *slay*
Thus live I daily in continual fear,
In sorrow, so despairing of redress
As every day I wish with hearty prayer
That he or I were taken forth the world.° *were dead*
GREENE Now trust° me, Mistress Alice, it grieveth me *believe*
So fair a creature should be so abused.
Why, who would have thought the civil sir so sullen?
He looks so smoothly. Now, fie upon him, churl!
An if he live a day he lives too long.
But frolic,° woman! I shall be the man *be cheerful*

Shall° set you free from all this discontent. — *Who will*
And if the churl deny my interest
And will not yield my lease into my hand,
I'll pay him home,° whatever hap to me. — *strike all the way*
ALICE But speak you as you think?
GREENE Ay, God's my witness, I mean plain dealing,
For I had rather die than lose my land.
ALICE Then, Master Greene, be counselèd by me:
Endanger not yourself for such a churl,
But hire some cutter° for to cut him short; — *cutthroat*
And here's ten pound to wager° them withal. — *hire at wages*
[*She gives money.*]
When he is dead you shall have twenty more,
And the lands whereof my husband is possessed
Shall be intitled as they were before.
GREENE Will you keep promise with me?
ALICE Or count me false and perjured whilst I live.
GREENE Then here's my hand. I'll have him so dispatched.
I'll up to London straight; I'll thither post,
And never rest till I have compassed° it. — *encompassed, achieved*
Till then, farewell.
ALICE Good fortune follow all your forward° thoughts! — *zealous*
And whosoever doth attempt the deed,
A happy hand I wish, and so farewell. *Exit Greene.*
All this goes well. Mosby, I long for thee,
To let thee know all that I have contrived.

Here enters Mosby and Clarke.

MOSBY How now, Alice, what's the news?
ALICE Such as will content thee well, sweetheart.
MOSBY Well, let them° pass awhile, and tell me, Alice, — *(the news)*
How have you dealt and tempered with° my sister? — *worked on*
What, will she have my neighbor Clarke, or no?
ALICE What, Master Mosby, let him woo himself.
Think you that maids look not for fair words?—
Go to her, Clarke; she's all alone within.
Michael, my man,° is clean out of her books.° — *servant / i.e., favor*
CLARKE I thank you, Mistress Arden. I will in,
And, if fair Susan and I can make a gree,° — *an agreement*
You shall command me to the uttermost,
As far as either goods or life may stretch. *Exit Clarke.*
MOSBY Now, Alice, let's hear thy news.
ALICE They be so good that I must laugh for joy
Before I can begin to tell my tale.
MOSBY Let's hear them, that I may laugh for company.
ALICE This morning, Master Greene—Dick Greene, I mean,
From whom my husband had° the abbey land— — *took away*
Came hither railing for° to know the truth, — *in order*
Whether my husband had the lands by grant.
I told him all, whereat he stormed amain° — *with might and main*
And swore he would cry quittance° with the churl, — *be even*
And, if he did deny his interest,° — *Greene's claim*
Stab him, whatsoever did befall himself.
Whenas° I saw his choler° thus to rise, — *When / anger*

I whetted on the gentleman with words.
And to conclude, Mosby, at last we grew
To composition° for my husband's death. *agreement*
I gave him ten pound to hire knaves
By some device to make away the churl;
When he is dead, he should have° twenty more, *is to have*
And repossess his former lands again.
On this we 'greed, and he is ridden straight
To London, to bring his death about.

MOSBY But call you this good news?

ALICE Ay, sweetheart, be they not?

MOSBY 'Twere° cheerful news to hear the churl were dead. *It would be*
But trust me, Alice, I take it passing° ill *exceedingly*
You would be so forgetful of our state° *(precarious) situation*
To make recount of it to every groom.
What, to acquaint each stranger with our drifts,° *intents, plots*
Chiefly in case of murder? Why, 'tis the way
To make it open unto Arden's self
And bring thyself and me to ruin, both.
Forewarned, forearmed: who° threats his enemy *whoever*
Lends him a sword to guard himself withal.

ALICE I did it for the best.

MOSBY Well, seeing 'tis done, cheerly let it pass.
You know this Greene; is he not religious?
A man, I guess, of great devotion?

ALICE He is.

MOSBY Then, sweet Alice, let it pass. I have a drift° *plan (that)*
Will quiet all, whatever is amiss.

Here enters Clarke and Susan.

ALICE How now, Clarke, have you found me false?
Did I not plead the matter hard for you?

CLARKE You did.

MOSBY And what, will't be a match?

CLARKE A match, i'faith, sir. Ay, the day is mine.
The painter lays his colors to the life;° *as they are in real life*
His pencil° draws no shadows in his love. *brush*
Susan is mine.

ALICE You make her blush.

MOSBY What, sister, is it Clarke must be the man?

SUSAN It resteth in your grant.° Some words are passed, *in your authority*
And haply° we be grown unto a match, *perchance; happily*
If you be willing that it shall be so.

MOSBY Ah, Master Clarke, it resteth at my grant!
You see my sister's yet at my dispose;° *disposal*
But, so° you'll grant me one thing I shall ask, *so long as*
I am content my sister shall be yours.

CLARKE What is it, Master Mosby?

MOSBY I do remember once, in secret talk,
You told me how you could compound by art
A crucifix impoisonèd,
That whoso look upon it should wax blind
And with the scent be stifled, that ere long
He should die poisoned that did view it well.
I would have you make me such a crucifix,

And then I'll grant my sister shall be yours.
CLARKE Though I am loath, because it toucheth life,° *is mortal, deadly*
Yet, rather or° I'll leave sweet Susan's love, *ere, before*
I'll do it, and with all the haste I may.
But for whom is it?
ALICE Leave that to us. Why, Clarke, is it possible
That you should paint and draw it out yourself,
The colors being baleful and impoisoned,
And no ways prejudice° yourself withal?° *endanger / with it*
MOSBY Well questioned, Alice.—Clarke, how answer you that?
CLARKE Very easily. I'll tell you straight
How I do work of these impoisoned drugs:
I fasten on my spectacles so close
As nothing can any way offend my sight;
Then, as I put a leaf within my nose,
So put I rhubarb to avoid the smell,
And softly as another work I paint.
MOSBY 'Tis very well, but against when° shall I have it? *but when*
CLARKE Within this ten days.
MOSBY 'Twill serve the turn.—
Now, Alice, let's in and see what cheer° you keep. *hospitality*
I hope, now Master Arden is from home,
You'll give me leave to play your husband's part.
ALICE Mosby, you know, who's° master of my heart, *that person who is*
He well may be the master of the house. *Exeunt.*

[Scene 2]

Here enters Greene and Bradshaw.

BRADSHAW See you them that comes yonder, Master Greene?
GREENE Ay, very well. Do you know them?

Here enters Black Will and Shakebag.

BRADSHAW The one I know not, but he seems a knave,
Chiefly for bearing the other company;
For such a slave,° so vile a rogue as he, *wretch*
Lives not again upon the earth;
Black Will is his name. I tell you, Master Greene,
At Boulogne[1] he and I were fellow soldiers,
Where he played such pranks
As all the camp feared him for his villainy.
I warrant you he bears so bad a mind
That for a crown° he'll murder any man. *gold coin*
GREENE [*aside*] The fitter is he for my purpose, marry!° *by Mary (an oath)*
BLACK WILL How now, fellow Bradshaw? Whither away so early?
BRADSHAW Oh, Will, times are changed. No fellows now,
Though we were once together in the field;° *field of battle*
Yet thy friend to do thee any good I can.
BLACK WILL Why, Bradshaw, was not thou and I fellow sol-

Scene 2. Kent, near Rochester.
1. Henry VIII captured Boulogne, on the French coast of the English Channel, in 1544; the French recaptured it in 1550, just before the events recorded in this play.

diers at Boulogne, where I was a corporal and thou but a base mercenary groom? "No fellows now" because you are a goldsmith and have a little plate° in your shop? You were glad to call me "fellow Will" and, with a curtsy° to the earth, "One snatch,° good corporal" when I stole the half ox from John the victualer° and domineered° with it amongst good fellows in one night.

gold or silver plate / *bow* / *morsel* / *tavern-keeper / reveled*

BRADSHAW Ay, Will, those days are past with me.

BLACK WILL Ay, but they be not past with me, for I keep that same honorable mind still. Good neighbor Bradshaw, you are too proud to be my fellow; but, were it not that I see more company coming down the hill, I would be fellows with you once more, and share crowns° with you too. But let that pass, and tell me whither you go.

i.e., booty of a robbery

BRADSHAW To London, Will, about a piece of service,
Wherein haply thou mayst pleasure me.

BLACK WILL What is it?

BRADSHAW Of late, Lord Cheyne lost some plate,
Which one did bring and sold it at my shop,
Saying he served Sir Antony Cooke.
A search was made, the plate was found with me,
And I am bound to answer at the 'size.° *assize, court trial*
Now Lord Cheyne solemnly vows,
If law will serve him, he'll hang me for his plate.
Now I am going to London upon hope
To find the fellow.° Now, Will, I know *i.e., the real thief*
Thou art acquainted with such companions.° *rascally fellows*

BLACK WILL What manner of man was he?

BRADSHAW A lean-faced, writhen° knave, *contorted*
Hawk-nosed and very hollow-eyed,
With mighty furrows in his stormy brows;
Long hair down his shoulders curled;
His chin was bare, but on his upper lip
A mutchado,° which he wound about his ear. *mustache*

BLACK WILL What apparel had he?

BRADSHAW A watchet° satin doublet all to-torn° *blue / torn to pieces*
(The inner side did bear the greater show),° *showed more*
A pair of threadbare velvet hose, seam rent,° *torn at the seam*
A worsted stocking rent above the shoe,
A livery cloak, but all the lace was off;
'Twas bad, but yet it served to hide the plate.

BLACK WILL Sirrah Shakebag, canst thou remember since we trolled° the bowl° at Sittingburgh, where I broke the tapster's head of the Lion° with a cudgel stick?

handed round / cup / *an inn*

SHAKEBAG Ay, very well, Will.

BLACK WILL Why, it was with the money that the plate was sold for.—Sirrah Bradshaw, what wilt thou give him that can tell thee who sold thy plate?

BRADSHAW Who, I pray thee, good Will?

BLACK WILL Why, 'twas one Jack Fitten. He's now in Newgate° for stealing a horse, and shall be arraigned the next 'size.

a London prison

BRADSHAW Why, then, let Lord Cheyne seek Jack Fitten forth, for I'll back and tell him who robbed him of his plate. This cheers my heart.—Master Greene, I'll leave you, for I must to the Isle of Sheppey° with speed. [*(in Kent)*]

GREENE [*giving a letter*] Before you go, let me entreat you to carry this letter to Mistress Arden of Faversham and humbly recommend me to herself.

BRADSHAW That will I, Master Greene, and so farewell.—
Here, Will, there's a crown for thy good news.
[*He gives money.*]

BLACK WILL Farewell, Bradshaw. I'll drink no water° for thy sake whilst this lasts. *Exit Bradshaw.* [*I'll drink wine instead*]
Now, gentleman, shall we have your company to London?

GREENE Nay, stay, sirs.
A little more I needs must use your help,
And in a matter of great consequence,
Wherein, if you'll be secret and profound,° [*cunning and secret*]
I'll give you twenty angels° for your pains. [*gold coins*]

BLACK WILL How? Twenty angels? Give my fellow George Shakebag and me twenty angels, and, if thou'lt have thy own father slain that thou mayst inherit his land, we'll kill him.

SHAKEBAG Ay, thy mother, thy sister, thy brother, or all thy kin.

GREENE Well, this it is: Arden of Faversham
Hath highly wronged me about the abbey land,
That° no revenge but death will serve the turn. [*So that*]
Will you two kill him? Here's the angels down,
And I will lay the platform° of his death. [*He offers money.*] [*scheme*]

BLACK WILL Plat me no platform![2] Give me the money, and I'll stab him as he stands pissing against a wall, but I'll kill him.

SHAKEBAG Where is he?

GREENE He is now at London, in Aldersgate Street.

SHAKEBAG He's dead as if he had been condemned by an act of Parliament, if once Black Will and I swear his death.

GREENE [*giving money*] Here is ten pound, and when he is dead
Ye shall have twenty more.

BLACK WILL My fingers itches to be at the peasant.° Ah, that I might be set a-work thus through the year, and that murder would grow to an occupation, that a man might° without danger of law! Zounds,° I warrant I should be warden of the company. Come, let us be going, and we'll bait° at Rochester, where I'll give thee a gallon of sack° to hansel° the match withal. *Exeunt.* [*i.e., wretch, rogue* / *might murder* / *By God's wounds* / *stop for food and rest* / *a white wine / confirm*]

[Scene 3]

Here enters Michael.

MICHAEL I have gotten such a letter as will touch° the painter, and thus it is: [*injure, lay a finger on*]

Here enters Arden and Franklin, and hears Michael read this letter.

2. Sarcastic wordplay: "Don't talk to me about 'platform'!"

Scene 3. London.

"My duty remembered, Mistress Susan, hoping in God you be in good health as I, Michael, was at the making hereof. This is to certify° you that, as the turtle° true, when she hath lost her mate, sitteth alone, so I, mourning for your absence, do walk up and down Paul's,[1] till one day I fell asleep and lost my master's pantofles.° Ah, Mistress Susan, abolish that paltry painter! Cut him off by the shins with a frowning look of your crabbed countenance, and think upon Michael, who, drunk with the dregs of your favor, will cleave as fast to your love as a plaster of pitch to a galled° horseback. Thus hoping you will let my passions penetrate, or rather impetrate° mercy of your meek hands, I end.

inform / turtledove — *slippers or galoshes* — *chafed* — *implore*

Yours,
Michael, or else not Michael."

ARDEN [*coming forward*] Why, you paltry knave,
Stand you here loitering, knowing my affairs,
What haste my business craves to send to Kent?

FRANKLIN Faith, friend Michael, this is very ill,
Knowing your master hath no more° but you; *no other servant*
And do ye slack his business for your own?

ARDEN Where is the letter, sirrah? Let me see it.
Then he [*Michael*] *gives him the letter.*
See, Master Franklin, here's proper stuff:
Susan my maid, the painter, and my man,
A crew of harlots° all in love, forsooth!— *whores and rascals*
Sirrah, let me hear no more of this.
Now, for thy life, once write to her a word.[2]

Here enters Greene, Will, and Shakebag [*unseen by Arden, Michael, and Franklin*].

Wilt thou be married to so base a trull?
'Tis Mosby's sister. Come I once at home,
I'll rouse her from remaining in my house.—
Now Master Franklin, let us go walk in Paul's.
Come, but a turn or two and then away.
Exeunt [*Arden, Franklin, and Michael*].

GREENE The first is Arden, and that's his man;
The other is Franklin, Arden's dearest friend.

BLACK WILL Zounds, I'll kill them all three.

GREENE Nay, sirs, touch not his man in any case;
But stand close, and take you fittest standing,° *best hiding place*
And, at his coming forth, speed him.° *do him in*
To the Nag's Head!° There's this coward's haunt. *a London tavern*
But now I'll leave you till the deed be done. *Exit Greene.*

SHAKEBAG If he be not paid his own,° ne'er trust Shakebag. *what's coming to him*

BLACK WILL Sirrah Shakebag, at his coming forth
I'll run him through, and then to the Blackfriars,° *area on the Thames*
And there take water° and away. *go by boat*

SHAKEBAG Why, that's the best, but see thou miss him not.

BLACK WILL How can I miss him, when I think on the forty angels I must have° more? *am to have*

1. The center aisle of St. Paul's Cathedral was a favorite meeting place.

2. Don't let me catch you writing again; your life depends on it.

Here enters a Prentice.

PRENTICE 'Tis very late; I were best shut up my stall,° for here will be old° filching when the press° comes forth of Paul's. — *bookstall, bookshop*; *plenty of / crowd*

Then lets he down his window, and it breaks° Black Will's head. — *wounds*

BLACK WILL Zounds! Draw,° Shakebag, draw! I am almost killed. — *Draw your sword*

PRENTICE We'll tame you, I warrant.

BLACK WILL Zounds, I am tame enough already,

Here enters Arden, Franklin, and Michael.

ARDEN What troublesome fray or mutiny is this?
FRANKLIN 'Tis nothing but some brabbling,° paltry fray, — *noisy, wrangling*
Devised to pick men's pockets in the throng.
ARDEN Is't nothing else? Come, Franklin, let us away.

Exeunt [Arden, Franklin, and Michael].

BLACK WILL What mends shall I have for my broken head?

PRENTICE Marry, this mends, that if you get you not away all the sooner, you shall be well beaten and sent to the Counter.° — *London prison*

BLACK WILL Well, I'll be gone, but look to your signs,° for I'll pull them down all. — *shop signs*

Exit Prentice.

Shakebag, my broken head grieves me not so much as by this means Arden hath escaped.

Here enters Greene.

I had a glimpse of him and his companion.

GREENE Why, sirs, Arden's as well as I. I met him and Franklin going merrily to the ordinary.° What, dare you not do it? — *tavern dining room*

BLACK WILL Yes, sir, we dare do it; but, were my consent to give again, we would not do it under ten pound more. I value every drop of my blood at a French crown.[3] I have had ten pound to steal a dog, and we have no more here to kill a man. But that° a bargain is a bargain, and so forth, you should do it yourself. — *Were it not that*

GREENE I pray thee, how came thy head broke?° — *wounded*

BLACK WILL Why, thou see'st it is broke, dost thou not?

SHAKEBAG Standing against a stall, watching Arden's coming, a boy let down his shop window and broke his head, whereupon arose a brawl, and in the tumult Arden escaped us and passed by unthought on. But forbearance is no acquittance;[4] another time we'll do it, I warrant thee.

GREENE I pray thee, Will, make clean thy bloody brow,
And let us bethink us on some other place
Where Arden may be met with handsomely.° — *handily, conveniently*
Remember how devoutly thou hast sworn
To kill the villain. Think upon thine oath.
BLACK WILL Tush, I have broken five hundred oaths.
But wouldst thou charm° me to effect this deed, — *bewitch*
Tell me of gold, my resolution's fee;[5]
Say thou see'st Mosby kneeling at my knees,

3. A French crown is both a gold coin and a reference to syphilis (the "French disease"), an effect of which was loss of hair from the "crown," or head.

4. Being spared for the time being is not the same as being allowed to go scot free.

5. The fee that steels my resolve.

Off'ring me service° for my high° attempt; — *homage / daring, lofty*
And sweet Alice Arden, with a lap° of crowns, — *lapful*
Comes with a lowly curtsy to the earth,
Saying, "Take this but for thy quarterage;° — *quarterly payment*
Such yearly tribute will I answer° thee"— — *recompense*
Why, this would steel soft-mettled cowardice,
The which Black Will was never tainted with.
I tell thee, Greene, the forlorn° traveler, — *lost*
Whose lips are glued with summer's parching heat,
Ne'er longed so much to see a running brook
As I to finish Arden's tragedy.
See'st thou this gore that cleaveth to my face?
From hence ne'er will I wash this bloody stain
Till Arden's heart be panting in my hand.

GREENE Why, that's well said. But what saith Shakebag?

SHAKEBAG I cannot paint my valor out with words;
But give me place and opportunity:
Such mercy as the starven lioness,
When she is dry-sucked of her eager young,
Shows to the prey that next encounters her,
On Arden so much pity would I take.

GREENE So should it fare with men of firm resolve.
And now, sirs, seeing this accident° — *happening*
Of meeting him in Paul's hath no success,
Let us bethink us on some other place
Whose earth may swallow up this Arden's blood.

Here enters Michael.

See, yonder comes his man; and wot° you what? — *know*
The foolish knave is in love with Mosby's sister,
And for her sake, whose love he cannot get
Unless Mosby solicit° his suit, — *plead*
The villain hath sworn the slaughter of his master.
We'll question him, for he may stead° us much.— — *profit*
How now, Michael, whither are you going?

MICHAEL My master hath new supped,
And I am going to prepare his chamber.

GREENE Where supped Master Arden?

MICHAEL At the Nag's Head, at the eighteenpence ordinary.[6]—How now, Master Shakebag?—What, Black Will! God's dear lady, how chance your face is so bloody?

BLACK WILL Go to, sirrah, there is a chance in it.° This sauciness in you will make you be knocked. — *i.e., it just happened*

MICHAEL Nay, an° you be offended, I'll be gone. — *if*
[*He starts to leave.*]

GREENE Stay, Michael! You may not scape us so.
Michael, I know you love your master well.

MICHAEL Why, so I do, but wherefore urge you that?

GREENE Because I think you love your mistress better.

MICHAEL So think not I. But say, i'faith, what if I should?

SHAKEBAG [*to Greene*] Come to the purpose.—Michael, we hear
You have a pretty love in Faversham.

6. A dining room charging a relatively high price.

MICHAEL Why, have I° two or three, what's that to thee? *suppose I have*
BLACK WILL [*to Shakebag*] You deal too mildly with the peasant.—Thus it is:
'Tis known to us you love Mosby's sister.
We know besides that you have ta'en your oath
To further Mosby to your mistress' bed
And kill your master for his sister's sake.° *so you can have Susan*
Now, sir, a poorer coward than yourself
Was never fostered in the coast° of Kent. *district, county*
How comes it, then, that such a knave as you
Dare swear a matter of such consequence?
GREENE Ah, Will—
BLACK WILL [*to Greene*] Tush, give me leave.—There's no more but this:
Sith° thou hast sworn, we dare discover° all; *Since / reveal (to you)*
And, hadst thou or shouldst thou utter it,
We have devised a complot° underhand, *conspiracy*
Whatever shall betide to any of us,
To send thee roundly° to the devil of hell. *with no further ado*
And therefore thus: I am the very man,
Marked in my birth hour by the Destinies,° *the Fates*
To give an end to Arden's life on earth;
Thou but a member,° but to whet the knife *assistant*
Whose edge must search° the closet of his breast. *probe, enter*
Thy office is but to appoint the place
And train° thy master to his tragedy; *lure*
Mine to perform it, when occasion serves.
Then be not nice,° but here devise with us *fastidious*
How and what way we may conclude his death.
SHAKEBAG So shalt thou purchase Mosby for thy friend
And by his friendship gain his sister's love.
GREENE So shall thy mistress be thy favorer,
And thou disburdened of the oath° thou made. *(of duty to Arden)*
MICHAEL Well, gentlemen, I cannot but confess,
Sith you have urged me so apparently,° *openly*
That I have vowed my master Arden's death;
And he whose kindly love and liberal hand
Doth challenge° naught but good deserts of me *ask, deserve*
I will deliver over to your hands.
This night, come to his house at Aldersgate;
The doors I'll leave unlocked against° you come. *anticipating when*
No sooner shall ye enter through the latch,
Over the threshold to the inner court,
But on your left hand shall you see the stairs
That leads directly to my master's chamber.
There take him and dispose him as ye please.
Now it were good we parted company.
What I have promisèd I will perform.
BLACK WILL Should you deceive us, 'twould go wrong with you.
MICHAEL I will accomplish all I have revealed.° *declared*
BLACK WILL Come, let's go drink. Choler makes me as dry as a dog. *Exeunt Will, Greene, and Shakebag.*
Manet Michael.° *Michael remains*
MICHAEL Thus feeds the lamb securely on the down,° *hillside*

Whilst through the thicket of an arbor brake° *clump of brushwood*
The hunger-bitten wolf o'erpries° his haunt *surveys, looks over*
And takes advantage to eat him up.
Ah, harmless Arden, how, how hast thou misdone,
That thus thy gentle life is leveled° at? *aimed*
The many good turns that thou hast done to me
Now must I quittance° with betraying thee. *repay*
I, that should take the weapon in my hand
And buckler° thee from ill-intending foes, *shield*
Do lead thee with a wicked fraudful smile,
As unsuspected, to the slaughterhouse.
So have I sworn to Mosby and my mistress;
So have I promised to the slaughtermen;
And, should I not deal currently° with them, *faithfully, as agreed*
Their lawless rage would take revenge on me.
Tush, I will spurn at° mercy for this once. *kick away, reject*
Let pity lodge where feeble women lie;
I am resolved, and Arden needs must die. *Exit Michael.*

[Scene 4]

Here enters Arden and Franklin.

ARDEN No, Franklin, no. If fear or stormy threats,
If love of me or care of womanhood,
If fear of God or common speech of men,
Who mangle credit° with their wounding words *good names, reputations*
And couch dishonor as dishonor buds,[1]
Might 'join° repentance in her wanton thoughts, *enjoin*
No question, then, but she would turn the leaf
And sorrow for her dissolution.° *dissolute ways*
But she is rooted in her wickedness,
Perverse and stubborn, not to be reclaimed;
Good counsel is to her as rain to weeds,
And reprehension° makes her vice to grow *censure*
As Hydra's head that plenished by decay.[2]
Her faults, methink, are painted in my face
For every searching eye to overread;° *plainly see*
And Mosby's name, a scandal unto mine,
Is deeply trenchèd° in my blushing brow. *entrenched, gashed*
Ah, Franklin, Franklin, when I think on this,
My heart's grief rends° my other powers *tears apart*
Worse than the conflict° at the hour of death. *soul's agony*
FRANKLIN Gentle Arden, leave this sad lament.
She will amend, and so your griefs will cease,
Or else she'll die, and so your sorrows end.
If neither of these two do haply fall,° *befall*
Yet let your comfort be that others° bear *other husbands*
Your woes twice doubled all with patience.
ARDEN My house is irksome; there I cannot rest.
FRANKLIN Then stay with me in London; go not home.

Scene 4. London. Franklin's house.
1. Who are quick to discredit wanton behavior with sharp reproof and denounce dishonorable conduct as soon as it appears.
2. The many-headed monster Hydra grew ("plenished") two new heads to replace any one that was cut off. (It was ultimately slain by Hercules.)

ARDEN Then that base Mosby doth usurp my room
And makes his triumph of my being thence.
At home, or not at home, where'er I be,
[*Pointing to his heart*] Here, here it lies, ah, Franklin here it lies,
That will not out till wretched Arden dies.

Here enters Michael.

FRANKLIN Forget your griefs awhile. Here comes your man.
ARDEN [*to Michael*] What o'clock is't, sirrah?
MICHAEL Almost ten.
ARDEN See, see how runs away the weary time!
Come, Master Franklin, shall we go to bed?
FRANKLIN I pray you, go before. I'll follow you.

Exeunt Arden and Michael. Manet Franklin.

Ah, what a hell is fretful jealousy!
What pity-moving words, what deep-fetched sighs,
What grievous groans and overlading° woes — *overloading*
Accompanies this gentle gentleman!
Now will he shake his care-oppressèd head,
Then fix his sad eyes on the sullen earth,
Ashamed to gaze upon the open world.
Now will he cast his eyes up towards the heavens,
Looking that ways for redress of wrong.
Sometimes he seeketh to beguile his grief
And tells a story with his careful° tongue; — *burdened-with-cares*
Then comes his wife's dishonor in his thoughts
And in the middle cutteth off his tale,
Pouring fresh sorrow on his weary limbs.
So woebegone, so inly° charged with woe, — *utterly*
Was never any lived and bare° it so. — *bore*

Here enters Michael.

MICHAEL My master would desire you come to bed.
FRANKLIN Is he himself already in his bed?
MICHAEL He is, and fain° would have the light away.° — *gladly / extinguished*

Exit Franklin. Manet Michael.

Conflicting thoughts encampèd in my breast
Awake me with the echo of their strokes,
And I, a judge to censure° either side, — *pass judgment on*
Can give to neither wishèd victory.
My master's kindness pleads to me for life,
With just demand, and I must grant it him.
My mistress, she hath forced me with an oath
For Susan's sake, the which I may not break,
For that is nearer than a master's love.
That grim-faced fellow, pitiless Black Will,
And Shakebag, stern in bloody stratagem—
Two rougher ruffians never lived in Kent—
Have sworn my death if I infringe my vow,
A dreadful thing to be considered of.
Methinks I see them with their boltered° hair, — *matted*
Staring and grinning in thy° gentle face, — *i.e., Arden's*
And in their ruthless hands their daggers drawn,

Insulting° o'er thee with a peck of oaths, — *Exulting*
Whilst thou, submissive, pleading for relief,
Art mangled by their ireful° instruments. — *angry*
Methinks I hear them ask where Michael is,
And pitiless Black Will cries, "Stab the slave!
The peasant will detect° the tragedy." — *disclose*
The wrinkles in his foul death-threat'ning face
Gapes open wide, like graves, to swallow men.
My death to him is but a merriment,
And he will murder me to make him sport.
He comes, he comes! Ah, Master Franklin, help!
Call up the neighbors, or we are but dead!

Here enters Franklin and Arden.

FRANKLIN What dismal outcry calls me from my rest?
ARDEN What hath occasioned such a fearful cry?
Speak, Michael, hath any injured thee?
MICHAEL Nothing, sir, but as I fell asleep
Upon the threshold, leaning to° the stairs, — *leaning against*
I had a fearful dream that troubled me,
And in my slumber thought I was beset
With murderer thieves that came to rifle° me. — *rob*
My trembling joints witness my inward fear.
I crave your pardons for disturbing you.
ARDEN So great a cry for nothing I ne'er heard.
What, are the doors fast locked and all things safe?
MICHAEL I cannot tell; I think I locked the doors.
ARDEN I like not this, but I'll go see myself.
[*He locks the doors.*]
Ne'er trust me° but the doors were all unlocked. — *believe me again*
This negligence not half contenteth me.
Get you to bed, and, if you love my favor,
Let me have no more such pranks as these.—
Come, Master Franklin, let us go to bed.
FRANKLIN Ay, by my faith. The air is very cold.—
Michael, farewell. I pray thee, dream no more. *Exeunt.*

[Scene 5]

Here enters Will, Greene, and Shakebag.

SHAKEBAG Black night hath hid the pleasures of the day,
And sheeting° darkness overhangs the earth — *covering like a sheet*
And with the black fold of her cloudy robe
Obscures us from the eyesight of the world,
In which sweet silence such as we° triumph. — *thieves like us*
The lazy minutes linger on their time,
Loath to give due audit to the hour,[1]
Till in the watch° our purpose be complete — *in our act of watching*
And Arden sent to everlasting night.
Greene, get you gone and linger hereabout,

Scene 5. London, Franklin's house.
1. Reluctant to let their numbers add up and make the total of the hour.

And at some hour hence come to us again,
Where we will give you instance° of his death. *proof*
GREENE Speed to my wish, whose will soe'er says no![2]
And so I'll leave you for an hour or two. *Exit Greene.*
BLACK WILL I tell thee, Shakebag, would this thing were done!
I am so heavy that I can scarce go.° *move, walk*
This drowsiness in me bodes little good.
SHAKEBAG How now, Will, become a precisian?° *Puritan*
Nay, then, let's go sleep, when bugs° and fears *bugbears, terrors*
Shall kill our courages with their fancy's work.° *work on the imagination*
BLACK WILL Why, Shakebag, thou mistakes me much
And wrongs me too in telling me of fear.
Were't not a serious thing we go about,
It should be slipped° till I had fought with thee, *postponed*
To let thee know I am no coward, I.
I tell thee, Shakebag, thou abusest me.
SHAKEBAG Why, thy speech bewrayed° an inly° kind of fear *betrayed / inward*
And savored° of a weak, relenting spirit. *showed traces of*
Go forward now in that we have begun,
And afterwards attempt me° when thou darest. *take me on*
BLACK WILL And if I do not, heaven cut me off!
But let that pass, and show me to this house,
Where thou shalt see I'll do as much as Shakebag.
SHAKEBAG This is the door. [*He tries the door.*] But soft!° *wait a minute* Methinks 'tis shut.
The villain Michael hath deceivèd us.
BLACK WILL Soft, let me see. [*He tries the door.*] Shakebag, 'tis shut indeed.
Knock with thy sword. Perhaps the slave will hear.
[*Shakebag knocks.*]
SHAKEBAG It will not be. The white-livered° peasant *cowardly*
Is gone to bed and laughs us both to scorn.
BLACK WILL And he shall buy his merriment as dear
As ever coistrel° bought so little sport. *horse groom, menial*
Ne'er let this sword assist me when I need,
But rust and canker° after I have sworn, *be ulcerated with rust*
If I, the next time that I meet the hind,° *i.e., peasant*
Lop not away his leg, his arm, or both.
SHAKEBAG And let me never draw a sword again,
Nor prosper in the twilight, cockshut light,° *twilight*
When I would fleece the wealthy passenger,° *traveler*
But lie and languish in a loathsome den,
Hated and spit at by the goers-by,
And in that death may die unpitièd,
If I, the next time that I meet the slave,
Cut not the nose from off the coward's face
And trample on it for this villainy.
BLACK WILL Come, let's go seek out Greene. I know he'll swear.
SHAKEBAG He were a villain an° he would not swear. *if*
'Twould make a peasant swear amongst his boys,

2. Success to my desires, whoever may wish to the contrary!

That ne'er durst say before but "yea" and "no,"
To be thus flouted of a coisterel.[3]
BLACK WILL Shakebag, let's seek out Greene, and in the morning,
At the alehouse 'butting° Arden's house, — *abutting*
Watch the out-coming of that prick-eared° cur; — *pointed-eared*
And then let me alone° to handle him. *Exeunt.* — *leave it to me*

[Scene 6]

Here enters Arden, Franklin, and Michael.

ARDEN [*to Michael*] Sirrah, get you back to Billingsgate° — *(on the Thames)*
And learn what time the tide will serve our turn.° — *suit us*
Come to us in Paul's.° First go make the bed, — *St. Paul's Cathedral*
And afterwards go hearken for the flood.° *Exit Michael.* — *flood tide*
Come, Master Franklin, you shall go with me.
This night I dreamed that, being in a park,
A toil was pitched° to overthrow the deer, — *A trap was set*
And I, upon a little rising hill,
Stood whistly° watching for the herd's approach. — *silently*
Even there, methoughts, a gentle slumber took me
And summoned all my parts to sweet repose.
But in the pleasure of this golden rest,
An ill-thewed foster° had removed the toil — *evil-natured forester*
And rounded° me with that beguiling home° — *surrounded / i.e., net*
Which late,° methought, was pitched to cast° the deer. — *a moment ago / trap*
With that he blew an evil-sounding horn,
And at the noise another herdman came,
With falchion° drawn, and bent° it at my breast, — *a curved sword / aimed*
Crying aloud, "Thou art the game we seek!"
With this I waked and trembled every joint,
Like one obscurèd° in a little bush — *hidden*
That sees a lion foraging about,
And, when the dreadful forest king is gone,
He pries about with timorous suspect° — *fear*
Throughout° the thorny casements° of the brake, — *From out / openings*
And will not think his person dangerless
But quakes and shivers though the cause be gone.
So, trust me, Franklin, when I did awake
I stood in doubt whether I waked or no,
Such great impression took this fond surprise.[1]
God grant this vision bedeem° me any° good! — *betoken / some*
FRANKLIN This fantasy doth rise from Michael's fear,
Who, being awakèd with the noise he made,
His troubled senses yet could take no rest;
And this, I warrant you, procured° your dream. — *prompted*
ARDEN It may be so. God frame° it to the best! — *bring about*
But oftentimes my dreams presage too true.
FRANKLIN To such as note their nightly fantasies,

3. This spelling indicates trisyllabic pronunciation. Cf. line 41 above.
Scene 6. London.

1. So great was the impression made by this foolish terror.

Some one in twenty may incur belief.
But use it not;[2] 'tis but a mockery.
ARDEN Come, Master Franklin, we'll now walk in Paul's,
And dine together at the ordinary,° *eating place*
And by my man's direction draw to° the quay, *head toward*
And with the tide go down to Faversham.
Say, Master Franklin, shall it not be so?
FRANKLIN At your good pleasure, sir; I'll bear you company.
Exeunt.

[Scene 7]

Here enters Michael at one door; here enters Greene, Will, and Shakebag at another door.

BLACK WILL Draw, Shakebag, for here's that villain Michael.
GREENE First, Will, let's hear what he can say.
BLACK WILL Speak, milksop slave, and never after speak.
MICHAEL For God's sake, sirs, let me excuse myself.
For here I swear, by heaven and earth and all,
I did perform the outmost° of my task *utmost*
And left the doors unbolted and unlocked.
But see the chance!° Franklin and my master *mischance*
Were very late conferring in the porch,
And Franklin left his napkin° where he sat, *handkerchief*
With certain gold knit in it, as he said.
Being in bed, he did bethink himself,
And coming down he found the doors unshut.
He locked the gates and brought away the keys,
For which offense my master rated° me. *berated*
But now I am going to see what flood it is;
For with the tide my master will away,
Where you may front° him well on Rainham Down— *confront*
A place well fitting such a stratagem.
BLACK WILL Your excuse hath somewhat mollified my choler.—
Why now, Greene, 'tis better now nor° e'er it was. *than*
GREENE But, Michael, is this true?
MICHAEL As true as I report it to be true.
SHAKEBAG Then, Michael, this shall be your penance:
To feast us all at the Salutation,° *a tavern*
Where we will plot our purpose throughly.° *thoroughly*
GREENE And, Michael, you shall bear no news of this tide,[1]
Because they two° may be in Rainham Down *So that Will and Shakebag*
Before your master.
MICHAEL Why, I'll agree to anything you'll have me,
So you will except of my company.° *Exeunt.* *excuse me from going*

2. But do not continue to attach significance to your dreams.
Scene 7. London.

1. Don't tell Arden about the tide (see line 17 above), so that he won't start so soon (see 6.43–44).

[Scene 8]

Here enters Mosby.

MOSBY Disturbèd thoughts drives me from company
And dries my marrow with their watchfulness.
Continual trouble of my moody brain
Feebles my body by excess of drink
And nips me as the bitter northeast wind
Doth check the tender blossoms in the spring.
Well fares the man, howe'er his cates° do taste, *delicacies*
That tables° not with foul suspicion; *dines*
And he but pines amongst his delicates° *delicacies*
Whose troubled mind is stuffed with discontent.
My golden time was when I had no gold;
Though then I wanted, yet I slept secure;
My daily toil begat me night's repose;
My night's repose made daylight fresh to me.
But since I climbed the top bough of the tree,
And sought to build my nest among the clouds,
Each gentle starry° gale doth shake my bed *celestial*
And makes me dread my downfall to the earth.
But whither doth contemplation carry me?
The way I seek to find where pleasure dwells
Is hedged behind me, that° I cannot back,° *so that / go back*
But needs must on, although to danger's gate.
Then, Arden, perish thou by that decree!
For Greene doth ear° the land and weed thee up, *plow*
To make my harvest nothing but pure corn.
And for his pains I'll heave him up awhile
And, after, smother him to have his wax.[1]
Such bees as Greene must never live to sting.
Then is there Michael and the painter too,
Chief actors to Arden's overthrow,
Who, when they shall see me sit in Arden's seat,
They will insult upon me for my meed
Or fright me by detecting of his end.[2]
I'll none of that, for I can cast a bone
To make these curs pluck out each other's throat,[3]
And then am I sole ruler of mine own.
Yet Mistress Arden lives; but she's myself,
And holy church rites makes us two but one.
But what for that?° I may not trust you, Alice; *of that*
You have supplanted Arden for my sake,
And will extirpen° me to plant another. *root out*
'Tis fearful sleeping in a serpent's bed,
And I will cleanly° rid my hands of her. *completely; deftly*

Here enters Alice [holding a prayer book].

But here she comes, and I must flatter° her.— *sweet-talk; deceive*
How now, Alice? What, sad and passionate?° *sorrowful*

Scene 8. Faversham. Arden's house.
1. I.e., I'll flatter Greene with promises a while, and then get rid of him, to enjoy what he obtained for me.
2. They will menace me if I don't reward them or frighten me by threatening to tell how Arden died.
3. I can use my sister, Susan, to foment a quarrel between the two of them, much as one throws a bone to two dogs.

Make me partaker of thy pensiveness;
Fire divided burns with lesser force.
ALICE But I will dam that fire in my breast
Till by the force thereof my part° consume. — *my heart*
Ah, Mosby!
MOSBY Such deep pathaires,° like to a cannon's burst — *sighs*
Discharged against a ruinated wall,
Breaks my relenting heart in thousand pieces.
Ungentle Alice, thy sorrow is my sore!
Thou know'st it well, and 'tis thy policy° — *stratagem*
To forge distressful looks to wound a breast
Where lies a heart that dies when thou art sad.
It is not love that loves to anger love.
ALICE It is not love that loves to murder love.
MOSBY How mean you that?
ALICE Thou knowest how dearly Arden lovèd me.
MOSBY And then?
ALICE And then—conceal the rest, for 'tis too bad,
Lest that my words be carried with the wind
And published° in the world, to both our shames. — *proclaimed*
I pray thee, Mosby, let our springtime wither!
Our harvest else will yield but loathsome weeds.
Forget, I pray thee, what hath passed betwixt us,
For now I blush and tremble at the thoughts.
MOSBY What, are you changed?
ALICE Ay, to my former happy life again:
From title of an odious strumpet's name
To honest Arden's wife—not Arden's honest wife.
Ha! Mosby, 'tis thou hast rifled me of that
And made me slanderous to all my kin.
Even in my forehead is thy name engraven:
A mean artificer,° that lowborn name. — *lowborn artisan*
I was bewitched. Woe worth° the hapless hour — *A curse upon*
And all the causes that enchanted me!
MOSBY Nay, if thou ban,° let me breathe curses forth! — *curse*
And if you stand so nicely at your fame,° — *on your reputation*
Let me repent the credit° I have lost. — *reputation*
I have neglected matters of import
That would have stated° me above thy state,° — *raised / your social rank*
Forslowed advantages, and spurned at time.[4]
Ay, Fortune's right hand Mosby hath forsook
To take a wanton giglot° by the left. — *whore*
I left the marriage of an honest maid,
Whose dowry would have weighed down° all thy wealth, — *outweighed*
Whose beauty and demeanor far exceeded thee.
This certain good I lost for changing° bad, — *in exchange for*
And wrapped my credit in thy company.
I was bewitched—that is no theme of thine![5]—
And thou, unhallowed,° hast enchanted me. — *accursed (like a witch)*
But I will break thy spells and exorcisms,
And put another sight upon° these eyes — *see more clearly with*
That showed my heart a raven for a dove.

4. I have wasted advantages and kicked away timely opportunities.

5. Don't think for a minute that you alone can claim to have been bewitched! (See line 78.)

Thou art not fair—I viewed thee not till now;
Thou art not kind—till now I knew thee not.
And, now the rain hath beaten off thy gilt,
Thy worthless copper shows thee counterfeit.
It grieves me not to see how foul thou art,
But mads me that ever I thought thee fair.
Go, get thee gone, a copesmate° for thy hinds!° *companion / servants*
I am too good to be thy favorite.

ALICE Ay, now I see, and too soon find it true
Which often hath been told me by my friends,
That Mosby loves me not but for my wealth,
Which, too incredulous, I ne'er believed.
Nay, hear me speak, Mosby, a word or two;
I'll bite my tongue if it speak bitterly.
Look on me, Mosby, or I'll kill myself;
Nothing shall hide me from thy stormy look.
If thou cry war, there is no peace for me;
I will do penance for offending thee
And burn this prayer book where° I here use° *wherein / comply with*
The holy word that had converted me.[6]
See, Mosby, I will tear away the leaves,
And all the leaves, and in this golden cover
Shall thy sweet phrases and thy letters dwell;
And thereon will I chiefly meditate,
And hold° no other sect but such devotion. *hold to, follow*
Wilt thou not look? Is all thy love overwhelmed?
Wilt thou not hear? What malice stops thine ears?
Why speaks thou not? What silence ties thy tongue?
Thou hast been sighted° as the eagle is, *keen-eyed*
And heard as quickly as the fearful hare,
And spoke as smoothly as an orator,
When I have bid thee hear, or see, or speak.
And art thou sensible° in none of these? *capable of sensation*
Weigh all thy good turns° with this little fault, *my favors to you*
And I deserve not Mosby's muddy looks.
A fount° once troubled is not thickened still;° *spring / always*
Be clear again, I'll ne'er more trouble thee.

MOSBY Oh, no, I am a base artificer;
My wings are feathered for a lowly flight.
Mosby? Fie, no, not for a thousand pound!
Make love to you? Why, 'tis unpardonable;
We beggars must not breathe where gentles° are. *gentlefolk*

ALICE Sweet Mosby is as gentle as a king,
And I too blind to judge him otherwise.
Flowers do sometimes spring in fallow lands,
Weeds in gardens, roses grow on thorns;
So, whatsoe'er my Mosby's father was,
Himself is valued gentle by his worth.° *innate worthiness*

MOSBY Ah, how you women can insinuate
And clear a trespass° with your sweet-set tongue! *clear away an offense*
I will forget this quarrel, gentle Alice,
Provided I'll be tempted° so no more. *provoked*

6. I will burn the prayer book for teaching me that to abandon my sinful ways I should leave you.

Here enters Bradshaw.

ALICE [*kissing Mosby*] Then with thy lips seal up this new-made match.
MOSBY Soft, Alice, for here comes somebody.
ALICE How now, Bradshaw, what's the news with you?
BRADSHAW I have little news, but here's a letter
That Master Greene importuned me to give you.
[*He presents a letter.*]
ALICE Go in, Bradshaw; call for a cup of beer.
'Tis almost suppertime; thou shalt stay with us.
Exit [*Bradshaw*].
Then she reads the letter.

"We have missed of our purpose at London, but shall perform it by the way. We thank our neighbor Bradshaw.[7]

Yours,
Richard Greene."

How likes my love the tenor of this letter?
MOSBY Well, were his date complete and expired.[8]
ALICE Ah, would it were! Then comes my happy hour;
Till then my bliss is mixed with bitter gall.
Come, let us in to shun suspicion.
MOSBY Ay, to the gates of death to follow thee. *Exeunt.*

[Scene 9]

Here enters Greene, Will, and Shakebag.

SHAKEBAG Come, Will, see thy tools be in a readiness.
Is not thy powder dank, or will thy flint strike fire?
BLACK WILL Then ask me if my nose be on my face,
Or whether my tongue be frozen in my mouth.
Zounds, here's a coil!° *fuss*
You were best swear me on the inter'gatories[1]
How many pistols I have took in hand,
Or whether I love the smell of gunpowder,
Or dare abide the noise the dag° will make, *pistol*
Or will not wink° at flashing of the fire. *blink*
I pray thee, Shakebag, let this answer thee:
That I have took more purses in this down° *upland expanse*
Than e'er thou handled'st pistols in thy life.
SHAKEBAG Ay, haply thou hast picked° more in a throng; *stolen*
But, should I brag what booties I have took,
I think the overplus that's more than thine[2]
Would mount to a greater sum of money
Than either thou or all thy kin are worth.
Zounds, I hate them as I hate a toad
That carry a muscado° in their tongue *i.e., sting*
And scarce a hurting weapon in their hand.
BLACK WILL [*to Greene*] Oh, Greene, intolerable!

7. Our thanks to our neighbor Bradshaw for delivering this letter.
8. I would like the letter well enough if the task were done and if Arden were in fact dead.
Scene 9. Between Rochester and Faversham, near Rainham Down.
1. Questions to be answered under oath.
2. I think that the amount that exceeds what you have done.

It is not for mine honor to bear this.—
Why, Shakebag, I did serve the King at Boulogne,
And thou canst brag of nothing that thou hast done.
SHAKEBAG Why, so can Jack of Faversham,° (*cf.* 2.69)
That sounded° for a fillip° on the nose, *swooned / punch*
When he that gave it him halloed in his ear,
And he° supposed a cannon bullet hit him. *Then they fight.* (*Jack*)
GREENE [*separating them*] I pray you, sirs, list° to Aesop's talk:° *listen* / *fable*
Whilst two stout° dogs were striving for a bone, *fierce*
There comes a cur and stole it from them both;
So, while you stand striving on these terms of manhood,
Arden escapes us and deceives us all.
SHAKEBAG Why, he begun.
BLACK WILL And thou shalt find I'll end.
I do but slip° it until better time. *postpone*
But, if I do forget— *Then he kneels down and holds up his hands to heaven.*
GREENE Well, take your fittest standings,° and once more *best spot for ambush*
Lime your twigs to catch this wary bird.[3]
I'll leave you, and at your dag's discharge
Make towards,° like the longing water dog *I'll come out of hiding*
That coucheth° till the fowling piece° be off, *lies hid / bird gun*
Then seizeth on the prey with eager mood.
Ah, might I see him stretching forth his limbs
As I have seen them° beat their wings ere now! (*waterfowl*)
SHAKEBAG Why, that thou shalt see if he come this way.
GREENE Yes, that he doth, Shakebag, I warrant thee.
But brawl not when I am gone in any case,
But, sirs, be sure to speed him° when he comes; *do him in*
And in that hope I'll leave you for an hour. *Exit Greene.*
[*Black Will and Shakebag take cover.*]

Here enters Arden, Franklin, and Michael.

MICHAEL 'Twere best that I went back to Rochester.
The horse halts downright;° it were not good *limps badly*
He traveled in such pain to Faversham.
Removing of a shoe may haply help it.
ARDEN Well, get you back to Rochester. But, sirrah,
See ye o'ertake us ere we come to Rainham Down,
For it will be very late ere we get home.
MICHAEL [*aside*] Ay, God he knows, and so doth Will and Shakebag,
That thou shalt never go further than that down,
And therefore have I pricked° the horse on purpose, *stabbed*
Because I would not view the massacre. *Exit Michael.*
ARDEN Come, Master Franklin, onwards with your tale.
FRANKLIN I assure you, sir, you task me much.
A heavy blood is gathered at my heart,
And on the sudden is my wind so short
As hindereth the passage of my speech.

3. Sticky lime was smeared on branches to catch birds.

So fierce a qualm yet ne'er° assailèd me. *never yet*
ARDEN Come, Master Franklin, let us go on softly.
The annoyance of the dust, or else some meat
You ate at dinner, cannot brook with you.° *sit well with you*
I have been often so, and soon amended.
FRANKLIN Do you remember where my tale did leave?° *leave off*
ARDEN Ay, where the gentleman did check° his wife. *correct, reprove*
FRANKLIN She being reprehended for the fact°— *deed*
Witness produced that took her with the deed,° *caught her in the act*
Her glove brought in which there she left behind,
And many other assurèd arguments°— *proofs*
Her husband asked her whether it were not so.
ARDEN Her answer, then? I wonder how she looked,
Having forsworn it with such vehement oaths,
And at the instant so approved upon° her. *proved against*
FRANKLIN First did she cast her eyes down to the earth,
Watching the drops that fell amain° from thence; *in profusion*
Then softly draws she forth her handkercher,
And modestly she wipes her tear-stained face;
Then hemmed she out,° to clear her voice should seem, *she cleared her throat*
And with a majesty addressed herself
To encounter all their accusations.—
Pardon me, Master Arden, I can no more;
This fighting at my heart makes short my wind.
ARDEN Come, we are almost now at Rainham Down.
Your pretty tale beguiles the weary way;
I would you were in state to tell it out.
SHAKEBAG [*aside*] Stand close, Will! I hear them coming.

Here enters Lord Cheyne with his men [*just as Shakebag and Black Will are about to attack*].

BLACK WILL [*aside*] Stand to it, Shakebag, and be resolute!
LORD CHEYNE Is it so near night as it seems,
Or will this black-faced evening have a shower?—
What, Master Arden? You are well met.
I have longed this fortnight's day to speak with you.
You are a stranger,° man, in the Isle of Sheppey. *i.e., I haven't seen you*
ARDEN Your Honor's always, bound to do you service.
LORD CHEYNE Come you from London, and ne'er a man with you?
ARDEN My man's coming after,
But here's my honest friend that came along with me.
LORD CHEYNE [*to Franklin*] My Lord Protector's° man, I take you to be? *(see 1.2 and n)*
FRANKLIN Ay, my good lord, and highly bound to you.
LORD CHEYNE You and your friend come home and sup with me.
ARDEN I beseech Your Honor pardon me.
I have made a promise to a gentleman,
My honest friend, to meet him at my house;
The occasion is great, or else would I wait on you.
LORD CHEYNE Will you come tomorrow and dine with me,
And bring your honest friend° along with you? *i.e., Franklin*
I have divers matters to talk with you about.
ARDEN Tomorrow we'll wait upon Your Honor.

LORD CHEYNE [*to his men*] One of you stay my horse at the top of the hill.
[*Seeing Black Will*] What, Black Will, for whose purse wait you?
Thou wilt be hanged in Kent, when all is done.
BLACK WILL Not hanged, God save Your Honor.
I am your beadsman,° bound to pray for you. *i.e., suppliant*
LORD CHEYNE I think thou ne'er saidest prayer in all thy life.
[*To his men*] One of you give him a crown.
[*Black Will is given a gold coin.*]
And, sirrah, leave this kind of life.
If thou be'st 'tainted° for a penny matter *arraigned, convicted*
And come in question, surely thou wilt truss.°— *hang*
Come, Master Arden, let us be going;
Your way and mine lies four mile together.
Exeunt. Manent Black Will and Shakebag.
BLACK WILL The devil break all your necks at four miles' end!
Zounds, I could kill myself for very anger.
His Lordship chops me in,° even when *interrupts*
My dag was leveled at his° heart. *(Arden's)*
I would his crown were molten down his throat!
SHAKEBAG Arden, thou hast wondrous holy luck.
Did ever man escape as thou hast done?
Well, I'll discharge my pistol at the sky,
For by this bullet Arden might not die.
[*He fires off his gun.*]

Here enters Greene.

GREENE What, is he down? Is he dispatched?° *killed; sent along*
SHAKEBAG Ay, in health towards Faversham, to shame us all.
GREENE The devil he is! Why, sirs, how escaped he?
SHAKEBAG When we were ready to shoot,
Comes my Lord Cheyne to prevent his death.
GREENE The Lord of heaven hath preservèd him.
BLACK WILL Preserved a fig!
The Lord Cheyne hath preservèd him,
And bids him to a feast, to his house at Shorlow.
But by the way once more I'll meet with him,
And if° all the Cheynes in the world say no, *even if*
I'll have a bullet in his breast tomorrow.
Therefore come, Greene, and let us to Faversham.
GREENE Ay, and excuse ourselves to Mistress Arden.
Oh, how she'll chafe when she hears of this!
SHAKEBAG Why, I'll warrant you she'll think we dare not do it.
BLACK WILL Why, then, let us go and tell her all the matter,
And plot the news to cut him off tomorrow. *Exeunt.*

[Scene 10]

Here enters Arden and his wife, Franklin, and Michael.

ARDEN See how the Hours, the guardant of heaven's gate,[1]
Have by their toil removed the darksome clouds,
That Sol° may well discern the trampled pace° *the sun / path*
Wherein he wont° to guide his golden car. *is accustomed*
The season fits.° Come, Franklin, let's away. *The time is suitable*
ALICE I thought you did pretend° some special hunt, *intend*
That made you thus cut short the time of rest.
ARDEN It was no chase that made me rise so early,
But, as I told thee yesternight, to go
To the Isle of Sheppey, there to dine
With my Lord Cheyne;
For so His Honor late° commanded me. *recently*
ALICE Ay, such kind husbands seldom want° excuses; *lack*
Home is a wild cat° to a wand'ring wit. *is ill-tempered, savage*
The time hath been—would God it were not past!—
That honors, title, nor a lord's command
Could once have drawn you from these arms of mine.
But my deserts or your desires decay,
Or both; yet if true love may seem desert,
I merit still to have thy company.
FRANKLIN Why, I pray you, sir, let her go along with us.
I am sure His Honor will welcome her,
And us the more, for bringing her along.
ARDEN Content. [*To Michael*] Sirrah, saddle your mistress' nag.
ALICE No, begged favor merits little thanks.
If I should go, our house would run away,
Or else be stol'n; therefore I'll stay behind.
ARDEN Nay, see how mistaking you are.
I pray thee go.
ALICE No, no, not now.
ARDEN Then let me leave thee satisfied in this:
That time nor place nor persons alter me
But that I hold thee dearer than my life.
ALICE That will be seen by your quick return.
ARDEN And that shall be ere night, an if° I live. *an if = if*
Farewell, sweet Alice. We mind° to sup with thee. *intend*
Exit Alice.
FRANKLIN Come, Michael, are our horses ready?
MICHAEL Ay, your horse° are ready, but I am not ready, for I have lost my purse with six-and-thirty shillings in it, with taking up of° my master's nag. *horses* / *catching (?)*
FRANKLIN [*to Arden*] Why, I pray you, let us go before,
Whilst he stays behind to seek his purse.
ARDEN [*to Michael*] Go to,° sirrah. *(expressing impatience)*
See you follow us to the Isle of Sheppey,
To my Lord Cheyne's, where we mean to dine.

Scene 10. Faversham. Arden's house.
1. The Hours, daughters of Jupiter and Themis, presided over the hours of the day and also the changing of the seasons. ("Guardant" means "guardian.")

MICHAEL So, fair weather after you!

Exeunt Arden and Franklin. Manet Michael.

[*To himself*] For before you lies Black Will and Shakebag, in the broom close,° to close for you. They'll be your ferrymen to long home.° — *enclosed gorse field*; *escort to the next life*

Here enters the painter [*Clarke, with a poisoned crucifix*].

But who is this? The painter, my corrival, that would needs° win Mistress Susan! — *wishes to*

CLARKE How now, Michael? How doth my mistress, and all at home?

MICHAEL Who, Susan Mosby? She is your mistress, too?

CLARKE Ay. How doth she, and all the rest?

MICHAEL All's well but Susan. She is sick.

CLARKE Sick? Of what disease?

MICHAEL Of a great fear.

CLARKE A fear? Of what?

MICHAEL A great fever.

CLARKE A fever? God forbid!

MICHAEL Yes, faith, and of a lurdan° too, as big as yourself. — *good-for-nothing*

CLARKE Oh, Michael, the spleen° prickles you. Go to, you carry an eye over° Mistress Susan. — *peevish temper*; *have an eye on*

MICHAEL Ay, faith, to keep her from the painter.

CLARKE Why more from a painter than from a serving creature like yourself?

MICHAEL Because you painters make but a painting-table° of a pretty wench and spoil her beauty with blotting.° — *painted picture*; *smearing, sullying*

CLARKE What mean you by that?

MICHAEL Why, that you painters paint lambs in the lining of wenches' petticoats, and we servingmen put horns to them to make them become sheep.[2]

CLARKE Such another word will cost you a cuff or a knock.

MICHAEL What, with a dagger made of a pencil?° Faith, 'tis too weak, and therefore thou too weak to win Susan. — *paintbrush*

CLARKE Would Susan's love lay upon this stroke!

Then he breaks Michael's head.° — *i.e., draws blood*

Here enters Mosby, Greene, and Alice.

ALICE I'll lay° my life, this is for Susan's love. — *bet*
[*To Michael*] Stayed you behind your master to this end?
Have you no other time to brabble° in — *brawl*
But now, when serious matters are in hand?—
Say, Clarke, hast thou done the thing thou promised?

CLARKE Ay, here it is—the very touch is death.

[*He shows the poisoned crucifix.*]

ALICE Then this, I hope, if all the rest do fail,
Will catch Master Arden
And make him wise in death, that lived a fool.
Why should he thrust his sickle in our corn?° — *i.e., spoil our harvest*
Or what hath he to do with thee, my love,
Or govern me that am to rule myself?
Forsooth, for credit° sake I must leave thee! — *reputation's*

2. Michael insinuates that servingmen are more virile than artists, whom they cuckold.

Nay, he° must leave to live, that we may love, *(Arden)*
May live, may love; for what is life but love?
And love shall last as long as life remains,
And life shall end before my love depart.

MOSBY Why, what's love without true constancy?
Like to a pillar built of many stones,
Yet neither with good mortar well compact
Nor cement to fasten it in the joints,
But that it shakes with every blast of wind
And, being touched, straight falls unto the earth
And buries all his° haughty pride in dust. *its*
No, let our love be rocks of adamant,° *diamondlike hardness*
Which time nor place nor tempest can asunder.° *put asunder*

GREENE Mosby, leave° protestations now, *leave off*
And let us bethink us what we have to do.
Black Will and Shakebag I have placed
In the broom close, watching Arden's coming.
Let's to them and see what they have done. *Exeunt.*

[Scene 11]

Here enters Arden and Franklin.

ARDEN Oh, ferryman, where art thou?

Here enters the Ferryman.

FERRYMAN Here, here! Go before to the boat, and I will follow you.

ARDEN We have great haste. I pray thee, come away.

FERRYMAN Fie, what a mist is here!

ARDEN This mist, my friend, is mystical,° *of mysterious origin*
Like to a good companion's smoky brain,
That was half-drowned with new ale overnight.

FERRYMAN 'Twere pity but° his skull were opened, to make more chimney room. *unless*

FRANKLIN Friend, what's thy opinion of this mist?

FERRYMAN I think 'tis like to a curst° wife in a little house, that never leaves her husband till she have driven him out at° doors with a wet pair of eyes. Then looks he as if his house were afire or some of his friends dead. *shrewish* / *of*

ARDEN Speaks thou this of thine own experience?

FERRYMAN Perhaps ay, perhaps no; for my wife is as other women are—that is to say, governed by the moon.° *changeable, fickle*

FRANKLIN By the moon? How, I pray thee?

FERRYMAN Nay, thereby lies a bargain, and you shall not have it fresh and fasting.° *i.e., too soon, too cheap*

ARDEN Yes, I pray thee, good ferryman.

FERRYMAN Then for this once let it be midsummer moon, but yet my wife has another moon.° *i.e., menstrual cycles*

FRANKLIN Another moon?

FERRYMAN Ay, and it hath influences and eclipses.

Scene 11. At the ferry crossing from the mainland to the Isle of Sheppey.

ARDEN Why, then, by this reckoning you sometimes play the man in the moon.

FERRYMAN Ay, but you had not best to meddle with that moon, lest I scratch you by the face with my bramble bush.[1]

ARDEN I am almost stifled with this fog. Come, let's away.

FRANKLIN And, sirrah, as we go, let us have some more of your bold yeomanry.° *homely plainspokenness*

FERRYMAN Nay, by my troth sir, but flat° knavery. *Exeunt.* *out and out*

[Scene 12]

Here enters Will at one door and Shakebag at another.

SHAKEBAG Oh, Will, where art thou?

BLACK WILL Here, Shakebag, almost in hell's mouth, where I cannot see my way for smoke.° *fog*

SHAKEBAG I pray thee, speak still,° that we may meet by the sound, for I shall fall into some ditch or other unless my feet see better than my eyes. *keep talking*

BLACK WILL Didst thou ever see better weather to run away with another man's wife, or play with a wench at potfinger?° *sexual foreplay*

SHAKEBAG No. This were a fine world for chandlers,° if this weather would last, for then a man should never dine nor sup without candlelight. But, sirrah Will, what horses are those that passed? *candle-makers*

BLACK WILL Why, didst thou hear any?

SHAKEBAG Ay, that I did.

BLACK WILL My life for thine,° 'twas Arden and his companion, and then all our labor's lost. *My life against yours*

SHAKEBAG Nay, say not so; for if it be they, they may haply lose their way as we have done, and then we may chance meet with them.

BLACK WILL Come, let us go on like a couple of blind pilgrims.

Then Shakebag falls into a ditch.

SHAKEBAG Help, Will, help! I am almost drowned.

Here enters the Ferryman.

FERRYMAN Who's that that calls for help?

BLACK WILL 'Twas none here; 'twas thou thyself.

FERRYMAN I came to help him that called for help. Why, how now? Who is this that's in the ditch? [*He helps Shakebag out.*] You are well enough served, to go° without a guide, such weather as this! *go walking*

BLACK WILL Sirrah, what companies hath passed your ferry this morning?

FERRYMAN None but a couple of gentlemen that went to dine at my Lord Cheyne's.

BLACK WILL Shakebag, did not I tell thee as much?

FERRYMAN Why, sir, will you have any letters carried to them?

BLACK WILL No, sir. Get you gone.

FERRYMAN Did you ever see such a mist as this?

1. A traditional accoutrement of the Man in the Moon, along with his dog and lantern.

Scene 12. The scene continues.

BLACK WILL No, nor such a fool as will rather be houghed° — *hamstrung, disabled*
than get his way.° — *go on his way*
FERRYMAN Why, sir, this is no Hough Monday;[1] you are
deceived. What's his name, I pray you, sir?
SHAKEBAG His name is Black Will.
FERRYMAN I hope to see him one day hanged upon a hill.
Exit Ferryman.
SHAKEBAG See how the sun hath cleared the foggy mist,
Now we have missed the mark of our intent.

Here enters Greene, Mosby, and Alice.

MOSBY Black Will and Shakebag, what make you° here? — *are you doing*
What, is the deed done? Is Arden dead?
BLACK WILL What could a blinded man perform in arms?° — *using weapons*
Saw you not how, till now, the sky was dark,
That neither horse nor man could be discerned?
Yet did we hear their horses as they passed.
GREENE Have they escaped you, then, and passed the ferry?
SHAKEBAG Ay, for awhile, but here we two will stay,
And at their coming back meet with them once more.
Zounds, I was ne'er so toiled° in all my life — *wearied*
In following so slight a task as this!
MOSBY [*to Shakebag*] How cam'st thou so berayed?° — *bespattered*
BLACK WILL With making false footing in the dark.
He needs would follow° them without a guide. — *insisted on following*
ALICE [*giving money*] Here's to pay for a fire and good
cheer.
Get you to Faversham to the Flower-de-Luce,
And rest yourselves until some other time.
GREENE Let me alone;° it most concerns my state. — *Leave this to me*
BLACK WILL Ay, Mistress Arden, this will serve the turn,
In case we fall into a second fog.
Exeunt Greene, Will, and Shakebag.
MOSBY These knaves will never do it. Let us give it over.
ALICE First tell me how you like my new device:
Soon, when my husband is returning back,
You and I both marching arm in arm,
Like loving friends, we'll meet him on the way
And boldly beard and brave° him to his teeth. — *defy and challenge*
When words grow hot and blows begin to rise,
I'll call those cutters forth° your tenement, — *cutthroats forth from*
Who, in a manner to take up the fray,
Shall wound my husband Hornsby° to the death. — *i.e., Mr. Cuckold*
MOSBY Ah, fine device! Why, this deserves a kiss.
[*He kisses her.*] *Exeunt.*

[Scene 13]

Here enters Dick Reede and a Sailor.

SAILOR Faith, Dick Reede, it is to little end.
His conscience is too liberal° and he too niggardly — *easy, slack*

1. The second Monday after Easter. The Ferryman is making a feeble pun on "Hough" and "houghed," in line 36.

Scene 13. Kent, near Arden's house in Faversham.

To part from anything may do thee good.
REEDE He is coming from Shorlow, as I understand;
Here I'll intercept him, for at his house
He never will vouchsafe to speak with me.
If prayers and fair entreaties will not serve,
Or make no batt'ry in his flinty breast,

Here enters Franklin, Arden, and Michael.

I'll curse the carl° and see what that will do. *churl, villain*
See where he comes, to further my intent.—
Master Arden, I am now bound to the sea.
My coming to you was about the plot of ground
Which wrongfully you detain from me.
Although the rent of it be very small,
Yet will it help my wife and children,
Which here I leave in Faversham, God knows,
Needy and bare. For Christ's sake, let them have it!
ARDEN Franklin, hearest thou this fellow speak?
That which he craves I dearly° bought of him, *expensively*
Although the rent of it was ever mine.[1]—
Sirrah, you, that ask these questions,
If with thy clamorous impeaching° tongue *accusing*
Thou rail on me, as I have heard thou dost,
I'll lay thee up so close a twelvemonth's day[2]
As° thou shalt neither see the sun nor moon. *That*
Look to it, for, as surely as I live,
I'll banish pity if thou use me thus.
REEDE What, wilt thou do me wrong and threat me too?
Nay, then, I'll tempt° thee, Arden; do thy worst. *provoke*
God, I beseech thee, show some miracle
On thee or thine in plaguing thee for this!
That plot of ground which thou detains from me—
I speak it in an agony of spirit—
Be ruinous and fatal unto thee!
Either there be butchered by thy dearest friends,
Or else be brought for men to wonder at;[3]
Or° thou or thine miscarry° in that place, *Either / come to harm*
Or there run mad and end thy cursèd days!
FRANKLIN Fie, bitter knave! Bridle thine envious tongue,
For curses are like arrows shot upright,
Which, falling down, light on the shooter's head.
REEDE Light where they will! Were I upon the sea,
As oft I have in many a bitter storm,
And saw a dreadful southern flaw° at hand, *squall*
The pilot quaking at the doubtful° storm *frightening*
And all the sailors praying on their knees,
Even in that fearful time would I fall down
And ask of God, whate'er betide of me,
Vengeance on Arden, or some mis-event,° *mischance*
To show the world what wrong the carl hath done.
This charge I'll leave with my distressful wife;

1. I.e., Although it was my property to rent as I pleased.
2. I'll lock you up so tight for a year.
3. Or else be made a public spectacle.

My children shall be taught such prayers as these.
And thus I go, but leave my curse with thee.
Exeunt Reede and Sailor.

ARDEN It is the railingest knave in Christendom,
And oftentimes the villain will be mad.
It greatly matters not what he says,
But I assure you I ne'er did him wrong.

FRANKLIN I think so, Master Arden.

ARDEN Now that our horses are gone home before,
My wife may haply meet me on the way,
For, God knows, she is grown passing° kind of late — *very*
And greatly changèd from the old humor° — *disposition*
Of her wonted frowardness,° — *usual shrewishness*
And seeks by fair means to redeem old faults.

FRANKLIN Happy the change that alters for the best!
But see in any case you make no speech
Of the cheer° we had at my Lord Cheyne's, — *hospitality*
Although most bounteous and liberal,
For that will make her think herself more wronged
In that we did not carry her along;
For sure she grieved that she was left behind.

ARDEN Come, Franklin, let us strain to mend° our pace, — *speed, improve*
And take her unawares playing the cook;

Here enters Alice and Mosby [arm in arm, unobserved by Arden and Franklin at first].

For I believe she'll strive to mend our cheer.° — *make us welcome*

FRANKLIN Why, there's no better creatures in the world
Than women are, when they are in good humors.

ARDEN Who is that? Mosby? What, so familiar?
Injurious strumpet, and thou ribald° knave, — *scurrilous*
Untwine those arms!

ALICE Ay, with a sugared kiss let them untwine.
[*She kisses Mosby.*]

ARDEN Ah, Mosby! Perjured beast! Bear this and all![4]

MOSBY And yet no hornèd beast. The horns are thine.

FRANKLIN Oh, monstrous! Nay, then, 'tis time to draw.
[*Arden, Franklin, and Mosby draw their swords.*]

ALICE Help, help! They murder my husband.

Here enters Will and Shakebag.

SHAKEBAG Zounds, who injures Master Mosby?
[*In the ensuing scuffle, Franklin wounds Shakebag and Arden wounds Mosby.*]
Help, Will! I am hurt.

MOSBY I may thank you, Mistress Arden, for this wound.
Exeunt Mosby, Will, and Shakebag.

ALICE Ah, Arden, what folly blinded thee?
Ah, jealous harebrain man, what hast thou done?
When we, to welcome thy intended sport,[5]
Came lovingly to meet thee on thy way,
Thou drew'st thy sword, enraged with jealousy,

4. Take that from me and still more!
5. When we, to welcome you home to the pleasures you intended. (Sometimes emended to "thee, intended sport.")

And hurt thy friend, whose thoughts were free from
  harm—
All for a worthless kiss and joining arms,
Both done but merrily° to try thy patience; *in jest*
And me unhappy that devised the jest,
Which, though begun in sport, yet ends in blood!

FRANKLIN Marry, God defend me from such a jest!

ALICE Couldst thou not see us friendly smile on thee
When we joined arms and when I kissed his cheek?
Hast thou not lately found me overkind?° *exceedingly kind*
Didst thou not hear me cry they murder thee?
Called I not help to set my husband free?
No, ears and all were witched.° Ah, me accurst, *bewitched*
To link in liking° with a frantic° man! *love / mad*
Henceforth I'll be thy slave, no more thy wife,
For with that name° I never shall content thee. *(the name of wife)*
If I be merry, thou straightways thinks me light;
If sad, thou sayest the sullens° trouble me; *sulks*
If well attired, thou thinks I will be gadding;
If homely,° I seem sluttish in thine eye. *plainly attired*
Thus am I still, and shall be while° I die, *until*
Poor wench, abused by thy misgovernment.

ARDEN But is it for truth that neither thou nor he
Intended'st malice in your misdemeanor?

ALICE The heavens can witness of our harmless thoughts!

ARDEN Then pardon me, sweet Alice, and forgive this fault;
Forget but this, and never see the like.
Impose me penance and I will perform it,
For in thy discontent I find a death—
A death tormenting more than death itself.

ALICE Nay, hadst thou loved me as thou dost pretend,
Thou wouldst have marked the speeches of thy friend,° *(Mosby)*
Who, going wounded from the place, he said
His skin was pierced only through my device;
And if sad sorrow taint° thee for this fault, *accuse*
Thou wouldst have followed him and seen him dressed,° *his wounds dressed*
And cried him mercy° whom thou hast misdone. *begged pardon of him*
Ne'er shall my heart be eased till this be done.

ARDEN Content thee, sweet Alice. Thou shalt have thy will,
Whate'er it be. For that° I injured thee *Because*
And wronged my friend, shame scourgeth my offense.
Come thou thyself and go along with me,
And be a mediator 'twixt us two.

FRANKLIN Why, Master Arden, know you what you do?
Will you follow him that hath dishonored you?

ALICE Why, canst thou prove I have been disloyal?

FRANKLIN Why, Mosby taunts your husband with the horn.° *cuckold's horn*

ALICE Ay, after he° had revilèd him° *(Arden) / (Mosby)*
By the injurious name of "perjured beast."
He knew no wrong could spite a jealous man
More than the hateful naming of the horn.

FRANKLIN Suppose 'tis true, yet is it dangerous
To follow him whom he hath lately hurt.

ALICE A fault confessed is more than half amends,
But men of such ill spirit as yourself

Work crosses° and debates 'twixt man and wife. *quarrels*
ARDEN I pray thee, gentle Franklin, hold thy peace.
I know my wife counsels me for the best.
I'll seek out Mosby where his wound is dressed
And salve this hapless quarrel if I may.
Exeunt Arden and Alice.
FRANKLIN He whom the devil drives must go perforce.
Poor gentleman, how soon he is bewitched!
And yet because his wife is the instrument,
His friends must not be lavish in their speech.
Exit Franklin.

[Scene 14]

Here enters Will, Shakebag, and Greene.

BLACK WILL Sirrah Greene, when was I so long in killing a man?
GREENE I think we shall never do it. Let us give it over.
SHAKEBAG Nay, zounds, we'll kill him, though we be hanged at his door for our labor.
BLACK WILL Thou knowest, Greene, that I have lived in London this twelve years, where I have made some go upon wooden legs for taking the wall on me,[1] divers with silver noses° for saying, "There goes Black Will." I have cracked as many blades as thou hast done nuts. *false noses of silver*
GREENE Oh, monstrous lie!
BLACK WILL Faith, in a manner I have. The bawdy houses have paid me tribute; there durst not a whore set up[2] unless she have agreed with me first for op'ning her shop windows. For a cross word of a tapster, I have pierced one barrel after another with my dagger and held him by the ears till all his beer hath run out. In Thames Street a brewer's cart was like to° have run over me; I made no more ado but went to the clerk and cut all the notches of his tallies[3] and beat them about his head. I and my company have taken the constable from his watch and carried him about the fields on a coltstaff.[4] I have broken a sergeant's head with his own mace,[5] and bailed° whom I list° with my sword and buckler. All the tenpenny alehouses° would stand every morning, with a quart pot in his hand, saying, "Will it please Your Worship drink?" He that had not done so had been sure to have had his sign° pulled down and his lattice[6] borne away the next night. To conclude, what have I not done? Yet cannot do this. Doubtless he is preserved by miracle. *was about to* / *freed from jail / wished* / *alehouse-keepers* / *tavern sign*

Here enters Alice and Michael [not seeing Black Will, Shakebag, and Greene at first].

GREENE Hence, Will! Here comes Mistress Arden.
ALICE Ah, gentle Michael, art thou sure they're friends?

Scene 14. Faversham. Arden's house.
1. Taking the side next to the wall and thus forcing me into the dirtier part of the street.
2. A whore wouldn't dare set up for business.
3. Notched sticks used to keep records of customers' accounts.
4. Cowlstaff, pole used to carry heavy burdens, borne on two persons' shoulders.
5. I have drawn blood from the head of an arresting officer with his own club.
6. Red lattices were a familiar sight on alehouse windows.

MICHAEL Why, I saw them when they both shook hands.
When Mosby bled, he° even wept for sorrow, *(Arden)*
And railed on Franklin, that was cause of all.
No sooner came the surgeon in at doors
But my master took to his purse and gave him money,
And, to conclude, sent me to bring you word
That Mosby, Franklin, Bradshaw, Adam Fowle,[7]
With divers of his neighbors and his friends,
Will come and sup with you at our house this night.

ALICE Ah, gentle Michael, run thou back again,
And, when my husband walks into the fair,° *fair of St. Valentine*
Bid Mosby steal from him and come to me;
And this night shall thou and Susan be made sure.° *be engaged*

MICHAEL I'll go tell him.

ALICE And as thou goest, tell John cook° of our guests, *John the cook*
And bid him lay it on; spare for no cost. *Exit Michael.*

BLACK WILL Nay, an° there be such cheer, we will bid ourselves.— *if*
Mistress Arden,
Dick Greene and I do mean to sup with you.

ALICE And welcome shall you be.—Ah, gentlemen,
How missed you of your purpose yesternight?

GREENE 'Twas long of° Shakebag, that unlucky villain. *because of*

SHAKEBAG Thou dost me wrong; I did as much as any.

BLACK WILL Nay, then, Mistress Alice, I'll tell you how it was. When he should have locked with both his hilts,[8] he° *(Arden)* in a bravery° *show of bravado* flourished[9] over his head. With that comes Franklin at him lustily° *vehemently* and hurts the slave;° *(Shakebag)* with that he slinks away. Now his way had been° *should have been* to have come hand and feet, one and two round° *roundly* at his costard.° *i.e., head* He, like a fool, bears his sword point half a yard out o'danger. I lie° *take up position* here for my life. [*He demonstrates a defensive stance.*] If the devil come, and he have no more strength than fence, he shall never beat me from this ward.° *defensive stance* I'll stand to it, a buckler° *shield* in a skillful hand is as good as a castle; nay, 'tis better than a sconce,° *small fort* for I have tried it. Mosby, perceiving this, began to faint.° *lose courage* With that comes Arden with his arming sword[1] and thrust him through the shoulder in a trice.

ALICE Ay, but I wonder why you both stood still.

BLACK WILL Faith, I was so amazed I could not strike.

ALICE Ah, sirs, had he yesternight been slain,
For every drop of his detested blood
I would have crammed in angels in thy fist,
And kissed thee, too, and hugged thee in my arms.

BLACK WILL Patient yourself; we cannot help it now.
Greene and we two will dog him through the fair,
And stab him in the crowd, and steal away.

Here enters Mosby [*with bandaged arm*].

ALICE It is unpossible. But here comes he
That will, I hope, invent some surer means.—

7. The host of the Flower-de-Luce Inn in Faversham (see 1.104.1 ff.).
8. When the time came for Shakebag to cross swords with his opponents up to the hilts.
9. Brandished his sword.
1. Waving the sword he was armed with.

Sweet Mosby, hide thy arm; it kills my heart!
MOSBY Ay, Mistress Arden, this is your favor.° *gift, love token*
ALICE Ah, say not so! For when I saw thee hurt,
I could have took the weapon thou let'st fall
And run at Arden, for I have sworn
That these mine eyes, offended with his sight,
Shall never close till Arden's be shut up.
This night I rose and walked about the chamber,
And twice or thrice I thought to have murdered him.
MOSBY What, in the night? Then had we been undone.
ALICE Why, how long shall he live?
MOSBY Faith, Alice, no longer than this night.—
Black Will and Shakebag, will you two
Perform the complot° that I have laid? *plot*
BLACK WILL Ay, or else think me as a villain.
GREENE And rather than you shall want,° I'll help° myself. *fail / offer assistance*
MOSBY You, Master Greene, shall single Franklin forth° *draw Franklin aside*
And hold him with a long tale of strange news,
That he may not come home till supper time.
I'll fetch Master Arden home, and we, like friends,
Will play a game or two at tables° here. *backgammon*
ALICE But what of all this? How shall he be slain?
MOSBY Why, Black Will and Shakebag, locked within the
countinghouse,° *business office*
Shall, at a certain watchword given, rush forth.
BLACK WILL What shall the watchword be?
MOSBY "Now I take you"—that shall be the word.
But come not forth before in any case.
BLACK WILL I warrant you. But who shall lock me in?
ALICE That will I do; thou'st° keep the key thyself. *you shall*
MOSBY Come, Master Greene, go you along with me.—
See all things ready, Alice, against° we come. *by the time that*
ALICE Take no care for° that; send you him home, *Don't worry about*
And if he e'er go forth again, blame me.
Exeunt Mosby and Greene.
Come, Black Will, that in mine eyes art fair;
Next unto Mosby do I honor thee.
Instead of fair words and large promises,
My hands shall play you golden harmony.° *reward you with gold*
How like you this? Say, will you do it, sirs?
BLACK WILL Ay, and that bravely° too. Mark my device: *splendidly*
Place Mosby, being a stranger,° in a chair, *guest*
And let your husband sit upon a stool,
That I may come behind him cunningly
And with a towel pull him to the ground,
Then stab him till his flesh be as a sieve.
That done, bear him behind the abbey,
That those that find him murdered may suppose
Some slave° or other killed him for his gold. *wretch*
ALICE A fine device! You shall have twenty pound,
And, when he is dead, you shall have forty more;
And, lest you might be suspected staying here,
Michael shall saddle you two lusty geldings.° *strong horses*
Ride whither you will, to Scotland or to Wales;
I'll see you shall not lack,° where'er you be. *need money*

BLACK WILL Such words would make one kill a thousand men.
Give me the key. Which is the countinghouse?
ALICE [*giving a key*] Here would I stay and still encourage you,
But that I know how resolute you are.
SHAKEBAG Tush, you are too fainthearted; we must do it.
ALICE But Mosby will be there, whose very looks
Will add unwonted courage to my thought
And make me the first that shall adventure on him.
BLACK WILL Tush, get you gone. 'Tis we must do the deed.
When this door opens next, look for his death.
[*Exeunt Black Will and Shakebag.*]
ALICE Ah, would he now were here, that it might open!
I shall no more be closed in Arden's arms,
That like the snakes of black Tisiphone[2]
Sting me with their embracings. Mosby's arms
Shall compass° me; and, were I made a star, *encompass*
I would have none other spheres but those.
There is no nectar but in Mosby's lips;
Had chaste Diana kissed him, she like me
Would grow lovesick, and from her wat'ry bower
Fling down Endymion[3] and snatch him° up. *(Mosby)*
Then blame not me that slay a silly man
Not half so lovely as Endymion.

Here enters Michael.

MICHAEL Mistress, my master is coming hard by.
ALICE Who comes with him?
MICHAEL Nobody but Mosby.
ALICE That's well, Michael.
Fetch in the tables, and, when thou hast done,
Stand before the countinghouse door.
MICHAEL Why so?
ALICE Black Will is locked within, to do the deed.
MICHAEL What, shall he die tonight?
ALICE Ay, Michael.
MICHAEL But shall not Susan know it?
ALICE Yes, for she'll be as secret as ourselves.
MICHAEL That's brave.° I'll go fetch the tables. *splendid*
[*He starts to leave.*]
ALICE But, Michael, hark to me a word or two:
When my husband is come in, lock the street door.
He shall be murdered or° the guests come in. *ere, before*
Exit Michael [*and returns shortly with the gaming tables*].

Here enters Arden and Mosby.

Husband, what mean you to bring Mosby home?
Although I wished you to be reconciled,
'Twas more for fear of you[4] than love of him.

2. One of the Furies, usually represented as winged women with serpent hair, who were intent on avenging crimes against kin. Tisiphone is known as the "blood avenger."

3. A shepherd loved by Diana (line 150), goddess of the moon.

4. (1) Fear for your safety; (2) fear and hatred of you.

Black Will and Greene are his companions,
And they are cutters° and may cut you short; *cutthroats*
Therefore I thought it good to make you friends.
But wherefore do you bring him hither now?
You have given me my supper[5] with his sight.

MOSBY Master Arden, methinks your wife would have me gone.

ARDEN No, good Master Mosby, women will be prating.—
Alice, bid him welcome; he and I are friends.

ALICE You may enforce me to it if you will,
But I had rather die than bid him welcome.
His company hath purchased° me ill friends, *gotten*
And therefore will I ne'er frequent it more.

MOSBY [*aside*] Oh, how cunningly she can dissemble!

ARDEN [*to Alice*] Now he is here you will not serve me so.° *i.e., disobey me*

ALICE I pray you be not angry or displeased;
I'll bid him welcome, seeing you'll have it so.—
You are welcome, Master Mosby. Will you sit down?

MOSBY [*sitting*] I know I am welcome to your loving husband,
But for yourself, you speak not from your heart.

ALICE And if I do not, sir, think I have cause.

MOSBY Pardon me, Master Arden, I'll away.

ARDEN No, good Master Mosby.

ALICE We shall have guests enough, though you go hence.

MOSBY I pray you, Master Arden, let me go.

ARDEN I pray thee, Mosby, let her prate her fill.

ALICE The doors are open, sir. You may be gone.

MICHAEL [*aside*] Nay, that's a lie, for I have locked the doors.

ARDEN [*to Michael*] Sirrah, fetch me a cup of wine. I'll make them friends. [*Exit Michael.*]
And, gentle Mistress Alice, seeing you are so stout,° *stubborn*
You shall begin.° Frown not; I'll have it so. *offer the first toast*

ALICE I pray you meddle with that you have to do.° *mind your own business*

ARDEN Why, Alice, how can I do too much for him
Whose life I have endangered without cause?

[*Enter Michael with wine.*]

ALICE 'Tis true, and, seeing 'twas partly through my means,
I am content to drink to him for this once.
[*Offering a toast*] Here, Master Mosby! And I pray you henceforth
Be you as strange to me as I to you.[6]
Your company hath purchased me ill friends,
And I for you, God knows, have undeserved° *undeservedly*
Been ill spoken of in every place;
Therefore henceforth frequent my house no more.

MOSBY I'll see your husband in despite of you.—
Yet, Arden, I protest to thee by heaven,
Thou ne'er shalt see me more after this night.[7]

5. (1) You've taken away my appetite; (2) you've fed my secret longing.
6. Stay away from me as much as I'll stay away from you. (With secret understanding that they will be inseparable.)
7. (1) I'll never visit you again; (2) you will be dead.

I'll go to Rome rather than be forsworn.
ARDEN Tush, I'll have no such vows made in my house.
ALICE Yes, I pray you, husband, let him swear;
And on that condition, Mosby, pledge me here.
MOSBY Ay, as willingly as I mean to live.
[He and Alice drink.]
ARDEN Come, Alice, is our supper ready yet?
ALICE It will by then° you have played a game at tables. *by the time*
ARDEN Come, Master Mosby, what shall we play for?
MOSBY Three games for a French crown, sir, an please you.° *if you please*
ARDEN Content. *[He sits opposite Mosby.]*
Then they play at the tables.

[Enter Black Will and Shakebag behind Arden.]

BLACK WILL [*aside*] Can he not take him° yet? What a spite is that! *take his pieces*
ALICE [*aside to him*] Not yet, Will. Take heed he see thee not.
BLACK WILL [*aside*] I fear he will spy me as I am coming.
MICHAEL [*aside*] To prevent that, creep betwixt my legs.
MOSBY [*throwing dice*] One ace, or else I lose the game.
ARDEN Marry, sir, there's two for failing.° *to prevent failing*
MOSBY Ah, Master Arden, "Now I can take you."
Then Will pulls him down with a towel.
ARDEN Mosby! Michael! Alice! What will you do?
BLACK WILL [*striking*] Nothing but take you up,° sir, nothing else. *settle matters with you*
MOSBY [*striking*] There's for the pressing iron° you told me of. *(see 1.314)*
SHAKEBAG [*striking*] And there's for the ten pound in my sleeve.° *i.e., as my reward*
ALICE What, groans thou?—Nay, then, give me the weapon.—
[*Striking*] Take this for hind'ring Mosby's love and mine.
MICHAEL Oh, mistress! *[Arden dies.]*
BLACK WILL Ah, that villain will betray us all.
MOSBY Tush, fear him not; he will be secret.
MICHAEL Why, dost thou think I will betray myself?
SHAKEBAG In Southwark dwells a bonny° northern lass, *attractive*
The widow Chambley. I'll to her house now,
And if she will not give me harborough,° *harbor, shelter*
I'll make booty of the quean,° even to her smock.° *rob the whore / petticoat*
BLACK WILL Shift for yourselves. We two will leave you now.
ALICE First, lay the body in the countinghouse.
Then they lay the body in the countinghouse.
BLACK WILL We have our gold. Mistress Alice, adieu;
Mosby, farewell, and Michael, farewell too!
Exeunt [Black Will and Shakebag.
Knocking is heard].

Enter Susan.

SUSAN Mistress, the guests are at the doors.
Hearken! They knock. What, shall I let them in?
ALICE Mosby, go thou and bear them company. *Exit Mosby.*
And, Susan, fetch water and wash away this blood.

SUSAN [*attempting to wash the floor*] The blood cleaveth to the ground and will not out.

ALICE But with my nails I'll scrape away the blood.
[*She tries to scrape away the blood.*]
The more I strive, the more the blood appears.

SUSAN What's the reason, mistress, can you tell?

ALICE Because I blush not at my husband's death.

Here enters Mosby.

MOSBY How now, what's the matter? Is all well?

ALICE Ay, well, if Arden were alive again.
In vain we strive, for here his blood remains.

MOSBY Why, strew rushes° on it, can you not? *a floor covering*
This wench doth nothing. [*To Susan*] Fall unto the work.

ALICE 'Twas thou that made me murder him.

MOSBY What of that?

ALICE Nay, nothing, Mosby, so° it be not known. *so long as*

MOSBY Keep thou it close,° and 'tis unpossible. *secret*

ALICE Ah, but I cannot. Was he not slain by me?
My husband's death torments me at the heart.

MOSBY It shall not long torment thee, gentle Alice.
I am thy husband; think no more of him.

Here enters Adam Fowle and Bradshaw.

BRADSHAW How now, Mistress Arden? What ail you weep?° *Why do you weep?*

MOSBY Because her husband is abroad so late.
A couple of ruffians threat'ned him yesternight,
And she, poor soul, is afraid he should be hurt.

ADAM Is't nothing else? Tush, he'll be here anon.

Here enters Greene.

GREENE Now, Mistress Arden, lack you any guests?

ALICE Ah, Master Greene, did you see my husband lately?

GREENE I saw him walking behind the abbey even now.

Here enters Franklin.

ALICE I do not like this being out so late.—
Master Franklin, where did you leave my husband?

FRANKLIN Believe me, I saw him not since morning.
Fear you not; he'll come anon. Meantime,
You may do well to bid his guests sit down.

ALICE Ay, so they shall.—Master Bradshaw, sit you there;
I pray you be content, I'll have my will.° *I insist*
Master Mosby, sit you in my husband's seat.
[*They sit. Michael and Susan converse in whispers.*]

MICHAEL Susan, shall thou and I wait on them?
Or, an thou say'st the word, let us sit down too.

SUSAN Peace! We have other matters now in hand.
I fear me, Michael, all will be bewrayed.° *revealed*

MICHAEL Tush, so it be known that I shall marry thee in the morning, I care not though I be hanged ere night. But to prevent the worst, I'll buy some ratsbane.° *rat poison*

SUSAN Why, Michael, wilt thou poison thyself?

MICHAEL No, but my mistress, for I fear she'll tell.

SUSAN Tush, Michael, fear not her; she's wise enough.

MOSBY Sirrah Michael, give 's a cup of beer.
Mistress Arden, here's to your husband.
[*He takes beer and offers a toast.*]
ALICE My husband?
FRANKLIN What ails you, woman, to cry so suddenly?
ALICE Ah, neighbors, a sudden qualm came over my heart.
My husband's being forth torments my mind.
I know something's amiss; he is not well,
Or else I should have heard of him ere now.
MOSBY [*aside*] She will undo us through her foolishness.
GREENE Fear not, Mistress Arden, he's well enough.
ALICE Tell not me. I know he is not well;
He was not wont for to stay thus late.—
Good Master Franklin, go and seek him forth,
And if you find him send him home to me,
And tell him what a fear he hath put me in.
FRANKLIN [*aside*] I like not this. I pray God all be well!—
I'll seek him out, and find him if I can.
Exeunt Franklin, Mosby, and Greene.
ALICE [*aside*] Michael, how shall I do to rid the rest away?
MICHAEL [*aside*] Leave that to my charge; let me alone.
[*Aloud*] 'Tis very late, Master Bradshaw,
And there are many false knaves abroad,
And you have many narrow lanes to pass.
BRADSHAW Faith, friend Michael, and thou sayest true.
Therefore I pray thee light 's forth[8] and lend 's a link.° *torch*
ALICE Michael, bring them to the doors, but do not stay;
You know I do not love to be alone.
Exeunt Bradshaw, Adam, and Michael.
Go, Susan, and bid thy brother come.
But wherefore should he come? Here is naught but fear.
Stay, Susan, stay, and help to counsel me.
SUSAN Alas, I counsel? Fear frights away my wits.
Then they open the countinghouse door and look upon Arden.
ALICE See, Susan, where thy quondam° master lies, *former*
Sweet Arden, smeared in blood and filthy gore.
SUSAN My brother, you, and I shall rue this deed.
ALICE Come, Susan, help to lift his body forth,
And let our salt tears be his obsequies.° *funeral prayers*
[*They bring forth Arden's body.*]

Here enters Mosby and Greene.

MOSBY How now, Alice, whither will you bear him?
ALICE Sweet Mosby, art thou come? Then weep that will;° *let those weep who want*
I have my wish in that I joy° thy sight. *rejoice in*
GREENE Well it 'hooves° us to be circumspect. *behooves*
MOSBY Ay, for Franklin thinks that we have murdered him.
ALICE Ay, but he cannot prove it for his life.
We'll spend this night in dalliance and in sport.

Here enters Michael.

8. Light us on our way.

MICHAEL Oh, mistress, the Mayor and all the watch
Are coming towards our house with glaives° and bills!° *broadswords / halberds*
ALICE Make the door fast; let them not come in.
MOSBY Tell me, sweet Alice, how shall I escape?
ALICE Out at the back door, over the pile of wood,
And for one night lie° at the Flower-de-Luce. *stay*
MOSBY That is the next° way to betray myself. *quickest*
GREENE Alas, Mistress Arden, the watch will take me here,
And cause suspicion where else would be none.
ALICE Why, take that way that Master Mosby doth.
But first convey the body to the fields.

Then they bear the body into the fields [*and return*].

MOSBY Until tomorrow, sweet Alice, now farewell;
And see you confess nothing in any case.
GREENE Be resolute, Mistress Alice; betray us not,
But cleave to us as we will stick to you.

Exeunt Mosby and Greene.

ALICE Now let the judge and juries do their worst;
My house is clear, and now I fear them not.
SUSAN As we went, it snowèd all the way,
Which makes me fear our footsteps will be spied.
ALICE Peace, fool! The snow will cover them again.
SUSAN But it had done° before we came back again. *stopped snowing*

[*Knocking is heard.*]

ALICE Hark, hark! They knock. Go, Michael, let them in.

[*Michael opens the door.*]

Here enters the Mayor and the watch.

How now, Master Mayor, have you brought my husband home?
MAYOR I saw him come into your house an hour ago.
ALICE You are deceived; it was a Londoner.
MAYOR Mistress Arden,
Know you not one that is called Black Will?
ALICE I know none such. What mean these questions?
MAYOR I have the Council's warrant to apprehend him.
ALICE [*aside*] I am glad it is no worse.—
Why, Master Mayor, think you I harbor any such?
MAYOR We are informed that here he is;
And therefore pardon us, for we must search.
ALICE Ay, search and spare you not, through every room.
Were my husband at home, you would not offer° this. *undertake, propose*

Here enters Franklin [*with a hand towel and a knife*].

Master Franklin, what mean you come so sad?
FRANKLIN Arden, thy husband and my friend, is slain.
ALICE Ah, by whom? Master Franklin, can you tell?
FRANKLIN I know not, but behind the abbey
There he lies, murdered in most piteous case.
MAYOR But, Master Franklin, are you sure 'tis he?
FRANKLIN I am too sure. Would God I were deceived!
ALICE Find out the murderers; let them be known.
FRANKLIN Ay, so they shall. Come you along with us.
ALICE Wherefore?

FRANKLIN Know you this hand towel and this knife?
SUSAN [*aside*] Ah, Michael, through this thy negligence
Thou hast betrayèd and undone us all!
MICHAEL [*aside*] I was so afraid I knew not what I did.
I thought I had thrown them both into the well.
ALICE [*to Franklin*] It is the pig's blood we had to° supper. *for*
But wherefore stay you? Find out the murderers.
MAYOR I fear me you'll prove one of them yourself.
ALICE I one of them? What mean such questions?
FRANKLIN I fear me he was murdered in this house
And carried to the fields, for from that place
Backwards and forwards may you see
The print of many feet within the snow.
And look about this chamber where we are,
And you shall find part of his guiltless blood;
For in his slipshoe° did I find some rushes, *slipper*
Which argueth he was murdered in this room.
MAYOR Look in the place where he was wont to sit.
[*They look.*]
See, see, his blood! It is too manifest.
ALICE It is a cup of wine that Michael shed.° *spilled*
MICHAEL Ay, truly.
FRANKLIN It is his blood, which, strumpet, thou hast shed.
But if I live, thou and thy complices,
Which have conspired and wrought his death, shall rue it.
ALICE Ah, Master Franklin, God and heaven can tell
I loved him more than all the world beside.
But bring me to him; let me see his body.
FRANKLIN [*to the watch, indicating Michael and Susan*] Bring
that villain and Mosby's sister too,
And one of you go to the Flower-de-Luce
And seek for Mosby, and apprehend him too. *Exeunt.*

[Scene 15]

Here enters Shakebag solus.° *alone*

SHAKEBAG The widow Chambley in her husband's days I
kept;° *kept as a mistress*
And, now he's dead, she is grown so stout° *haughty*
She will not know her old companions.
I came thither, thinking to have had
Harbor as I was wont,
And she was ready to thrust me out at doors.
But whether she would or no, I got me up,
And, as she followed me, I spurned° her down the stairs *kicked*
And broke her neck, and cut her tapster's throat;
And now I am going to fling them in the Thames.
I have the gold; what care I though it be known?
I'll cross the water and take sanctuary. *Exit Shakebag.*

Scene 15. London.

[Scene 16]

Here enters the Mayor, Mosby, Alice, Franklin, Michael, and Susan [attended by an armed guard. All gather before the body of Arden].

MAYOR See, Mistress Arden, where your husband lies.
Confess this foul fault and be penitent.
ALICE Arden, sweet husband, what shall I say?
The more I sound his name, the more he bleeds.
This blood condemns me and, in gushing forth,
Speaks as it falls and asks me why I did it.
Forgive me, Arden! I repent me now;
And, would my death save thine, thou shouldst not die.
Rise up, sweet Arden, and enjoy thy love,
And frown not on me when we meet in heaven!
In heaven I love thee, though on earth I did not.
MAYOR Say, Mosby, what made thee murder him?
FRANKLIN Study not° for an answer; look not down. *Don't make up excuses*
His purse and girdle° found at thy bed's head *belt*
Witness sufficiently thou didst the deed.
It bootless° is to swear thou didst it not. *unavailing*
MOSBY I hired Black Will and Shakebag, ruffians both,
And they and I have done this murd'rous deed.
But wherefore stay we? Come and bear me hence.
FRANKLIN Those ruffians shall not escape. I will
Up to London and get the Council's warrant
To apprehend them. *Exeunt [with the body].*

[Scene 17]

Here enters Will.

BLACK WILL Shakebag, I hear, hath taken sanctuary,
But I am so pursued with hues and cries° *outcries in pursuit*
For petty robberies that I have done
That I can come unto no sanctuary.
Therefore must I in some oyster boat
At last be fain to go aboard some hoy,° *small boat*
And so to Flushing.° There is no staying here. *(in the Netherlands)*
At Sittingburgh[1] the watch was like to° take me; *about to*
And, had I not with my buckler° covered my head *shield*
And run full blank at all adventures,[2]
I am sure I had ne'er gone further than that place,
For the constable had twenty warrants to apprehend me.
Besides that, I robbed him and his man once at Gad's Hill.
Farewell, England! I'll to Flushing now. *Exit Will.*

Scene 16. Faversham.
Scene 17. London, on the Thames.

1. Sittingbourne, near Faversham.
2. And run full tilt, the devil take the hindmost.

[Scene 18]

Here enters the Mayor; Mosby, Alice, Michael, Susan, and Bradshaw [under armed guard].

MAYOR [*to the watch*] Come, make haste, and bring away
the prisoners.
BRADSHAW Mistress Arden, you are now going to God,
And I am by the law condemned to die
About a letter I brought from Master Greene.
I pray you, Mistress Arden, speak the truth:
Was I ever privy to° your intent or no? *in on the secret of*
ALICE What should I say? You brought me such a letter,
But I dare swear thou knewest not the contents.
Leave° now to trouble me with worldly things, *Cease*
And let me meditate upon my Savior Christ,
Whose blood must save me for the blood I shed.
MOSBY How long shall I live in this hell of grief?
Convey me from the presence of that strumpet.
ALICE Ah, but for thee I had never been strumpet.
What cannot oaths and protestations do
When men have opportunity to woo?
I was too young to sound° thy villainies, *sound the depths of*
But now I find it and repent too late.
SUSAN [*to Mosby*] Ah, gentle brother, wherefore should I die?
I knew not of it till the deed was done.
MOSBY For thee I mourn more than for myself,
But let it suffice, I cannot save thee now.
MICHAEL [*to Susan*] And if your brother and my mistress
Had not promised me you in marriage,
I had ne'er given consent to this foul deed.
MAYOR Leave to accuse each other now,
And listen to the sentence I shall give:
Bear Mosby and his sister to London straight,
Where they in Smithfield[1] must be executed;
Bear Mistress Arden unto Canterbury,
Where her sentence is she must be burnt;
Michael and Bradshaw in Faversham must suffer death.
ALICE Let my death make amends for all my sins!
MOSBY Fie upon women!—This shall be my song.
But bear me hence, for I have lived too long.
SUSAN Seeing no hope on earth, in heaven is my hope.
MICHAEL Faith, I care not, seeing I die with Susan.
BRADSHAW My blood be on his head that gave the sentence!
MAYOR To speedy execution with them all! *Exeunt.*

[Epilogue]

Here enters Franklin.

FRANKLIN Thus have you seen the truth of Arden's death.
As for the ruffians Shakebag and Black Will,
The one° took sanctuary, and, being sent for out,° *(Shakebag) / to come out*

Scene 18. Faversham.
1. An open space northwest of London, just outside the city walls, sometimes used as a place of execution.

Was murderèd in Southwark as he passed
To Greenwich, where the Lord Protector° lay. *(see 1.2 and n)*
Black Will was burnt in Flushing on a stage;° *scaffold*
Greene was hanged at Osbridge° in Kent; *(near Faversham)*
The painter fled, and how he died we know not.
But this above the rest is to be noted:
Arden lay murdered in that plot of ground
Which he by force and violence held from Reede,
And in the grass his body's print was seen
Two years and more after the deed was done.
Gentlemen, we hope you'll pardon this naked tragedy,
Wherein no filèd points° are foisted in *smooth rhetoric*
To make it gracious to the ear or eye;
For simple truth is gracious enough
And needs no other points of glozing° stuff. [*Exit.*] *specious*

FINIS.

TEXTUAL NOTES

Arden of Faversham was entered in the Stationers' Register on April 3, 1592, and published in that same year by Edward White. Some obvious misprints were corrected in a second quarto of 1599 and again in 1633, each successive edition being a reprint of the previous. The first quarto, though based on copy that seems to have contained numerous repetitions, metrical irregularities, and errors, is the only authoritative edition we have. It serves as the basis of the present edition. Substantive departures from Q1 are noted here, using the following abbreviations:

Q1: The first quarto (London: Edward White, 1592)
Q2: The second quarto (London: Edward White, 1599)
Q3: The third quarto (London: Elizabeth Allde, 1633)
Southouse MS: A manuscript by the Kentish eighteenth-century antiquary Thomas Southouse. Huntington Library MS. HM1341
ed.: A modern editor's emendation

1.5 [and elsewhere] **Faversham** [Q1: *Feuershame*, also *Feuersham, Feueshame*] **15** [and elsewhere] **Mosby** [Q1: *Mosbie*] **37 ribald** [Q3] riball [Q1] **47, 118 raze** [Q1: race] **48** [and elsewhere] **jealous** [Q1: Jelyouse] **56, 247 Ho** [ed.] How [Q1] **56** [and elsewhere] **Alice** [Q1: Ales] **78 heard** [Q1: hard] **83 than** [Southouse ms.] there [Q1] **88** [and elsewhere] **Whilst** [ed.] Whilest [Q1] **89** [and elsewhere] **quay** [Q1: key] **125 won** [Q1: wan] **128 To come** [Q2] Come [Q1] **132 SD** [placement, ed.; after 131 in Q1] **135 narrow** [ed.] marrow [Q1] **142** [and elsewhere] **whither** [Q1: whether] **145 you** [Q2] yon [Q1] **155 hear** [Q1: heere] **160 As she** [ed.] As [Q1] **168 sheriff** [Q1: Shriefe] **192** [and elsewhere] **thee** [Q2] the [Q1] **214 lists** [Q3] list [Q1] **253** [and elsewhere] **off** [Q1: of] **290.1** [placement, ed.; after 292 in Q1] **353** [and elsewhere] **to** [Q2] too [Q1] **396** [and elsewhere] **Lest** [Q1: Least] **535 SD** [placement, ed.; after 533 in Q1] **595** [and elsewhere] **will't** [Q1: Wilt] **603** [and elsewhere] **haply** [ed.] happely [Q1] **614 scent** [Q1: sent] **639** [and elsewhere] **who's** [Q1: whose] **640 SD *Exeunt*** [Q1: *Eeunt*]

2.8 [and elsewhere] **Boulogne** [Q1: *Bulloine*] **23** [and elsewhere] **curtsy** [Q1: cursy] **25 victualer** [Q1: vitler] **58 worsted** [ed.] wosted [Q1] **82 SD** [placement, ed.; after 80 in Q1] **112 bait** [Q1: bate]

3.40 There's [Q1: ther'is] **64 SD** [placement, ed.; after 62 in Q1] **98 The** [ed.] With [Q1] **99 traveler** [Q1: trauailer] **118 wot** [Q1: wat] **138 MICHAEL** [Q2; not in Q1] **143 known** [Q2] kowne [Q1] **149 a knave** [Q1: aknaue] **155 complot** [Q2] complat [Q1] **193 haunt** [Q1: hant]

4.5 couch [Q1: cooch] **8 dissolution** [Q1: desolution] **13 plenished** [ed.] perisht [Q1] **21 FRANKLIN** [Q2] *Farn.* [Q1] **39.1** [placement, ed.; after 38 in Q1] **41 pity-moving** [Q2] pitty moning [Q1] **58.1** [placement, ed.; after 57 in Q1] **73 boltered** [ed.] bolstred [Q1] **76 thee** [Q3] there [Q1] **88 FRANKLIN** [Q2] *Eran.* [Q1] **107 FRANKLIN** [Q2] *Farn.* [Q1] **107 by** [Q2] be [Q1] **108 SD** [placement, Q2; after 107 in Q1]

5.0.1 [placement, Q2; after 1 in Q1] **2 sheeting** [Q1: sheting] **4 Obscures** [Q2] Obscure [Q1] **7 Loath** [Q1: Loth] **23 Were't** [Q1: Wert] **40** [and elsewhere] **buy** [Q2] by [Q1] **62 the** [Q2] thee [Q1]

6.1 Billingsgate [Q1: billensgate] **18 falchion** [Q1: Fauchon] **21 obscurèd** [Q2] oscured [Q1] **27 shivers** [Q3] shewers [Q1]

7.18 front [Q3] frons [Q1] **18 Rainham** [Q1: Raynum] **26** [and elsewhere] **plot** [Q1: plat]

8.12 Though [Q2] Thought [Q1] **17 starry** [ed.] stary [Q1] **24 ear** [Q1: erre] **43.1** ***Alice*** [ed.] *Aes* [Q1] **48 dam** [Q1: damne] **57 when** [Q2] where [Q1] **68 betwixt** [Q2] betwix [Q1] **90 demeanor** [Q1: demianor] **95 exorcisms** [Q1: excirsimes] **97 dove** [Q2] dowe [Q1] **133 fount once troubled** [ed.] fence of trouble [Q1] **139 gentles** [ed.] gentiles [Q1] **145 is valued** [ed.] valued [Q1] **156.1** [placement, Q2; after 155 in Q1] **166 MOSBY** [Q3] *Ales.* [Q1]

9.28 halloed [Q1: hollowed] **34 deceives** [Q2] deceaue [Q1] **43 seizeth** [Q1: ceazeth] **53 traveled** [Q1: trauailed] **67 fierce** [Q1: ferse] **70 ate** [Q3] eat [Q1] **70 brook with** [Q2] brooke [Q1] **127.1** ***Manent*** [ed.] *Manet* [Q1]

10.3 discern [Q3] deserue [Q1] **18 desires** [ed.] deserues [Q1] **39 master's** [Q1: M.] **45 weather** [Q1: whether] **45.1** [placement, ed.; after 44 in Q1] **61 lurdan** [Q1: lordaine] **97 cement** [Q3] semell [Q1]

11.20 Nay [Q3] Na [Q1] **24 has** [Q3] as [Q1]

12.18 lose [Q1: loose]

13.6 vouchsafe [Q2] vouchafe [Q1] **41 shooter's** [Q3] sutors [Q1] **51 my** [Q1: wy] **95 merrily** [Q2] mirrely [Q1] **112 while** [Q2] whill [Q1] **138 taunts your** [Q3] traunt you [Q1] **141 a jealous** [Q3] an Jelious [Q1] **151 this** [Southouse MS] his [Q1]

14.16 by [ed.] be [Q1] **17** [and elsewhere] **beer** [Q2] beare [Q1] **17** [and elsewhere] **Thames** [Q1: Temes] **19 tallies** [ed.] tales [Q1] **22 sergeant's** [Q1: Sariants] **27 sign** [Q1: Singne] **30** [and elsewhere] **Mistress** [Q1: M.] **47 cost** [Q2] coast [Q1] **73 crammed** [Q3] cramme [Q1] **112.1** [placement, ed.; after 111 in Q1] **123 sieve** [Q2] sine [Q1] **152 snatch** [Q2] snath [Q1] **163 shall** [ed.] shull [Q1] **171 Although** [Q2] Althought [Q1] **246 And** [Q2] Ind [Q1] **304 being** [Q3] deing [Q1] **315.1** [placement, ed.; after 314 in Q1] **324.1** [placement, ed.; after 322 in Q1]

18.16 woo [Q1: woe]

The Shoemaker's Holiday

No play better celebrates bourgeois London than *The Shoemaker's Holiday*, first staged in 1599. Its protagonist, Simon Eyre, is an ordinary citizen and guild member who rises to become Lord Mayor and the admired recipient of royal favor. His workers and family rise with him in wealth and social importance. At the same time, the play is fascinated with social and political conflict: between the nobility and powerful London guild members, between artisans and immigrant laborers, between Englishmen and foreigners, between owners and workers. Thomas Dekker's London breathes vitality and economic competitiveness. His characters are often partly heroic, partly humorous and flawed. The dramatist's point of view seems both laudatory and mildly satiric, and through this point of view, he offers his London audiences a mirror that is at once flattering and realistic.

The play's festive and celebratory mood of rising expectations puts a cheerful face on the end of a decade filled with uncertainties and unresolved problems. War with Spain had dragged on for more than twelve years. Attempts to suppress rebellion in Ireland were getting nowhere. Outbreaks of plague, bad harvests, inflation, and an influx of unemployed workers from the countryside added to social tensions.[1]

Dekker's approach to these contemporary issues is to dramatize and fictionalize the story of a historical figure, Simon Eyre, who had in fact been elected sheriff of London in 1434, then alderman, and finally Lord Mayor in 1445. Dekker got most of his supposedly factual information from Thomas Deloney's *The Gentle Craft* (1597), a collection of prose tales about shoemaking that included a life of Simon Eyre. The building of Leadenhall, one of Eyre's major achievements, is chronicled in Dekker's play. Yet Eyre was not a shoemaker; indeed, the shoemakers were too poor a guild to count for much in London's political arena. Tailors and shoemakers, trading in inexpensive, everyday goods, could not compete with the wealth and power of the goldsmiths or the Gentlemen Grocers. Dekker chooses unhistorically to glorify the "Gentle Craft" of shoemaking, perhaps because of its legends of hospitality and caring for the poor (see 4.46–47 and note). *The Shoemaker's Holiday* appeals to those who are relatively far down on the economic scale, providing them, especially those in London, with a dream of worldly advancement. Maybe for this reason the play was a great success.

Social and economic conflict are an inescapable feature of every aspect of the play, including its central romantic plot. The Lord Mayor at the start of the play, Sir Roger Oatley, of the Gentlemen Grocers (see 11.44–45), has a fair and virtuous daughter, Rose, who is in love with Rowland Lacy, nephew of the Earl of Lincoln. Oatley and Lincoln both deplore this match, but for different reasons. The Lord Mayor fears that the young aristocrat, having run through his money like most such young men, wishes to marry into bourgeois London wealth to recoup his fortunes. Lincoln, for his part,

Introduction, glosses, footnotes, and textual notes by David Bevington; text edited by David Bevington and checked by Eric Rasmussen.

1. Paul Seaver, "The Artisanal World," in *The Theatrical City: Culture, Theatre, and Politics in London, 1576–1649*, ed. David L. Smith, Richard Strier, and David Bevington (Cambridge and New York: Cambridge University Press, 1995). See also David Bevington's "Theatre as Holiday," in the same volume, and David Scott Kastan, "Workshop and/as Playhouse: Comedy and Commerce in *The Shoemaker's Holiday*," *Studies in Philology* 84 (1987): 324–37.

mistrusts the Lord Mayor and his daughter as parvenus attempting to buy their way into the respectability of the landed aristocracy through a socially advantageous marriage. The two older men are thus in agreement about preventing the marriage, and yet they cannot abide one another. Speaking of Oatley, Lincoln exclaims: "I know this churl, even in the height of scorn, / Doth hate the mixture of his blood with thine" (1.78–79). Lincoln condescendingly urges Oatley: "Then seek, my lord, some honest citizen / To wed your daughter to" (1.36–37). Oatley's opinion of Lincoln is no less contemptuous: "Well, fox, I understand your subtlety," he says in an aside (1.38). Young love must find a way to triumph over social and economic jealousies like these.

Lacy's decision to become a shoemaker is part romantic fiction: no nobleman's nephew, however greatly in need of funds, would stoop so low. The plot device is essential, on the other hand, to a number of Dekker's purposes. It lends to shoemaking an aura of respectability and adventure and makes the point that a willingness to do manual labor distinguishes ordinary people from the upper classes during this period. Moreover, it provides a cover for Lacy when, in order to escape being sent into France on military service, he disguises himself as a shoemaker in the employ of Simon Eyre. The device also has the structural advantage of uniting the play's plots: Lacy the wooer is also Lacy the presumed "Hans" of the Gentle Craft.

Eyre's shoemaking shop brims with vitality. Never is there a dull moment. Eyre busies himself about his workers. He does what he can to save one of his best men, Ralph, from military conscription and comforts Ralph's wife, Jane, when nothing can shield Ralph from the draft. He staves off work stoppages threatened when his employees register complaints about the interference of his wife, Margery, or when they insist on his hiring a foreign worker in the name of the solidarity of the shoemakers' trade. His dealings sometimes appear questionable, as for instance when he buys at bargain prices the merchandise of the merchant owner of a ship who dares not show his head in public. The story of this ship and its cargo betrays a contradictory though familiar attitude toward the wealth it represents. On the one hand, the play suggests that Eyre gets rich because he is such an ebullient person and a hard worker. On the other hand, the account of the ship bestows on him a fantasy source of wealth only tangentially related to his shoemaking trade. His ship literally comes in—almost as though he had won the lottery. The effect is to give Eyre's social advancement a kind of magical quality. Stuffed as it is with civet, almonds, cambric, and the like, the ship is rather like a child's notion of wealth and seems related to Eyre's mode of being mayor, which involves a lot of feasting and drinking; he runs London on a plan similar to that for his shop. His conception of wealth is unsophisticated: it has to do with what people who don't have money, and don't think about wealth in the long term, might imagine money will buy.

Simon Eyre, Lord Mayor of London, 1445–46, in aldermanic robes.

Eyre believes in his men and succeeds commercially in good part because he is so charismatic in his role as employer, and yet he has a sharp eye for profit margins and spends no more on employee costs than is necessary. When his journeymen threaten to walk out over working conditions, Eyre bribes them to stay with the offer of "a dozen cans of beer," but then adds, in an aside, that if the boy who is dispatched to buy the beer "fills any more than two, he pays for them" (7.74, 77–78). Such sharp dealing is a part of what Dekker portrays as so fascinating and even attractive in this larger-than-life figure.

"Prince am I none, yet am I princely born" is one version of the refrain that Eyre applies to himself (see 10.156 and 21.17, for example). It is his logo, his slogan. As a pithy emblem of self-fashioning, it bespeaks his pride in his social class. Competitive social advancement often took the form, in Elizabethan England, of newly wealthy men buying land as an entry into the ruling elite; some historians, such as J. H. Hexter, insist that England in the early modern period had no stable middle class worthy of the name.[2] Eyre, conversely, wishes to cling to his bourgeois London roots no matter how wealthy and powerful he may become. He is proud of his humble origins, his working-class wife, his journeymen; they will together celebrate their joint advancement. Rather than putting his origins behind him, Eyre insists on being who he is and on the role that people of his kind must play in England's political and economic destiny of the early modern period. He is not "middle class" in the nineteenth-century sense of the term, since his values remain stubbornly and proudly those of his artisan origins, yet he and his London compatriots represent a new power structure that must be reckoned with. The friendly endorsement he receives from the King at the play's end strongly reinforces the atmosphere of political and economic realignment then at hand. Loyal to the monarchy and supported by it, London's bourgeois class comes to occupy a new center in English politics and is prepared to rewrite its own history as a means of underscoring the political and historical significance of a social class too long underappreciated.

Dekker celebrates this revisionist view of history, but not without a wink and a nod. Eyre's ebullient jollity does not conceal the rough edges of a man who is evidently a master at political infighting. He outwits Oatley, his predecessor as Lord Mayor, whose motive in putting Eyre up for sheriff is that Eyre will have to "spend some of his thousands now" (9.71). Indeed, holding public offices of this sort could be ruinously expensive. Eyre manages this financial burden and moves up the ladder, from sheriff to alderman to Lord Mayor, taking advantage of the deaths of various office-holders along the way. Even though he may piously insist that he is "a handicraftsman" whose "heart is without craft" (21.10), we are invited to see him as the quintessential operator.

Firk, the most combative of Eyre's journeymen, is representative of a restive self-consciousness among workers about whether they enjoy any rights as employees. Firk is continually testing Eyre, pushing the limits, despite his fierce loyalty to his master and to his guild. His very name—suggesting variously a cheating trick or robbery, a dodge, a prank, a trouncing, and an aggressive sexual act—points toward the restless mobility of London's labor force, continually ready to walk out on the job (as Firk incessantly threatens but never in fact does). Not surprisingly, Firk is also the most verbal embodiment of a conflicted attitude toward immigrant workers. Such workers were in overabundant supply in London during the 1590s, owing to the exodus from the Netherlands of cloth workers and other artisans who were being persecuted for their Protestant faith by the soldiers of Philip II of Spain. Firk takes the lead in Eyre's shop in insisting that Eyre hire the German-speaking "Hans" (really Lacy in disguise). To Firk, this is partly a matter of solidarity among shoemakers, a kind of anticipation of international trade unionism. Never mind that Eyre has no present need of more employees; a shoemaker is in need of a job, and his fellow shoemakers will stick by him. At the same time, Firk is motivated by a wish to laugh at "Hans" for his funny way of speaking. Firk is pure xenophobe in his laughter at *"Yaw, yaw,"* and other foreign expressions (4.86ff). Dekker thus endearingly portrays human contradiction in his Londoners: kindness and hostility, generosity and resentment, welcoming of foreigners and blaming them for many of London's social ills.

Eyre's wife, Margery, is presented in a similarly ambivalent way. Eyre claims to have met her "selling tripes in Eastcheap" (7.67). He has taken her into his shop and

2. J. H. Hexter, "The Myth of the Middle Class in Tudor England," in *Reappraisals in History* (Evanston, Ill.: Northwestern University Press, 1961).

put rich clothes on her back. He takes pleasure in insulting her with his most colorful language: "Avaunt, kitchen-stuff! Rip, you brown-bread tannikin, out of my sight!" She is a "powder-beef quean," a "chitterling," an "Islington whitepot," a "hopper-arse," a "barley pudding full of maggots," a "broiled carbonado" (7.65–66, 70, 73, 20.51–53). The journeymen laugh at her social pretentiousness, and indeed she is ceaselessly concerned about where to find a "farthingale maker" or a "French hood maker"; once her husband has more money, she is determined to "enlarge my bum" and obtain "a false hair for my periwig" (10.37–38, 46–47). Her talk is laden with Puritan cant, by way of disclaiming her social longings: "Indeed, all flesh is grass" (10.43). Yet her hypocrisies are presented as innocent, almost childish. The sexual double entendres she utters appear to be unconscious (see, for example, 1.157ff. and 10.96–100). Despite all this, Eyre is fond, even proud, of her. She represents for him, and for us, an important part of London's bustling vitality and diversity that he is not willing to give up.

Dekker employs the kind of multiple plotting we find in so many Elizabethan comedies and does so with considerable skill. Ralph, the shoemaker who must go to war, is wounded and reported dead—or so, at least, his wife is told by a gentleman named Hammon, who wishes Jane for his own. We know that Ralph is actually alive and has returned from the Continent, lame but eager to find Jane again. His friends, the shoemakers, have lost track of Jane. Thus is set in motion a melodramatic plot of sorrow and apparent loss, quite different in texture from the love plot of Lacy and Rose or the story of Eyre's rise to fame. Hammon, "a proper gentleman" (6.59), has previously paid court to Rose and has received the avid encouragement of Rose's father, Oatley, who would vastly prefer such a prosperous and respectable gentleman to the down-at-the-heels young aristocrat Lacy. When Hammon receives no encouragement from Rose, he abandons that suit and shifts his attention to the war-widowed Jane. When he reports to her the news that Ralph has supposedly died in military action, does he know that the report is false? She suspects a forgery (12.95) but is still vulnerable to his attentions because she cannot prove that her husband is alive. Barely in time, a shoe comes to her rescue: as part of the wedding arrangements for the match with Hammon, Jane reluctantly orders a pair of new shoes and sends along with the servant bearing this order a shoe of her own as a sample. Ralph recognizes it and, accompanied by his companion shoemakers (especially Firk, who revels in the sport of outwitting those who oppose young love or marital happiness), reclaims his wife just in time.

This plot reinforces a number of cultural values underlying other parts of the play as well. Hammon, as a gentleman, is suspect; his mores are not those of the Gentle Craft. He attempts to violate the sanctity of marriage so earnestly protected by the right-minded shoemakers. His attempts to use money and position to force his will on a member of the London bourgeois class (as when he actually offers to buy Jane from Ralph, even after Ralph's return has proven to Hammon that Ralph is still alive [18.81–85]) put him in the position of being a figure who stands in the way of comic resolution. Comedy triumphs by outwitting him, just as it does with Rose and Lacy's successful undertaking to marry and thus outwit Lacy's aristocratic uncle. Aristocrat and gentleman alike (including Sir Roger Oatley) are figures of derision in this play, foiled in their own devices by the resourceful shoemakers, whose forthright moral position wins the day. Marriages in this play are sacred bonds of mutual commitment, strong enough to withstand the improper assaults mounted on them by an oppressive social hierarchy. As Jane declares, "Whom should my thoughts affect / But him whom heaven hath made to be my love?" (18.61–62). London bourgeois citizens, allied in sympathy and political ties with an idealized monarchy, outlast and outwit the self-interested machinations of the privileged few. As Hodge, Eyre's shop steward, triumphantly declares: "Shoemakers are steel to the back, men every inch of them, all spirit" (18.35–36).

Dekker's treatment of the war is attuned to his ironic and good-humored approach to other aspects of social conflict. The war simply exists in the background. Fictionally, we are led to understand that England is at war with France, since the nominal period of history being displayed is presumably around the years of the real-life Eyre and his career as sheriff and Lord Mayor in the 1430s and 1440s. Dekker's spectators are invited to think about their own decade of the 1590s and about war with Spain, mainly. But the exact time period doesn't really matter; wars occur, and young men go off to fight in them. The play offers very little moral fervor on the subject. We are never told why the two sides are fighting. The attitudes of Londoners are presented as endearingly contradictory: both Eyre and Hodge are ready to do what they can to save Ralph from going to France ("Ralph, thou'rt a gull, by this hand, an thou goest," insists Hodge [1.177]), until it appears that nothing can be done. At this point, Hodge sees nothing but good in Ralph's new mission. "Thou'rt a gull, by my stirrup, if thou dost not go," he urges (1.187). Eyre too shifts from pleading that young married men be allowed to remain at home to an eruption of patriotic commonplaces: "Well, let him go. He's a proper shot. Let him vanish.—Peace, Jane, dry up thy tears; they'll make his powder dankish. Take him, brave men. Hector of Troy was an hackney to him, Hercules and Termagant scoundrels; Prince Arthur's Round Table, by the Lord of Ludgate, ne'er fed such a tall, such a dapper swordsman" (1.167–72). Patriotism is a subject on which most people are comically confused. Lacy's draft-dodging in order to be near Rose does not seem very noble, but he is still presented to us as the young hero in the central love plot. The war is simply part of the fabric of this play about London; it merely functions in the plot. Only at the very last moment, in an atmosphere of reconciliation and good, hearty English feeling, can the King express a platitude that probably no one has any objection to: "Wars must right wrongs which Frenchmen have begun" (21.197).

Again and again in *The Shoemaker's Holiday,* conventional history is revised in favor of an emergent class. Yet all is done with good humor and a rich appreciation of human foibles. Dekker is no polemical apologist for the class of Londoners to which his play is chiefly offered. He is a dramatist, not a writer of tracts. His play is a celebration not of the shoemakers' new social destiny, or even of young love's triumphs over aged calculation, but of the rich pageantry of London life in all its complexity and amusing imperfections.

THOMAS DEKKER
The Shoemaker's Holiday

[THE PERSONS IN THE PLAY

The PROLOGUE
The KING of England
Simon EYRE, master shoemaker, then sheriff and Lord Mayor of London
MARGERY, his wife
HODGE, or Roger, his foreman
FIRK, a journeyman shoemaker
RALPH Damport, a journeyman shoemaker
JANE, Ralph's wife
Sir Roger OATLEY, Lord Mayor of London at the start of the play
ROSE, his daughter
SIBYL, her maid
The Earl of LINCOLN (Sir Hugh Lacy)
Rowland LACY, his nephew, in love with Rose, disguised as "Hans"
ASKEW, Lacy's cousin
HAMMON, a gentleman, wooer of Rose and then Jane
WARNER, his brother-in-law
LOVELL, a courtier
DODGER, serving the Earl of Lincoln
The Earl of CORNWALL
SCOTT, a friend of Oatley's
A Dutch SKIPPER
A boy in Eyre's shop
A BOY with the hunters
A PRENTICE employed by Oatley
A SERVINGMAN in Hammon's household
Noblemen, officers, soldiers, huntsmen, shoemakers, prentices, and servants

THE SCENE: London and Old Ford, a nearby village.]

The original 1600 title page reads "*The Shoemaker's Holiday, or The Gentle Craft.* With the humorous life of Simon Eyre, Shoemaker, and Lord Mayor of London. As it was acted before the Queen's most excellent Majesty on New Year's day at night last, by the right honorable the Earl of Nottingham, Lord High Admiral of England, his servants. Printed by Valentine Sims dwelling at the foot of Adling Hill, near Baynard's Castle, at the sign of the White Swan, and are there to be sold. 1600."

[The Epistle]

TO ALL GOOD FELLOWS, PROFESSORS° OF THE GENTLE CRAFT,° OF WHAT DEGREE SOEVER — *practitioners*; *shoemaking*

Kind gentlemen and honest boon companions, I present you here with a merry conceited° comedy called *The Shoemaker's Holiday*, acted by my Lord Admiral's Players this present Christmas° before the Queen's most excellent Majesty, for the mirth and pleasant matter by Her Highness graciously accepted, being indeed no way offensive. The argument° of the play I will set down in this epistle. Sir Hugh Lacy, Earl of Lincoln, had a young gentleman of his own name, his near kinsman, that loved the Lord Mayor's daughter of London, to prevent and cross which love the Earl caused his kinsman to be sent colonel of a company into France, who resigned his place to another gentleman his friend and came disguised like a Dutch shoemaker to the house of Simon Eyre in Tower Street, who served the Mayor and his household with shoes; the merriments that passed in Eyre's house, his coming to be mayor of London, Lacy's getting his love, and other accidents;° with two merry three-man's songs.° Take all in good worth that is well intended, for nothing is purposed but mirth. Mirth lengtheneth long life, which with all other blessings I heartily wish you.

fanciful, witty — *(1599–1600)* — *plot* — *happenings* — *(for three male voices)*

Farewell.

The First Three-Man's Song[1]

Oh, the month of May, the merry month of May,
So frolic, so gay, and so green, so green, so green!
Oh, and then did I unto my true love say:
"Sweet Peg, thou shalt be my summer's queen."

Now the nightingale, the pretty nightingale,
The sweetest singer in all the forest's quire,° — *choir*
Entreats thee, sweet Peggy, to hear thy true love's tale.
Lo, yonder she sitteth, her breast against a briar.[2]

But oh, I spy the cuckoo, the cuckoo, the cuckoo!
See where she sitteth. Come away, my joy.
Come away, I prithee; I do not like the cuckoo
Should sing where my Peggy and I kiss and toy.° — *dally*

Oh, the month of May, the merry month of May,
So frolic, so gay, and so green, so green, so green!
And then did I unto my true love say:
"Sweet Peg, thou shalt be my summer's queen."

The First Three-Man's Song.
1. Placement of these songs in performance is uncertain, but see note on the second song.
2. The nightingale was thought to lean its breast against a thorn in order to keep itself awake by the pain, so that it might sing its sad song.

The Second Three-Man's Song

(This is to be sung at the latter end.)[1]

Cold's the wind, and wet's the rain.
  Saint Hugh° be our good speed! *shoemakers' patron saint*
Ill is the weather that bringeth no gain,
  Nor helps good hearts in need.

Troll° the bowl, the jolly nut-brown bowl, *Pass around*
  And here, kind mate, to thee!
Let's sing a dirge for Saint Hugh's soul,
  And down it merrily.

Down-a-down, hey down-a-down,
  Hey-derry-derry down-a-down.
      Close with° the tenor boy. *Sing in unison with*
Ho! Well done. To me let come;
  Ring compass,° gentle joy. *Reach the fullest extent*

Trowl the bowl, the nut-brown bowl,
  And here, kind &c.
      As often as there be men to drink.

At last, when all have drunk, this verse:

Cold's the wind, and wet's the rain.
  Saint Hugh be our good speed!
Ill is the weather that bringeth no gain,
  Nor helps good hearts in need.

The Prologue,
as it was pronounced before the Queen's Majesty° *(on New Year's Day 1600)*

[*Enter the Prologue.*]

PROLOGUE As wretches in a storm, expecting day,
With trembling hands and eyes cast up to heaven,
Make prayers the anchor of their conquered hopes,
So we, dear goddess,° wonder of all eyes, *Queen Elizabeth*
Your meanest vassals,° through mistrust and fear *lowliest subjects*
To sink into the bottom° of disgrace *bottom of sea; hull*
By our imperfect pastimes, prostrate thus,
On bended knees, our sails of hope do strike,° *lower in salute*
Dreading the bitter storms of your dislike.

Since then—unhappy men—our hap° is such *lot*
That to ourselves ourselves no help can bring,
But needs must perish if your saintlike ears,
Locking the temple° where all mercy sits, *Shutting your mind*
Refuse the tribute of our begging tongues,
Oh, grant, bright mirror° of true chastity, *model*
From those life-breathing stars, your sunlike eyes,

The Second Three-Man's Song.
1. Possibly indicating that this song is to be sung as the last song (see note at 13.1).

One gracious smile; for your celestial breath
Must send us life or sentence us to death. [*Exit the Prologue.*]

[Scene 1]

Enter [*Sir Roger Oatley, the*] *Lord Mayor,* [*and the Earl of*] *Lincoln.*

LINCOLN My Lord Mayor, you have sundry times
Feasted myself and many courtiers more;
Seldom or never can we be so kind
To° make requital of your courtesy. *As to*
But leaving this, I hear my cousin° Lacy *i.e., kinsman, nephew*
Is much affected to° your daughter Rose. *in love with*

OATLEY True, my good lord, and she loves him so well
That I mislike her boldness in the chase.

LINCOLN Why, my Lord Mayor, think you it then a shame
To join a Lacy with an Oatley's name?

OATLEY Too mean° is my poor girl for his high birth. *of lower station*
Poor citizens must not with courtiers wed,
Who will in silks and gay apparel spend
More in one year than I am worth by far.
Therefore, Your Honor need not doubt° my girl. *be concerned about*

LINCOLN Take heed, my lord; advise you° what you do. *consider carefully*
A verier unthrift° lives not in the world *more out-and-out prodigal*
Than is my cousin, for I'll tell you what:
'Tis now almost a year since he requested
To travel countries for experience.
I furnished him with coin, bills of exchange,° *i.e., drafts, checks*
Letters of credit,[1] men to wait on° him, *attend, serve*
Solicited my friends in Italy
Well to respect him. But to see the end:° *to come to the point*
Scant° had he journeyed through half Germany *Scarcely*
But all his coin was spent, his men cast off,° *dismissed*
His bills embezzled,° and my jolly coz,° *frittered away / nephew*
Ashamed to show his bankrupt presence here,
Became a shoemaker in Wittenberg—
A goodly science° for a gentleman *occupation, skill*
Of such descent! Now judge the rest by this:
Suppose your daughter have a thousand pound;° *pounds (as dowry)*
He did consume me° more in one half year! *at my cost*
And make° him heir to all the wealth you have; *suppose you make*
One twelvemonth's rioting° will waste it all. *lavish living*
Then seek, my lord, some honest citizen
To wed your daughter to.

OATLEY I thank Your Lordship.
[*Aside*] Well, fox, I understand your subtlety.
[*To him*] As for your nephew, let Your Lordship's eye
But watch his actions and you need not fear,
For I have sent my daughter far enough.
And yet your cousin Rowland might do well,
Now he hath learned an occupation.
[*Aside*] And yet I scorn to call him son-in-law.

Scene 1. London.

1. Letters establishing financial credit.

LINCOLN Ay, but I have a better trade for him.
I thank His Grace,° he hath appointed him *the King*
Chief colonel of all those companies
Mustered in London and the shires about
To serve His Highness in those wars of France.
See where he comes.

Enter Lovell, Lacy, and Askew.

Lovell, what news with you?
LOVELL My lord of Lincoln, 'tis His Highness' will
That presently° your cousin ship for France *immediately*
With all his powers.° He would not for a million *armed forces*
But they[2] should land at Dieppe within four days.
LINCOLN Go certify His Grace it shall be done. *Exit Lovell.*
Now, cousin Lacy, in what forwardness° *state of readiness*
Are all your companies?
LACY All well prepared.
The men of Hertfordshire lie at Mile End;° *(east of London)*
Suffolk and Essex train in Tothill Fields;° *(in Westminster)*
The Londoners, and those of Middlesex,
All gallantly prepared in Finsbury,° *a training area north*
With frolic spirits long for their parting hour.
OATLEY They have their imprest,° coats, and furniture,° *advance pay / equipment*
And if it please your cousin Lacy come
To the Guildhall° he shall receive his pay, *i.e., city hall*
And twenty pounds besides my brethren° *fellow aldermen*
Will freely give him, to approve° our loves *prove, show*
We bear unto my lord your uncle here.
LACY I thank Your Honor.
LINCOLN Thanks, my good Lord Mayor.
OATLEY At the Guildhall we will expect your coming. *Exit.*
LINCOLN To approve your loves to me? No, subtlety![3]
Nephew, that twenty pound he doth bestow
For joy to rid you from his daughter Rose.
But, cousins both, now here° are none but friends, *now that here*
I would not have you cast an amorous eye
Upon so mean a project as the love
Of a gay, wanton, painted° citizen. *(with cosmetics)*
I know this churl, even in the height of scorn,
Doth hate the mixture of his blood with thine.
I pray thee do thou so. Remember, coz,
What honorable fortunes wait on thee.
Increase the King's love, which so brightly shines
And gilds thy hopes. I have no heir but thee—
And yet not thee, if with a wayward spirit
Thou start from the true bias[4] of my love.
LACY My lord, I will for honor—not desire
Of land or livings, or to be your heir—

2. It means more to the King than would a million pounds that Lacy and his troops.
3. No, cunning one! (Lincoln apostrophizes Oatley, who has just left.)
4. Swerve from the proper course. (A metaphor from the game of bowls, in which weighted bowling balls enabled the bowler to roll a curved path.)

So guide my actions in pursuit of France° — *the French*
As shall add glory to the Lacys' name.

LINCOLN [*giving money*] Coz, for those words here's thirty
portagues,° — *gold coins*
And, nephew Askew, there's a few for you.
Fair honor in her loftiest eminence
Stays in France for you till you fetch her thence.
Then, nephews, clap swift wings° on your designs. — *set swift sails*
Begone, begone! Make haste to the Guildhall;
There presently I'll meet you. Do not stay.° — *delay*
Where honor beckons, shame attends delay. *Exit.*

ASKEW How gladly would your uncle have you gone!

LACY True, coz, but I'll o'erreach° his policies.° — *outmaneuver / schemes*
I have some serious business for three days,
Which nothing but my presence can dispatch.
You therefore, cousin, with the companies
Shall haste to Dover. There I'll meet with you,
Or if I stay past my prefixèd time,
Away for France; we'll meet in Normandy.
The twenty pounds my Lord Mayor gives to me
You shall receive, and these ten portagues,
Part of mine uncle's thirty. Gentle coz,
Have care to our great charge.° I know your wisdom — *commission*
Hath tried itself in higher consequence.[5]

ASKEW Coz, all myself am yours. Yet have this care:
To lodge in London with all secrecy.
Our uncle Lincoln hath, besides his own,
Many a jealous° eye, that in your face — *mistrustful, vigilant*
Stares only to watch means for your disgrace.

LACY Stay, cousin, who be these?

Enter Simon Eyre, his wife [Margery], Hodge, Firk, Jane, and Ralph with a piece.° — *weapon*

EYRE Leave whining, leave whining. Away with this whimp'ring, this puling,° these blubb'ring tears, and these wet eyes! I'll get thy husband discharged, I warrant thee, sweet Jane. Go to!° — *whining* / *(an expostulation)*

HODGE Master, here be the captains.

EYRE Peace,° Hodge. Husht, ye knave, husht! — *Be quiet*

FIRK Here be the cavaliers° and the colonels, master. — *horse soldiers, knights*

EYRE Peace, Firk, peace, my fine Firk. Stand by with your pishery-pashery.° Away! I am a man of° the best presence. I'll speak to them an° they were popes.—Gentlemen, captains, colonels, commanders: brave men, brave leaders, may it please you to give me audience. I am Simon Eyre, the mad° shoemaker of Tower Street. This wench with the mealy mouth that will never tire is my wife, I can tell you. Here's Hodge, my man and my foreman; here's Firk, my fine firking journeyman;° and this is blubbered Jane. All we come to be suitors for° this honest Ralph. Keep him at home, and, as I am a true shoemaker and a gentleman of the Gentle Craft,° buy spurs yourself and I'll find° ye boots these seven years. — *foolish chatter / fit for* / *even if* / *irrepressible* / *rascally craftsman* / *on behalf of* / *shoemaking* / *provide*

5. Has been tested in even greater emergencies.

MARGERY Seven years, husband?
EYRE Peace, midriff,° peace! I know what I do. Peace. — *i.e., fatso*
FIRK [*to Lacy*] Truly, Master Cormorant,[6] you shall do God
good service to let Ralph and his wife stay together. She's a
young new-married woman. If you take her husband away
from her a-night,° you undo her—she may beg in the day- — *by nights*
time—for he's as good a workman at a prick and an awl[7] as
any is in our trade.
JANE Oh, let him stay, else I shall be undone!
FIRK Ay, truly, she shall be laid at° one side like a pair of old — *to*
shoes else, and be occupied for no use.
LACY Truly, my friends, it lies not in my power.
The Londoners are pressed,° paid, and set forth — *conscripted*
By the Lord Mayor. I cannot change a man.
HODGE Why, then, you were as good be a corporal as a colonel if you cannot discharge one good fellow; and I tell you
true, I think you do more than you can answer,° to press a — *justify*
man within a year and a day of his marriage.
EYRE Well said, melancholy° Hodge! Gramercy,° my fine — *pensive / Many thanks*
foreman!
MARGERY Truly, gentlemen, it were ill done for such as you
to stand so stiffly against a poor young wife, considering her
case.[8] She is new-married—but let that pass. I pray, deal not
roughly with her. Her husband is a young man and but newly
entered—but let that pass.
EYRE Away with your pishery-pashery, your pols and your
edepols.° Peace, midriff! Silence, Cecily Bumtrinket![9] Let — *senseless chatter*
your head° speak. — *head of household*
FIRK Yea, and the horns° too, master. — *(emblems of cuckoldry)*
EYRE Tawsoone,° my fine Firk, tawsoone. Peace, scoundrels! — *Be quiet! (Welsh)*
[*Pointing to Ralph*] See you this man? Captains, you will not
release him? Well, let him go. He's a proper shot.° Let him — *fine marksman*
vanish.—Peace, Jane, dry up thy tears; they'll make his powder dankish.° Take him, brave men. Hector of Troy was an — *gunpowder damp*
hackney° to him, Hercules and Termagant[1] scoundrels; — *hired horse, drudge*
Prince Arthur's Round Table, by the Lord of Ludgate,[2] ne'er
fed such a tall,° such a dapper° swordsman: by the life of — *brave / skillful*
Pharaoh, a brave, resolute swordman.—Peace, Jane.—I say
no more, mad knaves.
FIRK See, see, Hodge, how my master raves in commendation
of Ralph.
HODGE Ralph, thou'rt a gull, by this hand, an thou goest.[3]
ASKEW I am glad, good master Eyre, it is my hap° — *lot, chance*
To meet so resolute a soldier.
Trust me, for° your report and love to him, — *because of*
A common slight regard shall not respect him.° — *He'll be well regarded*
LACY Is thy name Ralph?

6. A ravenous seabird; Firk's insolent version of "colonel," pronounced in three syllables.
7. Piercing tools for shoemaking, here used with erotic double meaning ("awl" suggesting "hole") that continues in the following two speeches in "undone," "laid," and "occupied."
8. Margery is presumably unaware of the sexual double meaning in her "stand so stiffly" and "case" (i.e., female sexual anatomy). This continues in "deal not roughly" and "entered" (lines 158–60).
9. Eyre addresses his wife as "midriff," alluding presumably to her girth (as at line 137), and "Cecily Bumtrinket," pointing to her "bum."
1. A supposed Muslim blustering deity.
2. Eyre swears by "the Lord of Ludgate" presumably for its alliterative flavor. Ludgate was one of London's old city gates; there was no Lord of Ludgate historically.
3. Ralph, you're a fool, I swear, if you go.

RALPH Yes, sir.
LACY Give me thy hand.
Thou shalt not want, as I am a gentleman.
[*To Jane*] Woman, be patient. God, no doubt, will send
Thy husband safe again,° but he must go; *back again*
His country's quarrel says it shall be so.
HODGE Thou'rt a gull, by my stirrup,[4] if thou dost not go. I
will not have thee strike thy gimlet into these weak vessels.[5]
Prick thine enemies, Ralph.

Enter Dodger.

DODGER [*to Lacy*] My lord, your uncle on the Tower Hill
Stays° with the Lord Mayor and the aldermen, *Waits*
And doth request you with all speed you may
To hasten thither.
ASKEW Cousin, let us go.
LACY Dodger, run you before. Tell them we come.

Exit Dodger.

This Dodger is mine uncle's parasite,° *hanger-on, servant*
The arrant'st varlet° that e'er breathed on earth. *most flagrant rascal*
He sets more discord in a noble house
By one day's broaching° of his pickthank° tales *venting / sycophantic*
Than can be salved° again in twenty years, *healed*
And he, I fear, shall go with us to France,
To pry into our actions.
ASKEW Therefore, coz,
It shall behoove you to be circumspect.
LACY Fear not, good cousin.—Ralph, hie to your colors.° *ensign, standard*

[*Exeunt Lacy and Askew.*]

RALPH I must, because there's no remedy.
But, gentle master and my loving dame,
As you have always been a friend to me,
So in mine absence think upon my wife.
JANE Alas, my Ralph!
MARGERY She cannot speak for weeping.
EYRE Peace, you cracked groats, you mustard tokens!° Dis- *worthless coins*
quiet not the brave soldier.—Go thy ways, Ralph.
JANE Ay, ay, you bid him go. What shall I do when he is gone?
FIRK Why, be doing° with me, or my fellow Hodge; be not *(with bawdy suggestion)*
idle.
EYRE Let me see thy hand, Jane. [*He takes her hand.*] This
fine hand, this white hand, these pretty fingers must spin,
must card,° must work, work, you bombast-cotton-candle *comb unspun wool*
quean,[6] work for your living, with a pox° to you!—Hold thee, *syphilis; curse*
Ralph [*giving money*], here's five sixpences for thee. Fight
for the honor of the Gentle Craft, for the Gentlemen Shoemakers, the courageous cordwainers,° the flower of Saint *shoemakers*
Martin's,[7] the mad knaves of Bedlam,° Fleet Street, Tower *Bethlehem insane hospital*

4. A leather strap used to hold the shoe while it is being sewn.
5. I.e., It's time to stop puncturing leather with your leather-making tool; it's time to strike the French instead. (With bawdy undertone; women are conventionally the "weaker vessel." The sexual banter continues in "Prick.")
6. Eyre's abusive epithet for Jane characterizes her as a slut or wench ("quean") who works in cotton wool ("bombast") and expensive wax candles (instead of cheap ones made of kitchen fat).
7. Eyre points with pride to the area around the site of a former church of Saint Martin's-le-Grand, where many workers in shoe-leather were located.

Street, and Whitechapel. Crack me the crowns of the French knaves,[8] a pox on them! Crack them! Fight, by the Lord of Ludgate! Fight, my fine boy!

FIRK [*giving money*] Here, Ralph, here's three twopences. Two, carry into France; the third shall wash our souls° at parting, for sorrow is dry. For my sake, firk the *baisez-monculs*.[9] *i.e., buy us drinks*

HODGE [*giving money*] Ralph, I am heavy° at parting; but here's a shilling for thee. God send thee to° cram thy slops[1] with French crowns° and thy enemies' bellies with bullets! *sad* / *grant that you may* / *coins; bald heads*

RALPH I thank you, master, and I thank you all.—
Now, gentle wife, my loving lovely Jane,
Rich men at parting give their wives rich gifts,
Jewels and rings, to grace their lily hands.
Thou know'st our trade makes rings for women's heels.[2]
[*Giving her shoes*] Here, take this pair of shoes cut out by Hodge,
Stitched by my fellow Firk, seamed by myself,
Made up and pinked° with letters for thy name. *pricked, decorated*
Wear them, my dear Jane, for thy husband's sake,
And every morning, when thou pull'st them on,
Remember me, and pray for my return.
Make much of them, for I have made them so
That I can know them from a thousand mo.° *more, others*

Sound drum. Enter Lord Mayor [*Oatley*], *Lincoln, Lacy, Askew, Dodger, and soldiers. They pass over° the stage. Ralph falls in amongst them.* *cross over and exit*

Firk and the rest cry "Farewell!" etc., and so exeunt.

[Scene 2]

Enter Rose alone, making a garland.

ROSE Here sit thou° down upon this flow'ry bank, *(said to herself)*
And make a garland for thy Lacy's head.
These pinks, these roses, and these violets,
These blushing gillyflowers,° these marigolds, *carnations*
The fair embroidery of his coronet,° *this wreath (for Lacy)*
Carry not half such beauty in their cheeks
As the sweet count'nance of my Lacy doth.
Oh, my most unkind father! O my stars!
Why loured° you so at my nativity, *frowned*
To make me love, yet live robbed of my love?
Here as a thief am I imprisonèd,
For my dear Lacy's sake, within those walls
Which by my father's cost were builded up
For better purposes. Here must I languish
For him that doth as much lament, I know,
Mine absence as for him I pine in woe.

8. Eyre puns on cracked heads, cracked coins (which were worthless as currency), and bald heads produced by syphilis, "the French disease."
9. Sock it to the "kiss-my-asses"—i.e., the French.
1. Baggy breeches.
2. Shoemakers enclose women's heels in leather, as if fitting them with a ring.
Scene 2. Oatley's house at Old Ford.

Enter Sibyl.

SIBYL Good morrow, young mistress. I am sure you make that garland for me, against° I shall be Lady° of the Harvest.

anticipating when / Queen

ROSE Sibyl, what news at London?

SIBYL None but good: my Lord Mayor your father, and Master Philpot your uncle, and Master Scott your cousin, and Mistress Frigbottom, by° Doctors' Commons, do all, by my troth,° send you most hearty commendations.

living next to / *faith*

ROSE Did Lacy send kind greetings to his love?

SIBYL Oh, yes, out of cry.° By my troth, I scant knew him! Here 'a° wore a scarf, and here[1] a scarf, here a bunch of feathers, and here precious stones and jewels, and a pair of garters—oh, monstrous!—like one of our yellow silk curtains at home here in Old Ford° house, here in Master Bellymount's chamber. I stood at our door in Cornhill,° looked at him, he at me indeed; spake to him, but he not to me, not a word. "Marry gup,"° thought I, "with a wanion!"° He passed by me as proud—"Marry,° foh, are you grown humorous?"° thought I—and so shut the door, and in I came.

limitlessly / *he* / *village near London* / *a London thoroughfare* / *Hoity-toity / vengeance* / *By Mary / moody*

ROSE Oh, Sibyl, how dost thou my Lacy wrong!
My Rowland is as gentle as a lamb;
No dove was ever half so mild as he.

SIBYL Mild? Yea, as a bushel of stamped crabs.° He looked upon me as sour as verjuice.° "Go thy ways," thought I, "thou mayst be much in my gaskins, but nothing in my netherstocks."[2] This is your fault, mistress, to love him that loves not you. He thinks scorn° to do as he's done to; but if I were as you, I'd cry, "Go by, Jeronimo, go by!"[3]
I'd set mine old debts against my new driblets,
And the hare's foot against the goose giblets;[4]
For if ever I sigh° when sleep I should take,
Pray God I may lose my maidenhead when I wake.

crushed crab apples / *juice of unripe fruit* / *He disdains* / *sigh for love*

ROSE Will my love leave me, then, and go to France?

SIBYL I know not that, but I am sure I see° him stalk before the soldiers. By my troth, he is a proper° man; but he° is proper that proper doth.[5] Let him go snick up,° young mistress.

saw / *good-looking / (a person)* / *go hang*

ROSE Get thee to London, and learn perfectly
Whether my Lacy go to France or no.
Do this, and I will give thee for thy pains
My cambric° apron and my Romish° gloves,
My purple stockings, and a stomacher.°
Say, wilt thou do this, Sibyl, for my sake?

fine linen / Italian / *upper garment, vest*

SIBYL Will I, quotha?° At whose suit?° By my troth, yes, I'll go. A cambric apron, gloves, a pair of purple stockings, and a stomacher? I'll sweat in purple,[6] mistress, for you; I'll take anything that comes i'God's name.° Oh, rich! A cambric

forsooth / Need you ask? / *free*

1. The repeated "here" refers to various parts of Lacy's fancy outfit.
2. I.e., you may be an acquaintance of mine, but not a close friend. (Gaskins are a kind of breeches or hose; netherstocks are stockings, tighter than breeches.)
3. Based on a famous phrase from Kyd's *The Spanish Tragedy* (3.12.31), connoting impatient dismissal.
4. By these proverbial expressions, Sibyl offers her advice to Rose to weigh the possible advantages of loving Lacy against the manifest disadvantages. Driblets are small debts.
5. Handsome is as handsome does; judge by actions, not by appearances.
6. I.e., I'll suffer the discomfort of wearing heavy finery.

apron! Faith, then, have at uptails all.° I'll go jiggy-joggy to *i.e., here goes!*
London and be here in a trice, young mistress.

ROSE Do so, good Sibyl. *Exit [Sibyl].*
Meantime, wretched I
Will sit and sigh for his lost company. *Exit.*

[Scene 3]

Enter Rowland Lacy like a Dutch shoemaker.

LACY How many shapes have gods and kings devised,
Thereby to compass° their desirèd loves? *encompass*
It is no shame for Rowland Lacy, then,
To clothe his cunning with the Gentle Craft,
That, thus disguised, I may unknown possess
The only happy presence of my Rose.
For her have I forsook my charge in France,
Incurred the King's displeasure, and stirred up
Rough hatred in mine uncle Lincoln's breast.
O Love, how powerful art thou, that canst change
High birth to bareness,° and a noble mind *threadbare poverty*
To the mean° semblance of a shoemaker! *lowly*
But thus it must be; for her cruel father,
Hating the single union° of our souls, *union of two in one*
Hath secretly conveyed my Rose from London
To bar me of her presence; but I trust
Fortune and this disguise will further me
Once more to view her beauty, gain her sight.
Here in Tower Street, with Eyre the shoemaker,
Mean I awhile to work. I know the trade;
I learned it when I was in Wittenberg.
Then cheer thy drooping sprites;° be not dismayed; *spirits*
Thou canst not want. Do Fortune what she can,
The Gentle Craft is living for a man. *Exit.*

[Scene 4]

Enter Eyre, making himself ready.

EYRE Where be these boys, these girls, these drabs,° these *sluts*
scoundrels? They wallow in the fat brewis° of my bounty and *meat broth*
lick up the crumbs of my table, yet will not rise to see my
walks cleansed.° [*Calling*] Come out, you powder-beef *my pavement swept*
queans.° What, Nan! What, Madge Mumblecrust! Come *salted-beef whores*
out, you fat midriff-swag-belly° whores, and sweep me these *fat-bellied*
kennels,° that the noisome° stench offend not the nose of *gutters / noxious*
my neighbors. What, Firk, I say! What, Hodge! Open my
shop windows. What, Firk, I say!

Enter Firk.

FIRK Oh, master, is't you that speak bandog° and bedlam° this *like a mad dog / madly*
morning? I was in a dream, and mused what madman was

Scene 3. Near Eyre's shop in Tower Street (see line 19).

Scene 4. In front of Eyre's shop.

got into the street so early. Have you drunk this morning, that your throat is so clear?

EYRE Ah, well said, Firk, well said, Firk. To work, my fine knave, to work! Wash thy face, and thou'lt be more blessed.

FIRK Let them wash my face that will eat it. Good master, send for a souse-wife[1] if you'll have my face cleaner.

Enter Hodge.

EYRE Away, sloven! Avaunt,° scoundrel!—Good morrow, *Begone*
Hodge; good morrow, my fine foreman.

HODGE Oh, master, good morrow. You're an early stirrer. Here's a fair morning! Good morrow, Firk. I could have slept
this hour. Here's a brave° day towards!° *fine / at hand*

EYRE Oh, haste to work, my fine foreman, haste to work.

FIRK Master, I am dry as dust to hear my fellow Roger talk
of fair weather. Let us pray for good leather, and let clowns° *peasants*
and plowboys and those that work in the fields pray for brave days. We work in a dry shop; what care I if it rain?

Enter Eyre's wife [Margery].

EYRE How now, Dame Margery, can you see to rise?[2] Trip
and go;° call up the drabs your maids. *Trip along*

MARGERY See to rise? I hope 'tis time enough; 'tis early
enough for any woman to be seen abroad. I marvel° how *wonder*
many wives in Tower Street are up so soon? God's me,° 'tis *God's my life (an oath)*
not noon! Here's a yawling.° *wawling, yowling*

EYRE Peace, Margery, peace! Where's Cecily Bumtrinket,
your maid? She has a privy° fault: she farts in her sleep. Call *secret (with pun)*
the quean up. If my men want° shoe thread, I'll swinge° her *lack / thrash*
in a stirrup.° *with a strap*

FIRK Yet that's but a dry° beating. Here's still a sign of *bloodless; thirsty*
drought.

Enter Lacy [disguised as Hans], singing.

LACY [*as Hans*] *Der was een bore van Gelderland,*
Frolick si byen;
He was als dronck he could niet stand,
Upsee al sie byen.
Tap eens de canneken;
Drincke, schoene mannekin.[3]

FIRK Master, for my life, yonder's a brother of the Gentle Craft! If he bear not Saint Hugh's bones,[4] I'll forfeit my
bones. He's some uplandish° workman. Hire him, good mas- *foreign*
ter, that I may learn some gibble-gabble.° 'Twill make us *senseless chatter*
work the faster.

EYRE Peace, Firk. A hard world; let him pass, let him vanish. We have journeymen enough. Peace, my fine Firk.

1. A woman who pickled and sold various parts of the pig (feet, ears, etc.) and other animals for eating.

2. I.e., is it light enough for you to make your way out of bed? (Said sarcastically.)

3. There was a boor (peasant) from Gelderland; jolly they be. He was so drunk he couldn't stand; drunk they all be. Fill the cannikin; drink, my fine little man. (Lacy, disguised as Hans, speaks in a kind of stage German or Dutch dialect aimed at comic effect.)

4. According to legend, and as recorded by Thomas Deloney in *The Gentle Craft*, a certain Sir Hugh fell in love with a young woman named Winifred, suffered martyrdom with her (thus becoming a saint), and thereupon left his bones "to all the kind yeomen of the Gentle Craft," i.e., the shoemakers, who, wishing to make profitable use of the bones, converted them into shoemaking tools.

MARGERY Nay, nay, you're best follow your man's counsel.° You shall see what will come on't.° We have not men enough but we must entertain° every butter-box°—but let that pass.

(said ironically) / of it / hire / i.e., Dutchman

HODGE Dame, 'fore God, if my master follow your counsel, he'll consume little beef.° He shall be glad of men, an° he can catch them.

starve, not prosper / if

FIRK Ay, that he shall.

HODGE 'Fore God, a proper man, and I warrant a fine workman.
Master, farewell; dame, adieu.
If such a man as he cannot find work, Hodge is not for you.

Offer° to go.

Make as if, start

EYRE Stay, my fine Hodge!

FIRK Faith,° an your foreman go, dame, you must take a journey to seek a new journeyman. If Roger remove,° Firk follows. If Saint Hugh's bones shall not be set awork, I may prick mine awl in the walls° and go play. Fare ye well, master. God b'wi'you, dame. [*He starts to go.*]

In faith / leaves / i.e., put up my tools

EYRE Tarry, my fine Hodge, my brisk foreman! Stay, Firk! [*To Margery*] Peace, pudding° broth! By the Lord of Ludgate, I love my men as my life. Peace, you gallimaufry!°—Hodge, if he want work I'll hire him. One of you, to° him.—Stay, he comes to us.

fatty sausage / hodgepodge, hash / go to

LACY [*as Hans, approaching them*] *Goeden dach, meester, end you, vro, auch.*[5]

FIRK 'Nails,° if I should speak after° him without drinking, I should choke.—And you, friend Auch,° are you of the Gentle Craft?

By God's nails / like / Also; oak

LACY [*as Hans*] *Yaw yaw, ik bin den skomawker.*[6]

FIRK "*Den skomaker*," quotha!° And hark you, skomaker, have you all your tools: a good rubbing pin, a good stopper,° a good dresser,° your four sorts of awls, and your two balls of wax, your paring knife, your hand- and thumb-leathers, and good Saint Hugh's bones to smooth up your work?

says he, forsooth / crevice filler / trimmer

LACY [*as Hans*] *Yaw, yaw, be niet vorveard, ick hab all de dingen voour mack skoes groot and klene.*[7]

FIRK Ha, ha! Good master, hire him. He'll make me laugh so that I shall work more in mirth than I can in earnest.

EYRE [*to "Hans"*] Hear ye, friend: have ye any skill in the mystery° of cordwainers?

craft

LACY [*as Hans*] *Ick weet niet wat yow seg; ick verstaw you niet.*[8]

FIRK Why thus, man: [*He demonstrates the actions of a shoemaker.*] "*Ick verste yow niet,*" quotha!

LACY [*as Hans*] *Yaw, yaw, yaw, ick can dat well doen.*[9]

FIRK "*Yaw, yaw*"! He speaks yawing[1] like a jackdaw that gapes to be fed with cheese curds. Oh, he'll give a villainous pull at a can of double° beer, but Hodge and I have the vantage; we must drink first, because we are the eldest° journeymen.

extra strength / i.e., with most seniority

EYRE [*to "Hans"*] What is thy name?

5. Good day, master, and you, goodwife, also.
6. Yes, yes, I am a shoemaker.
7. Yes, yes, be not afraid. I have all the things for making shoes, great and small.
8. I know not what you say; I understand you not.
9. Yes, yes, yes, I can do that well.
1. With mouth agape. (Firk puns on Lacy's "*yaw.*")

LACY [*as Hans*] Hans. Hans Meulter.

EYRE Give me thy hand; thou'rt welcome. Hodge, entertain him. Firk, bid him welcome. Come, Hans. Run, wife; bid your maids, your trullibubs,[2] make ready my fine men's breakfasts. To him, Hodge.

HODGE Hans, thou'rt welcome. Use thyself friendly,° for we are good fellows; if not, thou shalt be fought with, wert thou bigger than a giant.

Be friendly

FIRK Yea, and drunk with, wert thou Gargantua.° My master keeps no cowards, I tell thee. [*Calling*] Ho, boy! Bring him an heel-block.[3] Here's a new journeyman.

Gargantuan in appetite

Enter boy.

LACY [*as Hans*] *Oh, ich verstaw yow. Ich moet een halve dossen cans betaelen.* [*Giving money*] Here, boy, *nempt dis skilling; tap eens freelick.*[4]

EYRE Quick, snippersnapper,° away! *Exit boy.*
Firk, scour thy throat; thou shalt wash it with Castilian° liquor.

whippersnapper
Spanish; Parnassan

Enter boy [*with beer*].

Come, my last of the fives,[5] give me a can. [*He takes a can and offers drinks around.*] Have to thee,° Hans! Here, Hodge; here, Firk. Drink, you mad Greeks,[6] and work like true Trojans, and pray for Simon Eyre the shoemaker. Here, Hans; and thou'rt welcome.

Here's to you

FIRK [*to Margery*] Lo, dame, you would have lost a good fellow that will teach us to laugh. This beer came hopping in well.

MARGERY Simon, it is almost seven.

EYRE Is't so, Dame Clapperdudgeon?[7] Is't seven o'clock and my men's breakfast not ready? Trip and go, you soused conger.° Away! Come, you mad Hyperboreans.[8] Follow me, Hodge; follow me, Hans; come after, my fine Firk. To work! To work awhile, and then to breakfast. *Exit.*

pickled eel

FIRK Soft! Yaw, yaw, good Hans. Though my master have no more wit but to call you afore me, I am not so foolish to go behind you, I being the elder° journeyman. *Exeunt.*

i.e., with more seniority

[Scene 5]

Holloing within. Enter Warner and Hammon, like hunters.

HAMMON Cousin, beat every brake.° The game's° not far.
This way with wingèd feet he fled from death,
Whilst the pursuing hounds, scenting his steps,

thicket / quarry is

2. Animal entrails; hence, fat persons. (Here a term of friendly abuse.)
3. A block used by shoemakers in working on the heel; also, seemingly, a colloquial way of requesting a round of drinks.
4. Oh, I understand you. I must pay for a half dozen cans. Here, boy, take this shilling; fill up once all around.
5. I.e., my little man. (Referring to a shoe "last," or form, used here for a small, size five foot, or perhaps to the "pinkie," or fifth finger.)
6. I.e., merry companions. (Anti-Greek bias in medieval accounts of the Trojan War equated the Greeks with hedonistic pleasure-seeking. In his next phrase, Eyre antithetically equates the Trojans with industriousness.)
7. Eyre implies with this name that Margery's tongue clatters incessantly, like the lid of wooden dishes clapped by beggars to gain attention from passersby.
8. Dwellers beyond Boreas (god of the north wind), legendarily peaceful and happy.
Scene 5. The meadows near Old Ford.

Find out his highway to destruction.
Besides, the miller's boy told me even now
He saw him take soil,[1] and he holloed him,
Affirming him so embossed° — *blown and exhausted*
That long he could not hold.° — *hold out*

WARNER If it be so,
'Tis best we trace° these meadows by Old Ford. — *traverse in pursuit*

A noise of hunters within.

Enter a Boy.

HAMMON How now, boy, where's the deer? Speak. Saw'st thou him?

BOY Oh, yea, I saw him leap through a hedge, and then over a ditch, then at my Lord Mayor's pale.° Over he skipped me° and in he went me,° and "Holla!" the hunters cried, and "There, boy, there, boy"; but there he is, i'mine honesty. — *fence / skipped*; *went*

HAMMON Boy, god-a-mercy.°—Cousin, let's away. — *thanks*
I hope we shall find better sport° today. *Exeunt.* — *(in courtship)*

[Scene 6]

Hunting within.° Enter Rose and Sibyl. — *Hunting sounds offstage*

ROSE Why, Sibyl, wilt thou prove° a forester? — *turn out to be*

SIBYL Upon some,° no! Forester, go by.[1] No, faith, mistress, the deer came running into the barn through the orchard, and over the pale. I wot° well I looked as pale[2] as a new cheese to see him. But "Whip!"° says Goodman Pinclose;° up with his flail, and our Nick with a prong,° and down he° fell, and they upon him, and I upon them. By my troth, we had such sport, and in the end we ended him; his throat we cut, flayed him, unhorned him, and my Lord Mayor shall eat of him anon° when he comes. *Horns sound within.* — *i.e., Upon my word*; *know*; *"Quick!" / Farmer Pinfold*; *pitchfork / (the deer)*; *shortly*

ROSE Hark, hark! The hunters come. You're best° take heed. — *You'd better*
They'll have a saying to you[3] for this deed.

Enter Hammon, Warner, huntsmen, and Boy.

HAMMON God save you, fair ladies.

SIBYL "Ladies"? Oh, gross![4]

WARNER Came not a buck this way?

ROSE No, but two does.° — *i.e., Rose and Sibyl*

HAMMON And which way went they? Faith, we'll hunt at those.

SIBYL At those? Upon some, no. When, can you tell?[5]

WARNER Upon some, ay![6]

SIBYL Good Lord!

WARNER 'Wounds,° then farewell. — *By God's wounds*

HAMMON Boy, which way went he?° — *(the deer)*

1. Take to water or a muddy marsh (as a way of throwing off the hounds by concealing its scent).

Scene 6. Old Ford.

1. Be on your way. (Said in apostrophe to the forester, who is not present.)
2. Punning on "pale" meaning "fence."
3. They'll have something to say to you (to rebuke you).
4. Sibyl is scornful of such flattery; she is no lady, even if Rose is.
5. Sibyl's colloquial sarcasm means, more or less, "You mean to pretend you're hunting deer? Upon my word, no. Tell me another one."
6. Warner insists that they too are hunting the two "does" that Rose mentioned in line 14.

BOY This way, sir, he ran.
HAMMON This way he ran, indeed. Fair Mistress Rose,
Our game was lately in your orchard seen.
WARNER Can you advise which way he took his flight?
SIBYL Follow your nose; his horns° will guide you right. *(a cuckold joke)*
WARNER Thou'rt a mad° wench. *irrepressible*
SIBYL Oh, rich!
ROSE Trust me,° not I. *Believe me*
It is not like° the wild forest deer *likely (that)*
Would come so near to places of resort.° *human habitation*
You are deceived; he fled some other way.
WARNER Which way, my sugar candy? Can you show?
SIBYL Come up, good honey-sops, upon some, no.[7]
ROSE Why do you stay, and not pursue your game?
SIBYL I'll hold° my life their hunting nags be lame. *bet*
HAMMON A deer more dear is found within this place.
ROSE But not the deer, sir, which you had in chase.
HAMMON I chased the deer, but this dear chaseth me.° *holds me in thrall*
ROSE The strangest hunting that ever I see!° *saw*
But where's your park?° *She offers° to go away.* *hunting ground / starts*
HAMMON 'Tis here. Oh, stay!
ROSE Impale me,[8] and then I will not stray.
WARNER [*to Sibyl*] They° wrangle, wench. We are more kind° than they. *(Hammon and Rose)* *loving*
SIBYL What kind of hart is that, dear heart, you seek?
WARNER A heart, dear heart.
SIBYL Who ever saw the like?
ROSE [*to Hammon*] To lose your hart: is't possible you can?
HAMMON My heart is lost.
ROSE Alack, good gentleman!
HAMMON This poor lost heart would I wish you might find.[9]
ROSE You by such luck might prove your hart a hind.[1]
HAMMON Why, luck had horns,[2] so have I heard some say.
ROSE Now God, an't be his will, send luck into your way!

Enter Lord Mayor [Oatley] and servants.

OATLEY What, Master Hammon! Welcome to Old Ford.
SIBYL [*to Warner*] God's pitikins,° hands off, sir![3] Here's my lord. *God's pity (an oath)*
OATLEY I hear you had ill luck, and lost your game.
HAMMON 'Tis true, my lord.
OATLEY I am sorry for the same.
[*Indicating Warner*] What gentleman is this?
HAMMON My brother-in-law.
OATLEY You're welcome both. Sith° fortune offers you *Since*
Into my hands, you shall not part from hence
Until you have refreshed your wearied limbs.—

7. I.e., Forget it, sugar daddy, upon my word, no. (Honey-sops are bread sops soaked in honey—a retort to "sugar candy.")
8. (1) Enclose me in a "pale," or enclosure. (Suggesting an embrace.) (2) Transfix me on a pointed stake. (With erotic suggestion.)
9. I wish you might rescue (by reciprocating affection) my poor lost heart.
1. If I were to find your heart within me, your "hart" (male deer) might prove to be a "hind" (a female deer). ("Hind" also suggests "servant," "rustic," or "boor.") This is a put-down.
2. Fortune (with its cornucopia) was horned like a male deer, not a "hind." (But this has unfortunate connotations of cuckold's horns, which are the point of Rose's pert riposte in the next line; she wishes he may become a cuckold.)
3. Warner is evidently attempting to embrace Sibyl.

Go, Sibyl, cover the board.°—You shall be guest *set the table*
To no good cheer, but even a hunter's feast.° *simple, rustic fare*
HAMMON I thank Your Lordship. [*Aside to Warner*] Cousin,° on my life, *Kinsman*
For our lost venison, I shall find a wife.
OATLEY In, gentlemen. I'll not be absent long.

Exeunt [*except for Oatley*].

This Hammon is a proper° gentleman, *true, real*
A citizen by birth, fairly allied.° *with good connections*
How fit an husband were he for my girl!
Well, I will in, and do the best I can
To match my daughter to this gentleman. *Exit.*

[Scene 7]

Enter Lacy [*as Hans*], *Skipper, Hodge, and Firk.*

SKIPPER *Ick sal yow wat seggen, Hans: dis skip dat comen from Candy is all fol, by Got's sacrament, van sugar, civet, almonds, cambric, end alle dingen—towsand towsand ding. Nempt it, Hans, nempt it vor your meester. Daer be de bils van laden. Yowr meester Simon Eyre sal hae good copen. Wat seggen yow, Hans?*[1]

FIRK *Wat seggen de reggen de copen, slopen*°—laugh, Hodge, laugh! *(nonsense mockery)*

LACY [*as Hans*] *Mine liever broder Firk, bringt Meester Eyre tot den signe van Swannekin. Daer sal yow finde dis skipper end me. Wat seggen yow, broder Firk? Do't, Hodge!*[2] Come, Skipper! *Exeunt* [*Lacy and the Skipper*].

FIRK Bring him, quoth you? Here's no knavery,° to bring my master to buy a ship worth the lading of° two or three hundred thousand pounds! Alas, that's nothing—a trifle, a bauble, Hodge. *(said ironically)* *with a cargo worth*

HODGE The truth is, Firk, that the merchant owner of the ship dares not show his head, and therefore this skipper that deals for him, for the love he bears to Hans, offers my master Eyre a bargain in the commodities.[3] He shall have a reasonable day of payment.° He may sell the wares by that time, and be an huge gainer himself. *time to raise the money*

FIRK Yea, but can my fellow Hans lend my master twenty porpentines° as an earnest-penny?° *porcupines / down payment*

HODGE "Portagues,"° thou wouldst say. Here they be, Firk. [*He shows money.*] Hark, they jingle in my pocket like Saint Mary Overy's° bells. *gold coins* *a church in Southwark*

Enter Eyre and his wife [*Margery, and a boy*].

FIRK Mum. Here comes my dame and my master. She'll scold, on my life, for loitering this Monday, but all's one;° let them all say what they can, Monday's our holiday. *no matter*

Scene 7. London. Eyre's shop.
1. I shall tell you what, Hans: this ship that came from Candy (Crete) is all full, by God's sacrament, of sugar, civet (used in perfumes), almonds, cambric (fine white linen), and all things—a thousand thousand things. Take it, Hans, take it for your master. There be the bills of lading (cargo). Your master Simon Eyre shall have a good bargain. What say you, Hans?
2. My dear brother Firk, bring Master Eyre to the sign of the Swan (a pub). There shall you find this skipper and me. What say you, brother Firk? Do it, Hodge!
3. Hodge hints that the owner is in trouble with the authorities in some way and is therefore interested in a quick sale.

MARGERY [*to Firk*] You sing, Sir Sauce,° but I beshrew° your heart,
I fear for this your singing we shall smart.[4] *Sir Impudence / curse*

FIRK Smart for me, dame? Why, dame, why?

HODGE Master, I hope you'll not suffer my dame to take down[5] your journeymen.

FIRK If she take me down, I'll take her up,° yea, and take her down too, a buttonhole lower. *take her up short*

EYRE Peace, Firk. Not I,° Hodge. By the life of Pharaoh, by the Lord of Ludgate, by this beard—every hair whereof I value at a king's ransom—she shall not meddle with you. [*To Margery*] Peace, you bombast-cotton-candle quean! Away, Queen of Clubs![6] Quarrel not with me and my men, with me and my fine Firk. I'll firk[7] you if you do. *I won't allow it*

MARGERY Yea, yea, man, you may use me as you please—but let that pass.

EYRE Let it pass, let it vanish away. Peace! Am I not Simon Eyre? Are not these my brave men, brave shoemakers, all gentlemen of the Gentle Craft? Prince am I none, yet am I nobly born, as being the sole° son of a shoemaker. Away, rubbish! Vanish, melt, melt like kitchen-stuff!° *(punning on sole of shoe)* *kitchen refuse*

MARGERY Yea, yea, 'tis well. I must be called rubbish, kitchen-stuff, for a sort° of knaves. *pack, bunch*

FIRK Nay, dame, you shall not weep and wail in woe for me.—Master, I'll stay no longer. Here's a venentory° of my shop tools. Adieu, master. Hodge, farewell. [*He starts to go.*] *i.e., inventory*

HODGE Nay, stay, Firk, thou shalt not go alone.

MARGERY I pray, let them go. There be more maids than Malkin,[8] more men than Hodge, and more fools than Firk.

FIRK Fools? 'Nails, if I tarry now, I would my guts might be turned to shoe thread.

HODGE And if I stay, I pray God I may be turned to a Turk and set in Finsbury for boys to shoot at.[9] Come, Firk.

EYRE Stay, my fine knaves, you arms of my trade, you pillars of my profession. What, shall a tittle-tattle's words make you forsake Simon Eyre? [*To Margery*] Avaunt, kitchen-stuff! Rip,° you brown-bread tannikin,[1] out of my sight! Move° me not. Have not I ta'en you from selling tripes° in Eastcheap, and set you in my shop, and made you hail-fellow° with Simon Eyre the shoemaker? And now do you deal thus with my journeymen? Look, you powder-beef quean, on the face of Hodge. Here's a face for a lord. *Be off with you / Anger* *entrails* *boon companion*

FIRK And here's a face for any lady in Christendom.[2]

4. In response to Firk's prediction that she will scold, Margery obliges with a satirical rhyming couplet characterizing Firk as one whose insolent singsong will bring grief to them all.
5. Rebuke—but with bawdy implications pursued in the following exchanges, in "take her down" (lines 36–37), "buttonhole" (line 37), "meddle" (line 40), "firk" (line 43), "use" (line 44), etc.
6. Another jovial insult. Margery is the queen, or perhaps "quean" (i.e., whore), of the apprentices, whose rallying cry when they were aroused was "Clubs!" meaning "Everyone grab your clubs!" Cf. 18.31–32.
7. Trounce; but with a suggestion, sometimes found elsewhere in "firk," of sexual assault. See note 5 above.
8. Malkin, or Mawkin, was a common girl's name. The expression is proverbial.
9. Figures of Turks were used as targets for archery practice in Finsbury Fields, a favorite training ground. The Turks were much feared and hated for their invasion of Europe.
1. Coarse Dutch bread—here an abusive epithet for Margery.
2. Firk scoffs ironically at Margery's affectation of fashionable looks.

EYRE [*to Margery*] Rip, you chitterling,° avaunt!—Boy, bid the tapster of the Boar's Head fill me a dozen cans of beer for my journeymen. — *pig's intestines*

FIRK A dozen cans? Oh, brave,° Hodge! Now I'll stay. — *excellent*

EYRE [*aside to the boy*] An° the knave fills any more than two, he pays for them. [*Exit boy.*] — *If*
[*Aloud*] A dozen cans of beer for my journeymen!

[*Enter the boy with two cans, and exit.*]

Here, you mad Mesopotamians, wash your livers with this liquor. Where be the odd ten?[3] [*To Margery*] No more, Madge, no more. [*To them*] Well said!° Drink and to work. [*They set to work.*] What work dost thou, Hodge? What work? — *Well done!*

HODGE I am a-making a pair of shoes for my Lord Mayor's daughter, Mistress Rose.

FIRK And I a pair of shoes for Sibyl, my lord's maid. I deal° with her. — *(with sexual hint)*

EYRE Sibyl? Fie, defile not thy fine, workmanly fingers with the feet of kitchen-stuff and basting ladles.° Ladies of the court, fine ladies, my lads, commit their feet to our appareling. Put gross work to Hans. Yerk and seam,° yerk and seam. — *i.e., servant maids*; *Sew away*

FIRK For yerking and seaming let me alone, an I come to't.[4]

HODGE Well, master, all this is from the bias.° Do you remember the ship my fellow Hans told you of? The skipper and he are both drinking at the Swan.° [*Offering money*] Here be the portagues to give earnest.° If you go through with it, you cannot choose but be° a lord at least. — *off the point (see 1.85)*; *a pub*; *make a down payment*; *can't help being*

FIRK [*to Margery*] Nay, dame, if my master prove not a lord, and you a lady, hang me.

MARGERY Yea, like° enough, if you may loiter and tipple thus. — *likely (ironic)*

FIRK Tipple, dame? No, we have been bargaining with Skellum-Skanderbag-can-you-Dutch-spreaken° for a ship of silk cypress,° laden with sugar candy. — *German-speaking skipper*; *a costly fabric*

EYRE Peace, Firk. Silence, tittle-tattle.° Hodge, I'll go through with it. Here's a seal ring,[5] and I have sent for a guarded° gown and a damask cassock. — *i.e., Margery*; *ornamented, trimmed*

Enter the boy with a velvet coat and an alderman's gown.

See where it comes. Look here, Maggy. (*Eyre puts it on.*) Help me, Firk. Apparel me, Hodge. Silk and satin, you mad Philistines,[6] silk and satin.

FIRK Ha, ha! My master will be as proud as a dog in a doublet,° all in beaten[7] damask and velvet. — *men's jacket*

EYRE Softly, Firk, for rearing of° the nap and wearing thread- — *so as not to rear up*

3. Eyre makes a show of asking for the extra beers that he has indicated privately he will not pay for. "Mesopotamians" (line 80) has a resonance like "Greeks" at 4.121, suggesting wild pleasure-seeking.

4. Leave it to me to excel at sewing, if I'm put to the test. (Firk also hints at sexual performance.)

5. A ring bearing a seal with which to affix impressions in wax in order to authenticate documents.

6. Another jolly epithet signifying merriment, like "Greeks" (4.121) and "Mesopotamians" (line 80).

7. Embroidered.

bare my garments. How dost thou like me, Firk? How do I look, my fine Hodge?

HODGE Why, now you look like yourself, master. I warrant you there's few in the city but will give you the wall,° and come upon you° with the "Right Worshipful."

i.e., yield precedence
address you

FIRK 'Nails, my master looks like a threadbare cloak new turned and dressed.[8] Lord, lord, to see what good raiment doth! Dame, dame, are you not enamored?

EYRE How say'st thou, Maggy, am I not brisk?° Am I not fine?

spruce

MARGERY Fine? By my troth, sweetheart, very fine. By my troth, I never liked thee so well in my life, sweetheart. But let that pass. I warrant there be many women in the city have not such handsome husbands, but only for[9] their apparel; but let that pass too.

Enter [Lacy as] Hans and [the] Skipper.

LACY [*as Hans*] *Godden day, meester; dis be de skipper dat heb de skip van marchandice. De commodity ben good. Nempt it, meester, nempt it.*[1]

EYRE God-a-mercy,° Hans. Welcome, Skipper. Where lies this ship of merchandise?

Thank you

SKIPPER *De skip ben in revere: dor be van sugar, civet, almonds, cambric, and a towsand towsand tings, Got's sacrament! Nempt it, meester; yow sal heb good copen.*[2]

FIRK To him, master. O sweet master! O sweet wares! Prunes, almonds, sugar candy, carrot-roots,° turnips—Oh, brave fatting meat!° Let not a man buy a nutmeg but yourself.

(for "cambric," 135)
fattening food

EYRE Peace, Firk. Come, Skipper, I'll go aboard with you. Hans, have you made him° drink?

given him

SKIPPER *Yaw, yaw, ick heb veale gedrunck.*[3]

EYRE Come, Hans, follow me. Skipper, thou shalt have my countenance° in the city.

patronage, protection

Exeunt [Eyre, the Skipper, and Lacy as Hans].

FIRK "*Yaw, heb veale gedrunck*," quotha!° They may well be called butter-boxes when they drink fat veal, and thick° beer too. But come, dame, I hope you'll chide us no more.

says he, indeed
strong

MARGERY No, faith, Firk. No, perdie,° Hodge. I do feel honor creep upon me, and, which is more, a certain rising in my flesh[4]—but let that pass.

by God, indeed

FIRK Rising in your flesh do you feel, say you? Ay, you may be with child; but why should not my master feel a rising in his flesh, having a gown and a gold ring on? But you are such a shrew, you'll soon pull him down.[5]

MARGERY Ha, ha! Prithee, peace, thou mak'st My Worship°

me, as I am now titled

8. Like an old cloak made like new by reversing the material and adorning it with decoration.
9. (1) Except only in; (2) if only in. The latter meaning, perhaps unintended, is not very complimentary.
1. Good day, master; this is the skipper that has the ship with merchandise. The commodity is good. Take it, master, take it.
2. The ship is in the river: there are sugar, civet, almonds, cambric, and a thousand thousand things, by God's sacrament! Take it, master; you shall have a good bargain.
3. Yes, yes, I have drunk much.
4. I.e., rising social distinction. (But with unintended bawdy meaning; Firk comically picks up on this sense in the next speech.)
5. (1) Beat him down with your shrewishness; (2) defeat his success in his career; (3) take him down sexually.

laugh—but let that pass. Come, I'll go in. Hodge, prithee go before me. Firk, follow me.

FIRK Firk doth follow. Hodge, pass out in state!° *Exeunt.* *exit ceremoniously*

[Scene 8]

Enter Lincoln and Dodger.

LINCOLN How now, good Dodger, what's the news in France?
DODGER My lord, upon the eighteen° day of May, *eighteenth*
The French and English were prepared to fight.
Each side with eager fury gave the sign
Of a most hot encounter. Five long hours
Both armies fought together; at the length,
The lot of victory fell on our sides.
Twelve thousand of the Frenchmen that day died,
Four thousand English, and no man of name° *gentlemanly title*
But Captain Hyam and young Ardington.
LINCOLN Two gallant gentlemen, I knew them well.
But, Dodger, prithee tell me, in this fight
How did my cousin Lacy bear himself ?
DODGER My lord, your cousin Lacy was not there.
LINCOLN Not there?
DODGER No, my good lord.
LINCOLN Sure thou mistakest.
I saw him shipped, and a thousand eyes beside
Were witnesses of the farewells which he gave,
When I with weeping eyes bid him adieu.
Dodger, take heed.
DODGER My lord, I am advised° *certain*
That what I spake is true. To prove it so,
His cousin Askew, that supplied° his place, *took*
Sent me for him from France,° that secretly *from France to fetch him*
He might convey himself thither.
LINCOLN Is't even so?
Dares he so carelessely venture his life
Upon the indignation of a king?
Hath he despised my love, and spurned those favors
Which I with prodigal hand poured on his head?
He shall repent his rashness with his soul.
Since of my love he makes no estimate,° *has no regard*
I'll make him wish he had not known my hate.
Thou hast no other news?
DODGER None else, my lord.
LINCOLN None worse I know thou hast. Procure the King[1]
To crown his giddy brows with ample honors,
Send him chief colonel, and all my hope
Thus to be dashed? But 'tis in vain to grieve;
One evil cannot a worse relieve.
Upon my life, I have found out his plot.
That old dog, Love—that fawned upon him so,
Love to that puling° girl, his fair-cheeked Rose, *whining*

Scene 8. Lincoln's place of residence.
1. I.e., I know you couldn't possibly have worse news. To think that I prevailed upon the King.

The Lord Mayor's daughter—hath distracted him,
And in the fire of that love's lunacy
Hath he burnt up himself, consumed his credit,° *reputation and wealth*
Lost the King's love, yea, and I fear, his life,[2]
Only to get a wanton to his° wife. *as his*
Dodger, it is so?

DODGER I fear so, my good lord.

LINCOLN It is so.—Nay, sure it cannot be.
I am at my wits' end. Dodger—

DODGER Yea, my lord?

LINCOLN Thou art acquainted with my nephew's haunts.
[*Giving money*] Spend this gold for thy pains; go seek him out.
Watch at my Lord Mayor's. There if he live,° *If he's staying there*
Dodger, thou shalt be sure to meet with him.
Prithee, be diligent.—Lacy, thy name
Lived once in honor, now dead in shame!—
Be circumspect. *Exit.*

DODGER I warrant° you, my lord. *Exit.* *assure*

[Scene 9]

Enter Lord Mayor [*Oatley*] *and Master Scott.*

OATLEY Good Master Scott, I have been bold with you
To be a witness to a wedding knot
Betwixt young Master Hammon and my daughter.
Oh, stand aside; see where the lovers come.
[*They stand aside.*]

Enter Hammon and Rose [*he holding Rose's hand*].

ROSE Can it be possible you love me so?
No, no; within those eyeballs I espy
Apparent likelihoods of flattery.
Pray now, let go my hand.

HAMMON Sweet Mistress Rose,
Misconstrue not my words, nor misconceive
Of my affection, whose devoted soul
Swears that I love thee dearer than my heart.

ROSE As dear as your own heart? I judge it right:
Men love their hearts best when they're out of sight.[1]

HAMMON I love you, by this hand.

ROSE [*withdrawing her hand*] Yet hands off, now.
If flesh be frail, how weak and frail's your vow?

HAMMON Then by my life I swear.

ROSE Then do not brawl.° *wrangle*
One quarrel loseth wife and life and all.[2]
Is not your meaning thus?

HAMMON In faith, you jest.

ROSE Love loves to sport. Therefore leave love, you're best.[3]

2. As a deserter, Lacy stands to be executed.

Scene 9. London. Oatley's house.

1. I.e., Men are too apt to be infatuated with the idea of being in love rather than with the reality of it. Cf. *Romeo and Juliet*, 2.2.

2. Rose teases Hammon for his hyperbolic oaths; if he were serious about staking his life on his oaths of love (line 16), then one falling-out would mean the end of everything.

3. Love loves playfulness. If you don't like it, you'd better leave off your suit.

OATLEY What, square° they, Master Scott? *quarrel*
SCOTT Sir, never doubt;° *fear*
Lovers are quickly in and quickly out.° *(with a bawdy pun)*
HAMMON Sweet Rose, be not so strange° in fancying me. *distant, standoffish*
Nay, never turn aside; shun not my sight.
I am not grown so fond° to fond° my love *foolish / bestow*
On any that shall quit° it with disdain. *requite, respond to*
If you will love me, so;° if not, farewell. *well and good*
OATLEY [*coming forward*] Why, how now, lovers, are you both agreed?
HAMMON Yes, faith, my lord.
OATLEY 'Tis well. Give me your hand.
Give me yours, daughter. [*They hesitate.*]
How now, both pull back?
What means this, girl?
ROSE I mean to live a maid.
HAMMON (*aside*) But not to die one. Pause ere° that be said. *before*
OATLEY [*to Rose*] Will you still cross me? Still be obstinate?
HAMMON Nay, chide her not, my lord, for doing well.
If she can live an happy virgin's life,
'Tis far more blessèd than to be a wife.
ROSE Say, sir, I cannot. I have made a vow;
Whoever be my husband, 'tis not you.
OATLEY Your tongue is quick. But, Master Hammon, know
I bade you welcome to another end.° *purpose*
HAMMON What, would you have me pule,° and pine, and pray, *whine*
With "lovely lady," "mistress of my heart,"
"Pardon your servant," and the rhymer play,° *play the versifier*
Railing on Cupid and his tyrant's dart?
Or shall I undertake some martial spoil,° *exploit, conquest*
Wearing your glove at tourney and at tilt,[4]
And tell how many gallants I unhorsed?
Sweet, will this pleasure you?
ROSE Yea. When wilt begin?
What, love rhymes, man? Fie on that deadly sin!° *(said mockingly)*
OATLEY If you will have her, I'll make her agree.
HAMMON Enforcèd love is worse than hate to me.
[*Aside*] There is a wench keeps shop in the Old Change.° *Royal Exchange*
To her will I. It is not wealth I seek;
I have enough, and will prefer her love
Before the world.—My good Lord Mayor, adieu.
[*Aside*] Old love for me; I have no luck with new. *Exit.*
OATLEY [*to Rose*] Now, mammet,° you have well behaved yourself.° *puppet* *(ironic)*
But you shall curse your coyness, if I live.
[*Calling*] Who's within there?

[*Enter a servant.*]

See you convey your mistress
Straight to th'Old Ford. [*To Rose*] I'll keep you strait° enough. *narrowly confined*
[*To himself*] 'Fore God, I would have sworn the puling girl

4. Wearing your glove in my hat as a love token as I take part in tournaments and jousting.

Would willingly accepted° Hammon's love. *have accepted*
But banish him° my thoughts. [*To Rose*] Go, minion.° In! *banish him from / hussy*
Exit Rose [*with servant*].
Now tell me, Master Scott, would you have thought
That Master Simon Eyre, the shoemaker,
Had been of wealth to buy such merchandise?
SCOTT 'Twas well, my lord, Your Honor and myself
Grew partners with him, for your bills of lading° *receipts for cargo*
Show that Eyre's gains in one commodity
Rise at the least to full three thousand pound,
Besides like gain in other merchandise.
OATLEY Well, he shall spend some of his thousands now,[5]
For I have sent for him to the Guildhall.° *city hall*

Enter Eyre.

See where he comes.—Good morrow, Master Eyre.
EYRE Poor Simon Eyre, my lord, your shoemaker.
OATLEY Well, well, it likes yourself° to term you so.° *pleases you / i.e., "poor"*

Enter Dodger.

Now, Master Dodger, what's the news with you?
DODGER I'd gladly speak in private to Your Honor.
OATLEY You shall, you shall.—Master Eyre and Master Scott,
I have some business with this gentleman.
I pray, let me entreat you to walk before
To the Guildhall; I'll follow presently.
Master Eyre, I hope ere noon to call you sheriff.
EYRE I would not care, my lord, if you might call me King of
Spain.—Come, Master Scott. [*Exeunt Eyre and Scott.*]
OATLEY Now, Master Dodger, what's the news you bring?
DODGER The Earl of Lincoln by me greets Your Lordship
And earnestly requests you, if you can,
Inform him where his nephew Lacy keeps.° *keeps himself*
OATLEY Is not his nephew Lacy now in France?
DODGER No, I assure Your Lordship, but disguised
Lurks here in London.
OATLEY London? Is't even so?
It may be, but, upon my faith and soul,
I know not where he lives, or whether he lives.
So tell my lord of Lincoln. Lurch° in London? *Lurk*
Well, Master Dodger, you perhaps may start him.° *rouse him from his lair*
Be but the means to rid° him into France, *remove*
I'll give you a dozen angels° for your pains, *gold coins*
So much I love His Honor, hate his nephew;
And prithee so inform thy lord from me.
DODGER I take my leave.
OATLEY Farewell, good Master Dodger.
Exit Dodger.
Lacy in London? I dare pawn my life
My daughter knows thereof, and for that cause
Denied young Master Hammon in his love.

5. A Londoner had to pay a lot of money for the privilege of becoming sheriff. Oatley relishes the thought of Eyre's incurring new financial burdens.

Well, I am glad I sent her to Old Ford.
God's Lord,° 'tis late! To Guildhall I must hie; — *Good Lord*
I know my brethren stay° my company. *Exit.* — *wait for*

[Scene 10]

Enter Firk, Eyre's wife [*Margery*], [*Lacy as*] *Hans, and Roger* [*Hodge*].

MARGERY Thou goest too fast for me, Roger.—Oh, Firk!

FIRK Ay, forsooth.

MARGERY I pray thee, run, do you hear? Run to Guildhall, and learn if my husband, Master Eyre, will take that worshipful vocation of Master Sheriff upon him. Hie thee, good Firk.

FIRK Take it? Well, I go. An° he should not take it, Firk swears to forswear° him.—Yes, forsooth, I go to Guildhall. — *If*; *renounce, leave*

MARGERY Nay, when!° Thou art too compendious and tedious. — *i.e., Get a move on!*

FIRK Oh, rare! Your Excellence is full of eloquence.[1] [*Aside*] How like a new cart wheel° my dame speaks! And she looks like an old musty ale bottle going to scalding.° — *i.e., squeakily*; *i.e., washing*

MARGERY Nay, when! Thou wilt make me melancholy.

FIRK God forbid Your Worship should fall into that humor!° I run. *Exit.* — *mood*

MARGERY Let me see now, Roger and Hans.

HODGE Ay, forsooth, dame—mistress, I should say, but the old term so sticks to the roof of my mouth I can hardly lick it off.

MARGERY Even what thou wilt, good Roger. "Dame" is a fair name for any honest Christian, but let that pass. How dost thou, Hans?

LACY [*as Hans*] *Mee tanck you, vro.*[2]

MARGERY Well, Hans and Roger, you see God hath blessed your master, and, perdie,° if ever he comes to be Master Sheriff of London (as we are all mortal), you shall see I will have some odd thing or other in a corner for you. I will not be your back friend,° but let that pass. Hans, pray thee, tie my shoe. — *by God, indeed*; *false friend*

LACY [*as Hans*] *Yaw, ick sal, vro.*[3] [*He does so.*]

MARGERY Roger, thou know'st the length of my foot. As it is none of the biggest, so I thank God it is handsome enough. Prithee, let me have a pair of shoes made: cork, good Roger, wooden heel too.

HODGE You shall.

MARGERY Art thou acquainted with never a farthingale° maker, nor a French hood maker? I must enlarge my bum.° Ha, ha! How shall I look in a hood, I wonder? Perdie, oddly, I think. — *hooped petticoat*; *(with a bumroll)*

HODGE [*aside*] As a cat out of° a pillory. [*Aloud*] Very well, I warrant you, mistress. — *whore looking out of*

Scene 10. Eyre's shop.

1. Firk mockingly praises Margery's eloquence: "compendious" (line 9), i.e., succinct, is the very opposite of what she meant to say.
2. I thank you, mistress.
3. Yes, I will, mistress.

MARGERY Indeed, all flesh is grass.° And, Roger, canst thou tell where I may buy a good hair?° *(see Isaiah 40.6)* *hairpiece*

HODGE Yes, forsooth, at the poulterer's[4] in Gracious Street.

MARGERY Thou art an ungracious wag. Perdie, I mean a false hair for my periwig.

HODGE Why, mistress, the next time I cut my beard, you shall have the shavings of it, but they are all true hairs.

MARGERY It is very hot. I must get me a fan, or else a mask.

HODGE [*aside*] So you had need, to hide your wicked° face. *ugly*

MARGERY Fie upon it, how costly this world's calling° is! Perdie, but that it is one of the wonderful works of God, I would not deal with it. Is not Firk come yet? Hans, be not so sad. Let it pass and vanish, as my husband's worship° says. *vocation of fashion* *my worshipful husband*

LACY [*as Hans*] *Ick bin vrolicke; lot see yow soo.*[5]

HODGE Mistress, will you drink° a pipe of tobacco? *smoke*

MARGERY Oh, fie upon it, Roger! Perdie, these filthy tobacco pipes are the most idle,° slavering baubles° that ever I felt. Out upon it! God bless us, men look not like men that use them. *useless / toys*

Enter Ralph, being lame.

HODGE What, fellow Ralph? Mistress, look here: Jane's husband! Why, how now, lame? Hans, make much of him; he's a brother of our trade, a good workman, and a tall° soldier. *brave*

LACY [*as Hans*] You be welcome, *broder*.° *brother*

MARGERY Perdie, I knew him not.—How dost thou, good Ralph? I am glad to see thee well.

RALPH I would God° you saw me, dame, as well
As when I went from London into France. *I wish to God*

MARGERY Trust me, I am sorry, Ralph, to see thee impotent.° Lord, how the wars have made him sunburnt!° The left leg is not well. 'Twas a fair gift of God the infirmity took not hold a litle higher, considering thou camest from France[6]—but let that pass. *lame; sexually impotent* *venereally diseased*

RALPH I am glad to see you well, and I rejoice
To hear that God hath blessed my master so
Since my departure.

MARGERY Yea, truly, Ralph, I thank my maker—but let that pass.

HODGE And, sirrah° Ralph, what news, what news in France? *(said to commoners)*

RALPH Tell me, good Roger, first, what news in England?
How does my Jane? When didst thou see my wife?
Where lives my poor heart? She'll be poor indeed
Now I want limbs to get whereon to feed.[7]

HODGE Limbs? Hast thou not hands, man? Thou shalt never see a shoemaker want bread, though he have but three fingers on a hand.

RALPH Yet all this while I hear not of my Jane.

MARGERY Oh, Ralph, your wife, perdie, we know not what's become of her. She was here awhile, and because she was

4. Poultry-seller's. (Hodge puns on "hair" and "hare"; one could buy hares at such a shop.)
5. I am merry; let's see you so.
6. Margery worries about syphilis, "the French disease," and about castration if the amputation had been higher.
7. Now that I lack the limbs I need to earn a living by.

married grew more stately° than became her. I checked° her, and so forth. Away she flung,° never returned, nor said bye nor bah.° And, Ralph, you know: "ka me, ka thee."[8] And so as I tell ye—Roger, is not Firk come yet?

proud / rebuked · *flounced, dashed* · *so much as "goodbye"*

HODGE No, forsooth.

MARGERY And so, indeed, we heard not of her; but I hear she lives in London—but let that pass. If she had wanted,° she might have opened her case[9] to me or my husband, or to any of my men; I am sure there's not any of them, perdie, but would have done her good to his power.[1] Hans, look if Firk be come. [*Ralph weeps.*]

been in need

LACY [*as Hans*] *Yaw, ick sal, vro.*[2] *Exit* [*Lacy as*] *Hans.*

MARGERY And so, as I said°—but Ralph, why dost thou weep? Thou knowest that naked we came out of our mother's womb, and naked we must return,° and therefore thank God for all things.

as I was saying · *(see Job 1.21)*

HODGE No, faith, Jane is a stranger here. But, Ralph, pull up° a good heart; I know thou hast one. Thy wife, man, is in London. One told me he saw her awhile ago very brave° and neat. We'll ferret her out, an London hold her.

pluck up · *handsome-looking*

MARGERY Alas, poor soul, he's overcome with sorrow! He does but as I do, weep for the loss of any good thing. But, Ralph, get thee in. Call for some meat and drink. Thou shalt find me worshipful° towards thee.

generous, gracious

RALPH I thank you, dame. Since I want limbs and lands,
I'll° to God, my good friends, and to these my hands.

I'll trust

Exit.

Enter [*Lacy as*] *Hans, and Firk, running.*

FIRK Run, good Hans. Oh, Hodge, oh, mistress! Hodge, heave up thine ears; mistress, smug up° your looks, on with your best apparel. My master is chosen, my master is called, nay, condemned,[3] by the cry of the country° to be sheriff of the city for this famous year now to come and time now being. A great many men in black gowns were asked for their voices° and their hands, and my master had all their fists° about his ears presently,° and they cried "Ay, ay, ay, ay," and so I came away.
Wherefore, without all other grieve,°
I do salute you Mistress Shrieve.°

smarten up · *general acclamation* · *votes / raised hands* · *immediately* · *without further ado* · *Sheriff's wife*

LACY [*as Hans*] *Yaw, my meester is de groot man, de shrieve.*[4]

HODGE Did not I tell you, mistress? Now I may boldly say, "Good morrow to Your Worship."

MARGERY Good morrow, good Roger. I thank you, my good people all. Firk, hold up thy hand. Here's a threepenny piece for thy tidings. [*She tips him.*]

FIRK 'Tis but three halfpence, I think.—Yes, 'tis threepence. I smell the rose.°

(embossed on the coin)

8. I.e., tit for tat, help me and I'll help you.
9. She might have talked about her problems. (With perhaps unintended bawdy meaning; see 1.156–58 and note.)
1. To the best of his ability. (Inadvertently continuing the sexual innuendo.)
2. Yes, I shall, madam.
3. Perhaps a malapropism for "confirmed," but election to the post of sheriff did commit the winner to a considerable financial outlay. (See 9.71 and note.)
4. Yes, my master is the great man, the sheriff.

HODGE But, mistress, be ruled by me and do not speak so pulingly.° [*affectedly*]

FIRK 'Tis Her Worship speaks so, and not she. No, faith, mistress, speak me in the old key: "To it, Firk," "There, good Firk," "Ply your business, Hodge"—"Hodge," with a full mouth[5]—"I'll fill your bellies with good cheer till they cry twang."° [*cry "Enough!"*]

Enter Simon Eyre wearing a gold chain [and carrying a French hood].

LACY [*as Hans*] *See, myn liever broder, heer compt my meester.*[6]

MARGERY Welcome home, Master Shrieve. I pray God continue you in health and wealth.

EYRE See here, my Maggy, a chain, a gold chain for Simon Eyre. I shall make thee a lady. Here's a French hood for thee. [*He presents her with the hood.*] On with it, on with it. Dress thy brows with this flap of a shoulder of mutton,° [*i.e., woolen hood*] to make thee look lovely. Where be my fine men? Roger, I'll make over° [*transfer ownership of*] my shop and tools to thee. Firk, thou shalt be the foreman. Hans, thou shalt have an hundred for twenty.° [*you'll prosper fivefold*] Be as mad knaves as your master Sim Eyre hath been, and you shall live to be sheriffs of London. How dost thou like me, Margery? Prince am I none, yet am I princely born. Firk, Hodge, and Hans!

ALL THREE Ay, forsooth, what says Your Worship, Master Sheriff?

EYRE Worship and honor, you Babylonion knaves,[7] for the Gentle Craft! But I forgot° [*have forgotten*] myself. I am bidden by my Lord Mayor to dinner to Old Ford. He's gone before; I must after. Come, Madge, on with your trinkets. Now, my true Trojans,[8] my fine Firk, my dapper Hodge, my honest Hans, some device, some odd crotchets, some morris[9] or suchlike, for the honor of the Gentle° [*Gentlemen*] Shoemakers. Meet me at Old Ford. You know my mind. Come, Madge. Away!
Shut up the shop, knaves, and make holiday.

Exeunt [Eyre and Margery].

FIRK Oh, rare!° Oh, brave!° [*excellent / fine*] Come, Hodge. Follow me, Hans.
We'll be with them for° [*We'll take part in*] a morris dance. *Exeunt.*

[Scene 11]

Enter Lord Mayor [Oatley], Eyre, his wife [Margery] in a French hood, [Rose], Sibyl, and other servants.

OATLEY [*to Eyre and Margery*] Trust me, you are as welcome to Old Ford
As I myself.

5. Firk characterizes Margery as speaking the name "Hodge" with a booming, baying voice, as though she were a hunting dog.
6. See, my dear brother, here comes my master.
7. Another of Eyre's expansive epithets, like "Greeks" (4.121), "Mesopotamians" (7.80), and "Philistines" (7.111).
8. One of Eyre's colorful epithets. See note 7 above.
9. Eyre calls for some entertainment, including music (crotchets are literally musical notes) and morris dancing (a country-dance).
Scene 11. Old Ford.

MARGERY Truly I thank Your Lordship.

OATLEY Would our bad cheer were worth the thanks you give.

EYRE Good cheer, my Lord Mayor, fine cheer, a fine house, fine walls, all fine and neat.

OATLEY Now, by my troth, I'll tell thee, Master Eyre,
It does me good, and all my brethren,° *fellow aldermen*
That such a madcap fellow as thyself
Is entered into our society.

MARGERY Ay, but, my lord, he must learn now to put on gravity.

EYRE Peace, Maggy. A fig for gravity! When I go to Guildhall in my scarlet gown, I'll look as demurely as a saint, and speak as gravely as a justice of peace; but now I am here at Old Ford, at my good Lord Mayor's house, let it go by, vanish, Maggy; I'll be merry. Away with flip-flap,° these fooleries, these gulleries!° What, honey? Prince am I none, yet am I princely born. What says my Lord Mayor? *i.e., gaudy finery* / *deceptive things*

OATLEY Ha, ha, ha! I had rather than a thousand pound
I had an heart but half so light as yours.

EYRE Why, what should I do, my lord? A pound of care pays not a dram° of debt. Hum, let's be merry whiles we are young. Old age, sack,° and sugar will steal upon us ere we be aware. *small amount* / *a Spanish white wine*

OATLEY It's well done.—Mistress Eyre, pray give good counsel to my daughter.

MARGERY I hope Mistress Rose will have the grace to take nothing that's bad.

OATLEY Pray God she do, for i'faith, Mistress Eyre,
I would bestow upon that peevish girl
A thousand marks° more than I mean to give her, *(worth 13s. 4d. each)*
Upon condition she'd be ruled by me.
The ape° still crosseth° me. There came of late *i.e., fool / resists*
A proper gentleman, of fair revenues,
Whom gladly I would call son-in-law;
But my fine cockney° would have none of him. *spoiled child*
[*To Rose*] You'll prove a coxcomb° for it ere you die. *simpleton*
A courtier or no man must please your eye.

EYRE Be ruled, sweet Rose; thou'rt ripe for a man. Marry not with a boy that has no more hair on his face than thou hast on thy cheeks. A courtier? Wash, go by!° Stand not upon pishery-pashery.[1] Those silken fellows are but painted images: outsides, outsides, Rose. Their inner linings are torn. No, my fine mouse,° marry me° with a Gentleman Grocer like my Lord Mayor your father. A grocer is a sweet trade. Plums, Plums! Had I a son or daughter should° marry out of the generation and blood of the shoemakers, he should pack.° What, the Gentle Trade is a living for a man through Europe, through the world. *(expressing contempt)* / *i.e., young lady / marry* / *who would* / *be sent packing*

A noise within of a tabor° and a pipe. *small drum*

OATLEY What noise is this?

1. Don't be taken in by showy appearances.

EYRE Oh, my Lord Mayor, a crew of good fellows that, for love to Your Honor, are come hither with a morris dance. [*Calling*] Come in, my Mesopotamians,° cheerly! *(see 7.80, 81 n)*

Enter Hodge, [Lacy as] Hans, Ralph, Firk, and other shoemakers in a morris. After a little dancing, the Lord Mayor speaks.

OATLEY Master Eyre, are all these shoemakers?
EYRE All cordwainers, my good Lord Mayor.
ROSE [*aside*] How like my Lacy looks yond shoemaker!
LACY [*aside*] Oh, that I durst° but speak unto my love! *only dared*
OATLEY Sibyl, go fetch some wine to make these drink.
[*Sibyl exits briefly and returns with wine.*]
You are all welcome.
ALL [THE SHOEMAKERS] We thank Your Lordship.
Rose takes a cup of wine and goes to Hans.
ROSE For his sake whose fair shape thou represent'st,° *closely resemble*
Good friend, I drink to thee. [*She offers a toast.*]
LACY [*as Hans*] *Ick bedancke, good frister.*[2]
MARGERY I see, Mistress Rose, you do not want° judgment. *lack*
You have drunk to the properest° man I keep. *best-looking*
FIRK Here be some have done their parts to be as proper as he.[3]
OATLEY Well, urgent business calls me back to London.
Good fellows, first go in and taste our cheer,
And, to make merry as you homeward go,
Spend these two angels in beer at Stratford Bow.° *a tavern near Old Ford*
[*He gives them coins.*]
EYRE [*giving a coin*] To these two, my mad lads, Sim Eyre adds another. Then cheerly, Firk, tickle it,° Hans, and all for the honor of shoemakers! *live it up*
All [the shoemakers] go dancing out.
OATLEY Come, Master Eyre, let's have your company.
Exeunt [Oatley, Eyre, and Margery].
ROSE Sibyl, what shall I do?
SIBYL Why, what's the matter?
ROSE That Hans the shoemaker is my love, Lacy,
Disguised in that attire to find me out.
How should I find the means to speak with him?
SIBYL What, mistress, never fear. I dare venture my maidenhead to nothing—and that's great odds—that Hans the Dutchman, when we come to London, shall not only see and speak with you, but, in spite of all your father's policies,° steal you away and marry you. Will not this please you? *stratagems*
ROSE Do this,
And ever be assurèd of my love.
SIBYL Away, then, and follow your father to London, lest your absence cause him to suspect something.
Tomorrow, if my counsel be obeyed,
I'll bind you prentice to the Gentle Trade. [*Exeunt.*]

2. I thank you, good maiden.
3. Firk combatively asserts his own deserving of attention as a male (with suggestion of sexual prowess).

[Scene 12]

Enter Jane in a sempster's shop,[1] *working, and Hammon, muffled, at another door. He stands aloof.*° — *to one side*

HAMMON Yonder's the shop, and there my fair love sits.
She's fair and lovely, but she is not mine.
Oh, would she were! Thrice have I courted her;
Thrice hath my hand been moistened with her hand,
Whilst my poor famished eyes do feed on that
Which made them famish. I am infortunate;
I still love one,° yet nobody loves me. — *always love someone*
I muse in other men what women see
That I so want?° Fine Mistress Rose was coy, — *lack*
And this° too curious.° Oh, no, she is chaste, — *(Jane) / choosy*
And, for° she thinks me wanton, she denies — *because*
To cheer my cold heart with her sunny eyes.
How prettily she works! Oh, pretty hand!
Oh, happy work!° It doth me good to stand — *needlework*
Unseen to see her. Thus I oft have stood,
In frosty evenings, a light burning by her,
Enduring biting cold, only to eye her.
One only look° hath seemed as rich to me — *A mere chance to look*
As a king's crown—such is love's lunacy.
Muffled I'll pass along, and by that try
Whether she know me. [*He approaches the shop.*]

JANE Sir, what is't you buy?
What is't you lack, sir? Calico, or lawn,° — *fine linen*
Fine cambric shirts, or bands°—what will you buy? — *hatbands, ruffs, etc.*

HAMMON [*aside*] That which thou wilt not sell. Faith, yet I'll try.—
How° do you sell this handkercher? — *For how much*

JANE Good cheap.° — *Cheaply*

HAMMON And how these ruffs?

JANE Cheap, too.

HAMMON And how this band?

JANE Cheap too.

HAMMON [*taking her hand*] All cheap. How sell you then this hand?

JANE My hands are not to be sold.

HAMMON To be given, then.
Nay, faith, I come to buy.

JANE But none knows when.

HAMMON Good sweet, leave work a little while. Let's play.

JANE I cannot live° by keeping holiday. — *earn my living*

HAMMON I'll pay you for the time which shall be lost.

JANE With me you shall not be at so much cost.

HAMMON Look how you wound° this cloth, so you wound me. — *Just as you prick*

JANE It may be so.

HAMMON 'Tis so.

Scene 12. A London shop.
1. The tailor's (sempster's) shop is discovered by the opening of a curtain in the back of the stage or else is thrust onstage at a stage door.

JANE What remedy?
HAMMON Nay, faith, you are too coy.
JANE Let go my hand.
HAMMON I will do any task at your command.
I would let go this beauty, were I not
Enjoined to disobey you by a power
That controls kings: I love you.
JANE So. Now part.
HAMMON With hands I may, but never with my heart.
In faith, I love you.
JANE I believe you do.
HAMMON Shall a true love in me breed hate in you?
JANE I hate you not.
HAMMON Then you must love.
JANE I do.
What, are you better now? I love not you.
HAMMON All this, I hope, is but a woman's fray,° *i.e., protestation*
That means "Come to me!" when she cries "Away!"
In earnest, mistress—I do not jest—
A true chaste love hath entered in my breast.
I love you dearly as I love my life;
I love you as a husband loves a wife.
That, and no other love, my love requires.
Thy wealth, I know, is little. My desires
Thirst not for gold. Sweet beauteous Jane, what's mine
Shall, if thou make myself thine,° all be thine. *your husband*
Say, judge, what is thy sentence: life, or death?
Mercy or cruelty lies in thy breath.
JANE Good sir, I do believe you love me well;
For 'tis a silly° conquest, silly° pride, *unworthy / foolish*
For one like you (I mean, a gentleman)
To boast that by his love tricks he hath brought
Such and such women to his amorous lure.
I think you do not so; yet many do,
And make it even a very trade° to woo. *veritable profession*
I could be coy, as many women be,
Feed you with sunshine smiles and wanton looks;
But I detest witchcraft. Say that I
Do constantly believe you constant have—
HAMMON Why dost thou not believe me?
JANE I believe you.
But yet, good sir, because I will not grieve you
With hopes to taste fruit which will never fall,
In simple truth, this is the sum of all:
My husband lives—at least I hope he lives.
Pressed° was he to these bitter wars in France; *Conscripted*
Bitter they are to me by wanting° him. *through lacking*
I have but one heart, and that heart's his due.
How can I then bestow the same on you?
Whilst he lives, his I live, be it ne'er so poor,
And rather be his wife than a king's whore.
HAMMON Chaste and dear woman, I will not abuse thee,
Although it cost my life if thou refuse me.
Thy husband pressed for France—what was his name?
JANE Ralph Damport.

HAMMON Damport.
[*He produces a letter.*] Here's a letter sent
From France to me, from a dear friend of mine,
A gentleman of place.° Here he doth write *authority, rank*
Their names that have been slain in every fight.
JANE I hope death's scroll contains not my love's name.
HAMMON Cannot you read?
JANE I can.
HAMMON Peruse the same.
To my remembrance, such a name I read
Amongst the rest. See here.
JANE [*reading the letter*] Ay me, he's dead!
He's dead! If this be true, my dear heart's slain.
HAMMON Have patience, dear love.
JANE [*weeping*] Hence, hence!
HAMMON Nay, sweet Jane,
Make not poor Sorrow proud with these rich tears.
I mourn thy husband's death because thou mourn'st.
JANE That bill° is forged. 'Tis signed by forgery. *document*
HAMMON I'll bring thee letters sent besides to many
Carrying the like report. Jane, 'tis too true.
Come, weep not. Mourning, though it rise from love,
Helps not the mournèd, yet hurts them that mourn.
JANE [*turning from him*] For God's sake, leave me.
HAMMON Whither dost thou turn?
Forget the dead; love them that are alive.
His love is faded; try how mine will thrive.
JANE 'Tis now no time for me to think on love.
HAMMON 'Tis now best time for you to think on love,
Because your love lives not.
JANE Though he be dead,
My love to him shall not be burièd.
For God's sake, leave me to myself alone.
HAMMON 'Twould kill my soul to leave thee drowned in moan.° *sorrow*
Answer me to my suit, and I am gone.
Say to me yea or no.
JANE No!
HAMMON Then farewell.
[*He starts to leave, then returns.*]
One farewell will not serve. I come again.
Come, dry these wet cheeks. Tell me, faith, sweet Jane,
Yea or no once more.
JANE Once more I say no.
Once more, be gone, I pray, else will I go.
HAMMON Nay, then I will grow rude. By this white hand,
Until you change that cold "no," here I'll stand
Till by your hard heart—
JANE Nay, for God's love, peace!
My sorrows by your presence more increase—
Not that° you thus are present, but all grief *because*
Desires to be alone. Therefore in brief
Thus much I say, and saying bid adieu:
If ever I wed man it shall be you.
HAMMON Oh, blessèd voice! Dear Jane, I'll urge no more.

Thy breath hath made me rich.

JANE Death makes me poor.

Exeunt.

[Scene 13]

Enter Hodge at his shop board, Ralph, Firk, [Lacy as] Hans, and a boy, at work.

ALL [*singing*] Hey down, a-down, down-derry.[1]

HODGE Well said,° my hearts! Ply your work today; we loitered yesterday. To it, pell-mell, that we may live to be lord mayors, or aldermen at least.
That's the spirit

FIRK [*singing*] Hey down-a-down derry.

HODGE Well said, i'faith! How say'st thou, Hans, doth not Firk tickle it?°
do it well

LACY [*as Hans*] *Yaw, meester.*°
Yes, master

FIRK Not so, neither. My organ pipe squeaks this morning for want of liquoring. [*He sings*] Hey down-a-down derry.

LACY [*as Hans*] *Forware, Firk, tow best un jolly yongster. Hort, ay, meester, ick bid yow cut me un pair vampies vor Meester Jeffrey's boots.*[2]

HODGE Thou shalt, Hans.

FIRK Master!

HODGE How now, boy?°
i.e., my foreman

FIRK Pray, now you are in the cutting vein, cut me out a pair of counterfeits,° or else my work will not pass current.[3] [*He sings*] Hey down-a-down.
copies

HODGE Tell me, sirs, are my cousin Mistress Priscilla's shoes done?

FIRK Your cousin? No, master, one of your aunts,° hang her. Let them alone.
slang for "whores"

RALPH I am in hand with them.° She gave charge° that none but I should do them for her.
working on them / orders

FIRK Thou do° for her? Then 'twill be a lame doing, and that she loves not. Ralph, thou mightst have sent her to me. In faith, I would have yerked and firked° your Priscilla. [*He sings*] Hey down-a-down derry.—This gear[4] will not hold.
i.e., perform sexually
(bawdy; see 7.43 n)

HODGE How say'st thou, Firk, were we not merry at Old Ford?

FIRK How, merry? Why, our buttocks went jiggy-joggy like a quagmire. Well, Sir Roger Oatmeal, if I thought all meal° of that nature, I would eat nothing but bagpuddings.[5]
every meal; oatmeal

RALPH Of all good fortunes, my fellow Hans had the best.

FIRK 'Tis true, because Mistress Rose drank to him.

HODGE Well, well, work apace. They say seven of the aldermen be dead, or very sick.

FIRK I care not. I'll be none.

RALPH No, nor I, but then my Master Eyre will come quickly to be mayor.

Scene 13. The shoemakers' shop.

1. The Second Three-Man's Song (p. 490 above) may have been sung here.

2. Indeed (German: *fürwahr*), Firk, thou art a jolly youngster. Listen, master, I bid you cut me a pair of vamps (boot fronts) for Master Jeffrey's boots. (Jeffrey is evidently a customer.)

3. Will not pass for valid currency. (Firk plays on the idea of "counterfeits.")

4. Business—shoe work, or sexual activity, or the singing.

5. Pudding boiled in a bag and made partly of oats. (Firk recalls the food at Old Ford.)

Enter Sibyl.

FIRK Whoop! Yonder comes Sibyl.
HODGE Sibyl, welcome, i'faith. And how dost thou, mad wench?
FIRK Sib-whore, welcome to London.
SIBYL God-a-mercy, sweet Firk.—Good Lord, Hodge, what a delicious° shop you have got! You tickle it,° i'faith. *delightful / do it well*
RALPH God-a-mercy,° Sibyl, for our good cheer at Old Ford. *Thanks*
SIBYL That you shall have, Ralph.[6]
FIRK Nay, by the Mass, we had tickling cheer, Sibyl. And how the plague° dost thou and Mistress Rose, and my Lord Mayor? I put the women in first. *how the devil*
SIBYL Well, God-a-mercy. But God's me,° I forget myself. Where's Hans the Fleming? *God save me*
FIRK Hark, butter-box, now you must yelp out some *spreken.*° *foreign talk*
LACY [*as Hans*] *Vat begay yow? Vat vod yow, frister?*[7]
SIBYL Marry, you must come to my young mistress, to pull on° her shoes you made last. *try for fit*
LACY [*as Hans*] *Vare ben your edle fro? Vare ben your mistress?*[8]
SIBYL Marry, here at our London house in Cornwall.° *Cornhill Street*
FIRK Will nobody serve her turn° but Hans? *(with bawdy suggestion)*
SIBYL No, sir.—Come, Hans. I stand upon needles.° *am on pins and needles*
HODGE Why, then, Sibyl, take heed of pricking.° *(with bawdy suggestion)*
SIBYL For° that, let me alone. I have a trick in my budget.[9]— Come, Hans. *As for*
LACY [*as Hans*] *Yaw, yaw, ick sall meet yow gane.*[1]
HODGE Go, Hans, make haste again.° *return quickly*

Exit [Lacy as] Hans, and Sibyl.

Come, who lacks work?
FIRK I, master, for I lack my breakfast; 'tis munching time, and past.
HODGE Is't so? Why, then, leave work. Ralph, to breakfast! Boy, look to the tools. Come, Ralph, come, Firk. *Exeunt.*

[Scene 14]

Enter a Servingman [with a shoe].

SERVINGMAN Let me see now: the sign of the last° in Tower Street. Mass,° yonder's the house. [*He calls.*] What ho! Who's within? *form used for shoemaking* / *By the Mass*

Enter Ralph.

RALPH Who calls there? What want you, sir?
SERVINGMAN Marry, I would have a pair of shoes made for a gentlewoman against° tomorrow morning. What, can you do them? *in time for*

6. Sibyl makes a disparaging or self-deprecating remark about the entertainment the shoemakers were given in scene 11; or perhaps she issues a facetious invitation that she, as servant, is not in a position to give seriously.
7. What do you want? What would you, girl?
8. Where is your noble lady? Where is your mistress?
9. I.e., I have a trick up my sleeve. (But with bawdy implications in "trick" and "budget," the latter meaning "bag" and hinting at the female sexual anatomy; these implications are suggested by "pricking" in line 62.)
1. Yes, yes, I will go with you.
Scene 14. At the door of the shoemakers' shop.

RALPH Yes, sir, you shall have them. But what length's her foot?

SERVINGMAN [*giving Ralph a shoe*] Why, you must make them in all parts like this shoe. But at any hand° fail not to do them, for the gentlewoman is to be married very early in the morning. (*on any account*)

RALPH How? By° this shoe must it be made? By this? Are you sure, sir? By this? (*Modeled on*)

SERVINGMAN How, "by this" am I "sure," "by this"? Art thou in thy wits? I tell thee I must have a pair of shoes; dost thou mark me? A pair of shoes, two shoes, made by this very shoe, this same shoe, against tomorrow morning by four o'clock. Dost understand me? Canst thou do't?

RALPH Yes, sir, yes. Ay, ay, I can do't. By this shoe, you say? [*Aside*] I should know this shoe.—Yes, sir, yes, by this shoe, I can do't. Four o'clock? Well, whither shall I bring them?

SERVINGMAN To the sign of the Golden Ball in Watling Street. Inquire for one Master Hammon, a gentleman, my master.

RALPH Yea, sir. By this shoe, you say.

SERVINGMAN I say Master Hammon at the Golden Ball. He's the bridegroom, and those shoes are for his bride.

RALPH They shall be done, by this shoe. Well, well, Master Hammon at the Golden Shoe—I would say the Golden Ball. Very well, very well. But I pray you, sir, where must Master Hammon be married?

SERVINGMAN At Saint Faith's Church, under° Paul's. But what's that to thee? Prithee, dispatch° those shoes; and so farewell. *Exit.* (*in the crypt of* / *hurry up with*)

RALPH By this shoe, said he? How am I amazed
At this strange accident! Upon my life,
This was the very shoe I gave my wife
When I was pressed for France, since when, alas,
I never could hear of her. It is the same,
And Hammon's bride no other but my Jane.

Enter Firk.

FIRK 'Snails,° Ralph, thou hast lost thy part of three pots a countryman° of mine gave me to° breakfast. (*By God's nails* / *neighbor / for*)

RALPH I care not. I have found a better thing.

FIRK A thing?° Away! Is it a man's thing, or a woman's thing? (*(with sexual suggestion)*)

RALPH Firk, dost thou know this shoe?

FIRK No, by my troth. Neither doth that know me. I have no acquaintance with it; 'tis a mere° stranger to me. (*utter*)

RALPH Why, then, I do. This shoe, I durst be sworn,
Once coverèd the instep of my Jane:
This is her size, her breadth. Thus trod my love.
These truelove knots° I pricked. I hold° my life, (*ornaments / bet*)
By this old shoe I shall find out my wife.

FIRK Ha, ha! Old shoe, that wert new—how a murrain° came this ague° fit of foolishness upon thee? (*plague* / *feverish*)

RALPH Thus, Firk: even now here came a servingman;
By this shoe would he have a new pair made
Against tomorrow morning for his mistress,
That's to be married to a gentleman.

And why may not this be my sweet Jane?
FIRK And why mayst not thou be my sweet ass? Ha, ha!
RALPH Well, laugh, and spare not.° But the truth is this: *all you want*
Against tomorrow morning I'll provide
A lusty° crew of honest shoemakers *merry; courageous*
To watch the going of the bride to church.
If she prove Jane, I'll take her in despite
From Hammon and the devil, were he by.
If it be not my Jane, what remedy?
Hereof am I sure: I shall live till I die,
Although I never with a woman lie. *Exit.*

FIRK Thou lie with a woman—to build nothing but Cripple-gates![1] Well, God sends fools fortune, and it may be he° may light upon his matrimony by such a device; for wedding and hanging goes by destiny. *Exit.* *(Ralph)*

[Scene 15]

Enter [Lacy dressed as] Hans, and Rose, arm in arm.

LACY How happy am I by embracing thee!
Oh, I did fear such cross° mishaps did reign *adverse*
That I should never see my Rose again.
ROSE Sweet Lacy, since fair Opportunity
Offers herself to further our escape,
Let not too overfond esteem of me[1]
Hinder that happy hour. Invent the means,
And Rose will follow thee through all the world.
LACY Oh, how I surfeit° with excess of joy, *am glutted*
Made happy by thy rich perfection!
But since thou pay'st sweet int'rest to my hopes,
Redoubling love on love, let me once more,
Like to a bold-faced debtor, crave° of thee *request*
This night to steal abroad,° and at Eyre's house— *out of your house*
Who now, by death of certain aldermen,
Is mayor of London, and my master once—
Meet thou thy Lacy, where, in spite of change,° *inconstant fortune*
Your father's anger, and mine uncle's hate,
Our happy nuptials will we consummate.

Enter Sibyl.

SIBYL Oh, God, what will you do, mistress? Shift for yourself. Your father is at hand; he's coming, he's coming! Master Lacy, hide yourself. In, my mistress! For God's sake, shift for yourselves.

LACY Your father come! Sweet Rose, what shall I do?
Where shall I hide me? How shall I escape?
ROSE A man, and want wit° in extremity? *lack resourcefulness*
Come, come: be Hans still; play the shoemaker.
Pull on my shoe.

1. Firk jokes about Ralph's lameness, rendering him capable only of siring children who are cripples and who might then beg at an ancient London gate known as a gathering place for crippled beggars.

Scene 15. Oatley's London house in Cornhill Street (see 13.59).

1. Do not let an infatuated fondness for me and concern about my reputation (which an elopement might well compromise).

LACY Mass, and that's well remembered.° *thought of*
SIBYL Here comes your father.

Enter [Oatley, the former] Lord Mayor.

LACY [*as Hans*] *Forware, metresse, 'tis un good skow; it sal vel dute, or ye sal neit betaelen.*[2]
ROSE Oh, God, it pincheth me. What will you do?
LACY [*aside*] Your father's presence pincheth, not the shoe.
OATLEY Well done. Fit my daughter well, and she shall please° thee well. *pay; reward*
LACY [*as Hans*] *Yaw, yaw, ick weit dat well. Forware, 'tis un good skoo; 'tis gimait van neit's leither; se ever, mine heer.*[3]
OATLEY I do believe it.

Enter a Prentice.

What's the news with you?
PRENTICE Please you, the Earl of Lincoln at the gate
Is newly lighted,° and would speak with you. *alighted from his coach*
OATLEY The Earl of Lincoln come to speak with me?
Well, well, I know his errand.—Daughter Rose,
Send hence your shoemaker. Dispatch, have done!—
Sib, make things handsome.—Sir boy, follow me.
Exit [Oatley with the Prentice, and Sibyl].
LACY Mine uncle come? Oh, what may this portend?
Sweet Rose, this of our love threatens an end.[4]
ROSE Be not dismayed at this. Whate'er befall,
Rose is thine own. To witness I speak truth,
Where thou appoints the place I'll meet with thee.
I will not fix a day° to follow thee, *some future day*
But presently° steal hence. Do not reply. *at once*
Love which gave strength to bear my father's hate
Shall now add wings to further our escape. *Exeunt.*

[Scene 16]

Enter [Oatley, the former] Lord Mayor, and Lincoln.

OATLEY Believe me, on my credit° I speak truth: *on my word*
Since first your nephew Lacy went to France
I have not seen him. It seemed strange to me
When Dodger told me that he stayed behind,
Neglecting the high charge the King imposed.
LINCOLN Trust me, Sir Roger Oatley, I did think
Your counsel had given head° to this attempt, *countenance*
Drawn to it by the love he bears your child.
Here I did hope to find him in your house,
But now I see mine error, and confess
My judgment wronged you by conceiving so.
OATLEY Lodge in my house, say you? Trust me, my lord,
I love your nephew Lacy too too dearly

2. Indeed, mistress, it is a good shoe; it will do well, or you shall not pay for it.
3. Yes, yes, I know that well. Indeed, it is a good shoe; it is made with neat's leather (cow leather); just look, my lord. (Lacy observes, in his Dutch-German dialect, that Oatley speaks truer than he realizes about Rose's "fitting" Lacy and "pleasing him well.")
4. This threatens an end to our love.
Scene 16. Oatley's London house still.

So much to wrong his honor, and he° hath done so° *(someone) / wronged him*
That° first gave him advice to stay from France. *Who*
To witness I speak truth, I let you know
How careful I have been to keep my daughter
Free from all conference or speech of° him— *communication with*
Not that I scorn your nephew, but in love
I bear Your Honor, lest your noble blood
Should by my mean° worth be dishonorèd. *lowly*

LINCOLN [*aside*] How far the churl's tongue wanders from his heart!—
Well, well, Sir Roger Oatley, I believe you,
With more than many thanks for the kind love
So much you seem to bear me. But, my lord,
Let me request your help to seek my nephew,
Whom, if I find, I'll straight embark° for France. *put on board ship*
So shall your Rose be free, my thoughts at rest,
And much care die which now lives in my breast.

Enter Sibyl.

SIBYL Oh, Lord, help, for God's sake! My mistress, oh, my young mistress!

OATLEY Where is thy mistress? What's become of her?

SIBYL She's gone, she's fled.

OATLEY Gone? Whither is she fled?

SIBYL I know not, forsooth. She's fled out of doors with Hans the shoemaker. I saw them scud,° scud, scud, apace, apace. *scuttle off*

OATLEY Which way? [*Calling*] What, John! Where be my men?—Which way?

SIBYL I know not, an it please Your Worship.

OATLEY Fled with a shoemaker? Can this be true?

SIBYL Oh, Lord, sir, as true as God's in heaven.

LINCOLN [*aside*] Her love turned shoemaker? I am glad of this.

OATLEY A Fleming butter-box, a shoemaker?
Will she forget her birth? Requite my care
With such ingratitude? Scorned she young Hammon
To love a honnikin,° a needy knave? *i.e., Flemish nobody*
Well, let her fly. I'll not fly after her.
Let her starve, if she will; she's none of mine.

LINCOLN Be not so cruel, sir.

Enter Firk, with shoes.

SIBYL [*aside*] I am glad she's scaped.

OATLEY I'll not account of her as of my child.
Was there no better object for her eyes
But a foul drunken lubber, swill-belly,
A shoemaker? That's brave!° *fine! (ironic)*

FIRK Yea, forsooth, 'tis a very brave shoe,[1] and as fit as a pudding.

OATLEY How now, what knave is this?—From whence comest thou?

FIRK No knave, sir. I am Firk the shoemaker, lusty Roger's chief lusty journeyman, and I come hither to take up° the *attend to (with bawdry)*

1. Firk saucily pretends that "brave!" (line 51) is said in admiration of his handiwork.

pretty leg of sweet Mistress Rose, and thus, hoping Your Worship is in as good health as I was at the making hereof, I bid you farewell. Yours, Firk.[2] [*He starts to leave.*]

OATLEY Stay, stay, sir knave!

LINCOLN Come hither, shoemaker.

FIRK [*returning*] 'Tis happy the "knave" is put before the "shoemaker,"[3] or else I would not have vouchsafed to come back to you. I am moved, for I stir.[4]

OATLEY [*to Lincoln*] My lord, this villain calls us knaves by craft.[5]

FIRK Then 'tis by the Gentle° Craft, and to call one "knave" gently is no harm. Sit Your Worship merry!° [*Aside to Sibyl*] Sib, your young mistress—I'll so bob° them, now my master, Master Eyre, is Lord Mayor of London! (*stressing "Gentle"*) (*a form of farewell*) (*hoodwink; flout, mock*)

OATLEY Tell me, sirrah,° whose man[6] are you? (*said to inferiors*)

FIRK I am glad to see Your Worship so merry. I have no maw° to this gear,° no stomach as yet to a red petticoat (*pointing to Sibyl*). (*stomach, appetite*) (*baggage (Sibyl)*)

LINCOLN [*to Firk*] He means not, sir, to woo you to° his maid, (*solicit you to woo*)
But only doth demand° whose man you are. (*ask*)

FIRK I sing now to the tune of "Rogero."° Roger my fellow is now my master. (*a popular ballad*)

LINCOLN Sirrah, know'st thou one Hans, a shoemaker?

FIRK Hans shoemaker? Oh, yes—stay°—yes, I have° him. I tell you what (I speak it in secret): Mistress Rose and he are by this time—no, not so,° but shortly—are to come over one another with "Can you dance the shaking of the sheets?"° It is that Hans. [*Aside*] I'll so gull° these diggers!° (*wait / recall*) (*not yet*) (*an erotic dance tune*) (*fool / information seekers*)

OATLEY Know'st thou then where he is?

FIRK Yes, forsooth. Yea, marry.

LINCOLN Canst thou, in sadness?° (*Do you know, seriously?*)

FIRK No, forsooth. No, marry.

OATLEY Tell me, good honest fellow, where he is,
And thou shalt see what I'll bestow of thee.° (*give you*)

FIRK "Honest fellow"? No, sir, not so, sir.[7] My profession is the Gentle Craft. I care not for seeing, I love feeling.[8] Let me feel it here—*aurium tenus*, ten pieces of gold, *genuum tenus*, ten pieces of silver[9]—and then Firk is your man in a new pair of stretchers.° (*shoe stretchers; lies*)

OATLEY [*offering money*] Here is an angel, part of thy reward
Which I will give thee. Tell me where he is.

FIRK No point.° Shall I betray my brother? No! Shall I prove Judas° to Hans? No! Shall I cry treason to my corporation?° (*Absolutely not*) (*(see Matthew 26) / guild*)

2. Firk cheekily concludes in the formal style of writing a complimentary close to a letter.

3. It's a good thing you corrected "knave" to "shoemaker." (On the double meaning in "put before," see note 5 below.)

4. (1) I have stirred from the spot where I was; (2) I am angry and stirred up.

5. Oatley senses the insult and insubordination in Firk's double meaning: by saying "the 'knave' is put before the 'shoemaker' " (lines 63–64), Firk implies that knaves are standing "before," in front of, him, the shoemaker. "Craft" means (1) cunning; (2) shoemakers' craft.

6. Servant—but Firk interprets it as "husband" and saucily answers as though he should marry the likes of Sibyl.

7. Firk proudly rejects the suggestion of being Oatley's "fellow," preferring his status as a shoemaker.

8. Firk wants tangible evidence of the money in his hand, not the mere promise of it. (The line contains a sexual hint as well.)

9. Firk suggests he will tell all for gold coins (*aurium tenus* means "up to the ears") but will tell less for silver (*genuum tenus* means "up to the knees").

No! I shall be firked and yerked,° then. But give me your *given a going-over*
angel; your angel shall tell you.

LINCOLN Do so, good fellow. 'Tis no hurt to thee.

FIRK [*taking the money*] Send simpering Sib away.

OATLEY Huswife,° get you in. *Exit Sibyl.* *Hussy*

FIRK Pitchers have ears, and maids have wide mouths. But
for Hans Prans,° upon my word, tomorrow morning he and *Prancing Hans*
young Mistress Rose go to this gear.° They shall be married *business; marriage*
together, by this rush,° or else turn Firk to a firkin° of butter *(an oath) / small cask*
to tan leather withal.° *with*

OATLEY But art thou sure of this?

FIRK Am I sure that Paul's steeple is a handful higher than
London Stone?° Or that the Pissing Conduit leaks nothing *a familiar landmark*
but pure Mother Bunch?[1] Am I sure I am lusty Firk? God's
nails, do you think I am so base to gull° you? *as to cheat*

LINCOLN Where are they married? Dost thou know the
church?

FIRK I never go to church, but I know the name of it. It is a
swearing church.[2] Stay awhile, 'tis "Ay, by the Mass." No,
no, 'tis "Ay, by my troth." No, nor that; 'tis "Ay, by my faith."
That, that! 'Tis "Ay, by my Faith's Church"—under Paul's
cross.° There they shall be knit like a pair of stockings in *(see 14.33)*
matrimony. There they'll be incony.[3]

LINCOLN [*to Oatley*] Upon my life, my nephew Lacy walks
In the disguise of this Dutch shoemaker.

FIRK [*interrupting them*] Yes, forsooth.

LINCOLN Doth he not, honest° fellow? *worthy*

FIRK No, forsooth.[4] I think Hans is nobody but Hans—no
spirit.

OATLEY [*to Lincoln*] My mind misgives me° now 'tis so *makes me suspect*
indeed.

LINCOLN My cousin speaks the language, knows the trade.

OATLEY Let me request your company, my lord.
Your honorable presence may, no doubt,
Refrain° their headstrong rashness, when myself, *Restrain*
Going alone, perchance may be o'erborne.° *defeated*
Shall° I request this favor? *May*

LINCOLN This, or what else.° *or anything else*

FIRK Then you must rise betimes,° for they mean to fall to *early*
their "heypass and repass, pindy-pandy, which hand will you
have?"[5] very early.

OATLEY My care shall every way equal their haste.
This night accept° your lodging in my house; *accept my offer of*
The earlier shall we stir, and at Saint Faith's
Prevent this giddy harebrained nuptial.
This traffic of hot love shall yield cold gains;
They ban° our loves, and we'll forbid their bains.[6] *Exit.* *reject; curse*

1. The Pissing Conduit, a public water supply, yielded a trickle of water, the brownish color of which may have resembled the ale sold at Mother Bunch's Tavern near the conduit in Cornhill Street.
2. It is a church that one might swear by in an oath—as Firk proceeds to demonstrate.
3. They'll be a happy couple. (With a vulgar suggestion also of "in cunny," meaning "in the cunt.")
4. Firk's reversing himself from "Yes" to "No" is part of his tactic to bewilder the two older men, as at line 84 ff. above.
5. Firk alludes to conjuring and cheating games of guessing which hand an object is being held in. This is his way of characterizing the exchanging of vows and hands in the marriage ceremony and the ensuing sexual consummation.
6. Banns (here "bains" for the rhyme) were public announcements in church of a proposed marriage, to

LINCOLN At Saint Faith's Church, thou say'st?

FIRK Yes, by their troth.[7]

LINCOLN Be secret, on thy life. [*Exit.*]

FIRK Yes, when I kiss your wife. Ha, ha! Here's no craft in the Gentle Craft! I came hither of purpose with shoes to Sir Roger's Worship,° whilst Rose his daughter be coney-catched° by Hans. Soft,° now: these two gulls will be at Saint Faith's Church tomorrow morning, to take Master Bridegroom and Mistress Bride napping, and they in the meantime shall chop up° the matter at the Savoy.[8] But the best sport is, Sir Roger Oatley will find my fellow, lame Ralph's wife, going to marry a gentleman, and then he'll stop her instead of his daughter. Oh, brave! There will be fine tickling° sport. Soft now, what have I to do? Oh, I know now: a mess° of shoemakers meet at the Woolsack° in Ivy Lane to cozen my gentleman° of lame Ralph's wife, that's true.

Alack, alack!
Girls, hold out tack,°
For now smocks for this jumbling
Shall go to wrack.[9] *Exit.*

His Worship Sir Roger / *taken by guile* / *Easy* / *settle* / *amusing* / *group* / *a tavern* / *to trick Hammon* / *stand firm*

[Scene 17]

Enter Eyre, his wife [*Margery*], [*Lacy dressed as*] *Hans,*[1] *and Rose.*

EYRE This is the morning, then—say, my bully,° my honest Hans—is it not?

fine fellow

LACY This is the morning that must make us two
Happy or miserable. Therefore, if you—

EYRE Away with these "if's" and "an's," Hans, and these etceteras. By mine honor, Rowland Lacy, none but the King shall wrong thee. Come, fear nothing. Am not I Sim Eyre? Is not Sim Eyre Lord Mayor of London? Fear nothing, Rose. Let them all say what they can. [*He sings.*] "Dainty, come thou to me."° Laughest thou?

a popular song

MARGERY Good my lord, stand° her friend in what thing you may.

act as (bawdy)

EYRE Why, my sweet Lady Madgy, think you Simon Eyre can forget his fine Dutch journeyman? No, vah!° Fie, I scorn it. It shall never be cast in my teeth that I was unthankful. Lady Madgy, thou hadst never covered thy Saracen's head with this French flap,[2] nor loaden° thy bum with this farthingale°—'tis trash, trumpery, vanity—Simon Eyre had never walked in a red petticoat,° nor wore a chain of gold, but for° my fine journeyman's portagues;° and shall I leave him? No. Prince am I none, yet bear a princely mind.

fie! / *loaded, clothed* / *petticoat* / *i.e., gown* / *were it not for* / *money*

---

provide an opportunity for the lodging of any objections.

7. Since Rose and Lacy are marrying, Firk comically swears by *their* "troth" (meaning "pledge" or "betrothal") rather than, more conventionally, by his own.

8. The Savoy, originally a palace, was rebuilt in 1505 as a poorhouse with a chapel.

9. I.e., For now maidenheads, as a result of this confusion, will be lost. ("Smocks," or petticoats, is a metonymy for women in a sexual sense.)

Scene 17. The shoemakers' shop.

1. Lacy dresses as Hans in this scene but speaks in his own voice, as Lacy.

2. Eyre amiably insults his wife by comparing her French-hooded head to an archery target or a tavern sign; a Saracen's head was used as a target in archery. Cf. 7.61–62 and note.

LACY My lord, 'tis time for us to part from hence.

EYRE Lady Madgy, Lady Madgy, take two or three of my pie-crust eaters,° my buff-jerkin varlets,[3] that do walk in black gowns at Simon Eyre's heels. Take them, good Lady Madgy, trip and go, my brown Queen of Periwigs,[4] with my delicate Rose and my jolly Rowland, to the Savoy. See them linked; countenance° the marriage; and when it is done, cling, cling together, you Hamborow turtledoves.[5] I'll bear you out.° Come to Simon Eyre; come dwell with me, Hans; thou shalt eat minced pies and marchpane.° Rose, away, cricket!° Trip and go, my Lady Madgy, to the Savoy. Hans, wed and to bed; kiss and away. Go, vanish!

ravenous workers / *witness* / *protect you* / *marzipan / (a pet name)*

MARGERY Farewell, my lord.

ROSE Make haste, sweet love.

MARGERY She'd fain the deed° were done. *the ceremony; sex*

LACY Come, my sweet Rose, faster than deer we'll run.

EYRE Go, vanish, vanish! Avaunt,° I say! *Begone*

They [all but Eyre] go out.

By the Lord of Ludgate, it's a mad life to be a lord mayor. It's a stirring life, a fine life, a velvet° life, a careful° life. Well, Simon Eyre, yet set a good face on it, in the honor of Saint Hugh. Soft, the King this day comes to dine with me, to see my new buildings.[6] His Majesty is welcome; he shall have good cheer, delicate cheer, princely cheer. This day my fellow prentices of London come to dine with me too; they shall have fine cheer, gentlemanlike cheer. I promised the mad Cappadocians,[7] when we all served at the Conduit together,[8] that if ever I came to be mayor of London, I would feast them all; and I'll do't, I'll do't, by the life of Pharaoh. By this beard, Sim Eyre will be no flincher. Besides, I have procured° that upon every Shrove Tuesday, at the sound of the pancake bell,[9] my fine dapper Assyrian lads° shall clap° up their shop windows and away. This is the day, and this day they shall do't, they shall do't.

cushy / full of cares / *contrived* / *(see n. 7) / shut*

Boys, that day are you free. Let masters care,°
And prentices shall pray for Simon Eyre. *Exit.*

worry, take care

[Scene 18]

Enter Hodge, Firk, Ralph, and five or six shoemakers, all with cudgels, or such weapons.

HODGE Come, Ralph. Stand to it, Firk. My masters,° as we are the brave bloods° of the shoemakers, heirs apparent to

good sirs / *brethren, comrades*

3. Leather-jacketed attendants, here wearing the garb of sheriff's officers and other such minor functionaries.
4. Eyre joshes Margery for her vanity in craving elaborate wigs (periwigs), or headdresses, such as were worn by ladies of fashion.
5. Hamburg (Germany) must have been known for its turtledoves.
6. Eyre refers especially to Leadenhall, a splendid building at the corner of Gracechurch Street and Cornhill, rebuilt in the fifteenth century by the historical Eyre. See 21.131–35.
7. Another of Erye's irrepressible epithets, like "Greeks," etc. See 10.160 and note, and "Assyrian lads" in line 51 below.
8. I.e., when we madcap companions gathered at the conduit, as servants, to draw water for the houses in which we served.
9. On the day before Ash Wednesday (modern Mardi Gras), the bell summoning Christians to church became known as the "pancake bell" because of the associations of the day with riotous feasting. Dekker's source, Thomas Deloney's *The Gentle Craft* (1597), attributes the institution of this custom to the real-life Mayor Simon Eyre.

Scene 18. Near the Woolsack Inn (see 16.158–59).

Saint Hugh, and perpetual benefactors to all good fellows, thou shalt have no wrong. Were Hammon a king of spades,[1] he should not delve in thy close° without thy sufferance.° But tell me, Ralph, art thou sure 'tis thy wife? *enclosure / consent*

RALPH Am I sure this is Firk? This morning, when I stroked° on her shoes, I looked upon her, and she upon me, and sighed, asked me if ever I knew one Ralph. "Yes," said I. "For his sake," said she, tears standing in her eyes, "and for° thou art somewhat like him, spend this piece of gold." I took it. [*He shows the gold piece.*] My lame leg and my travel beyond sea made me unknown. All is one° for that; I know she's mine. *eased, fitted* / *because* / *No matter*

FIRK Did she give thee this gold? Oh, glorious, glittering gold! She's thine own. 'Tis thy wife, and she loves thee, for, I'll stand to't, there's no woman will give gold to any man but she thinks better of him than she thinks of them she gives silver to. And for° Hammon, neither Hammon nor hangman shall wrong thee in London. Is not our old master, Eyre, Lord Mayor? Speak, my hearts.° *as for* / *comrades*

ALL Yes, and Hammon shall know it to his cost.

Enter Hammon, his [*Serving*]*man, Jane* [*with a mask*],[2] *and others* [*servants*].

HODGE Peace, my bullies,° yonder they come. *fine fellows*

RALPH Stand to't, my hearts! Firk, let me speak first.

HODGE No, Ralph, let me.—Hammon, whither away so early?

HAMMON Unmannerly rude° slave, what's that to thee? *ignorant, uncivil*

FIRK To him, sir? Yes, sir, and to me, and others.—Good morrow, Jane, how dost thou? Good Lord, how the world is changed with you, God be thanked!

[*The shoemakers unmask Jane and strive to take her from Hammon and his servants.*]

HAMMON Villains, hands off! How dare you touch my love?

ALL [THE SHOEMAKERS] Villains? Down with them! Cry "Clubs for prentices!"° [*The two sides prepare to fight.*] *(a rallying cry)*

HODGE Hold, my hearts!—Touch her, Hammon? Yea, and more than that, we'll carry her away with us.—My masters and gentlemen, never draw your bird-spits.° Shoemakers are steel to the back,° men every inch of them, all spirit. *rapiers (sarcastic)* / *from top to bottom*

ALL OF HAMMON'S SIDE Well, and what of all this?

HODGE I'll show you.—Jane, dost thou know this man? 'Tis Ralph, I can tell thee. Nay, 'tis he, in faith; though he be lamed by the wars, yet look not strange,° but run to him, fold him about the neck, and kiss him. *as if on a stranger*

JANE Lives then my husband? Oh, God, let me go!
Let me embrace my Ralph.

HAMMON What means my Jane?

JANE Nay, what meant you to tell me he was slain?

HAMMON Pardon me, dear love, for being misled.
[*To Ralph*] 'Twas rumored here in London thou wert dead.

1. The most powerful king in the deck. (Also introducing the metaphor of "delve," with its bawdy suggestion of delving into a woman's secret parts.)

2. Jane needs the mask again at line 106 ff. At present, Firk, Ralph, and the other shoemakers are not fooled because they know Hammon's plan to marry her.

FIRK Thou see'st he lives.—Lass, go pack° home with him.— *be off*
Now, Master Hammon, where's your mistress your wife?
SERVINGMAN [*to Hammon*] 'Swounds,° master, fight for her! *By God's wounds*
Will you thus lose her?
ALL [THE SHOEMAKERS] Down with that creature!° Clubs! *toady, creep*
Down with him! [*The two sides prepare to fight.*]
HODGE Hold, hold!
HAMMON [*to his Servingman*] Hold, fool!—Sirs, he shall do no wrong.
[*To Jane*] Will my Jane leave me thus, and break her faith?
FIRK Yea, sir, she must, sir, she shall, sir. What then? Mend it.° *Alter it if you can*
HODGE Hark, fellow Ralph. Follow my counsel: set the wench in the midst, and let her choose her man, and let her be his° woman. *(that man's)*
JANE Whom should I choose? Whom should my thoughts affect° *love*
But him whom heaven hath made to be my love?
[*To Ralph*] Thou art my husband, and these humble weeds° *your humble attire*
Makes thee more beautiful than all his wealth.
Therefore I will but put off his attire,[3]
Returning it into the owner's hand,
And after ever be thy constant wife.
HODGE Not a rag, Jane. The law's on our side; he that sows in another man's ground forfeits his harvest. Get thee home, Ralph; follow him, Jane. He shall not have so much as a busk point° from thee. *lace for tying bodice*
FIRK Stand to that, Ralph. The appurtenances[4] are thine own.—Hammon, look not at her.
SERVINGMAN Oh, 'swounds, no!
FIRK Bluecoat,[5] be quiet! We'll give you a new livery else;° we'll make Shrove Tuesday Saint George's Day for you.[6] Look not, Hammon; leer not—I'll firk you; for° thy head now—one glance, one sheep's eye,° anything at her. Touch not a rag, lest I and my brethren beat you to clouts.° *otherwise; at peril of; amorous glance; rags*
SERVINGMAN Come, Master Hammon, there's no° striving here. *no point in*
HAMMON Good fellows, hear me speak; and honest Ralph,
Whom I have injured most by loving Jane,
Mark what I offer thee. [*Laying down money*] Here in fair gold
Is twenty pound. I'll give it for thy Jane.
If this content thee not, thou shalt have more.
HODGE Sell not thy wife, Ralph; make her not a whore.
HAMMON [*to Ralph*] Say, wilt thou freely cease thy claim in her,
And let her be my wife?
ALL [THE SHOEMAKERS] No, do not, Ralph!

3. I.e., I will simply remove the wedding attire in which I was to have married Hammon (and which he has apparently paid for).
4. Things belonging to a larger property and passing in possession with it. (A legal term.)
5. Servants traditionally wore blue livery.
6. I.e., We'll beat you black and blue, showing our valor in honor of Saint George, the patron saint of England. (Saint George's Day was also traditionally the day when servants looked for new employment. On Shrove Tuesday, see 17.50–51 and note above.)

RALPH Sirrah[7] Hammon, Hammon, dost thou think a shoemaker is so base to be a bawd° to his own wife for commodity?° Take thy gold; choke with it! Were I not lame, I would make thee eat thy words. *pander* *profit*

FIRK A shoemaker sell his flesh and blood? Oh, indignity!

HODGE Sirrah, take up your pelf,° and be packing. *ill-gotten wealth*

HAMMON I will not touch one penny. But in lieu
Of that great wrong I offerèd thy Jane,
To Jane and thee I give that twenty pound.
Since I have failed of° her, during my life *failed to win*
I vow no woman else shall be my wife.
Farewell, good fellows of the Gentle Trade.
Your morning's mirth my mourning day hath made.

Exeunt [*Hammon and his men*].

FIRK [*to the departing Servingman*] Touch the gold, creature, if you dare! You're best be trudging. [*Exit Servingman.*] Here, Jane, take thou it. [*He picks up the gold and gives it to Jane.*] Now let's home, my hearts.

HODGE Stay, who comes here? Jane, on again with thy mask. [*She masks.*]

Enter Lincoln; [*Oatley, the former*] *Lord Mayor; and servants.*

LINCOLN Yonder's the lying varlet° mocked us so. *rascal, menial (who)*

OATLEY [*to Firk*] Come hither, sirrah.

FIRK Ay, sir, I am sirrah.° You mean me, do you not? *(see n. 7)*

LINCOLN Where is my nephew married?

FIRK Is he married? God give him joy! I am glad of it. They have a fair day, and the sign is in a good planet, Mars in Venus.[8]

OATLEY Villain, thou told'st me that my daughter Rose
This morning should be married at Saint Faith's.
We have watched there these three hours at the least,
Yet see we no such thing.

FIRK Truly I am sorry for't. A bride's a pretty thing.[9]

HODGE Come to the purpose. Yonder's the bride and bridegroom you look for, I hope. Though you be lords, you are not to bar by your authority men from women, are you?

OATLEY [*to Lincoln*] See, see: my daughter's masked!

LINCOLN True; and my nephew,
To hide his guilt, counterfeits him° lame. *himself to be*

FIRK Yea, truly, God help the poor couple! They are lame and blind.

OATLEY I'll ease her blindness.

LINCOLN I'll his lameness cure.

FIRK [*aside to his fellows*] Lie down, sirs, and laugh! My fellow Ralph is taken for Rowland Lacy, and Jane for Mistress Damask Rose.° This is all my knavery. *a variety of rose*

OATLEY [*to Jane*] What, have I found you, minion?° *hussy*

LINCOLN [*to Ralph*] Oh, base wretch!

7. A term ordinarily addressed to servants and social inferiors (as at 16.72), hence here an insult. See lines 108–9 below.

8. Firk means that Mars and Venus are in conjunction, representing the union of male valor and female beauty.

9. Firk cheekily interprets Oatley's "watched" (line 116) as meaning "looked at something," whereas Oatley of course meant "stood watch."

Nay, hide thy face; the horror of thy guilt
Can hardly be washed off. Where are thy powers?° *troops*
What battles have you made?° Oh, yes, I see *fought*
Thou fought'st with shame, and shame hath conquered
thee.
This lameness will not serve.

OATLEY [*to Jane*] Unmask yourself!

LINCOLN [*to Oatley*] Lead home your daughter.

OATLEY [*to Lincoln*] Take your nephew hence.

RALPH Hence? 'Swounds, what mean you? Are you mad? I hope you cannot enforce my wife from me. Where's Hammon?

OATLEY Your wife?

LINCOLN What Hammon?

RALPH Yea, my wife; and therefore the proudest of you that lays hands on her first, I'll lay my crutch 'cross° his pate.° *across / head*

FIRK To him, lame Ralph!—Here's brave sport!

RALPH Rose, call you her? Why, her name is Jane. Look here else. [*He unmasks Jane.*] Do you know her now?

LINCOLN [*to Oatley*] Is this your daughter?

OATLEY No, nor this your nephew.
My lord of Lincoln, we are both abused° *deceived*
By this base crafty varlet.

FIRK Yea, forsooth, no "varlet," forsooth;[1] no "base," forsooth. I am but mean.[2] No "crafty" neither, but of the Gentle Craft.

OATLEY Where is my daughter Rose? Where is my child?

LINCOLN Where is my nephew Lacy married?

FIRK Why, here is good laced mutton,[3] as I promised you.

LINCOLN Villain, I'll have thee punished for this wrong.

FIRK Punish the journeyman villain, but not the journeyman shoemaker.[4]

Enter Dodger.

DODGER My lord, I come to bring unwelcome news.
Your nephew Lacy, and [*to Oatley*] your daughter Rose
Early this morning wedded at the Savoy,
None being present but the Lady Mayoress.
Besides, I learnt among the officers,° *city officials*
The Lord Mayor vows to stand in their defense
'Gainst any that shall seek to cross the match.

LINCOLN Dares Eyre the shoemaker uphold the deed?

FIRK Yes, sir, shoemakers dare stand in a woman's quarrel, I warrant you, as deep as another, and deeper too.[5]

DODGER Besides, His Grace° today dines with the Mayor, *the King*
Who on his knees humbly intends to fall
And beg a pardon for your nephew's fault.

LINCOLN But I'll prevent him. Come, Sir Roger Oatley.
The King will do us justice in this cause.

1. Firk may be like a varlet, a menial worker, since he provides services for wages, but he insists he is not a varlet in the sense of being a scoundrel.
2. Musical puns: "base" also means "bass"; "mean" signifies the middle voice, as well as "lowly." Firk goes on punningly to say that he practices the shoemakers' "craft" but is not "crafty," meaning "scheming."
3. Firk jestingly refers to Jane as a whore ("laced mutton") in order to twit Oatley and Lincoln about having been hoodwinked. (With a pun on "laced"/"Lacy.")
4. More punning: Lincoln and Oatley can punish a "villein" (migrant worker or peasant) if they like, but Firk is a guild member and no "villain" (scoundrel).
5. Firk's bawdy wordplay is evident in "stand," "deep," and probably "quarrel" (since "quarry" can mean "vagina").

Howe'er their hands have made them man and wife,
I will disjoin the match, or lose my life.

Exeunt [Lincoln, Oatley, and Dodger].

FIRK Adieu, Monsieur Dodger! Farewell, fools! Ha ha! Oh, if they had stayed I would have so lammed° them with flouts!° O heart, my codpiece point[6] is ready to fly in pieces every time I think upon Mistress Rose—but let that pass, as my Lady Mayoress says. [*thrashed / mocks*]

HODGE This matter is answered.° Come, Ralph, home with thy wife. Come, my fine shoemakers, let's to our master's, the new Lord Mayor, and there swagger this Shrove Tuesday. I'll promise you wine enough, for Madge[7] keeps° the cellar. [*settled*; *presides over*]

ALL Oh, rare! Madge is a good wench.

FIRK And I'll promise you meat° enough, for simpering Susan keeps the larder. I'll lead you to victuals, my brave soldiers. Follow your captain. Oh, brave! (*Bell rings.*) Hark, hark! [*food*]

ALL The pancake bell° rings, the pancake bell! Tri-lill, my hearts! [*(see 17.51 n above)*]

FIRK Oh, brave! O sweet bell! O delicate pancakes! Open the doors, my hearts, and shut up the windows. Keep in° the house, let out the pancakes. Oh, rare, my hearts! Let's march together for the honor of Saint Hugh to the great new hall in Gracious° Street corner, which our master the new Lord Mayor hath built.° [*Lock up*; *Gracechurch*; *i.e., Leadenhall*]

RALPH Oh, the crew of good fellows that will dine at my Lord Mayor's cost today!

HODGE By the lord, my Lord Mayor is a most brave° man. How shall prentices be bound to pray for him and the honor of the Gentlemen Shoemakers! Let's feed and be fat with my lord's bounty. [*splendid*]

FIRK Oh, musical bell still! O Hodge, O my brethren! There's cheer for the heavens:[8] venison pasties° walk up and down piping hot like sergeants, beef and brewis° comes marching in dry fats,[9] fritters and pancakes comes trolling° in in wheelbarrows, lemons and oranges hopping in porters' baskets, collops and eggs° in scuttles,° and tarts and custards comes quavering in in malt shovels.° [*meat pies*; *broth*; *trundling*; *ham and eggs / platters*; *large shovels for malt*]

Enter more prentices.

ALL Whoop! Look here, look here!

HODGE How now, mad lads, whither away so fast?

FIRST PRENTICE Whither? Why, to the great new hall. Know you not why? The Lord Mayor hath bidden all the prentices in London to breakfast this morning.

ALL O brave shoemaker! O brave lord of incomprehensible° good fellowship! Hoo, hark you, the pancake bell rings. [*beyond one's imagination*]

Cast up caps.

FIRK Nay, more, my hearts: every Shrove Tuesday is our year of° jubilee, and when the pancake bell rings we are as free [*our annual*]

6. The lace used to attach to the breeches the baggy appendage covering the male genitals.
7. The name of a servant-class woman they all evidently know—probably not the "Madgy" who is Eyre's wife at 17.16.
8. There's good cheer enough to satisfy the heavens themselves.
9. Dry-goods vats.

as my Lord Mayor; we may shut up our shops and make holiday. I'll have it called Saint Hugh's Holiday.

ALL Agreed, agreed! Saint Hugh's Holiday!

HODGE And this shall continue forever.

ALL Oh, brave! Come, come, my hearts! Away, away!

FIRK Oh, eternal credit to us of the Gentle Craft! March fair, my hearts. Oh, rare! *Exeunt.*

[Scene 19]

Enter King and his train° [including Cornwall] over the stage. — *entourage*

KING Is our Lord Mayor of London such a gallant?

CORNWALL One of the merriest madcaps in your land,
Your Grace will think, when you behold the man;
He's rather a wild ruffian than a mayor.
Yet thus much I'll ensure° Your Majesty: — *assure*
In all his actions that concern his state° — *official capacity*
He is as serious, provident, and wise,
As full of gravity amongst the grave,
As any mayor hath been these many years.

KING I am with child° till I behold this huff-cap.° — *eager / swashbuckler*
But all my doubt° is, when we come in presence, — *worry*
His madness will be dashed clean out of countenance.

CORNWALL It may be so, my liege.

KING Which to prevent,
Let someone give him notice, 'tis our pleasure
That he put on his wonted° merriment. — *customary*
Set forward.

ALL On afore! *Exeunt.*

[Scene 20]

Enter Eyre, Hodge, Firk, Ralph, and other shoemakers, all with napkins on their shoulders.

EYRE Come, my fine Hodge, my jolly Gentlemen Shoemakers. Soft, where be these cannibals, these varlets my officers?° Let them all walk and wait upon my brethren, for my meaning is that none but shoemakers, none but the livery° of my company, shall in their satin hoods wait upon the trencher° of my sovereign. — *city officials* / *liverymen, members* / *serve at the dinner*

FIRK Oh, my lord, it will be rare.

EYRE No more, Firk. Come lively.° Let your fellow prentices want no cheer;° let wine be plentiful as beer, and beer as water. Hang these penny-pinching fathers° that cram wealth in innocent lambskins!° Rip,° knaves, avaunt! Look to my guests. — *Step lively* / *lack no refreshment* / *old skinflints* / *purses / Look sharp*

HODGE My lord, we are at our wits' end for room. Those hundred tables will not feast the fourth part of them.

EYRE Then cover me° those hundred tables again and again, till all my jolly prentices be feasted. Avoid,° Hodge; run, — *load up with food* / *Get going*

Scene 19. On the way to Leadenhall.
Scene 20. Leadenhall, Eyre's new building on Gracechurch Street (see 18.194–96).

Ralph; frisk about, my nimble Firk; carouse me fathom healths° to the honor of the shoemakers. Do they drink lively, Hodge? Do they tickle it,° Firk?

drink deep / *enjoy themselves*

FIRK Tickle it? Some of them have taken their liquor standing so long that they can stand no longer; but for° meat, they would eat it an they had it.

as for

EYRE Want they meat? Where's this swag-belly,° this greasy kitchen-stuff cook? Call the varlet to me. Want meat? Firk, Hodge, lame Ralph, run, my tall men, beleaguer the shambles,° beggar all Eastcheap, serve me whole oxen in chargers,° and let sheep whine upon the tables like pigs for want of good fellows to eat them. Want meat? Vanish, Firk! Avaunt, Hodge!

fat belly / *besiege the meat stalls* / *platters*

HODGE Your Lordship mistakes my man Firk. He means their bellies want meat, not the boards, for they have drunk so much they can eat nothing.[1]

Enter [Lacy dressed as] Hans, Rose, and [Eyre's] wife [Margery].

MARGERY Where is my lord?

EYRE How now, Lady Madgy?

MARGERY The King's most excellent Majesty is new° come; he sends me for Thy Honor.° One of his most worshipful peers bade me tell thou must be merry, and so forth—but let that pass.

newly, just / *sends me for you*

EYRE Is my sovereign come? Vanish, my tall shoemakers, my nimble brethren. Look to my guests, the prentices. Yet stay a little.—How now, Hans, how looks my little Rose?

LACY Let me request you to remember me.
I know Your Honor easily may obtain
Free pardon of the King for me and Rose,
And reconcile me to my uncle's grace.

EYRE Have done,° my good Hans, my honest journeyman. Look cheerly.° I'll fall upon both my knees till they be as hard as horn but° I'll get thy pardon.

Say no more / *cheerful* / *unless and until*

MARGERY Good, my lord, have a care what you speak to His Grace.

EYRE Away, you Islington whitepot![2] Hence, you hopper-arse,[3] you barley pudding° full of maggots, you broiled carbonado,° avaunt, avaunt! Avoid, Mephistopheles!° Shall Sim Eyre learn to speak of° you, Lady Madgy? Vanish, Mother Miniver-Cap,° vanish! Go, trip and go, meddle with your partlets° and your pishery-pashery, your flews° and your whirligigs!° Go, rub, out of mine alley![4] Sim Eyre knows how to speak to a pope, to Sultan Suleiman, to Tamburlaine,[5] an he were here; and shall I melt, shall I droop before my sovereign? No! Come, my Lady Madgy. Follow me, Hans. About your business, my frolic freebooters.° Firk, frisk about, and

sausage / *grilled meat / a devil* / *from* / *cap trimmed with ermine* / *neck linen, ruffs / flaps* / *frills* / *pirates; shoemakers*

1. Firk didn't mean (in lines 20–22) that more food was needed for the banqueting tables, as Eyre has supposed, but rather that the men are so full of liquor that they have no more room for food.
2. A dish of cream, eggs, etc., from a town near London often visited on outings from the city; here a phrase of affectionate abuse.
3. Hopper-shaped butt.
4. I.e., Get out of my way. (From the game of bowls, in which a "rub" is an obstacle.)
5. Eyre can stand up to a pope, or to Suleiman the Magnificent of the Ottoman Empire (reigned 1520–66; see 7.61–62 and note), or to the invincible protagonist of Marlowe's play *Tamburlaine*.

about, and about, for the honor of mad Simon Eyre, Lord Mayor of London.

FIRK Hey for the honor of the shoemakers! *Exeunt.*

[Scene 21]

A long flourish or two. Enter King, nobles [including Cornwall], Eyre, his wife [Margery], Lacy [in his proper attire, and] Rose [with officers and attendants]. Lacy and Rose kneel.

KING Well, Lacy, though the fact° was very foul [*deed*]
Of your revolting from our kingly love
And your own duty, yet we pardon you.
Rise both; and Mistress Lacy, thank my Lord Mayor
For your young bridegroom here. [*The couple rises.*]

EYRE So, my dear liege, Sim Eyre and my brethren the Gentlemen Shoemakers shall set Your sweet Majesty's image cheek by jowl by Saint Hugh for this honor you have done poor Simon Eyre. I beseech Your Grace pardon my rude behavior. I am a handicraftsman, yet my heart is without craft. I would be sorry at my soul that my boldness should offend my king.

KING Nay, I pray thee, good Lord Mayor, be even as merry
As if thou wert among thy shoemakers.
It does me good to see thee in this humor.

EYRE Say'st thou me so, my sweet Diocletian?° Then, hump! Prince am I none, yet am I princely born. By the Lord of Ludgate, my liege, I'll be as merry as a pie.° [*emperor 284–305*; *magpie*]

KING Tell me, in faith, mad Eyre, how old thou art.

EYRE My liege, a very boy, a stripling, a younker.° You see not a white hair on my head, not a gray in this beard. Every hair, I assure Thy Majesty, that sticks in this beard Sim Eyre values at the King of Babylon's ransom. Tamar Cham's° beard was a rubbing brush to't.° Yet I'll shave it off and stuff tennis balls with it to please my bully king. [*youth*; *Genghis Khan's*; *compared to it*]

KING But all this while I do not know your age.

EYRE My liege, I am six-and-fifty year old, yet I can cry "Hump!" with a sound heart for the honor of Saint Hugh. [*Indicating Margery*] Mark this old wench, my king. I danced the shaking of the sheets° with her six-and-thirty years ago, and yet I hope to get° two or three young lord mayors ere I die. I am lusty still, Sim Eyre still. Care and cold lodging brings white hairs. My sweet Majesty, let care vanish. Cast it upon thy nobles. It will make thee look always young, like Apollo, and cry "Hump!" Prince am I none, yet am I princely born. [*(see 16.83)*; *beget*]

KING Ha ha! Say, Cornwall, didst thou ever see his like?

CORNWALL Not I, my lord.

Enter Lincoln and [Oatley, the former] Lord Mayor.

KING Lincoln, what news with you?

LINCOLN My gracious lord, have care unto yourself,

Scene 21. Leadenhall.

For there are traitors here.
ALL Traitors? Where? Who?
EYRE Traitors in my house? God forbid. Where be my officers? I'll spend° my soul ere my king feel harm. *expend, sacrifice*
KING Where is the traitor, Lincoln?
LINCOLN [*indicating Lacy*] Here he stands.
KING Cornwall, lay hold on Lacy.
[*Cornwall and officers detain Lacy.*]
Lincoln, speak:
What canst thou lay unto thy nephew's charge?
LINCOLN This, my dear liege: Your Grace, to do me honor,
Heaped on the head of this degenerous° boy *degenerate*
Desertless° favors. You made choice of him *Undeserved*
To be commander over powers° in France, *troops, forces*
But he—
KING Good Lincoln, prithee pause awhile;
Even in thine eyes I read what thou wouldst speak.
I know how Lacy did neglect our love,
Ran himself deeply, in the highest degree,
Into vile treason.
LINCOLN Is he not a traitor?
KING Lincoln, he was. Now have we pardoned him.
[*Lacy is freed.*]
'Twas not a base want° of true valor's fire *lack*
That held him out of France, but love's desire.
LINCOLN I will not bear his shame upon my back.° *my family honor*
KING Nor shalt thou, Lincoln. I forgive you both.
LINCOLN Then, good my liege, forbid the boy to wed
One whose mean birth will much disgrace his bed.
KING Are they not married?
LINCOLN No, my liege.
BOTH [LACY *and* ROSE] We are.
KING Shall I divorce them, then? Oh, be it far
That any hand on earth should dare untie
The sacred knot knit by God's Majesty.
I would not for my crown disjoin their hands
That are conjoined in holy nuptial bands.
How say'st thou, Lacy? Wouldst thou lose thy Rose?
LACY Not for all India's wealth, my sovereign.
KING But Rose, I am sure, her Lacy would forgo.
ROSE If Rose were asked that question, she'd say no.
KING You hear them, Lincoln?
LINCOLN Yea, my liege, I do.
KING Yet canst thou find i'th'heart to part these two?
Who seeks, besides you, to divorce these lovers?
OATLEY I do, my gracious lord. I am her father.
KING [*to Cornwall*] Sir Roger Oatley, our last mayor, I think?
CORNWALL The same, my liege.
KING [*to Oatley*] Would you offend love's laws?
Well, you shall have your wills. You sue to° me *petition*
To prohibit the match. Soft, let me see.
You both are married, Lacy, art thou not?
LACY I am, dread sovereign.
KING Then upon thy life,

I charge thee not to call this woman wife.
OATLEY I thank Your Grace.
ROSE Oh, my most gracious lord!
Kneel.
KING Nay, Rose, never woo° me. I tell you true, *petition; seek love from*
Although as yet I am a bachelor,
Yet I believe I shall not marry you.
ROSE Can you divide the body from the soul,
Yet make the body live?
KING Yea, so profound?
I cannot, Rose, but you I must divide.
Fair maid, this bridegroom cannot be your bride.°— *spouse*
Are you pleased, Lincoln? Oatley, are you pleased?
BOTH Yes, my lord.
KING Then must my heart be eased;
For, credit° me, my conscience lives in pain *believe*
Till these whom I divorced be joined again.
Lacy, give me thy hand. Rose, lend me thine.
[*Rose rises. The King joins their hands.*]
Be what you would be. Kiss now. [*They kiss.*] So, that's fine.
At night, lovers, to bed. Now let me see,
Which of you all mislikes this harmony?
OATLEY Will you then take from me my child perforce?
KING Why, tell me, Oatley, shines not Lacy's name
As bright in the world's eye as the gay beams
Of any citizen?
LINCOLN Yea, but, my gracious lord,
I do mislike the match far more than he;
Her blood is too too base.
KING Lincoln, no more.
Dost thou not know that love respects no blood,
Cares not for difference of birth or state?
The maid is young, wellborn, fair, virtuous,
A worthy bride for any gentleman.
Besides, your nephew for her sake did stoop
To bare necessity, and, as I hear,
Forgetting honors and all courtly pleasures,
To gain her love became a shoemaker.
As for the honor which he lost in France,
Thus I redeem it.—Lacy, kneel thee down. [*Lacy kneels.*]
Arise Sir Rowland Lacy. [*Lacy rises.*] Tell me now,
Tell me in earnest, Oatley, canst thou chide,
Seeing thy Rose a lady and a bride?
OATLEY I am content with what Your Grace hath done.
LINCOLN And I, my liege, since there's no remedy.
KING Come on, then, all shake hands. I'll have you friends.
Where there is much love, all discord ends.
What says my mad Lord Mayor to all this love?
EYRE Oh, my liege, this honor you have done to my fine journeyman here, Rowland Lacy, and all these favors which you have shown to me this day in my poor house, will make Simon Eyre live longer by one dozen of warm summers more than he should.
KING Nay, my mad Lord Mayor—that shall be thy name—

If any grace of mine can length thy life,
One honor more I'll do thee. That new building
Which at thy cost in Cornhill is erected
Shall take a name from us. We'll have it called
The Leadenhall, because in digging it
You found the lead that covereth° the same. *provides a roof for*

EYRE I thank Your Majesty.

MARGERY God bless Your Grace!

KING Lincoln, a word with you.

[*The King and Lincoln confer privately.*]

Enter Hodge, Firk, Ralph, and more shoemakers.

EYRE How now, my mad knaves? Peace, speak softly; yonder is the King.

KING [*to Lincoln*] With the old troop which there we keep in pay
We will incorporate a new supply.
Before one summer more pass o'er my head,
France shall repent England was injurèd.—
What are all those?

LACY All shoemakers, my liege,
Sometimes° my fellows. In their companies *Formerly*
I lived as merry as an emperor.

KING My mad Lord Mayor, are all these shoemakers?

EYRE All shoemakers, my liege, all gentlemen of the Gentle Craft, true Trojans,° courageous cordwainers. They all kneel to the shrine of holy Saint Hugh. *(see 4.121–22 and n)*

ALL SHOEMAKERS [*kneeling*] God save Your Majesty!

KING Mad Simon, would they anything with us?[1]

EYRE [*to the shoemakers*] Mum, mad knaves! Not a word; I'll do't, I warrant you. [*Kneeling to the King*] They are all beggars, my liege, all for themselves; and I for them all on both my knees do entreat that for the honor of poor Simon Eyre and the good of his brethren, these mad knaves, Your Grace would vouchsafe some privilege to my new Leadenhall, that it may be lawful for us to buy and sell leather there two days a week.

KING Mad Sim, I grant your suit. You shall have patent
To hold two market days in Leadenhall.
Mondays and Fridays, those shall be the times.
Will this content you?

ALL Jesus bless Your Grace!

EYRE In the name of these my poor brethren shoemakers, I most humbly thank Your Grace. But before I rise, seeing you are in the giving vein,° and we in the begging, grant Sim Eyre one boon more. *mood*

KING What is it, my Lord Mayor?

EYRE Vouchsafe to taste of a poor banquet that stands sweetly waiting for your sweet presence.

KING I shall undo thee, Eyre, only with feasts.[2]
Already have I been too troublesome;
Say, have I not?

1. Do the shoemakers have any request to make to me?
2. I will impoverish you with this munificent feasting, let alone any further expenditures.

EYRE [*rising*] O my dear King, Sim Eyre was taken unawares
upon a day of shroving[3] which I promised long ago to the
prentices of London.
For, an't please Your Highness, in time past
I bare the water tankard,° and my coat (*see 17.46–47 and n. 8*)
Sits not a whit the worse upon my back.
And then upon a morning some mad boys—
It was Shrove Tuesday, e'en as 'tis now—
gave me my breakfast, and I swore then by the stopple° of *stopper*
my tankard, if ever I came to be Lord Mayor of London, I
would feast all the prentices. This day, my liege, I did it, and
the slaves° had an hundred tables five times covered.° They *rascals / (with food)*
are gone home and vanished.
Yet add more honor to the Gentle Trade:
Taste of Eyre's banquet, Simon's happy made.° *and I'll be happy*

KING Eyre, I will taste of thy banquet, and will say
I have not met more pleasure on a day.—
Friends of the Gentle Craft, thanks to you all.
Thanks, my kind Lady Mayoress, for our cheer.
Come, lords, awhile let's revel it at home.
When all our sports and banquetings are done,
Wars must right wrongs which Frenchmen have begun.
Exeunt.

FINIS.

3. On Shrove Tuesday (see line 183 below), a day of merriment and license immediately preceding Ash Wednesday and the beginning of Lent. See also 17.50–52, 18.76, 18.182–83, and 18.217–18.

TEXTUAL NOTES

The Shoemaker's Holiday was published in quarto in 1600, not having been previously entered in the Stationers' Register (though an entry in Henslowe's diary for 15 July 1599 does record "A Boocke of thomas dickers Called the gentle Craft"). The text, evidently based on an authorial manuscript, was carefully prepared for the printer and was printed with relatively few errors. Five subsequent quarto editions provide a few commonsense corrections, but seemingly without authorial revision. The present edition is based on the original quarto. Substantive departures from it are noted here, using the following abbreviations:

Q1: Published by Valentine Sims (London, 1600)
Q1 corr.: The corrected first quarto
Q1 uncorr.: The uncorrected first quarto
Q2: Published by John Wright (London, 1610)
Q3: Published by John Wright (London, 1618)
Q6: Published by William Gilbertson (London, 1657)
ed.: A modern editor's emendation

1.10 Oatley's [Q1: Otleys; elsewhere the name is variously spelled Otly, Otley, and Oteley] **41 have sent** [ed.] haue [Q1] **50 SD** [placement, ed.; after "with you" in 50 in Q1] **54 Dieppe** [ed.] Deepe [Q1] **59 Tothill** [Q1: Tuttle] **97 beckons** [ed.] becomes [Q1] **116.2** [and elsewhere] ***Ralph*** [Q1: *Rafe*] **145 at one** [Q1: atone] **162 midriff** [ed.] Midasse [Q1] **165 Tawsoone . . . tawsoone** [ed.] Too soone . . . too soone [Q1] **177** [and elsewhere] **Ralph** [Q1: Raph] **177 goest** [Q1] goest not [many eds.] **178 Eyre** [Q1: Ayre, used interchangeably throughout with Eyre] **193 let us** [ed.] lets [Q1] **194.1** [placement, ed.; after "thither" in 193 in Q1] **227–28** ***baisez-mon-culs*** [Q1: *Basa mon cues*]

2.16.1 [placement, ed.; after 15 in Q1] **26 wore a** [Q3] wore [Q1] **62 i'Gods** [Q1: a Gods] **65 SD** [placement, ed.; opposite 64 in Q1]

3.22 drooping [ed.] hoping [Q1]

4.42 ***could*** [Q1: cold] **43** ***Upsee al sie*** [ed.] vpsolce se [Q1] **45** ***schoene*** [ed.] scheue [Q1] **52** [and elsewhere] **enough** [Q1: enow] **69 b'wi'you** [Q1: buy] **76** ***you, vro, auch*** [ed.] v vro oak [Q1] **80** ***bin*** [ed.] vin [Q1] **92** ***verstaw*** [Q2] vestaw [Q1] **94** ***yow*** [Q1: v] **111 Ho** [Q1: how] **113** ***verstaw yow.*** [ed.] wersto, you [Q1] **116 SD** [placement, ed.; after 115 in Q1] **118.1** [placement, ed.; after "Have to" in 120 in Q1]

5.3 scenting [Q1: senting] **6 soil** [Q2] saile [Q1] **6 holloed** [Q1: hallowed] **15 i'mine** [Q1: a mine]

6.9 flayed [Q1: flead] **58.1** [placement, ed.; after 57 in Q1]

7.2 fol [Q1: wol] **4 your** [Q1: v] **10** ***tot*** [ed.] lot [Q1] **10** ***van*** [ed.] vn [Q1] **11** ***Do't*** [Q1: doot it] **81 Here** [Q1: heare] **108.1–2** [placement, ed.; after 105 in Q1] **109 SD** [placement, ed.; after 105 in Q1] **134** ***revere*** [ed.] rouere [Q1] **136 yow** [Q1: yo] **140 aboard** [Q3] abroade [Q1]

8.11 LINCOLN [placement, ed.; at 12 in Q1] **23 thither** [ed.] hither [Q1]

9.45 your glove [Q1 corr.] your gloue at gloue [Q1 uncorr.] **59 strait** [Q1: straight] **75.1** [placement, ed.; after 76 in Q1] **100.1** [placement, ed.; after "I take my leave" in Q1]

10.1 Oh, Firk! [Q3; not in Q1] **63 how now** [Q1 corr.] how [Q1 uncorr.] **102** ***ick*** [ed.] it [Q1] **102 SD** [placement, ed.; after 101 in Q1] **158 Master** [Q6] mistris [Q1]

11.0.1–2 ***wife . . . Sibyl*** [ed.] *wife, Sibill in a French hood* [Q1]

12.39 Enjoined [ed.] In mind [Q1] **101 dead** [Q2] deede [Q1]

13.11 ***Forware*** [ed.] Forward [Q1] **11–12** ***Hort, ay, meester*** [Q1] hort I mester **12** ***vampies*** [ed.] vāpres [Q1] **20 Mistress** [Q1: M.] **55** ***yow . . . yow*** [ed.] gon . . . gon [Q1] **58** ***edle*** [ed.] egle [Q1] **66.1** [placement, ed.; after 65 in Q1]

14.2 ho! [ed.] haw, [Q1] **21 Ay, ay** [ed.] I, I [Q1]

15.19 we [Q3] me [Q1] **22 yourself. In** [ed.] your selfe in [Q1] **29.1** [placement, ed.; after "Pull on my shoe" in 28 in Q1] **31** ***betaelen*** [Q1: betallen] **37** ***heer*** [Q1: here] **38 SD** [placement, ed.; after 37 in Q1] **41 come to** [ed.] come [Q1]

16.28 your . . . my [Q3] my . . . your [Q1] **29 lives** [ed.] dies [Q1] **70 them** [Q2] then [Q1] **143 SD** ***Exit*** [Q3] *exeunt* [Q1]

17.1 say [ed.] stay [Q1] **37.1** [placement, ed.; after 36 in Q1]

18.188 SD [placement, ed.; after "Hark, hark!" in Q1] **204 pasties** [Q2] pastimes [Q1] **207 lemons** [ed.] hennes [Q1]

19.2, 13 CORNWALL [ed.] *Noble man* [Q1] **4 ruffian** [Q1: ruffin]

20.54 learn [Q3] leaue [Q1]

21.23 Tamar Cham's [Q1: Tama Chams] **38 CORNWALL** [ed.] *Noble man* [Q1] **70 India's** [ed.] Indians [Q1] **78 CORNWALL** [ed.] *Nob* [Q1] **151** [Q3, subst.] *All* God saue your maiesty all shoomaker. [Q1]

The Malcontent

Like the title character in John Marston's *The Malcontent* (1604), who assumes multiple identities, Marston himself played a series of seemingly contradictory roles in his remarkable life. His early verse satires, published under the pseudonym W. Kinsayder, were banned and publicly burned in June of 1599 by order of the Bishop of London and the Archbishop of Canterbury. In September of that year, the theater owner Philip Henslowe recorded an advance of two pounds to "Mr. Marston, the new poet" (the term "poet" was routinely applied to dramatists). Despite the strenuous objections of his father, who wanted him to be a lawyer, Marston soon began writing for a newly formed company of child actors, Paul's Boys. Over the next decade, he composed a dozen plays for the children's companies, every one of which was published in quarto soon after it was written. Yet in 1608, Marston suddenly and unaccountably gave up playwriting, apparently leaving *The Insatiate Countess* unfinished and relinquishing his one-sixth ownership share in the Children of the Queen's Revels. He may have abjured the stage for religion, since he was ordained as an Anglican priest in 1609. He lived out the remaining twenty-five years of his life with no connection to the theater, even insisting that the publisher of *The Works of Mr. John Marston* (1633) remove all mention of his name from the collection, which was thus reissued with the anonymous title *Tragedies and Comedies Collected into One Volume*.

At the beginning of his career as a dramatist, Marston was distinguished by his ability to refashion old plays for performance by the children's companies. In the case of *The Malcontent*, on the other hand, Marston originally wrote the play for the Children of the Queen's Revels at Blackfriars and then revised it for performance by an adult company, the King's Men at the Globe, in collaboration with John Webster. The revision added an induction and 450 new lines of dialogue. Linguistic and stylistic tests indicate that Webster wrote the Induction and about half of the new passages and that Marston was responsible for the rest of the added material.

The Induction, in which a number of actors from the King's Men play themselves, offers a wealth of information about playhouse practices of the day. When a company actor named Will Sly, pretending to be a member of the audience, attempts to sit on the stage, an anonymous tire-man, or stagehand (played by another company actor), explains to him an important difference between the Globe Theater, where *The Malcontent* is about to begin, and the so-called private theaters, such as Blackfriars: at Blackfriars, spectators are allowed to sit onstage, but not here at the Globe. Sly will have to move. He is reluctant to do so, since he has seen *The Malcontent* in its previous incarnation, when it was played by boy actors, and reckons he can let the audience in on the way it was staged by the boys. It turns out that the boy actors and the Globe's adult company have been quarreling over this particular play. Sly engages other members of the King's Men, notably Richard Burbage, John Lowin, and Henry Condell, in a discussion about how the King's Men came to acquire the script of a play previously staged by the boy actors at Blackfriars:

Introduction by Eric Rasmussen; glosses, footnotes, and textual notes by David Bevington; text edited by Eric Rasmussen and David Bevington.

The folded arms of this gentleman and the face buried beneath the hat are conventional signs of melancholy. From Samuel Rowlands, *The Melancholy Knight* (1615).

SLY ... I would know how you came by this play.
CONDELL Faith, sir, the book was lost; and because 'twas pity so good a play should be lost, we found it and play it.
SLY I wonder you would play it, another company having interest in it.
CONDELL Why not Malevole in folio with us, as Jeronimo in decimo-sexto with them? They taught us a name for our play; we call it *One for Another*. (Induction 71–79)

Using a metaphor from book publishing, Condell compares the adult actors to large-format folio volumes and the boy actors to pint-sized decimo-sexto volumes in which the printing sheet contained many more small pages of print. The name Jeronimo, or Hieronimo, refers to the protagonist of Thomas Kyd's *The Spanish Tragedy*, an enormously popular play of the late 1580s still in the repertory. Condell's point is that the boy actors stole *The Spanish Tragedy*, an adult play. Why, then, should not the adult actors appropriate one of the boys' plays for their use? Condell's facetious title, *One for Another*, signifies a tit for tat. The present revival of *The Malcontent* is thus a major event in a competitive rivalry between the adult and the juvenile players.

Other details emerge from the Induction in a comparison of staging practices in the adult and boys' theaters. As a playgoer familiar with the boys' companies who has purportedly recorded most of the jokes from the original children's production of *The Malcontent* in his "table-book," or memorandum book, Sly is curious to know what revisions the King's Men have made to the text—a curiosity no doubt shared by members of the actual audience:

SLY What are your additions?
BURBAGE Sooth, not greatly needful, only as your sallet to your great feast, to entertain a little more time and to abridge the not-received custom of music in our theater. (Induction 80–83)

Burbage alludes to the practice of indoor playhouses such as Blackfriars to present musical interludes between the acts. Without these musical embellishments, *The Malcontent* apparently needed lengthening in order to fill the time for a customary afternoon's entertainment—what the opening chorus of *Romeo and Juliet* calls "the two-hours' traffic of our stage," though it was often closer to three hours. The added passages significantly expanded Malevole's role, no doubt to provide a more substantial part for the actor Burbage to play. The revision also created a new character, the bitter clown Passarello, presumably to make appropriate use of the talents of the company's comic actor, Robert Armin. The Induction also refers to some spectators who are standing, as would not have been the case in the boys' theaters, and to the hard seats in the galleries. The Induction breathes a theatrical vitality arising out of the economic competition among the theaters.

The play that follows, in the five acts of *The Malcontent*, is no less fascinated with role-playing than is the Induction. The identity of the leading figure, Malevole, turns out to be a fictional guise for Altofronto, the deposed duke of Genoa; having been deprived of power by the present duke, Pietro Jacomo, Malevole stays on at the Genoese court in a disguise that encourages him to speak out sharply and bitterly as a moral critic of the enervation he sees on every side. Disguise further enables Malevole to hoodwink Mendoza, the play's power-seeking and lustful villain. Presenting himself to Mendoza as an accomplice in a plot to oust Pietro as duke, Malevole soon finds himself being hired (once the ousting of Pietro has taken place) to woo his own virtuous wife, Maria, on behalf of the new duke, Mendoza, who wants to marry her in order to secure his hold on the dukedom. Malevole stages yet another deception when he pretends to have assassinated Pietro on behalf of Mendoza but instead provides Pietro with an improbable disguise as the "Hermit of the Rock" (4.3.16). These two disguised figures, vastly amused to discover that they have been commissioned by Mendoza to kill each other, engineer a richly deserved comeuppance for the villainous new duke. The final scene is one of multiple unmaskings in which Mendoza is brought face-to-face with his accusers; Maria is rejoined with her long-separated husband; and Pietro and Aurelia, Pietro's lascivious but now penitent duchess, are united in mutual forgiveness.

Disguised dukes and railing malcontents are, to be sure, staples in the drama of the period, most famously in Shakespeare's *Measure for Measure* and *As You Like It*. Marston offers his own remarkable variation on these dramatic types by combining them in Malevole to create an inscrutable character who resides at once both inside and outside the corrupt world on which he comments. The corruption of that courtly world is manifest from the very start of the play, in the opening stage direction calling for the *"vilest out-of-tune music"* (1.1.0.1). The noise is overwhelming, reminding its hearers of the cacaphony of the Tower of Babel. The room where the courtiers gather is "ill scented" (1.1.7), as though they are in a brothel. The perfume needed to counter this stench is a kind of mask, obscuring but not obliterating what lies beneath.

The stage name for the protagonist, "Malevole," reflects this pervasive corruption. The name means, literally, "the ill-wishing one." Malevole is, moreover, identified as a cynic, a word derived from the Greek word *kynikos*, meaning "doglike"; a cynic is one who snarls and bites. Malevole is also a malcontent, one who acts as a discontented, alienated social critic, having derived a satiric perspective on human folly from being deprived of his usual social role and thus being forced to stand outside of the world on which he comments. Having suffered huge reversals of fortune, he is in a position to see clearly what is so absurd about human strivings for power and sex. Malevole is also something of a fool, or court jester. The lineage of such a persona is ancient, going back for example to Socrates and to Diogenes, the so-called laughing cynic, who lived in a tub during the fourth century B.C.E. in Greece, from which vantage he could jibe at no less a figure than Alexander the Great.

Marston presents his railing satiric figure in as vividly nasty a way as possible. Malcontents and cynics prided themselves on being offensively plainspoken, claiming that their antisocial rudeness was justified by the extensiveness of the corruption they needed to excoriate. Malevole, as a dog-cynic, is ready to lift his leg and piss against the world: "Come down, thou ragged cur, and snarl here," Pietro calls to him in the play's opening act; "trot about and bespurtle whom thou pleasest" (1.2.10–12). Malevole's diatribes abound in scatological and vulgar imagery: the earth is "the very muckhill on which the sublunary orbs cast their excrements" (4.5.114–15); courtiers are like pigeon-houses, "smooth, round, and white without, and full of holes and stink within" (1.4.87–88); a typical courtier would "rather follow a drunkard and live by licking up his vomit than by servile flattery" (4.5.67–69). Malevole's splendidly vitriolic prose is punctuated by sardonic stuttering—" 'dieu, adieu, Duke" (4.3.93)—and energetically repeated phrases—"to fret, to fret . . . to suck up, to suck up" (1.2.14–15)—doublings that may serve as subtle reminders of his dual character as both Malevole and Altofronto.

We know little about the "real" Altofronto; he is a shadow in comparison with Malevole. Altofronto sees himself as an avenger, as a champion of morality and order, but as Malevole he is a troublemaker and schemer; "His highest delight is to procure others' vexation" (1.2.21–22). Indeed, Malevole delights in torturing Pietro with the news of his wife's adultery, a form of revenge that he sees as more devastating than murder: "The heart's disquiet is revenge most deep. / He that gets blood, the life of flesh but spills, / But he that breaks heart's peace, the dear soul kills" (1.3.158–60). Altofronto ultimately claims to be weary of playing the Malevole role: "how loathsome this toying is to me! That a duke should be forced to fool it!" (5.3.41–43). Even so, he clearly enjoys his status as an unsparing critic who can rail against sin, and even participate in it, without necessarily being responsible for rooting it out.

The Malcontent presents a tempestuous world where character is mutable and political stability is, at best, uncertain. The play was probably written sometime between late 1602 and early 1604—an extraordinarily unstable period in English history. Queen Elizabeth died early in 1603, passing the Crown to her Scottish cousin, James. Tensions between the English and the newly arrived Scots made court life volatile. Although Marston does not engage in direct jabs at the Crown—an undertaking that would have invited censorship, or even imprisonment[1]—a critique of the new king and his courtiers seems apparent in the derisive references to "bawbees" (Scottish pennies), i.e., the poor retainers who accompanied James to the English court (Induction 95); "Scotch barnacle" (3.1.48); "Scotch boot" (3.1.78); and "Signor Saint Andrew Jaques," a Scotsman (5.5.24).[2] The exchange in which Malevole asks, "What religion will you be of now?" to which the sycophant Bilioso replies, "Of the Duke's religion, when I know what it is" (4.5.94–95), probably reflects the atmosphere in which traditional Anglicans and zealously reforming Puritans jockeyed for position under the new Stuart regime.

The Induction identifies the target of the play's satire not as a specific political figure, but, more generally, as "such vices as stand not accountable to law"—ignorance, avarice, hypocrisy, sanctimoniousness, and lechery—which can be cured only "by casting ink upon them" (Induction 67–69). Marston crafts characters that we "love to hate" (1.6.29): the faithless duchess Aurelia, who is "only constant in inconstancy" (1.6.93–94); the reprehensible schemer Mendoza, who feigns love "but for a spurt" (1.6.20); the greedy Maquerelle, for whom "Honesty is but an art to seem so" (5.3.12). Although much ink is indeed spent upon these disreputable characters, Marston is more parsimonious with the admirable ones: Altofronto's trusted confidant, the nobly named Celso (*celso* is Italian for "noble"), has only thirty-eight lines in the play; the faithful duchess Maria, who is not only "truly modestly honorable" but avoids even the appearance of impropriety (5.2.85–87), has all of forty-six lines. Meantime, the manifestly unfaithful Aurelia has nearly three times that number, and the panderess Maquerelle has over two hundred. Vice is here vibrantly rendered, virtue merely sketched.

The Malcontent's frequent allusions to *Hamlet* seem calculated to highlight the differences between the two revenge plays, even as they attest to Marston's perhaps envious indebtedness to Shakespeare, his great contemporary.[3] Every major character

1. In 1605, Marston was imprisoned, along with fellow playwrights George Chapman and Ben Jonson, and threatened with mutilation because of the seditious elements in *Eastward Ho,* a play on which the three had collaborated.

2. The reference to "Signor Saint Andrew Jaques" appears only in the first edition, Q1 (see Textual Notes, 5.5.24). In subsequent editions, Q2 and Q3, the line is altered to read "Signor Saint Andrew"; perhaps Marston censored his own text in order to avoid royal disapproval. (Saint Andrew is the patron saint of Scotland, and Jaques is French for James).

3. Compare Malevole's "Illo, ho, ho, ho! Art there, old truepenny?" (3.3.38) with Hamlet's "Hillo, ho, ho . . . Art thou there, truepenny?" (1.5.119, 159). See also Aurelia's "Look where the base wretch comes"

in *Hamlet* is killed as an indirect or direct result of the revenge plot. In contrast, Altofronto carries out his revenge, frustrates multiple murder plots, and reassumes his regency without killing anyone, thereby foreshadowing the bloodless revenge of Prospero in *The Tempest*. In the final scene of restoration and reconciliation, Altofronto makes it clear that he does not have the stomach for bloodletting: "prostrate at my feet, / I scorn to hurt thee" (5.6.132–33). Mendoza is thus punished for his crimes of attempted murder and treason simply by being banished from the court.

To be sure, discordant elements remain. Although Pietro and Aurelia pledge to renew their vows of fidelity to each other and to spend their remaining years in contemplation, the speed of their conversions may leave the audience wondering about the permanence of the transformation. Bilioso is still a confirmed sycophant; Ferneze brazenly woos the married Bianca; Maquerelle returns to the brothels. Disorder is apparently a constituent part of the new order just as it was a part of the old in Marston's probing, unflattering, yet strangely appealing vision of the political and social degradation of his time.

when Mendoza enters *"reading a sonnet"* (1.6.65.1, 66) and Gertrude's "look where sadly the poor wretch comes reading" when Hamlet enters *"reading on a book"* (2.2.167.1, 168). Mendoza's "In body how delicate, in soul how witty, in discourse how pregnant, in life how wary" (1.5.44–45) may be compared with Hamlet's "in form and moving how express and admirable, in action how like an angel, in apprehension how like a god" (2.2.306–8).

JOHN MARSTON
The Malcontent

To the Reader

I am an ill orator, and, in truth, use to indite° more honestly than eloquently, for it is my custom to speak as I think and write as I speak.

am used to write

In plainness, therefore, understand that in some things I have willingly erred, as in supposing a duke of Genoa, and in taking names different from that city's families, for which some may wittily accuse me; but my defense shall be as honest as many reproofs unto me have been most malicious; since, I heartily protest, it was my care to write so far from reasonable offense that even strangers,° in whose state I laid my scene, should not from thence draw any disgrace to any, dead or living. Yet in despite of my endeavors, I understand some have been most unadvisedly overcunning in misinterpreting me, and, with subtlety as deep as hell, have maliciously spread ill rumors which, springing from themselves, might to themselves have heavily returned. Surely I desire to satisfy every firm spirit who, in all his actions, proposeth to himself no more ends than God and virtue do, whose intentions are always simple. To such I protest that, with my free understanding, I have not glanced at disgrace of any but of those whose unquiet studies labor innovation, contempt of holy policy, reverent comely superiority, and established unity. For the rest of my supposed tartness, I fear not, but unto every worthy mind it will be approved so general and honest as may modestly pass with the freedom of a satire. I would fain leave the paper.° Only one thing afflicts me, to think that scenes invented merely to be spoken should be enforcively published to be read, and that the least hurt I can receive is to do myself the wrong.° But since others otherwise would do me more, the least inconvenience is to be accepted. I have myself therefore set forth this comedy, but so° that my enforced absence must much rely upon the printer's discretion. But I shall entreat, slight errors in orthography may be as slightly overpassed, and that the

i.e., Italians

stop writing this

(of publishing)

in such a way

The 1604 title page reads "*The Malcontent,* augmented by Marston. With the additions played by the King's Majesty's Servants. Written by John Webster. 1604, at London. Printed by V[alentine] S[immes] for William Aspley, and are to be sold at his shop in Paul's Churchyard." A dedication follows (in Latin, here translated): "John Marston, disciple of the muses, gives and dedicates this his harsh comedy to Benjamin Jonson, the most profound and at the same time the most polished of poets, his true and heartfelt friend."

unhandsome shape which this trifle in reading presents may be pardoned for the pleasure it once afforded you when it was presented with the soul of lively action.

Sine aliqua dementia nullus Phoebus.[1]
J[ohn] M[arston]

DRAMATIS PERSONAE

[*Actors of the King's Men, at the Globe Theater, who appear in the Induction:*
TIRE-MAN° (stagehand)
Will SLY
John SINKLO
Richard BURBAGE
Henry CONDELL
John LOWIN

The play proper:
PROLOGUE]
Giovanni Altofronto, disguised MALEVOLE, sometime° (formerly) Duke of Genoa
PIETRO Jacomo, Duke of Genoa
MENDOZA, a minion to the Duchess of Pietro Jacomo
CELSO, a friend to Altofront
BILIOSO, an old choleric marshal
PREPASSO, a gentleman-usher
FERNEZE, a young courtier, and enamored on the Duchess [Aurelia]
FERRARDO, a minion to Duke Pietro Jacomo
EQUATO, GUERRINO } two courtiers
AURELIA, Duchess to Duke Pietro Jacomo
MARIA, Duchess to Duke Altofront
EMILIA, BIANCA [Bilioso's wife] } two ladies attending the Duchess [Aurelia]
MAQUERELLE, an old panderess
PASSARELLO, fool to Bilioso
[CAPTAIN of the Genoan citadel
MERCURY, presenter of the masque
EPILOGUE
Pages; a guard; four halberdiers; four suitors, or petitioners, to Mendoza

THE SCENE: Genoa.]

1. Without some madness there is no poetic power. (Source unknown.)

[Prologue]

An Imperfect Ode, Being But One Staff,° Spoken by the Prologue

stanza

[*Enter the Prologue.*]

PROLOGUE To wrest each hurtless thought to private sense
Is the foul use of ill-bred Impudence;[1]
Immodest censure now grows wild,
All overrunning.
Let Innocence be ne'er so chaste,
Yet at the last
She is defiled
With too nice-brainèd° cunning. *fastidiously witty*
O you of fairer soul,
Control
With an Herculean arm
This harm,
And once teach all old freedom of a pen,
Which still must write of fools, whiles 't writes of men.

[*Exit.*]

The Induction

Enter Will Sly,[1] a Tire-man° following him with a stool. *stagehand*

TIRE-MAN Sir, the gentlemen° will be angry if you sit here. *the audience*

SLY Why? We may sit upon the stage at the private house.° Thou dost not take me for a country gentleman,° dost? Dost think I fear hissing? I'll hold° my life thou took'st me for one of the players.° *Blackfriars Theater / country simpleton / bet / actors*

TIRE-MAN No, sir.

SLY By God's lid,° if you had, I would have given you but sixpence for your stool. Let them that have stale° suits sit in the galleries.° Hiss at me? He that will be laughed out of a tavern or an ordinary shall seldom feed well or be drunk in good company.[2] Where's Harry Condell, Dick Burbage, and Will Sly? Let me speak with some of them. [*He sits.*] *By God's eyelid / out-of-fashion / in the auditorium*

TIRE-MAN An't° please you to go in,° sir, you may. *If it / backstage*

SLY I tell you, no. I am one that hath seen this play often, and can give them intelligence for their action.[3] I have most of the jests here in my table-book.° *pocket notebook*

Enter Sinklo.° *(a minor actor)*

SINKLO Save you, coz.° *God save you, friend*

SLY Oh, cousin,° come, you shall sit between my legs here. *(any close friend)*

SINKLO No, indeed, cousin, the audience then will take me for a viol da gambo,° and think that you play upon me. *an early cello*

Prologue.
1. For an audience to misinterpret innocent dramatic writing as a personal attack is the worst sort of boorish impudence.

The Induction.
1. A minor actor in the King's Men, here playing an audience member, as does John Sinklo when he enters at 16.1. The other, better-known actors of the company named in this induction (Burbage, Lowin, and Condell) play themselves.
2. No one is going to laugh Sly out of taking a seat onstage, any more than he would give up a meal or a drink in a tavern or eating establishment just because of some scornful remark.
3. I can tell the audience how the play went in its original version.

SLY Nay, rather that I work upon you,° coz. [*use you sexually*]

SINKLO We stayed° for you at supper last night at my cousin Honeymoon's, the woolen-draper. After supper we drew cuts° for a score of apricots, the longest cut still to draw an apricot. By this light, 'twas Mistress Frank° Honeymoon's fortune still to have the longest cut.° I did measure for the women.—What be these, coz? [*waited*; *drew straws, lots*; *Frances*; *lot; vagina*]

Enter Dick Burbage, Harry Condell, [and] John Lowin.

SLY The players!—God save you!

BURBAGE You are very welcome.

SLY I pray you, know° this gentleman, my cousin. 'Tis Master Doomsday's son, the usurer. [*be acquainted with*]

CONDELL I beseech you, sir, be covered.° [*put your hat back on*]

SLY No, in good faith, for mine ease; look you, my hat's the handle to this fan. God's so,° what a beast was I, I did not leave my feather at home![4] Well, but I'll take an order with you.° *Puts his feather in his pocket.* [*(a vulgar oath)*; *I'll do as you say*]

BURBAGE Why do you conceal your feather, sir?

SLY Why? Do you think I'll have jests broken upon me in the play, to be laughed at? This play hath beaten all your gallants out of the feathers; Blackfriars hath almost spoiled Blackfriars for feathers.[5]

SINKLO God's so, I thought 'twas for somewhat° our gentlewomen at home counseled me to wear my feather to the play; yet I am loath to spoil it.° [*for some reason*; *(by putting it in pocket)*]

SLY Why, coz?

SINKLO Because I got it in the tiltyard. There was a herald broke my pate for taking it up,[6] but I have worn it up and down the Strand,° and met him forty times since, and yet he dares not challenge it. [*a fashionable street*]

SLY Do you hear, sir, this play is a bitter play.

CONDELL Why, sir, 'tis neither satire nor moral,° but the mean passage of a history.[7] Yet there are a sort of discontented creatures that bear a stingless envy to great ones, and these will wrest the doings of any man to their base, malicious applyment.[8] But should their interpretation come to the test, like your marmoset° they presently turn their teeth to their tail and eat it.° [*morality play*; *a kind of monkey*; *i.e., eat their words*]

SLY I will not go so far with you, but I say, any man that hath wit may censure—if he sit in the twelvepenny room° —and I say again, the play is bitter. [*expensive box seats*]

BURBAGE Sir, you are like a patron that, presenting a poor scholar to a benefice,° enjoins him not to rail against anything that stands within compass° of his patron's folly. Why [*church position*; *within the scope*]

4. Sly, posing as an audience member, affects the mannerism of fanning himself with the feather in his hat, pretending that the hat is simply a part of the fan; he professes to have brought the feather along quite by chance. (See next note.)

5. As a "gallant," or courtly gentleman, overly sensitive to not being dressed in the latest fashion, Sly senses that feathers are no longer the thing for gentlemen to wear. The satiric atmosphere of the Blackfriars private playhouse, he says, has almost ruined the feather trade located in the Blackfriars district (between Saint Paul's Cathedral and the Thames) by running feathers down as unfashionable.

6. There was a tournament officer who battered my head for picking up the feather (where it had fallen from the helmet of a tournament combatant in the tiltyard, an area in Whitehall Palace devoted to jousting).

7. But a plain narrative told as a story.

8. And these envious persons twist any account (as in a play) into a personal and malicious attack, imagining a slander where the author intended none.

should not we enjoy the ancient° freedom of poesy? Shall we protest to the ladies that their painting° makes them angels, or to my young gallant that his expense in the brothel shall gain him reputation? No, sir, such vices as stand not accountable to law should be cured as men heal tetters,° by casting ink upon them. Would you be satisfied in anything else, sir? *classical, time-honored* / *use of cosmetics* / *skin eruptions*

SLY Ay, marry,° would I. I would know how you came by this play. *by Mary (an oath)*

CONDELL Faith,° sir, the book° was lost; and because 'twas pity so good a play should be lost, we found it and play it. *In faith / promptbook*

SLY I wonder you would play it, another company having interest in it.[9]

CONDELL Why not Malevole in folio with us, as Jeronimo in decimo-sexto with them?[1] They taught us a name for our play; we call it *One for Another*.° Tit for Tat

SLY What are your additions?

BURBAGE Sooth,° not greatly needful, only as your sallet° to your great feast, to entertain° a little more time and to abridge the not-received custom of music in our theater.[2] I must leave you, sir. *Exit Burbage.* *In truth / salad* / *pass*

SINKLO Doth he play the malcontent?

CONDELL Yes, sir.

SINKLO I durst lay four of mine ears[3] the play is not so well acted as it hath been.° *been acted by boys*

CONDELL Oh, no, sir, nothing *ad Parmenonis suem*.[4]

LOWIN [*to Sinklo*] Have you lost your ears, sir, that you are so prodigal of laying them?[5]

SINKLO Why did you ask that, friend?

LOWIN Marry, sir, because I have heard of a fellow would° offer to lay° a hundred-pound wager, that° was not worth five bawbees;° and in this kind you might venture four of your elbows; yet God defend your coat should have so many.[6] *who would* / *bet / who* / *coins of little value*

SINKLO Nay, truly, I am no great censurer,° and yet I might have been one of the college of critics once. My cousin here hath an excellent memory indeed, sir. *judge, critic*

SLY Who, I? I'll tell you a strange thing of myself; and I can tell you, for one that never studied the art of memory, 'tis very strange, too.

CONDELL What's that, sir?

9. Marston originally wrote this play for a boys' company at Blackfriars. The adult actors, the King's Men, who acted regularly at the open-air Globe Theater, acquired an interest in the indoor Blackfriars Theater. Here they have appropriated and adapted Marston's play to their use.

1. Why shouldn't we adult actors (like large books printed in folio, with each printed sheet folded only once) act this play, when the boy actors (pint-sized, like the smallest common size of a printed book) took over Thomas Kyd's *The Spanish Tragedy*, a play that had belonged to the adult actors? (Jeronimo, or Hieronimo, is the protagonist of *The Spanish Tragedy*.)

2. And to make up for the entr'actes, or musical interludes, featured in the private theater, which we adult actors do not employ.

3. I would dare to bet four ears, if I had them. (Cropping of ears was a common punishment for such offenses as stealing.)

4. Nothing compared to Parmeno's pig—i.e., a skilled imitation of a pig's grunting, which some undiscerning appreciators of Parmeno preferred to the real thing. (The story is told by Plutarch, c. 46 C.E.)

5. That you are so recklessly ready to bet them? (Lowin implies a lack of good critical taste on Sinklo's part and also that Sinklo may have been punished for criminal offenses by having his ears cropped; see note 3 above.)

6. You could safely bet four elbows, having only two, just as a certain fellow could afford to bet a hundred pounds since he was virtually penniless; yet God forbid your coat of arms should display such a ridiculous emblem as four elbows.

SLY Why, I'll lay a hundred pound I'll walk but once down by the Goldsmiths' Row in Cheap,° take notice of the signs, and tell you them with a breath° instantly.

Cheapside, a shop area
in one breath

LOWIN 'Tis very strange.

SLY They begin as the world did, with Adam and Eve.° There's in all just five-and-fifty. I do use° to meditate much when I come to plays, too. What do you think might come into a man's head now, seeing all this company?°

a tavern
make it a practice
the audience

CONDELL I know not, sir.

SLY I have an excellent thought: if some fifty of the Grecians that were crammed in the horse belly° had eaten garlic, do you not think the Trojans might have smelt out their knavery?

the Trojan horse

CONDELL Very likely.

SLY By God, I would they had, for I love Hector horribly.

SINKLO Oh, but coz, coz:
"Great Alexander, when he came to the tomb of Achilles,
Spake with a big loud voice, 'O thou thrice blessèd and happy!'"[7]

SLY Alexander was an ass to speak so well of a filthy cullion.°

pervert (lit., "testicle")

LOWIN Good sir, will you leave the stage? I'll help you to a private room.°

box

SLY [*to Sinklo*] Come, coz, let's take° some tobacco. [*To Lowin*] Have you never a prologue?°

smoke
no prologue

LOWIN Not any, sir.

SLY Let me see, I will make one extempore. Come to them, and, fencing of a congé° with arms and legs, be round with them:[8] "Gentlemen, I could wish for the women's sakes you had all soft cushions; and gentlewomen, I could wish that for the men's sakes you had all more easy standings."[9] What would they wish more but the play now? And that they shall have instantly. [*Exeunt.*]

taking a grand bow

1.1

The vilest out-of-tune music being heard [*above*], *enter Bilioso and Prepasso.*

BILIOSO [*shouting to the musicians*] Why, how now! Are ye mad, or drunk, or both, or what?

PREPASSO Are ye building Babylon there?[1]

BILIOSO Here's a noise in court! You think you are in a tavern, do you not?

PREPASSO You think you are in a brothel-house, do you not? This room is ill scented.

7. In Alexander the Great's view, Achilles was fortunate in having Homer to immortalize him. Achilles was the greatest Greek warrior, and Hector the greatest Trojan warrior, in the Trojan War. Sly bemoans Hector's defeat at the hands of the Greeks in line 118. The English generally favored the Trojan side, since, according to legend, England was settled by a descendant of Aeneas of Troy.
8. Be plainspoken with the audience.
9. Places to stand; some of the audience at the Globe stood in the yard close to the stage. (With dirty jokes about women's "soft cushions," i.e., buttocks and genital area, and men's "standings," or erections.)
1.1. The court of the Duke of Genoa.
1. Genesis 11.1–9 describes how the descendants of Noah settled on a plain in the land of Shinar (i.e., Babylonia), where they built a city and a tower "whose top may reach unto heaven." The central building became known as the Tower of Babel "because the Lord did there confound the language of all the earth: and from thence did the Lord scatter them abroad upon the face of all the earth." This confusion of languages would have created a jumble of noise like that presently heard in the Genoese court.

Enter one [a page] with a perfume.

So, perfume, perfume; some upon me, I pray thee.—The Duke is upon instant entrance;° so, make place° there. *about to enter / room*

1.2

Enter the Duke Pietro; Ferrardo, Count Equato, [and] Count Celso before;° and Guerrino. *preceding as escorts*

PIETRO Where breathes that music?

BILIOSO The discord, rather than the music, is heard from the malcontent Malevole's chamber.° *(on the upper stage)*

FERRARDO [*calling*] Malevole!

MALEVOLE (*out of his chamber*) Yaugh! God-a'-man,° what dost thou there? Duke's Ganymede, Juno's jealous of thy long stockings.[1] Shadow° of a woman, what wouldst, weasel? Thou lamb o'court,° what dost thou bleat for? Ah, you smooth-chinned catamite!° *(an oath)* *Picture, imitation* *court-pet* *boy sexual partner*

PIETRO Come down, thou ragged° cur, and snarl here. I give thy dogged sullenness free liberty; trot about and bespurtle° whom thou pleasest. *shaggy* *piss on*

MALEVOLE [*out of his chamber*] I'll come among you, you goatish-blooded toderers,° as gum into taffeta, to fret, to fret.[2] I'll fall like a sponge into water to suck up, to suck up. Howl again!° I'll go to church and come to you. *lecherous old dodderers* *(said to the musicians)*

PIETRO This Malevole is one of the most prodigious affections that ever conversed with nature;[3] a man, or rather a monster, more discontent than Lucifer when he was thrust out of the presence.° His appetite is unsatiable as the grave, as far from any content as from heaven. His highest delight is to procure others' vexation, and therein he thinks he truly serves heaven; for 'tis his position,° whosoever in this earth can be contented is a slave° and damned; therefore does he afflict all in that to which they are most affected.[4] The elements struggle within him; his own soul is at variance within herself. His speech is halterworthy° at all hours. I like him, faith; he gives good intelligence to my spirit, makes me understand those weaknesses which others' flattery palliates.[5] Hark, they sing. *A song.*° *God's divine presence* *view, argument* *servile wretch* *worthy of hanging* *(missing)*

1.3

Enter Malevole [on the main stage] after the song.

See, he comes. Now shall you hear the extremity of a malcontent. He is as free as air; he blows over every man.—And, sir, whence come you now?

MALEVOLE From the public place of much dissimulation, the church.

1.2. The scene continues.
1. Jupiter's, or Zeus's, delight in Ganymede as his cupbearer and erotic male favorite was a source of jealousy for Jupiter's wife, Juno. Malevole suggests that Ferrardo's effeminate style of dressing in long stockings will have the same effect on Aurelia, Pietro's wife.
2. Gum used as a stiffener caused the cloth to rub and chafe. Malevole promises to chafe the courtiers.
3. Malevole has one of the most monstrous dispositions of any person ever to have been born.
4. Pietro sardonically characterizes Malevole as one who thinks his vexing people is a divine mission, since religion teaches that one should not become attached ("affected") to the things of this world.
5. Malevole gives me insight into my weaknesses, while other courtiers merely encourage and excuse those weaknesses with their flattery.
1.3. The scene continues.

PIETRO What didst there?

MALEVOLE Talk with a usurer; take up° at interest. *borrow*

PIETRO I wonder what religion thou art of?

MALEVOLE Of a soldier's religion.[1]

PIETRO And what dost thou think makes most infidels now?

MALEVOLE Sects, sects. I have seen seeming Piety change her robe so oft that sure none but some archdevil can shape her a new petticoat.° *i.e., an inner life*

PIETRO Oh, a religious policy!° *expediency*

MALEVOLE But damnation on a politic religion![2] I am weary; would I were one of the Duke's hounds now.

PIETRO But what's the common news abroad, Malevole? Thou dogg'st° rumor still.[3] *follow the trail of*

MALEVOLE Common news? Why, common words are, "God save ye, fare ye well"; common actions, flattery and cozenage;° common things, women and cuckolds.—And how does my little Ferrard? Ah, ye lecherous animal! My little ferret, he goes sucking up and down the palace into every hen's nest° like a weasel. And to what dost thou addict thy time to now, more than to those antique painted drabs° that are still affected of° young courtiers, Flattery, Pride, and Venery?° *cheating / i.e., woman's bed / whores / sought after by / Lechery*

FERRARDO I study languages. Who dost think to be the best linguist of our age?

MALEVOLE Phew! The devil. Let° him possess thee, he'll teach thee to speak all languages most readily and strangely; and great reason, marry: he's traveled greatly i'the world and is everywhere. *If you let*

FERRARDO Save° i'th'court. *Except*

MALEVOLE Ay, save i'th'court. (*To Bilioso*) And how does my old muckhill° overspread with fresh snow?° Thou half a man, half a goat, all a beast! How does thy young wife, old huddle?° *dunghill / white hair / miser*

BILIOSO Out,° you improvident rascal! *(expressing scorn)*

[*He kicks at Malevole.*]

MALEVOLE Do, kick, thou hugely horned° old duke's ox, good Master Make-Please!° *repeatedly cuckolded / a flatterer*

PIETRO How dost thou live nowadays, Malevole?

MALEVOLE Why, like the knight Sir Patrick Penlolians, with killing o'spiders for my lady's monkey.[4]

PIETRO How dost spend the night? I hear thou never sleep'st.

MALEVOLE Oh, no, but dream the most fantastical. Oh, heaven! Oh, fubbery,° fubbery! *deception*

PIETRO Dream! What dream'st?

MALEVOLE Why, methinks I see that signor° pawn his foot-cloth,° that metreza° her plate; this madam takes physic, that t'other monsieur may minister to her; here is a pander *sir / horse blanket / lady*

1. A religion like that of a mercenary soldier, who fights for the side that offers the most money.
2. My curse on a religion that practices Machiavellian deception!
3. The word "cynic" comes from the Greek word for dog. Pietro sees Malevole as "dogged" in his constant pursuit of human folly. Malevole would rather be a dog than a courtier; that way he could be fed by the Duke, and bark and snarl, without having to endure being human.
4. Malevole mockingly describes himself performing the most trivial of courtly tasks, like the knight who finds food for the pet monkey of the lady he self-abasingly serves and adores in a courtly love relationship. Pets of this sort were a common affectation. "Sir Patrick Penlolians" is an invented name for a foppish courtier.

jeweled;° there is a fellow in shift° of satin this day, that could not shift° a shirt t'other night; here a Paris supports that Helen; there's a Lady Guinevere bears up that Sir Lancelot.[5] Dreams, dreams, visions, fantasies, chimeras, imaginations, tricks, conceits!° (*To Prepasso*) Sir Tristram Trimtram, come aloft, jackanapes, with a whim-wham! Here's a knight of the land of Catito shall play at trap with any page in Europe,[6] do the sword dance with any morris dancer in Christendom, ride at the ring till the fin of his eyes look as blue as the welkin, and run the wild-goose chase even with Pompey the Huge.[7]

bejeweled / new outfit; change; fancies

PIETRO You run—

MALEVOLE To the devil! Now, Signor Guerrino, that thou from a most pitied prisoner shouldst grow a most loathed flatterer!—Alas, poor Celso, thy star's oppressed;° thou art an honest lord; 'tis pity.

your fate's in decline

EQUATO Is't pity?

MALEVOLE Ay, marry is't, philosophical Equato, and 'tis pity that thou, being so excellent a scholar by art,° shouldst be so ridiculous a fool by nature.—I have a thing to tell you, Duke. Bid 'em avaunt,° bid 'em avaunt.

learning; begone

PIETRO [*to his courtiers*] Leave us, leave us.

Exeunt all saving Pietro and Malevole.

Now, sir, what is't?

MALEVOLE Duke, thou art a *becco*,° a cornuto.°

horned goat / cuckold

PIETRO How?

MALEVOLE Thou art a cuckold.

PIETRO Speak! Unshell him° quick.

Identify the culprit

MALEVOLE With most tumblerlike° nimbleness.

acrobatlike

PIETRO Who? By whom? I burst with desire.

MALEVOLE Mendoza is the man makes thee a horned beast. Duke, 'tis Mendoza cornutes° thee.

who cuckolds

PIETRO What conformance?° Relate! Short,° short!

confirmation / Briefly

MALEVOLE As a lawyer's beard:

There is an old crone in the court,
Her name is Maquerelle;
She is my mistress, sooth to say,
And she doth ever tell me.

Blurt o'rhyme,° blurt o'rhyme! Maquerelle is a cunning bawd, I am an honest villain, thy wife is a close drab,° and thou art a notorious cuckold. Farewell, Duke.

i.e., I spit on rhyme; secret whore

PIETRO Stay, stay!

MALEVOLE Dull, dull Duke, can lazy patience make lame

5. Here one courtier plays the part of Paris, i.e., sleeping with another man's wife as Paris did with Helen when he abducted her to Troy; there a courtly lady plays the part of Guinevere, the adulterous wife of King Arthur, having an affair as Guinevere did with Lancelot and providing her lover with financial support.

6. You monkey, perform your trifling tricks! Here's a knight from the land of Cockaigne (an imaginary land of luxury and ease) who will play cat and trap (a bat-and-ball game) with any youngster. ("Sir Tristram Trimtram" is a mocking reference to ballad and romance material based on the story of Tristram, a knight of the Round Table; "jackanapes" means both "monkey" and "impudent fellow"; "whim-wham" is just an extravagant expostulation. Playing games with a youth would be comically undignified for a courtier.)

7. Here's a knight who will show his prowess at the sword dance and morris dance (both rustic folk dances socially inappropriate for a courtier), ride in a contest to spear a suspended ring on one's lance point (another inappropriate sport for a courtier) till his eyelids look as blue as the sky (from weariness), and play a children's chasing game with Pompey the Great, one of the giant figures of Roman history, who was defeated by Julius Caesar (again, an absurd thing calculated to make the courtier look foolish).

revenge? Oh, God, for a woman to make a man that which
God never created, never made!

PIETRO What did God never make?

MALEVOLE A cuckold. To be made a thing that's hoodwinked° *blindfolded*
with kindness, whilst every rascal fillips his brows;° to have *crowns him with horns*
a coxcomb with egregious horns pinned to a lord's back,° *(in blindman's buff)*
every page sporting himself with delightful laughter, whilst
he must be the last must know it—pistols and poniards,° *daggers*
pistols and poniards!

PIETRO Death and damnation!

MALEVOLE Lightning and thunder!

PIETRO Vengeance and torture!

MALEVOLE Catso!° *Penis! (a vulgar oath)*

PIETRO Oh, revenge!

MALEVOLE Nay, to select among ten thousand fairs° *handsome women*
A lady far inferior to the most
In fair proportion both of limb and soul;
To take her from austerer check° of parents, *more strict control*
To make her his by most devoutful rites,° *marriage rites*
Make her commandress of a better essence
Than is the gorgeous world even of a man;[8]
To hug her with as raised an appetite
As usurers do their delved-up° treasury *dug-up, found-again*
(Thinking none tells° it but his private self); *counts*
To meet her spirit in a nimble kiss,
Distilling panting ardor to her heart;
True to her sheets, nay, diets strong his blood,° *desire (for other women)*
To give her height of hymeneal° sweets— *nuptial*

PIETRO Oh, God!

MALEVOLE Whilst she lisps, and gives him some court
quelque chose° *trifle*
Made only to provoke, not satiate;
And yet even then the thaw of her delight
Flows from lewd heat of apprehension,° *anticipation*
Only from strange imagination's rankness,
That forms the adulterer's presence in her soul
And makes her think she clips the foul knave's loins.[9]

PIETRO Affliction to my blood's root!° *This cuts to my heart!*

MALEVOLE Nay, think, but° think what may proceed of this! *merely, only*
Adultery is often the mother of incest.

PIETRO Incest?

MALEVOLE Yes, incest. Mark: Mendoza of his° wife begets, *(the cuckold's)*
perchance, a daughter. Mendoza dies. His son marries this
daughter. Say you? Nay, 'tis frequent, not only probable, but
no question often acted, whilst ignorance, fearless ignorance, clasps his own seed.° *blood relative*

PIETRO Hideous imagination!

MALEVOLE Adultery? Why, next to the sin of simony,° 'tis the *selling church offices*
most horrid transgression under the cope of salvation.° *under the heavens*

PIETRO Next to simony?

8. To make his wife commandress of his soul, the part of him more essential than mere physical life.

9. Even in lawful sex with her husband, her warmth of delight stems from her fantasizing an embrace with her adulterous lover. (Malevole's implied diatribe against Duchess Aurelia spills over into antifeminist disgust at women generally. "Clips" means "embraces.")

MALEVOLE Ay, next to simony, in which our men° in next age shall not sin. *our countrymen*
PIETRO Not sin? Why?
MALEVOLE Because (thanks to some churchmen) our age will leave them nothing° to sin with. But adultery!—O dullness!°—should have exemplary punishment, that intemperate bloods may freeze but to think it. I would damn him° and all his generation;° my own hands should do it. Ha! I would not trust heaven with my vengeance anything.° *no wealth; O slow to revenge!; (the adulterer); progeny; at all*
PIETRO Anything, anything, Malevole! Thou shalt see instantly what temper my spirit holds. Farewell; remember I forget thee not; farewell. *Exit Pietro.*
MALEVOLE Farewell.
Lean thoughtfulness, a sallow meditation,[1]
Suck thy veins dry; distemperance° rob thy sleep! *mental disorder*
The heart's disquiet is revenge most deep.
He that gets blood, the life of flesh but spills,
But he that breaks heart's peace, the dear soul kills.[2]
Well, this disguise doth yet afford me that
Which kings do seldom hear or great men use—
Free speech; and though my state's° usurped, *my dukedom is*
Yet this affected strain° gives me a tongue *adopted mode of speech*
As fetterless as is an emperor's.
I may speak foolishly, ay, knavishly,
Always carelessly, yet no one thinks it fashion
To peise my breath;° for he that laughs and strikes *weigh my words*
Is lightly felt, or seldom struck again.[3]
Duke, I'll torment thee; now my just revenge
From thee than crown a richer gem shall part.[4]
Beneath God, naught's so dear as a calm heart.

1.4

Enter Celso.

CELSO My honored lord—
MALEVOLE Peace, speak low, peace! O Celso, constant lord,
Thou to whose faith I only rest discovered,[1]
Thou, one of full ten millions of men,
That lovest virtue only for itself,
Thou in whose hands old Ops may put her soul,[2]
Behold forever-banished Altofront,
This Genoa's last year's duke. O truly noble!
I wanted° those old instruments of state, *lacked*
Dissemblance and suspect. I could not time it,° Celso; *be a time-server*
My throne stood like a point in midst of a circle,
To all of equal nearness, bore with none;° *had no favorites*

1. May melancholy, a sickly yellow meditation characteristic of jealousy and anger. (Addressed to the departed duke.)
2. A man who sheds blood merely deprives his victim of life, but he who engenders emotional torment takes vengeance on the victim's very soul. (Based on Seneca, *Medea*, lines 19–25.)
3. He who uses satiric laughter as a weapon is not felt to wound deeply, nor is he struck at in return.
4. In exacting revenge from you, I'll take from you a jewel more valuable than a mere crown: peace of mind.

1.4. The scene continues.
1. You to whose loyalty I entrust the secret of my true identity.
2. Ops, wife of Saturn and mother of the gods, saved Jupiter, Neptune, and Pluto from being devoured by their father. Malevole means that he can trust Celso utterly, as one in whom even the inveterately suspicious Ops could place her trust.

Reigned° all alike, so slept in fearless° virtue, — *Ruled over / unfearing*
Suspectless,° too suspectless; till the crowd — *Unsuspecting*
(Still lickerous of° untried novelties), — *Always eager for*
Impatient with severer government,
Made strong with° Florence, banished Altofront. — *Backed by*
CELSO Strong with Florence! Ay, thence your mischief rose;
For when the daughter of the Florentine° — *the Duke of Florence*
Was matched once with this Pietro, now duke,
No stratagem of state untried was left,
Till you of all—
MALEVOLE Of all was quite bereft.
Alas, Maria, too close prisonèd,
My true-faithed duchess i'the citadel!
CELSO I'll still adhere; let's mutiny and die.
MALEVOLE Oh, no, climb not a falling tower, Celso;
'Tis well held° desperation, no zeal, — *wisely regarded as*
Hopeless to strive with fate. Peace! Temporize.
Hope, hope, that never forsak'st the wretched'st man,
Yet bidd'st me live and lurk in this disguise.
What, play I well the free-breathed° discontent? — *outspoken*
Why, man, we are all philosophical monarchs
Or natural fools.[3] Celso, the court's afire;
The Duchess' sheets will smoke for't ere it be long.
Impure Mendoza, that sharp-nosed lord that made
The cursèd match linked° Genoa with Florence, — *that linked*
Now broad-horns° the Duke, which he° now knows. — *cuckolds / (the Duke)*
Discord to malcontents is very manna;° — *heaven-sent food*
When the ranks are burst, then scuffle Altofront.[4]
CELSO Ay, but durst°— — *do you dare*
MALEVOLE 'Tis gone; 'tis swallowed like a mineral;° — *medicine; poison*
Some way 'twill work. Phewt!° I'll not shrink. — *(exclamation of disgust)*
He's resolute who can no lower sink.

Bilioso entering, Malevole shifteth° his speech. — *disguises*

[*Aside to Celso*] Oh, the father of maypoles!° Did you never — *skinny old fool*
see a fellow whose strength consisted in his breath,° respect — *his flatteries*
in his office, religion in his lord,[5] and love in himself? Why,
then, behold.
BILIOSO Signor—
MALEVOLE My right worshipful lord, your court nightcap
makes you have a passing high forehead.[6]
BILIOSO I can tell you strange news, but I am sure you know
them already. The Duke speaks much good of you.
MALEVOLE Go to,° then; and shall you and I now enter into a — *(expressing impatience)*
strict friendship?
BILIOSO Second° one another? — *Support*
MALEVOLE Yes.
BILIOSO Do one another good offices?
MALEVOLE Just.° What though I called thee old ox, egregious — *Exactly*

3. Either we make philosophy the monarch of our souls or we remain fools in the natural order of things.
4. When discord tears the court apart, the time for me to move will have come.
5. Who is respected only for the office he holds and whose only religion is service to the Duke.
6. Under the guise of complimenting Bilioso for his headgear, Malevole hints that Bilioso's obsequious life at court results in his being a cuckold. ("Passing" means "exceedingly.")

wittol,° broken-bellied coward, rotten mummy? Yet since I am in favor— *uncomplaining cuckold*

BILIOSO Words, of course, terms of disport.[7] [*Offering a gold chain*] His Grace presents you by me a chain, as his grateful remembrance for—I am ignorant for what; marry, ye may impart.[8] Yet howsoever—come—dear friend, dost know my son?

MALEVOLE Your son?

BILIOSO He shall eat woodcocks, dance jigs, make possets, and play at shuttlecock[9] with any young lord about the court. He has as sweet a lady too; dost know her little bitch?

MALEVOLE 'Tis a dog,° man. *male dog*

BILIOSO Believe me, a she-bitch! Oh, 'tis° a good creature; thou shalt be her servant.° I'll make thee acquainted with my young wife, too. What, I keep her not at court for nothing! 'Tis grown to supper time; come to my table; that, anything I have, stands open to thee.[1] *my son's sweet lady is* / *devoted admirer*

MALEVOLE (*to Celso*) How smooth to him that is in state of
grace,° *in princely favor*
How servile is the rugged'st courtier's face!
What profit, nay, what nature would keep down
Are heaved to them are minions to a crown.[2]
Envious ambition never sates his thirst
Till, sucking all, he swells and swells, and bursts.

BILIOSO I shall now leave you with my always-best wishes; only let's hold betwixt us a firm correspondence,° a mutual-friendly-reciprocal kind of steady-unanimous-heartily-leagued— *alliance, amity*

MALEVOLE Did Your Signorship ne'er see a pigeon-house that was smooth, round, and white without, and full of holes and stink within? Ha' ye not, old courtier?

BILIOSO Oh, yes, 'tis the form, the fashion of them all.

MALEVOLE Adieu, my true court-friend; farewell, my dear Castilio.[3] *Exit Bilioso.*

CELSO (*descries Mendoza*) Yonder's Mendoza.

MALEVOLE True, the privy key.[4]

CELSO I take my leave, sweet lord.

MALEVOLE 'Tis fit. Away! *Exit Celso.*

1.5

Enter Mendoza with three or four suitors.° *petitioners*

MENDOZA Leave your suits with me; I can and will.° Attend my secretary; leave me. [*Exeunt suitors.*] *will aid you*

7. Those were mere words that you were playing with, joshing me. ("Disport" means "amusement" or "game.")
8. You can share with me the reason for this favor shown by the Duke.
9. My son can hold his own in many courtly pastimes, eating rare dishes, dancing, making bedtime drinks of warm milk curdled with beer or ale (possets), playing at badminton. (Woodcocks are proverbially stupid birds; by implication, the son is stupid too.)
1. "Stands open" hints unawares at a sexual dimension in Bilioso's offer to let Malevole enjoy the company of his wife (Bianca) and of his son's "sweet lady."
2. All those gifts that self-interest and natural modesty would ordinarily repress are offered up in sycophantic spirit to royal favorites.
3. A model courtier—alluding to Baldassare Castiglione's *The Courtier*. (Malevole speaks ironically.)
4. The one with access to the Duke's privy chamber. (With bawdy and scatological implications.)
1.5. The scene continues.

MALEVOLE Mendoza, hark ye, hark ye. You are a treacherous villain. God b'wi'ye.

MENDOZA Out, you baseborn rascal!

MALEVOLE We are all the sons of heaven, though a tripe-wife° were our mother. Ah, you whoreson, hot-reined he-marmoset!° Aegisthus! Didst ever hear of one Aegisthus?[1]
street peddler of tripe / *lecherous monkey*

MENDOZA Gistus?

MALEVOLE Ay, Aegisthus. He was a filthy incontinent° flesh-monger, such a one as thou art.
lascivious

MENDOZA Out, grumbling rogue!

MALEVOLE Orestes, beware Orestes!°
(see 8 n)

MENDOZA Out, beggar!

MALEVOLE I once shall rise.

MENDOZA Thou, rise?

MALEVOLE Ay, at the Resurrection.
No vulgar seed° but once may rise and shall;
No king so huge but, 'fore he die, may fall. *Exit.*
humbly born man

MENDOZA Now, good Elysium,° what a delicious heaven is it for a man to be in a prince's favor! O sweet god! O Pleasure! O Fortune! O all thou best of life! What should I think? What say? What do? To be a favorite! A minion!° To have a general timorous respect observe° a man, a stateful° silence in his presence, solitariness in his absence, a confused hum and busy murmur of obsequious suitors training° him; the cloth° held up and way proclaimed before him; petitionary vassals licking the pavement with their slavish knees, whilst some odd palace lamprels° that engender with snakes and are full of eyes° on both sides, with a kind of insinuated° humbleness, fix all their delights upon his brow—oh, blessed state! What a ravishing prospect doth the Olympus° of favor yield! Death,° I cornute the Duke! Sweet women, most sweet ladies, nay, angels! By heaven, he is more accursed than a devil that hates you or is hated by you, and happier than a god that loves you or is beloved by you. You preservers of mankind, lifeblood of society: who would live, nay, who can live without you? O Paradise, how majestical is your austerer° presence! How imperiously chaste is your more modest face! But, oh, how full of ravishing attraction is your pretty, petulant, languishing, lasciviously composed countenance! These amorous smiles, those soul-warming, sparkling glances, ardent as those flames that singed the world by heedless Phaëthon![2] In body how delicate, in soul how witty, in discourse how pregnant,° in life how wary, in favors how judicious, in day how sociable, and in night how—oh, pleasure unutterable! Indeed, it is most certain, one man cannot deserve only° to enjoy a beauteous woman; but a duchess? In despite of Phoebus,° I'll write a sonnet instantly in praise of her. *Exit.*

the abode of the blessed / *favorite* / *revere / dignified* / *following* / *canopy of state* / *eel-like sycophants* / *i.e., gill openings* / *insinuating* / *the height* / *(an oath)* / *seemingly modest* / *pithy, quick-witted* / *alone* / *god of poetry*

1. Clytemnestra's lover, the cuckolder of Agamemnon, who together with Clytemnestra murdered Agamemnon on his return from the Trojan War. Agamemnon and Clytemnestra's son, Orestes, later killed them out of revenge.

2. Phaëthon "singed" (burned) the world by his "heedless" mismanagement of his father Helios' sun-chariot and horses.

1.6

Enter Ferneze ushering Aurelia, Emilia and Maquerelle bearing up her train, Bianca attending. All go out but Aurelia, Maquerelle, and Ferneze.

AURELIA And is't possible? Mendoza slight me? Possible?
FERNEZE Possible?
What can be strange in him that's drunk with favor,
Grows insolent with grace? Speak, Maquerelle, speak.
MAQUERELLE [*aside to Ferneze*] To speak feelingly, more,
more richly in solid sense° than worthless words, give me *i.e., deeds, gifts*
those jewels of your ears to receive my enforced duty. (*Ferneze privately feeds Maquerelle's hands with jewels during this speech.*) [*To Aurelia*] As for my part, 'tis well known I can
put up anything, can bear patiently with any man.[1] But when
I heard he° wronged your precious sweetness, I was enforced *(Mendoza)*
to take deep offense. 'Tis most certain he loves Emilia with high appetite, and as she told me (as you know we women impart our secrets one to another), when she repulsed his suit, in that he was possessed with your endeared grace,[2] Mendoza most ingratefully renounced all faith to you.
FERNEZE Nay, called you—speak, Maquerelle, speak.
MAQUERELLE By heaven, "witch," "dried biscuit," and con
tested° blushlessly he loved you but for a spurt° or so. *contended / ejaculation*
FERNEZE For maintenance.
MAQUERELLE Advancement and regard.[3]
AURELIA Oh, villain! Oh, impudent Mendoza!
MAQUERELLE Nay, he is the rustiest-jawed,° the foulest- *rudest-mouthed*
mouthed knave in railing against our sex. He will rail agen'° *against*
women—
AURELIA How? How?
MAQUERELLE I am ashamed to speak't, I.
AURELIA I love to hate him. Speak.
MAQUERELLE Why, when Emilia scorned his base unsteadi-
ness,° the black-throated rascal scolded, and said— *fickleness*
AURELIA What?
MAQUERELLE Troth,° 'tis too shameless. *In truth*
AURELIA What said he?
MAQUERELLE Why, that at four women were fools, at fourteen
drabs,° at forty bawds,° at fourscore witches, and a hundred, *whores / panderesses*
cats.° *witches' attendant spirits*
AURELIA Oh, unlimitable impudency!
FERNEZE But as for poor Ferneze's fixèd heart,
Was never° shadeless meadow drier parched *Never was there*
Under the scorching heat of heaven's dog
Than is my heart with your enforcing° eyes.[4] *compelling, ravishing*
MAQUERELLE [*aside*] A hot simile.

1.6. The scene is virtually continuous.
1. (1) I can endure patiently what any man says or does; (2) I can bear the weight of a man in sex.
2. When Emilia repulsed Mendoza's advances because, in her view, he should have remained loyal to Aurelia.
3. And said furthermore that he loved Aurelia solely for the financial support (maintenance) she had given him, her advancement of his interests, and her bestowing her favorable regard on him.
4. The sun is near the so-called Dog Star, Sirius, in the scorching days of summer. Ferneze means a compliment to the Duchess but uses a metaphor of parching under her withering gaze.

FERNEZE Your smiles have been my heaven, your frowns my hell.
Oh, pity, then! Grace should with beauty dwell.
MAQUERELLE [*aside*] Reasonable perfect,° by'r Lady! — *well recited*
AURELIA I will love thee, be it but in despite
Of that Mendoza. "Witch," Ferneze, "witch"!
Ferneze, thou art the Duchess's favorite.
Be faithful, private; but 'tis dangerous.
FERNEZE His love is lifeless that for love fears breath;
The worst that's due to sin, oh, would 'twere death![5]
AURELIA Enjoy my favor. I will be sick° instantly and take physic;° therefore, in depth of night, visit— — *pretend to be sick; medicine*
MAQUERELLE Visit her chamber, but conditionally° you shall not offend her bed. By this diamond! — *on condition that*
FERNEZE By this diamond. *Gives it to Maquerelle.*[6]
MAQUERELLE Nor tarry longer than you please. By this ruby!
FERNEZE By this ruby. *Gives again.*
MAQUERELLE And that the door shall not creak.
FERNEZE And that the door shall not creak.
MALEVOLE Nay, but swear.
FERNEZE By this purse. *Gives her his purse.*
MAQUERELLE Go to; I'll keep your oaths for you. Remember, visit.

Enter Mendoza reading a sonnet. [*He is unaware at first of their presence.*]

AURELIA "Dried biscuit"! Look where the base wretch comes.
MENDOZA "Beauty's life, heaven's model, love's queen"—
MAQUERELLE That's his Emilia.
MENDOZA "Nature's triumph, best on earth"—
MAQUERELLE Meaning Emilia.
MENDOZA "Thou only wonder that the world hath seen"—
MAQUERELLE That's Emilia.
AURELIA Must I then hear her praised, Mendoza?
MENDOZA [*seeing Aurelia*] Madam, Your Excellency is graciously encountered. I have been writing passionate flashes in honor of— *Exit Ferneze.*
AURELIA Out, villain, villain!
O judgment, where have been my eyes? What
Bewitched election° made me dote on thee? — *choice*
What sorcery made me love thee? But begone,
Bury thy head. Oh, that I could do more
Than loathe thee! Hence, worst of ill!
No reason ask; our° reason is our will. — *(my; women's)*
Exit with Maquerelle.
MENDOZA Women? Nay, Furies!° Nay, worse, for they torment only the bad, but women good and bad. Damnation of mankind! Breath, hast thou praised them for this? And is't you, Ferneze, are wriggled into smock-grace?[7] Sit sure! Oh, that I could rail against these monsters in nature, models of — *avenging deities*

5. I.e., It is shameful to fear for one's life, and cowardice is worse than death. Ferneze embraces the danger of being Aurelia's lover.
6. These gifts to Maquerelle are made privately (see 7–8 SD above) even though Aurelia is fully aware that Maquerelle is acting the part of a panderess.
7. A smock is a petticoat. Ferneze has wriggled himself into intimate sexual favor with Aurelia.

hell, curse of the earth—women that dare attempt anything, and what they attempt they care not how they accomplish: without all premeditation or prevention,° rash in asking, desperate in working, impatient in suffering, extreme in desiring, slaves unto appetite, mistresses° in dissembling, only constant in inconstancy, only perfect in counterfeiting. Their words are feigned, their eyes forged,° their sighs dissembled, their looks counterfeit, their hair false, their given hopes° deceitful, their very breath artificial. Their blood° is their only god. Bad clothes and old age are only the devils they tremble at. That° I could rail now!

prevention: anticipation / mistresses: experts / forged: cosmetically enhanced / given hopes: the promises they give / blood: desire / That: Would that

1.7

Enter Pietro, his sword drawn.

PIETRO A mischief fill thy throat, thou foul-jawed slave!
Say thy prayers.
MENDOZA I ha' forgot 'em.
PIETRO Thou shalt die.
MENDOZA So shalt thou. I am heart-mad.° *distracted*
PIETRO I am horn-mad.° *an enraged cuckold*
MENDOZA Extreme mad.
PIETRO Monstrously mad.
MENDOZA Why?
PIETRO Why? Thou—thou hast dishonorèd my bed.
MENDOZA I? Come, come, sit.
Here's my bare heart to thee, as steady
As is this center to the glorious world.[1]
And yet, hark, thou art a cornuto°—but by me? *cuckold*
PIETRO Yes, slave, by thee.
MENDOZA Do not, do not with tart and spleenful° breath *angry*
Lose him can loose thee.[2] I offend my duke?
Bear record, O ye dumb and raw-aired nights,
How vigilant my sleepless eyes have been
To watch the traitor! Record, thou spirit of truth,
With what debasement I ha' thrown myself
To under offices,° only to learn *menial tasks*
The truth, the party,° time, the means, the place, *guilty person*
By whom, and when, and where thou wert disgraced!
And am I paid with "slave"? Hath my intrusion
To places private and prohibited,
Only to observe the closer passages°— *secret goings-on*
Heaven knows with vows of revelation[3]—
Made me suspected, made me deemed a villain?
What rogue hath wronged us?
PIETRO Mendoza, I may err.
MENDOZA Err? 'Tis too mild a name; but err and err,
Run giddy with suspect,° 'fore through me thou know *suspicion*
That which most creatures save thyself do know.
Nay, since my service hath so loathed reject,° *rejection*
'Fore I'll reveal, shalt° find them clipped together.° *you will / embracing*

1.7. The scene continues.
1. As is the world, the center of the Ptolemaic system, to the entire cosmos.
2. Do not cast off the person who can ease you of your disgrace.
3. Having sworn to tell you all I learned.

PIETRO Mendoza, thou know'st I am a most plain-breasted° man. — *plainspoken*

MENDOZA The fitter to make a cuckold.[4] Would your brows were most plain° too! — *unhorned*

PIETRO Tell me; indeed I heard thee rail—

MENDOZA At women, true. Why, what cold phlegm° could choose, — *what apathetic person*
Knowing a lord so honest, virtuous,
So boundless-loving, bounteous, fair-shaped, sweet,
To be contemned,° abused, defamed, made cuckold! — *To see him be scorned*
Heart!° I hate all women for't. Sweet sheets, wax lights, antic° bedposts, cambric smocks, villainous° curtains, arras pictures,° oiled hinges, and all the tongue-tied lascivious witnesses of great creatures'° wantonness! What salvation can you expect?[5] — *By God's heart* / *carved / concealing* / *wall tapestries* / *noble persons'*

PIETRO Wilt thou tell me?° — *tell me who it is*

MENDOZA Why, you may find it yourself; observe, observe.

PIETRO I ha' not the patience. Wilt thou deserve me?° Tell, give it.° — *earn my favor* / *(the secret)*

MENDOZA Take't! Why Ferneze is the man, Ferneze. I'll prove't; this night you shall take him in your sheets. Will't serve?

PIETRO It will; my bosom's in some peace. Till night—

MENDOZA What?

PIETRO Farewell.

MENDOZA God, how weak a lord are you!
Why, do you think there is no more but so?° — *no more to it than that*

PIETRO Why?

MENDOZA Nay, then will I presume to counsel you.
It should be thus:
You, with some guard, upon the sudden break
Into the princess'° chamber; I stay behind, — *the Duchess's*
Without° the door through which he needs must pass. — *Outside*
Ferneze flies;° let him. To me he comes; he's killed — *flees*
By me; observe, by me. You follow; I rail,
And seem° to save the body. Duchess comes, — *pretend*
On whom (respecting her advancèd° birth — *noble*
And your fair nature) I know—nay, I do know—
No violence must be used. She comes; I storm;
I praise, excuse Ferneze, and still maintain
The Duchess' honor; she for this loves me;
I honor you, shall know her soul, you mine.[6]
Then naught shall she contrive in vengeance
(As women are most thoughtful° in revenge) — *cunning*
Of her Ferneze but you shall sooner know't
Than she can think't. Thus shall his death come sure;
Your Duchess brain-caught;° so, your life secure. — *tricked by deception*

PIETRO It is too well, my bosom and my heart.[7]
When nothing helps, cut off the rotten part. *Exit.*

4. The more likely, being plainspoken, to be cuckolded.
5. (1) What salvation is to be hoped for in such a morally corrupt world? (2) How can you expect that ordinary mortals could resist such temptations?
6. By seeming to save the Duchess's reputation, I earn her confidence and learn her innermost secrets, which you will know in turn.
7. The plan is all too sure to succeed, in that I must divorce her whom I adore as my innermost self. (Pietro may also mean that Mendoza is now his most intimate partner.)

MENDOZA Who° cannot feign friendship can ne'er produce — *He who*
the effects of hatred. Honest fool Duke, subtle lascivious
Duchess, silly° novice Ferneze, I do laugh at ye! My brain is — *naive*
in labor till it produce mischief, and I feel sudden throes,
proofs sensible,° the issue° is at hand. — *tangible / outcome*
As bears shape young,[8] so I'll form my device,
Which, grown, proves horrid;° vengeance makes men wise. — *terrible; shaggy*
[*Exit.*]

[1.8]

Enter Malevole and Passarello.

MALEVOLE Fool, most happily° encountered. Canst sing, fool? — *fortunately*
PASSARELLO Yes, I can sing, fool, if you'll bear the burden;° — *bass line; responsibility*
and I can play upon instruments, scurvily,° as gentlemen do. — *ineptly*
Oh, that I had been gelded!° I should then have been a fat — *castrated*
fool for a chamber, a squeaking° fool for a tavern, and a — *high-voiced*
private fool for all the ladies.
MALEVOLE You are in good case° since you came to court, — *situation; outfit*
fool. What, guarded,° guarded! — *trimmed with braid*
PASSARELLO Yes, faith, even as footmen and bawds wear velvet, not for an ornament of honor but for a badge of drudgery; for, now the Duke is discontented, I am fain° to fool — *obliged*
him asleep every night.
MALEVOLE What are his griefs?
PASSARELLO He hath sore eyes.
MALEVOLE I never observed so much.
PASSARELLO Horrible sore eyes; and so hath every cuckold, for the roots of the horns spring in the eyeballs, and that's the reason the horn of a cuckold is as tender as his eye, or as that growing in the woman's forehead twelve years since,[1] that could not endure to be touched. The Duke hangs down
his head like a columbine.° — *a drooping flower*
MALEVOLE Passarello, why do great men beg fools?[2]
PASSARELLO As the Welshman stole rushes° when there was — *a floor covering*
nothing else to filch: only to keep begging in fashion.
MALEVOLE Pooh! Thou givest no good reason; thou speakest like a fool.
PASSARELLO Faith, I utter small fragments as your knight° — *a typical knight*
courts your city widow with jingling of his gilt spurs, advancing his bush-colored° beard, and taking tobacco. This — *bushy red*
is all the mirror of their knightly compliments.[3] Nay, I shall talk when my tongue is a-going once; 'tis like a citizen° on — *an inept rider*
horseback, evermore in a false gallop.
MALEVOLE And how doth Maquerelle fare nowadays?
PASSARELLO Faith, I was wont to salute° her as our English — *accustomed to greet*
women are at their first landing in Flushing:[4] I would call
her whore; but now that antiquity° leaves her as an old piece — *old age*

8. According to legendary lore, mother bears licked their newborn cubs into the shape of young bears.
1.8. The Genoese court still.
1. A pamphlet of 1588 told of a woman with "a crooked horn of four inches long" growing out of her forehead.
2. Why do great men petition the Crown for the custody of fools (and thereby enjoy their revenues)?
3. The knight awkwardly jingles his spurs, etc., in order to avoid having to make conversation. Such are his skills in making compliments to ladies.
4. The women one would see in Flushing (in the Netherlands) might be expected to be camp followers of the English soldiers stationed there.

of plastic° t'work by, I only ask her how her rotten teeth fare every morning, and so leave her. She was the first that ever invented perfumed smocks for the gentlewomen and woolen shoes for fear of creaking° for the visitant.° She were an excellent lady, but that her face peeleth like Muscovy glass.°

(something easily worked) · *creaking floors / lover* · *mica*

MALEVOLE And how doth thy old lord,° that hath wit enough to be a flatterer and conscience enough° to be a knave?

(Bilioso) · *no conscience at all*

PASSARELLO Oh, excellent. He keeps, beside me, fifteen jesters to instruct him in the art of fooling, and utters their jests in private to the Duke and Duchess. He'll lie like to your Switzer° or lawyer; he'll be of° any side for most money.

Swiss mercenary / on

MALEVOLE I am in haste. Be brief.

PASSARELLO As your fiddler when he is paid. He'll thrive, I warrant you, while your young courtier stands, like Good Friday in Lent: men long to see it, because more fatting days come after it;[5] else he's the leanest and pitiful'st actor in the whole pageant. Adieu, Malevole.

MALEVOLE O world most vile, when thy loose vanities,
Taught by this fool, do make the fool seem wise![6]

PASSARELLO You'll know° me again, Malevole?

recognize

MALEVOLE Oh, ay, by that velvet.

PASSARELLO Ay, as a pettifogger° by his buckram bag. I am as common° in the court as an hostess's lips in the country; knights, and clowns, and knaves, and all share me;° the court cannot possibly be without me. Adieu, Malevole.

an inferior lawyer · *everyday; shared by all* · *all partake of folly*

[*Exeunt separately.*]

2.1

Enter Mendoza with a sconce° to observe Ferneze's entrance, who, whilst the act° is playing, enter unbraced,° two pages before him with lights, is met by Maquerelle, and conveyed in. The pages are sent away.

lantern · *entr'acte* · *with clothes unfastened*

MENDOZA He's caught. The woodcock's° head is i'th'noose! *a gullible bird*
Now treads Ferneze in dangerous path of lust,
Swearing his sense is merely° deified. *completely*
The fool grasps clouds, and shall beget centaurs;[1]
And now, in strength of° panting faint delight, *buoyed up by*
The goat° bids heaven envy him. Good goose, *lecher*
I can afford thee nothing but the poor
Comfort of calamity, pity.
Lust's like the plummets hanging on clock lines,
Will ne'er ha' done till all is quite undone.[2]
Such is the course salt° sallow lust doth run, *salacious*
Which thou° shalt try.° I'll be revenged. Duke, thy suspect,° *(Ferneze) / prove* · *suspicion*
Duchess, thy disgrace, Ferneze, thy rivalship
Shall have swift vengeance. Nothing so holy,

5. Bilioso will outlast younger courtiers as long as men prefer to be reminded, by his thinness, of fatter days to come with the arrival of Easter, after the fasting period of Lent. (Good Friday, the day of Christ's crucifixion, is just before Easter.)
6. How corrupt is this world, in which a fool can seem wise by preaching about worldly vanity!

2.1. Before the Duchess's bedchamber.
1. When Ixion sought to embrace Juno, he encountered a cloud in her shape. From their union came the centaurs, creatures that were half man and half horse.
2. Lust goes on ceaselessly, like time itself, propelled forward by the weights ("plummets") in a clock until the end of time.

No band° of nature so strong, *bond*
No law of friendship so sacred
But I'll profane, burst, violate,
'Fore I'll endure disgrace, contempt, and poverty.
Shall I, whose very "hum" struck all heads bare,° *made everyone uncover*
Whose face made° silence, creaking of whose shoe *commanded*
Forced the most private passages fly ope,
Scrape like a servile dog at some latched door?
Learn now to make a leg° and cry, "Beseech ye, *bow*
Pray ye, is such a lord within?" Be awed
At some odd usher's scoffed° formality? *fit to be scoffed at*
First sear my brains! *Unde cadis non quo refert.*[3]
My heart cries, "Perish all!" How? How? What fate
Can once avoid revenge that's desperate?° *driven to desperation*
I'll to the Duke. If all should ope,° if! Tush, *come out into the open*
Fortune still dotes on those who cannot blush.° [*Exit.*] *who are shameless*

2.2

Enter Malevole at one door, Bianca, Emilia, and Maquerelle at the other door.

MALEVOLE Bless ye, cast° o'ladies! Ha, Dipsas,[1] how dost thou, old coal? *pair*

MAQUERELLE Old coal?

MALEVOLE Ay, old coal. Methinks thou liest like a brand under these billets of green wood.[2] He that will inflame a young wench's heart, let him lay close to her an old coal that hath first been fired,° a panderess, my half-burnt lint,° who, though thou canst not flame thyself, yet art able to set a thousand virgins' tapers afire. [*To Bianca*] And how does Janivere[3] thy husband, my little periwinkle? Is 'a° troubled with the cough o'the lungs still? Does he hawk° o'nights still? He will not bite. *set afire / tinder* — *he* — *hack, cough*

BIANCA No, by my troth, I took him with his mouth empty of old teeth.

MALEVOLE And he took thee with thy belly full of young bones;° marry, he took his maim by the stroke of his enemy.[4] *i.e., pregnant*

BIANCA And I mine by the stroke of my friend.° *lover*

MALEVOLE The close stock!° O mortal wench! Lady, ha' ye now no restoratives for your decayed Jasons?[5] Look ye, crabs' guts baked, distilled ox pith, the pulverized hairs of a lion's upper lip, jelly of cock-sparrows, he-monkeys' marrow, or powder of fox-stones?[6] And whither are all you ambling now? *fencing thrust*

BIANCA Why, to bed, to bed.

3. Before that happens, may my brains dry up! What matters is where we fall from, not where we fall to. (Seneca, *Thyestes*, line 925.)

2.2. The scene continues.

1. Malevole addresses Maquerelle as Dipsas, a demeaning name for a bawd or old woman, as in John Lyly's *Endymion*.

2. Maquerelle is like an old coal in that, though old, she kindles lust in younger women ("green wood"). The "billets," or sticks of firewood, that she is here accused of igniting are Bianca and Emilia.

3. Janivere, or January, is an old husband (Bilioso) married to a young wife, May (Bianca).

4. I.e., he received his disgrace (literally, a blow) in the form of a (sexual) thrust delivered by his cuckolder to his wife, Bianca.

5. Jason's father was restored to youth by Medea, who was in love with Jason.

6. Malevole mockingly asks Bianca if she is well stocked in various aphrodisiacs, made out of bone marrow (e.g., "ox pith"), testicles ("stones"), or other body parts of animals associated with lecherousness.

MALEVOLE Do your husbands lie with ye?
BIANCA That were country° fashion, i'faith. *uncourtly*
MALEVOLE Ha' ye no foregoers[7] about you? Come, whither in good deed,° la,° now? *in truth / indeed*
BIANCA In good indeed, la, now, to eat the most miraculously, admirably, astonishable-composed posset with three curds, without any drink.[8] Will ye help me with a he-fox?[9] Here's the Duke. *The ladies go out.*
MALEVOLE (*to Bianca*) Fried frogs° are very good, and French-like too. *another aphrodisiac*

2.3

Enter Duke Pietro, Count Celso, Count Equato, Bilioso, Ferrardo, and Mendoza.

PIETRO The night grows deep and foul. What hour is't?
CELSO Upon the stroke of twelve.
MALEVOLE Save° ye, Duke. *God save*
PIETRO From thee. Begone! I do not love thee; let me see thee no more. We° are displeased. *(the royal "we")*
MALEVOLE Why, God b'wi'thee! Heaven hear my curse:
May thy wife and thee live long together.
PIETRO Begone, sirrah!° *(said to inferiors)*
MALEVOLE "When Arthur first in court began"—Agamemnon—Menelaus—was ever any duke a cornuto?[1]
PIETRO Begone, hence!
MALEVOLE What religion wilt thou be of next?[2]
MENDOZA Out with him!
MALEVOLE [*to Pietro*] With most servile patience. Time will come
When wonder of thy error will strike dumb
Thy bezzled° sense. *befuddled with drink*
Slaves i'favor! Ay, marry, shall he rise.[3]
Good God! How subtle hell doth flatter Vice,
Mounts him aloft, and makes him seem to fly,
As fowl the tortoise mocked, who to the sky
Th'ambitious shellfish raised.[4] Th'end of all
Is only that from height he might dead fall.
BILIOSO Why, when?° Out, ye rogue! Begone, ye rascal! *(expressing impatience)*
MALEVOLE I shall now leave ye with all my best wishes.
BILIOSO Out, ye cur!
MALEVOLE "Only let's hold together a firm correspondence"—
BILIOSO Out!

7. Gentleman-ushers, whom a lady like Bianca might employ to bring her lovers to her.
8. Bianca mockingly answers Malevole's insinuations by suggesting she's about to go to bed. A posset is a bedtime drink of warm milk curdled with ale or beer, as at 1.4.67. This one is to be special, with lots of curdled milk but without the ale or beer.
9. Will you help me find a fox's testicles (the "fox-stones" mentioned in line 22) to serve as an aphrodisiac? (Said mockingly. Perhaps "he-fox" also refers to the Duke, who enters right after this.)
2.3. The scene continues.
1. Malevole mockingly sings a fragment from the ballad "Sir Launcelot du Lake," sung also by Falstaff in *2 Henry IV*, 2.4.28, and then goes on to cite famous cuckolds from antiquity. Menelaus was the husband of Helen of Troy, who was abducted by Paris. For Agamemnon's story, see note at 1.5.8.
2. Have you changed your "faith" again as to whom to believe?
3. Servile wretches enjoying courtly favor! Yes, truly, men like Ferneze and Bilioso will rise one day (and fall the next).
4. Like the tortoise of a beast fable, who was lifted to a great height by an eagle only to be dashed onto the rocks and thus broken open. (The tortoise is called a shellfish because it has a shell and swims.)

MALEVOLE "A mutual-friendly-reciprocal perpetual kind of steady-unanimous-heartily-leagued"[5]—

BILIOSO Hence, ye gross-jawed peasantly!° Out, go! *bigmouthed peasant*

MALEVOLE Adieu, pigeon-house;° thou burr that only stickest to nappy[6] fortunes! The serpigo, the strangury, an eternal uneffectual priapism seize thee![7] *(see 1.4.86)*

BILIOSO Out, rogue!

MALEVOLE Mayst thou be a notorious, wittolly° pander to thine own wife, and yet get no office,° but live to be the utmost misery of mankind, a beggarly cuckold! *Exit.* *complaisant cuckold* / *preferment by it*

PIETRO [*to Mendoza*] It° shall be so. *(Your plan)*

MENDOZA It must be so, for where great states revenge,
'Tis requisite the parts which piety
And loft respect forbears be closely dogged;[8]
Lay one into his breast shall sleep with him,
Feed in the same dish, run in self-faction,[9]
Who may discover any shape of danger;
For once disgraced, displayèd in offense,
It makes man blushless,[1] and man is (all confess)
More prone to vengeance than to gratefulness.
Favors are writ in dust,° but stripes° we feel; *soon forgotten / blows*
Depravèd nature stamps in lasting steel.[2]

PIETRO You shall be leaguèd with the Duchess.[3]

EQUATO The plot is very good.

PIETRO You shall both kill, and seem the corse° to save.° *corpse / (see 1.7.65–70)*

FERRARDO A most fine brain trick.

CELSO (*tacitè*)° Of a most cunning knave. *silently, aside*

PIETRO My lords, the heavy action we intend
Is death and shame, two of the ugliest shapes
That can confound° a soul; think, think of it. *destroy*
I strike, but yet like him that 'gainst stone walls
Directs his shafts, rebounds° in his own face, *so that they rebound*
My lady's shame is mine; O God, 'tis mine!
Therefore, I do conjure° all secrecy; *implore, invoke*
Let it be as very little° as may be— *as small a disturbance*
Pray ye, as may be.
Make frightless entrance, salute her with soft eyes,
Stain naught with blood; only Ferneze dies,
But not before her brows.° Oh, gentlemen, *before her face*
God knows I love her! Nothing else but this:° *One last point*
I am not well. If grief, that sucks veins dry,
Rivels° the skin, casts ashes in men's faces,[4] *Wrinkles*
Bedulls the eye, unstrengthens all the blood,
Chance to remove me to another world—

5. Malevole mockingly recalls Bilioso's professions of friendship uttered at 1.4.83–85 in order to highlight the hypocrisy of those statements.
6. With a shaggy, rich pile, characteristic of expensive clothing.
7. May you be afflicted by skin infections like ringworm and herpes, painful urination, and a forever persistent but ineffective erection!
8. Where princes seek revenge, it is requisite that those factions that withhold duty and lofty, proud respect be closely watched.
9. The prince should choose as his agent of revenge one who shares everything with him, eats and sleeps with him, joins in conspiracy with him.
1. Such a man (Mendoza offers himself as such) can find out treason; for persons like the Duchess or Ferneze, when they are publicly disgraced and put on display as offenders, become shameless.
2. The depravity that is stamped in our very human nature responds only to violent and bloody chastisement.
3. You'll be placed in the Duchess's household (to carry out this plan). See 1.7.73–81, where Mendoza proposed this.
4. Makes ashen the complexion.

As sure I once° must die—let him° succeed. *sometime / (Mendoza)*
I have no child; all that my youth begot
Hath been your loves, which shall inherit me;° *be my legacy*
Which, as° it ever shall, I do conjure° it, *so that / beseech*
Mendoza may succeed; he's noble born,
With me of much desert.° *Deserving in my eyes*

CELSO (*tacitè*) Much!° *(expressing scorn)*

PIETRO Your silence answers, "ay."
I thank you. Come on, now. Oh, that I might die
Before her shame's displayed! Would I were forced
To burn my father's tomb, unhele° his bones, *exhume*
And dash them in the dirt, rather than this!
This both the living and the dead offends;
Sharp surgery where naught but death amends.[5]

Exit with the others.

2.4

Enter Maquerelle, Emilia, and Bianca, with the posset.° *(see 2.2.28–30)*

MAQUERELLE Even here it is: three curds in three regions individually distinct, most methodically, according to art composed, without any drink.

BIANCA Without any drink?

MAQUERELLE Upon my honor. Will ye sit and eat?

EMILIA Good, the composure,° the receipt,° how is't? *recipe / recipe*

MAQUERELLE 'Tis a pretty pearl; by this pearl (how dost with me?)[1] [*Emilia gives Maquerelle the pearl*], thus it is: seven-and-thirty yolks of Barbary hens' eggs, eighteen spoonfuls and a half of the juice of cock-sparrow bones, one ounce, three drams, four scruples,° and one quarter of the syrup of Ethiopian dates, sweetened with three quarters of a pound of pure candied Indian eryngoes,° strewed over with the powder of pearl of America, amber° of Cataia,° and lamb-stones° of Muscovia.[2] *tiny quantities / sea-holly roots / ambergris / China / testicles*

BIANCA Trust me, the ingredients are very cordial,° and no question° good, and most powerful in restoration. *stimulating / doubtless*

MAQUERELLE I know not what you mean by "restoration," but this it doth: it purifieth the blood, smootheth the skin, enliveneth the eye, strengtheneth the veins, mundifieth° the teeth, comforteth the stomach, fortifieth the back, and quickeneth the wit; that's all. *cleans*

EMILIA [*eating*] By my troth, I have eaten but two spoonfuls, and methinks I could discourse most swiftly and wittily already.

MAQUERELLE Have you the art to seem honest?° *chaste*

BIANCA I thank advice and practice.

MAQUERELLE Why, then, eat me° o'this posset, quicken your blood, and preserve your beauty. Do you know Doctor Plas- *eat some*

5. We can call it extreme surgery when death alone will suffice.
2.4. The scene is virtually continuous.
1. How does it become me? (Maquerelle seems to be begging Emilia's pearl in return for the recipe.)
2. Compare Maquerelle's list of supposed aphrodisiacs here with Malevole's at 2.2.19–22. The ones listed here come mainly from exotic faraway lands.

ter-face? By this curd, he is the most exquisite in forging of veins,[3] sprightening° of eyes, dyeing of hair, sleeking of skins, blushing of cheeks, surfling° of breasts, blanching and bleaching of teeth that ever made an old lady gracious by torchlight; by this curd, la.

brightening / *cosmetically painting*

BIANCA Well, we are resolved. What God has given us we'll cherish.

MAQUERELLE Cherish anything saving° your husband; keep him not too high,[4] lest he leap the pale.° But for° your beauty, let it be your saint; bequeath two hours to it every morning in your closet.° I ha' been young, and yet° in my conscience I am not above five-and-twenty; but believe me, preserve and use your beauty, for, youth and beauty once gone, we are like beehives without honey, out-o'-fashion apparel that no man will wear; therefore use me° your beauty.

save, except / *fence, bounds / as for* / *private room / even now* / *make use of*

EMILIA Ay, but men say—

MAQUERELLE Men say! Let men say what they will; life° o'woman, they are ignorant of our wants. The more in years, the more in perfection they grow; if they lose youth and beauty, they gain wisdom and discretion. But when our beauty fades, good night with us. There cannot be an uglier thing to see than an old woman; from which, O pruning,° pinching, and painting, deliver all sweet beauties!

by the life (an oath) / *preening; trimming*

[*Music within.*]

BIANCA Hark, music.

MAQUERELLE Peace, 'tis i'the Duchess' bedchamber. Good rest, most prosperously graced ladies.

EMILIA Good night, sentinel.

BIANCA 'Night, dear Maquerelle. *Exeunt all but Maquerelle.*

MAQUERELLE May my posset's operation send you my wit and honesty, and me your youth and beauty. The pleasing'st rest! *Exit Maquerelle.*

2.5

A song. Whilst the song is singing, enter Mendoza with his sword drawn, standing ready to murder Ferneze as he flies from the Duchess's chamber. Tumult within.

ALL [*within*] Strike, Strike!

AURELIA [*within*] Save my Ferneze! Oh, save my Ferneze!

Enter Ferneze in his shirt, and is received upon Mendoza's sword.

ALL [*within*] Follow! Pursue!

AURELIA [*within*] Oh, save Ferneze!

[*Mendoza*] *thrusts his rapier in Ferneze.*

MENDOZA Pierce, pierce! Thou shallow fool, drop there.
He that attempts a princess' lawless love
Must have broad hands, close heart, with Argus' eyes,
And back of Hercules,[1] or else he dies.

3. Painting artificial veins over the cosmetic base.
4. Don't overfeed your husband with rich food that will overexcite him sexually.
2.5. The scene is virtually continuous.
1. Must have strong hands, a quietly resolved heart, eyes everywhere, and the strength and sexual endurance of Hercules. (Argus was Hera's hundred-eyed watchman over Io, a mistress of her husband, Zeus.)

Enter Aurelia, Duke Pietro, Ferrardo, Bilioso, Celso, and Equato.

ALL Follow, follow! [*Mendoza bestrides the wounded body of Ferneze and seems to save him.*]

MENDOZA Stand off! Forbear, ye most uncivil lords!
PIETRO Strike!
MENDOZA Do not; tempt not a man resolved.
Would you, inhuman murderers, more than death?
AURELIA Oh, poor Ferneze!
MENDOZA Alas, now all defense too late.
AURELIA He's dead.
PIETRO [*to Aurelia*] I am sorry for our shame. Go to your bed;
Weep not too much, but leave some tears to shed
When I am dead.
AURELIA What, weep for thee? My soul no tears shall find.
PIETRO Alas, alas, that women's souls are blind!
MENDOZA Betray such beauty?
Murder such youth? Contemn civility?° *Spurn good manners?*
He loves him not that rails not at him.[2]
PIETRO Thou canst not move° us; we have blood° enough.— *anger / bloodshed*
An't° please you, lady, we have quite forgot *If it*
All your defects; if not, why then—
AURELIA Not.° *It does not please me*
PIETRO Not.° *Then I won't forget*
The best of rest.° Good night. *Sleep well*

Exit Pietro with other courtiers.

AURELIA Despite° go with thee! *Scorn*
MENDOZA Madam, you ha' done me foul disgrace.
You have wronged him much loves° you too much. *who loves*
Go to! Your soul knows you have.
AURELIA I think I have.
MENDOZA Do you but think so?
AURELIA Nay, sure I have. My eyes have witnessed thy love;
Thou hast stood too firm for me.° *for me to doubt you*
MENDOZA Why, tell me, fair-cheeked lady, who even in tears
Art powerfully beauteous, what unadvisèd° passion *ill-advised*
Struck ye into such a violent heat against me?
Speak. What mischief wronged us? What devil injured us?
Speak.
AURELIA That thing ne'er worthy of the name of man—Ferneze.
Ferneze swore thou lov'st Emilia,
Which to advance, with most reproachful breath
Thou both didst blemish and denounce my love.
MENDOZA [*to the prostrate Ferneze*] Ignoble villain, did I for this bestride
Thy wounded limbs? For this? Rank opposite[3]
Even to my sovereign? For this, O God, for this
Sunk all my hopes, and with my hopes my life,
Ripped bare my throat unto the hangman's ax?
Thou most dishonored trunk!°—Emilia? *(Ferneze's corpse)*

2. Anyone who really cares about Pietro should heap abuse on his faults in order to correct him. (Mendoza, as part of the plot he arranged with Pietro at 1.7.63–81, is pretending to defend Ferneze and implicate Pietro in the death of Ferneze in order to win the Duchess's confidence.)
3. For this deed have I taken a stand in opposition.

By life, I know her not.—Emilia?
Did you believe him?
AURELIA Pardon me. I did.
MENDOZA Did you? And thereupon you graced him?
AURELIA I did.
MENDOZA Took him to favor, nay, even clasped° with him? *embraced sexually*
AURELIA Alas, I did.
MENDOZA This night?
AURELIA This night.
MENDOZA And in your lustful twines the Duke took you?
AURELIA A most sad truth.
MENDOZA O God! O God! How we dull honest souls,
Heavy-brained° men, are swallowed in the bogs *Lacking in cunning*
Of a deceitful ground, whilst nimble bloods,
Light-jointed spirits, pent,° cut good men's throats *when hemmed in*
And scape. Alas, I am too honest for this age,
Too full of phlegm° and heavy steadiness, *Too slow to anger*
Stood still whilst this slave cast a noose about me;
Nay, then to stand in honor of him and her° *(Ferneze and Aurelia)*
Who had even sliced my heart!
AURELIA Come, I did err,
And am most sorry I did err.
MENDOZA Why, we are both but° dead. The Duke hates us, *as good as*
And, those whom princes do once groundly° hate, *rootedly*
Let them provide° to die, as sure as fate. *prepare*
Prevention is the heart of policy.
AURELIA Shall we murder him?
MENDOZA Instantly?
AURELIA Instantly. Before he casts a plot,
Or further blaze° my honor's much-known blot, *proclaims*
Let's murder him.
MENDOZA I would do much for you. Will ye marry me?
AURELIA I'll make thee duke. We are of Medicis,
Florence our friend; in court my faction
Not meanly° strengthful; the Duke then dead, *Not slightly*
We well prepared for change, the multitude
Irresolutely reeling, we in force,
Our party seconded,° the kingdom mazed°— *supported / bewildered*
No doubt of° swift success all shall be graced. *with*
MENDOZA You do confirm me; we are resolute.
Tomorrow look for change; rest confident.
'Tis now about the immodest waist° of night; *middle*
The mother of moist dew° with pallid light *(The moon)*
Spreads gloomy shades about the numbèd earth.
Sleep, sleep, whilst we contrive our mischief's birth.
This man I'll get inhumed.° Farewell, to bed; *buried*
Ay, kiss thy pillow, dream the Duke is dead.
So, so, good night. *Exit Aurelia.*

How Fortune dotes on impudence! I am in private the adopted son of yon good prince. I must be duke. Why, if I must, I must. Most silly lord, name me?[4] O heaven! I see God made honest fools to maintain crafty knaves. The

4. How silly of Pietro to name me heir! (See 2.3.67–76.)

Duchess is wholly mine too; must kill her husband to quit° — *clear, remove*
her shame.
Much!° Then marry her. Ay! — *(expressing scorn)*
Oh, I grow proud in prosperous treachery!
As wrestlers clip,° so I'll embrace you all, — *embrace*
Not to support, but to procure your fall.

Enter Malevole.

MALEVOLE God arrest° thee! — *rest; stop*
MENDOZA At whose suit?
MALEVOLE At the devil's. Ha, you treacherous, damnable
monster! How dost? How dost, thou treacherous rogue? Ha,
ye rascal, I am banished the court, sirrah.° — *(see 2.3.4–5)*
MENDOZA Prithee, let's be acquainted; I do love thee, faith.
MALEVOLE At your service, by the Lord, la. Shall 's° go to — *Shall we*
supper? Let's be once drunk together, and so unite a most
virtuously strengthened friendship; shall 's, Huguenot,[5]
shall 's?
MENDOZA Wilt fall upon° my chamber tomorrow morn? — *come to*
MALEVOLE As a raven to a dunghill. They say there's one dead
here, pricked for the pride of the flesh.° — *stabbed for lechery*
MENDOZA Ferneze. There he is; prithee, bury him.
MALEVOLE Oh, most willingly; I mean to turn pure Rochelle
churchman,[6] I.
MENDOZA Thou, churchman? Why? Why?
MALEVOLE Because I'll live lazily, rail upon authority, deny
kings' supremacy in things indifferent, and be a pope in mine
own parish.
MENDOZA Wherefore dost thou think churches were made?
MALEVOLE To scour plowshares.[7] I ha' seen oxen plow up
altars. *Et nunc seges ubi Sion fuit.*[8]
MENDOZA Strange!
MALEVOLE Nay, monstrous! I ha' seen a sumptuous steeple
turned to a stinking privy; more beastly, the sacred'st place° — *the sanctuary*
made a dog's kennel; nay, most inhuman, the stoned° coffins — *stone-made*
of long-dead Christians burst up and made hogs' troughs.
Hic finis Priami.[9] Shall I ha' some sack° and cheese at thy — *sweet white wine*
chamber? Good night, good mischievous, incarnate devil;
good night, Mendoza. Ha, ye inhuman villain, good night,
night, fub!° — *cheat, infamous one*
MENDOZA Good night. Tomorrow morn? *Exit Mendoza.*
MALEVOLE Ay, I will come, friendly damnation, I will come. I
do descry cross-points;° honesty and courtship straddle as — *tricky dance steps*
far asunder as a true Frenchman's legs.[1]
FERNEZE [*stirring*] Oh!

5. A Huguenot is a French Protestant, here used to suggest both a comrade in conspiracy and a hypocrite. Puritans were often the target of satire on the English stage.
6. Rochelle, in France, was a Huguenot center; see previous note. The satire of Puritans continues here in lines 123–29, stressing their hostility toward the authority of the state.
7. The churches, having fallen into ruins, will serve to burnish plow blades as they scrape against the stones of the wreckage.
8. And now fields of grain stand where Sion (Mount Zion, the old city of Jerusalem) once stood. (Ovid, *Heroides*, 1.53.)
9. Such is Priam's end. (Adapted from Virgil, *Aeneid*, 2.554. This line came to be a catchphrase for any violent dissolution. Priam was the King of Troy during the Trojan War.)
1. True honesty and courtiership are as far apart as the spread-apart legs of a Frenchman afflicted with syphilis.

MALEVOLE Proclamations, more proclamations!
FERNEZE Oh, a surgeon!
MALEVOLE Hark! Lust cries for a surgeon. What news from Limbo?° How does the grand cuckold, Lucifer? *i.e., the underworld*
FERNEZE Oh, help, help! Conceal and save me!
Ferneze stirs, and Malevole helps him up and conveys him away.
MALEVOLE Thy shame, more than thy wounds, do grieve me far.
Thy wounds but° leave upon thy flesh some scar, *merely*
But fame° ne'er heals, still rankles worse and worse; *infamy*
Such is of uncontrollèd lust the curse.
Think what it is in lawless sheets to lie,
But, oh, Ferneze, what in lust to die!
Then thou that shame respects,[2] oh, fly converse° *flee familiarity*
With women's eyes and lisping wantonness!
Stick candles 'gainst a virgin wall's white back;
If they not burn, yet at the least they'll black.[3]
Come, I'll convey thee to a private port,° *place of refuge*
Where thou shalt live (O happy man) from° court. *away from*
The beauty of the day begins to rise,
From whose bright form night's heavy shadow flies.
Now 'gins close° plots to work; the scene° grows full, *secret / story line*
And craves his eyes who hath a solid skull.[4] *Exeunt.*

3.1

Enter Pietro the Duke, Mendoza, Count Equato, and Bilioso.

PIETRO 'Tis grown to youth of day.° How shall we waste this light?° *morning* / *pass the time*
My heart's more heavy than a tyrant's crown.
Shall we go hunt? Prepare for field. *Exit Equato.*
MENDOZA Would ye could be merry!
PIETRO Would God I could! Mendoza, bid 'em haste. *Exit Mendoza.*
I would fain shift place. Oh, vain relief!
Sad souls may well change place, but not change grief;
As deer being struck fly thorough° many soils,° *through / pools of water*
Yet still the shaft sticks fast, so—
BILIOSO A good old simile, my honest lord.
PIETRO I am not much unlike to some sick man
That long desirèd hurtful drink; at last
Swills in and drinks his last, ending at once
Both life and thirst. Oh, would I ne'er had known
My own dishonor! Good God, that men should desire
To search out that which, being found, kills all
Their joy of life! To taste the tree of knowledge,
And then be driven from out paradise!
Canst give me some comfort?
BILIOSO My lord, I have some books which have been dedi-

2. Any persons hearing my voice (including the audience) who feel the force of shame.
3. I.e., Evil stands out in vivid contrast to good and darkens it even if it may not be able to destroy it entirely.
4. And requires close observation by a sharp-minded person.
3.1. The Genoese court.

cated to my honor, and I ne'er read 'em, and yet they had very fine names: *Physic for Fortune, Lozenges of Sanctified Sincerity*, very pretty works of curates, scriveners, and schoolmasters. Marry, I remember one Seneca, Lucius Annaeus Seneca—

PIETRO Out upon him! He writ of temperance and fortitude, yet lived like a voluptuous epicure, and died like an effeminate coward.[1] Haste thee to Florence.
Here, take our letters, see 'em sealed. Away!
[*He gives Bilioso letters.*]
Report in private to the honored duke
His daughter's forced disgrace. Tell him at length
We know too much; due compliments° advance. *courtly courtesies*
There's naught that's safe and sweet but ignorance.
Exit Duke [*Pietro*].

Enter Bianca.

BILIOSO Madam, I am going ambassador for Florence. 'Twill be great charges° to me. *expense*

BIANCA No matter, my lord, you have the lease of two manors come out° next Christmas; you may lay your tenants on the greater rack° for it; and when you come home again, I'll teach you how you shall get two hundred pounds a year by your teeth. *due to expire* / *i.e, up their rents*

BILIOSO How, madam?

BIANCA Cut off so much from housekeeping.° That which is saved by the teeth,° you know, is got by the teeth. *keeping an open house* / *by less eating*

BILIOSO 'Fore God, and so I may. I am in wondrous credit,° lady. *good favor, reputation*

BIANCA See the use of flattery! I did ever counsel you to flatter greatness, and you have profited well. Any man that will do so shall be sure to be like your Scotch barnacle, now a block, instantly a worm, and presently a great goose.[2] This it is to rot and putrefy in the bosom of greatness.

BILIOSO Thou art ever my politician!° Oh, how happy is that old lord that hath a politician to° his young lady! I'll have fifty gentlemen shall attend upon me; marry, the most of them shall be farmers' sons, because they shall bear their own charges,° and they shall go appareled thus: in seawater green suits, ash-color cloaks, watchet° stockings, and popinjay green° feathers. Will not the colors do excellent? *Machiavellian* / *as* / *pay their own way* / *pale blue* / *blue-green*

BIANCA Out upon't! They'll look like citizens riding to their friends at Whitsuntide, their apparel just so many several parishes.[3]

BILIOSO I'll have it so; and Passarello, my fool, shall go along with me; marry, he shall be in velvet.

BIANCA A fool in velvet?

BILIOSO Ay, 'tis common for your fool° to wear satin; I'll have mine in velvet. *a typical fool*

BIANCA What will you wear, then, my lord?

1. Seneca (c. 4 B.C.E.–65 C.E.) wrote Stoical treatises and plays. Despite what Pietro says of him, he lived comfortably until he was compelled by Nero to take his own life.
2. Barnacles were reputed to grow as stumps ("blocks") on trees by the seaside and to turn from wormlike creatures into geese as they fell into the water.
3. They'll be a jumble of color, like citizens on excursions during Whitsuntide, the week beginning with Whitsunday, the seventh Sunday after Easter.

BILIOSO Velvet, too; marry, it shall be embroidered, because I'll differ from the fool somewhat. I am horribly troubled with the gout; nothing grieves me but that my doctor hath forbidden me wine, and you know your ambassador° must drink. Didst thou ask thy doctor what was good for the gout? *an ambassador*

BIANCA Yes. He said ease, wine, and women were good for it.° *would increase it*

BILIOSO Nay, thou hast such a wit! What was good to cure it, said he?

BIANCA Why, the rack.° All your empirics° could never do the like cure upon the gout the rack did in England, or your Scotch boot.[4] The French harlequin[5] will instruct you. *torture / quack doctors*

BILIOSO Surely I do wonder how thou, having for the most part of thy lifetime been a country body, shouldst have so good a wit.

BIANCA Who, I? Why, I have been a courtier thrice two months.

BILIOSO So have I this twenty year, and yet there was a gentleman-usher called me coxcomb° t'other day, and to my face too. Was't not a backbiting rascal? I would I were better traveled, that I might have been better acquainted with the fashions of several countrymen;° but my secretary, I think he hath sufficiently instructed me. *conceited fool / men of different lands*

BIANCA How, my lord?

BILIOSO "Marry, my good lord," quoth he, "Your Lordship shall ever find amongst a hundred Frenchmen, forty hotshots;° amongst a hundred Spaniards, threescore braggarts; amongst a hundred Dutchmen, fourscore drunkards; amongst a hundred Englishmen, fourscore-and-ten madmen; and amongst an hundred Welshmen—" *hotheads*

BIANCA What, my lord?

BILIOSO "Fourscore-and-nineteen gentlemen."° *claiming gentle birth*

BIANCA But since you go about a sad° embassy, I would have you go in black, my lord. *serious*

BILIOSO Why, dost think I cannot mourn° unless I wear my hat in cypress° like an alderman's heir? That's vile, very old,° in faith. *appear serious / black crepe / old-fashioned*

BIANCA I'll learn of° you shortly. Oh, we should have a fine gallant of you, should not I instruct you. How will you bear yourself when you come into the Duke of Florence' court? *teach*

BILIOSO Proud enough, and 'twill do well enough. As I walk up and down the chamber, I'll spit frowns about me, have a strong perfume in my jerkin,° let my beard grow to make me look terrible, salute no man beneath the fourth button,° and 'twill do excellent. *a man's jacket / bow only slightly*

BIANCA But there is a very beautiful lady there. How will you entertain her?

BILIOSO I'll tell you that when the lady hath entertained me.° But to satisfy thee, here comes the fool. *taken me as lover*

4. A torture instrument designed to crush the leg. Bianca's witty point is that the only way to cure gout is to suffer torments of privation worse than the gout itself or to die from the torture.

5. The zany who usually accompanies the mountebank, or "empiric" (line 76), in the commedia dell'arte, Italian comedy improvised from stock characters and situations. Only a fool like this, says Bianca, can teach wisdom.

Enter Passarello.

Fool, thou shalt stand for the fair lady.

PASSARELLO Your fool will stand° for your lady most willingly and most uprightly. *(with a sexual pun)*

BILIOSO I'll salute her in Latin.

PASSARELLO Oh, your fool can understand no Latin.

BILIOSO Ay, but your lady can.

PASSARELLO Why, then, if your lady take down° your fool, your fool will stand no longer for your lady. *dress down; sleep with*

BILIOSO A pestilent fool! 'Fore God, I think the world be turned upside down too.

PASSARELLO Oh, no, sir; for then your lady, and all the ladies in the palace, should go with their heels upward, and that were a strange sight, you know.

BILIOSO There be many will repine at my preferment.° *advancement*

PASSARELLO Oh, ay, like the envy of an elder sister that hath her younger made a lady° before her. *married into the gentry*

BILIOSO The Duke is wondrous discontented.

PASSARELLO Ay, and more melancholic than a usurer having all his money out° at the death of a prince.[6] *loaned out*

BILIOSO Didst thou see Madam Floria today?

PASSARELLO Yes, I found her repairing her face today; the red upon the white showed as if her cheeks should have been served in for two dishes of barberries in stewed broth, and the flesh to them a woodcock.[7]

BILIOSO A bitter fool! Come, madam, this night thou shalt enjoy me freely, and tomorrow for Florence.

[*He withdraws.*] *Exit* [*Bianca*].

PASSARELLO What a natural fool is he that would be a pair of bodice to a woman's petticoat, to be trussed and pointed to them![8] Well, I'll dog° my lord, and the word is proper; for when I fawn upon him he feeds me; when I snap him by the fingers, he spits in my mouth.° If a dog's death were not strangling, I had rather be one than a servingman; for the corruption of coin is either the generation of a usurer, or a lousy beggar.[9] [*Exit Passarello. Bilioso remains onstage.*] *follow* *(a friendly gesture)*

3.2

Enter Malevole in some frieze° gown, whilst Bilioso reads his patent.° *coarse wool* *commission*

MALEVOLE I cannot sleep; my eyes' ill-neighboring lids
Will hold no fellowship. O thou pale sober° Night, *subdued, quiet*
Thou that in sluggish fumes all sense dost steep;
Thou that gives all the world full leave to play,° *to cease work*
Unbend'st° the feebled veins of sweaty labor! *Relaxes*
The galley-slave, that all the toilsome day
Tugs at his oar against the stubborn wave,
Straining his rugged veins, snores fast;

6. A newly crowned prince might be expected to cancel all debts.

7. Her cheeks looked like red berries in a dish of white broth made from cooked fowl. ("Woodcock" connotes stupidity; see 1.4.67–68 and note.)

8. What a fool is he who would wish to be tied to a woman's petticoat, laced in like a corset!

9. Money corruptly offers only the alternatives of being an extortionate usurer or a lice-infested beggar.

3.2. The scene continues.

The stooping scythe-man that doth barb° the field — *mow*
Thou makest wink° sure. In night all creatures sleep; — *shut his eyes*
Only the malcontent, that 'gainst his fate
Repines and quarrels, alas, he's Goodman Tell-Clock!° — *Sir Count-the-Clock*
His sallow jawbones sink with wasting moan;
Whilst others' beds are down,° his pillow's stone. — *down feather*

BILIOSO [*coming forward*] Malevole!

MALEVOLE (*to Bilioso*) Elder of Israel,[1] thou honest defect of wicked nature° and obstinate ignorance, when did thy wife let thee lie with her? — *unredeemed humanity*

BILIOSO I am going ambassador to Florence.

MALEVOLE Ambassador? Now, for thy country's honor, prithee do not put up mutton and porridge[2] i'thy cloak-bag. Thy young lady wife goes to Florence with thee too, does she not?

BILIOSO No, I leave her at the palace.

MALEVOLE At the palace? Now discretion shield man!° For God's love, let's ha' no more cuckolds. Hymen begins to put off his saffron robe.[3] Keep thy wife i'the state of grace. Heart o'truth, I would sooner leave my lady singled° in a bordello than in the Genoa palace. — *protect us from folly*; *alone*

Sin there° appearing in her sluttish shape — *(in the bordello)*
Would soon grow loathsome, even to blushless° sense; — *unblushing, shameless*
Surfeit° would choke intemperate appetite, — *Overabundance*
Make the soul scent the rotten breath of lust;
When° in an Italian lascivious palace, — *Whereas*
A lady guardianless,
Left to the push of all allurement,
The strongest incitements to immodesty—
To have her bound, incensed° with wanton sweets, — *garlanded and perfumed*
Her veins filled high with heating delicates,° — *arousing delicacies*
Soft rest, sweet music, amorous masquerers,
Lascivious banquets, sin itself gilt o'er,
Strong fantasy tricking up° strange delights, — *adorning artfully*
Presenting it dressed pleasingly to sense,
Sense leading it unto the soul, confirmed
With potent° example, impudent custom, — *noble, aristocratic*
Enticed by that great bawd Opportunity;
Thus being prepared, clap to her easy ear
Youth in good clothes, well shaped, rich,
Fair-spoken, promising-noble, ardent, blood-full,° — *passionate*
Witty, flattering—Ulysses absent,
O Ithaca, can chastest Penelope hold out?[4]

BILIOSO Mass,° I'll think on't. Farewell. — *By the Mass (an oath)*

MALEVOLE Farewell. Take thy wife with thee. Farewell.

Exit Bilioso.

To Florence, um? It may prove good, it may,
And we may once unmask our brows.° — *reveal my identity*

1. Malevole compares Bilioso to the scribes and Pharisees of Israel embodying the authoritarian and corrupt older ways described in the Gospels.
2. Lower-class fare (and glancing in "mutton" at a slang term for "whore").
3. Even Hymen, the god of marriage, puts aside his traditional priestly robes of saffron yellow (indicating that chaste marriage is out of fashion).
4. Ulysses' chaste wife, Penelope, living on their island of Ithaca, held out for years against the importunities of suitors for her hand, despite not knowing if Ulysses was alive or dead (see Homer's *Odyssey*). Malevole doubts that even a woman this chaste could hold out for long at the Genoese court.

3.3

Enter Count Celso.

CELSO My honored lord!
MALEVOLE Celso, peace! How is't? Speak low; pale fears
Suspect that hedges, walls, and trees have ears.
Speak, how runs all?
CELSO I'faith, my lord, that beast with many heads,
The staggering° multitude, recoils apace; *wavering*
Though thorough° great men's envy, most men's° malice, *through / the majority's*
Their much intemperate heat hath banished you,
Yet now they find envy and malice ne'er
Produce faint° reformation. *even faint*
The Duke, the too soft Duke, lies as a block° *a senseless thing*
For which two tugging factions seem to saw,° *seesaw*
But still the iron through the ribs they draw.[1]
MALEVOLE I tell thee, Celso, I have ever found
Thy breast most far from shifting° cowardice *wavering*
And fearful baseness. Therefore, I'll tell thee, Celso,
I find the wind begins to come about;° *reverse direction*
I'll shift my suit of fortune.
I know the Florentine—whose only force,° *whose power alone*
By marrying his proud daughter to this prince,
Both banished me and made this weak lord duke—
Will now forsake them all; be sure he will.
I'll lie in ambush for conveniency,
Upon their severance to confirm myself.[2]
CELSO Is Ferneze interred?
MALEVOLE Of that at leisure. He lives.
CELSO But how stands Mendoza? How is't with him?
MALEVOLE Faith, like a pair of snuffers:° snibs° filth in other men and retains it in himself. *candle snuffers / rebukes*
CELSO He does fly from public notice, methinks, as a hare does from hounds: the feet whereon he flies betrays him.° *leave tracks behind*
MALEVOLE I can track him, Celso.
Oh, my disguise fools him most powerfully.
For that° I seem a desperate malcontent, *Because*
He fain° would clasp° with me; he is the true slave *gladly / be close*
That will put on the most affected grace
For some vile second cause.[3]

Enter Mendoza.

CELSO He's here.
MALEVOLE Give place.
Celso [retires].
Illo, ho, ho, ho!° Art there, old truepenny? Where hast thou spent thyself this morning? I see flattery in thine eyes and damnation i'thy soul. Ha, ye huge rascal! *(cry used to call a hawk)*
MENDOZA Thou art very merry.

3.3. The scene continues.
1. The two contending factions continually wound and torture the body politic.
2. I'll wait until the coalition falls apart, providing an opportunity to strengthen my position.
3. He will feign friendship in order to employ me in villainy. ("Second cause" means "ulterior motive.")

MALEVOLE As a scholar *futuens gratis*.° How does the devil go with thee now? — *having free sex*

MENDOZA Malevole, thou art an arrant knave.

MALEVOLE Who, I? I have been a sergeant,° man. — *arresting officer*

MENDOZA Thou art very poor.

MALEVOLE As Job,[4] an alchemist, or a poet.

MENDOZA The Duke hates thee.

MALEVOLE As Irishmen do bum-cracks.° — *farts*

MENDOZA Thou hast lost his amity.

MALEVOLE As pleasing as maids lose their virginity.

MENDOZA Would thou wert of a lusty° spirit! Would thou wert noble!° — *vigorous; ambitious* / *honorable; resolved*

MALEVOLE Why, sure my blood gives° me I am noble;° sure I am of noble kind, for I find myself possessed with all their qualities: love dogs, dice, and drabs,° scorn wit in stuff-clothes,° have beat my shoemaker, knocked my seamstress, cuckold'° my pothecary, and undone° my tailor. Noble? Why not? Since the Stoic° said, *Neminem servum non ex regibus, neminem regem non ex servis esse oriundum*.[5] Only busy Fortune touses,° and the provident Chances blends them together. I'll give you a simile: did you e'er see a well with two buckets? Whilst one comes up full to be emptied, another goes down empty to be filled; such is the state of all humanity. Why, look you, I may be the son of some duke; for, believe me, intemperate lascivious bastardy makes nobility doubtful. I have a lusty, daring heart, Mendoza.° — *tells / nobly born*; *whores*; *coarse garments*; *cuckolded / bankrupted*; *(Seneca)*; *pulls roughly about*; *(answering 52–53)*

MENDOZA Let's grasp.° I do like thee infinitely. Wilt enact one thing for me? — *embrace, shake hands*

MALEVOLE Shall I get° by it? — *profit*

[*Mendoza*] *gives him his purse.*

Command me; I am thy slave beyond death and hell.

MENDOZA Murder the Duke.

MALEVOLE My heart's wish, my soul's desire, my fantasy's dream, my blood's longing, the only height of my hopes! How, O God, how? Oh, how my united spirits throng together, so strengthen my resolve!

MENDOZA The Duke is now a-hunting.

MALEVOLE Excellent, admirable, as the devil would have it! Lend me—lend me rapier, pistol, crossbow; so, so, I'll do it.

MENDOZA Then we agree?

MALEVOLE As Lent and fishmongers.[6] Come 'a cap-à-pie?[7] How in form?

MENDOZA Know that this weak-brained duke, who only stands
On Florence' stilts,° hath out of witless zeal — *Propped up by Florence*
Made me his heir, and secretly confirmed
The wreath° to me after his life's full point.° — *crown / end*

MALEVOLE Upon what merit?

4. The title figure of the Book of Job is tested by God with extreme poverty and suffering.

5. There is no slave not descended from kings, nor any king not descended from slaves. (Seneca, *Epistles*, 14, quoting Plato.)

6. Fish merchants liked Lent because of the restrictions on eating meat.

7. Is the Duke outfitted in armor, head to foot? ("Come 'a" means "Comes he.")

MENDOZA Merit? By heaven, I horn° him! — *cuckold*
Only Ferneze's death gave me state's life.[8]
Tut, we are politic;° he must not live now. — *cunning*
MALEVOLE No reason,° marry. But how must he die now? — *(for him to live)*
MENDOZA My utmost project is to murder the Duke, that I
might have his state,° because he makes me his heir; to ban- — *throne*
ish the Duchess, that I might be rid of a cunning Lacedaemonian,[9] because I know Florence will forsake her; and then
to marry Maria, the banished Duke Altofront's wife, that her
friends might strengthen me and my faction. This is all, la.
MALEVOLE Do you love Maria?
MENDOZA Faith, no great affection, but as wise men do love
great women, to ennoble their blood° and augment their rev- — *family, stock*
enue. To accomplish this now, thus now: the Duke is in the
forest next the sea; single him,° kill him, hurl him i'the — *separate him from others*
main,° and proclaim thou sawest wolves eat him. — *sea*
MALEVOLE Um, not so good. Methinks, when he is slain,
To get some hypocrite, some dangerous wretch
That's muffled o'er° with feignèd holiness — *concealed, disguised*
To swear he heard the Duke on some steep cliff
Lament his wife's dishonor, and, in an agony
Of his heart's torture, hurled his groaning sides
Into the swollen sea. This circumstance,° — *detailed account*
Well made, sounds probable; and hereupon
The Duchess—
MENDOZA May well be banished.
Oh, unpeerable° invention! Rare!° — *peerless / Excellent!*
Thou god of policy! It honeys° me. — *delights*
MALEVOLE Then fear not for the wife of Altofront.
I'll close to° her. — *come to terms with*
MENDOZA Thou shalt, thou shalt. Our Excellency is
pleased.° — *I am pleased*
Why wert not thou an emperor? When we are duke,
I'll make thee some great man, sure.
MALEVOLE Nay, make me some rich knave, and I'll make
myself some great man.
MENDOZA In thee be all my spirit!
Retain ten souls,° unite thy virtual° powers; — *Take ten men / effective*
Resolve. Ha, remember greatness![1] Heart, farewell.
The fate of all my hopes in thee doth dwell.
[*Exit Mendoza.*] *Celso* [*comes forward*].
MALEVOLE Celso, didst hear? O heaven, didst hear?
Such devilish mischief? Sufferest thou the world
Carouse° damnation even with greedy swallow, — *To drink down*
And still dost wink,° still does thy vengeance slumber? — *shut your eyes*
If now thy brows are clear,° when will they thunder? — *smooth, unfrowning*
Exeunt.

8. Only the plot to kill Ferneze kept my political schemes alive.
9. The Lacedaemonians, from the Peloponnese in southern Greece, had a reputation for deviousness and immorality (as did the Greeks generally, in English eyes; see Induction 120–22 and note).
1. Remember the greatness I've promised you!

3.4

Enter Pietro, Ferrardo, Prepasso, and three Pages. Cornets like horns.

FERRARDO The dogs are at a fault.° *losing the scent*

PIETRO Would God nothing but the dogs were at it! Let the deer pursue safety, the dogs follow the game, and do you follow the dogs. As for me, 'tis unfit one beast° should hunt another; I ha' one chaseth me. An't please you, I would be rid of ye a little. *(myself, a cuckold)*

FERRARDO Would your grief would as soon leave you as we to quietness!

PIETRO I thank you. *[Ferrardo and Prepasso] exeunt.* Boy, what dost thou dream of now?

PAGE Of a dry summer, my lord, for here's a hot world towards.° But, my lord, I had a strange dream last night. *coming on*

PIETRO What strange dream?

PAGE Why, methought I pleased you with singing, and then I dreamt you gave me that short sword.

PIETRO Prettily begged. Hold thee, I'll prove thy dream true; take't. *[He gives him the sword.]*

PAGE My duty.° But still I dreamt on, my lord, and methought, an't shall please Your Excellency, you would needs, out of your royal bounty, give me that jewel in your hat. *I offer dutiful thanks*

PIETRO Oh, thou didst but dream, boy; do not believe it. Dreams prove not always true; they may hold in a short sword, but not in a jewel. But now,° sir, you dreamt you had pleased me with singing; make that true as I ha' made the other. *Just now*

PAGE Faith, my lord, I did but dream; and dreams, you say, prove not always true. They may hold in a good sword, but not in a good song. The truth is, I ha' lost my voice.

PIETRO Lost thy voice? How?

PAGE With dreaming, faith. But here's a couple of sirenical° rascals shall enchant ye. What shall they sing, my good lord? *sirenlike, enchanting*

PIETRO Sing of the nature of women, and then the song shall be surely full of variety: old crotchets° and most sweet closes.° It shall be humorous,° grave, fantastic, amorous, melancholy, sprightly—one in all, and all in one. *quarter notes; whimsies* / *cadences / moody*

PAGE All in one?° *one song; one woman*

PIETRO By'r Lady, too many. Sing; my speech grows culpable of unthrifty idleness.° Sing. *Song.*[1] *idle chitchat*
Ah, so, so, sing. I am heavy;° walk off. I shall talk in my sleep; walk off. *[He sleeps.] Exeunt Pages.* *sleepy*

3.5

Enter Malevole with crossbow and pistol.

MALEVOLE Brief, brief! Who? The Duke? Good heaven, that fools should stumble upon greatness! Do not sleep, Duke. [*He wakens him.*] Give ye good morrow. Must be brief, Duke. I am fee'd to murder thee. Start not! Mendoza, Men-

3.4. A forest near the sea (see 3.3.101–2).
1. The song is missing.

3.5. The scene continues.

doza hired me; here's his gold, his pistol, crossbow, sword; 'tis all as firm as earth. Oh, fool, fool, choked with the common maze° of easy° idiots, credulity! Make him thine heir? What, thy sworn murderer? *delusion / gullible*

PIETRO Oh, can it be?

MALEVOLE Can!

PIETRO Discovered he not Ferneze?

MALEVOLE Yes, but why? But why? For love to thee? Much, much! To be revenged upon his rival, who had thrust his jaws awry,[1] who being slain, supposed° by thine own hands, defended by his° sword, made thee most loathsome, him most gracious with thy loose princess.° Thou, closely yielding egress° and regress to her, madest him heir, whose hot unquiet lust straight toused thy sheets,° and now would seize thy state. Politician! Wise man! Death,° to be led to the stake like a bull by the horns, to make even kindness cut a gentle throat![2] Life,° why art thou numbed?° Thou foggy dullness, speak! Lives not more faith in a home-thrusting tongue than in these fencing tip-tap courtiers?[3] *supposedly / (Mendoza's) / (Aurelia) / yielding secret entry / rumpled your wife's bed / By God's death / By God's life / mute*

Enter Celso with a hermit's gown and beard.

PIETRO Lord Malevole, if this be true—

MALEVOLE If? Come, shade° thee with this disguise. If? Thou shalt handle it; he shall thank thee for killing thyself. Come, follow my directions, and thou shalt see strange sleights.° *hide / tricks*

PIETRO World, whither wilt thou?

MALEVOLE Why, to the devil. Come, the morn grows late;
A steady quickness is the soul of state.° *Exeunt.* *statecraft*

4.1

Enter Maquarelle knocking at the ladies' door.

MAQUERELLE Medam,° medam, are you stirring, medam? If you be stirring, medam—if I thought I should disturb ye— *(affected pronunciation)*

[*Enter a Page.*]

PAGE My lady is up, forsooth.

MAQUERELLE A pretty boy, faith. How old art thou?

PAGE I think fourteen.

MAQUERELLE Nay, an ye be in the teens, are ye a gentleman born? Do you know me? My name is Medam Maquerelle; I lie° in the old Cunny Court.[1]—See, here, the ladies. *dwell*

[*The Page retires.*]

Enter Bianca and Emilia.

BIANCA A fair day to ye, Maquerelle.

EMILIA Is the Duchess up yet, sentinel?

MAQUERELLE Oh, ladies, the most abominable mischance! Oh, dear ladies, the most piteous disaster! Ferneze was taken

1. Oh, sure! To be revenged on Ferneze, who had put his (Mendoza's) nose out of joint (i.e., had put him out of favor with the Duke).
2. To offer your throat unprotestingly to be cut by a supposed friend!
3. Isn't an honest, blunt critic (like me) to be trusted more than a fashion-mongering fop (like Mendoza) who practices the newfangled style of fencing?

4.1. The Genoese court.
1. Literally, the Rabbit Warren, but with indecent punning on "cunny" and "cunt."

last night in the Duchess' chamber. Alas, the Duke catched him and killed him.

BIANCA Was he found in bed?

MAQUERELLE Oh, no, but the villainous certainty is, the door was not bolted, the tongue-tied hatch° *[oiled-hinged half door]* held his peace; so the naked truth is, he was found in his shirt, whilst I, like an arrant beast, lay in the outward chamber, heard nothing; and yet they came by me in the dark, and yet I felt° *[perceived]* them not, like a senseless creature as I was. Oh, beauties, look to your busk points,° *[corset stays, laces]* if not chastely, yet charily. Be sure the door be bolted.—Is your lord° *[husband]* gone to Florence?

BIANCA Yes, Maquerelle.

MAQUERELLE I hope you'll find the discretion to purchase a fresh gown 'fore his return. Now, by my troth, beauties, I would ha' ye once° *[once and for all]* wise. He loves ye, pish! He is witty, bubble!° Fair proportioned, mew! Nobly born, wind!° *[nonsense! / pish!]* Let this be still your fixed position: esteem me every man according to his good gifts,° *[rich gifts, bribes]* and so ye shall ever remain most dear, and most worthy to be most dear ladies.

EMILIA Is the Duke returned from hunting yet?

MAQUERELLE They say not yet.

BIANCA 'Tis now in midst of day.

EMILIA How bears° *[bears up]* the Duchess with this blemish now?

MAQUERELLE Faith, boldly; strongly defies defame,° *[infamy]* as one that has a duke to her father. And there's a note° *[observation]* to you: be sure of a stout° *[sturdy]* friend in a corner that may always awe your husband. Mark the 'havior of the Duchess, now; she dares defame,° cries, "Duke, do what thou canst, I'll quite° *[defies disgrace / clear]* mine honor." Nay, as one confirmed in her own virtue against ten thousand mouths that mutter her disgrace, she's presently° *[immediately]* for dances.

Enter Ferrardo.

BIANCA For dances?

MAQUERELLE Most true.

EMILIA Most strange. See, here's my servant,° *[courtly admirer]* young Ferrardo. How many servants think'st thou I have, Maquerelle?

MAQUERELLE The more, the merrier. 'Twas well said: use your servants as you do your smocks. Have many, use one,° *[one at a time]* and change often, for that's most sweet and courtlike.

FERRARDO Save ye, fair ladies. Is the Duke returned?

BIANCA Sweet sir, no voice of him as yet in court.

FERRARDO 'Tis very strange.

BIANCA And how like you my servant, Maquerelle?[2]

MAQUERELLE I think he could hardly draw Ulysses' bow;[3] but, by my fidelity, were his nose narrower, his eyes broader, his hands thinner, his lips thicker, his legs bigger, his feet lesser, his hair blacker, and his teeth whiter, he were a tolerable sweet youth, i'faith. An he will come to my chamber, I will read him the fortune of his beard.[4] *Cornets sound.*

2. Emilia spoke of Ferrardo as her "servant" in line 46; perhaps Bianca is competing for Ferrardo's affection.
3. Not one of Penelope's importunate suitors was strong enough to string or shoot her husband Ulysses' bow—the test posed for winning her hand. (See 3.2.50–51 and note.) Maquerelle may hint at a lack of male sufficiency in Ferrardo.
4. I'll show him the fortune he can expect when he comes to manhood. (With erotic suggestion.)

FERRARDO Not yet returned, I fear—but the Duchess approacheth.

4.2

Enter Mendoza supporting the Duchess [Aurelia], Guerrino. The ladies that are on the stage rise. Ferrardo ushers in the Duchess, and then takes a lady to tread a measure.° *do a stately dance*

AURELIA We will dance—music!—We will dance.

GUERRINO *Les quanto*, lady, *Pensez bien*, *Passa regis*, or *Bianca's brawl?°* *various dances*

AURELIA We have forgot the brawl.

FERRARDO So soon? 'Tis wonder.[1]

GUERRINO Why, 'tis but two singles° on the left, two on the right, three doubles forward, a traverse of six round; do this twice, three singles side, galliard trick of twenty, coranto-pace; a figure of eight, three singles broken down, come up, meet, two doubles, fall back, and then honor.° *dance steps* / *bow to your partner*

AURELIA O Daedalus, thy maze![2] I have quite forgot it.

MAQUERELLE Trust me, so have I, saving the falling back,° and then honor. *(in a bawdy sense)*

Enter Prepasso.

AURELIA Music, music!

PREPASSO Who saw the Duke? The Duke?

Enter Equato.

AURELIA Music!

EQUATO The Duke? Is the Duke returned?

AURELIA Music!

Enter Celso.

CELSO The Duke is either quite invisible, or else is not.

AURELIA We are not pleased with your intrusion upon our private retirement. We are not pleased. You have forgot yourselves.

Enter a Page.

CELSO Boy, thy master? Where's the Duke?

PAGE Alas, I left him burying° the earth with his spread joyless limbs. He told me he was heavy, would sleep; bade me walk off, for that° the strength of fantasy oft made him talk in his dreams. I straight obeyed, nor ever saw him since; but wheresoe'er he is, he's sad. *covering* / *because*

AURELIA Music! Sound high as is our heart, sound high!
[*Music plays.*]

4.2. The scene continues.

1. Ferrardo, responding to Aurelia's previous line, refers to the "brawl," or violent encounter, in Aurelia's bedchamber.

2. Aurelia compares the complexities of the dance to the famous labyrinth built by Daedalus for King Minos of Crete to house the monstrous Minotaur.

4.3

Enter Malevole, and Pietro disguised like an hermit.

MALEVOLE The Duke—peace! [*Music ceases.*]—the Duke is dead.
AURELIA Music!° *That's music to my ears!*
MALEVOLE Is't music?
MENDOZA Give proof.
FERRARDO How?
CELSO Where?
PREPASSO When?
MALEVOLE Rest in peace, as the Duke does; quietly sit. For my own part I beheld him but dead; that's all. Marry, here's one can give you a more particular account of him.
MENDOZA [*to Pietro*] Speak, holy father, nor let any brow° *frown*
Within this presence fright thee from the truth.
Speak confidently and freely.
AURELIA We attend.
PIETRO [*as the hermit*] Now had the mounting sun's all-ripening wings
Swept the cold sweat of night° from earth's dank breast, *the dew*
When I, whom men call Hermit of the Rock,
Forsook my cell and clambered up a cliff,
Against whose base the heady Neptune° dashed *violent god of the sea*
His high-curled brows.° There 'twas I eased my limbs, *pounding surf*
When, lo, my entrails melted with the moan
Someone, who far 'bove me was climbed, did make.—
I shall offend.
MENDOZA Not.
AURELIA On.
PIETRO [*as the hermit*] Methinks I hear him yet: "O female faith!
Go sow the ungrateful sand, and love a woman.[1]
And do I live to be the scoff of men?
To be the wittol-cuckold, even to hug
My poison? Thou knowest—oh, truth!—
Sooner hard steel will melt with southern wind,
A seaman's whistle calm the ocean,
A town on fire be extinct° with tears *extinguished*
Than women, vowed to blushless impudence,
With sweet behavior and soft minioning,° *caressing*
Will turn from that where appetite is fixed.
O powerful blood,° how thou dost slave° their soul! *sexual passion / enslave*
I washed an Ethiop,[2] who, for recompense
Sullied my name. And must I then be forced
To walk, to live thus black?° Must? Must? Fie! *blackened in name*
He that can bear with 'must,' he cannot die."° *is afraid to die*
With that he sighed so passionately deep
That the dull air even groaned. At last he cries,
"Sink shame in seas, sink deep enough!" so dies.
For then I viewed his body fall and souse° *plunge*
Into the foamy main. Oh, then I saw
That which methinks I see:° it was the Duke, *see in my mind's eye*

4.3. The scene continues.
1. I.e., It's as easy to grow crops in unyielding sand as to reap any reward from loving a woman.
2. "To wash an Ethiopian white" is a proverb meaning "to attempt the impossible."

Whom straight the nicer-stomached° sea belched up. *queasy-stomached*
But then—

MALEVOLE Then came I in, but 'las, all was too late,
For even straight he sunk.

PIETRO [*as the hermit*] Such was the Duke's sad fate.

CELSO A better fortune to our Duke Mendoza!

OMNES° Mendoza! *Cornets flourish.* *All*

MENDOZA A guard, a guard!

Enter a guard.

We,° full of hearty° tears *(royal "we") / heartfelt*
For our good father's loss—
For so we well may call him
Who did beseech your loves for our° succession— *your approval of my*
Cannot so lightly overjump° his death *pass over*
As leave his woes revengeless. (*To Aurelia*) Woman of shame,
We banish thee forever to the place
From whence this good man° comes; nor permit on death *(the hermit)*
Unto the body any ornament;[3]
But, base as was thy life, depart away.

AURELIA Ungrateful!

MENDOZA Away!

AURELIA Villain, hear me!

MENDOZA Begone! *Prepasso and Guerrino* [*assisted by the guard*] *lead away the Duchess.*
My lords,
Address to° public counsel; 'tis most fit, *Prepare for*
The train of Fortune is borne up by wit.[4]
Away! Our presence shall be sudden; haste.

All depart saving Mendoza, Malevole, and Pietro.

MALEVOLE Now, you egregious devil! Ha, ye murdering politician!° How dost, Duke? How dost look now? Brave Duke, i'faith! *schemer*

MENDOZA How did you kill him?

MALEVOLE Slatted° his brains out, then soused him in the briny sea. *Dashed*

MENDOZA Brained him and drowned him too?

MALEVOLE Oh, 'twas best, sure work. For he that strikes a great man, let him strike home,° or else 'ware,° he'll prove no man.° Shoulder not[5] a huge fellow unless you may be sure to lay him in the kennel.° *all the way / watch out* *he'll be done for* *gutter*

MENDOZA A most sound brainpan!° I'll make you both emperors. *intelligence*

MALEVOLE Make us Christians, make us Christians![6]

MENDOZA I'll hoist ye; ye shall mount.

MALEVOLE To the gallows, say ye? Come. *Praemium incertum petit certum scelus.*[7] How stands the progress?° *course of action*

MENDOZA Here, take my ring° unto the citadel; *(for proof of identity)*
Have entrance to Maria, the grave duchess

3. Nor, when you die, will we allow any ceremony in your funeral.
4. The sagacious mind takes advantage of every opportunity.
5. Don't try to shoulder aside.
6. Malevole perhaps reflects that because the ancient emperors were pagans and hence damned, Mendoza's gift might be a mixed blessing.
7. The prize being sought is uncertain, but the crime is clear. (Seneca, *Phoenissae*, line 632.)

Of banished Altofront. Tell her we° love her. *(the royal "we")*
Omit no circumstance° to grace our person. Do't. *detail*

MALEVOLE I'll make an excellent pander.[8] Duke, farewell; 'dieu, adieu, Duke.

MENDOZA Take Maquerelle with thee; for 'tis found,° *found to be true*
None cuts a diamond but a diamond.[9] *Exit Malevole.*
Hermit, thou art a man for me, my confessor.
O thou selected spirit, born for my good,
Sure thou wouldst make an excellent elder
In a deformed° church. Come, *irregular; Puritan*
We must be inward,° thou and I all one.° *intimate / together*

PIETRO [*as the hermit*] I am glad I was ordained for ye.

MENDOZA Go to, then. Thou must know that Malevole is a strange villain; dangerous, very dangerous. You see how broad 'a° speaks—a gross-jawed rogue. I would have thee poison him. He's like a corn upon my great toe; I cannot go for° him; he must be cored out, he must. Wilt do't, ha? *coarsely he* / *walk because of*

PIETRO [*as the hermit*] Anything, anything.

MENDOZA Heart of my life! Thus, then, to the citadel;
Thou shalt consort with° this Malevole; *keep company with*
There being at supper, poison him.
It shall be laid upon Maria, who yields love or dies.
Scud quick!

PIETRO [*as the hermit*] Like lightning. Good deeds crawl, but mischief flies. *Exit Pietro.*

Enter Malevole.

MALEVOLE Your Devilship's ring has no virtue.° The buff-captain, the sallow Westphalian gammon-faced zaza,[1] cries, "Stand out!° Must have a stiffer° warrant, or no pass into the Castle of Comfort." *effect* / *Stand back! / stronger*

MENDOZA Command our sudden letter.° Not enter? Sha't!° What place is there in Genoa but thou shalt? Into my heart, into my very heart. Come, let's love; we must love, we two, soul and body. *warrant / Thou shalt!*

MALEVOLE How didst like the hermit? A strange hermit, sirrah.

MENDOZA A dangerous fellow, very perilous. He must die.

MALEVOLE Ay, he must die.

MENDOZA Thou'st° kill him. We are wise; we must be wise. *Thou must*

MALEVOLE And provident.

MENDOZA Yea, provident. Beware an hypocrite;
A churchman once corrupted, oh, avoid!
A fellow that makes religion his stalking-horse,
Shoots under his belly.[2]
He breeds a plague. Thou shalt poison him.

MALEVOLE Ho, 'tis wondrous necessary. How?

8. Malevole privately appreciates the jest that he is being asked to pander his own wife, just as the disguised Pietro has savored Malevole's account to Mendoza (in lines 74–81) of how he, Malevole, killed Pietro.

9. I.e., Only a consummate panderess like Maquerelle can hope to prevail over the chaste Maria.

1. The leather-jacketed captain of the citadel, the pig-faced bully and military adventurer. (Westphalia, in Germany, was noted for its hams.)

2. Mendoza demonstrates what he means by "stalking-horse" by miming the action of shooting at game from protective cover, from under the belly of a trained horse used to move close to the hunted animal.

MENDOZA You both go jointly to the citadel;
There sup, there poison him. And Maria,
Because she is our opposite,° shall bear — *opponent*
The sad suspect,° on which she dies or loves us. — *grave suspicion*

MALEVOLE I run. *Exit Malevole.*

MENDOZA We that are great, our sole self-good still° moves us. — *incessantly*
They shall die both, for their deserts° craves more — *deservings*
Than we can recompense; their presence still
Imbraids° our fortunes with beholdingness,° — *Upbraids / obligation*
Which we abhor; like deed, not doer.[3] Then conclude:
They live not° to cry out ingratitude. — *must not live*
One stick burns t'other; steel cuts steel alone.
'Tis good trust few, but, oh, 'tis best trust none.
Exit Mendoza.

4.4

Enter Malevole and Pietro, still disguised, at several° doors. — *separate*

MALEVOLE How do you? How dost, Duke?

PIETRO Oh, let the last day° fall, drop, drop on our cursed heads! Let heaven unclasp itself, vomit forth flames! — *Judgment Day*

MALEVOLE Oh, do not rant, do not turn player;° there's more of them than can well live one by another already. What, art an infidel still?[1] — *(histrionic) actor*

PIETRO I am amazed, struck in a swoon with wonder! I am commanded to poison thee.

MALEVOLE I am commanded to poison thee, at supper.

PIETRO At supper?

MALEVOLE In the citadel.

PIETRO In the citadel?

MALEVOLE Cross-capers![2] Tricks! Truth o'heaven, he would discharge us as boys do eldern guns,° one pellet to strike out another. Of what faith art now?° — *popguns made of elder* / *Whom do you believe?*

PIETRO All is damnation, wickedness extreme; there is no faith in man.

MALEVOLE In none but usurers and brokers.° They deceive no man; men take 'em for bloodsuckers, and so they are. Now, God deliver° me from my friends! — *pawnbrokers* / *defend*

PIETRO Thy friends?

MALEVOLE Yes, from my friends, for from mine enemies I'll deliver myself. Oh, cutthroat friendship is the rankest villainy! Mark this Mendoza, mark him for a villain; but heaven will send a plague upon him for a rogue.

PIETRO O world!

MALEVOLE World! 'Tis the only region of death, the greatest shop of the devil, the cruel'st prison of men, out of the which none pass without paying their dearest breath for a fee.

3. I applaud the deeds they (Malevole and Pietro "the hermit") do for me, but not the doers.

4.4. The Genoese court still.

1. Don't you believe yet what I told you (about Mendoza)?

2. (1) Cross-steps (in dancing)! (2) Pranks at cross-purposes!

There's nothing perfect° in it but extreme, extreme calamity, such as comes yonder. *brought to completion*

4.5

Enter Aurelia, two halberds° before and two after, supported by Celso and Ferrardo; Aurelia in base° mourning attire. *guards with pikes* / *humble*

AURELIA To banishment! Lead on to banishment!
PIETRO [*as the hermit*] Lady, the blessedness of repentance to you.
AURELIA Why? Why? I can desire nothing but death,
Nor deserve anything but hell.
If heaven should give sufficiency of grace
To clear my soul, it would make heaven graceless;° *empty of grace*
My sins would make the stock of mercy poor.
Oh, they would tire heaven's goodness to reclaim them.
Judgment is just, yet° from that vast villain;° *even though / (Mendoza)*
But sure he shall not miss sad° punishment *heavy*
'Fore he shall rule. On to my cell of shame!
PIETRO [*as the hermit*] My cell 'tis, lady; where, instead of masques,
Music, tilts, tourneys,° and such courtlike shows, *jousts, tournaments*
The hollow murmur of the checkless° winds *unchecked*
Shall groan again, whilst the unquiet sea
Shakes the whole rock with foamy battery.° *battering*
There usherless° the air comes in and out; *unannounced*
The rheumy vault° will force your eyes to weep, *dank cave*
Whilst you behold true desolation;
A rocky barrenness shall pierce your eyes,
Where all at once° one reaches, where he° stands, *simultaneously / (one)*
With brows° the roof, both walls with both his° hands. *With one's head / (one's)*
AURELIA It is too good. Blessed spirit of my lord,° *(Pietro)*
Oh, in what orb° soe'er thy soul is throned, *heavenly sphere*
Behold me worthily° most miserable! *deservedly*
Oh, let the anguish of my contrite spirit
Entreat some reconciliation.
If not, O joy, triumph in my just grief![1]
Death is the end of woes, and tears' relief.
PIETRO [*as the hermit*] Belike° your lord not loved you, was unkind? *Perhaps*
AURELIA O heaven!
As the soul loves the body, so loved he;
'Twas death to him to part° my presence, *depart from*
Heaven to see me pleased.
Yet I, like to a wretch given o'er to hell,
Brake° all the sacred rites of marriage *Broke*
To clip° a base, ungentle,° faithless villain, *embrace / ignoble*
Oh, God, a very pagan reprobate!—
What should I say?—Ungrateful, throws° me out, *Mendoza throws*
For whom I lost soul, body, fame, and honor.

4.5. The scene continues.
1. If not, O heavens, rejoice in my penitence! (Since God rejoices at the true penitence of a sinner); or, if I am not contrite, let heaven triumph in my just punishment!

But 'tis most fit; why should a better fate
Attend on any who forsake chaste sheets,
Fly the embrace of a devoted heart,
Joined by a solemn vow 'fore God and man,
To taste the brackish° blood of beastly lust [*salty; salacious*]
In an adulterous touch? O ravenous immodesty,
Insatiate impudence of appetite!
Look, here's your end; for mark, what sap in dust,
What sin in good, even so much love in lust.[2]
Joy to thy ghost, sweet lord; pardon to me!

CELSO 'Tis the Duke's° pleasure this night you rest° in court. [*(Mendoza's) / remain*]

AURELIA Soul, lurk in shades;° run, shame, from brightsome skies! [*hide in shadows*]
In night the blind man misseth not his eyes.

Exit [Aurelia with Celso, Ferrardo, and halberds].

MALEVOLE Do not weep, kind° cuckold; take comfort, man. [*softhearted*] Thy betters have been *beccos*:° [*cuckolds*] Agamemnon, emperor of all the merry Greeks that tickled° [*tormented*] all the true Trojans, was a cornuto;° [*(see 1.5.8 and n)*] Prince Arthur, that cut off twelve kings' beards, was a cornuto;[3] Hercules, whose back bore up heaven, and got forty wenches with child in one night—

PIETRO Nay, 'twas fifty.

MALEVOLE Faith, forty's enough, o'conscience—yet was a cornuto.[4]
Patience; mischief grows proud;° be wise. [*overconfident*]

PIETRO Thou pinchest too deep, art too keen upon me.

MALEVOLE Tut, a pitiful° [*tenderhearted*] surgeon makes a dangerous sore; I'll tent thee° [*probe your wound*] to the ground. Thinkest I'll sustain myself by flattering thee because thou art a prince? I had rather follow a drunkard and live by licking up his vomit than by servile flattery.

PIETRO Yet great men ha' done't.

MALEVOLE Great slaves fear better than love, born naturally for a coal basket, though the common usher of princes' presence, Fortune, hath blindly given them better place.[5] I am vowed to be thy affliction.

PIETRO Prithee, be;
I love much misery, and be thou son to me.

MALEVOLE Because you are an usurping duke.[6]

Enter Bilioso.

(*To Bilioso*) Your Lordship's well returned from Florence.

BILIOSO Well returned, I praise my horse.

2. Here is what lust must come to; for note well, just so much moisture as is found in dust, or sin in goodness, even so much true love is to be found in lust.
3. Arthur is traditionally reported to have defeated the Saxon invaders in twelve battles in the sixth century. In Arthurian legend he is cuckolded by Lancelot.
4. Hercules was supposed to have impregnated in one night all, or all but one, of the fifty daughters of King Thespius. He held up the skies while Atlas fetched the golden apples from the Garden of the Hesperides, thus completing his eleventh labor. Although no account is to be found of Hercules as a cuckold, he was married several times and was enslaved to the Amazon Omphale; and Nessus did attempt to ravish Hercules' second wife, Deianira.
5. Even though Fortune, who commonly ushers in and out the occupants of princes' palaces, has blindly raised to eminence certain persons who were born naturally for servile tasks (such as carrying coals), these noble wretches rule through fear rather than love (and thus are often more unhappy than their subjects).
6. I.e., You are much enamored of misery because you have usurped the dukedom. (The stoical teaching of despising worldly things follows from Malevole's previous speech and note 5 above.)

MALEVOLE What news from the Florentines?

BILIOSO I will conceal the great duke's pleasure, only this was his charge: his pleasure is that his daughter die, Duke Pietro be banished for banishing his blood's dishonor,[7] and that Duke Altofront be reaccepted. This is all; but I hear Duke Pietro is dead.

MALEVOLE Ay, and Mendoza is Duke. What will you do?

BILIOSO Is Mendoza strongest?

MALEVOLE Yet° he is. *So far*

BILIOSO Then yet I'll hold with him.

MALEVOLE But if that Altofront should turn straight° again? *return at once*

BILIOSO Why, then I would turn° straight again. *go back to Altofront*
'Tis good run° still with him that has most might; *to go along*
I had rather stand with wrong than fall with right.

MALEVOLE What religion will you be of now?

BILIOSO Of the Duke's religion, when I know what it is.

MALEVOLE O Hercules!

BILIOSO Hercules? Hercules was the son of Jupiter and Alcmena.[8]

MALEVOLE Your Lordship is a very wittol.° *willing cuckold*

BILIOSO Wittol?

MALEVOLE Ay, all-wit.[9]

BILIOSO Amphitryo was a cuckold.

MALEVOLE Your Lordship sweats; your young lady will get you a cloth for Your old Worship's brows.° *Exit Bilioso.* *(horned) forehead*
Here's a fellow to be damned. This is his inviolable maxim: "Flatter the greatest, and oppress the least"—a whoreson flesh fly that still gnaws upon the lean, galled backs.[1]

PIETRO Why dost then salute° him? *converse with*

MALEVOLE Faith, as bawds go to church, for fashion° sake. *fashion's* Come, be not confounded;° *discomfited, confused* thou'rt but in danger to lose a dukedom. Think this: this earth is the only grave and Golgotha° *a burial place* wherein all things that live must rot; 'tis but the draught° *privy* wherein the heavenly bodies discharge their corruption, the very muckhill on which the sublunary° *beneath the moon* orbs cast their excrements. Man is the slime of this dung-pit, and princes are the governors of these men. For, for° *as for* our souls, they are as free as emperors', all of one piece;° *cut from the same cloth* there goes but a pair of shears betwixt an emperor and the son of a bagpiper—only the dyeing, dressing,° *finishing of the surface* pressing, glossing, makes the difference. Now, what art thou like° *likely* to lose?
A jailer's office to keep men in bonds,
Whilst toil and treason all life's good confounds.° *overthrows*

PIETRO I here renounce forever regency.° *rule*

7. That Aurelia die and Duke Pietro be banished for his part in Aurelia's disgraceful behavior that has dishonored the bloodline of the Duke of Florence. (Mendoza correctly predicted, at 3.3.95, that the Duke of Florence would abandon his own daughter. The Duke lent support originally to the banishment of Altofronto, but is obviously disillusioned with the result.)

8. Disguising himself in the likeness of Amphitryon, Jupiter slept with Amphitryon's wife, Alcmena, who subsequently gave birth to Hercules. Perhaps Bilioso wonders whether Malevole would call on Hercules if he knew that Hercules was a product of cuckoldry. See also line 102.

9. "All-wit" is essentially an anagram of "witoll" (or "wittol"), giving rise to a familiar jest; Malevole insults Bilioso by calling him a complacent cuckold and then passes the remark off as though he were praising Bilioso's wit. Cf. the name "Allwit" for the wittol in Thomas Middleton's *A Chaste Maid in Cheapside*.

1. Bilioso is a wretched parasite (literally, a maggot that feeds on meat) who continually gnaws on the chafed backs of his starved tenants.

O Altofront, I wrong thee to supplant thy right,
To trip thy heels up with a devilish sleight,° *trick*
For which I now from throne am thrown; world tricks
abjure,° *I swear off deceits*
For vengeance,° though't comes slow, yet it comes sure. *divine vengeance*
Oh, I am changed; for here, 'fore the dread power,° *heavenly power*
In true contrition I do dedicate
My breath to solitary holiness,
My lips to prayer, and my breast's care shall be
Restoring Altofront to regency.

MALEVOLE Thy vows are heard, and we accept thy faith.
Undisguiseth himself.

Enter Ferneze and Celso.

Altofront.° Ferneze, Celso, Pietro: *I am Altofront*
Banish amazement. Come, we four must stand° *withstand the*
Full shock of Fortune. Be not so wonder-stricken.

PIETRO Doth Ferneze live?

FERNEZE For your pardon.

PIETRO Pardon and love. Give leave to recollect° *Allow me to collect*
My thoughts, dispersed in wild astonishment.
My vows stand fixed in heaven, and from hence° *henceforth*
I crave all love and pardon.

MALEVOLE Who doubts of Providence
That sees this change? A hearty faith° to all! *offer of allegiance*
He needs must rise who can no lower fall,
For still impetuous vicissitude
Touseth° the world; then let no maze° intrude *Tosses about / amazement*
Upon your spirits. Wonder not I rise,
For who can sink that close can temporize?[2]
The time grows ripe for action; I'll detect° *reveal*
My privat'st plot, lest ignorance fear suspect.[3]
Let's close to° counsel, leave the rest to fate. *meet privately for*
Mature discretion is the life of state.° *Exeunt.* *essence of statecraft*

5.1

Enter Bilioso and Passarello.

BILIOSO Fool, how dost thou like my calf in a long stocking?° *(see 1.2.6–7 and n)*

PASSARELLO An excellent calf,° my lord. *part of leg; fool*

BILIOSO This calf hath been a reveler this twenty year. When Monsieur Gundi lay here ambassador,[1] I could have carried a lady up and down at arm's end in a platter; and I can tell you there were those at that time who, to try the strength of a man's back and his arm, would be coistered.[2] I have measured calves with most of the palace, and they come nothing near me; besides, I think there be not many armors in the

2. For who can fail to rise who knows the art of secretly biding one's time and seizing the right opportunity?
3. Lest ignorance of my secret plot should breed mistrust.
5.1. The Genoese court still.
1. Jeromo de Gondi, Count de Retz, came to England in 1578 as French Ambassador Extraordinary to plead for Mary, Queen of Scots.
2. This rare and puzzling word seems to mean either "coiled up into a small compass" or "inconvenienced," "put out." Bilioso is talking about male competitiveness in feats of strength.

arsenal will fit me, especially for the headpiece. I'll tell thee—

PASSARELLO What, my lord?

BILIOSO I can eat stewed broth as it comes seething off the fire, or a custard as it comes reeking° out of the oven; and I think there are not many lords can do it. A good pomander,° a little decayed in the scent, but six grains of musk ground with rose water and tempered with a little civet° shall fetch her° again presently. *steaming* / *perfume ball* / *civet cat musk* / *renew the scent*

PASSARELLO Oh, ay, as a bawd with aqua vitae.[3]

BILIOSO And, what, dost thou rail upon the ladies as thou wert wont?° *accustomed*

PASSARELLO I were better roast a live cat, and might do it with more safety. I am as secret as thieves to their painting.[4] There's Maquerelle, oldest bawd and a perpetual beggar. Did you never hear of her trick to be known in the city?

BILIOSO Never.

PASSARELLO Why, she gets all the picture-makers to draw her picture; when they have done, she most courtly° finds fault with them one after another, and never fetcheth them.° They, in revenge of this, execute her in pictures as they do in Germany, and hang her in their shops. By this means is she better known to the stinkards° than if she had been five times carted.[5] *fastidiously* / *picks the pictures up* / *rabble*

BILIOSO 'Fore God, an excellent policy.

PASSARELLO Are there any revels° tonight, my lord? *masques, entertainments*

BILIOSO Yes.

PASSARELLO Good my lord, give me leave to break° a fellow's pate that hath abused me. *knock*

BILIOSO Whose pate?

PASSARELLO Young Ferrard, my lord.

BILIOSO Take heed, he's very valiant. I have known him fight eight quarrels° in five days, believe it. *duels*

PASSARELLO Oh, is he so great a quarreler? Why, then, he's an arrant coward.

BILIOSO How prove you that?

PASSARELLO Why, thus. He that quarrels seeks to fight; and he that seeks to fight, seeks to die; and he that seeks to die, seeks never to fight more; and he that will quarrel and seeks means never to answer a man° more, I think he's a coward. *answer a challenge*

BILIOSO Thou canst prove anything.

PASSARELLO Anything but a rich knave,[6] for I can flatter no man.

BILIOSO Well, be not drunk, good fool. I shall see you anon° in the presence.° *Exeunt.* *presently* / *duke's reception room*

3. Bilioso boasts how he uses various perfumes as part of his male charm. Passarello wryly compares this desperate attempt at creating sex appeal to an old woman's using brandy to revive someone who has fainted.

4. I.e., I confidentially guard the secrets of their use of cosmetics. ("As thick as thieves" is proverbial.)

5. Dragged through the streets tied to or in a cart and whipped—a common punishment for bawds and prostitutes.

6. I might prove to be anything but a rich rascal. (Passarello playfully changes the meaning of Bilioso's "prove" in line 50, i.e., "demonstrate through proof," into "turn out to be.")

[5.2]

Enter Malevole [disguised] and Maquerelle, at several° doors opposite, singing. — *separate*

MALEVOLE The Dutchman for a drunkard,
MAQUERELLE The Dane for golden locks,
MALEVOLE The Irishman for usquebaugh,° — *whisky*
MAQUERELLE The Frenchman for the ( ).[1]

MALEVOLE Oh, thou art a blessed creature! Had I a modest woman to conceal, I would put her to thy custody, for no reasonable creature would ever suspect her to be in thy company. Ha, thou art a melodious Maquerelle, thou picture of a woman and substance of a beast!

Enter Passarello [with wine].

MAQUERELLE Oh, fool, will ye be ready anon to go with me to the revels? The hall will be so pestered° anon. — *crowded*

PASSARELLO Ay, as the country is with attorneys.

MALEVOLE What hast thou there, fool?

PASSARELLO Wine. I have learnt to drink since I went with my lord ambassador. I'll drink to the health of Madam Maquerelle.

MALEVOLE Why, thou wast wont to rail upon her.

PASSARELLO Ay, but since,° I borrowed money of her. I'll drink to her health now as gentlemen visit brokers,° or as knights send venison to the city,[2] either to take up° more money or to procure longer forbearance.° — *since that time; pawnbrokers; borrow; delay in repayment*

MALEVOLE Give me the bowl. I drink a health to Altofront, our deposed duke. *[He drinks.]*

PASSARELLO I'll take it; so.° Now I'll begin a health to Madam Maquerelle. *[He drinks.]* — *I'll drink that toast*

MALEVOLE Pew! I will not pledge her.

PASSARELLO Why, I pledged your lord.

MALEVOLE I care not.

PASSARELLO Not pledge Madam Maquerelle? Why, then will I spew up your lord again with this fool's finger.[3]

MALEVOLE Hold; I'll take it. *[He drinks.]*

MAQUERELLE Now° thou hast drunk my health, fool, I am friends with thee. — *Now that*

PASSARELLO Art? Art?
When Griffon saw the reconcilèd quean° — *hussy, whore*
Offering about his neck her arms to cast,
He threw off sword and heart's malignant stream,
And lovely her below the loins embraced.[4]—
Adieu, Madam Maquerelle. *Exit Passarello.*

MALEVOLE And how dost thou think o'this transformation of state° now? — *change of rulers*

MAQUERELLE Verily, very well; for we women always note, the

5.2. Before the citadel (see lines 73–77).
1. These parentheses indicate that a word is omitted; the omitted word is "pox," or syphilis, known in England as "the French disease." The omission invites the audience, who presumably know what is meant, to snicker.
2. Because hunting was controlled by large landowners, a gift of venison would be appreciated by merchant moneylenders in the city and might dispose them favorably toward a potential borrower. (This was true of London, but is here applied nominally to Genoa.)
3. I'll vomit up the pledge I just drank to Duke Altofronto by tickling my throat.
4. Passarello parodies, with bawdy flourishes, some lines from Ariosto's epic poem *Orlando Furioso*.

falling of the one is the rising of the other.° Some must be fat, some must be lean; some must be fools, and some must be lords; some must be knaves, and some must be officers; some must be beggars, some must be knights; some must be cuckolds, and some must be citizens. As for example, I have two court-dogs, the most fawning curs, the one called Watch, th'other Catch.[5] Now I, like Lady Fortune, sometimes love this dog, sometimes raise° that dog, sometimes favor Watch, most commonly fancy Catch. Now, that dog which I favor I feed, and he's so ravenous that what I give he never chaws it, gulps it down whole, without any relish of what he has, but with a greedy expectation of what he shall have. The other dog, now— *(with bawdy implication)* *favor, elevate*

MALEVOLE No more dog, sweet Maquerelle, no more dog. And what hope hast thou of the Duchess Maria? Will she stoop° to the Duke's lure?° Will she come, think'st? *swoop down* *(like a trained hawk)*

MAQUERELLE Let me see, where's the sign,° now? Ha' ye e'er a calendar? Where's the sign, trow you?° *zodiacal sign* *do you think?*

MALEVOLE Sign? Why, is there any moment° in that? *significance*

MAQUERELLE Oh, believe me, a most secret power. Look ye, a Chaldean or an Assyrian—I am sure 'twas a most sweet Jew—told me, court any woman in the right sign, you shall not miss. But you must take her in the right vein, then: as, when the sign is in Pisces, a fishmonger's wife is very sociable; in Cancer, a precisian's wife is very flexible; in Capricorn, a merchant's wife hardly holds out; in Libra, a lawyer's wife is very tractable, especially if her husband be at the term; only in Scorpio 'tis very dangerous meddling.[6] Has the Duke sent any jewel, any rich stones?

Enter Captain.

MALEVOLE Ay, I think those are the best signs to take a lady in. [*To Captain*] By your favor, signor, I must discourse with the Lady Maria, Altofront's duchess. I must enter for° the Duke. *on behalf of*

CAPTAIN She here shall give you interview. I received the guardship of this citadel from the good Altofront, and for his use I'll keep't till I am of no use.

MALEVOLE Wilt thou? [*Aside*] Oh, heavens, that a Christian should be found in a buff jerkin!° Captain Conscience, I love thee, Captain. [*Aloud*] We attend.° *Exit Captain.* And what hope hast thou of this duchess's easiness?° *leather jacket* *We'll wait here* *readiness to agree*

MAQUERELLE 'Twill go hard. She was a cold° creature ever; she hated monkeys,° fools, jesters, and gentlemen-ushers extremely. She had the vile trick on't not only to be truly modestly honorable in her own conscience, but she would avoid the least wanton carriage° that might incur suspect, as, God bless me, she had almost brought bed-pressing° out *chaste* *lecherous animals* *conduct* *sex*

5. The names Watch and Catch allude to court mannerisms of watching incessantly for any opportunity and catching at whatever chances to come up.

6. The zodiacal signs Maquerelle cites are comically appropriate in each case: a fish-seller's wife for the Fish; a sour and crabbed Puritan for the Crab; the wife of a cuckolded, and therefore horned, merchant for the horned Goat; a lawyer's wife for the Balance representing justice, especially when he is away for the law term; and sexual meddling that is dangerous (because of venereal disease) for the Scorpion with the sting in its tail.

of fashion; I could scarce get a fine° for the lease of a lady's favor° once in a fortnight. *fee* / *sexual favors*

MALEVOLE Now, in the name of immodesty, how many maidenheads hast thou brought to the block?[7]

MAQUERELLE Let me see. Heaven forgive us our misdeeds!—Here's the Duchess.

5.[3]

Enter Maria and Captain.

MALEVOLE God bless thee, lady.

MARIA Out of thy company.[1]

MALEVOLE We have brought thee tender° of a husband.° *offer / (Mendoza)*

MARIA I hope I have one already.

MAQUERELLE Nay, by mine honor, madam, as good ha' ne'er a husband as a banished husband; he's in another world now. I'll tell ye, lady, I have heard of a sect[2] that maintained, when the husband was asleep, the wife might lawfully entertain another man, for then her husband was as dead; much more when he is banished.

MARIA Unhonest° creature! *Unchaste*

MAQUERELLE Pish! Honesty is but an art to seem so. Pray ye, what's honesty, what's constancy but fables feigned, odd old fools' chat, devised by jealous fools to wrong our liberty?

MALEVOLE Molly,° he that loves thee is a duke, Mendoza; he will maintain thee royally, love thee ardently, defend thee powerfully, marry thee sumptuously, and keep thee in despite of Rosicleer or Dozel del Phoebo.[3] [*Offering jewels*] There's jewels. If thou wilt, so; if not, so. *(nickname for Maria)*

MARIA Captain, for God's sake, save poor wretchedness
From tyranny of lustful insolence!
Enforce me in the deepest dungeon dwell
Rather than here; here round about is hell.—
O my dear'st Altofront, where'er thou breathe,
Let my soul sink into the shades beneath° *the underworld*
Before I stain thine honor. This thou hast,° *You have my vow*
And, long° as I can die, I will live chaste. *as long*

MALEVOLE 'Gainst him that can enforce, how vain is strife!

MARIA She that can be enforced has ne'er a knife.[4]
She that through force her limbs with lust enrolls° *subscribes*
Wants° Cleopatra's asps and Portia's coals.[5] *Lacks*
God amend you. *Exit with Captain.*

MALEVOLE Now, the fear of the devil forever go with thee! Maquerelle, I tell thee, I have found an honest woman. Faith, I perceive when all is done, there is of women, as of all other things, some good, most bad; some saints, some

7. (1) Auction block; (2) execution block, where the hymen would, in a sense, be "beheaded."

5.3. The scene continues before the citadel still, although beginning at 64.1 the scene may be supposed to have shifted to the court.

1. I would be more hopeful of receiving God's blessing if I were not in your company.

2. The so-called Family of Love, accused of practicing sexual freedom in the name of religious inspiration.

3. Heroes of a popular Spanish romance, *The Mirror of Knighthood.*

4. A woman having a knife with which to kill herself can thus avoid rape, or at least the dishonor that would follow. (Maria compares herself to Lucrece, who was raped by Tarquinius Sextus and then stabbed herself to death.)

5. Cleopatra and Brutus's wife, Portia, both took their own lives to avoid dishonor, Cleopatra by means of poisonous snakes and Portia by taking burning coals in her mouth.

sinners. For as nowadays no courtier but has his mistress, no captain but has his cockatrice,° no cuckold but has his horns, and no fool but has his feather,[6] even so, no woman but has her weakness and feather too, no sex but has his—I can hunt the letter no farther.[7] [*Aside*] Oh, God, how loathsome this toying is to me! That a duke should be forced to fool it! Well, *stultorum plena sunt omnia;*[8] better play the fool lord than be the fool lord.—Now, where's your sleights, Madam Maquerelle?

whore; mistress

MAQUERELLE Why, are ye ignorant that 'tis said a squeamish, affected niceness° is natural to women, and that the excuse of their yielding is only, forsooth, the difficult obtaining?[9] You must put her to't; women are flax, and will fire° in a moment.

coyness
catch fire

MALEVOLE Why, was the flax put into thy mouth, and yet thou—thou set fire? Thou enflame her?[1]

MAQUERELLE Marry, but I'll tell ye now, you were too hot.

MALEVOLE The fitter to have enflamed the flax-woman.[2]

MAQUERELLE You were too boisterous, spleeny;° for indeed—

impetuous, abrupt

MALEVOLE Go, go, thou art a weak panderess; now I see.
Sooner earth's fire heaven itself shall waste°
Than all with heat can melt a mind that's chaste.
Go, thou the Duke's lime-twig![3] I'll make the Duke turn thee out of thine office. What, not get one touch of hope, and had her at such advantage!

destroy, consume

MAQUERELLE Now, o'my conscience, now I think, in my discretion, we did not take her in the right sign;° the blood was not in the true vein, sure. *Exit.*

zodiacal sign (5.2.59–70)

Enter Bilioso.

BILIOSO Make way there! The Duke returns from the enthronment. Malevole!

MALEVOLE Out, rogue!

BILIOSO Malevole!

MALEVOLE "Hence, ye gross-jawed peasantly! Out, go!"[0]

(quotes Bilioso at 2.3.30)

BILIOSO Nay, sweet Malevole, since my return I hear you are become the thing I always prophesied would be: an advanced° virtue, a worthily employed faithfulness, a man o'grace, dear friend. Come. What? *Si quoties peccant homines . . .*[4] If, as often as courtiers play the knaves, honest men should be angry.—Why, look ye, we must collogue° sometimes, forswear sometimes.

court-favored
converse

MALEVOLE Be damned sometimes.

BILIOSO Right. *Nemo omnibus horis sapit.*[5] No man can be honest at all hours. Necessity often depraves virtue.

6. The affectation practiced by gallants of wearing feathers is satirized earlier; see Induction 33–49 and notes.
7. To "hunt the letter" is to play alliterative word games.
8. All places are full of fools. (Cicero, *Epistolae ad Familiares*, 9.22.4.)
9. And that women pretend reluctance only to make their eventual yielding more delectable?
1. I.e., All your inflammatory talk did little to ignite Maria, did it?
2. All the better to have inflamed Maria if she were really ignitable, as you claim all women are.
3. I.e., Get out of here, you vile seducer! (Lime was smeared on branches to ensnare birds.)
4. If, as often as men sinned (Jupiter should hurl a thunderbolt, he would soon be weaponless). (Ovid, *Tristia*, 2.33–34. Bilioso modifies Ovid's phrasing to suit his purposes in his English paraphrase in the next lines.)
5. No one can be wise all the time. (Pliny, *Natural History*, 7.41.2.)

MALEVOLE I will commend thee to the Duke.

BILIOSO Do; let us be friends, man.

MALEVOLE And knaves, man.

BILIOSO Right; let us prosper and purchase;° our lordships shall live and our knavery be forgotten. *acquire titles*

MALEVOLE He that by any ways gets riches, his means never shames him.

BILIOSO True.

MALEVOLE For impudency and faithlessness are the mainstays to greatness.

BILIOSO By the Lord, thou art a profound lad.

MALEVOLE By the Lord, thou art a perfect knave. Out, ye ancient damnation!

BILIOSO Peace, peace! An thou wilt not be a friend to me as I am a knave, be not a knave to me as I am thy friend and disclose me.[6] [*Music is heard.*] Peace! Cornets!

5.[4]

Enter Prepasso and Ferrardo, two pages with lights, Celso and Equato, Mendoza in duke's robes, and Guerrino.

MENDOZA On, on. Leave us, leave us.

Exeunt all saving Malevole [*and Mendoza*].

Stay. Where is the hermit?° *(Pietro)*

MALEVOLE With Duke Pietro, with Duke Pietro.

MENDOZA Is he dead? Is he poisoned?

MALEVOLE Dead as the Duke is.

MENDOZA Good, excellent. He will not blab; secureness lives in secrecy. Come hither, come hither.

MALEVOLE Thou hast a certain strong villainous scent about thee my nature cannot endure.

MENDOZA Scent, man? What returns° Maria? What answer to our suit? *replies*

MALEVOLE Cold, frosty; she is obstinate.

MENDOZA Then she's but dead; 'tis resolute,° she dies. *resolved, determined*
Black deed only through black deed safely flies.[1]

MALEVOLE Pew! *Per scelera semper sceleribus tutum est iter.*

MENDOZA What, art a scholar? Art a politician? Sure thou art an arrant knave.

MALEVOLE Who, I? I have been twice an undersheriff, man.[2] Well, I will go rail upon some great man, that I may purchase the bastinado,° or else go marry some rich Genoan lady and instantly go travel. *earn a cudgeling*

MENDOZA Travel, when thou art married?

MALEVOLE Ay, 'tis your young lord's fashion to do so, though he was so lazy, being a bachelor, that he would never travel so far as the university; yet when he married her, tails off,° and catso,° for England! *turns tail* *(see 1.3.106)*

6. If you won't befriend me because you consider me a rascal, at least do not betray my friendly confidences to you.

5.4. The scene continues either at court or possibly still in front of the citadel; see note at 5.3 above.

1. Black crimes find safety only in further crimes. (Malevole scornfully replies in line 15 by quoting Seneca's original of this sentiment—from *Agamemnon*, line 115—an aphorism known by every schoolboy.)

2. A mocking answer; sheriff's deputies were doubtless suspected of being easily corrupted.

MENDOZA And why for England?
MALEVOLE Because there is no brothel-houses there.
MENDOZA Nor courtesans?
MALEVOLE Neither; your whore went down with the stews, and your punk came up with your Puritan.[3]
MENDOZA Canst thou empoison? Canst thou empoison?
MALEVOLE Excellently; no Jew,[4] pothecary, or politician better. Look ye, here's a box—Whom wouldst thou empoison?—here's a box [*giving it*] which, opened and the fume taken up in conduits° through which the brain purges itself, doth instantly for twelve hours' space bind up all show of life in a deep senseless sleep. Here's another [*giving it*] which, being opened under the sleeper's nose, chokes all the power of life, kills him suddenly. *the nostrils*
MENDOZA I'll try experiments; 'tis good not to be deceived.—
So, so; catso!

Seems to poison Malevole [*who falls as if dead*].

Who would fear that may destroy?
Death hath no teeth nor tongue;
And he that's great, to him are slaves
Shame, murder, fame, and wrong.[5]
[*Calling*] Celso!

Enter Celso.

CELSO My honored lord?
MENDOZA The good Malevole, that plain-tongued man,
Alas, is dead on sudden, wondrous strangely.
He held in our esteem good place. Celso,
See him buried, see him buried.
CELSO I shall observe ye.° *obey you*
MENDOZA And, Celso, prithee let it be thy care tonight
To have some pretty show to solemnize
Our high installment—some music, masquery.° *masques*
We'll give fair entertain° unto Maria, *welcome, entertainment*
The duchess to the banished Altofront.
Thou shalt conduct her from the citadel
Unto the palace. Think on some masquery.
CELSO Of what shape, sweet lord?
MENDOZA What shape? Why, any quick-done fiction—
As some brave spirits° of the Genoan dukes *ghosts*
To come out of Elysium,° forsooth, *the abode of the blessed*
Led in by Mercury, to gratulate° *greet, celebrate*
Our happy fortune—some such anything,
Some far-fet° trick, good for ladies, *clever, exotic*
Some stale toy° or other, *device, trifle*
No matter so't be of our devising.
Do thou prepare't; 'tis but for fashion sake;
Fear not, it shall be graced,° man; it shall take.° *applauded / succeed*
CELSO All service.° *I am all service*

3. The licensed "stews," or brothels, of Southwark were shut down in 1546 only to reemerge with the new name of "punks" for the prostitutes as a sop to Reformation hypocrisy.

4. Jews were accused of being poisoners.

5. Why fear someone when you can kill that person? The dead cannot blab; shame, murder, infamy, and injustice are all servants of great persons.

MENDOZA All thanks;
Our hand shall not be close° to thee. Farewell. *niggardly, closed*
[*Celso retires.*]
Now is my treachery secure, nor can we fall;
Mischief that prospers men do virtue call.
I'll trust no man; he that by tricks gets wreaths° *garlands, crowns*
Keeps them with steel;° no man securely breathes. *the sword*
Out of distunèd° ranks, the crowd will mutter, "Fool"; *discontented*
Who° cannot bear with spite, he cannot rule. *He who*
The chiefest secret for a man of state
Is to live senseless of° a strengthless hate. *Exit Mendoza.* *indifferent to*

MALEVOLE (*starts up and speaks*) Death of the damned thief! I'll make one i'the masque; thou shalt ha' some brave spirits of the antique dukes.

CELSO [*coming forward*] My lord, what strange delusion!

MALEVOLE Most happy, dear Celso; poisoned with an empty box! I'll give° thee all anon. My lady comes to court; there is a whirl of fate comes tumbling on; the castle's captain stands for me, the people pray for me, and the great leader of the just° stands for me. Then courage, Celso, *tell* *(God)*
For no disastrous chance can ever move him
That feareth nothing but a god above him. *Exeunt.*

[5.5]

Enter Prepasso and Bilioso, two pages before them; Maquerelle, Bianca, and Emilia.

BILIOSO Make room there, room for the ladies! Why, gentlemen, will not ye suffer the ladies to be entered in the great chamber? Why, gallants! And you, sir, to drop your torch° where the beauties must sit, too! *to allow pitch to drip*

PREPASSO And there's a great fellow° plays the knave. Why dost not strike him? *big-limbed servant*

BILIOSO Let him play the knave, i'God's name. Think'st thou I have no more wit than to strike a great fellow?—The music! More lights! Reveling! Scaffolds!° Do you hear? Let there be oaths° enough ready at the door; swear out the devil himself. Let's leave the ladies and go see if the lords be ready for them. *All save the ladies depart.* *Put up more bleachers!* *(to stop gate-crashers)*

MAQUERELLE And by my troth, beauties, why do you not put you° into the fashion? This is a stale cut;° you must come in fashion. Look ye, you must be all felt, felt and feather, a felt° upon your bare hair. Look ye, these tiring things° are justly out of request now. And—do ye hear?—you must wear falling-bands,° you must come into the falling fashion; there is such a deal o'pinning these ruffs, when the fine clean fall° is worth all. And again, if you should chance to take a nap in the afternoon, your falling-band requires no poting-stick° to recover his° form; believe me, no fashion to° the falling, I say. *yourselves / fashion* *hat* *headdresses* *turned-down collars* *(with sexual wordplay)* *iron for pleats* *its / compared with*

5.5. The Genoese court, the palace (see 5.4.54–60).

BIANCA And is not Signor Saint Andrew Jaques° a gallant fellow, now? *a Scotsman*

MAQUERELLE By my maidenhead, la, honor and he agrees as well together as a satin suit and woolen stockings.[1]

EMILIA But is not Marshall Make-Room, my servant in reversion,[2] a proper gentleman?

MAQUERELLE Yes, in reversion, as he had his office, as, in truth, he hath all things in reversion. He has his mistress in reversion, his clothes in reversion, his wit in reversion, and indeed is a suitor to me for my dog in reversion. But in good verity, la, he is as proper° a gentleman in reversion as—and indeed, as fine a man as may be, having a red beard and a pair of warped legs.[3] *handsome*

BIANCA But, i'faith, I am most monstrously in love with Count Quidlibet-in-Quodlibet.° Is he not a pretty, dapper, unidle° gallant? *Whichever-in-Whatever* *active*

MAQUERELLE He is even one of the most busy-fingered lords; he will put the beauties to the squeak most hideously.[4]

[*Enter Bilioso.*]

BILIOSO Room! Make a lane there! The Duke is entering. Stand handsomely, for beauty's sake; take up the ladies there. So, cornets, cornets! [*Music plays.*]

5.[6]

Enter Prepasso, joins to Bilioso; two pages with lights, Ferrardo, Mendoza; at the other door two pages with lights, and the Captain leading in Maria; the Duke meets Maria and closeth° with her. The rest fall back. *joins*

MENDOZA Madam, with gentle ear receive my suit.
A kingdom's safety should o'erpeise slight rites;[1]
Marriage is merely Nature's policy.° *stratagem, device*
Then, since unless our royal beds be joined,
Danger and civil tumult frights the state,
Be wise as you are fair; give way to fate.

MARIA What wouldst thou, thou affliction to our house?° *the house of Medici*
Thou ever devil, 'twas thou that banished'st
My truly noble lord.

MENDOZA I?

MARIA Ay, by thy plots, by thy black stratagems.
Twelve moons have suffered° change since I beheld *undergone*
The lovèd presence of my dearest lord.
O thou far worse than Death! He parts but soul
From a weak body, but thou soul from soul
Disseverest that which God's own hand did knit.

1. Woolen stockings are homely in appearance and style; a satin suit would require silk stockings, such as were fashionable in England. Satire of Scottish courtiers was commonplace in drama after the arrival of King James I and his entourage from Scotland in 1603.

2. I.e., the gentleman next in line to be my "servant," meaning "courtly admirer." Legally, reversion is the right of succeeding to the possession of something after another is done with it. Maquerelle, in her next speech, disparages the gentleman for having obtained everything secondhand.

3. This description is widely regarded as Marston's wry comment on his own appearance.

4. This gentleman is evidently fond of pinching ladies' behinds and hearing the ladies squeak in reaction.

5.6. The scene continues.

1. A kingdom's safety should outweigh your scruples about marrying me.

Thou scant of° honor, full of devilish wit! *lacking in*
MENDOZA We'll check your too intemperate lavishness;° *freedom of speech*
I can and will.
MARIA What canst?
MENDOZA Go to; in banishment thy husband dies.
MARIA He ever is at home that's ever wise.[2]
MENDOZA You'st° never meet more; reason should love control. *You must*
MARIA Not meet?
She that dear° loves, her love's still in her soul. *dearly*
MENDOZA You are but a woman, lady; you must yield.
MARIA Oh, save me, thou innated° bashfulness, *innate*
Thou only ornament of woman's modesty!
MENDOZA Modesty? Death,° I'll torment thee! *By God's death*
MARIA Do; urge° all torments, all afflictions try; *press forward*
I'll die my lord's,° as long as I can die. *still Altofronto's wife*
MENDOZA Thou obstinate, thou shalt die!—Captain,
That lady's life is forfeited to justice.
We have examined her,
And we do find she hath empoisonèd
The reverend hermit. Therefore, we command
Severest custody. Nay, if you'll do 's° no good, *do us*
You'st do 's no harm; a tyrant's peace is° blood. *is achieved by*
MARIA Oh, thou art merciful! O gracious devil,
Rather by much let me condemnèd be
For seeming murder than be damned for thee!° *for marrying you*
I'll mourn no more. Come, girt my brows with flowers;
Revel and dance. Soul, now thy wish thou hast;
Die like a bride;° poor heart, thou shalt die chaste. *wedded to virtue*

Enter Aurelia in mourning habit.

AURELIA "Life is a frost of cold felicity,
And death the thaw of all our vanity."[3]
Was't not an honest priest that wrote so?
MENDOZA Who let her in?
BILIOSO [*to Aurelia*] Forbear!
PREPASSO Forbear!
AURELIA Alas, calamity is everywhere.
Sad misery, despite your double doors,
Will enter even in court.
BILIOSO Peace!
AURELIA I ha' done. One word—take heed! I ha' done.

Enter Mercury with loud music.

MERCURY Cyllenian° Mercury, the god of ghosts, *Born on Mt. Cyllene*
From gloomy shades that spread° the lower coasts,° *extend over / regions*
Calls four high-famèd Genoan dukes to come
And make this presence° their Elysium, *reception room*
To pass away this high-triumphal night
With song and dances, court's more soft delight.
AURELIA Are you god of ghosts? I have a suit depending° *pending*

2. The wise person is at home anywhere, because that person rises above vicissitude. (A classical commonplace.)

3. Aurelia quotes an epigram by the cleric Thomas Bastard, from *Chrestoleros* (1598).

in hell betwixt me and my conscience; I would fain have thee help me to an advocate.

BILIOSO Mercury shall be your lawyer, lady.

AURELIA Nay, faith, Mercury has too good a face to be a right° lawyer. *proper*

PREPASSO Peace, forbear! Mercury presents° the masque. *acts as presenter for*

Cornets: the song to the cornets, which playing, the masque enters: Malevole, Pietro, Ferneze, and Celso in white robes, with dukes' crowns upon laurel wreaths, pistolets° and short swords under their robes. [*The men are masked.*] *pistols*

MENDOZA [*to disguised Malevole*] Celso, Celso, court Maria for our love.—Lady, be gracious, yet grace.[4]

Malevole takes his wife to dance.

MARIA [*to Malevole*] With me, sir?

MALEVOLE Yes, more lovèd than my breath;
With you I'll dance.

MARIA Why, then, you dance with death.
But come, sir, I was ne'er more apt to° mirth. *inclined to*
Death gives eternity a glorious birth.
Oh, to die honored, who would fear to die?

MALEVOLE They die in fear who live in villainy.

MENDOZA Yes, believe him, lady, and be ruled by him.

PIETRO [*to Aurelia*] Madam, with me?

Pietro takes his wife Aurelia to dance.

AURELIA Wouldst then be miserable?

PIETRO I need not wish.[5]

AURELIA Oh, yet forbear my hand. Away, fly, fly!
Oh, seek not her that only seeks to die.

PIETRO Poor lovèd soul!

AURELIA What, wouldst court misery?

PIETRO Yes.

AURELIA She'll° come too soon. Oh, my grieved heart! *Misery will*

PIETRO Lady, ha' done, ha' done.
Come, let's dance; be once from sorrow free.

AURELIA Art a sad man?

PIETRO Yes, sweet.

AURELIA Then we'll agree.

Ferneze takes Maquerelle, and Celso, Bianca; then the cornets sound the measure;° one change,° and rest. *dance* *round of dance*

FERNEZE (*to Bianca*) Believe it, lady; shall I swear? Let me enjoy you in private and I'll marry you, by my soul.

BIANCA I had rather you would swear by your body. I think that would prove the more regarded oath with you.

FERNEZE I'll swear by them both to please you.

BIANCA Oh, damn them° not both to please me, for God's sake. *(by forswearing)*

FERNEZE Faith, sweet creature, let me enjoy you tonight and I'll marry you tomorrow fortnight, by my troth, la.

4. Listen graciously to Celso as he woos you on my behalf. (Mendoza is fooled by Malevole's disguise as Celso.)

5. I don't need to wish to be miserable; I am so already.

MAQUERELLE On his troth, la! Believe him not. That kind of coney catching° is as stale as Sir Oliver Anchovy's perfumed jerkin. Promise of matrimony by a young gallant to bring a virgin lady into a fool's paradise, make her a great° woman, and then cast her off—'tis as common, as natural to a courtier as jealousy to a citizen, gluttony to a Puritan, wisdom° to an alderman, pride to a tailor, or an empty handbasket to one of those sixpenny damnations.° Of his troth, la! Believe him not; traps to catch polecats!° *knavery, tricks* / *noble; pregnant* / *pose of wisdom* / *streetwalkers* / *whores*

MALEVOLE (*to Maria* [*aside, as he reveals his identity to her*])
Keep your face constant. Let no sudden passion
Speak in your eyes.

MARIA [*aside to him*] O my Altofront!

PIETRO (*to Aurelia* [*as he reveals his identity to her*]) A tyrant's jealousies
Are very nimble; you receive° it all. *understand; suffer*

AURELIA (*to Pietro*) My heart, though not my knees, doth humbly fall
Low as the earth to thee.

MALEVOLE [*aside to Maria*] Peace. Next change.° No words. *round of dancing*

MARIA [*aside to him*] Speech to such? Ay. Oh, what will affords![6] *Cornets sound the measure over again, which danced, they unmask.*

MENDOZA Malevole?
They environ° Mendoza, bending° their pistols on him. *surround / aiming*

MALEVOLE No.

MENDOZA Altofront, Duke Pietro, Ferneze! Ha!

ALL Duke Altofront, Duke Altofront! *Cornets, a flourish.*

MENDOZA Are we surprised?° What strange delusions mock *Am I taken by surprise?*
Our senses? Do I dream? Or have I dreamt
This two days' space?° Where am I? *My time as duke*
They seize upon Mendoza.

MALEVOLE Where an archvillain is.

MENDOZA Oh, lend me breath, till I am fit to die!° *until I've confessed*
For peace with heaven, for your own souls' sake,
Vouchsafe me life!

PIETRO Ignoble villain, whom neither heaven nor hell,
Goodness of God or man, could once make good!

MALEVOLE Base, treacherous wretch, what grace canst thou expect,
That had grown impudent in gracelessness?

MENDOZA Oh, life!

MALEVOLE Slave, take thy life.
Wert thou defensèd,° through blood and wounds, *armed, defended*
The sternest horror of a civil fight,° *of civil strife*
Would I achieve° thee; but prostrate at my feet, *make an end of*
I scorn to hurt thee. 'Tis the heart of slaves
That deigns to triumph over peasants' graves—
For such thou art, since birth° doth ne'er enroll *noble ancestry*
A man 'mong monarchs, but a glorious soul.
Oh, I have seen strange accidents of state:
The flatterer, like the ivy, clip° the oak *embrace*

6. I.e., Why would I possibly want to speak to Mendoza? Oh, what liberties powerful men allow themselves!

And waste it to the heart; lust so confirmed
That the black act of sin itself not shamed
To be termed courtship.[7]
Oh, they that are as great° as be their sins, *noble; vast*
Let them remember that th'inconstant people° *multitude*
Love many princes merely for their faces
And outward shows, and they do covet more
To have a sight of these than of their virtues.
Yet thus much let the great ones still conceit:° *keep in mind*
When they observe not heaven's imposed conditions,
They are no kings, but forfeit their commissions.

MAQUERELLE O good my lord, I have lived in the court this twenty year; they that have been old courtiers and come to live in the city, they are spited at° and thrust to the walls like apricots,[8] good my lord. *scorned*

BILIOSO [*to Malevole*] My lord, I did know Your Lordship in this disguise; you heard me ever say if Altofront did return I would stand for him. Besides, 'twas Your Lordship's pleasure to call me wittol and cuckold; you must not think, but that° I knew you, I would have put it up° so patiently. *were it not that* / *put up with it*

MALEVOLE [*to the courtiers*] You o'erjoyed spirits, wipe your
long-wet eyes. *Kicks out Mendoza.*
Hence with this man! An eagle takes° not flies. *captures, subdues*
(*To Pietro and Aurelia*) You to your vows; (*to Maquerelle*)
and thou unto the suburbs.[9]
(*To Bilioso*) You to my worst friend I would hardly give;
Thou art a perfect old knave.—All-pleased, live,
(*To Celso and the Captain* [*embracing them*]) You two unto my breast;
(*to Maria* [*embracing her*]) thou to my heart.
The rest of idle° actors idly part. *unimportant*
And as for me, I here assume my right,° *dukedom*
To which I hope all's pleased; to all, good night.
Cornets, a flourish. Exeunt omnes.° *everyone*

FINIS.

Epilogue

[*Enter the Epilogue.*]

EPILOGUE Your modest silence, full of heedy° stillness, *attentive*
Makes me thus speak: a voluntary illness° *wrongdoing*
Is merely° 'scuseless, but unwilling error, *entirely*
Such as proceeds from too-rash youthful fervor,
May well be called a fault, but not a sin.
Rivers take names from founts where they begin.[1]
Then let not too severe an eye peruse
The slighter breaks° of our reformèd Muse, *flaws*
Who could herself herself of faults detect,
But that she knows 'tis easy to correct,

7. Lust so ingrained that adultery itself is not ashamed to be called courtliness.
8. Apricots are often grown against a south-facing wall to maximize their exposure to the sun.
9. Pietro and Aurelia are to retire to their marriage vows and a quiet life of meditation. The suburbs, to which Maquerelle is to be sent, contained many houses of prostitution; such was the case with the suburbs of London at any rate.

Epilogue.
1. I.e., Things must be judged by their origins and intents.

Though some men's labor.[2] Troth, to err fit,
As long as wisdom's not professed, but wit.[3]
Then till another's° happier Muse appears, *(Ben Jonson's)*
Till his Thalia° feast your learnèd ears, *Muse of comedy*
To whose desertful lamps pleased Fates impart
Art above Nature, Judgment above Art,[4]
Receive this piece, which hope nor fear yet daunteth;[5]
He that knows most, knows most how much he wanteth.° *he doesn't know*
[*Exit.*]

2. Though for some writers it is hard work.
3. Flaws can be excused if the writing is offered as witty entertainment, not as profound wisdom.
4. To whose well-deserving powers of illumination the Fates have given a power of art exceeding Nature itself, and a power of judgment even more exalted than that.
5. Which is not inhibited either by an unrealistic hope of great success or by the fear of utter failure.

TEXTUAL NOTES

The Malcontent was entered in the Stationers' Register on July 5, 1604, and printed three times in that same year. The third quarto (Q3), on which this present edition is based, contains additions not found in the earlier quartos (as well as a prologue and an epilogue added in Q2 and not in Q1). It also tidies up and clarifies the earlier printed versions, occasionally omitting something advertently and sometimes sophisticating usages (changing "ye" to "you," for example), so that in some instances where Q3 is simply reprinting the material of Q1 and Q2 (i.e., not revising or adding material), those earlier texts may be more reliably close to the author's manuscript. The following textual notes record significant departures from Q3 and, in a few instances, readings from Q1 and Q2 that may be of textual interest even where the Q3 reading is adopted, using the following abbreviations:

Q1: First quarto of 1604 (London: Valentine Sims for William Aspley; quires B–E were printed by a printer other than Simmes)
Q2: Second quarto of 1604 (London: Valentine Sims for William Aspley; quires B–E were printed by a printer other than Simmes)
Q3: Third quarto of 1604 (London: Valentine Sims for William Aspley)
Q3 corr.: The corrected third quarto
Q3 uncorr.: The uncorrected third quarto
ed.: A modern editor's emendation

Dramatis Personae [and occasionally elsewhere] **10 MENDOZA** [Q3: Mendozo] **21** [and elsewhere] **BIANCA** [Q3: Beancha]

Prologue [placement, ed.; follows act 5 and "FINIS" in Q3] **1 Prologue** [ed.; not in Q3]

Induction 0.1 *Will* [Q3: *W.*] **7 lid** [ed.] slid [Q3] **11 Condell** [Q3: Cundale] **11 Dick** [Q3: D:] **12 Will** [Q3: W:] **16.1 *Sinklo*** [Q3: *Sinkclow*] **17, 21** [and elsewhere] **coz** [Q3: Coose] **24 apricots** [Q3: Apricoks] **25 apricot** [Q3: Aprícoke] **27.1 *Dick*** [Q3: *D:*] **27.1 *Harry Condell*** [Q3: *H:* Cundale] **27.1 *John Lowin*** [Q3: *I. Lewin*] **35 feather** [ed.] father [Q3] **95 bawbees** [Q3: baubees] **95 venture** [Q3: venter] **118 they** [ed.] he [Q3]

1.1.7 [and elsewhere] **scented** [Q3: sented]

1.2.30 SD A *song* [not in Q3; after "*Scena Tertia*" ("Third Scene") in Q1, Q2]

1.3.4–5 the church [present in some copies of Q3, deleted in others] **10 thou** [Q1, Q2; not in Q3] **13 new** [Q1, Q2; not in Q3] **32 i'the** [Q1, Q2] in the [Q3] **41 Make-Please** [Q3: make-pleece] **64 Guerrino** [Q3: *Guerchino*] **73.1** [placement, ed.; after 74 in Q3] **78 Unshell** [Q3: vnshale] **89 Blurt** [Q3: Blirt] **108–**

49 Nay . . . think it [Q3; not in Q1, Q2] **112 rites** [Q3: rightes] **148 should have** [ed.] shue, should [Q3] **155–72** [Q3; not in Q1, Q2] **168 peise** [Q3: poize]

1.4.11 midst [Q3: middest] **15 lickerous** [Q3: liquorous] **20 this** [Q1, Q2] his [Q3] **33 afire** [Q3: afiar] **43.1–91 SD** [Q3; not in Q1, Q2] **46 in his lord** [ed.] on his Lord [Q3] **91 SD** [placement, ed.; after "Mendoza" in 92 in Q3] **92 SD** [placement, ed.; after "key" in 92 in Q3] **93 SD** [placement, ed.; after "sweet lord" in 93 in Q3]

1.6.9 put up [Q1] put [Q2, Q3] **23 jawed** [Q1, Q2: iawde] jade [Q3] **24 agen'** [Q1, Q2] against [Q3] **94 sighs** [ed.] sights [Q3]

1.7.17 [and elsewhere] **Lose** [Q3: Loose] **32 'fore** [Q1, Q2] for [Q3] **46 antic** [Q3: antique] **66 princess'** [Q3: Princes] **86 silly** [Q3: seely] **87 throes** [Q1: throws]

1.8.1–61 [Q3; not in Q1, Q2] **25 Pooh** [Q3: Pue] **30 compliments** [Q3: complements] **54** [and elsewhere] **vile** [Q3: vilde]

2.1.19 struck [Q1: strooke] **26 sear** [Q1, Q3 corr.] seate [Q3 uncorr.]

2.2.1 Dipsas [Q1: dip-sawce] **5 these** [Q1, Q2; not in Q3] **8 not** [Q1, Q2, Q3 corr.; not in Q3 uncorr.] **9 does** [Q1, Q2] dooth [Q3] **10 Is 'a** [Q1, Q2] is hee [Q3] **11 o'the** [Q1, Q2] of the [Q3] **22 all** [Q1, Q2; not in Q3] **23 Why** [Q1, Q2; not in Q3] **27, 28** [and elsewhere] **la** [Q3: law]

2.3.0.2 [and elsewhere] ***Ferrardo*** [Q3: Ferrard] **6 b'wi'thee** [ed.] buy thee [Q1, Q2] be with thee [Q3] **17 i'favor** [ed.] I fauour [Q3] **23–37** [Q3; not in Q1, Q2] **40 which** [ed.] with [Q3] **52 PIETRO** [ed.] *Mend.* [Q3] **52 corse** [Q3: course]

2.4.2 methodically [Q1, Q2] methodicall [Q3] **5 ye** [Q1, Q2] you [Q3] **17, 18 restoration** [Q3: restauration] **28 o'this** [Q1, Q2] of this [Q3] **35 Well** [Q1, Q2] We [Q3] **48 our** [Q1, Q2] your [Q3] **55 i'the** [Q1, Q2] in the [Q3]

2.5.0.3 *Tumult within* [Q1, Q2; not in Q3] **4.1** [placement, ed.; opposite 8 in Q3] **6 princess'** [ed.] Princes [Q3] **9 SD–9.1** [in margin in Q1, Q2; not in Q3] **25 An't** [Q3: And] **46–47 For . . . sovereign?** [Q1, Q2; not in Q3] **64 pent** [Q1, Q2] spent [Q3] **90 waist** [Q3: waste] **92** [and elsewhere] **numbèd** [Q3: nummed] **95 thy** [Q1, Q2] the [Q3] **96 SD** [placement, ed.; after 95 in Q3] **99 silly** [Q1, Q2] seely [Q3] **109, 110 Ha** [Q1, Q2] ah [Q3] **128 ha' seen** [Q1, Q2] haue seene [Q3] **137 Ha, ye** [Q1, Q2] ah you [Q3] **147 does** [Q1, Q2] dooth [Q3]

3.1.10 BILIOSO [Q3] *Mend.* [Q2] *Pietro* [Q1] **32 compliments** [Q3: complements] **33.2 *Bianca*** [ed.] Bilioso *and Bianca* [Q3; not in Q1, Q2] **87** [and elsewhere] **traveled** [Q3: trauaild] **102 cypress** [Q3: cipers] **115.1** [placement, ed.; after 116 in Q3] **141.1** [placement, ed.; at 139 in Q3] **143 bodice** [ed.] bodies [Q3]

3.2.21 i'thy [Q1, Q2] in thy [Q3] **31 blushless** [ed.] blushes [Q3] **32 choke** [ed.] cloke [Q3] **51 Ithaca, can** [Q1, Q2] *Ithacan* [Q3] **53.1** [placement, ed.; after 52 in Q3]

3.3.29 himself [Q1, Q2] it selfe [Q3] **37.1 *Celso* [*retires*]** [ed.] *Exit Celso* [Q3] **40 i'thy** [Q1, Q2] in thy [Q3] **40 ye** [Q1, Q2] thou [Q3] **42 does** [Q1, Q2] dooth [Q3] **102 i'the** [Q1, Q2] in the [Q3] **110 swollen** [Q3: swolne] **125.1** [ed.] *Enter* Celzo [after 124 in Q3] **130.1 *Exeunt*** [ed.] *Exit* [Q3]

3.4.3 safety [ed.] safely [Q3] **6 ye** [Q1, Q2] you [Q3] **9 SD** [placement, ed.; after 8 in Q3] **24 ha'** [Q1, Q2] haue [Q3]

3.5 [scene number placement, ed.; after "Sing" in 3.4.38 in Q3] **0.1** [placement, ed.; after SD in 3.4.38 in Q3] **3 Must** [Q1, Q2] you must [Q3] **5 sword** [Q1, Q2] and sword [Q3] **18** [and elsewhere] **straight** [Q3: strait] **24 PIETRO** [ed.] *Cel.* [Q3]

4.1.19 arrant [Q3: arrand] **26 'fore** [Q1, Q2] for [Q3]

4.2.0.1–4 [placement, ed.; preceding SCENA SECVNDA in Q3] **17 EQUATO** [Q1; not in Q2] *Pre:* [Q3] **25 bade** [Q1, Q2] bid [Q3]

4.3.54 SD [placement, ed.; before 54 in Q3] **59 SD** [placement, ed.; opposite 58 in

Q3] **67 SD** [placement, ed.; after 66 in Q3] **95 SD** [placement, ed.; after 93 in Q3] **113 Like lightning** [Q1; continuing the speech of *Men.* in Q3] **114 SD** [placement, ed.; to the right of "*Enter* Maleuole" in Q3]

4.4.4 rant [ed.] rand [Q2, Q3] raue [Q1] **18 MALEVOLE** [ed.] *Men.* [Q3]

4.5.0.1 *halberds* [Q3: *Holberts*] **1 Lead** [ed.] ledde [Q3] **33 soul loves** [ed.] soule lou'd [Q1, Q2, Q3] **77.1** [placement, ed.; after 76 in Q3] **90–98** [Q2, Q3; not in Q1] **99 wittol** [Q3: wittall] **104 SD *Bilioso*** [Q: *Biliosa*] **107 galled** [Q3: gawld] **109 Faith** [Q1, Q2] Yfaith [Q3] **110 thou'rt** [Q1, Q2] thou arte [Q3] **128 here, 'fore** [ed.] heerefore [Q3] **134** [as dialogue, ed.; as SD in Q3] **144 who** [Q1, Q2; not in Q3]

5.1.23 as thieves to [ed.] to thieues as [Q3] **54 SD *Exeunt*** [ed.] *Exit* [Q3]

5.2.10–39 [Q3; not in Q1, Q2] **58 come** [Q1, Q2] cowe [Q3] **81 SD *Exit Captain*** [placement, ed.; after "I love thee, Captain" in 80–81 in Q3]

5.3 [ed.] SCENA SECVNDA [Q3] **15 Molly** [Q3: *Mully*] **20 sake** [Q3] loue [Q1, Q2] **41 farther** [Q3: farder] **55 too** [Q3: to] **63.1** [Q3; not in Q1, Q2] **64–94** [Q3; not in Q1, Q2] **74 collogue** [Q3: collouge]

5.4 [ed.] SCENE TERTIA [Q3] **0.2 *and*** [ed.] Bilioso *and* [Q3] **1.1** [placement, ed.; before 1 in Q3] **14 deeds** [Q1, Q2] *deede* [Q3] **17 arrant** [Q3: arrand] **19–31** [Q3, with an alternative beginning seemingly meant to replace 1–12; not in Q1, Q2] **25 tails off** [Q3: tales of] **34, 35 here's** [Q3: her's] **36 conduits through** [Q3: condites, thorow] **38 senseless** [Q1, Q2] cẽnsles [Q3] **44 nor** [Q1, Q2] *or* [Q3] **47.1** [placement, ed.; at 40 in Q3] **62 What** [ed.] Why [Q3] **70 fashion** [Q1] a fashion [Q2, Q3] **79 distunèd** [Q1] *deserued* [Q2, Q3] **82 SD** [Q1, Q2; not in Q3] **93 feareth** [ed.] *leaueth* [Q3] **93 SD** [Q1; not in Q2, Q3]

5.5.10 enough [Q3: enow] **15 felt . . . felt** [Q3: fealt . . . fealt] **24 Jaques** [Q1; not in Q2, Q3] **36 warped** [Q1, Q2] wrapt [Q3]

5.6 [ed.] SCENA QVARTA [Q3] **0.1 *with*** [Q1, Q2] *and* [Q3] **33 forfeited** [Q1, Q2] forteified [Q3] **34 examined** [Q3: axamined] **37, 38 do 's** [Q3: dooes] **45 AURELIA** [Q2, Q3; assigned to Maria in Q1] **67 court** [Q1, Q2] count [Q3] **72 birth** [ed.] *breath* [Q3] **107 SD** [Q1; not in Q2, Q3] **111 MALEVOLE** [ed.] *Pietro* [Q3] **113.1, 119.1 *Mendoza*** [Q3: *Mendozo*] **144 princes** [Q3 uncorr.] men [Q3 corr.] **147 conceit** [ed.] conceale [Q3] **149 kings** [Q3 uncorr.] men [Q3 corr.] **153 apricots** [Q3: Apricokes] **159 MALEVOLE** [ed.; not in Q3] **159 SD *to the courtiers*** [ed.] *To Pietro & Aurelia* [Q3]

Epilogue [scene heading, ed.] *Epilogus* [Q2, Q3] **1 EPILOGUE** [ed.; not in Q3] **3 'scuseless** [Q2] *sensles* [Q3]

The Tragedy of Mariam

The Tragedy of Mariam occupies a unique position in this anthology in several respects. It is the only play written by a woman. It is the only play written by a member of England's privileged and wealthy class. It alone treats of Jewish history from the time of Herod and Salome. It alone is a "closet" play, designed for reading and not for performance. And it is the only tragedy written in the severely neoclassical Senecan style: with long, sententious speeches; banishment of all violence from the stage; a Nuntio, or messenger, who appears in the fifth act to narrate the tragic events of the catastrophe; and a disembodied classical chorus punctuating the acts with didactic commentary on the preceding action. These distinctive features of *Mariam* are interrelated.

The play's author, Elizabeth Cary (c. 1585–1639), was the daughter of a wealthy Oxfordshire lawyer. Privately educated and urged on by her own intellectual curiosity, she read in French, Spanish, Italian, Latin, and Hebrew. She translated Seneca's *Epistles* while still a girl. In 1602, she married Sir Henry Cary, and became Lady Falkland by virtue of his being named Viscount of Falkland in 1620. The marriage appears to have been distant and unsuccessful. He was staunchly Protestant; she was increasingly drawn to Roman Catholicism, though torn by doubts and seeking always to reconcile her faith with her duty to her husband and the established church of her country. She wrote *Mariam* sometime before 1612, perhaps 1603–8 (it was published in 1613), and another play, set in Syracuse, now lost; other works followed. Later, she was disinherited by her father, partly perhaps because of her conversion to Catholicism and partly because she mortgaged her property for her profligate husband. She and her husband seem to have been somewhat reconciled at the time of his death in 1633, but they had by then long lived apart. We learn much of this information from a biography by one of her daughters, probably Anne. It is the first biography of an English woman writer, written probably in 1643–50 though not published until 1861.

As the principal source for her first play, Cary chose two works by the Jewish historian Flavius Josephus: *History of the Jewish War* (75–79 C.E.) and *Antiquities of the Jews* (93 C.E.). Cary's primary interest was in Josephus' account of Herod the Great's difficult marriage with a Jewish woman of royal ancestry, Mariam, or Mariamne. Having been appointed King of Judaea by the Romans in 39 B.C.E., Herod divorced his first wife, Doris, some three years later in order to strengthen a needed alliance with the Jews through his marriage to Mariam. Conflict was inevitable. Mariam belonged to the family whose dynasty Herod had displaced. Having executed Mariam's grandfather, Hyrcanus, on a trumped-up charge of treason, Herod then staged an apparent accident in which Mariam's brother, Aristobulus, was drowned. Herod also attempted to destroy his political enemies, the sons of Babas, forcing them to conceal themselves under the protection of an Idumaean named Constabarus. When Mariam's mother, Alexandra, complained to Marc Antony about these crimes, Herod

Introduction, glosses, footnotes, and textual notes by David Bevington; text edited by David Bevington and checked by Eric Rasmussen.

Portrait of Elizabeth Cary, Viscountess Falkland (c. 1620) by Paul Van Somer.

was obliged to travel to Rome and give an account of himself.

The play picks up the story at the point when Herod is about to return from a second visit to Rome that was needed to settle his affairs with Octavian (originally Octavius, later Augustus), the victor over Herod's erstwhile patron, Marc Antony. Previous to this, Herod's vengeful sister, Salome, has arranged for her first husband, Josephus, to be executed for having betrayed to Mariam the secret that she would be killed if Herod died. Herod has arranged a second marriage for Salome to Constabarus, Governor of Idumaea and Gaza. Now, on his return from Rome, Herod finds himself with a wife distraught over the deaths of her kindred and a sister bent on destroying that wife. Deeply in love with Mariam but persuaded by Salome that she is conspiring to kill him and has been unfaithful, he consents to her execution and then is overwhelmed with remorse.

Why did Cary choose to dramatize this story? It cannot have been familiar to most English readers. Herod the Great was well known, of course, from the New Testament, as the king who had ordered the massacre of the infant children of Bethlehem in an attempt to kill Jesus (Matthew 2.1–16). A different, later Salome, daughter of Herodias, was infamous for having danced before her stepfather Herod Antipas, one of Herod the Great's sons, and then demanding the head of John the Baptist as a reward, as recorded in Matthew 14.1–11 and Mark 6.17–28—though even there the dancing woman is referred to only as Herodias' daughter; that her name was Salome is derived from Josephus' writings. Instead of these well-known stories, Cary chose from her wide-ranging and very scholarly reading an unfamiliar account that must have seemed personally and painfully relevant to her own life. Perhaps the writing of *Mariam* afforded Cary an opportunity to think seriously about her own marriage and choice of religion.

The Mariam of Cary's play believes herself to be descended from Jacob and thus to be a Jew in a pure line of descent. Herod, contrastingly, is an Idumaean, which is to say a descendant of Esau. Jacob, his mother's favorite, had personated his twin brother Esau in order to take from him their father Isaac's blessing, and he had also encouraged the pleasure-loving Esau to sell him, Jacob, his birthright for a mess of pottage (Genesis 25–27). In time, the quarrel between these brothers became the basis of a tradition of rivalry and hatred. Mariam's mother, Alexandra, fans these flames of antipathy in her conversations with Mariam. She appeals to "our forefather Abram" (i.e., Abraham) and is outraged that Herod, "Base Edomite, the damnèd Esau's heir," should "be set in David's chair" (1.2.6–10). Mariam is "of David's blood" and is thus rightful heir of the kingdom (David being descended from Jacob) (1.2.67). Herod is a usurper and murderer.

Cary's identification with the circumstances of Mariam's dilemma is clear. Like Cary, Mariam was unhappily married to a powerful and unpredictable man who did not share her spiritual allegiance. Though Herod and Mariam are of the same religious persuasion, being Jews (just as Cary and her husband were both Christians), their antagonisms are more acute than any shared tradition. The differences of situation are of course great: Herod is a king with the blood of Mariam's relatives on his hands, and he has a menacing sister. Cary's circumstances were not so dire. Even so, the story of Mariam was presumably meaningful to its author because Mariam's inner conflict was recognizably like that of Cary herself. Mariam must struggle with the strong sense of obligation imposed on her by the sacrament of marriage, even if she is married to a dangerously suspicious man.

The play thus centers, as its title implies, on Mariam and her troubled relationship with Herod. She argues unhappily with herself in soliloquy as the play begins. Rumor has it that Herod has been put to death by Octavian; the rumor turns out not to be true, but this false report gives Mariam occasion to think over her marriage. She confesses to having wished him dead. She loved him once, but "rage and scorn" soon "put [her] love to flight" (1.1.19). She acknowledges her wrong in this: "Hate hid his true affection from my sight, / And kept my heart from paying him his debt" (1.1.21–22). She concedes that Herod did love her and that it was her own hatred that prevented her from giving him his due in marriage. At the same time, she blames him for his jealousy, which prompted him to deprive her of her liberty, and for his terrible cruelties to her brother and grandfather. Now that he is dead (so she thinks), Mariam remembers Herod's love for her and cannot help shedding tears, even though his death brings genuine relief. She vacillates. "Hard-hearted Mariam!" she berates herself for not grieving more unfeignedly (1.1.63). These are the emotions with which Cary seems to have identified, feeling antipathy to her husband and yet at the same time chastising herself for being a reluctant wife.

The Chorus at the end of act 1 reinforces a strong impression of self-examination and even self-accusation on the part of the author. As a presumably impartial voice, the Chorus criticizes Mariam for her "wavering mind" (1 Chorus 6) and especially for her perversity in grieving for a thing she has long desired:

> Still Mariam wished she from her lord were free,
> For expectation of variety;
> Yet, now she sees her wishes prosperous be,
> She grieves because her lord so soon did die.
> (1 Chorus 25–28)

Mariam's impulsive longing for change, followed by remorse, is anathema to the Senecan chorus. Its teachings are deeply Stoic, urging the need for all humans to learn that they must never pin their hopes for happiness on the vicissitudes of Fortune: "To wish variety is sign of grief; / For if you like your state as now it is, / Why should an alteration bring relief?" (1 Chorus 19–21). The only way to find genuine happiness is to be "delighted in a settled state" (1 Chorus 24). Mariam, in the view of the Chorus of act 1, has a lot to learn.

Mariam never denies that a husband has a right to call himself his wife's "lord." To be sure, that lordship invites a rebellious response, especially when the "lord" in question is a tyrant. Mariam is heroic in her resistance to male tyranny; at the same time, she criticizes herself severely for exactly this resistance. As she faces the prospect of death, she blames herself for not having handled her end of the bad bargain of marriage with more grace. When husbands turn out to be brutes, wives bear the chief responsibility for salvaging the situation and the marriage itself.

As her end draws near, in act 4, Mariam perceives in soliloquy that she has been her own worst enemy. She berates herself for assuming that her beauty would protect her from the assaults of Salome and Herod. She, Mariam, believes she must bear a major part of the blame for her impending tragedy: "Had not myself against myself conspired, / No plot, no adversary from without / Could Herod's love from Mariam have retired" (4.8.9–11). The opposition she has encountered was potent indeed, but her handling of it should have been more skillful, diplomatic, and self-effacing:

> As well as fair, I might have proved me wise;
> But I did think, because I knew me chaste,
> One virtue for a woman might suffice.
> (4.8.36–38)

Humility and chastity, Mariam argues, are equally demanded of a woman if she is to be the "glory of our sex" (4.8.39). Mariam sets a high standard for herself; so, implicitly, did Cary in her analysis of her own marriage.

The other figure in the play who wavers most visibly in a struggle with his soul is Herod. He cannot make up his tortured mind, toward the end of the play, whether to order Mariam's execution or not. He loves her passionately and is obsessed by her sexually, but he is also driven by paranoid fears of betrayal. He is, like too many men in Elizabethan drama (one thinks of Othello, or Duke Ferdinand in *The Duchess of Malfi*), insanely vulnerable to the suspicion that women are inherently deceitful. Herod is a jealous husband, fearful of cuckoldry. He listens readily to reports that Mariam has been unfaithful to him with a virtuous counselor named Sohemus and is convinced that Mariam seeks to poison him. He rages at her and resolves to execute her along with Sohemus, egged on to do so by the spiteful Salome; then relents because of Mariam's beauty; then reverses himself once again. When the Nuntio brings him news of Mariam's public execution in act 5, describing her graceful calm, Herod curses the deed and curses himself for having destroyed his "better half" (5.1.134). Like Othello, he is too late convinced that his wife was spotless and realizes now that she has died an innocent victim.

Herod and Mariam are thus alike in regretting their actions. The portrait of Herod is given some sympathy by his divided soul and his admiration for Mariam. His tragedy is that he destroyed the most beautiful thing in his life through his own weak fears and suspicions; her tragedy is that she failed to meet the challenge of a deeply flawed marriage as she, a virtuous and courageous woman, ought to have done. Such is Cary's anatomy of a troubled marriage as nightmare fantasy.

Mariam and Herod are paired and contrasted in this play with a range of other characters who, for the most part, highlight differences between virtue and vice. Constabarus, the unhappy husband of Salome, is a model of selfless courage. He knows his wife to be a "light creature" but does not proceed against her (1.6.98), hoping only that heaven may see fit to forgive her sin. He virtuously admires Mariam, wishing her well and deploring the villainies of her accusers. His willingness to shelter Herod's political enemies, the sons of Babas, is fatal. They too are brave and incorruptible, intrepid fighters for justice who are oppressed by Herod's tyranny. Herod's brother, Pheroras, shows honorable decency in his love for Graphina despite her inability to bring wealth or social position to their hoped-for marriage. (To be sure, Pheroras allows Salome to blackmail him into telling Herod about Constabarus' sheltering of the sons of Babas, so that Salome can be freed from her unwelcome marriage; in return, Salome agrees to persuade her brother to permit Pheroras to marry Graphina.) Virtuous persons need all the stoic resolution they can muster to withstand misfortune, for life in Herod's Judaea offers little hope of social justice. The only reward for virtue, it seems, is the consolation of being true to oneself and to an ideal of courageous generosity. That reward, in the Chorus's view, is sufficient. One must be patient, eschew revenge, and expect nothing of Fortune.

Characters of lesser moral stature cannot absorb this hard lesson. Doris, Herod's rejected first wife, is a pathetic victim, understandably embittered for herself and her son, Antipater. Her bitterness leads her to curse the children of her hated rival and successor, Mariam. For her part, Mariam senses that heaven is about to punish her somehow, but hopes that Doris's curse may fall on her guiltless head and not on her children. Doris is implacable: she calls on the spirit of Moses to "Stretch thy revenging arm! Thrust forth thy hand / And plague the mother much, the children worse!" (4.8.91–92). Mariam's mother, Alexandra, is also remorseless in her hatred of her enemies. While such desire for heaven-sent revenge can be considered justifiable, it is plainly seen as counterproductive in this profoundly Stoic play, as the teachings of the Chorus especially make clear.

Vengeance in a just cause is understandable, but it prompts a consequent desire for vengeance in one's enemies. Salome embodies vindictive jealousy and vengeful hatred in this play: she represents everything the author especially deplores. Salome is her brother's evil genius, prompting him to violence and guile when his own feelings are mixed. She is a seductive temptress. She is everything that Cary seems to have disliked in a woman. For that reason, it is fascinating that Salome is made the play's spokeswoman for a woman's right to divorce. Tiring of her marriage to the virtuous Constabarus and his criticism of her unchaste behavior, Salome announces to him that she means to free herself of him "By a divorcing bill before I sleep" (1.6.46). She has no patience with his argument that such an inversion of male and female prerogatives will turn the universe itself upside down, "topsy-turvèd quite" (1.6.50). When he appeals to Jewish law and tradition granting authority only to the husband to put away his wife from him, she responds, "I mean not to be led by precedent. / My will shall be to me instead of law" (1.6.79–80).

A woman's right to initiate divorce is something that Cary must have pondered a great deal. Divorce was rare in early-seventeenth-century England; it certainly was not something to be taken as a matter of an individual woman's will. To seek to be freed from the encumbrance of a blameless husband such as Constabarus was unthinkable. Henry Cary was no Constabarus, certainly, but he had law and social convention on his side. The woman author of this play explores the touchy issue of a woman's right to divorce but does so by assigning the espousal of the cause to Salome, the play's most transgressive woman. Did Cary do this to indicate her moral disavowal of the very idea or to protect herself against criticism by denouncing the proposition even as she raised it as an issue?

The Chorus does not comment on the issue of divorce, but it is thoughtfully outspoken in its moral evaluation of the characters and their choices. The lessons propounded by the Chorus are sententious, much in the vein of Seneca: To wish for a change of fortune is to doom oneself to dissatisfaction with one's present lot. Rash judgments are prone to human error; prejudgment of a situation is sure to lead to a foolish understanding. Partiality is to be avoided at all costs. A wife must be not only spotless in her actions but above suspicion; appearances are as important as substance when it comes to a woman's reputation. And one must do everything to avoid being swayed by unruly passion. Above all, warns the Chorus, one must eschew any craving for revenge. "The fairest action of our human life," intones the Chorus at the end of act 4, "Is scorning to revenge an injury" (4 Chorus 1–2). To see an opportunity for revenge and yet rise above that temptation is a kind of victory over one's opponent. Proverbially, and paradoxically, the noblest revenge is forgiveness. This lesson and the others that accompany it apply with perhaps equal force to Mariam and Herod. They illustrate how deeply read Cary was in Seneca.

Cary's closet play was never acted and was not intended to be. In this it models itself once again on Seneca, whose tragedies, fashioned in imitation of the ancient Greek writers Aeschylus, Sophocles, and Euripides, were written only to be read. The Roman theater under Nero was in a state of frivolous decay; serious philosophical writing, even by Nero's tutor, Seneca, was not welcome. Writing a purely literary play permitted Seneca to indulge in long speeches with a minimum of stage action. His plays are quite untheatrical, even antitheatrical. They banish violence through the device of the Nuntio, or Nuntius, who appears in act 5 and describes the unseen violence as Sophocles does at the end of *Oedipus the King*, with the suicide of Jocasta and the self-blinding of Oedipus both occurring offstage. That his works were not to be performed allowed Seneca to tell tales of almost unimaginable horror about men devouring or madly slaying their own children.

A private, literary drama of this sort was well suited to the options Cary had as a woman. She had received a good classical education, even if not at one of the universities, and was well enough off that she could devote herself to serious writing without having to depend on revenue from it. Yet she could not write for the live theater. Women did not act in commercial plays in her time or belong to acting companies. No woman was ever commissioned to write a play for public performance. Other women of adequate financial means had translated plays before Cary, but not for the stage. Jane, or Joanna, Lumley, daughter of a Catholic nobleman, had translated Euripides' *Iphigenia at Aulis* around 1549. Mary Sidney, sister of the poet and statesman Sir Philip Sidney and, by marriage, Countess of Pembroke, had translated Robert Garnier's *Marc Antoine* (1578) in 1592. To this latter translation and to Samuel Daniel's *The Tragedy of Cleopatra* (1594), Cary was indebted; both were closet dramas and studiously classical in form.

Severely regular classical drama never took hold in England, as it did in Italy and France. (Spain was more like England in producing a drama that was markedly national and popular.) Marlowe, Shakespeare, Jonson, Webster, and Middleton wrote for paying audiences whose tastes needed to be taken into account. For better and for worse, Cary was insulated from that world of free-enterprise dramatic entertainment and its irrepressible experimentation. Dramatists from the more classically trained and genteel amateur tradition, to which Cary belonged, could afford to write in accordance with the classical "rules" practiced by Continental writers such as Garnier, in whose *Marc Antoine* the great events in the life of Antony and Cleopatra are told from the perspective of a single day at the end of the story.

Cary's dramaturgy is like that, and designedly so. Choosing with striking originality a story that no one, so far as is known, had ever before fictionalized, Cary arranged her materials in the form of a classical tragedy. The sprawling narrative of Josephus' Jewish histories, extending over many years and moving from one far-flung location to another (as in Shakespeare's *Antony and Cleopatra*), is restricted in Cary's play to a single day in Jerusalem—the day of Herod's return from Rome and also of Mariam's execution. The parts of the story preceding that day are narrated to us, first by an "argument," or summary, and then by what the characters say to one another. The plot is as unified as the time and place: the whole story revolves around Mariam and Herod, even the secondary love plot of Pheroras and Graphina and the plight of the sons of Babas.

The Tragedy of Mariam is a "what if" play. It invites us to ask what the plays of the English Renaissance would have been like if classically trained writers had had a large audience for the kind of "regular" drama that was to produce Corneille, Racine, and Molière in France. *Mariam* also invites us to wonder what sorts of plays Cary might have written if women had been encouraged to write for the theater. Given her limited options, her private classical training, and her attachment to the literary tradition championed earlier by Philip Sidney, Cary eschewed drama designed for public performance in favor of an elite, neoclassical, and learnedly Senecan tradition. To be sure, Seneca also left his unmistakable imprint on plays for the popular stage, such as *The Spanish Tragedy* and *The Revenger's Tragedy*, but in those plays and others of the same mixed genre, classicism is blended with dramatic forms that are distinctively English and popular. Cary's play permits us to consider what English theater might have been like if Seneca had taken hold in England as a rigorously classical model. *Mariam* is an instructive and powerful example of the road not taken.

ELIZABETH CARY

The Tragedy of Mariam

To Diana's earthly deputess, and my worthy sister,° Mistress Elizabeth Cary   *sister-in-law*

When cheerful Phoebus° his full course hath run,   *god of the sun*
  His sister's° fainter beams our hearts doth cheer;   *i.e., The moon's*
So your fair brother[1] is to me the sun,
  And you his sister as my moon appear.
You are my next beloved, my second friend;
  For, when my Phoebus' absence makes it night,
Whilst to th'antipodes° his beams do bend,   *opposite sides of world*
  From you, my Phoebe, shines my second light.
He like to Sol, clear-sighted, constant, free,
  You Luna-like, unspotted, chaste, divine;
He shone on Sicily; you destined be
  T'illumine the now-obscurèd Palestine.
    My first[2] was consecrated to Apollo;
    My second° to Diana[3] now shall follow.   *The present work*

E. C.

The Names of the Speakers

HEROD, King of Judaea
DORIS, his first wife
MARIAM, his second wife
SALOME, Herod's [and Pheroras'] sister
ANTIPATER, his son by Doris
ALEXANDRA, Mariam's mother
SILLEUS, Prince of Arabia
CONSTABARUS, husband to Salome
PHERORAS, Herod's [and Salome's] brother
GRAPHINA, his love
BABAS'S FIRST SON
BABAS'S SECOND SON

The 1613 title page reads "*The Tragedy of Mariam, the fair Queen of Jewry*. Written by that learned, virtuous, and truly noble lady, E[lizabeth] C[ary]. London: Printed by Thomas Creede for Richard Hawkins, and are to be sold at his shop in Chancery Lane, near unto Sergeant's Inn. 1613."

Dedication.

1. Either the author's husband, Henry Cary, who had a sister named Elizabeth, or Henry's brother, Sir Philip Cary, who married Elizabeth Bland.
2. An earlier (lost) tragedy by Cary. John Davies of Hereford praises Cary (in his dedication to *The Muses Sacrifice*, 1612) for making her muse "to mete [appraise, measure] / The scenes of Syracuse and Palestine."
3. Virgin huntress and goddess of the moon.

ANANELL [Ananelus], the high priest
SOHEMUS, a counselor to Herod
NUNTIO [a messenger]
BUTLER, another messenger
CHORUS, a company of Jews
[SILLEUS' MAN° *servant*
Herod's soldiers and attendants, a guard

THE SCENE: Jerusalem.]

The Argument

Herod, the son of Antipater, an Idumaean,[1] having crept by the favor of the Romans into the Jewish monarchy, married Mariam, the daughter° of Hyrcanus, the rightful king and priest, and for her (besides her high blood, being of singular beauty) he reputiated Doris, his former wife, by whom he had children.

granddaughter

This Mariam had a brother called Aristobulus, and, next° him and Hyrcanus his grandfather, Herod in his wife's right° had the best rule.° Therefore to remove them, he charged the first with treason and put him to death, and drowned the second under color of sport.[2] Alexandra, daughter to the one° and mother to the other,° accused him for their deaths before Antony.°

following after / *right of inheritance* / *title* / *Hyrcanus / Aristobulus* / *Marc Antony*

So when he° was forced to go answer this accusation at Rome, he left the custody of his wife to Josephus his uncle, that had married his° sister Salome, and out of a violent affection (unwilling any should enjoy her after him) he° gave strict and private commandment that if he were slain, she° should be put to death. But he returned with much honor, yet found his wife extremely discontented, to whom Josephus had (meaning it for the best, to prove Herod loved her) revealed his charge.

(Herod) / *(Herod's)* / *(Herod)* / *(Mariam)*

So by Salome's accusation he put Josephus to death, but was reconciled to Mariam, who still bare° the death of her friends° exceeding hardly.

bore / *relatives*

In this meantime Herod was again necessarily to revisit Rome, for Caesar, having overthrown Antony, his great friend, was likely to make an alteration of his fortune.[3]

In his absence, news came to Jerusalem that Caesar had put him to death. Their willingness it should be so, together with the likelihood, gave this rumor so good credit as° Sohemus, that had succeeded° Josephus' charge,° succeeded him likewise in revealing it. So at Herod's return, which was

that / *succeeded to / office*

The Argument.

1. An inhabitant of Idumaea, or Edom, the land given to Esau; therefore a descendant of Esau and not of Jacob, as the true Jews were considered to be, since Esau was disinherited when his brother Jacob tricked him out of their father's blessing (see Genesis 27).

2. Historically, Herod had Hyrcanus executed on a charge of treason; he also arranged for his henchmen to drown Aristobulus and make it look as though he had died in a swimming accident.

3. Historically, Herod served the Roman Empire well. When Caesar Octavianus (or Octavian) overthrew his former ally and fellow triumvir, Marc Antony, at the Battle of Actium in 31 B.C.E. and became Emperor Augustus in 29 B.C.E., Herod visited Rome to mend his political fences (he had previously allied himself with Antony). Many observers were convinced of the "likelihood" (line 31) that Herod would not survive the transition, though he in fact did.

speedy and unexpected, he found Mariam so far from joy that she showed apparent° signs of sorrow. He still desiring to win her to a better humor, she, being very unable to conceal her passion, fell to upbraiding him with her brother's death. As they were thus debating, came in a fellow with a cup of wine, who, hired by Salome, said first it was a love potion which Mariam desired to deliver to the King; but afterwards he affirmed that it was a poison and that Sohemus had told her somewhat which procured[4] the vehement hate in her.

manifest

The King hearing this, more moved with jealousy of Sohemus than with this intent of poison, sent her away, and presently after, by the instigation of Salome, she was beheaded. Which rashness was afterward punished in him with an intolerable and almost frantic passion° for her death.

sorrow

1.1

[*Enter Mariam.*]

MARIAM (*sola*)° How oft have I with public voice run on *alone*
To censure Rome's last hero for deceit
Because he wept when Pompey's life was gone,
Yet when he lived, he thought his name too great?[1]
But now I do recant, and, Roman lord,° *(Julius Caesar)*
Excuse too rash a judgment in a woman!
My sex pleads pardon; pardon then afford;° *grant*
Mistaking is with us° but too too common. *among us women*
Now do I find, by self-experience taught,
One object yields both grief and joy:
You wept indeed when on his° worth you thought, *(Pompey's)*
But joyed that slaughter did your foe destroy.
So at his death your eyes true drops did rain,
Whom, dead, you did not wish alive again.
When Herod lived, that now is done to death,
Oft have I wished that I from him were free;
Oft have I wished that he might lose his breath;
Oft have I wished his carcass dead to see.
Then rage and scorn had put my love to flight,
That love which once on him was firmly set;
Hate hid his true affection from my sight,
And kept my heart from paying him his debt.[2]
And blame me not, for Herod's jealousy
Had power even constancy itself to change;
For he, by barring me from liberty
To shun° my ranging, taught me first to range. *prevent*
But yet too chaste a scholar was my heart
To learn to love another than my lord.
To leave his love, my lesson's former part,
I quickly learned;[3] the other° I abhorred. *i.e., infidelity*

4. And that Sohemus had told Mariam something that induced.

1.1.
1. Julius Caesar ("Rome's last hero") defeated his former partner, Pompey the Great, at Pharsalia in 48 B.C.E., thereafter pursuing him to Egypt, where he learned that Pompey had been murdered.
2. My hatred for him blinded me to his true affection for me and kept my heart from yielding to him the love that was his due.
3. I quickly learned, taught by his jealous cruelty, to cease loving him.

But now his death to memory doth call
The tender love that he to Mariam bare,° *bore*
And mine to him; this makes those rivers fall,
Which by another thought unmoistened are:[4]
For Aristobulus, the loveliest youth
That ever did in angel's shape appear,
The cruel Herod was not moved to ruth.° *pity*
Then why grieves Mariam Herod's death to hear?
Why joy° I not the tongue no more shall speak *rejoice*
That yielded forth my brother's latest° doom? *final*
Both youth and beauty might thy° fury break, *i.e., Herod's*
And both in him° did ill befit a tomb. *(Aristobulus)*
And, worthy grandsire,° ill did he° requite *(Hyrcanus) / (Herod)*
His high ascent alone by thee procured,
Except° he murdered thee to free the sprite° *Unless / spirit, soul*
Which still he thought on earth too long immured.° *(said with bitter irony)*
How happy was it that Sohemus' mind
Was moved to pity my distressed estate!
Might Herod's life a trusty servant find,
My death to his had been unseparate.[5]
These thoughts have power his death to make me bear,
Nay, more, to wish the news may firmly hold;
Yet cannot this repulse° some falling tear *hold back*
That will, against my will, some grief unfold.
And more I owe him for his love to me,
The deepest love that ever yet was seen;
Yet had I rather much a milkmaid be
Than be the monarch of Judaea's queen.° *Than be Herod's queen*
It was for naught but love he wished his end
Might to my death but the vaunt-courier° prove; *forerunner*
But I had rather still be foe than friend
To him that saves° for hate and kills for love. *spares life*
Hard-hearted Mariam! At thy discontent
What floods of tears have drenched his manly face!
How canst thou then so faintly now lament
Thy truest lover's death, a death's disgrace?[6]
[*She weeps.*] Ay, now, mine eyes, you do begin to right
The wrongs of your admirer and my lord![7]
Long since you° should have put your smiles to flight; *(my eyes)*
Ill doth a widowed eye with joy accord.
Why, now methinks the love I bare him then,
When virgin freedom left me unrestrained,
Doth to my heart begin to creep again;
My passion now is far from being feigned.
[*She hears or sees Alexandra coming.*]
But, tears, fly back, and hide you in your banks!
You must not be to Alexandra seen,
For if my moan be spied, but little thanks
Shall Mariam have from that incensèd queen.

4. Which tears are quickly stopped when I think of another matter (the murder of Aristobulus).

5. Had Sohemus been Herod's trusty servant, my death would have followed the news of Herod's.

6. Disgracing Herod's death with such perfunctory mourning? (Or perhaps she means that his death is a disgrace to Death itself, because unjust.)

7. You, my weeping eyes, begin to right the wrongs done to Herod, your admirer and my lord and husband!

1.2

[*Enter*] *Alexandra.*

ALEXANDRA What means these tears? My Mariam doth mistake;
The news we heard did tell the tyrant's end.
What, weep'st thou for thy brother's murd'rer's sake?
Will ever wight° a tear for Herod spend? *a person, anyone*
My curse pursue his breathless trunk and spirit,
Base Edomite, the damnèd Esau's heir!
Must he ere° Jacob's child the crown inherit? *before*
Must he, vile wretch, be set in David's chair?[1]
No, David's soul, within the bosom placed
Of our forefather Abram,° was ashamed *i.e., set in eternal bliss*
To see his seat with such a toad disgraced,
That seat that hath by Judah's race[2] been famed.
Thou fatal enemy to royal blood,° *i.e., Herod*
Did not the murder of my boy° suffice *(Aristobulus)*
To stop thy cruel mouth that gaping stood,
But must thou dim the mild Hyrcanus' eyes,° *i.e., kill Hyrcanus*
My gracious father, whose too ready hand
Did lift this Idumaean from the dust?° *i.e., promoted Herod*
And he, ungrateful caitiff,° did withstand° *wretch / oppose*
The man° that did in him most friendly trust. *(Hyrcanus)*
What kingdom's right could cruel Herod claim?
Was he not Esau's issue, heir of hell?
Then what succession can he have but shame?
Did not his ancestor his birthright sell?[3]
Oh, yes, he doth from Edom's name derive
His cruel nature, which with blood is fed;[4]
That made him me of sire° and son deprive. *father (Hyrcanus)*
He ever thirsts for blood, and blood is red.
Weep'st thou because his love to thee was bent?
And read'st thou love in crimson° characters? *bloodred*
Slew he thy friends° to work thy heart's content? *relatives*
No. Hate may justly call that action hers.
He gave the sacred priesthood for thy sake
To Aristobulus, yet doomed° him dead° *sentenced / to death*
Before his back the ephod° warm could make, *priestly garment*
And ere the miter° settled on his head. *priest's headdress*
Oh, had he given my boy no less than right,
The double oil[5] should to his forehead bring
A double honor, shining doubly bright;
His birth anointed him both priest and king.
And say my father and my son he slew
To royalize by right your prince-born breath:[6]
Was love the cause? Can Mariam deem it true
That Mariam gave commandment for her° death? *their (?)*

1.2.
1. Alexandra considers herself a true Jew and the rightful inheritor of rule in Judaea ("David's chair") by virtue of her descent from Jacob; Herod, as a descendant of Esau, she considers a usurper. See Argument, note 1.
2. As the fourth son of Jacob (see Genesis 29.35, 35.22–23), Judah was the ancestor of one of the twelve tribes of Israel.
3. Esau sold his birthright to Jacob for a mess of pottage; see Genesis 25.29–34.
4. Esau (here equated with Edom, or Idumaea) is described in Genesis 25.27–28 as "a cunning hunter, a man of the field" who "did eat of his [Isaac's] venison."
5. Holy oil used to anoint both priests and kings.
6. And even if we were to suppose that Herod slew Hyrcanus and Aristobulus to recognize your royally born right of inheritance and to make your children lawful heirs.

I know by fits he showed some signs of love,
And yet not love, but raging lunacy;
And this his hate to thee may justly prove
That sure he hates Hyrcanus' family.
Who knows if he, unconstant wavering lord,
His love to Doris had renewed again,
And, that he might his bed to her afford,
Perchance he wished that Mariam might be slain?

MARIAM Doris? Alas, her time of love was past;
Those coals were raked in embers long ago
Of Mariam's love, and she was now disgraced,° *then repudiated*
Nor did I glory in her overthrow.
He not a whit his firstborn son esteemed,
Because as well as his he was not mine.[7]
My children only for his own he deemed,
These boys that did descend from royal line.
These did he style his heirs to David's throne;
My Alexander,° if he live, shall sit *My son Alexander*
In the majestic seat of Solomon.
To will it so did Herod think it fit.

ALEXANDRA Why, who can claim from Alexander's[8] brood
That gold-adornèd lion-guarded chair?
Was Alexander not of David's blood?
And was not Mariam Alexander's heir?
What more than right could Herod then bestow?
And who will think except for more than right
He did not raise them?[9] For they were not low,
But born to wear the crown in his despite.
Then send those tears away, that are not sent
To thee by reason, but by passion's power.
Thine° eyes to cheer, thy cheeks to smiles be bent, *Let thine*
And entertain with joy this happy hour.
Felicity, if, when she comes, she finds
A mourning habit° and a cheerless look, *garb*
Will think she is not welcome to thy mind,
And so perchance her lodging will not brook.° *put up with*
Oh, keep her° whilst thou hast her! If she go, *(Felicity, good fortune)*
She will not easily return again.
Full many a year have I endured in woe,
Yet still have sued her presence to obtain;[1]
And did not I to her as presents send
A table, that best art did beautify,
Of two, to whom heaven did best feature lend,
To woo her love by winning Antony?[2]
For when a prince's favor we do crave,
We first their minions' loves do seek to win;
So I, that sought Felicity to have,
Did with her minion Antony begin.

7. Because Antipater was not my son as well as his.
8. My husband Alexander's. (Mariam is the daughter of Alexander and Alexandra; her son is also Alexander.)
9. Alexandra argues that because Herod could not give his children by Mariam any greater right than they already inherited through her, he must have raised them with the intent of taking away that right.
1. Yet I have continually petitioned to have Felicity (good fortune) accompany me.
2. By way of wooing Felicity, or Fortune, Alexandra sent portraits on a board ("table," line 86) of Aristobulus and Mariam to Marc Antony in hopes that he would be tempted by their handsomeness to take one or both as his favorites, or lovers, and thus ally himself with Alexandra.

With double sleight° I sought to captivate *trickery*
The warlike lover, but I did not right;
For if my gift had borne but half the rate,[3]
The Roman had been overtaken quite.
But now he farèd like a hungry guest
That to some plenteous festival is gone;
Now this, now that he deems to eat were best;
Such choice doth make him let them all alone.
The boy's large forehead first did fairest seem;
Then glanced his eye upon my Mariam's cheek,
And that without comparison did deem.
What was in either but he most did leek?[4]
And thus distracted, either's beauty's might[5]
Within the other's excellence was drowned;
Too much delight did bare° him from delight, *strip; carry; bar*
For either's love the other's did confound.
Where° if thy portraiture had only gone,° *Whereas / only had gone*
His life from Herod Antony had taken.[6]
He would have loved thee, and thee alone,
And left the brown Egyptian° clean forsaken, *(Cleopatra)*
And Cleopatra then to seek had been° *would have had to seek*
So firm a lover of her wanèd face;
Then great Antonius' fall we had not seen
By her that fled to have him hold the chase.[7]
Then Mariam, in a Roman's chariot set,
In place of Cleopatra might have shown;° *been seen*
A mart° of beauties in her visage met, *market*
And part in this, that they were all her own.[8]

MARIAM Not° to be empress of aspiring Rome *Not even*
Would Mariam like to° Cleopatra live. *like to = like*
With purest body will I press my tomb,° *go to my grave*
And wish no favors Antony could give.

ALEXANDRA Let us retire us, that we may resolve
How now to deal in this reversèd° state. *topsy-turvy*
Great are th'affairs that we must now revolve,° *ponder*
And great affairs must not be taken late.° *too slowly; lightly*

[*They start to leave, but Salome intercepts them.*]

1.3

[*Enter*] *Salome.*

SALOME More plotting yet? Why, now you have the thing° *i.e., Herod's death*
For which so oft you spent your suppliant breath,
And Mariam hopes to have another king.
Her eyes do sparkle joy for Herod's death.

ALEXANDRA If she desired another king to have,
She might, before she came in Herod's bed,
Have had her wish. More kings than one did crave

3. If I had sent only one picture. ("Rate" means "value.")
4. What was there in either of them that could fail to please him most? ("Leek" means "like.")
5. The power of either's beauty.
6. Antony would have killed Herod (to have Mariam for himself).
7. Cleopatra fled the sea battle of Actium, in this account, to entice Antony (or Antonius) to chase after her. (See Shakespeare's *Antony and Cleopatra*, 3.10, and Argument, note 3, above.)
8. And part of the force of her beauties being that they are all her own (not cosmetic, as in Cleopatra's case). 1.3.

For leave° to set a crown upon her head. *permission*
I think with more than reason° she laments *understandably*
That she is freed from such a sad annoy.° *i.e., her marriage*
Who is't will weep to part from discontents?
And if she joy,° she did not causeless joy. *rejoice*

SALOME You durst not thus have given your tongue the rein
If noble Herod still remained in life.
Your daughter's betters far, I dare maintain,
Might have rejoiced to be my brother's wife.

MARIAM My betters far? Base woman, 'tis untrue.
You scarce have ever my superiors seen,
For Mariam's servants were as good as you
Before she came to be Judaea's queen.

SALOME Now stirs the tongue that is so quickly moved;
But more than once your choler° have I borne. *anger*
Your fumish° words are sooner said than proved, *irascible*
And Salome's reply is only scorn.

MARIAM Scorn those that are for thy companions held![1]
Though I thy brother's face had never seen,
My birth thy baser birth so far excelled,
I had to both of you the princess been.
Thou parti-Jew and parti-Edomite,
Thou mongrel, issued from rejected race!
Thy ancestors against the heavens did fight,
And thou like them wilt heavenly birth disgrace.

SALOME Still twit you me with nothing but my birth?
What odds° betwixt your ancestors and mine? *difference*
Both born of Adam, both were made of earth,
And both did come from holy Abraham's line.

MARIAM I favor thee when nothing else I say.
With thy black acts I'll not pollute my breath;
Else to thy charge I might full justly lay
A shameful life, besides a husband's° death. *i.e., Josephus'*

SALOME 'Tis true indeed, I did the plots reveal
That passed betwixt your favorites and you.
I meant not, I, a traitor to conceal.
Thus Salome your minion Joseph slew.[2]

MARIAM Heaven,° dost thou mean this infamy to smother? *(addressed to God)*
Let slandered Mariam ope thy closèd ear!
Self-guilt hath ever been Suspicion's mother,
And therefore I this speech with patience bear.
No, had not Salome's unsteadfast heart
In Josephus' stead her Constabarus placed,[3]
To free° herself she had not used the art *exculpate*
To slander hapless Mariam for unchaste.

ALEXANDRA Come, Mariam, let us go: it is no boot° *unavailing*
To let the head contend against the foot.[4]

[*Exeunt Mariam and Alexandra.*]

1. Save your scorn for those contemptible creatures that are reputed to be your companions!
2. In that sense, if you like, I was responsible for your lover Josephus' death (in that I denounced him to Herod as a traitor).
3. I.e., had not the inconstant Salome taken Constabarus as her lover after rejecting and in effect killing Josephus.
4. I.e., To encourage insubordination of a lesser subject against a queen.

1.4

SALOME (*sola*) Lives Salome to get° so base a style° *be given / title*
As "foot" to the proud Mariam? Herod's spirit
In happy time for her endured exile,[1]
For, did he live, she should not miss her merit.° *what's coming to her*
But he is dead, and, though he were my brother,
His death such store of cinders cannot cast
My coals of love to quench;[2] for, though they° smother *(the cinders)*
The flames awhile, yet will they out at last.
O blest Arabia, in best climate placed!
I by the fruit will censure of° the tree. *judge*
'Tis not in vain thy happy name thou hast,
If all Arabians like Silleus be.
Had not my fate been too too contrary,
When I on Constabarus first did gaze,[3]
Silleus had been object to mine eye,
Whose looks and personage must all eyes amaze.
But now, ill-fated Salome, thy tongue
To Constabarus by itself° is tied; *by the oath it spoke*
And now, except° I do the Hebrew° wrong, *unless / (Constabarus)*
I cannot be the fair Arabian bride.
What childish lets° are these? Why stand° I now *hindrances / adhere*
On honorable points?° 'Tis long ago *To codes of honor*
Since shame was written on my tainted brow,
And certain 'tis that shame is honor's foe.
Had I upon my reputation stood,
Had I affected° an unspotted life, *chosen to lead*
Josephus' veins had still been stuffed with blood,
And I to him had lived a sober° wife. *virtuous*
Then had I never° cast an eye of love *I never would have*
On Constabarus' now-detested face;
Then had I kept my thoughts without remove,° *wandering disloyalty*
And blushed at motion of the least disgrace.
But shame is gone, and honor wiped away,
And Impudency on my forehead sits.
She bids me work my will without delay,
And for my will I will employ my wits.
He° loves, I love; what then can be the cause *(Silleus)*
Keeps me from being the Arabian's wife?
It is the principles of Moses' laws,
For Constabarus still remains in life.
If he to me did bear as earnest hate
As I to him, for him there were an ease;° *he'd have an option*
A separating bill° might free his fate *bill of divorce*
From such a yoke that did so much displease.
Why should such privilege to man be given?
Or, given to them, why barred from women then?
Are men than we in greater grace with heaven?
Or cannot women hate as well as men?
I'll be the custom-breaker, and begin

1.4.
1. Luckily for Mariam, Herod's soul has left his body.
2. I.e., The sadness of Herod's death cannot quench my passion for Silleus, Prince of Arabia.
3. If fate had not caused me to meet Constabarus before Silleus.

To show my sex the way to freedom's door,
And with an off'ring will I purge my sin;
The law was made for° none but who° are poor. *to control / those who*
If Herod had lived, I might to him accuse
My present lord.° But for the future's sake *husband (Constabarus)*
Then would I tell the King he did refuse
The sons of Babas in his power to take.[4]
But now I must divorce him from my bed,
That my Silleus may possess his room.° *take Constabarus' place*
Had I not begged his life, he° had been dead. *(Constabarus)*
I curse my tongue, the hind'rer of his doom!
But then my wand'ring heart to him was fast,° *fixed*
Nor did I dream of change.—Silleus said
He would be here, and see, he comes at last!
Had I not named him, longer had he stayed.[5]

1.5

[*Enter*] *Silleus.*

SILLEUS Well found, fair Salome, Judaea's pride!
Hath thy innated° wisdom found the way *innate, inborn*
To make Silleus deem him deified° *think himself blessed*
By gaining thee, a more than precious prey?° *prize*
SALOME I have devised the best I can devise.
A more imperfect means was never found;
But what cares Salome? It doth suffice
If our endeavors with their end be crowned.
In this our land we have an ancient use,° *custom*
Permitted first by our lawgiver's head:° *by Moses' direction*
Who° hates his wife, though for no just abuse, *Whoever*
May with a bill divorce her from his bed.
But in this custom women are not free;
Yet I for once will wrest° it. Blame not thou *force; reinterpret*
The ill I do, since what I do's° for thee; *do is*
Though others blame, Silleus should allow.° *approve*
SILLEUS Thinks Salome Silleus hath a tongue
To censure her fair actions? Let my blood
Bedash my proper° brow for such a wrong! *own, very*
The being yours can make even vices good.—
Arabia, joy!° Prepare thy earth with green! *rejoice!*
Thou never happy wert indeed till now.
Now shall thy ground be trod by beauty's queen;
Her foot is destined to depress thy brow.—
Thou shalt, fair Salome, command as much
As if the royal ornament° were thine. *crown*
The weakness of Arabia's king is such,
The kingdom is not his so much as mine.
My mouth is our Obodas' oracle,[1]

4. Salome would tell Herod, if he were alive, that Constabarus disobeyed Herod's orders to arrest and execute the sons of Babas for their opposition to Herod; instead, Constabarus has concealed the two sons for twelve years.

5. Salome speaks as if she has the power to conjure Silleus.

1.5.

1. I speak for and control the ineffectual King Obodas of Arabia as though I were his oracle.

Who° thinks not aught but what Silleus will.° *i.e., Obodas / wishes*
And thou, rare° creature, Asia's miracle, *excellent, nonpareil*
Shalt be to me as it: Obodas' still.[2]
SALOME 'Tis not for glory I thy love accept;
Judaea yields me honor's worthy store.° *great store of honor*
Had not affection° in my bosom crept, *amorous desire*
My native country should my life deplore.[3]
Were not Silleus he with whom I go,
I would not change my Palestine for Rome;
Much less would I, a glorious state to show,° *to appear in splendor*
Go far to purchase an Arabian tomb.[4]
SILLEUS Far be it from Silleus so to think.
I know it is thy gratitude° requites *grace, favor*
The love that is in me, and shall not shrink
Till death do sever me from earth's delights.
SALOME [*hearing a sound*] But whist!° Methinks the wolf is in our talk.° *hush / someone's listening*
Begone, Silleus. Who doth here arrive?
'Tis Constabarus that doth hither walk;
I'll find a quarrel, him from me to drive.
SILLEUS Farewell! But, were it not for thy command,
In his despite° Silleus here would stand. [*Exit Silleus.*] *Defying Constabarus*

1.6

[*Enter*] *Constabarus.*

CONSTABARUS Oh, Salome, how much you wrong your name,
Your race, your country, and your husband most!
A stranger's private conference° is shame. *Talking with a stranger*
I blush for you, that° have your blushing lost. *you who*
Oft have I found, and found you to my grief,
Consorted with° this base Arabian here. *Keeping company with*
Heaven knows that you have been my comfort chief;
Then do not now my greater plague appear.
Now by the stately carvèd edifice° *the Temple of Jerusalem*
That on Mount Zion makes so fair a show,
And by the altar fit for sacrifice,
I love thee more than thou thyself dost know.
Oft with a silent sorrow have I heard
How ill Judaea's mouth doth censure thee;
And, did I not thine honor much regard,
Thou shouldst not be exhorted° thus for me. *admonished*
Didst thou but know the worth of honest fame,° *reputation*
How much a virtuous woman is esteemed,
Thou wouldst like hell eschew deservèd shame,
And seek to be both chaste and chastely deemed.
Our wisest prince° did say, and true he said: *(Solomon)*
A virtuous woman crowns her husband's head.
SALOME Did I for this uprear thy low estate?
Did I for this requital beg thy life

2. You will command me as my oracle, just as I command Obodas.
3. My whole being would grieve at having to depart from my native land.
4. Travel so far to spend the rest of my life in Arabia.
1.6.

That thou hadst forfeited to hapless fate,
To be to such a thankless wretch the wife?
This hand of mine hath lifted up thy head,
Which many a day ago had fall'n full low
Because the sons of Babas are not dead;[1]
To me thou dost both life and fortune owe.

CONSTABARUS You have my patience often exercised.° *tried, tested*
Use, make my choler keep within the banks![2]
Yet boast no more, but be by me advised;
A benefit upbraided° forfeits thanks. *Ingratitude*
I prithee, Salome, dismiss this mood.
Thou dost not know how ill it fits thy place.
My words were all intended for thy good,
To raise thine honor and to stop disgrace.

SALOME To stop disgrace? Take thou no care for me.
Nay, do thy worst! Thy worst I set not by.° *utterly disregard*
No shame of mine is like° to light on thee. *likely*
Thy love and admonitions I defy!
Thou shalt no hour longer call me wife;
Thy jealousy procures my hate so deep
That I from thee do mean to free my life
By a divorcing bill before I sleep.

CONSTABARUS Are Hebrew women now transformed to men?
Why do you not as well our battles fight,
And wear our armor? Suffer° this, and then *Permit*
Let all the world be topsy-turvèd quite!
Let fishes graze, beasts swim, and birds descend;
Let fire burn downwards whilst the earth aspires;° *ascends*
Let winter's heat and summer's cold offend;
Let thistles grow on vines, and grapes on briars!
Set us° to spin or sow, or at the best *us men*
Make us wood-hewers, water-bearing wights!° *persons, creatures*
For sacred service let us take no rest!
Use us as Joshua did the Gibeonites![3]

SALOME Hold on your talk, till it be time to end.[4]
For° me, I am resolved it shall be so. *As for*
Though I be first that to this course° do bend, *(divorcing a husband)*
I shall not be the last, full well I know.

CONSTABARUS Why, then, be witness, heav'n, the judge of sins;
Be witness, spirits that eschew the dark;
Be witness, angels; witness, cherubins,
Whose semblance sits upon the Holy Ark;° *the Ark of the Covenant*
Be witness, earth; be witness, Palestine;
Be witness, David's city,° if my heart *Jerusalem*
Did ever merit such an act of thine,
Or if the fault be mine that makes us part!
Since mildest Moses, friend unto the Lord,
Did work his wonders in the land of Ham° *Egypt*

1. Because you did not order the execution of Babas's two sons. (See 1.4.55–56 and note.)
2. May my habitual practice of calm teach me to control my anger!
3. Deny us the Sabbath as a day of rest! Enslave us! (See the Book of Joshua, where the Gibeonites are made bondsmen to Joshua and forced to be hewers of wood and drawers of water in Joshua's campaign to lead the Israelites back to the Holy Land.)
4. Keep on talking till you're finished.

And slew the firstborn babes without a sword—
In sign whereof we eat the Holy Lamb,[5]
Till now that fourteen hundred years are past
Since first the law° with us hath been in force— *Mosaic law*
You are the first, and will, I hope, be last
That ever sought her husband to divorce.

SALOME I mean not to be led by precedent.
My will shall be to me instead of law.

CONSTABARUS I fear me much you will too late repent
That you have ever lived so void of awe.° *respect for divine law*
This is Silleus' love that makes you thus
Reverse all order; you must next be his.
But if my thoughts aright the cause discuss,° *surmise correctly*
In winning you he gains no lasting bliss.
I was Silleus,° and not long ago *in Silleus' situation*
Josephus then was Constabarus now;
When you became my friend,° you proved his° foe, *lover / (Josephus')*
As now for him° you break to me your vow. *(Silleus)*

SALOME If once I loved you, greater is your debt;
For certain 'tis that you deserved it not,
And undeservèd love we soon forget,
And therefore that to me can be no blot.° *hindrance; disgrace*
But now fare ill,° my once-belovèd lord, *(instead of "farewell")*
Yet never more beloved than now abhorred. [*Exit.*]

CONSTABARUS Yet Constabarus biddeth thee farewell.
Farewell, light creature. Heaven forgive thy sin!
My prophesying spirit doth foretell
Thy wavering thoughts do yet but new begin.[6]
Yet I have better scaped than Joseph° did; *Josephus*
But if our Herod's death had been delayed,
The valiant youths° that I so long have hid *(Babas's sons; 1.4.55–56)*
Had been by her, and I for them, betrayed.
Therefore in happy hour did Caesar° give *Octavian*
The fatal blow to wanton Antony,
For, had he lived, our Herod then should live;
But great Antonius' death made Herod die.° *(see Argument 26–28 and n)*
Had he enjoyed his breath,° not I alone *continued to live*
Had been in danger of a deadly fall,
But Mariam had the way of peril gone,
Though by the tyrant most beloved of all—
The sweet-faced Mariam, as free from guilt
As heaven from spots, yet had her lord come back
Her purest blood had been unjustly spilt,
And Salome it was would work her wrack.[7]
Though all Judaea yield her° innocent, *grant Mariam to be*
She often hath been near to punishment. [*Exit.*]

5. To rescue the Israelites from captivity in Egypt, the Lord had Moses perform miracles to show the might of their God and sent ten plagues to force Pharaoh to let them go out of Egypt, the last of which "smote all the firstborn in the land of Egypt," including Pharaoh's own eldest child, but passed over the houses of the Israelites (see Exodus 11–12). In commemoration, Jews celebrate Passover each year, a time when they traditionally eat the Passover lamb ("the Holy Lamb").

6. I prophesy that your inconstancies will continue.

7. And Salome is the one who would have brought about Mariam's destruction.

1 Chorus

CHORUS Those minds that wholly dote upon delight,
Except° they only joy in inward good, *Unless*
Still hope at last to hop upon the right,[1]
And so from sand they leap in loathsome mud.
Fond° wretches, seeking what they cannot find, *Foolish*
For no content attends a wavering mind.

If wealth they do desire, and wealth attain,
Then wondrous fain° would they to honor leap. *gladly*
If mean° degree they do in honor gain, *moderate*
They would but wish a little higher step.
Thus step to step and wealth to wealth they add,
Yet cannot all their plenty make them glad.

Yet oft we see that some in humble state
Are cheerful, pleasant, happy, and content,
When those indeed that are of higher state
With vain additions do their thoughts torment.
Th'one would to his mind his fortune bind;
Th'other to his fortune frames his mind.[2]

To wish variety is sign of grief;
For if you like your state as now it is,
Why should an alteration bring relief?
Nay, change would then be feared as loss of bliss.
That man is only happy in his fate
That is delighted in a settled state.

Still Mariam wished she from her lord were free,
For expectation of variety;[3]
Yet, now she sees her wishes prosperous be,° *wishes are fulfilled*
She grieves because her lord so soon did die.
Who can those vast imaginations feed
Where in a property contempt doth breed?[4]

Were Herod now perchance to live again,
She would again as much be grieved at that.
All that she may,° she ever doth disdain; *All Mariam can attain*
Her wishes guide her to she knows not what.
And sad must be their looks, their honor sour,
That care for nothing being in their power.° *that they can achieve*

1 Chorus.
1. Such minds hope continually to leap upward toward better fortune.
2. The fool makes good fortune an essential condition of happiness; the wise person accepts what Fortune has brought.
3. I.e., In hopes that Herod's death would change things for the better.
4. When achievement of one's wish breeds contempt for it and desire for more?

2.1

[Enter] Pheroras and Graphina.

PHEROROS 'Tis true, Graphina, now the time draws nigh
Wherein the holy priest with hallowed rite
The happy long-desirèd knot shall tie,
Pheroras and Graphina to unite.
How oft have I with lifted hands implored
This blessèd hour, till now implored in vain,
Which hath my wishèd liberty restored,
And made my subject self my own again![1]
Thy love, fair maid, upon mine eye doth sit,
Whose nature hot doth dry the moisture all,
Which were, in nature and in reason, fit
For my monarchal brother's death to fall.[2]
Had Herod lived, he would have plucked my hand
From fair Graphina's palm perforce, and tied
The same in hateful and despisèd band,° *marriage bands*
For I had had° a baby to my bride.[3] *would have had*
Scarce can her infant tongue with easy voice
Her name distinguish° to another's ear; *make distinct*
Yet had he lived, his power and not my choice
Had made me solemnly the contract swear.
Have I not cause in such a change to joy?
What though she be my niece, a princess born?
Near blood's without respect, high birth a toy,
Since love can teach us blood and kindred's scorn.[4]
What booted it° that he did raise my head *What benefit was it*
To be his realm's copartner, kingdom's mate?
Withal,° he kept Graphina from my bed, *With that*
More wished by me than thrice Judaea's state.
Oh, could not he be skillful judge in love
That doted so upon his Mariam's face?
He, for his passion, Doris did remove;° *divorce*
I needed not a lawful wife displace.
It could not be but he had power to judge;
But he, that never grudged a kingdom's share,[5]
This well-known happiness to me did grudge,
And meant to be therein without compare.° *unrivaled*
Else had I been his equal in love's host;° *army*
For, though the diadem on Mariam's head
Corrupt the vulgar judgments,° I will boast *Wins popular approval*
Graphina's brows° as white, her cheeks as red. *brow*
Why speaks thou not, fair creature? Move thy tongue,
For silence is a sign of discontent.
It were to both our loves too great a wrong
If now this hour do find thee sadly bent.° *inclined*

GRAPHINA Mistake me not, my lord. Too oft have I
Desired this time to come with wingèd feet

2.1.
1. And made me my own master once again!
2. My hot love for you dries up in me the tears that should naturally and reasonably fall for my brother Herod's death.
3. Out of love for Graphina, Pheroras has refused to marry the eldest of Herod's young daughters.
4. Love can teach us to scorn noble birth and kinship as mere frivolities.
5. Undoubtedly Herod had the royal authority to act as he did; but he, who willingly made me copartner in power.

To be enwrapped with grief when 'tis too nigh.° *so near*
You know my wishes ever yours did meet.° *concur with*
If I be silent, 'tis no more but fear
That I should say too little° when I speak; *talk idly*
But since you will my imperfections bear,
In spite of doubt I will my silence break.
Yet might amazement° tie my moving tongue, *bewilderment*
But that I know before° Pheroras' mind. *beforehand*
I have admirèd° your affection long, *wondered at*
And cannot yet therein a reason find.
Your hand hath lifted me from lowest state
To highest eminency, wondrous grace,
And me, your handmaid, have you made your mate,
Though all but you alone do count me base.
You have preserved me pure° at my request, *a virgin*
Though you so weak a vassal might constrain
To yield to your high will. Then, last not best,° *not least*
In my respect a princess you disdain.
Then need not all these favors study crave,
To be requited by a simple maid?[6]
And study still, you know, must silence have.
Then be my cause for silence justly weighed.° *considered, understood*
But study cannot boot,° nor I requite, *avail*
Except° your lowly handmaid's steadfast love *Unless*
And fast° obedience may your mind delight; *firm*
I will not promise more than I can prove.° *demonstrate, manifest*

PHERORAS That study needs not.° Let Graphina smile, *is unnecessary*
And I desire no greater recompense.
I cannot vaunt me° in a glorious style, *sing boastful praises*
Nor show my love in far-fetched eloquence;
But this believe me: never Herod's heart
Hath held his prince-born beauty-famèd wife
In nearer place than thou, fair virgin, art
To him that holds thee glory of his life.
Should Herod's body leave the sepulchre
And entertain the severed ghost again,° *rejoin body and soul*
He should not be my nuptial hinderer,
Except he hindered it with dying pain.[7]
Come, fair Graphina, let us go in state,
This wish-endearèd° time to celebrate. [*Exeunt.*] *made precious by wishing*

2.2

[*Enter*] *Constabarus and Babas's Sons.*

BABAS'S FIRST SON Now, valiant friend, you have our lives redeemed,
Which lives, as saved by you, to you are due.
Command and you shall see yourself esteemed;
Our lives and liberties belong to you.
This twice six years, with hazard of your life,
You have concealed us from the tyrant's sword;
Though cruel Herod's sister were your wife,

6. Don't all these favors that you do me require ("crave") that I make an effort ("study") to requite them?

7. Unless he paid with his life for the attempt, or killed me.
2.2.

You durst, in scorn of fear, this grace afford.
In recompense we know not what to say;
A poor reward were thanks for such a merit.[1]
Our truest friendship at your feet we lay,
The best requital to a noble spirit.
CONSTABARUS Oh, how you wrong our friendship, valiant youth!
With friends there is not such a word as "debt";
Where amity is tied with bond of truth,° — *troth, fidelity*
All benefits are there in common set.[2]
Then is the golden age with them renewed;[3]
All names of properties° are banished quite; — *exclusive ownerships*
Division and distinction are eschewed;
Each hath to what belongs to others right.[4]
And 'tis not, sure, so full a benefit
Freely to give as freely to require.
A bounteous act hath glory following it;
They cause the glory that the act desire.[5]
All friendship should the pattern imitate
Of Jesse's son and valiant Jonathan,
For neither sovereign's nor father's hate
A friendship fixed on virtue sever can.[6]
Too much° of this; 'tis written in the heart, — *I've spoken too much*
And needs no amplifying with the tongue.
Now may you from your living tomb° depart, — *your secret hiding*
Where Herod's life hath kept you overlong—
Too great an injury to a noble mind,
To be quick buried;° you had purchased° fame — *buried alive / acquired*
Some years ago, but that you were confined,
While thousand meaner° did advance their name. — *of lesser worth*
Your best of life, the prime of all your years,
Your time of action, is from you bereft.
Twelve winters have you overpassed in fears;
Yet if you use it well, enough is left.
And who can doubt but you will use it well?
The sons of Babas have it by descent° — *heredity*
In all their thoughts each action to excel,
Boldly to act, and wisely to invent.° — *plan*
BABAS'S SECOND SON Had it not like the hateful cuckoo been,
Whose riper age his infant nurse doth kill,
So long we had not kept ourselves unseen;[7]
But Constabarus safely° crossed our will. — *desiring safety for us*
For, had the tyrant fixed his cruel eye
On our concealèd faces, wrath had swayed
His justice so that he had forced us die.
And dearer price than life we should have paid,

1. Mere thanks would be a poor reward for such goodness.
2. Among friends, all is held in common.
3. In the golden age, or first and best age of the world, as described by Ovid in *Metamorphoses*, Book 1, all things were held in common.
4. Each person has a right to whatever belongs to others.
5. It is no less important, surely, to know how to receive a gift graciously than to be the giver. An act of generosity reaps a benefit to the giver of being honored for his act; hence the need of the recipient is a cause of that honor. (See Seneca, *De Beneficiis*.)
6. Although King Saul sought to kill David (Jesse's son), the friendship between the King's son, Jonathan, and David remained strong (see 1 Samuel 18–19).
7. Babas's Second Son insists that if it would not have seemed ungrateful on their part in return for Constabarus' concealment of them, they would have disobeyed him by leaving. (The cuckoo lays its eggs in other birds' nests, and when the eggs hatch, the larger and more aggressive cuckoo chicks beat out the invaded chicks for survival; though they do not actually kill the parent birds, they do in effect kill their offspring.)

For you, our truest friend, had fall'n with us,
And we, much like a house on pillars set,
Had clean depressed our prop; and therefore thus
Our ready will with our concealment met.[8]
But now that you, fair lord, are dangerless,
The sons of Babas shall their rigor° show, *unyielding honor*
And prove it was not baseness did° oppress *that did*
Our hearts so long, but honor° kept them low. *duty (to Constabarus)*

BABAS'S FIRST SON Yet do I fear this tale of Herod's death
At last will prove a very tale indeed;
It gives me strongly in my mind,° his breath *I have a presentiment*
Will be preserved to make a number° bleed. *many people*
I wish not therefore to be set at large;
Yet peril to myself I do not fear.
Let us for some days longer be your charge,° *be under your protection*
Till we of Herod's state the truth do hear.

CONSTABARUS What, art thou turned a coward, noble youth,
That thou begin'st to doubt undoubted truth?

BABAS'S FIRST SON Were it my brother's tongue that cast this doubt,
I from his heart would have the question out
With this keen falchion!° But 'tis you, my lord, *curved broadsword*
Against whose head I must not lift a sword,
I am so tied in gratitude.

CONSTABARUS Believe
You have no cause to take it ill;
If any word of mine your heart did grieve,
The word dissented from the speaker's will.
I know it was not fear the doubt begun,
But rather valor and your care of me;
A coward could not be your father's son.
Yet know I doubts unnecessary be;
For who can think that in Antonius' fall,
Herod, his bosom friend, should scape unbruised?° *(see Argument 26–28 and n)*
Then, Caesar, we might thee an idiot call,
If thou by him° shouldst be so far abused.° *(Herod) / deceived*

BABAS'S SECOND SON Lord Constabarus, let me tell you this:
Upon submission Caesar will forgive.
And therefore, though the tyrant° did amiss, *(Herod)*
It may fall out that he° will let him live. *(Octavianus)*
Not many years agone it is since I,
Directed thither by my father's care,
In famous Rome for twice twelve months did lie,° *reside*
My life from Hebrews' cruelty to spare.
There, though I were but yet of boyish age,
I bent mine eye to mark, mine ears to hear,
Where I did see Octavius, then a page,
When first he did to Julius' sight appear.[9]
Methought I saw such mildness in his face,
And such a sweetness in his looks did grow,
Withal commixed with so majestic grace,

8. We would have utterly ruined the person on whom we have relied—Constabarus; therefore we readily consented to our concealment.

9. Octavius was Julius Caesar's great-nephew; when Octavius was a boy, Julius Caesar took great interest in him and made him his heir (whereupon he became Caesar Octavianus or Octavian).

His phys'nomy° his fortune did foreshow.° *face / prefigure*
For this I am indebted to mine eye,
But then mine ear received more evidence;
By that I knew his love to clemency,
How he with hottest choler could dispense.
CONSTABARUS But we have more than barely heard the news.[1]
It hath been twice confirmed. And though some tongue
Might be so false with false report t'abuse,
A false report hath never lasted long.
But be it so° that Herod have his life, *if it were so*
Concealment would not then a whit avail;
For certain 'tis that she that was my wife
Would not to set her accusation fail.[2]
And therefore now as good the venture give[3]
And free ourselves from blot of cowardice
As show a pitiful desire to live;
For who can pity but they must despise?[4]
BABAS'S FIRST SON I yield, but to necessity I yield.
I dare upon this doubt engage mine arm[5]
That Herod shall again this kingdom wield,
And prove his death to be a false alarm.
BABAS'S SECOND SON I doubt° it, too. God grant it be an error! *suspect, fear*
'Tis best without a cause to be in terror.[6]
And rather had I, though my soul be mine,
My soul should lie than prove a true divine.[7]
CONSTABARUS Come, come, let Fear go seek a dastard's° nest! *coward's*
Undaunted courage lies in noble breast. [*Exeunt*.]

2.3

[*Enter*] *Doris and Antipater.*

DORIS You royal buildings, bow your lofty side,° *sides, walls*
And stoop to her that is by right your queen!
Let your humility upbraid the pride
Of those in whom no due respect is seen![1]
Nine times have we with trumpets' haughty sound,
And banishing sour leaven from our taste,
Observed the feast that takes the fruit from ground,
Since I, fair city, did behold thee last.[2]
So long° it is since Mariam's purer cheek *i.e., Nine years*
Did rob from mine the glory, and so long
Since I returned my native town to seek,
And with me nothing but the sense of wrong.
And thee, my boy, whose birth, though great it were,
Yet have thy after-fortunes proved but poor.

1. But we have heard more than a single report of Herod's death.
2. Salome would not fail to press her accusation against us.
3. We might just as well take our chances now.
4. Pity breeds contempt. (Proverbial.)
5. (1) I'll bet my strong right arm I'm right; (2) I dare risk engagement despite my doubts.
6. It's best to fear the worst.
7. I'd rather be proved a liar, at peril to my soul, than be proved a true prophet in this.

2.3.
1. May you be humbled in such a way as to chastise the pride of arrogant persons (like Herod and Mariam)!
2. Doris complains that she has been banished from Jerusalem for nine years, while the trumpet has yearly proclaimed feasts bidding the Israelites to partake of the Passover lamb and to offer to God their firstfruits, or the earliest produce of the season. ("Sour leaven" refers to the yeast that is absent from the unleavened bread of the Passover meal.)

When thou wert born, how little did I fear
Thou shouldst be thrust from forth thy father's door!
Art thou not Herod's right-begotten son?
Was not the hapless Doris Herod's wife?
Yes, ere he had the Hebrew kingdom won,
I was companion to his private life.
Was I not fair enough to be a queen?
Why, ere thou wert to me, false monarch, tied,° *married*
My lack of beauty might as well be seen
As after I had lived five years thy bride.
Yet then° thine oaths came pouring like the rain, *(when Herod wooed)*
Which all affirmed my face without compare,
And that, if thou mightst Doris' love obtain,
For all the world besides thou didst not care.
Then was I young, and rich, and nobly born,
And therefore worthy to be Herod's mate;
Yet thou, ungrateful, cast me off with scorn,
When heaven's purpose raised your meaner fate.° *raised you from lowness*
Oft have I begged for vengeance for this fact,° *deed*
And with dejected° knees, aspiring hands, *bowed, humbled*
Have prayed the highest power to enact
The fall of her that on my trophy stands.[3]
Revenge I have according to my will,
Yet where I wished, this vengeance did not light;
I wished it should high-hearted Mariam kill,
But it against my whilom lord° did fight. *former husband (Herod)*
With thee, sweet boy, I came, and came to try
If thou before his bastards might be placed
In Herod's royal seat and dignity.
But Mariam's infants here are only graced,° *alone are graced*
And now for us there doth no hope remain.
Yet we will not return till Herod's end
Be more confirmed. Perchance he is not slain;
So° glorious fortunes may my boy attend. *In that case*
For if he live, he'll think it doth suffice
That he to Doris shows such cruelty,
For, as he did my wretched life despise,
So do I know I shall despisèd die.
Let him but prove as natural to thee
As cruel to thy miserable mother,
His cruelty shall not upbraided be
But in thy fortunes. I his faults will smother.[4]

ANTIPATER Each mouth within the city loudly cries
That Herod's death is certain. Therefore we
Had best some subtle hidden plot devise,
That Mariam's children might subverted be
By poisoned drink or else by murderous knife.
So we may be advanced, it skills not° how. *doesn't matter*
They are but bastards; you were Herod's wife,
And foul adultery blotteth Mariam's brow.

3. I have prayed for the fall of her (Mariam) who rises up on the spoils of my ruin.

4. I will upbraid him only for his treatment of you if he fails to give you your due. I'll forgive his wrongs to me.

DORIS They are too strong to be by us removed,
Or else Revenge's foulest spotted face
By our detested wrongs might be approved.[5]
But weakness must to greater power give place.
But let us now retire to grieve alone,
For solitariness best fitteth moan. [*Exeunt.*]

2.4

[*Enter*] *Silleus and Constabarus* [*meeting*].

SILLEUS Well met, Judaean lord, the only wight° *person*
Silleus wished to see! I am to call
Thy tongue to strict account.
CONSTABARUS For what despite?
I ready am to hear and answer all.
But if directly at the cause I guess
That breeds this challenge, you must pardon me,° *excuse me from fighting*
And now some other ground of fight profess,
For I have vowed; vows must unbroken be.
SILLEUS What may be your exception? Let me know.
CONSTABARUS Why, aught concerning Salome. My sword
Shall not be wielded for a cause so low;
A blow for her my arm will scorn t'afford.
SILLEUS It° is for slandering her unspotted name; *(My cause of challenge)*
And I will make thee, in thy vow's despite,
Suck up the breath that did my mistress blame,
And swallow it again to do her right.
CONSTABARUS I prithee, give some other quarrel ground
To find beginning. Rail against my name,
Or strike me first, or let some scarlet wound
Inflame my courage; give me words of shame;
Do thou our Moses' sacred laws disgrace;
Deprave our nation, do me some despite.
I'm apt enough to fight in any case,
But yet for Salome I will not fight.
SILLEUS Nor I for aught but Salome. My sword,
That owes his° service to her sacred name, *its*
Will not an edge for other cause afford;
In other fight I am not sure of fame.
CONSTABARUS For° her, I pity thee enough already; *As for, regarding*
For her, I therefore will not mangle thee.
A woman with a heart so most unsteady
Will of herself sufficient torture be.
I cannot envy for so light a gain,
Her mind with such unconstancy doth run;
As with a word thou didst her love obtain,
So with a word she will from thee be won.
So light as her possessions for most day
Is her affections lost; to me 'tis known;[1]
As good go hold the wind as make her stay;

5. Or else our taking dire revenge could be justified by the detestable wrongs done to us.

2.4.

1. Her affections are as lightly lost as possessions held for a day only; I'm all too familiar with that.

She never loves but till she call her own.[2]
She merely is a painted sepulchre,
That is both fair and vilely foul at once;
Though on her outside graces garnish her,
Her mind is filled with worse than rotten bones,
And ever ready lifted is her hand
To aim destruction at a husband's throat.
For proofs Josephus and myself do stand,
Though once on both of us she seemed to dote.
Her mouth, though serpentlike it never hisses,
Yet, like a serpent, poisons where it kisses.

SILLEUS Well, Hebrew, well, thou bark'st, but wilt not bite.

CONSTABARUS I tell thee still, for her I will not fight.

SILLEUS Why, then, I call thee coward.

CONSTABARUS From my heart
I give thee thanks. A coward's hateful name
Cannot to valiant minds a blot impart,
And therefore I with joy receive the same.
Thou know'st I am no coward. Thou wert by° *[nearby]*
At the Arabian battle th'other day,
And saw'st my sword with daring valiancy
Amongst the faint Arabians cut my way.
The blood of foes no more could let it shine,[3]
And 'twas enamelèd with some of thine.
But now, have at thee!° Not for Salome *[defend yourself!]*
I fight, but to discharge° a coward's style.° *[be rid of / name]*
Here 'gins the fight that shall not parted be
Before a soul or two endure exile.° [*They fight.*] *[separation from body]*

SILLEUS Thy sword hath made some windows for my blood,
To show a horrid crimson phys'nomy.° *[countenance]*
To breathe,° for both of us methinks 'twere good; *[pause]*
The day will give us time enough to die.

CONSTABARUS With all my heart, take breath. Thou shalt have time,
And, if thou list,° a twelvemonth. Let us end. *[prefer]*
Into thy cheeks there doth a paleness climb;
Thou canst not from my sword thyself defend.
What needest thou for Salome to fight?
Thou hast her, and mayst keep her; none strives for her.
I willingly to thee resign my right,
For in my very soul I do abhor her.
Thou see'st that I am fresh, unwounded yet;
Then not for fear I do this offer make.
Thou art, with loss of blood, to fight unfit,
For here is one, and there another take.[4]

SILLEUS I will not leave, as long as breath remains
Within my wounded body. Spare your words.° *[Shut up]*
My heart, in blood's stead, courage entertains;[5]
Salome's love no place for fear affords.

CONSTABARUS Oh, could thy soul but prophesy like mine,
I would not wonder thou shouldst long to die!

2. She loves only where she rules.
3. My sword was so covered with enemies' blood that one could not see the shine of the metal.
4. For here (on your body) is one wound, and there you will receive another in the give and take of combat (if we continue to fight).
5. Though short of blood, my heart is sustained by courage.

For Salome, if I aright° divine, — *correctly*
Will be than death a greater misery.
SILLEUS Then list:° I'll breathe° no longer. — *hear me / pause*
CONSTABARUS Do thy will.
I hateless fight, and charitably kill.
They fight. [*Silleus falls.*]
Ay, ay,
Pity° thyself, Silleus. Let not death — *Spare, save*
Intrude before his time into thy heart!—
Alas, it is too late, I fear; his breath
Is from his body now about to part.—
How far'st thou, brave Arabian?
SILLEUS Very well;
My leg is hurt, I can no longer fight.
It only grieves me that so soon I fell,
Before fair Salom's wrongs I came to right.° — *avenge*
CONSTABARUS Thy wounds are less than mortal. Never fear;
Thou shalt a safe and quick recovery find.
Come, I will thee unto my lodging bear;
I hate thy body, but I love thy mind.
SILLEUS Thanks, noble Jew. I see a courteous foe.
Stern enmity to friendship can no art.[6]
Had not my heart and tongue engaged me so,
I would from thee no foe, but friend, depart.
My heart to Salome is tied too fast
To leave her love for friendship; yet my skill
Shall be employed to make your favor last,° — *retain your good graces*
And I will honor Constabarus still.° — *always*
CONSTABARUS I ope my bosom to thee, and will take
Thee in, as friend, and grieve for thy complaint.° — *wounds*
But if we do not expedition make,° — *make haste*
Thy loss of blood, I fear, will make thee faint.
[*Exeunt, Constabarus helping Silleus.*]

2 Chorus

CHORUS To hear a tale with ears prejudicate,° — *prejudiced*
It spoils the judgment and corrupts the sense.
That human error, given to every state,° — *human condition*
Is greater enemy to innocence.[1]
It makes us foolish, heady, rash, unjust;
It makes us never try before we trust.[2]

It will confound the meaning, change the words,
For it our sense of hearing much deceives.
Besides, no time to judgment it affords
To weigh the circumstance our ear receives.
The ground of accidents° it never tries,° — *appearances / tests*
But makes us take for truth ten thousand lies.

6. I.e., Enmity cannot compare with friendship's transcendent power. ("To" means "compared to"; "can no art" means "knows no skill.")
2 Chorus.
1. Is especially severe in those who are naive.
2. It prompts us to fail to test our conclusions before we rely on them.

Our ears and hearts are apt to hold for good
That° we ourselves do most desire to be, *That which*
And then we drown objections in the flood
Of partiality. 'Tis that we see
  That makes false rumors long with credit passed,° *long accepted*
  Though they, like rumors, must conclude° at last. *die away*

The greatest part of us, prejudicate,
With wishing Herod's death do hold it true;[3]
The being once deluded doth not bate
The credit to a better likelihood due.[4]
  Those few that wish it not, the multitude
  Do carry headlong, so they doubts conclude.[5]

They not object[6] the weak uncertain ground
Whereon they° built this tale of Herod's end, *(the gullible majority)*
Whereof the author° scarcely can be found, *originator*
And all because their wishes that way bend.
  They think not of the peril that ensu'th
  If this should prove the contrary to truth.

On this same doubt,° on this so light a breath, *doubtful rumor*
They pawn their lives and fortunes, for they all
Behave them as the news of Herod's death
They did of most undoubted credit call.[7]
  But if their actions now do rightly hit,
  Let them commend their fortune, not their wit.[8]

3.1

[*Enter*] *Pheroras* [*and*] *Salome.*

PHERORAS Urge me no more Graphina to forsake.
Not twelve hours since I married her for love,
And do you think a sister's power can make
A resolute decree so soon remove?° *cancel itself*
SALOME Poor minds they are that honor not affects.[1]
PHERORAS Who° hunts for honor, happiness neglects. *Whoever*
SALOME You might have been both of felicity
And honor too in equal measure seized.° *possessed*
PHERORAS It is not you can tell so well as I
What 'tis can make me happy or displeased.
SALOME To match for neither beauty nor respects° *honorable station*
One mean° of birth, but yet of meaner mind, *lowly*
A woman full of natural defects—
I wonder what your eye in her could find.
PHERORAS Mine eye found loveliness, mine ear found wit,

3. Most of us, with our minds already made up, take our wish for Herod's death as evidence that it is so.
4. Having been deluded before does not lessen ("bate") our readiness to bestow a belief that might better be given to a likelier story.
5. The gullible multitude prevails over those wise few who are not deluded by wish-fulfillment fantasies, prompting the wise few to silence their doubts.
6. Those few do not protest against.
7. The multitude act as if they believe the rumor of Herod's death as a matter of undoubted credibility.
8. If the multitude should now happen to hit the mark in this, they can thank their lucky stars, not their intelligence.

3.1.
1. They are poor-spirited wretches who do not aspire to worldly honor.

To please the one and to enchant the other.
Grace on her eye, mirth on her tongue doth sit;
In looks a child, in wisdom's house a mother.
SALOME But say you thought her fair, as none thinks else,° *no one else thinks so*
Knows not Pheroras beauty is a blast,° *brief gust; blight*
Much like this flower which today excels,
But longer than a day it will not last?
PHERORAS Her wit exceeds her beauty.
SALOME Wit may show
The way to ill as well as good, you know.
PHERORAS But wisdom is the porter° of her head, *gatekeeper*
And bars all wicked words from issuing thence.
SALOME But of a porter, better were you sped
If she against their entrance made defense.[2]
PHERORAS But wherefore comes the sacred Ananell,
That hitherward his hasty steps doth bend?° *direct*

[*Enter*] *Ananell.*

Great sacrificer, you're arrivèd well!
Ill news from holy mouth I not attend.° *do not expect*

3.2

ANANELL My lips, my son, with peaceful tidings blest,
Shall utter honey to your list'ning ear.
A word of death comes not from priestly breast;
I speak of life. In life there is no fear.
And for the news I did the heavens salute,
And filled the Temple with my thankful voice;
For though that mourning may not me pollute,[1]
At pleasing accidents° I may rejoice. *unexpected events*
PHERORAS Is Herod then revived from certain death?
SALOME What? Can your news restore my brother's breath?
ANANELL Both so, and so.° The King is safe and sound, *Both are true*
And did such grace in royal Caesar meet
That he, with larger style° than ever crowned, *greater title*
Within this hour Jerusalem will greet.
I did but come to tell you, and must back
To make preparatives for sacrifice.
I knew his death your hearts like mine did rack,[2]
Though to conceal it° proved you wise. [*Exit.*] *(your sorrow)*
SALOME How can my joy sufficiently appear?
PHERORAS A heavier tale did never pierce mine ear.
SALOME Now Salome of happiness may boast.
PHERORAS But now Pheroras is in danger most.
SALOME I shall enjoy the comfort of my life.
PHERORAS And I shall lose it, losing of my wife.

2. You would be better served if some gatekeeper were there to prevent the entrance of wicked thoughts into her head in the first place.

3.2.

1. Ananell explains that he cannot defile ("pollute") himself by mourning the death of Herod because he is a priest and Herod is not his immediate kin. See Leviticus 21.1–6, where the Lord instructs Moses to tell the priests the rules for mourning: that no priest shall be defiled for the dead among his people (by shaving his head, cutting his flesh, etc.) except when mourning one who is his near kin.

2. I knew that the news of his death tortured your hearts, as it did mine.

SALOME Joy, heart, for Constabarus shall be slain!
PHERORAS Grieve, soul, Graphina shall from me be ta'en!
SALOME Smile, cheeks, the fair Silleus shall be mine!
PHERORAS Weep, eyes, for I must with a child combine!° *marry Herod's daughter*
SALOME Well, brother, cease your moans. On one condition
I'll undertake to win the King's consent;
Graphina still shall be in your tuition,° *safekeeping*
And her with you be ne'er the less content.
PHERORAS What's the condition? Let me quickly know,
That I as quickly your command may act,
Were it to see what herbs in Ophir grow,
Or that the lofty Tyrus might be sacked.[3]
SALOME 'Tis not so hard a task. It is no more
But tell the King that Constabarus hid
The sons of Babas, done° to death before; *sentenced*
And 'tis no more than Constabarus did.
And tell him more, that we,° for Herod's sake, *I*
Not able to endure our brother's foe,° *i.e., Babas's sons*
Did with a bill° our separation make, *bill of divorce*
Though loath from Constabarus else to go.
PHERORAS Believe this tale for told.° I'll go from hence, *as good as told*
In Herod's ear the Hebrew° to deface; *(Constabarus)*
And I, that never studied eloquence,
Do mean with eloquence this tale to grace. *Exit.*
SALOME This will be Constabarus' quick dispatch,° *death sentence*
Which from my mouth would lesser credit find.
Yet shall he not decease without a match,° *companion (in death)*
For Mariam shall not linger long behind.
First, jealousy; if that avail not, fear
Shall be my minister to work her end.
A common error moves not Herod's ear,[4]
Which doth so firmly to his Mariam bend.
She shall be chargèd with so horrid crime
As Herod's fear shall turn his love to hate:
I'll make some swear that she desires to climb,
And seeks to poison him for his estate.° *crown*
I scorn that she should live my birth t'upbraid,
To call me base and hungry Edomite.
With patient show her choler I betrayed,[5]
And watched the time to be revenged by sleight.° *stratagem*
Now, tongue of mine, with scandal load her name!
Turn hers° to fountains, Herod's eyes to flame! *(Mariam's eyes)*
Yet first I will begin Pheroras' suit,
That he my earnest business may effect,
And I of Mariam will keep me mute
Till first some other doth her name detect.° *expose to scandal*
[*Seeing a man approach*] Who's there? Silleus' man?

[*Enter Silleus' Man.*]

3. Ophir, in Arabia, was legendarily famous for gold, jewels, and perfumes. Tyre ("lofty Tyrus"), on the Mediterranean just north of Israel in what is today Lebanon, was a Phoenician city of wealth and commercial importance, fortified and often attacked.
4. An ordinary slander would not persuade Herod.
5. By pretended patience I goaded Mariam into intemperate anger (in her attacks on me).

How fares your lord,
That your aspects° do bear the badge of sorrow? *look, countenance*
SILLEUS' MAN He hath the marks of Constabarus' sword,
And for a while desires your sight to borrow.° *wishes to see you*
SALOME My heavy curse the hateful sword pursue!
My heavier curse on the more hateful arm
That wounded my Silleus! But renew
Your tale again. Hath he no mortal harm?
SILLEUS' MAN No sign of danger doth in him appear,
Nor are his wounds in place of peril° seen. *in a vital organ*
He bids you be assured you need not fear;
He hopes to make you yet Arabia's queen.
SALOME Commend my heart to be Silleus' charge.[6]
Tell him my brother's sudden coming now
Will give my foot no room to walk at large,
But I will see him yet ere night, I vow. [*Exeunt.*]

3.3

[*Enter*] *Mariam and Sohemus.*

MARIAM Sohemus, tell me what the news may be
That makes your eyes so full, your cheeks so blue?° *pale*
SOHEMUS I know not how to call them.° Ill for me *(the news)*
'Tis sure they are; not so, I hope, for you.
MARIAM Oh, what? Of Herod?
SOHEMUS Herod lives.
MARIAM How! Lives? What, in some cave or forest hid?
SOHEMUS Nay, back returned with honor. Caesar gives
Him greater grace than e'er Antonius did.
MARIAM Foretell the ruin of my family;
Tell me that I shall see our city burned,
Tell me I shall a death disgraceful die;
But tell me not that Herod is returned!
SOHEMUS Be not impatient, madam; be but mild;
His love to you again will soon be bred.
MARIAM I will not to his love be reconciled!
With solemn vows I have forsworn his bed.
SOHEMUS But you must break those vows.
MARIAM I'll rather break
The heart of Mariam. Cursèd is my fate!
But speak no more to me. In vain ye speak° *urge (me)*
To live with him I so profoundly hate.
SOHEMUS Great queen, you must to me your pardon give.
Sohemus cannot now your will obey.
If your command should me to silence drive,
It were not to obey, but to betray.[1]
Reject and slight my speeches, mock my faith,° *loyalty*
Scorn my observance,° call my counsel naught; *dutiful service*
Though you regard not what Sohemus saith,
Yet will I ever freely speak my thought.

6. Tell Silleus that my heart is entirely his.
3.3.
1. If I were to obey you now by remaining silent, it would not be true obedience, but a betrayal of my deepest loyalty to you.

I fear ere long I shall fair Mariam see
In woeful state, and by herself undone.
Yet for your issue's° sake more temp'rate be; *son's (Alexander's)*
The heart by affability is won.

MARIAM And must I to my prison turn again?
Oh, now I see I was an hypocrite:
I did this morning for his death complain,° *lament*
And yet do mourn because he lives ere night.
When I his death believed, compassion wrought,° *was at work*
And was the stickler° 'twixt my heart and him; *mediator, umpire*
But now that° curtain's drawn from off my thought, *now that that*
Hate doth appear again with visage grim,
And paints the face of Herod in my heart
In horrid colors with detested look.
Then Fear would come, but Scorn doth play her part,
And saith that Scorn with Fear can never brook.[2]
I know I could enchain him with a smile,
And lead him captive with a gentle word.
I scorn my look should ever man beguile,
Or other speech than meaning to afford.[3]
Else Salome in vain might spend her wind;
In vain might Herod's mother whet her tongue;
In vain had they complotted and combined,[4]
For I could overthrow them all ere long.
Oh, what a shelter is mine innocence,
To shield me from the pangs of inward grief!
'Gainst all mishaps it is my fair defense,
And to my sorrows yields a large relief.
To be° commandress of the triple earth,[5] *Even to be*
And sit in safety from a fall secure,
To have all nations celebrate my birth,
I would not that° my spirit were° impure. *would not allow / to be*
Let my distressèd state unpitied be;
Mine innocence is hope enough for me. *Exit.*

SOHEMUS Poor guiltless queen! Oh, that my wish might place
A little temper° now about thy heart! *moderation*
Unbridled speech is Mariam's worst disgrace,° *defect*
And will endanger her without desart.° *desert, deserving*
I am in greater hazard. O'er my head
The fatal ax doth hang unsteadily;
My disobedience, once discoverèd,
Will shake it down. Sohemus so shall die.
For when the King shall find we thought his death
Had been as certain as we see his life,
And marks withal I slighted so his breath° *command*
As to preserve alive his matchless wife—
Nay, more, to give to Alexander's° hand *(Mariam's son's)*
The regal dignity, the sovereign power,
How I had yielded up at her° command *(Mariam's)*
The strength of all the city, David's Tower—

2. My fear of Herod is not as strong as my scorn of him; i.e., Scorn banishes Fear. (Scorn and Fear are personified. "Brook" means "tolerate, put up with.")

3. I scorn that my speech should suggest something other than what I mean.

4. Otherwise, if I chose to smile beguilingly at Herod, Salome and Herod's mother would inveigh against me in vain; in vain would they have plotted and conspired against me.

5. Europe, Asia, and Africa.

What more than common death may I expect,
Since I too well do know his cruelty?
'Twere death a word of Herod's to neglect;
What then to do directly contrary?[6]
Yet, life, I quit thee with a willing spirit,
And think thou couldst not better be employed;
I forfeit thee for her that more doth merit.
Ten such° were better dead than she destroyed. *Ten men like myself*
But fare thee well, chaste queen! Well may I see
The darkness palpable, and rivers part,
The sun stand still—nay, more, retorted be—
But never woman with so pure a heart.[7]
Thine eyes' grave majesty keeps all in awe,
And cuts the wings° of every loose desire; *hinders the flight*
Thy brow is table to the modest law.[8]
Yet though we dare not love, we may admire.
And if I die, it shall my soul content,
My breath in Mariam's service shall be spent. [*Exit.*]

3 Chorus

CHORUS 'Tis not enough for one that is a wife
To keep her spotless from an act of ill,
But from suspicion she should free her life,
And bare° herself of power as well as will. *strip; bar*
'Tis not so glorious for her to be free
As by her proper° self restrained to be. *own*

When she hath spacious ground to walk upon,
Why on the ridge should she desire to go?
It is no glory to forbear alone
Those things that may her honor overthrow,
But 'tis thankworthy if she will not take
All lawful liberties for honor's sake.[1]

That wife her hand against her fame° doth rear *chaste reputation*
That more than to her lord alone will give
A private word to any second ear,° *to another man*
And, though she may with reputation live,
Yet though most chaste, she doth her glory blot
And wounds her honor, though she kills it not.

When to their husbands they themselves do bind,
Do they not wholly give themselves away?

6. It would virtually be a sentencing of oneself to die if one were merely to neglect some command of Herod's; what then can one expect if one were to disobey him openly?
7. Sohemus would expect to see a darkness that can be felt, or bodies of waters parted, or the sun arrested in its course or reversed ("retorted"), as did Moses in Egypt and Joseph at Gibeon (see Exodus 10.21–22 and 14.21–22 and Joshua 10.12–14), sooner than find another woman as pure-hearted as Mariam.
8. Mariam's forehead is like a tablet on which is engraved the Mosaic law forbidding adultery.

3 Chorus.

1. It is not a special distinction for such a woman merely to forbear things that would dishonor her (such as seeking power, wealth, or sexual pleasure), but it is certainly worthy of thanks if, for her honor's sake, she refuses to take up such pursuits that are lawful albeit morally questionable.

Or give they but their body, not their mind,
Reserving that, though best, for others' prey?[2]
No, sure, their thoughts no more can be their own,° *exclusively theirs*
And therefore should to none but one° be known. *but the husband*

Then she usurps upon another's° right *(her husband's)*
That seeks to be by public language graced;° *Who seeks public acclaim*
And, though her thoughts reflect with purest light,
Her mind, if not peculiar,° is not chaste. *limited to one man*
For in a wife it is no worse to find
A common° body than a common mind. *shared; debased*

And every mind, though free from thought of ill,
That out of glory seeks a worth to show,[3]
When any's ears but one° therewith they fill, *but her husband's*
Doth in a sort° her pureness overthrow. *in a sense*
Now Mariam had (but that to this she bent)[4]
Been free from fear, as well as innocent.

4.1

Enter Herod and his attendants. [*The attendants stand aside.*]

HEROD Hail, happy city! Happy in thy store,° *plenty*
And happy that thy buildings such we see!
More happy in the Temple where w'adore,
But most of all that Mariam lives in thee!

Enter Nuntio.

Art thou returned? How fares my Mariam now?

NUNTIO She's well, my lord, and will anon be here
As you commanded. [*Exit.*]

HEROD Muffle up thy brow,
Thou day's dark taper!° Mariam will appear, *i.e., the sun*
And where she shines we need not thy dim light.
Oh, haste thy steps, rare° creature! Speed thy pace, *splendid*
And let thy presence make the day more bright,
And cheer the heart of Herod with thy face.
It is an age since I from Mariam went;
Methinks our parting was in David's days,[1]
The hours are so increased by discontent.
Deep sorrow, Joshua-like, the season stays,[2]
But when I am with Mariam, time runs on.
Her sight can make months minutes, days of weeks;
An hour is then no sooner come than gone

2. Not giving to their husbands their minds, the most noble part of them, allowing their minds to be preyed on by other men?
3. That out of desire for vainglory and fame seeks to show off its intellectual prowess.
4. If it were not for her inclination in this direction.

4.1.
1. David, the second and greatest of the kings of Israel, ruled centuries before the events of this play, which occur shortly before the birth of Jesus. Herod uses this gap of time as a hyperbolic way of expressing his sense of a long separation.
2. Herod compares his sorrowful sense of the slow passage of the seasons to the time when Joshua commanded the sun and moon to stand still for a day while the Israelites avenged themselves on the Amorites (see Joshua 10.12–14).

When in her face mine eye for wonders seeks.
You world-commanding city,° Europe's grace, *(Rome)*
Twice hath my curious eye your streets surveyed,
And I have seen the statue-fillèd place
That once if not for grief had been betrayed.[3]
I all your Roman beauties have beheld,
And seen the shows your aediles[4] did prepare;
I saw the sum of what in you excelled,
Yet saw no miracle like Mariam rare.
The fair and famous Livia, Caesar's love,
The world's commanding mistress, did I see,
Whose beauties both the world and Rome approve;
Yet, Mariam, Livia is not like to thee.
Be patient but a little while, mine eyes;
Within your compassed° limits be contained; *circumscribed*
That object straight shall your desires suffice
From which you were so long a while restrained.
How wisely Mariam doth the time delay,
Lest sudden joy my sense should suffocate!
I am prepared; thou needst no longer stay.
[*He hears someone approaching.*]
Who's there? My Mariam? More than happy fate!
Oh, no, it is Pheroras.—Welcome, brother!
[*Aside*] Now for a while I must my passion smother.

4.2

[*Enter*] *Pheroras.*

PHERORAS All health and safety wait upon° my lord, *attend*
And may you long in prosperous fortunes live
With Rome-commanding Caesar at accord,
And have all honors that the world can give!
HEROD Oh, brother, now thou speak'st not from thy heart.
No, thou hast struck a blow at Herod's love;
That cannot quickly from my memory part,
Though Salome did me to pardon move.° *urged me to pardon*
Valiant Phasaelus,[1] now to thee farewell!
Thou wert my kind and honorable brother.
Oh, hapless hour, when you self-stricken fell,
Thou father's image, glory of thy mother!
Had I desired a greater suit of thee
Than to withhold thee from a harlot's° bed, *(such as Graphina's)*
Thou wouldst have granted it; but now I see
All are not like° that in a womb are bred. *alike*
Thou wouldst not, hadst thou heard of Herod's death,
Have made his burial time thy bridal hour;
Thou wouldst with clamors, not with joyful breath,
Have showed the news to be not sweet but sour.

3. That would have been overthrown on one occasion if the outcries of the grief-stricken inhabitants had not awakened remorse on the part of the invader (?). Or "grief" perhaps should read "geese," i.e., those sacred to Juno who, according to Livy's history of Rome (5.47), saved the city by giving a noisy alarm.

4. Officials in charge of public works and games.

4.2.

1. Another of Herod's brothers, who took his own life ("self-stricken fell," line 11) when captured in Herod's war against Antigonus, hoping that Herod would live to avenge him.

PHERORAS Phasaelus' great worth, I know, did stain° *i.e., put to shame*
Pheroras' petty valor; but they° lie *(people, any persons)*
(Excepting you yourself) that dare maintain
That he did honor Herod more than I.
For what I showed,° love's power constrained me show; *demonstrated, did*
And pardon loving faults for Mariam's sake.
HEROD Mariam? Where is she?
PHERORAS Nay, I do not know,
But absent use of her fair name I make.
You have forgiven greater faults than this;
For Constabarus, that against your will
Preserved the sons of Babas, lives in bliss,
Though you commanded him the youths to kill.
HEROD Go, take a present order for his death,
And let those traitors° feel the worst of fears! *(Babas's sons)*
Now Salome will whine to beg his breath,
But I'll be deaf to prayers and blind to tears.
PHERORAS He is, my lord, from Salome divorced,
Though her affection did to leave him grieve;
Yet was she by her love to you enforced
To leave the man that would your foes relieve.
HEROD Then haste them to their death. *Exit* [*Pheroras*].
I will requite
Thee, gentle Mariam—Salome, I mean.
The thought of Mariam doth so steal my sprite,° *spirit*
My mouth from speech of her I cannot wean.

4.3

[*Enter*] *Mariam* [*dressed in black*].

And here she comes indeed.—Happily met,
My best and dearest half! What ails my dear?
Thou dost the difference° certainly forget *incongruity*
'Twixt dusky habits° and a time so clear.° *garments / fair*
MARIAM My lord, I suit my garment to my mind,
And there no cheerful colors can I find.
HEROD Is this my welcome? Have I longed so much
To see my dearest Mariam discontent?
What is't that is the cause thy heart to touch?
Oh, speak, that I thy sorrow may prevent.
Art thou not Jewry's queen, and Herod's too?
Be my commandress, be my sovereign guide;
To be by thee directed I will woo,° *solicit*
For in thy pleasure lies my highest pride.
Or if thou think Judaea's narrow bound
Too strict a limit for thy great command,
Thou shalt be empress of Arabia crowned,
For thou shalt rule and I will win the land.
I'll rob the holy David's sepulchre
To give thee wealth, if thou for wealth do care;
Thou shalt have all they did with him inter,
And I for thee will make the Temple bare.
MARIAM I neither have of power nor riches want;° *need*

4.3.

I have enough, nor do I wish for more.
Your offers to my heart no ease can grant,
Except° they could my brother's life restore. (*Unless*)
No, had you wished the wretched Mariam glad,
Or had your love to her been truly tied—
Nay, had you not desired to make her sad—
My brother nor my grandsire had not died.

HEROD Wilt thou believe no oaths to clear thy lord?° (*to exculpate me*)
How oft have I with execration° sworn! (*imprecation, oath*)
Thou art by me beloved, by me adored,
Yet are my protestations heard with scorn.
Hyrcanus plotted to deprive my head
Of this long-settled° honor that I wear, (*time-honored*)
And therefore I did justly doom him dead° (*sentence him to death*)
To rid the realm from peril, me from fear.
Yet I for Mariam's sake do so repent
The death of one whose blood she did inherit,
I wish I had a kingdom's treasure spent,
So I had ne'er expelled Hyrcanus' spirit.
. . . .° (*a line is missing*)
As I affected° that same noble youth;° (*loved / (Aristobulus)*)
In lasting infamy my name enroll
If I not mourned his death with hearty truth.° (*genuine feeling*)
Did I not show to him my earnest love
When I to him the priesthood did restore,
And did for him a living priest remove,
Which never had been done but once before?

MARIAM I know that, moved by importunity,
You made him priest, and shortly after die.

HEROD I will not speak unless to be believed.
This froward humor° will not do you good; (*peevish mood*)
It hath too much already Herod grieved
To think that you on terms of hate have stood.
Yet smile, my dearest Mariam, do but smile,
And I will all unkind conceits° exile. (*thoughts*)

MARIAM I cannot frame° disguise, nor never taught (*concoct*)
My face a look dissenting from my thought.

HEROD By heav'n, you vex me! Build° not on my love. (*Presume*)

MARIAM I will not build on so unstable ground.

HEROD Naught is so fixed but peevishness may move.[1]

MARIAM 'Tis better slightest cause than none were found.[2]

HEROD Be judge yourself if ever Herod sought
Or would be moved a cause of change to find.[3]
Yet let° your look declare a milder thought, (*if you'd let*)
My heart again you shall to Mariam bind.
How oft did I for you my mother chide,
Revile my sister and my brother rate,° (*scold*)
And tell them all my Mariam they belied!
Distrust me still if these be signs of hate.

1. No love is so fixed that it cannot be dislodged or moved to anger by the sort of peevishness you are displaying. (Herod warns that his patience is wearing thin.)

2. I.e., You needed some excuse for being angry at me, and you've found this slight one.

3. Be honest and admit that I have never stooped to finding excuses for my changes of mind.

4.4

[*Enter Butler.*]

What hast thou here?
BUTLER A drink procuring love.
The Queen desired me to deliver it.
MARIAM Did I? Some hateful practice° this will prove; *plot*
Yet can it be no worse than heavens permit.
HEROD [*to the Butler*] Confess the truth, thou wicked instrument
To her outrageous will! 'Tis poison, sure.
Tell true and thou shalt scape the punishment,
Which, if thou do conceal, thou shalt endure.
BUTLER I know not, but I doubt° it be no less. *fear*
Long since the hate of you her heart did seize.[1]
HEROD Know'st thou the cause thereof?
BUTLER My lord, I guess:
Sohemus told the tale that did displease.
HEROD Oh, heaven! Sohemus false? Go, let him die;
Stay not to suffer him to speak a word. [*Exit Butler.*]
Oh, damnèd villain! Did he falsify
The oath he swore ev'n of his own accord?
Now do I know thy falsehood, painted devil,
Thou white° enchantress. Oh, thou art so foul *fair-seeming*
That hyssop[2] cannot cleanse thee, worst of evil.
A beauteous body hides a loathsome soul.
Your love Sohemus, moved by his affection,
Though he have ever heretofore been true,° *loyal*
Did blab, forsooth, that I did give direction,
If we° were put to death, to slaughter you; *I*
And you in black revenge attended° now *awaited opportunity*
To add a murder to your breach of vow.
MARIAM Is this a dream?
HEROD Oh, heaven, that 'twere no more!
I'll give my realm to who° can prove it so. *whoever*
I would I were like any beggar poor,
So° I for false my Mariam did not know— *Provided*
Foul pith containèd in the fairest rind° *bark; exterior*
That ever graced a cedar. Oh, thine eye
Is pure as heaven, but impure thy mind,
And for impurity shall Mariam die.
Why didst thou love Sohemus?
MARIAM They can tell
That say I loved him. Mariam says not so.
HEROD Oh, cannot impudence the coals expel
That for thy love in Herod's bosom glow?[3]
It is as plain as water, and denial
Makes of thy falsehood but a greater trial.° *demonstration*
Hast thou beheld thyself, and couldst thou stain
So rare perfection?[4] Even for love of thee

4.4.
1. Hatred of you seized her heart long ago.
2. A plant used in ritual purification.
3. Is my love for you so strong that even your impudence cannot extinguish the coals of passion in my bosom?
4. If you have examined your remarkable beauty, could you stain that perfection?

I do profoundly hate thee.[5] Wert thou plain,[6]
Thou shouldst the wonder of Judaea be,
But oh, thou art not; hell itself lies hid
Beneath thy heavenly show. Yet, wert thou chaste,
Thou mightst exalt, pull down, command, forbid,
And be above the wheel of Fortune placed.
Hadst thou complotted Herod's massacre,
That so thy son a monarch might be styled,
Not half so grievous such an action were
As once to think that Mariam is defiled.
Bright workmanship of nature sullied o'er
With pitchèd° darkness, now thine end shall be: *pitch-black*
Thou shalt not live, fair fiend, to cozen° more *deceive*
With heav'nly semblance, as thou coz'ned'st me.
Yet must I love thee in despite of death,
And thou shalt die in the despite of love;
For neither shall my love prolong thy breath,
Nor shall thy loss of breath my love remove.
I might have seen thy falsehood in thy face.
Where couldst thou get thy stars that served for eyes
Except by theft? And theft is foul disgrace.
This had appeared° before, were Herod wise, *been apparent*
But I'm a sot, a very sot, no better.
My wisdom long ago a-wand'ring fell;
Thy face, encount'ring it, my wit did fetter
And made me for delight my freedom sell.
Give me my heart, false creature! 'Tis a wrong
My guiltless heart should now with thine be slain;
Thou hadst no right to lock it up so long,
And with usurper's name I Mariam stain.

Enter Butler.

Have you designed° Sohemus to his end? *consigned*

BUTLER I have, my lord.

HEROD Then call our royal guard
To do as much for Mariam. [*Butler goes to the door.*]
They° offend *(Rulers)*
Leave° ill unblamed or good without reward. *Who leave*

[*Enter soldiers.*]

Here, take her to her death.
[*The soldiers start to take her away; Herod calls to them.*]
Come back, come back!
What meant I to deprive the world of light,
To muffle Jewry in the foulest black
That ever was an opposite to white?
Why, whither would you carry her?

A SOLDIER You bade
We should conduct her to her death, my lord.

HEROD Why, sure I did not. Herod was not mad.
Why should she feel the fury of the sword?

5. It is because I love what you should be that I hate you now.

6. Even if you were unhandsome.

Oh, now the grief returns into my heart,
And pulls me piecemeal. Love and Hate do fight,
And now hath Love acquired the greater part.
Yet now hath Hate affection conquered quite,
And therefore bear her hence. And, Hebrew,° why *(Herod himself)*
Seize you with lion's paws the fairest lamb
Of all the flock? She must not, shall not, die.
Without her I most miserable am,
And with her more than most.° Away, away! *most of all*
But bear her but to prison, not to death.
[*They start to leave.*]
And is she gone indeed? [*Calling*] Stay, villains, stay!
Her looks alone preserved your sovereign's breath.
Well, let her go. But yet she shall not die;
I cannot think she meant to poison me,
But certain 'tis she lived too wantonly,
And therefore shall she nevermore be free. [*Exeunt.*]

4.5

[*Enter Butler.*]

BUTLER Foul villain, can thy pitchy-colored soul
Permit thine ear to hear her causeless doom,° *unjust sentence*
And not enforce thy tongue that tale control° *to stop that story*
That must unjustly bring her to her tomb?
Oh, Salome, thou hast thyself repaid
For all the benefits that thou hast done!
Thou art the cause I have the Queen betrayed;
Thou hast my heart to darkest falsehood won.
I am condemned! Heav'n gave me not my tongue
To slander innocents, to lie, deceive,
To be the hateful instrument to wrong,
The earth of greatest glory to bereave.
My sin ascends and doth to heav'n cry;
It is the blackest deed that ever was;
And there doth sit an angel notary
That doth record it down in leaves of brass.
Oh, how my heart doth quake! Achitophel,
Thou found'st a means thyself from shame to free;[1]
And sure my soul approves thou didst not well.
All follow some, and I will follow thee.[2] [*Exit.*]

4.6

[*Enter*] *Constabarus, Babas's Sons, and their guard.*

CONSTABARUS Now here we step our last, the way to death;
We must° not tread this way a second time. *may*
Yet let us resolutely yield our breath;
Death is the only ladder, heav'n to climb.

4.5.
1. When Absalom rejected the counsel of Achitophel (Ahithophel) to wage a rebellion against Absalom's father, David, Achitophel hanged himself (see 2 Samuel 17.23).
2. I.e., Even though my soul disapproves of suicide, I will follow your example. (Or perhaps "didst not well" in line 19 should read "didst full well" or "didest well.")
4.6.

BABAS'S FIRST SON With willing mind I could myself resign;
But yet it grieves me with a grief untold
Our death should be accompanied with thine.
Our friendship we to thee have dearly sold.° *It's cost you dear*
CONSTABARUS Still wilt thou wrong the sacred name of friend?
Then shouldst thou never style° it friendship more, *call, name*
But base mechanic traffic° that doth lend, *vulgar commerce*
Yet will be sure they° shall the debt restore. *(the debtors)*
I could with needless compliment return.° *reply*
This for thy ceremony[1] I could say:
'Tis I that made the fire your house to burn,
For, but for° me she° would not you betray. *were it not for / (Salome)*
Had not the damnèd woman sought mine end,
You had not been the subject of her hate;
You never did her hateful mind offend,
Nor could your deaths have freed her nuptial fate.
Therefore, fair friends, though you were still unborn,
Some other subtlety devised should be° *should have been*
Whereby my life, though guiltless, should be torn.
Thus have I proved 'tis you that die for me,
And therefore should I weakly° now lament. *softly, sadly*
You have but done your duties; friends should die
Alone their friends' disaster to prevent,
Though not compelled by strong necessity.[2]
But now farewell, fair city! Nevermore
Shall I behold your beauty shining bright.
Farewell, of Jewish men the worthy store,° *stock, number*
But no farewell to any female wight.
You wavering crew,° my curse to you I leave! *false-hearted women*
You had but one to give you any grace,
And you yourselves will Mariam's life bereave;
Your commonwealth doth innocency chase,[3]
You creatures made to be the human curse,
You tigers, lionesses, hungry bears,
Tear-massac'ring° hyenas! Nay, far worse, *Weeping-while-killing*
For they for prey do shed their feignèd tears,
But you will weep, you creatures cross to° good, *at odds with*
For your unquenchèd thirst of human blood.[4]
You were the angels cast from heav'n for pride,
And still do keep your angels' outward show,
But none of you are inly beautified,
For still your heav'n-depriving pride doth grow.
Did not the sins of man require a scourge,
Your place on earth had been by this withstood;° *withheld, denied*
But since a flood no more the world must purge,
You stayed in office of° a second flood. *took the place of*
You giddy creatures, sowers of debate,
You'll love today, and for no other cause
But for° you yesterday did deeply hate, *because*
You are the wreak° of order, breach of laws. *destruction*

1. In response to your courteous self-blame.
2. Friends should be willingly ready to die in support of friends.
3. Your unholy alliance of vengeful women drives out the innocent (like Mariam).
4. You savage women weep only because your thirst for human blood cannot be quenched.

Your best are foolish, froward,° wanton, vain; *perverse*
Your worst adulterous, murderous, cunning, proud,
And Salome attends the latter train,° *group*
Or rather she their leader is allowed.° *is conceded to be*
I do the sottishness of men bewail,
That do with following you enhance your pride.
'Twere better that the human race should fail
Than be by such a mischief multiplied.
Cham's servile curse to all your sex was given,
Because in Paradise you did offend;[5]
Then do we not resist the will of heaven
When on your wills like servants we attend?
You are to nothing constant but to ill;
You are with naught but wickedness endued;
Your loves are set on nothing but your will;
And thus my censure I of you conclude.
You are the least of goods, the worst of evils;
Your best are worse than men, your worst than devils.

BABAS'S SECOND SON Come, let us to our death. Are we not blest?
Our death will freedom from these creatures give,
Those trouble-quiet° sowers of unrest. *disturbing-the-peace*
And this I vow: that, had I leave to live,
I would forever lead a single life
And never venture on a devilish wife. [*Exeunt.*]

4.7

[*Enter*] *Herod and Salome.*

HEROD Nay, she shall die. Die, quoth you? That she shall.
But for the means—the means! Methinks 'tis hard
To find a means to murder her withal;
Therefore I am resolved she shall be spared.

SALOME Why? Let her be beheaded.

HEROD That were well.° *(said ironically)*
Think you that swords are miracles like you?[1]
Her skin will ev'ry curtl'ax edge refell,° *repel*
And then your enterprise you well may rue.
What if the fierce Arabian notice take
Of this your wretched weaponless estate?
They° answer, when we bid resistance make, *(The men of Jerusalem)*
That Mariam's skin their falchions° did rebate.° *swords / blunt*
Beware of this! You make a goodly hand[2]
If you of weapons do deprive our land.

SALOME Why, drown her, then.

HEROD Indeed, a sweet device.° *(said ironically)*
Why, would not ev'ry river turn her° course *its*
Rather than do her beauty prejudice,° *harm*

5. Canaan, the son of Cham, or Ham, was cursed by Noah, Ham's father, and sentenced to servitude, thus inheriting the curse that God placed on Eve (see Genesis 3.16, 9.18–27).

4.7.

1. Do you think that swords can perform miracles of beheading here, when she is proof against such attacks? (See lines 7–8. Or perhaps "miracles" should read "merciles" ["merciless"].)

2. You play your hand well. (Said ironically, meaning its opposite. Herod madly supposes, in this speech, that Mariam's magical skin would blunt the weapons of all his soldiers in their attempts to execute her, leaving Judaea defenseless.)

And be reverted to the proper° source, *to its true*
So not a drop of water should be found
In all Judaea's quondam° fertile ground? *onetime, formerly*
SALOME Then let the fire devour her.
HEROD 'Twill not be.
Flame is from her derived° into my heart. *conveyed*
Thou nursest flame; flame will not murder thee,
My fairest Mariam, fullest of desert.° *deserving*
SALOME Then let her live, for me.° *for all I care*
HEROD Nay, she shall die.
But can you live without her?
SALOME Doubt you that?
HEROD I'm sure I cannot. I beseech you, try;
I have experience, but—I know not what.
SALOME How should I try?
HEROD Why, let my love be slain;
But if we cannot live without her sight,
You'll find the means to make her breathe again,
Or else you will bereave my comfort quite.
SALOME Oh, ay, I warrant you. [*Exit.*]
HEROD What, is she gone?
And gone to bid the world be overthrown?
What, is her heart's composure hardest stone?
To what a pass are cruel women grown!

[*Enter Salome.*]

She is returned already.—Have you done?
Is't possible you can command so soon
A creature's heart to quench the flaming sun
Or from the sky to wipe away the moon?
SALOME If Mariam be the sun and moon, it is,
For I already have commanded this.
HEROD But have you seen her cheek?
SALOME A thousand times.
HEROD But did you mark it too?
SALOME Ay, very well.
HEROD What is't?
SALOME A crimson bush, that ever limes[3]
The soul whose foresight doth not much excel.° *The unwary soul*
HEROD Send word she shall not die. Her cheek a bush?
Nay, then, I see indeed you marked° it not. *saw, noted*
SALOME 'Tis very fair, but yet will never blush,
Though foul dishonors do her forehead blot.° *stain, blemish*
HEROD Then let her die. 'Tis very true indeed,
And for this fault alone shall Mariam bleed.
SALOME What fault, my lord?
HEROD What fault is't? You that ask,
If you be ignorant I know of none.
To call her back from death shall be your task.
I'm glad that she for innocent is known,° *is known to be innocent*
For on the brow of Mariam hangs a fleece° *tresses*
Whose slenderest twine is strong enough to bind

3. I.e., entraps. (Sticky birdlime was smeared on the branches of bushes to ensnare birds.)

The hearts of kings; the pride and shame of Greece,
Troy-flaming Helen's not so fairly shined.[4]
SALOME 'Tis true indeed, she lays them° out for nets *(her tresses)*
To catch the hearts that do not shun a bait.
'Tis time to speak, for Herod sure forgets
That Mariam's very tresses hide deceit.
HEROD Oh, do they so? Nay, then, you do but well;
In sooth, I thought it had been hair.
Nets call you them? Lord, how they do excel!
I never saw a net that showed° so fair. *looked*
But have you heard her speak?
SALOME You know I have.
HEROD And were you not amazed?
SALOME No, not a whit.
HEROD Then 'twas not her you heard. Her life I'll save,
For Mariam hath a world-amazing wit.
SALOME She speaks a beauteous language, but within
Her heart is false as powder;° and her tongue *gunpowder; cosmetics*
Doth but allure the auditors to sin,
And is the instrument to do you wrong.
HEROD It may be so; nay, 'tis so. She's unchaste;
Her mouth will ope to ev'ry stranger's ear.
Then let the executioner make haste,
Lest she enchant him if her words he hear.
Let him be deaf, lest she do him surprise
That shall to free her spirit be assigned.[5]
Yet what boots° deafness if he have his eyes? *avails*
Her murderer must be both deaf and blind.
For if he see, he needs must see the stars° *i.e., eyes*
That shine on either side of Mariam's face,
Whose sweet aspect will terminate the wars
Wherewith he should a soul so precious chase.° *drive from the body*
Her eyes can speak, and in their speaking move.° *persuade*
Oft did my heart with reverence receive
The world's mandates.[6] Pretty tales of love
They utter, which can human bondage weave.° *which can enslave*
But shall I let this, heaven's model, die,
Which for a small self-portraiture she° drew? *(heaven)*
Her eyes like stars, her forehead like the sky,
She is like heaven, and must be heavenly true.
SALOME Your thoughts do rave with doting on the Queen.
Her eyes are ebon-hued,° and you'll confess *ebony-colored, black*
A sable star hath been but seldom seen.
Then speak of reason more, of Mariam less.
HEROD Yourself are held a goodly creature here,
Yet so unlike my Mariam in your shape
That, when to her you have approachèd near,
Myself hath often ta'en you for an ape.
And yet you prate of beauty! Go your ways.° *Get along with you*
You are to her a sunburnt blackamoor.

4. Mariam's tresses outshine the Golden Fleece sought by Jason and the Argonauts (which included many kings of Greece) and those of Helen of Sparta, whose beauty led to the burning of Troy.

5. Lest she turn the head of the executioner who is assigned to release her soul from her body.

6. Mariam's eyes have made me, king though I be, subject to the all-powerful mandates of love to which all the world owes obedience.

Your paintings° cannot equal Mariam's praise, *cosmetic appearance*
Her nature is so rich, you are so poor.
Let her be stayed from death, for if she die,
We do we know not what to stop her breath.[7]
A world cannot another Mariam buy.
Why stay you ling'ring? Countermand her death!
SALOME Then you'll no more remember what hath passed?
Sohemus' love and hers shall be forgot?
'Tis well, in truth. That fault may be her last,
And she may mend, though yet she love you not.
HEROD Oh, God, 'tis true! Sohemus—earth and heav'n,
Why did you both conspire to make me curst,
In coz'ning° me with shows and proofs unev'n?° *deceiving / illusory*
She showed° the best, and yet did prove the worst. *looked, appeared*
Her show was such as, had our singing° king, *psalm-writing*
The holy David, Mariam's beauty seen,
The Hittite had then felt no deadly sting,
Nor Bethsabe had never been a queen.[8]
Or had his son, the wisest man of men,° *the wise Solomon*
Whose fond delight did most consist in change,° *sexual variety*
Beheld her face, he had been stayed° again; *reined in*
No creature having her can wish to range.
Had Asuerus seen my Mariam's brow,
The humble Jew, she might have walked alone;[9]
Her beauteous virtue should have stayed below,° *(among ordinary mortals)*
Whiles Mariam mounted to the Persian throne.
But what avails it all? For in the weight° *when she's sized up*
She is deceitful, light as vanity.
Oh, she was made for nothing but a bait
To train° some hapless° man to misery. *entice / unlucky*
I am the hapless man that have been trained
To endless bondage. I will see her yet.
Methinks I should discern her if she feigned;
Can human eyes be dazed by woman's wit?
Once more these eyes of mine with hers shall meet,
Before the headsman do her life bereave.
Shall I forever part from thee, my sweet,
Without the taking of my latest° leave? *last*
SALOME You had as good° resolve to save her now. *might as well*
I'll stay° her death. 'Tis well determinèd,° *halt / decided*
For sure she nevermore will break her vow;
Sohemus and Josephus both are dead.
HEROD She shall not live, nor will I see her face.
A long-healed wound a second time doth bleed.
With Joseph I remember her disgrace;[1]
A shameful end ensues° a shameful deed. *follows*
Oh, that I had not called to mind anew
The discontent of Mariam's wavering heart![2]

7. We cannot foresee the consequences of killing Mariam.
8. Uriah the Hittite, husband of Bethsabe, or Bathsheba, was sent to his death so that King David might enjoy Bethsabe's love (see 2 Samuel 11).
9. If King Ahasuerus, or Xerxes I of Persia, had beheld my beautiful Mariam, the humble Jewish maiden Esther (whom Ahasuerus favored over all his concubines and made his queen) might have led an unmarried life (see the Book of Esther).
1. I remember how she disgraced herself with Josephus.
2. The discontent I felt at Mariam's wandering affections!

'Twas you, you foul-mouthed Ate,° none but you, *goddess of fury (Salome)*
That did the thought hereof to me impart.
Hence from my sight, my black tormenter, hence!
For, hadst not thou made Herod unsecure,
I had not doubted Mariam's innocence,
But still had held her in my heart for pure.

SALOME I'll leave you to your passion. 'Tis no time
To purge me° now, though of a guiltless crime. *excuse myself*
Exit [*Salome*].

HEROD Destruction take thee! Thou hast made my heart
As heavy as revenge.—I am so dull,
Methinks I am not sensible of smart,° *stings, blows*
Though hideous horrors at my bosom pull.
My head weighs downwards.° Therefore will I go *hangs heavy*
To try if I can sleep away my woe. [*Exit*.]

4.8

[*Enter Mariam*.]

MARIAM Am I the Mariam that presumed so much,
And deemed my face must needs preserve my breath?
Ay, I it was that thought my beauty such
As it alone could countermand my death.
Now Death will teach me; he can pale as well
A cheek of roses as a cheek less bright,
And dim an eye whose shine doth most excel
As soon as one that casts a meaner° light. *ignobler*
Had not myself against myself conspired,
No plot, no adversary from without
Could Herod's love from Mariam have retired,
Or from his heart have thrust my semblance° out. *image*
The wanton queen that never loved for love,
False Cleopatra, wholly set on gain,
With all her sleights did prove,° yet vainly prove, *try*
For her° the love of Herod to obtain; *herself*
Yet her allurements, all her courtly guile,
Her smiles, her favors, and her smooth deceit
Could not my face from Herod's mind exile,
But were with him of less than little weight.
That face and person that in Asia late° *lately*
For beauty's goddess, Paphos' queen,[1] was ta'en,
That face that did captive° great Julius' fate, *take captive*
That very face that was Antonius' bane,° *undoing*
That face that to be Egypt's pride was born,
That face that all the world esteemed so rare
Did Herod hate, despise, neglect, and scorn
When with the same he Mariam's did compare.
This made that I improvidently wrought,° *This made me reckless*
And on the wager even my life did pawn,
Because I thought—and yet but truly thought—
That Herod's love could not from me be drawn.

4.8.
1. Aphrodite, or Venus, was worshiped at the shrine of Paphos, on Cyprus. See also 5.1.231.

But now, though out of time,° I plainly see *too late*
It could be drawn, though never drawn from me
Had I but with humility been graced;
As well as fair, I might have proved me wise;
But I did think, because I knew me° chaste, *myself*
One virtue for a woman might suffice.
That mind for glory of our sex might stand
Wherein humility and chastity
Doth march with equal paces, hand in hand;[2]
But one, if single seen, who setteth by?° *pays any attention*
And I had singly one. But 'tis my joy
That I was ever innocent, though sour.° *acerbic, proud*
And therefore can they but my life destroy;
My soul is free from adversaries' power.

Enter Doris.

You princes great in power, and high in birth,
Be great and high! I envy not your hap.° *fortune*
Your birth must be from dust, your power on earth;
In heav'n shall Mariam sit in Sarah's lap.[3]

DORIS I'heav'n? Your beauty cannot bring you thither.
Your soul is black and spotted, full of sin;
You in adult'ry lived nine year together,
And heav'n will never let adult'ry in.

MARIAM What art thou that dost poor Mariam pursue?
Some spirit sent to drive me to despair?
Who sees for truth that Mariam is untrue?
If fair she be, she is as chaste as fair.

DORIS I am that Doris that was once beloved,
Beloved by Herod—Herod's lawful wife.
'Twas you that Doris from his side removed,
And robbed from me the glory of my life.

MARIAM Was that adult'ry? Did not Moses say
That he° that, being matched, did deadly hate *(any man)*
Might by permission put his wife away
And take a more beloved to be his mate?

DORIS What did he hate me for? For simple truth?° *loyalty*
For bringing° beauteous babes for love to him? *bringing forth*
For riches, noble birth, or tender youth?
Or for no stain did Doris' honor dim?[4]
Oh, tell me, Mariam, tell me, if you know,
Which fault of these made Herod Doris' foe.
These thrice three years have I, with hands held up
And bowèd knees fast nailèd to the ground,
Besought for thee the dregs of that same cup,
That cup of wrath that is for sinners found;
And now thou art to drink it. Doris' curse
Upon thyself did all this while attend,
But now it shall pursue thy children worse.

2. A mind or spirit in which humility and chastity go together, hand in hand, might well stand for the glory of the feminine race.

3. Unlike those great persons who—despite their brief enjoyment of earthly power—are born out of ashes and to ashes must eventually return, Mariam hopes to be gathered into the bosom of Sarah, Abraham's loyal wife, just as men might hope to rest eternally in the bosom of Abraham (see 1.2.9–10).

4. Or did Doris's fortunes decline through no fault of hers, for no reason at all?

MARIAM [*kneeling*] Oh, Doris, now to thee my knees I bend!
That heart that never bowed to thee doth bow.
Curse not mine infants! Let it thee suffice
That heav'n doth punishment to me allow.
Thy curse is cause that guiltless Mariam dies.

DORIS Had I ten thousand tongues, and every tongue
Inflamed with poison's power and steeped in gall,
My curses would not answer° for my wrong, *compensate*
Though I in cursing thee employed them all.
Hear, thou that didst Mount Gerizim command
To be a place whereon with cause to curse![5]
Stretch thy revenging arm! Thrust forth thy hand
And plague the mother much, the children worse!
Throw flaming fire upon the baseborn heads
That were begotten in unlawful beds!
But let them live till they have sense to know
What 'tis to be in miserable state.
Then be their nearest friends their overthrow;
Attended be they by suspicious hate!
And, Mariam, I do hope this boy of mine° *(Antipater)*
Shall one day come to be the death of thine. *Exit.*

MARIAM Oh, heaven forbid! I hope the world shall see
This curse of thine shall be returned on thee.
Now, earth, farewell! Though I be yet but young,
Yet I, methinks, have known thee too too long. *Exit.*

4 Chorus

CHORUS The fairest action of our human life
Is scorning to revenge an injury;
For who° forgives without a further strife, *whoever*
His adversary's heart to him doth tie,
And 'tis a firmer conquest truly said
To win the heart than overthrow the head.[1]

If we a worthy enemy do find,
To yield to worth, it must be nobly done;[2]
But if of baser metal be his mind,
In base revenge there is no honor won.
Who would a worthy courage overthrow,
And who would wrestle with a worthless foe?

We say our hearts are great and cannot yield;
Because they cannot yield, it proves them poor.[3]
Great hearts are tasked beyond their power but seld;
The weakest lion will the loudest roar.[4]

5. Doris apostrophizes Moses, to whom God announced that the twin mountains, Gerizim and Ebal, were the places for pronouncing blessings and curses, respectively. (In Deuteronomy 11.29, the pronouncing of curses is assigned to Ebal, not, as in this passage, to Gerizim.)

4 Chorus.

1. It can truly be said that it is greater to win by love and forgiveness than by overthrowing the spirit and mind of one's enemy. (Proverbially, the noblest revenge is forgiveness.)
2. Whenever worthy enemies meet, it is a noble act to yield to superior worth; there is no base revenge in this.
3. When we stubbornly insist that our hearts must never yield, we impoverish them.
4. Truly great and generous hearts are seldom taxed beyond their power of showing magnanimity; blustering vengefulness is characteristic of the cowardly wretch.

Truth's school for certain doth this same allow:
High-heartedness° doth sometimes teach to bow. *Generosity of spirit*

A noble heart doth teach a virtuous scorn:
To scorn to owe a duty overlong,
To scorn to be for benefits forborn,[5]
To scorn to lie, to scorn to do a wrong,
To scorn to bear an injury in mind,
To scorn a freeborn heart slavelike to bind.

But if for wrongs we needs revenge must have,
Then be our vengeance of the noblest kind.
Do we his body from our fury save,
And let our hate prevail against our mind?[6]
What can 'gainst him a greater vengeance be
Than make his foe more worthy far than he?[7]

Had Mariam scorned to leave a due unpaid,
She would to Herod then have paid her love,[8]
And not have been by sullen passion swayed.
To fix her thoughts all injury above° *above revenge*
Is virtuous pride. Had Mariam thus been proud,° *virtuously proud*
Long famous life to her had been allowed.

5.1

[*Enter Nuntio.*]

NUNTIO When, sweetest friend,° did I so far offend *Mariam (not present)*
Your heavenly self that you, my fault to quit,° *repay*
Have made me now relator of your end—
The end of beauty, chastity, and wit?
Was none so hapless in the fatal place
But I, most wretched, for the Queen to choose?
'Tis certain I have some ill-boding face
That made me culled° to tell this luckless news. *picked out*
And yet no news to Herod; were° it new, *even were*
To him unhappy 't had not been at all.[1]
Yet do I long to come within his view,
That he may know his wife did guiltless fall.
And here he comes.

Enter Herod.

Your Mariam greets you well.
HEROD What? Lives my Mariam? Joy, exceeding joy!
She shall not die.
NUNTIO Heav'n doth your will repel.° *repudiate*
HEROD Oh, do not with thy words my life destroy!
I prithee, tell no dying tale. Thine eye

5. To scorn to remain too long under an obligation without repaying it, to scorn to hold back from acknowledging benefits received.
6. Do we act rightly when we save an opponent's life and yet harbor a hatred of him, to the detriment of generosity of spirit?
7. What better vengeance can we take than, as his foe, to show ourselves more worthy in spirit than he? (Again, the noblest revenge is forgiveness.)
8. If Mariam had scorned to take the revenge that was her due, she could have learned charity enough to give to Herod the marriage rites and duties she owed him.
5.1.
1. Such news would not be unwelcome to Herod.

Without thy tongue doth tell but too too much.
Yet let thy tongue's addition make me die;
Death welcome comes to him whose grief is such.

NUNTIO I went amongst the curious gazing troop° *crowd*
To see the last of her that was the best,
To see if death had heart to make her stoop,
To see the sun-admiring phoenix' nest.[2]
When there I came, upon the way I saw
The stately Mariam not debased by fear.
Her look did seem to keep the world in awe,
Yet mildly did her face this fortune bear.

HEROD Thou dost usurp my right; my tongue was framed° *created, shaped*
To be the instrument of Mariam's praise.
Yet speak. She cannot be too often famed;
All tongues suffice not her sweet name to raise.

NUNTIO But as she came she Alexandra met,
Who did her death (sweet queen) no whit bewail,
But, as if nature she did quite forget,
She did upon her daughter loudly rail.° *heap abuse*

HEROD Why stopped you not her mouth? Where had she words
To darken that that heaven made so bright?
Our sacred tongue° no epithet affords *The Hebrew language*
To call her other than the world's delight.

NUNTIO She told her that her death was too too good,
And that already she had lived too long.
She said she shamed to have a part in blood
Of her that did the princely Herod wrong.

HEROD Base pickthank° devil! Shame? 'Twas all her glory, *telltale, officious*
That she to noble Mariam was the mother.
But never shall it live in any story;
Her° name, except to infamy, I'll smother. *(Alexandra's)*
What answer did her princely daughter make?

NUNTIO She made no answer, but she looked the while
As if thereof she scarce did notice take,
Yet smiled—a dutiful though scornful smile.

HEROD Sweet creature! I that look to mind do call.
Full oft hath Herod been amazed withal.
Go on.

NUNTIO She came, unmoved,° with pleasant grace, *calm*
As if to triumph her arrival were,
In stately habit and with cheerful face;
Yet ev'ry eye was moist but Mariam's there.
When justly° opposite to me she came, *exactly*
She picked me out from all the crew;
She beckoned to me, called me by my name,
For she my name, my birth, and fortune knew.

HEROD What, did she name thee? Happy, happy man!
Wilt thou not ever love that name the better?
But what sweet tune did this fair dying swan[3]
Afford thine ear? Tell all; omit no letter.

2. The phoenix, a mythical bird of regeneration, was fabled to live for five hundred years, at which point it would build a nest and set itself afire; from the ashes either it would rise again or a new phoenix would arise, to begin the cycle over again.

3. The swan was fabled to sing only once in its lifetime, at its death.

NUNTIO "Tell thou my lord," said she—
HEROD Me? Meant she me?
Is't true? The more my shame; I was her lord.
Were I not mad, her lord I still should be;
But now her name must be by me adored.
Oh, say, what said she more? Each word she said
Shall be the food whereon my heart is fed.
NUNTIO "Tell thou my lord thou saw'st me lose my breath."
HEROD Oh, that I could that sentence now control!° *overrule*
NUNTIO "If guiltily, eternal be my death"—
HEROD I hold her chaste ev'n in my inmost soul.
NUNTIO "By three days hence, if wishes could revive,
I know himself would make me oft alive."
HEROD Three days? Three hours, three minutes, not so much,
A minute in a thousand parts divide!
My penitency for her death is such
As in the first° I wished she had not died. *the first millisecond*
But forward in thy tale.
NUNTIO Why, on she went,
And, after she some silent prayer had said,
She died as if to die she were content;
And thus to heav'n her heav'nly soul is fled.
HEROD But art thou sure there doth no life remain?
Is't possible my Mariam should be dead?
Is there no trick to make her breathe again?
NUNTIO Her body is divided from her head.
HEROD Why, yet methinks there might be found by art
Strange ways of cure. 'Tis sure rare things are done
By an inventive head and willing heart.
NUNTIO Let not, my lord, your fancies idly run.
It is as possible it should be seen
That we should make the holy Abraham live,
Though he entombed two thousand years had been,
As breath again to slaughtered Mariam give.
But now for more assaults prepare your ears.
HEROD There cannot be a further cause of moan;
This accident° shall shelter me from fears. *terrible event*
What can I fear? Already Mariam's gone.
Yet tell ev'n what you will.
NUNTIO As I came by
From Mariam's death, I saw upon a tree
A man that to his neck a cord did tie,
Which cord he had designed his end to be.
When me he once discerned, he downwards bowed,
And thus with fearful voice he cried aloud:
"Go tell the King he trusted ere he tried;[4]
I am the cause that Mariam causeless died."
HEROD Damnation take him! For it was the slave
That said she meant with poison's deadly force
To end my life, that she the crown might have;
Which tale did Mariam from herself divorce.° *(soul from body)*
Oh, pardon me, thou pure unspotted ghost!
My punishment must needs sufficient be,

4. Go tell the King he was too credulous, not testing the truth of the accusations.

In missing that content I valued most,
Which was thy admirable face to see.
I had but one inestimable jewel,
Yet one I had no° monarch had the like, *had of which no*
And therefore may I curse myself as cruel;
'Twas broken by a blow myself did strike.
I gazed thereon, and never thought me blest
But when on it my dazzled eye might rest—
A precious mirror made by wondrous art.
I prized it ten times dearer than my crown,
And laid it up fast folded in my heart;
Yet I in sudden choler cast it down
And pashed° it all to pieces. 'Twas no foe *smashed*
That robbed me of it; no Arabian host,° *army*
Nor no Armenian guide,° hath used me so, *scout, spy*
But Herod's wretched self hath Herod crossed.° *thwarted*
She was my graceful moiety.° Me accurst, *my better half*
To slay my better half and save my worst!
But sure she is not dead. You did but jest
To put me in perplexity awhile.
'Twere well indeed if I could so be 'dressed.° *put straight, rebuked*
I see she is alive; methinks you smile.

NUNTIO If sainted Abel[5] yet deceasèd be,
'Tis certain Mariam is as dead as he.

HEROD Why, then, go call her to me. Bid her now
Put on fair habit,° stately ornament, *garments*
And let no frown o'ershade her smoothest brow.
In her doth Herod place his whole content.

NUNTIO She'll come in stately weeds° to please your sense, *garments*
If now she come attired in robe of heaven.
Remember you yourself did send her hence,
And now to you she can no more be given.

HEROD She's dead. Hell take her murderers! She was fair.
Oh, what a hand she had! It was so white,
It did the whiteness of the snow impair.
I never more shall see so sweet a sight.

NUNTIO 'Tis true, her hand was rare.

HEROD Her hand? Her hands.
She had not singly one of beauty rare,
But such a pair as, here where Herod stands,
He dares the world to make to both compare.
Accursèd Salome! Hadst thou been still,° *quiet*
My Mariam had been breathing by my side.
Oh, never had I, had I had my will,
Sent forth command that Mariam should have died.
But, Salome, thou didst with envy vex° *fret*
To see thyself outmatchèd in thy sex.
Upon your sex's forehead Mariam sat,
To grace you all like an imperial crown,
But you, fond fool, have rudely pushed° thereat, *chafed; thrust*
And proudly pulled your proper° glory down. *own*
One smile of hers—nay, not so much—a look
Was worth a hundred thousand such as you.

5. Abel, saintly as the victim of Cain.

Judaea, how canst thou the wretches brook° *tolerate*
That robbed from thee the fairest of the crew?
You dwellers in the now-deprivèd land
Wherein the matchless Mariam was bred,
Why grasp not each of you a sword in hand
To aim at me, your cruel sovereign's head?
Oh, when you think of Herod as your king
And owner of the pride of Palestine,
This act to your remembrance likewise bring;
'Tis I have overthrown your royal line.
Within her purer veins the blood did run
That from her grandam Sarah° she derived, *(see 4.8.50 n)*
Whose beldame age the love of kings hath won.[6]
Oh, that her issue° had as long been lived! *grandchild (Mariam)*
But can her eye be made by death obscure?
I cannot think but it must sparkle still.
Foul sacrilege, to rob those lights so pure
From out a temple made by heav'nly skill!
I am the villain that have done the deed,
The cruel deed, though by another's hand;
My word, though not my sword, made Mariam bleed.
Hyrcanus' grandchild died at my command—
That Mariam that I once did love so dear,
The partner of my now-detested bed.
Why shine you, sun, with an aspect so clear?
I tell you once again my Mariam's dead.
You could but shine if some Egyptian blowze
Or Ethiopian dowdy lose her life;
This was—then wherefore bend you not your brows?—
The King of Jewry's fair and spotless wife.[7]
Deny thy beams, and, moon, refuse thy light!
Let all the stars be dark; let Jewry's eye
No more distinguish which is day and night,
Since her best birth did in her bosom° die. *i.e., in Judaea*
Those fond° idolaters, the men of Greece, *foolish*
Maintain these orbs are safely governèd,
That each within themselves have gods apiece,[8]
By whom their steadfast course is justly led.
But were it so—as so it cannot be—
They all would put their mourning garments on;
Not one of them would yield a light to me,
To me that is the cause that Mariam's gone.
For though they° feign their Saturn melancholy, *(the Greeks)*
Of sour behaviors and of angry mood,
They fame° him likewise to be just and holy, *repute*
And justice needs must seek revenge for blood.
Their Jove, if Jove he were, would sure desire
To punish him that slew so fair a lass,
For Leda's beauty set his heart on fire,[9]

6. Abraham's wife Sarah, even in her later years, won the admiration of Pharaoh and of Abimelech, King of Gerar (see Genesis 12.10–20 and 20).
7. Your routine daily shining would be appropriate to mark the death of some Egyptian beggarly wench or slatternly Cleopatra; you should bend your brows in an eclipse to signal the death of the beautiful and virtuous Mariam.
8. The foolish Greeks maintain that each planet is governed by a single deity.
9. Leda's beauty inspired Jove (Jupiter, Greek Zeus) to take the shape of a swan in order to ravish her.

Yet she not half so fair as Mariam was.
And Mars would deem his Venus had been slain;
Sol° to recover her would never stick,° *god of the sun / hesitate*
For, if he want° the power her life to gain, *lack*
Then physic's god is but an emperic.[1]
The queen of love would storm for beauty's sake,[2]
And Hermes° too, since he bestowed her wit. *patron of eloquence*
The night's pale light° for angry grief would shake *The moon*
To see chaste Mariam die in age unfit.° *too young*
But oh, I am deceived! She passed° them all *surpassed*
In every gift, in every property;° *quality*
Her excellencies wrought her timeless° fall, *untimely*
And they° rejoiced, not grieved, to see her die. *(the gods)*
The Paphian goddess did repent her waste
When she to one such beauty did allow;[3]
Mercurius[4] thought her wit his wit surpassed,
And Cynthia° envied Mariam's brighter brow. *Diana, the moon*
But these are fictions; they are void of sense;
The Greeks but dream, and dreaming falsehoods tell.
They° neither can offend nor give defense, *(The Greek gods)*
And not by them it was my Mariam fell.
If she had been like an Egyptian, black,
And not so fair, she had been longer lived;
Her overflow of beauty turnèd back
And drowned the spring from whence it was derived.
Her heav'nly beauty 'twas that made me think
That it with chastity could never dwell;
But now I see that heav'n in her did link
A spirit and a person° to excel. *body*
I'll muffle up myself in endless night,
And never let mine eyes behold the light.
Retire thyself, vile monster, worse than he° *(Cain)*
That stained the virgin earth with brother's blood!
Still° in some vault or den enclosèd be, *Continually*
Where with thy tears thou mayst beget a flood,
Which flood in time may drown thee—happy day,
When thou at once shalt die and find a grave!
A stone upon the vault someone shall lay,
Which monument shall an inscription have,
And these shall be the words it shall contain:
"Here Herod lies, that hath his Mariam slain." [*Exeunt.*]

5 Chorus

CHORUS Whoever hath beheld with steadfast eye
The strange events of this one only day—
How many were deceived, how many die
That once today did grounds of safety lay°— *Who felt secure*
It will from them all certainty bereave,
Since twice six hours so many can deceive.

1. Then Apollo, god of medicine (and of the sun), would be only a quack.
2. Venus would rage at the destruction of such beauty.
3. Venus (who was worshiped at the shrine of Paphos, on Cyprus) repented her own prodigality in lavishing so much beauty on Mariam.
4. Mercury (or Hermes), patron of eloquence (see line 224 above).
5 Chorus.

This morning Herod held for° surely dead, *was thought to be*
And all the Jews on Mariam did attend,
And Constabarus rise° from Salom's bed, *did rise*
And neither dreamed of a divorce or end;
  Pheroras joyed° that he might have his wife, *rejoiced*
  And Babas' sons for° safety of their life. *rejoiced for*

Tonight our Herod doth alive remain;
The guiltless Mariam is deprived of breath;
Stout° Constabarus both° divorced and slain; *Brave / is both*
The valiant sons of Babas have their death;
  Pheroras sure his love to be bereft,
  If Salome her suit unmade had left.[1]

Herod this morning did expect with joy
To see his Mariam's much-belovèd face,
And yet ere night he did her life destroy,
And surely thought she did her name disgrace.
  Yet now again so short do humors° last, *fanciful ideas*
  He both repents her death and knows her chaste.

Had he with wisdom now her death delayed,
He at his pleasure might command her death;
But now he hath his power so much betrayed
As° all his woes cannot restore her breath. *That*
  Now doth he strangely, lunaticly rave,
  Because his Mariam's life he cannot save.

This day's events were certainly ordained
To be the warning to posterity,
So many changes are therein contained,
So admirably strange variety.
  This day alone our sagest Hebrews shall
  In aftertimes the school of wisdom call.

FINIS.

1. Pheroras would surely have been deprived of his beloved (Graphina) if Salome had not petitioned Herod on Pheroras' behalf (in return for Pheroras' informing against Constabarus).

TEXTUAL NOTES

The Tragedy of Mariam was entered in the Stationers' Register on December 17, 1612, and was published the following year by Richard Hawkins. No other early text is known. The present edition is based on the quarto of 1613. Substantive departures from it are noted here, using the following abbreviations:

Q: The quarto of 1613 (London: Thomas Creede for Richard Hawkins)
Q corr.: The corrected quarto
Q uncorr.: The uncorrected quarto
ed.: A modern editor's emendation

The Names of the Speakers 5 Doris [ed.] *Salome* [Q] **11, 12 BABAS'S** [ed.] *Babus* [Q] **16 BUTLER** [Q: *Bu.*]

1.1.35 loveliest [ed.] lowlyest [Q] **44 ascent** [Q: Assent] **47 mind** [ed.] maide [Q]

1.2.3 murd'rer's [ed.] murthers [Q] **12 Judah's** [Q: *Iudas*] **12 famed** [ed.] fain'd [Q] **53 MARIAM** [ed.] *Nun*: [Q] **55 Of** [ed.] If [Q] **81 whilst** [Q: whilest] **93** [and elsewhere] **sleight** [Q: slight]

1.3.11 discontents [ed.] discontent [Q] **13 rein** [Q: raine] **47 Suspicion's** [ed.] suspitious [Q]

1.4.16 all eyes [ed.] allyes [Q] **18** [and elsewhere] **tied** [Q: tide] **38 from** [ed.] for [Q]

1.5.4 prey [Q: pray] **37 whom** [ed.] home [Q]

1.6.25 to [ed.; not in Q] **51 swim** [ed.] swine [Q] **56 water-bearing** [ed.] Waters-bearing [Q] **79 precedent** [Q: president] **90 vow** [ed.] vowd [Q]

1 Chorus [and so at 2, 3, 4, and 5 Chorus: scene heading, ed.; not in Q] **8 leap** [Q: lep] **9 If** [ed.] Of [Q]

2.1.2 rite [Q: right] **12 monarchal** [ed.] monachall [Q] **24 us** [ed.; not in Q] **73 not. Let** [ed.] not let [Q] **80 thee** [ed.] the [Q]

2.2.30 needs [ed.] need [Q] **39 overpassed** [Q: operpast] **42 Babas** [Q: *Babus*] **66 fear** [ed.] leare [Q] **87 Constabarus** [Q: *Constab:*] **93 lie** [ed.] liue [Q] **98 Julius'** [Q: *Iulions*]

2.3.1 You [ed.] Your [Q] **2 stoop** [ed.] scope [Q] **25 oaths** [ed.] oath [Q] **61 poisoned** [ed.] poisons [Q]

2.4.9 exception [ed.] expectation [Q] **10 Salome** [ed.] *Salom* [Q] **11 wielded** [Q: welded] **92.1–93** ***They fight.* / Ay, ay** [ed.] I, I, they fight [as dialogue in Q] **96 I** [ed.] to [Q] **110 too** [ed.] so [Q]

2 Chorus 3 [and elsewhere] **human** [Q: humane] **10 weigh** [Q: way] **17 passed** [Q: past]

3.1.3 can make [Q: cane mak] **8 seized** [Q: seasde] **26 bars** [Q: bares]

3.2.24 losing [Q: loosing] **37 not** [ed.] no [Q] **38** [and elsewhere] **Constabarus** [Q: *Consta:*] **41 we** [ed.] he [Q] **42 our** [ed.] his [Q] **64 sleight** [Q: slite] **81 bids** [Q: bides]

3.3.5 MARIAM [ed.] *Herod. Mari.* [Q] **6 MARIAM** [ed.; not in Q] **83 quit** [ed.] quite [Q]

3 Chorus 22 prey [Q: pray]

4.1.4.1 [placement, ed.; at end of 5 in Q] **5 now?** [ed.; not in Q] **24 grief** [Q: griefe; query "geese"?] **33 little while,** [ed.] little, while [Q] **38 Lest** [Q: Least] **40 Who's** [Q: Whose]

4.2.30 your [ed.] you [Q] **37, 42 Salome** [ed.] *Salom* [Q] **41 SD** ***Exit*** [placement, ed.; at the end of 44 in Q] **43 sprite** [ed.] spirit [Q]

4.4.6 poison [ed.] passion [Q] **10 seize** [Q: cease] **31 contained** [Q: contain'd] **46 wert** [ed.] neuer wert [Q] **56 heav'nly** [ed.] heauy [Q] **62 stars** [Q: stares] **71 lock** [ed.] looke [Q] **81 A SOLDIER** [Q: *Sould:*] **83 Why** [Q: Wie] **87 Love** [ed.] boue [Q]

4.5.2 causeless [Q: caules] **18 found'st** [Q: founds]

4.6.13 compliment [Q: complement] **14 This** [ed.] Tis [Q] **20 her** [ed.] your [Q] **23 Whereby** [ed.] Were by [Q] **47 man** [ed.] many [Q] **55 Your** [ed.] You [Q] **58 she** [ed.] he [Q] **78 venture** [Q: venter]

4.7.12 falchions [Q: fanchions] **123 Hittite** [ed.] *Hittits* [Q]

4.8.4 As [ed.] At [Q] **89 Gerizim** [ed.] *Gerarim* [Q]

4 Chorus 12 wrestle [Q: wrastle] **35 proud** [ed.] prou'd [Q]

5.1.3 your [ed.] her [Q] **6 to choose** [ed.] t'chuse [Q] **13 SD** [placement, ed.; at the end of 13 in Q] **38 darken** [ed.] darke [Q] **55 Go on. / NUNTIO She** [ed.] *Nun.* Go on, she [Q] **69 mad, her lord I** [ed.] made her Lord, *I* [Q] **80 divide** [ed.] diuided [Q] **85, 190 died** [ed.] did [Q] **108 he** [ed.] she [Q] **195 blowze** [Q: blows] **211 feign** [Q corr.: faine] fame [Q uncorr.]

Volpone

By 1606, when Ben Jonson wrote *Volpone*, English dramatists had long realized that a charismatic outlaw makes an effective protagonist. He almost automatically generates momentum, since his plots become the play's plot. He elicits a complex response from spectators, who can by turns thrill to his cunning, deplore his ferocity, tremble at his recklessness, and applaud his predictably dire end. Often such characters, aptly if nonnaturalistically, simply walk onstage as their plays begin and frankly describe themselves and their plans to the audience. These self-introductions convey as much by their form as by their content. The long, uninterrupted opening speech not only showcases the hero's rhetorical mastery but suggests, as a conversational exchange could not, his isolation, egoism, and initiative. Volpone's bravura opening speech, like the soliloquies of Shakespeare's Richard III, Barabas in Marlowe's *The Jew of Malta*, or Vindice in *The Revenger's Tragedy*, makes vividly clear to the audience what will be at stake and who will be in charge.

Volpone's initial confidences, then, testify to important aspects of his character. We notice first his metaphysical daring. He is ostentatiously blasphemous: "Open the shrine that I may see my saint" (1.1.2). By worshiping gold, Volpone deliberately commits the sin of idolatry, replacing spiritual values with material ones and substituting an immediate good for a distant, less tangible one. As the speech continues, we recognize as well his cleverly deployed erudition. Like any Renaissance humanist, Volpone freely combines Christian and classical imagery, heaven and hell with Venus and Cupid. But while such juxtapositions ordinarily emphasize the benign harmony between the traditions, Volpone slyly inverts the usual uplifting message. Faith and learning conspire to reinforce his lust for riches. For example, though Ovid had claimed that the quasi-Edenic Golden Age predated the invention of money, for Volpone its very name testifies to the prestige of his deity. Throughout the play, Volpone will evidence an acute, if narrowly focused, sense of history: he is inspired by the examples of late-imperial Rome and of voluptuous "Oriental" courts, by Cleopatra dissolving and drinking a pearl worth ten million sesterces, by the mad emperor Caligula's wife, Lollia Paulina, "When she came in like starlight, hid with jewels / That were the spoils of provinces" (3.7.195–96). Jonson was as enthusiastic as any early modern writer about the Renaissance recovery of the classical past. But he was aware, too, that the classical legacy had a dark underbelly—and that the newly wealthy states of seventeenth-century Europe might revive not merely the civilizing aspects of classical culture but its potential for cruelty and greed.

In fact, Volpone's numerous references to decadence throughout history suggest that although he prides himself on his singularity—"I gain / No common way," he boasts (1.1.32–33)—he is less a monster than a symptom. He exemplifies a culture in which riches have become not a means to an end but an end in themselves. He has amassed his treasure by pretending to be near death in order to attract gifts from would-be heirs, the "carrion birds" Voltore, Corbaccio, and Corvino. This enterprise would

Introduction, glosses, footnotes, and textual notes by Katharine Eisaman Maus; text edited by Katharine Eisaman Maus and checked, along with the textual notes, by David Bevington and Eric Rasmussen.

fail if Volpone's victims did not share his cupidity. Volpone's uniqueness consists not in his greed but in the effectiveness with which he gets what he wants.

Jonson therefore depicts Volpone's cultural environment carefully. The play refers constantly to Venice's geography, landmarks, customs, and political institutions: this is hardly the throwaway "Italian city" in which so many English Renaissance plays are set. In Jonson's time, Venice was Europe's richest city. Its geographical location and naval might allowed it to control access to trade routes between Asia and Western Europe, and as this trade burgeoned during the late Middle Ages and early modern period, Venice flourished. English tourists, such as Jonson's friend Thomas Coryate, gaped at Venice's magnificent buildings and marveled at the sumptuous taste of its aristocracy. But they were not wholeheartedly admiring. They remarked as well on the Venetians' suspicious reserve, their unscrupulousness, and their appetite for elegant vice, best symbolized by the city's famed courtesans.

Since England was rapidly becoming a major naval power and owed an increasing proportion of her wealth to international trade, Venice seemed, for better or worse, to prophesy what England might become. Jonson mocks one possible result in the pseudo-sophisticated Sir Politic Would-be, who ineptly cites Machiavelli and boasts his facility with that Italianate novelty, the fork. What if Sir Pol's shrewder fellow countrymen, newly alive to the pleasures of opulence, were to replicate as well the graver offenses of Volpone and his rapacious clientele? While in our own time we are apt to approve of "rising standards of living," in the first decades of the seventeenth century the effects of new wealth on English society hardly seemed straightforwardly benign. The gap between rich and poor, and between wastefulness and penury, yawned ever wider, even as the craving for newly available luxuries encouraged many gentlemen and aristocrats to plunge into unprecedented amounts of debt. At King James's court, banquet tables groaned under the weight of delicacies; the entire first course was merely to be looked at, then discarded. Meanwhile, in the countryside, starving peasants rioted and were brutally subdued. Preachers and moralists warned that greed endangered individuals as well social groups, subordinating human affections to money concerns and isolating people from one another by encouraging selfishness and competition.

The terms of this critique—what the critic L. C. Knights long ago called Jonson's "anti-acquisitive attitude"[1]—pervade *Volpone*. Cloistered in his own house, since he cannot even go outdoors in his own person, Volpone abandons the Venetian magnifico's traditional civic role: he has nothing to do but "cocker up my genius, and live free / To all delights my fortune calls me to" (1.1.71–72). His isolation immunizes him against the traditional social discipline of shame. What need he care for his reputation? He makes money by representing himself as diseased, physically repulsive, sexually impotent—the antithesis of the impression most people attempt to project. The gulls are likewise impervious to shame: their perjuries succeed in act 4 because the court cannot believe that anyone would confess to being the husband of a whore or the father of a parricidal debaucher unless it were true. For Jonson the satirist, the possibility of a Volpone-like withdrawal from public evaluation is dangerous, insofar as the effectiveness of satire depends on the operation of shame and the importance of reputation. At the

Stock figures in the Italian commedia dell'arte: the zany (or zanni) and the pantalone. From G. Borgetto, *The Devil's Legend* (1595).

1. L. C. Knights, *Drama and Society in the Age of Jonson* (London: Chatto and Windus, 1937).

same time, shamelessness is part of Volpone's appeal. He could not be so disarmingly explicit about his own venality if he were awed by the specter of conventional morality. Moreover, his tremendous rhetorical and theatrical gifts, which make him so compelling onstage, are amplified by his utter lack of scruple. He plays his many parts with the panache of a born liar.

Despite his emotional detachment from the community at large, at the beginning of his play, Volpone—unlike Richard III, or Barabas in *The Jew of Malta*—does not come onto the stage alone. His servant Mosca accompanies him, obsequiously drawing aside a curtain to disclose Volpone's treasure. Because Volpone's plot requires that he himself remain physically passive, Mosca needs impressive executive skills; and Mosca rises to the challenge, coordinating the entrances and exits of the gulls, managing the attempted seduction of Celia, orchestrating the elaborate group perjury of act 4, and posing as Volpone's heir for most of act 5.

In Mosca, Jonson does not naturalize class difference as his contemporary Shakespeare so often does, by making the servant character speak an "inferior" dialect or betray his lower-class origins with comically uncouth habits. Mosca is at least as articulate, as sophisticated in his tastes, and as unscrupulous as his "betters," and he is also considerably more analytical and perceptive. He revels in this gap in awareness—between what he says and what his interlocutors believe he says. His technique is baldest with the literally deaf Corbaccio:

MOSCA Your Worship is a precious ass—
CORBACCIO What say'st thou?
MOSCA I do desire Your Worship to make haste, sir.
(1.4.130–31)

But there are plenty of subtler examples. When Volpone asks to clasp the hand of his "friend" Voltore, Mosca coolly substitutes Voltore's gift: "The plate is here, sir" (1.3.15). He is especially adept at knowing precisely how openly he can vent his feelings toward Volpone without Volpone's noticing. In act 1, scene 5, Mosca bellows insults into Volpone's ears, but because he frames this assault as a trick on Corvino, Volpone fails to comprehend his real hostility. Even while he pretends to regret Volpone's beating (2.4.33–34) or his sweating with fear (5.2.37–39, 98), Mosca, with his apparently sympathetic comments, repeatedly draws attention to Volpone's physical cowardice and to the abject position this proud and wealthy man's deceptions force him to occupy. Early in act 5, when Mosca and Volpone hastily settle the terms by which they will trick the "gulls" into believing that Volpone is dead, Mosca tries to anticipate possible reactions: "But, what, sir, if they ask / After the body?" "Say it was corrupted," replies Volpone, at which point Mosca elaborates just a little too vividly: "I'll say it stunk, sir, and was fain t'have it / Coffined up instantly and sent away" (5.2.76–79). Whether we interpret these comments as symptoms of a settled hostility or merely as flashes of ambivalence, they help prepare us for the moment when, given the opportunity, this servant betrays his master. If Volpone is in some ways an earthier, more sumptuous Faustus, Mosca resembles Mephistopheles, veiling his malicious power behind a deferential facade.

The nineteenth-century German philosopher G. W. F. Hegel argues that servants possess a more highly developed consciousness than their masters because the continual requirements of submission force them to acknowledge the existence of subjectivities other than their own. Ben Jonson, a poor man of humble birth professionally dependent upon the approval of fickle theater audiences and wealthy patrons, knew this truth three hundred years before Hegel, by experience rather than theory, and also knew well that poverty could tempt one to sycophancy. Arguably, in fact, Jonson intends his truculent statements of principle in his prefatory epistle and prologue to distance him from playwrights who, like Mosca, pander to the basest wishes of their customers. Still, like his master, Mosca is depicted with a certain sympathy. Once he is dressed in a nobleman's gown, Mosca is, as the furious gulls themselves acknowledge, indistinguishable from his social superiors. What, then, is the difference between master and servant? If it is purely a matter of social convention—as was beginning to seem possible in early modern England—not an innate, ineradicable distinction between highborn and lowborn, then anyone can rise in status merely by becoming rich. In that case, however, a competitive struggle—"every man for himself"—replaces ancient virtues of loyalty and service on the part of inferiors and noblesse oblige on the part of superiors.

Jonson's own attitudes toward such social changes are complex. Jonson the political and religious conservative can see that once class and social hierarchy no longer seem identical with the laws of God and nature, the social fabric may unravel calamitously. But Jonson the entrepreneurial professional can also see that for a humbly born, talented person like himself, a system that permits social and individual mobility has distinct advantages. However much his play may seem to deplore the loss of spiritual values and traditional hierarchical relationships, it also celebrates the dangerously liberated imagination: Volpone's preference for ingenuity over dull toil, Mosca's delight in his own clever fluidity, even Sir Politic's loopy entrepreneurial schemes. At the same time, Jonson's generic choices tell against this intuition of limitless possibility. The characters' names derive from the ancient genre of the beast fable, which diagnoses human behavior in terms of animals whose nature is circumscribed and predictable. The Italian dramatic tradition of commedia dell'arte, which is several times referred to in the action of the play and which influences Jonson's conception of character and situation in *Volpone*, features stock caricatures juxtaposed in brilliantly improvisatory ways. Novelty in this tradition is the effect not of character development but of the unexpected, farcical ways in which fixed characters interact. In such a dramatic context, personal uniqueness tends to become mere grotesquerie, and the dream of improving one's lot a mere illusion.

The culture of competitive accumulation puts women in an especially disadvantageous position. When Volpone avows that gold is "the best of things, and far transcending / All style of joy in children, parents, friends" (1.1.16–17), he depreciates the reproductive functions and familial alliances from which women traditionally derived their social power. Lady Would-be reacts to the virtual disappearance of a valued female role by trying to assume a masculine one. She asserts her sexual freedom, plunges into the game of legacy-hunting, and imitates the humanist rhetorical attainments that early modern culture restricted to men. But her endeavors to seduce Volpone, Peregrine, and Mosca fail ignominiously, she can't understand classic authors, and her attempts at the arts of discourse are long-winded and ostentatious. Most significantly, she is pathetically out of her depth in the competition for Volpone's favor. She offers him not a massive platter or a huge pearl but a crocheted cap, "A toy . . . of mine own work" (3.5.15). Like her husband's, her attempts to imitate the Italians founder on a lack of intellectual and material resources.

While Lady Would-be attempts to compete with men, Celia exemplifies age-old feminine excellences: beauty, chastity, and submissiveness. Unfortunately, in Jonson's Venice these qualities hardly improve her situation. Although some critics have complained that Celia seems ineffectual, almost irrelevant, in fact she is crucial for the plot, and her conflicts with her husband and would-be seducer raise important ethical issues. While Volpone's success as a theatrical protagonist depends on his willingness to lie and his craving for things that are vividly there onstage, Celia's pallid stage presence is partly due to her principled unwillingness to display herself theatrically. Her sincerity and innocence inhibit her from modifying her own behavior to suit her audience; thus in the courtroom scene, for instance, her genuine distress is ironically misread as hypocrisy. Moreover, Celia wants intangible spiritual rewards, not sensual gratification, and as a corollary stubbornly refuses to accept what most of the other characters see as true, obvious, or desirable. Her example suggests that the theatrical medium might be to blame for overvaluing the kind of superficial display at which Volpone and Mosca excel.

Celia's longest speeches are pleas that may seem to work violently counter to her own interests, since they incite already brutal men to visit even more agony upon her. "I will take down poison, / Eat burning coals, do anything," she assures Corvino (3.7.94–95). "Flay my face / Or poison it with ointments for seducing / Your blood to this rebellion," she urges Volpone (3.7.251–53). This is not ordinary masochism, for Celia does not, apparently, enjoy or eroticize pain. Rather, she sees herself in terms of a long tradition of suffering virtue. When Corvino proposes a bloody and humiliating punishment if she refuses to cooperate, she replies simply, "Sir, what you please, you may; I am your martyr" (3.7.107). Because she seems passive in the face of oppression, Celia, like all martyrs, may seem to lack effective agency, but in fact her resistance makes a clear statement. When Volpone lavishly recounts, sings, and dances the joys of voluptuous consumption and sensuous waste, Celia rejects him in a few brief words. Goods he imagines to be irresistible are, from her point of view, quite easily spurned, and despite her evident physical terror of Volpone, she remains morally unintimidated.

Celia's example suggests the possibility of a perspective on life wholly different from the one that most of *Volpone*'s characters share. Martyrdom never, however, offers the prospect of this-worldly satisfaction; the martyr can only look forward to the next world. In Jonson's theater, which restricts itself to the presentation of a debased here-and-now and often seems to draw its gusto from that debasement, the kind of recompense Celia seeks cannot be plausibly presented to her onstage.

The deep alienation of Jonson's Venice from ideals of truth or justice becomes evident in act 4. Celia and Bonario, her rescuer, prove no match for the determined perjury of her husband and his father, the artful advocacy of Voltore, and Volpone's anxious but successful pretense of mortal illness. Critics have often remarked on the corruption of *Volpone*'s legal system, but actual graft does not emerge until very late in the play, when one of the Avocatori proposes to marry his daughter to Mosca and thus obviously compromises his impartiality. In act 4, the Avocatori, confronted with incompatible testimony, come to incorrect conclusions that are, nonetheless, reasonable, given the evidence as it is presented to them. Although they ought perhaps to be more skeptical and less hasty to render judgment, their difficulties are not specific to the Venetian court but plague all systems of secular justice, based as they must be on probabilities and evidence. Courts, like theaters, prefer what can be easily seen and heard to what cannot be.

At the end of act 4, the action seems logically complete, though from a moralist's point of view the prospective conclusion is drastically improper. Jonson, who loudly announces his moral credentials in his prefatory epistle, eventually arranges for the guilty to be discovered and punished and the innocent to be freed. Yet the way in which he does so has occasioned many objections both to Volpone's apparently improbable change of heart and to the punitiveness of the final scene.

When Volpone announces his own death, he throws caution to the wind for a virtually suicidal joke. Even without Mosca's betrayal, it is hard to see how he believes he can possibly recommence his old schemes after this staged demise. Volpone's plan is surely impulsive: he hits on it while drunk, unnerved by an action that has escaped from his control. Nonetheless, his new plot is to some degree an absurd extension of what he has been doing all along—for Volpone's playing dead is not merely, as he believes, a ruse to deceive others; it incorporates a powerful element of self-deception as well. The gulls swarm around Volpone because they believe that a man without obvious heirs is going to die—and though they are wrong about the time frame, they are right about the basics. By refusing to take account of anything beyond the immediate pleasures of acquisition, possession, and consumption, Volpone avoids admitting that he is mortal, that "you can't take it with you," and that he has no loved one to whom to pass his wealth. To Volpone, utterly without either religious faith or the consolations of family perpetuation, the prospect of his own death is both scandalous and terrifying. His pretense of mortal illness continually rehearses that which he most fears, as if he could inoculate himself against death by ritually exposing himself to it.

So too, when he appears before Celia's window as a mountebank, his medical expertise seems to render him superior to, immune from, the bodily ills of his prospective customers. Similar displacements characterize Volpone's attempt to seduce Celia: he eagerly emphasizes that the ruinously costly things they will consume will be thereby destroyed, as if one could magically protect oneself against extinction by inducing it in something else. The culmination of his fantasy involves the mythical phoenix, which regenerates from its own ashes; since there is no need for a reproductive partner, it was supposed that only one phoenix existed at any one time. For Volpone, eating it would be a triumph of self-assertion: "Though nature lost her kind, she were our dish" (3.7.204). By the beginning of act 5, Volpone seems to forget that such playacting does not actually render him immune to disease, mortality, and devastation.

As Jonson acknowledged elsewhere, he typically writes "not of love."[2] *Volpone* is no exception. At the very end of the play, in what she undoubtedly would recognize as a providential intervention, Celia is finally rescued from the peril that surrounds her. But since divorce is impossible, there can be no romantic relationship between Celia and Bonario, or indeed between Celia and anybody else. Once sent "Home to her father with her dowry trebled" (5.12.144), Celia will enter a kind of social limbo, neither married nor unmarried, from which only Corvino's death might free her. Instead of emphasizing prospects of renewal or regeneration, Jonson concentrates on punishing evildoers. Mosca and Volpone receive the equivalent of a capital sentence. Life expectancy in the galleys to which Mosca is consigned was no more than a few months, and Volpone can expect an even shorter sojourn in the notoriously brutal conditions of a Venetian prison. Volpone and Mosca are guilty of many crimes—extortion, attempted rape, fraudulent impersonation, and perjury among them—but this is clearly harsher punishment than Volpone expected, or he would not have thrown off his disguise and confessed in order to escape a whipping. Lines 108–10 of Jonson's prefatory epistle suggest that the severity of the conclusion also shocked some members of *Volpone*'s original audience, accustomed though they were to the rigors of justice in early modern England. Formally, the lack of deaths in *Volpone* satisfies the primary criterion of comedy, but one cannot help thinking that a swift demise would be a happier fate than slow "mortification" in unpitied torment.

Why does Jonson treat his heroes so savagely? As we have seen, Volpone originally mobilizes the power of playacting and the glamor of sensually perceptible things in an attempt to forget his own mortality, and perhaps Jonson hopes that crushing Volpone will crush what he stands for. In that case, Volpone's punishment, as Jonson claims in his prefatory epistle, might exonerate the theater in the eyes of those among Jonson's contemporaries who objected to it precisely because, Volpone-like, the theater substitutes immediate, spectacular pleasures for more difficult and distant goals. If tricksters, sensualists, and idolaters, in other words, are more theatrically compelling than pious, truthful characters, perhaps the only way to make the theater serve moral objectives is to ensure that such evildoers suffer at last. But the excessiveness of *Volpone*'s ending suggests that the relationship between entertainment and edification remains uneasy. In the epilogue, "the fox" reminds spectators that his crimes have delighted them and that he deserves their applause. His irrepressibility and enduring glamor seem the play's final, most telling lesson.

2. "Why I Write Not of Love" is the first poem in Jonson's collection *The Forest* (1616).

BEN JONSON

Volpone, or The Fox

To the most noble and most equal° *(in merit)* sisters, the two famous universities,[1] for their love and acceptance shown to his poem in the presentation, Ben Jonson, the grateful acknowledger, dedicates both it and himself.

Never, most equal sisters, had any man a wit so presently° *immediately* excellent as that it could raise itself, but there must come both matter, occasion, commenders, and favorers[2] to it. If this be true, and that the fortune of all writers doth daily prove it, it behooves the careful to provide well toward these accidents,° *contingencies* and having acquired them, to preserve that part of reputation most tenderly wherein the benefit of a friend[3] is also defended. Hence it is that I now render myself grateful, and am studious° *eager* to justify the bounty of your act,° *approval* to which, though your mere authority° were satisfying,° *authority alone / sufficient* yet, it being an age wherein poetry and the professors° *practitioners* of it hear so ill on all sides, there will be a reason looked for in the subject.[4] It is certain, nor can it with any forehead° *confidence* be opposed, that the too much license of poetasters in this time hath much deformed their mistress;[5] that every day their manifold and manifest ignorance doth stick unnatural reproaches upon her. But for° *Were it not for* their petulancy, it were an act of the greatest injustice either to let the learned suffer, or so divine a skill—which indeed should not be attempted with unclean hands—to fall under the least contempt. For if men will impartially and not asquint look toward the offices and function of a poet, they will easily conclude to themselves the impossibility of any man's being the good poet without first being a good man.[6] He that is said to be able to inform° *instruct; shape* young men to all good disciplines, inflame grown men to all great virtues, keep old men in their best and supreme

The 1616 folio title page reads "*Volpone, or The Fox*. A comedy. Acted in the year 1605 by the King's Majesty's Servants. The author, B. J. / Horatius: *Simul et iucunda, et idonea dicere vitae*. London. Printed by William Stansby, 1616." Horace's *The Art of Poetry*, from which the title page quotation was taken, describes the goals of the good poet. Jonson's own translation of the poem (published 1640) renders the line as: "Mixing sweet and fit, teach life the right."

Prefatory Epistle.

1. Oxford and Cambridge, where *Volpone* was evidently performed shortly after its premier in London.
2. Subject matter, occasion to display his wit, people to praise the man and help him. Jonson's point is that no one succeeds purely by his own efforts; Oxford and Cambridge, by their favorable reception of *Volpone,* have helped "raise" Jonson, and he is therefore grateful to them.
3. A "commender" or "favorer." (See line 3 above).
4. I.e., people will ask why Jonson's poetry is worth supporting (and therefore he will attempt to justify his own practice). "Hear so ill" means "hear such bad things said about them."
5. That by taking too many freedoms, bad poets have ruined Poetry, their mistress.
6. Here, as elsewhere in the prefatory epistle, Jonson derived his aesthetic theory from the Roman poet Horace's *The Art of Poetry* and from Latin treatises on rhetoric by Cicero and Quintilian.

state, or, as they decline to childhood,° recover them to their first strength; that comes forth the interpreter and arbiter of nature, a teacher of things divine no less than human, a master in manners,[7] and can alone, or with a few,[8] effect the business of mankind: this, I take him,° is no subject for pride and ignorance to exercise their railing rhetoric upon.

But it will here be hastily answered that the writers of these days are other things; that not only their manners but their natures are inverted, and nothing remaining with them of the dignity of poet but the abused name, which every scribe usurps; that now, especially in dramatic or, as they term it, stage poetry, nothing but ribaldry, profanation, blasphemy, all license of offense to God and man is practiced. I dare not deny a great part of this (and am sorry I dare not), because in some men's abortive features° (and would they had never boasted the light)° it is overtrue. But that all are embarked in this bold adventure for hell is a most incharitable thought, and, uttered, a more malicious slander.

For my particular,° I can, and from a most clear conscience, affirm that I have ever trembled to think toward the least profaneness, have loathed the use of such foul and unwashed bawdry as is now made the food of the scene.° And howsoever I cannot escape, from some, the imputation of sharpness,° but that they will say I have taken a pride or lust to be bitter, and not my youngest infant° but hath come into the world with all his teeth,[9] I would ask of these supercilious politics[1] what nation, society, or general order or state I have provoked? What public person? Whether I have not, in all these, preserved their dignity, as mine own person, safe? My works are read, allowed° (I speak of those that are entirely mine). Look into them. What broad° reproofs have I used? Where have I been particular?° Where personal, except to a mimic, cheater, bawd, or buffoon, creatures for their insolencies worthy to be taxed?° Yet to which of these so pointingly as he might not either ingenuously have confessed or wisely dissembled his disease? But it is not rumor can make men guilty, much less entitle me to° other men's crimes. I know that nothing can be so innocently writ or carried but may be made obnoxious to construction;[2] marry,° whilst I bear mine innocence about me, I fear it not. Application[3] is now grown a trade with many, and there are that° profess to have a key for the deciphering of everything; but let wise and noble persons take heed how° they be too credulous, or give leave to these invading interpreters to be overfamiliar with their fames,° who cunningly and often utter their own virulent malice under other men's simplest meanings.

As for those that will (by faults which charity hath raked up° or common honesty° concealed) make themselves a name with the multitude, or, to draw their rude and beastly claps,° care not whose living faces they entrench° with their petulant styles:° may they do it without a rival, for me.° I choose rather

slip into senility
as I understand it
botched creations
come to light
part
served up in a play
satiric aggression
most recent play
licensed by the censor
indiscriminate; lewd
targeted individuals
reproved
impute to me
by Mary (an oath)
those who
lest
reputations
covered over / courtesy
applause
wound
pens / for my part

7. Not merely etiquette rules, but proper behavior more generally.
8. With the help of a few others.
9. The tyrannical king Richard III was supposed to have been born with teeth.
1. Arrogant, pseudo-sophisticated observers of current events.
2. Susceptible to misconstruction.
3. The practice of interpreting literary works as political allegories with veiled references to current events.

to live graved in obscurity than share with them in so preposterous a fame. Nor can I blame the wishes of those severe and wiser patriots who, providing° [foreseeing] the hurts these licentious spirits may do in a state, desire rather to see fools and devils,[4] and those antique relics of barbarism retrieved, with all other ridiculous and exploded° [discredited] follies, than behold the wounds of private men, of princes, and nations. For, as Horace makes Trebatius speak, among these, *Sibi quisque timet, quamquam est intactus, et odit.*[5] And men may justly impute such rages, if continued, to the writer as his sports. The increase of which lust in liberty, together with the present trade of the stage, in all their misc'line interludes[6] what learned or liberal soul doth not already abhor, where nothing but the filth of the time is uttered, and that with such impropriety of phrase, such plenty of solecisms, such dearth of sense, so bold prolepses,° [historical inaccuracies] so racked metaphors, with brothelry able to violate the ear of a pagan, and blasphemy to turn the blood of a Christian to water? I cannot but be serious in a cause of this nature, wherein my fame and the reputations of divers honest and learned are the question, when a name° [(the name of poet)] so full of authority, antiquity, and all great mark is, through their insolence, become the lowest scorn of the age, and those men subject to the petulancy of every vernaculous[7] orator that were wont to be the care° [protégés] of kings and happiest monarchs.

This it is that hath not only rapt me to present indignation, but made me studious heretofore, and by all my actions to stand off from them, which may most appear in this my latest work, which you, most learned arbitresses,° [judges (the universities)] have seen, judged, and to my crown, approved. Wherein I have labored, for their instruction and amendment, to reduce not only the ancient forms but manners of the scene:[8] the easiness, the propriety, the innocence, and last the doctrine, which is the principal end of poesy, to inform men in the best reason of living. And though my catastrophe° [ending] may, in the strict rigor of comic law,[9] meet with censure, as turning back to° [failing to keep] my promise, I desire the learned and charitable critic to have so much faith in me to think it was done of industry;° [on purpose] for with what ease I could have varied it nearer his scale,[1] but that I fear to boast my own faculty,° [facility] I could here insert. But my special aim being to put the snaffle° [horse's bit] in their mouths that cry out, "We never punish vice in our interludes," etc., I took the more liberty, though not without some lines of example drawn even in the ancients themselves, the goings-out° [endings] of whose comedies are not always joyful, but ofttimes the bawds, the servants, the rivals, yea, and the masters are mulcted,° [penalized] and fitly, it being the office of a comic poet to imitate justice and instruct to life, as well as purity of language, or stir up gentle affections. To which I shall take the occasion elsewhere to speak.

4. Stock characters in old-fashioned morality plays and burlesques.
5. Each man, although untouched himself, fears that he is hurt and hates such satires. (Horace, *Satires*, 2.1.23.)
6. Miscellaneous entertainments.
7. (1) Scurrilous; (2) unlearned (literally, "knowing only his native tongue").
8. To revive not only the formal properties of classical drama but its moral qualities.
9. Comedies were not supposed to end with deaths, as the punishments at the close of *Volpone* suggest will be the outcome.
1. Made it more to the taste of the spectator who prefers happy endings.

For the present, most reverenced sisters, as I have cared to be thankful for your affections past, and here made the understanding° acquainted with some ground of your favors, let me not despair their continuance to the maturing of some worthier fruits. Wherein, if my muses be true to me, I shall raise the despised head of poetry again, and, stripping her out of those rotten and base rags wherewith the times have adulterated her form, restore her to her primitive habit,° feature, and majesty, and render her worthy to be embraced and kissed of all the great and master spirits of our world. As for the vile and slothful, who never affected° an act worthy of celebration, or are so inward with° their own vicious natures as they worthily fear her, and think it a high point of policy to keep her in contempt with their declamatory and windy invectives: she shall out of just rage incite her servants, who are *genus irritabile*,° to spout ink in their faces that shall eat farther than their marrow, into their fames. And not Cinnamus the barber with his art shall be able to take out the brands,[2] but they shall live and be read till the wretches die, as things worst deserving of themselves in chief,° and then of all mankind.

discerning reader
original clothing
liked
intimate with; attached to
a quick-tempered sort
principally

THE PERSONS OF THE PLAY[1]

VOLPONE, a magnifico° — *Venetian nobleman*
MOSCA, his parasite° — *hanger-on*
NANO, a dwarf
ANDROGYNO, a hermaphrodite
CASTRONE, an eunuch
VOLTORE, an advocate° — *lawyer*
CORBACCIO, an old gentleman
BONARIO, a young gentleman [Corbaccio's son]
CORVINO, a merchant
CELIA, the merchant's wife
Servitore, a SERVANT [to Corvino]
[Sir] POLITIC Would-be, a knight
Fine Madame [LADY] WOULD-BE, the knight's wife
[Two] WOMEN [servants to Lady Would-be]
PEREGRINE, a gentleman traveler
AVOCATORI,° four magistrates — *public prosecutors*
Notario [NOTARY], the register° — *court recorder*
COMMENDATORI,° officers — *court deputies*
[Other court officials, litter-bearers]
Mercatori, three MERCHANTS
Grege [members of a CROWD]

THE SCENE: Venice.

2. Cinnamus is a barber-surgeon in the Roman poet Martial's *Epigrams*. Branding by a hot iron was a common criminal punishment, one suffered by Jonson himself in a homicide case. In this passage Jonson imagines branding by ink—not as fantastic as it might seem, since early modern ink was a corrosive substance.

The Persons of the Play.

1. Many of the characters have allegorically apt names. "Volpone" is defined in John Florio's 1598 Italian-English dictionary as "an old fox . . . a sneaking, lurking, wily deceiver." "Mosca" means "fly." "Nano" means "dwarf." "Voltore" means "vulture." "Corbaccio" means "raven." "Bonario" is derived from *bono*, meaning "good." "Corvino" means "crow." "Celia" means "heaven." "Politic" means "worldly-wise," or "temporizing." "Peregrine" means "traveler" or "small hawk." In many performances the symbolism of the animal names is reinforced by costuming.

The Argument[1]

V olpone, childless, rich, feigns sick, despairs,° — *is despaired of*
O ffers his state° to hopes of several heirs, — *estate*
L ies languishing; his parasite receives
P resents of all, assures, deludes, then weaves
O ther cross-plots, which ope themselves,° are told.° — *unfold / exposed*
N ew tricks for safety are sought; they thrive—when, bold,
E ach tempts th'other again, and all are sold.° — *betrayed*

Prologue

Now, luck yet send us, and a little wit
Will serve to make our play hit
According to the palates of the season.° — *fashionable taste*
Here is rhyme not empty of reason.
This we were bid to credit° from our poet, — *asked to believe*
Whose true scope,° if you would know it, — *aim*
In all his poems still hath been this measure,
To mix profit with your pleasure;[1]
And not as some—whose throats their envy failing°— — *not fully expressing*
Cry hoarsely, "all he writes is railing,"° — *personal insult*
And when his plays come forth think they can flout them
With saying he was a year about them.[2]
To these there needs no lie° but this his creature,° — *denial / creation*
Which was, two months since,° no feature;° — *ago / nonexistent*
And, though he dares give them° five lives to mend it, — *(his detractors)*
'Tis known five weeks fully penned it
From his own hand, without a coadjutor,° — *collaborator*
Novice, journeyman,° or tutor. — *apprentice*
Yet thus much I can give you, as a token
Of his play's worth: no eggs are broken,
Nor quaking custards with fierce teeth affrighted,[3]
Wherewith your rout° are so delighted; — *mob*
Nor hales he in a gull,° old ends° reciting, — *fool / saws*
To stop gaps in his loose writing,
With such a deal of monstrous and forced action
As might make Bethlehem a faction.[4]
Nor made he his play for jests stol'n from each table,° — *plagiarized jokes*
But makes jests to fit his fable,
And so presents quick° comedy, refined — *lively*
As best critics have designed.
The laws of time, place, persons he observeth;[5]
From no needful rule he swerveth.
All gall and copperas[6] from his ink he draineth;

The Argument.
1. Plot summary. Jonson imitates the acrostic "arguments" of the Latin playwright Plautus.

Prologue.
1. Rule, as laid down by Horace, that the poet ought both to please his audience and teach it something useful.
2. Thomas Dekker ridiculed the slow pace at which Jonson produced new work in *Satiromastix, or The Untrussing of the Humorous Poet* (1602), and John Marston did the same in *The Dutch Courtesan* (1605).
3. The satirist John Marston, in a line Jonson had previously ridiculed, boasted: "let custards [cowards] quake, my rage must freely run." Such custards were a staple feature of city feasts.
4. As might win approval from lunatics (who inhabited Bethlehem hospital in London).
5. He observes the unities of time and place and the consistency of character.
6. Ferrous sulfate, like gall a corrosive substance used in ink.

Only a little salt[7] remaineth
Wherewith he'll rub your cheeks, till, red with laughter,
They shall look fresh a week after.

1.1

[*Enter*] *Volpone* [*and*] *Mosca.*[1]

VOLPONE Good morning to the day, and, next, my gold!
Open the shrine that I may see my saint.
[*Mosca reveals the treasure.*][2]
Hail the world's soul,° and mine! More glad than is — *animating principle*
The teeming earth to see the longed-for sun
Peep through the horns of the celestial Ram[3]
Am I to view thy splendor darkening his,° — *outshining the sun's*
That, lying here amongst my other hoards,
Show'st like a flame by night, or like the day
Struck out of chaos, when all darkness fled
Unto the center.° O thou son of Sol[4]— — *center of the earth*
But brighter than thy father—let me kiss
With adoration thee and every relic
Of sacred treasure in this blessèd room.
Well did wise poets by thy glorious name
Title that age which they would have the best,[5]
Thou being the best of things, and far transcending
All style° of joy in children, parents, friends, — *kind*
Or any other waking dream on earth.
Thy looks when they to Venus did ascribe,
They should have giv'n her twenty thousand Cupids,[6]
Such are thy beauties and our loves.° Dear saint, — *our love of thee*
Riches, the dumb° god, that giv'st all men tongues, — *speechless*
That canst do naught and yet mak'st men do all things,
The price of souls; even hell, with thee to boot,° — *in the bargain*
Is made worth heaven! Thou art virtue, fame,
Honor, and all things else. Who° can get thee, — *Whoever*
He shall be noble, valiant, honest, wise—
MOSCA And what he will, sir. Riches are in fortune
A greater good than wisdom is in nature.
VOLPONE True, my belovèd Mosca. Yet I glory
More in the cunning purchase° of my wealth — *acquisition*
Than in the glad possession, since I gain
No common way. I use no trade, no venture;° — *risky commerce*
I wound no earth with plowshares; fat no beasts
To feed the shambles;° have no mills for iron, — *slaughterhouse*
Oil, corn, or men, to grind 'em into powder;
I blow no subtle[7] glass; expose no ships
To threat'nings of the furrow-facèd sea;

7. A traditional metaphor for satiric wit.
1.1. Volpone's house.
1. Alternatively, the play may begin with Volpone rising from his onstage bed.
2. The treasure is probably hidden behind a curtain in the alcove at the back of the stage.
3. Aries, the constellation ascendant in early spring.
4. Alchemists believed gold to have issued from the sun (Sol). Volpone blasphemously applies this metaphor to God's creation of the world in Genesis.
5. The mythical Golden Age (when, ironically, gold was not yet in use) was influentially described by Ovid in *The Metamorphoses*.
6. In Latin poetry, Venus was commonly described as *aurea*, meaning "golden." The throng of Cupids Volpone imagines around her suggests gold's irresistible, and for him highly sexual, appeal.
7. (1) Delicate; (2) artful. (Venice was and is renowned for its art glass.)

I turn° no moneys in the public bank, *exchange*
Nor usure° private— *lend money at interest*
MOSCA No, sir, nor devour
Soft prodigals.° You shall ha' some will swallow *spendthrifts*
A melting° heir as glibly as your Dutch *financially dwindling*
Will pills° of butter, and ne'er purge for't;[8] *morsels*
Tear forth the fathers of poor families
Out of their beds and coffin them alive
In some kind, clasping° prison, where their bones *manacling*
May be forthcoming° when the flesh is rotten. *protruding; carted away*
But your sweet nature doth abhor these courses;
You loathe the widow's or the orphan's tears
Should wash your pavements, or their piteous cries
Ring in your roofs and beat the air for vengeance.
VOLPONE Right, Mosca, I do loathe it.
MOSCA And besides, sir,
You are not like the thresher that doth stand
With a huge flail, watching a heap of corn,
And, hungry, dares not taste the smallest grain,
But feeds on mallows° and such bitter herbs; *unpalatable weeds*
Nor like the merchant who hath filled his vaults
With Romagnia and rich Candian wines,
Yet drinks the lees of Lombard's vinegar.[9]
You will not lie in straw whilst moths and worms
Feed on your sumptuous hangings° and soft beds. *bed curtains*
You know the use of riches, and dare give now
From that bright heap to me, your poor observer,° *follower*
Or to your dwarf, or your hermaphrodite,
Your eunuch, or what other household° trifle *menial*
Your pleasure allows maint'nance°— *You're pleased to support*
VOLPONE [*giving money*] Hold thee, Mosca,
Take of my hand; thou strik'st on truth in all,
And they are envious term° thee parasite. *who term*
Call forth my dwarf, my eunuch, and my fool,° *(Androgyno)*
And let 'em make me sport. [*Exit Mosca.*]
What should I do
But cocker up my genius,° and live free *indulge my appetite*
To all delights my fortune calls me to?
I have no wife, no parent, child, ally
To give my substance to, but whom I make° *he whom I designate*
Must be my heir, and this makes men observe° me. *flatter*
This draws new clients° daily to my house, *petitioners*
Women and men of every sex and age,
That bring me presents, send me plate,° coin, jewels, *gold or silver plate*
With hope that when I die—which they expect
Each greedy minute—it shall then return
Tenfold upon them; whilst some, covetous
Above the rest, seek to engross° me whole, *swallow; monopolize*
And counterwork,° the one unto the other, *compete; undermine*
Contend in gifts as they would seem in love;
All which I suffer,° playing with their hopes, *permit*

8. Never use a remedy for gastric distress. (The Dutch were notoriously fond of butter.)
9. Romagnia and rich Candian wines are expensive wines from Greece and Crete. The lees of Lombard's vinegar are the dregs of cheap Italian wine.

And am content to coin 'em into profit,
And look upon their kindness and take more,
And look on that, still bearing them in hand,° *leading them on*
Letting the cherry knock against their lips,
And draw it by their mouths and back again.[1]—
How now!

1.2

[*Enter*] *Mosca, Nano, Androgyno,* [*and*] *Castrone.*

NANO Now, room for fresh gamesters,° who do will you to know *entertainers*
They do bring you neither play nor university show,[1]
And therefore do entreat you that whatsoever they rehearse
May not fare a whit the worse for the false pace of the verse.[2]
If you wonder at this, you will wonder more ere we pass,
For know here [*indicating Androgyno*] is enclosed the soul
 of Pythagoras,[3]
That juggler° divine, as hereafter shall follow; *trickster*
Which soul (fast and loose, sir) came first from Apollo,
And was breathed into Aethalides,[4] Mercurius his° son, *Mercury's*
Where it had the gift to remember all that ever was done.
From thence it fled forth and made quick transmigration
To goldilocked Euphorbus,[5] who was killed in good fashion
At the siege of old Troy, by the cuckold of Sparta.[6]
Hermotimus[7] was next—I find it in my *charta*°— *record*
To whom it did pass, where no sooner it was missing
But with one Pyrrhus of Delos° it learned to go a-fishing; *another philosopher*
And thence did it enter the Sophist of Greece.° *Pythagoras*
From Pythagore she went into a beautiful piece° *slut*
Hight° Aspasia the meretrix;[8] and the next toss of her *Named*
Was again of a whore; she became a philosopher,
Crates the Cynic,[9] as itself doth relate it.
Since,° kings, knights, and beggars, knaves, lords, and *Since then*
 fools gat° it, *received*
Besides ox and ass, camel, mule, goat, and brock,° *badger*
In all which it hath spoke as in the cobbler's cock.[1]
But I come not here to discourse of that matter,
Or his one, two, or three, or his great oath, "By quater,"[2]

1. In the game of chop-cherry, one player dangles a cherry in front of another, who tries to bite it.

1.2. The scene continues.

1. University students performed classical plays or their imitations to hone their abilities in Latin oratory.
2. The four-stress meter of the skit Nano, Androgyno, and Castrone here perform was common in medieval drama but old-fashioned by Jonson's time.
3. Ancient Greek philosopher, mathematician, and music theorist who believed in the transmigration of souls and in the mystical properties of geometrical relationships (especially triangles [triangle = trigon]). His followers observed strict dietary restrictions and took five-year vows of silence. His thigh was rumored to be made of gold. Jonson adapts much of the career of Pythagoras' soul from *The Dialogue of the Cobbler and the Cock*, by the Greek satirist Lucian.
4. The herald of the Greek Argonauts and son of the god Mercury, who inherited his father's divine gift of memory. Thus, unlike other souls, which forget their previous lives, Aethalides' soul can recall its transmigrations.
5. Trojan youth who injured Achilles' beloved friend, Patroclus, in the *Iliad*.
6. Menelaus, the Spartan king whose wife, Helen, was stolen by the Trojan prince Paris.
7. Greek philosopher of about 500 B.C.E.
8. Whore. Aspasia was the mistress of the Athenian statesman Pericles.
9. Student of Diogenes, founder of the Cynic philosophy.
1. The speaker in Lucian's dialogue (see note 3 above).
2. A quater is an equilateral triangle the sides of which are evenly divisible by four.

His musics, his trigon, his golden thigh,° *(see 6 n)*
Or his telling how elements° shift; but I *earth, air, fire, water*
Would ask how of late thou hast suffered translation,° *metamorphosis*
And shifted thy coat in these days of reformation?° *religious change*
ANDROGYNO Like one of the reformed, a fool,[3] as you see,
Counting all old doctrine heresy.
NANO But not on thine own forbid meats hast thou ventured?
ANDROGYNO On fish, when first a Carthusian I entered.[4]
NANO Why, then thy dogmatical silence° hath left thee? *vow of silence*
ANDROGYNO Of that an obstreperous° lawyer bereft me. *noisy*
NANO Oh, wonderful change! When Sir Lawyer forsook thee,
For Pythagore's sake, what body then took thee?
ANDROGYNO A good dull mule.
NANO And how, by that means,
Thou wert brought to allow of the eating of beans?
ANDROGYNO Yes.
NANO But from the mule into whom didst thou pass?
ANDROGYNO Into a very strange beast, by some writers called an ass;
By others a precise, pure, illuminate brother[5]
Of those devour flesh and sometimes one another,° *prey on each other*
And will drop you° forth a libel° or a sanctified lie *drop / polemic*
Betwixt every spoonful of a Nativity pie.[6]
NANO Now quit thee, for heaven, of that profane nation,° *sect*
And gently report thy next transmigration.
ANDROGYNO To the same that I am.° *what I am now*
NANO A creature of delight?
And—what is more than a fool—an hermaphrodite?
Now pray thee, sweet soul, in all thy variation° *of all your shapes*
Which body wouldst thou choose to take up thy station?
ANDROGYNO Troth, this I am in, even here would I tarry.
NANO 'Cause here the delight of each sex thou canst vary?
ANDROGYNO Alas, those pleasures be stale and forsaken.
No, 'tis your fool wherewith I am so taken,
The only one creature that I can call blessèd,
For all other forms I have proved° most distressèd. *found to be*
NANO Spoke true, as° thou wert in Pythagoras still. *as if*
This learnèd opinion we celebrate will,
Fellow eunuch, as behooves us, with all our wit and art,
To dignify that° whereof ourselves are so great and special a part. *(folly)*
VOLPONE [*applauding*] Now, very, very pretty! Mosca, this
Was thy invention?
MOSCA If it please my patron,
Not else.
VOLPONE It doth, good Mosca.
MOSCA Then it was, sir.

3. The "reformed" are Protestants in general, but more specifically the Puritan wing of the Church of England. Jonson was a Catholic when he wrote *Volpone*.
4. Pythagoreans abstained from fish, but Carthusians, an order of Catholic monks, ate fish on fast days.
5. Puritan who claimed immediate, visionary knowledge of religious truth. Puritans did not observe the traditional fasting days (hence "devour flesh" in the following line).
6. Puritans substituted the term "Nativity" for "Christmas," to avoid reference to the Mass.

SONG

NANO *and* CASTRONE [*sing*]
Fools, they are the only nation° — *group*
Worth men's envy or admiration,
Free from care or sorrow-taking,
Selves° and others merry making; — *Themselves*
All they speak or do is sterling.
Your fool, he is your great man's dearling,° — *darling*
And your lady's sport and pleasure;
Tongue and bauble° are his treasure. — *fool's staff; penis*
E'en his face begetteth laughter,
And he speaks truth free from slaughter.° — *with impunity*
He's the grace of every feast,
And sometimes the chiefest guest,
Hath his trencher° and his stool, — *platter*
When wit waits upon the fool.
Oh, who would not be
He, he, he? *One knocks without.*

VOLPONE Who's that? Away! [*Exeunt Nano and Castrone.*]
Look, Mosca.

MOSCA Fool, begone!
[*Exit Androgyno.*]
'Tis Signor Voltore, the advocate;
I know him by his knock.

VOLPONE Fetch me my gown,
My furs, and nightcaps; say my couch is changing,[7]
And let him entertain himself awhile
Without i'th'gallery. [*Exit Mosca.*]
Now, now, my clients
Begin their visitation! Vulture, kite,
Raven, and gorcrow,° all my birds of prey — *carrion crow*
That think me turning carcass, now they come.
I am not for 'em° yet. — *ready to die*

[*Enter Mosca.*]

How now? The news?

MOSCA A piece of plate,° sir. — *gold platter*

VOLPONE Of what bigness?

MOSCA Huge,
Massy, and antique, with your name inscribed
And arms° engraven. — *coat of arms*

VOLPONE Good! And not a fox
Stretched on the earth, with fine delusive sleights° — *deceptive tricks*
Mocking a gaping crow?[8] Ha, Mosca?

MOSCA [*laughing*] Sharp, sir.

VOLPONE Give me my furs. Why dost thou laugh so, man?

MOSCA I cannot choose, sir, when I apprehend
What thoughts he has, without,° now, as he walks: — *outside*
That this might be the last gift he should° give; — *would have to*

7. My bedsheets are being changed.
8. In one of Aesop's *Fables*, the fox tricks the crow into dropping its cheese.

That this would fetch you;° if you died today — *bring you around*
And gave him all, what he should be tomorrow;
What large return would come of all his ventures;
How he should worshiped be and reverenced;
Ride with his furs and footcloths,[9] waited on
By herds of fools and clients; have clear way
Made for his mule, as lettered° as himself; — *educated*
Be called the great and learnèd advocate;
And then concludes there's naught impossible.
VOLPONE Yes, to be learnèd, Mosca.
MOSCA Oh, no, rich
Implies it.° Hood an ass with reverend purple,[1] — *wealth implies learning*
So you can hide his two ambitious° ears, — *aspiring; upraised*
And he shall pass for a cathedral doctor.° — *Doctor of Divinity*
VOLPONE My caps, my caps, good Mosca. Fetch him in.
MOSCA Stay, sir, your ointment for your eyes.
[*Mosca helps Volpone with his disguise.*]
VOLPONE That's true.
Dispatch,° dispatch! I long to have possession — *Hurry*
Of my new present.
MOSCA That, and thousands more
I hope to see you lord of.
VOLPONE Thanks, kind Mosca.
MOSCA And that, when I am lost in blended dust,
And hundred such as I am in succession—
VOLPONE Nay, that were too much, Mosca.
MOSCA —you shall live
Still, to delude these Harpies.[2]
VOLPONE Loving Mosca!
'Tis well. My pillow now, and let him enter.
[*Exit Mosca. Volpone lies down.*]
Now, my feignèd cough, my phthisic,° and my gout, — *consumption; asthma*
My apoplexy, palsy, and catarrhs,° — *mucus discharges*
Help with your forcèd functions this my posture,° — *imposture*
Wherein this three year I have milked their hopes.
He comes, I hear him. [*Coughing*] Uh, uh, uh, uh! Oh—

1.3

[*Enter*] Voltore [*with a platter, ushered by*] Mosca.

MOSCA [*to Voltore*] You still are what you were, sir. Only you,
Of all the rest, are he commands° his love; — *the one who possesses*
And you do wisely to preserve it thus
With early visitation and kind notes° — *tokens*
Of your good meaning to° him, which, I know, — *intentions toward*
Cannot but come most grateful. [*Loudly, to Volpone*] Patron, sir!
Here's Signor Voltore is come—

9. Ornamental cloths for the back of a horse.
1. Doctors of Divinity wore purple academic hoods.
2. Mythological ravenous monsters with women's heads and the bodies and claws of birds.
1.3. The scene continues.

VOLPONE [*weakly*] What say you?
MOSCA Sir, Signor Voltore is come this morning
To visit you.
VOLPONE I thank him.
MOSCA And hath brought
A piece of antique plate bought of Saint Mark,[1]
With which he here presents you.
VOLPONE He is welcome.
Pray him to come more often.
MOSCA Yes.
VOLTORE [*straining to hear*] What says he?
MOSCA He thanks you, and desires you see him often.
VOLPONE Mosca.
MOSCA My patron?
VOLPONE [*groping*] Bring him near. Where is he?
I long to feel his hand.
MOSCA [*guiding Volpone's hands toward the platter*] The plate
is here, sir.
VOLTORE How fare you, sir?
VOLPONE I thank you, Signor Voltore.
Where is the plate? Mine eyes are bad.
VOLTORE [*relinquishing the platter*] I'm sorry
To see you still thus weak.
MOSCA [*aside*] That he is not weaker.
VOLPONE You are too munificent.
VOLTORE No, sir, would to heaven
I could as well give health to you as that plate.
VOLPONE You give, sir, what you can. I thank you. Your love
Hath taste in° this, and shall not be unanswered. *Is suggested by*
I pray you see me often.
VOLTORE Yes, I shall, sir.
VOLPONE Be not far from me.
MOSCA [*aside to Voltore*] Do you observe that, sir?
VOLPONE Hearken unto me still. It will concern you.
MOSCA [*aside to Voltore*] You are a happy man, sir. Know your good.
VOLPONE I cannot now last long—
MOSCA (*aside to Voltore*) You are his heir, sir.
VOLTORE (*aside to Mosca*) Am I?
VOLPONE I feel me going, uh, uh, uh, uh!
I am sailing to my port, uh, uh, uh, uh!
And I am glad I am so near my haven.
[*He pretends to lapse into unconsciousness.*]
MOSCA Alas, kind gentleman! Well, we must all go—
VOLTORE But Mosca—
MOSCA Age will conquer.
VOLTORE Pray thee, hear me.
Am I inscribed his heir for certain?
MOSCA Are you?
I do beseech you, sir, you will vouchsafe
To write me i'your family.[2] All my hopes

1. Goldsmiths kept shop in the square of Saint Mark's Basilica.

2. Employ me in your household (after Volpone's death).

Depend upon Your Worship. I am lost
Except° the rising sun do shine on me. *Unless*
VOLTORE It shall both shine and warm thee, Mosca.
MOSCA Sir,
I am a man that have not done your love
All the worst offices:° here I wear your keys, *services*
See all your coffers and your caskets locked,
Keep the poor inventory of your jewels,
Your plate, and moneys, am your steward, sir,
Husband your goods here.
VOLTORE But am I sole heir?
MOSCA Without a partner, sir, confirmed this morning;
The wax° is warm yet, and the ink scarce dry *(of the seal)*
Upon the parchment.
VOLTORE Happy, happy me!
By what good chance, sweet Mosca?
MOSCA Your desert, sir;
I know no second cause.
VOLTORE Thy modesty
Is loath to know it.° Well, we shall requite it. *admit your role*
MOSCA He ever liked your course, sir; that first took him.
I oft have heard him say how he admired
Men of your large[3] profession, that could speak
To every cause, and things mere contraries,° *utterly contradictory*
Till they were hoarse again, yet all be law;
That with most quick agility could turn
And re-turn, make knots and undo them,
Give forkèd° counsel, take provoking gold *ambiguous*
On either hand, and put it up:[4] these men,
He knew, would thrive with their humility.° *obsequiousness*
And for his part, he thought he should be blessed
To have his heir of such a suffering° spirit, *long-suffering*
So wise, so grave, of so perplexed° a tongue, *bewildering*
And loud withal,° that would not wag nor scarce *besides*
Lie still without a fee, when every word
Your Worship but lets fall is a *cecchine!*° *Another knocks.* *gold coin*
Who's that? One knocks; I would not have you seen, sir.
And yet—pretend you came and went in haste;
I'll fashion an excuse. And, gentle sir,
When you do come to swim in golden lard,
Up to the arms in honey, that your chin
Is born up stiff with fatness of the flood,
Think on your vassal; but° remember me. *only*
I ha' not been your worst of clients.
VOLTORE Mosca—
MOSCA When will you have your inventory brought, sir?
Or see a copy of the will? [*More knocking.*] Anon!°— *Just a minute!*
I'll bring 'em to you, sir. Away, begone,
Put business i'your face.[5] [*Exit Voltore.*]
VOLPONE Excellent, Mosca!
Come hither, let me kiss thee.

3. Expansive, liberal (with the suggestion of "unscrupulous").
4. Take a bribe from each party to a suit and pocket it.
5. Look as if you were here on business.

MOSCA Keep you still, sir.
Here is Corbaccio.
VOLPONE Set the plate away.
The vulture's gone, and the old raven's come.

1.4

MOSCA [*to Volpone*] Betake you to your silence and your sleep; [*He puts up the plate.*]
Stand there and multiply.°—Now shall we see *beget more booty*
A wretch who is indeed more impotent
Than this° can feign to be, yet hopes to hop *(Volpone)*
Over his° grave. *(Volpone's)*

[*Enter*] *Corbaccio.*

Signor Corbaccio!
You're very welcome, sir.
CORBACCIO How does your patron?
MOSCA Troth, as he did, sir: no amends.
CORBACCIO What? Mends he?
MOSCA No, sir, he is rather worse.
CORBACCIO That's well. Where is he?
MOSCA Upon his couch, sir, newly fall'n asleep.
CORBACCIO Does he sleep well?
MOSCA No wink, sir, all this night,
Nor yesterday, but slumbers.° *dozes fitfully*
CORBACCIO Good! He should take
Some counsel of physicians. I have brought him
An opiate here, from mine own doctor—
MOSCA He will not hear of drugs.
CORBACCIO Why, I myself
Stood by while't was made, saw all th'ingredients,
And know it cannot but most gently work.
My life for his, 'tis but to make him sleep.
VOLPONE [*aside*] Ay, his last sleep, if he would take it.
MOSCA Sir,
He has no faith in physic.° *medicine*
CORBACCIO 'Say° you? 'Say you? *What say*
MOSCA He has no faith in physic. He does think
Most of your doctors[1] are the greater danger
And worse disease t'escape. I often have
Heard him protest that your physician
Should never be his heir.
CORBACCIO Not I his heir?
MOSCA Not your physician, sir.
CORBACCIO Oh, no, no, no,
I do not mean it.
MOSCA No, sir, nor their fees
He cannot brook.° He says they flay° a man *tolerate / skin*

1.4. The scene continues.
1. Not Corbaccio's doctors, but doctors generally. (Also in line 23.)

Before they kill him.

CORBACCIO Right, I do conceive° you. *understand*

MOSCA And then, they do it by experiment,[2]
For which the law not only doth absolve 'em,
But gives them great reward; and he is loath
To hire his death so.

CORBACCIO It is true, they kill
With as much license as a judge.

MOSCA Nay, more:
For he° but kills, sir, where the law condemns, *(the judge)*
And these° can kill him,° too. *(the doctors) / (the judge)*

CORBACCIO Ay, or me
Or any man. How does his apoplex?° *apoplexy, stroke*
Is that strong on him still?

MOSCA Most violent.[3]
His speech is broken and his eyes are set,° *fixed*
His face drawn longer than 'twas wont°— *than usual*

CORBACCIO How? How?
Stronger than he was wont?

MOSCA No, sir: his face
Drawn longer than 'twas wont.

CORBACCIO Oh, good.

MOSCA His mouth
Is ever gaping, and his eyelids hang.

CORBACCIO Good.

MOSCA A freezing numbness stiffens all his joints,
And makes the color of his flesh like lead.

CORBACCIO 'Tis good.

MOSCA His pulse beats slow and dull.

CORBACCIO Good symptoms still.

MOSCA And from his brain—

CORBACCIO Ha? How? Not from his brain?

MOSCA Yes, sir, and from his brain—

CORBACCIO I conceive you, good.

MOSCA —Flows a cold sweat with a continual rheum° *mucus discharge*
Forth the resolvèd° corners of his eyes. *watery; limp*

CORBACCIO Is't possible? Yet I am better, ha!
How does he with the swimming of his head?

MOSCA Oh, sir, 'tis past the scotomy;[4] he now
Hath lost his feeling, and hath left to snort;° *stopped snoring*
You hardly can perceive him that he breathes.

CORBACCIO Excellent, excellent. Sure I shall outlast him!
This makes me young again a score of years.

MOSCA I was a-coming for you, sir.

CORBACCIO Has he made his will?
What has he giv'n me?

MOSCA No, sir.

CORBACCIO Nothing? Ha?

MOSCA He has not made his will, sir.

2. By testing possible remedies on their patients.
3. In the following lines, Mosca attributes to Volpone a wide variety of symptoms that were, even occurring singly, considered sure signs of impending death.
4. Dizziness, accompanied by partial blindness.

CORBACCIO Oh, oh, oh.
What then did Voltore, the lawyer, here?
MOSCA He smelt a carcass, sir, when he but heard
My master was about his testament°— *making his will*
As I did urge him to it, for your good—
CORBACCIO He came unto him, did he? I thought so.
MOSCA Yes, and presented him this piece of plate.
CORBACCIO To be his heir?
MOSCA I do not know, sir.
CORBACCIO True,
I know it too.
MOSCA [*aside*] By your own scale,° sir. *scale of values*
CORBACCIO [*showing a bag of gold*] Well,
I shall prevent° him yet. See, Mosca, look, *forestall*
Here I have brought a bag of bright *cecchines*,
Will quite weigh down his plate.
MOSCA Yea, marry, sir!
This is true physic, this your sacred medicine;
No talk of opiates to° this great elixir.[5] *compared to*
CORBACCIO 'Tis *aurum palpabile*, if not *potabile*.[6]
MOSCA It shall be ministered to him in his bowl?
CORBACCIO Ay, do, do, do.
MOSCA Most blessed cordial!° *heart medicine*
This will recover him.
CORBACCIO Yes, do, do, do.
MOSCA I think it were not best, sir.
CORBACCIO What?
MOSCA To recover him.
CORBACCIO Oh, no, no, no; by no means.
MOSCA Why, sir, this
Will work some strange effect, if he but feel it.
CORBACCIO 'Tis true, therefore forbear, I'll take my venture.° *investment*
Give me 't again. [*He snatches for the bag.*]
MOSCA [*keeping it out of his reach*] At no hand.° Pardon me, *By no means*
You shall not do yourself that wrong, sir. I
Will so advise you, you shall have it all.
CORBACCIO How?
MOSCA All, sir, 'tis your right, your own; no man
Can claim a part. 'Tis yours without a rival,
Decreed by destiny.
CORBACCIO How? How, good Mosca?
MOSCA I'll tell you, sir. This fit he shall recover—
CORBACCIO I do conceive you.
MOSCA —and, on first advantage° *opportunity*
Of his gained sense, will I re-importune him
Unto the making of his testament,
And show him this.
CORBACCIO Good, good.
MOSCA 'Tis better yet,
If you will hear, sir.

5. In alchemy, a liquid thought to be capable of prolonging life indefinitely or changing base metal into gold.

6. It is gold that can be felt, if not drunk. (Latin.) Dissolved gold was used as a medicine.

CORBACCIO Yes, with all my heart.
MOSCA Now, would I counsel you, make home with speed;
There frame° a will, whereto you shall inscribe *devise*
My master your sole heir.
CORBACCIO And disinherit
My son?
MOSCA Oh, sir, the better, for that color° *appearance; fiction*
Shall make it much more taking.° *plausible; attractive*
CORBACCIO Oh, but color?° *it's only a ruse?*
MOSCA This will, sir, you shall send it unto me.
Now, when I come to enforce°—as I will do— *urge*
Your cares, your watchings, and your many prayers,
Your more than many gifts, your this day's present,
And last produce your will, where—without thought
Or least regard unto your proper issue,° *own offspring*
A son so brave° and highly meriting— *splendid*
The stream of your diverted love hath thrown you
Upon my master, and made him your heir,
He cannot be so stupid or stone dead
But out of conscience and mere gratitude—
CORBACCIO He must pronounce me his?
MOSCA 'Tis true.
CORBACCIO This plot
Did I think on before.
MOSCA I do believe it.
CORBACCIO Do you not believe it?
MOSCA Yes, sir.
CORBACCIO Mine own project.
MOSCA Which when he hath done, sir—
CORBACCIO Published me his heir?
MOSCA And you so certain to survive him—
CORBACCIO Ay.
MOSCA Being so lusty a man—
CORBACCIO 'Tis true.
MOSCA Yes, sir—
CORBACCIO I thought on that too. See how he° should be *(Mosca)*
The very organ to express my thoughts!
MOSCA You have not only done yourself a good—
CORBACCIO But multiplied it on my son?
MOSCA 'Tis right, sir.
CORBACCIO Still my invention.
MOSCA 'Las, sir, heaven knows,
It hath been all my study, all my care,
(I e'en grow gray withal) how to work things—
CORBACCIO I do conceive, sweet Mosca.
MOSCA You are he
For whom I labor here.
CORBACCIO Ay, do, do, do.
I'll straight about it. [*Corbaccio starts to leave.*]
MOSCA Rook go with you,[7] raven!
CORBACCIO I know thee honest.

7. May you be swindled ("rooked"). Playing on "rook" meaning "crow," "raven." This speech and Mosca's following lines, through line 130, could be considered asides since Corbaccio cannot hear them; but they need not be delivered sotto voce.

MOSCA You do lie, sir—
CORBACCIO And—
MOSCA Your knowledge is no better than your ears,° sir. *(which are deaf)*
CORBACCIO I do not doubt to be a father to thee.
MOSCA Nor I to gull my brother of his blessing.[8]
CORBACCIO I may ha' my youth restored to me, why not?
MOSCA Your Worship is a precious ass—
CORBACCIO What say'st thou?
MOSCA I do desire Your Worship to make haste, sir.
CORBACCIO 'Tis done, 'tis done, I go. [*Exit.*]
VOLPONE [*leaping from the bed*] Oh, I shall burst!
Let out my sides,° let out my sides— *Loosen my clothes*
MOSCA Contain
Your flux of laughter, sir. You know this hope
Is such a bait it covers any hook.
VOLPONE Oh, but thy working and thy placing it!
I cannot hold;° good rascal, let me kiss thee. *contain my delight*
I never knew thee in so rare a humor.° *so excellently witty*
MOSCA Alas, sir, I but do as I am taught:
Follow your grave instructions, give 'em words,° *deceptive speech*
Pour oil into their ears,° and send them hence. *Flatter them*
VOLPONE 'Tis true, 'tis true. What a rare° punishment *exquisite*
Is avarice to itself![9]
MOSCA Ay, with our help, sir.
VOLPONE So many cares, so many maladies,
So many fears attending on old age,
Yea, death so often called on,° as no wish *invoked*
Can be more frequent with 'em, their limbs faint,
Their senses dull, their seeing, hearing, going,° *ability to walk*
All dead before them;° yea, their very teeth, *before they die*
Their instruments of eating, failing them—
Yet this is reckoned life! Nay, here was one
Is now gone home that wishes to live longer!
Feels not his gout nor palsy, feigns himself
Younger by scores of years, flatters his age
With confident belying it,[1] hopes he may
With charms, like Aeson,[2] have his youth restored,
And with these thoughts so battens,° as if fate *gluts himself*
Would be as easily cheated on as he,
And all turns air!° *Another knocks.* *is illusory*
Who's that there, now? A third?
MOSCA Close,° to your couch again. I hear his voice. *Hide yourself*
It is Corvino, our spruce° merchant. *dapper*
VOLPONE [*lying down again*] Dead.° *I'll play dead*
MOSCA Another bout, sir, with your eyes.
[*He applies ointment.*]
Who's there?

8. If Corbaccio were Mosca's father, then Bonario would be his brother. A reference to Genesis 25, in which Jacob tricks his elder brother, Esau, into resigning his birthright, and Genesis 27, in which Jacob tricks their dying father, Isaac, into giving him the paternal blessing and property.

9. Quoting the Stoic philosopher Seneca's *Moral Epistles*, no. 115.

1. Deceives himself, and attempts to deceive others, about his age by vigorously refusing to admit the truth.

2. Father of the Greek hero Jason; his youth was restored by Medea, his sorceress daughter-in-law.

1.5

[*Enter*] *Corvino.*

Signor Corvino! Come° most wished for! Oh, *You come*
How happy were you if you knew it now!
CORVINO Why? What? Wherein?
MOSCA The tardy hour is come, sir.
CORVINO He is not dead?
MOSCA Not dead, sir, but as good;
He knows no man.
CORVINO How shall I do, then?
MOSCA Why, sir?
CORVINO I have brought him here a pearl.
MOSCA Perhaps he has
So much remembrance left as to know you, sir;
He still calls on you; nothing but your name
Is in his mouth. Is your pearl orient,[1] sir?
CORVINO Venice was never owner of the like.
VOLPONE [*weakly*] Signor Corvino—
MOSCA Hark.
VOLPONE Signor Corvino—
MOSCA He calls you. Step and give it him.—He's here, sir,
And he has brought you a rich pearl.
CORVINO [*to Volpone*] How do you, sir?
[*To Mosca*] Tell him it doubles the twelfth carat.[2]
[*He gives Volpone the pearl.*]
MOSCA [*to Corvino*] Sir,
He cannot understand. His hearing's gone;
And yet it comforts him to see you—
CORVINO Say
I have a diamond for him too.
MOSCA Best show't, sir.
Put it into his hand; 'tis only there
He apprehends; he has his feeling yet.
[*Corvino gives Volpone the diamond.*]
See how he grasps it!
CORVINO 'Las, good gentleman!
How pitiful the sight is!
MOSCA Tut, forget, sir.
The weeping of an heir should still° be laughter *always*
Under a visor.° *mask*
CORVINO Why, am I his heir?
MOSCA Sir, I am sworn; I may not show the will
Till he be dead. But here has been Corbaccio,
Here has been Voltore, here were others too,
I cannot number 'em they were so many,
All gaping here for legacies; but I,
Taking the vantage° of his naming you— *opportunity*

1.5. The scene continues.
1. Especially brilliant. (The most beautiful pearls came from the Indian Ocean.)
2. In the seventeenth century, a carat was between 1/144 and 1/150 of an ounce. A twenty-four-carat pearl was therefore very large, weighing roughly 1/6 of an ounce.

"Signor Corvino! Signor Corvino!"—took
Paper and pen and ink, and there I asked him
Whom he would have his heir? "Corvino." Who
Should be executor? "Corvino." And
To any question he was silent to,
I still interpreted the nods he made
Through weakness for consent, and sent home th'others,
Nothing bequeathed them but to cry and curse.

CORVINO Oh, my dear Mosca! (*They embrace.*) Does he not perceive us?

MOSCA No more than a blind harper.[3] He knows no man,
No face of friend, nor name of any servant,
Who 'twas that fed him last or gave him drink;
Not those he hath begotten or brought up
Can he remember.

CORVINO Has he children?

MOSCA Bastards,[4]
Some dozen or more, that he begot on beggars,
Gypsies and Jews and blackmoors,° when he was drunk. (*black Africans*)
Knew you not that, sir? 'Tis the common fable.° (*rumor*)
The dwarf, the fool, the eunuch are all his;
He's the true father of his family
In all save° me, but he has given 'em nothing. (*except*)

CORVINO That's well, that's well. Art sure he does not hear us?

MOSCA Sure, sir? Why, look you, credit your own sense.° (*believe your senses*)
[*Shouting at Volpone*] The pox° approach and add to your diseases (*syphilis*)
If it would send you hence the sooner, sir.
For° your incontinence, it hath deserved it (*As for*)
Throughly° and throughly, and the plague to boot. (*Thoroughly*)
[*To Corvino*] You may come near, sir. [*Shouting at Volpone again*] Would you would once close
Those filthy eyes of yours, that flow with slime
Like two frog-pits,° and those same hanging cheeks, (*mud puddles*)
Covered with hide instead of skin—nay, help, sir—
That look like frozen dishclouts° set on end! (*dishrags*)

CORVINO [*shouting at Volpone*] Or like an old smoked wall on which the rain
Ran down in streaks!

MOSCA Excellent, sir! Speak out;
You may be louder yet; a culverin° (*firearm*)
Dischargèd in his ear would hardly bore it.

CORVINO [*shouting*] His nose is like a common sewer, still° running. (*continually*)

MOSCA 'Tis good! And what his mouth?

CORVINO [*shouting*] A very draught!° (*cesspool; privy*)

MOSCA Oh, stop it up—

CORVINO By no means.

MOSCA Pray you let me.
Faith, I could stifle him rarely with a pillow

3. Harp players were often blind.
4. By law, ordinarily barred from the line of inheritance.

As well as any woman that should keep° him. *take care of*

CORVINO Do as you will, but I'll be gone.

MOSCA Be so;

It is your presence makes him last so long.

CORVINO I pray you, use no violence.

MOSCA No, sir? Why?

Why should you be thus scrupulous? Pray you, sir.

CORVINO Nay, at your discretion.

MOSCA Well, good sir, begone.

CORVINO I will not trouble him now to take my pearl?

MOSCA Pooh! Nor your diamond. What a needless care
Is this afflicts you? Is not all here yours?
Am not I here, whom you have made your creature?
That owe my being to you?

CORVINO Grateful Mosca!
Thou art my friend, my fellow, my companion,
My partner, and shalt share in all my fortunes.

MOSCA Excepting one.

CORVINO What's that?

MOSCA Your gallant° wife, sir. *splendid*

[*Exit Corvino.*]

Now is he gone. We had no other means
To shoot him hence but this.

VOLPONE My divine Mosca!
Thou hast today outgone thyself. *Another knocks.*
Who's there?
I will be troubled with no more. Prepare
Me music, dances, banquets, all delights.
The Turk[5] is not more sensual in his pleasures
Than will Volpone. [*Exit Mosca.*]
Let me see, a pearl?
A diamond? Plate? *Cecchines*? Good morning's purchase.° *haul*
Why, this is better than rob churches, yet,
Or fat by eating, once a month, a man.° *i.e., taking monthly interest*

[*Enter Mosca.*]

Who is't?

MOSCA The beauteous Lady Would-be, sir,
Wife to the English knight, Sir Politic Would-be—
This is the style, sir, is directed me[6]—
Hath sent to know how you have slept tonight,° *last night*
And if you would be visited.

VOLPONE Not now.
Some three hours hence—

MOSCA I told the squire° so much. *messenger*

VOLPONE When I am high with mirth and wine: then, then.
'Fore heaven, I wonder at the desperate° valor *reckless*
Of the bold English, that they dare let loose
Their wives to all encounters![7]

MOSCA Sir, this knight

5. Stereotyped as given to decadent luxuries.
6. This is the mode of address I've been told to use.
7. Married Englishwomen were reputed to enjoy more personal freedom than their southern European counterparts; Venetian wives in particular were much restricted, though Celia's situation is obviously extreme (see below, lines 118–26).

Had not his name for nothing. He is politic,° *canny*
And knows, howe'er his wife affect strange° airs, *foreign; bizarre*
She hath not yet the face[8] to be dishonest.° *unchaste*
But had she Signor Corvino's wife's face—
VOLPONE Has she so rare a face?
MOSCA Oh, sir, the wonder,
The blazing star[9] of Italy! A wench
O'the first year!° A beauty ripe as harvest! *Unflawed and in her prime*
Whose skin is whiter than a swan, all over,
Than silver, snow, or lilies! A soft lip,
Would° tempt you to eternity of kissing! *That would*
And flesh that melteth in the touch to blood![1]
Bright as your gold, and lovely as your gold!
VOLPONE Why had not I known this before?
MOSCA Alas, sir,
Myself but yesterday discovered it.
VOLPONE How might I see her?
MOSCA Oh, not possible.
She's kept as warily as is your gold:
Never does come abroad,° never takes air *outside*
But at a window. All her looks are sweet
As the first° grapes or cherries, and are watched *(of the season)*
As near° as they are. *closely*
VOLPONE I must see her—
MOSCA Sir,
There is a guard of ten spies thick upon her—
All his whole household—each of which is set
Upon his fellow, and have all their charge
When he goes out; when he comes in, examined.[2]
VOLPONE I will go see her, though but at her window.
MOSCA In some disguise, then.
VOLPONE That is true. I must
Maintain mine own shape still the same.[3] We'll think.
[*Exeunt.*]

2.1

[*Enter*] *Politic Would-be* [*and*] *Peregrine.*

POLITIC Sir, to a wise man all the world's his soil.[1]
It is not Italy, nor France, nor Europe
That must bound me if my fates call me forth.
Yet I protest° it is no salt° desire *insist / inordinate*
Of seeing countries, shifting a religion,[2]
Nor any disaffection to the state
Where I was bred—and unto which I owe
My dearest plots°—hath brought me out;° much less *projects / abroad*

8. (1) Beauty; (2) shamelessness.
9. Comet. (Rare and beautiful.)
1. (1) Blushes; (2) sexual responsiveness. (Mosca is evidently conjecturing here.)
2. Each member of the household spies on all the others; each gets his instructions when Corvino departs and is interrogated when he returns.
3. I must, in my own person, continue to pretend to be near death.
2.1. Saint Mark's Square.
1. Proverbial, like most of Sir Pol's "original" advice. "Soil" means "native land."
2. Throughout the sixteenth and seventeenth centuries, members of religious minorities throughout Europe sought refuge in lands more hospitable to their faiths.

That idle, antique, stale, gray-headed project
Of knowing men's minds and manners with Ulysses;[3]
But a peculiar humor° of my wife's — *whim*
Laid for this height° of Venice, to observe, — *latitude*
To quote,° to learn the language, and so forth.— — *jot things down*
I hope you travel, sir, with license?[4]

PEREGRINE Yes.

POLITIC I dare the safelier converse. How long, sir,
Since you left England?

PEREGRINE Seven weeks.

POLITIC So lately!
You ha' not been with my Lord Ambassador?

PEREGRINE Not yet, sir.

POLITIC Pray you, what news, sir, vents our climate?[5]
I heard last night a most strange thing reported
By some of my lord's° followers, and I long — *the ambassador's*
To hear how't will be seconded.° — *confirmed*

PEREGRINE What was't, sir?

POLITIC Marry, sir, of a raven that should build° — *reportedly built*
In a ship royal of the King's.

PEREGRINE [*aside*] This fellow,
Does he gull° me, trow?° Or is gulled?—Your name, sir? — *trick / do you suppose?*

POLITIC My name is Politic Would-be.

PEREGRINE [*aside*] Oh, that speaks° him.— — *characterizes*
A knight, sir?

POLITIC A poor knight, sir.[6]

PEREGRINE Your lady
Lies° here in Venice for intelligence° — *Stays / news*
Of tires° and fashions and behavior — *apparel*
Among the courtesans?[7] The fine Lady Would-be?

POLITIC Yes, sir, the spider and the bee ofttimes
Suck from one flower.

PEREGRINE Good Sir Politic,
I cry you mercy!° I have heard much of you. — *beg your pardon*
'Tis true, sir, of your raven.

POLITIC On your knowledge?

PEREGRINE Yes, and your lion's whelping in the Tower.[8]

POLITIC Another whelp!

PEREGRINE Another, sir.

POLITIC Now, heaven!
What prodigies° be these? The fires at Berwick! — *strange occurrences*
And the new star![9] These things concurring,° strange! — *happening together*
And full of omen! Saw you those meteors?

PEREGRINE I did, sir.

3. The hero of the *Odyssey*, an archetype of the wise traveler.
4. A passport. (English people could not travel abroad without permission.)
5. Comes from our part of the world?
6. In the first decade of the seventeenth century, King James I raised badly needed money by selling knighthoods to many whose birth, attainments, or wealth would not have previously merited a title.
7. Venice was famous for its elegant prostitutes.
8. A lioness kept at the Tower of London gave birth in 1604 and 1605.
9. The fires at Berwick were aurora borealis visible above Berwick, Northumberland, in 1605, said to resemble battling armies. The new star, a supernova, was described by the astronomer Johannes Kepler in 1604.

POLITIC Fearful! Pray you sir, confirm me:
Were there three porpoises seen above the bridge,[1]
As they give out?° *people report*
PEREGRINE Six, and a sturgeon, sir.
POLITIC I am astonished!
PEREGRINE Nay, sir, be not so.
I'll tell you a greater prodigy than these—
POLITIC What should these things portend!
PEREGRINE The very day—
Let me be sure—that I put forth from London,
There was a whale discovered in the river
As high° as Woolwich,[2] that had waited there— *far upstream*
Few know how many months—for the subversion° *scuttling*
Of the Stode Fleet.[3]
POLITIC Is't possible? Believe it,
'Twas either sent from Spain or the Archdukes.[4]
Spinola's[5] whale, upon my life, my credit!° *honor*
Will they not leave these projects? Worthy sir,
Some other news.
PEREGRINE Faith, Stone the fool is dead;
And they do lack a tavern-fool extremely.
POLITIC Is Mas' Stone dead?[6]
PEREGRINE He's dead, sir. Why, I hope
You thought him not immortal? [*Aside*] Oh, this knight,
Were he well known, would be a precious thing
To fit our English stage. He° that should write° *(Anyone) / write about*
But such a fellow should be thought to feign
Extremely, if not maliciously.
POLITIC Stone dead!
PEREGRINE Dead. Lord, how deeply, sir, you apprehend it!
He was no kinsman to you?
POLITIC That° I know of. *Not that*
Well, that same fellow was an unknown fool.[7]
PEREGRINE And yet you knew him, it seems?
POLITIC I did so. Sir,
I knew him one of the most dangerous heads
Living within the state, and so I held° him. *considered*
PEREGRINE Indeed, sir?
POLITIC While he lived, in action,° *subversive activities*
He has received weekly intelligence,
Upon my knowledge, out of the Low Countries,
For all parts of the world, in cabbages,° *(a Dutch import)*
And those dispensed again to ambassadors
In oranges, muskmelons, apricots,
Lemons, pome-citrons,° and suchlike—sometimes *grapefruitlike fruits*

1. A porpoise was found upstream of London Bridge in the Thames River the January before *Volpone* was first performed.
2. A town on the Thames, a bit to the east of London.
3. The English merchant adventurers' ships, which were harboring at Stade, in the mouth of the Elbe River.
4. The Archdukes Albert of Austria and his wife, Isabella, the Infanta of Spain, ruled the Netherlands in the name of Spain.
5. Ambrosio de Spinola was general of the Spanish army in the Netherlands.
6. "Mas'" means "master," a term of address for boys and fools. Stone, King James's outspoken court jester, was a well-known urban character. He was whipped the year before *Volpone*'s first performance for slandering the Lord Admiral. Politic is evidently unaware of the play on words in "Stone dead."
7. The person who said this was not commonly recognized as a spy; he used foolery as his cover.

In Colchester oysters, and your Selsey cockles.[8]
PEREGRINE You make me wonder!
POLITIC Sir, upon my knowledge.
Nay, I have observed him at your public ordinary° — *tavern*
Take his advertisement° from a traveler— — *information*
A concealed statesman—in a trencher° of meat, — *wooden plate*
And instantly before the meal was done
Convey an answer in a toothpick.[9]
PEREGRINE Strange!
How could this be, sir?
POLITIC Why, the meat was cut
So like his character,° and so laid as he — *code letters*
Must easily read the cipher.
PEREGRINE I have heard
He could not read, sir.
POLITIC So 'twas given out,° — *reported*
In polity,° by those that did employ him. — *Craftily*
But he could read, and had your languages,° — *knew foreign languages*
And to't° as sound a noddle°— — *in addition / head*
PEREGRINE I have heard, sir,
That your baboons were spies, and that they were
A kind of subtle nation near to China.
POLITIC Ay, ay, your *Mamuluchi.*[1] Faith, they had
Their hand in a French plot or two, but they
Were so extremely given to women as
They made discovery of° all. Yet I — *They revealed*
Had my advices° here, on Wednesday last, — *information*
From one of their own coat;° they were returned, — *kind*
Made their relations,° as the fashion is, — *reports*
And now stand fair° for fresh employment. — *ready*
PEREGRINE [*aside*] Heart!° — *By God's heart!*
This Sir Pol will be° ignorant of nothing. — *admit to being*
[*To Politic*] It seems, sir, you know all?
POLITIC Not all, sir. But
I have some general notions; I do love
To note and to observe. Though I live out,° — *abroad*
Free from the active torrent, yet I'd mark
The currents and the passages of things
For mine own private use, and know the ebbs
And flows of state.
PEREGRINE Believe it, sir, I hold
Myself in no small tie unto my fortunes° — *much obliged to my luck*
For casting me thus luckily upon you,
Whose knowledge—if your bounty equal it—
May do me great assistance in instruction
For my behavior and my bearing, which
Is yet so rude and raw—
POLITIC Why, came you forth
Empty of rules for travel?
PEREGRINE Faith, I had

8. Expensive delicacies, unlikely tavern fare.
9. Presumably by inserting a tiny note into a toothpick hollowed out for espionage use.
1. Mamluks, a class of warriors originally from Asia Minor, who ruled Egypt from 1250 to 1517.

Some common ones from out that vulgar grammar,[2]
Which he that cried° Italian to me taught me. *taught orally*
POLITIC Why, this it is that spoils all our brave bloods,° *fine young men*
Trusting our hopeful° gentry unto pedants, *promising*
Fellows of outside and mere bark.[3] You seem
To be a gentleman of ingenuous race°— *honorable family*
I not profess it,° but my fate hath been *don't declare it openly*
To be where I have been consulted with
In this high kind,° touching some great men's sons, *important matter*
Persons of blood° and honor— *noble birth*
PEREGRINE Who be these, sir?

2.2

[*Enter*] *Mosca* [*and*] *Nano* [*disguised as a mountebank's assistants*].

MOSCA Under that window, there't must be. The same.
[*Mosca and Nano set up a platform.*]
POLITIC Fellows to mount a bank!° Did your instructor *platform*
In the dear tongues[1] never discourse to you
Of the Italian mountebanks?
PEREGRINE Yes, sir.
POLITIC Why,
Here shall you see one.
PEREGRINE They are quacksalvers,° *quacks*
Fellows that live by venting° oils and drugs. *selling; spewing out*
POLITIC Was that the character he gave you of them?
PEREGRINE As I remember.
POLITIC Pity his ignorance.
They are the only knowing men of Europe!
Great general scholars, excellent physicians,
Most admired statesmen, professed favorites
And cabinet counselors° to the greatest princes! *close advisers*
The only languaged° men of all the world! *most eloquent*
PEREGRINE And I have heard they are most lewd° impostors, *ignorant*
Made all of terms° and shreds, no less beliers *jargon*
Of great men's favors than their own vile med'cines,
Which they will utter° upon monstrous oaths, *advertise for sale*
Selling that drug for twopence ere they part
Which they have valued at twelve crowns° before. *silver or gold coins*
POLITIC Sir, calumnies are answered best with silence.
Yourself shall judge. [*To Mosca and Nano*] Who is it
mounts, my friends?
MOSCA Scoto of Mantua,[2] sir.
POLITIC Is't he? [*To Peregrine*] Nay, then,
I'll proudly promise, sir, you shall behold
Another man than has been phant'sied° to you. *presented in imagination*
I wonder yet that he should mount his bank
Here in this nook, that has been wont t'appear
In face of° the piazza! Here he comes. *Facing*

2. Modern language textbook, which sometimes included travelers' tips.
3. Superficial accomplishments.
2.2. The scene continues.

1. Italian was called the "cara lingua," a phrase Sir Politic translates.
2. An Italian juggler and magician who visited England and performed before Elizabeth I in the 1570s.

[*Enter*] Volpone [*disguised as a mountebank, followed by*] *a crowd.*

VOLPONE [*to Nano*] Mount, zany.° — *clown; performer*

[*Volpone and Nano climb onto the platform.*]

CROWD Follow, follow, follow, follow, follow!

POLITIC See how the people follow him! He's a man
May write ten thousand crowns in bank here. Note,
Mark but his gesture. I do use° to observe — *make it my practice*
The state° he keeps, in getting up. — *stateliness*

PEREGRINE 'Tis worth it, sir.

VOLPONE Most noble gentlemen and my worthy patrons, it may seem strange that I, your Scoto Mantuano, who was ever wont to fix my bank in face of the public piazza near the shelter of the portico to the *procuratia,*[3] should now, after eight months' absence from this illustrious city of Venice, humbly retire myself into an obscure nook of the piazza.

POLITIC [*to Peregrine*] Did not I now object the same?° — *ask the same question*

PEREGRINE Peace, sir.

VOLPONE Let me tell you: I am not, as your Lombard proverb saith, cold on my feet,° or content to part with my commodities at a cheaper rate than I accustomed; look not for it. Nor that the calumnious reports of that impudent detractor and shame to our profession (Alessandro Buttone,° I mean) who gave out in public I was condemned a *'sforzato*° to the galleys for poisoning the Cardinal Bembo's—cook,[4] hath at all attached,° much less dejected me. No, no, worthy gentlemen. To tell you true, I cannot endure to see the rabble of these ground *ciarlitani,*[5] that spread their cloaks on the pavement as if they meant to do feats of activity° and then come in lamely with their moldy tales out of Boccaccio, like stale Tabarine,[6] the fabulist: some of them discoursing their travels and of their tedious captivity in the Turks' galleys, when indeed, were the truth known, they were the Christians' galleys, where very temperately they ate bread and drunk water as a wholesome penance, enjoined them by their confessors, for base pilferies.

cold on my feet: in desperate straits / Buttone: a rival mountebank / 'sforzato: prisoner / attached: stuck to / activity: acrobatics

POLITIC [*to Peregrine*] Note but his bearing and contempt of these.

VOLPONE These turdy-facy-nasty-paty-lousy-fartical rogues, with one poor groatsworth° of unprepared antimony,[7] finely wrapped up in several *scartoccios,*° are able very well to kill their twenty a week, and play;° yet these meager starved spirits, who have half stopped the organs of their minds with earthy oppilations,° want° not their favorers among your shriveled, salad-eating artisans, who are overjoyed that they may have their ha'p'orth° of physic; though it purge 'em into another world, 't makes no matter.

groatsworth: fourpenceworth / scartoccios: paper envelopes / play: as if it were a game / oppilations: obstructions / want: lack / ha'p'orth: halfpennyworth

POLITIC Excellent! Ha' you heard better language, sir?

VOLPONE Well, let 'em go.° And, gentlemen, honorable gen- — *say no more about them*

3. Arcade on the north side of the Piazza di San Marco.
4. Pietro Bembo (1470–1547) was a famous humanist, featured as a speaker in Castiglione's *Book of the Courtier* (1528). "Cook" is a teasing substitution for "whore."
5. Charlatans too poor to afford a "bank," or platform.
6. Boccaccio's *Decameron* is a storehouse of tales. Tabarine was a member of an Italian comic troupe that played in France and perhaps in England.
7. White metal used as an emetic and, in larger doses, a poison.

tlemen, know that for this time, our bank, being thus removed from the clamors of the *canaglia*,° shall be the scene of pleasure and delight. For I have nothing to sell, little or nothing to sell. *mob*

POLITIC I told you, sir, his end.

PEREGRINE You did so, sir.

VOLPONE I protest, I and my six servants are not able to make of this precious liquor so fast as it is fetched away from my lodging by gentlemen of your city, strangers of the *terra firma*,[8] worshipful merchants, ay, and senators too, who ever since my arrival have detained me to their uses by their splendidous liberalities. And worthily. For what avails your rich man to have his magazines° stuffed with *moscadelli*,° or of° the purest grape, when his physicians prescribe him (on pain of death) to drink nothing but water cocted° with anise seeds? Oh, health, health! The blessing of the rich! The riches of the poor! Who can buy thee at too dear a rate, since there is no enjoying this world without thee? Be not then so sparing of your purses, honorable gentlemen, as to abridge the natural course of life— *storehouses / wine* *wine of* *boiled*

PEREGRINE You see his end?

POLITIC Ay, is't not good?

VOLPONE For when a humid flux° or catarrh, by the mutability of air, falls from your head into an arm or shoulder or any other part, take you a ducat or your *cecchine* of gold and apply to the place affected; see what good effect it can work. No, no, 'tis this blessed *unguento*,° this rare extraction, that hath only power to disperse all malignant humors that proceed either of hot, cold, moist, or windy causes[9]— *runny discharge* *ointment*

PEREGRINE I would he had put in "dry," too.

POLITIC Pray you, observe.

VOLPONE To fortify the most indigest and crude° stomach, ay, were it of one that, through extreme weakness, vomited blood, applying only a warm napkin to the place after the unction and fricace;° for the *vertigine*° in the head putting but a drop into your nostrils, likewise behind the ears, a most sovereign° and approved remedy; the *mal caduco*, cramps, convulsions, paralyses, epilepsies, *tremor cordia*, retired nerves, ill vapors of the spleen, stoppings of the liver, the stone, the strangury, *hernia ventosa, iliaca passio;* stops a *dysenteria* immediately; easeth the torsion of the small guts; and cures *melancholia hypocondriaca*,[1] being taken and applied according to my printed receipt.° (*Pointing to his bill and his glass*)° For this is the physician, this the medicine; this counsels, this cures; this gives the direction, this works the effect; and in sum, both together may be termed an *upset* *massage / dizziness* *potent* *directions* *paper and flagon*

8. Mainland territory of Venice.

9. Renaissance medicine was based on the theory of the humors, four bodily fluids whose balance within the body determined both physical and mental health. Their qualities, in various combinations, were hot, cold, moist, and dry; hence Peregrine's comment in the next line.

1. Volpone's list of diseases includes "*mal caduco*," epilepsy; "*tremor cordia*," palpitations; "retired nerves," withered sinews; "ill vapors of the spleen," short temper; "stone," kidney stones; "strangury," painful urination; "*hernia ventosa*," a hernia containing air; "*iliaca passio*," intestinal cramps; "*dysenteria*," diarrhea; "torsion of the small guts," spasmodic bowel pain; and "*melancholia hypochondriaca*," depression.

abstract of the theoric and practic in the Aesculapian[2] art. 'Twill cost you eight crowns. And, Zan Fritatta,[3] pray thee sing a verse extempore in honor of it.

POLITIC How do you like him, sir?

PEREGRINE Most strangely, I!

POLITIC Is not his language rare?° — *unrivaled*

PEREGRINE But° alchemy — *Except for*
I never heard the like, or Broughton's books.[4]

SONG

NANO [*sings*] Had old Hippocrates or Galen,[5]
That to their books put med'cines all in,
But known this secret, they had never
(Of which they will be guilty ever)
Been murderers of so much paper,° — *Written so much*
Or wasted many a hurtless taper;° — *candle (working at night)*
No Indian drug had e'er been famed,
Tobacco, sassafras[6] not named,
Ne° yet of *guacum*[7] one small stick, sir, — *Nor*
Nor Raymond Lully's great elixir.
Ne had been known the Danish Gonswart
Or Paracelsus with his long sword.[8]

PEREGRINE All this yet will not do; eight crowns is high.

VOLPONE [*to Nano*] No more.—Gentlemen, if I had but time to discourse to you the miraculous effects of this my oil, surnamed *oglio del Scoto,* with the countless catalogue of those I have cured of th'aforesaid and many more diseases, the patents and privileges of all the princes and commonwealths of Christendom, or but the depositions of those that appeared on my part before the signory of the *Sanitá,*[9] and most learned College of Physicians, where I was authorized, upon notice taken of the admirable virtues of my medicaments and mine own excellency in matter of rare and unknown secrets, not only to disperse them publicly in this famous city but in all the territories that happily joy under the government of the most pious and magnificent states of Italy. But may some other gallant fellow say, "Oh, there be divers that make profession° to have as good and as experimented receipts as yours." Indeed, very many have assayed like apes in imitation of that which is really and essentially in me, to make of° this oil; bestowed great cost in furnaces, stills, alembics,[1] continual fires, and preparation of the ingredients (as indeed there goes to it six hundred several simples,° besides some quantity of human fat for the conglutination,° which we buy of the anatomists); but, when

that claim / *some of* / *different ingredients* / *to glue it together*

2. Medical. Aesculapius was the classical god of medicine.
3. Italian dialect for "Jack Omelet," the name of the zany (see line 28), here referring to Nano.
4. Hugh Broughton was a Puritan rabbinical scholar who wrote impenetrable treatises on scriptural matters.
5. Greek physicians (c. 460–377 B.C.E. and 129–c. 199 C.E., respectively) who developed the theory of humors.
6. New World plants, used medicinally.
7. The bark of a tropical tree, used medicinally.
8. Raymond Lully was a medieval astrologer rumored to have discovered the elixir of life. "Danish Gonswart" has not been positively identified. Paracelsus was an early sixteenth-century alchemist who developed an alternative to Galenic medicine; he carried his medicines in his sword pommel.
9. Venetian medical licensing board.
1. Vessels for purifying liquids.

these practitioners come to the last decoction,° blow, blow, puff, puff, and all flies *in fumo*.° Ha, ha, ha! Poor wretches! I rather pity their folly and indiscretion° than their loss of time and money; for those may be recovered by industry, but to be a fool born is a disease incurable. For myself, I always from my youth have endeavored to get the rarest secrets and book° them, either in exchange° or for money; I spared nor° cost nor labor where anything was worthy to be learned. And, gentlemen, honorable gentlemen, I will undertake, by virtue of chemical art, out of the honorable hat that covers your head to extract the four elements—that is to say, the fire, air, water, and earth—and return you your felt° without burn or stain. For, whilst others have been at the balloo° I have been at my book, and am now past the craggy paths of study and come to the flow'ry plains of honor and reputation.

boiling down / *up in smoke* / *lack of discernment* / *record* / *barter* / *neither* / *felt hat* / *Venetian ball game*

POLITIC I do assure you, sir, that is his aim.

VOLPONE But to our price.

PEREGRINE And that withal,° Sir Pol.

as well

VOLPONE You all know, honorable gentlemen, I never valued this *ampulla,* or vial, at less than eight crowns, but for this time I am content to be deprived of it for six; six crowns is the price, and less, in courtesy, I know you cannot offer me. Take it or leave it howsoever, both it and I am at your service. I ask you not as the value of the thing, for then I should demand° of you a thousand crowns; so the Cardinals Montalto, Fernese, the great Duke of Tuscany, my gossip,° with divers other princes, have given me. But I despise money. Only to show my affection to you, honorable gentlemen, and your illustrious state here, I have neglected the messages of these princes, mine own offices,° framed° my journey hither only to present you with the fruits of my travels. [*To Nano and Mosca*] Tune your voices once more to the touch of your instruments, and give the honorable assembly some delightful recreation.

ask / *buddy* / *duties* / *devised*

PEREGRINE What monstrous and most painful circumstance°
Is here, to get some three or four *gazets*!°
Some threepence, i'th'whole, for that 'twill come to.

beating around the bush / *small Venetian coins*

SONG

[*During the song, Celia appears at her window, above.*]

NANO [*sings*]° You that would last long, list to my song,
Make no more coil,° but buy of this oil.
Would you be ever fair and young?
Stout of teeth and strong of tongue?
Tart° of palate? Quick of ear?
Sharp of sight? Of nostril clear?
Moist of hand[2] and light of foot?
Or (I will come nearer to't)°
Would you live free from all diseases,
Do the act your mistress pleases,
Yet fright all aches° from your bones?
Here's a med'cine for the nones.°

(accompanied by Mosca) / *fuss* / *Keen* / *get to the point* / *venereal disease* / *occasion*

2. Associated with youth and sexual vigor.

VOLPONE Well, I am in a humor at this time to make a present
of the small quantity my coffer contains: to the rich in courtesy, and to the poor for God's sake.° Wherefore, now mark;   *charity*
I asked you six crowns, and six crowns at other times you
have paid me. You shall not give me six crowns, nor five, nor
four, nor three, nor two, nor one, nor half a ducat, no, nor
a *moccenigo*.° Six—pence it will cost you, or six hundred   *(worth ninepence)*
pound—expect no lower price, for by the banner of my
front,° I will not bate a *bagatine*,[3] that I will have only a   *displayed on my "bank"*
pledge of your loves, to carry something from amongst you
to show I am not contemned° by you. Therefore now, toss   *scorned*
your handkerchiefs cheerfully, cheerfully, and be advertised°   *notified*
that the first heroic spirit that deigns to grace me with a
handkerchief, I will give it a little remembrance of some-
thing beside, shall please° it better than if I had presented   *which will please*
it with a double *pistolet*.[4]

PEREGRINE Will you be that heroic spark,° Sir Pol?   *gallant*

Celia at the window throws down her handkerchief [with a coin tied inside it].

Oh, see! The window has prevented you.°   *beaten you to it*

VOLPONE Lady, I kiss your bounty, and, for this timely grace
you have done your poor Scoto of Mantua, I will return you,
over and above my oil, a secret of that high and inestimable
nature shall° make you forever enamored on that minute   *which will*
wherein your eye first descended on so mean,° yet not alto-   *lowly*
gether to be despised, an object. Here is a powder concealed
in this paper of which, if I should speak to the worth, nine
thousand volumes were but as one page, that page as a line,
that line as a word—so short is this pilgrimage of man, which
some call life, to° the expressing of it. Would I reflect on the   *compared to*
price, why, the whole world were but as an empire, that
empire as a province, that province as a bank, that bank as
a private purse, to the purchase of it. I will only tell you it is
the powder that made Venus a goddess, given her by Apollo,[5]
that kept her perpetually young, cleared her wrinkles, firmed
her gums, filled° her skin, colored her hair; from her derived   *filled out*
to Helen, and at the sack of Troy unfortunately lost; till now
in this our age it was as happily° recovered by a studious   *fortunately*
antiquary out of some ruins of Asia, who sent a moiety° of   *part*
it to the court of France (but much sophisticated)° where-   *adulterated*
with the ladies there now color their hair. The rest, at this
present, remains with me, extracted to a quintessence,° so   *refined concentrate*
that wherever it but touches, in youth it perpetually pre-
serves, in age restores the complexion; seats your teeth, did°   *even if*
they dance like virginal jacks,[6] firm as a wall; makes them
white as ivory that were black as—

2.3

[Enter] Corvino. He beats away the mountebank, etc.

CORVINO Spite o'the devil, and my shame! Come down here,
Come down! No house but mine to make your scene?°   *stage set*

3. I won't reduce the price by even a tiny coin.
4. Spanish gold coin worth about one English pound.
5. In his capacity as the god of health.
6. The virginal is a type of harpsichord; its "jacks" are quills that pluck strings when the keys are played, but the term was also sometimes used for the keys.

2.3. The scene continues.

Signor Flaminio, will you down, sir? Down!
What, is my wife your Franciscina, sir?[1]
No windows on the whole piazza here
To make your properties° but mine? But mine? *stage props*
Heart! Ere tomorrow I shall be new christened
And called the *pantalone di besogniosi*[2]
About the town. [*Exeunt Volpone, Nano, and Mosca, followed by Corvino and the crowd.*]

PEREGRINE What should this mean, Sir Pol?
POLITIC Some trick of state, believe it. I will home.
PEREGRINE It may be some design on you.
POLITIC I know not.
I'll stand upon my guard.
PEREGRINE It is your best,° sir. *best course of action*
POLITIC This three weeks, all my advices, all my letters,
They have been intercepted.
PEREGRINE Indeed, sir?
Best have a care.
POLITIC Nay, so I will. [*Exit.*]
PEREGRINE This knight,
I may not lose him,° for my mirth, till night. [*Exit.*] *I won't leave him*

2.4

[*Enter*] *Volpone* [*and*] *Mosca.*

VOLPONE Oh, I am wounded!
MOSCA Where, sir?
VOLPONE Not without;° *externally*
Those blows were nothing; I could bear them ever.
But angry Cupid, bolting° from her° eyes, *shooting darts / (Celia's)*
Hath shot himself into me like a flame,
Where now he flings about his burning heat,
As in a furnace an ambitious° fire *rising*
Whose vent is stopped.° The fight is all within me. *stopped up*
I cannot live except° thou help me, Mosca; *unless*
My liver[1] melts, and I, without the hope
Of some soft air from her refreshing breath,
Am but a heap of cinders.
MOSCA 'Las, good sir!
Would you had never seen her.
VOLPONE Nay, would thou
Hadst never told me of her.
MOSCA Sir, 'tis true;
I do confess I was unfortunate,
And you unhappy; but I'm bound in conscience
No less than duty to effect my best

1. Corvino imagines the scene in terms of a stock episode from the Italian commedia dell'arte, in which the young lover, conventionally named Flaminio after the famous actor Flaminio Scala, seduces Franciscina, the easygoing serving wench.
2. The *pantalone* is another stock figure in the commedia dell'arte, a decrepit old man suspicious of his desirable young wife. *Di besogniosi* is his jocular surname, meaning "descended from poor people."
2.4. Volpone's house.
1. Supposed to be the seat of lust.

To your release of torment, and I will, sir.
VOLPONE Dear Mosca, shall I hope?
MOSCA Sir, more than dear,
I will not bid you to despair of aught
Within a human compass.° *That's humanly possible*
VOLPONE Oh, there spoke
My better angel. Mosca, take my keys.
Gold, plate, and jewels, all's at thy devotion;° *disposal*
Employ them how thou wilt; nay, coin me too,[2]
So° thou in this but crown my longings. Mosca? *Provided that*
MOSCA Use but your patience.
VOLPONE So I have.[3]
MOSCA I doubt not
To bring success to your desires.
VOLPONE Nay, then,
I not repent me of my late disguise.
MOSCA If you can horn him,[4] sir, you need not.
VOLPONE True;
Besides, I never meant him for my heir.
Is not the color o'my beard and eyebrows[5]
To make me known?
MOSCA No jot.
VOLPONE I did it well.
MOSCA So well, would I could follow you in mine
With half the happiness!° And yet I would *success*
Escape your epilogue.° *(the beating)*
VOLPONE But were they gulled° *fooled*
With a belief that I was Scoto?
MOSCA Sir,
Scoto himself could hardly have distinguished!
I have not time to flatter you now. We'll part,
And, as I prosper, so applaud my art. [*Exeunt.*]

2.5

[*Enter*] *Corvino* [*and*] *Celia.*

CORVINO Death of mine honor, with the city's fool?
A juggling, tooth-drawing,[1] prating° mountebank? *chattering*
And at a public window? Where, whilst he
With his strained action° and his dole of faces[2] *overacting*
To his drug lecture draws your itching ears,
A crew of old, unmarried, noted lechers
Stood leering up like satyrs;° and you smile *lustful goat-men*
Most graciously! And fan your favors forth
To give your hot spectators satisfaction!
What, was your mountebank their call? Their whistle?[3]
Or were you enamored on his copper rings?
His saffron jewel with the toadstone° in't? *agatelike stone*
Or his embroidered suit with the cope-stitch,° *gaudy needlework*

2. Use my coins as well. (But also with the implication "make coins out of me," i.e., "turn my body into money.")
3. Punning on the original meaning of "patience," "enduring blows."
4. Cuckold him. (The husbands of adulterous wives were traditionally supposed to sprout horns.)
5. Red, because he is a fox.

2.5. Corvino's house.
1. Mountebanks, like barbers, performed dental work.
2. Small repertory of facial expressions.
3. Used to lure trained falcons.

Made of a hearse-cloth? Or his old tilt-feather?[4]
Or his starched beard? Well! You shall have him, yes.
He shall come home and minister unto you
The fricace for the mother.[5] Or, let me see,
I think you'd rather mount?[6] Would you not mount?
Why, if you'll mount, you may; yes truly, you may—
And so you may be seen down to th'foot.
Get you a cittern, Lady Vanity,[7]
And be a dealer with the virtuous° man; *virile*
Make one.[8] I'll but protest° myself a cuckold *proclaim*
And save your dowry.[9] I am a Dutchman, I!
For if you thought me an Italian,
You would be damned ere you did this, you whore.[1]
Thou'dst tremble to imagine that the murder
Of father, mother, brother, all thy race,° *kin*
Should follow as the subject of my justice!

CELIA Good sir, have patience!

CORVINO [*drawing a weapon*] What couldst thou propose
Less to thyself° than, in this heat of wrath *as your punishment*
And stung with my dishonor, I should strike
This steel unto° thee, with as many stabs *into*
As thou wert gazed upon with goatish° eyes? *lustful*

CELIA Alas, sir, be appeased! I could not think
My being at the window should more now
Move your impatience than at other times.

CORVINO No? Not to seek and entertain a parley° *have a conversation*
With a known knave? Before a multitude?
You were an actor with your handkerchief!
Which he most sweetly kissed in the receipt,
And might, no doubt, return it with a letter,
And 'point the place where you might meet—your sister's,
Your mother's, or your aunt's might serve the turn.° *occasion; sexual act*

CELIA Why, dear sir, when do I make these excuses?
Or ever stir abroad but to the church?
And that, so seldom—

CORVINO Well, it shall be less;
And thy restraint before was liberty
To° what I now decree: and therefore, mark me. *Compared with*
[*Pointing to the window*] First, I will have this bawdy light
dammed° up, *blocked*
And, till't be done, some two or three yards off
I'll chalk a line, o'er which if thou but chance
To set thy desp'rate foot, more hell, more horror,
More wild, remorseless rage shall seize on thee
Than on a conjurer that had heedless left
His circle's safety ere his devil was laid.[2]

4. The feather from a tilting (jousting) helmet. A hearse-cloth is a heavy cloth for draping over a coffin.
5. Womb massage; with obvious sexual innuendo. "The mother" was a term for the uterus, but also for a variety of ailments, from cramps to depression, that were supposed to originate there.
6. (1) Climb up on the mountebank's stage yourself; (2) take the top sexual position.
7. Allegorical character of a morality play representing pride and worldly pleasure. A cittern is a guitarlike instrument that conventionally was played by whores.
8. Join up with him. (With sexual innuendo.)
9. The husbands of proven adultresses could divorce them and keep their dowry.
1. The Dutch were proverbially phlegmatic, in contrast to Italians, who were stereotypically impetuous and vengeful.
2. Conjurers protected themselves from the devils who served them by staying inside a magical circle.

Then here's a lock which I will hang upon thee.
[*He shows a chastity belt.*]
And now I think on't, I will keep thee backwards;[3]
Thy lodging shall be backwards, thy walks backwards,
Thy prospect°—all be backwards; and no pleasure *view (see 58 n)*
That thou shalt know but backwards. Nay, since you force
My honest nature, know it is your own
Being too open makes me use you thus,
Since you will not contain your subtle° nostrils *delicate; crafty*
In a sweet° room, but they must snuff the air *sweet-smelling*
Of rank and sweaty passengers°— *Knock within.* *passersby*
One knocks.
Away, and be not seen, pain of thy life!° *on pain of death*
Not° look toward the window. If thou dost— *Do not*
[*Celia begins to exit.*]
Nay stay, hear this—let me not prosper, whore,
But I will make thee an anatomy,[4]
Dissect thee mine own self, and read° a lecture *deliver*
Upon thee to the city, and in public.
Away! [*Exit Celia.*]
Who's there?

[*Enter*] *Servitore* [*a Servant*].

SERVANT 'Tis Signor Mosca, sir.

2.6

CORVINO Let him come in. [*Exit Servant.*]
His master's dead! There's yet
Some good to help the bad.

[*Enter*] *Mosca.*

My Mosca, welcome!
I guess your news.
MOSCA I fear you cannot, sir.
CORVINO Is't not his death?
MOSCA Rather the contrary.
CORVINO Not his recovery?
MOSCA Yes, sir.
CORVINO I am cursed,
I am bewitched! My crosses° meet to vex me! *misfortunes*
How? How? How? How?
MOSCA Why, sir, with Scoto's oil.
Corbaccio and Voltore brought of° it *some of*
Whilst I was busy in an inner room—
CORVINO Death! That damned mountebank! But° for the law, *Were it not*
Now, I could kill the rascal. 'T cannot be
His oil should have that virtue.° Ha' not I *power*
Known him a common rogue, come fiddling in

3. In the back part of the house, lacking a view out onto the piazza; but with the suggestion of anal intercourse, supposedly favored by Italians.
4. Use you for anatomical research. (In the early modern period, physicians obtained the bodies of executed criminals upon which to perform dissections, often before large crowds.)
2.6. The scene continues.

To th'*osteria*° with a tumbling whore, *tavern (Italian)*
And, when he has done all his forced° tricks, been glad *contrived*
Of a poor spoonful of dead° wine with flies in't? *stale*
It cannot be. All his ingredients
Are a sheep's gall, a roasted bitch's marrow,
Some few sod° earwigs, pounded caterpillars, *boiled*
A little capon's grease, and fasting spittle:[1]
I know 'em to a dram.° *tiny amount*
MOSCA I know not, sir,
But some on't there they poured into his ears,
Some in his nostrils, and recovered him,
Applying but the fricace.° *massage*
CORVINO Pox o'that fricace!
MOSCA And since, to seem the more officious° *zealous*
And flatt'ring of his health, there they have had—
At extreme fees—the College of Physicians
Consulting on him how they might restore him;
Where one would have a cataplasm[2] of spices,
Another a flayed ape clapped to his breast,
A third would ha' it a dog, a fourth an oil
With wildcats' skins. At last, they all resolved
That to preserve him was no other means
But some young woman must be straight sought out,
Lusty° and full of juice, to sleep by him; *Vigorous; sexy*
And to this service—most unhappily
And most unwillingly—am I now employed,
Which here I thought to preacquaint you with,
For your advice, since it concerns you most,
Because I would not do that thing might cross
Your ends,[3] on whom I have my whole dependence, sir.
Yet if I do it not, they may delate[4]
My slackness to my patron, work me out
Of his opinion;° and there all your hopes, *favor*
Ventures, or whatsoever, are all frustrate.
I do but tell you, sir. Besides, they are all
Now striving who shall first present him. Therefore,
I could entreat you briefly, conclude somewhat;° *decide something*
Prevent° 'em if you can. *Forestall*
CORVINO Death to my hopes!
This is my villainous fortune! Best to hire
Some common courtesan.
MOSCA Ay, I thought on that, sir.
But they are all so subtle,° full of art,° *cunning / deceit*
And age again° doting and flexible, *old people moreover*
So as—I cannot tell—we may perchance
Light on a quean° may cheat us all. *whore (who)*
CORVINO 'Tis true.
MOSCA No, no; it must be one that has no tricks, sir,
Some simple thing, a creature made unto° it; *suited to; forced into*

1. Saliva of a fasting person (Scoto, who cannot afford anything to eat).
2. Poultice. (The substances described in the following lines were believed to work by absorbing the patient's infection, which bodes ill for the young woman prescribed for Volpone in lines 34–35.)
3. Do anything that might frustrate your purposes.
4. Report. (A legal term for making an accusation.)

Some wench you may command. Ha' you no kinswoman?
Godso°—think, think, think, think, think, think, think, sir. *(an oath)*
One o'the doctors offered there his daughter.
CORVINO How!
MOSCA Yes, Signor Lupo,° the physician. *Wolf (Italian)*
CORVINO His daughter?
MOSCA And a virgin, sir. Why, alas,
He knows the state of's body,° what it is, *of Volpone's body*
That naught can warm his blood, sir, but a fever,
Nor any incantation raise his spirit.° *vigor; semen*
A long forgetfulness hath seized that part.° *(his penis)*
Besides, sir, who shall know it? Some one or two—
CORVINO I pray thee give me leave.° [*He walks apart.*] If any man *give me a minute*
But I had had this luck—The thing in 'tself,
I know, is nothing.—Wherefore should not I
As well command my blood and my affections
As this dull doctor? In the point of honor
The cases are all one, of wife and daughter.
MOSCA [*aside*] I hear him coming.° *coming around*
CORVINO [*aside*] She shall do't.'Tis done.
'Slight,° if this doctor, who is not engaged, *By God's light (an oath)*
Unless 't be for his counsel (which is nothing),[5]
Offer his daughter, what should I, that am
So deeply in? I will prevent° him. Wretch! *forestall*
Covetous wretch!—Mosca, I have determined.
MOSCA How, sir?
CORVINO We'll make all sure. The party you wot° of *know (a circumlocution)*
Shall be mine own wife, Mosca.
MOSCA Sir, the thing
(But that I would not seem to counsel you)
I should have motioned° to you at the first. *proposed*
And, make your count,° you have cut all their throats. *rest assured*
Why, 'tis directly taking a possession![6]
And in his next fit we may let him go.
'Tis but to pull the pillow from his head
And he is throttled; 't had been done before,
But for your scrupulous doubts.
CORVINO Ay, a plague on't!
My conscience fools my wit.° Well, I'll be brief, *common sense*
And so be thou, lest they should be before us.
Go home, prepare him, tell him with what zeal
And willingness I do it; swear it was
On the first hearing (as thou mayst do, truly)
Mine own free motion.° *initiative*
MOSCA Sir, I warrant you,
I'll so possess° him with it that the rest *impress*
Of his starved clients shall be banished all,
And only you received. But come not, sir,
Until I send, for I have something else

5. Who is not financially involved, except for whatever slight fee he could expect for his advice.

6. A legal term for the heir's formal assumption of inherited property.

To ripen for your good; you must not know't.
CORVINO But do not you forget to send, now.
MOSCA Fear not.
[*Exit.*]

2.7

CORVINO Where are you, wife? My Celia? Wife?

[*Enter*] *Celia* [*weeping*].

What, blubbering?
Come, dry those tears. I think thou thought'st me in earnest?
Ha! By this light, I talked so but to try° thee. *test*
Methinks the lightness° of the occasion *triviality*
Should ha' confirmed thee.[1] Come, I am not jealous.
CELIA No?
CORVINO Faith, I am not, I, nor never[2] was;
It is a poor, unprofitable humor.
Do not I know if women have a will
They'll do 'gainst all the watches° o'the world? *despite the vigilance*
And that the fiercest° spies are tamed with gold? *even the fiercest*
Tut, I am confident in thee, thou shalt see't;
And see, I'll give thee cause too, to believe it.
Come, kiss me. Go and make thee ready straight
In all thy best attire, thy choicest jewels;
Put 'em all on, and, with 'em thy best looks.
We are invited to a solemn feast° *formal banquet*
At old Volpone's, where it shall appear
How far I am free from jealousy or fear. [*Exeunt.*]

3.1

[*Enter*] *Mosca.*

MOSCA I fear I shall begin to grow in love
With my dear self and my most prosp'rous parts,° *talents*
They do so spring and burgeon.° I can feel *swell; thrive*
A whimsy° i'my blood. I know not how, *giddiness*
Success hath made me wanton.° I could skip *sportive; reckless*
Out of my skin now like a subtle° snake, *agile; artful*
I am so limber. Oh, your parasite
Is a most precious thing, dropped from above,° *sent from heaven*
Not bred 'mongst clods and clodpolls° here on earth. *blockheads*
I muse the mystery was not made a science,
It is so liberally professed![1] Almost
All the wise world is little else in nature
But parasites or subparasites. And yet
I mean not those that have your bare town-art,[2]
To know who's fit to feed 'em; have no house,
No family, no care, and therefore mold

2.7. The scene continues.
1. Convinced you that I was not serious.
2. Double negatives are grammatical in Jacobean English.
3.1. The piazza.
1. I wonder why the craft was not made a subject for academic study, it is so frequently practiced! (Punning on the "liberal professions.")
2. Crude skills of ingratiation, sufficient only for getting free meals in taverns.

Tales for men's ears,° to bait° that sense; or get *tell juicy rumors / entice*
Kitchen-invention, and some stale receipts° *recipes*
To please the belly and the groin;° nor those, *(as aphrodisiacs)*
With their court-dog tricks, that can fawn and fleer,° *smile insincerely*
Make their revenue out of legs and faces,
Echo my lord, and lick away a moth;[3]
But your fine, elegant rascal, that can rise
And stoop almost together, like an arrow,
Shoot through the air as nimbly as a star,° *meteor*
Turn short as doth a swallow, and be here
And there and here and yonder all at once,
Present to any humor, all occasion,[4]
And change a visor° swifter than a thought! *mask; expression*
This is the creature had° the art born with him, *who had*
Toils not to learn it, but doth practice it
Out of most excellent nature;° and such sparks *innate ability*
Are the true parasites, others but their zanies.° *clownish imitators*

3.2

[*Enter*] *Bonario.*

[*Aside*] Who's this? Bonario? Old Corbaccio's son?
The person I was bound° to seek.—Fair sir, *on my way*
You are happ'ly° met. *fortunately*
BONARIO That cannot be by thee.
MOSCA Why, sir?
BONARIO Nay, pray thee know° thy way and leave me. *get on*
I would be loath to interchange discourse
With such a mate° as thou art. *fellow (contemptuous)*
MOSCA Courteous sir,
Scorn not my poverty.
BONARIO Not I, by heaven,
But thou shalt give me leave to hate thy baseness.
MOSCA Baseness?
BONARIO Ay. Answer me, is not thy sloth
Sufficient argument? Thy flattery?
Thy means of feeding?
MOSCA Heaven, be good to me!
These imputations are too common, sir,
And eas'ly stuck on virtue when she's poor.
You are unequal° to me, and howe'er *superior; unfair*
Your sentence° may be righteous, yet you are not, *verdict*
That, ere you know me, thus proceed in censure.
Saint Mark bear witness 'gainst you, 'tis inhuman.
[*He weeps.*]
BONARIO [*aside*] What? Does he weep? The sign is soft and good.
I do repent me that I was so harsh.
MOSCA 'Tis true that, swayed by strong necessity,
I am enforced to eat my careful° bread *hard-won*
With too much obsequy;° 'tis true, beside, *obsequiousness*

3. Make a living from bows and sycophantic looks, repeat anything a nobleman says, and fawn over him, fussing over every detail of his appearance.

4. Ready to respond to any mood or opportunity.

3.2. The scene continues.

That I am fain° to spin mine own poor raiment — *obliged*
Out of my mere observance,° being not born — *deferential service*
To a free° fortune. But that I have done — *i.e., inherited*
Base offices in rending friends asunder,
Dividing families, betraying counsels,
Whispering false lies, or mining° men with praises, — *undermining*
Trained° their credulity with perjuries, — *Lured on*
Corrupted chastity, or am in love
With mine own tender ease, but would not rather
Prove° the most rugged and laborious course — *Undergo*
That might redeem my present estimation,[1]
Let me here perish in all hope of goodness.

BONARIO [*aside*] This cannot be a personated° passion!— — *faked*
I was to blame, so to mistake thy nature;
Pray thee forgive me, and speak out thy business.

MOSCA Sir, it concerns you; and though I may seem
At first to make a main° offense in manners — *great*
And in my gratitude unto my master,
Yet for the pure love which I bear all right
And hatred of the wrong, I must reveal it.
This very hour your father is in purpose
To disinherit you—

BONARIO How!

MOSCA And thrust you forth
As a mere° stranger to his blood. 'Tis true, sir. — *utter*
The work no way engageth° me but as — *concerns*
I claim an interest in the general state
Of goodness and true virtue, which I hear
T'abound in you, and for which mere respect,° — *for which reason alone*
Without a second aim,° sir, I have done it. — *ulterior motive*

BONARIO This tale hath lost thee much of the late° trust — *recent*
Thou hadst with me. It is impossible.
I know not how to lend it any thought° — *believe that*
My father should be so unnatural.

MOSCA It is a confidence° that well becomes — *trustingness*
Your piety;° and formed, no doubt, it is — *filial loyalty*
From your own simple innocence, which makes
Your wrong° more monstrous and abhorred. But, sir, — *being wronged*
I now will tell you more. This very minute
It is or will be doing; and if you
Shall be but pleased to go with me, I'll bring you,
I dare not say where you shall see, but where
Your ear shall be a witness of the deed:
Hear yourself written bastard, and professed
The common issue of the earth.[2]

BONARIO I'm mazed!

MOSCA Sir, if I do it not, draw your just sword
And score your vengeance on my front° and face; — *brow*
Mark me your villain. You have too much wrong,
And I do suffer for you, sir. My heart
Weeps blood in anguish—

BONARIO Lead. I follow thee. [*Exeunt.*]

1. That might improve your current appraisal of me.

2. A bastard was called *filius terrae*, "son of the earth."

3.3

[*Enter*] *Volpone, Nano, Androgyno,* [*and*] *Castrone.*

VOLPONE Mosca stays long, methinks. Bring forth your sports
And help to make the wretched time more sweet.
NANO Dwarf, fool, and eunuch, well met here we be.
A question it were now, whether° of us three, *which*
Being all the known delicates° of a rich man, *playthings*
In pleasing him, claim the precedency can?
CASTRONE I claim for myself.
ANDROGYNO And so doth the fool.
NANO 'Tis foolish indeed; let me set you both to school.
First, for° your dwarf: he's little and witty, *as for*
And everything, as° it is little, is pretty; *insofar as*
Else why do men say to a creature of my shape,
So soon as they see him, "It's a pretty little ape"?
And why a pretty ape? But for pleasing imitation
Of greater men's action in a ridiculous fashion.
Beside, this feat° body of mine doth not crave *neat, trim*
Half the meat, drink, and cloth one of your bulks will have.
Admit your fool's face be the mother of laughter,
Yet for his brain, it must always come after;° *be lesser*
And though that do feed him,° it's a pitiful case,[1] *earns his keep*
His body is beholding° to such a bad face. *One knocks.* *beholden*
VOLPONE Who's there? My couch. [*He lies down.*] Away, look, Nano, see!
Give me my caps, first—go, inquire.
[*Exeunt Nano, Androgyno, and Castrone.*]
Now, Cupid
Send° it be Mosca, and with fair return!° *Grant / good results*

[*Enter Nano.*]

NANO It is the beauteous Madam—
VOLPONE Would-be—is it?
NANO The same.
VOLPONE Now, torment on me! Squire her in,
For she will enter or dwell here forever.
Nay, quickly, that° my fit were past! [*Exit Nano.*] *so that*
I fear
A second hell, too, that my loathing this
Will quite expel my appetite to the other.° *(Celia)*
Would she were taking, now, her tedious leave.
Lord, how it threats me what I am to suffer!

3.3. Volpone's house.

1. With a pun on "container."

3.4

[*Enter*] *Lady* [*Would-be and*] *Nano.*

LADY WOULD-BE [*to Nano*] I thank you, good sir. Pray you signify
Unto your patron I am here.[1] [*Regarding herself in a mirror*]
This band° *ruff*
Shows not my neck enough. I trouble you, sir.
Let me request you, bid one of my women
Come hither to me. [*Exit Nano.*]
In good faith, I am dressed
Most favorably today!° It is no matter; *(sarcastic)*
'Tis well enough.

[*Enter Nano and First*] *Woman.*

Look, see, these petulant things!° *her women; her curls*
How they have done this!
VOLPONE [*aside*] I do feel the fever
Ent'ring in at mine ears. Oh, for a charm
To fright it hence!
LADY WOULD-BE [*to First Woman*] Come nearer. Is this curl
In his° right place? Or this? Why is this higher *its*
Than all the rest? You ha' not washed your eyes yet?
Or do they not stand even° i'your head? *level; focused*
Where's your fellow? Call her. [*Exit First Woman.*]
NANO [*aside*] Now Saint Mark
Deliver us! Anon she'll beat her women
Because her nose is red.

[*Enter First and Second Women.*]

LADY WOULD-BE I pray you, view
This tire,° forsooth. Are all things apt or no? *headdress*
SECOND WOMAN One hair a little here sticks out, forsooth.
LADY WOULD-BE Does 't so, forsooth? [*To First Woman*] And where was your dear sight
When it did so, forsooth? What now? Bird-eyed?° *Startled (?); asquint (?)*
[*To Second Woman*] And you, too? Pray you both approach and mend it. [*They tend to her.*]
Now, by that light,° I muse you're not ashamed! *i.e., by heaven*
I, that have preached these things so oft unto you,
Read you the principles, argued all the grounds,
Disputed every fitness, every grace,
Called you to counsel of so frequent dressings—
NANO (*aside*) More carefully than of your fame° or honor. *reputation*
LADY WOULD-BE Made you acquainted what an ample dowry
The knowledge of these things would be unto you,
Able alone to get you noble husbands
At your return,° and you thus to neglect it? *(to England)*
Besides, you seeing what a curious° nation *fastidious*
Th'Italians are, what will they say of me?

3.4. The scene continues.
1. Much of Lady Would-be's dialogue in the following scene is adapted from Libanius of Antioch's *On Talkative Women.*

"The English lady cannot dress herself."
Here's a fine imputation to our country!
Well, go your ways, and stay i'the next room.
This fucus° was too coarse, too; it's no matter. *makeup*
[*To Nano*] Good sir, you'll give 'em entertainment?° *look after them*
[*Exeunt Nano and Women.*]
VOLPONE [*aside*] The storm comes toward me.
LADY WOULD-BE [*approaching the bed*] How does my Volp?
VOLPONE Troubled with noise. I cannot sleep; I dreamt
That a strange Fury° entered now my house, *avenging goddess*
And with the dreadful tempest of her breath
Did cleave my roof asunder.
LADY WOULD-BE Believe me, and I
Had the most fearful dream, could I remember't—
VOLPONE [*aside*] Out on° my fate! I ha' giv'n her the occasion *Curses on*
How to torment me: she will tell me hers.
LADY WOULD-BE Methought the golden mediocrity,° *golden mean*
Polite and delicate—
VOLPONE Oh, if you do love me,
No more! I sweat and suffer at the mention
Of any dream. Feel how I tremble yet.
LADY WOULD-BE Alas, good soul! The passion of the heart.° *heartburn*
Seed pearl were good now, boiled with syrup of apples,
Tincture of gold and coral, citron pills,
Your elecampane° root, myrobalans[2]— *perennial herb*
VOLPONE [*aside*] Ay me, I have ta'en a grasshopper by the wing!
LADY WOULD-BE Burnt silk and amber; you have muscadel
Good i'the house—
VOLPONE You will not drink and part?
LADY WOULD-BE No, fear not that. I doubt we shall not get
Some English saffron—half a dram would serve—
Your sixteen cloves, a little musk, dried mints,
Bugloss,° and barley-meal— *an herb*
VOLPONE [*aside*] She's in again.
Before I feigned diseases; now I have one.
LADY WOULD-BE And these applied with a right scarlet cloth—
VOLPONE [*aside*] Another flood of words! A very torrent!
LADY WOULD-BE Shall I, sir, make you a poultice?
VOLPONE No, no, no.
I'm very well; you need prescribe no more.
LADY WOULD-BE I have a little studied physic,° but now *medicine*
I'm all for music, save° i'the forenoons *except*
An hour or two for painting. I would have
A lady indeed t' have all letters and arts,
Be able to discourse, to write, to paint,
But principal, as Plato holds,° your music (*in* The Republic)
(And so does wise Pythagoras, I take it)
Is your true rapture, when there is concent° *harmony*
In face, in voice, and clothes, and is indeed

2. Dried tropical fruits.

Our sex's chiefest ornament.
VOLPONE The poet° *(Sophocles, in* Ajax*)*
As old in time as Plato, and as knowing,
Says that your highest female grace is silence.
LADY WOULD-BE Which o' your poets? Petrarch? Or Tasso?
Or Dante?
Guarini? Ariosto? Aretine?
Cieco di Hadria?[3] I have read them all.
VOLPONE [*aside*] Is everything a cause to my destruction?
LADY WOULD-BE [*searching her garments*] I think I ha' two or three of 'em about me.
VOLPONE [*aside*] The sun, the sea will sooner both stand still
Than her eternal tongue! Nothing can scape it.
LADY WOULD-BE Here's *Pastor Fido*[4]—
VOLPONE [*aside*] Profess obstinate silence,
That's now my safest.
LADY WOULD-BE All our English writers,
I mean such as are happy° in th'Italian, *fluent*
Will deign to steal out of this author mainly,
Almost as much as from Montaignié;° *French essayist*
He has so modern and facile° a vein, *graceful*
Fitting the time, and catching the court ear.
Your Petrarch is more passionate, yet he,
In days of sonneting, trusted 'em with much.[5]
Dante is hard, and few can understand him.
But for a desperate° wit, there's Aretine! *outrageous*
Only his pictures are a little obscene[6]—
You mark me not?
VOLPONE Alas, my mind's perturbed.
LADY WOULD-BE Why, in such cases we must cure ourselves,
Make use of our philosophy—
VOLPONE Ay me!
LADY WOULD-BE And, as we find our passions do rebel,
Encounter 'em with reason, or divert 'em
By giving scope unto some other humor
Of lesser danger—as in politic bodies° *political councils*
There's nothing more doth overwhelm the judgment
And clouds the understanding than too much
Settling and fixing and (as 'twere) subsiding° *(alchemical jargon)*
Upon one object. For the incorporating
Of these same outward things into that part
Which we call mental leaves some certain feces° *dregs*
That stop the organs and, as Plato says,
Assassinates our knowledge.
VOLPONE [*aside*] Now, the spirit
Of patience help me!
LADY WOULD-BE Come, in faith, I must

3. Lady Would-be juxtaposes major Italian writers with the minor di Hadria and the obscene Aretino.
4. A pastoral by Giovanni Guarini, translated into English in 1602.
5. When sonnet writing was popular, gave poets plenty to imitate.
6. The libertine poems of Aretine (Pietro Aretino, 1492–1556) were published with pornographic illustrations by Giulio Romano.

Visit you more o'days and make you well.
Laugh and be lusty.° — *merry*
VOLPONE [*aside*] My good angel save me!
LADY WOULD-BE There was but one sole man in all the world
With whom I e'er could sympathize, and he
Would lie you° often three, four hours together — *lie*
To hear me speak, and be sometime so rapt
As he would answer me quite from the purpose,
Like you—and you are like him, just. I'll discourse—
An't° be but only, sir, to bring you asleep— — *If it*
How we did spend our time and loves together
For some six years.
VOLPONE Oh, oh, oh, oh, oh, oh!
LADY WOULD-BE For we were *coaetani*° and brought up— — *the same age*
VOLPONE [*aside*] Some power, some fate, some fortune rescue me!

3.5

[*Enter*] *Mosca.*

MOSCA God save you, madam.
LADY WOULD-BE Good sir.
VOLPONE [*aside to Mosca*] Mosca? Welcome,
Welcome to my redemption.
MOSCA [*to Volpone*] Why, sir?
VOLPONE [*aside to Mosca*] Oh,
Rid me of this my torture quickly, there,
My madam with the everlasting voice!
The bells in time of pestilence ne'er made
Like noise, or were in that perpetual motion;[1]
The cockpit° comes not near it. All my house — *cockfighting arena*
But now steamed like a bath with her thick breath.
A lawyer° could not have been heard, nor scarce — *Even a lawyer*
Another woman, such a hail of words
She has let fall. For hell's sake, rid her hence.
MOSCA [*aside to Volpone*] Has she presented?° — *given a gift*
VOLPONE [*aside to Mosca*] Oh, I do not care.
I'll take her absence upon any price,
With any loss.
MOSCA Madam—
LADY WOULD-BE I ha' brought your patron
A toy,° a cap here, of mine own work— — *trifle; embroidered piece*
MOSCA [*taking it from her*] 'Tis well.
I had forgot to tell you, I saw your knight
Where you'd little think it—
LADY WOULD-BE Where?
MOSCA Marry,
Where yet, if you make haste, you may apprehend him,
Rowing upon the water in a gondole
With the most cunning courtesan of Venice.
LADY WOULD-BE Is't true?

3.5. The scene continues.
1. Church bells marked the deaths of parishioners; in times of plague they therefore rang almost constantly.

MOSCA Pursue 'em, and believe your eyes.
Leave me to make your gift. [*Exit Lady Would-be.*]
I knew 'twould take.° *do the trick*
For lightly,° they that use themselves most license *commonly*
Are still° most jealous. *always*
VOLPONE Mosca, hearty thanks
For thy quick fiction and delivery of me.
Now, to my hopes, what say'st thou?

[*Enter Lady Would-be.*]

LADY WOULD-BE But do you hear, sir?
VOLPONE [*aside*] Again! I fear a paroxysm.° *relapse*
LADY WOULD-BE Which way
Rowed they together?
MOSCA Toward the Rialto.° *commercial district*
LADY WOULD-BE I pray you, lend me your dwarf.
MOSCA I pray you, take him.
[*Exit Lady Would-be.*]
Your hopes, sir, are like happy blossoms: fair,
And promise timely fruit if you will stay
But the maturing. Keep you at your couch.
Corbaccio will arrive straight with the will;
When he is gone I'll tell you more. [*Exit.*]
VOLPONE My blood,
My spirits are returned. I am alive;
And like your wanton° gamester at primero,[2] *reckless; lustful*
Whose thought had whispered to him, not go° less, *don't gamble*
Methinks I lie, and draw—for an encounter.[3]
[*He gets into bed and closes the bed curtains.*]

3.6

[*Enter*] *Mosca* [*and*] *Bonario.* [*Mosca shows Bonario to a hiding place.*]

MOSCA Sir, here concealed you may hear all. But pray you
Have patience, sir. (*One knocks.*) The same's your father knocks.
I am compelled to leave you.
BONARIO Do so. Yet
Cannot my thought imagine this a truth.
[*He conceals himself.*]

3.7

[*Enter*] *Corvino* [*and*] *Celia. Mosca* [*crosses the stage to intercept them*].

MOSCA Death on me! You are come too soon. What meant you?
Did not I say I would send?
CORVINO Yes, but I feared
You might forget it, and then they prevent° us. *act more quickly than*

2. A card game.
3. (1) Winning play in primero; (2) sexual act.

3.6. The scene continues.
3.7. The scene continues.

MOSCA [*aside*] Prevent? Did e'er man haste so for his horns?° *cuckold's horns*
A courtier would not ply it so for a place.[1]
[*To Corvino*] Well, now there's no helping it, stay here;
I'll presently return. [*He crosses the stage to Bonario.*]
CORVINO Where are you, Celia?
You know not wherefore I have brought you hither?
CELIA Not well, except° you told me. *except what*
CORVINO Now I will.
Hark hither. [*Corvino and Celia talk apart.*]
MOSCA (*to Bonario*) Sir, your father hath sent word
It will be half an hour ere he come;
And therefore, if you please to walk the while
Into that gallery, at the upper end
There are some books to entertain the time;
And I'll take care no man shall come unto you, sir.
BONARIO Yes, I will stay there. [*Aside*] I do doubt this fellow.
[*He retires.*]
MOSCA There, he is far enough; he can hear nothing.
And for° his father, I can keep him off. *as for*
[*Mosca joins Volpone and opens his bed curtains.*]
CORVINO [*to Celia*] Nay, now, there is no starting back, and therefore
Resolve upon it; I have so decreed.
It must be done. Nor would I move't° afore, *suggest it*
Because I would avoid all shifts° and tricks *evasions*
That might deny me.
CELIA Sir, let me beseech you,
Affect° not these strange trials. If you doubt *Undertake*
My chastity, why, lock me up forever;
Make me the heir of darkness. Let me live
Where I may please° your fears, if not your trust. *satisfy*
CORVINO Believe it, I have no such humor, I.
All that I speak, I mean; yet I am not mad,
Not horn-mad,° see you? Go to, show yourself *crazy with jealousy*
Obedient, and a wife.
CELIA O heaven!
CORVINO I say it,
Do so.
CELIA Was this the train?° *scheme*
CORVINO I have told you reasons:
What the physicians have set down; how much
It may concern me; what my engagements are;
My means, and the necessity of those means
For my recovery. Wherefore, if you be
Loyal and mine, be won, respect my venture.° *support my endeavor*
CELIA Before your honor?
CORVINO Honor? Tut, a breath.
There's no such thing in nature; a mere term
Invented to awe fools. What is my gold

1. Work so hard for a position at court.

The worse for touching? Clothes for being looked on?
Why, this's no more. An old, decrepit wretch,
That has no sense,° no sinew; takes his meat — *sensory perception*
With others' fingers; only knows to gape
When you do scald his gums; a voice, a shadow.
And what can this man hurt you?
CELIA — Lord! What spirit
Is this hath entered him?° — *(Corvino)*
CORVINO — And for° your fame,° — *as for / reputation*
That's such a jig;° as if I would go tell it, — *joke*
Cry° it on the piazza! Who shall know it — *Advertise*
But he that cannot speak it,° and this fellow° — *(Volpone) / (Mosca)*
Whose lips are i'my pocket, save° yourself? — *except*
If you'll proclaim't, you may. I know no other
Should° come to know it. — *Who could*
CELIA — Are heaven and saints then nothing?
Will they be blind or stupid?
CORVINO — How?° — *What's this?*
CELIA — Good sir,
Be jealous still, emulate them, and think
What hate they burn with toward every sin.
CORVINO I grant you, if I thought it were a sin
I would not urge you. Should I offer this
To some young Frenchman, or hot Tuscan blood
That had read Aretine, conned° all his prints, — *learned by heart*
Knew every quirk within lust's labyrinth,
And were professed critic° in lechery, — *connoisseur*
And I would° look upon him and applaud him, — *if I were to*
This were a sin. But here 'tis contrary,
A pious work, mere charity, for physic,
And honest polity° to assure mine own. — *prudence*
CELIA O heaven! Canst thou suffer such a change?
VOLPONE [*aside to Mosca*] Thou art mine honor, Mosca, and my pride,
My joy, my tickling, my delight! Go, bring 'em.
MOSCA [*to Corvino*] Please you draw near, sir.
CORVINO [*dragging Celia toward Volpone*] Come on, what—
You will not be rebellious? By that light—
MOSCA [*to Volpone*] Sir, Signor Corvino here is come to see you.
VOLPONE Oh!
MOSCA — And, hearing of the consultation had
So lately for your health, is come to offer,
Or rather, sir, to prostitute—
CORVINO — Thanks, sweet Mosca.
MOSCA Freely, unasked or unentreated—
CORVINO — Well.
MOSCA As the true, fervent instance of his love,
His own most fair and proper wife, the beauty
Only of price° in Venice— — *Beyond compare*
CORVINO — 'Tis well urged.
MOSCA To be your comfortress and to preserve you.
VOLPONE Alas, I am past already! Pray you, thank him
For his good care and promptness. But for° that, — *as for*
'Tis a vain labor e'en to fight 'gainst heaven,
Applying fire to a stone (uh! uh! uh! uh!),

Making a dead leaf grow again. I take
His wishes gently,° though; and you may tell him — *kindly*
What I have done for him. Marry, my state is hopeless!
Will° him to pray for me, and t' use his fortune — *Ask*
With reverence when he comes to't.

MOSCA [*to Corvino*] Do you hear, sir?
Go to him with your wife.

CORVINO [*to Celia*] Heart of my father!° — *(an oath)*
Wilt thou persist thus? Come, I pray thee, come.
Thou see'st 'tis nothing. [*He threatens to strike her.*] Celia!
By this hand,
I shall grow violent. Come, do't, I say.

CELIA Sir, kill me, rather. I will take down poison,
Eat burning coals, do anything—

CORVINO Be damned!
Heart! I will drag thee hence, home, by the hair,
Cry thee a strumpet through the streets, rip up
Thy mouth unto thine ears, and slit thy nose
Like a raw rochet!°—Do not tempt me. Come, — *a fish, the red gurnard*
Yield! I am loath—Death!° I will buy some slave — *God's death! (an oath)*
Whom I will kill,[2] and bind thee to him alive,
And at my window hang you forth, devising
Some monstrous crime, which I in capital letters
Will eat into thy flesh with *aquafortis*° — *nitric acid*
And burning cor'sives° on this stubborn breast. — *corrosives*
Now, by the blood thou hast incensed, I'll do't.

CELIA Sir, what you please, you may; I am your martyr.

CORVINO Be not thus obstinate. I ha' not deserved it.
Think who it is entreats you. Pray thee, sweet!
Good faith, thou shalt have jewels, gowns, attires,
What° thou wilt think and ask. Do but go kiss him. — *Whatever*
Or touch him but. For my sake. At my suit.
This once. No? Not? I shall remember this.
Will you disgrace me thus? Do you thirst my undoing?

MOSCA Nay, gentle lady, be advised.

CORVINO No, no.
She has watched her time.[3] God's precious,[4] this is scurvy;
'Tis very scurvy, and you are—

MOSCA Nay, good, sir.

CORVINO An arrant locust,° by heaven, a locust. Whore, — *destroyer*
Crocodile,[5] that hast thy tears prepared,
Expecting° how thou'lt bid 'em flow! — *Anticipating*

MOSCA Nay, pray you, sir,
She will consider.

CELIA Would my life would serve
To satisfy—

CORVINO 'Sdeath, if she would but speak to him
And save my reputation, 'twere somewhat—
But spitefully to effect my utter ruin!

MOSCA Ay, now you've put your fortune in her hands.
Why, i'faith, it is her modesty; I must quit° her. — *absolve*

2. In the following lines, Corvino elaborates luridly upon the fate that the notorious rapist Tarquin promised the chaste Roman matron Lucretia if she did not capitulate; unlike Celia, Lucretia yielded to threats.

3. Waited for her chance (to ruin me).

4. God's precious blood. (An oath.)

5. Which was supposed to weep while preying upon its victims.

If you were absent she would be more coming,° *compliant*
I know it, and dare undertake for her.
What woman can before her husband? Pray you,
Let us depart and leave her here.

CORVINO Sweet Celia,
Thou mayst redeem all yet; I'll say no more.
If not, esteem yourself as lost.—Nay, stay there.
[*Exeunt Corvino and Mosca.*]

CELIA O God and his good angels! Whither, whither
Is shame fled human breasts, that with such ease
Men dare put off your° honors and their own? *(God's and the angels')*
Is that which ever was a cause of life° *(sex and wedlock)*
Now placed beneath the basest circumstance,° *lowest of concerns*
And modesty an exile made for money?
He [Volpone] leaps off from his couch.

VOLPONE Ay, in Corvino, and such earth-fed minds
That never tasted the true heav'n of love.
Assure thee, Celia, he that would sell thee
Only for hope of gain, and that uncertain,
He would have sold his part of paradise
For ready money, had he met a copeman.° *buyer*
Why art thou mazed to see me thus revived?
Rather applaud thy beauty's miracle;
'Tis thy great work, that hath, not now alone° *not only just now*
But sundry times raised me in several shapes,
And but this morning like a mountebank
To see thee at thy window. Ay, before
I would have left my practice° for thy love, *scheming*
In varying figures° I would have contended *shapes*
With the blue Proteus or the hornèd flood.[6]
Now art thou welcome.

CELIA Sir!

VOLPONE Nay, fly me not,
Nor let thy false imagination
That I was bedrid make thee think I am so.
Thou shalt not find it. I am now as fresh,
As hot, as high, and in as jovial plight° *robust condition*
As when—in that so celebrated scene,
At recitation of our comedy
For entertainment of the great Valois[7]—
I acted young Antinoüs,[8] and attracted
The eyes and ears of all the ladies present,
T'admire each graceful gesture, note, and footing.° *dance step*

SONG

[*He sings.*] Come, my Celia, let us prove,[9]
While we can, the sports of love.

6. Proteus is a shape-changing sea god with whom Menelaus wrestles in the *Odyssey*, Book 4. The "hornèd flood" is the river god Achelous, defeated by Hercules despite changing into an ox.

7. Henry of Valois, Duke of Anjou, and later King Henry III of France (1574–89), was sumptuously entertained at Venice in 1574. His sexual taste for men was widely remarked.

8. The beautiful homosexual favorite of the Roman emperor Hadrian.

9. Try out. (The song is an adaptation of the Roman poet Catullus' fifth ode.)

Time will not be ours forever;
He at length our good will sever.
Spend not then his gifts in vain.
Suns that set may rise again,
But if once we lose this light
'Tis with us perpetual night.
Why should we defer our joys?
Fame and rumor are but toys.° *trifles*
Cannot we delude the eyes
Of a few poor household spies?
Or his° easier ears beguile, *(Corvino's)*
Thus removèd by our wile?
'Tis no sin love's fruits to steal,
But the sweet thefts to reveal.
To be taken,° to be seen, *caught*
These have crimes accounted been.

CELIA Some serene° blast me, or dire lightning strike *poisonous mist*
This my offending face!

VOLPONE Why droops my Celia?
Thou hast in place of a base husband found
A worthy lover. Use thy fortune well,
With secrecy and pleasure. See, behold
What thou art queen of, not in expectation,° *merely in hope*
As I feed others, but possessed and crowned.
[*He reveals his treasure.*]
See here a rope of pearl, and each more orient° *brilliant*
Than that the brave Egyptian queen caroused;[1]
Dissolve and drink 'em. See, a carbuncle[2]
May° put out both the eyes of our Saint Mark;[3] *That could*
A diamond would° have bought Lollia Paulina[4] *that would*
When she came in like starlight, hid with jewels
That were the spoils of provinces. Take these,
And wear, and lose 'em; yet remains an earring
To purchase them again, and this whole state.
A gem but° worth a private patrimony *merely*
Is nothing; we will eat such at a meal.
The heads of parrots, tongues of nightingales,
The brains of peacocks and of ostriches
Shall be our food, and, could we get the phoenix,[5]
Though nature lost her kind,° she were our dish. *it became extinct*

CELIA Good sir, these things might move a mind affected
With such delights; but I, whose innocence
Is all I can think wealthy° or worth th'enjoying, *valuable*
And which once lost, I have naught to lose beyond it,
Cannot be taken with these sensual baits.
If you have conscience—

VOLPONE 'Tis the beggar's virtue.
If thou hast wisdom, hear me, Celia.
Thy baths shall be the juice of July flowers,° *gillyflowers, clove pinks*

1. Cleopatra dissolved and drank a pearl during a banquet with her lover, Marc Antony. "Brave" means "magnificent."
2. Ruby, thought to emit light.
3. Patron saint of Venice, whose statue stood in the basilica.
4. Third wife of the Roman emperor Caligula.
5. Mythical bird, of which it was supposed that only one existed at a time; it died in flames and was reborn from its own ashes.

Spirit° of roses, and of violets, *Extract*
The milk of unicorns, and panthers' breath[6]
Gathered in bags, and mixed with Cretan wines.
Our drink shall be preparèd gold and amber,
Which we will take° until my roof whirl round *drink*
With the vertigo; and my dwarf shall dance,
My eunuch sing, my fool make up the antic,[7]
Whilst we, in changèd shapes, act Ovid's tales:
Thou like Europa now and I like Jove,
Then I like Mars and thou like Erycine,[8]
So of the rest, till we have quite run through
And wearied° all the fables of the gods. *exhausted*
Then will I have thee in more modern forms,
Attirèd like some sprightly dame of France,
Brave Tuscan lady, or proud Spanish beauty;
Sometimes unto the Persian Sophy's° wife, *Shah of Persia's*
Or the Grand Signor's° mistress; and for change, *Sultan of Turkey's*
To one of our most artful courtesans,
Or some quick° Negro, or cold Russian. *energetic, lively*
And I will meet thee in as many shapes,
Where we may so transfuse° our wand'ring souls *pour into each other*
Out at our lips, and score up sums of pleasures,
[*He sings.*] That the curious shall not know
How to tell° them as they flow; *count*
And the envious, when they find
What their number is, be pined.° *tormented*

CELIA If you have ears that will be pierced, or eyes
That can be opened, a heart may be touched,
Or any part that yet sounds man[9] about you;
If you have touch of holy saints or heaven,
Do me the grace to let me scape. If not,
Be bountiful and kill me. You do know
I am a creature hither ill betrayed
By one whose shame I would forget it were.
If you will deign me neither of these graces,
Yet feed your wrath, sir, rather than your lust—
It is a vice comes nearer manliness—
And punish that unhappy crime of nature
Which you miscall my beauty. Flay my face
Or poison it with ointments for seducing
Your blood to this rebellion.° Rub these hands *sexual mutiny*
With what may cause an eating leprosy
E'en to my bones and marrow—anything
That may disfavor me,° save in my honor— *make me ugly*
And I will kneel to you, pray for you, pay down
A thousand hourly vows, sir, for your health,
Report and think you virtuous—

VOLPONE Think me cold,
Frozen, and impotent, and so report me?

6. Panthers were believed to use their sweet-smelling breath to lure prey.
7. Grotesque dance or pageant.
8. Ovid's *Metamorphoses* retells the pagan myths of transformation. Jove, king of the gods, became a bull to seduce the lovely Europa. The adulterous couple Mars, god of war, and Erycine (Venus), goddess of sexual love, were caught in a net by Vulcan, her husband.
9. That has a hint of manliness.

That I had Nestor's[1] hernia, thou wouldst think.
I do degenerate, and abuse my nation[2]
To play with opportunity thus long.
I should have done the act and then have parleyed.
Yield, or I'll force thee.

CELIA O just God!

VOLPONE [*seizing Celia*] In vain—

He [Bonario] leaps out from where Mosca had placed him.

BONARIO Forbear, foul ravisher, libidinous swine!
Free the forced lady or thou diest, impostor.
But° that I am loath to snatch thy punishment *Were it not*
Out of the hand of justice, thou shouldst yet
Be made the timely sacrifice of vengeance
Before this altar and this dross,° thy idol.— *(the treasure)*
Lady, let's quit the place. It is the den
Of villainy. Fear naught; you have a guard;
And he° ere long shall meet his just reward. *(Volpone)*
[*Exeunt Bonario and Celia.*]

VOLPONE Fall on me, roof, and bury me in ruin!
Become my grave, that wert my shelter! Oh!
I am unmasked, unspirited, undone,
Betrayed to beggary, to infamy—

3.8

[*Enter*] *Mosca* [*bloody*].[1]

MOSCA Where shall I run, most wretched shame of men,
To beat out my unlucky brains?

VOLPONE Here, here.
What! Dost thou bleed?

MOSCA Oh, that his well-driv'n sword
Had been so courteous to have cleft me down
Unto the navel, ere I lived to see
My life, my hopes, my spirits, my patron, all
Thus desperately engagèd° by my error! *placed at risk*

VOLPONE Woe on thy fortune!

MOSCA And my follies, sir.

VOLPONE Th'hast made me miserable.

MOSCA And myself, sir.
Who would have thought he would have hearkened° so? *eavesdropped*

VOLPONE What shall we do?

MOSCA I know not. If my heart
Could expiate the mischance, I'd pluck it out.
Will you be pleased to hang me, or cut my throat?
And I'll requite you, sir. Let's die like Romans,
Since we have lived like Grecians.[2] *They knock without.*

VOLPONE Hark, who's there?
I hear some footing: officers, the *Saffi*,° *arresting officers*

1. Nestor was the oldest of the Greek leaders in the Trojan War.
2. I fall away from my ancestors' virtues and abuse the Italian reputation for virility.
3.8. The scene continues.
1. Bonario apparently remembered Mosca's invitation, in 3.2.66–68, to punish him if he turns out to be lying: "draw your just sword / And score your vengeance on my front and face; / Mark me your villain."
2. Romans often committed suicide in adversity; Greeks were thought to be pleasure-loving.

Come to apprehend us! I do feel the brand
Hissing already at my forehead; now
Mine ears are boring.[3]

MOSCA To your couch, sir; you
Make that place good, however.[4] [*Volpone gets into bed.*]
Guilty men
Suspect° what they deserve still.° [*He opens the door.*] *Dread / always*
Signor Corbaccio!

3.9

[*Enter*] *Corbaccio* [*and converses with*] *Mosca; Voltore* [*enters unnoticed by them*].

CORBACCIO Why, how now, Mosca!
MOSCA Oh, undone, amazed, sir.
Your son—I know not by what accident—
Acquainted with your purpose to my patron
Touching° your will and making him your heir, *Concerning*
Entered our house with violence, his sword drawn,
Sought for you, called you wretch, unnatural,
Vowed he would kill you.
CORBACCIO Me?
MOSCA Yes, and my patron.
CORBACCIO This act shall disinherit him indeed.
Here is the will.
MOSCA [*taking it from him*] 'Tis well, sir.
CORBACCIO Right and well.
Be you as careful now for me.
MOSCA My life, sir,
Is not more tendered;° I am only yours. *cherished*
CORBACCIO How does he? Will he die shortly, think'st thou?
MOSCA I fear
He'll outlast May.
CORBACCIO Today?
MOSCA No, last out May, sir.
CORBACCIO Couldst thou not gi' him a dram?° *dose (of poison)*
MOSCA Oh, by no means, sir.
CORBACCIO Nay, I'll not bid you.
VOLTORE [*aside*] This is a knave, I see.
[*Voltore comes forward to speak privately with Mosca.*]
MOSCA [*aside*] How, Signor Voltore! Did he hear me?
VOLTORE Parasite!
MOSCA Who's that? Oh, sir, most timely welcome—
VOLTORE Scarce° *Only just in time*
To the discovery of your tricks, I fear.
You are his only? And mine also? Are you not?
MOSCA Who, I, sir? [*They speak out of Corbaccio's hearing.*]
VOLTORE You, sir. What device° is this *ruse*
About a will?

3. Branding was a common criminal punishment; ear-boring is described as an Italian torture in Thomas Nashe's *The Unfortunate Traveler* (1594).
4. (1) Defend that place, whatever happens; (2) maintain your invalid's role at all costs, since that role suits you.
3.9. The scene continues.

MOSCA A plot for you, sir.
VOLTORE Come,
Put not your foists° upon me. I shall scent 'em. *tricks; stenches*
MOSCA Did you not hear it?
VOLTORE Yes, I hear Corbaccio
Hath made your patron there his heir.
MOSCA 'Tis true,
By my device, drawn to it by my plot,
With hope—
VOLTORE Your patron should reciprocate?
And you have promised?
MOSCA For your good I did, sir.
Nay, more, I told his son, brought, hid him here
Where he might hear his father pass the deed,
Being persuaded to it by this thought, sir,
That the unnaturalness, first, of the act,
And then, his father's oft disclaiming in° him *disowning*
(Which I did mean t' help on) would sure enrage him
To do some violence upon his parent,
On which the law should take sufficient hold,
And you be stated° in a double hope. *installed*
Truth be my comfort and my conscience,
My only aim was to dig you a fortune
Out of these two old rotten sepulchres—
VOLTORE I cry thee mercy, Mosca.
MOSCA Worth your patience
And your great merit, sir. And see the change!
VOLTORE Why? What success?° *outcome*
MOSCA Most hapless!° You must help, sir. *unfortunate*
Whilst we expected th'old raven, in comes
Corvino's wife, sent hither by her husband—
VOLTORE What, with a present?
MOSCA No, sir, on visitation—
I'll tell you how, anon—and, staying long,
The youth, he grows impatient, rushes forth,
Seizeth the lady, wounds me, makes her swear—
Or he would murder her, that was his vow—
T'affirm my patron to have done her rape,
Which how unlike° it is, you see! And hence, *unlikely*
With that pretext, he's gone t'accuse his father,
Defame my patron, defeat you—
VOLTORE Where's her husband?
Let him be sent for straight.
MOSCA Sir, I'll go fetch him.
VOLTORE Bring him to the *Scrutineo*.° *Venetian law court*
MOSCA Sir, I will.
VOLTORE This must be stopped.
MOSCA Oh, you do nobly, sir.
Alas, 'twas labored all, sir, for your good;
Nor was there want of counsel° in the plot. *lack of wisdom*
But fortune can at any time o'erthrow
The projects of a hundred learnèd clerks,° sir. *scholars*
CORBACCIO [*striving to hear*] What's that?
VOLTORE [*to Corbaccio*] Will't please you, sir, to go along?
[*Exeunt Corbaccio and Voltore.*]

MOSCA Patron, go in and pray for our success.
VOLPONE [*rising*] Need makes devotion. Heaven your labor bless!
[*Exeunt.*]

4.1

[*Enter*] *Politic* [*and*] *Peregrine.*

POLITIC I told you, sir, it° was a plot. You see — *(the mountebank episode)*
What observation is! You mentioned me
For° some instructions; I will tell you, sir, — *As one who could give latitude*
Since we are met here, in this height° of Venice,
Some few particulars I have set down
Only for this meridian, fit to be known
Of your crude° traveler, and they are these. — *inexperienced*
I will not touch, sir, at your phrase or clothes,
For they are old.[1]
PEREGRINE Sir, I have better.
POLITIC Pardon,
I meant as they are themes.° — *topics for advice*
PEREGRINE Oh, sir, proceed.
I'll slander° you no more of wit, good sir. — *accuse*
POLITIC First, for your garb,[2] it must be grave and serious,
Very reserved and locked;° not° tell a secret — *guarded / do not*
On any terms, not to your father; scarce
A fable[3] but with caution. Make sure choice
Both of your company and discourse. Beware
You never speak a truth—
PEREGRINE How!
POLITIC Not to strangers,° — *foreigners*
For those be they you must converse with most;
Others° I would not know, sir, but at distance, — *Fellow countrymen*
So as I still might be a saver[4] in 'em.
You shall have tricks else passed upon you hourly.
And then, for° your religion, profess none, — *as for*
But wonder at the diversity of all,
And, for your part, protest,° were there no other — *insist that*
But simply the laws o'th'land, you could content you.
Nick Machiavel and Monsieur Bodin both
Were of this mind.[5] Then must you learn the use
And handling of your silver fork° at meals, — *(an Italian novelty)*
The metal° of your glass—these are main matters — *composition*
With your Italian—and to know the hour
When you must eat your melons and your figs.
PEREGRINE Is that a point of state,° too? — *statecraft*
POLITIC Here it is.
For your Venetian, if he see a man

4.1. The piazza.
1. I will not discuss those familiar ("old") topics: the language one ought to use or the clothes one ought to wear. In the next line, in an attempt at a joke, Peregrine deliberately misconstrues "your clothes" to refer to his own apparel, but Politic does not get it.
2. As for a traveler's bearing.
3. An apparently trivial story subject to political allegorization.
4. So that I might not be imposed upon. ("Be a saver" is a gambling term, meaning "to escape loss.")
5. Political theorists Niccolò Machiavelli (1469–1527) and Jean Bodin (1530–1596) argued that religious zeal was often politically inexpedient or divisive; as a result both were popularly thought to be atheists.

Preposterous in the least, he has° him straight; [*sees through*]
He has, he strips° him. I'll acquaint you, sir. [*ridicules; defrauds*]
I now have lived here—'tis some fourteen months;
Within the first week of my landing here,
All took me for a citizen of Venice,
I knew the forms so well—

PEREGRINE [*aside*] And nothing else.

POLITIC I had read Contarine,[6] took me a house,
Dealt with my Jews[7] to furnish it with movables°— [*household goods*]
Well, if I could but find one man, one man
To mine own heart, whom I durst trust, I would—

PEREGRINE What? What, sir?

POLITIC Make him rich, make him a fortune.
He should not think° again. I would command it. [*have to think*]

PEREGRINE As how?

POLITIC With certain projects° that I have— [*entrepreneurial schemes*]
Which I may not discover.° [*reveal*]

PEREGRINE [*aside*] If I had
But one° to wager with, I would lay odds, now, [*Someone*]
He tells me instantly.

POLITIC One is—and that
I care not greatly who knows—to serve the state
Of Venice with red herrings for three years,
And at a certain rate, from Rotterdam,[8]
Where I have correspondence. [*He shows Peregrine a paper.*] There's a letter
Sent me from one o'th'States,° and to that purpose; [*Dutch provinces*]
He cannot write his name, but that's his mark.

PEREGRINE [*examining the paper*] He is a chandler?[9]

POLITIC No, a cheesemonger.
There are some other° too, with whom I treat° [*others / deal*]
About the same negotiation;
And I will undertake it, for 'tis thus
I'll do't with ease; I've cast it all.° Your hoy[1] [*figured it all out*]
Carries but three men in her and a boy,
And she shall make me three returns° a year. [*round trips*]
So if there come but one of three, I save;° [*break even*]
If two, I can defalk.° But this is, now, [*pay off loans*]
If my main project fail.

PEREGRINE Then you have others?

POLITIC I should be loath to draw° the subtle air [*breathe*]
Of such a place without my thousand aims.
I'll not dissemble, sir: where'er I come,
I love to be considerative;° and 'tis true [*analytic*]
I have at my free hours thought upon
Some certain goods° unto the state of Venice, [*benefits*]
Which I do call my cautions,° and, sir, which [*precautions*]
I mean, in hope of pension,° to propound [*financial reward*]

6. An English translation of Gasparo Contarini's important book, *The Commonwealth and Government of Venice*, was published in 1599.

7. The usual Jews. (In Venice Jews served as money-lenders and pawnbrokers.)

8. Venice, on the Adriatic Sea, had little need to import pickled fish from afar.

9. Candlemaker. (Evidently the paper is grease-stained.)

1. Small vessel, not suitable for long voyages. Sir Pol's scheme is thus obviously impractical.

To the Great Council, then unto the Forty,
So to the Ten.[2] My means° are made already— *contacts*
PEREGRINE By whom?
POLITIC Sir, one that though his place b'obscure,
Yet he can sway and they will hear him. He's
A *commendatore*.
PEREGRINE What, a common sergeant?
POLITIC Sir, such as they are put it in their mouths
What they should say, sometimes, as well as greater.[3]
I think I have my notes to show you—
[*He searches in his garments.*]
PEREGRINE Good, sir.
POLITIC But you shall swear unto me on your gentry° *gentleman's honor*
Not to anticipate—
PEREGRINE I, sir?
POLITIC Nor reveal
A circumstance—My paper is not with me.
PEREGRINE Oh, but you can remember, sir.
POLITIC My first is
Concerning tinderboxes.° You must know *(for lighting fires)*
No family is here without its box.
Now, sir, it being so portable a thing,
Put case° that you or I were ill affected° *Suppose / disposed*
Unto the state; sir, with it in our pockets
Might not I go into the Arsenale?[4]
Or you? Come out again? And none the wiser?
PEREGRINE Except yourself, sir.
POLITIC Go to,° then. I therefore *(impatient expression)*
Advertise to° the state how fit it were *Warn*
That none but such as were known patriots,
Sound lovers of their country, should be suffered° *permitted*
T'enjoy them° in their houses, and even those *(tinderboxes)*
Sealed° at some office, and at such a bigness *Licensed; sealed shut*
As might not lurk in pockets.
PEREGRINE Admirable!
POLITIC My next is, how t'inquire and be resolved° *satisfied*
By present° demonstration whether a ship *immediate*
Newly arrived from Syria, or from
Any suspected part of all the Levant,° *Middle East*
Be guilty of the plague. And where they use° *are accustomed*
To lie out° forty, fifty days sometimes *at anchor*
About the Lazaretto,[5] for their trial,
I'll save that charge and loss unto the merchant,
And in an hour clear the doubt.
PEREGRINE Indeed, sir?
POLITIC Or—I will lose my labor.
PEREGRINE My faith, that's much.
POLITIC Nay, sir, conceive° me. 'Twill cost me in onions[6] *understand*

2. The Great Council was a large legislative group made up of wealthy Venetians; the Councils of Forty were much smaller groups that oversaw judicial affairs; the Council of Ten consisted of the elected Doge and his cabinet.
3. Common men, as well as those of higher status, may sometimes make suggestions to the government.
4. Shipyard where Venice built and repaired its naval vessels.
5. Quarantine hospital on an outlying island.
6. Onions were popularly supposed to absorb plague infection.

Some thirty livres°— *French coins*
PEREGRINE Which is one pound sterling.
POLITIC Beside my waterworks. For this I do, sir.
First I bring in your ship° 'twixt two brick walls— *a ship in question*
But those the state shall venture.° On the one *pay for*
I strain° me a fair tarpaulin, and in that *stretch*
I stick my onions cut in halves; the other
Is full of loopholes out at which I thrust
The noses of my bellows, and those bellows
I keep with° waterworks in perpetual motion[7]— *by means of*
Which is the easiest matter of a hundred.° *as easy as can be*
Now, sir, your onion, which doth naturally
Attract th'infection, and your bellows, blowing
The air upon him,° will show instantly *it (the onion)*
By his changed color if there be contagion,
Or else remain as fair as at the first.
Now 'tis known, 'tis nothing.° *there's nothing to it*
PEREGRINE You are right, sir.
POLITIC I would I had my note.
[*He searches again in his garments.*]
PEREGRINE Faith, so would I;
But, you ha' done well for once, sir.
POLITIC Were I false,° *traitorous*
Or would be made so,° I could show you reasons *made out to be so*
How I could sell this state now to the Turk,[8]
Spite of their galleys° or their— *warships*
PEREGRINE Pray you, Sir Pol.
POLITIC I have 'em° not about me. *(the notes)*
PEREGRINE That I feared.
They are there, sir? [*He indicates a book Politic is holding.*]
POLITIC No, this is my diary,
Wherein I note my actions of the day.[9]
PEREGRINE Pray you, let's see, sir. What is here? [*Reading*]
"*Notandum*,° *Be it noted*
A rat had gnawn my spur leathers;° notwithstanding *laces*
I put on new and did go forth, but first
I threw three beans over the threshold.° *Item*, *(for good luck)*
I went and bought two toothpicks, whereof one
I burst immediately in a discourse
With a Dutch merchant, 'bout *ragion' del stato*.° *political expediency*
From him I went, and paid a *moccinigo*° *small coin*
For piecing° my silk stockings; by the way *mending*
I cheapened sprats,[1] and at Saint Mark's I urined."
Faith, these are politic notes!
POLITIC Sir, I do slip° *let pass*
No action of my life thus but I quote° it. *without noting*
PEREGRINE Believe me, it is wise!
POLITIC Nay, sir, read forth.

7. Perpetual-motion machines were popular attractions in early modern England, but Jonson regarded them contemptuously. Since Venice is in flat marshland, there are no waterfalls to harness there, as Sir Pol proposes.
8. The Ottoman Turks, southeast of Venice along the Adriatic Sea, were maritime and religious rivals and a long-standing military threat.
9. Many Renaissance travel writers recommended that travelers keep a written record of their journeys.
1. Bargained over some small fish.

4.2

[*Enter*] *Lady* [*Would-be*], *Nano*, [*and the two*] *Women*.
[*They do not see Politic and Peregrine at first.*]

LADY WOULD-BE Where should this loose knight be, trow?° *do you suppose?*
Sure he's housed.° *in a brothel*
NANO Why, then he's fast.° *fast-moving; secure*
LADY WOULD-BE Ay, he plays both° with me. *both fast and loose*
I pray you, stay.° This heat will do more harm *wait*
To my complexion than his heart is worth.
I do not care° to hinder, but to take° him. *wish / catch*
[*She rubs her cheeks.*]
How it° comes off! *(the makeup)*
FIRST WOMAN [*pointing*] My master's yonder.
LADY WOULD-BE Where?
FIRST WOMAN With a young gentleman.
LADY WOULD-BE That same's the party,
In man's apparel![1] [*To Nano*] Pray you, sir, jog my knight.
I will be tender to his reputation,
However he demerit.° *deserves blame*
POLITIC [*seeing her*] My lady!
PEREGRINE Where?
POLITIC 'Tis she indeed, sir; you shall know her. She is,
Were she not mine,[2] a lady of that merit
For fashion and behavior; and for beauty
I durst° compare— *would dare*
PEREGRINE It seems you are not jealous,
That dare commend her.
POLITIC Nay, and for discourse—
PEREGRINE Being your wife, she cannot miss° that. *lack (sarcastic)*
POLITIC [*introducing Peregrine*] Madam,
Here is a gentleman; pray you use him fairly.
He seems a youth, but he is—
LADY WOULD-BE None?
POLITIC Yes, one
Has° put his face as soon° into the world— *Who has / so young*
LADY WOULD-BE You mean, as early? But° today? *Only*
POLITIC How's this!
LADY WOULD-BE Why, in this habit,° sir; you apprehend° me. *apparel / understand*
Well, Master Would-be, this doth not become you;
I had thought the odor, sir, of your good name
Had been more precious to you, that you would not
Have done this dire massacre on your honor—
One of your gravity and rank besides!
But knights, I see, care little for the oath
They make to ladies, chiefly their own ladies.
POLITIC Now, by my spurs—the symbol of my knighthood—
PEREGRINE (*aside*) Lord, how his brain is humbled[3] for an oath!
POLITIC —I reach° you not. *comprehend*

4.2. The scene continues.
1. Lady Would-be believes that Peregrine is the whore Mosca mentioned, in transvestite attire.
2. Even though I, her husband, say so.
3. Literally, "brought down" to his feet—where spurs, the appurtenances of a knight, are worn.

LADY WOULD-BE Right, sir, your polity° *cunning*
May bear° it through thus. [*To Peregrine*] Sir, a word with you. *bluff*
I would be loath to contest publicly
With any gentlewoman, or to seem
Froward° or violent; as *The Courtier*[4] says, *Bad-tempered*
It comes too near rusticity° in a lady, *ill breeding*
Which I would shun by all means. And however
I may deserve from Master Would-be, yet
T' have one fair gentlewoman° thus be made *i.e., Peregrine*
Th'unkind° instrument to wrong another, *cruel; unnatural*
And one she knows not, ay, and to persevere,
In my poor judgment is not warranted
From being a solecism° in our sex, *impropriety*
If not in manners.
PEREGRINE How is this?
POLITIC Sweet madam,
Come nearer to your aim.° *Speak more clearly*
LADY WOULD-BE Marry, and will, sir.
Since you provoke me with your impudence
And laughter of your light land-siren[5] here,
Your Sporus,[6] your hermaphrodite—
PEREGRINE What's here?
Poetic fury and historic storms![7]
POLITIC The gentleman, believe it, is of worth,
And of our nation.
LADY WOULD-BE Ay, your Whitefriars° nation! *London brothel district*
Come, I blush for you, Master Would-be, I,
And am ashamed you should ha' no more forehead° *shame*
Than thus to be the patron, or Saint George,[8]
To a lewd harlot, a base fricatrice,° *whore*
A female devil in a male outside.
POLITIC [*to Peregrine*] Nay,
An° you be such a one, I must bid adieu *If*
To your delights. The case appears too liquid.[9]
[*Politic starts to leave.*]
LADY WOULD-BE Ay, you may carry't clear, with your state-face!° *dignified expression*
But for your carnival concupiscence,° *lecherous strumpet*
Who here is fled for liberty of conscience° *licentious conduct*
From furious persecution of the marshal,[1]
Her will I disc'ple.° *discipline, whip*
[*Exit Politic. Lady Politic accosts Peregrine.*]
PEREGRINE This is fine, i'faith!
And do you use this° often? Is this part *act this way*

4. Baldassare Castiglione's famous handbook of gentility.
5. The Sirens were mythical sea creatures who lured sailors to their deaths by sitting on dangerous rocks and singing irresistibly. (Lady Would-be refers to Peregrine.)
6. A eunuch whom the emperor Nero dressed in drag and married.
7. Peregrine notes that even Lady Would-be's tantrums include literary allusions.
8. Patron saint of England, often pictured rescuing a damsel from a dragon.
9. Obvious. (Politic has become convinced that his wife is right in believing that Peregrine is a transvestite whore.)
1. Official charged with punishing prostitutes. Lady Would-be thinks that Peregrine has dressed as a man to flee prosecution.

Of your wit's exercise, 'gainst you have occasion?[2]
Madam—

LADY WOULD-BE Go to,° sir. *(impatient expression)*

PEREGRINE Do you hear me, lady?
Why, if your knight have set you to beg shirts,[3]
Or to invite me home, you might have done it
A nearer° way by far. *more direct*

LADY WOULD-BE This cannot work you
Out of my snare.

PEREGRINE Why, am I in it, then?
Indeed, your husband told me you were fair,
And so you are; only your nose inclines—
That side that's next the sun—to the queen-apple.[4]

LADY WOULD-BE This cannot be endured by any patience.

4.3

[*Enter*] *Mosca.*

MOSCA What's the matter, madam?

LADY WOULD-BE If the Senate° *Venetian government*
Right not my quest° in this, I will protest° 'em *petition / proclaim*
To all the world no aristocracy.

MOSCA What is the injury, lady?

LADY WOULD-BE Why, the callet° *prostitute*
You told me of, here I have ta'en disguised.

MOSCA Who, this? What means Your Ladyship? The creature
I mentioned to you is apprehended now
Before the Senate. You shall see her—

LADY WOULD-BE Where?

MOSCA I'll bring you to her. This young gentleman,
I saw him land this morning at the port.

LADY WOULD-BE Is't possible! How has my judgment wandered!
[*Releasing Peregrine*] Sir, I must, blushing, say to you I have erred,
And plead your pardon.

PEREGRINE What, more changes yet?

LADY WOULD-BE I hope you ha' not the malice to remember
A gentlewoman's passion. If you stay
In Venice here, please you to use me,[1] sir—

MOSCA Will you go, madam?

LADY WOULD-BE Pray you, sir, use me. In faith,
The more you see me, the more I shall conceive
You have forgot our quarrel.

[*Exeunt Mosca, Lady Would-be, Nano, and Women.*]

PEREGRINE This is rare!
Sir Politic Would-be? No, Sir Politic Bawd,
To bring me thus acquainted with his wife!
Well, wise Sir Pol, since you have practiced thus

2. To keep it ready for when it is really needed?
3. Peregrine pretends to believe that Lady Would-be is tearing off his shirt in order to give it to her husband. Probably she is just trying to prevent his leaving.
4. A bright red apple. See 3.4.15–16, where we learn that Lady Would-be is sensitive about her red nose.

4.3. The scene continues.
1. Make use of my services. (With a sexual innuendo continued in "The more you see me, the more I shall conceive" [line 18], where "conceive" means both "understand" and "conceive a child.")

Upon my freshmanship,[2] I'll try your salt-head,
What proof° it is against a counterplot. [*Exit.*] *How invulnerable*

4.4

[*Enter*] *Voltore, Corbaccio, Corvino,* [*and*] *Mosca.*

VOLTORE Well, now you know the carriage° of the business, *management*
Your constancy is all that is required
Unto the safety of it.
MOSCA Is the lie
Safely conveyed° amongst us? Is that sure? *agreed upon*
Knows every man his burden?° *refrain, tune*
CORVINO Yes.
MOSCA Then shrink not.
CORVINO [*aside to Mosca*] But knows the advocate the truth?
MOSCA [*aside to Corvino*] Oh, sir,
By no means. I devised a formal° tale *elaborate*
That salved your reputation. But be valiant, sir.
CORVINO I fear no one but him,° that this his pleading *(Voltore)*
Should make him° stand for a co-heir— *himself*
MOSCA Co-halter![1]
Hang him, we will but use his tongue, his noise,
As we do Croaker's,° here. *(Corbaccio's)*
CORVINO Ay, what shall he do?
MOSCA When we ha' done, you mean?
CORVINO Yes.
MOSCA Why, we'll think—
Sell him for *mummia;*[2] he's half dust already.
([*Aside*] *to Voltore*) Do not you smile to see this buffalo,[3]
How he doth sport it with his head? [*To himself*] I should,
If all were well and past. ([*Aside*] *to Corbaccio*) Sir, only you
Are he that shall enjoy the crop° of all, *harvest*
And these not know for whom they toil.
CORBACCIO Ay, peace!
MOSCA ([*aside*] *to Corvino*) But you shall eat it. [*To himself*]
Much!° (*Then to Voltore again*) Worshipful sir, *Sure you will!*
Mercury[4] sit upon your thund'ring tongue,
Or the French Hercules, and make your language
As conquering as his club,[5] to beat along,° *at full length*
As with a tempest, flat, our adversaries!
[*Aside to Corvino*] But much more yours,° sir. *(your adversaries)*
VOLTORE Here they come. Ha' done.° *Shut up*
MOSCA I have another witness° if you need, sir, *(Lady Would-be)*
I can produce.

2. Taken advantage of my inexperience. (Peregrine apparently believes that Sir Pol has deliberately involved him in a humiliating setup. "Salt-head," following, plays on both "salt" meaning "seasoned," "old," and "salt" meaning "lecherous.")
4.4. The Scrutineo, or Court of Law, in the Doge's palace.
1. Playing on "halter," a hangman's noose, to suggest that both Corbaccio and Voltore are being duped.
2. Powdered embalmed corpse, used medicinally.
3. Corvino, with his cuckold's horns.
4. May the god of rhetoric (and thieves).
5. After his tenth labor, according to some legendary accounts, Hercules, aged by now but powerfully eloquent, fathered the Celts in Gaul, or France. He was traditionally pictured with a club.

VOLTORE Who is it?

MOSCA Sir, I have her.

4.5

[*Enter*] *four Avocatori, Bonario, Celia, Notario* [*Notary*], *Commendatori*° [*and other court officials*]. *law court deputies*

FIRST AVOCATORE The like of this the Senate never heard of.

SECOND AVOCATORE 'Twill come most strange to them when we report it.

FOURTH AVOCATORE The gentlewoman has been ever held
Of unreprovèd name.

THIRD AVOCATORE So, the young man.

FOURTH AVOCATORE The more unnatural part that of his father.

SECOND AVOCATORE More of the husband.

FIRST AVOCATORE I not know to give
His act a name, it is so monstrous!

FOURTH AVOCATORE But the impostor,° he is a thing created *(Volpone)*
T'exceed example!° *precedent*

FIRST AVOCATORE And all aftertimes!° *later eras*

SECOND AVOCATORE I never heard a true voluptuary
Described but him.

THIRD AVOCATORE Appear yet those were cited?° *who were summoned*

NOTARY All but the old magnifico, Volpone.

FIRST AVOCATORE Why is not he here?

MOSCA Please Your Fatherhoods,° *reverend sirs*
Here is his advocate. Himself's so weak,
So feeble—

FOURTH AVOCATORE What are you?

BONARIO His parasite,
His knave, his pander! I beseech the court
He may be forced to come, that your grave eyes
May bear strong witness of his strange impostures.

VOLTORE Upon my faith and credit with your virtues,
He is not able to endure the air.

SECOND AVOCATORE Bring him, however.

THIRD AVOCATORE We will see him.

FOURTH AVOCATORE Fetch him.

[*Exit officers.*]

VOLTORE Your Fatherhoods' fit pleasures be obeyed,
But sure the sight will rather move your pities
Than indignation. May it please the court,
In the meantime he may be heard in me.
I know this place most void of prejudice,
And therefore crave it, since we have no reason
To fear our truth should hurt our cause.

THIRD AVOCATORE Speak free.

VOLTORE Then know, most honored fathers, I must now
Discover° to your strangely abusèd ears *Reveal*
The most prodigious and most frontless° piece *shameless*
Of solid° impudence and treachery *complete*
That ever vicious nature yet brought forth

4.5. The scene continues.

To shame the state of Venice. [*Indicating Celia*] This lewd woman,
That wants° no artificial looks or tears — *Who lacks*
To help the visor° she has now put on, — *(weeping) mask*
Hath long been known a close° adulteress — *secret; intimate*
To that lascivious youth there [*indicating Bonario*]; not suspected,
I say, but known, and taken in the act
With him; and by this man, the easy° husband, — *lenient*
Pardoned; whose timeless° bounty makes him now — *unseasonable; endless*
Stand here, the most unhappy, innocent person
That ever man's own goodness made accused.[1]
For these, not knowing how to owe° a gift — *acknowledge*
Of that dear grace but° with their shame, being placed — *other than*
So above all powers of their gratitude,[2]
Began to hate the benefit, and in place
Of thanks devise t'extirp° the memory — *to extirpate, wipe out*
Of such an act. Wherein I pray Your Fatherhoods
To observe the malice, yea, the rage of creatures
Discovered in their evils, and what heart° — *audacity*
Such take even from their crimes. But that anon
Will more appear. This gentleman, the father,
[*indicating Corbaccio*]
Hearing of this foul fact,° with many others — *deed*
Which daily struck at his too tender ears,
And grieved in nothing more than that he could not
Preserve himself a parent—his son's ills° — *evil deeds*
Growing to that strange flood—at last decreed
To disinherit him.

FIRST AVOCATORE These be strange turns!

SECOND AVOCATORE The young man's fame° was ever fair and honest. — *reputation*

VOLTORE So much more full of danger is his vice,
That can beguile so under shade of virtue.
But, as I said, my honored sires, his father
Having this settled purpose, by what means
To him° betrayed we know not, and this day — *(Bonario)*
Appointed for the deed, that parricide—
I cannot style him better°—by confederacy — *give him a better name*
Preparing this his paramour to be there,
Entered Volpone's house—who was the man,
Your Fatherhoods must understand, designed
For the inheritance—there sought his father.
But with what purpose sought he him, my lords?
I tremble to pronounce it, that a son
Unto a father, and to such a father,
Should have so foul, felonious intent:
It was to murder him. When, being prevented
By his more happy° absence, what then did he? — *Corbaccio's fortunate*
Not check his wicked thoughts; no, now new deeds—
Mischief doth ever end where it begins[3]—
An act of horror, fathers! He dragged forth

1. That ever had his own goodness turned against him.
2. Since the rare value of Corvino's forgiveness was so far beyond their powers of gratitude.
3. Wickedness is always persistent.

The agèd gentleman, that had there lain bedrid
Three years and more, out of his innocent couch;
Naked upon the floor there left him; wounded
His servant in the face, and with this strumpet,
The stale° to his forged practice,° who was glad — *decoy / plot*
To be so active—I shall here desire
Your Fatherhoods to note but my collections° — *deductions*
As most remarkable—thought at once to stop
His father's ends,° discredit his free choice — *aims*
In the old gentleman,° redeem themselves — *(Volpone)*
By laying infamy upon this man° — *(Corvino)*
To whom with blushing they should owe their lives.

FIRST AVOCATORE What proofs have you of this?

BONARIO Most honored fathers,
I humbly crave there be no credit given
To this man's mercenary tongue.

SECOND AVOCATORE Forbear.

BONARIO His soul moves in his fee.

THIRD AVOCATORE Oh, sir!

BONARIO This fellow,
For six sols° more, would plead against his Maker. — *halfpennies*

FIRST AVOCATORE You do forget yourself.

VOLTORE Nay, nay, grave fathers,
Let him have scope. Can any man imagine
That he will spare 's° accuser, that would not — *spare his*
Have spared his parent?

FIRST AVOCATORE Well, produce your proofs.

CELIA I would I could forget I were a creature!° — *living being*

VOLTORE [*calling a witness*] Signor Corbaccio!

FOURTH AVOCATORE What is he?

VOLTORE The father.

SECOND AVOCATORE Has he had an oath?

NOTARY Yes.

CORBACCIO What must I do now?

NOTARY Your testimony's craved.

CORBACCIO [*mishearing*] Speak to the knave?
I'll ha' my mouth first stopped with earth! My heart
Abhors his knowledge;° I disclaim in° him. — *knowing him / disavow*

FIRST AVOCATORE But for what cause?

CORBACCIO The mere portent of nature.[4]
He is an utter stranger to my loins.

BONARIO Have they made° you to this? — *worked, primed*

CORBACCIO I will not hear thee,
Monster of men, swine, goat, wolf, parricide!
Speak not, thou viper.

BONARIO Sir, I will sit down,
And rather wish my innocence should suffer
Than I resist the authority of a father.

VOLTORE [*calling a witness*] Signor Corvino!

SECOND AVOCATORE This is strange!

FIRST AVOCATORE Who's this?

NOTARY The husband.

FOURTH AVOCATORE Is he sworn?

4. A completely monstrous birth. (A deformed child was often considered to be a portent, or evil omen.)

NOTARY He is.
THIRD AVOCATORE Speak, then.
CORVINO This woman, please Your Fatherhoods, is a whore
Of most hot exercise, more than a partridge,[5]
Upon record°— *As is well attested*
FIRST AVOCATORE No more.
CORVINO Neighs like a jennet.° *mare (in heat)*
NOTARY Preserve the honor of the court.
CORVINO I shall,
And modesty of your most reverend ears.
And yet I hope that I may say these eyes
Have seen her glued unto that piece of cedar,
That fine well-timbered gallant;[6] and that here
[*Pointing to his forehead*] The letters may be read, thorough the horn,[7]
That make the story perfect.° *complete*
MOSCA [*aside to Corvino*] Excellent, sir!
CORVINO [*aside to Mosca*] There is no shame in this, now, is there?
MOSCA [*aside to Corvino*] None.
CORVINO [*to the court*] Or if I said I hoped that she were onward° *well on her way*
To her damnation, if there be a hell
Greater than whore and woman—a good Catholic
May make the doubt°— *May wonder*
THIRD AVOCATORE His grief hath made him frantic.
FIRST AVOCATORE Remove him hence. *She* [*Celia*] *swoons.*
SECOND AVOCATORE Look to the woman!
CORVINO [*taunting her*] Rare!
Prettily feigned! Again!
FOURTH AVOCATORE Stand from about her.
FIRST AVOCATORE Give her the air.
THIRD AVOCATORE [*to Mosca*] What can you say?
MOSCA My wound,
May't please Your Wisdoms, speaks for me, received
In aid of my good patron when he° missed *(Bonario)*
His sought-for father, when that well-taught dame
Had her cue given her to cry out a rape.
BONARIO Oh, most laid° impudence! Fathers— *premeditated*
THIRD AVOCATORE Sir, be silent.
You had your hearing free,° so must they theirs. *uninterrupted*
SECOND AVOCATORE I do begin to doubt th'imposture here.
FOURTH AVOCATORE This woman has too many moods.
VOLTORE Grave fathers,
She is a creature of a most professed
And prostituted lewdness.
CORVINO Most impetuous!
Unsatisfied,° grave fathers! *Insatiable*
VOLTORE May her feignings
Not take° Your Wisdoms! But° this day she baited *take in / Only*

5. A bird capable of numerous consecutive sexual acts and so a byword for lechery.
6. Excited by his jealousy into fantasizing about his wife making love to a good-looking man, Corvino sarcastically compliments Bonario as a strapping fellow to whom Celia no doubt wishes to cling. (The cedars of the Middle East are tall and stately.)
7. Children learned to read the alphabet from pages protected by transparent sheets of horn. (With an allusion to the cuckold's horn.)

A stranger, a grave knight, with her loose eyes
And more lascivious kisses. This man° saw 'em *(Mosca)*
Together on the water in a gondola.
MOSCA Here is the lady herself that saw 'em too,
Without;° who then had in the open streets *Waiting outside*
Pursued them, but for saving her knight's honor.
FIRST AVOCATORE Produce that lady.
SECOND AVOCATORE Let her come.
[*Exit Mosca.*]
FOURTH AVOCATORE These things,
They strike with wonder!
THIRD AVOCATORE I am turned a stone!

4.6

[*Enter*] *Mosca* [*and*] *Lady* [*Would-be*].

MOSCA Be resolute, madam.
LADY WOULD-BE Ay, this same is she.
[*To Celia*] Out, thou chameleon° harlot! Now thine eyes *deceitfully changeable*
Vie tears with the hyena.[1] Dar'st thou look
Upon my wrongèd face? [*To the Avocatori*] I cry° your pardons. *beg*
I fear I have forgettingly transgressed
Against the dignity of the court—
SECOND AVOCATORE No, madam.
LADY WOULD-BE And been exorbitant°— *excessive; improper*
SECOND AVOCATORE You have not, lady.
FOURTH AVOCATORE These proofs are strong.
LADY WOULD-BE Surely, I had no purpose
To scandalize your honors, or my sex's.
THIRD AVOCATORE We do believe it.
LADY WOULD-BE Surely, you may believe it.
SECOND AVOCATORE Madam, we do.
LADY WOULD-BE Indeed, you may. My breeding
Is not so coarse—
FOURTH AVOCATORE We know it.
LADY WOULD-BE —to offend
With pertinacy°— *stubborn resolution*
THIRD AVOCATORE Lady—
LADY WOULD-BE —such a presence;
No, surely.
FIRST AVOCATORE We well think it.
LADY WOULD-BE You may think it.
FIRST AVOCATORE [*to the other Avocatori*] Let her o'ercome.° *have the last word*
[*To Celia and Bonario*] What witnesses have you
To make good your report?
BONARIO Our consciences.
CELIA And heaven, that never fails the innocent.
FOURTH AVOCATORE These are no testimonies.
BONARIO Not in your courts,
Where multitude and clamor overcomes.

4.6. The scene continues.
1. A symbol of treachery, the hyena was supposed to be able to change its sex and the color of its eyes at will and to imitate human voices.

FIRST AVOCATORE Nay, then, you do wax insolent.

Volpone is brought in [on a litter], as impotent.° [Lady Would-be embraces him.]° — *disabled (see 5.2.97)*

VOLTORE Here, here
The testimony comes that will convince
And put to utter dumbness their bold tongues.
See here, grave fathers, here's the ravisher,
The rider on men's wives, the great impostor,
The grand voluptuary! Do you not think
These limbs should affect venery?[2] Or these eyes
Covet a concubine? Pray you, mark these hands:
Are they not fit to stroke a lady's breasts?
Perhaps he doth dissemble?
BONARIO So he does.
VOLTORE Would you ha' him tortured?
BONARIO I would have him proved.[3]
VOLTORE Best try him, then, with goads or burning irons;
Put him to the strappado.[4] I have heard
The rack[5] hath cured the gout; faith, give it him
And help him of a malady; be courteous.
I'll undertake, before these honored fathers,
He shall have yet as many left° diseases — *remaining*
As she has known° adulterers, or thou° strumpets. — *(carnally) / (Bonario)*
O my most equal° hearers, if these deeds, — *impartial*
Acts of this bold and most exorbitant strain,
May pass with sufferance,° what one citizen — *be permitted*
But owes the forfeit of his life, yea, fame
To him that dares traduce him?[6] Which of you
Are safe, my honored fathers? I would ask,
With leave of Your grave Fatherhoods, if their plot
Have any face or color° like to truth? — *appearance*
Or if unto the dullest nostril here
It smell not rank and most abhorrèd slander?
I crave your care of this good gentleman,
Whose life is much endangered by their fable;
And as for them, I will conclude with this:
That vicious persons, when they are hot, and fleshed[7]
In impious acts, their constancy° abounds. — *resoluteness*
Damned deeds are done with greatest confidence.
FIRST AVOCATORE Take 'em to custody, and sever them.
SECOND AVOCATORE 'Tis pity two such prodigies° should live. — *monsters*
[Exeunt Celia and Bonario, guarded.]
FIRST AVOCATORE Let the old gentleman be returned with care.
I'm sorry our credulity wronged him.
[Exeunt litter-bearers with Volpone.]
FOURTH AVOCATORE These are two creatures!° — *monsters*
THIRD AVOCATORE I have an earthquake in me!

2. Delight in sexual activity.
3. Tested for impotence, a regular court procedure in some divorce and rape cases. (Torture was another method sometimes used to extract confessions.)
4. Torture in which the victim's arms were tied behind his back; he was then hoisted up by the wrists and dropped.
5. Torture instrument that stretched the victim to the point of dislocating his joints.
6. What citizen is there whose life and reputation might not be forfeit to a slanderer?
7. Excited by the taste of blood, like hunting hounds.

SECOND AVOCATORE Their shame, even in their cradles, fled their faces.

FOURTH AVOCATORE [*to Voltore*] You've done a worthy service to the state, sir,
In their discovery.

FIRST AVOCATORE You shall hear ere night
What punishment the court decrees upon 'em.

VOLTORE We thank Your Fatherhoods.

[*Exeunt Avocatori, Notary, Commendatori.*]

[*To Mosca*] How like you it?

MOSCA Rare!
I'd ha' your tongue, sir, tipped with gold for this;
I'd ha' you be the heir to the whole city;
The earth I'd have want men ere you want living.° *lack income*
They're bound to erect your statue in Saint Mark's.—
Signor Corvino, I would have you go
And show yourself,[8] that you have conquered.

CORVINO Yes.

MOSCA [*aside to Corvino*] It was much better that you should profess
Yourself a cuckold thus, than that the other[9]
Should have been proved.

CORVINO Nay, I considered that.
Now it is her fault.

MOSCA Then it had° been yours. *would have*

CORVINO True. I do doubt° this advocate still. *mistrust*

MOSCA I'faith,
You need not; I dare ease you of that care.

CORVINO I trust thee, Mosca.

MOSCA As your own soul, sir.

[*Exit Corvino.*]

CORBACCIO Mosca!

MOSCA Now for your business, sir.

CORBACCIO How? Ha' you business?

MOSCA Yes, yours, sir.

CORBACCIO Oh, none else?

MOSCA None else, not I.

CORBACCIO Be careful, then.

MOSCA Rest you with both your eyes,° sir. *Rest assured*

CORBACCIO Dispatch it.[1]

MOSCA Instantly.

CORBACCIO And look that all
Whatever° be put in: jewels, plate, moneys, *Whatsoever*
Household stuff, bedding, curtains.

MOSCA Curtain rings, sir.
Only the advocate's fee must be deducted.

CORBACCIO I'll pay him, now; you'll be too prodigal.

MOSCA Sir, I must tender° it. *present*

CORBACCIO Two *cecchines* is well?

MOSCA No, six, sir.

8. Appear in public. (To indicate that he is not ashamed of having admitted to being a cuckold.)

9. The attempt to prostitute Celia to Volpone.

1. I.e., Hurry to make Volpone's will, since Corbaccio has already delivered on his half of the promise.

CORBACCIO 'Tis too much.
MOSCA He talked a great while,
You must consider that, sir.
CORBACCIO [*giving money*] Well, there's three—
MOSCA I'll give it him.
CORBACCIO Do so, and [*he tips Mosca*] there's for thee.
[*Exit Corbaccio.*]
MOSCA [*aside*] Bountiful bones! What horrid strange offense
Did he commit 'gainst nature in his youth
Worthy this age?° [*To Voltore*] You see, sir, how I work *To deserve this old age*
Unto your ends; take you no notice.° *leave it to me*
VOLTORE No,
I'll leave you.
MOSCA All is yours, [*Exit Voltore.*]
[*aside*] the devil and all,
Good advocate! [*To Lady Would-be*] Madam, I'll bring you home.
LADY WOULD-BE No, I'll go see your patron.
MOSCA That you shall not.
I'll tell you why. My purpose is to urge
My patron to reform° his will; and, for *revise*
The zeal you've shown today, whereas before
You were but third or fourth, you shall be now
Put in the first, which would appear as begged
If you were present. Therefore—
LADY WOULD-BE You shall sway me.
[*Exeunt.*]

5.1

[*Enter*] *Volpone* [*attended*].

VOLPONE Well, I am here, and all this brunt° is past. *crisis*
I ne'er was in dislike with my disguise
Till this fled° moment; here 'twas good, in private, *past*
But, in your public—*cavé*,° whilst I breathe. *watch out*
'Fore God, my left leg 'gan to have the cramp,
And I apprehended straight° some power had struck me *thought at once*
With a dead palsy.° Well, I must be merry *paralysis*
And shake it off. A many of these fears
Would put me into some villainous disease,
Should they come thick upon me. I'll prevent 'em.
Give me a bowl of lusty wine to fright
This humor from my heart.[1]—Hum, hum, hum! *He drinks.*
'Tis almost gone already; I shall conquer.° *overcome my fears*
Any device, now, of rare ingenious knavery,
That would possess me with a violent laughter,
Would make me up° again. So, so, so, so. *Drinks again.* *restore me*
This heat is life; 'tis blood by this time. [*Calling*] Mosca!

5.1. Volpone's house.
1. Wine was supposed to convert quickly to blood (see line 17), thus giving courage to the drinker.

5.2

[*Enter*] *Mosca.*

MOSCA How now, sir? Does the day look clear again?
Are we recovered and wrought out of error
Into our way, to see our path before us?
Is our trade free once more?
VOLPONE Exquisite Mosca!
MOSCA Was it not carried learnedly?
VOLPONE And stoutly.° *resolutely*
Good wits are greatest in extremities.
MOSCA It were a folly beyond thought to trust
Any grand act unto a cowardly spirit.
You are not taken° with it enough, methinks? *pleased*
VOLPONE Oh, more than if I had enjoyed the wench!
The pleasure of all womankind's not like it.
MOSCA Why, now you speak, sir. We must here be fixed;
Here we must rest.° This is our masterpiece. *rest on our laurels*
We cannot think to go beyond this.
VOLPONE True,
Th'hast played thy prize,[1] my precious Mosca.
MOSCA Nay, sir,
To gull° the court— *hoodwink*
VOLPONE And quite divert the torrent
Upon the innocent.
MOSCA Yes, and to make
So rare a music out of discords[2]—
VOLPONE Right.
That yet to me's the strangest, how th'ast borne it!° *brought it off*
That these,° being so divided 'mongst themselves, *these men*
Should not scent° somewhat, or° in me or thee, *suspect / either*
Or doubt their own side.° *position*
MOSCA True, they will not see't.
Too much light blinds 'em, I think. Each of 'em
Is so possessed and stuffed with his own hopes
That anything unto the contrary,
Never so true or never so apparent,
Never so palpable, they will resist it—
VOLPONE Like a temptation of the devil.
MOSCA Right, sir.
Merchants may talk of trade, and your great signors
Of land that yields well; but if Italy
Have any glebe° more fruitful than these fellows, *soil*
I am deceived. Did not your advocate rare?° *do brilliantly*
VOLPONE Oh!—"My most honored fathers, my grave fathers,
Under correction of Your Fatherhoods,
What face of truth is here? If these strange deeds
May pass, most honored fathers"—I had much ado

5.2. The scene continues.
1. Professional fencers "played the prize," i.e., competed for purses and titles, in virtuoso displays of swordsmanship.
2. To bring harmony out of various discordant elements was thought to be the highest achievement of art.

To forbear laughing.

MOSCA 'T seemed to me you sweat,° sir. *sweated (with fear)*

VOLPONE In troth, I did a little.

MOSCA But confess, sir,
Were you not daunted?

VOLPONE In good faith, I was
A little in a mist,° but not dejected;° *uncertain / overwhelmed*
Never but still myself.

MOSCA I think° it, sir. *believe*
Now, so truth help me, I must needs say this, sir,
And out of conscience for your advocate:
He's taken pains, in faith, sir, and deserved,
In my poor judgment—I speak it under favor,° *with your permission*
Not to contrary° you, sir—very richly— *contradict*
Well—to be cozened.° *cheated*

VOLPONE Troth, and I think so too,
By that° I heard him° in the latter end. *what / him say*

MOSCA Oh, but before, sir! Had you heard him first
Draw it to certain heads, then aggravate,[3]
Then use his vehement figures°—I looked still *figures of speech*
When he would shift[4] a shirt; and doing this
Out of pure love, no hope of gain—

VOLPONE 'Tis right.
I cannot answer° him, Mosca, as I would, *repay*
Not yet; but for thy sake, at thy entreaty,
I will begin ev'n now to vex 'em all,
This very instant.

MOSCA Good, sir.

VOLPONE Call the dwarf
And eunuch forth.

MOSCA [*calling*] Castrone, Nano!

[*Enter*] *Nano* [*and*] *Castrone.*

NANO Here.

VOLPONE Shall we have a jig, now?

MOSCA What you please, sir.

VOLPONE [*to Castrone and Nano*] Go,
Straight give out° about the streets, you two, *Immediately report*
That I am dead. Do it with constancy,° *conviction*
Sadly, do you hear? Impute it to the grief
Of this late slander. [*Exeunt Castrone and Nano.*]

MOSCA What do you mean, sir?

VOLPONE Oh,
I shall have instantly my vulture, crow,
Raven come flying hither on the news
To peck for carrion, my she-wolf° and all, *(Lady Would-be)*
Greedy and full of expectation—

MOSCA And then to have it ravished from their mouths?

VOLPONE 'Tis true. I will ha' thee put on a gown[5]
And take upon thee as° thou wert mine heir; *act as though*

3. Arrange his material under various headings, then bring charges.
4. Change (because his efforts made him sweat).
5. This must be the long black gown ordinarily worn by chief mourners, not the *clarissimo*'s (aristocrat's) garment, which Mosca dons later in the scene and which constitutes a different kind of insult to Voltore, Corbaccio, and Corvino.

Show 'em a will. Open that chest and reach
Forth one of those that has the blanks.° I'll straight — *blank spaces*
Put in thy name.
MOSCA [*fetching a blank will*] It will be rare, sir.
VOLPONE Ay,
When they e'en gape, and find themselves deluded—
MOSCA Yes.
VOLPONE And thou use them scurvily. Dispatch,
Get on thy gown.
[*Volpone signs the will Mosca has given him.*
Mosca puts on a mourning garment.]
MOSCA But, what, sir, if they ask
After the body?
VOLPONE Say it was corrupted.
MOSCA I'll say it stunk, sir, and was fain° t'have it — *I was obliged*
Coffined up instantly and sent away.
VOLPONE Anything; what thou wilt. Hold, here's my will.
Get thee a cap, a count-book,° pen and ink, — *an account book*
Papers afore thee; sit as° thou wert taking — *as if*
An inventory of parcels.° I'll get up — *items*
Behind the curtain on a stool, and hearken;
Sometime peep over, see how they do look,
With what degrees their blood doth leave their faces.
Oh, 'twill afford me a rare meal of laughter!
MOSCA Your advocate will turn stark dull° upon it. — *gloomy; insensible*
VOLPONE It will take off his oratory's edge.
MOSCA But your *clarissimo*,° old round-back, he — *aristocrat (Corbaccio)*
Will crump you° like a hog-louse with the touch. — *curl up on you*
VOLPONE And what Corvino?
MOSCA Oh, sir, look for him
Tomorrow morning with a rope and a dagger[6]
To visit all the streets; he must run mad.
My lady, too, that came into the court
To bear false witness for Your Worship—
VOLPONE Yes,
And kissed me 'fore the fathers, when my face
Flowed all with oils.° — *(see 4.6.20.1–2)*
MOSCA And sweat, sir. Why, your gold
Is such another° med'cine, it dries up — *so effective a*
All those offensive savors! It transforms
The most deformèd, and restores 'em lovely,
As 'twere the strange poetical girdle.[7] Jove
Could not invent t'himself a shroud more subtle
To pass Acrisius' guards.[8] It is the thing
Makes° all the world her grace, her youth, her beauty. — *That provides*
VOLPONE I think she loves me.
MOSCA Who? The lady, sir?
She's jealous of you.[9]

6. Traditional equipment of suicidal madmen, borne by the allegorical figure of Despair in Spenser's *Faerie Queene*, 1.9, and by the revenger Hieronimo in *The Spanish Tragedy*.
7. The girdle of Venus, the goddess of love, made its wearer irresistible.
8. King Acrisius shut his daughter Danaë in a tower, but the god Jove came to her in a shower of gold.
9. (1) Devoted to you; (2) covetous of your wealth.

VOLPONE Dost thou say so?

[*Knocking offstage.*]

MOSCA Hark,

There's some already.

VOLPONE Look.

MOSCA [*peeping out the door*] It is the vulture.

He has the quickest scent.

VOLPONE I'll to my place,

Thou to thy posture.° — *pose; imposture*

MOSCA I am set.

VOLPONE But, Mosca,

Play the artificer° now; torture 'em rarely. — *artist; trickster*

[*Volpone conceals himself.*]

5.3

[*Enter*] *Voltore.*

VOLTORE How now, my Mosca?

MOSCA [*pretending not to notice him, and reading from an inventory*] "Turkey carpets,° nine"— — *Oriental rugs*

VOLTORE Taking an inventory? That is well.

MOSCA "Two suits of bedding, tissue"[1]—

VOLTORE Where's the will?

Let me read that the while.° — *while you're busy*

[*Enter*] *Corbaccio* [*on a litter*].

CORBACCIO [*to the litter-bearers*] So, set me down

And get you home. [*Exeunt litter-bearers.*]

VOLTORE Is he come now to trouble us?

MOSCA "Of cloth-of-gold,[2] two more"—

CORBACCIO Is it done, Mosca?

MOSCA "Of several velvets,° eight"— — *separate velvet hangings*

VOLTORE [*aside*] I like his care.

CORBACCIO [*to Mosca*] Dost thou not hear?

[*Enter*] *Corvino.*

CORVINO Ha! Is the hour come, Mosca?

Volpone peeps from behind a traverse.° — *curtain*

VOLPONE [*aside*] Ay, now they muster.° — *assemble*

CORVINO What does the advocate here?

Or this Corbaccio?

CORBACCIO What do these here?

[*Enter*] *Lady* [*Would-be*].

LADY WOULD-BE Mosca,

Is his thread spun?[3]

MOSCA "Eight chests of linen"—

VOLPONE [*aside*] Oh,

5.3. The scene continues.

1. Sets of bedcovers and hangings, made of cloth with gold or silver threads interwoven. The fancy textiles Mosca mentions in this scene were extremely expensive to produce in the days before automation.

2. Cloth made of gold threads.

3. Is he dead? (In Greek mythology, the Fates spin out the thread of a human being's life and cut it at the time of death.)

My fine Dame Would-be, too!
CORVINO Mosca, the will,
That I may show it these, and rid 'em hence.
MOSCA "Six chests of diaper, four of damask"[4]—there.
[*He gives them the will.*]
CORBACCIO Is that the will?
MOSCA "Down beds and bolsters"—
VOLPONE [*aside*] Rare!
Be busy still. Now they begin to flutter;
They never think of me. Look, see, see, see!
How their swift eyes run over the long deed
Unto the name, and to the legacies,
What is bequeathed them there—
MOSCA "Ten suits of hangings"°— *sets of tapestries*
VOLPONE [*aside*] Ay, i' their garters,[5] Mosca. Now their hopes
Are at the gasp.° *last gasp*
VOLTORE Mosca the heir!
CORBACCIO What's that?
VOLPONE [*aside*] My advocate is dumb. Look to my merchant;
He has heard of some strange storm, a ship is lost,
He faints. My lady will swoon. Old glazen-eyes,[6]
He hath not reached his despair yet.
CORBACCIO All these
Are out of hope; I'm sure the man.
CORVINO But, Mosca—
MOSCA "Two cabinets"—
CORVINO Is this in earnest?
MOSCA "One
Of ebony"—
CORVINO Or do you but delude me?
MOSCA "The other, mother-of-pearl"—I am very busy.
Good faith, it is a fortune thrown upon me—
"Item, one salt° of agate"—not my seeking. *saltcellar*
LADY WOULD-BE Do you hear, sir?
MOSCA "A perfumed box"—pray you, forbear;
You see I am troubled°—"made of an onyx"— *busy*
LADY WOULD-BE How!
MOSCA Tomorrow or next day I shall be at leisure
To talk with you all.
CORVINO Is this my large hope's issue?° *outcome*
LADY WOULD-BE Sir, I must have a fairer answer.
MOSCA Madam!
Marry, and shall: pray you, fairly° quit my house. *positively*
Nay, raise no tempest with your looks, but hark you,
Remember what Your Ladyship offered me° *(implicitly, sexual favors)*
To put you in° an heir; go to, think on't, *your name in as*
And what you said e'en your best madams did
For maintenance,° and why not you? Enough. *financial support*
Go home and use the poor Sir Pol, your knight, well,

4. Two kinds of costly textile with interwoven motifs. Diaper was linen with a diamond pattern; damask could be linen or silk with floral or other designs.

5. "Go hang yourself in your own garters" was a common phrase of ridicule.

6. Corbaccio wears spectacles (see also line 63 below).

For fear I tell some riddles.° Go, be melancholic. *secrets*
[*Exit Lady Would-be.*]
VOLPONE [*aside*] Oh, my fine devil!
CORVINO Mosca, pray you a word.
MOSCA Lord! Will not you take your dispatch hence yet?
Methinks of all you should have been th'example.° *led the way*
Why should you stay here? With what thought? What promise?
Hear you, do not you know I know you an ass?
And that you would most fain have been a wittol° *willing cuckold*
If fortune would have let you? That you are
A declared cuckold, on good terms?° This pearl, *in good standing*
You'll say, was yours? Right. This diamond?
I'll not deny't, but thank you. Much here else?
It may be so. Why, think that these good works
May help to hide your bad. I'll not betray you.
Although you be but extraordinary° *in name only*
And have it° only in title, it sufficeth. *(the name of cuckold)*
Go home. Be melancholic too, or mad. [*Exit Corvino.*]
VOLPONE [*aside*] Rare, Mosca! How his° villainy becomes him! *(Mosca's)*
VOLTORE [*aside*] Certain he doth delude all these for me.
CORBACCIO [*finally making out the will*] Mosca the heir?
VOLPONE [*aside*] Oh, his four eyes have found it!
CORBACCIO I'm cozened, cheated by a parasite-slave!
Harlot,[7] th'ast gulled me.
MOSCA Yes, sir. Stop your mouth,
Or I shall draw the only tooth is left.
Are not you he, that filthy covetous wretch
With the three legs,° that here, in hope of prey, *(including his cane)*
Have, any time this three year, snuffed about
With your most grov'ling nose, and would have hired
Me to the pois'ning of my patron? Sir?
Are not you he that have today in court
Professed the disinheriting of your son?
Perjured yourself? Go home, and die, and stink.
If you but croak a syllable, all comes out.
Away and call your porters. Go, go stink! [*Exit Corbaccio.*]
VOLPONE [*aside*] Excellent varlet!° *servant; rascal*
VOLTORE Now, my faithful Mosca,
I find thy constancy—
MOSCA Sir?
VOLTORE Sincere.
MOSCA "A table
Of porphyry"—I mar'l° you'll be thus troublesome. *marvel*
VOLTORE Nay, leave off now, they are gone.
MOSCA Why, who are you?
What? Who did send for you? Oh, cry you mercy,° *beg your pardon*
Reverend° sir! Good faith, I am grieved for you, *Worthy*
That any chance° of mine should thus defeat *luck*
Your—I must needs say—most deserving travails.° *labors*
But I protest, sir, it was cast upon me,

7. A word used of wicked men as well as women.

And I could almost wish to be without it,
But that the will o'th'dead must be observed.
Marry, my joy is that you need it not;
You have a gift, sir—thank your education—
Will° never let you want,° while there are men — *Which will / go without*
And malice to breed causes.° Would I had — *lawsuits*
But half the like, for all my fortune, sir!
If I have any suits—as I do hope,
Things being so easy and direct,[8] I shall not—
I will make bold with your obstreperous° aid, — *vociferous*
Conceive me, for your fee,[9] sir. In meantime
You, that have° so much law, I know, ha' the conscience — *know*
Not to be covetous of what is mine.
Good sir, I thank you for my plate;° 'twill help — *(see 1.3.1–20)*
To set up a young man.° Good faith, you look — *set up my household*
As° you were costive;° best go home and purge, sir. — *As if / constipated*
[*Exit Voltore.*]

VOLPONE [*coming from behind the traverse*] Bid him eat let-
tuce° well. My witty mischief, — *(used as a laxative)*
Let me embrace thee! [*He hugs Mosca.*] Oh, that I could now
Transform thee to a Venus!° Mosca, go, — *(for Volpone's sexual use)*
Straight take my habit of *clarissimo*[1]
And walk the streets; be seen, torment 'em more.
We must pursue as well as plot. Who would
Have lost° this feast? — *missed*

MOSCA I doubt° it will lose them.° — *fear / (as dupes)*

VOLPONE Oh, my recovery shall recover all.[2]
That I could now but think on some disguise
To meet 'em in, and ask 'em questions.
How I would vex 'em still at every turn!

MOSCA Sir, I can fit you.

VOLPONE Canst thou?

MOSCA Yes, I know
One o'the *commendatori,*° sir, so like you, — *law court deputies*
Him will I straight make drunk, and bring you his habit.

VOLPONE A rare disguise, and answering thy brain!° — *suiting your wit*
Oh, I will be a sharp disease unto 'em.

MOSCA Sir, you must look for° curses— — *expect*

VOLPONE Till they burst!
The fox fares ever best when he is curst.° [*Exeunt.*] — *(proverbial wisdom)*

5.4

[*Enter*] *Peregrine* [*in disguise, and*] *three Mercatori* [*Merchants*].

PEREGRINE Am I enough disguised?

FIRST MERCHANT I warrant° you. — *assure*

PEREGRINE All my ambition is to fright him only.

8. The situation being so straightforward.
9. It being understood that I will pay you, of course.
1. Aristocrat. (By obeying this order, Mosca violates the sumptuary laws that restricted the wearing of distinctive high-status garments, such as the *clarissimo*'s robe, to persons of the appropriate rank.)
2. Volpone believes that by "undoing" his death, he will be able to resuscitate his scam.
5.4. The Would-bes' house.

SECOND MERCHANT If you could ship him away, 'twere excellent.
THIRD MERCHANT To Zante, or to Aleppo?[1]
PEREGRINE Yes, and ha' his
Adventures put i'th'book of voyages,[2]
And his gulled° story registered for truth? *erroneous*
Well, gentlemen, when I am in awhile,
And that you think us warm in our discourse,
Know° your approaches. *Make*
FIRST MERCHANT Trust it to our care.
[*Exeunt Merchants.*]

[*Peregine knocks. A*] *Woman* [*servant answers the door*].

PEREGRINE Save° you, fair lady. Is Sir Pol within? *God save*
WOMAN I do not know, sir.
PEREGRINE Pray you, say unto him
Here is a merchant upon earnest business
Desires to speak with him.
WOMAN I will see, sir.
PEREGRINE Pray you.
[*Exit Woman.*]
I see the family is all female here.

[*Enter Woman.*]

WOMAN He says, sir, he has weighty affairs of state
That now require him whole;° some other time *demand all his attention*
You may possess° him. *gain audience with*
PEREGRINE Pray you say again,
If those require him whole, these will exact him° *force him out*
Whereof I bring him tidings. [*Exit Woman.*]
What might be
His grave affair of state, now? How to make
Bolognian sausages here in Venice, sparing° *omitting*
One o'th'ingredients?

[*Enter Woman.*]

WOMAN Sir, he says he knows
By your word "tidings" that you are no statesman,[3]
And therefore wills you stay.° *wishes you to wait*
PEREGRINE Sweet, pray you return° him *reply to*
I have not read so many proclamations
And studied them for words as he has done,
But—here he deigns to come.

[*Enter*] *Politic.*

[*Exit Woman.*]

POLITIC Sir, I must crave
Your courteous pardon. There hath chanced today

1. Zante is an island off Greece under Venetian control; Aleppo, a big trading center, is in Syria.
2. An enlarged edition of Richard Hakluyt's *Principal Navigations, Voyages, Traffics, and Discoveries of the English Nation* was published in 1598–1600.
3. Government agent. (Sir Politic believes that a spy would use the word "intelligence.")

Unkind disaster 'twixt my lady and me,
And I was penning my apology
To give her satisfaction, as you came now.

PEREGRINE Sir, I am grieved I bring you worse disaster.
The gentleman you met at th'port today,
That told you he was newly arrived—

POLITIC Ay, was
A fugitive punk?° *prostitute*

PEREGRINE No, sir, a spy set on you;
And he has made relation to the Senate
That you professed to him to have a plot
To sell the state of Venice to the Turk.° *(see 4.1.128–30)*

POLITIC Oh, me!

PEREGRINE For which warrants are signed by this time
To apprehend you, and to search your study
For papers—

POLITIC Alas, sir, I have none but notes
Drawn out of playbooks°— *printed plays*

PEREGRINE All the better, sir.

POLITIC And some essays. What shall I do?

PEREGRINE Sir, best
Convey yourself into a sugar-chest;
Or, if you could lie round, a frail were rare,[4]
And I could send you aboard.

POLITIC Sir, I but talked so,
For discourse sake merely.° *They knock without.* *Just to be conversing*

PEREGRINE Hark, they are there!

POLITIC I am a wretch, a wretch!

PEREGRINE What will you do, sir?
Ha' you ne'er a currant-butt° to leap into? *casket for currants*
They'll put you to the rack; you must be sudden.

POLITIC Sir, I have an engine°— *contrivance*

THIRD MERCHANT [*without*] Sir Politic Would-be!

SECOND MERCHANT [*without*] Where is he?

POLITIC That I have thought upon beforetime.° *beforehand*

PEREGRINE What is it?

POLITIC I shall ne'er endure the torture!
Marry, it is, sir, of a tortoiseshell, [*producing the shell*]
Fitted for these extremities. Pray you sir, help me.
Here I have a place, sir, to put back my legs—
Please you to lay it on, sir—with this cap
And my black gloves. I'll lie, sir, like a tortoise
Till they are gone.

PEREGRINE [*laying the shell on Politic's back*] And call you this an engine?

POLITIC Mine own device—good sir, bid my wife's women
To burn my papers. [*Exit Peregrine.*]

They [*the Merchants*] *rush in.*

FIRST MERCHANT Where's he hid?

THIRD MERCHANT We must

4. If you could curl up, a fruit basket would be excellent.

And will, sure, find him.

SECOND MERCHANT Which is his study?

[*Enter Peregrine.*]

FIRST MERCHANT What

Are you, sir?

PEREGRINE I'm a merchant, that came here

To look upon this tortoise.

THIRD MERCHANT How?

FIRST MERCHANT Saint Mark!

What beast is this?

PEREGRINE It is a fish.

SECOND MERCHANT [*to Politic*] Come out here!

PEREGRINE Nay, you may strike him, sir, and tread upon him.

He'll bear a cart.

FIRST MERCHANT What, to run over him?

PEREGRINE Yes.

THIRD MERCHANT Let's jump upon him.

SECOND MERCHANT Can he not go?° *walk*

PEREGRINE He creeps, sir.

FIRST MERCHANT [*poking Politic*] Let's see him creep.

PEREGRINE No, good sir, you will hurt him.

SECOND MERCHANT Heart! I'll see him creep, or prick his guts.

THIRD MERCHANT [*to Politic*] Come out here!

PEREGRINE [*aside to Politic*] Pray you, sir, creep a little.

[*Politic creeps.*]

FIRST MERCHANT Forth!

SECOND MERCHANT Yet further.

PEREGRINE [*aside to Politic*] Good sir, creep.

SECOND MERCHANT We'll see his legs.

They pull off the shell and discover° him. *expose*

THIRD MERCHANT Godso, he has garters!

FIRST MERCHANT Ay, and gloves!

SECOND MERCHANT Is this

Your fearful tortoise?

PEREGRINE [*revealing himself*] Now, Sir Pol, we are even.

For your next project I shall be prepared.

I am sorry for the funeral of your notes, sir.

FIRST MERCHANT 'Twere° a rare motion to be seen in Fleet Street![5] *It would be*

SECOND MERCHANT Ay, i'the term.

FIRST MERCHANT Or Smithfield, in the fair.[6]

THIRD MERCHANT Methinks 'tis but a melancholic sight!

PEREGRINE Farewell, most politic tortoise.

[*Exeunt Peregine and Merchants.*]

[*Enter Woman.*]

POLITIC Where's my lady?

Knows she of this?

5. Puppet shows, called "motions," were frequently performed on London's Fleet Street, adjacent to the Inns of Court, where attorneys were trained and cases were argued during the three law terms.

6. Smithfield, just northwest of London, was the site every August of Bartholomew Fair; puppet shows were a prime entertainment there.

WOMAN I know not, sir.
POLITIC Inquire.
[*Exit Woman.*]
Oh, I shall be the fable of all feasts,° *talk of the town*
The freight of the *gazetti*, ship boys' tale,[7]
And, which is worst, even talk for ordinaries.° *taverns*

[*Enter Woman.*]

WOMAN My lady's come most melancholic home,
And says, sir, she will straight to sea for physic.° *her health*
POLITIC And I, to shun this place and clime forever,
Creeping with house on back, and think it well
To shrink my poor head in my politic shell. [*Exeunt.*]

5.5

[*Enter*] *Volpone* [*and*] *Mosca, the first in the habit of a commendatore, the other, of a clarissimo.*° *(see 5.3.104–15)*

VOLPONE Am I then like him?
MOSCA Oh, sir, you are he.
No man can sever° you. *distinguish*
VOLPONE Good.
MOSCA But what am I?
VOLPONE 'Fore heav'n, a brave° *clarissimo;* thou becom'st it! *fine*
Pity thou wert not born one.
MOSCA If I hold° *uphold*
My made one,° 'twill be well. *disguised identity*
VOLPONE I'll go and see
What news, first, at the court.
MOSCA Do so. [*Exit Volpone.*]
My fox
Is out on° his hole,[1] and ere he shall reenter *of*
I'll make him languish in his borrowed case,° *disguise*
Except he come to composition° with me. *Unless he makes a deal*
[*Calling*] Androgyno, Castrone, Nano!

[*Enter Androgyno, Castrone, and Nano.*]

ALL Here.
MOSCA Go recreate yourselves abroad;° go sport. *outside*
[*Exeunt Androgyno, Castrone, and Nano.*]
So, now I have the keys, and am possessed.° *in possession*
Since he will needs be dead afore his time,
I'll bury him or gain by him. I am his heir,
And so will keep me° till he share at least. *remain*
To cozen him of all were but a cheat
Well placed; no man would construe it a sin.
Let his sport pay for't.° This is called the Fox Trap. [*Exit.*] *for itself*

7. Topic of the newspapers and the gossip of boys serving on board ships.

5.5. Volpone's house.
1. Alluding to the children's game, fox-in-the-hole.

5.6

[Enter] Corbaccio [and] Corvino.

CORBACCIO They say the court is set.° *in session*
CORVINO We must maintain
Our first tale good, for both our reputations.
CORBACCIO Why, mine's no tale; my son would there have killed me.
CORVINO That's true; I had forgot. [*Aside*] Mine is,° I am sure.— *is a mere tale*
But for your will, sir.
CORBACCIO Ay, I'll come upon him° *(Mosca)*
For that hereafter, now his patron's dead.

[Enter] Volpone [disguised].

VOLPONE Signor Corvino! And Corbaccio! Sir,
Much joy unto you.
CORVINO Of what?
VOLPONE The sudden good
Dropped down upon you—
CORBACCIO Where?
VOLPONE And none knows how—
From old Volpone, sir.
CORBACCIO Out, arrant knave!
VOLPONE Let not your too much wealth, sir, make you furious.° *insane*
CORBACCIO Away, thou varlet!
VOLPONE Why, sir?
CORBACCIO Dost thou mock me?
VOLPONE You mock the world, sir.[1] Did you not change° wills? *exchange*
CORBACCIO Out, harlot!
VOLPONE [*to Corvino*] Oh, belike° you are the man, *perhaps*
Signor Corvino? Faith, you carry it° well; *carry it off*
You grow not mad withal. I love your spirit.
You are not overleavened° with your fortune. *too puffed up*
You should ha' some° would swell now like a wine-vat *Some people*
With such an autumn.° Did he gi' you all, sir? *harvest*
CORVINO Avoid,° you rascal! *Go away*
VOLPONE Troth, your wife has shown
Herself a very° woman. But you are well; *typical*
You need not care; you have a good estate
To bear it out,° sir, better by this chance— *carry it off*
Except° Corbaccio have a share? *Unless*
CORBACCIO Hence, varlet!
VOLPONE You will not be aknown,[2] sir; why, 'tis wise.
Thus do all gamesters° at all games dissemble. *gamblers*
No man will seem to win.° *admit he's winning*
[Exeunt Corbaccio and Corvino.]
Here comes my vulture,
Heaving his beak up i'the air and snuffing.

5.6. A street in Venice.
1. Volpone pretends to believe that Corbaccio is misleading people by refusing to admit to his good fortune.
2. You prefer not to be recognized (as heir).

5.7

[*Enter*] *Voltore.*

VOLTORE [*to himself*] Outstripped thus by a parasite? A slave
Would° run on errands, and make legs° for crumbs? *Who would / curtsies*
Well, what I'll do—
VOLPONE The court stays for° Your Worship. *awaits*
I e'en rejoice, sir, at Your Worship's happiness,
And that it fell into so learnèd hands
That understand the fingering[1]—
VOLTORE What do you mean?
VOLPONE I mean to be a suitor to Your Worship
For the small tenement, out of reparations[2]—
That° at the end of your long row of houses *The one*
By the *piscaria*.° It was in Volpone's time, *fish market*
Your predecessor, ere he grew diseased,
A handsome, pretty, customed° bawdy house *much-patronized*
As any was in Venice—none dispraised[3]—
But fell° with him; his body and that house *declined*
Decayed together.
VOLTORE Come, sir, leave your prating.° *chattering*
VOLPONE Why, if Your Worship give me but your hand,
That I may ha' the refusal,° I have done. *right of first refusal*
'Tis a mere toy to you, sir, candle-rents,[4]
As Your learned Worship knows—
VOLTORE What do I know?
VOLPONE Marry, no end of your wealth, sir, God
decrease° it. *(instead of "increase")*
VOLTORE Mistaking° knave! What, mock'st thou my *Misspeaking*
misfortune?
VOLPONE His° blessing on your heart, sir! Would 'twere more. *(God's)*
[*Exit Voltore.*]
Now, to my first[5] again, at the next corner.

5.8

[*Enter*] *Corbaccio* [*and*] *Corvino.* [*Enter*] *Mosca,*
passant° [*over the stage in* clarissimo*'s attire, and exit*]. *passing*

CORBACCIO See, in our habit! See the impudent varlet!
CORVINO That° I could shoot mine eyes at him, like *Would that*
gunstones!° *cannonballs*
VOLPONE But, is this true, sir, of the parasite?° *i.e., that Mosca is heir*
CORBACCIO Again t'afflict us? Monster!
VOLPONE In good faith, sir,
I'm heartily grieved a beard of your grave length° *so wise an old man*
Should be so overreached. I never brooked° *could stand*
That parasite's hair; methought his nose should cozen.° *he had a cheating nose*

5.7. The scene continues.
1. That understand how to handle money.
2. For the rental house in bad repair.
3. Not to disparage the others.
4. (1) Revenue from deteriorating property; (2) "pin money," money for incidentals.
5. The ones I was taunting earlier, Corvino and Corbaccio.
5.8. The scene continues.

There still° was somewhat in his look did promise — *always*
The bane° of a *clarissimo*. — *ruin*
CORBACCIO Knave—
VOLPONE [*to Corvino*] Methinks
Yet you that are so traded° i'the world, — *experienced*
A witty merchant, the fine bird Corvino,
That have such moral emblems[1] on your name,
Should not have sung your shame and dropped your cheese,
To let the fox laugh at your emptiness.[2]
CORVINO Sirrah, you think the privilege of the place,[3]
And your red saucy cap, that seems to me
Nailed to your jolt-head with those two *cecchines*,[4]
Can warrant° your abuses. Come you hither. — *sanction*
You shall perceive, sir, I dare beat you. Approach!
VOLPONE No haste, sir, I do know your valor well,
Since you durst publish° what you are, sir. — *make public*
[*Volpone makes as if to leave.*]
CORVINO Tarry!
I'd speak with you.
VOLPONE Sir, sir, another time—
CORVINO Nay, now.
VOLPONE Oh, God, sir! I were° a wise man — *would be (ironic)*
Would stand° the fury of a distracted cuckold. — *To withstand*

Mosca [*enters and*] *walks by 'em.*

CORBACCIO What! Come again?
VOLPONE [*aside to Mosca*] Upon 'em, Mosca; save me.
CORBACCIO The air's infected where he breathes.
CORVINO Let's fly him.
[*Exeunt Corvino and Corbaccio.*]
VOLPONE Excellent basilisk![5] Turn upon the vulture.

5.9

[*Enter*] *Voltore.*

VOLTORE [*to Mosca*] Well, flesh fly,° it is summer with you now; — *(translating Mosca's name)*
Your winter will come on.
MOSCA Good advocate,
Pray thee not rail, nor threaten out of place° thus; — *unsuitably*
Thou'lt make a solecism,° as madam says. — *(see 4.2.43)*
Get you a biggin[1] more; your brain breaks loose.
VOLTORE Well, sir. [*Exit Mosca.*]
VOLPONE Would you ha' me beat the insolent slave?
Throw dirt upon his first good clothes?

1. Mottoes accompanying symbolic engravings.
2. As in Aesop's fable; see 1.2.95–97 and note.
3. Violence was forbidden near the court.
4. The *commendatore*'s cap is decorated with gold buttons.
5. A legendary monster whose breath and glance were deadly.

5.9. The scene continues.
1. A larger skullcap (worn by lawyers).

VOLTORE This same° *(the disguised Volpone)*
Is doubtless some familiar!° *attendant devil*
VOLPONE Sir, the court,
In troth, stays for you. I am mad° a mule *furious (that)*
That never read Justinian[2] should get up
And ride an advocate. Had you no quirk° *trick*
To avoid gullage,° sir, by such a creature? *deception*
I hope you do but jest; he has not done't.
This's but confederacy to blind the rest.° *(Corvino and Corbaccio)*
You are the heir?
VOLTORE A strange, officious,
Troublesome knave! Thou dost torment me.
VOLPONE I know—
It cannot be, sir, that you should be cozened;
'Tis not within the wit of man to do it.
You are so wise, so prudent, and 'tis fit
That wealth and wisdom still should go together. [*Exeunt.*]

5.10

[*Enter*] *four Avocatori, Notario* [*Notary*], *Commendatori, Bonario* [*and*] *Celia* [*under guard*], *Corbaccio,* [*and*] *Corvino.*

FIRST AVOCATORE Are all the parties here?
NOTARY All but the advocate.
SECOND AVOCATORE And here he comes.
FIRST AVOCATORE Then bring 'em forth to sentence.

[*Enter*] *Voltore,* [*and*] *Volpone* [*still disguised as a commendatore*].

VOLTORE O my most honored fathers, let your mercy
Once win upon° your justice, to forgive— *prevail over*
I am distracted—
VOLPONE (*aside*) What will he do now?
VOLTORE Oh,
I know not which t'address myself to first,
Whether Your Fatherhoods or these innocents°— *(Celia and Bonario)*
CORVINO [*aside*] Will he betray himself?
VOLTORE Whom equally
I have abused, out of most covetous ends°— *motives*
CORVINO [*aside to Corbaccio*] The man is mad!
CORBACCIO What's that?
CORVINO He is possessed.
VOLTORE For which, now struck in conscience, here I prostrate
Myself at your offended feet for pardon.
[*He throws himself down.*]
FIRST AND SECOND AVOCATORI Arise!
CELIA O heav'n, how just thou art!
VOLPONE [*aside*] I'm caught
I' mine own noose—
CORVINO [*aside to Corbaccio*] Be constant, sir; naught now

2. The Roman law, codified under Emperor Justinian and still influential on the Continent. Lawyers traditionally rode mules to the courts; here the image is comically inverted.
5.10. The law court.

Can help but impudence. [*Voltore rises.*]
FIRST AVOCATORE [*to Voltore*] Speak forward.° *Continue*
COMMENDATORI [*to the courtroom*] Silence!
VOLTORE It is not passion° in me, reverend fathers, *madness*
But only conscience, conscience, my good sires,
That makes me now tell truth. That parasite,
That knave hath been the instrument of all.
SECOND AVOCATORE Where is that knave? Fetch him.
VOLPONE [*as commendatore*] I go. [*Exit.*]
CORVINO Grave fathers,
This man's distracted; he confessed it now;° *just now*
For, hoping to be old Volpone's heir,
Who now is dead—
THIRD AVOCATORE How?
SECOND AVOCATORE Is Volpone dead?
CORVINO Dead since,° grave fathers— *(since his appearance here)*
BONARIO O sure vengeance!
FIRST AVOCATORE Stay.
Then he was no deceiver?
VOLTORE Oh, no, none.
The parasite, grave fathers.
CORVINO He does speak
Out of mere° envy, 'cause the servant's made *pure*
The thing he gaped° for. Please Your Fatherhoods, *Voltore yearned*
This is the truth; though I'll not justify
The other,° but he may be somedeal° faulty. *(Mosca) / somewhat*
VOLTORE Ay, to your hopes as well as mine, Corvino;
But I'll use modesty.° Pleaseth° Your Wisdoms *self-control / May it please*
To view these certain notes, and but confer° them. *compare*
As I hope favor, they shall speak clear truth.
[*He gives documents to the Avocatori.*]
CORVINO The devil has entered him!
BONARIO Or bides in you.
FOURTH AVOCATORE We have done ill, by a public officer° *(Volpone as* commendatore*)*
To send for him, if he be heir.
SECOND AVOCATORE For whom?
FOURTH AVOCATORE Him that they call the parasite.
THIRD AVOCATORE 'Tis true;
He is a man of great estate now left.° *bequeathed to him*
FOURTH AVOCATORE [*to Notary*] Go you and learn his name,
and say the court
Entreats his presence here but to the clearing
Of some few doubts. [*Exit Notary.*]
SECOND AVOCATORE This same's a labyrinth!
FIRST AVOCATORE [*to Corvino*] Stand you unto° your first report? *Do you stand by*
CORVINO My state,° *status, estate*
My life, my fame°— *reputation*
BONARIO Where is't?[1]
CORVINO —are at the stake.
FIRST AVOCATORE [*to Corbaccio*] Is yours so too?
CORBACCIO The advocate's a knave,
And has a forkèd tongue—

1. Implying that Corvino has nothing of worth to lose.

SECOND AVOCATORE Speak to the point.
CORBACCIO So is the parasite, too.
FIRST AVOCATORE This is confusion.
VOLTORE I do beseech Your Fatherhoods, read but those.
CORVINO And credit nothing the false spirit hath writ.
It cannot be but he is possessed, grave fathers.
[*The Avocatori examine Voltore's papers.*]

5.11

[*Enter*] *Volpone* [*on a separate part of the stage*].

VOLPONE To make a snare for mine own neck! And run
My head into it willfully! With laughter!
When I had newly scaped, was free and clear!
Out of mere wantonness!° Oh, the dull devil — *caprice*
Was in this brain of mine when I devised it,
And Mosca gave it second.° He must now — *seconded it*
Help to sear up° this vein, or we bleed dead. — *cauterize*

[*Enter*] *Nano, Androgyno,* [*and*] *Castrone.*

How now, who let you loose? Whither go you now?
What, to buy gingerbread? Or to drown kitlings?° — *kittens*
NANO Sir, Master Mosca called us out of doors,
And bid us all go play, and took the keys.
ANDROGYNO Yes.
VOLPONE Did Master Mosca take the keys? Why, so!
I am farther in.° These are my fine conceits!° — *in trouble / notions*
I must be° merry, with a mischief to me! — *I insisted on being*
What a vile wretch was I, that could not bear
My fortune soberly! I must ha' my crotchets° — *perverse whims*
And my conundrums! Well, go you and seek him.
His meaning may be truer than my fear.[1]
Bid him he straight come to me, to the court.
Thither will I, and, if't be possible,
Unscrew° my advocate upon° new hopes. — *Dissuade / by means of*
When I provoked him, then I lost myself.
[*Exeunt Volpone and his entourage.*
The Avocatori and parties to the court-room proceedings remain onstage.]

5.12

FIRST AVOCATORE [*with Voltore's notes*] These things can ne'er be reconciled. He here
Professeth that the gentleman° was wronged, — *(Bonario)*
And that the gentlewoman was brought thither,
Forced by her husband, and there left.
VOLTORE Most true.
CELIA How ready° is heav'n to those that pray! — *responsive*
FIRST AVOCATORE But that
Volpone would have ravished her, he holds

5.11. A street. The courtroom characters remain visible onstage, perhaps in silent tableau, while Volpone is understood to be outside.

1. Mosca's intentions may be truer (more loyal) than my fear is true (accurate).

5.12. The courtroom.

Utterly false, knowing his impotence.
CORVINO Grave fathers, he is possessed; again I say,
Possessed. Nay, if there be possession
And obsession, he has both.
THIRD AVOCATORE Here comes our officer.

[*Enter Volpone, still disguised.*]

VOLPONE The parasite will straight be here, grave fathers.
FOURTH AVOCATORE You might invent some other name, sir varlet.
THIRD AVOCATORE Did not the notary meet him?
VOLPONE Not that I know.
FOURTH AVOCATORE His coming will clear all.
SECOND AVOCATORE Yet° it is misty. *As yet*
VOLTORE May't please Your Fatherhoods—
VOLPONE (*whispers* [*to*] *the advocate*) Sir, the parasite
Willed me to tell you that his master lives,
That you are still the man, your hopes the same;
And this was only a jest—
VOLTORE [*aside to Volpone*] How?
VOLPONE [*aside to Voltore*] Sir, to try
If you were firm, and how you stood affected.° *how loyal you were*
VOLTORE Art sure he lives?
VOLPONE Do I live,° sir? *He's as alive as I am*
VOLTORE Oh, me!
I was too violent.
VOLPONE Sir, you may redeem it.
They said you were possessed; fall down, and seem so.
I'll help to make it good. *Voltore falls.*
[*Aloud*] God bless the man!
[*Aside to Voltore*] Stop your wind hard, and swell.[1] [*Aloud*]
See, see, see, see!
He vomits crooked pins! His eyes are set
Like a dead hare's hung in a poulter's[2] shop!
His mouth's running away!° [*To Corvino*] Do you see, signor? *twitching spasmodically*
Now 'tis in his belly.
CORVINO Ay, the devil!
VOLPONE Now in his throat.
CORVINO Ay, I perceive it plain.
VOLPONE 'Twill out, 'twill out! Stand clear. See where it flies,
In shape of a blue toad with a bat's wings!
[*To Corbaccio*] Do not you see it, sir?
CORBACCIO What? I think I do.
CORVINO 'Tis too manifest.
VOLPONE Look! He comes t' himself!
VOLTORE Where am I?
VOLPONE Take good heart; the worst is past, sir.
You are dispossessed.
FIRST AVOCATORE What accident° is this? *unforeseen event*
SECOND AVOCATORE Sudden, and full of wonder!
THIRD AVOCATORE If he were

1. The details of Voltore's dispossession in the following lines resemble the fake exorcisms described in Samuel Harsnett's lively exposé, *A Discovery of the Fraudulent Practices of John Darrell* (1599). "Stop your wind" means "hold your breath."
2. Seller of poultry and small game.

Possessed, as it appears, all this° is nothing. *(Voltore's written statement)*
CORVINO He has been often subject to these fits.
FIRST AVOCATORE Show him that writing. [*To Voltore*] Do you know it, sir?
VOLPONE [*aside to Voltore*] Deny it, sir; forswear it; know it not.
VOLTORE Yes, I do know it well, it is my hand;° *handwriting*
But all that it contains is false.
BONARIO Oh, practice!° *deception*
SECOND AVOCATORE What maze is this!
FIRST AVOCATORE Is he not guilty, then,
Whom you there name the parasite?
VOLTORE Grave fathers,
No more than his good patron, old Volpone.
FOURTH AVOCATORE Why, he is dead!
VOLTORE Oh, no, my honored fathers.
He lives—
FIRST AVOCATORE How! Lives?
VOLTORE Lives.
SECOND AVOCATORE This is subtler yet!
THIRD AVOCATORE [*to Voltore*] You said he was dead?
VOLTORE Never.
THIRD AVOCATORE [*to Corvino*] You said so?
CORVINO I heard so.
FOURTH AVOCATORE Here comes the gentleman; make him way.° *room for him*

[*Enter Mosca.*]

THIRD AVOCATORE A stool!
FOURTH AVOCATORE [*aside*] A proper° man! And, were Volpone dead, *handsome*
A fit match for my daughter.
THIRD AVOCATORE Give him way.
VOLPONE [*aside to Mosca*] Mosca, I was almost lost; the advocate
Had betrayed all; but now it is recovered.
All's o'the hinge° again. Say I am living. *running smoothly*
MOSCA [*aloud*] What busy° knave is this? Most reverend fathers, *troublesome*
I sooner had attended your grave pleasures,
But that my order for the funeral
Of my dear patron did require me—
VOLPONE (*aside*) Mosca!
MOSCA Whom I intend to bury like a gentleman.
VOLPONE [*aside*] Ay, quick,° and cozen me of all.[3] *alive*
SECOND AVOCATORE Still stranger!
More intricate!
FIRST AVOCATORE And come about° again! *reversing direction*
FOURTH AVOCATORE [*aside*] It is a match; my daughter is bestowed.
MOSCA [*aside to Volpone*] Will you gi' me half?
VOLPONE [*aside to Mosca*] First, I'll be hanged.
MOSCA [*aside to Volpone*] I know
Your voice is good.° Cry not so loud. *strong*
FIRST AVOCATORE Demand° *Question*

3. Volpone sees that Mosca's pious pretense of burying the "dead" Volpone will mean an end to all of Volpone's hopes; he'll be cheated out of everything.

The advocate. [*To Voltore*] Sir, did not you affirm
Volpone was alive?
VOLPONE Yes, and he is;
This gent'man told me so. (*Aside to Mosca*) Thou shalt have half.
MOSCA Whose drunkard is this same? Speak, some that know him;
I never saw his face. (*Aside to Volpone*) I cannot now
Afford it you so cheap.
VOLPONE (*aside to Mosca*) No?
FIRST AVOCATORE [*to Voltore*] What say you?
VOLTORE The officer told me.
VOLPONE I did, grave fathers,
And will maintain he lives with mine own life,
And that this creature° told me. (*Aside*) I was born *(Mosca)*
With all good stars my enemies.
MOSCA Most grave fathers,
If such an insolence as this must pass° *be permitted*
Upon me, I am silent. 'Twas not this
For which you sent, I hope.
SECOND AVOCATORE [*pointing to Volpone*] Take him away.
VOLPONE (*aside to Mosca*) Mosca!
THIRD AVOCATORE Let him be whipped.
VOLPONE (*aside to Mosca*) Wilt thou betray me?
Cozen me?
THIRD AVOCATORE And taught to bear himself
Toward a person of his° rank. *(Mosca's)*
FOURTH AVOCATORE Away!
[*Officers seize Volpone.*]
MOSCA I humbly thank Your Fatherhoods.
VOLPONE Soft, soft. [*Aside*] Whipped?
And lose all that I have? If I confess,
It cannot be much more.
FOURTH AVOCATORE [*to Mosca*] Sir, are you married?
VOLPONE [*aside*] They'll be allied° anon; I must be resolute. *linked by marriage*
The fox shall here uncase.° *He puts off his disguise.* *reveal himself*
MOSCA (*aside*) Patron!
VOLPONE Nay, now
My ruins shall not come alone. Your match
I'll hinder sure; my substance shall not glue you
Nor screw you into a family.
MOSCA (*aside*) Why, patron!
VOLPONE I am Volpone, and [*pointing to Mosca*] this is my knave;
[*Pointing to Voltore*] This his own knave; [*pointing to Corbaccio*] this, avarice's fool;
[*Pointing to Corvino*] This, a chimera° of wittol, fool, and knave; *monstrous combination*
And, reverend fathers, since we all can hope
Naught but a sentence, let's not now despair it.° *be disappointed (ironic)*
You hear me brief.° *That's all I have to say*
CORVINO May it please Your Fatherhoods—
COMMENDATORE[4] Silence!

4. Not Volpone, of course, but one of the genuine Commendatori. They are probably the officers who strip Mosca at line 103.

FIRST AVOCATORE The knot is now undone by miracle!
SECOND AVOCATORE Nothing can be more clear.
THIRD AVOCATORE Or can more prove
These innocent.
FIRST AVOCATORE Give 'em their liberty.
[*Bonario and Celia are released.*]
BONARIO Heaven could not long let such gross crimes be hid.
SECOND AVOCATORE If this be held the highway to get riches,
May I be poor!
THIRD AVOCATORE This's not the gain, but torment.
FIRST AVOCATORE These possess wealth as sick men possess fevers,
Which trulier may be said to possess them.
SECOND AVOCATORE Disrobe that parasite.
[*Mosca is stripped of his clarissimo's robe.*]
CORVINO [*and*] MOSCA Most honored fathers!
FIRST AVOCATORE Can you plead aught to stay the course of justice?
If you can, speak.
CORVINO [*and*] VOLTORE We beg favor—
CELIA And mercy.
FIRST AVOCATORE [*to Celia*] You hurt your innocence, suing° for the guilty. *pleading*
[*To the others*] Stand forth; and, first, the parasite. You appear
T'have been the chiefest minister,° if not plotter, *agent*
In all these lewd° impostures, and now, lastly, *vile, obscene*
Have with your impudence abused the court
And habit° of a gentleman of Venice, *garb*
Being a fellow of no birth or blood;
For which our sentence is, first thou be whipped,
Then live perpetual prisoner in our galleys.
VOLPONE I thank you for him.
MOSCA Bane to° thy wolfish nature! *Curses on*
FIRST AVOCATORE Deliver him to the *saffi*.° [*Mosca is placed under guard.*] Thou, Volpone, *bailiffs*
By blood and rank a gentleman, canst not fall
Under like censure;° but our judgment on thee *the same sentence*
Is that thy substance° all be straight confiscate *wealth*
To the hospital of the *Incurabili*;[5]
And since the most was gotten by imposture,
By feigning lame, gout, palsy, and such diseases,
Thou art to lie in prison, cramped with irons,
Till thou be'st sick and lame indeed.—Remove him.
[*Volpone is placed under guard.*]
VOLPONE This is called mortifying[6] of a fox.
FIRST AVOCATORE Thou, Voltore, to take away the scandal
Thou hast giv'n all worthy men of thy profession,
Art banished from their fellowship and our state.° *(Venice)*
[*Voltore is placed under guard.*]
Corbaccio—bring him near.—We here possess
Thy son of all thy state,° and confine thee *estate*
To the monastery of San' Spirito,° *the Holy Spirit*
Where, since thou knew'st not how to live well here,

5. The Hospital of the Incurables was founded in Venice in 1522 to care for people terminally ill with syphilis.

6. (1) Hanging of meat to make it tender; (2) disciplining spiritually; (3) killing. (Volpone's sentence is almost certain to bring about his death.)

Thou shalt be learned° to die well. *taught*

CORBACCIO Ha! What said he?

COMMENDATORE You shall know anon,° sir. *soon enough*

[*Corbaccio is placed under guard.*]

FIRST AVOCATORE Thou, Corvino, shalt
Be straight embarked from thine own house and rowed
Round about Venice, through the Grand Canal,
Wearing a cap with fair° long ass's ears *handsome; clearly visible*
Instead of horns, and so to mount, a paper
Pinned on thy breast, to the *berlino*[7]—

CORVINO Yes,
And have mine eyes beat out with stinking fish,
Bruised fruit, and rotten eggs—'Tis well. I'm glad
I shall not see my shame yet.

FIRST AVOCATORE And to expiate
Thy wrongs done to thy wife, thou art to send her
Home to her father with her dowry trebled.[8]
And these are all your judgments—

ALL Honored fathers!

FIRST AVOCATORE Which may not be revoked. Now you begin,
When crimes are done and past and to be punished,
To think what your crimes are.—Away with them!

[*Mosca, Volpone, Voltore, Corbaccio, and Corvino retire to the back of the stage, guarded.*][9]

Let all that see these vices thus rewarded
Take heart,° and love to study 'em. Mischiefs feed *Take them to heart*
Like beasts, till they be fat, and then they bleed.

[*The Avocatori step back.*]

[*Volpone comes forward.*]

VOLPONE The seasoning of a play is the applause.
Now, though the fox be punished by the laws,
He yet doth hope there is no suff'ring due
For any fact° which he hath done 'gainst you. *crime*
If there be, censure him; here he, doubtful,° stands. *apprehensive*
If not, fare jovially, and clap your hands. [*Exeunt.*]

THE END.

This comedy was first acted in the year 1605[1] by the King's Majesty's Servants.

The principal comedians were:

Richard Burbage	John Heminges
Henry Condell	John Lowin
Will Sly	Alexander Cooke

With the allowance of the Master of Revels.

---

7. Pillory. Versions of such shaming punishments were commonly imposed for sexual and marital infractions. The offender typically had to wear a placard specifying his crimes; hence the paper pinned on Corvino's breast.

8. The judges grant Celia what was called "separation from bed and board." Such legal separations could be permitted to the innocent party in a case of adultery or, as here, to a victim of gross spousal abuse. Because legal separation entailed the finding of serious fault, the guilty spouse could also, as here, be forced to pay financial damages. Legal separation did not bring with it, however, the right of remarriage for either party.

9. Alternatively, the prisoners, and later the Avocatori and the others, could exit, and Volpone could return to speak the epilogue. The advantage of the staging preferred here is that almost all the players are onstage to receive the audience's applause.

1. I.e., early 1606.

TEXTUAL NOTES

First performed in 1606, *Volpone* was published twice during Jonson's lifetime. In 1607, Thomas Thorpe issued it in quarto (Q); in 1616, William Stansby printed it in *The Works of Benjamin Jonson,* a large folio volume (F1). Both texts were published with Jonson's approval, and while editors have disagreed about their relative authority, most of the differences between them are changes of spelling and punctuation that disappear in a modernized text. The most important distinction between the two texts is a significant number of stage directions found in F1 but not in Q. F1 is the copy-text for this edition.

Changes not marked here include modernized stage directions and punctuation. In these two areas Jonson's practices are not only unfamiliar to a modern reader but were idiosyncratic in his own time. As a result, though we applied the same rules for modernizing Jonson's texts that we applied to other plays in this volume, the modernized versions of all his plays differ in two striking ways from their old-spelling versions. In the case of stage directions, Jonson followed the precedent established in Latin plays as printed in his time. He begins a new scene whenever a new character enters, listing at the head of each scene all the characters that appear at any point therein. We have retained Jonson's scene divisions but rendered his stage directions in a more modern and accessible form. All editorially added stage directions are enclosed in brackets.

Jonson's punctuation was also quite distinctive. He used commas and colons very liberally both to indicate syntactic divisions within his sentences and to suggest moments where an actor might pause in his delivery. Although this punctuation has its own kind of eloquence once a reader gets used to it, its sheer density tends to impede a modern reader. We have opted to lighten Jonson's punctuation considerably and list punctuation variants only when there is a possible change of meaning.

Substantive departures from F1 are noted here, using the following abbreviations:

Q: The quarto of 1607 (London: Thomas Thorpe)
F1: *The Works of Benjamin Jonson* (London: William Stansby, 1616)
F2: The second folio edition of the *Works* (London: Richard Bishop, 1640)
F3: The third folio edition of the *Works* (London: Thomas Hodgkin for H. Herringman and others, 1692)
ed.: A modern editor's emendation

Dedicatory epistle 11–12 will be a reason [ed.] *will a reason bee* [F1] **83** ***quamquam*** [ed.] quanquam [F1]

The Persons of the Play [order, ed.; in two columns of ten in a different order in F1] **18** [and elsewhere] **COMMENDATORI** [F1: COMMANDADORI]

Prologue 26 Bethlehem [F1: *Bet'lem*] **33 copperas** [F1: coppresse]

1.1.1 VOLPONE [ed.; not in F1; speech headings at heads of scenes are omitted throughout F1] **33** [and elsewhere] **venture** [F1: venter] **36** [and elsewhere] **powder** [F1: poulder]

1.2.39, 42 [and elsewhere] **mule** [F1: *moyle*] **67 NANO *and* CASTRONE** [ed.; not in F1] **74 bauble** [F1: bable]

1.3.27–28 [here and at some other points, parenthetical remarks are indicated in F1 by parentheses]

1.5.34 to [F1: too] **48** [and elsewhere] **He's** [F1: H' is] **63 culverin** [F1: culuering] **120** [and elsewhere] **window** [F1: windore]

2.1.40 porpoises [F1: porcpisces] **41 and** [Q] and and [F1] **98 This** [Q] This, [F1]

2.2.27.2 *a crowd* [ed.] GREGE [at 0.2 in F1] **29 CROWD** [ed.] GRE. [F1] **31 ten thousand** [F1: 10000] **56 ate** [F1: *eate*] **67 ha'p'orth** [F1: *halfe-pe'rth*] **120, 191 NANO** [ed.; not in F1]

2.4.15 [and elsewhere] **I'm** [ed.] I'am [F1]
2.5.18 you'd [F1: you'had]
2.6.59 Godso [F1: Gods so] **88 throttled** [F1: thratled]
3.2.17 inhuman [F1: inhumane]
3.4.18 SECOND WOMAN [ed.] WOM. [F1] **37** [and elsewhere] **coarse** [F1: course] **100 Ay** [F1: O'y]
3.5.17 [and elsewhere] **Marry** [F1: Mary]
3.7.30 to [F1: too] **92 Celia** [ed.; as speech heading in F1] **118** [and elsewhere] **arrant** [F1: errant] **119 thy** [Q] thy thy [F1] **124 effect** [F1: affect] **125** [and elsewhere] **you've** [F3] you'haue [F1] **133 Whither, whither** [F1: whether, whether] **134 human** [F1: humane] **197** [and elsewhere] **lose** [F2] loose [F1] **202 ostriches** [F1: estriches] **219 antic** [F1: antique]
3.8.5 navel [F1: nauill]
3.9.22 [and elsewhere] **scent** [F1: sent] **61 Will't** [F1: Wilt]
4.1.17 speak [Q] spake [F1] **60 I've** [ed.] I'haue [F1] **78** [and elsewhere] ***commendatore*** [ed.] *commandadore* [Q, F1] **102 Syria** [ed.] *Soria* [F1]
4.2.6 off [F2] of [F1] **6, 7** FIRST WOMAN [F1: WOM.]
4.5.0.1 ***four Avocatori*** [F1: AVOCATORI, 4.] **9** FIRST ADVOCATORE [F2] AVOC. [F1] **81 lain bedrid** [F1: lien, bed-red] **82 of** [F1: off] **100 spare 's** [F1: spare'his]
4.6.7 SECOND AVOCATORE [ed.] Avo. 4 [F1] **67 They're** [F3] They'are [F1] **98 you've** [F1: you haue]
5.2.15 Th'hast [ed.] Thou'hast [F1] **15 prize** [F1: prise] **44 He's** [F1: He' has] **84 curtain** [F1: cortine]
5.3.7 velvets [F2] vellets [F1] **84 travails** [F1: trauels]
5.4.0.1 ***three Mercatori*** [F1: MERCATORI. 3] **49 currant-butt** [F1: curren-but] **72.1** ***off*** [F1: *of*]
5.6.18 wine-vat [F1: wine-fat]
5.7.3 Your [Q] you [F1]
5.8.13 your shame [Q] you shame [F1] **20 valor** [F1: valure]
5.10.0.1 ***four Avocatori*** [F1: AVOCATORI, 4] **2** FIRST AVOCATORE [F1: Avo.] **20** SECOND AVOCATORE [ed.] Avo. [F1]
5.12.1 FIRST AVOCATORE [ed.; not in F1, though implied by scene heading "AVOCATORI, & c."] **35** FIRST AVOCATORE [F1: ATO. I] **36** SECOND AVOCATORE [ed.] Avo. [F1] **42** BONARIO [F1: BON. 3]

Epicene

In 1609, the date of *Epicene*'s first performance, London was the largest city in Europe. Its population—about two hundred thousand—had doubled in only fifty years and was continuing to increase unabated as provincials and foreign nationals swarmed to the metropolis. Despite inadequate sanitation, rampant disease, and institutions often inadequate to the new burdens placed on them, London was a place of great vitality. Customers crowded into its shops and playhouses. Pedestrians, horses, coaches, and carts clogged its narrow streeets. London's river highway, the Thames, teemed with boat traffic.

In the late 1590s and early 1600s, a new dramatic genre, "city comedy," undertook to represent the pleasures and miseries of life in London for an audience of London inhabitants. City comedies are typically colloquial in their idiom and dense with references to the here and now: fads, in-jokes, current events, local landmarks. *Epicene* is full of allusions that seemed up-to-the-minute in 1609 but that often mystify a modern reader: to the New Exchange and the Bear Garden, to Saint Pulchre's and the Bankside, to Nomentack and Mary Ambree, to the seige of Ostend. The city playwrights' preoccupation with novel, parochial, and often ephemeral things testifies to their conviction that Jacobean London was, in important ways, unprecedented. London life could not properly be captured in terms designed for previous ages or other climes.

Ben Jonson initially avoided writing about London. Chronically under suspicion for making fun of recognizable individuals rather than mere types, he feared that explicit local references would make his satire seem even more pointed and personal. So he set his early plays not in London but in exotic locales—in Florence, ancient Rome, Venice, "Gargaphie." With *Epicene*, though, he began writing city comedy, a genre for which he was superbly equipped. He had been born and educated in London and spent most of his life there, and he had a gift for noticing what historians call "emergent social formations," new institutions and groups that suggest or are capable of producing important cultural change. All of Jonson's major London comedies—*Epicene, The Alchemist, Bartholomew Fair,* the revised *Every Man in His Humor, The Devil Is an Ass,* and *The Staple of News*—are radically original (and different from one another) in the way they respond to the problems and opportunities of the genre.

City comedies typically delight in urban bustle, and *Epicene* is no exception. The misanthropic, pathologically noise-hating Morose wants to beget a son in order to disinherit a hated nephew, Dauphine, who is next in line for Morose's estate if Morose dies without a child of his own. Early in the play, Morose believes he has found his dream partner, Epicene, an extremely shy and soft-spoken woman who, he hopes, will bear his child without disturbing his peace. To discourage Morose's plan, Dauphine and his friends Truewit and Clerimont conspire to visit turmoil on his previously hushed premises. The three men divert a large dinner party into Morose's house to "celebrate" Morose's wedding. Once there, they arrange for the aggressive Mrs. Otter

Introduction, glosses, footnotes, and textual notes by Katharine Eisaman Maus; glosses, footnotes, and textual notes checked by David Bevington; text checked by David Bevington and Eric Rasmussen.

Ben Jonson (ca. 1617) by Abraham van Blyenberch.

to overhear her husband's rebellious slanders of her; they abjectly humiliate the craven knights Daw and La Foole; and, finally, they arrange a noisy divorce consultation between two fake legal experts for the desperately unhappy Morose. The wedding festivities, drinking parties, marital quarrels, medical consultations, abortive duels, legal disputes, and endless conversations between compulsively talkative men and women produce one crescendo after another.

In at least one respect, however, *Epicene* is an atypical Renaissance city comedy. Most such plays—Jonson's in particular—are pointedly inclusive of different kinds and classes of people. *Epicene,* by contrast, focuses on affluent city dwellers. Its characters are gentlemen and ladies who are, or at least pretend to be, independently wealthy, for whom it would be a caste defilement to do useful work. With *Epicene,* Jonson practically single-handedly established the parameters for a durable genre, the "comedy of manners." This genre flourished in Restoration England in the works of Dryden, Behn, Wycherley, and Congreve and persisted into the nineteenth and twentieth centuries in such plays as Oscar Wilde's *The Importance of Being Earnest* and Noel Coward's *Private Lives.* In other words, while *Epicene*'s closest relatives in its own time seem to be other plays set in London, its influence upon later drama stems from its unprecedented focus on the leisure class.

In its concern with elite behavior, *Epicene* bears witness to an important social change in Jacobean England. Before the early part of the seventeenth century, the landed gentry typically lived on and administered the estates from which they derived their income, playing locally prominent political and judicial roles. But as London grew larger and more exciting, and as the royal court, centered nearby at Westminster, became more powerful, England's largest city became a magnet for the wellborn and well-to-do. They began entrusting their property to managers and betaking themselves to London. While in the countryside the gentry were thinly spread, the city concentrated their numbers, offering a larger group of social equals with whom to consort. The flight to the city alarmed the King and Parliament. How would the countryside be governed if the gentry did not live there? But laws attempting to restrict how long a provincial landowner could reside in London proved nearly unenforceable.

One of the great attractions of early modern London was a fascination cities still exert today: for affluent people, the city is a place of options. Externally imposed forms of affiliation—one's kinship group, one's inherited standing, one's traditional rivalries and obligations—become less important than voluntary affiliations among like-minded people. No wonder, then, that gentlemen and ladies should flock to London; nor, perhaps, that they should seek their community among one another, rejecting both the provinces they had fled and the workaday world of poorer city dwellers. Yet Jonson regards these apparent advantages with a jaundiced eye. He doubts that human beings, given free rein of their passions and the liberty to choose their own way of life, will create desirable or virtuous social arrangements. In *Epicene,* urbane leisure turns out to involve more difficulties than might be expected, and many of the supposed freedoms London offers turn out to be constraints in disguise.

Epicene begins with Clerimont getting ready to go out for the day, a scene much copied by Jonson's Restoration imitators. The opening moments immediately signal the important difference, in this play, between one's appearance and behavior within one's home and one's appearance and behavior outside it. Well-to-do people possessed, at the very least, a suite of rooms: a private space in which to prepare for public display. In consequence, appearing in public became a more or less artificial, calculated matter. The incentives for such artificiality were manifold. In an overcrowded city, the unavoidable proximity of other people's bodies demanded some attention to grooming and demeanor merely as an issue of politeness. But in *Epicene,* preparations for "going out" often seem motivated less by tact than by its apparent opposite, a self-aggrandizing impulse to impose oneself upon others. Since in London most people one meets are relative strangers, one is at liberty to adjust, to the extent of one's ability, the details of one's social presentation. All kinds of pretense and misrepresentation become possible. *Epicene*'s characters seize these opportunities with gusto, if not always with skill.

The play registers the moral complexities almost immediately, not merely in Clerimont's behavior but, once Truewit enters, in the two friends' debate over the uses of cosmetics. On the one hand, as Clerimont argues, cosmetics are a kind of fraud, and the connoisseur of female beauty ought to prefer "sweet neglect" (1.1.96). On the other hand, as Truewit maintains, cosmetics are essential to the lady's strategic self-presentation: "If she have good ears, show 'em; good hair, lay it out; good legs, wear short clothes; a good hand, discover it often; practice any art to mend breath, cleanse teeth, repair eyebrows, paint, and profess it" (1.1.103–6). The line between showcasing strong points and patching up defects is a blurry one, for bodies seem in continuous need of selective enhancement or concealment. Although both men agree that the process of applying cosmetics is disgusting, Truewit argues that "Many things that seem foul i'the doing do please, done" (1.1.109–10). Truewit conjures up a world divided into private and public domains: in the privacy of their homes, leisure-class individuals conduct noisome procedures for remediating their physical nastiness; in public, they aggressively exhibit their specious charms.

As the play continues, we realize why, in the world of *Epicene,* calculated self-presentation (and the self-withholding that necessarily accompanies it) is not merely possible but essential. In their former communities, members of the gentry were leading citizens; in London, deracinated from their traditional social function and kinship networks, they are cut off as well from the work of local government that had helped to give their lives structure and meaning. Truewit thus deplores gentlemanly time wasting but admits that he, too, can think of no better ways to spend his overabundant leisure.

People without an obvious social function must labor at self-creation, since nothing about their lives is predetermined by the requirements of their job or their station in life. This self-creation proves surprisingly difficult. For men, the traditional means of proving their masculinity—military prowess, political expertise, or skill at a job—are all proscribed. *Epicene*'s male characters attempt to demonstrate their manliness by writing love poems, participating in drinking contests, playing aggressive practical jokes, and bragging about their sexual exploits, and yet these displays often seem anxious and compensatory. Toward the end of the play, the reclusive Morose is manipulated into disparaging his own virility when he is put on trial for impotence and admits his "guilt." But he is not the play's only inadequate male, for one after another, all the men in this play find their manhood called into question.

If the London of *Epicene* puts gentry-class males in a difficult position, it puts ladies in a nearly impossible one, for two interconnected reasons. First, throughout the play, the men assuage their own anxieties by displacing them onto women—as when the men prattle on about female talkativeness or turn, as Clerimont and Truewit do in the opening scene, from the uncomfortable issue of masculine idleness to the safer topic of female cosmetic enhancement. Second, in early modern England generally, women's social options were more limited than men's, so they suffered more acutely from any further constriction. Traditionally, a woman's worth depended not on her achievements but on her fertility, her marital status, and her physical attractions. In the urbane world of well-to-do London, none of these prestige markers proves reliable. Just as *Epicene*'s men shrink from the military and political obligations that were incumbent upon them in previous generations, its women, recoiling from the prospect of childbearing, exchange "excellent receipts" for contraceptives: "Many births of a woman make her old," declares Madam Haughty, "as many crops make the earth barren" (4.3.54, 57–58). This avoidance of "labor" precludes women's taking pride in maternity. Nor is marriage an important emotional resource or status indicator. In the world of *Epicene*, where social identity is often contingent and voluntarily assumed, marriage indicates little about one's affections, one's conduct—or even, as the play's denouement suggests, whether one is male or female. Affection and loyalty become unmoored from ties of kinship; spinsterhood is no guarantee of virginity; marriage fails to indicate who cohabits with, sleeps with, or dominates whom. Attempting to compensate for this failure of traditional relationships, the protofeminist ladies invent a "College" modeled on a male prototype. But their experiment fails. Jonson, like Aristotle, considered women incapable of true friendship, and in the course of the play, his female characters prove congenitally unable to cooperate with one another.

Thus, in *Epicene*, physical attractiveness seems unnaturally momentous for women. But the youth and beauty on which the Collegiate Ladies pride themselves are hardly the accidents of age and genetic endowment. A lady's self-display, even more than a gentleman's, requires buying luxury items that simultaneously announce her class standing and amplify her sexual charms. Her reliance on purchased goods makes it unclear where the body ends and the commodity begins. "All her teeth were made i'the Blackfriars, both her eyebrows i'the Strand, and her hair in Silver Street," complains Otter of his wife (4.2.93–95). "She takes herself asunder still when she goes to bed, into some twenty boxes, and about next day noon is put together again like a great German clock" (4.2.98–100). Comments such as these suggest that women are nothing but assemblages of items procured here and there in the teeming metropolitan marketplace. Mrs. Otter is described not as attaching supplements to her body, but as compiling herself out of prophylaxes, like a Jacobean cyborg. When public appearance is so estranged from private truth, the supposedly immutable realities of gender difference retreat into invisibility, perhaps even nonexistence. The very beauty from which women acquire their tenuous social prestige itself becomes a target of suspicion, and all sexual attraction a form of fetishism. Because femininity is so thoroughly a matter of artful theatrical display, it is not wholly surprising to learn at the end of *Epicene* that the most "feminine" individual in the play, at first a shy virgin and then an assiduous housewife, is not genitally a woman at all. In a world in which commodities replace bodies, what would "cross-dressing" mean?

One understandable response to the grotesque artificiality of urbane life as Jonson portrays it is radical repudiation. In *Epicene,* that desire is incarnated in Morose, who goes to enormous lengths to insulate himself from London's chaos and inanity. Many critics have seen hints of Jonson in the quasi-stoic Morose, whose attempts to "collect and contain my mind, not suffering it to flow loosely" sound a little like the self-possession and autonomy Jonson admired in others and cultivated, not always successfully, in himself (5.3.46–47). Morose is hardly a self-portrait, though—at least not an admiring one. Morose combines hypersensitivity with an almost sublime imperceptiveness. He does not see, but we do, that his retreat is motivated by the same egoism that impels so many of his neighbors into noisy self-assertion. The supposed lover of silence is an indefatigible monologist. "[A]ll discourses but mine own afflict me," he intones, as he spins out lengthy fantasies of domestic despotism (2.1.3–4).

Morose's most important role in the plot is as the blocking agent—the imperious, usually elderly crank who in so many comedies stands between the young protagonists and their desires. But even while Jonson undercuts the ground on which Morose, that obstacle to comic gratification, stands, he also uses Morose's standpoint as a perspective from which the other characters might be criticized. Morose is ridiculous because he is rigidly behind the times in a city comedy, a play that prizes what is up-to-date. At the same time, his presence critiques the shallow novelty-seeking of the characters around him. Similarly, Morose's insistence on a silent wife is a butt of satire: silent women do not exist in Jacobean London, and he is stupid to think they do. Nonetheless, Morose's expectation that women will be silent and subordinate enables Jonson's satire of the play's assertive women, who so boisterously shatter the rule enjoining female reticence.

Epicene portrays a world in which most people's lives are pointless, non-goal-directed. Compared to the tightly plotted, continuously purposeful *Volpone* and *The Alchemist,* both plays that derive their momentum from the ferocious profit motive of their characters, *Epicene* seems to involve a lot of superficially aimless chatter and milling about. Actually, much of the apparent randomness is skillfully orchestrated by the trio of witty friends, Truewit, Clerimont, and Dauphine, who participate in the fashionable social world even while feeling, with some justification, superior to it. Because they work so well as a team, critics often discuss them collectively, but actually their individual modi operandi are quite distinct. For much of *Epicene,* Truewit seems the dominant member of the three, because he is the one who designs most of the play's elaborate practical jokes. Clerimont, the adaptable follower of others' leads, lacks Truewit's ironic inventiveness but is able to insinuate himself into his victims' confidences without exciting suspicion. Dauphine's habitual reserve contrasts with Truewit's extroverted theatrical flair.

Truewit's practical jokes have overtones of symbolic castration. Otter is beaten by his wife. Daw and La Foole relinquish their swords and submit to insults no knight was supposed to tolerate. Morose is induced to testify to his own sexual impotence. None of these revelations—Otter's resentful subservience, Daw's and La Foole's cowardice, or Morose's sexual inadequacy—is exactly surprising, and the targets of the jokes are already so abject that it is hard to disgrace them further, at least in their own eyes. Truewit hopes that his plot against the vainglorious Daw and La Foole will shame them into silence, "make 'em keep the peace for this remnant of the day, if not of the year" (4.5.32–33). But within minutes of what ought to have been an intensely humiliating experience, they are already irrepressibly boasting of their sexual exploits and slandering Epicene. The beaten Otter likewise almost immediately bounces back, inviting his "friends" to a future drinking party. Morose is so evidently desperate to be rid of his wife by act 5 that exacerbating that despair seems hardly necessary.

What, then, is Truewit's purpose in playing these jokes? Since so many scenes in the play depend on his initiative, the question of his motives naturally arises. His behavior is comprehensible only in an environment where the possibility for real achievement no longer exists; for in such an environment, publicly acknowledged criteria for worth and self-worth among gentlemen do not exist either. Truewit's plots constitute a desperate attempt to reinstate such criteria. Sir Amorous La Foole, Sir Jack Daw, and Tom Otter each instantiates, in grotesquely debased form, a traditional gentlemanly attribute: La Foole, a penchant for conspicuous consumption; Daw, an inclination for scholarly and literary pursuits; Otter, a love of drinking and sports. Otter, who marries merely for money, is less culpable, though no less sordid, than the other two; his torments are therefore relatively brief, and he can be rehabilitated into an accomplice of the wits by the final scenes. Daw and La Foole, on the other hand, have purchased their knighthoods—a common though widely criticized practice in Jacobean England. In other words, they attempt to buy honor just as, in this pervasively market-driven society, the women attempt to buy beauty. Neither Daw nor La Foole has any conception of what a knight's military career ought to involve, nor any sense of the chivalrous values a knight was supposed to defend. Truewit punishes them repeatedly, as ferociously as the decorum of a comedy of manners will allow, and finally banishes them from the world of the play.

The eagerness with which Truewit persecutes these poltroons is intensified by the fact that their flaws are, paradoxically, at once blatant and inconsequential. After all, for people who essentially do nothing, it is not obvious that learning, discernment, wit, or high principle are particularly important traits, or that the lack of them should matter. Such deficiencies certainly do not trouble the women for whose attention and favor the men purport to compete. The Collegiate Ladies fail to notice the transcendent stupidity of their "servants" until it is unmistakably laid bare to them, and then they incontinently court Dauphine, whom they mistakenly believe to be the engineer of this revelation. By the end of the play, "wit" seems to be the only socially acceptable and visible sign of the virility that has been so widely and abundantly interrogated in the course of *Epicene*. But the trio of intelligent men are, most of the time, merely showing off for one another. Their relationship proves by far the most durable bond in this fragile social universe.

Critics of *Epicene* are divided over how Jonson meant audiences to respond to the three wits. Some regard them as the conscience of the play, while others find them pointlessly cruel. Like Morose, Truewit represents a perspective that Jonson partly shares and partly condemns. Since Truewit's prime concern is the establishment of "authentic" gentility, his manifold plots are intended to humiliate unworthy pretenders publicly. His role in the play, in other words, is close to that of a satiric playwright. At the same time, Jonson suggests that Truewit's satiric stance sometimes amounts to little more than the pot calling the kettle black. The gregarious, compulsively talkative Truewit torments the vacuously chatty La Foole and Daw not merely because they differ from him but because, to a dangerous extent, they resemble him. If Morose makes himself ridiculous in his unqualified rejection of the fashionable urban world around him, Truewit seems at times too immersed in it.

Truewit is not, however, the only successful plotter in *Epicene*. At the end of the play, Truewit's machinations are revealed to have unwittingly furthered a heretofore secret plot of Dauphine's. All Jonson's comedies end unpredictably, but the final scene of *Epicene* is unusual even by Jonsonian standards. It strikingly defies that normal principle of drama: keep the audience informed. In the final lines of the play's last scene, Dauphine reveals—to onstage friends and rivals and to theater spectators alike—that he has entrapped Morose in a marriage to a boy. Instead of watching with an amused assurance of its own wider consciousness, the audience is compelled to admit that it, too, has succumbed to Dauphine's wiles. Jonson joked to his friend William Drummond that "The Silent Woman" proved a good subtitle because nobody applauded his play's initial performance, and some critics have suggested that *Epicene*'s first audience withheld its ovation either out of annoyance or bewilderment. The sense of exasperation must have been stronger among Jonson's original audiences than it would be at a modern performance, since those spectators in a sense "knew" that Epicene, like all female characters on the Renaissance stage, was actually a transvestite boy.

The final scene thus raises the question both of Jonson's motives and of Dauphine's, the heir apparent who has laid claim to the play's monetary spoils as well as to the Collegiate Ladies' dubious sexual favors. Superficially, Dauphine's aims contrast with Truewit's: Dauphine pursues the immediately intelligible objective of self-enrichment rather than a purportedly disinterested goal of social renovation. His means are different, too. In a world of pushy people, Dauphine gets what he wants by lying in wait and keeping his own counsel, even though his seeming passivity leaves him open to other people's condescension. His apparent helplessness in the face of Morose's threats encourages Morose's foolish overreaching; his apparent naïveté and bashfulness in love matters encourage Truewit to obtain the Collegiate Ladies for him. Both rival and friend unwittingly play into his hands. On the other hand, like Truewit, Dauphine scapegoats what is dangerously similar to himself: for Dauphine is truly the chilly, secretive, self-interested character that his victim, Morose, makes himself ridiculous by pretending to be. Dauphine's unfunny but substantial change in fortune contrasts with and supplements Truewit's extroverted, hilarious theatrical triumphs. Together, the two successful wits suggest a double basis for the brittle fabrication that is polite society: on the one hand, an obsession with self-presentation and one's reputation among one's peers; on the other, a necessary, if often hidden, concern for the money that underwrites that self-display.

BEN JONSON

Epicene, or The Silent Woman

To the truly noble, by all titles, Sir Francis Stuart[1]

THE PERSONS OF THE PLAY

MOROSE, a gentleman that loves no noise
DAUPHINE Eugenie,[1] a knight, his nephew
[Ned] CLERIMONT, a gentleman, his friend
TRUEWIT, another friend
EPICENE,[2] a young gentleman, supposed the silent woman
John DAW,[3] a knight, her servant° — *admirer*
Amorous LA FOOLE, a knight also
Tom OTTER,[4] a land and sea captain
CUTBEARD, a barber
MUTE, one of Morose his° servants — *Morose's*
Madam HAUGHTY, Madam CENTAUR,[5] Mistress MAVIS[6] } Ladies Collegiate
Mistress TRUSTY, the Lady Haughty's woman° — *attendant*
MRS. OTTER, the captain's wife
(Mistress TRUSTY and MRS. OTTER } pretenders[7])
PARSON
Pages [including Clerimont's BOY]
Servants
[Musicians, trumpeters, drummer]

THE SCENE: London.

The 1616 folio title page reads "*Epicoene, or the Silent Woman*. A comedy. Acted in the year 1609 by the Children of Her Majesty's Revels. The Author, B. J. / Horace: *Ut sis tu similis Caeli, Byrrhique latronum, / Non ego sim Capri, neque Sulci. Cur metuas me?* [Though you may be like the robbers Coelus and Byrrhus, I am not like those loudmouthed critics Caprius and Sulcius. Why do you fear me?] London. Printed by William Stansby, 1616." Jonson much admired the Roman poet Horace, who insisted that his satire differed from slander, in that it left readers free to decide whether his criticism applied to them or not.

Dedication.

1. The second son of the Earl of Moray, knighted in 1610; like Jonson and some other literary figures, he frequented the Mermaid Tavern in London.

The Persons of the Play.

1. "Dauphine" means "heir apparent"; "eugenie" means "wellborn." (French.)
2. Originally, a Latin word that was both masculine and feminine; by extension, a sexually ambiguous person.
3. A daw, or jackdaw, is a species of crow that can be taught to speak; also, a simpleton. "Jack" is a nickname for "John," so he is also called "Jack Daw."
4. Otters were believed to be intermediate between fish and mammals, because although they are furry, they live in water.
5. Centaurs have the bodies of horses and the torsos and heads of human beings; in Ovid's *Metamorphoses*, Book 12, they are violent guests at the wedding of Pirithous and Hippodame, which degenerates into a bloody battle.
6. Suggesting the French word *mauvais*, meaning "bad," or the Italian *malviso*, "ugly."
7. Aspirants to full membership in the Ladies' College.

Prologue

Truth says, of old the art of making plays
Was to content the people, and their praise
Was to the poet money, wine, and bays.[1]
But in this age a sect of writers are
That only for particular likings° care, *fastidious tastes*
And will taste nothing that is popular.
With such we mingle neither brains nor breasts;° *hearts; feelings*
Our wishes, like to those° make public feasts, *the wishes of those who*
Are not to please the cooks' tastes, but the guests'.
Yet if those cunning palates hither come,
They shall find guests' entreaty,° and good room; *invitation*
And though all relish not, sure there will be some
That, when they leave their seats, shall make 'em say,
Who° wrote that piece could so have wrote° a play, *He who / written*
But that he knew this was the better way.
For to present all custard or all tart,
And have no other meats° to bear a part, *foods*
Or to want° bread and salt, were but coarse art. *lack*
The poet prays you, then, with better thought
To sit; and when his cates° are all in brought, *dishes*
Though there be none far-fet, there will dear-bought
Be fit for ladies;[2] some for lords, knights, squires,
Some for your waiting-wench, and city-wires,[3]
Some for your men and daughters of Whitefriars.° *a brothel district*
Nor is it only while you keep your seat
Here that his feast will last; but you shall eat
A week at ordinaries° on his broken meat,° *taverns / leftovers*
If his muse be true
Who commends her° to you. *herself*

Another

Occasioned by some person's[1] impertinent exception

The ends of all who for the scene° do write *stage*
Are, or should be, to profit and delight.
And still 't hath been the praise of all best times,
So persons were not touched,[2] to tax° the crimes. *rebuke*
Then in this play, which we present tonight,
And make the object of your ear and sight,
On forfeit of yourselves think nothing true,
Lest so you make the maker to judge you,
For he knows poet never credit gained
By writing truths, but things like truths well feigned.
If any yet will (with particular sleight
Of application)[3] wrest what he doth write,

Prologue.
1. Laurel leaves, with which celebrated poets were crowned in ancient times.
2. Alluding to the proverb "Far-fetched and dear bought is good for ladies." "Far-fet" means "exotic."
3. Citizens' wives, who typically wore ruffs supported by wire.

Another (second prologue).
1. Probably Lady Arabella Stuart, a cousin of King James I, who took offense at a phrase in *Epicene* (5.1.22–23) that she believed referred to her.
2. Provided actual individuals were not attacked.
3. Application was the practice of interpreting literary texts as covertly alluding to well-known persons or to current political events (overt references were prohibited under the censorship laws).

And that he meant or° him or her, will say — *either*
They make a libel which he made a play.

1.1

[Enter] Clerimont, [accompanied by his] Boy.° He [Clerimont] comes out making himself ready. — *page*

CLERIMONT Ha' you got the song yet perfect° I ga' you, boy? — *memorized*

BOY Yes, sir.

CLERIMONT Let me hear it.

BOY You shall, sir, but, i'faith, let nobody else.

CLERIMONT Why, I pray?

BOY It will get you the dangerous name of a poet in town, sir, besides me a perfect deal of ill will at the mansion you wot° of, whose lady is the argument° of it, where now I am the welcom'st thing under° a man that comes there. — *know* / *subject* / *younger than*

CLERIMONT I think, and above° a man too, if the truth were racked° out of you. — *older than* / *tortured*

BOY No, faith, I'll confess before,° sir. The gentlewomen play with me, and throw me o'the bed, and carry me in to my lady; and she kisses me with her oiled face and puts a peruke° o'my head and asks me an° I will wear her gown, and I say no; and then she hits me a blow o'the ear and calls me innocent, and lets me go. — *before being tortured* / *wig / if*

CLERIMONT No marvel if the door be kept shut against your master, when the entrance is so easy to you. Well, sir, you shall go there no more, lest I be fain° to seek your voice in my lady's rushes a fortnight hence.[1] Sing, sir. *(Boy sings.)* — *obliged*

[Enter] Truewit.

TRUEWIT Why, here's the man that can melt away his time, and never feels it! What between his mistress abroad° and his ingle[2] at home, high fare, soft lodging, fine clothes, and his fiddle, he thinks the hours ha' no wings, or the day no post-horse.[3] Well, sir gallant, were you struck with the plague this minute, or condemned to any capital punishment tomorrow, you would begin then to think and value every article° o'your time, esteem it at the true rate, and give all for't. — *in town* / *bit*

CLERIMONT Why, what should a man do?

TRUEWIT Why, nothing; or that which, when 'tis done, is as idle.° Hearken after the next horse race or hunting match; lay wagers; praise Puppy or Peppercorn, Whitefoot, Franklin; swear upon Whitemane's° party; spend aloud,[4] that my lords may hear you; visit my ladies at night, and be able to give 'em the character° of every bowler or bettor o'the green.[5] These be the things wherein your fashionable men exercise themselves, and I for company. — *useless* / *(racehorses)* / *satirical sketch*

CLERIMONT Nay, if I have thy authority, I'll not leave° yet. — *leave off*

1.1. Clerimont's rooms.
1. Clerimont imagines the ladies' attention might hasten the boy's sexual maturation. Rushes were used as a floor covering.
2. Boy kept for homosexual use.
3. A metaphor for time pressure, since post-horses were stationed at intervals along the highways and were used in a relay fashion to deliver urgent messages.
4. Talk noisily, like a dog giving tongue.
5. Lawn bowling, sometimes accompanied by gambling, was a gentlemanly diversion.

Come, the other° are considerations when we come to have gray heads and weak hams, moist eyes and shrunk members.° We'll think on 'em then; then we'll pray and fast.

other occupations / *limbs; sexual parts*

TRUEWIT Ay, and destine° only that time of age to goodness which our want° of ability will not let us employ in evil?

devote / *lack*

CLERIMONT Why, then 'tis time enough.

TRUEWIT Yes, as if a man should sleep all the term[6] and think to effect his business the last day. Oh, Clerimont, this time, because it is an incorporeal thing and not subject to sense,° we mock ourselves the fineliest out of it, with vanity and misery indeed, not seeking an end of wretchedness but only changing the matter° still.

sensory perception / *circumstances*

CLERIMONT Nay, thou'lt not leave° now—

stop

TRUEWIT See but our common disease! With what justice can we complain that great men will not look upon us, nor be at leisure to give our affairs such dispatch° as we expect, when we will never do it to ourselves, nor° hear nor regard ourselves?

quick handling / *neither*

CLERIMONT Foh, thou hast read Plutarch's *Morals*[7] now, or some such tedious fellow, and it shows so vilely with thee. 'Fore God, 'twill spoil thy wit utterly. Talk me° of pins and feathers and ladies and rushes° and such things, and leave this stoicity[8] alone till thou mak'st sermons.

Talk to me / *i.e., trifles*

TRUEWIT Well, sir, if it will not take, I have learned to lose° as little of my kindness as I can. I'll do good to no man against his will, certainly. When were you at the College?

waste

CLERIMONT What college?

TRUEWIT As if you knew not!

CLERIMONT No, faith, I came but from court yesterday.

TRUEWIT Why, is it not arrived there yet, the news? A new foundation, sir, here i'the town, of ladies that call themselves the Collegiates, an order° between courtiers and country madams,[9] that live from° their husbands and give entertainment to all the wits and braveries[1] o'the time, as they call 'em, cry down or up° what they like or dislike in a brain or a fashion with most masculine—or rather hermaphroditical—authority, and every day gain to their College some new probationer.°

social class / *apart from* / *praise or criticize* / *applicant, novice*

CLERIMONT Who is the president?

TRUEWIT The grave and youthful matron, the Lady Haughty.

CLERIMONT A pox of her autumnal face, her pieced° beauty! There's no man can be admitted till she be ready, nowadays—till she has painted and perfumed and washed and scoured—but the boy here, and him she wipes her oiled lips upon like a sponge. I have made a song—I pray thee hear it—o'the subject.

pieced-together

BOY [*sings*] Still° to be neat, still to be dressed
As° you were going to a feast,

Always / *As if*

6. Period when law courts were in session.
7. An ancient Greek moral treatise. In fact, Truewit is paraphrasing *On the Shortness of Life*, by the Roman philosopher Seneca.
8. Strict philosophizing. The Stoics were an ancient philosophical school that taught that external things should neither be desired nor feared.
9. Truewit wryly observes that these ladies are neither ladies of the royal court nor the wives of country gentlemen.
1. The wits are young men who pride themselves on their intelligence; the braveries pride themselves on their fashionable dress.

Still to be powdered, still perfumed—
Lady, it is to be presumed,
Though art's hid causes are not found,
All is not sweet, all is not sound.

Give me a look, give me a face
That makes simplicity a grace,
Robes loosely flowing, hair as free:
Such sweet neglect more taketh me
Than all th'adulteries° of art. *adulterations*
They strike mine eyes, but not my heart.

TRUEWIT And I am clearly o'the other side: I love a good dressing before any beauty o'the world. Oh, a woman is then like a delicate garden, nor is there one kind of it; she may vary every hour, take often counsel of her glass,° and choose the best. If she have good ears, show 'em; good hair, lay it out; good legs, wear short clothes; a good hand, discover° it often; practice any art to mend breath, cleanse teeth, repair eyebrows, paint, and profess° it.[2] *mirror* / *reveal* / *openly admit*

CLERIMONT How? Publicly?

TRUEWIT The doing of it, not the manner: that must be private. Many things that seem foul i'the doing do please, done.° A lady should indeed study her face when we think she sleeps; nor, when the doors are shut, should men be inquiring; all is sacred within, then. Is it for us to see their perukes° put on, their false teeth, their complexion, their eyebrows, their nails? You see gilders° will not work but enclosed. They must not discover how little serves, with the help of art, to adorn a great deal. How long did the canvas hang afore Aldgate?[3] Were the people suffered° to see the city's *Love* and *Charity* while they were rude stone, before they were painted and burnished? No. No more should servants° approach their mistresses but when they are complete and finished. *when they are done* / *wigs* / *workers in gold leaf* / *allowed* / *male admirers*

CLERIMONT Well said, my Truewit.

TRUEWIT And a wise lady will keep a guard always upon the place, that she may do things securely. I once followed a rude° fellow into a chamber where the poor madam, for haste, and troubled, snatched at her peruke to cover her baldness and put it on the wrong way. *rustic, lower-class*

CLERIMONT Oh, prodigy!° *monstrous!*

TRUEWIT And the unconscionable knave held her in compliment° an hour with that reversed face, when I still° looked when she should talk from the t'other side. *chitchat / continually*

CLERIMONT Why, thou shouldst ha' relieved her.

TRUEWIT No, faith, I let her alone, as we'll let this argument,° if you please, and pass to another. When saw you Dauphine Eugenie? *subject for discussion*

CLERIMONT Not these three days. Shall we go to him this morning? He is very melancholic, I hear.

2. Truewit adapts his defense of female artifice from the worldly-wise *Art of Love*, by the Roman poet Ovid.
3. The east gate of London's city wall, rebuilt in 1606–9; the new entrance was flanked with *Love* and *Charity*, two allegorical statues.

TRUEWIT Sick o'the uncle,[4] is he? I met that stiff piece of formality, his uncle, yesterday, with a huge turban of night-caps on his head buckled over his ears.

CLERIMONT Oh, that's his custom when he walks abroad. He can endure no noise, man.

TRUEWIT So I have heard. But is the disease so ridiculous in him as it is made? They say he has been upon divers treaties with the fishwives and orange-women, and articles propounded between them; marry,° the chimney sweepers will not be drawn in.[5] *by Mary (an oath)*

CLERIMONT No, nor the broom-men: they stand out stiffly.[6] He cannot endure a costardmonger;° he swoons if he hear one. *apple-seller*

TRUEWIT Methinks a smith should be ominous.

CLERIMONT Or any hammer-man. A brazier° is not suffered to dwell in the parish, nor an armorer. He would have hanged a pewterer's prentice once upon a Shrove Tuesday's riot,[7] for being o'that trade when the rest were quit. *worker in brass*

TRUEWIT A trumpet should fright him terribly, or the hautboys.° *oboes*

CLERIMONT Out of his senses. The waits° of the city have a pension of him not to come near that ward. [*Indicating the Boy*] This youth practiced° on him one night like the bellman;[8] and never left till he had brought him down to the door with a long sword, and there left him him flourishing with° the air. *street musicians* / *played a trick* / *brandishing it in*

BOY Why, sir, he hath chosen a street to lie° in so narrow at both ends that it will receive no coaches nor carts, nor any of these common noises; and therefore, we that love him devise to bring him in such as we may now and then, for his exercise, to breathe° him. He would grow resty° else in his ease; his virtue would rust without action. I entreated a bear-ward° one day to come down with the dogs of some four parishes that way, and, I thank him, he did, and cried° his games under Master Morose's window till he was sent crying away, with his head made a most bleeding spectacle to the multitude. And another time, a fencer marching to his prize[9] had his drum most tragically run through for taking that street in his way at my request. *reside* / *exercise / sluggish* / *bear-trainer* / *announced*

TRUEWIT A good wag.° How does he for the bells? *wit, jester*

CLERIMONT Oh, i'the Queen's° time he was wont to go out of town every Saturday at ten o'clock, or on holiday eves.[1] But now, by reason of the sickness,[2] the perpetuity of ringing has made him devise a room with double walls and treble ceilings, the windows close shut and caulked; and there he lives by candlelight. He turned away a man° last week for having *Elizabeth's (1558–1603)* / *fired a servant*

4. Playing on a disorder called "the mother" because it supposedly originated in the uterus.
5. These trades walked through the city streets crying their wares. (Fishwives are women who sell fish.)
6. Refuse stubbornly. (Possibly with a phallic joke.)
7. Shrove Tuesday, the Tuesday before Lent, was traditionally a day of revelry and in early modern London a special time of liberty for apprentices, who sometimes became riotously violent.
8. Town crier, who loudly announced news and proclamations, sounded the hours, and shouted to awake those whose houses were afire or being burglarized.
9. Fencing competition. (Professional swordsmen obtained an audience by advertising the match loudly in the streets ahead of time.)
1. In order to avoid hearing the bells calling worshipers to church services the next morning.
2. Plague. (Because church bells sounded to mark a parishioner's death, they were constantly ringing during plague epidemics.)

a pair of new shoes that creaked. And this fellow° waits on him now in tennis-court socks, or slippers soled with wool; and they talk each to other in a trunk.° See who comes here.

(the new servant)
tube (see 2.1.1–3)

1.2

[*Enter*] *Dauphine.*

DAUPHINE How now, what ail you, sirs? Dumb?

TRUEWIT Struck into stone almost, I am here, with tales o'thine uncle! There was never such a prodigy heard of.

DAUPHINE I would you would once lose° this subject, my masters,° for my sake. They are such as you are that have brought me into that predicament I am with him.

abandon
good sirs

TRUEWIT How is that?

DAUPHINE Marry, that he will disinherit me, no more.° He thinks I and my company are authors of all the ridiculous acts and monuments[1] are told of him.

nothing more serious

TRUEWIT 'Slid,° I would be the author of more, to vex him. That purpose deserves it; it gives thee law of plaguing° him. I'll tell thee what I would do. I would make a false almanac, get it printed, and then ha' him drawn out on a Coronation Day to the Tower Wharf,[2] and kill him with the noise of the ordnance. Disinherit thee? He cannot, man. Art not thou next of blood, and his sister's son?

By God's eyelid
good reason to plague

DAUPHINE Ay, but he will thrust me out of it, he vows, and marry.

TRUEWIT How! That's a more portent.° Can he endure no noise, and will venture on a wife?

worse omen

CLERIMONT Yes. Why, thou art a stranger, it seems, to his best trick yet. He has employed a fellow this half year all over England to hearken him out a dumb° woman, be she of any form or any quality,° so° she be able to bear children. Her silence is dowry enough, he says.

silent
social rank / provided

TRUEWIT But I trust to God he has found none.

CLERIMONT No, but he has heard of one that's lodged i'the next street to him who is exceedingly soft-spoken, thrifty of her speech, that spends but six words a day. And her he's about now, and shall have her.

TRUEWIT Is't possible! Who is his agent i'the business?

CLERIMONT Marry, a barber, one Cutbeard, an honest fellow, one that tells Dauphine all here.

TRUEWIT Why, you oppress me with wonder! A woman and a barber, and love no noise![3]

CLERIMONT Yes, faith. The fellow trims him silently and has not the knack° with his shears or his fingers, and that continence in a barber he thinks so eminent a virtue as it has made him chief of his counsel.

snapping noise

TRUEWIT Is the barber to be seen? Or the wench?

CLERIMONT Yes, that they are.

TRUEWIT I pray thee, Dauphine, let's go thither.

1.2. The scene continues.
1. John Foxe's *Acts and Monuments*, also known as the *Book of Martyrs*, described the suffering of persecuted English Protestants.
2. The anniversary of King James's coronation was celebrated with cannon fire from the Tower of London.
3. Barbers, like women, were stereotyped as chatty.

DAUPHINE I have some business now. I cannot, i'faith.

TRUEWIT You shall have no business shall° make you neglect this, sir. We'll make her talk, believe it. Or if she will not, we can give out° at least so much as shall interrupt the treaty. We will break it. Thou art bound in conscience, when he suspects thee without cause, to torment him.

that will
circulate rumors

DAUPHINE Not I, by any means. I'll give no suffrage° to't. He shall never ha' that plea against me that I opposed the least fancy of his. Let it lie upon my stars° to be guilty; I'll be innocent.

permission
destiny

TRUEWIT Yes, and be poor and beg. Do, innocent,° when some groom of his has got him an heir, or this barber, if he himself cannot.[4] Innocent! I pray thee, Ned,° where lies° she? Let him be innocent still.

blameless one; fool
Clerimont / resides

CLERIMONT Why, right over against the barber's, in the house where Sir John Daw lies.

TRUEWIT You do not mean to confound° me!

astonish

CLERIMONT Why?

TRUEWIT Does he that would marry her know so much?

CLERIMONT I cannot tell.

TRUEWIT 'Twere enough of imputation to° her, with him.

to cast suspicion on

CLERIMONT Why?

TRUEWIT The only talking sir° i'th'town! Jack Daw! And he teach her not to speak! God b'w'you. I have some business, too.

chattiest guy

CLERIMONT Will you not go thither, then?

TRUEWIT Not with the danger to meet Daw, for mine ears.

CLERIMONT Why, I thought you two had been upon very good terms.

TRUEWIT Yes, of keeping distance.

CLERIMONT They say he is a very good scholar.

TRUEWIT Ay, and he says it first. A pox on him! A fellow that pretends only to learning, buys titles, and nothing else of books in him.

CLERIMONT The world reports him to be very learned.

TRUEWIT I am sorry the world should so conspire to belie him.

CLERIMONT Good faith, I have heard very good things come from him.

TRUEWIT You may. There's none so desperately ignorant to deny that. Would they were his own. God b'w'you, gentlemen.

CLERIMONT This is very abrupt! [*Exit Truewit.*]

1.3

DAUPHINE Come, you° are a strange open° man to tell everything thus.

(Truewit) / frank

CLERIMONT Why, believe it, Dauphine, Truewit's a very honest fellow.

4. Under English common law, all children born during a marriage were considered legitimate and therefore in the direct line of inheritance. In consequence, as Truewit notes, even if Morose is unable to make his wife pregnant, his barber or his menial servant (groom) may do so, and the resulting child would inherit Morose's estate in preference to his nephew, Dauphine. "Got" means "begot."

1.3. The scene continues.

DAUPHINE I think no other, but this frank nature of his is not for° secrets.
for keeping

CLERIMONT Nay, then, you are mistaken, Dauphine. I know where he has been well trusted, and discharged° the trust very truly and heartily.
carried out

DAUPHINE I contend not,° Ned, but with the fewer a business is carried, it is ever the safer. Now we are alone, if you'll go thither, I am for you.°
don't disagree / *I'll go with you*

CLERIMONT When were you there?

DAUPHINE Last night; and such a decameron of sport fallen out! Boccace never thought of the like.[1] Daw does nothing but court her, and the wrong way. He would lie with her, and praises her modesty; desires that she would talk and be free, and commends her silence in verses, which he reads, and swears are the best that ever man made. Then rails at his fortunes, stamps, and mutines why° he is not made a counselor and called to affairs of state.
complains that

CLERIMONT I pray thee, let's go. I would fain partake this.—Some water, boy. [*Exit Boy.*]

DAUPHINE We are invited to dinner together, he and I, by one that came thither to him, Sir La Foole.

CLERIMONT Oh, that's a precious manikin.°
little man

DAUPHINE Do you know him?

CLERIMONT Ay, and he will know you too, if e'er he saw you but once, though you should meet him at church in the midst of prayers. He is one of the braveries,° though he be none o'the wits. He will salute° a judge upon the bench and a bishop in the pulpit, a lawyer when he is pleading at the bar and a lady when she is dancing in a masque, and put her out.[2] He does give plays and suppers, and invites his guests to 'em aloud out of his window as they ride by in coaches—he has a lodging in the Strand[3] for the purpose—or to watch when ladies are gone to the china houses, or the Exchange,[4] that he may meet 'em by chance and give 'em presents, some two or three hundred pounds' worth of toys,° to be laughed at. He is never without a spare banquet° or sweetmeats in his chamber, for their women° to alight at and come up to, for a bait.
showy dressers / *greet* / *trifles* / *snack* / *the ladies' maids*

DAUPHINE Excellent! He was a fine youth last night, but now he is much finer! What is his Christian name? I ha' forgot.

[*Enter Boy.*]

CLERIMONT Sir Amorous La Foole.

BOY The gentleman is here below that owns that name.

CLERIMONT Heart,° he's come to invite me to dinner, I hold° my life.
By God's heart / bet

DAUPHINE Like° enough. Pray thee, let's ha' him up.
Likely

CLERIMONT Boy, marshal him.

BOY With a truncheon,[5] sir?

1. Boccaccio's *Decameron* is a collection of stories told by a group of patricians to entertain themselves while escaping from the plague in Florence.
2. Ruin her performance, throw her into confusion.
3. Fashionable street between the city of London and nearby Westminster, the seat of government.
4. China houses sold imported porcelain, a fashionable luxury; expensive textile goods were available at the New Exchange, a collection of shops on the south side of the Strand, first opened in 1609.
5. "Marshal him" means "show him in," but the Boy plays on "marshal," meaning "constable," someone who carried a truncheon, or cudgel, to enforce his authority.

CLERIMONT Away, I beseech you. [*Exit Boy.*] I'll make him tell us his pedigree now, and what meat he has to dinner, and who are his guests, and the whole course of his fortunes, with a breath.° *all in one breath*

1.4

[*Enter*] *La Foole.*

LA FOOLE 'Save,° dear Sir Dauphine, honored Master Clerimont. *God save you*

CLERIMONT Sir Amorous! You have very much honested° my lodging with your presence. *honored*

LA FOOLE Good faith, it is a fine lodging! Almost as delicate a lodging as mine.

CLERIMONT Not so, sir.

LA FOOLE Excuse me, sir, if it were i'the Strand, I assure you. I am come, Master Clerimont, to entreat you wait upon[1] two or three ladies to dinner today.

CLERIMONT How, sir! Wait upon 'em? Did you ever see me carry dishes?

LA FOOLE No, sir, dispense° with me; I meant, to bear 'em company. *bear*

CLERIMONT Oh, that I will, sir. The doubtfulness o'your phrase, believe it, sir, would breed you a quarrel once an hour with the terrible boys,[2] if you should but keep 'em fellowship a day.

LA FOOLE It should be extremely against my will, sir, if I contested with any man.

CLERIMONT I believe it, sir. Where hold you your feast?

LA FOOLE At Tom Otter's, sir.

DAUPHINE Tom Otter? What's he?

LA FOOLE Captain Otter, sir; he is a kind of gamester,° but he has had command both by sea and by land. *gambler*

DAUPHINE Oh, then he is *animal amphibium?*[3]

LA FOOLE Ay, sir. His wife was the rich china-woman[4] that the courtiers visited so often, that gave the rare entertainment.[5] She commands all at home.

CLERIMONT Then she is Captain Otter?

LA FOOLE You say very well, sir. She is my kinswoman, a La Foole by the mother side, and will invite any great ladies for my sake.

DAUPHINE Not of the La Fooles of Essex?

LA FOOLE No, sir, the La Fooles of London.

CLERIMONT [*aside to Dauphine*] Now he's in.° *launched on his topic*

LA FOOLE They all come out of our house,° the La Fooles o'the north, the La Fooles of the west, the La Fooles of the east and south—we are as ancient a family as any is in Europe—but I myself am descended lineally of the French *family*

1.4. The scene continues.

1. La Foole uses "wait upon" to mean "attend at dinner," but Clerimont pretends to understand the phrase as meaning "serve at table."

2. The "roaring boys," boisterous men who frequented London taverns and used any excuse for a fight.

3. An animal that lives in two places and combines two different natures.

4. A woman whose family made its fortune importing porcelain; but "china" most likely had a slang sexual meaning (cf. the "china scene" in William Wycherley's Restoration comedy, *The Country Wife*).

5. "Rare" means "fine." (With sexual suggestion.)

La Fooles, and we do bear for our coat yellow, or *or*, checkered azure and gules and some three or four colors more, which is a very noted coat,[6] and has sometimes been solemnly worn by divers nobility of our house—but let that go, antiquity is not respected now—I had a brace° of fat does sent me, gentlemen, and half a dozen of pheasants, a dozen or two of godwits,[7] and some other fowl which I would have eaten while they are good, and in good company—there will be a great lady or two, my Lady Haughty, my Lady Centaur, Mistress Doll Mavis—and they come o'purpose to see the silent gentlewoman, Mistress Epicene, that honest° Sir John Daw has promised to bring thither—and then Mistress Trusty, my lady's woman,° will be there too, and this honorable knight Sir Dauphine with yourself, Master Clerimont—and we'll be very merry, and have fiddlers, and dance—I have been a mad wag in my time, and have spent some crowns° since I was a page in court to my Lord Lofty, and after, my lady's gentleman-usher,[8] who got me knighted in Ireland,[9] since it pleased my elder brother to die—I had as fair a gold jerkin on that day as any was worn in the Island Voyage or at Caliz, none dispraised,[1] and I came over in it hither, showed myself to my friends in court, and after went down to my tenants in the country and surveyed my lands, let new leases, took their money, spent it in the eye° o'the land here, upon ladies—and now I can take up[2] at my pleasure.

pair / *worthy* / *waiting-woman* / *five-shilling coins* / *center (of London)*

DAUPHINE Can you take up ladies, sir?

CLERIMONT Oh, let him breathe; he has not recovered.

DAUPHINE Would I were your half in that commodity.[3]

LA FOOLE No, sir, excuse me, I meant money, which can take up anything. I have another guest or two to invite and say as much to, gentlemen. I'll take my leave abruptly, in hope you will not fail— your servant.[4] [*Exit.*]

DAUPHINE We will not fail you, Sir Precious La Foole;[5] but she° shall, that your ladies come to see, if I have credit afore° Sir Daw.

(Epicene) / with

CLERIMONT Did you ever hear such a wind-fucker° as this?

(lit., a kind of hawk)

6. La Foole's family "coat" is motley, the distinctive attire of the court jester. Or, azure, and gules are heraldic colors—yellow, blue, and red, respectively. La Foole's "French" background associates him, in the minds of an English audience, with affectation and lasciviousness.

7. Long-billed shore birds, considered delicacies.

8. Personal attendant; gentlemen-ushers were the butt of many bawdy jokes.

9. The Earl of Essex knighted his followers indiscriminately while on his disastrous campaign to quell rebellion in Ireland (1599–1600).

1. Two other expeditions headed by the Earl of Essex: a 1597 attack on Spanish treasure ships in the Azores and a successful capture of Caliz (i.e., Cádiz), in Spain, in 1596. Both ventures were popular with ambitious but indigent gentlemen whose attention to their appearance while on military campaign attracted censure. "None dispraised" means "not to say anything bad about anybody else's jerkin."

2. Borrow money. (But Dauphine pretends to understand "pick up" or "uncover.")

3. La Foole understands Dauphine to say, "I wish I were half as successful as you with the ladies," but Dauphine may mean, "I wish I had half as much breath as you do." Moneylenders got around laws against high interest on loans by giving the borrower part of the sum not in cash but in goods, called "commodity," which the borrower was supposed to sell to realize the balance of the amount borrowed. The commodity was typically nearly worthless and deliberately overvalued, so that the transaction constituted, in effect, a surcharge on the loan. Lavish spenders such as La Foole, desperate for cash, were especially vulnerable to such shady contracts.

4. "I am your obedient servant," a polite leave-taking. But in act 3, scene 7, La Foole will actually serve as a waiter at his own dinner party.

5. Said after La Foole as he leaves.

DAUPHINE Or such a rook° as the other,° that will betray his mistress to be seen! Come, 'tis time we prevented° it.

[*fool; crow / (Daw)* — *anticipated*]

CLERIMONT Go. [*Exeunt.*]

2.1

[Enter] Morose [holding a long tube for speaking through, and] Mute.

MOROSE Cannot I yet find out a more compendious° method than by this trunk to save my servants the labor of speech and mine ears the discord of sounds? Let me see: all discourses but mine own afflict me; they seem harsh, impertinent, and irksome. Is it not possible that thou shouldst answer me by signs, and I apprehend thee, fellow? Speak not, though I question you. You have taken the ring° off from the street door as I bade you? Answer me not by speech but by silence, unless it be otherwise (—)

At the breaches,° still the fellow makes legs° or signs.

Very good. And you have fastened on a thick quilt or flockbed° on the outside of the door, that if they knock with their daggers or with brickbats they can make no noise? But° with your leg your answer, unless it be otherwise. (—) Very good. This is not only fit modesty in a servant, but good state° and discretion in a master. And you have been with Cutbeard the barber to have him come to me? (—) Good. And he will come presently?° Answer me not but with your leg, unless it be otherwise; if it be otherwise, shake your head or shrug. (—) So. Your Italian and Spaniard are wise in these![1] And it is a frugal and comely gravity. How long will it be ere Cutbeard come? Stay, if an hour, hold up your whole hand; if half an hour, two fingers; if a quarter, one. (—) Good; half a quarter? 'Tis well. And have you given him a key to come in without knocking? (—) Good. And is the lock oiled, and the hinges, today? (—) Good. And the quilting of the stairs nowhere worn out and bare? (—) Very good. I see, by much doctrine° and impulsion,° it may be effected. Stand by. The Turk[2] in this divine discipline is admirable, exceeding all the potentates of the earth; still° waited on by mutes, and all his commands so executed; yea, even in the war, as I have heard, and in his marches, most of his charges and directions given by signs and with silence. An exquisite art! And I am heartily ashamed and angry oftentimes that the princes of Christendom should suffer a barbarian to transcend 'em in so high a point of felicity. I will practice it hereafter. (*One winds° a horn without.*) How now? Oh! Oh! What villain, what prodigy of mankind is that? Look!

[*efficient* — *knocker* — *dashes / bows* — *mattress* — *Only* — *dignity* — *immediately* — *teaching / coercion* — *always* — *blows*]

[*Exit Mute. Horn sounds*] *again.*

Oh! Cut his throat, cut his throat! What murderer, hellhound,° devil can this be?

[*watchdog of hell; fiend*]

[*Enter Mute.*]

2.1. Morose's house.

1. Italians and Spaniards were thought to use gestures more freely than the English but to be more guarded in their speech.

2. The Sultan of Turkey was considered a cruel despot by most Western Europeans.

MUTE It is a post° from the court— *messenger*

MOROSE Out,° rogue, and must thou blow thy horn, too? *(expressing anger)*

MUTE Alas, it is a post from the court, sir, that says he must speak with you, pain of death—

MOROSE Pain of thy life, be silent.

2.2

[*Enter*] *Truewit* [*carrying a horn and a noose*].

TRUEWIT By your leave, sir, I am a stranger here. Is your name Master Morose? Is your name Master Morose? Fishes! Pythagoreans all![1] This is strange. What say you, sir? Nothing? Has Harpocrates[2] been here with his club among you? Well, sir, I will believe you to be the man at this time; I will venture upon you, sir. Your friends at court commend 'em° to you, sir— *send their greetings*

MOROSE O men! O manners![3] Was there ever such an impudence?

TRUEWIT —and are extremely solicitous for° you, sir. *concerned about*

MOROSE Whose knave° are you? *servant (derogatory)*

TRUEWIT Mine own knave, and your compeer,° sir. *equal*

MOROSE [*to Mute*] Fetch me my sword—

TRUEWIT [*to Mute*] You shall taste the one half of my dagger if you do, groom, and [*to Morose*] you the other if you stir, sir. Be patient, I charge you, in the King's name, and hear me without insurrection. They say you are to marry! To marry! Do you mark, sir?[4]

MOROSE How then, rude companion!° *fellow (contemptuous)*

TRUEWIT Marry, your friends do wonder, sir, the Thames being so near, wherein you may drown so handsomely; or London Bridge at a low fall,° with a fine leap to hurry you down the stream; or such a delicate steeple i'the town as Bow° to vault from; or a braver height, as Paul's; or if you affected° to do it nearer home and a shorter way, an excellent garret window into the street, or a beam in the said garret with this halter° which they have sent, and desire that you would sooner commit your grave head to this knot (*He shows him a halter*) than to the wedlock noose; or take a little sublimate° and go out of the world like a rat, or a fly (as one said) with a straw i'your arse[5]—any way rather than to follow this goblin matrimony. Alas, sir, do you ever think to find a chaste wife in these times? Now? When there are so many masques, plays, Puritan preachings, mad folks,[6] and other strange sights to be seen daily, private and public? If you had lived in King Ethelred's time, or Edward the Confessor's,[7] you might perhaps have found in some cold country hamlet

tide · *St. Mary-le-Bow* · *desired* · *noose* · *poison*

2.2. The scene continues.

1. Fishes are, of course, mute; the disciples of Pythagoras took a vow of silence during their novitiate.

2. Son of the Egyptian god of the underworld, Osiris, shown with a finger to his lips and holding a club.

3. Loosely translating *O tempora, O mores!*, the Roman orator Cicero's famous lament for the degeneracy of his times, in *Against Catiline*, 1.2. (Literally, *tempora* means "these times.")

4. Much of Truewit's following "advice" is derived from Juvenal's misogynist Sixth Satire, with its local references updated to modern London.

5. Staged fights between spiders and flies were a low-level form of entertainment; the fly was controlled by a straw stuck into its tail.

6. Visiting the insane asylum, Saint Bethlehem's Hospital, or "Bedlam," was a popular pastime.

7. Ethelred and Edward the Confessor ruled England in 978–1016 and 1042–66, respectively.

then a dull, frosty wench would have been contented with one man. Now they will as soon be pleased with one leg or one eye. I'll tell you, sir, the monstrous hazards you shall run with a wife.

MOROSE Good sir, have I ever cozened° any friends of yours of their land? Bought their possessions? Taken forfeit of° their mortgage? Begged a reversion from 'em? Bastarded their issue?[8] What have I done that may deserve this?

cheated / *Foreclosed on*

TRUEWIT Nothing, sir, that I know, but your itch of marriage.

MOROSE Why, if I had made an assassinate° upon your father; vitiated° your mother, ravished your sisters—

murder / *violated*

TRUEWIT I would kill you, sir; I would kill you if you had.

MOROSE Why, you do more in this, sir. It were a vengeance centuple° for all facinorous° acts that could be named, to do that you do—

hundredfold / criminal

TRUEWIT Alas, sir, I am but a messenger; I but tell you what you must hear. It seems your friends are careful after° your soul's health, sir, and would have you know the danger—but you may do your pleasure, for all them; I persuade not, sir. If, after you are married, your wife do run away with a vaulter° or the Frenchman that walks upon ropes or him that dances the jig or a fencer for his skill at his weapon,° why, it is not their fault. They have discharged their consciences when you know what may happen. Nay, suffer valiantly, sir, for I must tell you all the perils that you are obnoxious° to. If she be fair, young, and vegetous,° no sweetmeats ever drew more flies; all the yellow doublets and great roses[9] i'the town will be there. If foul° and crooked, she'll be with them and buy those doublets and roses, sir. If rich, and that you marry her dowry, not her, she'll reign in your house as imperious as a widow.[1] If noble, all her kindred will be your tyrants. If fruitful, as proud° as May and humorous° as April; she must have her doctors, her midwives, her nurses, her longings every hour, though it be for the dearest morsel of man.° If learned, there was never such a parrot; all your patrimony° will be too little for the guests that must be invited to hear her speak Latin and Greek, and you must lie with her in those languages too if you will please her. If precise,° you must feast all the silenced brethren[2] once in three days, salute the sisters,° entertain the whole family or wood° of 'em, and hear long-winded exercises, singings, and catechizings, which you are not given° to, and yet must give° for, to please the zealous matron your wife, who for the holy cause will cozen you over and above. You begin to sweat, sir? But this is not half, i'faith. You may do your pleasure notwithstanding; as I said before, I come not to persuade you.—Upon my faith, master servingman, if you do stir, I will beat you. *The Mute is stealing away* [*but stops in his tracks*].

worried about / *acrobat* / *(with a phallic joke)* / *liable* / *flourishing* / *ugly* / *arrogant / changeable* / *(the penis)* / *inheritance* / *Puritan* / *Puritan women / group* / *inclined / pay*

MOROSE Oh, what is my sin! What is my sin?

TRUEWIT Then if you love your wife, or rather dote on her,

8. Secured the right to a job or to a piece of land they had been expecting to get? Had their children declared illegitimate (which would bar them from the line of inheritance)?

9. Gaudy doublets and fancy shoe ribbons gathered in a flowerlike shape, here worn by fops.

1. Widows, unlike married and never-married women, had the power to administer their own assets.

2. Clergy ejected from the Church of England for their radical views, and thus denied the forum of the pulpit.

sir, oh, how she'll torture you! And take pleasure i'your torments! You shall lie with her but° when she lists;° she will not hurt her beauty, her complexion; or it must be for that° jewel or that pearl, when she does; every half hour's pleasure must be bought anew, and with the same pain and charge° you wooed her at first. Then you must keep what servants she please, what company she will; that friend must not visit you without her license,° and him she loves most she will seem to hate eagerliest to decline° your jealousy, or feign to be jealous of you first and for that cause go live with her she-friend or cousin at the College, that can instruct her in all the mysteries° of writing letters, corrupting servants, taming spies; where she must have that° rich gown for such a great day, a new one for the next, a richer for the third; be served in silver; have the chamber filled with a succession of grooms, footmen, ushers, and other messengers, besides embroiderers, jewelers, tire-women,° sempsters,° feathermen, perfumers; while she feels not how the land drops away° nor the acres melt, nor foresees the change when the mercer° has your woods for her velvets; never weighs what her pride costs, sir, so° she may kiss a page or a smooth chin that has the despair of a beard; be a stateswoman,[3] know all the news, what was done at Salisbury, what at the Bath, what at court, what in progress;[4] or so she may censure° poets and authors and styles and compare 'em, Daniel with Spenser, Jonson with the tother youth,[5] and so forth; or be thought cunning in controversies or the very knots of divinity,[6] and have often in her mouth the state of the question,[7] and then skip to the mathematics and demonstration;° and answer in religion to one, in state° to another, in bawdry to a third.

only / pleases · *a certain* · *trouble and expense* · *permission* · *divert; avoid* · *arts* · *a certain* · *dressmakers / tailors* · *is sold off* · *textile dealer* · *provided that* · *pass judgment on* · *logic* · *politics*

MOROSE Oh, Oh!

TRUEWIT All this is very true, sir. And then her going in disguise to that conjurer and this cunning woman,° where the first question is, how soon you shall die? Next, if her present servant° love her? Next that, if she shall have a new servant? And how many? Which of her family would make the best bawd, male or female? What precedence[8] she shall have by her next match? And sets down the answers and believes 'em above the scriptures. Nay, perhaps she'll study the art.°

fortune-teller · *male admirer* · *(fortune-telling)*

MOROSE Gentle sir, ha' you done? Ha' you had your pleasure o' me? I'll think of these things.

TRUEWIT Yes, sir, and then comes reeking home of vapor and sweat with going afoot, and lies in[9] a month of a new face, all oil and birdlime,[1] and rises in ass's milk,[2] and is cleansed with a new fucus.° God b'w'you, sir. One thing more—which I had almost forgot. This too, with whom you are to marry,

cosmetic

3. Politically informed woman.
4. Salisbury and Bath were both places of fashionable resort: Salisbury for horse races, Bath for "taking the waters." The King's progress, or tour of his domains, was a major social expedition for many courtiers.
5. Samuel Daniel and Edmund Spenser were nondramatic poets of the English Renaissance. Jonson and the "tother youth" (perhaps Shakespeare, Marston, or Dekker) were presumably both dramatists.
6. Most difficult theological problems.
7. Principal issue in a controversy.
8. The right to go first in a group or pass first through an entryway, determined for women by their husbands' social rank.
9. Is confined to bed, like a childbearing woman.
1. Sticky substance spread on twigs to catch birds; here used as a term for gooey, opaque cosmetics spread on women's faces to make them attractive to suitors.
2. Used as a skin softener by ancient Roman empresses. (Some editors emend "rises" to "rinses.")

may have made a conveyance of her virginity aforehand, as your wise widows do of their states° before they marry, in trust to some friend, sir: who can tell?[3] Or if she have not done it yet she may do upon the wedding day or the night before, and antedate you cuckold. The like has been heard of in nature. 'Tis no devised impossible thing, sir. God b'w'you! I'll be bold to leave this rope with you, sir, for a remembrance. [*He leaves the noose behind.*] Farewell, Mute. [*Exit.*]

estates

MOROSE [*to Mute*] Come, ha'° me to my chamber, but first shut the door. (*The horn* [*sounds*] *again.*) Oh, shut the door, shut the door! Is he come again?

escort

[*Enter*] *Cutbeard.*

CUTBEARD 'Tis I, sir, your barber.

MOROSE O Cutbeard, Cutbeard, Cutbeard! Here has been a cutthroat with me. Help me in to my bed, and give me physic[4] with thy counsel. [*Exeunt.*]

2.3

[*Enter*] *Daw, Clerimont, Dauphine,* [*and*] *Epicene.*

DAW Nay, an° she will, let her refuse at her own charges.° 'Tis nothing to me, gentlemen. But she will not be invited to the like feasts or guests every day.

if / risk

They [*Clerimont and Dauphine*] *dissuade her privately.*

CLERIMONT [*aloud*] Oh, by no means, she may not refuse— [*aside to Epicene*]—to stay at home, if you love your reputation. 'Slight,° you are invited thither o'purpose to be seen and laughed at by the Lady of the College and her shadows.° This trumpeter° hath proclaimed you.

By God's light / *followers* / *(Jack Daw)*

DAUPHINE [*aside to Epicene*] You shall not go. Let him be laughed at in your stead for not bringing you, and put him to his extemporal faculty of fooling and talking loud to satisfy the company.

CLERIMONT [*aside to Dauphine*] He will suspect us; talk aloud.—Pray, Mistress Epicene, let's see your verses; we have Sir John Daw's leave.° Do not conceal your servant's merit and your own glories.

permission

EPICENE They'll prove my servant's glories if you have his leave so soon.

DAUPHINE His vainglories, lady!

DAW Show 'em, show 'em, mistress; I dare own° 'em.

acknowledge

EPICENE [*holding out papers to Clerimont and Dauphine*] Judge you what glories.

DAW [*taking the papers*] Nay, I'll read 'em myself, too; an author must recite his own works. It is a madrigal of modesty. [*He recites.*]

Modest and fair, for fair and good are near

3. In a legal maneuver called "conveyance," women, who under common law lost their property to their husbands upon marriage, could retain control of their assets by transferring them before marriage to a male trustee. Truewit warns Morose that the woman he chooses to marry may have similarly "conveyed" her virginity to another man before marriage.

4. Medicine. (Barbers doubled as physicians.)

2.3. Daw's house.

Neighbors, howe'er.—

DAUPHINE Very good.

CLERIMONT Ay, is't not?

DAW —No noble virtue ever was alone,
But two in one.—

DAUPHINE Excellent!

CLERIMONT That again, I pray, Sir John.

DAUPHINE It has something in't like rare° wit and sense. [*excellent; scarce*]

CLERIMONT Peace!° [*Silence!*]

DAW No noble virtue ever was alone,
But two in one.
Then when I praise sweet modesty, I praise
Bright beauty's rays;
And, having praised both beauty and modesty,
I have praised thee.

DAUPHINE Admirable!

CLERIMONT How it chimes and cries tink i'the close divinely!

DAUPHINE Ay, 'tis Seneca.

CLERIMONT No, I think 'tis Plutarch.[1]

DAW The *dor* on[2] Plutarch and Seneca! I hate it. They are mine own imaginations, by that° light. I wonder those fellows have such credit with gentlemen. [*heaven's*]

CLERIMONT They are very grave authors.

DAW Grave asses! Mere essayists!° A few loose sentences and that's all. A man would talk so his whole age. I do utter as good things every hour, if they were collected and observed, as either of 'em. [*(a very bad pun)*]

DAUPHINE Indeed, Sir John!

CLERIMONT He must needs, living among the wits and braveries too.

DAUPHINE Ay, and being president of 'em as he is.

DAW There's Aristotle, a mere commonplace fellow; Plato, a discourser; Thucydides and Livy, tedious and dry; Tacitus, an entire knot, sometimes worth the untying, very seldom.[3]

CLERIMONT What do you think of the poets, Sir John?

DAW Not worthy to be named for authors. Homer, an old tedious prolix° ass, talks of curriers and chines of beef. Virgil, of dunging of land and bees.[4] Horace, of I know not what. [*wordy*]

CLERIMONT [*aside*] I think so.° [*(that Daw knows nothing)*]

DAW And so Pindarus, Lycophron, Anacreon, Catullus, Seneca the tragedian, Lucan, Propertius, Tibullus, Martial, Juvenal, Ausonius, Statius, Politian, Valerius Flaccus, and the rest[5]—

1. Greek writer on the virtuous life. Seneca was a Roman moral philosopher who disapproved of sexual passion. (Dauphine knows that Clerimont will get the joke but that Daw is too ignorant to understand his irony.)
2. To the devil with. ("Dor" means "mock," "fool.")
3. Daw dismisses many of the classical texts upon which Renaissance education was based.
4. Homer mentions horse grooms (curriers) and sides (chines) of beef in the *Iliad*. Virgil writes of agricultural tasks in his *Georgics*.
5. Daw indiscriminately lists dramatists, lyric poets, historians, and satirists, and mixes classical writers with modern ones. Politian was an Italian Renaissance humanist; Valerius Flaccus wrote a poem about the Argonauts in the time of Augustus Caesar (see Clerimont's comment below, lines 74–75).

CLERIMONT [*aside to Dauphine*] What a sack full of their names he has got!

DAUPHINE [*aside to Clerimont*] And how he pours 'em out! Politian with Valerius Flaccus!

CLERIMONT [*aside to Dauphine*] Was not the character° right of him? *satiric description*

DAUPHINE [*aside to Clerimont*] As could be made, i'faith.

DAW And Persius,[6] a crabbed coxcomb,° not to be endured. *fool*

DAUPHINE Why, whom do you account for authors, Sir John Daw?

DAW *Syntagma juris civilis, Corpus juris civilis, Corpus juris canonici*, the King of Spain's Bible.[7]

DAUPHINE Is the King of Spain's Bible an author?

CLERIMONT Yes, and Syntagma.

DAUPHINE What was that Syntagma, sir?

DAW A civil lawyer, a Spaniard.

DAUPHINE Sure, Corpus was a Dutchman.

CLERIMONT Ay, both the Corpusses, I knew 'em; they were very corpulent authors.[8]

DAW And then there's Vatablus, Pomponatius, Symancha;[9] the other° are not to be received within the thought of a scholar. *others*

DAUPHINE [*to Epicene*] 'Fore God, you have a simple° learned servant, lady, in titles. *undoubted; simpleminded*

CLERIMONT I wonder that he is not called to the helm° and made a counselor! *the helm of state*

DAUPHINE He is one extraordinary.

CLERIMONT Nay, but in ordinary![1] To say truth, the state wants such.

DAUPHINE Why, that will follow.

CLERIMONT I muse a mistress can be so silent to the dotes° of such a servant. *love; endowments; idiocy*

DAW 'Tis her virtue, sir. I have written somewhat of her silence too.

DAUPHINE In verse, Sir John?

CLERIMONT What else?

DAUPHINE Why, how can you justify your own being of a poet, that so slight all the old poets?

DAW Why, every man that writes in verse is not a poet; you have of the° wits that write verses and yet are no poets. They are poets that live by it, the poor fellows that live by it. *there are some*

DAUPHINE Why, would not you live by your verses, Sir John?

CLERIMONT No, 'twere pity he should. A knight live by his verses? He did not make 'em to that end, I hope.

DAUPHINE And yet the noble Sidney lives by[2] his, and the noble family not ashamed.

6. Roman satirist with a notoriously difficult style.

7. The first two titles refer to *The Body of Civil Law* in different editions. (Daw has not noticed that they are the same book; in lines 82–83, Dauphine and Clerimont underscore the comic absurdity of Daw's referring to these works as authors.) Daw also lists *The Body of Canonical Law* and the multilingual Biblia Regia, revised in 1572 under the sponsorship of the Spanish king Philip II.

8. The English considered the Dutch overweight.

9. Vatablus was a Hebrew scholar and authority on Aristotle; Pomponatius (Pietro Pomponazzi), another Aristotelian, wrote a controversial treatise on the immortality of the soul; Symancha was a Spanish writer on canon law.

1. Holding a regular position at court. (A joking contrast to "extraordinary," which means both "remarkable" and "by special appointment.")

2. Punning on "makes a living" and "lives on after death in immortal poems." Sir Philip Sidney, the much-

CLERIMONT Ay, he professed himself,° but Sir John Daw has more caution; he'll not hinder his own rising i'the state so much! Do you think he will?—Your verses, good Sir John, and no poems.[3] *was open about it*

DAW [*reads*] Silence in woman is like speech in man,
Deny't who can.

DAUPHINE Not I, believe it. Your reason, sir.

DAW Nor is 't a tale[4]
That female vice should be a virtue male,
Or masculine vice a female virtue be.
You shall it see
Proved with increase:
I know to speak and she to hold her peace.

Do you conceive° me, gentlemen? *understand*

DAUPHINE No, faith, how mean you "with increase," Sir John?

DAW Why, "with increase" is when I court her for the common cause of mankind, and she says nothing but *consentire videtur,*[5] and in time is *gravida*.° *pregnant*

DAUPHINE Then this is a ballad of procreation?

CLERIMONT A madrigal[6] of procreation; you mistake.

EPICENE Pray give me my verses again, servant.

DAW If you'll ask 'em aloud,° you shall. *to be recited*

[*Daw and Epicene walk apart.*]

CLERIMONT See, here's Truewit again!

2.4

[*Enter*] *Truewit* [*with his horn*].

CLERIMONT Where hast thou been, in the name of madness, thus accoutered with thy horn?

TRUEWIT Where the sound of it might have pierced your senses with gladness had you been in ear-reach of it. Dauphine, fall down and worship me. I have forbid the banns,[1] lad. I have been with thy virtuous uncle and have broke the match.

DAUPHINE You ha' not, I hope.

TRUEWIT Yes, faith; an° thou shouldst hope otherwise, I should repent me. This horn got me entrance; kiss it. I had no other way to get in but by feigning to be a post,° but when I got in once I proved none, but rather the contrary, turned him into a post° or a stone or what is stiffer, with thundering into him the incommodities of a wife and the miseries of marriage. If ever Gorgon[2] were seen in the shape of a woman, he hath seen her in my description. I have put him off o'that scent forever. Why do you not applaud and adore *if* *messenger* *pole*

admired author of *Arcadia* and *Astrophil and Stella*, had died of battle wounds in 1586. Several of his surviving relatives were Jonson's friends and/or patrons.

3. Clerimont pretends that he is merely using Daw's preferred term, but implies that the "verses" are inartistic ("no poems").

4. Untrue. (With an unwitting suggestion of "tail.")

5. Seems to consent. (Silence was legally taken to signify consent; that is, any objections to a proposed policy or statute needed to be voiced at the time to be considered valid.)

6. The ballad is a popular song form; the madrigal, a courtly one preferred by the ambitious Daw.

2.4. The scene continues.

1. A betrothed couple had their intentions to marry announced in church in a procedure called "reading the banns," at which point anybody with objections could voice them.

2. Any of the three snaky-haired female monsters that changed anyone who saw them into stone.

me, sirs? Why stand you mute? Are you stupid?° You are not worthy o'the benefit.
dumbstruck

DAUPHINE [*to Clerimont*] Did not I tell you? Mischief!

CLERIMONT [*to Truewit*] I would you had placed this benefit somewhere else.

TRUEWIT Why so?

CLERIMONT 'Slight, you have done the most inconsiderate, rash, weak thing that ever man did to his friend.

DAUPHINE Friend! If the most malicious enemy I have had studied to inflict an injury upon me, it could not be a greater.

TRUEWIT Wherein? For God's sake, gentlemen, come to yourselves again.

DAUPHINE [*to Clerimont*] But I presaged thus much afore to you.

CLERIMONT Would my lips had been soldered when I spake on't.° [*To Truewit*] 'Slight, what moved you to be thus impertinent?
about Morose's plans

TRUEWIT My masters, do not put on this strange face to pay my courtesy. Off with this visor! Have good turns done you, and thank 'em this way?

DAUPHINE 'Fore heaven, you have undone me. That which I have plotted for and been maturing now these four months you have blasted° in a minute. Now° I am lost, I may speak. This gentlewoman was lodged here by me o'purpose, and, to be put upon my uncle, hath professed this obstinate silence for my sake, being my entire friend, and one that, for the requital of such a fortune as to marry him, would have made me very ample conditions; where now all my hopes are utterly miscarried by this unlucky accident.°
ruined / Now that
event

CLERIMONT Thus 'tis when a man will be ignorantly officious, do services, and not know his why.° I wonder what courteous itch possessed you! You never did absurder part i'your life, nor a greater trespass to friendship, to humanity.
the reason

DAUPHINE Faith, you may forgive it best; 'twas your cause° principally.
fault

CLERIMONT I know it; would it had not.

[*Enter*] *Cutbeard.*

DAUPHINE How now, Cutbeard? What news?

CUTBEARD The best, the happiest that ever was, sir. There has been a mad gentleman with your uncle this morning—I think this be the gentleman—that has almost talked him out of his wits with threatening him from marriage—

DAUPHINE On, I pray thee.

CUTBEARD And your uncle, sir, he thinks 'twas done by your procurement; therefore he will see the party you wot° of presently,° and if he like her, he says, and that she be so inclining to dumb as I have told him, he swears he will marry her today, instantly, and not defer it a minute longer.
know
immediately

DAUPHINE Excellent! Beyond our expectation!

TRUEWIT Beyond your expectation? By this light, I knew it would be thus.

DAUPHINE Nay, sweet Truewit, forgive me.

TRUEWIT No, I was "ignorantly officious," "impertinent." This was the absurd, weak part.

CLERIMONT Wilt thou ascribe that to merit now was° mere fortune? *which was*

TRUEWIT Fortune? Mere providence. Fortune had not a finger in't. I saw it must necessarily in nature fall out so; my genius[3] is never false to me in these things. Show me how it could be otherwise.

DAUPHINE Nay, gentlemen, contend not; 'tis well now.

TRUEWIT Alas, I let him go on with "inconsiderate" and "rash" and what° he pleased. *whatever*

CLERIMONT Away, thou strange justifier of thyself, to be wiser than thou wert by the event!

TRUEWIT Event! By this light, thou shalt never persuade me but I foresaw it as well as the stars themselves.

DAUPHINE Nay, gentlemen, 'tis well now. Do you two entertain Sir John Daw with discourse while I send her away with instructions.

TRUEWIT I'll be acquainted with her first, by your favor.° *by your leave*

[*Daw and Epicene come forward.*]

CLERIMONT [*to Epicene*] Master Truewit, lady, a friend of ours.

TRUEWIT I am sorry I have not known you sooner, lady, to celebrate this rare virtue of your silence.

CLERIMONT Faith, an you had come sooner you should ha' seen and heard her well celebrated in Sir John Daw's madrigals.

TRUEWIT Jack Daw, God save you. When saw you La Foole?

[*Exeunt Dauphine, Epicene, and Cutbeard.*]

DAW Not since last night, Master Truewit.

TRUEWIT That's miracle! I thought you two had been inseparable.

DAW He's gone to invite his guests.

TRUEWIT Gods so,° 'tis true! What a false memory have I towards that man! I am one;° I met him e'en now upon that he calls his delicate fine black horse, rid° into a foam with posting° from place to place and person to person, to give 'em the cue— *(an oath)* *(of the invitees)* *ridden* *rushing*

CLERIMONT Lest they should forget?

TRUEWIT Yes; there was never poor captain took more pains at a muster to show men° than he at this meal to show friends. *gather recruits*

DAW It is his quarter-feast,[4] sir.

CLERIMONT What, do you say so, Sir John?

TRUEWIT Nay, Jack Daw will not be out,° at the best friend's he has, to the talent° of his wit. Where's his mistress to hear and applaud him? Is she gone? *won't miss the party* *best*

DAW Is Mistress Epicene gone?

CLERIMONT Gone afore with Sir Dauphine, I warrant, to the place.° *(Captain Otter's)*

TRUEWIT Gone afore! That were a manifest injury, a disgrace and a half, to refuse him at such a festival time as this, being a bravery and a wit too.

CLERIMONT Tut, he'll swallow it like cream: he's better read

3. (1) Guardian spirit; (2) natural aptitude.

4. Feast to celebrate the receipt of his quarterly rents.

in *jure civili*[5] than to esteem anything a disgrace is° offered him from a mistress. *that is*

DAW Nay, let her e'en go; she shall sit alone and be dumb in her chamber a week together for John Daw,° I warrant her. Does she refuse me? *as far as I care*

CLERIMONT No, sir, do not take it so to heart. She does not refuse you, but a little neglect you.—Good faith, Truewit, you were to blame to put it into his head that she does refuse him.

TRUEWIT She does refuse him, sir, palpably, however you mince° it. An I were as he, I would swear to speak ne'er a word to her today for't. *make light of*

DAW By this light, no more I will not.

TRUEWIT Nor to anybody else, sir.

DAW Nay, I will not say so, gentlemen.

CLERIMONT [*aside to Truewit*] It had been an excellent happy condition for the company if you could have drawn him to it.

DAW I'll be very melancholic, i'faith.

CLERIMONT As a dog, if I were as you, Sir John.

TRUEWIT Or a snail or a hog-louse.° I would roll myself up for this day; in troth, they should not unwind me. *(tightly curled animals)*

DAW By this picktooth, so I will.

[*He picks his teeth aggressively.*]

CLERIMONT [*aside to Truewit*] 'Tis well done. He begins already to be angry with his teeth.

DAW Will you go, gentlemen?

CLERIMONT Nay, you must walk alone if you be right melancholic, Sir John.

TRUEWIT Yes, sir, we'll dog you; we'll follow you afar off.

[*Exit Daw.*]

CLERIMONT Was there ever such a two yards of knighthood measured out by time to be sold to laughter?

TRUEWIT A mere talking mole!° Hang him, no mushroom was ever so fresh.[6] A fellow so utterly nothing as° he knows not what he would be. *tumor; monstrous birth* *that*

CLERIMONT Let's follow him. But first let's go to Dauphine; he's hovering about the house to hear what news.

TRUEWIT Content. [*Exeunt.*]

2.5

[*Enter*] *Morose, Epicene, Cutbeard,* [*and*] *Mute.*

MOROSE Welcome, Cutbeard. Draw near with your fair charge and in her ear softly entreat her to unmask. [*Epicene unmasks.*] So. Is the door shut? [*Mute makes a bow.*] Enough. Now, Cutbeard, with the same discipline I use to my family,° I will question you. As I conceive, Cutbeard, this gentlewoman is she you have provided and brought, in hope she will fit me in the place and person of a wife? Answer me not but with your leg, unless it be otherwise. (—) Very well *household*

5. Civil law. (Punning on "the rules of civility," or etiquette.)

6. Newly sprung up into polite society, hence unsophisticated. (Mushrooms grow overnight.)

2.5. Morose's house.

done, Cutbeard. I conceive besides, Cutbeard, you have been preacquainted with her birth, education, and qualities, or else you would not prefer° her to my acceptance in the weighty consequence of marriage. (—) This I conceive, Cutbeard. Answer me not but with your leg, unless it be otherwise. (—) Very well done, Cutbeard. Give° aside now a little, and leave me to examine her condition and aptitude to my affection. (*He goes about her and views her.*) She is exceeding fair and of a special good favor,° a sweet composition or harmony of limbs; her temper° of beauty has the true height of my blood.° The knave hath exceedingly well fitted me without;° I will now try her within.—Come near, fair gentlewoman. Let not my behavior seem rude, though unto you, being rare,° it may haply° appear strange. (*She curtsies.*) Nay, lady, you may speak though Cutbeard and my man might not, for of all sounds, only the sweet voice of a fair lady has the just length of mine ears.[1] I beseech you say, lady, out of the first fire of meeting eyes, they say, love is stricken: do you feel any such motion suddenly shot into you from any part you see in me? Ha, lady? (*Curtsy.*) Alas, lady, these answers by silent curtsies from you are too courtless° and simple. I have ever had my breeding in court, and she that shall be my wife must be accomplished with courtly and audacious ornaments. Can you speak, lady?

recommend · *Stand* · *appearance* · *quality* · *arouses my desire* · *as far as externals go* · *unfamiliar / perhaps* · *uncourtly*

EPICENE (*she speaks softly*) Judge you, forsooth.

MOROSE What say you, lady? Speak out, I beseech you.

EPICENE Judge you, forsooth.

MOROSE O'my judgment, a divine softness! But can you naturally, lady, as I enjoin these° by doctrine and industry, refer yourself to the search of my judgment, and—not taking pleasure in your tongue, which is a woman's chiefest pleasure—think it plausible° to answer me by silent gestures so long as my speeches jump right° with what you conceive? (*Curtsy.*) Excellent! Divine! If it were possible she should hold out° thus! Peace,° Cutbeard, thou art made forever, as thou hast made me, if this felicity have lasting; but I will try her further.—Dear lady, I am courtly, I tell you, and I must have mine ears banqueted with pleasant and witty conferences, pretty girds,° scoffs, and dalliance in her that I mean to choose for my bed-fere.° The ladies in court think it a most desperate impair° to their quickness of wit and good carriage if they cannot give occasion for a man to court 'em, and, when an amorous discourse is set on foot, minister as good matter to continue it as himself.[2] And do you alone so much differ from all them, that what they with so much circumstance° affect° and toil for—to seem learned, to seem judicious, to seem sharp and conceited°—you can bury in yourself with silence? And rather trust your graces to the fair conscience° of virtue than to the world's or your own proclamation?

(Mute and Cutbeard) · *commendable; reasonable* · *agree* · *continue* · *Silence* · *mockery* · *bed partner* · *impairment* · *to-do / desire* · *witty* · *consciousness*

EPICENE [*speaking softly*] I should be sorry else.

MOROSE What say you, lady? Good lady, speak out.

1. Is perfectly adapted to my sense of hearing. (But unintentionally suggesting that Morose has long ears, like an ass.)

2. Be as sexually forward in their language as he is.

EPICENE I should be sorry else.

MOROSE That sorrow doth fill me with gladness! O Morose, thou art happy above mankind! Pray that thou mayst contain thyself. I will only put her to it once more, and it shall be with the utmost touch and test of their sex.—But hear me, fair lady, I do also love to see her whom I shall choose for my heifer[3] to be the first and principal in all fashions; precede all the dames at court by a fortnight; have her council of tailors, lineners,° lace-women, embroiderers, and sit with *linen-makers* 'em sometimes twice a day upon French intelligences;° and *the latest fashion news* then come forth varied like Nature, or oft'ner than she, and better by the help of Art, her emulous servant. This do I affect.° And how will you be able, lady, with this frugality of *desire* speech, to give the manifold but necessary instructions for that bodice, these sleeves, those skirts, this cut, that stitch, this embroidery, that lace, this wire, those knots, that ruff, those roses,° this girdle, that fan, the tother scarf, these *shoe ribbons* gloves? Ha! What say you, lady?

EPICENE [*softly*] I'll leave it to you, sir.

MOROSE How, lady? Pray you, rise a note.

EPICENE I leave it to wisdom and you, sir.

MOROSE Admirable creature! I will trouble you no more. I will not sin against so sweet a simplicity. Let me now be bold to print on those divine lips the seal of being mine. [*He kisses her.*] Cutbeard, I give thee the lease of thy house free—thank me not but with thy leg. (—) I know what thou wouldst say: she's poor and her friends° deceased. She has *kinsfolk* brought a wealthy dowry in her silence, Cutbeard, and in respect of her poverty, Cutbeard, I shall have her more loving and obedient, Cutbeard. Go thy ways and get me a minister presently with a soft, low voice to marry us, and pray him he will not be impertinent,° but brief as he can. Away! *digressive* Softly, Cutbeard. [*Exit Cutbeard.*]

[*To Mute*] Sirrah,° conduct your mistress into the dining *(said to inferiors)* room, your now-mistress. [*Exeunt Epicene and Mute.*]

Oh, my felicity! How I shall be revenged on mine insolent kinsman and his plots to fright me from marrying! This night I will get° an heir, and thrust him° out of my blood like a *beget / (Dauphine)* stranger. He would be knighted, forsooth, and thought by that means to reign over me; his title must do it. No, kinsman, I will now make you bring me the tenth lord's and the sixteenth lady's letter,[4] kinsman; and it shall do you no good, kinsman. Your knighthood itself shall come on its knees and it shall be rejected; it shall be sued for its fees to execution[5] and not be redeemed; it shall cheat at the twelvepenny ordinary,° it[6] knighthood, for its diet all the term-time, and tell *cheap tavern* tales for it in the vacation to the hostess;[7] or it knighthood

3. A cow that has not yet borne a calf—Morose's metaphor for "prospective virginal wife."

4. Letter of recommendation. Morose claims either that the previous lords and ladies declined to write on Dauphine's behalf or that they have written but Morose has ignored their appeals. In the lines following, Morose imagines various desperate and humiliating ways of raising money to which Dauphine will have to resort after Morose has disinherited him. Throughout the speech, he uses Dauphine's knighthood, which he resents, as a metonymy for Dauphine himself.

5. Sued for repayment until its goods are seized.

6. Old form of "its."

7. Morose fantasizes that during term-time, when the courts are in sesssion, Dauphine will support himself as a cardsharp, playing with the lawyers and suitors who flock to cheap taverns with money to gamble. During the vacations between court terms, when his usual vic-

shall do worse, take sanctuary in Cole Harbor° and fast. It shall fright all it friends with borrowing° letters, and when one of the fourscore hath brought it knighthood ten shillings, it knighthood shall go to the Cranes, or the Bear at the Bridge-foot,° and be drunk in fear. It shall not have money to discharge one tavern-reckoning, to invite the old creditors to forbear it knighthood, or the new that should be to trust it knighthood.[8] It shall be the tenth name in the bond to take up the commodity of pipkins and stone jugs,[9] and the part thereof shall not furnish it knighthood forth for the attempting of a baker's widow, a brown baker's widow.[1] It shall give it knighthood's name for a stallion° to all gamesome° citizens' wives, and be refused when the master of a dancing school or how-do-you-call-him, the worst reveler in the town, is taken.° It shall want clothes, and by reason of that, wit, to fool to lawyers. It shall not have hope to repair itself by Constantinople, Ireland, or Virginia;[2] but the best and last fortune to it knighthood shall be to make Doll Tearsheet or Kate Common[3] a lady, and so it knighthood may eat. [*Exit.*]

a debtors' refuge
dunning
(names of taverns)
sex partner
lustful
chosen instead

2.6

[*Enter*] *Truewit, Dauphine,* [*and*] *Clerimont.*

TRUEWIT Are you sure he° is not gone by? *(Cutbeard)*
DAUPHINE No, I stayed in the shop° ever since. *Cutbeard's barbershop*
CLERIMONT But he may take the other end of the lane.
DAUPHINE No, I told him I would be here at this end; I appointed him° hither. *told him to meet me*
TRUEWIT What a barbarian it° is to stay,° then! *he / delay*
DAUPHINE Yonder he comes.
CLERIMONT And his charge° left behind him, which is a very good sign, Dauphine. *(Epicene)*

[*Enter*] *Cutbeard.*

DAUPHINE How now, Cutbeard, succeeds it or no?
CUTBEARD Past imagination, sir, *omnia secunda;*[1] you could not have prayed to have had it so well. *Saltat senex,*[2] as it is i'the proverb; he does triumph in his felicity, admires the party! He has given me the lease of my house too! And I am now going for a silent minister to marry 'em, and away.

---

tims are out of town, Dauphine will have to entertain the tavern hostess with stories (and perhaps also provide sexual services) in return for food.

8. Your shabby knighthood won't have enough money to pay even your tavern bill, to stave off the demands for payment of the creditors to whom you already owe money, or to encourage prospective new creditors to extend you credit.

9. On "commodity," see note at 1.4.69. A pipkin is an earthenware pot; stone jugs are made of stoneware, coarse fired clay. Morose imagines Dauphine as the tenth in line to be paid off from any profits realized from the sale of these cheap goods.

1. And what you manage to glean in the way of ready cash after you have sold these nearly worthless commodities won't be enough to tempt a baker's widow into marrying you, not even the widow of a baker of brown bread. (Widows of shopkeepers controlled the estates they inherited and thus were desired as wives by fortune hunters, but socially such a marriage would be a step down for a gentleman. Bakers of brown bread served the lower orders and were poor themselves.)

2. Places where the financially desperate attempted to mend their fortunes.

3. Whores, who can support Dauphine by prostitution. The wife of Dauphine, a knight, would be called a lady irrespective of her profession.

2.6. A street near Cutbeard's barbershop.

1. All according to plan. (Latin.)

2. The old man leaps (for joy).

TRUEWIT 'Slight, get one o'the silenced ministers;[3] a zealous brother would torment him purely.° *thoroughly*

CUTBEARD *Cum privilegio,*[4] sir.

DAUPHINE Oh, by no means, let's do nothing to hinder it now; when 'tis done and finished I am for you, for any device of vexation.

CUTBEARD And that shall be within this half hour, upon my dexterity, gentlemen. Contrive what you can in the meantime, *bonis avibus.*[5] [*Exit.*]

CLERIMONT How the slave° doth Latin it! *wretch*

TRUEWIT It would be made a jest to posterity,° sirs, this day's mirth, if ye will.° *remember for generations / if you're willing*

CLERIMONT Beshrew his° heart that will not, I pronounce. *A curse on whoever's*

DAUPHINE And for my part. What is't?

TRUEWIT To translate° all La Foole's company and his feast hither today to celebrate this bride-ale.° *move / wedding feast*

DAUPHINE Ay, marry, but how will't be done?

TRUEWIT I'll undertake the directing of all the lady guests thither, and then the meat must follow.

CLERIMONT For God's sake, let's effect it. It will be an excellent comedy of affliction, so many several° noises. *various*

DAUPHINE But are they not at the other place° already, think you? *(Tom Otter's)*

TRUEWIT I'll warrant you for the College-honors:° one o'their faces has not the priming color° laid on yet, nor the other her smock sleeked.° *Collegiate Ladies / cosmetic base coat / petticoat ironed*

CLERIMONT Oh, but they'll rise earlier than ordinary to a feast.

TRUEWIT Best go see, and assure ourselves.

CLERIMONT Who knows the house?

TRUEWIT I'll lead you. Were you never there yet?

DAUPHINE Not I.

CLERIMONT Nor I.

TRUEWIT Where ha' you lived then? Not know Tom Otter!

CLERIMONT No. For God's sake, what is he?

TRUEWIT An excellent animal, equal with your Daw or La Foole if not transcendent, and does Latin it as much as your barber. He is his wife's subject; he calls her princess, and at such times as these follows her up and down the house like a page with his hat off, partly for heat, partly for reverence. At this instant he is marshaling of his bull, bear, and horse.

DAUPHINE What be those, in the name of Sphinx?[6]

TRUEWIT Why, sir, he has been a great man at the Bear Garden[7] in his time, and from that subtle sport has ta'en the witty denomination° of his chief carousing° cups. One he calls his bull, another his bear, another his horse. And then he has his lesser glasses that he calls his deer and his ape, and several degrees of 'em too, and never is well nor thinks *names / drinking*

3. See 2.2.75–81 and note. Puritans were notorious for long prayers and sermons.
4. "With privilege"; i.e., let's not interrupt my plan now.
5. If luck holds. (Literally, "the birds of omen being good," in Latin.)
6. Mythological riddling monster. (An oath.)
7. Bearbaiting arena. Bear- or bullbaiting involved tying a bear or bull to a stake by a loose chain and letting specially bred dogs, the ancestors of modern pit bulls, attack it. Variants of this popular sport involved horses, deer, monkeys, and other animals.

any entertainment perfect till these be brought out and set o'the cupboard.° *sideboard*

CLERIMONT For God's love! We should miss this if we should not go.

TRUEWIT Nay, he has a thousand things as good that will speak him° all day. He will rail on his wife with certain commonplaces behind her back, and to her face— *express his character*

DAUPHINE No more of him. Let's go see him, I petition you.

[*Exeunt.*]

3.1

[*Enter*] *Otter* [*and*] *Mrs. Otter.*

OTTER Nay, good princess, hear me *pauca verba.*° *a few words (Latin)*

MRS. OTTER By that light, I'll ha' you chained up with your bulldogs and bear-dogs if you be not civil the sooner. I'll send you to kennel, i'faith. You were best bait me with your bull, bear, and horse? Never a time that the courtiers or Collegiates come to the house but you make it a Shrove Tuesday!° I would have you get your Whitsuntide velvet cap and your staff i'your hand to entertain 'em;[1] yes, in troth, do. *(see 1.1.154–55 n)*

OTTER Not so, princess, neither, but under correction,[2] sweet princess, gi' me leave—these things I am known to the courtiers by. It is reported to them for my humor,° and they receive it so, and do expect it. Tom Otter's bull, bear, and horse is known all over England *in rerum natura.*° *idiosyncrasy* *in the nature of things*

MRS. OTTER 'Fore me, I will na-ture 'em over to Paris Garden° and na-ture you thither too, if you pronounce° 'em again.[3] Is a bear a fit beast, or a bull, to mix in society with great ladies—think, i'your discretion, in any good polity?° *a bearbaiting arena* *mention* *social group*

OTTER The horse, then, good princess.

MRS. OTTER Well, I am contented for the horse. They love to be well horsed,[4] I know. I love it myself.

[*Enter*] *Truewit, Clerimont,* [*and*] *Dauphine* [*unnoticed by the Otters*].

OTTER And it is a delicate fine horse, this. *Poetarum Pegasus.*[5] Under correction, princess, Jupiter did turn himself into a—*taurus,* or bull,[6] under correction, good princess.

MRS. OTTER By my integrity, I'll send you over to the Bankside,[7] I'll commit you to the Master of the Garden° if I hear but a syllable more. Must my house or my roof be polluted with the scent of bears and bulls when it is perfumed for great ladies? Is this according to the instrument° when I *chief bear-trainer* *contract*

3.1. Otter's house.

1. Otter apparently used to wear a fancy hat when baiting the bears before the court, common entertainment at Easter time and during Whitsuntide (the week beginning with Pentecost, or Whitsunday, the seventh Sunday after Easter). The staff is a bearbaiter's standard equipment, used to control the fighting between dogs and bears.

2. Subject to your correction. (A deferential formula used in addressing an authority.)

3. Mrs. Otter, unable to follow her husband's Latin, scornfully uses the word "nature" as if it meant "drive" or "beat."

4. (1) Provided with horses; (2) in the saddle sexually.

5. Pegasus of the Poets. (Latin.) Pegasus, the flying horse, was associated with poetic inspiration.

6. In his courtship of the mortal woman Europa, whom Jupiter abducted by assuming the form of a bull and carrying her on his back to Crete.

7. District on the south bank of the Thames where bearbaiting arenas (and theaters) were located.

married you? That I would be princess and reign in mine own house, and you would be my subject and obey me? What° did you bring me should make you thus peremptory? Do I allow you your half crown° a day to spend where you will among your gamesters, to vex and torment me at such times as these? Who gives you your maintenance, I pray you? Who allows you your horse meat[8] and man's meat? Your three suits of apparel a year? Your four pair of stockings, one silk, three worsted? Your clean linen, your bands,° and cuffs when I can get you to wear 'em? 'Tis mar'l° you ha 'em on now. Who graces you with courtiers or great personages to speak to you out of their coaches, and come home to your house? Were you ever so much as looked upon by a lord or a lady before I married you, but on the Easter or Whitsun holidays? And then out at the Banqueting House[9] window, when Ned Whiting or George Stone° were at the stake?

What financial assets
2s. 6d.
collars
a marvel
famous bears

TRUEWIT (*aside to Dauphine and Clerimont*) For God's sake, let's go stave her off him.[1]

MRS. OTTER Answer me to that. And did not I take you up from thence in an old greasy buff-doublet with points, and green velvet sleeves out at the elbows?[2] You forget this.

TRUEWIT (*aside to Dauphine and Clerimont*) She'll worry him,[3] if we help not in time.

MRS. OTTER Oh, here are some o'the gallants! Go to, behave yourself distinctly° and with good morality, or I protest I'll take away your exhibition.°

with distinction
allowance

3.2

Truewit, Clerimont, [*and*] *Dauphine* [*come forward*].

TRUEWIT By your leave, fair Mistress Otter, I'll be bold to enter these gentlemen in your acquaintance.

MRS. OTTER It shall not be obnoxious or *difficile*,° sir.

difficult (French)

TRUEWIT [*to Otter*] How does my noble captain? Is the bull, bear, and horse *in rerum natura*° still?

(see 3.1.13)

OTTER Sir, *sic visum superis.*[1]

MRS. OTTER [*to Otter*] I would you would but intimate° 'em, do. Go your ways in, and get toasts and butter made for the woodcocks.° That's a fit province for you.

dare mention (sarcastic)
fowl for eating

[*Exit Otter. The gentlemen speak privately.*]

CLERIMONT Alas, what a tyranny is this poor fellow married to!

TRUEWIT Oh, but the sport will be anon, when we get him loose.°

(from his wife)

DAUPHINE Dares he ever speak?

8. Food for horses. (The "instrument"—line 28—between Mrs. Otter and her husband has specifications normally found in a contract between an employer and a household servant.)
9. King James's palace, where bears were baited outside, below a balcony.
1. In bearbaiting, when the bear attacked the dogs too vehemently, it was beaten off with a heavy staff. (See note 1 on p. 808.)
2. Buff was a tough leather used in military garments; points were laces for attaching men's leggings, which were out of fashion by 1609. Mrs. Otter is emphasizing how marriage to her improved her husband's finances, and hence his clothes.
3. Chew him. (Continuing the bearbaiting analogy.)
3.2. The scene continues.
1. As it pleases the gods. (Latin.)

TRUEWIT No Anabaptist ever railed with the like license.[2] But mark her language in the meantime, I beseech you.

[*Mrs. Otter approaches them.*]

MRS. OTTER Gentlemen, you are very aptly come. My cousin, Sir Amorous, will be here briefly.° *shortly*

TRUEWIT In good time, lady. Was not Sir John Daw here to ask for him and the company?

MRS. OTTER I cannot assure° you, Master Truewit. Here was a very melancholy knight in a ruff that demanded my subject for° somebody, a gentleman, I think. *inform* / *asked Otter about*

CLERIMONT Ay, that was he, lady.

MRS. OTTER But he departed straight,° I can resolve° you. *right away / inform*

DAUPHINE What an excellent choice phrase this lady expresses in!

TRUEWIT Oh, sir, she is the only authentical courtier, that is not naturally bred one, in the city.

MRS. OTTER You have taken that report upon trust, gentlemen.

TRUEWIT No, I assure you, the court governs it so, lady, in your behalf.° *models itself on you*

MRS. OTTER I am the servant of the court and courtiers, sir.

TRUEWIT They are rather your idolaters.

MRS. OTTER Not so, sir.

[*Enter*] *Cutbeard.* [*He speaks privately with the three gentlemen.*]

DAUPHINE How now, Cutbeard? Any cross?° *impediment*

CUTBEARD Oh, no, sir: *omnia bene.*° 'Twas never better o'the hinges,° all's sure. I have so pleased him with a curate that he's gone to't almost with the delight he hopes for soon. *all is well* / *It works smoothly*

DAUPHINE What is he for a vicar?[3]

CUTBEARD One that has catched a cold, sir, and can scarce be heard six inches off, as if he spoke out of a bulrush that were not picked, or his throat were full of pith:° a fine quick fellow, and an excellent barber° of prayers. I came to tell you, sir, that you might *omnem movere lapidem*,[4] as they say, be ready with your vexation. *stuff* / *shortener*

DAUPHINE Gramercy,° honest Cutbeard. Be thereabouts with thy key to let us in. *Thanks*

CUTBEARD I will not fail you, sir. *Ad manum.*° [*Exit.*] *I'll be at hand*

TRUEWIT Well, I'll go watch° my coaches. *watch for*

CLERIMONT Do; and we'll send Daw to you if you meet him not. [*Exit Truewit.*]

MRS. OTTER Is Master Truewit gone?

DAUPHINE Yes, lady, there is some unfortunate business fallen out.

MRS. OTTER So I judged by the physiognomy° of the fellow that came in; and I had a dream last night too of the new pageant and my Lady Mayoress,[5] which is always very ominous to me. I told it my Lady Haughty t'other day, when Her *expression*

2. The Anabaptists were a radical Protestant sect often accused of political violence and subversion; since they did not accept the secular governance of religious practices, they allowed the concealment of one's true beliefs from interrogators. Cf. Otter, who pretends to accept his wife's authority but rails violently in her absence.

3. What kind of vicar is he?

4. Leave no stone unturned. (Latin.)

5. A pageant was performed annually on the investiture of the new Lord Mayor. The Lady Mayoress was his wife.

Honor came hither to see some china stuffs,° and she expounded it out of Artemidorus,[6] and I have found it since very true. It has done me many affronts.

porcelain

CLERIMONT Your dream, lady?

MRS. OTTER Yes, sir, anything I do but dream o'the city.[7] It stained me a damask tablecloth cost° me eighteen pound, at one time; and burnt me a black satin gown as I stood by the fire at my Lady Centaur's chamber in the College, another time. A third time, at the lord's masque, it dropped° all my wire[8] and my ruff with wax candle, that I could not go up to the banquet. A fourth time, as I was taking coach to go to Ware[9] to meet a friend, it dashed me a new suit all over—a crimson satin doublet[1] and black velvet skirts—with a brewer's horse, that I was fain to go in and shift me,° and kept° my chamber a leash of° days for the anguish of it.

which cost / *dripped on* / *change* / *kept to / three*

DAUPHINE These were dire mischances, lady.

CLERIMONT I would not dwell in the city an 'twere so fatal° to me.

ominous; perilous

MRS. OTTER Yes, sir, but I do take advice of my doctor to dream of it as little as I can.

DAUPHINE You do well, Mistress Otter.

[*Enter Daw, whom Clerimont takes aside.*]

MRS. OTTER Will it please you to enter the house farther, gentlemen?

DAUPHINE And° your favor, lady; but we stay to speak with a knight, Sir John Daw, who is here come. We shall follow you, lady.

And farther into

MRS. OTTER At your own time, sir. It is my cousin Sir Amorous his° feast.—

Amorous'

DAUPHINE I know it, lady.

MRS. OTTER And mine together. But it is for his honor, and therefore I take no name of° it, more than of the place.

credit for

DAUPHINE You are a bounteous kinswoman.

MRS. OTTER Your servant, sir. [*Exit.*]

3.3

Clerimont [*and*] *Daw* [*come forward to join*] *Dauphine.*

CLERIMONT Why, do not you know it, Sir John Daw?

DAW No, I am a rook° if I do.

dupe; jackdaw

CLERIMONT I'll tell you, then, she's married by this time. And whereas you were put i'the head° that she was gone with Sir Dauphine, I assure you Sir Dauphine has been the noblest, honestest friend to you that ever gentleman of your quality° could boast of. He has discovered° the whole plot, and made

made to imagine / *social rank* / *revealed*

6. Late classical Greek author of a book of dream symbolism.
7. The city of London (as contrasted with the more fashionable court). Mrs. Otter's dreams, which represent a series of social embarrassments, betray her anxiety about the figure she cuts in London society.
8. Used to support the ruff.
9. Ware, north of London, was a place of assignation.
1. Expensive and doubly inappropriate dress, since red satin was reserved for the upper aristocracy and a doublet was a man's upper garment. The first decade of the seventeenth century saw widespread flouting of the sumptuary laws, which were supposed to regulate attire by class and sex, and, from preachers and moralists, much inveighing against the violations.
3.3. The scene continues.

your mistress so acknowledging and indeed so ashamed of her injury to you that she desires you to forgive her and but grace her wedding with your presence today. She is to be married to a very good fortune, she says, his uncle, old Morose; and she willed me in private to tell you that she shall be able to do you more favors,° and with more security, now than before. *i.e., sexual favors*

DAW Did she say so, i'faith?

CLERIMONT Why, what do you think of me, Sir John! Ask Sir Dauphine.

DAW Nay, I believe you.—Good Sir Dauphine, did she desire me to forgive her?

DAUPHINE I assure you, Sir John, she did.

DAW Nay, then, I do with all my heart, and I'll be jovial.

CLERIMONT Yes, for look you, sir, this was the injury to you. La Foole intended this feast to honor her bridal day, and made you the property° to invite the College Ladies and promise to bring her, and then at the time she should have appeared as his friend, to have given you the *dor*.° Whereas now Sir Dauphine has brought her to a feeling° of it, with this kind of satisfaction, that you shall bring all the ladies to the place where she is and be very jovial, and there she will have a dinner, which shall be in your name,° and so disappoint La Foole to make you good again and, as it were, a saver[1] i'the main. *means* *humiliated you* *regret* *honor*

DAW As I am a knight, I honor her and forgive her heartily.

CLERIMONT About it then presently.° Truewit is gone before to confront the coaches and to acquaint you with so much if he meet you. Join with him, and 'tis well. *immediately*

[*Enter*] *La Foole.*

See, here comes your antagonist, but take you no notice, but be very jovial.

LA FOOLE Are the ladies come, Sir John Daw, and your mistress? [*Exit Daw.*] Sir Dauphine! You are exceeding welcome, and honest Master Clerimont. Where's my cousin?° Did you see no Collegiates, gentlemen? *(Mrs. Otter)*

DAUPHINE Collegiates! Do you not hear, Sir Amorous, how you are abused?

LA FOOLE How, sir?

CLERIMONT Will you speak so kindly to Sir John Daw, that has done you such an affront?

LA FOOLE Wherein, gentlemen? Let me be a suitor to you to know, I beseech you!

CLERIMONT Why, sir, his mistress is married today to Sir Dauphine's uncle, your cousin's neighbor, and he has diverted all the ladies and all your company thither, to frustrate your provision and stick a disgrace upon you. He was here now to have enticed us away from you too, but we told him his own,° I think. *told him off*

LA FOOLE Has Sir John Daw wronged me so inhumanly?

1. Gambler who avoids losses.

DAUPHINE He has done it, Sir Amorous, most maliciously and treacherously, but if you'll be ruled by us, you shall quit° *repay* him, i'faith.

LA FOOLE Good gentlemen! I'll make one,° *cooperate* believe it. How, I pray?

DAUPHINE Marry, sir, get me your pheasants and your godwits° and your best meat,° *edible fowl / food* and dish it in silver dishes of your cousin's presently, and say nothing, but clap me a clean towel about you like a sewer,[2] and, bareheaded, march afore it with a good confidence—'tis but over the way, hard by—and we'll second you, where you shall set it o'the board° *table* and bid 'em welcome to't, which shall show 'tis yours and disgrace his preparation utterly; and for° *as for* your cousin, whereas she should be troubled here at home with care of making and giving welcome, she shall transfer all that labor thither and be a principal guest herself, sit ranked with the College-honors and be honored, and have her health drunk as often, as bare,[3] and as loud as the best of 'em.

LA FOOLE I'll go tell her presently. It shall be done, that's resolved.° *settled* [*Exit.*]

CLERIMONT I thought he would not hear it out but 'twould take° *please; trick* him.

DAUPHINE Well, there be guests and meat now; how shall we do for music?

CLERIMONT The smell of the venison going through the street will invite one noise° *consort* of fiddlers or other.

DAUPHINE I would it would call the trumpeters thither.

CLERIMONT Faith, there is hope; they have intelligence° *news* of all feasts. There's good correspondence betwixt them and the London cooks. 'Tis twenty to one but we have 'em.

DAUPHINE 'Twill be a most solemn day for my uncle and an excellent fit of mirth for us.

CLERIMONT Ay, if we can hold up the emulation° *rivalry* betwixt Foole and Daw, and never bring them to expostulate.[4]

DAUPHINE Tut, flatter 'em both, as Truewit says, and you may take their understandings in a purse-net.[5] They'll believe themselves to be just such men as we make 'em, neither more nor less. They have nothing, not the use of their senses, but by tradition.° *what they're told*

[*La Foole*] *enters like a sewer.*

CLERIMONT See! Sir Amorous has his towel on already. [*To La Foole*] Have you persuaded your cousin?

LA FOOLE Yes, 'tis very feasible. She'll do anything, she says, rather than the La Fooles shall be disgraced.

DAUPHINE She is a noble kinswoman. It will be such a pestling[6] device, Sir Amorous! It will pound all your enemy's practices to powder, and blow him up with his own mine, his own train.[7]

2. Waiter (as a servant-class occupation, a serious loss of caste for a knight).
3. Bareheaded (out of respect for the person toasted).
4. Discuss the matter between themselves.
5. Small net bag for catching rabbits or fish.
6. Effective at grinding, like a pestle in a mortar.
7. (1) Track of gunpowder; (2) plot.

LA FOOLE Nay, we'll give fire, I warrant you.

CLERIMONT But you must carry it° privately, without any noise, and take no notice by any means— *bring it off*

[*Enter*] *Otter.*

OTTER Gentlemen, my princess says you shall have all her silver dishes, *festinate,*° and she's gone to alter her tire° a little and go with you— *right away / attire*

CLERIMONT And yourself too, Captain Otter.

DAUPHINE By any means, sir.

OTTER Yes, sir, I do mean it, but I would entreat my cousin Sir Amorous, and you gentlemen, to be suitors to my princess that I may carry my bull and my bear, as well as my horse.

CLERIMONT That you shall do, Captain Otter.

LA FOOLE My cousin will never consent, gentlemen.

DAUPHINE She must consent, Sir Amorous, to reason.

LA FOOLE Why, she says they are no *decorum*° among ladies. *suitable thing*

OTTER But they are *decora,*° and that's better, sir. *suitable things (plural)*

CLERIMONT Ay, she must hear argument. Did not Pasiphaë, who was a queen, love a bull? And was not Callisto, the mother of Arcas, turned into a bear and made a star, Mistress Ursula, i'the heavens?[8]

OTTER Oh, God, that I could ha' said as much! I will have these stories painted i'the Bear Garden, *ex Ovidii Metamorphosi.*[9]

DAUPHINE Where is your princess, Captain? Pray be our leader.

OTTER That I shall, sir.

CLERIMONT Make haste, good Sir Amorous. [*Exeunt.*]

3.4

[*Enter*] *Morose, Epicene, Parson,* [*and*] *Cutbeard.*

MOROSE [*to the Parson*] Sir, there's an angel° for yourself, and a brace of° angels for your cold. Muse° not at this manage° of my bounty. It is fit we should thank Fortune, double to° Nature, for any benefit she confers upon us; besides, it is your imperfection,° but my solace. *gold coin* *two / Wonder / handling* *partner to* *affliction*

PARSON (*speaks as having a cold*) I thank Your Worship, so is it mine, now.

MOROSE What says he, Cutbeard?

CUTBEARD He says, *praesto,*° sir, whensoever Your Worship needs him, he can be ready with the like. He got this cold with sitting up late and singing catches° with cloth workers.[1] *at your service* *rounds*

MOROSE No more. I thank him.

PARSON God keep Your Worship, and give you much joy with your fair spouse. (*He coughs.*) Umh, umh!

MOROSE Oh, oh! Stay, Cutbeard! Let him give me five shil-

8. Pasiphaë, Queen of Crete, had sex with a bull and gave birth to the Minotaur, a monster that was half bull and half human; Callisto, who was changed into a bear by Hera, was eventually set in the heavens as Ursa Major, the Great Bear.

9. Out of Ovid's *Metamorphoses*. (Latin.)

3.4. Morose's house, the setting of the remainder of the play.

1. English weavers had a long tradition of religious dissent; their numbers were augmented in the sixteenth century by zealous Protestant refugees from France. They were known for their hymn singing.

lings of my money back. As it is bounty to reward benefits, so is it equity to mulct° injuries. I will have it. What says he? *impose a fine for*

CUTBEARD He cannot change it, sir.

MOROSE It must be changed.

CUTBEARD [*aside to Parson*] Cough again.

MOROSE What says he?

CUTBEARD He will cough out the rest, sir.

PARSON (*again*) Umh, umh, umh.

MOROSE Away, away with him! Stop his mouth! Away! I forgive it—

[*He pushes the Parson out the door. Cutbeard follows.*]

EPICENE Fie, Master Morose, that you will use this violence to a man of the church!

MOROSE How!

EPICENE It does not become your gravity or breeding,° as you pretend, in court, to have offered this outrage on a waterman° or any more boisterous creature, much less on a man of his civil° coat. *upbringing* *Thames boatman* *sober, dignified*

MOROSE You can speak, then!

EPICENE Yes, sir.

MOROSE Speak out, I mean.

EPICENE Ay, sir. Why, did you think you had married a statue? Or a motion,° only? One of the French puppets, with the eyes turned with a wire?[2] Or some innocent° out of the hospital, that would stand with her hands thus, and a plaice° mouth, and look upon you? *marionette* *retarded person* *fishlike*

MOROSE Oh, immodesty! A manifest woman![3] [*Calls*] What, Cutbeard!

EPICENE Nay, never quarrel with Cutbeard, sir; it is too late now. I confess it doth bate° somewhat of the modesty I had when I writ simply maid,[4] but I hope I shall make it a stock still competent° to the estate and dignity of your wife. *diminish* *an amount sufficient*

MOROSE She can talk!

EPICENE Yes, indeed, sir.

MOROSE [*calling*] What, sirrah! None of my knaves there?

[*Enter Mute.*]

Where is this impostor Cutbeard? [*Mute points to the exit.*]

EPICENE Speak to him, fellow, speak to him. I'll have none of this coacted,° unnatural dumbness in my house, in a family where I govern. [*Exit Mute.*] *forced*

MOROSE She is my regent already! I have married a Penthesilea, a Semiramis, sold my liberty to a distaff![5]

2. Such puppets could be made to move their eyes by means of a thin wire controlled by the puppeteer.

3. "Manifest" means obvious, but the word was often used to refer to clearly guilty criminals; Morose means that Epicene is clearly evidencing the female vices deplored by the writers of misogynist tracts, such as talkativeness and a domineering nature. The joke is on Morose, however, since Epicene's gender is anything but "manifest."

4. When I styled myself simply as an unmarried woman.

5. Penthesilea and Semiramis were warrior queens of ancient times. A distaff is a spinning stick, often used metonymically to refer to a woman.

3.5

[*Enter*] *Truewit.*

TRUEWIT Where's Master Morose?

MOROSE Is he come again? Lord have mercy upon me!

TRUEWIT I wish you all joy, Mistress Epicene, with your grave and honorable match.

EPICENE I return you the thanks, Master Truewit, so° [*that so*] friendly a wish deserves.

MOROSE She has acquaintance, too!

TRUEWIT God save you, sir, and give you all contentment in your fair choice here. Before I was the bird of night to you, the owl,[1] but now I am the messenger of peace, a dove, and bring you the glad wishes of many friends to the celebration of this good hour.

MOROSE What hour, sir?

TRUEWIT Your marriage hour, sir. I commend your resolution, that—notwithstanding all the dangers I laid afore you, in the voice of a night-crow° [*owl*]—would yet go on and be yourself. It shows you are a man constant to your own ends and upright to your purposes, that would not be put off with left-handed° [*sinister*] cries.

MOROSE How should you arrive at the knowledge of so much?

TRUEWIT Why, did you ever hope, sir, committing the secrecy of it to a barber, that less than the whole town should know it? You might as well ha' told it the conduit or the bake-house, or the infantry that follow the court,[2] and with more security. Could your gravity forget so old and noted a remnant° [*literary quotation*] as *lippis et tonsoribus notum?*[3] Well, sir, forgive it yourself now, the fault, and be communicable with your friends. Here will be three or four fashionable ladies from the College to visit you presently, and their train of minions° [*favorites*] and followers.

MOROSE [*calling*] Bar my doors! Bar my doors! Where are all my eaters,° [*dependents*] my mouths now?

[*Enter servants.*]

Bar up my doors, you varlets!° [*menials; knaves*]

EPICENE He is a varlet that stirs to such an office. Let 'em stand open. I would see him that dares move his eyes° [*even his eyes*] toward it. Shall I have a *barricado*° [*barricade*] made against my friends, to be barred of any pleasure they can bring in to me with honorable visitation?

MOROSE Oh, Amazonian impudence![4]

TRUEWIT Nay, faith, in this, sir, she speaks but reason, and methinks is more continent° [*restrained*] than you. Would you go to bed so presently,° [*quickly*] sir, afore noon? A man of your head and hair° [*of your dignity*] should owe more to that reverend ceremony, and not mount

3.5. The scene continues.

1. Considered a bird of ill omen.

2. A conduit was a public water main where one could obtain water for the household; a bake-house was an oven where bread dough could be brought for baking. Both places, not surprisingly, were important sites for gossip. The infantry were hangers-on who followed the King and his court on "progress" (see 2.2.111 and note).

3. Known to the bleary-eyed and the barbers (that is, to everyone). (From Horace, *Satires*, 1.7.)

4. The Amazons were a mythical tribe of women warriors who dispensed with men except for breeding purposes.

the marriage-bed like a town bull or a mountain goat, but stay the due season, and ascend it then with religion and fear.° Those delights are to be steeped in the humor° and silence of the night, and give the day to other open pleasures and jollities of feast, of music, of revels, of discourse. We'll have all, sir, that may make your Hymen[5] high and happy. *awe / moisture; mood*

MOROSE Oh, my torment, my torment!

TRUEWIT Nay, if you endure the first half hour, sir, so tediously and with this irksomeness, what comfort or hope can this fair gentlewoman make to° herself hereafter, in the consideration of so many years as are to come— *anticipate for*

MOROSE Of my affliction. Good sir, depart, and let her do it alone.

TRUEWIT I have done, sir.

MOROSE That cursed barber!

TRUEWIT Yes, faith, a cursed wretch indeed, sir.

MOROSE I have married his cittern,[6] that's common to all men. Some plague above the plague—

TRUEWIT —All Egypt's ten plagues[7]—

MOROSE —revenge me on him!

TRUEWIT 'Tis very well, sir. If you laid on a curse or two more, I'll assure you he'll bear 'em. As, that he may get the pox° with seeking to cure it, sir? Or that while he is curling another man's hair, his own may drop off?[8] Or for burning some male bawd's lock,° he may have his brain beat out with the curling iron? *syphilis* / *lock of hair*

MOROSE No, let the wretch live wretched. May he get the itch, and his shop so lousy° as no man dare come at him, nor he come at no man! *full of head lice*

TRUEWIT Ay, and if° he would swallow all his balls° for pills, let not them purge him.° *even if / (of soap)* / *may he stay constipated*

MOROSE Let his warming pan be ever cold!

TRUEWIT A perpetual frost underneath it, sir.

MOROSE Let him never hope to see fire again—

TRUEWIT —But in hell, sir.

MOROSE His chairs be always empty, his scissors rust, and his combs mold in their cases!

TRUEWIT Very dreadful, that! And may he lose the invention, sir, of carving lanterns in paper.[9]

MOROSE Let there be no bawd carted that year to employ a basin of his,[1] but let him be glad to eat his sponge for bread!

TRUEWIT And drink lotium[2] to it, and much good do him.

MOROSE Or for want of bread—

TRUEWIT Eat earwax, sir. I'll help you. Or draw his own teeth, and add them to the lute string.[3]

MOROSE No, beat the old ones to powder, and make bread of them.

TRUEWIT Yes, make meal[4] o'the millstones.

5. Wedding. (Hymen was the Greek god of marriage.)
6. Stringed guitarlike instrument kept in barbershops to entertain waiting customers; also, often played by prostitutes.
7. Sent by God when Pharoah would not release the Hebrews from slavery.
8. Loss of hair is a symptom of syphilis.
9. Paper lanterns were for sale in barbershops.
1. Prostitutes were punished by being tied to a cart and whipped through the streets; someone preceded them, banging on a basin, to draw a crowd.
2. Stale urine (used as a hairdressing).
3. Barbers pulled teeth and hung them out on lute strings as an advertisement.
4. Flour (because he has nothing but the stone to eat).

MOROSE May all the botches° and burns that he has cured on others break out upon him! *scabs*

TRUEWIT And he now forget the cure of 'em in himself, sir, or if he do remember it, let him ha' scraped all his linen into lint for't, and have not a rag left him to set up with.[5]

MOROSE Let him never set up again, but have the gout in his hands forever! Now, no more, sir.

TRUEWIT Oh, that last was too high set!° You might go less with him, i'faith, and be revenged enough: as, that he be never able to new-paint his pole°— *extreme* / *barber's pole*

MOROSE Good sir, no more. I forgot myself.

TRUEWIT Or want credit to take up with° a comb-maker— *get an advance from*

MOROSE No more, sir.

TRUEWIT Or, having broken his glass° in a former despair, fall now into a much greater, of ever getting another— *mirror*

MOROSE I beseech you, no more!

TRUEWIT Or, that he never be trusted with trimming of any but chimney sweepers°— *(who are poor and filthy)*

MOROSE Sir—

TRUEWIT Or, may he cut a collier's[6] throat with his razor by chance-medley,° and yet hang for't. *accidental homicide*

MOROSE I will forgive him, rather than hear any more. I beseech you, sir!

3.6

[Enter] Daw, Haughty, Centaur, Mavis, [and] Trusty.

DAW This way, madam.

MOROSE Oh, the sea breaks in upon me! Another flood! An inundation! I shall be o'erwhelmed with noise. It beats already at my shores. I feel an earthquake in myself for 't.

DAW Give° you joy, mistress. *God give*

MOROSE Has she servants,° too! *male admirers*

DAW I have brought some ladies here to see and know you. (*She [Epicene] kisses them severally° as he presents them.*) My Lady Haughty; this my Lady Centaur; Mistress Doll Mavis; Mistress Trusty, my Lady Haughty's woman. Where's your husband? Let's see him. Can he endure no noise? Let me come to him. *each*

MOROSE What nomenclator° is this! *announcer of guests*

TRUEWIT Sir John Daw, sir, your wife's servant, this.

MOROSE A daw, and her servant! Oh, 'tis decreed, 'tis decreed of me,° an° she have such servants. [*He starts to exit.*] *my fate is sealed / if*

TRUEWIT [*intercepting him*] Nay, sir, you must kiss the ladies; you must not go away now; they come toward you to seek you out.

HAUGHTY I'faith, Master Morose, would you steal a marriage thus, in the midst of so many friends, and not acquaint us? Well, I'll kiss you, notwithstanding the justice of my quarrel. [*To Epicene*] You shall give me leave, mistress, to use a

5. To get back in business with. (Lint was a fluffy wound-dressing material made by unraveling and scraping linen rags; Truewit anticipates that Cutbeard will use up all his lint treating the "botches and burns" Morose has just wished upon him.)

6. Charcoal-seller or coal miner—like the chimney sweep, poor and dirty.

3.6. The scene continues.

becoming familiarity with your husband.

[*She kisses Morose.*]

EPICENE Your Ladyship does me an honor in it to let me know he is so worthy your favor, as you have done both him and me grace to visit so unprepared a pair to entertain you.

MOROSE Compliment! Compliment!

EPICENE But I must lay the burden of that upon my servant° here. — *i.e., Daw*

HAUGHTY It shall not need, Mistress Morose, we will all bear° rather than one shall be oppressed. — *(with sexual suggestion)*

MOROSE I know it; and you will teach her the faculty,° if she be to learn it. — *skill*

[*The Collegiate Ladies converse among themselves.*]

HAUGHTY Is this the silent woman?

CENTAUR Nay, she has found her tongue since she was married, Master Truewit says.

HAUGHTY Oh, Master Truewit! [*Truewit joins them.*] Save you. What kind of creature is your° bride here? She speaks, methinks. — *this*

TRUEWIT Yes, madam, believe it, she is a gentlewoman of very absolute[1] behavior, and of a good race.° — *family*

HAUGHTY And Jack Daw told us she could not speak.

TRUEWIT So it was carried in plot, madam, to put her upon this old fellow, by Sir Dauphine his nephew and one or two more of us; but she is a woman of an excellent assurance and an extraordinary happy° wit and tongue. You shall see her make rare° sport with Daw ere night. — *apt, quick*; *superb*

HAUGHTY And he brought us to laugh at her!

TRUEWIT That falls out° often, madam, that he that thinks himself the master wit is the master fool. I assure Your Ladyship, ye cannot laugh at her. — *happens*

HAUGHTY No, we'll have her to the College; an she have wit she shall be one of us. Shall she not, Centaur? We'll make her a Collegiate.

CENTAUR Yes, faith, madam, and Mavis and she will set up a side.° — *pair in a card game*

TRUEWIT Believe it, madam and Mistress Mavis, she will sustain her part.

MAVIS I'll tell you that when I have talked with her and tried° her. — *tested*

HAUGHTY Use her very civilly, Mavis.

MAVIS So I will, madam.

[*Mavis and Epicene whisper to one another.*]

MOROSE [*to himself*] Blessed minute, that they would whisper thus ever!

TRUEWIT [*aside to Haughty*] In the meantime, madam, would but Your Ladyship help to vex him a little? You know his disease; talk to him about the wedding ceremonies, or call for your gloves,° or— — *(see 3.6.90–91 n)*

HAUGHTY Let me alone.° Centaur, help me.—Master bridegroom, where are you? — *Leave it to me*

MOROSE [*to himself*] Oh, it was too miraculously good to last!

1. (1) Polished; (2) assertive.

HAUGHTY We see no ensigns° of a wedding here, no character of a bride-ale: where be our scarves and our gloves? I pray you, give 'em us. Let's know your bride's colors and yours, at least. *emblems*

CENTAUR Alas, madam, he has provided none.

MOROSE Had I known Your Ladyship's painter,° I would. *applier of cosmetics*

HAUGHTY He has given it you,° Centaur, i'faith. But, do you hear, Master Morose, a jest will not absolve you in this manner. You that have sucked the milk of the court, and from thence have been brought up to the very strong meats and wine of it—been a courtier from the biggin to the nightcap,[2] as we may say, and you to offend in such a high point of ceremony as this! And let your nuptials want all marks of solemnity! How much plate° have you lost today—if you had but regarded your profit—what gifts, what friends, through your mere rusticity?° *told you off* / *silverware and dishes* / *utter uncouthness*

MOROSE Madam—

HAUGHTY Pardon me, sir, I must insinuate° your errors to you. No gloves? No garters? No scarves? No epithalamium? No masque?[3] *tactfully suggest*

DAW Yes, madam, I'll make an epithalamium. I promised my mistress; I have begun it already. Will Your Ladyship hear it?

HAUGHTY Ay, good Jack Daw.

MOROSE Will it please Your Ladyship command a chamber, and be private with your friend? You shall have your choice of rooms to retire to after; my whole house is yours. I know it hath been Your Ladyship's errand into the city at other times,[4] however now you have been unhappily° diverted upon me; but I shall be loath to break any honorable custom of Your Ladyship's. And therefore, good madam— *unfortunately*

EPICENE Come, you are a rude bridegroom to entertain ladies of honor in this fashion.

CENTAUR He is a rude groom,° indeed. *fellow*

TRUEWIT By that light, you deserve to be grafted, and have your horns[5] reach from one side of the island° to the other. [*Aside to Morose*] Do not mistake me, sir; I but speak this to give the ladies some heart again, not for any malice to you. *(Great Britain)*

MOROSE [*pointing to Truewit*] Is this your *bravo*,[6] ladies?

TRUEWIT As God help me, if you utter such another word, I'll take mistress bride in, and begin to you in a very sad cup,[7] do you see? Go to,° know your friends and such as love you. *(expressing impatience)*

2. I.e., from infancy to old age. A biggin is a baby's cap; a nightcap is worn by old men.

3. Masques were specially commissioned theatrical performances, sometimes performed at the weddings of rich and prominent people; an epithalamium is a wedding poem. Gloves, garters, and scarves would be gifts for the guests; the "plate" in line 85 would be for the groom and bride.

4. That is, to find a room in which to consummate an affair.

5. Invisible horns were supposed to grow on a cuckold's forehead.

6. Male escort of prostitutes.

7. Get you off to a very bad start. (Literally, "make an unwelcome toast.")

3.7

[Enter] Clerimont [with musicians].

CLERIMONT By your leave, ladies. Do you want any music? I have brought you variety of noises.—Play, sirs, all of you.

Music of all sorts.

MOROSE Oh, a plot, a plot, a plot, a plot upon me! This day I shall be their anvil to work on; they will grate me asunder. 'Tis worse than the noise of a saw.

CLERIMONT No, they are hair, rosin, and guts.[1] I can give you the receipt.° *recipe*

TRUEWIT [*to the musicians*] Peace, boys.

CLERIMONT Play, I say.

TRUEWIT Peace, rascals! [*Music stops.*] You see who's your friend now, sir? Take courage; put on a martyr's resolution. Mock down all their attemptings with patience. 'Tis but a day, and I° would suffer heroically. Should an ass exceed me in fortitude? No. You betray your infirmity with your hanging dull ears, and make them insult.° Bear up bravely and constantly. *if I were you I* / *triumph*

La Foole passes over sewing the meat° [followed by servants], Dauphine, and Mrs. Otter. *serving in the food*

Look you here, sir, what honor is done you unexpected by your nephew: a wedding dinner come, and a knight-sewer[2] before it for the more reputation, and fine Mistress Otter, your neighbor, in the rump or tail of it.° *coming behind*

MOROSE Is that Gorgon, that Medusa[3] come? Hide me, hide me!

TRUEWIT I warrant you, sir, she will not transform you. Look upon her with a good courage. Pray you entertain her, and conduct your guests in. No? Mistress bride, will you entreat in the ladies? Your bridegroom is so shamefaced, here—

EPICENE Will it please Your Ladyship, madam?

HAUGHTY With the benefit of your company, mistress.

EPICENE [*to Daw*] Servant, pray you perform your duties.

DAW And glad to be commanded, mistress.

CENTAUR [*to Mavis*] How like you her wit, Mavis?

MAVIS Very prettily, absolutely well.

MRS. OTTER [*pushing Mavis aside*] 'Tis my place.[4]

MAVIS [*pushing Mrs. Otter back*] You shall pardon me, Mistress Otter.

MRS. OTTER Why, I am a Collegiate.

MAVIS But not in ordinary.[5]

MRS. OTTER But I am.

MAVIS We'll dispute that within.

[Exeunt Collegiate Ladies with Epicene and Daw.]

CLERIMONT Would this had lasted a little longer!

TRUEWIT And that they had sent for the heralds![6]

3.7. The scene continues.
1. The raw materials of string instruments. Rosin, a translucent resin produced from pine tar, is rubbed on the bow hairs.
2. Knight-waiter. (See 3.3.63–66 and note.)
3. Medusa was one of the three Gorgons, snake-haired monsters of Greek mythology; see 2.4.15 and note.
4. Mavis and Mrs. Otter are arguing about who is of higher status and thus gets to go first through the doorway.
5. A regular member, with all privileges.
6. To confirm their respective pedigrees, since precedence depended upon birth.

[*Enter*] *Otter.*

Captain Otter, what news?

OTTER I have brought my bull, bear, and horse in private, and yonder are the trumpeters without, and the drum,[7] gentlemen. *The drum and trumpets sound.*

MOROSE Oh, oh, oh!

OTTER And we will have a rouse° in each of 'em anon, for bold Britons, i'faith. *toast*

MOROSE Oh, oh, oh! [*Exit.*]

ALL Follow, follow, follow! [*Exeunt.*]

4.1

[*Enter*] *Truewit* [*and*] *Clerimont.*

TRUEWIT Was there ever poor bridegroom so tormented? Or man, indeed?

CLERIMONT I have not read of the like in the chronicles of the land.

TRUEWIT Sure, he cannot but go to a place of rest° after all this purgatory. *(in the afterlife)*

CLERIMONT He may presume it, I think.

TRUEWIT The spitting, the coughing, the laughter, the neezing,° the farting, dancing, noise of the music, and her masculine and loud commanding and urging the whole family, makes him think he has married a Fury.[1] *sneezing*

CLERIMONT And she carries it up bravely.° *off magnificently*

TRUEWIT Ay, she takes any occasion to speak; that's the height on't.° *best part*

CLERIMONT And how soberly Dauphine labors to satisfy him that it was none of his plot!

TRUEWIT And has almost brought him to the faith i'the article. Here he comes.

[*Enter*] *Dauphine.*

Where is he now? What's become of him, Dauphine?

DAUPHINE Oh, hold me up a little! I shall go away° i'the jest else. He has got on his whole nest of nightcaps and locked himself up i'the top o'the house, as high as ever he can climb from the noise. I peeped in at a cranny and saw him sitting over a crossbeam o'the roof, like him o'the saddler's horse in Fleet Street,[2] upright; and he will sleep there. *collapse; die*

CLERIMONT But where are your Collegiates?

DAUPHINE Withdrawn with the bride in private.

TRUEWIT Oh, they are instructing her i'the College grammar.° If she have grace with them she knows all their secrets instantly. *regulations*

CLERIMONT Methinks the Lady Haughty looks well today, for all my dispraise of her i'the morning. I think I shall come about to thee° again, Truewit. *your point of view*

7. In drinking bouts, a trumpet flourish and a drumroll marked the downing of each drink. Otter's bull, bear, and horse are his drinking cups (see 2.6.60–63).

4.1. Morose's house still.

1. In classical mythology, one of the three vengeful sisters who punished criminals.

2. Evidently a shop sign consisting of a horse and rider, located in Fleet Street, an important thoroughfare running west from Ludgate Hill into the Strand.

TRUEWIT Believe it, I told you right. Women ought to repair
the losses time and years have made i'their features with
dressings.[3] And an intelligent woman, if she know by° herself — *about*
the least defect, will be most curious° to hide it; and it — *careful*
becomes her. If she be short, let her sit much, lest when she
stands she be thought to sit. If she have an ill foot, let her
wear her gown the longer and her shoe the thinner. If a fat
hand and scald° nails, let her carve° the less and act in — *bad / gesture; cut meat*
gloves. If a sour breath, let her never discourse fasting,° and — *talk before eating*
always talk at her distance. If she have black and rugged
teeth, let her offer the less at laughter, especially if she laugh
wide and open.

CLERIMONT Oh, you shall have some° women, when they — *there are some*
laugh you would think they brayed, it is so rude and—

TRUEWIT Ay, and others, that will stalk i'their gait like an
estrich° and take huge strides. I cannot endure such a sight. — *ostrich*
I love measure° i'the feet and number° i'the voice: they are — *proportion / harmony*
gentlenesses that ofttimes draw° no less than the face. — *attract*

DAUPHINE How cam'st thou to study these creatures so
exactly? I would thou wouldst make me a proficient.

TRUEWIT Yes, but you must leave° to live i'your chamber then° — *cease / therefore*
a month together upon *Amadis de Gaule* or *Don Quixote*,° — *chivalric romances*
as you are wont, and come abroad where the matter is fre-
quent: to court, to tiltings,° public shows, and feasts, to — *tournaments*
plays, and church sometimes. Thither they come to show
their new tires° too, to see and to be seen. In these places a — *attires*
man shall find whom to love, whom to play with, whom to
touch once, whom to hold ever. The variety arrests his judgment. A wench to please a man comes not down dropping
from the ceiling as he lies on his back droning° a tobacco — *puffing on*
pipe. He must go where she is.

DAUPHINE Yes, and be never the near.° — *nearer*

TRUEWIT Out, heretic! That diffidence makes thee worthy it
should be so.

CLERIMONT He says true to you, Dauphine.

DAUPHINE Why?

TRUEWIT A man should not doubt to overcome any woman.
Think he can vanquish 'em, and he shall; for though they
deny, their desire is to be tempted. Penelope[4] herself cannot
hold out long. Ostend,[5] you saw, was taken at last. You must
persevere, and hold to your purpose. They would solicit us,
but that they are afraid. Howsoever, they wish in their hearts
we should solicit them. Praise 'em, flatter 'em; you shall
never want eloquence or trust. Even the chastest delight to
feel themselves that way rubbed. With praises you must mix
kisses too; if they take them, they'll take more. Though they
strive, they would be overcome.

CLERIMONT Oh, but a man must beware of force.

TRUEWIT It is to them° an acceptable violence, and has oft- — *(women)*
times the place of the greatest courtesy. She that might have

3. Truewit derives his account of deceptive wooing strategies, in the following passages, from Ovid's *The Art of Love*.

4. Wife of the Greek hero Odysseus; she successfully kept her many suitors at bay during her husband's long absence.

5. Town in present-day Belgium beseiged by the Spanish from 1601 to 1604.

been forced and you let her go free without touching, though she then seem to thank you, will ever hate you after, and, glad i'the face, is assuredly sad at the heart.

CLERIMONT But all women are not to be taken all ways.

TRUEWIT 'Tis true, no more than all birds or all fishes. If you appear learned to an ignorant wench, or jocund to a sad, or witty to a foolish, why, she presently begins to mistrust herself. You must approach them i'their own height, their own line,° [*(fencing term)*] for the contrary makes many that fear to commit themselves to noble and worthy fellows run into the embraces of a rascal. If she love wit, give verses, though you borrow 'em of a friend or buy 'em to have good. If valor, talk of your sword and be frequent in the mention of quarrels, though you be staunch° [*restrained*] in fighting. If activity, be seen o'your barbary° [*Arabian horse*] often, or leaping over stools, for the credit of your back.° [*strength; sexual vigor*] If she love good clothes or dressing, have your learned council about you every morning, your French tailor, barber, linener, etc. Let your powder, your glass, and your comb be your dearest acquaintance. Take more care for the ornament of your head than the safety, and wish the commonwealth rather troubled than a hair about you. That will take her. Then if she be covetous and craving, do you promise anything, and perform sparingly: so shall you keep her in appetite still. Seem as° [*as if*] you would give, but be like a barren field that yields little, or unlucky dice to foolish and hoping gamesters. Let your gifts be slight and dainty rather than precious. Let cunning be above cost. Give cherries at time of year,° [*in season*] or apricots, and say they were sent you out o'the country, though you bought 'em in Cheapside.° [*London market district*] Admire her tires; like her in all fashions; compare her in every habit° [*outfit*] to some deity; invent excellent dreams to flatter her, and riddles. Or, if she be a great one,° [*socially prominent*] perform always the second parts to her: like what she likes, praise whom she praises, and fail not to make the household and servants yours,° [*your dependents*] yea, the whole family, and salute 'em by their names—'tis but light cost if you can purchase 'em so—and make her physician your pensioner,[6] and her chief woman. Nor will it be out of your gain° [*unprofitable*] to make love to her° [*(the maid)*] too, so° [*provided*] she follow, not usher, her lady's pleasure. All blabbing is taken away° [*The maid won't talk*] when she comes to be a part of the crime.

DAUPHINE On what courtly lap hast thou late° [*lately*] slept, to come forth so sudden and absolute° [*perfect*] a courtling?

TRUEWIT Good faith, I should rather question you, that are so heark'ning after these mysteries.° [*secrets*] I begin to suspect your diligence, Dauphine. Speak, art thou in love in earnest?

DAUPHINE Yes, by my troth am I; 'twere ill dissembling before thee.

TRUEWIT With which of 'em, I pray thee?

DAUPHINE With all the Collegiates.

CLERIMONT Out on thee! We'll keep you at home, believe it, i'the stable, an you be such a stallion.° [*stud*]

TRUEWIT No. I like him well. Men should love wisely, and° [*and should love*] all women: some one for the face, and let her please the eye;

6. That is, dependent on your bribes.

another for the skin, and let her please the touch; a third for the voice, and let her please the ear; and where the objects mix, let the senses so too. Thou wouldst think it strange if I should make 'em all in love with thee afore night!

DAUPHINE I would say thou hadst the best philter° i'the world, and couldst do more than Madam Medea or Doctor Foreman.[7] *love potion*

TRUEWIT If I do not, let me play the mountebank° for my meat while I live, and the bawd for my drink. *seller of quack remedies*

DAUPHINE So be it, I say.

4.2

[Enter] Otter [with his cups, and with trumpeters and drummer], Daw, [and] La Foole.

OTTER Oh, lord, gentlemen, how my knights and I have missed you here!

CLERIMONT Why, Captain, what service?° What service? *how can we help?*

OTTER To see me bring up my bull, bear, and horse to fight.

DAW Yes, faith, the captain says we shall be his dogs to bait 'em.

DAUPHINE A good employment.

TRUEWIT Come on, let's see a course,[1] then.

LA FOOLE I am afraid my cousin will be offended if she come.

OTTER Be afraid of nothing. Gentlemen, I have placed the drum and the trumpets, and one to give 'em the sign when you are ready. [*Setting out his cups*] Here's my bull for myself, and my bear for Sir John Daw, and my horse for Sir Amorous. Now set your foot to mine, and yours to his, and—

LA FOOLE Pray God my cousin come not.

OTTER Saint George and Saint Andrew![2] Fear no cousins. Come, sound, sound! *Et rauco strepuerunt cornua cantu.*[3]

[*Trumpets sound. Drumroll. They drink.*]

TRUEWIT Well said, Captain, i'faith! Well fought at the bull!

CLERIMONT Well held at the bear!

TRUEWIT Loo, loo,° Captain. *(bearbaiting cheer)*

DAUPHINE Oh, the horse has kicked off his dog already.

LA FOOLE I cannot drink it, as I am a knight.° *on my honor (an oath)*

TRUEWIT Gods so, off with his spurs,° somebody. *(symbol of knighthood)*

LA FOOLE It goes again' my conscience. My cousin will be angry with it.

DAW [*finishing his cup*] I ha' done mine.

TRUEWIT You fought high and fair, Sir John.

CLERIMONT At the head.[4]

DAUPHINE Like an excellent bear-dog.

CLERIMONT [*aside to Daw*] You take no notice of the business,° I hope. *(La Foole's "insult")*

7. Medea was a mythical sorceress whose magical arsenal included an elixir that could restore youth. Simon Foreman (1552–1611) was a London magician who provided love potions and aphrodisiacs to his mostly female clientele.

4.2. The scene continues.

1. Round of drinking or bearbaiting. (Otter is staging a drinking contest on the model of a bearbaiting contest, using his animal-shaped cups.)

2. Patron saints of England and Scotland, respectively.

3. And the horns blared with hoarse song. (From Virgil, *Aeneid,* 8.2.)

4. Good bear-dogs attacked the bear's head rather than its flanks, a more dangerous but also more effective tactic.

DAW [*aside to Clerimont*] Not a word, sir; you see we are jovial.

OTTER Sir Amorous, you must not equivocate.° It must be pulled° down, for all "my cousin."°

make excuses / *drunk / i.e., Mrs. Otter*

CLERIMONT [*aside to La Foole*] 'Sfoot,° if you take not your drink, they'll think you are discontented with something; you'll betray all if you take the least notice.

God's foot (an oath)

LA FOOLE [*aside to Clerimont*] Not I, I'll both drink and talk then. [*He drinks.*]

OTTER You must pull the horse on his knees,° Sir Amorous. Fear no cousins! *Jacta est alea.*[5]

drink to the bottom

TRUEWIT [*aside to Clerimont*] Oh, now he's in his vein, and bold. The least hint given him of his wife now will make him rail desperately.°

recklessly

CLERIMONT [*aside to Truewit*] Speak to him of her.

TRUEWIT [*aside to Clerimont*] Do you, and I'll fetch her to the hearing of it. [*Exit.*]

DAUPHINE Captain he-Otter, your she-Otter is coming, your wife.

OTTER Wife! Buzz! *Titivilitium!*° There's no such thing in nature. I confess, gentlemen, I have a cook, a laundress, a house-drudge that serves my necessary turns,° and goes under that title. But he's an ass that will be so uxorious to tie his affections to one circle.° Come, the name dulls appetite. Here, replenish again; another bout. [*He refills the cups.*] Wives are nasty sluttish animals.

Balderdash! / *sexual and other needs* / *(with bawdy suggestion)*

DAUPHINE Oh, Captain.

OTTER As ever the earth bare,° *tribus verbis.*° Where's Master Truewit?

bore / in a few words

DAW He's slipped aside, sir.

CLERIMONT But you must drink and be jovial.

DAW Yes, give it me.

LA FOOLE And me, too.

DAW Let's be jovial.

LA FOOLE As jovial as you will.

OTTER Agreed. [*Redistributing the cups*] Now you shall ha' the bear, cousin, and Sir John Daw the horse, and I'll ha' the bull still. Sound, tritons[6] o'the Thames! *Nunc est bibendum, nunc pede libero.*[7] [*The trumpets sound.*]

[*Enter*] *Morose.* [*He*] *speaks from above, the trumpets sounding.*

MOROSE Villains, murderers, sons of the earth,° and traitors, what do you there?

bastards

CLERIMONT Oh, now the trumpets have waked him, we shall have his company.

OTTER A wife is a scurvy *clogdogdo;* an unlucky thing, a very foresaid bear whelp,[8] without any good fashion or breeding: *mala bestia.*°

vile beast

5. The die is cast. (Julius Caesar's words upon crossing the Rubicon to march on Rome.)
6. Sea gods with conch-shell trumpets.
7. Now is the time when we drink, now with light foot. (From Horace, *Odes*, 1.37.1.)
8. Newborn bear, thought to be shapeless until licked into a rough form by its mother. "*Clogdogdo*" is a nonce word, perhaps a combination of "clog," meaning "hindrance," and "dog."

His wife is brought out [by Truewit] to hear him. [Otter does not notice them.]

DAUPHINE Why did you marry one then, Captain?

OTTER A pox! I married with six thousand pound, I. I was in love with that. I ha' not kissed my Fury these forty weeks.

CLERIMONT The more to blame you, Captain.

TRUEWIT [*restraining her*] Nay, Mistress Otter, hear him a little first.

OTTER She has a breath worse than my grandmother's, *profecto.*° — *in truth*

MRS. OTTER [*aside to Truewit*] Oh, treacherous liar! Kiss me, sweet Master Truewit, and prove him a slandering knave.

TRUEWIT [*aside to her*] I'll rather believe you, lady.

OTTER And she has a peruke that's like a pound of hemp, made up in shoe threads.° — *shoelaces*

MRS. OTTER [*aside*] Oh, viper, mandrake!° — *a poisonous plant*

OTTER A most vile face! And yet she spends me forty pound a year in mercury and hogs' bones.° All her teeth were made i'the Blackfriars, both her eyebrows i'the Strand, and her hair in Silver Street.[9] Every part o'the town owns a piece of her.° — *cosmetics ingredients*; *(with sexual innuendo)*

MRS. OTTER [*aside*] I cannot hold.° — *keep quiet*

OTTER She takes herself asunder still when she goes to bed, into some twenty boxes, and about next day noon is put together again like a great German clock, and so comes forth and rings a tedious 'larum° to the whole house, and then is quiet again for an hour, but for her quarters.[1] Ha' you done me right,° gentlemen? *She falls upon him and beats him.* [*Exeunt Daw and La Foole.*] — *alarum, a call to arms*; *matched my drinking*

MRS. OTTER No, sir, I'll do you right° with my quarters, with my quarters! — *fix you*

OTTER Oh, hold, good princess!

TRUEWIT Sound, sound! [*Drum and trumpets.*]

CLERIMONT A battle, a battle!

MRS. OTTER You notorious stinkardly bear-ward, does my breath smell?

OTTER Under correction, dear princess.—Look to my bear and my horse, gentlemen.

MRS. OTTER Do I want° teeth and eyebrows, thou bulldog? — *lack*

TRUEWIT Sound, sound still! [*Drum and trumpets.*]

OTTER No, I protest, under correction—

MRS. OTTER Ay, now you are under correction, you protest, but you did not protest before correction, sir. Thou Judas,[2] to offer to betray thy princess! I'll make thee an example—

Morose descends with a long sword.

MOROSE I will have no such examples in my house, Lady Otter.

MRS. OTTER Ah—

9. Districts in London where such purchases might be made.

1. (1) Bells at quarter hours; (2) hindquarters, imagined as breaking wind.

2. Disciple who betrayed Jesus.

MOROSE Mistress Mary Ambree,[3] your examples are dangerous. [*Exit Mrs. Otter.*] Rogues, hellhounds, stentors,[4] out of my doors, you sons of noise and tumult, begot on an ill May Day, or when the galleyfoist is afloat to Westminster![5] A trumpeter could not be conceived but then! [*Exeunt trumpeters and drummer.*]

DAUPHINE What ails you, sir?

MOROSE They have rent my roof, walls, and all my windows asunder with their brazen throats. [*Exit.*]

TRUEWIT Best follow him, Dauphine.

DAUPHINE So I will. [*Exit.*]

CLERIMONT Where's Daw and La Foole?

OTTER They are both run away, sir. Good gentlemen, help to pacify my princess, and speak to the great ladies° for me. Now must I go lie with the bears this fortnight, and keep out o'the way till my peace be made, for this scandal° she has taken. [*Gathering up his drinking vessels*] Did you not see my bull-head,° gentlemen?

Collegiate Ladies / *offense* / *bull-headed cup*

CLERIMONT Is 't not on,[6] Captain?

TRUEWIT No, but he may make a new one by that is on.[7]

OTTER Oh, here 'tis. An you come over,° gentlemen, and ask for Tom Otter, we'll go down to Ratcliffe° and have a course,° i'faith, for all these disasters. There's *bona spes*° left.

(across the Thames) / *a tavern district / round* / *good hope (Latin)*

TRUEWIT Away, Captain! Get off while you are well. [*Exit Otter.*]

CLERIMONT I am glad we are rid of him.

TRUEWIT You had never been, unless we had put his wife upon him. His humor° is as tedious at last as it was ridiculous at first.

temperament

4.3

[*Enter*] *Haughty, Mrs. Otter, Mavis, Daw, La Foole, Centaur,* [*and*] *Epicene.* [*Truewit and Clerimont retire to one side.*]

HAUGHTY We wondered why you shrieked so, Mistress Otter.

MRS. OTTER Oh, God, madam, he° came down with a huge long naked weapon in both his hands, and looked so dreadfully! Sure he's beside himself.

(Morose)

MAVIS Why, what made you° there, Mistress Otter?

were you doing

MRS. OTTER Alas, Mistress Mavis, I was chastising my subject° and thought nothing of him.°

husband / (Morose)

DAW [*to Epicene*] Faith, mistress, you must do so too. Learn to chastise. Mistress Otter corrects her husband so he dares not speak but under correction.

3. English woman warrior of the late sixteenth century.
4. Stentor was a Greek fighter in the Trojan War, with a thunderous voice. The hellhound was the dog that guarded the underworld; also, a fiendish person.
5. May Day was a sexually licentious holiday; in 1517, in London, the festivities turned into a riot against foreigners by London apprentices. The galleyfoist was the barge on which the Lord Mayor rode from the city to Westminster during his investiture ceremony, another day of noisy citywide celebration.
6. Implying that Otter is a cuckold, with cuckold's horns.
7. Truewit continues Clerimont's joke by suggesting that Otter's cup, decorated with its horned bull, is likely to foment more quarreling between husband and wife and hence more incentive for cuckoldry. ("That" means "that which.")
4.3. The scene continues.

LA FOOLE And with his hat off to her; 'twould do you good to see.

HAUGHTY In sadness,° 'tis good and mature counsel. [*To Epicene*] Practice it, Morose. I'll call you "Morose" still now, as I call "Centaur" and "Mavis"; we four will be all one.

all seriousness

CENTAUR And you'll come to the College and live with us?

HAUGHTY Make him give milk and honey.°

i.e., pay up

MAVIS Look how you manage him at first, you shall have him ever after.

CENTAUR Let him allow you your coach and four horses, your woman, your chambermaid, your page, your gentleman-usher, your French cook, and four grooms.

HAUGHTY And go with us to Bedlam, to the china houses, and to the Exchange.°

(see 1.3.38 n, 2.2.34 n)

CENTAUR It will open the gate to your fame.

HAUGHTY Here's Centaur has° immortalized herself with taming of her wild male.

who has

MAVIS Ay, she has done the miracle of the kingdom.

EPICENE But, ladies, do you count it lawful to have such plurality of servants,° and do 'em all graces?

male admirers

HAUGHTY Why not? Why should women deny their favors to men? Are they the poorer, or the worse?

DAW Is the Thames the less for the dyer's water,[1] mistress?

LA FOOLE Or a torch for lighting many torches?

TRUEWIT Well said, La Foole! [*Aside*] What a new one° he has got!

metaphor (sarcastic)

CENTAUR They are empty losses women fear in this kind.

HAUGHTY Besides, ladies should be mindful of the approach of age, and let no time want his° due use. The best of our days pass first.

lack its

MAVIS We are rivers that cannot be called back, madam. She that now excludes her lovers may live to lie a forsaken beldame° in a frozen bed.

old woman

CENTAUR 'Tis true, Mavis; and who will wait on us° to coach then? Or write, or tell us the news then? Make anagrams of our names, and invite us to the Cockpit,[2] and kiss our hands all the play time, and draw their weapons for our honors?

escort us

HAUGHTY Not one.

DAW Nay, my mistress is not altogether unintelligent of these things; here be in presence° have tasted of her favors.

those present who

CLERIMONT [*aside to Truewit*] What a neighing hobbyhorse° is this!

buffoon; lustful person

EPICENE But not with intent to boast 'em again, servant. And have you those excellent receipts,° madam, to keep yourselves from bearing of children?

contraceptive recipes

HAUGHTY Oh, yes, Morose. How should we maintain our youth and beauty else? Many births of a woman make her old, as many crops make the earth barren.

1. Water that is returned, stained (by the dye), to the stream after use.

2. Theater where one could sit directly in front of the stage, in the company of fashionable gentlemen.

4.4

[Enter] Morose [and] Dauphine [conversing privately. Truewit joins them].

MOROSE O my cursed angel, that instructed° me to this fate!
appointed

DAUPHINE Why, sir?

MOROSE That I should be seduced by so foolish a devil as a barber will make!

DAUPHINE I would I had been worthy, sir, to have partaken your counsel; you should never have trusted it to such a minister.°
agent

MOROSE Would I could redeem it with the loss of an eye, nephew, a hand, or any other member!°
(bawdy)

DAUPHINE Marry, God forbid, sir, that you should geld° yourself to anger your wife.
castrate

MOROSE So° it would rid me of her! And that I did supererogatory° penance in a belfry at Westminster Hall, i'the Cockpit, at the fall of a stag, the Tower Wharf—what place is there else?—London Bridge, Paris Garden, Billingsgate, when the noises are at their height and loudest.[1] Nay, I would sit out a play that were nothing but fights at sea, drum, trumpet, and target!°
So long as · *extra* · *shield*

DAUPHINE I hope there shall be no such need, sir. Take patience, good uncle. This is but a day, and 'tis well worn° too, now.
advanced toward night

MOROSE Oh, 'twill be so forever, nephew, I foresee it, forever. Strife and tumult are the dowry that comes with a wife.

TRUEWIT I told you so, sir, and you would not believe me.

MOROSE Alas, do not rub those wounds, Master Truewit, to blood° again. 'Twas my negligence. Add not affliction to affliction. I have perceived the effect of it too late in Madam Otter.
to make them bleed

EPICENE *[approaching them]* How do you, sir?

MOROSE Did you ever hear a more unnecessary question? As if she did not see!—Why, I do as you see, empress, empress.[2]

EPICENE You are not well, sir. You look very ill. Something has distempered you.

MOROSE Oh, horrible, monstrous impertinencies! Would not one of these° have served? *[To Truewit]* Do you think, sir, would not one of these have served?
(Epicene's statements)

TRUEWIT Yes, sir, but these are but notes of female kindness, sir, certain tokens that she has a voice, sir.

MOROSE Oh, is't so? *[To Epicene]* Come, an't be no otherwise, what say you?

EPICENE How do you feel yourself, sir?

MOROSE Again, that!

TRUEWIT Nay, look you, sir: you would be friends with your wife upon unconscionable terms, her silence—

EPICENE *[to Morose]* They say you are run mad, sir.

MOROSE Not for love, I assure you, of you; do you see?

[He makes threatening gestures.]

4.4 The scene continues.

1. Some of these famously noisy places have been mentioned earlier. Billingsgate was an East London wharf frequented by notoriously raucous, foulmouthed fishwives. The killing of a deer was marked by repeated blasts of the hunting horn.

2. Sarcastically going Otter's "princess" one better.

EPICENE Oh, lord, gentlemen! Lay hold on him, for God's sake. [*The men restrain Morose.*] What shall I do? Who's his physician, can you tell, that knows the state of his body best, that I might send for him?—Good sir, speak. I'll send for one of my doctors else.

MOROSE What, to poison me, that I might die intestate° and leave you possessed of all?

having left no will

EPICENE Lord, how idly° he talks, and how his eyes sparkle! He looks green about the temples! Do you see what blue spots he has?

madly

CLERIMONT Ay, it's melancholy.

EPICENE Gentlemen, for heaven's sake, counsel me. Ladies! Servant,° you have read Pliny and Paracelsus;° ne'er a word now to comfort a poor gentlewoman? Ay me! What fortune had I to marry a distracted° man?

(Daw) / medical men

crazy

DAW I'll tell you, mistress—

TRUEWIT [*aside to Clerimont and Dauphine*] How rarely° she holds it° up!

superbly

(the pretense)

MOROSE [*struggling*] What mean you, gentlemen?

EPICENE [*to Daw*] What will you tell me, servant?

DAW The disease in Greek is called *mania,* in Latin *insania, furor, vel ecstasis melancholica,* that is, *egressio,* when a man *ex melancholico evadit fanaticus.*[3]

MOROSE Shall I have a lecture read upon me alive?[4]

DAW But he may be but *phreneticus*° yet, mistress, and *phrenetis* is only delirium, or so—

frenetic

EPICENE Ay, that is for the disease,° servant, but what is this to the cure? We are sure enough of the disease.

by way of diagnosis

MOROSE [*struggling*] Let me go!

TRUEWIT Why, we'll entreat her to hold her peace, sir.

MOROSE Oh, no. Labor not to stop her. She is like a conduit pipe that will gush out with more force when she opens again.

HAUGHTY [*to Epicene*] I'll tell you, Morose, you must talk divinity to him altogether, or moral philosophy.

LA FOOLE Ay, and there's an excellent book of moral philosophy, madam, of Reynard the Fox and all the beasts, called *Doni's Philosophy.*[5]

CENTAUR There is indeed, Sir Amorous La Foole.

MOROSE Oh, misery!

LA FOOLE I have read it, my Lady Centaur, all over to my cousin here.

MRS. OTTER Ay, and 'tis a very good book as any is, of the moderns.°

modern authorities

DAW Tut, he must have Seneca read to him, and Plutarch, and the ancients. The moderns are not for this disease.

CLERIMONT Why, you discommended them too today, Sir John.

3. Insanity, madness, or melancholic ecstasy, that is, loss of wits, when a man from a depressed state becomes raving mad.

4. In early modern Europe, physicians would dissect corpses publicly, giving lectures on them to curious crowds.

5. Anton Francesco Doni's Italian translation of the Fables of Bidpai, which had already passed from Sanskrit into Arabic and then into Greek, was itself translated into English by Thomas North in 1570. La Foole confuses it with the medieval tales of Reynard the Fox.

DAW Ay, in some cases; but in these they are best, and Aristotle's *Ethics*.

MAVIS Say you so, Sir John? I think you are deceived; you took it upon trust.[6]

HAUGHTY Where's Trusty, my woman? I'll end this difference.° I prithee, Otter,° call her. Her father and mother were both mad when they put her to° me. [*Exit Mrs. Otter.*] *dispute / (Mrs. Otter)* *to work for*

MOROSE I think so.—Nay, gentlemen, I am tame. This is but an exercise, I know, a marriage ceremony, which I must endure.

HAUGHTY And one of 'em—I know not which—was cured with *The Sick Man's Salve*; and the other with *Greene's Groatsworth of Wit*.[7]

TRUEWIT A very cheap cure, madam.

HAUGHTY Ay, it's very feasible.

[*Enter Mrs. Otter and*] *Trusty.*

MRS. OTTER My lady called for you, Mistress Trusty. You must decide a controversy.

HAUGHTY Oh, Trusty, which was it you said, your father or your mother, that was cured with *The Sick Man's Salve*?

TRUSTY My mother, madam, with the *Salve*.

TRUEWIT Then it was *The Sick Woman's Salve*.

TRUSTY And my father with the *Groatsworth of Wit*. But there was other means used. We had a preacher that would preach folk asleep still,° and so they were prescribed to go to church, by an old woman that was their physician, thrice a week— *all the time*

EPICENE To sleep?

TRUSTY Yes, forsooth; and every night they read themselves asleep on those books.

EPICENE Good faith, it stands with great reason.° I would I knew where to procure those books. *stands to reason*

MOROSE Oh!

LA FOOLE I can help you with one of 'em, Mistress Morose: the *Groatsworth of Wit*.

EPICENE But I shall disfurnish° you, Sir Amorous. Can you spare it? *deprive*

LA FOOLE Oh, yes, for a week or so; I'll read it myself to him.

EPICENE No, I must do that, sir; that must be my office.° *job*

MOROSE Oh, oh!

EPICENE Sure, he would do well enough if he could sleep.

MOROSE No, I should do well enough if you could sleep.—Have I no friend that will make her drunk? Or give her a little laudanum?° Or opium? *a narcotic*

TRUEWIT Why, sir, she talks ten times worse in her sleep.

MOROSE How!

CLERIMONT Do you not know that, sir? Never ceases all night.

TRUEWIT And snores like a porpoise.[8]

MOROSE Oh, redeem me, fate, redeem me, fate!—For how many causes may a man be divorced, nephew?

6. I.e., without having read it.

7. *The Sick Man's Salve*, a popular sixteenth-century treatise by Thomas Becon, discussed how Christians ought to behave in times of mortal illness. *Greene's Groatsworth of Wit Bought with a Million of Repentance*, written by the dramatist Robert Greene shortly before his death in 1592, described his prodigal life and subsequent repentance.

8. The porpoise exhales noisily through its blowhole.

DAUPHINE I know not truly, sir.

TRUEWIT Some divine must resolve you in° that, sir, or canon lawyer.[9] *inform you about*

MOROSE I will not rest, I will not think of any other hope or comfort, till I know. [*Exeunt Morose and Dauphine.*]

CLERIMONT Alas, poor man!

TRUEWIT You'll make him mad indeed, ladies, if you pursue this.

HAUGHTY No, we'll let him breathe° now, a quarter of an hour or so. *rest*

CLERIMONT By my faith, a large truce.

HAUGHTY Is that his keeper,° that is gone with him? *madman's caretaker*

DAW It is his nephew, madam.

LA FOOLE Sir Dauphine Eugenie.

CENTAUR He looks like a very pitiful° knight— *pitiable*

DAW As can be. This marriage has put him out of all.° *all hopes of inheritance*

LA FOOLE He has not a penny in his purse, madam—

DAW He is ready to cry all this day.

LA FOOLE A very shark.° He set me i'the nick t'other night at primero.[1] *true card shark*

TRUEWIT [*aside to Clerimont*] How these swabbers[2] talk!

CLERIMONT [*aside to Truewit*] Ay, Otter's wine has swelled their humors above a spring tide.

HAUGHTY [*to Epicene*] Good Morose, let's go in again. I like your couches exceeding well; we'll go lie and talk there.

EPICENE I wait on you,° madam. *I attend you*

[*Exeunt Haughty, Centaur, Mavis, Mrs. Otter, Trusty, Daw, and La Foole.*]

TRUEWIT [*to Clerimont*] 'Slight, I will have 'em° as silent as signs, and their posts too, ere I ha' done. [*Detaining Epicene, who is following Lady Haughty out*] Do you hear, lady bride? I pray thee now, as thou art a noble wench, continue this discourse of Dauphine within, but praise him exceedingly. Magnify him with all the height of affection thou canst—I have some purpose in't—and but beat off these two rooks, Jack Daw and his fellow, with any discontentment hither, and I'll honor thee forever. *(Daw and La Foole)*

EPICENE I was about it, here. It angered me to the soul to hear 'em begin to talk so malapert.° *impudently*

TRUEWIT Pray thee perform it, and thou winn'st me an idolater to thee everlasting.

EPICENE Will you go in and hear me do it?

TRUEWIT No, I'll stay here. Drive 'em out of your company; 'tis all I ask, which cannot be any way better done than by extolling Dauphine, whom they have so slighted.

EPICENE I warrant you. You shall expect one of 'em presently. [*Exit.*]

CLERIMONT What a cast of kestrels° are these, to hawk after ladies thus! *pair of small falcons*

TRUEWIT Ay, and strike at such an eagle as Dauphine.

CLERIMONT He will be mad when we tell him. Here he comes.

9. Expert in church law. (Most marital cases came under the jurisdiction of the ecclesiastical courts.)

1. He cheated at the card game primero. Since cheating at cards was very ungentlemanly, this slander is deeply insulting to Dauphine.

2. Unmannerly fellows. (Literally, sailors who mop a ship's deck.)

4.5

[*Enter*] *Dauphine.*

CLERIMONT Oh, sir, you are welcome.

TRUEWIT Where's thine uncle?

DAUPHINE Run out o'doors in's nightcaps to talk with a casuist[1] about his divorce. It works admirably.

TRUEWIT Thou wouldst ha' said so an thou hadst been here.° *(sarcastic)* The ladies have laughed at thee most comically since thou went'st, Dauphine.

CLERIMONT And asked if thou wert thine uncle's keeper.

TRUEWIT And the brace° *couple* of baboons answered yes, and said thou wert a pitiful poor fellow and didst live upon posts,[2] and hadst nothing but three suits of apparel and some few benevolences° that lords ga' thee to fool to 'em° and swagger. *handouts / entertain them*

DAUPHINE Let me not live, I'll° *if I don't* beat 'em. I'll bind 'em both to grand madam's bedposts, and have 'em baited with monkeys.° *(as in bearbaiting)*

TRUEWIT Thou shalt not need; they shall be beaten to thy hand,[3] Dauphine. I have an execution[4] to serve upon 'em, I warrant thee shall serve. Trust my plot.

DAUPHINE Ay, you have many plots! So you had one to make all the wenches in love with me.

TRUEWIT Why, if I do not yet afore night, as near as 'tis, and that they do not every one invite thee and be ready to scratch° for thee, take the mortgage of my wit.° *contend / my wit is forfeit*

CLERIMONT 'Fore God, I'll be his witness. Thou shalt have it, Dauphine; thou shalt be his fool forever if thou dost not.[5]

TRUEWIT Agreed. Perhaps 'twill be the better estate. Do you observe this gallery, or rather lobby, indeed? Here are a couple of studies, at each end one; here will I act such a tragicomedy between the Guelphs and the Ghibellines,[6] Daw and La Foole. Which of 'em comes out first will I seize on. You two shall be the chorus behind the arras,° *wall hangings* and whip out between the acts and speak. If I do not make 'em keep the peace[7] for this remnant of the day, if not of the year, I have failed once.° *for once* I hear Daw coming. Hide, and do not laugh, for God's sake. [*Dauphine and Clermont conceal themselves behind the arras.*]

[*Enter*] *Daw.*

DAW Which is the way into the garden,° trow?° *(to urinate) / do you think?*

TRUEWIT Oh, Jack Daw! I am glad I have met with you. In good faith, I must have this matter go no further between you. I must ha' it taken up.° *stopped*

DAW What matter, sir? Between whom?

TRUEWIT Come, you disguise it: Sir Amorous and you. If you

4.5. The scene continues.
1. Expert in ethical dilemmas.
2. Upon gambling winnings at cards. ("Posts" refers to "post and pair," a card game. Or perhaps this refers to small amounts of money dispatched by post.)
3. Into subjection without any effort on your part.
4. Plot. (Playing on the sense "enforcement of a legal judgment.")
5. You, Dauphine, will have the mortgage of Truewit's wit; you, Truewit, will serve as Dauphine's jester forever if your plots fail.
6. Rival factions in Renaissance Florence.
7. Make them refrain from disorderly conduct, i.e., shut them up and show their cowardice.

love me, Jack, you shall make use of your philosophy now, for this once, and deliver me your sword. [*He takes Daw's sword.*] This is not the wedding the centaurs[8] were at, though there be a she-one here. The bride has entreated me I will see no blood shed at her bridal; you saw her whisper me erewhile.°

just now

DAW As I hope to finish Tacitus,[9] I intend no murder.

TRUEWIT Do you not wait for Sir Amorous?

DAW Not I, by my knighthood.

TRUEWIT And your scholarship too?

DAW And my scholarship too.

TRUEWIT [*giving back the sword*] Go to; then I return you your sword and ask you mercy; but put it not up,° for you will be assaulted. I understood that you had apprehended it° and walked here to brave° him, and that you had held your life contemptible in regard of your honor.

don't sheathe it
(La Foole's anger)
defy

DAW No, no, no such thing, I assure you. He and I parted now as good friends as could be.

TRUEWIT Trust not you to that visor.° I saw him since dinner with another face. I have known many men in my time vexed with losses, with deaths, and with abuses, but so offended a wight° as Sir Amorous did I never see or read of. For taking away his guests, sir, today, that's the cause; and he declares it behind your back with such threatenings and contempts! He said to Dauphine you were the arrant'st ass—

mask, pretense
creature

DAW Ay, he may say his pleasure.

TRUEWIT And swears you are so protested° a coward that he knows you will never do him any manly or single right,° and therefore he will take his course.

noted
combat

DAW I'll give him any satisfaction, sir—but fighting.

TRUEWIT Ay, sir, but who knows what satisfaction he'll take? Blood he thirsts for and blood he will have; and whereabouts on you he will have it, who knows but himself?

DAW I pray you, Master Truewit, be you a mediator.

TRUEWIT Well, sir, conceal yourself then in this study till I return. (*He puts him up.*)° Nay, you must be content to be locked in; for, for mine own reputation I would not have you seen to receive a public disgrace while I have the matter in managing. Gods so,° here he comes. Keep your breath close,° that he do not hear you sigh. [*Pretending to address La Foole*] In good faith, Sir Amorous, he is not this way. I pray you be merciful; do not murder him; he is a Christian as good as you; you are armed as if you sought a revenge on all his race.—Good Dauphine, get him away from this place. I never knew a man's choler° so high but he would speak to his friends, he would hear reason.—Jack Daw, Jack Daw! Asleep?

behind a door
(an oath)
silent
anger

DAW [*within*] Is he gone, Master Truewit?

TRUEWIT Ay, did you hear him?

DAW Oh, God, yes.

TRUEWIT [*aside*] What a quick ear fear has!

DAW [*emerging from the study*] But is he so armed as you say?

8. See "The Persons of the Play," note 5.

9. Prolific Roman historian with a terse, difficult style.

TRUEWIT Armed? Did you ever see a fellow set out to take possession?[1]

DAW Ay, sir.

TRUEWIT That may give you some light to conceive of him, but 'tis nothing to the principal.° Some false brother° i'the house has furnished him° strangely. Or, if it were out o'the house, it was Tom Otter. *actuality / fellow* *(with weapons)*

DAW Indeed, he's a captain, and his° wife is his° kinswoman. *(Otter's) / (La Foole's)*

TRUEWIT He has got somebody's old two-hand sword to mow you off at the knees. And that sword hath spawned such a dagger! But then he is so hung with pikes, halberds, petronels, calivers, and muskets that he looks like a justice of peace's hall.[2] A man of two thousand a year is not 'sessed[3] at so many weapons as he has on. There was never fencer challenged at so many several foils.[4] You would think he meant to murder all Saint Pulchre's parish.[5] If he could but victual himself for half a year in his breeches,[6] he is sufficiently armed to overrun a country.

DAW Good lord, what means he, sir? I pray you, Master Truewit, be you a mediator.

TRUEWIT Well, I'll try if he will be appeased with a leg or an arm. If not, you must die once.° *at some point*

DAW I would be loath to lose my right arm for writing madrigals.

TRUEWIT Why, if he will be satisfied with a thumb or a little finger, all's one° to me. You must think I'll do my best. *it's all the same*

DAW Good sir, do.

He [Truewit] puts him up again, and then [Clerimont and Dauphine] come forth.

CLERIMONT What hast thou done?

TRUEWIT He will let me do nothing, man. He does all afore me; he offers his left arm.

CLERIMONT His left wing, for a Jack Daw.

DAUPHINE Take it, by all means.

TRUEWIT How, maim a man forever for a jest? What a conscience hast thou!

DAUPHINE 'Tis no loss to him: he has no employment for his arms but to eat spoon-meat.[7] Beside, as good maim his body as his reputation.

TRUEWIT He is a scholar and a wit, and yet he does not think so. But he loses no reputation with us, for we all resolved him an ass before. To your places again.

CLERIMONT I pray thee, let me be in at the other° a little. *help with La Foole*

TRUEWIT Look, you'll spoil all. These be ever your tricks.

1. Foreclose on a property (sometimes a violent affair).
2. Local militias stored their weapons with the justice of the peace; their arms might include pikes, shafted weapons with axlike heads; petronels, old-fashioned guns fired with their butts against the chest; and calivers, or small muskets.
3. Assessed. (Wealthy persons were required to contribute weapons to local and national arsenals.)
4. Fencers often specialized in the use of a particular variety of sword (foil, épée, saber, etc.), but especially skilled fencers might be prepared to accept a variety of challenges, and thus they carried a number of different weapons.
5. Saint Sepulchre's in London; perhaps chosen for its ominous-sounding name, or because it included Newgate Prison.
6. "Victual" means "store food for." Very voluminous breeches, such as La Foole is evidently wearing, were modish but often derided by more temperate dressers.
7. Soft food for babies or invalids.

CLERIMONT No, but I could hit of° some things that thou wilt miss, and thou wilt say are good ones.

upon

TRUEWIT I warrant you. I pray forbear; I'll leave it off, else.

DAUPHINE Come away, Clerimont.

[*Dauphine and Clerimont conceal themselves again.*]

[*Enter*] *La Foole.*

TRUEWIT Sir Amorous!

LA FOOLE Master Truewit.

TRUEWIT Whither were you going?

LA FOOLE Down into the court to make water.

TRUEWIT By no means, sir. You shall rather tempt your breeches.°

risk wetting your pants

LA FOOLE Why, sir?

TRUEWIT [*indicating the empty study*] Enter here, if you love your life.

LA FOOLE Why? Why?

TRUEWIT Question till your throat be cut, do; dally till the enraged soul find you.

LA FOOLE Who's that?

TRUEWIT Daw it is. Will you in?

LA FOOLE Ay, ay, I'll in. What's the matter?

TRUEWIT Nay, if he had been cool enough to tell us that, there had been some hope to atone° you, but he seems so implacably enraged.

reconcile

LA FOOLE 'Slight, let him rage. I'll hide myself.

TRUEWIT Do, good sir. But what have you done to him within that should provoke him thus? You have broke° some jest upon him afore the ladies—

made

LA FOOLE Not I, never in my life broke jest upon any man. The bride was praising Sir Dauphine, and he went away in snuff,° and I followed him—unless he took offense at me in his drink erewhile, that I would not pledge all the horse full.

in a huff

TRUEWIT By my faith, and that may be, you remember well. But he walks the round up and down through every room o'the house with a towel in his hand,[8] crying, "Where's La Foole? Who saw La Foole?" And when Dauphine and I demanded° the cause, we can force no answer from him, but "O revenge, how sweet art thou! I will strangle him in this towel!"—which leads us to conjecture that the main cause of his fury is for bringing your meat today, with a towel about you, to his discredit.

asked

LA FOOLE Like° enough. Why, an he be angry for that, I'll stay here till his anger be blown over.

Likely

TRUEWIT A good becoming° resolution, sir, if you can put it on o'the sudden.

suitable

LA FOOLE Yes, I can put it on. Or I'll away into the country presently.

TRUEWIT How will you get out o'the house, sir? He knows you are i'the house, and he'll watch you this se'ennight° but he'll have you. He'll outwait a sergeant[9] for you.

week

8. Like the hero of a Renaissance revenge tragedy, who typically carries a memento to keep his sense of injury fresh.

9. Officer entrusted with making arrests, who often had to wait outside a place of sanctuary for the offender to emerge, at which point he might legally seize him.

LA FOOLE Why, then I'll stay here.

TRUEWIT You must think how to victual yourself in time, then.

LA FOOLE Why, sweet Master Truewit, will you entreat my cousin Otter to send me a cold venison pasty,° a bottle or two of wine, and a chamber pot? *meat pie*

TRUEWIT A stool were better, sir, of Sir Ajax his invention.[1]

LA FOOLE Ay, that will be better indeed—and a pallet to lie on.

TRUEWIT Oh, I would not advise you to sleep by any means.

LA FOOLE Would you not, sir? Why, then, I will not.

TRUEWIT Yet there's another fear—

LA FOOLE Is there, sir? What is't?

TRUEWIT No, he cannot break open this door with his foot, sure.

LA FOOLE I'll set my back against it, sir. I have a good back.[2]

TRUEWIT But then if he should batter—

LA FOOLE Batter! If he dare, I'll have an action° of battery against him. *legal action*

TRUEWIT Cast you° the worst. He has sent for powder° already, and what he will do with it no man knows: perhaps blow up the corner o'the house where he suspects you are. Here he comes; in, quickly! (*He feigns as if one were present, to fright the other* [*La Foole*], *who is run in* [*to the study*] *to hide himself.*) I protest, Sir John Daw, he is not this way. What will you do? Before God, you shall hang no petard° here. I'll die rather. Will you not take my word? I never knew one but would be satisfied. [*Speaking through the study door*] Sir Amorous, there's no standing out.° He has made a petard of an old brass pot to force your door. Think upon some satisfaction or terms to offer him. *Expect / gunpowder* *bomb* *staying out of it*

LA FOOLE [*within*] Sir, I'll give him any satisfaction. I dare give any terms.

TRUEWIT You'll leave it to me, then?

LA FOOLE Ay, sir. I'll stand° to any conditions. *agree*

TRUEWIT (*call*[*ing*] *forth Clerimont and Dauphine* [*from behind the arras*]) How now, what think you, sirs? Were't not a difficult thing to determine which of these two feared most?

CLERIMONT Yes, but this fears the bravest.[3] The other a whiniling° dastard Jack Daw! But La Foole a brave heroic coward, and is afraid in a great look and a stout° accent! I like him rarely.° *whimpering* *manly* *extremely (ironic)*

TRUEWIT Had it not been pity these two should ha' been concealed?° *escaped detection*

CLERIMONT Shall I make a motion?° *proposal*

TRUEWIT Briefly. For I must strike while 'tis hot.

CLERIMONT Shall I go fetch the ladies to the catastrophe?° *climax, finale*

TRUEWIT Umh? Ay, by my troth.

DAUPHINE By no mortal means. Let them continue in the

1. Sir John Harington (1561–1612) contrived a kind of flush toilet and wrote an account of it with the mock-classical title *The Metamorphosis of Ajax* (1596). "Jakes" was slang for "privy."

2. To "have a good back" meant to "have sexual stamina"; here it suggests instead La Foole's cowardice, since he will use his strong back to prevent Daw from opening the door.

3. Most magnificently. (Playing on the meaning "most courageously.")

state of ignorance, and err still—think 'em wits and fine fellows, as they have done. 'Twere sin to reform them.° *set the ladies straight*

TRUEWIT Well, I will have 'em fetched, now I think on't, for a private purpose of mine. Do, Clerimont, fetch 'em, and discourse to 'em all that's passed, and bring 'em into the gallery here.

DAUPHINE This is thy extreme vanity, now. Thou think'st thou wert undone if every jest thou mak'st were not published.° *made public*

TRUEWIT Thou shalt see how unjust thou art presently.—Clerimont, say it was Dauphine's plot. [*Exit Clerimont.*] Trust me not if the whole drift be not for thy good. There's a carpet i'the next room: put it on, with this scarf over thy face and cushion o'thy head, and be ready when I call Amorous. Away! [*Exit Dauphine.*] [*Calling*]—John Daw!

[*Enter Daw from his study.*]

DAW What good news, sir?

TRUEWIT Faith, I have followed, and argued with him hard for you. I told him you were a knight and a scholar, and that you knew fortitude did consist *magis patiendo quam faciendo, magis ferendo quam feriendo.*[4]

DAW It doth so indeed, sir.

TRUEWIT And that you would suffer, I told him; so at first he demanded, by my troth, in my conceit,° too much. *judgment*

DAW What was it, sir?

TRUEWIT Your upper lip, and six o'your fore-teeth.

DAW 'Twas unreasonable.

TRUEWIT Nay, I told him plainly you could not spare 'em all. So after long argument (pro et con, as you know) I brought him down to your two butter-teeth,° and them he would have. *incisors*

DAW Oh, did you so? Why, he shall have 'em.

TRUEWIT But he shall not, sir, by your leave. The conclusion is this, sir: because° you shall be very good friends hereafter, and this never to be remembered or upbraided,° besides, that he may not boast he has done any such thing to you in his own person, he is to come here in disguise, give you five kicks in private, sir, take your sword from you,[5] and lock you up in that study during pleasure.° Which will be but a little while; we'll get it released presently. *in order that* / *uttered in reproach* / *as long as he wants*

DAW Five kicks? He shall have six, sir, to be friends.

TRUEWIT Believe me, you shall not overshoot yourself, to send him that word by me.

DAW Deliver it, sir. He shall have it with all my heart, to be friends.

TRUEWIT Friends? Nay, an he should not be so, and heartily too, upon these terms, he shall have me to enemy while I live.—Come, sir, bear it bravely.

DAW Oh, God, sir, 'tis nothing.

TRUEWIT True. What's six kicks to a man that reads Seneca?[6]

DAW I have had a hundred, sir.

4. More in suffering than in inflicting pain, more in enduring than in dealing blows.
5. A symbolic emasculation and, for a knight, the ultimate humiliation.
6. Seneca recommends patience in the face of misfortune.

Dauphine comes forth [*in disguise. Above, enter Clerimont with Haughty, Centaur, Mrs. Otter, Mavis, Epicene, and Trusty*].

TRUEWIT Sir Amorous! No speaking one to another, or rehearsing old matters.

[*Daw offers his backside to Dauphine, who*] *kicks him.*

DAW One, two, three, four, five. I protest,° Sir Amorous, you shall have six. *insist*

TRUEWIT Nay, I told you° should not talk. [*To Dauphine*] Come, give him six, an he will needs.° [*Dauphine gives him another kick.*] Your sword. [*Daw gives Dauphine his sword.*] Now return to your safe custody. You shall presently meet afore the ladies, and be the dearest friends one to another. *you that you* / *if he insists*

[*Daw returns to his study.*]

[*To Dauphine*] Give me the scarf now; thou shalt beat the other barefaced. [*Exit Dauphine.*]

[*Calling through the door of the other study*] Stand by, Sir Amorous.

[*La Foole emerges from his study.*]

LA FOOLE What's here, a sword?

TRUEWIT I cannot help it without° I should take the quarrel upon myself. Here he has sent you his sword[7]— *unless*

LA FOOLE I'll receive none on't.

TRUEWIT And he wills you to fasten it against a wall and break° your head in some few several places against the hilts. *bruise, cut*

LA FOOLE I will not. Tell him roundly,° I cannot endure to shed my own blood. *bluntly*

TRUEWIT Will you not?

LA FOOLE No. I'll beat it against a fair flat wall, if that will satisfy him. If not, he shall beat it himself, for Amorous.° *for all I care*

TRUEWIT Why, this is strange starting off,° when a man undertakes for you! I offered him another condition: will you stand to that? *refusal to cooperate*

LA FOOLE Ay, what is't?

TRUEWIT That you will be beaten in private.

LA FOOLE Yes, I am content, at the blunt.° *in short*

TRUEWIT Then you must submit yourself to be hoodwinked° in this scarf and be led to him, where he will take your sword from you, and make you bear a blow over the mouth, *gules*,[8] and tweaks by the nose *sans nombre*.[9] *blindfolded*

LA FOOLE I am content. But why must I be blinded?

TRUEWIT That's for your good, sir, because, if he should grow insolent upon this, and publish it hereafter to your disgrace (which I hope he will not do), you might swear safely, and protest he never beat you to your knowledge.

LA FOOLE Oh, I conceive.

TRUEWIT I do not doubt but you'll be perfect good friends upon't, and not dare to utter an ill thought one of another, in future.

7. The standard challenge to a duel.
8. Scarlet. (That is, drawing blood.)
9. Without number. (French, continuing the mock-heraldic terminology.)

LA FOOLE Not I, as God help me, of him.

TRUEWIT Nor he of you, sir. If he should—Come, sir. [*He blindfolds La Foole.*]—[*Calling*] All hid,[1] Sir John.

Dauphine enters to tweak him.

LA FOOLE Oh, Sir John, Sir John. Oh, o-o-o-o-o-oh—

TRUEWIT Good Sir John, leave tweaking; you'll blow his nose off. [*To La Foole*] 'Tis Sir John's pleasure you should retire into the study. Why, now you are friends. All bitterness between you, I hope, is buried; you shall come forth by and by Damon and Pythias[2] upon't, and embrace with all the rankness° of friendship that can be. *strength; foul smell*

[*La Foole returns to his study. The ladies and Clerimont exeunt above.*]

I trust we shall have 'em tamer i'their language hereafter. Dauphine, I worship thee. God's will, the ladies have surprised us!

4.6

[*Reenter, on the main stage,*] *Haughty, Centaur, Mavis, Mrs. Otter, Epicene, Trusty,* [*and Clerimont,*] *having discovered part of the past scene above.* [*The ladies talk among themselves.*]

HAUGHTY Centaur, how our judgments were imposed on by these adulterate° knights! *sham*

CENTAUR Nay, madam, Mavis was more deceived than we; 'twas her commendation uttered 'em[1] in the College.

MAVIS I commended but their wits, madam, and their braveries. I never looked toward their valors.

HAUGHTY Sir Dauphine is valiant and a wit too, it seems.

MAVIS And a bravery too.

HAUGHTY Was this his project?

MRS. OTTER So Master Clerimont intimates, madam.

HAUGHTY Good Morose, when you come to the College, will you bring him with you? He seems a very perfect gentleman.

EPICENE He is so, madam, believe it.

CENTAUR But when will you come, Morose?

EPICENE Three or four days hence, madam, when I have got me a coach and horses.

HAUGHTY No, tomorrow, good Morose; Centaur shall send you her coach.

MAVIS Yes, faith, do, and bring Sir Dauphine with you.

HAUGHTY She has promised that, Mavis.

MAVIS He is a very worthy gentleman in his exteriors, madam.

HAUGHTY Ay, he shows he is judicial° in his clothes. *judicious*

CENTAUR And yet not so superlatively neat° as some, madam, that have their faces set in a brake![2] *dandyish*

HAUGHTY Ay, and have every hair in form!° *place*

1. The "Ready!" cry of children in a game of a hide-and-seek.
2. Legendary friends who offered to die for one another.

4.6. The scene continues.
1. (1) Declared their character; (2) advertised them.
2. An immovable expression. (A brake is a wooden framework to confine a horse while it is shod.)

MAVIS That wear purer linen than ourselves, and profess more neatness than the French hermaphrodite![3]

EPICENE Ay, ladies; they, what they tell one of us, have told a thousand, and are the only thieves of our fame,° that think to take us with that perfume or with that lace, and laugh at us unconscionably when they have done. *reputation*

HAUGHTY But Sir Dauphine's carelessness° becomes him. *casual manner*

CENTAUR I could love a man for such a nose!

MAVIS Or such a leg!

CENTAUR He has an exceeding good eye, madam!

MAVIS And a very good lock!° *(of hair)*

CENTAUR Good Morose, bring him to my chamber first.

MRS. OTTER Please Your Honors to meet at my house, madam?

TRUEWIT [*aside to Dauphine*] See how they eye thee, man! They are taken, I warrant thee.

HAUGHTY [*approaching Dauphine and Truewit*] You have unbraced° our brace° of knights, here, Master Truewit. *exposed / pair*

TRUEWIT Not I, madam, it was Sir Dauphine's engine:° who, if he have disfurnished° Your Ladyship of any guard or service by it, is able to make the place good again in himself. *contrivance* *deprived*

HAUGHTY There's no suspicion of that, sir.

[*She kisses Dauphine.*]

CENTAUR God so, Mavis, Haughty is kissing.

MAVIS Let us go too, and take part.

[*They approach the gentlemen.*]

HAUGHTY But I am glad of the fortune—beside the discovery of two such empty caskets—to gain the knowledge of so rich a mine of virtue as Sir Dauphine.

CENTAUR We would be all glad to style him of our friendship° and see him at the College. *one of our company*

MAVIS He cannot mix with a sweeter society, I'll prophesy, and I hope he himself will think so.

DAUPHINE I should be rude to imagine otherwise, lady.

TRUEWIT [*aside to Dauphine*] Did not I tell thee, Dauphine? Why, all their actions are governed by crude opinion without reason or cause. They know not why they do anything, but as they are informed,° believe, judge, praise, condemn, love, hate, and—in emulation one of another—do all these things alike. Only they have a natural inclination sways 'em generally to the worst when they are left to themselves. But pursue it, now thou hast 'em. *(by gossip or rumor)*

HAUGHTY Shall we go in again, Morose?

EPICENE Yes, madam.

CENTAUR We'll entreat Sir Dauphine's company.

TRUEWIT Stay,° good madam, the interview of the two friends, Pylades and Orestes.[4] I'll fetch 'em out to you straight. *Wait for*

HAUGHTY Will you, Master Truewit?

DAUPHINE Ay, but, noble ladies, do not confess in your countenance or outward bearing to 'em any discovery° of their *awareness*

3. Perhaps referring to King Henry III of France, a notorious transvestite, or to a French castrato who visited England.

4. Like Damon and Pythias (see 4.5.332 and note), famous for their friendship.

follies, that we may see how they will bear up again, with what assurance and erection.[5]

HAUGHTY We will not, Sir Dauphine.

CENTAUR [*and*] MAVIS Upon our honors, Sir Dauphine.

TRUEWIT [*calling through the study door*] Sir Amorous, Sir Amorous, the ladies are here.

LA FOOLE [*within*] Are they?

TRUEWIT Yes, but slip° out by and by, as their backs are turned, and meet Sir John here as by chance, when I call you. [*Calling through the other study door*] Jack Daw! *simply slip*

DAW [*within*] What say you, sir?

TRUEWIT Whip out behind me suddenly, and no anger i'your looks to your adversary. Now, now.

[*La Foole and Daw emerge from their studies.*]

LA FOOLE Noble Sir John Daw! Where ha' you been?

DAW To seek you, Sir Amorous.

LA FOOLE Me! I honor you.

DAW I prevent you,° sir. *(by honoring you first)*

CLERIMONT They have forgot their rapiers!

TRUEWIT Oh, they meet in peace, man.

DAUPHINE Where's your sword, Sir John?

CLERIMONT And yours, Sir Amorous?

DAW Mine? My boy had it forth° to mend the handle, e'en now. *took it away*

LA FOOLE And my gold handle was broke too, and my boy had it forth.

DAUPHINE Indeed, sir? [*To Truewit and Clerimont*] How their excuses meet!

CLERIMONT What a consent there is i'the handles!

TRUEWIT Nay, there is so i'the points too, I warrant you.[6]

MRS. OTTER Oh, me! Madam, he comes again, the madman.° Away! [*Exeunt Daw, La Foole, and the Collegiate Ladies.*] *(Morose)*

4.7

[*Enter*] *Morose* [*with*] *the two swords* [*belonging to Daw and La Foole, which*] *he had found drawn within.*

MOROSE What make° these naked weapons here, gentlemen? *do*

TRUEWIT Oh, sir! Here hath like to° been murder since you went! A couple of knights fallen out[1] about the bride's favors; we were fain° to take away their weapons. Your house had been begged[2] by this time else— *was likely to have* *obliged*

MOROSE For what?

CLERIMONT For manslaughter, sir, as being accessory.

MOROSE And for her favors?

TRUEWIT Ay, sir, heretofore,° not present.—Clerimont, carry 'em their swords now. They have done all the hurt they will do. [*Exit Clerimont.*] *before the marriage*

5. Confidence. (With a phallic joke.)
6. I.e., they are equally harmless.
4.7. The scene continues.
1. Having quarreled.
2. Requested by a courtier after being forfeited to the Crown as the property of a felon. Truewit pretends that Morose would have been considered an accessory to the homicides committed by Daw and La Foole.

DAUPHINE Ha' you spoke with a lawyer, sir?

MOROSE Oh, no. There is such a noise i'the court that they have frighted me home with more violence than I went. Such speaking and counterspeaking with their several voices of citations, appellations, allegations, certificates, attachments, inter'gatories, references, convictions, and afflictions indeed among the doctors and proctors,[3] that the noise here is silence to't!° A kind of calm midnight! *compared with it*

TRUEWIT Why, sir, if you would be resolved indeed, I can bring you hither a very sufficient° lawyer and a learned divine° that shall inquire into every least scruple for you. *competent* *clergyman*

MOROSE Can you, Master Truewit?

TRUEWIT Yes, and are very sober grave persons that will dispatch it in a chamber with a whisper or two.

MOROSE Good sir, shall I hope this benefit from you and trust myself into your hands?

TRUEWIT Alas, sir! Your nephew and I have been ashamed and ofttimes mad since you went, to think how you are abused. Go in, good sir, and lock yourself up till we call you; we'll tell you more anon, sir.

MOROSE Do your pleasure with me, gentlemen; I believe in you, and that deserves no delusion.

TRUEWIT You shall find none, sir— [*Exit Morose.*] but heaped, heaped plenty of vexation.

DAUPHINE What wilt thou do now, wit?

TRUEWIT Recover° me hither Otter and the barber if you can by any means, presently.° *Bring* *right away*

DAUPHINE Why? To what purpose?

TRUEWIT Oh, I'll make the deepest divine and gravest lawyer out o'them two, for him—

DAUPHINE Thou canst not, man; these are waking dreams.° *delusions*

TRUEWIT Do not fear° me. Clap but a civil gown with a welt[4] o'the one, and a canonical cloak with sleeves o'the other, and give 'em a few terms i'their mouths. If there come not forth as able a doctor and complete a parson for this turn° as may be wished, trust not my election.° And I hope without wronging the dignity of either profession, since they are but persons put on and for mirth's sake,[5] to torment him. The barber smatters° Latin, I remember. *doubt* *purpose* *discretion; choice* *speaks a little*

DAUPHINE Yes, and Otter too.

TRUEWIT Well, then, if I make 'em not wrangle° out this case to his no-comfort, let me be thought a Jack Daw or La Foole, or anything worse. Go you to your ladies, but first send for them.° *(a legal term)* *(Cutbeard and Otter)*

DAUPHINE I will. [*Exeunt.*]

3. These are all legal terms. Attachments (lines 16–17) are (1) arrests; (2) seizures of property. Interrogatories are formal legal questioning. Doctors and proctors are legal scholars and attorneys.

4. Ornamental stripe indicating a doctor of civil law.

5. Jonson attempts to ward off the kind of criticism he had received for his satiric portrayal of soldiers in *Every Man Out of His Humour* (1599), courtiers in *Cynthia's Revels* (c. 1600), and actors in *Poetaster* (1601).

5.1

[Enter] La Foole, Clerimont, [and] Daw.

LA FOOLE Where had you our swords, Master Clerimont?

CLERIMONT Why, Dauphine took 'em from the madman.° *(Morose)*

LA FOOLE And he took 'em from our boys, I warrant you.

CLERIMONT Very like, sir.

LA FOOLE Thank you, good Master Clerimont. Sir John Daw and I are both beholden to you.

CLERIMONT Would I knew how to make you so, gentlemen.

DAW Sir Amorous and I are your servants, sir.

[Enter] Mavis.

MAVIS Gentlemen, have any of you a pen and ink? I would fain write out a riddle in Italian for Sir Dauphine to translate.

CLERIMONT Not I, in troth, lady. I am no scrivener.° *professional copyist*

DAW I can furnish you, I think, lady.

[Daw and Mavis confer privately.]

CLERIMONT He has it in the haft° of a knife, I believe! *handle*

LA FOOLE No, he has his box of instruments.

CLERIMONT Like a surgeon!

LA FOOLE For the mathematics: his squire,° his compasses, his brass pens, and black lead, to draw maps of every place and person where he comes. *square*

CLERIMONT How, maps of persons!

LA FOOLE Yes, sir, of Nomentack when he was here, and of the Prince of Moldavia, and of his mistress, Mistress Epicene.[1]

CLERIMONT Away! He has not found out her latitude, I hope.

LA FOOLE You are a pleasant° gentleman, sir. *jocular*

[Exit Mavis with pen and ink.]

CLERIMONT Faith, now we are in private, let's wanton it° a little and talk waggishly.—Sir John, I am telling Sir Amorous here that you two govern the ladies where'er you come; you carry the feminine gender afore you. *be sportive*

DAW They shall rather carry us afore them, if they will, sir.° *(an attempt at bawdry)*

CLERIMONT Nay, I believe that they do, withal!° But that you are the prime men in their affections, and direct all their actions— *as well*

DAW Not I; Sir Amorous is.

LA FOOLE I protest, Sir John is.

DAW As I hope to rise i'the state, Sir Amorous, you ha' the person.° *physique*

LA FOOLE Sir John, you ha' the person and the discourse° too. *conversational ability*

DAW Not I, sir. I have no discourse—and then you have activity° beside. *athletic ability*

LA FOOLE I protest, Sir John, you come as high from Tripoli° as I do every whit, and lift as many joint-stools,[2] and leap over 'em, if you would use it— *jump as high*

5.1. Morose's house still.

1. Nomentack was a Native American from the Virginia Colony, brought, as a curiosity of the New World, to England in 1608. The Prince of Moldavia was Stephano Janiculo, a fraud who claimed to be of royal origin and to be engaged to Lady Arabella Stuart (see second prologue, note 1). Arabella apparently interpreted the phrase "his mistress, Mistress Epicene" as a reference to herself, even though Jonson evidently meant that Epicene was Daw's mistress.

2. A routine way to show off strength.

CLERIMONT Well, agree on't together, knights; for between you, you divide the kingdom or commonwealth of ladies' affections; I see it, and can perceive a little how they observe you and fear you, indeed. You could tell strange stories, my masters, if you would, I know.

DAW Faith, we have seen somewhat, sir.

LA FOOLE That we have—velvet petticoats and wrought smocks,° or so. *embroidered petticoats*

DAW Ay, and—

CLERIMONT Nay, out with it, Sir John; do not envy your friend the pleasure of hearing, when you have had the delight of tasting.

DAW Why—ah—do you speak, Sir Amorous.

LA FOOLE No, do you, Sir John Daw.

DAW I'faith, you shall.

LA FOOLE I'faith, you shall.

DAW Why, we have been—

LA FOOLE In the great bed at Ware[3] together in our time. On, Sir John.

DAW Nay, do you, Sir Amorous.

CLERIMONT And these ladies with you, knights?

LA FOOLE No, excuse us, sir.

DAW We must not wound reputation.

LA FOOLE No matter—they were these, or others. Our bath[4] cost us fifteen pound when we came home.

CLERIMONT Do you hear, Sir John, you shall tell me but one thing truly, as you love me.

DAW If I can, I will, sir.

CLERIMONT You lay° in the same house with the bride, here? *resided*

DAW Yes, and conversed with her hourly, sir.

CLERIMONT And what humor is she of? Is she coming and open, free?

DAW Oh, exceeding open, sir. I was her servant, and Sir Amorous was to be.

CLERIMONT Come, you have both had favors from her? I know and have heard so much.

DAW Oh, no, sir.

LA FOOLE You shall excuse us, sir. We must not wound reputation.

CLERIMONT Tut, she is married now, and you cannot hurt her with any report, and therefore speak plainly. How many times, i'faith? Which of you led first, ha?

LA FOOLE Sir John had her maidenhead, indeed.

DAW Oh, it pleases him to say so, sir, but Sir Amorous knows what's what as well.

CLERIMONT Dost thou, i'faith, Amorous?

LA FOOLE In a manner, sir.

CLERIMONT Why, I commend you, lads. Little knows Don° Bridegroom of this. Nor shall he, for me.° *Sir* *for my part*

DAW Hang him, mad ox.° *i.e., cuckold*

3. A huge bed, capable of sleeping more than twelve people, in the Saracen's Head Inn at Ware (see 3.2.72 and note).

4. Medical remedy for venereal disease.

CLERIMONT Speak softly; here comes his nephew with the Lady Haughty. He'll get the ladies from you, sirs, if you look not to him in time.

LA FOOLE Why, if he do, we'll fetch 'em home again, I warrant you. [*Exeunt*.]

5.2

[*Enter*] *Haughty* [*and*] *Dauphine*.

HAUGHTY I assure you, Sir Dauphine, it is the price° and estimation of your virtue only that hath embarked me to this adventure, and I could not but make out to tell° you so; nor can I repent me of the act, since it is always an argument of some virtue in ourselves that we love and affect° it so in others. *worth* / *make a point of telling* / *admire*

DAUPHINE Your Ladyship sets too high a price on my weakness.

HAUGHTY Sir, I can distinguish gems from pebbles—

DAUPHINE [*aside*] Are you so skillful in stones?° *jewels; testicles*

HAUGHTY And, howsoever I may suffer in such a judgment as yours, by admitting equality of rank or society with Centaur or Mavis—

DAUPHINE You do not, madam; I perceive they are your mere foils.[1]

HAUGHTY Then are you a friend to truth, sir. It makes me love you the more. It is not the outward, but the inward man that I affect. They° are not apprehensive of an eminent perfection, but love flat and dully. *(Centaur and Mavis)*

CENTAUR [*within*] Where are you, my Lady Haughty?

HAUGHTY I come presently, Centaur.—My chamber, sir, my page shall show you; and Trusty, my woman, shall be ever awake for you. You need not fear to communicate anything with her, for she is a Fidelia.[2] I pray you wear this jewel for my sake, Sir Dauphine. [*She gives Dauphine a jewel*.]

[*Enter*] *Centaur*.

Where's Mavis, Centaur?

CENTAUR Within, madam, a-writing. I'll follow you presently. I'll but speak a word with Sir Dauphine. [*Exit Haughty*.]

DAUPHINE With me, madam?

CENTAUR Good Sir Dauphine, do not trust Haughty nor make any credit° to her, whatever you do besides. Sir Dauphine, I give you this caution: she is a perfect courtier[3] and loves nobody but for her uses, and for her uses she loves all. Besides, her physicians give her out to be none o'the clearest[4]—whether she pay 'em or no, heav'n knows—and she's above fifty, too, and pargets![5] See her in a forenoon.[6] *give any credence*

[*Enter*] *Mavis* [*with a paper*].

5.2. The scene is virtually continuous.
1. Literally, black backgrounds that add luster to a diamond.
2. Stock name for a faithful servant.
3. I.e., smoothly insincere and manipulative.
4. Report her to be tainted with venereal disease.
5. Plasters (herself with cosmetics).
6. In the morning, before she has applied her makeup.

Here comes Mavis, a worse face than she! You would not like this by candlelight. If you'll come to my chamber one o'these mornings early, or late in an evening, I'll tell you more.—Where's Haughty, Mavis?

MAVIS Within, Centaur.

CENTAUR What ha' you there?

MAVIS An Italian riddle for Sir Dauphine. (You shall not see it, i'faith, Centaur.) Good Sir Dauphine, solve it for me. I'll call for it anon. [*She gives the paper to Dauphine. Exeunt Centaur and Mavis.*]

[*Enter*] *Clerimont.*

CLERIMONT How now, Dauphine? How dost thou quit thyself of these females?

DAUPHINE 'Slight, they haunt me like fairies and give me jewels here; I cannot be rid of 'em.

CLERIMONT Oh, you must not tell, though.[7]

DAUPHINE Mass,° [*By the Mass (an oath)*] I forgot that! I was never so assaulted. One loves for virtue, and bribes me with this. Another loves me with caution, and so would possess me. A third brings me a riddle here; and all are jealous, and rail each at other.

CLERIMONT A riddle? Pray le' me see't. (*He reads the paper.*) "Sir Dauphine, I chose this way of intimation for privacy. The ladies here, I know, have both hope and purpose to make a Collegiate and servant of you. If I might be so honored as to appear at any end of so noble a work, I would enter into a fame of taking physic[8] tomorrow, and continue it four or five days or longer, for your visitation. Mavis." By my faith, a subtle one! Call you this a riddle? What's their plain dealing, trow?° [*do you suppose?*]

DAUPHINE We lack Truewit to tell us that.

CLERIMONT We lack him for somewhat else, too. His knights *reformados*° [*chastened (Spanish)*] are wound up as high and insolent as ever they were.

DAUPHINE You jest.

CLERIMONT No drunkards, either with wine or vanity, ever confessed such stories of themselves. I would not give a fly's leg in balance against all the women's reputations here, if they could be but thought to speak truth; and for° [*as for*] the bride, they have made their affidavit against her directly—

DAUPHINE What, that they have lien° [*lain*] with her?

CLERIMONT Yes, and tell times and circumstances, with the cause why and the place where. I had almost brought 'em to affirm that they had done it today.

DAUPHINE Not both of 'em!

CLERIMONT Yes, faith, with a "sooth"[9] or two more I had effected it. They would ha' set it down under their hands.° [*sworn it in writing*]

DAUPHINE Why, they will be our sport, I see, still, whether we will or no.

7. Because fairies' gifts vanished unless they were kept secret.
8. I would start a rumor that I was undergoing medical treatment.
9. Expression of surprise, admiration, or agreement, like "Really!"

5.3

[Enter] Truewit.

TRUEWIT Oh, are you here? Come, Dauphine. Go, call your uncle presently. I have fitted my divine and my canonist, dyed their beards and all. The knaves do not know themselves, they are so exalted and altered. Preferment° changes any man. Thou shalt keep one door, and I another, and then Clerimont in the midst, that he° may have no means of escape from their caviling when they grow hot once. And then the women—as I have given the bride her instructions—to break in upon him i'the *l'envoy*.° Oh, 'twill be full and twanging! Away, fetch him. *[Exit Dauphine.]*

Career advancement

(Morose)

postscript

[Enter] Cutbeard [disguised as a canon lawyer, and] Otter [as a parson].

Come, Master Doctor and Master Parson, look to your parts now, and discharge 'em bravely.° You are well set forth; perform it as well. If you chance to be out,° do not confess it with standing still or humming or gaping one at another, but go on and talk aloud and eagerly, use vehement action, and only remember your terms, and you are safe. Let the matter go where it will; you have many will do so.[1] But at first be very solemn and grave like your garments, though you loose yourselves° after and skip out like a brace of jugglers on a table. Here he comes! Set your faces and look superciliously while I present you.

carry them out well

at a loss

let yourselves go

[Enter] Dauphine [and] Morose.

MOROSE Are these the two learned men?

TRUEWIT Yes, sir. Please you salute° 'em. *greet*

MOROSE Salute 'em? I had rather do anything than wear out time so unfruitfully, sir. I wonder how these common forms, as "God save you," and "You are welcome," are come to be a habit in our lives! Or, "I am glad to see you!"—when I cannot see what the profit can be of these words, so long as it is no whit better with him whose affairs are sad and grievous that he hears this salutation.

TRUEWIT 'Tis true, sir. We'll go to the matter, then.—Gentlemen, Master Doctor and Master Parson, I have acquainted you sufficiently with the business for which you are come hither. And you are not now to inform yourselves in the state of the question, I know. This is the gentleman who expects your resolution, and therefore when you please, begin.

OTTER Please you, Master Doctor.

CUTBEARD Please you, good Master Parson.

OTTER I would hear the canon law[2] speak first.

CUTBEARD It must give place to positive divinity,[3] sir.

MOROSE Nay, good gentlemen, do not throw me into circumstances.° Let your comforts arrive quickly at me, those that are.° Be swift in affording me my peace, if so I shall hope

don't beat around the bush

such as they are

5.3. The scene continues.

1. Don't worry about the substance of what you say; lots of learned scholars don't.

2. Ecclesiastical law, supposedly Cutbeard's province.

3. Theology based directly on Scripture, Otter's area of expertise.

any. I love not your disputations or your court-tumults. And that it be not strange to you, I will tell you. My father, in my education, was wont to advise me that I should always collect and contain my mind, not suffering it to flow loosely; that I should look to what things were necessary to the carriage° of my life and what not, embracing the one and eschewing the other. In short, that I should endear myself to rest and avoid turmoil, which now is grown to be another nature to me, so that I come not to your public pleadings or your places of noise—not that I neglect those things that make for the dignity of the commonwealth, but for the mere avoiding of clamors and impertinencies of orators that know not how to be silent. And for the cause of noise am I now a suitor to you. You do not know in what a misery I have been exercised this day, what a torrent of evil! My very house turns round with the tumult! I dwell in a windmill! The perpetual motion is here and not at Eltham.[4] *conduct*

TRUEWIT Well, good Master Doctor, will you break the ice? Master Parson will wade after.

CUTBEARD Sir, though unworthy and the weaker, I will presume.

OTTER 'Tis no presumption, *Domine*° Doctor. *Master*

MOROSE Yet again!

CUTBEARD Your question is, for how many causes a man may have *divortium legitimum*,[5] a lawful divorce. First, you must understand the nature of the word "divorce," *a divertendo*°— *derived from "separate"*

MOROSE No excursions° upon words, good Doctor; to the question briefly. *digressions*

CUTBEARD I answer then: the canon law affords divorce but in few cases, and the principal is in the common case, the adulterous case. But there are *duodecim impedimenta*, twelve impediments, as we call 'em, all which do not *dirimere contractum*, but *irritum reddere matrimonium*, as we say in the canon law, not take away the bond but cause a nullity therein.

MOROSE I understood you before. Good sir, avoid your impertinency of translation.

OTTER He cannot open° this too much, sir, by your favor. *clarify*

MOROSE Yet more!

TRUEWIT Oh, you must give the learned men leave, sir. To your impediments, Master Doctor.

CUTBEARD The first is *impedimentum erroris*.° *the impediment of error*

OTTER Of which there are several species.

CUTBEARD Ay, as *error personae*.

OTTER If you contract yourself to one person, thinking her another.

CUTBEARD Then, *error fortunae*.

OTTER If she be a beggar and you thought her rich.

CUTBEARD Then, *error qualitatis*.

4. A royal palace nine miles south of Saint Paul's in which an inventor exhibited what he claimed was a perpetual motion machine.

5. Translated in the following phrase, as is much of the Latin in this scene. The points of ecclesiastical law are from Thomas Aquinas, much of whose body of marriage regulations had been adopted by the Church of England.

OTTER If she prove stubborn or headstrong that you thought obedient.

MOROSE How? Is that, sir, a lawful impediment? One at once,° I pray you, gentlemen. *a time*

OTTER Ay, *ante copulam*, but not *post copulam,*[6] sir.

CUTBEARD Master Parson says right. *Nec post nuptiarum benedictionem.*[7] It doth indeed but *irrita reddere sponsalia,* annul the contract;[8] after marriage it is of no obstancy.° *judicial opposition*

TRUEWIT Alas, sir, what a hope are we fall'n from, by this time!

CUTBEARD The next is *conditio:* if you thought her freeborn and she prove a bondwoman, there is impediment of estate and condition.

OTTER Ay, but Master Doctor, those servitudes are *sublatae*° now among us Christians. *laid aside*

CUTBEARD By your favor, Master Parson—

OTTER You shall give me leave, Master Doctor.

MOROSE Nay, gentlemen, quarrel not in that question; it concerns not my case. Pass to the third.

CUTBEARD Well, then, the third is *votum:* if either party have made a vow of chastity. But that practice, as Master Parson said of the other, is taken away among us, thanks be to discipline.[9] The fourth is *cognatio:* if the persons be of kin within the degrees.[1]

OTTER Ay; do you know what the degrees are, sir?

MOROSE No, nor I care not, sir. They offer me no comfort in the question, I am sure.

CUTBEARD But, there is a branch of this impediment may, which is *cognatio spiritualis.* If you were her godfather, sir, then the marriage is incestuous.

OTTER That comment is absurd and superstitious, Master Doctor. I cannot endure it. Are we not all brothers and sisters, and as much akin in that as godfathers and goddaughters?[2]

MOROSE Oh, me! To end the controversy, I never was a godfather, I never was a godfather in my life, sir. Pass to the next.

CUTBEARD The fifth is *crimen adulterii,*° the known case. The sixth, *cultus disparitas,* difference of religion. Have you ever examined her what religion she is of? *crime of adultery*

MOROSE No, I would rather she were of none than be put to the trouble of it.

OTTER You may have it done for you, sir.

MOROSE By no means, good sir. On to the rest. Shall you ever come to an end, think you?

TRUEWIT Yes, he has done half, sir. On to the rest! Be patient and expect,° sir. *wait*

6. Before copulation, but not after copulation.
7. Nor after the nuptial blessing has been pronounced.
8. That is, it is grounds for breaking an engagement.
9. Thanks to the religious reformation. (Protestants did not consider celibacy holier than marriage and discouraged vows of chastity.)
1. Degrees of forbidden relationships.
2. Rigorous Protestants objected to the elaborate incest taboos established in medieval ecclesiastical law and inherited by the Church of England; they also minimized the importance of godparents.

CUTBEARD The seventh is *vis:* if it were upon compulsion or force.

MOROSE Oh, no, it was too voluntary, mine; too voluntary.

CUTBEARD The eighth is *ordo:* if ever she have taken holy orders.

OTTER That's superstitious too.[3]

MOROSE No matter, Master Parson. Would she would go into a nunnery° yet! *convent; brothel*

CUTBEARD The ninth is *ligamen:* if you were bound, sir, to any other before.

MOROSE I thrust myself too soon into these fetters.

CUTBEARD The tenth is *publica honestas*, which is *inchoata quaedam affinitas.*[4]

OTTER Ay, or *affinitas orta ex sponsalibus*, and is but *leve impedimentum.*[5]

MOROSE I feel no air of comfort blowing to me in all this.

CUTBEARD The eleventh is *affinitas ex fornicatione.*[6]

OTTER Which is no less *vera affinitas*° than the other, Master Doctor. *true a relationship*

CUTBEARD True, *quae oritur ex legitimo matrimonio.*[7]

OTTER You say right, venerable Doctor. And *nascitur ex eo quod per conjugium duae personae efficiuntur una caro*[8]—

MOROSE Heyday, now they begin.

CUTBEARD I conceive you, Master Parson. *Ita per fornicationem aeque est verus pater, qui sic generat*[9]—

OTTER *Et vere filius qui sic generatur*[1]—

MOROSE What's all this to me?

CLERIMONT [*aside to Truewit and Dauphine*] Now it grows warm.

CUTBEARD The twelfth and last is, *si forte coire nequibis.*[2]

OTTER Ay, that is *impedimentum gravissimum.*° It doth utterly annul and annihilate, that. If you have *manifestam frigiditatem*° you are well, sir. *a most heavy impediment* / *obvious impotence*

TRUEWIT Why, there is comfort come at length, sir. Confess yourself but a man unable, and she will sue to be divorced first.

OTTER Ay, or if there be *morbus perpetuus et insanabilis,*[3] as paralysis, elephantiasis, or so—

DAUPHINE Oh, but *frigiditas* is the fairer way, gentlemen.

OTTER You say troth, sir, and as it is in the canon, Master Doctor.

CUTBEARD I conceive you, sir.

3. Because Protestant clergy did not take vows of celibacy and the Church of England did not maintain convents or monasteries.

4. "Public decency," the technical term for an impediment that arises once a betrothal is solemnized: the kin of the betrothed are no longer permitted to marry one another, even if the engagement is later broken off. *Inchoata quaedam affinitas*: "a kind of incomplete marriage relationship."

5. Relationship arising from marriage, and is but a light impediment. (The Church of England had a more restricted definition of incest than did the Roman Catholic Church. Technically marriages between distant in-laws could still be annulled as incestuous, but in practice such strictures were rarely invoked.)

6. Relationship through fornication. (One could not marry the kin of anyone with whom one had had an illicit relationship.)

7. Which arises from a legitimate marriage.

8. And originates in the fact that in marriage two persons become one flesh.

9. Thus he is just as true a father as one who produces offspring in this manner, through fornication.

1. And he is truly a son who is thus begotten.

2. If you cannot perform sexual intercourse.

3. An enduring and incurable disease. Elephantiasis (line 177) is a parastic infection of the lymphatic system that produces enormous swelling, especially in the legs and scrotum.

CLERIMONT [*aside*] Before he speaks.

OTTER That a boy, or child under years, is not fit for marriage because he cannot *reddere debitum.*[4] So your *omnipotentes*°—

all-powerful ones

TRUEWIT [*aside to Otter*] Your *impotentes,* you whoreson lobster.

OTTER Your *impotentes*, I should say, are *minime apti ad contrahenda matrimonium.*[5]

TRUEWIT [*aside to Otter*] *"Matrimonium"*? We shall have most unmatrimonial Latin with you.[6] *"Matrimonia,"* and be hanged!

DAUPHINE [*aside to Truewit*] You put 'em out,° man.

disconcert them

CUTBEARD But then there will arise a doubt, Master Parson, in our case, *post matrimonium:*° that *frigiditate praeditus*[7]—do you conceive me, sir?

after marriage

OTTER Very well, sir.

CUTBEARD Who cannot *uti uxore pro uxore*, may *habere eam pro sorore.*[8]

OTTER Absurd, absurd, absurd, and merely apostatical.°

heretical

CUTBEARD You shall pardon me, Master Parson, I can prove it.

OTTER You can prove[9] a will, Master Doctor, you can prove nothing else. Does not the verse of your own canon say, *"Haec socianda vetant conubia, facta retractant—"*[1]

CUTBEARD I grant you, but how do they *retractare,*° Master Parson?

make it invalid

MOROSE [*aside*] Oh, this was it I feared.

OTTER *In aeternum,*° sir.

Eternally

CUTBEARD That's false in divinity, by your favor.

OTTER 'Tis false in humanity to say so. Is he not *prorsus inutilis ad thorum?* Can he *praestare fidem datam?*[2] I would fain know.

CUTBEARD Yes; how if he do *convalere?*°

recover

OTTER He cannot *convalere*, it is impossible.

[*Morose attempts to exit but is intercepted by Truewit.*]

TRUEWIT Nay, good sir, attend the learned men; they'll think you neglect 'em else.

CUTBEARD Or, if he do *simulare* himself *frigidum, odio uxoris,*[3] or so?

OTTER I say, he is *adulter manifestus,*° then.

plainly an adulterer

DAUPHINE [*aside*] They dispute it very learnedly, i'faith.

OTTER And *prostitutor uxoris,*° and this is positive.

a prostitutor of his wife

MOROSE [*to Truewit*] Good sir, let me escape.

TRUEWIT You will not do me that wrong, sir?

OTTER And therefore, if he be *manifeste frigidus,* sir—

CUTBEARD Ay, if he be *manifeste frigidus,* I grant you—

OTTER Why, that was my conclusion.

4. Pay the (marital) debt.
5. Not at all able to contract marriage.
6. Because the genders of Otter's words are improper.
7. One suffering from impotence.
8. Use a wife as a wife, may have her for a sister.
9. In the sense of "probate."

1. "These associations prevent marrying, and if a marriage has already occurred, they render it invalid."
2. Is he not completely useless in the marriage-bed? Can he keep the promise he has made?
3. If he pretends himself frigid, out of hatred of his wife.

CUTBEARD And mine too.
TRUEWIT [*to Morose*] Nay, hear the conclusion, sir.
OTTER Then, *frigiditatis causa*[4]—
CUTBEARD Yes, *causa frigiditatis*—
MOROSE Oh, mine ears!
OTTER She may have *libellum divortii*° against you. *a bill of divorce*
CUTBEARD Ay, *divortii libellum* she will sure have.
MOROSE Good echoes, forbear.
OTTER If you confess it.
CUTBEARD Which I would do, sir—
MOROSE I will do anything.—
OTTER And clear myself *in foro conscientiae*[5]—
CUTBEARD Because you want indeed—
MOROSE Yet more?
OTTER *Exercendi potestate*.° *The power to raise it*

5.4

[*Enter*] *Epicene, Haughty, Centaur, Mavis, Mrs. Otter, Daw,* [*and*] *La Foole.*

EPICENE I will not endure it any longer. Ladies, I beseech you help me. This is such a wrong as never was offered to poor bride before. Upon her marriage day to have her husband conspire against her, and a couple of mercenary companions° to be brought in for form's sake to persuade a separation! If you had blood° or virtue in you, gentlemen, you would not suffer such earwigs[1] about a husband, or scorpions to creep between man and wife— *base fellows* / *breeding*
MOROSE Oh, the variety and changes of my torment!
HAUGHTY Let 'em be cudgeled out of doors by our grooms.
CENTAUR I'll lend you my footman.
MAVIS We'll have our men blanket 'em[2] i'the hall.
MRS. OTTER As there was one at our house, madam, for peeping in at the door.° *(as a Peeping Tom)*
DAW Content, i'faith.
TRUEWIT Stay, ladies and gentlemen, you'll hear before you proceed?
MAVIS I'd ha' the bridegroom blanketed, too.
CENTAUR Begin with him first.
HAUGHTY Yes, by my troth.
MOROSE O mankind generation!° *race of manlike women*
DAUPHINE Ladies, for my sake, forbear.
HAUGHTY Yes, for Sir Dauphine's sake.
CENTAUR He shall command us.
LA FOOLE He is as fine a gentleman of his inches,° madam, as any is about the town, and wears as good colors when he list.° *size (with bawdy pun)* / *wishes*
TRUEWIT [*to Morose*] Be brief, sir, and confess your infirmity; she'll be afire to be quit° of you; if she but hear that° named once, you shall not entreat her to stay. She'll fly you like one that had the marks° upon him. *rid / (impotence)* / *plague sores*

4. For the reason of frigidity.
5. In the forum of conscience. (Because permanent impotence was hard to prove in court.)
5.4. The scene continues.

1. Bad counselors. (Literally, insects believed to penetrate the brain through the ear.)
2. Toss them in blankets, a humiliating punishment.

MOROSE Ladies, I must crave all your pardons—

TRUEWIT Silence, ladies.

MOROSE For a wrong I have done to your whole sex in marrying this fair and virtuous gentlewoman—

CLERIMONT Hear him, good ladies.

MOROSE Being guilty of an infirmity which, before I conferred with these learned men, I thought I might have concealed—

TRUEWIT But now being better informed in his conscience by them, he is to declare it, and give satisfaction by asking your public forgiveness.

MOROSE I am no man, ladies.

ALL How!

MOROSE Utterly unabled in nature, by reason of frigidity, to perform the duties or any the least office of a husband.

MAVIS Now, out upon him, prodigious° creature! *monstrous*

CENTAUR Bridegroom uncarnate!° *lit., "without flesh"*

HAUGHTY And would you offer it° to a young gentlewoman? *(marriage)*

MRS. OTTER A lady of her longings?

EPICENE Tut, a device,° a device, this! It smells rankly, ladies. A mere comment° of his own. *trick* *fabrication*

TRUEWIT Why, if you suspect that, ladies, you may have him searched.

DAW As the custom is, by a jury of physicians.[3]

LA FOOLE Yes, faith, 'twill be brave.° *fine*

MOROSE Oh, me, must I undergo that!

MRS. OTTER No, let women search him, madam; we can do it ourselves.

MOROSE Out on me, worse!

EPICENE No, ladies, you shall not need. I'll take him with all his faults.

MOROSE Worst of all!

CLERIMONT Why, then, 'tis no divorce, Doctor, if she consent not?

CUTBEARD No, if the man be *frigidus*, it is *de parte uxoris*° that we grant *libellum divortii*, in the law. *on the part of the wife*

OTTER Ay, it is the same in theology.

MOROSE Worse, worse than worst!

TRUEWIT Nay, sir, be not utterly disheartened. We have yet a small relic of hope left, as near as our comfort is blown out.—Clerimont, produce your brace of knights. What was that, Master Parson, you told me *in errore qualitatis*,° e'en now? [*Aside to Dauphine*] Dauphine, whisper the bride that she carry it° as if she were guilty and ashamed. *(see 5.3.92–94)* *should act*

OTTER Marry, sir, *in errore qualitatis*, which Master Doctor did forbear to urge, if she be found *corrupta*, that is, vitiated° or broken up, that was *pro virgine desponsa*, espoused for a maid— *deflowered*

MOROSE What then, sir?

OTTER It doth *dirimere contractum*, and *irritum reddere*[4] too.

TRUEWIT If this be true, we are happy again, sir, once more.

3. On the Continent, though not in England, a group of physicians (or, alternatively, matrons) tested male defendants in divorce cases for impotence and reported their findings to the court.

4. Cancel the contract and render it void.

Here are an honorable brace of knights that shall affirm so much.

DAW Pardon us, good Master Clerimont.

LA FOOLE You shall excuse us, Master Clerimont.

CLERIMONT Nay, you must make it good now, knights; there is no remedy, I'll eat no words for you, nor no men; you know you spoke it to me!

DAW Is this gentlemanlike, sir?

TRUEWIT [*aside to Daw*] Jack Daw, he's° worse than Sir Amorous, fiercer a great deal. [*Aside to La Foole*] Sir Amorous, beware, there be ten Daws in this Clerimont. *Clerimont is*

LA FOOLE I'll confess it, sir.

DAW Will you, Sir Amorous? Will you wound reputation?

LA FOOLE I am resolved.

TRUEWIT So should you be too, Jack Daw. [*Aside to Daw*] What should keep you off? She is but a woman, and in disgrace. He'll° be glad on't. *Morose will*

DAW [*aside to Truewit*] Will he? I thought he would ha' been angry.

CLERIMONT You will dispatch, knights; it must be done, i'faith.

TRUEWIT Why, an it must it shall, sir, they say. They'll ne'er go back.° [*Aside to Daw and La Foole*] Do not tempt his patience. *retract their story*

DAW [*to Morose*] It is true indeed, sir.

LA FOOLE Yes, I assure you, sir.

MOROSE What is true, gentlemen? What do you assure me?

DAW That we have known your bride, sir—

LA FOOLE In good fashion. She was our mistress, or so—

CLERIMONT Nay, you must be plain, knights, as you were to me.

OTTER Ay, the question is, if you have *carnaliter*° or no. *carnally*

LA FOOLE *Carnaliter*? What else, sir?

OTTER It is enough: a plain nullity.° *annulment*

EPICENE I am undone! I am undone!

MOROSE Oh, let me worship and adore you, gentlemen!

EPICENE I am undone! [*She weeps.*]

MOROSE Yes, to my hand,° I thank these knights. Master Parson, let me thank you otherwise. [*He gives Otter money.*] *to my benefit*

CENTAUR And ha' they confessed?

MAVIS Now, out upon 'em, informers!

TRUEWIT You see what creatures you may bestow your favors on, madams.

HAUGHTY [*to Epicene, who is still weeping*] I would except° against 'em as beaten knights, wench, and not good witnesses in law.[5] *object*

MRS. OTTER Poor gentlewoman, how she takes it!

HAUGHTY Be comforted, Morose,° I love you the better for't. *i.e., Epicene*

CENTAUR So do I, I protest.

CUTBEARD But, gentlemen, you have not known her since *matrimonium*?

DAW Not today, Master Doctor.

LA FOOLE No, sir, not today.

5. Because the oaths of dishonorable men could not be trusted.

CUTBEARD Why, then I say, for any act before, the *matrimonium* is good and perfect, unless the worshipful bridegroom did precisely before witness demand if she were *virgo ante nuptias*.[6]

EPICENE No, that he did not, I assure you, Master Doctor.

CUTBEARD If he cannot prove that, it is *ratum conjugium*,° notwithstanding the premises. And they do no way *impedire*.° And this is my sentence, this I pronounce.

a valid marriage
impede

OTTER I am of Master Doctor's resolution too, sir, if you made not that demand *ante nuptias*.°

before the wedding

MOROSE O my heart, wilt thou break? Wilt thou break? This is worst of all worst worsts that hell could have devised! Marry a whore! And so much noise!

DAUPHINE Come, I see now plain confederacy in this doctor and this parson to abuse a gentleman. You study° his affliction. I pray begone, companions.° [*To Clerimont and Truewit*] And, gentlemen, I begin to suspect you for having parts° with 'em. [*To Morose*] Sir, will it please you hear me?

work to aggravate
rogues, fellows
for conspiring

MOROSE Oh, do not talk to me. Take not from me the pleasure of dying in silence, nephew.

DAUPHINE Sir, I must speak to you. I have been long your poor despised kinsman, and many a hard thought has strengthened you against me, but now it shall appear if either I love you or your peace,° and prefer them to all the world beside. I will not be long or grievous° to you, sir. If I free you of this unhappy match absolutely and instantly after all this trouble, and almost in your despair now—

tranquillity
burdensome

MOROSE It cannot be.

DAUPHINE —sir, that you be never troubled with a murmur of it more, what shall I hope for, or deserve of you?

MOROSE Oh, what thou wilt, nephew! Thou shalt deserve me, and have me.

DAUPHINE Shall I have your favor perfect to me, and love hereafter?

MOROSE That and anything beside. Make thine own conditions. My whole estate is thine. Manage it; I will become thy ward.[7]

DAUPHINE Nay, sir, I will not be so unreasonable.

EPICENE Will Sir Dauphine be mine enemy too?

DAUPHINE You know I have been long a suitor to you, uncle, that out of your estate, which is fifteen hundred° a year, you would allow me but five hundred during life, and assure the rest upon me after; to which I have often by myself and friends tendered you a writing to sign, which you would never consent or incline to. If you please but to effect it now—

(pounds)

MOROSE Thou shalt have it, nephew. I will do it and more.

DAUPHINE If I quit you not presently° and forever of this cumber,° you shall have power instantly, afore all these, to revoke your act, and I will become whose slave you will give me to, forever.

immediately
burden

6. A virgin before the wedding.
7. Person whose property was managed by a guardian—the usual arrangement when a minor inherited an estate.

MOROSE Where is the writing? I will seal to it, that or to a blank, and write thine own conditions.

EPICENE Oh, me, most unfortunate wretched gentlewoman!

HAUGHTY Will Sir Dauphine do this?

EPICENE Good sir, have some compassion on me.

MOROSE Oh, my nephew knows you, belike;° [probably] away, crocodile![8]

CENTAUR He does it not, sure, without good ground.

DAUPHINE [*giving Morose a paper*] Here, sir.

MOROSE Come, nephew, give me the pen. I will subscribe° [agree] to anything, and seal to what thou wilt for my deliverance. Thou art my restorer. [*He signs the paper and returns it to Dauphine.*] Here, I deliver it thee as my deed. If there be a word in it lacking or writ with false orthography, I protest before—I will not take the advantage.[9]

DAUPHINE Then here is your release, sir. (*He takes off Epicene's peruke.*) You have married a boy, a gentleman's son that I have brought up this half year at my great charges,° [expense] and for this composition° [settlement] which I have now made with you.—What say you, Master Doctor? This is *justum impedimentum*, I hope, *error personae*?[1]

OTTER Yes, sir, *in primo gradu*.° [in the first degree]

CUTBEARD *In primo gradu*.

DAUPHINE (*he pulls off their beards and disguise*) I thank you, good Doctor Cutbeard and Parson Otter. [*To Morose*] You are beholden to 'em, sir, that have taken this pains for you, and my friend, Master Truewit, who enabled 'em° [provided them means] for the business. Now you may go in and rest, be as private as you will, sir. I'll not trouble you till you trouble me with your funeral, which I care not how soon it come. [*Exit Morose.*] Cutbeard, I'll make your lease good. Thank me not but with your leg, Cutbeard. [*Cutbeard bows.*] And, Tom Otter, your princess shall be reconciled to you.—How now, gentlemen, do you look at me?

CLERIMONT A boy.

DAUPHINE Yes, Mistress Epicene.

TRUEWIT Well, Dauphine, you have lurched° [cheated] your friends of the better half of the garland° [(of victory)] by concealing this part of the plot! But much good do it thee, thou deserv'st it, lad. And, Clerimont, for thy unexpected bringing in these two to confession, wear my part of it° [(the garland)] freely.—Nay, Sir Daw and Sir La Foole, you see the gentlewoman that has done you the favors!° [sexual favors] We are all thankful to you, and so should the womankind here, specially for lying on° [about] her, though not with her! You meant so, I am sure? But that we have stuck it° [fastened dishonor] upon you today in your own imagined persons, and so lately, this Amazon, the champion of the sex, should beat you now thriftily° [thoroughly] for the common slanders which ladies receive from

8. Supposed to lure its prey by insincere tears. Morose complains that Dauphine and Epicene are in cahoots.

9. Although under early modern English law, trivial errors in the spelling or wording of a writ often provided material for a court challenge, Morose promises not to regard them. The sentence in F1 reads "I protest before—," and some editors take the dash to be a substitute for "God," a word that could not be spoken onstage. But since "before" can mean "beforehand" or "in advance," the sentence makes sense without this emendation.

1. A real impediment . . . an error of person?

such cuckoos[2] as you are. You are they that, when no merit or fortune can make you hope to enjoy their bodies, will yet lie with their reputations and make their fame suffer. Away, you common moths° of these and all ladies' honors. Go, travel[3] to make legs and faces, and come home with some new matter to be laughed at. You deserve to live in an air as corrupted as that wherewith you feed rumor. *i.e. destroyers*

[*Exeunt Daw and La Foole.*]

Madams, you are mute upon this new metamorphosis! But here stands she that has vindicated your fames. Take heed of such *insectae*[4] hereafter. And let it not trouble you that you have discovered° any mysteries to this young gentleman. He is almost of years,° and will make a good visitant° within this twelvemonth. In the meantime we'll all undertake for his secrecy, that° can speak so well of his silence. [*Coming forward to address the audience*] Spectators, if you like this comedy, rise cheerfully, and, now Morose is gone in, clap your hands. It may be that noise will cure him, at least please him. [*Exeunt.*] *revealed* *sexually of age / lover* *we who*

THE END.

This comedy was first acted in the year 1609 by the Children of Her Majesty's Revels. The principal comedians were Nathan Field, Giles Carie, Hugh Attwell, John Smith, William Barksted, William Penn, Richard Alleyn, John Blaney. With the allowance of the Master of Revels.

---

2. Noisy birds that lay their eggs in other bird's nests, traditionally associated with sexual slander.

3. (1) Go elsewhere; (2) work hard (travail). It was beginning to become fashionable for gentlemen to finish their education with a trip to France and Italy, but such travelers were sometimes scorned when they returned home for having acquired affected manners and "un-English" morals.

4. Insects. (Probably referring to Daw and La Foole, the "moths," or perhaps to the "metamorphosed" Epicene, since insects change form drastically in the course of development.)

TEXTUAL NOTES

Epicene was first performed between December 1609 and February 1610. Possibly it was first printed in quarto, but if so, no copy survives prior to the first folio; the first quarto printing was in 1620. The copy-text for this edition is the 1616 F collection of Jonson's *Works* (F1), the printing of which was overseen by the author himself. F1 contains a number of errors that were, according to usual early modern printing-house practice, sporadically corrected in the course of the printing, so that some bound copies of F1 contain pages with the errors and some do not. These textual notes list those places where the Norton text varies from the corrected F1 text or where the proper reading is unclear.

Later editions of the play include the 1620 quarto and reprintings of F1, which is the only authority for the text. In a few cases, the 1640 second folio of Jonson's *Works* corrected some F1 misprints.

For *Epicene*, most editorial emendations are uncontroversial. The only point in the text where there is some disagreement is at 1.3.41. Some modern editors, as here, prefer "for their," others "there." Either reading is possible, but the second involves a more tortuous word order.

The following abbreviations are used:

F1: *The Works of Benjamin Jonson* (London: William Stansby, 1616)
F1 corr.: The corrected state of F1
F1 uncorr.: The uncorrected state of F1
F2: *The Works of Benjamin Jonson*, vol. 1 (London: Richard Bishop, 1640)
ed.: A modern editor's emendation

Title [and throughout] **Epicene** [Fl: EPICOENE]
Prologue 18 coarse [F1: course]
1.1.64 [and elsewhere] **lose** [F1: loose] **87** BOY [ed.; not in Fl] **87 SD** ***sings*** [ed.] SONG [F1] **98 They** [F1 corr.] *Thy* [F1 uncorr.] **139 turban** [Fl: turbant] **158 waits** [Fl: Waights] **172** [and elsewhere] **window** [F1: windore] **179 holiday** [Fl: holy-day] **181–82 ceilings** [Fl: seelings]
1.2.2 Struck [Fl: Strooke] **16 ordnance** [Fl: ordinance] **21** [and elsewhere] **venture** [F1: venter] **52 fancy** [F1: phant'sie]
1.3.41 for their [some copies of F1] for there [some copies of F1] **44 Christian name** [F1: christen-name]
2.2.62 to [ed.] too [F1] **68 tyrants** [F1: tyrannes] **131 rises** [F1] rinses [some eds.]
2.3.123 DAW [ed.] DAV. [F1; the usual abbreviation for "DAUPHINE"] **137 you'll** [ed.] you you'll [F1]
2.4.16 have [ed.] hane [F1] **17** [and elsewhere] **scent** [Fl: sent] **53** CLERIMONT [ed.] DLE. [F1] **54** DAUPHINE [ed.] DAVP. [F1 corr.] CAVP. [F1 uncorr.] **128 to** [Fl: too]
2.5.1 your [F1 corr.] you [F1 uncorr.] **22 haply** [F1: happely] **48 bed-fere** [Fl: bedpheere] **67 heifer** [F1: heicfar] **75 bodice** [ed.] bodies [F1]
3.1.43 holidays [F1: holy-daies] **45–46, 50–51** [asides indicated in Fl by parentheses] **49** [and elsewhere] **velvet** [ed.] vellet [F1]
3.2.11 to [F1: too] **69 lord's** [F1: Lords]
3.3.1 Why, [ed.] Why [F1] **7** [and elsewhere] **of** [F1: off] **18** DAW [ed.] DAVP. [F1] **32 main** [ed.] man [F1] **57 in humanly** [Fl: in-humanely] **96.1** [***La Foole***] [ed.] He [Fl] **103** [and elsewhere] **powder** [F1: poulder]
3.4.6 SD ***speaks*** [ed.] *The parson speaks* [F1] **39 plaice** [F1: playse]
3.5.59, 62, 73–74, 76, 78, 81–82 ("And . . . paper"), 91 [ed., without indicating "aside"; these speeches of Truewit are in parens. in F1, a style normally indicating asides] **84 basin** [F1: bason]
3.6.27 Compliment! Compliment! [F1: Complement! complement!] **113 Go to** [ed.] Goe too [F1]
4.1.63 ceiling [Fl: seeling] **87 all ways** [F1: alwaies]
4.2.20 Loo, loo [F1: Low, low]
4.4.15 Billingsgate [F1: *Belins*-gate] **84** ***Doni's*** [F1: DONES] **140 porpoise** [F1: *porcpisce*]
4.5.66 arrant'st [F1: errandst] **120.2** ***come*** [ed.] *came* [F1] **142 Whither** [F1: Whether] **218** ***call*[*ing*]** [ed.] *He calls* [F1] **235 passed** [Fl: past] **280.1–3, 282.1–2** [ed.] *Dauphine comes forth, and kicks him* [in the right margin opposite 281–82 in F1]
4.7.0.1–2 [ed.] *He had found the two swords drawne within* [F1]
5.1.42 joint-stools [Fl: ioyn'd stooles] **85 led** [ed.] lead [F1]
5.3.125 akin [Fl: a kinne] **143 eighth** [F1: eight]
5.4.200 SD, 208 SD ***off*** [Fl: *of*] **237 travel** [F1: trauaile]

The Alchemist

While Ben Jonson's earlier play *Volpone* opens with a long monologue that suggests the hero's self-confident control over the events that follow, *The Alchemist* begins with a fight. Hurling insults and threats at one another, the two combatants, Subtle and Face, quickly acquaint the audience with the situation at the beginning of the action. Bubonic plague, which reached epidemic levels in early modern London in many years, has visited the city once again. Those who can afford to do so have fled to the countryside to avoid contagion. A butler, entrusted with the care of his master's house, sets up shop therein with a fake alchemist and a prostitute as partners. Together the three swindlers attract a wide range of customers who come to them for a variety of services, from fortune-telling and conjuring to tutoring in sophisticated London ways. But most are attracted by what they see as alchemy's chief promise: the possibility that base metals might somehow, by magic or by a secret physical process, be converted into gold so that its practitioners might become staggeringly rich.

The fight between Subtle and Face seems to bear out a point that Renaissance moral and political thinkers often emphasized: when hierarchical precedence is blurred and chains of command get tangled, turmoil ensues. The "venture tripartite" of Subtle, Face, and Doll (1.1.135), with its lack of clear leadership, is no exception to this rule. But in *The Alchemist,* disruption and opportunity go hand in hand. With the departure of the city's property-holding class, the group in which power traditionally rested, new social configurations are free to emerge—enterprises and alliances structured not by traditional bonds of kinship and class hierarchy, but by self-interest and the pursuit of profit. The "venture tripartite" seems an instance of what was happening all over England in the early seventeenth century, as pools of investors and entrepreneurs joined forces to finance undertakings ranging from the building of theaters to voyages of discovery. If the fray between Subtle and Face is comically appalling, it also highlights their verbal adroitness and improvisatory skill. Moreover, Jonson suggests, for better or worse, it heralds a future way of life.

Alchemy fascinated Jonson. Its lore permeates not only this play, first performed in 1610, but several of his masques for King James and his court. Alchemists sought to produce or discover a substance they called the "philosophers' stone," which could supposedly turn base metals into gold and confer immortality on its possessor. The aims of alchemy—endless wealth and eternal youth—are of course immensely ambitious and, in the early seventeenth century, disquieting as well as exciting, since nobody could be sure that alchemy would not work. In England, alchemical experimentation was illegal because, the government reasoned, if someone actually managed to produce precious metals from lead, the resulting disruption in the value of government-issued coinage would produce economic chaos.

In Jonson's play, the alchemist's first two customers, Dapper and Drugger, have ridiculously little conception of the enormous powers upon which they supposedly

Introduction by Katharine Eisaman Maus; glosses and footnotes by David Bevington; text edited by David Bevington and Eric Rasmussen.

call. Dapper initially wants a minor attendant devil to help him cheat at cards: "A rifling fly—none o'your great familiars" (1.2.84). Drugger requests some interior decorating hints and advice on the design of his shop sign. Face and Subtle, working together, attempt to create for these two dullards the imaginations they do not possess, improving upon their modest fantasy lives in order to extract more profit from their gullibility; for only if astounding success is prophesied them will they surrender the relatively paltry amounts of money they already have on hand. The customers that follow, Sir Epicure Mammon and the Puritan leaders Tribulation Wholesome and Ananias, are more aware of the possibilities. Mammon in particular considers himself learned in alchemical history and theory. His gullibility arises not from a failure of imagination but from a lurid excess: Jonson gives him impressive blank verse lines, full of mythic resonances and exotic allusions, modeled upon the language spoken by Christopher Marlowe's magniloquent heroes. In London as Jonson depicts it, grand appetites make one all the more susceptible to chicanery.

Alchemy is not, however, merely the get-rich-quick scheme most of Jonson's characters take it for. The alchemical worldview is centered upon positive metamorphosis. Indeed, the whole universe is supposed to be slowly trending toward perfection, a process that the alchemist might hasten, but does not originate. Just as the chick is latent with the egg, Subtle explains to Mammon's skeptical companion, Surly, so the perfection of gold is latent in "lead and other metals, / Which would be gold, if they had time" (2.3.135–36). Alchemy has, moreover, a strong tincture of mysticism, and its practitioners insisted upon deep and important analogies between the material and the spiritual world. The alchemist, working simultaneously on the materials of nature and his own spirit, is supposed to bring about a positive change in both interrelated realms. To gain the philosophers' stone, one needs not merely experimental facility but extraordinary spiritual discipline. Surly succinctly lists the requirements for the successful alchemist: "he must be *homo frugi*, / A pious, holy, and religious man, / One free from mortal sin, a very virgin" (2.2.97–99). In fact, alchemy's failure to obtain its end in previous ages was attributed to a lack of fit between eager experimentalists and what they sought. The only person qualified to discover the philosophers' stone would be free of the passion and desire for material things, and hence would have no motivation to search for it.

Even while his play subjects the claims of alchemy to skeptical critique, Jonson exploits for his own purposes the alchemical insistence that physical, social, and psychological realms are intimately linked. But he uses those interconnections to make

Alchemists used fairly elaborate equipment in their search for the "philosophers' stone," a substance reputed to have the property of changing other metals into gold and silver.

virtually the opposite claim: whereas alchemy attempts to spiritualize matter, Jonson's satiric language aggressively reverses this process, grounding the impulses of his characters in the materials of their bodies and continually ridiculing claims of transcendence. In Surly's curt account, alchemy's exotic substances turn out to be homely and disgusting: "piss and eggshells, women's terms, man's blood, / Hair o'the head, burnt clouts, chalk, merds, and clay, / Powder of bones, scalings of iron, glass" (2.3.194–96). The declaration "I fart at thee," in the first line of the play, and Face's opening fantasy about forcing Subtle to lick his hemorrhoids introduce a rich vein of scatological imagery: references to feces, the backside, the process of excretion, and the places where it occurs. Dapper is purified for his encounter with his supposed aunt, the Faery Queen, by a "fumigation" in a stinking privy (3.5.78–81). At last, Doll, dressed as the Faery Queen, arrives to bestow her blessings: as she leaves the stage Subtle instructs her "nephew" to "Kiss her departing part" (5.4.57).

Such persistent reductiveness suggests that high-flown declarations of love, intellectual commitment, or religious zeal are merely hypocritical covers for lust and greed; and the action of the play implies that raw greed itself is often a screen for an even more fundamental impulse. Even more than they want to be rich, Dapper, Drugger, and Mammon hunger for an assurance that they are *special*—magically marked out for a remarkable destiny by signs such as a newborn's caul (1.2.128) or a star in the forehead (1.3.45). The Puritans succumb to a different version of the same temptation. They believe they are God's chosen people, designated for salvation no matter how they behave; they believe they therefore have immediate access to the truth without any particular training or effort and can disregard the laws that apply to the rest of humanity. The Puritans collude uneasily with Subtle and Face, rightly seeing that alchemy both competes with and uncannily duplicates the doctrines of their faith.

The success of the "venture tripartite" suggests that the need to feel singled out is so universal as to be, paradoxically, anything but unique. It succeeds in deluding its victims, despite its obvious creakiness, because it so efficiently colludes with the gulls' wishful narcissism that they are willing to ignore its flagrant implausibilities. Moreover, the details of the gulls' fantasies suggest that the "individualism" they—and many of their descendants in the modern world—value so highly is inextricable from egotism and competitiveness. Jonson's satiric world is a zero-sum economy, in which one person's triumphant good fortune always implies another's deprivation or humiliation. Thus the gambling Dapper hopes to enrich himself by cheating his companions; the Puritans steal from widows and orphans; and the would-be "quarreler," Kastril, grounds his sense of self in senselessly aggressive posturing. In the ecstasies of Sir Epicure Mammon, especially, we see clearly how the deprivation of others is not merely an unfortunate by-product of self-enrichment but a perverse source of pleasure. In a particularly telling moment, he imagines himself dining on "the swelling unctuous paps / Of a fat pregnant sow newly cut off, / Dressed with an exquisite and poignant sauce" (2.2.83–85). The violence of "newly cut off," jarring in this pseudo-gourmet context, reminds us that the owner of the "swelling unctuous paps" lost her life to provide Mammon with a meal; that she was pregnant means, of course, that her piglets died with her. Swine are not only the displaced rivals here but, Jonson slyly implies, Mammon's true compeers.

Because Jonson keeps the "low" origins of "high" sentiments so plainly in view, the alchemical fraud often seems to work by substituting a merely linguistic alteration for the real-world one it cannot accomplish. Often both the alchemists and their clients substitute a more delicate or roundabout expression for a simpler original term, just as we call garbagemen "sanitary engineers" or old people "senior citizens." Much of the comedy of *The Alchemist* relies upon hilariously inappropriate terminological substitutions, as when the reek of a privy is renamed "fumigation" (3.5.81) or the Puritans conclude that "Casting of money may be lawful" even though "coining" is a capital crime (3.2.149–53). Jonson seems to recognize that rhetorical puffery—what we would call "advertising"—is a key feature of a market-driven society like early modern London, insofar as the value of everything in such a society depends not on its intrinsic worth but on what somebody can be induced to pay for it. It is obviously much easier to *say* one can make gold from lead than actually to do so, just as it is easier to claim that one's product is "new and improved" than actually to invent or improve it.

In *The Alchemist*, ordinary, or even disgusting, human activities can be redescribed to seem wonderful and strange, hence the allure of alchemical terms, of Puritan cant, of elaborate laws for "quarreling." Such jargons reinforce the characters' aspirations to uniqueness, since they typically have the effect of separating members of an in-group from the indiscriminate, uncomprehending masses. Some characters—Subtle and Face in particular—are acutely aware of how jargon, and the secret knowledge that seems to stand behind it, can become an important weapon in status competitions. They use rhetorical expertise as a weapon to dazzle innocents and intimidate skeptics. In the extreme case, jargon is so specialized that it can be understood, if at all, only by its speaker. In this category are the fairy language Face and Subtle jabber to the bewildered Dapper (3.5.33–57) and the Puritan writer Broughton's impenetrable biblical commentaries, quoted by the supposedly mad Doll Common to impress Mammon (4.5.1–32). Language, purportedly a medium of communication, here becomes a way to fend off everybody else. In a world in which people all believe themselves to be radically individual, solipsism and gibberish are the natural results.

Although Jonson's satire of jargon is scathing and often very funny, he is nonetheless aware that its pseudo-transformative rhetorical powers are close to those that poets claim for themselves. Philip Sidney, in his famous *Defense of Poetry* (1595), praised poets for making a golden world out of a brazen one: precisely what the "venture tripartite" pretends to be able to accomplish. When the skeptical Surly claims that alchemical writing is unnecessarily obscure, Subtle's reply echoes a standard Renaissance theory of poetry as an art that reveals the truth to discerning readers even while concealing it from the unworthy:

Was not all the knowledge
Of the Egyptians writ in mystic symbols?
Speak not the Scriptures oft in parables?
Are not the choicest fables of the poets,
That were the fountains and first springs of wisdom,
Wrapped in perplexèd allegories? (2.3.202–7)

Subtle's implicit distinction between those initiates who can penetrate "mystic symbols" and "perplexèd allegories" and the ignoramuses who cannot seems unnervingly similar to Jonson's own distinction, in his preface to *The Alchemist* ("To the Reader"), between a reader who is an "understander" and one who is "but a pretender" and thus "fair in the way to be cozened" (lines 1–4).

It is even easier to see the resemblance between the alchemical scam and a theatrical performance. The "venture tripartite" requires, of course, an extraordinary amount of role-playing. Jeremy, the servant left alone in his master's house, must impersonate both Captain Face and "Lungs," the alchemist's apprentice. Doll becomes an aristocratic madwoman and the Faery Queen. Even Subtle, a less virtuosic actor, is alternately a shrewd dealer in practical magic, the unworldly innocent whose virtue Sir Epicure Mammon assumes he can purchase, and "a Priest of Faery." If the alchemist and his co-conspirators are like playwrights and actors, their clients are comparable to theater spectators. As Mammon enters the house with Surly, he tells his friend:

Now you set your foot on shore
In Novo Orbe; here's the rich Peru,
And there within, sir, are the golden mines,
Great Solomon's Ophir! (2.1.1–4)

The willingness to believe that Lovewit's empty rooms are Peru or the mines of Solomon—just the kind of imagination that makes Mammon susceptible to Subtle, Face, and Doll—is akin to the imaginative faculty that make theater audiences take the bare wooden boards of the Globe or the Fortune for the exotic and varied locales of English Renaissance drama. Given the lack of scenery in the public theater, Mammon's "rich Peru" looks just like Marlowe's Malta or Damascus, Shakespeare's Forest of Arden or cliffs of Dover, Jonson's own Venice, Rome, or Gargaphie. In *The Alchemist*, Jonson makes the transaction between cheats and gulls seem close to the transaction between a theater company and the spectators who pay good money but get nothing more substantial in return than chimeras and fantasies.

But is alchemy, finally, a form of theatrical poetry or a travesty of true art? If the similarity between poetry and alchemy taints poetry, it can also elevate poetry, because its parodic resemblances throw into sharp relief the difference between Jonson's means and aims and those of his clever, but nonetheless criminal, protagonists. There is more than one way to make a golden world out of a brazen one. For Sidney, the poet's imagination was an idealizing one, which tidied up the moral messiness of history, animated the dry precepts of philosophy with rhetorical power, and gave readers and audiences grand examples to emulate. Jonson, anything but an idealist, does what might seem harder. He creates a superbly written, intricately constructed, and exquisitely funny play from squalid raw materials without denying their sordidness—indeed, while continually highlighting it.

Doll Common is crucial to the workings of the alchemical fraud. Although—especially late in the play—Subtle and Face conspire to minimize her knowledge of exactly what is going on, she wields significant executive power. Whores in Renaissance drama tend to be either demonized as corrupters of youth and threats to the sacred institution of marriage or else sentimentalized as eventually repentant "sinners." Doll fits neither stereotype. Jonson's refusal to spiritualize or romanticize sexual attraction works to her advantage. In the world of *The Alchemist,* where "love" seems merely a polite word for "sexual appetite," there is nothing singularly shocking about lust: it cannot "debase" or "pervert" a higher sentiment because there aren't really any higher sentiments. Moreover, the thoroughgoing commercialism of London as Jonson imagines it tends to blunt the force of the sexual double standard. Like everyone else in the play, Doll attempts to make a profit from the materials available to her. She is no better, but also no worse, than her comrades Subtle and Face. In her wit and theatrical verve, she contrasts favorably, too, with the naive, corruptible Dame Pliant.

When accepted social hierarchies distintegrate, Jonson suggests, comic disorder reigns; but through Doll, Jonson also suggests that those hierarchies were always artificial anyway. When Doll is otherwise occupied with Mammon and thus unavailable to consort with the "Spaniard" Surly, Subtle and Face substitute the wellborn, prosperous Dame Pliant; and as her name suggests, she hardly turns out to be unassailable. Meanwhile, when the baseborn Doll represents herself to Mammon as "a poor baron's daughter" (4.1.43), Mammon enthuses:

> There is a strange nobility i'your eye,
> This lip, that chin! Methinks you do resemble
> One o'the Austriac princes.
>
> . . . .
>
> The house of Valois just had such a nose,
> And such a forehead yet the Medici
> Of Florence boast. (4.1.54–60)

Of course the joke is partly on the naive Mammon, posing as a man of the world so much less effectively than Doll poses as a lady. But surely, too, the inappositeness of Mammon's "blood will tell" topos satirizes the idea that the aristocratic classes are, by their very birth, physically, mentally, or morally distinguishable from their inferiors.

Jonson was a social conservative of sorts but no essentialist about class difference: members of the elite, in his view, had to prove their worth in virtuous action, not merely embody it.

In act 4, it briefly looks as if *The Alchemist* is headed toward a rather predictable conclusion, in which the skeptical Surly disguises himself, penetrates the fraud, and reveals it in the play's final scene to receive a monetary and marital reward. But *The Alchemist* is hardly a conventional comedy. Instead, Lovewit, the owner of the house in which the conspirators have been practicing their scam, unexpectedly returns. The comedy veers off in an unexpected direction as he blithely appropriates both the thieves' spoils, such as they are, and a richer prize, Dame Pliant. Unlike the reckless Mosca in *Volpone,* Face has the sense to save his skin by allying himself with his powerful master, and thus Lovewit becomes, like the wellborn heroes of the Latin comedies by Plautus and Terence that Jonson knew and admired, the indulgent beneficiary of his witty servant.

Lovewit's final ascendancy, predicated as it is upon his ownership of the house in which the scam was conducted, seems to reimpose the feudal relationships of dependency and noblesse oblige that have been suspended for most of the play's duration. At the same time, the action of Jonson's play tends to undermine any claims about the naturalness or inherent rightness of traditional social hierarchies. Moreover, Lovewit's vivid sense of his own self-interest and his improvisatory willingness to take advantage of the situation despite "some small strain / Of his own candor" (5.5.151–52) suggest that his ultimate sympathies lie with the new, entrepreneurial mode of life Jonson has ambivalently delineated in the earlier parts of the play. The impecunious Surly had imagined himself as the chivalrous hero of a romance and Dame Pliant as the kind of virtuous and conveniently wealthy heroine who would remember and reward his courteous treatment of her in her "distress." But as Lovewit notes, Surly's restraint fails to pay off:

> Good faith, now, she does blame you extremely, and says
> You swore and told her you had ta'en the pains
> To dye your beard and umber o'er your face,
> Borrowed a suit and ruff, all for her love—
> And then did nothing. What an oversight
> And want of putting forward, sir, was this! (5.5.50–55)

Lovewit ends up with the play's rewards not because he deserves them but because he knows how to seize an opportunity when it presents itself. Or perhaps, in the world of *The Alchemist,* this sort of shrewdness is all "desert" amounts to.

Just as Lovewit's keen sense of his own self-interest overrides the expected judgment in the final scenes, so, Jeremy/Face suggests, the self-interest of the audience may dictate their response: amused rather than outraged, tolerant rather than scandalized. In the epilogue, Jeremy addresses the audience as "my country," that is, his jury in a court of law, trying him for his supposed offenses in the play. Half in character, half as a spokesman for the King's Men, he proposes a bribe:

> I put myself
> On you, that are my country; and this pelf
> Which I have got, if you do quit me, rests
> To feast you often, and invite new guests.
> (5.5.162–65)

The "pelf which I have got" refers to the profits of the "venture tripartite," but also, at the same time, to the theater receipts. Jeremy proposes, in other words, to bribe the audience with their own money, a swindle worthy of the con man he was and is. Here as earlier in the play, Jonson implies that the theater company gives spectators, in return for their cash, fantasies perhaps not so different from what Subtle, Face, and Doll have offered their clients. But by "quitting"—both "acquitting" and "requiting"—Jeremy with their applause, the spectators in turn suggest that unlike those clients, they collude knowingly with the trickeries of the theater and gladly approve of their own deception. And of course they are right to do so. They might not leave the theater laden with alchemist's gold, but Jonson has given them something precious nonetheless.

BEN JONSON

The Alchemist

To the lady most deserving her name and blood, Mary, Lady Wroth.[1]

The Persons of the Play

SUBTLE, the alchemist
FACE, the housekeeper
DOLL Common, their colleague
DAPPER, a clerk
[Abel] DRUGGER, a tobacco man
LOVEWIT, master of the house
[Sir] Epicure MAMMON, a knight
[Pertinax] SURLY, a gamester
TRIBULATION [Wholesome], a pastor of Amsterdam
ANANIAS, a deacon there
KASTRIL, the angry boy
Dame PLIANT, his sister, a widow
NEIGHBORS
OFFICERS
[A parson]
Mutes

THE SCENE: London. [A house in Blackfriars.]

To the Reader

If thou be'st more, thou art an understander,[1] and then I trust thee. If thou art one that tak'st up, and but a pretender, beware at what hands thou receiv'st thy commodity; for thou wert never more fair in the way to be cozened[2] (than in this age) in poetry, especially in plays, wherein, now, the concupiscence of° dances and antics° so reigneth, as° to run away from Nature

desire for
grotesqueries / that

The original 1616 title page reads "*The Alchemist*. A Comedy. Acted in the year 1610. By the King's Majesty's Servants. The Author B. J. / Lucret[ius]: —*petere inde coronam, / Unde prius nulli velarint tempora Musae* [To seek out the muses' garland where no one has won it before (Lucretius, *On the Nature of the Universe,* 4.1)]. London. Printed by William Stansby. M.DC.XVI [1616]."

Dedication.

1. The wife of Sir Robert Wroth and niece of Sir Philip Sidney, and an accomplished poet. Jonson spoke admiringly of her literary ability in his converstions with William Drummond.

To the Reader.

1. One who understands.
2. To take up a commodity is to accept usually shabby commodities in lieu of a cash loan and then be "cozened," or cheated, when one attempts to sell those goods for cash.

and be afraid of her is the only point of art that tickles the spectators. But how out of purpose and place do I name art? When the professors° are grown so obstinate contemners° of it, and presumers on their own naturals,° as° they are deriders of all diligence that way, and, by simple mocking at the terms, when they understand not the things, think to get off wittily with their ignorance. Nay, they are esteemed the more learned and sufficient° for this by the many,° through their excellent vice° of judgment. For they° commend writers as they do fencers or wrestlers, who, if they come in robustiously and put° for it with a great deal of violence, are received for the braver° fellows, when many times their own rudeness° is the cause of their disgrace, and a little touch of their adversary gives all that boisterous force the foil.° I deny not but that these men, who always seek to do more than enough, may sometime happen on some thing that is good and great; but very seldom, and when it comes it doth not recompense the rest of their ill.° It sticks out, perhaps, and is more eminent, because all is sordid and vile about it, as lights are more discerned in a thick darkness than a faint shadow. I speak not this out of a hope to do good on any man against his will; for I know, if it were put to the question° of theirs and mine, the worse would find more suffrages,° because the most° favor common errors. But I give thee this warning, that there is a great difference between those that (to gain the opinion of copy)° utter all they can, however unfitly, and those that use election and a mean.° For it is only the disease of the unskillful to think rude things greater than polished, or scattered more numerous than composed.

practitioners / scorners
capacities / that
judicious / multitude
viciousness / (the many)
strive
braver; showier
lack of polish
overthrow
bad work
put to a vote
votes / most people
copiousness
discriminate wisely

The Argument

T he sickness hot,° a master quit for fear — *Plague raging*
H is house in town, and left one servant there.
E ase° him corrupted, and gave means to know — *Lack of work*
A cheater and his punk,° who, now brought low,° — *whore / penniless*
L eaving their narrow° practice, were become — *small-time*
C oz'ners° at large; and, only wanting° some — *Con artists / lacking*
H ouse to set up, with him° they here contract — *(the servant)*
E ach for a share, and all begin to act.° — *play their parts*
M uch company they draw, and much abuse,° — *deception*
I n casting figures,° telling fortunes, news, — *devising horoscopes*
S elling of flies,° flat bawdry, with the stone[1]— — *familiar spirits*
T ill it and they and all in fume° are gone. — *smoke, vapor*

Prologue

Fortune, that favors fools, these two short hours
We wish away, both for your sakes and ours,
Judging spectators, and desire in place° — *instead*
To th'author justice, to ourselves but grace.° — *gracious acceptance*

The Argument.
1. The philosophers' stone, supposedly able to change other metals into gold or silver.

Our scene is London, 'cause we would make known
   No country's mirth is better than our own.
No clime breeds better matter for your whore,
   Bawd, squire,° impostor, many persons more, — *pander, pimp*
Whose manners, now called humors,[1] feed the stage,
   And which have still° been subject for the rage — *perennially*
Or spleen of comic writers. Though this pen
   Did never aim to grieve, but better,° men, — *correct, improve*
Howe'er the age he lives in doth endure
   The vices that she breeds above their cure.[2]
But when the wholesome remedies are sweet,
   And in their working gain and profit meet,
He hopes to find no spirit so much diseased
   But will with such fair correctives be pleased;
For here he doth not fear who can apply.[3]
   If there be any that will sit so nigh
Unto the stream to look what it doth run,
   They shall find things they'd think or wish were done,
They are so natural follies, but so shown
   As even the doers may see and yet not own.° — *admit to*

1.1

[Enter] Face [with a sword], Subtle [with a vial of acid, and] Doll Common.

FACE   Believe't, I will.
SUBTLE   Thy worst.° I fart at thee! — *Do your worst*
DOLL   Ha' you your wits? Why, gentlemen! For love—
FACE   Sirrah, I'll strip you°— — *cut you into strips*
SUBTLE   What to do? Lick figs° — *piles*
   Out at my—
FACE   Rogue, rogue, out of all your sleights!° — *stop your tricks!*
DOLL   Nay, look ye! Sovereign, General, are you madmen?
SUBTLE   Oh, let the wild sheep° loose.—I'll gum your silks° — *(Face) / silk stockings*
   With good strong water,° an° you come.° — *acid / if / approach*
DOLL   Will you have
   The neighbors hear you? Will you betray all?
   Hark, I hear somebody.
FACE   Sirrah°— — *(said to inferiors)*
SUBTLE   I shall mar
   All that the tailor has made,° if you approach. — *Your sham appearance*
FACE   You most notorious whelp,° you insolent slave, — *puppy*
   Dare you do this?
SUBTLE   Yes, faith,° yes, faith. — *in faith*
FACE   Why, who
   Am I, my mongrel? Who am I?
SUBTLE   I'll tell you,
   Since you know not yourself—

Prologue.
1. Dominant personality traits, supposedly derived from the varying proportions in the body of the four chief fluids: blood, bile, phlegm, and black bile.
2. However much this present age is more tolerant of vice than of moral chastisement.
3. In this theater and with this audience, the author doesn't worry about those who try to read personal satire into a play's characters and situations. To "apply" here means to interpret literary works as political allegories with veiled references to current events—something that Jonson professes to deplore.

1.1. Lovewit's house.

FACE   Speak lower, rogue.
SUBTLE   Yes. You were once (time's° not long past) the good,   *the time is*
  Honest, plain, livery-three-pound thrum[1] that kept
  Your master's worship's° house here in the Friars,[2]   *Your worshipful master's*
  For the vacations°—   *Between court terms*
FACE   Will you be so loud?
SUBTLE   Since, by my means, translated suburb-captain.°   *made into a pimp*
FACE   By your means, Doctor Dog?
SUBTLE   Within man's memory,
  All this I speak of.
FACE   Why, I pray you, have I
  Been countenanced° by you? Or you by me?   *supported*
  Do but collect,° sir, where I met you first.   *recollect*
SUBTLE   I do not hear well.
FACE   Not of this, I think it.
  But I shall put you in mind, sir: at Pie Corner,[3]
  Taking your meal of steam in from cooks' stalls,
  Where, like the father of hunger, you did walk
  Piteously costive,° with your pinched-horn nose   *constipated*
  And your complexion of the Roman wash,°   *(sallow, sickly)*
  Stuck full of black and melancholic worms,°   *blackheads*
  Like powder-corns° shot at th'artillery yard.[4]   *grains of gunpowder*
SUBTLE   I wish you could advance° your voice a little.   *raise (ironic)*
FACE   When you went pinned up in the several° rags   *various*
  You'd raked and picked from dunghills before day,
  Your feet in moldy slippers for your kibes,°   *chilblains*
  A felt of rug,° and a thin threaden° cloak   *coarse hat / shabby*
  That scarce would cover your no-buttocks°—   *emaciated butt*
SUBTLE   So, sir!
FACE   When all your alchemy and your algebra,
  Your minerals, vegetals, and animals,
  Your conjuring, cozening,° and your dozen of trades   *trickery*
  Could not relieve your corpse,° with so much linen   *body*
  Would make you tinder but to see a fire,[5]
  I ga' you count'nance,° credit for your coals,[6]   *endorsement*
  Your stills, your glasses,° your materials,   *Your beakers, your flasks*
  Built you a furnace, drew you customers,
  Advanced all your black arts; lent you, beside,
  A house to practice in—
SUBTLE   Your master's house.
FACE   Where you have studied the more thriving skill
  Of bawdry° since.   *running a brothel*
SUBTLE   Yes, in your master's house.
  You and the rats here kept possession.
  Make it not strange.° I know you were one could keep   *Don't feign ignorance*
  The buttery-hatch still locked and save the chippings,[7]

1. I.e., shabbily dressed, underfed menial. A thrum is a fringe of unwoven threads, hence coarse material a servant might wear.
2. Blackfriars, a London district where Jonson lived and where this play was performed.
3. A district of cooks' shops and petty crime where cooked food could be bought; near Smithfield, just outside the north wall of the city.
4. A practice range used by the citizen militia of London, who were much laughed at for amateur soldiership.
5. With underwear so tattered and shredded that it could be used as tinder to start a fire.
6. I supplied you with a line of credit, enabling you to buy coals for your furnace.
7. Bread scraps were distributed at the "buttery-hatch," a door whose top half could be opened separately.

Sell the dole-beer to *aqua-vitae* men,[8]
The which, together with your Christmas vails,° *tips*
At post and pair° your letting out of counters,[9] *a card game*
Made you a pretty stock, some twenty marks,[1]
And gave you credit to converse with cobwebs
Here since your mistress'° death hath broke up house. *the owner's wife's*
FACE You might talk softlier, rascal.
SUBTLE No, you scarab,° *dung beetle*
I'll thunder you in pieces. I will teach you
How to beware to tempt a Fury° again *avenging spirit*
That carries tempest in his hand and voice.
FACE The place has made you valiant.
SUBTLE No, your clothes.
Thou vermin, have I ta'en thee out of dung,
So poor, so wretched, when no living thing
Would keep thee company but a spider or worse?
Raised thee from brooms and dust and wat'ring pots?
Sublimed thee, and exalted thee, and fixed thee
I'the third region,[2] called our state of grace?
Wrought thee to spirit, to quintessence,° with pains *purest essence*
Would° twice have won me the philosophers' work?° *Which would / stone*
Put thee in words and fashion?[3] Made thee fit
For more than ordinary° fellowships? *commonplace; tavern*
Giv'n thee thy oaths, thy quarreling dimensions,° *rules for quarreling*
Thy rules to cheat at horse race, cockpit,° cards, *cockfighting*
Dice, or whatever gallant tincture° else? *touch of gallantry*
Made thee a second in mine own great art?
And have I this for thanks? Do you rebel?
Do you fly out° i'the projection?° *explode / climax*
Would you be gone, now?
DOLL Gentlemen, what mean you?
Will you mar all?
SUBTLE Slave,° thou hadst had no name— *Wretch*
DOLL Will you undo yourselves with civil war?
SUBTLE Never been known, past *equi clibanum*,° *heat of horse dung*
The heat of horse dung, underground, in cellars,
Or an alehouse darker than deaf John's;° been lost *an alehouse*
To all mankind but laundresses and tapsters,° *barkeeps*
Had not I been.
DOLL D'you know who hears you, sovereign?
FACE Sirrah—
DOLL Nay, General, I thought you were civil.
FACE I shall turn desperate if you grow thus loud.
SUBTLE And hang thyself, I care not.
FACE Hang thee, collier,° *filthy wretch*
And all thy pots and pans! In picture° I will, *graphic detail; a poster*
Since thou hast moved° me— *angered*
DOLL (*aside*) Oh, this'll o'erthrow all.

8. Sell to liquor distillers the leftover beer and wine of your master's household that should have been distributed to the poor.
9. Your renting to gamblers the metal disks used as "counters," or chips, in games of chance.
1. Helped you amass a respectable stake of about thirteen and one-third pounds.
2. Vaporized, concentrated, and stabilized you into the purest region of the air.
3. Taught you fashionable, elegant speech?

FACE Write thee up bawd in Paul's;° have all thy tricks — *St. Paul's Cathedral*
Of cozening with a hollow coal, dust, scrapings,
Searching for things lost with a sieve and shears,
Erecting figures in your rows of houses,
And taking in of shadows with a glass,
Told in red letters;[4] and a face cut for° thee — *engraved to resemble*
Worse than Gamaliel Ratsey's.[5]
DOLL Are you sound?° — *sane*
Ha' you your senses, masters?
FACE I will have
A book, but° barely reckoning thy impostures, — *only*
Shall prove a true philosophers' stone to printers.[6]
SUBTLE Away, you trencher-rascal!° — *gluttonous parasite*
FACE Out, you dog-leech,[7]
The vomit of all prisons—
DOLL Will you be
Your own destructions, gentlemen?
FACE Still spewed out
For lying too heavy o'the basket![8]
SUBTLE Cheater!
FACE Bawd!
SUBTLE Cowherd!
FACE Conjurer!
SUBTLE Cutpurse!° — *Pickpocket!*
FACE Witch!
DOLL Oh, me!
We are ruined! Lost! Ha' you no more regard
To your reputations? Where's your judgment? 'Slight,° — *By God's light*
Have yet some care of me, o'your republic°— — *i.e., fellowship*
FACE Away this brach!° I'll bring thee, rogue, within — *bitch*
The statute of sorcery, *tricesimo tertio*
Of Harry the Eighth,[9] ay, and perhaps thy neck
Within a noose, for laund'ring gold and barbing it.[1]
DOLL You'll bring your head within a coxcomb,° will you? — *make yourself a fool*
She catcheth out Face his° sword, — *Face's*
and breaks Subtle's glass.° — *beaker*
And you, sir, with your menstrue,° gather it up. — *solvent*
'Sdeath,° you abominable pair of stinkards, — *By God's death*
Leave off your barking and grow one° again, — *be reconciled*
Or, by the light that shines, I'll cut your throats.
I'll not be made a prey unto the marshal° — *police official*
For ne'er a snarling dog-bolt o'you both.[2]
Ha' you together cozened° all this while, — *cheated; "cousined"*

4. Expose your cheating tricks of filling a hollow coal with gold to create the impression that the dust and scrapings supposedly being transmuted to precious metal in the fire have turned to gold, your pretending to be able to locate lost items with a kind of divining rod consisting of an open pair of scissors suspended in a sieve so that the blades can "spin" to the "right" answers, your diagramming of planetary positions in the row of zodiacal signs in order to cast a horoscope, and your pretending to raise spirits or angels in a crystal ball or magic mirror, announced in the decorated red letters one sees in elegant books and manuscripts.
5. Ratsey was a notorious highwayman remembered especially for the grotesque mask he wore when he committed the robberies. He was hanged in 1605.
6. Which will be a gold mine of a best-seller.
7. (1) Mangy veterinarian; (2) quack; (3) dog's vermin.
8. For being so disgusting that even starving prisoners would vomit you up again if you were the food scraps sent in the alms-basket to the prison.
9. Statutes were normally dated by the year in the monarch's reign, here, in the thirty-third year of the reign of Henry VIII (c. 1542).
1. For washing gold coins in acid and clipping their edges for the gold fragments.
2. I'll not go to prison for the likes of you two snarling ne'er-do-wells. (A "dog-bolt" is literally a blunt-headed arrow, hence "servile and contemptible.")

And all the world,° and shall it now be said — *everyone*
You've made most courteous shift° to cozen yourselves? — *device*
[*To Face*] You will accuse him? You will bring him in
Within the statute? Who shall take your word?
A whoreson, upstart, apocryphal° captain, — *phony*
Whom not a Puritan in Blackfriars will trust
So much as for a feather![3] [*To Subtle*] And you, too,
Will give the cause, forsooth? You will insult,° — *brag insolently*
And claim a primacy in the divisions?° — *division of spoils*
You must be chief, as if you only had
The powder to project with,[4] and the work
Were not begun out of equality?
The venture tripartite? All things in common?
Without priority? 'Sdeath, you perpetual curs,
Fall to your couples° again, and cozen kindly — *Work as hunting dogs*
And heartily and lovingly, as you should,
And lose not the beginning of a term,° — *court term*
Or, by this hand, I shall grow factious too,
And take my part° and quit you. — *share*

FACE 'Tis his fault.
He ever murmurs, and objects his pains,° — *stresses his efforts*
And says the weight of all lies upon him.

SUBTLE Why, so it does.

DOLL How does it? Do not we
Sustain our parts?

SUBTLE Yes, but they are not equal.

DOLL Why, if your part exceed today, I hope
Ours may tomorrow match it.

SUBTLE Ay, they may.

DOLL "May," murmuring mastiff? Ay, and do. Death on me!
[*To Face*] Help me to throttle him. [*She seizes Subtle.*]

SUBTLE Dorothy, mistress Dorothy!
'Od's precious,° I'll do anything. What do you mean? — *By God's precious body*

DOLL Because o'your fermentation and cibation?[5]

SUBTLE Not I, by heaven—

DOLL Your Sol and Luna°— [*To Face*] Help me. — *gold and silver*

SUBTLE Would I were hanged, then! I'll conform myself.

DOLL Will you, sir? Do so, then, and quickly. Swear.

SUBTLE What should I swear?

DOLL To leave your faction,° sir, — *quarreling*
And labor kindly in the common work.

SUBTLE Let me not breathe if I meant aught beside.
I only used those speeches as a spur
To him.

DOLL I hope we need no spurs, sir. [*To Face*] Do we?

FACE 'Slid,° prove today who shall shark° best. — *By God's eyelid / cheat*

SUBTLE Agreed.

DOLL Yes, and work close and friendly.

SUBTLE 'Slight, the knot

3. A number of Puritans earned their living as feather merchants in the Blackfriars district.
4. As if you and no one else had the powdered elixir needed to cause the metals to be transmuted.
5. Because of your skills at bringing the transmutation of metal to its final two stages? (Cibation is the infusing of liquids into substances that have been dried.)

Shall grow the stronger for this breach, with me.° *for my part*
[*They shake hands.*]
DOLL Why so, my good baboons! Shall we go make
A sort° of sober, scurvy, precise° neighbors, *gang / puritanical*
That scarce have smiled twice sin' the king came in,° *since 1603*
A feast of laughter at our follies? Rascals
Would run themselves from breath to see me ride,
Or you t'have but a hole to thrust your heads in,
For which you should pay ear-rent?[6] No, agree.
And may Don Provost° ride a-feasting° long *the hangman / thrive*
In his old velvet jerkin° and stained scarves, *jacket*
My noble sovereign and worthy general,
Ere we contribute a new crewel garter
To his most worsted worship.[7]
SUBTLE Royal Doll!
Spoken like Claridiana,° and thyself. *a romance heroine*
FACE For which, at supper, thou shalt sit in triumph,
And not be styled Doll Common but Doll Proper,
Doll Singular. The longest cut,° at night, *straw drawn as a lot*
Shall draw thee for his Doll Particular.[8] [*A bell rings.*]
SUBTLE Who's that? One rings. To the window, Doll! Pray heav'n
The master do not trouble us this quarter.° *fall quarter*
[*Doll goes to investigate.*]
FACE Oh, fear not him. While there dies one a week
O'the plague, he's safe from thinking toward London.
Beside, he's busy at his hopyards° now; *hop gardens*
I had a letter from him. If he do,
He'll send such word for airing o'the house
As you shall have sufficient time to quit it.
Though° we break up a fortnight,° 'tis no matter. *Even if / in two weeks*
SUBTLE [*to Doll as she returns*] Who is it, Doll?
DOLL A fine young quodling.° *green apple, raw youth*
FACE Oh,
My lawyer's clerk I lighted on last night
In Holborn, at the Dagger.° He would have *a tavern*
(I told you of him) a familiar[9]
To rifle° with at horses and win cups. *raffle, gamble*
DOLL Oh, let him in.
SUBTLE Stay. Who shall do't?
FACE Get you
Your robes on. I will meet him, as° going out. *as if*
DOLL And what shall I do?
FACE Not be seen. Away! [*Exit Doll.*]
Seem you very reserved.
SUBTLE Enough. [*Exit.*]
FACE [*speaking loudly to Subtle offstage*] God b'w'you, sir.

6. Rascals who would run themselves breathless to see me carted in public humiliation for being a bawd (see 4.6, note 1) or to see you pilloried and your ears clipped off.
7. Before we contribute to the hangman's wardrobe (as executed persons regularly did). "Crewel" means "worsted" (punning on "cruel").
8. The grammatical terms in lines 177–79 ("Common," "Proper," "Singular," "Particular") resonate with sexual suggestion. "Common" hints at "promiscuous"; "proper" can mean "private property" as well as "regular," "excellent," "morally refined." Also, "cut" is slang for the female sex organ.
9. A demonic spirit acting at the command of a person, here supposedly providing Dapper with tips about horseracing, etc.

I pray you, let him know that I was here.
His name is Dapper. I would gladly have stayed, but—

1.2

DAPPER [*calling from offstage*] Captain, I am here.
FACE Who's that?
[*He shouts to Subtle*] He's come, I think, Doctor.

[*Enter*] *Dapper.*

[*To Dapper*] Good faith, sir, I was going away.
DAPPER In truth,
I'm very sorry, Captain.
FACE But I thought
Sure I should meet you.
DAPPER Ay, I'm very glad.
I had a scurvy writ° or two to make, — *wretched legal document*
And I had lent my watch last night to one
That dines today at the sheriff's, and so was robbed
Of my pass-time.° — *timepiece*

[*Enter*] *Subtle* [*in his robes. He stands apart, oblivious to Face and Dapper as they converse in hushed tones*].

Is this the cunning° man? — *learned in magic*
FACE This is His Worship.
DAPPER Is he a doctor?° — *man of learning*
FACE Yes.
DAPPER And ha' you broke° with him, Captain? — *broached the matter*
FACE Ay.
DAPPER And how?
FACE Faith, he does make the matter, sir, so dainty,° — *he has such scruples*
I know not what to say—
DAPPER Not so,° good Captain. — *Don't say that*
FACE Would I were fairly rid on't,° believe me. — *of it*
DAPPER Nay, now you grieve me, sir. Why should you wish so?
I dare assure you I'll not be ungrateful.
FACE I cannot think you will, sir. But the law
Is such a thing—and then, he says, Read's matter[1]
Falling° so lately— — *Occurring*
DAPPER Read? He was an ass,
And dealt, sir, with a fool.
FACE It was a clerk, sir.
DAPPER A clerk?
FACE Nay, hear me, sir. You know the law
Better, I think—
DAPPER I should, sir; and the danger.
You know I showed the statute to you?
FACE You did so.
DAPPER And will I tell, then? By this hand of flesh,
Would it might never write good court hand° more — *legal handwriting*

1.2. The scene continues.
1. Simon Read was indicted in 1607–8 for summoning spirits to recover stolen money.

If I discover.° What do you think of me, — *reveal*
That I am a chiaus?[2]

FACE What's that?

DAPPER The Turk was° here— — *who was*
As one would say, do you think I am a Turk?

FACE I'll tell the doctor so.

DAPPER Do, good sweet Captain.
[*They approach Subtle.*]

FACE Come, noble Doctor, pray thee, let's prevail.
This is the gentleman, and he is no chiaus.

SUBTLE Captain, I have returned° you all my answer. — *given in reply*
I would do much, sir, for your love—but this
I neither may nor can.

FACE Tut, do not say so.
You deal now with a noble fellow, Doctor,
One that will thank you richly, and he's no chiaus.
Let that, sir, move you.

SUBTLE Pray you, forbear—

FACE He has
Four angels° here— — *gold coins*

SUBTLE You do me wrong, good sir.

FACE Doctor, wherein? To tempt you with these spirits?

SUBTLE To tempt my art and love, sir, to my peril.
'Fore heav'n, I scarce can think you are my friend,
That so would draw me to apparent° danger. — *manifest*

FACE I draw you? A horse draw° you, and a halter,° — *(to execution) / noose*
You and your flies° together— — *familiar spirits*

DAPPER Nay, good Captain.

FACE That know no difference of men.

SUBTLE Good words,° sir. — *Speak moderately*

FACE Good deeds, Sir Doctor Dogs' Meat. 'Slight, I bring you
No cheating Clim o'the Cloughs, or Claribels,[3]
That look as big as five-and-fifty and flush,° — *a winning hand at cards*
And spit out secrets like hot custard—

DAPPER Captain!

FACE Nor any melancholic underscribe
Shall tell the vicar,[4] but a special gentle° — *gentleman*
That is the heir to forty marks° a year, — *nearly £27*
Consorts with the small poets of the time,
Is the sole hope of his old grandmother,
That knows the law and writes you six fair hands,[5]
Is a fine clerk and has his ciphering° perfect, — *bookkeeping*
Will take his oath o'the Greek Xenophon,[6]
If need be, in his pocket, and can court
His mistress out of Ovid.° — *Ovid's* The Art of Love

→ subverted in Arden of Faversham

DAPPER Nay, dear Captain.

FACE Did you not tell me so?

DAPPER Yes, but I'd ha' you

2. Cheat. Literally, "messenger." The title of the Turk Mustapha, who was reported to have cheated his English merchant hosts in 1607.
3. Clim of the Cloughs is an outlaw in "The Ballad of Adam Bell." Claribel is a lewd knight in Spenser's *The Faerie Queene*, 4.9.20.
4. Who will tattle to the vicar-general, an official of the ecclesiastical courts.
5. Dapper can write in court hand (see 1.2.24), English and French secretary hands, Italic, Roman, and chancery hands.
6. Greek historian, c. 431–352 B.C.E. Swearing by Xenophon is comically absurd. This folio reading is a substitute for the quarto's "*Testament*" (in Greek), which Jonson dropped to avoid the appearance of profanity in print.

Use Master Doctor with some more respect.
FACE Hang him, proud stag, with his broad velvet head![7]
But° for your sake, I'd choke ere I would change° *Were it not / exchange*
An article of breath with such a puck-fist!° *puffball, braggart*
Come, let's be gone. [*Face starts to leave.*]
SUBTLE Pray you, le' me speak with you.
DAPPER His Worship calls you, Captain.
FACE I am sorry
I e'er embarked myself in such a business.
DAPPER Nay, good sir. He did call you.
FACE Will he take,° then? *accept money*
SUBTLE First, hear me—
FACE Not a syllable, 'less you take.
SUBTLE Pray ye, sir—
FACE Upon no terms but an *assumpsit*.[8]
SUBTLE Your humor° must be law. *He takes the money.* *whim*
FACE Why now, sir, talk.
Now I dare hear you with mine honor. Speak.
So may this gentleman too.
SUBTLE [*pretending confidentiality*] Why, sir—
FACE No whisp'ring.
SUBTLE 'Fore heav'n, you do not apprehend the loss
You do yourself in this.
FACE Wherein? For what?
SUBTLE Marry,° to be so importunate for one *By Mary (an oath)*
That, when he has it, will undo you all:
He'll win up all the money i'the town.
FACE How!
SUBTLE Yes, and blow up° gamester° after gamester, *ruin / gambler*
As they do crackers° in a puppet play. *fireworks*
If I do give him a familiar,° *(see 1.1.192 n)*
Give you him all you play for; never set° him, *lay odds against*
For he will have it.
FACE You're mistaken, Doctor.
Why, he does ask one but for cups and horses,
A rifling fly°—none o'your great familiars. *familiar for gambling*
DAPPER Yes, Captain, I would have it for all games.
SUBTLE I told you so.
FACE [*drawing Dapper aside*] 'Slight, that's a new business!
I understood you, a tame bird,[9] to fly
Twice in a term or so, on Friday nights,
When you had left the office, for a nag
Of° forty or fifty shillings. *Worth*
DAPPER Ay, 'tis true, sir,
But I do think now I shall leave the law,
And therefore—
FACE Why, this changes quite the case!
D'you think that I dare move him?
DAPPER If you please, sir,
All's one to him,° I see. *He's not unwilling*
FACE What, for that money?

7. Subtle's velvet cap and staglike head suggest the horns of cuckoldry.
8. A verbal promise, legally confirmed by acceptance of a fee.
9. I understood you to want a simple little familiar spirit.

I cannot, with my conscience. Nor should you
Make the request, methinks.
DAPPER No, sir, I mean
To add consideration.° *a gratuity*
FACE Why, then, sir,
I'll try. [*To Subtle*] Say that it were for all games, Doctor?
SUBTLE I say, then, not a mouth shall eat for° him *because of*
At any ordinary° but o'the score, *tavern*
That is a gaming mouth, conceive me.[1]
FACE Indeed!
SUBTLE He'll draw you all the treasure of the realm,
If it be set him.° *If he's bet against*
FACE Speak you this from art?° *magical skill*
SUBTLE Ay, sir, and reason too—the ground° of art. *basis*
He's o'the only best complexion
The Queen of Faery loves.[2]
FACE What! Is he?
SUBTLE Peace!° *Quiet!*
He'll overhear you. Sir, should she but see him—
FACE What?
SUBTLE Do not you tell him.
FACE Will he win at cards too?
SUBTLE The spirits of dead Holland, living Isaac,[3]
You'd swear were in him—such a vigorous luck
As cannot be resisted. 'Slight, he'll put
Six o'your gallants to a cloak,[4] indeed.
FACE A strange success, that some man shall be born to!
SUBTLE He hears you, man—
DAPPER Sir, I'll not be ingrateful.
FACE Faith, I have a confidence in his good nature.
You hear, he says he will not be ingrateful.
SUBTLE Why, as you please; my venture follows yours.° *I'll play your game*
FACE Troth, do it, Doctor. Think him trusty, and make him.° *make his fortune*
He may make us both happy° in an hour— *i.e., rich*
Win some five thousand pound, and send us two on't.° *two shares*
DAPPER Believe it, and I will, sir.
FACE And you shall, sir.
You have heard all?
DAPPER No, what was't? Nothing, I, sir.
FACE Nothing? *Face takes him aside.*
DAPPER A little, sir.
FACE Well, a rare star
Reigned at your birth.
DAPPER At mine, sir? No!
FACE The doctor
Swears that you are—
SUBTLE Nay, Captain, you'll tell all, now.
FACE Allied° to the Queen of Faery. *Related*
DAPPER Who? That I am?
Believe it, no such matter.

1. In that case, I say that all gamblers had better be prepared to charge their meals at the eating houses, since he will have won so completely, believe me.
2. His temperament is of the sort that the Queen of Faery loves best.
3. Dutch alchemists of the early seventeenth century.
4. He'll reduce at least six gallants to their last garment.

FACE Yes, and that
You were born with a caul o'your head.[5]
DAPPER Who says so?
FACE Come,
You know it well enough, though you dissemble it.
DAPPER I'fac,° I do not. You are mistaken. *In faith*
FACE How!
Swear "by your fac," and in a thing so known
Unto the doctor? How shall we, sir, trust you
I'the other matter? Can we ever think,
When you have won five or six thousand pound,
You'll send us shares in't, by this rate?
DAPPER By Jove, sir,
I'll win ten thousand pound, and send you half.
"I'fac" 's no oath.[6]
SUBTLE [*to Face*] No, no, he did but jest.
FACE [*to Subtle*] Go to.°—Go, thank the doctor. He's your friend *(expressing impatience)*
To take it so.
DAPPER I thank His Worship.
FACE So?
Another angel.
DAPPER Must I?
FACE "Must you"? 'Slight,
What else is thanks? Will you be trivial?° [*Dapper gives gold to Subtle.*] Doctor, *penny-pinching*
When must he come for his familiar?
DAPPER Shall I not ha' it° with me? *take it*
SUBTLE Oh, good sir,
There must a world of ceremonies pass.° *take place*
You must be bathed and fumigated first.
Besides, the Queen of Faery does not rise
Till it be noon.
FACE Not if she danced tonight.° *last night*
SUBTLE And she must bless it.
FACE Did you never see
Her Royal Grace yet?
DAPPER Whom?
FACE Your aunt of Faery.
SUBTLE Not since she kissed him in the cradle, Captain,
I can resolve you that.° *answer that*
FACE Well, see Her Grace,
Whate'er it cost you, for a thing that I know.[7]
It will be somewhat hard to compass,° but, *accomplish*
However, see her. You are made, believe it,
If you can see her. Her Grace is a lone woman,
And very rich, and if she take a fancy,
She will do strange things. See her, at any hand.° *at any rate*
'Slid,° she may hap to leave you all she has! *By God's eyelid*

5. To be born with the inner membrane enclosing the fetus still wrapped around the head, like a cap, was considered good luck.
6. "In faith" is too mild to be binding as an oath; "By Jove" (line 135) is stronger.
7. Face hints at something secret and probably salacious.

It is the doctor's fear.
DAPPER How will't be done, then?
FACE Let me alone;° take you no thought. Do you — *Leave it to me*
But say to me, "Captain, I'll see Her Grace."
DAPPER Captain, I'll see Her Grace.
FACE Enough.
One knocks without.
SUBTLE Who's there?
[*Calling*] Anon! (*To Face*) Conduct him forth, by the back way.
[*To Dapper*] Sir, against° one o'clock, prepare yourself; — *in anticipation of*
Till when you must be fasting. Only take
Three drops of vinegar in at your nose,
Two at your mouth, and one at either ear;
Then, bathe your fingers' ends and wash your eyes,
To sharpen your five senses; and cry "hum"
Thrice, and then "buzz" as often; and then come. [*Exit.*]
FACE Can you remember this?
DAPPER I warrant° you. — *assure*
FACE Well, then, away. 'Tis but your bestowing
Some twenty nobles° 'mong Her Grace's servants; — *almost £7*
And put on a clean shirt. You do not know
What grace Her Grace may do you in clean linen.
[*Exeunt.*]

1.3

[*Enter*] *Subtle* [*with*] *Drugger.*

SUBTLE Come in. [*He calls offstage to imaginary persons.*]
Good wives, I pray you forbear me now;
Troth, I can do you no good till afternoon.—
What is your name, say you? Abel Drugger?
DRUGGER Yes, sir.
SUBTLE A seller of tobacco?
DRUGGER Yes, sir.
SUBTLE Umh!
Free of the Grocers?[1]
DRUGGER Ay, an't° please you. — *if it*
SUBTLE Well—
Your business, Abel?
DRUGGER This, an't please Your Worship:
I am a young beginner, and am building
Of a new shop, an't like° Your Worship, just — *please*
At corner of a street. Here's the plot° on't. — *ground plan*
[*He shows a diagram.*]
And I would know, by art, sir, of Your Worship,
Which way I should make my door, by necromancy,
And where my shelves, and which should be for boxes
And which for pots. I would be glad to thrive, sir.
And I was wished° to Your Worship by a gentleman, — *recommended*
One Captain Face, that says you know men's planets,

1.3. Lovewit's house still.
1. A member of the grocers' guild. Grocers were wholesale dealers in foods of all kinds.

And their good angels, and their bad.
SUBTLE I do,
If I do see 'em—

[*Enter*] *Face.*

FACE What! My honest Abel?
Thou art well met here!
DRUGGER Troth, sir, I was speaking,
Just as Your Worship came here, of Your Worship.
I pray you, speak for me to Master Doctor.
FACE He shall do anything.—Doctor, do you hear?
This is my friend Abel, an honest fellow.
He lets me have good tobacco, and he does not
Sophisticate° it with sack-lees° or oil, *Adulterate / dregs*
Nor washes it in muscadel° and grains,° *wine / spices*
Nor buries it in gravel, underground,
Wrapped up in greasy leather or pissed clouts,° *cloths, rags*
But keeps it in fine lily pots° that, opened, *ornamental jars*
Smell like conserve of roses or French beans.° *fragrant flowers*
He has his maple block, his silver tongs,
Winchester pipes, and fire of juniper.[2]
A neat, spruce, honest fellow, and no goldsmith.° *i.e., usurer*
SUBTLE He's a fortunate fellow, that I am sure on—
FACE Already, sir, ha' you found it?—Lo thee,° Abel! *i.e., You see?*
SUBTLE And in right way toward riches.
FACE Sir!
SUBTLE This summer
He will be of the clothing° of his company, *wearing the livery*
And next spring called to the scarlet.° Spend what he can. *named alderman*
FACE What, and so little beard?° *so young*
SUBTLE Sir, you must think
He may have a receipt° to make hair come. *recipe*
But he'll be wise, preserve his youth, and fine for't;[3]
His fortune looks for him another way.
FACE 'Slid, Doctor, how canst thou know this so soon?
I am amused° at that. *bemused, puzzled*
SUBTLE By a rule, Captain,
In metoposcopy,° which I do work by— *phrenology*
A certain star i'the forehead, which you see not.
Your chestnut- or your olive-colored face
Does never fail, and your long ear doth promise.
I knew't by certain spots too, in his teeth,
And on the nail of his mercurial finger.[4]
FACE Which finger's that?
SUBTLE [*taking Drugger's hand*] His little finger. Look.
You were born upon a Wednesday?
DRUGGER Yes, indeed, sir.
SUBTLE The thumb, in chiromanty,° we give Venus, *palm reading*
The forefinger to Jove, the midst to Saturn,
The ring° to Sol, the least to Mercury, *ring finger*

2. The tobacconist's equipment includes a maple block for shredding the tobacco, tongs for handling hot coals, and long-burning juniper wood to help customers light pipes.
3. He'll pay the fine for refusing to serve as sheriff or alderman (both of which entailed onerous financial responsibilities).
4. Long ears and spotted teeth were traditionally signs of foolishness and untidiness. The "mercurial" finger is the little finger.

Who was the lord, sir, of his horoscope,
His house of life being Libra,[5] which foreshowed
He should be a merchant and should trade with balance.
FACE Why, this is strange! Is't not, honest Nab?[6]
SUBTLE There is a ship now, coming from Ormuz,° *(on the Persian Gulf)*
That shall yield him such a commodity° *supply*
Of drugs— [*He points to the diagram.*] This is the west, and this the south?
DRUGGER Yes, sir.
SUBTLE And those are your two sides?
DRUGGER Ay, sir.
SUBTLE Make me° your door, then, south; your broad side, west; *Make me = Make*
And, on the east side of your shop, aloft,
Write *Mathlai, Tarmiel,* and *Baraborat;*
Upon the north part, *Rael, Velel, Thiel.*
They are the names of those mercurial spirits
That do fright flies from boxes.
DRUGGER Yes, sir.
SUBTLE And
Beneath your threshold bury me a lodestone° *bury a magnet*
To draw in gallants, that wear spurs. The rest,
They'll seem° to follow. *be seen*
FACE That's a secret, Nab!
SUBTLE And, on your stall a puppet with a vice° *mechanical doll*
And a court fucus,° to call city dames. *cosmetic used at court*
You shall deal much with minerals.
DRUGGER Sir, I have,
At home, already—
SUBTLE Ay, I know, you've arsenic,
Vitriol, sal tartar, argaile, alkali,
Cinoper:[7] I know all.—This fellow, Captain,
Will come in time to be a great distiller,
And give a say°—I will not say directly, *make an attempt, assay*
But very fair°—at the philosophers' stone. *with a good chance*
FACE Why, how now, Abel! Is this true?
DRUGGER [*taking Face aside*] Good Captain,
What must I give?
FACE Nay, I'll not counsel thee.
Thou hear'st what wealth (he says, spend what thou canst)
Thou'rt like to come to.
DRUGGER I would gi' him a crown.° *(worth 5s.)*
FACE A crown! And toward such a fortune? Heart,° *By God's heart*
Thou shalt rather gi' him thy shop. No gold about thee?
DRUGGER Yes, I have a portague° I ha' kept this half year. *valuable gold coin*
FACE Out on thee, Nab! 'Slight, there was such an offer!
'Shalt keep't no longer; I'll gi' it him for thee.
[*Face takes the coin and gives it to Subtle.*]
Doctor, Nab prays Your Worship to drink° this, and swears *buy drinks with*
He will appear more grateful as your skill
Does raise him in the world.

5. The zodiacal sign of the autumnal equinox, a balance.
6. Worthy Abel. ("Nab" is a nickname for "Abel.")
7. Sulfuric acid, carbonate of potash, cream of tartar, soda ash, cinnabar (red mercuric sulfide).

DRUGGER I would entreat
Another favor of His Worship.
FACE What is't, Nab?
DRUGGER But° to look over, sir, my almanac,° *Simply / horoscope*
And cross out my ill° days, that I may neither *unlucky*
Bargain nor trust° upon them. *extend credit*
FACE That he shall, Nab.
Leave it; it shall be done 'gainst° afternoon. *in time for*
SUBTLE And a direction for his shelves.
FACE Now, Nab,
Art thou well pleased, Nab?
DRUGGER Thank, sir, both Your Worships.
FACE Away! [*Exit Drugger.*]
Why, now, you smoky persecutor of nature!
Now, do you see that something's to be done
Beside your beech coal and your cor'sive waters,[8]
Your crosslets,° crucibles, and cucurbites?° *melting pots / retorts*
You must have stuff brought home to you to work on?
And yet you think I am at no expense
In searching out these veins, then following 'em,
Then trying 'em out. 'Fore God, my intelligence° *information*
Costs me more money than my share oft comes to
In these rare works.
SUBTLE You're pleasant,° sir. *joking*

1.4

[*Enter*] *Doll.*

How now?
What says my dainty Dollkin?
DOLL Yonder fishwife° *(an offstage client)*
Will not away. And there's your giantess,
The bawd of Lambeth.° *(an offstage client)*
SUBTLE Heart, I cannot speak with 'em.
DOLL Not afore night, I have told 'em, in a voice
Thorough° the trunk,° like one of your familiars. *Through / speaking tube*
But I have spied Sir Epicure Mammon—
SUBTLE Where?
DOLL Coming along at far end of the lane,
Slow of his feet, but earnest of his tongue
To one that's with him.
SUBTLE Face, go you and shift.° *change clothes*
[*Exit Face.*]
Doll, you must presently° make ready too. *at once*
DOLL Why, what's the matter?
SUBTLE Oh, I did look for him
With the sun's rising. Marvel he could sleep!
This is the day I am to perfect for him
The *magisterium*,° our great work, the stone, *masterwork*
And yield it, made, into his hands—of which
He has, this month, talked as° he were possessed; *as if*

8. A high grade of charcoal and acids used in alchemy. 1.4. The scene continues.

And now he's dealing pieces on't° away. *of his imagined wealth*
Methinks I see him ent'ring ordinaries,° *eating houses*
Dispensing for the pox, and plaguy-houses,° *houses for plague victims*
Reaching his dose; walking Moorfields for lepers,[1]
And off'ring citizens' wives pomander bracelets[2]
As his preservative, made of the elixir;° *stone in solution*
Searching the spital° to make old bawds young, *hospital*
And the highways for beggars to make rich.
I see no end of his labors. He will make
Nature ashamed of her long sleep, when art,
Who's but a stepdame,° shall do more than she, *stepmother*
In her best love to mankind, ever could.
If his dream last, he'll turn the age to gold.[3] [*Exeunt.*]

2.1

[*Enter*] *Mammon* [*and*] *Surly.*

MAMMON Come on, sir. Now you set your foot on shore
In *Novo Orbe;*° here's the rich Peru, *In the New World*
And there within, sir, are the golden mines,
Great Solomon's Ophir![1] He was sailing to't
Three years, but we have reached it in ten months.
This is the day wherein to all my friends
I will pronounce the happy word, "Be rich;
This day you shall be *spectatissimi.*"° *highly looked up to*
You shall no more deal with the hollow die° *loaded dice*
Or the frail card;° no more be at charge of keeping *crooked cards*
The livery-punk for the young heir that must
Seal at all hours in his shirt;[2] no more,
If he deny,° ha' him beaten to't, as he is *forfeit*
That brings him the commodity.[3] No more
Shall thirst of satin, or the covetous hunger
Of velvet entrails° for a rude-spun cloak, *lining*
To be displayed at Madam Augusta's,[4] make
The sons of sword and hazard° fall before *swashbuckling gamblers*
The golden calf and on their knees, whole nights,
Commit idolatry with wine and trumpets,
Or go a-feasting after drum and ensign.[5]
No more of this. You shall start up° young viceroys, *beget*
And have your punks and punketees,° my Surly. *young prostitutes*
And unto thee I speak it first, "Be rich."
[*Calling*] Where is my Subtle, there? Within, ho!
FACE (*within*) Sir,

1. I can imagine him (Mammon) entering eating houses, handing out doses of a supposed cure for syphilis and plague in the form of an elixir (a liquid concoction) made from the philosophers' stone, and seeking out lepers in Moorfields (north of London, where lepers were allowed to beg).
2. Bracelets with perfume balls thought to ward off plague.
3. The golden age was imagined to be the first and earliest of the world's four ages—a time of innocence and plenty, with no need for gold as wealth.
2.1. Lovewit's house still.
1. According to 1 Kings 9–10, Solomon built a navy to fetch gold from Ophir (in Arabia or East Africa). Later tradition supposes that Solomon used the philosophers' stone.
2. No more will you have to bear the expense of maintaining a prostitute as your accomplice in swindling a spendthrift young gentleman by tricking him into signing ("sealing") a promissory note in return for worthless goods.
3. Just as the person bringing the worthless goods also deserves to be whipped.
4. To be worn and shown off at a brothel.
5. Commit idolatrous worship of gold in scenes of dissipation, or enlist to repair a wasted fortune.

He'll come to you by and by.
MAMMON That's his firedrake,
His lungs, his Zephyrus,[6] he that puffs his coals
Till he firk° nature up in her own center. *stir*
You are not faithful,° sir. This night I'll change *attentive; believing*
All that is metal in my house to gold,
And early in the morning will I send
To all the plumbers and the pewterers,
And buy their tin and lead up, and to Lothbury[7]
For all the copper.
SURLY What, and turn that too?
MAMMON Yes, and I'll purchase Devonshire and Cornwall,° *counties with mines*
And make them perfect Indies! You admire° now? *marvel*
SURLY No, faith.
MAMMON But when you see th'effects of the great med'cine,
Of which one part projected on a hundred
Of Mercury, or Venus,° or the moon° *copper / silver*
Shall turn it to as many of the sun°— *gold*
Nay, to a thousand, so *ad infinitum*—
You will believe me.
SURLY Yes, when I see't I will.
But if my eyes do cozen° me so, and I *hoodwink*
Giving 'em no occasion, sure I'll have
A whore shall piss 'em out next day.[8]
MAMMON Ha! Why?
Do you think I fable with you? I assure you,
He that has once the flower of the sun,
The perfect ruby, which we call elixir,
Not only can do that, but by its virtue° *strength*
Can confer honor, love, respect, long life,
Give safety, valor, yea, and victory
To whom he will. In eight-and-twenty days
I'll make an old man of fourscore a child.
SURLY No doubt he's that° already. *i.e., he's childish*
MAMMON Nay, I mean
Restore his years, renew him, like an eagle,
To the fifth age;[9] make him get° sons and daughters, *beget*
Young giants, as our philosophers have done
(The ancient patriarchs° afore the flood), *(Abraham, Isaac, Jacob)*
But° taking, once a week on a knife's point, *And merely by*
The quantity of a grain of mustard of it,
Become stout Marses° and beget young Cupids. *mighty gods of war*
SURLY The decayed° vestals of Pict-hatch° would thank you, *diseased / a brothel area*
That keep the fire[1] alive there.
MAMMON 'Tis the secret
Of nature naturized[2] 'gainst all infections,
Cures all diseases coming of all causes:
A month's grief° in a day, a year's in twelve, *illness*

6. Face is Subtle's fiery dragon (i.e., the one who works the fire), his bellows operator, his west wind.
7. Street of workers in copper and other metals.
8. If I allow my eyes to deceive me like this without my active connivance, may some whore blind me by urinating in my eyes.
9. To manhood, the fifth of the seven ages of man.
1. The fire of lust and venereal infection.
2. Created nature, as distinguished from *natura naturans,* the creating power of nature and the Creator Himself.

And of what age soever in a month,
Past all the doses of your drugging doctors.
I'll undertake withal to fright the plague
Out o'the kingdom in three months.

SURLY And I'll
Be bound the players shall sing your praises then,
Without their poets.[3]

MAMMON Sir, I'll do't. Meantime
I'll give away so much unto my man° *servant*
Shall° serve th'whole city with preservative, *As shall*
Weekly, each house his dose, and at the rate—

SURLY As he that built the waterwork does with water?[4]

MAMMON You are incredulous.

SURLY Faith, I have a humor;° *whim*
I would not willingly be gulled.° Your stone *tricked*
Cannot transmute me.

MAMMON Pertinax, my Surly,
Will you believe antiquity? Records?
I'll show you a book where Moses and his sister
And Solomon have written of the art;
Ay, and a treatise penned by Adam—

SURLY How!

MAMMON O'the philosophers' stone, and in High Dutch.° *High German*

SURLY Did Adam write, sir, in High Dutch?

MAMMON He did,
Which proves it was the primitive tongue.

SURLY What paper?

MAMMON On cedar board.

SURLY Oh, that, indeed, they say,
Will last 'gainst worms.

MAMMON 'Tis like your Irish wood
'Gainst cobwebs. I have a piece of Jason's fleece,[5] too,
Which was no other than a book of alchemy,
Writ in large sheepskin, a good fat ram-vellum.° *parchment*
Such was Pythagoras' thigh,[6] Pandora's tub,° *box*
And all that fable of Medea's charms,
The manner of our work: the bulls, our furnace,
Still breathing fire; our *argent-vive*,° the dragon; *quicksilver*
The dragon's teeth,[7] mercury sublimate,
That keeps the whiteness, hardness, and the biting;
And they are gathered into Jason's helm,
Th'alembic,° and then sowed in Mars his° field,[8] *retort, flask / Mars's*
And thence sublimed° so often till they are fixed. *refined*
Both this, th'Hesperian garden,[9] Cadmus' story,

3. Ending the plague would benefit the players, who were forbidden to act in times of plague. They would not even need their dramatists to write praises for Sir Epicure.

4. Pumping stations and systems of lead pipes had been built in 1582 and 1594 to supply London with water from the Thames, and a new aqueduct was under construction in 1610.

5. When Jason sailed in quest of the Golden Fleece, Medea used her charms (line 93) to restore Jason's youth and to put a spell on the dragon (line 95) guarding the fleece, and Jason plowed with fire-eating bulls (line 94).

6. A legendarily golden thigh. See *Volpone*, 1.2.9 and note.

7. Cadmus (line 101) killed the dragon (line 95) of Thebes and sowed its teeth in "Mars his field" (line 99), which sprang up as armed men.

8. The "alembic," a retort or distilling flask, has a long beak (resembling Jason's helmet) by means of which the distillate is conveyed to the condenser, an iron vessel here named for Mars, the god of war.

9. Mythical garden of golden apples guarded by a dragon and by nymphs called the "Hesperides."

Jove's shower, the boon of Midas, Argus' eyes,[1]
Boccace his Demogorgon,[2] thousands more,
All abstract riddles° of our stone.— *allegories*

2.2

[*Enter*] *Face* [*as Lungs, the Alchemist's servant*].

How now?
Do we succeed? Is our day come? And holds it?
FACE The evening will set red upon you, sir.
You have color° for it, crimson; the red ferment *reason; red color*
Has done his° office. Three hours hence, prepare you *its*
To see projection.° *the climax*
MAMMON Pertinax, my Surly,
Again, I say to thee aloud, "Be rich."
This day thou shalt have ingots, and tomorrow
Give lords th'affront.[1]—Is it, my Zephyrus,° right? *(see 2.1.27 and n)*
Blushes the bolt's-head?° *long-necked flask*
FACE Like a wench with child, sir,
That were but now discovered° to her master. *revealed*
MAMMON Excellent witty Lungs! My only care is
Where to get stuff enough now to project on;° *transmute into gold*
This town will not half serve me.
FACE No, sir? Buy
The covering° off o'churches. *lead roofs*
MAMMON That's true.
FACE Yes.
Let 'em stand bare, as do their auditory,° *congregation*
Or cap 'em new with shingles.
MAMMON No, good thatch;
Thatch will lie light upo' the rafters, Lungs.
Lungs, I will manumit° thee from the furnace; *release*
I will restore thee thy complexion, Puff,
Lost in the embers, and repair this brain,
Hurt wi'the fume o'the metals.
FACE I have blown, sir,
Hard for Your Worship; thrown by° many a coal *aside*
When 'twas not beech;[2] weighed those I put in, just,° *exactly*
To keep your heat still° even. These bleared eyes *continually*
Have waked to read your several° colors, sir, *various*
Of the pale citron, the green lion, the crow,
The peacock's tail, the plumèd swan.[3]
MAMMON And lastly
Thou hast descried the flower, the *sanguis agni*?° *blood of the lamb*
FACE Yes, sir.
MAMMON Where's master?
FACE At 's prayers, sir, he;
Good man, he's doing his devotions

1. Jove wooed Danaë in a shower of gold; Midas requested that everything he touched be turned to gold; the hundred eyes of Argus became the eyes of the peacock's tail.
2. In Boccaccio's *Genealogy of the Gods,* Demogorgon is parent of all things.
2.2. The scene continues.

1. Look boldly in the face of any aristocrat.
2. Beech wood produces high-quality charcoal for a steady fire.
3. The color sequence symbolically here described in terms of various animals (the black crow, the white swan, etc.) spells out the desired sequence of alchemical steps toward the desired perfection.

For the success.
MAMMON Lungs, I will set a period° *make an end*
To all thy labors. Thou shalt be the master
Of my seraglio.° *harem*
FACE Good, sir.
MAMMON But do you hear?
I'll geld you, Lungs.[4]
FACE Yes, sir.
MAMMON For I do mean
To have a list of wives and concubines
Equal with Solomon,[5] who had the stone
Alike with me; and I will make me a back° *develop sexual potency*
With the elixir that shall be as tough
As Hercules, to encounter fifty a night.[6]
Thou'rt sure thou saw'st it blood?
FACE Both blood and spirit,° sir. *color and quality*
MAMMON I will have all my beds blown up,° not stuffed; *inflated*
Down is too hard. And then, mine oval room
Filled with such pictures as Tiberius took
From Elephantis, and dull Aretine[7]
But coldly imitated. Then my glasses° *mirrors*
Cut in more subtle angles, to disperse
And multiply the figures as I walk
Naked between my succubae.[8] My mists
I'll have of perfume, vapored 'bout the room,
To lose° ourselves in; and my baths like pits *abandon; loose, let go*
To fall into, from whence we will come forth
And roll us dry in gossamer and roses.—
Is it arrived at ruby?°—Where I spy *a red glow*
A wealthy citizen or rich lawyer
Have a sublimed° pure wife, unto that fellow *rarefied*
I'll send a thousand pound to be my cuckold.
FACE And I shall carry it?
MAMMON No. I'll ha' no bawds
But fathers and mothers. They will do it best,
Best of all others. And my flatterers
Shall be the pure° and gravest of divines *purest*
That I can get for money; my mere fools
Eloquent burgesses;° and then my poets *councilmen, MPs*
The same that writ so subtly of the fart,
Whom I will entertain° still for that subject. *retain, employ*
The few that would give out° themselves to be *boast*
Court- and town-stallions, and eachwhere belie° *everywhere slander*
Ladies who are known most innocent, for° them, *as for*
Those will I beg to make me eunuchs of;
And they shall fan me with ten ostrich tails
Apiece, made in a plume to gather wind.
We will be brave,° Puff, now we ha' the med'cine. *splendid*

4. Face is to be castrated so that he can guard Mammon's harem.
5. Solomon was reputed to have seven hundred wives and three hundred concubines (1 Kings 11.3).
6. Hercules impregnated in one night all but one of the fifty daughters of King Thespius.
7. Tiberius was Roman emperor (14–37 C.E.); Elephantis is mentioned by the poet Martial (c. 40–103 C.E.) and the biographer Suetonius (c. 69–after 122 C.E.) as an erotic writer; Aretine was an Italian sonneteer (1492–1556) who wrote erotic verse to accompany pornographic illustrations by Giulio Romano. (See *Volpone*, 3.4.)
8. I.e., paramours. Succubae are literally demons assuming female shape and having sex with men.

My meat shall all come in in Indian shells,
Dishes of agate set in gold and studded
With emeralds, sapphires, hyacinths,° and rubies. *jacinths (gems)*
The tongues of carps, dormice, and camels' heels,
Boiled i'the spirit of Sol° and dissolved pearl, *distillate of gold*
(Apicius' diet 'gainst the epilepsy)[9]—
And I will eat these broths with spoons of amber,
Headed° with diamond and carbuncle. *Festooned*
My footboy shall eat pheasants, calvered° salmons, *sliced alive*
Knots, godwits,° lampreys;° I myself will have *Wildfowl / eel-like fish*
The beards of barbels° served instead of salads, *carp*
Oiled mushrooms, and the swelling unctuous paps
Of a fat pregnant sow newly cut off,
Dressed with an exquisite and poignant sauce,
For which I'll say unto my cook, "There's gold;
Go forth, and be a knight."

FACE Sir, I'll go look
A little how it heightens.

MAMMON Do. [*Exit Face.*]
My shirts
I'll have of taffeta-sars'net,° soft and light *fine silk*
As cobwebs; and for° all my other raiment, *as for*
It shall be such as might provoke the Persian,[1]
Were he to teach the world riot° anew. *debauchery*
My gloves of fishes' and birds' skins, perfumed
With gums of Paradise and Eastern air°— *i.e., from Eden*

SURLY And do you think to have the stone with this?

MAMMON No, I do think t'have all this with the stone.

SURLY Why, I have heard he must be *homo frugi*,° *a temperate man*
A pious, holy, and religious man,
One free from mortal sin, a very virgin.

MAMMON That makes it, sir; he° is so. But I buy it; *(Subtle)*
My venture brings it me. He, honest wretch,
A notable, superstitious,° good soul, *extremely devout*
Has worn his knees bare and his slippers bald
With prayer and fasting for it; and, sir, let him
Do it alone, for me, still. Here he comes.
Not a profane word afore him; 'tis poison.—

2.3

[*Enter*] *Subtle.*

Good morrow, father.

SUBTLE Gentle son, good morrow,
And to your friend there. What is he is with you?

MAMMON An heretic that I did bring along
In hope, sir, to convert him.

SUBTLE Son, I doubt° *fear, suspect*

9. Apicius, a gourmet of the reign of Tiberius (14–37 C.E.), is reported to have eaten camels' heels and nightingales' tongues to ward off the plague. He is understandably confused with another Apicius who wrote a cookbook in the third century C.E.

1. Sardanapalus, legendary king of Assyria (c. 822 B.C.E.), whose name was a byword for decadent luxury.

2.3. The scene continues.

You're covetous, that thus you meet your time
I'the just point,° prevent your day[1] at morning. — *So exactly*
This argues° something worthy of a fear — *suggests, points to*
Of importune° and carnal appetite. — *importunate*
Take heed you do not cause the blessing leave you,
With your ungoverned haste! I should be sorry
To see my labors, now e'en at perfection,
Got by long watching° and large patience, — *vigilance*
Not prosper where my love and zeal hath placed 'em—
Which° (heaven I call to witness, with yourself, — *I who*
To whom I have poured my thoughts), in all my ends,° — *aims*
Have looked no way but unto public good,
To pious uses and dear charity,
Now grown a prodigy with men;[2] wherein
If you, my son, should now prevaricate,° — *swerve aside*
And to your own particular lusts employ
So great and catholic° a bliss, be sure — *universal*
A curse will follow, yea, and overtake
Your subtle and most secret ways.

MAMMON I know, sir;
You shall not need to fear° me. I but come — *worry about*
To ha' you confute this gentleman.

SURLY Who is,
Indeed, sir, somewhat costive° of belief — *niggardly*
Toward your stone—would not be gulled.

SUBTLE [*to Mammon*] Well, son,
All that I can convince him in is this:
The work is done; bright Sol° is in his robe.° — *gold / ready for climax*
We have a med'cine of the triple Soul,[3]
The glorified spirit. Thanks be to heaven,
And make us worthy of it! [*Calling offstage*] Ulenspiegel![4]

FACE [*within*] Anon, sir.

SUBTLE [*calling*] Look well to the register,° — *furnace air intake*
And let your heat still lessen by degrees,
To the aludels.° — *pots for distillation*

FACE [*within*] Yes, sir.

SUBTLE Did you look
O'the bolt's-head° yet? — *long-necked flask*

FACE [*within*] Which, on D, sir?

SUBTLE Ay.
What's the complexion?

FACE [*within*] Whitish.

SUBTLE Infuse vinegar,
To draw his volatile substance and his tincture,
And let the water in Glass E be filtered
And put into the gripe's egg.° Lute[5] him well, — *egg-shaped vessel*
And leave him closed in *balneo*.° — *a sand or water bath*

FACE [*within*] I will, sir.

SURLY What a brave language here is! Next to canting.[6]

1. You come before your time.
2. Charity has become abnormal among people today.
3. I.e., of the vital, natural, and animal spirits of liver, heart, and brain—all essential to the interconnectedness of body and soul.
4. Till Ulenspiegel (or Eulenspiegel), meaning "Owlglass" in German, was a peasant clown of the fourteenth century whose merry pranks were recorded in German jest books.
5. Bury in clay (to protect from the heat).
6. What fine lingo! Next best thing to thieves' slang. (Said sardonically.)

SUBTLE [*to Mammon*] I have another work you never saw, son,
That three days since passed the philosophers' wheel,° *alchemical cycle*
In the lent° heat of Athanor,[7] and 's become *slow, gentle*
Sulfur o'nature.[8]
MAMMON But 'tis for me?
SUBTLE What need you?
You have enough, in that is perfect.° *enough is a feast*
MAMMON Oh, but—
SUBTLE Why, this is covetise!° *covetousness*
MAMMON No, I assure you,
I shall employ it all in pious uses,
Founding of colleges° and grammar schools, *foundations*
Marrying° young virgins, building hospitals, *Giving in marriage*
And now and then a church.

[*Enter*] *Face.*

SUBTLE How now?
FACE Sir, please you,
Shall I not change the filter?
SUBTLE Marry, yes.
And bring me the complexion of Glass B. [*Exit Face.*]
MAMMON Ha' you another?
SUBTLE Yes, son. Were I assured
Your piety were firm, we would not want° *lack*
The means to glorify it. But I hope the best:
I mean to tinct C in sand-heat tomorrow,
And give him imbibition.° *soaking*
MAMMON Of white° oil? *mercury*
SUBTLE No, sir, of red.° F is come over the helm° too, *sulfur / flask cap*
I thank my Maker, in St. Mary's bath,° *a sand or water bath*
And shows *lac Virginis*.° Blessed be heaven! *virgin's milk, mercury*
I sent you of his feces° there, calcined;[9] *sediment*
Out of that calx° I ha' won the salt of mercury. *refined, powdery metal*
MAMMON By pouring on your rectified° water? *distilled*
SUBTLE Yes, and reverberating° in Athanor. *heating intensely*

[*Enter*] *Face.*

How now? What color says it?
FACE The ground black, sir.
MAMMON That's your crow's head?° *(see 2.2.26)*
SURLY Your coxcomb's,° is't not? *Your own fool's head*
SUBTLE No, 'tis not perfect. Would it were the crow!
That work wants something.
SURLY (*aside*) Oh, I looked for this.
The hay is a-pitching.° *snare is being set*
SUBTLE [*to Face*] Are you sure you loosed 'em
I'their own menstrue?° *solvent*
FACE Yes, sir, and then married° 'em, *blended*
And put 'em in a bolt's-head nipped to digestion,[1]
According as you bade me, when I set
The liquor of Mars° to circulation *molten iron*

7. Charcoal-fed furnace producing constant low heat.
8. A solution of pure sulfur supposed, when combined with mercury, to produce gold.
9. Made into powder.
1. And put them in a long-necked flask, sealed for gentle heating, in order to complete the chemical reaction.

In the same heat.
SUBTLE The process, then, was right.
FACE Yes, by the token,° sir, the retort brake,[2] *appearance of things*
And what was saved was put into the pelican,° *long-necked vessel*
And signed with Hermes' seal.° *hermetically sealed*
SUBTLE I think 'twas so.
We should have a new amalgama.[3]
SURLY (*aside*) Oh, this ferret
Is rank as any polecat!
SUBTLE But I care not.
Let him e'en die; we have enough beside,
In embryon.° H has his white shirt on? *the beginning stage*
FACE Yes, sir,
He's ripe for inceration;[4] he stands warm
In his ash-fire. I would not you should° let *I wish you wouldn't*
Any die now, if I might counsel, sir,
For luck's sake to the rest. It is not good.
MAMMON He says right.
SURLY (*aside*) Ay, are you bolted?° *driven into the net*
FACE Nay, I know't, sir;
I have seen th'ill fortune. What is[5] some three ounces
Of fresh materials?
MAMMON Is't no more?
FACE No more, sir,
Of gold, t'amalgam,[6] with some six of mercury.
MAMMON Away! Here's money. What will serve?
FACE [*indicating Subtle*] Ask him, sir.
MAMMON [*to Subtle*] How much?
SUBTLE Give him nine pound; you may gi' him ten.
SURLY [*aside*] Yes, twenty, and be cozened, do.
MAMMON [*giving money to Face*] There 'tis.
SUBTLE This needs not,° but that you will have it so *isn't necessary*
To see conclusions of all. For two
Of our inferior works are at fixation;° *stabilization*
A third is in ascension.° Go your ways.— *distillation*
Ha' you set the oil of *Luna*° in *kemia*?[7] *white elixir*
FACE Yes, sir.
SUBTLE And the philosophers' vinegar?° *mercury*
FACE Ay. [*Exit.*]
SURLY [*aside*] We shall have a salad![8]
MAMMON When do you make projection?
SUBTLE Son, be not hasty. I exalt° our med'cine *refine*
By hanging him in *balneo vaporoso*° *a vapor bath*
And giving him solution,° then congeal him *making it soluble*
And then dissolve him, then again congeal him;
For look how oft° I iterate the work, *no matter how often*
So many times I add unto his virtue.° *its strength*
As, if at first one ounce convert a hundred,
After his second loose° he'll turn a thousand; *loosening; solution*
His third solution, ten;° his fourth, a hundred;° *10,000 / 100,000*

2. The flask broke.
3. Mixture of other metals with mercury.
4. It's ready for slow mixing of dry matter with fluid to the consistency of wax.
5. I.e., Why worry about the added expense of.
6. Some gold is purportedly needed to amalgamate or combine with the mercury and other ingredients.
7. In the distilling flask for chemical analysis?
8. A "salad" in alchemical terms is composed of gold, salt, sulfur (the "oil"), and mercury (the "vinegar").

After his fifth, a thousand thousand ounces
Of any imperfect metal into pure
Silver or gold, in all examinations° *assays*
As good as any of the natural mine.
Get you your stuff here against° afternoon— *in preparation for*
Your brass, your pewter, and your andirons.

MAMMON Not those of iron?

SUBTLE Yes. You may bring them too.
We'll change all metals.

SURLY [*aside*] I believe you in that.

MAMMON Then I may send my spits?

SUBTLE Yes, and your racks.° *brackets for spits*

SURLY And dripping-pans and pot-hangers and hooks,
Shall he not?

SUBTLE If he please.

SURLY To be an ass.

SUBTLE How, sir!

MAMMON This gent'man you must bear withal.° *put up with*
I told you he had no faith.

SURLY And little hope, sir,
But much less charity, should I° gull myself. *lest I*

SUBTLE Why, what have you observed, sir, in our art
Seems so impossible?

SURLY But° your whole work, no more. *Merely*
That° you should hatch gold in a furnace, sir, *To suppose that*
As they do eggs in Egypt![9]

SUBTLE Sir, do you
Believe that eggs are hatched so?

SURLY If I should?

SUBTLE Why, I think that the greater miracle.
No egg but differs from a chicken more
Than metals in themselves.

SURLY That cannot be.
The egg's ordained by nature to that end,
And is a chicken *in potentia*.° *potentially*

SUBTLE The same we say of lead and other metals,
Which would be gold, if they had time.

MAMMON And that
Our art doth further.

SUBTLE Ay, for 'twere absurd
To think that nature, in the earth, bred gold
Perfect i'the instant. Something went before.
There must be remote° matter. *original, primeval*

SURLY Ay? What is that?

SUBTLE Marry, we say—

MAMMON Ay, now it heats. Stand, father;
Pound him to dust.

SUBTLE It is, of° the one part,° *on / hand*
A humid exhalation which we call
Materia liquida° or the unctuous° water; *Liquid matter / oily*
On th'other part, a certain crass° and viscous *dense*
Portion of earth; both which, concorporate,° *united into one mass*
Do make the elementary matter of gold,

9. The Egyptians practiced incubation. Sealed flasks were sometimes known as "philosophers' eggs."

Which is not yet *propria materia,*° *its truest substance*
But common to all metals and all stones.
For, where it is forsaken of that moisture
And hath more dryness, it becomes a stone;
Where it retains more of the humid fatness,
It turns to sulfur or to quicksilver,
Who are the parents of all other metals.
Nor can this remote matter suddenly
Progress so from extreme unto extreme
As to grow gold and leap o'er all the means.° *intermediate steps*
Nature doth first beget th'imperfect; then
Proceeds she to the perfect. Of that airy
And oily water, mercury is engendered;
Sulfur o'the fat and earthy part—the one
Which is the last° supplying the place of male, *latter*
The other of the female, in all metals.
Some do believe hermaphrodeity,
That both do act and suffer.° But these two *are active and passive*
Make the rest ductile, malleable, extensive.° *extensible*
And even in gold they are; for we do find
Seeds of them by our fire, and gold in them,
And can produce the species of each metal
More perfect thence than nature doth in earth.
Beside, who doth not see in daily practice
Art° can beget bees, hornets, beetles, wasps *Skill, ingenuity*
Out of the carcasses and dung of creatures—
Yea, scorpions of an herb,° being rightly placed?[1] *i.e., out of basil*
And these are living creatures, far more perfect
And excellent than metals.

MAMMON Well said, father!—
Nay, if he take you in hand, sir, with an argument,
He'll bray° you in a mortar. *pound into bits*

SURLY Pray you, sir, stay.
Rather than I'll be brayed, sir, I'll believe
That alchemy is a pretty kind of game,
Somewhat like tricks o'the cards, to cheat a man
With charming.° *incantation, magic*

SUBTLE Sir?

SURLY What else are all your terms,
Whereon no one o'your writers 'grees° with other? *agrees*
Of your elixir, your *lac virginis,*° *lit., "virgin's milk"*
Your stone, your med'cine, and your chrysosperm,° *seed of gold*
Your sal,° your sulfur, and your mercury, *salt*
Your oil of height,° your tree of life,[2] your blood, *basis of all salts*
Your marcasite,° your tutty,[3] your magnesia, *white iron pyrites*
Your toad, your crow, your dragon, and your panther,° *tinctures of black*
Your sun, your moon, your firmament,° your adrop,° *stone / lead*
Your lato, azoch, zernich, chibrit, heautarit,[4]
And then, your red man and your white woman,° *sulfur and mercury*

1. A reference to the theory of "spontaneous generation"—that living organisms could originate spontaneously from lifeless matter—believed from the Middle Ages through the seventeenth century (disproved by Francesco Redi in 1668 with his experiment with flies laying eggs on spoiled meat).

2. The philosophers' stone, or emblem of the seven basic metals.

3. Impure zinc oxide.

4. Your latten (a brasslike metal), quicksilver, trisulfate of arsenic, sulfur, mercury.

With all your broths, your menstrues,° and materials *solvents*
Of piss and eggshells, women's terms,° man's blood, *menstrual flow*
Hair o'the head, burnt clouts,° chalk, merds,° and clay, *clods of earth / feces*
Powder of bones, scalings of iron, glass,
And worlds of other strange ingredients,
Would burst a man to name?

SUBTLE And all these named
Intending° but one thing, which art our writers *Meaning*
Used to obscure° their art. *to veil in mystery*

MAMMON Sir, so I told him—
Because° the simple idiot should not learn it *In order that*
And make it vulgar.° *commonplace*

SUBTLE Was not all the knowledge
Of the Egyptians writ in mystic symbols?
Speak not the Scriptures oft in parables?
Are not the choicest fables of the poets,
That were the fountains and first springs of wisdom,
Wrapped in perplexèd allegories?

MAMMON I urged that,
And cleared° to him that Sisyphus was damned *made clear*
To roll the ceaseless stone only because
He would have made ours common.[5]—

Doll is seen.

Who is this?

SUBTLE God's precious, what do you mean? Go in, good lady,
Let me intreat you! [*Exit Doll.*]
Where's this varlet?° *knave, menial*

[*Enter*] *Face.*

FACE Sir?

SUBTLE You very° knave! Do you use° me thus? *arrant / treat*

FACE Wherein, sir?

SUBTLE Go in and see, you traitor. Go! [*Exit Face.*]

MAMMON Who is it, sir?

SUBTLE Nothing, sir, nothing.

MAMMON What's the matter, good sir?
I have not seen you thus distempered. Who is't?

SUBTLE All arts have still° had, sir, their adversaries, *always*
But ours the most ignorant.

Face returns.

What now?

FACE 'Twas not my fault, sir. She would speak with you.

SUBTLE Would she, sir? Follow me. [*Exit. Face starts to follow.*]

MAMMON Stay, Lungs!

FACE I dare not, sir.

MAMMON How! Pray thee, stay.

FACE She's mad, sir, and sent hither—

MAMMON Stay, man. What is she?

FACE [*still going*] A lord's sister, sir.

5. Sisyphus, in Greek myth, was condemned to roll a stone ceaselessly (line 209) uphill only to have it roll back again as a punishment for having dared to reveal, or make "common" (line 210), the gods' secrets. Sir Epicure compares those secrets with the mysteries of alchemy.

He'll° be mad, too. *Subtle will*
MAMMON I warrant thee.° Why sent hither? *No doubt you're right*
FACE Sir, to be cured.
SUBTLE [*shouting from within*] Why, rascal!
FACE Lo you!° *You see, I told you!*
[*Calling*] Here, sir!
He goes out.
MAMMON 'Fore God, a Bradamante,[6] a brave piece!° *handsome dame*
SURLY Heart,[7] this is a bawdy house! I'll be burnt° else. *burnt as a heretic*
MAMMON Oh, by this light, no. Do not wrong him. He's
Too scrupulous that way. It is his vice.
No, he's a rare° physician; do him right. *excellent*
An excellent Paracelsian,[8] and has done
Strange cures with mineral physic.° He deals all° *medicine / entirely*
With spirits, he. He will not hear a word
Of Galen[9] or his tedious recipes.—

Face again.

How now, Lungs!
FACE Softly, sir, speak softly. I meant
To ha' told Your Worship all. This° must not hear. *(Surly)*
MAMMON No, he will not be gulled; let him alone.
FACE You're very right, sir: she is a most rare scholar,
And is gone mad with studying Broughton's works.[1]
If you but name a word touching the Hebrew,
She falls into her fit and will discourse
So learnedly of genealogies
As you would run mad, too, to hear her, sir.
MAMMON How might one do t'have conference with her, Lungs?
FACE Oh, divers have run mad upon the conference.° *merely meeting her*
I do not know, sir. I am sent in haste
To fetch a vial.
SURLY Be not gulled, Sir Mammon.
MAMMON Wherein? Pray ye, be patient.
SURLY Yes, as you are,
And trust confederate° knaves and bawds and whores. *in cahoots*
MAMMON You are too foul,° believe it.—Come, here, Ulen.° *dirty-minded / (2.3.32)*
One word. [*He whispers in Face's ear.*]
FACE I dare not, in good faith. [*Going.*]
MAMMON Stay, knave.
FACE He's extreme angry that you saw her, sir.
MAMMON [*giving money*] Drink that. What is she when she's out of her fit?
FACE Oh, the most affablest creature, sir! So merry!
So pleasant! She'll mount you up like quicksilver
Over the helm, and circulate like oil,[2]
A very vegetal;[3] discourse of state,
Of mathematics, bawdry, anything—

6. Amazonian warrior in Ariosto's *Orlando Furioso*.
7. By God's heart. (A common oath.)
8. A follower of Paracelsus (1493–1541), who introduced alchemy into medical treatment.
9. The traditional medical authority (129–c. 199 C.E.), scorned by Paracelsians. His medical treatments tended to be herbal, not alchemical.
1. Hugh Broughton (1549–1612) was a Puritan minister and rabbinical scholar.
2. The metaphors in these lines play on alchemical and erotic senses of rising to a climax.
3. Face describes Doll as endowed with the vital energy of a growing organism.

MAMMON Is she no way accessible? No means,
No trick, to give a man a taste of her—wit—
Or so?
SUBTLE [*within*] Ulen!
FACE I'll come to you again, sir. [*Exit.*]
MAMMON Surly, I did not think one o'your breeding
Would traduce personages of worth.
SURLY Sir Epicure,
Your friend to use,[4] yet still loath to be gulled.
I do not like your philosophical bawds.
Their stone is lechery enough to pay for
Without this bait.
MAMMON Heart, you abuse yourself.
I know the lady, and her friends, and means,° *financial situation*
The original of this disaster.° Her brother *cause of her madness*
Has told me all.
SURLY And yet you ne'er saw her
Till now?
MAMMON Oh, yes, but I forgot. I have, believe it,
One o'the treacherous'st memories, I do think,
Of all mankind.
SURLY What call you her brother?
MAMMON My lord—
He wi' not have his name known, now I think on't.
SURLY A very treacherous memory!
MAMMON O'my faith—
SURLY Tut, if you ha' it not about you, pass it° *let it pass*
Till we meet next.
MAMMON Nay, by this hand, 'tis true.
He's one I honor, and my noble friend,
And I respect his house.° *family*
SURLY Heart! Can it be
That a grave sir, a rich, that has no need,° *financial need*
A wise sir, too, at other times, should thus
With his own oaths and arguments make hard means° *make every effort*
To gull himself? An° this be your elixir, *If*
Your *lapis mineralis*,° and your lunary,[5] *philosophers' stone*
Give me your honest trick yet at primero° *a card game*
Or gleek,° and take your *lutum sapientis*,[6] *another card game*
Your *menstruum simplex*!° I'll have gold before you, *plain solvent*
And with less danger of the quicksilver
Or the hot sulfur.[7]

[*Enter Face as Lungs.*]

FACE (*to Surly*) Here's one° from Captain Face, sir, *a messenger*
Desires you meet him i'the Temple Church[8]
Some half hour hence, and upon earnest business.
(*He whispers* [*to*] *Mammon.*) Sir, if you please to quit us now and come
Again within two hours, you shall have
My master busy examining o'the works,

4. I am your friend; call on me for anything.
5. (1) The fern moonwort; (2) mercury.
6. Paste or clay for sealing glass receptacles.
7. Cures for venereal infection.
8. A common site for business and legal appointments.

And I will steal you in unto the party,
That you may see her converse. [*Aloud to Surly*] Sir, shall I say
You'll meet the Captain's Worship?° *His Worship the captain*

SURLY Sir, I will.
[*Aside*] But by attorney,° and to a second purpose. *i.e., in disguise*
Now I am sure it is a bawdy house;
I'll swear it, were the marshal° here to thank me. *police official*
The naming this commander° doth confirm it. *captain*
Don Face! Why, he's the most authentic dealer
I'these commodities, the superintendent
To all the quainter[9] trafficers in town!
He is their visitor,° and does appoint *official inspector*
Who lies with whom, and at what hour, what price,
Which gown, and in what smock, what fall,° what tire.° *flat collar / headdress*
Him will I prove,° by a third person, to find *test*
The subtleties of this dark labyrinth,
Which if I do discover, dear Sir Mammon,
You'll give your poor friend leave, though no philosopher,
To laugh; for you that are, 'tis thought, shall weep.[1]

FACE Sir. He does pray you'll not forget.

SURLY I will not, sir.—
Sir Epicure, I shall leave you.

MAMMON I follow you straight.
[*Exit Surly.*]

FACE But do so, good sir, to avoid suspicion.
This gent'man has a parlous° head. *shrewd*

MAMMON But wilt thou, Ulen,
Be constant to thy promise?

FACE As my life, sir.

MAMMON And wilt thou insinuate what I am, and praise me,
And say I am a noble fellow?

FACE Oh, what else, sir?
And that you'll make her royal with the stone,
An empress, and yourself King of Bantam.[2]

MAMMON Wilt thou do this?

FACE Will I, sir?

MAMMON Lungs, my Lungs!
I love thee.

FACE Send your stuff, sir, that my master
May busy himself about projection.

MAMMON Th'hast witched me, rogue. [*Giving money*] Take, go.

FACE Your jack and all,[3] sir.

MAMMON Thou art a villain!° I will send my jack, *dear rogue*
And the weights too. Slave,° I could bite thine ear.° *Wretch / (love nip)*
Away! Thou dost not care for me.

FACE Not I, sir?

MAMMON Come, I was born to make thee,° my good weasel, *raise your fortunes*
Set thee on a bench, and ha' thee twirl a chain° *steward's insignia*
With the best lord's vermin° of 'em all. *underlings*

9. Craftier (with a pun on "quaint," meaning "vagina").
1. Surly recalls the familiar contrast between "the laughing philosopher," Democritus, and "the weeping philosopher," Heraclitus, to make his point that Sir Epicure, for all his seeming sagacity, is heading for a fall.
2. In Java. The East Indies were thought to be fabulously wealthy.
3. Don't forget to send your mechanical spit-turner and everything.

FACE Away, sir.
MAMMON A count, nay, a count palatine[4]—
FACE Good sir, go.
MAMMON Shall not advance thee better; no, nor faster.
[*Exit.*]

2.4

[*Enter*] *Subtle* [*and*] *Doll.*

SUBTLE Has he bit? Has he bit?
FACE And swallowed too, my Subtle.
I ha' giv'n him line, and now he plays,[1] i'faith.
SUBTLE And shall we twitch him?
FACE Thorough° both the gills. [*Through*]
A wench is a rare bait, with which a man
No sooner's taken but he straight firks mad.° [*goes wild*]
SUBTLE Doll, my Lord What's-um's sister, you must now
Bear yourself *statelich.*° [*in a stately manner*]
DOLL Oh, let me alone.° [*leave it to me*]
I'll not forget my race,° I warrant you. [*breeding; sex*]
I'll keep my distance, laugh, and talk aloud,
Have all the tricks of a proud, scurvy° lady, [*discourteous*]
And be as rude as her woman.° [*female attendant*]
FACE Well said, sanguine![2]
SUBTLE But will he send his andirons?
FACE His jack too,
And 's iron shoeing-horn; I ha' spoke to him. Well,
I must not lose my wary gamester° yonder. [*i.e., Surly*]
SUBTLE Oh, Monsieur Caution, that will not be gulled?° [*refuses to be tricked*]
FACE Ay, if I can strike a fine hook into him, now!
The Temple Church, there I have cast mine angle.° [*fishing line*]
Well, pray for me. I'll about it. *One knocks.*
SUBTLE What, more gudgeons?° [*gullible fish*]
Doll, scout, scout! [*Doll goes to the window.*]
Stay, Face, you must go to the door.
Pray God it be my Anabaptist.[3]—Who is't, Doll?
DOLL I know him not. He looks like a gold-end-man.[4]
SUBTLE Godso,° 'tis he! He said he would send—what call you him?— [*(a vulgar profanity)*]
The sanctified elder,° that should deal° [*pastor / bargain*]
For Mammon's jack and andirons. Let him in.
Stay, help me off first with my gown. Away,
Madam, to your withdrawing chamber.° [*private room*]
[*Exit Doll, and Face with Subtle's gown.*]
Now,
In a new tune, new gesture, but old language.
This fellow is sent from one° negotiates with me [*one who*]
About the stone, too, for the holy Brethren

4. One possessing royal prerogatives within his own domain.
2.4. The scene continues.
1. And now he exhausts himself by pulling at the line.
2. A "sanguine" person, in whom the "humor" of blood predominates, is typically cheerful, red-faced, and amorous.
3. A member of a German sect advocating adult baptism, common ownership of all wealth, and self-governance of their sect without state interference.
4. A peddler in odd bits of gold and silver.

Of Amsterdam,[5] the exiled Saints, that hope
To raise° their discipline° by it. I must use him — *strengthen / order*
In some strange fashion now, to make him admire me.

2.5

[*Enter*] *Ananias.* [*Subtle pretends not to see him.*]

SUBTLE [*calling*] Where is my drudge?

[*Enter*] *Face.*

FACE Sir?
SUBTLE Take away the recipient,° — *vessel for condensate*
And rectify your menstrue from the phlegma.
Then pour it o'the Sol in the cucurbite[1]
And let 'em macerate° together. — *steep and soften*
FACE Yes, sir.
And save the ground?° — *dregs*
SUBTLE No. *Terra damnata*° — *Dregs, sediment*
Must not have entrance in the work. [*To Ananias*] Who are you?
ANANIAS A faithful Brother, if it please you.
SUBTLE What's that?
A Lullianist? A Ripley? *Filius artis?*[2]
Can you sublime and dulcify? Calcine?
Know you the *sapor pontic? Sapor stiptic?*[3]
Or what is homogene or heterogene?° — *one or various kinds*
ANANIAS I understand no heathen language, truly.
SUBTLE Heathen, you Knipperdoling?[4] Is *Ars sacra*,
Or *chrysopoeia*, or *spagirica*,
Or the pamphysic or panarchic knowledge
A heathen language?[5]
ANANIAS Heathen Greek, I take it.
SUBTLE How? Heathen Greek?
ANANIAS All's heathen but the Hebrew.
SUBTLE [*to Face*] Sirrah, my varlet, stand you forth and speak to him
Like a philosopher;° answer i'the language.° — *alchemist / lingo*
Name the vexations° and the martyrizations° — *trials / sufferings*
Of metals in the work.
FACE Sir, putrefaction,° — *decomposition*
Solution, ablution,° sublimation, — *washing off impurities*
Cohobation,° calcination, ceration, and — *Redistillation*
Fixation.
SUBTLE [*to Ananias*] This is heathen Greek to you, now?—
And when comes vivification?

5. Home to many Anabaptists driven from Germany in the 1530s, and similarly home to English Puritans after 1604.
2.5. The scene continues.
1. And separate your solvent from the distilled product; then pour it over the gold in the gourd-shaped distilling flask.
2. A follower of Raymond Lully, a thirteenth-century Spanish alchemist, or of his fifteenth-century English disciple George Ripley, or a son of the art (*filius artis*: i.e., an alchemist). (Subtle deliberately misunderstands Ananias; "Brother" [line 7] means "Anabaptist," but was also a term applied to alchemists.)
3. Can you distill and purify, and neutralize the acidity? Do you know the sour and the less sour?
4. Bernt Knipperdollinck was a leader of the Anabaptist uprising in Münster in 1534–36.
5. Is the sacred art of alchemy, or the making of gold, or the process of repeatedly separating and combining ingredients, or all-ruling knowledge of all nature or all power a heathen language?

FACE After mortification.[6]
SUBTLE What's cohobation?
FACE 'Tis the pouring on
Your *aqua regis*[7] and then drawing him off
To the trine circle of the seven spheres.[8]
SUBTLE What's the proper passion° of metals? *special attribute*
FACE Malleation.° *Hammering*
SUBTLE What's your *ultimum supplicium auri?*
FACE Antimonium.[9]
SUBTLE This's heathen Greek to you?—And what's your mercury?
FACE A very fugitive;° he will be gone, sir. *volatile substance*
SUBTLE How know you him?
FACE By his viscosity,
His oleosity,° and his suscitability.° *oiliness / volatility*
SUBTLE How do you sublime° him? *vaporize*
FACE With the calce° of eggshells, *calx, powder*
White marble, talc.
SUBTLE Your *magisterium*,° now? *philosophers' stone*
What's that?
FACE Shifting, sir, your elements,
Dry into cold, cold into moist, moist into hot,
Hot into dry.
SUBTLE [*to Ananias*] This's heathen Greek to you still?—
Your *lapis philosophicus?*° *philosophers' stone*
FACE 'Tis a stone and not
A stone; a spirit, a soul, and a body,
Which, if you do dissolve, it is dissolved;
If you coagulate, it is coagulated;
If you make it to fly, it flieth.
SUBTLE Enough. [*Exit Face.*]
This's heathen Greek to you? What are you, sir?
ANANIAS Please you, a servant of the exiled Brethren,
That deal with° widows' and with orphans' goods, *trade in*
And make a just account unto the Saints[1]—
A deacon.
SUBTLE Oh, you are sent from Master Wholesome,
Your teacher?
ANANIAS From Tribulation Wholesome,
Our very zealous pastor.
SUBTLE Good. I have
Some orphans' goods to come here.
ANANIAS Of what kind, sir?
SUBTLE Pewter, and brass, andirons, and kitchenware,
Metals that we must use our med'cine on,
Wherein the Brethren may have a penn'orth,
For ready money.
ANANIAS Were the orphans' parents
Sincere professors?° *believers*

6. After the breakdown ("mortification") of a substance's active properties, "vivification" restores the erstwhile compound to pure metal.
7. A mixture of nitric and hydrochloric acids used as a solvent for the gold. (Literally, "royal water.")
8. By analogy with astronomy, alchemy has its firmament and seven planetary spheres, divided into three segments of 120 degrees each. Alchemical processes must be repeated three times.
9. What's your ultimate punishment for gold?—Antimony (which makes gold less malleable).
1. The puritan-elect, those Protestant reformers who believed themselves to be chosen by God.

SUBTLE Why do you ask?
ANANIAS Because
We then are to deal justly, and give, in truth,
Their utmost value.
SUBTLE 'Slid, you'd cozen else,° *cheat otherwise*
An if their parents were not of the faithful?
I will not trust you, now I think on't,
Till I ha' talked with your pastor. Ha' you brought money
To buy more coals?
ANANIAS No, surely.
SUBTLE No? How so?
ANANIAS The Brethren bid me say unto you, sir,
Surely they will not venture any more
Till they may see projection.° *transmutation*
SUBTLE How!
ANANIAS You've had,
For the instruments,° as° bricks, and loam, and glasses, *materials / such as*
Already thirty pound, and for materials,
They say, some ninety more; and they have heard since
That one at Heidelberg° made it of an egg *a Lutheran center*
And a small paper of pin dust.° *metal filings*
SUBTLE What's your name?
ANANIAS My name is Ananias.
SUBTLE Out, the varlet
That cozened the apostles![2] Hence, away!
Flee, mischief! Had your holy consistory° *assembly of elders*
No name to send me, of another sound,
Than wicked Ananias? Send your elders
Hither to make atonement for you quickly
And gi' me satisfaction, or out goes
The fire, and down th'alembics,° and the furnace, *(see 2.1.99)*
Piger Henricus,° or what not. Thou wretch, *Multiple furnace*
Both sericon and bufo° shall be lost, *red and black tincture*
Tell 'em. All hope of rooting out the bishops
Or th'anti-Christian hierarchy shall perish
If they stay threescore minutes.° The aqueity,° *an hour / moisture*
Terreity,° and sulfureity° *Earthiness / sulfurosity*
Shall run together again and all be annulled.° *spoiled*
Thou wicked Ananias! [*Exit Ananias.*]
This will fetch 'em
And make 'em haste towards their gulling more.
A man must deal like a rough nurse and fright
Those that are froward° to an appetite. *obstinate, willful*

2.6

[*Enter*] *Face* [*and*] *Drugger.*

FACE [*aside to Drugger*] He's busy with his spirits, but we'll upon him.
SUBTLE How now! What mates,° what Bayards[1] ha' we here? *wretches, rascals*

2. In Acts 5, Ananias attempts to swindle the apostles but is found out by Peter.
2.6. The scene continues.
1. I.e., blundering fools. Bayard was a magical horse given by Charlemagne to Rinaldo and his four brothers. This remarkable steed, famed for thrusting boldly in everywhere, was able to accommodate all four brothers at once.

FACE [*to Drugger*] I told you he would be furious.—Sir, here's Nab,
Has brought you another piece of gold to look on—
(*To Drugger*) We must appease him. Give it me— [*To Subtle*] and prays you
You° would devise— (*To Drugger*) What is it, Nab? — *That you*
DRUGGER A sign, sir.
FACE Ay, a good lucky one, a thriving sign, Doctor.
SUBTLE I was devising now.
FACE (*aside to Subtle*) 'Slight, do not say so;
He will repent he ga' you any more.—
[*Aloud*] What say you to his constellation,° Doctor? — *zodiacal sign*
The Balance?° — *Libra (see 1.3.56 n)*
SUBTLE No, that way is stale and common.
A townsman, born in Taurus, gives° the Bull, — *displays as a sign*
Or the Bull's head; in Aries, the Ram—
A poor device! No, I will have his name
Formed in some mystic character, whose *radii*,° — *rays*
Striking the senses of the passersby,
Shall, by a virtual influence,[2] breed affections° — *desire (for tobacco)*
That may result upon° the party owns° it, — *benefit / who owns*
As thus—
FACE Nab!
SUBTLE He first shall have a bell, that's Abel;
And by it standing one whose name is Dee,[3]
In a rug° gown; there's D, and rug, that's Drug; — *coarse woven*
And right anenst° him, a Dog snarling "er"— — *opposite*
There's Drugger, Abel Drugger. That's his sign.
And here's now mystery and hieroglyphic!
FACE Abel, thou art made.
DRUGGER [*bowing*] Sir, I do thank His Worship.
FACE Six o'thy legs° more will not do it, Nab.— — *bows*
He has brought you a pipe of tobacco, Doctor.
DRUGGER [*presenting the pipe to Subtle*] Yes, sir.
I have another thing I would impart—
FACE Out with it, Nab.
DRUGGER Sir, there is lodged hard° by me — *close*
A rich young widow—
FACE Good! A *bona roba*?[4]
DRUGGER But nineteen at the most.
FACE Very good, Abel.
DRUGGER Marry, sh' is not in fashion,° yet; she wears — *fashionable*
A hood, but 't stands a-cop.° — *atop the head*
FACE No matter, Abel.
DRUGGER And I do now and then give her a fucus°— — *cosmetic*
FACE What, dost thou deal,° Nab? — *deal in cosmetics*
SUBTLE I did tell you, Captain.
DRUGGER And physic° too sometime, sir, for which she trusts me — *medicine*
With all her mind. She's come up here° of purpose — *come to London*
To learn the fashion.
FACE Good! (His match° too!) On, Nab. — *equal in gullibility*

2. A powerful emanation thought to be emitted by celestial bodies and to influence human action.
3. English mathematician, astrologer, and occultist (1527–1608), who claimed to have discovered the secret of alchemy.
4. (1) A well-dressed woman; (2) a sexually available woman.

DRUGGER And she does strangely long to know her fortune.
FACE God's lid,° Nab, send her to the doctor, hither. *eyelid*
DRUGGER Yes, I have spoke to her of His Worship already;
But she's afraid it will be blown abroad° *spread around*
And hurt her marriage.° *chances to remarry*
FACE Hurt it? 'Tis the way
To heal it, if 'twere hurt—to make it more
Followed and sought. Nab, thou shalt tell her this.
She'll be more known, more talked of, and your widows
Are ne'er of any price till they be famous;
Their honor is their multitude of suitors.
Send her; it may be thy good fortune. What?
Thou dost not know?
DRUGGER No, sir, she'll never marry
Under a knight. Her brother has made a vow.
FACE What, and dost thou despair, my little Nab,
Knowing what the doctor has set down for thee,
And seeing so many o'the city dubbed?° *knighted*
One glass o'thy water,° with a madam I know, *urine (for love spell)*
Will have it done, Nab. What's her brother? A knight?
DRUGGER No, sir, a gentleman newly warm in his land, sir,
Scarce cold in his one-and-twenty,° that does govern *Barely twenty-one*
His sister here, and is a man himself
Of some three thousand a year, and is come up° *come to London*
To learn to quarrel and to live by his wits,
And will go down° again and die i'the country. *(to his estate)*
FACE How! To quarrel?
DRUGGER Yes, sir, to carry quarrels,
As gallants do, and manage 'em by line.° *by the rules*
FACE 'Slid, Nab, the doctor is the only man
In Christendom for him. He has made a table,
With mathematical demonstrations,
Touching° the art of quarrels. He will give him *Concerning*
An instrument° to quarrel by. Go, bring 'em both, *set of instructions*
Him and his sister. And, for° thee, with her *as for*
The doctor haply° may persuade. Go to! *perhaps*
Shalt° give His Worship a new damask suit *You shall*
Upon the premises.° *prospect*
SUBTLE Oh, good Captain!
FACE He shall;
He is the honestest fellow, Doctor.—Stay not,° *Don't delay*
No offers; bring the damask° and the parties. *damask suit (72)*
DRUGGER I'll try my power, sir.
FACE And thy will too, Nab.
SUBTLE [*smoking*] 'Tis good tobacco, this! What is't an ounce?
FACE He'll send you a pound, Doctor.
SUBTLE Oh, no.
FACE He will do't.
It is the goodest soul!—Abel, about it.
(*Aside to him*) Thou shalt know more anon. Away, be gone!
[*Exit Drugger.*]
A miserable rogue, and lives with cheese,[5]
And has the worms. That was the cause indeed

5. Cheese was regarded as drab fare and apt to give the eater worms.

Why he came now. He dealt with me in private
To get a med'cine for 'em.
SUBTLE And shall, sir. This works.
FACE A wife, a wife, for one on's,° my dear Subtle! *of us*
We'll e'en draw lots, and he that fails shall have
The more in goods, the other° has in tail.[6] *than the other*
SUBTLE Rather, the less. For she may be so light[7]
She may want grains.[8]
FACE Ay, or be such a burden
A man would scarce endure her for the whole.[9]
SUBTLE Faith, best let's see her first and then determine.
FACE Content. But Doll must ha' no breath on't.
SUBTLE Mum.
Away! You to your Surly yonder; catch him.
FACE Pray God I ha' not stayed too long.
SUBTLE I fear it.
[*Exeunt.*]

3.1

[*Enter*] *Tribulation* [*Wholesome and*] *Ananias.*

TRIBULATION These chastisements are common to the Saints,° *Puritan brethren*
And such rebukes we of the separation° *dissenting sect*
Must bear with willing shoulders as the trials
Sent forth to tempt our frailties.
ANANIAS In pure zeal,
I do not like the man. He is a heathen,
And speaks the language of Canaan,[1] truly.
TRIBULATION I think him a profane person, indeed.
ANANIAS He bears
The visible mark of the Beast[2] in his forehead.
And for° his stone, it is a work of darkness, *as for*
And with philosophy blinds the eyes of man.[3]
TRIBULATION Good brother, we must bend unto all means
That may give furtherance to the holy cause.
ANANIAS Which his cannot. The sanctified cause
Should have a sanctified course.
TRIBULATION Not always necessary.
The children of perdition are ofttimes
Made instruments even of the greatest works.
Beside, we should give somewhat to° man's nature, *make allowance for*
The place he lives in, still° about the fire *continually*
And fume of metals, that intoxicate
The brain of man and make him prone to passion.
Where have you greater atheists than your cooks?
Or more profane or choleric than your glassmen?° *glassblowers*

6. I.e., (1) entail: fixed possession that cannot be bequeathed at pleasure to another; (2) in "tail": the pudendum.
7. (1) The opposite of "heavy"; (2) wanton.
8. That she may be short in grains of weight to make up the value of the goods against which she is weighed. (With a pun on "groins.") The sexual punning continues in "burden," "scarce endure her," and "whole" (hole).
9. Could scarcely put up with her, even with the financial inducement of receiving her entire estate. (See previous note.)
3.1. Lovewit's house still.
1. And speaks the language of infidels. See Isaiah 19.18.
2. The mark of the damned. See Revelation 16.2, 19.20.
3. And with his alchemical pretended learning he blinds humans to the higher divine truth.

More anti-Christian than your bell-founders?° — *those who cast bells*
What makes the devil so devilish, I would ask you—
Satan, our common enemy—but his being
Perpetually about the fire and boiling
Brimstone and arsenic? We must give,° I say, — *make allowance*
Unto the motives° and the stirrers-up — *moving causes*
Of humors in the blood. It may be so.
Whenas° the work is done, the stone is made, — *When*
This heat of his may turn into a zeal
And stand up for the beauteous discipline° — *Puritanism*
Against the menstruous cloth and rag of Rome.[4]
We must await his calling and the coming
Of the good spirit. You did fault t'upbraid him
With the Brethren's blessing of Heidelberg,° weighing — *(see 2.5.70)*
What need we have to hasten on the work
For the restoring of the silenced° Saints, — *forbidden to preach*
Which ne'er will be but by the philosophers' stone.
And so a learnèd elder, one of Scotland,° — *a Puritan stronghold*
Assured me, *aurum potabile*[5] being
The only med'cine for the civil magistrate
T'incline him to a feeling of the cause,
And must be daily used in° the disease. — *against*
ANANIAS I have not edified° more, truly, by man, — *been edified*
Not since the beautiful light first shone on me;
And I am sad my zeal hath so offended.
TRIBULATION Let us call on him, then.
ANANIAS The motion's° good, — *inward prompting is*
And of the spirit. I will knock first. [*He knocks.*] Peace be within!

3.2

[*Enter*] *Subtle.*

SUBTLE Oh, are you come? 'Twas time. Your threescore minutes° — *(see 2.5.84)*
Were at the last thread, you see, and down had gone
Furnus acediae, turris circulatorius;[1]
'Lembic, bolt's-head, retort, and pelican° — *Distilling equipment*
Had all been cinders. Wicked Ananias!
Art thou returned? Nay then, it goes down yet.
TRIBULATION Sir, be appeased. He is come to humble
Himself in spirit, and to ask your patience
If too much zeal hath carried him aside
From the due path.
SUBTLE Why, this doth qualify!° — *mitigate the insult*
TRIBULATION The Brethren had no purpose, verily,
To give you the least grievance, but are ready
To lend their willing hands to any project
The spirit and you direct.
SUBTLE This qualifies more!

4. To Puritans, the Catholic Church, centered in Rome, was the scarlet Babylonian whore of the Book of Revelation, ornately vested in the trappings of a corrupt doctrine and liturgy.
5. Drinkable gold suspended in liquid, a medication here acting as a bribe.
3.2. The scene continues.
1. The furnace of sloth (a synonym for "Lazy Henry," the multiple furnace mentioned at 2.5.79–80), the circulation tower (i.e., "pelican," or still; see 2.3.78).

TRIBULATION And, for° the orphans' goods,° let them be valued, *as for / (see 2.5.47)*
Or what is needful else to the holy work,
It shall be numbered.° Here, by me, the Saints *reckoned*
Throw down their purse before you.
SUBTLE This qualifies most!
Why, thus it should be; now you understand.
Have I discoursed so unto you of our stone
And of the good that it shall bring your cause?
Showed you—beside the main° of hiring forces *main business*
Abroad, drawing the Hollanders, your friends,
From th'Indies, to serve you, with all their fleet[2]—
That even the med'cinal use shall make you a faction
And party° in the realm? As, put the case *influential*
That some great man in state,° he have the gout, *some statesman*
Why, you but send three drops of your elixir,
You help him straight;° there you have made a friend. *immediately*
Another has the palsy° or the dropsy;° *tremor / fluid retention*
He takes of your incombustible° stuff, *refined, purified*
He's young again; there you have made a friend.
A lady that is past the feat of body,° *sex*
Though not of mind,° and hath her face decayed *desire*
Beyond all cure of paintings,° you restore *cosmetics*
With the oil of talc;° there you have made a friend, *white elixir cosmetic*
And all her friends.° A lord that is a leper, *lovers*
A knight that has the boneache,° or a squire *i.e., syphilis*
That hath both these, you make 'em smooth and sound
With a bare fricace° of your med'cine; still *mere rubbing*
You increase your friends.
TRIBULATION Ay, 'tis very pregnant.° *full of possibility*
SUBTLE And then the turning of this lawyer's° pewter *some lawyer's*
To plate° at Christmas— *silver plate*
ANANIAS "Christ-tide,"[3] I pray you.
SUBTLE Yet,° Ananias? *What did I tell you*
ANANIAS I have done.
SUBTLE Or changing
His parcel gilt° to massy gold. You cannot *gold-plated ware*
But raise you friends. Withal, to be of power
To pay an army in the field, to buy
The King of France out of his realms, or Spain
Out of his Indies—what can you not do
Against lords spiritual or temporal° *lords of church or state*
That shall oppone° you? *oppose*
TRIBULATION Verily, 'tis true.
We may be temporal lords ourselves, I take it.
SUBTLE You may be anything, and leave off to make
Long-winded exercises° or suck up *prayers, sermons*
Your "ha!" and "hum!" in a tune.° I not deny *hymn singing*
But such as are not gracèd in a state° *are out of power*
May, for their ends, be adverse° in religion, *nonconformist*
And get a tune° to call the flock together— *adopt an anthem*

2. The Dutch offered refuge for Anabaptists fleeing Germany (after 1536) and England (since 1604) and protected trade with the West Indies from which Tribulation and other Puritans might hope to profit and become a power to be reckoned with.
3. Puritans insisted on saying "Christ-tide" to avoid the popish "mass" of "Christmas."

For, to say sooth, a tune does much with women
And other phlegmatic people; it is your bell.° *a drawing device*
ANANIAS Bells are profane. A tune may be religious.[4]
SUBTLE No warning with you? Then farewell my patience.
'Slight, it° shall down. I will not be thus tortured. *(the whole process)*
TRIBULATION I pray you, sir—
SUBTLE All shall perish. I have spoke it.
TRIBULATION Let me find grace, sir, in your eyes. The man,
He stands corrected. Neither did his zeal,
But as yourself, allow a tune, somewhere,[5]
Which now, being to'ard° the stone, we shall not need. *near to possessing*
SUBTLE No, nor your holy vizard,° to win widows *mask of piety*
To give you legacies, or make zealous wives
To rob their husbands for the common cause;° *the Puritan cause*
Nor take the start of bonds broke but one day
And say they were forfeited by Providence.[6]
Nor shall you need o'ernight to eat huge meals,
To celebrate your next day's fast the better,
The whilst the Brethren and the Sisters, humbled,
Abate the stiffness° of the flesh. Nor cast *obstinacy; erection*
Before your hungry hearers scrupulous bones:° *hairsplitting scruples*
As,° whether a Christian may hawk or hunt, *Such as*
Or whether matrons of the holy assembly
May lay their hair out,° or wear doublets, *use wire-framed wigs*
Or have that idol, starch, about their linen.
ANANIAS It is indeed an idol.
TRIBULATION [*to Subtle*] Mind him not, sir.—
I do command thee, spirit of zeal but trouble,
To peace within him!—Pray you, sir, go on.
SUBTLE Nor shall you need to libel 'gainst the prelates,
And shorten so your ears[7] against° the hearing *in anticipation of*
Of the next wiredrawn grace.° Nor of necessity *long-winded prayer*
Rail against plays to please the alderman[8]
Whose daily custard° you devour. Nor lie *(served at city feasts)*
With zealous rage till you are hoarse. Not one
Of these so singular arts! Nor call yourselves
By names of Tribulation, Persecution,
Restraint, Long-Patience, and suchlike, affected° *desired; falsely assumed*
By the whole family or wood° of you *group*
Only for glory and to catch the ear
Of the disciple.
TRIBULATION Truly, sir, they are
Ways that the godly Brethren have invented
For propagation of the glorious cause,
As very notable means, and whereby also
Themselves grow soon and profitably famous.
SUBTLE Oh, but the stone, all's idle to° it! Nothing! *useless compared with*
The art of angels, nature's miracle,

4. Bells are popish to Ananias, but he is eager to defend the congregational singing of nonconformist sects that Subtle has been satirizing.
5. I.e., Even though Ananias spoke sharply in his zeal, he's prepared to compromise on the issue of church music; his differences with you are easily overcome.
6. And you won't need any longer to foreclose on bonds just one day overdue, while claiming sanctimoniously that the foreclosing was the work of Providence.
7. Nor will you need to attack the bishops and so suffer the cropping of your ears and pillorying for disrespect to authority.
8. London aldermen were often sympathetic to Puritan hostility to the stage.

The divine secret that doth fly in clouds
From east to west, and whose tradition
Is not from men, but spirits.
ANANIAS I hate traditions.
I do not trust them—
TRIBULATION Peace!° *Quiet!*
ANANIAS They are popish all.
I will not peace. I will not—
TRIBULATION Ananias!
ANANIAS Please the profane to grieve the godly I may not.
SUBTLE Well, Ananias, thou shalt overcome.° *ruin everything*
TRIBULATION It is an ignorant zeal that haunts him, sir—
But truly, else, a very faithful Brother,
A botcher, and a man by revelation,[9]
That hath a competent° knowledge of the truth. *(enough for salvation)*
SUBTLE Has he a competent sum there i'the bag
To buy the goods within? I am made guardian,
And must, for charity and conscience' sake,
Now see the most be made° for my poor orphans— *get the best deal*
Though I desire the Brethren, too, good° gainers. *to be good*
There they are, within. When you have viewed and bought 'em,
And ta'en the inventory of what they are,
They are ready for projection; there's no more
To do. Cast on the med'cine° so much silver *(see 2.5.54)*
As there is tin there, so much gold as brass;
I'll gi' it you in by weight.[1]
TRIBULATION But how long time,
Sir, must the Saints expect,° yet? *be kept waiting*
SUBTLE Let me see:
How's the moon now? Eight, nine, ten days hence
He will be silver potate;° then three days *liquefied*
Before he citronize;° some fifteen days, *turn yellow*
The *magisterium*° will be perfected. *philosophers' stone*
ANANIAS About the second day of the third week
In the ninth month?[2]
SUBTLE Yes, my good Ananias.
TRIBULATION What will the orphans' goods arise to,° think you? *come to*
SUBTLE Some hundred marks;° as much as filled three cars,° *almost £67 / carts*
Unladed° now; you'll make six millions of 'em. *Unloaded*
But I must ha' more coals laid in.
TRIBULATION How!
SUBTLE Another load,
And then we ha' finished. We must now increase
Our fire to *ignis ardens;*° we are past *intensely hot fire*
Fimus equinus, balnei, cineris,[3]
And all those lenter° heats. If the holy purse *gentler*
Should with this draft° fall low, and that the Saints *order for payment*
Do need a present sum,° I have a trick *ready cash*
To melt the pewter you shall buy now instantly,
And with a tincture° make you as good Dutch dollars *a coloring agent*

9. A tailor who does repairs and alterations, and a man guided by the inner light.
1. I'll transmute the baser metal for you into gold, weight by weight.
2. Puritans rejected the pagan names for the days of the week and the months.
3. Heat produced, in rising stages of intensity, by horse dung, baths of ashes or sand, and ash-fire.

As any are in Holland.
TRIBULATION Can you so?
SUBTLE Ay, and shall bide the third examination.[4]
ANANIAS It will be joyful tidings to the Brethren.
SUBTLE But you must carry it° secret. *carry it off in*
TRIBULATION Ay, but stay.
This act of coining: is it lawful?
ANANIAS Lawful?
We know° no magistrate. Or, if we did, *acknowledge*
This's foreign coin.
SUBTLE It is no coining, sir.
It is but casting.
TRIBULATION Ha! You distinguish well.
Casting of money may be lawful.
ANANIAS 'Tis, sir.
TRIBULATION Truly, I take it so.
SUBTLE There is no scruple,
Sir, to be made of it. Believe Ananias;
This case of conscience he is studied° in. *learned*
TRIBULATION I'll make a question of it to the Brethren.
ANANIAS The Brethren shall approve it lawful, doubt not.
Where shall't be done?
SUBTLE For° that we'll talk anon. *Concerning*
Knock without.
There's some to speak with me. Go in, I pray you,
And view the parcels. [*He gives them a paper.*] That's the inventory.
I'll come to you straight. [*Exeunt Tribulation and Ananias.*]
[*Calling*] Who is it? Face! Appear!

3.3

[*Enter*] *Face* [*in his captain's uniform*].

How now? Good prize?
FACE Good pox!° Yond costive cheater° *(an oath) / i.e., Surly*
Never came on.° *showed up*
SUBTLE How then?
FACE I ha' walked the round
Till now, and no such thing.[1]
SUBTLE And ha' you quit him?
FACE Quit him? An hell would quit him too, he were happy.[2]
'Slight, would you have me stalk like a mill-jade,° *old mill horse*
All day, for one that will not yield us grains?° *bits (of money)*
I know him of old.° *I'm on to him*
SUBTLE Oh, but to ha' gulled him
Had been a maistry!° *masterstroke*
FACE Let him go, black boy!° *i.e., Subtle (?) Surly (?)*
And turn thee,° that some fresh news may possess thee. *turn your attention*
A noble count, a don of Spain (my dear
Delicious compeer and my party-bawd),° *fellow pimp*
Who is come hither private for his conscience° *religious convictions*

4. And are counterfeited accurately enough to pass repeated inspections.
3.3. The scene continues.
1. I've looked for him in the rotunda at the rear of the Temple Church (see 2.3.289), but with no results.
2. Have you given up looking for him?—Given up on him? If hell would be quit of him (i.e., if he could avoid hellfire), he'd be a happy man.

And brought munition° with him, six great slops,° — *supplies / wide breeches*
Bigger than three Dutch hoys,° beside round trunks,° — *ships / stuffed breeches*
Furnished with pistolets and pieces of eight,° — *Spanish coins*
Will straight be here, my rogue, to have thy bath° — *bathhouse; brothel*
(That is the color)° and to make his batt'ry° — *pretext / assault*
Upon our Doll, our castle, our Cinque Port,[3]
Our Dover pier, our what thou wilt. Where is she?
She must prepare perfumes, delicate linen,
The bath in chief,° a banquet, and her wit, — *especially*
For she must milk his epididymis.[4]
Where is the doxy?° — *harlot, wench*

SUBTLE I'll send her to thee,
And but dispatch my brace° of little John Leydens[5] — *pair*
And come again myself.

FACE Are they within, then?

SUBTLE Numb'ring the sum.

FACE How much?

SUBTLE A hundred marks, boy.
[*Exit.*]

FACE Why, this's a lucky day. Ten pounds of Mammon!
Three o'my clerk! A portague° o'my grocer! — *(see 1.3.87)*
This o'the Brethren! Beside reversions° — *future benefits*
And states° to come i'the widow and my count!° — *estates / i.e., Surly*
My share today will not be bought° for forty— — *I wouldn't sell my share*

[*Enter*] *Doll.*

DOLL What?

FACE Pounds, dainty Dorothy. Art thou so near?

DOLL Yes. Say, Lord General, how fares our camp?[6]

FACE As with the few that had entrenched themselves
Safe, by their discipline, against a world, Doll,
And laughed within those trenches, and grew fat
With thinking on the booties, Doll, brought in
Daily by their small parties.° This dear hour — *raiders*
A doughty don is taken with my Doll,
And thou mayst make his ransom what thou wilt,
My Dowsabell.[7] He shall be brought here, fettered
With thy fair looks before he sees thee, and thrown
In a down° bed as dark as any dungeon, — *feather*
Where thou shalt keep him waking with thy drum°— — *pounding sexual rhythm*
Thy drum, my Doll, thy drum—till he be tame
As the poor blackbirds were i'the great frost,[8]
Or bees are with a basin,[9] and so hive° him — *i.e., enclose*
I'the swanskin coverlid° and cambric sheets — *silky quilt*
Till he work honey and wax, my little God's-gift.[1]

DOLL What is he, General?

FACE An *adalantado*,° — *Spanish governor*

3. One of five strategic defensive towns on England's southeast coast; i.e., a valuable port of entry (with suggestion of sexual penetration).
4. Literally, a duct from the back of the testicles; a euphemism for the penis.
5. John of Leyden led an uprising of the Anabaptists at Münster in 1534.
6. Doll quotes from the opening line, after the opening chorus, of Kyd's *The Spanish Tragedy*.
7. *Douce et belle*: sweet and beautiful.
8. The Thames froze over in the winter of 1607–8.
9. Beating on a basin was supposed to induce bees to settle down in their hive.
1. A literal rendition of "Dorothea," Doll's more formal name. The don (really Surly) will be as malleable as wax and honey when Doll has worked him over.

A grandee, girl. Was not my Dapper here yet?
DOLL No.
FACE Nor my Drugger?
DOLL Neither.
FACE A pox on 'em,
They are so long a-furnishing![2] Such stinkards
Would° not be seen upon these festival days. *Should*

[*Enter*] *Subtle.*

How now! Ha' you done?
SUBTLE Done. They° are gone. The sum *(The Anabaptists)*
Is here in bank, my Face. I would we knew
Another chapman now would buy 'em[3] outright.
FACE 'Slid, Nab shall do't against° he ha' the widow, *preparing for the time*
To furnish household.
SUBTLE Excellent! Well thought on.
Pray God he come.
FACE I pray he keep away
Till our new business be o'erpast.
SUBTLE But Face,
How cam'st thou by this secret don?
FACE A spirit
Brought me th'intelligence in a paper here,
As I was conjuring yonder in my circle[4]
For Surly; I ha' my flies° abroad. Your bath *familiars; spies*
Is famous, Subtle, by my means.—Sweet Doll,
You must go tune your virginal,° no losing *spinet (with pun)*
O'the least time. And, do you hear? Good action.
Firk° like a flounder, kiss like a scallop, close, *Wiggle*
And tickle him with thy mother tongue. His great
Verdugoship[5] has not a jot of language°— *English*
So much the easier to be cozened, my Dolly.
He will come here in a hired coach, obscure,
And our own coachman, whom I have sent, as guide,
No creature else. (*One knocks.*) Who's that?
[*Doll goes to the window.*]
SUBTLE It i' not he?
FACE Oh, no, not yet this hour.
SUBTLE [*to Doll, as she returns*] Who is't?
DOLL Dapper,
Your clerk.
FACE God's will, then, Queen of Faery,
On with your tire!° And, Doctor, with your robes. *attire; headdress*
Let's dispatch° him, for God's sake. [*Exit Doll.*] *finish with*
SUBTLE 'Twill be long.
FACE I warrant you, take but the cues I give you,
It shall be brief enough. [*He goes to the window.*] 'Slight,
here are more!
Abel, and I think the angry boy,° the heir *quarrelsome youth*
That fain would° quarrel. *wants to learn to*

2. They're taking so long bringing the goods they promised to pay up.
3. I wish we knew another dealer now who would buy Mammon's ironwork.
4. Magician's circle—i.e., the "round" (line 2) that Face has been walking to try to find Surly.
5. A mock honorific: His great Hangmanship.

SUBTLE And the widow?

FACE No,
Not that I see. Away! [*Exit Subtle.*]

3.4

[*Enter*] *Dapper.*

Oh, sir, you are welcome.
The doctor is within, a-moving° for you; *pleading*
I have had the most ado to win him to it!
He swears you'll be the darling o'the dice;
He never heard Her Highness dote till now, he says.
Your aunt has giv'n you the most gracious words
That can be thought on.

DAPPER Shall I see Her Grace?

FACE See her, and kiss her too.—

[*Enter*] *Drugger* [*and*] *Kastril.*

What, honest Nab!
Hast brought the damask?° *(see 2.6.72–75)*

DRUGGER No, sir, here's tobacco.

FACE 'Tis well done, Nab. Thou'lt bring the damask too?

DRUGGER Yes. Here's the gentleman, Captain, Master Kastril,
I have brought to see the doctor.

FACE Where's the widow?

DRUGGER Sir, as he likes, his sister, he says, shall come.

FACE Oh, is it so? Good time.°—Is your name Kastril, sir? *All in good time*

KASTRIL Ay, and the best o'the Kastrils—I'd be sorry else—
By fifteen hundred a year. Where is this doctor?
My mad° tobacco-boy here tells me of one *madcap*
That can do things. Has he any skill?

FACE Wherein, sir?

KASTRIL To carry a business,° manage a quarrel fairly, *manage a duel*
Upon fit terms.

FACE It seems, sir, you're but young
About the town, that can make that a question.

KASTRIL Sir, not so young but I have heard some speech
Of the angry boys,° and seen 'em take° tobacco, *roisterers / smoke*
And in his shop; and I can take it too.
And I would fain be one of 'em, and go down
And practice i'the country.

FACE Sir, for° the duello, *as for*
The doctor, I assure you, shall inform you
To the least shadow of a hair, and show you
An instrument° he has of his own making, *set of instructions*
Wherewith no sooner shall you make report
Of any quarrel but he will take the height on't,° *seriousness of it*
Most instantly, and tell in what degree
Of safety it lies in, or mortality,
And how it may be borne, whether in a right line
Or a half circle, or may else be cast

3.4. The scene continues.

Into an angle blunt, if not acute[1]—
All this he will demonstrate. And then rules
To give and take the lie by.[2]
KASTRIL How? To take it?
FACE Yes, in oblique,° he'll show you, or in circle, *indirectly*
But never in diameter.° The whole town *directly*
Study his theorems, and dispute them ordinarily[3]
At the eating academies.
KASTRIL But does he teach
Living by the wits too?
FACE Anything whatever.
You cannot think that subtlety but he reads it.[4]
He made me a captain. I was a stark pimp,
Just o'your standing, 'fore I met with him;
It i' not two months since. I'll tell you his method.
First, he will enter° you at some ordinary. *introduce; enroll*
KASTRIL No, I'll not come there. You shall pardon me.
FACE For why, sir?
KASTRIL There's gaming° there, and tricks. *gambling*
FACE Why, would you be
A gallant, and not game?
KASTRIL Ay, 'twill spend a man.° *waste one's substance*
FACE Spend you? It will repair you when you are spent.
How do they live by their wits there, that have vented° *blown away*
Six times your fortunes?
KASTRIL What, three thousand a year?
FACE Ay, forty thousand.
KASTRIL Are there such?
FACE Ay, sir.
And gallants, yet. [*Indicating Dapper*] Here's a young gentleman
Is born to nothing—forty marks a year,
Which I count nothing. He's to be initiated
And have a fly° o'the doctor. He will win you *familiar spirit*
By unresistible luck, within this fortnight,
Enough to buy a barony. They will set him
Upmost,° at the groom-porter's,[5] all the Christmas, *At head of table*
And, for the whole year through, at every place
Where there is play,° present him with the chair, *gambling*
The best attendance,° the best drink, sometimes *service*
Two glasses of canary,° and pay nothing; *sweet wine*
The purest linen and the sharpest knife,
The partridge next his trencher,° and somewhere *wooden plate*
The dainty bed, in private, with the dainty.° *dainty whore*
You shall ha' your ordinaries° bid for him, *eating houses*
As playhouses for a poet, and the master° *eating-house host*
Pray him, aloud, to name what dish he affects,° *desires*
Which must be buttered shrimps; and those that drink

1. Face analyzes quarreling—i.e., issuing and responding to challenges to a duel, etc.—as though it were a mathematical science of geometrical dimensions. The language parodies actual treatises on quarreling that were in print.
2. Subtle will set forth rules of quarreling specifying in what circumstances a gentleman may give and respond to an insult or accusation of lying.
3. Customarily; with a pun on "ordinaries," meaning "eating places," or "eating academies" (line 41).
4. You can't imagine a subtle point that he does not study and is ready to lecture on.
5. Officer at court superintending card playing, dice, etc.

To no mouth else will drink to his, as being
The goodly, president° mouth of all the board. *presiding*
KASTRIL Do you not gull one?° *Aren't you kidding?*
FACE Od's° my life! Do you think it? *God's*
You shall have a cast commander° (can but get *cashiered officer*
In credit with a glover or a spurrier
For some two pair of either's ware aforehand)[6]
Will, by most swift posts,[7] dealing with him,
Arrive at competent means to keep himself,
His punk, and naked boy in excellent fashion,
And be admired for't.[8]
KASTRIL Will the doctor teach this?
FACE He will do more, sir: when your land is gone° *sold off*
(As men of spirit hate to keep earth long),
In a vacation,° when small money is stirring *(of the law courts)*
And ordinaries suspended till the term,
He'll show a perspective[9] where on one side
You shall behold the faces and the persons
Of all sufficient° young heirs in town, *moneyed*
Whose bonds are current for commodity;° *(see 2.1.13–14)*
On th'other side, the merchants' forms,° and others *benches*
That, without help of any second broker,
Who would expect a share, will trust such parcels;[1]
In the third square, the very street and sign
Where the commodity dwells and does but wait
To be delivered, be it pepper, soap,
Hops, or tobacco, oatmeal, woad,° or cheeses— *blue dye*
All which you may so handle to enjoy
To your own use and never stand obliged.
KASTRIL I'faith! Is he such a fellow?
FACE Why, Nab here knows him.
And then for making matches for rich widows,
Young gentlewomen, heirs, the fortunat'st man!
He's sent to, far and near, all over England,
To have his counsel and to know their fortunes.
KASTRIL God's will, my suster° shall see him. *(dialect speech)*
FACE I'll tell you, sir,
What he did tell me of Nab. It's a strange thing!
(By the way, you must eat no cheese, Nab, it breeds melancholy,
And that same melancholy breeds worms; but pass it.)° *let that pass*
He told me honest Nab here was ne'er at tavern
But once in's life.
DRUGGER Truth, and no more I was not.
FACE And then he was so sick—
DRUGGER Could he tell you that, too?
FACE How should I know it?° *know it otherwise*
DRUGGER In troth, we had been a-shooting,
And had a piece of fat ram-mutton to supper
That lay so heavy o'my stomach—

6. Whose credit line is limited to the cost of ordering two pairs of gloves or spurs.
7. Who will, with the speed of a post-horse.
8. The dismissed officer will swiftly recoup his fortune sufficiently through Subtle's tutelage to support himself while keeping a whore and a young boy as lovers and to be a part of good society.
9. A magic glass, or a picture made to take on differing appearances from different points of view.
1. Merchants who will be willing to extend credit on such parcels of goods without involving the expense of a usurer.

FACE And he has no head
To bear any wine; for, what with the noise o'the fiddlers,
And care of his shop, for he dares keep no servants—
DRUGGER My head did so ache—
FACE As he was fain to be brought home,
The doctor told me. And then, a good old woman—
DRUGGER Yes, faith, she dwells in Seacoal Lane°—did cure me (*a run-down district*)
With sodden° ale and pellitory o'the wall;° (*heated / an herb*)
Cost me but twopence. I had another sickness
Was worse than that.
FACE Ay, that was with the grief
Thou took'st for being 'sessed° at eighteen pence (*assessed*)
For the waterwork.° (*(see 2.1.76)*)
DRUGGER In truth, and it was like° (*likely*)
T'have cost me almost my life.
FACE Thy hair went off?[2]
DRUGGER Yes, sir. 'Twas done for spite.[3]
FACE Nay, so says the doctor.
KASTRIL Pray thee, tobacco-boy, go fetch my suster;
I'll see this learnèd boy° before I go, (*(Subtle)*)
And so shall she.
FACE Sir, he is busy now.
But if you have a sister to fetch hither,
Perhaps your own pains° may command her sooner, (*efforts*)
And he by that time will be free.
KASTRIL I go. [*Exit.*]
FACE Drugger, she's thine.[4] The damask! [*Exit Drugger.*]
(*Aside*) Subtle and I
Must wrestle for her.°—Come on, Master Dapper. (*(Kastril's sister)*)
You see how I turn clients here away
To give your cause dispatch.° Ha' you performed (*priority*)
The ceremonies were enjoined° you? (*that were urged upon*)
DAPPER Yes, o'the vinegar
And the clean shirt.
FACE 'Tis well. That shirt may do you
More worship° than you think. Your aunt's afire, (*honor, dignity*)
But° that she will not show it, t'have a sight on you. (*Except*)
Ha' you provided° for Her Grace's servants? (*provided tips*)
DAPPER Yes, here are six-score Edward shillings—
FACE Good.
DAPPER And an old Harry's° sovereign— (*reign of Henry VIII*)
FACE Very good.
DAPPER And three James shillings, and an Elizabeth groat;° (*worth 4d.*)
Just twenty nobles.° (*almost £7*)
FACE Oh, you are too just.° (*exact*)
I would you had had the other noble in Marys.
DAPPER I have some Philip and Marys.[5]
FACE Ay, those same
Are best of all. Where are they? Hark, the doctor.

2. Hair loss was a common result of treatment for syphilis.
3. Drugger believes that the amount was set so high out of someone's spite toward him. Face indicates, in his reply, that he and Subtle concur in this analysis.
4. The Queen of Faery (Dame Pliant) is thine.
5. Coins from the time of Queen Mary (r. 1553–58), who married Philip of Spain. Other coins mentioned here are from the reigns of Edward VI (1547–53), Henry VIII (1509–47), James I (1603–25), and Elizabeth I (1558–1603).

3.5

[Enter] Subtle disguised like a Priest of Faery [with a tattered robe].

SUBTLE Is yet Her Grace's cousin come?
FACE He is come.
SUBTLE And is he fasting?
FACE Yes.
SUBTLE And hath cried "hum"?
FACE [*to Dapper*] Thrice, you must answer.
DAPPER Thrice.[1]
SUBTLE And as oft "buzz"?
FACE [*to Dapper*] If you have, say.
DAPPER I have.
SUBTLE [*presenting Dapper the robe*] Then to her coz,° — *i.e., her favorite*
Hoping that he hath vinegared his senses
As he was bid, the Faeiry Queen dispenses,
By me, this robe, the petticoat° of Fortune, — *underskirt*
Which that he straight put on she doth importune.
And though to Fortune near be her petticoat,
Yet nearer is her smock,° the Queen doth note; — *innermost undergarment*
And therefore even of that a piece she hath sent,
Which, being° a child, to wrap him in was rent,° — *when he was / torn*
And prays him for a scarf he now will wear it
(With as much love as then Her Grace did tear it)
About his eyes,[2] to show he is fortunate.° — *(Fortune is blind)*
They blind him with a rag.
And, trusting unto her to make his state,° — *estate, fortune*
He'll throw away all worldly pelf° about him— — *wealth*
Which that he will perform, she doth not doubt him.
FACE She need not doubt him, sir. Alas, he has nothing
But what he will part withal as willingly,
Upon Her Grace's word (throw away your purse!)
As she would ask it. (Handkerchiefs and all!)
She cannot bid that thing but he'll° obey. — *anything he will not*
(If you have a ring about you, cast it off,
Or a silver seal° at your wrist; Her Grace will send — *charm*
Her fairies here to search you! Therefore deal
Directly° with Her Highness. If they find — *Candidly*
That you conceal a mite, you are undone.)
He throws away as they bid him.
DAPPER Truly, there's all.
FACE All what?
DAPPER My money, truly.
FACE Keep nothing that is transitory° about you.— — *of this transitory life*
(*Aside to Subtle*) Bid Doll play music.
Doll enters with a cittern.° They pinch him. — *guitarlike instrument*
Look, the elves are come
To pinch you if you tell not truth. Advise you.° — *Be warned*
DAPPER Oh, I have a paper with a spur-royal° in't. — *gold coin worth 15s.*

3.5. The scene continues.
1. I.e., Yes, I said "hum" thrice. (See 1.2.169–70.)
2. And bids him wear, as a scarf over his eyes, a piece torn off Fortune's undergarment to wrap Dapper in, as Fortune proverbially does for her favorite "children."

FACE *Ti, ti!*—
They knew't, they say.
SUBTLE *Ti, ti, ti, ti!* He has more yet.
FACE *Ti, ti-ti-ti!* I'the t'other pocket?
SUBTLE *Titi, titi, titi, titi!*
They must pinch him or he will never confess, they say.
DAPPER Oh, oh!
FACE Nay, pray you hold. He is Her Grace's nephew.—
Ti, ti, ti! What care you? Good faith, you shall care.[3]—
Deal plainly, sir, and shame the fairies. Show
You are an innocent.° *blameless; foolish*
DAPPER By this good light, I ha' nothing.
SUBTLE *Ti ti, ti ti to ta!* He does equivocate, she says—
Ti, ti do ti, ti ti do, ti da!—and swears by the light, when he is blinded.
DAPPER By this good dark, I ha' nothing but a half crown
Of gold about my wrist that my love gave me,
And a leaden heart I wore sin' she forsook me.
FACE I thought 'twas something. And would you incur
Your aunt's displeasure for these trifles? Come,
I had rather you had thrown away twenty half crowns.
[*He removes Dapper's coin bracelet.*]
You may wear your leaden heart still.—How now?
[*Subtle, Doll, and Face confer out of Dapper's hearing.*]
SUBTLE What news, Doll?
DOLL Yonder's your knight, Sir Mammon.
FACE God's lid, we never thought of him till now.
Where is he?
DOLL Here, hard by. He's at the door.
SUBTLE And you are not ready now? Doll, get his° suit. *(Face's)*
[*Exit Doll.*]
He must not be sent back.
FACE Oh, by no means.
What shall we do with this same puffin here,
Now he's o'the spit?[4]
SUBTLE Why, lay him back° awhile *back of the fire*
With some device.—

[*Enter Doll with the clothes Face wears as Lungs.*]

[*Aloud*] *Ti, ti ti, ti ti ti!* Would Her Grace speak with me?
I come.— [*Aside*] Help, Doll!
FACE (*He speaks through the keyhole, the other° knocking.*) *(Sir Epicure)*
Who's there? Sir Epicure,
My master's i'the way. Please you to walk
Three or four turns but till his back be turned,
And I am for° you. [*Aside*] Quickly, Doll! *ready for*
SUBTLE [*to Dapper*] Her Grace
Commends her kindly to you, Master Dapper.
DAPPER I long to see Her Grace.
SUBTLE She now is set

3. Face uses two "fairy" voices, one urging consideration of Dapper as the Queen's nephew, the other answering saucily, "Why should anyone care about that?"
4. Dapper is compared to a seabird being roasted on a spit.

At dinner, in her bed, and she has sent you,
From her own private trencher,° a dead mouse — *wooden plate*
And a piece of gingerbread to be merry withal
And stay° your stomach, lest you faint with fasting. — *quiet*
Yet if you could hold out till she saw you, she says,
It would be better for you.

FACE — Sir, he shall
Hold out, an 'twere this° two hours, for Her Highness; — *even if for*
I can assure you that. We will not lose
All we ha' done—

SUBTLE — He must nor see nor speak
To anybody till then.

FACE — For that we'll put, sir,
A stay° in 's mouth. — *i.e., gag*

SUBTLE — Of what?

FACE — Of gingerbread.
Make you it fit. He that hath pleased Her Grace
Thus far shall not now crinkle° for a little.— — *shrink, flinch*
Gape, sir, and let him fit you. [*They gag Dapper.*]

SUBTLE [*aside to Doll and Face*] Where shall we now
Bestow him?

DOLL [*to Subtle*] I'the privy.

SUBTLE [*aloud, to Dapper*] Come along, sir.
I now must show you Fortune's privy° lodgings. — *private; outhouse*
[*The rogues converse privately.*]

FACE Are they perfumed, and his bath ready?

SUBTLE — All.
Only the fumigation's somewhat strong.

FACE [*through the door*] Sir Epicure, I am yours, sir, by and by.° — *right away*
[*Exeunt Subtle and Doll with Dapper.*
Face changes to his disguise as Lungs.]

4.1

[*Enter*] *Mammon.*

FACE Oh, sir, you're come i'the only finest° time! — *absolutely the best*

MAMMON Where's master?

FACE — Now preparing for projection, sir.
Your stuff will b' all changed° shortly. — *transmuted*

MAMMON — Into gold?

FACE To gold and silver, sir.

MAMMON — Silver I care not for.

FACE Yes, sir, a little to give beggars.

MAMMON — Where's the lady?

FACE At hand here. I ha' told her such brave° things o'you, — *fine*
Touching° your bounty and your noble spirit— — *Regarding*

MAMMON — Hast thou?

FACE As° she is almost in her fit to see you. — *That*
But, good sir, no divinity i'your conference,° — *no talk of theology*
For fear of putting her in rage.° — *madness*

MAMMON — I warrant thee.

FACE Six men will not hold her down. And then

4.1. The scene continues.

If the old man° should hear or see you— *i.e., Subtle*
MAMMON Fear not.
FACE The very house, sir, would run mad. You know it,
How scrupulous he is and violent
'Gainst the least act of sin. Physic or mathematics,
Poetry, state,° or bawdry, as I told you, *politics*
She will endure and never startle; but
No word of controversy.
MAMMON I am schooled, good Ulen.
FACE And you must praise her house,° remember that, *family*
And her nobility.
MAMMON Let me alone.° *Leave it to me*
No herald, no, nor antiquary, Lungs,
Shall do it better. Go.
FACE [*aside*] Why, this is yet
A kind of modern happiness,° to have *everyday aptness*
Doll Common for a great lady. [*Exit.*]
MAMMON Now, Epicure,
Heighten° thyself. Talk to her all in gold; *Arouse, lift to climax*
Rain her as many showers as Jove did drops
Unto his Danaë;° show the god a miser, *(see 2.1.102 n)*
Compared with Mammon. What! The stone will do't.
She shall feel gold, taste gold, hear gold, sleep gold—
Nay, we will *concumbere*° gold. I will be puissant *couple sexually*
And mighty in my talk to her. Here she comes.

[*Enter*] *Face* [*with*] *Doll* [*richly dressed*].

FACE [*aside*] To him, Doll, suckle him.° [*Aloud*] This is the noble knight *nurse, suck him dry*
I told Your Ladyship—
MAMMON Madam, with your pardon,
I kiss your vesture.° *garment*
DOLL Sir, I were uncivil
If I would suffer° that. My lip to you, sir. [*She accepts a kiss.*] *permit*
MAMMON I hope my lord your brother° be in health, lady? *(see 2.3.221, 268–78)*
DOLL My lord my brother is, though I no lady, sir.
FACE (*aside to Doll*) Well said, my guinea bird.° *i.e., prostitute*
MAMMON Right noble madam—
FACE (*aside*) Oh, we shall have most fierce idolatry!
MAMMON 'Tis your prerogative.° *right to be so called*
DOLL Rather your courtesy.
MAMMON Were there nought else t'enlarge° your virtues to me, *make known*
These answers speak° your breeding and your blood. *proclaim*
DOLL Blood we boast none, sir; a poor baron's daughter.
MAMMON "Poor"! And gat° you? Profane not. Had your father *begat*
Slept all the happy remnant of his life
After that act, lain but there still and panted,
He'd done enough to make himself, his issue,° *offspring*
And his posterity noble.
DOLL Sir, although
We may be said to want the gilt and trappings,
The dress° of honor, yet we strive to keep *outward show*
The seeds and the materials.° *essential ingredients*
MAMMON I do see
The old ingredient, virtue, was not lost,

Nor the drug, money, used to make your compound.
There is a strange nobility i'your eye,
This lip, that chin! Methinks you do resemble
One o'the Austriac princes.[1]

FACE [*aside*] Very like!
Her father was an Irish costermonger.° *apple-seller*

MAMMON The house of Valois[2] just had° such a nose, *had just*
And such a forehead yet° the Medici *even today*
Of Florence boast.

DOLL Troth, and I have been lik'ned
To all these princes.

FACE [*aside*] I'll be sworn I heard it.

MAMMON I know not how, it is not any one,
But e'en the very choice of all their features.

FACE [*aside*] I'll in and laugh. [*Exit.*]

MAMMON A certain touch, or air,
That sparkles a divinity beyond
An earthly beauty!

DOLL Oh, you play the courtier.

MAMMON Good lady, gi' me leave—

DOLL In faith, I may not° *I won't allow you*
To mock me, sir.

MAMMON To burn i'this sweet flame;
The Phoenix[3] never knew a nobler death.

DOLL Nay, now you court the courtier,° and destroy *go beyond flattery*
What you would build. This art,° sir, i'your words *artifice*
Calls your whole faith in question.

MAMMON By my soul—

DOLL Nay, oaths are made o'the same air, sir.

MAMMON Nature
Never bestowed upon mortality
A more unblamed,° a more harmonious feature; *unblemished*
She played the stepdame° in all faces else. *Nature was niggardly*
Sweet madam, le' me be particular—

DOLL Particular,[4] sir? I pray you, know° your distance. *keep*

MAMMON In no ill sense, sweet lady, but to ask
How your fair graces pass the hours? I see
You're lodged here i'the house of a rare man,
An excellent artist—but what's that to you?

DOLL Yes, sir. I study here the mathematics° *(including astrology)*
And distillation.° *chemistry*

MAMMON Oh, I cry your pardon.
He's a divine instructor, can extract
The souls of all things by his art, call all
The virtues and the miracles of the sun
Into a temperate° furnace, teach dull Nature *well-regulated*
What her own forces are—a man the emp'ror
Has courted above Kelly,[5] sent his medals

1. The Habsburgs were known for their large lower lips and chins.
2. A royal and noble lineage of France.
3. A mythical bird that was supposed to exist only one at a time, to live for five hundred years, and then to burn itself to ashes on a pyre, from which arose a new phoenix; hence a symbol of regeneration.
4. Doll coyly interprets Mammon's "particular" to mean "intimate, personal." Cf. the dirty joking at 1.1.177–79.
5. The astrologer and alchemist Edward Kelly (1555–1595), who was an assistant to Dee (see 2.6.20, note 3) and who won the notice of the Emperor Rudolph II but failed to produce the philosophers' stone.

And chains° t'invite him. — *badges of office*
DOLL Ay, and for his physic,° sir— — *as for his medicine*
MAMMON Above the art of Aesculapius,
That drew the envy of the Thunderer![6]
I know all this, and more.
DOLL Troth, I am taken, sir,
Whole° with these studies that contemplate nature. — *Wholly*
MAMMON It is a noble humor. But this form° — *your beauty*
Was not intended to so dark a use!
Had you been crooked, foul, of some coarse mold,
A cloister had done well; but such a feature,
That might stand up° the glory of a kingdom, — *represent*
To live recluse is a mere solecism,° — *total impropriety*
Though in a nunnery. It must not be.
I muse° my lord your brother will permit it! — *am astonished*
You should spend half my land first, were I he.
Does not this diamond better on my finger
Than i'the quarry?
DOLL Yes.
MAMMON Why, you are like it.
You were created, lady, for the light!
[*He offers his diamond ring.*]
Here, you shall wear it; take it, the first pledge
Of what I speak: to bind you to believe me.
DOLL In chains of adamant?° — *the strongest iron*
MAMMON Yes, the strongest bands.
And take a secret, too: here, by your side,
Doth stand, this hour, the happiest man in Europe.
DOLL You are contented, sir?
MAMMON Nay, in true being:
The envy of princes, and the fear of states.
DOLL Say you so, Sir Epicure?
MAMMON Yes, and thou shalt prove° it, — *test, try*
Daughter of honor. I have cast mine eye
Upon thy form, and I will rear° this beauty — *elevate, privilege*
Above all styles.° — *fashions; titles*
DOLL You mean no treason, sir?° — *(see 146–50 below)*
MAMMON No, I will take away that jealousy.° — *suspicion*
I am the lord of the philosophers' stone,
And thou the lady.
DOLL How, sir! Ha' you that?
MAMMON I am the master of the maistry.° — magisterium *(1.4.14)*
This day the good old wretch here o'the house
Has made it for us. Now he's at projection.
Think therefore thy first wish, now; let me hear it,
And it shall rain into thy lap—no shower,° — *(see 26–27 above)*
But floods of gold, whole cataracts, a deluge,
To get a nation° on thee! — *beget multitudes*
DOLL You are pleased, sir,
To work on the ambition of our sex.
MAMMON I'm pleased the glory of her sex° should know — *i.e., Doll*
This nook here of the Friars° is no climate — *Blackfriars (1.1.17)*

6. Jove, the Thunderer, struck Aesculapius, the god of medicine, with lightning for his audacity in restoring the dead to life, lest humanity should become immortal.

For her to live obscurely in, to learn
Physic and surgery for° the constable's wife — *fit for*
Of some odd hundred° in Essex; but come forth — *county subdivision*
And taste the air of palaces; eat, drink
The toils of emp'rics,[7] and their boasted practice—
Tincture of pearl and coral, gold, and amber;
Be seen at feasts and triumphs;° have it asked — *celebrations*
What miracle she is; set all the eyes
Of court afire like a burning glass° — *magnifying glass*
And work 'em into cinders, when the jewels
Of twenty states° adorn thee and the light — *countries*
Strikes out the stars, that,° when thy name is mentioned, — *so that*
Queens may look pale, and, we but showing° our love, — *when we simply display*
Nero's Poppea[8] may be lost in story!° — *history*
Thus will we have it.

DOLL — I could well consent, sir.
But in a monarchy how will this be?
The prince will soon take notice, and both seize
You and your stone, it being a wealth unfit
For any private subject.

MAMMON — If he knew it.

DOLL — Yourself do boast it, sir.

MAMMON — To thee, my life.

DOLL — Oh, but beware, sir! You may come to end
The remnant of your days in a loathed prison
By speaking of it.

MAMMON — 'Tis no idle fear!
We'll therefore go with all,° my girl, and live — *leave with everything*
In a free state,° where we will eat our mullets — *republic*
Soused in high-country° wines, sup pheasants' eggs, — *from the hills*
And have our cockles° boiled in silver shells, — *clams, mollusks*
Our shrimps to swim again, as when they lived,
In a rare butter made of dolphins' milk,
Whose cream does look like opals; and, with these
Delicate meats,° set ourselves high° for pleasure, — *dishes / aroused*
And take us down° again, and then renew — *i.e., go to bed*
Our youth and strength with drinking the elixir,
And so enjoy a perpetuity
Of life and lust. And thou shalt ha' thy wardrobe
Richer than Nature's, still° to change thyself, — *constantly*
And vary oftener, for thy pride, than she,
Or Art, her wise and almost equal servant.

[*Enter*] *Face* [*dressed as Lungs*].

FACE — Sir, you are too loud. I hear you, every word,
Into the laboratory. Some fitter place:
The garden, or great chamber above. [*Aside to him*] How
like you her?

MAMMON [*aside to Face*] — Excellent, Lungs! There's for thee.
[*He gives money.*]

FACE [*aside to Mammon*] — But do you hear?
Good sir, beware, no mention of the rabbins.° — *rabbis (see 2.3.239–42)*

7. The results of the efforts of experimenters.
8. Poppaea Sabina, the beautiful woman whom Nero married after killing his first wife.

MAMMON [*aside to Face*] We think not on 'em.
FACE Oh, it is well, sir.
[*Exeunt Mammon and Doll.*]
[*Calling*] Subtle!

4.2

[*Enter*] *Subtle* [*as the Alchemist*].

Dost thou not laugh?
SUBTLE Yes. Are they gone?
FACE All's clear.
SUBTLE The widow is come.
FACE And your quarreling disciple?
SUBTLE Ay.
FACE I must to my captainship° again, then. *captain's uniform*
SUBTLE Stay, bring 'em in first.
FACE So I meant. What is she?
A bonnibel?° *bonny lass*
SUBTLE I know not.
FACE We'll draw lots.
You'll stand° to that? *agree*
SUBTLE What else?
FACE Oh, for a suit
To fall now, like a curtain: flap![1]
SUBTLE To th'door, man.
FACE You'll ha' the first kiss, 'cause I am not ready.
[*He goes to the door.*]
SUBTLE [*aside*] Yes, and perhaps hit you through both the nostrils.[2]

[*Enter*] *Kastril,* [*followed by*] *Dame Pliant.*

FACE Who would you speak with?[3]
KASTRIL Where's the Captain?
FACE Gone, sir,
About some business.
KASTRIL Gone?
FACE He'll return straight.
But Master Doctor, his lieutenant, is here. [*Exit.*]
SUBTLE Come near, my worshipful boy, my *terrae fili,*[4]
That is, my boy of land; make thy approaches.
Welcome. I know thy lusts° and thy desires, *wishes*
And I will serve and satisfy 'em. Begin;
Charge° me from thence, or thence, or in this line.° *Attack / direction*
Here is my center;° ground° thy quarrel. *stance / justify*
KASTRIL You lie!
SUBTLE How, child of wrath and anger! The loud lie?
For what, my sudden boy?
KASTRIL Nay, that look you to;
I am aforehand.[5]
SUBTLE Oh, this's no true grammar,

4.2. The scene continues.
1. Oh, for my captain's uniform to descend over me like a curtain, going "flap"!
2. Put your nose out of joint, make a fool of you.
3. Face adopts the persona here of Lungs, the alchemist's assistant, concealing from Kastril his identity as the "captain," whom Kastril has already met (3.4.10 ff.).
4. Son of earth; in alchemy, a spirit, but also a phrase meaning "bastard."
5. I.e., You figure that out; I spoke first. (In reply, Subtle uses the jargon of logic and rhetoric to expound the "rules" of quarreling. Cf. 3.4.36–41.)

And as ill logic! You must render causes, child,
Your first and second intentions, know your canons° *standards*
And your divisions, moods, degrees, and differences,
Your predicaments, substance, and accident,° *unplanned events*
Series extern and intern, with their causes
Efficient,° material, formal, final, *Immediate agency*
And ha' your elements° perfect. *principles*

KASTRIL What is this?
The angry tongue he talks in?

SUBTLE That false precept
Of being aforehand has deceived a number,° *many*
And made 'em enter quarrels oftentimes
Before they were aware, and afterward
Against their wills.

KASTRIL How must I do then, sir?

SUBTLE [*to Dame Pliant*] I cry this lady mercy.°—She should first *beg her pardon*
Have been saluted. I do call you "lady"
Because you are to be one ere't be long,
My soft and buxom widow. *He kisses her.*

KASTRIL Is she, i'faith?

SUBTLE Yes, or my art is an egregious liar.

KASTRIL How know you?

SUBTLE By inspection on her forehead
And subtlety of her lip, which must be tasted
Often, to make a judgment. *He kisses her again.*
[*Aside*] 'Slight, she melts
Like a myrobalan!°—Here is yet a line *plumlike fruit*
In *rivo frontis*° tells me he[6] is no° knight. *frontal vein / no mere*

PLIANT What is he then, sir?

SUBTLE [*to her*] Let me see your hand.
Oh, your *linea Fortunae*° makes it plain, *line of Fortune*
And *stella* here in *monte Veneris,*[7]
But most of all *junctura annularis:*° *joint of ring finger*
He is a soldier, or a man of art, lady,[8]
But shall have some great honor shortly.

PLIANT Brother,
He's° a rare man, believe me! *Subtle is*

[*Enter*] *Face* [*in his captain's uniform*].

KASTRIL Hold your peace.
Here comes the t'other rare man.—Save you,° Captain! *God save you*

FACE Good Master Kastril! Is this your sister?

KASTRIL Ay, sir.
Please you to kusse° her, and be proud to know her? *kiss (dialect)*

FACE I shall be proud to know you, lady. [*He kisses her.*]

PLIANT Brother,
He calls me lady, too.

KASTRIL Ay, peace. I heard it.

FACE [*taking Subtle aside*] The Count is come.

6. The man Dame Pliant is destined to marry.
7. Subtle points to a star on the mount of Venus (at the base of the thumb, but also alluding to the pubic area).
8. Subtle's bogus forecast suggests that Dame Pliant is to marry either a soldier (Face in his captain's disguise) or a man of learning (Subtle, the alchemist).

SUBTLE Where is he?
FACE At the door.
SUBTLE Why, you must entertain him.
FACE What'll you do
With these the while?° *meanwhile*
SUBTLE Why, have 'em up,° and show 'em *upstairs*
Some fustian° book, or the dark glass.[9] *worthless; bombastic*
FACE 'Fore God,
She is a delicate dabchick!° I must have her. [*Exit.*] *wading bird*
SUBTLE [*aside*] Must you? Ay, if your fortune will, you must.—
Come, sir, the captain will come to us presently.
I'll ha' you to my chamber of demonstrations,
Where I'll show you both the grammar and logic
And rhetoric of quarreling, my whole method
Drawn out in tables,° and my instrument *diagrams*
That hath the several scale upon't shall[1] make you
Able to quarrel at a straw's breadth by moonlight.° *the least provocation*
And, lady, I'll have you look in a glass,° *magic crystal (59)*
Some half an hour, but to clear your eyesight
Against you see° your fortune, which is greater *So you can see*
Than I may judge upon the sudden, trust me. [*Exeunt.*]

4.3

[*Enter*] *Face.*

FACE Where are you, Doctor?
SUBTLE [*within*] I'll come to you presently.
FACE I will ha' this same widow, now I ha' seen her,
On any composition.° *terms*

[*Enter*] *Subtle.*

SUBTLE What do you say?
FACE Ha' you disposed of them?
SUBTLE I ha' sent 'em up.° *upstairs*
FACE Subtle, in troth, I needs must have this widow.
SUBTLE Is that the matter?
FACE Nay, but hear me.
SUBTLE Go to!° *(expressing anger)*
If you rebel once, Doll shall know it all.
Therefore be quiet and obey your chance.° *take your chances*
FACE Nay, thou art so violent now. Do but conceive:° *understand*
Thou art old, and canst not serve°— *function sexually*
SUBTLE Who cannot? I?
'Slight, I will serve her with thee,° for a— *serve as well as you*
FACE Nay,
But understand: I'll gi' you composition.° *make you a deal*
SUBTLE I will not treat° with thee. What, sell my fortune? *bargain*
'Tis better than my birthright. Do not murmur.° *grumble*
Win her, and carry her.° If you grumble, Doll *Winner take all*
Knows it directly.
FACE Well, sir, I am silent.

9. A polished dark stone serving as a magic crystal.
1. And my instruction manual with various divisions in it that will.
4.3. Lovewit's house still.

Will you go help to fetch in Don in state?° — *ceremonially*
SUBTLE I follow you, sir. [*Exit Face.*]
We must keep Face in awe,
Or he will overlook° us like a tyrant. — *domineer over*

[*Enter*] *Face,* [*with*] *Surly like a Spaniard.* [*Subtle and Face continue to speak aloud, assuming that the don understands no English.*]

Brain of a tailor![1] Who comes here? Don John?° — *stock Spanish name*
SURLY *Señores, beso las manos a vuestras mercedes.*[2]
SUBTLE Would you had stooped a little and kissed our *anos.*° — *anus, ass*
FACE Peace, Subtle!
SUBTLE Stab me! I shall never hold,° man. — *keep from laughing*
He looks, in that deep ruff, like a head in a platter
Served in by a short cloak upon two trestles.° — *i.e., his legs*
FACE Or what do you say to a collar of brawn° cut down — *boar's neck meat*
Beneath the souse° and wriggled with a knife? — *ear*
SUBTLE 'Slud,° he does look too fat to be a Spaniard. — *God's blood*
FACE Perhaps some Fleming or some Hollander got° him — *begot*
In D'Alva's time—Count Egmont's bastard.[3]
SUBTLE [*to Surly*] Don,
Your scurvy, yellow, Madrid face is welcome.
SURLY *Gracias.*° — *Thank you*
SUBTLE He speaks out of a fortification.
Pray God he ha' no squibs° in those deep sets!° — *fireworks / ruff folds*
SURLY *Por dios, señores, muy linda casa!*[4]
SUBTLE What says he?
FACE Praises the house, I think.
I know no more but 's action.° — *gesture*
SUBTLE [*to Surly*] Yes, the *casa,*
My precious Diego,° will prove fair enough — *Spaniard*
To cozen you in. Do you mark? You shall
Be cozened, Diego.
FACE Cozened, do you see,
My worthy Donzel?° Cozened. — *little Don*
SURLY *Entiendo.*° — *I understand*
SUBTLE Do you intend it? So do we, dear Don.
Have you brought pistolets, or portagues,° — *gold coins*
My solemn Don?—Dost thou feel any?
FACE (*He feels his pockets.*) Full.
SUBTLE You shall be emptied, Don, pumped and drawn
Dry, as they say.
FACE Milked, in troth, sweet Don.
SUBTLE See all the monsters—the great lion of all, Don.[5]
SURLY *Con licencia, se puede ver a esta señora?*[6]
SUBTLE What talks he now?
FACE O'the *señora.*
SUBTLE O Don,
That is the lioness, which you shall see

1. Referring to Surly's outlandish dress. Tailors were often the subject of laughter for their supposed stupidity (along with dishonesty and effeminacy).
2. Gentlemen, I kiss Your Honors' hands.
3. The Duke of Alva, or Alba, was the hated Spanish governor of the Netherlands who ordered the death of the patriot Egmont in 1568.
4. By God, gentlemen, a very handsome house.
5. I.e., You'll be given the grand tour. (The lions in the Tower of London were a famous attraction.)
6. By your leave, may I see the lady?

Also, my Don.
FACE 'Slid, Subtle, how shall we do?
SUBTLE For what?
FACE Why, Doll's employed, you know.
SUBTLE That's true!
'Fore heav'n, I know not. He must stay,° that's all. *wait*
FACE Stay? That he must not by no means.
SUBTLE No? Why?
FACE Unless you'll mar all. 'Slight, he'll suspect it.
And then he will not pay, not half so well.
This is a traveled punk-master,° and does know *experienced whoremaster*
All the delays—a notable° hot rascal, *notorious*
And looks already rampant.° *reared up, aroused*
SUBTLE 'Sdeath, and Mammon
Must not be troubled.
FACE Mammon, in no case!
SUBTLE What shall we do, then?
FACE Think. You must be sudden.
SURLY *Entiendo que la señora es tan hermosa, que codicio tan a verla como la bien aventuranza de mi vida.*[7]
FACE *Mi vida*? 'Slid, Subtle, he puts me in mind o'the widow.
What dost thou say to draw her to't,° ha? *to meet the Don*
And tell her it is her fortune? All our venture
Now lies upon't. It is but one man more,
Which on 's° chance to have her; and beside, *Whichever of us*
There is no maidenhead to be feared° or lost. *concerned about*
What dost thou think on't, Subtle?
SUBTLE Who, I? Why—
FACE The credit of our house too is engaged.
SUBTLE You made me an offer for my share erewhile.° *just now*
What wilt thou gi' me, i'faith?
FACE Oh, by that light,
I'll not buy now. You know your doom° to me. *decision (13–15)*
E'en take your lot, obey your chance, sir; win her,
And wear her—out for me.[8]
SUBTLE 'Slight. I'll not work her,° then. *(as a whore)*
FACE It is the common cause; therefore bethink you.
Doll else must know it, as you said.
SUBTLE I care not.
SURLY *Señores, por qué se tarda tanto?*[9]
SUBTLE Faith, I am not fit, I am old.
FACE That's now no reason, sir.
SURLY *Puede ser de hacer burla de mi amor?*[1]
FACE You hear the don, too? By this air, I call,
And loose the hinges.°—Doll! *(of our partnership)*
SUBTLE A plague of hell—
FACE Will you then do?
SUBTLE You're a terrible rogue!
I'll think of° this. Will you, sir, call the widow? *I'll remember*
FACE Yes, and I'll take her too, with all her faults,
Now I do think on't better.

7. I understand that the lady is so beautiful that I am eager to see her as the height of my life's fortune.
8. And wear her out, for all I care.
9. Gentlemen, why such a delay?
1. Can it be that you are making fun of my love?

SUBTLE With all my heart, sir.
Am I discharged° o'the lot? — *freed from obligation*
FACE As you please.
SUBTLE Hands.
[*They shake hands.*]
FACE Remember now, that upon any change,° — *no matter what*
You never claim her.
SUBTLE Much good joy and health to you, sir.
Marry a whore? Fate, let me wed a witch first.
SURLY *Por estas honradas barbas*°— — *By this honored beard*
SUBTLE He swears by his beard.
Dispatch,° and call the brother too. [*Exit Face.*] — *Finish up*
SURLY *Tengo duda, señores,*
Que no me hagan alguna traición.[2]
SUBTLE How, issue on?[3] Yes, *presto, señor.*° Please you — *right away, sir*
Enthratha the *chambratha*, worthy Don,
Where, if it please the Fates, in your *bathada*[4]
You shall be soaked, and stroked, and tubbed, and rubbed,
And scrubbed, and fubbed,° dear Don, before you go. — *cheated*
You shall, in faith, my scurvy baboon Don,
Be curried, clawed, and flawed, and tawed,[5] indeed.
I will the heartilier° go about it now, — *more heartily*
And make the widow a punk° so much the sooner, — *whore*
To be revenged on this impetuous Face.
The quickly doing of it is the grace.° [*Exeunt.*] — *the best thing*

4.4

[*Enter*] *Face, Kastril,* [*and*] *Dame Pliant.*

FACE Come, lady. I knew the doctor would not leave° — *leave off*
Till he had found the very nick° of her fortune. — *turning point*
KASTRIL To be a countess, say you?
FACE A Spanish countess, sir.
PLIANT Why, is that better than an English countess?
FACE Better? 'Slight, make you that a question,° lady? — *can you doubt that*
KASTRIL Nay, she is a fool, Captain; you must pardon her.
FACE Ask from your courtier to your Inns of Court man,[1]
To your mere milliner: they will tell you all,
Your Spanish jennet° is the best horse, your Spanish — *small Spanish horse*
Stoop° is the best garb,° your Spanish beard — *Bow, curtsy / fashion*
Is the best cut, your Spanish ruffs are the best
Wear, your Spanish pavan° the best dance, — *a stately dance*
Your Spanish titillation° in a glove — *scent*
The best perfume; and for° your Spanish pike° — *as for / spear weapon*
And Spanish blade,° let your poor captain° speak.— — *Toledo sword / me*
Here comes the doctor.

[*Enter*] *Subtle* [*carrying a paper*].

2. I fear, gentlemen, that you are playing me some trick.
3. Subtle misinterprets the don's "*traición*" to mean that he is urgently asking that they "issue on," exit and move on quickly to what the don longs for.
4. Subtle attempts to lampoon the don's Spanish by pronouncing English words with phony Spanish cadences (especially by imitating the Castilian lisp): *Enthratha* (Enter), *chambratha* (chamber), *bathada* (bath).
5. Be soaked, beaten, and scraped, then flayed and softened with alum (as though in preparation for tanning).
4.4. Lovewit's house still.
1. Lawyer at the Inns of Court, legal residences in London.

SUBTLE My most honored lady,
For so I am now to style you, having found
By this my scheme° you are to undergo — *horoscope*
An honorable fortune very shortly,
What will you say now, if some—
FACE I ha' told her all, sir,
And her right worshipful brother here, that she shall be
A countess; do not delay 'em, sir. A Spanish countess.
SUBTLE Still, my scarce worshipful Captain, you can keep
No secret!—Well, since he has told you, madam,
Do you forgive him, and I do.
KASTRIL She shall do that, sir.
I'll look to't; 'tis my charge.° — *responsibility*
SUBTLE Well, then, naught rests° — *remains*
But that she fit her love now to her fortune.
PLIANT Truly, I shall never brook° a Spaniard. — *endure*
SUBTLE No?
PLIANT Never sin' eighty-eight° could I abide 'em, — *(year of the Spanish Armada)*
And that was some three year afore I was born, in truth.
SUBTLE Come, you must love him or be miserable;
Choose which you will.
FACE By this good rush,° persuade her; — *bit of floor covering*
She will cry strawberries° else within this twelvemonth. — *become a fruit-seller*
SUBTLE Nay, shads and mack'rel,° which is worse. — *become a fishwife*
FACE Indeed, sir?
KASTRIL God's lid, you shall love him, or I'll kick you.
PLIANT Why,
I'll do as you will ha' me, brother.
KASTRIL Do,
Or, by this hand, I'll maul you.
FACE Nay, good sir,
Be not so fierce.
SUBTLE No, my enragèd child,
She will be ruled.° What, when she comes to taste — *She'll obey*
The pleasures of a countess! To be courted—
FACE And kissed, and ruffled!° — *tousled*
SUBTLE Ay, behind the hangings.° — *tapestries*
FACE And then come forth in pomp!
SUBTLE And know her state!° — *social rank*
FACE Of keeping all th'idolaters o'the chamber° — *courtly sycophants*
Barer° to her than at their pray'rs! — *More bareheaded*
SUBTLE Is served
Upon the knee!° — *By kneeling servants*
FACE And has her pages, ushers,
Footmen, and coaches—
SUBTLE Her six mares—
FACE Nay, eight!
SUBTLE To hurry her through London to th'Exchange,
Bedlam, the china houses[2]—
FACE Yes, and have
The citizens gape at her, and praise her tires,° — *attires, headdresses*

2. Dame Pliant is to be seen at fashionable places, like the New Exchange in the Strand (which had opened in 1609, with dressmakers' and milliners' shops, etc.), Bethlehem hospital for the insane (often visited as a form of entertainment), and shops featuring Oriental luxuries.

And my lord's goose-turd bands,° that rides with her! *greenish yellow collars*
KASTRIL Most brave! By this hand, you are not my suster
If you refuse.
PLIANT I will not refuse, brother.

[*Enter*] *Surly.*

SURLY *Qué es esto, señores, que no se venga? Esta tardanza me mata!*[3]
FACE [*to Kastril and Pliant*] It is the Count come!
The doctor knew he would be here, by his art.
SUBTLE *En galanta madama, Don! Galantissima!*[4]
SURLY *Por todos los dioses, la más acabada hermosura, que he visto en mi vida!*[5]
FACE Is't not a gallant language that they speak?
KASTRIL An admirable language! Is't not French?
FACE No, Spanish, sir.
KASTRIL It goes like law-French,
And that, they say, is the courtliest language.
FACE List,° sir. *Listen*
SURLY *El Sol ha perdido su lumbre, con el resplandor, que trae esta dama. Válgame dios!*[6]
FACE [*to Kastril*] He admires your sister.
KASTRIL Must not she make curtsy?
SUBTLE 'Od's will, she must go to him, man, and kiss him.
It is the Spanish fashion for the women
To make first court.
FACE [*to Kastril*] 'Tis true he tells you, sir;
His art knows all.
SURLY *Por qué no se acude?*° *Why don't you come?*
KASTRIL He speaks to her, I think?
FACE That he does, sir.
SURLY *Por el amor de dios, que es esto, que se tarda?*[7]
KASTRIL Nay, see: she will not understand him!—Gull!
Noddy!° *Simpleton!*
PLIANT What say you, brother?
KASTRIL Ass, my suster,
Go kusse him, as the cunning° man would ha' you! *learned*
I'll thrust a pin i'your buttocks else.
FACE Oh, no, sir.
SURLY *Señora mía, mi persona muy indigna está a llegar a tanta hermosura.*[8] [*He kisses her.*]
FACE Does he not use° her bravely? *treat*
KASTRIL Bravely, i'faith!
FACE Nay, he will use° her better. *use sexually*
KASTRIL Do you think so?
SURLY *Señora, si será servida, entramos.*[9]
[*Exit with Dame Pliant.*]
KASTRIL Where does he carry° her? *escort*
FACE Into the garden, sir.

3. What is this, gentlemen, that she doesn't come? The delay is killing me.
4. A fine lady, Don! Very fine!
5. By all the gods, the most perfect beauty I've seen in my life!
6. The sun has lost his light with the splendor that this lady brings. God bless me!
7. For the love of God, why is it that she delays?
8. My lady, my person is all unworthy to approach such beauty.
9. Madam, if you please, let us go in.

Take you no thought;° I must interpret for her. *Don't worry*
SUBTLE [*aside to Face*] Give Doll the word.° [*Exit Face.*] *the cue to go mad*
Come, my fierce child, advance.
We'll to our quarreling lesson again.
KASTRIL Agreed.
I love a Spanish boy with all my heart.
SUBTLE Nay, and by this means, sir, you shall be brother
To a great count.
KASTRIL Ay, I knew that at first.
This match will advance the house of the Kastrils.
SUBTLE Pray God your sister prove but pliant!
KASTRIL Why,
Her name is so, by her other husband.
SUBTLE How!
KASTRIL The widow Pliant. Knew you not that?
SUBTLE No, faith, sir.
Yet, by erection of her figure[1] I guessed it.
Come, let's go practice.
KASTRIL Yes, but do you think, Doctor,
I e'er shall quarrel well?
SUBTLE I warrant you. [*Exeunt.*]

4.5

[*Enter*] *Doll* (*in her fit of talking*) [*and Sir Epicure*] *Mammon.*

DOLL For after Alexander's death—
MAMMON Good lady—
DOLL That Perdiccas and Antigonus were slain,
The two that stood, Seleuc' and Ptolomy[1]—
MAMMON Madam—
DOLL Made up the two legs, and the fourth beast,
That was Gog-north and Egypt-south, which after
Was called Gog Iron-leg and South Iron-leg—
MAMMON Lady—
DOLL And then Gog-hornèd. So was Egypt, too.
Then Egypt clay-leg and Gog clay-leg—
MAMMON Sweet madam—
DOLL And last Gog-dust, and Egypt-dust, which fall
In the last link of the fourth chain.° And these *historical period*
Be stars in story, which none see or look at—
MAMMON What shall I do?
DOLL For, as he says, except° *unless*
We call the rabbins° and the heathen Greeks— *(see 4.1.174)*
MAMMON Dear lady—
DOLL To come from Salem° and from Athens *Jerusalem*
And teach the people of great Britain—

[*Enter*] *Face* [*as Lungs*].

FACE What's the matter, sir?

1. By casting of her horoscope. (With sexual pun.)
4.5. Lovewit's house still.
1. Doll's garbled nonsense, taken from Hugh Broughton's *A Concent of Scripture* (1590), comes from Hebrew history about Alexander's four generals (interpreted by rabbinical scholars as the four kingdoms of Daniel's prophecy), etc.

DOLL To speak the tongue of Eber and Javan°— *Hebrew and Greek*
MAMMON Oh,
She's in her fit.
DOLL We shall know nothing—
FACE Death, sir,
We are undone.
DOLL Where, then, a learned linguist
Shall see the ancient used communion
Of vowels and consonants—
FACE My master will hear!
DOLL A wisdom which Pythagoras° held most high— *Greek philosopher*
MAMMON Sweet honorable lady!
DOLL To comprise
All sounds of voices, in few marks of letters—
FACE Nay, you must never hope to lay° her now. *quiet; sleep with*
They speak together.[2]
DOLL And so we may arrive by Talmud skill
And profane° Greek to raise the building up *pagan*
Of Helen's[3] house against the Ishmaelite,
King of Thogarma, and his habergeons° *coats of chain mail*
Brimstony, blue, and fiery; and the force
Of King Abaddon, and the beast of Cittim,
Which Rabbi David Kimchi, Onkelos,
And Aben-Ezra do interpret° Rome. *take to represent*
FACE How did you put her into't?
MAMMON Alas, I talked
Of a fifth monarchy° I would erect *millennial paradise*
With the philosophers' stone, by chance, and she
Falls on the other four straight.
FACE Out of Broughton!° *(see 2.3.238; 4.5, n. 1)*
I told you so. 'Slid, stop° her mouth. *gag*
MAMMON Is't best?
FACE She'll never leave° else. If the old man hear her, *leave off, cease*
We are but feces, ashes.
SUBTLE [*within*] What's to do there?
FACE Oh, we are lost! Now she hears him, she is quiet.
MAMMON Where shall I hide me?

Upon Subtle's entry they disperse.

[*Exeunt Doll and Face; Mammon tries to hide.*]

SUBTLE How! What sight is here?
Close° deeds of darkness, and that shun the light! *Secret*
Bring him again.[4] [*He pretends to discover Mammon.*] Who is he? What, my son!
Oh, I have lived too long!
MAMMON Nay, good, dear father,
There was no unchaste purpose.
SUBTLE Not? And flee me
When I come in?
MAMMON That was my error.

2. While Doll raves (lines 25–32), Face and Mammon confer urgently (lines 33–40). F1 prints these simultaneous actions in parallel columns (see Textual Notes).

3. "Helen's" is a mistake for "Heber's" (another name out of Broughton's obscure rabbinical treatise).

4. If Subtle is meant to say this to Face, the latter could exit a few lines later. ("Again" means "back.")

SUBTLE Error?
Guilt, guilt, my son. Give it the right name. No marvel
If I found check° in our great work within, *obstruction*
When such affairs as these were managing!° *going on*

MAMMON Why, have you so?

SUBTLE It has stood still this half hour,
And all the rest of our less works gone back.
Where is the instrument of wickedness,
My lewd, false drudge?° *(Ulen, Lungs)*

MAMMON Nay, good sir, blame not him.
Believe me, 'twas against his will or knowledge.
I saw her by chance.

SUBTLE Will you commit more sin,
T'excuse a varlet?

MAMMON By my hope,° 'tis true, sir. *hope of salvation*

SUBTLE Nay, then, I wonder less, if you, for whom
The blessing was prepared, would so tempt heaven,
And lose your fortunes.

MAMMON Why, sir?

SUBTLE This'll retard
The work a month at least.

MAMMON Why, if it do,
What remedy? But think it not, good father.
Our purposes were honest.° *chaste*

SUBTLE As they were,
So the reward will prove. (*A great crack and noise within.*)
How now? Ay me!
God and all saints be good to us! What's that?

[*Enter*] *Face* [*as Lungs still*].

FACE Oh, sir, we are defeated! All the works
Are flown *in fumo:*° every glass is burst; *in smoke*
Furnace and all rent down, as if a bolt
Of thunder had been driven through the house.
Retorts, receivers,° pelicans, bolt-heads, *(for distillate)*
All struck in shivers! *Subtle falls down as in a swoon.*
Help, good sir!—Alas,
Coldness and death invades him. Nay, Sir Mammon,
Do the fair offices of a man!° You stand *Be a man!*
As° you were readier to depart° than he.° *One knocks.* *As if / die / (Subtle)*
Who's there?—My lord her brother° is come. *(see 4.1.36)*

MAMMON Ha, Lungs?

FACE His coach is at the door. Avoid his sight,
For he's as furious as his sister is mad.

MAMMON Alas!

FACE My brain is quite undone with the fume, sir;
I ne'er must hope to be mine own man° again. *be myself*

MAMMON Is all lost, Lungs? Will nothing be preserved
Of all our cost?

FACE Faith, very little, sir.
A peck of coals or so, which is cold comfort, sir.

MAMMON Oh, my voluptuous mind! I am justly punished.

FACE And so am I, sir.

MAMMON Cast from all my hopes—

FACE Nay, certainties, sir.

MAMMON By mine own base affections.
Subtle seems [to] come to himself.
SUBTLE Oh, the curst fruits of vice and lust!
MAMMON Good father,
It was my sin. Forgive it.
SUBTLE Hangs my roof
Over us still, and will not fall, O Justice,
Upon us for this wicked man?
FACE [*to Mammon*] Nay, look, sir,
You grieve him now with staying in his sight.
Good sir, the nobleman will come too, and take you,
And that may breed a tragedy.[5]
MAMMON I'll go.
FACE Ay, and repent at home, sir. It may be,
For some good penance you may ha' it° yet; *(forgiveness)*
A hundred pound to the box° at Bedlam— *poor box*
MAMMON Yes.
FACE For the restoring such as ha' their wits.
MAMMON I'll do't.
FACE I'll send one to you to receive it.
MAMMON Do.
Is no projection left?
FACE All flown, or stinks, sir.
MAMMON Will naught be saved that's good for med'cine, think'st thou?
FACE I cannot tell, sir. There will be perhaps
Something about the scraping of the shards
Will cure the itch— [*aside*] though not your itch of mind, sir.—
It shall be saved for you, and sent home. Good sir,
This way, for fear the lord should meet you. [*Exit Mammon.*]
SUBTLE Face!
FACE Ay.
SUBTLE Is he gone?
FACE Yes, and as heavily
As° all the gold he hoped for were in his blood. *As if*
Let us be light, though.
SUBTLE Ay, as balls, and bound
And hit our heads against the roof for joy!
There's so much of our care now cast away.
FACE Now to our don.
SUBTLE Yes, your young widow by this time
Is made a countess, Face; she's has been in travail° *labor*
Of a young heir for you.
FACE Good, sir.
SUBTLE Off with your case,° *disguise as Lungs*
And greet her kindly, as a bridegroom should,
After these common hazards.
FACE Very well, sir.
Will you go fetch Don Diego off,° the while? *take Diego aside*
SUBTLE And fetch him over° too, if you'll be pleased, sir. *get the better of him*
Would Doll were in her place, to pick his pockets now!

5. Face pretends to worry that the supposedly noble brother (see line 74) of the pretend lady whom Mammon has been courting will burst in upon them and "take" ("catch") Mammon in a compromising situation, resulting in a fatal duel.

FACE Why, you can do it as well, if you would set to't.
I pray you, prove your virtue.° *try your skill*
SUBTLE For your sake, sir. [*Exeunt.*]

4.6

[*Enter*] *Surly* [*disguised still as a Spanish grandee, and*] *Dame Pliant.*

SURLY Lady, you see into what hands you are fall'n,
'Mongst what a nest of villains, and how near
Your honor was t'have catched a certain clap° *gonorrhea; harm*
Through your credulity, had I but been
So punctually forward,° as place, time, *ready to take advantage*
And other circumstance would ha' made a man;
For you're a handsome woman. Would you were wise, too!
I am a gentleman come here disguised,
Only to find° the knaveries of this citadel; *expose*
And where I might have wronged your honor, and have not,
I claim some interest in your love. You are,
They say, a widow, rich, and I am a bachelor,
Worth naught. Your fortunes may make me a man,
As mine ha' preserved you a woman. Think upon it,
And whether I have deserved you or no.
PLIANT I will, sir.
SURLY And for° these household rogues, let me alone *as for*
To treat° with them. *deal*

[*Enter*] *Subtle.*

SUBTLE How doth my noble Diego
And my dear madam Countess? Hath the count
Been courteous, lady, liberal, and open?
Donzel, methinks you look melancholic
After your coitum,° and scurvy! Truly, *sexual intercourse*
I do not like the dullness of your eye;
It hath a heavy cast; 'tis upsee Dutch,° *in Dutch fashion*
And says you are a lumpish° whoremaster. *dull*
Be lighter; I will make your pockets so.
He falls to picking of them.
SURLY [*disclosing himself*] Will you, Don bawd and pick-purse? [*He beats Subtle.*] How now? Reel you?
Stand up, sir. You shall find, since I am so heavy,
I'll gi' you equal weight.
SUBTLE Help, murder!
SURLY No, sir.
There's no such thing intended. A good cart
And a clean whip[1] shall ease you of that fear.
I am the Spanish Don, that should be cozened,
Do you see? Cozened? Where's your Captain Face,
That parcel-broker° and whole bawd, all rascal? *part pimp*

[*Enter*] *Face* [*in his captain's uniform*].

4.6. Lovewit's house still.
1. Being whipped through town while tied to the end of a cart was a standard punishment for minor offenses.

FACE How, Surly!
SURLY Oh, make your approach, good Captain.
I've found from whence your copper rings and spoons
Come now, wherewith you cheat abroad° in taverns. *around town*
'Twas here you learned t'anoint your boot with brimstone,° *sulfur*
Then rub men's gold on't for a kind of touch,° *touchstone for gold*
And say 'twas naught, when you had changed the color,
That you might ha't for nothing.[2] And this doctor,
Your sooty, smoky-bearded compeer, he
Will close° you so much gold in a bolt's-head,° *conceal / flask*
And, on a turn,° convey i'the stead another *presto, change-o*
With sublimed mercury that shall burst i'the heat
And fly out all *in fumo*.[3] Then weeps Mammon;
Then swoons His Worship. Or he is the Faustus,° *i.e., a magician*
[*Face slips out.*]
That casteth figures,° and can conjure, cures *horoscopes*
Plague, piles, and pox by the ephemerides,° *astrological almanacs*
And holds intelligence° with all the bawds *exchanges information*
And midwives of three shires, while you send in
(Captain? What, is he gone?) damsels with child,° *(for abortion)*
Wives that are barren, or the waiting-maid
With the greensickness.° [*He seizes Subtle as he tries to escape.*] Nay, sir, you must tarry, *anemia*
Though he be scaped, and answer by the ears,° sir. *ear-cropping in pillory*

4.7

[*Enter*] *Face* [*with*] *Kastril.*

FACE [*to Kastril*] Why, now's the time, if ever you will quarrel
Well, as they say, and be a trueborn child.° *knight-errant*
The doctor and your sister both are abused.° *insulted*
KASTRIL Where is he? Which is he? He is a slave,
Whate'er he is, and the son of a whore. [*To Surly*] Are you
The man, sir, I would know?
SURLY I should be loath, sir,
To confess so much.
KASTRIL Then you lie i'your throat.
SURLY How?
FACE [*to Kastril*] A very arrant rogue, sir, and a cheater,
Employed here by another conjuror
That does not love the doctor and would cross° him *thwart*
If he knew how.
SURLY [*to Kastril*] Sir, you are abused.° *you're being lied to*
KASTRIL You lie!
And 'tis no matter.
FACE Well said, sir. He is
The impudent'st rascal—
SURLY You are indeed.° [*To Kastril*] Will you hear me, sir? *indeed being lied to*

2. A hard, dark surface, such as dark leather, acting as touchstone ("touch"), would normally leave an authenticating trace when any gold was rubbed on it; a boot dressed with sulfur would not, enabling the con artist to declare the item worthless and pocket it for far less than its real value.
3. The explosion would enable the swindler to declare the experiment (like Mammon's) a failure and pocket the real gold, which was supposed to be used as part of the alchemical process but which the swindler has secretly removed and replaced with an explosive compound.
4.7. The scene continues.

FACE [*to Kastril*] By no means.° Bid him be gone. *Don't listen to him*
KASTRIL [*to Surly*] Begone, sir, quickly.
SURLY This's strange!—Lady, do you inform your brother.[1]
[*Dame Pliant whispers to Kastril.*]
FACE [*to Kastril*] There is not such a foist° in all the town. *another cheater*
The doctor had him presently,° and finds yet *found him out at once*
The° Spanish count will come here. [*Aside to Subtle*] Bear up,° Subtle. *The real* / *Back me up*
SUBTLE Yes, sir, he must appear within this hour.
FACE And yet this rogue° would come in a disguise, *i.e., Surly*
By the temptation of another spirit,° *an evil spirit*
To trouble our art, though he could not hurt it.
KASTRIL Ay,
I know. [*To Pliant*] Away! You talk like a foolish mauther.° *wench*
[*Exit Dame Pliant.*]
SURLY Sir, all is truth she says.
FACE [*to Kastril*] Do not believe him, sir.
He is the lying'st swabber!° [*To Surly*] Come your ways, sir. *seaman; rogue*
SURLY You are valiant out of company!° *when you have backers*
KASTRIL Yes, how then, sir?

[*Enter Drugger with a piece of damask.*]

FACE Nay, here's an honest fellow too that knows him
And all his tricks. (*Aside to Drugger*) Make good° what I say, Abel; *Back up*
This cheater would ha' cozened thee o'the widow.—
He owes this honest Drugger, here, seven pound
He has had on° him in twopenny'orths of tobacco. *from*
DRUGGER Yes, sir. And he's damned himself three terms° to pay me. *sworn falsely 9 months*
FACE And what does he owe for lotium?[2]
DRUGGER Thirty shillings, sir,
And for six syringes.
SURLY Hydra[3] of villany!
FACE [*aside to Kastril*] Nay, sir, you must quarrel him out o'the house.
KASTRIL I will.—
Sir, if you get not out o'doors, you lie,
And you are a pimp.
SURLY Why, this is madness, sir,
Not valor in you. I must laugh at this.
KASTRIL It is my humor. You are a pimp and a trig,° *coxcomb*
And an Amadis de Gaul, or a Don Quixote.[4]
DRUGGER Or a Knight o'the Curious Coxcomb, do you see?

[*Enter*] *Ananias.*

ANANIAS Peace to the household!
KASTRIL I'll keep peace for no man.
ANANIAS Casting° of dollars is concluded lawful. *Coining*
KASTRIL Is he the constable?
SUBTLE Peace, Ananias.
FACE [*to Kastril*] No, sir.

1. I.e., tell Kastril who I really am.
2. Stale urine used by barbers for hairdressing.
3. A many-headed water snake that could grow two new heads whenever one was cut off; hence a symbol for an evil that continues to grow. Hercules managed to vanquish the Hydra in the second of his twelve labors.
4. Jonson derides these heroes of romance.

KASTRIL Then you are an otter, and a shad,° a whit,° *herring / puny thing*
A very tim.° *tiny bit (?)*
SURLY You'll hear me, sir?
KASTRIL I will not.
ANANIAS What is the motive?
SUBTLE Zeal in the young gentleman
Against his Spanish slops°— *baggy breeches*
ANANIAS They are profane,
Lewd, superstitious, and idolatrous breeches.
SURLY New rascals!
KASTRIL Will you be gone, sir?
ANANIAS Avoid,° Satan! *Get out*
Thou art not of the light. That ruff of pride
About thy neck betrays thee, and is the same
With that which the unclean birds, in seventy-seven,[5]
Were seen to prank it° with on divers coasts.° *swagger / places*
Thou look'st like Antichrist in that lewd hat.
SURLY I must give way.
KASTRIL Begone, sir.
SURLY But I'll take
A course° with you— *turn*
ANANIAS Depart, proud Spanish fiend!
SURLY Captain and Doctor—
ANANIAS Child of perdition!
KASTRIL Hence, sir!
[*Exit Surly.*]
Did I not quarrel bravely?
FACE Yes, indeed, sir.
KASTRIL Nay, an I give my mind to't, I shall do't.
FACE Oh, you must follow, sir, and threaten him tame.° *until he's tame*
He'll turn again else.
KASTRIL I'll re-turn him, then. [*Exit.*]
FACE Drugger, this rogue prevented° us for thee; *forestalled*
We had determined that thou shouldst ha' come
In a Spanish suit and ha' carried° her so, and he, *prevailed with*
A brokerly slave,° goes, puts it on himself. *pimping wretch*
Hast brought the damask?
DRUGGER [*giving Face the damask*] Yes, sir.
FACE Thou must borrow
A Spanish suit. Hast thou no credit with the players?° *actors*
DRUGGER Yes, sir. Did you never see me play the fool?
FACE I know not, Nab. [*Aside*] Thou shalt, if I can help it.—
Hieronimo's[6] old cloak, ruff, and hat will serve;
I'll tell thee more when thou bring'st 'em. [*Exit Drugger.*]
ANANIAS (*Subtle hath whispered with him° this while*) Sir, I know *(Ananias)*
The Spaniard hates the Brethren, and hath spies
Upon their actions; and that this was one
I make no scruple.° But the holy Synod[7] *have no doubt*
Have been in prayer and meditation for it;

5. Although the Duke of Alba (see 4.3.30 and note) invaded the Netherlands in 1567, not 1577, the hated Spanish presence continued there through to the destruction of Antwerp in 1576 and subsequently. Or 1577 could be an error for 1588, the year of the Spanish Armada.
6. Hieronimo is the protagonist-avenger in Kyd's *The Spanish Tragedy*, for a revival of which Jonson seems to have written some scenes.
7. Puritan assembly.

And 'tis revealed no less to them than me
That casting of money is most lawful.

SUBTLE True.
But here I cannot do it; if the house
Should chance to be suspected, all would out° *be known*
And we be locked up in the Tower forever,
To make gold there for th'state, never come out;
And then are you defeated.

ANANIAS I will tell
This to the elders and the weaker Brethren,
That the whole company of the separation° *(see 3.1.2)*
May join in humble prayer again.

SUBTLE And fasting.

ANANIAS Yea, for some fitter place. The peace of mind
Rest with these walls!

SUBTLE Thanks, courteous Ananias.

[*Exit Ananias.*]

FACE What did he come for?

SUBTLE About casting dollars
Presently, out of hand.° And so I told him *at once*
A Spanish minister came here to spy
Against the faithful—

FACE I conceive.° Come, Subtle, *understand*
Thou art so down upon the least disaster!
How wouldst thou ha' done if I had not helped thee out?

SUBTLE I thank thee, Face, for the angry boy, i'faith.

FACE Who would ha' looked° it should ha' been that rascal *supposed, expected*
Surly? He had dyed his beard and all. Well, sir,
Here's damask come to make you a suit.

[*He shows Drugger's damask cloth.*]

SUBTLE Where's Drugger?

FACE He is gone to borrow me a Spanish habit;° *outfit*
I'll be the count now.

SUBTLE But where's the widow?

FACE Within, with my lord's° sister: Madam Doll *(see 4.1.36; 4.5.74)*
Is entertaining her.

SUBTLE By your favor, Face,
Now she is honest,° I will stand° again. *chaste / bid for her*

FACE You will not offer it!

SUBTLE Why?

FACE Stand to your word,
Or—here comes Doll. She knows°— *She'll be told*

SUBTLE You're tyrannous° still. *overbearing*

FACE Strict for my right.

[*Enter*] *Doll.*

How now, Doll? Hast told her
The Spanish count will come?

DOLL Yes, but another is come
You little looked for.

FACE Who's that?

DOLL Your master!
The master of the house.

SUBTLE How, Doll!

FACE She lies.

This is some trick.—Come, leave your quiblins,° Dorothy. *quibbles, tricks*
DOLL Look out and see. [*Face goes to the window.*]
SUBTLE Art thou in earnest?
DOLL 'Slight,
Forty o'the neighbors are about him, talking.
FACE [*returning*] 'Tis he, by this good day.
DOLL 'Twill prove ill day
For some on° us. *of*
FACE We are undone, and taken!° *caught in the act*
DOLL Lost, I'm afraid!
SUBTLE You said he would not come
While there died° one a week within the liberties.[8] *(of the plague)*
FACE No, 'twas within the walls.
SUBTLE Was't so? Cry you mercy;° *I beg your pardon*
I thought the liberties. What shall we do now, Face?
FACE Be silent; not a word, if he call or knock.
I'll into mine old shape again, and meet him,
Of Jeremy, the butler. I'the meantime,
Do you two pack up all the goods and purchase° *winnings, booty*
That we can carry i'the two trunks. I'll keep him
Off for today, if I cannot longer; and then
At night I'll ship you both away to Ratcliff,° *(downriver)*
Where we'll meet tomorrow, and there we'll share.
Let Mammon's brass and pewter keep° the cellar; *remain in*
We'll have another time for that. But, Doll,
Pray thee, go heat a little water quickly;
Subtle must shave me. All my captain's beard
Must off, to make me appear smooth Jeremy.
You'll do't?
SUBTLE Yes, I'll shave° you as well as I can. *shave (face); cheat*
FACE And not cut my throat, but trim me?
SUBTLE You shall see, sir.
[*Exeunt.*]

5.1

[*Enter*] *Lovewit* [*and*] *Neighbors.*

LOVEWIT Has there been such resort,° say you? *gathering*
FIRST NEIGHBOR Daily, sir.
SECOND NEIGHBOR And nightly, too.
THIRD NEIGHBOR Ay, some as brave° as lords. *showily dressed*
FOURTH NEIGHBOR Ladies and gentlewomen.
FIFTH NEIGHBOR Citizens' wives.
FIRST NEIGHBOR And knights.
SIXTH NEIGHBOR In coaches.
SECOND NEIGHBOR Yes, and oyster-women.° *women selling oysters*
FIRST NEIGHBOR Beside other gallants.
THIRD NEIGHBOR Sailors' wives.
FOURTH NEIGHBOR Tobacco men.
FIFTH NEIGHBOR Another Pimlico!° *a popular resort*

8. The districts of Whitefriars and Blackfriars, formerly church property, enjoyed a special status under the jurisdiction of the Crown. Though geographically within London's walls (line 117), they were spoken of as separate entities.

5.1. At the door of Lovewit's house.

LOVEWIT What should my knave advance° *propose, promote*
To draw this company? He hung out no banners
Of a strange calf with five legs to be seen,
Or a huge lobster with six claws?
SIXTH NEIGHBOR No, sir.
THIRD NEIGHBOR We had gone in then, sir.
LOVEWIT He has no gift
Of teaching i'the nose° that e'er I knew of. *(like a Puritan)*
You saw no bills set up that promised cure
Of agues or the toothache?
SECOND NEIGHBOR No such thing, sir.
LOVEWIT Nor heard a drum struck° for baboons or puppets? *(as advertisement)*
FIFTH NEIGHBOR Neither, sir.
LOVEWIT What device° should he bring forth now? *clever plot*
I love a teeming wit as I love my nourishment.
Pray God he ha' not kept such open house
That he hath sold my hangings° and my bedding! *tapestries*
I left him nothing else. If he have eat 'em,
A plague o'the moth, say I. Sure he has got
Some bawdy pictures to call all this ging:° *gang, company*
The Friar and the Nun, or the new motion° *puppet show*
Of the knight's courser covering° the parson's mare, *copulating with*
The boy of six year old with the great thing,
Or't may be he has the fleas that run at tilt
Upon a table, or some dog to dance?
When saw you him?
FIRST NEIGHBOR Who, sir, Jeremy?
SECOND NEIGHBOR Jeremy butler?
We saw him not this month.
LOVEWIT How!
FOURTH NEIGHBOR Not these five weeks, sir.
FIRST NEIGHBOR These six weeks, at the least.
LOVEWIT You amaze me, neighbors!
FIFTH NEIGHBOR Sure, if Your Worship know not where he is,
He's slipped away.
SIXTH NEIGHBOR Pray God he be not made away!
LOVEWIT Ha? It's no time to question, then. *He knocks.*
SIXTH NEIGHBOR About
Some three weeks since I heard a doleful cry,
As I sat up a-mending my wife's stockings.
LOVEWIT This's strange, that none will answer! Didst thou hear
A cry, say'st thou?
SIXTH NEIGHBOR Yes, sir, like unto a man
That had been strangled an hour and could not speak.
SECOND NEIGHBOR I heard it too, just this day three weeks,° at two o'clock *three weeks ago today*
Next° morning. *In the*
LOVEWIT These be miracles, or you make 'em so!
A man an hour strangled, and could not speak,
And both you heard him cry?
THIRD NEIGHBOR Yes, downward,° sir. *i.e., definitely*
LOVEWIT Thou art a wise fellow. Give me thy hand, I pray thee.
What trade art thou on?° *of*
THIRD NEIGHBOR A smith, an't° please Your Worship. *if it*

LOVEWIT A smith? Then lend me thy help to get this door open.
THIRD NEIGHBOR That I will presently, sir; but° fetch my tools— *merely*
[*Exit.*]
FIRST NEIGHBOR Sir, best to knock again, afore you break it.

5.2

LOVEWIT [*knocking again*] I will.

[*Enter*] *Face* [*in his butler's livery*].

FACE What mean you, sir?
FIRST, SECOND, FOURTH NEIGHBORS Oh, here's Jeremy!
FACE Good sir, come from the door.
LOVEWIT Why, what's the matter?
FACE Yet farther; you are too near, yet.
LOVEWIT I'the name of wonder!
What means the fellow?
FACE The house, sir, has been visited.
LOVEWIT What, with the plague? Stand thou then farther.
FACE No, sir,
I had it not.
LOVEWIT Who had it, then? I left
None else but thee i'the house.
FACE Yes, sir. My fellow,
The cat, that kept° the butt'ry, had it on her *guarded; occupied*
A week before I spied it; but I got her
Conveyed away i'the night. And so I shut
The house up for a month—
LOVEWIT How!
FACE Purposing then, sir,
T'have burnt rose-vinegar, treacle, and tar,
And ha' made it sweet, that you should ne'er ha' known it,
Because I knew the news would but afflict you, sir.
LOVEWIT Breathe less, and farther off. Why, this is stranger!
The neighbors tell me all here that the doors
Have still° been open— *continually*
FACE How, sir!
LOVEWIT Gallants, men and women,
And of all sorts, tag-rag,° been seen to flock here *rabble*
In threaves,° these ten weeks, as to a second Hoxton° *droves / a resort town*
In days of Pimlico and Eye-bright.° *famous resorts*
FACE Sir,
Their wisdoms[1] will not say so.
LOVEWIT Today they speak
Of coaches and gallants; one in a French hood
Went in, they tell me, and another was seen
In a velvet gown, at the window; divers more
Pass in and out.
FACE They did pass through the doors, then,
Or walls, I assure their eyesights and their spectacles;
For here, sir, are the keys, and here have been

5.2. The scene continues.
1. They in their great wisdom. (Said sarcastically, as if "Their wisdoms" were a title.)

In this my pocket now above twenty days.
And for° before, I kept the fort alone there. *as for*
But that° 'tis yet not deep i'the afternoon, *Were it not that*
I should believe my neighbors had seen double
Through the black pot,° and made these apparitions! *beer mug*
For, on my faith to Your Worship, for these three weeks
And upwards the door has not been opened.

LOVEWIT Strange!

FIRST NEIGHBOR Good faith, I think I saw a coach.

SECOND NEIGHBOR And I too,
I'd ha' been sworn.

LOVEWIT Do you but think it now?
And but one coach?

FOURTH NEIGHBOR We cannot tell, sir. Jeremy
Is a very honest fellow.

FACE Did you see me at all?

FIRST NEIGHBOR No. That we are sure on.

SECOND NEIGHBOR I'll be sworn o'that.

LOVEWIT Fine rogues, to have your testimonies built on!

[*Enter Third Neighbor with his tools.*]

THIRD NEIGHBOR Is Jeremy come?

FIRST NEIGHBOR Oh, yes. You may leave your tools;
We were deceived, he says.

SECOND NEIGHBOR He's had the keys,
And the door has been shut these three weeks.

THIRD NEIGHBOR Like° enough! *Likely*

LOVEWIT Peace, and get hence, you changelings.° *fickle ones; idiots*

FACE [*aside, seeing Surly and Mammon*] Surly come?
And Mammon made acquainted? They'll tell all.
How shall I beat them off? What shall I do?
Nothing's more wretched than a guilty conscience.

5.3

[*Enter*] *Surly* [*and Sir Epicure*] *Mammon.*

SURLY [*to Mammon*] No, sir, he was a great physician. This,
It was no bawdy house, but a mere chancel!° *an absolute church*
You knew the lord and his sister.

MAMMON Nay, good Surly—

SURLY The happy word, "Be rich"—

MAMMON Play not the tyrant—

SURLY Should be today pronounced to all your friends.
And where be your andirons now, and your brass pots,
That should ha' been golden flagons and great wedges?° *ingots of gold*

MAMMON Let me but breathe. What! They ha' shut their doors,
Methinks! *Mammon and Surly knock.*

SURLY Ay, now 'tis holiday with them.

MAMMON Rogues,
Cozeners, impostors, bawds!

FACE What mean you, sir?

MAMMON To enter if we can.

5.3. The scene continues.

FACE Another man's house?
Here is the owner, sir. Turn you to him
And speak your business.
MAMMON [*to Lovewit*] Are you, sir, the owner?
LOVEWIT Yes, sir.
MAMMON And are those knaves within your cheaters?
LOVEWIT What knaves? What cheaters?
MAMMON Subtle and his Lungs.
FACE The gentleman is distracted, sir. No lungs
Nor lights° ha' been seen here these three weeks, sir, *animal lungs*
Within these doors, upon my word.
SURLY Your word,
Groom arrogant?
FACE Yes, sir. I am the housekeeper,
And know the keys ha' not been out o'my hands.
SURLY This's a new Face?° *another impostor*
FACE You do mistake the house, sir.
What sign° was't at? *tavern sign*
SURLY You rascal!—This is one
O'the confederacy. Come, let's get officers,
And force the door.
LOVEWIT Pray you stay,° gentlemen. *hold on*
SURLY No, sir, we'll come with warrant.
MAMMON Ay, and then
We shall ha' your doors open. [*Exeunt Mammon and Surly.*]
LOVEWIT [*to Face*] What means this?
FACE I cannot tell, sir.
FIRST NEIGHBOR These are two o'the gallants
That we do think we saw.
FACE Two o'the fools?
You talk as idly as they.—Good faith, sir,
I think the moon has crazed 'em all.

[*Enter*] *Kastril.*

(*Aside*) Oh, me,
The angry boy come too? He'll make a noise,
And ne'er away till he have betrayed us all.
Kastril knocks.
KASTRIL What, rogues, bawds, slaves! You'll open the door anon,
Punk, cockatrice,° my suster! By this light, *basilisk; whore*
I'll fetch the marshal to you. You are a whore
To keep° your castle— *keep to, stay in*
FACE Who would you speak with, sir?
KASTRIL The bawdy doctor and the cozening captain,
And Puss, my suster.
LOVEWIT This is something, sure!
FACE Upon my trust, the doors were never open, sir.
KASTRIL I have heard all their tricks told me twice over
By the fat knight° and the lean gentleman.° *(Mammon) / (Surly)*
LOVEWIT Here comes another.

[*Enter*] *Ananias and Tribulation.*

FACE [*aside*] Ananias too?
And his pastor?

TRIBULATION The doors are shut against us.
They beat too at the door.
ANANIAS Come forth, you seed of sulfur, sons of fire!
Your stench, it is broke forth; abomination
Is in the house.
KASTRIL Ay, my suster's there.
ANANIAS The place,
It is become a cage of unclean birds.
KASTRIL Yes, I will fetch the scavenger[1] and the constable.
TRIBULATION You shall do well.
ANANIAS We'll join to weed them out.
KASTRIL You will not come, then, punk device,° my suster? *arrant whore*
ANANIAS Call her not sister.° She is a harlot, verily. *i.e., Puritan woman*
KASTRIL I'll raise the street.° *arouse the residents*
LOVEWIT Good gentlemen, a word.
ANANIAS Satan, avoid, and hinder not our zeal!
[*Exeunt Ananias, Tribulation, and Kastril.*]
LOVEWIT The world's turned Bedlam.
FACE These are all broke loose
Out of Saint Katherine's,° where they use[2] to keep *an insane asylum*
The better sort of madfolks.
FIRST NEIGHBOR [*to Lovewit*] All these persons
We saw go in and out here.
SECOND NEIGHBOR Yes, indeed, sir.
THIRD NEIGHBOR These were the parties.
FACE Peace, you drunkards!—Sir,
I wonder at it. Please you to give me leave
To touch the door, I'll try an° the lock be changed. *to see if*
LOVEWIT It mazes me!
FACE [*examining the door*] Good faith, sir, I believe
There's no such thing. 'Tis all *deceptio visus*.° *an optical illusion*
[*Aside*] Would I could get him away!
DAPPER (*cries out within*) Master Captain! Master Doctor!
LOVEWIT Who's that?
FACE (*aside*) Our clerk within, that I forgot!—I know not, sir.
DAPPER [*within*] For God's sake, when will Her Grace be at leisure?
FACE Ha!
Illusions, some spirit o'the air! (*Aside*) His gag is melted,
And now he sets out the throat.° *raises his voice*
DAPPER [*within*] I am almost stifled—
FACE (*aside*) Would you were altogether!
LOVEWIT 'Tis i'the house.
Ha! List!
FACE Believe it, sir, i'the air.
LOVEWIT Peace, you—
DAPPER [*within*] Mine aunt's Grace does not use me well.
SUBTLE [*within*] You fool,
Peace, you'll mar all!
FACE [*speaking through the keyhole*] Or you will else,[3] you rogue!

1. Functionary in charge of street cleaning.
2. Where the authorities make it their practice.
3. Or it will be you (Subtle) that ruins everything (by talking so loud).

LOVEWIT [*hearing Face*] Oh, is it so? Then you converse with spirits!
Come, sir. No more o'your tricks, good Jeremy.
The truth, the shortest way.
FACE Dismiss this rabble, sir.
[*Aside*] What shall I do? I am catched.
LOVEWIT Good neighbors,
I thank you all. You may depart. [*Exeunt Neighbors.*]
Come, sir,
You know that I am an indulgent master,
And therefore conceal nothing. What's your med'cine
To draw so many several° sorts of wildfowl? *different*
FACE Sir, you were wont to affect° mirth and wit— *fond of indulging in*
But here's no place to talk on't i'the street.
Give me but leave to make the best of my fortune,
And only pardon me th'abuse of your house;
It's all I beg. I'll help you to a widow,
In recompence, that you shall gi' me thanks for,
Will make you seven years younger, and a rich one.
'Tis but° your putting on a Spanish cloak. *It requires only*
I have her within. You need not fear the house;
It was not visited.° *afflicted by plague*
LOVEWIT But by me, who came
Sooner than you expected.
FACE It is true, sir.
Pray you forgive me.
LOVEWIT Well, let's see your widow. [*Exeunt.*]

5.4

[*Enter*] *Subtle* [*and*] *Dapper.*

SUBTLE How! Ha' you eaten your gag?
DAPPER Yes, faith, it crumbled
Away i'my mouth.
SUBTLE You ha' spoiled all, then.
DAPPER No!
I hope my aunt of Faery will forgive me.
SUBTLE Your aunt's a gracious lady; but in troth
You were to blame.
DAPPER The fume did overcome me,
And I did do't to stay° my stomach. Pray you *quiet*
So satisfy Her Grace.

[*Enter*] *Face* [*in his captain's uniform*].

Here comes the captain.
[*Face and Subtle confer privately.*]
FACE How now, is his mouth down?° *open*
SUBTLE Ay, he has spoken.
FACE A pox! I heard him, and you too. He's undone, then.
I have been fain° to say the house is haunted *obliged*
With spirits, to keep churl[1] back.
SUBTLE And hast thou done it?

5.4. Inside Lovewit's house.
1. Face speaks deprecatingly of his master Lovewit in order to catch Subtle off guard, using the word "churl" to signify one who resides in the country and tends his hopyards (see 1.1.184).

FACE Sure, for this night.
SUBTLE Why, then triumph and sing
Of Face so famous, the precious king
Of present° wits. *living*
FACE Did you not hear the coil° *fuss*
About the door?
SUBTLE Yes, and I dwindled° with it. *shrank (in dismay)*
FACE Show him his aunt, and let him be dispatched;
I'll send her to you. [*Exit.*]
SUBTLE Well, sir, your aunt Her Grace
Will give you audience presently, on my suit° *petition*
And the captain's word that you did not eat your gag
In any contempt of Her Highness.
DAPPER Not I, in troth, sir.

[*Enter*] *Doll like the Queen of Faery.*

SUBTLE Here she is come. Down o'your knees and wriggle!
She has a stately presence. [*Dapper kneels.*] Good. Yet nearer,
And bid, "God save you!"
DAPPER Madam—
SUBTLE And your aunt.
DAPPER And my most gracious aunt, God save Your Grace.
DOLL Nephew, we° thought to have been angry with you, *(the royal "we")*
But that sweet face of yours hath turned the tide,
And made it flow with joy that ebbed of love.
Arise, and touch our velvet gown.
SUBTLE The skirts,
And kiss 'em. So. [*Dapper kisses the hem of her skirt.*]
DOLL Let me now stroke that head.
Much, nephew, shalt thou win; much shalt thou spend;
Much shalt thou give away; much shalt thou lend.
SUBTLE (*aside*) Ay, much, indeed.—Why do you not thank
Her Grace?
DAPPER I cannot speak for joy.
SUBTLE See, the kind° wretch! *full of natural feeling*
Your Grace's kinsman right.° *true*
DOLL Give me the bird.°— *familiar spirit*
Here is your fly,° in a purse about your neck, cousin. *the bird*
[*She puts a purse on a chain around his neck.*]
Wear it, and feed it about this day sev'night,° *this time next week*
On your right wrist—
SUBTLE Open a vein with a pin
And let it suck but once a week.[2] Till then
You must not look on't.
DOLL No. And, kinsman,
Bear yourself worthy of the blood you come on.° *descend from*
SUBTLE Her Grace would ha' you eat no more Woolsack° pies, *a London tavern*
Nor Dagger frumenty.[3]
DOLL Nor break his fast
In Heaven and Hell.° *two Westminster taverns*
SUBTLE She's with you everywhere!
Nor play with costermongers at mumchance, tray-trip,

2. Familiars, or demonic spirits, were thought to feed on human blood.

3. A pudding made from hulled wheat, here served in the Dagger tavern (see 1.1.191).

God-make-you-rich (whenas your aunt has done it);[4] but keep
The gallant'st company and the best games—
DAPPER Yes, sir.
SUBTLE Gleek and primero;° and what you get, be true to us. *(see 2.3.284–85)*
DAPPER By this hand, I will.
SUBTLE You may bring 's a thousand pound
Before tomorrow night (if but three thousand
Be stirring),[5] an you will.
DAPPER I swear I will, then.
SUBTLE Your fly will learn° you all games. *teach*
FACE [*within*] Ha' you done there?
SUBTLE [*to Doll*] Your Grace will command him no more duties?
DOLL No;
But come and see me often. I may chance
To leave him three or four hundred chests of treasure,
And some twelve thousand acres of Faery land,
If he game well and comely° with good gamesters. *gambles stylishly*
SUBTLE There's a kind aunt! Kiss her departing part.° *her behind*
But you must sell your forty mark a year° now. *sell your land (1.2.51)*
DAPPER Ay, sir, I mean.° *mean to do so*
SUBTLE Or gi 't° away. Pox on't! *give it*
DAPPER I'll gi 't mine aunt. I'll go and fetch the writings.
SUBTLE 'Tis well. Away! [*Exit Dapper.*]

[*Enter*] *Face* [*with a cloak and hat*].

FACE Where's Subtle?
SUBTLE Here. What news?
FACE Drugger is at the door. Go take his suit° *(see 4.7.98)*
And bid him fetch a parson presently;
Say he shall marry the widow. Thou shalt spend° *earn, have to spend*
A hundred pound by° the service! [*Exit Subtle.*] *for*
Now, queen Doll,
Ha' you packed up all?
DOLL Yes.
FACE And how do you like
The lady Pliant?
DOLL A good, dull innocent.

[*Enter Subtle, with garments.*]

SUBTLE Here's your Hieronimo's cloak and hat.° *(see 4.7.71)*
FACE [*taking the garments*] Give me 'em.
SUBTLE And the ruff too?
FACE [*taking the ruff*] Yes. I'll come to you presently.
[*Exit.*]
SUBTLE Now he is gone about his project, Doll,
I told you of, for the widow.
DOLL 'Tis direct
Against our articles.° *articles of agreement*
SUBTLE Well, we'll fit him,° wench. *We'll settle his hash*
Hast thou gulled her of her jewels or her bracelets?

4. Dagger is bidden not to play lower-class games of chance at dice and backgammon with "costermongers" (fruit-sellers) and the like; the Queen of Faery offers a better model of gambling in elegant company.

5. Even if the whole wager amounts to only £3,000 (in which case winnings of £1,000 would be quite a killing).

DOLL No, but I will do't.
SUBTLE Soon at night, my Dolly,
When we are shipped and all our goods aboard,
Eastward for Ratcliff,° we will turn our course — *(see 4.7.125)*
To Brentford,° westward, if thou say'st the word, — *an upriver resort*
And take our leaves of this o'erweening rascal,
This peremptory Face.
DOLL Content. I'm weary of him.
SUBTLE Thou'st° cause, when the slave will run a-wiving, Doll, — *You have*
Against the instrument° that was drawn between us. — *agreement*
DOLL I'll pluck his bird° as bare as I can. — *i.e., Dame Pliant*
SUBTLE Yes, tell her
She must by any means address some present
To th'cunning man,° make him amends for wronging — *(Subtle the alchemist)*
His art with her suspicion, send a ring
Or chain of pearl; she will be tortured else
Extremely in her sleep, say, and ha' strange things° — *hallucinations*
Come to her. Wilt thou?
DOLL Yes.
SUBTLE My fine flittermouse,° — *bat*
My bird o'the night! We'll tickle it at the Pigeons,° — *a Brentford tavern*
When we have all, and may unlock the trunks,
And say, this's mine, and thine, and thine, and mine—
They kiss.

[*Enter*] *Face.*

FACE What now, a-billing?° — *wooing like doves*
SUBTLE Yes, a little exalted
In the good passage° of our stock affairs.° — *progress / business*
FACE Drugger has brought his parson. Take him in, Subtle,
And send Nab° back again to wash his face. — *Abel Drugger*
SUBTLE I will—and shave himself?
FACE If you can get him.
[*Exit Subtle.*]
DOLL You are hot upon it, Face, whate'er it is!
FACE A trick that Doll shall spend ten pound a month by.

[*Enter*] *Subtle.*

Is he gone?
SUBTLE The chaplain waits you i'the hall, sir.
FACE I'll go bestow him. [*Exit.*]
DOLL He'll now marry her instantly.
SUBTLE He cannot yet, he is not ready. Dear Doll,
Cozen her of all thou canst. To deceive him
Is no deceit, but justice, that° would break — *for him who*
Such an inextricable tie as ours was.
DOLL Let me alone to fit him.° — *(see 72 above)*

[*Enter*] *Face.*

FACE Come, my venturers,° — *partners*
You ha' packed up all? Where be the trunks? Bring forth.
SUBTLE [*producing the booty*] Here.
FACE Let's see 'em. Where's the money?
SUBTLE Here,
In this.

FACE [*counting the loot*] Mammon's ten pound; eight score before;
The Brethren's money, this; Drugger's and Dapper's.
What paper's that?
DOLL The jewel of the waiting-maid's,
That stole it from her lady, to know certain°— *for certain*
FACE If she should have precedence of her mistress?
DOLL Yes.
FACE What box is that?
SUBTLE The fishwife's rings, I think,
And th'alewife's single money.° Is't not, Doll? *small change*
DOLL Yes, and the whistle that the sailor's wife
Brought you to know an° her husband were with Ward.° *if / a noted pirate*
FACE We'll wet it° tomorrow, and our silver beakers *drink up the proceeds*
And tavern cups. Where be the French petticoats
And girdles and hangers?° *sword-loops on belts*
SUBTLE Here, i'the trunk,
And the bolts of lawn.° *rolls of fine linen*
FACE Is Drugger's damask there?
And the tobacco?
SUBTLE Yes.
FACE Give me the keys.
DOLL Why you the keys?
SUBTLE No matter, Doll, because
We shall not open 'em before he comes.
FACE 'Tis true, you shall not open them, indeed,
Nor have 'em forth.° Do you see? Not forth, Doll. *out of the house*
DOLL No?
FACE No, my smock-rampant.° The right is, my master *whore; roaring girl*
Knows all, has pardoned me, and he will keep 'em.
Doctor, 'tis true—you look°—for all your figures;° *stare / horoscopes*
I sent for him, indeed.° Wherefore, good partners, *(a lie)*
Both he and she, be satisfied, for here
Determines° the indenture tripartite *Concludes*
'Twixt Subtle, Doll, and Face. All I can do
Is to help you over the wall, o'the back-side,° *rear of the property*
Or lend you a sheet to save your velvet gown, Doll.
Here will be officers presently; bethink you
Of some course suddenly to scape the dock,° *i.e., courtroom*
For thither you'll come else.° (*Some knock.*) Hark you, thunder! *otherwise*
SUBTLE You are a precious fiend!
OFFICER [*without*]° Open the door! *outside the door*
FACE Doll, I am sorry for thee, i'faith. But hear'st thou?
It shall go hard but I will° place thee somewhere; *i.e., I'm sure to*
Thou shalt ha' my letter to Mistress Amo.° *a brothel-keeper*
DOLL Hang you—
FACE Or Madam Caesarean.° *another brothel-keeper*
DOLL Pox upon you, rogue!
Would I had but time to beat thee!
FACE Subtle,
Let's know where you set up next; I'll send you
A customer now and then, for old acquaintance.
What new course ha' you?
SUBTLE Rogue, I'll hang myself,

That I may walk a greater devil than thou
And haunt thee i'the flock-bed and the buttery.° [*Exeunt.*] *a butler's province*

5.5

[*Enter*] *Lovewit* [*in Spanish costume, with the parson. Knocking is heard at the door*].

LOVEWIT [*responding to the knocking*] What do you mean, my masters?° *my good people*
MAMMON [*without*] Open your door,
Cheaters, bawds, conjurers!
OFFICER [*without*] Or we'll break it open.
LOVEWIT What warrant have you?
OFFICER [*without*] Warrant enough, sir, doubt not,
If you'll not open it.
LOVEWIT Is there an officer there?
OFFICER [*without*] Yes, two, or three for° failing. *as insurance against*
LOVEWIT Have but patience,
And I will open it straight.

[*Enter*] *Face* [*as Jeremy the butler*].

FACE Sir, ha' you done?
Is it a marriage? Perfect?
LOVEWIT Yes, my brain.
FACE Off with your ruff and cloak, then; be yourself, sir.
[*Lovewit removes the Spanish costume.*]
SURLY [*without*] Down with the door!
KASTRIL [*without*] 'Slight, ding° it open! *break*
LOVEWIT [*opening the door*] Hold,
Hold, gentlemen. What means this violence?

[*Enter*] *Mammon, Surly, Kastril, Ananias, Tribulation,* [*and*] *Officers.*

MAMMON Where is this collier?° *filthy wretch*
SURLY And my Captain Face?
MAMMON These day-owls.
SURLY That are birding° in men's purses. *hunting; thieving*
MAMMON Madam Suppository.
KASTRIL Doxy,° my suster. *Harlot*
ANANIAS Locusts
Of the foul pit.
TRIBULATION Profane as Bel and the Dragon.[1]
ANANIAS Worse than the grasshoppers, or the lice of Egypt.° *(see Exodus 8.16–18)*
LOVEWIT Good gentlemen, hear me.—Are you officers,
And cannot stay° this violence? *halt*
OFFICER Keep the peace!
LOVEWIT Gentlemen, what is the matter? Whom do you seek?
MAMMON The chemical cozener.
SURLY And the captain pander.
KASTRIL The nun° my suster. *i.e., whore*
MAMMON Madam Rabbi.
ANANIAS Scorpions

5.5. Still inside Lovewit's house.

1. An apocryphal addition to the Book of Daniel.

And caterpillars.
LOVEWIT Fewer at once, I pray you.
OFFICER One after another, gentlemen, I charge you,
By virtue of my staff—
ANANIAS They are the vessels
Of pride, lust, and the cart.° *(see 4.6.29)*
LOVEWIT Good zeal, lie still
A little while.
TRIBULATION Peace, Deacon Ananias.
LOVEWIT The house is mine here, and the doors are open.
If there be any such persons as you seek for,
Use your authority; search on, o'God's name.
I am but newly come to town, and, finding
This tumult 'bout my door, to tell you true,
It somewhat mazed me; till my man, here, fearing
My more displeasure, told me he had done
Somewhat an insolent part, let out my house
(Belike° presuming on my known aversion *Probably*
From any air o'the town while there was sickness)° *plague*
To a doctor and a captain—who, what they are
Or where they be, he knows not.
MAMMON Are they gone?
LOVEWIT You may go in and search, sir.
They enter. [Mammon, Tribulation, Ananias, and the Officers disappear through stage doors as they begin their search of the house.]
Here I find
The empty walls worse than I left 'em, smoked,
A few cracked pots, and glasses, and a furnace,
The ceiling filled with poesies of the candle,[2]
And "Madam with a dildo"[3] writ o'the walls.
Only one gentlewoman I met here,
That is within, that said she was a widow—
KASTRIL Ay, that's my suster. I'll go thump her. Where is she?
[He goes in.]
LOVEWIT And should ha' married a Spanish count, but he,
When he came to't, neglected her so grossly
That I, a widower, am gone through with her.° *have married her*
SURLY How! Have I lost her, then?
LOVEWIT Were you the don, sir?
Good faith, now, she does blame you extremely, and says
You swore and told her you had ta'en the pains
To dye your beard and umber o'er your face,
Borrowed a suit and ruff, all for her love—
And then did nothing. What an oversight
And want of putting forward, sir, was this!
Well fare an old harquebusier,° yet, *musketeer*
Could° prime his powder, and give fire, and hit, *Who could*
All in a twinkling![4]
Mammon comes forth.

2. Patterns made by smoking candles.
3. Fragment of a smutty ballad about, or a picture of, a woman and a phallus.
4. Lovewit compliments himself as an old soldier who could fire his musket quickly, unlike the hesitant Surly. (With bawdy suggestion.)

MAMMON The whole nest are fled!
LOVEWIT What sort of birds were they?
MAMMON A kind of choughs,° — *crowlike birds*
Or thievish daws,° sir, that have picked my purse — *jackdaws*
Of eightscore and ten pounds within these five weeks,
Beside my first materials, and my goods,
That lie i'the cellar, which I am glad they ha' left.
I may have home° yet. — *take them home*
LOVEWIT Think you so, sir?
MAMMON Ay.
LOVEWIT By order of law,° sir, but not otherwise. — *With a warrant*
MAMMON Not mine own stuff?
LOVEWIT Sir, I can take no knowledge
That they are yours but by public means.° — *by course of law*
If you can bring certificate that you were gulled of 'em,
Or any formal writ out of a court
That you did cozen yourself, I will not hold them.
MAMMON I'll rather lose 'em.
LOVEWIT That you shall not, sir,
By me, in troth; upon these terms they are yours.
What, should they ha' been, sir, turned into gold all?
MAMMON No.
I cannot tell. It may be they should. What then?
LOVEWIT What a great loss in hope have you sustained!
MAMMON Not I; the commonwealth has.
FACE Ay, he would ha' built
The city new, and made a ditch about it
Of silver, should° have run with cream from Hoxton,[5] — *which would*
That every Sunday in Moorfields° the younkers° — *(see 1.4.20) / youths*
And tits° and tomboys° should have fed on, gratis. — *wenches / hoydens*
MAMMON I will go mount a turnip-cart and preach
The end o'the world within these two months.—Surly,
What! In a dream?° — *Lost in thought?*
SURLY Must I needs cheat myself
With that same foolish vice of honesty?
Come, let us go and hearken° out the rogues. — *inquire, search*
That Face I'll mark for mine if e'er I meet him.
FACE If I can hear of him, sir, I'll bring you word
Unto your lodging; for in troth they were strangers
To me. I thought 'em honest as myself, sir.
[*Exeunt Surly and Mammon.*]

They [*Tribulation and Ananias*] *come forth.*

TRIBULATION 'Tis well; the Saints shall not lose all yet. Go
And get some carts—
LOVEWIT For what, my zealous friends?
ANANIAS To bear away the portion of the righteous
Out of this den of thieves.
LOVEWIT What is that portion?
ANANIAS The goods, sometimes° the orphans', that the Brethren — *formerly*
Bought with their silver pence.
LOVEWIT What, those i'the cellar

5. A semirural village and popular resort north of London in Jonson's time. The original spelling, "Hogsden," suggests that it was once known for raising hogs. See 5.2.19.

The knight Sir Mammon claims?
ANANIAS I do defy
The wicked Mammon; so do all the Brethren,
Thou profane man! I ask thee with what conscience
Thou canst advance that idol against us
That have the seal?° Were not the shillings numbered — *mark of God's grace*
That made the pounds? Were not the pounds told° out — *counted*
Upon the second day of the fourth week,
In the eight month, upon the table dormant,° — *fixed side table*
The year of the last patience of the Saints,
Six hundred and ten?[6]
LOVEWIT Mine earnest, vehement botcher,° — *repair tailor*
And deacon also, I cannot dispute with you;
But, if you get you not away the sooner,
I shall confute you with a cudgel.
ANANIAS Sir!
TRIBULATION Be patient, Ananias.
ANANIAS I am strong,
And will stand up, well girt, against an host
That threaten Gad in exile.[7]
LOVEWIT I shall send you
To Amsterdam, to your cellar.
ANANIAS I will pray there
Against thy house. May dogs defile thy walls
And wasps and hornets breed beneath thy roof,
This seat of falsehood and this cave of coz'nage!
[*Exeunt Tribulation and Ananias.*]

Drugger enters, and he° beats him away. — *(Lovewit)*

LOVEWIT Another too?
DRUGGER Not I, sir; I am no Brother.
LOVEWIT Away, you Harry Nicholas![8] Do you talk?
[*Exit Drugger.*]
FACE No, this was Abel Drugger. (*To the parson*) Good sir, go
And satisfy him; tell him all is done;
He stayed too long a-washing of his face.
The doctor, he shall hear of him at Westchester,[9]
And of the captain, tell him, at Yarmouth, or
Some good port town else, lying° for a wind. [*Exit parson.*] — *waiting*
[*To Lovewit*] If you can get off° the angry child, now, sir— — *placate, satisfy*

[*Enter Kastril and Dame Pliant.*]

KASTRIL (*to his sister*) Come on, you ewe! You have matched most sweetly, ha' you not?
Did not I say I would never ha' you tupped° — *mated, topped*
But by a dubbed boy,° to make you a lady-tom? — *a knight*
'Slight, you are a mammet!° Oh, I could touse° you now. — *doll, puppet / thrash*
Death, mun° you marry, with a pox?[1] — *must*
LOVEWIT You lie, boy.

6. Ananias dates, in Puritan reckoning, the expected last millennium on earth. Cf. 3.2.131–32.
7. See Genesis 49.19: "Gad, a troop shall overcome him: but he shall overcome at the last."
8. Hendrick Niclaes founded the radical sect of the Anabaptists, known as the Family of Love, in the sixteenth century.
9. Drugger is to be told that he can hear news of Subtle being at Chester, a town far to the northwest of London on the Irish Sea. Yarmouth (line 122), on the Norfolk coast, is also a fair distance.
1. Kastril pronounces a familiar oath, "with a pox," meaning "a curse on you," to which Lovewit replies in lines 129–30 with wordplay, as though Kastril's oath meant "with a diseased man."

As sound° as you; and I am aforehand with you. *I'm as healthy*
KASTRIL Anon?° *How's that?*
LOVEWIT Come, will you quarrel? I will feeze you,° sirrah. *settle your hash*
Why do you not buckle to your tools?° *draw your weapon*
KASTRIL God's light!
This is a fine old boy as e'er I saw!
LOVEWIT What, do you change your copy° now? Proceed; *change your tune*
Here stands my dove.° Stoop at her,[2] if you dare. *Pliant; a sword*
KASTRIL 'Slight, I must love him! I cannot choose, i'faith,
An I should be hanged for't! Suster, I protest
I honor thee for this match.
LOVEWIT Oh, do you so, sir?
KASTRIL Yes. An thou canst take tobacco and drink,° old boy, *smoke tobacco*
I'll give her five hundred pound more to her marriage
Than her own state.° *estate*
LOVEWIT Fill a pipeful, Jeremy.
FACE Yes, but go in and take it, sir.
LOVEWIT We will.
I will be ruled by thee in anything, Jeremy.
KASTRIL 'Slight, thou art not hidebound! Thou art a jovy° boy! *jovial*
Come, let's in, I pray thee, and take our whiffs.
LOVEWIT Whiff in with your sister, brother boy.
[*Exeunt Kastril and Dame Pliant.*]
That master
That had received such happiness by a servant,
In such a widow, and with so much wealth,
Were very ungrateful if he would not be
A little indulgent to that servant's wit,
And help his fortune, though with some small strain
Of his own candor.° [*To the audience*] Therefore, gentlemen *honor, sincerity*
And kind spectators, if I have outstripped
An old man's gravity or strict canon,° think *rules of decorum*
What a young wife and a good brain° may do: *wit, intelligence*
Stretch age's truth sometimes, and crack it too.—
Speak for thyself, knave.
FACE So I will, sir.—Gentlemen,
My part a little fell in this last scene,
Yet 'twas decorum.[3] And though I am clean
Got off from Subtle, Surly, Mammon, Doll,
Hot Ananias, Dapper, Drugger, all
With whom I traded, yet I put myself
On you, that are my country;° and this pelf° *i.e., jury / loot*
Which I have got, if you do quit° me, rests° *acquit / remains*
To feast you often, and invite new guests. [*Exeunt.*]

THE END.

This comedy was first acted in the year 1610 by the King's Majesty's Servants. The principal comedians were Richard Burbage, John Lowin, Henry Condell, Alexander Cooke, Robert Armin, John Heminges, William Ostler, John Underwood, Nicholas Tooley, William Ecclestone. With the allowance of the Master of Revels.

---

2. Swoop down to catch her. (A term from falconry.)
3. It was appropriate to my character type.

TEXTUAL NOTES

The Alchemist was entered in the Stationers' Register on October 3, 1610, and was published in quarto in 1612. Jonson revised this text (not extensively) for his folio edition of 1616, and, though it contains some euphemisms for profanities that may be regarded with caution as the result of a kind of censorship, generally the folio alterations (few in number) are convincingly authorial. The present edition is based on that folio text. Substantive departures from it are noted here, along with some readings from Q1 not adopted in this present edition but for which a plausible argument (such as suspicion of censorship) can be made, using the following abbreviations:

Q1: Quarto of 1612 (London: Walter Burre)
Q1 corr.: The corrected version of this quarto
Q1 uncorr.: The uncorrected version of this quarto
F1: *The Works of Benjamin Jonson* (London: William Stansby, 1616)
F2: Folio of 1640 (London: Richard Bishop)
F3: Folio of 1692 (London)
ed.: A modern editor's emendation

To the Reader [Q1; not in F1] **12** [and elsewhere] **off** [F1: *of*]
1.1.51 you were [Q1] yo'were [F1] **78 thanks** [F2] thanke [F1] **92** [and elsewhere] ***aside*** [indicated by parentheses in F1] **113 Eighth** [F3] eight [F1] **122** [and elsewhere] **cozened** [F1: cossen'd] **133** [and elsewhere] **powder** [F1: poulder] **135** [and elsewhere] **venture** [F1: venter] **139** [and elsewhere] **lose** [F1: loose] **156 common** [F1: commune]
1.2.4 [and elsewhere] **I'm** [Q1] I'am [F1] **5** [and elsewhere] **I had** [F1: I'had] **15 you I'll** [Q1 uncorr.] you. I'll [Q1 corr., F1] **24 write** [F2] wright [F1] **29 pray** [F1: 'pray] **56 Xenophon** [F1] *Testament* [Q1] **93 D'you** [F1: Do' you] **113 born to** [ed.] borne too [F1] **135 Jove** [F1] Gad [Q1] **156 fancy** [F1: phant'sye] **168 bathe** [F2] bath [F1]
1.3.75 you've [F1: you'haue] **85 And** [Q1] 'nd [F1]
1.4.0 How now [placement, ed.; at the end of 2.1 in F1] **23 spital** [F1: spittle]
2.1.4 [and elsewhere] **Solomon's** [F1: Salomon's] **25 ho!** [F1: hough?] **25 face** [ed.; not in F1] **30 my** [Q1] thy [F1] **51 valor** [F1: valure] **79 my** [ed.; not in F1] **92 Pythagoras'** [F1: Pythagora's]
2.2.0 How now? [placement, ed.; at the end of 2.1 in F1] **14** [and elsewhere] **off** [F1: of] **33 *seraglio*** [F1: *seraglia*] **69 ostrich** [ed.] estrich [F1]
2.3.18 Now [F2] No [F1] **53 filter** [F1: *feltre*] **137 further** [F1: furder] **174 rightly** [F1: ritely] **209 roll** [F1: roule] **221–22** [order of lines as in Q1; transposed in F1] **246 vial** [F1: violl] **260 subtle** [ed.; not in F1] **272 surly** [ed.] Svb. [F1]
2.5.10 *stiptic* [F1: *stipstick*]
3.2.45 [and elsewhere] **gilt** [F1: guilt] **118 orphans** [ed.] orphane [F1] **142 a trick** [F2] trick [F1]
3.3.1 costive [Q1] caustiue [F1] **14 hoys** [F1: hoighs] **19 pier** [F1: pire] **42 sees** [F1: see's] **47 basin** [F1: bason] **56 bank** [F1: banque] **62 face** [F2; omitted in F1]
3.4.0 Oh . . . welcome [placement, ed.; at end of 3.3 in F1] **3 darling** [F1: dearling] **57** [and elsewhere] **He's** [F1: H'is] **75 Od's** [F1] God's [Q1]
3.5.74 in 's [F1: in'is]
4.1.1 [and elsewhere] **you're** [F1: yo'are] **46 lain** [F1: lyen] **98 coarse** [F1: course] **105 diamond** [F1: diamant]
4.2.7 curtain [F1: cortine] **20 to** [F1: too]
4.3.11 'Slight [F1] 'Sblood [Q1] **19** [and elsewhere] **tyrant** [F1: tyranne] **20 John** [F1: Ion] **21 *beso las*** [F1: *besolas*] **62 *verla*** [F1: *ver la*] **78 *tanto*** [ed.] *tanta*

[F1] **91** ***honradas*** [F1: *honrada's*] **92** ***Tengo*** [ed.] *Tiengo* [F1] **94** [and elsewhere] ***presto*** [F1: *praesto*] **99** [and elsewhere] **baboon** [F1: babioun]

4.4.3 FACE [Q1: FAC.; omitted in F1] **12 pavan** [F1: *Pauin*] **45 ushers** [F1: huishers] **48** [and elsewhere] **Bedlam** [F: *Bet'lem*] **53** ***no*** [ed.] *non* [F1] **65** ***Válgame*** [F1: *Valga me*] **77** ***a llegar*** [F1: *Alle gar*] **81** ***entramos*** [F1: *entremus*]

4.5.17 She's [F1: Sh'is] **25–40** [F1 prints Doll's speech in a left-hand column and the conversation of Face and Mammon in a parallel right-hand column] **33, 37 MAMMON** [Q1: MAM.] MAN. [F1] **34 fifth** [F1: fift] **70** [and elsewhere] **struck** [F1: strooke]

4.6.16 SURLY [Q1: SVR.] SVB. [F1]

4.7.8 arrant [F1: errant] **32 he's** [F1: h'has] **38 valor** [F1: valure] **64 We had** [F1: We'had] **104 SUBTLE** [Q1: SVB.] SVR. [F1]

5.1.29 FIRST NEIGHBOR [ed.] NEI. [F1]

5.2.3, 5, 15 farther [F1: farder] **19 Hoxton** [F1: *Hogs-den*] **24 window** [F1: windore] **42 He's** [F1: He'has] **46** [in parentheses in F1]

5.3.8 breathe [F1: breath] **9 holiday** [F1: holy-day]

5.4.58 your [Q1, F2] you [F1] **60 DAPPER** [F2] FAC. [F1] **77 Brentford** [F1: *Brainford*] **113 fishwife's** [F1: fish-wiues] **114 alewife's** [F1: ale-wiues] **142 Caesarean** [F1] *Imperiall* [Q1]

5.5.32 he [F2; not in F1] **41 ceiling** [F1: seeling] **56 harquebusier** [F1: Hargubuzier] **78 Hoxton** [F1: *Hogsden*] **99 idol** [F1] *Nemrod* [Q1] **124 can get** [Q1] get [F1] **125 ewe** [F1: yew]

Bartholomew Fair

Bartholomew Fair, first performed in 1614, is a play so rich, various, and conceptually original that it can be difficult to grasp at first reading. It relies less on story or character than, as its title may suggest, on the compelling evocation of a setting. In fact, for much of the action, Jonson seems deliberately to erode the forward momentum of the plot, replacing cause-and-effect narrative with a panoramic view of a multifarious urban landscape. Despite its structural complexity, however, *Bartholomew Fair* begins from a simple premise: a group of relatively affluent Londoners ventures to the fair held every year in Smithfield around August 24, Saint Bartholomew's Day. The trip is something of a slumming expedition, for the fair teems with itinerant performers, prostitutes, minor criminals, vendors of trashy merchandise, and providers of greasy food. The Londoners assume that they will experience the fair as tourists, from an emotional distance. But the shabby booths and dusty performance spaces have unexpectedly transformative effects on the visitors.

The first few scenes of *Bartholomew Fair* present a stock theme of comedy: the perverse regulation of marriage and sexuality. These scenes take place near the Arches, or London ecclesiastical courts, where John Littlewit works as a "proctor," preparing standard legal documents in much the way a modern paralegal would. In Jacobean England, marriage came under the purview of the ecclesiastical courts, so it is not surprising that Littlewit is preparing a marriage license. However, he does so not at the behest of a couple who wishes to wed but for Justice Overdo, who plans to marry his ward, Grace Wellborn, to his moronic brother-in-law, Bartholomew Cokes (the word "cokes" meant "fool").

Wardship was a controversial institution in Jacobean England. In an age when parents often died young, many minors from wealthy families inherited substantial amounts of property. Such orphans traditionally became wards of the monarch, who was supposed to provide a class-appropriate match when each child came of age. By the early seventeenth century the wardship system, originally designed to protect underage heirs, had degenerated into a cruelly coercive moneymaking scheme. An investor paid the king a handsome fee for the right to dispose of a ward in marriage, usually to one of the investor's close relatives. If the ward accepted the match, his or her property would augment the investor's own family fortune. A ward who refused the proposed marriage forfeited to the "guardian" his or her land and lost as well the social status that accompanied land ownership in the period. Thus Grace Wellborn correctly perceives herself to be little better than a slave sold to the highest bidder. Although she recoils from the prospect of marriage to an idiot, she apparently has no other option.

The other "courtship" in the opening scenes likewise owes more to legal technicalities than to sexual ardor. The cynical Quarlous remarks on how assiduously his impecunious friend Winwife courts wealthy older widows, such as John Littlewit's mother-in-law, Dame Purecraft: "There cannot be an ancient tripe or trillibub i'the

Introduction by Katharine Eisaman Maus; glosses, footnotes, and textual notes by David Bevington; text edited by David Bevington and checked by Eric Rasmussen.

town but thou art straight nosing it" (1.3.64–65). In early modern England, most single and married women were *femmes couvertes,* or "covered women"; that is, their legal and property rights were subsumed under their husbands' or fathers'. A widow, however, was not *couverte* unless and until she married again. Her legal independence gave her an unusual degree of autonomy in making marital and other choices. Early modern city comedy usually presents the transaction between young widow-hunter and elderly widow as a calculated trade. The impecunious youth brings to the table vigor and good looks, traits appealing to the sexually experienced widow. The superannuated widow, although no longer desirable in her person, offers her future husband the prospect of control over her financial assets.

Like the prospective marriage between Grace and Cokes, in other words, this arrangement sacrifices the prospect of intimacy and mutual pleasure on the altar of gain. The problem is that for the relatively affluent, supposedly respectable people we meet in the opening scenes, marriage seems the only path to enrichment. Unfortunately, in a world without divorce, marriage involves a lifetime connection that in this play seems oppressively immutable. Moreover, in the prosperous London of *Bartholomew Fair,* not only are family ties unbreakable, but they entail inflexible authority relations. The individual's status in the family is unchanging: once a child, always a child. Even the Littlewits, married adults, cannot go out without Dame Purecraft's permission—and in order to obtain it, they must pretend to have the perpetuation of the family as their motive. When they want to visit Bartholomew Fair, they get around her Puritan disapproval of its carnal pleasures by pretending that Win is suffering from an implausibly specific pregnancy-induced craving for the roast pork served at the fair. Genuine affection between married folks is not impossible in this world, as the banter between John and Win suggests, but it seems a form of foolery: "She's my match, indeed, and as little wit as I," chortles John (1.4.105). In this world, pleasure in marriage is incidental and fugitive, not one of its fundamental aims.

The fair contrasts sharply with the rigidly rule-bound world we see in act 1. The fair lasted only a few days a year, and in Jonson's play, its brevity affects everything

View of the Bear Garden, Southwark. In bearbaiting, a popular gambling entertainment in early modern England, a bear was tied to a post and then set on by a pack of dogs. The Hope Theater, built on the site of the Bear Garden when that building was torn down in 1613, served both as a bear-baiting arena and as the theater where *Bartholomew Fair* was publicly performed in 1614. See the Induction, lines 50–52.

about it. Land—the most permanent, least alienable possession for the prosperous classes—is rented at the fair. Although fair workers are not indigent by early modern standards, they own moveable chattels rather than real estate: easily disassembled booths, cooking equipment, puppets. What they sell is likewise designed for short-term enjoyment: pork, pears, gingerbread, cheap toys, puppet plays, the chance to see a freak or hear a ballad. Because nomads populate the fair, it must even have its own legal arrangements, for when no one is in residence for long, justice must be summarily dispensed. Justice Overdo thus presides over the Court of Piepowders, a court specially convened during the fair; "piepowders" is a corruption of the French phrase *pied poudreux* and refers to the dusty feet of people continually on the move.

The fair apparently recycles many of the same characters from year to year. Justice Overdo notes of the redoubtable Ursula, who supposedly makes her money selling roast pork but who also runs a brothel and serves as a receiver for stolen goods, that she "hath been before me, punk, pinnace, and bawd, any time these two-and-twenty years" (2.2.75–77). Similarly, Wasp remarks that "the bull with five legs and two pizzles . . . was a calf at Uxbridge Fair two years agone" (5.4.85–86). Still, the oppressively indestructible family ties that feature so prominently in *Bartholomew Fair*'s first act seem ill suited to this transitory place. Relationships are typically provisional: between seller and client, employer and employee, whore and john, performer and auditor, shark and gull, as well as between partners in crime and commercial competitors. Some connections are mutually advantageous, others antagonistic or victimizing, but all are short term. The characters are thus constantly shuffling themselves into new configurations. In the scenes at the fair, Jonson does not follow a single protagonist or group of characters for long, but instead interlaces numerous, apparently random moments of unexpected interaction among the various members of the play's enormous cast.

Quite possibly Jonson employed a staging technique common on the medieval stage but rare in his own time to facilitate these swift rearrangements of personnel. The various locations at the fair—the gingerbread basket, the toy stall, Ursula's booth, the stocks, and so on—were most likely all represented onstage at once for the last four acts of the play. Although at scene changes the focus shifts from one part of the stage to another, many of the characters are continually present. This staging not only effectively conveys a sense of tightly packed urban space but also enables almost effortless crosscutting between various subplots and groups of characters. We see such a moment in act 2, scene 5, when Ursula falls with the scalding pan and burns herself. The gingerbread-seller Joan Trash, who has not spoken or called attention to herself since the beginning of the previous scene but who is presumably sitting only a few feet away, instantly responds to her screams.

Not only groups and relationships but also selves are fluctuating and inconstant at the fair. As Ursula's customers drink more and more ale, they amuse themselves by playing the "game of vapors," in which each man contradicts what is said by the one before him (4.4.16–139). Although each participant is soon denying what he himself asserted only moments before, he fails to notice the inconsistency, because in this environment, consistency is not a trait to be desired. Consciousness narrows down to an intense experience of the present moment, from which awareness of a larger context is excluded: an experience of drunkenness, orgasm, aesthetic rapture, or acquisitive bliss. As Jonson notes in his stage direction, the result is "*nonsense*" (4.4.29.2)—a radical lack of continuity from moment to moment. Self-loss is perhaps both the scariest and the most alluring commodity the fair has on offer.

The fair's transitory quality poses a challenge to traditional ethics, which typically value durable human relationships more highly than casual, fleeting ones. In time-honored carnivalian fashion, the fair overturns "normal" hierarchies and assumptions. The common becomes absurd, the low dominates the high, mutability trumps permanence, and the everyday seems almost impossibly strange. In practical terms, many characters that thrive in the world of the London courts flounder at the fair, while incompetents flourish. The childish Bartholomew Cokes, for instance, is in his element, because he is easily distracted by novelty, has little memory for the past or concern for the future, and has no conception of long-range value. He rushes gleefully from one experience to the next, and though the pickpocket Edgeworth steals both his purses and almost all his valuable clothing, he cannot be dejected more than momentarily. Likewise, John Littlewit's limited intelligence suits him perfectly for writing the kind of puppet play that fairgoers enjoy.

Meanwhile, the fair chastens those who function, or would like to function, as authority figures: Zeal-of-the-land Busy, a Puritan preacher; the overweening Justice Overdo; and Humphrey Wasp, Bartholomew Cokes's caretaker. All of these elders attempt to ride herd on the young; all of them end the play publicly humiliated and stripped of their pretensions. Their failure to command respect at the fair is partly ascribable to the way carnival erodes incentives for obedience. Authorities typically either invoke the power of precedent, insist on their own power over the future, or both. Busy, for instance, threatens damnation and promises salvation. Overdo wields the power of secular punishment and plots a way to incorporate Grace and her money into his family. Wasp's supervision of the refractory Cokes retains vestiges of a humanist pedagogical agenda, in which the mentorship of an older, wiser man improves the mind and habits of a younger one. But in a world in which the past is hazy and the future hardly matters, these authority figures cannot obtain a purchase on the imaginations of their subjects. Only a madman, Troubleall, wanders through the fair searching for a "warrant," for the permission of an authority. For everyone else, the fair's attraction is that it makes warrants unnecessary.

Still, the irrelevance of reward and punishment in the world of the fair is not the only, or even the main, reason for the failure of authority. When only the present matters, the only motive to action is appetite—for food, for sex, for novelty, for triumph over others. The authority figures in the play, despite their pretensions, are at least as susceptible to such appetites as their subjects are. Wasp imagines grandiosely that "The whole care of [Cokes's] well-doing is now mine" (1.4.71–72), but at the fair, he abandons his vigilance and plunges, almost as enthusiastically as his protégé, into its various pleasures: quarreling, getting drunk, spewing profanity, enjoying the puppet play. Although Wasp accurately observes of Cokes that "If a leg or an arm on him did not grow on, he would lose it i'the press" (1.5.113–14), it is Wasp himself who, distracted by a brawl, fails to notice Edgeworth stealing the marriage license. When he learns, late in the play, that Cokes saw him set in the stocks—a humiliating punishment usually reserved for the lower orders—Wasp ruefully acknowledges, "I must think no longer to reign; my government is at an end. He that will correct another must want fault himself" (5.4.98–100).

Justice Overdo is, even more than Wasp, a casualty of his own overweening. While Wasp merely thinks he can chaperon a single young fool, Overdo believes he can effectively supervise the entire fair. Worried that the Court of Piepowders fails to curb the fair's "enormities," he plans not merely to punish offenses brought to his attention by others but actively to detect wrongdoing himself. Like the Duke in Shakespeare's *Measure for Measure,* he disguises himself and circulates incognito among his subjects. Armed by his secretly obtained knowledge, he imagines, he will bring all to rights. His illusions about himself and others derive from two sources: Roman history, which renders him patterns of heroic statesmanship, and contemporary plays, which afford him images of concealed truth and reversed fortunes. When he encounters adversity, as he does repeatedly—he is beaten, accused of stealing purses, and set in the stocks—he cheers himself up by quoting Stoic tags from Roman philosophers. Intoxicated by a combination of officiousness and a plethora of inapposite stories, he imagines that Edgeworth is a young gentleman led astray by debauched company, as Hal pretends to be in Shakespeare's *Henry IV* plays, and that Quarlous, disguised as the madman Troubleall, urgently needs his help to regain his wits. At the end of the play, he, like Wasp, must recognize his failure and, at the same time, relinquish his sense of his own superiority.

Busy, the most savagely satirized of the trio, combines Wasp's impetuousness with Overdo's delusions of self-importance. While the established church insisted that its clergy's religious authority be based on education and social position, radical Puritans like Busy claimed that such "external" qualifications had little to do with godliness. Instead, Busy bases his claim to spiritual leadership on his own supposedly immediate relationship with God, a relationship evidenced by his allegedly exemplary sanctity. However, he is a glutton who craves pig more helplessly than Win does. "[T]wo and a half he eat to his share!" marvels the horse-dealer Knockem. "And he has drunk a pailful. He eats with his eyes, as well as his teeth" (3.6.47–48). When Busy's pretense of sanctity fails, as it does so spectacularly in the course of *Bartholomew Fair,* his claim to religious authority necessarily collapses at the same time.

At the fair, then, the supremacy of appetite, the inescapability of bodily need, and the natural tendency to exaggerate one's own importance at the expense of others all give the lie to bourgeois and aristocratic hierarchies of value. Jonson is never sentimental about marriage, and in act 1 of *Bartholomew Fair,* the outright purchase of a ward, the hunting of widows, and the ambiguous byplay between Win Littlewit and her husband's friends already blur the distinction between marriage and whoredom. At the fair, the distinction is more than blurred; it is erased as the two London wives, Win and Mistress Overdo, are recruited as prostitutes. It would be easy to see the behavior of both women as self-interested—following rules, the first act suggests, avails women little in securing their own agency. But the women's capitulation is not a knowing choice; it is the mute insurgence of bodies incontinent in every sense of the word. Both men and women get drunk at the fair, but only the women urinate and vomit uncontrollably. Smithfield was originally a livestock market, and Knockem's mock blazon describes Win as a filly, physically delectable but apparently lacking any rational capacity whatsoever: a "delicate dark chestnut . . . with the fine lean head, large forehead, round eyes, even mouth, sharp ears, long neck, thin crest, close withers, plain back, deep sides, short fillets, and full flanks; with a round belly, a plump buttock, large thighs, knit knees, straight legs, short pasterns, smooth hoofs, and short heels" (4.5.20–26). Again and again in *Bartholomew Fair,* women are their bodies' victims. In a play that both celebrates and fears loss of control, perhaps women function as scapegoats, drawing off some of the more disturbingly dehumanizing aspects of carnival revelry.

Ursula, the pig-woman, both ratifies and challenges this misogynist state of affairs. The connection between femaleness and bestiality is especially obvious in her case: not only in her association with the pigs she roasts and sells but in the imagery associated with her first name. "Ursula" in Latin means "she-bear," and Ursula's customers and associates bait her as if she were one of those unfortunate animals that, in Jacobean England, were chained to a stake and made to fight mastiffs in sport. But like the best sort of bear, Ursula gives as good as she gets, or better. She has a gift for deriving agency and power from the very symbolic mechanisms that seem to deny her that power. Unlike the bourgeois women, Ursula not only embodies appetite but makes money from it: selling food, drink, and sex; exchanging stolen goods; profiting from what other people consider shameful. Gargantuan, sweaty, lowborn, foulmouthed, domineering, promiscuous, and uninhibited by anything resembling principle, Ursula represents everything early modern Englishmen ordinarily thought they despised, especially in a woman. But in the topsy-turvy world of the fair, the pig-woman rules. "Thou shalt sit i'thy chair, and give directions, and shine Ursa Major," declares the horse-dealer Knockem (2.5.186–87).

Standing a bit apart from this stew of appetite is the trio of Grace Wellborn, Winwife, and Quarlous. Grace eludes the degradation that engulfs the other women, but at a price. Her fastidiousness comes across, in this environment, less as good sense than as a priggish recoiling from pleasure. Nonetheless, she does, to some extent, recognize that when one comes to the fair one submits oneself to its preposterous rules. In the London world, her status as a ward gives her almost no scope for independent action. In the world of the fair, unlike the other women, Grace acquires a bit of autonomy, but she immediately deputizes her freedom, leaving her choice of husband to a madman. This dubious procedure, however, produces a satisfactory result. She ends the play coupled with her male counterpart, the class-conscious, slightly prissy Winwife, a romantic despite himself.

Quarlous is the character who most clearly prospers from his day at the fair. His success is due not to any authoritative status but to an entrepreneurial temperament—a combination of contentiousness, wit, observational acuity, and unabashed self-interest that suits him well for the opportunities the fair presents. We recognize his differences from the other bourgeois characters in his interactions with the pickpocket Edgeworth. Edgeworth entirely deludes Justice Overdo, who believes he is a gentleman led astray; the more discerning Winwife notices the pickpocket at work but merely takes an aesthetic pleasure in his skill. Quarlous, by contrast, is not content just to possess knowledge, but immediately figures out how to exploit it, and so blackmails Edgeworth into stealing Cokes's marriage license for him. A former law student, Quarlous has enough sense of the future to strategize, but he is inhibited neither by principle nor by a need for consistency. In act 5, he embarks on exactly the course of action he noisily deplored to Winwife in act 1: marriage to Dame Purecraft, the rich widow. It is an appropriate match, since Purecraft's commercial wiliness and veneer of respectability matches his own. Moreover, Quarlous's lack of emotional range prevents him from comprehending what he might be missing.

The scattered characters begin to reassemble in act 5, scene 4, as Leatherhead prepares to stage Littlewit's puppet play: a version of Hero and Leander "made . . . easy and modern for the times . . . As, for the Hellespont I imagine our Thames here; and then Leander I make a dyer's son, about Puddle Wharf; and Hero a wench o'the Bankside" (5.3.121–25). The classical love story is not only "Anglicized" but debased, as if, in the contemporary world, heroic possibility seems impossibly anachronistic. Like most plays within plays, this puppet show reflects on its dramatic context. In many ways it reproduces the fair world itself, with its untrammeled appetites, gratuitous violence, pointless verbosity, and lack of refined feeling. Just as Jonson, in the Induction to the play, raises the issue of decorum, of writing to the "meridian" of his audience (line 56), so Leatherhead and Littlewit must make those calculations too.

In the original Hero and Leander story, the presiding deities were Venus and Neptune, gods of love and the sea. In the puppet play the genius loci is, appropriately enough, Dionysius—the name not only of a famous tyrant of Syracuse, but also of the god of intoxication, partying, and excess. The debate between Busy and Puppet Dionysius about theatrical idolatry is one of several important climaxes toward the end of the play. The puppet defeats Busy, ironically, not by denying that he is an idol, but by proving that he is one: that he is a mere piece of wood, taken for real. Busy, in debating him, is himself an idolater, a person who imagines that inanimate things have the characteristics of human or divine beings. In other words, Dionysius does not attempt to argue that theater escapes idolatry, but rather that everyone is an idolater and that every activity has its idolatrous aspect. There is therefore no point in stigmatizing particular people or activities as especially reprehensible.

Dionysius' "plain demonstration" (5.5.106) effectively silences Busy because it strikes at the heart of the Puritan's most basic commitments. Busy belongs to a sect of Protestants that insists—unlike the Church of England, which welcomes almost everybody—that the church should consist only of the godly. This conviction is possible only for those confident of their ability to separate the good from the bad, the saved from the damned. But in the world of *Bartholomew Fair*, no one—least of all the people who set themselves up as authorities—has the capacity to make such judgments. The self-styled authorities are too deeply implicated in the very behaviors and attitudes they decry, and the situations they attempt to evaluate are too opaque.

We see the same radical skepticism about judgment in the last scene. Overdo, still in the grip of his fantasy of judicial omnipotence, begins to sort the characters into groups. He clearly believes that he is preparing for the kind of climactic final judgment that typically ends "ruler in disguise" plays, when the duke or king visits appropriate punishments on malefactors and demonstrates the ascendance of the proper authorities. But then his wife's drunken vomiting reveals her as one of the prostitutes in Knockem's stable, and he is shamed and silenced. The judgment scene turns into something quite different, as Overdo acknowledges his inability to judge. The play ends with his blanket invitation to dinner: "I will have none fear to go along" (5.6.120). The carnival world of the fair prepares to decamp, and its denizens to move into, or back into, the settled world of prosperous London, perhaps to undo some of its repressiveness.

Jonson's previous plays have each invariably ended in some kind of trial scene, and even when the revelations and punishments are partial or biased, the basic premise seems to be that some distinction can be made between the worthy and the unworthy. But *Bartholomew Fair* runs roughshod over ways of discriminating between kinds of people: over distinctions between wit and fool, saint and idolater, criminal and law-abider, gentleman and knave. A satiric play apparently devoted to the premise that judgment is impossible, *Bartholomew Fair* puts its author in a curious position. Satire is, by its very nature, a genre that passes judgment on others. Is the satiric artist somehow exempt from the laws to which all the characters in his play must submit? Or does the play's wholesale attack on authority and discrimination compromise the position of the "master poet," as Jonson, never one for false modesty, calls himself in the Induction? On the one hand, Jonson seems sympathetic to what the fair has to offer: pleasure in the present, distrust of permanence, disregard for law, disrespect for authority. On the other hand, his very representation of the fair's carnival anarchy requires him to be aware of an alternative. Only someone aware of the absurdities of the game of vapors—as its players are not—is in a position to call it "*nonsense*," Jonson's word for it in his stage direction (4.4.29.2).

Jonson, then, seems to stand outside the world he represents, but at the same time satirizes fantasies of self-exemption. In the much-abused authority figures in the play, we see traces of self-representation. Like Justice Overdo, Jonson was fond of seeing his own career in the heroic terms of classical precedent. Like Busy, he preached temperance but was in fact a man of strong appetites liberally indulged. Like Wasp, Jonson was the chaperone to a young scapegrace, the son of Sir Walter Raleigh. On a supposedly educational trip to the Continent, young "Wat," Jonson told his friend William Drummond, "caused him to be drunken and dead drunk," loaded him into a cart, and paraded him through the streets of Paris, "at every corner showing his governor stretched out, and telling them that it was a more lively image of the crucifix than any they had."[1] In *Bartholomew Fair,* Jonson seems to ridicule not only the world of the fair and the pretensions of the fairgoers but all those who would claim to evaluate and deplore it, including himself.

To some readers and audiences, *Bartholomew Fair* represents a welcome loosening of Jonson's more typically judgmental stance, while to others, the play has seemed less to celebrate human frailty than to accept it with disgusted resignation. Perhaps Jonson renounces his earlier moralism not because he doubts his own ability to diagnose human failings but because he no longer believes that his audience will reform its manners in response to his critique. Nine years before, in the prefatory epistle to *Volpone,* Jonson described what he then saw as the poet's function: to "inform young men to all good disciplines, inflame grown men to all great virtues, keep old men in their best and supreme state, or, as they decline to childhood, recover them to their first strength" (lines 24–27). In those days, Jonson imagined himself to be "the interpreter and arbiter of nature, a teacher of things divine no less than human, a master in manners, [who] can alone, or with a few, effect the business of mankind" (*Volpone,*

1. *Conversations with Drummond,* lines 247–51.

Prefatory Epistle, lines 27–30). By 1614, Jonson seems to have revised this heroic conception of the solitary genius, given the realities of the commercial, collaborative theater world in which he had to work. In the Induction to *Bartholomew Fair*, Jonson playfully replaces that vision of the poet's task with a mock contract that attempts to regulate what cannot be regulated: the spectator's unpredictable, uncontrollable responses, upon which the success or failure of the "master poet" will, finally, depend.

BEN JONSON

Bartholomew Fair

THE PERSONS OF THE PLAY

[PROLOGUE]
[STAGE-KEEPER° } [persons in the Induction] — *stagehand*
BOOK-HOLDER° — *prompter*
SCRIVENER]° — *scribe, copyist*
John LITTLEWIT, a proctor[1]
[SOLOMON, his manservant]
WIN[-the-fight] Littlewit, his wife
Dame PURECRAFT, her mother and a widow
Zeal-of-the-land BUSY, her suitor, a Banbury° man — *a Puritan center*
[Ned] WINWIFE, his rival, a gentleman
[Tom] QUARLOUS, his° companion, a gamester° — *(Winwife's) / rake*
Bartholomew COKES,° an esquire of Harrow — *"fool, coxcomb"*
Humphrey WASP, his man° — *servant*
[JUSTICE] Adam OVERDO, a justice of peace
DAME [Alice] OVERDO, his wife [and Cokes's sister]
GRACE Wellborn, his ward
Lantern LEATHERHEAD, a hobbyhorse-seller
JOAN TRASH, a gingerbread-woman
Ezekiel EDGEWORTH, a cutpurse
NIGHTINGALE, a ballad singer
URSULA, a pig-woman[2]
MOONCALF,° her tapster — *"congenital idiot"*
Jordan KNOCKEM, a horse-courser° and ranger[3] o'Turnbull — *horse-dealer*
Val CUTTING,° a roarer° — *"bullying" / brawler*
Captain WHIT, a bawd° — *pimp*
Punk° ALICE, mistress o'the game° — *whore / prostitute*
TROUBLEALL, a madman

The original title page reads "*Bartholomew Fair:* a comedy, acted in the year 1614. By the Lady Elizabeth's Servants, and then dedicated to King James, of most blessed memory, by the author, Benjamin Jonson.

Si foret in terris, rideret Democritus: nam
Spectaret populum ludis attentiùs ipsis,
Ut sibi praebentem, mimo spectacula plura.
Scriptores autem narrare putaret assello
Fabellam surdo.—Horace, Liber 2, Epist. 1.

London. Printed by J. B. for Robert Allot, and are to be sold at the sign of the Bear, in Paul's Churchyard, 1631."

(The quotation from Horace substitutes "*nam*" [either; whether] in the first line for Horace's "*seu*" [for], and then omits two lines in the Horace passage. A translation of the original is as follows: If Democritus [the so-called laughing philosopher] were still on earth, he would laugh: whether it were some hybrid monster, such as a panther bred with a camel [i.e., the giraffe, known as the cameleopard], or a white elephant that caught the eye of the crowd, he would center his attention more intently on the people than on the play itself, as yielding him the more rewarding spectacle. As for the authors, he would suppose them to be telling their story to a deaf ass.)

The Persons of the Play.
1. Agent or attorney to an ecclesiastical court.
2. A seller of pig meat. "Ursula" = "she-bear."
3. (1) Park-keeper; (2) lothario. Turnbull Street was a red-light district.

[Toby HAGGIS
Davy BRISTLE } watchmen, three
POACHER, a beadle]° — *underbailiff*
COSTERMONGER° — *fruit-seller*
MOUSETRAP-MAN
[NORTHERN, a] clothier
[CORN-CUTTER][4]
[PUPPY, a] wrestler
Porters
[FILCHER
SHARKWELL] } doorkeepers[5]
PUPPETS
[Passengers or passersby, boys or urchins]
[EPILOGUE]

[THE SCENE: London, and Smithfield, near London.]

The Prologue to the King's Majesty[1]

[*Enter the Prologue.*]

PROLOGUE Your Majesty is welcome to a fair.
Such place, such men, such language, and such ware
You must expect; with these, the zealous noise
Of your land's faction,° scandalized at toys,° — *the Puritans / trifles*
As babies,° hobbyhorses,[2] puppet plays, — *dolls, puppets*
And suchlike rage,° whereof the petulant ways — *senseless fury*
Yourself have known, and have been vexed with long.[3]
These for your sport, without particular wrong° — *individual satire*
Or just complaint of any private man
Who of himself or° shall think well or can,[4] — *either*
The maker° doth present, and hopes tonight — *dramatist, poet*
To give you, for a fairing,° true delight. [*Exit.*] — *gift bought at a fair*

The Induction on the Stage

[*Enter the*] *Stage-keeper.*

STAGE-KEEPER [*to the spectators*] Gentlemen, have a little patience; they are e'en upon° coming, instantly. He that should begin the play, Master Littlewit, the proctor, has a stitch new fall'n° in his black silk stocking; 'twill be drawn° up ere you can tell° twenty. He plays one o'the Arches,[1] that dwells about the hospital,° and he has a very pretty part. But for the whole play, will you ha' the truth on't? (I am looking, lest the poet hear me, or his man, Master Brome,[2] behind

just on the point of / *pulled loose / sewn* / *count* / *(St. Bartholomew's)*

4. One who trims corns on feet and toes; see 2.4.6.
5. Theater ticket-sellers. A "shark" is a card shark, or cardsharp.

The Prologue.
1. Performed at court, November 1, 1614, after opening at the Hope Theater on October 31.
2. Morris dancers costumed in wickerwork to look like horses.
3. King James I made no secret of his dislike of Puritan objections to holidays and playacting.
4. Who has just reason to think himself a decent person.

The Induction.
1. Legal practitioners in the ecclesiastical court known as Arches because of its location at a church with an arched steeple.
2. Richard Brome assisted Jonson and was later a playwright on his own.

the arras.)° It is like° to be a very conceited scurvy one, in plain English. When't comes to the fair once,° you were e'en as good go to Virginia, for anything there is of Smithfield.[3] He has not hit the humors;° he does not know 'em. He has not conversed with the Barthol'mew birds,° as they say. He has ne'er a sword-and-buckler man° in his fair, nor a little Davy[4] to take toll o'the bawds there, as in my time, nor a kind-heart,° if anybody's teeth should chance to ache in his play. Nor a juggler with a well-educated ape to come° over the chain for the King of England and back again for the Prince, and sit still on his arse for the Pope and the King of Spain. None o'these fine sights. Nor has he the canvas cut i'the night for a hobbyhorse-man° to creep in to his she-neighbor and take his leap° there. Nothing! No. An° some writer that I know had had but the penning o'this matter, he would ha' made you such a jig-a-jog i'the booths,[5] you should ha' thought an earthquake had been i'the fair. But these master poets, they will ha' their own absurd courses; they will be informed of nothing. He has, sir-reverence,° kicked me three or four times about the tiring-house,° I thank him, for but offering to put in° with my experience. I'll be judged by you, gentlemen, now, but° for one conceit° of mine. Would not a fine pump upon the stage ha' done well for a property, now? And a punk° set under upon her head, with her stern upward, and ha' been soused by my witty young masters o'the Inns o'Court?[6] What think you o'this for a show, now? He will not hear o'this. I am an ass, I! And yet I kept° the stage in Master Tarlton's[7] time, I thank my stars. Ho! An that man had lived to have played in *Barthol'mew Fair,* you should ha' seen him ha' come in and ha' been cozened° i'the cloth-quarter[8] so finely! And Adams,[9] the rogue, ha'° leaped and capered upon him, and ha' dealt his vermin° about as though they had cost him nothing. And then a substantial watch° to ha' stol'n in upon 'em and taken 'em away, with mistaking words,° as the fashion is in the stage practice.

tapestry hanging / likely
As for the fair
personality tics
Bartholomew denizens
swashbuckler
itinerant tooth-drawer
jump
woman-chaser
sexual pleasure / If
pardon my saying it
actors' dressing area
put in my oar, interfere
only / clever notion
whore
tended to
cheated, fleeced
would have
scattered his fleas
group of watchmen
comic malapropisms

[*Enter the*] *Book-holder*° [*and*] *Scrivener to him.*

prompter

BOOK-HOLDER How now? What rare° discourse are you fall'n upon, ha? Ha' you found any familiars° here, that you are so free? What's the business?

excellent (ironic)
chums; attendant devils

STAGE-KEEPER Nothing, but the understanding gentlemen o'the ground° here asked my judgment.

groundlings, spectators

BOOK-HOLDER Your judgment, rascal? For what? Sweeping the stage? Or gathering up the broken apples for the bears within?[1] Away, rogue! It's come to a fine degree° in these

state of affairs

3. The Stage-keeper complains that the play no more resembles Smithfield, the actual site of Bartholomew Fair, than does the newly established colony of Virginia.
4. A notorious London bully, here described as one who extorts money from the prostitutes he manages.
5. He would have set up quite a jiggling (from sexual activity) in the fair booths.
6. Residents of London's law school buildings were much given to rowdy entertainment. Here they are imagined as taking part in publicly humiliating a whore by dousing her, bottom side up, with a water pump set up onstage.
7. The leading comic actor of the Queen's Men in the 1580s—quite some time before this play.
8. Section of the fair for selling cloth—and where, according to a familiar anecdote, Tarlton was tricked out of his clothes.
9. John Adams also acted with the Queen's Men. See note 7 above.
1. The Hope Theater on the Bankside (the south bank of the Thames), where this play was publicly performed, also served as a bearbaiting arena.

spectacles when such a youth° as you pretend to a judgment. [*Exit Stage-keeper.*] — *(ironic)*

[*To the spectators*] And yet he may, i'the most o'this matter, i'faith, for the author hath writ it just to his meridian° and the scale of the grounded judgments° here, his playfellows in wit. Gentlemen, not for want° of a prologue, but by way of a new one, I am sent out to you here, with a scrivener and certain articles drawn out in haste between our author and you, which, if you please to hear, and as they appear reasonable to approve of, the play will follow presently.—Read, scribe. Gi' me the counterpane.[2]

level of understanding / *groundlings' taste* / *lack*

SCRIVENER [*reading*] Articles of agreement, indented,° between the spectators or hearers at the Hope on the Bankside, in the County of Surrey, on the one party,° and the author of *Barthol'mew Fair,* in the said° place and county, on the other party, the one-and-thirtieth day of October, 1614, and in the twelfth year of the reign of our sovereign lord, James, by the grace of God, King of England, France, and Ireland, Defender of the Faith, and of Scotland the seven-and-fortieth.

(see 63 n) / *side of the agreement* / *aforesaid*

Inprimis,° It is covenanted and agreed, by and between the parties abovesaid, that the said spectators and hearers, as well° the curious° and envious° as the favoring and judicious, as also the grounded° judgments and understandings, do for themselves severally° covenant and agree to remain in the places their money or friends have put them in, with patience, for the space of two hours and an half and somewhat more. In which time the author promiseth to present them, by us, with a new, sufficient° play called *Barthol'mew Fair,* merry, and as full of noise as sport, made to delight all and to offend none, provided they have either the wit or the honesty to think well of themselves.

Imprimis, first / *both / carping / hostile* / *well-set; groundling* / *individually* / *up-to-standard*

It is further agreed that every person here have his or their free will of censure,° to like or dislike at their own charge, the author having now departed with° his right. It shall be lawful for any man to judge his sixpenn'orth,[3] his twelvepenn'orth, so to his eighteenpence, two shillings, half a crown, to the value of his place, provided always his place get not above his wit.° And if he pay for half a dozen, he may censure for all them too, so° that he will undertake that they shall be silent. He shall put in for censures here, as they do for lots at the lottery.[4] Marry,° if he drop but sixpence at the door, and will censure a crown's worth, it is thought there is no conscience or justice in that.

judgment / *surrendered* / *intelligence* / *provided* / *By Mary (an oath)*

It is also agreed that every man here exercise his own judgment, and not censure by contagion,° or upon trust, from another's voice, or face, that sits by him, be he never so first in the commission of wit.° As also that he be fixed and settled in his censure, that what he approves or not approves today he will do the same tomorrow, and if tomor-

infectious influence / *a body of critics*

2. The counterpart of an indenture, which was written in duplicate and divided in two along a jagged line so that each party could prove partnership in the document.
3. This is rather higher than the penny charged for the least expensive admission at such theaters as the Globe in the 1600s.
4. Royally sponsored lotteries helped finance the Virginia plantation.

row, the next day, and so the next week if need be; and not to be brought about by any that sits on the bench° with him, though they indite and arraign plays daily. He that will swear *Jeronimo* or *Andronicus*[5] are the best plays yet shall pass unexcepted at° here as a man whose judgment shows it is constant and hath stood still these five-and-twenty or thirty years. Though it be an ignorance, it is a virtuous and staid° ignorance; and, next to truth, a confirmed error does well. Such a one the author knows where to find him.

seat; legal bench
unobjected to
steadfast; prim

It is further covenanted, concluded, and agreed that, how great soever the expectation be, no person here is to expect more than he knows or better ware than a fair will afford, neither to look back to the sword-and-buckler age of Smithfield, but content himself with the present. Instead of a little Davy to take toll o'the bawds,° the author doth promise a strutting horse-courser, with a leer° drunkard, two or three to attend him in as good equipage as you would wish. And then for° Kind-heart the tooth-drawer,° a fine oily pig-woman with her tapster to bid you welcome, and a consort of roarers° for music. A wise justice of peace *meditant*[6] instead of a juggler with an ape. A civil cutpurse *searchant*.° A sweet singer of new ballads *allurant*° and as fresh an hypocrite as ever was broached *rampant*.° If there be never a servant-monster[7] i'the fair, who can help it? he says; nor a nest of antics?° He is loath to make Nature afraid in his plays, like those that beget tales, tempests, and suchlike drolleries, to mix his head with other men's heels,[8] let the concupiscence of° jigs and dances reign as strong as it will amongst you. Yet if the puppets will please anybody, they shall be entreated to come in.

(see 14–15 and n)
sly
instead of / (see 16)
gang of brawlers
searching (for purses)
enticing (the gullible)
rearing up
weird dancers, clowns
popular demand for

In consideration of which it is finally agreed, by the foresaid hearers and spectators, that they neither in themselves conceal, nor suffer° by them to be concealed, any state decipherer or politic picklock[9] of the scene so solemnly ridiculous as to search out who was meant by the gingerbread-woman, who by the hobbyhorse-man, who by the costermonger—nay, who by their wares. Or that will pretend to affirm, on his own inspired ignorance, what Mirror of Magistrates[1] is meant by the justice, what great lady by the pig-woman, what concealed statesman by the seller of mousetraps, and so of the rest. But that such person or persons so found be left discovered to the mercy of the author, as a forfeiture to the stage and your laughter aforesaid.[2] As also, such as shall so desperately or ambitiously play the fool

permit

5. Shakespeare's *Titus Andronicus* (from perhaps as early as 1589). *Jeronimo* refers to Thomas Kyd's *The Spanish Tragedy* (from the 1580s, by the time of *Bartholomew Fair* an old-fashioned play).
6. Meditating. The articles of agreement here employ mock-heraldic terms to denote character types at the fair.
7. Caliban in Shakespeare's *The Tempest* is servant (and slave) to Prospero and is often called a monster because he appears strange to the Europeans. He is plainly alluded to here and in lines 127–28, along with *The Winter's Tale* and similar romances.
8. The playwright is loath to bring himself down to the level of kissing his audience's feet or being kicked at by them.
9. Officious would-be discoverer of hidden political meaning.
1. What a paragon of a magistrate. Named after an enduringly popular sixteenth-century lesson book for those in power, filled with object lessons of the abuse of authority.
2. Any such would-be decipherer is to be identified by the audience to the playwright and left to his tender mercies, as a fit punishment in the name of the stage and the audience's satirical laughter.

by his place aforesaid, to challenge° the author of scurrility — *accuse*
because the language somewhere savors of Smithfield, the
booth, and the pig broth, or of profaneness because a madman cries "God quit° you" or "bless you."[3] — *requite, reward*

In witness whereof, as° you have preposterously[4] put to — *inasmuch as*
your seals already (which is your money), you will now add
the other part of suffrage,° your hands.° The play shall pres- — *approval / applause*
ently begin. And though the fair be not kept in the same
region that some here perhaps would have it, yet think that
therein the author hath observed a special decorum,° the — *fitness*
place° being as dirty as Smithfield and as stinking every — *(Hope Theater)*
whit.° — *bit*

Howsoever, he prays you to believe his ware is still the
same;° else you will make him justly suspect that he° that is — *(as advertised) / (anyone)*
so loath to look on a baby° or an hobbyhorse here would be — *doll, puppet*
glad to take up a commodity of them,[5] at any laughter or
loss, in another place. [*Exeunt.*]

1.1

[*Enter*] *Littlewit.*

LITTLEWIT [*examining a marriage license he has just drawn up*] A pretty conceit,° and worth the finding! I ha' such — *word game, witticism*
luck to spin out these fine things still, and, like a silkworm,
out of myself. Here's Master Bartholomew Cokes, of Harrow
o'th'Hill, i'th' County of Middlesex, Esquire, takes forth his
license to marry Mistress Grace Wellborn of the said place
and county. And when does he take it forth? Today, the four-
and-twentieth of August: Barthol'mew Day! Barthol'mew
upon Barthol'mew! There's the device!° Who would have — *wordplay*
marked such a leapfrog chance° now? A very less than ames- — *long shot*
ace, on two dice.[1] Well, go thy ways,° John Littlewit, Proctor — *get along with you*
John Littlewit: one o'the pretty wits o'Paul's,[2] the Little Wit
of London (so thou art called) and something beside.° When — *other names too*
a quirk or a quiblin° does scape thee, and thou dost not — *quibble*
watch and apprehend it and bring it afore the constable of
conceit—there now, I speak quib° too—let 'em carry thee — *speak in word games*
out o'the Archdeacon's court° into his kitchen and make a — *Court of Arches*
jack° of thee instead of a John.—There I am again, la!° — *knave; spit-turner / indeed*

[*Enter*] *to him, Win* [*wearing a velvet cap*].

Win! Good morrow, Win. Ay, marry, Win, now you look
finely indeed, Win. This cap does convince!° You'd not ha' — *looks stunning*
worn it, Win, nor ha' had it velvet, but a rough country
beaver,° with a copper band, like the coney-skin woman of — *rustic beaver hat*
Budge Row.[3] Sweet Win, let me kiss it!° And her fine high — *kiss you (baby talk)*

3. The articles protest against the picayune way in which the act forbidding the naming of the Deity onstage (the Act to Restrain Abuses of Players, 1606) could be used to censor harmless colloquial speech.
4. In the wrong order. The spectators have paid before signing (i.e., before applauding at the end of the show), reversing the normal course of events in contracts.
5. Literally, would be willing to receive such trash as a loan instead of hard cash—a common swindle, since the goods would be worth far less than the nominal loan, which would have to be repaid in cash. The dramatist implies that his carping critics will have to go elsewhere for entertainment, where they are sure to be fleeced and made to look ridiculous.

1.1. London. The Littlewit household.
1. Truly less than throwing two aces, or ones, which is the lowest throw and doesn't come up very often.
2. The central aisle of Saint Paul's Cathedral was a meeting place for the wits about town.
3. Like the seller of rabbit skins on Budge Row (a street with many skinners' and furriers' shops). Budge is a kind of fur.

shoes, like the Spanish lady![4] Good Win, go° a little. I would fain see thee pace, pretty Win. By this fine cap, I could never leave° kissing on't.°

walk up and down / *leave off / you*

WIN Come, indeed, la, you are such a fool still!

LITTLEWIT No, but half a one, Win. You are the t'other half: man and wife make one fool, Win. (Good!)[5] Is there the proctor, or doctor° indeed, i'the diocese, that ever had the fortune to win him such a Win! (There I am again!)[6] I do feel conceits coming upon me, more than I am able to turn tongue to. A pox° o'these pretenders to wit, your Three Cranes, Mitre, and Mermaid men![7] Not a corn° of true salt nor a grain of right° mustard[8] amongst them all. They may stand° for places or so, again'° the next witfall, and pay two-pence in a quart more for their canary° than other men. But gi' me the man can start up a Justice of Wit out of six-shillings beer, and give the law to[9] all the poets and poet-suckers° i'town. Because they are the players' gossips?[1] 'Slid,° other men have wives as fine as the players and as well dressed. Come hither, Win. [*He kisses her.*]

person of learning / *A curse* / *grain* / *true* / *compete / anticipating* / *wine* / *fledgling poets* / *By God's eyelid*

1.2

[*Enter*] *Winwife.*

WINWIFE Why, how now, Master Littlewit, measuring of lips? Or molding of kisses? Which is it?

LITTLEWIT Troth, I am a little taken with my Win's dressing here. Does 't not fine, Master Winwife? How do you apprehend,° sir? She would not ha' worn this habit.[1] I challenge all Cheapside° to show such another—Moorfields, Pimlico Path, or the Exchange,[2] in a summer evening—with a lace to boot,° as this has.—Dear Win, let Master Winwife kiss you. He comes a-wooing to our mother, Win, and may be our father° perhaps, Win. There's no harm in him, Win.

Would you believe it / *a commercial district* / *trimming as well* / *stepfather*

WINWIFE None i'the earth, Master Littlewit. [*He kisses Win.*]

LITTLEWIT I envy° no man my delicates,° sir.

grudge / delicacies

WINWIFE Alas, you ha' the garden where they grow still: a wife here with a strawberry breath, cherry lips, apricot cheeks, and a soft velvet head like a melocoton.°

hybrid peach and quince

LITTLEWIT Good, i'faith! Now dullness upon me,° that I had not that° before him, that I should not light on't as well as he! "Velvet head"!

may I be struck dull / *that witticism*

WINWIFE But my taste, Master Littlewit, tends to fruit of a later kind: the sober matron, your wife's mother.

LITTLEWIT Ay, we know you are a suitor, sir. Win and I both wish you well. By this license° here, would you had her, that your two names were as fast in it as here are a couple!° Win

(see 1.1.1) / *(Cokes and Grace)*

4. High-heeled shoes were often vanity imports from Spain or Italy.
5. Littlewit admires his own verbal dexterity: man and wife are one in marriage and the result is a "fool," or baby.
6. There I go again, punning on "win" and "Win"!
7. Men who are seen in these most-frequented taverns of London.
8. "Salt" and "mustard" signify sharp, pungent wit.
9. Give me the man who can, when drunk on cheap beer selling for six shillings a barrel, prove himself the nonpareil of wits, and lay down the rules for.
1. Do they (the "pretenders to wit") think they are special simply because they are on familiar terms with the actors?

1.2. The scene continues.
1. Given her Puritan proclivities, Win-the-fight would not have chosen to dress herself in such finery.
2. Various locations in or near London where fashionable ladies might gather.

would fain have a fine young father-i'-law° with a feather,° that her mother might hood it and chain it with Mistress Overdo.[3] But you do not take the right course, Master Winwife.

stepfather / (sign of rank)

WINWIFE No, Master Littlewit? Why?

LITTLEWIT You are not mad enough.

WINWIFE How, is madness a right course?

LITTLEWIT I say nothing, but I wink upon Win. You have a friend, one Master Quarlous, comes here sometimes?

WINWIFE Why, he makes no love to her, does he?

LITTLEWIT Not a tokenworth° that ever I saw, I assure you. But—

i.e., tiny amount

WINWIFE What?

LITTLEWIT He is the more madcap° o'the two. You do not apprehend me.

zany

WIN [*to Littlewit*] You have a hot coal i'your mouth, now; you cannot hold.[4]

LITTLEWIT Let me out with it, dear Win.

WIN I'll tell him myself.

LITTLEWIT Do, and take all the thanks, and much good do° thy pretty heart, Win.

much good may it do

WIN Sir, my mother has had her nativity water cast[5] lately by the cunning men° in Cow Lane, and they ha' told her her fortune, and do ensure her she shall never have happy hour unless she marry within this sen'night,° and when it is, it must be a madman, they say.

fortune-tellers / *week*

LITTLEWIT Ay, but it must be a gentleman madman.

WIN Yes, so the tother man of Moorfields° says.

the other astrologer

WINWIFE But does she believe 'em?

LITTLEWIT Yes, and has been at Bedlam° twice since, every day, to inquire if any gentleman be there, or to come there, mad.

an insane asylum

WINWIFE Why, this is a confederacy,° a mere piece of practice° upon her, by these impostors!

conspiracy / *trickery*

LITTLEWIT I tell her so; or else say I that they mean some young madcap gentleman (for the devil can equivocate,° as well as a shopkeeper), and therefore would I advise you to be a little madder than Master Quarlous hereafter.

use double-talk

WINWIFE Where is she? Stirring yet?

LITTLEWIT Stirring! Yes, and studying an old elder,[6] come from Banbury, a suitor that puts in here at meal-tide° to praise the painful brethren or pray that the sweet singers may be restored;[7] says a grace as long as his breath lasts him. Sometime the spirit is so strong with him, it gets quite out of him, and then my mother, or Win, are fain to fetch° it again with malmsey° or *aqua coelestis*.°

mealtime (a Puritanism) / *restore, revive* / *a sweet wine / brandy*

WIN Yes, indeed, we have such a tedious° life with him for his diet—and his clothes too. He breaks his buttons and cracks seams at every saying he sobs out.

irksome

3. Might dress up in finery befitting her husband's rank so as to compete with the justice's wife.
4. You will insist on telling; you cannot keep a secret.
5. Had her horoscope told by means of urinalysis. (Win is confused about the method; for horoscopes one consults the planets, not the subject's urine.)
6. And taking instruction from an elder of a Puritan congregation.
7. To praise the assiduous and long-suffering or pray that those Puritan ministers who have been ejected from the church for their reforming extremism may be restored to their congregations.

LITTLEWIT He cannot abide my vocation, he says.

WIN No, he told my mother a proctor was a claw of the Beast,[8] and that she had little less than committed abomination in marrying me° so as she has done.

giving me in marriage

LITTLEWIT Every line, he says, that a proctor writes, when it comes to be read in the Bishop's Court, is a long black hair kembed° out of the tail of Antichrist.

combed

WINWIFE When came this proselyte?°

born-again convert

LITTLEWIT Some three days since.

1.3

[*Enter*] *Quarlous.*

QUARLOUS [*to Winwife*] Oh, sir, ha' you ta'en soil° here? It's well a man may reach you, after three hours' running, yet! What an unmerciful companion° art thou, to quit thy lodging at such ungentlemanly hours! None but a scattered covey° of fiddlers, or one of these rag-rakers in dunghills, or some marrowbone-man° at most would have been up when thou wert gone abroad, by all description.° I pray thee, what ailest thou, thou canst not sleep? Hast thou thorns i'thy eyelids, or thistles i'thy bed?

taken refuge in the hunt / *fellow; friend* / *flock* / *rag and bone collector* / *by all accounts*

WINWIFE I cannot tell. It seems you had neither i'your feet, that took this pain° to find me.

this effort

QUARLOUS No. An° I had, all the lyam-hounds° o'the city should have drawn after you by the scent rather.° —Master John Littlewit! God save you, sir. 'Twas a hot night with some of us last night, John. Shall we pluck a hair o'the same wolf° today, Proctor John?

If / bloodhounds / *sooner than I would* / *drink more of the same*

LITTLEWIT Do you remember, Master Quarlous, what we discoursed on last night?

QUARLOUS Not I, John. Nothing that I either discourse or do at those times I forfeit all to forgetfulness.°

I remember nothing

LITTLEWIT No? Not concerning Win? Look you, there she is, and dressed as I told you she should be. Hark you, sir, had you forgot?

QUARLOUS By this head, I'll beware how I keep you company, John, when I drink, an you have this dangerous° memory! That's certain.

dangerously good

LITTLEWIT Why, sir?

QUARLOUS Why? [*To Winwife*] We were all a little stained° last night, sprinkled with a cup or two, and I agreed with Proctor John here to come and do somewhat with Win (I know not what 'twas) today, and he puts me in mind on't now; he says he was coming to fetch me. [*To Littlewit*] Before truth,° if you have that fearful quality, John, to remember when you are sober, John, what you promise drunk, John, I shall take heed of you, John. For this once, I am content to wink at you.° Where's your wife?—Come hither, Win. (*He kisseth her.*)

befuddled with wine / *i.e., Upon my word* / *look the other way*

WIN Why, John! Do you see this, John? Look you! Help me, John!

8. The Beast of the Apocalypse, in the Book of Revelation, identified by Puritans with oppressive Catholic tyranny.
1.3. The scene continues.

LITTLEWIT Oh, Win, fie, what do you mean, Win? Be womanly, Win? Make an outcry to your mother, Win? Master Quarlous is an honest gentleman, and our worshipful° good friend, Win, and he is Master Winwife's friend, too. And Master Winwife comes a suitor to your mother, Win, as I told you before, Win, and may perhaps be our father, Win. They'll do you no harm, Win; they are both our worshipful good friends. Master Quarlous! You must know Master Quarlous, Win; you must not quarrel with Master Quarlous, Win.

worthy

QUARLOUS No, we'll kiss again and fall in.°

make up (and have sex)

[*He kisses her again.*]

LITTLEWIT Yes, do, good Win.

WIN I'faith, you are a fool, John.

LITTLEWIT A fool-John° she calls me. Do you mark that, gentlemen? Pretty Littlewit of velvet! A fool-John!

(an endearment)

QUARLOUS She may call you an apple-John, if you use this.[1]

[*Quarlous and Winwife converse apart.*]

WINWIFE Pray thee forbear, for my respect° somewhat.

sake

QUARLOUS Hoyday! How respective° you are become o'the sudden! I fear this family will turn you reformed° too. Pray you come about° again. Because she° is in possibility to be your daughter-in-law,° and may ask you blessing hereafter when she courts it to Tottenham[2] to eat cream—well, I will forbear, sir, but i'faith, would thou wouldst leave thy exercise of widow-hunting once, this drawing after an old reverend smock by the splayfoot.[3] There cannot be an ancient tripe or trillibub° i'the town but thou art straight nosing it. And 'tis a fine occupation thou'lt confine thyself to when thou hast got one: scrubbing a piece of buff as if thou hadst the perpetuity of Pannier Alley[4] to stink in, or perhaps, worse, currying° a carcass that thou hast bound thyself to alive. I'll be sworn, some of them that thou art, or hast been, a suitor to are so old as no chaste or married pleasure can ever become° 'em; the honest instrument of procreation has, forty years since, left° to belong to 'em. Thou must visit 'em° as thou wouldst do a tomb, with a torch, or three handfuls of link,° flaming hot, and so thou mayst hap to make 'em feel thee, and after come to inherit according to thy inches.° A sweet course for a man to waste the brand° of life for, to be still raking himself a fortune in an old woman's embers!° We shall ha' thee, after thou hast been but a month married to one of 'em, look like the quartan ague° and the black jaundice met in a face,° and walk as if thou hadst borrowed legs of a spinner° and voice of a cricket. I would endure to hear fifteen sermons a week for° her, and such coarse and

concerned about manners / *Puritan* / *turn back / (Win)* / *stepdaughter* / *entrails; bag of guts* / *rubbing down; flattering* / *suit; come to* / *ceased / come to their beds* / *burning torches* / *height; sexual prowess* / *torch, fire* / *decayed sexual body* / *high fever* / *all in one* / *spider* / *sooner than*

1. She may call you a shriveled apple, if you act in this foolish way. (Suggesting a lack of sexual potency, as in a withered old man.)

2. When she petitions in courtierlike fashion to go to Tottenham Court Road (where one could buy cakes and cream).

3. I wish you would leave off, once and for all, your occupation of fortune hunting through marrying a rich widow (and thus gaining, as the husband, control of all her wealth), this hunting after an old, respectable woman with clumsy flat feet. ("The splayfoot" could belong either to the hunter or the widow.)

4. An alley of leather-goods stores and basket-makers. Quarlous compares Winwife to the scrubber of an aging widow's hide, as though she were an old horse and he the "groom." "Perpetuity" means "perpetual tenure."

loud ones as some of 'em° must be. I would e'en desire of fate I might dwell in a drum, and take in my sustenance with an old broken tobacco pipe and a straw. Dost thou ever think to bring thine ears or stomach to the patience° of a dry° grace as long as thy tablecloth, and droned out by thy son,° here, that might be thy father, till all the meat o'thy board has forgot it was that day i'the kitchen?[5] Or to brook° the noise made, in a question of predestination, by the good laborers and painful° eaters assembled together, put to 'em by the matron, your spouse, who moderates° with a cup of wine ever and anon and a sentence° out of Knox[6] between? Or the perpetual spitting, before and after a sober, drawn° exhortation of six hours, whose better part was the hum-ha-hum? Or to hear prayers groaned out over thy iron chests,° as if they were charms to break 'em?[7] And all this° for the hope of two apostle spoons[8] to suffer, and a cup to eat a caudle[9] in! For that will be thy legacy. She'll ha' conveyed her state[1] safe enough from thee, an she be a right° widow.

(sermons; widows) / *enduring / dull; thirsty* / *son-in-law Littlewit* / *endure* / *assiduous* / *presides* / *solemn pronouncement* / *long, drawn-out* / *money chests* / *to suffer all this* / *true-to-form*

WINWIFE Alas, I am quite off that scent now.

QUARLOUS How so?

WINWIFE Put off by a brother° of Banbury, one that, they say, is come here and governs all already.

Puritan elder

QUARLOUS What do you call him? I knew divers of those Banburians when I was in Oxford.

WINWIFE [*turning to Littlewit*] Master Littlewit can tell us.

LITTLEWIT Sir!—Good Win, go in, and if Master Barthol'mew Cokes his man° come for the license—the little old fellow—let him speak with me. [*Exit Win.*]
What say you, gentlemen?

Cokes's servant

WINWIFE What call you the reverend elder you told me of, your Banbury man?

LITTLEWIT Rabbi[2] Busy, sir. He is more than an elder; he is a prophet, sir.

QUARLOUS Oh, I know him. A baker, is he not?

LITTLEWIT He was a baker, sir, but he does dream now and see visions. He has given over his trade.

QUARLOUS I remember that too, out of a scruple he took that (in spiced° conscience) those cakes he made were served to bride-ales, maypoles, morrisses,[3] and such profane feasts and meetings. His Christian name is Zeal-of-the-land.

overscrupulous

LITTLEWIT Yes, sir, Zeal-of-the-land Busy.

WINWIFE How? What a name's there!

LITTLEWIT Oh, they have all such names, sir. He was witness° for Win here (they will not be called godfathers), and named her Win-the-fight. You thought her name had been Winifred, did you not?

(Puritan for "godfather")

WINWIFE I did indeed.

5. Till all the food on your table has gotten cold through waiting for grace to be said.
6. John Knox, a Scottish reform preacher.
7. As if the prayers were incantations to break the money chests open.
8. Silver spoons were traditional christening gifts. Often their handles were engraved with figures of the apostles.
9. A warm, spiced bedtime drink.
1. She'll have made over her estate to a trustee or other person.
2. Puritans chose this Hebrew-derived term, "rabbi," to avoid the "popery" of the Catholic Church.
3. Wedding feasts (with ale drinking), Maytime festivities around a maypole, and morris dances—all deplored by Puritan reformers.

LITTLEWIT He would ha' thought himself a stark reprobate° if it had.

reprobate: one of the ungodly

QUARLOUS Ay, for there was a blue-starch woman[4] o'the name at the same time. A notable hypocritical vermin it is; I know him. One that stands upon his face[5] more than his faith at all times; ever in seditious motion,° and reproving for vainglory; of a most lunatic conscience and spleen, and affects the violence of singularity[6] in all he does. (He has undone° a grocer here, in Newgate Market, that broked° with him, trusted° him with currants, as arrant a zeal° as he; that's by the way.) By his profession,° he will ever be i'the state of innocence, though, and childhood; derides all antiquity;° defies any other learning than inspiration; and what discretion soever years should afford him, it is all prevented° in his original ignorance. Ha' not to do with him, for he is a fellow of a most arrogant and invincible dullness, I assure you.—Who is this?

seditious motion: stirring up strife / undone: bankrupted / broked: traded / trusted: gave credit to / zeal: zealot / profession: declaration of faith / antiquity: ancient learning / prevented: forestalled

1.4

[Enter] Wasp [carrying some parcels, escorted in by Win].

WASP By your leave, gentlemen, with all my heart to you. And God° you good morrow. Master Littlewit, my business is to you. Is this license ready?

God: God grant

LITTLEWIT *[showing the license]* Here, I ha' it for you in my hand, Master Humphrey.

WASP That's well. Nay, never open or read it to me; it's labor in vain, you know. I am no clerk.° I scorn to be saved by my book,[1] i'faith; I'll hang first. Fold it up, o'your word, and gi' it me. What must you ha'° for't?

clerk: cleric; scribe / ha': be paid

LITTLEWIT We'll talk of that anon, Master Humphrey.

WASP Now or not at all, good Master Proctor. I am for no anon's, I assure you.

LITTLEWIT *[to his wife]* Sweet Win, bid Solomon send me the little black box within, in my study.

WASP Ay, quickly, good mistress, I pray you, for I have both eggs o'the spit° and iron i'the fire. *[Exit Win.]* Say what you must have, good Master Littlewit.

eggs o'the spit: I'm in a hurry

LITTLEWIT Why, you know the price, Master Numps.°

Numps: i.e., Humphrey

WASP I know? I know nothing, I. What tell you me of knowing? Now I am in haste. Sir, I do not know, and I will not know, and I scorn to know, and yet, now I think on't, I will and do know, as well as another; you must have a mark° for your thing here, and eightpence for the box. I could ha' saved twopence i'that, an° I had bought it myself, but here's fourteen shillings for you. *[He gives money.]* Good Lord, how long your little wife stays! Pray God Solomon, your clerk, be

mark: 13s. 4d. / an: if

4. A laundress who uses starch to stiffen ruffs—the sort of finery objected to by Puritans.
5. Relies on brazen effrontery.
6. And is much inclined to be an aggressive dissenter from social norms (owing to his Puritan fixation on direct inspiration).

1.4. The scene continues.
1. An accused person could plead "benefit of clergy" by reading or reciting in Latin and thus be spared the gallows. (Jonson himself claimed this benefit when he was accused of manslaughter.)

not looking i'the wrong box,° Master Proctor. *container; vagina*

LITTLEWIT Good,° i'faith! No, I warrant you, Solomon is wiser than so,° sir. *Good witticism* / *than that*

WASP Fie, fie, fie, by your leave, Master Littlewit, this is scurvy, idle, foolish, and abominable. With all my heart, I do not like it.

WINWIFE [*aside to Littlewit*] Do you hear? Jack Littlewit, what business does thy pretty head think this fellow may have that he keeps such a coil° with? *makes such a fuss*

QUARLOUS [*joining their conversation*] More than buying of gingerbread i'the cloister here—for that we allow him—or a gilt pouch i'the fair?[2]

LITTLEWIT Master Quarlous, do not mistake him. He is his master's both-hands,° I assure you. *all-purpose servant*

QUARLOUS What? To pull on his boots a-mornings, or his stockings, does he?

LITTLEWIT Sir, if you have a mind to mock him, mock him softly, and look t'other way; for if he apprehend you flout° him, once, he will fly at you presently.° A terrible testy old fellow, and his name is Wasp too. *mock* / *immediately*

QUARLOUS Pretty insect! [*To Winwife*] Make much on him.° *Savor or coddle him*

[*They rejoin Wasp.*]

WASP A plague o'this box, and the pox too, and on him that made it, and her° that went for't, and all that should ha' sought it, sent it, or brought it! Do you see, sir? *(Win)*

LITTLEWIT Nay, good Master Wasp.

WASP Good Master Hornet, turd i'your teeth! Hold you your tongue. Do not I know you? Your father was a pothecary, and sold clysters, more than he gave, I wusse.[3] And turd i'your little wife's teeth too! Here she comes.

[*Enter Win with the box.*]

'Twill make her spit, as fine as she is, for all her velvet-custard on her head,[4] sir.

LITTLEWIT Oh, be civil, Master Numps.

WASP Why, say I have a humor° not to be civil; how then? Who shall compel me? You? *notion, whimsy*

LITTLEWIT [*offering the box*] Here is the box, now.

WASP Why a pox o'your box, once again! Let your little wife stale° in it, an she will. [*He takes the box, reluctantly.*] Sir, I would have you to understand, and these gentlemen too, if they please— *urinate*

WINWIFE With all our hearts, sir.

WASP That I have a charge,° gentlemen. *responsibility*

LITTLEWIT They do apprehend, sir.

WASP Pardon me, sir, neither they nor you can apprehend me yet. You are an ass! I have a young master; he is now upon his making and marring.[5] The whole care of his well-doing is now mine. His foolish schoolmasters have done nothing but run up and down the country with him to beg puddings° *sausages or puddings*

2. Quarlous wryly supposes that Wasp may at least be capable of shopping for trifles. (Booths might be set up in a cloister during a fair.)

3. Your father was a mere druggist, a shopkeeper who dispensed enemas, not one who practiced medicine. "I wusse" means "forsooth," "certainly."

4. My outspokenness will provoke her anger, for all her fancy ways and her pie-shaped velvet cap.

5. He is about to enter on adulthood, to succeed or fail.

and cake-bread of his tenants, and almost spoiled him; he has learned nothing but to sing catches and repeat "rattle bladder rattle" and "O Madge."[6] I dare not let him walk alone for fear of learning of vile tunes, which he will sing at supper and in the sermon-times. If he meet but a carman° i'the street, and I find him not talk to keep him off on him,[7] he will whistle him and all his tunes over at night in his sleep. He has a head full of bees!° I am fain° now, for this little time I am absent, to leave him in charge with° a gentlewoman. 'Tis true she is a justice of peace his° wife, and a gentlewoman o'the hood,[8] and his natural° sister; but what may happen under a woman's government,° there's the doubt.° Gentlemen, you do not know him; he is another manner of piece° than you think for! But° nineteen year old, and yet he is taller than either of you by the head,° God bless him.

carrier, carter / *zany notions / obliged* / *in the care of* / *peace's* / *blood-kin; foolish* / *control / worry* / *different sort* / *Only* / *a head taller*

QUARLOUS [*aside to Winwife*] Well, methinks this is a fine fellow!° *(said sarcastically)*

WINWIFE [*aside to Quarlous*] He has made his master a finer by this description, I should think.

QUARLOUS [*aside to Winwife*] Faith, much about one; it's cross and pile, whether for a new farthing.[9]

WASP I'll tell you, gentlemen—

LITTLEWIT Will't please you drink, Master Wasp?

WASP Why, I ha' not talked so long to be dry, sir. You see no dust or cobwebs come out o'my mouth, do you? You'd ha' me gone, would you?[1]

LITTLEWIT No, but you were in haste e'en now, Master Numps.

WASP What an I were? So I am still, and yet I will stay too. Meddle you with your match,° your Win, there; she has as little wit as her husband, it seems. I have others to talk to. *mate, wife*

LITTLEWIT She's my match, indeed, and as little wit as I. Good![2]

WASP We ha' been but a day and a half in town, gentlemen, 'tis true; and yesterday i'the afternoon we walked° London to show the city to the gentlewoman he shall marry, Mistress Grace; but afore I will endure such another half day with him, I'll be drawn with a good gib-cat through the great pond at home,[3] as his uncle Hodge was. Why, we could not meet that heathen thing all day but stayed him.[4] He would name you all the signs° over, as he went, aloud; and where he spied a parrot or a monkey, there he was pitched, with all the little long coats about him,[5] male and female; no getting him

walked about / *tavern and shop signs*

6. To sing rounds and children's nonsense verses or popular ballads.

7. And if I don't think of something to distract his attention from the carter. (Carters were famous for their whistling tunes.)

8. She is entitled to wear a French hood signifying the dignity of her husband's rank.

9. To tell the truth, it's a toss-up; it's heads or tails, not a farthing's worth of difference between them. ("Cross and pile" comes from the French phrase *croix et pile*, which refers to the emblems on the two sides of a French coin—French coins portrayed a cross on the back; "whether" means "no matter which of the two.")

1. Wasp touchily takes the offer of a drink as a signal for him to leave; it was customary to offer a drink to a departing guest.

2. Littlewit appreciates his own joke: as a "match," Win is both a married partner to Littlewit and well suited to him in her witlessness, as their last name suggests.

3. A popular practical joke was to bet a gullible country rube that a tomcat could drag him through a pond, whereupon the trickster's accomplices would pretend to be guiding the cat but would in fact haul on the rope and drag the victim through the water themselves.

4. We couldn't encounter any profane, godless trickster who didn't succeed in drawing him in.

5. And there he sat himself down, with a bunch of little ragamuffins in their long petticoats gathered around him.

away! I thought he would ha' run mad o'the black boy in Bucklersbury[6] that takes the scurvy, roguey tobacco there.

LITTLEWIT You say true, Master Numps. There's such a one indeed.

WASP It's no matter whether there be or no. What's that to you?

QUARLOUS [*aside to Winwife*] He will not allow of John's reading at any hand.[7]

1.5

[*Enter*] *Cokes, Mistress* [*Dame*] *Overdo,* [*and*] *Grace.*

COKES O Numps! Are you here, Numps? Look where I am, Numps, and Mistress Grace, too! Nay, do not look angerly, Numps. My sister° is here, and all; I do not come without her. *(Mistress Overdo)*

WASP What the mischief, do you come with her, or she with you?[1]

COKES We came all to seek you, Numps.

WASP To seek me? Why, did you all think I was lost? Or run away with your fourteen shillings' worth of small ware, here? Or that I had changed it i'the fair for hobbyhorses? 'S precious°—to seek me! *By God's precious body*

DAME OVERDO Nay, good Master Numps, do you show discretion, though he be exorbitant,° as Master Overdo says, an't be but for conservation of the peace. *out of orbit*

WASP Marry gip,° goody she-Justice, Mistress French-hood![2] Turd i'your teeth! And turd i'your French hood's teeth, too, to do you service,[3] do you see? Must you quote your Adam to me?[4] You think you are Madam Regent[5] still, Mistress Overdo, when I am in place? No such matter, I assure you. Your reign is out when I am in, dame. *By Mary Gipsy (an oath)*

DAME OVERDO I am content to be in abeyance, sir, and be governed by you; so should he° too, if he did well.° But 'twill be expected you should also govern your passions. *(Cokes) / behaved properly*

WASP Will't so, forsooth? Good Lord, how sharp you are! With being at Bedlam° yesterday? Whetstone[6] has set an edge upon you, has he? *(see 1.2.53)*

DAME OVERDO Nay, if you know not what belongs to° your dignity, I do yet to mine. *is appropriate to*

WASP Very well, then.

COKES Is this the license, Numps? For love's sake, let me see't. I never saw a license.

WASP Did you not so? Why, you shall not see't, then.

COKES An you love me, good Numps.

WASP Sir, I love you, and yet I do not love you i'these fooleries.

6. Depicted on a tobacconist's sign in Bucklersbury, a street frequented by grocers and apothecaries (who sold tobacco).
7. He won't allow Littlewit to get a word in edgewise under any circumstances.
1.5. The scene continues.
1. Who's in charge, you or your guardian?
2. See 1.4.84 and note. "Goody" means "goodwife," a title of address for women of ordinary citizen rank.
3. As a mark of respect for your social rank. (Said sarcastically.)
4. Do you think you can impress me by citing your husband, Adam Overdo?
5. A woman appointed to act in the name of an absent or minority ruler—here, acting as custodian of Cokes.
6. Probably the name of a keeper or a patient at Bethlehem Hospital for the insane. (With a pun on "whetstone" as a sharpener capable of setting "an edge.")

Set your heart at rest. There's nothing in't but hard words, and what would you see't for?

COKES I would see the length and the breadth on't, that's all; and I will see't now, so I will.

WASP You sha' not see it here.

COKES Then I'll see't at home, and I'll look upo' the case° here.

box

WASP Why, do so. [*To the others*] A man must give way to him a little in trifles, gentlemen. These are errors, diseases of youth, which he will mend when he comes to judgment and knowledge of matters. I pray you conceive° so, and I thank you. And I pray you pardon him, and I thank you again.

understand

[*Quarlous and Winwife confer aside.*]

QUARLOUS Well, this dry nurse, I say still, is a delicate man.[7]

WINWIFE And I am for the cosset,[8] his charge. Did you ever see a fellow's face more accuse him for an ass?

QUARLOUS Accuse him? It confesses him one without accusing. What pity 'tis yonder wench [*indicating Grace*] should marry such a cokes!°

Bartholomew Cokes; ninny

WINWIFE 'Tis true.

QUARLOUS She seems to be discreet, and as sober as she is handsome.

WINWIFE Ay, and if you mark her, what a restrained scorn she casts upon all his behavior and speeches!

COKES Well, Numps, I am now for another piece of business more, the fair, Numps, and then—

WASP Bless me! Deliver° me! Help, hold me! The fair?

Save

COKES Nay, never fidge° up and down, Numps, and vex itself.° I am resolute Barthol'mew in this. I'll make no suit on't to you;° 'twas all the end of my journey, indeed, to show Mistress Grace my fair. I call't my fair because of Barthol'mew: you know, my name is Barthol'mew, and Barthol'mew Fair.

fidget / yourself

I'll not beg you

LITTLEWIT That° was mine afore, gentlemen: this morning. I had that, i'faith, upon his license, believe me. There he comes after me.°

That witticism

imitates me

QUARLOUS Come, John, this ambitious wit of yours, I am afraid, will do you no good i'the end.

LITTLEWIT No? Why, sir?

QUARLOUS You grow so insolent° with it, and overdoing, John, that if you look not to it and tie it up, it will bring you to some obscure place in time, and there 'twill leave you.

extravagant

WINWIFE Do not trust it too much, John; be more sparing, and use it but now and then. A wit is a dangerous thing in this age; do not overbuy° it.

pay too much for

LITTLEWIT Think you so, gentlemen? I'll take heed on't hereafter.

WIN Yes, do, John.

COKES A pretty little soul, this same Mistress Littlewit. Would I might marry her!

7. I still maintain that Wasp is a marvelous specimen of odd humors worthy of our observation. ("Dry nurse" means "nanny.")

8. And I pick the spoiled child (literally, a hand-raised lamb), Cokes, as my interesting specimen.

GRACE [*aside*] So would I, or anybody else, so I might scape you.

COKES Numps, I will see it,° Numps, 'tis decreed. Never be melancholy for the matter. *(the fair)*

WASP Why, see it, sir, see it, do see it! Who hinders you? Why do you not go see it? 'Slid, see it.

COKES The fair, Numps, the fair.

WASP Would the fair, and all the drums and rattles in't, were i'your belly for me![9] They are already i'your brain. He that had the means to travel° your head, now, should meet finer sights than any are i'the fair, and make a finer voyage on't, to see it all hung with cockleshells,° pebbles, fine wheat straws, and here and there a chicken's feather and a cobweb. *travel through*; *mollusk shells*

QUARLOUS [*aside to Winwife*] Good faith, he° looks, methinks, an you mark him, like one that were made to catch flies, with his Sir Cranion° legs. *(Cokes)*; *daddy longlegs*

WINWIFE [*aside to Quarlous*] And his Numps, to flap 'em away.° *keep things from him*

WASP [*offering some of the trinkets to Cokes*] God be w'you, sir. There's your bee in a box,[1] and much good do't you.

COKES Why, your friend, and Barthol'mew, an you be so contumacious.[2]

QUARLOUS What mean you, Numps?

WASP I'll not be guilty, I, gentlemen.

DAME OVERDO You will not let him go, brother, and lose him?[3]

COKES Who can hold that will away?° I had rather lose him than the fair, I wusse.° *one who wishes to go*; *certainly*

WASP You do not know the inconvenience, gentlemen, you persuade to, nor what trouble I have with him in these humors. If he go to the fair, he will buy of everything, to a baby there,[4] and household stuff° for that too. If a leg or an arm on him did not grow on, he would lose it i'the press.° Pray heaven I bring him off with one stone!° And then he is such a ravener after fruit! You will not believe what a coil° I had, t'other day, to compound° a business between a Catherine-pear woman and him about snatching!° 'Tis intolerable, gentlemen. *doll paraphernalia*; *crowd*; *smidgen; testicle*; *fuss*; *settle*; *shoplifting*

WINWIFE Oh, but you must not leave him now to these hazards, Numps.

WASP Nay, he knows too well I will not leave him, and that makes him presume. [*To Cokes*] Well, sir, will you go now? If you have such an itch i'your feet to foot it° to the fair, why do you stop? Am I your tarriers?° Go! Will you go? Sir, why do you not go? *hasten*; *Am I stopping you?*

COKES Oh, Numps, have I brought you about?°—Come, Mistress Grace, and sister, I am resolute Bat,° i'faith, still. *around*; *Bartholomew*

GRACE Truly, I have no such fancy to the fair, nor ambition to see it. There's none goes thither of any quality° or fashion. *social standing*

9. Would the fair were consumed and done for, for all I care!

1. Evidently one of the parcels that Wasp has been carrying around for Cokes (see 1.4.0.1) is a bee in a box.

2. I.e., Well, goodbye then, if you're going to be so uppity. (Cokes mockingly uses a customary form of farewell, as if he were composing the complimentary close to a letter.)

3. And lose the services of your servant, Wasp?

4. Buy something of everything there, right down to the last doll or puppet.

COKES Oh, Lord, sir! You shall pardon me, Mistress Grace, we are enough of ourselves to make it a fashion. And for qualities,° let Numps alone; he'll find qualities.

as for character traits

[*Exeunt Cokes, Wasp, Dame Overdo, and Grace. Quarlous and Winwife confer privately.*]

QUARLOUS What a rogue in apprehension° is this, to understand her language no better!

poor comprehender

WINWIFE Ay, and offer° to marry to her! Well, I will leave the chase of my widow for today, and directly to the fair. These flies cannot, this hot season, but° engender us excellent creeping sport.

undertake / *help but*

QUARLOUS A man that has but a spoonful of brain would think so. [*Aloud, to Littlewit*] Farewell, John.

[*Exit with Winwife.*]

LITTLEWIT Win, you see 'tis in fashion to go to the fair, Win. We must to the fair too, you and I, Win. I have an affair i'the fair, Win, a puppet play of mine own making—say nothing—that I writ for the motion man,° which you must see, Win.

puppet master

WIN I would I might, John, but my mother will never consent to such a profane motion,° she will call it.

proposal

LITTLEWIT Tut, we'll have a device,° a dainty° one.—Now, wit, help at a pinch! Good wit, come, come, good wit, an't be thy will!—I have it, Win, I have it, i'faith, and 'tis a fine one. Win, long to eat of a pig, sweet Win, i'the fair; do you see? I'the heart o'the fair, not at Pie Corner.[5] Your mother will do anything, Win, to satisfy your longing, you know. Pray thee, long presently, and be sick° o'the sudden, good Win. I'll go in and tell her. Cut thy lace[6] i'the meantime, and play the hypocrite, sweet Win.

stratagem / nifty / *(from morning sickness)*

WIN No, I'll not make me unready° for it. I can be hypocrite enough, though I were never so straitlaced.°

undressed / *all laced up; prim*

LITTLEWIT You say true. You have been bred i'the family and brought up to't.[7] Our mother is a most elect° hypocrite, and has maintained us all this seven year with it, like gentlefolks.

chosen (a Puritanism)

WIN Ay. Let her alone, John; she is not a wise willful widow for nothing, nor a sanctified sister for a song.° And let me alone too. I ha' somewhat o'the mother° in me, you shall see. Fetch her, fetch her. [*She commences to groan on cue.*] Ah, ah!

Puritan to no avail / *my mother; hysteria*

[*Exit Littlewit.*]

1.6

[*Enter Dame*] Purecraft [*led by Littlewit*].

PURECRAFT Now, the blaze of the beauteous discipline° fright away this evil from our house! How now, Win-the-fight, child, how do you? Sweet child, speak to me!

godly Puritan faith

WIN Yes, forsooth.

PURECRAFT Look up, sweet Win-the-fight, and suffer not the enemy° to enter you at this door!° Remember that your edu-

the devil / (the belly)

5. Near the Pie, or Magpie, Inn.

6. Cut the lacings on your bodice (as a way of feigning faintness).

7. You've been brought up to practice hypocrisy, both by your own mother and by the Puritan sect.

1.6. The scene continues.

cation has been with the purest. What polluted one was it that named first the unclean beast, pig,° to you, child?

(see Leviticus 11.7)

WIN [*groaning*] Uh, uh!

LITTLEWIT Not I, o'my sincerity, mother. She longed above° three hours ere she would let me know it.—Who was it, Win?

more than

WIN A profane black thing with a beard, John.

PURECRAFT Oh, resist it, Win-the-fight! It is the tempter,° the wicked tempter! You may know it by the fleshly motion° of pig. Be strong against it and its foul temptations in these assaults, whereby it broacheth° flesh and blood, as it were, on the weaker° side, and pray against its carnal provocations, good child. Sweet child, pray!

devil (see Matthew 4.3)
urging, suggestion
pierces
feminine

LITTLEWIT Good mother, I pray you that she may eat some pig, and her bellyful, too; and do not you cast away your own child, and perhaps one of mine,° with your tale of the tempter.—How do you, Win? Are you not sick?

my unborn child

WIN Yes, a great deal, John. [*Groaning*] Uh, uh!

PURECRAFT What shall we do? [*To Littlewit*] Call our zealous brother Busy hither, for his faithful fortification in this charge of the adversary.° [*Exit Littlewit.*] Child, my dear child, you shall eat pig. Be comforted, my sweet child.

the devil

WIN Ay, but i'the fair, mother.

PURECRAFT I mean i'the fair, if it can be any way made or found lawful.

[*Littlewit returns.*]

Where is our brother Busy? Will he not come?—Look up, child.

LITTLEWIT Presently, mother, as soon as he has cleansed his beard. I found him, fast by the teeth i'the cold turkey pie, i'the cupboard, with a great white loaf on his left hand and a glass of malmsey on his right.

PURECRAFT Slander not the brethren, wicked one.

[*Enter*] *Busy.*

LITTLEWIT Here he is now, purified, mother.

PURECRAFT O brother Busy, your help here to edify and raise us up in a scruple!° My daughter Win-the-fight is visited with a natural disease° of women called a longing to eat pig.

matter of conscience
weakness

LITTLEWIT Ay, sir, a Barthol'mew-pig; and in the fair.

PURECRAFT And I would be satisfied from you, religiously-wise, whether a widow of the sanctified assembly, or a widow's daughter, may commit the act without offense to the weaker sisters.

BUSY Verily, for° the disease of longing, it is a disease, a carnal disease, or appetite, incident to women; and as it is carnal, and incident, it is natural, very natural. Now pig, it is a meat, and a meat that is nourishing and may be longed for, and so consequently eaten. It may be eaten, very exceeding well eaten. But in the fair, and as a Barthol'mew-pig, it cannot be eaten; for the very calling it a Barthol'mew-pig, and to eat

as for

it so, is a spice° of idolatry, and you make the fair no better than one of the high places.° This, I take it, is the state of the question. A high place.

species; trace / *places of idol worship*

LITTLEWIT Ay, but in state of necessity, place should give place,° Master Busy. (*Aside*) I have a conceit° left, yet.

yield precedence / pun

PURECRAFT Good brother Zeal-of-the-land, think to make it as lawful as you can.

LITTLEWIT Yes, sir, and as soon as you can; for it must be, sir. You see the danger my little wife is in, sir.

PURECRAFT Truly, I do love my child dearly, and I would not have her miscarry or hazard her firstfruits° if it might be otherwise.

firstborn (a Puritanism)

BUSY Surely, it may be otherwise, but it is subject to construction—subject, and hath a face° of offense with the weak, a great face, a foul face, but that face may have a veil put over it, and be shadowed, as it were. It may be eaten, and in the fair, I take it, in a booth, the tents of the wicked. The place is not much, not very much; we may be religious in midst of the profane, so° it be eaten with a reformed mouth, with sobriety and humbleness, not gorged in with gluttony or greediness. There's the fear;° for, should she go there as taking pride in the place or delight in the unclean dressing,° to feed the vanity of the eye or the lust of the palate, it were not well, it were not fit, it were abominable, and not good.

appearance / *provided* / *danger* / *meat preparation*

LITTLEWIT Nay, I knew that afore, and told her on't. [*To Win*] But courage, Win, we'll be humble enough; we'll seek out the homeliest booth i'the fair, that's certain; rather than fail, we'll eat it o'the ground.

PURECRAFT Ay, and I'll go with you myself, Win-the-fight; and my brother, Zeal-of-the-land, shall go with us too for our better consolation.

WIN [*groaning*] Uh, uh!

LITTLEWIT Ay, and Solomon too, Win. The more the merrier, Win. [*Aside to her*] We'll leave Rabbi Busy in a booth. [*Calling*] Solomon, my cloak.

[*Enter*] *Solomon* [*with the cloak*].

SOLOMON Here, sir.

BUSY In the way of comfort to the weak, I will go, and eat. I will eat exceedingly, and prophesy. There may be a good use made of it, too, now I think on't: by the public eating of swine's flesh, to profess our hate and loathing of Judaism, whereof the brethren stand taxed.[1] I will therefore eat; yea, I will eat exceedingly.

LITTLEWIT Good, i'faith! I will eat heartily too, because I will be no Jew; I could never away with° that stiff-necked[2] generation.° And truly, I hope my little one will be like me, that cries for pig so i'the mother's belly.

put up with / *race*

BUSY Very likely, exceeding likely, very exceeding likely.

[*Exeunt.*]

1. Eating pork will make clear that we Puritans are not sympathetic to the Jews (who are forbidden to eat pork), as we are often accused of being because of our love for the Old Testament.

2. Because they refuse to convert to Christianity.

2.1

[Enter] Justice Overdo [disguised as a fool, with a black book].

JUSTICE OVERDO Well, in justice' name and the King's, and for the commonwealth!° Defy all the world, Adam Overdo, for a disguise, and all story;[1] for thou hast fitted° thyself, I swear. Fain would I meet the Lynceus[2] now, that eagle's eye, that piercing Epidaurian serpent,[3] as my Quintus Horace calls him, that could discover a justice of peace, and lately of the quorum,[4] under this covering.° They may have seen many a fool in the habit° of a justice, but never till now a justice in the habit of a fool. Thus must we do, though, that wake° for the public good; and thus hath the wise magistrate done in all ages. There is a doing of right out of wrong, if the way be found. Never shall I enough commend a worthy worshipful man, sometime a capital° member of this city for his high wisdom in this point, who would take you now the habit of a porter, now of a carman, now of the dog°-killer in this month of August, and in the winter of a seller of tinderboxes.[5] And what would he do in all these shapes? Marry, go you° into every alehouse and down into every cellar; measure the length of puddings;° take the gauge° of black pots and cans, ay, and custards, with a stick, and their circumference with a thread; weigh the loaves of bread on his middle finger. Then would he send for 'em home, give the puddings to the poor, the bread to the hungry, the custards to his children; break the pots and burn the cans himself. He would not trust his corrupt officers; he would do't himself. Would all men in authority would follow this worthy precedent! For, alas, as we are public persons, what do we know? Nay, what can we know? We hear with other men's ears; we see with other men's eyes. A foolish constable or a sleepy watchman is all our information; he slanders a gentleman, by the virtue° of his place,° as he calls it, and we, by the vice of ours, must believe him—as, a while agone,° they made me, yea, me, to mistake an honest zealous pursuivant for a seminary[6] and a proper° young Bachelor of Music for a bawd.° This we are subject to that live in high place. All our intelligence° is idle° and most of our intelligencers knaves; and, by your leave, ourselves thought little better, if not arrant fools, for believing 'em. I, Adam Overdo, am resolved therefore to spare spy-money° hereafter and make mine own discoveries. Many are the yearly enormities of this fair, in whose Courts of Piepowders[7] I have had the honor

common good
outfitted, furnished
disguise
garb
we who are watchful
leading
(thought to carry plague)
he would go
sausages / capacity
authority / office
ago
handsome
pimp
information / unreliable
not to pay spies

2.1. The fair.
1. And a complete fabrication.
2. One of the Argonauts, whose eyesight was so keen that he could see through the earth.
3. One of the sharp-sighted serpents at the temple of Epidaurus, sacred to Aesculapius, the god of medicine; mentioned by the Roman poet Horace (Quintus Horatius Flaccus) in his *Satire,* 1.3.26–27. It is to be seen twined about Aesculapius' caduceus.
4. A panel of judges needed to constitute a bench.
5. Overdo refers to Thomas Middleton, Lord Mayor of London in 1613–14 (a relative of the dramatist Thomas Middleton), who was said to have visited taverns and places of resort in disguise as a means of seeking out violators.
6. To mistake an honest officer commissioned to summon persons before an ecclesiastical court for a Catholic priest trained on the Continent in a seminary for dangerous missionary work in England.
7. Summary courts held at fairs to administer justice among itinerant dealers. (From the French *pied poudreux,* meaning "dusty foot.")

during the three days sometimes to sit as judge. But this is the special day for detection of those foresaid enormities. Here is my black book for the purpose, this [*indicating his fool's disguise*] the cloud that hides me. Under this covert° I shall see and not be seen. On, Junius Brutus![8] And as I began, so I'll end: in justice' name and the King's, and for the commonwealth! [*He stands aside.*] [covert: *cover, disguise*]

2.2

[*Lantern*] *Leatherhead* [*and Joan*] *Trash* [*are discovered,° Leatherhead in his booth and Joan at her stand*]; *passengers.°* [discovered: *suddenly disclosed*; passengers: *passersby*]

LEATHERHEAD The fair's pestilence dead,° methinks; people come not abroad° today, whatever the matter is.—Do you hear, sister Trash, Lady o'the Basket? Sit farther with your gingerbread progeny there, and hinder not the prospect° of my shop, or I'll ha' it proclaimed i'the fair what stuff they are made on.° [pestilence dead: *plaguily inactive*; abroad: *from their houses*; prospect: *view*; on: *of*]

JOAN TRASH Why, what stuff are they made on, brother Leatherhead? Nothing but what's wholesome, I assure you.

LEATHERHEAD Yes, stale bread, rotten eggs, musty ginger, and dead honey, you know.

JUSTICE OVERDO [*aside*] Ay! Have I met with enormity° so soon? [enormity: *monstrous wickedness*]

LEATHERHEAD I shall mar your market, old Joan.

JOAN TRASH Mar my market, thou too-proud peddler? Do thy worst! I defy thee, ay, and thy stable of hobbyhorses. I pay for my ground° as well as thou dost, and thou wrong'st me, for all thou art parcel poet and an engineer.[1] I'll find a friend shall° right me and make a ballad of thee and thy cattle° all over. Are you puffed up with the pride of your wares, your arsedine?° [ground: *rental location*; shall: *who will*; cattle: *(trashy) stock*; arsedine: *fake gold leaf on toys*]

LEATHERHEAD Go to,° old Joan. I'll talk with you anon, and take you down,° too, afore Justice Overdo. He is the man must charm° you. I'll ha' you i'the Piepowders. [Go to: *(expressing annoyance)*; take you down: *down a peg*; charm: *subdue*]

JOAN TRASH Charm me? I'll meet thee face to face afore His Worship when thou dar'st! And though I be a little crooked o'my body, I'll be found as upright in my dealing as any woman in Smithfield, I. Charm me?

JUSTICE OVERDO [*aside*] I am glad to hear my name is their terror yet. This is doing of justice.

LEATHERHEAD [*to passersby*] What do you lack?° What is't you buy? What do you lack? Rattles, drums, halberds,° horses, babies° o'the best? Fiddles o'th'finest? [What do you lack: *(a familiar street cry)*; halberds: *(toy) pikes*; babies: *dolls*]

Enter Costermonger° [and] Nightingale. [Costermonger: *fruit-seller*]

COSTERMONGER Buy any pears, pears, fine, very fine pears!

JOAN TRASH Buy any gingerbread, gilt° gingerbread! [gilt: *decorated, frosted*]

NIGHTINGALE [*singing*]

8. A leader of an uprising against the Tarquins and one of the first two Roman consuls; a champion of liberty and justice. He disguised himself as an idiot and was impartial enough as a judge to sentence his own sons to death for crimes they committed.

2.2. The scene continues.

1. Even if you are an amateur part-time poet and deviser of shows.

Hey, now the fair's a-filling!
Oh, for a tune to startle
The birds o'the booths here billing° *billing and cooing*
Yearly with old Saint Bartle!° *Bartholomew*
The drunkards they are wading,° *awash with drink*
The punks and chapmen° trading; *merchants, peddlers*
Who'd see the fair without his lading?° *without purchasing*
Buy any ballads, new ballads?

Ursula [*is discovered at her booth*].

URSULA Fie upon't, who would wear out their youth and prime thus in roasting of pigs that had any cooler vocation? Hell's a kind of cold cellar to't,° a very fine vault,° o'my conscience. [*Calling*] What, Mooncalf!

compared with it / tomb

Mooncalf [*appears at the booth entrance*].

MOONCALF Here, mistress.

NIGHTINGALE How now, Ursula? In a heat, in a heat?

URSULA [*to Mooncalf*] My chair, you false faucet,° you, and my morning's draft, quickly, a bottle of ale, to quench me, rascal. [*Mooncalf disappears.*] [*To Nightingale*] I am all fire and fat, Nightingale. I shall e'en melt away to the first woman, a rib,[2] again, I am afraid. I do water the ground in knots,° as I go, like a great garden-pot; you may follow me by the S's° I make.

i.e., tapster / *crisscrossed lines* / *S-shaped drips*

NIGHTINGALE Alas, good Urs! Was Zekiel here this morning?

URSULA Zekiel? What Zekiel?

NIGHTINGALE Zekiel Edgeworth, the civil° cutpurse. You know him well enough: he that talks bawdy to you still.° I call him my secretary.°

well-mannered / *constantly* / *confidence man*

URSULA He promised to be here this morning. I remember.

NIGHTINGALE When he comes, bid him stay. I'll be back again presently.°

right away

URSULA Best take your morning's dew° in your belly, Nightingale.

eye-opener, drink

Mooncalf brings in the chair.

[*To Mooncalf*] Come, sir, set it here. Did not I bid you should get this chair let out o'the sides for me, that my hips might play?° You'll never think of anything till your dame be rump-galled.° 'Tis well, changeling:[3] because it can take in your grasshoppers' thighs, you care for no more. Now, you look as° you had been i'the corner o'the booth, fleaing° your breech with a candle's end, and set fire o'the fair. Fill, stoat,° fill! [*Mooncalf adjusts her chair and serves her a drink.*]

have room to move / *chafed in the fanny* / *as if / singeing fleas off* / *weasel; horse; stupid*

JUSTICE OVERDO [*aside*] This pig-woman do I know, and I will put her in° for my second enormity. She hath been before me, punk, pinnace,° and bawd, any time[4] these two-and-twenty years, upon record i'the Piepowders.

in my black book / *go-between, bawd, whore*

2. As written in Genesis 2.21–22, Eve was made of Adam's rib.
3. A mentally defective or deformed child supposedly left by fairies in exchange for a baby they stole.
4. Again and again.

URSULA [*to Mooncalf*] Fill again, you unlucky vermin.

MOONCALF [*serving her more liquor*] Pray you, be not angry, mistress. I'll ha' it° widened anon.

URSULA No, no, I shall e'en dwindle away to't° ere the fair be done, you think, now you ha' heated me. A poor vexed thing I am! I feel myself dropping° already, as fast as I can: two stone[5] o'suet a day is my proportion.° I can but hold life and soul together with this (here's to you, Nightingale)° and a whiff of tobacco, at most. [*To Mooncalf*] Where's my pipe now? Not filled? Thou arrant incubee!°

NIGHTINGALE Nay, Ursula, thou'lt gall° between the tongue and the teeth with fretting, now.

URSULA How can I hope that ever he'll discharge° his place° of trust—tapster, a man of reckoning[6] under me—that remembers nothing I say to him? [*Exit Nightingale.*] [*To Mooncalf*] But look to't, sirrah, you were best. Threepence a pipeful I will ha' made[7] of all my whole half pound of tobacco, and a quarter of a pound of coltsfoot° mixed with it too, to eke it out. I that have dealt so long in the fire will not be to seek° in smoke now. Then six-and-twenty shillings a barrel I will advance° o'my beer, and fifty shillings a hundred o'my bottle ale. I ha' told you the ways how to raise it: froth your cans well i'the filling, at length,° rogue, and jog your bottles o'the buttock, sirrah, then skink out° the first glass, ever, and drink with all companies,[8] though you be sure to be drunk; you'll misreckon° the better and be less ashamed on't. But your true trick, rascal, must be to be ever busy, and mis-take away° the bottles and cans in haste before they be half drunk off, and never hear anybody call, if they should chance to mark° you, till you ha' brought fresh, and be able to forswear 'em. Give me a drink of ale.

JUSTICE OVERDO [*aside*] This is the very womb and bed of enormity, gross as herself! This must all down for enormity, all, every whit on't.° [*He writes in his black book.*]

One knocks.

URSULA Look who's there, sirrah. [*Mooncalf goes to see.*] Five shillings a pig is my price, at least; if it be a sow-pig, sixpence more; if she° be a great-bellied° wife, and long for't, sixpence more for that.

JUSTICE OVERDO [*aside*] *O tempora! O mores!*[9] I would not ha' lost my discovery of this one grievance° for my place and worship° o'the bench. How is the poor subject° abused, here! Well, I will fall in with her, and with her Mooncalf, and wind out° wonders of enormity. [*Coming forward, to Ursula*] By thy leave, goodly woman, and the fatness of the fair, oily as the King's constable's lamp° and shining as his shoeing-horn! Hath thy ale virtue,° or thy beer strength, that the tongue of man may be tickled and his palate pleased in the morning? Let thy pretty nephew° here go search and see.

(the chair)
to fit the chair
dwindling; dripping
portion
(she drinks to him)
incubus, demon
chafe
perform / office
a tobacco extender
won't be lacking
raise
far below the spigot
pour out, draw
inflate the bill
mistakenly take away
notice
bit of it
(the customer) / pregnant
transgression
honor / citizen
smell out (in hunting)
oil-burning lamp
potency
i.e., Mooncalf

5. A measure of weight, officially now fourteen pounds.
6. (1) A man of destiny; (2) a barkeep who totes up the customers' expenses.
7. You'd better look sharp, my lad. I'll dispense my tobacco at threepence a pipeful. ("Sirrah" is a form of address used when speaking to inferiors.)
8. Drink with the customers (to encourage them to drink more and then be lacking in vigilance when you overcharge them).
9. What an age! What manners! (Cicero, *In Catilinam*, 1.1.2.)

URSULA [*to Mooncalf*] What new roarer° is this?
rowdy reveler

MOONCALF Oh, Lord, do you not know him, mistress? 'Tis mad Arthur of Bradley, that makes the orations. [*To Justice Overdo*] Brave master, old Arthur of Bradley, how do you? Welcome to the fair! When shall we hear you again, to handle your matters with your back again' a booth,[1] ha? I ha' been one o'your little disciples i'my days.

JUSTICE OVERDO Let me drink, boy, with my love, thy aunt,° here, that I may be eloquent; but of thy best, lest it be bitter in my mouth and my words fall foul on the fair.
sponsor; chum; whore

URSULA [*to Mooncalf*] Why dost thou not fetch him drink and offer him to sit?

MOONCALF Is't ale or beer, Master Arthur?

JUSTICE OVERDO Thy best, pretty stripling, thy best: the same thy dove° drinketh and thou drawest° on holy days.
(Ursula) / (from the keg)

URSULA [*to Mooncalf*] Bring him a sixpenny bottle of ale. They say a fool's handsel[2] is lucky.

JUSTICE OVERDO Bring both, child. Ale for Arthur, and beer for Bradley. Ale for thine aunt, boy. [*Exit Mooncalf.*] [*Aside*] My disguise takes° to the very wish and reach° of it. I shall, by the benefit of this, discover enough and more, and yet get off with the reputation of what I would be: a certain middling thing between a fool and a madman.
succeeds / full extent

2.3

[*Enter*] *Knockem to them* [*and Mooncalf with drink*].

KNOCKEM What, my little, lean Ursula, my she-bear!° Art thou alive yet, with thy litter of pigs to grunt out another Barthol'mew Fair? Ha!
("Ursula" means "she-bear")

URSULA Yes, and to amble afoot, when the fair is done, to hear you groan out of a cart up the heavy hill.[1]

KNOCKEM Of Holborn, Ursula, mean'st thou so? For what? For what, pretty Urs?

URSULA For cutting halfpenny purses or stealing little penny dogs° out o'the fair.
cheap utensils

KNOCKEM Oh, good words,° good words, Urs.
speak calmly

JUSTICE OVERDO [*aside*] Another special enormity. A cutpurse of° the sword, the boot, and the feather! Those are his marks.
wearing, identified by

URSULA You are one of those horse-leeches° that gave out I was dead, in Turnbull Street,° of a surfeit of bottle ale and tripes?°
bloodsuckers; vets
a red-light district
cooked stomachs

KNOCKEM No, 'twas better meat, Urs: cows' udders, cows' udders!

URSULA Well, I shall be meet with° your mumbling mouth one day.
be even with

KNOCKEM What, thou'lt poison me with a newt in a bottle of ale, wilt thou? Or a spider in a tobacco pipe, Urs? Come, there's no malice in these fat folks. I never fear thee, an I

1. To treat your various topics, using a booth as a backdrop. Arthur of Bradley is the clown-hero of an old ballad.
2. Something received first and kept as a token of good luck, such as a New Year's gift or the day's first money received.

2.3. The scene continues.
1. Holborn Hill, leading from Newgate Prison to the gallows at Tyburn. Felons were carted up this hill.

can scape thy lean Mooncalf here. Let's drink it out, good
Urs, and no vapors!° [*Exit Ursula into her booth.*] *quarreling; odd ways*

JUSTICE OVERDO [*taking Mooncalf aside*] Dost thou hear, boy?
[*Giving money*] There's for thy ale, and the remnant° for *change (as tip)*
thee. Speak in thy faith of a faucet,[2] now: is this goodly person before us here, this vapors,° a knight of the knife? *odd character*

MOONCALF What mean you by that, Master Arthur?

JUSTICE OVERDO I mean a child of the horn-thumb,° a babe *the cutpurse's thimble*
of booty, boy: a cutpurse.

MOONCALF Oh, Lord, sir! Far from it. This is Master Dan
Knockem—Jordan, the Ranger of Turnbull.[3] He is a horse-
courser,° sir. *horse-dealer*

JUSTICE OVERDO Thy dainty dame, though, called him cutpurse.

MOONCALF Like° enough, sir. She'll do forty such things in *Likely*
an hour, an you listen to her, for her recreation, if the toy
take her i'the greasy kerchief.[4] It makes her fat, you see. She
battens° with it. *fattens*

JUSTICE OVERDO [*aside*] Here might I ha' been deceived, now,
and ha' put a fool's blot° upon myself, if I had not played an *stigma, disgrace*
after-game° o'discretion. *reversing second set*

Ursula comes in again, dropping.° *dripping with sweat*

KNOCKEM Alas, poor Urs, this 's an ill season for thee.

URSULA Hang yourself, hackney-man!° *keeper of hired horses*

KNOCKEM How? How? Urs, vapors? Motion breed vapors?[5]

URSULA Vapors? Never tusk nor twirl your dibble,[6] good Jor-
dan; I know what you'll take° to a very drop. Though you be *take as an insult; drink*
captain o'the roarers, and fight well at the case of piss-pots,° *(playing on "pistols")*
you shall not fright me with your lion-chap,° sir, nor your *lion's jaw, whiskers*
tusks. You angry? You are hungry. Come, a pig's head will
stop your mouth and stay° your stomach at all times. *quiet, satisfy*

KNOCKEM Thou art such another° mad merry Urs still! Troth, *such a*
I do make conscience of° vexing thee, now i'the dog days,[7] *feel guilty about*
this hot weather, for fear of found'ring° thee i'the body and *laming*
melting down a pillar of the fair. Pray thee take thy chair
again, and keep state;° and let's have a fresh bottle of ale *preside*
and a pipe of tobacco, and no vapors. I'll ha' this belly o'thine
taken up° and thy grass scoured,[8] wench. Look, here's Eze- *reduced*
kiel Edgeworth, a fine boy of his inches° as any is i'the fair. *for his size*
H'as° still money in his purse, and will pay all, with a kind *He has*
heart and good vapors.

2.4

[*Enter*] *to them Edgeworth, Nightingale, Corn-cutter,*° *(see 6)*
Mousetrap-man, [*and*] *passengers.*

EDGEWORTH That I will, indeed, willingly, Master Knockem.
[*To Mooncalf*] Fetch some ale and tobacco.

2. On your honor as a barkeep.
3. Jordan Knockem, the "park-keeper" of the red-light district in Turnbull Street. ("Dan" is an honorific, like "Don"; "Jordan" means "chamberpot.")
4. If she gets a notion into her greasy head.
5. Is your exertion making you quarrelsome?
6. Don't bare your teeth in a sneer or twirl your mustache or spade-shaped beard at me.
7. The days of late summer, when the sun is near Sirius, the Dog Star.
8. Knockem speaks as though Ursula were one of his horses; he will purge or cleanse her feed.
2.4. The scene continues.

[*Mooncalf exits and returns shortly with ale and tobacco.*]

LEATHERHEAD What do you lack, gentlemen? Maid,° see a fine hobbyhorse for your young master! Cost you but a token° a week his provender.°

(a passerby) / (a tiny amount) / for his feed

CORN-CUTTER Ha' you any corns i'your feet and toes?

MOUSETRAP-MAN Buy a mousetrap, a mousetrap, or a tormentor° for a flea!

trap

JOAN TRASH Buy some gingerbread!

NIGHTINGALE Ballads, Ballads! Fine new ballads! [*He chants.*]

Hear for your love, and buy for your money,
A delicate ballad o' "The Ferret° and the Coney,"°
"A Preservative again' the Punk's Evil,"°
Another of "Goose-green° Starch and the Devil,"
"A Dozen of Divine Points,"° and "The Godly Garters,"
"The Fairing° of Good Counsel," of an ell[1] and three-
quarters.
What is't you buy?
"The Windmill Blown Down by the Witch's Fart,"
Or "Saint George, That Oh! Did Break the Dragon's Heart"?

swindler / dupe; venereal disease; yellowish green; maxims; clothes fasteners; buying at the fair

EDGEWORTH Master Nightingale, come hither. Leave your mart° a little.

trade

NIGHTINGALE Oh, my secretary!° What says my secretary?

confidence man

[*Nightingale and Edgeworth converse privately, joined by Ursula; meantime, Overdo confers apart with Mooncalf.*]

JUSTICE OVERDO Child o'the bottles, what's he? What's he?

MOONCALF A civil young gentleman, Master Arthur, that keeps company with the roarers,° and disburses all, still. He has ever money in his purse. He pays for them, and they roar° for him; one does good offices for another. They call him the secretary, but he serves nobody. A great friend of the ballad man's; they are never asunder.

rowdies; create an uproar

JUSTICE OVERDO What pity 'tis so civil a young man should haunt this debauched company! Here's the bane of the youth of our time apparent. A proper° penman, I see't in his countenance; he has a good clerk's look with him, and I warrant him a quick hand.°

handsome; presentable; nimble scribe

MOONCALF A very quick hand,° sir. [*Exit into the booth.*]

cutpurse, pickpocket

(*This* [*the following speeches*] *they* [*Edgeworth, Ursula, and Nightingale*] *whisper, that Overdo hears it not.*)

EDGEWORTH All the purses and purchase° I give you today by conveyance° bring hither to Ursula's presently. Here we will meet at night in her lodge and share. Look you choose good places for your standing i'the fair when you sing, Nightingale.

booty; sleight of hand

URSULA Ay, near the fullest passages; and shift 'em° often.

change places

EDGEWORTH And i'your singing you must use your hawk's eye nimbly, and fly the purse to a mark still[2]—where 'tis worn, and o'which side—that you may gi' me the sign with your beak,° or hang your head that way i'the tune.

nose

1. Forty-five inches.
2. And indicate to me by gesture where a purse is to be had. (Said in the language of hawking.)

URSULA Enough, talk no more on't. Your friendship, masters, is not now to begin. Drink your draft of indenture,[3] your sup° of covenant, and away! The fair fills apace, company begins to come in, and I ha' ne'er a pig ready yet. *sip*

KNOCKEM [*joining their company*] Well said! Fill the cups, and light the tobacco. Let's give fire i'th'works, and noble vapors.

EDGEWORTH And shall we ha' smocks,° Ursula, and good whimsies,° ha? *women* / *whores*

URSULA Come, you are i'your bawdy vein. The best the fair will afford, Zekiel, if bawd Whit keep his word.

[*Enter Mooncalf from the booth.*]

How do the pigs, Mooncalf?

MOONCALF Very passionate,° mistress. One on 'em has wept out an eye.[4] Master Arthur o'Bradley is melancholy, here; nobody talks to him.—Will you any tobacco, Master Arthur? *sorrowful*

JUSTICE OVERDO No, boy. Let my meditations alone.

MOONCALF [*to the others*] He's studying for an oration, now.

JUSTICE OVERDO [*aside*] If I can, with this day's travail and all my policy,° but rescue this youth here out of the hands of the lewd man° and the strange woman,° I will sit down at night and say with my friend Ovid, *Iamque opus exegi, quod nec Jovis ira, nec ignis,* etc.[5] *calculation, cunning* / *(Nightingale)* / *(Ursula)*

KNOCKEM [*offering a toast*] Here, Zekiel; here's a health to Ursula, and a kind vapor.° Thou hast money i'thy purse still, and store.° How dost thou come by it? Pray thee vapor° thy friends some in a courteous vapor. *and all good wishes* / *plenty of it* / *humor*

EDGEWORTH Half I have, Master Dan Knockem, is always at your service.

JUSTICE OVERDO [*aside*] Ha, sweet nature! What goshawk° would prey upon such a lamb? *short-winged hawk*

KNOCKEM Let's see what 'tis, Zekiel. Count it. [*To Mooncalf*] Come, fill him° to pledge me. *(Edgeworth)*

[*Drinks are poured. Exit Ursula into her booth.*]

2.5

[*Enter*] *Winwife* [*and*] *Quarlous to them* [*in front of the booths, not yet conversing with the denizens of the fair*].

WINWIFE [*to Quarlous*] We are here before 'em,° methinks. *(Cokes, Grace, etc.)*

QUARLOUS All the better. We shall see 'em come in now.

LEATHERHEAD What do you lack, gentlemen, what is't you lack? A fine horse? A lion? A bull? A bear? A dog or a cat? An excellent fine Barthol'mew-bird? Or an instrument? What is't you lack?

QUARLOUS [*to Winwife*] 'Slid, here's Orpheus among the beasts, with his fiddle, and all![1]

3. Your partnership, my good sirs, didn't begin just yesterday. Drink your pledge of agreement. (Punning on "draft," meaning "document.")
4. One of the roasted pigs' eyes has burst and let out its fluid, indicating that it is nearly done.
5. And now my work is finished, which neither the wrath of Jove, nor fire (nor sword, the gnawing tooth of time, will ever be able to undo). (Ovid, *Metamorphoses*, 15.871–72.)

2.5. The scene continues.
1. Orpheus was a legendary musician able to spellbind wild beasts with his playing. (Said ironically here.)

JOAN TRASH Will you buy any comfortable° bread, gentlemen? *tasty*

QUARLOUS [*to Winwife*] And Ceres[2] selling her daughter's picture in gingerwork!° *shaped gingerbread*

WINWIFE That these people should be so ignorant to think us chapmen° for 'em! Do we look as if we would buy gingerbread? Or hobbyhorses? *customers*

QUARLOUS Why, they know no better ware than they have, nor better customers than come. And our very being here makes us fit to be demanded,° as well as others. Would Cokes would come! There were a true customer for 'em. *solicited*

KNOCKEM [*looking at Edgeworth's haul*] How much is't? Thirty shillings? [*Seeing the new arrivals*] Who's yonder? Ned Winwife and Tom Quarlous, I think. Yes. [*To Edgeworth*] Gi' me it all, gi' me it all. [*To the gentlemen*] Master Winwife! Master Quarlous! Will you take a pipe of tobacco with us?— Do not discredit me now, Zekiel.

[*Winwife and Quarlous continue to speak privately.*]

WINWIFE Do not see him. He is the roaring horse-courser. Pray thee, let's avoid him. Turn down this way.

QUARLOUS 'Slud,° I'll see him, and roar with him, too, an° he roared as loud as Neptune.° Pray thee, go with me. *By God's blood / even if* *god of the sea*

WINWIFE You may draw me to as likely an inconvenience, when you please, as this.[3]

QUARLOUS Go to,° then, come along. We ha' nothing to do, man, but to see sights, now. [*They approach Knockem.*] *(expressing impatience)*

KNOCKEM Welcome, Master Quarlous and Master Winwife! Will you take any froth,° and smoke with us? *beer*

QUARLOUS Yes, sir, but you'll pardon us if we knew not of so much familiarity between us afore.

KNOCKEM As what, sir?

QUARLOUS To be so lightly invited to smoke and froth.

KNOCKEM A good vapor! Will you sit down, sir? This is old Ursula's mansion. How like you her bower? Here you may ha' your punk and your pig in state, sir, both piping hot.° *hot; venereally diseased*

QUARLOUS I had rather ha' my punk cold, sir.

JUSTICE OVERDO [*aside, as he writes*] There's for me:° punk! And pig! *for me to make note of*

She [*Ursula*] *calls within.*

URSULA What, Mooncalf? You rogue!

MOONCALF [*calling to her*] By and by. The bottle is almost off,° Mistress. [*He serves more liquor to Justice Overdo.*] Here, Master Arthur. *finished*

URSULA [*calling from within*] I'll part you and your playfellow there, i'the guarded[4] coat, an you sunder° not the sooner. *part company*

KNOCKEM Master Winwife, you are proud, methinks. You do not talk nor drink. Are you proud?

WINWIFE Not of the company I am in, sir, nor the place, I assure you.

KNOCKEM You do not except at° the company, do you? Are you in vapors, sir? *take exception to*

MOONCALF Nay, good Master Dan Knockem, respect my mis-

2. Roman goddess of agriculture and mother of Proserpine, or Persephone, wife of Hades.

3. Nothing could be a greater inconvenience and waste of time than this.

4. Trimmed, braided. (Referring to Justice Overdo's motley fool's coat.)

tress's bower, as you call it. For the honor of our booth, none o'your vapors here.

She [Ursula] comes out with a firebrand.° — *kindled stick*

URSULA [*to Mooncalf*] Why, you thin, lean polecat, you, an they have a mind to be i'their vapors, must you hinder 'em? What did you know,° vermin, if they would ha' lost a cloak or such a trifle? Must you be drawing the air of pacification here, while I am tormented, within, i'the fire, you weasel? — *know to the contrary*

MOONCALF Good mistress, 'twas in the behalf of your booth's credit° that I spoke. — *reputation*

URSULA Why, would my booth ha' broke° if they had fall'n out in't, sir? Or would their heat ha' fired° it? In, you rogue, and wipe° the pigs and mend the fire that they fall not,° or I'll both baste[5] and roast you, till your eyes drop out like 'em.° Leave the bottle behind you, and be curst awhile. — *gone bankrupt; fallen* / *set fire to* / *baste* / *(into the fire)* / *like the roasting pigs'*

[*Exit Mooncalf into the booth.*]

QUARLOUS Body o'the fair! What's this? Mother o'the bawds?

KNOCKEM No, she's mother o'the pigs, sir, mother o'the pigs.

WINWIFE Mother o'the Furies,° I think, by her firebrand. — *avenging goddesses*

QUARLOUS Nay, she is too fat to be a Fury; sure some walking sow of tallow. *She drinks this while.*

WINWIFE An inspired° vessel of kitchen-stuff!° — *inflated* / *grease*

QUARLOUS She'll make excellent gear° for the coach-makers, here in Smithfield, to anoint wheels and axletrees with. — *stuff, i.e., oil*

URSULA Ay, ay, gamesters,° mock a plain plump soft wench o'the suburbs, do, because she's juicy and wholesome.° You must ha' your thin pinched ware,° pent up i'the compass of a dog collar, or 'twill not do, that looks like a long laced conger° set upright, and a green feather, like fennel, i'the jowl on't. — *playboys* / *free of disease* / *i.e., whores* / *striped eel*

KNOCKEM Well said, Urs, my good Urs! To 'em, Urs!

QUARLOUS Is she your quagmire, Dan Knockem? Is this your bog?

NIGHTINGALE [*aside to Edgeworth*] We shall have a quarrel presently.

KNOCKEM How? Bog? Quagmire? Foul vapors! Hum'h!

QUARLOUS Yes, he that would venture for't, I assure him, might sink into her and be drowned a week ere any friend he had could find where he were.

WINWIFE And then he would be a fortnight weighing up° again. — *weighing anchor*

QUARLOUS 'Twere like falling into a whole shire° of butter; they had need a team of Dutchmen° should draw him out. — *region, district* / *noted butter-lovers*

KNOCKEM Answer 'em, Urs. Where's thy Barthol'mew wit now, Urs, thy Barthol'mew wit?

URSULA Hang 'em, rotten,° roguey cheaters! I hope to see 'em plagued one day (poxed° they are already, I am sure) with lean playhouse poultry° that has the bony rump sticking out like the ace of spades or the point of a partisan,° that every rib of 'em is like the tooth of a saw, and will so grate 'em — *syphilitic* / *venereally infected* / *theater whores* / *long-handled spear*

5. (1) Moisten during roasting; (2) thrash.

with their hips and shoulders as, take 'em altogether,° they were as good lie with a hurdle.°

all in all / *rail*

QUARLOUS Out upon her, how she drips! She's able to give a man the sweating sickness° with looking on her.

fever; syphilis

URSULA Marry, look off,° with a patch o'your face and a dozen i'your breech,[6] though they be o'scarlet,° sir! I ha' seen as fine outsides as either o'yours bring lousy linings to the brokers,[7] ere now, twice a week.

i.e., buzz off / *expensive cloth*

QUARLOUS Do you think there may be a fine new cucking stool[8] i'the fair to be purchased? One large enough, I mean. I know there is a pond of capacity° for her.

large enough

URSULA For your mother, you rascal. Out, you rogue, you hedge-bird,° you pimp, you pannier-man's bastard,[9] you!

thief, vagrant

QUARLOUS Ha, ha, ha!

URSULA Do you sneer, you dog's head,° you trundle-tail?° You look as you were begotten atop of a cart in harvesttime, when the whelp was hot and eager. Go, snuff after your brother's bitch, Mistress Commodity!° That's the livery you wear; 'twill be out at the elbows shortly. It's time you went to't, for the tother remnant.[1]

dog-faced baboon / cur / *Gain; goods for sale*

KNOCKEM Peace, Urs, peace, Urs.—They'll kill the poor whale, and make oil of her. [*To Ursula*] Pray thee go in.

URSULA I'll see 'em poxed first, and piled,[2] and double piled.

WINWIFE Let's away. Her language grows greasier than her pigs.

URSULA Does't so, snotty nose? Good Lord! Are you sniveling? You were engendered on a she-begger, in a barn, when the bald° thrasher,[3] your sire, was scarce warm.

hairless; wretched

WINWIFE [*to Quarlous*] Pray thee, let's go.

QUARLOUS No, faith, I'll stay the end of her, now. I know she cannot last long; I find by her similes she wanes apace.

URSULA Does she so? I'll set you gone.° [*Calling to Mooncalf*] Gi' me my pig pan hither a little.—I'll scald you hence, an you will not go. [*Exit.*]

i.e., get you moving

KNOCKEM Gentlemen, these are very strange vapors, and very idle vapors, I assure you.

QUARLOUS You are a very serious ass, we assure you.

KNOCKEM Hum'h! Ass? And serious? Nay, then pardon me my vapor. I have a foolish vapor, gentlemen: any man that does vapor me° the ass, Master Quarlous—

i.e., call me

QUARLOUS What then, Master Jordan?

KNOCKEM I do vapor him the lie.

QUARLOUS Faith, and to any man that vapors me the lie, I do vapor that. [*He strikes Knockem.*]

KNOCKEM [*striking back*] Nay, then, vapors upon vapors.

EDGEWORTH [*and*] NIGHTINGALE 'Ware the pan, the pan, the

6. With patches to cover your syphilis pox.
7. Ursula has seen seemingly well-dressed gentlemen obliged to bring their lice-infested undergarments to the used-clothes peddlers and pawnbrokers—her point being that you can't judge a book by its cover and that Quarlous and Winwife, for all their fine appearance, could be just as diseased as shabbily dressed men.
8. A chair used to punish offenders, such as dishonest tradespeople, scolds, and disreputable women, by ducking them in water.
9. A pannier-man is one who hawks wares from his pannier, or basket.
1. Ursula jeeringly suggests that the gallants may look fine but are lechers who "go to it" readily enough and are seen to be threadbare in short order.
2. (1) Worn threadbare; (2) hairless from syphilis, or "pox"; (3) suffering from piles.
3. (1) A farm laborer threshing grain; (2) a fornicator.

pan! She comes with the pan, gentlemen! God bless the woman!

Ursula comes in, with the scalding pan. They fight. She falls with it.

[*Exeunt Quarlous and Winwife.*]

[*Enter Mooncalf.*]

URSULA Oh!
JOAN TRASH What's the matter?
JUSTICE OVERDO Goodly woman!
MOONCALF Mistress!
URSULA Curse of hell, that ever I saw these fiends! Oh, I ha'
scalded my leg, my leg, my leg, my leg! I ha' lost a limb in
the service! Run for some cream and salad oil, quickly. [*To*
Mooncalf] Are you underpeering,° you baboon? Rip off my   *looking up my skirt*
hose, an you be men, men, men.
MOONCALF [*to Trash*] Run you for some cream, good mother
Joan. I'll look to your basket. [*Exit Trash.*]
LEATHERHEAD Best sit up i'your chair, Ursula. Help, gentlemen! [*They help her up into her chair.*]
KNOCKEM Be of good cheer, Urs. Thou hast hindered me the
currying of a couple of stallions here that abused the good
race-bawd o'Smithfield.[4] 'Twas time for 'em to go.
NIGHTINGALE I'faith, when the pan came; they had made you
run else. (*Aside to Edgeworth*) This had been a fine time for
purchase,° if you had ventured.   *picking of pockets*
EDGEWORTH [*aside to Nightingale*] Not a whit. These fellows
were too fine° to carry money.   *refined, smart*
KNOCKEM Nightingale, get some help to carry her leg out
o'the air. Take off her shoes. [*He examines her legs.*] Body
o'me, she has the malanders, the scratches, the crown-scab,
and the quitter-bone° i'the tother leg.   *horse leg diseases*
URSULA Oh, the pox! Why do you put me in mind o'my leg
thus, to make it prick and shoot?° Would you ha' me i'the   *suffer shooting pains*
hospital afore my time?[5]
KNOCKEM Patience, Urs. Take a good heart; 'tis but a blister
as big as a windgall.° I'll take it away with the white of an   *tumor of horse's leg*
egg, a little honey, and hog's grease, ha' thy pasterns° well   *feet above the hoof*
rolled,° and thou shalt pace° again by tomorrow. I'll tend thy   *bandaged / walk*
booth and look to thy affairs the while. Thou shalt sit i'thy
chair, and give directions, and shine Ursa Major.°   *i.e., the Big Dipper*

[*Knockem, Leatherhead, and Mooncalf carry Ursula, in her chair, into her booth. Leatherhead soon returns to his booth, and Trash returns from fetching some cream.*]

4. You have saved me the trouble of administering a drubbing to these studs here that have abused you, Ursula, our best breeder of bawds. ("Currying" is literally a brisk rubbing or cleaning of a horse's coat with a currycomb, hence a thrashing; "race-bawd" plays on "racehorse.")

5. Going to the hospital in early modern times was tantamount to being sent there to die.

2.6

[Enter] Cokes, Wasp, Mistress [Dame] Overdo, [and] Grace.

JUSTICE OVERDO These are the fruits of bottle ale and tobacco! The foam of the one and the fumes of the other! [*To Edgeworth*] Stay, young man, and despise not the wisdom of these few hairs that are grown gray in care of thee.

EDGEWORTH [*aside to Nightingale*] Nightingale, stay a little. Indeed, I'll hear some o'this.

COKES [*to Wasp*] Come, Numps, come, where are you?—Welcome into the fair, Mistress Grace.

EDGEWORTH [*aside to Nightingale*] 'Slight,° he° will call company, you shall see, and put us into doings[1] presently.

By God's light / (Cokes)

JUSTICE OVERDO [*to Edgeworth*] Thirst not after that frothy liquor, ale, for who knows, when he openeth the stopple,° what may be in the bottle? Hath not a snail, a spider, yea, a newt been found there? Thirst not after it, youth, thirst not after it.

stopper

COKES [*to Wasp*] This is a brave° fellow, Numps. Let's hear him.

fine

WASP 'Sblood, how brave is he? In a guarded° coat? You were best truck° with him, e'en strip and truck presently; it will become you. Why will you hear him? Because he is an ass, and may be akin to the Cokeses?

motley, fool's
deal, exchange coats

COKES Oh, good Numps!

JUSTICE OVERDO [*to Edgeworth*] Neither do thou lust after that tawny weed, tobacco.

COKES Brave words!

JUSTICE OVERDO Whose complexion is like the Indian's that vents it.°

puffs it out; sells it

COKES Are they not brave words, sister?

JUSTICE OVERDO And who can tell if, before the gathering and making up thereof, the alligarta° hath not pissed thereon?

alligator

WASP Heart,° let 'em be brave words, as brave as they will! An they were all the brave words in a country, how then? Will you away yet? Ha' you enough on him?—Mistress Grace, come you away, I pray you, be not you accessory.—If you do lose your license, or somewhat° else, sir, with list'ning to his fables, say Numps is a witch,° with all my heart, do, say so.

By God's heart
something
wizard, prophet

COKES Avoid,° i'your satin doublet, Numps!

Avaunt, begone

JUSTICE OVERDO The creeping venom of which subtle serpent, as some late writers° affirm, neither the cutting of the perilous plant, nor the drying of it, nor the lighting, or burning, can any way persway° or assuage.

(including James I)
lessen

COKES Good, i'faith! Is't not, sister?

JUSTICE OVERDO Hence it is that the lungs of the tobacconist° are rotted, the liver spotted, the brain smoked like the backside of the pig-woman's booth here, and the whole body within black as her pan you saw e'en now, without.

smoker

2.6. The scene continues.

1. He will give us the opportunity for picking pockets.

COKES A fine similitude, that, sir! [*To Edgeworth*] Did you see the pan?

EDGEWORTH Yes, sir.

JUSTICE OVERDO Nay, the hole in the nose° here of some tobacco-takers, or the third nostril, if I may so call it, which makes that they can vent the tobacco out, like the ace of clubs, or rather the fleur-de-lis,° is caused from the tobacco, the mere tobacco, when the poor innocent pox,° having nothing to do there, is miserably and most unconscionably slandered.

(an effect of syphilis)
heraldic lily
syphilis

COKES Who would ha' missed this, sister?

DAME OVERDO Not anybody but Numps.

COKES He does not understand.

EDGEWORTH [*aside*] Nor you feel. *He picketh his purse.*

COKES What would you have,° sister, of a fellow that knows nothing but a basket hilt and an old fox in't?[2] The best music i'the fair will not move a log.°

could you expect
i.e., stodgy old Wasp

EDGEWORTH [*aside to Nightingale, handing him the purse*] In to Ursula, Nightingale, and carry her comfort; see it told.° This fellow was sent to us by fortune for our first fairing.°

[*Exit Nightingale.*]

counted
fair purchase, booty

JUSTICE OVERDO But what° speak I of the diseases of the body, children of the fair?

why

COKES That's to us, sister. Brave, i'faith!

JUSTICE OVERDO Hark, O you sons and daughters of Smithfield, and hear what malady it doth the mind: It causeth swearing, it causeth swaggering, it causeth snuffling° and snarling, and now and then a hurt.

disdainful sniffing

DAME OVERDO [*aside to Cokes*] He hath something of° Master Overdo, methinks, brother.

somewhat resembles

COKES So methought, sister, very much of my brother° Overdo, and 'tis when he speaks.

brother-in-law

JUSTICE OVERDO Look into any angle° o'the town—the Straits, or the Bermudas°—where the quarreling lesson is read,[3] and how do they entertain° the time but with bottle ale and tobacco? The lecturer is o'one side and his pupils o'the other, but the seconds° are still bottle ale and tobacco, for which the lecturer reads° and the novices pay. Thirty pound a week in bottle ale! Forty in tobacco! And ten more in ale again! Then for a suit to drink in, so much,[4] and, that being slavered,° so much for another suit, and then a third suit, and a fourth suit! And still the bottle ale slavereth, and the tobacco stinketh!

corner
disreputable districts
employ, pass
props, standbys
lectures
slobbered on

WASP [*to Cokes*] Heart of a madman! Are you rooted here? Will you never away? What can any man find out in this bawling fellow to grow° here for?—He is a full handful higher sin' he heard him.[5]—Will you fix here? And set up a booth? Sir?

stay, be rooted

JUSTICE OVERDO I will conclude briefly—

2. The sort of fellow who wears an old-fashioned sword with a large basket-shaped hilt.
3. Where quarreling is taught, as if in a fencing academy.
4. A certain amount.
5. Cokes has grown six inches taller since Overdo began talking.

WASP Hold your peace, you roaring rascal! I'll run my head i'your chops° else. [*To Cokes*] You were best build a booth, and entertain° him; make your will, an you say the word, and him your heir! Heart, I never knew one taken with a mouth of a peck° afore. By this light, I'll carry you away o'my back, an you will not come. *He gets him up on pick-pack.*°

jaws · *hire* · *two-gallon capacity* · *pickaback, piggyback*

COKES Stay, Numps, stay, set me down! I ha' lost my purse, Numps. Oh, my purse! One o'my fine purses is gone!

DAME OVERDO Is't indeed, brother?

COKES Ay, as I am an honest man; would I were an arrant rogue else! A plague of all roguey, damned cutpurses for me!°

for my part

WASP Bless 'em with all my heart, with all my heart, do you see? Now, as I am no infidel that I know of, I am glad on't, I. I am; here's my witness! Do you see, sir? I did not tell you of his fables,[6] I? No, no, I am a dull malt-horse,° I; I know nothing. Are you not justly served, i'your conscience now? Speak, i'your conscience? Much good do you, with all my heart, and his good heart that has it,° with all my heart again!

workhorse · *(the purse)*

EDGEWORTH [*aside*] This fellow is very charitable. Would he had a purse too! But I must not be too bold all at a time.

COKES Nay, Numps, it is not my best purse.

WASP Not your best? Death! Why should it be your worst? Why should it be any, indeed, at all? Answer me to that. Gi' me a reason from you why it should be any?

COKES Nor my gold, Numps; I ha' that yet. [*He shows his money.*] Look here else,° sister.

if you don't believe me

WASP Why, so, there's all the feeling he has!

DAME OVERDO I pray you, have a better care of that, brother.

COKES Nay, so I will, I warrant you; let him catch this that catch can. I would fain° see him get this. Look you here.

gladly

WASP So, so, so, so, so, so, so, so! Very good.

COKES I would ha' him come again, now, and but offer at it.° Sister, will you take notice of a good jest? I will put it just where th'other was [*pocketing the money*], and, if we ha' good luck, you shall see a delicate fine trap to catch the cutpurse nibbling.

attempt pickpocketing

EDGEWORTH [*aside*] Faith, and he'll try ere you be out o'the fair.

COKES Come, Mistress Grace, prithee be not melancholy for my mischance. Sorrow wi' not keep it,° sweetheart.

bring the money back

GRACE I do not think on't, sir.

COKES 'Twas but a little scurvy white money,° hang it. It may hang the cutpurse one day. I ha' gold left to gi' thee a fairing° yet, as hard as the world goes. Nothing angers me but that nobody here looked like a cutpurse, unless 'twere Numps.

silver · *fair gift*

WASP How? I? I look like a cutpurse? Death! Your sister's a cutpurse! And your mother and father and all your kin were cutpurses! And here [*indicating Justice Overdo*] is a rogue is° the bawd° o'the cutpurses, whom I will beat to begin with.

who is · *confederate*

They speak all together; and Wasp beats the Justice.

COKES Numps, Numps!

DAME OVERDO Good Master Humphrey!

6. Didn't I warn you about the nonsense that this strange preacher has been spouting?

JUSTICE OVERDO Hold thy hand, child of wrath and heir of anger! Make it not Childermas Day[7] in thy fury, or the feast of the French Barthol'mew, parent of the massacre![8]

WASP You are the patrico,° are you? The patriarch of the cutpurses? You share,° sir, they say; let them share this with you. Are you i'your hot fit of preaching again? I'll cool you. *i.e., priest of thieves* / *share booty*

JUSTICE OVERDO Murder, murder, murder!

[*Exeunt all but Leatherhead and Trash.*]

3.1

[*Enter*] *Whit, Haggis,* [*and*] *Bristle. Leatherhead* [*is in his booth and*] *Trash* [*at her stand*].[1]

WHIT Nay, 'tish all gone, now! Dish 'tish, phen[2] tou vilt not be phitin° call, Master Offisher. Phat° ish a man te better to lishen out noishes for tee, an tou art in an oder° 'orld, being very shuffishient noishes and gallantsh too? One o'their brabblesh° woud have fed ush[3] all dish fortnight, but tou art so bushy° about beggersh still, tou hast no leshure to intend° shentlemen, an't be.° *within / What* / *other* / *brabbles, quarrels* / *busy / attend to* / *if you please*

HAGGIS Why, I told you, Davy Bristle.

BRISTLE Come, come, you told me a pudding,° Toby Haggis, a matter of nothing; I am sure it came to nothing. You said, "Let's go to Ursula's," indeed, but then you met the man with the monsters,° and I could not get you from him. An old fool! Not leave seeing° yet? *a load of tripe* / *fair freaks* / *leave off gazing*

HAGGIS Why, who would ha' thought anybody would ha' quarreled so early? Or that the ale o'the fair would ha' been up° so soon? *flowing*

WHIT Phy, phat a clock° toest tou tinke it ish, man? *Why, what o'clock*

HAGGIS I cannot tell.

WHIT Tou art a vishe° vatchman, i'te mean teeme.° *wise / in the meantime*

HAGGIS Why, should the watch go by the clock, or the clock by the watch, I pray?

BRISTLE One should go by another, if they did well.

WHIT Tou art right, now! Phen didst tou ever know or hear of a shuffishient vatchman but he did tell° the clock, phat bushiness soever he had? *call out; count*

BRISTLE Nay, that's most true, a sufficient watchman knows what o'clock it is.

WHIT Shleeping or vaking, ash well as te clock himshelf, or te jack° dat shtrikes him! *figure striking the bell*

BRISTLE Let's inquire of Master Leatherhead, or Joan Trash here.— Master Leatherhead, do you hear, Master Leatherhead?

WHIT If it be a Ledderhead, 'tish a very tick° Ledderhead, tat sho mush noish° vill not peirsh° him. *thick* / *so much noise / pierce*

LEATHERHEAD I have a little business now, good friends; do not trouble me.

7. The Feast of the Holy Innocents, December 28.

8. A massacre of French Huguenots on Saint Bartholomew's Day, August 24, 1572.

3.1. The fair.

1. Leatherhead and Trash have presumably been silently present at their places of business during the previous scene.

2. This 'tis, when. (Stage Irish—more a theatrical convention than an accurate representation of any particular Irish dialect.)

3. I.e., would have provided us with fees for quelling a disturbance.

WHIT Phat? Because o'ty wrought neet-cap and ty phelvet sherkin,[4] man? Phy? I have sheen tee in ty ledder sherkin ere now, mashter o'de hobbyhorses, as bushy and as stately as tou sheem'st to be.

JOAN TRASH Why, what an you have, Captain Whit? He has his choice of jerkins, you may see by that, and his caps too, I assure you, when he pleases to be either sick or employed.

LEATHERHEAD God-a-mercy, Joan! Answer for me.

WHIT [*to Haggis and Bristle*] Away! Be not sheen i'my company![5] Here be shentlemen and men of vorship.°

good name, renown

[*Exeunt Haggis and Bristle.*]

3.2

[*Enter*] *Quarlous* [*and*] *Winwife.*

QUARLOUS [*to Winwife*] We had wonderful° ill luck to miss this prologue o'the purse,° but the best is we shall have five acts of him° ere night. He'll be spectacle enough. I'll answer° for't.

extremely / i.e., robbing of Cokes / (Cokes) / vouch

WHIT Oh, Creesh!° Duke Quarlous, how dosht tou? Tou dosht not know me, I fear? I am te vishesht° man but° Justish Overdo in all Barthol'mew Fair, now. Gi' me twelvepence from tee, I vill help tee to a vife vorth forty marks° for't, an't be.

Christ! / wisest / other than / annual income of £26 14s.

QUARLOUS Away, rogue! Pimp, away!

WHIT And she shall show tee as fine cut'orke for't, in her shmock[1] too, as tou canst vish, i'faith. Vilt tou have her, vorshipful Vinvife? I vill help tee to her, here, be an't be,° in te pig-quarter.[2] Gi' me ty twel'pence from tee.

be it as it may be

WINWIFE [*giving money*] Why, there's twelvepence. Pray thee, wilt thou be gone?

WHIT Tou art a vorthy man, and a vorshipful man still.°

ever

QUARLOUS Get you gone, rascal.

WHIT I do mean it,° man. Prinsh Quarlous, if tou hasht need on me, tou shalt find me here at Ursula's. I vill see phat ale and punk° ish i'te pigshty for tee. Bless ty good vorship!

I mean to leave / whores

[*Exit.*]

[*Enter*] *Busy, John* [*Littlewit*], *Purecraft,* [*and*] *Win.* [*Winwife and Quarlous stand aside and comment as the others enter.*]

QUARLOUS Look who comes here: John Littlewit.

WINLIFE And his wife, and my widow, her mother—the whole family.

QUARLOUS 'Slight, you must gi' 'em all fairings, now.

WINWIFE Not I. I'll not see 'em.

QUARLOUS They are going a-feasting. What schoolmaster's that is with 'em?

WINWIFE That's my rival, I believe, the baker.

BUSY [*to the Littlewit party*] So, walk on in the middle way, foreright.° Turn neither to the right hand nor to the left. Let

straight ahead

4. Thy embroidered cap and velvet jerkin, or jacket.
5. I.e., Don't let on that I am an informer for the watch.
3.2. The scene continues.
1. She'll show you fine lacework in her petticoat. (With obscene suggestion.)
2. The area of the fair where roast pig is obtainable.

not your eyes be drawn aside with vanity, nor your ear with noises.

QUARLOUS [*aside to Winwife*] Oh, I know him by that start!° *twitch, sudden movement*

LEATHERHEAD What do you lack? What do you buy, pretty mistress? A fine hobbyhorse, to make your son a tilter?° A drum to make him a soldier? A fiddle to make him a reveler? What is't you lack? Little dogs for your daughters, or babies,° male or female? *jouster; lecher* / *dolls*

BUSY Look not toward them! Hearken not. The place is Smithfield, or the field of smiths, the grove of hobbyhorses and trinkets; the wares are the wares of devils. And the whole fair is the shop of Satan! They are hooks, and baits, very baits, that are hung out on every side, to catch you and to hold you, as it were, by the gills and by the nostrils, as the fisher doth. Therefore, you must not look nor turn toward them. The heathen man could stop his ears with wax against the harlot o'the sea; do you the like, with your fingers against the bells of the Beast.[3]

WINWIFE [*aside to Quarlous*] What flashes comes from him!

QUARLOUS [*aside to Winwife*] Oh, he has° those of° his oven. A notable hot baker 'twas, when he plied the peel.° He is leading his flock into the fair, now. *got / from* / *used a baker's shovel*

WINWIFE [*aside to Quarlous*] Rather, driving 'em to the pens,[4] for he will let 'em look upon nothing.

[*Enter*] *Knockem* [*and*] *Whit.*

KNOCKEM [*to Win and Purecraft*] Gentlewomen, the weather's hot! Whither walk you? Have a care o'your fine velvet caps; the fair is dusty. Take a sweet delicate° booth, with boughs, here, i'the way, and cool yourselves i'the shade, you and your friends. [*To Littlewit*] The best pig and bottle ale i'the fair, sir. Old Ursula is cook. There you may read: the pig's head speaks it. *delightful*

Littlewit is gazing at the sign, which is the pig's head with a large writing under it.

Poor soul, she has had a springhalt, the maryhinchco,° but she's prettily amended.° *horse leg diseases* / *feeling somewhat better*

WHIT A delicate show-pig,° little mistress, with shweet sauce, and crackling like de bay leaf i'de fire, la! Tou shalt ha' de clean side o'de tableclot and dy glass vashed with phatersh of Dame Annessh Cleare.[5] *sow-pig*

LITTLEWIT [*reading the sign*] This 's fine, verily: Here be the best pigs, and she does roast 'em as well as ever she did, the pig's head says.

KNOCKEM [*to Win*] Excellent, excellent, mistress, with fire o'juniper and rosemary branches.° [*To Littlewit*] The oracle of the pig's head, that,° sir. *(for fragrant smoke)* / *(the sign)*

PURECRAFT [*to Littlewit*] Son, were you not warned of the

3. Just as Odysseus resisted the charms of the Sirens, you must similarly stop your ears against the voices of the Beast of the Apocalypse. (The Sirens—Busy's "harlot o'the sea," line 48—were mythological bird-women who lured ships with their singing to destruction on rocks. Busy, in his Puritan contempt for a "heathen" hero like Odysseus, gets the story wrong; Odysseus had his sailors tie him to the mast of their ship so that he could hear the Sirens' song without being able to jump overboard. Revelation 4 describes four winged, monstrous beasts "full of eyes before and behind.")

4. He is herding them as if they were a "flock" (line 53) to be herded into cattle pens.

5. Waters of Annis Clare (who was reported to have drowned herself at Hoxton).

vanity of the eye? Have you forgot the wholesome admonition so soon?

LITTLEWIT Good mother, how shall we find a pig if we do not look about for't? Will it run off o'the spit into our mouths, think you, as in Lubberland,[6] and cry, "Wee, wee"?° *(pigs' squeal)*

BUSY No, but your mother, religiously wise, conceiveth it may offer itself by other means to the sense, as by way of steam, which I think it doth, here in this place. (*Busy scents after it like a hound.*) Huh, huh!° *(a snuffing sound)* Yes, it doth! And it were a sin of obstinacy, great obstinacy, high and horrible obstinacy, to decline or resist the good titillation of the famelic° *hunger-exciting* sense, which is the smell. Therefore be bold. [*He sniffs again.*] Huh, huh, huh! Follow the scent. Enter the tents of the unclean, for once, and satisfy your wife's frailty. Let your frail wife be° *Provided your wife is* satisfied, your zealous mother and my suffering self will also be satisfied.

LITTLEWIT Come, Win, as good winny° *stay (with pun on "Win")* here as go farther and see nothing.

BUSY We scape so much of the other vanities by our early ent'ring.

PURECRAFT It is an edifying consideration.

WIN [*aside to Littlewit*] This is scurvy, that we must come into the fair and not look on't.

LITTLEWIT [*aside to her*] Win, have patience, Win. I'll tell you more anon.

KNOCKEM Mooncalf, entertain within there: the best pig i'the booth, a porklike pig. These are Banbury-bloods,° *purebred of Banbury* o'the sincere stud,° *true breed* come a-pig-hunting. Whit, wait, Whit, look to your charge.° *(see 65–68)* [*Exit Whit.*]

BUSY A pig prepare presently. Let a pig be prepared to us.

[*Exeunt Busy, Littlewit, Win, and Purecraft into Ursula's booth.*]

[*Enter*] *Mooncalf* [*and*] *Ursula.*

MOONCALF 'Slight, who be these?

URSULA Is this the good service, Jordan, you'd do me?

KNOCKEM Why, Urs, why, Urs, thou'lt ha' vapors i'thy leg again presently. Pray thee, go in; 't may turn to the scratches° *scabs on legs* else.

URSULA Hang your vapors! They are stale and stink like you. Are these the guests o'the game° you promised to fill my pit° *sex-seekers / booth* withal today?

KNOCKEM Ay, what ail they, Urs?

URSULA Ail they? They are all sippers, sippers o'the city. They look as they would not drink off two penn'orth of bottle ale amongst 'em.

MOONCALF A body° may read that i'their small printed ruffs.° *person / (Puritan garb)*

KNOCKEM Away! Thou art a fool, Urs, and thy Mooncalf too, i'your ignorant vapors, now. Hence! Good guests, I say, right° *true* hypocrites, good gluttons. In, and set a couple o'pigs o'the board and half a dozen of the biggest bottles afore 'em, and call Whit. I do not love to hear innocents abused.° *slandered* Fine ambling hypocrites! And a stone° Puritan, with a sorrel° head *stallion / red-brown*

6. A mythical land of leisure and plenty, like the land of Cockaigne.

and beard, good-mouthed° gluttons, two to a pig. Away!

greedy, hungry

[*Exit Mooncalf.*]

URSULA Are you sure they are such?

KNOCKEM O'the right breed; thou shalt try 'em by the teeth,[7] Urs. Where's this Whit?

[*Enter Whit.*]

WHIT [*declaiming*] "Behold, man and see,
What a worthy man am ee!°
With the fury of my sword, and the shaking of my beard,
I will make ten thousand men afeard."

am I

KNOCKEM Well said, brave Whit! In, and fear° the ale out o'the bottles into the bellies of the brethren and the sisters.° Drink to the cause,° and pure vapors.

frighten, propel / *Puritan men and women* / *Puritan cause*

[*Exeunt Whit, Knockem, and Ursula.*]

QUARLOUS My roarer° is turned tapster, methinks. Now were a fine time for thee, Winwife, to lay aboard° thy widow. Thou'lt never be master of a better season or place; she that will venture herself into the fair and a pig box° will admit any assault, be assured of that.

i.e., Whit / *come alongside for attack* / *pig booth*

WINWIFE I love not enterprises of that suddenness, though.

QUARLOUS I'll warrant thee, then, no wife out o'the widow's hundred.[8] If I had but as much title to her as to have breathed once on that strait° stomacher of hers,[9] I would now assure myself to carry° her yet, ere she went out of Smithfield. Or she should carry° me, which were the fitter sight, I confess. But you are a modest undertaker, by circumstances and degrees;[1] come, 'tis disease in thee, not judgment. I should offer at° all together. Look, here's the poor fool° again that was stung by the wasp° erewhile.

closely fitting / *win* / *support; hold up in sex* / *have a go at* / *(Overdo) / by Wasp*

[*They stand aside.*]

3.3

[*Enter*] *Justice* [*Overdo*].

JUSTICE OVERDO [*to himself*] I will make no more orations shall draw on° these tragical conclusions. And I begin now to think that, by a spice° of collateral° justice, Adam Overdo deserved this beating. For I, the said Adam, was one cause—a by-cause°—why the purse was lost, and my wife's brother's purse too, which they know not of yet.[1] But I shall make very good mirth with it at supper (that will be the sport), and put my little friend Master Humphrey Wasp's choler quite out of countenance. When, sitting at the upper end o'my table, as I use,° and drinking to my brother Cokes, and Mistress Alice Overdo, as I will, my wife, for their good affection to old Bradley, I deliver° to 'em it was I that was cudgeled, and show 'em the marks. To see what bad events° may peep out

that will invite / *kind / concomitant* / *incidental cause* / *as is my custom* / *reveal* / *consequences*

7. (1) By how much they eat; (2) as one judges horses by the condition of their teeth.

8. I.e., I assure you that you'll win no propertied widow without taking the offensive. (A hundred is a subdivision of the English shire having its own court.)

9. If I could get so far as to make the first intimate advances. (A stomacher ornamentally covers the woman's bodice.)

1. But you are a timid venturer, moving cautiously.

3.3. The scene continues.

1. They don't yet know of my presence during the theft.

o'the tail of good purposes! The care I had of that civil young man I took fancy to this morning (and have not left it yet) drew me to that exhortation, which drew the company, indeed, which drew the cutpurse, which drew the money, which drew my brother Cokes his° loss, which drew on Wasp's anger, which drew on my beating: a pretty gradation! And they shall ha' it i'their dish, i'faith, at night, for fruit.° I love to be merry at my table. I had thought once, at one special blow he ga' me, to have revealed myself. But then (I thank thee, fortitude) I remembered that a wise man, and who is ever so great a part o'the commonwealth in himself,[2] for no particular° disaster ought to abandon a public good design. The husbandman° ought not, for one unthankful year, to forsake the plow; the shepherd ought not, for one scabbed sheep, to throw by his tar box;° the pilot ought not, for one leak i'the poop,° to quit the helm, nor the alderman ought not, for one custard more, at a meal to give up his cloak.[3] The constable ought not to break his staff and forswear the watch for one roaring° night, nor the piper o'the parish (*ut parvis componere magna solebam*)[4] to put up his pipes for one rainy Sunday. These are certain knocking° conclusions, out of which I am resolved, come what come can—come beating, come imprisonment, come infamy, come banishment, nay, come the rack,° come the hurdle,[5] welcome all!—I will not discover° who I am till my due time. And yet still all shall be, as I said ever, in justice' name, and the King's, and for the commonwealth. [*Exit.*]

- his: *Cokes's*
- for fruit: *as dessert*
- particular: *personal*
- husbandman: *farmer*
- tar box: *(to salve sheep sores)*
- poop: *stern*
- roaring: *riotous*
- knocking: *hard-hitting, confirming*
- rack: *torture rack*
- discover: *reveal*

WINWIFE What° does he talk to himself, and act so seriously? Poor fool!

- What: *Why*

QUARLOUS No matter what. Here's fresher argument;° intend° that.

- argument / intend: *subject matter / heed*

3.4

[Enter] Cokes, Wasp [carrying fair purchases], Mistress [Dame] Overdo, [and] Grace. Leatherhead [and Joan] Trash [are visible at their places of business].

COKES Come, Mistress Grace, come, sister, here's more fine sights yet, i'faith. God's lid,° where's Numps?

- God's lid: *By God's eyelid*

LEATHERHEAD What do you lack, gentlemen? What is't you buy? Fine rattles? Drums? Babies? Little dogs, and birds for ladies? What do you lack?

COKES Good honest Numps, keep afore.° I am so afraid thou'lt lose somewhat.° My heart was at my mouth when I missed thee.

- keep afore: *walk on ahead*
- somewhat: *something*

WASP You were best buy a whip i'your hand to drive me.

COKES Nay, do not mistake, Numps; thou art so apt to mis-

2. And who has a role to play in the governance of the state.
3. An alderman ought not to give up his cloak of office just because an extra guest at the banquet happens to require yet another custard. (The huge custards served at lord mayors' feasts were frequently a subject of ridicule.)
4. To compare great things with small. (Virgil, *Eclogues*, 1.23.) The "piper" is employed to play at church-ales and other festive parish occasions.
5. A frame on which traitors were drawn to execution.

3.4. The scene continues.

take. I would but watch the goods. Look you now, the treble fiddle was e'en almost like to be° lost.

on the verge of being

WASP Pray you take heed you lose not yourself. Your best way were e'en get up° and ride for more surety. Buy a token's worth of great pins to fasten yourself to my shoulder.

up on my shoulders

LEATHERHEAD What do you lack, gentlemen? Fine purses, pouches, pin cases, pipes? What is't you lack? A pair o'smiths[1] to wake you i'the morning? Or a fine whistling bird?

COKES Numps, here be finer things than any we ha' bought, by odds! And more delicate horses, a great deal! Good Numps, stay, and come hither.

WASP Will you scorse° with him? You are in Smithfield; you may fit yourself with a fine easygoing street nag for your saddle again' Michaelmas term,[2] do! Has he ne'er a little odd cart for you to make a caroche° on, i'the country, with four pied° hobbyhorses? Why the measles° should you stand here with your train,° cheaping of° dog, birds, and babies? You ha' no children to bestow 'em on, ha' you?

bargain, deal / *carriage* / *parti-colored / dickens* / *retinue / haggling for*

COKES No, but again'° I ha' children, Numps, that's all one.°

in case / all the same

WASP Do, do, do, do! How many shall you have, think you? An I were as you, I'd buy for all my tenants, too; they are a kind o'civil° savages, that will part with their children for rattles, pipes, and knives. You were best buy a hatchet or two, and truck° with 'em.

half-civilized / *bargain, deal*

COKES Good Numps, hold that little tongue o'thine and save it a labor. I am resolute Bat, thou know'st.

WASP A resolute fool you are, I know, and a very sufficient coxcomb, with all my heart. Nay, you have it,° sir; an you be angry, turd i'your teeth, twice (if I said it not once afore), and much good do you.

you have my reply

WINWIFE [*aside to Quarlous*] Was there ever such a self-affliction? And so impertinent?

QUARLOUS [*aside to Winwife*] Alas! His care will go near to crack° him. Let's in,° and comfort him.

craze / join the company

[*Winwife and Quarlous join the others.*]

WASP Would I had been set i'the ground, all but the head on me, and had my brains bowled at, or threshed out, when first I underwent this plague of a charge!

QUARLOUS How now, Numps? Almost tired i'your protectorship? Overparted?° Overparted?

Given too hard a role?

WASP Why, I cannot tell, sir, it may be I am. Does't grieve you?

QUARLOUS No, I swear does't not, Numps, to satisfy you.

WASP "Numps"? 'Sblood, you are fine and familiar! How long ha' we been acquainted, I pray you?

QUARLOUS I think it may be remembered, Numps, that? 'Twas since morning, sure.

WASP Why, I hope I know't well enough, sir. I did not ask to be told.

QUARLOUS No? Why, then?

WASP It's no matter why. You see with your eyes, now, what

1. Metal pieces forming the figure of a man (or blacksmith) that strike the bells on the outside of clocks.

2. In preparation for the fall court term.

I said to you today? You'll believe me another time?

QUARLOUS Are you removing° the fair, Numps? *leaving; carrying off*

WASP A pretty question, and a very civil one! Yes, faith, I ha' my lading,° you see, or shall have anon. You may know whose beast I am by my burden. If the pannier-man's jack were ever better known by his loins of mutton, I'll be flayed and feed dogs for him when his time comes.[3] *load*

WINWIFE [*to Quarlous*] How melancholy Mistress Grace is yonder! Pray thee, let's go enter ourselves in grace° with her. *ingratiate ourselves*

[*Winwife and Quarlous join Grace.*]

COKES [*to Leatherhead*] Those six horses,° friend, I'll have— *hobbyhorses*

WASP How!

COKES And the three Jews' trumps,° and half a dozen o'birds, and that drum (I have one drum already), and your smiths° (I like that device o'your smiths very pretty well), and four halberds,° and—le' me see—that fine painted great lady and her three women for state° I'll have. *Jews' harps* / *(see 17–18 and n)* / *long-handled spears* / *ceremonial show*

WASP No, the shop! Buy the whole shop, it will be best, the shop, the shop!

LEATHERHEAD If His Worship please.

WASP [*to Leatherhead*] Yes, and keep it during the fair, bobchin.° *blabbermouth*

COKES Peace, Numps!—Friend, do not meddle with him, an you be wise and would show your head above board.° He will sting thorough° your wrought° nightcap, believe me. A set of these violins I would buy too, for a delicate young noise° I have i'the country that are every one a size less than another, just like your fiddles. I would fain have a fine young masque at my marriage, now I think on't; but I do want° such a number o'things. And Numps will not help me now, and I dare not speak to him. *in company* / *through / woven* / *instrumental group* / *lack*

JOAN TRASH Will Your Worship buy any gingerbread, very good bread, comfortable bread? *He runs to her shop.*

COKES Gingerbread! Yes, let's see.

WASP There's the tother springe!° *the other trap*

LEATHERHEAD Is this well, Goody° Joan? To interrupt my market? In the midst? And call away my customers? Can you answer this at the Piepowders? *Goodwife*

JOAN TRASH Why, if His Mastership have a mind to buy, I hope my ware lies as open° as another's; I may show my ware as well as you yours. *(with sexual suggestion)*

COKES Hold your peace! I'll content you both: I'll buy up his shop and thy basket.

WASP Will you, i'faith?

LEATHERHEAD Why should you put him from it, friend?

WASP Cry you mercy!° You'd be sold too, would you? What's the price on you, jerkin,° and all as you stand? Ha' you any qualities?° *I beg your pardon!* / *you in the jacket* / *accomplishments*

JOAN TRASH Yes, goodman° angry man, you shall find he has qualities, if you cheapen° him. *my good sir* / *ask the price of*

3. If the jackass carrying burdens for his master (who hawks his wares in a "pannier," or basket) is ever better known by the loins of mutton in his packsaddle than I am known by this trumpery I'm carrying, I'll agree to be flayed alive and fed to the dogs in place of the jackass when its time comes. (Worn-out beasts of burden were regularly skinned and made into dog food.)

WASP Godso,° you ha' the selling of him! What are they? Will they be bought for love or money?

(an oath)

JOAN TRASH No, indeed, sir.

WASP For what, then? Victuals?

JOAN TRASH He scorns victuals, sir. He has bread and butter° at home, thanks be to God. And yet he will do more for a good meal, if the toy° take him i'the belly. Marry, then, they must not set him at lower end;° if they do, he'll go away, though he fast. But put him atop° o'the table, where his place is, and he'll do you forty fine things. He has not been sent for and sought out for nothing at your great city suppers, to put down Coryate and Cokeley,[4] and been laughed at for his labor. He'll play you° all the puppets i'the town over, and the players, every company, and his own company too. He spares nobody!

i.e., enough to eat / *fancy* / *lower end of the table* / *at the head* / *He'll mimic*

COKES I'faith?

JOAN TRASH He was the first, sir, that ever baited the fellow i'the bear's skin,[5] an't like° Your Worship; no dog ever came near him since. And for fine motions!°

if it please / *puppet shows*

COKES Is he good at those too? Can he set out a masque, trow?°

do you suppose?

JOAN TRASH Oh, Lord, master! Sought to° far and near for his inventions; and he engrosses° all. He makes all the puppets i'the fair.

He is resorted to / *monopolizes*

COKES [*to Leatherhead*] Dost thou, in troth, old velvet jerkin?° Give me thy hand.

(see 107 above)

JOAN TRASH Nay, sir, you shall see him in his velvet jerkin, and a scarf, too, at night,° when you hear him interpret° Master Littlewit's motion.

this evening / produce

COKES Speak no more, but shut up shop presently, friend. I'll buy both it and thee too, to carry down° with me, and her hamper, beside. Thy shop shall furnish out the masque, and hers the banquet. I cannot go° less, to set out anything with credit.° What's the price, at a word, o'thy whole shop, case and all as it stands?

down into the country / *do* / *creditably*

LEATHERHEAD Sir, it stands me in° six-and-twenty shillings sevenpence halfpenny, besides three shillings for my ground.°

costs me / *rental*

COKES Well, thirty shillings will do all, then.—And what comes yours to?

JOAN TRASH Four shillings and elevenpence, sir, ground and all, an't like Your Worship.

COKES [*giving money*] Yes, it does like My Worship very well, poor woman; that's five shillings more. What a masque shall I furnish out for forty shillings (twenty pound Scotch)![6] And a banquet of gingerbread! There's a stately thing. Numps? Sister? And my wedding gloves° too! (That I never thought on afore.) All my wedding gloves, gingerbread! Oh, me, what a device will there be, to make 'em eat their fingers' ends!° And delicate brooches for the bridemen° and all! And then

customary wedding favors / *lick their fingers* / *groomsmen*

4. Two famous jesters. Thomas Coryate, jester in Prince Henry's household, wrote *Coryate's Crudities* (1611), a travel account.

5. Joan Trash refers to the baiting of a fake bear at the Fortune Theater in 1612.

6. When James I became King of England in 1603, the Scottish pound was valued at one-twelfth of a pound sterling.

I'll ha' this posy° put to 'em: "For the best grace," meaning Mistress Grace, my wedding posy.

motto

GRACE I am beholden to you, sir, and to your Barthol'mew wit.°

(said ironically)

WASP [*to Cokes*] You do not mean this, do you? Is this your first purchase?

COKES Yes, faith, and I do not think, Numps, but thou'lt say it was the wisest act that ever I did in my wardship.°

period of minority

WASP Like enough. I shall say anything, I!

3.5

[*Enter*] *Edgeworth* [*and*] *Nightingale* [*followed by the disguised*] *Justice* [*Overdo, who stands aside, concealed*].

JUSTICE OVERDO I cannot beget a project, with all my political° brain, yet. My project is how to fetch off° this proper° young man° from his debauched company. I have followed him all the fair over, and still I find him with this songster;° and I begin shrewdly to suspect their familiarity, and the young man of a terrible taint, poetry! With which idle disease if he be infected, there's no hope of him in a state course.° *Actum est* of him for a commonwealth's man,[1] if he go to't in rhyme, once.

shrewd / *rescue / fine* / *(Edgeworth)* / *(Nightingale)* / *public career*

EDGEWORTH [*aside to Nightingale*] Yonder he° is, buying o'gingerbread. Set in quickly, before he part with too much on° his money.

(Cokes) / *of*

NIGHTINGALE [*singing*]

"My masters and friends and good people, draw near," etc.

COKES Ballads! Hark, hark! *He runs to the ballad man.* Pray thee, fellow, stay a little.—Good Numps, look to the goods.— What ballads hast thou? Let me see, let me see myself.

WASP Why, so! He's flown to another limebush;[2] there he will flutter as long more, till he ha' ne'er a feather left. Is there a vexation like this, gentlemen? Will you believe me now? Hereafter shall I have credit with° you?

be believed by

QUARLOUS Yes, faith, shalt thou, Numps, and thou art worthy on't, for thou sweatest for't. [*Aside to Winwife and Grace*] I never saw a young pimp-errant and his squire better matched.[3]

[*Quarlous, Winwife, and Grace continue to speak confidentially to one another.*]

WINWIFE Faith, the sister comes after 'em° well, too.

is like them

GRACE Nay, if you saw the justice her husband, my guardian, you were fitted for the mess.° He is such a wise one his way—

foursome

WINWIFE I wonder we see him not here.

GRACE Oh, he is too serious for this place, and yet better sport° than the other three, I assure you, gentlemen, where'er he is, though't be o'the bench.

subject of laughter

3.5. The scene continues.
1. His career as a useful citizen is finished.
2. A bush smeared with sticky lime to snare songbirds.
3. Quarlous sardonically compares Cokes and Wasp to a knight-errant and a squire from chivalric romance.

COKES [*examining Nightingale's ballads*] How° dost thou call it? "A Caveat against Cutpurses"? A good jest, i'faith. I would fain see that demon, your cutpurse you talk of, that delicate-handed devil; they say he walks hereabout. I would see him walk, now. (*He shows his purse boastingly.*) Look you, sister, here, here! Let him come, sister, and welcome.—Ballad man, does any cutpurses haunt hereabout? Pray thee raise me° one or two. Begin and show me one. *What* / *conjure*

NIGHTINGALE [*showing one of his ballads*] Sir, this is a spell against 'em, spick and span new, and 'tis made, as 'twere, in mine own person, and I sing it in mine own defense.° But 'twill cost a penny alone, if you buy it. *(against cutpurses)*

COKES No matter for the price. Thou dost not know me, I see. I am an odd Barthol'mew.

DAME OVERDO Has't a fine picture,° brother? *woodcut*

COKES Oh, sister, do you remember the ballads over the nursery chimney at home o'my own pasting up? There be brave pictures. [*To Nightingale*] Other manner of pictures than these, friend.

WASP Yet these will serve to pick the pictures° out o'your pockets, you shall see. *i.e., engraved coins*

COKES So I heard 'em° say.—Pray thee mind him not, fellow. He'll have an oar in everything. *(people)*

NIGHTINGALE It° was intended, sir, as if a purse should chance to be cut° in my presence, now, I may be blameless, though, as by the sequel will more plainly appear. *(The ballad)* / *i.e., stolen*

COKES We shall find that i'the matter.° Pray thee begin. *narrative*

NIGHTINGALE To the tune of "Paggington's Pound,"° sir. *a current tune*

COKES [*dancing and singing*] Fa, la la la, la la la, fa la la la! Nay, I'll put thee in tune,° and all. Mine own country-dance! Pray thee begin. *sing the tune for you*

NIGHTINGALE It is a gentle admonition, you must know,° sir, both to the purse-cutter and the purse-bearer. *understand*

COKES Not a word more out o'the tune,° an thou lov'st me. [*Singing*] Fa, la la la, la la la, fa la la la! Come, when?° *not in the song* / *i.e., start singing*

NIGHTINGALE [*singing*]
My masters and friends and good people, draw near,
And look to your purses, for that I do say.

COKES Ha, ha, this chimes!° Good counsel at first dash. *rings true; is fitting*

NIGHTINGALE [*singing*]
And though little money in them you do bear,
It cost more to get than to lose in a day.

COKES Good!

NIGHTINGALE [*singing*]
You oft have been told,
Both the young and the old,
And bidden beware of the cutpurse so bold.
Then if you take heed not, free me from the curse,
Who both give you warning, for and° the cutpurse. *and moreover*

COKES Well said! He were to blame that would not, i'faith.

NIGHTINGALE [*singing*]
Youth, youth, thou hadst better been starved by thy nurse
Than live to be hangèd for cutting a purse.

COKES Good, i'faith. How say you, Numps? Is there any harm i'this?

NIGHTINGALE [*singing*]
It hath been upbraided to men of my trade
That oftentimes we are the cause of this crime.
Alack and for pity, why should it be said?
As if they° regarded or° places or time. *(cutpurses) / either*

COKES The more coxcombs° they that did it, I wusse.° *fools / certainly*

NIGHTINGALE [*singing*]
Examples have been
Of some that were seen
In Westminster Hall,[4] yea, the pleaders between.° *amidst the lawyers*
Then why should the judges be free from this curse,
More than my poor self, for cutting the purse?

COKES God-a-mercy° for that! Why should they be more free, indeed? *Thanks*

NIGHTINGALE [*singing*]
Youth, youth, thou hadst better been starved by thy nurse
Than live to be hangèd for cutting a purse.

COKES That again, good ballad man, that again.
He sings the burden° with him. *refrain*

NIGHTINGALE *and* COKES [*singing*]
Youth, youth, thou hadst better been starved by thy nurse
Than live to be hangèd for cutting a purse.

COKES Oh, rare!° I would fain rub mine elbow° now, but I dare not pull out my hand. On, I pray thee. He that made this ballad shall be poet to° my masque. *fine! / hug myself for joy* *librettist for*

NIGHTINGALE [*singing*]
At Worc'ster, 'tis known well, and even i'the jail,
A knight of good worship° did there show his face *good name, renown*
Against the foul sinners in zeal for to rail,
And lost, *ipso facto*,° his purse in the place. *for that very reason*

COKES Is it possible?

NIGHTINGALE [*singing*]
Nay, once from the seat
Of judgment so great,
A judge there did lose a fair pouch of velvete.° *velvet*

COKES I'faith?° *Really?*

NIGHTINGALE [*singing*]
Oh, Lord, for thy mercy, how wicked or worse
Are those that so venture their necks for a purse!
Youth, youth, thou hadst better been starved by thy nurse
Than live to be hangèd for cutting a purse.

COKES [*singing with him*]
Youth, youth, thou hadst better been starved by thy nurse
Than live to be hangèd for cutting a purse.
Pray thee stay° a little, friend.—Yet o'thy conscience, *pause*
Numps, speak, is there any harm i'this?

WASP To tell you true, 'tis too good for you, 'less you had grace to follow it.

4. Site of the courts of Common Law, King's Bench, and Chancery.

JUSTICE OVERDO [*aside*] It doth discover enormity.° I'll mark it more. I ha' not liked a paltry piece of poetry so well a good while. *expose criminality*

COKES [*singing*]
Youth, youth, thou hadst better been starved by thy nurse
Than live to be hangèd for cutting a purse.

Where's this youth, now? A man must call upon him for his own good,[5] and yet he will not appear. (*He shows his purse.*) Look here, here's for him, handy-dandy,° which hand will he have? [*To Nightingale*] On, I pray thee, with the rest. I do hear of him, but I cannot see him, this Master Youth, the cutpurse. *guess which hand*

NIGHTINGALE [*singing*]
At plays and at sermons, and at the sessions,° *law court sessions*
'Tis daily their practice such booty to make;
Yea, under the gallows, at executions,
They stick not the stare-abouts' purses to take[6]—
Nay, one without grace,
At a far better place,
At court, and in Christmas, before the King's face.

COKES That was a fine fellow! I would have him,° now. *would like to see him*

NIGHTINGALE [*singing*]
Alack then for pity, must I bear the curse,
That only belongs to the cunning cutpurse?

COKES But where's their cunning, now, when they should use it? They are all chained now, I warrant you. [*Singing*]
Youth, youth, thou hadst better been starved by thy nurse
Than live to be hangèd for cutting a purse.

The rat-catcher's charm are all fools and asses to this![7] A pox on 'em,° that they will not come! That a man should have such a desire to a thing, and want it!° *(cutpurses)* *fail to have it*

QUARLOUS [*aside to Winwife*] 'Fore God, I'd give half the fair, an 'twere mine, for a cutpurse for him, to save° his longing. *satisfy*

COKES (*he shows his purse again*) Look you sister, here, here, where is't now? Which pocket is't in, for a wager?

WASP I beseech you leave your wagers, and let him° end his matter, an't may be. *(Nightingale)*

COKES Oh, are you edified,° Numps? *are you catching on*

JUSTICE OVERDO [*aside*] Indeed, he° does interrupt him° too much. There Numps spoke to purpose. *(Cokes) / (Nightingale)*

COKES ([*he shows his purse*] *again*) Sister, I am an ass, I cannot keep my purse.° [*To Nightingale*] On, on, I pray thee, friend. *(said ironically)*

NIGHTINGALE [*singing*]
But O you vile nation of cutpurses all,
Relent and repent, and amend and be sound,
And know that you ought not, by honest men's fall,
Advance your own fortunes, to die above ground.° *on the scaffold*

5. Where's this cutpurse we're singing about now? It's as though one must give open encouragement to the cutpurse to come and enrich himself.
6. They don't scruple to rob the purses of the onlookers staring at an execution.
7. The rat-catcher's magic spells, able to spirit away rats and other creatures (cf. the Pied Piper of Hamelin, Germany), are as nothing compared to these ballads!

Edgeworth gets up to him [Cokes] and tickles him in the ear with a straw twice to draw his hand out of his pocket.

WINWIFE [*aside to Quarlous*] Will you see sport? Look, there's a fellow gathers° up to him. Mark. *sidles*

QUARLOUS [*aside to Winwife*] Good, i'faith! Oh, he has lighted on the wrong pocket.

WINWIFE [*aside to Quarlous*] He has it.° 'Fore God, he is a brave fellow. Pity he should be detected. *(the purse)*

NIGHTINGALE [*singing*]

And though you go gay,
In silks as you may,
It is not the highway to heaven, as they say.
Repent then, repent you, for better, for worse,
And kiss not the gallows for cutting a purse.
Youth, youth, thou hadst better been starved by thy nurse
Than live to be hangèd for cutting a purse.

ALL An excellent ballad! An excellent ballad!

EDGEWORTH [*to Nightingale, as he covertly slips the purse to him*] Friend, let me ha' the first,° let me ha' the first, I pray you. *the first ballad*

COKES Pardon me, sir. First come, first served; and I'll buy the whole bundle too.

WINWIFE [*aside to Quarlous*] That conveyance was better than all; did you see't? He has given the purse to the ballad singer.

QUARLOUS [*aside to Winwife*] Has he?

EDGEWORTH [*to Cokes*] Sir, I cry you mercy; I'll not hinder the poor man's profit. Pray you, mistake me not.

COKES Sir, I take you for an honest gentleman, if that be mistaking; I met you today afore. [*He discovers the loss of his purse.*] Ha! Hum'h! Oh, God! My purse is gone! My purse, my purse! etc.

WASP Come, do not make a stir and cry yourself an ass thorough° the fair afore your time. *throughout*

COKES Why, hast thou it, Numps? Good Numps, how came you by it, I mar'l?° *marvel, wonder*

WASP I pray you, seek some other gamester° to play the fool with. You may lose it time enough,° for all your fair wit. *playmate* *soon enough*

COKES By this good hand, glove and all, I ha' lost it already, if thou hast it not. Feel else, and Mistress Grace's handkercher, too, out o'the tother pocket.

WASP Why, 'tis well, very well, exceeding pretty and well.° *(said ironically)*

EDGEWORTH Are you sure you ha' lost it, sir?

COKES Oh, God! Yes. As I am an honest man, I had it but e'en now, at "Youth, youth."

NIGHTINGALE I hope you suspect not me, sir.

EDGEWORTH Thee? That were a jest indeed! Dost thou think the gentleman is foolish? Where hadst thou hands, I pray thee? Away, ass, away! [*Exit Nightingale.*]

JUSTICE OVERDO [*aside*] I shall be beaten again, if I be spied. [*He attempts to sneak away.*]

EDGEWORTH [*to Cokes*] Sir, I suspect an odd fellow, yonder, is° stealing away. *who is*

DAME OVERDO Brother, it is the preaching fellow! You shall° suspect him. He was at° your tother purse, you know. [*To* *ought to, must* *at the taking of*

Overdo] Nay, stay, sir, and view the work you ha' done. An you be beneficed at the gallows, and preach there,[8] thank your own handiwork. [*Overdo is detained.*]

COKES [*to Overdo*] Sir, you shall take no pride in your preferment.[9] You shall be silenced quickly.

JUSTICE OVERDO What do you mean, sweet buds° of gentility?

youths

COKES To ha' my pennyworth's out on you, bud![1] No less than two purses a day serve you? I thought you a simple° fellow when my man Numps beat you i'the morning, and pitied you—

simpleminded

DAME OVERDO So did I, I'll be sworn, brother, but now I see he is a lewd° and pernicious enormity, as Master Overdo calls him.

wicked

JUSTICE OVERDO [*aside*] Mine own words turned upon me, like swords.

COKES Cannot a man's purse be at quiet for you, i'the master's pocket, but you must entice it forth and debauch it?

WASP [*to Cokes*] Sir, sir, keep your "debauch" and your fine Barthol'mew terms to yourself, and make as much on 'em as you please. But gi' me this [*indicating the license and its box*] from you i'the meantime. I beseech you, see if I can look to this.

COKES Why, Numps?

WASP Why? Because you are an ass, sir; there's a reason the shortest way,° an you will needs ha' it. Now you ha' got the trick of losing, you'd lose your breech, an't were loose. I know you, sir, come, deliver. (*Wasp takes the license from him.*) You'll go and crack the vermin you breed now, will you?[2] 'Tis very fine. Will you ha' the truth on't? They are such retchless° flies as you are that blow° cutpurses abroad in every corner; your foolish having of money makes° 'em. An there were no wiser than I, sir, the trade should lie open for you,[3] sir, it should, i'faith, sir. I would teach your wit to come to your head, sir, as well as your land to come into your hand,° I assure you, sir.

in the fewest words / *heedless / breed* / *breeds* / *possession*

WINWIFE Alack, good Numps!

WASP Nay, gentlemen, never pity me, I am not worth it. Lord send me at home once,[4] to Harrow o'the Hill° again, if I travel any more call me Coryate,[5] with all my heart.

(northwest of London)

[*Exeunt Cokes, Dame Overdo, and Wasp, leading out Justice Overdo. Edgeworth starts to leave.*]

QUARLOUS [*to Edgeworth*] Stay, sir, I must have a word with you in private. Do you hear?

EDGEWORTH With me, sir? What's your pleasure, good sir?

QUARLOUS Do not deny it: you are a cutpurse, sir. This gentleman here and I saw you. Nor do we mean to detect you,° though we can sufficiently inform ourselves toward° the dan-

give you away / *we fully understand*

8. If it turns out that your preaching is to be done at your own hanging. (A benefice is a church living.)

9. You'll not be proud of your being elevated (to the gallows).

1. I intend to have my pennyworth of revenge by apprehending you, you pimple! (Playing on "buds" in line 222.)

2. I.e., You wish to institute proceedings against the very pickpockets you encourage by your heedless ways, do you?

3. If I might have my way without the interference of the supposedly wise, you would be apprenticed to some trade. (Perhaps Wasp hints at the "trade" of cutting purses.)

4. If the good Lord would just send me home, once and for all.

5. I.e., the traveling fool. (See 3.4.122 and note.)

ger of concealing you. But you must do us a piece of service.

EDGEWORTH Good gentlemen, do not undo me! I am a civil° *respectable*
young man, and but a beginner, indeed.

QUARLOUS Sir, your beginning shall bring on your ending, for
us.° We are no catchpoles° nor constables. That you are to *for all we care / officers*
undertake is this: you saw the old fellow with the black box,
here?

EDGEWORTH The little old governor,° sir? *tutor*

QUARLOUS That same. I see you have flown him to a mark° *singled him out*
already. I would ha' you get away that box from him and
bring it us.

EDGEWORTH Would you ha' the box and all, sir, or only that
that is in't? I'll get you that, and leave him the box, to play
with still (which° will be the harder o'the two) because I *(getting license only)*
would gain Your Worships' good opinion of me.

WINWIFE [*to Quarlous*] He says well. 'Tis the greater mastery,° *masterstroke*
and 'twill make the more sport when 'tis missed.

EDGEWORTH Ay, and 'twill be the longer a-missing, to draw
on° the sport. *lengthen out*

QUARLOUS But look you do it now, sirrah, and keep your word,
or—

EDGEWORTH Sir, if ever I break my word with a gentleman,
may I never read word at my need.° Where shall I find you? *(see 1.4.8 n)*

QUARLOUS Somewhere i'the fair, hereabouts. Dispatch it
quickly. [*Exit Edgeworth.*]
I would fain see the careful fool° deluded. Of all beasts, I *officious Wasp*
love the serious ass: he that takes pains to be one, and plays
the fool with the greatest diligence that can be.

GRACE Then you would not choose, sir, but love my guardian,
Justice Overdo, who is answerable to that description in
every hair of him.

QUARLOUS So I have heard. But how came you, Mistress
Wellborn, to be his ward, or have relation to him, at first?

GRACE Faith, through a common calamity. He bought me,[6]
sir, and now he will marry me to his wife's brother, this wise
gentleman that you see, or else I must pay value o'my land.

QUARLOUS 'Slid, is there no device of disparagement,[7] or so?
Talk with some crafty fellow, some picklock o'the law.° *sharp lawyer*
Would I had studied a year longer i'the Inns of Court, an't
had been but i'your case![8]

WINWIFE Ay, Master Quarlous, are you proffering?° *proposing*

GRACE [*to Quarlous*] You'd bring but little aid, sir.

WINWIFE (*aside*) I'll look to° you, i'faith, gamester.—An unfor- *keep an eye on*
tunate foolish tribe you are fall'n into, lady. I wonder you
can endure 'em.

GRACE Sir, they that cannot work their fetters off must wear
'em.

WINWIFE You see what care they have on° you, to leave you *of*
thus.

6. I.e., He paid the Court of Wards for the profitable right of guardianship over me.

7. I.e., couldn't you plead that Overdo, in furthering this match with Cokes, is attempting to marry you to someone of lesser social rank? (A guardian could force a marriage only "without disparagement or inequality," according to the English jurist William Blackstone. If Grace were being forced into an unequal match, she would not have to forfeit her land.)

8. If only to be able to help with your legal case. (With a hint of sexual meaning in "case," meaning "vagina.")

GRACE Faith, the same they have of themselves, sir. I cannot greatly complain, if this were all the plea I had against 'em.

WINWIFE 'Tis true. But will you please to withdraw with us a little, and make them think they have lost you? I hope our manners ha' been such hitherto, and our language, as will give you no cause to doubt° yourself in our company. *fear for*

GRACE Sir, I will give myself no cause. I am so secure of° mine own manners as I suspect not yours. *confident in*

QUARLOUS Look where John Littlewit comes.

WINWIFE Away! I'll not be seen by him.

QUARLOUS No, you were not best.° He'd tell his mother, the widow. *you'd better not*

WINWIFE Heart, what do you mean?

QUARLOUS Cry you mercy, is the wind there?° Must not the widow be named? [*Exeunt Quarlous, Winwife, and Grace.*] *in that direction*

3.6

[*Enter, from Ursula's booth,*] *John* [*Littlewit and*] *Win. Trash* [*and*] *Leatherhead* [*remain visible at their places of business*].

LITTLEWIT Do you hear Win, Win?

WIN What say you, John?

LITTLEWIT While they are paying the reckoning, Win, I'll tell you a thing, Win: we shall never see any sights i'the fair, Win, except° you long still, Win. Good Win, sweet Win, long to see some hobbyhorses, and some drums, and rattles, and dogs, and fine devices, Win—the bull with the five legs, Win, and the great hog. Now you ha' begun with pig, you may long for anything, Win, and so for my motion,° Win. *unless* / *puppet show*

WIN But we sha' not eat o'the bull and the hog, John. How shall I long, then?

LITTLEWIT Oh, yes, Win, you may long to see as well as to taste, Win. How did the pothecary's wife, Win, that longed to see the anatomy,° Win? Or the lady, Win, that desired to spit i'the great lawyer's mouth° after an eloquent pleading? I assure you they longed, Win. Good Win, go in and long. *skeleton* / *(as a reward to him)*

[*Exeunt Littlewit and Win.*]

JOAN TRASH I think we are rid of our new customer,° brother Leatherhead. We shall hear no more of him. *i.e., Cokes*

They plot to be gone.

LEATHERHEAD All the better. Let's pack up all and be gone before he find us.

JOAN TRASH Stay a little; yonder comes a company. It may be we may take some more money.

[*Enter*] *Knockem* [*and*] *Busy.*

KNOCKEM Sir, I will take your counsel, and cut my hair,° and leave vapors. I see that tobacco, and bottle ale, and pig, and Whit, and very Ursula herself is all vanity. *(a sign of penance)*

BUSY Only pig was not comprehended° in my admonition; the rest were. For° long hair, it is an ensign of pride, a banner, *included* / *As for*

3.6. The scene continues.

and the world is full of those banners, very full of banners. And bottle ale is a drink of Satan's, a diet-drink° of Satan's, devised to puff us up and make us swell in this latter° age of vanity, as the smoke of tobacco to keep us in mist and error. But the fleshly woman which you call Ursula is above all to be avoided, having the marks upon her of the three enemies of man: the world, as being in the fair; the devil, as being in the fire; and the flesh, as being herself.

elixir — *modern*

[*Enter Dame*] *Purecraft.*

PURECRAFT Brother Zeal-of-the-land! What shall we do? My daughter Win-the-fight is fall'n into her fit of longing again.

BUSY For more pig? There is no more, is there?

PURECRAFT To see some sights i'the fair.

BUSY Sister, let her fly the impurity of the place swiftly, lest she partake of the pitch° thereof.—Thou art the seat of the Beast,° O Smithfield, and I will leave thee. Idolatry peepeth out on every side of thee.

contaminating tar — *Beast of the Apocalypse*

KNOCKEM [*aside*] An excellent right° hypocrite! Now his belly is full, he falls a-railing and kicking, the jade.° A very good vapor! I'll in and joy° Ursula with telling how her pig works; two and a half he eat to° his share! And he has drunk a pailful. He eats with his eyes, as well as his teeth. [*Exit.*]

true — *vicious horse* — *gladden* — *ate as*

LEATHERHEAD What do you lack, gentlemen? What is't you buy? Rattles, drums, babies—

BUSY Peace with thy apocryphal° wares, thou profane publican:° thy bells, thy dragons, and thy Toby's dogs![1] Thy hobbyhorse is an idol, a very idol, a fierce and rank idol, and thou the Nebuchadnezzar, the proud Nebuchadnezzar of the fair, that set'st it up for children° to fall down to and worship.[2]

spurious — *i.e., idolator* — *the chosen people*

LEATHERHEAD Cry you mercy, sir. Will you buy a fiddle to fill up your noise?[3]

[*Enter Littlewit and Win.*]

LITTLEWIT Look, Win. Do look, i'God's name, and save° your longing. Here be fine sights.

assuage

PURECRAFT Ay, child, so° you hate 'em, as our brother Zeal does, you may look on 'em.

provided

LEATHERHEAD Or what do you say to a drum, sir?

BUSY It is the broken belly of the Beast, and thy bellows there are his lungs, and these pipes are his throat, those feathers are of his tail, and thy rattles the gnashing of his teeth.

JOAN TRASH And what's my gingerbread, I pray you?

BUSY The provender that pricks him up.° Hence with thy basket of popery, thy nest of images, and whole legend° of gingerwork!

arouses the Beast — *(of saints' lives)*

LEATHERHEAD Sir, if you be not quiet the quicklier, I'll ha' you clapped fairly by the heels° for disturbing the fair.

put in the stocks

1. *The Book of Tobit* (in which a faithful dog follows Tobias) and *Bel and the Dragon* are apocryphal books repudiated by Puritan reformers.

2. Nebuchadnezzar II (605–562 B.C.E.), Chaldean ruler of Babylon, forced his subjects to worship idols (see Daniel 3).

3. Since "noise" can mean "a company or band of musicians," Leatherhead seems to be asking Busy if he wants to buy a fiddle to complete a musical set of instruments. He may also be offering a veiled comment on all the noise Busy is making.

BUSY The sin of the fair provokes me. I cannot be silent.

PURECRAFT [*trying to restrain him*] Good brother Zeal!

LEATHERHEAD Sir, I'll make you silent, believe it.

LITTLEWIT [*conferring aside with Leatherhead*] I'd give a shilling you could,° i'faith, friend. *if you could get help*

LEATHERHEAD Sir, give me your shilling. I'll give you my shop if I do not, and I'll leave it° in pawn with you i'the meantime. *(the booth)*

LITTLEWIT [*giving money*] A match, i'faith, but do it quickly, then. [*Exit Leatherhead.*]

BUSY (*he speaks to the widow*)° Hinder me not, woman! I was moved in spirit to be here this day, in this fair, this wicked and foul fair—and fitter may it be a called a foul than a fair—to protest against the abuses of it, the foul abuses of it, in regard of the afflicted saints,° that are troubled, very much troubled, exceedingly troubled, with the opening of the merchandise of Babylon again and the peeping of popery upon the stalls, here, here, in the high places. See you not Goldilocks,° the purple strumpet, there, in her yellow gown and green sleeves? The profane pipes, the tinkling timbrels? A shop of relics!° *(Dame Purecraft)* *Puritans* *(one of the puppets)* *venerated idols*

[*He attempts an assault on the hobbyhorse booth.*]

LITTLEWIT [*preventing him*] Pray you forbear. I am put in trust with 'em.

BUSY And this idolatrous grove of images, this flasket° of idols, which I will pull down— *container*

[*He*] *overthrows the gingerbread.*

JOAN TRASH Oh, my ware, my ware! God bless it!

BUSY —In my zeal and glory to be thus exercised.° *employed*

Leatherhead enters with officers.

LEATHERHEAD Here he is. Pray you lay hold on his zeal. We cannot sell a whistle, for° him, in tune. Stop his noise, first! *because of*

BUSY Thou canst not; 'tis a sanctified noise. I will make a loud and most strong noise, till I have daunted the profane enemy. And for this cause—

LEATHERHEAD Sir, here's no man afraid of you or your cause. You shall swear it° i'the stocks, sir. *do your swearing*

BUSY —I will thrust myself into the stocks, upon the pikes of the land.[4]

LEATHERHEAD [*to the officers*] Carry him away.

PURECRAFT What do you mean, wicked men?

BUSY Let them alone; I fear them not.

[*Exeunt officers escorting Busy;*
Dame Purecraft follows.]

LITTLEWIT Was not this shilling° well ventured, Win, for our liberty? Now we may go play and see° over the fair, where we list,° ourselves. My mother is gone after him, and let her e'en go and loose° us. *(see 76–81 above)* *look* *choose, desire* *release; lose track of*

WIN Yes, John, but I know not what to do.

LITTLEWIT For what, Win?

WIN For a thing I am ashamed to tell you, i'faith, and 'tis too far to go home.

LITTLEWIT I pray thee be not ashamed, Win. Come, i'faith,

4. I will martyr myself, falling upon the weapons of the enemy.

thou shall not be ashamed. Is it anything about the hobby-horse-man? An't be, speak freely.

WIN Hang him, base bobchin,° I scorn him. No, I have very great what-sha'-call-'em,° John.

rascal, chatterer
i.e., need to urinate

LITTLEWIT Oh, is that all, Win? We'll go back to Captain Jordan, to the pig-woman's, Win. He'll help us, or she with a dripping-pan, or an old kettle, or something. The poor greasy soul loves you, Win, and after we'll visit the fair all over, Win, and see my puppet play, Win; you know it's a fine matter, Win. [*Exeunt Littlewit and Win.*]

LEATHERHEAD Let's away. I counseled you to pack up afore, Joan.

JOAN TRASH A pox of his° Bedlam purity! He has spoiled half my ware. But the best is, we lose nothing, if we miss our first merchant.[5]

(Busy's)

LEATHERHEAD It shall be hard for him to find or know us when we are translated,° Joan. [*Exeunt.*][6]

moved and disguised

4.1

[*Enter*] *Troubleall,* [*meeting*] *Bristle* [*and*] *Haggis,* [*with*] *Cokes,* [*and*] *Justice* [*Overdo under arrest. A pair of stocks is brought onstage*].

TROUBLEALL My masters,° I do make no doubt but you are officers.

good sirs

BRISTLE What then, sir?

TROUBLEALL And the King's loving and obedient subjects.

BRISTLE Obedient, friend? Take heed what you speak, I advise you; Oliver° Bristle advises you. His loving subjects, we grant you, but not his obedient at this time, by your leave. We know ourselves a little better than so.° We are to command, sir, and such as you are to be obedient. Here's one of his obedient subjects going to the stocks, and we'll make you such another, if you talk.

(an error for "Davy"?)
than that

TROUBLEALL You are all wise enough i'your places,° I know.

offices

BRISTLE If you know it, sir, why do you bring it in question?

TROUBLEALL I question nothing; pardon me. I do only hope you have warrant for what you do, and so quit° you, and so multiply you.° *He goes away again.*

God requite, reward
give you many children

HAGGIS What's he? Bring him° up to the stocks there. Why bring you him not up?

(Overdo)

[*Troubleall*] *comes again.*

TROUBLEALL If you have Justice Overdo's warrant, 'tis well, you are safe; that is the warrant of warrants. I'll not give this button° for any man's warrant else.

badge; trifle

BRISTLE Like enough, sir, but let me tell you, an' you play° away your buttons thus, you will want° 'em ere night. For any store° I see about you, you might keep 'em and save pins, I wusse.° [*Troubleall*] *goes away.*

gamble
miss, need
supply
certainly

JUSTICE OVERDO [*aside*] What should° he be that doth so

might, can

5. If we can avoid meeting Cokes, our first customer (who bought them out but left his purchases behind). (See line 17 above.)

6. With the exits of Leatherhead and Trash, the stage is now cleared for the first time since the end of act 1.

4.1. The fair.

esteem and advance° my warrant? He seems a sober and discreet person. It is a comfort to a good conscience to be followed with a good fame° in his° sufferings. The world will have a pretty taste, by this, how I can bear adversity, and it will beget a kind of reverence toward me hereafter, even from mine enemies, when they shall see I carry my calamity nobly, and that it doth neither break me nor bend me.

extol — *reputation / one's*

HAGGIS Come, sir, here's a place for you to preach in. Will you put in your leg? *They put him in the stocks.*

JUSTICE OVERDO That I will, cheerfully.

BRISTLE O'my conscience, a seminary!° He kisses the stocks.

recusant priest (2.1.34 n)

COKES Well, my masters, I'll leave him with you. Now° I see him bestowed, I'll go look for my goods and Numps.

Now that

HAGGIS You may, sir, I warrant you. [*Exit Cokes.*] [*To Bristle*] Where's the tother bawler?° Fetch him too. You shall find 'em both fast enough.

(Busy)

JUSTICE OVERDO [*aside*] In the midst of this tumult, I will yet be the author of mine own rest,° and, not minding their fury, sit in the stocks in that calm as shall be able to trouble° a triumph.°

peace of mind; arrest — *mar* — *victory celebration*

[*Troubleall*] *comes again.*

TROUBLEALL Do you assure me upon your words? May I undertake for you, if I be asked the question, that you have this warrant?

HAGGIS What's this fellow, for God's sake?

TROUBLEALL Do but show me Adam Overdo, and I am satisfied. [*He*] *goes out.*

BRISTLE He is a fellow that is distracted, they say, one Troubleall. He was an officer in the Court of Piepowders here last year, and put out on° his place by Justice Overdo.

of

JUSTICE OVERDO [*aside*] Ha!

BRISTLE Upon which he took an idle conceit,° and 's run mad upon't. So that, ever since, he will do nothing but by Justice Overdo's warrant. He will not eat a crust, nor drink a little, nor make him in his apparel ready. His wife, sir-reverence,° cannot get him make his water° or shift° his shirt without his warrant.

foolish obsession — *pardon my saying so* — *urinate / change*

JUSTICE OVERDO [*aside*] If this be true, this is my greatest disaster! How am I bound to satisfy this poor man, that is, of so good a nature to° me, out of his wits, where there is no room left for dissembling!

owing to his respect for

[*Troubleall*] *comes in.*

TROUBLEALL If you cannot show me Adam Overdo, I am in doubt of you. I am afraid you cannot answer it.° [*He*] *goes again.*

justify yourselves

HAGGIS Before me,° neighbor Bristle—and now I think on't better—Justice Overdo is a very parantory° person.

(a mild oath) — *peremptory*

BRISTLE Oh, are you advised° of that? And a severe justicer, by your leave.

aware

JUSTICE OVERDO [*aside*] Do I hear ill o'that side,° too?

from that quarter

BRISTLE He will sit as upright o'the bench, an you mark him, as a candle i'the socket, and give light to the whole court in every business.

HAGGIS But he will burn blue° and swell like a boil (God bless us) an he be angry.

turn pale (a bad omen)

BRISTLE Ay, and he will be angry too, when he list,° that's° more; and when he is angry, be it right or wrong, he has the law on's side, ever. I mark that too.

wishes / what's

JUSTICE OVERDO [*aside*] I will be more tender hereafter. I see compassion may become a justice—though it be a weakness, I confess, and nearer a vice than a virtue.

HAGGIS Well, take him out o'the stocks again. We'll go a sure way to work;° we'll ha' the ace of hearts[1] of° our side, if we can. *They take the Justice out* [*of the stocks*].

play it safe / on

[*Enter*] *Poacher,* [*leading*] *Busy* [*under guard, followed by Dame*] *Purecraft.*

POACHER Come, bring him away to his fellow, there.—Master Busy, we shall rule your legs, I hope, though we cannot rule your tongue.

BUSY No, minister of darkness, no, thou canst not rule my tongue. My tongue it is mine own, and with it I will both knock and mock down your Barthol'mew abominations, till you be made a hissing° to the neighbor parishes round about.

object of derision

HAGGIS [*to Poacher*] Let him alone. We have devised better upon't.

PURECRAFT And shall he not into the stocks, then?

BRISTLE No, mistress, we'll have 'em both° to Justice Overdo, and let him do over 'em as is fitting. Then I and my gossip° Haggis and my beadle Poacher are discharged.°

(Overdo and Busy) / *partner* / *freed of responsibility*

PURECRAFT Oh, I thank you, blessed, honest men!

BRISTLE Nay, never thank us, but thank this madman that comes here. He put it in our heads.

[*Troubleall*] *comes again.*

PURECRAFT Is he mad? Now heaven increase his madness, and bless it, and thank it! [*To Troubleall*] Sir, your poor handmaid thanks you.

TROUBLEALL Have you a warrant? An you have a warrant, show it.

PURECRAFT Yes, I have a warrant out of the Word,° to give thanks for removing any scorn intended to the brethren.

the Bible

TROUBLEALL It is Justice Overdo's warrant that I look for. If you have not that, keep your word,° I'll keep mine. Quit ye, and multiply ye.

hold your tongue

[*Justice Overdo and Busy are led out by Haggis, Bristle, and Poacher with Purecraft following. Troubleall remains alone onstage.*]

4.2

[*Enter*] *Edgeworth* [*and*] *Nightingale.*

EDGEWORTH Come away, Nightingale, I pray thee.

TROUBLEALL Whither go you? Where's your warrant?

1. The winning trick. Haggis and Bristle will make sure of correct procedures by taking their culprit before the authorities.

4.2. The scene continues.

EDGEWORTH Warrant? For what, sir?

TROUBLEALL For what you go about. You know how fit it is. An you have no warrant, bless you, I'll pray for you, that's all I can do. *[He] goes out.*

EDGEWORTH What means he?

NIGHTINGALE A madman that haunts the fair. Do you not know him? It's marvel he has not more followers after his ragged heels.

EDGEWORTH Beshrew° him! He startled me. I thought he had known of our plot. Guilt's a terrible thing. Ha' you prepared° the costermonger?°

i.e., Curse
coached
fruit-seller

NIGHTINGALE Yes, and agreed for° his basket of pears. He is at the corner here, ready. And your prize,° he comes down, sailing, that way, all alone, without his protector. He is rid of him, it seems.

agreed on a price for
prey (Cokes)

EDGEWORTH Ay, I know. I should ha' followed His Protectorship for a feat I am to do upon him,[1] but this offered itself so i'the way° I could not let it scape. Here he comes. Whistle; be this sport called "Doring the Dotterel."[2]

opportunely

[Enter] Cokes.

NIGHTINGALE (*whistles*) Wh, wh, wh, wh, etc.

COKES By this light, I cannot find my gingerbread-wife nor my hobbyhorse-man in all the fair, now, to ha' my money again.° And I do not know the way out on't,° to go home for more. [*Noticing Nightingale*] Do you hear, friend, you that whistle: what tune is that you whistle?

back again / of the fair

NIGHTINGALE A new tune I am practicing, sir.

COKES Dost thou know where I dwell, I pray thee? Nay, on with thy tune; I ha' no such haste for an answer. I'll practice with thee.

[Enter the] Costermonger.

COSTERMONGER Buy any pears, very fine pears, pears fine!

Nightingale sets his foot afore him, and he falls with his basket.

COKES Godso, a muss,° a muss, a muss, a muss!

scramble

COSTERMONGER Good gentleman, my ware, my ware! I am a poor man. Good sir, my ware!

NIGHTINGALE [*to Cokes*] Let me hold your sword, sir; it troubles you.

COKES [*handing Nightingale his things*] Do, and my cloak, an thou wilt, and my hat, too.

Cokes falls a-scrambling whilst they run away with his things.

EDGEWORTH [*to Nightingale*] A delicate great boy!° Methinks he outscrambles 'em all. I cannot persuade myself but° he goes to grammar school yet, and plays the truant today.

overgrown child
but that

NIGHTINGALE Would he had another purse to cut, Zekiel!

EDGEWORTH Purse? A man might cut out his kidneys, I think, and he never feel 'em, he is so earnest at the sport.

1. I.e., I was supposed to follow Wasp (Cokes's "protector") in order to steal the license. ("His Protectorship" is a mock honorific title modeled on titles such as "His Worship.")

2. Let this game be called "Hoodwinking the Simpleton." (The "dotterel," or plover, is a bird easily taken.)

NIGHTINGALE His soul is halfway out on's body at the game.

EDGEWORTH Away, Nightingale! That way.

[*Nightingale runs off with Cokes's things.*]

COKES I think I am furnished for Cather'ne pears° for one undermeal.° Gi' me my cloak.

small early pears / snack

COSTERMONGER Good gentleman, give me my ware.°

my pears

COKES Where's the fellow I ga' my cloak to? My cloak? And my hat? Ha! God's lid, is he gone? Thieves, thieves! Help me to cry,° gentlemen. *He runs out.*

raise a hue and cry

EDGEWORTH Away, costermonger! Come to us to Ursula's.

[*Exit Costermonger.*]

Talk of him to have a soul? Heart, if he have any more than a thing given him instead of salt, only to keep him from stinking,[3] I'll be hanged afore my time, presently. Where should it be, trow? In his blood? He has not so much to'ard it° in his whole body as will maintain a good flea; and if he take this course,° he will not ha' so much land left as to rear a calf within this twelvemonth. Was there ever green plover° so pulled?° That° his little overseer had been here now, and been but tall enough to see him steal pears in exchange for his beaver hat and his cloak thus! I must go find him out next for his black box and his patent it seems he has, of his place,[4] which I think the gentleman° would have a reversion[5] of, that spoke to me for it so earnestly. [*Exit.*]

contributing to it / course of losing money / naive gull / plucked / Would that / (Quarlous)

He [*Cokes*] *comes again.*

COKES Would I might lose my doublet, and hose, too, as I am an honest man, and never stir, if I think there be anything but thieving and cozening i'this whole fair. Barthol'mew Fair, quoth he!° An ever any Barthol'mew had that luck in't that I have had, I'll be martyred for him, and in Smithfield,[6] too. I ha' paid for my pears. A rot on 'em! I'll keep 'em no longer. (*Throws away his pears.*) You were choke-pears° to me; I had been better ha' gone to mumchance[7] for° you, I wusse.° Methinks the fair should not have used me thus, an 'twere but° for my name's sake. I would not ha' used a dog o'the name so. Oh, Numps will triumph now!

forsooth! / inedible, bitter fruit / instead of / certainly / if only

Troubleall comes again.

Friend, do you know who I am, or where I lie?° I do not myself, I'll be sworn. Do but carry° me home, and I'll please° thee; I ha' money enough there. I ha' lost myself, and my cloak and my hat, and my fine sword, and my sister, and Numps, and Mistress Grace (a gentlewoman that I should ha'° married) and a cutwork° handkercher she ga' me, and two purses today. And my bargain° o'hobbyhorses and gingerbread, which grieves me worst of all.

dwell / escort / reward, tip / was to have / lace / purchase

TROUBLEALL By whose warrant, sir, have you done all this?

3. Edgeworth wryly alludes to the commonplace that the soul is the body's salt, preserving and enlivening it just as salt is a preservative of meat. Cokes is notably deficient in anything like a soul.

4. And the papers evidently appointing Wasp as Cokes's custodian.

5. Right of succession. (Edgeworth supposes that Quarlous would like to take the position of custodian away from Wasp.)

6. The site of numerous burnings of Protestant martyrs during the reign of Mary I (1553–58).

7. I.e., (1) to have played at dice; (2) to have preserved a dogged silence.

COKES Warrant? Thou art a wise fellow, indeed! As if a man need a warrant to lose anything with.

TROUBLEALL Yes, Justice Overdo's warrant a man may get and lose with, I'll stand to't.° *vouch for that*

COKES Justice Overdo? Dost thou know him? I lie° there. He is my brother-in-law; he married my sister. Pray thee show me the way. Dost thou know the house? *reside*

TROUBLEALL Sir, show me your warrant. I know nothing without a warrant, pardon me.

COKES Why, I warrant thee. Come along; thou shalt see I have wrought° pillows there, and cambric sheets, and sweet bags,[8] too. Pray thee guide me to the house. *embroidered, decorated*

TROUBLEALL Sir, I'll tell you: go you thither yourself first alone, tell your worshipful brother your mind, and but bring me three lines of his hand or his clerk's with "Adam Overdo" underneath. Here I'll stay° you; I'll obey you, and I'll guide you presently. *wait for*

COKES 'Slid, this is an ass! I ha' found him.° Pox upon me, what do I talking to such a dull fool? [*To Troubleall*] Farewell. You are a very coxcomb, do you hear? *found him out*

TROUBLEALL I think I am. If Justice Overdo sign to it, I am, and so we are all. He'll quit us all, multiply us all.

[*Exeunt. The stocks remain visible onstage.*]

4.3

[*Enter*] *Grace* [*with*] *Quarlous* [*and*] *Winwife. They enter with their swords drawn.*

GRACE Gentlemen, this is no way° that you take. You do but breed one another trouble and offense, and give me no contentment at all. I am no she that affects° to be quarreled for, or have my name or fortune made the question of men's swords. *not the right way* / *desires*

QUARLOUS 'S'lood,° we love you. *By God's blood*

GRACE If you both love me, as you pretend,° your own reason will tell you but one can enjoy me; and to that point there leads a directer line than by my infamy, which must follow if you fight. 'Tis true, I have professed it to you ingenuously that, rather than to be yoked with this bridegroom is° appointed me, I would take up any husband, almost, upon any trust—though subtlety would say to me, I know, he° is a fool, and has an estate, and I might govern him and enjoy a friend° beside. But these are not my aims. I must have a husband I must° love, or I cannot live with him. I shall ill make one of these politic° wives. *claim* / *who is* / *(Cokes)* / *lover* / *can and will* / *cunning*

WINWIFE Why, if you can like either of us, lady, say which is he, and the other shall swear instantly to desist.

QUARLOUS Content. I accord to that willingly.

GRACE Sure you think me a woman of an extreme levity, gentlemen, or a strange fancy, that—meeting you by chance in such a place as this, both at one instant, and not yet of two

8. Bags of sweet-smelling herbs to be placed in the linen.

4.3. The scene continues.

hours' acquaintance, neither of you deserving afore the other of me°—I should so forsake my modesty (though I might affect° one more particularly) as to say, "This is he," and name him.

in my estimation / *like*

QUARLOUS Why, wherefore should you not? What should hinder you?

GRACE If you would not give it to my modesty, allow it yet to my wit;° give me so much of woman and cunning as not to betray myself impertinently.° How can I judge of you, so far as to a choice, without knowing you more? You are both equal and alike to me yet, and so indifferently affected° by me as each of you might be the man if the other were away. For you are reasonable creatures; you have understanding and discourse. And if fate send me an understanding husband, I have no fear at all but mine own manners shall make him a good one.

intelligence / *unbecomingly* / *impartially regarded*

QUARLOUS Would I were put forth to making for° you, then!

apprenticed to

GRACE It may be you are; you know not what's toward° you. Will you consent to a motion° of mine, gentlemen?

in store for / *proposal*

WINWIFE Whatever it be, we'll presume reasonableness, coming from you.

QUARLOUS And fitness, too.

GRACE I saw one of you buy a pair of tables° e'en now.

writing tablet

WINWIFE [*showing a writing tablet*] Yes, here they be, and maiden ones too, unwritten in.

GRACE The fitter for what they may be employed in. You shall write, either° of you, here, a word, or a name, what you like best°—but of two or three syllables at most—and the next person that comes this way (because destiny has a high hand in business of this nature) I'll demand° which of the two words he or she doth approve, and according to that sentence° fix my resolution and affection without change.

each / *whichever you prefer* / *ask* / *decision, pronouncement*

QUARLOUS Agreed. My word is conceived already.

WINWIFE And mine shall not be long creating after.

GRACE But you shall promise, gentlemen, not to be curious to know which of you it is, is taken, but give me leave to conceal that till you have brought me either home or where I may safely tender° myself.

take care of; offer

WINWIFE Why that's but equal.°

only fair

QUARLOUS We are pleased.

GRACE Because I will bind both your endeavors to work together, friendly and jointly, each to the other's fortune, and have myself fitted with some means to make him that is forsaken a part of amends.°

some compensation

QUARLOUS These conditions are very courteous. Well, my word is out of the *Arcadia*, then: "Argalus."[1]

WINWIFE And mine out of the play, "Palemon."[2]

Troubleall comes again.

TROUBLEALL Have you any warrant for this, gentlemen?

QUARLOUS [*and*] WINWIFE Ha!

1. A lover in Philip Sidney's *Arcadia* (1580–81).
2. The rival of Arcite, in Shakespeare and Fletcher's *The Two Noble Kinsmen* and in Chaucer's *Knight's Tale*, for the hand of Emilia, where the name is spelled "Palamon."

TROUBLEALL There must be a warrant had, believe it.

WINWIFE For what?

TROUBLEALL For whatsoever it is, anything indeed, no matter what.

QUARLOUS 'Slight, here's a fine ragged prophet, dropped down i'the nick!°

nick of time

TROUBLEALL Heaven quit you, gentlemen.

[*He starts to leave.*]

QUARLOUS Nay, stay a little.—Good lady, put him to the question.

GRACE You are content, then?

WINWIFE [*and*] QUARLOUS Yes, yes.

GRACE [*to Troubleall*] Sir, here are two names written—

TROUBLEALL Is Justice Overdo one?

GRACE How,° sir? I pray you read 'em to yourself—it is for a wager between these gentlemen—and with a stroke or any difference° mark which you approve best.

What is that / *distinguishing mark*

TROUBLEALL They may be both worshipful names for aught I know, mistress, but Adam Overdo had been worth three of 'em, I assure you, in this place. That's in plain English.

GRACE This man amazes me!—I pray you, like° one of 'em, sir.

prefer, choose

TROUBLEALL I do like him there that has the best warrant. Mistress, to save your longing, and multiply him,[3] it may be this. [*He marks the writing tablet.*] But I am aye° still for Justice Overdo, that's my conscience.° And quit you. [*Exit.*]

always / *conviction*

WINWIFE Is't done, lady?

GRACE Ay, and strangely as ever I saw! What fellow is this, trow?

QUARLOUS No matter what; a fortune-teller we ha' made him. Which is't, which is't?

GRACE Nay, did you not promise not to inquire?

QUARLOUS 'Slid, I forgot that; pray you, pardon me.

[*Enter*] *Edgeworth.*

Look, here's our Mercury° come. The license arrives i'the finest time, too! 'Tis but scraping out Cokes his° name, and 'tis done.

god of thieves / *Cokes's*

WINWIFE How now, lime-twig? Hast thou touched?[4]

EDGEWORTH Not yet, sir; except° you would go with me and see't, it's not worth speaking on. The act is nothing without a witness. Yonder° he is, your man with the box, fall'n into the finest company, and so transported with vapors! They ha' got in° a northern clothier, and one Puppy, a western° man, that's come to wrestle before my Lord Mayor[5] anon, and Captain Whit, and one Val Cutting, that helps Captain Jordan to roar—a circling boy,° with whom your Numps is so taken that you may strip him of his clothes, if you will. I'll undertake to geld° him for you, if you had but a surgeon ready to sear° him. And Mistress Justice, there, is the good-

unless / *(Within Ursula's booth)* / *assembled* / *(from west)* / *roarer (see 4.4.132–36)* / *castrate* / *cauterize*

3. And increase Justice Overdo's authority.

4. How now, thief? Have you fingered the license? (A lime-twig, literally, is a branch smeared with sticky lime to snare songbirds.)

5. An important fair event in the afternoon of the opening day.

est woman! She does so love 'em all over, in terms of justice and the style of authority,[6] with her hood upright, that I beseech you come away,° gentlemen, and see't. [come along]

QUARLOUS 'Slight, I would not lose it for the fair. What'll you do, Ned?

WINWIFE Why, stay hereabout for you. Mistress Wellborn must not be seen.

QUARLOUS Do so, and find out a priest i'the meantime. I'll bring the license. [*To Edgeworth*] Lead. Which way is't?

EDGEWORTH Here, sir. You are o'the backside o'the booth already; you may hear the noise.

[*Exeunt Winwife and Grace. Quarlous and Edgeworth retire to one side, in the vicinity of Ursula's booth.*]

4.4

[*Enter, as from Ursula's booth,*] *Knockem, Northern, Puppy, Cutting, Whit,* [*Dame*] *Overdo,* [*and*] *Wasp.*

KNOCKEM Whit, bid Val Cutting continue the vapors for a lift,° Whit, for a lift. [theft]

NORTHERN I'll ne mare, I'll ne mare, the eale's too meeghty.[1]

KNOCKEM How now, my Galloway nag,° the staggers?[2] Ha! Whit, gi' him a slit i'the forehead. Cheer up, man; a needle and thread to stitch his ears. I'd cure him now, an I had it, with a little butter and garlic, long pepper, and grains. Where's my horn?° I'll gi' him a mash,° presently, shall take away this dizziness. [Scottish steed] [funnel / boiled grain]

PUPPY Why, where are you, zurs? Do you vlinch, and leave us i'the zuds, now?[3]

NORTHERN I'll ne mare. I is e'en as vull as a paiper's° bag, by my troth, I. [bagpiper's]

PUPPY Do my northern cloth zhrink i'the wetting,° ha? [(a common complaint)]

KNOCKEM Why, well said, old flea-bitten. Thou'lt never tire,° I see. [Old nags never tire]

They fall to their vapors° again. [(see 29.1–3 below)]

CUTTING No, sir, but he may tire, if it please him.

WHIT Who told dee sho?° That he vuld° never teer,° man? [so / would / tire]

CUTTING No matter who told him so, so long as he knows.

KNOCKEM Nay, I know nothing, sir; pardon me there.

EDGEWORTH [*aside to Quarlous*] They are at it still, sir, this they call "vapors."

WHIT [*to Cutting*] He shall not pardon dee, Captain; dou shalt not be pardoned. Pre'de,° shweetheart, do not pardon him. [Prithee, I pray you]

CUTTING 'Slight, I'll pardon him, an I list, whosoever says nay to't.

QUARLOUS [*aside to Edgeworth*] Where's Numps? I miss him.° [don't see him here]

6. Dame Overdo, inebriated, uses the legal language of her husband in her loving talk.

4.4. The scene continues.

1. I'll drink no more, the ale's too mighty (strong). (Northern speaks in a northern, or border, dialect, caricatured for comic stage speech.)

2. A horse disease causing the animal to stagger. Knockem goes on to specify his remedies, including head surgery and various herbs.

3. Why, what are you up to, sirs? Do you flinch (from our drinking and quarreling contest) and leave us holding the bag (literally, "in the suds," perhaps suggesting also "in the drink"), now? (Puppy's Cornish dialect, like Northern's border speech and Whit's Irish—see 3.1.1 ff.—is in a conventional stage diction exploiting regional difference for comic effect.)

WASP Why, I say nay to't.

QUARLOUS [*aside to Edgeworth*] Oh, there he is!

Here they continue their game of vapors, which is nonsense: every man to oppose the last man that spoke, whether it concerned him or no.

KNOCKEM [*to Wasp*] To what do you say nay, sir?

WASP To anything, whatsoever it is, so long as I do not like it.

WHIT Pardon me, little man, dou musht° like it a little. *thou must*

CUTTING No, he must not like it at all, sir. There you are i'the wrong.

WHIT I tink I be; he musht not like it, indeed.

CUTTING Nay, then he both must and will like it, sir, for all you.° *despite what you say*

KNOCKEM If he have reason, he may like it, sir.

WHIT By no meansh, Captain, upon reason. He may like nothing upon reason.

WASP I have no reason, nor I will hear of no reason, nor I will look for no reason, and he is an ass that either knows any or looks for't from me.

CUTTING Yes, in some sense you may have reason, sir.

WASP Ay, in some sense, I care not if I grant you.

WHIT Pardon me, thou ougsht to grant him nothing, in no shensh, if dou do love dyshelf, angry man.

WASP Why, then, I do grant him nothing, and I have no sense.

CUTTING 'Tis true, thou hast no sense indeed.

WASP 'Slid, but I have sense, now I think on't better, and I will grant him anything, do you see?

KNOCKEM He is i'the right, and does utter a sufficient vapor.

CUTTING Nay, it is no sufficient vapor, neither. I deny that.

KNOCKEM Then it is a sweet vapor.

CUTTING It may be a sweet vapor.

WASP Nay, it is no sweet vapor, neither, sir. It stinks, and I'll stand to't.° *stand by what I say*

WHIT Yes, I tink it doth shtink, Captain. All vapor dosh shtink.

WASP Nay, then it does not stink, sir, and it shall not stink.

CUTTING By your leave, it may, sir.

WASP Ay, by my leave, it may stink. I know that.

WHIT Pardon me, thou knowesht nothing. It cannot, by thy leave, angry man.

WASP How can it not?

KNOCKEM Nay, never question him, for he is i'the right.

WHIT Yesh, I am i'de right, I confesh it; so ish de little man too.

WASP I'll have nothing confessed that concerns me. I am not i'the right, nor never was i'the right, nor never will be i'the right, while I am in my right mind.

CUTTING Mind? Why, here's no man minds° you, sir, nor anything else. *They drink again.* *pays attention to*

PUPPY Vriend, will you mind this that we do?

QUARLOUS [*aside to Edgeworth*] Call you this "vapors"?° This is such belching of quarrel as I never heard. Will you mind your business,[4] sir? *(see 29.1–3 above)*

4. Will you get on with the business of stealing the license?

EDGEWORTH [*aside to Quarlous*] You shall see,° sir. *i.e., Watch me now*

NORTHERN I'll ne mair. My waimb° warks too mickle° with this auready.° *stomach / much* *already*

EDGEWORTH [*joining the company*] Will you take that,° Master Wasp, that nobody should mind you? *swallow that insult*

WASP Why, what ha' you to do?° Is't any matter to you? *what's it to you?*

EDGEWORTH No, but methinks you should not be unminded,° though. *ignored*

WASP Nor I wu' not be, now I think on't. [*To Cutting*] Do you hear, new acquaintance? Does no man mind me, say you?

CUTTING Yes, sir, every man here minds you, but how?

WASP Nay, I care as little how as you do. That was not my question.

WHIT No, noting° was ty question. Tou art a learned man, and I am a valiant man, i'faith, la. Tou shalt speak for me, and I vill fight for tee. *paying heed; nothing*

KNOCKEM Fight for him, Whit? A gross vapor. He can fight for himself.

WASP It may be I can, but it may be I wu' not. How then?

CUTTING Why, then you may choose.° *have it your way*

WASP Why, and I'll choose whether I'll choose or no.

KNOCKEM I think you may, and 'tis true, and I allow it for a resolute vapor.

WASP Nay, then, I do think you do not think, and it is no resolute vapor.

CUTTING Yes, in some sort he° may allow you. *(Knockem, as umpire)*

KNOCKEM In no sort, sir, pardon me, I can allow him nothing. You mistake the vapor.

WASP He mistakes nothing, sir, in no sort.

WHIT [*to Knockem*] Yes, I pre dee now, let him mistake.

WASP A turd i'your teeth! Never "pre dee" me, for I will have nothing mistaken.

KNOCKEM Turd? Ha, turd? A noisome° vapor. Strike, Whit! *disagreeable, offensive*

They fall by the ears.° [*During the commotion, Edgeworth steals the license out of the black box, and exits.*] *They fight*

DAME OVERDO Why, gentlemen, why, gentlemen, I charge you upon my authority, conserve the peace. In the King's name, and my husband's, put up your weapons! I shall be driven to commit° you myself, else. *send to prison*

QUARLOUS [*laughing out loud*] Ha, ha, ha!

WASP Why do you laugh, sir?

QUARLOUS Sir, you'll allow me my Christian liberty. I may laugh, I hope.

CUTTING In some sort you may, and in some sort you may not, sir.

KNOCKEM Nay, in some sort,° sir, he may neither laugh nor hope in this company. *fashion; company*

WASP Yes, then he may both laugh and hope in any sort, an't please him.

QUARLOUS Faith, and I will, then, for it doth please me exceedingly.

WASP No exceeding° neither, sir. *going too far*

KNOCKEM No, that vapor is too lofty.

QUARLOUS Gentlemen, I do not play well at your game of vapors. I am not very good at it, but—

CUTTING Do you hear, sir? I would speak with you° in circle. *dare you to fight me*

He draws a circle on the ground.

QUARLOUS In circle, sir? What would you with me in circle?

CUTTING Can you lend me a piece, a Jacobus,° in circle? *gold coin (another dare)*

QUARLOUS 'Slid, your circle will prove more costly than your vapors, then. Sir, no, I lend you none.

CUTTING Your beard's not well turned up,° sir. *(a grave insult)*

QUARLOUS How, rascal? Are you playing° with my beard? I'll break circle with you. *trifling*

They draw all, and fight.

PUPPY [*and*] NORTHERN Gentlemen, gentlemen!

KNOCKEM [*aside to Whit*] Gather up, Whit, gather up, Whit! Good vapors. [*Whit furtively picks up cloaks, etc., and exits.*]

DAME OVERDO What mean you? Are you rebels?° Gentlemen! Shall I send out a sergeant at arms,° or a writ o'rebellion,° against you? I'll commit you, upon my womanhood, for a riot, upon my justicehood, if you persist. *rioters* / *arresting officer / riot*

WASP Upon your justicehood? Marry, shit o'your hood! You'll commit?° Spoke like a true justice of peace's wife, indeed, and a fine female lawyer! Turd i'your teeth for a fee,° now. *send to jail; fornicate* / *arresting fee*

DAME OVERDO Why, Numps, in Master Overdo's name, I charge you.

WASP Good Mistress Underdo,° hold your tongue. *(with sexual insult)*

DAME OVERDO Alas, poor Numps!

WASP "Alas!" And why "Alas!" from you, I beseech you? Or why "poor Numps," Goody Rich?[5] Am I come to be pitied by your tuftaffeta° now? Why, mistress, I knew Adam, the clerk, your husband when he was Adam scrivener and writ for twopence a sheet, as high as he bears his head now, or you your hood, dame. *expensive silk fabric*

[*Exeunt Knockem, Quarlous, and Cutting.*]

The watch [*Bristle and others*] *comes in* [*accompanied by Whit,° who is holding the cloaks still*]. *(see 3.1.45–46 and n)*

What are you, sir?

BRISTLE We be men, and no infidels. What is the matter here, and the noises? Can you tell?

WASP Heart, what ha' you to do?° Cannot a man quarrel in quietness but he must be put out on't° by you? What are you? *what's it to you?* / *made to desist*

BRISTLE Why, we be His Majesty's watch, sir.

WASP Watch? 'Sblood, you are a sweet watch, indeed. A body would think, an you watched° well o'nights, you should be contented to sleep at this time o'day. Get you to your fleas and your flock-beds,° you rogues, your kennels, and lie down close.° *stood watch* / *stuffed mattresses* / *quiet*

BRISTLE Down? Yes, we will down, I warrant you.—Down with him in His Majesty's name! Down, down with him, and carry him away to the pigeonholes!° *i.e., stocks*

[*They take Wasp into custody.*]

DAME OVERDO I thank you, honest friends, in the behalf o'the

5. The Rich family held the rights to and received tolls from part of Bartholomew Fair. (On "goody," see note at 1.5.15.)

Crown, and the peace, and in Master Overdo's name, for suppressing enormities.

[*The watch starts to leave with Wasp.*]

WHIT [*pointing to Northern and Puppy*] Stay, Bristle, here ish anoder brash° o'drunkards, but very quiet, special drunkards, will pay dee five shillings[6] very well. Take 'em to dee, in de graish° o'God. One of 'em° does change cloth for ale in the fair, here; te toder° ish a strong man, a mighty man, my Lord Mayor's man, and a wrastler. He has wrashled so long with the bottle, here, that the man with the beard hash almosht streek up hish heelsh.[7]

brash: brace, pair; graish: grace; 'em: (Northern); toder: the other (Puppy)

BRISTLE 'Slid, the clerk o'the market has been to cry him all the fair over, here, for my lord's service.[8]

WHIT [*to Bristle*] Tere he ish. Pre de,° taik him hensh, and make ty best on° him.

Pre de: Prithee; make ty best on: do what you can with

[*Exeunt the watch with Wasp, Northern, and Puppy.*]

[*To Dame Overdo*] How now, woman o'shilk,° vat ailsh ty shweet faish?° Art tou melancholy?

shilk: silk; faish: face

DAME OVERDO A little distempered with these enormities. Shall I entreat a courtesy of you, Captain?

WHIT Entreat a hundred, velvet voman, I vill do it. Shpeak out.

DAME OVERDO I cannot with modesty speak it out, but—

[*She whispers to him.*]

WHIT I vill do it, and more, and more, for dee. [*Calling out*] What, Ursula! An't be,° bitch, an't be, bawd, an't be!

An't be: i.e., Where are you?

[*Enter*] *Ursula* [*from her booth*].

URSULA How now, rascal? What roar you for, old pimp?

WHIT [*furtively giving her the cloaks he picked up*] Here, put up° de cloaks, Ursh; de purchase.° Pre dee now, shweet Ursh, help dis good brave voman to a jordan,° an't be.°

put up: conceal; purchase: booty; jordan: chamberpot; an't be: if possible

URSULA 'Slid, call your Captain Jordan to her, can you not?

WHIT Nay, pre dee, leave dy consheits,° and bring the velvet woman to de—

consheits: your witticisms

URSULA I bring her? Hang her! Heart, must I find a common pot for every punk i'your purlieus?°

purlieus: string of brothels

WHIT Oh, good voordsh,° Ursh. It ish a guest o'velvet, i'fait, la.

voordsh: words; speak gently

URSULA Let her sell her hood and buy a sponge,° with a pox to her! My vessel is employed, sir. I have but one, and 'tis the bottom of an old bottle. An honest proctor and his wife are at it° within. If she'll stay her time, so.° [*Exit.*]

sponge: (to soak up urine); at it: using it; so: well and good

WHIT As soon ash tou cansht, shwet Ursh. Of° a valiant man I tink I am the patientsh man i'the world, or in all Smithfield.

Of: For

[*Enter Knockem.*]

KNOCKEM How now, Whit? Close vapors?° Stealing your leaps? Covering in corners, ha?[9]

Close vapors: Secret dealing?

6. The arresting of whom will earn you a five-shilling fee.
7. That the potbellied drinking jug (decorated with a bearded face) has almost struck up his heels, i.e., knocked him over. ("The man with the beard" may also refer to Quarlous; see lines 137–38.)
8. The city official responsible for inspecting the market has been all over the fair paging Puppy to wrestle before the Lord Mayor. (See 4.3.113–14.)
9. Knockem, in his usual horse lingo, jocularly asks Whit what sorts of fornicating tricks he's up to. ("Covering" is the term used for the copulating of a stallion with a mare.)

WHIT No, fait, Captain. Dough° tou beesht a vishe° man, dy vit is a mile hence,° now. I vas procuring a shmall courtesy for a woman of fashion here.
Though / wise *you're way off*

DAME OVERDO Yes, Captain, though I am justice of peace's wife, I do love men of war and the sons of the sword when they come before my husband.

KNOCKEM Say'st thou so, filly? Thou shalt have a leap° presently. I'll horse thee myself, else.
horse leap; sex

[*Enter Ursula.*]

URSULA [*to Whit*] Come, will you bring her in now and let her take her turn?

WHIT Gramercy,° good Ursh, I tank dee.
Many thanks

DAME OVERDO Master Overdo shall thank her.

[*Exit into the booth, escorted by Whit, who returns immediately.*]

4.5

[*Enter from the booth*] *John* [*Littlewit and*] *Win.*

LITTLEWIT Good gammer° Urs, Win and I are exceedingly beholden to you, and to Captain Jordan and Captain Whit.—Win, I'll be bold to leave you i'this good company, Win, for half an hour or so, Win, while I go and see how my matter goes forward and if the puppets be perfect,° and then I'll come and fetch you, Win.
old woman *know their parts*

WIN Will you leave me alone with two men, John?

LITTLEWIT Ay, they are honest° gentlemen, Win, Captain Jordan and Captain Whit; they'll use you very civilly, Win. God b'w'you, Win. [*Exit.*]
respectable

[*Ursula confers privately with Knockem and Whit.*]

URSULA What, 's her husband gone?

KNOCKEM On his false, gallop, Urs, away.[1]

URSULA An you be right Barthol'mew birds, now show yourselves so. We are undone for want of fowl° i'the fair, here. Here will be Zekiel Edgeworth and three or four gallants with him at night, and I ha' neither plover nor quail° for 'em. Persuade this,° between you two, to become a bird o'the game while I work the velvet woman° within, as you call her.
lack of whores *no wenches* *her (Win)* *(Dame Overdo)*

KNOCKEM I conceive° thee, Urs. Go thy ways. [*Exit Ursula.*] Dost thou hear, Whit? Is't not pity my delicate dark chestnut° here—with the fine lean head, large forehead, round eyes, even mouth, sharp ears, long neck, thin crest, close withers,[2] plain back, deep sides, short fillets,° and full flanks; with a round belly, a plump buttock, large thighs, knit knees, straight legs, short pasterns,° smooth hoofs, and short heels—should lead a dull honest° woman's life, that might live the life of a lady?
understand *(Win)* *loins* *feet above the hoof* *chaste*

WHIT Yes, by my fait and trot,° it is, Captain. De honesht woman's life is a scurvy dull life, indeed, la.
faith and truth

WIN How, sir? Is an honest woman's life a scurvy life?

4.5. The scene continues.
1. Littlewit is cantering off on some sly pretext or other.
2. Thin neck ridge along the mane, a tight back between the shoulders.

WHIT Yes, fait, shweetheart, believe him, de leef of a bond-woman! But if dou vilt hearken to me, I vill make tee a free woman and a lady. Dou shalt live like a lady, as te captain saish.

KNOCKEM Ay, and be honest too, sometimes: have her wires,° and her tires,° her green gowns,[3] and velvet petticoats. *ruff stiffeners* / *headdresses*

WHIT Ay, and ride to Ware and Rumford[4] i'dy coash,° shee° de players,° be in love vit 'em; sup vit gallantsh, be drunk, and cost dee noting.° *in your coach / see* / *actors* / *nothing*

KNOCKEM Brave vapors!

WHIT And lie by twenty on 'em, if dou pleash, shweetheart.

WIN What, and be honest° still? That were fine sport. *chaste*

WHIT 'Tish common, shweetheart. Tou mayst do it, by my hand; it shall be justified to ty husband's faish,° now. Tou shalt be as honesht as the skin between his hornsh,° la! *face* / *(cuckolds') horns*

KNOCKEM Yes, and wear a dressing, top and topgallant, to compare with e'er a husband on 'em all, for a foretop.[5] It is the vapor of spirit in the wife to cuckold nowadays, as it is the vapor of fashion in the husband not to suspect. Your° prying cat-eyed citizen is an abominable vapor. *Your typical*

WIN Lord, what a fool have I been!

WHIT Mend,° then, and do everyting like a lady hereafter; never know° ty husband from another man. *Mend your ways* / *distinguish, recognize*

KNOCKEM Nor any one man from another but i'the dark.

WHIT Ay, and then it ish no dishgrash to know° any man. *have sex with*

[*Enter Ursula.*]

URSULA Help, help here!

KNOCKEM How now? What vapor's there?

URSULA Oh, you are a sweet ranger,° and look well to your walks!° Yonder is your punk of Turnbull,[6] ramping Alice, has fall'n upon the poor gentlewoman within, and pulled her hood over her ears and her hair through it. *i.e., pimp* / *turf*

Alice enters, beating the Justice's wife.

DAME OVERDO Help, help, i'the King's name!

ALICE A mischief on you! They are such as you are° that undo us and take our trade from us, with your tuftaffeta haunches.° *It's women like you* / *elegant padded hips*

KNOCKEM How now, Alice!

ALICE The poor common whores can ha' no traffic° for° the privy[7] rich ones. Your caps and hoods of velvet call away our customers and lick the fat from us. *trade / because of*

URSULA Peace, you foul ramping jade, you—

ALICE Od's foot,° you bawd in grease,[8] are you talking? *By God's foot*

KNOCKEM Why, Alice, I say!

ALICE Thou sow of Smithfield, thou!

URSULA Thou tripe° of Turnbull! *entrails, "fatty"*

3. Whores traditionally wore green.
4. Towns north and northeast of London; convenient retreats for assignations. ("Rumford" is Romford.)
5. Yes, and wear a headdress as elaborate as a ship under full sail, making you more than a fit match for your cuckolded husband. (The top is the topsail; the topgallant is above the topmast; the "foretop" is the top of the foremast, likened here to a husband's branded forehead.)
6. Your typical whore of Turnbull Street, a red-light district. "Ramping" means unrestrained; thieving.
7. (1) Clandestine; (2) private, exclusive.
8. You fat pimp, like an animal ready for slaughter.

KNOCKEM Catamountain° vapors! Ha! *Wildcat*

URSULA You know where you were tawed° lately. Both lashed and slashed you were, in Bridewell.° *i.e., whipped* / *a London prison*

ALICE Ay, by the same token, you rid that week and broke out the bottom o'the cart, night-tub.[9]

KNOCKEM Why, lion face! Ha! Do you know who I am? Shall I tear ruff, slit waistcoat, make rags of petticoat?[1] Ha! Go to, vanish, for fear of vapors.—Whit, a kick, Whit, in the parting vapor.° [*They kick Alice out.*] *i.e., rear end*
[*To Win*] Come, brave woman, take a good heart; thou shalt be a lady, too.

WHIT Yes, fait, dey shall all both be ladies and write° "Madam." I vill do't myself for dem. "Do"° is the vord, and "D" is the middle letter of "Madam." D D: put 'em together and make deeds, without which all words are alike, la.[2] *sign themselves* / *Fornicate*

KNOCKEM 'Tis true.—Ursula, take 'em in, open thy wardrobe, and fit 'em to their calling. Green gowns,° crimson petticoats, green women! My Lord Mayor's green women![3] Guests o'the game,° true bred! I'll provide you a coach to take the air in. *(see 36 and n)* / *prostitution*

WIN But do you think you can get one?

KNOCKEM Oh, they are as common as wheelbarrows where there are great dunghills. Every pettifogger's° wife has 'em, for first he buys a coach that he may marry, and then he marries that he may be made cuckold in't. For if their wives ride not to their cuckolding, they do 'em° no credit. Hide and be hidden, ride and be ridden,° says the vapor of experience. [*Exeunt Ursula into the booth with Win and Dame Overdo. Knockem and Whit remain. The stocks are still onstage.*] *cheap lawyer's* / *(their husbands)* / *be mounted sexually*

4.6

[*Enter*] *Troubleall.*

TROUBLEALL By what warrant does it say so?

KNOCKEM Ha! Mad child o'the Piepowders, art thou there? [*Calling*] Fill us a fresh can, Urs, we° may drink together. *which we; so that we*

TROUBLEALL I may not drink without a warrant, Captain.

KNOCKEM 'S'lood, thou'll not stale° without a warrant, shortly.—Whit, give me pen, ink, and paper. I'll draw him a warrant presently.° *urinate* / *right away*

TROUBLEALL It must be Justice Overdo's.

KNOCKEM I know, man.—Fetch the drink, Whit.

WHIT [*bringing drink and writing materials*] I pre dee now, be very brief, Captain, for de new ladies stay for dee.

KNOCKEM [*writing*] Oh, as brief as can be. Here 'tis already. [*Reading what he has written*] "Adam Overdo."

9. You rode that week as you were carted through the streets (in the form of punishment and public exposure devised especially for bawds and whores), and you were so heavy that you broke through the bottom of the cart, you tub of excrement.

1. Am I going to have to tear your clothes off, you whore? (A waistcoat, if worn by a woman without a covering gown, would identify her as a "waistcoat," or prostitute.)

2. Whit prefers deeds of putting together (i.e., sex) to mere words (such as "write 'Madam,'" lines 86–87) that are essentially abstract and undifferentiated signs.

3. (1) Loose women; (2) the female opposites of "green men" (wild men) in the Lord Mayor's show. (See also 4.5.36 and note.)

4.6. The scene continues.

TROUBLEALL Why, now I'll pledge you, Captain.

KNOCKEM Drink it off. [*They drink.*] I'll come to thee anon, again. [*Exeunt, Knockem and Whit into Ursula's booth, Troubleall in another direction.*]

[*Enter*] *Quarlous* [*and*] *Edgeworth.*

QUARLOUS (*to the cutpurse*) Well, sir, you are now discharged. Beware of being spied° hereafter.

observed in crime

EDGEWORTH Sir, will it please you enter in here, at Ursula's, and take part of a silken gown,° a velvet petticoat, or a wrought smock?° I am promised such, and I can spare any gentleman a moiety.°

partake of a whore
finely dressed whore
half, share

QUARLOUS Keep it for your companions in beastliness; I am none of 'em, sir. If I had not already forgiven you a greater trespass, or thought you yet worth my beating, I would instruct your manners,° to whom you made your offers. But go your ways; talk not to me. The hangman is only° fit to discourse with you; the hand of beadle° is too merciful a punishment for your trade of life. [*Exit Edgeworth.*] I am sorry I employed this fellow, for he thinks me such;° *Facinus quos inquinat, aequat.*[1] But it was for sport. And would I make it serious,° the getting of this license is nothing to me without° other circumstances concur. I do think how impertinently° I labor if the word be not mine that the ragged fellow° marked, and what advantage I have given Ned Winwife in this time now, of working her,° though° it be mine. He'll go near to form° to her what a debauched rascal I am, and fright her out of all good conceit° of me. I should do so by him, I am sure, if I had the opportunity. But my hope is in her temper,° yet; and it must needs be next to despair that is grounded on any part of a woman's discretion. I would give, by my troth, now, all I could spare (to° my clothes and my sword) to meet my tattered soothsayer again who was my judge i'the question, to know certainly whose word he has damned or saved. For till then I live but under a reprieve. I must seek him. Who be these?

teach you a lesson
alone is
whipper of offenders
the same as he
take it seriously
unless
pointlessly
(Troubleall)
working on Grace / even if
explain, picture
opinion
temperament
right down to

Enter Wasp with the officers [*Bristle and another*].

WASP [*to Bristle*] Sir, you are a Welsh cuckold, and a prating runt,° and no constable.

stunted animal; oaf

BRISTLE You say very well.—Come, put in his leg in the middle roundel, and let him hole° there.

occupy a hole

[*They put Wasp in the stocks.*]

WASP You stink of leeks, metheglin,° and cheese,[2] you rogue.

Welsh mead

BRISTLE Why, what is that to you, if you sit sweetly in the stocks in the meantime? If you have a mind to stink too, your breeches sit close enough to your bum. Sit you merry, sir.

QUARLOUS How now, Numps?

WASP It is no matter how. Pray you look off.°

avert your gaze

QUARLOUS Nay, I'll not offend you, Numps. I thought you had sat there to be seen.

1. Crime levels distinctions among those it corrupts. (Lucan, *Pharsalia*, 5.290.)

2. Reputedly favorite Welsh foods.

WASP And to be sold,° did you not? Pray you mind your business, an you have any. *sold like a slave*

QUARLOUS Cry you mercy, Numps. Does your leg lie high enough?

[*Enter*] *Haggis.*

BRISTLE How now, neighbor Haggis, what says Justice Overdo's Worship° to the other offenders? *His Worship Justice Overdo*

HAGGIS Why, he says just nothing. What should he say? Or where should he say? He is not to be found, man. He ha' not been seen i'the fair, here, all this livelong day, never since seven o'clock i'the morning. His clerks know not what to think on't. There is no Court of Piepowders yet.—Here they be returned.

[*Enter others of the watch with*] *Justice* [*Overdo in disguise still, and*] *Busy.*

BRISTLE What shall be done with 'em, then, in your discretion?° *judgment*

HAGGIS I think we were best put 'em in the stocks, in discretion (there they will be safe, in discretion) for the valor of an hour,[3] or such a thing, till His Worship come.

BRISTLE It is but a hole matter if we do, neighbor Haggis. [*To Wasp*] Come, sir, here is company for you. [*To the watchmen*] Heave° up the stocks. *Lift*

WASP [*aside*] I shall put a trick upon your Welsh diligence, perhaps. *As they open the stocks, Wasp puts his shoe on his hand and slips it in for his leg.*

BRISTLE [*to Busy*] Put in your leg, sir. *They bring Busy and put him in.*

QUARLOUS [*aside*] What, Rabbi Busy! Is he come?

BUSY I do obey thee. The lion may roar, but he cannot bite. I am glad to be thus separated from the heathen of the land, and put apart in the stocks, for the holy cause.

WASP What are you, sir?

BUSY One that rejoiceth in his affliction, and sitteth here to prophesy the destruction of fairs and May-games, wakes, and Whitsun ales,[4] and doth sigh and groan for the reformation of these abuses.

[*Justice Overdo is put in the stocks. The watchmen stand aside, not attentive to the ensuing action.*]

WASP [*to Justice Overdo*] And do you sigh and groan too, or rejoice in your affliction?

JUSTICE OVERDO I do not feel it, I do not think of it; it is a thing without me.° [*He apostrophizes himself.*] Adam, thou art above these batt'ries,° these contumelies.° *In te manca ruit Fortuna,*[5] as thy friend Horace says; thou art one *quem neque pauperies, neque mors, neque vincula terrent.*[6] And *outside of me* *blows / insults*

3. Haggis responds to Bristle's "in your discretion" with multiple wordplay on "discretion": we can put these men in the stocks prudently, and at a discreet distance from one another, for the value or length of an hour.
4. Traditional rural festivals objected to by many Puritans.
5. Fortune cripples herself when she assaults you. (Horace, *Satires*, 2.7.88.)
6. Whom neither poverty, nor death, nor chains can affright. (Horace, *Satires*, 2.7.83–84.)

therefore, as another friend of thine says (I think it be thy friend Persius), *Non te quaesiveris extra.*[7]

QUARLOUS [*aside*] What's here? A stoic i'the stocks? The fool is turned philosopher.

BUSY [*to Justice Overdo*] Friend, I will leave° to communicate my spirit with you if I hear any more of those superstitious relics, those lists° of Latin, the very rags of Rome and patches of popery.

cease
remnants, shreds

WASP Nay, an you begin to quarrel, gentlemen, I'll leave you. I ha' paid for quarreling too lately.° Look you, a device: but° shifting in° a hand for a foot. God b'w'you. *He gets out.*

recently / merely
substituting

BUSY Wilt thou then leave thy brethren in tribulation?

WASP For this once, sir. [*Exit.*]

BUSY [*calling after Wasp*] Thou art a halting° neutral—stay him there, stop him!—that will not endure the heat of persecution.

wavering (doctrinally)

BRISTLE [*hearing the commotion*] How now, what's the matter?

BUSY He is fled, he is fled, and dares not sit it out.

BRISTLE What, has he made an escape? Which way? Follow, neighbor Haggis! [*Exeunt Bristle and Haggis.*]

[*Enter Dame*] *Purecraft.*

PURECRAFT Oh, me! In the stocks! Have the wicked prevailed?

BUSY Peace, religious sister, it is my calling. Comfort yourself. An extraordinary calling, and done for my better standing, my surer standing, hereafter.

The madman [*Troubleall*] *enters.*

TROUBLEALL By whose warrant, by whose warrant, this?

QUARLOUS [*aside*] Oh, here's my man dropped in I° looked for.

whom I

JUSTICE OVERDO Ha!

PURECRAFT [*to Troubleall*] O good sir, they have set the faithful here to be wondered at, and provided holes for the holy of the land.

TROUBLEALL Had they warrant for it? Showed they Justice Overdo's hand? If they had no warrant, they shall answer it.

[*Enter Bristle and Haggis.*]

BRISTLE Sure you did not lock the stocks sufficiently, neighbor Toby.

HAGGIS No? See if you can lock 'em better.

BRISTLE [*examining the locks on the stocks*] They are very sufficiently locked, and truly, yet something is in the matter.

TROUBLEALL True, your warrant is the matter that is in question. By what warrant?

BRISTLE Madman, hold your peace! I will put you in his° room else, in the very same hole, do you see?

(Wasp's, or Overdo's)

QUARLOUS [*aside*] How, is he° a madman?

(Troubleall)

7. Look to no one outside yourself. (Persius, *Satires*, 1.7.)

TROUBLEALL Show me Justice Overdo's warrant, I obey° you. *and I'll obey*

HAGGIS You are a mad fool. Hold your tongue.

[*Haggis and Bristle walk aside.*]

TROUBLEALL (*shows his can*) In Justice Overdo's name, I drink to you, and here's my warrant.° *(see 4.6.3–15)*

JUSTICE OVERDO [*aside*] Alas, poor wretch, how it earns° my heart for him! *grieves*

QUARLOUS [*aside*] If he be mad, it is in vain to question him. I'll try, though. [*Aloud to Troubleall*] Friend, there was a gentlewoman showed you two names some hour since, "Argalus" and "Palemon," to mark° in a book. Which of 'em was it you marked? *write*

TROUBLEALL I mark° no name but Adam Overdo. That is the name of names; he only is the sufficient magistrate, and that name I reverence. Show it me. *heed*

QUARLOUS [*aside*] This fellow's mad indeed. I am further off now than afore.

JUSTICE OVERDO [*aside*] I shall not breathe in peace till I have made him some amends.

QUARLOUS [*aside*] Well, I will make another use of him is° come in my head. I have a nest° of beards in my trunk,[8] one something like his. *that has* *collection*

The watchmen [*Bristle, Haggis, and perhaps others*] *come back again.*

BRISTLE This mad fool has made me that I know not whether I have locked the stocks or no. I think I locked 'em.

TROUBLEALL Take Adam Overdo in your mind, and fear nothing.

BRISTLE 'Slid, madness itself. Hold thy peace, and take that!

[*He strikes Troubleall.*]

TROUBLEALL Strikest thou without a warrant? Take thou that!

The madman fights with 'em, and they leave open the stocks.

BUSY We are delivered by miracle! Fellow in fetters, let us not refuse the means; this madness was of the spirit. The malice of the enemy hath mocked itself.

[*Exeunt Busy, Justice Overdo, and Troubleall.*]

PURECRAFT Mad do they call him? The world is mad in error, but he is mad in truth. I love him° o'the sudden (the cunning man[9] said all true), and shall love him more and more. How well it becomes a man to be mad in truth! Oh, that I might be his yokefellow, and be mad with him! What a many° should we draw to madness in truth with us! *Troubleall* *What a crowd*

[*Exit.*] *The watch, missing them, are affrighted.*

BRISTLE How now? All scaped? Where's the woman? It is witchcraft! Her velvet hat is a witch, o'my conscience, or my key,[1] t'one.° The madman was a devil, and I am an ass; so bless° me, my place, and mine office! [*Exeunt.*] *one or the other* *may God protect*

8. Trunk hose, knee-length trousers, were roomy enough to accommodate something, such as a set of beards for masking.

9. Fortune-teller. See 1.2.45–49.

1. Or perhaps my key to the stocks is bewitched.

5.1

[Enter, in his puppet-theater booth, Leatherhead, as] Lantern *[the puppet master, with]* Filcher *[and]* Shark-well.

LEATHERHEAD Well, luck and Saint Barthol'mew! Out with the sign of our invention,° in the name of wit, and do you beat the drum the while. [*Filcher and Sharkwell display a banner, to the accompaniment of drumming.*] All the foul° i'the fair, I mean all the dirt in Smithfield (that's one of Master Littlewit's carriwitchets° now), will be thrown at our banner today if the matter does not please the people. Oh, the motions° that I, Lantern Leatherhead, have given light to i'my time, since my Master Pod° died! "Jerusalem" was a stately thing, and so was "Nineveh," and "The City of Norwich," and "Sodom and Gomorrah,"[1] with the rising o'the prentices and pulling down the bawdy houses there upon Shrove Tuesday.[2] But "The Gunpowder Plot"[3]—there was a get-penny!° I have presented that to an eighteen- or twenty-pence audience nine times in an afternoon. Your home-born projects° prove ever the best; they are so easy and familiar. They° put too much learning i'their things nowadays, and that, I fear, will be the spoil o'this.° Littlewit? I say, Micklewit, if not too mickle!°—Look to your gathering° there, Goodman Filcher.

banner for our show; filth; fowl; whores; puns (fowl/foul); puppet shows; a puppet master; moneymaker; homegrown shows; (Poets, playwrights); (this puppet show); much / taking money

FILCHER I warrant you, sir.

LEATHERHEAD An there come any gentlefolks, take twopence apiece, Sharkwell.

SHARKWELL I warrant you, sir, threepence an we can.

[*They stand aside, Leatherhead still in his puppet theater.*]

5.2

The Justice comes in like a porter.

JUSTICE OVERDO This later° disguise I have borrowed of a porter shall carry me out to° all my great and good ends, which, however interrupted, were never destroyed in me. Neither is the hour of my severity yet come to reveal myself, wherein, cloudlike, I will break out in rain and hail, lightning and thunder, upon the head of enormity. Two main works I have to prosecute first. One is to invent some satisfaction for the poor, kind wretch who is out of his wits for my sake; and yonder I see him coming.[1] I will walk aside and project° for it.

most recent; enable me to do; plan

[*He stands aside.*]

[*Enter*] Winwife [*and*] Grace.

5.1. The fair. At the pupper-theater booth.

1. These puppet shows told stories of the destruction of Jerusalem by the Roman Titus in 70 C.E.; how on his way to Nineveh to prophesy the destruction of that city, Jonah was swallowed by "a great fish" (see the Book of Jonah); about Norwich, a city raised in an hour, according to legend; and about the cities of Sodom and Gomorrah, which were destroyed by God because of their debauchery (see Genesis 19).

2. The day before Lent, which was a traditional time for rioting.

3. About the infamous Catholic plot to blow up both houses of Parliament on November 5, 1605.

5.2. The scene continues.

1. Overdo is misled by seeing Quarlous disguised as Troubleall.

WINWIFE I wonder where Tom Quarlous is, that he returns not. It may be he is struck° in here to seek us.

has gone

GRACE See, here's our madman again.

[Enter] Quarlous [and Dame] Purecraft. Quarlous, in the habit of the madman, is mistaken by Mistress [Dame] Purecraft.

QUARLOUS [*aside*] I have made myself as like him as his gown and cap will give me leave.°

allow me

PURECRAFT Sir, I love you, and would be glad to be mad with you in truth.

WINWIFE [*aside*] How? My widow in love with a madman?

PURECRAFT Verily, I can be as mad in spirit as you.

QUARLOUS By whose warrant? Leave your canting,° gentlewoman. Have I found you?° Save ye, quit ye, and multiply ye. (*He desires to see the book of Mistress Grace.*) Where's your book? 'Twas a sufficient name I marked. Let me see't; be not afraid to show't me.

pious jargon
found you out

GRACE What would you with it, sir?

QUARLOUS Mark it again and again, at your service.

GRACE [*showing him her book*] Here it is, sir. This was it you marked.

QUARLOUS [*reading*] "Palemon"?° Fare you well, fare you well.

Winwife's word (4.3.70)

WINWIFE How, "Palemon"!

GRACE Yes, faith, he has discovered it to you now, and therefore 'twere vain to disguise it longer. I am yours, sir, by the benefit° of your fortune.

agency

WINWIFE And you have him, mistress, believe it, that shall never give you cause to repent her° benefit, but make you rather to think that in this choice she[2] had both her eyes.

(Fortune's)

GRACE I desire to put it to no danger of protestation.°

dissent, objection

[*Exeunt Winwife and Grace.*]

QUARLOUS [*aside*] "Palemon" the word, and Winwife the man?

PURECRAFT Good sir, vouchsafe a yokefellow in your madness. Shun not one of the sanctified sisters that would draw° with you in truth.

work together

QUARLOUS Away! You are a herd of hypocritical proud ignorants, rather wild than mad, fitter for woods and the society of beasts than houses and the congregation of men. You are the second part° of the society of canters, outlaws to order and discipline, and the only privileged church-robbers of Christendom. Let me alone! [*Aside*] "Palemon" the word, and Winwife the man?

i.e., past masters

PURECRAFT [*aside*] I must uncover myself unto him, or I shall never enjoy him, for all the cunning men's° promises.—Good sir, hear me. I am worth six thousand pound. My love to you is become my rack.° I'll tell you all, and the truth, since you hate the hypocrisy of the parti-colored brotherhood.° These seven years I have been a willful holy widow only to draw feasts and gifts from my entangled suitors. I am also, by office, an assisting sister of the deacons, and a devourer, instead of a distributor, of the alms. I am a special maker of marriages for our

fortune-tellers'
torture rack
i.e., the Puritans

2. Fortune, traditionally depicted as female and blindfolded.

decayed brethren° with our rich widows, for a third part of their wealth, when they are married, for the relief of the poor elect;[3] as also our poor handsome young virgins with our wealthy bachelors or widowers, to make them steal from their husbands when I have confirmed them in the faith and got all put into their custodies.[4] And if I ha' not my bargain, they may sooner turn a scolding drab° into a silent minister[5] than make me leave pronouncing reprobation° and damnation unto them. Our elder, Zeal-of-the-land, would have had me, but I know him to be the capital° knave of the land, making himself rich by being made feoffee° in trust to deceased brethren, and coz'ning their heirs by swearing the absolute gift of their inheritance.[6] And thus, having eased my conscience and uttered my heart with the tongue of my love: enjoy all my deceits together,° I beseech you. I should not have revealed this to you but that in time° I think you are mad, and I hope you'll think me so too, sir?

impoverished Puritans / *wench, slut* / *eternal damnation* / *chief* / *trustee* / *take me for what I am* / *propitiously*

QUARLOUS Stand aside; I'll answer you presently. (*He considers with himself of it.*) Why should not I marry this six thousand pound, now I think on't? And a good trade,° too, that she has beside, ha? The tother wench Winwife is sure of; there's no expectation for me there. Here I may make myself some saver° yet, if she continue mad—there's the question. It is money that I want; why should I not marry the money when 'tis offered me? I have a license and all; it is but razing° out one name and putting in another. There's no playing° with a man's fortune. I am resolved! I were truly mad an I would not. [*To her*] Well, come your ways, follow me. An you will be mad, I'll show you a warrant.

business / *make up for losses* / *scraping* / *shilly-shallying*

PURECRAFT Most zealously. It is that I zealously desire.

He takes her along with him [and is about to leave]. The Justice calls him.[7]

JUSTICE OVERDO Sir, let me speak with you.

QUARLOUS By whose warrant?

JUSTICE OVERDO [*taking Quarlous privately aside*] The warrant that you tender° and respect so: Justice Overdo's. I am the man, friend Troubleall, though thus disguised (as the careful° magistrate ought) for the good of the republic,° in the fair, and the weeding out of enormity. Do you want a house, or meat, or drink, or clothes? Speak; whatsoever it is, it shall be supplied you. What want you?

have regard for / *caring / commonwealth*

QUARLOUS Nothing but your warrant.

JUSTICE OVERDO My warrant? For what?

QUARLOUS To be gone, sir.

JUSTICE OVERDO Nay, I pray thee stay. I am serious, and have not many words nor much time to exchange with thee. Think what may do thee good.

QUARLOUS Your hand and seal will do me a great deal of good; nothing else in the whole fair that I know.°

know of

3. As part of the marriage contract, one-third of the man's wealth acquired through marriage to a rich widow went to the relief of poor Puritans. The elect are those predestined for salvation.

4. Young Puritan women were married to rich men to convert the men to Puritanism and then take custody of their wealth.

5. A Puritan minister removed from his office for non-compliance with Anglican practice.

6. Cheating their heirs by swearing under oath that the inheritance had unconditionally been deeded to him.

7. Overdo, standing aside till now, has not heard Purecraft's conversation with Quarlous.

JUSTICE OVERDO If it were to any end, thou shouldst have it willingly.

QUARLOUS Why, it will satisfy me; that's end enough to look on.° An you will not gi' it me, let me go. *sufficient reason*

JUSTICE OVERDO Alas! Thou shalt ha' it presently. I'll but step into the scrivener's hereby and bring it. Do not go away.

The Justice goes out.

QUARLOUS [*aside*] Why, this madman's shape will prove a very fortunate one, I think! Can a ragged robe produce these effects? If this be the wise Justice, and he bring me his hand, I shall go near° to make some use on't. He is come already! *make every attempt*

And [*Justice Overdo*] *returns* [*with a document*].

JUSTICE OVERDO Look thee, here is my hand and seal: "Adam Overdo." If there be anything to be written above in the paper that thou want'st now, or at any time hereafter, think on't; it is my deed, I deliver it so. Can your friend write?

QUARLOUS Her hand for a witness, and all is well.

He urgeth Mistress [*Dame*] *Purecraft* [*to sign; she does so*].

JUSTICE OVERDO [*taking the document*] With all my heart.

QUARLOUS [*aside*] Why should not I ha' the conscience° to make this a bond of a thousand pound, now, or what I would else? *effrontery; good sense*

JUSTICE OVERDO [*giving the document*] Look you, there it is; and I deliver it as my deed again.

QUARLOUS [*to Purecraft*] Let us now proceed in madness.

He takes her in with him [*and so exeunt*].

JUSTICE OVERDO Well, my conscience is much eased. I ha' done my part; though° it doth him no good, yet Adam hath offered satisfaction. The sting is removed from hence. Poor man, he is much altered with his affliction; it has brought him low! Now for my other work, reducing the young man° I have followed so long in love from the brink of his bane° to the center of safety. Here, or in some suchlike vain° place, I shall be sure to find him. I will wait the good time.° *even if* / *leading back Edgeworth* / *ruin* / *given to vanities* / *for the right moment*

[*He stands aside.*]

5.3

[*Enter*] *Cokes,* [*followed by urchins, encountering*] *Sharkwell* [*and*] *Filcher* [*at Leatherhead's theater*].

COKES How now, what's here to do?° Friend, art thou the master of the monuments?[1] *what's going on here?*

SHARKWELL 'Tis a motion, an't please Your Worship.

JUSTICE OVERDO [*aside*] My fantastical brother-in-law, Master Barthol'mew Cokes!

COKES A motion? What's that? (*He reads the bill.*)° "The Ancient Modern History of Hero and Leander, otherwise called The Touchstone of True Love, with as true a trial of *announcement, banner*

5.3. The scene continues.

1. Are you in charge of this exhibition? (Cokes speaks as though Sharkwell were a guide taking visitors around Westminster Abbey.)

friendship between Damon and Pythias, two faithful friends o'the Bankside."[2] Pretty, i'faith. What's the meaning on't? Is't an interlude?° Or what is't? — *dramatic entertainment*

FILCHER Yes, sir. Please you come near, we'll take your money within.

COKES Back with these children! They do so follow me up and down. *The boys o'the fair follow him.*

[*Enter*] *John* [*Littlewit*].

LITTLEWIT [*to Filcher*] By your leave, friend.

FILCHER You must pay, sir, an you go in.

LITTLEWIT Who, I? I perceive thou know'st not me. Call the master o'the motion.

SHARKWELL What, do you not know the author, fellow Filcher? You must take no money of him; he must come in gratis. Master Littlewit is a voluntary; he is the author.

LITTLEWIT Peace, speak not too loud! I would not have any notice taken that I am the author till we see how it passes.° — *is received*

COKES Master Littlewit, how dost thou?

LITTLEWIT Master Cokes! You are exceeding well met. What, in your doublet and hose, without a cloak or a hat?

COKES I would I might never stir, as I am an honest man, and by that fire,° I have lost all i'the fair, and all my acquaintance too. Didst thou meet anybody that I know, Master Littlewit? My man Numps, or my sister Overdo, or Mistress Grace? Pray thee, Master Littlewit, lend me some money to see the interlude here. I'll pay thee again,° as I am a gentleman. If thou'lt but carry° me home, I have money enough there. — *fire in Ursula's booth*; *back*; *escort*

LITTLEWIT Oh, sir, you shall command it. What, will a crown° serve you? — *five shillings*

COKES I think it well.° [*To Filcher and Sharkwell*] What do we pay for coming in, fellows? — *I think so, indeed*

FILCHER Twopence, sir.

COKES Twopence? [*Giving a shilling*] There's twelvepence, friend. Nay, I am a gallant, as simple° as I look now, if you see me with my man about me, and my artillery,° again. — *humbly outfitted*; *trappings, equipment*

LITTLEWIT Your man was i'the stocks e'en now, sir.

COKES Who, Numps?

LITTLEWIT Yes, faith.

COKES For what, i'faith? I am glad o'that. Remember to tell me on't anon; I have enough,° now! What manner of matter is this, Master Littlewit? What kind of actors ha' you? Are they good actors? — *enough to think about*

LITTLEWIT Pretty youths, sir, all children, both old and young. [*Pointing to Leatherhead, who is visible at his puppet theater*] Here's the master of 'em—

LEATHERHEAD (*whispers to Littlewit*) Call me not Leatherhead, but Lantern.

2. Littlewit's puppet play ludicrously combines two familiar stories, transferring their locales to the two shores of the Thames River in London. One, narrated by Ovid and further immortalized in an amorous poem by Christopher Marlowe in 1598, tells of Leander of Abydos, who drowned to death as he attempted to swim the Hellespont to Sestos (see lines 112–14), where his beloved Hero served as a priestess of Aphrodite. The other is about the philosophers Damon and Pythias, who were devoted friends in the time of the tyrant Dionysius of Syracuse; their willingness to die for each other moved the hard heart of the tyrant. (See note at 5.4.308.) Richard Edwards wrote a play on the subject in about 1565–71.

LITTLEWIT Master Lantern, that gives light to the business.

COKES In good time,° sir. I would fain see 'em; I would be glad drink° with the young company. Which is the tiring-house?°

(a polite greeting) · *to drink* · *dressing area*

LEATHERHEAD Troth, sir, our tiring-house is somewhat little; we are but beginners yet. Pray pardon us; you cannot go upright° in't.

walk without stooping

COKES No? Not now my hat is off? What would you have done with me if you had had me, feather and all, as I was once today? Ha' you none of your pretty impudent boys, now, to bring stools, fill tobacco, fetch ale, and beg money, as they have at other houses?° Let me see some o'your actors.

theaters

LITTLEWIT Show him 'em, show him 'em. Master Lantern, this is a gentleman that is a favorer of the quality.°

acting profession

JUSTICE OVERDO [*aside*] Ay, the favoring of this licentious quality is the consumption° of many a young gentleman—a pernicious enormity.

financial ruin

He [*Leatherhead*] *brings them* [*the puppets*] *out in a basket.*

COKES What, do they live in baskets?

LEATHERHEAD They do lie in a basket, sir. They are o'the small players.

COKES These be players minors,° indeed. Do you call these players?

juvenile actors

LEATHERHEAD They are actors, sir, and as good as any—none dispraised°—for dumb shows. Indeed, I am the mouth of 'em all.

not to disparage others

COKES Thy mouth will hold 'em all. I think one tailor[3] would go near to beat all this company with a hand bound behind him.

LITTLEWIT Ay, and eat 'em all, too, an they were in° cake-bread.

baked in

COKES I thank you for that, Master Littlewit. A good jest! [*To Leatherhead*] Which is your Burbage[4] now?

LEATHERHEAD What mean you by that, sir?

COKES Your best actor, your Field?[5]

LITTLEWIT Good, i'faith! You are even° with me, sir.

even in jesting

LEATHERHEAD [*showing his puppets in turn*] This is he that acts young Leander, sir. He is extremely beloved of the womenkind. They do so affect his action, the green gamesters that come here![6] And this is lovely Hero; this with the beard, Damon; and this pretty Pythias. This is the ghost of King Dionysius in the habit° of a scrivener, as you shall see anon, at large.°

garb · *at length*

COKES Well, they are a civil company; I like 'em for that. They offer not to fleer,° nor jeer, nor break jests, as the great players do. And then there goes not so much charge° to the

They don't scoff · *expense*

3. (1) Clothes tailor, often laughed at as effeminate; (2) John Taylor, the often-scorned "Water Poet"; (3) Joseph Taylor, member of the Lady Elizabeth's Men (and also the King's Men) and perhaps acting in this play.

4. Richard Burbage, lead actor in Shakespeare's company.

5. Nathan Field, lead actor in the Lady Elizabeth's Men.

6. They do so adore his acting, the young whores who come here!

feasting of 'em, or making 'em drunk, as to the other, by reason of their littleness. Do they use to play perfect?° Are they never flustered?

know their lines

LEATHERHEAD No, sir, I thank my industry, and policy° for it; they are as well governed a company, though I say it—and here is young Leander, is as proper an actor of his inches,° and shakes his head like an hostler.°

management / *for his size* / *horse groom*

COKES But do you play it according to the printed book?[7] I have read that.

LEATHERHEAD By no means, sir.

COKES No? How then?

LEATHERHEAD A better way, sir; that is too learned and poetical for our audience. What do they know what Hellespont is? "Guilty of true love's blood"? Or what Abydos is? Or "the other Sestos hight"?[8]

COKES Thou'rt i'the right. I do not know myself.

LEATHERHEAD No, I have entreated Master Littlewit to take a little pains to reduce it to a more familiar strain for our people.

COKES How, I pray thee, good Master Littlewit?

LITTLEWIT It pleases him to make a matter° of it, sir. But there is no such matter, I assure you. I have only made it a little easy and modern for the times, sir, that's all. As, for the Hellespont I imagine our Thames here; and then Leander I make a dyer's son, about Puddle Wharf;° and Hero a wench o'the Bankside,° who, going over one morning to old Fish Street, Leander spies her land at Trig Stairs° and falls in love with her. Now do I introduce Cupid, having metamorphosed himself into a drawer,° and he strikes Hero in love with° a pint of sherry. And other pretty passages there are, o'the friendship,° that will delight you, sir, and please you of judgment.

a big deal / *(on north bank of Thames)* / *(on the south bank)* / *(on the north bank)* / *tapster / by means of* / *(of Damon and Pythias)*

COKES I'll be sworn they shall! I am in love with the actors already, and I'll be allied° to them presently. (They respect gentlemen, these fellows.) Hero shall be my fairing;° but which of my fairings? Le' me see: i'faith, my fiddle! And Leander, my fiddlestick; then Damon, my drum; and Pythias, my pipe; and the ghost of Dionysius, my hobbyhorse. All fitted.

closely linked / *fair purchase*

5.4

[Enter] to them Winwife [and] Grace. [They stand aside, unnoticed by the others.]

WINWIFE [*aside to Grace*] Look, yonder's your Cokes gotten in among his playfellows. I thought we could not miss him at such a spectacle.

GRACE [*aside to Winwife*] Let him alone. He is so busy he will never spy us.

LEATHERHEAD [*to Cokes*] Nay, good sir.

Cokes is handling the puppets.

7. Marlowe's *Hero and Leander* (pub. 1598). See note 2 above.

8. Leatherhead quotes from the beginning of *Hero and Leander*. On Abydos and Sestos, see note 2 above. "Hight" means "is called."

5.4. The scene continues.

COKES I warrant thee, I will not hurt her,° fellow. What, dost think me uncivil? I pray thee, be not jealous; I am toward° a wife. *(Hero)* / *about to take, marry*

LITTLEWIT Well, good Master Lantern, make ready to begin, that I may fetch my wife. And look you be perfect; you undo me else i'my reputation.

LEATHERHEAD I warrant you, sir, do not you breed too great an expectation of it among your friends; that's the only hurter of these things.

LITTLEWIT No, no, no. [*Exit.*]

COKES I'll stay here and see. Pray thee, let me see.

[*Cokes disappears from view inside.*]

WINWIFE [*aside to Grace*] How diligent and troublesome he is!

GRACE [*aside to Winwife*] The place becomes him, methinks.

JUSTICE OVERDO [*aside*] My ward, Mistress Grace, in the company of a stranger? I doubt° I shall be compelled to discover° myself before my time. *fear / reveal*

[*Enter*] *Knockem, Whit, Edgeworth, Win,* [*and*] *Mistress* [*Dame*] *Overdo.* [*The women are masked.*] *The doorkeepers speak.*

FILCHER Twopence apiece, gentlemen! An excellent motion.

KNOCKEM Shall we have fine fireworks, and good vapors?

SHARKWELL Yes, Captain, and waterworks,° too. *water pageants; tears*

WHIT I pree dee, take a care o'dy shmall lady,° there, Edgeworth; I will look to dish tall lady° myself. *(Win)* / *(Dame Overdo)*

LEATHERHEAD Welcome, gentlemen, welcome, gentlemen.

WHIT Predee, mashter o'de monshtersh,° help a very sick lady, here, to a chair, to shit in. *(he means "motions")*

LEATHERHEAD Presently, sir.

They bring Mistress [*Dame*] *Overdo a chair.*

WHIT Good fait now, Ursula's ale and aqua vitae° ish to blame for't. [*To Dame Overdo*] Shit down, shweetheart, shit down and shleep a little. *brandy, spirits*

[*Dame Overdo, put in the chair, soon falls asleep.*]

EDGEWORTH [*to Win*] Madam, you are very welcome hither.

KNOCKEM Yes, and you shall see very good vapors.

JUSTICE OVERDO [*aside*] (*by*° *Edgeworth*) Here is my care come! I like to see him in so good company; and yet I wonder that persons of such fashion should resort hither. *referring to; close to*

EDGEWORTH [*to Win*] This is a very private house, madam.

The cutpurse [*Edgeworth*] *courts Mistress Littlewit.*

LEATHERHEAD [*to Win*] Will it please Your Ladyship sit, madam?

WIN Yes, good man. [*To Edgeworth*] They do so all-to-be-madam me,° I think they think me a very lady! *keep calling me madam*

EDGEWORTH What else, madam?

WIN Must I put off my mask to him?

EDGEWORTH Oh, by no means.

WIN How should my husband know me, then?

KNOCKEM Husband? An idle vapor. He must not know you, nor you him; there's the true vapor.

JUSTICE OVERDO [*aside*] Yea, I will observe more of this. [*To Whit*] Is this a lady, friend?

WHIT Ay, and dat [*indicating Dame Overdo*] is anoder lady, shweetheart. If dou hasht a mind to 'em, give me twelvepence from tee, and dou shalt have eder-oder on° 'em. *one or the other of*

JUSTICE OVERDO I? [*Aside*] This will prove my chiefest enormity. I will follow this.

EDGEWORTH [*to Win*] Is not this a finer life, lady, than to be clogged° with a husband? *encumbered*

WIN Yes, a great deal. When will they begin, trow,° in the name o'the motion? *do you think*

EDGEWORTH By and by, madam. They stay but for company.

KNOCKEM Do you hear, puppet master, these are tedious vapors. When begin you?

LEATHERHEAD We stay but for Master Littlewit, the author, who is gone for his wife; and we begin presently.

WIN [*aside to Edgeworth*] That's I, that's I.

EDGEWORTH [*aside to Win*] That was you, lady; but now you are no such poor thing.

KNOCKEM Hang the author's wife! A running vapor. Here be ladies will stay for ne'er a Delia[1] o'em all.

WHIT But hear me now, here ish one o'de ladish ashleep. Stay till she but vake, man.

[*Enter*] *to them, Wasp.*

WASP How now, friends? What's here to do?

The doorkeepers [*speak*] *again.*

FILCHER Twopence apiece, sir, the best motion in the fair.

WASP I believe you lie. If you do, I'll have my money again,° and beat you. *refunded*

WINWIFE [*aside to Grace*] Numps is come!

WASP Did you see a master of mine come in here, a tall young squire of Harrow o'the Hill, Master Barthol'mew Cokes?

FILCHER I think there be such a one within.

WASP Look° he be, you were best; but it is very likely. I wonder I found him not at all the rest.° I ha' been at the eagle, and the black wolf, and the bull with the five legs and two pizzles° (he was a calf at Uxbridge Fair two years agone)°, and at the dogs that dance the morris, and the hare o'the tabor,° and missed him at all these! Sure this must needs be some fine sight that holds him so, if it have him. *See if* / *the other sideshows* / *penises* / *ago* / *playing a small drum*

[*Cokes and Leatherhead appear from the puppet-theater booth.*]

COKES Come, come, are you ready now?

LEATHERHEAD Presently, sir.

WASP Hoyday,° he's at work in his doublet and hose. [*To Cokes*] Do you hear, sir? Are you employed,° that you are bareheaded and so busy? *Heyday (an exclamation)* / *hired as a worker*

COKES Hold your peace, Numps. You ha' been i'the stocks, I hear.

WASP Does he know that? Nay, then the date° of my authority *term*

1. The imaginary woman to whom Samuel Daniel's sonnet sequence *Delia* (1592) is addressed. By "running vapor" (line 71), Knockem expressed impatience at Littlewit's notion to run after his wife; the ladies present, he protests, have no wish to hold up the proceedings for the woman whom the poet Littlewit may choose to idealize in this way.

is out.° I must think no longer to reign; my government is at an end. He that will correct another must want° fault in himself. — *expired*; *lack*

WINWIFE [*aside to Grace*] Sentientious Numps! I never heard so much° from him before. — *so much good sense*

LEATHERHEAD Sure, Master Littlewit will not come. [*To Wasp*] Please you take your place, sir, we'll begin.

COKES I pray thee, do; mine ears long to be at it, and my eyes too. Oh, Numps, i'the stocks, Numps? Where's your sword, Numps?

WASP I pray you intend° your game, sir. Let me alone. — *pay attention to*

COKES Well, then we are quit° for all. Come, sit down, Numps; I'll interpret to thee. Did you see Mistress Grace? It's no matter, neither, now I think on't; tell me anon. — *even, quits*

WINWIFE [*aside to Grace*] A great deal of love and care he expresses!

GRACE [*aside to Winwife*] Alas, would you have him to express more than he has? That were tyranny.

COKES [*to the assembly*] Peace, ho! Now, now.

LEATHERHEAD Gentles,° that no longer your expectations may wander, — *Gentlefolk*
Behold our chief actor, amorous Leander,

[*Enter Leander on the puppet stage.*]

With a great deal of cloth lapped about him like a scarf,
For he yet serves his father, a dyer at Puddle Wharf,
Which place we'll make bold with to call it our Abydus,° — *Abydos (comic rhyme)*
As the Bankside is our Sestos,° and let it not be denied us. — *(see 5.3.10 n)*
Now, as he is beating, to make the dye take° the fuller, — *take effect*
Who chances to come by but fair Hero in a sculler?° — *rowboat*

[*Leatherhead mimes with his puppets the arrival of Hero and Cole, a waterman, in his boat.*]

And seeing Leander's naked leg and goodly calf,
Cast at him, from the boat, a sheep's eye and a half.° — *an amorous look*
Now she is landed, and the sculler come back.[2]
By and by you shall see what Leander doth lack.° — *desire*

PUPPET LEANDER *Cole, Cole, old Cole!*[3]

LEATHERHEAD That is the sculler's° name, without control.° — *boatman's*; *without doubt*

PUPPET LEANDER *Cole, Cole, I say, Cole!*

LEATHERHEAD *We do hear you.*

PUPPET LEANDER *Old Cole!*

LEATHERHEAD *"Old Cole"? Is the dyer turned collier? How° do you sell?* — *For how much*

PUPPET LEANDER *A pox o'your manners! Kiss my hole here, and smell.*

LEATHERHEAD *Kiss your hole and smell? There's manners, indeed.*

PUPPET LEANDER *Why, Cole, I say, Cole!*

LEATHERHEAD *It's the sculler you need.*

2. The boatman, Cole, has landed Hero at Trig Stairs (see line 138), not far from Puddle Wharf, where Leander spied her in the boat. Having landed her, Cole returns to Puddle Wharf, while Hero proceeds to a room at the Swan Inn (line 147). Leander then hires the boatman to carry him after Hero (lines 146–47). A boat would hardly be necessary for so short a trip, but it is part of the absurd story.

3. All the speeches of the puppet play and the puppets are set in italics. "Old cole" could also mean "pander."

PUPPET LEANDER *Ay, and be hanged!*
LEATHERHEAD *Be hanged! [To Cole] Look you yonder,*
Old Cole, you must go hang with Master Leander.
PUPPET COLE *Where is he?*
PUPPET LEANDER *Here, Cole. What fairest of fairs*
Was that fare that thou landed'st but° now at Trig Stairs? just
COKES [*to Leatherhead*] What was that, fellow? Pray thee tell me, I scarce understand 'em.
LEATHERHEAD Leander does ask, sir, what fairest of fairs
Was the fare that he landed but now at Trig Stairs?
PUPPET COLE [*to Leander*] *It is lovely Hero.*
PUPPET LEANDER *Nero?*
PUPPET COLE *No, Hero.*
LEATHERHEAD It is Hero
Of the Bankside, he saith, to tell you truth without erring,
Is° come over into Fish Street to eat some fresh herring. Who is
Leander says no more, but as fast as he can
Gets on all his best clothes, and will after to the Swan.
[*During this dialogue, Hero makes her way to a room at the Swan.*]
COKES Most admirable good, is't not?
LEATHERHEAD *Stay, sculler.*
PUPPET COLE *What say you?*
LEATHERHEAD *You must stay for Leander,*
And carry him to the wench.
PUPPET COLE *You rogue, I am no pander.*
COKES He says he is no pander. 'Tis a fine language; I understand it now.
LEATHERHEAD *Are you no pander, Goodman Cole? Here's no man says you are.*
You'll grow a hot Cole,° it seems. Pray you stay for your fare. Cole; coal
PUPPET COLE *Will he come away?*
LEATHERHEAD *What do you say?*
PUPPET COLE *I'd ha' him come away.*
LEATHERHEAD *Would you ha' Leander come away? Why, pray, sir, stay.*
You are angry, Goodman Cole. I believe the fair maid
Came over w'you o'trust.° Tell us, sculler, are you paid? on credit
PUPPET COLE *Yes, Goodman Hogrubber o'Pickt-hatch.*[4]
LEATHERHEAD *How, Hogrubber o'Pickt-hatch?*
PUPPET COLE *Ay, Hogrubber o'Pickt-hatch.*
Take you that! (*The puppet strikes him over the pate.*)
LEATHERHEAD *Oh, my head!*
PUPPET COLE *Harm watch, harm catch.*[5]
COKES "Harm watch, harm catch," he says. Very good, i'faith!
The sculler had like to ha' knocked you,° sirrah. nearly did you in
LEATHERHEAD Yes, but that his fare called him away.
PUPPET LEANDER [*getting in the boat*] *Row apace, row apace, row, row, row, row, row!*

4. Master Swineherd of Pickt-hatch, a crime-ridden neighborhood.

5. Do harm and you'll suffer harm. (A proverb.)

LEATHERHEAD [*to Cole*] *You are knavishly loaden, sculler; take heed where you go.*

PUPPET COLE *Knave i'your face, goodman rogue.*

PUPPET LEANDER [*to Cole*] *Row, row, row, row, row, row!*

[*In mime, Cole rows Leander in pursuit of Hero. Leander lands and makes his way to Hero's room during the ensuing dialogue. Exit Cole.*]

COKES [*to Leatherhead*] He said "knave i'your face," friend.

LEATHERHEAD Ay, sir, I heard him. But there's no talking to these watermen; they will ha' the last word.

COKES God's my life! I am not allied to° the sculler, yet; he — *haven't adopted*
shall be Dauphin my boy.[6] But my fiddlestick° does fiddle in — *(Leander)*
and out too much; I pray thee speak to him on't.° Tell him — *about it*
I would have him tarry in my sight more.

LEATHERHEAD I pray you, be content; you'll have enough on° — *of*
him, sir.—
Now, gentles, I take it here is none of you so stupid
But that you have heard of a little god of love called Cupid,
Who, out of kindness to Leander, hearing he but saw her,
This present day and hour doth turn himself to a drawer.° — *tapster, barkeep*

[*Enter, onto the puppet stage, Cupid disguised as Jonas, the tapster.*]

And because he would have their first meeting to be merry,
He strikes Hero in love to him with a pint of sherry,
Which, he tells her, from amorous Leander is sent her,
Who after him° into the room of Hero doth venter.° — *(Cupid) / venture*

(*Puppet Leander goes into Mistress Hero's room.*)

PUPPET JONAS *A pint of sack! Score a pint of sack i'the Coney!*[7]

COKES Sack? You said but e'en now it should be sherry.

PUPPET JONAS Why, so it is.—*Sherry, sherry, sherry!*

[*The puppets remain in Hero's room during the ensuing dialogue.*]

COKES Sherry, sherry, sherry! By my troth, he makes me
merry. I must have a name for Cupid, too. Let me see. Thou
mightst help me now an thou wouldest, Numps, at a dead
lift,° but thou art dreaming o'the stocks still. Do not think — *at a pinch*
on't; I have forgot it. 'Tis but a nine days' wonder,° man; let — *a passing event*
it not trouble thee.

WASP I would the stocks were about your neck, sir, condition° — *on condition that*
I hung by the heels in them till the wonder were off from
you, with all my heart.

COKES Well said, resolute Numps. [*To Leatherhead*] But hark you, friend, where is the friendship all this while between my drum, Damon, and my pipe, Pythias?

LEATHERHEAD You shall see by and by, sir.

COKES You think my hobbyhorse° is forgotten, too; no, I'll see — *(Dionysius)*
'em all enact° before I go. I shall not know which to love — *act*
best, else.

6. Cokes gives the name of a lost ballad or song to the sculler, or boatman, who thus becomes one of Cokes's collection of toys. (See 5.3.133–38.)

7. Cupid, given the name of "Jonas" in his role as tapster, calls out to the tavern owner his orders for drinks: "A pint of sack (a strong sweet wine)! Charge a pint of sack to the customers in the tavern room called the 'Rabbit'!" (Cf. the tapster Francis in *1 Henry IV*, 2.4.)

KNOCKEM [*aside to Whit*] This gallant has interrupting vapors, troublesome vapors, Whit. Puff with° him. *Quarrel with, bully*

WHIT [*aside to Knockem*] No, I pre dee, Captain, let him alone. He is a child, i'faith, la.

LEATHERHEAD Now, gentles, to° the friends, who in number are two, *let us turn to*
And lodged in that alehouse in which fair Hero does do.° *work; provide sex*
Damon, for some kindness done him the last week,
Is come fair Hero in Fish Street this morning to seek.
Pythias does smell the knavery of the meeting,
And now you shall see their true friendly greeting.

[*Enter Damon and Pythias on the puppet stage.*]

PUPPET PYTHIAS [*to Damon*] *You whoremasterly slave, you!*

COKES "Whoremasterly slave, you"? Very friendly and familiar, that.

PUPPET DAMON [*to Pythias*] *Whoremaster i'thy face!*
Thou hast lien° with her thyself. I'll prove't i'this place. *lain, had sex*

COKES Damon says Pythias has lien with her himself; he'll prove't in this place.

LEATHERHEAD They are whoremasters both, sir, that's a plain case.

PUPPET PYTHIAS *You lie, like a rogue!*

LEATHERHEAD *Do I lie like a rogue?*

PUPPET PYTHIAS *A pimp and a scab.°* *scoundrel*

LEATHERHEAD *A pimp and a scab?*
I say, between you you have both but one drab.° *whore*

PUPPET DAMON *You lie again.*

LEATHERHEAD *Do I lie again?*

PUPPET DAMON *Like a rogue again.*

LEATHERHEAD *Like a rogue again?*

PUPPET PYTHIAS *And you are a pimp again.*

COKES "And you are a pimp again," he says.

PUPPET DAMON *And a scab again.*

COKES "And a scab again," he says.

LEATHERHEAD *And I say again you are both whoremasters again,*
And you have both but one drab again. (*They fight.*)

PUPPETS DAMON [*and*] PYTHIAS *Dost thou, dost thou, dost thou?*

LEATHERHEAD *What, both at once?*[8]

PUPPET PYTHIAS *Down with him, Damon!*

[*They attack Leatherhead.*]

PUPPET DAMON *Pink° his guts, Pythias!* *Stab*

LEATHERHEAD *What, so malicious?*
Will ye murder me, masters° both, i'mine own house? *good sirs*

COKES Ho! Well acted, my drum! Well acted, my pipe! Well acted still!

WASP Well acted, with all my heart.

LEATHERHEAD *Hold, hold your hands!*

COKES Ay, both your hands, for my sake, for you ha' both done well.

PUPPET DAMON *Gramercy, pure Pythias.*

PUPPET PYTHIAS *Gramercy, dear Damon.*

COKES Gramercy to you both, my pipe and my drum.

8. (1) What, are you both attacking me at once? (2) What, am I having to speak both puppets' parts at once?

PUPPET PYTHIAS *Come, now, we'll together to breakfast to° Hero.* *with*
LEATHERHEAD *'Tis well, you can now go to breakfast to Hero.*
You have given me my breakfast, with a 'hone and 'honero.° *alas! (Gaelic)*
[*Damon and Pythias make their way to Hero's room during the ensuing dialogue.*]
COKES [*to Leatherhead*] How is't, friend? Ha' they hurt thee?
LEATHERHEAD Oh, no.
Between you and I, sir, we do but make show.—
Thus, gentles, you perceive, without any denial,
'Twixt Damon and Pythias here, friendship's true trial.
Though hourly they quarrel thus, and roar each with other,
They fight you° no more than does brother with brother, *They fight*
But, friendly together, at the next man they meet,
They let fly their anger, as here you might see't.
COKES Well, we have seen't, and thou hast felt it, whatsoever thou sayest. What's next? What's next?
LEATHERHEAD This while° young Leander with fair Hero is drinking, *All this while*
And Hero grown drunk, to any man's thinking!
Yet was it not three pints of sherry could flaw her° *make her drunk*
Till Cupid, distinguished° like Jonas the drawer, *disguised*
From under his apron, where his lechery lurks,
Put love in her sack.° Now mark how it works. *white wine; vagina*
[*Hero, Leander, and Jonas are seen in Hero's room on the puppet stage.*]
PUPPET HERO *O Leander, Leander, my dear, my dear Leander!*
I'll forever be thy goose, so° thou'lt be my gander. *provided*
COKES Excellently well said, fiddle!—She'll ever be his goose, so he'll be her gander. Was't not so?
LEATHERHEAD Yes, sir, but mark his answer, now.
PUPPET LEANDER *And sweetest of geese, before I go to bed*
I'll swim o'er the Thames, my goose, thee to tread.° *to have sex with you*
COKES Brave!° He will swim o'er the Thames and tread his goose tonight, he says. *Excellent!*
LEATHERHEAD Ay. Peace, sir! They'll be angry if they hear you eavesdropping, now they are setting their match.° *arranging to meet*
PUPPET LEANDER *But lest the Thames should be dark, my goose, my dear friend,*
Let thy window be provided of° a candle's end. *with*
PUPPET HERO *Fear not, my gander. I protest I should handle*
My matters very ill, if I had not a whole candle.° *(with erotic suggestion)*
PUPPET LEANDER *Well, then, look to't, and kiss me to boot.°* *besides*
[*They kiss.*]
LEATHERHEAD Now, here come the friends again, Pythias and Damon,
And under their cloaks they have of bacon a gammon.° *a side of bacon*

Damon and Pythias enter [*Hero's room at the inn*].

PUPPET PYTHIAS [*to Cupid*] *Drawer, fill some wine here.*
LEATHERHEAD *How, some wine there?*
There's company already, sir. Pray forbear!
PUPPET DAMON *'Tis Hero.*
LEATHERHEAD *Yes, but she will not be taken,*

After sack and fresh herring, with your Dunmow bacon.[9]

PUPPET PYTHIAS *You lie, it's Westfabian.*

LEATHERHEAD *"Westphalian,"° you should say.* — *in Germany*

PUPPET DAMON *If you hold not your peace, you are a coxcomb, I would say.* *(Leander and Hero are kissing.)*

PUPPET PYTHIAS *What's here? What's here? Kiss, kiss upon kiss?*

LEATHERHEAD *Ay. Wherefore should they not? What harm is in this? 'Tis Mistress Hero.*

PUPPET DAMON *Mistress Hero's a whore.*

LEATHERHEAD *Is she a whore? Keep you quiet, or, sir knave, out of door.°* — *out you go*

PUPPET DAMON *Knave, out of door?*

PUPPET HERO *Yes, knave, out of door.*

PUPPET DAMON *Whore, out of door!*

PUPPET HERO *I say, knave out of door!*

(Here the puppets quarrel and fall together by the ears.)° — *fall to fighting*

PUPPET DAMON *I say, whore, out of door!*

PUPPET PYTHIAS *Yea, so say I too.*

PUPPET HERO *Kiss the whore o'the arse.*

LEATHERHEAD *Now you ha' something to do:*
You must kiss her o'the arse, she says.

PUPPETS DAMON [*and*] PYTHIAS *So we will, so we will.*

[*They kick her.*]

PUPPET HERO *Oh, my haunches! Oh, my haunches! Hold, hold!*

LEATHERHEAD *Stand'st thou still?*
Leander, where art thou? Stand'st thou still like a sot,
And not offer'st to break° both their heads with a pot? — *knock*
See who's at thine elbow, there: Puppet Jonas and Cupid!° — *Cupid dressed as Jonas*

PUPPET JONAS *Upon 'em, Leander! Be not so stupid.*

(They fight.)

PUPPET LEANDER *You goat-bearded slave!*

PUPPET DAMON *You whoremaster knave!*

PUPPET LEANDER *Thou art a whoremaster.*

PUPPET JONAS *Whoremasters all!*

[*The puppets retire from view.*]

LEATHERHEAD See, Cupid with a word° has ta'en up the brawl. — *i.e., "whoremaster"*

KNOCKEM These be fine vapors!

COKES By this good day, they fight bravely! Do they not, Numps?

WASP Yes, they lacked but you to be their second° all this while. — *backup in a duel*

LEATHERHEAD This tragical encounter falling out thus to busy us,
It raises up the ghost of their friend Dionysius,[1]

[*Enter Puppet Dionysius.*]

9. "To fetch a flick of bacon from Dunmow" was a proverbial phrase for marital harmony, since the married couples of that Essex town were awarded a side of bacon if they could prove that they had passed a year without quarreling. Leatherhead implies his opinion that Hero, flush with wine and sexual desire, is in no mood for Damon's or Pythias' tame offers of fidelity and constancy.

1. This tyrant of Syracuse (367–356 and 347–344 B.C.E.), as portrayed in Richard Edwards's play *Damon and Pythias* (c. 1565–71), was so moved by the example of friendship in the two young men that he pardoned the treason he had wrongly suspected. Tradition reports that he abdicated and became a schoolmaster.

Not like a monarch, but the master of a school,
In a scrivener's furred gown, which shows he is no fool,
For therein he hath wit enough to keep himself warm.° *(proverbial)*
"O Damon," he cries, "and Pythias, what harm
Hath poor Dionysius done you in his grave
That after his death you should fall out thus and rave,
And call amorous Leander whoremaster knave?"

PUPPET DIONYSIUS *I cannot, I will not, I promise you, endure it!*

5.5

[*Enter*] *to them, Busy.*

BUSY Down with Dagon,° down with Dagon! 'Tis I will no longer endure your profanations. *god of the Philistines*

LEATHERHEAD What mean you, sir?

BUSY I will remove Dagon there, I say, that idol, that heathenish idol, that remains (as I may say) a beam, a very beam, not a beam of the sun, nor a beam of the moon, nor a beam of a balance,° neither a house beam nor a weaver's beam,[1] but a beam in the eye,° in the eye of the brethren; a very great beam, an exceeding great beam; such as are your stage-players, rhymers, and morris dancers, who have walked hand in hand in contempt of the brethren and the cause, and been borne out° by instruments of no mean countenance.° *weighing scales* / *(see Matthew 7.3–5)* / *supported / authority*

LEATHERHEAD Sir, I present nothing but what is licensed by authority.

BUSY Thou art all license, even licentiousness itself, Shimei!° *(see 2 Samuel 16.5–13)*

LEATHERHEAD I have the Master of the Revels'° hand for't, sir. *licenser of plays'*

BUSY The Master of Rebels' hand, thou hast: Satan's! Hold thy peace! Thy scurrility° shut up thy mouth! Thy profession is damnable, and in pleading for it thou dost plead for Baal.[2] I have long opened my mouth wide, and gaped; I have gaped as the oyster for the tide after thy destruction, but cannot compass it° by suit or dispute, so that I look for a bickering ere long and then a battle. *May your scurrility* / *bring it about*

KNOCKEM Good Banbury vapors.

COKES Friend, you'd have an ill match on't if you bicker with him here.° Though he be no man o'the fist,° he has friends that will go to cuffs for him.—Numps, will not you take our side? *(Leatherhead) / fisticuffs*

EDGEWORTH Sir, it shall not need. In my mind, he° offers him° a fairer course, to end it by disputation. [*To Leatherhead*] Hast thou nothing to say for thyself, in defense of thy quality?° *(Busy) / (Leatherhead)* / *(acting) profession*

LEATHERHEAD Faith, sir, I am not well studied in these controversies between the hypocrites° and us. But here's one of my motion, Puppet Dionysius, shall undertake him,° and I'll venture° the cause on't. *Puritans* / *who'll take Busy on* / *wager*

COKES Who? My hobbyhorse? Will he dispute with him?

5.5. The scene continues.
1. Wooden roller or cylinder in a loom, on which the warp of lengthwise threads is wound before weaving.
2. Busy is citing Judges 6.25–32, which describes how God commanded Gideon to throw down the altar of the heathen god Baal and erect an altar to God in its place.

LEATHERHEAD Yes, sir, and make a hobby-ass of him, I hope.

COKES That's excellent! Indeed, he looks like the best scholar of 'em all. [*To Busy*] Come, sir, you must be as good as your word, now.

BUSY I will not fear to make my spirit and gifts known. Assist me, zeal! Fill me, fill me, that is, make me full!

WINWIFE [*aside to Grace*] What a desperate, profane wretch is this! Is there any ignorance or impudence like his? To call his zeal to fill him against a puppet?

GRACE [*aside to Winwife*] I know no fitter match than a puppet to commit° with an hypocrite. [*The debate begins.*] *do battle*

BUSY [*to Dionysius*] First, I say unto thee, idol, thou hast no calling.[3]

PUPPET DIONYSIUS *You lie. I am called Dionysius.*

LEATHERHEAD The motion says you lie; he is called Dionysius i'the matter,° and to that calling he answers. *puppet show*

BUSY I mean, no vocation, idol, no present lawful calling.

PUPPET DIONYSIUS *Is yours a lawful calling?*

LEATHERHEAD The motion asketh if yours be a lawful calling?

BUSY Yes, mine is of the spirit.

PUPPET DIONYSIUS *Then idol is a lawful calling.*

LEATHERHEAD He says, then idol is a lawful calling. For you called him idol, and your calling is of the spirit.

COKES Well disputed, hobbyhorse!

BUSY [*to Cokes*] Take not part with the wicked, young gallant. He neigheth and hinnyeth; all is but hinnying sophistry. I call him idol again. Yet,° I say, his calling, his profession is profane. [*To Dionysius*] It is profane, idol! *Yet again*

PUPPET DIONYSIUS *It is not profane!*

LEATHERHEAD It is not profane, he says.

BUSY It is profane!

PUPPET DIONYSIUS *It is not profane!*

BUSY It is profane!

PUPPET DIONYSIUS *It is not profane!*

LEATHERHEAD Well said! Confute him with "not," still. [*To Busy*] You cannot bear him down with your base° noise, sir. *vile; bass*

BUSY Nor he me, with his treble° creaking, though he creak like the chariot wheels of Satan. I am zealous for the cause— *with boy actor's voice*

LEATHERHEAD As a dog for a bone.

BUSY And I say it is profane, as being the page of Pride and the waiting-woman of Vanity.

PUPPET DIONYSIUS *Yea? What say you to your tire-women,° then?* *dressmakers*

LEATHERHEAD Good.

PUPPET DIONYSIUS *Or feather-makers i'the Friars, that are o'your faction of faith?*[4] *Are not they, with their perukes° and their puffs, their fans and their huffs,° as much pages of Pride and waiters upon Vanity? What say you? What say you? What say you?* *wigs* *shoulder pads*

BUSY I will not answer for them.

3. (1) Lawful occupation; (2) religious vocation. But Puppet Dionysius then punningly insists that he is indeed "called": he is called Dionysius. (Dionysus is the god of wine and revelry, both of which this puppet defends. Dionysius was the famous tyrant of Syracuse.)

4. Many feather-makers and dressmakers in the Blackfriars district were Puritans.

PUPPET DIONYSIUS *Because you cannot, because you cannot. Is a bugle-maker° a lawful calling? Or the confect-maker's?*[5] *Such you have there.° Or your French fashioner?° You'd have all the sin within yourselves, would you not? Would you not?*

maker of glass beads
among Puritans / tailor

BUSY No, Dagon.

PUPPET DIONYSIUS *What then, Dagonet?*[6] *Is a puppet worse than these?*

BUSY Yes, and my main argument against you is that you are an abomination; for the male among you putteth on the apparel of the female, and the female of the male.

PUPPET DIONYSIUS *You lie, you lie abominably.*

COKES Good, by my troth, he has given him the lie thrice.

PUPPET DIONYSIUS *It is your old stale argument against the players,° but it will not hold against the puppets; for we have neither male nor female amongst us. And that thou mayst see, if thou wilt, like a malicious purblind zeal° as thou art!*

actors
blind fanatic

(*The puppet takes up his garment.*)

EDGEWORTH By my faith, there he has answered you, friend, by plain demonstration.

PUPPET DIONYSIUS *Nay, I'll prove, against e'er a rabbin° of 'em all, that my standing° is as lawful as his, that I speak by inspiration as well as he, that I have as little to do with learning as he, and do scorn her° helps as much as he.*

rabbi, Puritan cleric
profession
(learning's)

BUSY I am confuted. The cause hath failed me!

PUPPET DIONYSIUS *Then be converted, be converted.*

LEATHERHEAD Be converted, I pray you, and let the play go on.

BUSY Let it go on. For I am changed, and will become a beholder with you.

COKES That's brave, i'faith! Thou hast carried it away,° hobbyhorse.—On with the play!

won the day

JUSTICE OVERDO Stay, now do I forbid. (*The Justice discovers° himself.*) I, Adam Overdo! Sit still, I charge you.

reveals

COKES What, my brother-i'-law!

GRACE My wise guardian!

EDGEWORTH Justice Overdo!

JUSTICE OVERDO It is time to take enormity by the forehead and brand it, for I have discovered enough.

5.6

[*Enter*] *to them Quarlous* (*like the madman*), [*followed by Dame*] *Purecraft.*

QUARLOUS [*to Dame Purecraft*] Nay, come, mistress bride. You must do as I do, now. You must be mad with me, in truth. I have here Justice Overdo° for it.

Overdo's warrant

JUSTICE OVERDO Peace, good Troubleall! Come hither, and you shall trouble none. I will take the charge of you, and your friend° too. (*To the cutpurse and Mistress Littlewit*) You

(Dame Purecraft)

5. Makers of sweetmeats and confections. (Busy himself had been a baker; see 1.3.115–19, 3.2.51–52.) Puritans also took up glass-bead-making and tailoring.

6. King Arthur's fool. (With wordplay on "Dagon," line 93.)

5.6. The scene continues.

also, young man,[1] shall be my care. Stand there.

EDGEWORTH [*aside*] Now, mercy upon me!

The rest [Knockem and Whit] are stealing away.

KNOCKEM [*aside to Whit*] Would we were away, Whit. These are dangerous vapors! Best fall off° with our birds,° for fear o'the cage.°

slip away / women
prison

JUSTICE OVERDO [*to Knockem and Whit*] Stay! Is not my name your terror?

WHIT Yesh, faith, man, and it ish for tat° we would be gone, man.

for that reason

[*Enter*] *John* [*Littlewit*].

LITTLEWIT O gentlemen, did you not see a wife of mine? I ha' lost my little wife, as I shall be trusted:° my little pretty Win! I left her at the great woman's house in trust yonder, the pig-woman's, with Captain Jordan and Captain Whit, very good men, and I cannot hear of her. Poor fool, I fear she's stepped aside.°—Mother, did you not see Win?

as I hope to be saved
gone astray

JUSTICE OVERDO [*indicating Dame Purecraft*] If this grave matron be your mother, sir, stand by her, *et digito compesce labellum*.[2] I may perhaps spring[3] a wife for you anon.—Brother° Barthol'mew, I am sadly sorry to see you so lightly given, and such a disciple of enormity, with your grave governor Humphrey. But stand you both there in the middle place; I will reprehend you in your course.°—Mistress Grace, let me rescue you out of the hands of the stranger.

Brother-in-law
turn

WINWIFE Pardon me, sir, I am a kinsman of hers.

JUSTICE OVERDO Are you so? Of what name, sir?

WINWIFE Winwife, sir.

JUSTICE OVERDO Master Winwife? I hope you have won no wife of her, sir. If you have, I will examine the possibility of it at fit leisure. Now, to my enormities. Look upon me, O London, and see me, O Smithfield! The example of justice and Mirror of Magistrates,[4] the true top of formality° and scourge of enormity! Hearken unto my labors, and but observe my discoveries; and compare Hercules with me, if thou dar'st, of old, or Columbus, Magellan, or our countryman Drake° of later times. Stand forth, you weeds of enormity and spread!° (*To Busy*) First, Rabbi Busy, thou superlunatical hypocrite! (*To Lantern* [*Leatherhead*]) Next, thou other extremity, thou profane professor of puppetry, little better than poetry! (*To* [*Knockem,*] *the horse-courser*) Then, thou strong debaucher and seducer of youth—witness this easy° and honest young man! [*Indicating Edgeworth, the*] (*cutpurse*). (*Then Captain Whit*) Now, thou esquire of dames, madams, and twelvepenny ladies! (*And Mistress Littlewit*) Now my green madam herself, of the price![5] Let me unmask Your Ladyship.

legal procedure
Sir Francis Drake
widespread enormity
credulous

[*He unmasks Win-the-fight Littlewit.*]

1. Edgeworth, whom Overdo has seen paired with Win-the-fight Littlewit.
2. And put your fingers to your lips, be silent. (Juvenal, *Satires*, 1.160.)
3. Flush from cover, like a game bird.
4. Overdo alludes to *The Mirror for Magistrates*, a popular treatise offering instructive examples for rulers; see Induction 140–41 and note.
5. Overdo assumes that Win is for sale as a whore, since she is dressed in green, the traditional color for prostitutes (see 4.5.36, 91–92 and notes).

LITTLEWIT Oh, my wife, my wife, my wife!

JUSTICE OVERDO Is she your wife? *Redde te Harpocratem!*[6]

Enter Troubleall.

TROUBLEALL By your leave, stand by, my masters. Be uncovered.[7]

[*Enter*] *to them Ursula and Nightingale.*

URSULA Oh, stay him,° stay him! Help to cry, Nightingale! My pan, my pan! — *detain Troubleall*

JUSTICE OVERDO What's the matter?

NIGHTINGALE He has stol'n gammer° Ursula's pan. — *old woman*

TROUBLEALL Yes, and I fear no man but Justice Overdo.

JUSTICE OVERDO Ursula? Where is she? Oh, the sow of enormity, this! (*To Ursula and Nightingale*) Welcome. Stand you there; you, songster, there.

URSULA An please Your Worship, I am in no fault. A gentleman stripped him° in my booth, and borrowed his gown and his hat; and he ran away with my goods, here, for it.° — *(Troubleall)* — *in retaliation*

JUSTICE OVERDO Then this is the true madman, and (*to Quarlous*) you are the enormity!

QUARLOUS [*revealing his identity*] You are i'the right. I am mad but from the gown outward.

JUSTICE OVERDO Stand you there.

QUARLOUS Where you please, sir.

Mistress [*Dame*] *Overdo* [*who has been drunkenly asleep in her chair all this while*] *is sick, and her husband is silenced.*

DAME OVERDO Oh, lend me a basin! I am sick, I am sick. Where's Master Overdo? Bridget,[8] call hither my Adam.

JUSTICE OVERDO How?

WHIT [*unmasking her*] Dy very own wife, i'fait, worshipful Adam.

DAME OVERDO Will not my Adam come at° me? Shall I see him no more, then? — *to*

QUARLOUS Sir, why do you not go on with the enormity? Are you oppressed with° it? I'll help you. [*Privately to him*] Hark you, sir, i'your ear: your "innocent young man" you have ta'en such care of all this day is a cutpurse that hath got all your brother Cokes his° things, and helped you to your beating and the stocks. If you have a mind to hang him now and show him your magistrate's wit, you may, but I should think it were better recovering the goods and to save your estimation in him.[9] I thank you, sir, for the gift of your ward, Mistress Grace:[1] look you [*showing the warrant*], here is your hand and seal, by the way.—Master Winwife, give° you joy! You are Palemon, you are possessed o'the gentlewoman, but she must pay me value; here's warrant for it.[2] [*To Troubleall,* — *overwhelmed by* — *Cokes's* — *may God give*

6. Make yourselves like Harpocrates (the god of silence)!

7. Show respect by doffing your hats.

8. Dame Overdo presumably calls for her maid, who is not actually present.

9. It would be better to restore the stolen property to its rightful owners and save your reputation (by not prosecuting Edgeworth, whom you have misjudged and who might tell on you).

1. I'm grateful for the guardianship of Grace that I now enjoy, thanks to the warrant signed by you.

2. Quarlous, in possession of the marriage license, or "warrant," can act as Grace's guardian to demand that she pay him the value of her land if she marries Winwife instead of Cokes. In effect, he is splitting the proceeds with Winwife; Winwife gets Grace, Quarlous gets her fortune. See 3.5.293–97.

giving him his gown and cap] And, honest madman, there's thy gown and cap again; I thank thee for my wife. (*To the widow* [*Dame Purecraft*]) Nay, I can be mad, sweetheart, when I please, still; never fear° me.—And careful° Numps, where's he? I thank him for my license.

doubt / worrier

Wasp misseth° the license.

realizes he is missing

WASP How!

QUARLOUS 'Tis true, Numps.

WASP I'll be hanged, then.

QUARLOUS Look i'your box, Numps. [*To Justice Overdo*] Nay, sir, stand not you fixed here, like a stake in Finsbury[3] to be shot at, or the whipping post i'the fair, but get your wife out o'the air; it will make her worse else. And remember you are but Adam, flesh and blood! You have your frailty;° forget your other name of Overdo, and invite us all to supper. There you and I will compare our discoveries, and drown the memory of all enormity in your bigg'st bowl at home.

i.e., Adam's fall

COKES [*to Wasp, who is looking frantically in the box for the deed*] How now, Numps, ha' you lost it? I warrant 'twas when thou wert i'the stocks. Why dost not speak?

WASP I will never speak while I live, again, for aught I know.

JUSTICE OVERDO Nay, Humphrey, if I be patient, you must be so too. [*To them all*] This pleasant-conceited gentleman° hath wrought upon my judgment, and prevailed. I pray you take care of your sick friend, Mistress Alice,° and my good friends all—

(Quarlous, full of jests)

Alice Overdo

QUARLOUS And no enormities.

JUSTICE OVERDO I invite you home with me to my house, to supper. I will have none fear to go along, for my intents are *ad correctionem, non ad destructionem; ad aedificandum, non ad diruendum.*[4] So, lead on.

COKES Yes, and bring the actors along. We'll ha' the rest o'the play at home. [*Exeunt.*]

THE END.

The Epilogue°

(for court performance)

[*Enter the Epilogue.*]

EPILOGUE Your Majesty hath seen the play, and you
Can best allow° it from your ear and view. *sanction, approve*
You know the scope of writers, and what store
Of leave° is given them, if they take not more *permission*
And turn it into license.° You can tell *unwarranted liberty*
If we have used that leave you gave us well,
Or whether we to rage or license break,
Or be profane, or make profane men speak.
This is your power to judge, great sir, and not
The envy of a few.[1] Which° if we have got, *Which royal approval*

3. A sporting ground north of the city, used for archery contests.
4. For correction, not destruction; for building up, not tearing down. (Horace, *Epistles*, 1.1.100.)

Epilogue.
1. There are many carping, small-minded critics who envy you that power of judgment and us whom you favor.

We value less what their dislike° can bring, *the dislike of the envious*
If it° so happy° be t'have pleased the King. [*Exit.*] *(the play) / fortunate*

TEXTUAL NOTES

Bartholomew Fair was first printed in the second folio of 1631–40. This edition was not printed as carefully as was the first folio of 1616, which did not include *Bartholomew Fair*, but it is at all events the authoritative edition on which the present text, like other modern editions, must be based. The following notes indicate departures from the second folio, using these abbreviations:

F2: The second folio (London: John Beale, 1631). This second folio edition was then included in *The Works of Benjamin Jonson*, vol. 2 (London: Richard Meighen, 1640)
F2 corr.: The corrected second folio
F2 uncorr.: The uncorrected second folio
F3: The third folio edition of the *Works* (London: Thomas Hodgkin for H. Herringman and others, 1692)
ed.: A modern editor's emendation

The Persons of the Play 21 [and elsewhere] **URSULA** [F2: VRSLA] **31** [and elsewhere] **COSTERMONGER** [F2: COSTARD-monger]
Prologue 1 PROLOGUE [ed.; not in F2]
Induction 1 STAGE-KEEPER [ed.; not in F2; throughout, the first speaker in a scene is not provided with a speech heading] **32** [and elsewhere] **punk** [F2: *Punque*] **74 abovesaid, that** [ed.] abouesaid, and [F2] **94** [and elsewhere] **Marry** [F2: mary] **127 antics** [F2: *Antiques*]
1.1.17.1 [placement, ed.; at 0.1 in F2] **32 to** [F2: too]
1.2.43 good do [ed.] do good [F2] **62 WINWIFE** [ed.] WIN [F2]
1.3.12 lyam-hounds [F2: Lime-hounds] **13** [and elsewhere] **scent** [F2: sent] **25 drink** [ed.] drunke [F2] **43 friend, too** [ed.] friends, too [F2] **83 coarse** [F2: course] **123 Christian name** [F2: Christen-name] **139 broked** [ed.] broke [F2] **140 currants** [F2: Currans] **140** [and elsewhere] **arrant** [F2: errant]
1.4.13 [and elsewhere] **Solomon** [F2: *Salomon*] **54 clysters** [F2: glisters]
1.5.25 Bedlam [F2: *Bet'lem*] **92 your** [F2 corr.] you [F2 uncorr.] **107, 108 lose** [F2: loose] **132 enough** [F2: inow] **159 straitlaced** [F2: straight lac'd]
1.6.61 [and occasionally elsewhere: aside, indicated in F2 by parentheses]
2.1.21 thread [F2: thrid] **27 precedent** [F2: president] **40 of this** [ed.] of of this [F2] **41** [and elsewhere] **Piepowders** [F2: *Pye-pouldres*]
2.2.17 engineer [F2: Inginer] **34 gilt** [F2: guilt] **72 stoat** [ed.] *Stote* [F2] **96 eke** [F3: eech] itch [F2] **119 wind** [ed.] winne [F2]
2.3.20 newt [F2: neuft] **21 wilt** [F2: will't] **61 H'as** [F2: has]
2.4.0.2 ***Mousetrap-man*** [ed.] *Tinder-box-man* [F2] **7 MOUSETRAP-MAN** [ed.] TIN. [F2] **23 What's** [ed.] what [F2] **63 travail** [F2: trauell]
2.5.85 jowl [F2: Ioll] **121 atop** [F2: a'top] **155 JOAN TRASH** [ed.] ERA. [F2]
2.6.14 newt [F2: Neuft] **54 fleur-de-lis** [F2: Flower-de-lice] **91 Will** [ed.] well [F2] **97 chops** [F2: chaps] **137 COKES** [ed.] COOK [F2]
3.2.141 WINWIFE [ed.] WIN. [F2] 144 strait [F2: streight]
3.4.67 flayed [F2: flead] 85 [and elsewhere] **thorough** [F2: thorow] **161, 162 posy** [F2: poesie]
3.5.31 than [ed.] then then [F2] **100–101** [ed.; not in F2] **116–17, 118–19, 127–28** [ed.] *Youth, youth, etc.* [F2] **140 far better** [ed.] *better* [F2] **147–48** [ed.] *Youth, youth, thou hadst better, etc.* [F2] **186 WINWIFE** [ed.] WIN. [F2] **242**

an't were [F2: an't 'twere] **243–44 SD** [placement, ed.; opposite 238–39 in F2 **290 choose** [F2: chose]

3.6.35 and [ed.] and and [F2] **59 i'God's** [F2: a Gods]

4.1.77 boil [F2: bile] **79 he list** [ed.] his list [F2]

4.2.15 prize [F2: Prise] **39.1–2 SD** [placement, ed.; opposite 36–42 in F2] **78.1** [placement, ed.; opposite 87 in F2]

4.3.59 is, is [ed.] is, [F2] **85 Justice** [ed.] *Iudice* [F2] **96 aye** [F2: I] **113** [and elsewhere] **northern** [F2: Northren]

4.4.29.1–3 [placement, ed.; opposite 27–40 in F2] **147 shit** [F2: shite] **211 vessel is** [ed.] vessell, [F2] **227 take** [ed.] talke [F2]

4.5.39 dee [F2: de] **90 wardrobe** [F2: wardrope]

4.6.165 I have [ed.] I I haue [F2]

5.2.75–76 SD *considers* [ed.] consider [F2]

5.4.74.1 [ed.] *And to them* Waspe [F2, at 5.4.0.2] **79 winwife** [ed.] Win. [F2] **138 *at*** [ed.] *a* [F2] **142 that he** [ed.] *thhe* [F2] **156 leatherhead** [ed.] Lea. [F2] **195 were** [F2]; wore [some eds.] **230 SD *They fight*** [placement, ed.; at 229 in F2] **237 *Hold*** [ed.] *Hld* [F2] **244 *me my*** [ed.] *mmy* [F2] **270 They'll** [F2: the'll] **285 puppet pythias** [F2: Pvp.]

5.5.15 busy [ed.] Bas. [F2] **48 grace** [ed.] Qva. [F2] **94, 112 puppet dionysius** [ed.] Pvs. [F2]

5.6.0.2. *Purecraft* [ed.] Pvrecraft. (*a while after*) Iohn. *to them* Trovble-all. Vrsla. Nightigale. [F2] **15.1 *John*** [ed.] (*a while after*) Iohn. [at 0.2 in F2] **55.1** [ed.] *to them* Trovble-all. Vrsla. Nightigale. [F2 at 5.6.0.2] **73 basin** [F2: bason]

Epilogue 1 epilogue [ed.; not in F2]

The Knight of the Burning Pestle

Francis Beaumont reportedly wrote *The Knight of the Burning Pestle* in eight days, in 1607, for performance by a boys' acting company, the Children of the Queen's Revels, at the second Blackfriars Theater. The dramatist with whom Beaumont frequently collaborated, John Fletcher, may have contributed something to this play, but the first two acts are undoubtedly Beaumont's, and so is most or all of the rest. Initially the play was a failure, but since then it has become something of a classic. Today it provides us with a wonderfully funny send-up of London's theater world in the early seventeenth century.

It helps to know that the play was performed by boy actors in an indoor theater. Such theaters were known as private theaters because they catered to an exclusive clientele. The price of admission could be as much as six times that at public theaters such as the Globe or the Swan. Attendance was not private in the sense of having to belong to a club, but public audiences generally preferred both the price of admission and the bill of fare at the open-air theaters.

The private theaters specialized in satire and not infrequently got in trouble as a result. Both the Crown and the London authorities were wary of topical political commentary. Sexual innuendo in the boys' plays was often offensive to the morals of ordinary citizens. Religious reformers and angry pamphleteers, unhappy about theaters anyway, took a dim view of plays that satirized London's citizenry. Thomas Dekker's *The Shoemaker's Holiday* (1599), performed by an adult company (the Admiral's Men), could get away with its genial laughter at mayors, aldermen, and shoemakers because of its friendly and embracing comic approach, but Ben Jonson's *Epicene* (1609), performed by the same boys' company (the Children of the Queen's Revels) that had acted *The Knight of the Burning Pestle* only a short time before, was another matter. The boys' companies had been shut down in the early 1590s because of their scandalously satiric productions and were not allowed to reopen until 1599. Once back in business, they went on with what they had been doing before, thumbing their noses at figures of authority and at London's citizens.

A chief instrument of the satiric comedy in *The Knight of the Burning Pestle* is the presence, in the audience and then onstage, of the Citizen and his Wife, along with their servant Rafe. People of this social class did not go to the private theaters. When the Citizen and his Wife call for homely dramatic fare of the sort they enjoy, what they get turns out to be hilariously inappropriate for their avant-garde surroundings. The comedy focuses on their disappointment with what the private theaters have to offer and the inappropriateness of their thinking they have the right to request something more to their liking. We are invited to view their lack of sophistication with polite condescension. They are amusing, even endearing, in their jollity and their affection for each other, but (speaking from the point of view of a well-to-do audience member) one would never invite these people into one's home. They have wandered into the wrong pew. At the same time, their impatience with private-theater fare can be seen

Introduction, glosses, footnotes, and textual notes by David Bevington; text edited by David Bevington and checked by Eric Rasmussen.

as a form of protest against the private theaters by those the theaters were wont to ridicule.

The juxtaposition of a sophisticated, courtly world with one that is ineffably bourgeois affords Beaumont a delicious opportunity to play with theatrical illusion. The Citizen, his Wife, and Rafe are seated in the audience as the play is about to begin, presumably not identified as members of the acting company. The audience, not forewarned that anything unusual is about to happen, suddenly becomes aware of a commotion in its midst. Two spectators, a man and his wife (Rafe not yet being called on to take his part), interrupt the Prologue and speaker of the Induction of the play that is nominally about to begin and clamor up onto the stage, where gentlemen are already seated (the private houses sometimes allowed such seating onstage). The Citizen and his Wife have already heard enough of the Induction, with its namby-pamby blank verse, to know that they do not like it. They want their own play.

These good people have just broken a primary convention of theatergoing: audience members stay in their seats and remain silent. The whole point of traditional theater is that it is fiction, a mimesis that occupies its own imaginative space. The front edge of the stage (the "fourth wall") is a barrier between the illusory world of the theater and the daily world to which the audience will return once the play is finished. The Citizen and his Wife do not know this, or at least refuse to acknowledge it. They are not going to wait till the end of the play to comment. They want to change things right now.

The breaking of theatrical illusion is an old trick, to be sure. Aristophanes revels in it in *The Clouds, The Birds*, and other satiric comedies of the fifth century B.C.E. Shakespeare, Jonson, Middleton, Marston, and other Renaissance dramatists similarly remind us that we are in the theater watching an illusion, as when the title figure of *Epicene* turns out to be a boy actor rather than a marriageable young woman, or when Zeal-of-the-land Busy in *Bartholomew Fair* inveighs against the theater for permitting men to dress as women only to be put down by a puppet-actor who is not demonstrably either male or female. Both Face in *The Alchemist* and Volpone in the play named for him drop their masks as characters when they come before the audience as speakers of the epilogue. Revenge and the ghost of Don Andrea serve as choric audience to the main action of *The Spanish Tragedy*. Like his fellow dramatists, Beaumont celebrates the idea of a play as an illusion, by allowing the Citizen and his Wife to enter into the very play they have come to watch. They do so with a naive delight that we are invited to regard with both amused sympathy and sophisticated condescension; we see that the Citizen and his Wife keenly appreciate an evening's dramatic entertainment, and yet we also see what is absurd about the kinds of drama that they, and presumably other Londoners as well, prefer.

Though the Citizen and his Wife violate all the decorums of expected audience behavior, they also know what they are about. The Citizen does not wait long before interrupting the billed program, because after hearing only the first three lines he knows what to expect. He has been keeping an eye on these private theaters, he tells the Prologue, for seven years at least, and in all that time, he complains, "you have still girds at citizens" (Induction 7–8). The very title of the scheduled entertainment, *The London Merchant*, promises more of the same. The Citizen will have none of it. Why cannot a London theater make dramatic capital out of London's own history? Why not a play called *The Legend of Whittington*, about the mayor who was famous for his cat, or *The Life and Death of Sir Thomas Gresham, with the Building of the Royal Exchange*, in celebration of the wealthy merchant who financed the erection of a famous mercantile center in 1566–68? Beaumont's contemporary Thomas Heywood had indeed written plays just like this, including *The Four Prentices of London* (c. 1600); and the Gresham play touted by the Citizen is probably a reference to part 2 of Heywood's *If You Know Not Me You Know Nobody, with the Building of the Royal Exchange and the Famous Victory of Queen Elizabeth in the Year 1588* (1606). The idea of a play about the building of a merchandise mart must have amused the Blackfriars audience. Yet the Citizen is serious. He has had enough of jeering at him and his kind on the private stages.

The Wife has something else in mind: she wants her servant Rafe to play a part in the evening's entertainment. What better way to infiltrate a decadently sophisticated boys' acting company than to introduce into their midst an apprentice to the Grocer's Guild? Robust, innocent, poorly educated but brimming with expectation, Rafe is ready for anything. Moreover, he nurtures a budding thespian talent: as the Wife proudly reports, he has been known to "act you sometimes at our house, that all the neighbors cry out on him" (Induction 69–70). When called on to demonstrate his skills as an actor, Rafe is ready with a few choice lines of Hotspur's in Shakespeare's *1 Henry IV*. Beaumont and his well-to-do audience are undoubtedly aware that many of London's best-known actors came from the ranks of the artisanal trades, much as Bottom the weaver joins with a tinker, a carpenter, a joiner, a tailor, and a bellows-mender to form an acting company in *A Midsummer Night's Dream*. Rafe's credentials for public acting are more plausible than one might at first suppose. In addition, Beaumont's audience is presumably attuned also to the erotic implications of the Wife's wanting Rafe to star in her play: she betrays ambivalently maternal and sexual feelings toward both Rafe and the boy-actors in the company, reminding us of often-heard jokes about apprentices being too familiar with their masters' wives.

The London Merchant, or as much of it as we get before the Citizen and his Wife manage to derail it, turns out to be what these Londoners warily expected. The characters in the opening scene—a merchant (Venturewell) in his shop and his apprentice (Jasper)—seem promising enough, but it is soon apparent that virtue as the Citizen and his Wife see it is not going to triumph. Despite Venturewell's having taken in Jasper as his apprentice out of "charitable love," redeeming him from a "fall of fortune" and giving him a chance to be respectably employed (1.1.2–3), Jasper has had the effrontery to fall in love with the merchant's daughter, Luce. The Citizen does not like the looks of this sneaky apprentice or the merchant's daughter either, for that matter. "Fie upon 'em, little infidels!" he grumbles chorically to his Wife in something a good deal louder than a stage whisper; "Well, I'll be hanged for a halfpenny if there be not some abomination knavery in this play" (1.1.62–64). His Wife agrees with his concern, but reassures him that Rafe will set all to rights: "Rafe will find all out, I warrant you, an they were older than they are" (1.1.67–68). The couple's disapproval of the way the merchant-apprentice plot is going is a major reason for their continual intervention in the show.

Needless to say, the Citizen and his Wife heartily approve of Master Humphrey, the nincompoop whom Venturewell wishes to foist on his daughter. Humphrey is a friend of the merchant, no doubt a merchant himself. He plies Luce with gifts and makes sure she knows how much he has paid for them. The Citizen and his Wife cannot be expected, in their ignorance about drama, to know that Humphrey is the blocking figure in this romantic plot, the unwelcome wooer, a descendant of the lean old dotard in classical and neoclassical comedy whom the young lovers must outwit. The lovers must also outmaneuver the girl's overprotective father, another recognizable type from neoclassical drama. The dramatic function of blocking figures of this sort is to serve as obstacles in the conventional plot of romantic love; managerial parents and wealthy rival wooers deserve to be foiled in their attempts to prevent the fulfillment of romantic happiness. The Citizen and his Wife, however, see this traditional plot structure inside out. The Wife genially concludes of Humphrey that he is "e'en the kindest young man that ever trod on shoe-leather" (1.2.130–31). In her eyes, he deserves the lady and Jasper deserves a good whipping.

Jasper's ways as a prodigal son are exacerbated by a conflict within his own family. His father, old Merrythought, is just what his name implies, a carefree and utterly irresponsible parent who cannot manage his own affairs and whose dereliction of duty as a husband goads his wife into seeking her fortune somewhere other than his household. Left to his own devices, not a whit sorry for having lost his wife's company,

Merrythought spends day and night singing and drinking with his companions. His wife, meantime, looks after her younger son, Michael, who is as boringly dutiful as Jasper is inventively feckless. This dysfunctional family, in other words, splits along the divergent lines of hedonism and its opposite: Jasper is his father's son, Michael is his mother's.

The Citizen and his Wife cannot be expected to appreciate these niceties. Functioning as what we begin to understand as a kind of counterchorus or antichorus, the Citizen and his Wife are as solicitous of Michael as they are censorious of Jasper. We can confirm our own judgments of the characters in the play by contrasting them with those of this upstanding bourgeois couple sitting on the stage and offering their maudlin evaluations of everything they see and hear.

Increasingly, the Citizen and his Wife are interested most in how Rafe can spice up a floundering evening at the theater. They want a new play entirely, with Rafe as its star. Their choice of a genre is entirely predictable, given their social orientation as London bourgeoisie and given Beaumont's amusement at their culturally deprived taste: they want a fairy-tale romance, with knights in armor, ladies in distress, ogres, magical effects, and last-minute rescues. This is the stuff of popular fictional romance in late-sixteenth-century England, both onstage and in narrative prose accounts, with roots going back well into medieval times.

The immensely popular tale of Guy of Warwick can provide an instance. As the son of the steward of Warwick Castle, Guy falls in love with the Earl's daughter Felice only to learn that she will not allow him to woo her until he has proven himself the most renowned knight in the world. This demand sets in motion a narrative of martial exploits across Europe and against the Saracens of Constantinople, followed by a crusade to the Holy Land to atone for a life of profane service to the cause of erotic desire. Eventually, Guy disguises himself as a pilgrim and returns to Warwick, where he is recognized by means of a birthmark and reunited with Felice. This splendid concoction, or part of it at least, was made into a play, *The Tragical History of Guy of Warwick*, perhaps in the late 1580s.

Francis Beaumont may have known the story of Guy of Warwick, as well as others in the same popular genre. Another possibility is that he may have known Cervantes' *Don Quixote*, in which the picaresque adventures of the good Don and Sancho Panza also satirize the romance tradition. Although Thomas Shelton's English translation of the first part of Cervantes' novel did not appear in print until 1612, scholars speculate that Beaumont may have read part of the translation in manuscript by 1607 or that he read the novel in Spanish. In any case, tales of wandering knights and their trusty squires were legion and had become a staple of homespun theatrical entertainments.

In his genial satire of popular romance, Beaumont caters to the tastes of his urbane, upper-class audience, inviting them to laugh at popular culture. Part of the audience's pleasure is to be found in parsing Beaumont's witty analogies between knightly adventures and the banal realities they represent. For instance, Rafe takes as his fictional identity the title of the Knight of the Burning Pestle. Why a pestle? Presumably it is the mundane implement used in the grocer's trade to pound or grind various substances in a mortar. The implication, one supposes, is that Rafe will pulverize his enemies. Still, the pestle is surely a ludicrous weapon, and, given its phallic shape, especially as displayed in heraldic emblems, the implement may bring to mind a pun on "pizzle," both a flogging instrument and the penis of an animal.

One of Rafe's most notable adventures takes place at the Bell Inn in Waltham, north of London. George, the junior apprentice who serves as Rafe's dwarf, announces the prospect as it looms into view:

> Take courage, valiant knight, damsel, and squire.
> I have discovered, not a stone's cast off,
> An ancient castle held by the old knight

Of the most holy Order of the Bell,
Who gives to all knights-errant entertain.
(2.5.31–35)

The "damsel" is Mistress Merrythought, the lady in distress whom Rafe is chivalrously escorting through the imagined dangers of Waltham Forest. The "squire" is Rafe's other apprentice, Tim. The inn they have come upon is nothing more than a public house and tavern, but George's description invests it with all the wonders of a medieval keep. A "squire" named Chamberlino will see to their beds; Tapstero will fill their drinking vessels; and Ostlero will look after their "palfreys." Rafe solemnly announces himself to be a wandering knight seeking refuge for the night in a castle. All goes well until next morning, when the Tapster and the Host are so crass as to demand that the reckoning be paid. Rafe, utterly immersed in his fictional world of romantic adventure, supposes that he need only thank them for their gracious hospitality. The Citizen and his Wife, concerned for Rafe's welfare, intervene by paying the tab. The boundary between fiction and humdrum reality is broached and anatomized, not only in Rafe's chivalric fantasy world and the commonplace "real" world it overlays (which is of course no more real than anything else being depicted onstage), but also in the way in which the Citizen and his Wife so easily enter and exit the romance plot. We perceive three layers of fiction in all this: the imagined "real" world of common people (a tapster, a barber, etc.), the imagined chivalric and romantic world inhabited by Rafe and his companions, and the imagined world of the commenting Citizen and his Wife. Where does fiction end and reality begin?

Rafe's encounter with a giant in the guise of a barber provides, in burlesque, the climactic confrontation that every romantic adventure story worth its salt must include. The extended analogy here is both witty and invitingly off-color. The giant, Barbaroso, wields a "naked lance of purest steel" and wears a garment to protect his clothes from the blood of the knights he massacres (3.2.99–102). We understand from this that he is actually a barber-surgeon, licensed to let blood for medical purposes and to practice dentistry. He sets his victims down in his "enchanted chair" (the barber's chair), claws at them with a formidable forty-toothed "engine" (his comb), and "snaps" their hair off to the accompaniment of a "most hideous noise" (3.2.108–16). (Barbers were noted for snapping their fingers and for being incorrigibly chatty.)

Syphilis victim in tub. Frontispiece to the play *Cornelianum Dolium* (1638), possibly authored by Thomas Randolph. The tub inscription translates as "I sit on the throne of love, I suffer in the tub"; and the banner as "Farewell O sexual pleasures and lusts."

Rafe is determined to fight this giant and does so, managing in the process to free from the giant's lair various captives who suffer from symptoms markedly identifiable as those of venereal disease. One inmate, named Sir Pockhole, a knight of French extraction (since syphilis was known in England as "the French disease"), has come to Barbaroso complaining of aching bones (a symptom of syphilis) only to have the giant cut away the gristle of his nose and place a velvet plaster in its stead, thus branding him with still more recognizable signs of advanced venereal infection. Another rescued knight describes his adventures on Turnbull Street, a notable red-light district in London, and the sweating hot-tub treatment to which he has been subjected. And so it goes. Rafe has stumbled into an underworld of sexual misadventures in the guise of a giant's cave in a romance plot.

Eventually this plotline loses what little coherence it can initially lay claim to. Abetted by the Citizen and his Wife, Rafe assembles the apprentices of London at Mile End for military drill. Mile End was notorious as a training ground for the inept and was much laughed at by sophisticates for the bumbling Londoners' aspirations to military preparedness. Rafe delivers an inspirational address to the troops that reads like a send-up of Henry V's exhortations to his army at Agincourt, incongruously mingled with echoes of Richard III's address to his troops before his defeat at Bosworth Field:

> Gentlemen, countrymen, friends, and my fellow soldiers, I have brought you this day from the shops of security and the counters of content to measure out, in these furious fields, honor by the ell and prowess by the pound. Let it not, oh, let it not, I say, be told hereafter, the noble issue of this city fainted! But bear yourselves in this fair action like men—valiant men and free men. Fear not the face of the enemy nor the noise of the guns, for, believe me, brethren, the rude rumbling of a brewer's cart is far more terrible, of which you have a daily experience. Neither let the stink of powder offend you, since a more valiant stink is nightly with you. (5.2.54–65)

Repeatedly in this speech, lofty sentiments dive down precipitously into banalities of bourgeois London life—brewer's carts and the nightly stink of inadequate sanitation facilities or lack of personal hygiene. Deeds are measured by the "ell," a craftsman's or tailor's way of doling out goods. Alliterative effects ("shops of security," "counters of content," "furious fields") betray a striving after hyperbole and rant. Rafe calls his men from the shops of his artisanal world to defend England against her enemies, though who those enemies are remains unclear. This muddled warmongering is a perfect target of ridicule in a play so vastly amused at the untidy excesses of the London popular stage.

Yet despite the pervasive satire directed at popular entertainment, Beaumont does not simply adopt the presumed point of view of his sophisticated audience at the expense of the Citizen and his Wife. Instead he balances his satire of popular culture with a quizzical look at the other side of the debate between popular and elite. The "high" play *The London Merchant* is so painfully clichéd that it deserves what it gets at the hands of the Citizen and his Wife. They are right to suspect it of animus against popular culture. If they were more critically eloquent, they might go on to point out its absurdities. The scene in which Jasper threatens Luce's life to test her constancy is as hilariously unmotivated and implausible as the comparable sequences in *Friar Bacon and Friar Bungay* and *The Woman's Prize*. The resurrection scene at the end of *The London Merchant*, in which Jasper opens the lid of his own coffin to reclaim Luce as his bride-to-be, is as much a parody of high culture as Rafe's soliloquizing with an arrow through his head is a parody of low culture. If *The London Merchant* is supposed to represent sophisticated taste—the resurrection scene is so hilariously like the comic resolution of Thomas Middleton's *A Chaste Maid in Cheapside* that one would swear it is a satire of that play if *A Chaste Maid* had not been written later—then sophisticated taste may have its own limitations and imperfections.

Increasingly, as we watch the Citizen and his Wife react in naive dismay at the play they are watching, we come to realize that they are far more affectionate to each other than are the members of Jasper's unhappy family onstage. The Citizen and his Wife are more down to earth, less pretentious, heartier, and more generous. Does the seeming satire of "uxorious" Londoners question the attitude of the gentry in the select audience of the private theaters by wondering if those privileged viewers regard marital affection as something a little indecent, something too embarrassing for a good play?

A droll inversion seems to be taking place. Maybe the Citizen and his Wife are on to something that the urbane spectators are missing. The Citizen and his Wife are so caught up in the theatrical illusion that they mistake it for reality and enter into its sphere. They want to change the events onstage because those events are not just entertainment to them. Perhaps the Citizen and his Wife are proper playgoers after all.

"Come, Nell, shall we go?" asks the Citizen (Epilogue 1), after Rafe has delivered the closing soliloquy *"with a forked arrow through his head"* (5.3.128.1), in a delightful spoof of tragic death scenes of the Renaissance stage. The Wife, however, has one more piece of business: she must speak the epilogue, thanking for their courtesy the gentlemen with whom she has seen the show. The bond between this quaint chorus and the audience is remarkable. The Wife especially has pestered the audience with noisy asides. She and her husband have misapprehended the play set before them in an epic display of unsophisticated taste—albeit in a way that calls into question the artificiality of *The London Merchant* as well. They have drained the entertainment of its original purpose and have brought back into the theater every childish abuse of storytelling that sophisticated audiences had long deplored. Perhaps that is why *The Knight of the Burning Pestle* failed in its first production; the audience at Blackfriars did not know what to make of it. Perhaps also the initial audience was uncomfortably aware that it too was being satirized. From the safe distance of several hundred years, we today are in a better position to see how incisively and amusingly *The Knight of the Burning Pestle* comments on issues of theatrical illusion and on the delicate matter of judging a work of art.

FRANCIS BEAUMONT

The Knight of the Burning Pestle

To His Many-Ways-Endeared Friend, Master Robert Keysar[1]

Sir, this unfortunate child, who in eight days (as lately I have learned) was begot and born, soon after was by his parents (perhaps because he was so unlike his brethren) exposed to the wide world,[2] who, for want of judgment, or not understanding the privy° mark of irony about it (which showed it was no offspring of any vulgar brain), utterly rejected it;[3] so that for want of acceptance it was even ready to give up the ghost, and was in danger to have been smothered in perpetual oblivion, if you (out of your direct antipathy to ingratitude) had not been moved both to relieve and cherish it, wherein I must needs commend both your judgment, understanding, and singular love to good wits. You afterwards sent it to me, yet being an infant and somewhat ragged.[4] I have fostered it privately in my bosom these two years, and now, to show my love, return it to you, clad in good lasting clothes,° which scarce memory will wear out, and able to speak for itself; and withal, as it telleth me, desirous to try his fortune in the world, where, if yet it be welcome, father, foster father, nurse, and child,[5] all have their desired end. If it be slighted or traduced, it hopes his father will beget him a younger brother,° who shall revenge his quarrel and challenge the world either of fond° and merely° literal interpretation or illiterate misprision.° Perhaps it will be thought to be of the race of *Don Quixote*. We both may confidently swear it is his elder brother above a year, and therefore may (by virtue of his birthright) challenge the wall of him.[6] I doubt not but they will meet in their adventures, and I

concealed

i.e., bound now as a book

another play by Beaumont

foolish / utterly

misinterpretation

The 1613 title page reads "*The Knight of the Burning Pestle. / Quod si / Iudicium subtile videndis artibus illud / Ad libros et ad haec Musarum dona vocares, / Boeotum in crasso iurares aere natos* [But call that judgment, so nice for viewing works of art, to books and to these gifts of the Muses, and you'd swear that he'd been born in Boeotia's heavy air]. / Horat[ius], in Epist. ad Oct[avius] Aug[ustus] / London. Printed for Walter Burre, and are to be sold at the sign of the Crane in Paul's Churchyard. 1613."

Dedication.

1. Theater manager of the Children of the Queen's Revels, who performed *The Knight of the Burning Pestle* at the second Blackfriars Theater in 1607.
2. The play was evidently completed and produced in a hurry, but unsuccessfully, perhaps because it was so unlike other plays by Beaumont and Fletcher ("his [the play's] brethren").
3. The play failed owing to lack of critical understanding of its satiric allegory.
4. The play was somewhat in need of further rewriting or other preparation for publication.
5. Beaumont, Keysar, Walter Burre (who published the play in 1613 and wrote this dedication), and the play itself.
6. Cervantes' *Don Quixote* first appeared in 1605, and its first part was translated into English by Thomas Shelton around 1612. Burre here claims that Beaumont's play predates Cervantes' great novel. The likelihood is that Beaumont derived at least some ideas from

hope the breaking of one staff will make them friends;[7] and perhaps they will combine themselves and travel through the world to seek their adventures. So I commit him to his good fortune and myself to your love.

Your assured friend,
W[alter] B[urre]

The Prologue[1]

Where the bee can suck no honey, she leaves her sting behind; and where the bear cannot find origanum° to heal his grief,° he blasteth° all other leaves with his breath. We fear it is like° to fare so with us, that, seeing you cannot draw from our labors sweet content, you leave behind you a sour mislike, and with open reproach blame our good meanings because you cannot reap the wonted mirth. Our intent was at this time to move inward delight, not outward lightness, and to breed (if it might be) soft smiling, not loud laughing, knowing it to the wise to be as great pleasure to hear counsel mixed with wit as to the foolish to have sport mingled with rudeness.° They were banished the theater of Athens, and from Rome hissed, that brought parasites on the stage with apish actions, or fools with uncivil habits, or courtesans with immodest words. We have endeavored to be as far from unseemly speeches to make your ears glow° as we hope you will be free from unkind reports, or mistaking the author's intention (who never aimed at anyone particular in this play), to make our cheeks blush. And thus I leave it and thee to thine own censure,° to like or dislike. *Vale.*°

a healing herb
wound / withers
likely
coarseness
blush
judging / Farewell

THE SPEAKERS' NAMES

The PROLOGUE
Then a CITIZEN [George] }
The citizen's WIFE [Nell] } sitting below amidst the spectators
And RAFE,° her man° }
[VENTUREWELL,] a rich merchant
JASPER, his apprentice [in love with Luce]
Master HUMPHREY, a friend to the merchant [and suitor to Luce]
LUCE, the merchant's daughter
MISTRESS MERRYTHOUGHT, Jasper's mother
MICHAEL, a second son of Mistress Merrythought
Old Master [Charles] MERRYTHOUGHT
[TIM,] a squire }
[GEORGE,] a dwarf } [apprentices to Rafe]
A TAPSTER
A BOY that danceth and singeth
An HOST
A BARBER

Ralph / servant

Cervantes, though without verbal borrowings. To "challenge the wall" is to claim the better position in walking on the street so as not to be forced out into the gutter.
7. I hope that one brief encounter of jousting will lead to a friendship.

The Prologue.
1. This prologue is borrowed, with minor changes, from the prologue to John Lyly's *Sappho and Phao,* which was presented at the first Blackfriars Theater in 1584.

Three [captive] KNIGHTS
[A captive WOMAN]
A SERGEANT
SOLDIERS
[A BOY who helps Jasper
Other BOYS
A SERVANT to Venturewell
William HAMMERTON, a pewterer
George GREENGOOSE, a poulterer
LADY POMPIONA, daughter of the King of Moldavia
Coffin-carriers, men

THE SCENE: London, Waltham Forest, Moldavia, etc.]

[Induction]

[Several gentlemen are sitting onstage, on stools. The Citizen, his Wife, and Rafe are below, among the spectators.]

Enter Prologue.

PROLOGUE From all that's near the court, from all that's great,
Within the compass of the city walls,° — *London's ancient walls*
We now have brought our scene—

Enter Citizen [climbing onstage from among the spectators].

CITIZEN Hold your peace, goodman boy!° — *i.e., young rascal*
PROLOGUE What do you mean, sir?
CITIZEN That you have no good meaning. This seven years there hath been plays at this house,° I have observed it, you have still girds° at citizens; and now you call your play *The London Merchant*. Down with your title,° boy, down with your title! — *playhouse; always taunts; sign hung onstage*
PROLOGUE Are you a member of the noble city?
CITIZEN I am.
PROLOGUE And a freeman?[1]
CITIZEN Yea, and a grocer.
PROLOGUE So, grocer, then, by your sweet favor, we intend no abuse to the city.
CITIZEN No, sir? Yes, sir. If you were not resolved to play the jacks,° what need you study for new subjects, purposely to abuse your betters? Why could not you be contented, as well as others, with *The Legend of Whittington*,[2] or *The Life and Death of Sir Thomas Gresham, with the Building of the Royal Exchange*?[3] Or *The Story of Queen Eleanor*,[4] *with the Rearing of London Bridge upon Woolsacks*?[5] — *play the knaves*

Induction.
1. One who posseses the "freedom," i.e., the privileges of full citizenship, of the city of London, usually granted after the completion of an apprenticeship and entry into membership of a guild.
2. Lord Mayor of London (died 1423), legendarily famous for his cat.
3. Sir Thomas Gresham, a wealthy merchant, founded and built the Royal Exchange at his own expense in 1566–68.
4. Edward I's queen, from Spain, much hated in England.
5. The rebuilding of London Bridge was financed by a duty on wool.

PROLOGUE You seem to be an understanding man. What would you have us do, sir?

CITIZEN Why, present something notably in honor of the commons of the city.

PROLOGUE Why, what do you say to *The Life and Death of Fat Drake, or the Repairing of Fleet Privies*?[6]

CITIZEN I do not like that; but I will have a citizen, and he shall be of my own trade.

PROLOGUE Oh, you should have told us your mind a month since. Our play is ready to begin now.

CITIZEN 'Tis all one for that.° I will have a grocer, and he shall do admirable things. *No matter for that*

PROLOGUE What will you have him do?

CITIZEN Marry,° I will have him— *By Mary (an oath)*

WIFE (*below*) Husband, husband!

RAFE (*below*) Peace, mistress!

WIFE Hold thy peace, Rafe. I know what I do, I warrant tee.°—Husband, husband! *thee*

CITIZEN What say'st thou, cunny?° *bunny (pet name)*

WIFE Let him kill a lion with a pestle, husband. Let him kill a lion with a pestle.

CITIZEN So he shall.—I'll have him kill a lion with a pestle.

WIFE Husband! Shall I come up, husband?

CITIZEN Ay, cunny.—Rafe, help your mistress this way.—Pray, gentlemen, make her a little room. I pray you, sir, lend me your hand to help up my wife. [*She is helped up to the stage.*] I thank you, sir.—So.

WIFE By your leave, gentlemen all; I'm something troublesome. I'm a stranger here; I was ne'er at one of these plays, as they say, before. But I should have seen *Jane Shore* once,[7] and my husband hath promised me any time this twelvemonth to carry me to *The Bold Beauchamps*,[8] but in truth he did not. I pray you bear with me.

CITIZEN [*to the Prologue*] Boy, let my wife and I have a couple stools, and then begin, and let the grocer do rare° things. *remarkable*

[*Stools are brought.*]

PROLOGUE But sir, we have never a boy° to play him. Everyone hath a part already. *no boy actor*

WIFE Husband, husband, for God's sake, let Rafe play him. Beshrew me° if I do not think he will go beyond them all. *Curse me*

CITIZEN Well remembered, wife.—Come up, Rafe.—I'll tell you, gentlemen, let them but lend him a suit of reparel° and necessaries, and, by Gad, if any of them all blow wind in the tail on him,° I'll be hanged. *apparel* / *breathe down his neck*

[*Rafe, in his apron of tradesman's blue, jumps up onto the stage.*]

WIFE [*to the Prologue*] I pray you, youth, let him have a suit of reparel.—I'll be sworn, gentlemen, my husband tells you

6. Sir Francis Drake (c. 1540–1596) was a famous mariner and buccaneer. The privies overhanging Fleet Ditch, an open sewer, were notable as sources of pollution and stench. The title reads like a burlesque of the plays the Citizen asks for in lines 20–24 above and seems not overly respectful of Drake, popularly remembered in 1607 and afterward as a hero.

7. I.e., I was once to have seen a play (presumably Thomas Heywood's *Edward IV*) about Jane Shore, the mistress of Edward IV.

8. A lost play about Thomas Beauchamp and his Yorkist kindred; he served bravely in Normandy in 1346.

true. He will act you° sometimes at our house, that all the — *He'll act*
neighbors cry out on him. He will fetch you up a couraging° — *saber-rattling*
part so in the garret that we are all as feared, I warrant you,
that we quake again. We'll fear° our children with him; if — *frighten*
they be never so unruly, do but cry, "Rafe comes, Rafe
comes!" to them, and they'll be as quiet as lambs.—Hold up
thy head, Rafe; show the gentlemen what thou canst do.
Speak a huffing° part; I warrant you the gentlemen will — *ranting*
accept of it.

CITIZEN Do, Rafe, do.

RAFE [*reciting*] "By heaven, methinks it were an easy leap
To pluck bright honor from the pale-faced moon,
Or dive into the bottom of the sea,
Where never fathom line touched any ground,
And pluck up drownèd honor from the lake of hell."[9]

CITIZEN How say you, gentlemen, is it not as I told you?

WIFE Nay, gentlemen, he hath played before, my husband
says, *Mucedorus*[1] before the wardens° of our company. — *officers*

CITIZEN Ay, and he should have played Jeronimo[2] with a shoemaker for a wager.

PROLOGUE He shall have a suit of apparel, if he will go in.° — *enter the tiring-house*

CITIZEN In, Rafe, in, Rafe, and set out the Grocery° in their — *the Grocers*
kind,° if thou lov'st me. [*Exit Rafe.*] — *in their livery*

WIFE I warrant our Rafe will look finely when he's dressed.

PROLOGUE But what will you have it called?

CITIZEN *The Grocer's Honor.*

PROLOGUE Methinks *The Knight of the Burning Pestle*° were — *(see 43–44 above)*
better.

WIFE I'll be sworn, husband, that's as good a name as can be.

CITIZEN Let it be so.—Begin, begin; my wife and I will sit
down.

PROLOGUE I pray you, do.

CITIZEN What stately music have you? You have shawms?° — *oboelike instruments*

PROLOGUE Shawms? No.

CITIZEN No? I'm a thief if my mind did not give° me so. Rafe — *tell*
plays a stately part, and he must needs have shawms. I'll be
at the charge° of them myself rather than we'll be without — *take on the expense*
them.

PROLOGUE So you are like to be.[3]

CITIZEN Why, and so I will be. There's two shillings. [*He gives
money.*] Let's have the waits° of Southwark. They are as rare° — *musicians / excellent*
fellows as any are in England; and that will fetch them all
o'er the water° with a vengeance,° as if they were mad. — *the Thames / in force*

PROLOGUE You shall have them. Will you sit down, then?

CITIZEN Ay.—Come, wife.

WIFE Sit you merry all, gentlemen. I'm bold to sit amongst
you for my ease. [*She and her husband sit.*]

PROLOGUE [*to the audience*] From all that's near the court,
from all that's great,
Within the compass of the city walls,

9. Misquoted slightly (especially in the final phrase) from Hotspur's speech in *1 Henry IV*, 1.3.201–5.

1. An enduringly popular romantic comedy of the 1590s.

2. The hero (also spelled Hieronimo) of *The Spanish Tragedy* by Thomas Kyd—another warhorse.

3. You are likely to bear the expense yourself, or you'll have to do without.

We now have brought our scene. Fly far from hence,
All private taxes,° immodest phrases, *personal satire*
Whate'er may but show like vicious![4]
For wicked mirth never true pleasure brings,
But honest minds are pleased with honest things.—
[*To Citizen and Wife*] Thus much for that° we do. But for *that which*
Rafe's part you must answer for yourself.
CITIZEN Take you no care for° Rafe. He'll discharge himself,[5] *Don't worry about*
I warrant you. [*Exit Prologue.*]
WIFE I'faith, gentlemen, I'll give my word for Rafe.

1.1

Enter merchant [Venturewell] and Jasper his prentice.

VENTUREWELL Sirrah,° I'll make you know you are my prentice, *(said to inferiors)*
And whom my charitable love redeemed
Even from the fall of fortune; gave thee heat° *shelter*
And growth° to be what now thou art; new-cast° thee, *food / remade*
Adding the trust of all I have at home,
In foreign staples° or upon the sea, *markets*
To thy direction; tied the good opinions
Both of myself and friends to thy endeavors.
So fair were thy beginnings. But with these,
As I remember, you had never charge° *commission, authorization*
To love your master's daughter—and even° then *particularly*
When I had found a wealthy husband for her.
I take it, sir, you had not. But, however,
I'll break the neck of that commission,
And make you know you are but a merchant's factor.° *agent*
JASPER Sir,
I do liberally confess I am yours,
Bound both by love and duty to your service,
In which my labor hath been all my profit.
I have not lost in bargain,° nor delighted *in matters of trade*
To wear your honest gains upon my back,[1]
Nor have I given a pension° to my blood,° *penchant / passions*
Or lavishly in play° consumed your stock. *gambling*
These, and the miseries that do attend them,
I dare with innocence proclaim are strangers
To all my temperate actions.[2] For° your daughter, *As for*
If there be any love to my deservings
Borne by her virtuous self, I cannot stop it,
Nor am I able to refrain° her wishes. *curb*
She's private to herself, and best of knowledge[3]
Whom she'll make so happy as to sigh for.
Besides, I cannot think you mean to match her
Unto a fellow of so lame a presence,
One that hath little left of nature° in him. *vitality*
VENTUREWELL 'Tis very well, sir. I can tell Your Wisdom° *(a mock title)*

4. Whatever may give the slightest appearance of immodesty!
5. He'll acquit himself handsomely.
1.1. Venturewell's shop.
1. Nor have I taken to enriching my wardrobe out of your hard-earned income.
2. These vices are unknown to me, temperate as I am.
3. She is discreetly independent, and best knows.

How all this shall be cured.
JASPER Your care becomes you.° *does you honor*
VENTUREWELL And thus it must be, sir: I here discharge you
My house and service. Take your liberty;
And when I want a son, I'll send for you. *Exit.*
JASPER These be the fair rewards of them that love!
Oh, you that live in freedom never prove° *may you never experience*
The travail of a mind led by desire!

Enter Luce.

LUCE Why, how now, friend, struck with my father's thunder?
JASPER Struck, and struck dead, unless the remedy
Be full of speed and virtue.° I am now— *strength*
What I expected long—no more your father's.
LUCE But mine.
JASPER But yours, and only yours, I am;
That's all I have to keep me from the statute.[4]
You dare be constant still?
LUCE Oh, fear me not!
In this I dare be better than a woman.
Nor shall his anger nor his offers move me,
Were they both equal to a prince's power.
JASPER You know my rival?
LUCE Yes, and love him dearly—
Even as I love an ague° or foul weather. *fever*
I prithee, Jasper, fear him not.
JASPER Oh, no,
I do not mean to do him so much kindness.
But to our own desires: you know the plot
We both agreed on?
LUCE Yes, and will perform
My part exactly.
JASPER I desire no more.
Farewell! And keep my heart; 'tis yours.
LUCE I take it.
He° must do miracles makes° me forsake it. *Exeunt.* *(A person) / who makes*

CITIZEN Fie upon 'em, little infidels! What a matter's here now? Well, I'll be hanged for a halfpenny if there be not some abomination knavery in this play. Well, let 'em look to't. Rafe must come, and if there be any tricks a-brewing—
WIFE Let 'em brew, and bake too, husband, i'God's name. Rafe will find all out, I warrant you, an° they were older than they are.— *even if*

[*Enter Boy.*]

I pray, my pretty youth, is Rafe ready?
BOY He will be presently.
WIFE Now, I pray you, make my commendations unto him, and withal° carry him this stick of licorice. Tell him his mis- *in addition*

4. The statute mandating punishment for beggars, vagabonds, and apprentices who have left their parishes without authorization.

tress sent it him, and bid him bite a piece. 'Twill open his pipes the better, say. [*Exit Boy.*]

[1.2]

Enter merchant [Venturewell] and Master Humphrey.

VENTUREWELL Come, sir, she's yours; upon my faith, she's yours.
You have my hand.° For other idle lets° *promise / hindrances*
Between your hopes and her, thus with a wind
They are scattered and no more. My wanton prentice,
That like a bladder blew° himself with love, *puffed up*
I have let out,° and sent him to discover *let go*
New masters yet unknown.

HUMPHREY I thank you, sir;
Indeed I thank you, sir; and, ere I stir,
It shall be known, however you do deem,
I am of gentle blood and gentle seem.° *act like a gentleman*

VENTUREWELL Oh, sir, I know it, certain.

HUMPHREY Sir, my friend,
Although, as writers say, all things have end,
And that° we call a pudding° hath his two,° *what / sausage / two ends*
Oh, let it not seem strange, I pray, to you,
If in this bloody simile I put
My love, more endless than frail things or gut.[1]

WIFE Husband, I prithee, sweet lamb, tell me one thing, but tell me truly— [*To the actors*] Stay,° youths, I beseech you, till I question my husband. *Wait*

CITIZEN What is it, mouse?° *(a term of endearment)*

WIFE Sirrah, didst thou ever see a prettier child? How it behaves itself, I warrant ye, and speaks and looks, and perts° up the head? [*To the actor who plays Humphrey*] I pray you, brother, with your favor:° were you never none of Master Moncaster's scholars?[2] *perks, cocks / begging your pardon*

CITIZEN Chicken,° I prithee heartily, contain thyself. The childer° are pretty childer, but when Rafe comes, lamb— *(a pet name) / children*

WIFE Ay, when Rafe comes, cunny!—Well, my youth, you may proceed.

VENTUREWELL [*to Humphrey*] Well, sir, you know my love, and rest,° I hope, *remain*
Assured of my consent; get but my daughter's,
And wed her when you please. You must be bold,
And clap in close unto her.° Come, I know *woo her avidly*
You have language good enough to win a wench.

WIFE A whoreson° tyrant! He's been an old stringer° in's days, I warrant him. *rascally / fornicator*

1.2. Venturewell's shop.
1. Intestines used to make a "pudding," or blood sausage.
2. I.e., a student of Richard Mulcaster, a renowned schoolmaster and the sponsor of a boys' acting company.

HUMPHREY I take your gentle offer, and withal
Yield love again for love reciprocal.
VENTUREWELL [*calling*] What, Luce! Within there!

Enter Luce.

LUCE Called you, sir?
VENTUREWELL I did.
Give entertainment° to this gentleman, *welcome*
And see you be not froward.°—To her, sir. *refractory*
My presence will but be an eyesore to you. *Exit.*
HUMPHREY Fair Mistress Luce, how do you? Are you well?
Give me your hand, and then, I pray you, tell
How doth your little sister and your brother?
And whether you love me or any other?
LUCE Sir, these are quickly answered.
HUMPHREY So they are,
Where women are not cruel. But how far
Is it now distant from this place we are in
Unto that blessèd place, your father's warren?[3]
LUCE What makes you think of that, sir?
HUMPHREY Even that face;° *that face of yours*
For, stealing rabbits whilom° in that place, *once upon a time*
God Cupid, or the keeper, I know not whether,° *which of the two*
Unto my cost and charges brought you thither,
And there began—
LUCE Your game,[4] sir.
HUMPHREY Let no game,
Or anything that tendeth to the same,
Be evermore remembered, thou fair killer,° *slayer of hearts*
For whom I sat me down and brake my tiller.° *broke my crossbow*

WIFE There's a kind gentleman, I warrant you. When will you do as much for me, George?

LUCE Beshrew me,° sir, I am sorry for your losses, *(a mild oath)*
But, as the proverb says, I cannot cry.
I would you had not seen me.
HUMPHREY So would I,
Unless you had more maw° to do me good. *stomach, desire*
LUCE Why, cannot this strange passion be withstood?
Send for a constable and raise the town.[5]
HUMPHREY Oh, no, my valiant love will batter down
Millions of constables, and put to flight
Even that great watch of Midsummer Day at night.[6]
LUCE Beshrew me, sir, 'twere good I yielded, then.
Weak women cannot hope, where valiant men
Have no resistance.° *Are relentless*
HUMPHREY Yield, then! I am full

3. A piece of land used for breeding rabbits and other hunting game.
4. (1) Your hunting; (2) your chasing after me.
5. Raise the citizens in pursuit of a wrongdoer.
6. The so-called Marching Watch was an annual ceremonial muster of London citizens to provide a militia and constabulary for the upcoming year; it is here described as being held on Midsummer Eve, June 21, the summer solstice, when the days are longest. Humphrey's hyperbolic claim is that his love could vie with even that army of constables.

Of pity, though I say it, and can pull
Out of my pocket thus a pair of gloves.° *(a betrothal gift)*
[*He offers a pair of gloves.*]
Look, Lucy, look. The dog's tooth nor the dove's
Are not so white as these; and sweet they be,
And whipped° about with silk, as you may see. *ornamented*
If you desire the price, shoot from your eye
A beam to this place, and you shall espy
"F. S.,"° which is to say, my sweetest honey, *"Fine Silk" (?)*
They cost me three and twopence, or no money.° *i.e., no less*

LUCE [*taking the gloves*] Well, sir, I take them kindly, and I thank you.
What would you more?

HUMPHREY Nothing.

LUCE Why, then, farewell.

HUMPHREY Nor so, nor so. For, lady, I must tell,
Before we part, for what° we met together. *why*
God grant me time and patience and fair weather!

LUCE Speak, and declare your mind in terms so brief.

HUMPHREY I shall. Then, first and foremost, for relief
I call to you, if that you can afford it.
I care not at what price, for, on my word, it
Shall be repaid again, although it cost me
More than I'll speak of now; for love hath tossed me
In furious blanket like a tennis ball,
And now I rise aloft, and now I fall.

LUCE Alas, good gentleman, alas the day!

HUMPHREY I thank you heartily, and, as I say,
Thus do I still continue without rest—
I'th'morning like a man, at night a beast,
Roaring and bellowing mine own disquiet,
That much I fear forsaking of my diet
Will bring me presently to that quandary
I shall bid all adieu.° *i.e., I'll die*

LUCE Now, by Saint Mary,
That were great pity!

HUMPHREY So it were, beshrew me.
Then ease me, lusty° Luce, and pity show me. *jolly, pretty*

LUCE Why, sir, you know my will is nothing worth
Without my father's grant. Get his consent,
And then you may with assurance try me.

HUMPHREY The worshipful your sire will not deny me,
For I have asked him, and he hath replied:
"Sweet Master Humphrey, Luce shall be thy bride."

LUCE Sweet Master Humphrey, then I am content.

HUMPHREY And so am I, in truth.

LUCE Yet take me with you.° *understand me fully*
There is another clause must be annexed,
And this it is—I swore, and will perform it:
No man shall ever joy° me as his wife *enjoy*
But he that stole me hence. If you dare venture,
I am yours. You need not fear; my father loves you.
If not, farewell forever. [*She starts to leave.*]

HUMPHREY Stay, nymph, stay!

I have a double gelding, colored bay,[7]
Sprung by his father from Barbarian kind;° — *of Barbary breed*
Another for myself, though somewhat blind,
Yet true as trusty tree.

LUCE I am satisfied,
And so I give my hand. Our course must lie
Through Waltham Forest,° where I have a friend — *(north of London)*
Will entertain us. So farewell, Sir Humphrey,
And think upon your business. *Exit Luce.*

HUMPHREY Though I die,
I am resolved to venture life and limb
For one so young, so fair, so kind, so trim.
Exit Humphrey.

WIFE By my faith and troth, George, and as I am virtuous,° it is e'en the kindest young man that ever trod on shoe-leather.—Well, go thy ways.° If thou hast her not, 'tis not thy fault, i'faith.

chaste; *get along with you*

CITIZEN I prithee, mouse, be patient. 'A° shall have her, or I'll make some of 'em smoke° for't.

He; *suffer blows*

WIFE That's my good lamb, George.—Fie, this stinking tobacco kills men! Would there were none in England.—Now I pray, gentlemen, what good does this stinking tobacco do you? Nothing, I warrant. You make chimneys o'your faces.—Oh, husband, husband, now, now there's Rafe, there's Rafe!

[1.3]

Enter Rafe, like a grocer in 's shop, with two prentices [Tim and George], reading Palmerin of England.[1]

CITIZEN Peace, fool! Let Rafe alone.—Hark you, Rafe, do not strain yourself too much at the first.—Peace!—Begin, Rafe.

RAFE [*reading*] "Then Palmerin and Trineus, snatching their lances from their dwarfs, and clasping their helmets, galloped amain° after the giant, and Palmerin, having gotten a sight of him, came posting° amain, saying, 'Stay, traitorous thief! For thou mayst not so carry away her that is worth the greatest lord in the world'; and with these words gave him a blow on the shoulder that he struck him besides° his elephant. And Trineus, coming to the knight that had Agricola° behind him, set him soon besides his horse, with his neck broken in the fall, so that the princess, getting out of the throng, between joy and grief, said, 'All-happy° knight, the mirror° of all such as follow arms, now may I be well assured of the love thou bearest me.' "—I wonder why the kings do not raise an army of fourteen or fifteen hundred thousand men, as big as the army that the Prince of Portigo brought

with might and main; *hastening*; *off*; *(an error for "Agriola")*; *All-fortunate*; *paragon*

7. A reddish brown castrated male horse capable of carrying two riders.
1.3. Rafe's grocer's shop.
1. Anthony Munday translated *Palmerin of England* (a sixteenth-century Portuguese romance) in 1581. The present passage is actually a condensed and somewhat varied rendition of a passage from *Palmerin de Oliva*, to which *Palmerin of England* was a sequel.

against Rosicleer,[2] and destroy these giants? They do much hurt to wandering damsels that go in quest of their knights.[3]

WIFE Faith, husband, and Rafe says true, for they say the King of Portugal cannot sit at his meat but the giants and the ettins° will come and snatch it from him.

giants

CITIZEN Hold thy tongue!—On, Rafe.

RAFE And certainly those knights are much to be commended, who, neglecting their possessions, wander with a squire and a dwarf through the deserts° to relieve poor ladies.

wildernesses

WIFE Ay, by my faith, are they, Rafe; let 'em say what they will, they are indeed. Our knights neglect their possessions well enough, but they do not the rest.

RAFE There are no such courteous and fair well-spoken knights in this age; they will call one "the son of a whore" that Palmerin of England would have called "fair sir"; and one that Rosicleer would have called "right beautiful damsel" they will call "damned bitch."

WIFE I'll be sworn will they, Rafe. They have called me so an hundred times about a scurvy pipe of tobacco.

RAFE But what brave spirit could be content to sit in his shop with a flappet° of wood and a blue apron before him, selling mithridatum and dragon's water[4] to visited° houses, that might pursue feats of arms, and through his noble achievements procure° such a famous history to be written of his heroic prowess?

hinged counter
plague-visited
cause

CITIZEN Well said, Rafe! Some more of those words, Rafe!

WIFE They go finely, by my troth.

RAFE Why should not I then pursue this course, both for the credit of myself and our company? For amongst all the worthy books of achievements, I do not call to mind that I yet read of a grocer-errant.[5] I will be the said knight.—Have you heard of any that hath wandered unfurnished of° his squire and dwarf? My elder prentice Tim shall be my trusty squire, and little George my dwarf. Hence, my blue apron! [*He casts his apron aside.*] Yet in remembrance of my former trade, upon my shield shall be portrayed a burning pestle, and I will be called the Knight o'the Burning Pestle.

unprovided with

WIFE Nay, I dare swear thou wilt not forget thy old trade. Thou wert ever meek.

2. Rosicleer is the hero of a Spanish romance by Diego Ortunez de Calahorra (1555), which was translated, along with continuations of the romance by other authors, as *The Mirror of Princely Deeds and Knighthoods* by Margaret Tyler and others between 1587 and 1601.

3. A comic error: Rafe means "wandering knights that go in quest of their damsels."

4. Various nostrums against the plague.

5. A grocer-errant would be a wandering grocer, like a wandering knight (meaning a knight in quest of honor and adventure; cf. "knight-errant" in line 72)—an absurd analogy when applied to a grocer.

RAFE [*calling*] Tim!

TIM Anon! [*He and George come to see what Rafe has to say.*]

RAFE My beloved squire, and George my dwarf, I charge you that from henceforth you never call me by any other name but "the right courteous and valiant Knight of the Burning Pestle," and that you never call any female by the name of a woman or wench, but "fair lady," if she have her desires; if not, "distressed damsel"; that you call all forests and heaths "deserts," and all horses "palfreys."

WIFE This is very fine, faith.—Do the gentlemen like Rafe, think you, husband?

CITIZEN Ay, I warrant thee. The players would give all the shoes in their shop for him.

RAFE My beloved squire Tim, stand out. [*Tim steps forward.*] Admit° this were a desert,° and over it a knight-errant pricking,° and I should bid you inquire of his intents. What would you say? *Suppose / wilderness* *spurring*

TIM Sir, my master sent me to know whither you are riding.

RAFE No, thus: "Fair sir, the right courteous and valiant Knight of the Burning Pestle commanded me to inquire upon what adventure you are bound, whether to relieve some distressed damsel or otherwise."

CITIZEN Whoreson° blockhead cannot remember! *Good-for-nothing*

WIFE I'faith, and Rafe told him on't before. All the gentlemen heard him.—Did he not, gentlemen? Did not Rafe tell him on't?

GEORGE Right courteous and valiant Knight of the Burning Pestle, here is a distressed damsel to have a halfpennyworth of pepper.

WIFE That's a good boy! See, the little boy can hit it.° By my troth, it's a fine child. *get it right*

RAFE Relieve her with all courteous language. Now shut up shop; no more my prentice, but my trusty squire and dwarf. I must bespeak° my shield and arming° pestle. *arrange for / heraldic*

[*Exeunt Tim and George.*]

CITIZEN Go thy ways, Rafe. As I'm a true man, thou art the best on° 'em all. [*Rafe starts to leave.*] *of*

WIFE Rafe, Rafe!

RAFE What say you, mistress?

WIFE I prithee come again quickly, sweet Rafe.

RAFE By and by. *Exit Rafe.*

[1.4]

Enter Jasper and his mother, Mistress Merrythought.

MISTRESS MERRYTHOUGHT Give thee my blessing? No, I'll ne'er give thee my blessing. I'll see thee hanged first; it shall ne'er be said I gave thee my blessing. Thou'rt thy father's own son, of the right° blood of the Merrythoughts. I may curse the time that e'er I knew thy father. He hath spent all his own, and mine too. And when I tell him of it, he laughs, and dances, and sings, and cries, "A merry heart lives long-a!" And thou art a wastethrift, and art run away from thy master that loved thee well, and art come to me; and I have laid up a little for my younger son, Michael, and thou think'st to bezzle° that, but thou shalt never be able to do it. [*Calling*] Come hither, Michael!

true

embezzle, make off with

Enter Michael.

Come, Michael, down on thy knees. Thou shalt have my blessing.

MICHAEL [*kneeling*] I pray you, mother, pray to God to bless me.

MISTRESS MERRYTHOUGHT God bless thee! [*Michael rises.*] But Jasper shall never have my blessing. He shall be hanged first, shall he not, Michael? How say'st thou?

MICHAEL Yes, forsooth, mother, and grace of God.

MISTRESS MERRYTHOUGHT That's a good boy.

WIFE I'faith, it's a fine-spoken child.

JASPER Mother, though you forget a parent's love,
I must preserve the duty of a child.
I ran not from my master, nor return
To have your stock° maintain my idleness.

store of goods

WIFE Ungracious child, I warrant him! Hark how he chops logic° with his mother!—Thou hadst best tell her she lies. Do, tell her she lies.

argues sophistically

CITIZEN If he were my son, I would hang him up by the heels, and flay him, and salt him, whoreson halter-sack!°

gallows bait

JASPER My coming only is to beg your love,
Which I must ever, though I never gain it;
And, howsoever you esteem of me,
There is no drop of blood hid in these veins
But I remember well belongs to you
That brought me forth, and would be glad for you
To rip them all again and let it out.

MISTRESS MERRYTHOUGHT I'faith, I had sorrow° enough for thee, God knows; but I'll hamper° thee well enough. Get thee in, thou vagabond, get thee in, and learn of thy brother Michael. [*Exeunt Jasper and Michael.*]

pain in childbirth

fetter

1.4. Merrythought's house.

MERRYTHOUGHT ([*singing*] *within*)

Nose, nose, jolly red nose,
And who gave thee this jolly red nose?

MISTRESS MERRYTHOUGHT Hark, my husband! He's singing and hoiting,° and I'm fain to cark° and care, and all little enough. [*Calling*] Husband! Charles! Charles Merrythought!

making merry / labor

Enter old Merrythought.

MERRYTHOUGHT [*singing*]

Nutmegs and ginger, cinnamon and cloves,
And they gave me this jolly red nose.

MISTRESS MERRYTHOUGHT If you would consider your state,° you would have little list° to sing, iwis.°

estate

desire / God knows

MERRYTHOUGHT It should never be considered, while it were an estate, if I thought it would spoil my singing.

MISTRESS MERRYTHOUGHT But how wilt thou do, Charles? Thou art an old man, and thou canst not work, and thou hast not forty shillings left, and thou eatest good meat,° and drinkest good drink, and laughest.

food

MERRYTHOUGHT And will do.

MISTRESS MERRYTHOUGHT But how wilt thou come by it, Charles?

MERRYTHOUGHT How? Why, how have I done hitherto this forty years? I never came into my dining room but at eleven and six o'clock I found excellent meat and drink o'th'table; my clothes were never worn out but next morning a tailor brought me a new suit; and without question it will be so ever. Use makes perfectness. If all should fail, it is but a little straining myself extraordinary, and laugh myself to death.

WIFE It's a foolish old man, this, is not he, George?

CITIZEN Yes, cunny.

WIFE Give me a penny i'th'purse while I live, George.

CITIZEN Ay, by Lady,° cunny. Hold thee there.[1]

by Our Lady

MISTRESS MERRYTHOUGHT Well, Charles, you promised to provide for Jasper, and I have laid up for Michael. I pray you, pay Jasper his portion.° He's come home, and he shall not consume Michael's stock. He says his master turned him away, but I promise you truly I think he ran away.

inheritance

WIFE No, indeed, Mistress Merrythought; though he be a notable gallows,° yet I'll assure you his master did turn him away, even in this place.° 'Twas, i'faith, within this half hour, about his daughter. My husband was by.°

destined for hanging

in this theater

present

CITIZEN Hang him, rogue! He served him well enough. Love his master's daughter! By my troth, cunny, if there were a thousand boys, thou wouldst spoil them all with taking their parts. Let his mother alone° with him.

Let her manage

WIFE Ay, George, but yet truth is truth.

1. (1) Cling to that precept; (2) rest assured.

MERRYTHOUGHT Where is Jasper? He's welcome, however.° *at all events*
Call him in; he shall have his portion. Is he merry?
MISTRESS MERRYTHOUGHT Ay, foul chive° him, he is too merry. *ill befall*
[*She calls*] Jasper! Michael!

Enter Jasper and Michael.

MERRYTHOUGHT Welcome, Jasper. Though thou run'st away, welcome! God bless thee! 'Tis thy mother's mind thou shouldst receive thy portion. Thou hast been abroad,° and, I hope, hast learned experience enough to govern it. Thou art of sufficient years. Hold thy hand: [*giving money*] one, two, three, four, five, six, seven, eight, nine, there's ten shillings for thee. Thrust thyself into the world with that, and take some settled course. If Fortune cross° thee, thou hast a retiring place. Come home to me; I have twenty shillings left. Be a good husband,° that is, wear ordinary clothes, eat the best meat, and drink the best drink; be merry, and give to the poor, and, believe me, thou hast no end of thy goods. *out in the world* *thwart* *manager*

JASPER Long may you live free from all thought of ill,
And long have cause to be thus merry still!
But, father—

MERRYTHOUGHT No more words, Jasper. Get thee gone. Thou hast my blessing: thy father's spirit upon thee! Farewell, Jasper. [*He sings.*]
But yet, or ere you part (oh, cruel!),
Kiss me, kiss me, sweeting, mine own dear jewel.
So, now begone. No words. *Exit Jasper.*

MISTRESS MERRYTHOUGHT So, Michael, now get thee gone too.

MICHAEL Yes, forsooth, mother, but I'll have my father's blessing first.

MISTRESS MERRYTHOUGHT No, Michael, 'tis no matter for his blessing. Thou hast my blessing; begone. I'll fetch my money and jewels, and follow thee. I'll stay no longer with him, I warrant thee. [*Exit Michael.*]
Truly, Charles, I'll be gone too.

MERRYTHOUGHT What, you will not?

MISTRESS MERRYTHOUGHT Yes, indeed will I.

MERRYTHOUGHT [*singing*]
Heigh-ho, farewell, Nan!
I'll never trust wench more again, if I can.

MISTRESS MERRYTHOUGHT You shall not think, when all your own is gone, to spend that° I have been scraping up for Michael. *that which*

MERRYTHOUGHT Farewell, good wife! I expect it not. All I have to do in this world is to be merry—which I shall, if the ground be not taken from me. And if it be, [*singing*]
When earth and seas from me are reft,
The skies aloft for me are left. *Exeunt.*

[*Enter*] *Boy* [*and*] *danceth. Music.*

Finis actus primi.° *End of act 1*

[Interlude 1]

WIFE I'll be sworn he's a merry old gentleman, for all that.
Hark, hark, husband! Hark, fiddles, fiddles! Now surely they
go finely. They say 'tis present° death for these fiddlers to — *immediate*
tune their rebecs° before the great Turk's grace,[1] is't not, — *stringed instruments*
George? But look, look, here's a youth dances!—Now, good
youth, do a turn o'th'toe.—Sweetheart, i'faith, I'll have Rafe
come and do some of his gambols.°—He'll ride the wild — *capers*
mare,[2] gentlemen, 'twould do your hearts good to see him.
[*To the Boy*] I thank you, kind youth. Pray bid Rafe come.

CITIZEN Peace, cunny.—Sirrah, you scurvy boy, bid the players send Rafe, or, by God's—,° an they do not, I'll tear some — *(the actor improvises)*
of their periwigs beside° their heads. This is all riffraff.° — *off / worthless stuff*

[*Exit Boy.*]

2.1

Enter merchant [Venturewell] and Humphrey.

VENTUREWELL And how, faith, how goes it now, son Humphrey?
HUMPHREY Right worshipful and my belovèd friend
And father dear, this matter's at an end.
VENTUREWELL 'Tis well; it should be so. I'm glad the girl
Is found so tractable.
HUMPHREY Nay, she must whirl° — *i.e., elope*
From hence, and you must wink°—for so, I say, — *shut your eyes*
The story° tells—tomorrow before day. — *elopement plan*

WIFE George, dost thou think, in thy conscience now, 'twill be
a match? Tell me but what thou think'st, sweet rogue. Thou
see'st the poor gentleman, dear heart, how it labors and
throbs, I warrant you, to be at rest. I'll go move° the father — *urge*
for't.

CITIZEN No, no, I prithee sit still, honeysuckle; thou'lt spoil
all. If he deny him,° I'll bring half a dozen good fellows — *(Humphrey)*
myself, and in the shutting of an evening knock't up,[1] and
there's an end.

WIFE I'll buss° thee for that, i'faith, boy. Well, George, well, — *kiss*
you have been a wag in your days, I warrant you. But God
forgive you! And I do with all my heart.

VENTUREWELL How was it, son? You told me that tomorrow,
Before daybreak, you must convey her hence.
HUMPHREY I must, I must; and thus it is agreed:
Your daughter rides upon a brown-bay steed,
I on a sorrel, which I bought of Brian,
The honest host of the Red Roaring Lion° — *an inn*
In Waltham situate. Then, if you may,
Consent in seemly sort,° lest, by delay, — *fashion*

Interlude 1.
1. In the presence of the Turkish sultan Amurath, or Murad, who was known and feared for his impatience with the tuning of instruments.
2. A child's game, like leapfrog.

2.1. Venturewell's shop.
1. And late in the evening quickly finish the business.

The Fatal Sisters come and do the office,[2]
And then you'll sing another song.

VENTUREWELL Alas,
Why should you be thus full of grief° to me, *complaint*
That do as willing as yourself agree
To anything, so° it be good and fair? *provided*
Then steal her when you will, if such a pleasure
Content you both. I'll sleep and never see it,
To make your joys more full. But tell me why
You may not here perform your marriage?

WIFE God's blessing o'thy soul, old man! I'faith, thou art loath to part true hearts. I see 'a has her, George, and I'm as glad on't. Well, go thy ways, Humphrey, for a fair-spoken man. I believe thou hast not thy fellow within the walls of London; an I should say the suburbs too, I should not lie.—Why dost not rejoice with me, George?

CITIZEN If I could but see Rafe again, I were as merry as mine host,° i'faith. *an innkeeper*

HUMPHREY The cause you seem to ask, I thus declare.
Help me, O Muses nine! Your daughter sware
A foolish oath, the more it was the pity;
Yet none but myself within this city
Shall dare to say so, but a bold defiance
Shall meet him, were he of the noble science.° *the art of fencing*
And yet she sware, and yet why did she swear?
Truly I cannot tell, unless it were
For her own ease, for, sure, sometimes an oath,
Being sworn, thereafter is like cordial° broth. *restorative*
And this it was: she swore never to marry
But such a one whose mighty arm could carry
(As meaning me, for I am such a one)
Her bodily away through stick and stone,
Till both of us arrive, at her request,
Some ten miles off in the wild Waltham Forest.

VENTUREWELL If this be all, you shall not need to fear
Any denial in your love. Proceed;
I'll neither follow nor repent the deed.

HUMPHREY Good night. Twenty good nights, and twenty more,
And twenty more good nights! That makes threescore.

Exeunt.

[2.2]

Enter Mistress Merrythought [with a casket] and her son Michael.

MISTRESS MERRYTHOUGHT Come, Michael, art thou not weary, boy?

MICHAEL No, forsooth, mother, not I.

2. I.e., lest some mishap occur. (The Fatal Sisters are those who spin, measure, and cut the thread of life.)

2.2. Waltham Forest.

MISTRESS MERRYTHOUGHT Where be we now, child?

MICHAEL Indeed, forsooth, mother, I cannot tell, unless we be at Mile End.[1] Is not all the world Mile End, mother?

MISTRESS MERRYTHOUGHT No, Michael, not all the world, boy; but I can assure thee, Michael, Mile End is a goodly matter. There has been a pitched field, my child, between the naughty Spaniels° and the Englishmen, and the Spaniels ran away, Michael, and the Englishmen followed.[2] My neighbor Coxstone was there, boy, and killed them all with a birding piece.°

Spaniards / *bird shotgun*

MICHAEL Mother, forsooth—

MISTRESS MERRYTHOUGHT What says my white° boy?

fair-haired

MICHAEL Shall not my father go with us too?

MISTRESS MERRYTHOUGHT No, Michael, let thy father go snick up;° he shall never come between a pair of sheets with me again while he lives. Let him stay at home and sing for his supper, boy. Come, child, sit down, and I'll show my boy fine knacks° indeed. [*They sit. She opens the casket.*] Look here, Michael: here's a ring, and here's a brooch, and here's a bracelet, and here's two rings more, and here's money, and gold by th'eye,° my boy.

go hang / *knickknacks* / *unlimited*

MICHAEL Shall I have all this, mother?

MISTRESS MERRYTHOUGHT Ay, Michael, thou shalt have all, Michael.

CITIZEN How lik'st thou this, wench?

WIFE I cannot tell. I would have Rafe, George; I'll see no more else indeed, la.° And I pray you let the youths° understand so much by word of mouth, for I tell you truly, I'm afraid o'my boy.° Come, come, George, let's be merry and wise; the child's a fatherless child, and say they should put him into a strait pair of gaskins,[3] 'twere worse than knotgrass;[4] he would never grow after it.

indeed / boy actors / *for Rafe*

Enter Rafe [*in ridiculous armor, wearing the pestle as his badge*], *squire* [*Tim*], *and dwarf* [*George*].

CITIZEN Here's Rafe, here's Rafe!

WIFE How do you, Rafe? You are welcome, Rafe, as I may say. It's a good boy. Hold up thy head and be not afraid; we are thy friends, Rafe. The gentlemen will praise thee, Rafe, if thou play'st thy part with audacity. Begin, Rafe, i'God's name.

RAFE My trusty squire, unlace my helm; give me my hat. Where are we, or what desert may this be?

GEORGE [*as dwarf*] Mirror of knighthood, this is, as I take it, the perilous Waltham Down, in whose bottom stands the enchanted valley.

MISTRESS MERRYTHOUGHT [*seeing Rafe and his attendants*] Oh,

1. Site of the drilling of the London militia.
2. Sham battles of this sort were enacted at Mile End.
3. Breeches tight at the buttocks and wide at the knees.
4. A concoction derived from a weed that was thought to inhibit growth.

Michael, we are betrayed, we are betrayed! Here be giants.
Fly, boy! Fly, boy, fly!
Exeunt mother and Michael [leaving the casket].

RAFE Lace on my helm again. What noise is this?
A gentle lady flying the embrace
Of some uncourteous knight? I will relieve her.
Go, squire, and say the knight that wears this pestle
In honor of all ladies swears revenge
Upon that recreant° coward that pursues her. *cowardly; traitorous*
Go comfort her, and that same gentle squire
That bears her company.

TIM [*as squire*] I go, brave knight. [*Exit.*]

RAFE My trusty dwarf and friend, reach me my shield,
And hold it while I swear. First by my knighthood,
Then by the soul of Amadis de Gaul,[5]
My famous ancestor; then by my sword,
The beauteous Brionella[6] girt about me;
By this bright burning pestle, of mine honor
The living trophy; and by all respect
Due to distressèd damsels, here I vow
Never to end the quest of this fair lady
And that forsaken squire till by my valor
I gain their liberty.

GEORGE [*as dwarf*] Heaven bless the knight
That thus relieves poor errant gentlewomen!
Exit [with Rafe].

WIFE Ay, marry, Rafe, this has some savor in't; I would see the proudest of them all offer to carry his books after him.[7] But George, I will not have him go away so soon; I shall be sick if he go away, that I shall. Call Rafe again, George, call Rafe again. I prithee, sweetheart, let him come fight before me, and let's ha' some drums and some trumpets, and let him kill all that comes near him, an thou lov'st me, George.

CITIZEN Peace a little, bird. He shall kill them all, an they were twenty more on° 'em than there are. *of*

Enter Jasper.

JASPER Now, Fortune, if thou be'st not only ill,
Show me thy better face, and bring° about *turn*
Thy desperate wheel, that I may climb at length
And stand. This is our place of meeting,
If love have any constancy. O age,
Where only wealthy men are counted happy!
How shall I please thee? How deserve thy smiles,
When I am only rich in misery?
My father's blessing, and this little coin
Is my inheritance—a strong revenue!
From earth thou art, and to the earth I give thee.
[*He throws away his ten shillings.*]° *(see 1.4.96–98)*
There grow and multiply, whilst fresher air

5. Titular hero of the most popular of the chivalric romances; translated from the Spanish by Anthony Munday beginning c. 1590.

6. Named for a character in *Palmerin*; see 1.3.0.2 and note above.

7. I.e., play second fiddle to Rafe.

Breeds me a fresher fortune. (*Spies the casket.*) How! Illusion?
What, hath the devil coined himself before me?° *before my eyes*
[*He examines the ring, bracelet, etc.*]
'Tis metal good; it rings well. I am waking,
And taking° too, I hope. Now, God's dear blessing *comprehending*
Upon his heart that left it here! 'Tis mine!
These pearls, I take it, were not left for swine.
Exit [*with the casket*].

WIFE I do not like that this unthrifty youth should embezzle away the money; the poor gentlewoman his mother will have a heavy heart for it, God knows.

CITIZEN And reason good, sweetheart.

WIFE But let him go. I'll tell Rafe a tale in's ear shall fetch him again with a wanion,° I warrant him, if he be above ground; and besides, George, here are a number of sufficient° gentlemen can witness, and myself, and yourself, and the musicians, if we be called in question. But here comes Rafe, George. Thou shalt hear him speak an° he were an emperal.°

with a vengeance | *reliable* | *as if* | *emperor*

[2.3]

Enter Rafe and dwarf [*George*].

RAFE Comes not Sir Squire again?
GEORGE [*as dwarf*] Right courteous knight,
Your squire doth come, and with him comes the lady,

Enter Mistress Merrythought and Michael, and squire [*Tim*].

For and° the Squire of Damsels, as I take it. *And also*
RAFE Madam, if any service or devoir° *duty*
Of a poor errant knight may right your wrongs,
Command it. I am prest° to give you succor, *ready*
For to that holy end I bear my armor.

MISTRESS MERRYTHOUGHT Alas, sir, I am a poor gentlewoman, and I have lost my money in this forest.

RAFE "Desert," you would say, lady; and not lost
Whilst I have sword and lance. Dry up your tears,
Which ill befits the beauty of that face,
And tell the story, if I may request it,
Of your disastrous fortune.

MISTRESS MERRYTHOUGHT Out,° alas, I left a thousand pound, a thousand pound, e'en all the money I had laid up for this youth, upon the sight of Your Mastership—you looked so grim, and, as I may say it, saving your presence,° more like a giant than a mortal man.

(expression of dismay) | *begging your pardon*

RAFE I am as you are, lady; so are they° *i.e., my squire and dwarf*
All mortal. But why weeps this gentle squire?

MISTRESS MERRYTHOUGHT Has he not cause to weep, do you think, when he hath lost his inheritance?

2.3. The forest.

RAFE [*to Michael*] Young hope of valor, weep not. I am here
That will confound thy foe, and pay it dear
Upon his coward head[1] that dares deny
Distressèd squires and ladies equity.° *justice*
I have but one horse, on which shall ride
This lady fair behind me, and, before,
This courteous squire. Fortune will give us more
Upon our next adventure. Fairly speed
Beside us, squire and dwarf, to do us need! *Exeunt.*

CITIZEN Did not I tell you, Nell, what your man would do? By the faith of my body, wench, for clean° *adroit* action and good delivery they may all cast their caps at him.[2]

WIFE And so they may, i'faith, for—I dare speak it boldly—the twelve companies of London cannot match him, timber for timber.° *man for man* Well, George, an he be not inveigled by some of these paltry players, I ha' much marvel.° *I'll be surprised* But George, we ha' done our parts, if the boy have any grace to be thankful.

CITIZEN Yes, I warrant thee, duckling.

[2.4]

Enter Humphrey and Luce.

HUMPHREY Good Mistress Luce, however I in fault am
For your lame horse, you're welcome unto Waltham.
But which way now to go, or what to say,
I know not truly till it be broad day.

LUCE Oh, fear not, Master Humphrey, I am guide
For this place good enough.[1]

HUMPHREY Then up and ride,
Or, if it please you, walk for your repose,
Or sit, or, if you will, go pluck a rose°— *i.e., urinate*
Either of which shall be indifferent
To your good friend and Humphrey,[2] whose consent
Is so entangled ever to your will
As the poor harmless horse is to the mill.

LUCE Faith, an you say the word, we'll e'en sit down
And take a nap.

HUMPHREY 'Tis better in the town,
Where we may nap together; for, believe me,
To sleep without a snatch[3] would mickle° grieve me. *greatly*

LUCE You're merry, Master Humphrey.

HUMPHREY So I am,
And have been ever merry from my dam.° *mother; birth*

LUCE Your nurse had the less labor.[4]

HUMPHREY Faith, it may be,
Unless it were by chance I did beray me.° *befoul myself*

Enter Jasper.

1. Upon the head of that coward.
2. The other actors will salute Rafe by throwing up their caps in recognition of his taking the prize.
2.4. The forest.
1. Luce is confident that she can find their way.
2. To Humphrey, your good friend.
3. (1) A snack; (2) a little sex (hence Luce's reply in line 17).
4. Your nurse had an easy time of it with such a merry infant.

JASPER Luce! Dear friend Luce!
LUCE Here, Jasper.
JASPER You are mine.
HUMPHREY If it be so, my friend, you use me fine.° *(said ironically)*
What do you think I am?
JASPER An arrant noddy.° *nitwit*
HUMPHREY A word of obloquy!° Now, by God's body, *abuse, detraction*
I'll tell thy master, for I know thee well.
JASPER Nay, an you be so forward for to tell,
Take that, and that! [*He beats him.*] And tell him, sir, I gave it,
And say I paid you well.
HUMPHREY Oh, sir, I have it,
And do confess the payment. Pray be quiet.
JASPER Go, get you to your nightcap and the diet° *usual nostrum*
To cure your beaten bones.
LUCE Alas, poor Humphrey,
Get thee some wholesome broth, with sage and comfrey,° *healing herbs*
A little oil of roses and a feather
To 'noint thy back withal.
HUMPHREY When I came hither,
Would I had gone to Paris with John Dorry![5]
LUCE Farewell, my pretty Nump.[6] I am very sorry
I cannot bear thee company.
HUMPHREY Farewell!
The devil's dam was ne'er so banged in hell.
Exeunt [*Luce and Jasper*]. *Manet*° *Humphrey.* *Remains onstage*

WIFE This young Jasper will prove me another thing,[7] o'my conscience, an he may be suffered.° George, dost not see, George, how 'a swaggers, and flies at the very heads o' folks, as° he were a dragon? Well, if I do not do his lesson° for wronging the poor gentleman, I am no true woman. His friends° that brought him up might have been better occupied, iwis,° than ha' taught him these fegaries.° He's e'en in the highway to the gallows, God bless him. *allowed to continue* / *as if* / *teach him a lesson* / *relations* / *certainly / vagaries, tricks*

CITIZEN You're too bitter, cunny. The young man may do well enough for all this.

WIFE Come hither, Master Humphrey. Has he hurt you? Now beshrew his fingers for't! Here, sweetheart, here's some green ginger° for thee. Now, beshrew my heart, but 'a has peppernel° in's head as big as a pullet's egg! Alas, sweet lamb, how thy temples beat! Take the peace on him,[8] sweetheart, take the peace on him. *an herbal remedy* / *a lump*

Enter a Boy.

CITIZEN No, no, you talk like a foolish woman. I'll ha' Rafe fight with him, and swinge° him up well-favoredly.°—Sirrah boy, come hither. Let Rafe come in and fight with Jasper. *thrash / handsomely*

WIFE Ay, and beat him well. He's an unhappy° boy. *mischievous*

5. The hero of a popular song.
6. (1) A nickname for Humphrey; (2) a simpleton.
7. Jasper will turn out to be something else, i.e., in a heap of trouble.
8. Take him (Jasper) to the law to enjoin him to desist.

BOY Sir, you must pardon us; the plot of our play lies contrary, and 'twill hazard the spoiling of our play.

CITIZEN Plot me no plots!° I'll ha' Rafe come out. I'll make your house° too hot for you else. *(cf. But me no buts!)* *playhouse*

BOY Why, sir, he shall, but if anything fall out of order, the gentlemen must pardon us.

CITIZEN Go your ways, goodman boy! [*Exit Boy.*]
I'll hold° him a penny he shall have his belly full of fighting now.—Ho, here comes Rafe! No more. *bet*

Enter Rafe, Mistress Merrythought, Michael, squire [*Tim*], *and dwarf* [*George*].

RAFE What knight is that, squire? Ask him if he keep° *guard*
The passage,° bound by love of lady fair, *castle entrance*
Or else but prickant.° *only spurring quickly by*
HUMPHREY Sir, I am no knight,
But a poor gentleman, that this same night
Had stol'n from me, on yonder green,
My lovely wife, and suffered (to be seen
Yet extant on my shoulders) such a greeting
That, whilst I live, I shall think of that meeting.

WIFE Ay, Rafe, he beat him unmercifully, Rafe. An thou spar'st him,° Rafe, I would thou wert hanged. *(Jasper)*

CITIZEN No more, wife, no more.

RAFE Where is the caitiff wretch° hath done this deed? *wicked wretch who*
[*To Mistress Merrythought*] Lady, your pardon, that I may proceed
Upon the quest of this injurious knight.
[*To Michael*] And thou, fair squire, repute me not the worse
In leaving the great venture of the purse
And the rich casket till some better leisure.

Enter Jasper and Luce.

HUMPHREY Here comes the broker hath° purloined my treasure! *pimp who has*
RAFE Go, squire, and tell him I am here,
An errant knight-at-arms, to crave delivery
Of that fair lady to her own knight's arms.
If he deny, bid him take choice of ground,° *place to fight*
And so defy him.
TIM [*as squire, to Jasper*] From the knight that bears
The golden pestle, I defy thee, knight,
Unless thou make fair restitution
Of that bright lady.
JASPER Tell the knight that sent thee
He is an ass, and I will keep the wench
And knock his headpiece.
RAFE Knight, thou art but dead
If thou recall° not thy uncourteous terms. *take back*
[*Rafe and Jasper prepare to fight.*]

WIFE Break 's pate, Rafe! Break 's pate, Rafe, soundly!

JASPER Come, knight, I am ready for you. Now your pestle
(Snatches away his pestle.)
Shall try what temper, sir, your mortar's of.° *cap is of*
"With that he stood upright in his stirrups,
And gave the Knight of the Calfskin such a knock
[*He knocks Rafe down.*]
That he forsook his horse, and down he fell;
And then he leaped upon him, and, plucking off his helmet—"[9]

HUMPHREY Nay, an my noble knight be down so soon,
Though I can scarcely go,° I needs must run. *walk*
Exit Humphrey and Rafe.

WIFE Run, Rafe, run, Rafe! Run for thy life, boy! Jasper comes, Jasper comes!

JASPER Come, Luce, we must have other arms for you.[1]
Humphrey and golden pestle, both adieu! *Exeunt.*

WIFE Sure the devil, God bless us, is in this springald!° Why, George, didst ever see such a firedrake?° I am afraid my boy's miscarried.° If he be, though he° were Master Merrythought's son a thousand times, if there be any law in England I'll make some of them smart for't. *youngster* / *fiery dragon* / *come to grief / (Jasper)*

CITIZEN No, no, I have found out the matter, sweetheart. Jasper is enchanted. As sure as we are here, he is enchanted. He could no more have stood in Rafe's hands[2] than I can stand in my Lord Mayor's. I'll have a ring° to discover all enchantments, and Rafe shall beat him yet. Be no more vexed, for it shall be so. *magic ring*

[2.5]

Enter Rafe, squire [*Tim*], *dwarf* [*George*], *Mistress Merrythought, and Michael.*

WIFE Oh, husband, here's Rafe again.—Stay, Rafe, let me speak with thee. How dost thou, Rafe? Art thou not shrewdly° hurt? The foul great lungis° laid unmercifully on thee. There's some sugar candy for thee. Proceed; thou shalt have another bout with him. *seriously / lout*

CITIZEN If Rafe had him at the fencing school, if he did not make a puppy° of him, and drive him up and down the school, he should ne'er come in my shop more. *coward*

MISTRESS MERRYTHOUGHT Truly, Master Knight of the Burning Pestle, I am weary.

MICHAEL Indeed, la, mother, and I am very hungry.

RAFE Take comfort, gentle dame, and you, fair squire.
For in this desert there must needs be placed
Many strong castles, held by courteous knights,

9. Jasper parodies the style of a chivalric romance.
1. I.e., take my arms rather than the chivalric arms borne by Rafe.
2. He could no more have held his own against Rafe.
2.5. In front of the Bell Inn, Waltham.

And till I bring you safe to one of those
I swear by this my order° ne'er to leave you. *order of knighthood*

WIFE Well said, Rafe.—George, Rafe was ever comfortable,° was he not? *comforting, supportive*

CITIZEN Yes, duck.

WIFE I shall ne'er forget him. When we had lost our child—you know it was strayed almost, alone, to Puddle Wharf,° *(on the Thames)* and the criers were abroad for it,[1] and there it had drowned itself but for a sculler°—Rafe was the most comfortablest to *oarsman* me. "Peace, mistress," says he, "let it go. I'll get° you another *find; beget* as good." Did he not, George? Did he not say so?

CITIZEN Yes, indeed, did he, mouse.

GEORGE [*as dwarf*] I would we had a mess of pottage° and a pot of drink, squire, and were going to bed. *thick soup*

TIM [*as squire*] Why, we are at Waltham town's end, and that's the Bell Inn.

GEORGE [*as dwarf*] Take courage, valiant knight, damsel,
and squire.
I have discovered, not a stone's cast off,
An ancient castle held by the old knight
Of the most holy Order of the Bell,
Who gives to all knights-errant entertain.° *hospitality*
There plenty is of food, and all prepared
By the white hands of his own lady dear.
He hath three squires that welcome all his guests:
The first, hight° Chamberlaino, who will see *called*
Our beds prepared, and bring us snowy sheets,
Where never footman stretched his buttered hams;[2]
The second, hight Tapstero, who will see
Our pots full fillèd, and no froth therein;
The third, a gentle squire, Ostlero hight,
Who will our palfreys slick° with wisps of straw, *groom our saddle horses*
And in the manger put them oats enough,
And never grease their teeth with candle-snuff.[3]

WIFE That same dwarf's a pretty boy, but the squire's a groutnoll.° *blockhead*

RAFE Knock at the gates, my squire, with stately lance.
[*Tim, as squire, knocks.*]

Enter Tapster.

TAPSTER Who's there? You're welcome, gentlemen. Will you see a room?

GEORGE [*as dwarf, to Rafe*] Right courteous and valiant Knight of the Burning Pestle, this is the Squire Tapstero.

RAFE Fair Squire Tapstero, I, a wand'ring knight,
Hight of the Burning Pestle, in the quest

1. Those who make public announcements were calling out his name everywhere.
2. Footmen used to grease their thighs to prevent chafing as they ran alongside the carriage.
3. Greasing horses' feed was a common trick of unscrupulous hostlers to discourage the horses from eating.

Of this fair lady's casket and wrought° purse, *embroidered*
Losing myself in this vast wilderness,
Am to this castle well by fortune brought,
Where, hearing of the goodly entertain
Your knight of holy Order of the Bell
Gives to all damsels and all errant knights,
I thought to knock, and now am bold to enter.

TAPSTER An't please you see a chamber, you are very welcome. *Exeunt.*

WIFE George, I would have something done, and I cannot tell what it is.

CITIZEN What is it, Nell?

WIFE Why, George, shall Rafe beat nobody again? Prithee, sweetheart, let him.

CITIZEN So he shall, Nell; and if I join with him we'll knock them all.

[2.6]

Enter Humphrey and merchant [*Venturewell*].

WIFE Oh, George, here's Master Humphrey again now, that lost Mistress Luce, and Mistress Luce's father. Master Humphrey will do somebody's errand,° I warrant him. *come to the rescue*

HUMPHREY Father, it's true, in arms I ne'er shall clasp her,
For she is stol'n away by your man Jasper.

WIFE I thought he would tell him.

VENTUREWELL Unhappy that I am, to lose my child!
Now I begin to think on Jasper's words,
Who oft hath urged to me thy foolishness.
Why didst thou let her go? Thou lov'st her not,
That wouldst bring home thy life,° and not bring her. *save your own life*

HUMPHREY Father, forgive me. Shall I tell you true?
Look on my shoulders; they are black and blue.
Whilst to and fro fair Luce and I were winding,
He came and basted me with a hedge binding.[1]

VENTUREWELL Get men and horses straight;° we will be there *at once*
Within this hour. You know the place again?

HUMPHREY I know the place where he my loins did swaddle.° *beat*
I'll get six horses, and to each a saddle.

VENTUREWELL Meantime I'll go talk with Jasper's father.
Exeunt.

WIFE George, what wilt thou lay° with me now that Master Humphrey has not Mistress Luce yet? Speak, George, what wilt thou lay with me? *wager*

CITIZEN No, Nell, I warrant thee, Jasper is at Puckeridge° with her by this.° *(in Hertfordshire)* *by this time*

WIFE Nay, George, you must consider Mistress Luce's feet

2.6. Venturewell's house.

1. A stake or timber from a hedgerow.

are tender, and besides, 'tis dark; and I promise you truly, I do not see how he should get out of Waltham Forest with her yet.

CITIZEN Nay, cunny, what wilt thou lay with me that Rafe has her not yet?

WIFE I will not lay against Rafe, honey, because I have not spoken with him.—But look, George; peace! Here comes the merry old gentleman again.

[2.7]

Enter old Merrythought.

MERRYTHOUGHT [*singing*]

When it was grown to dark midnight,
And all were fast asleep,
In came Margaret's grimly° ghost — *grim-looking*
And stood at William's feet.

I have money, and meat, and drink beforehand, till tomorrow at noon; why should I be sad? Methinks I have half a dozen jovial spirits within me. [*He sings.*]

I am three merry men, and three merry men!

To what end should any man be sad in this world? Give me a man that, when he goes to hanging, cries, "Trowl the black bowl to me!"[1] and a woman that will sing a catch° in her travail.° I have seen a man come by my door, with a serious face, in a black cloak, without a hatband, carrying his head as if he looked for pins in the street;[2] I have looked out of my window half a year after, and have spied that man's head upon London Bridge.[3] 'Tis vile. Never trust a tailor that does not sing at his work; his mind is of nothing but filching.°

round / *labor of childbirth* / *stealing*

WIFE Mark this, George, 'tis worth noting: Godfrey, my tailor, you know, never sings, and he had fourteen yards to make this gown; and, I'll be sworn, Mistress Pennistone, the draper's wife, had one made with twelve.[4]

MERRYTHOUGHT [*singing*]

'Tis mirth that fills the veins with blood,
More than wine, or sleep, or food.
Let each man keep his heart at ease;
No man dies of that disease.
He that would his body keep
From diseases must not weep,
But whoever laughs and sings
Never he his body brings
Into fevers, gouts, or rheums,° — *colds*
Or ling'ringly his lungs consumes,
Or meets with achès in the bone,
Or catarrhs, or griping stone,° — *painful kidney stone*

2.7. Merrythought's house.
1. "Pass me the drinking cup!" (Called "black" for the dark color of the ale.)
2. I.e., with his head down, abstracted by worry.
3. Traitors' and heretics' heads were erected on poles on London Bridge as a warning to other potential offenders.
4. Tailors were proverbially dishonest, charging for more material than they used.

But contented lives for aye.
The more he laughs, the more he may.

WIFE Look, George, how say'st thou by this, George? Is't not a fine old man?—Now God's blessing o'thy sweet lips!—When wilt thou be so merry, George? Faith, thou art the frowning'st little thing, when thou art angry, in a country.

Enter merchant [*Venturewell*].

CITIZEN Peace, cunny. Thou shalt see him taken down too, I warrant thee.—Here's Luce's father come now.

MERRYTHOUGHT [*singing*]
As you came from Walsingham,
From that Holy Land,
There met you not with my true love
By the way as you came?

VENTUREWELL Oh, Master Merrythought, my daughter's gone!
This mirth becomes you not. My daughter's gone!

MERRYTHOUGHT [*singing*]
Why, an if she be, what care I?
Or let her come, or go, or tarry.

VENTUREWELL Mock not my misery. It is your son,
Whom I have made my own when all forsook him,
Has stol'n my only joy, my child, away.

MERRYTHOUGHT [*singing*]
He set her on a milk-white steed,
And himself upon a gray.
He never turned his face again,
But he bore her quite away.

VENTUREWELL Unworthy of the kindness I have shown
To thee, and thine! Too late, I well perceive
Thou art consenting to my daughter's loss.

MERRYTHOUGHT Your daughter? What a stir's here wi' your daughter? Let her go; think no more on her, but sing loud. If both my sons were on the gallows, I would sing

[*He sings.*]

Down, down, down: they fall
Down, and arise they never shall.

VENTUREWELL Oh, might I behold her once again,
And she once more embrace her agèd sire!

MERRYTHOUGHT Fie, how scurvily this goes! "And she once more embrace her agèd sire"? You'll make a dog on her,[5] will ye? She cares much for her agèd sire, I warrant you.

[*He sings.*]

She cares not for her daddy,
Nor she cares not for her mammy.
For she is, she is, she is, she is
My Lord of Lowgave's lassie.

VENTUREWELL For this thy scorn I will pursue
That son of thine to death.

MERRYTHOUGHT Do, and when you ha' killed him,

[*He sings.*]

5. The word "sire," to Merrythought, suggests the siring or breeding of animals.

Give him flowers enow,° palmer,° give
him flowers enow;
Give him red and white, and blue,
green, and yellow. *enough / pilgrim*

VENTUREWELL I'll fetch my daughter.

MERRYTHOUGHT I'll hear no more o'your daughter; it spoils my mirth.

VENTUREWELL I say I'll fetch my daughter.

MERRYTHOUGHT [*singing*]

Was never man for lady's sake,
Down, down,
Tormented as I, poor Sir Guy,
De derry down,
For Lucy's sake, that lady bright,
Down, down,
As ever men beheld with eye?
De derry down.

VENTUREWELL I'll be revenged, by heaven. *Exeunt.*

Music.

Finis actus secundi.° *End of act 2*

[Interlude 2]

WIFE How dost thou like this, George?

CITIZEN Why this is well, cunny; but if Rafe were hot° once, thou shouldst see more. *aroused*

WIFE The fiddlers go again, husband.

CITIZEN Ay, Nell, but this is scurvy music. I gave the whoreson gallows° money, and I think he has not got me the waits° of Southwark. If I hear 'em not anon, I'll twinge him by the ears. [*Calling*] You musicians, play "Baloo"!° *one destined for hanging / musicians / a ballad refrain*

WIFE No, good George, let's ha' "Lachrymae."° *lute song by Dowland*

CITIZEN Why this is it, cunny.

WIFE It's all the better, George. Now, sweet lamb, what story is that painted upon the cloth?° *The Confutation*[1] *of Saint Paul*? *imitation tapestry*

CITIZEN No, lamb, that's *Rafe and Lucrece.*[2]

WIFE *Rafe and Lucrece*? Which Rafe? Our Rafe?

CITIZEN No, mouse, that was a Tartarian.[3]

WIFE A Tartarian? Well, I would the fiddlers had done, that we might see our Rafe again.

3.1

Enter Jasper and Luce.

JASPER Come, my dear. Though we have lost our way,
We have not lost ourselves.° Are you not weary
With this night's wand'ring, broken from your rest, *We have each other*

Interlude 2.
1. The Wife's comic blunder for "Conversion."
2. The Citizen means *The Rape of Lucrece*.
3. The Citizen ignorantly confounds an inhabitant of Tartarus, the lowest region of the underworld (also a cant term for "thief"), with Tarquin, whose son Sextus Tarquinius raped Lucrece.

3.1. The forest.

And frighted with the terror that attends
The darkness of this wild, unpeopled place?

LUCE No, my best friend, I cannot either fear
Or entertain a weary thought whilst you,
The end of all my full desires, stand by me.
Let them that lose their hopes, and live to languish
Amongst the number of forsaken lovers,
Tell° the long, weary steps, and number time,° *Count / count minutes*
Start° at a shadow, and shrink up their blood, *Be startled*
Whilst I, possessed with all content and quiet,
Thus take my pretty love, and thus embrace him.
[*She embraces Jasper.*]

JASPER You have caught me, Luce, so fast, that whilst I live
I shall become your faithful prisoner,
And wear these chains forever. Come, sit down,
And rest your body, too too delicate
For these disturbances. [*They sit.*] So, will you sleep?
Come, do not be° more able than you are; *try to be*
I know you are not skillful in these watches,° *keeping awake*
For women are no soldiers. Be not nice,° *foolish; fastidious*
But take it.° Sleep, I say. *acquiesce, agree*

LUCE I cannot sleep.
Indeed I cannot, friend.

JASPER Why, then, we'll sing,
And try how that will work upon our senses.

LUCE I'll sing, or say, or anything but sleep.

JASPER Come, little mermaid, rob me of my heart
With that enchanting voice.

LUCE You mock me, Jasper.

SONG

JASPER Tell me, dearest, what is love?

LUCE 'Tis a lightning from above,
'Tis an arrow, 'tis a fire,
'Tis a boy they call Desire.
'Tis a smile
Doth beguile

JASPER The poor hearts of men that prove.° *experience it*

Tell me more: are women true?

LUCE Some love change, and so do you.

JASPER Are they fair, and never kind?

LUCE Yes, when men turn with the wind.

JASPER Are they froward?

LUCE Ever toward
Those that love, to love anew.

JASPER Dissemble it no more. I see the god
Of heavy sleep lay on his heavy mace
Upon your eyelids.

LUCE I am very heavy. [*She lies down.*]

JASPER Sleep, sleep, and quiet rest crown thy sweet thoughts!
Keep from her fair blood distempers, startings,
Horrors, and fearful shapes! Let all her dreams
Be joys and chaste delights, embraces, wishes,
And such new pleasures as the ravished soul

Gives to the senses! [*She sleeps.*] So; my charms have took.
Keep her, you powers divine, whilst I contemplate
Upon the wealth and beauty of her mind!
She is only° fair and constant, only kind, *alone*
And only to thee, Jasper. Oh, my joys!
Whither will you transport me? Let not fullness
Of my poor buried hopes come up together
And overcharge my spirits! I am weak.
Some say (however ill)° the sea and women *disparagingly*
Are governed by the moon; both ebb and flow,
Both full of changes. Yet to them that know
And truly judge, these but opinions are,
And heresies, to bring on pleasing war
Between our tempers, that without these were
Both void of after-love and present fear,[1]
Which are the best of Cupid. O thou child° *i.e., Mistrust*
Bred from despair, I dare not entertain thee,
Having a love° without the faults of women, *sweetheart*
And greater in her perfect goods than men—
Which to make good,° and please myself the stronger, *to prove*
Though certainly I am certain of her love,
I'll try° her, that the world and memory *test*
May sing to aftertimes her constancy.
[*He unsheathes his sword.*]
Luce! Luce, awake!

LUCE [*awakening*] Why do you fright me, friend,
With those distempered looks? What makes your sword
Drawn in your hand? Who hath offended you?
I prithee, Jasper, sleep. Thou art wild with watching.° *staying awake*

JASPER Come, make your way to heaven, and bid the world,
With all the villainies that stick upon it,
Farewell. You're for another life.

LUCE Oh, Jasper,
How have my tender years committed evil,
Especially against the man I love,
Thus to be cropped untimely?[2]

JASPER Foolish girl,
Canst thou imagine I could love his daughter° *the daughter of him*
That flung me from my fortune into nothing,
Dischargèd me his service, shut the doors
Upon my poverty, and scorned my prayers,
Sending me, like a boat without a mast,
To sink or swim? Come, by this hand you die.
I must have life and blood to satisfy
Your father's wrongs.

WIFE Away, George, away! Raise the watch at Ludgate,° *gate of the old city* and bring a mittimus° *arrest warrant* from the justice for this desperate villain.—Now I charge you, gentlemen, see the King's peace° *law and order* kept.—Oh, my heart, what a varlet's this, to offer manslaughter upon the harmless gentlewoman!

1. And that without these difficulties between the sexes we would be deprived of the fears of jealousy and the pleasures of making up.

2. What have I done at my tender age to offend the man I love so terribly that I am to be plucked prematurely, like unripe fruit?

CITIZEN I warrant thee, sweetheart, we'll have him hampered.° *arrested, detained*

LUCE Oh, Jasper, be not cruel!
If thou wilt kill me, smile and do it quickly,
And let not many deaths appear before me.
I am a woman, made of fear and love,
A weak, weak woman. Kill not with thy eyes;
They shoot me through and through. Strike! I am ready,
And, dying, still I love thee.

Enter merchant [Venturewell], Humphrey, and his men.

VENTUREWELL Whereabouts?
JASPER [*aside*] No more of this. Now to myself again.
HUMPHREY There! There he stands, with sword, like martial knight,
Drawn in his hand; therefore beware the fight,
You that are wise. For, were I good Sir Bevis,
I would not stay his coming, by your leaves.[3]
VENTUREWELL [*to Jasper*] Sirrah, restore my daughter.
JASPER Sirrah, no.
VENTUREWELL [*to the men*] Upon him, then!
[*The men attack Jasper.*]

WIFE So, down with him, down with him, down with him!
Cut him i'th'leg, boys, cut him i'th'leg!

[*The men take Luce away from Jasper.*]

VENTUREWELL Come your ways, minion.° I'll provide a cage *hussy*
For you, you're grown so tame.—Horse° her away. *Carry on horseback*
HUMPHREY Truly, I'm glad your forces have the day.
Exeunt. Manet Jasper.
JASPER They are gone, and I am hurt; my love is lost,
Never to get° again. Oh, me unhappy!° *be had / unfortunate*
Bleed, bleed, and die! I cannot. Oh, my folly,
Thou hast betrayed me! Hope, where art thou fled?
Tell me, if thou be'st anywhere remaining.
Shall I but see my love again? Oh, no!
She will not deign to look upon her butcher,
Nor is it fit she should; yet I must venture.
O Chance, or Fortune, or whate'er thou art
That men adore for° powerful, hear my cry, *as*
And let me loving live, or losing die! *Exit.*

WIFE Is 'a gone, George?
CITIZEN Ay, cunny.
WIFE Marry, and let him go, sweetheart. By the faith o'my body, 'a has put me into such a fright that I tremble (as they say) as 'twere an aspen leaf. Look o'my little finger, George, how it shakes! Now, i'truth, every member of my body is the worse for't.

3. Even if I were Sir Bevis (the hero of a popular fourteenth-century chivalric romance called *Sir Bevis of Hampton*), I wouldn't take Jasper on single-handed, I can tell you.

CITIZEN Come, hug in mine arms, sweet mouse. He shall not fright thee any more. Alas, mine own dear heart, how it quivers!

[3.2]

Enter Mistress Merrythought, Rafe, Michael, squire [Tim], dwarf [George], Host, and a Tapster.

WIFE Oh, Rafe, how dost thou, Rafe? How hast thou slept tonight?° Has the knight used thee well? *last night*

CITIZEN Peace, Nell, let Rafe alone.

TAPSTER Master, the reckoning° is not paid. *bill*

RAFE Right courteous knight—who, for the order's sake
Which thou hast ta'en, hang'st out the holy bell,
As I this flaming pestle bear about—
We render thanks to your puissant° self, *mighty*
Your beauteous lady, and your gentle squires
For thus refreshing of our wearied limbs,
Stiffened with hard achievements in wild desert.

TAPSTER Sir, there is twelve shillings to pay.

RAFE Thou merry Squire Tapstero, thanks to thee
For comforting our souls with double jug;
And if adventurous Fortune prick thee forth,
Thou jovial squire, to follow feats of arms,
Take heed thou tender° every lady's cause, *treat with care*
Every true knight, and every damsel fair;
But spill the blood of treacherous Saracens
And false enchanters that with magic spells
Have done to death full many a noble knight.

HOST Thou valiant Knight of the Burning Pestle, give ear to me. There is twelve shillings to pay, and, as I am a true knight, I will not bate° a penny. *deduct, remit*

WIFE George, I pray thee tell me, must Rafe pay twelve shillings now?

CITIZEN No, Nell, no, nothing but the old knight is merry with Rafe.

WIFE Oh, is't nothing else? Rafe will be as merry as he.

RAFE Sir Knight, this mirth of yours becomes you well.
But to requite this liberal courtesy,
If any of your squires will follow arms,
He shall receive from my heroic hand
A knighthood, by the virtue of this pestle.

HOST Fair knight, I thank you for your noble offer.
Therefore, gentle knight,
Twelve shillings you must pay, or I must cap° you. *arrest*

WIFE Look, George, did not I tell thee as much? The Knight of the Bell is in earnest. Rafe shall° not be beholding° to him. Give him his money, George, and let him go snick up.° *must / beholden* *go hang*

3.2. The Bell Inn.

CITIZEN Cap Rafe? No.—Hold your hand, Sir Knight of the Bell; there's your money. [*He pays the bill.*] Have you anything to say to Rafe now? Cap Rafe?

WIFE I would you should know it, Rafe has friends that will not suffer him to be capped for ten times so much, and ten times to the end of° that.—Now take thy course, Rafe.

in addition to

MISTRESS MERRYTHOUGHT Come, Michael, thou and I will go home to thy father. He hath enough left to keep us a day or two, and we'll set fellows abroad to cry[1] our purse and our casket. Shall we, Michael?

MICHAEL Ay, I pray, mother. In truth, my feet are full of chilblains with traveling.

WIFE Faith, and those chilblains are a foul trouble, Mistress Merrythought. When your youth comes home, let him rub all the soles of his feet, and the heels, and his ankles, with a mouse skin; or, if none of your people can catch a mouse, when he goes to bed let him roll his feet in the warm embers, and I warrant you he shall be well. And you may make him put his fingers between his toes and smell to° them; it's very sovereign° for his head, if he be costive.°

sniff
curative / constipated

MISTRESS MERRYTHOUGHT Master Knight of the Burning Pestle, my son Michael and I bid you farewell. I thank Your Worship heartily for your kindness.

RAFE Farewell, fair lady, and your tender squire.
If, pricking through these deserts, I do hear
Of any traitorous knight who, through his guile,
Hath light° upon your casket and your purse, *alighted, come*
I will despoil him of them and restore them.

MISTRESS MERRYTHOUGHT I thank Your Worship.

Exit with Michael.

RAFE Dwarf, bear my shield. Squire, elevate my lance.
And now farewell, you Knight of Holy Bell.

CITIZEN Ay, ay, Rafe, all is paid.

RAFE But yet before I go, speak, worthy knight,
If aught you do of sad° adventures know, *important*
Where errant knight may through his prowess win
Eternal fame, and free some gentle souls
From endless bounds of steel and ling'ring pain.

HOST [*aside to the Tapster*] Sirrah, go to Nick the Barber, and bid him prepare himself, as I told you before, quickly.

TAPSTER I am gone, sir. *Exit Tapster.*

HOST Sir Knight, this wilderness affordeth none
But the great venture, where full many a knight
Hath tried his prowess and come off with shame,
And where I would not have you lose your life
Against no man, but furious fiend of hell.

RAFE Speak on, Sir Knight. Tell what he is, and where.
For here I vow, upon my blazing badge,

1. We'll hire criers to announce publicly the loss of.

Never to blaze° a day in quietness, *i.e., consume*
But bread and water will I only eat,
And the green herb and rock shall be my couch
Till I have quelled° that man, or beast, or fiend *killed*
That works such damage to all errant knights.

HOST Not far from hence, near to a craggy cliff
At the north end of this distressèd town,
There doth stand a lowly house
Ruggedly builded, and in it a cave
In which an ugly giant now doth won° *dwell*
Yclepèd° Barbaroso. In his hand *Called*
He shakes a naked lance of purest steel,
With sleeves turned up, and him before° he wears *in front of him*
A motley garment to preserve his clothes
From blood of those knights which he massacres,
And ladies gent.° Without° his door doth hang *gentle, noble / Outside*
A copper basin, on a prickant spear;° *i.e., barber pole*
At which, no sooner gentle knights can knock
But the shrill sound fierce Barbaroso hears,
And, rushing forth, brings in the errant knight
And sets him down in an enchanted chair.
Then with an engine,° which he hath prepared *instrument; comb*
With forty teeth, he claws his courtly crown,
Next makes him wink,° and underneath his chin *shut his eyes*
He plants a brazen piece° of mighty bord,° *basin / rim*
And knocks his bullets° round about his cheeks, *soap pellets*
Whilst with his fingers, and an instrument
With which he snaps his hair off, he doth fill
The wretch's ears with a most hideous noise.
Thus every knight adventurer he doth trim,° *clip hair; thrash*
And now no creature dares encounter him.

RAFE In God's name, I will fight with him. Kind sir,
Go but before me to this dismal cave
Where this huge giant Barbaroso dwells,
And by that virtue that brave Rosicleer[2]
That damnèd brood of ugly giants slew,
And Palmerin Frannarco[3] overthrew,
I doubt not but to curb this traitor foul,
And to the devil send his guilty soul.

HOST Brave-sprighted° knight, thus far I will perform *Brave-spirited*
This your request: I'll bring you within sight
Of this most loathsome place, inhabited
By a more loathsome man; but dare not stay,
For his main° force swoops all he sees away. *brute*

RAFE Saint George° set on before! March, squire and page. *patron saint of England*
Exeunt.

WIFE George, dost think Rafe will confound° the giant? *overthrow, slay*

CITIZEN I hold° my cap to a farthing he does. Why, Nell, I saw him wrestle with the great Dutchman,° and hurl him. *bet* *a strongman in a fair*

WIFE Faith, and that Dutchman was a goodly man, if all things were answerable° to his bigness. And yet they say *corresponding*

2. And by the power through which the hero of *The Mirror of Knighthood*.

3. A giant who is overthrown in the Palmerin story.

there was a Scotchman higher° than he, and that they two and a knight met and saw one another for nothing.° But of all the sights that ever were in London, since I was married, methinks the little child that was so fair grown about the members° was the prettiest—that and the hermaphrodite.

taller
fought inconclusively
sexual members

CITIZEN Nay, by your leave, Nell, Ninivie[4] was better.

WIFE Ninivie? Oh, that was the story of Joan and the wall,[5] was it not, George?

CITIZEN Yes, lamb.

[3.3]

Enter Mistress Merrythought.

WIFE Look, George, here comes Mistress Merrythought again! And I would have Rafe come and fight with the giant; I tell you true, I long to see't.

CITIZEN Good Mistress Merrythought, begone, I pray you, for my sake. I pray you, forbear a little. You shall have audience presently. I have a little business.

WIFE Mistress Merrythought, if it please you to refrain your passion a little till Rafe have dispatched the giant out of the way, we shall think ourselves much bound to you. I thank you, good Mistress Merrythought.

Exit Mistress Merrythought.

Enter a Boy.

CITIZEN Boy, come hither. Send away° Rafe and this whoreson giant quickly.

out onto the stage

BOY In good faith, sir, we cannot. You'll utterly spoil our play and make it to be hissed, and it cost money. You will not suffer us to go on with our plot.—I pray, gentlemen, rule° him.

control

CITIZEN Let him come now and dispatch this, and I'll trouble you no more.

BOY Will you give me your hand of° that?

on

WIFE Give him thy hand, George, do, and I'll kiss him. I warrant thee the youth means plainly.°

honestly, sincerely

BOY I'll send him to you presently.°

right away

WIFE [*kissing him*] I thank you, little youth. *Exit Boy.* Faith, the child hath a sweet breath, George, but I think it be troubled with the worms. *Carduus Benedictus*[1] and mare's milk were the only thing in the world for't.—Oh, Rafe's here, George!—God send thee good luck, Rafe!

4. A puppet show about Jonah and the whale and Jonah preaching at Nineveh.
5. The Wife's comic approximation of "Jonah and the whale."
3.3. The forest.
1. Blessed Thistle, a cure-all.

[3.4]

Enter Rafe, Host, squire [Tim], and dwarf [George]. [A barber's basin and spear and a string of teeth are displayed.]

HOST Puissant knight, yonder his mansion is.
Lo, where the spear and copper basin are!
Behold the string on which hangs many a tooth,
Drawn from the gentle jaw of wand'ring knights!
I dare not stay to sound;° he will appear. *Exit Host.* *sound a challenge*
RAFE Oh, faint not, heart! Susan, my lady dear,
The cobbler's maid in Milk Street, for whose sake
I take these arms, oh, let the thought of thee
Carry thy knight through all adventurous deeds,
And in the honor of thy beauteous self
May I destroy this monster Barbaroso!—
Knock, squire, upon the basin, till it break
With the shrill strokes, or till the giant speak.
[*Tim, as squire, knocks on the barber's basin.*]

Enter Barber.

WIFE Oh, George, the giant, the giant!—Now, Rafe, for thy life!

BARBER What fond,° unknowing wight° is this that dares *foolish / person*
So rudely knock at Barbaroso's cell,
Where no man comes but leaves his fleece behind?
RAFE I, traitorous caitiff, who am sent by Fate
To punish all the sad enormities
Thou hast committed against ladies gent
And errant knights. Traitor to God and men,
Prepare thyself! This is the dismal hour
Appointed for thee to give strict account
Of all thy beastly, treacherous villainies.
BARBER Foolhardy knight, full soon thou shalt aby° *pay for*
This fond reproach. Thy body will I bang,
(*He takes down his pole.*)
And lo, upon that string thy teeth shall hang.
Prepare thyself, for dead soon shalt thou be.
RAFE Saint George for me!
BARBER Gargantua for me! *They fight.*

WIFE To him, Rafe, to him! Hold up° the giant! Set out thy leg before, Rafe! *Keep back*
CITIZEN Falsify° a blow, Rafe, falsify a blow! The giant lies open on the left side. *Feint*
WIFE Bear't off,° bear't off still! There, boy!—Oh, Rafe's almost down, Rafe's almost down! *Fend it off*

RAFE Susan inspire me! Now have up° again! *up I go*

WIFE Up, up, up, up, up! So, Rafe! Down with him, down with him, Rafe!
CITIZEN Fetch him o'er the hip, boy!

3.4. A barbershop, Waltham.

[*Rafe knocks the Barber down.*]

WIFE There, boy. Kill, kill, kill, kill, kill, Rafe!
CITIZEN No, Rafe, get all out of him° first. *relieve his prisoners*

RAFE Presumptuous man, see to what desperate end
Thy treachery hath brought thee! The just gods,
Who never prosper those that do despise them,
For all the villainies which thou hast done
To knights and ladies now have paid° thee home° *punished / fully*
By my stiff arm, a knight adventurous.
But say, vile wretch, before I send thy soul
To sad Avernus,° whither it must go, *underworld entrance*
What captives hold'st thou in thy sable° cave? *dark*
BARBER Go in and free them all. Thou hast the day.° *the victory*
RAFE Go, squire and dwarf: search in this dreadful cave,
And free the wretched prisoners from their bonds.
Exit squire [*Tim*] *and dwarf* [*George*].
BARBER I crave for mercy, as thou art a knight
And scorn'st to spill the blood of those that beg.
RAFE Thou showed'st no mercy, nor shalt thou have any.
Prepare thyself, for thou shalt surely die.

Enter squire [*Tim*], *leading one* [*the First Knight*] *winking,*[1] *with a basin under his chin.*

TIM [*as squire*] Behold, brave knight, here is one prisoner,
Whom this wild man hath usèd as you see.

WIFE This is the first wise word I heard the squire speak.

RAFE Speak what thou art, and how thou hast been used,
That I may give him condign° punishment. *fitting*
FIRST KNIGHT I am a knight that took my journey post° *in haste*
Northward from London; and in courteous wise
This giant trained° me to his loathsome den, *lured*
Under pretense of killing of the itch,
And all my body with a powder strewed
That smarts and stings, and cut away my beard
And my curled locks wherein were ribbons tied,
And with a water washed my tender eyes—
Whilst up and down about me still he skipped—
Whose virtue is that, till mine eyes be wiped
With a dry cloth, for this my foul disgrace
I shall not dare to look a dog i'th'face.

WIFE Alas, poor knight!—Relieve him, Rafe. Relieve poor knights whilst you live.

RAFE My trusty squire, convey him to the town,
Where he may find relief.—Adieu, fair knight.
Exit [*First*] *Knight* [*with Tim, who then reenters*].

Enter dwarf [*George*], *leading one* [*the Second Knight*] *with a patch o'er his nose.*[2]

1. I.e., shutting his eyes from the soapy water; see lines 71–75.

2. A common sign of advanced syphilis, since syphilis eats away at the nose.

GEORGE [*as dwarf*] Puissant knight, of the Burning Pestle hight,
See here another wretch, whom this foul beast
Hath scorched and scored[3] in this inhuman wise.
RAFE Speak me thy name, and eke° thy place of birth, *also*
And what hath been thy usage in this cave.
SECOND KNIGHT I am a knight. Sir Pockhole° is my name, *(suggesting syphilis)*
And by my birth I am a Londoner,
Free by my copy,[4] but my ancestors
Were Frenchmen[5] all; and riding hard this way
Upon a trotting horse, my bones did ache,[6]
And I, faint knight, to ease my weary limbs,
Light° at this cave, when straight° this furious fiend, *Alighted / at once*
With sharpest instrument of purest steel,
Did cut the gristle of my nose away,
And in the place this velvet plaster° stands. *patch*
Relieve me, gentle knight, out of his hands!

WIFE Good Rafe, relieve Sir Pockhole and send him away, for in truth his breath stinks.[7]

RAFE Convey him straight after the other knight.—
Sir Pockhole, fare you well.
SECOND KNIGHT Kind sir, good night.
Exit [*with George, who then reenters*].
Cries within.
THIRD KNIGHT [*within*] Deliver us!
WOMAN [*within*] Deliver us!

WIFE Hark, George, what a woeful cry there is! I think some woman lies in there.

THIRD KNIGHT [*within*] Deliver us!
WOMAN [*within*] Deliver us!
RAFE What ghastly noise is this? Speak, Barbaroso,
Or, by this blazing steel, thy head goes off.
BARBER Prisoners of mine, whom I in diet° keep. *on a diet (for syphilis)*
Send lower down into the cave,
And in a tub that's heated smoking hot[8]
There may they find them and deliver them.
RAFE Run, squire and dwarf! Deliver them with speed.
Exeunt squire [*Tim*] *and dwarf* [*George*].

WIFE But will not Rafe kill this giant? Surely I am afeard, if he let him go, he will do as much hurt as ever he did.
CITIZEN Not so, mouse, neither, if he could convert him.
WIFE Ay, George, if he could convert him; but a giant is not so soon converted as one of us ordinary people. There's a pretty tale of a witch that had the devil's mark° about her, God bless us, that had a giant to° her son, that was called *brand, birthmark* / *as*

3. Scratched and cut (in treatment for syphilitic chancres).
4. I am a free citizen of London, enjoying traditional rights. (See Induction, line 13 and note.)
5. Syphilis was known to the English as "the French disease."
6. More syphilitic symptoms. The "horse" suggests "whore" or "whores."
7. An effect of mercury treatment for syphilis.
8. A standard treatment for syphilis.

Lob-lie-by-the-fire.[9] Didst never hear it, George?

Enter squire [Tim], leading a man [the Third Knight] with a glass of lotion in his hand, and the dwarf [George] leading a Woman, with diet bread[1] and drink.

CITIZEN Peace, Nell, here comes the prisoners.

GEORGE [*as dwarf*] Here be these pinèd° wretches, manful knight, *wasted*
That for these six weeks have not seen a wight.
RAFE Deliver° what you are, and how you came *Say, report*
To this sad cave, and what your usage was?
THIRD KNIGHT I am an errant knight that followed arms° *practiced knighthood*
With spear and shield, and in my tender years
I stricken was with Cupid's fiery shaft,
And fell in love with this my lady dear,
And stole her from her friends in Turnbull Street,° *a red-light district*
And bore her up and down from town to town,
Where we did eat and drink and music hear,
Till at the length at this unhappy town
We did arrive, and, coming to this cave,
This beast us caught and put us in a tub,° *(see 110 and n)*
Where we this two months sweat, and should have done
Another month if you had not relieved us.
WOMAN This bread and water hath our diet been,
Together with a rib cut from a neck
Of burnèd mutton; hard hath been our fare.
Release us from this ugly giant's snare!
THIRD KNIGHT This hath been all the food we have received,
But only twice a day, for novelty,
He gave a spoonful of this hearty broth° *i.e., enema*
(*Pulls out a syringe.*)
To each of us, through this same slender quill.
RAFE From this infernal monster you shall go,
That useth knights and gentle ladies so.—
Convey them hence. *Exeunt man [Third Knight] and Woman [escorted by Tim and George, who then reenter].*

CITIZEN Cunny, I can tell thee the gentlemen like Rafe.
WIFE Ay, George, I see it well enough.—Gentlemen, I thank you all heartily for gracing° my man Rafe, and I promise you you shall see him oft'ner. *being gracious to*

BARBER Mercy, great knight! I do recant my ill,
And henceforth never gentle blood will spill.
RAFE I give thee mercy, but yet thou shalt swear
Upon my burning pestle to perform
Thy promise uttered.
BARBER I swear and kiss.
RAFE Depart, then, and amend.
[*Exit Barber.*]
Come, squire and dwarf, the sun grows towards his set,
And we have many more adventures yet. *Exeunt.*

9. A giant of popular oral tradition.

1. A bread specially prepared for invalids.

CITIZEN Now Rafe is in this humor, I know he would ha' beaten all the boys in the house° if they had been set on him.

theater

WIFE Ay, George, but it is well as it is. I warrant you the gentlemen do consider what it is to overthrow a giant.—But look, George, here comes Mistress Merrythought and her son Michael.—Now you are welcome, Mistress Merrythought! Now Rafe has done, you may go on.

[3.5]

Enter Mistress Merrythought and Michael.

MISTRESS MERRYTHOUGHT Mick,° my boy?

Michael

MICHAEL Ay, forsooth, mother?

MISTRESS MERRYTHOUGHT Be merry, Mick. We are at home now, where, I warrant you, you shall find the house flung out at the windows.° [*Music and sounds of merriment within*] Hark! Hey, dogs, hey! This is the old world,° i'faith, with my husband. If I get in among 'em, I'll play 'em such a lesson that they shall have little list° to come scraping° hither again. [*Calling*] Why, Master Merrythought! Husband! Charles Merrythought!

i.e., in disorder
the usual way
appetite / fiddling

MERRYTHOUGHT ([*singing*] *within*)

If you will sing, and dance, and laugh,
And halloo, and laugh again,
And then cry, "There, boys, there!" why, then,
One, two, three, and four,
We shall be merry within this hour.

MISTRESS MERRYTHOUGHT [*calling*] Why, Charles, do you not know your own natural wife? I say, open the door, and turn me out° those mangy companions! 'Tis more than time that they were fellow and fellowlike with you.[1] You are a gentleman, Charles, and an old man, and father of two children; and I myself, though I say it, by my mother's side niece to a worshipful° gentleman and a conductor°—he has been three times in His Majesty's service at Chester,° and is now the fourth time, God bless him and his charge,° upon his journey.

throw out on my behalf
honorable / captain
(en route to Ireland)
his soldiers

MERRYTHOUGHT [*singing at the window*]

Go from my window, love, go;
Go from my window, my dear.
The wind and the rain
Will drive you back again;
You cannot be lodgèd here.

Hark you, Mistress Merrythought, you that walk upon adventures° and forsake your husband because he sings with never a penny in his purse: what, shall I think myself the worse? Faith, no, I'll be merry. You come not here. Here's none but lads of mettle, lives of a hundred years and upwards.[2] Care never drunk° their bloods, nor want made 'em warble, [*singing*]

wander about
shriveled up

Heigh-ho, my heart is heavy!

3.5. In front of Merrythought's house.
1. I.e., They've been your boon companions for far too long.
2. Lads who seem young forever.

[*He leaves the window.*]

MISTRESS MERRYTHOUGHT Why, Master Merrythought, what am I that you should laugh me to scorn thus abruptly? Am I not your fellow feeler,° as we may say, in all our miseries? Your comforter in health and sickness? Have I not brought you children? Are they not like you, Charles? Look upon thine own image, hard-hearted man! And yet, for all this— *of fellow feeling*

MERRYTHOUGHT ([*singing*] *within*)

Begone, begone, my Juggy,° my puggy,° *Joanie / pet*
Begone, my love, my dear.
The weather is warm,
'Twill do thee no harm,
Thou canst not be lodgèd here.

[*To his companions*] Be merry, boys! Some light music, and more wine!

WIFE He's not in earnest, I hope, George, is he?

CITIZEN What if he be, sweetheart?

WIFE Marry, if he be, George, I'll make bold to tell him he's an ingrant° old man to use his bedfellow so scurvily. *ignorant; ungrateful*

CITIZEN What! How does he use her, honey?

WIFE Marry, come up,° Sir Saucebox! I think you'll take his part, will you not? Lord, how hot you are grown! You are a fine man, an you had a fine dog;[3] it becomes you sweetly. *i.e., come off it*

CITIZEN Nay, prithee, Nell, chide not, for, as I am an honest man and a true Christian grocer, I do not like his doings.

WIFE I cry you mercy,° then, George. You know we are all frail and full of infirmities. [*Calling*] D'ye hear, Master Merrythought? May I crave a word with you? *beg your pardon*

MERRYTHOUGHT (*within*) Strike up lively, lads!

WIFE [*calling to him*] I had not thought, in truth, Master Merrythought, that a man of your age and discretion (as I may say), being a gentleman, and therefore known by your gentle conditions,° could have used so little respect to the weakness of his wife; for your wife is your own flesh, the staff of your age, your yokefellow, with whose help you draw through the mire of this transitory world. Nay, she's your own rib.° And again— *qualities; station* *(see Genesis 2.21–24)*

MERRYTHOUGHT [*singing within*]° *(perhaps at a window)*

I come not hither for thee to teach;
I have no pulpit for thee to preach;
I would thou hadst kissed me under the breech,° *kissed my ass*
As thou art a lady gay.

WIFE [*calling to Merrythought*] Marry, with a vengeance! I am heartily sorry for the poor gentlewoman, but if I were thy wife, i'faith, graybeard, i'faith—

CITIZEN I prithee, sweet honeysuckle, be content.

WIFE Give me such words, that am a gentlewoman born! Hang him, hoary rascal! Get me some drink, George. I am almost molten with fretting. Now, beshrew his knave's heart for it! [*The Citizen goes to find something to drink.*]

3. You don't cut quite as fine a figure as you think.

MERRYTHOUGHT [*within, to the musicians*] Play me a light lavolto!° [*To his guests*] Come, be frolic. [*To servants*] Fill the good fellows wine! *a lively dance*

MISTRESS MERRYTHOUGHT [*calling*] Why, Master Merrythought, are you disposed to make me wait here? You'll open, I hope. I'll fetch them that shall open else.

MERRYTHOUGHT [*within*]° Good woman, if you will sing, I'll give you something; if not— *(perhaps at a window)*

SONG

You are no love for me, Marg'ret,
I am no love for you.
[*To his guests*] Come aloft, boys, aloft!

MISTRESS MERRYTHOUGHT [*calling*] Now a churl's fart in your teeth, sir!—Come, Mick, we'll not trouble him; 'a shall not ding° us i'th'teeth with his bread and his broth,[4] that he shall not! Come, boy. I'll provide for thee, I warrant thee. We'll go to Master Venturewell's, the merchant. I'll get his letter to mine host of the Bell in Waltham; there I'll place° thee with the tapster. Will not that do well for thee, Mick? And let me alone for° that old, cuckoldly knave, your father. I'll use him in his kind,° I warrant ye. [*Exeunt.*] *knock* / *apprentice* / *let me deal with* / *as he deserves*

[Interlude 3]

[*The Citizen returns with the beer.*]

WIFE Come, George, where's the beer?

CITIZEN Here, love.

WIFE This old fornicating fellow will not out of my mind yet.—Gentlemen, I'll begin to you all, and I desire more of your acquaintance, with all my heart. [*She drinks.*] Fill the gentlemen some beer, George.

[*He provides some refreshment for the gentlemen onstage.*]

Music.

Finis actus tertii.° *End of act 3*

[*Enter*] *Boy* [*and*] *danceth.*

WIFE Look, George, the little boy's come again. Methinks he looks something like the Prince of Orange in his long stocking,[1] if he had a little harness° about his neck. George, I will have him dance "Fading."°—"Fading" is a fine jig, I'll assure you, gentlemen. [*To the Boy*] Begin, brother.—Now 'a capers, sweetheart.—Now a turn o'th'toe, and then tumble.° Cannot you tumble, youth? *armor* / *an Irish dance* / *somersault*

BOY No, indeed, forsooth.

WIFE Nor eat fire?

BOY Neither.

WIFE Why, then, I thank you heartily. [*Giving money*] There's twopence to buy you points[2] withal. [*Exit Boy.*]

4. I.e., I won't let him taunt us thus with our having to depend on him.

Interlude 3.

1. A portrait of Maurice of Nassau, Prince of Orange and son of William the Silent, in long stockings was well known.

2. Laces to secure breeches to the upper garment.

4.1

Enter Jasper [with a letter] and [a] Boy.

JASPER [*giving the letter*] There, boy, deliver this; but do it well.
Hast thou provided me four lusty° fellows, *strong*
Able to carry me? And art thou perfect° *thoroughly rehearsed*
In all thy business?
BOY Sir, you need not fear;
I have my lesson here and cannot miss it.
The men are ready for you, and what else
Pertains to this employment.
JASPER [*giving money*] There, my boy,
Take it, but buy no land.[1]
BOY Faith, sir, 'twere rare
To see so young a purchaser.[2] I fly,
And on my wings carry your destiny.
JASPER Go, and be happy!° *Exit [Boy].* *fortunate*
Now, my latest° hope, *last*
Forsake me not, but fling thy anchor out
And let it hold! Stand fixed, thou rolling stone,° *(the earth)*
Till I enjoy my dearest! Hear me, all
You powers that rule in men celestial![3] *Exit.*

WIFE Go thy ways. Thou art as crooked a sprig as ever grew in London. I warrant him he'll come to some naughty° end or other, for his looks say no less. Besides, his father (you know, George) is none of the best. You heard him take me up like a flirt-gill,° and sing bawdy songs upon me. But i'faith, if I live, George— [*naughty*: *wicked*; *flirt-gill*: *coquette*]

CITIZEN Let me alone,° sweetheart. I have a trick in my head shall lodge him in the Arches° for one year and make him sing *Peccavi*° ere I leave him, and yet he shall never know who hurt him neither. [*Let me alone*: *Leave it to me*; *Arches*: *an ecclesiastical court*; *Peccavi*: *I have sinned*]

WIFE Do, my good George, do.

[*Enter a Boy.*]

CITIZEN [*to the Boy*] What shall we have Rafe do now, boy?

BOY You shall have what you will, sir.

CITIZEN Why so, sir, go and fetch me him, then, and let the Sophy of Persia come and christen him° a child. [*christen him*: *serve as godparent to*]

BOY Believe me, sir, that will not do so well. 'Tis stale; it has been had before at the Red Bull.[4]

WIFE George, let Rafe travel over great hills, and let him be very weary, and come to the King of Cracovia's° house covered with velvet, and there let the King's daughter stand [*Cracovia's*: *Poland's*]

4.1. Location unspecified.

1. I.e., but don't spend it all at once. (Said sardonically, since the amount of money is small; with an allusion also to rapid turnovers in the ownership of land in the early seventeenth century, resulting in marked changes in the composition of the gentry class.)

2. The Boy answers in the wry spirit of Jasper's observation: It would be unusual for an apprentice like myself to be able to purchase land. "Purchaser" has the negative connotation of one who "feathers his nest," i.e., one who aims to acquire possessions.

3. Hear me, you heavenly powers that govern us humans.

4. A cock-and-bull play called *The Travels of Three English Brothers,* by John Day, William Rowley, and George Wilkins, had been acted at the Red Bull Theater in 1607. In it the Sophy, or Shah, of Persia stood as godfather to an illegitimate grandniece.

in her window, all in beaten° gold, combing her golden locks with a comb of ivory, and let her spy Rafe and fall in love with him, and come down to him and carry him into her father's house, and then let Rafe talk with her. *hammered*

CITIZEN Well said, Nell. It shall be so.—Boy, let's ha't done quickly.

BOY Sir, if you will imagine all this to be done already, you shall hear them talk together; but we cannot present a house covered with black velvet and a lady in beaten gold.

CITIZEN Sir boy, let's ha't as you can,° then. *as best you can*

BOY Besides, it will show ill-favoredly° to have a grocer's prentice to court a king's daughter. *look indecorous*

CITIZEN Will it so, sir? You are well read in histories:° I pray you, what was Sir Dagonet?[5] Was not he prentice to a grocer in London? Read the play of *The Four Prentices of London*, where they toss their pikes so.[6] I pray you fetch him in, sir, fetch him in. *plays and stories*

BOY It shall be done. [*To the audience*] It is not our fault, gentlemen. *Exit.*

WIFE Now we shall see fine doings, I warrant 'ee, George.—Oh, here they come. How prettily the King of Cracovia's daughter is dressed!

[4.2]

Enter Rafe and the Lady [*Pompiona*], *squire* [*Tim*], *and dwarf* [*George*].

CITIZEN Ay, Nell, it is the fashion of that country, I warrant 'ee.

LADY POMPIONA Welcome, Sir Knight, unto my father's court,
King of Moldavia,° unto me, Pompiona, *(in modern-day Romania)*
His daughter dear! But, sure, you do not like
Your entertainment,° that° will stay with us *welcome / you who*
No longer but a night.

RAFE Damsel right fair,
I am on many sad° adventures bound, *serious*
That call me forth into the wilderness.
Besides, my horse's back is something galled,° *somewhat chafed*
Which will enforce me ride a sober pace.
But many thanks, fair lady, be to you
For using errant knight with courtesy.

LADY POMPIONA But say, brave knight: what is your name and birth?

RAFE My name is Rafe. I am an Englishman,

5. The King's fool in Thomas Malory's *Le Morte d'Arthur*. The Citizen reproves the Boy for not knowing his history, but in fact the Citizen is relying on his knowledge of archery exhibits at Mile End (see 2.2.5–13 and notes 1 and 2 there) in which London citizens played the parts of the Knights of the Round Table. These shows were often lampooned for the sorts of things the Citizen especially admires, such as the playing of King Arthur's famous fool by a grocer's apprentice.

6. Thomas Heywood's play of about 1600, *The Four Prentices of London, with the Conquest of Jerusalem*, features (along with two others) a grocer's apprentice named Eustace and a goldsmith's apprentice named Guy who, though nobly born and eager to reclaim their earldoms, think it no scorn to practice trades in London. At one point these two toss and catch pikes as tests of strength.

4.2. The court of the King of Moldavia.

As true as steel, a hearty Englishman,
And prentice to a grocer in the Strand,° *a fashionable street*
By deed indent, of which I have one part.[1]
But Fortune calling me to follow arms,° *serve as a knight*
On me this holy order I did take
Of Burning Pestle, which in all men's eyes
I bear, confounding° ladies' enemies. *overthrowing*

LADY POMPIONA Oft have I heard of your brave countrymen,
And fertile soil, and store of wholesome food.
My father oft will tell me of a drink
In England found, and nippitato° called, *strong ale*
Which driveth all the sorrow from your hearts.

RAFE Lady, 'tis true; you need not lay your lips
To better nippitato than there is.

LADY POMPIONA And of a wild fowl he will often speak,
Which powdered°-beef-and-mustard callèd is; *salted*
For there have been great wars 'twixt us and you.
But truly, Rafe, it was not long of° me. *on account of*
Tell me then, Rafe, could you contented be
To wear a lady's favor° in your shield? *love token*

RAFE I am a knight of religious order,
And will not wear a favor of a lady's
That trusts in Antichrist and false traditions.

CITIZEN Well said, Rafe! Convert her if thou canst.

RAFE Besides, I have a lady of my own
In merry England, for whose virtuous sake
I took these arms, and Susan is her name—
A cobbler's maid in Milk Street, whom I vow
Ne'er to forsake whilst life and pestle last.

LADY POMPIONA Happy that cobbling° dame, whoe'er she be, *(punning on "bungling")*
That for her own, dear Rafe, hath gotten thee!
Unhappy I, that ne'er shall see the day
To see thee more, that bear'st my heart away!

RAFE Lady, farewell. I needs must take my leave.

LADY POMPIONA Hard-hearted Rafe, that ladies dost deceive!

CITIZEN Hark thee, Rafe, there's money for thee. [*He gives Rafe money.*] Give something in the King of Cracovia's house; be not beholding° to him. *beholden*

RAFE Lady, before I go, I must remember
Your father's officers, who, truth to tell,
Have been about me very diligent.
Hold up thy snowy hand, thou princely maid.
[*He gives her the money just received from the Citizen.*]
There's twelvepence for your father's chamberlain,
And another shilling for his cook—
For, by my troth, the goose was roasted well—
And twelvepence for your father's horse-keeper

1. An indenture was torn in two parts along an irregular line so that each partner to the deal could prove the validity of the document by matching the halves together.

For 'nointing my horse' back, and for his butter[2]
There is another shilling. To the maid
That washed my boot-hose,° there's an English groat,° *upper leggings / fourpence*
And twopence to the boy that wiped my boots.
And last, fair lady, there is for yourself
Threepence to buy you pins at Bumbo Fair.[3]

LADY POMPIONA Full many thanks, and I will keep them safe
Till all the heads° be off, for thy sake, Rafe. *pinheads*

RAFE Advance,° my squire and dwarf! I cannot stay. *Move on ahead*

LADY POMPIONA Thou kill'st my heart in parting thus away.
Exeunt.

WIFE I commend Rafe yet that he will not stoop to a Cracovian; there's properer° women in London than any are there, iwis.—But here comes Master Humphrey and his love again now, George. *handsomer*

CITIZEN Ay, cunny. Peace!

[4.3]

Enter merchant [Venturewell], Humphrey, Luce [weeping], and a Boy.

VENTUREWELL [*to Luce*] Go get you up.° I will not be entreated. *upstairs; standing*
And, gossip° mine, I'll keep you sure hereafter *gadabout*
From gadding out again with boys and unthrifts.° *spendthrifts*
Come, they are women's tears. I know your fashion.
[*To Boy*] Go, sirrah, lock her in, and keep the key
Safe as you love your life. *Exeunt Luce and Boy.*
Now, my son° Humphrey, *son-in-law*
You may both rest assurèd of my love
In this, and reap your own desire.

HUMPHREY I see this love you speak of, through your daughter,
Although the hole be little,[1] and hereafter
Will yield the like in all I may or can,
Fitting a Christian and a gentleman.

VENTUREWELL I do believe you, my good son, and thank you,
For 'twere an impudence to think you flattered.

HUMPHREY It were indeed. But shall I tell you why?
I have been beaten twice about the lie.° *for lying*

VENTUREWELL Well, son, no more of compliment.° My daughter *polite chitchat*
Is yours again; appoint the time and take her.
We'll have no stealing° for it. I myself *elopement; niggardliness*
And some few of our friends will see you married.

HUMPHREY I would you would, i'faith, for, be it known,
I ever was afraid to lie alone.

VENTUREWELL Some three days hence, then.

HUMPHREY Three days! Let me see:
'Tis somewhat of the most,° yet I agree, *rather too long*

2. Butter could be used as a liniment, but was also mixed into the horses' feed by unscrupulous hostlers so that the horses would eat less feed. (See 2.5.47 and note.)

3. Named for a rum drink sold at fairs.

4.3. Venturewell's shop.

1. I can catch only the merest glimpse of love in Luce's behavior toward me. ("Hole" glances bawdily at Luce's sexual anatomy.)

Because I mean, against° the appointed day, *in expectation of*
To visit all my friends in new array.

Enter Servant.

SERVANT Sir, there's a gentlewoman without° would speak with Your Worship. *outside*

VENTUREWELL What is she?

SERVANT Sir, I asked her not.

VENTUREWELL Bid her come in.

Enter Mistress Merrythought and Michael.

MISTRESS MERRYTHOUGHT Peace be to Your Worship! I come as a poor suitor to you, sir, in the behalf of this child.

VENTUREWELL Are you not wife to Merrythought?

MISTRESS MERRYTHOUGHT Yes, truly. Would I had ne'er seen his eyes! He has undone me and himself and his children, and there he lives at home, and sings and hoits° and revels among his drunken companions; but, I warrant you, where to get a penny to put bread in his mouth, he knows not. And therefore, if it like° Your Worship, I would entreat your letter to the honest host of the Bell in Waltham, that I may place my child under the protection of his tapster, in some settled course of life. *is noisily mirthful* *please*

VENTUREWELL I'm glad the heavens have heard my prayers.
Thy husband,
When I was ripe in sorrows, laughed at me.
Thy son, like an unthankful wretch, I having
Redeemed him from his fall and made him mine,
To show his love again, first stole my daughter,
Then wronged this gentleman,° and last of all *(Humphrey)*
Gave me that grief had° almost brought me down *which would have*
Unto my grave, had not a stronger hand° *i.e., divine aid*
Relieved my sorrows. Go, and weep as I did,
And be unpitied, for I here profess
An everlasting hate to all thy name.

MISTRESS MERRYTHOUGHT Will you so, sir? How say you by that?[2]—Come, Mick, let him keep his wind to cool his porridge. We'll go to thy nurse's, Mick; she knits silk stockings, boy, and we'll knit too, boy, and be beholding to none of them all. *Exeunt Michael and mother.*

Enter a Boy with a letter.° *(see 4.1.1)*

BOY Sir, I take it you are the master of this house.

VENTUREWELL How then, boy?

BOY Then to yourself, sir, comes this letter.

VENTUREWELL From whom, my pretty boy?

BOY From him that was your servant, but no more
Shall that name ever be, for he is dead.
Grief of your purchased anger[3] broke his heart.
I saw him die, and from his hand received
This paper with a charge to bring it hither.
Read it, and satisfy yourself in all.

2. How do you like that?

3. Your anger incurred by him. (See lines 70–72.)

LETTER

VENTUREWELL [*reading*] "Sir, that I have wronged your love I must confess, in which I have purchased° to myself, besides mine own undoing, the ill opinion of my friends. Let not your anger, good sir, outlive me, but suffer me to rest in peace with your forgiveness. Let my body—if a dying man may so much prevail with you—be brought to your daughter, that she may truly know my hot flames are now buried, and withal receive a testimony of the zeal I bore her virtue. Farewell forever, and be ever happy! Jasper." *acquired*
God's hand is great in this! I do forgive him;
Yet I am glad he's quiet, where I hope
He will not bite again.—Boy, bring the body,
And let him have his will, if that be all.
BOY 'Tis here without,° sir. *outside*
VENTUREWELL So, sir; if you please,
You may conduct it in. I do not fear it.
HUMPHREY I'll be your usher, boy, for, though I say it,
He owed me something once, and well did pay it. *Exeunt.*

Enter Luce alone.

LUCE If there be any punishment inflicted
Upon the miserable more than yet I feel,
Let it together° seize me, and at once *altogether*
Press down my soul! I cannot bear the pain
Of these delaying tortures.—Thou that art
The end of all and the sweet rest of all,
Come, come, O Death! Bring me to thy peace,
And blot out all the memory I nourish
Both of my father and my cruel friend!—
O wretched maid, still living to be wretched,
To be a say[4] to Fortune in her changes
And grow to number times° and woes together, *count passages of time*
How happy had I been, if, being born,
My grave had been my cradle!

Enter Servant.

SERVANT By your leave,
Young mistress, here's a boy hath brought a coffin.
What 'a would say, I know not; but your father
Charged me to give you notice. Here they come.

Enter [*with the Boy*] *two* [*or more*[5] *coffin-carriers*]
bearing a coffin, Jasper in it.

LUCE For me, I hope, 'tis come; and 'tis most welcome.
BOY Fair mistress, let me not add greater grief
To that great store you have already. Jasper—
That whilst he lived was yours, now dead
And here enclosed—commanded me to bring
His body hither, and to crave a tear
From those fair eyes (though he deserve not pity)

4. An assay, subject of testing.
5. At 4.1.2–3, Jasper bid the Boy to provide four carriers.

To deck° his funeral; for so he bid me — *bedeck, adorn*
Tell her for whom he died.

LUCE He shall have many.°— — *many tears*
Good friends, depart a little, whilst I take
My leave of this dead man, that once I loved.

Exeunt coffin-carrier[*s*] *and Boy* [*and Servant*].

Hold yet a little, life, and then I give thee
To thy first heavenly being.[6] O my friend!
Hast thou deceived me thus, and got before me?
I shall not long be after. But believe me,
Thou wert too cruel, Jasper, 'gainst thyself,
In punishing the fault I could have pardoned,
With so untimely death. Thou didst not wrong me,
But ever wert most kind, most true, most loving,
And I the most unkind, most false, most cruel.
Didst thou but ask a tear? I'll give thee all—
Even all my eyes can pour down, all my sighs
And all myself. Before thou goest from me
There are but sparing° rites; but if thy soul — *meager*
Be yet about this place, and can behold
And see what I prepare to deck thee with,
It shall go up, borne on the wings of peace,
And satisfied. First will I sing thy dirge,
Then kiss thy pale lips, and then die myself,
And fill one coffin and one grave together.

SONG

Come, you whose loves are dead,
And, whiles I sing,
Weep, and wring
Every hand, and every head
Bind with cypress and sad yew,
Ribbons black and candles blue,
For him that was of men most true.

Come with heavy moaning,
And on his grave
Let him have
Sacrifice of sighs and groaning.
Let him have fair flowers enow,° — *enough*
White and purple, green and yellow,
For him that was of men most true.

Thou sable cloth, sad cover of my joys,
I lift thee up, and thus I meet with death.

[*As she lifts the cloth, Jasper emerges from the coffin.*]

JASPER And thus you meet the living.

LUCE Save me, heaven!

JASPER Nay, do not fly me, fair; I am no spirit.
Look better on me. Do you know me yet?

LUCE O thou dear shadow° of my friend! — *departed spirit*

JASPER Dear substance,
I swear I am no shadow.[7] Feel my hand;

6. And then I give back my life to God.
7. Dear flesh and blood person, I swear I too am flesh and blood, no departed spirit.

It is the same it was. I am your Jasper,
Your Jasper that's yet living and yet loving.
Pardon my rash attempt, my foolish proof
I put in practice of your constancy;
For sooner should my sword have drunk my blood
And set my soul at liberty than drawn
The least drop from that body. For which boldness,
Doom me to anything: if death, I take it
And willingly.

LUCE [*kissing him*] This death I'll give you for it.
So, now I am satisfied: you are no spirit,
But my own truest, truest, truest friend.
Why do you come thus to me?

JASPER First, to see you,
Then to convey you hence.

LUCE It cannot be,
For I am locked up here, and watched at all hours,
That 'tis impossible for me to scape.

JASPER Nothing more possible. Within this coffin
Do you convey yourself. Let me alone;° *Leave it to me*
I have the wits of twenty men about me.
Only I crave the shelter of your closet° *private room*
A little, and then fear me not.° Creep in, *don't fret about me*
That they may presently convey you hence.
Fear nothing, dearest love. I'll be your second.° *supporter*
[*She gets in the coffin.*]
Lie close.° So. All goes well yet. [*Calling*] Boy! *hidden*

[*Enter Boy and coffin-carriers.*]

BOY At hand, sir.

JASPER Convey away the coffin, and be wary.

BOY 'Tis done already.° *i.e., as good as done*

JASPER Now must I go conjure.° *Exit.* *(see 5.1.4–34)*
[*The Boy and the coffin-carriers start to leave.*]

Enter merchant [*Venturewell*].

VENTUREWELL Boy! Boy!

BOY Your servant, sir.

VENTUREWELL Do me this kindness, boy—hold, here's a crown° [*tipping him*] —before thou bury the body of this fellow, carry it to his old merry father and salute him from me, and bid him sing. He hath cause. *gold coin*

BOY I will, sir.

VENTUREWELL And then bring me word what tune° he is in, and have another crown; but do it truly. I have fitted him a bargain, now, will vex him. *mood*

BOY God bless Your Worship's health, sir!

VENTUREWELL Farewell, boy.
Exeunt [*the Boy and the coffin-carriers in one direction, Venturewell in another*].

[4.4]

Enter Master Merrythought.

WIFE Ah, old Merrythought, art thou there again? Let's hear some of thy songs.

MERRYTHOUGHT [*singing*]
Who can sing a merrier note
Than he that cannot change a groat?

Not a denier° left, and yet my heart leaps. I do wonder yet, as old as I am, that any man will follow a trade, or serve, that may sing and laugh, and walk the streets. My wife and both my sons are I know not where; I have nothing left, nor know I how to come by meat° to supper; yet am I merry still, for I know I shall find it upon the table at six o'clock. Therefore, hang thought! [*He sings.*]

small coin

food

I would not be a servingman
To carry the cloak-bag still,
Nor would I be a falconer,
The greedy hawks to fill.
But I would be in a good house,
And have a good master too;
But I would eat and drink of the best,
And no work would I do.

This is it that keeps life and soul together: mirth. This is the philosophers' stone[1] that they write so much on, that keeps a man ever young.

Enter a Boy.

BOY Sir, they[2] say they know all your money is gone, and they will trust you for no more drink.

MERRYTHOUGHT Will they not? Let 'em choose! The best is, I have mirth at home, and need not send abroad for that. Let them keep their drink to themselves. [*He sings.*]

For Jillian of Berry, she dwells on a hill,
And she hath good beer and ale to sell,
And of good fellows she thinks no ill.
And thither will we go now, now, now, now,
And thither will we go now.

And when you have made a little stay,
You need not ask what is to pay,
But kiss your hostess and go your way.
And thither will we go now, now, now, now,
And thither will we go now.

Enter another Boy.

SECOND BOY Sir, I can get no bread for supper.

MERRYTHOUGHT Hang bread and supper! Let's preserve our mirth, and we shall never feel hunger, I'll warrant you. Let's have a catch. Boy, follow me; come.

4.4. Merrythought's house.

1. The alchemical quintessence, supposedly able to transmute all metals into gold and to provide its owner with perpetual youth.

2. I.e., the tavern people to whom Merrythought has sent for drink.

[*Merrythought and the two Boys*]
sing this catch [*together*].

Ho, ho, nobody at home!
Meat, nor drink, nor money ha' we none.
Fill the pot, Eedy,
Never more need I.

MERRYTHOUGHT So, boys, enough. Follow me! Let's change our place,° and we shall laugh afresh. *Exeunt.* *go somewhere else*

[Interlude 4]

WIFE Let him go, George; 'a shall not have any countenance° from us, nor a good word from any i'th'company, if I may strike stroke° in't. *acceptance* / *if I have my say*

CITIZEN No more 'a sha' not, love. But Nell, I will have Rafe do a very notable matter now, to the eternal honor and glory of all grocers. [*Calling*] Sirrah! You there, boy! Can none of you hear?

[*Enter Boy.*]

BOY Sir, your pleasure?

CITIZEN Let Rafe come out on May Day in the morning, and speak upon a conduit,° with all his scarves about him, and his feathers, and his rings, and his knacks.° *cistern, aqueduct* / *trinkets*

BOY Why, sir, you do not think of our plot. What will become of that, then?

CITIZEN Why, sir, I care not what become on't. I'll have him come out, or I'll fetch him out myself. I'll have something done in honor of the city. Besides, he hath been long enough upon adventures. Bring him out quickly, or, if I come in amongst you—

BOY Well, sir, he shall come out; but if our play miscarry, sir, you are like° to pay for't. *likely; liable*

CITIZEN Bring him away, then. *Exit Boy.*

WIFE This will be brave,° i'faith! George, shall not he dance the morris° too, for the credit of the Strand? *fine* / *a country-dance*

CITIZEN No, sweetheart, it will be too much for the boy.—Oh, there he is, Nell!

Enter Rafe [*dressed as the Lord of the May,*[1] *in scarfs, feathers, rings, etc., and with a gilded staff*].

He's reasonable well in reparel, but he has not rings enough.

RAFE London, to thee I do present° the merry month of May. *represent*
Let each true subject be content to hear me what I say;
For from the top of conduit head, as plainly may appear,
I will both tell my name to you and wherefore I came here.
My name is Rafe, by due descent though not ignoble I,
Yet far inferior to the flock of gracious grocery;[2]
And by the common counsel of my fellows in the Strand,

Interlude 4.

1. Also known as the May King; in the Middle Ages, the male counterpart of the May Queen, both of whom presided over the activities of May Day. They were usually chosen by the townspeople—the "common counsel" in line 33.

2. Lines 31–32 here are a parody of the opening speech by the ghost of Andrea in Thomas Kyd's *The Spanish Tragedy* (1.1.5–7).

With gilded staff and crossèd° scarf, the May Lord here I stand. *diagonal*
Rejoice, O English hearts, rejoice! Rejoice, O lovers dear!
Rejoice, O city, town, and country! Rejoice eke° every shire! *also*
For now the fragrant flowers do spring and sprout in seemly sort;
The little birds do sit and sing, the lambs do make fine sport.
And now the birchen tree doth bud, that makes the schoolboy cry;[3]
The morris rings, while hobbyhorse doth foot it featously.[4]
The lords and ladies, now abroad° for their disport and play, *outdoors*
Do kiss sometimes upon the grass, and sometimes in the hay.
Now butter with a leaf of sage is good to purge the blood;
Fly Venus and phlebotomy,[5] for they are neither good.
Now little fish on tender stone begin to cast their bellies,° *spawn*
And sluggish snails, that erst° were mute, do creep out of their shellies. *formerly*
The rumbling rivers now do warm, for little boys to paddle;
The sturdy steed now goes to grass, and up they hang his saddle.
The heavy hart, the bellowing buck, the rascal and the pricket[6]
Are now among the yeoman's pease, and leave the fearful thicket.[7]
And be like them, O you, I say, of this same noble town,
And lift aloft your velvet heads,[8] and, slipping off your gown,
With bells on legs, and napkins° clean unto your shoulders tied, *handkerchiefs*
With scarves and garters[9] as you please, and "Hey for our town!" cried,
March out and show your willing minds, by twenty and by twenty,
To Hoxton or to Newington, where ale and cakes are plenty.
And let it ne'er be said, for shame, that we, the youths of London,
Lay thrumming of° our caps at home, and left our custom undone. *decorating with tufts*
Up, then, I say, both young and old, both man and maid a-Maying,
With drums and guns that bounce° aloud, and merry tabor° playing! *bang* / *a small drum*
Which to prolong, God save our King, and send his country peace,
And root out treason from the land! And so, my friends, I cease.
[*Exit.*]

Finis actus 4.° *End of act 4*

5.1

Enter merchant [Venturewell], solus.° *alone*

VENTUREWELL I will have no great store of company at the wedding—a couple of neighbors and their wives—and we will have a capon in stewed broth, with marrow,° and a good piece of beef, stuck° with rosemary. *squash; bone marrow* / *seasoned (as with cloves)*

Enter Jasper, his face mealed.° *whitened with flour*

JASPER Forbear thy pains,° fond° man! It is too late. *efforts / foolish*
VENTUREWELL Heaven bless me! Jasper?

3. Birch rods were used to whip schoolboys.
4. Hobbyhorses, shaped out of wickerwork to resemble a horse, were fastened around the waists of morris dancers, who pranced and curveted nimbly ("featously") in circle dances ("morris rings") in May Day festivities.
5. Avoid sexual intercourse and bloodletting.
6. The young deer and the yearling buck.
7. And leave the thicket where the deer regularly seek shelter, to eat peas in the farmer's field. ("Pease" is the old singular form of the modern "pea.")
8. Heads with velvet caps, resembling new antlers (and unconsciously suggesting cuckolds' horns).
9. Bells, scarves, and garters were worn by morris dancers.
5.1. Venturewell's shop.

JASPER Ay, I am his ghost,
Whom thou hast injured for° his constant love. *as payment for*
Fond worldly wretch, who dost not understand
In death that true hearts cannot parted be!
First, know thy daughter is quite borne away
On wings of angels through the liquid air
To far out of thy reach, and never more
Shalt thou behold her face; but she and I
Will in another world enjoy our loves,
Where neither father's anger, poverty,
Nor any cross° that troubles earthly men *vexation*
Shall make us sever our united hearts.
And never shalt thou sit or be alone
In any place but I will visit thee
With ghastly looks, and put into thy mind
The great offenses which thou didst to me.
When thou art at thy table with thy friends,
Merry in heart and filled with swelling wine,
I'll come in midst of all thy pride and mirth,
Invisible to all men but thyself,
And whisper such a sad tale in thine ear
Shall make thee let the cup fall from thy hand
And stand as mute and pale as Death itself.
VENTUREWELL Forgive me, Jasper! Oh, what might I do,
Tell me, to satisfy thy troubled ghost?
JASPER There is no means; too late thou think'st of this.
VENTUREWELL But tell me what were best for me to do?
JASPER Repent thy deed, and satisfy° my father, *compensate*
And beat fond Humphrey out of thy doors. *Exit Jasper.*

Enter Humphrey.

WIFE Look, George, his very ghost would have folks beaten.

HUMPHREY Father, my bride is gone, fair Mistress Luce!
My soul's the fount of vengeance, mischief's sluice.[1]
VENTUREWELL Hence, fool, out of my sight with thy fond passion!° *foolish grief*
Thou hast undone me. [*He beats Humphrey.*]
HUMPHREY Hold, my father dear,
For Luce thy daughter's sake, that had no peer!
VENTUREWELL [*beating him again*] Thy father, fool? There's some blows more. Begone!—
Jasper, I hope thy ghost be well appeased
To see thy will performed. Now will I go
To satisfy thy father for thy wrongs.° *Exit.* *the wrongs done you*
HUMPHREY What shall I do? I have been beaten twice,
And Mistress Luce is gone. Help me, device!° *some plan*
Since my true love is gone, I never more,
Whilst I do live, upon the sky will pore,° *gaze*
But in the dark will wear out my shoe soles
In passion,° in Saint Faith's Church under Paul's.[2] *Exit.* *sorrow*

1. The channel of mischief. (With a pun on "mischief is loose.")

2. A parish church underneath the choir of Saint Paul's Cathedral.

WIFE George, call Rafe hither. If you love me, call Rafe hither. I have the bravest° thing for him to do, George! Prithee call him quickly. *(finest)*

CITIZEN [*calling*] Rafe! Why, Rafe, boy!

Enter Rafe.

RAFE Here, sir.

CITIZEN Come hither, Rafe. Come to thy mistress, boy.

WIFE Rafe, I would have thee call all the youths together in battle 'ray,° with drums, and guns, and flags, and march to Mile End° in pompous° fashion, and there exhort your soldiers to be merry and wise, and to keep their beards from burning,° Rafe; and then skirmish, and let your flags fly, and cry, "Kill, kill, kill!" My husband shall lend you his jerkin,° Rafe, and there's a scarf; for the rest, the house° shall furnish you, and we'll pay for't. Do it bravely, Rafe, and think before whom you perform and what person you represent. *(array; (see 2.2.6 n) / ceremonious; (from gunpowder); men's jacket; theater)*

RAFE I warrant you, mistress, if I do it not for the honor of the city and the credit of my master, let me never hope for freedom.[3]

WIFE 'Tis well spoken, i'faith. Go thy ways, thou art a spark° indeed. *(stylish youth)*

CITIZEN Rafe, Rafe, double your files bravely,[4] Rafe.

RAFE I warrant you, sir. *Exit Rafe.*

CITIZEN Let him look narrowly° to his service;° I shall take° him else. I was there myself a pikeman° once, in the hottest of the day, wench, had my feather shot sheer away, the fringe of my pike burned off with powder, my pate broken with a scouring stick,° and yet I thank God I am here. *(sharp / maneuvers; scold / pike-carrier; gun-barrel cleaner)*

Drum within.

WIFE Hark, George, the drums!

CITIZEN Ran tan, tan, tan, ran tan! Oh, wench, an thou hadst but seen little Ned of Aldgate, Drum° Ned, how he made it° roar again, and laid on like a tyrant, and then struck softly till the ward° came up, and then thundered again, and together we go! "Sa, sa, sa! Bounce!"° quoth the guns. "Courage, my hearts!" quoth the captains; "Saint George!" quoth the pikemen; and withal here they lay,° and there they lay. And yet for all this I am here, wench. *(Drummer / (the drum); detachment of troops; Bang!; (fallen in battle))*

WIFE Be thankful for it, George, for indeed 'tis wonderful.

[5.2]

Enter Rafe and his company with drums and colors.

RAFE March fair, my hearts! Lieutenant, beat the rear up.[1]—Ancient,° let your colors fly; but have a great care of the butchers' hooks at Whitechapel;° they have been the death of many a fair ancient.°—Open your files,[2] that I may take a view both of your persons and munition.—Sergeant, call a muster. *(Ensign-bearer; a London parish; ensign)*

3. Full membership in the Grocers' Guild, freeing him from his apprenticeship.
4. Execute your drill maneuvers smartly.
5.2. Mile End.
1. Beat the drum at the rear of the company, keeping the rear closed up.
2. Spread out your ranks of soldiers for inspection.

SERGEANT A stand!°—William Hammerton, pewterer!
Line up! Attention!

HAMMERTON [*stepping forward*] Here, Captain.

RAFE [*inspecting him*] A corselet° and a Spanish pike; 'tis well. Can you shake it with a terror?
body armor

HAMMERTON I hope so, Captain.

RAFE Charge upon me. [*Hammerton charges upon Rafe with his pike.*] 'Tis with the weakest.° Put more strength, William Hammerton, more strength!—As you were again.—Proceed, Sergeant.
extremely weak

SERGEANT George Greengoose, poulterer!°
poultry merchant

GREENGOOSE [*stepping forward*] Here!

RAFE Let me see your piece, neighbor Greengoose. [*He inspects Greengoose's firearm.*] When was she shot in?°
When was she fired?

GREENGOOSE An't like you,° Master Captain, I made a shot even now, partly to scour her, and partly for audacity.
If you please

RAFE It should seem so, certainly, for her breath is yet inflamed. Besides, there is a main° fault in the touchhole;[3] it runs and stinketh; and I tell you, moreover, and believe it: ten such touchholes would breed the pox[4] in the army. Get you a feather, neighbor, get you a feather, sweet oil, and paper,[5] and your piece may do well enough yet. Where's your powder?
serious

GREENGOOSE [*producing his gunpowder*] Here.

RAFE What, in a paper? As I am a soldier and a gentleman, it craves a martial court;° you ought to die for't. Where's your horn?° Answer me to that.
court-martial
powder horn

GREENGOOSE An't like you sir, I was oblivious.°
(He means "forgetful")

RAFE It likes me not you should be so; 'tis a shame for you, and a scandal to all our neighbors, being a man of worth and estimation, to leave your horn behind you. I am afraid 'twill breed example. But let me tell you no more on't.[6] [*To the others*] Stand, till I view you all. [*To the Third Soldier*] What's become o'th'nose[7] of your flask?°
powder horn

THIRD SOLDIER Indeed, la, Captain, 'twas blown away with powder.

RAFE Put on a new one at the city's charge.° [*To the Fourth Soldier*] Where's the stone[8] of this piece?
expense

FOURTH SOLDIER The drummer took it out to light tobacco.

RAFE 'Tis a fault, my friend; put it in again. You [*to the Third Soldier*] want° a nose, and you [*to the Fourth Soldier*] a stone.—Sergeant, take a note on't, for I mean to stop it in the pay. [*To them all*] Remove,° and march! [*They march.*] Soft and fair,° gentlemen, soft and fair. Double your files! As you were! Faces about!° Now, you with the sodden° face, keep in,° there!—Look to your match,[9] sirrah; it will be in your fellow's flask anon!—So; make a crescent now. Advance° your pikes! [*They conclude their close-order drill.*]
lack
Get a move on
Easy does it
About-face! / stewed
keep in line
Lift high

3. The hole where fire was applied to the powder. (This and many terms in this passage—"runs and stinketh," "piece," "nose," "powder," "stone," "tacklings"—have scatological double meanings, having to do with the anus, testicles, etc.)

4. I.e., would raise Cain. (With the suggestion too of spreading syphilis.)

5. Materials used to clean a weapon.

6. But don't let me have to tell you this again.

7. Mouth, neck. (Ruined noses were an effect of advanced syphilis, as at 3.4.79.3 above. "Powder" [lines 28 and 41] also suggests the treatment of syphilis.)

8. Firing flint. (Also suggesting the testicles.)

9. Flammable material used to ignite gunpowder.

Stand and give ear. Gentlemen, countrymen, friends, and my fellow soldiers, I have brought you this day from the shops of security[1] and the counters° of content to measure out, in these furious fields, honor by the ell° and prowess by the pound. Let it not, oh, let it not, I say, be told hereafter, the noble issue° of this city fainted!° But bear yourselves in this fair action like men—valiant men and free[2] men. Fear not the face of the enemy nor the noise of the guns, for, believe me, brethren, the rude rumbling of a brewer's cart is far more terrible, of which you have a daily experience. Neither let the stink of powder offend you, since a more valiant stink is nightly with you.[3] To a resolved° mind his home is everywhere. I speak not this to take away the hope of your return, for you shall see—I do not doubt it, and that very shortly—your loving wives again, and your sweet children, whose care doth bear you company in baskets.[4] Remember, then, whose cause you have in hand, and, like a sort° of trueborn scavengers, scour me this famous realm of enemies. I have no more to say but this: stand to your tacklings,° lads, and show to the world you can as well brandish a sword as shake an apron.° Saint George, and on, my hearts![5]

shop counters / *45 inches, a shop measure* / *sons / were afraid* / *resolute* / *company, band* / *stick to your guns* / *shopkeeper's apron*

OMNES° Saint George! Saint George! *Exeunt.* *All*

WIFE 'Twas well done, Rafe! I'll send thee a cold capon afield, and a bottle of March beer,° and, it may be, come myself to see thee. *strong beer*

CITIZEN Nell, the boy has deceived me much; I did not think it had been in him. He has performed such a matter, wench, that, if I live, next year I'll have him captain of the galley foist,[6] or I'll want my will.° *not get my way*

[5.3]

Enter old Merrythought.

MERRYTHOUGHT Yet, I thank God, I break° not a wrinkle more than I had. Not a stoup,° boys? Care, live with cats; I defy thee. My heart is as sound as an oak; and, though I want° drink to wet my whistle, I can sing. [*He sings.*]

show, form / *tankard of ale* / *lack*

Come no more there, boys, come no more there.
For we shall never, whilst we live, come any more there.

Enter a Boy with a coffin [*borne by the coffin-carriers*].

BOY God save you, sir.

MERRYTHOUGHT It's a brave° boy. Canst thou sing? *fine*

BOY Yes, sir, I can sing, but 'tis not so necessary at this time.

1. From your secure and confidence-inspiring shops.
2. (1) Men not in bondage or servitude; (2) men not subject to arbitrary or tyrannical governmental authority; (3) men enjoying full privileges as London citizens and guild members (see Induction, line 13 and note, and 3.4.86–87 and note).
3. I.e., the stink of unflushed sewers in the street. (With the suggestion of bowel elimination.)
4. Whose concern for you manifests itself in the baskets of food they have sent with you.
5. Rafe's rousing speech parodies *Henry V*, 3.1.1–34, and *Richard III*, 5.3.313 ff. See introduction.
6. A barge used on ceremonial civic occasions.
5.3. Merrythought's house.

MERRYTHOUGHT [*singing*]
Sing we and chant it,
Whilst love doth grant it.

BOY Sir, sir, if you knew what I have brought you, you would have little list° to sing. *desire*

MERRYTHOUGHT [*singing*]
Oh, the minion round,° *plainspoken wench*
Full long, long I have thee sought.
And now I have thee found,
And what hast thou here brought?

BOY A coffin, sir, and your dead son Jasper in it.
[*The Boy and the coffin-carriers withdraw.*]

MERRYTHOUGHT Dead? [*He sings.*]
Why, farewell he!
Thou wast a bonny boy,
And I did love thee.

Enter Jasper.

JASPER Then I pray you, sir, do so still.

MERRYTHOUGHT Jasper's ghost? [*He sings.*]
Thou art welcome from Stygian lake° so soon. *from the underworld*
Declare to me what wondrous things in Pluto's court are done.

JASPER By my troth, sir, I ne'er came° there. 'Tis too hot for me, sir. *went*

MERRYTHOUGHT A merry ghost, a very merry ghost!
[*He sings.*]
And where is your true love? Oh, where is yours?

JASPER Marry, look you, sir.
Heaves up the [*lid of the*] *coffin.* [*Luce emerges.*]

MERRYTHOUGHT Aha! Art thou good at that, i'faith?
[*Singing*] With hey, trixy, terlery-whiskin,
The world it runs on wheels.
When the young man's—° *hand's a-friskin (?)*
Up goes the maiden's heels.

Mistress Merrythought and Michael within.

MISTRESS MERRYTHOUGHT [*within*] What, Master Merrythought, will you not let 's in? What do you think shall become of us?

MERRYTHOUGHT What voice is that that calleth at our door?

MISTRESS MERRYTHOUGHT [*within*] You know me well enough. I am sure I have not been such a stranger to you.

MERRYTHOUGHT [*singing*]
And some they whistled, and some they sung,
"Hey, down, down!"
And some did loudly say,
Ever as the Lord Barnet's horn blew,
"Away, Musgrave, away!"

MISTRESS MERRYTHOUGHT [*within*] You will not have us starve here, will you, Master Merrythought?

JASPER Nay, good sir, be persuaded. She is my mother. If her offenses have been great against you, let your own love remember she is yours, and so forgive her.

LUCE Good Master Merrythought, let me entreat you. I will not be denied.

MISTRESS MERRYTHOUGHT [*within*] Why, Master Merrythought, will you be a vexed° thing still? *ill-tempered*

MERRYTHOUGHT Woman, I take you to my love again, but you shall sing before you enter. Therefore, dispatch your song, and so come in.

MISTRESS MERRYTHOUGHT [*within*] Well, you must have your will, when all's done. [*To her son*] Mick, what song canst thou sing, boy?

MICHAEL [*within*] I can sing none, forsooth, but "A Lady's Daughter of Paris" properly.

SONG

MISTRESS MERRYTHOUGHT [*and* MICHAEL *sing*]
"It was a lady's daughter," etc.

[*Merrythought opens the door. Enter Mistress Merrythought and Michael.*]

MERRYTHOUGHT Come, you're welcome home again.
[*He sings.*]
If such danger be in playing,° *flirtation*
And jest must to earnest turn,
You shall go no more a-Maying.

VENTUREWELL (*within*) Are you within, sir, Master Merrythought?

JASPER It is my master's voice! [*To his father*] Good sir, go hold him in talk whilst we convey ourselves into some inward room. [*Exeunt Jasper and Luce.*]

MERRYTHOUGHT [*calling to Venturewell*] What are you? Are you merry? You must be very merry if you enter.

VENTUREWELL [*within*] I am, sir.

MERRYTHOUGHT Sing, then.

VENTUREWELL Nay, good sir, open to me.

MERRYTHOUGHT Sing, I say, or, by the merry heart, you come not in.

VENTUREWELL Well sir, I'll sing. [*He sings.*]
Fortune my foe, etc.

[*Merrythought opens the door. Enter Venturewell.*]

MERRYTHOUGHT You are welcome, sir, you are welcome. You see your entertainment; pray you be merry.

VENTUREWELL Oh, Master Merrythought, I am come to ask you
Forgiveness for the wrongs I offered you
And your most virtuous son! They're infinite;
Yet my contrition shall be more than they.
I do confess my hardness broke his heart,
For which just heaven hath given me punishment
More than my age can carry. His wand'ring spirit,
Not yet at rest, pursues me everywhere,
Crying, "I'll haunt thee for thy cruelty."
My daughter, she is gone, I know not how,
Taken invisible, and whether living
Or in grave, 'tis yet uncertain to me.

Oh, Master Merrythought, these are the weights
Will sink me to my grave! Forgive me, sir.

MERRYTHOUGHT Why, sir, I do forgive you; and be merry.
And if the wag in's lifetime played the knave,
Can you forgive him too?

VENTUREWELL With all my heart, sir.

MERRYTHOUGHT Speak it again, and heartily.

VENTUREWELL I do, sir.
Now, by my soul, I do.

MERRYTHOUGHT [*singing*]
With that came out his paramour;
She was as white as the lily flower.
Hey troll, trolly, lolly!

Enter Luce and Jasper.

With that came out her own dear knight;
He was as true as ever did fight, etc.
Sir, if you will forgive 'em, clap° their hands together. There's no more to be said i'th'matter. *join*

VENTUREWELL I do, I do. [*All embrace.*]

CITIZEN I do not like this. Peace, boys! Hear me, one of you: everybody's part is come to an end but Rafe's, and he's left out.

BOY 'Tis long of° yourself, sir. We have nothing to do with his part. *on account of*

CITIZEN [*calling offstage*] Rafe, come away! [*To the acting company*] Make on him° as you have done of° the rest, boys. Come! *Do with him / with*

WIFE Now, good husband, let him come out and die.

CITIZEN He shall, Nell. [*Calling*] Rafe, come away quickly and die, boy.

BOY 'Twill be very unfit he should die, sir, upon no occasion,° and in a comedy too. *without cause*

CITIZEN Take you no care for that, sir boy. Is not his part at an end, think you, when he's dead? [*Calling*] Come away, Rafe!

Enter Rafe, with a forked° arrow through his head. *barbed*

RAFE When I was mortal, this my costive° corpse[1] *reluctant; constipated*
Did lap up figs and raisins° in the Strand, *laxative fruits*
Where, sitting, I espied a lovely dame,
Whose master wrought with lingel° and with awl, *waxed thread*
And under ground he vampied many a boot.[2]
Straight did her love prick forth me,° tender sprig, *urge me forth*
To follow feats of arms in warlike wise
Through Waltham Desert, where I did perform
Many achievements, and did lay on ground
Huge Barbaroso, that insulting° giant, *vaunting*
And all his captives soon set at liberty.
Then honor pricked me from my native soil
Into Moldavia, where I gained the love

1. Rafe's final speech parodies ghost scenes in *The Spanish Tragedy*, *Richard III*, and *Eastward Ho!*

2. In his basement shop, this shoemaker supplied new uppers for many a boot.

Of Pompiona, his° belovèd daughter, *(the King's)*
But yet proved constant to the black-thumbed maid,
Susan, and scorned Pompiona's love.
Yet liberal I was, and gave her pins,
And money for her father's officers.
I then returnèd home, and thrust myself
In action, and by all men chosen was
Lord of the May, where I did flourish it,[3]
With scarves and rings, and posy° in my hand. *bouquet*
After this action I preferrèd° was, *promoted*
And chosen city captain at Mile End,
With hat and feather, and with leading staff,° *staff of office*
And trained my men, and brought them all off clear,° *unharmed*
Save one man that berayed him° with the noise. *befouled himself*
But all these things I, Rafe, did undertake
Only for my belovèd Susan's sake.
Then coming home, and sitting in my shop
With apron blue,° Death came unto my stall *(the tradesman's color)*
To cheapen aqua vitae;° but ere I *bargain for brandy*
Could take the bottle down and fill a taste,
Death caught a pound of pepper in his hand,
And sprinkled all my face and body o'er,
And in an instant vanishèd away.

CITIZEN 'Tis a pretty fiction, i'faith.

RAFE Then took I up my bow and shaft in hand
And walked into Moorfields° to cool myself. *(north of London)*
But there grim cruel Death met me again,
And shot this forkèd arrow through my head,
And now I faint. Therefore be warned by me,
My fellows every one, of forkèd heads.° *cuckolds' horns*
Farewell, all you good boys in merry London!
Ne'er shall we more upon Shrove Tuesday[4] meet,
And pluck down houses of iniquity.°— *prostitution*
My pain increaseth.—I shall never more
Hold open, whilst another pumps both legs,[5]
Nor daub° a satin gown with rotten eggs. *bespatter*
Set up a stake,[6] oh, never more I shall!
I die. Fly, fly my soul to Grocers' Hall!
Oh, oh, oh, etc.

WIFE Well said, Rafe! Do your obeisance° to the gentlemen, and go your ways. Well said, Rafe! *Exit Rafe.* *bow*

MERRYTHOUGHT [*to his assembled friends*] Methinks all we, thus kindly and unexpectedly reconciled, should not depart without a song.

VENTUREWELL A good motion.° *proposal*

MERRYTHOUGHT Strike up, then!

3. Where I moved about with a flourish, boasting triumphantly.
4. A traditional day of revelry (and riot) for the London apprentices.
5. I.e., plays at leapfrog or a similar game.
6. I.e., Tie up young roosters to stakes as targets.

SONG

Better music ne'er was known
Than a choir of hearts in one.
Let each other° that hath been *everyone*
Troubled with the gall or spleen
Learn of us to keep his brow
Smooth and plain as ours are now.
Sing, though before the hour of dying;
He° shall rise, and then be crying, *(Each person)*
"Heigh ho, 'tis naught but mirth
That keeps the body from the earth!"° *from burial*

Exeunt omnes.

Epilogus° *(Latin for "Epilogue")*

CITIZEN Come, Nell, shall we go? The play's done.

WIFE Nay, by my faith, George, I have more manners than so. I'll speak to these gentlemen first.—I thank you all, gentlemen, for your patience and countenance to° Rafe, a poor fatherless child; and, if I might see you at my house, it should go hard but[1] I would have a pottle° of wine and a pipe of tobacco for you; for truly I hope you do like the youth, but I would be glad to know the truth. I refer it to your own discretions, whether you will applaud him or no, for I will wink,° and whilst° you shall do what you will. I thank you with all my heart. God give you good night!—Come, George. [*Exeunt.*]

moral support of / *two-quart measure* / *shut my eyes / meantime*

FINIS.

Epilogus.
1. I.e., you can rest assured that.

TEXTUAL NOTES

The Knight of the Burning Pestle was first published in quarto in 1613, without having been previously entered in the Stationers' Register. This quarto serves as the primary authority for the present edition. A second quarto did not appear until 1635, long after Beaumont's death in 1616. A third quarto was printed after 1650, and the play was subsequently included in the second folio edition of the plays of Beaumont and Fletcher (1679). Substantive departures from the first quarto are noted here, using the following abbreviations:

Q1: Quarto of 1613 (London: Walter Burre)
Q1 corr.: The corrected 1613 quarto
Q1 uncorr.: The uncorrected 1613 quarto
Q2: Quarto of 1635 (London: John Spencer)
Q3: Quarto dated 1635 but printed after 1650
F2: The second folio edition of the plays of Beaumont and Fletcher (London: Martyn and Herringman, 1679)
ed.: A modern editor's emendation

Dedication 18–19 welcome . . . all have [Q1 corr.] *welcome, both father and foster-father, nurse and child, have* [Q1 uncorr.]
Prologue 1–20 [Q2; not in Q1] **10 as** [Lyly's *Sappho and Phao*; see Prologue, note 1] as a [Q2]
The Speakers' Names 1–28 [Q2; not in Q1] **18 Three** [ed.] Two [Q2, followed, on next line, by *A Captaine*]
Induction 1 PROLOGUE [ed.; not in Q1]
1.1.42 [and elsewhere] **travail** [Q1: trauell] **62 'em** [Q2] am [Q1]
1.2.22 looks, and perts [Q1 corr.] looke how it pearts [Q1 uncorr.] **35 He's** [Q1: has] **39 SD** ***Enter Luce*** [placement, ed.; opposite 38 in Q1] **78 shoot** [ed.] sute [Q1] **89 you, if** [Q2] you, I if [Q1] **116** [and elsewhere] **venture** [Q1: venter] **126 SD** ***Exit Luce*** [placement, ed.; opposite 125 in Q1] **134 of 'em** [Q2] 'em [Q1]
1.3.9 struck [Q1: stroake] **18 Rosicleer** [ed.] *Rocicler* [Q1] **52 apron** [Q1: Aporne] **54 shield** [Q1: shiled] **75** [and elsewhere] **whither** [Q1: whether] **75 you** [Q2] your [Q1] **78 you** [Q2] your [Q1]
1.4.12.1 [placement, ed.; opposite 14 in Q1] **31 flay** [Q1: flea] **52 list** [Q1 corr.] lust [Q1 uncorr.] **91.1** [ed.; after 89 in Q1] **117 no matter** [Q2] now matter [Q1]
2.2.9 pitched field [F2: pitcht field] pitch-field [Q1] **22 brooch** [Q1: Bruch] **30** [and elsewhere] **la** [Q1: law] **34 strait** [Q1: streight] **44** [and elsewhere] **GEORGE** [ed.] *Dwarfe* [Q1] **57** [and elsewhere] **TIM** [ed.] *Squire* [Q1] **93 metal** [Q1: mettle] **97 embezzle** [Q1: embecell] **106 hear** [Q1: here]
2.4.30 get you [Q2] get [Q1] **39 thing** [ed.] Things [Q1] **96 thou** [Q2] thou thou [Q1] **99 of** [Q2] off [Q1] **103 off** [Q3] of [Q1]
2.5.39 hight [ed.] high [Q1] **39 Chamberlaino** [Q2] Chamberlino [Q1] **42 Tapstero** [ed.] *Tastero* [Q1] *Tapstro* [Q2] **58** [and elsewhere] **Losing** [Q1: Loosing]
2.6.2, 26 Luce's [Q1: *Lucies*] **3 errand** [ed.] errant [Q1]
2.7.11 catch [Q2] cath [Q1] **31 lungs** [Q3] longs [Q1] **60 wi' your** [ed.] wee yer [Q1] **70 cares** [Q2] cares cares [Q1] **77 enow . . . enow** [Q1: i'now . . . i'now]
Interlude 2 7 'em [ed.] him [Q1] **7 anon** [Q1: anan] **17 I would** [Q1: I'wood]
3.1.1 dear [Q3] deere deere [Q1] **5 this** [Q2] these [Q1] **17 wear** [Q2] were [Q1] **28.1 SONG** [Q1 corr.] *Sung.* [Q1 uncorr.] **42 anew** [ed.] *a new* [Q1] **100 smile** [Q1: mile]
3.2.18 true [Q2] truery true [Q1] **18 fair** [Q2] faire faire [Q1] **35 your** [Q1 corr.; not in Q1 uncorr.] **75 knight** [ed.] Knights [Q1] **104** [and elsewhere] **basin** [Q1: bason] **107 brings** [Q2] bings [Q1] **119 with** [Q2; not in Q1] **131 swoops** [Q2] soopes [Q1]
3.3.8 dispatched [Q2] dispatch [Q1] **23 SD** ***Exit Boy*** [placement, ed.; opposite 22 in Q1] **24 Faith** [Q1: feth]
3.4.17 Barbaroso's [ed.] *Barbarossa's* [Q1] **30 SD** [placement, ed.; opposite "Saint . . . me!" in 30 in Q1] **35 off still** [Q1: of still] **63 That** [Q2] That that [Q1] **63 him condign** [Q2] condigne [Q1] **70** [and elsewhere] **ribbons** [Q1: ribands] **100, 104, 126, 142 THIRD KNIGHT** [ed.] *Man.* [Q1] **120 hear** [Q1: here]
3.5.12 [and elsewhere] **halloo** [Q1: hollow] **22 he** [Q2] ha [Q1] **63 D'ye** [ed.] Dee [Q1]
4.1 [location of scene indicator, ed.; after Interlude 3 6.4 in Q1] **11 SD** ***Exit*** [placement, ed.; opposite 10 in Q1] **55 warrant 'ee** [Q1: warrant tee]
4.2.1–2 warrant 'ee [Q1: warrant tee] **17 Strand** [Q1: strond]
4.3.6 SD ***Exeunt*** [ed.] *Exit* [opposite 5 in Q1] **17 compliment** [Q1: complement] **36 He** [Q3] ha [Q1] **37 hoits** [Q1: hoights] **56–57 porridge** [Q1: Porrage] Pottage [Q3] **89 seize** [Q1: ceaze] **104 hope** [Q2] hop't [Q1] **110 deserve** [Q3] deseru'd [Q1] **122 wert** [ed.] wer't [Q1] **141 moaning** [ed.] *mourning* [Q1]

4.4.1 hear [Q1: here] **25 'em** [Q2] am [Q1] **36–37** [ed.] And thither, &c. [Q1] **41.2** ***sing this catch*** [ed.; preceded by extra space but printed as a continuation of Merrythought's speech in Q1]

Interlude 4 21 SD [placement, ed.; after 20 in Q1] **25.1** ***Enter Rafe*** [placement, ed.; after 26 in Q1] **52 off** [Q1: *of*] **56 Hoxton** [Q1: *Hogsdon*]

5.1.21 which [Q2] wich [Q1] **80 Aldgate** [Q1: Algate]

5.2.20 An't [ed.] And [Q1] **40 THIRD** [ed.] 1. [Q1] **44 FOURTH** [ed.] 2. [Q1] **63 cart** [ed.] Carre [Q1]

5.3.14 minion [ed.] Mimon [Q1] **110 'em** [Q3] ham [Q1] **111 said** [Q2] sad [Q1] **132 awl** [Q1: All] **144 Pompiona's** [Q1: *Pompianaes*] **150 posy** [Q1 corr.: Posie] poesie [Q1 uncorr.] **154 off** [Q1 corr.] of [Q1 uncorr.] **189 choir** [Q1: *quire*]

The Maid's Tragedy

The writing team of Francis Beaumont and John Fletcher is one of the most celebrated in English literature. Though Beaumont and Fletcher also worked independently, their names are paired for all time, like Gilbert and Sullivan or Rodgers and Hammerstein. Playwriting partnerships were common in Elizabethan and Jacobean England: Thomas Nashe, Thomas Dekker, Thomas Heywood, Thomas Middleton, Ben Jonson, George Chapman, and many others formed a number of temporary alliances. At the end of his writing career, Shakespeare collaborated with Fletcher, his successor as chief dramatist for the King's Men, in writing the lost play *Cardenio* (1612) and *The Two Noble Kinsmen* (1613), and very probably on *Henry VIII* (1613) as well. Shakespeare also had a hand in revising *Sir Thomas More* by Anthony Munday and others, and may have shared the work on several plays usually ascribed solely to him.

The Maid's Tragedy was probably written in 1610–11 and performed soon afterward at the Blackfriars Theater (an indoor theater for well-to-do, sophisticated spectators) by the King's Men. It also received the accolade of a commission for performance at court. Beaumont probably shaped its major themes and controlled the final copy; Fletcher seems to have contributed act 2, scene 2; act 4, scene 1; and act 5, scenes 1 and 2. These scenes excel in the kinds of theatrical sudden reversals and surprising character motivations for which Fletcher became famous.

Beaumont and Fletcher achieved their notable success as partners by creating a strikingly new kind of drama, one that was to become a staple of courtly drama throughout the rest of the seventeenth century. Aimed at courtly and would-be courtly audiences, the plays presented novel, dramatically surprising situations based on the conflict of ideologies in courtly settings. Eschewing conventional narrative sources such as those provided by Plutarch, Holinshed, and Italianate short fiction, as well as the sensational real-life stories favored by John Webster, Beaumont and Fletcher turned to romances—Philip Sidney's *Arcadia* and familiar works by Torquato Tasso, Lodovico Ariosto, Jorge de Montemayor, John Lyly, Thomas Lodge, Robert Greene, Anthony Munday, and others—for inspiration. Deriving their fictional worlds and narrative techniques from those romances, Beaumont and Fletcher wrote plays governed by refined sentiment and chivalric loyalties; dramatic suspense in their plays centers on the conflicts that arise from the characters' attempts to follow incompatible chivalric ideals. With this focus, these two dramatists continually find new ways to surprise and delight the audience with a sophisticated kind of metatheatrical self-awareness of the artifice of their theater.

The chief premise of *The Maid's Tragedy* is that an absolute monarch has charged one of his chief courtiers, Amintor, to marry not the bride of his choice, Aspatia, but another of the King's choosing, Evadne. His reasons for this demand are soon apparent: the King (known in the play only by this title) is having an affair with Evadne and insists on a suitably aristocratic marriage for her to provide a cover for their continued affair. The thorny consequences of this assertion of royal will impinge heavily not only

Introduction, glosses, footnotes, and textual notes by David Bevington; text edited by David Bevington and checked by Eric Rasmussen.

on the bridegroom, the bride, and the rejected bride-to-have-been but on Aspatia's garrulous old father, Calianax; on Evadne's brothers, Melantius and Diphilus; and on the King's brother, Lysippus. All these figures find themselves in conflict at one time or other as to how, and to what extent, they ought to countenance the abuses of royal power. Should such a king be obeyed and abetted? A strong commitment to the ideology of royal absolutism repeatedly puts the persons of the play face-to-face with what appear to be impossible choices.

No less central to the play's focus on conflicting loyalties inherent in the values of chivalry is the fact that Melantius and Amintor are devoted friends. As a soldier just returned from campaigning in the field to discover that his sister is newly married to Amintor, Melantius is caught in a bind. He wishes all joy in marriage to his friend, whom he admires for his valor, temperance, chivalric idealism, and readiness to sacrifice his life in the name of friendship if necessary. At the same time, Melantius admires the beauty and wit of the rejected Aspatia and is sorry to learn of her plight. Aspatia's unhappy situation exacerbates a quarrel between Melantius and her father, Calianax. Melantius is only the first of several characters to find himself in a situation of torn loyalties and conflicting chivalric ideals.

Overwhelming all other problems for the courtiers is the King's absolute power and his abuse of it. "The breath of kings is like the breath of gods," declares the King's brother, Lysippus (1.1.16), and no courtier dares openly disagree, not even when the King is discovered to be the ruin of his subjects' personal lives. This universal acknowledgment of an absolutist ideology is not the product of dictatorial power. The King in this play employs no dungeons or threats of violence; he need not do so, for his courtiers consider that his will may be questioned only under the most extreme circumstances, and then only by secret conspiracy. The donnée of the play is that the King is to have Evadne if he wants her. She chooses not to resist this high demand, and though her husband and brothers do eventually resist the King's abuse of power, they do so only with a considerable agony of spirit. They must configure their constantly changing relationships around the immutable and axiomatic condition that kings belong to a different moral sphere, one otherwise inhabited only by the gods. Even when circumstances demand the virtually unthinkable alternative of acting against the King, the impiety of such a move has lasting consequences. The tragic action finally turns against the protagonists themselves as much as against the King who has wronged them.

The tyranny of the King is entirely a matter of his immoral sexual conduct. He is not guilty of unjust taxation or abuse of military power, nor is he subjected to the paranoid suspicion of those he rules. His court is seemingly free of corruption, unlike so many Italianate courts in Jacobean tragedy. In the play's never-never land called Rhodes, an imagined place bearing little resemblance to the real-life Mediterranean island of that name, Beaumont and Fletcher construct an idealized court where the courtiers aspire to chivalric ideals even as they confront adultery, seduction, and betrayal. Lacking the grand motives and human flaws one finds in the imagined worlds of Marlowe, Shakespeare, or Webster, *The Maid's Tragedy* is less interested in exploring human psychology than in engaging aristocratic audiences in plot twists and dramatic surprises. Audiences could count on the absolute power of the monarch being affirmed in the end, even if the last lines of the play do offer a conventional moral pronouncement against royal lust.

Consider, for example, Amintor's plight. His first ethical difficulty is the unpleasantness of having to jilt Aspatia. His excuse, of course, is that he has been commanded to do so by the King, and the absoluteness of that royal command appears to leave him no alternative. Yet to act this way toward a guiltless and noble lady is to behave not as a gentleman should. As is typical in this play, his dilemma is not couched in terms of personal feeling. Whereas Juliet, deeply in love with Romeo, will have nothing to do with an arranged marriage with Paris, we do not know in *The Maid's Tragedy* if Amintor feels similarly torn by the anguish of true desire. He is regretfully aware that "I did that lady wrong" (2.1.127), meaning Aspatia, but his discomfiture is a matter of his having behaved less than honorably, not because he cannot bear to lose her. He is as ready for a night of pleasure with Evadne as he presumably was before with Aspatia.

Amintor fatally wounds Aspatia, who is dressed "*in man's apparel*" as the supposed brother of Aspatia; see 5.3.0.1 ff. From the title page of the first quarto (1619) and appearing also on the title page of the second quarto (1622).

Amintor's problem is not that he is forced into a loveless marriage but that his bride refuses to go to bed with him on their marriage night. This surprising development leads to a litany of dirty jokes. Although this marriage is the beginning of the play's tragic action, it is presented at first with a kind of comic irreverence. Courtiers and attendants alike tease Amintor and his bride Evadne in the traditional way of wedding celebrations, with bawdy jest upon bawdy jest. Evadne's attendant ladies, helping her to dress for bed in act 2, scene 1, speak of "naked" wars and recommend that she leave some of her undressing to her presumably eager bridegroom. These circumstances set up, then, what is in some ways a comic bedroom scene with Evadne. The bridegroom is delighted with her physical charms and eager for consummation. When he learns to his astonishment that she has sworn that she will not go to bed with him, he assumes at first that "this is but the coyness of a bride" (2.1.159). Upon her insistence that she has serious reasons for her oath, he moves at once to the next gentlemanly assumption: that some man has compromised her, requiring that he act according to the code of gentlemanly honor. "Who has done thee wrong?" he questions Evadne. "Name me the man, and by thyself I swear, / Thy yet unconquered self, I will revenge thee" (2.1.170–72). His vow to kill the man she hates leads to the next surprise: Evadne declares that she hates Amintor, and bids him kill himself (2.1.183–84).

Her reasons for hating him are again not psychologically what we expect: she means simply that he is an obstacle to the fulfillment of an obligation she cannot explain to him. She would rather lie down in "the beds of snakes" than with Amintor (2.1.209–12), but not because she finds him unattractive, and not because she is in love with the King. Rather, the dilemmas of love and honor have placed her in an untenable situation, to which she must respond according to the aristocratic code governing behavior in this play.

The situation is extraordinary. "Was ever such a marriage night as this?" Amintor marvels (2.1.242). He has done as the King has demanded and is now being denied the rights of a bridegroom without any explanation he can comprehend. He offers violence to overcome Evadne's presumed reticence only to be told by her that she does not lack sexual desire. What then can possibly be the explanation? There must be another man; if so, then Amintor's path lies clear: he must cut this man's body into little bits and scatter them "before the northern wind" (2.1.299–300).

He has not stopped to consider what he might do, however, if that sexual rival should turn out to be the one human being he feels he may not touch: the King. When Evadne informs him that she is the King's mistress, everything changes:

> Oh, thou hast named a word that wipes away
> All thoughts revengeful. In that sacred name,

"The King," there lies a terror. What frail man
Dares lift his hand against it? (2.1.307–10)

Amintor's response to this shattering news is entirely correct in terms of Renaissance political orthodoxy: he knows that he must let the gods themselves correct regal truancy if it is to be corrected at all. "Let the gods / Speak to him [the King] when they please; till when, let us / Suffer and wait," he says (2.1.310–12). This is the doctrine of passive obedience, setting forth the Tudor and Stuart monarchs' carefully considered defense against treasonous activity of any kind. The premise of monarchical rule depends on the absolute distinction of the monarch from all of his subjects, for if the subjects can challenge royal behavior or even think of replacing the royal figure, monarchy is no longer monarchy. The problem comes up again and again in the period, in many plays and other literary works, since many regal figures do behave reprehensibly. The conservative, palliative answer is to rely on religious doctrine: God will surely punish all malfeasance, including that of monarchs, in this life or the next. When mere humans intervene in God's providence, therefore, they commit sacrilege. Subjects may offer sharp advice, but they must leave the ultimate determination of justice in God's hands.

Beaumont and Fletcher avail themselves of this truism here and do so in a way that must have been pleasing to the courtly and royal set for which they chiefly wrote. The play appears equally interested in bolstering royal orthodoxy and creating dramatic surprise. Amintor finds himself in a classic dilemma of gentlemanly conduct. Confronted eventually by the King himself, Amintor feels obliged to accept his role as cuckold and surrender Evadne to the King's adulterous amorousness. All his gentlemanly instincts to protect the lady and his own honor in such a situation are thwarted by the royal imperative.

The situation places all three of the participants in this ménage à trois in an extraordinary position if judged by ordinary codes of moral behavior or even by the standards of other Jacobean plays. Evadne confesses that she has become the King's lover at least partly out of ambition, to be the consort of one so powerful, and warns that she would forsake him if he were supplanted by some other ruler (3.1.183–88), and yet she is an elegant and high-minded lady responsive to the noblest of chivalric ideas of womanhood. Amintor is a cuckold, but he is not the wittol, or complacent cuckold, of many a Jacobean city comedy (Allwit in *A Chaste Maid in Cheapside,* for example), eager to prosper by letting his wife sleep with some wealthy and influential man. The King is an adulterer, but not a deplorable and laughably inept lecher like the Duke in *The Revenger's Tragedy.* The characters of *The Maid's Tragedy* make their way through an increasingly intricate plot driven not by familiar human responses but by turns in the maze of action that are exploited by the dramatists for their very unpredictability.

For Amintor, upholding the pretense of being happily married is deeply painful. It turns out that he plays his charade so successfully, however, that the King flies into a jealous rage, in another of the play's nearly comic surprises. Evadne then is prompted to appease the King's jealousy by quarreling with Amintor in the King's presence and declaring her hatred for him to prove that she has not slept with Amintor after all. This move satisfies the King but makes Amintor's situation more untenable still, prompting him to consider the virtually unthinkable alternative of challenging the King to a duel. When he goes so far as to reach for his sword, however, he realizes the impossibility of such an act. "But there is / Divinity about you that strikes dead / My rising passions," he says to the King. "As you are my king, / I fall before you and present my sword / To cut mine own flesh, if it be your will" (3.1.251–55). The realization that he must continue to accede to the King's adultery with Evadne galls him, but the King is now satisfied that Evadne has not actually slept with her husband, and that, apparently, is what matters most to him.

Melantius, the soldierly brother of Evadne, also faces an interlocking set of ethical dilemmas. Amintor is now his brother-in-law and has long been his friend. Friendship is the stronger of the two claims, Melantius insists: "we are friends, / And that is nearer"

(3.1.43–44). Amintor is drawn, in turn, to one who has been his mentor and closest companion. Indeed, friendship is portrayed in *The Maid's Tragedy* with a genuineness of feeling denied to heterosexual attachments, marital obligations, or even family ties. Accordingly, Melantius is anxious to know what explanation there can be for Amintor's sadness and scornful mien. Friendship demands that they bare their souls to one another; can Amintor share his terrible secret? To do so is, of course, to betray the King's best interests, but the call of loyalty ultimately compels him to tell Melantius that Melantius' sister has "given her honor up" to the King to live "in whoredom with him" (3.2.126–27).

Melantius' response is perhaps as surprising as the news itself: he turns on Amintor for impugning his family name and demands satisfaction in a duel. A whirlwind of conflicts and about-faces ensues. Amintor refuses to draw but willingly offers to end his unhappy existence if Melantius will simply execute him. Melantius can do nothing so base and ignoble as to kill an undefended gentleman and accuses his friend of simple cowardice in his unwillingness to draw. This accusation elicits a readiness on Amintor's part to fight after all, and it is only because Melantius thereupon recalls to himself that "The name of friend is more than family / Or all the world besides" that bloodshed is avoided (3.2.169–70). This breathless sequence of surprising reversals is typical of the play's method. The changes are too rapid to be psychologically plausible; they are driven instead by courtly attitudes in conflict with one another and by the audience's presumed delight in kaleidoscopic reversals of plot.

The play's rapid movement from this point onward toward catastrophe accelerates the basic motif of incessant reversal. And in this catastrophe, the women must suffer most of all, since they are the passive objects of male infatuation and possessive desire even as they are also called on to uphold their culture's most cherished ideals of loyalty and honor. Melantius' readiness to defend his friend Amintor's honor at all costs prompts him to conceive a plot against the King. Evadne joins him in this conspiracy, even though in doing so she commits herself to a process that will end in her own death; she will choose to kill herself rather than outlive the disgrace of having committed adultery and regicide. Tortured by her brother's accusations to confess to him what he already knows, and newly penitent to her wronged husband, Evadne agrees to take the King's life in a bedchamber scene (5.1) that sensationally combines eroticism with bloodletting.

Evadne acts thus out of the noble if conflicting ideals that drive all the major characters. She attacks her royal lover, stabbing him with wounds that betoken the many wrongs he has done: "This for my lord Amintor, / This for my noble brother, and this stroke / For the most wronged of women" (5.1.110–12). The act is "treason" (5.1.126–28), of course, and subverts the play's earlier insistent enunciation of the principle of passive obedience to royal absolutism. Conflicting ideologies dominate the play without easily determining where our loyalties as observers should lie.

To a degree remarkable even in Jacobean tragedy, the major figures of this play take their own lives rather than falling victim to a revenge plot. Aspatia, longing for death, disguises herself as her own brother and challenges Amintor to a duel in which she, as a woman and unschooled in dueling, is sure to be fatally wounded. As is appropriate to such an exculpatory end, she does not die until she is reconciled with the man who unwillingly deserted her in marriage. Evadne dies an expiatory suicide, at peace with herself and with the husband she feels she has wronged. Amintor, heartbroken, follows these two women by killing himself. Melantius, successful in his rebellion against tyranny but ready to yield monarchical authority to the King's brother, Lysippus, attempts suicide; when restrained, he vows to starve himself to death. Thus the protagonists die nobly in an edifying spirit of loyalty, self-abnegation, contrition, and resignation to providential will. Monarchy is restored (necessarily so in order to forestall the mass rebellion hinted at in 5.2.60–61), even though the violent act of taking a king's life has been sympathetically portrayed in full view of the audience.

The Maid's Tragedy is thus a tragedy in the classical sense that its highborn figures are brought low by malignant fortune and die at the end. Moreover, the play observes the unities of place and time: the action, limited to Rhodes, moves continuously through events that could well be contained within twenty-four hours. The play's action is also unified. A charming masque gracing the first act is plainly justified in the main plot by the aristocratic wedding it serves to celebrate. The sometimes comic business involving the quarrel of Melantius with old Calianax is integrally related to Melantius' resistance to royal tyranny. Even the construction of a series of dramatic surprises and improbable situations has a plausible classical antecedent, if not a direct source, in the tragedies of Euripides.

At the same time, the play does not center on a single tragic protagonist. To ask who is the tragic hero or heroine of *The Maid's Tragedy* is to realize, despite the play's title and its seeming reference to Aspatia, that the play is no less concerned with the tragic dilemmas of Evadne, Amintor, Melantius, and perhaps also the King. The court itself is perhaps the most plausible tragic protagonist in that the outcome seems dictated (despite all the clever reversals and surprises) by the conflicts inherent in a society that idealizes its own neochivalric fantasies and attempts, however fitfully and unsuccessfully, to live by them.

FRANCIS BEAUMONT AND JOHN FLETCHER

The Maid's Tragedy

SPEAKERS

KING
LYSIPPUS, brother to the King
AMINTOR, a noble gentleman
EVADNE, wife to Amintor
MELANTIUS } brothers to Evadne
DIPHILUS }
ASPATIA, trothplight wife° to Amintor — *engaged to be married*
CALIANAX, an old humorous° lord and father to Aspatia — *temperamental*
CLEON } gentlemen
STRATO }
DIAGORAS, a servant
ANTIPHILA } waiting-gentlewomen to Aspatia
OLYMPIAS }
DULA, a lady [attending on Evadne]
[A MESSENGER
A GENTLEMAN attendant on the King
FIRST GENTLEMAN
SECOND GENTLEMAN
FIRST LADY attendant on Evadne
SERVANT to Amintor
A lady with Melantius
Ladies, lords, attendants, servants, guards]

NIGHT }
CYNTHIA° } — *moon goddess*
NEPTUNE° } — *god of the sea*
AEOLUS° } masquers — *god of the winds*
[Proteus° and other sea deities } — *shape-changing sea god*
Favonius and other winds }

THE SCENE: Rhodes.]

The 1622 title page reads "*The Maid's Tragedy.* As it hath been divers times acted at the Blackfriars by the King's Majesty's Servants. Newly perused, augmented, and enlarged, this second impression. London: Printed for Francis Constable and are to be sold at the White Lion in Paul's churchyard. 1622."

1.1

Enter Cleon, Strato, Lysippus, [*and*] *Diphilus.*

CLEON The rest° are making ready, sir. — *(The courtly masquers)*
STRATO So let them. There's time enough.
DIPHILUS You are the brother to the King, my lord;
We'll take your word.
LYSIPPUS Strato, thou hast some skill in poetry.
What think'st thou of a masque? Will it be well?
STRATO As well as masques can be.
LYSIPPUS As masques can be?
STRATO Yes. They must commend their king and speak
In praise of the assembly, bless the bride
And bridegroom in person of some god.
They're tied to rules of flattery.

Enter Melantius.

CLEON See, good my lord, who is returned!
LYSIPPUS Noble Melantius, the land
By me welcomes thy virtues home to Rhodes,
Thou that with blood° abroad buyest us our peace. — *shedding your blood*
The breath of kings is like the breath of gods;
My brother wished thee here, and thou art here.
He will be too kind, and weary thee
With often welcomes; but the time° doth give thee — *the wedding time*
A welcome above his or all the world's.
MELANTIUS My lord, my thanks; but these scratched limbs of mine
Have spoke my love and truth° unto my friends — *fidelity*
More than my tongue e'er could. My mind's the same
It ever was to you; where I find worth,
I love the keeper° till he let it go, — *possessor*
And then I follow it.[1]
DIPHILUS Hail, worthy brother!
He that rejoices not at your return
In safety is mine enemy forever.
MELANTIUS I thank thee, Diphilus. But thou art faulty:
I sent for thee to exercise thine arms° — *use your weapons*
With me at Patria;° thou cam'st not, Diphilus. — *Patras (in Greece)*
'Twas ill.
DIPHILUS My noble brother, my excuse
Is my king's strict command—[*to Lysippus*] which you, my lord,
Can witness with me.
LYSIPPUS 'Tis most true, Melantius.
He might not come till the solemnities
Of this great match° were past. — *(Amintor's wedding)*
DIPHILUS Have you heard of it?
MELANTIUS Yes, and I have given cause to those that here
Envy my deeds abroad to call me gamesome.° — *frivolous*
I have no other business here at Rhodes.

1.1. The palace at Rhodes.
1. I love the person who practices true worthiness until he ceases to do so, at which point I no longer cherish him but give up his company just as his worthiness has done.

LYSIPPUS We have a masque tonight, and you must tread
A soldier's measure.° *stately dance*
MELANTIUS These soft and silken wars are not for me.
The music° must be shrill and all confused *music of battle*
That stirs my blood, and then I dance with arms.
But is Amintor wed?
DIPHILUS This day.
MELANTIUS All joys upon him! For he is my friend.
Wonder not that I call a man so young my friend.
His worth is great; valiant he is, and temperate,
And one that never thinks his life his own
If his friend need it. When he was a boy,
As oft as I returned (as, without boast,
I brought home conquest) he would gaze upon me
And view me round, to find in what one limb
The virtue° lay to do those things he heard.° *strength / heard about*
Then would he wish to see my sword, and feel
The quickness° of the edge, and in his hand *keenness*
Weigh it. He oft would make me smile at this.
His youth did promise much, and his ripe years
Will see it all performed.—

Enter Aspatia, passing by [attended].

Hail, maid and wife!
Thou fair Aspatia, may the holy knot
That thou hast tied today last till the hand
Of age undo't! Mayst thou bring a race° *family*
Unto Amintor that may fill the world
Successively with soldiers!
ASPATIA My hard fortunes
Deserve not scorn, for I was never proud
When they were good. *Exit Aspatia [with attendants].*
MELANTIUS How's this?
LYSIPPUS You are mistaken,
For she is not married.
MELANTIUS You said Amintor was.
DIPHILUS 'Tis true, but—
MELANTIUS Pardon me, I did receive
Letters at Patria from my Amintor
That he should° marry her. *was to*
DIPHILUS And so it stood
In all opinion long; but your arrival
Made me imagine you had heard the change.
MELANTIUS Who has he taken, then?
LYSIPPUS A lady, sir,
That bears the light about her,[2] and strikes dead
With flashes of her eye: the fair Evadne,
Your virtuous sister.
MELANTIUS Peace of heart betwixt them!
But this is strange.
LYSIPPUS The King my brother did it
To honor you, and these solemnities

2. Who carries the light on her person (like the evening star or morning star, Venus).

Are at his charge.[3]
MELANTIUS 'Tis royal, like himself. But I am sad
My speech bears so infortunate a sound
To beautiful Aspatia. There is rage
Hid in her father's breast, Calianax,
Bent long against me, and 'a should not° think, *I wouldn't want him to*
If I could call it back, that I would take
So base revenges as to scorn the state
Of his neglected daughter. Holds he still
His greatness° with the King? *influence*
LYSIPPUS Yes. But this lady
Walks discontented, with her wat'ry eyes
Bent on the earth. The unfrequented woods
Are her delight; and, when she sees a bank
Stuck full of flowers, she with a sigh will tell
Her servants what a pretty place it were° *would be*
To bury lovers in, and make her maids
Pluck 'em and strow° her over like a corse.° *strew / corpse*
She carries with her an infectious grief
That strikes° all her beholders; she will sing *afflicts*
The mournful'st things that ever ear hath heard,
And sigh, and sing again; and when the rest
Of our young ladies, in their wanton blood,° *lively spirits*
Tell mirthful tales in course° that fill the room *in turn*
With laughter, she will with so sad a look
Bring forth a story of the silent death
Of some forsaken virgin, which her grief
Will put in such a phrase that, ere she end,
She'll send them weeping one by one away.
MELANTIUS She has a brother under my command
Like her—a face as womanish as hers,
But with a spirit that hath much outgrown
The number of his years.

Enter Amintor.

CLEON My lord the bridegroom!
MELANTIUS [*embracing Amintor*] I might run fiercely,° not more hastily, *more fiercely*
Upon my foe. I love thee well, Amintor;
My mouth is much too narrow for my heart.
I joy to look upon those eyes of thine;
Thou art my friend—but my disordered speech
Cuts off my love.
AMINTOR Thou art Melantius;
All love is spoke in that. A sacrifice° *Let's have a sacrifice*
To thank the gods Melantius is returned
In safety! Victory sits on his sword
As she was wont. May she build there and dwell,
And may thy armor be as it hath been,
Only thy valor and thine innocence![4]
What endless treasures would our enemies give

3. Are ordered by him and at his expense.
4. And may your valor and innocence be all the armor that you need, as has been true till now!

That I might hold thee still thus![5]
MELANTIUS I am poor
In words; but credit me, young man, thy mother
Could do no more but weep for joy[6] to see thee
After long absence. All the wounds I have
Fetched not so much away,° nor all the cries — *Didn't cause such tears*
Of widowèd mothers. But this is peace,
And that was war.
AMINTOR Pardon, thou holy god
Of marriage-bed,° and frown not I° am forced, — *Hymen / that I*
In answer of such noble tears as those,° — *those of Melantius*
To weep upon my wedding day!
MELANTIUS I fear thou art grown too fickle, for I hear
A lady mourns for thee, men say, to death,
Forsaken of thee—on what terms° I know not. — *in what circumstances*
AMINTOR She had my promise, but the King forbade it,
And made me make this worthy change, thy sister,
Accompanied with graces all about her,
With whom I long to lose° my lusty youth — *expend*
And grow old in her arms.
MELANTIUS Be prosperous!

Enter Messenger.

MESSENGER My lord, the masquers rage° for you. — *clamor*
LYSIPPUS We are gone.
CLEON, STRATO, *and* DIPHILUS We'll all attend you.
[*Exeunt Lysippus, Cleon, Strato, and Diphilus.*]
AMINTOR We shall trouble you
With our solemnities.° — *festivities*
MELANTIUS Not so, Amintor.
But if you laugh at my rude carriage° — *rough demeanor*
In peace, I'll do as much for you in war
When you come thither. But I have a mistress[7]
To bring to your delights, rough though I am.
I have a mistress, and she has a heart,
She says, but, trust me, it is stone, no better;
There is no place that I can challenge° in't. — *lay claim to*
But you stand still, and here my way lies.[8]
Exit [*one way, Amintor the other*].

[1.2]

Enter Calianax with Diagoras.

CALIANAX Diagoras, look to the doors better, for shame! You let in all the world, and anon° the King will rail at me. Why, very well said.° By Jove, the King will have the show i'th'court.° — *right away* / *well done* / *courtyard*

DIAGORAS Why do you swear so,[1] my lord? You know he'll have it here.° — *here in the hall*

5. What wouldn't the enemy give to have me hold you like this always, keeping you thus from battle!
6. Not even your mother could weep more joyfully.
7. The lady Melantius escorts to the masque at 1.2.29.1. He wryly characterizes her here in lines 150–52 as disdainful of him. He sees himself as a soldier, not a ladies' man.
8. But I am interrupting what you have to do, and I must be off in another direction.
1.2. A hall in the palace. Ladies may be visible in the gallery over the stage (see line 31).
1. Why do you swear that the King wants the masque to be in the courtyard?

CALIANAX By this light,° if he be wise, he will not.
(an oath)

DIAGORAS And if he will not be wise, you are forsworn.

CALIANAX One may swear his heart out, and get thanks on no side. I'll be gone; look to't° who will.
see to the arrangements

DIAGORAS My lord, I shall never° keep them out. Pray stay. Your looks will terrify them.
never be able to

CALIANAX My looks terrify them, you coxcombly° ass, you? I'll be judged by all the company° whether thou hast not a worse face than I.
foolish / *(including the audience)*

DIAGORAS I mean, because they know you and your office.°
official function

CALIANAX Office! I would I could put it off. I am sure I sweat quite through my office.[2] I might have made room° at my daughter's wedding; they ha' near° killed her amongst them. And now I must do service for him that hath forsaken her. Serve that will![3] *Exit Calianax.*
cleared a way as usher / *have nearly*

DIAGORAS He's so humorous° since his daughter was forsaken! *Knock within.* Hark, hark! There, there! So, so! Coads,° coads! What now?
crotchety / *(a mild oath)*

MELANTIUS (*within*) Open the door!

DIAGORAS Who's there?

MELANTIUS [*within*] Melantius.

DIAGORAS I hope Your Lordship brings no troop° with you, for if you do I must return° them. [*He opens the door.*]
company / *refuse entrance to*

Enter Melantius and a lady.

MELANTIUS None but this lady, sir.

DIAGORAS The ladies are all placed above,° save those that come in the King's troop; the best of Rhodes sit there, and there's room.°
(in the gallery) / *up there there's room*

MELANTIUS I thank you, sir. [*To the lady*] When I have seen you placed, madam, I must attend the King; but, the masque done, I'll wait on you° again.
attend to you

[*Exit Melantius and the lady at the other door*[4] *as Diagoras opens it for them.*]

DIAGORAS [*to those within*] Stand back there! Room for my lord Melantius! Pray bear° back. This is no place for such youths and their trulls.° Let the doors shut again. Ay, do your heads itch? I'll scratch them for you. [*He shuts the door.*] So, now thrust and hang.° [*More knocking*] Again? Who is't now? I cannot blame my lord Calianax for going away. Would he were here! He would run raging amongst them, and break° a dozen wiser heads than his own in the twinkling of an eye.—What's the news now?
move / *wenches* / *be hanged* / *strike*

A VOICE (*within*) I pray you, can you help me to the speech of° the master cook?
to speak with

DIAGORAS If I open the door, I'll cook some of your calves'° heads. Peace, rogues! [*Knocking within*] Again? Who is't?
fools'

MELANTIUS (*within*) Melantius.

Enter Calianax.

2. Calianax responds to Diagoras' "office" (line 16) as though he meant "gown."

3. Now I must officiate at the wedding of the very man (Amintor) who has deserted my daughter, Aspatia. Let whoever wants to serve at court do it!

4. Melantius and the lady have entered by one of two stage doors. They now exit through the other door as though to take their places for the entertainment.

CALIANAX Let him not in.
DIAGORAS Oh, my lord, 'a° must. [*To those within, as he opens the door*] Make room there for my lord! *he*

Enter Melantius.

Is your lady placed?
MELANTIUS Yes sir, I thank you.—
My lord Calianax, well met.
Your causeless hate to me, I hope, is buried.
CALIANAX Yes. I do service for your sister here,
That brings mine own poor child to timeless° death; *untimely*
She loves your friend Amintor, such another
False-hearted lord as you.
MELANTIUS You do me wrong,
A most unmanly one; and I am slow
In taking vengeance, but be well advised.° *take care*
CALIANAX It may be so. Who placed the lady there
So near the presence of the King?
MELANTIUS I did.
CALIANAX My lord, she must not sit there.
MELANTIUS Why?
CALIANAX The place is kept for women of more worth.° *social importance*
MELANTIUS More worth than she? It misbecomes your age
And place to be thus womanish.° Forbear! *i.e., petty*
What you have spoke I am content to think
The palsy shook your tongue to.
CALIANAX Why, 'tis well
If I stand here to place men's wenches.
MELANTIUS I
Shall forget this place, thy age, my safety,
And through all cut that poor sickly week
Thou hast to live away from thee.
CALIANAX Nay, I know you can fight for your whore.
MELANTIUS Bate me the King, and, be he flesh and blood,
'A lies that says it.[5] Thy mother at fifteen
Was black and sinful to° her. *compared with*
DIAGORAS Good my lord—
MELANTIUS Some god pluck threescore years from that fond° man, *foolish*
That I may kill him and not stain mine honor!
It is the curse of soldiers that in peace
They shall be braved° by such ignoble men *insulted*
As, if the land were troubled,° would with tears *attacked*
And knees beg succor from 'em. Would that blood,
That sea of blood that I have lost in fight,
Were running in thy veins, that it might make thee
Apt to say less, or able to maintain,° *back up your words*
Shouldst thou say more! This Rhodes, I see, is naught
But a place privileged to do men wrong.[6]
CALIANAX Ay, you may say your pleasure.° *say what you want*

Enter Amintor.

5. Setting aside the King, if any living person were to dare offer me an insult like the one you've just uttered, he should die at my hands.

6. As far as I can see, Rhodes is nothing but a place where men are privileged to insult other men with complete impunity.

AMINTOR What vile injury
Has stirred my worthy friend, who is as slow
To fight with words as he is quick of hand?
MELANTIUS That heap of age, which I should reverence
If it were temperate, but testy years
Are most contemptible.
AMINTOR Good sir, forbear.
CALIANAX There is just such another as yourself.° *You're two of a kind*
AMINTOR [*to Melantius*] He will wrong you, or me, or any man,
And talk as if he had no life to lose,
Since this our match.° The King is coming in; *wedding*
I would not for more wealth than I enjoy
He should perceive you raging. He did hear
You were at difference° now, which hastened him. *quarreling*
CALIANAX [*to those within*] Make room there!
Hautboys° *play within.* *Oboes*

Enter King, Evadne, Aspatia, lords, and ladies.

KING Melantius, thou art welcome, and my love
Is with thee still;° but this is not a place *always*
To brabble° in.—Calianax, join hands. *squabble*
CALIANAX He shall not have mine hand.
KING This is no time
To force you to't; I do love you both.
Calianax, you look well to your office,
And you, Melantius, are welcome home.—
Begin the masque.
MELANTIUS Sister, I joy to see you and your choice.
You looked with my eyes when you took that man;
Be happy in him. *Recorders* [*play within*].
EVADNE O my dearest brother!
Your presence is more joyful than this day
Can be unto me.

THE MASQUE

Night rises in mists.

NIGHT Our reign is come, for in the quenching sea
The Sun is drowned, and with him fell the Day.
Bright Cynthia,° hear my voice! I am the Night, *the Moon*
For whom thou bear'st about thy borrowed light.
Appear! No longer thy pale visage shroud,
But strike thy silver horns quite through a cloud,
And send a beam upon my swarthy face
By which I may discover all the place
And persons, and how many longing eyes
Are come to wait on our solemnities.

Enter Cynthia.

How dull and black am I! I could not find
This beauty[7] without thee, I am so blind.
Methinks they show like to those eastern streaks
That warn us hence before the morning breaks.

7. The beauty of the court ladies onstage who are watching the masque.

Back, my pale servant, for these eyes° know how *(of the court ladies)*
To shoot far more and quicker rays than thou.

CYNTHIA Great queen, they be a troop for whom alone
One of my clearest moons I have put on—
A troop that looks as if thyself and I
Had plucked our reins in and our whips laid by,[8]
To gaze upon these mortals that appear
Brighter than we.

NIGHT Then let us keep 'em here,
And nevermore our chariots drive away,
But hold our places and outshine the Day.

CYNTHIA Great queen of shadows, you are pleased to speak
Of more than may be done. We may not break
The gods' decrees, but, when our time is come,
Must drive away and give the Day our room.
Yet whilst our reign lasts, let us stretch our power
To give our servants° one contented hour, *(the stage audience)*
With such unwonted solemn grace and state
As may forever after force them hate
Our brother's° glorious beams, and wish° the Night, *(The Sun's) / wish for*
Crowned with a thousand stars and our cold light;
For almost all the world their service bend
To Phoebus,° and in vain my light I lend, *god of the sun*
Gazed on unto° my setting from my rise *until*
Almost of none but of unquiet° eyes. *restless, sleepless*

NIGHT Then shine at full, fair queen, and by thy power
Produce a birth,° to crown this happy hour, *i.e., Provide a show*
Of nymphs and shepherds. Let their songs discover,° *reveal, show*
Easy and sweet,° who is a happy lover; *Flowing and mellifluous*
Or, if thou woot,° then call thine own Endymion *wilt (will)*
From the sweet flow'ry bed he lies upon
On Latmos' top;[9] thy pale beams draw away,
And of his long night let him make this day.[1]

CYNTHIA Thou dream'st, dark queen. That fair boy was not mine,
Nor went I down to kiss him. Ease° and wine *Sloth*
Have bred these bold tales. Poets, when they rage,° *write in poetic furor*
Turn gods to men, and make an hour an age;
But I will give a greater state and glory,
And raise to time° a nobler memory *for all time*
Of what these lovers° are. [*Calling*] Rise, rise, I say, *true lovers*
Thou power of deeps,° thy surges laid away, *the deep, the ocean*
Neptune, great king of waters, and by me
Be proud to be commanded!

Neptune rises.

NEPTUNE Cynthia, see,
Thy word hath fetched me hither. Let me know
Why I ascend.

CYNTHIA Doth this majestic show° *(of the stage audience)*

8. The reins and whips refer to the chariots (line 139) in which Night and Cynthia have arrived or are imagined to have arrived.

9. The standard myth reports that Cynthia, in love with the shepherd Endymion, cast him into a deep sleep atop Mount Latmos (in what is now southeast Turkey) in order to be able to visit him freely.

1. And let him end his long night of sleep by contributing to the happiness of this special day.

Give thee no knowledge yet?

NEPTUNE Yes, now I see
Something intended, Cynthia, worthy thee.° *worthy of you*
Go on; I'll be a helper.

CYNTHIA Hie thee, then,
And charge the wind god,° from his rocky den, *Aeolus*
Let loose his subjects; only Boreas,° *the north wind*
Too foul° for our intentions as he was, *stormy*
Still keep him fast chained. We must have none here
But vernal° blasts and gentle winds appear, *springtime*
Such as blow flowers° and through the glad boughs sing *make flowers bloom*
Many soft welcomes to the lusty spring.
These are our music. Next, thy wat'ry race° *your oceanic followers*
Bring on in couples. We are pleased to grace,
This noble night, each° in their richest things *each couple*
Your own deeps or the broken vessel° brings. *a sunken ship*
Be prodigal, and I shall be as kind,
And shine at full upon you.

NEPTUNE [*calling*] Ho! The wind-
Commanding Aeolus!

Enter Aeolus out of a rock.

AEOLUS Great Neptune?

NEPTUNE He.

AEOLUS What is thy will?

NEPTUNE We do command thee free
Favonius and thy milder winds to wait
Upon our Cynthia, but tie Boreas straight;° *at once; tightly*
He's too rebellious.

AEOLUS I shall do it.

NEPTUNE Do.

[*Exit Aeolus into the rock.*]

AEOLUS [*within*] Great master of the flood and all below,° *the sea and its depths*
Thy full command has taken.° [*Calling*] Ho! The Main!° *taken effect / The Sea!*
Neptune!

[*Enter Aeolus, followed by Favonius and other winds.*]

NEPTUNE Here.

AEOLUS Boreas has broke his chain,
And, struggling with the rest, has got away.

NEPTUNE Let him alone. I'll take him up° at sea; *recapture him*
He will not long be thence.° Go once again, *away from Aeolus' cave*
And call out of° the bottoms of the main *from*
Blue Proteus and the rest; charge them put on
Their greatest pearls and the most sparkling stone
The beaten° rock breeds, till this night is done, *wave-beaten*
By me, a solemn honor° to the Moon. *high ceremony*
Fly like a full sail!

AEOLUS I am gone. [*Exit.*]

CYNTHIA Dark Night,
Strike a full silence! Do a thorough right° *thoroughly due ceremony*
To this great chorus, that our music may
Touch high as heaven, and make the east break day
At midnight. *Music.*

[*Enter Proteus and other sea deities.*]

[FIRST] SONG

Cynthia, to thy power and thee
We obey.
Joy to this great company!
And no day
Come to steal this night away,
Till the rites of love are ended
And the lusty° bridegroom say, — *vigorous; desirous*
"Welcome, light, of all befriended!"° — *greeted as a friend*

Pace out,° you wat'ry powers below! — *Dance*
Let your feet,
Like the galleys'° when they row, — *galleys' "feet," or oars*
Even beat.° — *Beat evenly*
Let your unknown measures,° set — *strange dances*
To the still winds,[2] tell to all
That gods are come, immortal, great,
To honor this great nuptial. *The measure.*° — *stately dance*

SECOND SONG

Hold back thy hours, dark Night, till we have done.
The Day will come too soon;
Young maids will curse thee if thou steal'st away
And leav'st their blushes open to the Day.
Stay, stay, and hide
The blushes of the bride.

Stay, gentle Night, and with thy darkness cover
The kisses of her lover.
Stay, and confound° her tears and her shrill cryings, — *defeat*
Her weak denials, vows, and often dyings!° — *frequent swoonings*
Stay, and hide all,
But help not, though she call.

[*Another stately dance.*]

NEPTUNE Great queen of us and heaven, hear what I bring
To make this hour a full one.
CYNTHIA Speak, sea's king.
NEPTUNE The tunes my Amphitrite° joys to have, — *Neptune's queen*
When she will dance upon the rising wave,
And court me as she sails.—My Tritons,[3] play
Music to lay° a storm. I'll lead the way. — *calm*

[THIRD] SONG

To bed, to bed! Come, Hymen,° lead the bride, — *god of marriage*
And lay her by her husband's side.
Bring in the virgins every one
That grieve to lie alone,
That they may kiss while they may say° a maid; — *profess still to be*
Tomorrow 'twill be other,° kissed and said. — *otherwise*

2. Set to the music of the calm winds (who are singing this song).

3. The merman Triton was the son of Neptune (Greek Poseidon) and Amphitrite. In later mythology Neptune was credited with having had many sons.

Hesperus,° be long a-shining, — *the evening star*
Whilst these lovers are a-twining. *Measure.*

[*Enter Aeolus.*]

AEOLUS Ho! Neptune!
NEPTUNE Aeolus?
AEOLUS The sea goes high;
Boreas hath raised a storm. Go and apply
Thy trident;° else, I prophesy, ere day — *three-pronged spear*
Many a tall° ship will be cast away. — *stately*
Descend, with all the gods and all their power,
To strike a calm.
CYNTHIA A thanks to everyone;
My favor° to you all. To gratulate° — *blessing / reward*
So great a service done at my desire,
Ye shall have many floods,° fuller and higher — *tides*
Than you have wished for, and no ebb shall dare
To let the Day see where your dwellings are.[4]
Now back unto your governments° in haste, — *your offices*
Lest your proud charge° should swell above the waste° — *(the ocean) / its bed*
And win upon the island.° — *And flood Rhodes*
NEPTUNE We obey.
Neptune descends, and the sea gods.
[*Exeunt Aeolus and the winds into the rock.*]
CYNTHIA Hold up thy head, dead° Night. See'st thou not Day? — *sound asleep*
The east begins to lighten. I must down
And give my brother° place. — *(the Sun, Day)*
NIGHT Oh, I could frown
To see the Day, the Day, that flings his light
Upon my kingdom and contemns° old Night! — *scorns*
Let him go on and flame! I hope to see
Another wildfire in his axletree,
And all fall drenched.[5]—But I forget. Speak, queen.
The day grows on; I must no more be seen.
CYNTHIA Heave up thy drowsy head again and see
A greater light, a greater majesty,° — *(the King's majesty)*
Between our sect° and us! Whip up thy team; — *followers*
The day breaks here,° and yon same flashing stream — *(in the King's presence)*
Shot from the south. Say, wilt thou go? Which way?
NIGHT I'll vanish into mists.
CYNTHIA I into day.
Exeunt [*Night and Cynthia*]. *Finis masque.*
KING [*to attendants*] Take lights there!—Ladies, get the bride to bed.
[*To Evadne*] We will not see you laid.° [*To Amintor*] Good night, Amintor; — *laid to bed*
We'll ease you of that tedious ceremony.
Were it my case, I should think time run° slow. — *ran*
If thou be'st noble, youth, get° me a boy — *beget*
That may defend my kingdoms from my foes.

4. I.e., To expose to view the bottom of the sea, where you dwell.
5. A recollection of the story of Phaëthon, who could not control the chariot of his father, the sun god Phoebus (or Helios), and so was struck down by Zeus, falling to his death.

AMINTOR All happiness to you!
KING Good night, Melantius. *Exeunt.*

2.1

Enter Evadne, Aspatia [with a willow garland],° Dula, and other ladies. (to show love forsaken)

DULA [*to Evadne*] Madam, shall we undress you for this fight?
The wars are naked that you must make tonight.
EVADNE You are very merry, Dula.
DULA I should be
Far merrier, madam, if it were with me
As it is with you.
EVADNE How's that?
DULA That I might go
To bed with him wi'th'credit° that you do. *virtue of wifehood*
EVADNE Why, how now, wench?
DULA Come, ladies, will you help?
EVADNE I am soon undone.° *undressed*
DULA And as soon done.° *sexually possessed*
Good store of clothes will trouble you at both.
EVADNE Art thou drunk, Dula?
DULA Why, here's none but we.
EVADNE Thou think'st, belike,° there is no modesty *perhaps*
When we're alone?
DULA Ay, by my troth, you hit my thoughts aright.
EVADNE [*to the First Lady*] You prick° me, lady. *(while undressing her)*
FIRST LADY 'Tis against my will.
DULA Anon you must endure more, and lie still.
You're best° to practice. *You'd do well*
EVADNE [*to the others*] Sure this wench is mad.
DULA No, faith,° this is a trick° that I have had *in faith / quirk*
Since I was fourteen.
EVADNE 'Tis high time to leave it.
DULA Nay, now I'll keep it till the trick° leave me. *i.e., sexual desire*
A dozen wanton words put in your head
Will make you livelier in your husband's bed.
EVADNE Nay, faith, then take it.° *take it or leave it*
DULA Take it, madam? Where?
We all, I hope, will take it that are here.° *(including the audience)*
EVADNE Nay, then, I'll give you o'er.° *give up on you as hopeless*
DULA So will I make
The ablest man in Rhodes, or his heart ache.
EVADNE Wilt take my place° tonight? *(at cards; in bed)*
DULA I'll hold your cards
Against any two I know.
EVADNE What wilt thou do?
DULA Madam, we'll do't, and make 'em leave play too.[1]
EVADNE Aspatia, take her part.° *back her up*

2.1. Outside Evadne's bedchamber.
1. I.e., we'll wear them out sexually. (Dula's metaphor throughout this part of the scene compares the game of sex to a card game. Here she speaks as though she and Evadne are to be partners against an opposite pair or else take on separate opponents—in a card game or in sex.)

DULA I will refuse it.° *(to be her partner)*
She will pluck down a side; she does not use it.[2]
EVADNE [*to Aspatia*] Why, do, I prithee.
DULA [*to Evadne*] You will find the play
Quickly, because your head lies well that way.[3]
EVADNE I thank thee, Dula. Would thou couldst instill
Some of thy mirth into Aspatia!
Nothing but sad thoughts in her breast do dwell;
Methinks a mean° betwixt you would do well. *middle way*
DULA She is in love. Hang me if I were so
But I could run my country.[4] I love too
To do those things that people in love do.
ASPATIA It were a timeless smile should prove my cheek.[5]
It were° a fitter hour for me to laugh *would be*
When at the altar the religious priest
Were pacifying the offended powers° *gods*
With sacrifice, than now. This should have been
My night, and all your hands have° been employed *should have*
In giving me, a spotless° offering, *virgin*
To young Amintor's bed, as we are now
For you. Pardon, Evadne! Would my worth
Were great as yours, or that the King, or he,° *(Amintor)*
Or both, thought so! Perhaps he found me worthless,
But, till he did so, in these ears of mine,
These credulous ears, he poured the sweetest words
That art or love could frame.° If he were false, *devise*
Pardon it, heaven! And if I did want° *lack*
Virtue, you° safely may forgive that too, *you gods*
For I have lost none that I had from you.
EVADNE Nay, leave this sad talk, madam.
ASPATIA Would I could! Then should I leave the cause.
EVADNE See if you have not spoiled all Dula's mirth.
ASPATIA [*to Dula*] Thou think'st thy heart hard,° but, if thou *invulnerable*
be'st caught,° *caught by love*
Remember me; thou shalt perceive a fire
Shot suddenly into thee.
DULA That's not so good.
Let 'em° shoot anything but fire; I fear 'em not. *(men in love)*
ASPATIA Well, wench, thou mayst be taken.° *be caught by love*
EVADNE Ladies, good night. I'll do the rest° myself. *finish undressing*
DULA Nay, let your lord do some!
ASPATIA [*sings*]
Lay a garland on my hearse
Of the dismal yew—
EVADNE That's one of your sad songs, madam.
ASPATIA Believe me, 'tis a very pretty one.
EVADNE How is it, madam?

2. (1) She'll cause our side to lose; (2) she's not a practiced player. (With the suggestion also of sexual play.)
3. You, Evadne, will catch on quickly in playing the game (i.e., sex), because you've a natural aptitude for it. ("Head" plays on "maidenhead.")
4. I'll be hanged if, being in love, I couldn't follow up a scent, run in pursuit. (Alternatively, "run my country" may mean "take charge of the affair" or "provide a means of escape," with a sexual pun on "country" and "cunt.")
5. A smile upon my cheek, given my sad condition, would be untimely and out of place.

SONG

ASPATIA [*sings*]

Lay a garland on my hearse
Of the dismal yew.
Maidens, willow branches bear;
Say I died true.
My love was false, but I was firm
From my hour of birth.
Upon my buried body
Lay lightly, gentle earth!

EVADNE Fie on't, madam! The words are so strange, they are able to make one dream of hobgoblins.—"I could never have the power"—sing that, Dula.

DULA [*sings*]

I could never have the power
To love one above an hour
But my heart would prompt mine eye
On some other man to fly.
Venus, fix mine eyes fast,° *make me constant*
Or if not, give me all that I shall see at last.[6]

EVADNE So, leave me now.

DULA Nay, we must see you laid.° *laid in bed*

ASPATIA Madam, good night. May all the marriage joys
That longing maids imagine in their beds
Prove so unto you! May no discontent
Grow 'twixt your love and you! But if there do,
Inquire of me, and I will guide your moan,° *complaint*
And teach you an artificial° way to grieve, *artful*
To keep your sorrow waking.° Love your lord *awake, alive*
No worse than I; but, if you love so well,
Alas, you may displease him! So did I.
This is the last time you shall look on me.—
Ladies, farewell. As soon as I am dead,
Come all and watch° one night about my hearse; *keep a vigil*
Bring each a mournful story and a tear
To offer at it when I go to earth;
With flattering° ivy clasp my coffin round; *clinging*
Write on my brow my fortune;[7] let my bier
Be borne by virgins that shall sing by course° *by turns*
The truth° of maids and perjuries of men. *constancy*

EVADNE Alas, I pity thee!

OMNES° Madam, good night. *Exit Evadne.* *All (the ladies)*

FIRST LADY Come, we'll let in the bridegroom.

DULA Where's my lord?

Enter Amintor.

FIRST LADY [*to Amintor*] Here, take this light.

DULA You'll find her in the dark.

FIRST LADY Your lady's scarce abed yet. You must help her.

ASPATIA Go, and be happy in your lady's love!

6. Or, if not, give me all the men my heart desires.
7. Place on my forehead a paper on which is written my sad story.

May all the wrongs that you have done to me
Be utterly forgotten in my death!
I'll trouble you no more. Yet I will take
A parting kiss, and will not be denied. [*She kisses him.*]
You'll come, my lord, and see the virgins weep
When I am laid in earth, though you yourself
Can know no pity? Thus I wind myself
Into this willow garland, and am prouder
That I was once your love, though now refused,
Than to have had another true to me.
So with my prayers I leave you, and must try
Some yet unpracticed way to grieve and die. *Exit Aspatia.*
DULA Come, ladies, will you go?
OMNES Good night, my lord.
AMINTOR Much happiness unto you all!
Exeunt [*Dula and*] *ladies.*
I did that lady wrong. Methinks I feel
Her grief shoot suddenly through all my veins;
Mine eyes run. This is strange at such a time!
It was the King first moved me to't, but he
Has not my will in keeping.° Why do I — *Does not own my will*
Perplex myself thus? Something whispers me,
"Go not to bed." My guilt is not so great
As mine own conscience, too sensible,° — *sensitive*
Would make me think; I only brake° a promise, — *broke*
And 'twas the King that forced me. Timorous flesh,
Why shak'st thou so? Away, my idle fears!

Enter Evadne.

Yonder is she, the luster of whose eye
Can blot away the sad remembrance
Of all these things. [*To her*] Oh, my Evadne, spare
That tender body! Let it not take cold!
The vapors of the night shall not fall here.
To bed, my love! Hymen will punish us
For being slack performers of his rites.
Cam'st thou to call me?
EVADNE No.
AMINTOR Come, come, my love,
And let us lose° ourselves to one another. — *give way, loose*
Why art thou up so long?
EVADNE I am not well.
AMINTOR To bed, then! Let me wind thee in these arms
Till I have banished sickness.
EVADNE Good my lord,
I cannot sleep.
AMINTOR Evadne, we'll watch.° — *stay awake*
I mean° no sleeping. — *intend*
EVADNE I'll not go to bed.
AMINTOR I prithee, do.
EVADNE I will not for the world.
AMINTOR Why, my dear love?
EVADNE Why? I have sworn I will not.
AMINTOR Sworn!
EVADNE Ay.

AMINTOR How, sworn, Evadne?
EVADNE Yes, sworn, Amintor, and will swear again
If you will wish to hear me.
AMINTOR To whom have you sworn this?
EVADNE If I should name him, the matter were not great.° *Never mind who*
AMINTOR Come, this is but the coyness of a bride.
EVADNE The coyness of a bride?
AMINTOR How prettily
That frown becomes thee!
EVADNE Do you like it so?
AMINTOR Thou canst not dress thy face in such a look
But I shall like it.
EVADNE What look likes° you best? *pleases*
AMINTOR Why do you ask?
EVADNE That I may show you one less pleasing to you.
AMINTOR How's that?
EVADNE That I may show you one less pleasing to you.
AMINTOR I prithee, put thy jests in milder looks.
It shows as° thou wert angry. *as though*
EVADNE So perhaps
I am indeed.
AMINTOR Why, who has done thee wrong?
Name me the man, and by thyself I swear,
Thy yet unconquered° self, I will revenge thee. *virgin*
EVADNE Now I shall try thy truth.° If thou dost love me, *constancy*
Thou weighest not anything compared with me.
Life, honor, joys eternal, all delights
This world can yield, or hopeful people feign,° *desire*
Or in the life to come, are light as air
To a true lover when his lady frowns
And bids him "Do this." Wilt thou kill this man?
Swear, my Amintor, and I'll kiss the sin° *(of swearing to kill)*
Off from thy lips.
AMINTOR I wo' not° swear, sweet love, *will not*
Till I do know the cause.
EVADNE I would thou wouldst.
Why, it is thou that wrong'st me. I hate thee.
Thou shouldst have killed thyself.
AMINTOR If I should know that,° I should quickly kill *that I wronged you*
The man you hated.
EVADNE Know it, then, and do't.
AMINTOR Oh, no! What look soe'er thou shalt put on
To try my faith, I shall not think thee false;
I cannot find one blemish in thy face
Where falsehood should abide. Leave,° and to bed! *Leave off this talk*
If you have sworn to any of the virgins
That were your old companions to preserve
Your maidenhead a night, it may be done
Without this means.
EVADNE A maidenhead, Amintor,
At my years?[8]
AMINTOR [*aside*] Sure she raves. [*To her*] This cannot be
Thy natural temper.° Shall I call thy maids? *disposition*

8. Me, a virgin, at my age? (It takes a little while for this to sink in; Amintor would rather think that she is raving.)

Either thy healthful sleep hath left thee long,
Or else some fever rages in thy blood.
EVADNE Neither, Amintor. Think you I am mad
Because I speak the truth?
AMINTOR Is this the truth?
Will you not lie with me tonight?
EVADNE Tonight?
You talk as if you thought I would hereafter.
AMINTOR Hereafter? Yes, I do.
EVADNE You are deceived.° *mistaken*
Put off amazement, and with patience mark
What I shall utter, for the oracle
Knows nothing truer. 'Tis not for a night
Or two that I forbear thy bed, but ever.
AMINTOR I dream.—Awake, Amintor!
EVADNE You hear right.
I sooner will find out the beds of snakes,
And with my youthful blood warm their cold flesh,
Letting them curl themselves about my limbs,
Than sleep one night with thee. This is not feigned,
Nor sounds it like the coyness of a bride.
AMINTOR Is flesh so earthly to endure all this?[9]
Are these the joys of marriage? Hymen, keep
This story, that will make succeeding° youth *future generations of*
Neglect thy ceremonies, from all ears!
Let it not rise up for thy shame and mine
To after ages; we will scorn thy laws
If thou no better bless them. Touch the heart
Of her that thou hast sent me, or the world
Shall know there's not an altar that will smoke
In praise of thee; we will adopt us sons;
Then virtue shall inherit, and not blood.[1]
If we do lust, we'll take the next we meet,
Serving ourselves as other creatures do,
And never take note of the female more,
Nor of her issue.[2] [*Aside*] I do rage in vain;
She can but jest.° [*Aloud*] Oh, pardon me, my love! *She must be joking*
So dear the thoughts are that I hold of thee
That I must break forth. Satisfy° my fear; *Free from doubt*
It is a pain beyond the hand of death
To be in doubt. Confirm it with an oath,
If this be true.
EVADNE Do you invent the form.
Let there be in it all the binding words
Devils and conjurers can put together,
And I will take it.° I have sworn before, *(the oath)*
And here, by all things holy, do again,
Never to be acquainted with thy bed.
Is your doubt over now?
AMINTOR I know too much. Would I had doubted still!

9. Can human flesh be expected to endure anything like this?
1. We will leave our inheritances to sons adopted for their virtue rather than to naturally born children.
2. Like male animals, we will couple sexually with females and then have nothing to do with them or their offspring.

Was ever such a marriage night as this?
You powers above, if you did ever mean
Man should be used thus, you have° thought a way — *if ever you have*
How he may bear° himself and save his honor, — *conduct*
Instruct me in it, for to my dull eyes
There is no mean,° no moderate course to run. — *middle way*
I must live scorned, or be a murderer.° — *(of Evadne or her lover)*
Is there a third? Why is this night so calm?
Why does not heaven speak in thunder to us,
And drown her° voice? — *(Evadne's)*
EVADNE This rage will do no good.
AMINTOR Evadne, hear me. Thou hast ta'en an oath,
But such a rash one that to keep it were
Worse than to swear it. Call it back to thee!
Such vows as those never ascend the heaven;
A tear or two will wash it quite away.
Have mercy on my youth, my hopeful youth,
If thou be pitiful; for (without boast)
This land was proud of me. What lady was there
That men called fair and virtuous in this isle
That would have shunned my love? It is in thee
To make me hold this worth.[3] Oh, we vain men,
That trust all our reputation
To rest upon the weak and yielding hand
Of feeble woman! But thou art not stone;
Thy flesh is soft, and in thine eyes doth dwell
The spirit of love; thy heart cannot be hard.
Come, lead me from the bottom of despair
To all the joys thou hast—I know thou wilt—
And make me careful,° lest the sudden change — *caring of myself*
O'ercome my spirits.
EVADNE When I call back this oath,
The pains° of hell environ° me! — *May the pains / encircle*
AMINTOR I sleep,° and am too temperate. Come to bed, — *I neglect my cause*
Or, by those hairs which, if thou hadst a soul
Like to thy locks,° were threads for kings to wear — *As lovely as your hair*
About their arms—
EVADNE Why, so perhaps they are.
AMINTOR I'll drag thee to my bed and make thy tongue
Undo this wicked oath, or on thy flesh
I'll print a thousand wounds to let out life!
EVADNE I fear thee not. Do what thou dar'st to me.
Every ill-sounding word or threat'ning look
Thou showest to me will be revenged at full.
AMINTOR It will not, sure, Evadne.
EVADNE Do not you hazard° that. — *chance, risk*
AMINTOR Ha' ye your champions?° — *avengers*
EVADNE Alas, Amintor, think'st thou I forbear
To sleep with thee because I have put on
A maiden's strictness?° Look upon these cheeks, — *prudery*
And thou shalt find the hot and rising blood
Unapt for such a vow. No, in this heart
There dwells as much desire and as much will

3. It's within your power to enable me to sustain the respect that I have enjoyed till now.

To put that wished act in practice as ever yet
Was known to woman, and they have been shown
Both.[4] But it was the folly of thy youth
To think this beauty, to what hand soe'er
It shall be called, shall stoop to any second.[5]
I do enjoy the best,° and in that height — *a lover of highest rank*
Have sworn to stand or die. You guess the man.
AMINTOR No. Let me know the man that wrongs me so,
That I may cut his body into motes° — *atoms*
And scatter it before the northern wind.
EVADNE You dare not strike him.
AMINTOR Do not wrong me so.
Yes, if his body were a poisonous plant
That it were death to touch, I have a soul
Will throw me on him.
EVADNE Why, 'tis the King.
AMINTOR The King!
EVADNE What will you do now?
AMINTOR 'Tis not the King!
EVADNE What did he make this match for, dull Amintor?
AMINTOR Oh, thou hast named a word that wipes away
All thoughts revengeful. In that sacred name,
"The King," there lies a terror. What frail man
Dares lift his hand against it? Let the gods
Speak to him° when they please; till when, let us — *Chastise the King*
Suffer and wait.
EVADNE Why should you fill yourself so full of heat,
And haste so to my bed? I am no virgin.
AMINTOR What devil hath put it in thy fancy, then,
To marry me?
EVADNE Alas, I must have one
To father children and to bear the name
Of husband to me, that my sin may be
More honorable.
AMINTOR What a strange thing° am I! — *monster; cuckold*
EVADNE A miserable one, one that myself
Am sorry for.
AMINTOR Why, show it then in this:
If thou hast pity, though thy love be none,
Kill me, and all true lovers that shall live
In after ages crossed° in their desires — *thwarted*
Shall bless thy memory and call thee good,
Because such mercy in thy heart was found
To rid° a ling'ring wretch. — *do away with*
EVADNE I must have one
To fill thy room° again, if thou wert dead; — *place*
Else, by this night, I would. I pity thee.
AMINTOR These strange and sudden injuries have fall'n
So thick upon me that I lose all sense
Of what they are. Methinks I am not wronged,
Nor is it aught, if from the censuring world

4. My heart has known both instinctual desire for sex and a conscious wish to act on that desire.
5. Evadne compares herself to a hawk, trained to "stoop," or fly down, to its master's gloved hand and not to any other man's.

I can but hide it.—Reputation,
Thou art a word, no more! [*To her*] But thou hast shown
An impudence so high that to the world
I fear thou wilt betray or shame thyself.

EVADNE To cover shame I took thee. Never fear
That I would blaze° myself. *proclaim*

AMINTOR Nor let the King
Know I conceive he wrongs me. Then° mine honor *If you do*
Will thrust me into action; that° my flesh *(the secret arrangement)*
Could bear with patience. And it is some ease
To me in these extremes that I know this
Before I touched thee; else, had all the sins
Of mankind stood betwixt me and the King,
I had gone through 'em to his heart and thine.
I have left one desire. 'Tis not his crown
Shall buy me to thy bed,[6] now I resolve° *am convinced*
He has dishonored thee. Give me thy hand.° *Shake hands on this*
Be careful of thy credit,° and sin close;° *reputation / secretly*
'Tis all I wish. Upon thy chamber floor
I'll rest tonight, that morning visitors
May think we did as married people use.° *are accustomed to do*
And, prithee, smile upon me when they come,
And seem to toy,° as if thou hadst been pleased *dally fondly*
With what we did.

EVADNE Fear not; I will do this.

AMINTOR Come, let us practice; and, as wantonly° *amorously*
As ever loving bride and bridegroom met,
Let's laugh and enter here.

EVADNE I am content.

AMINTOR Down, all the swellings of my troubled heart!
When we walk thus entwined, let all eyes see
If ever lovers better did agree. *Exit* [*with Evadne*].

[2.2]

Enter Aspatia, Antiphila, [*and*] *Olympias.*

ASPATIA Away! You are not sad. Force it° no further. *Pretend grief*
Good gods, how well you look! Such a full color
Young bashful brides put on. Sure, you are new married.

ANTIPHILA Yes, madam, to your grief.° *married to your grief*

ASPATIA Alas, poor wenches!
Go learn to love first, learn to lose yourselves,
Learn to be flattered, and believe, and bless
The double° tongue that did it; make a faith *deceitful*
Out of the miracles of ancient lovers,
Such as spake truth and died in't; and, like me,
Believe all faithful, and be miserable.
Did you ne'er love yet, wenches? Speak, Olympias.
Thou hast an easy temper, fit for stamp.° *readily impressionable*

OLYMPIAS Never.

ASPATIA Nor you, Antiphila?

6. Not all the King's wealth could persuade me to sleep with you.

2.2. Calianax's house.

ANTIPHILA Nor I.
ASPATIA Then, my good girls, be more than women, wise.
At least be more than I was; and be sure
You credit anything the light gives life to° — *anything on earth*
Before a man. Rather believe the sea
Weeps for the ruined merchant° when he° roars; — *merchant ship / (the sea)*
Rather° the wind but courts the pregnant° sails — *Rather believe / swelling*
When the strong cordage° cracks; rather the sun — *rigging, tackle*
Comes but to kiss the fruit in wealthy autumn
When all falls blasted.° If you needs must love, — *blighted*
Forced by ill fate, take to your maiden bosoms
Two dead-cold aspics,° and of them make lovers. — *asps (poisonous snakes)*
They cannot flatter nor forswear; one kiss
Makes a long peace for all.° But man— — *forever*
Oh, that beast man! Come, let's be sad, my girls.
That downcast of thine eye, Olympias,
Shows a fine sorrow.—Mark, Antiphila,
Just such another was the nymph Oenone's
When Paris brought home Helen.[1] [*To Olympias*] Now a tear,
And then thou art a piece expressing° fully — *picture representing*
The Carthage queen,[2] when from a cold sea rock,
Full with her sorrow, she tied fast her eyes
To the fair Trojan ships, and, having lost them,° — *lost sight of them*
Just as thine° does, down stole a tear.—Antiphila, — *your eye*
What would this wench° do if she were Aspatia? — *(Olympias)*
Here she would stand till some more pitying god
Turned her to marble.—'Tis enough, my wench.
[*To Antiphila*] Show me the piece of needlework you wrought.
ANTIPHILA Of Ariadne,[3] madam?
ASPATIA Yes, that piece.
[*Antiphila shows it.*]
This should be Theseus. H'as a cozening° face. — *He has a deceiving*
You meant him for a man?
ANTIPHILA He was so, madam.
ASPATIA Why, then, 'tis well enough.—Never look back;° — *back to Naxos*
You have a full wind and a false heart, Theseus.—
Does not the story say his keel was split,
Or his masts spent,° or some kind rock or other — *worn to breaking*
Met with his vessel?
ANTIPHILA Not as I remember.
ASPATIA It should ha' been so. Could the gods know this,
And not, of all their number, raise a storm?[4]
But they° are all as ill. This false smile — *(men)*
Was well expressed; just such another caught me.—
[*To Theseus*] You shall not go° so.— — *escape*
Antiphila, in this place° work a quicksand, — *(in the needlework)*
And over it a shallow smiling water,

1. Paris deserted the nymph Oenone in order to carry off Menelaus' wife, Helen, to Troy.
2. Dido, Queen of Carthage, was deserted by Aeneas, a prince of Troy, when destiny ordered him to go on to Rome; she committed suicide out of grief. (Virgil, *Aeneid*, Book 4.)
3. Theseus deserted Ariadne, daughter of Minos, King of Crete, after she helped him escape the labyrinth at Crete and he fled with her to the island of Naxos. (Ovid, *Metamorphoses*, Book 8.)
4. And was not one of all the gods willing to raise a storm?

And his ship plowing it, and then a Fear.° *personification of Fear*
Do that Fear to the life,° wench. *in a lifelike way*
ANTIPHILA 'Twill wrong the story.
ASPATIA 'Twill make the story, wronged by wanton poets,
Live long and be believed. But where's the lady?
ANTIPHILA [*pointing to her work*] There, madam.
ASPATIA Fie, you have missed it here, Antiphila.
You are much mistaken, wench.
These colors are not dull and pale enough
To show a soul so full of misery
As this sad lady's was. Do it by me;° *modeled on me*
Do it again by me, the lost Aspatia,
And you shall find all true but the wild island.° *(Naxos; see 41 n)*
And think I stand upon the sea breach° now, *edge of the surf*
Mine arms thus,° and mine hair blown with the wind, *(she gestures)*
Wild as that desert, and let all° about me *everything*
Tell that I am forsaken. Do my face
(If thou hadst ever feeling of a sorrow)
Thus, thus, Antiphila. Strive to make me look
Like Sorrow's monument;° and the trees about me, *statue*
Let them be dry and leafless; let the rocks
Groan with continual surges, and behind me
Make all a desolation. Look, look, wenches,
A miserable life° of this poor picture! *A living embodiment*
OLYMPIAS Dear madam—
ASPATIA I have done. Sit down, and let us
Upon that point fix all our eyes, that point there.
Make a dumb silence, till you feel a sudden sadness
Give us new souls. [*They sit.*]

Enter Calianax.

CALIANAX [*to himself*] The King may do this, and he may not do it.[5]
My child is wronged, disgraced.—Well, how now, huswives?° *hussies*
What, at your ease? Is this a time to sit still?
Up, you young, lazy whores, up, or I'll swinge° you. *thrash*
OLYMPIAS Nay, good my lord—
CALIANAX You'll lie down shortly. Get you in and work!
What, are you grown so resty?° You want heats.° *indolent / need exercise*
We shall have some of the court boys° do that office. *pages, young courtiers*
ANTIPHILA My lord, we do no more than we are charged.° *ordered*
It is the lady's pleasure we be thus in grief;
She is forsaken.
CALIANAX There's a rogue,° too, *(Amintor)*
A young dissembling slave!° Well, get you in. *wretch*
I'll have a bout with that boy; 'tis high time
Now to be valiant. I confess my youth
Was never prone° that way. What, made an ass? *inclined*
A court stale?° Well, I will be valiant, *laughingstock*
And beat some dozen of these whelps. And there's
Another of 'em, a trim cheating soldier.° *(Melantius)*
I'll maul that rascal! He's outbraved° me twice; *faced me down, defied*

5. The King has the absolute power to do this (i.e., to take Amintor away from Aspatia), but not the moral right.

But now, I thank the gods, I am valiant.° *I'm ready for him*
Go, get you in. I'll take a course° with all. *take steps to deal*
Exeunt omnes.

3.1

Enter Cleon, Strato, [and] Diphilus.

CLEON Your sister is not up yet.

DIPHILUS Oh, brides must take their morning's rest. The night is troublesome.

STRATO But not tedious.

DIPHILUS What odds° he has not my sister's maidenhead tonight? *What do you bet*

STRATO None. It's odds against any bridegroom living; he ne'er gets it while he lives.[1]

DIPHILUS You're merry with my sister. You'll please to allow me the same freedom with your mother.

STRATO She's at your service.

DIPHILUS Then she's merry enough of herself; she needs no tickling.—Knock at the door.

STRATO We shall interrupt them.

DIPHILUS No matter; they have the year before them.
[*Diphilus calls through the door, as they knock.*]
Good morrow, sister! Spare yourself today;
The night will come again.

Enter Amintor [dressing].

AMINTOR Who's there, my brother?° I am no readier yet. *brother-in-law*
Your sister is but now up.

DIPHILUS You look as you had lost your eyes tonight;° *last night*
I think you ha' not slept.

AMINTOR I'faith, I have not.

DIPHILUS You have done better, then.

AMINTOR We ventured for a boy. When he is twelve,
'A° shall command against the foes of Rhodes. *He*
Shall we be merry?

STRATO You cannot. You want sleep.

AMINTOR 'Tis true. (*Aside*) But she,
As if she had drunk Lethe, or had made
Even with heaven,[2] did fetch so still a sleep,
So sweet and sound—

DIPHILUS What's that?

AMINTOR Your sister frets
This morning, and doth turn her eyes upon me,
As people on their headsman.° She does chafe,° *executioner / fret*
And kiss, and chafe again, and clap my cheeks—
She's in another world.

DIPHILUS Then I had° lost. I was about to lay° *would have / bet*
You had not got her maidenhead tonight.

3.1. Outside Evadne's bedchamber.

1. I.e., The odds are that any new husband will find no maidenhead to take on the marriage night.

2. As if she had drunk from the waters of oblivion (Lethe was one of the rivers of the underworld), or had settled her spiritual account with heaven in preparation for dying.

AMINTOR [*aside*] Ha! Does he not mock me? [*Aloud*] You'd
lost indeed;
I do not use° to bungle. *make it a practice*
CLEON You do deserve her.
AMINTOR I laid my lips to hers, and that wild breath
(*Aside*) That was so rude and rough to me last night
[*Aloud*] Was sweet as April. I'll be guilty too,
If these be the effects.[3]

Enter Melantius.

MELANTIUS Good day, Amintor—for to me the name
Of brother° is too distant; we are friends, *brother-in-law*
And that is nearer.
AMINTOR Dear Melantius,
Let me behold thee. Is it possible?
MELANTIUS What sudden gaze is this?
AMINTOR 'Tis wondrous strange.
MELANTIUS Why does thine eye desire so strict° a view *scrutinizing*
Of that it knows so well? There's nothing here
That is not thine.[4]
AMINTOR I wonder much, Melantius,
To see those noble looks that make me think
How virtuous thou art; and, on the sudden,
'Tis strange to me thou shouldst have worth and honor,
Or not be base, and false, and treacherous,
And every ill. But—
MELANTIUS Stay, stay, my friend;
I fear this sound will not become° our loves. *befit*
No more. Embrace me. [*They embrace.*]
AMINTOR Oh, mistake me not;
I know thee to be full of all those deeds
That we frail men call good; but by the course
Of nature thou shouldst be as quickly changed
As are the winds, dissembling as the sea
That now wears brows as smooth as virgins' be,
Tempting the merchant° to invade his face, *merchant ship*
And in an hour calls his billows up,
And shoots 'em at the sun,° destroying all *high in the air*
'A° carries on him. (*Aside*) Oh, how near am I *He*
To utter my sick thoughts!
MELANTIUS But why, my friend, should I be so by nature?
AMINTOR I have wed thy sister, who hath virtuous thoughts
Enough for one whole family, and it is strange
That you should feel no want.
MELANTIUS Believe me, this is compliment too cunning for me.
DIPHILUS What should I be, then, by the course of nature,
They° having both robbed me of so much virtue?[5] *(My brother and sister)*
STRATO Oh, call the bride, my lord Amintor,
That we may see her blush and turn her eyes down.
It is the prettiest sport!

3. I'll gladly pay for such pleasure. (With an undertone of hidden darker meaning, of embracing her evil.)
4. I am yours entirely (and so you should not be puzzled by anything in me).
5. Diphilus objects to Amintor's strange hypothesis that virtue is of a limited quantity in any given family, so that one member's virtue is necessarily at the others' expense.

AMINTOR [*calling offstage*] Evadne!
EVADNE (*within*) My lord?
AMINTOR [*calling offstage*] Come forth, my love.
Your brothers do attend to wish you joy.
EVADNE [*within*] I am not ready yet.
AMINTOR [*calling to her*] Enough,° enough! *Enough of these delays*
EVADNE [*within*] They'll mock me.
AMINTOR [*calling to her*] Faith, thou shalt come in.

Enter Evadne.

MELANTIUS Good morrow, sister. He that understands
Whom you have wed need not to wish you joy.
You have enough; take heed you be not proud.
DIPHILUS Oh, sister, what have you done?
EVADNE I done! Why, what have I done?
STRATO My lord Amintor swears you are no maid now.
EVADNE Push!° *Pshaw!*
STRATO I'faith, he does.
EVADNE I knew I should be mocked.
DIPHILUS With a truth.
EVADNE If 'twere to do again, in faith, I would not marry.
AMINTOR (*aside*) Nor I, by heaven!
DIPHILUS Sister, Dula swears she heard you cry two rooms off.
EVADNE Fie, how you talk!
DIPHILUS Let's see you walk, Evadne. By my troth, you're spoiled.
MELANTIUS Amintor!
AMINTOR Ha!
MELANTIUS Thou art sad.
AMINTOR Who, I? I thank you for that. Shall Diphilus, thou, and I sing a catch?° *round*
MELANTIUS How!
AMINTOR Prithee, let's.
MELANTIUS Nay, that's too much the other way.° *too mirthful*
AMINTOR I am so lightened with my happiness!
[*To Evadne*] How dost thou, love? Kiss me.
EVADNE I cannot love you. You tell tales of me.[6]
AMINTOR Nothing but what becomes° us.—Gentlemen, *does credit to, suits*
Would you had all such wives, and all the world,
That I might be no wonder!° You're all sad. *happy exception*
What, do you envy me? I walk, methinks,
On water and ne'er sink, I am so light.
MELANTIUS 'Tis well you are so.
AMINTOR Well? How can I be other
When she looks thus?—Is there no music there?
Let's dance.
MELANTIUS Why, this is strange, Amintor.
AMINTOR I do not know myself; yet I could wish
My joy were less.[7]
DIPHILUS I'll marry too, if it will make one thus.
EVADNE (*aside*) Amintor, hark.

6. Said with playful, teasing irony, as part of Evadne and Amintor's act to appear happily married.
7. Amintor speaks hyperbolically of being beside himself, and so happy that he finds it almost unbearable. (Or "yet . . . less" could be said as an aside.)

AMINTOR [*aside to her*] What says my love? [*To himself*] I must obey.

EVADNE [*aside to him*] You do it scurvily. 'Twill be perceived.

CLEON [*to Amintor*] My lord, the King is here.

Enter King and Lysippus.

AMINTOR Where?

STRATO And his brother.

KING Good morrow, all.
Amintor, joy on joy fall thick upon thee!—
And, madam, you are altered since I saw you.
I must salute° you; you are now another's. [*He kisses her.*] *greet with a kiss*
How liked you your night's rest?

EVADNE Ill, sir.

AMINTOR Indeed, she took but little.

LYSIPPUS You'll let her take more, and thank her too, shortly.

KING Amintor, wert thou truly honest° *chaste*
Till thou wert married?

AMINTOR Yes, sir.

KING Tell me, then, how shows° the sport unto thee? *seems*

AMINTOR Why, well.

KING What did you do?

AMINTOR No more nor less than other couples use.° *practice*
You know what 'tis; it has but a coarse name.

KING But, prithee, I should think, by her black° eye *dark, seductive*
And her red cheek, she should be quick and stirring
In this same business, ha?

AMINTOR I cannot tell.
I ne'er tried other, sir, but I perceive
She is as quick° as you delivered.° *lively; pregnant / said*

KING Well, you'll trust me then, Amintor,
To choose a wife for you again?

AMINTOR No, never, sir.

KING Why? Like you this° so ill? *this wife*

AMINTOR So well I like her,
For this° I bow my knee in thanks to you, *That for this wife*
And unto heaven will pay my grateful tribute
Hourly, and do hope we shall draw out
A long contented life together here,
And die both, full of gray hairs, in one day,
For which the thanks is yours; but if the powers
That rule us please to call her first away,
Without pride spoke,° this world holds not a wife *I speak without boast*
Worthy to take her room.

KING [*aside*] I do not like this.—
All forbear° the room but you, Amintor, *leave*
And your lady. I have some speech with you
That may concern your after living well.° *your subsequent welfare*
[*Exeunt all but the King, Amintor, and Evadne.*]

AMINTOR [*aside*] 'A will not tell me that he lies with her?
If he do, something heavenly stay° my heart! *restrain*
For I shall be apt to thrust this arm of mine
To acts unlawful.

KING You will suffer me
To talk with her, Amintor, and not have
A jealous pang?
AMINTOR Sir, I dare trust my wife
With whom she dares to talk, and not be jealous.
[*He withdraws.*]
KING How do you like Amintor?
EVADNE As I did, sir.
KING How's that?
EVADNE As one that, to fulfill your will and pleasure,
I have given leave to call me wife and love.
KING I see there is no lasting faith in sin;
They that break word with heaven will break again
With all the world, and so dost thou with me.
EVADNE How, sir?
KING This subtle woman's ignorance[8]
Will not excuse you. Thou hast taken oaths,
So great that methought they did misbecome
A woman's mouth, that thou wouldst ne'er enjoy
A man but me.
EVADNE I never did swear so.
You do me wrong.
KING Day and night have heard it.
EVADNE I swore indeed that I would never love
A man of lower place; but, if your fortune
Should throw you from this height, I bade you trust° *understand*
I would forsake you, and would bend° to him *incline; submit*
That won your throne. I love with my ambition,
Not with my eyes. But if I ever yet
Touched any other, leprosy light here
Upon my face, which for your royalty[9]
I would not stain!
KING Why, thou dissemblest, and it is in me° *in my power*
To punish thee.
EVADNE Why, it is in me, then,
Not to love you, which will more afflict
Your body than your punishment can mine.
KING But thou hast let Amintor lie with thee?
EVADNE I ha' not.
KING Impudence! He says himself so.
EVADNE 'A lies.
KING 'A does not.
EVADNE By this light he does,
Strangely and basely, and I'll prove it so!
I did not only shun him for a night,° *for one night only*
But told him I would never close° with him. *embrace, unite*
KING Speak lower. 'Tis false.
EVADNE I am no man
To answer with a blow, or, if I were,
You are the King. But urge° not, 'tis most true. *press, importune me*
KING Do not I know the uncontrollèd thoughts
That youth brings with him, when his blood is high
With expectation and desire of that

8. This ignorance that women subtly put on.

9. Which in order to be worthy of your royal rank.

He long hath waited for? Is not his° spirit, *(Amintor's)*
Though he be temperate, of a valiant° strain *of as valiant a*
As this our age hath known? What could he do,
If such a sudden speech had met his blood,[1]
But ruin° thee forever, if he had not killed thee? *disfigure*
He could not bear it thus; he is as we,
Or any other wrongèd man.

EVADNE It is° dissembling. *i.e., Amintor is*

KING Take him! Farewell. Henceforth I am thy foe,
And what disgraces I can blot thee with, look for.
[*He starts to leave.*]

EVADNE Stay, sir. [*Calling*] Amintor! [*To the King*] You shall hear.—Amintor!

AMINTOR [*coming forward*] What, my love?

EVADNE Amintor, thou hast an ingenious° look, *ingenuous, innocent*
And shouldst be virtuous. It amazeth me
That thou canst make such base, malicious lies.

AMINTOR What, my dear wife?

EVADNE Dear wife! I do despise thee.
Why, nothing can be baser than to sow
Dissension amongst lovers.

AMINTOR Lovers! Who?

EVADNE The King and me—

AMINTOR Oh, God!

EVADNE Who should live long, and love without distaste,° *unpleasantness*
Were it not for such pickthanks° as thyself! *talebearers; sycophants*
Did you lie with me? Swear now, and be punished° *(for perjury)*
In hell for this.

AMINTOR [*aside*] The faithless sin° I made *sin of faithlessness*
To fair Aspatia is not yet revenged;
It follows me. [*To the King*] I will not loose° a word *let loose*
To this vile woman; but to you, my king,
The anguish of my soul thrusts out this truth:
You're a tyrant, and not so much to wrong
An honest man thus as to take a pride
In talking with him of it.

EVADNE [*to the King*] Now, sir, see how loud this fellow lied.

AMINTOR [*to the King*] You that can know to° wrong should know how men *know how to*
Must right themselves. What punishment is due
From me to him that shall abuse my bed?° *marriage-bed*
Is it not death? Nor can that satisfy,
Unless I send your limbs through all the land,
To show how nobly I have freed myself.
[*He reaches for his sword.*]

KING Draw not thy sword. Thou know'st I cannot fear
A subject's hand; but thou shalt feel the weight
Of this, if thou dost rage. [*The King reaches for his sword.*]

AMINTOR The weight of that?
If you have any worth, for heaven's sake think
I fear not swords; for, as you are mere man,
I dare as easily kill you for this deed

1. If your unexpected refusal to sleep with him had thwarted his desire.

As you dare think to do it. But there is
Divinity about you that strikes dead
My rising passions. As you are my king,
I fall before you and present my sword
To cut mine own flesh, if it be your will.
Alas, I am nothing but a multitude
Of waking° griefs! Yet, should I murder you, — *unsleeping; unceasing*
I might before the world take the excuse
Of madness; for, compare° my injuries, — *examine*
And they will well appear too sad° a weight — *heavy*
For reason to endure. But fall I° first, — *may I fall dead*
Amongst my sorrows, ere my treacherous hand
Touch holy things! But why—I know not what
I have to say—why did you choose out me
To make thus wretched? There were thousands, fools,
Easy to work on, and of state° enough — *estate, rank*
Within the island.

EVADNE I would not have a fool;
It were no credit for° me. — *wouldn't reflect well on*

AMINTOR Worse and worse!
Thou that dar'st talk unto thy husband thus,
Profess thyself a whore, and, more than so,
Resolve to be so still, it is my fate
To bear and bow beneath a thousand griefs
To keep that little credit with the world.[2]
But there were wise ones too; you might have ta'en
Another.

KING No; for I believed thee honest° — *as honest, loyal*
As thou wert valiant.

AMINTOR All the happiness
Bestowed upon me turns into disgrace.
Gods, take your honesty again, for I
Am loaden with it!—Good my lord the King,
Be private in it.

KING Thou mayst live, Amintor,
Free as thy king, if thou wilt wink at this
And be a means that we may meet in secret.

AMINTOR A bawd! Hold, hold, my breast! A bitter curse
Seize me if I forget not all respects° — *considerations*
That are religious,° on another word — *enjoined by religion*
Sounded like that,[3] and through a sea of sins
Will wade to my revenge, though I should call° — *call down*
Pains here and after life[4] upon my soul!

KING Well, I am resolute° you lay not with her; — *convinced, satisfied*
And so I leave you. *Exit King.*

EVADNE You must needs be prating,° — *would insist on talking*
And see what follows!

AMINTOR Prithee, vex me not.
Leave me. I am afraid some sudden start° — *fit of passion*
Will pull a murder on me.° — *prompt me to murder*

2. In order to preserve merely the outward semblance of reputation.
3. If anyone ever says a word again about my acting as a bawd to my own wife.
4. Torments in this life and the next.

EVADNE I am gone.
I love my life well. *Exit Evadne.*
AMINTOR I hate mine as much.
This 'tis to break a troth!° I should be glad — *promise (to Aspatia)*
If all this tide of grief would make me mad. *Exit.*

[3.2]

Enter Melantius.

MELANTIUS I'll know the cause of all Amintor's griefs,
Or friendship shall be idle.° — *useless*

Enter Calianax.

CALIANAX Oh, Melantius,
My daughter will die!
MELANTIUS Trust me, I am sorry.
Would thou hadst ta'en her room!° — *died in her place*
CALIANAX Thou art a slave,
A cutthroat slave, a bloody, treacherous slave!
MELANTIUS Take heed, old man. Thou wilt be heard to rave,
And lose thine offices.
CALIANAX I am valiant grown
At all these years, and thou art but a slave.
MELANTIUS Leave!° — *Cease your chatter!*
Some company will come, and I respect
Thy years, not thee, so much that I could wish
To laugh at thee alone.
CALIANAX I'll spoil your mirth.
I mean to fight with thee. There lie, my cloak!
[*He casts aside his cloak and draws his sword.*]
This was my father's sword, and he durst fight.
Are you prepared?
MELANTIUS Why, wilt thou dote thyself
Out of thy life?[1] Hence! Get thee to bed.
Have careful looking to,° and eat warm things, — *nursing*
And trouble not me; my head is full of thoughts
More weighty than thy life or death can be.
CALIANAX You have a name° in war, where you stand safe — *reputation*
Amongst a multitude; but I will try
What you dare do unto a weak old man
In single fight. You'll give ground, I fear.
Come, draw!
MELANTIUS I will not draw, unless thou pull'st thy death
Upon thee with a stroke.° There's no one blow — *unless you strike first*
That thou canst give hath° strength enough to kill me. — *that has*
Tempt me not so far, then! The power of earth
Shall not redeem thee.[2]
CALIANAX [*aside*] I must let him alone.
He's stout° and able, and, to say the truth, — *fierce, brave*
However I may set a face° and talk, — *make threatening faces*

3.2. The palace.
1. Will you endanger your life with this foolishness?
2. No power on earth will be able to save you.

I am not valiant. When I was a youth,
I kept my credit with a testy trick
I had[3] 'mongst cowards, but durst never fight.

MELANTIUS I will not promise to preserve your life
If you do stay.

CALIANAX [*aside*] I would give half my land
That I durst fight with that proud man a little.
If I had men to hold him, I would beat him
Till he asked me mercy.

MELANTIUS Sir, will you be gone?

CALIANAX [*aside*] I dare not stay, but I will go home and beat my servants all over for this. *Exit Calianax.*

MELANTIUS This old fellow haunts me,
But the distracted carriage° of mine Amintor *behavior*
Takes deeply on me.° I will find the cause; *Affects me deeply*
I fear his conscience cries he wronged Aspatia.

Enter Amintor.

AMINTOR [*to himself*] Men's eyes are not so subtle° to perceive *aren't subtle enough*
My inward misery; I bear my grief
Hid from the world. How art thou° wretched, then? *(said to himself)*
For aught I know, all husbands are like me,
And every one I talk with of his wife
Is but a well° dissembler of his woes *skillful*
As I am. Would I knew it! For the rareness° *uniqueness of my case*
Afflicts me now.

MELANTIUS Amintor, we have not enjoyed our friendship of late, for we were wont to change° our souls in talk. *exchange*

AMINTOR Melantius, I can tell thee a good jest of Strato and a lady the last day.° *yesterday*

MELANTIUS How was't?

AMINTOR Why, such an odd one!

MELANTIUS I have longed to speak with you, not of an idle jest that's forced, but of matter you are bound to utter to me.

AMINTOR What is that, my friend?

MELANTIUS I have observed your words fall from your tongue
Wildly, and all your carriage
Like one that strove to show his merry mood,
When he were ill disposed. You were not wont
To put such scorn into your speech, or wear
Upon your face ridiculous jollity.
Some sadness sits here,° which your cunning would *(in your face)*
Cover o'er with smiles, and 'twill not be.° *but unsuccessfully*
What is it?

AMINTOR A sadness here? What cause
Can fate provide for me to make me so?
Am I not loved through all this isle? The King
Rains greatness on me. Have I not received
A lady to my bed that in her eye
Keeps mounting fire and on her tender cheeks
Inevitable° color, in her heart *Irresistible*
A prison for all virtue? Are not you,

3. I maintained a reputation (for bravery) by a trick I had of acting fierce.

Which is above all joys, my constant friend?
What sadness can I have? No, I am light,
And feel the courses of my blood more warm
And stirring than they were. Faith, marry too,
And you will feel so unexpressed° a joy — *inexpressible*
In chaste embraces that you will indeed
Appear another.° — *Seem a changed man*

MELANTIUS You may shape, Amintor,
Causes to cozen the whole world withal,[4]
And yourself too; but 'tis not like a friend
To hide your soul from me. 'Tis not your nature
To be thus idle.° I have seen you stand — *trifling*
As° you were blasted° midst of all your mirth, — *As if / thunderstruck*
Call thrice aloud, and then start, feigning joy
So coldly.[5] World,° what do I here? A friend — *In the world's name*
Is nothing.[6] Heaven! I would ha' told that man° — *i.e., Amintor*
My secret sins. I'll search° an unknown land, — *search out*
And there plant friendship; all is withered here.
Come with a compliment![7] I would have fought
Or told my friend 'a lied, ere soothed° him so. — *before I blandished*
Out of my bosom!

AMINTOR But there is nothing.[8]

MELANTIUS Worse and worse! Farewell.
From this time have° acquaintance, but no friend. — *have me as an*
[*He starts to leave.*]

AMINTOR Melantius, stay! You shall know what that° is. — *(the matter)*

MELANTIUS See how you played with friendship! Be advised
How you give cause unto yourself to say
You ha' lost a friend.

AMINTOR Forgive what I ha' done,
For I am so o'ergone° with injuries — *overwhelmed*
Unheard of that I lose consideration° — *the power to judge*
Of what I ought to do.—Oh!—Oh! [*He weeps.*]

MELANTIUS Do not weep.
What is't? May I once but know the man
Hath turned° my friend thus— — *Who has transformed*

AMINTOR I had spoke at first,
But that—

MELANTIUS But what?

AMINTOR I held it most unfit
For you to know. Faith, do not know° it yet. — *wish to know*

MELANTIUS [*weeping*] Thou see'st my love, that will keep company
With thee in tears. Hide nothing, then, from me,
For, when I know the cause of thy distemper,
With mine own armor I'll adorn myself,
My resolution,[9] and cut through thy foes
Unto thy quiet,° till I place thy heart — *For your peace of mind*
As peaceable as spotless innocence.

4. You can go ahead and devise, Amintor, reasons for your supposed happiness to fool everyone else with.
5. And then suddenly come to yourself and resume your calculated feigning of joy.
6. My being your friend evidently counts for nothing.
7. How could you reward our friendship by coming to me as you did (at lines 79–80) with a mere formal compliment?
8. But there's nothing I haven't told you.
9. I'll bedeck myself in my familiar armor of brave resolution.

What is it?
AMINTOR Why, 'tis this—it is too big
To get out. Let my tears make way awhile.
MELANTIUS Punish me strangely, heaven, if he scape
Of° life or fame,° that brought this youth to this! *With / reputation*
AMINTOR Your sister—
MELANTIUS Well said.° *i.e., Yes, go on*
AMINTOR You'll wish't unknown
When you have heard it.
MELANTIUS No.
AMINTOR —is much to blame,
And to the King has given her honor up,
And lives in whoredom with him.
MELANTIUS How's this?
Thou art run mad with injury indeed;
Thou couldst not utter this else. Speak again,
For I forgive it freely. Tell thy griefs.
AMINTOR She's wanton; I am loath to say "a whore,"
Though it be true.
MELANTIUS Speak yet again, before mine anger grow
Up beyond throwing° down. What are thy griefs? *Too high to be thrown*
AMINTOR By all our friendship, these.
MELANTIUS What, am I tame?
After mine actions,° shall the name of friend *Given my soldiership*
Blot° all our family, and strike the brand *Disgrace, stain*
Of whore upon my sister, unrevenged?
My shaking flesh, be thou a witness for me
With what unwillingness I go to scourge
This railer,° whom my folly hath called friend! *reviler*
I will not take thee basely. [*He draws his sword.*] Thy sword
Hangs near thy hand; draw it, that I may whip
Thy rashness to repentance. Draw thy sword!
AMINTOR Not on thee, did thine anger go as high
As troubled waters. Thou shouldst do me ease
Here and eternally[1] if thy noble hand
Would cut me from my sorrows.
MELANTIUS This is base
And fearful!° They that use° to utter lies *cowardly / are accustomed*
Provide not blows but words to qualify° *mollify, appease*
The men they wronged. Thou hast a guilty cause.
AMINTOR Thou pleasest me, for so much more like this° *of the same talk*
Will raise my anger up above my griefs,
Which is a passion easier to be borne,
And I shall then be happy.
MELANTIUS Take, then, more
To raise thine anger. 'Tis mere cowardice
Makes thee not draw; and I will leave thee dead
However.[2] But if thou art so much pressed° *oppressed*
With guilt and fear as not to dare to fight,
I'll make thy memory loathed, and fix a scandal
Upon thy name forever.
AMINTOR [*drawing his sword*] Then I draw,

1. In this life and the next (since I long to die in a way that will free me of the mortal sin of suicide).
2. I'll run you through whether you draw your sword or not.

As justly as our magistrates their swords
To cut offenders off. I knew before
'Twould grate your ears; but it was base in you
To urge a weighty secret from your friend
And then rage at it. I shall be at ease
If I be killed, and if you fall by me
I shall not long outlive you.° *i.e., I'll take my life*

MELANTIUS Stay awhile.
The name of friend is more than family
Or all the world besides. I was a fool.
Thou searching° human nature, that didst wake *officious, nosy*
To do me wrong, thou art inquisitive,° *too inquisitive*
And thrusts me upon questions that will take
My sleep away. Would I had died ere known
This sad dishonor! Pardon me, my friend.
[*He sheathes his sword.*]
If thou wilt strike, here is a faithful heart;
Pierce it, for I will never heave my hand
To thine.° Behold the power thou hast in me: *Against your heart*
I do believe my sister is a whore,
A leprous one. Put up thy sword, young man.

AMINTOR [*sheathing his sword*] How should I bear it, then,
she being so?
I fear, my friend, that you will lose me shortly,
And I shall do a foul act on myself° *I'll commit suicide*
Through these disgraces.

MELANTIUS Better half the land
Were buried quick° together. No, Amintor, *alive*
Thou shalt have ease. Oh, this adulterous king
That drew her to't! Where got he the spirit
To wrong me so?

AMINTOR What is it then to me,[3]
If it be wrong to you!

MELANTIUS Why, not so much.
The credit of our house° is thrown away. *family*
But from his iron den I'll waken Death,
And hurl him on this king. My honesty
Shall steel my sword, and on my horrid point
I'll wear my cause, that shall amaze the eyes
Of this proud man and be too glitt'ring
For him to look on.

AMINTOR I have quite undone my fame.° *reputation*

MELANTIUS Dry up thy wat'ry eyes,
And cast a manly look upon my face,
For nothing is so wild as I thy friend
Till I have freed thee. Still this° swelling breast. *Quiet your*
I go thus from thee, and will never cease
My vengeance till I find thy heart at peace.
[*He starts to leave.*]

AMINTOR It must not be so. Stay! Mine eyes would° tell *wish to, are about to*
How loath I am to this; but, love and tears,
Leave me awhile, for I have hazarded
All that this world calls happy. Thou hast wrought

3. How much greater, then, is the injury to me.

A secret from me, under name of friend,
Which art° could ne'er have found, nor torture wrung *artful questioning*
From out my bosom. Give it me again,
For I will find it, wheresoe'er it lies,
Hid in the mortal'st part.° Invent a way *i.e., in your heart*
To give it back.

MELANTIUS Why would you have it back?
I will to death pursue him° with revenge. *(the King)*

AMINTOR Therefore I call it from thee; for I know
Thy blood so high° that thou wilt stir in this *passion so strong*
And shame me to posterity. Take to thy weapon!
[*He draws his sword.*]

MELANTIUS Hear thy friend, that bears more years than thou.

AMINTOR I will not hear. But° draw, or I— *Either*

MELANTIUS Amintor!

AMINTOR Draw, then, for I am full° as resolute *fully*
As fame and honor can enforce me be.
I cannot linger. Draw!

MELANTIUS [*drawing his sword*] I do. But is not
My share of credit equal with thine,
If I do stir?[4]

AMINTOR No; for it will be called
Honor in thee to spill thy sister's blood
If she her birth° abuse, and on the King *family name*
A brave revenge; but on me, that have walked
With patience in it, it will fix the name
Of fearful cuckold—Oh, that word! Be quick.

MELANTIUS Then join° with me. *join in revenge*

AMINTOR I dare not do a sin, or else I would.
Be speedy.

MELANTIUS Then dare not fight with me, for that's a sin.
[*Aside*] His grief distracts him. [*To him*] Call thy thoughts
again,
And to thyself pronounce the name of friend,
And see what that will work. I will not fight.
[*He sheathes his sword.*]

AMINTOR You must.

MELANTIUS I will be killed first. Though my passions
Offered the like to you, 'tis not this earth
Shall buy my reason to it.[5] Think awhile,
For you are (I must weep when I speak that)
Almost besides° yourself. *beside*

AMINTOR [*sheathing his sword*] Oh, my soft temper!° *yielding disposition*
So many sweet words from thy sister's mouth,
I am afraid, would make me take her
To embrace and pardon her. I am mad indeed,
And know not what I do. Yet have a care
Of me in what thou dost.

MELANTIUS Why, thinks my friend
I will forget his honor, or, to save
The bravery° of our house, will lose his fame,[6] *splendor*

4. But won't we deserve equal blame or credit if I take revenge (on the King and Evadne)?
5. Though I did draw on you in anger, not for the world would I fight with you in a resonable frame of mind.
6. Will destroy his reputation.

And fear to touch the throne of majesty?
AMINTOR A curse will follow that;° but rather live *i.e., regicide*
And suffer with me.
MELANTIUS I will do what worth° *virtue*
Shall bid me, and no more.
AMINTOR [*leaning on Melantius*] Faith, I am sick,
And desperately, I hope;° yet, leaning thus, *think; fear*
I feel a kind of ease.
MELANTIUS Come, take again
Your mirth about you.° *i.e., be cheerful*
AMINTOR I shall never do't.
MELANTIUS I warrant you. Look up; we'll walk together.
Put thine arm here; all shall be well again.
AMINTOR Thy love (O wretched I!), thy love, Melantius—
Why, I have nothing else.
MELANTIUS Be merry, then. *Exeunt.*

Enter Melantius again.

MELANTIUS This worthy young man may do violence
Upon himself, but I have cherished him
As well as I could, and sent him smiling from me
To counterfeit again. Sword, hold thine edge!
My heart will never fail me.—

Enter Diphilus.

Diphilus!
Thou com'st as sent.° *sent for; heaven-sent*
DIPHILUS Yonder has been such laughing!
MELANTIUS Betwixt whom?
DIPHILUS Why, our sister and the King.
I thought their spleens° would break; they laughed us all *(seat of mirth)*
Out of the room.
MELANTIUS They must weep, Diphilus.
DIPHILUS Must they?
MELANTIUS They must.
Thou art my brother, and, if I did believe
Thou hadst a base thought, I would rip it out,
Lie where it durst.
DIPHILUS You should not. I would first
Mangle myself and find it.
MELANTIUS That was spoke
According to our strain.° Come, join thy hands to mine, *family, breeding*
And swear a firmness to what project I
Shall lay before thee.
DIPHILUS You do wrong us both.
People hereafter shall not say there passed
A bond more than our loves to tie our lives
And deaths together.[7]
MELANTIUS It is as nobly said as I would wish.
Anon I'll tell you wonders: we are wronged.
DIPHILUS But I will tell you now, we'll right ourselves.
MELANTIUS Stay not.° Prepare the armor in my house; *Make no delay*

7. People will have no occasion to say hereafter that we needed to bind ourselves by oaths to live and die together, since our mutual loves are sufficient for that.

And what friends you can draw unto our side,
Not knowing° of the cause, make ready too. *Without their knowing*
Haste, Diphilus! The time requires it. Haste!
Exit Diphilus.
I hope° my cause is just. I know my blood *believe, trust*
Tells me it is, and I will credit° it. *believe*
To take revenge, and lose° myself withal, *destroy, undo*
Were idle;° and to scape impossible, *Would be foolish*
Without° I had the fort, which (misery!), *Unless*
Remaining in the hands of my old enemy
Calianax—but I must have it.

Enter Calianax.

See
Where he comes shaking by me. [*To him*] Good my lord,
Forget your spleen° to me. I never wronged you, *anger*
But would have peace with every man.

CALIANAX 'Tis well.° *That's all very well*
If I durst fight, your tongue would lie at quiet.° *be still*

MELANTIUS You're touchy without all cause.

CALIANAX Do,° mock me. *Go ahead*

MELANTIUS By mine honor, I speak truth.

CALIANAX Honor? Where is't?

MELANTIUS See what starts° *leaps*
You make into your idle hatred, to° *in response to*
My love and freedom° to you. I am come *liberality; candor*
With resolution to obtain a suit
Of you.

CALIANAX A suit of me! 'Tis very like° *likely*
It should be granted, sir.° [*He starts to leave.*] *(said ironically)*

MELANTIUS Nay, go not hence.
'Tis this: you have the keeping of the fort,
And I would wish you, by the love you ought
To bear unto me, to deliver it
Into my hands.

CALIANAX I am in hope° thou art mad, *It's my belief*
To talk to me thus.

MELANTIUS But there is a reason
To move you to it: I would kill the King
That wronged you and your daughter.

CALIANAX Out,° traitor! [*He starts to leave.*] *(conveying indignation)*

MELANTIUS Nay, but stay. I cannot scape,
The deed once done, without I have this fort.

CALIANAX And should I help thee? Now thy treacherous mind
Betrays itself.

MELANTIUS Come, delay me not.
Give me a sudden° answer, or already *quick*
Thy last° is spoke. Refuse not offered love *last word*
When it comes clad in secrets.

CALIANAX [*aside*] If I say
I will not, he will kill me; I do see't
Writ in his looks. And should I say I will,
He'll run and tell the King. [*To him*] I do not shun
Your friendship, dear Melantius, but this cause
Is weighty. Give me but an hour to think.

MELANTIUS Take it. [*Aside*] I know this goes° unto the King, *will be told*
But I am armed.° *Exit Melantius.* *prepared*
CALIANAX Methinks I feel myself
But twenty now again. This fighting fool
Wants policy.° I shall revenge my girl *Lacks cunning*
And make her red° again. I pray my legs *healthy of color*
Will last° that pace that I will carry them! *hold out*
I shall want° breath before I find the King. [*Exit.*] *be out of*

4.1

Enter Melantius, Evadne, and ladies.

MELANTIUS God save you!
EVADNE Save you, sweet brother.
MELANTIUS In my blunt eye methinks you look, Evadne—
EVADNE Come, you would make me blush.° *blush in modesty*
MELANTIUS I would, Evadne. I shall displease my ends else.[1]
EVADNE You shall, if you commend° me; I am bashful. *flatter, praise*
Come, sir, how do I look?
MELANTIUS I would not have your women hear me
Break into commendations of you; 'tis not seemly.
EVADNE [*to her ladies*] Go wait me° in the gallery. *wait for me*
Exeunt ladies.
Now speak.
MELANTIUS I'll lock the door first. [*He does so.*]
EVADNE Why?
MELANTIUS I will not have your gilded things, that dance
In visitation with their Milan skins,
Choke up my business.[2]
EVADNE You are strangely disposed, sir.
MELANTIUS Good madam, not° to make you merry. *my purpose is not*
EVADNE No, if you praise me, 'twill make me sad.
MELANTIUS Such a sad commendation I have for you.
EVADNE Brother, the court has made you witty,
And learn to° riddle. *And taught you to*
MELANTIUS I praise the court for't. Has it learned° you *taught*
nothing?
EVADNE Me?
MELANTIUS Ay, Evadne. Thou art young and handsome,
A lady of a sweet complexion
And such a flowing carriage° that it cannot *graceful bearing*
Choose but inflame a kingdom.
EVADNE Gentle° brother! *Courteous; wellborn*
MELANTIUS 'Tis yet in° thy repentance, foolish woman, *in the power of*
To make me gentle.° *mild*
EVADNE How is this?
MELANTIUS 'Tis base,
And I could blush at these years,° through all *even at my age*
My honored scars, to come to such a parley.
EVADNE I understand ye not.

4.1. Evadne's apartment.
1. I.e., I do wish to make you blush, Evadne (but from guiltiness, not modesty). Otherwise I will offend the cause to which I am committed.
2. I don't want the court butterflies who flutter about you, dancing attendance in their imported fashions, to interrupt what I have to say to you.

MELANTIUS You dare not, fool;
They that commit thy faults fly the remembrance.[3]
EVADNE My faults, sir? I would have you know I care not
If they were written here, here in my forehead.
MELANTIUS Thy body is too little for the story,
The lusts of which would fill another woman,
Though she had twins within her.
EVADNE This is saucy.
Look° you intrude no more. There's your way.° *See to it that / the door*
MELANTIUS Thou art my way, and I will tread upon thee
Till I find truth out.
EVADNE What truth is that you look for?
MELANTIUS Thy long-lost honor. Would the gods had set me
Rather to grapple with the plague, or stand° *withstand*
One of their loudest bolts!° Come, tell me quickly, *thunderbolts*
Do it without enforcement, and take heed
You swell me not above my temper.[4]
EVADNE How, sir!
Where got you this report?
MELANTIUS Where there was people:
In every place.
EVADNE They and the seconds° of it *upholders, repeaters*
Are base people. Believe them not; they lied.
MELANTIUS Do not play with mine anger, do not, wretch!
[*He seizes her.*]
I come to know° that desperate fool that drew thee *learn the name of*
From thy fair° life. Be wise, and lay him open.° *spotless / say who he is*
EVADNE Unhand me, and learn manners! Such another
Forgetfulness forfeits your life.
MELANTIUS Quench me this mighty humor,[5] and then tell me
Whose whore you are; for you are one, I know it.
Let all mine honors perish but I'll find him,
Though he lie locked up in thy blood.[6] Be sudden;
There is no facing it.[7] And be not flattered;° *self-deceived*
The burnt air, when the Dog reigns,[8] is not fouler
Than thy contagious° name, till thy repentance *morally infectious*
(If the gods grant thee any) purge thy sickness.
EVADNE Begone! You are my brother; that's your safety.
MELANTIUS I'll be a wolf first.° 'Tis, to be thy brother, *I'd rather be a wolf*
An infamy below the sin of coward.
I am as far from being part of thee
As thou art from thy virtue. Seek a kindred
'Mongst sensual beasts, and make a goat° thy brother; *(a type of lechery)*
A goat is cooler.° Will you tell me yet? *less lascivious*
EVADNE If you stay here and rail thus, I shall tell you,
I'll ha' you whipped. Get you to your command,
And there preach to your sentinels, and tell them
What a brave man you are. I shall laugh at you.
MELANTIUS You're grown a glorious° whore. Where be your *haughty*
fighters?° *champions*

3. Those who commit such sins as you commit do not wish to remember.
4. Take heed you don't make me swell with ungovernable rage.
5. Quench this affectation of mightiness.
6. I.e., Even if I have to kill you to learn his name.
7. There's no point in trying to (1) brave the matter out; (2) put on a deceptive face.
8. The hot and humid air of late summer, when the Dog Star (Sirius) rises with the sun.

What mortal fool durst raise thee to this daring,° *audacity*
And I alive?° By my just sword, he'd safer *While I yet live*
Bestride a billow when the angry north° *north wind*
Plows up the sea, or made heaven's fire his food.[9]
Work° me no higher. Will you discover° yet? *Goad / reveal the name*
EVADNE The fellow's mad. Sleep, and speak sense.° *recover your wits*
MELANTIUS Force my swoll'n heart no further. I would save
thee.
Your great maintainers are not here; they dare not.° *dare not come here*
Would they were all,° and armed! I would speak loud; *all here*
Here's one should thunder to 'em.[1] Will you tell me?
Thou hast no hope to scape. He that dares most,
And damns away his soul to do thee service,
Will sooner snatch meat from a hungry lion
Than come to rescue thee. Thou hast death about thee.
He's undone thine honor, poisoned thy virtue,
And, of a lovely rose, left thee a canker.° *dog rose; blight*
EVADNE Let me consider.
MELANTIUS Do: whose child thou wert,
Whose honor thou hast murdered, whose grave opened,
And so pulled on° the gods that in their justice *provoked*
They must restore him° flesh again and life, *(our father)*
And raise his dry bones to revenge this scandal.
EVADNE The gods are not of my mind. They had better
Let 'em° lie sweet still in the earth; they'll stink here. *(his bones)*
MELANTIUS Do you raise mirth out of my easiness?° *leniency*
Forsake me, then, all weaknesses of nature
That make men women!
[*He draws his sword and forces her to her knees.*]
Speak, you whore, speak truth,
Or, by the dear soul of thy sleeping father,
This sword shall be thy lover.[2] Tell, or I'll kill thee;
And, when thou hast told all, thou wilt deserve it.° *deserve death anyway*
EVADNE You will not murder me!
MELANTIUS No, 'tis a justice,° and a noble one, *justice, not murder*
To put the light° out of such base offenders. *light of life*
EVADNE [*calling*] Help!
MELANTIUS By thy foul self, no human help shall help thee
If thou criest. When I have killed thee—as I
Have vowed to do if thou confess not—naked
As thou hast left thine honor will I leave thee,
That on thy branded° flesh the world may read *branded with infamy*
Thy black shame and my justice. Wilt thou bend° yet? *yield*
EVADNE Yes.
MELANTIUS [*raising her*] Up, and begin your story.
EVADNE Oh, I am miserable!
MELANTIUS 'Tis true, thou art. Speak truth still.
EVADNE I have offended, noble sir. Forgive me!
MELANTIUS With what secure slave?° *overconfident wretch*
EVADNE Do not ask me, sir.
Mine own remembrance is a misery

9. Or swallow a thunderbolt. (Q1's "foe" in place of Q2's "food" would suggest defying the heavens; see Textual Notes.)

1. Here I am, the person who would menace them terribly.

2. This sword will enter your heart.

Too mighty for me.

MELANTIUS Do not fall back° again; *back into secretiveness*
My sword's unsheathèd yet.

EVADNE What shall I do?

MELANTIUS Be true,° and make your fault less. *Be truthful*

EVADNE I dare not tell.

MELANTIUS Tell, or I'll be this day° a-killing thee. *the whole day*

EVADNE Will you forgive me, then?

MELANTIUS Stay, I must ask
Mine honor first. I have too much foolish nature
In me; speak.

EVADNE Is there none else here?

MELANTIUS None but a fearful conscience; that's too many.
Who is't?

EVADNE Oh, hear me gently! It was the King.

MELANTIUS No more! My worthy father's and my services
Are liberally rewarded. King, I thank thee;
For all my dangers and my wounds, thou hast paid me
In my own metal: these are soldiers' thanks.°— *(said in bitter irony)*
How long have you lived thus, Evadne?

EVADNE Too long.

MELANTIUS Too late you find it. Can you be sorry?

EVADNE Would I were half as blameless![3]

MELANTIUS Evadne, thou wilt to thy trade again.

EVADNE First to my grave.

MELANTIUS Would gods thou hadst been so blest![4]
Dost thou not hate this King now? Prithee, hate him.
Couldst thou not curse him? I command thee, curse him!
Curse till the gods hear and deliver him
To thy just wishes. Yet I fear, Evadne,
You had rather play your game out.° *i.e., continue your sin*

EVADNE No, I feel
Too many sad confusions here° to let in *(in my heart)*
Any loose flame hereafter.

MELANTIUS Dost thou not feel, amongst all those,° one brave anger *those confused thoughts*
That breaks out nobly and directs thine arm
To kill this base king?

EVADNE All the gods forbid it!

MELANTIUS No, all the gods require it.
They are dishonored in him.

EVADNE 'Tis too fearful.

MELANTIUS You're valiant in his bed, and bold enough
To be a stale° whore and have your madam's° name *worn out / ladyship's*
Discourse° for grooms and pages, and hereafter, *A subject of gossip*
When his cool° majesty hath laid you by, *satiated*
To be at pension° with some needy sir *To become dependent*
For meat and coarser clothes; thus far you knew° *have known*
No fear. Come, you shall kill him.

EVADNE Good sir!

MELANTIUS An 'twere° to kiss him dead, thou'dst smother him. *If it were*

3. Would I were half as blameless as I am sorry!
4. Would you had been so blessed as to have died before you fell into shameful sin!

Be wise and kill him. Canst thou live and know
What noble minds shall make thee,° see thyself — *make of you*
Found out with every finger,° made the shame — *Pointed at by all*
Of all successions,° and in this great ruin — *succeeding times*
Thy brother and thy noble husband broken?° — *ruined in reputation*
Thou shalt not live thus. Kneel and swear to help me
When I shall call thee to it, or, by all
Holy in heaven and earth, thou shalt not live
To breathe a full hour longer, not a thought.° — *not a moment*
Come, 'tis a righteous oath. [*She kneels.*] Give me thy hand,
And, both to heaven held up, swear by that wealth° — *wealth of reputation*
This lustful thief stole from thee, when I say it,
To let his foul soul out.

EVADNE Here I swear it,
And, all you spirits of abusèd ladies,
Help me in this performance!

MELANTIUS Enough. [*Raising her*] This must be known to none
But you and I, Evadne—not to your lord,° — *husband*
Though he be wise and noble, and a fellow
Dare° step as far into a worthy action — *Who dares*
As the most daring, ay, as far as justice.° — *carrying out justice*
Ask me not why. Farewell. *Exit Melantius.*

EVADNE Would I could say so° to my black disgrace! — *say farewell*
Gods, where have I been all this time? How friended,° — *befriended*
That I should lose myself thus desperately,
And none for pity show me how I wandered?
There is not in the compass of the light° — *anywhere under the sun*
A more unhappy creature. Sure I am monstrous,
For I have done those follies, those mad mischiefs,
Would dare° a woman. O my loaden soul, — *Which would daunt*
Be not so cruel to me! Choke not up
The way to my repentance!

Enter Amintor.

O my lord!

AMINTOR How now?

EVADNE My much abusèd lord! *Kneel.*

AMINTOR This cannot be.° — *i.e., Do not kneel*

EVADNE I do not kneel to live; I dare not hope it;
The wrongs I did are greater. Look upon me,
Though I appear with all my faults!

AMINTOR Stand up.
This is a new way to beget more sorrows.
Heaven knows I have too many! Do not mock me;
Though I am tame and bred up with° my wrongs, — *inured to; akin to*
Which are my foster brothers, I may leap,
Like a hand-wolf,° into my natural wildness, — *hand-tamed wolf*
And do an outrage. Prithee, do not mock me.

EVADNE My whole life is so leprous it infects
All my repentance. I would buy your pardon,
Though at the highest set,° even with my life— — *stake*
That slight contrition that's no sacrifice° — *that can scarcely atone*
For what I have committed.

AMINTOR Sure, I dazzle.° — *I am bewildered*

There cannot be a faith in that foul woman
That knows no god° more mighty than her mischiefs.° *no higher law / sins*
Thou dost still worse, still number on° thy faults, *add to*
To press° my poor heart thus. Can I believe *oppress*
There's any seed of virtue in that woman
Left to shoot up,° that dares go on in sin *thrive, grow*
Known, and so known, as thine is? Oh, Evadne!
Would there were any safety° in thy sex,° *trustworthiness / women*
That I might put a thousand sorrows off
And credit° thy repentance! But I must not; *believe in*
Thou hast brought me to that dull° calamity, *sensibility-dulling*
To that strange misbelief of all the world
And all things that are in it, that I fear
I shall fall like a tree, and find my grave,
Only rememb'ring that I grieve.

EVADNE My lord,
Give me° your griefs. You are an innocent, *Let me share*
A soul as white as heaven. Let not my sins
Perish° your noble youth. I do not fall° here *Cause to perish / kneel*
To shadow° my dissembling with my tears, *hide*
As all say women can, or to make less
What my hot will hath done, which heaven and you
Knows to be tougher° than the hand of time *more persistent*
Can cut from man's remembrance. No, I do not.
I do appear the same, the same Evadne,
Dressed in the shames I lived in, the same monster.
But these are names of honor to° what I am; *compared with*
I do present myself the foulest creature,
Most poisonous, dangerous, and despised of men° *by men*
Lerna e'er bred, or Nilus.[5] I am hell
Till you, my dear lord, shoot your light into me,
The beams of your forgiveness. I am soul-sick,
And wither with the fear of one condemned
Till I have got your pardon.

AMINTOR Rise, Evadne.
Those heavenly powers that put this good into thee
Grant a continuance of it! I forgive thee.
Make thyself worthy of it, and take heed,
Take heed, Evadne, this be serious.
Mock not the powers above, that can and dare° *won't hesitate to*
Give thee° a great example of their justice *Present you as*
To all ensuing ages, if thou play'st
With thy repentance, the best sacrifice.

EVADNE I have done nothing good to win belief,
My life hath been so faithless. All the creatures
Made for heaven's honors have their ends,° and good ones— *purposes*
All but the cozening crocodiles, false women.[6]
They reign here like those plagues, those killing sores° *bubonic pustules*
Men pray against; and when they die, like tales

5. The marshes of Lerna bred the terrifying many-headed Hydra that Hercules slew in one of his twelve labors. The Nile was famous for its crocodiles (see line 247 below).

6. Crocodile tears (false tears supposedly shed by crocodiles as they devour their prey) were often compared to women's deceptive ("cozening") tears.

Ill told and unbelieved, they pass away
And go to dust forgotten. But, my lord,
Those short days I shall number to my rest° *final rest, death*
(As many must not see me)° shall, though too late, *As I won't have many*
Though in my evening, yet perceive° I will— *perceive that*
Since I can do no good because a woman—
Reach constantly at something that is near it.° *something like goodness*
I will redeem one minute of my age,° *part of my life*
Or, like another Niobe, I'll weep
Till I am water.[7]

AMINTOR I am now dissolved.
My frozen soul melts. May each sin thou hast
Find a new mercy! Rise, I am at peace. [*She rises.*]
Hadst thou been thus, thus excellently good,
Before that devil king tempted thy frailty,
Sure thou hadst made° a star. Give me thy hand. *would have become*
From this time I will know° thee, and, as far *acknowledge as my wife*
As honor gives me leave, be thy Amintor.
When we meet next, I will salute thee fairly,
And pray the gods to give thee happy days.
My charity° shall go along with thee, *loving kindness*
Though my embraces must be far from thee.
I should ha' killed° thee, but this sweet repentance *I intended to kill*
Locks up my vengeance, for which thus I kiss thee—
[*He kisses her.*]
The last kiss we must take; and would to heaven
The holy priest that gave our hands together
Had given us equal virtues! Go, Evadne;
The gods thus part our bodies. Have a care
My honor falls no further; I am well then.

EVADNE All the dear joys here, and above hereafter,
Crown thy fair soul! Thus I take leave, my lord,
And never shall you see the foul Evadne
Till she have tried all honored means that may
Set her in rest and wash her stains away.
Exeunt [*in different directions*].

[4.2]

Hautboys° play within. [*A*] *banquet°* [*is carried in by servants*]. *Enter King* [*and*] *Calianax.* *Oboes / dessert*

KING I cannot tell how I should credit this
From you that are his enemy.

CALIANAX I am sure
He said it to me, and I'll justify it
What° way he dares oppose, but with my sword. *Whatever*

KING But did he break,° without all circumstance,° *he disclose / without ado*
To you his foe, that he would have the fort
To kill me, and then scape?

CALIANAX If he deny it,

7. When Niobe boasted of her superiority to Leto in having fourteen children (or twelve, or twenty, depending on the account) to Leto's two, those two children of Leto, Apollo and Artemis, killed all of Niobe's children. She was subsequently transformed into a weeping column of stone by Zeus.

4.2. The palace.

I'll make him blush.
KING It sounds incredibly.
CALIANAX Ay, so does everything I say of late.
KING Not so, Calianax.
CALIANAX Yes, I should sit
Mute, whilst a rogue with strong arms cuts your throat.° *(said ironically)*
KING Well, I will try° him, and if this be true *test*
I'll pawn° my life I'll find it;° if't be false, *bet / (the truth)*
And that you clothe your hate in such a lie,
You shall hereafter dote° in your own house, *play the fool*
Not in the court.
CALIANAX Why, if it be a lie,
Mine ears are false, for I'll be sworn I heard it.
Old men are good for nothing; you were best
Put me to death for hearing, and free him
For meaning° it. You would ha' trusted me *intending*
Once, but the time is altered.
KING And will still,
Where I may do with justice to the world.
You have no witness?
CALIANAX Yes, myself.
KING No more,
I mean, there were that heard it?
CALIANAX How? No more?
Would you have more? Why, am not I enough
To hang a thousand rogues?
KING But so° you may *that way*
Hang honest men too, if you please.
CALIANAX I may;
'Tis like° I will do so! There are a hundred *likely (ironic)*
Will swear it for a need, too, if I say it.
KING Such witnesses we need not.
CALIANAX And 'tis hard
If my word cannot hang a boisterous knave.
KING Enough.—Where's Strato?

Enter Strato.

STRATO Sir?
KING Why, where's all the company? Call Amintor and
Evadne. Where's my brother, and Melantius?
Bid him come too, and Diphilus. Call all
That are without there. *Exit Strato.*
If he° should desire *(Melantius)*
The combat° of you, 'tis not in the power *A duel*
Of all our laws to hinder it, unless
We mean to quit 'em.° *abandon the laws*
CALIANAX Why, if you do think
'Tis fit an old man and a counselor
To fight for what he says, then you may grant it.

Enter Amintor, Evadne, Melantius, Diphilus, Lysippus, Cleon, [and] Strato.

KING Come, sirs.—Amintor, thou art yet a bridegroom,
And I will use thee so. Thou shalt sit down.—
Evadne, sit, and you, Amintor, too;

This banquet is for you, sir. Who has brought
A merry tale about him, to raise laughter
Amongst our wine? Why, Strato, where art thou?
Thou wilt chop out with them° unseasonably *blurt out tales*
When I desire 'em not.

STRATO 'Tis my ill luck, sir, so to spend° them then. *expend; relate*

KING Reach me a bowl of wine, Melantius.
[*To Amintor*] Thou art sad.

AMINTOR I should be, sir, the merriest here,° *(being the bridegroom)*
But I ha' ne'er a story of mine own
Worth telling at this time.

KING Give me the wine.
[*He is handed a bowl of wine.*]
Melantius, I am now considering
How easy 'twere for any man we trust
To poison one of us in such a bowl.

MELANTIUS I think it were not hard sir, for a knave.

CALIANAX [*aside*] Such as you are.

KING I'faith, 'twere easy. It becomes° us well *befits*
To get plain-dealing men about ourselves,
Such as you all are here.—Amintor, to thee
And to thy fair Evadne! [*He drinks a toast.*]

MELANTIUS (*aside* [*to Calianax*]) Have you thought
Of this,[1] Calianax?

CALIANAX [*aside to Melantius*] Yes, marry,° have I. *indeed (lit., "by Mary")*

MELANTIUS [*aside to Calianax*] And what's your resolution?

CALIANAX [*aside to Melantius*] Ye shall have it—
[*To himself*] Soundly, I warrant you.

KING Reach to Amintor, Strato.
[*Strato passes the bowl to Amintor.*]

AMINTOR [*drinking to Evadne and then passing her the bowl*]
Here, my love,
This wine will do thee wrong, for it will set
Blushes° upon thy cheeks, and, till thou dost *(betokening shame)*
A fault, 'twere pity. [*Evadne drinks.*]

KING Yet I wonder much
Of° the strange desperation of these men *At*
That dare attempt such acts here in our state;
He could not scape that did it.

MELANTIUS Were he known,
Unpossible.

KING It would be known, Melantius.

MELANTIUS It ought to be. If he got then away,
He must wear all our lives upon his sword.° *i.e., must kill us all*
He need not fly the island; he must leave
No one alive.

KING No, I should think no man
Could kill me and scape clear but that old man.
[*The King indicates Calianax.*]

CALIANAX But I? Heaven bless me! I? Should I, my liege?

KING I do not think thou wouldst, but yet thou mightst,° *you would be able to*
For thou hast in thy hands the means to scape,
By keeping of the fort.—He has, Melantius,

1. I.e., Have you thought of my proposal that you turn over the fort to me?

And he has kept it well.
MELANTIUS From cobwebs, sir;
'Tis clean swept. I can find no other art
In keeping of it now. 'Twas ne'er besieged
Since he commanded.
CALIANAX I shall be sure
Of your good word,[2] but I have kept it safe
From such as you.
MELANTIUS Keep your ill temper in.
I speak no malice; had my brother kept it
I should ha' said as much.
KING [*to the banquet guests*] You are not merry.
[*To Lysippus*] Brother, drink wine.—Sit you all still!
[*The King takes Calianax*] *aside* [*in private conversation, while the others remain seated.*] Calianax,
I cannot trust thus.° I have thrown out words *trust what you've said*
That would have fetched warm blood upon the cheeks
Of guilty men, and he is never moved.
He knows no such thing.
CALIANAX [*aside to the King*] Impudence may scape
When feeble virtue is accused.
KING [*aside to Calianax*] 'A must,
If he were guilty, feel an alteration° *discomfort*
At this our whisper, whilst we point at him.
You see he does not.
CALIANAX [*aside to the King*] Let him hang himself.
What care I what he does? This he did say.
KING [*beckoning Melantius to join them*] Melantius, you can easily conceive
What I have meant, for men that are in fault
Can subtly apprehend when others aim
At what they do amiss. But I forgive
Freely before this man.[3] Heaven do so too!
I will not touch thee so much as with shame
Of telling it.[4] Let it be so no more.
CALIANAX [*aside*] Why, this is very fine!° *(ironic)*
MELANTIUS [*to the King*] I cannot tell
What 'tis you mean, but I am apt enough
Rudely to thrust into ignorant fault.° *to err unknowingly*
But let me know it; happily° 'tis naught *haply, perchance*
But misconstruction, and, where I am clear,
I will not take forgiveness of the gods,[5]
Much less of you.
KING Nay, if you stand so stiff,° *are so stubborn*
I shall call back my mercy.
MELANTIUS I want° smoothness *lack*
To thank a man for pardoning of a crime
I never knew.° *conceived of*
KING Not to instruct your knowledge, but to show you
My ears° are everywhere: you meant to kill me, *spies*

2. I can always count on you to put in a good word for me. (Said sarcastically.)
3. The guilty can guess what is said about them, whereas others who are innocent miss entirely in trying to interpret what is being said. But I forgive you freely for the offense with which Calianax has charged you.
4. I won't shame you by so much as mentioning it directly.
5. I won't allow even to the gods that there is anything for which I need to be forgiven.

And get the fort to scape.
MELANTIUS Pardon me, sir;
My bluntness will be° pardoned. You preserve — *insists on being*
A race° of idle people here about you, — *group, tribe*
Eaters and talkers, to defame the worth
Of those that do things worthy. The man that uttered this
Had perished without food,° be't who it will, — *Would have starved*
But for this° arm that fenced° him from the foe. — *my / protected*
And, if I thought you gave a faith° to this, — *credence*
The plainness of my nature would speak more.
Give me a pardon° (for you ought to do't) — *dispensation*
To kill him that spake this.
CALIANAX [*aside*] Ay, that will be
The end of all: then I am fairly paid
For all my care and service.
MELANTIUS That old man,° — *Even Calianax*
Who calls me enemy, and of whom I
(Though I will never match my hate so low)
Have no good thought, would yet, I think, excuse me,
And swear he thought me wronged in this.
CALIANAX Who, I?
Thou shameless fellow! Didst thou not speak to me
Of it thyself?
MELANTIUS [*to the King*] Oh, then it came from him?
CALIANAX From me! Who should it come from but from me?
MELANTIUS Nay, I believe your malice is enough,° — *great enough*
But I ha' lost my anger. [*To the King*] Sir, I hope
You are well satisfied.
KING [*to those at the table*] Lysippus, cheer
Amintor and his lady; there's no sound
Comes from you. I will come and do't myself.
AMINTOR You have done already,[6] sir, for me, I thank you.
KING Melantius, I do credit this from him,° — *(Calianax)*
How slight soe'er you make't.
MELANTIUS 'Tis strange you should.
CALIANAX 'Tis strange 'a should believe an old man's word,
That never lied in's life.
MELANTIUS I talk not to thee.—
[*To the King*] Shall the wild words of this distempered man,
Frantic with age and sorrow, make a breach
Betwixt Your Majesty and me? 'Twas wrong
To hearken to him, but to credit him
As° much, at least, as I have power° to bear. — *Is as / strength*
But pardon me (whilst I speak only truth,
I may commend myself), I have bestowed
My careless blood with you,[7] and should be loath
To think° an action that would make me lose — *Even to contemplate*
That° and my thanks too. When I was a boy, — *(My blood)*
I thrust myself into my country's cause,
And did a deed that plucked five years from time,
And styled me man, then, and for you, my King.[8]

6. You've already cheered us up. (But with a bitter hidden meaning: You've already destroyed my happiness.)
7. I have bled, without concern for my own life, to serve you.
8. My heroism made me a man five years ahead of my time, and I did all this in your royal service.

Your subjects all have fed by virtue of
My arm. This sword of mine hath plowed the ground
And reaped the fruit in peace,
And you yourself have lived at home in ease.
So terrible° I grew that without swords — *terrifying*
My name hath fetched you conquest, and my heart
And limbs are still the same, my will as great
To do you service. Let me not be paid
With such a strange distrust.

KING Melantius,
I held it great injustice to believe
Thine enemy, and did not; if I did,
I do not.° Let that satisfy. [*To those at the table*] What, struck — *I do not now*
With sadness, all? More wine! [*He rejoins the table.*]

CALIANAX [*to Melantius*] A few fine words
Have overthrown my truth. Ah, thou'rt a villain!

MELANTIUS (*aside* [*to him*]) Why, thou wert better let me have the fort.
Dotard, I will disgrace thee thus forever.
There shall no credit lie upon thy words.° — *No one will believe you*
Think better, and deliver it.

CALIANAX [*to the King*] My liege,
He's at me now again to do it. [*To Melantius*] Speak!
Deny it if thou canst. [*To the King*] Examine him
Whilst he is hot, for if he cool again
He will forswear it.

KING This is lunacy,
I hope,° Melantius. — *trust*

MELANTIUS He hath lost himself° — *become distracted*
Much since his daughter missed the happiness
My sister gained; and, though he call me foe,
I pity him.

CALIANAX Ha, pity? A pox upon you!

MELANTIUS Mark his disordered words; and at the masque
Diagoras knows° he raged and railed at me, — *can witness that*
And called a lady "whore" so° innocent — *who was so*
She understood him not. But it becomes
Both you and me to forgive distraction.
Pardon him, as I do.

CALIANAX I'll not speak for thee,[9]
For all thy cunning. [*To the King*] If you will be safe,
Chop off his head, for there was never known
So impudent a rascal.

KING [*to those nearby*] Some that love him,° — *(Calianax)*
Get him to bed. Why, pity should not let
Age make itself contemptible; we must be
All old. Have him away.

MELANTIUS Calianax,
The King believes you.° Come, you shall go home — *(said to humor Calianax)*
And rest; you ha' done well. [*Aside to him*] You'll give it° up — *(the fort)*
When I have used you thus a month, I hope.

CALIANAX [*to the King*] Now, now, 'tis plain, sir, he does move° me still! — *solicit; anger*

9. I.e., I refuse to play your game.

He says he knows I'll give him up the fort
When he has used me thus a month. I am mad,
Am I not, still?
OMNES° Ha, ha, ha! *All (at the table)*
CALIANAX I shall be mad indeed if you do thus.
Why should you trust a sturdy° fellow there *rebellious, defiant*
(That has no virtue in him; all's in his sword)
Before me? Do but take his weapons from him
And he's an ass; and I am a very fool,
Both with 'em° and without 'em, as you use me. *(weapons)*
OMNES Ha, ha, ha!
KING 'Tis well, Calianax; but if you use° *behave like*
This once again, I shall entreat some other
To see your offices be well discharged.
[*To those at the table*] Be merry, gentlemen!—It grows somewhat late.—
Amintor, thou wouldst be abed again.
AMINTOR Yes, sir.
KING And you, Evadne.—Let me take
Thee in my arms, Melantius, and believe
Thou art, as thou deservest to be, my friend
Still and forever.—Good Calianax,
Sleep soundly. It will bring thee to thyself.° *to your right mind*
Exeunt omnes. Manent° Melantius and Calianax. *Remain onstage*
CALIANAX Sleep soundly! I sleep soundly now, I hope;
I could not be thus else.—How dar'st thou stay
Alone with me, knowing how thou hast used me?
MELANTIUS You cannot blast° me with your tongue, *strike (like lightning)*
And that's the strongest part you have about ye.
CALIANAX I do look for some great punishment for this,[1]
For I begin to forget all my hate,
And take't unkindly that mine enemy
Should use me so extremely scurvily.
MELANTIUS I shall melt° too, if you begin to take *soften into tears*
Unkindnesses.[2] I never meant you hurt.
CALIANAX Thou'lt anger me again. Thou wretched rogue,
"Meant me no hurt"! Disgrace me with the King,
Lose all my offices—this is no hurt,
Is it? I prithee, what dost thou call hurt?
MELANTIUS To poison men because they love me not;
To call the credit of men's wives in question;
To murder children betwixt me and land°— *inheritance of land*
This I call hurt.
CALIANAX All this, thou think'st, is sport,
For mine° is worse. But use thy will with me, *the injury done me*
For betwixt grief and anger I could cry.
MELANTIUS Be wise, then, and be safe. Thou mayst revenge.
CALIANAX Ay, o'th'King! I would revenge of thee.
MELANTIUS That you must plot yourself.
CALIANAX I am a fine plotter![3]
MELANTIUS The short° is, I will hold thee with the King *The long and the short*
In this perplexity till peevishness

1. I expect heaven to punish this behavior.
2. If you begin to take my words the wrong way.
3. I'm no plotter (as you are). (Said with bitter irony.)

And thy disgrace have laid thee in thy grave.
But if thou wilt deliver up the fort,
I'll take thy trembling body in my arms
And bear thee over dangers. Thou shalt hold
Thy wonted state.° *accustomed high rank*

CALIANAX If I should tell the King,
Canst thou deny't again?

MELANTIUS Try, and believe.° *Try and see*

CALIANAX Nay, then, thou canst bring anything about.
Melantius, thou shalt have the fort.

MELANTIUS Why, well.
Here let our hate be buried, and this hand
Shall right us both. Give me thy agèd breast
To compass.° [*He offers to embrace Calianax.*] *encompass, embrace*

CALIANAX Nay, I do not love thee yet.
I cannot well endure to look on thee,
And, if I thought it were a courtesy,
Thou shouldst not have it. But I am disgraced;
My offices are to be ta'en away;
And if° I did but hold this fort a day, *even if*
I do believe the King would take it from me
And give it thee, things are so strangely carried.° *managed*
Ne'er thank me for't; but yet the King shall know
There was some such thing in't I told him of,
And that I was an honest man.

MELANTIUS He'll buy
That knowledge very dearly.—

Enter Diphilus.

Diphilus,
What news with thee?

DIPHILUS This were a night indeed
To do it° in; the King hath sent for her.° *(our plot) / (Evadne)*

MELANTIUS She shall perform it, then. Go, Diphilus,
And take from this good man, my worthy friend,
The fort; he'll give it thee.

DIPHILUS Ha' you got that?

CALIANAX Art thou of the same breed? Canst thou deny
This to the King too?

DIPHILUS With a confidence° *boldness*
As great as his.° *(Melantius')*

CALIANAX Faith, like° enough. *likely*

MELANTIUS [*to Diphilus*] Away! And use him kindly.

[*Diphilus offers to take Calianax's arm.*]

CALIANAX Touch not me!
I hate the whole strain.° If thou follow me *stock, breed*
A great way off, I'll give thee up the fort—
And hang yourselves!

MELANTIUS [*to Diphilus*] Begone.

DIPHILUS [*aside to Melantius*] He's finely wrought.° *worked on; agitated*

Exeunt Calianax [and] Diphilus.

MELANTIUS This is a night, spite of astronomers,° *despite astrologers*
To do the deed in. I will wash the stain
That rests upon our house off with his° blood. *(the King's)*

Enter Amintor [with drawn sword].

AMINTOR Melantius, now assist me. If thou be'st
That which thou say'st, assist me. I have lost
All my distempers, and have found a rage
So pleasing! Help me.
MELANTIUS Who can see him° thus — (Amintor)
And not swear vengeance? —What's the matter, friend?
AMINTOR Out with thy sword, and, hand in hand with me,
Rush to the chamber of this hated king,
And sink him with the weight of all his sins
To hell forever.
MELANTIUS 'Twere a rash attempt,
Not to be done with safety. Let your reason
Plot your revenge, and not your passion.
AMINTOR If thou refusest me in these extremes,
Thou art no friend. He sent for her to me—
By heaven, to me, myself! And I must tell ye
I love her as a stranger.° There is worth — *i.e., without sex*
In that vile woman, worthy things, Melantius;
And she repents. I'll do't myself alone,
Though I be slain. Farewell. [*He starts to go.*]
MELANTIUS [*aside*] He'll overthrow
My whole design with madness.—Amintor,
Think what thou dost. I dare as much as valor;° — *as valor dares, permits*
But 'tis the King, the King, the King, Amintor,
With whom thou fightest. (*Aside*) I know he's honest,° — *loyal*
And this will work with him.
AMINTOR [*letting fall his sword*] I cannot tell
What thou hast said,° but thou hast charmed my sword — *What magic you spoke*
Out of my hand, and left me shaking here
Defenseless.
MELANTIUS I will take it up for thee.
[*He picks up Amintor's sword and hands it to him.*]
AMINTOR What a wild beast is uncollected° man! — *out-of-control*
The thing that we call honor bears us all
Headlong unto sin, and yet itself is nothing.° — *a mere word*
MELANTIUS Alas, how variable are thy thoughts!
AMINTOR Just like my fortunes. I was run to° that — *was on the verge of*
I purposed to have chid thee for. Some plot
I did distrust° thou hadst against the King, — *suspect*
By that old fellow's carriage.° But take heed; — *Calianax's behavior*
There's not the least limb growing° to a king — *accruing*
But carries thunder in't.
MELANTIUS I have none° — *no bad intentions*
Against him.
AMINTOR Why, come, then, and still remember
We may not think revenge.
MELANTIUS I will remember. *Exeunt.*

5.1

Enter Evadne and a Gentleman.

EVADNE Sir, is the King abed?
GENTLEMAN Madam, an hour ago.
EVADNE Give me the key, then, and let none be near;
'Tis the King's pleasure.
GENTLEMAN I understand you, madam. Would 'twere mine!
I must not wish good rest unto Your Ladyship.
EVADNE You talk,° you talk. *You're joshing me*
GENTLEMAN 'Tis all I dare do, madam; but the King
Will wake, and then—
EVADNE Saving° your imagination, pray, good night, sir. *Sparing me*
GENTLEMAN A good night be it, then, and a long one, madam!
I am gone. *Exit.*
EVADNE The night grows horrible, and all about me,
Like my black purpose. Oh, the conscience
Of a lost virgin! Whither wilt thou pull me?
To what things dismal as the depth of hell
Wilt thou provoke me? Let no woman dare
From this hour be disloyal, if her heart
Be flesh, if she have blood and can fear. 'Tis a daring
Above that desperate fool's that left his peace° *peace and quiet*
And went to sea to fight; 'tis so many sins
An age cannot repent 'em, and so great
The gods want° mercy for. Yet I must through 'em. *lack*
I have begun a slaughter on my honor,
And I must end it there.

[Evadne draws the bedcurtains, and discovers the] King abed.

'A sleeps. O God,
Why give you peace to this untemperate beast
That hath so long transgressed you? I must kill him,
And I will do't bravely; the mere° joy *sheer*
Tells me I merit° in it. Yet I must not *acquire merit*
Thus tamely do it as he sleeps; that were
To rock him to another world.° My vengeance *send his soul to heaven*
Shall take him waking, and then lay before him
The number of his wrongs and punishments.
I'll shape his sins like furies,° till I waken *avenging spirits*
His evil angel, his sick conscience,
And then I'll strike him dead.—King, by your leave!
Ties his arms to the bed.
I dare not trust your strength; Your Grace and I
Must grapple upon even terms no more.° *Must not couple sexually*
So; if he rail° me not from my resolution, *chide*
I shall be strong enough.—
[*Waking him*] My lord the King! My lord! [*Aside*] 'A sleeps
As if he meant to wake no more. [*Aloud*] My lord!
[*Aside*] Is he not dead already? [*Aloud*] Sir! My lord!
KING Who's that?

5.1. The King's bedchamber, which is understood to be at the back of the stage, in a "discovery space," curtained off as the scene begins.

EVADNE Oh, you sleep soundly, sir!
KING My dear Evadne,
I have been dreaming of thee. Come to bed.
EVADNE I am come at length, sir; but how welcome?° *how welcome am I?*
KING What pretty new device is this, Evadne?
What, do you tie me to you? By my love,
This is a quaint one. Come, my dear, and kiss me.
I'll be thy Mars. To bed, my Queen of Love!
Let us be caught together, that the gods may see
And envy our embraces.[1]
EVADNE Stay, sir, stay.
You are too hot, and I have brought you physic° *medicine*
To temper your high veins.° *To abate your fever*
KING Prithee, to bed, then. Let me take it warm;
Here thou shalt know the state of my body better.
EVADNE I know you have a surfeited, foul body,
And you must bleed. [*She draws a knife.*]
KING Bleed!
EVADNE Ay, you shall bleed. Lie still, and if the devil,
Your lust, will give you leave, repent. This steel
Comes to redeem the honor that you stole,
King: my fair name, which nothing but thy death
Can answer to the world.
KING How's this, Evadne?
EVADNE I am not she, nor bear I in this breast
So much cold spirit° to be called a woman. *timidity*
I am a tiger; I am anything
That knows not pity. Stir not! If thou dost,
I'll take thee unprepared,° thy fears upon thee *spiritually unready*
That make thy sins look double, and so send thee
(By my revenge, I will!) to look° those torments *find out*
Prepared for such black souls.
KING Thou dost not mean this; 'tis impossible.
Thou art too sweet and gentle.
EVADNE No, I am not.
I am as foul as thou art, and can number
As many such hells here.° I was once fair, *(in my heart)*
Once I was lovely, not a blowing rose
More chastely sweet,[2] till thou, thou, thou foul canker,° *cankerworm*
(Stir not!) didst poison me. I was a world of virtue
Till your curst court and you (hell bless you for't!),
With your temptations on temptations,
Made me give up mine honor; for which, King,
I am come to kill thee.
KING No!
EVADNE I am.
KING Thou art not.
I prithee, speak not these things. Thou art gentle,
And wert not meant thus rugged.° *meant to be harsh*
EVADNE Peace, and hear me!

1. In Book 8 of the *Odyssey,* Homer relates how Aphrodite and Ares (the goddess of love and the god of war, Roman Venus and Mars) were discovered to be having an affair by Aphrodite's jealous husband, Hephaestus (Roman Vulcan), who then trapped them in a bronze net while they slept. When they were thus exposed, the gods came by to laugh at their expense. The story turns up elsewhere in classical literature also.
2. No full-blooming rose was ever more chastely sweet than I.

Stir nothing but your tongue, and that° for mercy — *and use it to beg*
To those° above us, by whose lights° I vow, — *(the gods) / stars*
Those blessèd fires° that shot to see our sin, — *shooting stars*
If thy hot soul had substance with° thy blood, — *were as material as*
I would kill that too—which, being past° my steel, — *beyond the reach of*
My tongue shall reach. Thou art a shameless villain,
A thing out of the overcharge of nature,° — *i.e., a monster*
Sent like a thick cloud to disperse a plague
Upon weak, catching° women—such a tyrant — *easily infected*
That for his lust would sell away his subjects,
Ay, all his heaven hereafter.

KING Hear, Evadne,
Thou soul of sweetness, hear! I am thy king.

EVADNE Thou art my shame. Lie still; there's none about you
Within° your cries; all promises of safety — *Within earshot of*
Are but deluding dreams. Thus, thus, thou foul man,
Thus I begin my vengeance. *Stabs him.*

KING Hold, Evadne!
I do command thee, hold!

EVADNE I do not mean, sir,
To part so fairly° with you. We must change° — *gently / exchange*
More of these love tricks yet.

KING What bloody villain
Provoked thee to this murder?

EVADNE Thou, thou monster! [*Stabs him.*]

KING Oh!

EVADNE Thou kept'st me brave° at court, and whored me, King, — *richly dressed*
Then married me to a young noble gentleman,
And whored me still.

KING Evadne, pity me!

EVADNE Hell take me, then! [*She stabs repeatedly.*] This for my lord Amintor,
This for my noble brother, and this stroke
For the most wronged of women! *Kills him.*

KING Oh, I die!

EVADNE Die all our faults together! I forgive thee. *Exit.*

Enter two [*Gentlemen*] *of the bedchamber.*

FIRST GENTLEMAN Come, now she's gone, let's enter. The King expects it, and will be angry.° — *angry if we're late*

SECOND GENTLEMAN 'Tis a fine wench. We'll have a snap° at her one of these nights, as she goes from him. — *snatch*

FIRST GENTLEMAN Content. How quickly he had done with her! I see kings can do no more that way than other mortal people.

SECOND GENTLEMAN How fast° he is! I cannot hear him breathe. — *fast asleep*

FIRST GENTLEMAN Either the tapers give a feeble light,
Or he looks very pale.

SECOND GENTLEMAN And so he does. Pray heaven he be well!
Let's look. [*He examines the King.*] Alas! He's stiff, wounded and dead.
[*Calling*] Treason, treason!

FIRST GENTLEMAN Run forth and call.
SECOND GENTLEMAN [*as he leaves*] Treason, treason!
Exit [the Second] Gentleman.
FIRST GENTLEMAN This will be laid on us. Who can believe
A woman could do this?

Enter Cleon and Lysippus.

CLEON How now, where's the traitor?
FIRST GENTLEMAN Fled, fled away; but there her woeful act
Lies still.
CLEON Her act! A woman?
LYSIPPUS Where's the body?
FIRST GENTLEMAN There.
LYSIPPUS Farewell, thou worthy man! There were two bonds
That tied our loves, a brother and a king,
The least of which might fetch a flood of tears;
But such the misery of greatness° is, *important persons*
They have no time to mourn. Then pardon me![3]—

Enter Strato.

Sirs, which way went she?
STRATO Never follow her,
For she, alas, was but the instrument.
News is now brought in that Melantius
Has got the fort and stands upon the wall,
And with a loud voice calls those few that pass
At this dead time of night, delivering° *proclaiming*
The innocence of this act.
LYSIPPUS Gentlemen,
I am your king.
STRATO We do acknowledge it.
LYSIPPUS I would I were not! Follow, all, for this
Must have a sudden stop. *Exeunt.*

5.2

Enter Melantius, Diphilus, [and] Calianax on the walls.

MELANTIUS If the dull people can believe,° I am armed. *grasp my motive*
Be constant, Diphilus. Now we have time
Either to bring our banished honors home° *restore our lost honor*
Or to create new ones in our ends.° *our honorable deaths*
DIPHILUS I fear not;
My spirit lies not that way.°—Courage, Calianax! *isn't fearful*
CALIANAX Would I had any, you should quickly know it.[1]
MELANTIUS Speak to the people; thou art eloquent.
CALIANAX 'Tis a fine eloquence to come to the gallows.
You were born to be my end.° The devil take you! *to be my undoing*
Now must I hang for company.° 'Tis strange *I must hang with you*
I should be old, and neither wise nor valiant.

3. Pardon the brevity of my mourning.
5.2. The walls of the fort. Melantius and the others appear in the gallery at the rear of the stage, looking down on the main stage as though from atop the walls.
1. If I did have courage, you'd feel the consequences of my wrath.

Enter [on the main stage below] Lysippus, Diagoras,
Cleon, Strato, [and a] guard.

LYSIPPUS See where he° stands, as boldly confident — *(Melantius)*
As if he had his full command° about him. — *his whole troop*
STRATO He looks as if he had the better cause.° Sir, — *a worthy cause*
Under your gracious pardon, let me speak it:
Though he be mighty-spirited and forward° — *eager*
To all great things, to all things of that danger
Worse men shake at the telling of,[2] yet certainly
I do believe him noble, and this action
Rather pulled on° than sought. His mind was ever — *forced on him*
As worthy as his hand.° — *his deeds*
LYSIPPUS 'Tis my fear, too.
Heaven forgive all!—Summon him, Lord Cleon.
CLEON [*calling*] Ho, from the walls there!
MELANTIUS Worthy Cleon, welcome.
We could ha' wished you here,° lord; you are honest. — *(on our side)*
CALIANAX (*aside*) Well, thou art as flattering a knave,
Though I dare not tell thee so.
LYSIPPUS Melantius!
MELANTIUS Sir?
LYSIPPUS I am sorry that we meet thus; our old love
Never required such distance. Pray° to heaven — *I pray*
You have not left yourself,° and sought this safety — *abandoned your best self*
More out of fear than honor! You have lost° — *destroyed*
A noble master, which your faith,° Melantius, — *whom your loyalty*
Some think might have preserved. Yet you know best.
CALIANAX [*aside*] When time was, I was mad.[3] Some that dares fight,
I hope, will pay° this rascal. — *give what's due to*
MELANTIUS [*to Lysippus*] Royal young man, those tears look lovely on thee.
Had they been shed for a deserving one,
They had been lasting monuments. Thy brother,
Whilst he was good, I called him king, and served him
With that strong faith, that most unwearied valor,
Pulled people from the farthest sun[4] to seek him
And buy° his friendship. I was then his soldier. — *earn*
But since his hot pride drew him to disgrace me,
And brand my noble actions with his lust
(That never-cured dishonor of my sister,
Base stain of whore, and, which is worse,
The joy to make it still so),[5] like myself° — *being my truest self*
Thus I have flung him off with° my allegiance, — *along with*
And stand here, mine own justice,° to revenge — *dispenser of justice*
What I have suffered in him, and this old man
Wronged almost to lunacy.
CALIANAX Who, I?
You would draw me in.° I have had no wrong; — *into your quarrel*
I do disclaim ye all.
MELANTIUS The short° is this: — *The long and the short*

2. Though he is quick to embrace dangers that mean-spirited men would quail at the very mention of.
3. There was a time when I was considered a madcap.
4. That drew people from the opposite side of the world.
5. The King's desire to keep Evadne as his mistress.

'Tis no ambition to lift up myself
Urgeth° me thus. I do desire again — *That urges*
To be a subject, so° I may be free; — *provided that*
If not, I know my strength, and will unbuild° — *level to the ground*
This goodly town. Be speedy and be wise
In a reply.

STRATO [*to Lysippus*] Be sudden, sir, to tie
All up again.° What's done is past recall, — *make a reconciliation*
And past you to revenge; and there are thousands
That wait for such a troubled hour as this.[6]
Throw him the blank.° — *uncompleted document*

LYSIPPUS [*throwing down a document*] Melantius, write in that thy choice.
My seal is at it.

MELANTIUS It was our honors drew° us to this act, — *that drew*
Not gain; and we will only work our pardons.[7]

CALIANAX Put my name in too.

DIPHILUS You disclaimed us all
But now,° Calianax. — *Just now*

CALIANAX That's all one.° — *Never mind that*
I'll not be hanged hereafter by a trick;
I'll have it° in. — *(my name)*

MELANTIUS You shall, you shall.
[*To Lysippus*] Come to the back gate, and we'll call you king,
And give you up the fort.

LYSIPPUS [*to his supporters*] Away, away! *Exeunt omnes.*

[5.3]

Enter Aspatia in man's apparel.

ASPATIA This is my fatal hour. Heaven may° forgive — *May heaven*
My rash attempt, that causelessly hath laid
Griefs on me that will never let me rest,
And put a woman's heart into my breast!
It is more honor for you° that I die, — *you gods*
For she that can endure the misery
That I have on me, and be patient too,
May live and laugh at all that you can do.—

Enter Servant.

God save you, sir.

SERVANT And you, sir. What's your business?

ASPATIA With you, sir, now, to do me the fair office
To help me to° your lord. — *to speak with*

SERVANT What, would you serve him?

ASPATIA I'll do him any service; but, to haste°— — *to be brief*
For my affairs are earnest—I desire
To speak with him.

SERVANT Sir, because you are in such haste, I would be loath to delay you longer: you cannot.

ASPATIA It shall become you,° though, to tell your lord. — *befit your office*

6. There are thousands just waiting for this kind of turmoil as an opportunity to rebel.

7. And we seek nothing more than a pardon.

5.3. Outside Amintor's apartment at the palace.

SERVANT Sir, he will speak with nobody.
ASPATIA This is most strange.
Art thou goldproof? [*She gives money.*] There's for thee;
help me to him.
SERVANT Pray be not angry, sir. I'll do my best. *Exit.*
ASPATIA How stubbornly this fellow answered me!
There is a vile dishonest trick in man,
More than in women. All the men I meet
Appear thus to me, are harsh and rude,
And have a subtlety° in everything, *guile, cunning*
Which love could never know; but we fond° women *foolish, innocent*
Harbor the easiest and the smoothest thoughts,
And think all shall go° so. It is unjust *that all people act*
That men and women should be matched together.

Enter Amintor and his man [the Servant].

AMINTOR Where is he?
SERVANT There, my lord.
AMINTOR [*to Aspatia*] What would you, sir?
ASPATIA Please it Your Lordship to command your man
Out of the room, I shall deliver things
Worthy your hearing.
AMINTOR [*to the Servant*] Leave us. [*Exit Servant.*]
ASPATIA (*aside*) Oh, that that shape
Should bury falsehood in it!
AMINTOR Now, your will, sir?
ASPATIA When you know me, my lord, you needs must guess
My business; and I am not hard to know,
For, till the chance of war marked this smooth face
With these few blemishes, people would call me
My sister's picture, and her mine. In short,
I am the brother to the wronged Aspatia.
AMINTOR The wronged Aspatia! Would thou wert so too
Unto the wronged Amintor![1] Let me kiss
That hand of thine in honor that I bear
Unto the wronged Aspatia. Here I stand
That did it.° Would I could not![2] Gentle youth, *(the wrong)*
Leave me, for there is something in thy looks
That calls my sins in a most hideous form
Into my mind, and I have grief enough
Without thy help.
ASPATIA I would I could with credit.[3]
Since I was twelve years old I had not seen
My sister till this hour I now arrived.
She sent for me to see her marriage—
A woeful one,° but they that are above° *occasion / (the gods)*
Have ends° in everything. She used few words, *purposes*
But yet enough to make me understand
The baseness of the injury you did her.
That little training I have had is war;

1. Would you were my brother-in-law! (Amintor expresses regret at not having married Aspatia and at having been "wronged" by being forced to marry Evadne instead.)
2. Would that I did not have to stand here thus guilty!
3. I wish I could leave honorably. (But I must instead challenge you to a duel.)

I may behave myself rudely in peace;
I would not, though. I shall not need to tell you
I am but young, and would be loath to lose
Honor that is not easily gained again.
Fairly I mean to deal. The age is strict
For single combats,° and we shall be stopped — *Concerning dueling*
If it be published.° If you like your sword, — *made public*
Use it; if mine appear a better to you,
Change; for the ground is this,° and this the time — *this is the place*
To end our difference.° [*Aspatia draws.*] — *quarrel*

AMINTOR Charitable youth,
If thou be'st such, think not I will maintain° — *defend*
So strange° a wrong; and, for thy sister's sake, — *outlandish*
Know that I could not think that desperate thing
I durst not do.[4] Yet, to enjoy this world,° — *for all the world*
I would not see her, for, beholding thee,
I am I know not what.° If I have aught — *I'm strangely moved*
That may content thee, take it and be gone,
For death is not so terrible as thou;
Thine eyes shoot guilt into me.

ASPATIA Thus she swore
Thou wouldst behave thyself and give me words
That would fetch tears into my eyes, and so
Thou dost indeed. But yet she bade me watch° — *take care*
Lest I were cozened,° and be sure to fight — *tricked*
Ere I returned.

AMINTOR That must not be with me.
For her I'll die directly,° but against her — *unhesitatingly*
Will never hazard it.

ASPATIA You must be urged.
I do not deal uncivilly with those
That dare to fight, but such a one as you
Must be used thus. *She strikes him.*

AMINTOR I prithee, youth, take heed!
Thy sister is a thing to me so much
Above mine honor that I can endure
All this—Good gods! A blow I can endure—
But stay not, lest thou draw a timeless° death — *untimely*
Upon thyself.

ASPATIA Thou art some prating fellow,
One that has studied out a trick to talk
And move softhearted people; to be kicked, *She kicks him.*
Thus to be kicked! (*Aside*) Why should he be so slow
In giving me my death?

AMINTOR A man can bear
No more and keep his flesh.[5] Forgive me, then;
I would endure yet if I could. [*He draws.*] Now show
The spirit thou pretendest, and understand
Thou hast no hour° to live. *They fight.* [*She is wounded.*] — *not another hour*
What dost thou mean?
Thou canst not fight; the blows thou mak'st at me
Are quite besides,° and those I offer at thee — *off target, to one side*

4. Please understand that there is nothing so unimaginably desperate that I would not do for your sister.

5. Flesh and blood can stand only so much.

Thou spread'st thine arms and tak'st upon thy breast,
Alas, defenseless.
ASPATIA I have got enough,° *enough to die from*
And my desire. There is no place so fit
For me to die as here. [*She falls.*]

Enter Evadne, her hands bloody, with a knife.

EVADNE Amintor, I am loaden with events
That fly° to make thee happy! I have joys *come quickly*
That in a moment can call back° thy wrongs *restore*
And settle thee in thy free state again.
It is Evadne still that follows thee,
But not her mischiefs.
AMINTOR Thou canst not fool me to believe again;
But thou hast looks and things° so full of news *(blood and the knife)*
That I am stayed.° *halted*
EVADNE Noble Amintor, put off thy amaze;° *amazement*
Let thine eyes loose,° and speak. Am I not fair? *Look at me*
Looks not Evadne beauteous with these rites° now? *(blood and the knife)*
Were these hairs° half so lovely in thine eyes *these unbound tresses*
When our hands met before the holy man?° *the priest*
I was too foul within to look fair then;
Since I knew ill, I was not free till now.[6]
AMINTOR There is presage of some important thing
About thee which, it seems, thy tongue hath lost.
Thy hands are bloody, and thou hast a knife.
EVADNE In this consists thy happiness and mine.
Joy to Amintor, for the King is dead!
AMINTOR Those have most power to hurt us that we love;
We lay our sleeping lives within their arms.
Why, thou hast raised up mischief to his° height, *its*
And found one to outname° thy other faults. *surpass*
Thou hast no intermission of thy sins,
But all thy life is a continued ill.
Black is thy color now, disease thy nature.
"Joy to Amintor"? Thou hast touched a life
The very name of which had power to chain
Up all my rage and calm my wildest wrongs.
EVADNE 'Tis done; and since I could not find a way
To meet thy love so clear as through his life,
I cannot now repent it.
AMINTOR Couldst thou procure° the gods to speak to me, *prevail upon*
To bid me love this woman° and forgive, *(Evadne)*
I think I should fall out with them. Behold,
Here lies a youth whose wounds bleed in my breast,° *cut me to the quick*
Sent by his violent fate to fetch his death
From my slow° hand; and, to augment my woe, *unwilling*
You now are present, stained with a king's blood
Violently shed! This keeps night here,
And throws an unknown wilderness about me.
ASPATIA Oh, oh, oh!

6. Ever since I knew evil (with the King), I have not been free of guilt till now.

AMINTOR [*to Evadne*] No more! Pursue me not.
[*He starts to leave.*]
EVADNE [*trying to restrain him*] Forgive me, then,
And take me to thy bed. We may not part.
AMINTOR Forbear! Be wise, and let my rage go this way.
EVADNE 'Tis you that I would stay, not it.° *(your rage)*
AMINTOR Take heed!
It will return with me.
EVADNE If it must be,
I shall not fear to meet it. Take me home.
AMINTOR Thou monster of cruelty, forbear!
EVADNE For heaven's sake, look more calm! Thine eyes are sharper
Than thou canst make thy sword. [*She kneels.*]
AMINTOR Away, away!
Thy knees are° more to me than violence. *kneeling is*
I am worse than sick to see knees follow me
For that° I must not grant. For God's sake, stand! *that which*
EVADNE Receive me, then.
AMINTOR I dare not stay° thy language. *stay to hear*
In midst of all my anger and my grief,
Thou dost awake something that troubles me
And says I loved thee once. I dare not stay;
There is no end of woman's reasoning. *Leaves her.*
EVADNE [*rising*] Amintor, thou shalt love me now again.
Go; I am calm. Farewell, and peace forever!
Evadne, whom thou hat'st, will die for thee. *Kills herself.*
AMINTOR (*returns*) I have a little human nature yet
That's left for thee, that bids me stay thy hand.
EVADNE Thy hand was welcome, but it came too late.
Oh, I am lost! The heavy sleep makes haste. *She dies.*
ASPATIA Oh, oh, oh!
AMINTOR This earth° of mine doth tremble, and I feel *flesh*
A stark, affrighted motion in my blood.
My soul grows weary of her house,° and I *body*
All over am a trouble to myself.
There is some hidden power in these dead things° *bodies*
That calls my flesh unto 'em; I am cold.
Be resolute, and bear 'em company!
There's something yet which I am loath to leave.
There's man enough in me to meet the fears
That death can bring, and yet would it were done!° *over with*
I can find nothing in the whole discourse
Of° death I durst not meet the boldest way; *About*
Yet still, betwixt the reason and the act,° *thought and deed*
The wrong I to Aspatia did stands up.° *stands out*
I have not such another fault to answer.
Though she may justly arm herself with scorn
And hate of me, my soul will part less troubled
When I have paid to her in tears my sorrow.
I will not leave this act unsatisfied° *unpaid for*
If all that's left in me can answer it.
ASPATIA Was it a dream? There stands Amintor still,
Or I dream still.

AMINTOR How dost thou? Speak; receive my love and help.
Thy blood climbs up to his old place again;[7]
There's hope of thy recovery.
ASPATIA Did you not name Aspatia?
AMINTOR I did.
ASPATIA And talked of tears and sorrow unto her?
AMINTOR 'Tis true; and, till these happy signs° in thee *signs of recovery*
Stayed my course, it was thither° I was going. *(to Aspatia)*
ASPATIA Thou art there already, and these wounds are hers.
Those threats I brought with me sought not revenge,
But came to fetch this blessing from thy hand.
I am Aspatia yet.
AMINTOR Dare my soul ever look abroad° again? *face the world*
ASPATIA I shall sure live, Amintor; I am well.
A kind of healthful joy wanders within me.
AMINTOR The world wants loveliness to excuse thy loss.[8]
Come, let me bear thee to some place of help.
ASPATIA Amintor, thou must stay.° I must rest here; *stop trying to help*
My strength begins to disobey my will.
How dost thou, my best soul? I would fain live
Now, if I could. Wouldst thou have loved me, then?° *if we'd married*
AMINTOR Alas,
All that I am's not worth a hair from thee.
ASPATIA Give me thine hand. Mine hands grope up and down,
And cannot find thee. I am wondrous sick.
Have I thy hand, Amintor?
AMINTOR Thou greatest blessing of the world, thou hast.
ASPATIA I do believe thee better than my sense.° *sense of touch*
Oh! I must go. Farewell! [*She dies.*]
AMINTOR She swoons.—Aspatia!—Help! For God's sake, water,
Such as may chain life forever to this frame!°— *body*
Aspatia, speak!—What, no help? Yet I fool;° *I'm being useless still*
I'll chafe her temples. Yet there nothing stirs.
Some hidden power tell her Amintor calls,
And let her answer me!—Aspatia, speak!—
I have heard, if there be any life, but bow° *simply bend*
The body thus, and it will show itself.
[*He tries to resuscitate her.*]
Oh, she is gone! I will not leave her° yet. *leave her for dead*
Since out of justice we must challenge° nothing, *can demand, claim*
I'll call it mercy if you'll pity me,
You heavenly powers, and lend forth some few years
The blessèd soul to this fair seat° again. *dwelling, body*
No comfort comes; the gods deny me too.
I'll bow the body once again.—Aspatia!—
The soul is fled forever, and I wrong
Myself, so long to lose her company.
Must I talk° now? Here's to be with thee, love! *waste time talking*
Kills himself.

Enter Servant.

7. Your blood returns to your face; you're no longer pale.

8. The world is too unlovely a place to get along without you.

SERVANT This is a great grace to my lord, to have the new king come to him. I must tell him he is entering. [*He sees the body.*] Oh, God! Help, help!

Enter Lysippus, Melantius, Calianax, Cleon, Diphilus, [and] Strato.

LYSIPPUS Where's Amintor?
STRATO Oh, there, there!
LYSIPPUS How strange is this!
CALIANAX What should we do here?
MELANTIUS These deaths are such acquainted things with me
That yet my heart dissolves not. May I stand
Stiff here forever! Eyes, call up your tears!
This is Amintor. Heart, he was my friend;
Melt! [*He weeps.*] Now it flows.—Amintor, give a word
To call me to thee.° *to you in death*
AMINTOR Oh!
MELANTIUS Melantius calls his friend Amintor. [*He embraces Amintor.*] Oh,
Thy arms are kinder to me than thy tongue.
Speak, speak!
AMINTOR What?
MELANTIUS That little word was worth all the sounds
That ever I shall hear again.
DIPHILUS Oh, brother,
Here lies your sister slain! You lose yourself
In sorrow there.
MELANTIUS Why, Diphilus, it is
A thing to laugh at in respect of° this. *in comparison with*
Here° was my sister, father, brother, son, *Here in Amintor*
All that I had.—Speak once again. What youth
Lies slain there by thee?
AMINTOR 'Tis Aspatia.
My last is said. Let me give up my soul
Into thy bosom. [*He dies in Melantius' arms.*]
CALIANAX What's that? What's that? Aspatia?
MELANTIUS I never did repent the greatness of
My heart till now. It will not burst at need.
CALIANAX My daughter dead here too! And you have all fine new tricks to grieve, but I ne'er knew any but direct crying. [*He weeps.*]
MELANTIUS I am a prattler, but no more.
[*He starts to kill himself.*]
DIPHILUS [*restraining him*] Hold, brother!
LYSIPPUS Stop him!
DIPHILUS Fie, how unmanly was this offer° in you! *attempt*
Does this become our strain?° *family*
CALIANAX I know not what the matter is, but I am grown very kind, and am friends with you all now. You have given me that among you will° kill me quickly, but I'll go home and live as long as I can. [*Exit.*] *that will*
MELANTIUS His° spirit is but poor that can be kept *(Any person's)*
From death for want of weapons.
Is not my hands a weapon sharp enough
To stop my breath? Or, if you tie down those,

I vow, Amintor, I will never eat,
Or drink, or sleep, or have to do with that
That may preserve life! This I swear to keep.

LYSIPPUS [*to the others*] Look to him, though, and bear those bodies in.
May this a fair example be to me
To rule with temper!° For on lustful kings *self-restraint*
Unlooked-for sudden deaths from God are sent;
But curst is he that is their instrument. [*Exeunt.*]

FINIS.

TEXTUAL NOTES

The Maid's Tragedy was entered in the Stationers' Register on April 28, 1619. A first quarto (Q1) appeared in that same year, with variant title pages, some naming Richard Higginbotham as publisher and some naming Francis Constable; the printer was Nicholas Okes, though some of the printing was not done in his shop. A second quarto (Q2) appeared in 1622, printed by George Purslowe for Francis Constable. It adds some eighty lines of undoubted authority, along with numerous changes in wording and punctuation. A second manuscript appears to have been consulted, but Q2 was printed from a copy of Q1 that had been annotated for the printer; at times it reproduces Q1's errors and is therefore in need of emendation. The Q1 readings are sometimes more defensible. Both manuscripts appear to have been in Beaumont's hand. Neither early quarto names an author on the title page; the first ascription to Beaumont and Fletcher is to be found in the third quarto (Q3), which appeared in 1630. Q2 serves as the basis for the present edition. Substantive departures from it are noted here, using the following abbreviations:

Q1: Quarto of 1619 (London: Nicholas Okes [in part] for Richard Higginbotham and Francis Constable)
Q1 corr.: The corrected first quarto
Q1 uncorr.: The uncorrected first quarto
Q2: Quarto of 1622 (London: George Purslowe for Francis Constable)
Q3: Quarto of 1630 (London: A. Mathewes for Richard Hawkins)
Q4: Quarto of 1638 (London: E. Griffin for H. Sheperd)
Q5: Quarto of 1641 (London: Elizabeth Purslowe for William Leake)
Q6: Quarto of 1650(?), 1660 (London)
Q7: Quarto of 1686 (London: R. Bentley and S. Magnes)
ed.: A modern editor's emendation

Speakers 3 a noble gentleman [Q3; not in Q1, Q2]

1.1.6 thou [Q1; not in Q2] **11.1** [placement, ed.; after "Noble Melantius" in 13 in Q2] **34 most** [Q1; not in Q2] **35 solemnities** [Q1] solemnitie [Q2] **37 and I** [ed.] and [Q1] I [Q2] **37 here** [Q1; not in Q2] **74 has** [Q1] hath [Q2] **82 infortunate** [Q1] vnfortunate [Q2] **85 'a** [Q1] he [Q2] **127 do** [Q1; not in Q2] **140 all** [ed.; not in Q1, Q2] **144 CLEON, STRATO, *and* DIPHILUS** [ed.] *Cleon, Strato, Diphilus. / Amint.* [Q2] **152 challenge in't.** [Q3] challenge gentlemen, [Q1] challenge: [Q2]

1.2.4 i'th' [Q3] i'th the [Q1, Q2] **9 may swear his heart out** [ed.] must sweat out his heart with swearing [Q1] may sweare his heart out with swearing [Q2] **14 judged** [Q3] iudge [Q1, Q2] **19 near** [Q2: nere] **23 SD** [placement, ed.; after 24 in Q2] **24 Coads** [Q2: codes] **25 SD *within*** [placement, ed.; after 24 in Q2]

46 A VOICE [ed.; not in Q2] **50.1** ***Enter Calianax*** [Q1] *Enter Calianax to Melantius* [Q2] **53.1** [Q1; not in Q2] **70 to** [Q2: too] **76 me** [Q1; not in Q2] **90** [and elsewhere] **vile** [Q2: vilde] **91 stirred** [Q2: sturd] **117 quenching** [Q1] raging [Q2] **140 hold** [Q1] keepe [Q2] **149 wish** [Q3] with [Q2; not in Q1] **161 draw** [ed.] drawne [Q1, Q2] **162 his** [Q1] this [Q2] **168 nobler** [Q1] noble [Q2] **178 wind god** [ed.] winde goe [Q1, Q2] winde flie [Q3] **179 his** [Q1] thy [Q2] **190 Ho!** [ed.] Oh, [Q2] **191 SD** [placement, ed.; opposite 190 in Q2] **193 Favonius** [Q3] *Fanonius* [Q1, Q2] **196** AEOLUS [placement, ed.; before "O! the Maine" in 197 in Q1, Q2] **197 Ho!** [ed.] O! [Q2] **241 full one** [Q1] full one, / If not her measure [Q2] **242 The** [ed.] Thy [Q2] **242 Amphitrite** [Q3] *Amphitrites* [Q2; not in Q1] **243 she** [ed.] they [Q2] **244 she** [ed.] the [Q2] **245 lay** [ed.] lead [Q2; not in Q1] **253 SD** [placement, ed.; after "Song," 245.1, in Q2] **260 My . . . gratulate** [Q1] and to gratulate [Q2] **263 and no** [Q1] no [Q2] **264 dwellings** [Q1] dwelling [Q2] **265 governments** [Q1] gouernment [Q2] **272 kingdom** [Q1] Kingdomes [Q2] **281 Say . . . way?** [ed.] say, which way wilt thou goe? [Q2] **282.1** ***Exeunt*** [placement, ed.; after "mists" in 282 in Q2]

2.1.2 naked [Q2: nak't] **5–6 How's . . . do** [Q1; not in Q2] **6 wi'th'** [Q1: with] **12 we're** [Q1: we'are] we are [Q2] **14–15** FIRST LADY **'Tis . . . will. /** DULA **Anon** [Q1] *Dul.* 'Tis . . . will, / Anon [Q2] **31 I prithee** [Q1; not in Q2] **40 cheek** [Q1] checke [Q2] **79 gentle** [Q4] gently [Q2; not in Q1] **105 bier** [Q2: beere] **108 SD** [placement, ed.; opposite "I pity thee" in 108 in Q2] **109.1** [placement, ed.; opposite "Here . . . light" in 110 in Q2] **123 my** [Q3; not in Q1, Q2] **124 SD** [placement, ed.; after "will you goe?" in 125 in Q2] **138 is she** [Q1] she is [Q2] **142 shall** [Q1] will [Q2] **146** [and elsewhere] **lose** [Q2: loose] **200 Is . . . truth?** [Q1; not in Q2] **202 you thought** [Q1; not in Q2] **266 doth** [Q3] doe [Q1, Q2] **274 hadst** [ed.] hast [Q1, Q2] **294 hand** [ed.] land [Q1, Q2] **300 northern** [Q2: Northren] **347 left** [Q1] lost [Q2] **351 floor** [Q2: floure]

2.2.9 spake [ed.] speake [Q2; not in Q1] **11** [placement, ed.; after 8 in Q2] **19 but courts** [ed.] courts but [Q2; not in Q1] **42** [and elsewhere] **H'as** [Q2: has] **68** [ed.] Suppose I stand vpon the Sea, breach now [Q1] I stand vpon the sea breach now, and thinke [Q2] **99 whelps. And** [Q1] whelps I will, and [Q2]

3.1.7 None [Q1] No [Q2] **18** [and elsewhere] **Who's** [Q2: Whose] **30 doth** [Q1] does [Q2] **36 Does he** [Q1] he does [Q2] **56 more. Embrace** [ed.] more embrace [Q2] **69 Enough** [Q2: enow] **71 compliment** [Q2: complement] **98 walk, Evadne. By** [ed.] walke. / *Euad.* By [Q1, Q2] **141 coarse** [Q2: course] **233 vile** [ed.] wilde [Q1, Q2] **242 Is it** [ed.] It is [Q1, Q2] **243 limbs** [ed.] liues [Q2; not in Q1] **275 believed** [ed.] beleeue [Q1] beleue [Q2]

3.2.34 'mongst [Q1] Amongst [Q2] **39 asked** [Q1: askt] aske [Q2] **55 change** [ed.] charge [Q1, Q2] **202 thy** [Q1] my [Q2] **214 it from** [Q1] it backe from [Q2] **263 SD** [placement, ed.; after "as sent" in 264 in Q2] **300 idle** [Q1; not in Q2] **301 am** [Q1; not in Q2]

4.1.0.1 ***ladies*** [ed.] a *Lady* [Q1, Q2] **1 God** [Q1; not in Q2] **5 commend** [ed.] command [Q1, Q2] **9 SD** ***Exeunt ladies*** [placement, ed.; opposite 10 in Q2] **18 commendation** [Q6] commendations [Q1, Q2] **74 he'd** [Q1: h'ad] ha'd [Q2] **76 food** [Q2] foe [Q1] **84 damns** [Q2: dams] **87 He's** [ed.] has [Q2; not in Q1] **138 thou** [Q3] thee [Q2] **154 coarser** [Q2: courser] **164 shalt** [Q1] shall [Q2] **187 SD** [placement, ed.; opposite 186 in Q2] **192 a . . . sorrows** [Q1] no . . . sorrow [Q2] **201 slight** [Q2: sleight] **201 that's** [Q3] that; [Q2] **205** [and elsewhere] **dost** [Q2: doest] **221 my** [ed.] by [Q1, Q2] **242 ages** [ed.] eies [Q1, Q2] **247 cozening** [Q2: cousening] **254 I** [Q7] a [Q1, Q2]

4.2.20 [and elsewhere] **ha'** [Q2: a] **34 and** [ed.] in [Q2] **37 SD** [placement, ed.; opposite 36 in Q2] **42.2** ***Strato*** [Q1] *Stra. Diag.* [Q2] **92 ha' said** [Q2: ha sed] **178 truth. Ah, thou'rt** [Q2: truth, / A th'art] **179 SD** ***aside*** [placement, ed.; opposite 180 in Q2] **190 Ha, pity?** [Q2: A pittie] **192 Diagoras** [ed.] *Mel.*

Diagoras [Q2] **216 'em . . . 'em** [ed.] him . . . him [Q1, Q2] **232 ye** [Q1] you [Q2] **236 extremely** [Q1] extraordinarily [Q2] **250 o'th'King** [Q5] oth' the King [Q1, Q2] **261 Melantius** [Q1; not in Q2] **275 SD** [placement, ed.; opposite "What news with thee?" in 276 in Q2]

5.1.18 daring [Q2] madness [Q1] **21 repent 'em** [Q1] preuent'm [Q2] **24 SD** ***King abed*** [opposite 13 in Q1, Q2] **24 O God** [Q1] good heauens [Q2] **35 strike** [Q1] strick [Q2] **36 Your Grace** [Q1] you Grace [Q2] **56 Here** [Q1] There [Q2] **113 SD** ***Exit*** [ed.] *Exeunt* [Q1, Q2] **128.1** [placement, ed.; opposite 127 in Q2] **138.1** [placement, ed.; opposite "Sirs . . . she?" in 139 in Q2]

5.2.24 could ha' [Q2: could a] **28 to** [Q1; not in Q2] **51 would** [Q2: wud] **66 Not** [Q6] No [Q1, Q2]

5.3.8.1 [placement, ed.; opposite "God save you, sir," in 9 in Q2] **9 God** [Q1] Cod [Q2] **18 nobody** [Q2] no body, but in particular, I haue in charge about no waightie matters [Q1] **45 I** [ed.] he [Q1, Q2] **80 cozened** [Q2: cossen'd] **118 these hairs** [ed.] those houres [Q1, Q2] **173 heavy** [Q1] heauiest [Q2] **180 unto** [Q1] into [Q2] **211 loveliness** [ed.] lines [Q1, Q2] **225 swoons** [Q2: sounds] **281 you all now** [Q1] you [Q2]

The Woman's Prize

Written and first performed in 1611, *The Woman's Prize* marks a significant development in John Fletcher's career. Fletcher had previously written plays primarily in collaboration with Francis Beaumont; their productions of 1609–11—*The Maid's Tragedy*, *Philaster*, and *A King and No King*—are Fletcher's best-known works. The consensus among his friends, critics, and peers who contributed commendatory verses to the 1647 Beaumont and Fletcher folio was that Fletcher was a creative genius, but one who needed the judicious editing that a collaborator such as Beaumont could provide. *The Woman's Prize*, a sequel to Shakespeare's *The Taming of the Shrew*, was Fletcher's first solo effort after his partnership with Beaumont abruptly and unaccountably ended in 1611. The play proved enormously successful on stage and remained a staple in the repertoire of the King's Men for more than two decades.[1] Shakespeare, for his part, collaborated with Fletcher on the lost play *Cardenio* (1612) and *The Two Noble Kinsmen* (1613), and very probably on *Henry VIII* (1613) as well, apparently grooming the talented younger playwright to take over his position as chief dramatist for the King's Men.

The Woman's Prize, or The Tamer Tamed continues, but also reverses, the action of *The Taming of the Shrew;* whereas Shakespeare's play tells the story of how Petruchio (or Petruccio) tames his first wife, Fletcher's sequel describes how Petruchio's second wife tames him. In the fictional time that has elapsed between *The Taming of the Shrew* and *The Woman's Prize*, Petruchio's first wife, Kate—who is frequently alluded to but never named in Fletcher's play—has evidently died. Despite his fearsome reputation as a wife-tamer, Petruchio has nightmares that his shrewish wife will return from the dead and dominate him; he even hides his breeches for fear that "her ghost / Should walk and wear 'em yet" (1.1.35–36). Accordingly, instead of undertaking to tame another shrew, Petruchio has wooed Maria, who everyone agrees is naturally sweet and submissive. The kind of absolute control Petruchio attempted to establish over Kate has become the defining feature of his hoped-for relationship with Maria: "She must do nothing of herself—not eat, / Drink, say 'Sir, how do ye,' make her ready, piss— / Unless he bid her," says Petruchio's friend Tranio (1.1.45–47). The gentlemen returning from the wedding in the opening scene predict that the delicate Maria's chances of survival are slim. "He will bury her," says one, "within these three weeks" (1.1.47–48).

The brilliant comic irony of Fletcher's play is that Petruchio finds his greatest fear realized: his "safe" second choice turns out to be as tempestuous as his first, and considerably more successful in getting her way. Maria resolves to stand up to Petruchio and take control of her body. "I am no more the gentle, tame Maria," she proclaims. "I have a new soul in me / Made of a north wind, nothing but tempest" (1.2.70–72). She intends to transform Petruchio and make him "easy as a child / And

Introduction by Eric Rasmussen; glosses, footnotes, and textual notes by David Bevington; text edited by David Bevington and checked by Eric Rasmussen.

1. As recorded in the Master of the Revels book in 1633, the Master of the Revels ordered that a public performance of the play be canceled and the playbook brought to him to be "purged of oaths, profaneness, and ribaldry." The play—presumably suitably censored—was then presented at court on November 28, 1633.

tame as fear" (1.2.113–14). She also hopes, more broadly, to improve the situation of all women, thereby laying the "Foundations" of rights and equality that will still be in place "An hundred year hence" (1.2.193, 2.2.82). Although Maria asserts that her motives are basically public-spirited, in defense of women's rights—that she has "Leaped into this gulf of marriage" in order "to redeem my country" (1.2.66, 67)—she acknowledges that her act of self-liberation will inevitably bring with it fame and recognition. Just as Petruchio has "been famous for a woman-tamer" (1.3.278), her status as a husband-tamer "Will make me ever famous" (1.2.192). "Thou wilt be chronicled," says Maria's cousin Bianca, whom the men rightly suspect of masterminding Maria's plot; Maria emphatically agrees: "That's all I aim at" (1.2.175).

The first two acts are physical and farcical, rife with innuendo and broad comedy. In scenes reminiscent of Aristophanes' *Lysistrata*, in which the women of Greece barricade themselves in the Parthenon on the Acropolis and refuse to have sex with their husbands until they give up the practice of war, the female characters in Fletcher's play barricade themselves in Maria's room, thereby preventing Petruchio from consummating the marriage. They form a sisterhood of women who have, at least temporarily, shaken themselves free of patriarchal bonds: to enter their citadel each woman must take "What fond obedience ye have living in you, / Or duty to a man" and "Fling it away" (2.2.120–22). Yet despite the women's high-minded view of their "noble cause" (2.2.80), the scene in Maria's chamber resembles nothing so much as an out-of-control sorority party. A scandalized servant, Jaques, describes to the frustrated men how the women engage in heavy drinking, assertive bragging, and lewd dancing to a song with a refrain that invites onlookers to kiss their rear ends:

> Dance with their coats tucked up to their bare breeches,
> And bid the kingdom kiss 'em, that's the burden.
> They have got metheglin, and audacious ale,
> And talk like tyrants. (2.6.39–42)

An unmistakable gender inversion has taken place, with the women figuratively wearing the pants: ("let's all wear breeches," declares Maria's sister, Livia [1.2.145]). This is the realization of Petruchio's worst nightmares. Maria's and Livia's father, Petronius, gives voice to male anxieties about this transformation by predicting that the women may soon urinate while standing, marking their territory: "They'll sooner / Draw upon walls, as we do" (2.1.55–56).

A circus atmosphere prevails during the siege of Maria's chamber, with the men placing bets on how long the women can hold out and the women hurling the contents of chamber pots at their opponents. Amid this ludicrous bombardment, Maria and Petruchio engage in a serious battle of wills—one rendered particularly complex by repeated acknowledgments of their deep and abiding, if unaccountable, love for each other. Their first exchange, in which Petruchio insists on obedience and Maria replies by redefining the nature of obedience, sets the stage for their interactions throughout the play. Confronted with Petruchio's demand, "by that duty you owe to me, Maria, / Open the door, and be obedient," Maria replies, "I owe no more / Than you owe back again" (1.3.203–4, 208–9). Her serious point is that both affection and duty need to be mutual in a companionate marriage—an ideal that the English reformed church had been urging for several decades.

Although Petruchio is not above threatening his wife with violence ("I should now drag thee to thy duty" [3.3.126]), he soon realizes that such threats are getting him nowhere. Nor can he prevail by reasoned argument, given Maria's superior rhetorical skills. As a last desperate expedient, Petruchio attempts to test his wife by offering to travel abroad and even by pretending to be dead. Throughout, she continues to maintain the upper hand by acting as though she believes all his fabrications—extolling the virtues of travel with such eloquence that the onlookers suggest she should be a writer—and by delivering an extraordinarily dismissive eulogy at his purported funeral:

Cucking stool, used to discipline scolds, shrews, and witches. From T. N. Brushfield, *Chester Archaeological and Historic Society Journal* (1855–62). See *The Woman's Prize,* 2.1.57–59: "We'll ship 'em out in cuck-stools; there they'll sail / As brave Columbus did, till they discover / The Happy Islands of obedience."

"To think what this man was, to think how simple, / How far below a man, how far from reason, / From common understanding" (5.4.23–25). This dazzling perversion of Hamlet's "What a piece of work is a man" speech is Maria's decisive gambit. Having scored her final point, she thereupon declares, "I have done my worst, and have my end" (5.4.44).

Significantly, however, the taming of the tamer does not ultimately result in an inverted hierarchy with the woman dominant. "I have tamed ye," Maria tells Petruchio, "And now am vowed your servant" (5.4.45–46). Petruchio, for his part, recognizes that Maria has succeeded in transforming him as she had hoped and that he has indeed been "born again" (5.4.60). Fletcher enables his audience to have it both ways: the women defy their men only to submit once they have made their point. The equine imagery that figures prominently throughout—permitting numerous jokes on "mount," with women imagined in a position of subjection to men—is subtly sustained in Petruchio's final speech, where he boasts, "I have my colt again, and now she carries" (5.4.88). The "she" of this speech is a compliant mount at Petruchio's service; the double entendre on "carries" implies that the marriage will at last be consummated, thereby awarding Petruchio the prize of sexual possession that he has sought all along. Yet even as Petruchio asserts his triumph, he acknowledges Maria's victory as well: it is she who has carried the day.

The inverted wife-taming plot of Petruchio and Maria is not the only plot of this captivating sexual comedy. Interwoven into their story is the saga of Maria's sister, Livia, and her anxious lover, Rowland. As in Shakespeare's *The Taming of the Shrew*, with its plot of Kate's sister, Bianca, and her wooer Lucentio, there is a rival wooer to contend with: a rich old man whom the father favors because of his wealth. The rival in *The Woman's Prize* is Moroso. Like old Gremio in Shakespeare's play, this rival wooer is a stock figure from classical and neoclassical comedy: the pantaloon. Both plays' sympathies naturally favor the young wooer. The plotting in this situation is the generic one of a trick to outwit age and bourgeois respectability in the name of romantic, young love. As in Shakespeare's play, a neatly turned yet conventional neoclassical story is set off against a thoroughly English and modern battle of the sexes that is rife with antifeminist humor. The advantage of the double plotting is to be found in the juxtapositions that repeatedly emerge. Maria and her sister Livia differ markedly in their views on marriage and obedience, much like the sisters Adriana and Luciana in Shakespeare's *The Comedy of Errors*, one of whom defends marriage, while the other resists yielding to male attempts at domination. The serious debate between the two sisters is also reminiscent of that between Antigone and Ismene in Sophocles' *Antigone*, where Ismene counsels acquiescense to male authority, while Antigone refuses to compromise.

To his Shakespearean model, Fletcher provides a new twist in this second plot. Drawn by sympathy with her sister's rebellion against men, Livia joins forces with the barricaded ladies. Even more threatening from a male perspective, she awakens in Rowland a fear that she is disloyal to him. When she speaks haughtily to him while Moroso eavesdrops on their conversation and then pretends to accept Moroso's marriage proposal, doing so solely as a ruse to hoodwink the old man and stall for time, Rowland is misled into believing the worst of Livia and of women generally. His antifeminist dismay prompts him to bet a friend, Tranio, that no amount of money could bribe him to be reconciled with Livia. His unexpressed hope that he will lose this bet ultimately bears fruit; he gladly pays up to Tranio and is rejoined with his Livia, to the discomfiture of Moroso. In this plot, then, as in the Maria-Petruchio battle of the sexes, a happy resolution gives the lie to men's worst fears about women. The women themselves seem to have entertained no similar fears; they are plucky, self-knowing, amused at male folly, loyal despite their playful teasing, and ready at last to forgive their wooers for their self-punishing foolishness and anxieties.

The Woman's Prize appeared at the beginning of a decade in which women's place in society was a matter of intense debate. The battle lines were clearly drawn by Joseph Swetnam's misogynistic *The Arraignment of Lewd, Idle, Froward, and Unconstant Women* (1615) and the numerous feminist replies it occasioned. Fletcher's astutely ambiguous play, written in the decade while this debate was flourishing, capitalized on the debate while resisting easy classification as either pro- or antifeminist. *The Woman's Prize* can be read as a decidedly feminist document, one in which women are empowered and win the battle of the sexes—the Prologue announces to the "Ladies" that "The victory's yours" (Prologue 1, 4)—one that presents a surprisingly modern paradigm of equality between marriage partners, and one with an explicitly didactic purpose, "meant / To teach both sexes due equality" (Epilogue 6–7). On the other hand, one could argue that the play undermines its principled calls for equality by deriving the thrust of its humor from an unrelenting series of gags—told by men for men—about the novel absurdity of dominant and assertive women. Fletcher challenges his audience to adjudicate between the play's avowed ideological stance and its status as a popular entertainment. The play may ultimately exploit the theme of women's equality without being genuinely committed to it.

JOHN FLETCHER

The Woman's Prize, or The Tamer Tamed

THE PERSONS REPRESENTED IN THE PLAY

[*Men*:]
MOROSO, an old rich doting citizen, suitor to Livia
SOPHOCLES, TRANIO } two gentlemen, friends to Petruchio
PETRUCHIO, an Italian gentleman, husband to Maria
ROWLAND, a young gentleman, in love with Livia
PETRONIUS, father to Maria and Livia
JACQUES, PEDRO } two witty servants to Petruchio
DOCTOR
Apothecary
WATCHMEN
Porters
[Servants]

Women:
MARIA, a chaste witty lady; LIVIA, mistress to Rowland } the two masculine daughters of Petronius
BIANCA, their cousin and commander in chief
CITY WIVES, COUNTRY WIVES, MAIDS } to the relief of the ladies, of which two were drunk° (*see* 2.6.57 *ff.*)

[PROLOGUE
EPILOGUE]

THE SCENE: London [the houses of Petronius and Petruchio].

Prologue

[*Enter Prologue.*]

PROLOGUE Ladies, to you, in whose defense and right
Fletcher's brave Muse prepared herself to fight

The original title page reads "*The Woman's Prize; or, The Tamer Tamed.*" The play was first published in a collected folio volume with the title page "*Comedies and Tragedies* written by Francis Beaumont and John Fletcher, Gentlemen. Never printed before, and now published by the authors' original copies. *Si quid habent veri Vatum praesagia, vivam* [If the sayings of the poets have any share of truth, I shall live (final line of Ovid's *Metamorphoses*)]. London: Printed for Humphrey Robinson, at the Three Pigeons, and for Humphrey Moseley at the Prince's Arms in St. Paul's Churchyard. 1647."

A battle without blood ('twas well fought, too;
(The victory's yours, though got with much ado),
We do present this comedy, in which
A rivulet of pure wit flows, strong and rich
In fancy, language, and all parts that may
Add grace and ornament to a merry play;
Which this may prove. Yet not to go too far
In promises from this our female war,
We do entreat the angry men would not
Expect the mazes of a subtle plot,
Set speeches, high expressions, and (what's worse
In a true comedy) politic discourse.
The end we aim at is to make you sport,
Yet neither gall the city nor the court.
Hear and observe his comic strain, and when
You're sick of melancholy, see't again.
'Tis no dear physic,° since 'twill quit° the cost; *costly medicine / repay*
Or his intentions, with our pains, are lost. [*Exit.*]

1.1

Enter Moroso, Sophocles, and Tranio, with rosemary,° as from a wedding. *(in a bouquet)*

MOROSO God give 'em joy!
TRANIO Amen!
SOPHOCLES Amen, say I, too.
The pudding's now i'th'proof. Alas, poor wench,° *(Maria)*
Through what a mine° of patience must thou work *store*
Ere thou know'st good hour more!
TRANIO 'Tis too true. Certain,
Methinks, her father has dealt harshly with her,
Exceeding harshly, and not like a father,
To match her to this dragon.° I protest° *(Petruchio) / declare*
I pity the poor gentlewoman.
MOROSO Methinks now
He's not so terrible as people think him.
SOPHOCLES [*aside to Tranio*] This old thief flatters, out of mere devotion,
To please the father for° his second daughter. *in hopes of winning*
TRANIO [*aside to Sophocles*] But shall he have her?
SOPHOCLES [*aside to Tranio*] Yes, when I have Rome.° *i.e., never*
And yet the father's for him.
MOROSO I'll assure ye,
I hold him° a good man. *hold Petruchio to be*
SOPHOCLES Yes, sure, a wealthy,
But whether a good woman's man is doubtful.
TRANIO Would 'twere no worse.
MOROSO What though his other wife,° *first wife (Kate)*
Out of her most abundant stubbornness,
Out of her daily hue and cries upon him
(For sure she was a rebel), turned° his temper, *returned, answered*

1.1. Before Petronius' house (see lines 70–71).

And forced him blow as high° as she? Does 't follow — *rage as loud*
He must retain that long-since-buried tempest
To this soft maid?[1]

SOPHOCLES I fear it.

TRANIO So do I, too,
And so far that if God had made me woman,
And his wife that must be—

MOROSO What would you do, sir?

TRANIO I would learn to eat coals° with an angry cat, — *i.e., become fiery*
And spit fire at him. I would, to prevent him,
Do all the ramping,° roaring tricks a whore — *extravagant*
Being drunk and tumbling ripe° would tremble at. — *ready to tumble in bed*
There is no safety else, nor moral wisdom,
To be a wife, and his.

SOPHOCLES So I should think, too.

TRANIO For yet the bare remembrance of his first wife
(I tell ye on my knowledge, and a truth, too)
Will make him start in's sleep, and very often
Cry out for cudgels, cowlstaffs,° anything, — *carrying poles*
Hiding his breeches out of fear her ghost
Should walk and wear 'em yet. Since his first marriage,
He is no more the still° Petruchio — *quiet, calm*
Than I am Babylon.[2]

SOPHOCLES He's a good fellow,
And, by my troth, I love him; but to think
A fit match for this tender soul—

TRANIO His very frown, if she but say her prayers
Louder than men talk treason, makes him tinder;° — *ready to ignite*
The motion of a dial,° when he's testy, — *clock or sundial*
Is the same trouble to him as a waterwork.° — *(noisy) water pump*
She must do nothing of° herself—not eat, — *by*
Drink, say "Sir, how do ye," make her ready, piss—
Unless he bid her.

SOPHOCLES He will bury her,
Ten pound to twenty shillings,° within these three weeks. — *i.e., 10 to 1*

TRANIO I'll be your half.° — *be partner in the bet*

Enter Jaques with a pot of wine.

MOROSO He loves her most extremely,
And so long 'twill be honeymoon.—Now, Jaques,
You are a busy man, I am sure.

JAQUES Yes, certain,
This old sport must have eggs°— — *food, delicacies*

SOPHOCLES Not yet this ten days.° — *Not any time soon*

JAQUES Sweet gentlemen, with muscatel.° — *a sweet wine*

TRANIO That's right, sir.

MOROSO This fellow broods his master.°—Speed ye, Jaques. — *looks after Petruchio*

SOPHOCLES We shall be for you presently.° — *We'll join you shortly*

JAQUES Your Worships
Shall have it rich and neat,° and, o'my conscience, — *undiluted*
As welcome as Our Lady Day.[3] [*To Moroso*] Oh, my old sir,

1. Does it follow that he must vent his long-forgotten fury against his first wife by storming and raging against Maria?
2. Tranio recalls the metrical version of Psalm 137. In the King James Version, the psalm reads, "By the still rivers of Babylon."
3. A feast day honoring the Virgin Mary.

When shall we see Your Worship run at ring?[4]
That hour a standing° were worth money. — *place to stand*
MOROSO — So, sir.
JAQUES — Upon my little honesty, your mistress,° — *(Livia)*
If I have any speculation,° must think — *perception*
This single thrumming of a fiddle
Without a bow[5] but ev'n poor sport.
MOROSO — You're merry.
JAQUES — Would I were wise too! So, God bless Your Worships! *Exit Jaques.*
TRANIO [*to Moroso*] — The fellow tells you true.
SOPHOCLES [*to Moroso*] — When is the day, man?
Come, come, you'd steal a marriage.° — *elope*
MOROSO — Nay, believe me;
But when her father pleases I am ready,
And all my friends shall know it.
TRANIO — Why not now?
One charge° had served for both.° — *expense / both marriages*
MOROSO — There's reason in't.
SOPHOCLES [*aside*] — Called Rowland.[6]
MOROSO — Will ye walk?° They'll think we are lost. — *walk in*
Come, gentlemen. [*Exit.*]
TRANIO — You have wiped him° now. — *put him down*
SOPHOCLES — So will he never the wench,° I hope. — *never put her down*
TRANIO — I wish it.
Exeunt.

1.2

Enter Rowland and Livia.

ROWLAND — Now, Livia, if you'll go away° tonight, — *elope*
If your affections be not made of words—
LIVIA — I love you, and you know how dearly, Rowland.
(Is there none near us?)° My affections ever — *Is no one listening?*
Have been your servants. With what superstition° — *veneration*
I have ever sainted° you— — *worshiped*
ROWLAND — Why, then, take this way.° — *elope*
LIVIA — 'Twill be a childish and a less prosperous course
Than his that knows not care.[1] Why should we do
Our honest and our hearty love such wrong,
To overrun our fortunes?
ROWLAND — Then you flatter.° — *deceive*
LIVIA — Alas, you know I cannot.
ROWLAND — What hope's left else
But flying, to enjoy ye?
LIVIA — None, so far,
For, let it be admitted° we have time, — *even supposing*
And all things now in other expectation,° — *everything else ready*
My father's bent against us. What but ruin

4. When will we see you tilt, or joust, in a tournament? (With the suggestion of sexual performance.)
5. I.e., This feeble sexual performance.
6. Moroso's rival for Livia's affection.
1.2. Petronius' house.
1. Elopement would be even more reckless than the course taken by an irresponsible person. (The reading of F1 and F2, "his," seems more plausible than MS's "this"; see Textual Notes.)

Can such a byway° bring us? If your fears — *indirect course*
Would let you look with my eyes, I would show you,
And certain, how our staying here would win us
A course, though somewhat longer, yet far surer.

ROWLAND And then Moroso has ye.

LIVIA No such matter.
For hold this certain: begging, stealing, whoring,
Selling (which is a sin unpardonable)
Of counterfeit cods, or musty English craccus,
Switches, or stones for th'toothache sooner finds me
Than that drawn fox, Moroso.[2]

ROWLAND But his money,
If wealth may win you—

LIVIA If a hog may be
High priest among the Jews.[3] His money, Rowland?
Oh, Love° forgive me, what a faith hast thou? — *Cupid*
Why, can his money kiss me?

ROWLAND Yes.

LIVIA Behind,
Laid out upon a petticoat?° Or grasp me — *Lying nearly naked?*
While I cry, "Oh, good, thank you"? O'my troth,
Thou mak'st me merry with thy fear. Or lie with me,
As you may do? Alas, what fools you men are!
His moldy money? Half a dozen riders,
That cannot sit but stamped fast to their saddles?[4]
No, Rowland, no man shall make use of me;
My beauty was born free, and free I'll give it
To him that loves, not buys, me. You yet doubt me.

ROWLAND I cannot say I doubt ye.

LIVIA Go thy ways,° — *Get along with you*
Thou art the prettiest puling piece of passion!° — *whining crybaby*
I'faith, I will not fail thee.

ROWLAND I had rather—

LIVIA Prithee, believe me. If I do not carry it° — *carry it off*
For both our goods—

ROWLAND But—

LIVIA What but?

ROWLAND I would tell you.

LIVIA I know all you can tell me. All's but this:
You would have me, and lie with me. Is't not so?

ROWLAND Yes.

LIVIA Why, you shall; will that content you? Go.

ROWLAND I am very loath to go.

Enter Bianca and Maria [not seeing Livia and Rowland at first].

LIVIA Now, o'my conscience,
Thou art an honest fellow. Here's my sister.
Go, prithee, go. This kiss and, credit° me, — *believe*

2. Livia would find begging, stealing, prostitution, the selling of adulterated perfume bags (cods) or musty tobacco (craccus) or bogus cures for the toothache (switches or stones, perhaps some sort of mineral treatment) more attractive than marrying Moroso, who is as withered as an eviscerated fox.

3. An impossible condition, since pigs are considered unclean in Judaism.

4. Gold coins showing the figure of horsemen—in this case, very inept riders, who would be thrown off if they were not fixed to their saddles in the stamping of the coin. (Suggesting Moroso's sexual incompetence.)

Ere I am three nights older, I am for thee. [*He kisses her.*]
You shall hear what I do.
ROWLAND I had rather feel it.
LIVIA Farewell!
ROWLAND Farewell! *Exit Rowland.*
LIVIA [*to herself*] Alas, poor fool, how it° looks! *i.e., babyish Rowland*
It would ev'n hang itself, should I but cross° it. *contradict*
For pure love to the matter I must hatch it.° *hatch a plan*
[*Bianca and Maria converse together, not seeing Livia.*]
BIANCA Nay, never look for merry hour, Maria,
If now ye make it not; let not your blushes,
Your modesty, and tenderness of spirit
Make you continual anvil to his anger.
Believe me, since his first wife set him going,
Nothing can bind his rage. Take your own counsel;
You shall not say that I persuaded you.
But if you suffer° him— *permit*
MARIA Stay, shall I do it?
BIANCA Have you a stomach to't?
MARIA I never showed it.° *I was never shrewish*
BIANCA 'Twill show the rarer and the stranger° in you. *more remarkable*
But do not say I urged you.
MARIA I am perfect.° *I know my part*
Like Curtius, to redeem my country, have I
Leaped into this gulf of marriage,[5] and I'll do it.
Farewell, all poorer thoughts but spite and anger,
Till I have wrought a miracle! Now, cousin,
I am no more the gentle, tame Maria.
Mistake me not; I have a new soul in me
Made of a north wind, nothing but tempest;
And like a tempest shall it make all ruins
Till I have run my will out.° *had my way completely*
BIANCA This is brave,° now, *excellent*
If you continue it; but your° own will lead you. *may your*
MARIA Adieu, all tenderness! I dare continue;
Maids that are made of fears and modest blushes,
View me, and love example.
BIANCA [*seeing Livia*] Here is your sister.
MARIA Here is the brave old man's° love. *(Morose's)*
BIANCA That° loves the young man. *She who*
MARIA [*to Livia*] Ay, and hold thee there, wench.° What a grief of heart is't, *(familiar form of address)*
When Paphos' revels should uprouse old night,[6]
To sweat against a cork, to lie and tell
The clock o'th'lungs, to rise sport-starved?[7]
LIVIA Dear sister,
Where have you been, you talk thus?

5. When an ominous chasm opened in the Roman forum and the soothsayers prophesied that the chasm would never close until the chief strength of Rome was sacrificed to it, Marcus Curtius leaped into it fully armed and on horseback, thus satisfying the terms of the prophecy.
6. When Venus's revels should enliven the night. (Paphos, in Cyprus, was famous as the seat of worship of Venus.)
7. To be condemned instead to be bedded down with a withered old man, to lie next to him and count his heavy breaths as if he were the clock, and to rise in the morning starved of sexual pleasure?

MARIA Why, at church, wench,
Where I am tied° to talk thus. I am a wife now. *yoked in marriage*
LIVIA It seems so, and a modest.° *(said ironically)*
MARIA You're an ass.
When thou art married once,° thy modesty *Once you're married*
Will never buy thee pins.° *Will be worthless*
LIVIA Bless me!° *God shield me!*
MARIA From what?
BIANCA From such a tame fool as our cousin Livia!
LIVIA You are not mad?
MARIA Yes, wench, and so must you be,
Or none of our acquaintance—mark me, Livia—
Or indeed fit for our sex.[8] 'Tis bedtime.
Pardon me, yellow Hymen,[9] that I mean
Thine off'rings to protract, or to keep fasting
My valiant bridegroom.
LIVIA [*to Bianca*] Whither will this woman?
BIANCA You may perceive her end.° *intent*
LIVIA Or rather fear it.
MARIA Dare you be partner in't?
LIVIA Leave it, Maria.
I fear I have marked° too much. For goodness, leave it; *seen*
Divest you° with obedient hands to bed. *Undress yourself*
MARIA To bed? No, Livia, there are comets hang
Prodigious° over that yet. There's a fellow *Ominous*
Must yet, before I know that heat (ne'er start,° wench), *don't be startled*
Be made a man, for yet he is a monster;
Here [*pointing to herself*] must his head be, Livia.
LIVIA Never hope it.
'Tis as easy with a sieve to scoop the ocean as
To tame Petruchio.
MARIA Stay.—Lucina,° hear me! *goddess of childbirth*
Never unlock the treasure of my womb
For human fruit, to make it capable,
Nor never with thy secret hand make brief
A mother's labor to me, if I do
Give way unto my married husband's will,
Or be a wife in anything but hopes!
Till I have made him easy° as a child *compliant*
And tame as fear, he shall not win a smile
Or a pleased look from this austerity,
Though it would pull another jointure° from him *marriage settlement*
And make him ev'ry day another man;[1]
And when I kiss him, till I have my will,
May I be barren of delights and know
Only what pleasures are in dreams and guesses!
LIVIA A strange exordium!
BIANCA All the several° wrongs *various*
Done by imperious husbands to their wives
These thousand years and upwards, strengthen thee!

8. Yes, I am ready to behave outrageously, Livia, and so must you, or you are not fit for our company, or indeed fit to belong to the female sex.
9. Hymen, the god of marriage, is traditionally outfitted in yellow.
1. And turn him daily into quite a different (and thus more agreeable) husband.

Thou hast a brave cause.
MARIA And I'll do it bravely,
Or may I knit my life out ever after![2]
LIVIA In what part of the world got she this spirit?
Yet pray, Maria, look before you,° truly; *look to the future*
Besides the disobedience of a wife,
Which you will find a heavy imputation,° *accusation*
Which yet I cannot think your own, it shows° *appears*
So distant from your sweetness.
MARIA 'Tis,° I swear. *It's my true nature*
LIVIA Weigh but the person° and the hopes you have *i.e., Petruchio*
To work this desperate cure.
MARIA A weaker subject° *subservient woman*
Would shame the end° I aim at, disobedience. *betray the cause*
You talk too tamely. By the faith I have
In mine own noble will, that childish woman
That lives a prisoner to her husband's pleasure
Has lost her making,° and becomes a beast, *betrayed her creation*
Created for his use, not fellowship.
LIVIA His first wife said as much.
MARIA She was a fool,
And took a scurvy° course. Let her be named *unworthy*
'Mongst those that wish for things but dare not do 'em.
I have a new dance for him, and a mad one.
LIVIA Are you of this faith?
BIANCA Yes, truly, and will die in't.
LIVIA Why, then, let's all wear breeches.
BIANCA That's a good wench.
MARIA Now thou com'st near the nature of a woman.
Hang these tame-hearted eyases° that no sooner *untrained hawks*
See the lure out and hear their husband's "Holla!"
But cry like kites° upon 'em! The free haggard[3] *scavenger hawks*
(Which is that woman that has wing and knows it,
Spirit, and plume) will make an hundred checks° *false stoops*
To show her freedom, sail in ev'ry air,
And look° out ev'ry pleasure, not regarding *seek*
Lure nor quarry till her pitch° command *height of ascent*
What she desires, making her foundered° keeper *hobbled, thwarted*
Be glad to fling out trains,° and golden ones, *lures of meat*
To take her down again.
LIVIA You are learnèd, sister;
Yet I say still, take heed.
MARIA A witty saying.
I'll tell thee, Livia, had this fellow tired
As many wives as horses under him
With spurring of their patience; had he got
A patent,° with an office° to reclaim us *license / commission*
Confirmed by Parliament; had he all the malice
And subtlety of devils, or of us,
Or anything that's worse than both—
LIVIA Hey, hey, boys, this is excellent!
MARIA Or could he

2. Or may I spend the rest of my life doing women's needlework!

3. An adult hawk caught wild.

Cast his wives new again, like bells, to make 'em
Sound to his will; or had the fearful name° *reputation*
Of the first breaker of wild women: yet,
Yet would I undertake° this man, thus single,° *take on / single-handed*
And, spite of all the freedom he has reached to,° *attained*
Turn him and bend him as I list,° and mold him *wish*
Into a babe again, that° agèd women, *that even*
Wanting° both teeth and spleen, may master him. *Lacking*
BIANCA Thou wilt be chronicled.
MARIA That's all I aim at.
LIVIA I must confess, I do with all my heart
Hate an imperious husband, and in time
Might be so wrought° upon— *prevailed*
BIANCA To make him cuckold?
MARIA If he deserve it.
LIVIA Then I'll leave ye, ladies.
BIANCA Thou hast not so much noble anger in thee.
MARIA Go sleep, go sleep. What we intend to do
Lies not for such starved souls as thou hast, Livia.
LIVIA Good night. The bridegroom will be with you presently.
MARIA That's more than you know.° *i.e., You'd be surprised*
LIVIA If ye work upon him,
As ye have promised, ye may give example,
Which no doubt will be followed.
MARIA So.
BIANCA Good night. We'll trouble you no further.
MARIA If you intend no good, pray do no harm.
LIVIA None, but pray for ye.
BIANCA 'Cheer,° wench! *Exit Livia.* *Good cheer*
MARIA Now, Bianca,
Those wits we have, let's wind 'em to the height.
My rest is up,[4] wench, and I pull for that° *that which*
Will make me ever famous. They that lay
Foundations are half builders, all men say.

Enter Jaques.

JAQUES My master, forsooth.° *Petruchio is waiting*
MARIA Oh, how does thy master? Prithee commend me to him.
JAQUES How's this? My master stays,° forsooth. *is waiting*
MARIA Why, let him stay. Who hinders him, forsooth?
JAQUES The revel's ended now,° to visit you. *Now the wedding's over*
MARIA I am not sick.
JAQUES I mean, to see his chamber, forsooth.
MARIA Am I his groom? Where lay he last night, forsooth?
JAQUES In the low matted° parlor. *spread with mats*
MARIA There lies his way, by the long gallery.
JAQUES I mean your chamber. You're very merry, mistress.
MARIA 'Tis a good sign I am sound-hearted, Jaques.
But if you'll know where I lie, follow me;
And what thou see'st, deliver° to thy master. *report*
BIANCA Do, gentle Jaques. *Exeunt [Maria and Bianca].*
JAQUES Ha, is the wind in that door?° *quarter*

4. I'm fully resolved. (The metaphor may be from gambling with cards.)

By'r Lady, we shall have foul weather, then.
I do not like the shuffling of these women;
They are mad beasts when they knock their heads together.
I have observed 'em all this day—their whispers
One in another's ear, their signs and pinches
And breaking often into violent laughters—
As if the end they purposed were their own.
Call you this weddings? Sure this is a knavery,
A very trick and dainty knavery,
Marvelous finely carried, that's the comfort!
What would these women do in ways of honor,
That are such masters this way? Well, my sir
Has been as good at finding out these toys° *tricks*
As any living; if he lose it now,
At his own peril be it. I must follow. *Exit.*

1.3

Enter servants with lights, Petruchio, Petronius, Moroso, Tranio, and Sophocles.

PETRUCHIO You that are married, gentlemen, have at ye° *I challenge you*
For a round° wager now! *sizable*
SOPHOCLES Of this night's stage?° *action*
PETRUCHIO Yes.
SOPHOCLES I am your first man: a pair of gloves of° twenty shillings. *worth*
PETRUCHIO Done. Who takes me up next? I am for all bets.
MOROSO Faith, lusty Laurence, were but my night now,[1]
Old as I am, I would make you clap on spurs° *use spurs*
But I would reach° you, and bring you to your trot[2] too; *catch up with*
I would, gallants.
PETRUCHIO Well said, good Will! But where's the stuff, boy, ha?
Old father Time, your hourglass is empty.° *i.e., you're impotent*
TRANIO [*to Moroso*] A good tough train° would break thee all to pieces; *bouncy trot*
Thou hast not breath enough to say thy prayers.
PETRONIUS [*to Moroso*] See how these boys despise us!° [*To Petruchio*] Will you to bed, son? *us old men*
This pride will have a fall.
PETRUCHIO Upon your daughter;
But I shall rise° again, if there be truth *be erect*
In eggs and buttered parsnips.° *(aphrodisiacs)*
PETRONIUS Will you to bed, son, and leave° talking? *leave off*
Tomorrow morning we shall have you look,
For all your great words, like Saint George at Kingston,
Running a-footback from the furious dragon,[3]
That with her angry tail belabors him
For being lazy.

1.3. Petronius' house.
1. In faith, jolly friar, if it were my turn to consummate a marriage tonight. ("Laurence" in line 6 and "Will" in line 10 are presumably names from Robin Hood legend, suggesting a kind of folk heroism in the act of possessing a woman sexually.)
2. (1) Horse trot; (2) old woman, hag.
3. Petronius refers to a satiric inn sign at Kingston depicting Saint George on foot fleeing from the dragon.

SOPHOCLES His warlike lance
Bent like a crossbow lath,° alas the while! *bending part of crossbow*

TRANIO His courage quenched, and so far quenched—

PETRUCHIO 'Tis well, sir.

TRANIO That any private saint, even small Saint Davy,
May lash him with a leek.[4]

PETRUCHIO What then?

SOPHOCLES "Fly, fly!" quoth then the fearful dwarf;
"Here is no place for living man."[5]

PETRUCHIO Well, my masters,° if I do sink under my business, as I find 'tis very possible, I am not the first that has miscarried; so that's my comfort. What may be done without impeach° or waste, I can and will do. *good sirs* / *hindrance; injury*

Enter Jaques.

How now, is my fair bride abed?

JAQUES No, truly, sir.

PETRONIUS Not abed yet? Body o'me! We'll up and rifle° her. *despoil, strip*
Here's a coil with° a maidenhead. 'Tis not entailed,[6] is it? *fuss about*

PETRUCHIO If it be, I'll try all the law i'th'land but I'll cut it off.[7] Let's up,° let's up, come. *go upstairs*

JAQUES That you cannot neither.

PETRUCHIO Why?

JAQUES Unless you'll drop through the chimney like a daw,° or force a breach i'th'windows. You may untile the house, 'tis possible. *jackdaw, small crow*

PETRUCHIO What dost thou mean?

JAQUES A moral, sir. The ballad will express it:

The wind and the rain
Has turned you back again;
Ye cannot be lodged there.

The truth is, all the doors are barricadoed; not a cat-hole but holds a murd'rer° in't. She's victualed° for this month. *small cannon / provisioned*

PETRUCHIO Art not thou drunk?

SOPHOCLES He's drunk, he's drunk. Come, come, let's up.

JAQUES Yes, yes, I am drunk. Ye may go up, ye may, gentlemen, but take heed to your heads. I say no more.

SOPHOCLES I'll try that. *Exit Sophocles.*

PETRONIUS How dost thou say? The door fast locked, fellow?

JAQUES Yes, truly, sir, 'tis locked, and guarded too, and two as desperate tongues planted behind it as e'er yet battered.° They stand upon their honors, and will not give up without strange composition,° I'll assure you; marching away with their pieces cocked and bullets in their mouths will not satisfy them. *assaulted (verbally)* / *harsh terms*

PETRUCHIO How's this? How's this? They are? Is there another with her?

JAQUES Yes, marry,° is there, and an engineer. *by Mary (an oath)*

4. The Welsh were proud of their favorite saint, Saint Davy, and reputedly fond of onionlike leeks; in *Henry V*, 5.1, the Welsh Fluellen gives the cowardly Pistol a drubbing and forces him to eat a leek. The implication here is that Petruchio must be daunted by the prospect of Maria's fierceness.

5. In Spenser's *The Faerie Queene*, 1.1.13, lines 8–9, Una's dwarf warns the Redcross Knight to flee the perils of the den of Error. The implication is that Petruchio is facing a greater danger in Maria than he may realize.

6. Bestowed as an unalienable possession. (With a bawdy wordplay on "tail.")

7. (1) I'll cancel it; (2) I'll deflower it.

MOROSO Who's that, for heaven's sake?
JAQUES Colonel Bianca. She commands the works.° Spinola's — *defenses*
but a ditcher to her; there's a half-moon.[8] I am but a poor
man, but, if you'd give me leave, I'll venture a year's wages,
draw° all your force before it and mount your ablest piece — *even if you muster*
of battery,° you shall not enter in't these three nights yet. — *ordnance*

Enter Sophocles.

PETRUCHIO I should laugh at that, good Jaques.
SOPHOCLES Beat back again! She's fortified forever.
JAQUES Am I drunk now, sir?° — *(see 53–56 above)*
SOPHOCLES He that dares most, go up now, and be cooled.° — *put down, suppressed*
I have scaped° a pretty scouring. — *barely escaped*
PETRUCHIO What, are they mad? Have we another Bedlam?° — *a hospital for the insane*
She doth not talk, I hope?
SOPHOCLES Oh, terribly, extremely fearful. The noise at London Bridge is nothing near her.
PETRUCHIO How got she tongue?
SOPHOCLES As you got tail: she was born to't.
PETRUCHIO Locked out o'doors, and on my wedding night?
Nay, an° I suffer this, I may go graze.° — *if / be put to pasture*
Come, gentlemen, I'll batter.° Are these virtues? — *make assault*
SOPHOCLES Do, and be beaten off with shame, as I was. I went
up, came to th'door, knocked; nobody answered; knocked
louder, yet heard nothing; would have broke in by force, when
suddenly a waterwork° flew from the window with such vio- — *urine in a chamber pot*
lence that, had I not ducked quickly like a friar, *cetera quis*
nescit?[9] The chamber's nothing but a mere Ostend,° in every — *(see 69–70 and n)*
window pewter cannons° mounted. You'll quickly find with — *i.e., chamber pots*
what they are charged,° sir. — *loaded*
PETRUCHIO Why, then, tantara° for us! — *a call to arms*
SOPHOCLES And all the lower works° lined sure with small — *fortifications*
shot, long tongues with firelocks that at twelvescore blank
hit to the heart.[1] Now, an ye dare, go up.

Enter Maria and Bianca above.° — *(gallery over the stage)*

MOROSO The window opens. Beat° a parley first. I am so — *Sound on drums*
much amazed my very hair stands.
PETRONIUS Why, how now, daughter? What, entrenched?° — *guarded by trenches*
MARIA A little guarded for my safety, sir.
PETRUCHIO For your safety, sweetheart? Why, who offends
you? I come not to use violence.
MARIA I think you cannot, sir. I am better fortified.
PETRUCHIO I know your end.° You would fain reprieve your — *aim*
maidenhead a night or two.
MARIA Yes, or ten, or twenty, or say an hundred; or, indeed,
till I list° lie with you. — *wish to*
SOPHOCLES That's a shrewd saying. From this present hour,
I never will believe a silent woman.

8. Spinola, the Italian general who commanded the Spanish army when it captured Ostend, in the Netherlands, in September 1604, is seen to be as far inferior to the intrepid Bianca as a lowly ditchdigger is to a commanding officer. The half-moon is a curved military formation.

9. Who knows what would have happened otherwise? (Friars were often satirized for ducking, i.e., bowing and genuflecting.)

1. That hit the center of the target even at 240 feet. Sophocles is perhaps describing the women's tongues as weapons.

When they break out, they are bonfires.

PETRONIUS [*to Maria*] Till you list lie with him? Why, who are you, madam?

BIANCA [*interrupting*] That trim gentleman's° wife, sir. *(Petruchio's)*

PETRUCHIO Cry ye mercy.° Do ye command too? *I beg your pardon*

MARIA Yes, marry, does she, and in chief.

BIANCA [*to Petruchio*] I do command, and you shall go without—I mean your wife,° for this night. *do without your wife*

MARIA And for the next too, wench, and so as 't follows.

PETRONIUS Thou wilt not, wilt 'a?° *wilt thou?*

MARIA Yes, indeed, dear father, and, till he seal° to what I shall set down,° for anything I know, forever. *i.e., sign, agree* / *write down*

SOPHOCLES By'r Lady, these are bug's-words.° *words to terrify*

TRANIO You hear, sir, she can talk, God be thanked.

PETRUCHIO I would I heard it not, sir.

SOPHOCLES I find that all the pity bestowed upon this woman makes but an anagram of an ill wife, for she was never virtuous.

PETRUCHIO [*to Maria*] You'll let me in, I hope, for all this jesting.

MARIA Hope still, sir.

PETRONIUS You will come down, I am sure.

MARIA I am sure I will not.

PETRONIUS I'll fetch you, then.

BIANCA The power of the whole country cannot, sir, unless we please to yield, which yet I think we shall not. Charge when you please; you shall hear quickly from us.

MOROSO Heaven bless° me from a chicken° of thy hatching! *shield / i.e., child*
Is this wiving?

PETRUCHIO Prithee, Maria, tell me what's the reason—
And do it freely—you deal thus strangely with me?
You were not forced to marry; your consent
Went equally with mine, if not before it.
I hope you do not doubt° I want° that mettle *fear / lack*
A man should have to keep a woman waking;° *to give sexual pleasure*
I would be sorry to be such a saint yet.
My person, as it is not excellent,
So 'tis not old, nor lame, nor weak with physic,° *medicine*
But well enough to please an honest woman
That keeps her house and loves her husband.

MARIA 'Tis so.

PETRUCHIO My means and my conditions° are no shamers *financial status*
Of him that owes 'em;[2] all the world knows that;
And my friends no reliers on my fortunes.[3]

MARIA All this I believe, and none of all these parcels° *items, particulars*
I dare except against;° nay, more, so far *take exception to*
I am from making these the ends I aim at—
These idle outward things, these women's fears°— *things women worry over*
That, were I yet unmarried, free to choose
Through all the tribes of man, I'd take Petruchio
In's shirt, with one ten groats° to pay the priest, *(worth fourpence)*
Before the best man living, or the ablest° *most manly*

2. My means do not shame their owner.
3. And my relatives are not dependent on me for support.

That ev'r leaped out of Lancashire, and they are right ones.[4]
PETRONIUS Why do you play the fool, then, and stand prating
Out of the window like a broken° miller? *bankrupt, unemployed*
PETRUCHIO If you will have me credit° you, Maria, *trust, think well of*
Come down, and let your love confirm it.
MARIA Stay there, sir. That bargain's yet to make.
BIANCA [*to Maria*] Play sure, wench. The pack's in thine own hand.
SOPHOCLES Let me die lousy° if these two wenches *lice-infested*
Be not brewing knavery to stock° a kingdom. *enough to fill up*
PETRUCHIO Death,° this is a riddle! *By God's death*
"I love ye, and I love ye not."
MARIA It is so;
And till your own experience do untie it,
This distance I must keep.
PETRUCHIO If you talk more,
I am angry, very angry.
MARIA I am glad on't, and I will talk.
PETRUCHIO Prithee, peace!
Let me not think thou art mad. I tell thee, woman,
If thou goest forward, I am still Petruchio.
MARIA And I am worse: a woman that can fear
Neither Petruchio Furius,[5] nor his fame,° *reputation*
Nor anything that tends to our allegiance.° *ties of obligation*
There's a short method° for ye; now you know me. *ordering of argument*
PETRUCHIO If you can carry't° so, 'tis very well. *carry it off*
BIANCA [*interrupting*] No, you shall carry it,° sir. *bear the burden*
PETRUCHIO Peace, gentle lowbell!° *bellwether, leading ram*
PETRONIUS [*to Maria*] Use no more words, but come down instantly,
I charge thee by the duty of a child.
PETRUCHIO Prithee, come, Maria. I forgive all.
MARIA [*to Petronius*] Stay there. That duty that you charge me by
(If you consider truly what you say)
Is now another man's; you gave't away
I'th'church, if you remember, to my husband.
So, all you can exact now is no more
But only a due reverence to your person,
Which thus I pay: your blessing,° and I am gone *I ask your blessing*
To bed for this night.
PETRONIUS This is monstrous.
That blessing that Saint Dunstan gave the devil,
If I were near thee, I would give thee—
Pull thee down by th'nose.[6]
BIANCA Saints should not rave, sir;
A little rhubarb° now were excellent. *a purgative medicine*
PETRUCHIO Then by that duty you owe to me, Maria,

4. Lancashire men were fabled for their athletic skill and strength.
5. Maria satirically models her name for Petruchio after *Orlando Furioso*, the popular epic by the Italian poet Ariosto (1532).
6. Legend has it that when the devil tempted Saint Dunstan (924–988), coming to him in the shape of a beautiful woman, Dunstan seized the apparition by the nose with a pair of red-hot tongs.

Open the door, and be obedient. I am quiet yet.
MARIA I do confess that duty; make your best on't.
PETRUCHIO Why, give me leave, I will.
BIANCA Sir, there's no learning° *teaching*
An old stiff jade° to trot. You know the moral. *worn-out horse*
MARIA Yet as I take it, sir, I owe no more
Than you owe back again.
PETRUCHIO You will not article?° *agree to terms*
All I owe, presently, let me but up, I'll pay.
MARIA You're too hot, and such prove jades at length.
You do confess a duty or respect to me from you again
That's very near, or full the same, with mine?
PETRUCHIO Yea.
MARIA Then by that duty, or respect, or what
You please to have it, go to bed and leave me,
And trouble me no longer with your fooling;
For know, I am not for you.
PETRUCHIO Well, what remedy?
PETRONIUS A fine smart cudgel. Oh, that I were near thee!
BIANCA If you had teeth now, what a case were we in![7]
MOROSO These are the most authentic rebels, next Tyrone,[8]
I ever read of.
MARIA A week hence, or a fortnight, as you bear ye,° *conduct yourself*
And as I find my will observed,° I may, *my wishes heeded*
With intercession of some friends, be brought
Maybe to kiss you, and so quarterly
To pay a little rent by composition.° *mutual agreement*
You understand me?
SOPHOCLES Thou boy,° thou! *i.e., impertinent*
PETRUCHIO Well, there are more maids than Maudlin,° that's my comfort. *there are other women*
MARIA Yes, and more men than Michael.
PETRUCHIO I must not to bed with this stomach and no meat, lady.
MARIA Feed where you will, so° it be sound and wholesome; *provided*
Else live at livery,[9] for I'll none with ye.
BIANCA You had best back° one of the dairymaids; they'll carry. *embrace sexually*
But take heed to your girths; you'll get a bruise else.
PETRUCHIO Now if° thou wouldst come down and tender me *even if*
All the delights due to a marriage-bed,
Study° such kisses as would melt a man, *Practice*
And turn thyself into a thousand figures
To add new flames unto me, I would stand
Thus heavy,° thus regardless,° thus despising *stolid / inattentive*
Thee and thy best allurings—all the beauty
That's laid upon your bodies, mark me well.
For without doubt your minds are miserable;
You have no masks for them. All this rare beauty,
Lay but the painter° and the silkworm by, *cosmetician*
The doctor with his diets, and the tailor,

7. How terrifying you'd be with teeth instead of being a toothless old man! (Said with mock horror.)
8. Hugh O'Neill, the second Earl of Tyrone, a powerful Irish rebel chieftain in 1595–1601.
9. Otherwise, live on the food allowance allotted to liveried servants.

And you appear like flayed cats, not so handsome.
MARIA And we appear like her that sent us hither,° *into the world*
That only excellent and beauteous Nature—
Truly ourselves, for men to wonder at,
But too divine to handle. We are gold,
In our own natures pure; but when we suffer
The husbands' stamp upon us, then alloys,
And base ones of you men, are mingled with us,
And make us blush like copper.
PETRUCHIO Then° and never *When married*
Till then are women to be spoken of,
For till that time you have no souls, I take it.
Good night. Come, gentlemen; I'll fast for this night,
But by this hand—well. I shall come up yet?
MARIA No.
PETRUCHIO There will I watch thee like a withered Jewry.° *I'll guard you churlishly*
Thou shalt neither have meat, fire, nor candle,
Nor anything that's easy.° Do you rebel so soon? *comforting*
Yet take° mercy. *accept*
BIANCA Put up your pipes.° To bed, sir; I'll assure you, *Stop talking*
A month's siege will not shake us.
MOROSO Well said, Colonel!° *(said ironically)*
MARIA To bed, to bed, Petruchio! Good night, gentlemen.
You'll make my father sick with sitting up.
Here you shall find us any time these ten days,
Unless we may march off with our contentment.° *with what we want*
PETRUCHIO I'll hang first.
MARIA And I'll quarter if I do not.[1]
I'll make ye know and fear a wife, Petruchio;
There my cause lies.
You have been famous for a woman-tamer,
And bear the feared name of a brave wife-breaker;
A woman now shall take those honors off,
And tame you. Nay, never look so big;° she shall, believe me, *threatening*
And I am she. What think ye? Good night to all.
Ye shall find sentinels.
BIANCA If ye dare sally.° *Exeunt above.* *venture forth*
PETRONIUS The devil's in 'em, ev'n the very devil, the downright devil!
PETRUCHIO I'll devil 'em, by these ten bones° I will. I'll bring it to the old proverb: no sport, no pie.[2] Death, taken down i'th'top of all my speed? This is fine dancing. Gentlemen, stick to me. You see our freehold's° touched, and, by this light, we will beleaguer 'em, and either starve 'em out or make 'em recreant.° *fingers* / *male privilege is* / *i.e., cry for mercy*
PETRONIUS I'll see all passages° stopped but those about 'em. If the good women of the town dare succor 'em, we shall have wars indeed. *passageways*
SOPHOCLES I'll stand perdu° upon 'em. *sentinel*
MOROSO My regiment shall lie before.° *set down before them*
JAQUES I think so; 'tis grown too old to stand.° *to be erect*

1. The sentence for treason included hanging and quartering, i.e., dismembering the body.
2. I.e., Nothing ventured, nothing gained.

PETRUCHIO Let's in, and each provide his tackle.° *gear; sexual gear*
We'll fire 'em out, or make 'em take° their pardons— *beg*
Hear what I say—on their bare knees, I vow.
Am I Petruchio, feared and spoken of,
And on my wedding night am I thus jaded?° *Exeunt omnes.* *scorned, mocked*

1.4

Enter Rowland and Pedro, at several° doors. *separate*

ROWLAND Now, Pedro?
PEDRO Very busy, Master Rowland.
ROWLAND What haste, man?
PEDRO I beseech you pardon me;
I am not mine own man.° *I am at another's command*
ROWLAND Thou art not mad?
PEDRO No; but believe me, as hasty—
ROWLAND The cause, good Pedro?
PEDRO There be a thousand, sir. You are not married?
ROWLAND Not yet.
PEDRO Keep yourself quiet, then.
ROWLAND Why?
PEDRO You'll find a fiddle that never will be tuned else.
From all such women, God deliver me! *Exit.*
ROWLAND What ails the fellow, trow?°—Jaques! *do you suppose?*

Enter Jaques.

JAQUES Your friend, sir.
But very full of business.
ROWLAND Nothing but business?
Prithee the reason. Is there any dying?
JAQUES I would there were, sir.
ROWLAND But thy business?
JAQUES I'll tell you in a word. I am sent to lay
An imposition° upon souse° and puddings, *heavy tax / pickled meat*
Pasties,° and penny custards, that the women *Meat pies*
May not relieve yon rebels.[1] Fare ye well, sir.
[*He starts to go.*]
ROWLAND How does my mistress?
JAQUES Like a resty jade.° *restive horse*
She's spoiled for riding. *Exit Jaques.*
ROWLAND What a devil ail they?

Enter Sophocles [*in haste*].

Custards, and penny pasties, fools and fiddles?
What's this to'th'purpose? [*To Sophocles*] Oh, well met.
SOPHOCLES Now, Rowland,
I cannot stay to talk long.
ROWLAND What's the matter?
Here's stirring, but to what end? Whither go you?
SOPHOCLES To view the works.
ROWLAND What works?

1.4. Petronius' house still.
1. So that the female servants may not bring in food to the rebellious women.

SOPHOCLES The women's trenches.
ROWLAND Trenches? Are such to see?
SOPHOCLES I do not jest, sir.
ROWLAND I cannot understand you.
SOPHOCLES Do not you hear
In what a state of quarrel the new bride
Stands with her husband?
ROWLAND Let him stand° with her, *i.e., be erect*
And there's an end.
SOPHOCLES It should be, but, by'r Lady,
She holds him out at pike's end,° and defies him, *at weapon's point*
And now is fortified. Such a regiment of rutters[2]
Never defied men braver. I am sent
To view their preparation.
ROWLAND This is news
Stranger than armies in the air.° You saw not *i.e., blown up*
My gentle mistress?
SOPHOCLES Yes, and meditating
Upon some secret business. When she had found it
She leapt for joy, and laughed, and straight° retired *immediately*
To shun Moroso.
ROWLAND This may be for me.
SOPHOCLES Will you along?° *come with us*
ROWLAND No.
SOPHOCLES Farewell.
ROWLAND Farewell, sir.
Exit Sophocles.
What should her musing mean, and what her joy in't,
If not for my advantage?

Enter Livia at one door, and Moroso at another, hearkening.

Stay ye;° may not *Wait a minute*
That bobtail jade Moroso, with his gold,
His gew-gauds,° and the hope she has to send him *gewgaws, gaudy trifles*
Quickly to dust,° excite this? Here she comes, *to the grave*
And yonder walks the stallion to discover.° *intent on overhearing*
Yet I'll salute° her.—Save° you, beauteous mistress. *greet / God save*
LIVIA [*aside*] The fox is kenneled° for me.—Save you, sir. *Moroso is hiding*
ROWLAND Why do you look so strange?
LIVIA I use to look, sir,
Without examination.[3]
MOROSO [*aside*] Twenty spur-royals for that word.[4]
ROWLAND Belike,° then, *Perhaps*
The object° discontents you? *i.e., Seeing me*
LIVIA Yes, it does.
ROWLAND Is't come to this? You know me, do you not?
LIVIA Yes, as I may know many by repentance.° *to my sorrow*
ROWLAND Why do ye break your faith?
LIVIA I'll tell you that too:
You are underage, and no band holds upon you.° *you're too unrestrained*

2. (1) German troops; (2) lustful persons.
3. I prefer not to be examined on the way I look.
4. Moroso, taken in by Livia's show of hauteur toward Rowland, values her words as worth twenty fifteen-shilling gold coins.

MOROSO [*aside*] Excellent wench!
LIVIA Sue out your understanding,° *Seek to be wiser*
And get more hair to cover your bare knuckle
(For boys were made for nothing but dry° kisses), *chaste*
And, if you can, more manners.
MOROSO [*aside*] Better still.
LIVIA And then if I want° Spanish gloves, or stockings, *lack*
A ten-pound° waistcoat, or a nag to hunt on, *i.e., expensive*
It may be I shall grace you to accept° 'em. *by accepting*
ROWLAND Farewell! And when I credit° women more, *believe, have faith in*
May I to Smithfield,° and there buy a jade *a livestock market*
(And know him to be so) that breaks my neck.
LIVIA Because I have known you, I'll be thus kind to you:
Farewell, and be a man, and I'll provide you,
Because I see you're desperate, some staid° chambermaid *steady, settled*
That may relieve your youth with wholesome doctrine.
MOROSO [*aside*] She's mine, from° all the world. [*Coming forward*] Ha, wench! *before*
LIVIA Ha, chicken!
Gives him a box o'th'ear, and exit.
MOROSO [*aside*] How's this? I do not love these favors.
[*To Rowland*] Save you!
ROWLAND The devil take thee! *Wrings him by th' nose.*
MOROSO Oh!
ROWLAND There's a love token for you. Thank me now. *Exit.*
MOROSO I'll think on some of ye, an if° I live. *an if = if*
My nose alone shall not be played withal.[5] *Exit.*

2.1

Enter Petronius and Moroso.

PETRONIUS A box o'th'ear, do you say?
MOROSO Yes, sure, a sound one,
Beside my nose blown to my hand.[1] If Cupid
Shoot arrows of that weight, I'll swear devoutly
He's sued his livery,[2] and is no more a boy.
PETRONIUS You gave her some ill language?
MOROSO Not a word.
PETRONIUS Or might be you were fumbling?° *groping*
MOROSO Would I had, sir;
I had been aforehand° then. But to be baffled,° *prepared / disgraced*
And have no feeling° of the cause— *understanding*
PETRONIUS Be patient.
I have a medicine clapped to her back° will cure her. *i.e., as a poultice*
MOROSO No, sure, it must be afore,° sir. *applied to the front*
PETRONIUS O'my conscience,
When I got° these two wenches (who till now *begot*
Ne'er showed their riding)[3] I was drunk with bastard,° *a sweet wine*
Whose nature is to form things like itself,
Heady and monstrous. Did she slight him° too? *(Rowland)*

5. No one is to be allowed to play with my nose like that.
2.1. Petronius' house still.
1. Besides being wrung by the nose.
2. Cupid has come to maturity. (Literally, he is in a position to claim possession of an inheritance.)
3. Never revealed their true nature, formed at the moment of conception. (To "ride" is to copulate.)

MOROSO That's all my comfort: a mere hobbyhorse
She made child Rowland.[4] 'Sfoot,° she would not know him, *By God's foot*
Not give him a free° look, not reckon him *willing*
Among her thoughts, which I held more than wonder.° *thought strange*
I having seen her within's° three days kiss him *within these*
With such an appetite as though she would eat him.
PETRONIUS There is some trick in this. How did he take it?
MOROSO Ready to cry; he ran away.
PETRONIUS I fear° her. *suspect*
And yet, I tell you, ever to° my anger *in response to*
She is as tame as innocency. It may be
This blow was but a favor.° *love pat, love token*
MOROSO I'll be sworn
'Twas well tied on,° then. *administered*
PETRONIUS Go to.° Pray forget it. *(a phrase of protest)*
I have bespoke° a priest, and within's two hours *arranged for, engaged*
I'll have ye married. Will that please you?
MOROSO Yes.
PETRONIUS I'll see it done myself, and give the lady
Such a sound exhortation for this knavery,
I'll warrant you, shall make her smell this month on't.° *from the beating*
MOROSO Nay, good sir, be not violent.
PETRONIUS Neither.° *I won't*
MOROSO It may be,
Out of her earnest love, there grew a longing
(As you know women have such toys),° in kindness, *tricks*
To give me a box o'th'ear or so.
PETRONIUS It may be.
MOROSO I reckon for the best still. This night, then,
I shall enjoy her?
PETRONIUS You shall handsel° her. *use for the first time*
MOROSO Old as I am, I'll give her one blow for't
Shall make her groan° this twelvemonth. *(in childbirth)*
PETRONIUS Where's your jointure?° *marriage settlement*
MOROSO I have a jointure° for her. *i.e., a sexual joining*
PETRONIUS Have your counsel° *lawyers*
Perused it yet?
MOROSO No counsel° but the night and your sweet daughter *witnesses, advisers*
Shall e'er peruse that jointure.
PETRONIUS Very well, sir.
MOROSO I'll no demurrers° on't nor no rejoinders.° *objections / answers*
The other's° ready sealed. *The contract is*
PETRONIUS Come, then, let's comfort
My son Petruchio. He's like little children
That lose their baubles,° crying ripe.° *playthings / tearful*
MOROSO Pray tell me,
Is this stern woman° still upon the flaunt *(Maria)*
Of bold defiance?
PETRONIUS Still, and still she shall be
Till she be starved out. You shall see such justice
That women shall be glad, after this tempest,

4. She made a complete fool of Rowland. (Mockingly named "child Rowland" after a figure in a ballad that is cited in *King Lear*, 3.4.170. "Child" here refers to a wellborn youth.)

To tie their husbands' shoes and walk their horses.
MOROSO That were a merry world. Do you hear the rumor?
They say the women are in insurrection,
And mean to make a—
PETRONIUS They'll sooner
Draw upon walls, as we do.[5] Let 'em, let 'em!
We'll ship 'em out in cuck-stools;[6] there they'll sail
As brave Columbus did, till they discover
The Happy Islands of obedience.
We stay too long. Come.
MOROSO Now Saint George° be with us! *England's patron saint*
Exeunt.

2.2

Enter Livia alone [with food and drink].

LIVIA Now if I can but get in° handsomely, *into Maria's apartments*
Father, I shall deceive you, and this night,° *I'll do so tonight*
For all your private plotting. I'll no wedlock;
I have shifted sail, and find my sister's safety° *stronghold*
A sure retirement. Pray to heaven that Rowland
Do not believe too far what I said to him!
For yon old foxcase° forced me. That's my fear. *(Moroso; see 1.2.25)*
Stay, let me see. This quarter fierce Petruchio
Keeps with his Myrmidons.[1] I must be sudden.
If he° seize on me, I can look for nothing *(Moroso)*
But martial law.° To this place have I scaped him.— *military justice*
[*Calling*] Above there!

Enter Maria and Bianca above.

MARIA *Qui va là?*° *Who goes there?*
LIVIA A friend.
BIANCA Who are you?
LIVIA Look out and know.
MARIA Alas, poor wench! Who sent thee?
What weak fool made thy tongue his orator?
I know ye come to parley.° *negotiate*
LIVIA You're deceived.
Urged by the goodness of your cause, I come
To do as you do.
MARIA You're too weak, too foolish,
To cheat us with your smoothness. Do not we know
Thou hast been kept up tame?[2]
LIVIA Believe me.
MARIA No, prithee, good Livia,
Utter thy eloquence somewhere else.
BIANCA [*to Livia*] Good cousin,
Put up your pipes;° we are not for your palate. *Stop talking*
Alas, we know who sent you.

5. I.e., The next thing you know, women will urinate standing up, as we men do. (The dash in the previous speech indicates an indecency of the same sort.)
6. Chairs in which offenders (such as scolds) were ducked in a pond or river as punishment.

2.2. Petronius' house still.
1. Petruchio guards this part of the house with his armed followers (named here for those who served under Achilles in the Trojan War).
2. You've been tamed like a hawk.

LIVIA O'my faith—
BIANCA Stay° there. You must not think your "faith," or "troth," — *Stop*
Or "by your maidenhead," or such Sunday oaths
Sworn after evensong,° can inveigle us — *the evening service*
To loose° our handfast.° Did their wisdoms think, — *loosen / firm grip*
That sent you hither, we would be so foolish
To entertain our gentle Sister Sinon
And give her credit, while the Wooden Jade,
Petruchio, stole upon us?[3] No, good sister,
Go home, and tell the merry Greeks that sent you
Ilium° shall burn; and I, as did Aeneas, — *Troy*
Will, on my back, spite of the Myrmidons,
Carry this warlike lady,° and through seas — *(Maria)*
Unknown and unbelieved seek out a land
Where, like a race of noble Amazons,° — *female warriors*
We'll root ourselves, and to our endless glory
Live, and despise base men.[4]
LIVIA I'll second ye.
BIANCA How long have you been thus?
LIVIA That's all one,° cousin. — *all the same*
I stand for freedom now.
BIANCA Take heed of lying;
For, by this light, if we do credit° you, — *believe*
And find you tripping,° his infliction — *making false steps*
That killed the Prince of Orange[5] will be sport
To° what we purpose. — *Compared with*
LIVIA Let me feel the heaviest.[6]
MARIA Swear by thy sweetheart Rowland (for by your maidenhead
I fear 'twill be too late to swear)[7] you mean
Nothing but fair and safe, and honorable
To us and to yourself.
LIVIA I swear.
BIANCA Stay yet.
Swear as you hate Moroso—that's the surest°— — *the surest oath*
And as you have a Christian° fear to find him — *devout*
Worse than a poor dried jack,° full of more aches — *dried fish*
Than autumn has; more knavery, and usury,
And foolery, and brokery than Dog's-ditch;[8]
As you do constantly° believe he's nothing — *steadfastly*
But an old empty bag with a grey beard,
And that beard such a bobtail° that it looks — *a horse's tail cut short*
Worse than a mare's tail eaten off with fillies;[9]
As you acknowledge that young handsome wench

3. The Greek Sinon, posing as a deserter, inveigled the Trojans to admit the Trojan horse ("Wooden Jade") into Troy (*Aeneid*, Book 2). "Give her credit" means "believe her."
4. As Aeneas tells the story to Dido in Virgil's *Aeneid*, Book 2, Aeneas fled from the burning Troy on the command of Venus, carrying his father, Anchises, on his shoulders and leading his son, Julus Ascanius, by the hand. Aeneas eventually went on to found Rome. The Myrmidons were followers of Achilles; see note 1 above.
5. The execution of the assassin of the Prince of Orange in 1584 was unusually gruesome.
6. Punish me extremely if I'm lying.
7. I fear you have no virginity left to swear by.
8. Than one might find in Houndsditch, a London district tenanted by dealers (brokers) in old clothes.
9. Colts were reputed to have a fondness for eating the tails off older horses.

That lies by such a bilbo blade, that bends
With ev'ry pass he makes to'th'hilts, most miserable,
A dry nurse to his coughs,[1] a fewterer° *lowly attendant*
To such a nasty fellow, a robbed thing
Of all delights youth looks for; and, to end,
One cast away on coarse beef,[2] born to brush
That everlasting cassock that has worn
As many servants out as the Northeast passage
Has consumed sailors:[3] if ye swear this, and truly
Without the reservation of° a gown *Without holding back*
Or any meritorious petticoat,
'Tis like° we shall believe you. *likely*
LIVIA I do swear it.
MARIA Stay yet a little. Came this wholesome motion° *proposal*
(Deal truly, sister) from your own opinion,
Or some suggestion of the foe?
LIVIA Nev'r fear me,
For, by that little faith I have in husbands,
And the great zeal I bear your cause, I come
Full of that liberty you stand for, sister.
MARIA If we believe, and you prove recreant,° Livia, *unfaithful*
Think what a maim you give the noble cause
We now stand up for! Think what women shall,
An hundred year hence, speak° thee, when examples *say about*
Are looked for, and so great ones, whose relations
Spoke as we do 'em, wench, shall make new customs![4]
BIANCA If ye be false, repent, go home, and pray,
And to the serious° women of the city *pious, puritanical*
Confess yourself; bring not a sin so heinous,
To load thy soul, to this place. Mark me, Livia:
If thou be'st double° and betray'st our honors, *false*
And we fail in our purpose, get thee where
There is no women living, nor no hope
There ever shall be.
MARIA If a mother's daughter
That ever heard the name of stubborn husband
Find thee, and know thy sin—
BIANCA Nay, if old age,° *an old woman*
One that has worn away the name of woman,° *lost her sexuality*
And no more left to know her by but railing°— *her scolding*
No teeth, nor eyes, nor legs, but wooden ones—
Come but i'th'windward of° thee—for sure she'll smell thee, *Get scent of*
Thou'lt be so rank—she'll ride thee like a nightmare,
And say her prayers backward° to undo thee; *say a curse*
She'll curse thy meat and drink, and, when thou marriest,

1. As you acknowledge that the handsome young woman who must sleep with such a pretend gentleman who bows obsequiously to every courtier he passes is bound to be utterly miserable, condemned as she is to serve as his caretaker in his fits of coughing. (A bilbo, line 61, is a sword noted for the temper of its blade, hence here meaning "swashbuckling" and probably intended to be ironic; Bianca is imagining a marriage to an old fuddy-duddy who wears a sword but is really only a sycophant.)

2. I.e., One who is thrown away on a tough old geezer.

3. The long-sought ship passage north of Russia to east Asia, like the better-known Northwest Passage above Canada, was the graveyard of many a sailor. Bianca imagines a young woman having to care for a garment that her aged husband has worn forever, exhausting many servants with the brushing of it.

4. And such great examples, the story of which will set new precedents!

Clap a sound spell forever on thy pleasures.° — *sexual pleasures*
MARIA Children of five year old, like little fairies,
Will pinch thee into motley.° All that ever — *i.e., black-and-blue*
Shall live, and hear of thee—I mean all women—
Will, like so many Furies,° shake their keys, — *avenging deities*
And toss their flaming distaffs° o'er their heads, — *spinning staffs*
Crying "Revenge!" Take heed; 'tis hideous.
Oh, 'tis a fearful office! If thou hadst
(Though thou be'st perfect° now) when thou cam'st hither — *say the right things*
A false imagination,° get thee gone, — *secret thought*
And, as my learnèd cousin said, repent.
This place is sought by soundness.[5]
LIVIA So I seek it,
Or let me be a most despised example.
MARIA I do believe thee. Be thou worthy of it.
You come not empty?
LIVIA No. Here's cakes and cold meat,
And tripe of proof.° Behold, here's wine, and beer. — *good quality*
Be sudden; I shall be surprised else.° — *captured otherwise*
MARIA Meet at the low parlor door; there lies a close° way. — *secret*
What fond° obedience ye have living in you, — *foolish*
Or duty to a man, before you enter
Fling it away; 'twill but defile our off'rings.° — *votive offerings*
BIANCA Be wary as you come.
LIVIA I warrant ye.
Exeunt [*Maria and Bianca above, Livia from the main stage*].

2.[3]

Enter Rowland and Tranio at several doors.

TRANIO Now, Rowland?
ROWLAND How do you?
TRANIO How dost thou, man?
Thou look'st ill.
ROWLAND Yes. Pray, can you tell me, Tranio,
Who knew the devil first?
TRANIO A woman.° — *i.e., Eve*
ROWLAND So,
Were they not well acquainted?
TRANIO Maybe so,
For they had certain dialogues together.
ROWLAND He sold her fruit,° I take it? — *(see Genesis 3)*
TRANIO Yes, and cheese
That choked all mankind after.[1]
ROWLAND Canst thou tell me
Whether that woman ever had a faith[2]
After she had eaten?
TRANIO That's a great school° question. — *scholastic, theological*

5. You need to be sound, i.e., reliable and true, to join us and enter here.

2.3. Petronius' house still.

1. Tranio refers wryly to cheese as something that is traditionally served with fruit—in this case the infamous fruit that Satan persuaded Eve to eat in the Garden of Eden, thus introducing death and suffering into the world. Hence this cheese "choked all mankind" forever after.

2. Whether Eve was restored to obedience toward God and Adam.

ROWLAND No, 'tis no question,° for believe me, Tranio, — *it's a certainty*
That cold fruit, after eating, bred naught in her
But windy promises and colic° vows — *colicky; choleric*
That broke out both ways.° Thou hast heard, I am sure, — *upward and downward*
Of Aesculapius,° a far-famed surgeon, — *god of medicine*
One that could set together quartered° traitors — *(see 1.3.275 n)*
And make 'em honest° men. — *whole; unblemished*

TRANIO How dost thou, Rowland?[3]

ROWLAND Let him° but take (if he dare do a cure — *(Aesculapius)*
Shall° get him fame indeed) a faithless woman— — *That will*
There will be credit for him, that will speak° him— — *proclaim*
A broken° woman, Tranio, a base woman, — *faithless, inconstant*
And if he can cure such a rack° of honor — *wreck, ruin*
Let him come here and practice.

TRANIO Now for heaven's sake,
Why, what ail'st thou, Rowland?

ROWLAND I am ridden, Tranio,
And spur-galled to the life of patience[4]
(Heaven keep my wits together!) by a thing
Our worst thoughts are too noble for: a woman.

TRANIO Your mistress has a little frowned, it may be?

ROWLAND She was my mistress.

TRANIO Is she not?

ROWLAND No, Tranio.
She has done me such disgrace, so spitefully,
So like a woman bent to my undoing,
That henceforth a good horse shall be my mistress,
A good sword, or a book; and if you see her,
Tell her, I do beseech you, even for love's sake.
Our old love and our friendship—

TRANIO I will, Rowland.

ROWLAND She may sooner count° the good I have thought her, — *reckon up*
Shed one true tear, mean one hour constantly,° — *be true for an hour*
Be old and honest, married and a maid° — *(impossible conditions)*
Than make me see her more, or more believe her.
And now I have met a messenger, farewell, sir. *Exit.*

TRANIO Alas, poor Rowland! I will do it for thee.
This is that dog Moroso, but I hope
To see him cold i'th'mouth° first ere he enjoy her. — *cold on the scent*
I'll watch this young man. Desperate thoughts may seize him,
And, if my purse or counsel can, I'll ease him. *Exit.*

2.[4]

Enter Petruchio, Petronius, Moroso, and Sophocles.

PETRUCHIO For look you, gentlemen, say that I grant her,
Out of my free and liberal love, a pardon,
Which you and all men else know she deserves not
(*Teneatis amici*),° can all the world leave laughing? — *Grasp this, friends*

3. Tranio repeats his question of line 1 out of concern that Rowland's wits are deserting him.

4. And spur-chafed to the limit of my patience.

2.4. Petronius' house still.

PETRONIUS I think not.
PETRUCHIO No, by this hand, they cannot;
For pray consider: have you ever read,
Or heard of, or can any man imagine
So stiff° a tomboy, of so set a malice, *stubborn*
And such a brazen resolution,
As this young crab tree?° And then answer me, *i.e., shrew*
And mark but this too, friends: without a cause,
Not a foul word comes 'cross her, not a fear
She justly can take hold on, and do you think
I must sleep out my anger, and endure it,
Sew pillows to her ease, and lull her mischief?° *appease her quarrels*
Give me a spindle° first. No, no, my masters, *Give me woman's work*
Were she as fair as Nell° o'Greece, and housewife *Helen*
As good as the wise sailor's wife,° and young still, *(Penelope, Odysseus' wife)*
Never above fifteen, and these tricks to it,° *in addition*
She should ride the wild mare[1] once a week, she should.
Believe me, friends, she should. I would tabor° her *beat as on a drum*
Till all the legions° that are crept into her *legions of devils*
Flew out with fire i'th'tails.
SOPHOCLES Methinks you err now,
For to me seems° a little sufferance° *it seems that / patience*
Were a far surer cure.
PETRUCHIO Yes, I can suffer,
Where I see promises of peace and amendment.
MOROSO Give her a few conditions.° *terms of settlement*
PETRUCHIO I'll be hanged first.
PETRONIUS Give her a crab-tree cudgel.
PETRUCHIO So I will;
And after it a flock-bed° for her bones, *lumpy mattress*
And hard eggs, till they brace° her like a drum. *i.e., constipate*
She shall be pampered with—
She shall not know a stool° in ten months, gentlemen. *chair; toilet*
SOPHOCLES This must not be.

Enter Jaques.

JAQUES Arm, arm! Out with your weapons,
For all the women in the kingdom's on ye.° *are attacking you*
They swarm like wasps, and nothing can destroy 'em
But stopping° of their hive and smothering of 'em. *stopping up, plugging*

Enter Pedro.

PEDRO Stand to your guard, sir! All the devils extant
Are broke upon us, like a cloud of thunder.
There are more women marching hitherward
In rescue of my mistress than e'er turned tail
At Stourbridge Fair[2]—and, I believe, as fiery.
JAQUES The forlorn hope's° led by a tanner's wife; *The desperate cause is*
I know her by her hide—a desperate woman.
She flayed her husband in her youth and made
Reins of his hide to ride the parish. Her placket° *petticoat slit*

1. She should be made to ride a wooden frame used as a form of punishment.
2. A famous annual fair in Stourbridge, near Cambridge, where there would be women turning tricks, or running away from their husbands or families, or doing turns in a dance (all possible meanings of "turn tail").

Looks like the straits of Gibraltar, still wider
Down to the gulf. All sunburnt Barbary° *northwest Africa*
Lies in her breech. Take 'em all together,
They are a genealogy of jennets,° gotten° *Spanish horses / begotten*
And born thus by the boisterous breath of husbands;[3]
They serve sure,° and are swift to catch Occasion *act decisively*
(I mean their foes, or husbands) by the forelocks,[4]
And there they hang like favors.° Cry they can, *love tokens; lovelocks*
But more for noble spite than fear; and, crying
Like the old giants that were foes to heaven,[5]
They heave ye stool on stool, and fling main° potlids *heavy*
Like massy rocks, dart° ladles, toasting irons, *throw*
And tongs like thunderbolts, till, overlaid,° *overcome*
They fall beneath the weight, yet still aspiring
At those imperious codheads that would tame 'em.[6]
There's ne'er a one of these, the worst and weakest,
Choose where you will, but dare attempt the raising,
Against the sovereign peace of Puritans,
A maypole and a morris, maugre mainly
Their zeal and dudgeon daggers;[7] and yet more,
Dares plant a stand of batt'ring ale against 'em
And drink 'em out o'th'parish.[8]

PEDRO There's one° brought in the bears against the canons° *one who / regulations*
Of two churchwardens, made it good, and fought 'em,° *put on a bearbaiting*
And in the churchyard after evensong.[9]

JAQUES Another, to her everlasting fame, erected
Two alehouses of ease,° the quarter sessions *hospitality; whoring*
Running against her roundly,[1] in which business
Two of the disannullers° lost their nightcaps; *would-be abolishers*
A third stood excommunicate° by the cudgel. *i.e., evicted*
The constable, to her eternal glory,
Drunk° hard, and was converted, and the victor.[2] *Drank*

PEDRO Then are they victualed° with pies and puddings *supplied*
(The trappings of good stomachs), noble ale
(The true defender),° sausages, and smoked ones, *encourager of spirits*
If need be, such as serve for pikes,° and pork *are skewered on spits*
(Better the Jews never hated); here and there
A bottle of metheglin, a stout Britain
That will stand to 'em.[3] What else they want, they war for.

SOPHOCLES Lo ye, fierce Petruchio,
This comes of your impatience.

PETRUCHIO Come to council.° *Let's consult*

3. And formed thus at birth by the boisterous outpouring of the spirit of fathers. (Men were generally credited with stamping their form on children; women were considered the passive carriers of the infant.)

4. Based on the proverb "Take Occasion by the forelock."

5. The Giants of Greek mythology were monstrous beings, partly human, who rose up against the gods and were confined in the earth for their rebellion, becoming transformed into volcanoes such as Mount Etna.

6. The men who seek to tame women are here disparagingly referred to as "codheads," since "cod" was a slang term for the penis and/or testicles.

7. There's not a woman among them, no matter how weak, who would not dare to erect a maypole or dance a morris dance in defiance of the Puritans, for all their zealotry and wooden (i.e., ineffectual) daggers.

8. Dares engage in church-ales (parish gatherings) and other kinds of drinking bouts as a means of chasing away the Puritans.

9. The popular sport of bearbaiting was much deplored by the Puritans and would have been especially offensive in a churchyard.

1. I.e., one step ahead of the law. (The quarter sessions were court sessions held four times a year.)

2. The constable was won over and joined in the fun, to the eternal glory of the alehouse woman (lines 71–72).

3. Metheglin, or spiced mead, is here described as a stout Celtic beverage (from "Britain") that will stand by them, stand the wives in good stead.

SOPHOCLES Now ye must grant conditions, or the kingdom
Will have no other talk but this.
PETRONIUS Away, then,
And let's advise the best.° *consider what's best*
SOPHOCLES [*to Moroso*] Why do you tremble?
MOROSO Have I lived thus long to be knocked o'th'head
With half a washing beetle?[4] Pray be wise, sir.
PETRUCHIO Come, something I'll do, but what it is I know not.
SOPHOCLES To council, then, and let's avoid° their follies. *refute, quash*
Guard all the doors, or we shall not have a cloak left.
Exeunt.

2.[5]

Enter three Maids at several doors.

FIRST MAID How goes the business, girls?
SECOND MAID A foot, and fair.° *i.e., Promisingly*
THIRD MAID If fortune favor us. Away to your strength!° *stronghold*
The country forces are arrived; begone!
We are discovered else.
FIRST MAID Arm, and be valiant!
SECOND MAID Think of our cause.
THIRD MAID Our justice.
FIRST MAID 'Tis sufficient.
Exeunt.

2.[6]

Enter Petronius, Petruchio, Moroso, Sophocles, and Tranio.

PETRONIUS I am indifferent, though I must confess
I had rather see her carted.[1]
TRANIO No more of that, sir.
SOPHOCLES Are ye resolved to give her fair conditions?
'Twill be the safest way.
PETRUCHIO I am distracted.
Would I had run my head into a halter° *noose*
When I first wooed her! If I offer peace,
She'll urge her own conditions, that's the devil.° *that's the hell of it*
SOPHOCLES Why, say° she do? *suppose*
PETRUCHIO Say I am made an ass, then.
I know her aim. May I with reputation
(Answer me this), with safety of mine honor—
After the mighty manage° of my first wife, *struggle for control*
Which was indeed a fury to° this filly, *compared with*
After my twelve strong labors to reclaim her,
Which would have made Don Hercules horn-mad,
And hid him in his hide[2]—suffer this Cecily,° *i.e., woman*
Ere she have warmed my sheets, ere grappled with me,

4. A staff used in pressing linen during washing—hence a woman's weapon.
2.5. Petronius' house still.
2.6. Petronius' house still.
1. Punished by being carted through the streets, as was done to whores.
2. Which would have driven even Sir ("Don") Hercules as mad as a cuckold, and compelled him to conceal himself in the hide he tore from the Nemean lion in one of his twelve labors.

This pink, this painted foist, this cockle boat,[3]
To hang her fights out[4] and defy me, friends,
A well known man-of-war? If this be equal,° — *just*
And I may suffer, say,° and I have done.° — *say so / I'll subside*
PETRONIUS I do not think you may.° — *ought to capitulate*
TRANIO You'll make it worse, sir.
SOPHOCLES Pray hear me, good Petruchio. But ev'n now° — *Just now*
You were contented to give all conditions,° — *grant concessions*
To try how far she would carry.° 'Tis a folly, — *go*
And you will find it so, to clap the curb on° — *curb this foal*
Ere ye be sure it proves a natural wildness
And not a forced. Give her conditions,
For on my life this trick is put into her.° — *she's put up to it*
PETRONIUS I should believe so, too.
SOPHOCLES And not her own.° — *her own idea*
TRANIO You'll find it so.
SOPHOCLES Then if she flounder° with you, — *struggle*
Clap spurs on, and in this you'll deal with temperance,
Avoid the hurry of the world.° — *Avoid being too rash*
TRANIO And lose— *Music above.*
MOROSO No honor, on my life, sir.
PETRUCHIO I will do it.
PETRONIUS It seems they are very merry.

Enter Jaques.

PETRUCHIO Why, God hold it.° — *God grant it go well*
MOROSO Now, Jaques?
JAQUES They are i'th'flaunt,° sir. — *flaunting their power*
SOPHOCLES Yes, we hear 'em.
JAQUES They have got a stick of fiddles,° and they firk° it — *fiddlers / dance, flaunt*
In wondrous ways. The two grand capitanos
(They brought the auxiliary regiments)
Dance with their coats tucked up to their bare breeches,
And bid the kingdom kiss 'em, that's the burden.° — *refrain*
They have got metheglin, and audacious ale,
And talk like tyrants.
PETRONIUS How knowest thou?
JAQUES I peeped in
At a loose lansket.[5]
TRANIO Hark!
PETRONIUS A song. Pray, silence.

SONG

A health for all this day
To the woman that bears the sway
And wears the breeches!
Let it come, let it come.
Let this health° be a seal:° — *toast / covenant*
For the good of the commonweal
The women shall wear the breeches.

3. Petruchio compares Maria to various small boats and barges, all of them inferior to a man-of-war (line 19).

4. To hang clothes about the deck in order to conceal the combatants.

5. "Lansket" might signify "lancet," a kind of window.

Let's drink, then, and laugh it
And merrily, merrily quaff it,
And tipple and tipple a round.
Here's to thy fool,
And to my fool.
Come, to all fools,
Though it cost us, wench, many a pound.

[*Enter*] *all the women* [*Maria, Bianca, a City Wife, a Country Wife, and three Maids*] *above.*

MOROSO They look out.
PETRUCHIO [*calling up*] Good ev'n, ladies.
MARIA Good° you good ev'n, sir. *God give*
PETRUCHIO How have you slept tonight?
MARIA Exceeding well, sir.
PETRUCHIO Did you not wish me with you?
MARIA No, believe me,
I never thought upon you.
COUNTRY WIFE [*to Bianca*] Is that he?
BIANCA Yes.
COUNTRY WIFE [*to Petruchio*] Sir?
SOPHOCLES She has drunk hard; mark her hood.° *i.e., wobbling head*
COUNTRY WIFE [*to Petruchio*] You are—
SOPHOCLES Learnedly drunk; I'll hang else. Let her utter.° *talk, babble*
COUNTRY WIFE [*to Petruchio*] And I must tell you, *viva voce*,° friend, *i.e., face-to-face*
A very foolish fellow.
TRANIO There's an ale figure.° *drunken expression*
PETRUCHIO [*to Country Wife*] I thank you, Susan Brotes.° *(a satiric name)*
CITY WIFE [*to Country Wife*] Forward, sister.
COUNTRY WIFE [*to Petruchio*] You have espoused here a hearty woman,
A comely, and courageous.
PETRUCHIO Well, I have so.
COUNTRY WIFE And, to the comfort of distressèd damsels,
Women out-worn in wedlock, and such vessels,
This woman has defied you.
PETRUCHIO It should seem so.
COUNTRY WIFE And why?
PETRUCHIO Yes, can you tell?
COUNTRY WIFE For thirteen causes.
PETRUCHIO Pray, by your patience,° mistress. *please go on (ironic)*
CITY WIFE Forward, sister.
PETRUCHIO Do you mean to treat of° all these? *discuss*
CITY WIFE Who shall let° her? *hinder*
PETRONIUS [*to Country Wife*] Do you hear, velvet hood?[6]
We come not now
To hear your doctrine.
COUNTRY WIFE For° the first,° I take it, *As for / first cause*
It doth divide itself into seven branches.
PETRUCHIO Hark you, good Maria,
Have you got a catechizer here?

6. High-ranking London citizens often wore velvet hoods.

TRANIO Good zeal!° — *Puritan zeal!*
SOPHOCLES [*to Country Wife*] Good three-piled predica-
tion,[7] will you peace,° — *be quiet*
And hear the cause we come for?
COUNTRY WIFE Yes, bobtails,° — *i.e., rogues (2.2.58)*
We know the cause you come for. Here's the cause,° — *i.e., Maria*
But never hope to carry her;° never dream — *win her over, take her*
Or flatter your opinions with a thought
Of base repentance in her.
CITY WIFE Give me sack,° — *white wine*
By this,° and next strong ale. — *(an oath)*
COUNTRY WIFE Swear forward,° sister. — *Go ahead and swear*
CITY WIFE By all that's cordial,° in this place we'll bury — *heart-stimulating*
Our bones, fames,° tongues, our triumphs, and ev'n all — *reputations*
That ever yet was chronicled of woman,
But° this brave wench, this excellent despiser,° — *Unless / despiser of men*
This bane of dull obedience, shall inherit° — *obtain*
Her liberal will,° and march off with conditions — *All her wishes*
Noble, and worth herself.
COUNTRY WIFE She shall, Tom Tilers,[8]
And brave° ones too. My hood° shall make a hearsecloth, — *fine / (see 76)*
And I lie under it, like Joan o'Gaunt,[9]
Ere I go less,° my distaff stuck up by me — *settle for less*
For the eternal trophy of my conquests;
And loud fame at my head, with two main° bottles, — *huge*
Shall fill° to all the world the glorious fall — *toast*
Of old Don Gillian.° — *(a derisive name)*
CITY WIFE Yet a little further:
We have taken° arms in rescue of this lady,° — *taken up / (Maria)*
Most just and noble. If ye beat us off
Without conditions, and we recreant,° — *if we desert*
Use us as we deserve. And first degrade° us — *demote, deprive*
Of all our ancient chamb'ring;° next that — *bedchamber rights*
The symbols of our secrecy, silk stockings;
Hew off our heels; our petticoats of arms[1]
Tear off our bodies, and our bodkins° break — *hairpins*
Over our coward heads.
COUNTRY WIFE And ever after,
To make the tainture° most notorious, — *defilement*
At all our crests, *videlicet* our plackets,
Let laces hang,[2] and we return again
Into our former titles: dairymaids.
PETRUCHIO No more wars. Puissant° ladies, show conditions, — *Powerful*
And freely I accept 'em.
MARIA [*to the ladies*] Call in Livia;
She's in the treaty too.° — *(see 145–47 below)*

Enter Livia above.

7. One given to preaching or loudly proclaiming, dressed in velvet of the thickest nap ("three-piled") and thus highest quality. (Said scornfully.)
8. A derisive name for henpecked husbands, as in the anonymous play of 1560 called *Tom Tyler and His Wife*.
9. The Country Wife plays on the name John of Gaunt, Duke of Lancaster and father of Henry IV, to characterize an extremely lean and starved condition.
1. The City Wife speaks of petticoats as if they were coats of arms.
2. Let our heraldic crests—i.e., the slits in our petticoats—hang open and unlaced. ("*Videlicet*" means "that is to say.")

MOROSO How, Livia?
MARIA Hear you that, sir?
[*Articles are presented to Petruchio.*][3]
There's the conditions for ye. Pray peruse 'em.
PETRONIUS Yes, there she° is. 'T had been no right° rebellion *(Livia) / true*
Had she held off. [*To Moroso*] What think you, man?
MOROSO Nay, nothing.
I have enough o'th'prospect. O'my conscience,
The world's end and the goodness of a woman
Will come together.[4]
PETRONIUS [*to Livia*] Are you there, sweet lady?
LIVIA Cry you mercy,° sir, I saw you not. Your blessing. *I beg your pardon*
PETRONIUS Yes, when I bless a jade° that stumbles with me. *worthless horse; whore*
[*To Petruchio*] How are the articles?
LIVIA [*to Moroso*] This is for you, sir;[5]
And I shall think upon't.
MOROSO You have used me finely.° *(said ironically)*
LIVIA There's no other use of thee now extant
But to be hung up, cassock, cap, and all,
For some strange monster at apothecary's.[6]
PETRONIUS I hear you, whore.
LIVIA It must be his, then, sir,
For need will then compel me.[7]
CITY WIFE Blessing on thee!
LIVIA He will undo me in mere pans of coals
To make him lusty.[8]
PETRONIUS There's no talking to 'em.—
[*To Petruchio*] How are they,° sir? *(the articles)*
PETRUCHIO As I expected. (*Reads.*) Liberty and clothes,
When and in what way she will; continual moneys,
Company, and all the house at her dispose;
No tongue to say, "Why is this, or whither will it?"° *where are you going?*
New coaches and some buildings she appoints° here; *stipulates*
Hangings,° and hunting horses; and for plate° *Tapestries / silver-plated dishes*
And jewels for her private use, I take it,
Two thousand pound in present.° Then for music, *present payment*
And women to read° French— *tutor in*
PETRONIUS This must not be.
PETRUCHIO And at the latter end a clause put in
That Livia shall by no man be importuned,
This whole month yet, to marry.
PETRONIUS This is monstrous.
PETRUCHIO This shall be done. I'll humor her awhile.
If nothing but repentance and undoing° *backing down*
Can win her love, I'll make a shift° for one. *give it a try*
SOPHOCLES [*aside to Petruchio*] When ye are once abed, all these conditions
Lie under your own seal.° *under your control*

3. Perhaps a servant hands the articles to Petruchio, on the main stage, on behalf of Maria and Livia, in the gallery above.
4. I.e., No good woman will be found as long as the world lasts.
5. This set of articles contains terms that are addressed to you as well, Moroso (as specified in lines 145–47 below).
6. Apothecaries sometimes displayed wonders such as preserved alligators.
7. Livia implies that if her father insists on her marrying Moroso, she will of necessity become a whore—either Moroso's or by taking her own lover.
8. I will be driven to endless cost and effort in a fruitless attempt to kindle Moroso's feeble lust.

MARIA [*to Petruchio*] Do ye like 'em?
PETRUCHIO Yes.
And, by that faith° I gave ye 'fore the priest, *promise, oath*
I'll ratify 'em.
COUNTRY WIFE Stay. What pledges?° *hostages*
MARIA No, I'll take° that oath; *accept, trust*
[*To Petruchio*] But have a care ye keep it.
CITY WIFE 'Tis not now
As when Andrea lived.[9]
COUNTRY WIFE If you do juggle,° *quibble*
Or alter but a letter of this creed
We have set down, the selfsame persecution—
MARIA Mistrust him not.
PETRUCHIO By all my honesty—
MARIA Enough. I yield.
PETRONIUS [*looking at the articles*] What's this inserted here?
SOPHOCLES [*looking also*] That the two valiant women that command here
Shall have a supper made 'em,° and a large one, *for them*
And liberal entertainment without grudging,
And pay for all their soldiers.° *supporting women*
PETRUCHIO That shall be too;
And if a tun° of wine will serve to pay 'em, *barrel*
They shall have justice. I ordain ye all
Paymasters, gentlemen.
TRANIO Then we shall have sport, boys.
MARIA We'll meet ye in the parlor. [*Exeunt above.*]
PETRUCHIO [*to Petronius*] Ne'er look sad, sir,
For I will do it.
SOPHOCLES There's no danger in't.
PETRUCHIO [*to Petronius*] For° Livia's article, you shall observe° it. *As for* / *honor*
I have tied° myself. *obligated*
PETRONIUS I will.
PETRUCHIO Along, then! Now
Either I break,° or this stiff plant must bow.[1] *Exeunt.* *relent, give in*

3.1

Enter Tranio and Rowland.

TRANIO Come, ye shall take my counsel.
ROWLAND I shall hang first.
I'll no more love, that's certain. 'Tis a bane,° *poison*
Next that° they poison rats with, the most mortal.° *to that which / deadly*
No, I thank heaven, I have got my sleep again,
And now begin to write sense; I can walk ye° *can walk*
A long hour in my chamber like a man,
And think of something that may better me—
Some serious point of learning, or my state.° *state of affairs*
No more ay-me's and *misereri*'s,° Tranio, *have-mercy-on-me's*
Come near my brain. I'll tell thee, had the devil

9. The City Wife recalls *The Spanish Tragedy*, 3.12.11, in which Andrea's murder sets in motion the revenge tragedy. Here the implication is of a long-lost chivalric world now nearly forgotten in an age of chicanery.
1. A bawdy reference to a male erection.
3.1. Petronius' house still.

But any essence in him of a man,
And could be brought to love, and love a woman,
'Twould make his head ache worser than his horns do,
And firk° him with a fire he never felt yet, *strike*
Would° make him dance. I tell thee, there is nothing *Which would*
(It may be thy case, Tranio, therefore hear me)
Under the sun (reckon° the mass of follies *if we reckon up*
Crept into th'world with man) so desperate,
So mad, so senseless, poor, and base, so wretched,
Roguey, and scurvy—

TRANIO Whither wilt thou,° Rowland? *Where is this leading*

ROWLAND As 'tis to be in love.

TRANIO And why, for heaven's sake?

ROWLAND "And why, for heaven's sake?" Dost thou not
conceive° me? *understand*

TRANIO No, by my troth.

ROWLAND Pray then, and heartily,
For fear thou fall into 't. I'll tell thee why, too,
For I have hope to save thee. When thou lovest,
And first begin'st to worship the gilt° calf, *golden*
Imprimis,° thou hast lost thy gentry,° *First / male birthright*
And like a prentice flung away thy freedom.
Forthwith thou art a slave.

TRANIO That's a new doctrine.

ROWLAND Next, thou art no more man.

TRANIO What, then?

ROWLAND A frippery;° *showily-dressed person*
Nothing but braided hair and penny ribbon,
Glove, garter, ring, rose,° or at best a swabber.° *ornamental knot / mop*
If thou canst love so near to keep thy making,[1]
Yet thou wilt lose thy language.° *babble like an idiot*

TRANIO Why?

ROWLAND Oh, Tranio,
Those things° in love ne'er talk as we do. *creatures, lovers*

TRANIO No?

ROWLAND No. Without doubt, they sigh and shake the head,
And sometimes whistle dolefully.

TRANIO No tongue?

ROWLAND Yes, Tranio, but no truth in't, nor no reason,
And when they cant° (for 'tis a kind of canting), *speak in love clichés*
Ye shall hear, if you reach° to understand 'em *strive*
(Which you must be a fool first, or you cannot),
Such gibberish! Such "Believe me, I protest, sweet,"
And "Oh, dear heavens, in which such constellations
Reign at the births of lovers"—This is too well—
And "Deign me, lady, deign me, I beseech ye,
Your poor unworthy lump," and then she licks him.[2]

TRANIO Oh, pox° on't, this is nothing. *i.e., a curse*

ROWLAND Thou hast hit it.° *the nail on the head*

1. Even if you can love so prudently as to be true to yourself.

2. And "Deign to receive my unworthy self as your worshiper," whereupon the woman caresses ("licks") and fondles her servant, or lover, much as a mother bear was said to lick her newborn, unformed cubs ("lumps") into the shape of bears.

Then talks she ten times worse, and wries° and wriggles — *twists*
As though she had the itch (and so it may be).

TRANIO Of what religion are they?

ROWLAND Good old Catholics;
They deal by intercession all.[3] They keep
A kind of household gods called chambermaids,
Which, being prayed to, and their offerings brought,
(Which are in gold, yet some observe the old law
And give 'em flesh),[4] *probatum est,*° you shall have — *it is proven*
As good love for your money and as tidy
As e'er you turned° your leg o'er, and that ended— — *threw*

TRANIO Why, thou art grown a strange discoverer.° — *social critic*

ROWLAND Of mine own follies, Tranio.

TRANIO Wilt thou, Rowland,
Certain ne'er love again?

ROWLAND I think so, certain,
And if I be not dead drunk, I shall keep it.° — *keep my word*

TRANIO Tell me but this: what dost thou think of women?

ROWLAND Why, as I think of fiddles: they delight me
Till their strings break.

TRANIO What strings?

ROWLAND Their modesties,
Faiths, vows, and maidenheads, for they are like kits;° — *small fiddles*
They have but four strings to 'em.

TRANIO What° wilt thou — *What odds in betting*
Give me for ten pound now, when thou next lovest,
And the same woman still?

ROWLAND Give me the money;
A hundred, and my bond for't.[5]

TRANIO But pray hear me.
I'll work all means I can to reconcile ye.

ROWLAND Do, do. Give me the money.

TRANIO [*giving money*] There.

ROWLAND Work, Tranio.

TRANIO You shall go sometimes where she is.

ROWLAND Yes, straight.° — *at once*
This[6] is the first good I e'er got by woman.

TRANIO You would think it strange now, if another beauty
As good as hers, say better—

ROWLAND Well?

TRANIO Conceive me,
This is no point o'th'wager.[7]

ROWLAND That's all one.° — *all the same*

TRANIO Love ye as much, or more, than she now hates ye.[8]

ROWLAND 'Tis a good hearing. Let 'em love! Ten pound° more — *I bet £100 to your £10*
I never love that woman.° — *such another woman*

TRANIO [*putting down £10 more*] There it is;

3. The godlike women are to be approached only through the intercession of their servants, who, like saints in Catholic theology, must be implored to for assistance and given offerings (i.e., bribes).
4. Sometimes the lovers pay off the maids by sleeping with them—analogous to the old Mosaic law demanding animal sacrifice ("flesh").
5. Rowland bets ten to one he will not love the same woman (Livia) again. He offers a promissary note for his one hundred pounds, and Tranio puts down his ten pounds in cash.
6. The bet that Rowland thinks he will win.
7. What I'm about to say is not what we bet about.
8. You'd think it strange if another beautiful woman were to love you as intensely as Livia now hates you.

And so an hundred,° if ye lose. *you forfeit £100*

ROWLAND 'Tis done.
Have ye another to put in?

TRANIO No, no, sir.

ROWLAND I am very sorry. Now will I erect
A new game and go hate for th'bell;[9] I am sure
I am in excellent case to win.

TRANIO I must have leave° *permission*
To tell ye, and tell truth too, what she is,
And how she suffers for you.

ROWLAND Ten pound more
I never believe ye.

TRANIO No, sir, I am stinted.° *finished betting*

ROWLAND Well, take your best way,[1] then.

TRANIO Let's walk. I am glad
Your sullen fever's off.

ROWLAND Shalt° see me, Tranio, *Thou shalt*
A monstrous merry man now. Let's to the wedding,[2]
And, as we go, tell me the general hurry° *commotion*
Of these mad wenches and their works.

TRANIO I will.

ROWLAND And do thy worst.

TRANIO Something I'll do.

ROWLAND Do, Tranio.
Exeunt.

3.2

Enter Pedro and Jaques.

PEDRO A pair of stocks bestride 'em!° Are they gone? *May they be punished!*

JAQUES Yes, they are gone, and all the pans i'th'town
Beating before 'em. What strange admonitions
They gave my master, and how fearfully
They threatened if he broke 'em!

PEDRO O'my conscience,
He's found his full match now.

JAQUES That I believe, too.

PEDRO How did she entertain° him? *Maria receive*

JAQUES She looked on him—

PEDRO But scurvily.

JAQUES Faith, with no great affection
That I saw; and I heard some say he kissed her,
But 'twas upon a treaty, and some copies° *reports*
Say but her cheek.

PEDRO Faith, Jaques, what wouldst thou give
For such a wife now?

JAQUES Full as many prayers
As the most zealous Puritan conceives

9. Rowland proposes to win the prize in a contest of hating women. ("Th'bell" signifies victory.)
1. (1) Be on your way; (2) make the best of it.
2. I.e., the wedding of Livia and Moroso. Rowland thinks this is still going to happen.
3.2. Petronius' house still.

Out of the meditation of fat veal,
Or birds of prey, crammed capons, against players,[1]
And to as good a tune, too—but against° her, *against my having*
That heaven would bless° me from her. Mark it, Pedro: *shield*
If this house be not turned within this fortnight
With the foundation upward, I'll be carted.° *(see 2.6.2 n)*
My comfort is yet that those Amorites° *Canaanites, heathens*
That came to back her cause, those heathen whores,
Had their hoods hallowèd with sack.° *i.e., were sick drunk*

PEDRO How dev'lish drunk they were!

JAQUES And how they tumbled,° Pedro! Didst thou mark *stumbled*
The country *cavaliero*?° *wife*

PEDRO Out upon her,° *i.e., Deuce take her*
How she turned down the bragget!° *downed the honey ale*

JAQUES Ay, that sunk her.

PEDRO That drink was well put to her. What a somersault,
When the chair fell, she fetched,° with her heels upward! *took*

JAQUES And what a piece of landscape° she discovered!° *sexual anatomy / revealed*

PEDRO Didst mark her when her hood fell in the posset?° *hot bedtime drink*

JAQUES Yes, and there rid,° like a Dutch hoy, the tumbrel,[2] *rode*
When she had got her ballasse.° *ballast, balance*

PEDRO That I saw too.

JAQUES How fain she would have drawn on Sophocles
To come aboard,° and how she simpered it! *come alongside; mount*

PEDRO I warrant her, she has been a worthy striker.° *fornicator*

JAQUES I'th'heat of summer there had been some hope on't,° *pleasure in it*
For then old women are cool cellars.° *i.e., sexually cold*

PEDRO Hang her!

JAQUES She offered him a Harry groat,[3] and belched out—
Her stomach being blown with ale—such courtship,
Upon my life, has giv'n him twenty stools° since. *bowel movements*
Believe my calculation: these old women,
When they are tippled and a little heated
Are like new wheels; they'll roar you° all the town o'er *make grating noises*
Till they be greased.

PEDRO The city cinquepace,
Dame Toast-and-Butter, had her bob too?[4]

JAQUES Yes,
But she was sullen drunk, and given to filching.
I see° her offer at° a spoon. [*Seeing Petruchio and Sophocles approach*] My master! *saw / try to steal*
I do not like his look. I fear he's fasted,° *had no sex*
For° all this preparation. Let's steal by him. *Exeunt.* *Despite*

1. As many prayers as a zealous Puritan, meditating greedily on fine delicacies for the table, composes in his mind against actors. (Puritans were satirized for their hypocritical gluttony and objection to the theater and actors. "Crammed" means "stuffed.")
2. A hoy is a small sailing vessel; a tumbrel is a flat-bottomed boat or barge and also a dung-cart.
3. A small silver coin worth fourpence, coined in the reign of Henry VIII.
4. Pedro asks amusedly if the City Wife also displayed a sportful trick or two (a "bob"). (The cinquepace is a fast, energetic five-step dance. "Toast-and-Butter" may suggest one who is overly fond of toast and ale; toast was often served in alcoholic beverages.)

3.3

Enter Petruchio and Sophocles.

SOPHOCLES Not let you touch her all this night?
PETRUCHIO Not touch her.
SOPHOCLES Where was your courage?
PETRUCHIO Where was her obedience?
Never poor man was shamed so; never rascal
That keeps a stud° of whores was used so basely. *harem*
SOPHOCLES Pray tell me one thing truly: do you love her?
PETRUCHIO I would° I did not, upon that condition *wish*
I passed thee half my land.[1]
SOPHOCLES It may be, then,
Her modesty required a little violence?
Some women love to struggle.
PETRUCHIO She had it,° *I used violence*
And so much that I sweat° for't, so I did, *sweated*
But to no end; I washed an Ethiop.[2]
She swore my force might weary her, but win her
I never could, nor should, till she consented;
And I might take her body prisoner,
But for° her mind or appetite— *as for*
SOPHOCLES 'Tis strange.
This woman is the first I ever read of
Refused° a warranted occasion, *Who refused*
And standing° on so fair terms. *(with an erotic pun)*
PETRUCHIO I shall quit° her. *requite, pay back*
SOPHOCLES Used you no more art?
PETRUCHIO Yes, I swore unto her,
And by no little ones,° if presently, *by no small oaths*
Without more disputation on the matter,
She grew not nearer to me, and dispatched me
Out of the pain I was°—for I was nettled— *was in*
And willingly, and eagerly, and sweetly,
I would to° her chambermaid, and in her hearing *turn to*
Begin her such a hunt's-up.[3]
SOPHOCLES Then she started?° *jumped from cover*
PETRUCHIO No more than I do now. Marry, she answered,
If I were so disposed, she could not help it;
But there was one called Jaques, a poor butler,
One that might well content a single woman.
SOPHOCLES And he should tilt° her? *i.e., have sex with*
PETRUCHIO To that sense;° and last *effect*
She bade me yet these six nights look for° nothing, *expect*
Nor strive to purchase° it, but fair good night, *acquire*
And so good morrow, and a kiss or two
To close° my stomach, for her vow had sealed° it, *appease / confirmed*
And she would keep it constant.
SOPHOCLES Stay ye,° stay ye. *Wait a minute*

3.3. Petruchio's house.
1. I'd give up half my land to you to be freed of loving her.
2. From the proverb "To wash an Ethiopian white"; i.e., to attempt the impossible.
3. I'd sound the hunting cry. ("Hunt's-up" is literally a song to awaken hunters.)

Was she thus when you wooed° her? *(before marriage)*
PETRUCHIO Nothing, Sophocles,
More keenly eager. I was oft afraid
She had been light and easy,° she would shower *wanton*
Her kisses so upon me.
SOPHOCLES Then I fear
Another spoke's i'th'wheel.° *There's new trouble*
PETRUCHIO Now thou hast found me;° *found my sore point*
There gnaws my devil, Sophocles. Oh, patience
Preserve me, that I make her not example
By some unworthy way, as° flaying her, *such as*
Boiling, or making verjuice,° drying her! [*A noise is heard.*] *sour juice*
SOPHOCLES I hear her.
PETRUCHIO Mark her, then, and see the heir° *true child*
Of spite and prodigality. She has studied
A way to beggar 's° both, and, by this hand, *impoverish us*
She shall be, if I live, a doxy.° *beggar's wench*
SOPHOCLES Fie, sir!

[*Enter*] *Maria at the door, and servant and woman.*° *maidservant*
[*Petruchio and Sophocles stand aside.*]

MARIA [*to the servants*] I do not like that dressing;° 'tis too poor. *outfit*
Let me have six gold laces, broad and massy,
And betwixt ev'ry lace a rich embroid'ry.
Line the gown through with plush, perfumed, and purfle° *embroider*
All the sleeves down with pearl.
PETRUCHIO [*aside to Sophocles*] What think you, Sophocles?
In what point stands my state° now? *state of affairs*
MARIA [*to the servants*] For° those hangings,° *As for / tapestries*
Let 'em be carried where I gave appointment°— *where I specified*
They are too base for my use—and bespeak° *commission*
New pieces° of the civil wars of France. *tapestries*
Let 'em be large and lively, and all silk work,
The borders gold.
SOPHOCLES [*aside to Petruchio*] Ay, marry, sir, this cuts it.° *maims your estate*
MARIA [*to the servants*] That fourteen yards of satin, give my woman.
I do not like the color, 'tis too civil;° *sedate, somber*
There's too much silk i'th'lace, too. Tell the Dutchman
That brought the mares he must with all speed send me
Another suit° of horses, and by all means *set*
Ten cast° of hawks for th'river. I much care not° *couples / don't much care*
What price they bear, so° they be sound,° and flying. *so long as / healthy*
For the next winter, I am for the country,
And mean to take my pleasure. Where's the horse, man?
PETRUCHIO [*aside to Sophocles*] She means to ride a great horse.
SOPHOCLES [*aside to Petruchio*] With a sidesaddle?
PETRUCHIO [*aside to Sophocles*] Yes, and she'll run a-tilt[4] within this twelvemonth.
MARIA [*to the manservant*] Tomorrow I'll begin to learn. But pray, sir,

4. She'll compete in a tournament—an activity that, like riding a great horse, women would not ordinarily undertake.

Have a great care he be an easy doer;° *gentle mount*
'Twill spoil a scholar° else. *beginner*
SOPHOCLES [*aside to Petruchio*] An easy doer.° *i.e., easily seduced*
Did you hear that?
PETRUCHIO [*aside to Sophocles*] Yes, I shall meet her morals° *intent; loose morals*
Ere it be long, I fear not.
MARIA [*seeing Petruchio and Sophocles*] Oh, good morrow.
SOPHOCLES Good morrow, lady. How is't now?
MARIA Faith, sickly.
This house stands in an ill air—
PETRUCHIO [*aside*] Yet more charges?° *expenses*
MARIA Subject to rots and rheums. Out on't, 'tis nothing
But a tiled fog.° *a fog with a roof over it*
PETRUCHIO What think you of the lodge,° then? *smaller house*
MARIA I like the seat,° but 'tis too little. Sophocles, *location*
Let me have thy opinion; thou hast judgment.
PETRUCHIO 'Tis very well.° *It's fine as it is*
MARIA What if I pluck it down
And built a square upon it, with two courts° *courtyards*
Still rising° from the entrance? *Leading in succession*
PETRUCHIO [*aside*] And i'th'midst
A college for young scolds.
MARIA And to the southward
Take in° a garden of some twenty acres, *Include*
And cast it off° the Italian fashion, hanging.° *design it in / sloping*
PETRUCHIO [*aside*] And you could cast° yourself so, too.— *cast away; defeat*
Pray, lady,
Will not this cost much money?
MARIA Some five thousand,
Say six. I'll have it battled° too. *with parapets*
PETRUCHIO And gilt. Maria,
This is a fearful course you take; pray think on't.
You are a woman now, a wife, and his
That must, in honesty and justice, look for
Some due obedience from you.
MARIA That bare word
Shall cost you many a pound more; build upon't.° *count on it*
Tell me of due obedience? What's a husband?
What are we married for? To carry sumpters?° *saddlebags*
Are we not one piece with you, and as worthy
Our own intentions as you yours?
PETRUCHIO Pray hear me.
MARIA Take two small drops of water, equal weighed:
Tell me which is the heaviest, and which ought
First to descend in duty?
PETRUCHIO You mistake me.
I urge not service from you, nor obedience
In way of duty, but of love and credit;° *faith*
All I expect is but a noble care
Of what I have brought you, and of what I am,
And what our name may be.
MARIA That's in my making.° *what I'll make of it*
PETRUCHIO 'Tis true, it is so.
MARIA Yes, it is, Petruchio.
For there was never man without our molding,

Without our stamp upon him, and our justice,
Left anything three ages after him
Good, and his own.[5]

SOPHOCLES Good lady, understand him.

MARIA I do too much, sweet Sophocles; he's one
Of a most spiteful self-condition,
Never at peace with anything but age° *i.e., old men*
That has no teeth left to return his anger.
A bravery° dwells in his blood yet, of abusing *bravado*
His first good wife; he's sooner fire than powder,
And sooner mischief.[6]

PETRUCHIO If I be so sudden,° *quick to anger*
Do not you fear me?

MARIA No, nor yet care for you,
And, if it may be lawful, I defy you.

PETRUCHIO Does this become° you now? *suit*

MARIA It shall become me.° *This is who I'll be*

PETRUCHIO Thou disobedient, weak, vainglorious woman,
Were I but half so willful as thou spiteful,
I should now drag thee to thy duty.

MARIA Drag me?

PETRUCHIO But I am friends again. Take all your pleasure.° *Have it your way*

MARIA Now you perceive him, Sophocles.

PETRUCHIO I love thee
Above thy vanity,[7] thou faithless creature.

MARIA [*to Sophocles*] Would I had been so happy, when I married,
But to have met an honest man like thee,
For I am sure thou art good. I know thou art honest,
A handsome, hurtless man, a loving man,
Though never a° penny with him, and those eyes, *not so much as*
That face, and that true heart. [*Giving him a favor*] Wear this for my sake,
And, when thou think'st upon me, pity me;
I am cast away.° *Exit Maria.* *shipwrecked; rejected*

SOPHOCLES Why, how now, man?

PETRUCHIO Pray leave me,
And follow your advices.° *inclinations*

SOPHOCLES The man's jealous.

PETRUCHIO I shall find a time, ere it be long, to ask you
One or two foolish questions.

SOPHOCLES I shall answer
As well as I am able, when you call me.° *call me out to duel*
If she mean true, 'tis but a little killing,° *i.e., duel*
And if I do not venture it, rot take me!° *may I rot in hell!*
Farewell, sir.

PETRUCHIO Pray, farewell. *Exit Sophocles.*
Is there no keeping
A wife to one man's use? No wintering
These cattle without straying? 'Tis hard dealing,

5. For never was there a man who, without our molding him and leaving our indelible impression upon him, as well as our sense of true justice, left any legacy of goodness that could last three generations beyond his own.

6. His hair-trigger temper ignites quicker than gunpowder and is even quicker to cause trouble.

7. I love you despite your vainglorious pride.

Very hard dealing, gentlemen,° strange dealing. *(the audience)*
Now, in the name of madness, what star reigned,
What Dog Star, Bull, or Bear Star,[8] when I married
This second wife, this whirlwind, that takes all
Within her compass? Was I not well warned
(I thought I had,° and I believe I know it) *had been warned*
And beaten to repentance in the days
Of my first doting? Had I not wife enough
To turn my tools to? Did I want° vexation, *lack*
Or any special care to kill my heart?
Had I not ev'ry morning a rare breakfast,
Mixed with a learnèd lecture of ill language,
Louder than Tom o'Lincoln,[9] and at dinner
A diet of the same dish? Was there evening
That e'er passed over us without "Thou knave"
Or "Thou whore" for digestion? Had I ever
A pull° at this same poor sport° men run mad for, *A go / (sex)*
But like a cur I was fain to show my teeth first,
And almost worry her?[1] And did heaven forgive me,
And take this serpent from me?° And am I *take Kate to heaven*
Keeping tame devils° now again? My heart aches. *i.e., wives*
Something I must do speedily: I'll die,
If I can handsomely, for that's the way
To make a rascal[2] of her. I am sick,
And I'll go very near it but I'll perish.[3] *Exit.*

3.4

Enter Livia, Bianca, Tranio, and Rowland.

LIVIA [*to Rowland*] Then I must be content, sir, with my fortune.
ROWLAND And I with mine.
LIVIA I did not think a look,
Or a poor word or two, could have displanted
Such a fixed constancy, and for your end too.[1]
ROWLAND Come, come, I know your courses.° There's your gewgaws,° *tricks* *trinkets*
Your rings, and bracelets, and the purse you gave me,
The moneys spent in entertaining you
At plays and cherry gardens. [*He returns gifts to her.*]
LIVIA [*giving a chain*] There's your chain too.
But if you'll give me leave, I'll wear the hair° still; *hair in a locket*
I would yet remember you.
BIANCA Give him his love, wench;
The young man has employment for't.° *He'll find someone else*

8. Petruchio appeals to astrological configurations in which the sun is near the Dog Star, Sirius (in late summer, a hot season), the Bull, Taurus (in May), or the Bear Star (perhaps an extravagant idea, since the sun never approaches Ursa Major, the Great Bear or Big Dipper, circling around the North Pole).
9. The great bell in Lincoln Cathedral.
1. Wasn't my experience in marriage such that I practically had to seize by the throat the quarry I had chased?
2. (1) Rogue, wretch; (2) inferior deer (continuing the metaphor of the hunt).
3. And I'm very close to dying.
3.4. Petronius' house.
1. I didn't think a mere quarrel could have caused you to forget your loyalty to me, especially when the few words I spoke were in your best interests.

TRANIO Fie, Rowland!
ROWLAND You cannot "fie" me out a hundred pound° *(see 3.1.66 ff.)*
With this poor plot. Yet let me ne'er see day more° *let me not live*
If something do not struggle strangely in me.
BIANCA Young man, let me talk with you.
ROWLAND Well, young woman?
BIANCA This was your mistress once.
ROWLAND Yes.
BIANCA Are ye honest?
I see you are young, and handsome.
ROWLAND I am honest.
BIANCA Why, that's well said; and there's no doubt your judgment
Is good enough and strong enough to tell you
Who are your foes and friends. Why did you leave her?
ROWLAND She made a puppy° of me. *coxcomb, fool*
BIANCA Be that granted.
She must do so sometimes, and oftentimes;
Love were too serious else.
ROWLAND A witty woman.
BIANCA Had ye loved me—
ROWLAND I would I had.
BIANCA And dearly;
And I had° loved you so. You may° love worse, sir, *would have / might*
But that is not material.
ROWLAND I shall lose.[2]
BIANCA Some time or other, for variety,
I should have called ye fool, or boy, or bid ye
Play with the pages,° but have loved you still, *boys*
Out of all question, and extremely too;
You are a man made to be loved.
ROWLAND [*aside*] This woman
Either abuses° me or loves me dearly. *deceives*
BIANCA I'll tell you one thing: if I were to choose
A husband to mine own mind, I should think
One of your mother's making would content me,
For o'my conscience she makes good ones.
ROWLAND Lady,
I'll leave you to your commendations.° *compliments*
[*Aside*] I am in° again. The devil take their tongues! *in love*
[*He starts to leave.*]
BIANCA You shall not go.
ROWLAND I will. Yet thus far, Livia:
Your sorrow may induce me to forgive ye,
But never love again. If I stay longer,
I have lost two hundred pound. [*Again he starts to leave.*]
LIVIA Good sir, but thus much—
TRANIO [*to Rowland*] Turn, if thou be'st a man.
LIVIA But one kiss of ye;
One parting kiss, and I am gone too.
ROWLAND Come,

2. I.e., I shall lose my bet. (Rowland fears that he will lose because he is falling in love again, this time with Bianca—see line 38 below—and so will lose the bet he made with Tranio never to love another woman.)

I shall kiss fifty pound away at this clap.° [*He kisses her.*] *stroke; kiss*
We'll have one more, and then farewell.
[*Another kiss, and he starts to go.*]
LIVIA Farewell, sir.
BIANCA Well, go thy ways. Thou bear'st a kind heart with thee.
TRANIO He's made a stand.° *He's stopped*
BIANCA A noble, brave young fellow,
Worthy a wench, indeed.
ROWLAND I will; I will not. *Exit Rowland.*
TRANIO He's gone, but shot again.[3] Play you but your part,
And I will keep my promise: forty angels° *gold coins*
In fair gold, lady. Wipe your eyes; he's yours,
If I have any wit.
LIVIA I'll pay the forfeit.[4]
BIANCA Come, then, let's see your sister, how she fares now,
After her skirmish; and be sure Moroso
Be kept in good hand.° Then all's perfect, Livia. *Exeunt.* *under control*

3.5

Enter Jaques and Pedro.

PEDRO Oh, Jaques, Jaques, what becomes of us?
Oh, my sweet master!
JAQUES Run for a physician
And a whole peck of pothecaries, Pedro.
He will die, diddle, diddle die,[1] if they come not quickly,
And bring all empirics° straight, and mountebanks *quacks*
Skillful in lungs and livers. Raise the neighbors,
And all the aqua vitae° bottles extant; *brandy*
And, oh, the parson, Pedro! Oh, the parson!
A little of his comfort, never so little.° *as much as can be*
Twenty to one you find him at the Bush;° *a tavern*
There's the best ale.
PEDRO I fly. *Exit Pedro.*

Enter Maria, and servants carrying out household-stuff and trunks.

MARIA Out with the trunks, ho!
Why are you idle? Sirrah,° up to th'chamber, *(said to inferiors)*
And take the hangings° down, and see the linen *tapestries*
Packed up and sent away within this half hour.
What, are the carts come yet? Some honest body° *worthy fellow*
Help down the chests of plate, and some the wardrobe.
Alas, we are undone else!
JAQUES Pray, forsooth,
And I beseech ye, tell me, is he dead yet?
MARIA No, but is drawing on.°—Out with the armor! *nearly so*
JAQUES Then I'll go see him.

3. He's shot again with Cupid's love arrows.
4. I'll pay up if I forfeit by not playing my part successfully.

3.5. Petruchio's house.
1. Jaques plays with "die" as though it were part of a jingling refrain, like "Hey, diddle, diddle."

MARIA Thou art undone, then, fellow.
No man that has been near him come near me.

Enter Sophocles and Petronius.

SOPHOCLES Why, how now, lady, what means this?
PETRONIUS Now, daughter,
How does my son?° — *son-in-law*
MARIA [*to the servants*] Save all ye can, for heaven's sake!

Enter Livia, Bianca, and Tranio.

LIVIA Be of good comfort, sister.
MARIA Oh, my casket!
PETRONIUS How does thy husband, woman?
MARIA Get ye gone,
If you mean to save your lives! The sickness°— — *plague*
PETRONIUS Stand further off, I prithee.
MARIA Is i'th'house, sir. My husband has it now.
Alas, he is infected, and raves extremely.
Give me some counsel, friends.
BIANCA Why, lock the doors up,
And send him in a woman to attend him.
MARIA I have bespoke° two women, and the city — *engaged*
Has sent a watch° by this time. Meat nor money — *door guards*
He shall not want,° nor prayers. — *lack*
PETRONIUS How long is't
Since it first took him?
MARIA But within this three hours.

Enter Watch.

I am frighted from my wits.—Oh, here's the watch.—
Pray do your office. Lock the doors up, friends,
And patience be his angel! *They lock the doors.*
TRANIO This comes unlooked for.
MARIA I'll to the lodge. Some that are kind and love me,
I know, will visit me.
PETRUCHIO (*within*) Do you hear, my masters?° — *good sirs*
Ho, you that lock the doors up!
PETRONIUS 'Tis his voice.
TRANIO Hold, and let's hear him.
PETRUCHIO [*within*] Will ye starve me here?
Am I a traitor, or an heretic,
Or am I grown infectious?
PETRONIUS [*calling*] Pray, sir, pray.
PETRUCHIO [*within*] I am as well as you are, goodman puppy.
MARIA Pray have patience. You shall want nothing, sir.
PETRUCHIO [*within*] I want a cudgel, and thee, thou wickedness!
PETRONIUS He speaks well enough.
MARIA 'Had° ever a strong heart, sir. — *He had*
PETRUCHIO [*within*] Will ye hear me? First be pleased
To think I know ye all, and can distinguish
Ev'ry man's several° voice. You that spoke first, — *individual*
I know my father-in-law; the other Tranio,
And I heard Sophocles; the last, pray mark me,
Is my damned wife Maria. Gentlemen,

If any man misdoubt me for° infected, — *fear that I am*
There is mine arm; let any man look on't.[2]

Enter Doctor and pothecary.

DOCTOR Save° ye, gentlemen. — *God save*
PETRONIUS Oh, welcome, Doctor!
Ye come in happy time.° Pray, your opinion: — *opportunely*
What think you of his pulse?
DOCTOR It beats with busiest,° — *It beats fast*
And shows a general inflammation,
Which is the symptom of a pestilent fever.
Take twenty ounces° from him. — *ounces of blood*
PETRUCHIO [*within*] Take a fool!
Take an ounce from mine arm, and, Doctor Deuce-ace,[3]
I'll make a closestool of your velvet costard.[4]
Death,° gentlemen, do ye make a May-game on° me? — *By God's death / of*
I tell ye once again, I am as sound,
As well, as wholesome, and as sensible° — *sane*
As any of ye all. Let me out quickly,
Or, as I am a man, I'll beat the walls down,
And the first thing I light upon shall pay for't.
Exit Doctor and pothecary.
PETRONIUS Nay, we'll go with you, Doctor.
MARIA 'Tis the safest;
I saw the tokens,° sir. — *plague-spots*
PETRONIUS Then there is but one way.
PETRUCHIO [*within*] Will it please ye open?
TRANIO His fit grows stronger still.
MARIA Let's save ourselves, sir;
He's past all worldly cure.
PETRONIUS [*to the Watch*] Friends, do your office.
And what he wants, if money, love, or labor,
Or any way may win it, let him have it.
Farewell, and pray, my honest friends.
Exeunt. Manent° Watchmen. — *Remain*
PETRUCHIO [*within*] Why, rascals!
Friends! Gentlemen! Thou beastly wife! Jaques!
None hear me? Who's at the door there?
FIRST WATCH Think, I pray, sir,
Whither ye are going,° and prepare yourself. — *(on Judgment Day)*
SECOND WATCH These idle thoughts disturb ye. The good gentlewoman
Your wife has taken care ye shall want nothing.
PETRUCHIO [*within*] The blessing of her grandam° Eve light on her! — *grandmother, forebear*
Nothing but thin fig leaves to hide her knavery.° — *(see Genesis 3.7)*
Shall I come out in quiet? Answer me,
Or shall I charge a fowling piece° and make — *load a shotgun*
Mine own way? Two of ye I cannot miss,
If I miss three.[5] Ye come here to assault me.

2. The "tokens" (line 72), or plague-spots, would be visible on Petruchio's arm.

3. A contemptuous name, from an unlucky throw in dice.

4. I'll make a chamber pot stool of your velvet-capped head. (Costard, literally, is a kind of apple.)

5. Even if I don't hit all three.

FIRST WATCH There's onions° roasting for your sore, sir. *(used in a poultice)*
PETRUCHIO [*within*] People,
I am as excellent well, I thank heav'n for't,
And have as good a stomach at this instant—
SECOND WATCH That's an ill sign.
FIRST WATCH Ay, he draws on;° he's a dead man. *grows worse*
PETRUCHIO [*within*] And sleep as soundly. Will ye look upon me?
FIRST WATCH Do ye want pen and ink? While ye have sense, sir,
Settle your state.° *Write your will*
PETRUCHIO [*within*] Sirs, I am as well as you are,
Or any rascal living.
SECOND WATCH Would ye were, sir.
PETRUCHIO [*within*] Look to yourselves, and, if you love your lives,
Open the door and fly° me, for I shoot else.° *flee from / otherwise*
I swear I'll shoot, and presently, chain bullets;[6]
And under four I will not kill.° *I'll kill at least 4*
FIRST WATCH Let's quit° him. *leave*
It may be it is a trick; he's dangerous.
SECOND WATCH The devil take the hindmost, I cry.
Exit Watch, running.

Enter Petruchio with a piece° and forces the door open. *gun*

PETRUCHIO Have among ye!° *Here I come!*
The door shall open too. I'll have a fair shoot.
Are ye all gone? Tricks in my old days? Crackers° *Firecrackers*
Put now upon me? And by Lady Green-sleeves?[7]
Am I grown so tame after all my triumphs?
But that° I should be thought mad if I railed *Were it not that*
As much as they deserve against these women,
I would now rip up, from the primitive cuckold,[8]
All their° archvillainies and all their doubles,° *(women's) / evasions*
Which are more than a hunted hare e'er thought on.
When a man has the fairest and the sweetest
Of all their sex, and, as he thinks, the noblest,
What has he, then? And I'll speak modestly:° *without exaggeration*
He has a quartern ague° that shall shake *virulent fever*
All his estate to nothing, never cured
Nor never dying. H'as° a ship to venture *He has*
His fame and credit in, which, if he man not
With more continual labor than a galley° *rowed vessel*
To make her tight, either she grows° a tumbrel *becomes*
Not worth the cloth she wears, or springs more leaks
Than all the fame° of his posterity *good name*
Can ever stop° again.[9] Out on 'em, hedgehogs!° *plug up / prickly things*
He that shall touch 'em has a thousand thorns

6. I.e., chain shot, formed of two balls or half balls connected by a chain and fired from cannons in naval warfare to destroy masts, rigging, and sails.
7. The name given to an inconstant ladylove in a ballad of 1580, here bitterly applied to Maria.
8. I would now invoke, from the story of the very first cuckold in history.
9. Petruchio's ship metaphors in lines 118–24—"man," "labor," "tight," "tumbrel," "springs more leaks," "stop," etc.—are all laden with sexual double meaning, hinting at a woman's leaky virtue. A tumbrel (line 121) is both a barge and a person loaded with drink. "The cloth she wears" (line 122) refers to both the sail a ship carries and the garment a woman wears.

Runs through his fingers. If I were unmarried,
I would do anything below° repentance—   *short of*
Any base dunghill slavery, be a hangman—
Ere I would be a husband. Oh, the thousand,
Thousand, ten thousand ways they have to kill us!
Some fall with too much stringing of the fiddles,°   *i.e., too much sex*
And those are fools; some, that they are not suffered,°   *permitted sex*
And those are maudlin° lovers; some, like scorpions,   *plaintive, tearful*
They° poison with their tails, and those are martyrs;   *(Women)*
Some die with doing good, those benefactors,
And leave 'em land to leap away.[1] Some few—
For those are rarest—they are said to kill
With kindness and fair usage; but what they are
My catalogue discovers not, only 'tis thought
They are buried in old walls with their heels upward.[2]
I could rail twenty days together now.
I'll seek 'em out, and, if I have not reason,
And very sensible, why this was done,
I'll go a-birding° yet, and some shall smart for't. *Exit.*   *hunting (for revenge)*

4.1

Enter Moroso and Petronius.

MOROSO That I do love her is without all question,
And most extremely, dearly, most exactly;
And that I would ev'n now, this present Monday,
Before all others—maids, wives, women, widows,
Of what degree or calling—marry her,
As° certain too. But to be made a whim-wham,°   *Is as / plaything*
A jibcrack, and a gentleman o'th'first house°   *an object of ridicule*
For all my kindness to her!
PETRONIUS How you take it!
Thou get a wench, thou get a dozen nightcaps.[1]
Wouldst have her come and lick thee like a calf,
And blow thy nose, and buss° thee?   *kiss*
MOROSO Not so, neither.
PETRONIUS What wouldst thou have her do?
MOROSO Do as she should do:
Put on a clean smock, and to church, and marry,
And then to bed, i'God's name. This is fair play,
And keeps the King's peace.° Let her leave her bobs°—   *keeps order / tricks*
I have had too many of them—and her quillets.°   *quibbles; quirks*
She is as nimble that way as an eel;
But in the way she ought° to me especially,   *duty she owes*
A sow of lead is swifter.[2]
PETRONIUS Quote° your griefs down.   *Note; quiet*
MOROSO Give fair quarter.° I am old and crazy,°   *Make allowances / feeble*

1. And leave their wives an inheritance to lose through fleshly indulgence.
2. They are buried in the tradition of some earlier cultures, head downward. (Here comically suggesting a sexual position.)
4.1. Petronius' house.
1. For Moroso to marry would be to acquire for himself a host of worries and the danger of cuckoldry.
2. Moroso observes glumly that a heavy ingot ("sow") of lead would move more quickly than Livia when she ought to fulfill her duty to Moroso.

And subject to much fumbling, I confess it;
Yet something I would have that's warm, to hatch me.[3]
But understand me I would have it so° — *in such a way that*
I buy not more repentance in the bargain
Than the ware's worth I have.° If you allow me — *receive*
Worthy° your son-in-law, and your allowance — *Worthy to be*
Do it i'way of credit, let me show so,° — *appear worthy*
And not be troubled in my visitations
With blows, and bitterness, and downright railings,
As if we were to couple like two cats,
With clawing and loud clamor.

PETRONIUS Thou fond° man, — *foolish*
Hast thou forgot the ballad "Crabbèd age"?[4]
Can May and January match together,
And nev'r a storm between 'em? Say° she abuse° thee; — *Suppose / scold*
Put case° she do. — *Suppose*

MOROSO Well.

PETRONIUS Nay, believe° she does. — *imagine*

MOROSO I do believe° she does. — *think truly*

PETRONIUS And dev'lishly;
Art thou a whit the worse?

MOROSO That's not the matter.
I know, being old, 'tis fit I am abused;
I know 'tis° handsome, and I know moreover — *she is*
I am to love her for't.

PETRONIUS Now you come to me.° — *Now you talk sense*

MOROSO Nay, more than this; I find too, and find certain,
What gold I have, pearl, bracelets, rings, or ouches,° — *brooches*
Or what° she can desire—gowns, petticoats, — *whatever*
Waistcoats, embroidered stockings, scarfs, cauls,° feathers, — *hairnets*
Hats, five-pound° garters, muffs, masks, ruffs, and ribbons— — *costly*
I am to give her for't.

PETRONIUS 'Tis right, you are so.

MOROSO But when I have done all this, and think it duty,
Is't requisite another bore my nostrils?° — *i.e., cuckold me*
Riddle me that.

PETRONIUS Go, get you gone, and dream
She's thine within these two days, for she is so.
The boy's beside the saddle.° Get warm broths, — *i.e., All's ready*
And feed apace. Think not of worldly business;
It cools the blood. Leave off your tricks;° they are hateful, — *mannerisms*
And mere forerunners of the ancient measures.[5]
Contrive your beard o'th'top cut like *verdugo*'s;° — *narrow-bladed in shape*
It shows you would be wise. And burn your nightcap;
It looks like half a winding-sheet,° and urges — *shroud*
From a young wench nothing but cold repentance.
You may eat onions, so° you'll not be lavish. — *provided*

MOROSO I am glad of that.

PETRONIUS They purge the blood, and quicken;° — *enliven*

3. Morose longs for a warm-blooded young wife to keep him warm, as a hen does its eggs, to hatch him and thereby make him youthful again.
4. The ballad begins, "Crabbèd age and youth cannot live together. / Youth is full of pleasance, age is full of care."
5. Your mannerisms precede even the style of the old dance; they are antiquated.

But after 'em, conceive° me, sweep° your mouth, *understand / cleanse*
And where there wants° a tooth, stick in a clove. *is missing*

MOROSO Shall I hope once again? Say't.

PETRONIUS You shall, sir,
And you shall have your hope.

Enter Bianca and Tranio [speaking privately].

MOROSO [*to Petronius*] Why, there's a match, then.

BIANCA [*to Tranio*] You shall not find me wanting. Get you gone.
Here's the old man; he'll think you are plotting else
Something against his new son.[6] *Exit Tranio.*

MOROSO [*to Petronius*] Fare ye well, sir.
Exit Moroso.

BIANCA [*singing*] An° ev'ry buck had his doe, *If*
And ev'ry cuckold a bell at his toe,
Oh, what sport should we have then, then, boys, then,
Oh, what sport should we have then!

PETRONIUS [*aside*] This is the spirit° that inspires 'em° all. *free spirit / (the ladies)*

BIANCA [*starting to go*] Give you good ev'n.

PETRONIUS A word with you, sweet lady.

BIANCA I am very hasty,° sir. *in haste*

PETRONIUS So you were ever.° *You were always hasty*

BIANCA Well, what's your will?

PETRONIUS Was not your skillful hand
In this last stratagem? Were not your mischiefs
Eking° the matter on? *Urging*

BIANCA In's° shutting up? *In Petruchio's*
Is that it?

PETRONIUS Yes.

BIANCA I'll tell you.

PETRONIUS Do.

BIANCA And truly.
Good old man, I do grieve exceeding much;
I fear, too much.

PETRONIUS I am sorry for your heaviness.° *grief*
Belike° you can repent, then? *Perhaps*

BIANCA There you are wide° too. *wide of the mark*
Not that the thing was done (conceive me rightly)
Does any way molest° me. *bother*

PETRONIUS What then, lady?

BIANCA But that I was not in't, there's my sorrow. There,
Now you understand me. For I'll tell you,
It was so sound a piece,° and so well carried,° *plot / carried off*
And, if you mark the way, so handsomely,
Of such a height° and excellence and art, *excellent quality*
I have not known a braver.° For, conceive me, *finer*
When the gross fool her husband would be sick—

PETRONIUS Pray, stay.

BIANCA Nay, good, your patience; and no sense for't[7]—
Then stepped your daughter in.

6. Something against Moroso, Petronius' prospective son-in-law.

7. Have patience; and when there was no adequate explanation for his behavior.

PETRONIUS By your appointment.° — *direction*
BIANCA I would it had, on that condition
I had but one half smock,[8] I like it so well;
And, like an excellent cunning woman,° cured me — *witch*
One madness with another,[9] which was rare,° — *remarkable*
And, to our weak beliefs, a wonder.
PETRONIUS Hang ye!
For surely, if your husband look not to ye,
I know what will.[1]
BIANCA I humbly thank Your Worship.
And so I take my leave.
PETRONIUS You have a hand, I hear, too—
BIANCA I have two,[2] sir.
PETRONIUS In my young daughter's business.
BIANCA You will find there
A fitter hand than mine to reach her frets,[3]
And play down-diddle[4] to her.
PETRONIUS I shall watch ye.
BIANCA Do.
PETRONIUS And I shall have justice.
BIANCA Where?
PETRONIUS That's all one;° — *Never you mind*
I shall be with you at a turn° henceforward. — *be even with you*
BIANCA Get you a posset,° too; and so good ev'n, sir. — *hot bedtime drink*
Exeunt.

[4.2]

Enter Petruchio, Jaques, and Pedro.

JAQUES And, as I told Your Worship, all the hangings:
Brass, pewter, plate, ev'n to the very pisspots.
PEDRO And that that hung for our defense, the armor,
And the march beer,° was going too. Oh, Jaques, — *strong beer*
What a sad sight was that!
JAQUES Even the two rundlets,° — *small barrels*
The two that was our hope, of muscatel° — *a sweet wine*
(Better nev'r tongue tripped over), those two cannons,
To batter brawn withal[1] at Christmas, sir,
Ev'n those two lovely twins, the enemy
Had almost cut off clean.
PETRUCHIO Go trim the house up,
And put the things in order as they were.
Exit Pedro and Jaques.
I shall find time for all this. Could I find her
But constant any way, I had done my business;
Were she a whore directly, or a scold,
An unthrift, or a woman made to hate me,

8. I.e., I'd gladly be reduced to having only a half petticoat to have been the director of that business.
9. Cured one zany plot with a counterplot.
1. I.e., If you don't find a husband to tame your spirit, you'll receive your comeuppance even so.
2. Bianca saucily interrupts Petronius' assertion that she has "a hand" in Livia's affairs by replying in the literal sense: I have two hands.
3. (1) Ridges on the fingerboard of a stringed instrument; (2) fretful behavior. Bianca hints that Livia has some other young man—Rowland, not Moroso—who can handle her.
4. A ballad tune. (With sexual suggestion.)
4.2. In front of Petruchio's house.
1. To drink with roast pig. The barrels of wine are compared jokingly to heavy artillery in the arsenal of revelry.

I had° my wish, and knew which way to rein her. *would have*
But while she shows all these, and all their losses[2]—
A kind of linsey-woolsey,° mingled mischief *i.e., medley*
Not to be guessed at, and whether true or borrowed,
Not certain neither—what a hap° had I! *what chance*

Enter Maria [apart].

And what a tidy fortune, when my fate
Flung me upon this bear whelp!°—Here she comes. *young bear*
[*He stands aside.*]
Now if she have a color°—for the fault is *a show of excuse*
A cleanly° one—upon my conscience, *honest, chaste*
I shall forgive her yet, and find a something
Certain I married for: her wit. I'll mark her.

MARIA [*to herself*] Not let his wife come near him in his sickness,
Not come to comfort him? She that all laws
Of heaven and nations have ordained his second,° *support, partner*
Is she refused? And two old paradoxes,° *i.e., old crones*
Pieces° of five-and-fifty, without faith *Elderly women*
Clapped in upon him?[3] H'as a little pet,° *peevish humor*
That all young wives must follow necessary,° *obligatorily*
Having their maidenheads—

PETRUCHIO [*aside*] This is an axiom° *proposition, maxim*
I never heard before.

MARIA Or say rebellion,° *my wifely rebellion*
If we durst be so foul°—which two fair words, *disobedient, sinful*
Alas, win us from, in an hour, an instant,
We are so easy[4]—make him so forgetful
Both of his reason, honesty, and credit° *reputation*
As to deny his wife a visitation?
His wife, that,° though she was a little foolish, *who*
Loved him—Oh, heaven forgive her for't!—nay, doted,
Nay, had run mad had she not married him?

PETRUCHIO [*aside*] Though I do know this falser than the devil,
I cannot choose but love it.

MARIA What do I know
But those that came to keep him° might have killed him? *But that his nurses*
In what a case had I been then? I dare not
Believe him such a base, deboshed companion° *debauched wretch*
That one refusal of a tender maid° *refusal by me*
Would make him feign this sickness out of need,
And take a keeper to him of fourscore° *80 years old*
To play at billiards—one that mewed content
And all her teeth together. Not come near him?[5]

2. But when she blends together all these bad qualities and their manifest shortcomings.

3. Maria complains that Petruchio is being nursed by two old women who have been unceremoniously assigned to take care of him. (Maria's statement of seeming unhappiness here is part of her witty stratagem of placing Petruchio in the wrong, as though she were not perfectly aware that she herself had him locked up as a supposed plague victim and arranged to have these women look after him; see 3.5.31–32.)

4. A rebelliousness that a few kind words could easily persuade us to abandon, we are so pliant. (Maria is pretending to regret that her little insubordination has led to his refusal to see her.)

5. One who molted, or lost, life's contentment and her teeth at the same time. And am I not allowed to come near him?

PETRUCHIO [*aside*] This woman would have made a most
rare° Jesuit; — *remarkable*
She can prevaricate on anything.[6]
There was not to be thought a way to save her
In all imagination, beside this.[7]
MARIA His unkind dealing—which was worst of all
In sending, heaven knows whither, all the plate
And all the household-stuff—had I not crossed° it, — *thwarted*
By a great providence and my friends' assistance,
Which he will thank me one day for! Alas,
I could have watched as well as they,° have served him — *(his keepers)*
In any use, better, and willinger.
The law commands me to do it, love commands me,
And my own duty charges me.
PETRUCHIO [*aside*] Heav'n bless me!
And, now I have said my prayers, I'll go to her.—
Are you a wife for any man?
MARIA For you, sir.
If I were worse, I were better.[8] That ye are well—
At least, that ye appear so—I thank heaven.
Long may it hold! And that you are here, I am glad too.
But that you have abused me wretchedly,
And such a way that shames the name of husband,
Such a malicious, mangy way, so mingled
(Never look strangely on me, I dare tell you)
With breach of honesty, care, kindness, manners—
PETRUCHIO Holla!° Ye kick too fast. — *Whoa!*
MARIA Was I a stranger?
Or had I vowed perdition° to your person? — *harm*
Am I not married to you? Tell me that?
PETRUCHIO I would I could not tell you.[9]
MARIA Is my presence,
The stock I come of, which is worshipful°— — *honorable, of good family*
If I should say right worshipful, I lied not;
My grandsire was a knight—
PETRUCHIO O'the shire?
MARIA A soldier,
Which none of all thy family e'er heard of° — *could boast of*
But one conductor° of thy name, a grazier[1] — *bearer*
That ran away with pay°—or am I grown — *with the payroll*
(Because I have been a little peevish to you,
Only to try° your temper) such a dog-leech[2] — *test*
I could not be admitted to your presence?
PETRUCHIO If I endure° this, hang me. — *put up with*
MARIA And two death's heads,
Two Harry groats,° that had their faces worn, — *small coins (see 3.2.38 n)*
Almost their names away too.[3]
PETRUCHIO Now hear me,

6. Jesuits were notorious in England for equivocating, using ambiguous language with an intent to mislead or deceive.
7. One could not possibly imagine a story to excuse her behavior that could compare with this.
8. If I were more of a scold to you than I am, I'd be more the wife that you really need.
9. I wish I didn't have to tell you what is undeniably true.
1. One who feeds cattle to ready them for market.
2. (1) A veterinarian who treats dogs; (2) an inferior medical practitioner, or quack; here, one whom Petruchio evidently regards as too inept to treat his presumed condition.
3. Maria continues to disparage Petruchio's aged nurses as virtually faceless and beneath notice.

For I will stay° no longer. *hold back; remain here*
MARIA This you shall:° *shall stay and hear*
However you shall think to flatter me
For this offense,° which no submission *For your rejecting me*
Can ever mediate° for, you'll find it so, *atone*
Whatever ye shall do by intercession,
What° ye can offer, what your land can purchase, *Whatever*
What all your friends or families can win,
Shall be but this: not to forswear your knowledge,
But ever to forbear it.[4] Now, your will,° sir. *say what you wish*
PETRUCHIO Thou art the subtlest woman, I think, living;
I am sure the lewdest.° Now be still, and mark me: *most unmannerly*
Were I but any way addicted to the devil,
I should now think I had met a playfellow
To profit by, and that way the most learnèd
That ever taught to murmur.[5] Tell me, thou,
Thou most poor, paltry, spiteful whore—do you cry?
I'll make you roar before I leave.° *leave off*
MARIA Your pleasure.° *Say what you want*
PETRUCHIO Was it not sin enough, thou fruiterer° *i.e., you Eve*
Full of the fall° thou eat'st, thou devil's broker, *sin*
Thou seminary of all sedition,
Thou sword of veng'ance with a thread hung o'er us,[6]
Was it not sin enough, and wickedness
In full abundance? Was it not vexation
At all points, cap-à-pie°—nay, I shall pinch ye— *from head to foot*
Thus like a rotten rascal to abuse
The name of heaven, the tie of marriage,
The honor of thy friends,° the expectation *kinsfolk*
Of all that thought thee virtuous, with rebellion,
Childish and base rebellion, but continuing
After forgiveness too; and worse, your mischief,
And against him—setting the hope of heaven by,
And the dear reservation° of his honor— *preservation*
Nothing above ground° could have won to hate thee? *Whom nothing on earth*
Well, go thy ways.
MARIA Yes.
PETRUCHIO You shall hear me out first.
What punishment mayst thou deserve, thou thing,
Thou idle thing of nothing, thou pulled° primrose *plucked*
That two hours after art a weed and withered,
For this last flourish on° me? Am I one *waving of a sword over*
Selected, out of all the husbands living,
To be so ridden by a tit of tenpence?° *two-bit hussy*
Am I so blind and bedrid? I was mad,
And had the plague, and no man must come near me?
I must be shut up, and my substance bezzled,° *embezzled, stolen*
And an old woman watch me?
MARIA Well, sir, well.

4. Not to deny falsely your knowledge of your wronging me, but to refrain from doing so henceforth.
5. If I were intent on pursuing evil in every way, I would now think I had met the most cunning and eloquent instructor in deviltry that ever taught rebellion.
6. Maria is likened to the sword of Damocles. Damocles was seated at a banquet with a sword hanging over his head by a single hair, thus representing ever-present peril.

You may well glory in't.° — *Enjoy your victory*
PETRUCHIO And when it comes to opening, 'tis my plot;[7]
I must undo myself, forsooth. Dost hear me?
If I should beat thee now, as much may be,° — *as I'm likely to do*
Dost thou not well deserve it, o'thy conscience?
Dost thou not cry, "Come, beat me"?
MARIA I defy you!
And my last° loving tears, farewell! The first stroke, — *recent*
The very first you give me, if you dare strike,
Try me, and you shall find it so, forever
Never to be recalled. I know you love me,
Mad till you have enjoyed° me. I do turn — *possessed sexually*
Utterly from you, and what° man I meet first — *whatever*
That has but spirit to deserve a favor°— — *a sexual favor*
Let him bear any shape, the worse the better—
Shall kill you, and enjoy me. What I have said
About your foolish sickness, ere you have me
As you would have me, you shall swear is certain,[8]
And challenge any man that dares deny it,
And in all companies approve my actions.
And so farewell for this time. *Exit Maria.*
PETRUCHIO Grief go with thee!
If there be any witchcrafts, herbs, or potions,
Saying my prayers backward, fiends, or fairies
That can again unlove me,° I am made. *Exit.* — *stop me from loving you*

4.[3]

Enter Bianca and Tranio.

TRANIO Faith, mistress, you must do it.
BIANCA Are the writings
Ready I told ye of?
TRANIO Yes, they are ready,
But to what use I know not.
BIANCA You're an ass.
You must have all things construed.° — *expounded*
TRANIO Yes, and pierced° too, — *parsed; pierced sexually*
Or I find little pleasure.
BIANCA Now you are knavish.° — *naughty*
Go to,° fetch Rowland hither presently; — *(expressing impatience)*
Your twenty pound lies bleeding° else. She is married — *You'll lose your bet*
Within these twelve hours if we cross° it not; — *thwart*
And see the papers of one size.[1]
TRANIO I have° ye. — *understand*
BIANCA And for° disposing of 'em. — *arrange for the*
TRANIO If I fail ye,
Now I have found the way,° use martial law — *understood the plot*
And cut my head off with a handsaw.

7. And when it comes time to reveal everything that has been going on, your game is to have it appear as if my being locked up with the plague was my plot, not yours.
8. Before you can have me as your wife, you must swear that what I have said about your being sick with the plague is absolutely true.
4.3. In front of Petronius' house.
1. And see to it that the papers look alike. (This is part of the plot of deception; see 5.1.103–52, 5.3.1–13.)

BIANCA Well, sir.
Petronius and Moroso I'll see sent for.
About your business; go.

TRANIO I am gone. *Exit Tranio.*

BIANCA [*calling*] Ho, Livia!

Enter Livia.

LIVIA Who's that?

BIANCA A friend of yours. Lord, how you look now,
As if you had lost a carrack!° *large cargo ship*

LIVIA Oh, Bianca,
I am the most undone, unhappy woman!

BIANCA Be quiet, wench. Thou shalt be done, and done,
And done, and double done, or all shall split° for't. *be shipwrecked*
No more of these minced° passions; they are mangy, *affected, mincing*
And ease thee of nothing but a little wind;
An apple° will do more. Thou fear'st Moroso? *(to ease flatulence)*

LIVIA Even as I fear the gallows.

BIANCA Keep thee there° still. *Hold to that*
And you love Rowland? Say.

LIVIA If I say "not,"
I am sure I lie.

BIANCA What wouldst thou give that woman,
In spite of all his° anger and thy fear, *(Moroso's)*
And all thy father's policy,° that could *plotting*
Clap° ye within these two nights quietly *Put, join*
Into a bed together?

LIVIA How?

BIANCA Why, fairly,
At half sword,[2] man and wife. Now the red blood° comes. *blushing*
Ay, marry, now the matter's changed.

LIVIA Bianca,
Methinks you should not mock me.

BIANCA Mock a pudding!° *Pooh!*
I speak good honest English and good meaning.

LIVIA I should not be ungrateful to that woman.

BIANCA I know thou wouldst not. Follow but my counsel,
And, if thou hast him not, despite of fortune,° *fickle Lady Fortune*
Let me nev'r know a good night more! You must
Be° very sick o'th'instant. *Pretend to be*

LIVIA Well, what follows?

BIANCA And in that sickness send for all your friends,
Your father, and your fever,[3] old Moroso,
And Rowland shall be there too.

LIVIA What of these?

BIANCA Do ye not twitter yet? Of this shall follow
That that shall make thy heart leap and thy lips
Venture as many kisses as the merchants
Do dollars to the East Indies. You shall know all.
But first, walk in and practice; pray be sick.

LIVIA I do believe ye, and I am sick.

BIANCA So.

2. Close together, like opponents at half a sword's length.

3. (1) Your affliction; (2) your feverish wooer.

To bed, then, come. I'll send away your servants,
Post° for your fool° and father; and good fortune, *Send / (Moroso)*
As we mean honestly, now strike an upshot![4] *Exeunt.*

4.[4]

Enter Tranio and Rowland.

TRANIO Nay, on my conscience, I have lost my money,° *lost my bet*
But that's all one;° I'll never more persuade ye. *never mind*
I see you are resolute, and I commend ye.
ROWLAND But did she send for me?
TRANIO Ye dare believe me?
ROWLAND I cannot tell; you have your ways for profit
Allowed ye, Tranio, as well as I
Have, to avoid 'em, fear.[1]
TRANIO No, on my word, sir,
I deal directly with ye.

Enter Servant.

ROWLAND How now, fellow,
Whither post you so fast?
SERVANT Oh, sir, my master!° *(Moroso)*
Pray, did you see my master?
ROWLAND Why your master?
SERVANT Sir, his jewel—
ROWLAND With the gilded button?° *(a flippant answer)*
SERVANT My pretty mistress Livia—
ROWLAND What of her?
SERVANT Is fall'n sick o'th'sudden.
ROWLAND How, o'th'sullens?[2]
SERVANT O'th'sudden, sir, I say, and very sick.
ROWLAND It seems she hath got the toothache with raw apples.[3]
SERVANT It seems you have got the headache. Fare ye well, sir.
You did not see my master?
ROWLAND Who told you so?
TRANIO No, no, he did not see him.
ROWLAND Farewell, bluebottle.[4]
Exit Servant.
What should her sickness be?
TRANIO For you, it may be.
ROWLAND Yes, when my brains are out, I may believe it;
Never before, I am sure. Yet I may see her;
'Twill be a point of honesty.° *decency, courtesy*
TRANIO It will so.
ROWLAND It may be not, too. You would fain be fing'ring° *You long to collect*
This old sin-off'ring of two hundred,° Tranio. *The £200 I bet*
How daintily and cunningly you drive me

4. May good fortune strike a final blow for us!
4.4. Petronius' house.
1. You have a financial motive for what you might say, just as I have my anxieties about winning the bet (and thus losing Livia).
2. I.e., melancholy. (Playing on "sullens" / "sudden.")
3. Rowland sarcastically hints that Livia is feigning illness. (Eating raw apples might help dislocate or irritate teeth already in an unhealthy condition, and dentistry in the early modern period was truly primitive.) The servant sardonically suggests in line 16 that Rowland is being overly critical.
4. In his blue livery appropriate to his status, the Servant reminds Rowland (facetiously) of a bluebottle, a type of fly.

Up like a deer to th'toil!° Yet I may leap it, — *trap, snare*
And what's the woodman,° then? — *hunter*
TRANIO A loser, by° ye. — *according to*
Speak, will you go or not? To me 'tis equal.° — *it's all the same*
ROWLAND Come, what goes less?° — *how about a lesser bet?*
TRANIO Nay, not a penny, Rowland.
ROWLAND Shall I have liberty of conscience,° — *freedom to act*
Which, by interpretation, is ten kisses?
Hang me if I affect° her. Yet it may be — *love, desire*
This whoreson manners will require a struggling° — *contest (of kisses)*
Of two-and-twenty, or, by'r Lady, thirty.[5]
TRANIO By'r Lady, I'll require my wager,° then, — *call in my bet*
For, if you kiss so often, and no kindness,° — *with no encouragement*
I have lost my speculation.° I'll allow ye— — *not received what I won*
ROWLAND Speak like a gamester° now. — *gambler*
TRANIO It may be two.° — *two kisses*
ROWLAND Under a dozen, Tranio, there's no setting.° — *placing of bets*
You shall have forty shillings; wink at small faults.
Say I take twenty?° Come, by all that's honest, — *20 kisses*
I do it but to vex her.
TRANIO I'll no by-blows.° — *I'll take no side bets*
If you can love her, do; if ye can, hate her,
Or any else that loves ye.
ROWLAND Prithee, Tranio.
TRANIO Why, farewell twenty pound! 'Twill not undo° me. — *bankrupt*
You have my resolution.° — *guarantee*
ROWLAND And your money,
Which, since you are so stubborn,° if I forfeit, — *insistent*
Make me a Jack-a-Lent, and break my shins
For untagged points and counters.[6] I'll go with you,
But if thou get'st a penny by the bargain—
A parting kiss is lawful?
TRANIO I allow it.
ROWLAND Knock out my brains with apples; yet a bargain.° — *our bet is still on*
TRANIO I tell you, I'll no bargains. Win and wear it.[7]
ROWLAND Thou art the strangest fellow!
TRANIO That's all one.° — *Never mind*
ROWLAND Along,° then. Twenty pound more, if thou dar'st. — *Come along*
I give her not a good word.[8]
TRANIO Not a penny. *Exeunt.*

4.[5]

Enter Petruchio, Jaques, and Pedro.

PETRUCHIO Prithee, entreat her come. I will not trouble her
Above a word or two. *Exit Pedro.*
Ere I endure
This life, and with a woman, and a vowed one° — *one who is committed*

5. Rowland, eager to kiss Livia but unwilling to admit it openly, bets Tranio as to the number of kisses Rowland will give Livia—purportedly out of kindness. He proposes as many as thirty.
6. I.e., Make fun of me and humiliate me. A Jack-a-Lent is a puppet figure of a man set up to be pelted, a butt of ridicule; striking on the shins is an especially humiliating way of administering such a drubbing. Untagged points (clothes fasteners lacking their metal tips) and counters (disks used in lieu of currency) are items of contemptibly small value.
7. It's yours if you can win it, not before.
8. I haven't anything good to say of her.
4.5. Petruchio's house.

To all the mischiefs she can lay upon me,
I'll go to plow again, and eat leek porridge.
Begging's a pleasure to't not to be numbered!° *incalculable*
No, there be other countries, Jaques, for me,
And other people, yea, and other women.
If I have need, here's money; there's your ware,° *there's commerce*
Which is fair dealing;° and the sun, they say, *an honest pursuit*
Shines as warm there as here; and, till I have lost
Either myself or her—I care not whether° *which*
Nor which first—

JAQUES Will Your Worship hear me?

PETRUCHIO And° utterly outworn the memory *And till I have*
Of such a curse as this, none of my nation
Shall ever know me more.

JAQUES Out, alas, sir,
What a strange way do you run?° *pursue*

PETRUCHIO Any way,° *I'll run anywhere*
So I outrun this rascal.° *wretch (Maria)*

JAQUES Methinks now
If Your good Worship could but have the patience—

PETRUCHIO The patience? Why the patience?

JAQUES Why, I'll tell you.
Could you but have the patience—

PETRUCHIO Well, the patience—

JAQUES To laugh at all she does, or, when she rails,
To have a drum beaten o'th'top o'th'house
To give the neighbors warning of her 'larm,° *(military) excursion*
As I do when my wife rebels—

PETRUCHIO Thy wife?
Thy wife's a pigeon to° her, a mere slumber; *compared with*
The dead of night's not stiller.

JAQUES Nor an iron mill.[1]

PETRUCHIO But thy wife is certain.° *steadfast, loyal*

JAQUES That's false doctrine;
You never read yet of a certain woman.

PETRUCHIO Thou know'st her way.

JAQUES I should do, I am sure.
I have ridden it, night and day, this twenty year.

PETRUCHIO But mine is such a drench of balderdash,° *dose of jumbled liquors*
Such a strange carded° cunningness! The rainbow, *i.e., mixed*
When she hangs bent in heaven, sheds not her colors
Quicker and more than this deceitful woman
Weaves in her dyes of wickedness.

Enter Pedro.

What says she?

PEDRO Nay, not a word, sir, but she pointed to me
As though she meant to follow. Pray, sir, bear it
Ev'n° as you may. I need not teach Your Worship, *As calmly*
The best men have their crosses;° we are all mortal. *crosses to bear*

PETRUCHIO What ails the fellow?

PEDRO And no doubt she may, sir—

PETRUCHIO What may she, or what does she, or what is she?

1. Nor is an iron mill more quiet than she is.

Speak, and be hanged.° — *i.e., curses on you*

PEDRO She's mad, sir.

PETRUCHIO Heaven continue it!

PEDRO Amen, if't be His pleasure.

PETRUCHIO How mad is she?

PEDRO As mad as heart can wish, sir. She has dressed herself
(Saving Your Worship's reverence)[2] just i'th'cut° — *style*
Of one of those that multiply i'th'suburbs° — *Of a prostitute*
For single money,° and as dirtily. — *small change*
If any speak to her, first she whistles,
And then begins her compass° with her fingers, — *she draws a circle*
And points to what she would have.

PETRUCHIO What new way 's this?

PEDRO There° came in Master Sophocles— — *At that point*

PETRUCHIO And what
Did Master Sophocles when he came in?
Get my trunks ready, sirrah; I'll be gone straight.

PEDRO He's here to tell you.

Enter Sophocles.

She's horn-mad, Jaques.

SOPHOCLES Call ye this a woman?

PETRUCHIO Yes sir, she's a woman.

SOPHOCLES Sir, I doubt it.

PETRUCHIO I had thought you had made experience.° — *tested it*

SOPHOCLES Yes, I did so,
And almost with° my life. — *at the cost of*

PETRUCHIO You rid° too fast, sir. — *rode, moved*

SOPHOCLES Pray, be not mistaken. By this light,
Your wife's as chaste and honest as a virgin,
For anything I know.° 'Tis true she gave me — *know to the contrary*
A ring.

PETRUCHIO For rutting.° — *fornicating*

SOPHOCLES You are much deceived still.
I swear I never kissed her since, and now,
Coming in visitation like a friend,
I think she is mad, sir. Suddenly she started,° — *recoiled*
And snatched the ring away, and drew her knife out—
To what intent I know not.

PETRUCHIO Is this certain?

SOPHOCLES As I am here, sir.

PETRUCHIO I believe ye honest.

Enter Maria.

And pray continue so.

SOPHOCLES She comes.

PETRUCHIO [*to Maria*] Now, damsel,
What will your beauty do, if I forsake you?
Do you deal by signs and tokens? As I guess, then,
You'll walk abroad this summer and catch captains,° — *whoremasters*
Or hire a piece of holy ground i'th'suburbs,° — *a place of prostitution*
And keep a nest of nuns?° — *i.e., whores*

SOPHOCLES Oh, do not stir° her! — *agitate*

2. Begging your pardon for my saying so.

You see in what a case she is.
PETRUCHIO She is dogged,° *stubborn, obstinate*
And in a beastly case, I am sure. I'll make her,
If she have any tongue, yet tattle. Sophocles,
Prithee observe this woman seriously
And eye her well, and, when thou hast done, but° tell me *simply*
(For thou hast understanding) in what case
My sense was when I chose this thing.
SOPHOCLES I'll tell ye:
I have seen a sweeter—
PETRUCHIO An hundred times cry "oysters!"[3]
There's a poor beggar-wench about Blackfriars° *a London district*
Runs on her breech may be an empress to her.[4]
SOPHOCLES Nay, now you are too bitter.
PETRUCHIO Nev'r a whit,° sir. *Not a bit*
[*To Maria*] I'll tell thee, woman—for, now I have day to see thee,
And all my wits about me, and I speak
Not out of passion, neither (leave your mumping!),° *mumbling*
I know you're well° enough. [*Aside*] Now would I give *handsome*
A million but to vex her. [*Aloud*] When I chose thee
To make a bedfellow, I took° more trouble *took upon myself*
Than twenty terms° can come to, such a cause, *law court terms*
Of such a title, and so everlasting
That Adam's genealogy may be ended
Ere any law find thee.[5] I took a leprosy,
Nay worse, the plague, nay, worse yet, a possession,° *being possessed*
And had° the devil with thee, if not more; *took, received*
And yet worse; was a beast, and like a beast
Had my reward, a jade to fling° my fortunes. *fling away*
For who° that had but reason to distinguish *who is there*
The light from darkness, wine from water, hunger
From full satiety, and fox from fern bush
That would have married thee?
SOPHOCLES She is not so ill.° *wicked; bad-looking*
PETRUCHIO She's worse than I dare think of. She's so lewd,° *wicked*
No court is strong enough to bear her cause.° *carry her case*
She hath neither manners, honesty, behavior,
Wifehood, nor womanhood, nor any moral
Can force me think she had a mother. No,
I do believe her steadfastly, and know her
To be a woman-wolf by transmigration;
Her first form was a ferret's, underground.
She kills the memories of men. Not yet?[6]
SOPHOCLES Do you think she's sensible° of this? *aware, conscious*
PETRUCHIO I care not.
Be° what she will. The pleasure I take in her, *Let her be*
Thus I blow off;° the care I took to love her, *blow away*
Like this point° I untie, and thus I loose it. *clothes fastener*
The husband I am to her, thus I sever.

3. Women oyster-sellers were notoriously loud and brazen.
4. Who, though dressed in unsightly breeches, is an empress when compared with Maria.
5. I.e., The world will come to an end before the case against you can be resolved in law. The genealogy of Adam presented in Genesis 5 is a long one and furthermore may be understood here to include all of humankind.
6. Do you think I've finished yet?

My vanity, farewell! Yet, for° you have been *because*
So near me as to bear the name of wife,
My unquenched charity shall tell you thus much:
Though you deserve it well, you shall not beg.
What I ordained your jointure,° honestly *marriage settlement*
You shall have settled on you, and half my house;
The other half shall be employed in prayers.
(That meritorious charge° I'll be at° also *expense / undertake*
Yet to confirm ye Christian.) Your apparel,
And what belongs to build up such a folly,
Keep, I beseech ye; it infects our uses.° *pollutes the house we use*
And now I am for travel.

MARIA Now I love ye,
And, now I see ye are a man, I'll talk to ye,
And I forget your bitterness.

SOPHOCLES How now, man?

PETRUCHIO O Pliny,[7] if thou wilt be ever famous,
Make but this woman all thy wonders!

MARIA Sure, sir,
You have hit upon a happy course,° a blessed, *plan of travel*
And what will make you virtuous.

PETRUCHIO She'll ship me![8]

MARIA A way of understanding I long wished for,
And, now 'tis come, take heed you fly not back,° sir. *don't retreat*
Methinks you look a new man to me now,
A man of excellence, and now I see
Some great design set in ye. You may think now
(And so may most that know me) 'twere my part
Weakly to weep your loss, and to resist ye,° *urge you to stay*
Nay, hang about your neck and like a dotard° *one who dotes*
Urge my strong tie upon ye. But I love ye—
And all the world shall know it—beyond woman,[9]
And more prefer the honor of your country,
Which chiefly you are born for and may perfect—
The uses you may make of other nations,
The ripening of your knowledge, conversation,
The full ability and strength of judgment—
Than any private love or wanton kisses.
Go, worthy man, and bring home understanding!

SOPHOCLES [*to Petruchio*] This were an excellent woman to breed schoolmen.[1]

MARIA For if the merchant through unknown seas plow
To get his wealth, then, dear sir, what must you
To gather wisdom? Go, and go alone,
Only your noble mind for your companion;
And if a woman may win credit with you,° *persuade you*
Go far. Too far you cannot; still the farther,
The more experience finds° you. And go sparing; *comes to*
One meal a week will serve you, and one suit,
Through all your travels; for you'll find it certain,

7. Pliny the Elder (23–79 C.E.), author of an encyclopedia of natural science containing many wonders.
8. (1) She'll send me on my travels; (2) she wants me to leave.
9. More than any woman ever loved a man.
1. Maria is such an expert at sophistry that she could breed a whole new generation of academic disputants.

The poorer and the baser ye appear,
The more you look through still.[2]
PETRUCHIO [*to Sophocles*] Dost hear her?
SOPHOCLES Yes.
PETRUCHIO What would this woman do, if she were suffered,° — *permitted*
Upon a new religion?
SOPHOCLES Make us pagans.
I wonder that she writes° not. — *writes treatises*
MARIA Then when time
And fullness of occasion have new-made you
And squared° you from a sot° into a signor, — *transformed / fool*
Or, nearer, from a jade into a courser,[3]
Come home an agèd man, as did Ulysses,
And I your glad Penelope.
PETRUCHIO That must have
As many lovers as I languages,
And what she does with one i'th'day, i'th'night
Undo it with another.[4]
MARIA Much that way,° sir; — *Essentially right*
For in your absence, it must be my honor—
That that° must make me spoken of hereafter— — *That which*
To have temptations, and not little ones,
Daily and hourly offered me, and strongly,
Almost believed against me,° to set off[5] — *to my detriment*
The faith and loyalty of her that loves ye.
PETRUCHIO [*to Sophocles*] What should I do?
SOPHOCLES Why, by my troth, I would travel.
Did not you mean so?
PETRUCHIO Alas, no, nothing less,° man. — *anything but*
I did it but to try her.° She's the devil, — *test her*
And now I find it, for she drives me; I must go.
[*Calling to servants*] Are my trunks down there, and my horses ready?
MARIA Sir, for° your house, an if you please to trust me — *as for*
With that you leave behind—
PETRUCHIO [*calling to servants*] Bring down the money.
MARIA As I am able, and to° my poor fortunes, — *to the extent of*
I'll govern as a widow. I shall long
To hear of your well-doing and your profit;
And when I hear not from you once a quarter,
I'll wish you in the Indies, or Cataya;° — *Cathay, old name for China*
Those are the climes must make you.° — *make you rich*
PETRUCHIO How's the wind?—
She'll wish me out o'th'world anon.
MARIA For France.[6]
'Tis very fair;° get ye aboard tonight, sir, — *a good wind*
And lose no time. You know the tide stays° no man. — *waits for*

2. The more you'll discover the things that really matter.
3. Or, more precisely, from a broken-down horse into a racehorse.
4. Out of loyalty to her husband Ulysses (or Odysseus), Penelope undid the weaving of her father-in-law's shroud each night to delay her suitors' demands for her hand in marriage. (She had promised to choose a husband once she had completed it.) Petruchio wryly interprets this story as one of womanly double-dealing.
5. To highlight. (Maria argues playfully that the temptations that will assail her during Petruchio's absence will show her to advantage when she remains loyal to him.)
6. The wind is favorable for sailing to France.

I have cold meats ready for you.
PETRUCHIO Fare thee well.
Thou hast fooled° me out o'th'kingdom with a vengeance, *tricked*
And thou canst fool me in again.
MARIA Not I, sir;
I love you better.° Take your time and pleasure. *better than that*
I'll see you horsed.° *on horseback*
PETRUCHIO I think thou wouldst see me hanged too,
Were I but half as willing.
MARIA Anything
That you think well of, I dare look upon.
PETRUCHIO [*to Sophocles*] You'll bear me to the land's end,° *frontier, border*
Sophocles,
And other of my friends, I hope?
MARIA Nev'r doubt, sir;
Ye cannot want° companions for your good. *lack*
I am sure you'll kiss me ere I go. I have business,
And stay long here I must not.
PETRUCHIO Get thee going,
For, if thou tarriest but another dialogue,° *verbal exchange*
I'll kick thee to thy chamber.
MARIA Fare you well, sir,
And bear yourself—I do beseech ye once more,
Since you have undertaken doing wisely—
Manly and worthily. 'Tis for my credit;° *reputation*
And for° those flying fames° here of your follies, *as for / rumors*
Your gambols and ill breeding of your youth,
For which I understand you take this travel
(Nothing should make me leave you° else), I'll deal *let you go*
So like a wife that loves your reputation
And the most large addition of your credit
That those° shall die. If ye want lemon-water,° *those rumors / lemonade*
Or anything to take the edge o'th'sea off,° *to cure scurvy*
Pray speak and be provided.
PETRUCHIO Now the devil,
That was your first good master, shower his blessing
Upon ye all! Into whose custody—
MARIA I do commit your reformation,
And so I leave you to your *Stilo novo*.[7] *Exit Maria.*
PETRUCHIO I will go; yet I will not. Once more, Sophocles,
I'll put her to the test.
SOPHOCLES You had better go.
PETRUCHIO I will go, then. Let's seek my father° out, *father-in-law*
And all my friends, to see me fair aboard.
Then, women, if there be a storm at sea
Worse than your tongues can make, and waves more broken
Than your dissembling faiths are, let me feel
Nothing but tempests, till they crack my keel. *Exeunt.*

7. Your new style (of dating letters according to the reformed Gregorian calendar, introduced in 1582 but not adopted in England until the mid-eighteenth century).

5.1

Enter Petronius, and Bianca with four papers.

BIANCA Now whether I deserve that blame you gave me,
Let all the world discern, sir.
PETRONIUS If this motion
(I mean this fair repentance of my daughter)
Spring from your good persuasion, as it seems so,
I must confess I have spoke too boldly of you,
And I repent.
BIANCA The first touch° was her own, *touch of remorse*
Taken no doubt from disobeying you;
The second I put to her° when I told her *induced in her*
How good and gentle, yet with free contrition,
Again you might be purchased.° Loving woman, *reclaimed*
She heard me and, I thank her, thought me worthy
Observing° in this point. Yet all my counsel *Of being heeded*
And comfort in this case could not so heal her
But that Grief got his share too, and she sickened.
PETRONIUS I am sorry she's so ill, yet glad her sickness
Has got so good a ground.° *moral justification*

Enter Moroso.

BIANCA Here comes Moroso.
PETRONIUS Oh, you are very welcome.
Now you shall know your happiness.
MOROSO I am glad on't.
What makes this lady here?° *Why is Bianca here?*
BIANCA A dish° for you, sir, *(Maria's repentance)*
You'll thank me for hereafter.
PETRONIUS True, Moroso.
Go get you in and see your mistress.
BIANCA She is sick, sir,
But you may kiss her whole.° *heal her with kisses*
MOROSO How?
BIANCA Comfort her.
MOROSO Why, am I sent for, sir?
PETRONIUS Will you in and see?
BIANCA Maybe she needs confession.
MOROSO By Saint Mary,
She shall have absolution then and penance,
But not above her carriage.[1]
PETRONIUS Get you in, fool. *Exit Moroso.*
BIANCA Here comes the other, too.

Enter Rowland and Tranio.

PETRONIUS Now, Tranio.
[*To Rowland*] Good e'en to you too, and you're welcome.
ROWLAND Thank you.
PETRONIUS I have a certain daughter.
ROWLAND Would you had, sir.[2]

5.1. Petronius' house.
1. But not above what her deportment deserves. (Said as a clumsy attempt at sexual humor; "carriage" suggests supporting the weight of a man in sexual intercourse.)
2. Would that Livia were indeed "certain," meaning "steadfast," "true."

PETRONIUS No doubt you know her well.
ROWLAND Nor never shall,[3] sir.
She is a woman, and the ways into her
Are like the finding of a certain path
After a deep-fall'n snow.[4]
PETRONIUS Well, that's by th'by still.° *never mind that*
This daughter that I tell you of is fall'n
A little crop-sick,° with the dangerous surfeit *sick to the stomach*
She took of your affection.
ROWLAND Mine, sir?
PETRONIUS Yes, sir.
Or rather, as it seems, repenting. And there
She lies within, debating° on't. *reflecting*
ROWLAND Well, sir.
PETRONIUS I think 'twere well you would see her.
ROWLAND If you please, sir;
I am not squeamish of my visitation.
PETRONIUS But this I'll tell you: she is altered much.
You'll find her now another Livia.
ROWLAND I had enough o'th'old, sir.
PETRONIUS No more fool,
To look gay babies in your eyes,[5] young Rowland,
And hang about your pretty neck.
ROWLAND I am glad on't,
And thank my fates I have scaped such execution.° *such hard fate*
PETRONIUS And buss° you till you blush again. *kiss*
ROWLAND That's hard, sir.
She must kiss shamefully ere I blush at it;
I never was so boyish.° Well, what follows? *prone to blush*
PETRONIUS She's mine now, as I please to settle her,° *give her in marriage*
At my command, and where I please to plant her.
Only she would take a kind of farewell of ye,
And give you back a wand'ring vow or two
You left in pawn; and two or three slight oaths
She lent you, too, she looks for.
ROWLAND She shall have 'em
With all my heart, sir, and, if you like it better,
A free release in writing.
PETRONIUS That's the matter;° *business at hand*
And you from her, you shall have another,° Rowland, *another release*
And then turn tail to tail, and peace be with you.° *good-bye*
ROWLAND Why, so be it.—Your twenty pound sweats, Tranio.
TRANIO 'Twill not undo me,° Rowland. Do your worst. *bankrupt me*
ROWLAND Come, shall we see her, sir?
BIANCA Whate'er she says
You must bear manly, Rowland, for her sickness
Has made her somewhat teatish.° *peevish*
ROWLAND Let her talk
Till her tongue ache, I care not. By this hand,
Thou hast a handsome face, wench, and a body

3. If I don't know her now, I never will.
4. I.e., women are all too knowable, like finding highly visible footprints in snow. (Playing on the sense of carnal knowledge.)
5. I.e., This new Livia is no mere wanton to gaze lovingly into your eyes with babyish looks.

Daintily mounted. Now do I feel an hundred° *£100 (see 3.1.74–80)*
Running directly from me, as° I pissed it. *as if*

Enter Livia discovered° abed, and Moroso by her. *(by drawn curtains)*
[*Petronius draws open the curtains.*]

BIANCA Pray draw 'em softly. The least hurry, sir,
Puts her to much impatience.
PETRONIUS How is't, daughter?
LIVIA Oh, very sick, very sick! Yet somewhat
Better, I hope; a little lightsomer,° *more cheerful*
Because this good man° has forgiven me. *(Moroso)*
Pray set me higher. Oh, my head!
BIANCA [*aside*] Well done, wench.
LIVIA Father, and all good people that shall hear me,
I have abused this man perniciously;
Was never old man humbled so. I have scorned him
And called him nasty names; I have spit at him,
Flung candles' ends in's beard, and called him harrow,
That must be drawn to all he does;[6] contemned° him, *scorned*
For methought then he was a beastly fellow
(Oh, God, my side!), a very beastly fellow;
And gave it out° his cassock was a barge cloth, *reported that*
Pawned to his predecessor by a sculler,° *boatman*
The man yet extant. I gave him purging comfits[7]
At a great christ'ning once
That spoiled his camlet° breeches; and one night *a costly fabric*
I strewed the stairs with peas as he passed down;
And the good gentleman (woe worth me° for't!), *bad luck to me*
Ev'n with his reverend head, this head of wisdom,
Told° two-and-twenty stairs, good and true, *Counted*
Missed not a step, and, as we say verbatim,
Fell to the bottom, broke his casting-bottle,° *perfume bottle*
Lost a fair toadstone[8] of some eighteen shillings,
Jumbled his joints together, had two stools,° *bowel movements*
And was translated.° All this villainy *delirious*
Did I—I, Livia, I alone, untaught.
MOROSO And I, unasked, forgive it.
LIVIA Where's Bianca?
BIANCA Here, cousin.
LIVIA Give me drink.
BIANCA [*giving drink*] There.
LIVIA Who's that?
MOROSO Rowland.
LIVIA O my dissembler, you and I must part.
Come nearer, sir.
ROWLAND I am sorry for your sickness.
LIVIA Be sorry for yourself, sir; you have wronged me,
But I forgive ye. [*To Bianca*] Are the papers ready?° *(see 5.1.0.1 above)*
BIANCA I have 'em here. [*To Petronius*] Will't please you view 'em?

6. Livia has compared Moroso to a piece of agricultural equipment used to smoothe out plowed land, implying that he has to be pulled reluctantly along on whatever he does (including sexual performance).
7. Sweetmeats that induce diarrhea.
8. A valuable stone or jewel likened to a toad in color or shape and supposed to be produced by a toad; often worn as an amulet because it was thought to possess therapeutic properties.

PETRONIUS Yes.
LIVIA Show 'em the young man too; I know he's willing
To shift his sails° too. 'Tis for his more advancement. *change course*
Alas, we might have beggared° one another; *impoverished*
We are young both, and a world of children
Might have been left behind to curse our follies.
We had been undone, Bianca, had we married,
Undone forever. I confess I loved him—
I care not who shall know it—most entirely;
And once, upon my conscience, he loved me.
But farewell that; we must be wiser, cousin.
Love must not leave us to the world.[9] [*To Rowland*] Have
ye done?° *finished reading*
ROWLAND Yes, and am ready to subscribe.° *sign*
LIVIA Pray stay,° then. *wait*
Give me the papers and let me peruse 'em,
And° so much time as may afford a tear *And give me*
At our last parting.
BIANCA [*to the gentlemen*] Pray retire and leave her.
I'll call ye presently.
PETRONIUS Come, gentlemen,
The shower° must fall. *shower of tears*
ROWLAND Would I had never seen her!
Exeunt all but Bianca and Livia.
BIANCA Thou hast done bravely,° wench. *excellently*
LIVIA Pray heaven it prove so!
BIANCA [*giving papers*] There are the other papers; when
they° come, *(the men)*
Begin you first, and let the rest subscribe
Hard by your side; give 'em as little light
As drapers do their wares.[1]
LIVIA Didst mark Moroso,
In what an agony he was, and how he cried most
When I abused him most?
BIANCA That was but reason.° *only just*
LIVIA Oh, what a stinking thief is this!
Though I was but to counterfeit,° he made me *only pretending*
Directly sick indeed. Thames Street to him
Is a mere pomander.[2]
BIANCA Let him be hanged.
LIVIA Amen!
BIANCA And lie you° still, *stay in bed*
And once more to your business.
LIVIA Call 'em in.
Now if there be a power that pities lovers,
Help now, and hear my prayers!

Enter Petronius, Rowland, Tranio, [and] Moroso.

PETRONIUS Is she ready?
BIANCA She has done her lamentations. Pray go to her.

9. We mustn't allow our love to bring us to penury in a world that will be indifferent to our suffering.
1. It was often suspected that cloth merchants' shops were dimly lit in order to cheat the customers.
2. I.e., Compared with Moroso, the stinking smell of fish and other produce in Thames Street, near the river, is like a pomander, a bag or box of aromatic substances used to perfume the air and ward off infection.

LIVIA Rowland, come near me, and, before you seal,° *sign*
Give me your hand. Take it again; now kiss me.
[*He kisses her.*]
This is the last acquaintance we must have;
I wish you ever happy. There's the paper.
[*She gives him a document.*]
ROWLAND [*weeping*] Pray stay a little.
PETRONIUS Let me never live more
But I do begin to pity this young fellow.
How heartily he weeps!
BIANCA [*to Rowland*] There's pen and ink, sir.
LIVIA [*showing Rowland where to sign*] Ev'n here, I pray you. 'Tis a little emblem
How near° you have been to me. *dear*
ROWLAND [*signing*] There.
BIANCA [*to Petronius and Moroso*] Your hands too,
As witnesses.
PETRONIUS [*signing*] By any means. [*To Moroso*] To th'book,° son. *the deed*
MOROSO [*signing*] With all my heart.
BIANCA [*to Rowland*] You must deliver it.
ROWLAND [*giving Livia the document*] There, Livia, and a better love light on thee![3]
I can no more.
BIANCA [*to Petronius and Moroso*] To this you must be witness too.
PETRONIUS We will.
BIANCA [*to Livia*] Do you deliver it now.
LIVIA Pray set me up.
[*She gives Rowland the document.*]
There, Rowland, all thy old love back; and may
A new to come exceed mine, and be happy!
I must no more.
ROWLAND Farewell!
LIVIA A long farewell! *Exit Rowland.*
BIANCA Leave her by any means, till this wild passion
Be off her head. Draw all the curtains close.
[*The bedcurtains are closed.*]
A day hence you may see her; 'twill be better.
She is now for little company.
PETRONIUS Pray tend her.
I must to horse straight. [*To Moroso*] You must needs along too,
To see my son° aboard. Were but his wife *(Petruchio)*
As fit for pity as this wench, I were happy.
BIANCA Time must do that too. Fare ye well! [*To Moroso*] Tomorrow
You shall receive a wife to quit° your sorrow. *Exeunt.* *recompense; end*

3. May you find better happiness in love than you have known with me!

5.2

Enter Jaques, Pedro, and porters, with a trunk and hampers.

JAQUES Bring 'em away, sirs.
PEDRO Must the great trunk go too?
JAQUES Yes, and the hampers. Nay, be speedy, masters;
He'll be at sea before us else.
PEDRO Oh, Jaques,
What a most blessed turn° hast thou! *turn of luck*
JAQUES I hope so.
PEDRO To have the sea between thee and this woman!
Nothing can drown her tongue but a storm.
JAQUES By your leave,
We'll get us up to Paris with all speed,
For, on my soul, as far as Amiens
She'll carry blank.[1] Away to Lyon quay° *(for departure to Lyon)*
And ship 'em presently! We'll follow ye.
PEDRO Now could I wish her in that trunk.
JAQUES God shield,° man, *forbid*
I had rather have a bear in't.
PEDRO Yes, I'll tell ye:
For in the passage° if a tempest take ye, *voyage*
As many do, and you lie beating° for it, *sailing upwind*
Then, if it pleased the Fates, I would have the master,
Out of a powerful providence, to cry,
"Lighten the ship of all hands, or we perish!"
Then this,° for one, as best spared, should by all means *this trunk (with Maria)*
Overboard presently.
JAQUES O'that condition,
So° we were certain to be rid of her, *Provided*
I would wish her with us. But believe me, Pedro,
She would spoil the fishing on this coast forever,
For none would keep her company but dogfish,° *small sharks*
As currish as herself, or porpoises,
Made to all fatal uses.[2] The two Fish Streets,[3]
Were she but once arrived amongst the whitings,° *a kind of fish*
Would sing a woeful *misereri*,° Pedro, *have mercy on us*
And mourn in Poor John,° till her memory *salted dried hake*
Were cast ashore again, with a strong sea breach.° *surf*
She would make god Neptune and his fire-fork,° *trident*
And all his demigods and goddesses,
As weary of the Flemish° Channel, Pedro, *English*
As ever boy was of the school. 'Tis certain,
If she but meet him° fair,° and were well angered, *(Neptune) / one-on-one*
She would break his godhead.
PEDRO Oh, her tongue, her tongue!
JAQUES Rather, her many tongues.
PEDRO Or rather, strange tongues.
JAQUES Her lying tongue.
PEDRO Her lisping tongue.

5.2. Petruchio's house.
1. She'll hit us with deadly accuracy. (Amiens is about seventy miles north of Paris—a long distance over which to shoot point-blank or in a level trajectory.)
2. Porpoises were believed to be able to predict storms.
3. London streets where fish was sold.

JAQUES Her long tongue.
PEDRO Her lawless tongue.
JAQUES Her loud tongue.
PEDRO And her lick'rish°— *lustful*
JAQUES Many other tongues, and many stranger tongues
Than ever Babel had to tell his ruins,[4]
Were women raised withal, but never a true one.

Enter Sophocles.

SOPHOCLES Home with your stuff again! The journey's ended.° *canceled*
JAQUES What does Your Worship mean?
SOPHOCLES Your master! Oh, Petruchio! Oh, poor fellows!
PEDRO Oh, Jaques, Jaques!
SOPHOCLES Oh, your master's dead!
His body coming back. His wife, his devil;
The grief of° her— *caused by*
JAQUES Has killed him?
SOPHOCLES Killed him, killed him.
PEDRO Is there no law to hang her?
SOPHOCLES Get ye in,
And let her know her misery. I dare not,
For fear impatience seize me, see her more;
I must away again. Bid her for wifehood,
For honesty, if she have any in her,
Even to avoid the shame that follows her,
Cry if she can. Your weeping cannot mend it.
The body will be here within this hour, so tell her,
And all his friends to curse her. Farewell, fellows!
Exit Sophocles.

PEDRO Oh, Jaques, Jaques!
JAQUES Oh, my worthy master!
PEDRO Oh, my most beastly mistress! Hang her!
JAQUES Split° her! *Shipwreck*
PEDRO Drown her directly!
JAQUES Starve her!
PEDRO Stink upon her!
JAQUES Stone her to death! May all she eat be eggs,° *(aphrodisiacs)*
Till she run kicking mad for men!
PEDRO And he,
That man that gives her remedy, pray heav'n
He may, ev'n ipso facto,° lose his fadings![5] *by that very fact*
JAQUES Let's go discharge ourselves;° and he that serves her, *quit as servants*
Or speaks a good word of her from this hour,
A Sedgley curse[6] light on him, which is, Pedro,
"The fiend ride through him booted and spurred, with a scythe at's back!" *Exeunt.*

4. God punished the builders of the Tower of Babel for their hubris by confounding their speech, so that they no longer spoke one tongue (see Genesis 11.1–9).

5. I.e., lose his male potency! (A fading is an Irish dance.)

6. A familar curse, named after a town in Staffordshire.

5.3

Enter Rowland [with a paper], and Tranio stealing behind him.

ROWLAND What a dull ass was I to let her go thus!
Upon my life, she loves me still. Well, paper,
Thou only monument of what I have had,
Thou all the love now left me and now lost,
Let me yet kiss her hand,° yet take my leave — *handwriting*
Of what I must leave ever. Farewell, Livia!
Oh, bitter words! I'll read ye once again,
And then forever study° to forget ye. [*He reads.*] — *strive*
How's this? Let me look better on't. A contract?° — *marriage contract*
By heaven, a contract, sealed and ratified,
Her father's hand set to it, and Moroso's!
I do not dream, sure. Let me read again. [*He reads again.*]
The same still! 'Tis a contract.
TRANIO [*coming forward*] 'Tis so, Rowland;
And by the virtue of the same, you pay me
Two hundred pound tomorrow.
ROWLAND Art sure, Tranio,
We are both alive now?
TRANIO Wonder not, ye have lost.° — *lost the bet*
ROWLAND If this be true, I grant it.
TRANIO 'Tis most certain.
There's a ring[1] for you too. You know it?
ROWLAND Yes.
TRANIO When shall I have my money?
ROWLAND Stay ye, stay ye,
When shall I marry her?
TRANIO Tonight.
ROWLAND Take heed now
You do not trifle with me; if you do,
You'll find more payment° than your money comes to. — *i.e., sword blows*
Come, swear; I know I am a man, and find
I may deceive myself. Swear faithfully,
Swear me directly: am I Rowland?
TRANIO Yes.
ROWLAND Am I awake?
TRANIO Ye are.
ROWLAND Am I in health?
TRANIO As far as I conceive.
ROWLAND Was I with Livia?
TRANIO You were, and had this contract.
ROWLAND And shall I enjoy her?
TRANIO Yes, if ye dare.
ROWLAND Swear to all these.
TRANIO I will.
ROWLAND As thou art honest, as thou hast a conscience,
As that may wring° thee if thou liest: all these — *distress, torture*
To be no vision, but a truth, and serious.
TRANIO Then by my honesty, and faith, and conscience,

5.3. Petronius' house.
1. Probably a seal made by a seal ring used to authenticate the marriage contract. Rowland recognizes the identity of the seal.

All this is certain.
ROWLAND Let's remove our places.° [*They do so.*] *trade places*
Swear it again.
TRANIO I swear by heaven 'tis true.
ROWLAND I have lost, then, and heaven knows I am glad on't!
Let's go, and tell me all, and tell me how,
For yet I am a pagan° in it. *unbelieving*
TRANIO I have a priest too,
And all shall come as even as two testers.° *Exeunt.* *coins worth sixpence*

5.4

Enter Petronius, Sophocles, Moroso, and Petruchio borne in a coffin [*by servants*].

PETRONIUS Set down the body, and one call her out.
[*A servant goes to the door.*]

Enter Maria in black, Jaques, [*and*] *Pedro.*

You are welcome to the last cast° of your fortunes. *throw (as of dice)*
There lies your husband, there your loving husband,
There he that was Petruchio, too good for ye;
Your stubborn and unworthy way has killed him
Ere he could reach the sea. If ye can weep,
Now ye have cause, begin, and after death
Do something yet to th'world to think° ye honest. *to give cause to think*
So many tears had° saved him, shed in time; *would have*
And as they are (so° a good mind go with 'em), *provided*
Yet they may move compassion.
MARIA Pray ye all hear me,
And judge me as I am, not as you covet,° *are inclined to think*
For that would make me yet more miserable.
'Tis true I have cause to grieve, and mighty cause;
And truly and unfeignedly I weep it.° *for it*
SOPHOCLES I see there's some good nature yet left in her.
MARIA But what's the cause? Mistake me not. Not this man,
As he is dead, I weep for—heaven defend° it, *forbid*
I never was so childish—but his life,
His poor, unmanly, wretched, foolish life,
Is that° my full° eyes pity; there's my mourning. *that which / tear-filled*
PETRONIUS Dost thou not shame?° *Aren't you ashamed?*
MARIA I do, and even to water,° *tears*
To think what this man was, to think how simple,
How far below a man, how far from reason,
From common understanding and all gentry,° *courtesy, breeding*
While he was living here he walked amongst us.
He had a happy turn he died.° I'll tell ye, *He was fortunate to die*
These are the wants I weep for, not his person.
The memory of this man, had he lived
But two years longer, had begot more follies
Than wealthy autumn flies.[1] But let him rest.
He was a fool, and farewell he—not pitied,
I mean in way of life or action

5.4. Petruchio's house.

1. Than autumn, rich with harvest, begets flies.

By any understanding man that's honest,
But only in's posterity, which I,
Out of the fear his ruins might outlive him
In some bad issue,° like a careful woman, *offspring*
Like one indeed born only to preserve him,
Denied him means to raise.

Petruchio rises out of the coffin.

PETRUCHIO Unbutton me!
By heaven, I die indeed else. Oh, Maria,
Oh, my unhappiness, my misery!

PETRONIUS [*to Maria*] Go to him, whore. By heaven, if he perish,
I'll see thee hanged myself.

PETRUCHIO Why, why, Maria!

MARIA I have done my worst, and have my end.° Forgive me! *am done*
From this hour, make me what you please. I have tamed ye,
And now am vowed your servant. Look not strangely,
Nor fear what I say to you. Dare you kiss me?
Thus I begin my new love. [*They kiss.*]

PETRUCHIO Once again?

MARIA With all my heart, sir. [*They kiss.*]

PETRUCHIO Once again, Maria!
Oh, gentlemen, I know not where I am.

SOPHOCLES Get ye to bed, then. There you'll quickly know, sir.

PETRUCHIO [*to Maria*] Never no more your old tricks?

MARIA Never, sir.

PETRUCHIO You shall not need, for, as I have a faith,° *as I'm a Christian*
No cause shall give occasion.

MARIA As I am honest,° *chaste*
And as I am a maid yet, all my life
From this hour, since ye make so free profession,
I dedicate in service to your pleasure.

SOPHOCLES Ay, marry, this goes roundly off.° *this ends well*

PETRUCHIO Go, Jaques,
Get all the best meat may be bought for money,
And let the hogsheads blood.[2] I am born again.
Well, little England, when I see a husband
Of any other nation stern or jealous,
I'll wish him but a woman of thy breeding,
And if he have not butter to his bread
Till his teeth bleed, I'll never trust my travel.[3]

Enter Rowland, Livia, Bianca, and Tranio as from marriage.

PETRONIUS What have we here?

ROWLAND Another morris,° sir, *morris dance*
That you must pipe to.[4]

TRANIO A poor married couple
Desire an offering,° sir. *peace offering; dowry*

2. Let hogs be slaughtered for the feast. A hogshead is also a large cask; the word is of uncertain derivation, but is related to "hog's head."

3. I'll wish for that man a wife just like Maria, and if he doesn't find that he has more than enough to satisfy his appetite, I'll never trust my years of experience.

4. That you must also (1) play the tune for; (2) pay the piper for.

BIANCA [*to Petronius*] Never frown at it;
You cannot mend it now. There's your own hand,° *signature*
And yours, Moroso, to confirm the bargain.
PETRONIUS My hand?
MOROSO Or mine?
BIANCA You'll find it so.
PETRONIUS A trick!
By heaven, a trick!
BIANCA Yes, sir, we tricked ye.
LIVIA Father!
PETRONIUS Hast thou lain with him? Speak.
LIVIA Yes, truly, sir.
PETRONIUS [*to Rowland*] And hast thou done the deed, boy?
ROWLAND I have done, sir,
That that° will serve the turn, I think. *That which*
PETRUCHIO A match, then.
I'll be the maker-up° of this. Moroso, *peacemaker*
There's now no remedy, you see. Be willing;
For be or be not,° he must have the wench. *come what may*
MOROSO Since I am overreached,° let's in to dinner, *outdone, outwitted*
And if I can I'll drink't away.
TRANIO That's well said.
PETRONIUS [*to Rowland*] Well, sirrah, ye have played a trick, look to't,
And let me be a grandsire within's twelvemonth,
Or, by this hand, I'll curtail half your fortunes.° *dowry*
ROWLAND There shall not want° my labor, sir. [*Giving money to Tranio*] Your money; *lack*
Here's one has undertaken.[5]
TRANIO Well, I'll trust her,
And glad I have so good a pawn.[6]
ROWLAND I'll watch ye.[7]
PETRUCHIO Let's in, and drink of all hands,° and be jovial. *all hands round*
I have my colt again, and now she carries;° *carries her rider (me)*
And, gentlemen, whoever marries next,
Let him be sure he keep him to his text.° *Exeunt.* *bargain; contract*

Epilogue

[*Enter Epilogue.*]

EPILOGUE The tamer's tamed, but so as nor° the men *neither*
Can find one just cause to complain of, when
They fitly do consider° in their lives *consider that*
They should not reign as tyrants o'er their wives;
Nor can the women from this precedent
Insult° or triumph, it being aptly meant *Boast scornfully*
To teach both sexes due equality,
And, as they stand bound,° to love mutually. *are obligated*
If this effect, arising from a cause
Well laid and grounded, may deserve applause,

5. I.e., Here's one woman (Livia) who (by marrying me) has completed the terms specified in our bet.
6. I.e., I'm glad to win the bet with such assurances.
7. Rowland jocosely suggests that Tranio might give him cause for jealousy.

We something more than hope our honest ends
Will keep the men, and women too, our friends.[1] [*Exit.*]

FINIS.

Epilogue.
1. I.e., We expect, with an assurance that goes beyond mere hope, that our honest efforts will receive the approbation of both the men and the women in the audience. (Or "than" could be "then," the folio spelling.)

TEXTUAL NOTES

The Woman's Prize was entered in the Stationers' Register on September 4, 1646, and was first published in the Beaumont and Fletcher 1647 folio. It exists also in manuscript, evidently a "favor," or presentation, copy of a promptbook, now housed in the Folger Shakespeare Library, Washington, D.C. The present edition is based on the folio text, with recourse to the manuscript for some significant restorations whose omissions in the folio were, in some cases, the result of censorship. (The play was suppressed by the Master of the Revels, and was then, presumably in an altered form, acted at court on November 28, 1633.) The textual notes here indicate substantive departures from the folio text, using the following abbreviations:

F1: The folio edition of the plays of Beaumont and Fletcher (London: H. Robinson and Humphrey Mosley, 1647)
F2: The second folio edition of the plays of Beaumont and Fletcher (London: Martyn and Herringman, 1679)
MS: The so-called Lambarde manuscript, now in the Folger Shakespeare Library
ed.: A modern editor's emendation

The Persons Represented in the Play [F2; not in F1]
Prologue 1–20 [Prologue printed at the end of the play in F1] **1 PROLOGUE** [ed.; not in F1]
1.1.1 too [F1: to] **17 stubbornness** [MS] sobernesse [F1] **18 hue** [F1: huy] **39 by my troth** [MS] on my word [F1] **46 piss** [MS] unready [F1] **64 Worships** [MS] worship [F1] **66 you'd** [MS] you'l [F1] **71 wiped him now** [F1] impt him [MS]
1.2.8 his [F1, F2] this [MS] **20 has** [F1: h'as] **23 craccus** [F1: Cracus] Crocus [MS] **25 fox,** [MS] Fox and [F1] **28 a faith** [MS] faith [F1] **30 Laid** [MS] Lasd [F1] **47.1** [and elsewhere] ***Bianca*** [F1: *Byancha*] **51 ROWLAND I . . . it** [MS; not in F1] **56 ye** [MS] you [F1] **64 stranger** [MS] stronger [F1] **81 revels** [MS] Rebels [F1] **83 lungs** [MS] longs [F1] **85 tied** [F1: tide] **86 You're** [MS: Y'are] You are [F1] **89** [and elsewhere] **cousin** [F1: cozen, cosen] **94 or** [F1] and [MS] **95** [and elsewhere] **Whither** [F1: Whether] **128 disobedience** [MS] obedience [F1] **143 him, and a mad one** [MS] him [F1] **145 BIANCA That's . . . wench** [MS; not in F1] **150 has** [MS] hath [F1] **185 ye have** [MS] you have [F1] **189 ye** [MS] you [F1] **189 SD** [placement, ed.; after "None . . . ye (you)" in F1] **214 'em** [MS] them [F1]
1.3.1 have [MS] home [F1] **6 Faith** [MS] Well [F1] **10 stuff** [MS] staffe [F1] **23–24 SOPHOCLES His . . . while!** [MS; not in F1] **26–27 TRANIO That . . . leek** [MS; not in F1] **47 ballad** [F1: Ballat] **50 Ye** [MS] *And you* [F1] **71 you'd** [MS] you'l [F1] **73 in't** [MS] it [F1] **80 She doth** [MS] They doe [F1] **117** [twice], **175** [twice], **185, 223, 236, 276 ye** [MS] you [F1] **125 By'r Lady** [MS] Indeed [F1] **140 Heaven bless** [MS] Blesse [F1] **174 Death** [MS] Why [F1] **245 the** [MS] thy [F1] **251** [and elsewhere] **flayed** [F1: flead] **257**

alloys [F1: alayes] **258 you men, are** [F1: you, men are] **287 Death** [MS] — [F1] **300 I vow** [MS] — [F1]

1.4.8 all . . . me! [MS] all women — [F1] **33 armies** [MS] Armes [F1] **38.1** [placement, ed.; after "SOPHOCLES Farewell" in F1] **53 ye** [MS] you [F1] **73 SD** [MS; not in F1]

2.1.4 [and elsewhere] **He's** [F1: Has] **4 is** [F2; not in F1] **47** [and elsewhere] **lose** [F1: loose] **47 baubles** [F1: Bables] **53 MOROSO** [F2; not in F1]

2.2.13 *Qui va là?* [MS] *Cheval'a* [F1] **16, 69, 85, 120 ye** [MS] you [F1] **24 faith** [MS] word [F1] **25 "faith," or "troth"** [MS] word [F1] **52 Christian** [MS] certaine [F1] **64 robbed** [F2] rob'd [F1] **66 coarse** [F1: course] **84 'em** [MS] th'em [F1] **94 Find** [MS] Found [F1]

2.3 [scene indicator, ed.] *Scaena quarta* [F1]; entire scene not in MS; preceded in F1 by what is 2.5 in this present edition and headed *Scaena Tertia* **1 do** [F1: yoe] **3–4 ROWLAND So . . . acquainted?** [MS] *Row.* Thou hast heard I am sure of *Esculapius.* / So were they not well acquainted? [F1] **9 great** [MS; not in F1, F2] **11 bred** [F1: bread] **13 Thou** [MS] *Row.* Thou [F1] **22 heaven's** [MS: heavens] honours [F1] **33 love's** [MS] love [F1] **34 Our . . . friendship** [placement, MS; after 35 in F1]

2.4 [scene indicator, ed.] *Scaena quinta* [F1] **5 by this hand** [MS] by— [F1] **15 Sew** [MS] Sow [F1] **36.1** [placement, ed.; opposite 34 in F1] **45 Reins** [F1: Raynes] **45–48 Her . . . breech** [MS; not in F1] **57 toasting** [MS: tosting] tossing [F1] **67** [MS; followed in F1 by lines 85–86, "Lo . . . impatience"] **69 two churchwardens** [MS] the Town [F1] **70** [MS; not in F1] **85–86 SOPHOCLES Lo . . . impatience** [placement, MS; after 67 in F1] **85, 87 ye** [MS] you [F1]

2.5 [scene indicator, ed.; marked *Scaena Tertia* in F1, where this short scene is placed after 2.2; it then reappears nearly verbatim at the end of what F1 marks as *Scaena quinta*, i.e., 2.4 in this present edition] **0.1 *at several doors*** [second version only in F1]

2.6 [scene indicator, ed.] *Scaena tertia* [F1] **15 Cecily** [F: Sicely] **26, 153, 156, 169 ye** [MS] you [F1] **40 the kingdom** [MS] them [F1] **44–57** [F2; song not in MS, F1] **89 ev'n** [MS] then [F1] **93 Her** [MS] His [F1] **104 recreant** [MS] recant [F1] **109 off** [F1: of] **152 ye** [MS] yo [F1] you [F2] **158 this creed** [MS] these Articles [F1]

3.1.1, 77 [twice], **80, 81, 85, 87 ye** [MS] you [F1] **9 *misereri's*** [ed.] miseries [F1] mistrisses [MS] **21 heaven's** [MS: heavens] vertue [F1] **22 heaven's** [MS: heavens] vertues [F1] **26 gilt calf** [F1] calfe with the white face [MS] **31** [and elsewhere] **ribbon** [F1: riband] **46 Your** [MS] You [F1] **47 Oh, pox** [MS] A— [F1] **50–57 TRANIO Of . . . ended—** [MS; not in F1]

3.2.6 He's [F1: Has] **8, 11 Faith** [MS; not in F1] **20 Amorites** [MS] Amorities [F1] **26 bragget** [MS] Bagget [F1] **27 somersault** [F2] sober salt [F1] Somersett [MS] **37 For . . . cellars** [MS; not in F1] **45 Toast-** [MS: Tost] tosse [F1] **45 her** [MS] he [F1]

3.3.5 Pray [MS] Pray you [F1] **7 passed** [F1: past] **19 unto** [MS] to [F1] **44 flaying** [F1: fleaing] **79 rheums** [MS: rhumes] hewms [F1] **80 you** [MS; not in F1] **143 it, rot take me!** [MS] its— [F1] **144 SD** [placement, ed.; after "Farewell, sir" in F1] **155 tools** [MS] love [F1] **155 to** [F2] too [F1, MS]

3.4.5 your gewgaws [MS] no gew-gaws [F1] **7 moneys** [ed.] money's [MS, F1] **24, 28** [twice], **40, 43 ye** [MS] you [F1] **32 dearly** [MS] deadly [F1] **46 sir** [MS; not in F1] **48** [and elsewhere] **He's** [F1: H'as]

3.5.5 empirics . . . mountebanks [MS] people that are [F1] **11 SD *carrying . . . trunks*** [MS; not in F1] **23, 25, 73, 81, 82, 83, 95** [twice], **97 ye** [MS] you [F1] **23 heaven's** [MS: heavens] Heaven [F1] **33 Has** [MS] Hath [F1] **38 SD** [MS; not in F1] **54 Gentlemen** [MS; not in F1] **62 from** [F1: frow] **65 Death** [MS]—[F1] **78 SD *Manent Watchmen*** [MS; not in F1] **80 Who's** [MS] who [F1] **84–85** [MS; not in F1] **90 FIRST . . . People,** [MS; not in F1] **93 Ay** [MS:

I; not in F1] **96 as well** [MS] wel [F1] **100 I swear** [MS] — [F1] **102 is a** [F2] is [F1] 'tis a [MS] **103.2–3 *and . . . open*** [MS; not in F1] **121 tight** [F1: tith] **124 again** [MS] againe: I could raile twenty daies [F1] **128 dunghill** [F1: dunhill]

4.1.9 a dozen [F2] dozen [F1] **19 Quote** [F1: Quoat] **31 and** [MS] add [F1] **32 ballad** [F1: Ballard] **44 cauls** [F1: Cals] **74 you** [F2] your [F1] **77 Eking** [F1: Eeking]

4.2.2 pisspots [MS] looking-glasses [F1] **6 muscatel** [F1: Muskadell] **7 those** [MS] these [F1] **59 heaven** [MS] who [F1] **69, 70, 77, 97, 98, 116 ye** [MS] you [F1] **84 heard of** [F1: heard off] **88 dog-leech** [MS] dogge-latch [F1]

4.3 [scene indicator, ed.] *Scaena Secunda* [F1] **1 Faith** [MS; not in F1] **2, 10, 42, 47 ye** [MS] you [F1] **40 fever** [F1: feavor] **43 That that** [MS] That which [F1] **47 So.** [MS] Doe [F1] **50 honestly** [MS] honesty [F1]

4.4 [scene indicator, ed.] *Scaena Tertia* [F1] **2, 3, 4, 6, 8, 16, 27, 37, 43, 44 ye** [MS] you [F1] **14 and** [MS; not in F1] **27 loser** [F1: looser] **42 by-blows** [MS] by-lowes [F1] **48 my** [MS; not in F1] **49 counters** [F1: Compters]

4.5 [scene indicator, ed.] *Scaena quarta* [F1] **29 yet** [MS; not in F1] **57 she's** [MS] she is [F1] **58 made** [MS] make [F1] **60 light** [MS] hand [F1] **64 I swear** [MS] Beleeve me [F1] **69, 82, 127, 129, 130, 131** [twice], **141, 143, 145** [twice], **164, 182, 197, 208, 213, 222 ye** [MS] you [F1] **93 to** [F1: too] **167 religion** [MS] adventure [F1] **167 pagans** [MS] nothing [F1] **183 troth** [MS] — [F1] **185 her** [MS] sir [F1] **200 out** [MS; not in F1] **212 Fare** [F1: Far] **222 lemon-water** [MS] Limon-waters [F1]

5.1.4 seems [F1: sems] **28 Good e'en** [MS: Goodde'n] Good ev'n [F1] **28 you're** [MS: y'are] you are [F1] **31 into** [MS] unto [F1] **43 had** [MS] have [F1] **52, 103, 115 ye** [MS] you [F1] **59 be** [MS] by [F1] **60 Why** [MS; not in F1] **85 extant** [MS] living [F1] **90 reverend** [F1: reverent] **121.1** [MS; not in F1]

5.2.0.1 *a trunk* [MS] *Chest* [F1] **1 trunk** [MS] Trunks [F1] **24 porpoises** [F1: Porpisces] **63 fadings** [MS] longings [F1] **66 Sedgley** [F2: Sedgly] seagly [F1, MS]

5.3.10 By heaven [ed.] I swear [MS] — [F1] **15 Two** [ed.] An [F1] a [MS] **21 with** [MS; not in F1] **28 this** [MS] his [F1] **35 I swear by heaven** [ed.] By— [F1] I sweare [MS]

5.4.1.2 *Jaques,* [*and*] *Pedro* [MS: Jaques, Pedro] *and Jaques* [F1] **13 yet** [MS] ye [F1] **39 SD** [MS; not in F1] **40 By heaven** [MS] — [F1] **42 By heaven** [ed.] — [F1, F2] I sweare [MS] **49 sir** [MS; not in F1] **56 hour, since** [MS] houre since, since [F1] **64, 65 his** [MS] thy [F1] **65.1–2 *as from marriage*** [MS; not in F1] **66 to** [F1: too] **72 By heaven** [ed.] By— [F1, F2] I sweare [MS] **73 lain** [F1: lyen] **81 ye** [MS] you [F1]

Epilogue 1 epilogue [ed.; not in F1] **5 precedent** [F1: *president*]

The Revenger's Tragedy

Savage and funny, often at the same time, *The Revenger's Tragedy* organizes itself around two social and moral issues: private revenge as an ethically dubious mode of action and the deep-seated and widespread social corruption that might justify it. Set in an Italian court—never named, but indebted for some plot elements to Florence in the 1530s—the play treats the consequences of two crimes. The first occurred at a time well before the events of the play, when the Duke poisoned Gloriana, the chaste and beautiful fiancée of Vindice. Vindice carries her skull around with him and periodically reinvigorates his thirst for vengeance by speaking to it. Additionally, Vindice's father, disgraced by the Duke, "Fell sick upon the infection of [the Duke's] frowns" (3.5.172), and has recently died in melancholic silence (3.5.175), leaving Vindice the head of a family that has few prospects because of the present ruler's dislike. The second crime occurs in the days before the play opens, when the Duchess's youngest son, Junior Brother, rapes the chaste and beautiful wife of a virtuous courtier, Lord Antonio, during a masked banquet. In the early scenes, Junior Brother is imprisoned, brazenly acknowledges the crime in court, and is about to be sentenced to death when the Duke at his wife's persuasion delays the proceedings and sends his stepson back to jail to await either sentencing or reprieve. Antonio's dishonored wife commits suicide, and a group of outraged nobles gathers around Antonio and, led by Vindice's brother, Hippolito, swears vengeance if Junior Brother is not sentenced and executed at the next meeting of the court.

The play thus presents two separate though related vengeance plots, one personal and familial, pursued by Vindice and his brother, Hippolito, alone and in secret; the other semipublic and, by the end of the play, involving "five hundred gentlemen" and nobles who band together to mount a coup against the tyranny of the Duke and that of his son Lussurioso, who has succeeded him (5.2.28). Though he has let his fiancée's and father's deaths go unrevenged for some time, Vindice proves an active and ingenious private revenger. By the end of the play, he has, helped by their own inept murderousness, swept away the Duke and most of his family, leaving Antonio to take over the dukedom without any ducal blood on his hands. Antonio, an old man, has himself been passive throughout. The contrast between Vindice and Antonio seems intended to structure the play's treatment of revenge.

"Revenge is sweet"; "Revenge is a dish that should be eaten cold"; " 'Vengeance is mine; I will repay,' saith the Lord" (Romans 12.19); "Living well is the best revenge." These general statements—three aphorisms and a biblical quotation—reflect different attitudes toward revenge that circulate in the play, as indeed in Renaissance drama and Western culture generally. The first two, which we could associate with Vindice, suggest that we should desire and appreciate revenge and that successful revenge often requires patience and strategy. The next two, which we could associate with Antonio, give reasons for hesitation in the pursuit of private vengeance: in religious terms, revenge usurps a role that God reserves for Himself; in philosophic terms, the best

Introduction by Lars Engle; glosses, footnotes, and textual notes by David Bevington and checked by Lars Engle; text edited by David Bevington and checked by Eric Rasmussen and Lars Engle.

way to achieve revenge on one's oppressors is stoically to live well despite them. Government sided with the latter positions: both Queen Elizabeth and King James campaigned against dueling and private revenge.

This division, while helpful in sorting out the moral treatment of revenge in the play, considerably simplifies an astonishingly complex set of murderous plots—plots that, in their profusion, illustrate the pervasive corruption of the Duke's court. The Duchess swears revenge on the Duke for failing to release Junior Brother from prison instantly, and she enlists help from the Duke's bastard son, Spurio (whom she fancies); Spurio in turn swears revenge on his father for illegitimately conceiving him. The Duke's elder stepsons, Ambitioso and Supervacuo, wish to do away with the Duke's son Lussurioso in order to inherit the dukedom; Supervacuo intends to murder Ambitioso for the same reason, and vice versa. Spurio wants all the legitimate sons to die.

Amid this welter of murderous intentions, dangerous (and entertaining) errors naturally are made. While Spurio, on advice from misinformed followers, attempts to catch his half-brother Lussurioso seducing Vindice's sister Castiza, Lussurioso, on advice from the misinformed Vindice, rushes to his father's bedroom to apprehend Spurio in flagrante delicto with his stepmother, the Duchess. But the Duke is in his own bed, for once, with his own wife. In the resulting confusion, the Duke sentences Lussurioso to the same prison where Junior Brother languishes, but then quickly changes his mind and releases him. Ambitioso and Supervacuo, not knowing that Lussurioso has been reprieved and hoping to eliminate the legitimate heir, carry a false death warrant for their "brother" to an officer, who then obediently has Junior Brother executed and brings his head to them. Having stumbled into this disaster, Ambitioso remarks, "I see now there is nothing sure in mortality but mortality. / Well, no more words. Shalt be revenged, i'faith" (3.6.101–3). Vengefulness in this play is among other things the last refuge of the incompetent.

Such bumbling vengefulness is vastly entertaining in a play that both follows and spoofs the conventions of Renaissance revenge tragedy. At the same time, the code of vengeance poses a serious ethical dilemma for the revenger. That person, usually male, must react to an offense against the life and honor of his family, often including both a murder and an assault on the chastity of a female relative. In such tragedies, the law offers the revenger no respite, usually because, as in *The Revenger's Tragedy* and *Hamlet*, the offender is himself a ruler and thus has institutional authority on his side. In combining a personal imperative to cleanse the family's honor in blood with a social imperative to remove a wicked per-

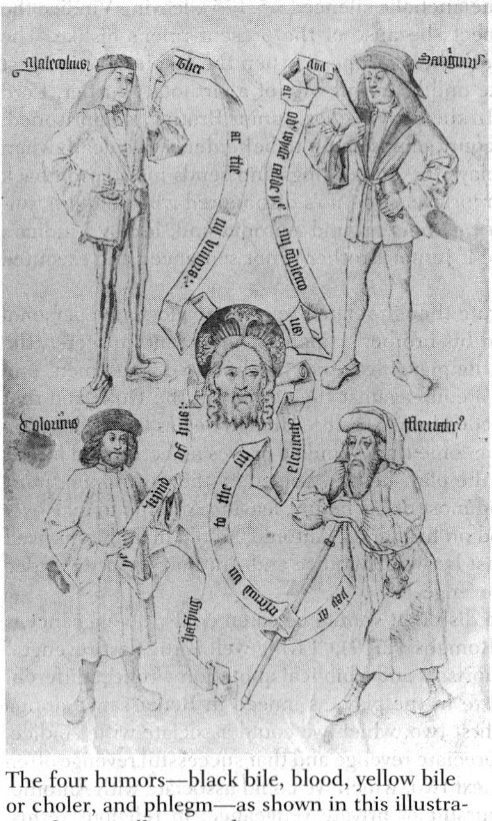

The four humors—black bile, blood, yellow bile or choler, and phlegm—as shown in this illustration from an illuminated manuscript, were believed to govern the human personality by producing a disposition toward melancholic, sanguine, choleric, or phlegmatic temperaments. See Spurio's comment at 2.2.133 and note.

son who stands at the top of a hierarchical social order and corrupts it, revenge tragedy engages a widespread human suspicion: that the social order does not protect the weak from the strong but rather empowers the strong to prey on the weak. The weak are forced to break the rules and take the law into their own hands. When they do so, however, they become like those against whom they act: violent, lawless, self-regarding.

The Revenger's Tragedy conforms to these norms of revenge tragedy in a number of ways, though the play is so funny, satiric, and parodic that it stretches the boundaries of the genre. In killing the corrupt Duke, Vindice acts to purge the state as well as to take private vengeance. Yet his manner of doing so is flamboyantly and comically outrageous. Having tricked the old Duke into a poison kiss that has eaten away the outer parts of his mouth, Vindice and his brother nail down with a knife what remains of the Duke's tongue, hold another knife to his heart, and force him to witness the incestuous embraces of the Duchess and Spurio, threatening to tear off his eyelids if he blinks and to "make his eyes, like comets, shine through blood" (3.5.205), so that the Duke finally dies only after he has fully agonized over his cuckoldry. Because of this gruesome scene and others like it, twentieth-century readers have seen the play as a model for the theater of cruelty, which uses over-the-top violence to prompt awareness of the omnipresence of power and oppression. The play similarly anticipates black comedy, which aims at a mixture of horror and amusement. Vindice's moralization, "When the bad bleeds, then is the tragedy good" (3.5.206), provokes the question: Does he mean "good" in a moral sense or a theatrical one?

The question reminds us that revenge, however engrossing to watch or engage in, cannot insulate itself from the criminality it punishes. Certainly the play's retributive mayhem shows how, as a social code, revenge presents problems for public order. Without some mechanism of adjudication, the cycle of revenge can end only when all those in the families or groups involved die or disappear; a society full of private wars cannot organize its affairs rationally. Private revenge cannot therefore responsibly be encouraged, and for this reason, among others, it is a central convention of Renaissance revenge tragedy that the revenger himself must die. Moreover, Vindice, like many revengers, kills a ruler; only his own prompt execution by a self-protective and legitimate duke at the play's end keeps the play from appearing to be a handbook for the revolutionary removal of immoral monarchs. *The Revenger's Tragedy*, first performed in 1606–7, appeared at a moment of particular sensitivity to such political issues; it was staged in the aftermath of the Gunpowder Plot, the Catholic conspiracy of 1605 to blow up the King and Parliament, which was justified by the claim that King James was a heretical tyrant. Yet even tyranny does not, in most Renaissance political theory, justify regicide: political writers of the time largely agreed that moral errors by rulers did not justify revolt on the part of subjects, even as Renaissance moral theorists agreed that vengeance for wrongs should be left to God and the law.

The play's risky relationship to sensitive issues of political ethics is matched by the complexity of Vindice's personal relationship to private morality. As he improvises brilliantly in several disguises to be revenged on the Duke and Lussurioso, Vindice pursues a personal moral agenda to expose the corruption of the social world he inhabits. Indeed, he often provokes others to evil in order to expose or test them; his own mother provides the most spectacular case when she agrees at Vindice's urging to help seduce her daughter and then repents at the point of his knife (in one of the many moments in which *The Revenger's Tragedy* echoes *Hamlet*). These testings are made all the more strikingly theatrical by Vindice's repeated awareness that he is acting as a kind of playwright within the play. When, for example, he calls for heavenly thunder at a key point in the action, he is answered by thunder as a sound effect (4.2.203–4), and he later responds to stage thunder by saying, "Dost know thy cue, thou big-voiced crier?" (5.3.44).

Vindice tries to maintain the propriety of his risky role-playing and scripting by offering moral commentary on it, as when, costumed as a pander, he is first presented to Lussurioso and seeks to whet Lussurioso's already hot appetite for sexual misbehavior. As a potential employer, Lussurioso naturally asks about Vindice's experience and qualifications: "Then thou know'st / I'th'world strange lust?" (1.3.55–56). Vindice replies, "Oh, Dutch lust, fulsome lust!" (1.3.56), and goes on to itemize the lust he has encountered, but then adds a disquieting moral note:

Oh, hour of incest!
Any kin now, next to the rim o'th'sister,
Is man's meat in these days; and in the morning
When they are up and dressed, and their mask on,
Who can perceive this, save that eternal eye
That sees through flesh and all? (1.3.61–66)

The speech both anatomizes and, in its way, encourages incestuous sexual promiscuity (along familiar "everybody's doing it" lines), yet at the end suggests that God will eventually damn those who engage in it. The closing reference to a panoptic deity does not entirely efface the nihilism and prurience that come before. Moreover, the sententiousness—the production of neat moral sayings, often in rhymed couplets—that so often makes Vindice seem his own chorus is a feature of the play as a whole. Even the obviously wicked offer brilliant maxims of immorality. Thus Lussurioso describes his preference for adultery over marriage:

I'm one of that number can defend
Marriage is good, yet rather keep a friend.
Give me my bed by stealth; there's true delight.
What breeds a loathing in't but night by night?
(1.3.103–6)

The play's sententious moralizing thus serves as a kind of debased currency of moral commentary in an immoral society, similar in this respect to the way private vengeance serves as a debased form of justice.

The play analyzes the corruption of its society in several ways. The ruler, his wife, his son, his stepsons, and his bastard are all wicked, and since they dominate, their court follows them in wickedness even if it may reform itself ultimately when they are gone. At the same time, the play also suggests that courtliness itself, with its focus on expensive display and consumption, may be corrupt and that sexual desire is intimately linked to these wasteful and decadent practices. When Vindice, holding Gloriana's skull, evokes her lost beauty, he does it in a peculiar way:

Oh, she was able to ha' made a usurer's son
Melt all his patrimony in a kiss,
And what his father fifty years told
To have consumed, and yet his suit been cold.
(1.1.26–29)

Female beauty, it seems, can be measured by the accumulated wealth that lustful men hastily spend in their attempts to enjoy sexual favors; chastity consists in making such spendthrift behavior unsuccessful, not in living outside the environment in which such exchanges are normal.

No named characters in *The Revenger's Tragedy* actually sell their patrimonies to woo a beautiful woman or to dress themselves and their mistresses luxuriously, so that the women "Walk with a hundred acres on their backs, / Fair meadows cut into green foreparts" (2.1.219–20). The idea of acres-for-velvets expenditure, though, recurs so insistently that one remembers such transactions as central to the play. Vindice invokes this idea as he poisons Gloriana's skull, sets it on a framework, and dresses the deadly dummy in sumptuous clothing and a mask to tempt the Duke:

> Does the silkworm expend her yellow labors
> For thee? For thee does she undo herself?
> Are lordships sold to maintain ladyships
> For the poor benefit of a bewitching minute?
> (3.5.71–74)

This complex reflection unites moral awareness of the transitory nature of fleshly life and beauty with economic awareness of how compulsive sexual desire concentrates and uses up the products of toil. Moral ideas are treated in economic terms. Lussurioso, plotting his seduction of Castiza, describes her "chastity" as "the portion of her soul"—that is, her soul's dowry—and he orders Vindice to "bring it into expense" and so destroy it (1.3.113–15). The play, then, treats court festivity and sexual license as forms of what the French theorist Georges Bataille calls "expenditure,"[1] a conspicuous waste undertaken for the purpose of symbolic display, and it views expenditure with a mixture of fascination and moral disapproval.

The disapproval stems in part from the play's unusually explicit presentation of a more or less universal truth: that particular environments, in this case luxurious court entertainments, can take over the lives of the people in them and subject them to the spirit of the occasion. Thus Spurio claims that he owes his bastardy not simply to a wicked Duke's lust, but also to the food and drink his father and mother consumed on the night of his conception:

> Faith, if the truth were known, I was begot
> After some gluttonous dinner; some stirring dish
> Was my first father. When deep healths went round,
> And ladies' cheeks were painted red with wine,
> Their tongues as short and nimble as their heels,
> Uttering words sweet and thick, and, when they rose,
> Were merrily disposed to fall again—
> In such a whisp'ring and withdrawing hour,
> When base male bawds kept sentinel at stair-head,
> Was I stol'n softly. (1.2.180–89)

This remarkably intense evocation of drunken sexual susceptibility to a complex and in some ways enticing social situation makes courtly festivity in general, not particular people, the cause of crime. Such passages, in showing how individual action may be scripted by the imperatives of a social occasion, complicate the ethics of vengeance considerably. Taking vengeance involves assigning individual responsibility for actions—you need a particular offender on whom to take revenge—and so dispersing the responsibility for immoral behavior onto something outside of and larger than the individual both deepens and blurs the play's treatment of morality and of human action. If corruption inheres in eating, drinking, feeling sexual desire, and enjoying the display of wealth and power, how can one revenger hope to do away with it? Vindice himself captures the enervating nature of this difficulty when, in disguise, he attempts to persuade his sister Castiza to become Lussurioso's mistress (fervently hoping that she will resist his blandishments, as indeed she does):

> Oh, think upon the pleasure of the palace:
> Securèd ease and state; the stirring meats
> Ready to move out of the dishes
> That e'en now quicken when they're eaten;

1. Georges Bataille, "The Notion of Expenditure," in *Visions of Excess: Selected Writings 1927–1938*, trans. A. Stoekl with C. Lovitt and D. Leslie, ed. Allan Stoekl (Minneapolis: University of Minnesota Press, 1985), p. 123. See also Thorstein Veblen, *The Theory of the Leisure Class* (New York: Macmillan, 1899).

Banquets abroad by torchlight; music, sports;
Bareheaded vassals, that had ne'er the fortune
To keep on their own hats, but let horns wear 'em;
Nine coaches waiting—hurry, hurry, hurry!
(2.1.201–8)

If, moreover, we consider together the play's many accounts of festivity as a corrupt and corrupting environment, they raise questions about theater itself and about this particular play: a festive representation of violent immorality put on display in a licentious pleasure zone in the suburbs of Renaissance London. Are theaters, in fact, demoralizing environments, as antitheatrical writers such as Philip Stubbs and William Prynne insisted? Does attending plays like *The Revenger's Tragedy* dispose audiences to vice, filling them with images of lust, violence, and self-surrender? If the play not only fulfills the conventions of revenge tragedy but also outdoes them almost to the point of parody, does it mock the genre's pretensions to moral seriousness as well?

Such questions are raised anew by the play's brilliant metatheatrical ending, in which Vindice completely rewrites the revels scripted for Lussurioso's accession to the dukedom. In Vindice's version, all his enemies get killed, either by him or by each other, and no one realizes who is in control. All the confusion, though deadly, is also comic: participants in a social order as decadent as this one deserve whatever deaths fall on their heads. Nonetheless, this masque of death certainly suggests that theater is not necessarily good for its audiences, and Vindice in organizing it seems very close to the playwright who wrote *The Revenger's Tragedy*.

The beneficiary of some happy coincidences, Vindice has also been the agent of much successful mayhem, and could at the end get away with everything just by keeping his mouth shut. But when Antonio wonders how the old Duke died, Vindice cannot refrain from a self-congratulatory confession: " 'Twas somewhat witty carried, though we say it. / 'Twas we two murdered him" (5.3.117–18). Antonio, about to become duke himself, needs no experienced duke-slayers in his court, and so he promptly sends Vindice and Hippolito off to be executed. Vindice takes this final reversal with nihilistic good cheer, moralizing on his confirmation of the adage that " 'time / Will make the murderer bring forth himself' " (5.3.137–38), and offering the consolation that he and Hippolito will die having achieved some definite good—and die in highborn company: "We're well, our mother turned, our sister true; / We die after a nest of dukes. Adieu" (5.3.145–46). In short, they die having made some mark on the world and having completed an existential project—morally dubious, but theatrically very satisfying.

Given the play's participation in the corruption it exposes, and given also Vindice's representation of the dangers of authoring vengeance dramas, it is both appropriate and ironic that the play (like many others) was published anonymously and has remained uncertain in authorship.[2] Even though in the past twenty-five years a near consensus on Middleton's authorship has emerged, time has in this case been slow to "make the murderer bring forth himself." Unlike Vindice, the author or authors of *The Revenger's Tragedy* kept their mouths shut about what they so wittily carried out.

2. Although scholarship used to assign this play to Cyril Tourneur, author of *The Atheist's Tragedy*, on the basis of an unreliable document from 1656 and the apparent similarity of the plays' titles, *The Revenger's Tragedy* is now more commonly ascribed to Thomas Middleton. In the view of the editors of this anthology, the resemblance to *The Atheist's Tragedy* is superficial at best. The case for Middleton's authorship is strong, even if it is necessarily based on internal evidence and is still sometimes disputed. Collaborative authorship remains a possibility.

THOMAS MIDDLETON (?)

The Revenger's Tragedy

[The Persons in the Play

VINDICE,[1] son of Gratiana and brother of Castiza and Hippolito; sometimes disguised as Piato
HIPPOLITO, brother of Vindice and Castiza
CASTIZA, sister of Vindice and Hippolito
MOTHER (Gratiana), mother of Vindice, Hippolito, and Castiza
DONDOLO, Gratiana's gentleman-usher

The DUKE
LUSSURIOSO, his son and heir by a previous marriage
NENCIO, SORDIDO } followers of Lussurioso
SPURIO, a bastard son of the Duke

The DUCHESS
AMBITIOSO, her eldest son
SUPERVACUO, her second son
JUNIOR BROTHER, her youngest son

ANTONIO, PIERO } noblemen in the Duke's court

Two JUDGES
Two SERVANTS attending Spurio
Four NOBLES
Three OFFICERS
KEEPER of a prison
Officers of the guard, gentlemen, servants

THE SCENE: An unidentified Italian court.]

The original 1607 title page reads "*The Revenger's Tragedy.* As it hath been sundry times acted by the King's Majesty's Servants. At London. Printed by G. Eld, and are to be sold at his house in Fleet Lane at the sign of the Printers' Press. 1607." (Some copies show a date of 1608.)

The Persons in the Play.

1. The Italian names here are often suggestively meaningful: Vindice, the revenger of wrongs; Piato, the hidden man; Castiza, the chaste one; Gratiana, the woman of grace; Dondolo, the gull, or fool; Lussurioso, the lecherous and dissolute man; Nencio, the fool, or idiot; Sordido, the sordid wretch; Spurio, the bastard; Ambitioso, the ambitious man; Supervacuo, the superfluous and vain man.

1.1

Enter Vindice [holding a skull and watching as] the
Duke, Duchess, Lussurioso his son, Spurio the Bastard,
with a train,° pass over the stage with torchlight. — *entourage*

VINDICE Duke, royal lecher! Go, grey-haired adultery,
And thou his son, as impious steeped° as he, — *evilly inclined*
And thou his bastard, true-begot in evil,
And thou his duchess, that will do° with devil— — *have sex*
Four excellent characters! Oh, that marrowless age
Would stuff the hollow bones with damned desires,
And, 'stead of heat, kindle infernal fires
Within the spendthrift veins of a dry duke,
A parched and juiceless luxur![1] Oh, God! One
That has scarce blood enough to live upon;
And he to riot it like a son and heir?
Oh, the thought of that
Turns my abusèd heartstrings into fret.[2]
[*To the skull*] Thou sallow picture of my poisoned love,
My study's ornament,[3] thou shell of death,
Once the bright face of my betrothèd lady
When life and beauty naturally filled out
These ragged imperfections,
When two heaven-pointed diamonds° were set — *i.e., eyes*
In those unsightly rings°—then 'twas a face — *eye sockets*
So far beyond the artificial shine
Of any woman's bought° complexion — *i.e., cosmetic*
That the uprightest man (if such there be,
That sin but seven times a day) broke custom
And made up eight with looking after° her. — *upon*
Oh, she was able to ha' made a usurer's son
Melt all his patrimony° in a kiss, — *inherited wealth*
And what his father fifty years told° — *counted in his hoard*
To have consumed, and yet his suit° been cold.° — *wooing / in vain*
But oh, accursèd palace!
Thee° when thou wert appareled in thy flesh — *(The dead Gloriana)*
The old Duke poisoned,
Because thy purer part would not consent
Unto his palsy° lust; for old men lustful — *i.e., quavering*
Do show like young men, angry, eager, violent,
Outbid like their limited performances.[4]
Oh, 'ware° an old man hot and vicious!° — *beware / given to vice*
Age, as in gold, in lust is covetous.
Vengeance, thou murder's quit-rent, and whereby
Thou show'st thyself tenant to Tragedy,[5]
Oh, keep thy day, hour, minute, I beseech,
For those thou hast determined![6] Hum, whoe'er knew
Murder unpaid? Faith, give Revenge her due;

1.1. At the ducal court.
1. How deplorable that the aged Duke is filled with hot desires instead of proper vital heat—desires that will damn him as an old lecher!
2. Fretfulness, anger. (With a wordplay on the fret of a stringed instrument.)
3. (1) The ornament of my study or room; (2) the object of my study.
4. Lustful old men may seem impetuous and violent like young men, but this show of lustfulness is far in excess of their sexual performance.
5. Vengeance shows itself in the service of Tragedy; vengeance must repay murder. (Quit-rent is payment made by a tenant in lieu of services required.)
6. Keep your promise to punish those whom you have marked for vengeance!

Sh' has kept touch° hitherto. Be merry, merry; *kept the faith*
Advance thee,° O thou terror to fat° folks, *(the skull) / rich; fat*
To have their costly three-piled° flesh worn off *thick-piled velvet*
As bare as this.° For banquets, ease, and laughter *As bare as a skull*
Can make great men, as greatness goes by clay,[7]
But wise men little are more great than they.[8]

Enter his brother, Hippolito.

HIPPOLITO Still sighing o'er death's vizard?° *mask*
VINDICE Brother, welcome.
What comfort bring'st thou? How go things at court?
HIPPOLITO In silk and silver, brother; never braver.° *more showily*
VINDICE Pooh,
Thou play'st upon my meaning. Prithee say:
Has that bald madam, Opportunity,[9]
Yet thought upon's? Speak, are we happy° yet? *fortunate*
Thy wrongs and mine are for one scabbard fit.
HIPPOLITO It may prove happiness.° *turn out lucky*
VINDICE What is't may prove?
Give me to taste.
HIPPOLITO Give me your hearing, then.
You know my place at court.
VINDICE Ay, the Duke's chamber;
But 'tis a marvel thou'rt not turned out yet.
HIPPOLITO Faith, I have been shoved at, but 'twas still my hap
To hold by th'Duchess' skirt—you guess at that;
Whom° such a coat keeps up can ne'er fall flat. *Anyone whom*
But to the purpose:
Last evening, predecessor unto this,
The Duke's son° warily inquired for me, *(Lussurioso)*
Whose pleasure I attended. He began
By policy° to open and unhusk me *cunning*
About the time and common rumor;
But I had so much wit° to keep my thoughts *intelligence*
Up in their built houses,° yet afforded him *i.e., To myself*
An idle satisfaction without danger.
But the whole aim and scope of his intent
Ended in this, conjuring me in private
To seek some strange-digested° fellow forth, *disaffected*
Of ill-contented nature, either disgraced
In former times, or by new grooms displaced
Since his stepmother's nuptials;[1] such a blood,° *roisterer*
A man that were for evil only good;
To give you the true word, some base-coined° pander. *debased, counterfeit*
VINDICE I reach° you, for I know his° heat is such, *understand / (Lussurioso's)*
Were there as many concubines as ladies
He would not be contained, he must fly out.
I wonder how ill featured, vile proportioned

7. Banquets, indolence, and laughter can make aristocrats great, i.e., fat (see line 45), since this superficial kind of greatness is a matter of the flesh only. ("Clay" is flesh, as in Job 10.9.)
8. Wise men, being not fat and of low expectations, are better than the indolent fat (materially successful) men. (Or perhaps "little" means that the wise men are only somewhat better.)
9. Opportunity (or Occasion—see line 99 below) was proverbially portrayed as a goddess to be seized by the forelock, since she was bald on the back of the head and therefore could not be pulled back again by the hair.
1. Or by new lowborn fellows thrust aside, because of his stepmother's remarrying, from his hopes of inheriting a fortune.

That one° should be, if she were made for° woman, *one woman / fashioned as a*
Whom at the insurrection of his lust
He would refuse for once? Heart,° I think none. *By God's heart*
Next to a skull, though more unsound than one,
Each face he meets he strongly dotes upon.[2]

HIPPOLITO Brother, you've truly spoke° him. *described*
He knows not you, but I'll swear you know° him. *understand*

VINDICE And therefore I'll put on that knave for once,[3]
And be a right° man, then, a man o'th'time, *fit, conforming*
For to be honest is not to be i'th'world.
Brother, I'll be that strange-composèd fellow.

HIPPOLITO And I'll prefer° you, brother. *recommend*

VINDICE Go to, then;
The small'st advantage fattens wrongèd men.
It may point out Occasion; if I meet her,
I'll hold her by the foretop° fast enough, *forelock (see 55 and n)*
Or, like the French mole, heave up hair and all.[4]
I have a habit° that will fit it quaintly.° *costume / cunningly*
Here comes our mother.

HIPPOLITO And sister.

VINDICE We must coin.° *counterfeit, pretend*

[*Enter Mother and Castiza.*]

[*Aside to Hippolito*] Women are apt, you know, to take false money,
But I dare stake my soul for these two creatures,
Only excuse excepted—that they'll swallow
Because their sex is easy in belief.[5]

MOTHER What news from court, son Carlo?[6]

HIPPOLITO Faith,° mother, *In faith*
'Tis whispered there the Duchess' youngest son
Has played a rape on Lord Antonio's wife.

MOTHER On that religious lady!

CASTIZA Royal blood! Monster, he deserves to die,
If° Italy had no more hopes but he. *Even if*

VINDICE Sister, you've sentenced most direct and true;
The law's a woman, and would she were you.[7]
Mother, I must take leave of you.

MOTHER Leave? For what?

VINDICE I intend speedy travel.

HIPPOLITO That he does, madam.

MOTHER Speedy indeed!

VINDICE For since my worthy father's funeral
My life's unnatural to me, e'en compelled° *forced on me*
As if I lived now when I should be dead.

MOTHER Indeed, he was a worthy gentleman,
Had his estate been fellow to° his mind. *matched to*

2. Lussurioso is infatuated with each women he meets—even though she may be more rotten (with venereal disease) than the skull of a dead person.
3. And therefore I'll disguise myself as that disaffected fellow that Lussurioso was asking you to find (see lines 74–81).
4. Or uproot everything in my path. ("French" signifies syphilis, known in England as "the French disease"; it resulted in hair loss.)
5. The one exception allowed being that, as women, they are naturally credulous.
6. "Carlo" may have been the dramatist's first idea of a name for Hippolito; it does not reappear in the play.
7. I wish that Justice, that female personification of true law, were embodied in you.

VINDICE The Duke did much deject him.° *force him down*
MOTHER Much!
VINDICE Too much.
And through disgrace, oft smothered in his spirit
When it would mount, surely I think he died
Of discontent, the nobleman's consumption.
MOTHER Most sure he did.
VINDICE Did he? 'Lack, you know all;
You were his midnight secretary.° *i.e., confidant*
MOTHER No,
He was too wise to trust me with his thoughts.
VINDICE I'faith, then, father, thou wast wise indeed.
Wives are but made to go to bed and feed.° *eat; nurse*
Come, mother, sister.—You'll bring me onward,° brother? *see me on my way*
HIPPOLITO I will.
VINDICE [*aside to Hippolito*] I'll quickly turn into another.
Exeunt.

[1.2]

Enter the old Duke; Lussurioso, his son; the Duchess; [Spurio] the Bastard; the Duchess's two sons, Ambitioso and Supervacuo; the third [Junior Brother], her youngest, brought out with officers [of the guard] for the rape; [and] two Judges.

DUKE Duchess, it is your youngest son; we're sorry.
His violent act has e'en drawn° blood of honor *shed*
And stained our honors,
Thrown ink upon the forehead of our state,
Which envious spirits will dip their pens into
After our death, and blot° us in our tombs; *stain; eclipse*
For that which would seem treason in our lives
Is laughter when we're dead. Who dares now whisper
That dares not then° speak out, and e'en proclaim *after our deaths*
With loud words and broad pens our closest° shame? *most secret*
FIRST JUDGE Your Grace hath spoke like to your silver years,
Full of confirmed gravity; for what is it to have
A flattering false insculption° on a tomb, *carved inscription*
And in men's hearts reproach? The boweled° corpse *disemboweled*
May be cered in,° but with free tongue I speak: *wrapped in shrouds*
The faults of great men through their cerecloths° break. *shrouds*
DUKE They do. We're sorry for't; it is our fate
To live in fear and die to live in hate.° *be hated in death*
I leave him to your sentence—doom° him, lords, *sentence*
The fact° is great—whilst I sit by and sigh. *deed, crime*
DUCHESS [*kneeling*] My gracious lord, I pray be merciful.
Although his trespass far exceed his years,
Think him to be your own, as I am yours;
Call him not son-in-law.° The law, I fear, *stepson*
Will fall too soon upon his name and him.
Temper his fault with pity!

1.2. A courtroom.

LUSSURIOSO Good my lord,
Then 'twill not taste so bitter and unpleasant
Upon the judges' palate,[1] for offenses
Gilt o'er with mercy show° like fairest women, *look*
Good only for their beauties, which, washed off,
No sin is uglier.
AMBITIOSO I beseech Your Grace,
Be soft and mild; let not relentless Law
Look with an iron forehead° on our brother. *stern frown*
SPURIO [*aside*] He° yields small comfort yet; hope he° shall die. *(The Duke) / I hope Junior*
And if a bastard's wish might stand in force,
Would all the court were turned into a corse!° *corpse*
DUCHESS No pity yet? Must I rise fruitless, then,
A wonder in a woman?[2] Are my knees
Of such low metal° that without respect— *worthless substance*
FIRST JUDGE Let the offender stand forth.
[*Junior Brother is brought forward.*]
'Tis the Duke's pleasure that impartial doom° *judgment*
Shall take fast hold of his unclean attempt.° *vile assault*
A rape! Why, 'tis the very core of lust,
Double° adultery. *Twice as bad as*
JUNIOR BROTHER So, sir.
SECOND JUDGE And, which was worse,
Committed on the lord Antonio's wife,
That general-honest° lady. Confess, my lord, *utterly chaste*
What moved you to't?
JUNIOR BROTHER Why, flesh and blood, my lord.
What should move men unto a woman else?
LUSSURIOSO Oh, do not jest° thy doom! Trust not an ax *jest about*
Or sword too far; the law is a wise serpent
And quickly can beguile thee of thy life.
Though marriage only has made thee my brother,° *stepbrother*
I love thee so far;° play not with thy death. *only enough to say this*
JUNIOR BROTHER I thank you, troth.° Good admonitions, 'faith, *in truth*
If I'd the grace now to make use of them.
FIRST JUDGE That lady's name has spread such a fair wing° *spread so widely*
Over all Italy that, if our tongues
Were sparing toward the fact,° judgment itself *crime*
Would be condemned and suffer in men's thoughts.
JUNIOR BROTHER Well, then, 'tis done, and it would please me well
Were it to do again. Sure she's a goddess,
For I'd no power to see her and to live;[3]
It falls out° true in this, for I must die. *turns out*
Her beauty was ordained to be my scaffold,
And yet methinks I might be easier 'sessed;° *assessed; ceased*
My fault being sport, let me but die in jest.
FIRST JUDGE This be the sentence—

1. If you relent and grant pardon, you will relieve the judges of their unpleasant (but necessary) duty.
2. It is a strange thing indeed to see a pleading woman not granted her wish. (With a wordplay on the idea of a woman rising from sex without having been made pregnant—a wonder in nature.)
3. Having seen her, I could not have lived without having her.

DUCHESS Oh, keep't upon your tongue! Let it not slip;° *slip out*
Death too soon steals out of a lawyer's lip.
Be not so cruel-wise!
FIRST JUDGE Your Grace must pardon us;
'Tis but the justice of the law.
DUCHESS The law
Is grown more subtle than a woman should be.° *(cf. 1.1.114–15 and n)*
SPURIO [*aside*] Now, now he dies; rid 'em° away! *(my brothers)*
DUCHESS Oh, what it is to have an old-cool duke
To be as slack in tongue as in performance!° *sexual performance*
FIRST JUDGE Confirmed, this be the doom irrevocable—
DUCHESS Oh!
FIRST JUDGE Tomorrow early—
DUCHESS Pray be abed, my lord.
FIRST JUDGE Your Grace much wrongs° yourself. *dishonors*
AMBITIOSO No, 'tis that tongue,
Your too much right,° does do us too much wrong. *excessive righteousness*
FIRST JUDGE Let that offender—
DUCHESS Live, and be in health.
FIRST JUDGE Be on a scaffold—
DUKE Hold, hold, my lord!
SPURIO [*aside*] Pox° on't, *(a curse); syphilis*
What makes my dad speak now?
DUKE We will defer the judgment till next sitting.
In the meantime let him be kept close prisoner.—
Guard, bear him hence.
AMBITIOSO [*aside to Junior Brother*] Brother, this makes for thee;° *helps you*
Fear not, we'll have a trick to set thee free.
JUNIOR BROTHER [*aside to Ambitioso*] Brother, I will expect it
from you both,
And in that hope I rest.
SUPERVACUO [*aside to Junior Brother*] Farewell; be merry.
Exit [Junior Brother] with a guard.
SPURIO [*aside*] Delayed, deferred!
Nay, then, if judgment have cold blood,
Flattery and bribes will kill it.
DUKE About it then, my lords, with your best powers.° *abilities*
More serious business calls upon our hours.
Exeunt. Manet° Duchess. *Remains onstage*
DUCHESS Was't ever known stepduchess was so mild
And calm as I? Some now would plot his° death *(the Duke's)*
With easy° doctors, those loose-living men, *easily bribed*
And make His withered Grace° fall to his grave *the old Duke*
And keep church better.[4]
Some second wife[5] would do this, and dispatch
Her double-loathèd lord at meat° and sleep. *food, meals*
Indeed, 'tis true an old man's twice a child.
Mine° cannot speak; one of his single words *My husband*
Would quite have freed my youngest dearest son
From death or durance,° and have made him walk *imprisonment*
With a bold foot upon the thorny law,
Whose prickles should bow under him; but 'tis not,° *it's not to be*

4. I.e., And be in better attendance at church (being buried in the graveyard) than he was during his life.

5. Many a second wife, in a position like mine.

And therefore wedlock faith shall be forgot.
I'll kill him in his forehead, hate there feed;[6]
That wound is deepest, though it never bleed.

[*Enter Spurio, not seeing her at first.*]

And here comes he whom my heart points unto:
His bastard son, but my love's true-begot.
Many a wealthy letter have I sent him,
Swelled up with jewels, and the timorous man
Is yet but coldly kind.
That jewel's mine that quivers in his ear,
Mocking his° master's chillness and vain fear. *its*
He's spied me now.

SPURIO Madam, Your Grace so private?
My duty° on your hand. [*He kisses her hand.*] *My dutiful kiss*

DUCHESS Upon my hand, sir! Troth, I think you'd fear
To kiss my hand too, if my lip stood there.

SPURIO Witness I would not, madam. [*He kisses her lips.*]

DUCHESS 'Tis a wonder,
For ceremony has made many fools.
It is as easy way unto a duchess
As to a hatted dame (if her love answer),
But that by timorous honors, pale respects,
Idle degrees of fear, men make their ways
Hard of themselves.[7] What have you thought of me?

SPURIO Madam, I ever think of you in duty,
Regard, and—

DUCHESS Pooh, upon my love, I mean.

SPURIO I would 'twere love, but 't has a fouler name
Than lust;° you are my father's wife. Your Grace *i.e., incest*
May guess now what I could call it.

DUCHESS Why, thou'rt his son but falsely.
'Tis a hard question whether he begot thee.

SPURIO I'faith, 'tis true too; I'm an uncertain man, of more uncertain woman. Maybe his groom o'th'stable begot me; you know, I know not. He could ride a horse well—a shrewd suspicion, marry.° He was wondrous tall; he had his length, i'faith, for peeping over half-shut holiday windows. Men would desire him 'light. When he was afoot, he made a goodly show under a penthouse, and when he rid, his hat would check the signs and clatter barbers' basins.[8] *by Mary (an oath)*

DUCHESS Nay, set you a-horseback once, you'll ne'er light off.

SPURIO Indeed, I am a beggar.[9]

DUCHESS That's more the sign thou'rt great.[1] But to our love:
Let it stand firm, both in thought and mind,
That the Duke was thy father, as no doubt then
He bid fair for't;° thy injury is the more, *gave it his all*

6. I'll cuckold him, and feed my hatred there.
7. A duchess (provided she is attracted to her wooer) might be seduced as easily as an ordinary gentlewoman, were it not that men are intimidated by rank and make things hard for themselves.
8. He was so tall that on horseback he was able to peer over half-shut windows like a Peeping Tom, prompting men to insist that he dismount. Even when on foot, he made quite a show under a shop awning, and when he rode, his hat would hit against the shop signs and clatter the shaving basins hung in front of barbers' shops.
9. Compare the proverb "Set a beggar on horseback, and he will never alight."
1. The Duchess jokes that many prominent men turn out, through their own extravagance, to be beggars; if Spurio is a beggar, he must be a great man.

For, had he cut thee a right diamond,[2]
Thou hadst been next set in the dukedom's ring,
When his worn self, like age's easy slave,
Had dropped out of the collet° into th'grave. *socket, jewel setting*
What wrong can equal this? Canst thou be tame
And think upon't?

SPURIO No, mad° and think upon't. *mad with anger*

DUCHESS Who would not be revenged of° such a father, *on*
E'en in the worst way? I would thank that sin
That could most injury° him, and be in league with it. *injure*
Oh, what a grief 'tis that a man should live
But once i'th'world, and then to live a bastard,
The curse o'the womb, the thief of nature,
Begot against the seventh commandment,° *(forbidding adultery)*
Half-damned in the conception by the justice
Of that unbribèd° everlasting law! *uncorrupted*

SPURIO Oh, I'd a hot-backed° devil to° my father. *horny / as*

DUCHESS Would not this mad e'en patience, make blood rough?[3]
Who but an eunuch would not sin, his bed
By one false minute disinherited?

SPURIO Ay, there's the vengeance that my birth was wrapped in.
I'll be revenged for all! Now, hate, begin;
I'll call foul incest but a venial sin.

DUCHESS Cold still? In vain then must a duchess woo?

SPURIO Madam, I blush to say what I will do.

DUCHESS Thence° flew sweet comfort. [*She kisses him.*] *i.e., From your blush*
Earnest,[4] and farewell.

SPURIO [*aside*] Oh, one incestuous kiss picks open hell!

DUCHESS Faith, now, old Duke, my vengeance shall reach high;
I'll arm thy brow with woman's heraldry.° *Exit.* *with cuckold's horns*

SPURIO Duke, thou didst do me wrong, and by thy act
Adultery is my nature.
Faith, if the truth were known, I was begot
After some gluttonous dinner; some stirring° dish *sexually arousing*
Was my first father. When deep healths° went round, *toasts*
And ladies' cheeks were painted red with wine,
Their tongues as short° and nimble as their heels, *lisping; perky*
Uttering words sweet and thick,° and, when they rose, *blurred, inarticulate*
Were merrily disposed to fall° again— *(into bed)*
In such a whisp'ring and withdrawing° hour, *(to bedchambers)*
When base male bawds kept sentinel at stair-head,
Was I stol'n° softly. Oh, damnation met *secretly begotten*
The sin of feasts, drunken adultery.
I feel it swell me; my revenge is just;
I was begot in impudent wine and lust.
Stepmother, I consent to thy desires.
I love thy mischief well, but I hate thee

2. I.e., if he had conceived you legitimately.
3. Would not this madden patience itself, and stir the blood to rage?
4. Take this kiss in earnest (as a promise of more to come).

And those three cubs, thy sons, wishing confusion,° *destruction*
Death, and disgrace may be their epitaphs.
As for my brother the Duke's only son,° *legitimate son*
Whose birth is more beholding to report° *beholden to reputation*
Than mine, and yet perhaps as falsely sown
(Women must not be trusted with their own),
I'll loose my days upon him, hate all, I.[5]
Duke, on thy brow I'll draw my bastardy.[6]
For indeed a bastard by nature should make cuckolds,
Because he is the son of a cuckold-maker. *Exit.*

[1.3]

Enter Vindice and Hippolito, Vindice in disguise to attend Lord Lussurioso, the Duke's son.

VINDICE What, brother, am I far enough from myself?[1]
HIPPOLITO As if another man had been sent whole
Into the world, and none wist° how he came. *knew*
VINDICE It will confirm me bold, the child o'th'court.° *a perfect courtier*
Let blushes dwell i'th'country.° Impudence, *away from court*
Thou goddess of the palace, mistress of mistresses,
To whom the costly perfumed people pray,
Strike thou my forehead into dauntless marble,
Mine eyes to steady sapphires! Turn° my visage, *Transform*
And, if I must needs glow,° let me blush inward, *blush*
That this immodest season° may not spy *time, age*
That scholar in my cheeks, fool-bashfulness,
That maid in the old time,° whose flush of grace *old-fashioned maiden*
Would never suffer° her to get good clothes. *allow*
Our maids° are wiser, and are less ashamed; *Maidens today*
Save° Grace the bawd, I seldom hear grace named. *Except for*
HIPPOLITO Nay, brother, you reach out o'th'verge° now.— *you go too far*
'Sfoot,° the Duke's son! Settle your looks. *By God's foot*
VINDICE Pray let me not be doubted.° *don't worry about me*

[*Enter Lussurioso.*]

HIPPOLITO My lord—
LUSSURIOSO Hippolito? [*To Vindice*] Be absent; leave us.
[*Vindice stands aside.*]
HIPPOLITO My lord, after long search, wary inquiries,
And politic siftings,° I made choice of yon fellow, *astute questioning*
Whom I guess rare° for many deep employments; *outstanding*
This our age swims within him, and if Time
Had so much hair, I should take him for Time,[2]
He is so near kin to this present minute.
LUSSURIOSO 'Tis enough.

5. I'll devote all my time and energy to pursuing him and hating everyone.
6. I'll give you, Duke, cuckold's horns in revenge for my bastardy.
1.3. The court.
1. Am I sufficiently disguised?
2. The corrupt ways of our times are second nature to him, and if Time were not bald behind, like Opportunity or Occasion (see 1.1.55 and note, and 1.1.99–100), I would mistake him for Time. (In order to deceive Lussurioso into hiring Vindice as a villain, Hippolito implies that Vindice is an opportunist. Presumably Vindice has a full head of hair.)

We thank thee; yet words are but great men's blanks;° *worthless vouchers*
Gold, though it be dumb, does utter the best thanks.
[*He gives Hippolito money.*]
HIPPOLITO Your plenteous Honor!—An excellent fellow, my lord.
LUSSURIOSO So, give us leave.° *leave us*
[*Exit Hippolito; Vindice approaches.*]
Welcome. Be not far off; we must be better
Acquainted. Push!° Be bold with us; thy hand. *Pish!*
VINDICE With all my heart, i'faith. [*They embrace.*] How
dost, sweet musk-cat?° *i.e., perfumed fop*
When shall we lie together?
LUSSURIOSO [*aside*] Wondrous knave!
Gather him into boldness?[3] 'Sfoot, the slave's
Already as familiar as an ague,° *fever*
And shakes me[4] at his pleasure.—Friend, I can
Forget myself° in private, but elsewhere, *i.e., my social station*
I pray, do you remember me.° *remember who I am*
VINDICE Oh, very well, sir. I conster° myself saucy. *construe, understand*
LUSSURIOSO What hast been, of what profession?
VINDICE A bonesetter.
LUSSURIOSO A bonesetter?
VINDICE A bawd, my lord, one that sets bones together.° *i.e., acts as a pander*
LUSSURIOSO Notable bluntness!
Fit, fit for me, e'en trained up to my hand.°— *to serve my purposes*
Thou hast been scrivener° to much knavery, then? *i.e., confidant, agent*
VINDICE Fool to abundance,[5] sir. I have been witness to the surrenders of a thousand virgins, and not so little.° I have seen patrimonies washed a-pieces, fruit fields turned into bastards, and, in a world of acres, not so much dust due to the heir 'twas left to as would well gravel a petition.[6] *and even more*
LUSSURIOSO [*aside*] Fine villain! Troth, I like him wondrously.
He's e'en shaped for my purpose.—Then thou know'st
I'th'world strange lust?
VINDICE Oh, Dutch lust,[7] fulsome lust!
Drunken procreation, which begets so many drunkards.
Some father dreads not (gone to bed in wine)
To slide from the mother and cling° the daughter-in-law; *embrace*
Some uncles are adulterous with their nieces,
Brothers with brothers' wives. Oh, hour of incest!
Any kin now, next to the rim° o'th'sister, *womb; outer limit*
Is man's meat in these days; and in the morning
When they are up and dressed, and their mask° on, *(for sun protection)*
Who can perceive this, save that eternal eye
That sees through flesh and all? Well, if anything
Be damned, it will be twelve o'clock at night;
That twelve will never scape;
It is the Judas of the hours,[8] wherein

3. I.e., Did I think I needed to encourage him to be familiar with me?
4. (1) Shakes hands with me; (2) shakes me like a fever.
5. I have played the accessory, the fool, to rich folk and their abundant knavery.
6. I have seen inheritances washed away in drunken license, orchards sold to pay for sexual pleasure, and land sold until not even enough dirt remained to sprinkle as ink-drying sand on a petition to recover the lost property. (Sand was used as an ink blotter.)
7. Drunken lust. (The Dutch and Germans were much satirized for their heavy drinking.)
8. Midnight is considered the hour of betrayal, just as Judas, one of the twelve disciples, betrayed Jesus to the Jewish chief priests, according to the Gospels.

Honest salvation is betrayed to sin.
LUSSURIOSO In troth it is, too; but let this talk glide.° *pass to another topic*
It is our blood° to err, though hell gaped loud; *passionate nature*
Ladies know Lucifer fell, yet still are proud.
Now, sir, wert thou as secret as thou'rt subtle,
And deeply fathomed into° all estates,° *acquainted with / sorts*
I would embrace thee for a near° employment, *of intimate concern*
And thou shouldst swell in money, and be able
To make lame beggars crouch to thee.
VINDICE My lord,
Secret? I ne'er had that disease o'th'mother,° *blabbing; hysteria*
I praise° my father. Why are men made close,° *thank / secret*
But to keep thoughts in best? I grant you this:
Tell but some woman a secret overnight,
Your doctor may find it in the urinal i'th'morning.
But, my lord—
LUSSURIOSO So, thou'rt confirmed in me,° *in my trust*
And thus I enter thee.° [*He gives Vindice money.*] *take you to me*
VINDICE This Indian devil[9]
Will quickly enter any man—but a usurer;
He prevents that by ent'ring the devil first.
LUSSURIOSO Attend me; I am past my depth in lust,
And I must swim or drown. All my desires
Are leveled° at a virgin not far from court, *aimed*
To whom I have conveyed by messenger
Many waxed lines,° full of my neatest spirit,[1] *sealed letters*
And jewels that were° able to ravish her *should have been*
Without the help of man; all which and more
She, foolish-chaste, sent back, the messengers
Receiving frowns for answers.
VINDICE Possible?° *Is that possible?*
'Tis a rare phoenix, whoe'er she be.[2]
If your desires be such, she so repugnant,° *resistant*
In troth, my lord, I'd be revenged and marry her.
LUSSURIOSO Push!
The dowry of her blood° and of her fortunes *family*
Are both too mean°—good enough to be bad withal.[3] *inferior, lowly*
I'm one of that number can defend[4]
Marriage is good, yet rather keep a friend.° *lover*
Give me my bed by stealth; there's true delight.
What breeds a loathing in't but night by° night? *after*
VINDICE [*aside*] A very fine religion!
LUSSURIOSO Therefore thus:
I'll trust thee in the business of my heart
Because I see thee well experienced
In this luxurious day° wherein we breathe. *lecherous time*
Go thou, and with a smooth enchanting tongue
Bewitch her ears and cozen° her of all grace. *cheat*
Enter upon the portion° of her soul, *dowry*
Her honor, which she calls her chastity,

9. I.e., gold from the Indies.
1. My most intense feeling.
2. In her unique virtue, the virgin that Lussurioso desires is compared to the phoenix, a legendary bird, only one of which was believed to live at a time.
3. Worthy only to be the object of lust.
4. I am one of those who are ready to argue that.

And bring it into expense,° for honesty *make her spend it*
Is like a stock of money laid to sleep,
Which, ne'er so little broke,° does never keep. *broken open*
VINDICE You have giv'n 't the tang,° i'faith, my lord. *expressed its essence*
Make known the lady to me, and my brain
Shall swell with strange invention; I will move it° *urge your suit*
Till I expire with speaking, and drop down
Without a word to save me;° but I'll work— *a final prayer*
LUSSURIOSO We thank thee, and will raise° thee. Receive her name: it is the only daughter to Madam Gratiana, the late widow.° *advance* *recently widowed*
VINDICE [*aside*] Oh, my sister, my sister!
LUSSURIOSO Why dost walk aside?
VINDICE My lord, I was thinking how I might begin, as thus: "O lady"—or twenty hundred devices her very bodkin° will put a man in.[5] *hairpin*
LUSSURIOSO Ay, or the wagging of her hair.
VINDICE No, that shall put you in, my lord.[6]
LUSSURIOSO Shall't? Why, content. Dost know the daughter, then?
VINDICE Oh, excellent well by sight.
LUSSURIOSO That was her brother that did prefer° thee to us. *recommend*
VINDICE My lord, I think so; I knew I had seen him somewhere—
LUSSURIOSO And therefore prithee let thy heart to him
Be as a virgin, close.° *secret*
VINDICE Oh, my good lord!
LUSSURIOSO We may laugh at that simple age within him.[7]
VINDICE Ha, ha, ha!
LUSSURIOSO Himself being made the subtle instrument
To wind up° a good fellow— *involve, incite*
VINDICE That's I, my lord.
LUSSURIOSO That's thou—
To entice and work° his sister. *prevail on*
VINDICE A pure novice!
LUSSURIOSO 'Twas finely managed.
VINDICE Gallantly carried.° *managed*
[*Aside*] A pretty-perfumed° villain! *(see 1.3.34)*
LUSSURIOSO I've bethought me:
If she prove chaste still and immovable,
Venture upon the mother, and with gifts,
As I will furnish thee, begin with her.
VINDICE Oh, fie, fie, that's the wrong end, my lord. 'Tis mere° impossible that a mother by any gifts should become a bawd to her own daughter! *simply*
LUSSURIOSO Nay, then, I see thou'rt but a puny° in the subtle mystery of a woman. Why, 'tis held now no dainty dish. *novice*
The name° *The name of "bawd"*
Is so in league with age° that nowadays *mature years*
It does eclipse three-quarters of a mother.

5. Will prompt a man how to begin.
6. Vindice playfully changes his own "put a man in" (line 130) to emphasize a sexual meaning: The suggestive wagging of her hair (line 131) will arouse you and put *you* in as her sexual partner, my lord, not me.
7. We may laugh at Hippolito's youthful gullibility. (Lussurioso instructs Vindice not to confide in Hippolito, since he is Castiza's brother.)

VINDICE Does't so, my lord?
Let me alone,° then, to eclipse the fourth. *Leave it to me*
LUSSURIOSO Why, well said! Come, I'll furnish thee, but first
Swear to be true in all.
VINDICE True?
LUSSURIOSO Nay, but swear.
VINDICE Swear?
I hope Your Honor little doubts my faith.
LUSSURIOSO Yet for my humor's° sake, 'cause I love swearing. *whimsy's*
VINDICE 'Cause you love swearing, 'slud,° I will. *by God's blood*
LUSSURIOSO Why, enough.
Ere long look to be made of better stuff.° *wealthier*
VINDICE That will do well, indeed, my lord.
LUSSURIOSO Attend° me. *Follow, wait on*
[*Exit.*]
VINDICE Oh,
Now let me burst! I've eaten noble poison.
We are made strange fellows,° brother, innocent villains. *accomplices*
Wilt not be angry when thou hear'st on't, think'st thou?
I'faith, thou shalt. Swear me to foul° my sister! *debauch*
Sword, I durst make a promise of him to thee;
Thou shalt disheir him;[8] it shall be thine honor.
And yet, now angry froth is down° in me, *subsided*
It would not prove the meanest policy° *worst stratagem*
In this disguise to try the faith of both;° *(mother and sister)*
Another might have had the selfsame office,° *assignment*
Some slave,° that would have wrought effectually, *villain*
Ay, and perhaps o'erwrought° 'em. Therefore I, *prevailed on*
Being thought traveled, will apply myself
Unto the selfsame form,[9] forget my nature,
As if no part about me were kin to 'em,
So touch° 'em—though I durst almost for good *test*
Venture my lands in heaven upon their blood.[1] *Exit.*

[1.4]

Enter the discontented Lord Antonio, whose wife the Duchess's youngest son ravished; he discovering[1] *the body of her dead to certain lords* [*including Piero*] *and Hippolito.*

ANTONIO Draw nearer, lords, and be sad witnesses
Of a fair comely building newly fall'n,
Being falsely undermined. Violent rape
Has played a glorious act. Behold, my lords,
A sight that strikes man out of me.° *unmans me*
PIERO That virtuous lady!
ANTONIO Precedent° for wives! *Example*
HIPPOLITO The blush° of many women, whose chaste presence *blush of rebuke*
Would e'en call shame up to their cheeks and make

8. You, my sword, will make him no longer heir (by killing him).
9. Vindice resolves to adopt the "form," i.e., shape or guise, of the "slave" in line 179; since he is presumed to be away on his travels (see 1.1.116–17), he will succeed in passing himself off to his mother and sister as a stranger.
1. Though I would almost dare to risk, once and for all (or, in the name of virtue), my hopes of eternal salvation on their chaste temperament.
1.4. The court.
1. Revealing by pulling back a curtain.

Pale wanton sinners have good colors.° *blush for shame*
ANTONIO Dead!
Her honor first drunk poison, and her life,
Being fellows in one house, did pledge her honor.[2]
PIERO Oh, grief of many!
ANTONIO I marked not this before:
A prayer book the pillow to her cheek—
This was her rich confection°—and another *spiritual medicine*
Placed in her right hand, with a leaf tucked up,
Pointing to these words:
"Melius virtute mori quam per dedecus vivere."[3]
True and effectual it is indeed.
HIPPOLITO My lord, since you invite us to° your sorrows, *to share*
Let's truly taste 'em, that with equal comfort
As to ourselves° we may relieve your wrongs. *As if the cause were ours*
We have grief too, that yet walks without tongue:
"Curae leves loquuntur, maiores stupent."[4]
ANTONIO You deal with truth,° my lord. *speak truly*
Lend me but your attentions, and I'll cut
Long grief into short words. Last reveling night,
When torchlight made an artificial noon
About the court, some courtiers in the masque,
Putting on better faces° than their own, *masks*
Being full of fraud and flattery—amongst whom
The Duchess' youngest son, that moth to honor,° *i.e., eater of honor*
Filled up a room°—and with long lust to eat *place*
Into my wearing,° amongst all the ladies *i.e., my wife's honor*
Singled out that dear form,° who ever lived *(my wife)*
As cold in lust as she is now in death
(Which that stepduchess' monster° knew too well); *monstrous son*
And therefore, in the height of all the revels,
When music was heard loud'st, courtiers busiest,
And ladies great with laughter—oh, vicious minute,
Unfit but for relation to be spoke of![5]—
Then with a face more impudent than his vizard
He harried° her amidst a throng of panders *violated*
That live upon damnation of both kinds,[6]
And fed the ravenous vulture of his lust.
Oh, death to think on't! She, her honor forced,
Deemed it a nobler dowry for her name
To die with poison than to live with shame.
HIPPOLITO A wondrous lady, of rare fire compact![7]
She's made her name an empress by that act.
PIERO My lord, what judgment follows the offender?
ANTONIO Faith, none, my lord; it cools and is deferred.
PIERO Delay the doom° for rape? *sentencing*
ANTONIO Oh, you must note who 'tis should die:
The Duchess' son. She'll look to be a saver.° *(of her son's life)*

2. After her honor was forced to drink the poison of Junior Brother's rape, her life, as a fellow inhabitant of her body, drank literal poison (and died), thus matching her honor drink for drink.
3. Better to die in virtue than live in shame.
4. Small cares speak, great ones remain silent. (Seneca, *Hippolytus*, line 607.)
5. Unfit to mention, were it not for my need to tell this story!
6. Who sin in their own persons and corrupt others as well.
7. Composed of the most ethereal and chaste qualities!

Judgment in this age is near kin to favor.° *influence, favoritism*

HIPPOLITO Nay, then, step forth, thou bribeless officer.

[*He draws his sword.*]

I bind you all in steel to bind you surely;
Here let your oaths meet, to be kept and paid,
Which else will stick like rust and shame the blade.
Strengthen my vow, that if, at the next sitting° *court session*
Judgment speak all in gold° and spare the blood *is influenced by money*
Of such a serpent, e'en before their seats
To let his soul out,[8] which long since was found
Guilty in heaven.

ALL We swear it and will act it.

ANTONIO Kind gentlemen, I thank you in mine ire.

HIPPOLITO 'Twere pity
The ruins of so fair a monument° *(Antonio's wife's corpse)*
Should not be dipped in the defacer's blood.

PIERO Her funeral shall be wealthy, for her name
Merits a tomb of pearl. My lord Antonio,
For this time wipe your lady from your eyes;
No doubt our grief and yours may one day court it,° *be seen at court*
When we are more familiar with revenge.

ANTONIO That is my comfort, gentlemen, and I joy
In this one happiness above the rest,
Which will be called a miracle at last:
That being an old man, I'd a wife so chaste. *Exeunt.*

2.1

Enter Castiza, the sister.

CASTIZA How hardly° shall that maiden be beset *severely*
Whose only fortunes are her constant thoughts,
That has no other child's part° but her honor *share of inheritance*
That keeps her low and empty in estate!
Maids and their honors are like poor beginners;
Were not sin rich, there would be fewer sinners.[1]
Why had not virtue a revenue? Well,
I know the cause: 'twould have impoverished hell.

[*Enter Dondolo.*]

How now, Dondolo?

DONDOLO Madonna, there is one—as they say, a thing of flesh and blood, a man, I take him, by his beard—that would very desirously mouth to mouth with you.

CASTIZA What's that?

DONDOLO Show his teeth in your company.

CASTIZA I understand thee not.

DONDOLO Why, speak with you, madonna.

CASTIZA Why, say so, madman, and cut off a great deal of dirty way.° Had it not been better spoke in ordinary words, that one would speak with me? *muddy path; tediousness*

8. Vow to kill the Duchess's youngest son in the very presence of those sitting justices who have corruptly let him off.

2.1. Gratiana's house, not far from court.

1. Without the temptation of great wealth, few persons would sin.

DONDOLO Ha, ha! That's as ordinary as two shillings. I would strive a little to show myself in my place;° a gentleman-usher scorns to use the phrase and fancy° of a servingman. *office, rank* / *idiom*

CASTIZA Yours be your own,[2] sir. Go direct him hither.

[*Exit Dondolo.*]

I hope some happy tidings from my brother,
That lately traveled, whom my soul affects.° *loves*
Here he comes.

Enter Vindice, her brother, disguised.

VINDICE Lady, the best of wishes to your sex:
Fair skins and new gowns. [*He presents a letter to her.*]
CASTIZA Oh, they° shall thank you, sir. *(other women)*
Whence this?
VINDICE Oh, from a dear and worthy friend,
Mighty!
CASTIZA From whom?
VINDICE The Duke's son.
CASTIZA Receive that!

A box o'th'ear to her brother.

I swore I'd put anger in my hand,
And pass the virgin limits of myself[3]
To him that next appeared in that base office,
To be his° sin's attorney. Bear to him *(Lussurioso's)*
That figure of my hate upon thy cheek
Whilst 'tis yet hot, and I'll reward thee for't.
Tell him my honor shall have a rich name
When several harlots shall share his with shame.
Farewell. Commend me to him in my hate. *Exit.*
VINDICE It is the sweet'st box[4] that e'er my nose came nigh,
The finest drawnwork cuff[5] that e'er was worn!
I'll love this blow forever, and this cheek
Shall still henceforward take the wall of this.[6]
Oh, I'm above my tongue!° Most constant sister, *i.e., speechless*
In this thou hast right honorable shown.
Many are called by their honor° that have none; *addressed as "honorable"*
Thou art approved forever in my thoughts.
It is not in the power of words to taint thee!
And yet, for the salvation of my oath,° *(see 1.3.147–65)*
As my resolve in that point, I will lay
Hard siege unto my mother, though I know
A Siren's tongue could not bewitch her so.[7]
Mass,° fitly here she comes. Thanks, my disguise! *By the Mass*

[*Enter the Mother, Gratiana.*]

Madam, good afternoon.
MOTHER You're welcome, sir.

2. Choose the phrases that best suit you. (Said with decorous irony.)
3. And exceed the limits of decorum normally restraining a virgin like myself.
4. Box on the ear, but also with the suggestion of a box of sweet-smelling fragrance.
5. Blow, but also suggesting a decorated sleeve cuff and perhaps female genitalia.
6. To "take the wall" is literally to take the safer and cleaner place on a street, next to the wall; hence, here, Vindice yields precedence and honor to the cheek that has suffered this gratifying blow.
7. The Sirens were mythological creatures whose bewitching singing lured sailors to their destruction on rocks.

VINDICE The next° of Italy commends him to you, *heir apparent*
Our mighty expectation, the Duke's son.
[*He presents a letter to her.*]
MOTHER I think myself much honored that he pleases
To rank° me in his thoughts. *place*
VINDICE So may you, lady:
One that is like to be our sudden° duke— *is likely soon to be our*
The crown gapes for him every tide°—and then *hour*
Commander o'er us all. Do but think on him.
How blest were they now that could pleasure him
E'en with anything almost!
MOTHER Ay, save their honor.° *chastity*
VINDICE Tut, one would let a little of that go too,
And ne'er be seen° in't; ne'er be seen in't, mark you. *And be unobserved*
I'd wink° and let it go— *shut the eyes*
MOTHER Marry, but I would not.
VINDICE Marry, but I would, I hope; I know you would too,
If you'd that blood° now which you gave your daughter. *passion; lineage*
To her indeed 'tis this wheel° comes about; *wheel of Fortune*
That man that must be all this,° perhaps ere morning *must be duke*
(For his white° father does but mold away), *white-haired*
Has long desired your daughter.
MOTHER Desired?
VINDICE Nay, but hear me:
He desires now that will command hereafter.
Therefore be wise. I speak as more a friend
To you than him. Madam, I know you're poor,
And, 'lack the day,° *alas*
There are too many poor ladies already.
Why should you vex° the number? 'Tis despised. *worsen by adding to*
Live wealthy; rightly understand the world,
And chide away that foolish country girl
Keeps° company with your daughter: chastity. *Who keeps*
MOTHER Oh, fie, fie!
The riches of the world cannot hire a mother
To such a most unnatural task!
VINDICE No, but a thousand angels[8] can.
Men have no power; angels must work you to't.
The world descends into such baseborn evils
That forty angels can make fourscore devils.
There will be fools still, I perceive, still fools.
Would I be poor, dejected,° scorned of greatness, *humbled in fortune*
Swept from the palace, and see other daughters
Spring with the dew o'th'court, having mine own° *my own daughter*
So much desired and loved by the Duke's son?
No, I would raise my state° upon her breast *estate, status*
And call her eyes my tenants.[9] I would count
My yearly maintenance° upon her cheeks, *allowance*
Take coach upon her lip, and all her parts
Should keep men after men,° and I would ride *lots of servants*
In pleasure upon pleasure.
You took great pains for her, once when it was;° *once upon a time*

8. (1) Gold coins; (2) evil angels or devils.
9. I would gain wealth through her beautiful eyes, as if they were rent-paying tenants.

Let her requite it now, though it be but some.° *only in part*
You brought her forth; she may well bring you home.° *i.e., enrich you*
MOTHER O heavens!
This overcomes me.
VINDICE [*aside*] Not, I hope, already?
MOTHER [*aside*] It is too strong for me. Men know, that know us,[1]
We are so weak their words can overthrow us.
He touched me nearly, made my virtues bate,° *abate, weaken*
When his tongue struck upon° my poor estate. *spoke of*
VINDICE [*aside*] I e'en quake to proceed. My spirit turns edge.° *loses its keenness*
I fear me she's unmothered,° yet I'll venture. *made unmotherly*
That woman is all male whom none can enter.[2]
[*To her*] What think you now, lady? Speak. Are you wiser?
What said Advancement to you? Thus it said:
"The daughter's fall lifts up the mother's head."
Did it not, madam? But I'll swear it does,
In many places. Tut, this age fears° no man; *frightens, daunts*
'Tis no shame to be bad, because 'tis common.
MOTHER Ay, that's the comfort on't.
VINDICE The comfort on't?
I keep the best for last. Can these persuade you
To forget heaven—and— [*He gives her money.*]
MOTHER Ay, these are they—
VINDICE [*aside*] Oh!
MOTHER That enchant our sex,
These are the means that govern our affections.
That woman
Will not be troubled with the mother[3] long
That sees the comfortable shine of you.° *i.e., gold*
I blush to think what for your sakes I'll do.
VINDICE [*aside*] O suff'ring heaven, with thy invisible finger
E'en at this instant turn the precious side
Of both mine eyeballs inward, not to see myself!
MOTHER Look you, sir.
VINDICE Holla!
MOTHER [*tipping him*] Let this thank your pains.° *efforts*
VINDICE Oh, you're a kind madam.° *matron; bawd*
MOTHER I'll see how I can move.° *persuade*
VINDICE Your words will sting.
MOTHER If she be still chaste, I'll ne'er call her mine.
VINDICE [*aside*] Spoke truer than you meant it.
MOTHER [*calling*] Daughter Castiza!

[*Enter Castiza.*]

CASTIZA Madam?
VINDICE Oh, she's yonder; meet her.
[*Aside*] Troops of celestial soldiers guard her heart!
Yon dam° has devils enough to take her part. *(My mother)*
CASTIZA Madam, what makes° yon evil-officed man *does*
In presence of you?
MOTHER Why?

1. Who know us for what we are.
2. Any woman a man cannot seduce is no longer a woman. ("Enter" suggests sexual penetration.)
3. (1) Motherly feeling; (2) hysteria (cf. 1.3.79).

CASTIZA He lately brought
Immodest writing sent from the Duke's son
To tempt me to dishonorable act.
MOTHER Dishonorable act? Good honorable fool,
That wouldst be honest° 'cause thou wouldst be so, *chaste*
Producing no one reason but thy will!
And't° has a good report, prettily commended; *And chastity*
But pray, by whom? Mean° people, ignorant people. *Inferior*
The better sort, I'm sure, cannot abide it,
And by what rule should we square out° our lives *frame, plan*
But by our betters' actions? Oh, if thou knew'st
What 'twere to lose it,° thou would never keep it. *(chastity)*
But there's a cold curse laid upon all maids;
Whilst others clip° the sun, they clasp the shades. *embrace*
Virginity is Paradise locked up.
You cannot come by yourselves° without fee, *be fully yourselves*
And 'twas decreed that man should keep the key.
Deny advancement? Treasure? The Duke's son?
CASTIZA I cry you mercy, lady, I mistook you.
Pray, did you see my mother? Which way went she?
Pray God I have not lost her.[4]
VINDICE [*aside*] Prettily put by.° *parried*
MOTHER Are you as proud to me as coy to him?
Do you not know me now?
CASTIZA Why, are you she?
The world's so changed, one shape into another,
It is a wise child now that knows her mother.
VINDICE [*aside*] Most right, i'faith.
MOTHER I owe your cheek my hand° *I ought to slap you*
For that presumption now, but I'll forget it.
Come, you shall leave those childish 'haviors,
And understand your time.° Fortunes flow to you; *opportunity*
What, will you be a girl?
If all feared drowning that spy waves ashore,° *from the shore*
Gold would grow rich, and all the merchants poor.[5]
CASTIZA It is a pretty saying of° a wicked one, *by*
But methinks now
It does not show so well out of your mouth;
Better in his.
VINDICE [*aside*] Faith, bad enough in both,
Were I in earnest, as I'll seem no less.
[*Aloud*] I wonder, lady, your own mother's words
Cannot be taken,° nor stand in full force. *taken at face value*
'Tis honesty° you urge; what's honesty? *chastity*
'Tis but heaven's beggar;° and what woman *virtuous poverty*
Is so foolish to keep honesty
And be not able to keep° herself? No, *support, maintain*
Times are grown wiser and will keep less charge;[6]
A maid that has small portion° now intends° *dowry / decides*
To break up house and live upon her friends.

4. Castiza speaks with heavy irony.
5. Wealth would pile up unused for lack of merchant-venturing.
6. (1) Will incur fewer costs; (2) will care less about virtue.

How blest are you! You have happiness alone;
Others° must fall° to thousands, you to one, — *Other women / yield*
Sufficient in himself to make your forehead
Dazzle the world with jewels, and petitionary people° — *courtiers urging suits*
Start° at your presence. — *Jump up obediently*

MOTHER Oh, if I were young,
I should be ravished!° — *dazzled; seduced*

CASTIZA Ay, to lose your honor.

VINDICE 'Slid,° how can you lose your honor — *By God's eyelid*
To deal with my lord's grace?° — *my gracious lord*
He'll add more honor to it by his title.
Your mother will tell you how.

MOTHER That I will.

VINDICE Oh, think upon the pleasure of the palace:
Securèd ease and state;° the stirring° meats — *social status / arousing*
Ready to move out of the dishes
That e'en now quicken when they're eaten;[7]
Banquets abroad° by torchlight; music, sports; — *outdoors*
Bareheaded vassals, that had ne'er the fortune
To keep on their own hats, but let horns wear 'em;[8]
Nine coaches waiting—hurry, hurry, hurry!

CASTIZA Ay, to the devil.

VINDICE [*aside*] Ay, to the devil.—To th'Duke, by my faith.

MOTHER Ay, to the Duke. Daughter, you'd scorn to think
o'th'devil an° you were there once. — *if*

VINDICE [*aside*] True, for most there are as proud
As he° for his heart, i'faith. — *(the devil)*
[*To Castiza*] Who'd sit at home in a neglected room,
Dealing her short-lived beauty to the pictures[9]
That are as useless as old men, when those
Poorer in face and fortune than herself
Walk with a hundred acres on their backs,[1]
Fair meadows cut into green foreparts[2]—Oh,
It was the greatest blessing ever happened to women
When farmers' sons agreed, and met again,° — *agreed in concert*
To wash their hands and come up gentlemen;[3]
The commonwealth has flourished ever since.
Lands that were mete by the rod,[4] that labor's spared;
Tailors ride down and measure 'em by the yard.[5]
Fair trees, those comely foretops° of the field, — *tall trees; forelocks*
Are cut to maintain head-tires°—much untold.[6] — *headdresses*
All thrives but Chastity; she lies a-cold.
Nay, shall I come nearer to you?° Mark but this: — *press the point*
Why are there so few honest women, but° because 'tis the — *unless*

7. That are replenished as soon as eaten, with ingredients so fresh that they seem alive still, with the power to sexually arouse those who consume them.
8. Persons of inferior social rank standing bareheaded in the presence of their superiors and thus revealing themselves, by their cuckolds' horns, to be the husbands of unfaithful wives.
9. Making use of her beauty of youth only by (1) being fruitlessly pictured in a painting; or (2) by sharing her beauty with those painted representations of other women.
1. Wear clothes costing the value of a hundred acres of land.
2. Meadows having been sold to pay for "foreparts," or stomachers worn under the bodice. (Suggesting also the park in front of a manor house.)
3. To abandon their farms for the life of courtiers and come up to London in order to become gentlemen.
4. Lands that were measured out in length of rods (5½ yards each) or in area (160 rods to the acre).
5. Tailors, riding down from London, invade the countryside and turn land into clothes.
6. (1) Countless; (2) much more might be said.

poorer profession? That's accounted best that's best followed; least in trade,° least in fashion; and that's not honesty, believe it.[7] And do but note the low and dejected° price of it: *in demand* / *depressed*
Lose but a pearl, we search and cannot brook it,° *bear its loss*
But that° once gone, who is so mad to look° it? *(chastity) / look for*

MOTHER Troth, he says true.

CASTIZA False! I defy you both.
I have endured you with an ear of fire;° *with blushes*
Your tongues have struck hot irons on my face.
Mother, come from that poisonous woman there![8]

MOTHER Where?

CASTIZA Do you not see her? She's too inward,° then. *interior; invisible*
[*To Vindice*] Slave, perish in thy office!—You heavens, please
Henceforth to make the mother a disease,
Which first begins with me, yet I've outgone you.[9] *Exit.*

VINDICE [*aside*] O angels, clap your wings upon the skies,
And give this virgin crystal plaudities!° *heavenly applause*

MOTHER Peevish, coy, foolish! But return this answer:
My lord shall be most welcome when his pleasure
Conducts him this way. I will sway mine own;° *my daughter*
Women with women can work best alone. *Exit.*

VINDICE Indeed, I'll tell him so.
Oh, more uncivil, more unnatural
Than those base-titled creatures that look downward![1]
Why does not heaven turn black, or with a frown
Undo the world? Why does not earth start up
And strike the sins that tread upon't? Oh,
Were't not for gold and women, there would be no damnation;
Hell would look like a lord's great kitchen without fire in't.
But 'twas decreed before the world began
That they should be the hooks to catch at man. *Exit.*

[2.2]

Enter Lussurioso with Hippolito, Vindice's brother.

LUSSURIOSO I much applaud thy judgment. Thou
Art well read in a fellow,[1]
And 'tis the deepest art to study man.
I know this, which I never learnt in schools:
The world's divided into knaves and fools.

HIPPOLITO [*aside*] "Knave" in your face, my lord, behind your back.

LUSSURIOSO And I much thank thee that thou hast preferred° *recommended*
A fellow of discourse—well mingled,° *with many qualities*
And whose brain time hath seasoned.

HIPPOLITO True, my lord.
[*Aside*] We shall find season once,[2] I hope. Oh, villain!
To make such an unnatural slave of me! But—

LUSSURIOSO Mass, here he comes.

7. And believe me, chastity is not what is most in fashion.
8. Separate your better self from the go-between or procuress that your actions too much resemble.
9. Castiza, feeling herself near hysteria, implores the heavens to forgive her excess of emotion and to recognize a vital distinction between this kind of virtuous panic and "the mother," a common synonym for hysteria (see 1.3.79 and line 128 above) but now associated in Castiza's mind with her morally corrupt mother.
1. Than the animals, which do not stand upright!
2.2. The court.
1. You are skillful in interpreting human behavior.
2. We will find a time to settle matters with you.

[*Enter Vindice, disguised.*]

HIPPOLITO [*aside to Vindice*] And now shall I have free leave
to depart.
LUSSURIOSO [*to Hippolito*] Your absence;° leave us. — *Be absent*
HIPPOLITO [*aside to Vindice*] Are not my thoughts true?
I must remove, but, brother, you may stay.
Heart, we are both made bawds a new-found way! *Exit.*
LUSSURIOSO Now we're an even number; a third man's
dangerous,
Especially her brother. Say, be free:° — *candid*
Have I a pleasure toward?° — *in prospect*
VINDICE Oh, my lord!
LUSSURIOSO Ravish me in thine answer. Art thou rare?° — *i.e., Did you succeed?*
Hast thou beguiled her of salvation,
And rubbed hell o'er with honey? Is she a woman?
VINDICE In all but in desire.
LUSSURIOSO Then she's in nothing.
I bate in courage° now. — *slacken in desire*
VINDICE The words I brought° — *brought to her*
Might well have made indifferent-honest naught;
A right good woman in these days is changed
Into white money° with less labor far. — *silver*
Many a maid has turned to Mahomet° — *Muhammad*
With easier working. I durst undertake
Upon the pawn and forfeit of my life
With half those words to flat° a Puritan's wife. — *i.e., seduce*
But she is close° and good. Yet 'tis a doubt — *Castiza is strict*
By this time—Oh, the mother, the mother!
LUSSURIOSO I never thought their sex had been a wonder
Until this minute. What fruit° from the mother? — *results*
VINDICE [*aside*] Now must I blister my soul, be forsworn,
Or shame the woman that received me first.° — *gave birth to me*
I will be true; thou liv'st not to proclaim;[3]
Spoke to a dying man, shame has no shame.[4]
[*To Lussurioso*] My lord!
LUSSURIOSO Who's that?[5]
VINDICE Here's none but I, my lord.
LUSSURIOSO What would thy haste utter?
VINDICE Comfort.
LUSSURIOSO Welcome.
VINDICE The maid being dull, having no mind to travel
Into unknown lands, what did me I straight° — *did I do at once*
But set spurs to the mother—golden spurs,
Will° put her to a false gallop in a trice. — *That will*
LUSSURIOSO Is't possible that in this
The mother should be damned before the daughter?
VINDICE Oh, that's good manners, my lord. The mother, for
her age, must go foremost,° you know. — *Age before beauty*
LUSSURIOSO Thou'st spoke that true. But where comes in
this comfort?

3. I will keep my word to test my mother and Castiza (see 1.3.160–85); you, Lussurioso, won't live long enough to be able to boast of your conquest.
4. Since Lussurioso is condemned to die, my otherwise shameful action is not shameful.
5. Lussurioso, absorbed in his thoughts, is surprised by Vindice's sudden speaking.

VINDICE In a fine place, my lord. The unnatural mother
Did with her tongue so hard beset her° honor *(Castiza's)*
That the poor fool° was struck to silent wonder. *innocent*
Yet still the maid, like an unlighted taper,
Was cold and chaste, save that her mother's breath
Did blow fire on her cheeks. The girl departed,
But the good ancient madam, half mad, threw me
These promising words, which I took deeply note of:
"My lord shall be most welcome—"
LUSSURIOSO Faith, I thank her.
VINDICE "When his pleasure conducts him this way."
LUSSURIOSO That shall be soon, i'faith.
VINDICE "I will sway mine own."
LUSSURIOSO She does the wiser; I commend her for't.
VINDICE "Women with women can work best alone."
LUSSURIOSO By this light, and so they can, give 'em their due; men are not comparable to 'em.
VINDICE No, that's true, for you shall have one woman knit more in an hour than any man can ravel° again in seven-and-twenty year. *unravel*
LUSSURIOSO Now my desires are happy; I'll make 'em freemen° now. *give them free rein*
Thou art a precious fellow; faith, I love thee.
Be wise and make it thy revenue: beg, leg.° *make a leg, bow*
What office couldst thou be ambitious for?
VINDICE Office, my lord? Marry, if I might have my wish, I would have one that was never begged yet.
LUSSURIOSO Nay, then, thou canst have none.[6]
VINDICE Yes, my lord, I could pick out another office yet, nay, and keep a horse and drab upon't.[7]
LUSSURIOSO Prithee, good bluntness, tell me.
VINDICE Why, I would desire but this, my lord: to have all the fees behind the arras, and all the farthingales that fall plump about twelve o'clock at night upon the rushes.[8]
LUSSURIOSO Thou'rt a mad apprehensive° knave. Dost think to make any great purchase° of that? *quick-apprehending* / *profit*
VINDICE Oh, 'tis an unknown thing,° my lord; I wonder 't has been missed so long. *missed opportunity*
LUSSURIOSO Well,
This night I'll visit her, and 'tis till then
A year in my desires. Farewell. Attend;
Trust me with thy preferment.
VINDICE My loved lord!
Exit [Lussurioso].
[Vindice draws his sword.]
Oh, shall I kill him o'th'wrong side° now? No! *from the back*
Sword, thou wast never a backbiter[9] yet.
I'll pierce him to his face; he shall die looking upon me.
Thy° veins are swelled with lust; this shall unfill 'em. *(Lussurioso's)*

6. I.e., No place at court was ever gotten without begging.
7. And maintain a horse and mistress on the income.
8. Vindice whimsically proposes to get rich on all the chicanery and fees connected with assignations conducted behind wall hangings, with the unfastening of hooped petticoats and the dropping of them onto the floor coverings ("rushes") at midnight.
9. (1) Attacker from the rear; (2) slanderer.

Great men were° gods if beggars could not kill 'em. *would be*
Forgive me, heaven, to call my mother wicked!
Oh, lessen not my days upon the earth!
I cannot honor her. By this,° I fear me, *By this time*
Her tongue has turned my sister into use.
I was a villain not to be forsworn
To this our lecherous hope,° the Duke's son; *heir apparent*
For lawyers, merchants, some divines, and all
Count beneficial° perjury a sin small. *in a good cause*
It shall go hard yet but I'll° guard her honor *I'll not fail to*
And keep the ports° sure. *gates (of chastity)*

Enter Hippolito.

HIPPOLITO Brother,
How goes the world? I would know news of you,
But I have news to tell you.
VINDICE What, in the name of knavery?
HIPPOLITO Knavery, 'faith.
This vicious old Duke's worthily abused:
The pen° of his bastard writes him cuckold! *pen; penis*
VINDICE His bastard?
HIPPOLITO Pray believe it. He and the Duchess
By night meet in their linen; they have been seen
By stair-foot panders.[1]
VINDICE Oh, sin foul and deep!
Great faults are winked at when the Duke's asleep.[2]
See, see, here comes the Spurio.

[*Enter Spurio, with two Servants, whispering. Vindice and Hippolito stand aside, unseen by Spurio and unable to hear him.*]

HIPPOLITO [*to Vindice*] Monstrous luxur!° *lecher*
VINDICE [*to Hippolito*] Unbraced;° two of his valiant bawds with him. *Partly undressed*
Oh, there's a wicked whisper; hell is in his ear.
Stay, let's observe his passage.
SPURIO [*to the Servants*] Oh, but are you sure on't?
FIRST SERVANT My lord, most sure on't, for 'twas spoke by one
That is most inward° with the Duke's son's lust: *intimately acquainted*
That he intends within this hour to steal
Unto Hippolito's sister, whose chaste life
The mother has corrupted for his use.
SPURIO Sweet word, sweet occasion! Faith, then, brother,° *(Lussurioso)*
I'll disinherit you° in as short time *get you disinherited*
As I was when I was begot in haste;
I'll damn you at your pleasure. Precious deed!
After your lust, oh, 'twill be fine to bleed.[3]
Come, let our passing out be soft and wary.
Exeunt [*Spurio and Servants*].
VINDICE Mark, there, there, that step! Now to the Duchess.

1. By panders keeping watch at the foot of the stairs.
2. Sin thrives when authority sleeps.
3. (1) To undergo a common medical procedure to correct an imbalance of the humors (the four bodily fluids believed to determine, by their relative proportions, a person's health and temperament) in the blood; (2) to receive a fatal wound.

This their second meeting writes the Duke cuckold
With new additions, his horns newly revived.
Night,° thou that look'st like funeral heralds' fees[4] *O Night*
Torn down betimes° i'th'morning, thou hang'st fitly *early*
To grace° those sins that have no grace° at all. *adorn / virtue*
Now 'tis full sea° abed over the world; *high tide (sexually)*
There's juggling of° all sides. Some that were maids *hanky-panky on*
E'en at sunset are now perhaps i'th'toll-book.° *register (of sinners)*
This woman,° in immodest thin apparel, *One woman*
Lets in her friend by water;° here, a dame, *lover from the river*
Cunning, nails leather° hinges to a door *i.e., noiseless*
To avoid proclamation.° *being proclaimed a sinner*
Now cuckolds are a-coining,° apace, apace, apace, apace; *being mass-produced*
And careful sisters° spin that thread i'th'night *industrious whores*
That does maintain them and their bawds i'th'day.

HIPPOLITO You flow well,° brother. *You're in fine fettle*

VINDICE Pooh, I'm shallow yet,
Too sparing and too modest.° Shall I tell thee? *moderate*
If every trick were told that's dealt by night,
There are few here° that would not blush outright. *(in the theater)*

HIPPOLITO I am of that belief too.

VINDICE Who's this comes?

[*Enter Lussurioso.*]

The Duke's son up so late? Brother, fall back,
And you shall learn some mischief.
[*Hippolito stands aside.*]
My good lord!

LUSSURIOSO Piato!° Why, the man I wished for. Come, *(Vindice's disguise name)*
I do embrace this season° for the fittest *time*
To taste of that young lady.

VINDICE [*aside*] Heart and hell!

HIPPOLITO [*aside*] Damned villain!

VINDICE [*aside*] I ha' no way now to cross° it but to kill him. *thwart*

LUSSURIOSO Come, only thou and I.

VINDICE My lord, my lord!

LUSSURIOSO Why dost thou start us?° *startle me*

VINDICE I'd almost forgot;
The Bastard!

LUSSURIOSO What of him?

VINDICE This night, this hour,
This minute, now—

LUSSURIOSO What? What?

VINDICE Shadows° the Duchess— *He covers (sexually)*

LUSSURIOSO Horrible word!

VINDICE And like strong poison eats
Into the Duke your father's forehead.

LUSSURIOSO Oh!

VINDICE He makes horn-royal.° *a royal cuckold*

LUSSURIOSO Most ignoble slave!

VINDICE This is the fruit of two beds.° *more beds than one*

LUSSURIOSO I am mad!

4. Fees paid to those who devise funeral trappings and decorations; also the decorations themselves.

VINDICE That passage he trod warily.
LUSSURIOSO He did?
VINDICE And hushed his villains every step he took.[5]
LUSSURIOSO His villains? I'll confound° them. *destroy*
VINDICE Take 'em° finely, finely, now. *(the lovers)*
LUSSURIOSO The Duchess' chamber door shall not control me.
Exeunt [*Lussurioso and Vindice*].
HIPPOLITO Good, happy, swift! There's gunpowder i'th'court,
Wildfire° at midnight. In this heedless fury *Flammable stuff*
He may show violence to cross° himself. *so as to thwart*
I'll follow the event.° *Exit.* *outcome*

[2.3]

Enter again [*Lussurioso, his sword drawn, and Vindice. A curtained bed is thrust out° containing the Duke and the Duchess, hidden from view by the bed curtains*]. *onto the stage*

LUSSURIOSO Where is that villain?
VINDICE Softly, my lord, and you may take 'em twisted.[1]
LUSSURIOSO I care not how!
VINDICE Oh, 'twill be glorious
To kill 'em doubled,° when they're heaped. Be soft,° my lord. *coupling / gentle*
LUSSURIOSO Away! My spleen° is not so lazy. Thus and thus *i.e, anger*
I'll shake their eyelids ope, and with my sword
Shut 'em again forever.—Villain! Strumpet!
[*He tears open the bed curtains and discovers the Duke and Duchess abed.*]
DUKE [*calling*] You upper guard,° defend us! *private guard*
DUCHESS Treason, treason!
DUKE Oh, take me not° in sleep! I have great sins; *don't take my life*
I must have days,
Nay, months, dear son, with penitential heaves,° *sighs, groans; liftings*
To lift 'em out, and not to die unclear.° *unabsolved*
Oh, thou wilt kill me both in heaven and here!
LUSSURIOSO I am amazed to death.
DUKE Nay, villain, traitor,
Worse than the foulest epithet, now I'll grip thee
Ee'n with the nerves° of wrath, and throw thy head *sinews*
Amongst the lawyers.—Guard!

Enter [*the guard, followed by Hippolito,*] *Nobles, and* [*the Duchess's*] *sons* [*Ambitioso and Supervacuo. The guard seizes Lussurioso*].

FIRST NOBLE How comes the quiet of Your Grace disturbed?
DUKE This boy, that should be myself° after me, *i.e., duke*
Would be myself before me, and in heat
Of that ambition bloodily rushed in,
Intending to depose me in my bed.
SECOND NOBLE Duty and natural° loyalty forfend!° *i.e., filial / forbid*
DUCHESS He called his father villain, and me strumpet—
A word that I abhor to file° my lips with. *defile*

5. See line 134 above, where Spurio admonishes his servants to be "soft and wary" as they exit. "Villains" are servants.

2.3. The Duke and Duchess's bedchamber.
1. You may apprehend the Duchess and Spurio entwined in each other's arms.

AMBITIOSO That was not so well done, brother.
LUSSURIOSO I am abused°— *hoodwinked, deceived*
I know there's no excuse can do me good.
VINDICE [*aside to Hippolito*] 'Tis now good policy° to be from sight; *stratagem*
His vicious purpose to our sister's honor
Is crossed beyond our thought.[2]
HIPPOLITO [*aside to Vindice*] You little dreamt
His father slept here.
VINDICE [*aside to Hippolito*] Oh, 'twas far beyond me.
But since it fell° so, without frightful word,[3] *fell out, happened*
Would he° had killed him!° 'Twould have eased our swords. *(Lussurioso) / (the Duke)*
[*Vindice and Hippolito*] *dissemble a flight*.° *steal away*
DUKE Be comforted, our duchess; he shall die.
[*Exit Duchess*.]
LUSSURIOSO Where's this slave-pander° now? Out of mine eye,[4] *i.e., "Piato"*
Guilty of this abuse!

Enter Spurio with his villains [*two Servants. They converse among themselves*].

SPURIO You're villains, fablers!° *liars*
You have knaves' chins and harlots' tongues! You lie,
And I will damn you with° one meal a day![5] *sentence you to*
FIRST SERVANT Oh, good my lord!
SPURIO 'Sblood, you shall never sup!° *never eat again*
SECOND SERVANT Oh, I beseech you, sir!
SPURIO To let my sword
Catch cold so long and miss him!° *(Lussurioso)*
FIRST SERVANT Troth, my lord,
'Twas his intent to meet there.
SPURIO [*aside, seeing Lussurioso*] Heart, he's yonder.
Ha? What news here? Is the day out o'th'socket,° *out of joint*
That it is noon at midnight? The court up?° *awake and out of bed*
How comes the guard so saucy with his elbows?[6]
LUSSURIOSO [*aside*] The Bastard here?
Nay, then, the truth of my intent shall out.°— *be publicly known*
My lord and father, hear me.
DUKE [*to the guard*] Bear him hence!
LUSSURIOSO I can with loyalty excuse—
DUKE Excuse?—To prison with the villain!
Death shall not long lag after him.
SPURIO [*aside*] Good, i'faith. Then 'tis not much amiss.
LUSSURIOSO Brothers, my best release lies on your tongues.
I pray, persuade for me.
AMBITIOSO It is our duties;
Make yourself sure of us.° *Count on us*
SUPERVACUO We'll sweat in pleading.
LUSSURIOSO And I may live to thank you.
Exeunt [*Lussurioso and the guard, followed by the Nobles*].

2. Is thwarted better than we could have hoped.
3. Without confrontation that would have been frightful.
4. He has disappeared from sight.
5. Spurio is furious with his servants for having told him that Lussurioso planned to seduce Castiza this night (see 2.2.123–28), since it now appears not to be true.
6. Spurio observes that the guard is roughly restraining Lussurioso by the arms.

AMBITIOSO [*aside*] No, thy death
Shall thank me better.
SPURIO [*aside*] He's gone. I'll after him,
And know his trespass, seem to bear a part
In all his ills, but with a puritan heart.[7]
Exit [*with his Servants*].
AMBITIOSO [*aside to Supervacuo*] Now, brother, let our hate and love be woven
So subtly together that in speaking
One word for his life we may make three for his death.
The craftiest pleader gets most gold for breath.
SUPERVACUO [*aside to Ambitioso*] Set on. I'll not be far behind you, brother.
DUKE Is't possible a son should be disobedient as far as the sword?
It is the highest; he can go no farther.
AMBITIOSO My gracious lord, take pity—
DUKE Pity, boys?
AMBITIOSO Nay, we'd be loath to move Your Grace too much.
We know the trespass is unpardonable,
Black, wicked, and unnatural.
SUPERVACUO In a son? Oh, monstrous!
AMBITIOSO Yet, my lord,
A duke's soft hand strokes the rough head of law,
And makes it lie smooth.
DUKE But my hand shall ne'er do't.
AMBITIOSO That as you please, my lord.
SUPERVACUO We must needs confess
Some father would have entered into hate
So deadly pointed° that before his eyes *sharp-pointed*
He would ha' seen the execution sound,° *fully completed*
Without corrupted favor.[8]
AMBITIOSO But, my lord,
Your Grace may live the wonder of all times,
In pard'ning that offense which never yet
Had face° to beg a pardon. *i.e., effrontery*
DUKE [*aside*] Honey?[9] How's this?
AMBITIOSO Forgive him, good my lord; he's your own son—
And, I must needs say, 'twas the vilelier° done. *more vilely*
SUPERVACUO He's the next heir—yet this true reason gathers:
None can possess° that dispossess their fathers. *inherit*
Be merciful—
DUKE [*aside*] Here's no stepmother's wit.[1]
I'll try 'em both upon their love and hate.
AMBITIOSO Be merciful—although—
DUKE You have prevailed.
My wrath like flaming wax hath spent itself.
I know 'twas but some peevish moon° in him.— *fit of lunacy*

7. Puritans were often accused of being hypocrites in their excessive religiosity; a prime example of this stereotype can be found in the character Zeal-of-the-land Busy in Ben Jonson's *Bartholomew Fair*.
8. Without allowing a corrupt plea for mercy to be heard.
9. Sweet words? (The Duke expected hostility toward Lussurioso from the Duchess's sons.)
1. I.e., These stepsons lack their mother's cleverness. (The Duke sees through their pretended solicitude for Lussurioso.)

Go, let him be released.
SUPERVACUO [*aside to Ambitioso*] 'Sfoot, how now, brother?
AMBITIOSO Your Grace doth please to speak beside your spleen.° *forgetting your anger*
I would it were so happy.[2]
DUKE Why, go release him.
SUPERVACUO Oh, my good lord, I know the fault's too weighty
And full of general loathing; too inhuman,
Rather by all mens' voices worthy death.
DUKE 'Tis true, too.
Here, then, receive this signet;° doom shall pass. *seal of judgment*
[*He hands them an authenticated document.*]
Direct it to the judges; he shall die
Ere many days. Make haste.
AMBITIOSO All speed that may be.
We could have wished his burden not so sore;
We knew Your Grace did but delay before.
Exeunt [*Ambitioso and Supervacuo*].
DUKE [*alone onstage*] Here's envy with a poor thin cover o'er 't,
Like scarlet hid in lawn, easily spied through.[3]
This their ambition by the mother's side
Is dangerous, and for safety must be purged.
I will prevent° their envies. Sure it was *forestall*
But some mistaken fury in our son,
Which these aspiring boys would climb upon.
He shall be released suddenly.° *quickly*

Enter [*two*] *Nobles.*

FIRST NOBLE Good morning to Your Grace.
DUKE Welcome, my lords.
SECOND NOBLE Our knees shall take away the office of our feet forever
Unless Your Grace bestow a father's eye
Upon the clouded fortunes of your son,
And in compassionate virtue grant him that
Which makes e'en mean° men happy: liberty. *lowly*
DUKE [*aside*] How seriously their loves and honors woo
For that which I am about to pray them do,
Which— [*To them*] Rise, my lords; your knees sign his release.
We freely pardon him.
FIRST NOBLE We owe Your Grace much thanks, and he much duty.
Exeunt [*Nobles*].
DUKE It well becomes that judge to nod at crimes
That does commit greater himself and lives.
I may forgive a disobedient error,
That° expect pardon for adultery *I who*
And in my old days am a youth in lust.
Many a beauty have I turned to poison° *caused to be poisoned*
In the denial,° covetous of all. *For denying me*
Age hot° is like a monster to be seen; *Lecherous old age*
My hairs are white, and yet my sins are green.° [*Exit.*] *young and fresh*

2. I wish matters were as satisfactory as all that.
3. Like rich velvet showing through a thin veil of white lace.

3.1

Enter Ambitioso and Supervacuo.

SUPERVACUO Brother, let my opinion sway you once;
I speak it for the best, to have him die,
Surest and soonest. If the signet come
Unto the judges' hands, why then his doom
Will be deferred till sittings° and court days, *court sessions*
Juries, and further. Faiths are bought and sold;
Oaths in these days are but the skin of gold.[1]
AMBITIOSO In troth, 'tis true too.
SUPERVACUO Then let's set by° the judges *disregard*
And fall to the officers.° 'Tis but mistaking *apply to the jailers*
The Duke our father's meaning, and, where he named
"Ere many days," 'tis but forgetting that
And have him die i'th'morning.
AMBITIOSO Excellent!
Then am I heir—duke in a minute.
SUPERVACUO [*aside*] Nay,
An he were once puffed out,[2] here is a pin° *i.e, sword*
Should quickly prick your bladder.
AMBITIOSO Blest occasion!
He being packed,° we'll have some trick and wile *packed off, disposed of*
To wind our younger brother out of prison
That lies in for the rape. The lady's dead,
And people's thoughts will soon be burièd.
SUPERVACUO We may with safety do't, and live and feed;
The Duchess' sons are too proud to bleed.
AMBITIOSO We are, i'faith, to say true. Come, let's not linger.
I'll to the officers; go you before,
And set an edge upon the executioner.[3]
SUPERVACUO Let me alone to grind him.
AMBITIOSO Meet!° Farewell. *That's most fitting!*
Exit [*Supervacuo*].
I am next, now; I rise just in that place
Where thou'rt° cut off—upon thy neck, kind brother. *you, Lussurioso, are*
The falling of one head lifts up another. *Exit.*

[3.2]

Enter, with the Nobles, Lussurioso from prison.

LUSSURIOSO My lords,
I am so much indebted to your loves
For this, oh, this delivery.
FIRST NOBLE But° our duties, *Merely*
My lord, unto the hopes that grow in you.
LUSSURIOSO If e'er I live to be myself,° I'll thank you. *i.e., duke*
O Liberty, thou sweet and heavenly dame!
But "hell" for prison is too mild a name. *Exeunt.*

3.1. The court.
1. Promises are broken for money; such oaths carry no validity these days and serve merely as a cover for commercial dealings.
2. If Lussurioso were snuffed out.
3. Go sharpen (get ready) the executioner (as if he were himself the fatal ax).
3.2. The court.

[3.3]

Enter Ambitioso and Supervacuo, with Officers.

AMBITIOSO [*presenting a warrant*] Officers,
Here's the Duke's signet, your firm warrant, brings° — *that brings*
The command of present° death along with it — *immediate*
Unto our brother, the Duke's son. We are sorry
That we are so unnaturally employed
In such an unkind° office, fitter far — *cruel; unnatural*
For enemies than brothers.
SUPERVACUO But you know
The Duke's command must be obeyed.
FIRST OFFICER It must and shall, my lord. This morning, then,
So suddenly?
AMBITIOSO Ay, alas, poor, good soul,
He must break fast betimes;° the executioner — *quickly*
Stands ready to put forth his cowardly° valor. — *unchivalric*
SECOND OFFICER Already?
SUPERVACUO Already, i'faith. Oh, sir, destruction hies,° — *hastens on, draws near*
And that is least impudent soonest dies.[1]
FIRST OFFICER Troth, you say true. My lord, we take our leaves.
Our office shall be sound;° we'll not delay — *well carried out*
The third part of a minute.
AMBITIOSO Therein you show
Yourselves good men and upright officers.
Pray let him die as private as he may;
Do him that favor, for the gaping° people — *staring openmouthed*
Will but trouble him at his prayers, and make
Him curse, and swear, and so die black.° Will you — *blackened in soul*
Be so far kind?
FIRST OFFICER It shall be done, my lord.
AMBITIOSO Why, we do thank you. If we live to be,° — *If I live to be duke*
You shall have a better office.
SECOND OFFICER Your good Lordship!
SUPERVACUO Commend us to the scaffold in our tears.
FIRST OFFICER We'll weep, and do your commendations.
Exeunt [*Officers*].
AMBITIOSO Fine fools in office!
SUPERVACUO Things fall out so fit!
AMBITIOSO So happily! Come, brother, ere next clock,
His head will be made serve a bigger block.[2] *Exeunt.*

[3.4]

Enter, in prison, Junior Brother.

JUNIOR BROTHER Keeper!

[*Enter Keeper.*]

KEEPER My lord?
JUNIOR BROTHER No news lately from our brothers?
Are they unmindful of us?

3.3. Near the prison.
1. And even the least impudence is quickly rewarded with death.
2. (1) Chopping block; (2) mold for blocking a hat.
3.4. The prison.

KEEPER My lord, a messenger came newly in,
And brought this from 'em. [*He gives a letter.*]

JUNIOR BROTHER Nothing but paper comforts?
I looked for my delivery before this,
Had they been worth their oaths—prithee be from us.
[*Exit Keeper.*]

Now, what say you, forsooth? Speak out, I pray. ([*He reads the*] *letter.*) "Brother be of good cheer." 'Slud, it begins like a whore, with good cheer!° "Thou shalt not be long a prisoner." Not five-and-thirty year, like a bankrupt; I think so. "We have thought upon a device to get thee out by a trick." By a trick? Pox o'your trick, an it be so long a-playing! "And so rest comforted; be merry and expect it suddenly." Be merry? Hang, merry! Draw and quarter merry![1] I'll be mad. Is't not strange that a man should lie in[2] a whole month for a woman? Well, we shall see how sudden our brothers will be in their promise. I must expect still a trick! I shall not be long a prisoner. [*He tears the letter.*] *merrymaking, carousing*

[*Enter Keeper.*]

How now, what news?

KEEPER Bad news, my lord: I am discharged of you.

JUNIOR BROTHER Slave, call'st thou that bad news?—I thank you, brothers.

KEEPER My lord, 'twill prove so.° Here come the officers *bad news*
Into whose hands I must commit you.

[*Enter three Officers.*]

JUNIOR BROTHER Ha!
Officers? What, why?

FIRST OFFICER You must pardon us, my lord.
Our office must be sound.° Here is our warrant: *validly executed*
The signet from the Duke. You must straight suffer.

JUNIOR BROTHER Suffer?
I'll suffer° you to be gone. I'll suffer you *permit*
To come no more. What would you have me suffer?

SECOND OFFICER My lord, those words were better changed to prayers.
The time's but brief with you. Prepare to die.

JUNIOR BROTHER Sure, 'tis not so.

THIRD OFFICER It is too true, my lord.

JUNIOR BROTHER I tell you 'tis not, for the Duke my father
Deferred me till next sitting,° and I look *court session*
E'en every minute, threescore times an hour,
For a release, a trick wrought by my brothers.

FIRST OFFICER A trick, my lord? If you expect such comfort,
Your hope's as fruitless as a barren woman.
Your brothers were the unhappy° messengers *sad; ill-boding*
That brought this powerful token for your death.

JUNIOR BROTHER My brothers? No, no.

SECOND OFFICER 'Tis most true, my lord.

JUNIOR BROTHER My brothers to bring a warrant for my death?

1. The punishment for high treason was to be hanged, drawn (disemboweled), and torn apart into quarters.

2. Be imprisoned; but the phrase also describes the confinement of a woman during childbirth.

How strange this shows!° *appears*
THIRD OFFICER There's no delaying time.
JUNIOR BROTHER Desire 'em hither; call 'em up. My brothers?
They shall deny it to your faces.
FIRST OFFICER My lord,
They're far enough by this,° at least at court, *by this time*
And this most strict command they left behind 'em.
When grief swum in their eyes, they showed° like brothers, *looked*
Brimful of heavy sorrow; but the Duke
Must have his pleasure.
JUNIOR BROTHER His pleasure?
FIRST OFFICER These were their last words which my memory bears:
"Commend us to the scaffold in our tears."
JUNIOR BROTHER Pox dry their tears! What should I do with tears?
I hate 'em worse than any citizen's son
Can hate salt water.° Here came a letter now, *i.e., shipboard life*
New-bleeding from their pens, scarce stinted° yet— *stanched; blotted*
Would I'd been torn in pieces when I tore it!
[*He finds a scrap of the letter.*]
Look you, officious whoresons, words of comfort:
"Not long a prisoner."
FIRST OFFICER It says true in that, sir, for you must suffer presently.
JUNIOR BROTHER A villainous duns upon the letter! Knavish exposition![3] [*He finds another scrap of the letter.*] Look you then here, sir: "We'll get thee out by a trick," says he.
SECOND OFFICER That may hold too, sir, for you know a trick is commonly four cards, which was meant by° us four officers.[4] *signified*
JUNIOR BROTHER Worse and worse dealing![5]
FIRST OFFICER The hour beckons us;
The headsman waits. Lift up your eyes to heaven.
JUNIOR BROTHER I thank you, faith; good, pretty, wholesome counsel.° *(said ironically)*
I should look up to heaven, as you said,
Whilst he° behind me cozens° me of my head. *(the hangman) / cheats*
Ay, that's the trick.
THIRD OFFICER You delay too long, my lord.
JUNIOR BROTHER Stay, good authority's bastards.° Since I must *i.e., low creatures*
Through brothers' perjury die, oh, let me venom° *envenom*
Their souls with curses.
FIRST OFFICER Come, 'tis no time to curse.
JUNIOR BROTHER Must I bleed, then, without respect of sign?[6]
Well—
My fault was sweet sport, which the world approves;
I die for that which every woman loves. *Exeunt.*

3. Junior Brother is exasperated by the letter's sophistic quibbling and hairsplitting in the vein of Duns Scotus and other medieval scholastics. He uses the name "duns" as if it were a swearword.
4. Either four officers are present, one of them remaining silent, or else the hangman is being counted as one of the four. (The card trick is probably from the game of primero.)
5. (1) Handling of matters; (2) card dealing.
6. It was Renaissance surgical practice to consult astrological signs before letting blood.

[3.5]

Enter Vindice [disguised as Piato] with Hippolito, his brother.

VINDICE Oh, sweet, delectable, rare, happy, ravishing!
HIPPOLITO Why, what's the matter, brother?
VINDICE Oh, 'tis able
To make a man spring up and knock his forehead
Against yon silver ceiling!° *sky; theater roof*
HIPPOLITO Prithee tell me.
Why may not I partake with you? You vowed once
To give me share to° every tragic thought. *in*
VINDICE By th'Mass, I think I did too.
Then I'll divide it to° thee: the old Duke, *share it with*
Thinking my outward shape and inward heart
Are cut out of one piece (for he that prates° *blabs*
His secrets, his heart stands o'th'outside),
Hires me by price to greet him with a lady
In some fit place veiled from the eyes o'th'court,
Some darkened blushless angle° that is guilty *nook*
Of his forefathers' lusts and great folks' riots;° *wanton revels*
To which I easily (to maintain my shape)° *disguise*
Consented, and did wish His impudent Grace
To meet her here in this unsunnèd lodge,
Wherein 'tis night at noon; and here the rather
Because unto the torturing of his soul
The Bastard and the Duchess have appointed
Their meeting too in this luxurious° circle— *lecherous*
Which most afflicting sight will kill his eyes
Before we kill the rest of him.
HIPPOLITO 'Twill, i'faith! Most dreadfully digested.° *awesomely arranged*
I see not how you could have missed me,° brother. *failed to tell me*
VINDICE True, but the violence of my joy forgot it.
HIPPOLITO Ay, but where's that lady now?
VINDICE Oh, at that word
I'm lost again; you cannot find me° yet; *catch up with me*
I'm in a throng of happy apprehensions.° *anticipations*
He's suited for° a lady; I have took care *provided with*
For a delicious lip, a sparkling eye.
You shall be witness, brother.
Be ready; stand with your hat off.° *Exit.* *(showing deference)*
HIPPOLITO Troth, I wonder
What lady it should be. Yet 'tis no wonder,
Now I think again, to have a lady
Stoop to a duke that stoops unto his men.[1]
'Tis common to be common° through the world; *to be a prostitute*
And there's more private common shadowing vices[2]
Than those° who are known both by their names and prices. *those whores*
'Tis part° of my allegiance to stand bare° *the duty / bareheaded*
To the Duke's concubine—and here she comes.

3.5. A secluded lodge near the court.
1. Submit to a duke who degrades himself to the level of his unworthiest servants.
2. And there are more women practicing vices secretively.

Enter Vindice, with the skull of his love dressed up in tires.° — *attires, headdresses*

VINDICE Madam, His Grace will not be absent long.
Secret? Ne'er doubt us, madam. 'Twill be worth
Three velvet gowns to Your Ladyship. Known?[3]
Few ladies respect that! Disgrace? A poor thin shell;
'Tis the best grace you have to do it well.[4]
I'll save your hand that labor;° I'll unmask you. — *labor of unmasking*
[*He uncovers the skull.*]
HIPPOLITO Why, brother, brother!
VINDICE Art thou beguiled now? Tut, a lady can,
At such,° all hid,[5] beguile a wiser man. — *such games*
Have I not fitted the old surfeiter° — *(the Duke)*
With a quaint° piece of beauty? Age and bare bone — *ingenious*
Are e'er allied in action.[6] Here's an eye
Able to tempt a great man—to serve God;
A pretty hanging lip, that has forgot now to dissemble.
Methinks this mouth should make a swearer tremble,
A drunkard clasp his teeth° and not undo 'em — *shut his mouth*
To suffer wet damnation° to run through 'em. — *alcoholic drink*
Here's a cheek keeps her color, let the wind go whistle.[7]
Spout, rain! We fear thee not; be hot or cold,
All's one° with us. And is not he absurd — *All's the same*
Whose fortunes are upon their faces set,
That fear no other god but wind and wet?[8]
HIPPOLITO Brother, you've spoke that right.
Is this the form that, living, shone so bright?
VINDICE The very same.
And now methinks I could e'en chide myself
For doting on her beauty, though her death
Shall be revenged after no common action.° — *in no ordinary way*
Does the silkworm expend her yellow labors
For thee? For thee does she undo herself?[9]
Are lordships° sold to maintain ladyships — *estates*
For the poor benefit of a bewitching minute?
Why does yon fellow falsify highways° — *turn highwayman*
And put his life between the judge's lips,[1]
To refine such a thing?° Keeps horse and men — *To pamper a woman*
To beat° their valors for her? — *i.e., exhaust*
Surely we're all mad people, and they
Whom we think are,° are not; we mistake those; — *think are mad*
'Tis we are mad in sense, they but in clothes.
HIPPOLITO Faith, and in clothes too we;[2] give us our due.
VINDICE Does every proud and self-affecting° dame — *self-loving*
Camphor her face for this?° And grieve her Maker — *for eventual death*

3. You worry that the affair may become known?
4. Disgrace is a mere matter of reputation without substance. You'll grace yourself best by playing your sexual part best.
5. "All hid" is a refrain in the children's game of hide-and-seek.
6. Old age and this skull have much in common, as they always do.
7. That keeps its color no matter what weather (or time) may do.
8. Isn't a person absurd whose happiness and success depend on cosmetics, which are so easily washed off? (Perhaps "he" in line 62 should read "she.")
9. Does the silkworm spin her yellow (gold-colored) cocoon just for you? Does she spin out her entrails for you? (Addressed to all worldlings.)
1. At the discretion of the judge.
2. We too are infatuated and insane in our preoccupation with clothes and mere appearances.

In sinful baths of milk, when many an infant starves
For her superfluous outside—all for this?[3]
Who now bids° twenty pound a night, prepares — *i.e., spends*
Music, perfumes, and sweetmeats? All are hushed;° — *ended in death*
Thou mayst lie chaste° now. It were fine, methinks, — *sleep alone*
To have thee seen at revels, forgetful° feasts, — *oblivion-inducing*
And unclean brothels; sure 'twould fright the sinner
And make him a good coward, put a reveler
Out of his antic amble,° — *grotesque stagger*
And cloy an epicure with empty dishes.[4]
Here might a scornful and ambitious woman
Look through and through herself.—See, ladies, with false
 forms° — *appearances*
You deceive men, but cannot deceive worms.
Now to my tragic business. Look you, brother,
I have not fashioned this only for show
And useless property;° no, it shall bear a part — *stage props*
E'en in it° own revenge. This very skull, — *its*
Whose mistress° the Duke poisoned, with this drug, — *owner (Gloriana)*
[*He shows a vial of poison.*]
The mortal curse of the earth, shall be revenged
In the like strain,° and kiss his lips to death. — *manner*
As much as the dumb thing° can, he shall feel; — *silent poison; the Duke*
What fails in poison, we'll supply in steel.

HIPPOLITO Brother, I do applaud thy constant vengeance,
The quaintness° of thy malice, above thought.[5] — *cleverness*

VINDICE [*poisoning the skull's lips*] So, 'tis laid on. Now
 come and welcome, Duke;
I have her for thee. I protest it,° brother: — *declare*
Methinks she makes almost as fair a sign° — *show, figure*
As some old gentlewoman in a periwig.
[*To the skull*] Hide thy face now, for shame! Thou hadst
 need have a mask now;
'Tis vain when beauty flows, but when it fleets
This would become graves better than the streets.[6]

HIPPOLITO You have my voice° in that. Hark, the Duke's come. — *agreement*

VINDICE Peace! Let's observe what company he brings,
And how he does absent° 'em, for you know — *dismiss*
He'll wish all private. Brother, fall you back
A little with the bony lady.

HIPPOLITO That I will.

[*He stands aside, and arranges Gloriana's skull and attires so that she resembles a beautiful lady.*]

VINDICE So, so—
Now nine years' vengeance crowd into a minute!

[*Enter the Duke and some gentlemen.*]

DUKE You shall have leave to leave us, with this charge,° — *commandment*
Upon your lives: if we be missed by th'Duchess

3. All just to provide her with artificial beauty, when her fate eventually is to be no better than a skull?
4. And take away the appetite of an epicure with your empty eye sockets.
5. More than I can imagine or say.
6. A mask is unnecessary on a beautiful woman, but when beauty is gone and only the skull is left, it is better hidden in the grave than publicly displayed on the streets.

Or any of the nobles, to give out° *let it be known*
We're privately rid forth.° *ridden from the court*
VINDICE [*aside*] Oh, happiness!
DUKE With some few honorable gentlemen, you may say.
You may name those that are away from court.
GENTLEMEN Your will and pleasure shall be done, my lord.
[*Exeunt gentlemen.*]
VINDICE [*aside*] Privately rid forth?
He strives to make sure work on't.° [*Coming forward*] Your good Grace! *of it*
DUKE Piato! Well done. Hast brought her? What lady is't?
VINDICE Faith, my lord, a country lady, a little bashful at first, as most of them are, but after the first kiss, my lord, the worst is past with them. Your Grace knows now what you have to do; sh' has somewhat a grave° look with her, but— *solemn; dead*
DUKE I love that best. Conduct her.
VINDICE [*aside*] Have at all!° *Here goes!*
DUKE In gravest looks the greatest faults seem less.
Give me that sin that's robed in holiness.
VINDICE [*aside to Hippolito*] Back with the torch! Brother, raise the perfumes.
DUKE How sweet can a duke breathe! Age has no fault.[7]
Pleasure should meet in a perfumèd mist.
Lady, sweetly encountered. I came from court;
I must be bold with you. [*He kisses the skull.*] Oh, what's this? Oh!
VINDICE Royal villain, white° devil! *white-haired*
DUKE Oh!
VINDICE [*to Hippolito*] Brother,
Place the torch here, that his affrighted eyeballs
May start° into those hollows.—Duke, dost know *dart, leap*
Yon dreadful vizard? View it well; 'tis the skull
Of Gloriana, whom thou poisoned'st last.° *last of your victims*
DUKE Oh, 't has poisoned me!
VINDICE Didst not know that till now?
DUKE What are you two?
VINDICE Villains all three![8] The very ragged bone
Has been sufficiently revenged.
DUKE Oh, Hippolito? Call treason.
HIPPOLITO Yes, my good lord.—Treason, treason, treason!
Stamping on him.
DUKE Then I'm betrayed.
VINDICE Alas, poor lecher, in the hands of knaves!
A slavish duke is baser than his slaves.
DUKE My teeth are eaten out!
VINDICE Hadst any left?
HIPPOLITO I think but few.
VINDICE Then those that did eat are eaten.° *dissolved by poison*
DUKE Oh, my tongue!
VINDICE Your tongue? 'Twill teach you to kiss closer,
Not like a slobbering Dutchman.° You have eyes still: *i.e., drunkard*

7. I.e., My old age brings no physical inadequacies with it.
8. Vindice mockingly corrects the Duke's "two" to "three" to include Gloriana's skull. Or he may be counting the Duke.

Look, monster, what a lady hast thou made me,° *for me*
My once bethrothèd wife.
DUKE Is it thou, villain? Nay, then—
VINDICE 'Tis I, 'tis Vindice, 'tis I.
HIPPOLITO And let this comfort thee: our lord and father
Fell sick upon the infection of thy frowns,
And died in sadness. Be that thy hope of life.
DUKE Oh!
VINDICE He had his tongue, yet grief made him die speechless.
Pooh, 'tis but early yet; now I'll begin
To stick thy soul with ulcers. I will make
Thy spirit grievous sore; it shall not rest,
But, like some pestilent° man, toss in thy breast. *plague-infected*
Mark me, Duke:
Thou'rt a renownèd, high, and mighty cuckold.
DUKE Oh!
VINDICE Thy bastard, thy bastard rides a-hunting° in thy brow. *i.e., cuckolding*
DUKE Millions° of deaths! *I suffer millions*
VINDICE Nay, to afflict thee more,
Here in this lodge they meet for damnèd clips.° *embraces*
Those eyes shall see the incest of their lips.
DUKE Is there a hell besides this, villains?
VINDICE Villain!° *Villain yourself!*
Nay, heaven is just; scorns are the hires° of scorns. *reward*
I ne'er knew yet adulterer without horns.° *cuckold's horns*
HIPPOLITO Once° ere they die, 'tis quitted.° [*Music is heard.*] *At some time / requited*
VINDICE Hark, the music!
Their banquet is prepared; they're coming—
DUKE Oh, kill me not with that sight!
VINDICE Thou shalt not lose that sight for all thy dukedom.
DUKE Traitors, murderers!
VINDICE What? Is not thy tongue eaten out yet?
Then we'll invent a silence.—Brother, stifle the torch.
DUKE Treason, murder!
VINDICE Nay, faith, we'll have you hushed. [*To Hippolito*]
Now with thy dagger
Nail down his tongue, and mine shall keep possession
About his heart. If he but gasp, he dies.
We dread not death to quittance° injuries. *requite*
[*They silence the Duke by nailing down his tongue.*]
Brother,
If he but wink,° not brooking° the foul object,[9] *blink / enduring*
Let our two other hands tear up his lids° *eyelids*
And make his eyes, like comets, shine through blood.
When the bad bleeds, then is the tragedy good.
[*Music is heard again.*]
HIPPOLITO Whist,° brother! Music's at our ear; they come. *Hush*
[*Vindice and Hippolito stand aside.*]

Enter the Bastard [*Spurio*], *meeting the Duchess* [*attended by servants with torches, who stand aside. Spurio and the Duchess kiss*].

9. The detested object of sight (i.e., Spurio and the Duchess's kisses).

SPURIO Had not that kiss a taste of sin, 'twere sweet.
DUCHESS Why, there's no pleasure sweet but° it is sinful. *unless*
SPURIO True; such a bitter sweetness fate hath given.
Best side to us is the worst side to heaven.[1]
DUCHESS Push, come. 'Tis the old Duke, thy doubtful° father; *putative*
The thought of him rubs heaven in thy way.[2]
But I protest, by yonder waxen fire,° *torches*
Forget him, or I'll poison him.
SPURIO Madam, you urge a thought which ne'er had life.[3]
So deadly do I loathe him for my birth
That, if he took me hasped° within his bed, *clasped in embrace*
I would add murder to adultery,
And with my sword give up his years to death.° *shorten his life*
DUCHESS Why, now thou'rt sociable; let's in and feast.—
Loud'st music, sound! Pleasure is banquest's guest.
[*Music.*] *Exeunt* [*Duchess, Spurio, and servants with torches*].
DUKE I cannot brook°— [*He dies.*] *cannot endure*
VINDICE The brook is turned to blood.
HIPPOLITO Thanks to loud music.
VINDICE 'Twas our friend indeed.[4]
'Tis state in music for a duke to bleed.[5]
The dukedom wants° a head, though yet unknown;[6] *lacks*
As fast as they° peep up, let's cut 'em down. *Exeunt.* *(ducal claimants)*

[3.6]

Enter the Duchess's two sons, Ambitioso and Supervacuo.

AMBITIOSO Was not his execution rarely plotted?
We are the Duke's sons now.
SUPERVACUO Ay, you may thank
My policy° for that. *cunning; stratagem*
AMBITIOSO Your policy?
For what?
SUPERVACUO Why, was 't not my invention, brother,
To slip° the judges, and, in lesser compass,° *bypass / scope*
Did not I draw the model° of his death, *plan*
Advising you to sudden° officers, *swift-acting*
And e'en extemporal° execution? *immediate*
AMBITIOSO Heart, 'twas a thing I thought on too.
SUPERVACUO You thought on't too! 'Sfoot, slander not your thoughts
With glorious untruth. I know 'twas from you.° *not your idea*
AMBITIOSO Sir, I say, 'twas in my head.
SUPERVACUO Ay, like your brains, then,
Ne'er to come out as long as you lived.[1]

1. What delights us most offends heaven most grievously.
2. The thought of him brings heavenly justice to your mind as a deterrent to seizing pleasure. (A rub is an obstacle in the game of bowls.)
3. Your notion that I am deterred by thoughts of heavenly justice never entered my head.
4. I.e., Music has befriended us by drowning out the Duke's last words.
5. Stately music ought to sound for a duke's death. (Said sardonically.)
6. Though that need is not yet publicly known.
3.6. The court.
1. Supervacuo scoffs that Ambitioso may have a brain, but not an idea coming from it.

AMBITIOSO You'd have the honor on't, forsooth, that your wit
Led him to the scaffold.
SUPERVACUO Since it is my due,
I'll publish't,° but° I'll ha 't in spite of you. *proclaim it / only*
AMBITIOSO Methinks you're much too bold. You should a little
Remember us, brother, next to be honest duke.[2]
SUPERVACUO Ay, it shall be as easy for you to be duke
As to be honest, and that's never, i'faith.
AMBITIOSO Well, cold he° is by this time; and because *(Lussurioso)*
We're both ambitious, be it our amity,° *let's be friends*
And let the glory be shared equally.
SUPERVACUO I am content to that.
AMBITIOSO This night our younger brother shall out of prison;
I have a trick.
SUPERVACUO A trick? Prithee, what is't?
AMBITIOSO We'll get him out by a wile.
SUPERVACUO Prithee, what wile?
AMBITIOSO No, sir, you shall not know it till't be done,
For then you'd swear 'twere yours.

[*Enter an Officer, carrying a severed head.*]

SUPERVACUO [*to Ambitioso*] How now, what's he?
AMBITIOSO One of the officers.
SUPERVACUO Desirèd news!
AMBITIOSO [*to the Officer*] How now, my friend?
OFFICER My lords, under your pardon, I am allotted
To that desertless° office, to present you *thankless*
With the yet bleeding head—
SUPERVACUO [*aside to Ambitioso*] Ha, ha, excellent!
AMBITIOSO [*aside to Supervacuo*] All's sure our own.° *going our way*
Brother, canst weep, think'st thou?
'Twould grace our flattery much. Think of some dame;[3]
'Twill teach thee to dissemble.
SUPERVACUO [*aside to Ambitioso*] I have thought.
Now for yourself. [*They pretend to weep.*]
AMBITIOSO [*aloud*] Our sorrows are so fluent,
Our eyes o'erflow our tongues. Words spoke in tears
Are like the murmurs of the waters; the sound
Is loudly heard, but cannot be distinguished.
SUPERVACUO How died he, pray?
OFFICER Oh, full of rage and spleen.
SUPERVACUO He died most valiantly, then; we're glad
To hear it.
OFFICER We could not woo° him once to pray. *persuade*
AMBITIOSO He showed himself a gentleman in that;
Give him his due.
OFFICER But in the stead° of prayer, *place*
He drew forth oaths.
SUPERVACUO Then° did he pray, dear heart, *In that case*
Although you understood him not.
OFFICER My lords,

2. Remember that I am the honorable heir to the dukedom.

3. Weeping would give a plausible appearance to our show of sorrow. Imitate the deceptive ways of women.

E'en at his last, with pardon be it spoke,[4]
He cursed you both.
SUPERVACUO He cursed us? 'Las, good soul!
AMBITIOSO It was not in our powers, but the Duke's pleasure.
[*Aside*] Finely dissembled o'both sides! Sweet fate!
Oh, happy opportunity!

Enter Lussurioso.

LUSSURIOSO Now, my lords—
BOTH [AMBITIOSO *and* SUPERVACUO] Oh!
LUSSURIOSO Why do you shun me, brothers?
You may come nearer now;
The savor° of the prison has forsook me. *scent*
I thank such kind lords as yourselves, I'm free.
AMBITIOSO Alive!
SUPERVACUO In health!
AMBITIOSO Released?
We were both e'en amazed with joy to see it.
LUSSURIOSO I am much to thank you.
SUPERVACUO Faith,
We spared no tongue unto my lord the Duke.
AMBITIOSO I know your delivery, brother,
Had not been half so sudden but for us.
SUPERVACUO Oh, how we pleaded!
LUSSURIOSO Most deserving, brothers!
In my best studies I will think of it.° *Exit Lussurioso.* *I'll ponder a reward*
AMBITIOSO Oh, death and vengeance!
SUPERVACUO Hell and torments!
AMBITIOSO [*to the Officer*] Slave, cam'st thou to delude us?
OFFICER Delude you, my lords?
SUPERVACUO Ay, villain. Where's this head now?
OFFICER Why, here, my lord.
[*He shows them Junior Brother's head, unrecognizable at first.*]
Just after his delivery,° you both came *Lussurioso's release*
With warrant from the Duke to behead your brother.
AMBITIOSO Ay, our brother, the Duke's son.
OFFICER The Duke's son, my lord, had his release before you came.
AMBITIOSO Whose head's that, then?
OFFICER His whom you left command for: your own brother's.
AMBITIOSO Our brother's? Oh, Furies!° *avenging goddesses*
SUPERVACUO Plagues!
AMBITIOSO Confusions!
SUPERVACUO Darkness!
AMBITIOSO Devils!
SUPERVACUO Fell it out so accursedly?
AMBITIOSO So damnedly?
SUPERVACUO Villain, I'll brain thee with it.
OFFICER Oh, my good lord! [*Exit.*]
SUPERVACUO The devil overtake thee!
AMBITIOSO Oh, fatal!

4. Please excuse my saying this.

SUPERVACUO Oh, prodigious° to our bloods! *ominous*
AMBITIOSO Did we dissemble?
SUPERVACUO Did we make our tears women for thee?[5]
AMBITIOSO Laugh and rejoice for thee?
SUPERVACUO Bring warrant for thy death?
AMBITIOSO Mock off thy head?
SUPERVACUO You had a trick; you had a wile, forsooth.
AMBITIOSO A murrain meet 'em,° there's none of these wiles that ever come to good. I see now there is nothing sure in mortality but mortality.[6] *A plague on them*
Well, no more words. Shalt° be revenged, i'faith. *You, Junior, will*
Come, throw off clouds° now, brother. Think of vengeance *moodiness*
And deeper settled hate.—Sirrah,[7] sit fast;
We'll pull down all but thou shalt down at last. *Exeunt.*

4.1

Enter Lussurioso with Hippolito.

LUSSURIOSO Hippolito!
HIPPOLITO My lord? Has Your good Lordship
Aught to command me in?
LUSSURIOSO I prithee leave us.
HIPPOLITO [*aside*] How's this? Come, and leave us?
LUSSURIOSO Hippolito!
HIPPOLITO Your Honor, I stand ready for any duteous employment.
LUSSURIOSO Heart, what mak'st thou° here? *are you doing*
HIPPOLITO [*aside*] A pretty lordly humor!° *whim*
He bids me to be present, to° depart. *only to bid me*
Something has stung his honor.
LUSSURIOSO Be nearer, draw nearer.
You're not so good,° methinks; I'm angry with you. *i.e., clever*
HIPPOLITO With me, my lord? I'm angry with myself for't.
LUSSURIOSO You did prefer° a goodly fellow to me; *recommend*
'Twas wittily elected,° 'twas. I thought *cleverly chosen*
'Had been a villain, and he proves a knave,[1]
To me a knave.
HIPPOLITO I chose him for the best, my lord.
'Tis much my sorrow if neglect in him
Breed discontent in you.
LUSSURIOSO Neglect? 'Twas will.° Judge of it: *willfulness*
Firmly to tell of an incredible act,
Not to be thought, less to be spoken of,
'Twixt my stepmother and the Bastard, oh,
Incestuous sweets between 'em.
HIPPOLITO Fie, my lord!
LUSSURIOSO I, in kind° loyalty to my father's forehead, *loving; filial*
Made this a desperate arm,[2] and in that fury
Committed treason on the lawful bed,

5. Did we weep like dissembling women, instead of weeping genuine tears for you, our brother?
6. There's nothing sure in mortal life except death.
7. "Sirrah" is an insulting way to refer to the absent Lussurioso, since it is normally used to address social inferiors.
4.1. The court.
1. I thought he was one who could do my dirty work, and instead he proves to be a rascal.
2. Lussurioso gestures with his sword arm.

And with my sword e'en razed° my father's bosom, *grazed*
For which I was within a stroke of death.
HIPPOLITO Alack, I'm sorry.

Enter Vindice [*disguised as Piato*].

[*Aside*] 'Sfoot, just upon the stroke
Jars in° my brother. 'Twill be villainous music. *Jarringly enters*
VINDICE My honored lord!
LUSSURIOSO Away!
Prithee forsake° us. Hereafter we'll not know thee. *leave*
VINDICE Not know me, my lord? Your Lordship cannot
choose.° *can't help knowing me*
LUSSURIOSO Begone, I say! Thou art a false knave.
VINDICE Why, the easier to be known, my lord.
LUSSURIOSO Push,° I shall prove too bitter, with a word *Pooh*
Make thee a perpetual prisoner,
And lay this iron age[3] upon thee.
VINDICE [*aside*] Mum!
For there's a doom would make a woman dumb.[4]
Missing the Bastard, next him, the wind's come about.[5]
Now 'tis my brother's turn to stay, mine to go out.
Exit Vindice.
LUSSURIOSO He's greatly moved° me. *angered*
HIPPOLITO Much to blame, i'faith.
LUSSURIOSO But I'll recover, to his ruin. 'Twas told me lately,
I know not whether falsely, that you'd a brother.
HIPPOLITO Who, I? Yes, my good lord, I have a brother.
LUSSURIOSO How chance the court ne'er saw him? Of what
nature?
How does he apply his hours?° *occupy his time*
HIPPOLITO Faith, to curse Fates,
Who, as he thinks, ordained him to be poor;
Keeps at home, full of want and discontent.
LUSSURIOSO There's hope in him, for discontent and want
Is the best clay to mold a villain of.
Hippolito, wish him repair to us.° *bid him come to me*
If there be aught in him to please our blood,° *temper*
For thy sake we'll advance him, and build fair
His meanest° fortunes; for it is in us° *lowest / lies in my power*
To rear up towers from cottages.
HIPPOLITO It is so, my lord. He will attend Your Honor;
But he's a man in whom much melancholy dwells.
LUSSURIOSO Why, the better. Bring him to court.
HIPPOLITO With willingness and speed.
[*Aside*] Whom he cast off e'en now, must now succeed.[6]
Brother, disguise must off;
In thine own shape now I'll prefer° thee to him. *recommend*
How strangely does himself work to undo him!° *Exit.* *himself, Lussurioso*

3. I.e., sword or leg irons; referring also to the mythological concept of the iron age, the present and most degenerate of the four ages (gold, silver, bronze, and iron) of human history described by Hesiod and other Greek poets.

4. Lussurioso's threat would stun even a woman into silence. (Women are proverbially talkative.)

5. I.e., I have failed thus far to kill Spurio and then Lussurioso; now Lussurioso is probably suspicious of, or at least impatient with, Piato. ("The wind's come about" is a hunting term, meaning that the prey can scent the hunter and is thus alarmed.)

6. Vindice, whom Lussurioso just cashiered, must now succeed himself (and thus succeed in his plan).

LUSSURIOSO This fellow will come fitly. He shall kill
That other slave° that did abuse my spleen° — *(Piato) / anger*
And made it swell to treason.° I have put — *a treasonous act*
Much of my heart into him;[7] he must die.
He that knows great men's secrets and proves slight,° — *untrustworthy*
That man ne'er lives to see his beard turn white.
Ay, he° shall speed him.° I'll employ the brother. — *(Vindice) / kill Piato*
Slaves° are but nails to drive out one another. — *Wretches, villains*
He being of black° condition, suitable — *melancholic*
To want° and ill content, hope of preferment — *poverty*
Will grind him to an edge—

The Nobles enter [two at first].

FIRST NOBLE Good days unto Your Honor!
LUSSURIOSO My kind lords, I do return the like.
SECOND NOBLE Saw you my lord the Duke?
LUSSURIOSO My lord and father? Is he from court?
FIRST NOBLE He's sure from court,
But where, which way, his pleasure took we know not,
Nor can we hear on't.
LUSSURIOSO Here come those should tell.° — *who can tell*

[Enter two more Nobles.]

Saw you my lord and father?
THIRD NOBLE Not since two hours before noon, my lord,
And then he privately rid forth.° — *(see 3.5.122–25)*
LUSSURIOSO Oh, he's rode forth?
FIRST NOBLE 'Twas wondrous privately.
SECOND NOBLE There's none i'th'court had any knowledge on't.
LUSSURIOSO His Grace is old, and sudden.° 'Tis no treason — *capricious*
To say the Duke my father has a humor,° — *whimsy*
Or such a toy° about him. What in us — *quirk*
Would appear light,° in him seems virtuous. — *frivolous*
THIRD NOBLE 'Tis oracle,° my lord. *Exeunt.* — *God's truth*

[4.2]

Enter Vindice and Hippolito, Vindice out of his disguise.

HIPPOLITO So, so, all's as it should be; you're yourself.
VINDICE How that great villain puts me to my shifts!° — *stratagems; disguises*
HIPPOLITO He that did lately in disguise reject thee
Shall, now thou art thyself, as much respect thee.
VINDICE 'Twill be the quainter fallacy.° But brother, — *cleverer misconception*
'Sfoot, what use will he put me to now, think'st thou?
HIPPOLITO Nay, you must pardon me in that;[1] I know not.
H'as some employment for you, but what 'tis
He and his secretary° the devil knows best. — *confidant*
VINDICE Well, I must suit my tongue to his desires,
What color° soe'er they be, hoping at last — *sort*
To pile up all my wishes on his breast.[2]

7. I have confided frankly in Piato.
4.2. The court.
1. You must excuse my not answering that.
2. (1) To press him to death under my vengeful desires; (2) to release my unfulfilled wishes at last on his dead body.

HIPPOLITO Faith, brother, he himself shows the way.
VINDICE Now the Duke is dead, the realm is clad in clay:° *the regime is dead*
His death being not yet known, under his name
The people still are governed. Well, thou his son° *(Lussurioso)*
Art not long-lived; thou shalt not joy° his death. *live to enjoy*
To kill thee, then, I should most honor thee,
For 'twould stand firm in every man's belief
Thou'st° a kind child, and only died'st with grief. *Thou wast*
HIPPOLITO You fetch about well, but let's talk in present.[3]
How will you appear in fashion° different, *manner of speech*
As well as in apparel, to make all things possible?
If you be but once tripped, we fall forever.
It is not the least policy to be doubtful.[4]
You must change tongue; familiar was your first.
VINDICE Why, I'll bear me in some strain of melancholy,
And string myself with heavy-sounding wire,
Like such an instrument that speaks
Merry things sadly.
HIPPOLITO Then 'tis as I meant;
I gave you out at first in discontent.[5]
VINDICE I'll turn myself,° and then— *transform my speech*
HIPPOLITO 'Sfoot, here he comes. Hast thought upon't?
VINDICE Salute him. Fear not me.

[*Enter Lussurioso. Vindice stands apart.*]

LUSSURIOSO Hippolito!
HIPPOLITO Your Lordship?
LUSSURIOSO What's he yonder?
HIPPOLITO 'Tis Vindice, my discontented brother,
Whom, 'cording to your will, I've brought to court.
LUSSURIOSO Is that thy brother? Beshrew me,° a good presence. *(a mild curse)*
I wonder he's been from the court so long.
[*To Vindice*] Come nearer.
HIPPOLITO Brother, Lord Lussurioso, the Duke's son.
[*Vindice approaches,*] *snatches off his hat and makes legs° to him.* [*Hippolito stands aside.*] *bows, curtsies*
LUSSURIOSO Be more near to us. Welcome. Nearer yet.
VINDICE How don you? God you god den.[6]
LUSSURIOSO We thank thee.
How strangely such a coarse, homely salute
Shows in the palace, where we greet in fire!
Nimble and desperate° tongues, should we name *reckless*
God in a salutation, 'twould ne'er be stood on't.[7] Heaven!
Tell me, what has made thee so melancholy?
VINDICE Why, going to law.
LUSSURIOSO Why, will that make a man melancholy?
VINDICE Yes, to look long upon ink and black buckram.[8] I went me to law in *anno quadragesimo secundo*, and I waded out of it in *anno sextagesimo tertio*.[9]

3. That was a nice rhetorical turn, but let's get down to business.
4. It is not unwise to be cautious.
5. From the first I described you as a malcontent. (See 4.1.61.)
6. How do you do? Good evening. (Colloquial rustic speech.)
7. No one would pay any heed. (Vindice did name God in his salutation, in line 43, although in a conventional phrase such as "God you god den," any remembrance of God is usually forgotten.)
8. A stiff linen often used in making lawyers' bags.
9. I began a lawsuit in the forty-second year of the present regime and emerged from it in the sixty-third

LUSSURIOSO What, three-and-twenty years in law?
VINDICE I have known those that have been five-and-fifty, and
all about pullen° and pigs. *poultry*
LUSSURIOSO May it be possible such men should breathe,° *exist*
To vex the terms° so much? *law-court terms*
VINDICE 'Tis food to some, my lord. There are old men at the
present that are so poisoned with the affectation of law
words (having had many suits canvassed)° that their com- *brought for investigation*
mon talk is nothing but Barbary° Latin. They cannot so *barbarous*
much as pray but in law, that their sins may be removed
with a writ of error[1] and their souls fetched up to heaven
with a sasarara.[2]
LUSSURIOSO It seems most strange to me.
Yet all the world meets round in the same bent;° *way, tendency*
Where the heart's set, there goes the tongue's consent.[3]
How dost apply thy studies, fellow?
VINDICE Study? Why, to think how a great rich man lies a-
dying, and a poor cobbler tolls the bell for him; how he cannot
depart the world,[4] and sees the great chest° stand before him, *chest for valuables*
when he lies speechless; how he will point you readily to all
the boxes, and when he is past all memory, as the gossips° *friends and relations*
guess, then thinks he of forfeitures and obligations;° nay, *legal dealings*
when to all men's hearings he whurls° and rattles in the *rumbles, gurgles*
throat, he's busy threat'ning his poor tenants; and this would
last me now some seven years thinking or thereabouts. But
I have a conceit a-coming in picture upon this;[5] I draw it
myself, which, i'faith, la, I'll present to Your Honor. You shall
not choose but like° it, for Your Lordship shall give me noth- *can't help liking*
ing for it.
LUSSURIOSO Nay you mistake me, then,
For I am published° bountiful enough. *reputed to be*
Let's taste of your conceit.
VINDICE In picture, my lord?
LUSSURIOSO Ay, in picture.
VINDICE Marry, this it is: A usuring father to be boiling in
hell, and his son and heir with a whore dancing over him.
HIPPOLITO [*aside*] He's pared him to the quick.
LUSSURIOSO The conceit's pretty, i'faith,
But, take't upon my life,° 'twill ne'er be liked. *take my word for it*
VINDICE No? Why, I'm sure the whore will be liked well
enough.
HIPPOLITO [*aside*] Ay, if she were out o'th'picture he'd like her
then himself.[6]
VINDICE And as for the son and heir, he shall be an eyesore
to no young revelers, for he shall be drawn in cloth-of-gold[7]
breeches.
LUSSURIOSO And thou hast put my meaning in the pockets,
And canst not draw that out.[8] My thought was this:

---

year. (Lussurioso subtracts 42 from 63 and gets 23. Either his arithmetic or his Latin is faulty. The figures are historically fanciful in any case.)

1. A writ seeking the reversal of a judgment on the basis of an error.

2. A certiorari, an appeal to a higher court.

3. Compare the proverb "What the heart thinks the tongue speaks."

4. How the rich man cannot bear to think of dying.

5. A clever idea for an emblematic picture is taking shape in my mind.

6. If she were a flesh-and-blood whore, not a mere picture, Lussurioso would like her.

7. Cloth of interwoven silk and gold thread.

8. I.e., You won't get any bounty (lines 81–84) from me that way; the money remains firmly placed in my pockets.

To see the picture of a usuring father
Boiling in hell, our rich men would ne'er like it.

VINDICE Oh, true! I cry you heartily mercy.° I know the reason, for some of 'em had rather be damned indeed than damned in colors.° *beg your pardon / in a painting*

LUSSURIOSO [*aside*] A parlous° melancholy! H'as wit enough *keen, shrewd*
To murder any man, and I'll give him means.—
I think thou art ill-monied.° *impoverished*

VINDICE Money? Ho, ho!
'T has been my want so long, 'tis now my scoff.
I've e'en forgot what color silver's of.

LUSSURIOSO [*aside*] It hits° as I could wish. *goes, occurs*

VINDICE I get good clothes
Of those that dread my humor, and, for table room,
I feed on those that cannot be rid of me.[9]

LUSSURIOSO [*giving money*] Somewhat to set thee up withal.° *with*

VINDICE Oh, mine eyes!

LUSSURIOSO How now, man?

VINDICE Almost struck blind.
This bright unusual shine to me seems proud;
I dare not look till the sun be in a cloud.

LUSSURIOSO I think I shall affect° his melancholy.— *take a fancy to*
How are they° now? *(your eyes)*

VINDICE The better for your asking.

LUSSURIOSO You shall be better yet, if you but fasten
Truly on my intent. [*He beckons Hippolito to join them.*]
Now you're both present,
I will unbrace° such a close° private villain *lay open / secret*
Unto your vengeful swords, the like ne'er heard of,
Who hath disgraced you much and injured us.° *me*

HIPPOLITO Disgraced us, my lord?

LUSSURIOSO Ay, Hippolito.
I kept it here° till now, that both your angers *(in my bosom or mind)*
Might meet him at once.

VINDICE I'm covetous
To know the villain.

LUSSURIOSO [*to Hippolito*] You know him: that slave-pander,
Piato, whom we threatened last
With irons in perpetual prisonment.° *(see 4.1.39–41)*

VINDICE [*aside*] All this is I.

HIPPOLITO Is't he, my lord?

LUSSURIOSO I'll tell you,
You first preferred him to me.

VINDICE Did you, brother?

HIPPOLITO I did indeed.

LUSSURIOSO And the ingrateful villain,
To quit° that kindness, strongly wrought° with me— *requite / prevailed*
Being,° as you see, a likely man for pleasure— *I being*
With jewels to corrupt your virgin sister.

HIPPOLITO Oh, villain!

VINDICE He shall surely die that did it.

LUSSURIOSO I, far from thinking any virgin harm—

9. Vindice describes how, as a typical malcontent and parasite, he sponges off those he castigates.

Especially knowing her to be as chaste
As that part which scarce suffers to be touched,
Th'eye[1]—would not endure him.
VINDICE Would you not,
My lord? 'Twas wondrous honorably done.
LUSSURIOSO But with some fine frowns kept him out.
VINDICE Out, slave!° *(expressing contempt)*
LUSSURIOSO What did me he° but, in revenge of that, *What did he do to me*
Went of his own free will to make infirm
Your sister's honor, whom I honor with my soul
For chaste respect;° and, not prevailing there *respect for chastity*
(As 'twas but desperate folly to attempt it),
In mere spleen, by the way, waylays your mother,
Whose honor being a coward, as it seems,
Yielded by little force.
VINDICE Coward indeed!
LUSSURIOSO He, proud of this advantage (as he thought),
Brought me these news for happy,° but I, *as promising success*
Heaven forgive me for't—
VINDICE What did Your Honor?
LUSSURIOSO In rage pushed him from me,
Trampled beneath his throat, spurned him,[2] and bruised;
Indeed I was too cruel, to say troth.
HIPPOLITO Most nobly managed!
VINDICE [*aside*] Has not heaven an ear?
Is all the lightning wasted?° *expended*
LUSSURIOSO If I now
Were so impatient in a modest° cause, *lesser, limited*
What should you be?
VINDICE Full mad. He shall not live
To see the moon change.° *To see a month pass*
LUSSURIOSO He's about the palace.—
Hippolito, entice him this way, that thy brother
May take full mark° of him. *observation*
HIPPOLITO Heart, that shall not need,° my lord. *be necessary*
I can direct him so far.
LUSSURIOSO Yet, for my hate's sake,
Go wind° him this way. I'll see him bleed myself. *i.e., lure*
HIPPOLITO [*aside to Vindice*] What now, brother?
VINDICE [*aside to Hippolito*] Nay, e'en what you will. You're put to't,° brother. *on your mettle*
HIPPOLITO [*aside to Vindice*] An impossible task, I'll swear,
To bring him hither that's already here. *Exit Hippolito.*
LUSSURIOSO Thy name? I have forgot it.
VINDICE Vindice,° my lord. *"revenger of wrongs"*
LUSSURIOSO 'Tis a good name, that.
VINDICE Ay, a revenger.
LUSSURIOSO It does betoken courage. Thou shouldst be valiant,
And kill thine enemies.
VINDICE That's my hope, my lord.
LUSSURIOSO This slave° is one. *(Piato)*
VINDICE I'll doom him.

1. Lussurioso leads his listeners to expect him to refer to the woman's sexual anatomy, but then demurely corrects that impression with "Th'eye."
2. Trampled on his body and kicked him.

LUSSURIOSO Then I'll praise thee.
Do thou observe° me best, and I'll best raise thee. *adhere to, humor*

Enter Hippolito.

VINDICE Indeed, I thank you.
LUSSURIOSO Now, Hippolito,
Where's the slave-pander?
HIPPOLITO Your good Lordship
Would have a loathsome sight of him, much offensive;
He's not in case[3] now to be seen, my lord.
The worst of all the deadly sins is in him:
That beggarly damnation, drunkenness.
LUSSURIOSO Then he's a double slave.
VINDICE [*aside to Hippolito*] 'Twas well conveyed,° *handled, improvised*
Upon a sudden wit.° *quick thinking*
LUSSURIOSO What, are you both
Firmly resolved? I'll see him dead myself.[4]
VINDICE Or else let not us live.
LUSSURIOSO You may direct
Your brother to take note of him.
HIPPOLITO I shall.
LUSSURIOSO Rise but in this, and you shall never fall.
VINDICE Your Honor's vassals!
LUSSURIOSO [*aside*] This was wisely carried;
Deep policy in us makes fools of such.° *(Vindice and Hippolito)*
Then must a slave die when he knows too much.

Exit Lussurioso.

VINDICE O thou almighty Patience!° 'Tis my wonder *patient God*
That such a fellow, impudent and wicked,
Should not be cloven° as he stood, *split by lightning*
Or with a secret wind burst open!
Is there no thunder left, or is't kept up
In stock for heavier vengeance? [*Thunder is heard.*] There it goes!
HIPPOLITO Brother, we lose° ourselves. *overreach*
VINDICE But I have found it;° *(the way)*
'Twill hold, 'tis sure. Thanks, thanks to any spirit
That mingled it 'mongst my inventions!
HIPPOLITO What is't?
VINDICE 'Tis sound and good; thou shalt partake it.
I'm hired to kill myself.
HIPPOLITO True.
VINDICE Prithee mark it:
And the old Duke being dead but not conveyed°— *carried off*
For he's already missed too, and you know
Murder will peep out of the closest° husk— *most tightly shut*
HIPPOLITO Most true.
VINDICE What say you then to this device:
If we dressed up the body of the Duke—
HIPPOLITO In that disguise of yours?
VINDICE You're quick, you've reached° it. *grasped*
HIPPOLITO I like it wondrously.
VINDICE And being in drink, as you have published° him, *declared, described*

3. (1) In any condition; (2) in a suit of clothes.
4. I wish to see the dead body (as proof of death).

To lean him on his elbow, as if sleep had caught him,
Which claims most interest in such sluggy° men. — *sluggish*
HIPPOLITO Good yet. But here's a doubt:
We, thought by th'Duke's son° to kill that pander,° — *(Lussurioso) / (Piato)*
Shall, when he is known, be thought to kill the Duke.
VINDICE Neither. Oh, thanks! It is substantial;[5]
For, that disguise being on him which I wore,
It will be thought I, which he calls the pander,
Did kill the Duke and fled away in his apparel, leaving him
so disguised to avoid swift pursuit.
HIPPOLITO Firmer and firmer!
VINDICE Nay, doubt not 'tis in grain.° — *fast dyed, firm*
I warrant it hold color.
HIPPOLITO Let's about it.
VINDICE But by the way, too, now I think on't, brother,
Let's conjure° that base devil out of our mother. *Exeunt.* — *exorcise, expel*

[4.3]

Enter the Duchess, arm in arm with the Bastard [Spurio]. He seemeth lasciviously to [look upon] her. After them, enter Supervacuo, running, with a rapier. His brother [Ambitioso] stops him.

SPURIO Madam, unlock yourself.° Should it be seen, — *let go your arm*
Your arm would be suspected.
DUCHESS Who is't that dares suspect or this or these?° — *(kisses or hugs)*
May not we deal our favors where we please?
SPURIO I'm confident you may.
Exeunt [Spurio and the Duchess].
AMBITIOSO 'Sfoot, brother, hold!
SUPERVACUO Wouldst° let the Bastard shame us? — *Would you*
AMBITIOSO Hold, hold, brother!
There's fitter time than now.
SUPERVACUO Now, when I see it?
AMBITIOSO 'Tis too much seen already.
SUPERVACUO Seen and known;
The nobler she's,° the baser is she grown. — *higher in rank she is*
AMBITIOSO If° she were bent° lasciviously, the fault — *Even if / inclined*
Of mighty women that sleep soft—oh, death!—
Must she needs choose such an unequal° sinner, — *socially inferior*
To make all worse?
SUPERVACUO A bastard, the Duke's bastard!
Shame heaped on shame!
AMBITIOSO Oh, our disgrace!
Most women have small waist the world throughout,
But their desires are thousand miles about.
SUPERVACUO Come, stay not here; let's after, and prevent,
Or else they'll sin faster than we'll repent.° *Exeunt.* — *regret not acting*

5. Not to worry. Thank goodness! I have a rock-solid solution.

4.3. The court.

[4.4]

Enter Vindice and Hippolito, bringing out their Mother, one by one shoulder and the other by the other, with daggers in their hands [*which they point at her breast*].

VINDICE O thou for whom no name is bad enough!
MOTHER What means my sons? What, will you murder me?[1]
VINDICE Wicked, unnatural parent!
HIPPOLITO Fiend of women!
MOTHER Oh, are sons turned monsters? Help!
VINDICE In vain.
MOTHER Are you so barbarous to set iron nipples° *i.e., daggers*
Upon the breast that gave you suck?
VINDICE That breast
Is turned to quarlèd° poison. *curdled*
MOTHER Cut not° your days for't. Am not I your mother? *Don't cut short*
VINDICE Thou dost usurp that title now by fraud,
For in that shell of mother breeds a bawd.
MOTHER A bawd? Oh, name far loathsomer than hell!
HIPPOLITO It should be so, knew'st thou thy office° well. *(as bawd or mother)*
MOTHER I hate it.° *(the name "bawd")*
VINDICE Ah, is't possible? Thou only?[2]—You powers on high,
That women should dissemble when they die!° *are about to die*
MOTHER Dissemble?
VINDICE Did not the Duke's son direct
A fellow of the world's condition° hither, *A worldling (Piato)*
That did corrupt all that was good in thee,
Made thee uncivilly° forget thyself, *barbarously*
And work our sister to his lust?
MOTHER Who, I?
That had been° monstrous. I defy that man *would have been*
For any such intent. None lives so pure
But shall be soiled with slander. Good son, believe it not.
VINDICE Oh, I'm in doubt whether I'm myself or no.
Stay, let me look again upon this face.
Who shall be saved, when mothers have no grace?
HIPPOLITO 'Twould make one half despair.
VINDICE [*to his mother*] I was the man.
Defy me now! Let's see, do't modestly.
MOTHER Oh, hell unto my soul!
VINDICE In that disguise, I, sent from the Duke's son,
Tried° you, and found you base metal,° *Tested / metal; mettle*
As any villain might have done.
MOTHER Oh, no,
No tongue but yours could have bewitched me so.
VINDICE Oh, nimble in damnation, quick in tune!
There is no devil could strike fire so soon.[3]
I am confuted in a word.

4.4. Gratiana's house, near the court.
1. This line is borrowed from *Hamlet*, 3.4.21, where Queen Gertrude responds in alarm to Hamlet's strange behavior after his sudden and brusque entry into her chamber; her outcry prompts the hidden Polonius to call for help, leading to Hamlet's mistaken killing of him.
2. I.e., You, of all women?
3. Vindice credits his mother with a brilliant stroke of blame-shifting, but also implies that only someone worse than a devil could so skillfully reassign guilt in such a circumstance.

MOTHER [*kneeling*] Oh, sons,
Forgive me! To myself I'll prove more true.
You that should honor me, I kneel to you. [*She weeps.*]
VINDICE A mother to give aim to her own daughter![4]
HIPPOLITO True, brother. How far beyond nature 'tis!
Though many mothers do't.
VINDICE [*to his dagger*] Nay, an° you draw tears once, go you to bed.[5] [*He sheathes his dagger.*] — *if*
Wet will make iron blush° and change to red. — *i.e., rust*
Brother, it rains.° 'Twill spoil your dagger; house it. — *i.e., she weeps*
HIPPOLITO [*sheathing his dagger*] 'Tis done.
VINDICE I'faith, 'tis a sweet shower; it does much good.
The fruitful grounds and meadows of her soul
Has been long dry. Pour down, thou blessèd dew!
Rise, mother. Troth, this shower has made you higher.
MOTHER [*rising*] O you heavens,
Take this infectious° spot out of my soul! — *infected*
I'll rinse it in seven waters of mine eyes.
Make my tears salt° enough to taste of grace! — *i.e., stinging*
To weep is to our sex naturally given,
But to weep truly, that's a gift from heaven.
VINDICE Nay, I'll kiss you now. Kiss her, brother.
[*They kiss her.*]
Let's marry her to our souls, wherein's no lust,
And honorably love her.
HIPPOLITO Let it be.° — *Let it be so*
VINDICE For honest women are so seld° and rare, — *infrequent*
'Tis good to cherish those poor few that are.
O you° of easy wax,° do but imagine, — *(mother) / too pliable*
Now the disease has left you, how leprously
That office would have clinged unto your forehead!
All mothers that had any graceful hue
Would have worn masks to hide their face at you.
It would have grown to this: at your foul name,
Green-colored maids[6] would have turned red with shame.
HIPPOLITO And then our sister, full of hire and baseness.[7]
VINDICE There had been boiling lead° again. — *punishments of hell*
The Duke's son's great concubine,
A drab of state, a cloth-o'-silver slut,[8]
To have her train borne up, and her soul trail i'th'dirt;
Great!° — *Such is greatness!*
HIPPOLITO To be miserably great, rich to be
Eternally wretched!
VINDICE Oh, common[9] madness!
Ask but the thriving'st harlot in cold blood;° — *when sober and unaroused*
She'd give the world to make her honor good.
Perhaps you'll say, but only to'th'Duke's son
In private; why, she first begins with one
Who afterward to thousand proves a whore.
Break ice in one place, it will crack in more.

4. To think of a mother guiding the aim of men to her own daughter, as if to a target!
5. Seeing his mother's tears, Vindice relents.
6. Maidens pale with greensickness, a kind of anemia.
7. And our sister too would have been shamed. ("Hire" means "payment for services," here as a whore.)
8. I.e., Castiza, having become Lussurioso's concubine, is imagined now as the state or royal whore expensively dressed in cloth of woven gold and silver threads.
9. (1) Frequently occurring; (2) cheap, disgusting.

MOTHER Most certainly applied.° *applied as a maxim*
HIPPOLITO Oh, brother, you forget our business.
VINDICE And well remembered. Joy's a subtle elf;
I think man's happiest when he forgets himself.—
Farewell, once dried,° now holy-watered mead;° *withered / meadow*
Our hearts wear feathers, that before wore lead.° *i.e., were heavy*
MOTHER I'll give° you this, that one I never knew *grant*
Plead better for, and 'gainst, the devil than you.
VINDICE You make me proud on't.
HIPPOLITO Commend us in all virtue to our sister.
VINDICE Ay, for the love of heaven, to that true maid.
MOTHER With my best words.
VINDICE Why, that was motherly said.
Exeunt [*Vindice and Hippolito*].
MOTHER I wonder now what fury did transport me?
I feel good thoughts begin to settle in me.
Oh, with what forehead° can I look on her, *i.e., effrontery*
Whose honor I've so impiously beset?
And here she comes.

[*Enter Castiza.*]

CASTIZA Now, mother, you have wrought° with me so strongly, *prevailed*
That what for° my advancement as to calm *as much for*
The trouble of your tongue, I am content.
MOTHER Content? To what?
CASTIZA To do as you have wished me:
To prostitute my breast to the Duke's son,
And put myself to common usury.° *commercial use*
MOTHER I hope you will not so.
CASTIZA Hope you will not?
That's not the hope you look to be saved in.[1]
MOTHER Truth, but it is.
CASTIZA Do not deceive yourself;
I am, as you, e'en out of marble wrought.° *impervious to shame*
What would you now? Are ye not pleased yet with me?
You shall not° wish me to be more lascivious *cannot*
Than I intend to be.
MOTHER Strike not me cold.
CASTIZA How often have you charged me on your blessing
To be a cursèd woman? When you knew
Your blessing had no force to make me lewd,
You laid your curse upon me. That did more.
The mother's curse is heavy; where that fights,
Suns° set in storm, and daughters lose their lights.[2] *Suns; sons*
MOTHER Good child, dear maid, if there be any spark
Of heavenly intellectual° fire within thee, *spiritual*
Oh, let my breath revive it to a flame!
Put not all out with woman's willful follies.
I am recovered of that foul disease
That haunts too many mothers. Kind,° forgive me; *Kind one; child*

1. I.e., That's not the way you hope to be saved from poverty. (With an added ironic sense: That's certainly not the way you have proceeded thus far as a means of saving your immortal soul.)
2. Daughters lose their moral guiding lights.

Make me not sick in health. If then
My words prevailed when they were wickedness,
How much more now when they are just and good!
CASTIZA I wonder what you mean? Are not you she
For° whose infect° persuasions I could scarce — *Because of / tainted*
Kneel out my prayers, and had much ado
In three hours' reading° to untwist so much — *devotional reading*
Of the black serpent as you wound about me?
MOTHER 'Tis unfruitful, held tedious to repeat
What's past. I'm now your present mother.° — *really your mother now*
CASTIZA Push,° now 'tis too late. — *Pooh*
MOTHER Bethink° again; — *Consider*
Thou know'st not what thou say'st.
CASTIZA No?
Deny advancement? Treasure? The Duke's son?
MOTHER Oh, see,
I spoke those words,° and now they poison me. — *(see 2.1.162)*
What will the deed do, then?
Advancement, true—as high as shame can pitch!
For° treasure, whoe'er knew a harlot rich? — *As for*
Or could build, by the purchase° of her sin, — *profit*
An hospital° to keep their bastards in? — *orphanage*
The Duke's son?[3] Oh, when women are young courtiers,
They are sure to be old beggars.
To know the miseries most harlots taste,
Thoud'st wish thyself unborn when thou art unchaste.
CASTIZA [*embracing her*] Oh, mother, let me twine about your neck,
And kiss you till my soul melt on your lips!
I did but this to try you.
MOTHER Oh, speak truth![4]
CASTIZA Indeed I did not,° for no tongue has force — *didn't mean to sin*
To alter me from honest.
If maidens would,° men's words could have no power. — *would be virtuous*
A virgin honor is a crystal tower,
Which, being weak, is guarded with good spirits;
Until she basely yields, no ill inherits.° — *takes possession*
MOTHER Oh, happy child! Faith and thy birth hath saved me.
'Mongst thousand daughters, happiest of all others,
Be thou a glass° for maids, and I for mothers. *Exeunt.* — *mirror, model*

[5.1]

Enter Vindice and Hippolito [with the Duke's body dressed as Piato. They arrange the body as if it were in a drunken sleep, leaning head on elbow].

VINDICE So, so, he leans well. Take heed you wake him not, brother.
HIPPOLITO I warrant you, my life for yours.° — *I bet my life*
VINDICE That's a good lay,° for I must kill myself. Brother, — *bet*

3. I.e., Do you really expect Lussurioso to make you wealthy and keep you so?

4. I.e., Are you kidding me now?

5.1. A private room at court.

that's I; that sits for me.[1] Do you mark it? And I must stand ready here to make away myself yonder—I must sit to be killed, and stand to kill myself.[2] I could vary it not so little as thrice over again; 't has some eight returns, like Michaelmas term.[3]

HIPPOLITO That's enough, o'conscience.° *(on my conscience)*

VINDICE But sirrah, does the Duke's son come single?

HIPPOLITO No, there's the hell on't, his faith's too feeble to go alone. He brings flesh flies[4] after him, that will buzz against° supper time, and hum for his coming out. *(in anticipation of)*

VINDICE Ah, the fly-flap° of vengeance beat 'em to pieces! Here was the sweetest occasion, the fittest hour, to have made my revenge familiar with him, shown° him the body of the Duke his father and how quaintly° he died, like a politician in hugger-mugger;° made° no man acquainted with it, and, in catastrophe,[5] slain° him over his father's breast; and oh, I'm mad to lose such a sweet opportunity! *(may the flyswatter; to have shown; ingeniously; secrecy / to have made; to have slain)*

HIPPOLITO Nay, push, prithee be content. There's no remedy present. May not hereafter times open in as fair faces as this?[6]

VINDICE They may, if they can paint° so well. *(i.e., dissemble)*

HIPPOLITO Come, now to avoid all suspicion, let's forsake this room, and be going to meet the Duke's son.

VINDICE Content; I'm for any weather.° [*They start to leave.*] Heart! Step close;° here he comes. *(ready for anything; Look out)*

Enter Lussurioso.

HIPPOLITO My honored lord!

LUSSURIOSO Oh, me! You both present?

VINDICE E'en newly, my lord, just as Your Lordship entered now. About this place we had notice given he° should be, but in some loathsome plight or other. *((Piato))*

HIPPOLITO Came Your Honor private?

LUSSURIOSO Private enough for this; only a few
Attend my coming out.

HIPPOLITO [*aside*] Death rot those few!

LUSSURIOSO [*seeing the body*] Stay! Yonder's the slave.[7]

VINDICE Mass, there's the slave indeed, my lord.
[*Aside*] 'Tis a good child; he calls his father slave.

LUSSURIOSO Ay, that's the villain, the damned villain! Softly,
Tread easy. [*They approach the body.*]

VINDICE Pooh, I warrant you, my lord,
We'll stifle in° our breaths. *(hold)*

LUSSURIOSO That will do well.—
Base rogue, thou sleepest thy last! [*Aside*] 'Tis policy° *(craftiness)*
To have him killed in's sleep, for if he waked
He would betray all to them.

1. That body of the duke is my look-alike (in my role as Piato).
2. My look-alike, the dead duke, must assume a reclining position, while I am commanded (as Vindice) to kill my disguised self, Piato.
3. I could even play as many as eight variations on this conundrum, like writs issued over eight weeks in Michaelmas term (the fall law-court term).
4. Blowflies, which lay eggs in dead flesh; hence, fawning courtiers.
5. In conclusion (as of a tragedy).
6. May not some later occasion give as good opportunity?
7. Lussurioso thinks he sees Piato.

VINDICE But my lord—
LUSSURIOSO Ha? What say'st?
VINDICE Shall we kill him now he's drunk?
LUSSURIOSO Ay, best of all.
VINDICE Why, then he will ne'er live to be sober.
LUSSURIOSO No matter; let him reel to hell.
VINDICE But being so full of liquor, I fear he will put out all the fire.° *hellfire*
LUSSURIOSO Thou art a mad beast![8]
VINDICE [*aside*] And leave none to warm Your Lordship's golls° withal. [*Aloud*] For he that dies drunk falls into hellfire like a bucket o'water, qush, qush. *hands*
LUSSURIOSO Come, be ready. Nake° your swords, think of your wrongs. This slave has injured you. *Unsheathe*
VINDICE Troth, so he has, [*aside*] and he has paid well for't.
LUSSURIOSO Meet with° him now. *Encounter*
VINDICE You'll bear us out,° my lord? *back us up*
LUSSURIOSO Pooh, am I a lord for nothing, think you? Quickly, now. [*Vindice and Hippolito stab the Duke's body.*]
VINDICE Sa, sa, sa; thump!° There he lies. *(cries in fencing)*
LUSSURIOSO Nimbly done. [*He recognizes the Duke.*] Ha?
Oh, villains, murderers!
'Tis the old Duke my father!
VINDICE That's a jest.° *You must be kidding*
LUSSURIOSO What, stiff and cold already?
[*To them*] Oh, pardon me to call you from your names![9]
'Tis none of your deed. That villain Piato,
Whom you thought now to kill, has murdered him
And left him thus disguised.
HIPPOLITO And not unlikely.
VINDICE Oh, rascal! Was he not ashamed
To put the Duke into a greasy doublet?° *man's jacket*
LUSSURIOSO He has been cold and stiff, who knows how long?
VINDICE [*aside*] Marry, that do I.
LUSSURIOSO No words, I pray, of anything intended.[1]
VINDICE Oh, my lord![2]
HIPPOLITO I would fain° have Your Lordship think that we have small reason to prate. *gladly*
LUSSURIOSO Faith, thou say'st true. I'll forthwith send to court
For all the nobles, Bastard, Duchess, all,
How here by miracle we found him dead,
And in his raiment that foul villain fled.[3]
VINDICE That will be the best way, my lord, to clear us all; let's cast about° to be clear. *find a way*
LUSSURIOSO [*calling*] Ho, Nencio, Sordido, and the rest!

Enter all [*his followers attending him without, including Sordido and Nencio*].

SORDIDO My lord?
NENCIO My lord?

8. Lussurioso laughs appreciatively at Vindice's witticism.
9. Forgive my calling you "villains, murderers" (line 65), when you are none.
1. Of anything commanded by me.
2. I.e., How can you imagine we would say anything?
3. And that the foul villain Piato has fled in the Duke's clothes.

LUSSURIOSO Be witnesses of a strange spectacle:
Choosing for private conference that sad° room, *gloomy, dark*
We found the Duke my father gealed° in blood. *congealed*
SORDIDO My lord the Duke?—Run, hie thee, Nencio!
Startle the court by signifying so much. [*Exit Nencio.*]
VINDICE [*aside to Hippolito*] Thus much by wit a deep revenger can:° *can do*
When murder's known, to be the clearest° man. *least suspected*
We're furthest off, and with as bold an eye
Survey his body as the standers-by.
LUSSURIOSO My royal father, too basely let blood
By a malevolent slave!
HIPPOLITO [*aside to Vindice*] Hark, he calls thee slave again.
VINDICE [*aside to Hippolito*] He's lost, he may.[4]
LUSSURIOSO Oh, sight! Look hither, see, his lips are gnawn
With poison.
VINDICE How, his lips? [*Examining*] By th'Mass, they be.
LUSSURIOSO Oh, villain! Oh, rogue! Oh, slave! Oh, rascal!
HIPPOLITO [*aside to Vindice*] Oh, good deceit! He quits him with like terms.[5]

[*Enter Nobles, along with Ambitioso and Supervacuo.*]

FIRST NOBLE Where?
SECOND NOBLE Which way?
AMBITIOSO Over what roof hangs this prodigious° comet *ominous*
In deadly fire?
LUSSURIOSO Behold, behold, my lords:
The Duke my father's murdered by a vassal
That owes this habit,° and here left disguised. *owns these clothes*

[*Enter Duchess and Spurio.*]

DUCHESS My lord and husband!
SECOND NOBLE Reverend Majesty!
FIRST NOBLE I have seen these clothes,[6]
Often attending on him.° *(the Duke)*
VINDICE [*aside to Hippolito*] That nobleman
Has been i'th'country, for he does not lie.[7]
SUPERVACUO [*aside to Ambitioso*] Learn of our mother; let's dissemble too.
I am glad he's vanished;° so, I hope, are you? *deceased*
AMBITIOSO [*aside to Supervacuo*] Ay, you may take my word for't.
SPURIO [*aside*] Old dad, dead?
I, one of his cast sins, will send the Fates
Most hearty commendations by his own son.[8]
I'll tug in the new stream till strength be done.[9]
LUSSURIOSO Where be those two that did affirm to us

4. Since he's lost the game, I am prepared to let him say whatever he wants.
5. Lussurioso lashes out at the supposed Piato ("quits him" means "requites him," or "pays him back") using much the same terms he used against Vindice and Hippolito at line 65.
6. I have often seen someone dressed in these clothes the dead Duke now wears.
7. I.e., The nobleman speaks more truly than he realizes, like a person who has been living away from court, is unaware of the goings-on there, and so unintentionally touches in his speech on some point of controversy or delicacy. The line may also play on the truism that country-folk speak more honestly than courtiers.
8. I, a by-product of his lechery, will kill Lussurioso and employ him as an ambassador to the goddesses of destiny.
9. I'll force my way against the currents of this new situation as long as my strength holds out.

My lord the Duke was privately rid forth?
FIRST NOBLE Oh, pardon us, my lords. He gave that charge
Upon our lives, if he were missed at court,
To answer so. He rode not anywhere;
We left him private with that fellow° here. (Piato; see 3.5.122–28)
VINDICE [*aside*] Confirmed!
LUSSURIOSO Oh, heavens! That false charge was his death.
Impudent beggars, durst you to our face
Maintain such a false answer?—Bear him straight
To execution.
FIRST NOBLE My lord!
LUSSURIOSO Urge me no more.
In this, the excuse may be called half the murder.[1]
VINDICE You've sentenced well.
LUSSURIOSO Away! See it be done.
[*Exit First Noble, under guard.*]
VINDICE [*aside*] Could you not stick?[2] See what confession doth!
Who would not lie, when men are hanged for truth?
HIPPOLITO [*aside to Vindice*] Brother, how happy is our vengeance!
VINDICE [*aside to Hippolito*] Why, it hits° *i.e., succeeds*
Past the apprehension of indifferent wits.° *ordinary intelligences*
LUSSURIOSO [*to a noble*] My lord, let post-horse° be sent *swift couriers*
Into all places to entrap the villain.
VINDICE [*aside*] Post-horse! Ha, ha!
SECOND NOBLE [*to Lussurioso*] My lord, we're something bold to know our duty.[3]
Your father's accidentally° departed; *unexpectedly*
The titles that were due to him meet you.
LUSSURIOSO Meet me? I'm not at leisure, my good lord;
I've many griefs to dispatch out o'th'way.
[*Aside*] Welcome, sweet titles! [*Aloud*] Talk to me, my lords,
Of sepulchres and mighty emperors' bones;
That's thought for me.
VINDICE [*aside*] So, one may see by this
How foreign markets go:[4]
Courtiers have feet o'th'nines, and tongues o'th'twelves;[5]
They flatter dukes, and dukes flatter themselves.° *deceive themselves*
SECOND NOBLE My lord, it is your shine must° comfort us. *radiance that must*
LUSSURIOSO Alas, I shine in tears like the sun in April.
SORDIDO You're now my lord's grace.° *my gracious lord*
LUSSURIOSO My lord's grace? I perceive you'll have it so.
SORDIDO 'Tis but your own.° *merely your due*
LUSSURIOSO Then heavens give me grace to be so!
VINDICE [*aside*] He prays well for himself!
THIRD NOBLE [*to the Duchess*] Madam, all sorrows
Must run their circles into° joys. No doubt but time *give way in time to*
Will make the murderer bring forth himself.
VINDICE [*aside*] He were an ass then, i'faith.
THIRD NOBLE In the mean season,° *In the meantime*

1. The First Noble's excuse makes him an accomplice in the murder.
2. Couldn't you keep silent? (Said as a comment on the departed First Noble.)
3. We're rather eager to know to whom we now owe obedience.
4. I.e., How courtiers adapt themselves to courtly flattering ways. ("Foreign" suggests effete imported fashions.)
5. Courtiers have voluble, huge tongues, larger even than their size nine feet.

Let us bethink° the latest° funeral honors — *consider / final*
Due to the Duke's cold body—and, withal,
Calling to memory our new happiness
Spread in° his royal son.°—Lords, gentlemen, — *by / son; sun*
Prepare for revels.
VINDICE [*aside*] Revels!
THIRD NOBLE Time hath several falls;° — *changes, reversals*
Griefs lift up joys, feasts put down funerals.
LUSSURIOSO Come, then, my lords; my favors to you all.
[*Aside*] The Duchess is suspected foully bent;° — *rumored to be corrupt*
I'll begin dukedom with her banishment.
Exeunt Duke [*Lussurioso*], *Nobles, and Duchess.*
HIPPOLITO [*to Vindice*] Revels!
VINDICE [*to Hippolito*] Ay, that's the word; we are firm° yet. — *safe, unsuspected*
Strike one strain more,° and then we crown our wit. — *Play one more tune*
Exeunt brothers [*Vindice and Hippolito*].
SPURIO [*aside*] Well, have at the fairest mark![6] So said the
Duke when he begot me;
And if I miss his heart or near about,
Then have at any; a bastard scorns to be out.° [*Exit.*] — *out of the action*
SUPVERVACUO Note'st thou that Spurio, brother?
AMBITIOSO Yes, I note him, to our shame.
SUPERVACUO He shall not live; his hair shall not grow much
longer. In this time of revels, tricks may be set afoot. See'st
thou yon new moon? It shall outlive the new duke by much.
This hand shall dispossess him; then we're mighty.
A masque is treason's license, that build upon;
'Tis murder's best face when a vizard's on.[7]
Exit Supervacuo.
AMBITIOSO Is't so? 'Tis very good!
And do you think to be duke then, kind brother?
I'll see fair play; drop one, and there lies t'other.[8]
Exit Ambitioso.

[5.2]

Enter Vindice and Hippolito, with Piero and other lords [*Nobles*].

VINDICE My lords, be all of music! Strike old griefs
Into other countries
That flow in too much milk and have faint livers,[1]
Not daring to stab home° their discontents. — *all the way*
Let our hid flames break out, as fire, as lightning,
To blast this villainous dukedom vexed with sin.
Wind up your souls to their full height again!
PIERO How?
FIRST NOBLE Which way?
SECOND NOBLE Any way. Our wrongs are such,
We cannot justly be revenged too much.

6. (1) Have a go at the best target, i.e., Lussurioso; (2) here's to sexual success with the most attractive wench.
7. A masque is a fine occasion for treachery—build on that idea; murder thrives under cover of disguise.
8. Eliminate one player (Supervacuo) and another is standing ready—I myself.
5.2. A banqueting room at court.
1. Banish all former griefs to foreign lands where the inhabitants lack manliness. (The liver was thought to be the seat of courage and other strong emotions.)

VINDICE You shall have all enough. Revels are toward,° *imminent*
And those few nobles that have long suppressed you
Are busied to° the furnishing of a masque, *with*
And do affect° to make a pleasant tale on't; *undertake, propose*
The masquing suits are fashioning.° Now comes in *being fashioned*
That which must glad us all: we to take pattern° *copy the pattern*
Of all those suits, the color, trimming, fashion,
E'en to an undistinguished hair almost;[2]
Then, ent'ring first, observing the true form,° *order of the dance*
Within a strain° or two we shall find leisure *musical tune, air*
To steal our swords out handsomely,
And, when they think their pleasure sweet and good,
In midst of all their joys, they shall sigh blood.

PIERO Weightily, effectually.

THIRD NOBLE Before the t'other masquers come—

VINDICE We're gone, all done and past.

PIERO But how for° the Duke's guard? *what to do about*

VINDICE Let that alone;° *Don't fret*
By one and one their strengths shall be drunk down.° *disabled by drink*

HIPPOLITO There are five hundred gentlemen in the action
That will apply themselves and not stand idle.

PIERO Oh, let us hug your bosoms!

VINDICE Come, my lords,
Prepare for deeds; let other times have words.° *Exeunt.* *talk some other time*

[5.3]

In a dumb show, the possessing° of the young Duke [Lussurioso] with all his Nobles. Then, sounding music. A furnished table is brought forth. Then enters the Duke and his Nobles to the banquet. A blazing star° appeareth. *installation* / *comet*

FIRST NOBLE Many harmonious hours and choicest pleasures
Fill up the royal numbers of your years!

LUSSURIOSO My lords, we're pleased to thank you—though we know
'Tis but your duty now to wish it so.

FIRST NOBLE That shine° makes us all happy. *smiling aspect*

THIRD NOBLE [*aside*] His Grace frowns.

SECOND NOBLE [*aside*] Yet we must say he smiles.

FIRST NOBLE [*aside*] I think we must.

LUSSURIOSO [*aside*] That foul, incontinent° Duchess we have banished; *unchaste*
The Bastard shall not live. After these revels,
I'll begin strange ones; he and the stepsons
Shall pay their lives for the first subsidies.[1]
We must not frown so soon,° else 't had been now. *so early in my dukedom*

FIRST NOBLE My gracious lord, please you prepare for pleasure;
The masque is not far off.

LUSSURIOSO We are for pleasure.
[*He sees the comet.*]
Beshrew° thee, what art thou? Thou mad'st me start. *A curse on*
Thou hast committed treason! A blazing star!

2. Even to the tiniest detail.
5.3. The court.

1. Will die as the first installment of the retribution that must be paid.

FIRST NOBLE A blazing star? Oh, where, my lord?
LUSSURIOSO Spy out.
SECOND NOBLE See, see, my lords, a wondrous dreadful one.
LUSSURIOSO I am not pleased at that ill-knotted fire,[2]
That bushing,° flaring star. Am not I duke? *bushy-tailed*
It should not quake me now. Had it appeared
Before, it I might then have justly feared;
But yet they say, whom art and learning weds,[3]
When stars wear locks,° they threaten great men's heads. *i.e., comet trails*
Is it so? You are read,° my lords. *learned*
FIRST NOBLE May it please Your Grace,
It shows great anger.
LUSSURIOSO That does not please Our Grace.° *i.e., me, the Duke*
SECOND NOBLE Yet here's the comfort, my lord: many times,
When it seems most,° it threatens farthest off. *greatest*
LUSSURIOSO Faith, and I think so too.
FIRST NOBLE Beside, my lord,
You're gracefully established, with the loves
Of all your subjects; and, for° natural death, *as for*
I hope it will be threescore years a-coming.
LUSSURIOSO True.—No more but threescore years?
FIRST NOBLE Fourscore, I hope, my lord.
SECOND NOBLE And fivescore, I.
THIRD NOBLE But 'tis my hope, my lord, you shall ne'er die.
LUSSURIOSO [*to Third Noble*] Give me thy hand. These others I rebuke.
He that hopes so is fittest for° a duke. *as adviser for*
Thou shalt sit next me.—Take your places, lords;
We're ready now for sports.° Let 'em set on!— *i.e., masquing*
You thing,° we shall forget you quite anon. *i.e., the comet*
THIRD NOBLE I hear 'em coming, my lord.

Enter the masque of revengers: the two brothers [*Vindice and Hippolito*] *and two lords* [*Nobles*] *more.*

LUSSURIOSO Ah, 'tis well.
[*Aside*] Brothers, and Bastard, you dance next in hell.

The revengers dance. At the end, steal out their swords, and these four kill the four at the table, in their chairs.[4] *It thunders.*

VINDICE Mark, thunder!
Dost know thy cue, thou big-voiced crier?
Dukes' groans are thunder's watchwords.° *signals for attack*
HIPPOLITO So, my lords, you have enough.
VINDICE Come, let's away, no ling'ring.
HIPPOLITO Follow, go!

Exeunt [*all the masquers except Vindice*].

VINDICE No power is angry when the lustful die;
When thunder claps, heaven likes the tragedy.

Exit Vindice.

2. Comet with an ominous protuberance at its tail.
3. But yet those who combine practical wisdom with their learning say.
4. Vindice, Hippolito, and two accomplices kill Lussurioso and the three noblemen.

Enter the other masque of intended murderers: step-sons [Ambitioso and Supervacuo], Bastard [Spurio], and a fourth man [the Fourth Noble] coming in dancing. The Duke [Lussurioso] recovers a little in voice, and groans, calls, "A guard! Treason!"° At which they all start out of their measure,° and, turning towards the table, they find them all to be murdered. (see 51–53) dance

LUSSURIOSO Oh, oh!
SPURIO Whose groan was that?
LUSSURIOSO Treason! A guard!
AMBITIOSO How now, all murdered?
SUPERVACUO Murdered!
FOURTH NOBLE And those his nobles!
AMBITIOSO [*aside to Supervacuo*] Here's a labor saved.
I thought to have sped° him. 'Sblood, how came this? killed
SUPERVACUO [*aloud*] Then I proclaim myself. Now I am duke.
AMBITIOSO Thou duke? Brother, thou liest.
[*He stabs Supervacuo.*]
SPURIO Slave, so dost thou. [*He stabs Ambitioso.*]
FOURTH NOBLE Base villain, hast thou slain my lord and master?
[*He stabs Spurio.*]

Enter the first men [Vindice, Hippolito, and the two lords or Nobles in the first masque of revengers, now in their usual attire].

VINDICE Pistols! Treason! Murder! Help! Guard my lord the Duke!

[*Enter Antonio, with a guard.*]

HIPPOLITO Lay hold upon this traitor!
[*The Fourth Noble is seized.*]
LUSSURIOSO Oh!
VINDICE Alas, the Duke is murdered!
HIPPOLITO And the nobles!
VINDICE Surgeons, surgeons! [*Aside*] Heart, does he breathe so long?
ANTONIO A piteous tragedy, able to make
An old man's eyes bloodshot.
LUSSURIOSO Oh!
VINDICE Look to my lord the Duke! [*Aside*] A vengeance throttle him!
[*To Fourth Noble*] Confess, thou murd'rous and unhallowed man,
Didst thou kill all these?
FOURTH NOBLE None but the Bastard, I.
VINDICE How came the Duke slain, then?
FOURTH NOBLE We found him so.
LUSSURIOSO Oh, villain!
VINDICE Hark!
LUSSURIOSO Those in the masque did murder us.
VINDICE [*to Fourth Noble*] La you now, sir.[5]
Oh, marble° impudence! Will you confess now? i.e., hardened
FOURTH NOBLE 'Slud, 'tis all false.

5. I.e., Well, sir, what Lussurioso just said pretty much demolishes your claim that you found the Duke slain.

ANTONIO Away with that foul monster,
Dipped in a prince's blood!
FOURTH NOBLE Heart, 'tis a lie!
ANTONIO Let him have bitter execution.
[*Exit the Fourth Noble, guarded.*]
VINDICE New marrow!° No, I cannot be expressed.[6] *food (for revenge)*
How fares my lord the Duke?
LUSSURIOSO Farewell to all!
He that climbs highest has the greatest fall.
My tongue is out of office.
VINDICE Air, gentlemen, air!
[*He whispers in Lussurioso's ear.*]
Now thou'lt not prate on't, 'twas Vindice murdered thee—
LUSSURIOSO Oh!
VINDICE Murdered thy father—
LUSSURIOSO Oh!
VINDICE And I am he. Tell nobody. [*Lussurioso dies.*] So, so.
[*Aloud*] The Duke's departed.
ANTONIO It was a deadly hand that wounded him.[7]
The rest,° ambitious who should rule and sway, *(The Duchess's sons, etc.)*
After his death were so made all away.° *similarly slain*
VINDICE My lord was unlikely.° *unfit (for rule)*
HIPPOLITO [*to Antonio*] Now the hope
Of Italy lies in your reverend years.
VINDICE [*to Antonio*] Your hair will make the silver age again,[8]
When there was fewer but more honest men.
ANTONIO The burden's weighty and will press age down.° *burden my old age*
May I so rule that heaven may keep° the crown! *protect*
VINDICE The rape of your good lady has been quited° *requited*
With death on death.
ANTONIO Just is the law above!
But of all things it puts me most to wonder
How the old Duke came murdered.
VINDICE Oh, my lord!
ANTONIO It was the strangeliest carried!° I not heard of the like. *carried out, managed*
HIPPOLITO 'Twas all done for the best, my lord.
VINDICE All for Your Grace's good. We may be bold to speak it now.
'Twas somewhat witty° carried, though we say it. *cleverly*
'Twas we two murdered him.
ANTONIO You two?
VINDICE None else, i'faith, my lord. Nay, 'twas well managed.
ANTONIO [*to the guard*] Lay hands upon those villains!
VINDICE How? On us?
[*Vindice and Hippolito are seized.*]
ANTONIO Bear 'em to speedy execution.
VINDICE Heart, was't not for your good, my lord?
ANTONIO My good?
Away with 'em! Such an old man as he;[9]

6. I cannot give voice to my feelings; my desire for revenge is inexpressible.
7. Antonio asserts that the as-yet-unknown assassin of Lussurioso is dangerous and must be brought to justice.
8. Your silver hair will bring back the silver age (mythologically, the second age of the world, following the golden age; see note at 4.1.41).
9. I.e., The Duke was an old man like me.

You that would murder him would murder me.
VINDICE Is't come about?[1]
HIPPOLITO 'Sfoot, brother, you begun.
VINDICE May not we set° as well as the Duke's son? *set like the sun (son)*
Thou hast no conscience.° Are we not revenged? *sense of right*
Is there one enemy left alive amongst those?
'Tis time to die when we are ourselves our foes.
When murd'rers shut deeds close,° this curse does seal 'em: *try to conceal murder*
If none disclose 'em, they themselves reveal 'em.
This murder might have slept in tongueless brass° *i.e., remained unknown*
But for ourselves, and the world died an ass.° *i.e., in ignorance*
Now I remember, too, here was Piato
Brought forth a knavish sentence° once: *saying, maxim*
"No doubt," said he, "but time
Will make the murderer bring forth himself."
'Tis well he died; he was a witch.° *prophesier, wizard*
And now, my lord, since we are in forever,
This work was ours, which else might have been slipped;
And, if we list, we could have nobles clipped
And go for less than beggars; but we hate
To bleed so cowardly.[2] We have enough, i'faith:
We're well, our mother turned,° our sister true; *converted*
We die after a nest of dukes. Adieu.
Exeunt [*Vindice and Hippolito, under guard*].
ANTONIO How subtly was that murder closed!° Bear up *hidden*
Those tragic bodies; 'tis a heavy season.
Pray heaven their° blood may wash away all treason! *(the revengers')*
Exit [*with others carrying the dead*].

FINIS.

1. Has the wheel of Fortune (and thus our luck) turned?
2. And now, my lord, since we are convicted without hope of reprieve, take note that we alone deserve the blame that might otherwise have been more widely distributed or else unnoticed; if we wished, we could have chosen to take nobles along with us in death and thus die side by side with wealthy men, but we have chosen to die without throwing blame around like cowards.

TEXTUAL NOTES

The Revenger's Tragedy was entered in the Stationers' Register on October 7, 1607, and was printed in quarto that same year, though some extant copies from the first printing show a date of 1608. This is the sole authoritative early edition; it exists, however, in three states, or phases, of correction. The present text is based on that quarto, as corrected. Substantive departures from it are noted below, using the following abbreviations:

Q: Quarto of 1607 (London: G. Eld)
Q corr.: The corrected quarto in the first of two states of correction
Q corr. state 2: The corrected quarto in the second of two states of correction
Q uncorr.: The uncorrected quarto
ed.: A modern editor's emendation

1.1.0.1 ***Vindice*** [ed.] Vendici [Q, and variously spelled at other places] **0.2 *his*** [ed.] *her* [Q] **5** [and elsewhere] **excellent** [Q: exlent] **15 study's** [Q: studies] **46** [and elsewhere] **off** [Q: of] **49.1 *his*** [ed.] *her* [Q] **50 death's** [Q corr.: deaths] death [Q uncorr.] **53** [and elsewhere] **Pooh** [Q: Puh] **85 vile** [Q: vilde] **97 to** [Q: too] **103 coin** [Q: quoyne] **117 travel** [Q: trauaile] **120 unnatural** [ed.] vnnaturally [Q] **124, 130 Too** [Q: To]

1.2.11 FIRST JUDGE [Q: *Iud.*] **15 cered** [Q: seard] **16 cerecloths** [ed.] searce clothes [Q] **19 doom** [Q: dome] **36 corse** [Q: coarse] **39 metal** [Q: mettall] **42 fast** [ed.] first [Q] **52 made** [Q: mad] **65 methinks** [ed.] my thinks [Q] **65 'sessed** [ed.] ceast [Q] **82 Pox** [ed.] Pax [Q] **131 't has** [ed.] 'tus [Q] **138 shrewd** [Q: shrowd] **143 basins** [Q: Basons] **151 dukedom's** [Q: Duke-doomes] **169 SPURIO** [ed.] *Spi.* [Q] **185 rose** [ed.] rise [Q]

1.3.6 mistress of mistresses [Q: Mistrs of Mistesses] **53 to** [ed.] too [Q] **88 depth** [Q: depht] **112 cozen** [Q: Couzen] **118 giv'n 't** [Q: gint] **127 walk** [Q: wa'ke] **138 my** [ed.] me [Q] **158 Does't** [Q: Dost] **181 traveled** [Q: trauayld] **185 blood** [ed.] good [Q]

1.4.6 Precedent [Q: President] **15 Placed** [Q: Plastc'd] **31 Duchess'** [Q: Ducheses] **38 heard** [ed.] hard [Q] **55 near** [Q: nere] **68 Should** [ed.] Sould [Q] **76 miracle** [Q: miralce]

2.1.22 fancy [Q: fanzye] **23 own** [ed.] one [Q] **25 traveled** [Q: trauayld] **66 seen in't, mark** [ed.] seene it, marke [Q] **93 still fools** [ed.] still foole [Q] **135 madam** [ed.] Mad-man [Q] **154 should** [ed.] shouldst [Q] **156** [and elsewhere] **lose** [Q: loose] **158 others** [ed.] other [Q] **164 she** [ed.] you [Q] **204 they're** [Q: their] **205 music** [ed.] Musicks [Q] **207 wear** [Q: were] **225 mete** [Q: meat] **234 low** [ed.] loue [Q]

2.2.40 [and elsewhere] **Who's** [Q: Whose] **56 cheeks** [ed.] checkes [Q] **69 an hour** [Q: a hower] **80 upon't** [Q: vppont] **92.1 *Exit*** [placement, ed.; after "preferment" in 92 in Q] **124 FIRST** [ed.; not in Q] **132** [and elsewhere] **damn** [Q: dam] **143 toll-book** [Q: Toale-booke]

2.3.4 they're [ed.] their [Q] **5 spleen** [Q: pleene] **15 grip** [Q1: gripe] **82 Honey?** [Q: Hunny,] **84 vilelier** [Q: vildlier] **98 inhuman** [Q: inhumaine]

3.1.15 Blest [ed.] Blast [Q] **25.1 *Exit*** [placement, ed.; opposite "grind him" in 25 in Q]

3.3.10 Ay [Q: I]

3.4.12 bankrupt [Q: banqrout]

3.5.54 e'er [Q: ere] **68 could** [Q: cold] **84 Camphor** [Q: Camphire] **93 of** [ed.] off [Q] **111 sign** [ed.] sine [Q] **166 slobbering** [ed.] Flobbering [Q] **178 not** [Q corr.] nor [Q uncorr.]

3.6.15 Led [ed.] Lead [Q] **25 our** [ed.] out [Q] **45 woo** [Q: woe] **47 stead** [Q: steed]

4.1.29 razed [Q: rac'd] **31 SD *Enter Vindice*** [placement, ed.; opposite 33 in Q] **43 come** [ed.] comes [Q] **45 He's** [Q: Has] **54 of** [ed.] off [Q] **74 the** [ed.] thee [Q] **78.1 *The Nobles enter*** [ed.; as a continuation of Lussurioso's speech in Q] **89 rode** [ed.] rod [Q]

4.2.41 Duke's [ed.] Duke [Q] **41.1 *off*** [Q: of] **66 LUSSURIOSO** [ed.] *Hip.* [Q] **72 sees** [ed.] see [Q] **76 rattles** [ed.] rotles [Q] **81 choose** [Q: chose] **104 heartily** [Q: heartly] **111 silver's of** [Q: siluers off] **112 clothes** [Q: cloths] **146 fine** [ed.] fiue [Q] **155 this** [ed.] their [Q] **221 We, thought** [ed.] Me thought [Q] **222 Shall** [Q corr.] Shalt [Q uncorr.]

4.3.6 Wouldst [ed.] Woult [Q] **15 waist** [Q: waste] **16 their** [ed.] there [Q] **17–18** [order of lines, Q corr.; reversed in Q uncorr.] **18 SD** [Q corr.; not in Q uncorr.; placement, ed.; opposite 16 in Q]

4.4.0.1 *their* [ed.] *there* [Q] **3 parent** [ed.] Parents [Q] **12 knew'st** [Q corr.: knewst] knowst [Q uncorr.] **19 thee** [Q corr.] the [Q uncorr.] **40 'tis** [Q corr.] to't [Q uncorr.] **43 Wet . . . iron** [Q corr. state 2] Wee . . . you [Q uncorr.] Wet . . . you [Q corr.] **52 rinse** [Q: rence] **59 seld** [ed.] sild [Q] **70 The Duke's** [Q corr.: The dukes] Dukes [Q uncorr.] **74 To be** [Q corr.] Too [Q uncorr.] **117 Suns** [ed.] Sonnes [Q] **158 Be** [ed.] Buy [Q]

5.1.10 enough [Q: enow] **12 faith's** [Q corr.] faith [Q uncorr.] **15 fly-flap** [Q: fly-flop] **17 shown** [ed.] show [Q] **18 died** [Q corr.] did [Q uncorr.] **53 beast** [Q uncorr.] brest [Q corr.] **57 Nake** [Q corr.] make [Q uncorr.] **76 of** [Q: off] **87, 92 SORDIDO** [ed.] 1. [Q] **88 NENCIO** [ed.] 2. [Q] **96 furthest** [Q: fordest] **106, 113, 124, 132 FIRST NOBLE** [ed.] 1. [Q] **107, 112 SECOND NOBLE** [ed.] 2. [Q] **142, 153 SECOND NOBLE** [ed.] *Nob.* [Q] **155, 157 SORDIDO** [ed.] *Nobl.* [Q] **155 You're** [Q: Your] **159, 170 THIRD NOBLE** [ed.] *Nobl.* [Q] **163 THIRD NOBLE** [ed.] Nob. [Q] **178 have at** [ed.] haue [Q] **190 'Tis** [ed.] 'ts [Q]

5.2.8 FIRST NOBLE [ed.] 1. [Q] **8 SECOND NOBLE** [ed.] 3. [Q] **13 tale** [Q: taile] **24 THIRD NOBLE** [ed.] 3. [Q]

5.3.1 FIRST NOBLE [ed.] *Noble* [Q] **5 FIRST NOBLE** [ed.] Nob. [Q] **14 Thou mad'st** [ed.] madst [Q] **21 Before, it I** [Q: Before it, I] **23 wear** [ed.] were [Q] **48.1 *Exeunt*** [placement, ed.; opposite 47 in Q] **50.2–9** [placement, ed.; after 51 in Q] **59 SUPERVACUO** [ed.] *Spur.* [Q] **64 traitor** [ed.] Traytors [Q] **69 make** [ed.] wake [Q] **73 unhallowed** [Q: vnhollowed] **81 La** [Q: Law] **83 'Slud** [ed.] Sloud [Q] **107 heaven may** [ed.] heauen nay [Q] **112 heard** [ed.] hard [Q] **122 to** [ed.] two [Q] **131 murd'rers** [ed.] murders [Q] **134 died** [ed.] dyed [Q]

The Roaring Girl

In 1611, when Thomas Middleton and Thomas Dekker based the swaggering, cross-dressed heroine of *The Roaring Girl* on an actual woman, Mary Frith, or "Moll Cutpurse," they were trying something new. Early modern censorship laws prohibited the theatrical depiction of politically powerful, socially prominent people. Unsurprisingly, then, the first positively identifiable living person to be translated into a quasi-fictional dramatic realm was someone the authorities had no interest in protecting. The real Moll Cutpurse was well known in London for dressing in men's apparel, brawling in the streets, and consorting with ruffians and prostitutes. In the first decade of the seventeenth century, she was repeatedly brought to court on charges of theft and burglary but never convicted. She died in 1659 at the age of seventy-five; three years later *The Life and Death of Mrs. Mary Frith*, purportedly her autobiography, regaled a new generation with tales of her exploits.

The indefatigable letter-writer John Chamberlain, describing one of Frith's escapades to his friend Dudley Carleton, allows us to catch a glimpse of the shameless flair that must have originally attracted Middleton and Dekker to her story. Frith was a natural target for the ecclesiastical courts, which punished disorderly conduct by various shaming punishments: typically offenders were made to express their repentance publicly on a raised platform before an assembled crowd while a clergyman fulminated against the sin thus exemplified (fornication, blasphemy, scolding, or the like). Penance was supposed to be intensely humiliating, and occasionally it was physically dangerous as well, since the spectators sometimes hurled fruit, dung, or stones at the transgressor. Chamberlain writes: "This last Sunday Moll Cutpurse, a notorious baggage that used to go in man's apparel and challenged the field of diverse gallants, was brought to [Paul's Cross], where she wept bitterly and seemed very penitent, but it is since doubted she was maudlin drunk, being discovered to have tippled of three quarts of sack before she came to her penance." A clergyman named Ratcliff was scheduled to give the sermon on her misdeeds to the assembled crowd, Chamberlain continues, but "he did extreme badly, and so wearied the audience that the best part went away, and the rest tarried rather to hear Moll Cutpurse than him."[1] Performing remorse with a tipsy, carnival-like extravagance, Moll converted what ought to have been an episode of abject subordination into an opportunity for subversive self-display.

Perhaps it is anachronistic to call Moll a "celebrity" in the modern sense, for both the word and the concept were alien to Jacobean England, but the cultural role that was assigned to her has some of the same features. Whether she was treated indignantly—as in Chamberlain's letter—or admiringly—as in *The Roaring Girl*—praise and blame had a way of becoming an equivocal fascination with her fame for its own sake. For Moll—as surely as for Elvis Presley or Marilyn Monroe or Princess Diana—the boundaries between the real person and the image blurred and wavered in a disconcerting way. Moreover, like modern celebrities, Moll played an unusually fraught

Introduction by Katharine Eisaman Maus; glosses, footnotes, and textual notes by David Bevington; text edited by David Bevington and checked by Eric Rasmussen.

1. Norman Egbert, ed., *The Letters of John Chamberlain* (Philadelphia: American Philosophical Society, 1939), p. 334.

cultural role. On the one hand, she was defined as unique: in order to attract public attention in the first place, celebrities need to seem singularly beautiful, gifted, or eccentric. On the other hand, in Jacobean accounts, she figures as both spectacularly deviant and somehow symptomatic of contemporary social possibilities, both good and bad: celebrity appeal typically draws its power from widely shared fantasies and anxieties. "A notorious baggage," she showed (as Chamberlain's anecdote suggests) scant respect for her social betters, derided their attempts to discipline her, and flouted the usual constraints on the behavior of baseborn women. But she seems more extreme, not different in kind, from many of her contemporaries. Early modern England witnessed enormous social upheaval: among the poor, changing agricultural practices produced a dramatic rise in vagrancy; among the higher orders, inflation and economic disturbances reshuffled traditional class categories. Given this turmoil, the old rules governing one's behavior toward people of a higher or lower status seemed obsolete. Moll's insouciant refusal to know her place thus appeared to be not merely an outlandish whim but a kind of social statement. Her habitual transvestism was part of this refusal, implicitly declaring gender to be just as permeable or optional a category as rank. And once again, though the openness of Moll's defiance was unusual, she was not alone. Fashionable Jacobean ladies pushed the sartorial envelope, wearing traditionally male garments such as a broad-brimmed hat or a doublet atop their feminine skirts, and some clergymen and other conservative spokesmen, including King James I, saw their behavior as part of a larger challenge to the distinction between the genders and the ideology of female subordination. The title of Middleton and Dekker's play, *The Roaring Girl*, itself carries a witty suggestion of gender transgression, since the expression "roaring boy," which referred to an urban brawler, did not normally have a female equivalent.

Of course, Middleton and Dekker's Moll is a fictional creation, not a real person, as Middleton acknowledges in his prefatory epistle: "Worse things, I must needs confess, the world has taxed her for than has been written of her; but 'tis the excellency of a writer to leave things better than he finds 'em" (Epistle 20–22). The significance of their heroine, and the particular ways in which the playwrights "improve on" their model, cannot be isolated from the play in which they situate her. In his epistle, Middleton half-facetiously claims that the "spruceness" of *The Roaring Girl* ought to appeal to its audience because "single plots" and "quaint conceits" have replaced "huge bombasted plays" just as closely cut Jacobean styles of clothing have replaced larger-scale Elizabethan ones (Epistle 2–9). *The Roaring Girl* is, however, structurally complex, interlacing two main plots with a variety of subsidiary actions. In the first act, young Sebastian Wengrave, whose marriage to his beloved Mary Fitzallard has been stymied by his grasping father, Sir Alexander, announces an elaborate scheme: he will counterfeit an infatuation with the outrageous Moll Cutpurse, in the hope of making a match with his original betrothed look good by comparison. Sir Alexander takes the bait but does not initially react as Sebastian had hoped; instead he plans to ruin Moll by hiring the unscrupulous Trapdoor to lure her into committing a capital crime. The second act introduces the other important line of action, in which the ne'er-do-well gentlemen Laxton and Goshawk attempt to seduce two shopkeepers' wives. Along the way, Laxton attempts to hire Moll for sex (she beats him soundly in a sword fight); Sir Alexander's comrade in avarice, Sir Davy Dapper, attempts to have his own son arrested for debt (Moll rescues the prisoner); and Moll, with her erstwhile betrayer Trapdoor, teaches the elements of canting, the code language of criminals and vagrants, to the son's gentlemen friends.

The two plots and the incidents loosely attached to them implicate a wide social range of characters, from prosperous knights to citizen shopkeepers to cutpurses and beggars. The kaleidoscopic arrangement and rearrangement of a diverse set of characters is one of the primary pleasures of *The Roaring Girl*, and in its more optimistic moments the play presents London as a place of benign variousness, its many classes and occupations attractively juxtaposed. When, for instance, Jack Dapper and his well-to-do comrades delightedly learn canting, it seems as if the city's differences can be appreciated in a spirit of toleration and wonder. Even the stage set, which provides the backdrop for much of the action—the apothecary, feather-seller, and sempster shops cheek by jowl—suggests an environment of picturesque heterogeneity. But threatening this sentimental outlook on urban diversity is a view of the city as a place of economic and personal competition: "All that live in the world are but great fish and little fish, and feed upon one another," says the sergeant who comes to arrest Jack Dapper (3.3.145–46). Almost every character in the play, both sympathetic and unsympathetic, is involved in some kind of trickery. Profit motives endanger the connections between individuals and threaten particularly the love and loyalty among family members. Alexander Wengrave blocks his son's love match for financial reasons, and Davy Dapper likewise rides roughshod over the claims of kinship: "If he were sure his father's skin would yield him any money, he would, when he dies, flay it off and sell it to cover drums for children at Barthol'mew Fair," says the sergeant (3.3.162–65). The London shop owners use their comely wives to sell their wares; their gentlemen customers target the wives for seduction not because they desire them sexually, but because they hope the women will bankroll their expensive tastes.

The Roaring Girle.
OR
Moll Cut-Purse.
As it hath lately beene Acted on the Fortune-stage by
the Prince his Players.
Written by T. Middleton and T. Dekkar.
My case is alter'd, I must worke for my liuing.
Printed at London for Thomas Archer, and are to be sold at his
shop in Popes head-pallace, neere the Royall
Exchange. 1611.

Title page of the 1611 quarto of *The Roaring Girl*.

The ambivalent presentation of urban life in *The Roaring Girl* is possibly traceable to the different viewpoints of the play's two authors: Dekker's typically sunny outlook collides with Middleton's more cynical one. At any rate, in this equivocal setting, Moll Cutpurse's unconventional behavior seems a natural, if surprising, adaptation to an environment in which people cannot afford to trust one another. Among London's various classes and subcultures, she "slips from one company to another like a fat eel between a Dutchman's fingers" (2.1.213–14). As the eel simile suggests, Moll is literally "a loose woman" who goes everywhere and knows everything worth knowing about life in the city. She couches her defense of herself in terms of preserving her independence: "I have no humor to marry," she declares. "I love to lie o'both sides o'th'bed myself" (2.2.37–38). Her autonomy and freedom of movement conflict with conventional ideas about female virtue, which are usually construed in terms of innocence, aversion to risk, and dependence on males. But the ubiquity of deception and competitiveness in London life makes naïveté obviously dangerous. In such an environment, Moll's self-reliance appears reasonable and prudent.

Moreover, knowing, Moll emphasizes, is not the same as doing, or approving: "must you have / A black ill name because ill things you know?" (5.1.343–44). Moll describes herself as vice's spectator, the student of the city who watches how pickpockets work and learns how thieves speak to one another, but she insists that she is not a criminal herself. Perhaps her surprising incorruptibility constitutes an implicit defense of the playwrights, who bear witness to London's quirks and flaws without necessarily endorsing them. Be that as it may, while Moll plays at transgression—making dirty jokes, playing the viola da gamba between her legs in an unladylike way—she commits no real improprieties. Middleton and Dekker take particular pains to show her, in two closely parallel scenes, resisting first an invitation to prostitute herself and then the temptation to steal valuable goods. Despite her whorish reputation, she is notably prim. She reacts violently less to Laxton's sexual overture than to his blithe assumption that she is his for the asking. She expresses shock at the apparent sight of two men kissing and declares herself willing to bring Sebastian and Mary Fitzallard together only on the condition that their loves are "honest" (4.1.43–44). By the end of *The Roaring Girl*, Moll's negative traits of aggression and deviancy have been redefined as boldness and self-reliance, her vagrancy as a form of ingenuity, her questionable cunning as innocuous autodidacticism. Her characterization seems designed to redeem the individualism that in characters such as Laxton, Goshawk, the elder Wengrave, or Prudence Gallipot is so selfish and predatory.

However, while Moll's behavior is excusable and even admirable, she is not a model for others. Not only is she inimitable, but she wants to remain so. Whereas in Jonson's *Epicene*, the transvestite, straddling the boundaries between male and female, symbolizes a more general crisis of gender norms, Moll represents no real threat to the status quo. As long as eligible young men like Sebastian Wengrave yearn to marry sweet, conventional women like Mary Fitzallard, women like Moll may emphatically disqualify themselves from the marriage market but the fundamental structures of society will remain safe. At the end of the play, Moll is thoroughly accepted and appreciated by the people around her. But the play applauds her not because she is what she initially seems to be—a symptom of social revolution—but because, paradoxically, the unique deviant actually safeguards the social order she appears to threaten.

One by-product of Moll's independence is a refusal to bother too much about what other people think. Moll insists that she concerns herself with substance, not appearance: whereas her outward outlandishness conceals an inner integrity, the respectability and specious charms of the conventionally feminine citizen's wives are "but outside" and eventually convince Openwork that "this whole world [is] but a gilt rotten pill" (4.2.234, 241). There are a few lessons here, one obvious and the other more implicit. The first—it might be called the moral of *The Roaring Girl*, insofar as it has one—is that people ought not be judged on hearsay or reputation, because they may be better (or worse) than they seem. But the other, covert lesson is that duplicity, though practiced by both sexes, is nonetheless metaphorically associated with femininity and its "wiles," and so Moll asks, "How many are whores in small ruffs and still looks? / How many chaste, whose names fill Slander's books?" (5.1.346–47). Toward the end of the play, the chastened Sir Alexander remarks:

> I'll nevermore
> Condemn by common voice, for that's the whore
> That deceives man's opinion, mocks his trust,
> Cozens his love, and makes his heart unjust.
> (5.2.256–59)

All his animus against Moll, who had seemed the very incarnation of the cozener and whore, is displaced onto "common voice," or mere rumor. Yet his imagery not only fails to challenge but actually reinforces the network of assumptions that links women as a class to artifice and untrustworthiness. Similarly, Moll defends her freedom of spirit by citing a deeply conservative analogy between mind and body, husband and wife:

> Base is that mind that kneels unto her body,
> As if a husband stood in awe on 's wife!
> My spirit shall be mistress of this house
> As long as I have time in't. (3.1.138–41)

While exempting herself from the rules that confine and subordinate most women, Moll pointedly invokes those rules: a man who defers to his wife is, she insists, debased. Elsewhere, even while proclaiming her own chastity, she deplores most women's lack of integrity: "I am of that certain belief there are more queans in this town of their own making than of any man's provoking. Where lies the slackness then?" (2.1.329–31).

Today's feminists, because they want to improve the situation of women in general, reject the kind of exceptionalist argument Moll makes for herself here. Some recent critics of the play, therefore, have argued that the terms of the fictional Moll's triumph, as the playwrights construct it for her, undermine any revolutionary potential suggested by her real-life prototype. But Moll's attitude is perhaps less surprising, given *The Roaring Girl*'s ambivalence about the social advantages and costs of individualism, and its uncertainty about the relationship of individuals to the groups to which they apparently belong. On the one hand, Moll's refusal to accept a group identity seems to be part of the playwrights' project of encouraging spectators to avoid hasty generalizations about other people: "He hates unworthily that by rote contemns," argues Sir Alexander's son (2.2.175). On the other hand, and apparently undercutting this point, every character in *The Roaring Girl* besides Moll is a highly predictable type, familiar from innumerable other city comedies: the two rich, avaricious fathers; their respectively amorous and prodigal sons; the linguistically pretentious servant; the sexually unscrupulous gentlemen; the scheming citizens' wives and their gullible, uxorious husbands. Situating the remarkable Moll among these stereotypes highlights her difference but at the same time seems to limit her charisma to her idiosyncratic case alone. In most situations, contemning (or praising) by rote seems perfectly appropriate.

Moreover, even in Moll's case, what might sympathetically be called myth or unsympathetically be called stereotype lurks just beneath the surface of her characterization. Representing their heroine as quintessentially independent and incorruptible requires a good deal of economic romanticism from the authors of the play. Moll declares roundly that "she that has wit and spirit / May scorn to live beholding to her body for meat / Or for apparel" (3.1.134–36). But how then *does* she support herself? In the play, we see her acquiring money from Laxton in a fair fight and from the Wengraves as a reward for facilitating Sebastian's plot. But surely such opportunities do not occur regularly enough to provide her with a predictable income. Moll is, in fact, a version of the Amazon, a type naturally popular in the reign of Elizabeth I, which had ended only a few years before this play was first produced; Elizabeth famously declared herself "endued with such qualities that if I were turned out of the realm in my petticoat I were able to live in any place of Christendom."[2] Middleton and Dekker's Moll, in her resolute impenetrability, her chivalrous cast of mind, and her magical self-sufficiency, owes something to the example of Edmund Spenser's Britomart in *The Faerie Queene*, who was herself an allegorical rendering of the redoubtable virgin queen.

When *The Roaring Girl* was first performed, Elizabeth had been dead for eight years and Spenser for twelve, so the influence of their mythology on a self-consciously up-to-the-minute city comedy might seem unlikely were it not that Moll is so closely associated with a potent strain of nostalgia. When she revolts against the status quo, it is often to profess beliefs that seem nearly lost in the modern city: the importance, for instance, of a strict code of personal honor associated with old-fashioned chivalry and pointedly disconnected from any profit motive. In this resuscitation of values that predate the rise of the metropolitan marketplace, she is abetted by Middleton and Dekker, who so often in *The Roaring Girl* represent the energies of comic renovation as issuing from a place outside the city. When the authors want to cultivate sympathy for Gallipot, Openwork, and Tiltyard, they display the citizen husbands shutting up

2. Leah Marcus, Janel Mueller, and Mary Beth Rose, eds., *Elizabeth I: Collected Works* (Chicago: University of Chicago Press, 2000), p. 97.

shop to go duck hunting, implicitly contrasting their traditional, wholesome blood sport with the sexual predation of the gentlemen seducers. The rogues' company evoked in the canting scene likewise seems innocent, even endearing, insofar as it summons up a romance of the open road—sleeping under hedges, "niggling" in fields, drinking by the side of the highway. At the end of the play, Sir Alexander sagely if somewhat incongruously, given his erstwhile role as an urban chiseler, advises his son, "The best joys / That can in worldly shapes to man betide / Are fertile lands and a fair fruitful bride" (5.2.207–9). He encourages the newlyweds to look forward to agricultural bounty and the propagation of children—the supposed natural rewards of a rural way of life. *The Roaring Girl* reminds us not only how close in early modern England the countryside still was geographically to the metropolis, but also how even in a city comedy performed before sophisticated urbanites, the imagined locus of purity and renewal was still, typically, a pastoral one.

THOMAS MIDDLETON AND THOMAS DEKKER

The Roaring Girl

[The Epistle]

To the Comic Play Readers: Venery° and Laughter

good hunting (sexual)

The fashion of playmaking I can properly compare to nothing so naturally as the alteration in apparel. For in the time of the great-crop doublet,[1] your huge bombasted° plays, quilted with mighty words to lean purpose, was only then in fashion; and as the doublet fell,[2] neater inventions began to set up. Now in the time of spruceness, our plays follow the niceness° of our garments: single plots, quaint conceits,° lecherous jests, dressed up in hanging° sleeves; and those are fit for the times and the termers.[3] Such a kind of light-color summer stuff, mingled with divers colors, you shall find this published comedy—good to keep you in an afternoon from dice, at home in your chambers. And for venery, you shall find enough for sixpence, but well couched,° an° you mark it. For Venus, being a woman, passes through the play in doublet and breeches—a brave° disguise and a safe one, if the statute untie not her codpiece point![4] The book I make no question but is fit for many of your companies, as well as the person itself, and may be allowed both gallery room at the playhouse and chamber room at your lodging. Worse things, I must needs confess, the world has taxed her for° than has been written of her; but 'tis the excellency of a writer to leave things better than he finds 'em. Though some obscene fellow, that cares not what he writes against others, yet keeps a mystical° bawdy house himself, and entertains drunkards to make use of° their pockets and vent his private bottle ale[5] at midnight—though such a one would have ripped up° the most nasty vice that ever hell belched forth and presented it to a modest assembly, yet we rather

padded; overblown
neatness / notions
long, drooping
hidden; expressed / if
showy; courageous
accused her of
secret
i.e., pick
exposed

The original 1611 title page reads "*The Roaring Girl, or Moll Cutpurse.* As it hath lately been acted on the Fortune stage by the Prince his Players. Written by T. Middleton and T. Dekker. Printed at London for Thomas Archer, and are to be sold at his shop in Pope's Head Palace, near the Royal Exchange. 1611."

The Epistle.

1. A padded short jacket.
2. (1) Lengthened; (2) fell out of fashion.
3. People involved in legal or other business during the law terms in London.
4. If the statute forbidding indecency does not reveal her sexual identity by disattaching her codpiece, the flap covering the male genitals in men's breeches of the time. The codpiece was held in place by "points," or metal-tagged laces.
5. And sell his illegal homemade brew. ("Vent" also means "discharge"; bottled homemade brew can open with explosive force.)

wish in such discoveries, where reputation lies bleeding, a slackness of truth than fullness of slander.[6]

Thomas Middleton

DRAMATIS PERSONAE

[The PROLOGUE]
SIR ALEXANDER Wengrave and NEATFOOT,° his man — *an ox's foot (as food)*
SIR ADAM Appleton
SIR DAVY Dapper
SIR BEAUTEOUS Ganymede[1]
[SIR THOMAS Long]
LORD NOLAND
Young [SEBASTIAN] Wengrave [Sir Alexander's son]
JACK DAPPER[2] [Sir Davy's son] and GULL,° his page — *"simpleton"*
GOSHAWK° — *a short-winged hawk*
GREENWIT° — *"gullible one"*
LAXTON

TILTYARD [a feather-seller][3]
[Hippocrates] OPENWORK [a sempster][4]
GALLIPOT[5] [an apothecary]
} *cives*° — *citizens*

[MRS. TILTYARD]
[MRS. Rosamond OPENWORK]
[MRS. Prudence GALLIPOT]
} *uxores*° — *(citizens') wives*

MOLL [Cutpurse],° the Roaring Girl — *a pickpocket*
[Ralph] TRAPDOOR
[TEARCAT]° — *"blusterer"*

SIR GUY Fitzallard
MARY Fitzallard, his daughter

CURTALAX,° a sergeant, and — *a cutlass*
HANGER,° his yeoman — *a sword strap*

Ministri° [including a SERVANT to Sir Alexander] — *servants*
[A FELLOW with a long rapier
A PORTER
A TAILOR
A COACHMAN
Several CUTPURSES
Gentlemen

[SCENE: London.]

6. We would rather give a charitable picture of our subject and avoid damaging reputations.

Dramatis Personae.

1. Ganymede was Jove's cupbearer. He was also Jove's lover and so this name has homoerotic connotations, which do not necessarily apply to the character in this play but may suggest a comic reference to the court of King James I, since James was criticized for relying on personal favorites and his court was noted for its extravagance and looseness.

2. An inversion of "dapper jack," a deprecatory term for a young man who is attempting to be fashionable. Jack's father, Davy Dapper (line 4), is presumably also attempting to pass himself off as a dashing gallant.

3. At a tiltyard, or tournament arena, young men festooned with feathers were present in abundance.

4. Hippocrates (c. 460–c. 377 B.C.E.) is known as the father of medicine. Openwork is knitting or other needlework, as appropriate to a sempster, or tailor. It also suggests sexual availability.

5. A small earthen glazed pot, especially one used by apothecaries for ointments and medicines; also, a druggist.

Prologus

[*Enter the Prologue.*]

PROLOGUE A play expected long makes the audience look
For wonders, that each scene should be a book,
Composed to all perfection. Each one° comes *(audience member)*
And brings a play in's head with him; up he sums
What he would of a roaring girl have writ;
If that he finds not here, he mews° at it. *makes catcalls*
Only we entreat you think our scene
Cannot speak high,° the subject being but mean.° *in lofty tones / ordinary*
A roaring girl (whose notes till now never were)° *never were heard*
Shall fill with laughter our vast theater;° *(the Fortune)*
That's all which I dare promise. Tragic passion
And such grave stuff is this day out of fashion.
I see Attention sets wide ope her gates
Of hearing, and with covetous° list'ning waits *eager, greedy*
To know what girl this roaring girl should be,
For of that tribe are many. One is she
That roars at midnight in deep tavern bowls,
That beats the watch,° and constables controls;° *night watch / challenges*
Another roars i'th'daytime, swears, stabs, gives braves,° *shouts defiance*
Yet sells her soul to the lust of fools and slaves.° *wretches*
Both these are suburb roarers.[1] Then there's besides
A civil city roaring girl, whose pride,
Feasting, and riding, shakes her husband's state,° *financial status*
And leaves him roaring through an iron grate.° *(of a debtors' prison)*
None of these roaring girls is ours: she flies
With wings more lofty. Thus her character lies.
Yet what need characters, when to give a guess
Is better than the person to express?[2]
But would you know who 'tis? Would you hear her name?
She is called Mad° Moll; her life our acts proclaim. [*Exit.*] *Eccentric, wild*

1.1

Enter Mary Fitzallard, disguised like a sempster,° with a case for bands,[1] and Neatfoot, a servingman, with her, with a napkin on his shoulder, and a trencher° in his hand, as from table. *seamstress* / *wooden dish*

NEATFOOT The young gentleman, our young master, Sir Alexander's son—is it into his ears, sweet damsel, emblem of fragility, you desire to have a message transported, or to be transcendent?[2]

MARY A private word or two, sir, nothing else.

NEATFOOT You shall fructify° in that which you come for; your pleasure shall be satisfied to your full contentation.° I will, fairest tree of generation,° watch when our young master is *be fruitful* / *contentment* / *procreation*

Prologus.
1. Brawlers in the suburban areas surrounding London, which were noted for lawlessness, including prostitution.
2. Why give away the "character" of Moll now, under the (false) assumption that such an abstract speculation would be better than letting Moll enact her own story in her own person?

1.1. Sir Alexander Wengrave's house.
1. A box for neck-bands, or collars.
2. To be delivered? (Neatfoot's affectation is to use grandiose, Latinate terms of vague and repetitive meaning—sometimes bawdy, as in lines 6 and 8–9.)

erected,° that is to say, up, and deliver him to this your most white hand.°

risen from the table / *fair handwriting*

MARY Thanks, sir.

NEATFOOT And withal° certify him that I have culled out for him, now his belly is replenished, a daintier bit or modicum than any lay upon his trencher at dinner.° Hath he notion of your name, I beseech your chastity?

moreover / *the midday meal*

MARY One, sir, of whom he bespake falling-bands.°

ordered neck-bands

NEATFOOT Falling-bands: it shall so be given° him. If you please to venture your modesty in the hall amongst a curl-pated° company of rude° servingmen and take such as they can set before you, you shall be most seriously and ingeniously° welcome—

delivered to / *curly-haired / simple* / *ingenuously, heartily*

MARY I have dined indeed already, sir.

NEATFOOT Or will you vouchsafe to kiss the lip of a cup of rich Orleans° in the buttery° amongst our waiting-women?

a French wine / pantry

MARY Not now, in truth, sir.

NEATFOOT Our young master shall then have a feeling° of your being here presently.° It shall so be given him.

sense / *at once*

MARY I humbly thank you, sir. *Exit Neatfoot.*
But that° my bosom *Were it not that*
Is full of bitter sorrows, I could smile
To see this formal° ape play antic tricks; *overly polite*
But in my breast a poisoned arrow sticks,
And smiles cannot become me. Love woven slightly,° *slackly, loosely*
Such as thy° false heart makes, wears out as lightly; *i.e., Sebastian's*
But love being truly bred i'th'soul, like mine,
Bleeds even to death at the least wound it takes.
The more we quench this fire, the less it slakes.° *slackens, dies down*
Oh, me!

Enter Sebastian Wengrave with Neatfoot.

SEBASTIAN A sempster speak with me, say'st thou?

NEATFOOT Yes, sir, she's there, viva voce,° to deliver her auricular confession.

i.e., in person

SEBASTIAN [*to Mary*] With me, sweetheart? What is't?

MARY I have brought home your bands, sir.

SEBASTIAN Bands?—Neatfoot!

NEATFOOT Sir?

SEBASTIAN Prithee look in,° for all the gentlemen are upon rising.[3]

into the dining room

NEATFOOT Yes, sir. A most methodical attendance shall be given.

SEBASTIAN And dost hear, if my father call for me, say I am busy with a sempster.

NEATFOOT Yes, sir. He shall know it that you are busied with a needlewoman.

SEBASTIAN In's ear, good Neatfoot.

NEATFOOT It shall be so given him. *Exit Neatfoot.*

SEBASTIAN Bands? You're mistaken, sweetheart, I bespake none. When, where, I prithee, what bands? Let me see them.

MARY Yes, sir, a bond fast sealed, with solemn oaths,
Subscribed unto (as I thought) with your soul,

3. About to rise from the table.

Delivered as your deed in sight of heaven.
Is this bond canceled? Have you forgot me?

SEBASTIAN Ha! Life of my life! Sir Guy Fitzallard's daughter!
What has transformed my love to this strange shape?
Stay: make all sure. [*He tests the doors.*] So: now speak and be brief,
Because the wolf's at door that lies in wait
To prey upon us both. Albeit mine eyes
Are blessed by thine,[4] yet this so strange disguise
Holds me with fear and wonder.

MARY Mine's a loathed sight.[5]
Why from it are you banished else so long?

SEBASTIAN I must cut short my speech. In broken language,
Thus much, sweet Moll:° I must thy company shun; — *(nickname for "Mary")*
I court another Moll. My thoughts must run
As a horse runs that's blind, round in a mill,
Out° every step, yet keeping one path still. — *Stumbling*

MARY Umh! Must you shun my company? In one knot
Have both our hands by th'hands of heaven been tied,
Now to be broke? I thought me once your bride;
Our fathers did agree on the time when.
And must another bedfellow fill my room?

SEBASTIAN Sweet maid, let's lose no time. 'Tis in heaven's book
Set down that I must have thee; an oath we took
To keep our vows. But when the knight your father
Was from mine parted, storms began to sit
Upon my covetous father's brow, which fell
From them° on me. He reckoned up what gold — *(my father's brows)*
This marriage would draw from him, at which he swore,
To lose so much blood could not grieve him more.
He then dissuades me from thee, called thee not fair,
And asked, "What is she but a beggar's heir?"
He scorned thy dowry of five thousand marks.° — *(each worth ⅔ of a pound)*
If such a sum of money could be found,
And I would match° with that, he'd not undo it,° — *marry / (the marriage)*
Provided his bags° might add nothing to it, — *moneybags*
But vowed, if I took thee—nay, more, did swear it—
Save birth° from him I nothing should inherit. — *family name*

MARY What follows then? My shipwreck?

SEBASTIAN Dearest, no.
Though wildly in a labyrinth I go,
My end is to meet thee. With a side wind° — *Indirectly; on a tack*
Must I now sail, else I no haven can find,
But both must sink forever. There's a wench
Called Moll, Mad Moll, or Merry Moll—a creature
So strange in quality, a whole city takes
Note of her name and person. All that affection
I owe to thee, on her, in counterfeit passion,
I spend to mad° my father. He believes — *madden*
I dote upon this roaring girl, and grieves
As it becomes a father for a son

4. Are blessed by your gazing into my eyes, by your presence.

5. I must be loathsome in your sight.

That could be so bewitched. Yet I'll go on
This crooked way, sigh still for her, feign dreams,
In which I'll talk only of her. These streams° *currents*
Shall, I hope, force my father to consent
That here° I anchor, rather than be rent° *(with you) / torn apart*
Upon a rock so dangerous. Art thou pleased,
Because thou see'st we are waylaid, that I take
A path that's safe, though it be far about?

MARY My prayers with heaven guide thee!

SEBASTIAN Then I will on.
My father is at hand; kiss and be gone.
Hours shall be watched for meetings. I must now,
As men for fear, to a strange idol bow.

MARY Farewell!

SEBASTIAN I'll guide thee forth. When next we meet,
A story of Moll shall make our mirth more sweet. *Exeunt.*

[1.2]

Enter Sir Alexander Wengrave, Sir Davy Dapper, Sir Adam Appleton, Goshawk, Laxton, and gentlemen.

OMNES° Thanks, good Sir Alexander, for our bounteous cheer. *All*

SIR ALEXANDER Fie, fie! In giving thanks you pay too dear.

SIR DAVY When bounty spreads the table, faith,° 'twere sin, *in faith*
At going off,° if thanks should not step in. *departing*

SIR ALEXANDER No more of thanks, no more. Ay, marry,° sir, *by Mary (an oath)*
Th'inner room was too close.° How do you like *stuffy*
This parlor, gentlemen?

OMNES Oh, passing° well. *exceedingly*

SIR ADAM What a sweet breath the air casts here, so cool!

GOSHAWK I like the prospect best.

LAXTON See how 'tis furnished.

SIR DAVY A very fair sweet room.

SIR ALEXANDER Sir Davy Dapper,
The furniture that doth adorn this room
Cost many a fair gray groat° ere it came here; *(worth fourpence)*
But good things are most cheap° when they're most dear.° *the best value / cherished*
Nay, when you look into my galleries,[1]
How bravely° they are trimmed up,° you all shall swear *handsomely / decorated*
You're highly pleased to see what's set down° there: *portrayed*
Stories of men and women, mixed together
Fair ones with foul, like sunshine in wet weather.
Within one square° a thousand heads are laid *picture frame*
So close that all of heads the room seems made;
As many faces there, filled with blithe looks,
Show° like the promising titles of new books *Look*
Writ merrily, the readers being their own eyes,
Which seem to move and to give plaudities;° *bursts of applause*
And here and there, whilst with obsequious ears

1.2. Sir Alexander's house still.

1. Sir Alexander's description in the following lines of the tapestries in his gallery contains an implied analogy to the theater audience, with its "Thronged heaps" of expectant spectators (line 26), cutpurses (pickpockets) in the crowd (lines 25–27), and the stage itself an island surrounded on three sides by a sea of faces (lines 30–32).

Thronged heaps do listen, a cutpurse thrusts and leers
With hawk's eyes for his prey. I need not show him;° — *point him out*
By a hanging villainous look yourselves may know him,
The face is drawn so rarely.° Then, sir, below, — *excellently*
The very floor, as 'twere, waves to and fro,
And like a floating island seems to move
Upon a sea bound in with shores above.

Enter Sebastian and Master Greenwit.

OMNES These sights are excellent.
SIR ALEXANDER I'll show you all;
Since we are met, make our parting comical.° — *happy*
SEBASTIAN This gentleman, my friend, will take his leave, sir.
SIR ALEXANDER Ha? Take his leave, Sebastian? Who?
SEBASTIAN This gentleman.
SIR ALEXANDER [*to Greenwit*] Your love,° sir, has already given me some time, — *courtesy*
And if you please to trust my age° with more, — *indulge an old man*
It shall pay double interest. Good sir, stay.
GREENWIT I have been too bold.
SIR ALEXANDER Not so, sir. A merry day
'Mongst friends being spent is better than gold saved.—
Some wine, some wine! Where be these knaves I keep?° — *employ as servants*

Enter three or four servingmen and Neatfoot.

NEATFOOT At your worshipful elbow, sir.
SIR ALEXANDER You are
Kissing my maids, drinking, or fast asleep.
NEATFOOT Your Worship has given it us° right. — *described us*
SIR ALEXANDER You varlets, stir!
Chairs, stools, and cushions.
[*The servants fetch chairs and wine.*]
Prithee, Sir Davy Dapper,
Make that chair thine.
SIR DAVY 'Tis but an easy gift,
And yet I thank you for it, sir. I'll take it.
SIR ALEXANDER [*to servants*] A chair for old Sir Adam Appleton.
NEATFOOT [*providing a chair*] A backfriend° to Your Worship. — *chair*
SIR ADAM Marry, good Neatfoot,
I thank thee for it. Backfriends° sometimes are good. — *Supporters; false friends*
SIR ALEXANDER Pray make that stool your perch, good Master Goshawk.
GOSHAWK I stoop to your lure,[2] sir.
SIR ALEXANDER Son Sebastian,
Take Master Greenwit to you.
SEBASTIAN [*to Greenwit*] Sit, dear friend.
SIR ALEXANDER Nay, Master Laxton. [*To servants*] Furnish Master Laxton
With what he wants: a stone.—A stool, I would say, a stool.[3]

2. I fly down to the food put out as a lure, as it were. (A technical phrase from hawking, appropriate to Goshawk's name, since a goshawk is a type of hawk.)

3. Sir Alexander's perhaps deliberate malapropism calls satiric attention to Laxton's name: lack-stone, suggesting the absence of testicles and of land.

LAXTON I had rather stand, sir.
SIR ALEXANDER I know you had, good Master Laxton. So, so.
Exeunt [*Neatfoot and*] *servants.*
Now here's a mess° of friends, and, gentlemen, *company of four*
Because time's glass° shall not be running long, *hourglass*
I'll quicken it with a pretty tale.
SIR DAVY Good tales do well
In these bad days, where vice does so excel.
SIR ADAM Begin, Sir Alexander.
SIR ALEXANDER Last day° I met *Yesterday*
An agèd man upon whose head was scored
A debt of just so many years as these
Which I owe to my grave. The man you all know.
OMNES His name, I pray you, sir?
SIR ALEXANDER Nay, you shall pardon me.
But when he saw me, with a sigh that brake,
Or seemed to break, his heartstrings, thus he spake:
"Oh my good knight," says he—and then his eyes
Were richer even by that which made them poor,
They had spent so many tears they had no more—
"Oh, sir," says he, "you know it, for you ha' seen
Blessings to rain upon mine house and me;
Fortune, who slaves° men, was my slave; her wheel *enslaves*
Hath spun me golden threads, for, I thank heaven,
I ne'er had but one cause to curse my stars."
I asked him then what that one cause might be.
OMNES So, sir.
SIR ALEXANDER He paused, and—as we often see
A sea so much becalmed there can be found
No wrinkle on his brow,° his waves being drowned *the sea's surface*
In their own rage; but when th'imperious winds
Use strange invisible tyranny to shake
Both heaven's and earth's foundation at their noise,
The seas, swelling with wrath to part that fray,
Rise up and are more wild, more mad than they—
Even so this good old man was by my question
Stirred up to roughness. You might see his gall° *bile, bitterness*
Flow even in's eyes; then grew he fantastical.° *bizarre*
SIR DAVY Fantastical? Ha, ha!
SIR ALEXANDER Yes, and talked oddly.
SIR ADAM Pray, sir, proceed.
How did this old man end?
SIR ALEXANDER Marry, sir, thus:
He left his wild fit to read o'er his cards;° *i.e., his fortunes*
Yet then, though age cast snow on all his hairs,
He joyed because, says he, "The god of gold
Has been to me no niggard; that disease
Of which all old men sicken, avarice,
Never infected me."
LAXTON [*aside*] He means not himself, I'm sure.
SIR ALEXANDER "For, like a lamp
Fed with continual oil, I spend and throw
My light to all that need it, yet have still
Enough to serve myself. Oh, but," quoth he,

"Though heaven's dew fall thus on this agèd tree,
I have a son that's like a wedge doth° cleave — *that does*
My very heart root."

SIR DAVY — Had he such a son?

SEBASTIAN [*aside*] — Now I do smell a fox strongly.

SIR ALEXANDER — Let's see: no, Master Greenwit is not yet
So mellow in years as he; but as like Sebastian,
Just like my son Sebastian—such another.

SEBASTIAN [*aside*] — How finely like a fencer my father fetches his by-blows° to hit me! But if I beat you not at your own weapon of subtlety— — *sideswipes*

SIR ALEXANDER — "This son," saith he, "that should be
The column and main arch unto my house,
The crutch unto my age, becomes a whirlwind
Shaking the firm foundation."

SIR ADAM — 'Tis some prodigal.

SEBASTIAN [*aside*] — Well shot, old Adam Bell![4]

SIR ALEXANDER — No city monster neither, no prodigal,
But sparing,° wary, civil, and—though wifeless— — *thrifty*
An excellent husband,° and such a traveler, — *thrifty householder*
He has more tongues° in his head than some have teeth. — *languages*

SIR DAVY — I have but two in mine.

GOSHAWK — So sparing and so wary,
What then could vex his father so?

SIR ALEXANDER — Oh, a woman.

SEBASTIAN [*aside*] — A flesh fly.[5] That can vex any man.

SIR ALEXANDER — A scurvy woman,
On whom the passionate old man swore he° doted. — *(the son)*
"A creature," saith he, "nature hath brought forth
To mock the sex of woman." It is a thing
One knows not how to name; her birth began
Ere she was all made. 'Tis woman more than man,
Man more than woman,[6] and—which to none can hap°— — *happen*
The sun gives her two shadows to one shape.
Nay, more, let this strange thing walk, stand, or sit,
No blazing star° draws more eyes after it. — *comet*

SIR DAVY — A monster. 'Tis some monster.

SIR ALEXANDER — She's a varlet.

SEBASTIAN [*aside*] — Now is my cue to bristle.

SIR ALEXANDER — A naughty pack.° — *bad character*

SEBASTIAN [*aloud*] — 'Tis false!

SIR ALEXANDER — Ha, boy?

SEBASTIAN — 'Tis false.

SIR ALEXANDER — What's false? I say she's naught.° — *wicked*

SEBASTIAN — I say that° tongue — *any*
That dares speak so, but yours, sticks in the throat
Of a rank villain. Set yourself aside—

SIR ALEXANDER — So, sir, what then?

SEBASTIAN — Any here else had lied.[7]
(*Aside*) I think I shall fit you.° — *prove a match for you*

4. A celebrated archer and fencer. (Said as a sarcastic observation on Sir Adam's feeble comment.)
5. A fly whose maggots feed on rotting meat.
6. To Sir Alexander, this imagined woman (really Moll) is both man and woman, having been born with the imperfectly formed genitals of a hermaphrodite.
7. Setting aside yourself, anyone else saying that is a liar.

SIR ALEXANDER Lie?
SEBASTIAN Yes.
SIR DAVY Doth this concern him?[8]
SIR ALEXANDER Ah, sirrah° boy, *(said to inferiors)*
Is your blood heated? Boils it? Are you stung?
I'll pierce you deeper yet.—Oh, my dear friends,
I am that wretched father, this that son
That sees his ruin, yet headlong on doth run.
SIR ADAM [*to Sebastian*] Will you love such a poison?
SIR DAVY Fie, fie!
SEBASTIAN You're all mad.
SIR ALEXANDER Thou'rt sick at heart, yet feel'st it not. Of all these,
What gentleman but thou, knowing his disease
Mortal, would shun the cure?—Oh, Master Greenwit,
Would you to such an idol bow?
GREENWIT Not I, sir.
SIR ALEXANDER Here's Master Laxton. Has he mind to a woman
As thou hast?
LAXTON No, not I, sir.
SIR ALEXANDER Sir, I know it.
LAXTON Their good parts are so rare,° their bad so common, *scarce; excellent*
I will have naught° to do with any woman. *nothing; sexual dalliance*
SIR DAVY 'Tis well done, Master Laxton.
SIR ALEXANDER Oh, thou cruel boy,
Thou wouldst with lust an old man's life destroy.
Because thou see'st I'm halfway in my grave,
Thou shovel'st dust upon me. Would thou mightest have
Thy wish, most wicked, most unnatural!
SIR DAVY Why, sir, 'tis thought Sir Guy Fitzallard's daughter
Shall wed your son Sebastian.
SIR ALEXANDER Sir Davy Dapper,
I have upon my knees wooed this fond° boy *foolish*
To take that virtuous maiden.
SEBASTIAN Hark you a word, sir.
You on your knees have cursed that virtuous maiden,
And me for loving her, yet do you now
Thus baffle° me to my face? Wear° not your knees *challenge / Wear out*
In such entreats!° Give me Fitzallard's daughter. *entreaties*
SIR ALEXANDER I'll give thee ratsbane° rather! *rat poison*
SEBASTIAN Well, then, you know
What dish I mean to feed upon.° *(see 124–25 and n)*
SIR ALEXANDER Hark, gentlemen,
He swears to have this cutpurse drab° to spite my gall. *whore*
OMNES Master Sebastian!
SEBASTIAN I am deaf to you all.
I'm so bewitched, so bound to my desires,
Tears, prayers, threats, nothing can quench out those fires
That burn within me. *Exit Sebastian.*
SIR ALEXANDER Her blood shall quench it, then.
[*To them*] Lose him not.° Oh, dissuade him, gentlemen! *Don't give up on him*
SIR DAVY He shall be weaned, I warrant you.

8. Does Sir Alexander's story point to Sebastian?

SIR ALEXANDER Before his eyes
Lay down his shame, my grief, his miseries.

OMNES No more, no more! Away!

Exeunt all but Sir Alexander.

SIR ALEXANDER I wash a Negro,° *attempt the impossible*
Losing both pains and cost. But take thy flight;
I'll be most near thee when I'm least in sight.° *when you least expect me*
Wild buck, I'll hunt thee breathless; thou shalt run on,
But I will turn thee° when I'm not thought upon. *force you about*

Enter Ralph Trapdoor [bowing and scraping].

Now, sirrah, what are you? Leave your ape's tricks and speak.

TRAPDOOR A letter from my captain° to Your Worship. *(former) commanding officer*

SIR ALEXANDER Oh, oh, now I remember. 'Tis to prefer° thee into my service. *recommend*

TRAPDOOR To be a shifter under Your Worship's nose of a clean trencher, when there's a good bit upon't.[9]

SIR ALEXANDER Troth, honest fellow. [*Aside*] Humh—ha—
let me see:
This knave shall be the ax to hew that down
At which I stumble. H'as° a face that promiseth° *He has / shows signs of*
Much of a villain. I will grind his wit,° *sharpen his cunning*
And if the edge prove fine, make use of it.—
Come hither, sirrah. Canst thou be secret, ha?

TRAPDOOR As two crafty attorneys plotting the undoing of their clients.

SIR ALEXANDER Didst never, as thou hast walked about this town, hear of a wench called Moll, Mad, Merry Moll?

TRAPDOOR Moll Cutpurse, sir.

SIR ALEXANDER The same. Dost thou know her, then?

TRAPDOOR As well as I know 'twill rain upon Simon and Jude's day[1] next. I will sift all the taverns i'th'city, and drink half-pots with all the watermen o'th'Bankside,[2] but if you will, sir, I'll find her out.

SIR ALEXANDER That task is easy; do't, then. Hold thy hand up. [*Examining his hand*] What's this, is't burnt?° *branded for a felony*

TRAPDOOR No, sir, no, a little singed with making fireworks.

SIR ALEXANDER [*giving money*] There's money. Spend it. That being spent, fetch more.

TRAPDOOR Oh, sir, that all the poor soldiers in England had such a leader! For fetching, no water spaniel is like me.

SIR ALEXANDER This wench we speak of strays so from her kind,° *natural state*
Nature repents she made her. 'Tis a mermaid
Has tolled° my son to shipwreck. *Who has lured*

TRAPDOOR I'll cut her comb° for you. *i.e., lower her pride*

SIR ALEXANDER I'll tell° out gold for thee then. Hunt her forth; *count*
Cast out a line hung full of silver hooks
To catch her to thy company. Deep spendings

9. I aim to clean up after your dinner and devour the leftovers.

1. October 28, a festival day, when rain would spoil the procession.

2. Oarsmen transporting passengers on the Thames. The Bankside is on the southern bank, in Southwark.

May draw her that's most chaste° to a man's bosom. *the chastest woman*
TRAPDOOR The jingling of golden bells, and a good fool with a hobbyhorse,[3] will draw all the whores i'th'town to dance in a morris.° *a country-dance*
SIR ALEXANDER Or rather, for that's best (they say sometimes
she goes in breeches), follow her as her man.° *manservant*
TRAPDOOR And when her breeches are off,° she shall follow me. *i.e., when she's naked*
SIR ALEXANDER Beat all thy brains° to serve her. *Tax your ingenuity*
TRAPDOOR Zounds,° sir, as country wenches beat cream till butter comes. *By God's wounds*
SIR ALEXANDER Play thou the subtle spider; weave fine nets
To ensnare her very life.
TRAPDOOR Her life?
SIR ALEXANDER Yes, suck
Her heart-blood if thou canst. Twist thou but cords
To catch her, I'll find law to hang her up.
TRAPDOOR Spoke like a worshipful bencher.° *worthy magistrate*
SIR ALEXANDER Trace° all her steps; at this she-fox's den *Follow*
Watch what lambs enter. Let me play the shepherd
To save their throats from bleeding, and cut hers.
TRAPDOOR This is the goll° shall do't. *hand*
SIR ALEXANDER Be firm, and gain me
Ever thine own. This done, I entertain° thee. *take into service*
How is thy name?
TRAPDOOR My name, sir, is Rafe° Trapdoor, honest Rafe. *(nickname for "Ralph")*
SIR ALEXANDER Trapdoor, be like thy name, a dangerous step
For her to venture on; but unto me—
TRAPDOOR As fast as your sole to your boot or shoe, sir.
SIR ALEXANDER Hence, then. Be little seen here as thou canst.
I'll still be at thine elbow.
TRAPDOOR The trapdoor's set.
Moll, if you budge, you're gone. This me shall crown:
A roaring boy° the roaring girl puts down. *swaggerer*
SIR ALEXANDER God-a-mercy.° Lose no time. *Exeunt.* *Thanks*

[2.1]

The three shops open in a rank:° the first a pothecary's shop,[1] the next a feather shop, the third a sempster's shop; Mistress Gallipot in the first, Mistress Tiltyard in the next, Master Openwork and his wife in the third. To them enters Laxton, Goshawk, and Greenwit. *row*

MRS. OPENWORK Gentlemen, what is't you lack? What is't you buy? See fine bands and ruffs, fine lawns, fine cambrics.° What is't you lack, gentlemen, what is't you buy? *fine linens*
LAXTON Yonder's the shop.
GOSHAWK Is that she?° *(Mrs. Gallipot)*
LAXTON Peace!° *Quiet!*
GREENWIT She that minces° tobacco? *cuts up finely*

3. Wickerwork made into the shape of a horse and fastened around the dancer's waist.
2.1. A London street.
1. An apothecary's shop could sell drugs and medicines, including tobacco.

LAXTON Ay. She's a gentlewoman born, I can tell you, though it be her hard fortune now to shred Indian potherbs.°
i.e., tobacco

GOSHAWK Oh, sir, 'tis many a good woman's fortune, when her husband turns bankrupt, to begin with pipes° and set up again.
tobacco pipes

LAXTON And indeed the raising of the woman is the lifting up of the man's head at all times;[2] if one flourish, t'other will bud as fast, I warrant ye.

GOSHAWK Come, thou'rt familiarly acquainted there, I grope° that.
grasp

LAXTON An° you grope° no better i'th'dark, you may chance lie i'th'ditch when you're drunk.
If / find your way

GOSHAWK Go, thou'rt a mystical° lecher.
covert, secret

LAXTON I will not deny but my credit° may take up an ounce of pure smoke.
good standing

GOSHAWK May take up an ell of pure smock![3] Away, go. [*Aside*] 'Tis the closest striker!° Life, I think he commits venery° forty foot deep; no man's aware on't. I, like a palpable smockster,° go to work so openly with the tricks of art that I'm as apparently° seen as a naked boy in a vial;[4] and were it not for a gift of treachery that I have in me to betray my friend when he puts most trust in me—mass,° yonder he[5] is too—and by his injury° to make good my access to her, I should appear as defective in courting as a farmer's son the first day of his feather,[6] that doth nothing at court but woo the hangings and glass windows[7] for a month together and some broken° waiting-woman forever after. I find those imperfections in my venery that, were't not for flattery and falsehood, I should want° discourse and impudence; and he that wants impudence among women is worthy to be kicked out at bed's feet.—He° shall not see me yet.
most secret lecher; sexual indulgence; petticoat-chaser; clearly; by the mass (an oath); by cuckolding him; penniless; defiled; lack; (Openwork)

[*He stands aside.*]

GREENWIT [*at the tobacco shop*] Troth, this is finely shred.

LAXTON Oh, women are the best mincers.°
shredders; word-mincers

MRS. GALLIPOT 'T had been° a good phrase for a cook's wife, sir.
That would have been

LAXTON But 'twill serve generally, like the front of a new almanac;° as thus: calculated for the meridian of cooks' wives, but generally for all Englishwomen.
astrology book

MRS. GALLIPOT Nay, you shall ha't,[8] sir; I have filled it for you. *She puts it to the fire.*

LAXTON The pipe's in a good hand, and I wish mine always so.°
(with bawdy suggestion)

GREENWIT But not to be used i'that fashion!°
i.e., put to the fire

LAXTON Oh, pardon me, sir, I understand no French.° [*To Goshawk*] I pray be covered.° Jack, a pipe of rich smoke?
French fashions; bawdry; put on your hat

2. Sexual double entendres run throughout this passage, in "pipes," "lifting up of the man's head," "grope," etc.

3. To Laxton's insistence in lines 21–22 that he is creditworthy enough to buy a supply of good tobacco, Goshawk replies with smutty wordplay on "take up" and "smoke/smock," with the implied meaning being "You're more likely to lift up a woman's smock, or petticoat." An ell is a cloth measure of forty-five inches.

4. An aborted fetus preserved in a glass jar.

5. Openwork, whose wife Goshawk would like to seduce.

6. I.e., as a son of a prosperous farmer trying to impress city sophisticates with the gaudy finery he has bought.

7. Does nothing but practice his bows to the wall hangings and windows.

8. (1) You shall have the pipe you ordered; (2) please go ahead. (Presumably Laxton has gestured a polite refusal of a first offer.)

GOSHAWK Rich smoke; that's sixpence a pipe, is't?

GREENWIT To me,° sweet lady. [*The men smoke.*]

Now serve me

MRS. GALLIPOT [*aside to Laxton*] Be not forgetful; respect my credit; seem strange.[9] Art and wit makes a fool of suspicion; pray be wary.

LAXTON [*aside to her*] Push,° I warrant you.—Come, how is't, gallants?

Pooh

GREENWIT Pure and excellent.

LAXTON I thought 'twas good, you were grown so silent. You are like those that love not to talk at victuals, though they make a worse noise i'the nose than a common fiddler's prentice, and discourse a whole supper with snuffling. [*Aside to Mrs. Gallipot*] I must speak a word with you anon.

MRS. GALLIPOT [*aside to him*] Make your way wisely, then.

[*They stand aside and converse privately.*]

GOSHAWK [*to Greenwit*] Oh, what else, sir? He's° perfection itself, full of manners, but not an acre of ground belonging to 'em.°

Laxton is; *his manners; his manors*

GREENWIT Ay, and full of form.° H'as ne'er a good stool in's chamber.

style; bench

GOSHAWK But above all, religious: he prayeth daily upon elder brothers.[1]

GREENWIT And valiant above measure: he's run three streets from a sergeant.°

one who arrests for debt

LAXTON Pooh, pooh. *He blows tobacco in their faces.*

GREENWIT [*and*] GOSHAWK Oh, pooh, ho, ho!

[*They move away. Laxton and Mrs. Gallipot resume their private conversation.*]

LAXTON So, so.

MRS. GALLIPOT What's the matter now, sir?

LAXTON I protest I'm in extreme want of money. If you can supply me now with any means, you do me the greatest pleasure, next to the bounty of your love, as ever poor gentleman tasted.°

experienced

MRS. GALLIPOT What's the sum would pleasure ye, sir? Though you deserve nothing less at my hands.

LAXTON Why, 'tis but for want of opportunity, thou know'st. [*Aside*] I put her off with opportunity° still. By this light, I hate her, but for means to keep me in fashion with gallants; for what I take from her I spend upon other wenches, bear her in hand° still. She has wit enough to rob her husband, and I ways enough to consume the money. [*To Goshawk and Greenwit, who are coughing*] Why, how now? What, the chin-cough?°

excuses; *lead her on*; *whooping cough*

GOSHAWK Thou hast the cowardliest trick to come before a man's face and strangle him ere he be aware! I could find in my heart to make a quarrel in earnest.

LAXTON Pox, an thou dost, thou know'st I never use° to fight with my friends; thou'll but lose thy labor in't.

am accustomed

Enter Jack Dapper and his man Gull.

9. Guard my reputation by acting as though you don't know me.

1. (1) He prays with Puritan elders; (2) he preys on heirs to fortunes.

Jack Dapper!

GREENWIT Monsieur Dapper, I dive down to your ankles.°

i.e., bow deeply

JACK DAPPER Save° ye, gentlemen, all three, in a peculiar° salute.

God save / special

GOSHAWK He were ill to make a° lawyer; he dispatches three at once.

would make a bad

LAXTON [*receiving a purse from Mrs. Gallipot*] So, well said.° But is this of the same tobacco, Mistress Gallipot?[2]

well done

MRS. GALLIPOT The same you had at first, sir.

LAXTON I wish it no better. This will serve to drink° at my chamber.

smoke

GOSHAWK Shall we taste a pipe on't?

LAXTON Not of this, by my troth, gentlemen. I have sworn before you.

GOSHAWK What, not Jack Dapper?[3]

LAXTON Pardon me, sweet Jack. I'm sorry I made such a rash oath, but foolish oaths must stand. [*Dapper starts to move away.*] Where art going, Jack?

JACK DAPPER Faith, to buy one feather.

LAXTON One feather? [*Aside*] The fool's peculiar still.

JACK DAPPER [*to his servant*] Gull!

GULL Master?

JACK DAPPER [*giving coin*] Here's three halfpence for your ordinary,° boy. Meet me an hour hence in Paul's.°

meal / Cathedral

[*Dapper makes his way to the feather shop.*]

GULL [*to himself*] How? Three single halfpence? Life,° this will scarce serve a man in sauce.[4] A ha'p'orth° of mustard, a ha'p'orth of oil, and a ha'p'orth of vinegar; what's left then for the pickle° herring? This shows° like small° beer i'th'morning after a great surfeit of wine o'ernight.° He could spend his three pound last night in a supper amongst girls and brave bawdy-house boys. I thought his pockets cackled not for nothing; these are the eggs of three pound.[5] I'll go sup 'em up presently.° *Exit Gull.*

(an oath) / *halfpennyworth* / *pickled / looks / weak* / *the night before* / *right away*

LAXTON [*aside, as he counts the money*] Eight, nine, ten angels.° Good wench, i'faith, and one that loves darkness well; she puts out a candle with the best tricks of any drugster's° wife in England. But that which mads her: I rail upon opportunity[6] still, and take no notice on't. The other night she would needs lead me into a room with a candle in her hand to show me a naked picture,° where no sooner entered but the candle was sent of an errand.° Now I, not intending to understand her, but like a puny at the inns of venery,[7] called for another light innocently. Thus reward I all her cunning with simple mistaking. I know she cozens° her husband to keep° me, and I'll keep her honest° as long as I can, to make the poor man some part of amends. An honest mind

gold coins / *apothecary's* / *picture of a nude figure* / *extinguished* / *hoodwinks* / *maintain / chaste*

2. Laxton pretends that the money pouch holds tobacco.

3. Isn't Jack Dapper to be allowed to smoke? (Laxton cannot share his tobacco, since it is really money.)

4. This will scarcely provide a person with enough to buy condiments, much less solid food to eat.

5. These threepence are the poor leftovers of three pounds spent by Jack Dapper in dissipation.

6. I complain of a lack of opportunity to make love to her.

7. Like a beginning student in lechery. (Playing on "Inns of Court," where a puny would be a freshman law student.)

of a whoremaster! [*To the gallants*] How think you amongst you? What, a fresh pipe? Draw in a third man.

GOSHAWK No, you're a hoarder; you engross° by th'ounces. *monopolize*

At the feather shop now.

JACK DAPPER [*examining a feather*] Pooh, I like it not.

MRS. TILTYARD What feather is't you'd have, sir? These are most worn and most in fashion amongst the beaver gallants, the stone riders,[8] the private stage's audience, the twelve-penny-stool gentlemen; I can inform you, 'tis the general° feather. *widely fashionable*

JACK DAPPER And therefore I mislike it. Tell me of general! Now a continual Simon and Jude's rain° beat all your feathers as flat down as pancakes! Show me—a—spangled feather. *October rain (1.2.205–6)*

MRS. TILTYARD Oh, to go a-feasting with! You'd have it for a henchboy.° You shall. *page*

At the sempster's shop now.

OPENWORK [*to his wife*] Mass, I had quite forgot. His Honor's° footman was here last night, wife. Ha' you done with my lord's shirt? *Some nobleman's*

MRS. OPENWORK What's that to you, sir? I was this morning at His Honor's lodging ere such a snail as you crept out of your shell.

OPENWORK Oh, 'twas well done, good wife.

MRS. OPENWORK I hold it better, sir, than if you had done't yourself.

OPENWORK Nay, so say I. But is the countess's smock almost done, mouse?° *(a term of affection)*

MRS. OPENWORK Here lies the cambric, sir, but wants,° I fear me. *needs some work*

OPENWORK I'll resolve you of that° presently. *take care of that*

[*He takes the work and retires.*]

MRS. OPENWORK Heyday! Oh, audacious groom,° *lackey (Openwork)*
Dare you presume to noblewomen's linen?
Keep you your yard° to measure shepherds' holland!° *yardstick; penis / cloth*
I must confine you, I see that.

At the tobacco shop now.

GOSHAWK [*as they smoke*] What say you to this gear?° *business (of smoking)*

LAXTON I dare the arrant'st° critic in tobacco to lay one fault upon't. *most audacious*

Enter Moll in a frieze jerkin and a black safeguard.[9]

GOSHAWK Life, yonder's Moll!

LAXTON Moll? Which Moll?

GOSHAWK Honest Moll.

LAXTON Prithee, let's call her.—Moll!

ALL Moll, Moll, psst, Moll!

MOLL How now, what's the matter?

GOSHAWK A pipe of good tobacco, Moll?

8. Among gallants in fashionable beaver hats and riders of stallions.

9. A coarse men's jacket and a black riding skirt.

MOLL I cannot stay.

GOSHAWK Nay, Moll, pooh! Prithee hark, but one word, i'faith.

MOLL Well, what is't?

GREENWIT Prithee come hither, sirrah.°

[sirrah: *i.e., Moll*]

LAXTON [*aside*] Heart,° I would give but too much money to be nibbling with that wench. Life, sh' has the spirit of four great parishes, and a voice that will drown all the city! Methinks a brave captain might get° all his soldiers upon her, and ne'er be beholding° to a company of Mile End[1] milksops, if he could come on and come off[2] quick enough. Such a Moll were a marrowbone° before an Italian; he would cry "*bona-roba*"° till his ribs were nothing but bone. I'll lay hard siege to her. Money is that aqua fortis° that eats into many a maidenhead. Where the walls are flesh and blood, I'll ever pierce through with a golden auger.°

[Heart: *By God's heart*; get: *beget*; beholding: *beholden*; marrowbone: *an aphrodisiac*; bona-roba: *"whore"*; aqua fortis: *nitric acid*; auger: *hole-boring tool*]

GOSHAWK [*offering tobacco*] Now, thy judgment, Moll. Is't not good?

MOLL Yes, faith, 'tis very good tobacco. How° do you sell an ounce? Farewell. God buy° you, Mistress Gallipot. [*She starts to go.*]

[How: *For how much*; buy: *be with*]

GOSHAWK Why, Moll, Moll!

MOLL I cannot stay now, i'faith. I am going to buy a shag° ruff. The shop will be shut in presently. [*She heads for the other shops.*]

[shag: *worsted*]

GOSHAWK 'Tis the maddest, fantastical'st girl! I never knew so much flesh and so much nimbleness put together.

LAXTON She slips from one company to another like a fat eel between a Dutchman's fingers. [*Aside*] I'll watch my time for her.

MRS. GALLIPOT Some will not stick° to say she's a man, and some, both man and woman.

[stick: *hesitate*]

LAXTON That were excellent. She might first cuckold the husband and then make him do as much for the wife.

The feather shop again.

MOLL [*as she approaches*] Save° you! How does Mistress Tiltyard?

[Save: *God save*]

JACK DAPPER Moll!

MOLL Jack Dapper!

JACK DAPPER How dost, Moll?

MOLL I'll tell thee by and by. I go but to th'next shop.

JACK DAPPER Thou shalt find me here this hour about a feather.

MOLL Nay, an a feather hold you in play a whole hour, a goose° will last you all the days of your life. [*She moves on.*]

[goose: *(a foolish bird)*]

The sempster shop.

Let me see a good shag ruff.

OPENWORK Mistress Mary, that shalt thou, i'faith, and the best in the shop.

MRS. OPENWORK How now, greetings? Love terms, with a pox,

1. The location of a training ground for citizen militia.
2. If he could execute military maneuvers of advancing and retiring. (With bawdy suggestion.)

between you? Have I found out one of your haunts? I send you for hollands, and you're i'th' Low Countries, with a mischief. I'm served with good ware by th'shift that makes it lie dead° so long upon my hands I were as good shut up shop, for when I open it I take nothing.[3] *unasked for*

OPENWORK Nay, an you fall a-ringing° once, the devil cannot stop you. I'll out of the belfry as fast as I can.—Moll! *scolding loudly*

[*He goes to join Goshawk and the others.*]

MRS. OPENWORK [*to Moll*] Get you from my shop!

MOLL I come to buy.

MRS. OPENWORK I'll sell ye nothing. I warn ye° my house and shop. *warn you away from*

MOLL You, Goody° Openwork, you that prick out a poor living *Goodwife*
And sews many a bawdy skin-coat° together, *coat of skins*
Thou private pand'ress between shirt and smock,° *i.e., man and woman*
I wish thee for a minute but a man;
Thou shouldst never use more shapes. But as th'art,
I pity my revenge.[4] Now my spleen's° up, *anger is*
I would not mock it willingly.° Ha! Be thankful. *if I were you*
Now I forgive thee.

MRS. OPENWORK Marry, hang thee! I never asked forgiveness in my life.

Enter a Fellow with a long rapier by his side.

MOLL [*to the Fellow, as she draws her sword*] You, goodman swine's face!

FELLOW What, will you murder me?

MOLL You remember, slave, how you abused° me t'other night in a tavern? *insulted*

FELLOW Not I, by this light.

MOLL No, but by candlelight you did. You have tricks to save° your oaths, reservations, have you? And I have reserved somewhat for you. [*She strikes him.*] As you like that, call for more. You know the sign again. *avoid fulfilling*

FELLOW [*to himself*] Pox on't, had I brought any company along with me to have borne witness on't,[5] 'twould ne'er have grieved me; but to be struck and nobody by, 'tis my ill fortune still. Why, tread upon a worm, they say 'twill turn tail, but indeed a gentleman should have more manners.[6]

Exit Fellow.

LAXTON Gallantly performed, i'faith, Moll, and manfully! I love thee forever for't. Base rogue! Had he offered but the least counterbuff,° by this hand, I was prepared for him. *return blow*

MOLL You prepared for him? Why should you be prepared for him? Was he any more than a man?[7]

3. The Low Countries, or the Netherlands, suggest Moll's sexual anatomy. Holland is a kind of cloth (with a suggestion of Openwork's wishing to hunt around in Moll's personal linen). Mrs. Openwork gets nothing from Openwork, she says, but "good ware" (line 236), i.e., inadequate sexual performance, and so she threatens to "shut up shop" (line 237), i.e., refuse to have sex, since when she does "open it" (line 238), meaning her sexual anatomy, nothing comes of it. ("By th'shift," in line 236, suggests both evasiveness and the use of petticoats, or "shifts.") "Take nothing" also means "have no customers."

4. If you were a man for just a minute, I'd settle your hash. But, being what you are, I take pity and withhold revenge.

5. To have testified in a trial as to Moll's actions of assault and battery.

6. The Fellow's excuse for not fighting is that he is too much the gentleman to strike a lady.

7. Moll stresses "you": "Why do you assume that *you* should be the one to respond to this fellow's blows? Was he anything more than a man, in which case I could

LAXTON No, nor so much by a yard and a handful, London measure.

MOLL Why do you speak this, then? Do you think I cannot ride a stone horse° unless one lead him by th'snaffle?° *stallion / bit*

LAXTON Yes, and sit him bravely; I know thou canst, Moll. 'Twas but an honest mistake, through love, and I'll make amends for't any way. Prithee, sweet plump Moll, when shall thou and I go out o'town together?

MOLL Whither? To Tyburn,° prithee? *a place of execution*

LAXTON Mass, that's out o'town indeed. Thou hang'st so many jests upon thy friends still. I mean honestly to Brentford, Staines, or Ware.[8]

MOLL What to do there?

LAXTON Nothing but be merry and lie together. I'll hire a coach with four horses.

MOLL I thought 'twould be a beastly° journey. You may leave out one well; three horses will serve, if I play the jade° myself. *animal-driven; nasty* *worthless horse; hussy*

LAXTON Nay, push,° thou'rt such another° kicking wench! Prithee be kind and let's meet. *pooh / such a*

MOLL 'Tis hard but we shall° meet, sir. *We're sure to*

LAXTON Nay, but appoint the place, then. [*He offers money.*] There's ten angels in fair gold, Moll; you see I do not trifle with you. Do but say thou wilt meet me, and I'll have a coach ready for thee.

MOLL Why, here's my hand I'll meet you, sir.

LAXTON [*aside*] Oh, good gold!—The place, sweet Moll?

MOLL It shall be your appointment.° *You name the place*

LAXTON Somewhat near Holborn,[9] Moll.

MOLL In Gray's Inn Fields, then.

LAXTON A match.° *Agreed*

MOLL I'll meet you there.

LAXTON The hour?

MOLL Three.

LAXTON That will be time enough to sup at Brentford.

Fall from them to the other.[1]

OPENWORK [*to Goshawk*] I am of such a nature sir, I cannot endure the house when she scolds. Sh' has a tongue will be heard further in a still morning than Saint Antholin's° bell. She rails upon me for foreign wenching, that I, being a freeman, must needs keep a whore i'th'suburbs and seek to impoverish the liberties.[2] When we fall out,° I trouble you still to make all whole with my wife. *church in Watling Street* *quarrel*

GOSHAWK No trouble at all. 'Tis a pleasure to me to join things together.[3]

OPENWORK Go thy ways.° [*Aside*] I do this but to try° thy honesty, Goshawk. *Get on with you / test*

have handled him?" Laxton replies flippantly, in lines 275–76: "He wasn't much of a man." ("A yard and a handful" means "a generous measure," with bawdy wordplay on "yard," meaning "penis.")

8. These places to the west and north of London were favorite spots for excursions and assignations. Tyburn (line 283) was similarly outside London, but served a grimmer purpose.

9. A main road flanked by the Inns of Court, including Gray's Inn (line 304).

1. Laxton and Moll join other groups onstage.

2. Mrs. Openwork scolds her husband for patronizing whores outside of London when he might enjoy the "liberties" of London and his standing as a "free" citizen of the city.

3. It's a pleasure (1) to reconcile husband and wife; (2) to join my flesh with that of Mrs. Openwork.

The feather shop.

JACK DAPPER [*trying on feathers*] How lik'st thou this, Moll?

MOLL Oh, singularly; you're fitted now for a bunch. [*Aside*] He looks for all the world with those spangled feathers like a nobleman's bedpost.[4] The purity of your wench° would I fain try; she seems like Kent unconquered, and I believe as many wiles are in her.[5] Oh, the gallants of these times are shallow lechers! They put not their courtship home° enough to a wench; 'tis impossible to know what woman is throughly° honest, because she's ne'er thoroughly tried. I am of that certain belief there are more queans° in this town of their own making than of any man's provoking. Where lies the slackness then? Many a poor soul would down,° and there's nobody will push 'em.
Women are courted but ne'er soundly tried;
As many walk in spurs that never ride.[6]

(Mrs. Tiltyard) — *all the way* — *thoroughly* — *whores* — *fall into sin*

The sempster's shop.

MRS. OPENWORK Oh, abominable!

GOSHAWK Nay, more: I tell you in private, he° keeps a whore i'th'suburbs. *(Openwork)*

MRS. OPENWORK Oh, spittle° dealing! I came to him a gentlewoman born. I'll show you mine arms° when you please, sir. *i.e., foul, sick* — *coat of arms; upper limbs*

GOSHAWK [*aside*] I had rather see your legs, and begin that way.

MRS. OPENWORK 'Tis well known he took me from a lady's service where I was well beloved of the steward. I had my Latin tongue and a spice of the French° before I came to him, and now doth he keep a suburbian whore[7] under my nostrils.° *(language; sexual disease)* — *right under my nose*

GOSHAWK There's ways enough to cry quit° with him. Hark in thine ear. [*He whispers to her.*] *get even*

MRS. OPENWORK There's a friend worth a million.

[*The feather shop.*]

MOLL [*aside*] I'll try one spear against your chastity, Mistress Tiltyard, though it prove too short by the burr.[8]

Enter Ralph Trapdoor.

TRAPDOOR [*seeing Moll*] Mass, here she is. I'm bound already to serve her, though it be but a sluttish° trick. [*To Moll*] Bless my hopeful° young mistress with long life and great limbs! Send her the upper hand of° all bailiffs and their hungry adherents!° *i.e., mean-spirited* — *whom I hope to serve* — *over* — *ill-paid subalterns*

MOLL How now, what art thou?

TRAPDOOR A poor ebbing° gentleman that would gladly wait for the young flood° of your service. *declining (in wealth)* — *flood tide, bounty*

4. A nobleman's bedpost might be ornamented with feathers.
5. Kent, in southeast England, proudly boasted of never having been conquered. The "wiles" refers playfully to the "wealds," or wilds, for which Kent was also justly famous.
6. Many men wear spurs, as though claiming to be riders (of women), but without ever actually having made a conquest. Hence women are seldom tested.
7. The suburbs were notorious as places of assignation or prostitution; see also Prologue, line 21 and note. The spelling "suburbian" ("subberbian" in Q) was common at this time.
8. The iron ring on a tilting lance. Moll wonders to herself if Mistress Tiltyard's defenses of her chastity will prove adequate.

MOLL My service? What should move you to offer your service to me, sir?

TRAPDOOR The love I bear to your heroic spirit and masculine womanhood.

MOLL So, sir, put case we° should retain you to us. What parts° are there in you for a gentlewoman's service? *let's suppose I* *qualities*

TRAPDOOR Of two kinds, Right Worshipful: movable and immovable—movable to run of° errands, and immovable to stand when you have occasion to use° me. *on* *(with bawdy suggestion)*

MOLL What strength have you?

TRAPDOOR Strength, Mistress Moll? I have gone up into a steeple and stayed° the great bell as't has been ringing; stopped a windmill going. *stopped*

MOLL And never struck down yourself?

TRAPDOOR Stood as upright as I do at this present.

Moll trips up his heels; he falls.

MOLL Come, I pardon you for this. It shall be no disgrace to you; I have struck up the heels of the high German's[9] size ere now.—What, not stand?

TRAPDOOR I am of that nature where I love, I'll be at my mistress's foot to do her service.

MOLL Why, well said. But say your mistress should receive injury: have you the spirit of fighting in you? Durst° you second° her? *Dare* *support, defend*

TRAPDOOR Life, I have kept° a bridge myself, and drove seven at a time before me. *defended*

MOLL Ay?

TRAPDOOR (*aside*) But they were all Lincolnshire bullocks,[1] by my troth.

MOLL Well, meet me in Gray's Inn Fields between three and four this afternoon, and upon better consideration we'll retain you.[2]

TRAPDOOR I humbly thank Your good Mistress-ship. [*Aside*] I'll crack your neck for this kindness! *Exit Trapdoor.*

Moll meets Laxton.

LAXTON Remember: three.

MOLL Nay, if I fail you, hang me.

LAXTON Good wench, i'faith.

Then [Moll meets] Openwork.

MOLL Who's this?

OPENWORK 'Tis I, Moll.

MOLL Prithee, tend thy shop and prevent bastards.° *i.e., stop whoring*

OPENWORK We'll have a pint of the same wine,° i'faith, Moll. *("bastard" was a wine)*

[*Exeunt Openwork and Moll.*] *The bell rings.*

GOSHAWK Hark! The bell rings. Come, gentlemen. Jack Dapper, where shall 's° all munch? *shall we*

JACK DAPPER I am for Parker's ordinary.° *eating place*

9. Referring to a tall German fencer who was well known in London.

1. Trapdoor, recalling a time when he served as a shepherd, privately confesses to us that he drove seven herd animals before him, not seven of the enemy as his vaunting speech in lines 384–85 is meant to imply. Cf. the intrepid tailor in the French folktale who was famed and feared for having killed *"sept à un coup"* (seven at a blow) when what he had actually done was to swat seven flies at one stroke.

2. When I've had time to reflect on this, I'll hire you.

LAXTON [*aside to the others*] He's a good guest to 'm, he deserves his board. He draws all the gentlemen in a term-time thither.[3]—We'll be your followers, Jack; lead the way.— Look you, by my faith, the fool has feathered his nest well.[4]
Exeunt gallants.

Enter Master Gallipot, Master Tiltyard, and servants with water spaniels and a duck.° *decoy or live duck*

TILTYARD Come, shut up your shops. Where's Master Openwork?

MRS. OPENWORK Nay, ask not me, Master Tiltyard.

GALLIPOT Where's his water-dog? Pooh—psst!—hur—hur—psst!° *(calls to the dog)*

TILTYARD Come, wenches, come, we're going all to Hoxton.° *a village near London*

MRS. GALLIPOT To Hoxton, husband?

GALLIPOT Ay, to Hoxton, pigsney.° *(a term of affection)*

MRS. TILTYARD I'm not ready, husband.

TILTYARD Faith, that's well. (*Spits in the dog's mouth.*)° *(a friendly gesture)* Hum—psst! psst!

GALLIPOT Come, Mistress Openwork, you are so long.

MRS. OPENWORK I have no joy of my life, Master Gallipot.

GALLIPOT Push, let your boy lead his water spaniel along, and we'll show you the bravest° sport at Parlous Pond.° Hey, *finest / (near Hoxton)* Trug, hey, Trug, hey, Trug! Here's the best duck in England, except my wife. Hey, hey, hey!
Fetch, fetch, fetch! Come, let's away.
Of all the year, this is the sportful'st day. [*Exeunt.*]

[2.2]

Enter Sebastian solus.° *alone*

SEBASTIAN If a man have a free will, where should the use
More perfect shine than in his will to love?
All creatures have their liberty in that;

Enter Sir Alexander and listens to him.

Though else kept under servile yoke and fear,
The very bondslave has his freedom there.° *(in love)*
Amongst a world of creatures voiced and silent,
Must my desires wear fetters? [*Aside, spying his father*]
Yea, are you
So near? Then I must break with my heart's truth,
Meet grief at a back way.[1] [*Aloud*] Well, why, suppose
The two-leaved° tongues of slander or of truth *forked-tongued, two-timing*
Pronounce Moll loathsome; if before my love° *in my adoring eyes*
She appear fair, what injury have I?
I have the thing I like. In all things else
Mine own eye guides me, and I find 'em prosper;° *my affairs prosper*

3. Jack Dapper is such a good customer and attracts so many customers to the eating house, especially during the term-time (when the law courts are sitting), that he deserves free meals.
4. Jack Dapper has outfitted himself with enough feathers to resemble a foolish nesting bird. (With a joke on "feathering one's nest," i.e., accumulating wealth.)
2.2. Another street.
1. Then I must break off my heart's true lament and commune with my grief on some other, more private occasion.

Life, what should ail it° now? I know that man — *why blame my eyesight*
Ne'er truly loves—if he gainsay't° he lies— — *deny it*
That winks° and marries with his father's eyes. — *shuts his eyes*
I'll keep mine own wide open.

Enter Moll and a Porter with a viol° on his back. — *viola da gamba*

SIR ALEXANDER [*aside*] Here's brave° willfulness! — *fine (ironic)*
A made match.° Here she comes; they met o'purpose. — *arranged meeting*

PORTER Must I carry this great fiddle to your chamber, Mistress Mary?

MOLL Fiddle, goodman hog-rubber?° [*Aside*] Some of these porters bear so much for others they have no time to carry wit for themselves. — *swineherd*

PORTER To your own chamber, Mistress Mary?

MOLL [*to the audience*] Who'll hear an ass speak?—Whither else, goodman pageant-bearer?[2]—They're people of the worst memories.° *Exit Porter.* — *Porters are so forgetful*

SEBASTIAN Why, 'twere too great a burden, love, to have them carry things in their minds and o'their backs together.

MOLL Pardon me, sir, I thought not you so near.

SIR ALEXANDER [*aside*] So, so, so.

SEBASTIAN I would be nearer to thee, and in that fashion that makes the best part of all creatures honest.[3] No otherwise I wish it.

MOLL Sir, I am so poor to requite you,° you must look for nothing but thanks of me. I have no humor° to marry. I love to lie o'both sides o'th'bed myself; and again,° o'th'other side,° a wife, you know, ought to be obedient, but I fear me I am too headstrong to obey; therefore I'll ne'er go about it.° I love you so well, sir, for your good will, I'd be loath you should repent your bargain after, and therefore we'll ne'er come together at first. I have the head now of myself,° and am man enough for a woman. Marriage is but a chopping and changing, where a maiden loses one head and has a worse i'th'place.[4] — *I can offer you so little* / *inclination* / *besides* / *on the other hand* / *undertake it* / *I'm my own boss*

SIR ALEXANDER [*aside*] The most comfortablest answer from a roaring girl that ever mine ears drunk in!

SEBASTIAN This were enough now to affright a fool forever from thee, when 'tis the music that I love thee for.

SIR ALEXANDER [*aside*] There's a boy spoils all again!

MOLL Believe it, sir, I am not of that disdainful temper but I could love you faithfully.

SIR ALEXANDER [*aside*] A pox on you for that word! I like you not now. You're a cunning roarer;° I see that already. — *rowdy*

MOLL But sleep upon this once more, sir. You may chance shift a mind tomorrow. Be not too hasty to wrong yourself. Never, while you live, sir, take a wife running;° many have run out at heels° that have done't. You see, sir, I speak against myself, and if every woman would deal with their — *in haste* / *i.e., into poverty*

2. A porter officiating at a civic pageant or procession.
3. I.e., I wish to join with you in marriage, which, for the most virtuous persons, makes possible the fulfillment of chaste love.
4. In marriage, a young woman exchanges her maidenhead for a new, worse head: her husband, her lord and master.

suitor so honestly, poor younger brothers would not be so often gulled with old cozening widows that turn o'er all their wealth in trust to some kinsman and make the poor gentleman work hard for a pension.[5] Fare you well, sir.

[*She starts to leave.*]

SEBASTIAN Nay, prithee one word more!

SIR ALEXANDER [*aside*] How do I wrong this girl! She puts him off still.

MOLL Think upon this in cold blood, sir; you make as much haste as if you were a-going upon a sturgeon voyage. Take deliberation, sir; never choose a wife as if you were going to Virginia.[6] [*She moves away from him.*]

SEBASTIAN [*declaiming*] And so we parted. My too cursèd fate! [*He stands aside.*]

SIR ALEXANDER [*aside*] She is but cunning, gives him longer time in't.

Enter a Tailor.

TAILOR Mistress Moll, Mistress Moll! Soho ho, soho!° *(a hunting call)*

MOLL There, boy,° there, boy. What, dost thou go a-hawking *(a call to dogs)* after me with a red clout° on thy finger? *red pincushion*

TAILOR I forgot to take measure on you for your new breeches.

SIR ALEXANDER [*aside*] Heyday, breeches! What, will he marry a monster with two trinkets?° What age is this![7] If the wife *i.e., testicles* go in breeches, the man must wear long coats like a fool.

[*The Tailor takes measurements on Moll.*]

MOLL What fiddling's here! Would not the old pattern have served your turn?

TAILOR You change the fashion. You say you'll have the great Dutch slop,° Mistress Mary. *baggy breeches*

MOLL Why, sir, I say so still.

TAILOR Your breeches then will take up a yard more.[8]

MOLL Well, pray look it be put in, then.

TAILOR It shall stand round and full, I warrant you.

MOLL Pray make 'em easy enough.

TAILOR I know my fault now; t'other was somewhat stiff between the legs. I'll make these open enough, I warrant you.

SIR ALEXANDER [*aside*] Here's good gear towards![9] I have brought up my son to marry a Dutch slop and a French doublet—a codpiece daughter.

TAILOR So, I have gone as far as I can go.

MOLL Why, then, farewell.

TAILOR If you go presently to your chamber, Mistress Mary, pray send me the measure of your thigh, by some honest body.° *person*

5. Younger brothers, lacking inheritances, are apt to seek rich widows in marriage and may be easily fooled by them.
6. Do not choose a wife in desperation as if you were about to go on a long voyage to Russia (where one might fish for sturgeon) or the Americas.
7. What is this age coming to?
8. This passage (lines 88–105) bawdily plays on "yard" (meaning "penis"), "put in," "stand round and full," "stiff between the legs," "open," "gear," "as far as I can go," "lusty," "back ache," etc.
9. Here's a fine state of affairs! (Ironic.)

MOLL Well, sir, I'll send it by a porter presently. *Exit Moll.*
TAILOR So you had need; it is a lusty one. Both of them° would make any porter's back ache in England. *Exit Tailor.* *(her thighs)*
SEBASTIAN [*to himself*] I have examined the best part of man—
Reason and judgment—and in love, they tell me,
They leave me uncontrolled.° He that is swayed *out of control*
By an unfeeling blood, past heat of love,
His springtime must needs err; his watch ne'er goes right
That sets his dial by a rusty clock.[1]
SIR ALEXANDER [*coming forward*] So, and which is that rusty clock, sir? You?
SEBASTIAN The clock at Ludgate,° sir. It ne'er goes true. *an old London gate*
SIR ALEXANDER But thou goest falser. Not thy father's cares
Can keep thee right, when that insensible work
Obeys the workman's art, lets off the hour,
And stops again when time is satisfied;
But thou run'st on, and judgment, thy main wheel,
Beats by all stops, as if the work would break,[2]
Begun with long pains, for a minute's ruin,° *ruinous pleasure*
Much like a suffering man brought up with care,
At last bequeathed to shame and a short prayer.° *(before execution)*
SEBASTIAN I taste you bitterer than I can deserve, sir.
SIR ALEXANDER Who has bewitched thee, son? What devil or drug
Hath wrought upon the weakness of thy blood
And betrayed all her° hopes to ruinous folly? *(your blood's, passion's)*
Oh, wake from drowsy and enchanted shame,
Wherein thy soul sits with a golden dream,
Flattered and poisoned! I am old, my son;
Oh, let me prevail quickly,
For I have weightier business° of mine own *(preparing for death)*
Than to chide thee. I must not to my grave
As a drunkard to his bed, whereon he lies
Only to sleep, and never cares to rise;
Let me dispatch° in time. Come no more near her. *finish up*
SEBASTIAN Not honestly, not in the way of marriage?
SIR ALEXANDER What say'st thou? Marriage? In what place, the sessions house?° *courthouse*
And who shall give the bride, prithee? An indictment?[3]
SEBASTIAN Sir, now ye take part with the world to wrong her.
SIR ALEXANDER Why, wouldst thou fain marry to be pointed at?
Alas, the number's° great; do not o'erburden't. *number of fools is*
Why, as good marry a beacon on a hill,
Which all the country fix their eyes upon,
As her thy folly dotes on. If thou long'st

1. (1) A person who is too controlled by judgment, waiting until it is too late for the heated passion of love, loses his chance at the springtime of his life; he is out of step with time; (2) an older person (like my father) whose desires have cooled with age is incapable of understanding youthful passion; he is, as it were, governed by a rusty clock. (Sebastian, knowing his father to be listening, speaks with deliberate ambiguity.)

2. A good clock acts as its maker intended, striking the hours and then ceasing; but you let your erratic judgments override the delicate balancing of the human mechanism set in motion by "the workman's art" (line 117), i.e., "thy father's cares" (line 115).

3. A formal accusation in a trial would replace the form of the marriage ceremony, in which the bride is "given" to the groom by her father.

To have the story of thy infamous fortunes
Serve for discourse in ordinaries and taverns,
Thou'rt in the way;° or to confound thy name, *on the right track*
Keep on, thou canst not miss it; or to strike
Thy wretched father to untimely coldness,° *death*
Keep the left° hand still, it will bring thee to't. *sinister, evil*
Yet if no tears wrung from thy father's eyes,
Nor sighs that fly in sparkles° from his sorrows, *sparks*
Had power to alter what is willful in thee,
Methinks her very name should fright thee from her,
And never trouble me.

SEBASTIAN Why, is the name of Moll so fatal, sir?

SIR ALEXANDER Many one, sir, where suspect is entered,[4]
Forseek° all London from one end to t'other *Seek out*
More whores of that name than of any ten other.

SEBASTIAN What's that to her? Let those blush for themselves.
Can any guilt in others condemn her?
I've vowed to love her. Let all storms oppose me
That ever beat against the breast of man;
Nothing but death's black tempest shall divide us.

SIR ALEXANDER Oh, folly, that can dote on naught but shame!

SEBASTIAN Put case° a wanton itch runs through one name *Even supposing*
More than another, is that name the worse
Where honesty sits possessed in't? It should rather
Appear more excellent, and deserve more praise,
When through foul mists a brightness it can raise.
Why, there are of the devil's,° honest gentlemen, *the devil's disciples*
And well descended, keep° an open house, *who keep*
And some o'th'good man's° that are arrant knaves. *Jesus' followers*
He° hates unworthily that by rote contemns,° *(A person) / scorns*
For the name neither saves nor yet condemns.
And for° her honesty,° I have made such proof on't, *as for / chastity*
In several forms, so nearly° watched her ways, *closely*
I will maintain that strict° against an army, *rigorously*
Excepting you, my father. Here's her worst:
Sh' has a bold spirit that mingles with mankind,° *the male sex*
But nothing else comes near it,[5] and oftentimes
Through° her apparel somewhat shames her birth; *By means of*
But she is loose in nothing but in mirth.
Would all Molls were no worse!

SIR ALEXANDER [*turning away*] This way I toil in vain and
give but aim° *merely provide a target*
To infamy and ruin. He will fall;
My blessing cannot stay him. All my joys
Stand at the brink of a devouring flood
And will be willfully swallowed, willfully!
But why so vain let all these tears be lost?
I'll pursue her to shame, and so all's crossed.° *thwarted*

Exit Sir Alexander.

SEBASTIAN He is gone with some strange purpose, whose effect

4. Many a constable, sir, when the hunt is on for a suspect.

5. But in no other way does she flirt with vice.

Will hurt me little if he shoot so wide
To think I love so blindly.[6] I but feed
His heart to this match to draw on th'other,[7]
Wherein my joy sits with a full wish crowned—
Only his mood excepted,[8] which must change
By opposite policies,° courses indirect; *stratagems*
Plain dealing in this world takes no effect.
This mad girl I'll acquaint with my intent,
Get her assistance, make my fortunes° known; *prospects, plans*
'Twixt lovers' hearts she's a fit instrument,
And has the art to help them to their own.° *own wishes*
By her advice—for in that craft she's wise—
My love and I may meet, spite° of all spies. *Exit Sebastian.* *in spite*

[3.1]

Enter Laxton in Gray's Inn Fields with the Coachman.

LAXTON Coachman!

COACHMAN Here, sir.

LAXTON There's a tester° more. Prithee drive thy coach to the hither end of Marybone Park°—a fit place for Moll to get in. *sixpence* *(now Regents Park)*

COACHMAN Marybone Park, sir?

LAXTON Ay, it's in our way, thou know'st.

COACHMAN It shall be done, sir. [*He starts to leave.*]

LAXTON Coachman!

COACHMAN Anon, sir.

LAXTON Are we fitted with good frampold jades?° *spirited horses*

COACHMAN The best in Smithfield,° I warrant you, sir. *a livestock market*

LAXTON May we safely take the upper hand of any coached velvet cap or tuftaffety jacket?[1] For they keep a vile swaggering in coaches nowadays; the highways are stopped with them.

COACHMAN My life for yours, and baffle 'em[2] too, sir. Why, they are the same jades, believe it, sir, that have drawn all your famous whores to Ware.° *(see 2.1.286 n)*

LAXTON Nay, then, they know their business; they need no more instructions.

COACHMAN They're so used to such journeys, sir, I never use whip to 'em; for if they catch but the scent of a wench once, they run like devils. *Exit Coachman with his whip.*

LAXTON Fine Cerberus![3] That rogue will have the start° of a thousand ones, for whilst others trot afoot he'll ride prancing to hell upon a coach horse.—Stay, 'tis now about the hour of her appointment, but yet I see her not. (*The clock strikes three.*) Hark, what's this? One, two, three: three by the clock at Savoy.° This is the hour, and Gray's Inn Fields the place, she swore she'd meet me. Ha! Yonder's two Inns o'Court *head start, advantage* *a building on the Thames*

6. If my father is so wide of the mark as to suppose that I really love Moll with such a blind passion.
7. I merely feed my father with suspicions about Moll in order to hasten my marriage to Mary Fitzallard.
8. Except for my father's angry opposition.
3.1. Gray's Inn Fields, at the Inns of Court.
1. May we safely overtake any richly dressed folk in other coaches? ("Coached" means "embroidered with gold thread or the like.")
2. I'd bet my life on it, and humiliate them and block their way.
3. The three-headed dog that guarded the gates of Hades.

men with one wench, but that's not she; they walk toward Islington° out of my way. I see none yet dressed like her. I must look for a shag ruff, a frieze jerkin, a short sword, and a safeguard,° or I get none. Why, Moll, prithee make haste, or the coachman will curse us anon.

Islington: a northern suburb
safeguard: (see 2.1.180.1)

Enter Moll like° a man. — *like: dressed like*

MOLL [*aside*] Oh, here's my gentleman. If they would keep their days as well with their mercers[4] as their hours with their harlots, no bankrupt would give sevenscore pound for a sergeant's place.[5] For, would you know a catchpole° rightly derived, the corruption of a citizen is the generation of a sergeant.[6] How his eye hawks for venery![7] [*To Laxton*] Come, are you ready, sir?

catchpole: arresting officer

LAXTON Ready for what, sir?

MOLL Do you ask that now, sir? Why was this meeting 'pointed?° — *appointed*

LAXTON I thought you mistook me, sir.
You seem to be some young barrister.
I have no suit in law; all my land's sold,
I praise heaven for't; 't has rid me of much trouble.

MOLL Then I must wake you, sir. Where stands the coach?

LAXTON Who's this? Moll? Honest Moll?

MOLL So young and purblind?° You're an old wanton in your eyes, I see that. — *purblind: partly or wholly blind*

LAXTON Thou'rt admirably suited° for the Three Pigeons at Brentford.° I'll swear I knew thee not. — *suited: dressed; fitted* — *Three Pigeons at Brentford: a famous tavern*

MOLL I'll swear you did not; but you shall know me now.
[*She starts to remove her cloak.*]

LAXTON No, not here. We shall be spied, i'faith. The coach is better; come. [*He starts to go.*]

MOLL Stay! *She puts off her cloak and draws* [*her sword*].

LAXTON What, wilt thou untruss a point,° Moll? — *unfasten your clothes*

MOLL Yes, here's the point that I untruss.[8] 'T has but one tag;[9] 'twill serve enough to tie up a rogue's tongue.

LAXTON How?

MOLL [*showing money*] There's the gold
With which you hired your hackney;° here's her pace. — *hackney: hired horse; whore*
She racks hard,[1] and perhaps your bones will feel it.
Ten angels of mine own I've put to thine;
Win 'em and wear 'em![2]

LAXTON Hold, Moll! Mistress Mary—

MOLL Draw, or I'll serve an execution upon thee
Shall° lay thee up till doomsday. — *Shall: That will*

LAXTON Draw upon a woman? Why, what dost mean, Moll?

4. If they would pay their debts as promptly to cloth merchants.
5. No one in bankruptcy would have to pay a hefty fee to become an arresting officer (as a way out of poverty, since arresting officers were paid for their services by the complainant).
6. Many an arresting officer was once a citizen merchant made bankrupt by unpaid bills.
7. How his eye hunts for game—i.e., women!
8. I.e., The only undressing I'm going to do is to unsheathe my sword.
9. The metal binding on the end of a lace.
1. This is how she moves; she gallops hard. (Moll mockingly refers to herself, the hackney [line 65] that Laxton thought he would hire for his lust; Moll promises she will give him a rough ride.)
2. A proverbial phrase. Moll challenges Laxton to a duel for the money he gave her (at 2.1.296–99) plus ten angels (line 67), or gold coins, that she has added to the pot.

MOLL To teach thy base thoughts manners. Thou'rt one of those
That thinks each woman thy fond° flexible whore. — *foolish; infatuated*
If she but cast a liberal° eye upon thee, — *wanton; generous*
Turn back her head, she's thine; or, amongst company,
By chance drink first to thee, then she's quite gone,
There's no means to help her; nay, for a need,° — *in case of need*
Wilt° swear unto thy credulous fellow lechers — *Thou wilt*
That thou'rt more in favor with a lady
At first sight than her monkey° all her lifetime. — *pet monkey*
How many of our sex by such as thou
Have their good thoughts paid° with a blasted° name — *repaid / blighted*
That never deserved loosely or did trip
In path of whoredom beyond cup and lip?[3]
But for the stain of conscience and of soul,
Better had women fall into the hands
Of an act silent than a bragging nothing;[4]
There's no mercy in't.° What durst move you, sir, — *Rumor is remorseless*
To think me whorish?—a name which I'd tear out
From the high German's° throat, if it lay ledger° there — *(see 2.1.377) / ambassador*
To dispatch privy° slanders against me! — *secret*
In thee I defy all men, their worst hates
And their best flatteries, all their golden witchcrafts
With which they entangle the poor spirits of fools,° — *innocent women*
Distressed needlewomen and trade-fall'n° wives. — *unprosperous*
Fish that must needs bite or themselves be bitten,
Such hungry things as these may soon be took
With a worm fast'ned on a golden hook;
Those are the lecher's food, his prey. He watches
For quarreling wedlocks and poor shifting sisters;[5]
'Tis the best fish he takes. But why, good fisherman,
Am I thought meat for you, that never yet
Had angling rod cast towards me? 'Cause, you'll say,
I'm given to sport, I'm often merry, jest?
Had mirth no kindred in the world but lust?
Oh, shame take all her° friends, then! But howe'er — *(Mirth's)*
Thou and the baser world censure my life,
I'll send 'em° word by thee, and write° so much — *(my critics) / carve*
Upon thy breast, 'cause° thou shalt bear't in mind: — *so that*
Tell them 'twere base to yield where I have conquered.
I scorn to prostitute myself to a man,
I that can prostitute a man to me,
And so I greet thee.° [*She draws her sword.*] — *say farewell*

LAXTON [*drawing in defense*] Hear me!

MOLL Would° the spirits — *Would that*
Of all my slanderers were clasped in thine,
That I might vex an army at one time!
They fight. [*Moll wounds Laxton.*]

3. Beyond toasting a man with a cup of wine or kissing him? (The phrase alludes to a betrothal.)

4. If it weren't for the sin, a woman would be better off having sex secretly with a man than being talked of by a bragging nonperformer.

5. The lecher preys on women who are unhappy in marriage and ready to deceive their husbands. ("Wedlocks" are wives; "shifting" means "deceitful," or perhaps "managing with meager resources.")

LAXTON I do repent me. Hold!
MOLL You'll die the better Christian, then.[6]
LAXTON I do confess I have wronged thee, Moll.
MOLL Confession is but poor amends for wrong,
Unless a rope° would follow. *hangman's noose*
LAXTON I ask thee pardon.
MOLL I'm your hired whore, sir!
LAXTON I yield both purse and body.
MOLL Both are mine and now at my disposing.
LAXTON Spare my life!
MOLL I scorn to strike thee basely.
LAXTON Spoke like a noble girl, i'faith. [*Aside*] Heart, I think
I fight with a familiar,[7] or the ghost of a fencer! She's
wounded me gallantly. Call you this a lecherous voyage?° *assignation*
Here's blood would have served me this seven year in bro-
ken° heads and cut fingers, and it now runs all out together. *bleeding*
Pox o'the Three Pigeons! I would the coach were here now
to carry me to the chirurgeon's.° *Exit Laxton.* *surgeon's*
MOLL If I could meet my enemies one by one thus,
I might make pretty shift° with 'em in time, *deal handily*
And make 'em know, she that has wit and spirit
May scorn to live beholding° to her body for meat° *beholden / food*
Or for apparel, like your common dame
That makes shame get her clothes to cover shame.[8]
Base is that mind that kneels unto her body,
As if a husband stood in awe on 's° wife! *of his*
My spirit shall be mistress of this house° *i.e., my body*
As long as I have time in't.° *As long as I live*

Enter Trapdoor [*not recognizing Moll*].

Oh,
Here comes my man° that would be; 'tis his hour.° *servant / appointed time*
Faith, a good well-set° fellow, if his spirit *well-built*
Be answerable to his umbles.[9] He walks stiff,
But whether he will stand to't° stiffly, there's the point. *face an opponent*
'Has a good calf for't, and ye shall have many a woman
Choose him she means to make her head° by his calf; *i.e., husband*
I do not know their tricks in't.° Faith, he seems *Their tricks are infinite*
A man without;° I'll try what he is within. *by his appearance*
TRAPDOOR She told me Gray's Inn Fields 'twixt three and four.
I'll fit° Her Mistress-ship with a piece of service; *furnish*
I'm hired to rid the town of one mad girl.
She jostles him.
[*To Moll*] What a pox ails you, sir?
MOLL [*aside*] He begins like a gentleman.
TRAPDOOR Heart, is the field so narrow, or your eyesight?
(*She comes toward him.*) Life, he comes back again![1]

6. Mary plays with Laxton's "repent me" (line 117), by which he meant "apologize." Her joke is that his soul will be assisted spiritually by repentance, a necessary condition for salvation.
7. An attendant spirit or demon in the shape of an animal.
8. Like a wanton woman who performs shameful acts of sex to pay for clothes to cover her nakedness.
9. I.e., if he's as brave as his talk; if he has guts. (Umbles are literally the edible organs of a deer or another animal.)
1. Trapdoor, who thought he was entitled to complain sharply of having been jostled by this apparent stranger, now realizes that the matter is getting serious.

MOLL Was this spoke to me, sir?

TRAPDOOR I cannot tell, sir.[2]

MOLL Go, you're a coxcomb!° — *fool*

TRAPDOOR Coxcomb?

MOLL You're a slave!

TRAPDOOR I hope there's law° for you, sir! — *laws against assault*

MOLL Yea, do you see, sir? *Turn his hat.*[3]

TRAPDOOR Heart, this is no good dealing. Pray let me know what house you're of.

MOLL One of the Temple,° sir. *Fillips him.*[4] — *of the Inns of Court*

TRAPDOOR Mass, so methinks.

MOLL And yet sometimes I lie about Chick Lane.° — *a rough neighborhood*

TRAPDOOR I like you the worse because you shift your lodging so often. I'll not meddle with you for° that trick, sir. — *because of*

MOLL A good shift,° but it shall not serve your turn. — *evasion*

TRAPDOOR You'll give me leave to pass about my business, sir?

MOLL Your business? I'll make you wait on me before I ha' done, and glad to serve me, too.

TRAPDOOR How, sir, serve you? Not if there were no more men in England.

MOLL But if there were no more women in England, I hope you'd wait upon your mistress then.

[*Moll reveals her identity.*]

TRAPDOOR Mistress!

MOLL Oh, you're a tried spirit° at a push, sir. — *experienced fighter*

TRAPDOOR What would Your Worship have me do?

MOLL You a fighter?

TRAPDOOR No, I praise heaven, I had better grace and more manners.

MOLL As how, I pray, sir?

TRAPDOOR Life, 't had been a beastly part° of me to have drawn my weapons upon my mistress. All the world would ha' cried shame of° me for that. — *action*; *reproached*

MOLL Why, but you knew me not.

TRAPDOOR Do not say so, mistress. I knew you by your wide straddle as well as if I had been in your belly.

MOLL Well, we shall try you further. I'th'meantime we give you entertainment.° — *employment*

TRAPDOOR Thank Your good Mistress-ship.

MOLL How many suits have you?

TRAPDOOR No more suits than backs, mistress.

MOLL Well, if you deserve, I cast off this° next week, and you may creep into't. — *(the suit I'm wearing)*

TRAPDOOR Thank Your good Worship.

MOLL Come, follow me to Saint Thomas Apostles.° I'll put a livery cloak° upon your back, the first thing I do. — *a church near clothiers*; *servant's uniform*

TRAPDOOR I follow my dear mistress. *Exeunt omnes.*

2. Trapdoor tries to weasel out.
3. Moll taunts Trapdoor by turning around the hat on his head.
4. Moll flicks Trapdoor with her nails, in another insulting gesture.

[3.2]

Enter Mistress Gallipot as from supper, her husband after her.

GALLIPOT What, Pru! Nay, sweet Prudence!

MRS. GALLIPOT What a pruing keep you![1] I think the baby° would have a teat, it kyes° so. Pray be not so fond of me; leave your city humors.° I'm vexed at you to see how like a calf you come bleating after me. *(Gallipot)* *cries* *uxoriousness*

GALLIPOT Nay, honey Pru, how does your rising up before all the table show?[2] And flinging° from my friends so uncivilly? Fie, Pru, fie. Come. *turning*

MRS. GALLIPOT Then up and ride,° i'faith. *(a bawdy taunt)*

GALLIPOT Up and ride? Nay, my pretty Pru, that's far from my thought, duck. Why, mouse,° thy mind is nibbling at something. What is't? What lies upon° thy stomach? *(terms of affection)* *is upsetting*

MRS. GALLIPOT Such an ass as you! Heyday, you're best turn midwife or physician; you're a pothecary already, but I'm none of your drugs.° *medicines; drudges*

GALLIPOT Thou art a sweet drug, sweetest Pru, and the more thou art pounded, the more precious.[3]

MRS. GALLIPOT Must you be prying into a woman's secrets? Say ye?

GALLIPOT Woman's secrets?

MRS. GALLIPOT What? I cannot have a qualm° come upon me but your teeth waters till your nose hang over it. *nausea*

GALLIPOT It is my love, dear wife.

MRS. GALLIPOT Your love? Your love is all words; give me deeds. I cannot abide a man that's too fond over me—so cookish!° Thou dost not know how to handle a woman in her kind.[4] *womanish*

GALLIPOT No, Pru? Why, I hope I have handled—

MRS. GALLIPOT Handle a fool's head of your own. Fie, fie!

GALLIPOT Ha, ha, 'tis such a wasp! It does me good now to have her sting me, little rogue.

MRS. GALLIPOT Now, fie, how you vex me! I cannot abide these apron husbands. Such cotqueans!° You overdo your things; they become you scurvily. *domesticated men*

GALLIPOT [*aside*] Upon my life, she breeds.° Heaven knows how I have strained myself to please her, night and day! I wonder why we citizens should get° children so fretful and untoward° in the breeding, their fathers being for the most part as gentle as milch kine.°—Shall I leave thee, my Pru? *is pregnant* *beget* *refractory* *milk cattle*

MRS. GALLIPOT Fie, fie!

GALLIPOT Thou shalt not be vexed no more, pretty kind rogue. Take no cold, sweet Pru. *Exit Master Gallipot.*

MRS. GALLIPOT As your wit has done!°—Now, Master Laxton, show your head. [*She takes out a letter.*] What news from you? Would any husband suspect that a woman crying "Buy any scurvy grass"° should bring love letters amongst her *taken cold, is sluggish* *medicinal herb*

3.2. The Gallipots' establishment.
1. What a caterwauling you keep up, sounding my name!
2. How does your leaving the table before all the dinner guests look?
3. Drugs were pounded into powder to mix the ingredients. (With a sexual double entendre.)
4. As a woman ought to be handled.

herbs to his wife? Pretty trick, fine conveyance!° Had jeal- *stratagem*
ousy a thousand eyes, a silly° woman with scurvy grass blinds *helpless; simple*
them all.
Laxton, with bays° *laurel leaves*
Crown I thy wit for this; it deserves praise.
This makes me affect° thee more; this proves thee wise. *love*
'Lack, what poor shift° is love forced to devise?— *cunning device*
To th'point. *She reads the letter.*
"O sweet creature," (a sweet beginning!) "pardon my long
absence, for thou shalt shortly be possessed with my presence. Though Demophoon was false to Phyllis, I will be to
thee as Pan-da-rus was to Cres-sida; though Aeneas made
an ass of Dido, I will die to thee ere I do so.[5] O sweetest
creature, make much of me, for no man beneath the silver
moon shall make more of° a woman than I do of thee. Fur- *dote more on; profit by*
nish me therefore with thirty pounds; you must do it of
necessity for me. I languish till I see some comfort come
from thee, protesting° not to die in thy debt, but rather to *beseeching*
live so, as hitherto I have and will,
Thy true Laxton, ever."
Alas, poor gentleman! Troth, I pity him.
How shall I raise this money? Thirty pound?
'Tis thirty, sure, a three before an O;
I know his threes too well. My childbed linen?
Shall I pawn that for him? Then if my mark° *(in place of a signature)*
Be known, I am undone! It may be thought
My husband's bankrupt. Which way shall I turn?
Laxton, what with my own fears and thy wants,
I'm as a needle 'twixt two adamants.° *i.e., magnets*

Enter Master Gallipot hastily.

GALLIPOT Nay, nay, wife, the women are all up.° [*Aside*] Ha? *have risen from the table*
How? Reading o' letters? I smell a goose. A couple of capons
and a gammon of bacon from her mother out of the country,
I hold° my life. Steal°—steal— [*He sneaks up behind her.*] *bet / Steal up behind her*
MRS. GALLIPOT Oh, beshrew° your heart! *the devil take*
GALLIPOT What letter's that? I'll see't. *She tears the letter.*
MRS. GALLIPOT Oh, would thou hadst no eyes to see the
downfall of me and thyself! I'm forever, forever I'm undone!
GALLIPOT What ails my Pru? What paper's that thou tear'st?
MRS. GALLIPOT Would I could tear
My very heart in pieces! For my soul
Lies on the rack of shame that tortures me
Beyond a woman's suffering.
GALLIPOT What means this?
MRS. GALLIPOT Had you° no other vengeance to throw down, *(the heavens)*
But even in height of all my joys—
GALLIPOT Dear woman!
MRS. GALLIPOT When the full sea of pleasure and content
Seemed to flow over me?

5. The letter cites old stories of love ending unhappily through desertion. Mrs. Gallipot stumbles over the names of Pandarus (who was actually Cressida's uncle and the go-between in her affair with Troilus) and Cressida.

GALLIPOT As thou desirest to keep me out of Bedlam,° tell *a madhouse*
what troubles thee. Is not thy child at nurse° fall'n sick, or *thy nursing child*
dead?
MRS. GALLIPOT Oh, no!
GALLIPOT Heavens bless me, are my barns and houses
Yonder at Hockley Hole° consumed with fire? *a village near London*
I can build more, sweet Pru.
MRS. GALLIPOT 'Tis worse, 'tis worse.
GALLIPOT My factor broke, or is the *Jonas* sunk?[6]
MRS. GALLIPOT Would all we had were swallowed in the waves,
Rather than both should be the scorn of slaves!° *wretches*
GALLIPOT I'm at my wit's end!
MRS. GALLIPOT Oh, my dear husband,
Where° once I thought myself a fixèd star, *Whereas*
Placed only in the heaven of thine arms,
I fear now I shall prove a wanderer.° *planet; untrue wife*
O Laxton, Laxton, is it then my fate
To be by thee o'erthrown?
GALLIPOT Defend me, wisdom,
From falling into frenzy! On my knees,
Sweet Pru, speak! What's that Laxton who so heavy lies
On thy bosom?[7]
MRS. GALLIPOT I shall sure run mad.
GALLIPOT I shall run mad for company,° then. Speak to me; *to keep you company*
I'm Gallipot thy husband.—Pru! Why, Pru!
Art sick in conscience for some villainous deed
Thou wert about to act? Didst mean to rob me?
Tush, I forgive thee. Hast thou on my bed
Thrust my soft pillow under another's head?
I'll wink° at all faults, Pru; 'las,° that's no more *shut my eyes / alas*
Than what some neighbors near thee have done before.
Sweet honey Pru, what's that Laxton?
MRS. GALLIPOT Oh!
GALLIPOT Out with him!
MRS. GALLIPOT Oh, he's born to be my undoer!
This hand which thou call'st thine to him was given;
To him was I made sure i'th'sight of heaven.° *I was betrothed*
GALLIPOT I never heard this thunder!° *I'm thunderstruck!*
MRS. GALLIPOT Yes, yes, before
I was to thee contracted, to him I swore.
Since last I saw him twelve months three times told
The moon hath drawn through her light silver bow,[8]
For o'er the seas he went, and it was said
(But rumor lies) that he in France was dead.
But he's alive, oh, he's alive! He sent
That letter to me, which in rage I rent,° *tore*
Swearing° with oaths most damnably to have me *He swearing*
Or tear me from this° bosom. O heavens, save me! *(my husband's)*
GALLIPOT My heart will break. Shamed and undone forever!

6. Has my agent financially ruined us, or has one of my merchant ships sunk?
7. Who troubles you so? (But suggesting also "lies with you.")
8. A florid way of saying that three years have passed.

MRS. GALLIPOT So black a day, poor wretch,° went o'er thee never! — *(she means herself)*
GALLIPOT If thou shouldst wrestle with him at the law,
Thou'rt sure to fall; no odd sleight, no prevention.° — *no trick can save you*
I'll tell him thou'rt with child.
MRS. GALLIPOT Umh!
GALLIPOT Or give out° — *let it be known*
One of my men was ta'en abed with thee.
MRS. GALLIPOT Umh, umh!
GALLIPOT Before I lose thee, my dear Pru,
I'll drive it to that push.
MRS. GALLIPOT Worse and worse still!
You embrace a mischief to prevent an ill.
GALLIPOT I'll buy thee of him, stop his mouth with gold.
Think'st thou 'twill do?
MRS. GALLIPOT Oh, me! Heavens grant it would!
Yet, now my senses are set more in tune,
He writ, as I remember in his letter,
That he in riding up and down had spent,
Ere he could find me, thirty pounds. Send that;
Stand not on° thirty with him. — *Don't balk at*
GALLIPOT Forty, Pru.
Say thou the word, 'tis done. We venture lives° — *risk our lives*
For wealth, but must do more to keep our wives.
Thirty or forty, Pru?
MRS. GALLIPOT Thirty, good sweet;
Of an ill bargain let's save what we can.
I'll pay it him with my tears. He was a man,
When first I knew him, of a meek spirit;
All goodness is not yet dried up, I hope.
GALLIPOT He shall have thirty pound. Let that stop all;
Love's sweets taste best when we have drunk down gall.

Enter Master Tiltyard and his wife, Master Goshawk, and Mistress Openwork.

Godso,° our friends! Come, come, smooth your cheek; — *(a mild oath)*
After a storm, the face of heaven looks sleek.
TILTYARD Did I not tell you these turtles° were together? — *turtledoves*
MRS. TILTYARD [*to Mrs. Gallipot*] How dost thou, sirrah?° Why, sister Gallipot! — *(see 178 and n)*
MRS. OPENWORK Lord, how she's changed!
GOSHAWK [*to Gallipot*] Is your wife ill, sir?
GALLIPOT Yes, indeed, la, sir, very ill, very ill, never worse.
MRS. TILTYARD How her head burns! Feel how her pulses work!
MRS. OPENWORK [*to Mrs. Gallipot*] Sister, lie down a little. That always does me good.
MRS. TILTYARD In good sadness,° I find best ease in that too. — *all seriousness*
Has she laid some hot thing to her stomach?
MRS. GALLIPOT No, but I will lay something anon.
TILTYARD [*to Mrs. Tiltyard*] Come, come, fools, you trouble her.—Shall 's° go, Master Goshawk? — *Shall we*
GOSHAWK Yes, sweet Master Tiltyard.
[*He talks privately with Mrs. Openwork.*]

Sirrah Rosamond,[9] I hold° my life Gallipot hath vexed his wife. *bet*

MRS. OPENWORK She has a horrible high color, indeed.

GOSHAWK We shall have your face painted with the same red soon at night, when your husband comes from his rubbers[1] in a false alley; thou wilt not believe me that his bowls run with a wrong bias.[2]

MRS. OPENWORK It cannot sink into me° that he feeds upon stale mutton° abroad, having better and fresher at home. *I can't believe* / *i.e., whores*

GOSHAWK What if I bring thee where thou shalt see him stand at rack and manger?° *at his feed*

MRS. OPENWORK I'll saddle him in's kind° and spur him till he kick again. *according to his nature*

GOSHAWK Shall thou and I ride our journey,[3] then?

MRS. OPENWORK Here's my hand.

GOSHAWK No more. [*Aloud*] Come, Master Tiltyard, shall we leap into the stirrups with our women and amble home?

TILTYARD Yes, yes.—Come, wife.

MRS. TILTYARD [*to Mrs. Gallipot*] In troth, sister, I hope you will do well for° all this. *despite*

MRS. GALLIPOT I hope I shall. Farewell, good sister, sweet Master Goshawk.

GALLIPOT Welcome,° brother; most kindly welcome, sir. *i.e., I'm glad you came*

OMNES Thanks, sir, for our good cheer.

Exeunt all but Gallipot and his wife.

GALLIPOT It shall be so, because a crafty knave
Shall not outreach me, nor walk by my door
With my wife arm in arm as 'twere his whore.
I'll give him a golden coxcomb: thirty pound.
Tush, Pru, what's thirty pound? Sweet duck, look cheerly.

MRS. GALLIPOT Thou art worthy of my heart; thou buy'st it dearly.

Enter Laxton, muffled.

LAXTON [*aside*] Ud's° light, the side's° against me. A pox of *God's* / *odds are*
Your Pothecaryship! Oh, for some glister° to set him going! *enema suppository*
'Tis one of Hercules' labors to tread° one of these city hens, because their cocks are still° crowing over them. There's no turning tail here; I must on. *copulate with* / *continually*

MRS. GALLIPOT Oh, husband, see, he comes!

GALLIPOT Let me deal with him.

LAXTON Bless you, sir.

GALLIPOT Be you blessed too, sir, if you come in peace.

LAXTON Have you any good pudding-tobacco,° sir? *sausage-shaped tobacco*

MRS. GALLIPOT Oh, pick no quarrels, gentle sir! My husband
Is not a man of weapon, as you are.
He knows all; I have opened all before him
Concerning you.

9. "Sirrah" could be used to address women as well as men, as in line 163 above; see also 4.2.10 and note. The instance at 2.1.192 may be exceptional, since Moll is treated as a man there.
1. Set of three bowling balls, from the game of bowls. (Here playing on a sexual meaning that runs throughout the passage.)
2. Bias weights in bowling balls enabled the bowler to throw curves. (With the suggestion here of sexual infidelity.)
3. Shall we (1) have a fling; (2) go see Openwork engaging in infidelity.

LAXTON [*aside*] Zounds, has she shown my letters?
MRS. GALLIPOT Suppose my case were yours, what would you do,
At such a pinch, such batteries, such assaults,
Of father, mother, kindred, to dissolve
The knot you tied, and to be bound to him?
How could you shift this storm off?
LAXTON [*aside*] If I know, hang me.
MRS. GALLIPOT Besides, a story of your death was read
Each minute to me.
LAXTON [*aside*] What a pox means this riddling?
GALLIPOT Be wise, sir. Let not you and I be tossed
On lawyers' pens; they have sharp nibs° and draw *pen points*
Men's very heart-blood from them. What need you, sir,
To beat the drum of° my wife's infamy, *To publicize*
And call your friends together, sir, to prove
Your precontact, when sh' has confessed it?
LAXTON Umh, sir—
Has she confessed it?
GALLIPOT Sh' has, faith, to me, sir,
Upon your letter sending.
MRS. GALLIPOT I have, I have.
LAXTON [*aside*] If I let this iron cool, call me slave.—
Do you hear, you dame Prudence? Think'st thou, vile woman,
I'll take these blows and wink?° *close my eyes*
MRS. GALLIPOT Upon my knees—
LAXTON Out, impudence!
GALLIPOT Good sir—
LAXTON You goatish° slaves, *lecherous*
No wild fowl to cut up but mine?[4]
GALLIPOT Alas, sir,
You make her flesh to tremble. Fright her not;
She shall do reason, and what's fit.
LAXTON [*to Mrs. Gallipot*] I'll have thee,
Wert thou more common° than an hospital *used by one and all*
And more diseased—
GALLIPOT But one word, good sir.
LAXTON So, sir.
GALLIPOT I married her, have lain with her, and got
Two children on her body; think but on that.
Have you so beggarly an appetite,
When I upon a dainty dish have fed,
To dine upon my scraps, my leavings? Ha, sir?
Do I come near you° now, sir? *Am I getting to you*
LAXTON By' Lady,° you touch me. *By Our Lady (an oath)*
GALLIPOT Would not you scorn to wear my clothes, sir?
LAXTON Right, sir.
GALLIPOT Then pray, sir, wear not her, for she's a garment
So fitting for my body I'm loath
Another should put it on; you will undo both.
Your letter, as she said, complained you had spent

4. I.e., Could you find no loose woman to satisfy your lust, choosing instead to deprive me of my intended wife?

In quest of her some thirty pound; I'll pay it.
Shall that, sir, stop this gap up 'twixt you two?
LAXTON Well, if I swallow this wrong,[5] let her thank you.
The money being paid, sir, I am gone;
Farewell. Oh, women! Happy's he° trusts none. *Happy the man who*
MRS. GALLIPOT Dispatch him hence,[6] sweet husband.
GALLIPOT Yes, dear wife.—
Pray, sir, come in. [*To his wife*] Ere Master Laxton part,
Thou shalt in wine drink to him.
MRS. GALLIPOT With all my heart.
Exit Master Gallipot.
How dost thou like my wit?
LAXTON Rarely! That wile
By which the serpent did the first woman° beguile *(Eve)*
Did ever since all women's bosoms fill;
You're apple eaters all, deceivers still. *Exeunt.*

[3.3]

Enter Sir Alexander Wengrave, Sir Davy Dapper, [and] Sir Adam Appleton at one door, and Trapdoor at another door.

SIR ALEXANDER Out with your tale, Sir Davy, to Sir Adam.
A knave is in mine eye deep in my debt.[1]
SIR DAVY Nay, if he be a knave, sir, hold him fast.
[*Sir Alexander takes Trapdoor aside and speaks privately.*]
SIR ALEXANDER Speak softly: what egg is there hatching now?
TRAPDOOR A duck's egg, sir, a duck that has eaten a frog.° I have cracked the shell, and some villainy or other will peep out presently. The duck that sits is the bouncing ramp,° that roaring girl, my mistress; the drake° that must tread° is your son, Sebastian. *swallowed the bait* / *shamefaced woman* / *male duck / copulate*
SIR ALEXANDER Be quick.
TRAPDOOR As the tongue of an oyster-wench.° *seller of oysters*
SIR ALEXANDER And see thy news be true.
TRAPDOOR As a barber's° every Saturday night. Mad Moll— *(a source of gossip)*
SIR ALEXANDER Ah!
TRAPDOOR Must be° let in without knocking at your back gate. *Is to be*
SIR ALEXANDER So.
TRAPDOOR Your chamber will be made bawdy.
SIR ALEXANDER Good.
TRAPDOOR She comes in a shirt of mail.
SIR ALEXANDER How, shirt of mail?
TRAPDOOR Yes, sir, or a male shirt, that's to say in man's apparel.
SIR ALEXANDER To my son.
TRAPDOOR Close to your son; your son and her moon will be in conjunction, if all almanacs lie not. Her black safeguard° is turned into a deep slop,° the holes of her upper body° to buttonholes, her waistcoat to a doublet, her placket° to the *riding skirt* / *breeches / bodice* / *slit in a petticoat*

5. If I put up with this insult.
6. Pay the money and send him on his way.
3.3. Holborn; see 185 below.

1. Sir Alexander pretends to have to speak to Trapdoor about money that the "knave" owes him, in order to be able to confer privately with him.

ancient seat of a codpiece,° and you shall take 'em both with standing° collars. — *(see Epistle 15–16 n)* / *high*

SIR ALEXANDER Art sure of this?

TRAPDOOR As every throng is sure of a pickpocket, as sure as a whore is of the clients all Michaelmas term° and of the pox° after the term. — *the autumn law term* / *syphilis*

SIR ALEXANDER The time of their tilting?° — *tournament; sex*

TRAPDOOR Three.

SIR ALEXANDER The day?

TRAPDOOR This.

SIR ALEXANDER Away, ply it.° Watch her. — *do it diligently*

TRAPDOOR As the devil doth for the death of a bawd.° I'll watch her; do you catch her. — *(waiting for his victim)*

SIR ALEXANDER She's fast.° Here, weave thou the nets. Hark! — *as good as caught*

TRAPDOOR They are made.° — *made fast*

SIR ALEXANDER I told them° thou didst owe me money. Hold it up; maintain't.° — *(the gentlemen here)* / *back up my story*

TRAPDOOR Stiffly, as a Puritan does contention: "Fox, I owe thee not the value of a halfpenny halter!"[2]

SIR ALEXANDER "Thou shalt be hanged in't ere thou scape° so. Varlet, I'll make thee look through a grate!"° — *escape* / *(of a prison window)*

TRAPDOOR "I'll do't presently: through a tavern grate. Drawer! Pish!"[3] *Exit Trapdoor.* [*Sir Alexander rejoins the others.*]

SIR ADAM Has the knave vexed you, sir?

SIR ALEXANDER Asked him° my money; — *I asked him for*
He swears my son received it. Oh, that boy
Will ne'er leave heaping sorrows on my heart
Till he has broke it quite!

SIR ADAM Is he still wild?

SIR ALEXANDER As is a Russian bear.

SIR ADAM But he has left
His old haunt° with that baggage?° — *companionship / hussy*

SIR ALEXANDER Worse still and worse.
He lays on me his shame, I on him my curse.

SIR DAVY My son Jack Dapper then shall run with him
All in one pasture.° — *i.e., will share his fate*

SIR ADAM Proves your son bad too, sir?

SIR DAVY As villainy can make him. Your Sebastian
Dotes but on one drab, mine on a thousand.
A noise° of fiddlers, tobacco, wine, and a whore, — *consort*
A mercer that will let him take up more,° — *buy more on credit*
Dice, and a water spaniel with a duck—oh,
Bring him abed with these![4] When his purse jingles,
Roaring boys follow at 's tail. Fencers and ningles°— — *homosexuals*
Beasts Adam ne'er gave name to°—these horse-leeches suck — *(see Genesis 2.19–20)*
My son; he being drawn dry, they all live on smoke.° — *vapors; tobacco smoke*

SIR ALEXANDER Tobacco?

SIR DAVY Right, but I have in my brain
A windmill going that shall grind to dust

2. Playing the part Sir Alexander has ordered him to play, Trapdoor mimics a contentious debtor, pretending to deny that he owes Sir Alexander money. Sir Alexander answers in kind, threatening incarceration for the unpaid debt. (A halter is a hangman's noose.)

3. Continuing the charade, Trapdoor arrogantly insists that he would prefer a tavern, with its characteristic red lattices, to a prison with its heavily barred windows. (A drawer is a tapster or waiter.)

4. I wish he could be cured of these hangers-on!

The follies of my son, and make him wise,
Or a stark fool. Pray lend me your advice.
SIR ALEXANDER *and* SIR ADAM That shall you, good Sir Davy.
SIR DAVY Here's the springe°   *trap*
I ha' set to catch this woodcock° in: an action   *a stupid bird*
In a false name—unknown to him—is entered
I'th'Counter° to arrest Jack Dapper.   *a debtors' prison*
SIR ALEXANDER *and* SIR ADAM Ha, ha, he!
SIR DAVY Think you the Counter cannot break him?
SIR ADAM Break him?
Yes, and break 's heart too, if he lie° there long.   *reside*
SIR DAVY I'll make him sing a countertenor,[5] sure.
SIR ADAM No way to tame him like it. There he shall learn
What money is indeed, and how to spend it.
SIR DAVY He's° bridled there.   *He'll be*
SIR ALEXANDER Ay, yet knows not how to mend it.
Bedlam cures not more madmen in a year
Than one of the counters does; men pay more dear
There for their wit than anywhere. A counter,
Why, 'tis an university. Who not sees?
As scholars there, so here men take degrees
And follow the same studies—all alike.
Scholars learn first logic and rhetoric;
So does a prisoner. With fine honeyed speech,
At 's first coming in, he doth persuade, beseech
He may be lodged with one that is not itchy,
To lie in a clean chamber, in sheets not lousy;
But when he has no money, then does he try,
By subtle logic and quaint° sophistry,   *ingenious*
To make the keepers trust° him.   *extend credit to*
SIR ADAM Say they do?
SIR ALEXANDER Then he's a graduate.
SIR DAVY Say they trust him not.
SIR ALEXANDER Then is he held a freshman and a sot,
And never shall commence,° but, being still barred,   *take advanced degree*
Be expulsed from the Master's Side to th'Twopenny Ward,
Or else i'th'Hole be placed.[6]
SIR ADAM When, then, I pray,
Proceeds° a prisoner?   *Goes to a higher degree*
SIR ALEXANDER When, money being the theme,
He can dispute with his hard creditors' hearts
And get out clear, he's then a Master of Arts.
Sir Davy, send your son to Wood Street° College;   *site of a debtors' prison*
A gentleman can nowhere get more knowledge.
SIR DAVY There gallants study hard.
SIR ALEXANDER True: to get money.
SIR DAVY 'Lies by th' heels,° i'faith. Thanks, thanks; I ha' sent   *He lies in irons*
For a couple of bears shall paw him.°   *who'll rough him up*

Enter Sergeant Curtalax and Yeoman Hanger.

5. I'll make him sing a new tune. ("Countertenor" is appropriate to the debtors' prison called the Counter. London had at least two such prisons; hence "counters" in line 86.)

6. Graded accommodations in a prison, for which the inmates had to pay, ranged from the high-priced Master's Side to the Hole for the destitute. (With a play on "Master of Arts.")

SIR ADAM Who comes yonder?
SIR DAVY They look like puttocks.° These should be they. *kites, birds of prey*
SIR ADAM I know 'em;
They are officers. Sir, we'll leave you.
SIR DAVY My good knights,
Leave me. You see I'm haunted now with sprites.° *spirits; sergeants*
SIR ALEXANDER *and* SIR ADAM Fare you well, sir.
Exeunt Alexander and Adam.

CURTALAX [*to Hanger*] This old muzzle chops° should be he, by the fellow's° description.—Save you, sir. *big mouth and nose* / *(Sir Davy's servant's)*

SIR DAVY Come hither, you mad° varlets. Did not my man° tell you I watched° here for you? *zany / servant* / *was waiting*

CURTALAX One in a blue° coat, sir, told us that in this place an old gentleman would watch for us—a thing contrary to our oath, for we are to watch° for every wicked member in a city. *(color for servants)* / *act as the town watch*

SIR DAVY You'll watch then for ten thousand. What's thy name, honesty?° *my good fellow*

CURTALAX Sergeant Curtalax, I, sir.

SIR DAVY An excellent name for a sergeant, Curtalax.° *cutlass*
Sergeants indeed are weapons of the law.
When prodigal ruffians far in debt are grown,
Should not you° cut them, citizens were° o'erthrown. *If you didn't / would be*
Thou dwell'st hereby in Holborn, Curtalax?

CURTALAX That's my circuit, sir; I conjure most in that circle.° *district; magic circle*

SIR DAVY And what young toward whelp° is this? *promising puppy*

HANGER Of the same litter; his yeoman, sir. My name's Hanger.° *sword strap*

SIR DAVY Yeoman Hanger!
One pair of shears, sure, cut out both your coats;° *i.e., You're a pair*
You have two names most dangerous to men's throats.
You two are villainous loads on gentlemen's backs;° *(see n. 8 below)*
Dear ware,° this Hanger and this Curtalax. *Expensive gear*

CURTALAX We are as other men are, sir. I cannot see but he who makes a show of honesty and religion, if his claws can fasten to his liking, he draws blood.[7] All that live in the world are but great fish and little fish, and feed upon one another. Some eat up whole men; a sergeant cares but for the shoulder of a man.[8] They call us knaves and curs, but many times he that sets us on worries° more lambs one year than we do in seven. *harasses*

SIR DAVY Spoke like a noble Cerberus.° Is the action entered?[9] *the doorkeeper of Hades*

HANGER His name is entered in the book of unbelievers.

SIR DAVY What book's that?

CURTALAX The book where all prisoners' names stand; and not one amongst forty, when he comes in, believes to come out in haste.

SIR DAVY Be as dogged to him as your office allows you to be.

CURTALAX *and* HANGER Oh, sir!° *i.e., But of course!*

7. Even supposedly upright citizens are ruthless when they fasten on their prey.
8. Arresting officers seized their victims by the shoulder.
9. Is the lawsuit officially entered in the register?

SIR DAVY You know the unthrift Jack Dapper?

CURTALAX I? Ay, sir, that gull? As well as I know my yeoman.

SIR DAVY And you know his father too, Sir Davy Dapper?

CURTALAX As damned a usurer as ever was among Jews. If he were sure his father's skin would yield him any money, he would, when he dies, flay it off and sell it to cover drums for children at Barthol'mew Fair.° *a famous annual fair*

SIR DAVY [*aside*] What toads are these, to spit poison on a man to his face! [*To them*] Do you see, my honest rascals? Yonder Grayhound[1] is the dog he hunts with; out of that tavern Jack Dapper will sally. Sa, sa! Give the counter![2] On, set upon him!

CURTALAX *and* HANGER We'll charge him upo' th'back,° sir. *shoulder (see n. 8 above)*

SIR DAVY Take no bail; put mace enough into his caudle![3] Double your files! Traverse your ground!° *(drill commands)*

CURTALAX *and* HANGER Brave,° sir. *Righto*

SIR DAVY Cry arm, arm, arm!° *Take up arms!*

CURTALAX *and* HANGER Thus, sir.

[*They ineptly execute the manual of arms.*]

SIR DAVY There, boy, there, boy,° away! Look to your prey, my true English wolves, and—and so I vanish. *Exit Sir Davy.* *(a call to hunting dogs)*

CURTALAX Some warden of the sergeants[4] begat this old fellow, upon my life. Stand close.° *hidden*

HANGER Shall the ambuscado lie in one place?[5]

CURTALAX No. Nook° thou yonder. [*They hide separately.*] *Hide*

Enter Moll and Trapdoor.

MOLL Ralph?

TRAPDOOR What says my brave captain, male and female?

MOLL This Holborn is such a wrangling street.

TRAPDOOR That's because lawyers walks to and fro in't.

MOLL Here's such jostling, as if everyone we met were drunk and reeled.

TRAPDOOR Stand,° mistress! Do you not smell carrion? *Stop*

MOLL Carrion? No, yet I spy ravens.

TRAPDOOR Some poor wind-shaken° gallant will anon fall into sore labor, and these men-midwives must bring him to bed i'the Counter; there all those that are great with child with debts lie in.[6] *agitated (by debt)*

MOLL Stand up.° *i.e., Back me up*

TRAPDOOR Like your° new maypole. *the proverbial*

HANGER [*signaling to Curtalax*] Whist! Whew!

CURTALAX [*signaling back*] Hump, no!° *i.e., No, not yet!*

MOLL Peeping? It shall go hard, huntsmen, but I'll spoil your game.[7] [*To Trapdoor*] They look for all the world like two

1. Sir Davy points to a stage door as though to a tavern door.
2. "Sa, sa!" is a cry accompanying a thrust in fencing; also a shout to urge on hunting hounds. To "give the counter" is to parry with a thrust; also a hunting term for taking a direction opposite to that of the game.
3. Put spice enough in his drink; i.e., give him the full treatment. (A mace is also a sergeant's staff; a caudle is a warm drink of wine or ale mixed with thin gruel, often for invalids.)
4. The official in charge of the arresting officers.
5. Shall the two of us hide in ambush in one spot?
6. (1) Lie in debtors' prison; (2) lie in childbirth. Trapdoor compares incarceration in debtors' prison to lying in childbirth, with the arresting officers as the midwives.
7. I'll have no trouble foiling your sport. (Said as though to the arresting officers.)

infected maltmen coming muffled up in their cloaks in a frosty morning to London.[8]

TRAPDOOR A course,° Captain! A bear comes to the stake.[9] *(I see) the hunted animal*

Enter Jack Dapper and Gull.

MOLL It should be so, for the dogs° struggle to be let loose. *i.e., the sergeants*

HANGER [*signaling*] Whew!

CURTALAX Hemp!° *(see 198)*

MOLL Hark, Trapdoor, follow your leader.° *i.e., follow me*

JACK DAPPER Gull?

GULL Master?

JACK DAPPER Didst ever see such an ass as I am, boy?

GULL No, by my troth, sir, to lose all your money, yet have false dice of your own, why, 'tis as I saw a great fellow used t'other day: he had a fair sword and buckler,° and yet a butcher dry-beat° him with a cudgel. *small round shield* *beat without drawing blood*

MOLL *and* TRAPDOOR Honest sergeant!—Fly, fly, Master Dapper! You'll be arrested else![1]

[*Moll and Trapdoor detain the sergeants.*]

JACK DAPPER Run, Gull, and draw!

GULL Run, master! Gull follows you. *Exit Dapper and Gull.*

CURTALAX [*to Moll*] I know you well enough. You're but a whore to hang upon any man.

MOLL Whores then are like sergeants,[2] so now hang you! [*To Trapdoor*] Draw, rogue, but strike not. For a broken pate, they'll keep their beds and recover twenty marks damages.[3]

CURTALAX You shall pay for this rescue![4] [*To Hanger*] Run down Shoe Lane° and meet him. *(near Fleet Street)*

TRAPDOOR Shoo!° Is this a rescue, gentlemen, or no? *(an exclamation)*

[*Exeunt Curtalax and Hanger.*]

MOLL Rescue? A pox on 'em, Trapdoor. Let's away.
I'm glad I have done perfect one good work today.
If any gentleman be in scrivener's bands,° *in debt*
Send but for Moll; she'll bail him, by these hands. *Exeunt.*

[4.1]

Enter Sir Alexander Wengrave solus.° *alone*

SIR ALEXANDER Unhappy in the follies of a son
Led against judgment, sense, obedience,
And all the powers of nobleness and wit!
Oh, wretched father!

Enter Trapdoor.

Now, Trapdoor, will she come?

TRAPDOOR In man's apparel, sir. I am in her heart° now, *in her confidence*
And share in all her secrets.

8. Maltmen were in the business of bringing malt into London. They often handled old bags and other rags, which made them peculiarly susceptible to becoming infected with the plague.

9. Bears were tethered to a stake in the sport of bear-baiting.

1. Moll and Trapdoor call to one of the officers to distract him, then yell to Dapper telling him to get away fast.

2. Both whores and arresting officers hang on men.

3. If these officers were to suffer a minor indignity, such as a cut forehead, like lazy cowards they'd pretend a more serious injury and haul you into court on a charge of battery instead of fighting bravely.

4. The forcible taking of a person out of legal custody.

4.1. Sir Alexander's house (see line 61).

SIR ALEXANDER Peace, peace, peace!
Here, take my German watch. Hang't up in sight,
That I may see her hang in English° for't. *under English law*
[*He give a watch.*]

TRAPDOOR I warrant you for that, now; next sessions° rids her, *court term*
sir. This watch will bring her in, better than a hundred constables.° *i.e., "the watch"*

SIR ALEXANDER Good Trapdoor, say'st thou so? Thou cheer'st my heart
After a storm of sorrow. My gold chain, too.
Here, take a hundred marks in yellow links.
[*He gives a gold chain.*]

TRAPDOOR That will do well to bring the watch to light, sir,
and worth a thousand of your headborough's° lanterns. *night watchman's*

SIR ALEXANDER Place that o' the court-cupboard.° Let it lie *sideboard*
Full in the view of her thief-whorish eye.
[*Trapdoor places the objects on a sideboard.*]

TRAPDOOR She cannot miss it, sir. I see't so plain that I could steal't myself.

SIR ALEXANDER Perhaps thou shalt, too—
That or something as weighty. What she leaves,
Thou shalt come closely° in and filch away, *secretly*
And all the weight° upon her back I'll lay. *burden of guilt*

TRAPDOOR You cannot assure that, sir.

SIR ALEXANDER No? What lets° it? *hinders*

TRAPDOOR Being a stout° girl, perhaps she'll desire pressing;[1] then all the weight must lie upon her belly. *spirited*

SIR ALEXANDER Belly or back, I care not so I've one.[2]

TRAPDOOR You're of my mind for that,° sir. *We agree on that*

SIR ALEXANDER Hang up my ruff band° with the diamond at it; *ruff collar*
It may be she'll like that best.

TRAPDOOR [*aside*] It's well for her that she must have her choice; he thinks nothing too good for her! [*To him*] If you hold on this mind° a little longer, it shall be the first work I do to turn thief myself. Would° do a man good to be hanged when he is so well provided for. *hold to your purpose* *It would*
[*The ruff collar is hung up in plain view.*]

SIR ALEXANDER So, well said.° All hangs well; would she hung so too! *well done*
The sight would please me more than all their glisterings.
Oh, that my mysteries° to such straits should run, *skills*
That I must rob myself to bless my son! *Exeunt.*

Enter Sebastian, with Mary Fitzallard like a page, and Moll [*dressed as a man*].

SEBASTIAN [*to Moll*] Thou hast done me a kind office,° without touch *service*
Either of sin or shame; our loves are honest.

MOLL I'd scorn to make such shift° to bring you together else. *effort*

SEBASTIAN [*to Mary*] Now have I time and opportunity,

1. (1) Pressing to death—a torture inflicted on those who refused to plead when charged with a crime; (2) bearing the weight of a man in sex.

2. (1) So long as I get a share of the sexual action; (2) so long as we apprehend Moll for thieving. (Arresting officers seized their victims by the shoulder or back.)

Without all fear, to bid thee welcome, love. [*They*] *kiss.*
MARY Never with more desire and harder venture!
MOLL How strange this shows,° one man to kiss another! *looks*
SEBASTIAN I'd kiss such men to choose,° Moll. *by choice*
Methinks a woman's lip tastes well in a doublet.° *men's jacket*
MOLL Many an old madam has the better fortune, then,
Whose breaths grew stale before the fashion came.
If that will help 'em, as you think 'twill do,
They'll learn in time to pluck on the hose too.[3]
SEBASTIAN The older they wax, Moll. Troth, I speak seriously:[4]
As some have a conceit° their drink tastes better *notion (that)*
In an outlandish° cup than in our own, *unfamiliar; foreign*
So methinks every kiss she gives me now
In this strange form is worth a pair of two.° *is worth two*
Here we are safe, and furthest from the eye
Of all suspicion. This is my father's chamber,
Upon which floor he never steps till night.
Here he mistrusts° me not, nor I his coming. *suspects*
At mine own chamber he still° pries unto me; *continually*
My freedom is not there at mine own finding,° *as I would prefer*
Still checked and curbed. Here he shall miss his purpose.
MOLL And what's your business, now you have your mind,° sir? *have your wish*
At your great suit° I promised you to come; *earnest petition*
I pitied her for name's sake that a Moll° *(nickname for "Mary")*
Should be so crossed° in love, when there's so many *thwarted*
That owes nine lays apiece, and not so little.[5]
My tailor fitted her. How like you his work?
SEBASTIAN So well, no art can mend it for this purpose.
But to thy wit and help we're chief in debt,
And must live still beholding.° *eternally beholden*
MOLL Any honest pity
I'm willing to bestow upon poor ringdoves.° *i.e., innocent lovers*
SEBASTIAN I'll offer no worse play.[6]
MOLL Nay, an° you should, sir, *if*
I should draw first and prove the quicker man.
SEBASTIAN Hold, there shall need no weapon at this meeting.
But 'cause° thou shalt not loose thy fury idle,° *in order that / in vain*
Here, take this viol. [*He takes down and hands her a viola da gamba.*] Run upon the guts
And end thy quarrel singing.[7]
MOLL Like a swan above bridge;[8]

3. Moll jests that old bawds, despite their characteristic bad breath, were more likely to attract customers in the usual way before this new business of men kissing men became fashionable; now, if Sebastian is right, they'll have to learn how to dress as men in order to be desirable. (Hose are breeches.)
4. Sebastian concedes the wit of Moll's fanciful notion about aging bawds but insists that he is not joking when he says that he finds it delicious to kiss Mary in her strange guise.
5. I.e., when so many others flourish and practice immorality with impunity (?). ("Lays" may refer to prizes or to lodgings used for fornication.)
6. I'll propose no worse sport than what you suggest. (This amiable quarrel is laden with sexual innuendo, through line 101, in "weapon," "put us together," "instrument," "hang by the walls," "offered," "took down," "close," "broadly," "sit wider," etc.)
7. Play on the gut strings of this viola da gamba, thus ending the friendly quarrel in a song. ("Run upon the guts" also suggests running through one's opponent with a weapon.)
8. Swans were fabled to sing only once, just before they died. Moll puns on a bridge over a stream and the one on a musical instrument.

For, look you, here's the bridge and here am I.

SEBASTIAN Hold on,° sweet Moll. *Hold forth*

MARY I've heard her much commended, sir, for one that was ne'er taught.

MOLL I'm much beholding to 'em. Well, since you'll needs put us together, sir, I'll play my part as well as I can. It shall ne'er be said I came into a gentleman's chamber and let his instrument hang by the walls!

SEBASTIAN Why, well said, Moll, i'faith. It had been° a shame for that gentleman, then, that would have let it hang still and ne'er offered thee it. *It would have been*

MOLL There it should have been still, then, for Moll,[9] for, though the world judge impudently of me, I ne'er came into that chamber yet where I took down the instrument myself.

SEBASTIAN Pish, let 'em prate abroad.° Thou'rt here where thou art known and loved. There be a thousand close° dames that will call the viol an unmannerly instrument for a woman, and therefore talk broadly° of thee, when you shall have them sit wider to a worse quality.[1] *gossip around the town* *prudish* *coarsely*

MOLL Push,° I ever fall asleep and think not of 'em, sir; and thus I dream. *Pish*

SEBASTIAN Prithee, let's hear thy dream, Moll.

THE SONG

MOLL [*sings*] I dream there is a mistress,
And she lays out the money.
She goes unto her sisters;° *neighbors; whores*
She never comes at any.[2]

Enter Sir Alexander behind them.

She says she went to th'Burse° for patterns; *the Royal Exchange*
You shall find her at Saint Kathern's,° *a dockside district*
And comes home with never a penny.

SEBASTIAN That's a free° mistress, faith. *generous; loose*

SIR ALEXANDER [*aside*] Ay, ay, ay,
Like her that sings it, one of thine own choosing.

MOLL But shall I dream again?

[*She sings.*] Here comes a wench will brave ye,° *who'll challenge you*
Her courage was so great;
She lay with one o'the navy,
Her husband lying i'the Fleet.° *navy; Fleet Prison*
Yet oft with him she caviled.° *found fault*
I wonder what she ails?° *what ails her*
Her husband's ship lay graveled° *beached, stranded*
When hers could hoise° up sails; *hoist*
Yet she began, like all my foes,
To call "whore" first; for so do those.° *(all my foes)*
A pox of all false tails![3]

9. As far as I, Moll, am concerned.
1. I.e., when such women will all too often spread their legs for a more debased reason than playing a viola da gamba.
2. (1) She never arrives at any money; (2) she never comes to sexual fulfillment.
3. A plague on all unreliable women ("tails" suggests "cunts") and all false tales! Moll's song is sexually suggestive throughout, as in the reference to a sexually insufficient husband and a wife lifting her skirts (lines 122–23).

SEBASTIAN Marry, amen, say I.
SIR ALEXANDER [*aside*] So say I, too.
MOLL [*returning the viola da gamba*] Hang up the viol now,
sir; all this while I was in a dream. One shall lie rudely° then; *i.e., with legs apart*
but being awake, I keep my legs together.°—A watch! What's *(see 101 and n)*
o'clock here?
SIR ALEXANDER [*aside*] Now, now she's trapped.
MOLL Between one and two? Nay, then, I care not. A watch
and a musician are cousin-germans° in one thing: they must *first cousins*
both keep time well or there's no goodness in 'em.[4] The one
else° deserves to be dashed against a wall, and t'other to have *otherwise*
his brains knocked out with a fiddle case. [*She sees the other displayed objects.*] What, a loose chain and a dangling diamond? Here were a brave booty for an evening thief now.
There's many a younger brother would be glad to look twice
in at a window for't, and wriggle in and out, like an eel in a
sandbag.[5] Oh, if men's secret youthful faults should judge
'em, 'twould be the general'st execution that e'er was seen
in England! There would be but few left to sing the ballads.° *(about the executions)*
There would be so much work, most of our brokers° would *pimps*
be chosen for hangmen! A good day for them: they might
renew their wardrobes of free cost then.[6]
SEBASTIAN [*to Mary*] This is the roaring wench must do us good.
MARY [*to Sebastian*] No poison, sir, but serves us for some use,
Which is confirmed in her.
SEBASTIAN Peace, peace!
Foot,° I did hear him, sure, where'er he be. *By God's foot*
MOLL Who did you hear?
SEBASTIAN My father;
'Twas like a sigh of his. I must be wary.
SIR ALEXANDER [*aside*] No? Will't not be?° Am I alone so wretched *Won't it work?*
That nothing takes?° I'll put him to his plunge° for't. *takes effect / crisis*
SEBASTIAN [*seeing Sir Alexander*] Life, here he comes.
[*Aloud to Moll*] Sir, I beseech you take it.° *(money)*
Your way of teaching° does so much content me, *teaching music*
I'll make it four pound. Here's forty shillings, sir.
[*He offers money.*]
I think I name it° right. [*Aside to Moll*] Help me, good Moll. *(the amount)*
[*Aloud*] Forty in hand.° *as partial payment*
MOLL Sir, you shall pardon me;
I have more of the meanest scholar I can teach.
This pays me more than you have offered yet.[7]
SEBASTIAN At the next quarter,
When I receive the means my father 'lows me,
You shall have t'other forty.

4. Moll evidently notes that the watch does not keep good time (since her appointment to be here was for three o'clock, according to 3.3.35, but the watch says it is between one and two), and therefore she is not tempted to steal it in any case.
5. Younger brothers did not inherit their fathers' fortunes and hence were perenially in financial need. Moll imagines how such a person might sneak in at a window to commit a larceny.
6. Hangmen traditionally were given the clothes of the executed person.
7. I receive better payment than this from the poorest students that I teach. And even at that, what you've just offered is more than you've offered me up to this time. (Said as part of the charade to deceive Sir Alexander, stressing Sebastian's financial needs.)

SIR ALEXANDER [*aside*] This were well° now, *would be believable*
Were't to a man whose sorrows had blind eyes,
But mine behold his follies and untruths
With two clear glasses. [*He comes forward.*]
[*To Sebastian*] How now?
SEBASTIAN Sir?
SIR ALEXANDER What's he° there? *i.e., Moll*
SEBASTIAN You're come in good time, sir. I've a suit to you;
I'd crave your present kindness.
SIR ALEXANDER What is he there?
SEBASTIAN A gentleman, a musician, sir, one of excellent fingering.° *lute playing; pilfering*
SIR ALEXANDER Ay, I think so. [*Aside*] I wonder how they scaped her?[8]
SEBASTIAN 'Has the most delicate stroke,[9] sir.
SIR ALEXANDER [*aside*] A stroke indeed; I feel it at my heart.
SEBASTIAN Puts down° all your famous musicians. *She excels*
SIR ALEXANDER [*aside*] Ay, a whore may put down° a hundred of 'em. *seduce*
SEBASTIAN Forty shillings is the agreement, sir, between us.
Now, sir, my present means mounts but to half on't.
SIR ALEXANDER And he stands upon° the whole. *insists upon*
SEBASTIAN Ay, indeed, does he, sir.
SIR ALEXANDER [*aside*] And will do still; he'll ne'er be in other tale.° *never change his story*
SEBASTIAN Therefore I'd stop his mouth,° sir, an I could. *silence him; kiss him*
SIR ALEXANDER H'm, true. [*Aside*] There is no other way, indeed.
His folly hardens; shame must needs succeed.° *follow*
[*To Moll*] Now, sir, I understand you profess° music. *claim expertise in*
MOLL I am a poor servant to that liberal science,° sir. *liberal art*
SIR ALEXANDER Where is it you teach?
MOLL Right against Clifford's Inn.[1]
SIR ALEXANDER [*aside*] H'm, that's a fit place for it. [*To Moll*]
You have many scholars?
MOLL And some of worth, whom I may call my masters.
SIR ALEXANDER [*aside*] Ay, true, a company of whoremasters.
[*To Moll*] You teach to sing, too?
MOLL Marry, do I, sir.
SIR ALEXANDER I think you'll find an apt scholar of my son, especially for prick-song.[2]
MOLL I have much hope of him.
SIR ALEXANDER [*aside*] I am sorry for't; I have the less for that.
[*To Moll*] You can play any lesson?
MOLL At first sight, sir.
SIR ALEXANDER There's a thing called "The Witch."[3] Can you play that?
MOLL I would be sorry anyone should mend° me in't. *improve on, outdo*

8. I wonder how the jewels that were set out escaped being taken by her?
9. She has the most delicate bowing stroke. (With sexual suggestion that continues in "put down," "mounts," "stands," "whole" [hole], "do," "tale" [tail], etc.)
1. Right next to Clifford's Inn. (One of the oldest of the Inns of Chancery, Clifford's Inn stood in a neighborhood to the north of Fleet Street, which was noted for prostitution; hence Sir Alexander's wry observation in the next line that Moll belongs in such a place.)
2. Music sung from a written (pricked down) score. (With a bawdy pun.)
3. Evidently a contemporary ballad or song.

SIR ALEXANDER [*aside*] Ay, I believe thee. Thou hast so bewitched my son,
No care will mend the work that thou hast done.
I have bethought myself, since my art fails,
I'll make her policy° the art to trap her. *stratagem*
[*He produces four coins.*]
Here are four angels marked with holes in them,
Fit for his cracked° companions. Gold he will give her; *flawed; madcap*
These will I make induction° to her ruin, *prologue*
And rid shame from my house, grief from my heart.
[*To Sebastian*] Here, son; in what you take content and pleasure,
Want° shall not curb you. Pay the gentleman *Financial need*
His latter half° in gold. [*He gives Sebastian the money.*] *(see 159, 164–66)*

SEBASTIAN I thank you, sir.

SIR ALEXANDER [*aside*] Oh, may the operation on't end three:
In her, life; shame in him; and grief in me! *Exit Alexander.*

SEBASTIAN [*giving Moll the money*] Faith, thou shalt have 'em. 'Tis my father's gift.
Never was man beguiled with better shift!° *trick*

MOLL He that can take me for a male musician,
I cannot choose but make him my instrument
And play upon him. *Exeunt omnes.*

[4.2]

Enter Mistress Gallipot and Mistress Openwork.

MRS. GALLIPOT Is then that bird of yours, Master Goshawk, so wild?

MRS. OPENWORK A goshawk? A puttock,° all for prey! He angles for fish, but he loves flesh better. *kite, bird of prey*

MRS. GALLIPOT Is't possible his smooth face should have wrinkles in't, and we not see them?

MRS. OPENWORK Possible? Why, have not many handsome legs in silk stockings villainous splay feet° for all their great roses?° *feet turned outward* *shoe ornaments*

MRS. GALLIPOT Troth, sirrah,[1] thou say'st true.

MRS. OPENWORK Didst never see an archer, as thou 'ast walked by Bunhill,° look asquint when he drew his bow? *a London street*

MRS. GALLIPOT Yes. When his arrows have fline° toward Islington,° his eyes have shot clean contrary towards Pimlico.° *flown* *(north)* *(northeast)*

MRS. OPENWORK For all the world so does Master Goshawk double with° me. *hoodwink, two-time*

MRS. GALLIPOT Oh, fie upon him! If he double once, he's not for me.

MRS. OPENWORK Because Goshawk goes in a shag-ruff band,° with a face sticking up in't which shows like an agate set in a cramp-ring,° he thinks I'm in love with him. *fancy collar* *(used to ward off cramps)*

MRS. GALLIPOT 'Las, I think he takes his mark amiss in thee.[2]

4.2. The Gallipots' establishment.
1. As at 3.2.163 and 178, "sirrah" could be used to address women as well as men. The usage recurs in lines 36, 47, and 69 below.
2. I think he misses the mark in aiming at you; he goes about it the wrong way.

MRS. OPENWORK He has, by often beating into° me, made me believe that my husband kept a whore. *bearing down on*

MRS. GALLIPOT Very good.

MRS. OPENWORK Swore to me that my husband this very morning went in a boat, with a tilt° over it, to the Three Pigeons at Brentford, and his punk° with him under his tilt. *awning* / *whore*

MRS. GALLIPOT That were wholesome!

MRS. OPENWORK I believed it; fell a-swearing at him, cursing of harlots, made me ready to hoise up sail° and be there as soon as he. *make ready*

MRS. GALLIPOT So, so.

MRS. OPENWORK And for that voyage Goshawk comes hither incontinently.° But, sirrah, this water spaniel dives after no duck but me; his hope is having me° at Brentford to make me cry quack. *any moment now* / *having me as his lover*

MRS. GALLIPOT Art sure of it?

MRS. OPENWORK Sure of it? My poor innocent Openwork came in as I was poking° my ruff. Presently hit I him i'the teeth° with the Three Pigeons. He forswore all. I up and opened° all, and now stands he, in a shop hard by,° like a musket on a rest,° to hit Goshawk i'the eye when he comes to fetch me to the boat. *stiffening the pleats of* / *I confronted him* / *told / close at hand* / *supported for firing*

MRS. GALLIPOT Such another lame gelding° offered to carry me through thick and thin—Laxton, sirrah—but I am rid of him now. *castrated horse*

MRS. OPENWORK Happy is the woman can be rid of 'em all. 'Las, what are your whisking° gallants to° our husbands, weigh 'em rightly, man for man? *brisk / compared with*

MRS. GALLIPOT Troth, mere shallow things.

MRS. OPENWORK Idle simple things, running heads.° And yet let 'em run over us never so fast, we shopkeepers, when all's done, are sure to have 'em in our purse-nets[3] at length, and when they are in, Lord, what simple animals they are! Then they hang the head. *footmen, lackeys*

MRS. GALLIPOT Then they droop.

MRS. OPENWORK Then they write letters.

MRS. GALLIPOT Then they cog.° *cheat; wheedle*

MRS. OPENWORK Then deal they underhand with us, and we must ingle° with our husbands abed, and we must swear they° are our cousins and able to do us a pleasure° at court. *fondle; cajole* / *(our lovers) / a favor*

MRS. GALLIPOT And yet when we have done our best, all's but put into a riven° dish; we are but frumped at° and libeled upon. *broken / mocked*

MRS. OPENWORK Oh, if it were the good Lord's will, there were a law made no citizen should trust any of 'em all!

Enter Goshawk.

MRS. GALLIPOT [*in a lowered voice*] Hush, sirrah. Goshawk flutters.

GOSHAWK [*to Mrs. Openwork*] How now, are you ready?

3. Bag-shaped nets. (With a bawdy reference to the female sexual anatomy; the bawdy punning continues in the ensuing dialogue in "are in," "hang the head," "droop.")

MRS. OPENWORK Nay, are you ready? A little thing, you see, makes us ready.
GOSHAWK Us? Why, must she make one° i'the voyage? *join the company*
MRS. OPENWORK Oh, by any° means. Do I know how my husband will handle me?[4] *all*
GOSHAWK [*aside*] Foot, how shall I find water to keep these two mills going?[5] [*To them*] Well, since you'll needs be clapped under hatches,[6] if I sail not with you both till all split,° hang me up at the main yard° and duck me.[7] [*Aside*] *goes to pieces / mainsail*
It's but liquoring° them both soundly, and then you shall see *supplying with liquor*
their cork heels fly up high, like two swans when their tails are above water and their long necks under water diving to catch gudgeons.° [*To them*] Come, come! Oars stand ready; *small fish*
the tide's with us. On with those false faces.° Blow winds, *masks*
and [*to Mrs. Openwork*] thou shalt take thy husband casting out his net to catch fresh salmon° at Brentford. *i.e., whores*
MRS. GALLIPOT [*as they put on masks*] I believe you'll eat of a cod's head of your own dressing before you reach half way thither.[8]
GOSHAWK So, so, follow close. Pin° as you go. *Pin your masks*
[*They start to leave.*]

Enter Laxton, muffled.

LAXTON Do you hear? [*He takes Mrs. Gallipot aside.*]
MRS. GALLIPOT Yes, I thank my ears.
LAXTON I must have a bout° with Your Pothecaryship. *talk; sexual encounter*
MRS. GALLIPOT At what weapon?
LAXTON I must speak with you.
MRS. GALLIPOT No.
LAXTON No? You shall.
MRS. GALLIPOT Shall? Away, soused sturgeon,° half fish, half flesh! *pickled fish*
LAXTON Faith, gib,° are you spitting? I'll cut your tail, pusscat, for this. *castrated male cat*
MRS. GALLIPOT 'Las, poor Laxton! I think thy tail's cut° already. Your worst!° *i.e., you're emasculated* / *Do your worst!*
LAXTON If I do not— *Exit Laxton.*
GOSHAWK [*to Mrs. Gallipot*] Come, ha' you done?

Enter Master Openwork.

[*Aside to Mrs. Openwork*] 'Sfoot, Rosamond, your husband!
OPENWORK How now? Sweet Master Goshawk, none more welcome!
I have wanted° your embracements. When friends meet, *lacked*
The music of the spheres sounds not more sweet
Than does their conference. Who is this? Rosamond?
Wife? [*To Mrs. Gallipot*] How now, sister?
GOSHAWK [*aside to Mrs. Openwork*] Silence, if you love me!

4. I.e., Don't you see that having Mrs. Gallipot along will allay my husband's suspicions?
5. I.e., How can I satisfy these two women at once?
6. Stowed safely aboard. (With added sexual meaning that runs throughout the passage.)
7. Drop me into the water. (Perhaps with the suggestion of keelhauling, hauling a person under the keel of a ship as punishment or torture.)
8. A cod's head is cheap, quite unlike salmon. Mrs. Gallipot predicts that Goshawk will be foiled by his own machinations.

OPENWORK Why masked?
MRS. OPENWORK Does a mask grieve you, sir?
OPENWORK It does.
MRS. OPENWORK Then you're best get you a-mumming.[9]
GOSHAWK [*aside to Mrs. Openwork*] 'Sfoot, you'll spoil all!
MRS. GALLIPOT May not we cover our bare faces with masks as well as you cover your bald heads with hats?
OPENWORK No masks! Why, they're thieves to beauty, that rob eyes
Of admiration in which true love lies.
Why are masks worn? Why good? Or why desired?
Unless by their gay covers wits are fired
To read the vilest looks. Many bad faces,
Because rich gems are treasured up in cases,
Pass by their privilege current;[1] but as caves
Damn misers' gold,[2] so masks are beauties' graves.
Men ne'er meet women with such muffled eyes
But they curse her that first did masks devise,
And swear it was some beldame.° Come, off with't. *hag*
MRS. OPENWORK I will not.
OPENWORK Good faces masked are jewels kept by sprites.° *guarded by demons*
Hide none but bad ones, for they poison men's sights;
Show them as shopkeepers do their broidered stuff,
By owl-light.[3] Fine wares cannot be open enough.
Prithee, sweet Rose, come, strike this sail.° *doff this mask*
MRS. OPENWORK Sail?
OPENWORK Ha?
Yes, wife, strike sail, for storms are in thine eyes.
MRS. OPENWORK They're here, sir, in my brows, if any rise.° *i.e., I'm indeed angry*
OPENWORK Ha, brows? [*To Mrs. Gallipot*] What says she,
friend? [*To them both*] Pray tell me why
Your two flags° were advanced? The comedy? *i.e., masks*
Come, what's the comedy?
MRS. GALLIPOT *Westward Ho.*[4]
OPENWORK How?
MRS. OPENWORK 'Tis *Westward Ho*, she says.
GOSHAWK Are you both mad?
MRS. OPENWORK Is't market day at Brentford, and your ware not sent up yet?
OPENWORK What market day? What ware?
MRS. OPENWORK A pie with three pigeons in't. 'Tis drawn° and *pulled from the oven*
stays° your cutting up. *awaits*
GOSHAWK [*aside to Mrs. Openwork*] As you regard my credit°— *reputation*
OPENWORK [*to Mrs. Openwork*] Art mad?
MRS. OPENWORK Yes, lecherous goat! Baboon!
OPENWORK Baboon? Then toss me in a blanket.[5]

9. Since mummings were without dialogue, Mrs. Openwork is impudently telling her husband to shut up.
1. Many unattractive faces pass for handsome when masked, because the viewer supposes the outward casing to conceal some rich jewel.
2. But just as hoarding wealth cancels out its value (because the wealth is not seen or used).
3. Hide only ugly faces, for they are poisonous to men's sights; display such faces only darkly and imperfectly, the way shopkeepers display their inferior cloth wares only in dim lighting.
4. The name of a play of 1604 by Dekker and Webster; also, a cry of a boatman offering transportation westward on the Thames. (Mrs. Openwork alludes here to their intended journey westward to Brentford.)
5. A humiliating punishment. (Openwork is denying his wife's insinuation.)

MRS. OPENWORK [*aside to Mrs. Gallipot*] Do I it well?
MRS. GALLIPOT [*aside to Mrs. Openwork*] Rarely!° *Excellently!*
GOSHAWK [*to Openwork*] Belike,° sir, she's not well; best leave her. *Perhaps*
OPENWORK No,
I'll stand the storm now, how fierce soe'er it blow.
MRS. OPENWORK Did I for this lose all my friends?° Refuse *family; connections*
Rich hopes and golden fortunes, to be made
A stale° to a common whore? *A ridiculed woman*
OPENWORK This does amaze me.
MRS. OPENWORK Oh, God, oh, God, feed at reversion° now? *leftovers*
A strumpet's leaving?
OPENWORK Rosamond!
GOSHAWK [*aside*] I sweat. Would I lay in Cold Harbor![6]
MRS. OPENWORK Thou hast struck ten thousand daggers through my heart!
OPENWORK Not I, by heaven, sweet wife.
MRS. OPENWORK Go, devil, go! That which thou swear'st by° damns thee. *i.e., heaven*
GOSHAWK [*aside to Mrs. Openwork*] 'Sheart, will you undo me?
MRS. OPENWORK [*to Openwork*] Why stay you here? The star by which you sail
Shines yonder above Chelsea; you lose your shore.[7]
If this moon° light you, seek out your light° whore. *i.e., star / wanton*
OPENWORK Ha?
MRS. GALLIPOT Push! Your western pug!° *harlot*
GOSHAWK [*aside*] Zounds, now hell roars!
MRS. OPENWORK With whom you tilted in a pair of oars° this very morning. *boat with two rowers*
OPENWORK Oars?
MRS. OPENWORK At Brentford, sir.
OPENWORK Rack° not my patience.—Master Goshawk, some slave has buzzed this into her, has he not?—I run a-tilt in Brentford with a woman? 'Tis a lie. What old bawd tells thee this? 'Sdeath,° 'tis a lie. *Torture, test* / *By God's death*
MRS. OPENWORK 'Tis one° to thy face shall justify all that I speak. *someone who*
OPENWORK Ud's soul,° do but name that rascal. *God bless my soul*
MRS. OPENWORK No, sir, I will not.
GOSHAWK [*aside*] Keep thee there, girl. [*To them*] Then!° *That's enough!*
OPENWORK [*to Mrs. Gallipot*] Sister, know you this varlet?° *the seducer (Goshawk)*
MRS. GALLIPOT Yes.
OPENWORK Swear true:
Is there a rogue so low damned? A second Judas?° *Jesus' betrayer*
A common hangman? Cutting a man's throat?
Does it to his face? Bite° me behind my back? *i.e., Vilify*
A cur dog? Swear if you know this hellhound.
MRS. GALLIPOT In truth, I do.
OPENWORK His name?
MRS. GALLIPOT Not for the world;
To have you to stab him.

6. Cold Harbor (or Coleharbour) is both a seedy area of London along the Thames River and a place suggestive of a cold river where a sweating person could cool off.

7. I.e., You are delaying your chance to direct your course westward by boat beyond Chelsea for your assignation.

GOSHAWK [*aside*] Oh, brave girls! Worth gold!
OPENWORK A word, honest° Master Goshawk. *worthy*
Draw[s] out his sword.
GOSHAWK What do you mean, sir?
OPENWORK Keep off, and if the devil can give a name
To this new Fury,° holla it through my ear, *avenging goddess*
Or wrap it up in some hid character.° *secret code*
I'll ride to Oxford, and watch out mine eyes,[8]
But I'll hear the Brazen Head[9] speak; or else
Show me but one hair of his° head or beard, *(the seducer's)*
That I may sample it. If the fiend I meet
In° mine own house, I'll kill him—the street, *Even in*
Or at the church door. There, 'cause he seeks to untie
The knot God fastens,° he deserves most to die. *The marriage bond*
MRS. OPENWORK [*to Mrs. Gallipot*] My husband titles him![1]
OPENWORK Master Goshawk, pray, sir,
Swear to me that you know him or know him not,
Who makes° me at Brentford to take up a petticoat *accuses*
Besides my wife's.
GOSHAWK By heaven, that man I know not.
MRS. OPENWORK Come, come, you lie.
GOSHAWK [*to Mrs. Openwork*] Will you not have all out?[2]
By heaven, I know no man beneath the moon
Should do° you wrong, but if I had his name, *Who may have done*
I'd print it in text letters.° *large capitals*
MRS. OPENWORK Print thine own, then.
Didst not thou swear to me he kept his whore?
MRS. GALLIPOT And that in sinful Brentford they would commit
That which our lips did water° at, sir? Ha? *salivate*
MRS. OPENWORK Thou spider, that hast woven thy cunning web
In mine own house t'ensnare me, hast not thou
Sucked nourishment even underneath this roof
And turned it all to poison, spitting it
On thy friend's face, my husband—he, as 'twere, sleeping°— *unsuspecting*
Only to leave him ugly to mine eyes,
That they might glance on thee?
MRS. GALLIPOT Speak, are these lies?
GOSHAWK Mine own shame me confounds.
MRS. OPENWORK No more, he's stung.
Who'd think that in one body there could dwell
Deformity and beauty, heaven and hell?
Goodness, I see, is but outside; we all set,
In rings of gold, stones° that be counterfeit. *precious stones*
I thought you none.
GOSHAWK Pardon me.

8. I'll keep watch till my eyes give out.
9. A famous prophetic speaking head of Brasenose College, Oxford. It figures prominently in Robert Greene's *Friar Bacon and Friar Bungay.*
1. (1) My husband addresses the very seducer he seeks! or (2) He gives the seducer fancy titles, like "devil" and "fiend" (lines 203, 209)!
2. Don't you want the whole truth? (Goshawk is putting on a bold show of innocence, or else says this as an aside to Mrs. Openwork in a desperate attempt to get her to stay quiet.)

OPENWORK Truth, I do.
This blemish grows in nature,° not in you, *human nature*
For man's creation stick even moles in scorn
On fairest cheeks.[3]—Wife, nothing is perfect born.

MRS. OPENWORK I thought you had been born perfect.

OPENWORK What's this whole world but a gilt rotten pill?
For at the heart lies the old core° still. *innate depravity*
I'll tell you, Master Goshawk, ay, in your eye
I have seen wanton fire; and then to try
The soundness of my judgment, I told you
I kept a whore, made you believe 'twas true
Only to feel how your pulse beat, but find
The world can hardly yield a perfect friend.
Come, come, a trick of youth, and 'tis forgiven.
This rub° put by, our love shall run more even. *obstacle (in a game of bowls)*

MRS. OPENWORK You'll deal upon° men's wives no more? *try to prevail upon*

GOSHAWK No. You teach me a trick for that.

MRS. OPENWORK Troth, do not; they'll o'erreach thee.

OPENWORK [*to Goshawk*] Make my house yours, sir, still.

GOSHAWK No.

OPENWORK I say you shall.
Seeing, thus besieged, it° holds out, 'twill never fall. *(our marriage)*

Enter Master Gallipot, and Greenwit like a summoner[4] [*in a wig*]; *Laxton muffled, aloof off.*° [*Greenwit seizes Gallipot by the shoulder in a gesture of arrest.*] *at a distance*

OMNES How now?

GALLIPOT [*to Greenwit*] With me, sir?

GREENWIT You, sir. I have gone snuffling up and down by your door this hour to watch for you.

MRS. GALLIPOT What's the matter, husband?

GREENWIT I have caught a cold in my head, sir, by sitting up late in the Rose Tavern, but I hope you understand my speech.[5]

GALLIPOT So, sir.

GREENWIT I cite you by the name of Hippocrates Gallipot, and you by the name of Prudence Gallipot, to appear upon *Crastino*, do you see, *Crastino sancti Dunstani*,[6] this Easter term, in Bow Church.

GALLIPOT Where, sir?—What says he?

GREENWIT Bow: Bow Church, to answer to a libel° of precontract on the part and behalf of the said Prudence and another.° You're best, sir, take a copy of the citation; 'tis but twelvepence. [*He holds out a citation.*] *accusation* / *i.e., Laxton*

OMNES A citation?

GALLIPOT You pocky-nosed° rascal, what slave fees you to this? *syphilitic-nosed*

LAXTON [*coming forward*] Slave? [*Aside to Goshawk*] I ha' nothing to do with you, do you hear, sir?

GOSHAWK [*aside*] Laxton, is't not? What vagary° is this? *detour, new twist*

3. For the creator that fashions humankind puts moles on even the most beautiful cheeks, as though to remind us of our imperfections.
4. A summoning officer for an ecclesiastical court.
5. Greenwit is talking through his nose, pretending to have a cold in order to disguise his voice.
6. The morrow after Saint Dunstan's Day, May 19.

GALLIPOT [*to Laxton*] Trust me, I thought, sir, this storm long ago had been full laid, when, if you be remembered, I paid you the last fifteen pound, besides the thirty you had first; for then you swore—

LAXTON Tush, tush, sir, oaths—
Truth, yet I'm loath to vex you. Tell you what;
Make up the money I had an hundred pound,[7]
And take your bellyful of her.

GALLIPOT An hundred pound?

MRS. GALLIPOT What, an hundred pound? He gets none.
What, an hundred pound?

GALLIPOT Sweet Pru, be calm. The gentleman offers thus:
If I will make the moneys that are past
An hundred pound, he will discharge all courts
And give his bond never to vex us more.

MRS. GALLIPOT An hundred pound? 'Las, take, sir, but threescore.
[*Aside to Laxton*] Do you seek my undoing?

LAXTON I'll not bate° *give up, deduct*
One sixpence. [*Aside to Mrs. Gallipot*] I'll maul you, puss, for spitting.

MRS. GALLIPOT [*aside to Laxton*] Do thy worst! [*Aloud*] Will fourscore stop thy mouth?

LAXTON No.

MRS. GALLIPOT You're a slave!
Thou cheat, I'll now tear money from thy throat.—
Husband, lay hold on yonder tawny coat.[8]

GREENWIT Nay, gentlemen, seeing your women are so hot, I must lose my hair in their company, I see. [*He removes his wig.*]

MRS. OPENWORK His hair sheds off,° and yet he speaks not so much in the nose as he did before. *(a symptom of syphilis)*

GOSHAWK He has had the better chirurgeon.[9]—Master Greenwit, is your wit so raw as to play no better a part than a summoner's?

GALLIPOT I pray, who plays *A Knack to Know an Honest Man*[1] in this company?

MRS. GALLIPOT Dear husband, pardon me. I did dissemble,
Told thee I was his precontracted wife.
When letters came from him for thirty pound,
I had no shift° but that. *stratagem*

GALLIPOT A very clean shift,° but able to make me lousy. On.° *undergarment / Go on*

MRS. GALLIPOT Husband, I plucked—when he had tempted me to think well of him—gelt° feathers from thy wings, to make him fly more lofty. *gilt*

GALLIPOT O'the top of you,° wife. On. *i.e., as sexual partner*

MRS. GALLIPOT He, having wasted them, comes now for more,
Using me as a ruffian° doth his whore *pimp*

7. Increase the amount you gave me already to a hundred pounds.
8. Greenwit, dressed in a summoner's tawny coat.
9. Goshawk implies that Greenwit has had a fake nose put on by a surgeon (chirurgeon) to replace the one that disintegrated as a result of syphilis.
1. An anonymous play of 1594. Gallipot quotes the title to suggest that it would take quite a knack to find an honest man in the present situation.

Whose sin keeps him in breath.° By heaven, I vow, *provides his livelihood*
Thy bed he never wronged more than he does now.
GALLIPOT My bed? Ha, ha, like° enough! A shop board will serve *likely*
To have a cuckold's coat cut out upon.[2]
Of that we'll talk hereafter. [*To Laxton*] You're a villain!
LAXTON Hear me but speak, sir. You shall find me none.
OMNES Pray, sir, be patient and hear him.
GALLIPOT I am muzzled for° biting, sir. Use me how you will. *to prevent*
LAXTON The first hour that your wife was in my eye,
Myself with other gentlemen sitting by
In your shop tasting smoke,° and speech being used *smoking*
That men who have fairest wives are most abused
And hardly scaped the horn,° your wife maintained *cuckoldry*
That only such spots in city dames were stained
Justly but by men's slanders.[3] For her own part,
She vowed that you had so much of her heart,
No man,° by all his wit, by any wile, *That no man*
Never so fine spun, should yourself beguile° *could cheat you*
Of what in her was yours.
GALLIPOT Yet, Pru, 'tis well.°— *Thus far I'm satisfied*
Play out your game at Irish,[4] sir. Who wins?
MRS. OPENWORK The trial is when she comes to bearing.[5]
LAXTON I scorned one° woman thus should brave° all men, *that one / mock, defy*
And, which more vexed me, a she-citizen.
Therefore I laid siege to her. Out she held,
Gave many a brave repulse, and me compelled
With shame to sound retreat to my hot lust.
Then, seeing all base desires raked up in dust,° *smothered*
And that to tempt her modest ears I swore
Ne'er to presume again, she said her eye
Would ever give me welcome honestly;
And, since I was a gentleman, if it run° low, *if money ran*
She would my state° relieve, not to° o'erthrow *finances / not so as to*
Your own and hers; did° so. Then, seeing I wrought° *she did / prevailed*
Upon her meekness,° me she set at naught;° *kindness / she scorned me*
And yet to try if I could turn that tide,
You see what stream I strove with. But, sir, I swear,
By heaven and by those hopes men lay up there,
I neither have nor had a base intent
To wrong your bed. What's done is merriment.
Your gold I pay back with this interest:
When I had most power to do't I wronged you least.
GALLIPOT If this no gullery° be, sir— *trickery*
OMNES No, no, on my life.
GALLIPOT Then, sir, I am beholden—not to you, wife,
But, Master Laxton, to your want° of doing ill, *lack*
Which it seems you have not.—Gentlemen,
Tarry and dine here all.

2. I.e., Instead of my bed, you may have practiced your adultery on the shop counter used to cut cloth.

3. I.e., your wife insisted that accusations of adultery leveled against city wives were just only if not the result of men's slanders. ("But" probably means "if not.")

4. I.e., Finish your story. ("Irish" is a lengthy board game, like backgammon.)

5. The test comes at the end of the game, when a piece is removed from the board. (With a pun on "childbearing.")

OPENWORK Brother, we have a jest
As good as yours to furnish out° a feast. *supply refreshment for*
GALLIPOT We'll crown our table with it. Wife, brag no more
Of holding out. Who° most brags is most whore. *Whoever*
Exeunt omnes.

[5.1]

Enter Jack Dapper, Moll, Sir Beauteous Ganymede, and Sir Thomas Long.

JACK DAPPER But prithee, Master Captain Jack,° be plain and perspicuous° with me: was it your Meg of Westminster's courage[1] that rescued me from the Poultry puttocks,[2] indeed? *i.e., Moll* / *clear*

MOLL The valor of my wit, I ensure you, sir, fetched you off° bravely, when you were i'the forlorn hope° among those desperates.° Sir Beauteous Ganymede here and Sir Thomas Long heard that cuckoo,° my man Trapdoor, sing the note of your ransom from captivity. *rescued you* / *in imminent danger* / *i.e., arresting officers* / *i.e., fool; intruder*

SIR BEAUTEOUS Uds so,° Moll, where's that Trapdoor? *God save my soul*

MOLL Hanged, I think, by this time. A justice° in this town, that speaks nothing but "Make a mittimus!° Away with him to Newgate!,"° used that rogue like a firework to run upon a line betwixt him and me.[3] *(Sir Alexander)* / *"Send him to prison!"* / *a famous prison*

OMNES How, how?

MOLL Marry, to lay trains[4] of villainy to blow up my life. I smelt the powder, spied what linstock° gave fire to shoot against the poor captain of the galley foist,[5] and away slid I my man like a shovel-board shilling.[6] He struts up and down the suburbs, I think, and eats up whores, feeds upon a bawd's garbage.[7] *staff for holding a match*

SIR THOMAS Sirrah Jack Dapper—

JACK DAPPER What say'st, Tom Long?

SIR THOMAS Thou hadst a sweet-faced boy hail-fellow° with thee to° your little Gull. How is he spent?[8] *on intimate terms* / *in the person of*

JACK DAPPER Troth, I whistled the poor little buzzard° off o'my fist,[9] because when he waited upon me at the ordinaries,° the gallants hit me i'the teeth still° and said I looked like a painted alderman's tomb, and the boy at my elbow like a death's-head.° Sirrah Jack, Moll[1]— *inferior hawk* / *eating houses* / *teased me incessantly* / *skull, memento mori*

MOLL What says my little Dapper?

SIR BEAUTEOUS Come, come, walk and talk, walk and talk.

JACK DAPPER Moll and I'll be i'the midst.

MOLL These knights° shall have squires' places,[2] belike, then. *(Beauteous and Thomas)*

5.1. A London street.
1. Dapper compares Moll's courage with that of Meg of Westminster, a legendary London heroine.
2. Officers of the Poultry Counter, a prison. Puttocks are kites, or small hawks. On the counters as prisons, see note at 3.3.81.
3. Used Trapdoor like a trail of gunpowder to lead to me.
4. (1) Stratagems; (2) lines of gunpowder.
5. Moll humorously characterizes herself as the captain of a state barge used in lord mayors' shows being assaulted by fireworks.
6. I quickly got my man, Trapdoor, out of the way, like a player at the game of shovel-board sliding (shuffling) his coin along the board.
7. He pimps for whores and devours their earnings, sponging off prostitution.
8. (1) Used up, consumed; (2) employed.
9. I.e., I dismissed him. (Terms from falconry.)
1. Dapper addresses Moll by both male and female names. (Cf. lines 1 and 55.)
2. They'll have places on the outside at both ends, where squires are supposed to stand.

Well, Dapper, what say you?

JACK DAPPER Sirrah Captain Mad Mary, the gull my own father—Dapper, Sir Davy—laid these London boot-halers,° the catchpoles,° in ambush to set upon me. *brigands* / *sergeants*

OMNES Your father? Away,° Jack! *i.e., You're kidding*

JACK DAPPER By the tassels of this handkercher, 'tis true; and what was his warlike stratagem, think you? He thought, because a wicker cage tames a nightingale, a lousy prison could make an ass of me.

OMNES A nasty plot.

JACK DAPPER Ay, as though a counter, which is a park in which all the wild beasts of the city run head by head, could tame me.[3]

Enter the Lord Noland.

MOLL Yonder comes my Lord Noland.

OMNES Save you, my lord.

LORD NOLAND Well met, gentlemen all, good Sir Beauteous Ganymede, Sir Thomas Long. And how does Master Dapper?

JACK DAPPER Thanks, my lord.

MOLL No tobacco, my lord?

LORD NOLAND No, faith, Jack.° *(Moll's male name)*

JACK DAPPER My Lord Noland, will you go to Pimlico° with us? We are making a boon° voyage to that nappy° land of spice-cakes. *the Pimlico Inn, Hoxton* / *prosperous / heady*

LORD NOLAND Here's such a merry ging,° I could find in my heart to sail to the World's End° with such company. Come, gentlemen, let's on. *gang* / *a tavern (with a pun)*

JACK DAPPER Here's most amorous° weather, my lord. *lovely*

OMNES Amorous weather? *They walk.*

JACK DAPPER Is not "amorous" a good word?

Enter Trapdoor, like a poor soldier, with a patch o'er one eye, and Tearcat with him, all tatters.

TRAPDOOR [*to Tearcat*] Shall we set upon the infantry, these troops of foot?[4] Zounds, yonder comes Moll, my whorish master and mistress. Would I had her kidneys between my teeth!

TEARCAT I had rather have a cow-heel.° *stewed cow foot (food)*

TRAPDOOR Zounds, I am so patched up she cannot discover° me. We'll on. *recognize*

TEARCAT *Alla corago,°* then. *Take courage*

TRAPDOOR [*to the group*] Good Your Honors and Worships, enlarge the ears of commiseration, and let the sound of a hoarse military organ-pipe penetrate your pitiful bowels to extract out of them so many small drops of silver° as may give a hard straw-bed lodging to a couple of maimed soldiers. *i.e., coins*

JACK DAPPER Where are you maimed?

TEARCAT In both our nether limbs.

MOLL Come, come, Dapper, let's give 'em something. 'Las,

3. Dapper's analogy compares a "counter," or prison, to a zoo. See 3.3.81 and note.

4. Trapdoor compares the persons he intends to hoodwink to enemy soldiers.

poor men! What money have you? By my troth, I love a soldier with my soul.

SIR BEAUTEOUS Stay, stay.—Where have you served?

SIR THOMAS In any part of the Low Countries?

TRAPDOOR Not in the Low Countries, if it please your manhood, but in Hungary against the Turk at the siege of Belgrade.

LORD NOLAND Who served there with you, sirrah?

TRAPDOOR Many Hungarians, Moldavians, Valachians, and Transylvanians, with some Sclavonians; and retiring home, sir, the Venetian galleys took us prisoners, yet freed us, and suffered us to beg up and down the country.

JACK DAPPER You have ambled all over Italy, then?

TRAPDOOR Oh, sir, from Venice to Roma, Vecchio,° Bononia, Romania, Bologna, Modena, Piacenza, and Tuscana° with all her cities, as Pistoia, Valteria, Mountepulchena,° Arrezzo, with the Siennois,° and divers others.

Vecchia / *Toscana* / *Montepulciana* / *citizens of Siena*

MOLL Mere rogues. Put spurs to 'em once more.

JACK DAPPER [*to Tearcat*] Thou look'st like a strange creature, a fat butter-box,° yet speak'st English. What are thou?

i.e., Dutchman

TEARCAT *Ick, mine here? Ick bin den ruffling Tearcat, den brave soldado. Ick bin dorick all Dutchlant gewesen. Der shellum das meere ine beasa, ine woert gaeb. Ick slaag um stroakes ou tom cop, dastick, den hundred touzun divell halle; frollick, mine here.*[5]

SIR BEAUTEOUS Here, here, let's be rid of their jabbering.

[*He starts to offer money to the beggars.*]

MOLL Not a cross,° Sir Beauteous.—You base rogues, I have taken measure of you, better than a tailor can, and I'll fit you,[6] as you—monster with one eye—have fitted me.

a coin of small value

TRAPDOOR Your Worship will not abuse a soldier!

MOLL Soldier? Thou deserv'st to be hanged up by that tongue which dishonors so noble a profession. Soldier, you skeldering° varlet? Hold, stand; there should be a trapdoor hereabouts. *Pull off his patch.*

begging; swindling

TRAPDOOR The balls of these glaziers° of mine—mine eyes—shall be shot° up and down in any hot piece of service for my invincible mistress.

eyes / *(like cannonballs)*

JACK DAPPER I did not think there had been such knavery in black patches as now I see.

MOLL Oh, sir, he hath been brought up in the Isle of Dogs,[7] and can both fawn like a spaniel and bite like a mastiff as he finds occasion.

LORD NOLAND [*to Tearcat*] What are you, sirrah? A bird of this feather too?

TEARCAT A man beaten from the wars, sir.

SIR THOMAS I think so, for you never stood° to fight.

stood your ground

JACK DAPPER What's thy name, fellow soldier?

5. I, good sir? I am the ruffling Tearcat, the brave soldier. I've traveled all over Germany. Whoever speaks angrily to me is a scoundrel. I give him blows to the head, enough for a hundred thousand devils; be merry, sir. (Stage German.)

6. (1) I'll settle your hash; (2) I'll measure you for clothes.

7. A lawless area downstream from London; also, the name of a lost satiric comedy by Thomas Nashe and others (1597).

TEARCAT I am called, by those that have seen my valor, Tearcat.

OMNES Tearcat?

MOLL A mere whip-jack,° and that is, in the commonwealth of rogues, a slave that can talk of sea-fight, name all your chief pirates, discover° more countries to you than either the Dutch, Spanish, French, or English ever found out; yet indeed all his service is by land, and that is to rob a fair, or some such venturous exploit. Tearcat! Foot, sirrah, I have your name, now I remember me, in my book of horners—horns for the thumb,[8] you know how.

bogus sailor; beggar / *make known*

TEARCAT No, indeed, Captain Moll—for I know you by sight—I am no such nipping° Christian, but a maunderer° upon the pad,° I confess; and meeting with honest° Trapdoor here, whom you had cashiered° from bearing arms, out at elbows under your colors,° I instructed him in the rudiments of roguery, and by my map made him sail over any country you can name, so that now he can maunder° better than myself.

purse-snatching / beggar / *road / worthy* / *dismissed from service* / *in tattered livery* / *beg*

JACK DAPPER So, then, Trapdoor, thou art turned soldier now.

TRAPDOOR Alas, sir, now there's no wars, 'tis the safest course of life I could take.

MOLL I hope then you can cant,° for by your cudgels, you, sirrah, are an upright man.°

speak underworld slang / *sturdy second-in-command*

TRAPDOOR As any walks the highway, I assure you.

MOLL And, Tearcat, what are you? A wild rogue, an angler, or a ruffler?[9]

TEARCAT Brother to this upright man, flesh and blood, ruffling Tearcat is my name, and a ruffler is my style, my title, my profession.

MOLL Sirrah, where's your doxy? Halt not° with me.

Don't hold back

OMNES Doxy, Moll? What's that?

MOLL His wench.

TRAPDOOR My doxy? I have, by the solomon,° a doxy that carries a kinchin-mort in her slate° at her back, besides my dell° and my dainty wild dell, with all whom I'll tumble this next darkmans° in the strommel,° and drink ben booze,° and eat a fat gruntling cheat, a cackling cheat, and a quacking cheat.[1]

mass / *little girl in a sheet* / *young girl* / *night / straw* / *good drink*

JACK DAPPER Here's old° cheating!

great, abundant

TRAPDOOR My doxy stays for me in a boozing ken, brave Captain.

MOLL He says his wench stays for him in an alehouse. [*To Trapdoor and Tearcat*] You are no pure rogues.°

beggars only

TEARCAT Pure rogues? No, we scorn to be pure rogues, but if you come to our libken,° or our stalling ken,[2] you shall find neither him nor me a queer cuffin.°

sleeping quarters / *churl, tramp*

MOLL So, sir, no churl of you.°

you're no tramp, then

TEARCAT No, but a ben cove,° a brave cove, a gentry cuffin.°

good chap / gentleman

LORD NOLAND Call you this canting?

8. A purse-snatcher would use horn thimbles to protect his thumb from his knife blade. (Also with a joke on cuckolding.)

9. A thief working independently, one who steals with a hooked pole, or a swaggering vagabond?

1. And eat a fat pig, a young rooster, and a duck. (Trapdoor is using underworld lingo.)

2. Our place for receiving stolen goods.

JACK DAPPER Zounds, I'll give a schoolmaster half a crown a week and° teach me this peddler's French. *if he*

TRAPDOOR Do but stroll, sir, half a harvest° with us, sir, and you shall gabble your bellyful. *thieving season*

MOLL Come, you rogue, cant with me.

SIR THOMAS Well said, Moll.—Cant with her, sirrah, and you shall have money; else not a penny.

TRAPDOOR I'll have a bout, if she please.

MOLL Come on, sirrah.

TRAPDOOR Ben mort, shall you and I heave a booth, mill a ken, or nip a bung? And then we'll couch a hogshead under the ruffmans, and there you shall wap with me, and I'll niggle with you.° *(translated at 195 ff.)*

MOLL Out, you damned impudent rascal! [*She flails at him.*]

TRAPDOOR Cut benar whids, and hold your fambles and your stamps![3]

LORD NOLAND Nay, nay, Moll, why art thou angry? What was his gibberish?

MOLL Marry, this, my lord. Says he: "Ben mort"—good wench —"shall you and I heave a booth, mill a ken, or nip a bung?"—shall you and I rob a house, or cut a purse?

OMNES Very good!

MOLL "And then we'll couch a hogshead under the ruff mans"—and then we'll lie under a hedge.

TRAPDOOR That was my desire, Captain, as 'tis fit a soldier should lie.° *i.e., in bivouac*

MOLL "And there you shall wap with me, and I'll niggle with you"—and that's all.

SIR BEAUTEOUS Nay, nay, Moll, what's that "wap"?

JACK DAPPER Nay, teach me what "niggling" is. I'd fain be niggling.

MOLL Wapping and niggling is all one. The rogue my man can tell you.

TRAPDOOR 'Tis fadoodling,° if it please you. *having sex*

SIR BEAUTEOUS This is excellent! One fit° more, good Moll. *stanza, canto*

MOLL Come, you rogue, sing with me.

THE SONG

MOLL A gage of ben Rom-booze° *quart pot of good wine*
In a boozing ken° of Rom-ville° *alehouse / London*
TEARCAT Is benar° than a caster,° *better / cloak*
Peck, pannam, lap, or poplar° *Food, bread, liquor, milk*
Which we mill° in Deuce-a-ville.° *steal / the country*
MOLL *and* TEARCAT Oh, I would lib° all the lightmans.° *lie / day*
Oh, I would lib all the darkmans,° *night*
By the solomon,° under the ruffmans,° *mass / woods*
By the solomon, in the harmans,° *stocks*
TEARCAT And scour the queer cramp-ring,° *wear fetters*
And couch till a palliard docked my dell,° *beggar screwed my girl*
So my boozy nab° might skew° Rome-booze well. *head / drink*

3. Speak civilly, and keep back your hands and your feet!

MOLL *and* TEARCAT Avast,° to the pad° let us bing,°
Avast, to the pad let us bing.[4] *Ahoy / road / go*

OMNES Fine knaves, i'faith.

JACK DAPPER The grating of ten new cart-wheels and the gruntling of five hundred hogs coming from Romford° market cannot make a worse noise than this canting language does in my ears. Pray, my Lord Noland, let's give these soldiers their pay. *(12 miles northeast)*

SIR BEAUTEOUS Agreed, and let them march.

LORD NOLAND [*giving money*] Here, Moll.

MOLL [*to Trapdoor and Tearcat*] Now I see that you are stalled to the rogue° and are not ashamed of your professions. Look you, my Lord Noland here and these gentlemen bestows upon you two two bords° and a half: that's two shillings sixpence. [*She gives them each money.*] *installed as rogues / shillings*

TRAPDOOR Thanks to Your Lordship.

TEARCAT Thanks, heroical Captain.

MOLL Away!

TRAPDOOR We shall cut ben whids° of your masters and mistress-ship wheresoever we come. *speak good words*

MOLL [*to Trapdoor*] You'll maintain, sirrah, the old justice's° plot to his face? *(Sir Alexander's)*

TRAPDOOR Else trine° me on the cheats:° hang me. *hang / gallows*

MOLL Be sure you meet me there.

TRAPDOOR Without any more maundering° I'll do't.—Follow, brave Tearcat. *muttering; begging*

TEARCAT *I prae, sequor.*° Let us go, mouse. *Go ahead, I'll follow*

Exeunt they two; manet the rest.° *the rest remain*

LORD NOLAND Moll, what was in that canting song?

MOLL Troth, my lord, only a praise of good drink, the only milk which these wild beasts love to suck; and thus it was:

A rich cup of wine,
Oh, it is juice divine,
More wholesome for the head
Than meat, drink, or bread.
To fill my drunken pate
With that, I'd sit up late;
By the heels would I lie,
Under a lousy hedge die,
Let a slave have a pull
At my whore, so I be full
Of that precious liquor—

and a parcel of such stuff, my lord, not worth the opening.° *unfolding*

Enter a Cutpurse very gallant, with four or five men after him, one with a wand.° *walking stick*

LORD NOLAND What gallant comes yonder?

SIR THOMAS Mass, I think I know him; 'tis one of Cumberland.° *a northern county*

FIRST CUTPURSE [*aside to his companions*] Shall we venture to shuffle in amongst yon heap of gallants, and strike?° *pick purses*

SECOND CUTPURSE 'Tis a question whether there be any silver

4. Moll paraphrases this song below in lines 255–65.

shells° amongst them, for all their satin outsides. *coins*

ALL THE CUTPURSES Let's try.

MOLL [*to the gentlemen*] Pox on him! A gallant? Shadow me? I know him: 'tis one that cumbers° the land indeed. If he swim near to the shore of any of your pockets, look to your purses. *burdens, troubles*

ALL THE GENTLEMEN Is't possible?

MOLL This brave fellow is no better than a foist.

ALL THE GENTLEMEN Foist? What's that?

MOLL A diver with two fingers: a pickpocket. All his train° study the figging law,° that's to say, cutting of purses and foisting. One of them is a nip;° I took him once i'the two-penny gallery at the Fortune.° Then there's a cloyer, or snap,[5] that dogs any new brother in that trade, and snaps will have half in any booty. He with the wand is both a stale,° whose office is to face° a man i'the streets whilst shells° are drawn by another; and then, with his black conjuring rod in his hand, he, by the nimbleness of his eye and juggling stick, will, in cheaping° a piece of plate at a goldsmith's stall, make four or five rings mount from the top of his caduceus,° and, as if it were at leapfrog, they skip into his hand presently. *crew* / *code of the cutpurse* / *cutpurse* / *a Bankside theater* / *decoy* / *chat with / coins* / *haggling over* / *wand*

SECOND CUTPURSE Zounds, we are smoked!° *smoked out, discovered*

ALL THE CUTPURSES Ha?

SECOND CUTPUSE We are boiled.° Pox on her! See Moll, the roaring drab.° *Our goose is cooked* / *whore*

FIRST CUTPURSE All the diseases of sixteen hospitals boil° her! Away! [*They start to leave, but Moll intercepts them.*] *inflame, infect*

MOLL [*to the First Cutpurse*] Bless you, sir.

FIRST CUTPURSE And you, good sir.

MOLL Dost not ken° me, man? *know*

FIRST CUTPURSE No, trust° me, sir. *believe*

MOLL Heart, there's a knight to whom I'm bound for many favors, lost his purse at the last new play i'the Swan°—seven angels° in't. Make it good, you're best;[6] do you see? No more. *a Bankside theater* / *gold coins*

FIRST CUTPURSE A synagogue[7] shall be called, Mistress Mary. Disgrace me not. *Pacus palabros.* I will conjure[8] for you; farewell. [*Exeunt Cutpurses.*]

MOLL Did not I tell you, my lord?

LORD NOLAND I wonder how thou cam'st to the knowledge of these nasty villains.

SIR THOMAS And why do the foul mouths of the world call thee Moll Cutpurse? A name, methinks, damned and odious.

MOLL Dare any step forth to my face and say,
"I have ta'en thee doing so,° Moll"? I must confess, *such and such*
In younger days, when I was apt to stray,
I have sat amongst such adders, seen their stings—
As any here might—and in full playhouses
Watched their quick-diving hands, to bring to shame
Such rogues, and in that stream met an ill name.[9]

5. The one who receives the stolen purse.
6. You'd be well advised to return the money.
7. A meeting (of thieves, to discuss what Moll has demanded).
8. Few words suffice. I will perform wonders. ("*Pacus palabros*" is the First Cutpurse's approximation of the Spanish *pocas palabras.*)
9. And in the course of events I acquired a bad reputation. (Moll insists that her only reason for keeping company with thieves was to expose them.)

When next, my lord, you spy any one of those,
So he be in his art a scholar,[1] question him,
Tempt him with gold to open the large book
Of his close° villainies; and you yourself shall cant — *secret*
Better than poor Moll can, and know more laws
Of cheaters, lifters, nips, foists, puggards, curbers,° — *pickpockets and thieves*
Withal the devil's black guard,° than it is fit — *attendant guard in black*
Should be discovered to a noble wit.
I know they have their orders, offices,° — *functions*
Circuits, and circles, unto which they are bound,
To raise° their own damnation in. — *conjure up*

JACK DAPPER How dost thou know it?

MOLL As you do. I show it you; they to me show it.
Suppose, my lord, you were in Venice.

LORD NOLAND Well.

MOLL If some Italian pander there would tell
All the close tricks of courtesans, would not you
Hearken to such a fellow?

LORD NOLAND Yes.

MOLL And here,
Being come from Venice, to a friend most dear
That were to travel thither, you would proclaim
Your knowledge in those villainies to save
Your friend from their quick danger: must you have
A black ill name because ill things you know?
Good troth, my lord, I am made Moll Cutpurse so.
How many are whores in small° ruffs and still° looks? — *puritanical / demure*
How many chaste, whose names fill Slander's books?
Were all men cuckolds whom gallants in their scorns
Call so, we should not walk for goring horns.[2]
Perhaps for my mad going° some reprove me; — *zany goings-on*
I please myself, and care not else who loves me.

ALL THE GENTLEMEN A brave mind, Moll, i'faith!

SIR THOMAS Come, my lord, shall 's to the ordinary?° — *eating house*

LORD NOLAND Ay, 'tis noon, sure.

MOLL Good my lord, let not my name° condemn me to you or to the world. A fencer, I hope,° may be called a coward; is he so for that? If all that have ill names in London were to be whipped and to pay but twelvepence apiece to the beadle, I would rather have his office than a constable's.[3] — *reputation / expect*

JACK DAPPER So would I, Captain Moll. 'Twere° a sweet tickling° office, i'faith! *Exeunt.* — *It would be / gratifying*

[5.2]

Enter Sir Alexander Wengrave, Goshawk, and Greenwit, and others.

SIR ALEXANDER My son marry a thief? That impudent girl
Whom all the world stick their worst eyes upon?

1. Provided he be proficient in his calling.
2. We would be wary of walking about, out of fear of being wounded by the horns on so many cuckolds' heads.
3. If all those who have unsavory reputations were sentenced to receive whippings and then pay a fine of twelvepence to the minor official (the beadle) whose menial job it is to whip offenders against the law, then I would rather be that beadle than a higher-ranking constable.
5.2. Sir Alexander's house.

GREENWIT How will your care prevent it?
GOSHAWK 'Tis impossible.
They marry close;° they're gone, but none knows whither. *secretly*
SIR ALEXANDER Oh, gentlemen, when has a father's heartstrings
Held out so long from breaking?

Enter a Servant.

Now, what news, sir?
SERVANT They were met upo' th'water an hour since, sir,
Putting in towards the Sluice.[1]
SIR ALEXANDER The Sluice? Come, gentlemen,
'Tis Lambeth works against us. [*Exit Servant.*]
GREENWIT And that Lambeth joins more mad matches than your six wet towns 'twixt that and Windsor Bridge, where fares lie soaking.[2]
SIR ALEXANDER Delay no time, sweet gentlemen! To Blackfriars!° We'll take a pair of oars° and make after 'em. *a river landing / rowers*

Enter Trapdoor.

TRAPDOOR Your son, and that bold masculine ramp,° my mistress, are landed now at Tower.° *hussy* / *the Tower of London*
SIR ALEXANDER Heyday, at Tower?
TRAPDOOR I heard it now reported. [*He retires.*]
SIR ALEXANDER Which way, gentlemen, shall I bestow my care?
I'm drawn in pieces betwixt deceit and shame.

Enter Sir [Guy] Fitzallard.

SIR GUY Sir Alexander,
You're well met, and most rightly served:
My daughter was a scorn° to you. *object of scorn*
SIR ALEXANDER Say not so, sir.
SIR GUY A very abject she, poor gentlewoman!
Your house had been° dishonored. Give you joy, sir, *would have been*
Of your son's gaskin-bride.° You'll be a grandfather shortly *bride in knee breeches*
To a fine crew of roaring sons and daughters;
'Twill help to stock the suburbs° passing° well, sir. *(see 2.1.346 n) / very*
SIR ALEXANDER Oh, play not with the miseries of my heart!
Wounds should be dressed and healed, not vexed or left
Wide open, to the anguish of the patient,
And scornful air° let in; rather let pity *(thought bad for wounds)*
And advice charitably help to refresh 'em.° *heal the wounds*
SIR GUY Who'd place his charity so unworthily,
Like one that gives alms to a cursing beggar?
Had I but found one spark of goodness in you
Toward my deserving child, which then grew fond
Of your son's virtues, I had eased° you now. *would have relieved*
But I perceive both fire of youth and goodness
Are raked up° in the ashes of your age, *smothered*

1. The Sluice and Lambeth Marsh (line 9) are across the Thames from London.
2. The "wet," or river, towns upstream from London were frequently sought out by eloping or adulterous couples because of lax regulations there. River taxi customers (called "fares") might also get wet from their travel on the rivers, or they might soak in hot tubs in the river towns to cure syphilis.

Else no such shame should have come near your house,
Nor such ignoble sorrow touch your heart.
SIR ALEXANDER If not for worth,° for pity's sake assist me! *my deserving*
GREENWIT You urge a thing past sense. How can he help you?
All his assistance is as frail as ours,
Full as uncertain. Where's the place that holds 'em?° *Where are they?*
One brings us water news; then comes another
With a full-charged mouth, like a culverin's° voice, *cannon's*
And he reports the Tower. Whose sounds are truest?
GOSHAWK [*to Sir Guy*] In vain you flatter him.°—Sir Alexander— *raise his hopes*
SIR GUY I flatter him? Gentlemen, you wrong me grossly.
GREENWIT [*aside to Goshawk*] He does it well,[3] i'faith.
SIR GUY Both news are false,
Of Tower or water. They took no such way yet.
SIR ALEXANDER Oh, strange! Hear you this, gentlemen? Yet more plunges?° *crises*
SIR GUY They're nearer than you think for,° yet more close *suppose*
Than if they were further off.
SIR ALEXANDER How am I lost in these distractions!
SIR GUY For° your speeches, gentlemen, *As for*
In taxing° me for rashness: 'fore you all, *criticizing*
I will engage° my state to half his° wealth, *pledge / (Sir Alexander's)*
Nay, to his son's revenues, which are less,
And yet nothing at all till they come from him,[4]
That I could, if my will stuck to my power,° *if I could effect my wish*
Prevent this marriage yet, nay, banish her° *(the bride)*
Forever from his thoughts, much more his arms.
SIR ALEXANDER Slack not° this goodness, though you heap upon me *Do not hold back*
Mountains of malice and revenge hereafter!
I'd willingly resign up half my state° to him, *estate*
So° he would marry the meanest° drudge I hire. *Provided / lowliest*
GREENWIT [*to Sir Alexander*] He talks impossibilities, and you believe 'em!
SIR GUY I talk no more than I know how to finish;
My fortunes else are his that dares stake with me.[5]
The poor young gentleman I love and pity;
And to keep shame from him—because the spring
Of his affection was my daughter's first,° *first love*
Till his° frown blasted all—do but estate him[6] *(Sir Alexander's)*
In those possessions which your love and care
Once pointed out° for him, that he may have room *designated*
To entertain fortunes of noble birth,
Where now his desperate wants casts him upon her;[7]
And if I do not, for his own sake chiefly,
Rid him of this disease[8] that now grows on him,

3. Sir Guy does well at playing the role of the injured father. (All are in on a trick to fool Sir Alexander.)
4. And entirely valueless until his father dies and he actually inherits.
5. If I'm not as good as my word, my entire fortune goes to that man who dares to bet with me.
6. I propose that you, Sir Alexander, vest him with full legal title.
7. His needs cast Sebastian on Moll, making him dependent on her.
8. The disease of Moll; also, of this financial need.

I'll forfeit my whole state, before these gentlemen.
GREENWIT Troth, but you shall not undertake such matches.
We'll persuade° so much with you. *plead*
SIR ALEXANDER [*giving a ring to Sir Guy*] Here's my ring;
He will believe this token. 'Fore these gentlemen,
I will confirm it fully: all those lands
My first love° 'lotted him he shall straight possess *My love originally*
In that refusal.° *When he refuses Moll*
SIR GUY If I change it not,[9]
Change me into a beggar.
GREENWIT Are you mad, sir?
SIR GUY 'Tis done.° *It's a deal*
GOSHAWK Will you undo yourself by doing,
And show a prodigal° trick in your old days? *extravagant; youthful*
SIR ALEXANDER 'Tis a match, gentlemen.
SIR GUY Ay, ay, sir, ay.
I ask no favor, trust to you for none.
My hope rests in the goodness of your son. *Exit Fitzallard.*
GREENWIT [*aside to Goshawk*] He holds it up° well yet. *Sir Guy plays his part*
GOSHAWK [*aside to Greenwit*] Of an old knight, i'faith.
SIR ALEXANDER Curst be the time I laid his first love barren,° *thwarted his first love*
Wilfully barren, that before this hour
Had° sprung forth fruits of comfort and of honor! *Would have*
He loved a virtuous gentlewoman.

Enter Moll [*dressed as a man*].

GOSHAWK Life, here's Moll.
GREENWIT Jack!
GOSHAWK How dost thou, Jack?
MOLL How dost thou, gallant?
SIR ALEXANDER [*to Moll*] Impudence, where's my son?
MOLL Weakness, go look° him. *look for*
SIR ALEXANDER Is this your wedding gown?[1]
MOLL The man talks monthly.° *(like a lunatic)*
Hot broth and a dark chamber° for the knight; *(cures for madmen)*
I see he'll be stark mad at our next meeting. *Exit Moll.*
GOSHAWK Why, sir, take comfort now, there's no such matter;
No priest will marry her, sir, for a woman,
Whiles that shape's on; and it was never known
Two men were married and conjoined in one.
Your son hath made some shift° to love another. *device; change*
SIR ALEXANDER Whate'er she be, she has my blessing with her.
May they be rich and fruitful, and receive
Like comfort to their issue° as I take in them! *in their children*
He's pleased me now, marrying not this;° *(Moll)*
Through a whole world he could not choose amiss.
GREENWIT Glad you're so penitent for your former sin, sir.

9. If I don't prevent this marriage to Moll.
1. Sir Alexander is outraged to think that Moll would marry in men's apparel.

GOSHAWK Say he should take a wench with her smock-dowry,[2]
No portion° with her but her lips and arms? *dowry*
SIR ALEXANDER Why, who thrive better, sir? They have most blessing,
Though other have more wealth, and least repent.[3]
Many that want most° know the most content. *are most in need*
GREENWIT Say he should marry a kind youthful sinner?
SIR ALEXANDER Age will quench that. Any offense but theft
And drunkenness—nothing but death can wipe away;
Their sins are green even when their heads are gray.[4]
Nay, I despair not now; my heart's cheered, gentlemen.
No face can come unfortunately° to me. *can be unwelcome*

Enter a Servant.

Now, sir, your news?
SERVANT Your son with his fair bride
Is near at hand.
SIR ALEXANDER Fair may their fortunes be!
GREENWIT Now you're resolved,° sir, it was never she?° *satisfied / (Moll)*
SIR ALEXANDER I find it in the music of my heart.

Enter Moll [dressed as a woman], masked, in Sebastian's hand,° and [Sir Guy] Fitzallard. *her hand in his*

See where they come.
GOSHAWK A proper lusty° presence, sir. *pleasing, cheerful*
SIR ALEXANDER Now has he pleased me right. I always counseled him
To choose a goodly personable creature.
Just of her pitch° was my first wife, his mother. *height*
SEBASTIAN [*kneeling*] Before I dare discover° my offense, *reveal, declare*
I kneel for pardon.
SIR ALEXANDER My heart gave it thee
Before thy tongue could ask it.
Rise. Thou hast raised my joy to greater height
Than to that seat where grief dejected it.° [*Sebastian rises.*] *cast it down*
Both welcome to my love and care forever!
Hide not my happiness too long; all's pardoned.
Here are our friends.—Salute her, gentlemen.
They unmask her.
OMNES Heart, who's this, Moll?
SIR ALEXANDER Oh, my reviving shame! Is't I must live,
To be struck blind? Be it the work of sorrow,
Before age take't in hand![5]
SIR GUY [*to Sir Alexander*] Darkness and death!
Have you deceived me thus? Did I engage
My whole estate for this?
SIR ALEXANDER You asked no favor,
And you shall find as little. Since my comforts

2. I.e., with a dowry consisting of her clothes only.
3. And they least regret their marriage.
4. Age will correct youthful sins, all but theft and drunkenness—nothing but death can wipe away these sins; they stay fresh even in gray-headed old age.
5. Let sorrow blind me (with tears) and end my life before age does its work!

Play false with me, I'll be as cruel to thee
As grief to fathers' hearts.
MOLL Why, what's the matter with you,
'Less° too much joy should make your age forgetful? *Unless*
Are you too well, too happy?
SIR ALEXANDER With a vengeance!
MOLL Methinks you should be proud of such a daughter—
As good a man as your son.
SIR ALEXANDER Oh, monstrous impudence!
MOLL You had no note° before, an unmarked° knight; *reputation / unregarded*
Now all the town will take regard on you,
And all your enemies fear you for my sake.
You may pass where you list,° through crowds most thick, *please, choose*
And come off bravely with your purse unpicked.
You do not know the benefits I bring with me:
No cheat dares work upon you, with thumb or knife,
While you've a roaring girl to your son's wife.
SIR ALEXANDER A devil rampant!° *rearing up fiercely*
SIR GUY [*to Sir Alexander*] Have you so much charity
Yet to release me of my last rash bargain,
An° I'll give in° your pledge? *If / release you from*
SIR ALEXANDER No, sir, I stand to't.
I'll work upon advantage, as all mischiefs
Do upon me.[6]
SIR GUY Content.—Bear witness all, then:
His° are the lands, and so contention ends. *(Sebastian's)*
Here comes your son's bride, 'twixt two noble friends.

Enter the Lord Noland and Sir Beauteous Ganymede, with Mary Fitzallard between them, the citizens [Tiltyard, Openwork, Gallipot] and their wives with them.

MOLL [*to Sir Alexander*] Now are you gulled as you would be.° Thank me for't; *would wish to be*
I'd a forefinger in't.
SEBASTIAN [*kneeling*] Forgive me, father.
Though there before your eyes my sorrow feigned,
This° still was she for whom true love complained. *(Mary)*
SIR ALEXANDER Blessings eternal, and the joys of angels,
Begin your peace here, to be signed in heaven!
[*Sebastian rises.*]
How short my sleep of sorrow seems now to me
To° this eternity of boundless comforts, *Compared with*
That finds no want but utterance and expression!° *That words can't express*
[*To Lord Noland*] My lord, your office here appears so honorably,
So full of ancient° goodness, grace, and worthiness, *venerable*
I never took more joy in sight of man
Than in your comfortable presence now.
LORD NOLAND Nor I more delight in doing grace to virtue
Than in this worthy gentlewoman, your son's bride,
Noble Fitzallard's daughter, to whose honor
And modest fame° I am a servant vowed; *reputation*

6. I'll take whatsoever advantage I can, since evils similarly conspire against me.

So is this knight.° (Sir Beauteous)
SIR ALEXANDER Your loves make my joys proud.
[*To Servant*] Bring forth those deeds of land my care laid
ready, [*The Servant fetches the deeds.*]
[*To Sir Guy*] And which, old knight, thy nobleness may
challenge,° *lay claim to*
Joined with thy daughter's virtues, whom I prize now
As dearly as that flesh I call mine own.
[*To Mary*] Forgive me, worthy gentlewoman; 'twas my blindness.
When I rejected thee, I saw thee not;
Sorrow and willful rashness grew like films
Over the eyes of judgment, now so clear
I see the brightness of thy worth appear.
MARY Duty and love may I deserve in those,° *in your eyes*
And all my wishes have a perfect close.
SIR ALEXANDER That tongue can never err, the sound's so sweet.
[*He gives Sebastian the deeds.*]
Here, honest son, receive into thy hands
The keys of wealth, possession of those lands
Which my first care provided; they're thine own.
Heaven give thee a blessing with 'em! The best joys
That can in worldly shapes to man betide
Are fertile lands and a fair fruitful bride,
Of which I hope thou'rt sped.° *provided*
SEBASTIAN I hope so too, sir.
MOLL Father and son, I ha' done you simple service here.
SEBASTIAN For which thou shalt not part, Moll, unrequited.
SIR ALEXANDER Thou art a mad girl, and yet I cannot now
Condemn thee.
MOLL Condemn me? Troth, an you should, sir,
I'd make you seek out one to hang in my room:
I'd give you the slip at gallows, and cozen° the people. *cheat*
[*To Lord Noland*] Heard you this jest, my lord?
LORD NOLAND What is it, Jack?
MOLL He was in fear his son would marry me,
But never dreamt that I would ne'er agree.
LORD NOLAND Why? Thou hadst a suitor once. Jack, when
wilt marry?
MOLL Who I, my lord? I'll tell you when, i'faith:
When you shall hear
Gallants void from sergeants' fear,° *fear of arrest*
Honesty and truth unslandered,
Woman manned° but never pandered, *provided with a man*
Cheaters booted but not coached,[7]
Vessels° older ere they're broached.° *Drinking vessels / opened*
If my mind be then not varied,
Next day following, I'll be married.
LORD NOLAND This sounds like doomsday.
MOLL Then were marriage best,
For if I should repent, I were soon at rest.[8]
SIR ALEXANDER In troth, thou'rt a good wench. I'm sorry now

7. Thieves outfitted with (stolen) boots but not with luxurious carriages.

8. Doomsday is the best time to marry, since a mistake will soon be over.

The opinion was so hard I conceived of thee.
Some wrongs I've done thee.

Enter Trapdoor.

TRAPDOOR [*aside*] Is the wind there, now?[9]
'Tis time for me to kneel and confess first,
For fear it come too late, and my brains feel it.°— *my head is beaten*
Upon my paws I ask you pardon, mistress. [*He kneels.*]
MOLL Pardon? For what, sir? What has Your Rogueship done now?
TRAPDOOR I have been from time to time hired to confound you, by this old gentleman.° *(Sir Alexander)*
MOLL How?
TRAPDOOR [*rising*] Pray forgive him;
But, may I counsel you, you should never do't.[1]
Many a snare to entrap Your Worship's life
Have I laid privily—chains, watches, jewels—
And when he saw nothing could mount you up,° *up to the gallows*
Four hollow-hearted angels° he then gave you, *gold coins*
By which he meant to trap you, I to° save you. *whereas I meant to*
SIR ALEXANDER To all which shame and grief in me cry guilty.
Forgive me now! I cast the world's eyes° from me, *worldly opinion*
And look upon thee freely with mine own.
I see the most of many wrongs before thee° *displayed before you*
Cast from the jaws of Envy and her people,° *her retinue*
And nothing foul but that. I'll nevermore
Condemn by common voice, for that's the whore
That deceives man's opinion, mocks his trust,
Cozens his love, and makes his heart unjust.
MOLL [*showing money*] Here be the angels, gentlemen; they were given me
As a musician. I pursue° no pity; *seek*
Follow the law. An you can cuck me,[2] spare not!
Hang up my viol by me, and I care not.
SIR ALEXANDER So far I'm sorry, I'll thrice double 'em° *(the gold coins)*
To make thy wrongs amends.—
Come, worthy friends, my honorable lord,
Sir Beauteous Ganymede, and noble Fitzallard,
And you, kind gentlewomen,° whose sparkling presence *(the citizens' wives)*
Are glories set in marriage—beams° of society, *rays of light*
For all your loves give luster to my joys.
The happiness of this day shall be remembered
At the return of every smiling spring;
In my time now 'tis born, and may no sadness
Sit on the brows of men upon that day,
But as I am, so all go pleased away![3] [*Exeunt, except Moll.*]

9. Trapdoor sees at once the new state of affairs. He may have been lurking backstage only to come forward at this point; what is marked in this edition at line 18 as his retiring from view is not in the quarto edition, and his movements are uncertain.

1. But on second thought, my advice is that you shouldn't forgive him after all.

2. If you can set me in the cucking stool. (Used as a punishment for scolding women and minor lawbreakers—in this case, for holding counterfeit coins.)

3. Let everyone (including the audience) go away as pleased as I am!

Epilogus

MOLL A painter having drawn with curious° art *[intricate]*
The picture of a woman—every part
Limned° to the life—hung out the piece to sell. *[Drawn]*
People who passed along, viewing it well,
Gave several° verdicts on it. Some dispraised *[various]*
The hair; some said the brows too high were raised;
Some hit her o'er the lips, misliked their color;
Some wished her nose were shorter; some, the eyes fuller;
Others said roses on her cheeks should grow,
Swearing they looked too pale; others cried no.
The workman still, as fault was found, did mend it,
In hope to please all; but this work being ended
And hung open at stall, it was so vile,
So monstrous, and so ugly, all men did smile
At the poor painter's folly. Such we doubt° *[fear]*
Is this our comedy. Some perhaps do flout° *[condemn]*
The plot, saying, 'tis too thin, too weak, too mean;° *[lowly; slender]*
Some for the person° will revile the scene, *[(Moll)]*
And wonder that a creature of her being
Should be the subject of a poet, seeing,
In the world's eye, none weighs so light; others look
For all those base tricks published in a book—
Foul as his brains they flowed from—of cutpurses,
Of nips and foists, nasty, obscene discourses,
As full of lies, as empty of worth or wit,
For any honest ear, or eye unfit.
And thus,
If we to every brain that's humorous° *[notional]*
Should fashion scenes, we, with the painter, shall,
In striving to please all, please none at all.
Yet for such faults as either the writer's wit
Or negligence of the actors do commit,
Both crave your pardons. If what both have done
Cannot full pay your expectation,
The Roaring Girl herself, some few days hence,
Shall on this stage give larger recompence;
Which mirth that you may share in, herself does woo you,
And craves this sign: your hands° to beckon her to you. *[applauding hands]*
[*Exit.*]

FINIS.

TEXTUAL NOTES

The Roaring Girl was entered in the Stationers' Register on February 18, 1612, having been published in quarto in the previous year. The printer, not named on the title page, was Nicholas Okes. The publisher was Thomas Archer. A friend of his named Ambrose Garbrand was fined for having the book printed before it was officially entered in the Stationers' Register. The 1611 quarto is the only known early edition of the play and is the basis of this present edition. Substantive departures from it are noted here, using the following abbreviations:

Q: The quarto (London: Thomas Archer, 1611)
Q corr.: The corrected quarto
Q uncorr.: The uncorrected quarto
ed.: A modern editor's emendation

Dramatis Personae [placement, ed.; after Prologue in Q] **2, 8 Wengrave** [Q: *Wentgraue*] 2 NEATFOOT [Q: *Neats-foot*] **14–17 *cives . . . uxores*** [Q: Ciues & Vxores]

Prologus 1 PROLOGUE [ed.; not in Q]

1.1.22 dined [ed.] dyed [Q] 28 SD [placement, ed.; after 27 in Q] **32 slightly** [ed.] sleightly [Q] **34 i'th'soul** [Q: ith the soule] **36 fire** [ed.; not in Q] **38 say'st** [Q corr.: saist] saith [Q uncorr.] **79** [and elsewhere] **lose** [Q: loose]

1.2.0.2 *Goshawk* [Q: Goshake] **2 too** [Q: to] **4** [and elsewhere] **off** [Q: of] **23 merrily** [Q: merily] **30 floor** [ed.] flowre [Q] **58.1** [placement, ed.; opposite 57 in Q] **83 winds** [ed.] wind, [Q] **91 talked** [ed.] talke [Q] **156 Their . . . their** [Q: There . . . there] **161** [and elsewhere] **Would** [Q: wod] **165 wooed** [Q: wood] **169 Wear** [Q: were] **195 H'as** [Q: has] **245 Rafe . . . Rafe** [Q: *Raph . . . Raph*]

2.1.11 [and elsewhere] **bankrupt** [Q: bankrout] **32** [and elsewhere] **woo** [Q: woe] **74 he's** [Q: h'as] **98.1** [placement, ed.; opposite 99 in Q] **139** [and elsewhere] **errand** [Q: arrant] **149** MRS. [Q: *M.*] **159 henchboy** [Q: hinch boy] **164 snail** [ed.] snake [Q] **174 Heyday** [Q: Haida] **179 arrant'st** [Q: arrants] **189 pooh** [Q: puh] **199 marrowbone** [Q: maribone] **206 an** [ed.] an an [Q] **229.1** [placement, ed.; opposite 230 in Q] **235 i'th'** [Q: ith the] **254.1** [placement, ed.; opposite 250 in Q] **283** [and elsewhere] **Whither** [Q1: Whether] **285** [and throughout] **Brentford** [Q: *Brainford*] **312 heard** [ed.] hard [Q] **312 Antholin's** [Q: Antlings] **348 quit** [Q: quite] **352 burr** [Q: burgh] **352.1** [placement, ed.; opposite "Mass . . . is" in 353 in Q] **375.1** [placement, ed.; opposite 373 in Q] **375.1 *Moll*** [ed.] Mols [Q] **393.1** [placement, ed.; opposite 394 in Q] **397** [and elsewhere] **Who's** Whose **410** MRS. OPENWORK [Q 2nd stage corr.: *Mist Open.*] *Mist. Gal.* [Q 1st stage corr. and uncorr.] **411** GALLIPOT [Q 2nd stage corr.: *Maist. Gal.*] *Maist. Tilt.* [Q 1st stage corr. and uncorr.] **413, 417** TILTYARD [Q 2nd stage corr.: *Maist. Tilt.*] *Maist. Gal.* [Q 1st stage corr. and uncorr.] **413, 414, 415 Hoxton** [Q: Hogsden] **417 SD** [placement, ed.; opposite 416 in Q] **422–24 Hey** [Q: he]

2.2.18.1 [and elsewhere] *viol* [Q: *viall*] **27 They're** [Q: the're] **80 Heyday** [Q: Hoyda] **125 bewitched** [ed.] bewitch [Q] **159 Forseek** [ed.] For seeke [Q]

3.1.10 frampold [Q: phrampell] **11 you** [ed.] your [Q] **13** [and elsewhere] **vile** [Q: vilde] **22 scent** [Q: sent] **59 SD** [placement, ed.; after 60 in Q] **93 their** [Q: there] **115 slanderers** [ed.] slanders [Q] **116.1** [placement, ed.; opposite 117 in Q] **127 voyage** [Q: viage] **163 Yea** [Q: Ye] **166 SD *Fillips*** [Q: *Philips*]

3.2.12 What is't [ed.] whats ist [Q] **13 Heyday** [Q: hoyda] **29 Fie, fie!** [Q: fih—fih] **31 sting** [ed.] sing [Q] **57 Demophoon** [Q: Demophon] **80 beshrew** [Q: beshrow] **137 wrestle** [Q: wrastle] **138 sleight** [Q: slight] **160 smooth** [Q: smoth] **250 lain** [Q: line] **255 By' Lady** [Q: Be Lady] **268.1 *Exit Master Gal-***

lipot [ed.] *Exit* Maister Gallipot *and his wife* [after "him" in 268 in Q] **272 SD** ***Exeunt*** [ed.] *Exit Laxton* [Q]

3.3.19, 20 mail [Q: male] **66 tail** [Q: tale] **73, 77, 116 SIR ALEXANDER *and* SIR ADAM** [ed.] *Both* [Q] **87 their** [Q: there] **103 be placed** [ed.] beg plac't [Q] **115 sprites** [ed.] spirits [Q] **158, 171, 174, 176 CURTALAX *and* HANGER** [ed.] *Both* [Q] **164 flay** [Q: flea] **190 Carrion?** [Q: Carry on?] **215 MOLL *and* TRAPDOOR** [ed.] *Both* [Q] **215 sergeant** [Q: Serieant] **226 Shoo** [Q: Shu]

4.1.4 SD [placement, ed.; opposite 3 in Q] **16 lanterns** [Q: lanthornes] **40 straits** [Q: streights] **92 hang** [ed.] hung [Q] **104.1 THE SONG** [placement, ed.; opposite 106 in Q] **145 ballads** [Q: ballets] **148 wardrobes** [Q: wardrops] **154 sigh** [ed.] sight [Q] **155 Will't** [ed.] wilt [Q]

4.2.21 agate [Q: agget] **56 Then** [ed.] *Mist.Open.* Then [Q] **57 the head** [Q uncorr.] head [Q corr.] **61 deal they** [Q 1st stage uncorr.] they deale [Q corr.] **81 liquoring** [Q: lickering] **125 vilest** [Q: vild'st] **133 sprites** [ed.] spirits [Q] **135 them** [ed.] then [Q] **145 MRS. GALLIPOT** [ed.] *Mist. Open.* [Q] **190 Ud's** [Q: Vd'] **216 Besides** [Q uncorr.] beside [Q corr.] **242 core** [ed.] chore [Q] **243 ay** [Q: I] **255.1 *summoner*** [Q: *Somner*] **258 snuffling** [ed.] snaffling [Q] **279 vagary** [Q: fagary] **289, 290, 293, 295 an hundred** [Q: a 100] **318 gelt** [ed.] Get [Q]

5.1.19 struts [Q: stroutes] **102 *gewesen*** [ed.] *Gueresen* [Q] **106 jabbering** [Q: iobbering] **161 kinchin** [ed.] kitchin [Q] **161 slate** [Q: slat] **164 booze** [ed.] baufe [Q] **173, 222** [and elsewhere] **queer** [Q: quire] **175 cove . . . cove** [Q: caue . . . caue] **212.1 THE SONG** [placement, ed.; opposite 218 in Q] **213 MOLL** [ed.; not in Q] **216 pannam** [Q: pennam] **216 lap** [ed.] lay [Q] **218, 225 MOLL *and* TEARCAT** [ed.; not in Q] **221 harmans** [ed.] Hartmans [Q] **229 Romford** [Q: Rumford] **235 stalled** [Q: stal'd] **274, 295 ALL THE CUTPURSES** [ed.] *Omnes* [Q] **279, 281, 352 ALL THE GENTLEMEN** [ed.] *Omnes* [Q]

5.2.6 SD [placement, ed.; after 5 in Q] **17 Heyday** [Q: Hoyda] **26 gaskin-bride** [Q: Gaskoyne-Bride] **126 Their . . . their** [Q: There . . . there] **128.1** [placement, ed.; opposite "news?" in 129 in Q] **145 who's this, Moll?** [ed.] who this *Mol*? [Q] **206 they're** [Q: thei'r] **227 Cheaters** [ed.] Cheates [Q] **254 thee** [ed.] hee [Q] **263 viol** [Q: vyall] **268 gentlewomen** [ed.] Gentlewoman [Q]

Epilogus 1 MOLL [ed.; not in Q] **3 Limned** [Q: Limb'd] **37 woo** [Q: woe]

A Chaste Maid in Cheapside

A Chaste Maid in Cheapside was produced in 1613 by an adult acting company, unlike most of Thomas Middleton's earlier comedies, which were written for boy actors in the private theaters.[1] This may help us understand why the play is so richly colorful and broad-gauge as a snapshot of London. The play is, exuberantly, a city comedy, celebrating and also laughing at the varied bustle of that thriving metropolis. It pokes fun at prosperous shopkeepers, at their talkative and poorly educated wives, at their witless sons who have been sent up to Cambridge to study, at hapless cuckolded husbands whose wives serve as mistresses to the rich, at younger sons of the gentry forced by lack of inherited wealth to live by their wits, at social regulations like those forbidding the eating of meat during Lent, and above all at the increasingly visible presence of Puritans in the social landscape. Much of this comic bustle centers around Cheapside, the chief commercial street running east from Saint Paul's Cathedral through the heart of old London.

The play's satire of Puritans suggests something of weighty importance that was happening in the London theater. The city itself was generally sympathetic to reform movements in, or even separate from, the English church. Puritan-leaning pamphleteers had long been uneasy with a theater that indulged in a kind of hedonistic irreverence at the expense of sobriety, religiosity, and hard work. London's civic and ecclesiastical authorities did what they could to restrict theatrical activity, by censorship and by taking advantage of times of unusual plague activity to close theaters. Had it not been for the support of highly placed patrons such as the Lady Elizabeth (see note 1) and other members of the royal family, the theater would scarcely have been able to defend itself against its vociferous critics.

Under these circumstances, the theater in London focused increasingly on attracting courtly and sophisticated audiences. The satire that had been the special purview of the boy companies in the so-called private theaters increasingly became the stock in trade of the adult actors as well. Ben Jonson's *The Alchemist*, acted in 1610 by the King's Men, is unsparing in its attack on Tribulation Wholesome, chief elder of a Puritan sect from Amsterdam. Jonson's *Bartholomew Fair*, acted in 1614 by the Lady Elizabeth's Men, includes a scathing caricature of a pompous Puritan hypocrite, Zeal-of-the-land Busy. At the same time, for economic reasons the adult actors did not want to alienate their city audiences unnecessarily. Because they were walking a fine line, some of their liveliest plays balance a satire of religious hypocrisy with a warm and generous celebration of London life in all its fullness. *The Roaring Girl*, by Middleton

Introduction, glosses, footnotes, and textual notes by David Bevington; text edited by David Bevington and checked by Eric Rasmussen.

1. According to the title page of its first publication in 1630, Thomas Middleton's *A Chaste Maid in Cheapside* was "often acted at the Swan on the Bankside, by the Lady Elizabeth her Servants." Lady Elizabeth, the eldest daughter of King James I and Queen Anne, married Frederick, the Elector Palatine, in 1613. Her acting company had already come into existence, in 1611; *A Chaste Maid* may have been one of its first plays. The Swan Theater stood somewhat to the west of the Globe and the Rose on the Bankside, or southern shore of the Thames River, across from Saint Paul's Cathedral. The sketch of that theater by a foreign visitor from about 1596 is the only one we have of the interior of a public stage from this era. (For a reproduction of this sketch, see the general introduction to this volume, p. li.)

and Thomas Dekker (published in 1611 and probably acted in that same year), is one manifestation of this heterogeneity. *A Chaste Maid* is certainly another.

The leading citizen in this play is Master Yellowhammer, a successful shopkeeper like the feather-seller, tailor, and apothecary we meet as a trio in *The Roaring Girl*. He and his wife, Maudlin, are discovered in their goldsmith's shop, along with their daughter Moll (or Mary), by the unveiling of a stage structure resembling a London shop. Such a stage device was by this time a commonplace of city comedy; we see it, for example, in *The Roaring Girl*, in *Bartholomew Fair*, and earlier in the domestic tragedy *Arden of Faversham*. Yellowhammer's name is a giveaway of the satiric caricature: he hammers at gold. We see him dealing with a gentleman customer over a gold chain or fashioning a wedding ring for another customer, Touchwood Junior, who, it turns out, is secretly in love with Yellowhammer's own daughter. This romantic motif is another staple of city comedy, present, for example, in Dekker's *The Shoemaker's Holiday* and in Francis Beaumont's send-up of this kind of drama in *The Knight of the Burning Pestle*.

Appropriately enough, Yellowhammer is the heavy, or "blocking" character, in this romantic story. Young love must eventually have its way, overcoming the traditional obstacles of parental objection and social distance between the lovebirds. We know from the start of the play that eventually young Touchwood will win Moll as his bride, if for no other reason than that she is innocently loyal and he is her intrepid protector. The devices of intrigue needed for an elopement are an important source of suspense in this dramatic entertainment. The shape of this familiar plot paces audience expectations as to when the lovers' tribulations will end and thus signal the conclusion of the play as well.

Yellowhammer's family is a study in comic absurdity. Maudlin, the wife, reminds us of Margery in *The Shoemaker's Holiday* with her pietisms and her splendid ignorance of learning. She is immensely proud to have a son studying at Cambridge; the family's ability to afford higher education for the son and heir is a mark of their upward social mobility. She smothers Tim with motherly solicitude when he comes home, accompanied by his tutor. She is eager to introduce Tim to her lady friends so that she can show how smart he has become. Tim has indeed learned some Latin at Cambridge, enough that he and his tutor are able to debate such empty topics as whether a fool is or is not a rational creature. Their use of syllogism demonstrates hilariously how such formal arguments can be made to prove anything without manifesting the least relevance about anything that matters. Tim is, moreover, terminally shy with women and is comfortable only in the boyish, adoring friendship he shares with his tutor. The play's look at education in Cambridge, seen from a London perspective, suggests that it amounts to exactly nothing. Yet Maudlin could not be more proud of her Tim. Cambridge is making a gentleman of him, and that is more than enough for her.

Both Maudlin and her husband hope that Moll will marry into the gentry. They have their eye set on Sir Walter Whorehound, whose name is hardly reassuring as to his husbandly qualities. Indeed, Sir Walter arrives in town with his Welsh mistress, known only in the play as the Welsh Gentlewoman. She has pretensions to gentry, although her wealth appears to be mainly in mountains and livestock. Rural provincialism was always an inviting topic for satire from London's urban and urbane perspective, and no part of Britain was more provincial to Londoners than Wales. Sir Walter hopes to marry this lady off, as the gentry often did in the Britain of this era; when they tired of a mistress, or inconveniently got her pregnant, gentlemen often would arrange financially for the woman to find a husband and thus gain respectability. As Sir Walter says privately to the Welsh Gentlewoman, "Here you must pass for a pure virgin"; meantime, we are assured by Sir Walter's servant Davy in an aside that "She lost her maidenhead in Brecknockshire" (1.1.111–14).

This lady turns out to be the perfect mate for Tim in the play's hilarious dissection of the marriage game; she is nominally of the gentry class and has an inheritance of sorts. Never mind that she is the cast-off mistress of Sir Walter; the marriage will be a step up socially for the Yellowhammer clan, and in any case, Tim can use his Latin casuistry to "prove a whore an honest woman" (5.4.108–9). Such are the inestimable advantages of a university education.

Middleton's approach to Sir Walter is largely one of tolerant amusement, though the play's ultimate punishment of him may strike us as a sop to conventions of morality. Not only does Sir Walter bring with him his about-to-be-cast-off mistress from Wales; it turns out that he also has a mistress in London and a whole household to boot. Mrs. Allwit has been Sir Walter's mistress long enough to have produced at least two bastard sons, Wat and Nick, and another child is on the way. Like other gentlemen of the early modern period, Sir Walter is willing to support an entire household as a part of the price of his philandering. Indeed, we sense a kind of domestic felicity in it all. The boys are eager to tip their caps to their wealthy and influential father. Sir Walter always presides when he is onstage; he exudes power and money. He appears to be fond of Mrs. Allwit, and she of him. What more could domesticity hope to provide?

This woodcut, from *Roxburghe Ballads* (published in 1871 by the Roxburghe Club, a society dedicated to the reprinting of rare pieces of ancient literature and popular culture), shows the Elizabethan interest in comic and serious representations of the cuckold's horns.

Moreover, the husband, Master Allwit, seems not to mind. To the contrary, he persuades himself that all is going well and that no one is as lucky as he. In a brilliant comic soliloquy, Allwit details for us the many advantages that have accrued to him from the benificence of the man he calls the Founder. Sir Walter keeps them all in food, lodging, and domestic help. Fires glow in the fireplaces. The coal house is full, and the woodpile in back of the house is as high as a small mountain. Mrs. Allwit is showered with gifts from expensive shops. What more could one want? Yet Allwit knows that he is the object of ridicule. Even the servants laugh at him behind his back, knowing as they do who is paying the bills and whose children are bouncing on Sir Walter's knees. Allwit is a vivid instance of the wittol, or complacent cuckold. His name is a transparent near anagram of "wittol." Eventually, when the remorseful Sir Walter turns on Allwit and his wife as the authors of his own moral degradation, they admit to themselves their unhappiness with the arrangement that has supported them all these years. Perhaps, they speculate, they can hold on to some of the household furnishings they have accumulated, let out lodgings, and take a house on the Strand, a fashionable London street. Middleton thus ends by revealing the evident unhappiness of Sir Walter's ménage à trois, but not before he has had a great deal of fun exploring the seemingly emancipated dimensions of an irregular sexual liaison.

The plot involving Touchwood Senior and the Kixes takes another look at the ménage à trois by observing a comic symmetry. Touchwood Senior is, despite being an older brother and thus traditionally an heir, a man without much family fortune. What is more, his libidinal drive together with his wife's rampant fertility have combined to burden them with an unending succession of offspring, more than they can afford. Reluctantly, they decide to live apart. Sir Oliver Kix, on the other hand, is caught in a literally sterile marriage; he and Lady Kix cannot produce offspring to whom to bequeath the wealth they hope to inherit from Sir Walter. What is more, they will not inherit that wealth at all if Sir Walter marries the goldsmith's daughter and produces heirs himself. (Sir Oliver is probably Sir Walter's first cousin, in line to inherit if Sir

Walter dies childless.) Middleton thus presents us with two contrasting marriages, one that is sterile and one that is sexually overproductive. The only question is how the two couples' needs can be fitted together.

Middleton's portrait of the Kixes as mismatched husband and wife is rich in details of their quarreling. Another comic symmetry is to be observed here: Kix is unable to sire children, while Lady Kix is desperate for an adequate male with whom to share her bed. Sir Oliver has spared for no cost at the apothecaries in buying drugs that might help with infertility. Husband and wife accuse each other, of course, of being responsible for their barrenness (in the early modern period, medical knowledge on the subject was minimal), but in the sexual comedy of their scenes together, the overall effect is to suggest that Sir Oliver is an inadequate male. He is a spiritual cousin of Master Allwit as the male who cannot perform and who is therefore subjected to the scorn visited on cuckolds.

Sir Oliver is virtually asking to be made a cuckold. That is the upshot of this story, at any rate, for Touchwood Senior's device is to offer them medical counseling with a program of exercise for Sir Oliver that will conveniently remove him from the house while Touchwood Senior tends to Lady Kix. How is her medicine to be taken? she asks Touchwood Senior. The answer is that she must take it "abed," either in her bed itself or in their coach. (Coaches were notorious as places for assignations.) Lady Kix is anything but unwilling. "The physic [medicine] must needs please," she concludes (3.3.171). Again, we see Middleton's delight in exploring an unorthodox sexual situation. We sense very little moral denunciation in this portrayal; instead it is amusing, droll. Why should anyone object? All partners get what they want; it's a neat match.

Even the satire of the Puritans in this play is relatively good-natured, though one wonders if Puritan-leaning audiences would have subjected themselves to the indignity of witnessing *A Chaste Maid*. Probably they did not. The Puritan episode is, in a sense, gratuitous: it centers on the christening of Mrs. Allwit's latest child and could easily be cut from production since it does not impinge on any of the play's main plotlines. To cut the scene would be, however, to leave out a wonderful vignette of London life of the time. Allwit is present as the anxious though only putative father; Sir Walter presides as the benefactor and actual sire of the newborn infant. Mrs. Allwit is at the center of it all, in her bed, which is *"thrust out upon the stage, Allwit's wife in it"* (3.2.0.1).

Among the guests are Puritan women. Some are identified simply as "gossips," that is, neighbors and well-wishers; two speak as "FIRST PURITAN" and "SECOND PURITAN." Their speeches use the cadences of Puritan speech, at least as parodied on the London stage. "Give you joy of your fine girl, sir!" says one of them to Allwit, the supposed father. "Grant that her education may be pure, / And become one of the faithful!" (2.3.19–21). The speaker hopes that the child will grow up to be of the Puritan persuasion. These women are concerned that the child be christened "i'the right way, / Without idolatry or superstition, / After the pure manner of Amsterdam" (3.2.3–5). As in *The Alchemist*, these religious reformers come from a city in the Netherlands that had become a center of religious zeal. They are constantly on the watch for what they regard as idolatrous images, such as one might encounter in seemingly innocent objects like spoons carved with figures of the apostles. The Puritan women object to red as "not the sisters' color" (3.2.56), partly at least because of its association with Judas's presumedly red hair (Judas being the apostle who betrayed Jesus). The women guests jostle for precedence in entering or leaving a room, and they are positively voracious in their appetite for the catered sweets of the christening feast. These are harmless enough hypocrisies; again, we see that Middleton is tolerantly amused rather than angrily denunciatory. Yet the play surely aims to please an audience largely composed of other than the elect. By the time of this play, the theater had, by and large, given up on that clientele.

Another comic sequence in *A Chaste Maid* that is extraneous to a tightly managed plot has to do with regulations forbidding the consumption of meat during Lent except for medical reasons. Two so-called promoters, or informers, look sharply around them for violators they can arrest, or, more profitably, coerce into turning over to them any illegally obtained meat. Observers like Allwit know well enough that these promoters are mainly interested in what they can get out of the business rather than in trying to enforce a code aimed at improving public morality. Middleton seems to be amused at the notion that abstinence of this sort during Lent might be good for the soul; he is much more intent on dramatizing for us the way opportunists work a racket. It is all part of the London scene, which the dramatist depicts as endlessly captivating and alive.

Men are often infantilized by women in this engaging play. The country Wench outwits the two promoters by leaving them with an unwanted child. "Women had need of wit if they'll shift here, and she that hath wit may shift anywhere," she meditates in soliloquy (2.2.154–55). The promoters are left to reflect glumly on how they will have to play nursemaid, spending half their income in "sugar-sops and nurses' wages now, besides many a pound of soap and tallow" (2.2.202–4). Sir Oliver Kix and Allwit are made to accommodate themselves to their wives' need for sexual fulfillment that they cannot satisfy. Mrs. Allwit, in her bed, surrounded by her friends, is an embodiment of domestic abundance. Her body is ever present, and it is often a messy body with its fluids, its appetites, its leaking. Allwit is revolted, at the christening, by the women's voracious appetite for sweetmeats. He has "heard a citizen complain once that his wife's belly only broke his back" (3.2.74–75)—that is, the wife's appetite and endless reproductive capacity drove him into bankruptcy. Men are dependent on women and then victimized by that dependency. Tim cannot bear being kissed by his mother's acquaintances. "Oh, this is horrible!" he confides to his tutor. "She wets as she kisses. Your handkercher, sweet tutor, to wipe them off, as fast as they come on!" (3.2.181–83). Eventually, with comic fitness, Tim finds himself tricked into a marriage with a whore. Such, perhaps, is the fate of most men, according to this satiric vision.

Money dominates most of the human relationships in the London of this play. Yellowhammer and his wife try to auction their daughter off to the wealthy Sir Walter and are suitably repaid by being outwitted by Moll's admirer, the younger Touchwood. Even here, in the romantic plot, elements of commercial and social rivalry predominate in the mating of a shopkeeper's daughter and a wellborn if impecunious gentleman; her inherited wealth will support him, and his social qualifications will satisfy a desire on her family's part to move up the social scale. Inheritance is an ingredient in virtually every plot. The Kixes need a son to outmaneuver Sir Walter's marriage plans, which are essentially dynastic in intent. Commodification of sex through money is especially evident in the use Sir Walter makes of Mrs. Allwit: she provides him with sex and bastard children in return for a comfortable way of life. London is a city of commerce, so much so that its denizens' most intimate personal concerns are responsive to that commerce.

Middleton's affectionate sketch of London life is further enriched by the boatmen who help Touchwood Junior and Moll with their elopement, by a porter arriving from Cambridge, and by servants wryly observing the strange behavior of their nominal social betters. The ironic tone is deft and friendly. Middleton anatomizes ways in which sex is commodified and commerce is eroticized. In terms of its genre as well, the play is inclusive. Much of it is city comedy, and yet that satiric vein is played off against the melodrama of Moll's escape from her family and the sermonizing that accompanies Sir Walter's belated determination to be freed of his own sinful ways. At times, the melodrama even seems to laugh at itself, as when Touchwood Junior and Moll rise up from their coffins, reborn into their new life as a happily married couple. Middleton is a theatrical master at having things both ways, providing both satiric laughter and a forgiving comic resolution bolstered by conventional moral observations. The characters are as varied and as pungent as London itself. That great city found in Thomas Middleton a portrait painter who insisted on showing warts and all.

THOMAS MIDDLETON

A Chaste Maid in Cheapside

The Names of the Principal Persons

Master YELLOWHAMMER, a goldsmith
MAUDLIN,[1] his wife
TIM, their son
MOLL, their daughter [sometimes called Mary]
TUTOR to Tim
SIR WALTER Whorehound, a suitor to Moll
SIR OLIVER Kix[2] and
His wife [LADY KIX] } kin to Sir Walter
Master [Jack] ALLWIT[3] and
His wife [MRS. ALLWIT], whom Sir Walter keeps
WELSH GENTLEWOMAN, Sir Walter's whore
WAT and NICK, his bastards [by Mrs. Allwit]
DAVY Dahumma,[4] his man° — *servant*
TOUCHWOOD[5] SR., a decayed° gentleman — *financially ruined*
And his wife [MRS. TOUCHWOOD]
TOUCHWOOD JR., another suitor to Moll
Two PROMOTERS° — *informers*
SERVANTS [in the Allwit, Kix, and Yellowhammer households]
[Three or four] WATERMEN° — *Thames boatmen*
[A MAID to Sir Oliver and Lady Kix
A PORTER
A GENTLEMAN
A country WENCH
A DRY NURSE to Mrs. Allwit's baby
A WET NURSE to Mrs. Allwit's baby
Two MEN, one named OLIVER, with meat in their baskets
Two PURITAN women
Five GOSSIPS° — *neighbors; godparents*
A midwife
A PARSON

The original 1630 title page reads "*A Chaste Maid in Cheapside.* A pleasant conceited comedy, never before printed. As it hath been often acted at the Swan on the Bankside, by the Lady Elizabeth her Servants. By Thomas Middleton Gent[leman]. London, Printed for Francis Constable dwelling at the sign of the Crane in Paul's Churchyard. 1630."

The Names of the Principal Persons.

1. Maudlin, or Maudline, as Middleton normally spells it, represents the traditional English pronunciation of "Magdalene."
2. Kix is a dry, hollow plant stalk; hence, a dried up, sapless person.
3. "Allwit" is a near anagram of "wittol," a willing cuckold.
4. "Come hither" in stage dialect Welsh; hence, a name for a servant.
5. Touchwood is tinder, easily ignited, here with implications of sexual desire.

Sir Walter's other bastard children
SUSAN, a maid to Moll

THE SCENE: London.]

1.1

Enter Maudlin and Moll, a shop being discovered.° — *revealed onstage*

MAUDLIN Have you played over all your old lessons o'the virginals?° — *an early harpsichord*

MOLL [*weeping*] Yes.

MAUDLIN "Yes"? You are a dull maid alate.° Methinks you had — *of late, recently*
need have somewhat to quicken° your greensickness°—do — *revive / anemia*
you weep?—a husband. Had not such a piece of flesh° been — *a mortal; a penis*
ordained, what had us wives been good for? To make° salads, — *be ingredients in*
or else cried up and down for samphire.[1] To see the difference of these seasons![2] When I was of your youth, I was
lightsome and quick° two years before I was married. You, — *lively; pregnant*
fit for a knight's bed? Drowsy-browed, dull-eyed, drossy-spirited?° I hold° my life you have forgot your dancing. When — *heavy-spirited / bet*
was the dancer with you?

MOLL The last week.

MAUDLIN Last week! When I was of your bord,° he missed me — *age and size*
not a night. I was kept at it;[3] I took delight to learn and he
to teach me. Pretty brown° gentleman, he took pleasure in — *dark-complected*
my company. But you are dull; nothing comes nimbly from you; you dance like a plumber's daughter, and deserve two
thousand pound in lead to° your marriage, and not in gold- — *as dowry for*
smith's ware.° — *i.e., gold*

Enter Yellowhammer.

YELLOWHAMMER Now what's the din betwixt mother and daughter, ha?

MAUDLIN Faith,° small: telling your daughter Mary of her errors. — *In faith*

YELLOWHAMMER "Errors"? Nay, the city cannot hold° you, wife, — *satisfy*
but you must needs fetch words from Westminster.[4] I ha' done, i'faith. Has no attorney's clerk been here alate and changed
his half-crown piece his mother sent him, or rather cozened° — *cheated*
you with a gilded° twopence, to bring the word in fashion — *(to appear to be gold)*
for her *faults* or *cracks*° in duty and obedience? Term 'em — *failures*
e'en so,° sweet wife.[5] — *Call 'em that*
As there is no woman made without a flaw,
Your purest lawns° have frays, and cambrics bracks.° — *linens / flaws*

1.1. At Yellowhammer's shop, London.

1. Or else be proclaimed for sale in the market as samphire, a kind of seaweed used as a relish for meat. (Samphire was thought to induce urinating and menstruation.)

2. How times have changed!

3. Sexual double entendres run throughout this passage, in "missed . . . not a night," "kept at it," "took pleasure," etc.

4. You insist on using fancy frenchified legal talk, like that used in the courts at Westminster.

5. The word Yellowhammer refers to, in line 30, is "errors" (lines 25 and 26), to which he objects as highfalutin; its technical meaning is "mistakes in matters of law." "Faults" and "cracks" are good English words, in his view, and his wife should use them instead.

MAUDLIN But 'tis a husband solders up all cracks.[6]
MOLL What, is he come, sir?
YELLOWHAMMER Sir Walter's come.
He was met at Holborn Bridge,° and in his company — *main bridge from the west*
A proper° fair young gentlewoman, which I guess, — *handsome, fine*
By her red hair and other rank° descriptions, — *overabundant; lustful*
To be his landed° niece brought out of Wales, — *landowning*
Which Tim our son, the Cambridge boy, must° marry. — *is to*
'Tis a match of Sir Walter's own making
To bind us to him, and our heirs, forever.

MAUDLIN We are honored, then, if this baggage° would be humble and kiss him with devotion when he enters. I cannot get her, for my life, to instruct her hand thus, before and after [*she demonstrates*], which a knight will look for, before and after.[7] I have told her still, 'tis the waving° of a woman does often move a man and prevails strongly. But, sweet, ha' you sent° to Cambridge? Has Tim word on't?° — *hussy (Moll)*; *wriggling of hips, etc.*; *sent a message / of it*

YELLOWHAMMER Had° word just the day after, when you sent him the silver spoon to eat his broth in the hall amongst the gentlemen commoners.° — *He received*; *wealthy students*

MAUDLIN Oh, 'twas timely.

Enter Porter.

YELLOWHAMMER How now?

PORTER A letter from a gentleman in Cambridge.

YELLOWHAMMER [*taking the letter*] Oh, one of Hobson's porters.[8] Thou art welcome.—I told thee, Maud, we should hear from Tim. [*He reads.*] *"Amantissimis charissimisque ambobus parentibus patri et matri."*[9]

MAUDLIN What's the matter?° — *content; fuss*

YELLOWHAMMER Nay, by my troth, I know not. Ask not me; he's grown too verbal. This learning is a great witch.

MAUDLIN Pray let me see it. I was wont° to understand him. [*She takes the letter and reads as though construing its Latin.*] "*Amantissimus charissimus,*" he has sent the carrier's man, he says, "*ambobus parentibus,*" for a pair of boots; "*patri et matri,*" pay the porter, or it makes no matter.° — *accustomed*; *or not, if you please*

PORTER Yes, by my faith, mistress, there's no true construction° in that. I have took a great deal of pains, and come from the Bell° sweating. Let me come to't, for I was a scholar forty years ago. [*He takes the letter.*] 'Tis thus, I warrant you: "*Matri,*" it makes no matter, "*ambobus parentibus,*" for a pair of boots; "*patri,*" pay the porter; "*amantissimis charissimis,*" he's the carrier's man, and his name is Sims.—And there he says true, forsooth; my name is Sims indeed. I have not forgot all my learning. A money matter; I thought I should hit on't.° — *you've misconstrued*; *a London inn*; *get that part right*

YELLOWHAMMER [*tipping him*] Go, thou art an old fox. There's a tester° for thee. — *sixpenny piece*

6. With sexual double entendre: the husband fills up the female genitals.
7. The mother shows her daughter how to do a proper curtsy, with one hand forward and the other back. (With a bawdy undertone that is presumably reinforced by the actor's gestures.)
8. Hobson was a famous Cambridge messenger.
9. To both my loving and beloved parents, my father and mother.

PORTER If I see Your Worship at Goose Fair, I have a dish of birds for you.

YELLOWHAMMER Why, dost dwell at Bow?

PORTER All my lifetime, sir; I could ever say boo to a goose.[1] Farewell to Your Worship. *Exit Porter.*

YELLOWHAMMER A merry porter!

MAUDLIN How can he choose but be so, coming with Cambridge letters from our son Tim?

YELLOWHAMMER [*reading*] What's here? *"Maximus diligo"*?[2] Faith, I must to my learned counsel with this gear;° 'twill ne'er be discerned else. — *business*

MAUDLIN Go to my cousin, then, at Inns of Court.[3]

YELLOWHAMMER Fie! They are all for French; they speak no Latin.

MAUDLIN The parson, then, will do it.

Enter a Gentleman with a chain.

YELLOWHAMMER Nay, he disclaims it, calls Latin "papistry";° he will not deal with it.—What is't you lack,° gentleman? — *Roman Catholicism* / *Can I help you*

GENTLEMAN Pray weigh this chain.

[*Yellowhammer weighs it.*]

Enter Sir Walter Whorehound, Welsh Gentlewoman, and Davy Dahumma [*not seeing Yellowhammer and his family in the shop at first*].

SIR WALTER Now, wench, thou art welcome to the heart of the city of London!

WELSH GENTLEWOMAN *Dugat a whee.*° — *God keep you (Welsh)*

SIR WALTER You can thank me in English, if you list.° — *please*

WELSH GENTLEWOMAN I can, sir, simply.

SIR WALTER 'Twill serve to pass,° wench. — *It will suffice*
'Twas° strange that I should lie with thee so often, — *It would be*
To leave thee without English; that were unnatural.
I bring thee up° to turn thee into gold, wench, — *up to London*
And make thy fortune shine like your bright trade.[4]
A goldsmith's shop sets out° a city maid.— — *shows to advantage*
Davy Dahumma, not a word.

DAVY Mum, mum, sir.

SIR WALTER [*to the Welsh Gentlewoman*] Here you must pass for a pure virgin.

DAVY [*aside*] Pure Welsh virgin! She lost her maidenhead in Brecknockshire.

SIR WALTER I hear you mumble, Davy.

DAVY I have teeth, sir. I need not mumble yet this forty years.

SIR WALTER The knave bites plaguily!

YELLOWHAMMER [*to the Gentleman*] What's your price, sir?

GENTLEMAN A hundred pound, sir.

YELLOWHAMMER A hundred marks° the utmost; 'tis not for me else. [*Seeing the others*] What, Sir Walter Whorehound! — *a mark = ⅔ of a pound*

MOLL Oh, death! *Exit Moll.*

1. Stratford atte Bow, just east of London, was the site of a fair during Whitsuntide, seven weeks after Easter, where young (green) geese were sold. The Porter plays on the words "Bow" and "boo" here: being unable to "say boo to a goose" was proverbial for timidity.

2. I.e., *Maxime diligo*, I esteem most greatly.

3. Institutions in London for the study of law.

4. I.e., like goldsmithing and prostitution. ("Your" is impersonal, meaning "one's.")

MAUDLIN [*calling after her*] Why, daughter!—Faith, the baggage!
[*To Sir Walter*] A bashful girl, sir; these young things are
shamefast.° *modest, shy*
Besides, you have a presence, sweet Sir Walter,
Able to daunt a maid° brought up i'the city. *even a maiden*

Enter Mary.° *Moll*

A brave court-spirit makes our virgins quiver
And kiss with trembling thighs. Yet see, she comes, sir.

SIR WALTER [*to Moll*] Why, how now, pretty mistress? Now
I have caught you. [*He catches her by the hand.*]
What, can you injure so your time to stray
Thus from your faithful servant?° *male admirer*

YELLOWHAMMER Pish! Stop your words, good knight—'twill make her blush else—which sound too high for the daughters of the freedom.[5] "Honor" and "faithful servant"? They are compliments for the worthies of Whitehall or Greenwich;° *royal palaces* e'en plain, sufficient, subsidy° *bourgeois, commercial* words serves us, sir. And is this gentlewoman [*indicating the Welsh Gentlewoman*] your worthy niece?

SIR WALTER You may be bold with her on these terms; 'tis she, sir, heir to some nineteen mountains.

YELLOWHAMMER Bless us all! You overwhelm me, sir, with love and riches.

SIR WALTER And all as high as Paul's.° *St. Paul's Cathedral*

DAVY Here's work, i'faith!

SIR WALTER How sayest thou, Davy?

DAVY Higher, sir, by far; you cannot see the top of 'em.

YELLOWHAMMER What, man?—Maudlin, salute° *greet, kiss, welcome* this gentlewoman—our daughter,° *daughter-in-law* if things hit right.

Enter Touchwood Junior.

TOUCHWOOD JR. [*aside*] My knight, with a brace° *pair* of footmen, is come, and brought up his ewe mutton° *strumpet* to find a ram at London. I must hasten it,[6] or else peak° *grow thin, starve* o' famine; her blood's mine, and that's the surest.[7] Well, knight, that choice spoil° *prize (Moll)* is only kept for me.

[*He whispers privately to Moll and gives her a letter.*]

MOLL [*aside to him*] Sir?

TOUCHWOOD JR. [*aside to her*] Turn not to me till thou mayst lawfully;[8] it but whets my stomach,° *appetite* which is too sharp-set already. Read that note carefully; keep me from suspicion still, nor know my zeal but in thy heart. Read and send but thy liking° *inclination* in three words; I'll be at hand to take it.

YELLOWHAMMER [*to Sir Walter*] Oh, Tim, sir, Tim. A poor plain boy, an university man; proceeds next Lent to a bachelor of art. He will be called Sir° *Dominus, Master* Yellowhammer then over all Cambridge, and that's half a knight.

5. The freedom of the city was a license to trade, extended only to privileged citizens.
6. I must act fast to marry Moll.
7. Moll's desire matches mine, and that's my surest advantage.
8. Don't turn around now (i.e., don't let it be seen that you know me) until you are lawfully entitled through marriage to turn to me as a wife does to her husband.

MAUDLIN [*to Sir Walter*] Please you draw near and taste the welcome of the city, sir?

YELLOWHAMMER Come, good Sir Walter, and your virtuous niece here.

SIR WALTER 'Tis manners to take kindness.° *accept hospitality*

YELLOWHAMMER Lead 'em in, wife.

SIR WALTER Your company, sir.

YELLOWHAMMER I'll give't you instantly.

[*Exeunt Sir Walter, Maudlin, Davy, and the Welsh Gentlewoman.*]

TOUCHWOOD JR. [*aside*] How strangely busy is the devil and riches!
Poor soul,° kept in too hard! Her mother's eye *i.e., Moll*
Is cruel toward her, being kind to him.° *(Sir Walter or Yellowhammer)*
'Twere a good mirth now to set him° a-work *(Yellowhammer)*
To make her wedding ring. I must about it.
Rather than the gain should fall to a stranger,
'Twas° honest in me to enrich my father. *It would be*

YELLOWHAMMER [*aside*] The girl is wondrous peevish. I fear nothing
But that she's taken with some other love.
Then all's quite dashed; that must be narrowly° looked to. *carefully*
We cannot be too wary in our children.
[*To Touchwood Junior*] What is't you lack?

TOUCHWOOD JR. [*aside*] Oh, nothing now. All that I wish° is present. *i.e., Moll*
[*To Yellowhammer*] I would have a wedding ring made for a gentlewoman, with all speed that may be.

YELLOWHAMMER Of what weight, sir?

TOUCHWOOD JR. [*showing a diamond*] Of some half ounce; stand° fair and comely with the spark° of a diamond. Sir, 'twere pity to lose the least grace. *I'd have it stand* / *shining body*

YELLOWHAMMER Pray let's see it. [*He examines the diamond.*] Indeed, sir, 'tis a pure one.

TOUCHWOOD JR. So is the mistress.

YELLOWHAMMER Have you the wideness of her finger, sir?

TOUCHWOOD JR. Yes, sure, I think I have her measure about me. [*He searches his pockets.*] Good faith, 'tis down.[9] I cannot show't you; I must pull too many things out to be certain. Let me see: long, and slender, and neatly jointed. Just such another gentlewoman that's your daughter,° sir. *as your daughter is*

[*He indicates Moll.*]

YELLOWHAMMER And therefore, sir, no gentlewoman.[1]

TOUCHWOOD JR. I protest I never saw two maids handed° more alike. I'll ne'er seek farther, if you'll give me leave, sir. *with hands*

YELOWHAMMER If you dare venture by her finger, sir.

TOUCHWOOD JR. Ay, and I'll bide all loss,° sir. *guarantee payment*

YELLOWHAMMER Say you so, sir? [*To Moll*] Let's see hither, girl.

9. I.e., it is deep down in the pocket. (The bawdy suggestion of detumescence introduces a passage in which the references to rings and fingers are erotically suggestive.)

1. Moll, a citizen's daughter, is not a member of the gentry class.

TOUCHWOOD JR. Shall I make bold with your finger, gentlewoman?

MOLL Your pleasure, sir.

TOUCHWOOD JR. [*using Moll's finger to test the size of a ring*] That fits her to a hair, sir.

YELLOWHAMMER What's your posy° now, sir? *motto (for engraving)*

TOUCHWOOD JR. Mass,° that's true. Posy, i'faith? Ev'n thus, sir: *By the Mass*
Love that's wise
Blinds parents' eyes.

YELLOWHAMMER How, how? If I may speak without offense, sir, I hold° my life— *bet*

TOUCHWOOD JR. What, sir?

YELLOWHAMMER Go to. You'll pardon me?[2]

TOUCHWOOD JR. Pardon you? Ay, sir.

YELLOWHAMMER Will you, i'faith?

TOUCHWOOD JR. Yes, faith, I will.

YELLOWHAMMER You'll steal away some man's daughter. Am I near you?[3] Do you turn aside? You gentlemen are mad wags.° *brash young devils*
I wonder things can be so warily carried,° *secretly carried on*
And parents blinded so; but they're served right
That have two eyes and wear so dull a sight.° *see so little*

TOUCHWOOD JR. [*aside*] Thy doom take hold of thee![4]

YELLOWHAMMER Tomorrow noon
Shall show your ring well done.

TOUCHWOOD JR. Being so, 'tis soon.[5]
Thanks, and your leave,° sweet gentlewoman. *I take my leave*

MOLL Sir, you are welcome. *Exit* [*Touchwood Junior*].
[*Aside*] Oh, were I made of wishes, I went° with thee! *would go*

YELLOWHAMMER Come now, we'll see how the rules° go within. *revels; agreements*

MOLL [*aside*] That robs my joy; there I lose all I win.

Exeunt.

[1.2]

Enter Davy and Allwit severally.° *at separate entrances*

DAVY [*aside*] Honesty wash my eyes! I have spied a wittol.° *willing cuckold (Allwit)*

ALLWIT What, Davy Dahumma! Welcome from North Wales, i'faith. And is Sir Walter come?

DAVY New come to town, sir.

ALLWIT In° to the maids,° sweet Davy, and give order his chamber be made ready instantly. My wife's as great° as she can wallow, Davy, and longs for nothing but pickled cucumbers and his coming; and now she shall ha't, boy. *Go in / maids' quarters* *pregnant*

DAVY She's sure of them, sir.

ALLWIT Thy very sight will hold my wife in pleasure
Till the knight come himself. Go in, in, in, Davy.

Exit [*Davy*].

The Founder's° come to town! I am like a man *Our patron is*
Finding a table furnished to his hand° *use, benefit*
As mine is still to me, prays° for the Founder: *who prays*
"Bless the Right Worshipful the good Founder's life!"

2. Come, come. You'll excuse my saying what I have to say?
3. Have I found you out?
4. May you fulfill your own prophecy!
5. That would be soon indeed, if well done.
1.2. Allwit's house.

I thank him, he's maintained my house this ten years;
Not only keeps my wife, but 'a° keeps me — *he*
And all my family. I am at his table;
He gets me° all my children, and pays the nurse — *supports; begets*
Monthly or weekly; puts me to nothing,° — *to no expense*
Rent, nor church duties, not so much as the scavenger.[1]
The happiest state that ever man was born to!
I walk out in a morning, come to breakfast,
Find excellent cheer; a good fire in winter;
Look in my coal house about Midsummer Eve,
That's full, five or six chaldron° new laid up; — *a chaldron = 32 bushels*
Look in my backyard, I shall find a steeple° — *i.e., high pile*
Made up with Kentish fagots° which o'erlooks° — *firewood / towers over*
The water house and the windmills. I say nothing,
But smile and pin° the door. When she lies in°— — *bolt / in childbirth*
As now she's even upon the point of grunting—
A lady lies not in° like her: there's her embossings,° — *No lady lies in / finery*
Embroid'rings, spanglings,° and I know not what, — *glittering fabrics*
As if she lay with all the gaudy shops
In Gresham's Burse° about her; then her restoratives, — *a famous mart*
Able to set up° a young pothecary° — *(in business) / druggist*
And richly stock the foreman of a drug shop;
Her sugar by whole loaves, her wines by runlets.° — *large casks*
I see these things, but like a happy man
I pay for none at all, yet fools think 's mine;° — *think it's mine*
I have the name,° and in his gold I shine. — *reputation*
And where some merchants would in soul kiss hell
To buy a paradise for their wives, and dye
Their conscience in the bloods of prodigal heirs
To deck their night-piece,[2] yet, all this being done,
Eaten with jealousy to the inmost bone—
As what affliction nature more constrains
Than feed the wife plump for another's veins?[3]—
These torments stand I freed of. I am as clear
From jealousy of a wife as from the charge.° — *cost; imputation*
Oh, two miraculous blessings! 'Tis the knight
Hath took that labor all out of my hands.
I may sit still and play; he's jealous for me,
Watches her steps, sets spies. I live at ease;
He has both the cost and torment. When the strings
Of his heart frets, I feed, laugh, or sing:
[*He sings.*] La dildo, dildo la dildo, la dildo dildo de dildo.

Enter two Servants.

FIRST SERVANT [*to Second Servant*] What, has he got a singing in his head now?

SECOND SERVANT Now 's° out of work, he falls to making dildos. — *Now that he's*

ALLWIT Now, sirs, Sir Walter's come.

FIRST SERVANT Is our master come?

1. Person who repairs and cleans pavements, streets, furnaces, and chimneys.
2. And stain their consciences by victimizing spendthrift sons in order to adorn the bodies of their bedfellows or mistresses. (A night-piece is literally a painting of a night-scene; here, figuratively, a mistress, playing on "piece" as a vulgar way to refer sexually to a woman.)
3. As indeed what affliction more distresses most men than to provide for the comfort of a wife who is sleeping with another man?

ALLWIT Your master? What am I?

FIRST SERVANT Do not you know, sir?

ALLWIT Pray, am not I your master?

FIRST SERVANT Oh, you are but our mistress's husband.

ALLWIT Ergo,° knave, your master. *Therefore*

Enter Sir Walter and Davy.

FIRST SERVANT *Negatur argumentum.*° [*Aside to Second Servant*] Here comes Sir Walter. Now 'a° stands bare° as well as we. Make the most of him; he's but one pip° above a servingman, and so much his horns make him.[4] *I deny your argument* / *(Allwit) / bareheaded* / *spot on dice; a bit*

SIR WALTER [*to Allwit*] How dost, Jack?

ALLWIT Proud of Your Worship's health, sir.

SIR WALTER How does your wife?

ALLWIT E'en after your own making,° sir. She's a tumbler, i'faith; the nose and belly meets. *doing*

SIR WALTER They'll part in time again.[5]

ALLWIT At the good hour they will, an't° please Your Worship. *if it*

SIR WALTER [*to a Servant*] Here, sirrah,° pull off my boots. [*To Allwit*] Put on,° put on, Jack. *(said to inferiors)* / *Put your hat back on*

ALLWIT I thank Your kind Worship, sir.

SIR WALTER Slippers! Heart,° you are sleepy. *By God's heart*

[*A Servant fetches slippers.*]

ALLWIT [*aside*] The game begins already.

SIR WALTER Pish, put on, Jack.

ALLWIT [*aside*] Now I must do it, or he'll be as angry now as if I had put it on at first bidding. 'Tis but observing— [*putting on his hat*] 'tis but observing a man's humor° once, and he may ha'° him by the nose all his life. *whimsy* / *lead*

SIR WALTER [*to First Servant*] What entertainment has lain
open° here? *been evident*
No strangers in my absence?

FIRST SERVANT Sure, sir, not any.

ALLWIT [*aside*] His jealousy begins. Am not I happy now
That can laugh inward whilst his marrow melts?° *he melts in jealousy*

SIR WALTER How do you satisfy me?

FIRST SERVANT Good sir, be patient.

SIR WALTER For two months' absence I'll be satisfied.

FIRST SERVANT No living creature entered—

SIR WALTER Entered? Come, swear!

FIRST SERVANT You will not hear me out, sir.

SIR WALTER Yes, I'll hear't out, sir.

FIRST SERVANT Sir, he° can tell himself. *(Allwit)*

SIR WALTER Heart, "He can tell"!
Do you think I'll trust him? As a usurer
With forfeited lordships.[6] Him? Oh, monstrous injury!
Believe him? Can the devil speak ill of darkness?[7]
[*To Allwit*] What can you say, sir?

4. And that is the only way he seems higher: by his cuckold's horns.

5. When she has been delivered of her baby, her nose and belly will no longer be close to touching, as is now the case with her very full pregnancy. "Tumbler," line 76, means (1) an acrobat in her ability to touch nose to belly; (2) a lively sexual partner.

6. I'd trust him as much as I would trust a usurer to whom mortgaged estates are forfeit on nonpayment of a loan.

7. I'd as soon trust him to speak truly as I would expect the devil to admit the terrible truth about the darkness of hell (to those persons he is tempting to evil).

ALLWIT Of° my soul and conscience, sir, she's a wife as honest of her body to me as any lord's proud lady can be. *On*
SIR WALTER Yet, by your leave, I heard you were once off'ring° to go to bed to her. *proposing*
ALLWIT No, I protest, sir!
SIR WALTER Heart, if you do, you shall take all.[8] I'll marry.
ALLWIT Oh, I beseech you, sir!
SIR WALTER [*aside*] That wakes the slave° and keeps his
flesh in awe. *wretch*
ALLWIT [*aside*] I'll stop that gap
Where'er I find it open. I have poisoned
His hopes in marriage already,
Some old rich widows and some landed° virgins— *landowning*

Enter two children [*Wat and Nick*].

And I'll fall to work still before I'll lose him.
He's yet too sweet to part from.
WAT God-den,° father. *Good day*
ALLWIT Ha, villain,° peace!° *rascal / hush*
NICK God-den, father.
ALLWIT Peace, bastard! [*Aside*] Should he° hear 'em! [*Aloud*] These are two foolish children; they do not know the gentleman that sits there. *If Sir Walter should*
SIR WALTER Oh, Wat! How dost, Nick? Go to school, ply your books, boys, ha?
ALLWIT Where's your legs,° whoresons?°—They should kneel indeed if they could say their prayers. *bows / rascals*
SIR WALTER [*aside*] Let me see, stay:° *wait a minute*
How shall I dispose of these two brats now
When I am married? For they must not mingle
Amongst my children that I get° in wedlock; *beget*
'Twill make foul work, that, and raise many storms.
I'll bind Wat prentice to a goldsmith—my father° Yellowhammer, as fit as can be! Nick with some vintner. Good: goldsmith and vintner! There will be wine in bowls, i'faith.[9] *father-in-law-to-be*

Enter Allwit's wife.

MRS. ALLWIT Sweet knight,
Welcome! I have all my longings now in town.
Now welcome the good hour!
SIR WALTER [*embracing her*] How cheers my mistress?
MRS. ALLWIT Made lightsome e'en by him that made me heavy.° *sorrowful; pregnant*
SIR WALTER Methinks she shows gallantly,° like a moon at full, sir. *looks full, splendid*
ALLWIT True, and if she bear a male child, there's the man in the moon, sir.
SIR WALTER 'Tis but the boy in the moon yet, goodman calf.° *sir idiot*
ALLWIT There was a man; the boy had never been there else.[1]
SIR WALTER It shall be yours, sir.
ALLWIT No, by my troth,

8. I.e., you shall take her and nothing else.
9. That way we'll have golden bowls made by Wat in which to serve Nick's wine.
1. There must have been a man in the moon to begin with (to sire the boy), or else there could be no boy there. (With an erotic suggestion of the man being inside the woman during sex and the boy inside her during pregnancy.)

I'll swear it's none of mine; let him that got° it — *begot*
Keep it. [*Aside*] Thus do I rid myself of fear,
Lie soft, sleep hard,° drink wine, and eat good cheer. — *soundly*
[*Exeunt.*]

2.1

Enter Touchwood Senior and his wife.

MRS. TOUCHWOOD 'Twill be so tedious, sir, to live from° you, — *away from*
But that necessity must be obeyed.

TOUCHWOOD SR. I would it might not, wife. The tediousness
Will be the most part mine, that° understand — *I who*
The blessings I have in thee; so to part,
That drives the torment to a knowing° heart. — *knowing my felicity*
But, as thou say'st, we must give way to need
And live awhile asunder; our desires
Are both too fruitful for our barren fortunes.
How adverse runs the destiny of some creatures!
Some only can get riches and no children;
We only can get children and no riches.
Then 'tis the prudent'st part to check our wills° — *control our appetites*
And, till our state° rise, make our bloods° lie still. — *situation / desires*
Life,° every year a child, and some years two! — *By God's life*
Besides drinkings abroad,° that's never reckoned. — *i.e., adulteries*
This gear° will not hold out. — *business; sexual gear*

MRS. TOUCHWOOD Sir, for a time
I'll take° the courtesy° of my uncle's house, — *accept / hospitality*
If you be pleased to like on't,° till prosperity — *approve of it*
Look with a friendly eye upon our states.

TOUCHWOOD SR. Honest wife, I thank thee. I ne'er knew
The perfect treasure thou brought'st with thee more
Than at this instant minute. A man's happy
When° he's at poorest that has matched his soul — *Even when*
As rightly as his body. Had I married
A sensual fool° now—as 'tis hard to scape it — *thoughtless sensualist*
'Mongst gentlewomen of our time[1]—she would ha' hanged
About my neck and never left her hold
Till she had kissed me into wanton businesses,° — *making love*
Which at the waking of my better judgment
I should have cursed most bitterly,
And laid a thicker vengeance on my act° — *sexual act*
Than misery of the birth°—which were enough — *the birth of a child*
If it were born to greatness,° whereas mine — *high social status*
Is sure of beggary, though it were got in wine.° — *begotten in drink*
Fullness of joy showeth the goodness in thee;
Thou art a matchless wife. Farewell, my joy!

MRS. TOUCHWOOD I shall not want° your sight? — *lack*

TOUCHWOOD SR. I'll see thee often,
Talk in mirth, and play at kisses with thee—
Anything, wench, but what may beget beggars.
There I give o'er the set,° throw down the cards, — *abandon the game*

2.1. Near Touchwood Senior's house (?).
1. As indeed it's not easy to escape ruinously marrying for lust, given the women of quality one meets nowadays.

And dare not take them up.

MRS. TOUCHWOOD Your will be mine, sir. *Exit.*

TOUCHWOOD SR. This does not only make her honesty° perfect, — *chastity*
But her discretion, and approves° her judgment. — *confirms*
Had° her desires been wanton, they'd been blameless — *Even had*
In being lawful° ever; but of all creatures — *justified by marriage*
I hold that wife a most unmatchèd treasure
That can unto her fortunes fix her pleasure
And not unto her blood.° This is like wedlock: — *passion*
The feast of marriage is not lust, but love
And care of the estate. When I please blood,
Merely I sing and suck out others';[2] then
'Tis many a wise man's fault. But of all men
I am the most unfortunate in that game
That ever pleased both genders. I ne'er played yet
Under a bastard.[3] The poor wenches curse me
To the pit° where'er I come; they were ne'er served so, — *To hell*
But used to have more words than one to a bargain.[4]
I have such a fatal finger in such business
I must forth with't, chiefly for country wenches.
For every harvest I shall hinder hay-making;[5]

Enter a [*country*] *Wench with a child.*

I had no less than seven lay in last progress[6]
Within three weeks of one another's time.

WENCH Oh, snaphance,[7] have I found you?

TOUCHWOOD SR. How? Snaphance?

WENCH [*showing him the child*] Do you see your workmanship? Nay, turn not from it, nor offer° to escape, for if you do I'll cry° it through the streets and follow you. Your name may well be called Touchwood. A pox on you! You do but touch and take.° Thou hast undone me. I was a maid before; I can bring a certificate for it from both the churchwardens. — *try* / *proclaim* / *and burst into flame*

TOUCHWOOD SR. I'll have the parson's hand,° too, or I'll not yield to't. — *signature*

WENCH Thou shalt have more, thou villain! Nothing grieves me but° Ellen, my poor cousin in Derbyshire. Thou hast cracked her marriage quite; she'll have a bout° with thee. — *as much as* / *law suit*

TOUCHWOOD SR. Faith, when she will. I'll have a bout° with her. — *sexual encounter*

WENCH A law bout, sir, I mean.

TOUCHWOOD SR. True, lawyers use such bouts as other men do. And if that be all thy grief, I'll tender° her a husband. I keep of° purpose two or three gulls in pickle° to eat such mutton° with, and she shall choose one. Do but in courtesy, — *offer, provide* / *on* / *dupes in reserve* / *whores*

2. When I enjoy sex, I merely give in to sensual pleasure and exploit others. (If "sing" is a misprint for "sting," the image is of sucking the blood of one's victim like a lecherous flesh fly, a fly whose maggots feed on flesh; but "sing" can mean "indulge in idle pleasure.")
3. I never yet engaged in the game of sex without begetting at least one bastard. ("Bastard" is also a card still held in the hand and counted against the player in the scoring of a card game like rummy.)
4. The women complain that they were never so badly treated; they used to have a say in the matter (of becoming pregnant) and could expect to enjoy several sexual encounters before becoming pregnant. ("Pit," "come," "served," line 57, "finger," line 59, and "country," line 60, all have sexual double meanings.)
5. I get so many country girls pregnant that I slow up harvesting.
6. No fewer than seven women were in childbirth during my last "royal tour."
7. "Snaphance" can mean "thief, marauder, or trifling person"; also a musket; a flintlock; or a device to ignite the "touchwood," or tinder, in the touchhole of a musket. (With sexual implication here.)

faith, wench, excuse me of this half yard of flesh,° in which — *baby*
I think it wants° a nail or two. — *comes up short*

WENCH No, thou shalt find, villain, it hath right shape and
all the nails it should have.[8]

TOUCHWOOD SR. Faith, I am poor. Do a charitable deed,
wench; I am a younger brother, and have nothing.[9]

WENCH Nothing? Thou hast too much,° thou lying villain! — *too much libido*
Unless thou wert more thankful.

TOUCHWOOD SR. I have no dwelling;
I brake° up house° but this morning. Pray thee, pity me; — *broke / housekeeping*
I am a good fellow, faith, have been too kind
To people of your gender; if I ha't
Without my belly, none of your sex shall want it.[1]
[*Aside*] That word° has been of force° to move a woman. — *promise / efficacious*
[*To her*] There's tricks enough to rid thy hand on't,° wench: — *of the child*
Some rich man's porch, tomorrow before day,
Or else anon i'the evening—twenty devices.
[*Giving money*] Here's all I have, i'faith; take purse and all.
[*Aside*] And would I were rid of all the ware i'the shop° so! — *of my other bastards*

WENCH Where I find manly dealings, I am pitiful.° — *full of pity*
This° shall not trouble you. — *This child*

TOUCHWOOD SR. And I protest, wench,
The next I'll keep myself.

WENCH Soft,° let it be got° first! — *Gently / begotten*
[*Aside*] This is the fifth; if e'er I venture more,
Where I now go for a maid, may I ride for a whore![2] *Exit.*

TOUCHOOD SR. What shift° she'll make now with this piece — *stratagem*
of flesh
In this strict time of Lent, I cannot imagine;[3]
Flesh dare not peep abroad° now. I have known — *out of the house*
This city now above this seven years,
But I protest, in better state of government
I never knew it yet, nor ever heard of.
There has been more religious wholesome laws
In the half circle of a year° erected — *six months*
For common good than memory ever knew of,

Enter Sir Oliver Kix and his Lady.

Setting apart° corruption of promoters° — *Except for / informers*
And other poisonous officers that infect
And with a venomous breath taint every goodness.

LADY KIX Oh, that e'er I was begot, or bred, or born!

SIR OLIVER Be content, sweet wife.

TOUCHWOOD SR. [*aside*] What's here to do,° now? — *What's going on here*
I hold° my life she's in deep passion — *bet*

8. Fingernails are sometimes lacking in children with congenital syphilis.

9. Younger brothers often lacked an inheritance, since by English law and custom estates normally passed intact to the eldest son. In fact, Touchwood Senior is the elder son but is here lying in an attempt to beg for relief from the financial burden of supporting a child. The Wench sees through his ruse.

1. (1) If I have food not yet eaten and thus not yet in my own belly, I freely give it to needy women; (2) whatever sexual gear I may possess I freely donate to any desirous woman.

2. This is my fifth child; if I get myself pregnant again, may I be hauled through the streets to prison like a convicted prostitute instead of passing for a virgin as I do now! ("Go" means "pass for" and also "walk as," playing on an antithesis of "go" [walk] and "ride.")

3. Regulations forbade the eating of meat during Lent, the weeks before Easter. Touchwood Senior implies that the Wench might try to sell the baby as flesh.

For the imprisonment of veal and mutton
Now kept in garrets, weeps for some calf's head now.
Methinks her husband's head might serve, with bacon.[4]

Enter Touchwood Junior.

LADY KIX Hist!° — *Look! Hush!*
SIR OLIVER Patience, sweet wife. [*They converse privately.*]
TOUCHWOOD JR. Brother, I have sought you strangely.° — *urgently*
TOUCHWOOD SR. Why, what's the business?
TOUCHWOOD JR. With all speed thou canst,
Procure a license for me.[5]
TOUCHWOOD SR. How, a license?
TOUCHWOOD JR. Cud's foot,° she's lost else! I shall miss her ever. — *By God's foot*
TOUCHWOOD SR. Nay, sure thou shalt not miss so fair a mark° — *target; coin, 13s. 4d.*
For thirteen shillings fourpence. [*He gives money.*]
TOUCHWOOD JR. Thanks by hundreds. *Exit.*
[*Touchwood Senior stands aside as the Kixes converse.*]
SIR OLIVER Nay, pray thee, cease. I'll be at more cost° yet; — *spend more*
Thou know'st we are rich enough.
LADY KIX All but in blessings,° — *children*
And there the beggar° goes beyond us. Oh! Oh! Oh! — *even a beggar*
To be seven years a wife, and not a child,
Oh, not a child!
SIR OLIVER Sweet wife, have patience.
LADY KIX Can any woman have a greater cut?° — *blow; vagina*
SIR OLIVER I know 'tis great, but what of that, wife?
I cannot do withal.° There's things making, — *I'm helpless, impotent*
By thine own doctor's advice, at pothecary's.
I spare for nothing,° wife. No, if the price — *spare no expense*
Were forty marks a spoonful,
I'd give a thousand pound to purchase fruitfulness.
'Tis but bating° so many good works — *cutting back on*
In the erecting of Bridewells and spital houses,[6]
And so fetch it up° again; for, having none, — *raise money; be erect*
I mean to make good deeds my children.[7]
LADY KIX Give me but those good deeds, and I'll find children.[8]
[*Touchwood Senior silently exits.*]
SIR OLIVER Hang thee, thou hast had too many![9]
LADY KIX Thou liest, brevity.[1]
SIR OLIVER Oh, horrible, dar'st thou call me "brevity"?
Dar'st thou be so short with me?
LADY KIX Thou deservest worse.

4. Touchwood Senior is willing to bet anything that Lady Kix is distressed at the unavailability of meat, since it is shut up during Lent in attics and hidden rooms. She longs for delicacies like calves' brains, with a hint also that what she really longs for is the "meat" of a lover's genital organs. Sir Oliver, by contrast, can be served up to her only as a fool's head, complete with cuckold's horns, as if he were a fancy dish garnished with bacon.

5. A license to marry without banns. (A special license was required to marry quickly, without the customary reading of the banns—public announcement in church of a proposed marriage—on three succcessive Sundays.)

6. Houses of correction for prostitutes and other offenders and hospitals for lepers and those with venereal diseases.

7. For, having no children, I mean to be remembered for my good deeds.

8. By "good deeds," Lady Kix implies sexual performance; if her husband were an adequate male, she would produce children readily enough. Alternatively, his money might enable her to find a lover.

9. You have had too much from me already (and no doubt from other men) in the way of sex; I haven't the appetite for more!

1. "Brevity" suggests both miserliness and sexual inadequacy. The sexual punning continues in "short" (line 153).

Think but upon the goodly lands and livings
That's kept back through want on't.[2]
SIR OLIVER Talk not on't, pray thee.
Thou'lt make me play the woman and weep too.
LADY KIX 'Tis our dry barrenness puffs up Sir Walter.
None gets° by your not getting but that knight; *No one prospers*
He's made by th'means,° and fats his fortunes shortly *by your infertility*
In a great dowry with a goldsmith's daughter.
SIR OLIVER They may be all deceived.
Be but you patient, wife.
LADY KIX I have suffered a long time.
SIR OLIVER Suffer thy heart out, a pox° suffer thee! *lit., "syphilis"*
LADY KIX Nay, thee, thou desertless slave!° *undeserving wretch*
SIR OLIVER Come, come, I ha' done.
You'll to the gossiping° of Master Allwit's child? *christening feast*
LADY KIX Yes, to my much joy.° *(said sarcastically)*
Everyone gets° before me. There's my sister *begets children*
Was married but at Barthol'mew Eve[3] last,
And she can have two children at a birth.
Oh, one of them, one of them would ha' served my turn!
SIR OLIVER Sorrow consume thee! Thou art still crossing° me, *contradicting*
And know'st my nature.

Enter a Maid.

MAID Oh, mistress,
Weeping or railing, that's our house harmony.[4]
LADY KIX What say'st, Jug?° *i.e., Joan*
MAID The sweetest news!
LADY KIX What is't, wench?
MAID Throw down your doctor's drugs; they're all
But heretics.° I bring certain remedy *Unworthy of belief*
That has been taught and proved,° and never failed. *tested*
SIR OLIVER Oh, that, that, that or nothing!
MAID There's a gentleman—
I haply° have his name too—that has got *by luck; happily*
Nine children by one water° that he useth. *medicine; semen*
It never misses; they come so fast upon him
He was fain° to give it over. *obliged*
LADY KIX His name, sweet Jug?
MAID One Master Touchwood, a fine gentleman,
But run behindhand° much with getting children. *into debt*
SIR OLIVER Is't possible?
MAID Why, sir, he'll undertake,
Using that water, within fifteen year,
For° all your wealth, to make you a poor man, *Despite*
You shall so swarm with children.
SIR OLIVER I'll venture that, i'faith.
LADY KIX That shall you, husband.
MAID But I must tell you first, he's very dear.° *expensive*

2. I.e., Think of all the landed inheritance we lose through lack of children if Sir Walter produces an heir. (Sir Oliver and his wife are related to Sir Walter in such a way that if Sir Walter, who evidently has no brother as a potential heir, were to die childless, his inheritance would pass to them; perhaps Sir Oliver is the eldest son of Sir Walter's father's younger brother.)

3. Eve of Saint Bartholomew Day, August 24.

4. The only harmony in our house is sentimental weeping and scolding. (The Maid has evidently been talking with Touchwood Senior, as the ensuing dialogue suggests.)

SIR OLIVER No matter. What serves wealth for?
LADY KIX True, sweet husband.
SIR OLIVER There's land to come. Put case his water stands me
In some five hundred pound a pint,
'Twill fetch a thousand, and a kersten soul.[5]
LADY KIX And that's worth all, sweet husband.
SIR OLIVER I'll about it.° *I'll get to work*
Exeunt.

[2.2]

Enter Allwit.

ALLWIT I'll go bid gossips° presently myself. *godparents; friends*
That's all the work I'll do; nor need I stir,
But that it is my pleasure to walk forth
And air myself a little. I am tied
To nothing in this business; what I do
Is merely recreation, not constraint.
Here's running to and fro: nurse upon nurse,
Three charwomen,° besides maids and neighbors' children. *cleaning women*
Fie, what a trouble have I rid my hands on!° *of*
It makes me sweat to think on't.

Enter Sir Walter Whorehound.

SIR WALTER How now, Jack?
ALLWIT I am going to bid gossips for Your Worship's child, sir: a goodly girl, i'faith. Give you joy on her! She looks as if she had two thousand pound to her portion° and run away with a tailor.[1] A fine, plump black-eyed slut. Under correction,° sir, I take delight to see her. [*Calling*] Nurse! *dowry* / *Pardon my saying so*

Enter Dry Nurse.

DRY NURSE Do you call, sir?
ALLWIT I call not you, I call the wet nurse hither.
Give me the wet nurse.[2] *Exit* [*Dry Nurse*].

Enter Wet Nurse [*with the baby*].

Ay, 'tis thou. Come hither, come hither.
Let's see her once again. [*He kisses the baby.*] I cannot choose
But buss° her thrice an hour. *kiss*
WET NURSE You may be proud on't, sir.
'Tis the best piece of work that e'er you did.
ALLWIT Think'st thou so, nurse? What sayest to Wat and Nick?
WET NURSE They're pretty children both, but here's a wench
Will be a knocker.° *a knockout*
ALLWIT [*dandling the child*] Pup!°—Say'st thou me so?—Pup, little countess! *(baby talk)*

5. I.e., We stand to inherit much land if we can manage to have children. (See note 2, line 156, above.) Suppose his medicine costs me as much as £500 a pint; even so, it will yield a return to us of £1,000 in land, and a christened baby to boot.

2.2. Allwit's house and vicinity.
1. Because she has such fine clothes.
2. A wet nurse gives suck to an infant; a dry nurse tends to it otherwise.

[To Sir Walter] Faith, sir, I thank Your Worship for this girl
Ten thousand times and upward.
SIR WALTER I am glad I have her for you, sir.
ALLWIT Here, take her in, nurse; wipe her, and give her
spoon-meat.° — *soft spoon-fed food*
WET NURSE Wipe your mouth, sir. *Exit [with the baby].*
ALLWIT And now about these gossips.
SIR WALTER Get but two. I'll stand for one myself.
ALLWIT To your own child, sir?
SIR WALTER The better policy; it prevents suspicion.
'Tis good to play with rumor at all weapons.[3]
ALLWIT Troth, I commend your care, sir; 'tis a thing
That I should ne'er have thought on.
SIR WALTER *[aside]* The more slave!
When man turns base, out goes his soul's pure flame;
The fat of ease o'erthrows the eyes of shame.
ALLWIT I am studying° who to get for godmother — *considering*
Suitable to Your Worship. Now I ha' thought on't.
SIR WALTER I'll ease you of that care, and please myself in't.
[Aside] My love, the goldsmith's daughter. If I send,
Her father will command her. *[Calling]* Davy Dahumma!

Enter Davy.

ALLWIT I'll fit Your Worship then with a male partner.° — *fellow godparent*
SIR WALTER What is he?
ALLWIT A kind proper gentleman, brother to Master Touchwood.
SIR WALTER I know Touchwood. Has he a brother living?
ALLWIT A neat° bachelor. — *elegant*
SIR WALTER Now we know him, we'll make shift° with him. — *make do*
Dispatch! The time draws near.—Come hither, Davy.
Exit [with Davy].
ALLWIT In troth, I pity him. He ne'er stands still.
Poor knight, what pains he takes! Sends this way one,
That way another, has not an hour's leisure.
I would not have thy toil for all thy pleasure.

Enter two Promoters.° — *informers*

[Aside] Ha, how now? What are these that stand so close° — *furtively*
At the street corner, pricking up their ears
And snuffing up their noses like rich men's dogs
When the first course goes in?° By the Mass, promoters! — *into the dining room*
'Tis so, I hold° my life; and planted there — *bet*
To arrest the dead corpse° of poor calves and sheep, — *carcasses*
Like ravenous creditors that will not suffer
The bodies of their poor departed debtors
To go to th'grave, but e'en in death to vex
And stay the corpse with bills of Middlesex.[4]
This Lent will fat the whoresons° up with sweetbreads, — *fatten the promoters*
And lard their whores with lamb-stones;° what their golls° — *an aphrodisiac / hands*
Can clutch goes presently to their Molls and Dolls.

3. It's a good idea to combat rumor by whatever means possible. (By standing as godfather, Sir Walter will undertake to mislead those who suspect him of fathering the child.)

4. A legal nicety used to extend the jurisdiction of the King's Bench by issuing warrants on fictitious charges in Middlesex County that could then be extended to cover other areas. Allwit here compares promoters, who pursue carcasses of animals, to creditors who continue to pursue their debtors even after the debtors have died.

The bawds will be so fat with what they earn,
Their chins will hang like udders by Easter Eve,
And, being stroked, will give the milk of witches.
How did the mongrels hear my wife lies in?° *is in childbirth*
Well, I may baffle° 'em gallantly. [*To them*] By your favor, *foil, humiliate*
gentlemen. I am a stranger both unto the city and to her
carnal strictness.° *meat regulations*

FIRST PROMOTER Good. Your will, sir?

ALLWIT Pray tell me where one dwells that kills° this Lent. *slaughters meat*

FIRST PROMOTER How, kills? [*Aside to his companion*] Come
hither, Dick. A bird,° a bird! *An easy victim*

SECOND PROMOTER [*to Allwit*] What is't that you would have?

ALLWIT Faith, any flesh, but I long especially for veal and
green sauce.° *vinegar sauce*

FIRST PROMOTER [*aside*] Green goose,° you shall be sauced.° *Fool / cheated*

ALLWIT I have half a scornful° stomach; no fish will be admitted. *queasy*

FIRST PROMOTER Not this Lent, sir?

ALLWIT Lent? What cares colon° here for Lent? *belly; appetite*

FIRST PROMOTER You say well, sir. Good reason that the
colon of a gentleman—as you were lately pleased to term
Your Worship,° sir—should be fulfilled° with answer- *yourself / filled*
able° food, to sharpen blood, delight health, and tickle *suitable*
nature.° Were you directed hither to this street, sir? *craving*

ALLWIT That I was, ay, marry.° *by Mary; indeed*

SECOND PROMOTER And the butcher, belike,° should kill and *it seems*
sell close° in some upper room? *furtively*

ALLWIT Some apple loft, as I take it, or a coal house; I know
not which, i'faith.

SECOND PROMOTER Either will serve. This butcher shall kiss
Newgate,[5] 'less he turn up the bottom of the pocket of his
apron.° You go to seek him? *i.e., pays a bribe*

ALLWIT Where you shall not find him. I'll buy, walk by your
noses with my flesh, sheep-biting mongrels, handbasket
freebooters![6] My wife lies in.[7] A foutra° for promoters! *(an obscenity)*
Exit.

FIRST PROMOTER That shall not serve your turn.°—What a *That excuse won't do*
rogue's this! How cunningly he came over° us! *outwitted*

Enter a Man with meat in a basket.

SECOND PROMOTER Husht! Stand close. [*They stand aside.*]

MAN I have scaped well thus far. They say the knaves are
wondrous hot and busy.

FIRST PROMOTER [*approaching the Man*] By your leave, sir, we
must see what you have under your cloak there.

MAN Have? I have nothing.

FIRST PROMOTER No? Do you tell us that? What makes this
lump stick out, then? We must see, sir.

MAN What will you see, sir? A pair of sheets and two of my
wife's foul smocks° going to the washers? *dirty petticoats*

SECOND PROMOTER Oh, we love that sight well; you cannot
please us better. [*They search his basket and find meat.*]

5. I.e., go to jail. (Newgate was one of London's main prisons.)
6. You cheating rascals and highwaymen preying on poor victims with handbaskets!
7. Pregnant women were exempt from Lenten restrictions on meat.

What? Do you gull° us? Call you these shirts and smocks? *cheat*

MAN Now a pox choke you! You have cozened° me and five of my wife's kindred of a good dinner. We must make it up now with herrings and milk pottage. *Exit.* *cheated*

FIRST PROMOTER [*examining the basket*] 'Tis all veal.

SECOND PROMOTER All veal? Pox! The worse luck. I promised faithfully to send this morning a fat quarter of lamb to a kind gentlewoman in Turnbull Street[8] that longs,° and how I'm crossed!° *craves because pregnant* *thwarted*

FIRST PROMOTER Let's share this, and see what hap comes next, then.

Enter another [Master Oliver] with a basket.

SECOND PROMOTER Agreed. Stand close again. Another booty! What's he?

FIRST PROMOTER [*accosting Oliver*] Sir, by your favor.

OLIVER Meaning me, sir?

FIRST PROMOTER Good Master Oliver, cry thee mercy,° i'faith! What hast thou there? *I beg your pardon*

OLIVER A rack of mutton, sir, and half a lamb. You know my mistress's diet.

FIRST PROMOTER Go, go, we see thee not. Away, keep close! [*To his partner*] Heart, let him pass. Thou'lt never have the wit to know our benefactors.[9] [*Exit Master Oliver.*]

SECOND PROMOTER I have forgot him.

FIRST PROMOTER 'Tis Master Beggarland's man—the wealthy merchant that is in fee with° us. *who makes payoffs to*

SECOND PROMOTER Now I have a feeling of him.° *Now I know who you mean*

FIRST PROMOTER You know, he purchased the whole Lent together,[1] gave us ten groats° apiece on Ash Wednesday.[2] *fourpenny pieces*

SECOND PROMOTER True, true.

Enter a [country] Wench with a basket, and a child in it under a loin of mutton.

FIRST PROMOTER A wench!

SECOND PROMOTER Why, then, stand close indeed. [*They conceal themselves.*]

WENCH [*to herself*] Women had need of wit if they'll shift° here, and she that hath wit may shift anywhere. *survive, get by*

FIRST PROMOTER [*aside to his companion*] Look, look! Poor fool, she has left the rump uncovered, too, more to betray her. This is like a murd'rer that will outface the deed with a bloody band.[3]

SECOND PROMOTER [*accosting her*] What time of the year is't,° sister? *i.e., Isn't it Lent*

WENCH Oh, sweet gentlemen! I am a poor servant; let me go.

FIRST PROMOTER You shall, wench, but this [*indicating the basket*] must stay with us.

8. A notorious brothel district.
9. You're never smart enough to recognize those who supply us with bribes.
1. He paid a bribe for all of Lent.
2. The first day of Lent.
3. Like a murderer who will try to talk his or her way out of an accusation of murder when the blood shows on the murderer's neck-band or cuff.

WENCH Oh, you undo me, sir! 'Tis for a wealthy gentlewoman that takes physic,° sir; the doctor does allow my mistress mutton. Oh, as you tender° the dear life of a gentlewoman, I'll bring my master to you; he shall show you a true authority from the higher powers, and I'll run every foot.

medicine
have a regard for

SECOND PROMOTER Well, leave your basket, then, and run and spare not.°

don't slow down

WENCH Will you swear then to me to keep it till I come?

FIRST PROMOTER Now, by this light I will.

WENCH [*to Second Promoter*] What say you, gentleman?

SECOND PROMOTER What a strange wench 'tis! Would we might perish else.°

May we die if we don't

WENCH Nay, then, I run, sir. *Exit* [*leaving the basket*].

FIRST PROMOTER And ne'er return, I hope.

SECOND PROMOTER A politic baggage!° She makes us swear to keep it. I prithee, look what market° she hath made.

cunning hussy
purchase

FIRST PROMOTER [*inspecting the basket*] Imprimis,° sir, a good fat loin of mutton. What comes next under this cloth? Now for a quarter of lamb.

First of all

SECOND PROMOTER Now for a shoulder of mutton.

FIRST PROMOTER Done!°

i.e., It's a bet!

SECOND PROMOTER Why, done, sir!

FIRST PROMOTER [*searching further*] By the Mass, I feel I have lost; 'tis of more weight, i'faith.

SECOND PROMOTER Some loin of veal?

FIRST PROMOTER No, faith, here's a lamb's head; I feel that plainly. Why, yet I'll win my wager.

SECOND PROMOTER Ha?

FIRST PROMOTER 'Swounds,° what's here?

By God's wounds

SECOND PROMOTER A child.

FIRST PROMOTER A pox of all dissembling cunning whores!

SECOND PROMOTER Here's an unlucky breakfast.

FIRST PROMOTER What shall 's° do?

shall we

SECOND PROMOTER The quean° made us swear to keep it, too.

whore

FIRST PROMOTER We might leave it else.°

otherwise

SECOND PROMOTER Villainous strange! Life, had she none to gull but poor promoters that watch° hard for a living?

spy

FIRST PROMOTER Half our gettings° must run° in sugar-sops and nurses' wages now, besides many a pound of soap and tallow. We have need to get loins of mutton still, to save suet to change for candles.[4]

earnings / be spent

SECOND PROMOTER Nothing mads me but this was a lamb's head with you;[5] you felt it! She has made calves' heads° of us.

fools

FIRST PROMOTER Prithee, no more on't. There's time to get it up;° it is not come to Mid-Lent Sunday yet.

make up the loss

SECOND PROMOTER I am so angry I'll watch no more today.

FIRST PROMOTER Faith, nor I neither.

SECOND PROMOTER Why, then, I'll make a motion.°

proposal

FIRST PROMOTER Well, what is't?

4. To make candles of. (The candles—made cheaply of suet, or animal fat—would be needed to tend to the baby at night. Sugar-sop, line 201, is soaked and sweetened bread, which could be fed to the baby.)

5. Nothing angers me so much as that you mistook this for a lamb's head—a delicacy we could profit from.

SECOND PROMOTER Let's e'en go to the Checker at Queenhithe° *an inn on the Thames*
and roast the loin of mutton till young flood,° then send the *turning of the tide*
child to Brentford.° [*Exeunt.*] *a town west of London*

[2.3]

Enter Allwit in one of Sir Walter's suits, and Davy trussing him.° *tying his laces*

ALLWIT 'Tis a busy day at our house, Davy.
DAVY Always the kurs'ning day,[1] sir.
ALLWIT Truss, truss me, Davy.
DAVY [*aside*] No matter an° you were hanged,[2] sir. *if*
ALLWIT How does this suit fit me, Davy?
DAVY Excellent neatly. My master's things were ever fit for you, sir, e'en to a hair, you know.
ALLWIT Thou hast hit it right, Davy.
We ever jumped in one,° this ten years, Davy. *agreed; shared my wife*
So, well said.

Enter a Servant with a box.

What art thou?
SERVANT Your comfit-maker's° man, sir. *preserved-fruit-maker's*
ALLWIT Oh, sweet youth, in to the nurse quick, quick!
'Tis time, i'faith. Your mistress° will be here? *(The comfit-maker's wife)*
SERVANT She was setting forth, sir. [*Exit.*]

Enter two Puritans.

ALLWIT Here comes our gossips now.
Oh, I shall have such kissing work today!—
Sweet Mistress Underman, welcome, i'faith.
FIRST PURITAN Give you joy of your fine girl, sir!
Grant that her education may be pure,
And become° one of the faithful! *may she become*
ALLWIT Thanks to your sisterly wishes, Mistress Underman.
SECOND PURITAN Are any of the brethren's° wives yet come? *Puritan men's*
ALLWIT There are some wives within, and some at home.
FIRST PURITAN Verily, thanks, sir. *Exeunt* [*Puritans*].
ALLWIT Verily, you are an ass, forsooth!
I must fit all these times,° or there's no music. *dance to others' tunes*

Enter two Gossips.

Here comes a friendly and familiar pair.
Now, I like these wenches well.
FIRST GOSSIP How dost, sirrah?
ALLWIT Faith, well, I thank you, neighbor. And how dost thou?
SECOND GOSSIP Want° nothing but such getting,° sir, as thine. *I lack / offspring*
ALLWIT My gettings,° wench? They are poor. *income; offspring*
FIRST GOSSIP Fie, that thou'lt say so!
Th' hast as fine children as a man can get.
DAVY [*aside*] Ay, as a man can get—and that's my master.

2.3. Allwit's house.

1. It's always busy on the christening day. (Since Sir Walter begets so many bastards, these are pretty regular events.)

2. By "Truss, truss me" in line 3, Allwit means "Help me to dress, help me with the laces that fasten my clothes." Davy, speaking aside, then plays on "truss" in the sense of "hang."

ALLWIT They are pretty foolish things, put to making° In minutes. I ne'er stand long about 'em.[3] — *begotten*
Will you walk in, wenches? [*Exeunt Gossips.*]

Enter Touchwood Junior [*with a ring*] *and Moll.*

TOUCHWOOD JR. [*aside to Moll*] The happiest meeting that our souls could wish for!
Here's the ring ready. I am beholding° — *beholden, indebted*
Unto your father's haste; he's kept his hour.

MOLL He never kept it better.

Enter Sir Walter Whorehound.

TOUCHWOOD JR. [*aside to Moll*] Back! Be silent.

SIR WALTER [*offering a toast to Moll and Touchwood Junior*] Mistress and partner, I will put you both
Into one cup.[4]

DAVY [*aside*] Into one cup! Most proper.
A fitting compliment for a goldsmith's daughter.

ALLWIT Yes, sir, that's he must be° Your Worship's partner — *he who is to be*
In this day's business, Master Touchwood's brother.

SIR WALTER [*to Touchwood Junior*] I embrace your acquaintance, sir.

TOUCHWOOD JR. It vows your service,° sir. — *Your obedient servant*

SIR WALTER It's near high time.° Come, Master Allwit. — *the christening time*

ALLWIT Ready, sir.

SIR WALTER Will't please you walk?

TOUCHWOOD JR. Sir, I obey your time.° *Exeunt.* — *I'll do as you say*

[2.4]

Enter midwife with the child, [*Maudlin, the two Puritans,*] *and the* [*five*] *Gossips to the kurs'ning.* [*The midwife, with the child, begins to lead the ceremonial procession offstage.*]

FIRST GOSSIP [*offering precedence*] Good Mistress Yellowhammer.

MAUDLIN In faith, I will not.

FIRST GOSSIP Indeed, it° shall be yours. — *(first place)*

MAUDLIN I have sworn, i'faith.

FIRST GOSSIP I'll stand still, then.

MAUDLIN So will you let the child go without company and make me forsworn.

FIRST GOSSIP You are such another creature!° — *You're something!*

SECOND GOSSIP Before me? I pray, come down° a little. — *be humbler*

THIRD GOSSIP Not a whit. I hope I know my place.

SECOND GOSSIP Your place? Great wonder, sure! Are you any better than a comfit-maker's wife?

THIRD GOSSIP And that's as good at all times as a pothecary's.

SECOND GOSSIP Ye lie! Yet I forbear° you too. — *show forbearance to*

FIRST PURITAN Come, sweet sister, we go in unity, and show the fruits of peace, like children of the spirit.

3. (1) I take little time in the act of procreation; (2) I had nothing to do with it. ("Stand" suggests "am erect.")
4. I drink to you both: my bride-to-be and my fellow godparent.
2.4. The scene is virtually continuous.

SECOND PURITAN I love lowliness.
FOURTH GOSSIP True, so say I. Though they° strive more, *(those in front)*
There comes as proud behind as goes before.[1]
FIFTH GOSSIP Every inch, i'faith. *Exeunt.*

3.1

Enter Touchwood Junior and a Parson.

TOUCHWOOD JR. Oh, sir, if ever you felt the force of love,
Pity it in me!
PARSON Yes. Though I ne'er was married, sir,
I have felt the force of love from good men's daughters,
And some that will be maids° yet three years hence. *virgins*
Have you got a license?° *(see 2.1.129)*
TOUCHWOOD JR. [*showing the license*] Here, 'tis ready, sir.
PARSON That's well.
TOUCHWOOD JR. The ring and all things perfect,° *being ready*
She'll steal hither.
PARSON She shall be welcome, sir.
I'll not be long a-clapping you together.

Enter Moll and Touchwood Senior.

TOUCHWOOD JR. Oh, here she's come, sir.
PARSON What's he?
TOUCHWOOD JR. My honest brother.
TOUCHWOOD SR. Quick, make haste, sirs.
MOLL You must dispatch with all the speed you can,
For I shall be missed straight. I made hard shift° *had difficulty*
For this small time I have.
PARSON Then I'll not linger.
Place that ring upon her finger.
This the finger plays the part,
Whose master vein shoots from the heart.
Now join hands—

Enter Yellowhammer and Sir Walter.

YELLOWHAMMER Which I will sever,
And so ne'er again meet, never.
MOLL Oh, we are betrayed!
TOUCHWOOD SR. Hard fate!
SIR WALTER I am struck with wonder.
YELLOWHAMMER [*to Moll*] Was this the politic fetch, thou mystical baggage,[1]
Thou disobedient strumpet? [*To Sir Walter*] And were you
So wise to send for her to such an end?
SIR WALTER Now I disclaim the end.° You'll make me mad. *any such motive*
YELLOWHAMMER [*to Touchwood Junior*] And what are you, sir?
TOUCHWOOD JR. An° you cannot see *If*
Without those two glasses,° put on a pair more. *spectacles*
YELLOWHAMMER I dreamt of anger still![2] Here, take your ring, sir. [*He takes the ring off Moll's finger.*]

1. People in back of the line can be just as proud as those in front.
3.1. A church (?).

1. Was this the cunning device, you secretive hussy.
2. I had a premonition of this in my recurring dreams!

Ha, this? Life, 'tis the same! Abominable!
Did not I sell this ring?
TOUCHWOOD JR. I think you did;
You received money for't.
YELLOWHAMMER Heart! Hark you, knight;
Here's no inconscionable villainy:[3]
Set me a-work to make the wedding ring,
And come with an intent to steal my daughter!
Did ever runaway match it?
SIR WALTER [*to Touchwood Senior*] This° your brother, sir? *Is this*
TOUCHWOOD SR. He can tell that as well as I.
YELLOWHAMMER The very posy mocks me to my face:
"Love that's wise
Blinds parents' eyes."
I thank your wisdom, sir, for blinding of us;
We have good hope to recover our sight shortly.
In the meantime I will lock up this baggage° *hussy*
As carefully as my gold. She shall see
As little sun, if a close° room or so *confined*
Can keep her from the light on't.
MOLL O sweet father,
For love's sake, pity me!
YELLOWHAMMER Away!
MOLL [*to Touchwood Junior*] Farewell, sir.
All content bless thee. And take this for comfort:
Though violence keep me, thou canst lose me never;
I am ever thine, although we part forever.
YELLOWHAMMER Ay, we shall part you, minx.
Exit [*with Moll*].
SIR WALTER [*to Touchwood Junior*] Your acquaintance, sir,
Came very lately, yet it came too soon.[4]
I must hereafter know you for no friend,
But one that I must shun like pestilence
Or the disease of lust.
TOUCHWOOD JR. Like° enough, sir. *Likely*
You ha' ta'en me at the worst time for words
That e'er ye picked out. Faith, do not wrong° me, sir. *Exit.* *misjudge*
TOUCHWOOD SR. [*to Sir Walter*] Look after him and spare
not.[5] There he walks
That never yet received baffling.° You're blest *public humiliation*
More than e'er I knew.[6] Go, take your rest. *Exit.*
SIR WALTER I pardon you. You are both losers. *Exit.*

[3.2]

A bed thrust out upon the stage, Allwit's wife in it. Enter [*the Puritans, Maudlin, Lady Kix, a Nurse holding the infant, and*] *all the Gossips.*

FIRST GOSSIP How is't, woman? We have brought you home
A kursen soul.° *Christian baby*

3. Here's a fine trick!
4. Though we've just met, I am sorry we met at all.
5. Watch out for my brother and spare no pains in being careful.
6. You're a lucky man so far—more lucky than I've ever been.
3.2. Allwit's house.

MRS. ALLWIT Ay, I thank your pains.° *you for your trouble*
FIRST PURITAN And, verily, well kursened, i'the right way,
Without idolatry or superstition,
After the pure manner of Amsterdam.° *a Puritan center*
MRS. ALLWIT Sit down, good neighbors.—Nurse!
NURSE At hand, forsooth.
MRS. ALLWIT Look° they have all low stools. *See to it that*
NURSE They have, forsooth.
SECOND GOSSIP Bring the child hither, nurse.—How say you now,
Gossip, is't not a chopping° girl, so like the father? *strapping*
THIRD GOSSIP As if it had been spit out of his mouth:° *The spitting image*
Eyed, nosed, and browed as like a girl can be,
Only indeed it has the mother's mouth.
SECOND GOSSIP The mother's mouth up and down, up and down.° *head to foot*
THIRD GOSSIP 'Tis a large child; she's but a little woman.
FIRST PURITAN No, believe me,
A very spiny° creature, but all heart, *skinny*
Well mettled,° like the faithful, to endure *Full of spirit*
Her tribulation here and raise up seed.° *breed, offspring*
SECOND GOSSIP She had a sore labor on't, I warrant you.
You can tell, neighbor.
THIRD GOSSIP Oh, she had great speed.° *it went well with her*
We were afraid once, but she made us all
Have joyful hearts again. 'Tis a good soul, i'faith.
The midwife found her a most cheerful daughter.
FIRST PURITAN 'Tis the spirit. The sisters° are all like her. *Puritan women*

Enter Sir Walter with two spoons and plate,° and Allwit. *silver plate*

SECOND GOSSIP Oh, here comes the chief gossip,° neighbors. *godparent*
[*The Nurse retires, with the infant.*]
SIR WALTER The fatness° of your wishes to you all, ladies. *choicest morsel*
THIRD GOSSIP Oh, dear sweet gentleman! What fine words he has: "The fatness of our wishes"!
SECOND GOSSIP Calls us all "ladies"!
FOURTH GOSSIP I promise you, a fine gentleman, and a courteous.
SECOND GOSSIP Methinks her husband shows° like a clown to° him. *looks* / *compared with*
THIRD GOSSIP I would not care what clown my husband were, too, so° I had such fine children. *so long as*
SECOND GOSSIP She's° all fine children, gossip. *She has*
THIRD GOSSIP Ay, and see how fast they come.
FIRST PURITAN Children are blessings, if they be got with zeal
By the brethren,° as I have five at home. *Puritan men*
SIR WALTER [*to Mrs. Allwit*] The worst is past, I hope now, gossip.
MRS. ALLWIT So I hope too, good sir.
ALLWIT [*aside*] Why, then, so hope I too for company;° I have nothing to do else. *to be part of the group*
SIR WALTER [*giving cup and spoon*] A poor remembrance, lady,
To the love of the babe. I pray, accept of it.

MRS. ALLWIT Oh, you are at too much charge,° sir. *you're too generous*
SECOND GOSSIP Look, look, what has he given her? What is't, gossip?
THIRD GOSSIP Now, by my faith, a fair high standing cup° *legged cup*
And two great 'postle spoons,[1] one of them gilt.
FIRST PURITAN Sure that was Judas, then, with the red beard.[2]
SECOND PURITAN I would not feed my daughter with that spoon
For all the world, for fear of coloring her hair.
Red hair the brethren like not; it consumes
Them much;° 'tis not the sisters' color. *it angers them*

Enter Nurse with comfits and wine.

ALLWIT Well said,° nurse. *Well done*
About,° about with them amongst the gossips! *Move about*
[*The Nurse serves comfits to the guests.*]
[*Aside*] Now out comes all the tasseled handkerchers;
They are spread abroad between their knees already.
Now in goes the long fingers that are washed
Some thrice a day in urine;° my wife uses it. *(used as a cosmetic)*
Now we shall have such pocketing!
See how they lurch at the lower end.[3]
FIRST PURITAN Come hither, nurse.
ALLWIT [*aside*] Again? She has taken twice already.
FIRST PURITAN [*taking comfits*] I had forgot a sister's child that's sick.
ALLWIT [*aside*] A pox! It seems your purity loves sweet things well, that puts in° thrice together. Had this been all my cost, now, I had been beggared. These women have no consciences at sweetmeats, where'er they come; see an they have not culled out all the long plums° too. They have left nothing here but short wriggle-tail° comfits, not worth mouthing. No mar'l° I heard a citizen complain once that his wife's belly only broke his back.[4] Mine had been all in fitters° seven years since but for this worthy knight, that with a prop upholds my wife and me and all my estate buried in Bucklersbury.[5] [*The Nurse serves wine to the guests.*] *you who help yourselves* / *sugar plums* / *twisted* / *It's no marvel (that)* / *little bits*
MRS. ALLWIT [*pledging them*] Here, Mistress Yellowhammer, and neighbors: To you all that have taken pains with me, all the good wives at once!
FIRST PURITAN I'll answer for them:
They wish all health and strength,
And that you may courageously go forward
To perform the like and many such,
Like a true sister, with motherly bearing.
ALLWIT [*aside*] Now the cups troll° about to wet the gossips' whistles. It pours down, i'faith; they never think of payment. *circulate*

1. Apostle spoons, silver spoons whose handles are engraved, each with the figure of one of the various apostles.
2. Judas, who betrayed Jesus, was traditionally represented as having red hair and a red beard. The color gold, achieved here by gilding, was regarded as reddish in hue.
3. See how they snitch sweets down at the end of the room opposite to the host.
4. That his wife's extravagant appetite, all by itself, pushed him beyond the limits of endurance, sexually and otherwise.
5. Sir Walter's generosity has supported the extravagance of my wife and all the consequent bills we have run up at the grocers' and apothecaries' shops in Bucklersbury (a London shop district).

FIRST PURITAN Fill again, nurse.

ALLWIT [*aside*] Now bless thee, two at once! I'll stay no longer; it would kill me an if° I paid for't. [*To Sir Walter*] Will it please you to walk down and leave the women? *an if = if*

SIR WALTER With all my heart, Jack.

ALLWIT Troth, I cannot blame you.

SIR WALTER Sit you all merry, ladies.

ALL GOSSIPS Thank Your Worship, sir.

FIRST PURITAN Thank Your Worship, sir.

ALLWIT [*aside*] A pox twice tipple ye!° You are last and lowest. *topple you over*

Exit [with Sir Walter].

FIRST PURITAN Bring hither that same cup, nurse. I would fain drive away this—hup!°—anti-Christian grief. *hiccup!*

[*The Nurse provides more drink.*]

THIRD GOSSIP See, gossip, an she° lies not in like a countess. Would I had such a husband for my daughter! *(Mrs. Allwit)*

FOURTH GOSSIP Is not she toward marriage?° *about to be married*

THIRD GOSSIP Oh, no, sweet gossip.

FOURTH GOSSIP Why, she's nineteen.

THIRD GOSSIP Ay, that she was, last Lammas.° But she has a fault, gossip, a secret fault. *August 1, harvest festival*

FOURTH GOSSIP A fault? What is't?

THIRD GOSSIP I'll tell you when I have drunk.

FOURTH GOSSIP [*aside*] Wine can do that, I see, that friendship cannot.

THIRD GOSSIP And now I'll tell you, gossip: she's too free.

FOURTH GOSSIP Too free?

THIRD GOSSIP Oh, ay, she cannot lie dry in her bed.° *she wets her bed*

FOURTH GOSSIP What, and nineteen?

THIRD GOSSIP 'Tis as I tell you, gossip.

[*Enter Nurse, and hands a note to Maudlin.*]

MAUDLIN Speak with me, nurse? Who is't?

NURSE A gentleman from Cambridge. I think it be your son, forsooth.

MAUDLIN 'Tis my son Tim, i'faith. Prithee call him up among the women. [*Exit Nurse.*]
'Twill embolden him well, for he wants° nothing but audacity. Would the Welsh gentlewoman at home were here now! *lacks*

LADY KIX Is your son come, forsooth?

MAUDLIN Yes, from the university, forsooth.

LADY KIX 'Tis great joy on ye.

MAUDLIN There's a great marriage towards° for him. *in the making*

LADY KIX A marriage?

MAUDLIN Yes, sure, a huge heir in Wales, at least to nineteen mountains, besides her goods and cattle.° *livestock; wealth*

Enter Tim [with the Nurse].

TIM Oh, I'm betrayed! *Exit.*

MAUDLIN What, gone again?—Run after him, good nurse.

[*Exit Nurse.*]

He's so bashful; that's the spoil° of youth. In the university they're kept still to men and ne'er trained up to women's company. *ruination*

LADY KIX 'Tis a great spoil of youth, indeed.

Enter Nurse and Tim.

NURSE [*to Tim*] Your mother will have it so.

MAUDLIN Why, son, why, Tim, what, must I rise and fetch you? For shame, son!

TIM Mother, you do entreat like a freshwoman. 'Tis against the laws of the university for any that has answered under bachelor[6] to thrust 'mongst married wives.

MAUDLIN Come, we'll excuse you here.

TIM Call up my tutor, mother, and I care not.° *I don't mind staying*

MAUDLIN What, is your tutor come? Have you brought him up?° *up to London*

TIM I ha' not brought him up;° he stands at door.° *Negatur.*[7] There's logic to begin with you, mother. *upstairs / downstairs*

MAUDLIN Run, call the gentleman, nurse. He's my son's tutor. [*Exit Nurse.*]
[*To Tim*] Here, eat some plums.

TIM Come I from Cambridge, and offer me six plums?

MAUDLIN Why, how now, Tim? Will not your old tricks yet be left?

TIM Served like a child, when I have answered under bachelor?

MAUDLIN You'll never lin° till I make your tutor whip you. You know how I served you once at the free school in Paul's Churchyard?° *cease* / *St. Paul's School*

TIM Oh, monstrous absurdity! Ne'er was the like in Cambridge since my time. Life, whip a bachelor? You'd be laughed at soundly. Let not my tutor hear you. 'Twould be a jest through the whole university. No more words, mother.

Enter Tutor.

MAUDLIN Is this your tutor, Tim?

TUTOR Yes, surely, lady. I am the man that brought him in league with logic and read° the Dunces[8] to him. *interpreted*

TIM That did he, mother, but now I have 'em all in my own pate,° and can as well read 'em to others. *head*

TUTOR That can he, mistress, for they flow naturally° from him. *spontaneously; foolishly*

MAUDLIN I'm the more beholding to your pains,° sir. *the trouble you've taken*

TUTOR *Non ideo sane.*[9]

MAUDLIN True, he was an idiot indeed, when he went out of London, but now he's well mended. Did you receive the two goose pies I sent you?

TUTOR And ate them heartily, thanks to Your Worship.

MAUDLIN [*to the Gossips*] 'Tis my son Tim. I pray bid him welcome, gentlewomen.

TIM "Tim"! Hark you: "Timothius," mother, "Timothius."

6. For any person who has met the requirements for the bachelor's degree.
7. Your point is refuted.
8. Followers of John Duns Scotus, a Scottish theologian (c. 1265–c. 1308) whose scholasticism was deemed arid and pedantic by many Renaissance writers. The word "dunce," meaning "stupid," comes from his name.
9. Not for that reason, indeed. (In the next line, Mrs. Allwit misunderstands *ideo*, meaning "for that reason," taking it to mean "idiot.")

MAUDLIN How, shall I deny your name? "Timothius," quoth he? Faith, there's a name! 'Tis my son Tim, forsooth.

LADY KIX You're welcome, Master Tim. *Kiss.*

TIM [*aside to Tutor*] Oh, this is horrible! She wets as she kisses. Your handkercher, sweet tutor, to wipe them off, as fast as they come on!

SECOND GOSSIP Welcome from Cambridge. *Kiss.*

TIM [*aside to Tutor*] This is intolerable. This woman has a villainous sweet breath, did she not stink of comfits. Help me, sweet tutor, or I shall rub my lips off.

TUTOR [*aside to Tim*] I'll go kiss the lower end[1] the whilst.

TIM [*aside to Tutor*] Perhaps that's the sweeter, and we shall dispatch° the sooner. — *finish up*

FIRST PURITAN Let me come next. Welcome from the well-spring of discipline that waters all the brethren![2]

Reels and falls.

TIM Hoist,° I beseech thee! — *Lift yourself (or her) up*

THIRD GOSSIP Oh, bless the woman!—Mistress Underman!

FIRST PURITAN 'Tis but the common affliction of the faithful; we must embrace our falls.[3]

TIM [*aside*] I'm glad I scaped it. It was some rotten kiss, sure; it dropped down before it came at me.

Enter Allwit and Davy.

ALLWIT [*aside*] Here's a noise. Not parted° yet? Heyday, a looking glass!° They have drunk so hard in plate° that some of them had need of other vessels.° [*Aloud*] Yonder's the bravest° show. — *departed* / *i.e., piss-pot / cups* / *piss-pots* / *finest*

ALL GOSSIPS Where? Where, sir?

ALLWIT Come along presently by the Pissing Conduit,[4] with two brave drums and a standard-bearer.

ALL GOSSIPS Oh, brave!

TIM Come, tutor. *Exit [with his Tutor].*

ALL GOSSIPS [*to Mrs. Allwit*] Farewell, sweet gossip!

MRS. ALLWIT I thank you all for your pains.

Exeunt [Gossips].

FIRST PURITAN Feed and grow strong.

Exeunt [Puritans, Mrs. Allwit in her bed, Maudlin, and Lady Kix].

ALLWIT [*in the direction of the departed company*] You had more need to sleep than eat. Go take a nap with some of the brethren, go,[5] and rise up a well edified, boldified sister! Oh, here's a day of toil well passed o'er,° able to make a citizen hare-mad![6] How hot they have made the room with their thick bums! Dost not feel it, Davy? — *thankfully ended*

DAVY Monstrous strong, sir.

ALLWIT What's here under the stools?

1. I'll go kiss the ladies at the lower end of the hall (see line 63 above). With an unaware suggestion also of kissing their lower ends.
2. The First Puritan cordially welcomes Tim from Cambridge because it was known as a hotbed of Calvinism and of the zealous reform movement in the English church known popularly as Puritanism.
3. We must accept our fallen nature. (With added unconscious sexual suggestion.)
4. A famous water fountain in London at the junction of Cornhill and Threadneedle Streets.
5. Allwit scoffs at the Anabaptist contention that it was all right for any man and woman to lie together so long as they were asleep.
6. As mad as a March hare.

DAVY Nothing but wet, sir; some wine spilt here, belike.° *probably*
ALLWIT Is't no worse,° think'st thou? Fair needlework stools cost nothing with them,° Davy. *i.e., urine* / *to them*
DAVY [*aside*] Nor you neither, i'faith.[7]
ALLWIT Look how they have laid them,° e'en as they lie themselves, with their heels up!° How they have shuffled up the rushes° too, Davy, with their short, figging, little shittle-cork heels![8] These women can let nothing stand as they find it. But what's the secret thou'st° about to tell me, my honest Davy? *(the stools)* / *up in the air* / *a floor covering* / *thou wast*
DAVY If you should disclose it, sir—
ALLWIT Life, rip my belly up to the throat, then, Davy.
DAVY My master's upon° marriage. *on the verge of*
ALLWIT Marriage, Davy? Send me to hanging rather![9]
DAVY [*aside*] I have stung him.
ALLWIT When, where? What is she, Davy?
DAVY E'en the same was gossip and gave the spoon.[1]
ALLWIT I have no time to stay, nor scarce can speak!
I'll stop those wheels, or all the work will break.° *Exit.* *my hopes will be ruined*
DAVY I knew 'twould prick. Thus do I fashion still
All mine own ends by him° and his rank° toil. *(Allwit) / sweaty*
'Tis my desire to keep him° still from marriage; *(Sir Walter)*
Being his poor nearest kinsman, I may fare° *inherit*
The better at his death.[2] There my hopes build,
Since my Lady Kix is dry° and hath no child. *Exit.* *barren*

[3.3]

Enter both the Touchwoods.

TOUCHWOOD JR. You're in the happiest way to enrich yourself
And pleasure me, brother, as man's feet can tread in;
For, though she be locked up, her vow is fixed
Only to me. Then time shall never grieve me;
For by that vow, e'en absent I enjoy her,
Assuredly confirmed that none else shall,
Which will make tedious years seem gameful° to me. *diverting, sportive*
In the mean space,° lose you no time, sweet brother. *meantime*
You have the means to strike at this knight's° fortunes *(Sir Oliver Kix's)*
And lay him level with his bankrupt merit.° *give him what he deserves*
Get but his wife with child; perch at treetop
And shake the golden fruit into her lap.° *make her pregnant*
About it, before she weep herself to a dry ground° *to dry infertility*
And whine out all her goodness.° *fecundity*
TOUCHWOOD SR. Prithee, cease.
I find a too much aptness in my blood

7. I.e., You won't be paying for them either (since Sir Walter buys all such things for this household).
8. With their short, fussy, worthless little cork high heels like shuttlecocks (which were made with cork). The image of women with their heels high in the air is sexually suggestive; and the description of women who "can let nothing stand," in the following sentence, suggests sexual conquering of the men.
9. Cf. the proverb, "Hanging and wedding go by destiny" (see also 3.3.59–60 below). Sir Walter's proposed marriage is bad news for Allwit.
1. Even she who served as godparent (Moll) and in whose name (perhaps) a spoon was presented by Sir Walter. (See 3.2.24.1ff.)
2. Davy, Sir Walter's servant, claims some kind of relationship to his master that would entitle him to inherit. Cf. Mosca's hopes of inheriting from his master in Jonson's *Volpone*.
3.3. The Kixes' house.

For such a business without provocation.
You might' well° spared this banquet of eryngoes, *might as well have*
Artichokes, potatoes, and your buttered crab;[1]
They were fitter kept for your own wedding dinner.

TOUCHWOOD JR. Nay, an you'll follow my suit° and save my purse too, *respond to my plea*
Fortune dotes on me. He's in happy case
Finds such an honest friend i'the common place.° *i.e., in time of need*

TOUCHWOOD SR. Life, what makes thee so merry? Thou hast no cause that I could hear of lately since thy crosses,° unless there be news come with new additions. *setbacks*

TOUCHWOOD JR. Why, there thou hast it right. I look for her this evening, brother.

TOUCHWOOD SR. How's that, look for her?

TOUCHWOOD JR. I will deliver you of the wonder straight,[2] brother. By the firm secrecy and kind assistance of a good wench i'the house,[3] who, made of pity, weighing the case her own, she's° led through gutters, strange hidden ways, which none but love could find or ha' the heart to venture. I expect her where you would little think. *Moll is*

TOUCHWOOD SR. I care not where, so she be safe, and yours.

TOUCHWOOD JR. Hope tells me so,
But from your love and time my peace° must grow. *peace of mind*

TOUCHWOOD SR. You know the worst, then,[4] brother.

Exit [Touchwood Junior].

Now to my Kix, the barren he and she. They're i'the next room. But to say which of their two humors[5] hold them now at this instant, I cannot say truly.

SIR OLIVER (*to his Lady within*) Thou liest, barrenness!

TOUCHWOOD SR. Oh, is't that time of day? Give you joy of your tongue! There's nothing else good in you.—This their life the whole day, from eyes open to eyes shut, kissing or scolding, and then must be made friends; then rail the second part of the first fit° out, and then be pleased again, no man knows which way; fall out like giants, and fall in° like children. Their fruit[6] can witness as much. *stanza; paroxysm* / *in each other's arms*

Enter Sir Oliver Kix and his Lady.

SIR OLIVER 'Tis thy fault.

LADY KIX Mine, drought and coldness?

SIR OLIVER Thine. 'Tis thou art barren.

LADY KIX I barren? O life, that I durst but speak now in mine own justice, in mine own right! I barren? 'Twas otherways with me when I was at court; I was ne'er called so till I was married.

SIR OLIVER I'll be divorced.

LADY KIX Be hanged! I need not wish it; that will come too soon to thee. I may say, marriage and hanging goes by destiny,° for all the goodness I can find in't yet. *(see 3.2.232 and n)*

1. Artichokes were regarded as an aphrodisiac, as were eryngoes (candied sea-holly root), potatoes, etc.
2. (1) I'll tell you the news at once; (2) I'll rescue you from your wonderment immediately.
3. With the help of a maid in the Yellowhammer household.
4. I.e., Then you know that you can count on me in any case.
5. Their two whimsical behaviors (which are quarreling and making up).
6. Their fruitlessness, childlessness.

SIR OLIVER [*to Touchwood Senior*] I'll give up house and keep some fruitful whore, like an old bachelor in a tradesman's chamber; she and her children shall have all.

LADY KIX [*taunting Sir Oliver*] Where be they?

TOUCHWOOD SR. [*to them both*] Pray, cease!
When there are friendlier courses took° for you — *taken*
To get and multiply within your house,
At your own proper° costs, in spite of censure,° — *personal / quarrels*
Methinks an honest peace might be established.

SIR OLIVER What, with her? Never.

TOUCHWOOD SR. Sweet sir—

SIR OLIVER You work all in vain.

LADY KIX [*to Sir Oliver*] Then he doth all like thee.[7]

TOUCHWOOD SR. Let me entreat, sir.

SIR OLIVER Singleness confound her! I took her with one smock.[8]

LADY KIX But, indeed, you came not so single when you came from shipboard.[9]

SIR OLIVER [*aside*] Heart, she bit sore there. [*To Touchwood Senior*] Prithee, make 's friends.

TOUCHWOOD SR. [*aside*] Is't come to that? The peal[1] begins to cease.

SIR OLIVER I'll sell all at an outcry.° — *auction*

LADY KIX Do thy worst, slave!—Good sweet sir, bring us into love again.

TOUCHWOOD SR. [*aside*] Some would think this impossible to compass.°—Pray, let this storm fly over. — *encompass, accomplish*

SIR OLIVER Good sir, pardon me. I'm master of this house, which I'll sell presently. I'll clap up bills° this evening. — *put up posters*

TOUCHWOOD SR. Lady, friends,° come! — *be friends*

LADY KIX If e'er ye loved woman, talk not on't, sir. What, friends with him? Good faith, do you think I'm mad? With one that's scarce the hinder quarter of a man?

SIR OLIVER Thou art nothing of a woman.

LADY KIX Would I were less than nothing! [*She*] *weeps.*

SIR OLIVER Nay, prithee, what dost mean?

LADY KIX I cannot please you.

SIR OLIVER I'faith, thou art a good soul; he lies that says it.° Buss,° buss, pretty rogue! [*He attempts to kiss her.*] — *otherwise* / *Kiss*

LADY KIX You care not for me.

TOUCHWOOD SR. [*aside*] Can any man tell now which way° they came in? By this light, I'll be hanged, then. — *how they behaved when*

SIR OLIVER Is the drink come?

TOUCHWOOD SR. (*aside*) Here's a little vial of almond milk that stood me in° some threepence. [*He produces a vial.*] — *cost me*

SIR OLIVER I hope to see thee, wench, within these few years,
Circled with children, pranking up° a girl, — *dressing up*
And putting jewels in their little ears.
Fine sport, i'faith!

7. If he (Touchwood Junior) works in vain, then he does just like you; he works in vain as a lover.
8. May divorce and single life be her punishment! I took her with only one petticoat to her name.
9. I.e., You didn't come to me empty-handed; on the contrary, you brought an infestation of lice (from shipboard). Or, you came with several "smocks," or loose women.
1. The jangling of bells—i.e., quarreling.

LADY KIX Ay, had you been aught,° husband, it had been done ere this time. *of any worth*

SIR OLIVER Had I been aught? Hang thee! Hadst thou been aught! But° a cross thing I ever found thee. *Nothing but*

LADY KIX Thou art a grub to say so.

SIR OLIVER A pox on thee!

TOUCHWOOD SR. [*aside*] By this light, they are out again at the same door, and no man can tell which way!—Come, here's your drink, sir.

SIR OLIVER I will not take it now, sir, an° I were sure to get three boys ere midnight. *even if*

LADY KIX Why, there thou show'st now of what breed thou com'st, to hinder generation.° O thou villain, that knows how crookedly the world goes with us for want of heirs, yet put by° all good fortune! *procreation* *sets aside*

SIR OLIVER Hang, strumpet! I will take it now in spite.° *to spite you*

TOUCHWOOD SR. Then you must ride upon't five hours.[2]

SIR OLIVER I mean so. [*Calling*] Within, there!

Enter a Servant.

SERVANT Sir?

SIR OLIVER Saddle the white mare. [*Exit Servant.*]
I'll take a whore along and ride to Ware.° *(north of London)*

LADY KIX Ride to the devil!

SIR OLIVER I'll plague you every way.
Look ye, do you see, 'tis gone. *Drinks.*

LADY KIX A pox go with it!

SIR OLIVER Ay, curse and spare not now.

TOUCHWOOD SR. Stir° up and down, sir; *Keep moving*
You must not stand.

SIR OLIVER Nay I'm not given to standing.[3]

TOUCHWOOD SR. So much the better, sir, for the—

SIR OLIVER I never could stand long in one place yet;
I learned it of my father, ever figient.° *fidgety*
How if I crossed this,[4] sir? *Capers.*

TOUCHWOOD SR. Oh, passing° good, sir, and would show well a-horseback. When you come to your inn, if you leaped over a joint-stool° or two, 'twere not amiss— (*aside*) although you brake your neck, sir. *very* *well-built stool*

SIR OLIVER What say you to a table thus high, sir?

TOUCHWOOD SR. Nothing better, sir, [*aside*] if it be furnished with good victuals.—You remember how the bargain runs about this business?

SIR OLIVER Or else I had a bad head:° you must receive, sir, four hundred pounds of me at four several° payments; one hundred pound now in hand. *memory* *separate*

TOUCHWOOD SR. Right. That I have, sir.

SIR OLIVER Another hundred when my wife is quick;° the third when she's brought abed;° and the last hundred when the child cries. For if it should be stillborn, it doth no good, sir. *pregnant* *(in childbirth)*

2. Then you must ride on horseback (as a form of vigorous exercise) for five hours. (This is Touchwood Senior's device to get Sir Oliver out of the house, while Touchwood Senior "rides" Lady Kix in her husband's stead.)

3. I'm not much in the habit of standing upright in one place. (With the suggestion of a failed erection.)

4. How about if I jumped over this (stool)?

TOUCHWOOD SR. All this is even still.° A little faster, sir. [*exactly right*]

SIR OLIVER Not a whit, sir. I'm in an excellent pace for any physic.° [*medicine*]

Enter a Servant.

SERVANT Your white mare's ready.

SIR OLIVER I shall up° presently.—One kiss, and farewell. [*mount*]

LADY KIX Thou shalt have two, love. [*They kiss.*]

SIR OLIVER Expect me about three.

LADY KIX With all my heart, sweet. *Exit* [*Sir Oliver*].

TOUCHWOOD SR. [*aside*] By this light, they have forgot their anger since,° and are as far in again as e'er they were. Which way the devil came they? Heart, I saw 'em not.[5] Their ways are beyond finding out.—Come, sweet lady. [*just now*]

LADY KIX How must I take mine,° sir? [*my medicine*]

TOUCHWOOD SR. Clean contrary:° yours must be taken lying. [*A different way*]

LADY KIX Abed, sir?

TOUCHWOOD SR. Abed, or where you will for your own ease. Your coach will serve.[6]

LADY KIX The physic must needs please.

Exeunt.

4.1

Enter Tim and Tutor.

TIM *Negatur argumentum*, tutor.

TUTOR *Probo tibi*, pupil: *stultus non est animal rationale.*

TIM *Falleris sane.*

TUTOR *Quaso ut taceas. Probo tibi—*

TIM *Quomodo probas, domine?*

TUTOR *Stultus non habet rationem, ergo non est animal rationale.*

TIM *Sic argumentaris, domine: stultus non habet rationem, ergo non est animal rationale. Negatur argumentum* again, tutor.

TUTOR *Argumentum iterum probo tibi, domine: qui non participat de ratione, nullo modo potest vocari rationalis;* but *stultus non participat de ratione, ergo stultus nullo modo potest dici rationalis.*

TIM *Participat.*

TUTOR *Sic disputas. Qui participat, quomodo participat?*

TIM *Ut homo. Probabo tibi in syllogismo.*

TUTOR *Hunc proba.*

TIM *Sic probo, domine: stultus est homo sicut tu et ego sumus; homo est animal rationale, sicut stultus est animal rationale.*[1]

5. I.e., How the devil did they change so quickly? These changes in mood happened too fast for me to follow.

6. Coaches were often used for assignations.

4.1. Yellowhammer's house.

1. TIM Your proof is denied, tutor.
TUTOR I prove to you, pupil: a fool is not a rational creature.
TIM You won't succeed.
TUTOR Please be quiet. I prove to you—
TIM How do you prove it, master?
TUTOR A fool has no reasoning ability; therefore he is not a rational animal.
TIM Thus you argue, master: a fool has no reasoning ability; therefore he is not a rational animal. Your proof is denied once again, tutor.
TUTOR Again I prove my argument to you, sir: he who does not take part in rational thought can in no way be said to be rational; but the fool does not take part in rational thought; therefore the fool can in no way be said to be rational.
TIM But he does take part in it.

Enter Maudlin.

MAUDLIN Here's nothing but disputing all the day long with 'em!

TUTOR *Sic disputas: stultus est homo sicut tu et ego sumus; homo est animal rationale, sicut stultus est animal rationale.*[2]

MAUDLIN Your reasons are both good, whate'er they be; pray give them o'er. Faith, you'll tire yourselves. What's the matter between you?

TIM Nothing but reasoning about a fool, mother.

MAUDLIN About a fool, son? Alas, what need you trouble your heads about that? None of us all but knows what a fool is.

TIM Why, what's a fool, mother? I come to you° now. *pose you a question*

MAUDLIN Why, one that's married before he has wit.

TIM 'Tis pretty, i'faith, and well guessed of a woman never brought up at the university; but bring forth what fool you will, mother, I'll prove him to be as reasonable a creature as myself or my tutor here.

MAUDLIN Fie, 'tis impossible.

TUTOR Nay, he shall do't, forsooth.

TIM 'Tis the easiest thing to prove a fool by logic. By logic I'll prove anything.

MAUDLIN What, thou wilt not!° *i.e., No, really?*

TIM I'll prove a whore to be an honest woman.

MAUDLIN Nay, by my faith, she must prove that herself, or logic will never do't.

TIM 'Twill do't, I tell you.

MAUDLIN Some in this street would give a thousand pounds that you could prove their wives so.

TIM Faith, I can, and all their daughters too, though they had three bastards. When comes your tailor hither?

MAUDLIN Why, what of him?

TIM By logic I'll prove him to be a man, let him come when he will.[3]

MAUDLIN [*to the Tutor*] How hard at first was learning to him! Truly, sir, I thought he would never ha' took the Latin tongue. How many accidences do you think he wore out ere he came to his grammar?[4]

TUTOR Some three or four.

MAUDLIN Believe me, sir, some four-and-thirty.

TIM Pish, I made haberdines[5] of 'em in church porches.

MAUDLIN He was eight years in his grammar, and stuck horribly at a foolish place there called *as in praesenti.*[6]

TUTOR So you claim. Who takes part in it, and in what way?
TIM As a man. I will prove it to you by a syllogism.
TUTOR Go ahead, prove it.
TIM I prove it thus, master: a fool is a man just like you and me; a man is a rational animal; therefore a fool is a rational animal.

2. Thus you argue: a fool is a man just like you and me; a man is a rational animal; therefore a fool is a rational animal.

3. Ladies' tailors were proverbially effeminate. Tim will undertake to prove the opposite.

4. Accidences introduced pupils to the basics of Latin inflection before the pupils went on to their grammars, dealing with the complexities of syntax.

5. Dried cod. (Perhaps Tim has cut his textbooks up into paper fish. In any case, he belittles the many accidences he has had.)

6. "*As* in the present tense"—a familiar phrase from William Lily's widely used Latin grammar, here dealing with the endings of verbs of the first conjugation. "*As*" puns pedantically on the Latin *-as* (a verbal ending for the second person singular in the present tense, as in *amas,* "you love") and the English "ass," so that Maudlin unintentionally appears to be saying, "an ass in (my) presence."

TIM [*tapping his forehead*] Pox, I have it here now.

MAUDLIN He so shamed me once before an honest gentleman that knew me when I was a maid.[7]

TIM These women must have all out.°

tell everything

MAUDLIN "*Quid est grammatica?*"° says the gentleman to him (I shall remember by a sweet, sweet token), but nothing could he answer.

What is grammar?

TUTOR How now pupil, ha? *Quid est grammatica?*

TIM *Grammatica?* Ha, ha, ha!

MAUDLIN Nay, do not laugh, son, but let me hear you say it now. There was one word went so prettily off the gentleman's tongue, I shall remember it the longest day of my life.

TUTOR Come, *Quid est grammatica?*

TIM Are you not ashamed, tutor? *Grammatica?* Why, *Recte scribendi atque loquendi ars*,[8] sir-reverence of my mother.

MAUDLIN That was it,° i'faith! Why now, son, I see you are a deep scholar. And, Master Tutor, a word, I pray. [*Aside to him*] Let us withdraw a little into my husband's chamber. I'll send in the North Wales gentlewoman to him. She looks for° wooing. I'll put together both, and lock the door.

"Ars" was the word

expects

TUTOR I give great approbation to your conclusion.

Exeunt [*Maudlin and Tutor*].

TIM I mar'l° what this gentlewoman should be that I should have° in marriage. She's a stranger to me. I wonder what my parents mean, i'faith, to match me with a stranger so—a maid that's neither kiff° nor kin to me. Life, do they think I have no more care of my body than to lie with one that I ne'er knew, a mere stranger, one that ne'er went to school with me neither, nor ever playfellows together? They're mightily o'erseen° in't, methinks. They say she has mountains to her marriage;° she's full of cattle, some two thousand runts.° Now what the meaning of these runts should be, my tutor cannot tell me. I have looked in Rider's Dictionary° for the letter R, and there I can hear no tidings of these runts neither; unless they should be Romford° hogs, I know them not.

wonder

am to have

kith, neighbor

mistaken

as her dowry

small cattle

(published in 1598)

a town in Essex

Enter Welsh Gentlewoman.

And here she comes. If I know what to say to her now in the way of marriage, I'm no graduate! Methinks, i'faith, 'tis boldly done of her to come into my chamber, being but a stranger. She shall not say I'm so proud yet but I'll speak° to her. Marry, as I will order it, she shall take no hold of my words, I'll warrant her.[9] [*The Welsh Gentlewoman curtsies.*] She looks, and makes a cur'sey. [*To her*] *Salve tu quoque,*

as not to speak

7. "Knew" hints at sexual knowledge. The punning is carried forward in "sweet, sweet token" (line 67).

8. The art of writing and speaking correctly. (Tim adds "sir-reverence," "begging pardon," by way of apologizing for the seemingly offensive "*ars*," meaning "art" in Latin but suggesting "arse" in English.)

9. Wanting to be sure that the Welsh Gentlewoman will understand him and assuming she cannot understand English because she is a foreigner, Tim (absurdly) chooses Latin because it is the universal learned language of Western Europe. "Shall take no hold of" means "will not misconstrue."

puella pulcherrima! Quid vis nescio nec sane curo[1]—Tully's° own phrase to a heart.° — Cicero's / learned by heart

WELSH GENTLEWOMAN [*aside*] I know not what he means. A suitor, quotha?° I hold° my life he understands no English. — indeed / bet

TIM *Fertur, mehercule, tu virgo, Wallia ut opibus abundas maximis.*[2]

WELSH GENTLEWOMAN [*aside*] What's this *fertur* and *abundundis*? He mocks me, sure, and calls me a bundle of farts.

TIM I have no Latin word now for their runts. I'll make some shift° or other: [*To her*] *Iterum dico, opibus abundas maximis montibus et fontibus et, ut ita dicam, rontibus; attamen vero homunculus ego sum natura simul et arte baccalareus, lecto profecto non paratus.*[3] — expedient

WELSH GENTLEWOMAN This is most strange. Maybe he can speak Welsh. [*To him*] *Avedera whee comrage, der due cog foginis.*[4]

TIM [*aside*] *Cog foggin?* I scorn to cog° with her. I'll tell her so, too, in a word near her own language. [*To her*] *Ego non cogo.*[5] — cheat; wheedle

WELSH GENTLEWOMAN *Rhegosin a whiggin harle ron corid ambre.*[6]

TIM [*aside*] By my faith, she's a good scholar, I see that already. She has the tongues, plain. I hold my life she has traveled. What will folks say? "There goes the learned couple." Faith, if the truth were known, she hath proceeded.° — taken her degree

Enter Maudlin.

MAUDLIN How now, how speeds your business?

TIM [*aside*] I'm glad my mother's come to part us.

MAUDLIN How do you agree, forsooth?° — indeed

WELSH GENTLEWOMAN As well as e'er we did before we met.

MAUDLIN How's that?

WELSH GENTLEWOMAN You put me to a man I understand not. Your son's no Englishman, methinks.

MAUDLIN No Englishman? Bless my boy, and born i'the heart of London?

WELSH GENTLEWOMAN I ha' been long enough in the chamber with him, and I find neither Welsh nor English in him.

MAUDLIN Why, Tim, how have you used the gentlewoman?

TIM As well as a man might do, mother, in modest Latin.

MAUDLIN Latin, fool?

TIM And she recoiled in Hebrew.

MAUDLIN In Hebrew, fool? 'Tis Welsh.

1. Hail to you, beautiful maiden! What you want I do not know, nor, truly, do I care.

2. It is said, by Hercules, O maiden, that you abound with great wealth in Wales. (Tim's Latin is so shaky that one cannot be certain to what extent the quarto text should be regularized. See textual notes. He may mean here that Wales abounds in great wealth.)

3. Again I say, you abound in great mountains and springs and, if I may coin a term, "runts"; yet truly I am a little man by nature and at the same time a bachelor of arts, not well suited for the bed (of love).

4. The first part of this phrase may be a rough approximation of the Welsh *A fedrych chwi Gymraeg?*, "Can you speak Welsh?" The second phrase is unintelligible and serves mainly as an opportunity for Tim to pun on "cog," meaning "cheat," in the next line. Middleton's phonetic stage Welsh is approximate at best.

5. Nonsense Latin for "I won't cog." More accurately, *cogo* means "I collect," "I come together" (with you).

6. Some cheese and whey after taking a walk.

TIM All comes to one,° mother. *It's all the same*

MAUDLIN She can speak English too.

TIM Who told me so much? Heart, an she can speak English, I'll clap to° her. I thought you'd marry me to a stranger.° *embrace / foreigner*

MAUDLIN [*to the Welsh Gentlewoman*] You must forgive him. He's so inured to Latin, he and his tutor, that he hath quite forgot to use the Protestant tongue.[7]

WELSH GENTLEWOMAN 'Tis quickly pardoned, forsooth.

MAUDLIN Tim, make amends and kiss her. [*To the Welsh Gentlewoman*] He makes towards° you, forsooth. *approaches*

TIM [*aside, kissing her*] Oh, delicious! One may discover her country by her kissing. 'Tis a true saying, "There's nothing tastes so sweet as your Welsh mutton."° [*To the Welsh Gentlewoman*] It was reported you could sing. *meat; whore*

MAUDLIN Oh, rarely,° Tim, the sweetest British° songs! *excellently / Celtic*

TIM And 'tis my mind,° I swear, before I marry, I would see all my wife's good parts° at once, to view how rich I were. *intent* *qualities; body parts*

MAUDLIN Thou shalt hear sweet music, Tim. [*To the Welsh Gentlewoman*] Pray,° forsooth. *Music, and Welsh song.* *Please begin*

THE SONG

WELSH GENTLEWOMAN

Cupid is Venus' only joy,
But he is a wanton boy,
A very, very wanton boy.
He shoots at ladies' naked breasts;
He is the cause of most men's crests°— *cuckolds' horns*
I mean upon the forehead,
Invisible but horrid.
'Twas he first thought upon the way
To keep a lady's lips in play.

Why should not Venus chide her son
For the pranks that he hath done,
The wanton pranks that he hath done?
He shoots his fiery darts so thick
They hurt poor ladies to the quick—
Ah, me!—with cruel wounding.
His darts are so confounding
That life and sense would soon decay
But that he keeps their lips in play.

Can there be any part of bliss
In a quickly fleeting kiss,
A quickly fleeting kiss?
To one's pleasure, leisures are but waste;[8]
The slowest kiss makes too much haste
. . . .° *(a line is missing)*
And lose it ere we find it.

7. As opposed to Latin, the language of the Catholic Church.

8. Delay only slows one's pleasure in love.

The pleasing sport they only know° *only they know*
That close above and close below.[9]

TIM I would not change my wife for a kingdom! I can do somewhat too in my own lodging.° *i.e., on my own*

Enter Yellowhammer and Allwit [posing as a country cousin].

YELLOWHAMMER Why, well said, Tim! The bells go merrily. I love such peals o'life!—Wife, lead them in awhile; here's a strange° gentleman desires private conference. *unknown*

[*Exeunt Maudlin, Tim, and the Welsh Gentlewoman.*]

[*To Allwit*] You're welcome, sir, the more for your name's sake. Good Master Yellowhammer! I love my name well. And which o'the Yellowhammers take you descent from, if I may be so bold with you? Which, I pray?

ALLWIT The Yellowhammers in Oxfordshire, near Abingdon.° *(on the Thames)*

YELLOWHAMMER And those are the best Yellowhammers, and truest bred. I came from thence myself, though now a citizen.° I'll be bold with you; you are most welcome. *Londoner*

ALLWIT I hope the zeal I bring with me shall deserve it.

YELLOWHAMMER I hope no less. What is your will, sir?

ALLWIT I understand by rumors you have a daughter, which my bold love shall henceforth title "cousin."

YELLOWHAMMER I thank you for her, sir.

ALLWIT I heard of her virtues and other confirmed graces.

YELLOWHAMMER A plaguey° girl, sir. *troublesome*

ALLWIT Fame sets her out with richer ornaments than you are pleased to boast of. 'Tis done modestly. I hear she's towards° marriage. *on the verge of*

YELLOWHAMMER You hear truth, sir.

ALLWIT And with a knight in town, Sir Walter Whorehound.

YELLOWHAMMER The very same, sir.

ALLWIT I am the sorrier for't.

YELLOWHAMMER The sorrier? Why, cousin?

ALLWIT 'Tis not too far past, is't? It may be yet recalled?

YELLOWHAMMER Recalled? Why, good sir?

ALLWIT Resolve° me in that point, ye shall hear from me. *If you can satisfy*

YELLOWHAMMER There's no contract passed.

ALLWIT I am very joyful, sir.

YELLOWHAMMER But he's the man must bed her.

ALLWIT By no means, coz.° She's quite undone, then, and you'll curse the time that e'er you made the match. He's an arrant whoremaster, consumes his time and state— [*He whispers, then speaks aloud again*] whom in my knowledge he hath kept° this seven years. Nay, coz, another man's wife too. *cousin* / *kept as a mistress*

YELLOWHAMMER Oh, abominable!

ALLWIT Maintains the whole house, apparels the husband, pays servants' wages, not so much but—

[*He whispers again.*]

YELLOWHAMMER Worse and worse! And doth the husband know this?

9. Who embrace with lips and body.

ALLWIT Knows? Ay, and glad he may, too. 'Tis his living, as other trades thrive—butchers by selling flesh, poulters by venting conies,[1] or the like, coz.

YELLOWHAMMER What an incomparable wittol's° this! — *complacent cuckold is*

ALLWIT Tush, what cares he for that? Believe me, coz, no more than I do.

YELLOWHAMMER What a base slave is that!

ALLWIT All's one to him. He feeds and takes his ease,
Was ne'er the man that ever broke his sleep
To get° a child yet, by his own confession, — *beget*
And yet his wife has seven.

YELLOWHAMMER What, by Sir Walter?

ALLWIT Sir Walter's like to° keep 'em and maintain 'em — *is disposed to*
In excellent fashion; he dares do no less, sir.

YELLOWHAMMER Life, has he children too?

ALLWIT Children? Boys thus high, in their Cato and Cordelius.[2]

YELLOWHAMMER What? You jest, sir.

ALLWIT Why, one can make a verse,° and is now at Eton College.[3] — *write Latin verse*

YELLOWHAMMER Oh, this news has cut into my heart, coz.

ALLWIT It had eaten nearer° if it had not been prevented: one Allwit's wife. — *caused more grief*

YELLOWHAMMER Allwit? Foot,° I have heard of him. He had a girl kurs'ned lately? — *By God's foot*

ALLWIT Ay, that work did cost the knight above a hundred mark.° — *more than £67*

YELLOWHAMMER I'll mark° him for a knave and villain for't. A thousand thanks and blessings! I have done with him. — *note; strike*

ALLWIT [*aside*] Ha, ha, ha! This knight will stick by my ribs° still; — *give me sustenance*
I shall not lose him yet. No wife will come;
Where'er he woos, I find him still at home.[4]
Ha, ha! *Exit.*

YELLOWHAMMER Well, grant all this; say now his deeds are black:
Pray, what serves marriage but to call him back?° — *rescue him from sin*
I have kept a whore myself, and had a bastard,
By Mistress Anne, in *anno*—° — *in the year—*
I care not who knows it. He's° now a jolly fellow, — *My bastard son is*
He's been twice warden.[5] So may his° fruit be; — *(Sir Walter's)*
They were but base begot, and so was he.° — *(my bastard son)*
The knight is rich; he shall be my son-in-law.
No matter, so the whore he keeps be wholesome;° — *free of syphilis*
My daughter takes no hurt, then. So, let them wed.
I'll have him sweat° well ere they go to bed. — *(to cure syphilis)*

1. As poultry merchants thrive by selling rabbits. (Poulters, or poulterers, dealt in hares and other small game as well as poultry.)
2. Cato's *Distichs*, a famous medieval textbook containing moral precepts, and Mathurin Cordier's *Colloquia Scholastica* were staples of the curriculum, with a Puritan emphasis. "Cordelius" may be Allwit's error for "Corderius," the Latin form of "Cordier."
3. A famous precollegiate school (what Americans would call a "private" school and the British a "public" school), richly endowed and elite.
4. Despite Sir Walter's attempts to acquire a wife, I'll fix it so that he stays close to my hearth and home (where his children live).
5. (1) A churchwarden; or (2) a member of a governing body of a city company—in either case, a position of respectability.

Enter Maudlin.

MAUDLIN Oh, husband, husband!
YELLOWHAMMER How now, Maudlin?
MAUDLIN We are all undone! She's gone, she's gone!
YELLOWHAMMER Again? Death! Which way?
MAUDLIN Over the houses.° Lay° the waterside; she's gone forever, else. *Over rooftops / Search*
YELLOWHAMMER Oh, vent'rous baggage!° *Exeunt.* *brazen hussy*

[4.2]

Enter Tim and Tutor.

TIM Thieves, thieves! My sister's stol'n! Some thief hath got her. Oh, how miraculously did my father's plate° scape! 'Twas all left out, tutor. *silver plate*
TUTOR Is't possible?
TIM Besides three chains of pearl and a box of coral. My sister's gone. Let's look at Trig Stairs[1] for her. My mother's gone to lay° the common° stairs at Puddle Wharf, and at the dock below° stands my poor silly° father. Run, sweet tutor, run! *Exeunt.* *search / public* *downstream / hapless*

[4.3]

Enter both the Touchwoods.

TOUCHWOOD SR. I had been taken, brother, by eight sergeants,° *sheriff's officers*
But for° the honest watermen;[1] I am bound to them. *Were it not for*
They are the most requitefull'st[2] people living;
For, as they get their means° by gentlemen, *means of livelihood*
They are still the forwardest° to help gentlemen. *always readiest*
You heard how one scaped out of the Blackfriars,° *Blackfriars Theater*
But awhile since, from two or three varlets
Came° into the house° with all their rapiers drawn, *Who came / theater*
As if they'd dance the sword dance on the stage,
With candles in their hands like chandlers'° ghosts, *candle-makers'*
Whilst the poor gentleman so pursued and bandied° *knocked about*
Was, by an honest pair of oars,° safely landed. *oarsmen*
TOUCHWOOD JR. I love them with my heart for't.

Enter three or four Watermen.

FIRST WATERMAN Your first man,° sir. *(a bid for customers)*
SECOND WATERMAN Shall I carry you gentlemen with a pair of oars?
TOUCHWOOD SR. These be the honest fellows. Take one pair and leave the rest for her.
TOUCHWOOD JR. Barn Elms.° *manor house on Thames*
TOUCHWOOD SR. No more,° brother. *Say no more*
FIRST WATERMAN Your first man.

4.2. Yellowhammer's house still.
1. A set of stairs going down to the Thames. Puddle Wharf (line 7) and Paul's Wharf (4.3.32) are similar points of embarkation. Blackfriars (4.3.6) is near the river.

4.3. A boat landing on the Thames.
1. Boatmen employed in ferrying customers.
2. Most eager to return favors.

SECOND WATERMAN Shall I carry Your Worship?

TOUCHWOOD JR. Go.

[*Exit Touchwood Senior with the First Waterman.*]

And you honest watermen that stay: here's a French crown° for you. [*He gives money.*] There comes a maid with all speed to take° water; row her lustily° to Barn Elms after me. *(worth 5 shillings)* *be carried by / vigorously*

SECOND WATERMAN To Barn Elms, good sir?—Make ready the boat, Sam.—We'll wait below. *Exeunt* [*Watermen*].

Enter Moll.

TOUCHWOOD JR. What made you stay so long?

MOLL I found the way more dangerous than I looked for.

TOUCHWOOD JR. Away, quick! There's a boat waits for you, and I'll take water at Paul's Wharf and overtake you.

MOLL Good sir, do. We cannot be too safe.° [*Exeunt.*] *prudent*

[4.4]

Enter Sir Walter, Yellowhammer, Tim, and Tutor.

SIR WALTER Life, call you this close keeping?° *careful guarding*

YELLOWHAMMER She was kept under a double lock.

SIR WALTER A double devil!

TIM [*to Tutor*] That's a buff sergeant, tutor; he'll ne'er wear out.[1]

YELLOWHAMMER How would you have women locked?

TIM With padlocks, father. The Venetian uses° it; my tutor reads it. *Venetians practice*

SIR WALTER Heart, if she were so locked up, how got she out?

YELLOWHAMMER There was a little hole looked into° the gutter, but who would have dreamt of that? *that opened into*

SIR WALTER A wiser man would.

TIM He says true, father; a wise man for love will seek every hole.° My tutor knows it. *(with bawdy implications)*

TUTOR *Verum poeta dicit.*° *The poet says true*

TIM *Dicit Virgilius,*[2] father.

YELLOWHAMMER Prithee, talk of thy jills° somewhere else; she's played the jill° with me. Where's your wise mother now? *(mishearing "Virgilius")* *minx, wanton*

TIM Run mad, I think. I thought she would have drowned herself. She would not stay for oars, but took a smelt boat.° Sure I think she be gone a-fishing for her. *fishing boat*

YELLOWHAMMER She'll catch a goodly dish of gudgeons now will serve us all to supper.[3]

Enter Maudlin, drawing Moll by the hair, and Watermen.

MAUDLIN I'll tug thee home by the hair.

FIRST WATERMAN Good mistress, spare her!

MAUDLIN Tend your own business.

4.4. Near Yellowhammer's house.

1. I.e., With restraint like that, Moll is not likely to escape again. (Arresting officers wore a durable buff-jerkin, or cowhide upper garment. The reference is to a leather chastity belt.)

2. Virgil says it. (Virgil did not, in fact, say anything as trite as what is attributed to him here.)

3. I.e., She'll be thoroughly shamed, and we'll all look foolish. (A gudgeon is a small fish used as bait; "to swallow gudgeons" was proverbial for being fooled. "To" means "for.")

SECOND WATERMAN You are a cruel mother.
Exeunt [*Watermen*].

MOLL Oh, my heart dies!

MAUDLIN I'll make thee an example for all the neighbors' daughters.

MOLL Farewell, life!

MAUDLIN You that have tricks can counterfeit.[4]

YELLOWHAMMER Hold, hold, Maudlin!

MAUDLIN [*to Yellowhammer*] I have brought your jewel by the hair.

YELLOWHAMMER [*to Sir Walter*] She's here, knight.

SIR WALTER Forbear, or I'll grow worse.° *angrier still*

TIM Look on her, tutor. She° hath brought her from the water like a mermaid.° She's but half my sister now; as far as the flesh goes, the rest may be sold to fishwives.° *(Maudlin)* *(slang for "whore")* *i.e., bawds*

MAUDLIN [*to Moll*] Dissembling, cunning baggage!

YELLOWHAMMER Impudent strumpet!

SIR WALTER Either give over both, or I'll give over.[5]
[*To Moll*] Why have you used me thus, unkind mistress?
Wherein have I deserved?

YELLOWHAMMER You talk too fondly,° sir. We'll take another course and prevent all; we might have done't long since. We'll lose no time now, nor trust to't° any longer. Tomorrow morn as early as sunrise we'll have you joined. *indulgently; madly* *trust to luck*

MOLL Oh, bring me death tonight, love-pitying Fates!
Let me not see tomorrow up upon the world!

YELLOWHAMMER Are you content, sir, till then she shall be watched?

MAUDLIN Baggage, you shall. *Exit* [*Maudlin, with Moll*].

TIM Why, father, my tutor and I will both watch° in armor. *stand guard*
[*Exit Yellowhammer.*]

TUTOR How shall we do for weapons?

TIM Take you no care for that. If need be, I can send for conquering metal, tutor, ne'er lost day yet;[6] 'tis but at Westminster. I am acquainted with him that keeps the monuments;[7] I can borrow Harry the Fifth's sword. 'Twill serve us both to watch with. *Exit* [*with Tutor*].

SIR WALTER I never was so near my wish
As this chance makes me! Ere tomorrow noon
I shall receive two thousand pound in gold,
And a sweet maidenhead worth forty.

Enter Touchwood Junior with a [*First*] *Waterman.*

TOUCHWOOD JR. [*to the Waterman*] Oh, thy news splits me!° *shipwrecks me*

FIRST WATERMAN Half drowned. She cruelly tugged her by the hair, forced her disgracefully, not like a mother.

TOUCHWOOD JR. Enough. Leave me, like my joys.
Exit [*First*] *Waterman.*
[*To Sir Walter*] Sir, saw you not a wretched maid pass this way?
[*Recognizing him*] Heart, villain, is it thou?

4. I.e., A deceiver like you can also feign heartbreak.
5. Stop, both of you, or I'll back out of the wedding.
6. I can send for weapons that have never yet lost a battle.
7. I know the custodian of the tombs and relics of the royal family.

SIR WALTER Yes, slave, 'tis I. *Both draw and fight.*
TOUCHWOOD JR. I must break through thee, then. There is no stop° — *barrier*
That checks my tongue° and all my hopeful fortunes, — *silences my wooing*
That breast excepted,[8] and I must have way.° — *be let through*
SIR WALTER Sir, I believe 'twill hold your life in play.[9]
[*He wounds Touchwood Junior.*]
TOUCHWOOD JR. So, you'll gain the heart in my breast at first?[1]
SIR WALTER There is no dealing,° then. Think on the dowry — *coming to terms*
For two thousand pounds.[2]
TOUCHWOOD JR. [*wounding Sir Walter*] Oh, now 'tis quit,° sir. — *your blow is repaid*
SIR WALTER And being of even hand,° I'll play no longer. — *the score being even*
TOUCHWOOD JR. No longer, slave?
SIR WALTER I have certain things to think on
Before I dare go further. [*Exit.*]
TOUCHWOOD JR. But one bout?
I'll follow thee to death, but ha't out.° *Exit.* — *have it out with you*

5.1

Enter Allwit, his wife, and Davy Dahumma.

MRS. ALLWIT A misery of a house!
ALLWIT What shall become of us?
DAVY I think his° wound be mortal. — *(Sir Walter's)*
ALLWIT Think'st thou so, Davy?
Then am I mortal too, but° a dead man, Davy; — *no better than*
This is no world for me, whene'er he goes.
I must e'en truss up[1] all and after him, Davy;
A sheet with two knots,[2] and away.

Enter Sir Walter led in, hurt [*by two Servants*].

DAVY Oh, see, sir,
How faint he goes! Two of my fellows lead him.
MRS. ALLWIT Oh, me! [*She faints.*]
ALLWIT Heyday, my wife's laid down too! Here's like° to be — *likely (ironic)*
A good house kept, when we are altogether down.
Take pains with her, good Davy, cheer her up there.
Let me come to His Worship, let me come.
[*He approaches Sir Walter where he lies.*]
SIR WALTER Touch me not, villain! My wound aches at thee,
Thou poison to my heart!
ALLWIT He raves already.
His senses are quite gone; he knows me not.—
Look up, an't like° Your Worship! Heave° those eyes. — *if it please / Lift up*
Call me to mind. Is your remembrance left?° — *lost*
Look in my face. Who am I, an't like Your Worship?
SIR WALTER If anything be worse than slave or villain,
Thou art the man.

8. Except for the stubborn heart inside your chest, at which I may aim my weapon.
9. Your challenging me is enough to put your life at risk.
1. So, you'd like to stab me to the heart with the first thrust, would you?
2. Either Sir Walter says this to himself by way of stiffening his resolve to have the dowry or offers Touchwood Junior the possibility of sharing the dowry.
5.1. Allwit's house.
1. (1) I must pack up; (2) I must hang myself.
2. (1) A sheet tied into knots with which to escape out a window or hang oneself; (2) a shroud, tied at head and foot.

ALLWIT Alas, His poor Worship's weakness!
He will begin to know me by little and little.
SIR WALTER No devil can be like thee!
ALLWIT Ah, poor gentleman!
Methinks the pain that thou endurest—
SIR WALTER Thou know'st me to be wicked, for thy baseness
Kept the eyes open still on all my sins.
None knew the dear° account my soul stood charged with *costly*
So well as thou, yet, like hell's flattering angel,
Wouldst never tell me on't, let'st me go on
And join with death in sleep, that if I had not
Waked now by chance, even by a stranger's pity,[3]
I had everlastingly slept out all hope
Of grace and mercy.
ALLWIT Now he is worse and worse.—
Wife, to him, wife; thou wast wont to do good on him.
MRS. ALLWIT [*to Sir Walter*] How is't with you, sir?
SIR WALTER Not as with you,[4]
Thou loathsome strumpet!—Some good pitying man
Remove my sins° out of my sight a little! *reminders of my sins*
I tremble to behold her; she keeps back
All comfort while she stays.—Is this a time,
Unconscionable woman, to see thee?
Art thou so cruel to the peace of man
Not to give liberty° now? The devil himself *freedom to my soul*
Shows a far fairer reverence and respect
To goodness than thyself. He dares not do this,[5]
But parts in time of penitence, hides his face;
When man withdraws from him, he leaves the place.
Hast thou less manners and more impudence
Than thy instructor?° Prithee show thy modesty, *i.e., the devil*
If the least grain be left, and get thee from me.
Thou shouldst be rather locked many rooms hence
From the poor miserable sight of me,
If either love or grace had part in thee.
MRS. ALLWIT [*weeping*] He is lost forever!
ALLWIT Run, sweet Davy, quickly,
And fetch the children hither. Sight of them
Will make him cheerful straight.° [*Exit Davy.*] *straightaway*
SIR WALTER Oh, death! Is this
A place for you to weep? What tears are those?
Get you away with them! I shall fare the worse;
As long as they are a-weeping, they work against me.
There's nothing but thy appetite° in that sorrow. *sexual appetite*
Thou weep'st for lust; I feel it in the slackness
Of comforts° coming towards me. I was well *divine comforts*
Till thou began'st to undo me. This shows° like *looks*
The fruitless sorrow of a careless° mother *uncaring*
That brings her son with dalliance to the gallows
And then stands by and weeps to see him suffer.

Enter Davy with the children [*Nick, Wat, and others*].

3. If I had not been awakened just now to an awareness of my sinful state by my brush with death and by Touchwood Junior's sparing me.

4. My spiritual state is not as perilous as yours.

5. Even the devil doesn't dare hover as you do over the man he has tempted to sin.

DAVY There are the children, sir, an't like Your Worship;
Your last° fine girl. In troth, she smiles; *latest*
Look, look, in faith, sir.
SIR WALTER Oh, my vengeance!° *God's vengeance on me!*
Let me forever hide my cursèd face
From sight of those that darkens all my hopes
And stands between me and the sight of heaven!
Who° sees me now, her too and those so near me, *Whoever*
May rightly say I am o'ergrown with sin.
Oh, how my offenses wrestle with my repentance!
It hath scarce breath;
Still my adulterous guilt hovers aloft
And with her black wings beats down all my prayers
Ere they be halfway up. What's he knows° now *Who can tell*
How long I have to live? Oh, what comes then?
My taste grows bitter; the round world all gall now;
Her pleasing pleasures now hath poisoned me,
Which I exchanged my soul for.
Make way, a hundred sighs, at once for me![6]
ALLWIT Speak to him, Nick.
NICK I dare not. I am afraid.
ALLWIT Tell him he hurts his wounds, Wat, with making moan.
SIR WALTER Wretched, death of seven![7]
ALLWIT [*to the others*] Come, let's be talking somewhat to keep him alive.—Ah, sirrah Wat, and did my lord° bestow that jewel on thee for an epistle thou mad'st in Latin? Thou art a good forward° boy; there's great joy on thee. *(some mighty person)* *promising*
SIR WALTER Oh, sorrow!
ALLWIT Heart, will nothing comfort him?
If he be so far gone, 'tis time to moan.
[*To him*] Here's pen and ink and paper, and all things ready.
Will't please Your Worship for to make your will?
SIR WALTER My will? Yes, yes, what else? Who writes apace now?
ALLWIT That can your man Davy, an't like Your Worship: a fair, fast, legible hand.
SIR WALTER Set it down, then: [*Davy writes.*]
Imprimis,° I bequeath to yonder wittol *First*
Three times his weight in curses.
ALLWIT How?
SIR WALTER All plagues of body and of mind.
ALLWIT Write them not down, Davy.
DAVY It is his will; I must.
SIR WALTER Together also
With such a sickness ten days ere his death.
ALLWIT There's a sweet legacy! I am almost choked with't.
SIR WALTER Next, I bequeath to that foul whore, his wife,
All barrenness of joy, a drought of virtue,
And dearth of all repentance; for her end,
The common misery of an English strumpet,
In French and Dutch,° beholding ere she dies *venereal diseases*
Confusion° of her brats before her eyes, *Destruction*
And never shed a tear for it.

6. Clear my way to heaven, you my many sighs!
7. (1) Wretched sevenfold death! (One for each bastard.) (2) Oh, wretched me, facing death with seven children!

Enter a Servant.

FIRST SERVANT Where's the knight?—Oh, sir, the gentleman you wounded is newly departed!
SIR WALTER Dead? Lift,° lift! Who helps me? *Lift me up*
ALLWIT Let the law lift° you now, that must have all; *arrest*
I have done lifting on° you, and my wife too. *helping; robbing for*
FIRST SERVANT [*to Sir Walter*] You were best lock yourself close.
ALLWIT Not in my house, sir!
I'll harbor no such persons as men-slayers.
Lock yourself where you will.
SIR WALTER What's this?
MRS. ALLWIT Why, husband!
ALLWIT I know what I do, wife.
MRS. ALLWIT You cannot tell yet, for, having killed the man in his defense, neither his life nor estate will be touched, husband.
ALLWIT Away, wife! Hear a fool! His lands will hang him.[8]
SIR WALTER Am I denied a chamber? [*To Mrs. Allwit*] What say you, forsooth?
MRS. ALLWIT Alas, sir, I am one that would have all well,
But must obey my husband. [*To Allwit*] Prithee, love,
Let the poor gentleman stay, being so sore wounded.
There's a close chamber° at one end of the garret *hidden room*
We never use; let him have that, I prithee.
ALLWIT We never use? You forget sickness, then,
And physic times; is't not a place for easement?[9]

Enter a [Second] Servant.

SIR WALTER Oh, death! Do I hear this with part
Of former life in me?—What's the news now?
SECOND SERVANT Troth, worse and worse: you're like to lose your land, if° the law save your life, sir, or the surgeon. *even if*
ALLWIT [*aside to Mrs. Allwit*] Hark you there, wife.[1]
SIR WALTER Why, how, sir?
SECOND SERVANT Sir Oliver Kix's wife is new quickened;° *pregnant*
That child undoes you,° sir. *defeats your hopes*
SIR WALTER All ill at once!
ALLWIT I wonder what he makes here with his consorts?[2]
Cannot our house be private to ourselves
But we must have such guests?—I pray, depart, sirs,° *(Sir Walter's servants)*
And take your murderer along with you.
Good° he were apprehended ere he go; *It would be best if*
He's killed some honest gentleman. Send for officers!
SIR WALTER I'll soon save you that labor.° *i.e., I'll leave, or die*
ALLWIT I must tell you, sir,
You have been somewhat bolder in my house
Than I could well like of. I suffered° you *put up with*

8. Hear the fool talk! A wealthy landowner like him has enemies who will be sure that he is found guilty. (A guilty verdict would mean that his lands would be forfeited to the Crown.)

9. (1) A place for comfortable resting of the sick; (2) a privy.

1. I.e., What did I tell you, wife, about his losing his land? (Allwit is presumably worried both about the loss to him and his family if Sir Walter loses his estates and about the danger to them of having harbored a fugitive from the law.)

2. I wonder what Sir Walter thinks he's doing here with his hangers-on?

Till it stuck here at my heart. I tell you truly
I thought you had been familiar with my wife once.

MRS. ALLWIT With me? I'll see him hanged first. I defy him and all such gentlemen in the like extremity!

SIR WALTER If ever eyes were open, these are they.[3]
Gamesters,° farewell. I have nothing left to play. — *Gamblers; lechers*
Exit [carried by Servants].

ALLWIT [*to Davy*] And therefore get you gone, sir.

DAVY [*to Allwit*] Of all wittols
Be thou the head! [*To Mrs. Allwit*] Thou, the grand whore of spitals!° *Exit.* — *VD hospitals*

ALLWIT So, since he's like° now to be rid of all,° I am right glad I am so well rid of him. — *likely / all wealth*

MRS. ALLWIT I knew he durst not stay when you named officers.

ALLWIT That stopped his spirits straight. What shall we do now, wife?

MRS. ALLWIT As we were wont to do.

ALLWIT We are richly furnished, wife, with household-stuff.

MRS. ALLWIT Let's let out lodgings, then, and take a house in the Strand.° — *a fashionable street*

ALLWIT In troth, a match,° wench. We are simply stocked with cloth-of-tissue° cushions to furnish out bay windows. Push,° what not that's quaint° and costly, from the top to the bottom? Life, for° furniture, we may lodge a countess. There's a closestool° of tawny velvet too, now I think on't, wife. — *it's a deal / fine silk cloth / Pooh / handsome / as for / a stool for a chamber pot*

MRS. ALLWIT There's that° should be, sir; your nose must be in everything. — *Everything's as it*

ALLWIT I have done, wench.
And let this stand° in every gallant's chamber: — *be posted*
"There's no gamester like a politic sinner,
For, whoe'er games, the box is sure a winner."[4] *Exeunt.*

[5.2]

Enter Yellowhammer and his wife.

MAUDLIN Oh, husband, husband, she° will die, she will die! — *(Moll)*
There is no sign but death.

YELLOWHAMMER 'Twill be our shame, then.

MAUDLIN Oh, how she's changed in compass of an hour!

YELLOWHAMMER Ah, my poor girl!—Good faith, thou wert too cruel to drag her by the hair.

MAUDLIN You would have done as much, sir, to curb her of her humor.

YELLOWHAMMER 'Tis curbed sweetly![1] She catched her bane° o'th' water. — *i.e., death*

Enter Tim.

3. If ever a person's eyes were opened to the perfidy of others, I am that person.

4. Like a clever gambler, the wise sinner knows when to confess his sins and quit while he is ahead, since (in life as in gambling) no matter who gambles, the house is sure to win. (The "box" is the percentage taken by the gambling establishment.)

5.2. Yellowhammer's house.

1. (1) How sweetly you have gone about checking her disposition! (2) A fit rebuke! (Said ironically.)

MAUDLIN How now, Tim?

TIM Faith, busy, mother, about an epitaph upon my sister's death.

MAUDLIN Death! She is not dead, I hope?

TIM No, but she means to be, and that's as good; and when a thing's done, 'tis done. You taught me that, mother.

YELLOWHAMMER What is your tutor doing?

TIM Making one too, in principal° pure Latin culled out of Ovid° *de Tristibus*.[2] — *choice* / *Ovid's*

YELLOWHAMMER How does your sister look? Is she not changed?

TIM Changed? Gold into white money° was never so changed as is my sister's color into paleness. — *silver coins*

Enter Moll [carried in sick by Servants].

YELLOWHAMMER Oh, here she's brought. See how she looks like death!

TIM Looks she like death, and ne'er a word° made yet? — *(of my elegy)*
I must go beat my brains against a bedpost
And get before my tutor.° [*Exit.*] — *see my tutor for help*

YELLOWHAMMER [*to Moll*] Speak. How dost thou?

MOLL I hope I shall be well, for I am as sick at heart
As I can be.

YELLOWHAMMER 'Las, my poor girl!
The doctor's making a most sovereign° drink for thee, — *efficacious*
The worst° ingredients dissolved pearl and amber; — *least costly*
We spare no cost, girl.

MOLL Your love comes too late,
Yet timely° thanks reward it. What is comfort, — *prompt; not too late*
When the poor patient's heart is past relief?
It is no doctor's art can cure my grief.

YELLOWHAMMER All is cast away,° then! Prithee, look upon me cheerfully. — *wasted, in vain*

MAUDLIN Sing but a strain° or two; thou wilt not think° — *stanza / can't imagine*
How 'twill revive thy spirits. Strive with thy fit,[3]
Prithee, sweet Moll.

MOLL You shall have my good will,° mother. — *my best effort*

MAUDLIN Why, well said, wench.

THE SONG

MOLL [*singing*]
Weep, eyes, break, heart!
My love and I must part.
Cruel fates true love do soonest sever.
Oh, I shall see thee, never, never, never!
Oh, happy is the maid whose life takes end
Ere it knows parents' frown or loss of friend!
Weep, eyes, break, heart!
My love and I must part.

Enter Touchwood Senior with a letter
[unnoticed by Yellowhammer's family at first].

2. Ovid's *Tristia* consists of elegaic poems written as epistles to the poet's wife and friends during his exile from Rome (8–c. 17 C.E.)—a properly lugubrious book for a house in mourning.

3. (1) Attack of melancholy; (2) stanza of music.

MAUDLIN Oh, I could die with music. Well sung, girl!
MOLL If you call it so, it was.
YELLOWHAMMER She plays the swan
And sings herself to death.[4]
TOUCHWOOD SR. [*to Yellowhammer*] By your leave, sir.
YELLOWHAMMER What are you, sir? Or what's your business, pray?
[*Moll and Maudlin do not hear the following conversation.*]
TOUCHWOOD SR. I may be now admitted, though the brother
Of him your hate pursued. It spreads no further;
Your malice sets° in death, does it not, sir? *ends (like the sun)*
YELLOWHAMMER In death?
TOUCHWOOD SR. He's dead. 'Twas a dear° love to him; *sweet; costly*
It cost him but his life, that was all, sir.
He paid enough, poor gentleman, for his love.
YELLOWHAMMER [*aside*] There's all our ill removed, if she were well now.—
Impute not, sir, his end to any hate
That sprung from us; he had a fair° wound brought that. *fairly given; large*
TOUCHWOOD SR. That helped him forward, I must needs confess;
But the restraint° of love, and your unkindness, *withholding*
Those were the wounds that from his heart drew blood.
But being past help, let words forget it too.
Scarcely three minutes ere his eyelids closed
And took eternal leave of this world's light,
He wrote this letter [*showing it*], which by oath he bound me
To give to her own hands. That's all my business.
YELLOWHAMMER You may perform it, then. There she sits.
TOUCHWOOD SR. Oh, with a following[5] look!
YELLOWHAMMER Ay, trust me, sir,
I think she'll follow him quickly.
TOUCHWOOD SR. Here's some gold
He willed me to distribute faithfully
Amongst your servants. [*He gives gold to the Servants.*]
YELLOWHAMMER 'Las, what doth he mean, sir?
TOUCHWOOD SR. How cheer you,° mistress? *How are you*
MOLL I must learn of you, sir.
TOUCHWOOD SR. Here's a letter from a friend of yours.
[*He gives Moll the letter.*]
And where that fails in satisfaction,
I have a sad tongue ready to supply.
MOLL How does he, ere I look on't?
TOUCHWOOD SR. Seldom better. H'as a contented health now.[6]
MOLL I am most glad on't. [*She reads.*]
MAUDLIN [*aside to her husband*] Dead, sir?
YELLOWHAMMER [*aside to her*] He is. Now, wife, let's but get the girl upon her legs again, and to church roundly° with her. *without further ado*
MOLL [*reading*] Oh, sick to death, he tells me! How does he after this?
TOUCHWOOD SR. Faith, feels no pain at all. He's dead, sweet mistress.

4. According to popular legend, the swan, normally mute, sang once, at the hour of its death.
5. (1) Longing; (2) about to follow in death.
6. (1) He's doing fine; (2) all his troubles are past. (Moll does not immediately catch the latter meaning.)

MOLL Peace close mine eyes! [*She faints.*]

YELLOWHAMMER The girl! Look to the girl, wife!

MAUDLIN Moll! Daughter! Sweet girl, speak! Look but once up, thou shalt have all the wishes of thy heart that wealth can purchase!

YELLOWHAMMER Oh, she's gone forever! That letter broke her heart.

TOUCHWOOD SR. As good now, then, as let her lie in torment and then break it.

Enter Susan.

MAUDLIN Oh, Susan, she thou loved'st so dear is gone!

SUSAN Oh, sweet maid!

TOUCHWOOD SR. [*to the others*] This is she that helped her° still.—I've a reward here for thee. [*He gives Susan a note.*] *(Moll)*

YELLOWHAMMER [*indicating Moll*] Take her in;
Remove her from our sight, our shame and sorrow.

TOUCHWOOD SR. Stay, let me help thee. 'Tis the last cold kindness
I can perform for my sweet brother's sake.

[*Exeunt Touchwood Senior, with Susan and Servants, carrying Moll.*]

YELLOWHAMMER All the whole street will hate us, and the world
Point me out cruel. It is our best course, wife,
After we have given order for the funeral,
To absent ourselves till she be laid in ground.

MAUDLIN Where shall we spend that time?

YELLOWHAMMER I'll tell thee where, wench:
Go to some private church, and marry Tim
To the rich Brecknock gentlewoman.

MAUDLIN Mass, a match!° *agreed; a wedding*
We'll not lose all at once; somewhat we'll catch.° *Exeunt.* *we'll salvage something*

[5.3]

Enter Sir Oliver and [four] Servants.

SIR OLIVER Ho, my wife's quickened!° I am a man forever! *pregnant*
I think I have bestirred my stumps, i'faith.—
Run, get your fellows all together instantly,
Then to the parish church and ring the bells.

FIRST SERVANT It shall be done, sir. [*Exit.*]

SIR OLIVER Upon my love, I charge you, villain, that you make a bonfire before the door at night.

SECOND SERVANT A bonfire, sir?

SIR OLIVER A thwacking one, I charge you.

SECOND SERVANT [*aside*] This is monstrous. [*Exit.*]

SIR OLIVER Run, tell° a hundred pound out for the gentleman that gave my wife the drink, the first thing you do. *count*

THIRD SERVANT A hundred pounds, sir?

SIR OLIVER A bargain! As our joys grows,
We must remember still from whence it flows,

5.3. The Kixes' house.

Or else we prove ungrateful multipliers.° — *breeders; profiteers*
[*Exit Third Servant.*]
The child is coming, and the land comes after!
The news of this will make a poor Sir Walter.
I have struck it home, i'faith.

FOURTH SERVANT That you have, marry, sir. But will not Your Worship go to the funeral of both these lovers?

SIR OLIVER Both? Go both together?

FOURTH SERVANT Ay, sir, the gentleman's brother° will have it so. 'Twill be the pitifullest sight! There's such running, such rumors, and such throngs! A pair of lovers had never more spectators, more men's pities or women's wet eyes. — *(Touchwood Senior)*

SIR OLIVER My wife helps° the number, then? — *augments*

FOURTH SERVANT There's such a drawing out of handkerchers!
And those that have no handkerchers lift up aprons.

SIR OLIVER Her parents may have joyful hearts at this.[1]
I would not have my cruelty so talked on
To any child of mine for a monopoly.[2]

FOURTH SERVANT I believe you, sir.
'Tis cast° so, too, that both their coffins meet, — *arranged*
Which will be lamentable.

SIR OLIVER Come, we'll see it. *Exeunt.*

[5.4]

Recorders dolefully playing. Enter at one door the coffin of the gentleman [Touchwood Junior], solemnly decked, his sword upon it, attended by many in black [among whom are Sir Oliver Kix, Allwit, and a Parson], his brother being the chief mourner; at the other door, the coffin of the virgin [Moll], with a garland of flowers, with epitaphs pinned on't, attended by maids and women [among whom are Lady Kix, Mrs. Allwit, and Susan]. Then set them down, one right over against° the other. While all the company seem to weep and mourn, there is a sad song in the music room. — *alongside*

TOUCHWOOD SR. Never could death boast of a richer prize
From the first parent!° Let the world bring forth[1] — *Since Adam's time*
A pair of truer hearts. To speak but truth
Of this departed gentleman, in a brother
Might, by hard censure,° be called flattery, — *severe judgment*
Which makes me rather silent in his right
Than so to be delivered to the thoughts
Of any envious hearer, starved in° virtue — *lacking in*
And therefore pining° to hear others thrive. — *disliking*
But for° this maid, whom Envy cannot hurt — *as for*
With all her poisons, having left to ages
The true, chaste monument of her living name,
Which no time can deface, I say of her
The full truth freely, without fear of censure.

1. Perhaps her parents can take comfort in such a public display.
2. Even for a grant of royal privilege to monopolize the use of some commodity, such as salt or tin—a privilege that was notoriously profitable under King James I.

5.4. Yellowhammer's house (?).
1. I challenge the world to find anywhere.

What nature could there shine, that might redeem
Perfection home to woman, but in her
Was fully glorious?[2] Beauty set° in goodness — *set like a jewel*
Speaks° what she was. That jewel so infixed, — *Expresses*
There was no want° of anything of life — *lack*
To make these virtuous precedents° man and wife. — *exemplars*

ALLWIT Great pity of their deaths!

ALL Ne'er more pity!

LADY KIX It makes a hundred weeping eyes, sweet gossip.

TOUCHWOOD SR. I cannot think there's anyone amongst you
In this full fair assembly—maid, man, or wife—
Whose heart would not have sprung with joy and gladness
To have seen their marriage day.

ALL It would have made
A thousand joyful hearts.

TOUCHWOOD SR. [*to Touchwood Junior and Moll*] Up then, apace,
And take your fortunes. Make these joyful hearts;
Here's none but friends. [*Touchwood Junior and Moll rise up out of their coffins.*]

ALL Alive, sir? Oh, sweet dear couple!

TOUCHWOOD SR. Nay, do not hinder 'em now; stand from about 'em.
If she be caught again, and have this time,° — *and lose this chance*
I'll ne'er plot further for 'em, nor this honest chambermaid° — *(Susan)*
That helped all at a push.° — *critical moment*

TOUCHWOOD JR. [*to the Parson*] Good sir, apace.

PARSON Hands join now, but hearts forever,
Which no parents' mood shall sever.
[*To Touchwood Junior*] You shall forsake all widows, wives, and maids;
[*To Moll*] You, lords, knights, gentlemen, and men of trades.
And if in haste any article misses,
Go interline it with a brace of kisses.[3] [*The couple kiss.*]

TOUCHWOOD SR. Here's a thing trolled° nimbly. Give you joy, brother! Were't not better thou shouldst have her than the maid should die? — *rolled off the tongue*

MRS. ALLWIT To you, sweet mistress bride!

ALL Joy, joy to you both!

TOUCHWOOD SR. [*pointing to the funeral shrouds*] Here be your wedding sheets you brought along with you. You may both go to bed when you please to.

TOUCHWOOD JR. My joy wants utterance.° — *goes beyond speech*

TOUCHWOOD SR. Utter° all at night, then, brother. — *Speak; ejaculate*

MOLL I am silent with delight.

TOUCHWOOD SR. Sister, delight will silence any woman, but you'll find your tongue again, among maidservants, now you keep house, sister.

ALL Never was hour so filled with joy and wonder.

TOUCHWOOD SR. To tell you the full story of this chamber-

2. What qualities could shine forth, able to restore women to the state of due perfection before the Fall, that she did not embody in their full glory?

3. And if in my hasty recitation of the marriage ceremony (in lines 36–37) I have omitted any article, go insert the additional clauses with a pair of kisses. (The Parson's metaphor is from the drawing up of legal documents.)

maid, and of her kindness in this business to us, 'twould ask an hour's discourse. In brief, 'twas she
That wrought it to this purpose cunningly.

ALL We shall all love her for't.

Enter Yellowhammer and his wife.

ALLWIT See who comes here now!

TOUCHWOOD SR. A storm, a storm! But we are sheltered for it.

YELLOWHAMMER I will prevent° you all, and mock you thus,
You and your expectations. I stand happy,
Both in your lives and your hearts' combination.

stop; anticipate

TOUCHWOOD SR. Here's a strange day again!

YELLOWHAMMER The knight's° proved villain. All's come out now: his niece an arrant baggage; my poor boy Tim is cast away this morning, even before breakfast, married a whore next to his heart.°

Sir Walter is / *closest in love*

ALL A whore?

YELLOWHAMMER His° "niece," forsooth.

(Sir Walter's)

ALLWIT [*aside to Mrs. Allwit*] I think we rid our hands in good time of him.

MRS. ALLWIT [*aside to Allwit*] I knew he was past the best when I gave him over. [*To Yellowhammer*] What is become of him, pray, sir?

YELLOWHAMMER Who, the knight? He lies i'th'knight's ward.[4] [*To Lady Kix*] Now your belly, lady, begins to blossom, there's no peace for him, his creditors are so greedy.

SIR OLIVER [*to Touchwood Senior*] Master Touchwood, hear'st thou this news? I am so endeared to thee for my wife's fruitfulness that I charge you both, your wife and thee, to live no more asunder for the world's frowns. I have purse and bed and board for you. Be not afraid to go to your business° roundly. Get children, and I'll keep° them.

have sex / support

TOUCHWOOD SR. Say you so, sir?

SIR OLIVER Prove° me with three at a birth, an thou dar'st now.

Try

TOUCHWOOD SR. Take heed how you dare a man, while you live, sir, that has good skill at his weapon.°

i.e., sexual prowess

Enter Tim and Welsh Gentlewoman [*and Tutor*].

SIR OLIVER Foot, I dare you, sir.

YELLOWHAMMER Look, gentlemen, if ever you saw the picture of the unfortunate marriage, yonder 'tis.

WELSH GENTLEWOMAN Nay, good sweet Tim.

TIM Come from the university to marry a whore in London, with my tutor too? *O tempora! O mores!*[5]

TUTOR Prithee, Tim, be patient.

TIM I bought a jade° at Cambridge. I'll let her out to execution, tutor, for eighteen pence a day, or Brentford horse races;[6] she'll serve to carry seven miles out of town well. Where be these mountains? I was promised mountains, but

worthless horse; whore

4. He is incarcerated in a comfortable section of a debtors' prison.

5. O times! O manners! (Cicero, *Against Catiline*, 1.1.)

6. I'll hire her out for performance of duties to pay off her debt to me, like a broken-down whore, or as a horse carrying customers to assignations in suburban places like Brentford. (The suburbs were popular places for assignations and were also considered places of prostitution.)

there's such a mist I can see none of 'em. What are become of those two thousand runts?° Let's have a bout with them in the meantime. A vengeance runt° thee! *cattle (see 4.1.90–92)* *reprove, berate*

MAUDLIN Good sweet Tim, have patience.

TIM *Flectere si nequeo superos, Acheronta movebo,*[7] mother.

MAUDLIN I think you have married her in logic, Tim. You told me once, by logic you would prove a whore an honest woman. Prove her so, Tim, and take her for thy labor.

TIM Troth, I thank you. I grant you I may prove another man's wife so, but not mine own.

MAUDLIN There's no remedy now, Tim. You must prove her so as well as you may.

TIM Why, then, my tutor and I will about° her as well as we can. *Uxor non est meretrix, ergo falleris.*[8] *set about, deal with*

WELSH GENTLEWOMAN Sir, if your logic cannot prove me honest, there's a thing called marriage, and that makes me honest.

MAUDLIN Oh, there's a trick beyond your logic, Tim.

TIM I perceive, then, a woman may be honest according to the English print,° when she is a whore in the Latin.[9] So much for marriage and logic! I'll love her for her wit; I'll pick out my runts there. And for my mountains, I'll mount° upon—[1] *spelling* *mount sexually*

YELLOWHAMMER So Fortune seldom deals two marriages
With one hand, and both lucky. The best is,
One feast will serve them both. Marry, for room,° *to have enough room*
I'll have the dinner kept° in Goldsmiths' Hall, *held*
To which, kind gallants, I invite you all. [*Exeunt.*]

FINIS.

7. If I cannot move the gods, I will appeal to the lower world. (Virgil, *Aeneid*, 7.312. Acheron was a river in Hades.)

8. A wife is not a whore, therefore you are mistaken.

9. Tim plays on *meretrix* (Latin for "whore") and "merry tricks."

1. The omitted word here is probably "cunts," to rhyme with "runts."

TEXTUAL NOTES

A Chaste Maid in Cheapside was entered in the Stationers' Register on April 8, 1630, and was printed in quarto in that same year by Francis Constable. It is apparently the only early edition, and it serves as the basis of the present edition. The lineation of the original appears to treat the distinction between prose and verse with a fair degree of inconsistency, and modern editors have varied considerably in their handling of this feature of the text. The present edition prints as prose all passages other than those in which the lineation as verse is reasonably persuasive and not hypermetrical. Substantive departures from the quarto are noted below, using the following abbreviations:

Q: The quarto (London: Francis Constable, 1630)
MSS: Manuscripts containing the song in act 4, scene 1
ed.: A modern editor's emendation

The Names of the Principal Persons 14–15 [ed.] TVCHWOOD SENIOR, and his Wife, *A decayed Gentleman.* [Q]
1.1.7 salads [Q: Sallets] **8 samphire** [Q: Sampier] **12 spirited** [ed.] sprited [Q]

20 pound [some copies of Q] pounds [some copies of Q] **32 e'en** [ed.] eeue [Q] **35 solders** [Q: sowders] **83 boo** [Q: Bo] **91** [and elsewhere] **cousin** [Q: Cousen] **97.3** [and elsewhere] ***Dahumma*** [ed.] *Dahanna* [Q] **134 sound too** [ed.] wound to [Q] **136** [and elsewhere] **compliments** [Q: complements] **152 peak** [ed.] picke [Q] **154 spoil** [ed.] spoy [Q] **161 Tim, sir, Tim** [ed.] turne Sir, turne [Q] **175 kind** [ed.; not in Q] **227 wear** [Q: were] **231 SD** [placement, ed.; after 230 in Q] **234** [and elsewhere] **lose** [Q: loose] **234.1** [and elsewhere] ***Exeunt*** [ed.] *Exit* [Q]

1.2.7–8 cucumbers [Q: Concombers] **26 chaldron** [Q: Chaldorne] **68.1** [placement, ed.; after 67 in Q] **71 pip** [ed.] peepe [Q] **81 Put on, put on** [ed.] Put on, but on [Q] **122 WAT** [Q: I *Boy.*] **124 NICK** [Q: 2 *Boy.*] **139 bowls** [Q: Boles]

2.1.13 prudent'st [ed.] prudents [Q] **45 desires** [ed.] desire [Q] **52 Merely** [ed.] Meerely [Q] **140 withal** [Q: with all] **161 fortunes** [some copies of Q] fortune [some copies of Q] **197 SIR OLIVER** [ed.; not in Q] **200 LADY KIX** [ed.; not in Q] **200 SIR OLIVER** [ed.; not in Q] **200 I'll about it** [placement, ed.; after 199 in Q]

2.2.16.1 [placement, ed.; after "portion" in 14 in Q] **17 DRY NURSE** [Q: *Nurse*] **19 SD** [placement, ed.; opposite 17 in Q] **19.1** [placement, ed.; after 18 in Q] **23, 26, 35 WET NURSE** [ed.] *Nurse* [Q] **136, 139 OLIVER** [ed.] *Man* [Q] **183 Now** [ed.] Not [Q] **190 I'll** [ed.; not in Q] **213 Queenhithe** [Q: Queene-hiue] **215 Brentford** [Q: Branford]

2.3.10.1 [placement, ed.; after 9 in Q] **22 Mistress** [ed.] Mr [Q]

3.1.22 you [ed.; not in Q] **36 posy** [Q: Poesie] **49 minx** [Q: Minkes]

3.2.3 [and throughout scene, except for 52] **FIRST PURITAN** [Q: *Pur.*] **11 Eyed** [ed.] Ey's [Q] **42 too, good** [Q: to good] **174 ate** [Q: eat] **194 Mistress** [ed.] Mr [Q] **199 Heyday** [ed.] Hyda [Q]

3.3.5 I [ed.; not in Q] **10 bankrupt** [Q: bankrout] **17 banquet of eryngoes** [Q: banket of Oringoes] **18 Artichokes** [Q: Hartechokes] **38.1** *Exit* [placement, ed.; opposite 37 in Q] **42 SD** [ed.] *Kix to his Lady within* [Q] **151 wife** [ed.] Wifes [Q] **162 SD** [placement, ed.; after 161 in Q]

4.1.12 *rationalis* [ed.] *rationalibus* [Q] **14 *dici*** [ed.] *dicere* [Q] **16, 23 *disputas*** [ed.] *disputus* [Q] **19, 23 *sumus*** [ed.] *sum* [Q] **61 *as*** [Q: *Asse*] **95 Romford** [Q: Rumford] **108 *Fertur*** [ed.] *Ferter* [Q] **108 *abundas*** [ed.] *abundis* [Q] **113 *abundas*** [ed.] *abundat* [Q] **115 *homunculus*** [ed.] *homauculus* [Q] **115 *simul et*** [ed.] *simule* [Q] **116 *paratus*** [ed.] *parata* [Q] **162 hear** [Q: here] **164** [SH preceding line] **WELSH GENTLEWOMAN** [ed.; not in Q] **171 thought** [MSS] *taught* [Q] **200 Abingdon** [Q: Abbington] **222 passed** [Q: past] **225** [and elsewhere] **coz** [Q: cus, cous]

4.2.5 coral [ed.] Curral [Q]

4.3.11 bandied [Q: banded]

4.4.4 wear [Q: were] **26 FIRST** [ed.; not in Q] **28 SECOND** [ed.; not in Q] **68 FIRST** [ed.; not in Q] **78 So** [ed.] Sir [Q]

5.1.46 parts [ed.] part [Q] **73 her too** [ed.] ho to [Q] **101 Imprimis** [Q: *Inprimis*]

5.2.31 ingredients [ed.] Ingredience [Q] **32 too** [Q: to] **43 MOLL** [ed.; not in Q] **79 fails in satisfaction,** [ed.] fayles, in satisfaction [Q]

5.3.3 all together [ed.] altogether [Q] **5 FIRST SERVANT** [ed.] *Seru.* [Q] **8, 10 SECOND SERVANT** [ed.] *Seru.* [Q] **13 THIRD SERVANT** [ed.] *Seru.* [Q] **20, 23, 28, 33 FOURTH SERVANT** [ed.] *Seru.* [Q] **28 such a** [some copies of Q] such [some copies of Q]

5.4.20 precedents [Q: presidents] **33 TOUCHWOOD JR.** [ed.] *T.S.* [Q] **40 trolled** [Q: trould] **47 please to** [Q: please too] **60 ALLWIT** [ed.] *All.* [Q] **77–78 ward. [*To Lady Kix*] Now your** [ed.] ward now. / Your [Q] **92 saw** [ed.] say [Q] **96 *mores*** [ed.] *Mors* [Q] **99 Brentford** [Q: Brainford] **106 *nequeo*** [ed.] *neguro* [Q] **106 *movebo*** [ed.] *mourbo* [Q] **115 *falleris*** [ed.] *falacis* [Q]

Women Beware Women

No Jacobean tragedy explores sexual obsessions more darkly than Thomas Middleton's *Women Beware Women* (c. 1620–24). In its varied portrayals of men and women controlled by forbidden desires and self-destructive impulses, the play continually reminds us of its great contemporaries, *The White Devil, The Duchess of Malfi, The Changeling,* and *'Tis Pity She's a Whore.* Its particular themes are graphically characteristic of Jacobean tragedy as a genre: imprudent elopements, enforced marriages of young women to foolish wealthy suitors, incestuous desire between close family members, royal or ducal seduction of young women, seductions engineered by managerial older women, sexual passion violently aroused in defiance of rational self-control. Happy thoughts of marital bliss and companionship are evoked again and again only to highlight the onrush of forbidden sexual desire.

What distinguishes *Women Beware Women* is the brilliance of its multiple plotting on the theme of obsessive desire. Middleton weaves together two sources: a partly historical account of a tragic love affair between Francesco de' Medici (1541–1587), second Grand Duke of Tuscany, and the Venetian-born Bianca Cappello, who became his mistress and eventually his consort; and a novella translated from the French in 1627 (and quite possibly known to Middleton in the French original) about an incestuous love affair between Hippolito and his niece Isabella, daughter of a Neapolitan magistrate, Fabricio, under cover of Isabella's marriage to the ungainly Pompeio. Adopting a technique of double plotting that was widespread in Renaissance drama, Middleton links his source stories in such a way as to allow each to intensify the moral dilemmas faced by his characters.

Middleton's dramatization of these two narratives is equally unsparing of both men and woman in their insistent desire for coupling. A Florentine commercial agent of distinctly bourgeois origins, Leantio, persuades the daughter of a great Venetian family, Bianca, to elope with him to Florence. (The historical Bianca Cappello did in fact elope in 1563 with a young Florentine named Pietro Buonaventure.) Shortly after they reach Florence, however, Leantio loses the loyalty of his bride when the Duke of Florence happens one day to spy Bianca at her window and desires to have her for his own. Simultaneously, a doddering old Florentine, Fabritio, enters into negotiations to marry his daughter, Isabella, to the foolish Ward and nephew of the politically well-connected Guardiano. Yet Isabella is far more contented with the company of her uncle, Hippolito. The dread of incest that bids her hesitate in this relationship is seemingly dispelled for her when her aunt, Livia, misleadingly tells her that she is not Hippolito's blood relative after all. Isabella and Hippolito thereupon agree to a secret love affair under cover of her marriage to the foolish Ward; incest may be a barrier for her, but adultery seemingly is not. The Ward is too infatuated with his own childish pleasures to catch on that he is being cuckolded. The widow Livia, for her part, takes an active role in the seduction of Bianca for the Duke's pleasure and then falls helplessly in love with Leantio when that unfortunate man is on the rebound from having

Introduction, glosses, footnotes, and textual notes by David Bevington; text edited by David Bevington and checked by Eric Rasmussen.

lost the affection of his wife, Bianca. Leantio's mother plays an unwitting but nonetheless inglorious role in the ducal seduction of her daughter-in-law occurring practically before her very eyes. No one is spared; the play's characters are all dupes or go-betweens or seducers, it appears. Innocence gives way to utter cynicism and the abandonment of moral restraint.

Middleton's title, *Women Beware Women*, calls particular attention to the perfidy of women, most of all toward one another. Bianca makes the point in the play's closing moments: "Oh, the deadly snares / That women set for women, without pity / Either to soul or honor!" Women have no enemy "Like our own sex" (5.2.213–17). No doubt the men could say the same thing of one another, and the two sexes have little to thank from each other, but the theme of woman versus woman does occupy a special prominence. And more than any other, Livia qualifies as the woman who is most at enmity with her own sex. Livia is implicitly the title figure of *Women Beware Women*.

Named for an infamous royal woman in the dissolute days of the Roman emperors Tiberius, Claudius, and Nero, and translated here to Florence as the Italian city-state famous for Machiavelli and the Medici dukes (and where the events on which the main plot of this tragedy was loosely based took place), Livia is a study in dramatic contrasts. She is no mere villainess; if she were, the play would lose much of its fascination. When we first see her, in fact, she is taking her niece Isabella's part against the matter-of-fact negotiations between Fabritio and Guardiano over the proposed marriage of Isabella to the doltish Ward. The men would be unjust, she insists, to force Isabella's love "to one she never saw. / Maids should both see and like"; if, upon seeing each other, both partners love truly, all is well (1.2.33–35). As one who has been twice widowed, Livia knows all too well that the marriage contract endures till death, and that if one were to ask most wives "at three years' end" their opinion of marriage, one would see well enough "how the game goes" (1.2.38–39). Men are also tied in mar-

Two gallants fight a duel in the street. From George Wither, *A Collection of Emblemes* (1635).

riage, but enjoy a greater freedom. Livia herself intends never to marry again; a third husband, she says, "shall never bury me" (1.2.54). Livia comes before us, then, as witty, self-possessed, wary, and sympathetic to the woman's plight in marriage.

When Livia learns of her brother Hippolito's incestuous desire for their niece, Isabella, her first instincts are to urge her brother to a morally sanctioned pursuit of some other woman. Yet when Hippolito persists, Livia's penchant for promoting erotic entanglements takes control. Confident in her ability to win any young woman away from chastity when the need arises, and assured that Isabella loathes her intended husband the Ward, Livia simply lies to Isabella about her parentage by inventing a supposed love affair between Isabella's mother (Livia's sister-in-law) and a roving Spanish marquis (2.1.136–58). Middleton takes this plot device from the novella he used as his source for the Isabella-Hippolito story line, but goes much further in a complex exploration of Livia's possible motives for telling such a lie. To be sure, Livia sympathizes with the plight of Isabella, and she loves her brother Hippolito, evidently taking his view (like that of Giovanni in *'Tis Pity She's a Whore*) that incest is an artificial social constraint interfering with young love. At the same time, Livia's pleasure in deceiving and manipulating is manifest. Our own responses to her machinations are in conflict as we watch Isabella's joy in being able to love Hippolito after all—a joy that is premised on her aunt's having lied to her.

Most of the play's seductions take place in Livia's house. The longest and most brilliant such scene is act 2, scene 2. In partnership with Guardiano, who hopes to win the Duke's favor thereby (2.2.39–40, 407–8), Livia lures Bianca to her house by a flattering invitation to Bianca's mother-in-law and a request that Bianca be brought along too. The Mother, as unofficial custodian of Bianca during her son Leantio's business trips, is easily inveigled into spending an evening with Livia; the invitation holds out the prospect of social advancement. Livia, for her own part, is curious to see the young beauty who has turned the head of the Duke of Florence (2.2.35–36); as an aging beauty, Livia seems to take vicarious pleasure in the sacrifice of such chastity. The seduction itself is arranged with a theatrical eye to visual juxtapositions: Livia and the Mother play chess on the main stage, while Bianca is shown the art treasures of the house by Guardiano, so that she may be surprised and vanquished by the Duke in the gallery over the main stage. The double entendres comparing the moves on the chessboard with those "*above*" heighten the dismaying sense of calculated strategy and entrapment of the innocent by the wary (2.2.298–422). Bianca appears to have no chance when Livia, Guardiano, and the Duke all conspire against her. Bianca's mother-in-law is no better than a pawn in the endgame leading to Bianca's being checkmated.

The play invites us to see a kind of poetic justice in Livia's own falling in love. It comes upon her unexpectedly and irrationally, as she presides over a banquet in her house in honor of the Duke and his new mistress, Bianca. Livia confides to us in soliloquy that she has never "truly felt the power of love / And pity to a man, till now" (3.3.65–66). The object of this sudden and vehement attachment is none other than Leantio, the cuckolded husband of Bianca. Livia's passion is awakened perhaps by Leantio's vulnerable status, perhaps partly by Livia's realization that she is wealthy enough to buy anything she desires, and perhaps most of all by a compulsive desire to compete for the affection of a man who is hopelessly in love with another woman (3.3.67–68, 261–75). That the choice could scarcely be less fortunate only intensifies her will to have Leantio. The man is below her in social station; he is a hapless misfit and failed husband; and he is capable of vengeful violence. Leantio is at first swept away by the prospect of such good fortune as Livia holds out to him, but he remains more intent on avenging his own cuckoldry than on returning Livia's passion. Livia is all too aware of the irrationality of her choice—"Where's my discretion now, my skill, my judgment?"—and yet she is unable to help herself. "I'm cunning in all arts but my own love," she realizes (3.3.321–22). When her brother Hippolito finds out about her affair with a lowly "factor," or commercial agent (4.1.163), the tragic consequences of her love choice become unavoidable.

The other women in the play are no less doomed, both by circumstances they cannot control and by character traits that compound their tragedies. Bianca, the innocent victim of the Duke's lust, turns whore indeed once her chastity has been vanquished. To her mother-in-law and unhappy husband she now reveals herself to be selfish, mercenary, mercurial, and dissatisfied with every aspect of the humble life they have provided for her, which, until now, she has accepted with willing grace (3.1–2). She is bitter toward the men who have wronged her, especially Guardiano and the Duke, and yet she acts out her new status with a consuming passion for the material comforts that through sin she has unwillingly bought. The Duke's plan to appoint her cuckolded husband to the captainship of Rouen citadel (3.3.42–47) in order to have him safely out of the way is a transparent replay of King David's disposing of Bathsheba's husband in order that he might enjoy her adulterously (2 Samuel 11). In their last, sad meeting, the faithless wife and the disappointed husband exchange bitter taunts that express the emptiness and fragility of their now separate quests for material advancement (4.1.41–104).

The seeming suddenness of Bianca's conversion from the lovingly dutiful wife of Leantio to the hardened mistress of the Duke and the thoroughly selfish despiser of Leantio's frugal hospitality catches everyone (including many critics) by surprise. We seem to be presented with two Biancas; as the "puzzled" Mother laments, there seems to be "no cause" for the abrupt change (3.1.65). Yet critics William Empson and Ronnie Mulryne may well be right in rejecting the necessity of any developmental continuity in the study of Bianca's character. We do not have to postulate a callous aspect of her personality that remains unseen until she is tested by circumstance; once the Duke has seduced her, she becomes a different person.[1] The play's very tragic conception of human behavior, both male and female, is apparent in this radical instability, for it manifests itself in the other characters as well.

Isabella, in a parallel instance, responds to her entrapment and betrayal with bitterness of spirit previously unseen in her. Auctioned off to the Ward by her father and the Ward's calculating uncle, Guardiano, Isabella submits with caustic irony to a marriage that will allow her to continue to enjoy Hippolito as her lover. Conceding that she has the advantage over the foolish Ward, in that he is simply gulled in the marriage while she has a secret partner, Isabella nonetheless suffers under the marital arrangement as "an infernal torment" (3.4.33, 35). It is unbearable to her to be "Thus bought and sold, and turned and pried into" (3.4.35). Indeed, the Ward and his charmingly idiotic servant, Sordido, proceed to scan her gait, peer up under her dress, and inspect her teeth as though they were buying a horse (3.4.44–132). The resulting comic blazon of her charms is hilarious but also degrading. Isabella can only suppose that her circumstances are at their lowest possible ebb until Livia takes vengeance for her loss of Leantio by informing Isabella that she is Hippolito's true niece after all. A knowing adulteress, Isabella now learns that she has also committed incest.

A failed quest for the cleansing experience of remorse and penance is a major component of the play's denouement, along with the predictable features of a tragedy of revenge. The Duke, confronted by his brother, the Cardinal, with his sins, resolves to do better—by marrying the woman he has stolen from her husband. Such penance will not do; the play's tragic figures are no more able to purge themselves of sin than they were able to avoid sinning in the first place. The Cardinal's role is prominent in labeling such actions as sin, as defined by the church, and the Duke readily confesses that he is a sinner (4.1.252–58). Hippolito knows himself to be "Monstrously guilty" (4.2.6). Livia confesses her lying and sees at last that "My own ambition pulls me down to ruin" (5.2.134). Isabella, however unknowing part of her sin may have been, con-

1. William Empson, *Some Versions of Pastoral* (London: Chatto and Windus, 1935), p. 55; J. R. Mulryne, ed., *Women Beware Women* (London: Methuen; Manchester: Manchester University Press, 1975), p. lxvi. See also Robert Ornstein, *The Moral Vision of Jacobean Tragedy* (Madison: University of Wisconsin Press, 1960).

cedes that she has committed "sin enough to make a whole world perish" (4.2.132). The grand ending, in a masque before the Duke and his court, emblematizes a fallen world in which splendor and wealth mask, but do not successfully conceal, the realities of forbidden desire.

The Cardinal (based on the historical Ferdinand de' Medici, who became his brother's successor as Grand Duke of Tuscany) is given the play's concluding lines to stress a seeming moral object lesson that sin and lust lead to ruin: "Sin, what thou art these ruins show too piteously" (5.2.225). Bianca too sees that "Pride, greatness, honors, beauty, youth, ambition, / You must all down together; there's no help for't" (5.2.221–22). Yet the greatness of this tragedy lies far more in the complexity with which its characters face, and are defeated by, the promptings of blood and desire than in any simple moral object lesson. Tragic sympathy arises to the extent that we are invited to see ourselves as fallen creatures struggling with human passions that are all too likely to undo us in our failed quest for self-understanding.

THOMAS MIDDLETON

Women Beware Women

[THE PERSONS IN THE PLAY]

DUKE of Florence
Lord CARDINAL, brother to the Duke
Two cardinals more
A LORD
FABRITIO, father to Isabella
HIPPOLITO, brother to Fabritio [and Livia]
GUARDIANO, uncle to the foolish Ward
The WARD, a rich young heir
LEANTIO, a factor,° husband to Bianca — *commercial agent*
SORDIDO, the Ward's man

LIVIA, sister to Fabritio [and Hippolito]
ISABELLA, niece to Livia [and Hippolito, and daughter to Fabritio]
BIANCA, Leantio's wife
Widow, his MOTHER

States° of Florence — *Rulers*
CITIZENS
A PRENTICE
BOYS
[A] MESSENGER [to the Duke]
A SERVANT [to Livia]
Two LADIES attending Bianca
[A PAGE to Leantio]
[HEBE, HYMEN, GANYMEDE, figures in the masque, along with nymphs, Isabella appearing as one; Hippolito and Guardiano appearing as shepherds, Livia as Juno, and pages as Cupids
Lords, ladies, cardinals, gentlemen, knights, pages, servants, torchbearers, attendants, guards]

THE SCENE: Florence.

The original 1657 title page reads *"Two New Plays, viz. More Dissemblers Besides Women* [*and*] *Women Beware Women.* Written by Tho. Middleton, Gent. London, Printed for Humphrey Moseley and are to be sold at his shop at the Prince's Arms in St. Pauls Churchyard. 1657." The individual play title on p. 85 of the octavo reads: *"Women Beware Women.* A Tragedy, by Tho. Middleton, Gent. London: Printed for Humphrey Moseley, 1657."

1.1

Enter Leantio with Bianca and Mother.
[*Bianca stands aside.*]

MOTHER Thy sight was never yet more precious to me.
Welcome, with all the affection of a mother
That comfort can express° from natural love! *call forth, elicit*
Since thy birth-joy—a mother's chiefest gladness,
After she's undergone her curse of sorrows°— *pain of childbirth*
Thou wast not more dear to me than this hour
Presents thee to my heart. Welcome again.

LEANTIO [*aside*] 'Las,° poor affectionate soul, how her joys *Alas*
speak to° me! *affect, move*
I have observed it often, and I know it is
The fortune commonly of knavish children
To have the loving'st mothers.

MOTHER [*indicating Bianca*] What's this gentlewoman?

LEANTIO Oh, you have named the most unvalued'st purchase° *inestimable acquisition*
That youth of man had ever knowledge of!
As often as I look upon that treasure,
And know it to be mine—there lies the blessing—
It joys me that I ever was ordained
To have a being° and to live 'mongst men; *To be alive*
Which is a fearful living, and a poor one;
Let a man truly think on't.[1]
To have the toil and griefs of fourscore years
Put up in a white sheet, tied with two knots[2]—
Methinks it should strike earthquakes in adulterers,[3]
When e'en the very sheets they commit sin in
May prove, for aught they know, all their last garments.
Oh, what a mark° were there for women then! *object lesson*
But beauty able to content a conqueror
(Whom earth could scarce content) keeps me in compass;° *content; within limits*
I find no wish in me bent sinfully
To this man's sister or to that man's wife.
In love's name, let 'em keep their honesties,° *chastities*
And cleave to their own husbands; 'tis their duties.
Now when I go to church, I can pray handsomely,
Not come like gallants° only to see faces, *fashionable gentlemen*
As if lust went to market still on Sundays.
I must confess I am guilty of one sin, mother,
More than I brought into the world with me,° *Besides original sin*
But that I glory in: 'tis theft,° but noble *stealing a marriage*
As ever greatness yet shot up withal.[4]

MOTHER How's that?

LEANTIO Never to be repented, mother,
Though sin be death;[5] I had died if I had not sinned.
And here's my masterpiece; do you now behold her!
Look on her well; she's mine. Look on her better.
Now say if't be not the best piece of theft

1.1. Leantio's house.
1. Leantio reflects piously that life is a vale of tears.
2. Laid into the grave in a shroud or winding-sheet tied at head and foot.
3. It should put the fear of God in adulterers.
4. But it is at least as noble as the kinds of theft used by great persons to get ahead in the world.
5. Cf. "For the wages of sin is death" (Romans 6.23).

That ever was committed! And I have my pardon for't;
'Tis sealed° from heaven by marriage. *approved*
MOTHER Married to her!
LEANTIO You must keep counsel,° mother, I am undone else; *keep my secret*
If it be known, I have lost her. Do but think now
What that loss is; life's but a trifle to't.
From Venice, her consent and I have brought her
From parents great in wealth, more now in rage.
But let storms spend their furies; now° we have got *now that*
A shelter o'er our quiet innocent loves,
We are contented. Little money she's brought me;
View but her face, you may see all her dowry,
Save that which lies locked up in hidden virtues,
Like jewels kept in cabinets.
MOTHER You're to blame—
If your obedience will give way to a check[6]—
To wrong such a perfection.
LEANTIO How?
MOTHER Such a creature,
To draw her° from her fortune—which no doubt, *take her away*
At the full time,° might have proved rich and noble— *In the fullness of time*
You know not what you have done. My life° can give you *My current income*
But little helps, and my death° lesser hopes; *what you will inherit*
And hitherto your own means has but made shift° *barely sufficed*
To keep you single,[7] and that hardly too.
What ableness have you to do her right, then,
In maintenance fitting her birth and virtues?
Which ev'ry woman of necessity looks for,
And most to go above it,° not confined *want more than that*
By their conditions, virtues, bloods, or births,[8]
But flowing to affections, wills, and humors.[9]
LEANTIO Speak low, sweet mother. You are able to spoil as many° *as many women*
As come within the hearing; if it be not
Your fortune to mar all, I have much marvel.[1]
I pray, do not you teach her to rebel,
When she's in a good way to obedience—
To rise with other women in commotion° *rebellion*
Against their husbands for six gowns a year,
And so maintain their cause, when they're once up,° *aroused, defiant*
In all things else that require cost enough.[2]
They are all of 'em a kind of spirits soon raised,
But not so soon laid,[3] mother. As for example,
A woman's belly is got up in a trice—
A simple charge[4] ere it be laid down again.
So° ever in all their quarrels and their courses.° *Thus / personal affairs*
And I'm a proud man; I hear nothing of 'em.
They're very still, I thank my happiness,
And sound asleep; pray let not your tongue wake 'em.

6. If the obedience you owe your mother will suffer you to accept a rebuke. ("Check" is also a chess term.)
7. To support you in your unmarried state.
8. Not content to be confined to their social station and family.
9. But giving free rein to their desires and fancies.
1. If you don't manage to spoil everything, I'll be much surprised.
2. In all sorts of expensive ways.
3. (1) Exorcized, laid to rest. (Said of spirits raised from the dead.) (2) Laid abed sexually.
4. A small cost. (Said ironically; the cost would be great.)

If you can but rest° quiet, she's contented *keep*
With all conditions that my fortunes bring her to:
To keep close° as a wife that loves her husband; *To stay at home*
To go after the rate of my ability,° *stay within my means*
Not the licentious swinge° of her own will, *inclination*
Like some of her old schoolfellows. She intends
To take out other works in a new sampler,[5]
And frame[6] the fashion of an honest love,
Which knows no wants,[7] but, mocking poverty,
Brings forth more children—to make rich men wonder
At divine Providence, that feeds mouths of infants,
And sends them none to feed,[8] but stuffs their rooms
With fruitful bags,° their beds with barren wombs. *moneybags*
Good mother, make not you things worse than they are
Out of your too much openness—pray take heed on't—
Nor imitate the envy of old people,
That strive to mar good sport because they are perfect.[9]
I would have you more pitiful° to youth, *full of pity*
Especially to your own flesh and blood.
I'll prove an excellent husband, here's my hand;° *my vow*
Lay° in provision, follow my business roundly,[1] *I'll lay*
And make you a grandmother in forty weeks.° *(term of pregnancy)*
Go, pray salute° her, bid her welcome cheerfully. *greet*

MOTHER [*approaching Bianca*] Gentlewoman, thus much is a debt of courtesy
Which fashionable strangers pay each other
At a kind meeting. [*She kisses Bianca.*] Then there's more than one
Due to the knowledge I have of your nearness;° *family connection*
I am bold to come again, and now salute you
By th'name of daughter, which may challenge° more *claim*
Than ordinary respect. [*She kisses her again.*]

LEANTIO [*aside*] Why, this is well, now,
And I think few mothers of threescore° will mend° it. *sixty / improve on*

MOTHER What I can bid you welcome to is mean;° *scanty*
But make it all your own. We are full of wants° *needs*
And cannot welcome worth.[2]

LEANTIO [*aside*] Now this is scurvy,° *shabby*
And spake as if a woman lacked her teeth.[3]
These old folks talk of nothing but defects,
Because they grow so full of 'em themselves.

BIANCA Kind mother, there is nothing can be wanting
To her that does enjoy all her desires.
Heaven send a quiet peace with this man's love,
And I am as rich as virtue can be poor,[4]
Which were enough after the rate of mind° *in the virtuous mind*
To erect temples for content placed here.° *(in this marriage)*
I have forsook friends, fortunes, and my country,
And hourly I rejoice in't; here's my friends,

5. She intends to pursue virtuous endeavors, such as embroidery, and live a new life accordingly.
6. Devise. (With suggestion of an embroidery frame.)
7. Which is content with a bare sufficiency.
8. And sends rich people no children to be fed.
9. Who interfere with youthful pleasure because, having lost their own sexual desire, they regard themselves as free of that sin.
1. (1) I'll work diligently; (2) I'll sire children energetically.
2. And cannot provide the welcome you are worth.
3. And spoken as if by a toothless, senile old woman.
4. And I shall be rich in much the way that virtuous persons can be content with the little they have.

And few is the good number. Thy successes,
Howe'er they look,° I will still name my fortunes; *Whatever fortune you have*
Hopeful or spiteful, they shall all be welcome.
Who° invites many guests has of all sorts, *Whoever*
As he that traffics much drinks of all fortunes;[5]
Yet they° must all be welcome, and used well. *(the guests; all fortunes)*
I'll call this place the place of my birth now,
And rightly too; for here my love was born,
And that's the birthday of a woman's joys.
[*To Leantio*] You have not bid me welcome since I came.

LEANTIO That I did, questionless.

BIANCA No, sure, how was't?
I have quite forgot it.

LEANTIO [*kissing her*] Thus.

BIANCA Oh, sir, 'tis true,
Now I remember well. I have done thee wrong.
Pray take't again, sir. [*They kiss again.*]

LEANTIO How many of these "wrongs"
Could I put up in an hour, and turn up° the glass° *turn over / hourglass*
For twice as many more!

MOTHER Will't please you to walk in, daughter?

BIANCA Thanks, sweet mother.
The voice of her that bare° me is not more pleasing. *gave birth to*
Exeunt [*Mother and Bianca*].

LEANTIO Though my own care and my rich master's trust
Lay their commands both on my factorship,° *role as a merchant's agent*
This day and night I'll know no other business
But her and her dear welcome. 'Tis a bitterness
To think upon tomorrow: that I must leave her
Still to the sweet hopes of the week's end.
That° pleasure should be so restrained and curbed, *How regrettable that*
After the course° of a rich work-master *Following the practice*
That never pays till Saturday night! Marry,° *By Mary (an oath)*
It° comes together in a round sum then, *(The week's pay)*
And does more good, you'll say. O fair-eyed Florence,
Didst thou but know what a most matchless jewel
Thou now art mistress of, a pride would take° thee *overwhelm, infect*
Able to shoot destruction through the bloods
Of all thy youthful sons.[6] But 'tis great policy° *stratagem*
To keep choice treasures in obscurest places;
Should we show° thieves our wealth, 'twould make 'em bolder. *If we showed*
Temptation is a devil will not stick° *that won't scruple*
To fasten upon a saint; take heed of that.
The jewel° is cased up° from all men's eyes; *Any jewel / encased*
Who could imagine now a gem were kept
Of that great value under this plain roof?
But how in times of absence?° What assurance *my absence*
Of this restraint then? Yes, yes, there's one° with her.° *(my mother) / (Bianca)*
Old mothers know the world, and such as these,
When sons lock chests, are good to look to° keys. *Exit.* *look after*

5. Just as the person who trades extensively experiences good and evil fortune.

6. Able to drive young Venetian men into self-destructive passions.

1.2

Enter Guardiano, Fabritio, and Livia.

GUARDIANO What, has your daughter seen him° yet? Know you that? *(my nephew and ward)*
FABRITIO No matter, she shall love him.
GUARDIANO Nay, let's have fair play.
He has been now my ward some fifteen year,
And 'tis my purpose, as time calls upon me,
By custom seconded and such moral virtues,
To tender° him a wife. Now, sir, this wife *provide for*
I'd fain° elect out of a daughter of yours; *gladly*
You see my meaning's fair. If now this daughter
So tendered (let me come to your own phrase, sir)
Should offer° to refuse him, I were hanselled.[1] *undertake*
[*Aside*] Thus am I fain to calculate all my words
For the meridian° of a foolish old man, *middle intelligence*
To take° his understanding. [*To him*] What do you answer, sir? *catch*
FABRITIO I say still she shall love him.
GUARDIANO Yet again?
And shall she have no reason for this love?
FABRITIO Why, do you think that women love with reason?
GUARDIANO [*aside*] I perceive fools are not at all hours foolish,
No more than wise men wise.
FABRITIO I had a wife;
She ran mad for me. She had no reason for't,
For aught I could perceive. [*To Livia*] What think you, lady sister?
GUARDIANO [*aside*] 'Twas a fit match, that, being both
Out of their wits. [*To him*] A loving wife! It seemed
She strove to come as near[2] you as she could.
FABRITIO And if her daughter prove not mad for love too,
She takes not after her; nor after me,
If she prefer reason before my pleasure.° *my wishes in this*
[*To Livia*] You're an experienced widow, lady sister.
I pray, let your opinion come amongst us.
LIVIA I must offend you, then, if truth will do't,
And take my niece's part, and call't injustice
To force her love to one she never saw.
Maids should both see and like; all little enough;[3]
If they love truly after that, 'tis well.
Counting the° time, she takes one man till death; *Considering the brief*
That's a hard task, I tell you. But one may
Inquire at three years' end amongst young wives
And mark how the game goes.
FABRITIO Why, is not man
Tied to the same observance,° lady sister, *ordinance*
And in one woman?
LIVIA 'Tis enough for him;
Besides, he tastes of many sundry dishes

1.2. Livia's house.
1. I.e., that would be a fine beginning! (Guardiano speaks ironically; usually a handsel is an auspicious gift given at the beginning of a new enterprise or new year.)
2. (1) Be as close to; (2) be as like.
3. Arranged matches and formal, constrained courtship give little enough occasion for either seeing or liking.

That we poor wretches never lay our lips to—
As obedience, forsooth, subjection, duty, and such kickshaws,° *fancy dishes; trifles*
All of our making, but served in to them.[4]
And if we lick a finger[5] then sometimes,
We are not to blame; your best cooks use° it. *practice*

FABRITIO Thou'rt a sweet lady, sister, and a witty—

LIVIA A witty! Oh, the bud of commendation
Fit for a girl of sixteen. I am blown,° man; *in full bloom (or past)*
I should be wise by this time; and for instance,
I have buried my two husbands in good fashion,
And never mean more to marry.

GUARDIANO No? Why so, lady?

LIVIA Because the third shall never bury me.
I think I am more than witty. [*To Fabritio*] How think you, sir?

FABRITIO I have paid often fees to a counselor
Has° had a weaker brain. *Who has*

LIVIA Then I must tell you,
Your money was soon parted.[6]

GUARDIANO [*to Fabritio*] Light her now, brother.[7]

LIVIA Where is my niece? Let her be sent for straight,° *at once*
If you have any hope 'twill prove a wedding.
'Tis fit, i'faith, she should have one sight of him,
And stop° upon't, and not be joined in haste, *pause; reflect*
As if they went to stock a newfound land.° *an overseas colony*

FABRITIO Look out her uncle,° and you're sure of her. *Look for Hippolito*
Those two are ne'er asunder; they've been heard
In argument at midnight. Moonshine nights
Are noondays with them; they walk out their sleeps,° *(instead of sleeping)*
Or rather at those hours appear like those
That walk in 'em,° for so they did to me. *like sleepwalkers*
Look you, I told you truth; they're like a chain:
Draw but one link, all follows.

Enter Hippolito, and Isabella, the niece.

GUARDIANO Oh, affinity,° *kinship*
What piece of excellent workmanship art thou!
'Tis work clean wrought,° for there's no lust, but love in't, *done purely; neatly*
And that abundantly, when in stranger things° *love between strangers*
There is no love at all but what lust brings.

FABRITIO [*to Isabella*] On with your mask, for 'tis your part to see now
And not be seen. Go to,° make use of your time; *(an expostulation)*
See what you mean to like; nay, and I charge you,
Like what you see. Do you hear me? There's no dallying;
The gentleman's almost twenty, and 'tis time
He were getting° lawful heirs, and you a-breeding on° 'em. *begetting / of*

ISABELLA Good father!

FABRITIO Tell not me of tongues° and rumors. *gossip*

4. Husbands get to taste various delicacies—such as a wife's obedience, subjection, etc.—that are denied us. We make these pleasures for them by serving in our duty to them.

5. I.e., if we taste pleasure by having an extramarital affair. (Good cooks are proverbially those that can lick their fingers.)

6. Cf. the proverb "A fool and his money are soon parted." Fabritio has wasted his money.

7. Perhaps Guardiano suggests that Isabella, the subject of their conversation, be lighted in, i.e., escorted in with a torch. "Brother" is a general term of relationship in anticipation of the marriage.

You'll say the gentleman is somewhat simple—
The better for a husband, were you wise,
For those that marry fools live ladies' lives.° *enjoy sexual freedom*
On with the mask. I'll hear no more. He's rich;
The fool's hid under bushels.° *bushels of money*

LIVIA Not so hid, neither,
But here's a foul great piece of him, methinks;
What will he be when he comes altogether?° *comes fully of age*

Enter the Ward with a trap-stick,[8] and Sordido, his man.° *servant*
[*The others stand aside and observe. Isabella masks.*]

WARD Beat him?° I beat him out o'th'field with his own cat- *(imaginary opponent)*
stick, yet gave him the first hand.° *stroke*

SORDIDO Oh, strange!

WARD I did it. Then he set jacks° on me. *lowbred fellows*

SORDIDO What, my lady's tailor?

WARD Ay, and I beat him too.

SORDIDO Nay, that's no wonder. He's used to beating.

WARD Nay, I tickled° him when I came once to my tippings.° *beat / (part of the game)*

SORDIDO Now you talk on 'em, there was a poulterer's° wife *chicken-seller's*
made a great complaint of you last night to your guardianer,° *guardian (uncle)*
that you struck a bump in her child's head as big as an egg.

WARD An egg may prove a chicken; then in time the poulterer's
wife will get° by't. When I am in game,° I am furious; came my *profit / fighting*
mother's eyes in my way, I would not lose a fair end.° No, *chance; shot*
were she alive, but with one tooth in her head, I should
venture the striking out of that. I think of nobody when I
am in play,° I am so earnest. [*Seeing the others*] Coads me,° *fighting / (an oath)*
my guardianer! Prithee lay up my cat and cat-stick° safe. *(see nn. 8 and 9)*

SORDIDO Where, sir, i'th'chimney-corner?

WARD Chimney-corner!

SORDIDO Yes, sir, your cats are always safe i'th'chimney-
corner, unless they burn their coats.[9]

WARD Marry, that I am afraid on!

SORDIDO Why, then I will bestow your cat i'th'gutter, and
there she's safe, I am sure.

WARD If I but live to keep a house, I'll make thee a great° *eminent; fat*
man, if meat and drink can do't. I can stoop gallantly, and
pitch out when I list;° I'm dog at° a hole.[1] I mar'l my guar- *wish / I'm skilled at*
dianer does not seek a wife for me; I protest° I'll have a bout° *declare / sexual encounter*
with the maids else, or contract myself at midnight to the
larder-woman,[2] in presence of a fool, or a sack-posset.[3]

GUARDIANO [*calling*] Ward!

WARD [*to Sordido*] I feel myself after any exercise horribly
prone.° Let me but ride, I'm lusty; a cockhorse° straight, i'faith. *horny / hobbyhorse; whore*

GUARDIANO Why, Ward, I say!

WARD I'll forswear eating eggs-in-moonshine[4] 'nights.° *a-nights*
There's ne'er a one I eat but turns into a cock° in four-and- *makes me randy*

8. A wooden object to be struck in a children's game; also called a "cat-stick" (see lines 90–91).

9. With sexual innuendo: "cat" suggests "whore"; "safe" means "free from infection"; and "burn" is to suffer the effects of syphilis.

1. The Ward's terms here ("stoop," "pitch out," "hole") are probably from his favorite game of cat; they probably also involve sexual wordplay that may be unconscious on his part ("pitch out" suggests ejaculation, and "hole" the vagina).

2. The woman servant presiding over the "larder," or pantry.

3. The witnesses required for a marriage contract here absurdly consist of a "fool" (a clotted-cream trifle) or hot milk curdled with wine and spices.

4. An egg dish regarded as an aphrodisiac.

twenty hours; if my hot blood be not took down in time, sure 'twill crow° shortly. *i.e., ejaculate*

GUARDIANO Do you hear, sir? Follow me. I must new school you.[5]

WARD School me? I scorn that now; I am past schooling. I am not so base to° learn to write and read; I was born to better fortunes in my cradle.[6] *as to*

Exit [Guardiano, with the Ward and Sordido].

FABRITIO How do you like him, girl? This is your husband.
Like him or like him not, wench, you shall have him,
And you shall love him.

LIVIA Oh, soft° there, brother! Though you be a justice, *gently*
Your warrant cannot be served out of your liberty;[7]
You may compel out of° the power of father *on the basis of*
Things merely° harsh to a maid's flesh and blood, *altogether*
But when you come to love, there the soil° alters; *terrain*
You're in another country, where your laws
Are no more set by° than the cacklings *heeded*
Of geese in Rome's great Capitol.[8]

FABRITIO Marry him she shall, then;
Let her agree upon love afterwards.

LIVIA You speak now, brother, like an honest mortal° *like an ordinary mortal*
That walks upon th'earth with a staff;° you were *That is like other men*
Up i'th'clouds before. You'd command love—
And so do most old folks that go without it.

Exit [Fabritio].

[*To Hippolito*] My best and dearest brother, I could dwell here;° *(in your company)*
There is not such another seat on earth
Where all good parts better express themselves.

HIPPOLITO You'll make me blush anon.

LIVIA 'Tis but like saying grace before a feast, then,
And that's most comely; thou art all a feast,
And she° that has thee a most happy° guest. *(any woman) / lucky*
Prithee cheer up thy niece with special counsel. *[Exit.]*

HIPPOLITO [*aside*] I would 'twere fit to speak to her what I would; but
'Twas not a thing ordained. Heaven has forbid it;
And 'tis most meet° that I should rather perish *fitting*
Than the decree° divine receive least blemish. *(against incest)*
Feed inward, you my sorrows! Make no noise;
Consume me silent;° let me be stark dead *in silence*
Ere the world know I'm sick. You see my honesty;
If you befriend me, so.[9]

ISABELLA [*aside*] Marry a fool!
Can there be greater misery to a woman
That means to keep her days true to her husband
And know no other man? So virtue wills it.
Why, how can I obey and honor him° *(the Ward)*
But I must needs commit idolatry?[1]

5. I must counsel you again. (But the Ward interprets it literally as schooling, in lines 131–33.)
6. The indifference to learning of some wellborn people was a standard joke at the time.
7. Your written authority cannot be enforced outside your immediate jurisdiction.
8. Sacred geese were to be seen on Capitoline Hill in ancient Rome.
9. You (my sorrow) alone know me for what I truly am; if you alone are to be my companion, so be it.
1. Without making my husband a kind of god?

A fool is but the image° of a man, — *mere semblance*
And that but ill made neither.° Oh, the heartbreakings — *not even well made*
Of miserable maids, where love's enforced!
The best condition is but bad enough.
When women have their choices, commonly
They do but buy their thraldoms,° and bring great portions° — *servitude / dowries*
To men to keep 'em° in subjection— — *(the wives)*
As if a fearful prisoner should bribe
The keeper to be good to him, yet lies in° still, — *remains in jail*
And glad of a good usage, a good look sometimes.
By'r Lady, no misery surmounts a woman's!
Men buy their slaves, but women buy° their masters. — *(with dowries)*
Yet honesty and love makes all this° happy, — *(marriage)*
And, next to angels', the most blest estate.
That Providence that has made ev'ry poison
Good for some use, and sets four warring elements° — *water, air, earth, fire*
At peace in man, can make a harmony
In things that are most strange to human reason.
Oh, but this marriage! [*To Hippolito*] What, are you sad
too, uncle?
Faith,° then there's a whole household down° together! — *In faith / depressed*
Where shall I go to seek my comfort now
When my best friend's distressed?
What is't afflicts you, sir?

HIPPOLITO Faith, nothing but one grief that will not leave me,
And now 'tis welcome.[2] Ev'ry man has something
To bring him to his end, and this will serve,
Joined with your father's cruelty to you;
That helps it forward.

ISABELLA Oh, be cheered, sweet uncle!
How long has't been upon you? I ne'er spied it;
What a dull sight have I! How long, I pray, sir?

HIPPOLITO Since I first saw you, niece, and left Bologna.

ISABELLA And could you deal so unkindly with my heart
To keep it up so long hid from my pity?
Alas, how shall I trust your love hereafter?
Have we passed through so many arguments° — *subjects of discussion*
And missed of that still, the most needful one?
Walked out whole nights together in discourses,
And the main point forgot? We are to blame both;
This is an obstinate willful forgetfulness,
And faulty on both parts. Let's lose no time now:
Begin, good uncle, you that feel't, what is it?

HIPPOLITO You of all creatures, niece, must never hear on't;
'Tis not a thing ordained for you to know.

ISABELLA Not I, sir? All my joys that word cuts off.
You made profession once you loved me best;
'Twas but profession!° — *an empty vow*

HIPPOLITO Yes, I do't too truly,
And fear I shall be chid for't. Know the worst then:
I love thee dearlier than an uncle can.

ISABELLA Why so you ever said, and I believed it.

HIPPOLITO [*aside*] So simple is the goodness of her thoughts,

2. Hippolito welcomes a grief that will hasten the end of a life from which he longs to be released.

They understand not yet th'unhallowed language
Of a near° sinner! I must yet be forced — *would-be; related*
(Though blushes be my venture)[3] to come nearer.° — *be more blunt*
[*To her*] As a man loves his wife so love I thee.

ISABELLA What's that?
Methought I heard ill news come toward me,
Which commonly we understand too soon,
Then overquick at hearing.[4] I'll prevent° it. — *anticipate; deflect*
Though my joys fare the harder, welcome it;[5]
It shall ne'er come so near mine ear again.
Farewell all friendly solaces and discourses!
I'll learn to live without ye, for your dangers
Are greater than your comforts. What's become
Of truth in love, if such we cannot trust—
When blood° that should be love is mixed with lust? *Exit.* — *affinity; kinship*

HIPPOLITO The worst can be but death, and let it come;
He that lives joyless, ev'ry day's his doom. *Exit.*

1.3

Enter Leantio alone.

LEANTIO Methinks I'm e'en as dull now at departure
As men observe great gallants the next day
After a revels;° you shall see 'em look — *masked entertainment*
Much of my fashion, if you mark 'em well.
'Tis e'en a second hell to part from pleasure
When man has got a smack on't.° As° many holidays — *taste of it / Just as*
Coming together makes your poor heads° idle — *workers*
A great while after, and are said to stick
Fast in their fingers' ends,[1] e'en so does game° — *sex*
In a new-married couple: for the time
It spoils all thrift,° and indeed lies abed — *industry*
To invent all the new ways for great expenses.[2]

[*Enter*] *Bianca and Mother above.*° — *on the upper stage*

See an° she be not got on purpose now — *if*
Into the window to look after me!° — *watch my going*
I have no power to go now, an I should be hanged.
Farewell all business! I desire no more
Than I see yonder. Let the goods at quay° — *at the dock*
Look to themselves; why should I toil my youth out?
It is but begging° two or three year sooner, — *falling into poverty*
And stay with her continually—is't a match?° — *bargain*
Oh fie, what a religion° have I leaped into! — *woman worship*
Get out again, for shame! Then man loves best
When his care's most;[3] that° shows his zeal to love. — *(his "care," or industry)*
Fondness is but the idiot to affection,[4]

3. At the risk of blushing.
4. Our sense of hearing being all too quick to detect such bad news.
5. Though my joy will suffer for this, I bid a sad welcome to adversity.
1.3. Outside Leantio's house.

1. I.e., and are said to lessen their enthusiasm for regular work.
2. And lolls about inventing new extravagances.
3. A man shows his love best by being industrious.
4. Doting uxoriousness is an absurd caricature of true affection.

That plays at hot-cockles[5] with rich merchants' wives—
Good to make sport withal° when the chest's° full   *with / money chest is*
And the long warehouse cracks.° 'Tis time of day   *is full to bursting*
For us to be more wise; 'tis early with us;
And if they° lose the morning of their affairs   *(people)*
They commonly lose the best part of the day.
Those that are wealthy, and have got enough,
'Tis after sunset with 'em; they may rest,
Grow fat with ease, banquet and toy and play,
When such as I enter the heat o'th'day;
And I'll do't cheerfully. [*He starts to leave.*]
BIANCA [*calling after him*] I perceive, sir,
You're not gone yet; I have good hope you'll stay now.
LEANTIO Farewell! I must not.
BIANCA Come, come, pray return;
Tomorrow, adding but a little care more,°   *working a bit more*
Will dispatch all as well; believe me 'twill, sir.
LEANTIO I could well wish myself where you would have me.
But love that's wanton must be ruled awhile
By that that's careful,° or all goes to ruin.   *By prudence*
As fitting is a government in love
As in a kingdom; where 'tis all mere lust°   *willful desire*
'Tis like an insurrection in the people
That, raised in self-will, wars against all reason.
But love that is respective for increase°   *thinks about profit*
Is like a good king that keeps all in peace.
Once more, farewell.
BIANCA But° this one night, I prithee.   *Only*
LEANTIO Alas, I'm in for twenty if I stay,
And then for forty more. I have such luck to flesh,[6]
I never bought a horse but he bore double.[7]
If I stay any longer I shall turn
An everlasting spendthrift. As you love
To be maintained° well, do not call me again,   *supported financially*
For then I shall not care which end goes forward.°   *what I do*
Again, farewell to thee!
BIANCA Since it must, farewell too! *Exit* [*Leantio*].
MOTHER Faith, daughter, you're to blame; you take the course
To make him an ill husband, troth you do.
And that disease° is catching, I can tell you,   *amorous idleness*
Ay, and soon taken° by a young man's blood,   *caught*
And that with little urging. Nay, fie, see now,
What cause have you to weep? Would I had no more,° || *no more cause*
That have lived threescore years—there° were a cause,   *(being 60 years old)*
An° 'twere well thought on.° Trust me, you're to blame.   *If / considered*
His absence cannot last five days at utmost.
Why should those tears be fetched forth? Cannot love
Be e'en as well expressed in a good look,
But it must see her face still in a fountain?[8]
It shows like a country maid dressing her head

5. A foolish game in which one player kneels with head buried in another's lap and guesses who strikes him or her.
6. (1) With horseflesh; (2) in matters of fleshly desire.
7. (1) Doubled my costs; (2) bore two riders. (With the suggestion of cuckoldry.)
8. Cannot love express itself smilingly without turning the face into a fountain of tears?

By a dish of water.[9] Come, 'tis an old° custom — *silly old*
To weep for love.

Enter two or three Boys, and a Citizen or two, with an Apprentice.

BOYS Now they come, now they come!
SECOND BOY The Duke!
THIRD BOY The state!° — *The ruling nobility!*
CITIZEN How near, boy?
FIRST BOY I'th'next street, sir, hard at hand.
CITIZEN [*to the Apprentice*] You, sirrah, get a standing° for your mistress,[1] — *station; stool*
The best in all the city.
APPRENTICE I have't for her, sir.
'Twas a thing I provided for her overnight;
'Tis ready at her pleasure.° — *(with sexual punning)*
CITIZEN Fetch her to't, then.
Away, sir! [*Exit the Apprentice.*]
BIANCA What's the meaning of this hurry,
Can you tell, mother?
MOTHER What a memory
Have I! I see by that, years come upon me.[2]
Why, 'tis a yearly custom and solemnity,° — *ceremony*
Religiously observed by th'Duke and state,
To Saint Mark's Temple, the fifteenth of April.
See if my dull brains had not quite forgot it.
'Twas happily questioned of thee; I had gone down° else, — *(from the upper stage)*
Sat like a drone below, and never thought on't.
I would not, to be ten years younger again,
That you had lost the sight! Now you shall see
Our Duke, a goodly gentleman of his years.
BIANCA Is he old, then?
MOTHER About some fifty-five.
BIANCA That's no great age in man; he's then at best
For wisdom and for judgment.
MOTHER The Lord Cardinal,
His noble brother, there's a comely gentleman,
And greater° in devotion than in blood.° — *even greater / birth*
BIANCA He's worthy to be marked.
MOTHER You shall behold
All our chief states° of Florence. You came fortunately — *statesmen*
Against° this solemn day. — *In time for*
BIANCA I hope so, always. *Music.*
MOTHER I hear 'em near us now. Do you stand easily?
BIANCA Exceeding well, good mother.
MOTHER Take this stool.
BIANCA I need it not, I thank you.
MOTHER Use your will,° then. — *Have it your way*

Enter in great solemnity six knights bareheaded, then two cardinals, and then the Lord Cardinal, then the

9. It looks like a country wench doing her coiffure by pouring water all over her hair.
1. The Citizen, probably on the main stage with others in the crowd, orders the Apprentice to find a good station for the Citizen's wife so that she can watch the procession. Bianca and her mother-in-law remain above, watching.
2. That tells me I'm getting old.

Duke; after him the states of Florence by two and two,
with variety of music and song.

Exit [the procession, followed by the crowd].

How like you, daughter?
BIANCA 'Tis a noble state.
Methinks my soul could dwell upon the reverence° *solemnity*
Of such a solemn and most worthy custom.
Did not the Duke look up? Methought he saw us.
MOTHER That's ev'ryone's conceit° that sees a duke; *idea*
If he look steadfastly, he looks straight at them,
When he, perhaps, good careful° gentleman, *full of cares*
Never minds° any, but the look he casts *has in mind*
Is at his own intentions, and his object
Only the public good.
BIANCA Most likely so.
MOTHER Come, come, we'll end this argument° below. *discussion*

Exeunt [above].

2.1

Enter Hippolito, and Lady Livia, the widow.

LIVIA A strange affection, brother! When I think on't,
I wonder how thou cam'st by't.
HIPPOLITO E'en as easily
As man comes by destruction, which ofttimes
He wears in his own bosom.
LIVIA Is the world
So populous in women, and creation
So prodigal in beauty and so various,
Yet does love turn thy point° to thine own blood? *compass needle point*
'Tis somewhat too unkindly.° Must thy eye *unnatural; cruel*
Dwell evilly on the fairness of thy kindred,
And seek not where it should? It is confined
Now in a narrower prison than was made for't.
It is allowed a stranger;° and where bounty *non–blood relation*
Is made the great man's honor, 'tis ill husbandry
To spare, and servants shall have small thanks for't.[1]
So he heaven's bounty seems to scorn and mock
That spares free means and spends of his own stock.[2]
HIPPOLITO Never was man's misery so soon summed up,
Counting how truly.° *If truly reckoned*
LIVIA Nay, I love you so
That I shall venture much to keep a change° from you *calamity*
So fearful as this grief will bring upon you.
Faith, it even kills me when I see you faint
Under a reprehension,° and I'll leave it,° *reprimand / say nothing*
Though I know nothing can be better for you.
Prithee, sweet brother, let not passion° waste *sorrow, suffering*
The goodness of thy time° and of thy fortune. *your best years*

2.1. Livia's house.
1. Whereas liberality redounds to a great man's credit, it is false economy to be stingy, and servants won't be thanked for it either.
2. A man (like Hippolito) seems to mock heaven's bounty when he passes up the women freely available to him in favor of his own (forbidden) family members.

Thou keep'st° the treasure of that life I love *You preserve in yourself*
As dearly as mine own; and if you think
My former words too bitter, which were ministered
By truth and zeal, 'tis but a hazarding
Of grace and virtue, and I can bring forth
As pleasant fruits as sensuality wishes
In all her teeming longings.[3] This I can do.

HIPPOLITO Oh, nothing that can make my wishes perfect![4]

LIVIA I would that love of yours were pawned to't, brother,
And as soon lost that way as I could win.[5]
Sir, I could give as shrewd a lift to chastity
As any she that wears a tongue in Florence.[6]
She'd need be a good horsewoman, and sit fast,
Whom my strong argument could not fling° at last. *unseat*
Prithee, take courage, man. Though I should counsel
Another to despair, yet I am pitiful
To thy afflictions, and will venture hard—
I will not name for what, 'tis not handsome.° *decent*
Find you the proof, and praise me.[7]

HIPPOLITO Then I fear me
I shall not praise you in haste.° *any time soon*

LIVIA This is the comfort:
You are not the first, brother, has° attempted *who has*
Things more forbidden than this seems to be.
I'll minister all cordials° now to you *heart stimulants*
Because I'd° cheer you up, sir. *I wish to*

HIPPOLITO I am past hope.

LIVIA Love, thou shalt see me do a strange cure, then,
As e'er was wrought on a disease so mortal,
And near akin to shame. When shall you see her?

HIPPOLITO Never in comfort more.

LIVIA You're so impatient, too.

HIPPOLITO Will you believe? 'Death,° she's forsworn my company, *By God's death*
And sealed° it with a blush. *confirmed*

LIVIA So, I perceive
All lies upon my hands, then. Well, the more glory
When the work's finished.

Enter Servant.

How now, sir, the news?

SERVANT Madam, your niece, the virtuous Isabella,
Is lighted° now to see you. *alighted (from coach)*

LIVIA [*to Hippolito*] That's great fortune.
Sir, your stars bless.° [*To Servant*] You, simple,° lead her in. *bless your stars / fool*

Exit Servant.

HIPPOLITO What's this to° me? *What does this ask of*

LIVIA Your absence, gentle brother;
I must bestir my wits for you.

3. If my true and zealous advice earlier was too bitter, at the mere risk of losing eternal salvation I can cater to your teeming lascivious wishes as much as you want.
4. Oh, but nothing that you do can completely satisfy me!
5. I.e., I wish that love of yours were staked (as a bet) on my promise to help, and that you could forget your love (for Isabella) as easily as I could win her to love you if I chose.
6. I could as deftly unseat chastity as any smooth-tongued woman in Florence.
7. When you see the results, then praise me.

HIPPOLITO Ay, to great purpose.
Exit Hippolito.
LIVIA Beshrew you,° would I loved you not so well! *(a mild curse)*
I'll go to bed, and leave this deed undone.
I am the fondest where I once affect,[8]
The carefull'st of their healths and of their ease,° forsooth, *pleasure, happiness*
That I look still° but slenderly to mine own.° *continually / own case*
I take a course to pity him so much now
That I have none left for modesty and myself.
This 'tis to grow so liberal!° You've few sisters *generous*
That love their brothers' ease° 'bove their own honesties; *pleasure*
But if you question my affections,
That will be found my fault.

Enter Isabella, the niece.

Niece, your love's welcome.° *you're lovingly welcome*
Alas, what draws that paleness to thy cheeks?
This enforced marriage towards?° *in prospect*
ISABELLA It helps, good aunt,
Amongst some other griefs; but those I'll keep
Locked up in modest silence, for they're sorrows
Would° shame the tongue more than they grieve the thought. *Which would*
LIVIA Indeed the Ward is simple.° *simpleminded*
ISABELLA Simple! That were well;
Why, one might make good shift° with such a husband. *arrangement*
But he's a fool entailed;° he halts downright[9] in't. *i.e., congenital*
LIVIA And knowing this, I hope 'tis at your choice
To take or refuse, niece.
ISABELLA You see it is not.
I loathe him more than beauty can hate death
Or age, her spiteful neighbor.[1]
LIVIA Let 't appear,° then. *Show your revulsion*
ISABELLA How can I, being born with that obedience
That must submit unto a father's will?
If he command, I must of force° consent. *perforce*
LIVIA Alas, poor soul! Be not offended, prithee,
If I set by° the name of niece awhile, *put aside*
And bring in pity in a stranger fashion—
It lies here in this breast—would cross° this match. *which would thwart*
ISABELLA How, cross it, aunt?
LIVIA Ay, and give thee more liberty
Than thou hast reason yet to apprehend.
ISABELLA Sweet aunt, in goodness keep not hid from me
What may befriend my life!
LIVIA Yes, yes, I must.
When I return to° reputation, *recall*
And think upon the solemn vow I made
To your dead mother, my most loving sister°— *(actually, sister-in-law)*
As long as I have her memory 'twixt mine eyelids,° *in my mind*
Look for no pity now.
ISABELLA Kind, sweet, dear aunt—
LIVIA No, 'twas a secret I have took special care of,

8. I am so foolishly solicitous once I feel strong affection.

9. (1) He limps; (2) he stops, goes no further.

1. Age and death are nearly allied.

Delivered by your mother on her deathbed.
That's nine years now, and I'll not part from't yet—
Though ne'er was fitter time, nor greater cause for't.
ISABELLA As you desire the praises of a virgin[2]—
LIVIA Good sorrow![3] I would do thee any kindness
Not wronging secrecy or reputation.
ISABELLA Neither of which, as I have hope of fruitfulness,° *bearing children*
Shall receive wrong from me.
LIVIA Nay, 'twould be your own wrong,° *you'd suffer most*
As much as any 's, should it come to that once.° *ever*
ISABELLA I need no better means to work persuasion, then.[4]
LIVIA Let it suffice you may refuse this fool° *(the Ward)*
Or you may take him, as you see occasion
For your advantage; the best wits° will do't. *cleverest women*
You've liberty enough in your own will;
You cannot be enforced. There grows the flower,
If you could pick it out, makes° whole life sweet to you. *that makes*
That which you call your father's command 's nothing;° *is without validity*
Then your obedience must needs be as little.
If you can make shift° here to taste your happiness, *devise*
Or pick out aught that likes° you, much good do you.° *pleases / may it do you*
You see your cheer; I'll make you no set dinner.[5]
ISABELLA And trust me, I may starve for all the good
I can find yet in this. Sweet aunt, deal plainlier.
LIVIA Say I should trust you now upon an oath,
And give you, in a secret, that° would start° you, *that which / startle*
How am I sure of you, in faith and silence?
ISABELLA Equal assurance may I find in mercy
As you for that in me.[6]
LIVIA It shall suffice.
Then know: however custom has made good,° *asserted*
For reputation's sake, the names of niece
And aunt 'twixt you and I, we're nothing less.° *nothing of the sort*
ISABELLA How's that?
LIVIA I told you I should start your blood.
You are no more allied to any of us,
Save° what the courtesy of opinion casts *Excepting*
Upon your mother's memory and your name,
Than the merest stranger is, or one begot
At Naples when the husband lies at Rome,
There's so much odds° betwixt us. Since your knowledge *distance*
Wished more instruction, and I have your oath
In pledge for silence, it makes me talk the freelier:
Did never the report of that famed Spaniard,
Marquis of Coria, since your time was ripe° *since you were old enough*
For understanding, fill your ear with wonder?
ISABELLA Yes, what of him? I have heard his deeds of honor
Often related when we lived in Naples.
LIVIA You heard the praises of your father, then.

2. If you wish to earn the thankful praise of me, virgin that I am.
3. Livia addresses Isabella as the embodiment of sorrow.
4. I.e., If I am the one who would suffer chiefly through revelation of this secret, let that persuade you to tell me.
5. You see what provisions are set before you; the choice is yours.
6. May I be assured of heavenly mercy to my soul in equal measures as you may be assured of my secrecy.

ISABELLA My father!
LIVIA That was he. But all the business
So carefully and so discreetly carried° *managed*
That fame° received no spot by't, not a blemish. *reputation*
Your mother was so wary to her end° *till her death*
None knew it but her conscience and her friend,° *lover*
Till penitent confession made it mine,
And now my pity yours.° It had been long° else; *makes it yours / long hid*
And I hope care and love alike in you,
Made good by oath, will see it° take no wrong now. *(the secret; reputation)*
How weak his commands now, whom you call father!
How vain all his enforcements, your obedience!
And what a largeness in your will and liberty,
To take, or to reject, or to do both!
For fools will serve to father wise men's children.[7]
All this you've time to think on. Oh, my wench,
Nothing o'erthrows our sex but indiscretion;
We might do well else of a brittle people[8]
As any under the great canopy.° *the sky*
I pray, forget not but to call me aunt still;
Take heed of that, it may be marked° in time else.° *noticed / otherwise*
But keep your thoughts to yourself, from all the world,
Kindred, or dearest friend—nay, I entreat you,
From him that all this while you have called uncle;
And though you love him dearly, as I know
His deserts claim as much e'en from a stranger,
Yet let not him know this. I prithee, do not;
As ever thou hast hope of second pity,[9]
If thou shouldst stand in need on't, do not do't.
ISABELLA Believe my oath, I will not.
LIVIA Why, well said.
[*Aside*] Who° shows more craft t'undo a maidenhead, *Any woman who*
I'll resign my part to her.

Enter Hippolito.

[*Aside to him*] She's thine own, go.
Exit [*Livia*].
HIPPOLITO [*aside*] Alas, fair flattery° cannot cure my sorrows! *flattering hopes*
ISABELLA [*aside*] Have I passed so much time in ignorance,
And never had the means to know myself
Till this blest hour? Thanks to her virtuous pity
That brought it now to light! Would I had known it
But one day sooner! He had then received
In favors what, poor gentleman, he took
In bitter words—a slight and harsh reward
For one of his deserts.
HIPPOLITO [*aside*] There seems to me now
More anger and distraction in her looks.
I'm gone.° I'll not endure a second storm; *I'll be gone*
The memory of the first is not past yet.
ISABELLA [*aside*] Are you returned, you comforts of my life,

7. Fools sometimes serve as fathers to children who are in fact born of more clever men. (Fabritio is by implication a fool.)

8. We women might do well enough otherwise as specimens of frail humanity.

9. (1) Of my helping you again; (2) of divine mercy.

In this man's presence? I will keep you fast now,
And sooner part eternally from the world
Than my good joys in you. [*To him*] Prithee, forgive me;
I did but chide in jest. The best loves use° it — *practice*
Sometimes; it sets an edge upon° affection. — *it sharpens*
When we invite our best friends to a feast,
'Tis not all sweetmeats that we set before them;
There's somewhat sharp and salt, both to whet appetite
And make 'em taste their wine well. So methinks
After a friendly, sharp, and savory chiding
A kiss tastes wondrous well, and full o'th'grape.
[*She kisses him.*]
How think'st thou, does't not?

HIPPOLITO 'Tis so excellent
I know not how to praise it, what to say to't.

ISABELLA This marriage shall go forward.

HIPPOLITO With the Ward?
Are you in earnest?

ISABELLA 'Twould be ill for us else.

HIPPOLITO [*aside*] For us? How means she that?

ISABELLA [*aside*] Troth, I begin
To be so well, methinks, within this hour,
For all this match able to kill one's heart,[1]
Nothing can pull me down now. Should my father
Provide a worse fool yet, which I should think
Were a hard thing to compass,° I'd have him either.° — *encompass / just as soon*
The worse, the better; none can come amiss now,
If he want wit enough.° So discretion love me, — *If he is dumb enough*
Desert, and judgment, I have content sufficient.[2]
[*To him*] She that comes once to be a housekeeper° — *housewife*
Must not look every day to fare well, sir,
Like a young waiting-gentlewoman in service;
For she° feeds commonly as her lady does; — *(the waiting-gentlewoman)*
No good bit passes her but she gets a taste on't.
But when she° comes to keep house for herself, — *(the plain housewife)*
She's glad of some choice cates° then once a week, — *delicacies, confections*
Or twice at most, and glad if she can get 'em;[3]
So must affection learn to fare with thankfulness.
Pray make your love no stranger, sir, that's all.
[*Aside*] Though you be one yourself,[4] and know not on't,
And I have sworn you must not. *Exit.*

HIPPOLITO This is beyond me!
Never came joys so unexpectedly
To meet desires in man. How came she thus?
What has she° done to her, can any tell? — *(Livia)*
'Tis beyond sorcery, this! Drugs, or love-powders—
Some art that has no name, sure, strange° to me — *more strange*
Of° all the wonders I e'er met withal — *Than*
Throughout my ten years' travels; but I'm thankful for't.

1. For all the seeming heartbreak of this enforced marriage (to the Ward).
2. So long as I am loved by a man (Hippolito) of discretion, deserving, and judgment, I'll be happy enough.
3. Once she is married to the Ward, Isabella suggests, she will have to content herself with occasional meetings with Hippolito, like a wife in charge of her own household and limited to occasional "cates," or delicacies; she will no longer be like a waiting-gentlewoman, eating daily what her mistress eats.
4. Though you are in fact a stranger yourself, in the sense of being unrelated by blood.

This marriage now must of necessity forward;° *proceed*
It is the only veil wit can devise
To keep our acts hid from sin-piercing eyes. *Exit.*

2.2

Enter Guardiano and Livia.

LIVIA How, sir, a gentlewoman° so young, so fair *(Bianca; see 1.3)*
As you set forth, spied° from the widow's window! *seen as she watched*
GUARDIANO She!° *(The mother-in-law)*
LIVIA Our Sunday-dinner woman?
GUARDIANO And Thursday-supper woman, the same still.[1]
I know not how she came by her, but I'll swear
She's the prime gallant° for a face in Florence; *handsomest person*
And no doubt other parts follow their leader.° *are like the face*
The Duke himself first spied her at the window,° *(see 1.3.109)*
Then in a rapture, as if admiration
Were poor when it were single,° beckoned me, *unshared*
And pointed to the wonder warily
As one that feared she would draw in her splendor
Too soon, if too much gazed at. I ne'er knew him
So infinitely taken with a woman,
Nor can I blame his appetite, or tax° *censure*
His raptures of slight folly.° She's a creature *as unworthy dotage*
Able to draw a state° from serious business, *statesman*
And make it their best piece° to do her service. *achievement*
What course shall we devise? He's° spoke twice now. *The Duke has*
LIVIA Twice?
GUARDIANO 'Tis beyond your apprehension
How strangely that one look has catched his heart.
'Twould prove but too much worth° in wealth and favor *untold worth*
To those should work° his peace.° *who'd satisfy / craving*
LIVIA And if I do't not,
Or at least come as near it—if your art
Will take a little pains and second me—
As any wench in Florence of my standing,° *social standing*
I'll quite give o'er,° and shut up shop in cunning. *resign*
GUARDIANO 'Tis for the Duke, and if I fail your purpose,° *to aid your scheme*
All° means to come by riches or advancement *May all*
Miss me and skip me over!
LIVIA Let the old woman° then *(Leantio's mother)*
Be sent for with all speed; then I'll begin.
GUARDIANO A good° conclusion follow, and a sweet one, *May a good*
After this stale beginning with old ware!°— *i.e., the aged widow*
[*Calling*] Within there!

Enter Servant.

SERVANT Sir, do you call?
GUARDIANO Come near, list° hither. *listen*
[*He talks aside with the Servant.*]
LIVIA I long myself to see this absolute° creature, *consummate*

2.2. Livia's house.
1. Leantio's mother, as a penniless and dependent widow, presumably took meals with her genteel acquaintance, or helped to cater such meals. Guardiano is a guest in Livia's house; see lines 147 and 173 below.

That wins the heart of love and praise so much.
GUARDIANO [*to the Servant*] Go, sir, make haste.
LIVIA Say I entreat her company;
Do you hear, sir?
SERVANT Yes, madam. *Exit.*
LIVIA That brings her quickly.
GUARDIANO I would 'twere done! The Duke waits the good hour,
And I wait the good fortune that may spring from't.
I have had a lucky hand these fifteen year
At such court passage with three dice in a dish.[2]

Enter Fabritio.

Signor Fabritio!
FABRITIO Oh, sir, I bring an alteration° in my mouth now. *news of a change*
GUARDIANO An alteration? [*Aside*] No wise speech, I hope;[3]
He means not to talk wisely, does he, trow?° *do you think?*
[*To him*] Good! What's the change, I pray, sir?
FABRITIO A new change.
GUARDIANO [*aside*] Another yet! Faith, there's enough already.[4]
FABRITIO My daughter loves him now.
GUARDIANO What does she, sir?
FABRITIO Affects° him beyond thought—who but the Ward, forsooth! *She loves*
No talk but of the Ward; she would have him
To choose° 'bove all the men she ever saw. *As her choice*
My will goes not so fast as her consent now;
Her duty gets before° my command still. *goes ahead of*
GUARDIANO Why, then, sir, if you'll have me speak my thoughts,
I smell 'twill be a match.
FABRITIO Ay, and a sweet young couple,
If I have any judgment.
GUARDIANO [*aside*] Faith, that's little.
[*To him*] Let her be sent tomorrow before noon,
And handsomely tricked up;° for 'bout that time *outfitted*
I mean to bring her in and tender her to him.
FABRITIO I warrant you for handsome.[5] I will see
Her things laid ready, every one in order,
And have some part of her° tricked up tonight. *(with sexual wordplay)*
GUARDIANO Why, well said.
FABRITIO 'Twas a use° her mother had, *practice*
When she was invited to an early wedding:
She'd dress her head o'er night, sponge up herself,
And give her neck three lathers—
GUARDIANO [*aside*] Ne'er a halter?[6]
FABRITIO On with her chain of pearl, her ruby bracelets,
Lay ready all her tricks, and jiggam-bobs°— *thingamabobs*
GUARDIANO So must your daughter.
FABRITIO I'll about it straight, sir.
Exit Fabritio.
LIVIA How he sweats in the foolish zeal of fatherhood
After° six ounces an hour, and seems *At the rate of*

2. (1) A gambling game played with three dice; (2) an amorous encounter.
3. Guardiano wryly jests that wise speech from Fabritio would be a change indeed.
4. Guardiano mocks Fabritio for redundancy; any change is a "new" change. (This may also be a reference to the New Exchange opened in London in 1609.)
5. I guarantee she'll look handsome.
6. A noose—suggested by Fabritio's "neck," around which a noose might be placed. "Lathers" suggests the "ladders" of a gallows.

To toil as much as if his cares were wise ones!
GUARDIANO You've let his folly blood in the right vein,[7] lady.
LIVIA And here comes his sweet son-in-law that shall be.
They're both allied in wit before the marriage;
What will they be hereafter, when they are nearer?° *closer*
Yet they can go no further than the fool;° *absolute folly*
There's the world's end° in both of 'em. *outer limit*

Enter Ward and Sordido, one with a shuttlecock,° the other a battledore.° *badminton bird* / *racket*

GUARDIANO Now, young heir!
WARD What's the next business after shuttlecock now?
GUARDIANO Tomorrow you shall see the gentlewoman must be° your wife. *who is to be*
WARD [*aside*] There's e'en another thing too must be kept up with a pair of battledores.[8] [*To Guardiano*] My wife! What can she do?
GUARDIANO Nay, that's a question you should ask yourself, Ward, when you're alone together.
[*Livia and Guardiano talk apart.*]
WARD That's as I list.° A wife's to be asked anywhere, I hope; I'll ask her in a congregation, if I have a mind to't, and so save a license.[9] My guardianer has no more wit than an herb-woman that sells away all her sweet herbs and nosegays° and keeps a stinking breath for her own pottage.° *wish* / *bouquets* / *to cool her soup*
SORDIDO Let me be at the choosing of your beloved, if you desire a woman of good parts.° *(see 63 and gloss)*
WARD Thou shalt, sweet Sordido.
SORDIDO I have a plaguy° guess. Let me alone° to see what she is; if I but look upon her—'way,° I know all the faults to a hair that you may refuse her for. *shrewd / Leave it to me* / *away, leave it to me*
WARD Dost thou? I prithee let me hear 'em, Sordido.
SORDIDO Well, mark 'em, then; I have 'em all in rhyme:
The wife your guardianer ought to tender
Should be pretty, straight and slender;
Her hair not short, her foot not long,
Her hand not huge, nor too too loud her tongue;
No pearl° in eye, nor ruby° in her nose, *cataract / pimple*
No burn or cut° but what the catalogue shows. *(suggesting syphilis)*
She must have teeth, and that no black ones,
And kiss most sweet when she does smack° once; *kiss*
Her skin must be both white and plumped,° *nicely filled out*
Her body straight, not hopper-rumped,° *with funnel-shaped butt*
Or wriggle sideways like a crab;
She must be neither slut nor drab,° *whore*
Nor go too splay-foot° with her shoes, *flat-footed*
To make her smock° lick up the dews. *petticoat*
And two things more, which I forgot to tell ye:
She neither must have bump in back nor belly.° *pregnant belly*
These are the faults that will not make her pass.

7. You've treated his foolish humor with just the right diagnosis. (With the figurative use of bleeding as a medical procedure and with wordplay on "vein" both as a satiric strain and as a blood vessel.)
8. I.e., Sex is like badminton.
9. To "ask" is to ask the banns, i.e., announce a forthcoming wedding in order to allow any objections to it to be brought forward. If the banns were not "asked," one had to obtain a license to marry from the church.

WARD And if I spy not these, I am a rank ass.
SORDIDO Nay, more: by right, sir, you should see her naked,
for that's the ancient order.° *ritual, ceremony*
WARD See her naked? That were good sport, i'faith. I'll have the books turned over,° *examined* and if I find her naked on record, she shall not have a rag on. But stay, stay, how if she should desire to see me so too? I were in a sweet case° *predicament; garment* then, such a foul skin.
SORDIDO But you've a clean shirt, and that makes amends, sir.
WARD I will not see her naked for that trick, though.[1]
Exit [Ward].
SORDIDO Then take her with all faults, with her clothes on!
And they may hide a number with a bum-roll.° *hip cushion under skirt* Faith, choosing of a wench in a huge farthingale° *hooped petticoat* is like the buying of ware under a great penthouse:[2]
What with the deceit of one,° *(the woman)*
And the false light of th'other,° mark my speeches, *(the shop)*
He may have a diseased wench in 's bed
And rotten stuff[3] in 's breeches. *Exit.*
GUARDIANO It may take° handsomely. *succeed*
LIVIA I see small hindrance.

Enter [Servant, followed by] Mother.

[*To Servant*] How now, so soon returned?
GUARDIANO She's come.
LIVIA That's well.
[Exit Servant.]
[*To Mother*] Widow, come, come, I have a great quarrel to you;
Faith, I must chide you, that you must be sent for!
You make yourself so strange,° never come at us, *distant, unsociable*
And yet so near a neighbor, and so unkind.
Troth, you're to blame. You cannot be more welcome
To any house in Florence, that I'll tell you.
MOTHER My thanks must needs acknowledge so much, madam.
LIVIA How can you be so strange, then? I sit here
Sometime whole days together without company,
When business draws this gentleman from home,° *(see 172–73)*
And should be happy in society
Which I so well affect as that of yours.[4]
I know you're alone too. Why should not we,
Like two kind neighbors, then supply the wants
Of one another, having tongue-discourse,° *gossip*
Experience in the world, and such kind helps
To laugh down time and meet age° merrily? *grow old*
MOTHER Age? Madam, you speak mirth.° *you're joking* 'Tis at my door,
But a long journey from Your Ladyship yet.
LIVIA My faith, I'm nine-and-thirty, ev'ry stroke,° *every bit of it* wench;
And 'tis a general observation
'Mongst knights' wives, or widows: we account ourselves
Then old when young men's eyes leave° *leave off* looking at 's.
'Tis a true rule amongst us, and ne'er failed yet

1. I.e., the trick that she be able to demand that I appear naked in turn.
2. Covered shop front (the effect of which would be to darken the interior of the shop itself).
3. (1) Inferior cloth purchased in a dimly lit shop; (2) venereal disease.
4. And would be happy to spend time with somone whose company I desire as much as I do yours.

In any but in one that I remember—
Indeed, she had a friend° at nine-and-forty; *lover*
Marry, she paid well for him, and in th'end
He kept a quean° or two with her own money, *whore*
That robbed her of her plate,° and cut her throat. *gold or silver plate*
MOTHER She had her punishment in this world, madam,
And a fair warning to all other women
That they live chaste at fifty.
LIVIA Ay, or never, wench.
Come, now I have thy company I'll not part with't
Till after supper.
MOTHER Yes, I must crave pardon, madam.
LIVIA I swear you shall stay supper. We have no strangers, woman,
None but my sojourners° and I, this gentleman *houseguests*
And the young heir his ward; you know our company.
MOTHER Some other time I will make bold with you, madam.
GUARDIANO Nay, pray stay, widow.
LIVIA Faith, she shall not go.
Do you think I'll be forsworn?° *(see 172)*
Table and chess [*are brought on by servants*].
MOTHER 'Tis a great while
Till supper time; I'll take my leave then now, madam,
And come again i'th'evening, since Your Ladyship
Will have it so.
LIVIA I'th'evening! By my troth, wench,
I'll keep you while I have you. You have great business, sure,
To sit alone at home; I wonder strangely° *exceedingly*
What pleasure you take in't. Were't to me° now, *my case*
I should be ever at one neighbor's house
Or other all day long. Having no charge,° *responsibility*
Or none to chide you if you go or stay,
Who may live merrier, ay, or more at heart's ease?
Come, we'll to chess, or draughts;° there are an hundred tricks *checkers*
To drive out time till supper, never fear't, wench.
MOTHER I'll but make one step home, and return straight, madam.
LIVIA Come, I'll not trust you; you use more excuses
To your kind friends than ever I knew any.
What business can you have, if you be sure
You've locked the doors? And that being all you have,
I know you're careful on't. One° afternoon *Is one*
So much to spend here? Say I should entreat you now
To lie° a night or two, or a week, with me, *sleep here*
Or leave your own house for a month together,
It were a kindness that long neighborhood° *neighborliness*
And friendship might well hope to prevail in.
Would you deny such a request? I'faith,
Speak truth, and freely.
MOTHER I were then uncivil, madam.
LIVIA [*indicating the chess table*] Go to, then, set your men;° *chess pieces*
we'll have whole nights
Of mirth together ere we be much older, wench.
MOTHER [*aside*] As good now tell her, then, for she will know't;
I have always found her a most friendly lady.
LIVIA Why, widow, where's your mind?° *thoughts*
MOTHER Troth, e'en at home, madam.

To tell you truth, I left a gentlewoman
E'en sitting all alone, which is uncomfortable,
Especially to young bloods.° *temperaments*
LIVIA Another excuse!
MOTHER No, as I hope for health, madam, that's a truth;
Please you to send and see.
LIVIA What gentlewoman? Pish.
MOTHER Wife to my son, indeed, but not known, madam,
To any but yourself.
LIVIA Now I beshrew° you, *curse*
Could you be so unkind to her and me
To come and not bring her? Faith, 'tis not friendly.
MOTHER I feared to be too bold.
LIVIA Too bold? Oh, what's become
Of the true hearty love was wont to be
'Mongst neighbors in old time?
MOTHER And she's a stranger,° madam. *i.e., non-Florentine*
LIVIA The more should be her welcome. When is courtesy
In better practice than when 'tis employed
In entertaining strangers? I could chide, i'faith—
Leave her behind, poor gentlewoman, alone too!
Make some amends, and send for her betimes,° go. *quickly*
MOTHER Please you command one of your servants, madam.
LIVIA [*calling*] Within there!

Enter Servant.

SERVANT Madam?
LIVIA Attend the gentlewoman.
MOTHER [*aside*] It must be carried° wondrous privately *carried out*
From my son's knowledge; he'll break out in storms else.
[*To Servant*] Hark you, sir.
[*They talk apart; exit Servant.*]
LIVIA [*aside to Guardiano*] Now comes in the heat° of your part. *most critical aspect*
GUARDIANO [*aside to her*] True, I know it, lady, and if I be out° *forget my lines*
May the Duke banish me from all employments,
Wanton or serious.
LIVIA [*to Mother*] So, have you sent, widow?
MOTHER Yes, madam, he's almost at home by this.° *by this time*
LIVIA And, faith, let me entreat you that henceforward
All such unkind faults may be swept from friendship,
Which does but dim the luster. And think thus much:
It is a wrong to me, that have ability
To bid friends welcome, when you keep 'em from me.
You cannot set greater dishonor near me,
For bounty is the credit and the glory
Of those that have enough.° I see you're sorry, *are wealthy*
And the good 'mends is made by't.
MOTHER Here she 's, madam.

Enter Bianca and Servant.

BIANCA [*aside*] I wonder how she comes to send for me now?
[*Exit Servant.*]
LIVIA Gentlewoman, you're most welcome—trust me, you are—
As courtesy can make one, or respect
Due to the presence of you.

BIANCA I give you thanks, lady.
LIVIA I heard you were alone, and't had appeared
An ill condition° in me, though I knew you not, *Bad manners*
Nor ever saw you—yet humanity
Thinks ev'ry case her own[5]—to have kept your company° *i.e., the Mother*
Here from you, and left you all solitary.
I rather ventured upon boldness then
As the least fault, and wished your presence here—
A thing most happily motioned of° that gentleman, *proposed by*
Whom I request you, for his care and pity,
To honor and reward with your acquaintance:
A gentleman that ladies' rights stands for,[6]
That's his profession.° *what he believes in*
BIANCA 'Tis a noble one,
And honors my acquaintance.
GUARDIANO All my intentions
Are servants to such mistresses.[7]
BIANCA 'Tis your modesty,
It seems, that makes your deserts° speak so low, sir. *deservings*
LIVIA Come, widow. [*To Bianca*] Look you, lady, here's our
business.[8] [*She indicates the chess table.*]
Are we not well employed, think you? An old quarrel
Between us, that will never be at an end.
BIANCA No, and methinks there's men° enough to part you, lady. *chess pieces*
LIVIA Ho! But they set us on, let us come off
As well as we can, poor souls; men care no farther.[9]
I pray, sit down, forsooth, if you have the patience
To look upon two weak and tedious gamesters.
GUARDIANO Faith, madam, set these by till evening;
You'll have enough on't then. The gentlewoman,
Being a stranger, would take more delight
To see your rooms and pictures.
LIVIA Marry, good sir,
And well remembered. I beseech you, show 'em her;
That will beguile time well. Pray heartily, do, sir;
I'll do as much for you. Here, take these keys.
[*She gives keys.*]
Show her the monument° too—and that's a thing *a carved memorial*
Everyone sees not.—You can witness that, widow.
MOTHER And that's worth sight indeed, madam.
BIANCA Kind lady,
I fear I came to be a trouble to you.
LIVIA Oh, nothing less,° forsooth. *nothing could be less*
BIANCA And to this courteous gentleman,[1]
That wears a kindness in his breast so noble
And bounteous to the welcome of a stranger.
GUARDIANO If you but give acceptance to my service,
You do the greatest grace and honor to me
That courtesy can merit.

5. Yet anyone can gauge the needs of another person by examining her own feelings.
6. A gentleman who stands up for ladies' interests. (With erotic suggestion.)
7. My fondest hopes are to serve such fine ladies; my best endeavors serve them.
8. The chess game that Livia and the Mother play, and their discussion of it, involves an extended wordplay, much of which the Mother is not clued in to.
9. But men stir us up to competition, however well we may fare in it; that's all men care about. (Implying sexual rivalries.)
1. And I fear I'm a trouble to Guardiano as well.

BIANCA I were to blame else,° *if I did not*
And out of fashion° much. I pray you lead, sir. *impolite, ungracious*
LIVIA After a game or two, we're for you,° gentlefolks. *we'll join you*
GUARDIANO We wish no better seconds° in society *supports, aids*
Than your discourses, madam, and your partner's there.
MOTHER I thank your praise. I listened to you, sir,
Though when you spoke there came a paltry rook[2]
Full in my way, and chokes up all my game.
Exit Guardiano and Bianca.
LIVIA Alas, poor widow, I shall be too hard for thee.
MOTHER You're cunning at the game,° I'll be sworn, madam. *chess; intrigue*
LIVIA It will be found so, ere I give you over.° *am finished with you*
She that can place her man° well— *i.e., the Duke*
MOTHER As you do, madam.
LIVIA As I shall, wench, can never lose her game.
Nay, nay, the black king's° mine. *i.e., the Duke is*
MOTHER Cry you mercy, madam.
LIVIA And this my queen.° *i.e., Livia*
MOTHER I see't now.
LIVIA Here's a duke° *rook; Duke of Florence*
Will strike a sure stroke for the game anon—
Your pawn° cannot come back to relieve itself. *i.e., Bianca*
MOTHER I know that, madam.
LIVIA You play well the whilst.° *the while*
How she belies her skill! I hold° two ducats° *bet / gold coins*
I give you check and mate to your white king°— *i.e., Leantio*
Simplicity itself, your saintish king there.
MOTHER Well, ere now, lady,
I have seen the fall of subtlety.[3] Jest on.
LIVIA Ay, but simplicity receives two for one.[4]
MOTHER What remedy but patience?

Enter, above, Guardiano and Bianca.

BIANCA Trust me, sir,
Mine eye ne'er met with fairer ornaments.
GUARDIANO Nay, livelier, I'm persuaded, neither Florence
Nor Venice can produce.
BIANCA Sir, my opinion
Takes your part° highly. *Endorses your view*
GUARDIANO There's a better piece
Yet than all these.

[*Enter*] *Duke above* [*behind Guardiano and Bianca*].

BIANCA Not possible, sir!
GUARDIANO Believe it;
You'll say so when you see't. Turn but your eye now;
You're upon't presently. *Exit.*
BIANCA [*seeing the Duke*] Oh, sir!
DUKE [*embracing her*] He's gone, beauty.
Pish, look not after him. He's but a vapor
That, when the sun appears, is seen no more.

2. The rook is one of the chess pieces; also called "castle" or "duke."
3. I have often seen cunning overreach and undo itself.
4. But simplicity receives two blows for one, and is therefore often the loser.

BIANCA Oh, treachery to honor!
DUKE Prithee, tremble not.
I feel thy breast shake like a turtle° panting *turtledove*
Under a loving hand that makes much on't.° *attentively strokes it*
Why art so fearful? As I'm friend to brightness,° *beauty*
There's nothing but respect and honor near thee.
You know me, you have seen me; here's a heart
Can witness I have seen thee.
BIANCA The more's my danger.
DUKE The more's thy happiness. Pish, strive not, sweet;
This strength were excellent employed in love now,
But here 'tis spent amiss. Strive not to seek
Thy liberty, and keep me still in prison.° *forever in your arms*
[*He draws her arms round him.*]
I'faith, you shall not out till I'm released now.
We'll be both freed together, or stay still° by't; *always; unmoving*
So is captivity pleasant.
BIANCA Oh, my lord!
DUKE I am not here in vain;° have but the leisure *for nothing*
To think on that, and thou'lt be soon resolved.° *decided*
The lifting of thy voice is but like one
That does exalt his enemy, who, proving high,
Lays all the plots to confound him that raised him.[5]
Take warning, I beseech thee. Thou seem'st to me
A creature so composed of gentleness
And delicate meekness—such as bless the faces
Of figures that are drawn for° goddesses *used as models for*
And makes art proud to look upon her work—
I should be sorry the least force should lay
An unkind touch upon thee.
BIANCA Oh, my extremity!
My lord, what seek you?
DUKE Love.
BIANCA 'Tis gone already;
I have a husband.
DUKE That's a single° comfort; *solitary; slender*
Take a friend to° him. *in addition to*
BIANCA That's a double mischief,
Or else there's no religion.
DUKE Do not tremble
At fears of thine own making.
BIANCA Nor, great lord,
Make me not bold with death° and deeds of ruin *spiritual death*
Because they fear° not you; me they must fright. *frighten*
Then am I best in health; should thunder speak
And none regard it, it had lost the name,
And were as good be still.[6] I'm not like those
That take their soundest sleeps in greatest tempests;
Then wake I most, the weather fearfullest,
And call for strength to virtue.° *to be virtuous*

5. Your cries of help would only undo you, like a courtier who, having urged the promotion of another, is plotted against by that ungrateful person.
6. I'm in best spiritual health when I have an honest fear of divine wrath and of Jove's thunder; if those warnings go unheeded, they might as well have remained silent.

DUKE Sure I think
Thou know'st the way to please me. I affect° — *am aroused by*
A passionate pleading 'bove an easy yielding,
But never pitied any—they deserve none—
That will not pity me. I can command;
Think upon that. Yet if thou truly knewest
The infinite pleasure my affection takes
In gentle, fair entreatings, when love's businesses
Are carried courteously 'twixt heart and heart,
You'd make more haste to please me.

BIANCA Why should you seek, sir,
To take away that° you can never give? — *i.e., chaste honor*

DUKE But I give better in exchange: wealth, honor.
She that is fortunate in a duke's favor
Lights on a tree that bears all women's wishes.
If your own mother saw you pluck fruit there,
She would commend your wit and praise the time
Of your nativity. Take hold of glory.
Do not I know you've cast away your life
Upon necessities, means merely° doubtful — *extremely*
To keep you in indifferent health and fashion?—
A thing I heard too lately,° and soon pitied. — *only recently*
And can you be so much your beauty's enemy
To kiss away a month or two in wedlock,
And weep whole years in wants for ever after?
Come, play the wise wench, and provide for ever;
Let storms come when they list,° they find thee sheltered. — *wish*
Should any doubt arise, let nothing trouble thee;
Put trust in our° love for the managing — *(the royal "we")*
Of all to thy heart's peace. We'll walk together,
And show a thankful joy for both our fortunes.

Exit [with Bianca] above.

LIVIA Did not I say my duke[7] would fetch you over,° widow? — *win the advantage*

MOTHER I think you spoke in earnest when you said it, madam.

LIVIA And my black king° makes all the haste he can, too. — *(also the Duke)*

MOTHER Well, madam, we may meet with him in time yet.

LIVIA I have given thee blind mate° twice. — *checkmate*

MOTHER You may see, madam,
My eyes begin to fail.

LIVIA I'll swear they do, wench.

Enter Guardiano.

GUARDIANO [*aside*] I can but smile as often as I think on't:
How prettily the poor fool° was beguiled, — *innocent*
How unexpectedly! It's a witty age.
Never were finer snares for women's honesties
Than are devised in these days; no spider's web
Made of a daintier thread than are now practiced
To catch love's flesh fly° by the silver wing. — *flesh-feeding fly*
Yet to prepare her stomach° by degrees — *appetite*
To Cupid's feast, because I saw 'twas queasy,
I showed her naked pictures by the way,
A bit to stay° the appetite. Well, advancement, — *whet; partly satisfy*

7. (1) My rook, or castle (a chess piece); (2) the Duke of Florence.

I venture hard to find thee. If thou com'st
With a greater title set upon thy crest,[8]
I'll take that first cross° patiently, and wait — *burden (ironic)*
Until some other comes greater than that;
I'll endure all.

LIVIA The game's e'en at the best now; you may see, widow,
How all things draw to an end.

MOTHER E'en so do I, madam.[9]

LIVIA I pray, take some of your neighbors along with you.[1]

MOTHER They must be those are almost twice your years, then,
If they be chose° fit matches for my time,° madam. — *chosen / (old) age*

LIVIA Has not my duke bestirred himself?

MOTHER Yes, faith, madam,
He's done me all the mischief in this game.

LIVIA He's showed himself in 's kind.° — *in his true colors*

MOTHER In 's kind, call you it?
I may swear that.° — *that to be true*

LIVIA Yes, faith, and keep your oath.[2]

GUARDIANO [*aside*] Hark, list!° There's somebody coming down; 'tis she. — *listen*

Enter Bianca.

BIANCA [*aside*] Now bless° me from a blasting!° I saw that now[3] — *shield / infection*
Fearful for any woman's eye to look on.
Infectious mists and mildews hang at 's° eyes; — *at the Duke's*
The weather of a doomsday dwells upon him.
Yet since mine honor's leprous, why should I
Preserve that fair° that caused the leprosy? — *beauty*
Come poison all at once! [*Aside to Guardiano*] Thou in whose baseness
The bane° of virtue broods,° I'm bound in soul — *ruin; poison / hatches*
Eternally to curse thy smooth-browed° treachery, — *smiling*
That wore the fair veil of a friendly welcome,
And I a stranger. Think upon't; 'tis worth it;
Murders piled up upon a guilty spirit
At his last breath will not lie heavier
Than this betraying act upon thy conscience.
Beware of off'ring the firstfruits to sin![4]
His weight is deadly who commits with strumpets
After they have been abased and made for use;
If they offend to th'death, as wise men know,
How much more they then that first make 'em so?[5]
I give thee that to feed on.° I'm made bold now; — *chew on*
I thank thy° treachery, sin and I'm acquainted; — *Thanks to your*
No couple greater. And I'm like that great one° — *(any aristocrat)*
Who, making politic° use of a base villain, — *crafty*
He likes the treason° well, but hates the traitor. — *treachery*

8. If you come with promise of even greater favors signaled on your shield. (Advancement [line 407] is allegorized as a figure in heraldry.)
9. (1) I see that, indeed; (2) I draw toward an end myself.
1. Don't forget the other Florentine women (including myself) who are also aging.
2. You won't be forsworn.
3. I saw just now what would be.
4. Beware of the moral crime of initiating a person into sin.
5. The moral responsibility of any man having sex with women who have already been turned into whores is bad enough; if such men are committing moral crimes, as wise people know they are, then how much more heinous is the crime of those who first introduce those women into a life of sin?

So I hate thee, slave.
GUARDIANO [*aside*] Well, so° the Duke love me, *provided that*
I fare not much amiss, then. Two great feasts
Do seldom come together in one day;
We must not look for 'em.
BIANCA What, at it still, mother?
MOTHER You see we sit by't.° Are you so soon returned? *are at our game*
LIVIA [*aside*] So lively and so cheerful! A good sign, that.
MOTHER You have not seen all since, sure?
BIANCA That have I, mother,
The monument and all. I'm so beholding° *beholden*
To this kind, honest, courteous gentleman,
You'd little think it, mother, showed° me all, *who showed*
Had me from place to place, so fashionably—
The kindness of some people, how't exceeds!
Faith, I have seen that° I little thought to see *that which*
I'th'morning when I rose.
MOTHER Nay, so I told you
Before you saw't, it would prove worth your sight.—
I give you great thanks for my daughter, sir,
And all your kindness towards her.
GUARDIANO Oh, good widow!
Much good may't do her—[*aside*] forty weeks° hence, i'faith. *(term of pregnancy)*

Enter Servant.

LIVIA Now, sir.
SERVANT May't please you, madam, to walk in?
Supper's upon the table.
LIVIA Yes, we come. [*Exit Servant.*]
[*To Bianca*] Will't please you, gentlewoman?
BIANCA Thanks, virtuous lady.
[*Aside to Livia*] You're a damned bawd.° [*To Guardiano*] I'll follow you, forsooth; *procuress*
Pray take my mother in. [*Aside to Livia*] An old ass° go with you! *i.e., My mother-in-law*
[*Aloud*] This gentleman and I vow not to part.
LIVIA Then get you both before.
BIANCA [*aside*] There lies his art.° *i.e., procuring*
LIVIA Widow, I'll follow you.
Exeunt [*Bianca, Guardiano, and Mother*].
Is't so, damned bawd?° *whore (Bianca)*
Are you so bitter? 'Tis but want° of use— *lack*
Her tender modesty is seasick a little,
Being not accustomed to the breaking billow
Of woman's wavering faith, blown with temptations.
'Tis but a qualm° of honor; 'twill away; *nausea*
A little bitter for the time,° but lasts not. *the time being*
Sin tastes at the first draft like wormwood water,° *absinthe*
But, drunk again, 'tis nectar ever after. *Exit.*

3.1

Enter Mother.

MOTHER I would my son would either keep at home,
Or I were in my grave!
She was but one day abroad,° but ever since — *out of the house*
She's grown so cutted° there's no speaking to her. — *querulous*
Whether the sight of great cheer at my lady's° — *(Livia's)*
And such mean° fare at home work discontent in her, — *lean, lowly*
I know not, but I'm sure she's strangely altered.
I'll ne'er keep daughter-in-law i'th'house with me
Again, if I had an hundred. When read I of any
That agreed long together, but she and her mother
Fell out in the first quarter—nay, sometime
A grudging or a scolding the first week, by'r Lady?[1]
So takes° the new disease, methinks, in my house. — *catches, spreads*
I'm weary of my part.° There's nothing likes° her; — *for my part / pleases*
I know not how to please her here a-late.° — *lately*
And here she comes.

Enter Bianca.

BIANCA This is the strangest house
For all defects as ever gentlewoman
Made shift withal° to pass away her love in. — *Contrived*
Why is there not a cushion-cloth of drawnwork,[2]
Or some fair cutwork° pinned up in my bedchamber, — *openwork embroidery*
A silver-and-gilt casting-bottle° hung by't? — *perfume-sprinkling bottle*
Nay, since I am content to be so kind to you
To spare you for[3] a silver basin and ewer,° — *pitcher*
Which one of my fashion looks for of duty°— — *as her due*
She's never offered under,° where she sleeps— — *anything less*

MOTHER [*aside*] She talks of things here my whole state's° not worth. — *estate is*

BIANCA Never a green silk quilt is there i'th'house, mother,
To cast upon my bed?

MOTHER No, by troth, is there,
Nor orange tawny° neither. — *(a prideful color)*

BIANCA Here's a house
For a young gentlewoman to be got with child in!° — *(said sarcastically)*

MOTHER Yes, simple though you make it, there has been three
Got° in a year in't, since you move me to't;° — *Begotten / to say it*
And all as sweet-faced children, and as lovely,
As you'll be mother of. I will not spare you.
What, cannot children be begot, think you,
Without gilt casting-bottles?° Yes, and as sweet ones: — *(see 21)*
The miller's daughter brings forth as white° boys — *fair-haired*
As she that bathes herself with milk and bean-flour.
'Tis an old saying: one may keep good cheer
In a mean house. So may true love affect° — *find contentment*
After the rate of princes,° in a cottage. — *On a princely scale*

3.1. Leantio's house.

1. When have I ever heard of a mother and daughter-in-law who could get along for long without the two of them quarreling during the first three months—indeed, sometimes with a foretaste of a scolding in the very first week, by Our Lady?

2. A cushion cover done in needlework.

3. Not to demand from you.

BIANCA Troth, you speak wondrous well for your old house here!
'Twill shortly fall down at your feet to thank you,
Or stoop° when you go to bed, like a good child *bow*
To ask you blessing. Must I live in want
Because my fortune matched me with your son?
Wives do not give away themselves to husbands
To the end° to be quite cast away; they look *With the intention*
To be the better used, and tendered° rather, *treated tenderly*
Highlier respected, and maintained the richer.
They're well rewarded else for the free gift
Of their whole life to a husband. I ask less now
Than what I had at home when I was a maid,° *virgin*
And at my father's house; kept short° of that *I am deprived*
Which a wife knows she must have, nay, and will—
Will, mother, if she be not a fool born.
And report went° of me that I could wrangle *rumor reported*
For what I wanted when I was two hours old,
And by that copy, this land still I hold.[4]
You hear me, mother. *Exit.*

MOTHER Ay, too plain, methinks!
And were I somewhat deafer when you spake,
'Twere ne'er a whit the worse for my quietness.
'Tis the most sudden'st, strangest alteration,
And the most subtlest that e'er wit at threescore° *60 years of age*
Was puzzled to find out.° I know no cause for't; but *explain*
She's no more like the gentlewoman at first[5]
Than I am like her° that never lay with man yet; *(a woman)*
And she's a very young thing, where'er she be.[6]
When she first lighted° here, I told her then *alighted, arrived*
How mean she should find all things; she was pleased, forsooth,
None better. I laid open all defects to her;
She was contented still. But the devil's in her;
Nothing contents her now. Tonight my son
Promised to be at home; would he were come once,° *now*
For I'm weary of my charge,° and life too. *responsibility*
She'd be served all in silver by her good will,° *if she had her way*
By night and day; she hates the name of pewter
More than sick men the noise, or diseased bones
That quake at fall o'th'hammer, seeming to have
A fellow feeling with't at every blow.
What course shall I think on? She frets me so! [*Exit.*]

[3.2]

Enter Leantio.

LEANTIO How near am I now to a happiness
That earth exceeds not! Not another like it;
The treasures of the deep are not so precious
As are the concealed comforts of a man,
Locked up in woman's love. I scent the air
Of blessings when I come but near the house.

4. And I claim the same privilege still, like one legally entitled to property.
5. She's no more like the Bianca I first met.
6. And such a virgin, if one could find one, would have to be very young indeed.
3.2. Outside Leantio's house.

What a delicious breath marriage sends forth!
The violet bed's not sweeter. Honest wedlock
Is like a banqueting-house built in a garden
On which the spring's chaste flowers take delight
To cast their modest odors, when° base lust, *whereas*
With all her powders,° paintings, and best pride° *cosmetics / finery*
Is but a fair house built by a ditch side.
When I behold a glorious dangerous strumpet,
Sparkling in beauty and destruction too,
Both at a twinkling, I do liken straight
Her beautified body to a goodly temple
That's built on vaults° where carcasses lie rotting; *crypts*
And so by little and little I shrink back again,
And quench desire with a cool meditation;
And I'm as well, methinks. Now for a welcome
Able to draw men's envies upon man:
A kiss now that will hang upon my lip
As sweet as morning dew upon a rose,
And full as long. After a five days' fast
She'll be so greedy now, and cling about me,
I take care how I shall be rid of her;[1]

[*Enter Bianca and Mother.*]

And here't begins.
BIANCA Oh, sir, you're welcome home.
MOTHER Oh, is he come? I am glad on't.
LEANTIO [*aside*] Is that all?
Why, this's° as dreadful now as sudden death *this is*
To some rich man, that flatters° all his sins *beguiles, puts off*
With promise of repentance when he's old,
And dies in the midway before he comes to't.—
Sure you're not well, Bianca. How dost, prithee?
BIANCA I have been better than I am at this time.
LEANTIO Alas, I thought so.
BIANCA Nay, I have been worse too
Than now you see me, sir.
LEANTIO I'm glad thou mend'st yet;
I feel my heart mend too. How came it to thee?
Has anything disliked° thee in my absence? *offended*
BIANCA No, certain, I have had the best content
That Florence can afford.
LEANTIO Thou makest the best° on't.— *You put the best face*
Speak, mother, what's the cause? You must needs know.
MOTHER Troth, I know none, son; let her speak herself.
[*Aside*] Unless it be the same gave° Lucifer *same cause that gave*
A tumbling cast:° that's pride. *fall from heaven*
BIANCA Methinks this house stands nothing to my mind;° *not as I would wish*
I'd have some pleasant lodging i'th'high street, sir,
Or if 'twere near the court, sir, that were much better.
'Tis a sweet recreation for a gentlewoman
To stand in a bay window and see gallants.
LEANTIO Now, I have another temper,° a mere° stranger *inclination / total*
To that of yours, it seems: I should delight

1. I'll need to strive to extricate myself from her embraces (in order to get work done).

To see none but yourself.
BIANCA I praise not that;
Too fond° is as unseemly as too churlish. *foolishly doting*
I would not have a husband of that proneness
To kiss me before company, for a world.
Beside, 'tis tedious to see one thing still,° sir, *constantly*
Be it the best that ever heart affected;° *desired*
Nay, were't yourself—whose love had power, you know,
To bring me from my friends°—I would not stand thus *To make me elope*
And gaze upon you always. Troth, I could not, sir;
As good be blind and have no use of sight
As look on one thing still. What's the eye's treasure[2]
But change of objects? You are learnèd, sir,
And know I speak not ill;° 'tis full° as virtuous *untruth / fully*
For woman's eye to look on several men
As for her heart, sir, to be fixed on one.
LEANTIO Now thou com'st home to me. A kiss for that word.
BIANCA No matter for a kiss, sir; let it pass.
'Tis but a toy;° we'll not so much as mind it.° *trifle / think of it*
Let's talk of other business, and forget it.
What news now of the pirates?[3] Any stirring?
Prithee discourse a little.
MOTHER [*aside*] I am glad he's here yet
To see her tricks himself; I had lied[4] monstrously
If I had told 'em first.
LEANTIO Speak, what's the humor,° sweet, *whim*
You make your lip so strange?° This was not wont. *To make you deny kisses*
BIANCA Is there no kindness betwixt man and wife
Unless they make a pigeon-house of friendship
And be still billing?° 'Tis the idlest fondness *billing and cooing*
That ever was invented, and 'tis pity
It's grown a fashion for poor gentlewomen;
There's many a disease kissed in a year by't,
And a French curtsy made to't.[5] Alas, sir,
Think of the world, how we shall live. Grow serious!
We have been married a whole fortnight now.
LEANTIO How, a whole fortnight? Why, is that so long?
BIANCA 'Tis time to leave off dalliance. 'Tis a doctrine
Of your own teaching, if you be remembered,
And I was bound to obey it.[6]
MOTHER [*aside*] Here's one fits him;
This was well catched, i'faith, son,[7] like a fellow
That rids another country of a plague,
And brings it home with him to his own house.
Knock within.
Who knocks?
LEANTIO Who's there now? Withdraw you, Bianca.

2. What is most precious to the eye.
3. Pirates were a hot topic at the time the play was produced, in the early 1620s.
4. He would have thought I lied.
5. Bianca's complaint against elaborate French courtly manners includes a warning against venereal disease, especially the so-called French disease, syphilis. Perhaps Bianca is thinking that she might pass on a venereal infection (caught from the Duke) to Leantio. Cf. lines 90–92 below.
6. Bianca twits Leantio about his attempts to teach her the virtues of industriousness.
7. You brought that rebuke on yourself, son.

Thou art a gem no stranger's eye must see,
Howe'er thou please now to look dull on me.[8]
Exit [Bianca].

Enter Messenger.

You're welcome, sir. To whom your business, pray?
MESSENGER To one I see not here now.° — *i.e., To Bianca*
LEANTIO Who should that be, sir?
MESSENGER A young gentlewoman I was sent to.
LEANTIO A young gentlewoman?
MESSENGER Ay, sir, about sixteen.
Why look you wildly, sir?
LEANTIO At your strange error.
You've mistook the house, sir. There's none such here,
I assure you.
MESSENGER I assure you too,
The man that sent me cannot be mistook.
LEANTIO Why, who is't sent you, sir?
MESSENGER The Duke.
LEANTIO The Duke?
MESSENGER Yes. He entreats her company at a banquet
At Lady Livia's house.
LEANTIO Troth, shall I tell you, sir,
It is the most erroneous business
That e'er your honest pains was abused with.
I pray, forgive me if I smile a little—
I cannot choose, i'faith, sir—at an error
So comical as this. I mean no harm, though.
His Grace has been most wondrous ill informed;
Pray so return it,° sir. What should her name be? — *return this answer*
MESSENGER That I shall tell you straight too: Bianca
Capella.° — *i.e., Cappello*
LEANTIO How, sir, Bianca? What do you call th'other?° — *(the last name)*
MESSENGER Capella. Sir, it seems you know no such, then?
LEANTIO Who should this be? I never heard o'th'name.
MESSENGER Then 'tis a sure mistake.
LEANTIO What if you inquired
In the next street, sir? I saw gallants there
In the new houses that are built of late.
Ten to one, there you find her.
MESSENGER Nay, no matter.
I will return° the mistake, and seek no further. — *take back news of*
LEANTIO Use your own will and pleasure, sir. You're welcome.
Exit Messenger.
What shall I think of first? [*Calling*] Come forth, Bianca!

Enter Bianca.

Thou art betrayed, I fear me.
BIANCA Betrayed! How, sir?
LEANTIO The Duke knows thee.
BIANCA Knows me! How know you that, sir?
LEANTIO He's got thy name.

8. (1) To look unexcitedly at me; (2) to lack the brilliant luster of a gem (see line 94).

BIANCA [*aside*] Ay, and my good name° too, *reputation*
That's worse o'th'twain.
LEANTIO How comes this work about?
BIANCA How should the Duke know me?—Can you guess, mother?
MOTHER Not I, with all my wits. Sure we kept house close.° *kept within doors*
LEANTIO Kept close! Not all the locks in Italy
Can keep you women so; you have been gadding,
And ventured out at twilight to th'court-green yonder,
And met the gallant bowlers° coming home— *players at lawn bowling*
Without your masks too, both of you, I'll be hanged else.
Thou hast been seen, Bianca, by some stranger;
Never excuse it.
BIANCA I'll not seek the way,° sir. *I won't even try*
Do you think you've married me to mew° me up *cage (as in hawking)*
Not to be seen? What would you make of me?
LEANTIO A good wife, nothing else.
BIANCA Why, so are some
That are seen ev'ry day, else the devil take 'em.
LEANTIO No more, then. I believe all virtuous in thee
Without an argument. 'Twas but thy hard chance° *misfortune*
To be seen somewhere; there lies all the mischief.
But I have devised a riddance.
MOTHER Now I can tell you, son,
The time and place.
LEANTIO When, where?
MOTHER What wits have I?° *Let me think*
When you last took your leave, if you remember,
You left us both at window.
LEANTIO Right, I know that.
MOTHER And not the third part of an hour after,
The Duke passed by in a great solemnity° *ceremoniousness*
To Saint Mark's Temple, and to my apprehension° *way of thinking*
He looked up twice to th'window.
LEANTIO Oh, there quickened° *was conceived*
The mischief of this hour!
BIANCA [*aside*] If you call't mischief.
It is a thing I fear I am conceived° with. *made pregnant*
LEANTIO Looked he up twice, and could you take no warning?
MOTHER Why, once may do as much harm, son, as a thousand.
Do not you know one spark has fired an house
As well as a whole furnace?
LEANTIO My heart flames for't.
Yet let's be wise and keep all smothered closely.
I have bethought a means. Is the door fast?
MOTHER I locked it myself after him.° *(the messenger)*
LEANTIO You know, mother,
At the end of the dark parlor there's a place
So artificially contrived for a conveyance,° *secret passage*
No search could ever find it. When my father
Kept in° for manslaughter, it was his sanctuary. *Stayed in hiding*
There will I lock my life's best treasure up:
Bianca.
BIANCA Would you keep me closer yet?
Have you the conscience? You're best e'en choke me up, sir!
You make me fearful of your health and wits,

You cleave to such wild courses. What's the matter?
LEANTIO Why, are you so insensible of your danger
To ask that now? The Duke himself has sent for you
To Lady Livia's, to a banquet, forsooth.
BIANCA Now I beshrew° you heartily! Has he so? *curse*
And you the man would° never yet vouchsafe *who would*
To tell me on't till now! You show your loyalty
And honesty at once; and so farewell, sir.
LEANTIO Bianca, whither now?
BIANCA Why to the Duke, sir.
You say he sent for me.
LEANTIO But thou dost not mean
To go, I hope.
BIANCA No? I shall prove unmannerly,
Rude, and uncivil, mad, and imitate you.—
Come, mother, come, follow his humor no longer.
We shall be all executed for treason° shortly. *(for disobeying the Duke)*
MOTHER Not I,° i'faith. I'll first obey the Duke, *I'll not be executed*
And taste of a good banquet; I'm of thy mind.
I'll step but up and fetch two handkerchiefs
To pocket up some sweetmeats, and o'ertake thee. *Exit.*
BIANCA [*aside*] Why, here's an old wench would trot into[9] a bawd now
For some dry sucket, or a colt in marchpane.[1] *Exit.*
LEANTIO O thou the ripe time of man's misery, wedlock,
When all his thoughts, like overladen trees,
Crack with the fruits they bear, in cares, in jealousies!
Oh, that's° a fruit that ripens hastily, *jealousy is*
After 'tis knit° to marriage; it begins *bound*
As soon as the sun shines upon the bride
A little to show color.[2] Blessèd Powers,
Whence comes this alteration? The distractions,
The fears and doubts it brings are numberless,
And yet the cause I know not. What a peace
Has he that never marries! If he knew
The benefit he enjoyed, or had the fortune
To come and speak with me, he should know then
The infinite wealth he had, and discern rightly
The greatness of his treasure by my loss.
Nay, what a quietness has he 'bove mine
That wears his youth out in a strumpet's arms,[3]
And never spends more care upon a woman
Than at the time of lust, but walks away,
And, if he find her dead at his return,
His pity is soon done; he breaks a sigh
In many parts, and gives her but a piece on't!
But all the fears, shames, jealousies, costs, and troubles,
And still renewed cares of a marriage bed
Live in the issue,[4] when the wife is dead.

9. Turn into. (With wordplay on "trot," meaning "old woman.")
1. Candied sweets, one of them marzipan formed in a mold to resemble a young horse.
2. To show a little color of ripening fruit—the color of jealousy.
3. How much better off than a married man is a young whoremaster.
4. Live on in the consequences of marriage—most of all, the children.

Enter Messenger.

MESSENGER A good perfection to your thoughts.[5]
LEANTIO The news, sir?
MESSENGER Though you were pleased of late to pin an error
on me,° — *(see 99ff. above)*
You must not shift another in your stead too:[6]
The Duke has sent me for you.
LEANTIO How, for me, sir?
[*Aside*] I see then 'tis my theft; we're both betrayed.[7]
Well, I'm not the first has stol'n away° a maid; — *eloped with*
My countrymen have used° it. [*To him*] I'll along with you, sir. — *practiced*
Exeunt.

3.[3]

A banquet prepared. Enter Guardiano and Ward.

GUARDIANO Take you especial note of such a gentlewoman;° — *(Isabella)*
She's here on purpose; I have invited her,
Her father, and her uncle, to this banquet.
Mark her behavior well; it does concern you,
And what her good parts are, as far as time
And place can modestly require a knowledge of,
Shall be laid open to your understanding.
You know I'm both your guardian and your uncle;
My care of you is double, ward and nephew,
And I'll express° it here. — *show*
WARD Faith, I should know her now by her mark° among a thousand women. A little pretty deft° and tidy thing, you say. — *distinctive features*; *dainty; smart-looking*
GUARDIANO Right.
WARD With a lusty° sprouting sprig in her hair. — *lively; large*
GUARDIANO Thou goest the right way° still. Take one mark more: — *on the right track*
Thou shalt ne'er find her hand out of her uncle's,
Or else his out of hers, if she be near him.
The love of kindred never yet stuck closer
Than theirs to one another; he that weds her
Marries her uncle's heart too.
WARD Say you so, sir? Then I'll be asked° i'th'church to both of them. — *ask the banns (2.2.90)*
Cornets [sound].
GUARDIANO Fall back! Here comes the Duke.
WARD [*aside*] He brings a gentlewoman. I should fall forward° rather. — *i.e., fall on her*

Enter Duke, Bianca, Fabritio, Hippolito, Livia, Mother, Isabella, [gentlemen,] and attendants.

DUKE Come, Bianca,
Of purpose sent into the world to show
Perfection once in woman. I'll believe
Henceforward they° have ev'ry one a soul too, — *(women)*

5. I.e., I come to report a happy conclusion to what you told me before (at lines 100–121 above).
6. You mustn't try to put another person in your own place.
7. I see it's the elopement (see 1.1.44–45) I'm summoned to explain; someone has informed on Bianca and me.
3.3. At Livia's house. (See 3.2.105–6.)

'Gainst all the uncourteous opinions
That man's uncivil rudeness ever held of 'em.[1]
Glory of Florence, light° into mine arms! [*They embrace.*] *alight, leap*

Enter Leantio.

BIANCA Yon comes a grudging man will chide you, sir;
The storm is now in 's heart, and would get nearer,
And fall here if it durst°—it pours down yonder. *dared*
DUKE If that be he, the weather shall soon clear.
List, and I'll tell thee how. [*He whispers in her ear.*]
LEANTIO [*aside*] A-kissing too?
I see 'tis plain lust now, adultery boldened.
What will it prove anon when 'tis stuffed full
Of wine and sweetmeats, being so impudent fasting?° *before dining*
DUKE [*to Leantio*] We have heard of your good parts,° sir, which we honor *qualities*
With our embrace and love. [*To gentlemen*] Is not the captainship
Of Rouen citadel, since the late deceased,[2]
Supplied° by any yet? *Filled*
A GENTLEMAN By none, my lord.
DUKE [*to Leantio*] Take it. The place is yours, then, and as faithfulness
And desert° grows, our favor shall grow with't. *deserving*
[*Leantio kneels.*]
Rise now the captain of our fort at Rouen.
LEANTIO [*rising*] The service of whole life give Your Grace thanks![3]
DUKE Come sit, Bianca.
LEANTIO [*aside*] This is some good yet,
And more than e'er I looked for; a fine bit
To stay° a cuckold's stomach. All preferment° *appease / promotion*
That springs from sin and lust, it shoots up quickly,
As gardeners' crops do in the rotten'st grounds;
So is all means° raised from base prostitution *gain, resources*
E'en like a sallet° growing upon a dunghill. *salad vegetable*
I'm like a thing that never was yet heard of,
Half merry and half mad—much like a fellow
That eats his meat° with a good appetite, *food*
And° wears a plague-sore that would fright a country; *And yet*
Or rather like the barren,° hardened ass *unproductive; stupid*
That feeds on thistles till he bleeds again;° *as a result*
And such is the condition of my misery.
LIVIA [*indicating Leantio*] Is that your son, widow?
MOTHER Yes. Did Your Ladyship
Never know that till now?
LIVIA No, trust me, did I,
[*Aside*] Nor ever truly felt the power of love
And pity to a man, till now I knew him!
I have enough to buy me my desires,
And yet to spare; that's one good comfort. [*To Leantio*] Hark you,
Pray let me speak with you, sir, before you go.
LEANTIO With me, lady? You shall. I am at your service.

1. Whether women possessed souls was a much-debated topic.
2. Since the death of the recent incumbent.
3. May my entire life be one of thankful service to Your Grace!

[*Aside*] What will she say now, trow? More goodness° yet? — *gifts of fortune*
WARD [*to himself*] I see her now, I'm sure. The ape's° so little, I — *(a term of endearment)*
shall scarce feel her. I have seen almost as tall as she sold in
the fair for ten pence. See how she simpers it,° as if marma- — *smiles self-consciously*
lade would not melt in her mouth! She might have the kind-
ness, i'faith, to send me a gilded bull[4] from her own trencher°— — *wooden plate*
a ram, a goat, or somewhat° to be nibbling. These women, — *something*
when they come to sweet things once, they forget all their
friends, they grow so greedy—nay, oftentimes their husbands.
DUKE Here's a health° now, gallants, — *a toast*
To the best beauty at this day in Florence.
BIANCA Whoe'er she be, she shall not go unpledged,° sir. — *untoasted*
DUKE Nay, you're excused for this.[5]
BIANCA Who, I, my lord?
DUKE Yes, by the law of Bacchus. Plead your benefit:° — *Claim your exemption*
You are not bound to pledge your own health, lady.
BIANCA That's a good way, my lord, to keep me dry.
DUKE Nay, then I will not offend Venus so much.[6]
Let Bacchus seek his 'mends in another court.[7]
Here's to thyself, Bianca. [*He toasts her.*]
BIANCA Nothing comes
More welcome to that name than Your Grace.[8]
LEANTIO [*aside*] So, so.
Here stands the poor thief° now that stole the treasure,° — *(Leantio) / eloped*
And he's not thought on. Ours[9] is near kin now
To a twin misery born into the world:
First the hard-conscienced worldling,° he hoards wealth up, — *miser*
Then comes the next,° and he feasts all upon't; — *his heir*
One's damned for getting,° th'other for spending on't. — *acquiring wealth*
O equal justice, thou hast met my sin
With a full weight![1] I'm rightly now oppressed;
All her friends' heavy hearts lie in my breast.[2]
DUKE Methinks there is no spirit amongst us, gallants,
But what divinely sparkles from the eyes
Of bright Bianca; we sat° all in darkness — *would be sitting*
But for that splendor. Who was't told us lately
Of a matchmaking right, a marriage tender?° — *betrothal*
GUARDIANO 'Twas I, my lord.
DUKE 'Twas you indeed. Where is she?
GUARDIANO [*presenting Isabella*] This is the gentlewoman.
FABRITIO My lord, my daughter.
DUKE Why, here's some stirring° yet. — *excitement*
FABRITIO She's a dear child to me.
DUKE That must needs be; you say she is your daughter.
FABRITIO Nay, my good lord, dear° to my purse, I mean, — *expensive*
Beside my person; I ne'er reckoned that.[3]
She has the full qualities of a gentlewoman:

4. Molded marzipan shaped as a bull; see 3.2.189.
5. Bianca is excused from drinking a pledge because the toast is to her.
6. The Duke wittily replies that it would be an offense to Venus (who is associated with hot and moist, not dry), and to Bianca as her mortal embodiment, to forbid her to drink.
7. The rule of Bacchus as to the ritual of offering toasts will just have to seek legal remedy elsewhere and yield precedence to Venus and Bianca.
8. No one speaking my name is more welcome to me than yourself, Duke.
9. My situation and that of other men like me.
1. Impartial justice, you have given me what I deserve: cuckoldry as a payment for elopement.
2. The sadness of her deprived kinsfolk lies heavy on my conscience.
3. As well as to me personally; I wasn't counting that.

I have brought her up to music, dancing, what not
That may commend her sex and stir her husband.
DUKE And which is he, now?
GUARDIANO [*presenting the Ward*] This young heir, my lord.
DUKE What is he brought up to?
HIPPOLITO [*aside*] To cat-and-trap.° *(see 1.2.89.1)*
GUARDIANO My lord, he's a great ward, wealthy, but simple;° *simpleminded*
His parts° consist in acres. *best qualities*
DUKE Oh, wiseacres.
GUARDIANO You've spoke him in a word, sir.
BIANCA 'Las, poor gentlewoman!
She's ill bestead,° unless she's dealt the wiselier *badly helped, matched*
And laid in more provision for her youth.
Fools[4] will not keep in summer.
LEANTIO [*aside*] No, nor such wives
From whores° in winter. *From becoming whores*
DUKE [*talking with Fabritio*] Yea, the voice too, sir!
FABRITIO Ay, and a sweet breast° too, my lord, I hope, *singing voice*
Or I have cast away my money wisely.° *foolishly (ironic)*
She took her pricksong[5] earlier, my lord,
Than any of her kindred ever did—
A rare child, though I say't. But I'd not have
The baggage° hear so much; 'twould make her swell straight; *hussy*
And maids of all things must not be puffed up.[6]
DUKE Let's turn us to a better banquet, then,
For music bids the soul of man to a feast,
And that's indeed a noble entertainment
Worthy Bianca's self. [*To Bianca*] You shall perceive, beauty,
Our Florentine damsels are not brought up idly.
BIANCA They're wiser of themselves, it seems, my lord,
And can take gifts when goodness offers 'em. *Music.*
LEANTIO [*aside*] True, and damnation has taught you that wisdom;
You can take gifts too. Oh, that music mocks me!
LIVIA [*aside*] I am as dumb to any language now
But love's as one that never learned to speak.
I am not yet so old but he° may think of me; *(Leantio)*
My own fault. I have been idle° a long time, *(in seeking a lover)*
But I'll begin the week, and paint° tomorrow, *use cosmetics*
So follow my true labor° day by day— *i.e., seduction*
I never thrived so well as when I used° it. *practiced*

SONG

ISABELLA [*sings*] What harder chance can fall to woman,
Who was born to cleave to some man,
Than to bestow her time, youth, beauty,
Life's observance,° honor, duty, *dutiful service*
On a thing° for no use good *a man*
But to make physic° work, or blood *medicine*
Force fresh in an old lady's cheek?[7]
She that would be

4. (1) Idiots like the Ward; (2) clotted-cream delicacies; cf. 1.2.120.
5. Harmony written down. (With bawdy wordplay.)
6. (1) Swollen with pride; (2) swollen in pregnancy.
7. I.e., A husband like the Ward would be good for nothing other than to provide mild excitement and amusement, thereby increasing the working effect of medicine and bringing a blush to an old lady's cheek by his inanities.

Mother of fools,
Let her compound° with me. *join*

WARD [*to himself*] Here's a tune indeed! Pish, I had rather hear one ballad sung i'th'nose° now, of the lamentable drowning of fat sheep and oxen, than all these simpering tunes played upon cats' guts[8] and sung by little kitlings.° *nasally* *i.e., young women*

FABRITIO [*to the Duke*] How like you her breast° now, my lord? *voice (as at 123)*

BIANCA [*aside to the Duke*] Her breast?
He talks as if his daughter had given suck
Before she were married, as her betters have;[9]
The next he praises sure will be her nipples.

DUKE [*aside to Bianca*] Methinks now, such a voice to° such a husband *given to*
Is like a jewel of unvalued° worth *priceless*
Hung at a fool's ear.

FABRITIO May it please Your Grace
To give her leave to show another quality?

DUKE Marry, as many good ones as you will, sir;
The more, the better welcome.

LEANTIO [*aside*] But the less,
The better practiced. That soul's black indeed
That cannot commend virtue; but who keeps° it? *practices*
The extortioner will say to a sick beggar,
"Heaven comfort thee!" though he give none himself;
This good° is common. *empty charity*

FABRITIO [*to Guardiano*] Will it please you now, sir,
To entreat your ward to take her by the hand
And lead her in a dance before the Duke?

GUARDIANO That will I, sir; 'tis needful.—Hark you, nephew.

FABRITIO Nay, you shall see, young heir, what y' have for your money, without fraud or imposture.

WARD Dance with her? Not I, sweet guardianer. Do not urge my heart to't; 'tis clean against my blood.° Dance with a stranger? Let whoso will do't; I'll not begin first with her. *inclination*

HIPPOLITO [*aside*] No, fear't not, fool. She's took a better order.[1]

GUARDIANO Why, who shall take her, then?

WARD Some other gentleman. Look, there's her uncle, a fine-timbered° reveler; perhaps he knows the manner of her dancing too. I'll have him do't before me. I have sworn, guardianer. Then may I learn the better. *well-built*

GUARDIANO Thou'lt be an ass still.

WARD Ay, all that, uncle, shall not fool me out.° Pish, I stick closer to myself than so.[2] *out of my wish*

GUARDIANO [*to Hippolito*] I must entreat you, sir, to take your niece
And dance with her. My ward's a little willful;
He would have you show him the way.

HIPPOLITO Me, sir? He shall command it at all hours; pray tell him so.

GUARDIANO I thank you for him; he has not wit himself, sir.

8. Used for strings on stringed instruments.

9. Bianca suggests that many a better-born woman than Isabella has experienced premarital sex and pregnancy.

1. I.e., She has "danced" with me first—in bed.

2. I look out for myself better than that.

HIPPOLITO [*to Isabella*] Come, my life's peace.
[*Aside*] I have a strange office on't here!° — *duty here*
'Tis some man's luck to keep the joys he likes
Concealed for his own bosom, but my fortune
To set 'em out now, for another's liking,[3]
Like the mad misery of necessitous man
That parts from his good horse with many praises,
And goes on foot himself.[4] Need must be obeyed
In ev'ry action; it mars man and maid.[5]

Music. A dance [by Hippolito and Isabella], making honors° to the Duke and curtsy to themselves, both before and after. — *bows*

DUKE Signor Fabritio, you're a happy father.
Your cares and pains are fortunate, you see;
Your cost° bears noble fruits.—Hippolito, thanks. — *pains of child-raising*
FABRITIO Here's some amends for all my charges yet;
She wins both prick and praise,[6] where'er she comes.
DUKE How lik'st, Bianca?
BIANCA All things well, my lord;
But this poor gentlewoman's fortune, that's the worst.
DUKE There is no doubt, Bianca, she'll find leisure
To make that good enough;° he's rich and simple. — *To improve her lot*
BIANCA She has the better hope o'th'upper hand, indeed,
Which women strive for most.
GUARDIANO [*to Ward*] Do't when I bid you, sir.
WARD I'll venture but a hornpipe° with her, guardianer, or some such married man's dance. — *(see n. 8 below)*
GUARDIANO Well, venture something, sir.
WARD I have rhyme for what I do.
GUARDIANO [*aside*] But little reason, I think.
WARD Plain men dance the measures,° the cinquepace,° the gay;[7] — *slow dance / galliard*
Cuckolds dance the hornpipe,[8] and farmers dance the hay.° — *country dance*
Your soldiers dance the round,[9] and maidens that grow big;
Your drunkards the canaries,° your whore and bawd the jig. — *Spanish dance; wine*
Here's your eight kind of dancers. He that finds the ninth, let him pay the minstrels.
DUKE Oh, here he appears once in his own person.
I thought he would have married her by attorney,° — *by proxy*
And lain with her so too.
BIANCA Nay, my kind lord,
There's very seldom any found so foolish
To give away his part there.
LEANTIO [*aside*] Bitter scoff!
Yet I must do't.° With what a cruel pride — *suffer it*
The glory of her sin strikes by my afflictions![1]

3. But my fortune is to show my joys of love publicly and as though to please the Ward.
4. Like one who makes a virtue out of necessity by taking pleasure in walking when he has been obliged to sell his good horse.
5. Necessity must be obeyed; it presses its stern requirements on us all.
6. I.e., She is "pricked," or marked down for highest praise, like the center of a target in archery. (With bawdy wordplay.)
7. I.e., any sprightly dance.
8. A sailors' dance, the name of which here suggests cuckolds' horns.
9. Round dances are appropriate to soldiers "of the round," i.e., on sentinel patrol.
1. With what cruel pride does she, in the boastful splendor of her sinful state, thrust aside me and my afflictions!

Music. The Ward and Isabella dance;
he ridiculously imitates Hippolito.

DUKE This thing° will make shift,° sirs, to make a husband, *(The Ward) / attempt*
For aught I see in him.—How think'st, Bianca?
BIANCA Faith, an ill-favored shift,° my lord, methinks; *attempt; undergarment*
If he would take some voyage when he's married,
Dangerous, or long enough, and scarce be seen
Once in nine year together, a wife then
Might make indifferent shift to be content with him.
DUKE A kiss! [*He kisses Bianca.*] That wit deserves to be made much on.
Come, our caroch.° *coach*
GUARDIANO Stands ready for Your Grace.
DUKE My thanks to all your loves.—Come, fair Bianca,
We have took special care of you, and provided
Your lodging near us now.
BIANCA Your love is great, my lord.
DUKE Once more, our thanks to all.
OMNES° All blest honors guard you! *All*
Cornets flourish.
Exeunt all but Leantio and Livia.
LEANTIO [*aside*] Oh, hast thou left me then, Bianca, utterly?
Bianca, now I miss thee! Oh, return,
And save the faith of woman. I ne'er felt
The loss of thee till now; 'tis an affliction
Of greater weight than youth was made to bear,
As if a punishment of afterlife
Were fall'n upon man here. So new it is
To flesh and blood, so strange, so insupportable
A torment, e'en mistook,° as if a body *inappropriate*
Whose death° were drowning must needs therefore suffer it *death sentence*
In scalding oil.
LIVIA Sweet sir!
LEANTIO [*aside*] As long as mine eye saw thee,
I half enjoyed thee.
LIVIA Sir!
LEANTIO [*aside*] Canst thou forget
The dear pains my love took? How it has watched° *stayed awake*
Whole nights together, in all weathers, for thee,
Yet stood° in heart more merry than the tempests *remained*
That sung about mine ears—like dangerous flatterers
That can set all their mischief to sweet tunes—
And then received thee from thy father's window
Into these arms at midnight, when we embraced
As if we had been statues only made for't,° *for embracing*
To show art's life,[2] so silent were our comforts,
And kissed as if our lips had grown together!
LIVIA [*aside*] This makes me madder° to enjoy him now. *more madly desirous*
LEANTIO [*aside*] Canst thou forget all this? And better joys
That we met after this, which then new kisses
Took pride to praise?[3]
LIVIA [*aside*] I shall grow madder yet. [*To him*] Sir!
LEANTIO [*aside*] This[4] cannot be but of some close° bawd's working. *secret*

2. Showing art itself what kissing lovers might look like if a statue were carved on the subject.
3. And can you forget the even better happinesses that we enjoyed subsequently, which our new kisses celebrated?
4. Bianca's infidelity to me.

[*To Livia*] Cry mercy,° lady. What would you say to me? *I beg your pardon*
My sorrow makes me so unmannerly,
So comfort bless me,° I had quite forgot you. *As I hope to be saved*
LIVIA Nothing but[5] e'en in pity to that passion
Would° give your grief good counsel. *I would*
LEANTIO Marry, and welcome, lady!
It never could come better.
LIVIA Then first, sir,
To make away all your good thoughts at once of her,
Know most assuredly she is a strumpet.
LEANTIO Ha? Most assuredly? Speak not a thing
So vile so certainly; leave it more doubtful.
LIVIA Then° I must leave all truth, and spare° my knowledge— *In that case / withhold*
A sin which I too lately found and wept for.[6]
LEANTIO Found you it?
LIVIA Ay, with wet eyes.
LEANTIO Oh, perjurious friendship![7]
LIVIA You missed your fortunes when you met with her, sir.
Young gentlemen that only love for beauty,
They love not wisely. Such a marriage rather
Proves the destruction of affection;
It brings on want, and want's the key of whoredom.[8]
I think y' had small means° with her. *got a small dowry*
LEANTIO Oh, not any, lady.
LIVIA Alas, poor gentleman! What meant'st thou, sir,
Quite to undo thyself with thine own kind heart?
Thou art too good and pitiful to woman.
Marry, sir, thank thy stars for this blest fortune
That rids the summer of thy youth so well
From many beggars that had lain a-sunning
In thy beams only else,[9] till thou hadst wasted
The whole days of thy life in heat and labor.° *sex and hard work*
What would you say now to a creature found° *woman found to be*
As pitiful to you, and as it were
E'en sent on purpose from the whole sex general° *all womankind*
To requite all that kindness you have shown to't?
LEANTIO What's that, madam?
LIVIA Nay, a gentlewoman, and one able
To reward good things; ay, and bears a conscience to't.[1]
Couldst thou love such a one, that, blow all fortunes,[2]
Would never see thee want?° *let you be in need*
Nay, more, maintain° thee to thine enemies' envy? *support*
And shalt° not spend a care for't, stir a thought, *thou shalt*
Nor break a sleep; unless love's music waked thee,
No storm of fortune should. Look upon me,
And know that woman.
LEANTIO Oh, my life's wealth, Bianca!
LIVIA [*aside*] Still with her name? Will nothing wear it out?

5. I wish to say nothing other than . . .
6. I have all too recently learned the cost of not telling the truth.
7. Leantio cries out against Bianca's deserting him and perhaps too in implied sympathy for Livia's plight.
8. Imprudent marriage brings on financial need, which in turn leads to the selling of sexual favors.
9. Thank your stars for the separation that will spare you the begetting of penniless children.
1. And who bestows rewards as a virtuous duty.
2. Let windy Fortune blow whichever way she chooses.

[*To him*] That deep sigh went but for a strumpet, sir.
LEANTIO It can go for no other that loves me.[3]
LIVIA [*aside*] He's vexed in mind; I came too soon to him.
Where's my discretion now, my skill, my judgment?
I'm cunning in all arts but my own love.
'Tis as unseasonable to tempt him now,
So soon, as for a widow to be courted
Following her husband's corse,° or to make bargain *corpse (to burial)*
By the graveside, and take a young man there.
Her° strange departure stands like a hearse[4] yet *(Bianca's)*
Before his eyes, which time will take down shortly. *Exit.*
LEANTIO Is she my wife till death, yet no more mine?
That's a hard measure; then what's marriage good for?
Methinks by right I should not now be living,
And then 'twere all well. What a happiness
Had I been made of, had I never seen her!
For nothing makes man's loss grievous to him
But knowledge of the worth of what he loses;
For what he never had he never misses.
She's gone forever, utterly! There is
As much redemption of a soul from hell
As a fair woman's body from his° palace. *(the Duke's)*
Why should my love last longer than her truth?° *Bianca's faithfulness*
What is there good in woman to be loved,
When only that which makes her so° has left her? *When her virtue*
I cannot love her now but° I must like *unless*
Her sin, and my own shame too, and be guilty
Of law's breach with her, and mine own abusing[5]—
All which were monstrous. Then my safest course
For health of mind and body is to turn
My heart, and hate her, most extremely hate her;
I have no other way. Those virtuous° Powers *heavenly*
Which were chaste witnesses of both our troths
Can witness she breaks° first. And I'm rewarded *breaks her vows*
With captainship o'th'fort—a place of credit,° *honor*
I must confess, but poor; my factorship
Shall not exchange means with't.[6] He that died last° in't, *most recently*
He was no drunkard, yet he died a beggar
For° all his thrift. Besides, the place not fits me— *Despite*
It suits my resolution, not my breeding.[7]

Enter Livia.

LIVIA [*aside*] I have tried all ways I can, and have not power
To keep from sight of him. [*To him*] How are you now, sir?
LEANTIO I feel a better ease, madam.
LIVIA Thanks to blessedness!° *Thank goodness!*
You will do well, I warrant you. Fear it not, sir;
Join but your own good will to't. He's not wise

3. There is no other woman for whom I might sigh, even if she pined for me.
4. An ornamental wooden structure erected for a certain length of time in the deceased's parish church.
5. I.e., unless I practice a kind of bigamy, insulting my male honor by sharing her with another man. (Or Leantio may envisage practicing adultery on his own, to sin like her.)
6. I.e., my earnings as a mercantile agent are more than equal in value to the income from the captainship of the fort.
7. The office suits my courage and determination well enough, but my low birth does not qualify me to be commander of a fort.

That loves his pain or sickness, or grows fond
Of a disease whose property is to vex him
And spitefully drink his blood up. Out upon't,° sir, *(an exclamation of dismay)*
Youth knows no greater loss. I pray, let's walk, sir;
You never saw the beauty of my house yet,
Nor how abundantly fortune has blessed me
In worldly treasure. Trust me, I have enough, sir,
To make my friend° a rich man in my life, *lover*
A great man at my death;° yourself will say so. *(by inheritance)*
If you want anything, and spare° to speak, *fail*
Troth, I'll condemn you for a willful man, sir.

LEANTIO Why, sure this can be but the flattery of some dream.

LIVIA Now by this kiss, my love, my soul, and riches,
'Tis all true substance. [*She kisses him.*]
Come, you shall see my wealth; take what you list;° *desire*
The gallanter you go,° the more you please me. *dress*
I will allow you, too, your page and footman,
Your racehorses, or any various pleasure
Exercised° youth delights in; but to me *Athletic*
Only, sir, wear your heart of constant stuff.° *be constant of heart*
Do but you love enough, I'll give enough.

LEANTIO Troth, then, I'll love enough, and take enough.

LIVIA Then we are both pleased enough. *Exeunt.*

3.[4]

Enter Guardiano and Isabella at one door, and the Ward and Sordido at another.

GUARDIANO Now, nephew, here's the gentlewoman again.

WARD Mass,° here she's come again. Mark her now, Sordido. *By the Mass (an oath)*

GUARDIANO This is the maid my love and care has chose° *chosen*
Out for your wife, and so I tender her to you.
Yourself has been eyewitness of some qualities
That speak° a courtly breeding, and are costly. *bespeak*
I bring you both to talk together now;
'Tis time you grew familiar in your tongues.
Tomorrow you join hands, and one ring ties you,
And one bed holds you, if you like the choice.
Her father and her friends° are i'th'next room, *relatives*
And stay to see the contract° ere they part. *marriage contract*
Therefore dispatch, good Ward, be sweet and short.
Like her, or like her not, there's but two ways;
And one your body, th'other your purse pays.[1]

WARD I warrant you, guardianer, I'll not stand all day thrumming,° *idling*
But quickly shoot my bolt at your next coming.[2]

GUARDIANO Well said. Good fortune to your birding,° then! *bird-shooting, fowling*
[*Exit Guardiano.*]

WARD I never missed mark yet.

SORDIDO Troth, I think, master, if the truth were known, you

3.4. Livia's house.
1. (1) You can pay bodily by joining with her in marriage, or financially by a fine on your estate if you refuse. (Guardians had the authority to make such demands.) (2) If you like sex, she will please you physically; even if you don't, your purse will benefit by the dowry you'll receive.
2. I.e., I'll quickly give my decision, as in shooting an arrow at a bird. (With a suggestion too of ejaculation.) Proverbially, "A fool's bolt is soon shot."

never shot at any but the kitchen-wench, and that was a she-woodcock, a mere innocent, that was oft lost and cried at eight-and-twenty.[3]

WARD No more of that meat,° Sordido. Here's eggs o'th'spit now;[4] we must turn gingerly. Draw out the catalogue of all the faults of women. — *i.e., stuff*

SORDIDO How, all the faults? Have you so little reason° to think so much paper will lie in my breeches?[5] Why, ten carts will not carry it, if you set down but° the bawds. All the faults? Pray let's be content with a few of 'em; an if° they were less, you would find 'em enough, I warrant you. Look you, sir. [*They scrutinize her intently.*] — *common sense* / *only* / *even if*

ISABELLA [*aside*] But that I have th'advantage of the fool,[6]
As much as woman's heart can wish and joy at,
What an infernal torment 'twere to be
Thus bought and sold, and turned and pried into,
When, alas, the worst bit is too good for him!
And the comfort is
H'as° but a cater's° place on't, and provides — *He has / provider's*
All for another's table. Yet how curious° — *fastidious*
The ass is, like some nice professor° on't, — *professed expert*
That buys up all the daintiest food i'th'markets,
And seldom licks his lips after a taste on't!

SORDIDO Now to her, now you've scanned all her parts over.

WARD But at which end shall I begin now, Sordido?

SORDIDO Oh, ever at a woman's lip, while you live, sir. Do you ask that question?

WARD Methinks, Sordido, sh' has but a crabbed face, to begin with.

SORDIDO A crabbed face? That will save money.

WARD How! Save money, Sordido?

SORDIDO Ay, sir, for, having a crabbed face of her own, she'll eat the less verjuice[7] with her mutton; 'twill save verjuice at year's end, sir.

WARD Nay, an your jests begin to be saucy[8] once,° I'll make you eat your meat without mustard. — *now*

SORDIDO And that in some kind is a punishment.

WARD [*to Isabella*] Gentlewoman, they say 'tis your pleasure to be my wife, and you shall know shortly whether it be mine or no to be your husband; and thereupon thus I first enter upon° you. [*He kisses her.*] Oh, most delicious scent! [*Aside*] Methinks it tasted as if a man had stepped into a comfit-maker's° shop to let a cart go by, all the while I kissed her. [*To her*] It is reported, gentlewoman, you'll run mad for me if you have me not. — *greet, accost* / *maker of sweetmeats'*

ISABELLA I should be in great danger of my wits, sir— [*Aside*]
For being so forward, should this ass kick backward now.

3. And she was a twenty-eight-year-old village half-wit who often strayed and had to be publicly announced as lost by the town crier.
4. Here's a matter requiring careful attention. (Cooking eggs on a skewer requires constant turning.)
5. Men sometimes carried writing materials, food, and other items in their capacious breeches.
6. Were it not that I have the advantage over the Ward (in having a lover).
7. Tart crab-apple sauce (punning on "crabbed," meaning "harsh and disagreeable," and "crab apple").
8. (1) Impudent; (2) dealing in sauces.

WARD Alas, poor soul! And is that hair your own?

ISABELLA Mine own? Yes, sure, sir, I owe nothing for't.[9]

WARD 'Tis a good hearing;° I shall have the less to pay when I have married you. [*To Sordido*] Look, does her eyes stand well?°

It's good to hear that / *are they well placed?*

SORDIDO They cannot stand better than in her head, I think; where would you have them? And for° her nose, 'tis of a very good last.°

as for / *shape*

WARD I have known as good as that has not lasted a year, though.

SORDIDO That's in the using of a thing. Will not any strong bridge fall down in time, if we do nothing but beat at the bottom?[1] A nose of buff° would not last always, sir, especially if it came into th'camp once.[2]

durable leather

WARD But, Sordido, how shall we do to make her laugh, that I may see what teeth she has? For I'll not bate her a tooth,[3] nor take a black one into th'bargain.

SORDIDO Why, do but you fall in talk with her, you cannot choose but one time or other make her laugh, sir.

WARD It shall go hard but I will.° [*To her*] Pray, what qualities have you beside singing and dancing? Can you play at shuttlecock, forsooth?

I'll surely do that

ISABELLA Ay, and at stool-ball[4] too, sir; I have great luck at it.

WARD Why, can you catch a ball well?

ISABELLA I have catched two° in my lap at one game.

(suggesting testicles)

WARD What, have you, woman? I must have you learn to play at trap° too; then you're full and whole.

cat-and-trap

ISABELLA Anything that you please to bring me up to I shall take pains to practice.

WARD [*aside to Sordido*] 'Twill not do, Sordido. We shall never get her mouth opened wide enough.

SORDIDO No, sir? That's strange! Then here's a trick for your learning. (*He yawns.*) [*Isabella yawns also.*] Look now, look now; quick, quick there.

WARD Pox of that scurvy mannerly trick with handkerchief![5] It hindered me a little. But I am satisfied. When a fair woman gapes and stops her mouth so, it shows° like a cloth-stopple° in a cream-pot. I have fair hope of her teeth now, Sordido.

looks / *cloth stopper*

SORDIDO Why, then y' have all well, sir; for aught I see she's right and straight enough now as she stands. They'll commonly lie crooked; that's no matter. Wise gamesters never find fault with that; let 'em lie still so.

WARD I'd fain mark how she goes,° and then I have all. For of all creatures I cannot abide a splay-footed woman. She's an unlucky thing to meet in a morning; her heels keep together so as if she were beginning an Irish dance still,° and

walks / *continually*

9. (1) I paid nothing for it; (2) I am not beholden to other women or to animal hair for a wig. (Also a reference to a familiar joke about hair loss as a symptom of syphilis.)

1. The Ward and Sordido joke about the effects of advanced syphilis in caving in the nose.

2. Syphilis was common in military camps; soldiers often wore "buff."

3. I'll not allow her to have any teeth missing.

4. A game in which a player defends her or his stool from a ball thrown by an opponent. Played often by women.

5. Isabella's polite use of a handkerchief to cover her yawn almost defeats the purpose of Sordido's trick.

the wriggling of her bum playing the tune to't. But I have bethought a cleanly shift° to find it: dab° down as you see me, and peep of one side, when her back's toward you. I'll show you the way. [*The Ward demonstrates.*] — *honest device / duck*

SORDIDO And you shall find me apt enough to peeping. I have been one of them has seen mad sights under your scaffolds.[6]

WARD [*to Isabella*] Will it please you walk, forsooth, a turn or two by yourself? You are so pleasing to me, I take delight to view you on both sides.

ISABELLA I shall be glad to fetch a walk to your love,° sir; 'twill get affection° a good stomach,° sir. [*Aside*] Which I had need have, to fall to such coarse victuals. — *to please you* / *give love / appetite*

[*They peep under her dress.*]

WARD Now go thy ways for a clean-treading wench[7] as ever man in modesty peeped under!

SORDIDO I see° the sweetest sight to please my master! Never went Frenchman righter upon ropes° than she on Florentine rushes.° — *saw* / *tightropes* / *floor covering*

WARD [*to Isabella*] 'Tis enough, forsooth.

ISABELLA And how do you like me now, sir?

WARD Faith, so well I never mean to part with thee, sweetheart, under° some sixteen children, and all boys. — *short of*

ISABELLA You'll be at simple pains, if you prove kind,
And breed 'em all in your teeth.[8]

WARD Nay, by my faith, what serves your belly for? 'Twould make my cheeks look like blown bagpipes.[9]

Enter Guardiano.

GUARDIANO How now, ward and nephew, gentlewoman and niece! Speak, is it so or not?

WARD 'Tis so, we are both agreed, sir.

GUARDIANO In to your kindred, then. There's friends, and wine, and music waits to welcome you.

WARD Then I'll be drunk for joy.

SORDIDO And I for company. I cannot break my nose in a better action.[1] *Exeunt.*

4.1

Enter Bianca attended by two Ladies.

BIANCA How goes your watches, ladies? What's o'clock now?[1]
FIRST LADY By mine, full nine.
SECOND LADY By mine, a quarter past.
FIRST LADY I set mine by Saint Mark's.
SECOND LADY Saint Anthony's, they say,
Goes truer.
FIRST LADY That's but your opinion, madam,
Because you love a gentleman o'th'name.

6. Scaffolds were erected for public spectacles or plays.
7. You take the prize for the woman with the straightest and truest gait.
8. Toothache was thought to be a proper sympathetic response on the husband's part to his wife's pain during childbirth.
9. The Ward considers the idea of breeding children in the mouth from a literal point of view and finds the idea alarming.
1. I can't imagine a cause more worth suffering for.
4.1. The Duke's court (see line 42).
1. Good timekeeping, in the ensuing conversation, becomes a metaphor for proper sexual behavior. Clocks were not very accurate.

SECOND LADY He's a true gentleman, then.
FIRST LADY So may he be
That comes to me tonight, for aught you know.
BIANCA I'll end this strife straight. I set mine by the sun.° *i.e., the Duke*
I love to set by th'best; one shall not then
Be troubled to set often.
SECOND LADY You do wisely in't.
BIANCA If I should set my watch, as some girls do,
By ev'ry clock i'th'town,° 'twould ne'er go true; *By taking many lovers*
And too much turning of the dial's point,
Or tamp'ring with the spring, might in small time
Spoil the whole work too. Here it wants of nine° now. *is before 9 A.M.*
FIRST LADY It does indeed, forsooth; mine's nearest truth yet.
SECOND LADY Yet I have found her lying° with an advocate, *falsifying; sleeping*
which showed like two false clocks together in one parish.
BIANCA So now I thank you, ladies; I desire
Awhile to be alone.
FIRST LADY And I am nobody, methinks, unless I have one or other with me. Faith, my desire and hers will ne'er be sisters.
Exeunt Ladies.
BIANCA How strangely woman's fortune comes about!
This° was the farthest way to come to me, *(My recent fortune)*
All would have judged, that knew me born in Venice,
And there with many jealous eyes brought up,[2]
That never thought they had me sure° enough *secure*
But when they were upon me.° Yet my hap° *looking at me / lot was*
To meet it° here, so far off from my birthplace, *(my fortune)*
My friends, or kindred. 'Tis not good, in sadness,° *seriously*
To keep a maid so strict in her young days;
Restraint breeds wand'ring thoughts, as many fasting days° *days breed*
A great desire to see flesh° stirring again. *meat; sexual desire*
I'll ne'er use any girl of mine so strictly;
Howe'er they're kept, their fortunes find 'em out.
I see't in me. If they be got° in court, *conceived*
I'll never forbid 'em the country; nor the court,
Though they be born i'th'country. They will come to't
And fetch their falls° a thousand mile about, *falling in sin*
Where one would little think on't.

Enter Leantio [elegantly dressed, not seeing Bianca at first].

LEANTIO [*to himself*] I long to see how my despiser looks,
Now she's come here to court. These are her lodgings;
She's simply° now advanced. I took her out *greatly*
Of no such window, I remember, first;
That was a great deal lower, and less carved.
BIANCA How now? What silkworm's° this, i'th'name of pride? *dandy is*
What, is it he?
LEANTIO [*to her*] A bow i'th'ham° to your greatness! *in the thighs*
You must have now three legs,° I take it, must you not? *bows*
BIANCA Then I must take another;° I shall want° else *another lover / lack*
The service I should have. You have but two there.[3]
LEANTIO You're richly placed.
BIANCA Methinks you're wondrous brave,° sir. *handsomely dressed*

2. And raised there by many suspicious-eyed relatives. 3. Bianca implies that Leantio lacks sexual potency.

LEANTIO A sumptuous lodging.
BIANCA You've an excellent suit there.
LEANTIO A chair of velvet!
BIANCA Is your cloak lined through,° sir? — *throughout*
LEANTIO You're very stately here.
BIANCA Faith, something proud,[4] sir.
LEANTIO Stay, stay, let's see your cloth-of-silver slippers.
BIANCA Who's your shoemaker? He's made you a neat boot.
LEANTIO Will you have a pair? The Duke will lend you spurs.
BIANCA Yes, when I ride.° — *ride horse; have sex*
LEANTIO 'Tis a brave life you lead.
BIANCA I could ne'er see you in such good clothes
In my time.
LEANTIO In your time?
BIANCA Sure I think, sir,
We both thrive best asunder.
LEANTIO You're a whore.
BIANCA Fear nothing,° sir. — *Don't worry about it*
LEANTIO An impudent, spiteful strumpet!
BIANCA Oh, sir, you give me thanks for your captainship;
I thought you had forgot all your good manners.[5]
LEANTIO And to spite thee as much, look there. [*He shows her a letter.*] There read,
Vex, gnaw;° thou shalt find there I am not love-starved. — *eat your heart out*
The world was never yet so cold or pitiless
But there was ever still more charity found out
Than at one proud fool's door;[6] and 'twere hard, faith,
If I could not pass° that. Read to thy shame there; — *surpass*
A cheerful and a beauteous benefactor too,
As e'er erected° the good works of love. — *(with sexual wordplay)*
BIANCA [*aside*] Lady Livia!
Is't possible? Her Worship° was my pandress.° — *Her Ladyship / procuress*
She dote, and send, and give, and all to him!
Why, here's a bawd plagued home.[7] [*To him*] You're simply° happy, sir, — *utterly*
Yet I'll not envy you.
LEANTIO No, court-saint,° not thou! — *one venerated at court*
You keep some friend° of a new fashion. — *lover*
There's no harm in your devil, he's a suckling;
But he will breed teeth shortly, will he not?[8]
BIANCA Take heed you play not, then, too long with him.[9]
LEANTIO Yes, and the great one° too. I shall find time — *the devil*
To play a hot religious bout with some of you,
And perhaps drive you and your course of sins[1]
To their eternal kennels. I speak softly now;
'Tis manners in a noble woman's lodgings,
And I well know all my degrees of duty.° — *duty owing to rank*
But come I to your everlasting parting once,[2]

4. Your appearance is altogether splendid (and proud).
5. With mock politeness, Bianca speaks of Leantio as though his insulting speech were a form of expressing thanks for his promotion.
6. I.e., Things aren't so bad that you, in your hard-hearted folly, are my only hope.
7. This bawd is getting a taste of her own medicine.
8. I.e., He may be gentle now, but your lover will turn nasty in time, don't you realize?
9. Don't you take chances messing, then, with the Duke.
1. And your sinful career. (Leantio uses the language of chasing after animals in a hunt.)
2. But when I come to see your death and damnation.

Thunder shall seem soft music to° that tempest. *compared to*
BIANCA 'Twas said last week there would be change of weather,[3]
When the moon hung° so, and belike° you heard it. *hovered / perhaps*
LEANTIO Why, here's sin made, and ne'er a conscience put to't[4]—
A monster with all forehead and no eyes.[5]
Why do I talk to thee of sense or virtue,
That art as dark as death? And as much madness° *it's just as crazy*
To set light before thee as to lead blind folks
To see the monuments, which they may smell as soon
As they behold—marry, ofttimes their heads,
For want of light, may feel the hardness of 'em.[6]
So shall thy blind pride° my revenge and anger, *pride feel*
That canst not see it now; and it may fall
At such an hour when thou least see'st of all.° *when you're least aware*
So to an ignorance darker than thy womb
I leave thy perjured soul. A plague will come. *Exit.*
BIANCA Get you gone first, and then I fear no greater;
Nor thee will I fear long. I'll have this sauciness
Soon banished from these lodgings, and the rooms
Perfumed well after the corrupt air it leaves.
His breath has made me almost sick, in troth.
A poor base start-up!° Life![7] Because he's got *upstart*
Fair clothes by foul means, comes to rail,° and show 'em. *scold abusively*

Enter the Duke.

DUKE Who's that?
BIANCA Cry you mercy,° sir. *I beg your pardon*
DUKE Prithee, who's that?
BIANCA The former thing, my lord, to whom you gave
The captainship. He eats his meat with grudging still.
DUKE Still!
BIANCA He comes vaunting here of his new love,
And the new clothes she gave him: Lady Livia.
Who but she now his mistress?
DUKE Lady Livia?
Be sure of what you say.
BIANCA He showed me her name, sir,
In perfumed paper, her vows, her letter,
With an intent to spite me; so his heart said,
And his threats made it good; they were as spiteful
As ever malice uttered, and as dangerous,
Should his hand follow the copy.[8]
DUKE But that must not.° *must not be allowed*
Do not you vex your mind. Prithee, to bed, go;
All shall be well and quiet.
BIANCA I love peace, sir.
DUKE And so do all that love. Take you no care for't;
It shall be still provided to your hand.° *Exit [Bianca].* *as you wish*
[*Calling*] Who's near us, there?

3. Bianca sarcastically responds to Leantio's talk of heavenly thunder as if it were a weather report.
4. Here's sin, and yet no conscience is troubled by it.
5. A monster who is all effrontery and no scruples of conscience.
6. Blind people have to perceive (albeit more bluntly) with their other senses.
7. By God's life! (An oath.)
8. (1) If his handwriting should follow the copybook used to teach penmanship; (2) if he should violently act as he has threatened.

Enter Messenger.

MESSENGER My lord?
DUKE Seek out Hippolito,
Brother to Lady Livia, with all speed.
MESSENGER He was the last man I saw, my lord.
DUKE Make haste.
Exit [Messenger].
He is a blood° soon stirred, and as he's quick — *young gallant*
To apprehend a wrong; he's bold and sudden
In bringing forth a ruin.° I know likewise — *destruction*
The reputation of his sister's honor's
As dear to him as lifeblood to his heart.
Beside, I'll flatter him with a goodness° to her, — *by giving a benefit*
Which I now thought on, but ne'er meant to practice,
Because I know her base;° and that wind drives him.[9] — *lowborn*
The ulcerous° reputation feels the poise° — *diseased / weight*
Of lightest wrongs, as sores are vexed with flies.

Enter Hippolito.

He comes.—Hippolito, welcome.
HIPPOLITO My loved lord!
DUKE How does that lusty° widow, thy kind sister? — *merry; lustful*
Is she not sped yet of a second husband?[1]
A bedfellow she has—I ask not that—
I know she's sped of him.
HIPPOLITO Of him, my lord?
DUKE Yes, of a bedfellow. Is the news so strange to you?
HIPPOLITO I hope 'tis so to all.
DUKE I wish it were, sir,
But 'tis confessed too fast.° Her ignorant pleasures, — *all too manifest*
Only by lust instructed, have received
Into their services an impudent boaster,
One that does raise his glory from her shame
And tells the midday sun what's done in darkness;
Yet, blinded with her appetite, wastes° her wealth, — *she wastes*
Buys her disgraces at a dearer rate
Than bounteous housekeepers purchase their honor.
Nothing sads° me so much as that in love — *saddens*
To thee, and to thy blood,° I had picked out — *family*
A worthy match for her, the great Vincentio,
High in our favor and in all men's thoughts.
HIPPOLITO O thou destruction of all happy fortunes,
Unsated blood!°—Know you the name, my lord, — *desire*
Of her abuser?
DUKE One Leantio.
HIPPOLITO He's a factor.° — *commercial agent*
DUKE He ne'er made so brave a voyage
By his own talk.[2]
HIPPOLITO The poor old widow's son!—
I humbly take my leave.

(lust/love - differentiation?)

9. That will drive him forward, like a ship before the wind.
1. (1) Has she yet succeeded in acquiring a second husband? (2) Has she been done in by one? (Actually, Livia has had two husbands already; see 1.2.52.)
2. Even in his bravado about himself, he never imagined a rich journey like winning the love of Livia.

DUKE [*aside*] I see 'tis done.
[*To him*] Give her good counsel; make her see her error.
I know she'll hearken to you.
HIPPOLITO Yes, my lord.
I make no doubt as I shall take the course
Which she shall never know till it be acted,
And when she wakes to honor,[3] then she'll thank me for't.
I'll imitate the pities of old surgeons
To this lost limb,° who, ere they show their art,[4] *i.e., Leantio*
Cast° one asleep, then cut the diseased part. *Put*
So, out of love to her I pity most,
She shall not feel him going till he's lost;
Then she'll commend the cure. *Exit.*
DUKE The great cure's past;[5]
I count this done already. His° wrath's sure, *(Hippolito's)*
And speaks° an injury deep. Farewell, Leantio! *bespeaks*
This place will never hear thee murmur more.

Enter Lord Cardinal attended [*by torchbearers*].

Our noble brother, welcome!
CARDINAL [*to the torchbearers*] Set those lights down;
Depart till you be called. [*Exeunt torchbearers.*]
DUKE [*aside*] There's serious business
Fixed in his look; nay, it inclines a little
To the dark color of a discontentment.
[*To him*] Brother, what is't commands your eye so powerfully?
Speak, you seem lost.° *lost in thought*
CARDINAL The thing I look on seems so,[6]
To my eyes lost forever.
DUKE You look on me.
CARDINAL What a grief 'tis to a religious feeling
To think a man should have a friend so goodly,
So wise, so noble—nay, a duke, a brother—
And all this certainly damned!
DUKE How?
CARDINAL 'Tis no wonder,
If your great sin can do't.[7] Dare you look up° *up to heaven*
For thinking of a vengeance?° Dare you sleep *divine vengeance*
For fear of never waking but to death,° *spiritual death*
And dedicate unto a strumpet's love
The strength of your affections, zeal, and health?
Here you stand now; can you assure your pleasures
You shall once more enjoy her, but once more?[8]
Alas, you cannot. What a misery 'tis then
To be more certain of eternal death
Than of a next embrace! Nay, shall I show you
How more unfortunate you stand in sin
Than the low private man? All his offenses,
Like enclosed grounds, keep but about himself° *concern only himself*

3. And when she becomes conscious of the threat to her reputation.
4. Before they practice their surgical skill.
5. I.e., The cutting off of Leantio is as good as done already.
6. The person on whom I look (yourself) seems spiritually lost.
7. If a man of your greatness can sin so dreadfully, then it's no wonder that such things happen.
8. Can you be sure that you won't die or that a profligate woman won't desert you tomorrow?

And seldom stretch beyond his own soul's bounds;
And when a man grows miserable, 'tis some comfort
When he's no further charged than with himself;° — *than with his own sin*
'Tis a sweet ease to wretchedness. But, great man,
Ev'ry sin thou commit'st shows like a flame
Upon a mountain. 'Tis seen far about,
And with a big wind made of popular breath° — *gossip*
The sparkles° fly through cities; here one takes,° — *sparks / ignites*
Another catches there, and in short time
Waste all to cinders. But remember still:
What burnt the valleys first came from the hill.
Ev'ry offense draws his° particular pain, — *produces its*
But 'tis example° proves the great man's bane. — *being an example (that)*
The sins of mean° men lie like scattered parcels° — *lowly / items*
Of an unperfect° bill; but when such° fall, — *incomplete / (great men)*
Then comes example, and that sums up all.
And this your reason grants.° If men of good lives, — *must grant*
Who by their virtuous actions stir up others
To noble and religious imitation,
Receive the greater glory after death—
As sin must needs confess—what may they° feel — *(sinful great men)*
In height of torments and in weight of vengeance,
Not only they themselves not doing well,
But sets a light up to show men to hell?

DUKE If you have done,° I have; no more, sweet brother. — *finished*

CARDINAL I know time spent in goodness° is too tedious; — *in hearing my lecture*
This had not been a moment's space in lust now.[9]
How dare you venture on eternal pain,
That° cannot bear a minute's reprehension?° — *You who / censure*
Methinks you should endure to hear that talked of
Which you so strive to suffer. Oh, my brother!
What were you, if you were taken° now! — *taken by Death*
My heart weeps blood to think on't. 'Tis a work
Of infinite mercy you can never merit
That yet you are not death-struck,[1] no, not yet—
I dare not stay° you long, for fear you should not — *detain*
Have time enough allowed you to repent in.
There's but this wall betwixt you and destruction,
When you're at strongest, and but poor thin clay.[2]
Think upon't, brother; can you come so near it° — *(damnation)*
For a fair strumpet's love? And fall into
A torment that knows neither end nor bottom,
For beauty but the deepness of a skin,
And that not of their own neither?[3] Is she a thing
Whom sickness dare not visit, or age look on,
Or death resist? Does the worm shun her grave?
If not, as your soul knows it, why should lust
Bring man to lasting pain for rotten dust?

DUKE Brother of spotless honor, let me weep
The first of my repentance in thy bosom,

9. The time you've devoted to hearing my speech would have seemed to you to pass by in an instant if spent in lovemaking.

1. It's a mercy given by God, in order to allow time for penitence, that you have not died already.

2. Even when you seem strongest, there's only a poor thin barrier of flesh ("clay") walling you off from damnation.

3. I.e., (1) And is a false beauty manufactured by cosmetics? or, (2) And is not an inherent part of who they are?

And show the blest fruits of a thankful spirit;
And if I e'er keep woman more° unlawfully, *henceforth*
May I want° penitence at my greatest need! *be incapable of*
And wise men know there is no barren place
Threatens more famine than a dearth in grace.

CARDINAL Why, here's a conversion is° at this time, brother, *that is*
Sung for a hymn in heaven! And at this instant
The powers of darkness groan, makes all hell sorry.
First, I praise heaven, then in my work I glory.—
[*Calling*] Who's there attends without?

Enter servants.

SERVANTS My lord?

CARDINAL Take up those lights; there was a thicker darkness
When they came first. The peace of a fair soul
Keep with my noble brother!

DUKE Joys be with you, sir!

Exit Cardinal, etc. [*servants with torches*].

She lies alone tonight for't, and must still,
Though it° be hard to conquer; but I have vowed *(desire)*
Never to know her° as a strumpet more, *know her carnally*
And I must save° my oath. If fury fail not, *keep, honor*
Her husband dies tonight, or at the most
Lives not to see the morning spent tomorrow.
Then will I make her lawfully mine own,
Without this sin and horror. Now I'm chidden
For what I shall enjoy then unforbidden,
And I'll not freeze in stoves.[4] 'Tis but a while,
Live° like a hopeful bridegroom, chaste from flesh; *To live*
And pleasure then will seem new, fair, and fresh. *Exit.*

4.2

Enter Hippolito.

HIPPOLITO The morning so far wasted, yet his baseness
So impudent? See if the very sun
Do not blush at him!
Dare he do thus much, and know me alive?
Put case° one must be vicious,° as I know myself *Suppose / sinful*
Monstrously guilty, there's a blind time° made for't;° *darkness / for sex*
He might use only that, 'twere conscionable;° *reasonable, just*
Art,° silence, closeness,° subtlety, and darkness *Cunning / secrecy*
Are fit for such a business. But there's no pity
To be bestowed on an apparent° sinner, *egregious, flagrant*
An impudent daylight lecher. The great zeal
I bear° to her° advancement in this match *have, feel / (Livia's)*
With Lord Vincentio, as the Duke has wrought it
To the perpetual honor of our house,
Puts fire into my blood to purge the air
Of this corruption, fear° it spread too far *for fear*
And poison the whole hopes of this fair fortune.

4. I.e., I'll not freeze when I might be warm. (Stoves are heated rooms.)

4.2. Outside Livia's chambers.

I love her good° so dearly that no brother *good fortune*
Shall venture farther for a sister's glory
Than I for her preferment.° *advancement*

Enter Leantio [not seeing Hippolito].

LEANTIO Once again
I'll see that glist'ring whore, shines° like a serpent *who shines*
Now the court sun's° upon her. [*Calling*] Page! *royal favor is*
PAGE [*within*] Anon, sir!
LEANTIO I'll go in state too.

[*Enter Page.*]

See the coach be ready.
I'll hurry away presently. [*Exit Page.*]
HIPPOLITO [*coming forward*] Yes, you shall hurry,
And the devil after you! [*He strikes Leantio.*] Take that at setting forth![1]
Now, an° you'll draw, we are upon equal terms, sir. *if*
Thou took'st advantage of my name in honor
Upon my sister; I ne'er saw the stroke
Come till I found my reputation bleeding,
And therefore count it I no sin to valor
To serve thy lust so.[2] Now we are of even hand,° *on equal terms*
Take your best course against me. You must die.
LEANTIO How close sticks envy to man's happiness!
When I was poor, and little cared for life,
I had no such means offered me to die;
No man's wrath minded° me. [*He draws his sword.*] Slave, I turn this to thee *paid attention to*
To call thee to account for a wound lately
Of a base stamp[3] upon me.
HIPPOLITO 'Twas most fit
For a base mettle.[4] Come and fetch one° now *receive one wound*
More noble, then, for I will use thee fairer
Than thou hast done thine own soul, or our° honor. *our family's*
[*They fight, and Leantio falls.*]
And there I think 'tis for thee.° *i.e., you're paid*
WITHIN Help, help! Oh, part 'em!
LEANTIO False wife! I feel now th' hast prayed heartily for me.° *(said ironically)*
Rise, strumpet,° by my fall! Thy lust may reign now; *whore (Bianca)*
My heartstring and the marriage-knot that tied thee
Breaks both together. [*He dies.*]
HIPPOLITO There I heard the sound on't,
And never liked string° better. *the sound of a string*

Enter Guardiano, Livia, Isabella, Ward, and Sordido.

LIVIA 'Tis my brother.—
Are you hurt, sir?
HIPPOLITO Not anything.
LIVIA Blessed fortune!
Shift for thyself.° What is he thou hast killed? *Make your own escape*
HIPPOLITO Our honor's enemy.

1. (1) As you start off; (2) to begin with.
2. Hippolito rationalizes his striking without warning by claiming that Leantio struck his family honor first.
3. I.e., Of a cowardly sort. (With reference to counterfeiting, stamping coins with false impressions.)
4. (1) Temperament; (2) metal.

GUARDIANO [*indicating Leantio*] Know you this man, lady?
LIVIA [*seeing the dead Leantio*] Leantio? My love's joy? [*To Hippolito*] Wounds stick upon thee
As deadly as thy sins! Art thou not hurt?
The devil take that fortune! And he dead?
Drop plagues into thy bowels without voice,° *unannounced*
Secret and fearful! [*To the others*] Run for officers!
Let him be apprehended with all speed,
For fear he scape° away. Lay hands on him! *escape*
We cannot be too sure. 'Tis willful murder;
You do heaven's vengeance and the law just service.
You know him not as I do; he's a villain,
As monstrous as a prodigy° and as dreadful. *portent*
HIPPOLITO Will you but entertain a noble patience
Till you but hear the reason, worthy sister?
LIVIA The reason! That's a jest hell falls a-laughing at.
Is there a reason found for the destruction
Of our more lawful loves? And was there none
To kill the black lust 'twixt thy niece and thee,
That has kept close° so long? *concealed*
GUARDIANO How's that, good madam?
LIVIA Too true, sir. There she stands; let her deny't.
The deed° cries shortly in the midwife's arms, *i.e., child, offspring*
Unless the parents' sins strike it stillborn;
And if you be not deaf and ignorant° *willfully heedless*
You'll hear strange notes° ere long. [*To Isabella*] Look upon me, wench! *infant cries*
'Twas I betrayed thy honor subtly to him° *(Hippolito)*
Under a false tale; it lights° upon me now; *alights as punishment*
His arm has paid me home° upon thy breast, *all the way, fatally*
My sweet beloved Leantio!
GUARDIANO Was my judgment
And care in choice so dev'lishly abused,
So beyond shamefully? All the world will grin at me.
WARD Oh, Sordido, Sordido, I'm damned, I'm damned!° *doomed to wear horns*
SORDIDO Damned? Why, sir?
WARD One of the wicked. Dost not see't? A cuckold, a plain, reprobate cuckold.
SORDIDO Nay, an you be damned for that, be of good cheer, sir; you've gallant company of all professions. I'll have a wife next Sunday too, because I'll along with you myself.
WARD That will be some comfort yet.
LIVIA [*to Guardiano*] You, sir, that bear your load of injuries,
As I of sorrows, lend me your grieved strength
To this sad burden, who in life wore actions;° *who was a man of action*
Flames were not nimbler. We will talk of things
May° have the luck to break our hearts together. *That may*
GUARDIANO I'll list to nothing but revenge and anger,
Whose counsels I will follow.
Exeunt Livia and Guardiano [*bearing Leantio's body*].
SORDIDO A wife, quotha!° *forsooth*
Here's a sweet plum-tree of your guardianer's graffing!° *grafting*
WARD Nay, there's a worse name belongs to this fruit yet, an you could hit on't—a more open one. For he that marries a whore looks like a fellow bound all his lifetime to a medlar-

tree;[5] and that's good stuff. 'Tis no sooner ripe but it looks
rotten—and so do some queans° at nineteen. A pox on't, I *whores*
thought there was some knavery abroach,° for something *i.e., afoot*
stirred in her belly the first night I lay with her.

SORDIDO What, what, sir?

WARD This is she° brought up so courtly, can sing, and *she who was*
dance—and tumble° too, methinks. I'll never marry wife *tumble in bed*
again that has so many qualities.

SORDIDO Indeed, they are seldom good, master; for likely
when they are taught so many, they will have one trick more
of their own finding out. Well, give me a wench but with° *with but*
one good quality, to lie with none but her husband, and
that's bringing-up enough for any woman breathing.

WARD This was the fault when she was tendered to me. You
never looked to this.

SORDIDO Alas, how would you have me see through a great
farthingale,° sir? I cannot peep through a millstone, or in the *hooped petticoat*
going,[6] to see what's done i'th'bottom.° *(with sexual wordplay)*

WARD Her father praised her breast. Sh' had the voice, forsooth; I marveled she sung so small indeed, being no maid.[7]
Now I perceive there's a young chorister in her belly. This
breeds a singing in my head, I'm sure.

SORDIDO 'Tis but the tune of your wife's cinquepace,° danced *galliard (see 3.3.224)*
in a featherbed. Faith, go lie down, master; but take heed your
horns do not make holes in the pillowbeers.° [*Aside*] I would *pillowcases*
not batter brows with him[8] for a hogshead of angels!° He *barrel of gold coins*
would prick my skull as full of holes as a scrivener's sandbox.[9]

Exeunt Ward and Sordido.

ISABELLA [*aside*] Was ever maid so cruelly beguiled,
To the confusion° of life, soul, and honor, *destruction*
All of one woman's murd'ring![1] I'd fain bring
Her name no nearer to my blood than woman,
And 'tis too much of that.[2] Oh, shame and horror!
In that small° distance from yon man to me *i.e., incestuous*
Lies sin enough to make a whole world perish.
[*Aside to Hippolito*] 'Tis time we parted, sir, and left the sight
Of one another; nothing can be worse
To hurt repentance;[3] for our very eyes
Are far more poisonous to religion° *piety*
Than basilisks to them.[4] If any goodness
Rest° in you, hope of comforts, fear of judgments, *Remains*
My request is I ne'er may see you more;
And so I turn me from you everlastingly,
So is my hope to miss you. [*Aside*] But for her° *(Livia)*
That durst so dally with a sin so dangerous,

5. The medlar pear turned partly rotten before it was ripe to be eaten. A common metaphor for female sexual anatomy and for promiscuous women.
6. (1) Into the mill's turning; (2) into Isabella's walking.
7. A young virgin might be presumed to sing in a high ("small") voice.
8. Banging heads together is a kind of sport for young nitwits like the Ward and Sordido. But with (cuckold's) horns on his head, the Ward would be a formidable adversary.
9. A box containing sand and with a perforated lid for shaking out the sand to dry ink on paper.
1. Livia has destroyed Isabella's life, soul, and honor.
2. I wish that Livia were no more related to me than in our sex, and even that is too much.
3. I.e., nothing could be more inimical to true repentance than our continuing to see each other.
4. Than basilisks are to eyes. (These fabled serpents were believed to be fatal to anyone viewing them.)

And lay a snare so spitefully for my youth,
If the least means but favor my revenge,[5]
That° I may practice the like cruel cunning *So that*
Upon her life as she has on mine honor,
I'll act it without pity.
HIPPOLITO [*aside*] Here's a care
Of reputation and a sister's fortune
Sweetly rewarded by her![6] Would a silence
As great as that which keeps among the graves
Had everlastingly chained up her tongue!
My love to her has made mine miserable.[7]

Enter Guardiano and Livia [*and talk aside*].

GUARDIANO If you can but dissemble your heart's griefs now,
Be but a woman so far.° *i.e., Dissemble now*
LIVIA Peace! I'll strive, sir.
GUARDIANO As° I can wear my injuries in a smile, *Insofar as, since*
Here's an occasion offered that gives anger
Both liberty and safety to perform
Things worth the fire° it holds, without the fear *anger, fury*
Of danger or of law; for mischiefs acted
Under the privilege of a marriage-triumph
At the Duke's hasty nuptials will be thought
Things merely accidental—all's by chance,
Not got of° their own natures. *conceived out of*
LIVIA I conceive° you, sir, *understand*
Even to a longing for performance on't;
And here behold some fruits. [*She kneels.*]
[*To Hippolito and Isabella*] Forgive me both!
What I am now returned to, sense and judgment,
Is not the same rage and distraction
Presented lately to you; that rude form
Is gone forever. I am now myself,
That speaks all peace and friendship; and these tears
Are the true springs of hearty penitent sorrow.
For° those foul wrongs which my forgetful fury *As for*
Slandered your virtues with, this gentleman° *(Guardiano)*
Is well resolved° now. *satisfied*
GUARDIANO I was never otherways.° *otherwise*
I knew, alas, 'twas but your anger spake it,
And I ne'er thought on't more.
HIPPOLITO Pray rise, good sister. [*She rises.*]
ISABELLA [*aside*] Here's e'en as sweet amends made for a wrong now
As one that gives a wound and pays the surgeon;
All the smart's° nothing—the great loss of blood *sting, pain is*
Or time of hindrance.° Well, I had a mother; *i.e., slow recovery*
I can dissemble too.[8] [*To Livia*] What wrongs have slipped
Through anger's ignorance, aunt, my heart forgives.
GUARDIANO Why, this's tuneful now!

5. If any means, no matter how small, aid in my revenge.
6. Hippolito reflects with bitter irony on Livia's having rewarded his loyalty to her and his concern for her reputation with her betrayal of his secret.
7. My love to Livia has led only to misery. (Or, possibly, My love for Isabella has made my life miserable.)
8. I.e., My mother was a woman, too, and she taught me the dissembling that women generally practice.

HIPPOLITO [*to Livia*] And what I did, sister,
Was all for honor's cause, which time to come
Will approve° to you. *prove*
LIVIA Being awaked to goodness,
I understand so much, sir, and praise now
The fortune of your arm and of your safety;[9]
For by his death you've rid me of a sin
As costly as e'er woman doted on.
'T has pleased the Duke so well too, that behold, sir,
He's sent you here your pardon° [*giving Hippolito a letter*], which I kissed *pardon for manslaughter*
With most affectionate comfort. When 'twas brought,
Then was my fit just past; it came so well, methought,
To glad my heart.
HIPPOLITO I see His Grace thinks on me.
LIVIA There's no talk now but of the preparation
For the great marriage.
HIPPOLITO Does he marry her, then?
LIVIA With all speed, suddenly, as fast as cost° *expensive preparation*
Can be laid on with many thousand hands.
This gentleman° and I had once a purpose *(Guardiano)*
To have honored the first marriage of the Duke
With an invention° of his° own. 'Twas ready, *masque / (Guardiano's)*
The pains° well past, most of the charge° bestowed on't. *effort / expenditure*
Then came the death of your good mother, niece,
And turned the glory of it all to black.[1]
'Tis a device° would fit these times so well too, *masque*
Art's treasury not better.[2] If you'll join,
It shall be done. The cost shall all be mine.
HIPPOLITO You've my voice° first. 'Twill well approve° my thankfulness *consent / prove*
For the Duke's love and favor.
LIVIA What say you, niece?
ISABELLA I am content to make one.° *take a part*
GUARDIANO The plot's full,° then. *The cast is complete*
Your pages, madam, will make shift for° Cupids. *improvise as*
LIVIA That will they, sir.
GUARDIANO You'll play your old part still.
LIVIA What is't? Good troth, I have e'en forgot it.
GUARDIANO Why, Juno Pronuba,° the marriage-goddess. *goddess of marriage*
LIVIA 'Tis right indeed.
GUARDIANO [*to Isabella*] And you shall play the nymph
That offers sacrifice to appease her wrath.
ISABELLA Sacrifice, good sir?
LIVIA Must I be appeased then?
GUARDIANO That's as you list ° yourself, as you see cause. *wish*
LIVIA Methinks 'twould show the more state° in her deity *majesty*
To be incensed.
ISABELLA 'Twould, but my sacrifice
Shall take a course to appease you, or I'll fail in't—
[*Aside*] And teach a sinful bawd to play a goddess.

9. I.e., I praise your taking arms against Leantio in a cause of honor.
1. Once Isabella's mother had died, the family could not decorously cast aside mourning black to take part in the Duke's wedding (to some unnamed woman).
2. I.e., The treasury of all art affords no finer masque with which to celebrate this marriage.

GUARDIANO [*to Hippolito*] For° our parts, we'll not be ambitious,° sir. — *As for* / *contentious*
Please you walk in, and see the project° drawn, — *plan for the masque*
Then take your choice.
HIPPOLITO I weigh not,° so° I have one. — *don't care / provided*
Exeunt [Isabella, Guardiano, and Hippolito].
LIVIA How much ado have I to restrain fury
From breaking into curses! Oh, how painful 'tis
To keep great sorrow smothered! Sure I think
'Tis harder to dissemble grief than love.
Leantio, here° the weight of thy loss lies, — *i.e., on my heart*
Which nothing but destruction can suffice. *Exit.*

4.3

Hoboys.° Enter in great state the Duke and Bianca, richly attired, with lords, cardinals, ladies, and other attendants; they pass solemnly° over. Enter Lord Cardinal in a rage, seeming° to break off the ceremony. — *Shawms, oboes* / *ceremoniously* / *intending*

CARDINAL Cease, cease! Religious honors done to sin
Disparage virtue's reverence, and will pull
Heaven's thunder upon Florence. Holy ceremonies
Were made for sacred uses, not for sinful.
Are these the fruits of your repentance, brother?
Better it had been you had never sorrowed
Than to abuse the benefit and return
To worse than where sin left you.
Vowed you then never to keep strumpet more,
And are you now so swift in your desires
To knit your honors and your life fast to her?
Is not sin sure enough to wretched man
But he must bind himself in chains to't? Worse,
Must marriage, that immaculate robe of honor,
That renders virtue glorious, fair, and fruitful
To her great master,° be now made the garment — *To God*
Of leprosy and foulness? Is this penitence,
To sanctify hot lust? What is it otherways
Than worship done to devils? Is this the best
Amends that sin can make after her riots?° — *reveling*
As if a drunkard, to appease heaven's wrath,
Should offer up his surfeit° for a sacrifice! — *overindulgence*
If that be comely,° then lust's offerings are — *decent*
On wedlock's sacred altar.
DUKE Here you're bitter
Without cause, brother. What I vowed, I keep
As safe as you your conscience, and this needs not;° — *scolding is unnecessary*
I taste more wrath in't than I do religion,
And envy° more than goodness. The path now — *enmity; jealousy*
I tread is honest, leads to lawful love,
Which Virtue in her strictness would not check.
I vowed no more° to keep a sensual woman; — *no longer*
'Tis done. I mean to make a lawful wife of her.

4.3. The Duke's court.

CARDINAL He° that taught you that craft, *(The devil)*
Call him not master long; he will undo you.
Grow not too cunning for your soul, good brother;
Is it enough to use adulterous thefts,° *to steal others' wives*
And then take sanctuary in marriage?
I grant, so long as an offender keeps
Close in a privileged temple, his life's safe;[1]
But if he ever venture to come out,
And so be taken, then he surely dies for't.
So now you're safe; but when you leave this body,
Man's only privileged temple upon earth,
In which the guilty soul takes sanctuary,
Then you'll perceive what wrongs chaste vows endure
When lust usurps the bed that should be pure.

BIANCA Sir, I have read you over° all this while *observed you*
In silence, and I find great knowledge in you,
And severe° learning; yet 'mongst all your virtues *serious; censorious*
I see not charity written, which some call
The firstborn of religion, and I wonder
I cannot see't in yours. Believe it, sir,
There is no virtue can be sooner missed
Or later welcomed;[2] it begins the rest,
And sets 'em all in order. Heaven and angels
Take great delight in a converted sinner;
Why should you then, a servant and professor,° *professed Christian*
Differ so much from them? If ev'ry woman
That commits evil should be therefore kept
Back in desires of goodness, how should virtue
Be known and honored? From a man that's blind
To take a burning taper, 'tis no wrong,
He never misses it; but to take light
From one that sees, that's injury and spite.
Pray,° whether is religion better served *Pray tell me*
When lives that are licentious are made honest
Than when they still run through a sinful blood?[3]
'Tis nothing° virtue's temples to deface; *all too easy*
But build° the ruins, there's a work of grace. *to rebuild*

DUKE I kiss thee for that spirit; thou hast praised thy wit
A modest way.[4]—On, on there!

Hoboys. [*Exeunt Duke, Bianca, and attendants.*]

CARDINAL Lust is bold,
And will° have vengeance speak ere't be controlled. *Exit.* *must*

5.1

Enter Guardiano [*with a weapon*] *and Ward.*

GUARDIANO Speak, hast thou any sense of thy abuse?° *the wrong done you*
Dost thou know what wrong's done thee?

WARD I were an ass else. I cannot wash my face but I am feeling on't.[1]

1. Criminals could seek protection from arrest in the sanctuary offered by the church.
2. No virtue is sooner noted in its absence or welcomed however late than Christian love and forgiveness.
3. Than when lives are given over to sinful desire?
4. You have modestly shown a witty ability in debate.
5.1. At court.
1. I.e., I feel cuckold's horns every time I touch my forehead.

GUARDIANO [*giving weapon*] Here, take this galtrop,° then; *multipointed weapon*
convey it secretly into the place I showed you. Look you, sir,
this is the trapdoor to't.

WARD I know't of old, uncle, since the last triumph.° Here *marriage pageant*
rose up a devil with one eye, I remember, with a company° *cluster*
of fireworks at 's tail.

GUARDIANO Prithee leave squibbing[2] now; mark me, and fail
not. But when thou hear'st me give a stamp, down with't°— *with the trapdoor*
the villain's caught then.

WARD If I miss you,° hang me; I love to catch a villain, and *miss your signal*
your stamp shall go current,[3] I warrant you. But how shall I
rise up and let him down too, all at one hole? That will be a
horrible puzzle. You know I have a part in't; I play Slander.

GUARDIANO True, but never make you ready for't.

WARD No? My clothes are bought and all, and a foul fiend's
head with a long contumelious° tongue i'th'chaps° on't—a *despiteful / jaws*
very fit shape for Slander i'th'out-parishes.[4]

GUARDIANO It shall not come so far;[5] thou understand'st it not.

WARD Oh, oh!

GUARDIANO He° shall lie deep enough ere that time, and stick *(Hippolito)*
first upon those.° *(the galtrop's prongs)*

WARD Now I conceive you, guardianer.

GUARDIANO Away! List to the privy° stamp, that's all thy part. *secret*

WARD Stamp° my horns in a mortar if I miss you, and give *Grind*
the powder in white wine to sick cuckolds[6]—a very present° *efficacious*
remedy for the headache. *Exit Ward.*

GUARDIANO If this should any way miscarry now—
As, if the fool be nimble enough, 'tis certain°— *certain to succeed*
The pages that present° the swift-winged Cupids *act the parts of*
Are taught to hit him° with their shafts of love *(Hippolito)*
(Fitting his part)° which I have cunningly poisoned. *i.e., lovesick shepherd*
He cannot scape° my fury; and those ills *escape*
Will be laid all on fortune, not our wills.
That's all the sport on't;° for who will imagine *of it*
That at the celebration of this night
Any mischance that haps can flow from spite? *Exit.*

5.2

Flourish. Enter, above,° Duke, Bianca, Lord Cardinal, Fabritio, and other cardinals, lords and ladies in state, [attended by pages]. *in the gallery*

DUKE Now, our fair duchess, your delight shall witness
How you're beloved and honored; all the glories
Bestowed upon the gladness of this night
Are done for your bright sake.

BIANCA I am the more
In debt, my lord, to loves and courtesies

2. (1) Stop talking foolishly; (2) stop talking of squibs, or fireworks.
3. Your foot stamping will be understood. (With added wordplay on serving as valid currency with an authorized stamp.)
4. Outside the city walls (where, in London, the theaters stood).
5. The masque won't proceed to that point.
6. Powdered horn was used medicinally as an aphrodisiac, often mixed with wine.
5.2. At court.

That offer up themselves so bounteously
To do me honored grace, without my merit.
DUKE A goodness set in greatness;[1] how it sparkles
Afar off, like pure diamonds set in gold!
How perfect° my desires were, might I witness *complete*
But a fair noble peace 'twixt your two spirits!° *(the Cardinal and Bianca)*
The reconcilement would be more sweet to me
Than longer life to him that fears to die.
[*To Lord Cardinal*] Good sir!
CARDINAL I profess peace, and am content.
DUKE I'll see the seal upon't, and then 'tis firm.
CARDINAL You shall have all you wish. [*He kisses Bianca.*]
DUKE I have all indeed, now.
BIANCA [*aside*] But I have made surer work; this shall not blind me;
He that begins so early to reprove,
Quickly rid° him or look for little love. *get rid of*
Beware a brother's envy; he's next heir too.[2]
Cardinal, you die this night; the plot's laid surely.
In time of sports° death may steal in securely; *entertainments*
Then 'tis least thought on.
For he that's most religious, holy friend,
Does not at all hours think upon his end;
He has his times of frailty, and his thoughts
Their transportations too through flesh and blood[3]
(For all his zeal, his learning, and his light)° *spiritual light*
As well as we poor souls that sin by night.
[*Fabritio gives the Duke a paper.*]
DUKE What's this, Fabritio?
FABRITIO Marry, my lord, the model° *plot, abstract*
Of what's presented.
DUKE Oh, we thank their loves.
Sweet Duchess, take your seat; list to the argument.° *plot*
(*Reads*) "There is a nymph that haunts the woods and springs,
In love with two at once, and they with her.
Equal it runs; but to decide these things,
The cause to mighty Juno they refer,
She being the marriage-goddess. The two lovers,
They offer sighs, the nymph a sacrifice,
All to please Juno, who by signs discovers° *reveals*
How the event° shall be; so that strife dies. *outcome*
Then springs a second;° for the man refused *second strife*
Grows discontent and, out of love abused,° *misused, wronged*
He raises Slander up, like a black fiend,
To disgrace th'other, which pays him° i'th'end." *who kills him*
BIANCA In troth, my lord, a pretty, pleasing argument,
And fits th'occasion well. Envy and slander
Are things soon raised against two faithful lovers;
But comfort is, they° are not long unrewarded. *Music.* *(envy and slander)*
DUKE This music shows they're upon entrance° now. *about to enter*
BIANCA [*aside*] Then enter all my wishes.[4]

1. I.e., You are modest virtue itself contained in a person of great social rank.
2. As brother and heir, the Cardinal might well be expected to be wary of Bianca's capacity for producing a young heir with a prior claim.
3. The Cardinal's thoughts no doubt have their times of being occupied with fleshly imaginings.
4. Bianca has prepared a poisoned cup for the Cardinal, to be presented in an "antemasque" (see line 69), a short masque preceeding the main spectacle, which

Enter [above] Hymen in yellow, Ganymede in a blue robe powdered with stars, and Hebe in a white robe with golden stars,[5] with covered° cups in their hands. They dance a short dance; then, bowing to the Duke, etc., Hymen speaks. — lidded

HYMEN [*giving Bianca a cup*] To thee, fair bride, Hymen offers up
Of nuptial joys this the celestial cup.
Taste it, and thou shalt ever find
Love in thy bed, peace in thy mind.
BIANCA We'll taste you, sure; 'twere pity to disgrace
So pretty a beginning.
DUKE 'Twas spoke nobly.
GANYMEDE Two cups of nectar have we begged from Jove.—
Hebe, give that to Innocence,° I this to Love.° — the Cardinal / the Duke
[*In a mix-up, the Duke is given the poisoned cup.*]
Take heed of stumbling more; look to your way;
Remember still the *Via Lactea*.[6]
HEBE Well, Ganymede, you have more faults, though not so known;
I spilled one cup, but you have filched many a one.
HYMEN No more! Forbear, for Hymen's sake;
In love we met, and so let's parting take.
Exeunt [masquers].
DUKE But soft!° Here's no such persons in the argument — wait a minute
As these three, Hymen, Hebe, Ganymede.
The actors that this model° here discovers° — plot / reveals
Are only four: Juno, a nymph, two lovers.
BIANCA This is some antemasque belike,° my lord, — seemingly
To entertain time.° [*Aside*] Now my peace is perfect. — pass the time
[*Aloud*] Let sports come on apace. Now is their time, my lord.
Music.
Hark you, you hear from 'em!
DUKE The nymph, indeed.

Enter [on the main stage] two dressed like nymphs, bearing two tapers lighted; then Isabella° dressed with flowers and garlands, bearing a censer with fire in it. They set the censer and tapers on Juno's altar with much reverence, this ditty being sung in parts.° — (as a nymph) / (by the nymphs)

DITTY

NYMPHS Juno, nuptial-goddess,
Thou that rul'st o'er coupled bodies,
Tiest man to woman, never to forsake her,
Thou only powerful marriage-maker,
Pity this amazed° affection; — perplexed
I° love both, and both love me, — (the chief nymph)
Nor know I where to give rejection,
My heart likes so equally,
Till thou set'st right my peace of life

---

she has inserted in the festivities at this point. (The "antimasque," as distinguished from an "antemasque," is usually comic and comes later.)

5. The three entering figures represent the god of marriage, Jove's cupbearer, and a daughter of Jove who also served as cupbearer.

6. According to one myth, the cupbearer Hebe, stumbling on a star, spilled her cup's contents and thereby created the *Via Lactea*, or Milky Way.

And with thy power conclude this strife.
ISABELLA [*to the other nymphs*] Now, with my thanks,
depart you to the springs,
I to these wells° of love. [*Exeunt the other nymphs.*] *springs*
[*Imploring Juno*] Thou sacred goddess
And queen of nuptials, daughter to great Saturn,
Sister and wife to Jove, imperial Juno,
Pity this passionate conflict in my breast,
This tedious war 'twixt two affections!
Crown one with victory, and my heart's at peace.

Enter [*on the main stage*] *Hippolito and Guardiano, like shepherds.*

HIPPOLITO [*as a shepherd*] Make me that happy man, thou mighty goddess!
GUARDIANO [*as the other shepherd*] But I live most in hope, if truest love
Merit the greatest comfort.
ISABELLA [*as the nymph*] I love both
With such an even and fair affection
I know not which to speak for, which to wish for,
Till thou, great arbitress 'twixt lovers' hearts,
By thy auspicious grace, design° the man; *designate*
Which pity I implore.
BOTH [HIPPOLITO *and* GUARDIANO] We all implore it.

Livia descends° like Juno [*attended by pages as Cupids*]. *(in a chariot by a winch)*

ISABELLA [*as the nymph*] And after sighs, contrition's truest odors,
I offer to thy powerful deity
This precious incense; may it ascend peacefully—
[*The incense ascends as poisoned smoke.*]
[*Aside*] And if it keep true touch,° my good aunt Juno, *prove trustworthy*
'Twill try° your immortality ere't be long. *sorely test*
I fear you'll never get so nigh heaven again,
When you're once down.° *fallen dead*
LIVIA [*as Juno*] Though you and your affections
Seem all as dark to° our illustrious brightness *compared to*
As night's inheritance, hell,[7] we pity you,
And your requests are granted. You ask signs;
They shall be given you; we'll be gracious to you.
He of those twain which we determine for you,
Love's arrows shall wound twice. The later wound
Betokens love in age, for so are all
Whose love continues firmly all their lifetime
Twice wounded at their marriage; else affection
Dies when youth ends. [*Aside*] This savor° overcomes me. *(of the poisoned incense)*
[*As Juno*] Now for a sign of wealth and golden days,
Bright-eyed prosperity, which all couples love,
Ay, and makes° love, take that! *which creates*
[*She throws flaming gold upon Isabella, who falls dead.*]
Our° brother Jove *My*
Never denies us of his burning treasure
T'express bounty.

7. I.e., as hell, the child of night.

DUKE She falls down upon't.
What's the conceit° of that? *meaning*
FABRITIO As overjoyed, belike.° *perhaps*
Too much prosperity overjoys us all,
And she has her lapful, it seems, my lord.
DUKE This swerves a little from the argument, though.
Look you, my lords. [*He shows them the plot.*]
GUARDIANO [*aside*] All's fast.° Now comes my part to toll° *in place / lure, entice*
him° hither; *(Hippolito)*
Then, with a stamp given, he's dispatched as cunningly.
HIPPOLITO [*discovering that Isabella is dead*] Stark dead. Oh,
treachery! Cruelly made away!
[*Guardiano falls through the trapdoor.*][8]
How's that?° *What's happened now?*
FABRITIO Look, there's one of the lovers dropped away too.
DUKE [*examining the plot*] Why, sure this plot's drawn false.
Here's no such thing.
LIVIA Oh, I am sick to th'death! Let me down quickly;
This fume is deadly.
[*Livia is taken from the chariot in which she descended.*]
Oh, 't has poisoned me!
My subtlety is sped.[9] Her° art has quitted° me; *(Bianca's) / repaid*
My own ambition pulls me down to ruin. [*She dies.*]
HIPPOLITO Nay, then I kiss thy° cold lips, and applaud *(Isabella's)*
This thy revenge in death. [*He kisses Isabella.*]
FABRITIO Look, Juno's down too!
What makes she° there? Her pride should keep aloft. *is she doing*
She was wont to scorn the earth in other shows;° *masques*
Methinks her peacocks' feathers are much pulled.
[*Pages dressed as*] *Cupids, shoot* [*at Hippolito*].
HIPPOLITO Oh, death runs through my blood, in a wild flame too!
Plague of° those Cupids! Some° lay hold on 'em; *on / Someone*
Let 'em not scape! They have spoiled° me; the shaft's deadly. *killed*
DUKE I have lost myself in this quite.° *I'm utterly bewildered*
HIPPOLITO My great lords, we are all confounded.
DUKE How?
HIPPOLITO [*pointing to Isabella's body*] Dead; and I worse.° *i.e., damned*
FABRITIO Dead? My girl dead? I hope
My sister Juno has not served me so.[1]
HIPPOLITO Lust and forgetfulness° has been amongst us, *moral obtuseness*
And we are brought to nothing. Some blest charity
Lend me the speeding° pity of his sword *helping; dispatching*
To quench this fire in blood! Leantio's death
Has brought all this upon us—now I taste it—
And made us lay plots to confound° each other. *destroy*
The event° so proves it, and man's understanding *outcome*
Is riper at his fall than all his lifetime.
She° in a madness for her lover's death *(Livia)*
Revealed a fearful lust in our near bloods,

8. The Ward, evidently not on stage, has sprung the trapdoor ineptly, perhaps misled by some loud stamping onstage, doing in his guardian rather than Hippolito, as planned.

9. Done for, dispatched.

1. Fabritio's sister, Livia, playing the part of Juno, has killed Fabritio's daughter.

For which I am punished dreadfully and unlooked for;° *unexpectedly*
Proved° her own ruin too. Vengeance met vengeance, *It proved to be*
Like a set match,[2] as if the plagues of sin
Had been agreed to meet here all together.
But how her fawning partner° fell I reach° not, *(Guardiano) / understand*
Unless caught by some springe° of his own setting; *trap*
For, on my pain,[3] he never dreamed of dying.
The plot was all his own, and he had cunning
Enough to save himself; but 'tis the property° *quality, tendency*
Of guilty deeds to draw your wise men downward.
Therefore the wonder ceases. Oh, this torment!

DUKE [*calling*] Our guard below there!

Enter [on the main stage] a Lord with a guard.

LORD My lord?

HIPPOLITO [*to himself*] Run and meet death, then,
And cut off time and pain.
[*He runs on a guard's halberd, and dies.*]

LORD Behold, my lord,
He's run his breast upon a weapon's point.

DUKE Upon the first night of our nuptial honors,
Destruction plays her triumph,° and great mischiefs *spectacle*
Mask° in expected pleasures. 'Tis prodigious! *Disguise selves; masque*
They're things most fearfully ominous; I like 'em not.
[*To guard*] Remove these ruined bodies from our eyes.

BIANCA [*aside*] Not yet? No change? When falls he° to the earth?[4] *(the Cardinal)*

LORD [*presenting a paper*] Please but Your Excellence to peruse that paper,
Which is a brief confession from the heart
Of him that fell first,° ere his soul departed; *Of Guardiano*
And there the darkness of these deeds speaks plainly.
'Tis the full scope, the manner, and intent.
His ward, that ignorantly let him down,° *fall into the trap*
Fear put to present flight° at the voice of him. *made the ward flee quickly*

BIANCA [*aside*] Nor yet?

DUKE [*to the Cardinal*] Read, read; for I am lost in sight and strength. [*He falls.*]

CARDINAL My noble brother!

BIANCA Oh, the curse of wretchedness!
My deadly hand is fallen upon my lord.[5]
Destruction take me to thee! Give me way;° *Don't hinder me*
The pains and plagues of a lost soul upon him
That hinders me a moment!

DUKE My heart swells bigger yet. Help here, break't ope!° *tear open my clothes*
My breast flies open next. [*He dies.*]

BIANCA Oh, with the poison
That was prepared for thee, thee, Cardinal!
'Twas meant for thee.

CARDINAL Poor prince!

BIANCA Accursèd error!

2. As if by an agreement (such as a setup for a highway robbery).
3. On my dying pains. (An oath.)
4. Bianca poisoned a cup intended for the Cardinal, but it was handed by mistake to the Duke; see 58.1.
5. I.e., I have killed the Duke by mistake.

[*To the Duke*] Give me thy last breath, thou infected bosom,
And wrap two spirits in one poisoned vapor.
[*She kisses the dead Duke.*]
Thus, thus reward thy murderer, and turn death
Into a parting kiss. My soul stands ready at my lips,
E'en vexed to stay one minute after thee.

CARDINAL The greatest sorrow and astonishment
That ever struck the general peace of Florence
Dwells in this hour.

BIANCA So, my desires are satisfied.
I feel death's power within me.
Thou hast prevailed in something, cursèd poison,
Though thy chief force was spent in my lord's bosom;
But my deformity in spirit's more foul;
A blemished face best fits a leprous soul.[6]
What make I° here? These are all strangers to me, *am I doing*
Not known but by their malice, now thou'rt° gone; *that you (the Duke) are*
Nor do I seek their pities.
[*She drinks from the poisoned cup.*]

CARDINAL Oh, restrain
Her ignorant willful hand!

BIANCA Now do; 'tis done.
Leantio, now I feel the breach of marriage
At my heartbreaking. Oh, the deadly snares
That women set for women, without pity
Either to soul or honor! Learn by me
To know your foes. In this belief I die:
Like our own sex, we have no enemy,[7]
No enemy!

LORD See, my lord,
What shift° she's made to be her own destruction! *stratagem*

BIANCA Pride, greatness, honors, beauty, youth, ambition,
You must all down together; there's no help for't.
Yet this my gladness is, that I remove,° *die*
Tasting the same death in a cup of love. [*She dies.*]

CARDINAL Sin, what thou art these ruins show too piteously.
Two kings on one throne cannot sit together,
But one must needs down, for his title's wrong;
So where lust reigns, that prince cannot reign long. *Exeunt.*

FINIS.

6. The poison is eating into Bianca's face.
7. We women have no enemy that can compare with other women.

TEXTUAL NOTES

Women Beware Women was not entered in the Stationers' Register until September 9, 1653. An octavo edition appeared in 1657 entitled *Two New Plays . . . Written by Thomas Middleton*; it included *More Dissemblers Besides Women.* The text appears to have been printed from a legible and orderly manuscript. The present edition is based on that octavo. Substantive departures from it are noted here, using the following abbreviations:

O: Octavo (London: Humphrey Moseley, 1657)
ed.: A modern editor's emendation

The Persons in the Play 9, 13 [and elsewhere] **Bianca** [ed.] *Brancha* [O] **20 A SERVANT** [ed.] Servants [O]

1.1.57 [and elsewhere] **to blame** [ed.] too blame [O] **150 Will't** [ed.] Wilt [O]

1.2.21 [and elsewhere] **e'en** [O: ev'n] **40 Tied** [O: Tide] **65** [and elsewhere] **ne'er** [O: nev'r] **150.1** [placement, ed.; after 146 in O] **158 thy** [ed.] that [O] **229 Then** [O] Than [some eds.]

1.3.17 quay [O: Key] **22 Then** [ed.] the [O] **58 SD** ***Exit*** [placement, ed.; after 57 in O]

2.1.17 summed [ed.] sow'd [O] **49 I'd** [ed.] I'll [O] **54 she's** [O: sh'has] **57 SD** [placement, ed.; after 57 in O] **73 SD** [placement, ed.; after "marriage towards?" in 75 in O] **109 fruitfulness** [ed.] fruit-/ness [O] **139 merest** [O: meer'st] **180 SD** ***Enter Hippolito*** [placement, ed.; after 180.1 in O] **205 does't** [ed.] do'st [O]

2.2.21 strangely [O: strangly] **42.1** [placement, ed.; after 43 in O] **79.1** [and elsewhere] ***shuttlecock*** [ed.] *Shittlecock* [O] **89 asked** [ed.] ask [O] **91** [and elsewhere] **guardianer** [O: Guardiner *or* Gardiner] **104 Her** [ed.] Heir [O] **110 plumped** [ed.] plump [O] **136.1** [placement, ed.; after "returned" in 137 in O] **154 merrily** [ed.] meerly [O] **159 account** [O: accompt] **246 you are** [ed.] y'are [O] **318 SD** [in right-hand margin in O] **385 wise** [ed.] wife [O] **427 why** [ed.] who [O] **464 may't** [ed.] may [O] **467 Will't** [ed.] Wilt [O] **472 SD** ***Exeunt*** [ed.; after 471 in O]

3.1.12 or [ed.] of [O] **20 pinned** [O: pin'd] **39 good** [ed.] gook [O] **77 pewter** [ed.] Pew-terer [O]

3.2 [scene numbering, ed.; not in O] **5 scent** [O: sent] **30 this's** [ed.] this? [O] **65 'tis** [ed.] 'till [O] **95 please** [ed.] pleas'd [O] **124.1** [placement, ed.; after "I fear me" in 125 in O] **127 He's** [ed.] Has [O] **178 whither** [O: whether]

3.3 [scene numbering, ed.; "Scaen. 2." in O] **22 SD** [in right-hand margin opposite 20 in O] **43, 47 Rouen** [O: *Rouans*] **44 Supplied** [ed.] Suppli' [O] **83 you're** [ed.] your [O] **131 of man** [ed.] of a man [O] **146 ISABELLA** [ed.; not in O] **146–55** [side by side with 156–59 in O] **182 whoso** [ed.] who's [O] **206.1–3** [in right-hand margin opposite 207–9 in O] **221 Well** [ed.] We'll [O] **227 Your . . . your** [ed.] You . . . you [O] **236.1–2** [placement, ed.; printed opposite 235–37 in O] **249.1–2** [ed.] *Exe. all but* Leantio *and* Livia; *Cornets flourish* [O] **280 to** [ed.] too, [O] **286 vile** [O: vilde] **324 for** [ed.; not in O] **325 corse** [O: course]

3.4 [scene numbering, ed.; "Scaen 3." in O] **45 which** [ed.; not in O] **115 the** [ed.] he [O] **126 coarse** [O: course]

4.1.22.1 ***Exeunt*** [ed.] *Exit* [O] **87 know** [ed.] knew [O] **110 he's** [O: has] **127 SD** [placement, ed.; opposite 125 in O] **130.1** [placement, ed.; after "my lord" in 130 in O] **134 honor's** [ed.] honor [O] **140.1** [placement, ed.; after "welcome" in 141 in O] **179.1** [placement, ed.; after "welcome" in 180 in O] **202 low** [ed.] love [O] **266.1** [placement, ed.; after "brother" in 266 in O]

4.2.20 SD [ed.] *Enter* Leantio, *and a Page* [O] **23 LEANTIO** [placement, ed.; at the head of 24 in O] **41 own** [ed.; not in O] **119 chorister** [O: Querister] **183 this's** [ed.] thus [O] **191 He's** [O: Has] **225.1** ***Exeunt*** [ed.] *Exit* [O] **231 Exit** [ed.] *Exeunt* [O]

4.3.72 ***Exit*** [ed.] *Exeunt* [O]

5.2.0.1 ***Flourish*** [placement, ed.; preceding the scene indicator in O] **29 we poor souls** [ed.] we, poor soul, [O] **64 parting take** [ed.] part [O] **73 NYMPHS** [ed.; not in O] **89 one** [ed.] me [O] **97.1** ***Livia . . . Juno*** [placement, ed.; in right margin opposite 98 in O] **102 be long** [ed.] belong [O] **114 savor** [ed.] favor [O] **139.1** [placement, ed.; in right margin opposite 136–37 in O] **159 plagues** [ed.] plague [O] **172 plays** [ed.] play [O]

The Changeling

Thomas Middleton and William Rowley's *The Changeling* enacts the fall of its central characters with startling immediacy and moral power. It focuses relentlessly on hidden changes in the mental states and moral situations of particular characters and on how these changes undermine the social order. Although for most readers the word "changeling" has a single meaning—that of a child switched (traditionally by fairies) at birth for another, as in *A Midsummer Night's Dream*—this is the meaning that is least helpful in explaining the title of Middleton and Rowley's play. More pertinent are the following senses, also current in 1622, when *The Changeling* first appeared: a person who is given to change, a fickle or inconstant person; a person or thing put in exchange for another, surreptitiously or otherwise; a half-witted person, an idiot or imbecile. Antonio, listed as "the changeling" in the Dramatis Personae when the play was first published in 1653, surreptitiously impersonates an idiot and moves in and out of this assumed role throughout the play; he is thus a changeling in all three of these senses. Beatrice, hastily shifting her preference in act 1 from Alonzo to Alsemero, is a changeling in the first sense. And because the play deals repeatedly in deceptive substitutions, many characters are changelings in the second sense, notably Beatrice's maid Diaphanta, who substitutes for Beatrice in the marriage bed; De Flores, who substitutes for Alsemero as Beatrice's first sexual partner; Franciscus, who smuggles himself into the madhouse as a lunatic; and Alsemero, who substitutes for Alonzo as Beatrice's bridegroom.

The play also uses the idea of change to draw its parts together. It closes with a litany of the changes brought about since "that moon / . . . last changed on us" (5.3.206–7): Alsemero, standing over the bodies of De Flores and Beatrice, comments, "Here's beauty changed / To ugly whoredom; here, servant obedience / To a master sin, imperious murder" (5.3.207–9). He continues by noting that he himself "changed [exchanged] embraces / With wantonness" in having sex with Diaphanta, thinking she was Beatrice, and he tells Tomazo, who has lost his brother Alonzo, "Your change is come too" (5.3.210–11, 212). Then Antonio and Franciscus both say, "I was changed" (5.3.214, 218); Isabella says to Alibius, "Your change is still behind" (5.3.220); and Alibius promises that he "will change now / Into a better husband" (5.3.224–25). This final change, the reclamation of a marriage, makes sense, since all the changes in the play involve marriage and sexual choices.

Renaissance culture, by making much of female virginity, by making marriage settlements the most important property transactions that wealthy families undertook, and by recognizing in literature and moral theory that marriage frequently brought on a battle of wills between parents anxious to secure obedience and children eager to make their own choices, ensured that marriage, especially the first marriage of a well-born daughter, was fraught with the kind of change that had dramatic power. For women and (at least theoretically) for men as well, marriage was the only socially sanctioned path along which sexual desire could find fulfillment. For that reason,

Introduction by Lars Engle; glosses, footnotes, and textual notes by David Bevington and checked by Lars Engle; text edited by David Bevington and checked by Lars Engle and Eric Rasmussen.

female sexuality could rarely be framed in a positive light except through marriage (and was not always positively regarded even in that context). Because divorce was difficult to obtain, marriage normally lasted till death, and even formal betrothal was broken only with difficulty. Marriage was, then, an institution haunted by the problem that though law and religion declared it irrevocable and men were often able to arrange it without consulting women, women's inner compliance was still required to make it real. Thus marriages, especially forced marriages, unorthodox marriages, and marriages across boundaries of race, religion, class, or nationality, had huge dramatic potential, tragically fulfilled in such plays as William Shakespeare's *Othello*, John Webster's *The Duchess of Malfi*, and Thomas Middleton's *Women Beware Women*, as well as *The Changeling*. In each of these plays, a woman's insistence that marriage bring her emotional and sexual fulfillment creates a situation in which the woman is destroyed, though in the first two of these plays the woman is entirely guiltless, and in the third she is only slightly less innocent.

In *The Changeling*, by contrast, Beatrice's pursuit of her desires leads her to conceive and initiate a series of crimes that eventually destroys her. It also leads her to a very different introduction to sexual life from the one she wants and expects: she is obliged to sleep with a man she loathes, her father's servant De Flores. Both Beatrice and De Flores fall, and fall without hesitation, in order to gratify impulses that are, in the first instance, sexual, though they also express a more general desire for independence in daughters and servants under the control of fathers and masters.

With one plot set mostly in a fortified castle and the other in a private asylum in which mentally retarded and insane people are confined, *The Changeling* richly represents institutions of social control run by fathers, husbands, and masters in order to prevent or contain change. On the whole, nevertheless, the play shows how such institutions fail despite the anxious care of the men who run them. As Beatrice's father, Vermandero, says when the actions of Beatrice and De Flores come to light, "An host of enemies entered my citadel / Could not amaze like this" (5.3.156–57). Similarly, the medicine that Alsemero thinks will allow him to certify the chastity of his bride proves fallible: when he gives it to her, Beatrice is able to fake the yawning, sneezing, and laughter that mark a virgin's reaction to his potion, and she uses Alsemero's system to check the virginity of her maid Diaphanta, whom she then substitutes for herself on her marriage night. Alibius' strategy of confining his young wife, Isabella, to shield her from temptation also fails to the extent that two young men, masquerading as an idiot and a lunatic, are able to gain admission to his asylum; though they do not seduce Alibius' wife, it is her virtue, not his vigilance, that thwarts them. Thus the castle, guarding a boundary between "native" and "strangers" (1.1.164–69); the medicine cabinet, with its potions to police the boundary between female unchastity and female purity; and the asylum, caging the mentally deficient or unhealthy to protect or entertain everyone else, all prove fallible.

Where institutions and devices fail, ordinary human observation works quite well in detecting the central problems of the play, though it does not avert them. Tomazo de Piracquo can see from Beatrice's expression that she does not love his brother Alonzo and urges him to delay the wedding. Jasperino warns Alsemero that Beatrice seems too intimate with De Flores and convinces him to test her virginity. And Jasperino leads Alsemero to "The prospect from the garden" (5.3.2) that finally convinces Alsemero of his new wife's unfaithfulness and prompts him to force her confession. No one in the play has a science to prevent transgression, no one save De Flores can credit its human depths and powers, but even De Flores cannot conceal it for long.

The central scenes of transgression involving Beatrice and De Flores have the special energy that comes when playwrights find their way through layers of convention—in this case, conventions of courtship and of the representation of sexual attraction—to get at what they take to be raw truths. The two characters are vital people with unusually strong desires, few scruples, and the willingness to express their impulses clearly and to act promptly and boldly on them. Their contest to make use of each other and De Flores' victory in this contest set Beatrice on a harrowing journey of moral and social discovery.

Though the play registers the structures of gender and class that mark Beatrice as a daughter caught in a marriage transaction determined by men and De Flores as a servant dependent on the will of others, it focuses more closely on the idiosyncratic emotions and local changes in circumstance that propel them to mutual dependence in crime and sweep away the social barriers between them. Beatrice, made intensely uncomfortable by De Flores but too naive to recognize that what bothers her is his ugly version of the sexual interest she has been pleased to arouse in Alsemero, plans to "get him quite discarded" during "The next good mood I find my father in" (2.1.93–94). She does not connect De Flores with her problems of sexual choice except as a distraction: "Oh, I was / Lost in this small disturbance, and forgot / Affliction's fiercer torrent" (2.1.94–96). Yet when Alsemero proposes to dispose of his rival Alonzo by challenging him to a duel, Beatrice makes the connection without conscious design through an association of words. Alsemero, she says, is too beloved and too beautiful to face the physical, legal, and moral risks of a sword fight: "Blood-guiltiness becomes a fouler visage— / [*Aside*] And now I think on one!" (2.2.40–41). It is, of course, De Flores' foul visage she has thought of, and she resolves to employ him to murder Alonzo and pay him to flee. Having done so, she comments in another aside that she will "rid myself / Of two inveterate loathings at one time, / Piracquo and his dog-face" (2.2.148–50). Throughout, the asides contrast the amoral brutality of her inner thoughts with the virtuous though ardent femininity she presents to Alsemero.

This engraving of about 1662, later adapted to serve as frontispiece to Francis Kirkman's *The Wits, or Sport upon Sport* (a collection of short comedies privately acted during the Puritan ban of theater from 1642 to 1660; published in 1672), depicts onstage a changeling and a simpleton along with Falstaff and Mistress Quickly. Note the curtained "discovery" space, the candelabras for lighting the stage, and the spectators in the gallery above.

Beatrice's plan undermines the social barriers that separate and protect her from De Flores: it is socially rash as well as morally wrong. She acts on it immediately. We know much better than she, however, that De Flores is a dangerous man for her to use, because through a similar set of extraordinarily effective asides, we know how he has been thinking about her. Early on, when Beatrice rails at him, De Flores comments that this abuse may eventually help him enjoy her: "I ha' seen / Women have chid themselves abed to men" (2.1.88–89). Fully conscious of his own unattractiveness, he nevertheless remains sexually self-confident, aware that "Some women are odd feeders"

(2.2.157). In keeping with the play's theme of change, he emphasizes the mutable, transformable value of his own ugliness. And like Beatrice, De Flores reveals a hidden self through his asides, a self whose obsessive passion and cynical realism contrast markedly with the cheerful readiness to serve that "Honest De Flores" (4.2.37) presents in dialogue with most other characters. *The Changeling*'s powerful depiction of public and private selves suggests that the outwardly polite behavior of both servants and women may actually mask violent and insubordinate desires for change.

Decorousness clashes again with roughness in the male characters' attitudes toward female sexuality. De Flores' frank assessment of female sexual appetites contrasts with Alsemero's more conventional idealization of Beatrice; it also contrasts with the male sexual insecurities suggested by Alsemero's pregnancy and virginity tests. Indeed, Beatrice's unfolding relationship with De Flores parodies the semi-decorous love she professes to Alsemero. She flirts with Alsemero and gains his devotion; when she decides to employ De Flores, she flirts with him as well, alleging that his complexion has improved and hinting that she needs him for "service" (2.2.93), a word with sexual implications. De Flores eagerly plays along: "It's a service that I kneel for to you"; "How sweet it were to me to be employed / In any act of yours" (2.2.119, 123–24). While Beatrice is delighted when Alsemero expresses sexual interest by embracing and kissing her in 2.2, she naively fails to hear De Flores' sexual double meanings, because she cannot imagine that a servant could have such designs on her.[1] Her relation to De Flores changes at her instigation but in ways she does not see, because despite her criminal enterprise she remains bound by social conventions. When De Flores returns from the murder of Alonzo, bearing Alonzo's finger with Beatrice's ring on it as a token of the deed, he assaults those conventions directly. De Flores demands her virginity, commenting that in their shared blood guilt they "should stick together" (3.4.84)—a nice example of how his speech combines simplicity and suggestiveness. She cannot imagine that he would be "so wicked" as "To make [Alonzo's] death the murderer of my honor" (3.4.120, 122). "Honor," for her, consists in her virginity and her gentility, "the distance that creation / Set 'twixt thy [De Flores'] blood and mine" (3.4.130–31). De Flores responds with shattering moral force:

> Look but into your conscience; read me there;
> 'Tis a true book. You'll find me there your equal.
> Push, fly not to your birth, but settle you
> In what the act has made you; you're no more now.
> You must forget your parentage to me.
> You're the deed's creature; by that name
> You lost your first condition. (3.4.132–38)

De Flores' "You're the deed's creature" emphasizes the moral priority of Beatrice's immediate context—the context she has created by her actions—over the social matrix in which she has grown up. Part of the play's power comes from its enactment of such a change—from the comforts of the habitual (Beatrice's sense of her own family, beauty, and purity) to the terrifying dominance of the immediate (here localized in De Flores and his sexual demand). In a hierarchical culture ruled by elaborate rituals of deference, the refusal of De Flores to be a tool and his insistence on Beatrice's maidenhead as a guarantee of his future cooperation—his aspiration to replace her "parentage" by their shared act—touch on explosive social material.[2] Beatrice's "first

1. See Christopher Ricks, "The Moral and Poetic Structure of *The Changeling*," *Essays in Criticism* 10, no. 3 (1960): 302, for a persuasive discussion of "Beatrice's tragic failure to see puns"; the essay offers an excellent account of sexual double meanings in the play.

2. It also had a topical point. By 1622, it was clear that Frances Carr, née Howard, married first to the Earl of Essex and then to Robert Carr, the Earl of Somerset, was not going to be executed for the crime of poisoning Sir Thomas Overbury in reprisal for his having opposed her projected marriage to Carr. Her

condition"—innocence and high social rank—has been lost, and De Flores' line likens her fall from the protections of rank to mankind's fall into sin. Beatrice returns to this allusion, focusing on Eve's relationship with the serpent in the Garden of Eden; with horror, she accepts that she must sleep with him to preserve her life: "Was my creation in the womb so curst / It must engender with a viper first?" (3.4.165–66). De Flores has used shared sin to level social barriers. The process may be seen as primarily moral or primarily social, though it must to some degree be both.

The explanation of these scenes that has until recently dominated critical discussion of them claims that there is a permanent moral lesson in Beatrice's fall, that of an "unmoral nature, suddenly trapped in the inexorable toils of morality—of morality not made by man but by Nature—and forced to take the consequences of an act which it had planned lightheartedly."[3] While this comment of T. S. Eliot's accounts well for the way Beatrice's world comes crashing in on her, it oddly casts De Flores as an instrument of a natural moral order. De Flores uses the language of conscience to overcome Beatrice, but he does so out of an amoral desire to have sex with her. While he "falls," in that he had been a faithful servant and becomes a murderer, adulterer, and betrayer of his master's trust, he does not appear to struggle with any moral inhibitions. Later in the play, he is startled but not substantially altered or made repentant by a direct encounter with the ghost of the man he murdered. In contrast to *Macbeth*, which influenced these scenes, *The Changeling* shows a morally insightful villain who masters his own conscience and is largely unmoved by supernatural solicitations.

Thus when De Flores calls Beatrice "the deed's creature," we can either, with Eliot, see the comment as her introduction to a moral order that forbids murder, or, with De Flores, see it as a revelation of the fragility of the social privilege that protected her from his sexual designs. The two views are not incompatible, but they move in different interpretive directions. Interpreters of a religious or metaphysical bent, who view morality as a foundational structure underlying social change, take this moment as one in which a shallow character suddenly collides with moral bedrock. Interpreters of a skeptical or historicizing bent, who view morality as a deep and strong but not immutable social structure, and as only one social structure among others, see this moment as exploring the vulnerability and artificiality of a social order that tries to contain human violence and sexuality through law, morality, and marriage.

Beatrice, having lost her comfortable place in this social order, expresses her situation in moral terms: "Murder, I see, is followed by more sins" (3.4.164). As in *Macbeth*, it is. Beatrice uses Diaphanta to deceive her husband, then connives with De Flores to murder Diaphanta when Diaphanta overstays her appointed time in Alsemero's bed. Beatrice seems to be growing more and more dependent on De Flores, that "wondrous necessary man" (5.1.93), even as she remains pathetically committed to Alsemero, with whom, despite all her criminal efforts, she never gets to have sex.

---

servants, who had actually carried out the poisoning that she confessed to having ordered, were hanged, while she and Carr were convicted but then pardoned. She was released from the Tower in 1622 and permitted to live in the country. She had first attained notoriety by suing successfully to annul her marriage to the Earl of Essex, claiming nonconsummation due to his impotence, and appearing veiled in court to have her virginity investigated by "the forewoman of a female jury," as Diaphanta puts it in a clear allusion to the case (4.1.102). It was widely believed that Frances Howard sent a substitute to the courtroom, since she had already had sex with the royal favorite Robert Carr, the man she was divorcing Essex to marry. In showing a woman of high birth forced to endure the same fate as her servant, Middleton and Rowley in one way describe the fate of Frances Howard (whose trial followed the conviction and execution of her servant accomplices). They also, however, may reprove by contrast the ways in which Frances Howard remained able to rely on her "first condition" to protect her from execution. Moreover, since Middleton contributed a masque, now lost, to the celebration of Frances Howard's marriage to Robert Carr in 1613, the allusions to Howard in *The Changeling* may demystify a set of marital, sexual, and criminal relations that Middleton himself, along with other major dramatists, had helped to mystify nine years earlier. See David Lindley, *The Trials of Frances Howard: Fact and Fiction at the Court of King James* (London: Routledge, 1993), for an account of her life and some discussion of *The Changeling* and of Middleton's lost masque.

3. T. S. Eliot, "Thomas Middleton," in *Selected Essays* (New York: Harcourt Brace Jovanovich, 1950), p. 142.

As De Flores says to Beatrice's husband and father in the shattering final scene, having stabbed Beatrice and preparing to stab himself,

> her honor's prize
> . . . .
> . . . was so sweet to me
> That I have drunk up all, left none behind
> For any man to pledge me. (5.3.177–81)

Thus De Flores dies making clear that he has not only gratified a sexual obsession but also triumphed over male rivals.

De Flores' final speech was, we believe, written by Rowley, not Middleton. Scholars have been able with considerable confidence to divide the scenes between the two authors on the basis of stylistic affinities with their other writings and have determined that Rowley set up and finished both plots and wrote the entire madhouse plot, while Middleton wrote the heart of the tragic plot involving Beatrice and De Flores.[4] The intricate relations between the two plots suggest, however, careful planning and collaboration. This matters, both because *The Changeling* often serves as evidence in a case for Middleton as a great author (but almost never as evidence for greatness in Rowley) and because collaborative authorship is such an important and under-discussed feature of Renaissance drama.

The Changeling allows us to observe a partnership in action. Middleton wrote both the scene in which Beatrice solicits the aid of De Flores and the scene in which De Flores demands her maidenhead as payment; but Rowley's writing in the first act anticipates and thus enables some of the most distinctive characteristics of these extraordinary scenes, such as the use of extended asides for psychological depth (e.g., Beatrice and Jasperino at 1.1.83–92, De Flores at 1.1.100–107, Alsemero at 1.1.204–5 and 213) and the complex, demystified understanding De Flores has of the compulsive nature of his attraction to Beatrice and her antipathy to him. Rowley has De Flores remark, as he fondles a glove Beatrice discarded because he touched it, "I know she had rather wear my pelt tanned / In a pair of dancing pumps than I should thrust my fingers / Into her sockets here" (1.1.241–43). Rowley thus prefigures the sexual satisfaction De Flores will obtain from her attempt to make use of him and then cast him off as she might a soiled glove. Rowley also contributed the sequence at the play's end in which Beatrice, confined in Alsemero's chamber with De Flores after the revelation of her guilt, cries out, "Oh! Oh! Oh!" either at being stabbed or in sexual climax (5.3.148–49). The moment brings to culmination the extensive nonlinguistic noise-making in both the tragic plot and the madhouse plot: compare Alonzo's "Oh! Oh! Oh!" when De Flores runs him through from behind (3.2.18), Antonio's sad "Oh!" (1.2.143) and repeated happy "He, he" (1.2.101, 3.3.102, etc.), Diaphanta's "Ha, ha, ha!" during the virginity test (4.1.112, 115), and the bird and animal cries of the madmen (3.3.197–99). Rowley, in writing the final scene, thus tied up a theme of both plots: the fragility of the distinction between human and animal. The consistent focus by both authors on human changefulness suggests not only collaboration but also mutual inspiration.

In larger ways, the madhouse plot provides both an obvious and a subtle foil to the tragic plot. Isabella retains her chastity despite being ill-treated by her husband and courted by handsome young men. She points out that in their unsanctioned love for her, Antonio and Franciscus act like the fool and the madman they impersonate. Her wisdom and self-control thus counterpoise Beatrice's impetuous criminal folly. At the same time, her tactics resemble Beatrice's, and through her the play shows subtly that subjected women may need to turn to crime in order to get what they want, even when what they want is to remain virtuous. In her weak position—in many productions she

4. For a precise account of the division, see N. W. Bawcutt, ed., *The Changeling* (Manchester: Manchester University Press, 1998), pp. 2–3.

is literally caged by Lollio, the servant who also pursues her sexually—Isabella makes threats that resemble the crimes Beatrice actually carries out, telling Lollio that if he continues to harass her, she will bribe Antonio with sex to cut Lollio's throat. To protect her, Lollio goads Antonio and Franciscus into planning to attack one another during the abortive dance of fools and madmen scheduled for the end of Beatrice and Alsemero's wedding celebration. Only by threatening violence, and only by driving Lollio to exploit the male rivalry that in the tragic plot proves so deadly, can Isabella remain chaste.

More broadly yet, the madhouse plot provides a disturbing metatheatrical parallel with *The Changeling* itself. In Renaissance culture generally, people enjoyed viewing madmen and fools, frequently in the sort of event that Alibius has contracted to provide for Vermandero, where a group of mad dancers will perform an antimasque symbolizing disorder to set off the supposed order represented by marriage. Isabella, contrastingly, finds madness "too full of pity / To be laughed at" (3.3.44–45). Her attitude, idiosyncratic at the time, has become universal today, so that the broad comedy of the madhouse scenes may be offensive to a modern audience. One may deal with this cultural shift by viewing the madhouse plot as a dark meditation on confinement, cruelty, and the enforcement of norms. Yet in doing so we lose sight of another important though subtle aspect of the play. When Jasperino tells Diaphanta he is a "mad wag," she replies, "we have a doctor in the city that undertakes the cure of such" (1.1.137, 139–40). Alibius runs a school for fools and madmen in his madhouse, in which Lollio alleges that he will help the apparent fool Antonio move toward normality, possibly to the extent that he will be able to marry. And though the madhouse is a profit-making enterprise that confines its mentally ill and retarded inmates with brutality and exhibits them with cynical opportunism, in Lollio's affectionate treatment of Antonio we can also see some attempt to educate or rehabilitate. Alibius may thus to some degree deserve Diaphanta's description of him as a man who aims to return his inmates to normal social life, though this purpose seems part of a more general desire for gain. When Isabella describes the noises made by the madmen to Antonio, she says they "act their fantasies in any shapes / Suiting their present thoughts" (3.3.194–95). "Sometimes," she adds, "they imitate the beasts and birds, / Singing, or howling, braying, barking—all / As their wild fancies prompt 'em" (3.3.197–99). In the tragic plot, wild fancies have, as we have seen, prompted animal behavior as well as animal noises. The many artful parallels between the madhouse plot and the tragic plot, and the metatheatrical parallels between the madhouse plot and the play as a whole, thus cut two ways. On one hand, they underline the ubiquity of madness and folly, and on the other they remind us that theater as an institution has often claimed to exhibit human failings in order to treat them. *The Changeling*, like Alibius' institution, provides lucrative entertainment by exhibiting insanity and deficiency. Like the madhouse, *The Changeling* may also do good, but only if we accept as real a hope the play offers as a faint one: though prone to change toward folly and madness, people may also, if suitably schooled, change back.

THOMAS MIDDLETON AND WILLIAM ROWLEY

The Changeling

Dramatis Personae

VERMANDERO, father to Beatrice
TOMAZO de Piracquo, a noble lord
ALONZO de Piracquo, his brother, suitor to Beatrice [and later a ghost]
ALSEMERO, a nobleman, afterwards married to Beatrice
JASPERINO, his friend
ALIBIUS, a jealous doctor
LOLLIO, his man° — *servant*
PEDRO, friend to Antonio
ANTONIO, the changeling
FRANCISCUS, the counterfeit madman
DE FLORES, servant to Vermandero
MADMEN [and fools]
SERVANTS
[Gallants, gentlemen, and gentlewomen in a dumb show]
BEATRICE [Beatrice-Joanna], daughter to Vermandero
DIAPHANTA, her waiting-woman
ISABELLA, wife to Alibius

THE SCENE: Alicante.

1.1

Enter Alsemero.

ALSEMERO 'Twas in the temple where I first beheld her,
And now again the same; what omen yet
Follows of that? None but imaginary.
Why should my hopes or fate be timorous?
The place is holy, so is my intent:
I love her beauties to the holy purpose,° — *with intent to marry*
And that, methinks, admits comparison
With man's first creation, the place blest,
And is his right home back, if he achieve it.[1]

The original 1653 title page reads "*The Changeling*. As it was Acted (with great applause) at the private house in Drury Lane and Salisbury Court. Written by Thomas Middleton and William Rowley, gent[lemen]. Never printed before. London, printed for Humphrey Moseley, and are to be sold at his shop at the sign of the Prince's Arms in St. Paul's Churchyard, 1653."

1.1. Alicante, on Spain's southeast coast. A temple.

1. Marriage can restore man to the Garden of Eden, where humankind was created and given the blessing of matrimony.

The church hath first begun our interview,° *seeing each other*
And that's the place must join us into one,
So there's beginning and perfection too.

Enter Jasperino.

JASPERINO Oh, sir, are you here? Come, the wind's fair with you.° *favorable for leaving*
You're like° to have a swift and pleasant passage. *likely*
ALSEMERO Sure you're deceived, friend; 'tis contrary,
In my best judgment.
JASPERINO What, for Malta?
If you could buy a gale amongst the witches,
They could not serve you such a lucky pennyworth
As comes i'God's name.[2]
ALSEMERO Even now I observed
The temple's vane° to turn full in my face; *weather vane*
I know 'tis against me.
JASPERINO Against you?
Then you know not where you are.
ALSEMERO Not well indeed.
JASPERINO Are you not well, sir?
ALSEMERO Yes, Jasperino,
Unless there be some hidden malady
Within me that I understand not.
JASPERINO And that
I begin to doubt,° sir. I never knew *fear*
Your inclinations to travels at a pause
With any cause to hinder it, till now.
Ashore you were wont to call your servants up
And help to trap° your horses for the speed.° *harness / for haste*
At sea I have seen you weigh the anchor with 'em,
Hoist sails for fear to lose the foremost breath,
Be in continual prayers for fair winds;
And have you changed your orisons?° *prayers*
ALSEMERO No, friend,
I keep the same church, same devotion.
JASPERINO Lover I'm sure you're none; the stoic
Was found in you long ago; your mother° *neither your mother*
Nor best friends, who have set snares of beauty,
Ay, and choice ones too, could never trap you that way.
What might be the cause?
ALSEMERO Lord, how violent
Thou art! I was but meditating of
Somewhat° I heard within the temple. *Something*
JASPERINO Is this violence? 'Tis but idleness
Compared with your haste yesterday.
ALSEMERO I'm all this while a-going, man.

Enter Servants.

JASPERINO Backwards, I think, sir. Look, your servants.
FIRST SERVANT The seamen call. Shall we board° your trunks? *put aboard*
ALSEMERO No, not today.

2. Even the witches (reputed to be able to control the winds) could not give you such a fine bargain as this present wind that comes as a gift of God.

JASPERINO 'Tis the critical° day, — *astrologically crucial*
It seems, and the sign in Aquarius.[3]

SECOND SERVANT [*aside to his fellow*] We must not to sea today. This smoke will bring forth fire.[4]

ALSEMERO Keep all on shore. I do not know the end
(Which needs I must do) of an affair in hand
Ere I can go to sea.

FIRST SERVANT Well, your pleasure.° — *as you wish*

SECOND SERVANT [*aside to his fellow*] Let him e'en take his leisure too. We are safer on land. *Exeunt Servants.*

Enter Beatrice-Joanna, Diaphanta, and Servants.
[*Alsemero greets and kisses Beatrice.*]

JASPERINO [*aside*] How now? The laws of the Medes are changed, sure.[5] Salute° a woman? He kisses too: wonderful! Where learned he this? And does it perfectly too; in my conscience° he ne'er rehearsed it before. Nay, go on; this will be stranger and better news at Valencia than if he had ransomed half Greece from the Turk.[6] — *Greet*; *on my word*

BEATRICE [*to Alsemero*] You are a scholar, sir?

ALSEMERO A weak one, lady.

BEATRICE Which of the sciences° is this love you speak of? — *learned subjects*

ALSEMERO From your tongue I take it to be music.

BEATRICE You are skillful in't, can sing at first sight.° — *sight-read (in love)*

ALSEMERO And I have showed you all my skill at once.
I want° more words to express me further, — *lack*
And must be forced to repetition:
I love you dearly.

BEATRICE Be better advised,° sir. — *Take care*
Our eyes are sentinels unto our judgments,
And should give certain judgment what they see;
But they are rash sometimes, and tell us wonders
Of common things which, when our judgments find,
They can then check° the eyes and call them blind. — *correct, rebuke*

ALSEMERO But I am further,° lady; yesterday — *further along*
Was mine eyes' employment, and hither now
They brought my judgment, where are both agreed.
Both houses[7] then consenting, 'tis agreed;
Only there wants the confirmation
By the hand royal.[8] That's your part, lady.

BEATRICE Oh, there's one above me,° sir. [*Aside*] For five — *(my father; God)*
days past° — *(since the engagement)*
To be recalled! Sure, mine eyes were mistaken;
This was the man was meant° me. That he should come — *that was meant for*
So near his time, and miss it!

JASPERINO [*aside*] We might have come by the carriers° from Valencia, I see, and saved all our sea provision; we are at farthest,° sure. Methinks I should do something too; — *land transport*; *far from our goal*
I meant to be a venturer in this voyage.

3. A zodiacal constellation, the Water Bearer—appropriate to sea voyaging.
4. Where there's smoke, there's fire; i.e., more consequences are in store.
5. A wonder! (According to Daniel 6.8, the law of the Medes and Persians "altereth not.")
6. In the early seventeenth century, Greece was under Turkish rule.
7. Houses of the brain. (With wordplay on "houses of Parliament.")
8. (1) By your gracious hand; (2) by the King's signature.

Yonder's another vessel;° I'll board her. *(Diaphanta)*
If she be lawful prize,° down goes her topsail.[9] *i.e., unmarried*
[*He approaches Diaphanta; they converse privately.*]

Enter De Flores.

DE FLORES Lady, your father—
BEATRICE Is in health, I hope.
DE FLORES Your eye shall instantly instruct you, lady.
He's coming hitherward.
BEATRICE What needed° then *What need was there for*
Your duteous preface? I had rather
He had come unexpected. You must stall° *forestall, anticipate*
A good presence° with unnecessary blabbing; *A desired arrival*
And how welcome for your part you are,
I'm sure you know.
DE FLORES [*aside*] Will't never mend, this scorn,
One side nor other?° Must I be enjoined *One way or another*
To follow still whilst she flies from me? Well,
Fates do your worst! I'll please myself with sight
Of her at all opportunities,
If but to spite her anger. I know she had
Rather see me dead than living, and yet
She knows no cause for't but a peevish will.
ALSEMERO You seem displeased, lady, on the sudden.
BEATRICE Your pardon, sir. 'Tis my infirmity,
Nor can I other reason render you
Than his or hers,° of some particular thing *one person or another's*
They must abandon as a deadly poison,
Which to a thousand other tastes were° wholesome; *would be*
Such to mine eyes is that same fellow there,
The same that report speaks of the basilisk.[1]
ALSEMERO This is a frequent frailty in our nature.
There's scarce a man amongst a thousand found
But hath his imperfection:° one distastes *idiosyncrasy*
The scent of roses, which to infinites° *i.e., most people*
Most pleasing is and odoriferous;
One° oil, the enemy° of poison; *One dislikes / antidote*
Another wine, the cheerer of the heart
And lively refresher of the countenance.
Indeed this fault (if so it be) is general;
There's scarce a thing but is both loved and loathed.
Myself, I must confess, have the same frailty.
BEATRICE And what may be your poison, sir? I am bold with you.
ALSEMERO What might be your desire, perhaps: a cherry.[2]
BEATRICE I am no enemy to any creature
My memory has° but yon gentleman. *That I can think of*
[*She indicates De Flores.*]
ALSEMERO He does ill to tempt your sight, if he knew it.[3]
BEATRICE He cannot be ignorant of that, sir.
I have not spared to tell him so, and I want

9. Jasperino's amorous "voyage" will lead him to "board" the "vessel" (striking up a conversation with Diaphanta) and oblige her to lower her "topsail" as a token of surrender.
1. A legendary monster, the mere sight of which was fatal.
2. Something perhaps that you like: a cherry.
3. If he is aware of your dislike, he does wrong to offend your sight.

To help myself,[4] since he's a gentleman
In good respect° with my father, and follows° him. *favor / serves*
ALSEMERO He's out of his place, then, now.
[*They talk apart.*]
JASPERINO [*to Diaphanta*] I am a mad wag,° wench. *jolly chap*
DIAPHANTA So methinks; but for your comfort I can tell you, we have a doctor in the city that undertakes the cure of such.[5]
JASPERINO Tush, I know what physic° is best for the state of mine own body. *medicine*
DIAPHANTA 'Tis scarce a well-governed state,[6] I believe.
JASPERINO I could show thee such a thing with an ingredient that we two would compound together,[7] and if it did not tame the maddest blood i'th'town for two hours after, I'll ne'er profess physic° again. *claim medical expertise*
DIAPHANTA A little poppy,° sir, were° good to cause you sleep. *opium / would be*
JASPERINO Poppy! I'll give thee a pop i'th'lips for that first, and begin there. [*He kisses her.*] Poppy is one simple° indeed, and cuckoo what-you-call't[8] another. I'll discover° no more now; another time I'll show thee all.[9] *herbal ingredient* / *reveal*
BEATRICE [*to Alsemero*] My father, sir.

Enter Vermandero and Servants.

VERMANDERO Oh, Joanna, I came to meet thee.
Your devotion's ended?
BEATRICE For this time, sir.
[*Aside*] I shall change my saint,[1] I fear me; I find
A giddy turning in me. [*To her father*] Sir, this while
I am beholding° to this gentleman, *beholden, indebted*
Who left his own way° to keep me company, *intended journey*
And in discourse I find him much desirous
To see your castle. He hath deserved it, sir,
If ye please to grant it.
VERMANDERO [*to Alsemero*] With all my heart, sir.
Yet there's an article between:° I must know *a stipulation first*
Your country. We use not° to give survey *are not accustomed*
Of our chief strengths° to strangers;° our citadels *fortifications / foreigners*
Are placed conspicuous to outward view
On promonts'° tops, but within are secrets. *promontories'*
ALSEMERO A Valencian, sir.
VERMANDERO A Valencian!
That's native, sir. Of what name, I beseech you?
ALSEMERO Alsemero, sir.
VERMANDERO Alsemero; not the son of John de Alsemero?
ALSEMERO The same, sir.
VERMANDERO My best love bids you welcome.
BEATRICE [*aside*] He was wont to call me so,° and then he speaks *i.e., "best love"*

4. I lack authority in my own name to aid myself in this.
5. Diaphanta responds saucily as though "mad" (line 137) should be taken to mean "insane."
6. (1) Healthy condition; (2) orderly and wisely ruled kingdom.
7. Jasperino's pharmacological metaphor of mixing ingredients conveys an erotic proposition.
8. An herbal remedy; hinting at cuckoldry.
9. (1) I'll tell you everything; (2) I'll appear naked to you.
1. I'll shift my object of devotion—in two senses, religious and amorous.

A most unfeignèd truth.[2]
VERMANDERO Oh, sir, I knew your father.
We two were in acquaintance long ago
Before our chins were worth Iulan Down,[3]
And so continued till the stamp of time
Had coined us into silver.[4] Well, he's gone;
A good soldier went with him.
ALSEMERO You went together° in that, sir. *were equals*
VERMANDERO No, by Saint Jaques,[5] I came behind him.
Yet I have done somewhat too. An unhappy° day *unlucky*
Swallowed him at last at Gibraltar
In fight with those rebellious Hollanders;[6]
Was it not so?
ALSEMERO Whose death I had° revenged, *would have*
Or followed him in fate, had not the late league[7]
Prevented° me. *Forestalled*
VERMANDERO Ay, ay, 'twas time to breathe.°— *pause*
Oh, Joanna, I should ha' told thee news:
I saw Piracquo lately.
BEATRICE [*aside*] That's ill news.
VERMANDERO He's hot preparing for this day of triumph;
Thou must be a bride within this sevennight.° *week*
ALSEMERO [*aside*] Ha!
BEATRICE [*to her father*] Nay, good sir, be not so violent;
With speed
I cannot render satisfaction
Unto the dear companion of my soul,
Virginity, whom I thus long have lived with,
And part with it so rude and suddenly.
Can such friends divide, never to meet again,
Without a solemn farewell?
VERMANDERO Tush, tush, there's a toy.° *trifle*
ALSEMERO [*aside*] I must now part, and never meet again
With any joy on earth. [*To Vermandero*] Sir, your pardon;
My affairs call on me.
VERMANDERO How, sir? By no means.
Not changed° so soon, I hope? You must see my castle *changed your mind*
And her best entertainment ere we part;
I shall think myself unkindly used else.
Come, come, let's on. I had good hope your stay
Had been awhile with us in Alicant;
I might have bid you to my daughter's wedding.
ALSEMERO [*aside*] He means to feast me, and poisons me beforehand.—
I should be dearly glad to be there, sir,
Did my occasions suit as I could wish.
BEATRICE I shall be sorry if you be not there
When it is done, sir—but not so suddenly.

change induced by circumstance — not intrinsic
views Alsemero as changeling - ignorant of circumstances

2. My father speaks more truth than he realizes when he says that Alsemero is welcome as a "best love."
3. I.e., Before our chins had grown beards. (Aeneas' son Ascanius was surnamed Iulus [Virgil, *Aeneid*, 1.267]—a name possibly derived from the Greek ἴουλοσ, "first growth of beard.")
4. Had silvered our beards and hair.
5. Saint James the Greater, Spain's patron saint. His shrine is at Santiago de Compostela.
6. A Dutch fleet decisively defeated a larger Spanish fleet at Gibraltar on April 25, 1607.
7. A treaty signed at the Hague on April 9, 1609, arranged a truce between Spain and the Dutch. See previous note.

VERMANDERO I tell you, sir, the gentleman's complete,° *a perfect gentleman*
A courtier and a gallant, enriched
With many fair and noble ornaments.° *qualities, achievements*
I would not change° him for a son-in-law *exchange*
For any he in Spain, the proudest he—
And we have great ones, that you know.° *you know that*
ALSEMERO He's much bound° to you, sir. *obliged*
VERMANDERO He shall be bound° to me as fast as this tie *tied by marriage*
Can hold him; I'll want my will° else. *fail to get my way*
BEATRICE [*aside*] I shall want mine if you do it.
VERMANDERO But come. By the way° I'll tell you more of him. *As we go*
ALSEMERO [*aside*] How shall I dare to venture in his castle,
When he discharges murderers at the gate?[8]
But I must on, for back I cannot go.
BEATRICE [*aside*] Not this serpent° gone yet? *(De Flores)*
[*She drops a glove.*]
VERMANDERO Look, girl, thy glove's fall'n.
Stay, stay.—De Flores, help a little.
[*Exeunt Vermandero, Alsemero, Jasperino, and Servants.*]
DE FLORES [*picking up the glove*] Here, lady.
BEATRICE Mischief° on your officious forwardness! *i.e., A curse*
Who bade you stoop? They touch my hand no more.
There, for t'other's sake I part with this.
[*She removes and throws down her other glove.*]
Take 'em and draw thine own skin off with 'em.[9]
Exeunt [*Beatrice and Diaphanta*].
DE FLORES [*picking up the other glove*] Here's a favor° *love token (ironic)*
come, with a mischief! Now
I know she had rather wear my pelt tanned
In a pair of dancing pumps° than I should thrust my fingers *dancing shoes*
Into her sockets° here. I know she hates me, *glove fingers (bawdy)*
Yet cannot choose but love her.
No matter. If but to vex her, I'll haunt her still;
Though I get nothing else, I'll have my will. *Exit.*

[1.2]

Enter Alibius and Lollio.

ALIBIUS Lollio, I must trust thee with a secret,
But thou must keep it.
LOLLIO I was ever close to a secret,° sir. *closemouthed*
ALIBIUS The diligence that I have found in thee,
The care and industry already past,
Assures me of thy good continuance.
Lollio, I have a wife.
LOLLIO Fie, sir, 'tis too late to keep her secret; she's known to be married all the town and country over.
ALIBIUS Thou goest too fast, my Lollio. That knowledge,
I allow, no man can be barred it;

8. (1) When he employs cannons ("murderers") to defend his castle; (2) when he kills all my hopes at the start.
9. May your own skin come off with these gloves when you remove them. (De Flores suffers from a disfiguring skin ailment.)
1.2. Alibius' insane asylum.

But there is a knowledge° which is nearer, *i.e., carnal knowledge*
Deeper and sweeter, Lollio.

LOLLIO Well, sir, let us handle° that between you and I. *(with sexual suggestion)*

ALIBIUS 'Tis that I go about,° man. Lollio, *That's my point*
My wife is young.

LOLLIO So much the worse to be kept secret, sir.

ALIBIUS Why, now thou meet'st the substance of the point.
I am old, Lollio.

LOLLIO No sir, 'tis I am old Lollio.

ALIBIUS Yet why may not this° concord and sympathize? *(youth and age)*
Old trees and young plants often grow together,
Well enough agreeing.

LOLLIO Ay, sir, but the old trees raise themselves higher and broader than the young plants.[1]

ALIBIUS Shrewd application!° There's the fear, man; *A painful analogy!*
I would wear my ring on my own finger.° *(with sexual suggestion)*
Whilst it is borrowed it is none of mine,
But his that useth it.

LOLLIO You must keep it on still,° then; if it but lie by, one or other will be thrusting into't. *constantly*

ALIBIUS Thou conceiv'st° me, Lollio. Here thy watchful eye *You understand*
Must have employment; I cannot always be at home.

LOLLIO I dare swear you cannot.

ALIBIUS I must look out.° *tend to business*

LOLLIO I know't, you must look out, 'tis every man's case.[2]

ALIBIUS Here, I do say, must thy employment be:
To watch her treadings,[3] and in my absence
Supply my place.[4]

LOLLIO I'll do my best, sir, yet surely I cannot see who you should have cause to be jealous of.

ALIBIUS Thy reason for that, Lollio? 'Tis a comfortable° question. *reassuring*

LOLLIO We have but two sorts of people in the house, and both under° the whip, that's fools and madmen; the one has not wit enough to be knaves, and the other not knavery enough to be fools.[5] *governed by*

ALIBIUS Ay, those are all my patients, Lollio.
I do profess the cure of either sort;
My trade, my living 'tis, I thrive by it.
But here's the care that mixes with my thrift:° *industry*
The daily visitants that come to see
My brainsick patients I would not have
To see my wife. Gallants I do observe
Of quick enticing eyes, rich in habits,° *garments*
Of stature and proportion very comely;
These are most shrewd temptations, Lollio.

LOLLIO They may be easily answered, sir. If they come to see the fools and madmen, you and I may serve the turn,° and let my mistress alone; she's of neither sort. *serve their purposes*

1. Lollio hints at the danger of cuckoldry to an older man; the cuckold's horns will raise his height above that of his young wife.
2. Every man has to watch out not to be cuckolded. ("Case" can mean "vagina.")
3. (1) Her comings and goings; (2) her sexual activity ("tread" is a verb used of bird copulation).
4. Act as my spy. (But with the unconscious sense of "take my place as my wife's lover.")
5. Fools are not clever enough to be rascals, and madmen are too innocent to be guilty of folly.

ALIBIUS 'Tis a good ward.° Indeed, come they to see — *defensive move (fencing)*
Our madmen or our fools. Let 'em see no more
Than what they come for; by that consequent° — *logic*
They must not see her. I'm sure she's no fool.

LOLLIO And I'm sure she's no madman.

ALIBIUS Hold that buckler° fast, Lollio; my trust — *defensive shield*
Is on thee, and I account it firm and strong.
What hour is't, Lollio?

LOLLIO Towards belly hour, sir.

ALIBIUS Dinnertime? Thou mean'st twelve o'clock.

LOLLIO Yes, sir, for every part° has his° hour. We wake at six and look about us, that's eye hour; at seven we should pray, that's knee hour; at eight walk, that's leg hour; at nine gather flowers and pluck a rose,° that's nose hour; at ten we drink, that's mouth hour; at eleven lay about us° for victuals, that's hand hour; at twelve go to dinner, that's belly hour. — *body part / its* — *urinate, defecate* — *bestir ourselves*

ALIBIUS Profoundly, Lollio. It will be long
Ere all thy scholars learn this lesson, and
I did look to have a new one entered.°—Stay, — *admitted*
I think my expectation is come home.° — *has arrived*

Enter Pedro, and Antonio like an idiot.

PEDRO Save you,° sir. My business speaks itself; — *God save you*
This sight takes off the labor of my tongue.

ALIBIUS Ay, ay, sir, 'tis plain enough, you mean him for my patient.

PEDRO And if your pains° prove but commodious,° to give but some little strength to his sick and weak part of nature in him, [*giving money*] these are but patterns° to show you of the whole pieces° that will follow to you, beside the charge° of diet, washing, and other necessaries fully defrayed. — *efforts / beneficial* — *samples* — *large coins / expense*

ALIBIUS Believe it, sir, there shall no care be wanting.° — *lacking*

LOLLIO Sir, an officer in this place may deserve something. The trouble will pass through my hands.

PEDRO 'Tis fit something should come to your hands, then, sir. [*He tips Lollio.*]

LOLLIO Yes, sir, 'tis I must keep him sweet,° and read to him. What is his name? — *clean*

PEDRO His name is Antonio. Marry, we use but half to him, only Tony.

LOLLIO Tony, Tony, 'tis enough, and a very good name for a fool.—What's your name, Tony?

ANTONIO He, he, he! Well, I thank you, cousin, he, he, he!

LOLLIO Good boy. Hold up your head.—He can laugh; I perceive by that he is no beast.° — *(animals don't laugh)*

PEDRO Well, sir,
If you can raise him but to any height,
Any degree of wit,° might he attain — *intelligence*
(As I might say) to creep but on all four
Towards the chair of wit, or walk on crutches,
'Twould add an honor to your worthy pains,
And a great family might pray for you,
To which he should be heir, had he discretion
To claim and guide his own. Assure you, sir,

He is a gentleman.

LOLLIO Nay, there's nobody doubted that; at first sight I knew him for a gentleman. He looks no other yet.

PEDRO Let him have good attendance° and sweet lodging. *be well attended*

LOLLIO As good as my mistress lies in, sir, and, as you allow us time and means, we can raise him to the higher degree of discretion.

PEDRO Nay, there shall no cost want,° sir. *no cost will be spared*

LOLLIO He will hardly be stretched up to the wit of a magnifico.° *magistrate, judge*

PEDRO Oh, no, that's not to be expected; far shorter will be enough.

LOLLIO I'll warrant you I'll make him fit to bear office in five weeks; I'll undertake to wind him up to the wit of constable.[6]

PEDRO If it be lower than that, it might serve turn.° *suffice*

LOLLIO No, fie, to level him with a headborough, beadle,° or watchman were but little better than he is. Constable I'll able him;° if he do come to be a justice afterwards, let him thank the keeper. Or I'll go further with you: say I do bring him up to my own pitch, say I make him as wise as myself? *parish officers* *make him fit for*

PEDRO Why, there I would have it.

LOLLIO Well, go to,° either I'll be as arrant a fool as he, or he shall be as wise as I, and then I think 'twill serve his turn. *(expressing remonstrance)*

PEDRO Nay, I do like thy wit passing° well. *exceedingly*

LOLLIO Yes, you may. Yet if I had not been a fool, I had had more wit than I have too; remember what state you find me in.[7]

PEDRO I will, and so leave you. Your best cares,° I beseech you. *Use your best efforts*

ALIBIUS Take you none with you; leave 'em all with us.[8]

Exit Pedro.

ANTONIO Oh, my cousin's gone. Cousin, cousin! Oh!

LOLLIO Peace, peace, Tony! You must not cry, child; you must be whipped if you do. Your cousin is here still; I am your cousin, Tony.

ANTONIO He, he! Then I'll not cry, if thou be'st my cousin. He, he, he!

LOLLIO [*to Alibius*] I were best try his wit° a little, that I may know what form° to place him in. *test his intelligence* *class in school*

ALIBIUS Ay, do, Lollio, do.

LOLLIO I must ask him easy questions at first.—Tony, how many true° fingers has a tailor on his right hand? *honest*

ANTONIO As many as on his left, cousin.

LOLLIO Good; and how many on both?

ANTONIO Two less than a deuce,[9] cousin.

LOLLIO Very well answered. I come to you again, cousin Tony. How many fools goes to° a wise man? *goes to make up*

ANTONIO Forty in a day sometimes, cousin.[1]

LOLLIO Forty in a day? How prove you that?

6. On the early modern stage, constables were often the subject of ridicule for their dullness of wit.

7. I.e., bear in mind that you find me as a keeper of fools and madmen.

8. Alibius takes "cares" (line 140) to mean "worries."

9. I.e., None. (Tailors had a reputation for dishonesty.)

1. Antonio answers as though "goes to" (line 158) meant "visit, call on."

ANTONIO All that fall out amongst themselves and go to a lawyer to be made friends.[2]

LOLLIO A parlous° fool. He must sit in the fourth form at least, I perceive that.—I come again, Tony. How many knaves make° an honest man? *shrewd* / *make up; create*

ANTONIO I know not that, cousin.

LOLLIO No, the question is too hard for you. I'll tell you, cousin. There's three knaves may make an honest man: a sergeant,° a jailer, and a beadle; the sergeant catches him, the jailer holds him, and the beadle lashes him; and if he be not honest then, the hangman must cure him. *arresting officer*

ANTONIO Ha, ha, ha! That's fine sport, cousin.

ALIBIUS This was too deep a question for the fool, Lollio.

LOLLIO Yes, this might have served yourself, though I say't.—Once more, and you shall go play, Tony.

ANTONIO Ay, play at pushpin,° cousin, ha, he! *a child's game*

LOLLIO So thou shalt. Say how many fools are here—

ANTONIO Two, cousin, thou and I.

LOLLIO Nay, you're too forward there, Tony. Mark my question: how many fools and knaves are here? A fool before° a knave, a fool behind a knave, between every two fools a knave:[3] how many fools, how many knaves? *in front of*

ANTONIO I never learnt so far, cousin.

ALIBIUS Thou put'st too hard questions to him, Lollio.

LOLLIO I'll make him understand it easily.—Cousin, stand there.

ANTONIO Ay, cousin. [*Lollio arranges them in a line, Alibius in the middle.*][4]

LOLLIO Master, stand you next the fool.

ALIBIUS Well, Lollio.

LOLLIO Here's my place. Mark now, Tony: there a fool before a knave.

ANTONIO That's I, cousin.

LOLLIO Here's a fool behind a knave, that's I, and between us two fools there is a knave, that's my master. 'Tis but we three,[5] that's all.

ANTONIO We three, we three, cousin.

Madmen [*are heard*] *within.*

FIRST MADMAN (*within*) Put 's° head i'th'pillory! The bread's too little.° *Put the baker's* / *scant*

SECOND MADMAN (*within*) Fly, fly, and he catches the swallow.

THIRD MADMAN (*within*) Give her[6] more onion, or the devil put the rope° about her crag.° *noose (of onions) / neck*

LOLLIO You may hear what time of day it is; the chimes of Bedlam° goes. *an insane asylum*

ALIBIUS [*calling out*] Peace, peace! Or the wire° comes. *wire whip*

2. In his mad wisdom, Antonio argues that only fools would go to a lawyer to reconcile a quarrel.

3. I.e., If you put a fool in front and another behind, with a knave in between.

4. This arrangement makes Alibius the knave between two fools, but the reality is closer to that of two knaves trying to make a fool of Alibius.

5. I.e., We're really just three fools. (Lollio is thinking of the well-known joke picture depicting two fools and labeled "We three," inviting the viewer to insert himself as the third.)

6. Me. (The Third Madman is Welsh, as seen in his dialectical "her" for "me" and "my," lines 201–2, and his stereotypical fondness for onions, or leeks, and cheese, which he madly imagines has been eaten by a mouse, line 211, because of a negligent cat, line 206.)

THIRD MADMAN (*within*) Cat whore, cat whore! Her permasant,° her permasant! *My Parmesan cheese*

ALIBIUS Peace, I say!—Their hour's come; they must be fed, Lollio.

LOLLIO There's no hope of recovery of that Welsh madman, was° undone by a mouse, that spoiled him° a permasant; lost his wits for't. *who was / robbed him of*

ALIBIUS Go to your charge,° Lollio, I'll to mine. *the madmen you care for*

LOLLIO Go you to your madmen's ward; let me alone with your fools.

ALIBIUS And remember my last charge,° Lollio. *Exit.* *exhortation*

LOLLIO Of which° your patients do you think I am?—Come, Tony, you must amongst your schoolfellows now. There's pretty° scholars amongst 'em, I can tell you; there's some of 'em at *stultus, stulta, stultum.*[7] *Which of* / *fine, clever*

ANTONIO I would see the madmen, cousin, if they would not bite me.

LOLLIO No, they shall not bite thee, Tony.

ANTONIO They bite when they are at dinner, do they not, coz?° *cousin*

LOLLIO They bite at dinner indeed, Tony. Well, I hope to get credit by thee. I like thee the best of all the scholars that ever I brought up, and thou shalt prove a wise man, or I'll prove a fool myself. *Exeunt.*

2.1

Enter Beatrice and Jasperino severally.° *by separate doors*

BEATRICE Oh, sir, I'm ready now for that fair service
Which makes the name of friend sit glorious on you.
Good angels and this conduct° be your guide! *set of directions*
[*She gives him a paper.*]
Fitness of time and place is there set down, sir.

JASPERINO The joy I shall return° rewards my service. *Exit.* *carry back with me*

BEATRICE How wise is Alsemero in his friend!
It is a sign he makes his choice with judgment.
Then I appear in nothing more approved° *justified*
Than making choice of him; for 'tis a principle,
He that can choose
That bosom° well who of his thoughts partakes *bosom friend*
Proves most discreet in every choice he makes.
Methinks I love now with the eyes of judgment,
And see the way to merit, clearly see it.
A true deserver like a diamond sparkles;
In darkness you may see him, that's in absence,
Which is the greatest darkness falls° on love, *that can fall*
Yet is he best discernèd then
With intellectual eyesight. What's Piracquo
My father spends° his breath for? And his° blessing *expends / (my father's)*
Is only mine as I regard his name;° *accept his authority*
Else it° goes from me, and turns head against me, *(the blessing)*
Transformed into a curse. Some speedy way

7. The inmates are learning to decline the Latin word for "foolish," giving the masculine, feminine, and neuter forms.

2.1. Vermandero's castle.

Must be remembered.° He's so forward,° too, *thought of / persistent*
So urgent that way, scarce allows me breath
To speak to my new comforts.

Enter De Flores.

DE FLORES [*aside*] Yonder's she.
Whatever ails me, now alate° especially? *recently*
I can as well be hanged as refrain seeing her.
Some twenty times a day, nay, not so little,° *not so few*
Do I force° errands, frame ways and excuses *invent*
To come into her sight, and I have small reason for't
And less encouragement; for she baits° me still *taunts*
Every time worse than other, does profess herself
The cruellest enemy to my face in town;
At no hand° can abide the sight of me, *On no account*
As if danger or ill luck hung in my looks.
I must confess my face is bad enough,
But I know far worse has better fortune,
And not endured alone,° but doted on; *merely endured*
And yet such pick-haired° faces—chins like witches', *spiky-haired*
Here and there five hairs whispering in a corner
As if they grew in fear one of another,
Wrinkles like troughs where swine° deformity swills° *swinish / devours*
The tears of perjury that lie there like wash° *watery discharge; swill*
Fallen from the slimy and dishonest eye—
Yet such a one plucked sweets° without restraint, *has taken women's favors*
And has the grace of beauty to his sweet.° *to go with sweet sex*
Though my hard fate has thrust me out to servitude,
I tumbled into th'world a gentleman.
She turns her blessèd eye upon me now,
And I'll endure all storms before I part with't.

BEATRICE [*aside*] Again!
This ominous ill-faced fellow more disturbs me
Than all my other passions.

DE FLORES [*aside*] Now't begins again.
I'll stand this storm of hail, though the stones pelt me.

BEATRICE [*to him*] Thy business? What's thy business?

DE FLORES [*aside*] Soft and fair.° I cannot part so soon now.[1] *Gently*

BEATRICE [*aside*] The villain's fixed!° [*To him*] Thou standing° toad-pool! *unmovable / stagnant*

DE FLORES [*aside*] The shower falls amain° now. *full force*

BEATRICE Who sent thee? What's thy errand? Leave my sight.

DE FLORES My lord your father charged° me to deliver *ordered*
A message to you.

BEATRICE What, another since?° *since the last one*
Do't and be hanged, then. Let me be rid of thee.

DE FLORES True service merits mercy.

BEATRICE What's thy message?

DE FLORES Let beauty settle but in patience,
You shall hear all.

BEATRICE A dallying, trifling torment!

1. I cannot be gotten rid of that easily.

DE FLORES Signor Alonzo de Piracquo, lady,
Sole brother to Tomazo de Piracquo—
BEATRICE Slave,° when wilt make an end? *Wretch*
DE FLORES [*aside*] Too soon I shall.
BEATRICE What all this while of him?
DE FLORES The said Alonzo,
With the foresaid Tomazo—
BEATRICE Yet again?
DE FLORES Is new alighted.
BEATRICE Vengeance° strike the news! *May divine vengeance*
Thou thing most loathed, what cause was there in this
To bring thee to my sight?
DE FLORES My lord your father
Charged me to seek you out.
BEATRICE Is there no other
To send his errand by?
DE FLORES It seems 'tis my luck
To be i'th'way still.° *always at hand*
BEATRICE Get thee from me.
DE FLORES So.
[*Aside*] Why, am not I an ass to devise ways
Thus to be railed at? I must see her still!
I shall have a mad qualm° within this hour again, *fit*
I know't, and like a common Garden bull[2]
I do but take breath to be lugged° again. *pulled by the ears*
What this may bode,° I know not. I'll despair the less *foretell*
Because there's daily precedents of bad faces
Beloved beyond all reason; these foul chops° *jaws; face*
May come into favor one day 'mongst his fellows.
Wrangling has proved the mistress of good pastime;[3]
As children cry themselves asleep, I ha' seen
Women have chid themselves abed to men.[4] *Exit De Flores.*
BEATRICE I never see this fellow but I think
Of some harm towards me. Danger's in my mind still;
I scarce leave trembling of° an hour after. *for*
The next good mood I find my father in,
I'll get him quite discarded.° Oh, I was *dismissed*
Lost in this small disturbance, and forgot
Affliction's fiercer torrent that now comes
To bear down all my comforts.

Enter Vermandero, Alonzo, [and] Tomazo.

VERMANDERO You're both welcome,
[*To Alonzo*] But an especial one belongs to you, sir,
To whose most noble name our love presents
The addition° of a son, our son Alonzo. *title, form of address*
ALONZO The treasury of honor cannot bring forth
A title I should more rejoice in, sir.
VERMANDERO You have improved it well.[5]—Daughter, prepare;
The day will steal upon thee suddenly.

2. A bull to be baited by dogs at Paris Garden or the Bear Gardens (both names were used), in Southwark. Bull- and bearbaiting were popular entertainments.
3. Quarreling is sometimes the prelude to amorous pleasure.
4. Women who have quarreled themselves right into bed with a man.
5. You augment such honor as I bestow on you by your own noble conduct and speech.

BEATRICE [*aside*] Howe'er, I will be sure to keep the night,
If it should come so near me.[6]
[*Beatrice and Vermandero talk apart.*
Tomazo and Alonzo speak privately.]

TOMAZO Alonzo!

ALONZO Brother?

TOMAZO In troth, I see small welcome in her eye.

ALONZO Fie, you are too severe a censurer
Of love in all points; there's no bringing on you.° *bringing you around*
If lovers should mark everything a fault,
Affection would be like an ill-set° book, *badly set into type*
Whose faults° might prove as big as half the volume. *misprints*

BEATRICE [*to her father*] That's all I do entreat.

VERMANDERO It is but reasonable;
I'll see what my son says to't.—Son Alonzo,
Here's a motion° made but to reprieve *proposal*
A maidenhead three days longer. The request
Is not far out of reason, for indeed
The former time is pinching.° *is very tight*

ALONZO Though my joys
Be set back so much time as I could wish
They had been forward, yet, since she desires it,
The time is set as pleasing as before;
I find no gladness wanting.° *lacking*

VERMANDERO May I ever meet it in that point still![7]
You're nobly welcome, sirs.
Exeunt Vermandero and Beatrice.

TOMAZO So, did you mark the dullness° of her parting now? *lack of enthusiasm*

ALONZO What dullness? Thou art so exceptious° still. *taking exception*

TOMAZO Why, let it go, then. I am but a fool
To mark° your harms so heedfully. *note*

ALONZO Where's the oversight?° *What have I missed?*

TOMAZO Come, your faith's cozened° in her, strongly cozened. *deceived*
Unsettle° your affection with all speed *Detach*
Wisdom can bring it to; your peace is ruined else.
Think what a torment 'tis to marry one
Whose heart is leapt into another's bosom!
If ever pleasure° she receive from thee, *sexual pleasure*
It comes not in thy name, or of thy gift.
She lies but with another in thine arms,
He the half father unto all thy children
In the conception; if° he get° 'em not, *even if / beget*
She helps to get 'em for him in his passions,[8] and how
dangerous
And shameful her restraint may go in time to,[9]
It is not to be thought on without sufferings.

ALONZO You speak as if she loved some other, then.

TOMAZO Do you apprehend so slowly?

ALONZO Nay, an° that *if*
Be your fear only, I am safe enough.

6. Beatrice resolves to keep herself solely for her hoped-for nights with Alsemero. ("Keep" means "be prepared against.")
7. May I always be able to satisfy you in that!
8. She undertakes to conceive childen for her lover as if fulfilling his ecstasy.
9. And how shamefully she may behave in time if too much restraint is placed on her.

Preserve your friendship and your counsel, brother,
For times of more distress. I should depart
An enemy, a dangerous, deadly one
To any but thyself[1] that should but think
She knew the meaning of inconstancy,
Much less the use and practice; yet we're friends.[2]
Pray, let no more be urged. I can endure
Much, till I meet an injury° to her; *insult*
Then I am not myself. Farewell, sweet brother;
How much we're bound to heaven to depart lovingly![3]
Exit.

TOMAZO Why, here is love's tame madness! Thus a man
Quickly steals into his vexation. *Exit.*

[2.2]

Enter Diaphanta and Alsemero.

DIAPHANTA The place is my charge;° you have kept your hour, *in my custody*
And the reward of a just meeting bless you![1]
I hear my lady coming. Complete° gentleman, *All-accomplished*
I dare not be too busy with my praises;
They're dangerous things to deal with. *Exit.*

ALSEMERO
This goes well.
These women are the ladies' cabinets;° *i.e., trusted custodians*
Things of most precious trust are locked into 'em.

Enter Beatrice.

BEATRICE I have within mine eye all my desires.
Requests that holy prayers ascend heaven for,
And brings 'em down to furnish our defects,[2]
Come not more sweet to our necessities
Than thou unto my wishes.

ALSEMERO [*embracing her*] We're so like
In our expressions, lady, that unless I borrow
The same words I shall never find their equals.[3]

BEATRICE How happy were this meeting, this embrace,
If it were free from envy!° This poor kiss, *malice*
It has an enemy, a hateful one,
That wishes poison to't.[4] How well were I now
If there were none such name known as Piracquo,
Nor no such tie as the command of parents!
I should be but too much blessed.

→ does not acknowledge previous affections—blinded?

ALSEMERO
One good service
Would strike off° both your fears, and I'll go near it,° too, *cancel / undertake it*
Since you are so distressed. Remove the cause,° *i.e., Alonzo*
The command° ceases; so there's two fears blown out *Your father's command*
With one and the same blast.° *puff; stroke*

BEATRICE
Pray let me find° you, sir. *understand*
What might that service be, so strangely happy?° *yielding a happy result*

1. I would part company now as a deadly enemy to anyone other than you.
2. Yet because it is you I forgive your speaking as you did; we're still friends.
3. How much we are obliged by heavenly edict to make up our quarrel before we part company!

2.2. The castle.
1. And may you be blessed in a well-deserved meeting!
2. And answer our prayers by furnishing what we lack.
3. I.e., You took the words right out of my mouth.
4. I.e., Alonzo, enemy to our happiness, would poison our kiss (if he knew).

ALSEMERO The honorablest piece 'bout° man, valor. — *attribute of*
I'll send a challenge to Piracquo instantly.
BEATRICE How? Call you that extinguishing of fear
When 'tis the only way to keep it flaming?
Are not you ventured° in the action, — *put at risk*
That's° all my joys and comforts? Pray, no more, sir. — *You who are*
Say you prevailed, you're danger's° and not mine then; — *a hostage to danger*
The law would claim you from me, or obscurity° — *going into hiding*
Be made the grave to bury you alive.
I'm glad these thoughts come forth. Oh, keep not one° — *don't harbor one thought*
Of this condition,° sir! Here was° a course — *sort / would be*
Found to bring sorrow on her way to death;[5]
The tears would ne'er ha' dried, till dust° had choked 'em. — *dust of the grave*
Blood-guiltiness becomes° a fouler visage— — *suits*
[*Aside*] And now I think on one!° I was to blame; — *(De Flores' face)*
I ha' marred so good a market° with my scorn. — *spoiled an opportunity*
'T had been done,° questionless; the ugliest creature — *He'd have done it*
Creation framed for some use, yet to see
I could not mark so much where it° should be! — *(the practical use)*
ALSEMERO Lady—
BEATRICE [*aside*] Why, men of art° make much of poison, — *learning*
Keep one to expel another. Where was my art?° — *skill, cunning*
ALSEMERO Lady, you hear not me.
BEATRICE [*to him*] I do especially, sir.
The present times are not so sure of° our side — *securely on*
As those hereafter may be; we must use 'em° then — *(opportunities)*
As thrifty folks their wealth, sparingly now
Till the time opens.° — *is more propitious*
ALSEMERO You teach wisdom, lady.
BEATRICE [*calling*] Within there! Diaphanta!

Enter Diaphanta.

DIAPHANTA Do you call, madam?
BEATRICE Perfect° your service, and conduct this gentleman — *Fulfill, complete*
The private way you brought him.
DIAPHANTA I shall, madam.
ALSEMERO My love's as firm as love e'er built upon.
Exeunt Diaphanta and Alsemero.

Enter De Flores.

DE FLORES [*aside*] I have watched this meeting, and do wonder much
What shall become of t'other;° I'm sure both — *(Alonzo)*
Cannot be served unless she transgress. Happily° — *Perhaps; if all goes well*
Then I'll put in° for one; for if a woman — *put myself forward*
Fly from one point, from him she makes a husband,
She spreads and mounts then like arithmetic—
One, ten, a hundred, a thousand, ten thousand[6]—
Proves in time sutler° to an army royal. — *caterer; camp follower*
Now do I look to be most richly railed at,
Yet I must see her.
BEATRICE [*aside*] Why, put case° I loathed him — *suppose*

5. Sure to bring on sorrow and then death.
6. De Flores compares women to hawks when they fly away from their masters, ascending in widening arcs. "Mounts" hints at sexual mounting.

As much as youth and beauty hates a sepulchre,
Must I needs show it? Cannot I keep that secret,
And serve my turn upon him?°—See, he's here. *make use of him*
[*To him*] De Flores!

DE FLORES [*aside*] Ha, I shall run mad with joy!
She called me fairly by my name, De Flores,
And neither "rogue" nor "rascal."

BEATRICE What ha' you done
To your face alate?° You've met with some good physician. *of late, lately*
You've pruned° yourself, methinks; you were not wont *preened; decked out*
To look so amorously.° *desirable; like a lover*

DE FLORES [*aside*] Not I;
'Tis the same physnomy,° to a hair and pimple, *physiognomy, face*
Which she called scurvy° scarce an hour ago. *diseased; vile*
How is this?

BEATRICE Come hither. Nearer, man.

DE FLORES [*aside*] I'm up to the chin in heaven!

BEATRICE [*examining his face*] Turn, let me see.
Faugh, 'tis but the heat° of the liver, *inflammation*
I perceive't; I thought it had been worse.

DE FLORES [*aside*] Her fingers touched me! She smells all
amber.° *of ambergris, perfume*

BEATRICE I'll make a water° for you shall° cleanse this *lotion / that will*
Within a fortnight.

DE FLORES With your own hands, lady?

BEATRICE Yes, mine own, sir. In a work of cure,
I'll trust no other.

DE FLORES [*aside*] 'Tis half an act of pleasure° *sex*
To hear her talk thus to me.

BEATRICE When we're used
To a hard° face, 'tis not so unpleasing. *ugly*
It mends° still in opinion, hourly mends; *improves*
I see it by experience.

DE FLORES [*aside*] I was blest
To light upon this minute! I'll make use on't.

BEATRICE Hardness becomes the visage of a man well;
It argues service, resolution, manhood,
If cause were of° employment. *If there were cause for*

DE FLORES 'Twould be soon seen,[7]
If e'er Your Ladyship had cause to use it.
I would but wish the honor of a service
So happy as that mounts to.[8]

BEATRICE We shall try you. Oh, my De Flores!

DE FLORES [*aside*] How's that?
She calls me hers already, *my* De Flores!
[*To her*] You were about to sigh out somewhat,° madam. *something*

BEATRICE No, was I? I forgot—Oh!

DE FLORES There 'tis again, the very fellow on't.° *of it*

BEATRICE You are too quick, sir.

DE FLORES There's no excuse for't now; I heard it twice,
madam.
That sigh would fain have utterance; take pity on't,

7. I.e., My resolution and desire to serve would soon be manifest.

8. As fortunate as my devotion and manhood aspire to.

And lend it a free word.° 'Las, how it labors *free expression*
For liberty! I hear the murmur yet
Beat at your bosom.
BEATRICE Would creation—
DE FLORES Ay, well said, that's it.
BEATRICE Had formed me man.
DE FLORES Nay, that's not it.
BEATRICE Oh, 'tis the soul of freedom!
I should not then be forced to marry one
I hate beyond all depths; I should have power
Then to oppose my loathings, nay, remove 'em
Forever from my sight.
DE FLORES [*aside*] Oh, blest occasion!° *opportunity*
[*To her*] Without change to your sex, you have your wishes.
Claim so much man in me.
BEATRICE In thee, De Flores?
There's small cause for that.
DE FLORES Put it not from me;
It's a service that I kneel for to you. [*He kneels.*]
BEATRICE You are too violent° to mean faithfully. *vehement; violent*
There's horror in my service, blood and danger;
Can those be things to sue° for? *beg*
DE FLORES If you knew
How sweet it were to me to be employed
In any act of yours, you would say then
I failed and used not reverence enough
When I receive the charge on't.
BEATRICE [*aside*] This is much, methinks;° *i.e., He seems sincere*
Belike° his wants are greedy, and to such *Probably*
Gold tastes like angels' food.° [*To him*] Rise. *manna*
DE FLORES I'll have the work first.
BEATRICE [*aside*] Possible° his need *Possibly*
Is strong upon him. [*She gives him money.*] There's to
encourage thee:
As thou art° forward and thy service dangerous, *To the extent you are*
Thy reward shall be precious.
DE FLORES That I have thought on.
I have assured myself of that beforehand,
And know it will be precious; the thought ravishes.
BEATRICE Then take him to thy fury.
DE FLORES I thirst for him.
BEATRICE Alonzo de Piracquo.
DE FLORES His end's upon him. He shall be seen no more.
BEATRICE How lovely now dost thou appear to me! [*He rises.*]
Never was man dearlier rewarded.
DE FLORES I do think of that.
BEATRICE Be wondrous careful in the execution.
DE FLORES Why, are not both our lives upon the cast?° *the throw of the dice*
BEATRICE Then I throw all my fears upon thy service.
DE FLORES They ne'er shall rise to hurt you.
BEATRICE When the deed's done,
I'll furnish thee with all things for thy flight;
Thou may'st live bravely° in another country. *handsomely*
DE FLORES Ay, ay, we'll talk of that hereafter.
BEATRICE [*aside*] I shall rid myself

Of two inveterate loathings at one time,
Piracquo and his dog-face.[9] *Exit.*

DE FLORES Oh, my blood!
Methinks I feel her in mine arms already,
Her wanton fingers combing out this beard,
And, being pleased, praising this bad face.
Hunger and pleasure, they'll commend sometimes
Slovenly dishes, and feed heartily on 'em—
Nay, which is stranger, refuse daintier for 'em.
Some women are odd feeders.—I'm too loud.
Here comes the man goes° supperless to bed, *who goes*
Yet shall not rise tomorrow to his dinner.

believes BJ has changed & sees imminent fulfilment of desires

Enter Alonzo.

ALONZO De Flores!
DE FLORES My kind honorable lord!
ALONZO I am glad I ha' met with thee.
DE FLORES Sir?
ALONZO Thou canst show me the full strength of the castle?
DE FLORES That I can, sir.
ALONZO I much desire it.
DE FLORES And if the ways and straits° of some of the passages be not too tedious for you, I will assure you, worth your time and sight, my lord. *narrow parts*
ALONZO Pah,° that shall be no hindrance. *Pooh*
DE FLORES I'm your servant, then. 'Tis now near dinnertime; 'gainst Your Lordship's rising° I'll have the keys about me. *before you finish dinner*
ALONZO Thanks, kind De Flores.
DE FLORES [*aside*] He's safely thrust upon me beyond hopes.
Exeunt.

(In the act-time° De Flores hides a naked rapier.) *interval between acts*

3.1

Enter Alonzo and De Flores.

DE FLORES Yes, here are all the keys. I was afraid, my lord,
I'd wanted° for the postern;° this is it. *lacked a key / back door*
I've all, I've all, my lord: this for the sconce.° *small fort, earthwork*
ALONZO 'Tis a most spacious and impregnable fort.
DE FLORES You'll tell me more,° my lord. This descent *be even more praising*
Is somewhat narrow; we shall never pass
Well with our weapons; they'll but trouble us.
ALONZO Thou say'st true.
DE FLORES Pray let me help Your Lordship.
[*He helps Alonzo unarm.*]
ALONZO 'Tis done. Thanks, kind De Flores.
DE FLORES Here are hooks, my lord, to hang such things on purpose. [*De Flores hangs up their swords.*]
ALONZO Lead. I'll follow thee. *Exit at one door*

9. (1) De Flores' ugly face; (2) His Honor the Dog-face (a mock title).

3.1. A narrow passageway in the castle.

[3.2]

and enter at the other.

DE FLORES All this is nothing; you shall see anon° *shortly*
A place you little dream on.
ALONZO I am glad
I have this leisure. All your master's house° *household persons*
Imagine I ha' taken a gondola.
DE FLORES All but myself, sir, [*aside*] which makes up my safety.°— *gives me an alibi*
My lord, I'll place you at a casement° here *window*
Will° show you the full strength of all the castle. *That will*
Look, spend your eye awhile upon that object.
ALONZO Here's rich variety, De Flores.
DE FLORES Yes, sir.
ALONZO Goodly munition.
DE FLORES Ay, there's ordnance sir,
No bastard° metal, will° ring you a peal like bells *debased / which will*
At great men's funerals. Keep your eye straight, my lord.
Take special notice of that sconce before you;
There you may dwell° awhile. [*He takes up the rapier he hid at the end of act* 2.] *pause*
ALONZO I am upon't.° *I see it*
DE FLORES And so am I.° [*He stabs Alonzo.*] *I am about my task*
ALONZO De Flores! Oh, De Flores,
Whose malice hast thou put on?[1]
DE FLORES Do you question
A work of secrecy? I must silence you. [*He stabs again.*]
ALONZO Oh! Oh! Oh!
DE FLORES [*stabbing repeatedly*] I must silence you.
So, here's an undertaking well accomplished.
This vault serves to good use now.—Ha! What's that
Threw sparkles in my eye? Oh, 'tis a diamond
He wears upon his finger. It was well found;
This will approve° the work. [*He tries to remove the ring.*] *confirm*
What, so fast on?
Not part in death? I'll take a speedy course, then;
Finger and all shall off. [*He cuts off the finger.*] So, now I'll clear
The passages from all suspect or fear. *Exit with body.*

[3.3]

Enter Isabella and Lollio.

ISABELLA Why, sirrah,° whence have you commission *(said to inferiors)*
To fetter the doors against me? If you keep
Me in a cage, pray whistle to me;[1]
Let me be doing something.
LOLLIO You shall be doing, if it please you.[2] I'll whistle to you if you'll pipe after.° *i.e., play my tune*

3.2. A narrow passageway in the castle.
1. Alonzo assumes that De Flores has been suborned to kill him by some great man.
3.3. The insane asylum.
1. Whistle as though to a caged bird, to encourage my singing.
2. Lollio interprets her "doing" as suggestive of sex.

ISABELLA Is it your master's pleasure, or your own,
To keep me in this pinfold?° *animal enclosure*

LOLLIO 'Tis for my master's pleasure, lest, being taken in another man's corn,° you might be pounded[3] in another place. *grainfield*

ISABELLA 'Tis very well, and he'll prove very wise.[4]

LOLLIO He says you have company enough in the house, if you please to be sociable, of all sorts of people.

ISABELLA Of all sorts? Why, here's none but fools and madmen.

LOLLIO Very well. And where will you find any other, if you should go abroad?° There's my master and I to boot, too. *out of doors*

ISABELLA Of either sort one:° a madman and a fool. *One of each kind*

LOLLIO I would ev'n participate of° both, then, if I were as you. I know you're half mad already; be half foolish° too. *share, enjoy in common* / *i.e., a fool for love*

ISABELLA You're a brave,° saucy rascal! Come on, sir, *fine*
Afford me then the pleasure of your bedlam.° *madhouse*
You were commending once today to me
Your last-come lunatic, what a proper° *handsome*
Body there was without brains to guide it,
And what a pitiful delight appeared
In that defect, as if your wisdom had found
A mirth in madness. Pray, sir, let me partake,
If there be such a pleasure.° *If one can enjoy madness*

LOLLIO If I do not show you the handsomest, discreetest madman, one that I may call the understanding madman, then say I am a fool.

ISABELLA Well, a match.° I will say so. *agreed*

LOLLIO When you have a taste of the madman, you shall, if you please, see Fools' College, o'th'side.° I seldom lock there; 'tis but shooting a bolt° or two, and you are amongst 'em. *other side of the asylum* / *sliding a doorbolt*
Exit.
[*Speaking offstage*] Come on, sir, let me see how handsomely you'll behave yourself now.

Enter Lollio, [*leading*] *Franciscus.*

FRANCISCUS How sweetly she looks! Oh, but there's a wrinkle in her brow as deep as philosophy. Anacreon, drink to my mistress' health, I'll pledge it. Stay, stay, there's a spider in the cup! No, 'tis but a grape-stone; swallow it, fear nothing, poet.[5] So, so, lift higher.

ISABELLA Alack, alack, 'tis too full of pity
To be laughed at. How fell he mad? Canst thou tell?

LOLLIO For love, mistress. He was a pretty poet, too, and that set him forwards° first; the Muses then forsook him; he ran mad for a chambermaid, yet she was but a dwarf neither.° *started him off* / *only a dwarf at that*

FRANCISCUS Hail, bright Titania!° *queen of fairies*
Why stand'st thou idle on these flow'ry banks?
Oberon° is dancing with his dryades;° *king of fairies / nymphs*
I'll gather daisies, primrose, violets,
And bind them in a verse of poesy.

3. (1) Impounded as a stray; (2) pounded in sex.
4. Isabella wryly suggests that Alibius' jealousy may turn out to be a self-fulfilling prophecy.
5. According to legend, the Greek poet Anacreon choked to death on a grape seed while drinking wine.

LOLLIO [*to Franciscus*] Not too near! You see your danger.
[*Lollio shows his whip.*]

FRANCISCUS Oh, hold thy hand, great Diomed! Thou feed'st
Thy horses well; they shall obey thee.
Get up; Bucephalus kneels.[6]

LOLLIO [*to Isabella*] You see how I awe my flock. A shepherd has not his dog at more obedience.

ISABELLA His° conscience is unquiet; sure that was — *(Franciscus')*
The cause of this. A proper gentleman.

FRANCISCUS Come hither, Aesculapius;° hide the poison.° — *god of healing / the whip*

LOLLIO Well, 'tis hid.° — *put away*

FRANCISCUS Didst thou never hear of one Tiresias,° — *a blind Greek seer*
A famous poet?

LOLLIO Yes, that kept tame wild geese.

FRANCISCUS That's he. I am the man.

LOLLIO No!

FRANCISCUS Yes; but make no words on't.° I was a man — *say nothing about it*
Seven years ago.

LOLLIO A stripling I think you might.° — *A youngster, perhaps*

FRANCISCUS Now I'm a woman, all feminine.

LOLLIO I would I might see that.° — *Show me the proof*

FRANCISCUS Juno struck me blind.[7]

LOLLIO I'll ne'er believe that; for a woman, they say, has an eye° more than a man. — *i.e., vagina*

FRANCISCUS I say she struck me blind.

LOLLIO And Luna° made you mad; you have two trades[8] to beg with. — *Moon*

FRANCISCUS Luna is now big-bellied,° and there's room — *full; pregnant*
For both of us to ride with Hecate;° — *witch-goddess of night*
I'll drag thee up into her silver sphere,
And there we'll kick the dog and beat the bush[9]
That barks against the witches of the night;
The swift lycanthropi[1] that walks the round,
We'll tear their wolvish skins and save the sheep.
[*He makes a menacing gesture.*]

LOLLIO Is't come to this? Nay, then, my poison° comes forth again. Mad slave,° indeed, abuse° your keeper! — *whip* / *rascal / to attack*

ISABELLA I prithee, hence with him, now he grows dangerous.

FRANCISCUS (*sing*) Sweet love pity me!
Give me leave to lie with thee.

LOLLIO No, I'll see you wiser first. To your own kennel!

FRANCISCUS No noise! She° sleeps. Draw all the curtains round; — *(The Moon)*
Let no soft sound molest the pretty soul
But love, and love creeps in at a mouse hole.

6. Diomedes, King of the Bistonians, in Thrace, fed his horses human flesh. One of Hercules' labors was to kill Diomedes, after which Hercules fed Diomedes' body to his horses. Bucephalus was Alexander the Great's favorite and legendary horse, which only he could ride. "Get up" means "mount."

7. According to some accounts, Juno struck Tiresias blind because when he was called on to arbitrate a dispute between her and her husband, Jupiter, over who enjoyed sex more, men or women (since Tiresias was a man who had been changed into a woman and then back again), he contradicted Juno, who argued that men enjoyed the advantage.

8. I.e., blindness and madness. (Both are "trades" in the sense that blind persons and mad folk could become beggars, seeking assistance in their affliction.)

9. Traditionally, the man in the moon was thought to be accompanied by a dog and to carry a thornbush, as in *A Midsummer Night's Dream*, 5.1.240–55.

1. Sufferers of lycanthropy, or lycanthropia, the delusion that one has become a wolf (as in the case of Duke Ferdinand in *The Duchess of Malfi*, 5.2).

LOLLIO I would you would get into your hole.
Exit Franciscus.
Now, mistress, I will bring you another sort; you shall be
fooled° another while. [*He calls.*] Tony! Come hither, Tony. *entertained by a fool*

Enter Antonio.

Look who's yonder, Tony.
ANTONIO Cousin, is it not my aunt?° *whore; aunt*
LOLLIO Yes, 'tis one of 'em, Tony.
ANTONIO He, he! How do you, uncle?
LOLLIO Fear him not, mistress, 'tis a gentle nidget;° you may *idiot, fool*
play with him, as safely with him as with his bauble.° *fool's baton (bawdy)*
ISABELLA [*to Antonio*] How long hast thou been a fool?
ANTONIO Ever since I came hither, cousin.
ISABELLA Cousin? I'm none of thy cousins, fool.
LOLLIO Oh, mistress, fools have always so much wit as to
claim their kindred.
MADMAN (*within*) Bounce,° bounce! He falls, he falls! *Bang*
ISABELLA Hark you, your scholars in the upper room
Are out of order.
LOLLIO [*calling*] Must I come amongst you there?—Keep you
the fool, mistress; I'll go up and play left-handed Orlando[2]
amongst the madmen. *Exit.*
ISABELLA [*to Antonio*] Well, sir.
ANTONIO [*dropping his disguise*] 'Tis opportuneful now,
sweet lady! Nay,
Cast no amazing° eye upon this change. *amazed*
ISABELLA Ha!
ANTONIO This shape of folly shrouds° your dearest love, *conceals*
The truest servant to your powerful beauties,
Whose magic had this force thus to transform me.
ISABELLA You are a fine fool indeed.
ANTONIO Oh, 'tis not strange.
Love has an intellect that runs through° all *explores*
The scrutinous sciences,° and, like *inquisitive learning*
A cunning poet, catches a quantity
Of every knowledge, yet brings all home
Into one mystery,° into one secret *arcane practice*
That he proceeds in.
ISABELLA You're a parlous° fool. *shrewd, mischievous*
ANTONIO No danger in me; I bring naught but love,
And his soft-wounding shafts° to strike you with. *Cupid's arrows*
Try but one arrow; if it hurt you,
I'll stand° you twenty back in recompense. *stand obligated to give*
[*He tries to kiss her.*]
ISABELLA A forward° fool too! *audacious, pert*
ANTONIO This was Love's teaching;
A thousand ways he° fashioned out my way, *(Cupid)*
And this I found the safest and nearest
To tread the Galaxia° to my star. *Milky Way*
ISABELLA Profound, withal!° Certain, you dreamed of this; *besides*
Love never taught it waking.

2. The hero of the Italian poet Ludovico Ariosto's epic poem, *Orlando Furioso*, whose "fury" is appropriate here to a madhouse; "left-handed" because Lollio is only ineptly modeled on that great hero.

ANTONIO Take no acquaintance° *Pay no attention*
Of° these outward follies;° there is within *To / fool's clothes*
A gentleman that loves you.
ISABELLA When I see him,
I'll speak with him; so in the meantime
Keep your habit,° it becomes you well enough. *garb; habit of speech*
As you are a gentleman, I'll not discover you;° *reveal your identity*
That's all the favor that you must expect.
When you are weary, you may leave the school,
For all this while you have but played the fool.° *wasted your time*

Enter Lollio.

ANTONIO And must again.°—He, he! I thank you, cousin; *must play the fool again*
I'll be your Valentine tomorrow morning.
LOLLIO How do you like the fool, mistress?
ISABELLA Passing° well, sir. *Very*
LOLLIO Is he not witty, pretty well for a fool?
ISABELLA If he hold on° as he begins, he is like° *continue / likely*
To come to something.
LOLLIO Ay, thank a good tutor. You may put him to't;° he begins to answer pretty hard questions.—Tony, how many is five times six? *question him*
ANTONIO Five times six is six times five.
LOLLIO What arithmetician could have answered better?—How many is one hundred and seven?
ANTONIO One hundred and seven is seven hundred and one, cousin.
LOLLIO [*to Isabella*] This is no wit to speak on!° Will you be rid of the fool now? *(said with proud irony)*
ISABELLA By no means. Let him stay a little.
MADMEN (*within*) Catch there, catch the last couple in hell![3]
LOLLIO Again? Must I come amongst you? Would my master were come home! I am not able to govern both these wards° together. *Exit.* *(fools' and madmen's)*
ANTONIO Why should a minute of love's hour be lost?
ISABELLA Fie, out° again! I had rather you kept *out of your role*
Your other posture; you become not your tongue
When you speak from your clothes.[4]
ANTONIO How can he freeze,° *any man be unresponsive*
Lives° near so sweet a warmth? Shall I alone *Who lives*
Walk through the orchard of the Hesperides,
And, cowardly, not dare to pull an apple?[5]
This with the red cheeks I must venture for.[6]
[*He tries to kiss her.*]

Enter Lollio above [*unseen by Isabella and Antonio*].

ISABELLA Take heed, there's giants keep 'em.[7]
LOLLIO [*aside*] How now, fool, are you good at that? Have you

3. The madmen are playing barley-break, a country game. "Hell" is the space in the center of a circle where the couple who are "it" are confined.
4. Your fool's costume does not suit you when you address me in these serious terms as a wooer.
5. One of Hercules' labors was to take the golden apples from the Garden of the Hesperides; the apples were guarded by the Hesperides, nymphs, with the assistance of a dragon. "Pull" means "pluck."
6. Rose-cheeked Isabella is like an apple in the Garden of the Hesperides.
7. Isabella warns that she, the apple Antonio desires, is guarded by two dangerous overseers, Lollio and Alibius.

read Lipsius? He's past *Ars Amandi.*[8] I believe I must put harder questions to him; I perceive that.

ISABELLA You are bold without fear, too.

ANTONIO What should I fear,
Having all joys about me? Do you smile,° *Do but smile*
And Love shall play the wanton on your lip,
Meet and retire, retire and meet again.
Look you but cheerfully, and in your eyes
I shall behold mine own deformity
And dress myself up fairer. I know this shape
Becomes me not, but in those bright mirrors° *your eyes*
I shall array me handsomely.

LOLLIO [*aside*] Cuckoo,° Cuckoo! *Exit.* *(hinting at cuckoldry)*

[*Enter*] *Madmen above, some as° birds, others as beasts.* *acting like*

ANTONIO What are these?

ISABELLA Of fear enough° to part us; *Frightening enough*
Yet are they but our schools of lunatics,
That act their fantasies in any shapes
Suiting their present thoughts. If sad, they cry;
If mirth be their conceit,° they laugh again. *fancy, mood*
Sometimes they imitate the beasts and birds,
Singing, or howling, braying, barking—all
As their wild fancies prompt 'em.

[*Exeunt Madmen above.*]

Enter Lollio [*below*].

ANTONIO These are no fears.

ISABELLA But here's a large one:° my man. *a real threat*

ANTONIO [*resuming his mad disguise*] Ha, he! That's fine sport indeed, cousin.

LOLLIO [*to himself*] I would my master were come home. 'Tis too much for one shepherd to govern two of these flocks; nor can I believe that one churchman can instruct two benefices at once; there will be some incurable mad of° the one side, and very° fools on the other.—Come, Tony. *on* *utter*

ANTONIO Prithee, cousin, let me stay here still.

LOLLIO No, you must to your book now you have played sufficiently.

ISABELLA Your fool is grown wondrous witty.

LOLLIO Well, I'll say nothing; but I do not think but he will put you down[9] one of these days.

Exeunt Lollio and Antonio.

ISABELLA Here the restrainèd current might make breach,
Spite of the watchful bankers.° Would a woman stray, *dike-makers*
She need not gad abroad to seek her sin!
It would be brought home one ways or other.
The needle's° point will to the fixèd north; *compass needle's*
Such drawing arctics° women's beauties are. *north poles*

Enter Lollio.

8. Lollio wryly notes that Antonio appears to be getting ahead as a scholar in the art of love, being well read in Lipsius, a famous jurist (with a play of words on "lips"), and advancing even beyond Ovid's *Ars Amatoria,* or *Ars Amandi,* a notorious handbook for lovers.

9. (1) Best you in argument; (2) bed you.

LOLLIO How dost thou, sweet rogue?
ISABELLA How now?[1]
LOLLIO Come, there are degrees; one fool may be better than another.
ISABELLA What's the matter?
LOLLIO Nay, if thou giv'st thy mind to fool's flesh, have at thee!° [*He tries to kiss her.*] *here I come!*
ISABELLA You bold slave, you!
LOLLIO I could follow now, as t'other fool did:° *speak as Antonio did*
"What should I fear,
Having all joys about me? Do you but smile,
And Love shall play the wanton on your lip,
Meet and retire, retire and meet again.
Look you but cheerfully, and in your eyes
I shall behold my own deformity
And dress myself up fairer. I know this shape
Becomes me not—" And so as it follows; but is not this the more foolish way?° Come, sweet rogue; kiss me, my little Lacedaemonian.[2] Let me feel how thy pulses beat. Thou hast a thing° about thee would do a man pleasure, I'll lay° my hand on't. *foolish courtliness* *vagina / bet; place*
ISABELLA Sirrah, no more! I see you have discovered
This love's knight-errant,[3] who hath made adventure
For purchase of° my love. Be silent, mute, *To acquire*
Mute as a statue, or his injunction° *my command to him*
For me enjoying° shall be to cut thy throat. *enjoying me sexually*
I'll do it, though for no other purpose,° *(than to be rid of you)*
And be sure he'll not refuse it.
LOLLIO My share, that's all! I'll have my fool's part with you.
ISABELLA No more! Your master.

Enter Alibius.

ALIBIUS Sweet, how dost thou?
ISABELLA Your bounden° servant, sir. *dutiful; constrained*
ALIBIUS Fie, fie, sweetheart,
No more of that.
ISABELLA You were best° lock me up. *You'd better*
ALIBIUS In my arms and bosom, my sweet Isabella,
I'll lock thee up most nearly.°—Lollio, *tightly*
We have employment, we have task in hand.
At noble Vermandero's, our castle captain,
There is a nuptial to be solemnized
(Beatrice-Joanna, his fair daughter-bride)
For which the gentleman hath bespoke our pains:° *commissioned our efforts*
A mixture of our madmen and our fools,
To finish, as it were, and make the fag° *fag end, last part*
Of all the revels, the third night from° the first. *after*
Only an unexpected passage over,° *foray into the hall*
To make a frightful pleasure, that is all,

1. I.e., What warrant have you to address me so familiarly?
2. I.e., my little wanton. (Lacedaemon, or Sparta, was an ancient city in the Peloponnese, in southern Greece. The Greeks were widely supposed by the English to have been deceitful and hedonistic.)
3. This knight-errant in the service of love.

But not the all I aim at. Could we so act it
To teach it in a wild, distracted measure,[4]
Though out of form and figure, breaking time's head,° — *not keeping time*
It were no matter, 'twould be healed again
In one age or other° if not in this.° — *Sooner or later / now*
This,° this, Lollio! There's a good reward begun,° — *This is it / promised*
And will beget a bounty,° be it known. — *generous gift*

LOLLIO This is easy, sir, I'll warrant you. You have about° you fools and madmen that can dance very well, and 'tis no wonder; your best dancers are not the wisest men—the reason is, with often jumping they jolt their brains down into their feet, that° their wits lie more in their heels than in their heads. — *about: near, with* / *that: so that*

ALIBIUS Honest Lollio, thou giv'st me a good reason,° — *reason to go ahead*
And a comfort in it.

ISABELLA You've a fine trade on't;° — *in it*
Madmen and fools are a staple commodity.° — *in plentiful supply*

ALIBIUS Oh, wife, we must eat, wear clothes, and live.
Just at the lawyers' haven we arrive;
By madmen and by fools we both do thrive.[5] *Exeunt.*

[3.4]

Enter Vermandero, Alsemero, Jasperino, and Beatrice.

VERMANDERO [*to Alsemero*] Valencia speaks so nobly of you, sir,
I wish I had a daughter now for you.

ALSEMERO The fellow of this creature° were a partner — *A woman like Beatrice*
For a king's love.

VERMANDERO I had her fellow° once, sir, — *(Beatrice's mother)*
But heaven has married her to joys eternal;
'Twere sin to wish her in this vale° again. — *vale of tears, earth*
Come, sir, your friend and you shall see the pleasures
Which my health chiefly joys in.

ALSEMERO I hear the beauty of this seat largely.° — *residence widely praised*

VERMANDERO It falls much short of that.

Exeunt. Manet° Beatrice. — *Remains onstage*

BEATRICE So, here's one step
Into my father's favor. Time will fix him.° — *(as a favorite)*
I have got him now the liberty of the house;
So wisdom by degrees works out her freedom.[1]
And if that eye° be darkened° that offends me — *i.e., Alonzo / slain*
(I wait but that eclipse), this gentleman
Shall soon shine glorious in my father's liking,
Through the refulgent virtue° of my love. — *radiant strength*

Enter De Flores.

DE FLORES [*aside*] My thoughts are at a banquet° for the deed. — *feasting in anticipation*
I feel no weight° in't; 'tis but light and cheap — *weight of conscience*

4. If we could manage it so as to teach our madmen and fools to perform a wild, crazy dance.
5. Alibius, perhaps remembering Antonio's comments at 1.2.161–62, plans to prosper as lawyers do, from the madness and folly of others.
3.4. The castle.
1. Thus careful planning slowly provides opportunity.

For the sweet recompense that I set down° for't. *have determined*
BEATRICE De Flores!
DE FLORES Lady?
BEATRICE Thy looks promise cheerfully.° *promise good news*
DE FLORES All things are answerable°—time, circumstance, *apt*
Your wishes, and my service.
BEATRICE Is it done, then?
DE FLORES Piracquo is no more.
BEATRICE [*weeping*] My joys start at mine eyes! Our sweet'st delights
Are evermore born weeping.
DE FLORES I've a token for you.
BEATRICE For me?
DE FLORES But it was sent somewhat unwillingly.
I could not get the ring without the finger.
[*He presents her with the bloody finger.*]
BEATRICE Bless me! What hast thou done?
DE FLORES Why is that more
Than killing the whole man? I cut his heartstrings.
A greedy hand thrust in a dish at court
In a mistake hath had as much as this.[2]
BEATRICE 'Tis the first token my father made me send him.
DE FLORES And I made him send it back again
For his last token. I was loath to leave it,
And I'm sure dead men have no use of jewels.
He was as loath to part with't, for it stuck
As if the flesh and it were both one substance.
BEATRICE At the stag's fall the keeper has his fees.[3]
'Tis soon applied;° all dead men's fees are yours, sir. *applied to this case*
I pray, bury the finger, but the stone
You may make use on shortly; the true value,
Take't of my truth,° is near three hundred ducats.° *Believe me / gold coins*
DE FLORES 'Twill hardly buy a capcase° for one's conscience, though, *traveling case*
To keep it from the worm,° as fine as 'tis. *the worm of conscience*
Well, being my fees, I'll take it;
Great men have taught me that,[4] or else my merit° *sense of injured merit*
Would scorn the way on't.° *this manner of reward*
BEATRICE It might justly,° sir. *justly be scorned*
Why, thou mistak'st, De Flores; 'tis not given
In state of° recompense. *In lieu of further*
DE FLORES No, I hope so, lady.
You should soon witness my contempt to't then!
BEATRICE Prithee, thou look'st as if thou wert offended.
DE FLORES That were strange, lady; 'tis not possible
My service should draw such a cause° from you. *cause of offense*
Offended? Could you think so? That were much° *would be inappropriate*
For one of my performance, and so warm
Yet in my service.
BEATRICE 'Twere misery° in me to give you cause, sir. *wretched ingratitude*
DE FLORES I know so much, it were° so—misery *would be*

2. Might mistakenly lose a finger to some knife in this fashion.
3. The gamekeeper was traditionally given a share of the fallen animal in a hunt.
4. Have taught me that one must accept gifts from great persons without a show of pride.

In her most sharp condition.
BEATRICE 'Tis resolved, then.
[*Offering money*] Look you, sir, here's three thousand golden florins;° *gold coins*
I have not meanly° thought upon thy merit. *ungenerously*
DE FLORES What, salary? Now you move° me. *anger*
BEATRICE How, De Flores?
DE FLORES Do you place me in the rank of verminous° fellows *vermin-like*
To destroy things for wages? Offer gold?
The lifeblood of man! Is anything
Valued too precious for my recompense?
BEATRICE I understand thee not.
DE FLORES I could ha' hired
A journeyman° in murder at this rate, *wage earner*
And mine own conscience might have slept at ease,
And have had the work brought home.° *reported back to me*
BEATRICE [*aside*] I'm in a labyrinth.
What will content him? I would fain be rid of him.
[*To him*] I'll double the sum, sir.
DE FLORES You take a course
To double my vexation, that's the good° you do. *that's all the good*
BEATRICE [*aside*] Bless me! I am now in worse plight than I was;
I know not what will please him. [*To him*] For my fear's sake,
I prithee make away° with all speed possible. *get away*
And if thou be'st so modest not to name
The sum that will content thee, paper blushes not;
Send thy demand in writing, it shall follow thee.
But prithee take thy flight.
DE FLORES You must fly too, then.
BEATRICE I?
DE FLORES I'll not stir a foot else.
BEATRICE What's your meaning?
DE FLORES Why, are not you as guilty, in (I'm sure)
As deep as I? And we should stick together.
Come, your fears counsel you but ill. My absence
Would draw suspect° upon you instantly; *suspicion*
There were no rescue for you.
BEATRICE [*aside*] He speaks home.° *to the point*
DE FLORES Nor is it fit we two, engaged so jointly,
Should part and live asunder. [*He tries to kiss her.*]
BEATRICE How now, sir?
This shows° not well. *looks*
DE FLORES What makes your lip so strange?° *unwelcoming*
This must not be betwixt us.
BEATRICE [*aside*] The man talks wildly.
DE FLORES Come, kiss me with a zeal now.
BEATRICE [*aside*] Heaven, I doubt° him! *fear, mistrust*
DE FLORES I will not stand so long to beg 'em° shortly. *(kisses, favors)*
BEATRICE Take heed, De Flores, of forgetfulness;° *forgetting your place*
'Twill soon betray us.
DE FLORES Take you heed first.
Faith, you're grown much forgetful;° you're to blame in't. *forgetful of my service*
BEATRICE [*aside*] He's bold, and I am blamed for't!
DE FLORES I have eased you

Of your trouble; think on't. I'm in pain,
And must be eased of you;° 'tis a charity. *by you*
Justice invites your blood° to understand me. *passions, sexuality*

BEATRICE I dare not.

DE FLORES Quickly!

BEATRICE Oh, I never shall!
Speak it yet further off, that I may lose° *forget; not hear*
What has been spoken and no sound remain on't.
I would not hear so much offense° again *offensive talk*
For such another deed.

DE FLORES Soft,° lady, soft. *Gently, not so fast*
The last° is not yet paid for. Oh, this act *The deed I just did*
Has put me into spirit! I was as greedy on't
As the parched earth of moisture when the clouds weep.
Did you not mark? I wrought myself into't,° *maneuvered to do it*
Nay, sued° and kneeled for't. Why was all that pains took? *begged*
You see I have thrown contempt upon your gold—
Not that I want it not, for I do piteously;
In order° I will come unto't, and make use on't, *In due course*
But 'twas not held so precious to begin with.
For I place wealth after the heels of° pleasure, *subservient to*
And, were I not resolved in my belief
That thy virginity were perfect in thee,
I should but take my recompense with grudging,
As if I had but half my hopes I agreed for.

BEATRICE Why, 'tis impossible thou canst be so wicked,
Or shelter such a cunning cruelty,
To make his death the murderer of my honor!
Thy language is so bold and vicious,
I cannot see which way I can forgive it
With any modesty.

DE FLORES Push,° you forget yourself. *Pish*
A woman dipped in blood, and talk of modesty?

BEATRICE Oh, misery of sin! Would I had been bound
Perpetually unto my living hate
In that Piracquo than to hear these words.
Think but upon the distance that creation° *God's ordered hierarchy*
Set 'twixt thy blood° and mine, and keep thee there. *inherited rank*

DE FLORES Look but into your conscience; read me there;
'Tis a true book. You'll find me there your equal.
Push, fly not to your birth, but settle you
In what the act has made you; you're no more now.
You must forget your parentage to me.° *in favor of me*
You're the deed's creature;° by that name *creation; slave*
You lost your first condition,° and I challenge° you, *your innocence / claim*
As peace and innocency has turned you out° *ousted you*
And made you one with me.

BEATRICE With thee, foul villain?

DE FLORES Yes, my fair murd'ress. Do you urge° me? *provoke*
Though thou writ'st maid,° thou whore in thy affection! *call yourself virgin*
'Twas changed from thy first love, and that's a kind
Of whoredom in thy heart; and he's changed° now, *i.e., dead*
To bring thy second on, thy Alsemero,
Whom (by all sweets that ever darkness tasted),
If I enjoy thee not, thou ne'er enjoy'st.

I'll blast the hopes and joys of marriage.
I'll confess all; my life I rate° at nothing. *value*
BEATRICE De Flores!
DE FLORES I shall rest from all lovers' plagues then.° *(when I'm executed)*
I live in pain now; that shooting eye° *your provocative eye*
Will burn my heart to cinders.
BEATRICE Oh, sir, hear me!
DE FLORES She that in life and love refuses me
In death and shame my partner she shall be.
BEATRICE Stay, hear me once for all! I make thee master
Of all the wealth I have in gold and jewels;
Let me go poor unto my bed with honor,
And I am rich in all things.
DE FLORES Let this silence thee:
The wealth of all Valencia shall not buy
My pleasure from me.
Can you weep fate from its determined purpose?
So soon may you weep me.
BEATRICE Vengeance begins;
Murder, I see, is followed by more sins.
Was my creation in the womb so curst
It must engender with a viper first?
DE FLORES Come, rise, and shroud° your blushes in my bosom. *hide*
Silence is one of pleasure's best receipts.° *recipes*
Thy peace is wrought° forever in this yielding. *made*
'Las, how the turtle° pants! Thou'lt love anon *turtledove*
What thou so fear'st and faint'st to venture on. *Exeunt.*

4.1

[DUMB SHOW]

Enter gentlemen, Vermandero meeting them with action of wonderment at the flight of Piracquo. Enter Alsemero, with Jasperino and gallants. Vermandero points to him, the gentlemen seeming to applaud the choice. Alsemero, Jasperino, and gentlemen [start to leave in procession], Beatrice the bride following in great state, accompanied with Diaphanta, Isabella, and other gentlewomen; De Flores after all, smiling at the accident.° Alonzo's ghost appears to De Flores in the midst of his smile, startles him, showing him the hand whose finger he had cut off. They pass over° in great solemnity.° (accident: *turn of events*; pass over: *cross and exit*; solemnity: *ceremoniousness*)

Enter Beatrice.

BEATRICE This fellow has undone me endlessly!
Never was bride so fearfully distressed.
The more I think upon th'ensuing night,
And whom I am to cope with in embraces—

4.1. The castle. Alsemero's chambers.

One that's ennobled both in blood and mind,
So clear in understanding (that's my plague now),[1]
Before whose judgment will my fault appear
Like malefactors' crimes before tribunals.
There is no hiding on't—the more I dive
Into my own distress. How a wise man
Stands for a great calamity![2] There's no venturing
Into his bed, what course soe'er I light upon,
Without my shame, which may grow up to° danger. *increase to*
He cannot but in justice strangle me
As I lie by him, as a cheater° use me. *adulteress; cardsharp*
'Tis a precious° craft to play with a false die° *costly; risky / dice*
Before a cunning gamester. Here's his closet,° *private room; cabinet*
The key left in't, and he abroad i'th'park.
Sure 'twas forgot. I'll be so bold as look in't.
[*She opens the door.*]
Bless me! A right° physician's closet 'tis, *veritable*
Set round with vials, every one her mark° too. *its label*
Sure he does practice physic° for his own use, *medicine*
Which may be safely called your great man's wisdom.[3]
What manuscript lies here? "The Book of Experiment,
Called Secrets in Nature." So 'tis, 'tis so.
[*She consults the table of contents.*]
"How to know whether a woman be with child or no."
I hope I am not yet; if he should try,° though! *test me*
Let me see, folio forty-five. Here 'tis;
The leaf° tucked down upon't, the place suspicious. *page*

"If you would know whether a woman be with child or not, give her two spoonfuls of the white water° in glass C—" where's that Glass C? Oh, yonder, I see't now—"and if she be with child, she sleeps full twelve hours after; if not, not." *liquid*

None of that water comes into my belly.
I'll know you from a hundred. I could break you now,
Or turn you into° milk, and so beguile *replace you with*
The master of the mystery,° but I'll look to° you. *secret / be wary of*
Ha! That which is next is ten times worse.
"How to know whether a woman be a maid or not."
If that should be applied,° what would become of me? *put to the test*
Belike° he has a strong faith of my purity, *Probably*
That° never yet made proof. But this he calls [*she reads*] *He who*

"A merry sleight,° but true experiment, the author Antonius Mizaldus. Give the party you suspect the quantity of a spoonful of the water in the glass M, which, upon her that is a maid, makes three several° effects: 'twill make her incontinently gape,° then fall into a sudden sneezing, last into a violent laughing, else° dull, heavy, and lumpish." *trick* *distinct* *immediately yawn* *otherwise*

1. Alsemero's clear understanding of things is my greatest worry.
2. How a wise man looms as a disaster! (Beatrice fears that Alsemero is too intelligent to be deceived. "Stands for" means "represents.")
3. A man is wise to master the practice of medicine. (Alsemero's manuscript, lines 24–25, appears to be derived from various authorities and from popular lore. Lines 44–45 cite Antonius Mizaldus [1520–1578], French author of *De Arcanis Naturae* [Secrets in Nature]; the pregnancy and virginity tests here described are actually to be found in other works by this author and elsewhere. They are scornfully dismissed in Robert Burton's *The Anatomy of Melancholy* [1621].)

Where had I been?[4]
I fear it; yet 'tis seven hours to bedtime.

Enter Diaphanta.

DIAPHANTA Cuds,° madam, are you here? *i.e., God's (an oath)*
BEATRICE [*aside*] Seeing that wench now,
A trick comes in my mind; 'tis a nice piece
Gold cannot purchase.[5] [*To Diaphanta*] I come hither, wench,
To look° my lord. *look for*
DIAPHANTA [*aside*] Would I had such a cause to look him too!
[*To Beatrice*] Why, he's i'th'park, madam.
BEATRICE There let him be.
DIAPHANTA Ay, madam, let him compass° *range through*
Whole parks and forests, as great rangers° do; *park-keepers; lotharios*
At roosting time a little lodge[6] can hold 'em.
Earth-conquering Alexander, that thought the world
Too narrow for him, in the end had but his pit-hole.° *grave; vagina*
BEATRICE I fear thou art not modest, Diaphanta.
DIAPHANTA Your thoughts are so unwilling to be known,° *are inscrutable*
madam!
'Tis ever the bride's fashion towards bedtime
To set light by her joys, as if she owed° 'em not. *owned*
BEATRICE Her joys? Her fears, thou wouldst say.
DIAPHANTA Fear of what?
BEATRICE Art thou a maid, and talk'st so to a maid?
You leave a blushing business behind,[7]
Beshrew your heart for't!
DIAPHANTA Do you mean good sooth,° madam? *Are you in earnest*
BEATRICE Well, if I'd thought upon the fear at first,
Man should have been unknown.° *I'd never have married*
DIAPHANTA Is't possible?
BEATRICE I will give a thousand ducats to that woman
Would° try what my fear were, and tell me true *Who would*
Tomorrow, when she gets from't;° as she likes, *disengages from sex*
I might perhaps be drawn to't.
DIAPHANTA Are you in earnest?
BEATRICE Do you get the woman, then challenge me,
And see if I'll fly from't. But I must tell you
This by the way: she must be a true maid,° *virgin*
Else there's no trial. My fears are not hers,° else. *Our fears are unalike*
DIAPHANTA Nay, she that I would put into your hands, madam,
Shall be a maid.
BEATRICE You know I should be shamed else,
Because she lies° for me. *makes love; deceives*
DIAPHANTA 'Tis a strange humor!° *caprice*
But are you serious still? Would you resign
Your first night's pleasure, and give money too?
BEATRICE As willingly as live. [*Aside*] Alas, the gold
Is but a by-bet° to wedge in the honor. *side bet, incidental*

4. Where would I have been if I hadn't found this?
5. It's a virtuous young woman indeed that gold cannot corrupt.
6. Hunting lodge. (But with the suggestion of a warm place to lodge his sexual organ.)
7. You speak lightly of the first night of marriage as though it were not a blushing matter.

DIAPHANTA I do not know how the world goes abroad° *generally*
For faith or honesty; there's both required in this.
Madam, what say you to me, and stray° no further? *search*
I've a good mind, in troth, to earn your money.
BEATRICE You're too quick,° I fear, to be a maid. *vivacious; wanton*
DIAPHANTA How? Not a maid? Nay, then, you urge° me, madam. *provoke*
Your honorable self is not a truer,
With all your fears upon you—
BEATRICE [*aside*] Bad enough,° then. *That's not very chaste*
DIAPHANTA Than I, with all my lightsome° joys about me. *cheerful*
BEATRICE I'm glad to hear't. Then you dare put your honesty° *chastity*
Upon an easy trial?
DIAPHANTA Easy? Anything.
BEATRICE I'll come to you straight.
[*She goes to the door of Alsemero's private room.*]
DIAPHANTA [*aside*] She will not search me, will she,
Like the forewoman of a female jury?[8]
BEATRICE Glass M: ay, this is it.—Look, Diaphanta,
You take no worse than I do. [*She drinks.*]
DIAPHANTA And in so doing
I will not question what 'tis, but take it. [*She drinks.*]
BEATRICE [*aside*] Now, if the experiment be true, 'twill praise itself,° *proclaim its own worth*
And give me noble ease. [*Diaphanta yawns.*] Begins already!
There's the first symptom. [*Diaphanta sneezes.*] And what haste it makes
To fall into the second, there by this time!
Most admirable secret! On the contrary
It stirs not me a whit, which most concerns it.° *I whom it concerns most*
DIAPHANTA [*laughing*] Ha, ha, ha!
BEATRICE [*aside*] Just in all things and in order
As if 'twere circumscribed!° One accident° *specified / symptom*
Gives way unto another.
DIAPHANTA Ha, ha, ha!
BEATRICE How now, wench?
DIAPHANTA Ha, ha, ha! I am so so light at heart—ha, ha, ha!—so pleasurable!
But one swig more, sweet madam.
BEATRICE Ay, tomorrow;
We shall have time to sit by't.° *sit and enjoy it*
DIAPHANTA Now I'm sad again.
BEATRICE [*aside*] It lays itself° so gently too!—Come, wench, *subsides*
Most honest Diaphanta I dare call thee now.
DIAPHANTA Pray tell me, madam, what trick call you this?
BEATRICE I'll tell thee all hereafter. We must study
The carriage° of this business. *carrying out*
DIAPHANTA I shall carry't well,[9]
Because I love the burden.

8. During a notorious trial in 1613, in which the Countess of Essex sued for divorce on the grounds of nonconsummation, she was examined by women to determine if her hymen was still intact. See also introduction, note 2.
9. I.e., carry the weight of the man well.

BEATRICE About midnight
You must not fail to steal forth gently,
That I may use° the place. *occupy*

DIAPHANTA Oh, fear not, madam,
I shall be cool by that time. [*Aside*] The bride's place,
And with a thousand ducats! I'm for a justice now.
I bring a portion with me; I scorn small fools.[1] *Exeunt.*

[4.2]

Enter Vermandero and Servant.

VERMANDERO I tell thee, knave, mine honor is in question,
A thing till now free from suspicion,
Nor ever was there cause. Who of my gentlemen are absent?
Tell me, and truly, how many and who.

SERVANT Antonio, sir, and Franciscus.

VERMANDERO When did they leave the castle?

SERVANT Some ten days since, sir, the one intending° to *intending to go*
Briamata,[1] th'other for Valencia.

VERMANDERO The time° accuses 'em. A charge of murder *The suspicious timing*
Is brought within my castle gate, Piracquo's murder;
I dare not answer faithfully° their absence. *justify in good faith*
A strict command of apprehension° *arrest*
Shall pursue 'em suddenly,° and either wipe *quickly*
The stain off clear or openly discover° it. *disclose*
Provide me wingèd warrants for the purpose. *Exit Servant.*

Enter Tomazo.

See, I am set on° again. *beset by dangers*

TOMAZO I claim a brother of you.

VERMANDERO You're too hot.
Seek him not here.

TOMAZO Yes, 'mongst your dearest bloods,[2]
If my peace° find no fairer satisfaction. *peace of mind*
This is the place must° yield account for him, *that must*
For here I left him, and the hasty tie
Of this snatched° marriage gives strong testimony *hastily arranged*
Of his most certain ruin.

VERMANDERO Certain falsehood!
This is the place indeed; his° breach of faith *(Alonzo's)*
Has too much marred° both my abusèd love— *injured, wronged*
The honorable love I reserved for him—
And mocked my daughter's joy. The prepared morning
Blushed at his infidelity; he left
Contempt and scorn to throw upon those friends
Whose belief hurt 'em.[3] Oh, 'twas most ignoble
To take his flight so unexpectedly,
And throw such public wrongs on those that loved him!

1. With a thousand ducats as my dowry, I intend to marry a justice of the peace; no small fry for me.

4.2. The castle.

1. An estate belonging to Vermandero, roughly forty miles from Alicante (according to the principal source for this play, John Reynolds's *The Triumph of God's Revenge against . . . Murder* [1621]).

2. Yes, among those closest to you, and in your own blood (which I intend to shed).

3. Whose belief in him came back to embarrass them.

TOMAZO Then this is all your answer?
VERMANDERO 'Tis too fair° [*too good an answer*]
For one of his alliance;° and I warn you [*kindred*]
That this place no more see you.° *Exit.* [*Not to come here again*]

Enter De Flores.

TOMAZO The best is,
There is more ground to meet a man's revenge on.[4]—
Honest De Flores!
DE FLORES That's my name indeed.
Saw you the bride? Good sweet sir, which way took she?
TOMAZO I have blessed° mine eyes from seeing such a false one. [*shielded*]
DE FLORES [*aside*] I'd fain get off. This man's not for my company;
I smell his brother's blood when I come near him.
TOMAZO Come hither, kind and true one; I remember
My brother loved thee well.
DE FLORES Oh, purely,° dear sir! [*cordially*]
[*Aside*] Methinks I am now again a-killing on him,
He brings it so fresh to me.
TOMAZO Thou canst guess, sirrah
(One honest friend has an instinct of jealousy),[5]
At some foul guilty person?
DE FLORES 'Las, sir, I am so charitable, I think none
Worse than myself.—You did not see the bride, then?
TOMAZO I prithee name her not. Is she not wicked?
DE FLORES No, no, a pretty, easy, round-packed° sinner, [*graciously plump*]
As your most ladies are,° else you might think [*As most ladies are*]
I flattered her; but sir, at no hand° wicked, [*by no means*]
Till they're so old their chins and noses meet,
And they salute° witches.—I am called,° I think, sir. [*consort with / summoned*]
[*Aside*] His company ev'n o'erlays° my conscience! *Exit.* [*oppresses*]
TOMAZO That De Flores has a wondrous honest heart.
He'll bring it° out in time, I'm assured on't. [*(the truth)*]
Oh, here's the glorious° master of the day's joy. [*(said ironically)*]
'Twill not be long till he and I do reckon.° [*settle accounts*]

Enter Alsemero.

Sir!
ALSEMERO You are most welcome.
TOMAZO You may call that word back.
I do not think I am, nor wish to be.
ALSEMERO 'Tis strange you found the way to this house, then.
TOMAZO Would I'd ne'er known the cause![6] I'm none of those, sir,
That come to give you joy and swill your wine;
'Tis a more precious liquor° that must lay° [*(blood) / allay, quench*]
The fiery thirst I bring.
ALSEMERO Your words and you

4. (1) The best thing about this expulsion from the house is that it gives me a further reason to exact revenge; (2) revenge can be pursued anywhere and everywhere. There are other ways of obtaining revenge.
5. As one who was a good friend of Alonzo's (see lines 42–43), you surely must have an instinctive suspicion of someone.
6. I wish I'd never known the cause of our coming in the first place—that is, the proposed marriage to Beatrice.

Appear to me great strangers.° *at odds; unexpected*

TOMAZO Time and our swords
May make us more acquainted. This the business:
I should have a brother in your place.° *here; in place of you*
How treachery and malice have disposed of him,
I'm bound to inquire of him which holds his right,[7]
Which never could come fairly.° *could have come honestly*

ALSEMERO You must look
To answer° for that word, sir. *answer with your sword*

TOMAZO Fear you not;
I'll have it ready drawn[8] at our next meeting.
Keep your day solemn.° Farewell; I disturb it not. *Celebrate your wedding*
I'll bear the smart° with patience for a time. *Exit.* *insult; pain, grief*

ALSEMERO 'Tis somewhat ominous, this, a quarrel entered
Upon this day! My innocence relieves me;
I should be wondrous sad else.

Enter Jasperino.

Jasperino!
I have news to tell thee, strange news.

JASPERINO I ha' some too,
I think as strange as yours. Would I might keep° *keep back*
Mine, so° my faith and friendship might be kept in't! *so long as*
Faith, sir, dispense a little with my zeal,
And let it cool in this.[9]

ALSEMERO This puts me on,° *piques my interest*
And blames thee for thy slowness.

JASPERINO All may prove nothing;
Only a friendly fear that leapt from me, sir.

ALSEMERO No question it may prove nothing. Let's partake° it, though. *partake of*

JASPERINO 'Twas Diaphanta's chance—for to that wench
I pretend° honest love, and she deserves it— *profess*
To leave me in a back part of the house,
A place we chose for private conference.
She was no sooner gone but instantly
I heard your bride's voice in the next room to me;
And lending more attention, found De Flores
Louder than she.

ALSEMERO De Flores? Thou art out° now. *mistaken*

JASPERINO You'll tell me more° anon. *You'll sing another tune*

ALSEMERO Still I'll prevent thee.[1]
The very sight of him is poison to her.

JASPERINO That made me stagger° too, but Diaphanta *hesitate in doubt*
At her return confirmed it.

ALSEMERO Diaphanta!

JASPERINO Then fell we both° to listen, and words passed *we both proceeded*
Like those that challenge interest° in a woman. *claim a right*

ALSEMERO Peace, quench thy zeal! 'Tis dangerous to thy bosom.

JASPERINO Then truth is full of peril.

7. I'm bound to inquire of him who possesses the woman to whom Alonzo had the right—you, Alsemero.
8. (1) I'll have my answer drafted; (2) I'll have my sword drawn from its sheath.
9. Let me be a little less zealous than usual and keep back this news.
1. I'll explain once again her feelings about De Flores in order to counter your improbable news.

ALSEMERO Such truths are.
Oh, were she the sole glory of the earth,
Had eyes that could shoot fire into kings' breasts,
And touched,° she sleeps not here! Yet I have time, *tainted, unchaste*
Though night be near, to be resolved° hereof; *made certain*
And prithee do not weigh me by my passions.° *judge me by my outburst*
JASPERINO I never weighed friend so.
ALSEMERO Done charitably. [*He gives a key.*]
That key will lead thee to a pretty° secret, *ingenious*
By a Chaldean° taught me, and I've made *astrologer, seer*
My study upon some. Bring from my closet
A glass inscribed there with the letter M,
And question not my purpose.
JASPERINO It shall be done, sir. *Exit.*
ALSEMERO How can this hang together? Not an hour since,
Her woman came pleading her lady's fears,
Delivered her for° the most timorous virgin *Reported her to be*
That ever shrunk at man's name, and so modest,
She charged her° weep out her° request to me *(Diaphanta) / (Beatrice's)*
That she might come obscurely° to my bosom. *under cover of darkness*

Enter Beatrice.

BEATRICE [*aside*] All things go well. My woman's preparing yonder
For her sweet voyage, which grieves me to lose.
Necessity compels it; I lose all else.
ALSEMERO [*aside*] Push, modesty's shrine is set in yonder forehead.
I cannot be too sure, though. [*To her*] My Joanna!
BEATRICE Sir, I was bold to weep a message° to you. *send a tearful message*
Pardon my modest fears.
ALSEMERO [*aside*] The dove's not meeker.
She's abused,° questionless.° *slandered / beyond doubt*

Enter Jasperino [with a vial].

Oh, are you come, sir?
BEATRICE [*aside*] The glass, upon my life! I see the letter.
JASPERINO Sir, this is M.
ALSEMERO 'Tis it.
BEATRICE [*aside*] I am suspected.
ALSEMERO How fitly our bride comes to partake with us!
[*He offers her the liquid to drink.*]
BEATRICE What is't, my lord?
ALSEMERO No hurt.
BEATRICE Sir, pardon me;
I seldom taste of any composition.° *concoction*
ALSEMERO But this upon my warrant° you shall venture on. *guarantee*
BEATRICE I fear 'twill make me ill.
ALSEMERO Heaven forbid that!
BEATRICE [*aside*] I'm put now to my cunning. Th'effects I know,
If I can now but feign 'em handsomely. [*She drinks.*]
ALSEMERO [*aside to Jasperino*] It has that secret virtue—it ne'er missed, sir—

Upon a virgin.
JASPERINO Treble qualitied?° *Having three effects?*
[*Beatrice yawns, then sneezes.*]
ALSEMERO By all that's virtuous, it takes° there, proceeds! *takes effect*
JASPERINO This is the strangest trick to know a maid by!
BEATRICE [*laughing*] Ha, ha, ha!
You have given me joy of heart to drink, my lord.
ALSEMERO No, thou hast given me such joy of heart
That never can be blasted.° *withered*
BEATRICE What's the matter, sir?
ALSEMERO [*to Jasperino*] See, now 'tis settled in a melancholy,
Keeps both the time and method. [*To her*] My Joanna!
Chaste as the breath of heaven, or morning's womb° *the dawn*
That brings the day forth: thus my love encloses thee.
[*He embraces her.*] *Exeunt.*

[4.3]

Enter Isabella [with a letter] and Lollio.

ISABELLA O heaven! Is this the waxing moon?° *time of growing lunacy*
Does love turn fool, run mad, and all at once?
Sirrah, here's a madman,° akin to the fool too: *(Franciscus)*
A lunatic lover.
LOLLIO No, no, not he I brought the letter from.
ISABELLA Compare his inside° with his out,° and tell me. *its contents / its outside*
[*She gives him the letter.*]

LOLLIO The out's mad, I'm sure of that; I had a taste on't. [*He reads.*] "To the bright Andromeda,[1] chief chambermaid to the Knight of the Sun,[2] at the sign of Scorpio, in the middle region,[3] sent by the bellows-mender of Aeolus.° Pay the post."° This is stark madness. *god of winds* / *letter carrier*

ISABELLA Now mark the inside. [*She takes the letter and reads.*] "Sweet lady, having now cast off this counterfeit cover of a madman, I appear to your best judgment a true and faithful lover of your beauty."

LOLLIO He is mad still.

ISABELLA "If any fault you find, chide those perfections in you which have made me imperfect;° 'tis the same sun that causeth to grow and enforceth to wither—" *i.e., foolish*

LOLLIO Oh, rogue!

ISABELLA "—shapes and transshapes, destroys and builds again. I come in winter to you dismantled of my proper ornaments;° by the sweet splendor of your cheerful smiles, I spring and live a lover." *my usual attire*

LOLLIO Mad rascal still!

ISABELLA "Tread him not under foot that shall appear an honor to° your bounties. I remain—mad till I speak with you, from whom I expect my cure. Yours all, or one beside himself,° Franciscus." *will heap honor on* / *beside himself in love*

4.3. The insane asylum.
1. Andromeda was saved by Perseus from a sea monster sent by Poseidon. Franciscus' letter hints at a similar rescue for Isabella from her old husband.
2. The hero of a Spanish chivalric romance.
3. Scorpio is the zodiacal sign represented by a scorpion and traditionally associated with the genital area ("middle region").

LOLLIO You are like° to have a fine time on't. My master and — *likely*
I may give over our professions; I do not think but° you can — *I am confident that*
cure fools and madmen faster than we, with little pains too.
ISABELLA Very likely.
LOLLIO One thing I must tell you, mistress. You perceive that
I am privy to° your skill. If I find you minister once and set — *in on the secret of*
up the trade,° I put in for my thirds; I shall be mad or fool — *i.e., take on a lover*
else.
ISABELLA The first place is thine, believe it, Lollio;
If I do fall°— — *fall in virtue*
LOLLIO I fall upon° you. — *mount sexually*
ISABELLA So.
LOLLIO Well, I stand to my venture.[4]
ISABELLA But thy counsel now. How shall I deal with 'em?
LOLLIO Why, do you mean to deal° with 'em? — *deal sexually*
ISABELLA Nay, the fair understanding:° how to use 'em. — *understand me decently*
LOLLIO Abuse° 'em. That's the way to mad the fool and make — *Hoodwink*
a fool of the madman, and then you use 'em kindly.° — *according to kind; gently*
ISABELLA 'Tis easy; I'll practice.° Do thou observe it. — *do it*
The key° of thy wardrobe. — *Give me the key*
LOLLIO [*giving a key*] There. Fit yourself for 'em, and I'll fit
'em both for you.
ISABELLA Take thou no further notice than the outside.[5]

Exit.

LOLLIO Not an inch; I'll put you to the inside.[6]

Enter Alibius.

ALIBIUS Lollio, art there? Will all be perfect,° think'st thou? — *Will our show go well*
Tomorrow night, as if to close up the solemnity,° — *end the festivities*
Vermandero expects us.
LOLLIO I mistrust° the madmen most. The fools will do well — *am worried about*
enough; I have taken pains with them.
ALIBIUS Tush, they cannot miss; the more absurdity,
The more commends it, so° no rough behaviors — *provided*
Affright the ladies. They are nice° things, thou know'st. — *delicate, fastidious*
LOLLIO You need not fear, sir; so long as we are there with
our commanding pizzles,[7] they'll be as tame as the ladies
themselves.
ALIBIUS I will see them once more rehearse before they go.
LOLLIO I was about it, sir; look you to the madmen's morris,° — *a country-dance*
and let me alone with the other.° There is one or two that I — *leave the other to me*
mistrust their fooling; I'll instruct them, and then they shall
rehearse the whole measure.° — *dance*
ALIBIUS Do so; I'll see the music prepared. But Lollio,
By the way, how does my wife brook° her restraint? — *tolerate*
Does she not grudge at it?
LOLLIO So, so. She takes some pleasure in the house; she
would abroad else. You must allow her a little more length;° — *latitude*
she's kept too short.° — *restrained*
ALIBIUS She shall along to Vermandero's with us;

4. (1) I intend to pursue my hopes; (2) I am erect.
5. Act as though you know nothing about me other than my appearance (as a madwoman).
6. Lollio agrees to Isabella's request but hopes to take advantage of his inside knowledge of her scheme and be inside her body.
7. Whips made of bulls' penises.

That will serve her for a month's liberty.

LOLLIO What's that on your face, sir?

ALIBIUS Where, Lollio? I see nothing.

LOLLIO Cry you mercy,° sir, 'tis your nose; it showed like the trunk of a young elephant. — *I beg your pardon*

ALIBIUS Away, rascal! I'll prepare the music, Lollio.

LOLLIO Do, sir, and I'll dance the whilst.° *Exit Alibius.* [*Calling*] Tony! Where art thou, Tony? — *meanwhile*

Enter Antonio.

ANTONIO Here, cousin. Where art thou?

LOLLIO Come, Tony, the footmanship I taught you.

ANTONIO I had rather ride,[8] cousin.

LOLLIO [*aside*] Ay, a whip take you! But I'll keep you out.° [*To him*] Vault in. Look you, Tony: Fa, la, la, la, la! — *i.e., from your pleasure*

[*Lollio demonstrates a leaping dance.*]

ANTONIO [*imitating Lollio*] Fa, la, la, la, la!

LOLLIO There, an honor.° — *make a bow*

ANTONIO [*bowing*] Is this an honor, coz?

LOLLIO Yes, an it please Your Worship.

ANTONIO Does honor bend in the hams, coz?

LOLLIO Marry does it, as low as worship, squireship, nay, yeomanry itself sometimes, from whence it first stiffened.° There rise, a caper.° — *stiffly arose (bawdy)*; *make a dancing leap*

ANTONIO Caper after an honor, coz?

LOLLIO Very proper; for honor is but a caper, rises as fast and high, has a knee° or two, and falls to th'ground again.[9] You can remember your figure,° Tony? — *is kneeled or bowed to*; *dance pattern or step*

ANTONIO Yes, cousin; when I see thy figure, I can remember mine.[1] *Exit [Lollio].*

Enter Isabella [like a madwoman].

ISABELLA Hey, how he° treads the air! Shoo, shoo! T'other way! — *(Icarus)*
He burns his wings else.—Here's wax enough below, Icarus,[2]
More than will be canceled[3] these eighteen moons.° — *months*
He's down, he's down! What a terrible fall he had!
Stand up, thou son of Cretan Daedalus,
And let us tread the lower labyrinth;
I'll bring thee to the clue.[4]

ANTONIO [*to Isabella*] Prithee, coz, let me alone.

ISABELLA Art thou not drowned?
About thy head I saw a heap of clouds
Wrapped like a Turkish turban; on thy back,
A crook'd chameleon-colored° rainbow hung, — *many-colored; shifting*
Like a tiara down unto thy hams.

8. Antonio probably has a sexual meaning in mind: to ride a woman (Isabella) sexually. See lines 152–53 below.

9. Honor capers and rises for a brief time, has its moment of ceremonious respect, and declines. (With an erotic suggestion of sexual arousal and detumescence, following "stiffened" in line 96.)

1. I.e., when I see your foolish face, I'm reminded to keep up my disguise by looking and acting foolish. (Antonio plays on Lollio's "figure," meaning "dance pattern"; here it means "face.")

2. Son of Daedalus, who devised the famous labyrinth for King Minos of Crete to house the monstrous Minotaur. When son and father escaped imprisonment at Crete by using wings they made of wax, Icarus rashly flew too near the sun and melted the wax, causing him to fall into the Aegean Sea.

3. Used up, like sealing wax used on legal deeds.

4. By means of a "clue," or ball, of thread given him by the lovesick Ariadne, daughter of King Minos, Theseus made his way out of the Cretan labyrinth after slaying the Minotaur.

Let me suck out those billows° in thy belly. *waves*
Hark how they roar and rumble in the straits!
Bless thee° from the pirates! *May heaven protect you*

ANTONIO Pox upon you, let me alone!

ISABELLA Why shouldst thou mount so high as Mercury,° *messenger of the gods*
Unless thou hadst reversion° of his place? *assurance of succession*
Stay in the moon with me, Endymion,[5]
And we will rule these wild rebellious waves
That would have drowned my love.

ANTONIO I'll kick thee if again thou touch me,
Thou wild unshapen antic!° I am no fool, *misshapen grotesquerie*
You bedlam.° *lunatic*

ISABELLA But you are, as sure as I am, mad.
Have I put on this habit of a frantic,° *mad person*
With love as full of fury to beguile
The nimble eye of watchful jealousy,
And am I thus rewarded? [*She reveals her identity.*]

ANTONIO Ha! Dearest beauty!

ISABELLA No, I have no beauty now,
Nor never had, but what was in my garments.
You a quick-sighted lover? Come not near me.
Keep your caparisons;° you're aptly clad. *(fool's) adornments*
I came a feigner° to return stark mad. *Exit.* *one feigning madness*

Enter Lollio.

ANTONIO [*to the departing Isabella*] Stay! Or I shall change condition
And become as you are.° [*He starts to follow her.*] *i.e., truly mad*

LOLLIO Why, Tony, whither now? Why, fool!

ANTONIO Whose fool, usher° of idiots? You coxcomb!° *keeper / fool*
I have fooled too much.

LOLLIO You were best° be mad another while, then. *You'd better*

ANTONIO So I am, stark mad. I have cause enough,
And I could throw the full effects on thee,
And beat thee like a Fury!° *avenging goddess*

LOLLIO Do not, do not; I shall not forbear° the gentleman under the fool,° if you do. Alas, I saw through your fox skin before now. Come, I can give you comfort: my mistress loves you, and there is as arrant a madman i'th'house as you are a fool, your rival, whom she loves not. If after the masque we can rid her of him, you earn her love, she says, and the fool° shall ride her.° *I won't spare* *the real Tony* *(you) / ride her sexually*

ANTONIO May I believe thee?

LOLLIO Yes, or you may choose whether you will or no.

ANTONIO She's eased of him;° I have a good quarrel on't. *I'll do him in for her*

LOLLIO Well, keep your old station yet, and be quiet.

ANTONIO Tell her I will deserve her love.

LOLLIO And you are like° to have your desire. *likely, assured*
[*Exit Antonio.*]

Enter Franciscus.

5. A handsome shepherd with whom the moon fell in love.

FRANCISCUS [*singing*] "Down, down, down a-down a-down,
and then with a horse trick,
To kick Latona's forehead, and break her bowstring."[6]

LOLLIO [*aside*] This is t'other counterfeit. I'll put him out of his humor. [*He takes out a letter and reads aloud.*] "Sweet lady, having now cast off this counterfeit cover of a madman, I appear to your best judgment a true and faithful lover of your beauty." This is pretty well for a madman.

FRANCISCUS Ha! What's that?

LOLLIO "Chide those perfections in you which have made me imperfect."

FRANCISCUS [*aside*] I am discovered° to the fool.° *revealed / (Lollio)*

LOLLIO "I hope to discover the fool in you,[7] ere I have done with you. Yours all, or one beside himself, Franciscus." This madman will mend, sure.

FRANCISCUS What do you read, sirrah?

LOLLIO Your destiny, sir. You'll be hanged for this trick, and another that I know.

FRANCISCUS Art thou of counsel with° thy mistress? *in the confidence of*

LOLLIO Next her apron strings.° *i.e., Very close indeed*

FRANCISCUS Give me thy hand.

LOLLIO Stay, let me put yours° in my pocket first. [*He puts away the letter.*] Your hand is true, is it not?[8] It will not pick?° I partly fear it because I think it does lie. *your handwriting / pick pockets*

FRANCISCUS Not in a syllable.

LOLLIO So, if you love my mistress so well as you have handled the matter here, you are like to be cured of your madness.

FRANCISCUS And none but she can cure it.

LOLLIO Well, I'll give you over,° then, and she shall cast your water° next. *stop tending to you / diagnose your urine*

FRANCISCUS [*giving money*] Take for thy pains past.

LOLLIO I shall deserve more, sir, I hope. My mistress loves you, but must have some proof of your love to her.

FRANCISCUS There I meet my wishes.° *That's my ardent desire*

LOLLIO That will not serve; you must meet her enemy and yours.

FRANCISCUS He's dead° already! *as good as dead*

LOLLIO Will you tell me that, and I parted but now° with him? *just now*

FRANCISCUS Show me the man.

LOLLIO Ay, that's a right course, now; see° him before you kill him in any case. And yet it needs not go so far, neither; 'tis but a fool that haunts the house and my mistress in the shape of an idiot. Bang but his fool's coat well-favoredly,° and 'tis well. *identify / Thrash the fool soundly*

FRANCISCUS Soundly, soundly!

LOLLIO Only reserve° him till the masque be past, and if you find him not now in the dance yourself, I'll show you.—In! In! My master! *spare*

Enter Alibius.

6. Franciscus, in pretended madness, confuses Latona, mother of Apollo and Diana, with the huntress Diana, whose bowstring Franciscus vows to break.

7. I hope you will make a fool of yourself (in love).

8. (1) Your letter speaks the truth, doesn't it? (2) You're no pickpocket, are you?

FRANCISCUS [*pretending madness*] He handles him like a feather.—Hey! [*Exit dancing.*]

ALIBIUS Well said!° In a readiness, Lollio? *Well done!*

LOLLIO Yes, sir.

ALIBIUS Away, then, and guide them in, Lollio.
Entreat your mistress to see this sight.
[*Lollio starts to leave.*]
Hark, is there not one incurable fool
That might be begged? I have friends.[9]

LOLLIO I have him° for you, one that shall deserve it too. *(Antonio)*

ALIBIUS Good boy, Lollio. [*Exit Lollio.*]

[*Lollio returns, leading Isabella, Madmen, and fools.*]
The Madmen and fools dance.

'Tis perfect! Well, fit but once these strains,[1]
We shall have coin and credit for our pains. *Exeunt.*

5.1

Enter Beatrice. A clock strikes one.

BEATRICE One struck, and yet she lies by't. Oh, my fears!
This strumpet serves her own ends, 'tis apparent now,
Devours the pleasure with a greedy appetite,
And never minds my honor or my peace,° *peace of mind*
Makes havoc of my right; but she pays dearly for't.
No trusting of her life with such a secret,
That cannot rule her blood° to keep her promise! *passions*
Beside, I have some suspicion of her faith to me,° *keeping my secrets*
Because I was suspected of my lord,° *by Alsemero*
And it must come from her. *Strike two.*
Hark! By my horrors,
Another clock strikes two.

Enter De Flores.

DE FLORES Psst! Where are you?

BEATRICE De Flores?

DE FLORES Ay. Is she not come from him yet?

BEATRICE As I am a living soul, not.

DE FLORES Sure the devil
Hath sowed his itch within her. Who'd trust
A waiting-woman?

BEATRICE I must trust somebody.

DE FLORES Push, they are termagants,° *brawling women*
Especially when they fall upon their masters
And have their ladies' first fruits.[1] They're mad whelps;
You cannot stave 'em off from game royal.[2] Then

9. Alibius needs another fool for the planned entertainment and hopes his friends and family can help him get custody of one.

1. Well, if we can adapt the dancing to the music.

5.1. The castle.

1. Especially when (like Diaphanta) they make sexual advances to the masters of their households and take away from the ladies of those houses the right of the first sexual embrace in marriage, to which brides are entitled. (First fruits are literally the first gathered harvest, offered to God in thankful acknowledgment of the gift of fruitfulness; hence, the earliest product of any undertaking.)

2. They're like frenzied dogs that cannot be beaten back from the deer they have quarried in the King's preserve.

You are so harsh and hardy,° ask no counsel,° *foolhardy / advice*
And I could have helped you to an apothecary's daughter
Would have fall'n off° before eleven, and thanked you too. *Who'd have left off*

BEATRICE Oh, me, not yet? This whore forgets herself.

DE FLORES The rascal fares so well. Look, you're undone;
The daystar, by this hand! See Phosphorus° plain yonder. *the morning star, Venus*

BEATRICE Advise me now to fall upon some ruin;° *to devise some catastrophe*
There is no counsel safe else.

DE FLORES Peace, I ha't now,
For we must force a rising;[3] there's no remedy.

BEATRICE How? Take heed of that.

DE FLORES Tush, be you quiet,
Or else give over all.° *give up entirely*

BEATRICE Prithee, I ha' done,° then. *i.e., I'll be quiet*

DE FLORES This is my reach:° I'll set some part afire *bright idea*
Of Diaphanta's chamber.

BEATRICE How? Fire, sir?
That may endanger the whole house.

DE FLORES You talk of danger when your fame's° on fire? *reputation is*

BEATRICE That's true. Do what thou wilt now.

DE FLORES Push, I aim
At a most rich success, strikes all dead sure.° *which'll make all sure*
The chimney being afire, and some light parcels
Of the least danger° in her chamber only, *danger of a general fire*
If Diaphanta should be met by chance then,
Far from her lodging, which is now suspicious,[4]
It would be thought her fears and affrights then
Drove her to seek for succor; if not seen
Or met at all, as that's the likeliest,
For her own shame she'll hasten towards her lodging.
I will be ready with a piece high charged,° *heavily loaded firearm*
As 'twere to cleanse the chimney.[5] There 'tis proper now,° *That will seem fitting*
But she shall be the mark.° *target*

BEATRICE I'm forced to love thee now,
'Cause thou provid'st so carefully for my honor.

DE FLORES 'Slid,° it concerns the safety of us both, *By God's eyelid (an oath)*
Our pleasure and continuance.

BEATRICE One word now, prithee:
How for the servants?

DE FLORES I'll dispatch them
Some one way, some another, in the hurry,
For buckets, hooks, ladders. Fear not you;
The deed° shall find its time, and I've thought since *(Killing Diaphanta)*
Upon a safe conveyance for the body too.
How this fire purifies wit! Watch you your minute.° *time to rejoin Alsemero*

BEATRICE Fear keeps my soul upon't;° I cannot stray from't. *focused on it*

Enter Alonzo's ghost.

DE FLORES Ha! What art thou that tak'st away the light

3. We must do something that will get everyone out of bed.

4. Diaphanta's being seen away from her lodging at night would normally awaken suspicion, in the absence of some extraordinary circumstance (such as a fire in her room).

5. Cleaning the chimney this way would have the beneficial effect of helping to put out a chimney fire—a common problem in older houses.

'Twixt that star and me? I dread thee not;
'Twas but a mist of conscience.—All's clear again. *Exit.*

BEATRICE Who's that, De Flores? Bless me! It slides by.
[*Exit ghost.*]
Some ill thing haunts the house; 't has left behind it
A shivering sweat upon me. I'm afraid now.
This night hath been so tedious. Oh, this strumpet!
Had she a thousand lives, he should not leave her[6]
Till he had destroyed the last. *Struck three o'clock.*
List! Oh, my terrors!
Three struck by Saint Sebastian's!° — *the church clock*

WITHIN Fire, fire, fire!

BEATRICE Already! How rare° is that man's speed! — *superb; unusual*
How heartily he serves me! His face loathes° one, — *revolts*
But look upon his care,° who would not love him? — *the care he takes*
The east° is not more beauteous than his service. — *The dawn*

WITHIN Fire, fire, fire!

Enter De Flores. Servants pass over.° Ring a bell. — *cross the stage*

DE FLORES Away! Dispatch!° Hooks, buckets, ladders! That's well said.° — *Hurry!* / *well done*
The fire bell rings, the chimney works. My charge;° — *Now to my assignment*
The piece° is ready. *Exit.* — *firearm*

BEATRICE Here's a man worth loving—

Enter Diaphanta.

Oh, you're a jewel!

DIAPHANTA Pardon frailty, madam.
In troth, I was so well° I ev'n forgot myself. — *happy*

BEATRICE You've made trim° work. — *fine (said sarcastically)*

DIAPHANTA What?

BEATRICE Hie quickly to your chamber;
Your reward follows you.

DIAPHANTA I never made
So sweet a bargain. *Exit.*

Enter Alsemero.

ALSEMERO O my dear Joanna,
Alas, art thou risen too? I was coming,
My absolute treasure.

BEATRICE When I missed you,
I could not choose but follow.

ALSEMERO Thou'rt all sweetness!
The fire is not so dangerous.

BEATRICE Think you so, sir?

ALSEMERO I prithee, tremble not. Believe me, 'tis not.

Enter Vermandero [and] Jasperino.

VERMANDERO Oh, bless my house and me!

ALSEMERO [*to Beatrice*] My lord your father.

Enter De Flores with a piece.

6. De Flores must not leave off killing Diaphanta.

VERMANDERO Knave, whither goes that piece?
DE FLORES To scour the chimney.
Exit.

VERMANDERO Oh, well said, well said.
That fellow's good on all occasions.
BEATRICE A wondrous necessary man, my lord.
VERMANDERO He hath a ready wit; he's worth 'em all, sir.
Dog at° a house afire. I ha' seen him singed ere now. *Adept at*
The piece goes off.

Ha! There he goes.
BEATRICE [*aside*] 'Tis done.
ALSEMERO Come, sweet, to bed now; alas, thou wilt get cold.
BEATRICE Alas, the fear keeps that out.
My heart will find no quiet till I hear
How Diaphanta my poor woman fares;
It is her chamber, sir, her lodging chamber.
VERMANDERO How should the fire come there?
BEATRICE As good a soul as ever lady countenanced,° *favored; retained*
But in her chamber negligent and heavy.° *slovenly; sluggish*
She scaped a mine twice.[7]
VERMANDERO Twice?
BEATRICE Strangely twice, sir.
VERMANDERO Those sleepy sluts are dangerous in a house,
An° they be ne'er so good.° *Even if / good servants*

Enter De Flores.

DE FLORES Oh, poor virginity!
Thou hast paid dearly for't.
VERMANDERO Bless us! What's that?
DE FLORES A thing[8] you all knew once—Diaphanta's burnt.
BEATRICE My woman, oh, my woman!
DE FLORES Now the flames are
Greedy of her: burnt, burnt, burnt to death, sir!
BEATRICE Oh, my presaging soul!
ALSEMERO Not a tear more,
I charge you, by the last embrace I gave you
In bed before this raised us.
BEATRICE Now you tie° me. *constrain*
Were it my sister, now she gets no more.

Enter Servant.

VERMANDERO How now?
SERVANT All danger's past. You may now take your rests, my lords;
The fire is throughly° quenched. Ah, poor gentlewoman, *thoroughly*
How soon was she stifled!
BEATRICE De Flores, what is left of her inter,
And we as mourners all will follow her.[9]
I will entreat that honor to° my servant, *for, on behalf of*

7. I.e., She twice slept right through a near accident.
8. Possibly De Flores is carrying Diaphanta's body, referring to it as "a thing" (i.e., a once-animate person) in response to Vermandero's question, "What's that?" Yet at lines 56–57, De Flores told Beatrice that he had thought of some "safe conveyance" for Diaphanta's body, meaning evidently to spirit it out of the way. "What's that?" in line 109 could well mean "What are you saying?" rather than "What are you carrying?"
9. All will follow her corpse to burial.

Ev'n of my lord himself.° *(Alsemero)*
ALSEMERO Command it, sweetness.
BEATRICE Which of you spied the fire first?
DE FLORES 'Twas I, madam.
BEATRICE And took such pains in't too? A double goodness!
'Twere well he were rewarded.
VERMANDERO He shall be.—
De Flores, call upon me.° *call upon my support*
ALSEMERO And upon me, sir.
Exeunt. [*De Flores remains.*]
DE FLORES Rewarded? Precious,° here's a trick beyond me! *By God's precious body*
I see in all bouts, both of sport and wit,
Always a woman strives for the last hit. *Exit.*

[5.2]

Enter Tomazo.

TOMAZO I cannot taste the benefits of life
With the same relish I was wont to do.
Man I grow weary of, and hold his fellowship
A treacherous bloody friendship; and because
I am ignorant in whom my wrath should settle,
I must think all men villains, and the next
I meet, whoe'er he be, the murderer
Of my most worthy brother—Ha! What's he?

Enter De Flores, passes over the stage [*and exit*].

Oh, the fellow that some call honest De Flores;
But methinks honesty was hard bestead° *hard pressed*
To come there for a lodging, as if a queen
Should make her palace of a pesthouse.° *plague hospital*
I find a contrariety in nature
Betwixt that face and me; the least occasion
Would give me game upon° him. Yet he's so foul *incite me to fight*
One would scarce touch him with a sword he° loved *(the sword's owner)*
And made account of—so most deadly venomous
He would go near to poison° any weapon *almost poison*
That should draw blood on him. One must resolve
Never to use that sword again in fight,
In way of honest manhood, that strikes him.
Some river must devour't; 'twere not fit
That any man should find it.—What, again?

Enter De Flores.

He walks o'purpose by, sure, to choke me up,
To infect my blood.
DE FLORES My worthy noble lord!
TOMAZO Dost offer° to come near and breathe upon me? *dare, venture*
[*He strikes De Flores.*]
DE FLORES [*drawing his sword*] A blow?
TOMAZO [*drawing his sword*] Yea, are you so prepared?
I'll rather, like a soldier, die by th'sword

5.2. The castle.

Than, like a politician,° by thy poison. — *intriguer*
DE FLORES Hold, my lord, as you are honorable!
TOMAZO All slaves° that kill by poison are still cowards. — *wretches*
DE FLORES [*aside*] I cannot strike; I see his brother's wounds
Fresh bleeding in his eye, as in a crystal.° — *crystal ball*
[*To Tomazo*] I will not question this.° I know you're noble; — *call you to account*
I take my injury with thanks given, sir,
Like a wise lawyer,[1] and as a favor
Will wear it for the worthy hand that gave it.[2]
[*Aside*] Why this from him, that yesterday appeared
So strangely loving to me?
Oh, but instinct is of a subtler strain;
Guilt must not walk so near his lodge again.[3]
He came near me° now. *Exit.* — *almost found me out*
TOMAZO All league° with mankind I renounce forever, — *alliance*
Till I find this murderer! Not so much
As common courtesy but I'll lock up;[4]
For in the state of ignorance I live in,
A brother may salute his brother's murderer
And wish good speed to th'villain in a greeting.

Enter Vermandero, Alibius, and Isabella.

VERMANDERO Noble Piracquo!
TOMAZO Pray keep on your way, sir;
I've nothing to say to you.
VERMANDERO Comforts bless you, sir!
TOMAZO I have forsworn compliment,° in troth I have, sir. — *everyday courtesies*
As you are merely man,[5] I have not left
A good wish for you nor any here.
VERMANDERO Unless you be so far in love with grief
You° will not part from't upon any terms, — *That you*
We bring that news will° make a welcome for us. — *that will*
TOMAZO What news can that be?
VERMANDERO Throw no scornful smile
Upon the zeal I bring you; 'tis worth more, sir.
Two of the chiefest men I kept about me
I hide not from the law, or your just vengeance.° — *private vengeance*
TOMAZO Ha!
VERMANDERO To give your peace more ample satisfaction,
[*Indicating Alibius and Isabella*] Thank these discoverers.
TOMAZO If you bring that calm,
Name but the manner I shall ask forgiveness in[6]
For that contemptuous smile upon you.
I'll perfect° it with reverence that belongs — *complete*
Unto a sacred altar. [*He kneels.*]
VERMANDERO [*raising him*] Good sir, rise.
Why, now you overdo as much o'this hand
As you fell short o' t'other.—Speak, Alibius.
ALIBIUS 'Twas my wife's fortune (as she is most lucky
At a discovery) to find out lately

1. A wise lawyer avoids dueling, forbidden by law; instead, he might claim damages.
2. And I will wear this mark you've given me as though it were a token or favor from a worthy man.
3. A guilty man must not return to the scene of the crime (lest he betray his guilt).
4. I'll refuse even the most common courtesy.
5. Since you are part of mankind (which I have renounced).
6. Tell me how I shall ask forgiveness.

Within our hospital of fools and madmen
Two counterfeits slipped into these disguises;
Their names, Franciscus and Antonio.
VERMANDERO Both mine,° sir, and I ask no favor° for 'em. *my followers / leniency*
ALIBIUS Now that which draws suspicion to their habits,° *disguised appearances*
The time of their disguisings agrees justly° *exactly*
With the day of the murder.
TOMAZO Oh, blest revelation!
VERMANDERO Nay more, nay more, sir—I'll not spare mine own
In way of justice—they both feigned a journey
To Briamata, and so wrought out their leaves;° *got permission to go*
My love° was so abused in't. *My trust in them*
TOMAZO Time's too precious
To run in waste now; you have brought a peace
The riches of five kingdoms could not purchase.
Be my most happy conduct;° I thirst for 'em. *guide*
Like subtle lightning will I wind about 'em,
And melt their marrow in 'em.[7] *Exeunt.*

[5.3]

Enter Alsemero and Jasperino.

JASPERINO Your confidence, I'm sure, is now of proof.° *armored against attack*
The prospect from the garden has showed
Enough for deep suspicion.[1]
ALSEMERO The black mask
That so continually was worn upon't
Condemns the face for ugly ere't be seen—
Her despite to him, and so seeming bottomless.[2]
JASPERINO Touch it home,° then. 'Tis not a shallow probe *Probe to the bottom of it*
Can search this ulcer soundly; I fear you'll find it
Full of corruption.° 'Tis fit I leave you. *evil; pus*
She meets you opportunely from that walk;
She took the back door at his° parting with her. *(De Flores')*
Exit Jasperino.
ALSEMERO Did my fate wait for this unhappy stroke
At my first sight of woman?—She's here.

Enter Beatrice.

BEATRICE Alsemero!
ALSEMERO How do you?
BEATRICE How do I?
Alas! How do you? You look not well.
ALSEMERO You read me well enough. I am not well.
BEATRICE Not well, sir? Is't in my power to better you?
ALSEMERO Yes.
BEATRICE Nay, then, you're cured° again. *consider yourself cured*
ALSEMERO Pray resolve° me one question, lady. *answer*

7. Lightning was thought to melt the marrow in the victim's bones without harming the skin—a subtle and nearly invisible form of destruction.
5.3. The castle. Alsemero's chambers.
1. Evidently Jasperino and Alsemero have just witnessed a tête-à-tête in the castle garden between Beatrice and De Flores, convincing Alsemero that his testing of Beatrice's virginity in act 4, scene 2, was somehow defeated by her cunning. They are now waiting for her to come from that meeting.
2. The extreme effort to cover up this relationship condemns it as guilty even before its true nature is known—that effort being Beatrice's pretense of seemingly bottomless spite toward De Flores.

BEATRICE If I can.
ALSEMERO None can so sure. Are you honest?° *chaste*
BEATRICE Ha, ha, ha! That's a broad question, my lord.
ALSEMERO But that's not a modest answer, my lady.
Do you laugh? My doubts are strong upon me.
BEATRICE 'Tis Innocence that smiles, and no rough° brow *furrowed in anger*
Can take away the dimple in her° cheek. *(Innocence's)*
Say I should strain° a tear to fill the vault,° *force / sky, heavens*
Which would you give the better faith to?
ALSEMERO 'Twere but hypocrisy of a sadder° color, *darker, more grave*
But the same stuff.° Neither your smiles nor tears *cloth, material*
Shall move or flatter me from my belief:
You are a whore.
BEATRICE What a horrid sound it hath!
It blasts° a beauty to deformity; *withers*
Upon what face soever that breath° falls, *sound, word*
It strikes it ugly. Oh, you have ruined
What you can ne'er repair again.
ALSEMERO I'll all demolish and seek out truth within you,
If there be any left. Let your sweet tongue
Prevent your heart's rifling; there I'll ransack
And tear out my suspicion.[3]
BEATRICE You may, sir,
'Tis an easy passage.[4] Yet, if you please,
Show me the ground° whereon you lost your love. *basis; place*
My spotless virtue may but tread° on that *stand firmly*
Before I perish.
ALSEMERO Unanswerable!° *Unchallengeable grounds!*
A ground you cannot stand on; you fall down
Beneath all grace and goodness, when you set
Your ticklish° heel on't. There was a visor *unsteady, fickle; randy*
O'er that cunning face, and that became you;
Now impudence in triumph rides upon't.
How comes this tender reconcilement else
'Twixt you and your despite,° your rancorous loathing, *a man you despised*
De Flores? He that your eye was sore at sight of,
He's now become your arm's supporter, your lip's saint.[5]
BEATRICE Is there the cause?° *grounds of accusation*
ALSEMERO Worse: your lust's devil, your adultery.
BEATRICE Would any but yourself say that,
'Twould turn him to a villain.
ALSEMERO 'Twas witnessed by the counsel of your bosom,° *your close confidant*
Diaphanta.
BEATRICE Is your witness dead, then?
ALSEMERO 'Tis to be feared
It was the wages of her knowledge;° poor soul, *what she got for knowing*
She lived not long after the discovery.
BEATRICE Then hear a story of not much less horror
Than this your false suspicion is beguiled with.
To° your bed's scandal, I stand up innocent, *In refutation of*
Which even the guilt of one black other deed

3. Tell the truth so that I won't have to rifle through your heart to get it.
4. You may do that easily, and the truth will be plain to see; I can offer little resistance.
5. He's become your supporter and the one you kiss and pray to.

Will stand for proof of: your love° has made me — *my love for you*
A cruel murd'ress.

ALSEMERO Ha!

BEATRICE A bloody one.
I have kissed poison for't, stroked a serpent.
That thing of hate,° worthy in my esteem — *(De Flores)*
Of no better employment, and him most worthy
To be so employed, I caused to murder
That innocent Piracquo, having no
Better means than that worst to assure
Yourself to me.

ALSEMERO Oh, the place itself e'er since
Has crying been° for vengeance—the temple — *been crying*
Where blood° and beauty first unlawfully — *sexual desire*
Fired their devotion and quenched the right one![6]
'Twas in my fears at first; 'twill have it now.[7]
Oh, thou art all deformed!

BEATRICE Forget not, sir,
It for your sake was done. Shall greater dangers
Make the less welcome?[8]

ALSEMERO Oh, thou shouldst have gone
A thousand leagues about° to have avoided — *To any lengths*
This dangerous bridge of blood!° Here we are lost. — *crossing over to murder*

BEATRICE Remember I am true unto your bed.

ALSEMERO The bed itself's a charnel,° the sheets shrouds — *vault for human bones*
For murdered carcasses. It must ask pause° — *I must reflect*
What I must do in this. Meantime you shall
Be my prisoner only. Enter my closet;
I'll be your keeper yet.

Exit Beatrice [into Alsemero's private room].

Oh, in what part
Of this sad story shall I first begin?

Enter De Flores.

Ha!
This same fellow has put me in.° [*To him*] De Flores! — *put me in mind*

DE FLORES Noble Alsemero!

ALSEMERO I can tell you news, sir. My wife has her commended to you.° — *sent you her greetings*

DE FLORES That's news indeed, my lord. I think she would
Commend me to the gallows if she could.
She ever loved me so well, I thank her.° — *(said ironically)*

ALSEMERO What's this blood upon your band,° De Flores? — *neck-band or cuff*

DE FLORES Blood? No, sure, 'twas washed since.

ALSEMERO Since when, man?

DE FLORES Since t'other day° I got a knock — *day when*
In a sword-and-dagger school; I think 'tis out.° — *washed out*

ALSEMERO Yes, 'tis almost out,° but 'tis perceived, though. — *discovered*

6. Fired up a passion (for sex and beauty) and quenched the virtuous love (of morality and truth)!
7. (1) What I most feared is now confirmed; (2) the temple where I sinned in thought will now claim its due.
8. Shouldn't the greater danger of punishment for murder prompt us to welcome the lesser danger of concealing that fact in our love for each other?

I had forgot my message. This it is:
What price goes murder?
DE FLORES How, sir?
ALSEMERO I ask you, sir.
My wife's behindhand with° you, she tells me, *still in debt to*
For a brave bloody blow you gave for her sake
Upon Piracquo.
DE FLORES Upon? 'Twas quite through him, sure.[9]
Has she confessed it?
ALSEMERO As sure as death to both of you,
And much more than that.
DE FLORES It could not be much more;
'Twas but one thing, and that she's a whore.
ALSEMERO It could not choose but follow. Oh, cunning devils!
How should blind men° know you from fair-faced saints? *men blinded by passion*
BEATRICE (*within*) He lies! The villain does belie me!
DE FLORES Let me go to her, sir.
ALSEMERO Nay, you shall to her.
[*Calling to her*] Peace, crying crocodile![1] Your sounds are heard.
[*To him*] Take your prey to you. Get you in to her, sir.
Exit De Flores [*into Alsemero's private room*].
[*To them*] I'll be your pander now. Rehearse again
Your scene of lust, that you may be perfect° *perfect in your roles*
When you shall come to act it to the black audience° *devils in hell*
Where howls and gnashings shall be music to you.
Clip° your adult'ress freely; 'tis the pilot *Embrace*
Will guide you to the *Mare Mortuum*,° *Dead Sea, i.e., hell*
Where you shall sink to fathoms bottomless.

Enter Vermandero, Alibius, Isabella, Tomazo, Franciscus, and Antonio.

VERMANDERO Oh, Alsemero, I have a wonder for you.
ALSEMERO No, sir, 'tis I, I have a wonder for you.
VERMANDERO I have suspicion near as proof itself
For Piracquo's murder.
ALSEMERO Sir, I have proof
Beyond suspicion for Piracquo's murder.
VERMANDERO Beseech you hear me. [*Indicating Antonio and Franciscus*] These two have been disguised
E'er since the deed was done.
ALSEMERO I have two other
That were more close° disguised than your two could be, *secretly, indiscernibly*
E'er since the deed was done.
VERMANDERO You'll hear me! These mine own servants—
ALSEMERO Hear me! Those nearer° than your servants, *nearer linked by blood*
That shall acquit them° and prove them guiltless. *(Antonio and Franciscus)*
FRANCISCUS That may be done with easy truth, sir.
TOMAZO How is my cause bandied° through your delays! *tossed about*
'Tis urgent in blood, and calls for haste.
Give me a brother alive or dead;

9. I did more than strike a blow upon his body. I stabbed right through him.

1. You who cry crocodile tears.

Alive, a wife° with him; if dead, for both, — *(Beatrice)*
A recompense for murder and adultery.[2]
BEATRICE (*within*) Oh! Oh! Oh!
ALSEMERO [*to Tomazo*] Hark, 'tis° coming to you. — *revenge is*
DE FLORES (*within*) Nay, I'll along for company.
BEATRICE (*within*) Oh! Oh!
VERMANDERO What horrid sounds are these?
ALSEMERO Come forth, you twins of mischief!
[*He unlocks the door of his private room.*]

Enter De Flores, bringing in Beatrice [*wounded*].

DE FLORES Here we are. If you have any more
To say to us, speak quickly; I shall not
Give you the hearing else. I am so stout° yet, — *resolute, strong*
And so, I think, that broken rib of mankind.[3]
VERMANDERO An host of enemies entered° my citadel — *having entered*
Could not amaze like this.—Joanna! Beatrice-Joanna!
BEATRICE Oh, come not near me, sir; I shall defile you.
I am that of your blood was taken from you
For your better health.[4] Look no more upon't,
But cast it to the ground regardlessly;° — *without regard*
Let the common sewer take it from distinction.° — *mix it with all waste*
Beneath the stars, upon yon meteor[5]
Ever hung my fate, 'mongst things corruptible;° — *in the sublunary world*
I ne'er could pluck it° from him. My loathing — *(my fate)*
Was prophet to the rest, but ne'er believed;° — *I ignored the warnings*
Mine honor fell with him, and now my life.
Alsemero, I am a stranger to your bed;
Your bed was cozened° on the nuptial night, — *cheated*
For which your false bride died.
ALSEMERO Diaphanta!
DE FLORES Yes, and the while° I coupled with your mate — *meanwhile*
At barley-break; now we are left in hell.° — *(see 3.3.166 n)*
VERMANDERO We are all there; it circumscribes° us here. — *surrounds*
DE FLORES I loved this woman in spite of her heart;
Her love I earned out of Piracquo's murder.
TOMAZO Ha! My brother's murderer!
DE FLORES Yes, and her honor's prize° — *her virginity*
Was my reward. I thank life for nothing
But that pleasure; it was so sweet to me
That I have drunk up all, left none behind
For any man to pledge° me. — *offer a toast to*
VERMANDERO Horrid villain!—
Keep life in him for further tortures.
DE FLORES No!
I can prevent° you; here's my penknife still. — *forestall*
It is but one thread° more [*stabbing himself*] —and now 'tis cut. — *heartstring*

2. Tomazo sees the marriage of Beatrice to Alsemero as a kind of adultery, since she was engaged to Alonzo.
3. De Flores speaks of Beatrice as a descendant of Eve, the first sinning woman, whom God fashioned out of one of Adam's ribs (Genesis 2.21–22). The rib is "broken" as a token both of its having been taken from Adam's body and of Eve's sin.
4. Being a blood relation of Vermandero, Beatrice is metaphorically like contaminated blood that has been drained from him in what was then a common medical procedure to improve one's (spiritual) health.
5. I.e., De Flores. (Because they are unlike the seemingly fixed and immutable stars, meteors were considered ominous signs of flux and instability.)

Make haste, Joanna, by that token to thee.
Canst not forget, so lately put in mind;
I would not go to leave thee far behind.[6] *Dies.*
BEATRICE Forgive me, Alsemero, all forgive!
'Tis time to die when 'tis a shame to live. *Dies.*
VERMANDERO Oh, my name is entered now in that record° *book of shame*
Where till this fatal hour 'twas never read!
ALSEMERO Let it be blotted out, let your heart lose° it, *forget*
And it can never look you in the face,
Nor tell a tale behind the back of life,° *behind your back*
To your dishonor. Justice hath so right° *rightly*
The guilty hit that innocence is quit° *acquitted*
By proclamation, and may joy° again. *rejoice*
[*To Tomazo*] Sir, you are sensible° of what truth hath done; *aware*
'Tis the best comfort that your grief can find.
TOMAZO Sir, I am satisfied; my injuries° *the injuries done to me*
Lie dead before me.° I can exact no more, *Are paid by these deaths*
Unless my soul were loose° and could o'ertake *freed from my body*
Those black fugitives that are fled from thence,[7]
To take a second vengeance; but there are wraths° *divine punishments*
Deeper than mine, 'tis to be feared, about 'em.° *pursuing them*
ALSEMERO What an opacous° body had that moon *opaque (a bad sign)*
That last changed on us!° Here's beauty changed *During its last cycle*
To ugly whoredom; here, servant obedience
To a master sin, imperious murder;[8]
I, a supposed husband, changed° embraces *exchanged*
With wantonness, but that was paid before.° *(by Diaphanta's death)*
[*To Tomazo*] Your change is come too, from an ignorant wrath
To knowing friendship. Are there any more on's?° *of us*
ANTONIO Yes, sir, I was changed too, from a little ass as I was to a great fool as I am, and had like° to ha' been changed to the gallows but that you know my innocence° always excuses me. *was likely* *guiltlessness; idiocy*
FRANCISCUS I was changed from a little wit to be stark mad,
Almost for the same purpose.
ISABELLA [*to Alibius*] Your change is still behind,° *still to come*
But deserve best your transformation.[9]
You are a jealous coxcomb, keep schools of folly,
And teach your scholars how to break your own head.° *i.e., cuckold you*
ALIBIUS I see all apparent, wife, and will change now
Into a better husband, and never keep scholars
That shall be wiser than myself.
ALSEMERO [*to Vermandero*] Sir, you have yet a son's duty living;° *my duty as a living son*
Please you accept it. Let that your sorrow,° *that sorrow of yours*
As it goes° from your eye, go from your heart. *flows in tears*
Man and his sorrow at the grave must part.

6. Make haste in dying, Joanna, in keeping with my killing of myself as a token of commitment to you. You cannot forget our promises, having this so recent reminder; I would not wish to die and leave you behind.
7. I.e., and could overtake the blackened souls that have fled from those bodies lying before us.
8. (1) Insolent murder; (2) murder of a master by a servant.
9. Show yourself worthy of transformation.

Epilogue

ALSEMERO All we can do, to comfort one another,
To stay° a brother's sorrow for a brother, *bring to an end*
To dry a child° from the kind father's eyes, *tears for a child*
Is to no purpose; it rather multiplies.
Your only smiles° have power to cause relive *Only your smiles*
The dead again, or in their rooms to give
Brother a new brother, father a child;
If these appear, all griefs are reconciled.
Exeunt omnes.

FINIS.

TEXTUAL NOTES

The Changeling was entered in the Stationers' Register on October 19, 1652, and published the next year by Humphrey Moseley. A subsequent printing in 1668 consisted only of a newly printed title page added to leftover sheets from Q1 for the rest of the book, some sheets still in their uncorrected state; it has no independent authority. The quarto of 1653 is accordingly the basis of the present edition. Substantive departures from it are listed below, using the following abbreviations:

Q1: The first quarto (London: Humphrey Moseley, 1653)
Q1 corr.: The corrected first quarto
Q1 uncorr.: The uncorrected first quarto
ed.: A modern editor's emendation

Dramatis Personae THE SCENE [and elsewhere] **Alicante** [Q1: *Allegant*]

1.1.57.1 ***Beatrice-Joanna, Diaphanta, and Servants.*** [ed.] *Beatrice, Diaphanta, and Servants, Joannna.* [Q1] **100 Will't** [ed.] Wilt [Q1] **111 of** [ed.] or [Q1] **115 The** [Q1: Ahe] **117 found** [ed.] sound [Q1] **128 What** [ed.] And what [Q1] **151** [and elsewhere] **cuckoo** [Q1: Cuckow]

1.2.11 barred [Q1: bar'd] **125 I'll make** [ed.] make [Q1] **134** [and elsewhere] **arrant** [Q1: errant] **142.1** [placement, ed.; after 141 in Q1]

2.1.69 wilt [ed.] wil't [Q1] **84 precedents** [Q1: presidents] **133 to** [Q1: too] **152 we're** [Q1 corr.: w'are] we are [Q1 uncorr.]

2.2.7 locked [ed.] lock [Q1] **33 you're** [ed.] your [Q1] **56.1** ***Exeunt*** [ed.] *Ex.* [Q1] **80 Faugh** [ed.] vauh [Q1] **133 of** [Q1 corr.; not in Q1 uncorr.] **174.2** [placement, ed.; after 3.1.0.1 in Q1]

3.3.36.1 ***Exit*** [ed.] *Ex.Enter presently* [Q1] **98.1** [placement, ed.; after 99 in Q1] **101 one** [Q1: on] **103 nidget** [Q1: nigget] **135 he** [ed.] she [Q1] **177 venture** [Q1: venter]

3.4.70 slept at ease [ed.; not in Q1] **96 to** [Q1: too] **102 off** [Q1: of] **112 it not** [ed.] it [Q1] **163 you** [ed.; not in Q1]

4.1.5 that's [ed.] both [Q1] **15 by** [ed.] by by [Q1] **21 vials** [Q1: viols] **29 down** [ed.] dow [Q1]

4.2.15 SD [placement, ed.; opposite 16 in Q1] **15.1** [placement, ed.; after 16 in Q1] **54 chins and noses** [ed.] sins and vices [Q1] **60 'Twill** [ed.] I will [Q1] **60.1** [placement, ed.; after 61 in Q1] **81 SD** [placement, ed.; after 80 in Q1] **89 though** [Q1 uncorr.: tho] thou [Q1 corr.] **113 made** [ed.; not in Q1] **130 SD** [placement, ed.; after 130 in Q1] **149 Keeps** [ed.] Keep [Q1]

4.3.1 waxing [ed.] waiting [Q1] **2 at** [ed.; not in Q1] **18 have** [ed.] *have have*

[Q1] **44 Why, do** [ed.] We do [Q1] **83 SD** [placement, ed.; opposite 82 in Q1] **99 rises** [ed.] rise [Q1] **103 SD** [placement, ed.; opposite 101 in Q1] **104 he** [ed.] she [Q1] **104 Shoo, shoo**! [Q1: shough, shough] **118 straits** [ed.] streets [Q1] **164 off** [ed.; not in Q1] **168 have** [ed.; not in Q1] **207.1** [placement, ed.; after 209 in Q1]

5.1.10 SD [placement, ed.; opposite 11 in Q1] **23 an** [ed.] a [Q1] **24 thanked** [ed.] thank [Q1] **27 Phosphorus** [ed.] *Bosphorus* [Q1] **68 SD** [placement, ed.; opposite 69 in Q1] **78.1** [placement, ed.; after "ready. *Exit*" in 78 in Q1] **95 afire** [Q1: of fire] **116.1** [placement, ed.; opposite 117 in Q1]

5.2.16 him [ed.; not in Q1] **18 near** [ed.] ne'er [Q1] **41 near** [ed.] neer [Q1] **42 near** [ed.] ne're [Q1] **81 Briamata** [Q1: *Bramata*]

5.3.65 innocent [ed.] innocence [Q1] **91 SD** [placement, ed.; opposite 90 in Q1] **92.1** [placement, ed.; after 94 in Q1] **117 It** [ed.] I [Q1] **162 sewer** [Q1: shewer] **164 hung** [ed.] hang [Q1] **173 us** [ed.; not in Q1]

The White Devil

John Webster based *The White Devil*, first performed in early 1612 at the Red Bull Theater, on a real-life incident that occurred in Italy some thirty years earlier. The story was notorious. The Duke of Bracciano, in league with his lover, Vittoria, had conspired to murder both Vittoria's husband (who was the nephew of a powerful cardinal) and the Duke's own innocent wife. Captured and arraigned for the murders, Vittoria was imprisoned but escaped to Padua to marry Bracciano. To avenge the murders of their kin, the Cardinal and other powerful relatives brought about the deaths of Bracciano and Vittoria. Her brother Flamineo, serving as Bracciano's secretary, also paid with his life for his role in furthering the affair. Webster had several accounts at his disposal and seems to have availed himself of at least three.

The story provided him with gripping material—adulterous passion, intrigue, vengeful violence—for a theatrical tragedy. It also enabled him to show his London audiences the corrupting effects of power politics in the service of greed, ambition, jealousy, and vengefulness, corruption that many Londoners might recognize in their own world. The play was not a success in its day, owing, in the author's view, to poor timing and the location of the performance and to an uncomprehending, philistine audience (see "To the Reader"), but today it takes its place as one of the truly great revenge tragedies of the early modern theater.

As in Webster's other great tragedy, *The Duchess of Malfi* (1613–14), a woman stands at the center of *The White Devil* and is its title figure. The title captures a marked element of paradox in Vittoria, suggesting that she is diabolical and yet somehow transcends that evil. Outwardly, the case for evil is not hard to establish. By relating to her lover a dream of a "goodly yew tree" in a churchyard that is attacked by Bracciano's wife, Isabella, and by Vittoria's husband, Camillo, and that in turn strikes both of them dead (1.2.229–55), Vittoria artfully signals to Bracciano her desire that he murder Isabella and Camillo, as the historical Vittoria Accoramboni and her lover had done in Webster's source. The identification of the yew tree with Bracciano is scarcely veiled under the insistent punning on "yew" and "you." Vittoria's desire for these two deaths is coded in her dream in such a way that we cannot prove she understands what she is asking, but her brother Flamineo, who has been listening, entertains no doubt in an aside to the audience: "Excellent devil! / She hath taught him in a dream / To make away his duchess and her husband" (1.2.256–58). Bracciano's explication of the dream is more diplomatic and circumspect: he sees it as a bid for him simply to "protect" her from "the fevers of a jealous husband" and "the poor envy of our phlegmatic duchess" (1.2.260–62). What means he should use to "protect" her is thus left open to interpretation. Yet Bracciano hesitates not at all in pursuing the deaths of Isabella and Camillo, and Vittoria never upbraids him with having misinterpreted her dream.

Camillo is portrayed as the idiotic duped cuckold, forced on Vittoria in an arranged marriage. As a comic type found frequently in Elizabethan and Jacobean drama, he

Introduction, glosses, footnotes, and textual notes by David Bevington; text edited by David Bevington and checked by Eric Rasmussen.

invites little sympathy. At the same time, his murder, on a gymnasium floor, is shockingly brutal. Camillo is about to go over a vaulting horse when Flamineo, under instructions from Bracciano, "*pitcheth him upon his neck, and, with the help of the rest* [*four captains there to assist Camillo*], *writhes his neck about*" (2.2.37.7–8). The display of this gruesome murder in a dumb show dramatizes the violence for us, with the added touch that Bracciano is watching too. He is a connoisseur of violent death. However ridiculous Camillo may be as a husband, the heartless butchery of his murder portrays Bracciano and Flamineo in a bad light. And although Vittoria is not there to witness the murder, the impression is inescapable that she, like Beatrice in *The Changeling,* is eager to pursue an affair of the heart by the removal of a man who happens to be inconveniently in the way. The less she knows about the manner in which that death is arranged, the better; all that matters to her is that she have her will.

Although Camillo forfeits some of our sympathy by being such a dupe, Isabella is another matter. She is an obedient and loyal wife to Bracciano, indeed to the extraordinary extent of being ready to take upon herself the blame for their divorce when her husband insists on one. Bracciano's behavior toward her is callous in the extreme. He refuses a single kiss after their two months' separation, accusing her instead of coming to Rome in order to meet some "amorous gallant" (2.1.177). In response to his unfeeling announcement that they are to live together no longer, she volunteers to become "the author of your cursèd vow" in order to keep the peace between Bracciano and Isabella's powerful brother, Francisco, Duke of Florence (2.1.219). Bracciano coolly allows her to do so, at the cost of directing her brother's anger against her, and rewards her for her self-sacrifice by arranging her murder.

This dismaying event also appears in a dumb show staged by the Conjuror, and in such a way as to underscore Isabella's long-suffering loyalty and her husband's cruelty. We see her kneeling in prayer before a portrait of her husband as she prepares to retire for the night, kissing his picture as her last act of silent devotion. The canvas is poisoned. She dies as a direct result of worshiping the husband who has arranged her murder. Bracciano, witnessing the dumb show, offers no comment other than to ask the Conjuror if he saw Count Lodowick (Lodovico) in the scene as well. Bracciano is assured that the banished Lodovico was indeed there and that he dotes virtuously on Isabella.

The vivid injustice of Isabella's murder sticks to Vittoria as well as to Bracciano, even though she does not see the dumb show, since this murder too stems from her yew-tree dream and its implicit request for the death of Isabella as one who obstructs the attainment of Vittoria's desires. That Isabella's position closely resembles Vittoria's own—in a loveless marriage with the possibility of an alternative love interest—lessens any claim on audience sympathy that Vittoria might wish to make as one who is powerless because she is a woman. The contrast of Isabella and Vittoria is all the more striking in that Isabella does not encourage Lodovico as her potential lover, nor does Lodovico ask her to be his mistress. Isabella offers a model, albeit a very otherworldly one, of how a woman, even in the man's world of Italian court politics and sexual scandals, can hold on to her virtue and integrity. The price of such integrity, it seems, is death, but for Isabella at least it offers a viable alternative to dishonor.

Webster's profound achievement is to create in Vittoria a character who is fully human in her contradictions: profoundly flawed, selfish, manipulative, but also impressively strong and self-possessed. As a counterpoint to Isabella, the emblem of traditional womanly virtue, Vittoria is a disturbing and threatening figure, especially to men, but she is by that same token a new sort of woman, the kind that challenges and adopts for her own use the things that men do. She plays power politics with the best of them. The very title of the play, *The White Devil*, captures this combination of political and rhetorical skill and courage—the gender-role-trandscending part of her—with diabolical and self-serving motivations.

Vittoria is, then, one of the truly remarkable, unruly women in Renaissance drama. At her arraignment and trial for the murders, she defends herself brilliantly. Surrounded by men, she proceeds to make fools of them. A lawyer mouths his Latin and obfuscating terms to such an oppressive degree that Vittoria succeeds in having him dismissed from the case. Cardinal Monticelso, uncle of the murdered Camillo and presiding officer at the trial, is a more considerable foe, but even with him, Vittoria has little difficulty in exposing his bias in the case. Isabella's brother Francisco is plainly vulnerable on the same charge of prejudice. Because their motives for proceeding against her are so self-interested, Vittoria scores a telling point when she insists,

For your names
Of whore and murd'ress, they proceed from you
As if a man should spit against the wind;
The filth returns in 's face. (3.2.150–53)

Vittoria argues that by law she cannot be found guilty merely because Bracciano loves her. "Sum up my faults, I pray," she concludes,

and you shall find
That beauty and gay clothes, a merry heart,
And a good stomach to a feast are all,
All the poor crimes that you can charge me with.
(3.2.209–12)

Even if this is disingenuous, or simply not true, she is certainly right that the proceedings are stacked against her and that no evidence is brought forward to substantiate the assertions of men who hate her. She loses the case, of course, because the men are in charge of the legal proceedings, but she leaves the papal courtroom having established herself as a courageous, beleaguered woman, strong-minded, eloquent, resourceful with language, and unfazed by male bluster.

This scene, in which a woman exposes the gender bias of her country's legal and social structures, stands as one of the great feminist moments in English Renaissance drama. Indeed, throughout *The White Devil,* Webster's iconoclastic exploration of customary social structures, by means of the plot and also in the wry observations of Flamineo, makes the play an especially powerful vehicle for pointing out areas of systematic injustice. The play raises issues of gender, of race (especially in the depiction of Zanche, Vittoria's Moorish attendant), and of class (since both Flamineo and Vittoria find themselves at a disadvantage in a world dominated by aristocratic wealth and power). As part of Webster's larger social critique, the arraignment of Vittoria is emblematically central to the play: what might have been simply a shocking murder trial becomes instead the trial of a woman who is at once guilty and victimized.

After the trial as well, Vittoria gains sympathy, largely through contrast with the vicious behavior of the men of the play. Confined now to a house of correction for prostitutes, she can only watch as Machiavellian plotting and counterplotting swirl about her. Francisco, driven to the brink of madness by what has happened (so much so that in his disturbed imagination he sees the ghost of his murdered sister, Isabella, prompting him to revenge), hits on the scheme, in act 4, scene 1, of sending a letter to Vittoria as her professed lover, offering to free her and take her to Florence as his duchess or mistress. The bearer of the letter is to deliver it to Vittoria when Bracciano or some of his followers are at hand. The ruse works, resulting in a scene of confrontation in which Bracciano reveals all his jealous mistrust, while Vittoria vents her bitterness at her involvement in an affair that has gained nothing for her but infamy. She, after all, is incarcerated, while he enjoys the freedom that aristocratic men customarily enjoy. "Go, go brag / How many ladies you have undone, like me," she taunts him (4.2.119–20). Whatever her guilt, Bracciano's is greater, and yet she is having to pay a much higher price. The scene strongly suggests that he was the importunate wooer in their relationship, that it was not her idea in the first place, and, more generally, that women are pawns in the world of powerful men.

Richard Perkins was a leading actor of "the Queen's Majesty's Servants," i.e., Queen Anne's Men. Though Webster felt the first performance of *The White Devil* was a failure, due to bad weather, a dark theater, and an unappreciative audience, at the end of the first quarto (1612) he praised the actors, specifically recalling the "well-approved industry of my friend Master Perkins" and noting that "the worth of his action did crown both the beginning and end." Perkins probably played Flamineo. (From an engraving after a portrait in the Dulwich Picture Gallery)

The quarreling lovers make up, to be sure, and engineer an escape to Bracciano's palace in Padua. Yet even this is part of Francisco's plot. When news comes to Francisco of Bracciano's having removed Vittoria from the house of correction, he can scarcely contain his glee; Francisco in fact had sent a letter to Bracciano instructing him to do just this (4.3.54–55). Francisco knows that the lovers' guilty flight and marriage will turn all respectable opinion against them. The elopement sets in motion a plot whereby Francisco, aided by Count Lodovico, the virtuous admirer of Isabella, will close in on Bracciano, using all the usual disguise tricks of a revenge play. An articulate mistress of her own fate earlier in the play, Vittoria now becomes a disempowered victim of aristocratic vendettas between men.

Vittoria nearly dies at the hands of her brother Flamineo. Like Bosola in *The Duchess of Malfi*, Flamineo is both criminally flawed and charismatic. The best thinker in the play, he vies with his sister in offering the most astute criticisms of social injustice. He uses the most pungent metaphors; paradoxically, though he normally speaks in prose, he is the play's best poet. Like Bosola, he is obliged by his limited social credentials to serve as secretary or assistant to great men and is both appalled and attracted by what he sees as the necessary and deadly game he must play if he wants to get ahead. Great men assert their power through unethical means; ordinary persons can hope for advancement, it seems, only by carrying out the depraved commands of the powerful. Yet Flamineo, like Bosola, knows too that the ends do not justify the means and that crime will ultimately not lead one to prosper. He tests the system, sardonically aware of its huge flaws. Thus he anatomizes what we as the audience see and feel.

Flamineo's actions heavily implicate him in the crimes that are plotted by his social betters. He serves as a kind of pimp for his sister's affair with Bracciano, cynically manipulating the cuckold Camillo in the process. He comments sotto voce on Vittoria's dream in a way that lays bare its criminal intent far more revealingly than speech out loud would allow. He finds a quack doctor able to compound poisons for the murder of Isabella and takes charge of the seeming accident in which Camillo's neck is broken. He acts mad to throw off suspicion of his crimes. He breaks with his virtuous younger brother, Marcello, and runs him through from behind with his sword, driving their poor mother into true madness. And, finally, he threatens to kill Vittoria, and Zanche for good measure, because Vittoria has refused to reward him for his villainies now that his chief patron, Bracciano, lies dead of a poisoned helmet.

Such a record of reprehensible deeds marks Flamineo as the play's agent for others' villainies, again like Bosola in *The Duchess of Malfi*. Yet Webster consistently gives him the most philosophical lines. His comment on the life he has known is predominantly stoical. The illusion of easy prosperity, he says, bewitches men into ignoring the imminence of misfortune, as the merry foam of waves breaking on rocks distracts men from the danger those rocks pose (5.6.251–52). The only way not to be Fortune's slave is to "cease to die, by dying," he argues—that is, to remedy the fear of dying by ceasing to live (5.6.254). The "busy trade of life" he sees as a vanity of vanities in which human beings seek comforts when they should embrace the eternal rest of death, finding through the brief painfulness of death an oblivion that will end all pain (5.6.274–75). Such utterances are often densely elliptical, but their very paradoxes aim at a kind of general truth that can rise above the sordid specificities of the play's narrative account.

Giovanni, Bracciano's son by his virtuous first wife, takes his father's place as duke at the end of the play. Throughout, his appearances demonstrate moral courage and right-mindedness that afford a useful if highly conventional yardstick by which to measure the fallen protagonists. His first utterance is to claim a horse and armor of his uncle Francisco (2.1.6–7). His fervent ambition is to be a soldier and lead an army against the French with himself at the very head of the advancing force. He vows that he will set free all the prisoners he takes in his first year of service, without asking ransom (2.1.128–30). As his father observes, he is a "Forward lapwing," a precocious young person (2.1.126). He mourns in black for his dead mother and is loyal to the memory of his father as well. He takes an instant dislike to Flamineo, bidding him say his prayers and be penitent (5.4.20).

All these manifestations are signs that Giovanni will be the instrument of closure in the play, entering upon the final scene of carnage in time to apprehend Lodovico and his associates for their gangland executions of Vittoria, Zanche, and Flamineo. In the play's traditional final speech, which serves to reassert moral order, Giovanni calls for punishment of the offenders and observes that crime does not ultimately pay. Such a figure can, however, do only so much to restore a sense of order; overwhelmingly, the play explores our fallen human natures, and Giovanni can offer little redress other than the philosophical longings for a better view of the human predicament than most of the characters in this play have been able to fashion for themselves. Giovanni serves mainly as a plaintive reminder of what virtuous ambitions can sound like, and as a slender hope that as life renews itself it can find a better way.

JOHN WEBSTER
The White Devil

To the Reader

In publishing this tragedy, I do but challenge to° myself that liberty which other men have ta'en before me. Not that I affect° praise by it, for *nos haec novimus esse nihil;*[1] only, since it was acted in so dull a time of winter, presented in so open° and black° a theater that it wanted° (that which was the only grace and setting out of a tragedy)[2] a full and understanding auditory;° and that since that time, I have noted, most of the people that come to that playhouse° resemble those ignorant asses who, visiting stationers'° shops, their use° is not to inquire for good books but new books. I present it to the general° view with this confidence:

claim for / *seek, aim at* / *unroofed* / *unlit; bleak* / *lacked* / *audience* / *(the Red Bull)* / *booksellers'* / *custom* / *public*

Nec rhoncos metues, maligniorum,
Nec scombris tuicas, dabis molestas.[3]

If it be objected that this is no true dramatic poem,[4] I shall easily confess it; *non potes in nugas dicere plura meas ipse ego quam dixi;*[5] willingly, and not ignorantly, in this kind have I faulted. For, should a man present to such an auditory the most sententious° tragedy that ever was written, observing all the critical laws, as° height of style and gravity of person, enrich it with the sententious chorus, and, as it were, liven death in the passionate and weighty *nuntius,*[6] yet, after all this divine rapture, O *dura messorum ilia,*[7] the breath that comes from the uncapable multitude is able to poison it, and, ere it be acted, let the author resolve to fix to every scene this of Horace:

deeply meaningful / *such as*

—Haec hodie porcis comedenda relinques.[8]

The original 1612 title page reads "*The White Devil*, or, the Tragedy of Paulo Giordano Ursini, Duke of Brachiano, with the life and death of Vittoria Corombona, the famous Venetian courtesan. Acted by the Queen's Majesty's Servants. Written by John Webster. *Non inferiora secutus* [Engaged in no less noble service; following no ignoble theme (Virgil, *Aeneid*, 6.170)]. London: printed by N[icholas] O[kes] for Thomas Archer, and are to be sold at his shop in Pope's Head Palace, near the Royal Exchange. 1612."

To the Reader.

1. We know these things to be nothing. (Martial, *Epigrams*, 13.2.8.)
2. That which should have been the most essential features and adornments of a tragedy.
3. You (my book) need not fear the turned-up noses of the malicious, nor will you be used for wrapping mackerel (literally, "give robes of torture to mackerel"). (Martial, *Epigrams*, 4.86.7–8.)
4. I.e., that this play fails to observe "all the critical laws." (See lines 18–19.)
5. You cannot say more against my trifles than I myself have said. (Martial, *Epigrams*, 13.2.4–5.)
6. And make death itself full of life by the deeply serious utterances of the messenger.
7. O strong stomachs of harvesters (with such a fondness for garlic)! (Horace, *Epodes*, 3.4.)
8. What you leave today will go to feed the pigs. (Horace, *Epodes*, 1.7.19.)

To those who report I was a long time in finishing this tragedy, I confess I do not write with a goose-quill winged with two feathers; and, if they will needs make it my fault, I must answer them with that of Euripides to Alcestides, a tragic writer. Alcestides objecting that Euripides had only in three days composed three verses, whereas himself had written three hundred: "Thou tell'st truth," quoth he,° "but here's the difference: thine shall only be read for three days, whereas mine shall continue three ages."

(Euripides)

Detraction is the sworn friend to ignorance.[9] For mine own part, I have ever truly cherished my good opinion of other men's worthy labors, especially of that full and heightened style of Master Chapman, the labored and understanding works of Master Jonson, the no less worthy composures° of the both worthily excellent Master Beaumont and Master Fletcher, and, lastly, without wrong last to be named,[1] the right happy and copious industry of Master Shakespeare, Master Dekker, and Master Heywood, wishing what I write may be read by their light; protesting that, in the strength of mine own judgment, I know them so worthy that, though I rest silent in° my own work, yet to most of theirs I dare without flattery fix that of Martial:

compositions

in relation to

—non norunt haec monumenta mori.[2]

[THE PERSONS IN THE PLAY, IN ORDER OF APPEARANCE

Count LODOVICO
ANTONELLI }
GASPARO } friends of Lodovico
The Duke of BRACCIANO, Paulo Giordano Orsini, husband of Isabella and then of Vittoria
CAMILLO, husband of Vittoria and nephew of Monticelso
FLAMINEO, brother of Vittoria and Marcello and secretary to Bracciano
VITTORIA Corombona, wife of Camillo and then of Bracciano
ZANCHE the Moor, servant to Vittoria
CORNELIA, mother of Vittoria, Flamineo, and Marcello
FRANCISCO de Medici, Duke of Florence, Isabella's brother
Cardinal MONTICELSO, later Pope Paul IV, Camillo's uncle
MARCELLO, brother of Flamineo and Vittoria, member of Bracciano's household
ISABELLA, wife of Bracciano and sister of Francisco
GIOVANNI, son of Bracciano and Isabella
JULIO, a doctor
A CONJUROR
Christopher, assistant to Julio
A chancellor
A register° — *registrar*
A LAWYER

9. Carping criticism is inseparably linked to ignorance.
1. Meaning no wrong by naming them last.
2. These monuments do not know how to die. (Martial, *Epigrams,* 10.2.12.)

The SAVOY AMBASSADOR
The FRENCH AMBASSADOR
The ENGLISH AMBASSADOR
The Spanish ambassador
Two other lords ambassadors
A SERVANT at the trial of Vittoria
Isabella's ghost
A SERVANT to Francisco
The MATRON of the house of convertites
A CARDINAL
Cardinal of ARRAGON
HORTENSIO, CARLO, PEDRO } members of Bracciano's household
Farnese
A YOUNG LORD
Two women in attendance with Zanche
A PAGE
An ARMORER
Two PHYSICIANS
A COURTIER
Three other LADIES
Bracciano's ghost
Guards, attendants, captains, lords, servants

THE SCENE: Rome and, in act 5, Padua.]

[1.1]

Enter Count Lodovico, Antonelli, and Gasparo.

LODOVICO Banished?
ANTONELLI It grieved me much to hear the sentence.
LODOVICO Ha, ha! O Democritus,[1] thy gods
That govern the whole world! Courtly reward
And punishment! Fortune's a right° whore. *an out-and-out*
If she give aught, she deals it in small parcels,
That she may take away all at one swoop.
This 'tis to have great enemies, God quit° them! *requite, punish*
Your wolf no longer seems to be a wolf
Than when she's hungry.[2]
GASPARO You term those enemies
Are° men of princely rank. *Who are*
LODOVICO Oh, I pray for them.
The violent thunder is adored by those
Are pashed° in pieces by it. *Who are smashed*
ANTONELLI Come, my lord,
You are justly doomed.° Look but a little back *sentenced*

1.1. Rome.
1. A Greek philosopher (c. 460–370 B.C.E.), known as "the laughing philosopher" because he laughed at the follies of men. He regarded the gods as mortal and expounded an atomistic and mechanical system in which desire for reward and fear of punishment govern human behavior.
2. I.e., Predatory men of power are ruthless and dangerously deceptive; they look harmless but strike when moved to do so.

Into your former life. You have in three years
Ruined the noblest earldom—

GASPARO Your followers
Have swallowed you like mummia,[3] and, being sick
With such unnatural and horrid physic,° *medicine*
Vomit you up i'th'kennel.° *gutter*

ANTONELLI All the damnable degrees
Of drinkings have you staggered through. One citizen
Is lord of two fair manors, called you master
Only for caviar.[4]

GASPARO Those noblemen
Which were invited to your prodigal feasts,
Wherein the phoenix[5] scarce could scape your throats,
Laugh at your misery, as foredeeming° you *prejudging, condemning*
An idle° meteor which, drawn forth the earth, *chance*
Would be soon lost i'th'air.[6]

ANTONELLI Jest° upon you, *Men make jests*
And say you were begotten in an earthquake,
You have ruined such fair lordships.° *estates*

LODOVICO Very good.
This well goes with two buckets; I must tend
The pouring out of either.[7]

GASPARO Worse than these,
You have acted° certain murders here in Rome, *carried out*
Bloody and full of horror.

LODOVICO 'Las, they were flea-bitings.
Why took they not my head,° then? *didn't they behead me*

GASPARO Oh, my lord,
The law doth sometimes mediate, thinks it good
Not ever° to steep violent sins in blood. *always*
This gentle penance° may both end your crimes *i.e., Your banishment*
And in the example° better these bad times. *by setting an example*

LODOVICO So. But I wonder then some great men scape° *escape*
This banishment. There's Paulo Giordano Orsini,
The Duke of Bracciano, now lives in Rome,
And by close° panderism seeks to prostitute *secret*
The honor of Vittoria Corombona—
Vittoria, she that might have got my pardon
For one kiss to the Duke.

ANTONELLI Have a full man within you.° *Be a man*
We see that trees bear no such pleasant fruit
There where they grew first as where they are new-set.° *transplanted*
Perfumes, the more they are chafed, the more they render° *emit, give out*
Their pleasing scents, and so affliction
Expresseth° virtue fully, whether true *Presses out*
Or else adulterate.[8]

3. A distasteful preparation, originally of the substance of mummies but also made out of pitch, used medicinally and touted as a remedy for many ills.
4. An ordinary citizen has become wealthy enough to buy two manor houses simply on what he has gained from catering to your extravagant longing for caviar.
5. A mythical bird, of which it was supposed that only one existed at any given time; hence, an unparalleled luxury.
6. Meteors were thought to be exhalations drawn forth from the earth by the sun, flying up into the sky and there disappearing in a moment.
7. Criticized from two sides by Antonelli and Gasparo, Lodovico sees himself as like a man coping single-handedly with two buckets in a well, one descending empty and one always rising full.
8. Affliction, by its severe testing of character, makes clear the difference between true and sham virtue.

LODOVICO Leave your painted° comforts. *specious*
I'll make Italian cutworks° in their guts *lace embroidery*
If ever I return.

GASPARO Oh, sir!

LODOVICO I am patient.
I have seen some ready to be executed
Give pleasant looks and money, and grown familiar
With the knave hangman. So do I, I thank them,
And would account them nobly merciful
Would they dispatch me quickly.

ANTONELLI Fare you well.
We shall find time, I doubt not, to repeal
Your banishment.

LODOVICO I am ever bound to you.
A sennet° sounds. *trumpet flourish*
This is the world's alms;[9] pray make use of it:
Great men sell sheep thus to be cut in pieces° *butchered*
When first they have shorn them bare and sold their fleeces. *Exeunt.*

[1.2]

Enter Bracciano, Camillo, Flamineo, Vittoria Corombona, [and attendants with torches].

BRACCIANO Your best of rest.° *Sleep well*

VITTORIA Unto my lord the Duke
The best of welcome.—More lights! Attend the Duke.
[*Exeunt Camillo and Vittoria.*]

BRACCIANO Flamineo.

FLAMINEO My lord?

BRACCIANO Quite lost, Flamineo.

FLAMINEO Pursue your noble wishes; I am prompt
As lightning to your service. O my lord!
(*Whisper*) The fair Vittoria, my happy sister,
Shall give you present audience.°—Gentlemen, *Will receive you now*
Let the caroche° go on, and 'tis his pleasure *Bracciano's coach*
You put out all your torches and depart.
[*Exeunt attendants.*]

BRACCIANO Are we so happy?° *fortunate*

FLAMINEO Can't be otherwise?
Observed you not tonight, my honored lord,
Which way soe'er you went she threw her eyes?
I have dealt already with her chambermaid,
Zanche the Moor, and she is wondrous proud
To be the agent for so high a spirit.° *so spirited a nobleman*

BRACCIANO We are happy above thought, because 'bove merit.° *more than I deserve*

FLAMINEO 'Bove merit! We may now talk freely. 'Bove merit?
What is't you doubt,° her coyness? That's but the superficies° *fear / outward appearance*
of lust most women have. Yet why should ladies blush to

9. The following maxim is a bit of worldly wisdom that the world bestows on us.

1.2. Camillo's house.

hear that named which they do not fear to handle?° Oh, they are politic;° they know our desire is increased by the difficulty of enjoying, whereas satiety is a blunt, weary, and drowsy passion. If the buttery-hatch° at court stood continually open, there would be nothing so° passionate crowding, nor hot suit after° the beverage.

touch; talk about / *cunning, wise* / *storeroom half-door* / *not nearly so much* / *urgent begging for*

BRACCIANO Oh, but her jealous husband.

FLAMINEO Hang him! A gilder° that hath his brains perished with quicksilver° is not more cold in the liver.° The great barriers moulted not more feathers than he hath shed hairs,[1] by the confession of his doctor. An Irish gamester that will play himself naked, and then wage all downward at hazard,[2] is not more venturous.° So unable to please a woman that, like a Dutch doublet,° all his back is shrunk into his breeches.

one who gilds objects / *mercury fumes / impotent* / *at risk; ridiculous* / *tight-fitting jacket*

Shroud° you within this closet,° good my lord. — *Hide / small room*
Some trick now must be thought on to divide
My brother-in-law from his fair bedfellow.

BRACCIANO Oh, should she fail to come!

FLAMINEO I must not have Your Lordship thus unwisely amorous. I myself have loved a lady and pursued her with a great deal of underage° protestation, whom some three or four gallants that have enjoyed would with all their hearts have been glad to have been rid of. 'Tis just like a summer bird-cage in a garden: the birds that are without° despair to get in, and the birds that are within despair and are in a consumption° for fear they shall never get out. Away, away, my lord! [*Exit Bracciano.*]

adolescent / *outside* / *a wasting disease*

Enter Camillo.

[*Aside*] See, here he comes. This fellow by his apparel
Some men would judge a politician,° — *man of the world*
But, call his wit in question, you shall find it
Merely an ass in's footcloth.° [*To Camillo*] How now, brother,° — *cloth over ass's back* / *brother-in-law*
What, traveling° to bed to your kind wife? — *going; laboring*

CAMILLO I assure you, brother, no. My voyage lies
More northerly, in a far colder clime.
I do not well remember, I protest,° — *I asssure you*
When I last lay with her.

FLAMINEO Strange you should lose your count.° — *reckoning; cunt*

CAMILLO We never lay together but ere morning
There grew a flaw° between us. — *squall; crack*

FLAMINEO T'had been° your part — *It should have been*
To have made up that flaw.° — *filled that vagina*

CAMILLO True, but she loathes
I should be seen in't.

1. Camillo's baldness (often a symptom of syphilis) is like the fluttering down of innumerable feather plumes falling from the contestants' helmets in a tournament fought at the "barriers," a low fence separating the charging combatants on horseback.

2. An Irish gambler who will gamble at dice till he's lost all his clothes, and then wager on the parts of his body—especially his genitals, toenails, etc., i.e., anything that can be cut off.

FLAMINEO Why, sir, what's the matter?
CAMILLO The Duke your master visits me—I thank him—
And I perceive how like an earnest bowler
He very passionately leans that way
He should have his bowl run.
FLAMINEO I hope you do not think—
CAMILLO That noblemen bowl booty?[3] Faith,° his cheek — *In faith*
Hath a most excellent bias; it would fain
Jump with my mistress.
FLAMINEO Will you be an ass,
Despite your Aristotle,° or a cuckold — *i.e., pretense at learning*
Contrary to your ephemerides,° — *astronomical almanacs*
Which shows you under what a smiling planet
You were first swaddled?° — *(i.e., at birth)*
CAMILLO Pew wew,° sir, tell not me — *Pooh pooh*
Of planets nor of ephemerides.
A man may be made cuckold in the daytime
When the stars' eyes are out.° — *are invisible*
FLAMINEO Sir God buy you.° — *God be with you*
I do commit you to your pitiful pillow
Stuffed with horn shavings.° — *(hinting at cuckoldry)*
CAMILLO Brother—
FLAMINEO God refuse me,° — *damn me*
Might I advise you now, your only course
Were to lock up your wife.
CAMILLO 'Twere very good.
FLAMINEO Bar her the sight of revels.
CAMILLO Excellent.
FLAMINEO Let her not go to church but° like a hound — *unless*
In leon° at your heels. — *Leashed in*
CAMILLO 'Twere for her honor.
FLAMINEO And so you should be certain in one fortnight,
Despite her chastity or innocence,
To be cuckolded, which yet is in suspense.[4]
This is my counsel, and I ask no fee for't.
CAMILLO Come, you know not where my nightcap wrings me.° — *pinches my horns*
FLAMINEO Wear it o'th'old fashion: let your large ears° come through, it will be more easy. Nay, I will be bitter: bar your wife of her entertainment. Women are more willingly and more gloriously chaste when they are least restrained of their liberty. It seems you would be a fine, capricious,° mathematically jealous coxcomb. Take the height of your own horns with a Jacob's staff° afore they are up. These politic enclosures for paltry mutton° makes more rebellion in the — *i.e., your ass's ears* — *whimsical; horned* — *(for measuring heights)* — *whores*

3. In the continuing metaphor from bowls, a bowling game played on a grassy green with a target ball called the "mistress," to "bowl booty" is for two players to combine to outmaneuver a third player. The "bias" (line 67) is the weight in the "cheek," or side, of the bowl enabling it to follow a curved path and thus join cleverly with ("Jump with") the "mistress" (line 68), as Bracciano hopes to do with Vittoria.
4. Flamineo sardonically suggests to Camillo that the surest way to prompt his wife to cuckold him (something that may not yet have happened) is to impose unwelcome restraints on her. Flamineo's tactic is to encourage Camillo this way to leave his wife unguarded (so that Flamineo can then arrange the affair between Vittoria and Bracciano). Flamineo goes on, in lines 88–97, to urge that restraint will only encourage Vittoria to be wanton.

flesh than all the provocative electuaries° doctors have uttered° since last jubilee.°

aphrodisiacs / sold / i.e., since 1600

CAMILLO This doth not physic° me.

cure

FLAMINEO It seems you are jealous. I'll show you the error of it by a familiar example. I have seen a pair of spectacles fashioned with such perspective art° that, lay down but one twelvepence o'th'board,° 'twill appear as if there were twenty. Now, should you wear a pair of these spectacles and see your wife tying her shoe, you would imagine twenty hands were taking up of your wife's clothes, and this would put you into a horrible, causeless fury.

optical illusion / on the table

CAMILLO The fault there, sir, is not in the eyesight.

FLAMINEO True, but they that have the yellow jaundice think all objects they look on to be yellow.° Jealousy is worser; her fits present to a man, like so many bubbles in a basin of water, twenty several° crabbed faces, many times makes his own shadow° his cuckold-maker.

(the color of jealousy) / various / reflection

Enter [Vittoria] Corombona.

[*Flamineo speaks privately to Camillo.*] See, she comes. What reason have you to be jealous of this creature? What an ignorant ass or flattering knave might he be counted° that should write sonnets to her eyes, or call her brow the snow of Ida,° or ivory of Corinth, or compare her hair to the blackbird's bill when 'tis liker the blackbird's feather?° This is all: be wise. I will make you friends, and you shall go to bed together. Marry,° look you, it shall not be your seeking; do you stand° upon that by any means. Walk you aloof; I would not have you seen in't. [*To Vittoria*] Sister, [*aside to her*] my lord attends° you in the banqueting-house. [*Aloud*] Your husband is wondrous discontented.

accounted / mountain near Troy / i.e., black, not yellow / By Mary (an oath) / insist / waits for

VITTORIA I did nothing to displease him. I carved to° him at supper time.

served

FLAMINEO [*aside to her*] You need not have carved° him, in faith. They say he is a capon° already. I must now seemingly fall out° with you. [*Aloud*] Shall a gentleman so well descended° as Camillo— [*aside*] a lousy slave that within this twenty years rode with the black guard° in the Duke's carriage° 'mongst spits and dripping-pans—

castrated / castrated cock, eunuch / quarrel / of such good family / lowly servants / household, retinue

CAMILLO [*to himself*] Now he begins to tickle° her.

arouse

FLAMINEO [*aloud*] An excellent scholar—[*aside*] one that hath a head filled with calves' brains without any sage° in them—[*aloud*] come crouching in the hams° to you for a night's lodging, [*aside*] that hath an itch° in's hams which, like the fire at the glasshouse,° hath not gone out this seven years? [*Aloud*] Is he not a courtly gentleman? [*Aside*] When he wears white satin, one would take him by his black muzzle to be no other creature than a maggot. [*Aloud*] You are a goodly foil,° I confess, well set out, [*aside*] but covered with a false stone: yon conterfeit diamond.°

seasoning; sagacity / bowing and scraping / craving; infection / glass factory / setting for a jewel / i.e., Camillo

CAMILLO [*to himself*] He will make her know what is in me.

FLAMINEO Come, my lord° attends you. Thou shalt go to bed to my lord—

(Camillo; Bracciano)

CAMILLO [*to himself*] Now he comes to't.

FLAMINEO With a relish as curious° as a vintner going to taste new wine. [*Aside to Camillo*] I am opening your case hard.[5] *keen*

CAMILLO A virtuous brother, o'my credit!° *on my word*

FLAMINEO [*to Vittoria*] He will give thee a ring with a philosophers' stone in it.[6]

CAMILLO Indeed, I am studying alchemy.

FLAMINEO [*to Vittoria*] Thou shalt lie in a bed stuffed with turtles'° feathers, swoon in perfumed linen like the fellow was° smothered in roses. So perfect shall be thy happiness that, as men at sea think land and trees and ships go that way they go, so both heaven and earth shall seem to go your voyage. Shalt meet him, 'tis fixed, with nails of diamonds° to inevitable necessity. *turtledoves' who was everlasting nails*

VITTORIA [*aside to Flamineo*] How shall 's° rid him hence? *shall we*

FLAMINEO [*aside to Vittoria*] I will put breeze° in's tail, set him gadding presently.° [*Aside to Camillo*] I have almost wrought her to it; I find her coming.° But, might I advise you now, for this night I would not lie with her. I would cross her humor° to make her more humble. *a gadfly at once forward, aroused thwart her mood*

[*The two men continue to talk privately.*]

CAMILLO Shall I, shall I?

FLAMINEO It will show in you a supremacy of judgment.

CAMILLO True, and a mind differing from the tumultuary° opinion, for *quae negata grata*.° *random, hasty what's denied is wanted*

FLAMINEO Right. You are the adamant° shall draw her to you, though you keep distance off. *lodestone, magnet*

CAMILLO A philosophical° reason. *wise*

FLAMINEO Walk by her o'the nobleman's fashion, and tell her you will lie with her at the end of the progress.° *state journey*

CAMILLO [*aloud*] Vittoria, I cannot be induced, or, as a man would say, incited—

VITTORIA To do what, sir?

CAMILLO To lie with you tonight. Your silkworm useth to fast° every third day, and the next following spins the better. Tomorrow at night I am for you. *Silkworms normally fast*

VITTORIA You'll spin a fair thread, trust to't.° *(with sexual overtones)*

[*The men converse privately.*]

FLAMINEO But do you hear? I shall have you steal to her chamber about midnight.

CAMILLO Do you think so? Why, look you, brother, because you shall not think I'll gull you, take the key, lock me into the chamber, and say you shall be sure of me.

[*He gives a key.*]

FLAMINEO In troth, I will. I'll be your jailer once. But have you ne'er a false door?

CAMILLO A pox on't! As I am a Christian.° Tell me tomorrow how scurvily° she takes my unkind parting. *i.e., I swear I don't ill-humoredly*

FLAMINEO I will.

CAMILLO Didst thou not mark the jest of the silkworm? Good night. In faith, I will use this trick often.

FLAMINEO Do, do, do. *Exit Camillo.*

5. (1) I am pleading your case; (2) I am getting your wife's "case" (vagina) ready for your "hard" entry.

6. The quintessence supposed to turn all metals into gold. "Stone" also means "testicle."

So, now you are safe. Ha, ha, ha! Thou° entanglest thyself *(Camillo)*
in thine own work, like a silkworm.

Enter Bracciano.

Come, sister, darkness hides your blush. Women are like
curst° dogs: civility keeps them tied all daytime, but they are *fierce; shrewish*
let loose at midnight; then they do most good or most mis-
chief.—My lord, my lord!

BRACCIANO Give credit:° I could wish time would stand still *Believe me*
And never end this interview this hour!
But all delight doth itself soon'st devour.

Zanche brings out a carpet, spreads it, and lays on it two fair cushions. Enter Cornelia. [*She stands aside, unobserved.*]

Let me into your bosom, happy lady,
Pour out, instead of eloquence, my vows.
Lose me not, madam, for if you forgo° me *forsake*
I am lost eternally.

VITTORIA Sir, in the way of pity
I wish you heart-whole.° *undismayed*

BRACCIANO You are a sweet physician.

VITTORIA Sure, sir, a loathed cruelty in ladies
Is as to doctors many funerals;
It takes away their credit.° *reputation*

BRACCIANO Excellent creature!
We call the cruel° fair. What name for you *beauties who deny us*
That are so merciful? [*He embraces her.*]

ZANCHE [*to Flamineo*] See now they close.° *embrace*

FLAMINEO Most happy union!

CORNELIA [*aside*] My fears are fall'n upon me. Oh, my heart!
My son the pander. Now I find our house° *family*
Sinking to ruin. Earthquakes leave behind,
Where they have tyrannized, iron, or lead, or stone;
But, woe to ruin! Violent lust leaves none.

BRACCIANO [*seeing a jewel she wears*] What value is this jewel?

VITTORIA 'Tis the ornament
Of a weak fortune.

BRACCIANO In sooth,° I'll have it. Nay, I will but change *truth*
My jewel for your jewel. [*He exchanges their jewels.*]

FLAMINEO [*aside*] Excellent!
His jewel for her jewel. Well put in, Duke.

BRACCIANO Nay, let me see you wear it.

VITTORIA [*pinning on his jewel*] Here, sir.

BRACCIANO Nay, lower. You shall wear my jewel lower.

FLAMINEO [*aside*] That's better. She must wear his jewel lower.

VITTORIA To pass away the time, I'll tell Your Grace
A dream I had last night.

BRACCIANO Most wishedly.

VITTORIA A foolish, idle dream.
Methought I walked, about the mid of night,
Into a churchyard, where a goodly yew tree
Spread her large root in ground. Under that yew,
As I sat sadly leaning on a grave,

Checkered with cross-sticks,[7] there came stealing in
Your duchess and my husband. One of them
A pickax bore, th'other a rusty spade,
And in rough terms they gan° to challenge me *began*
About this yew.° *yew tree; you*
BRACCIANO That tree.
VITTORIA This harmless yew.
They told me my intent was to root up
That well-grown yew, and plant i'th'stead of it
A withered blackthorn,[8] and for that they vowed
To bury me alive. My husband straight° *at once*
With pickax gan to dig, and your fell° duchess *fierce, cruel*
With shovel, like a Fury,° voided out *avenging deity*
The earth and scattered bones. Lord, how methought
I trembled! And yet for all this terror
I could not pray.
FLAMINEO [*aside*] No, the devil was in your dream.
VITTORIA When to my rescue there arose, methought,
A whirlwind, which let fall a massy° arm *massive*
From that strong plant,
And both were struck dead by that sacred yew
In that base shallow grave that was their due.
FLAMINEO [*aside*] Excellent devil!
She hath taught him in a dream
To make away his duchess and her husband.
BRACCIANO Sweetly shall I interpret this your dream.
You are lodged within his arms who shall protect you
From all the fevers of a jealous husband,
From the poor envy of our phlegmatic duchess.
I'll seat you above law and above scandal,
Give to your thoughts the invention of delight
And the fruition, nor shall government° *princely duties*
Divide me from you longer than a care
To keep you great. You shall to me at once
Be dukedom, health, wife, children, friends, and all.
CORNELIA [*coming forward*] Woe to light° hearts! They still forerun our fall. *inconstant*
FLAMINEO What Fury raised thee up?—Away, away!
Exit Zanche.[9]
CORNELIA What make you here, my lord, this dead of night?
Never dropped mildew on a flower here
Till now.
FLAMINEO I pray, will you go to bed, then,
Lest you be blasted?° *blighted, struck down*
CORNELIA Oh, that this fair garden
Had with all poisoned herbs of Thessaly° *(famed for poison herbs)*
At first been planted, made a nursery

7. With cross-hatchings of weathered stone (?). (A difficult image.) Yew trees were, and still are, common in English churchyards.
8. From a morally conventional perspective, the dream represents Vittoria uprooting marital happiness and substituting for it a blighted love affair. From an unconventional perspective, presented in lines 251–55 and 260–62, the yew is like Bracciano in protecting and avenging her.
9. Zanche, whose role has been to assist Flamineo in facilitating the assignation, is simply in the way now that Cornelia has unexpectedly appeared. Perhaps Flamineo says "Away, away!" to her.

For witchcraft, rather than a burial plot
For both your honors!
VITTORIA [*kneeling*] Dearest mother, hear me.
CORNELIA Oh, thou dost make my brow bend to the earth
Sooner than nature.° See the curse of children! *natural aging*
In life they keep us frequently in tears,
And in the cold grave leave us in pale fears.
BRACCIANO Come, come, I will not hear you.
VITTORIA Dear my lord!
CORNELIA Where is thy Duchess now, adulterous Duke?
Thou little dreamd'st this night she is come to Rome.
FLAMINEO How? Come to Rome?
VITTORIA The Duchess?
BRACCIANO She had been better—
CORNELIA The lives of princes should like dials° move, *sundials*
Whose regular example is so strong
They make the times by them go right or wrong.
FLAMINEO So, have you done?° *finished*
CORNELIA Unfortunate Camillo!
VITTORIA I do protest if any chaste denial,
If anything but blood could have allayed
His long suit to me—
CORNELIA [*kneeling*] I will join with thee,
To the most woeful end e'er mother kneeled:
If thou dishonor thus thy husband's bed,
Be thy life short as are the funeral tears
In great men's!° *In noblemen's funerals*
BRACCIANO Fie, fie, the woman's mad.
CORNELIA Be thy act Judas-like: betray in kissing.[1]
Mayst thou be envied during his short breath,° *Bracciano's short life*
And pitied like a wretch after his death!
VITTORIA Oh, me accurst! *Exit Vittoria.*
FLAMINEO [*to Cornelia*] Are you out of your wits?—My lord,
I'll fetch her back again.
BRACCIANO No, I'll to bed.
Send Doctor Julio to me presently.
[*To Cornelia*] Uncharitable woman, thy rash tongue
Hath raised a fearful and prodigious° storm. *ominous; enormous*
Be thou the cause of all ensuing harm! *Exit Bracciano.*
[*Cornelia rises.*]
FLAMINEO Now, you that stand so much upon your honor,
Is this a fitting time o'night, think you,
To send a duke home without e'er a man?° *unattended*
I would fain know where lies the mass of wealth
Which you have hoarded for my maintenance,
That I may bear my beard out of the level
Of my lord's stirrup.[2]
CORNELIA What? Because we are poor,
Shall° we be vicious? *Must*

1. A reference to Matthew 26.48–49, in which Judas betrays Jesus: "Now he [Judas] that betrayed him gave them [the priests and elders] a sign, saying, 'Whomsoever I shall kiss, that same is he: hold him fast.' And forthwith he came to Jesus, and said, 'Hail, Master'; and kissed him."
2. So that I will no longer have to walk beside my horseback-mounted lord as his attendant.

FLAMINEO Pray, what means have you
To keep me from the galleys, or the gallows?
My father proved himself a gentleman,[3]
Sold all 's land, and like a fortunate fellow
Died ere the money was spent. You brought me up,
At Padua,° I confess, where I protest, *a distinguished university*
For want of means—the university judge me—
I have been fain to heel° my tutor's stockings *obliged to mend*
At least seven years. Conspiring with a beard° *Coming of age*
Made me a graduate; then to this duke's service.
I visited the court, whence I returned,
More courteous,° more lecherous by far, *fashionable*
But not a suit° the richer. And shall I, *suit of clothes; petition*
Having a path so open and so free
To my preferment, still retain your milk
In my pale forehead?[4] No, this face of mine
I'll arm and fortify with lusty° wine *strong*
'Gainst shame and blushing.
CORNELIA Oh, that I ne'er had born thee!
FLAMINEO So would I.
I would the common'st courtesan in Rome
Had been my mother rather than thyself.
Nature is very pitiful° to whores *compassionate*
To give them but few children, yet those children
Plurality of fathers; they are sure
They shall not want.° Go, go, *go in need*
Complain unto my great Lord Cardinal;° *Cardinal Monticelso*
Yet may be he will justify the act.[5]
Lycurgus[6] wondered much° men would provide *was amazed that*
Good stallions for their mares, and yet would suffer
Their fair wives to be barren.
CORNELIA Misery of miseries! *Exit Cornelia.*
FLAMINEO The Duchess come to court! I like not that.
We are engaged to mischief and must on.
As rivers, to find out the ocean,
Flow with crook° bendings beneath forcèd° banks, *crooked / constraining*
Or as we see, to aspire° some mountain's top, *attain to*
The way ascends not straight, but imitates
The subtle foldings of a winter's° snake, *i.e., slow-moving*
So who° knows policy° and her true aspect *whoever / cunning*
Shall find her ways winding and indirect. *Exit.*

[2.1]

Enter Francisco de Medici, Cardinal Monticelso, Marcello, Isabella, [*and*] *young Giovanni* [*with attendants*].

FRANCISCO Have you not seen your husband since you arrived?
ISABELLA Not yet, sir.

3. I.e., My father ruined himself financially by extravagance, as gentlemen usually do.
4. Shall I . . . remain a pale-faced mama's boy?
5. Yet it may be that the Cardinal will sanction my behavior that you so criticize.
6. A legendary Spartan lawgiver (c. 600 B.C.E.). The episode is reported in Plutarch's *Life of Lycurgus*, in chapter 4.
2.1. Rome still.

FRANCISCO Surely he is wondrous kind.
If I had such a dovehouse° as Camillo's *nest of lovebirds*
I would set fire on't, were't but to destroy
The polecats that haunt° to't. [*To Giovanni*] My sweet cousin! *have resort*
GIOVANNI Lord uncle, you did promise me a horse
And armor.
FRANCISCO That I did, my pretty cousin.°— *kinsman*
Marcello, see it fitted.
MARCELLO My lord, the Duke is here.
FRANCISCO Sister, away!
You must not yet be seen.
ISABELLA I do beseech you
Entreat him mildly; let not your rough tongue
Set us at louder variance. All my wrongs° *the wrongs done me*
Are freely pardoned, and I do not doubt
As° men, to try the precious unicorn's horn, *That just as*
Make of the powder a preservative circle
And in it put a spider,[1] so these arms
Shall charm his poison, force it to obeying
And keep him chaste from an infected° straying. *diseased; immoral*
FRANCISCO I wish it may. Begone! *Exit* [*Isabella*].

Enter Bracciano and Flamineo.

Void° the chamber. *Clear, leave*
[*Exeunt all but Francisco, Monticelso, and Bracciano.*]
You are welcome. Will you sit? [*To Monticelso*] I pray, my lord,
Be you my orator; my heart's too full.
I'll second you anon.
MONTICELSO [*to Bracciano*] Ere I begin,
Let me entreat Your Grace forgo all passion
Which may be raisèd by my free discourse.
BRACCIANO As silent as i'th'church. You may proceed.
MONTICELSO It is a wonder to your noble friends
That you, that have as 'twere entered the world
With a free° scepter in your able hand, *unrestrained*
And have to th'use of nature well applied
High gifts of learning,[2] should in your prime age° *prime of life*
Neglect your awful° throne for the soft down *awe-inspiring*
Of an insatiate bed. Oh, my lord,
The drunkard, after all his lavish cups,
Is dry, and then is sober; so at length,
When you awake from this lascivious dream,
Repentance then will follow, like the sting
Placed in the adder's tail. Wretched are princes
When Fortune blasteth but a petty flower[3]
Of their unwieldy crowns, or ravisheth
But° one pearl from their scepter. But alas, *All but*
When they to willful shipwreck lose good fame,° *reputation*
All princely titles perish with their name.° *good name*

1. A supposed test of the authenticity of unicorn's horn (a magical potion derived from the single horn of that mythical beast) was to place a spider inside a ring of the powdered horn and see if the spider could escape.

2. And have ably applied a capacity for learning to your natural abilities.

3. When Fortune blights and ruins all but one tiny jewel.

BRACCIANO You have said, my lord—
MONTICELSO Enough to give you taste
How far I am from flattering your greatness.
BRACCIANO [*to Francisco*] Now you that are his second, what say you?
Do not, like young hawks, fetch a course about;° *turn tail*
Your game flies fair and for you.
FRANCISCO Do not fear it.
I'll answer you in your own hawking phrase:
Some eagles, that should gaze upon the sun,
Seldom soar high, but take their lustful ease,
Since they from dunghill birds their prey can seize.
You know Vittoria.
BRACCIANO Yes.
FRANCISCO You shift° your shirt there *change*
When you retire from tennis.
BRACCIANO Happily.° *Perhaps so; contentedly*
FRANCISCO Her husband is lord of a poor fortune,
Yet she wears cloth of tissue.[4]
BRACCIANO What of this?
Will you urge° that, my good Lord Cardinal, *inquire closely into*
As part of her confession at next shrift,° *confession*
And know from whence it sails?° *i.e., comes*
FRANCISCO She is your strumpet.
BRACCIANO Uncivil sir, there's hemlock° in thy breath *poison*
And that black slander. Were she a whore of mine,
All thy loud cannons and thy borrowed Switzers,° *Swiss mercenaries*
Thy galleys, nor thy sworn confederates,
Durst° not supplant° her. *Dare / dispossess*
FRANCISCO Let's not talk on thunder.
Thou hast a wife, our° sister. Would I had given *my*
Both her white hands to death, bound and locked fast
In her last winding-sheet,° when I gave thee *shroud*
But one!
BRACCIANO Thou hadst given a soul to God, then.
FRANCISCO True.
Thy ghostly father, with all 's absolution,
Shall ne'er do so by thee.[5]
BRACCIANO Spit thy poison.
FRANCISCO I shall not need. Lust carries her sharp whip
At her own girdle. Look to't, for our anger
Is making thunderbolts.
BRACCIANO Thunder? In faith,
They are but crackers.° *mere firecrackers*
FRANCISCO We'll end this with the cannon.° *with warfare*
BRACCIANO Thou'lt get naught by it but iron in thy wounds
And gunpowder in thy nostrils.
FRANCISCO Better that
Than change perfumes for plasters.[6]

4. A rich fabric, often interwoven with gold or silver thread (which Camillo's fortune alone would not enable him to afford).
5. Your confessor, with all his powers of forgiveness of sins, will never get you into heaven.
6. Better war than have sexual dalliance turn into the venereal disease it produces. (Plasters are medicated dressings.)

BRACCIANO Pity on thee.
'Twere good you'd show your slaves or men condemned
Your new-plowed forehead.[7] Defiance!° And I'll meet thee, *Take my defiance!*
Even in a thicket of thy ablest men.
MONTICELSO My lords, you shall not word° it any further *argue hotly*
Without a milder limit.
FRANCISCO Willingly.
BRACCIANO Have you proclaimed a triumph, that you bait
A lion thus?[8]
MONTICELSO My lord!
BRACCIANO I am tame, I am tame, sir.
FRANCISCO We send unto the Duke° for conference *(Bracciano)*
'Bout levies 'gainst the pirates; my lord Duke
Is° not at home. We come ourself in person; *Pretends to be*
Still my lord Duke is busied. But we fear,
When Tiber to each prowling passenger° *passerby*
Discovers° flocks of wild ducks,° then, my lord— *Reveals / whores*
'Bout molting time,[9] I mean—we shall be certain
To find you sure enough and speak with you.
BRACCIANO Ha?
FRANCISCO A mere tale of a tub;° my words are idle. *cock-and-bull story*
But to express the sonnet by natural reason:[1]
When stags grow melancholic,[2] you'll find the season.

Enter Giovanni [in his new suit of armor].

MONTICELSO No more, my lord. Here comes a champion
Shall end the difference between you both:
Your son, the Prince Giovanni. See, my lords,
What hopes you store in him! This is a casket
For both your crowns, and should be held like dear.° *dear by both of you*
Now is he apt for knowledge. Therefore know
It is a more direct and even° way *straightforward*
To train to virtue those of princely blood
By examples than by precepts. If by examples,
Whom should he rather strive to imitate
Than his own father? Be his pattern, then;
Leave him a stock° of virtue that may last, *ancestral line; supply*
Should fortune rend his sails and split his mast.
BRACCIANO Your hand, boy. Growing to a soldier?
GIOVANNI Give me a pike.° *long-handled weapon*
FRANCISCO What, practicing your pike so young, fair coz?° *"cousin," nephew*
GIOVANNI Suppose me one of Homer's frogs, my lord,
Tossing my bulrush thus.[3] Pray, sir, tell me:
Might not a child of good discretion° *judgment*
Be leader to an army?
FRANCISCO Yes, cousin, a young prince
Of good discretion° might. *prudent self-protection*
GIOVANNI Say you so?

7. I.e., Your furrowed brow of anger might impress lowly wretches or condemned criminals, but not me. (Said sarcastically.)
8. Are you enraging a lion (i.e., myself) thus to fight in a Roman spectacle in an amphitheater or in a triumphal processional entry into the city?
9. I.e., (1) When the mating season is over; or (2) when the hair begins to fall out as a result of syphilis.
1. But to put the matter simply and in rhyme.
2. Deer were thought to become melancholic late in the rut cycle.
3. In the mock-Homeric *The Battle of Frogs and Mice*, the frogs comically arm themselves with bulrushes.

Indeed, I have heard 'tis fit a general
Should not endanger his own person oft,
So° that he make a noise when he's a-horseback, *In such a way*
Like a Dansk° drummer. Oh, 'tis excellent! *Danish*
He need not fight; methinks his horse as well
Might lead an army for him. If I live,
I'll charge the French foe in the very front
Of all my troops, the foremost man.

FRANCISCO What, what?

GIOVANNI And will not bid my soldiers up, and follow,° *follow them*
But bid them follow me.

BRACCIANO Forward lapwing!
He flies with the shell on 's head.[4]

FRANCISCO Pretty cousin!

GIOVANNI The first year, uncle, that I go to war,
All prisoners that I take I will set free
Without their ransom.

FRANCISCO Ha, without their ransom?
How then will you reward your soldiers
That took those prisoners for you?

GIOVANNI Thus, my lord:
I'll marry them to all the wealthy widows
That falls° that year. *happen*

FRANCISCO Why, then, the next year following
You'll have no men to go with you to war.

GIOVANNI Why, then, I'll press° the women to the war, *impress, conscript*
And then the men will follow.

MONTICELSO Witty prince!

FRANCISCO See, a good habit makes a child a man,
Whereas a bad one makes a man a beast.
[*To Bracciano*] Come, you and I are friends.

BRACCIANO Most wishedly,
Like bones which, broke in sunder and well set,
Knit the more strongly.

FRANCISCO [*to attendants offstage*] Call Camillo hither.—
You have received the rumor how Count Lodowick° *Lodovico*
Is turned a pirate?

BRACCIANO Yes.

FRANCISCO We are now preparing
Some ships to fetch him in.° *take him into custody*

[*Enter Isabella.*]

Behold your duchess.
We now will leave you, and expect from you
Nothing but kind entreaty.° *treatment*

BRACCIANO You have charmed° me. *put a spell on*

Exeunt Franciso, Monticelso, [*and*] *Giovanni.*

You are in health, we see.

ISABELLA And above health
To see my lord well.

BRACCIANO So. I wonder much
What amorous whirlwind hurried you to Rome.

ISABELLA Devotion, my lord.

4. As a type of precocity, the lapwing (a ploverlike bird) was reputed to fly as soon as hatched.

BRACCIANO Devotion?
Is your soul charged with any grievous sin?
ISABELLA 'Tis burdened with too many, and I think
The oft'ner that we cast our reckonings up,° *reckon up our sins*
Our sleeps will be the sounder.
BRACCIANO Take your chamber.
ISABELLA Nay, my dear lord, I will not have you angry.
Doth not my absence from you two months
Merit one kiss?
BRACCIANO I do not use° to kiss. *make it a practice*
If that will dispossess your jealousy,
I'll swear it to you.
ISABELLA O my lovèd lord,
I do not come to chide. My jealousy?
I am to learn° what that Italian means. *I'm ignorant*
You are as welcome to these longing arms
As I to you a virgin. [*She attempts to kiss him.*]
BRACCIANO Oh, your breath!
Out upon sweetmeats° and continued physic!° *candy / medicine*
The plague is in them.
ISABELLA You have oft for these two lips
Neglected cassia° or the natural sweets *fragrant cinnamon*
Of the spring violet; they° are not yet much withered. *(my lips)*
My lord, I should be merry; these your frowns
Show in a helmet lovely, but on me,
In such a peaceful interview, methinks
They are too too roughly knit.
BRACCIANO Oh, dissemblance!
Do you bandy° factions 'gainst me? Have you learnt *instigate*
The trick of impudent baseness, to complain
Unto your kindred?
ISABELLA Never, my dear lord.
BRACCIANO Must I be haunted out, or was't your trick
To meet some amorous gallant here in Rome
That must supply our discontinuance?° *supplant me*
ISABELLA I pray, sir, burst my heart, and in my death
Turn to your ancient° pity, though not love. *former*
BRACCIANO Because your brother is the corpulent duke,
That is the great duke, 'sdeath,° I shall not shortly *by God's death*
Racket away five hundred crowns at tennis
But it shall rest upon record.[5] I scorn him
Like a shaved Polack.° All his reverend wit *i.e., As contemptible*
Lies in his wardrobe;[6] he's a discreet° fellow *impressive*
When he's made up in his robes of state.
Your brother the great duke, because h'as galleys,
And now and then ransacks a Turkish flyboat° *small sailing vessel*
(Now all the hellish Furies take his soul!),
First made this match. Accursèd be the priest
That sang the wedding mass, and even my issue!° *cursed be my own son*
ISABELLA Oh, too too far you have cursed.
BRACCIANO [*kissing her hand*] Your hand I'll kiss;

5. I won't so much as lose a wager at tennis without its being set down to my discredit.

6. All his admired intelligence is simply a matter of the way he dresses.

This is the latest° ceremony of my love. *last*
Henceforth I'll never lie with thee, by this,
This wedding ring. [*He returns the ring.*] I'll ne'er more lie with thee,
And this divorce shall be as truly kept
As if the judge had doomed° it. Fare you well; *passed sentence on*
Our sleeps are severed.

ISABELLA Forbid it, the sweet union
Of all things blessèd! Why, the saints in heaven
Will knit their brows at that.

BRACCIANO Let not thy love
Make thee an unbeliever.[7] This my vow
Shall never, on my soul, be satisfied° *fully discharged*
With my repentance. Let thy brother rage
Beyond° a horrid° tempest or sea-fight; *Worse than / dreadful*
My vow is fixèd.

ISABELLA O my winding-sheet,
Now shall I need thee shortly!—Dear my lord,
Let me hear once more what I would not hear—
Never?

BRACCIANO Never.

ISABELLA O my unkind lord, may your sins find mercy,
As I upon a woeful widowed bed
Shall pray for you, if not to turn your eyes
Upon your wretched wife and hopeful son,
Yet that in time you'll fix them upon heaven.

BRACCIANO No more. Go, go, complain to the great duke.

ISABELLA No, my dear lord, you shall have present° witness *immediate*
How I'll work peace between you. I will make
Myself the author of your cursèd vow;
I have some cause to do it, you have none.
Conceal it, I beseech you, for the weal° *well-being*
Of both your dukedoms, that you wrought the means
Of such a separation; let the fault
Remain with my supposèd jealousy,
And think with what a piteous and rent heart
I shall perform this sad ensuing part. [*She weeps.*]

Enter Francisco, Flamineo, Monticelso, [*and*] *Marcello.*

BRACCIANO Well, take your course.—My honorable brother!° *brother-in-law*

FRANCISCO Sister,—This is not well, my lord.—Why, sister!—
She merits not this welcome.

BRACCIANO Welcome, say?° *say you?*
She hath given a sharp welcome.

FRANCISCO [*to Isabella*] Are you foolish?
Come, dry your tears. Is this a modest course
To better what is naught,° to rail and weep? *wicked; worthless*
Grow to a reconcilement, or, by heaven,
I'll ne'er more deal between you.

ISABELLA Sir, you shall not,
No, though Vittoria upon that condition

7. I.e., Don't put your faith in me and in the saints to a test that will surely fail (since the saints will not be able to make me return to you).

Would become honest.[8]
FRANCISCO Was your husband loud° *angry*
Since we departed?
ISABELLA By my life, sir, no;
I swear by that I do not care to lose.° *(chastity)*
Are all these ruins of my former beauty
Laid out for a whore's triumph?
FRANCISCO Do you hear?
Look upon other women, with what patience
They suffer these slight wrongs, with what justice
They study° to requite them; take that course. *endeavor*
ISABELLA Oh, that I were a man, or that I had power
To execute my apprehended° wishes! *strongly felt*
I would whip some with scorpions.° *whips of knotted cords*
FRANCISCO What? Turned Fury?
ISABELLA To dig the strumpet's eyes out, let her lie
Some twenty months a-dying, to cut off
Her nose and lips, pull out her rotten teeth,
Preserve her flesh like mummia,° for trophies *(see 1.1.16 n)*
Of my just anger! Hell to° my affliction *compared with*
Is mere snow water. By your favor, sir,
Brother, draw near, and my Lord Cardinal.
[*To Bracciano*] Sir, let me borrow of you but one kiss;
Henceforth I'll never lie with you, by this,
This wedding ring.
FRANCISCO How? Ne'er more lie with him?
ISABELLA And this divorce shall be as truly kept
As if in throngèd court a thousand ears
Had heard it, and a thousand lawyers' hands
Sealed to the separation.
BRACCIANO Ne'er lie with me?
ISABELLA Let not my former dotage
Make thee an unbeliever. This my vow
Shall never, on my soul, be satisfied
With my repentance,[9] *manet alta mente repostum.*[1]
FRANCISCO Now, by my birth, you are a foolish, mad,
And jealous woman.
BRACCIANO You see 'tis not my seeking.
FRANCISCO Was this your circle of pure unicorn's horn
You said should charm your lord?° Now, horns upon thee![2] *(see 12–18 above)*
For jealousy deserves them. Keep your vow,
And take your chamber.
ISABELLA No, sir, I'll presently to Padua;
I will not stay a minute.
MONTICELSO Oh, good madam!
BRACCIANO 'Twere best to let her have her humor;° *whim*
Some half day's journey will bring down her stomach,° *pride, anger*

8. I refuse all attempts at reconciliation, even if Vittoria were to vow to behave chastely. (Isabella, despite her determination to take the guilt on herself, cannot resist making this hint as to where the fault truly lies.)
9. Isabella consciously repeats, in an ironic new context, the cruel words that Bracciano said to her at lines 201–4 above, substituting "my former dotage" for Bracciano's "thy love."
1. It remains treasured up deep in my mind. (Virgil, *Aeneid*, 1.26.)
2. I.e., Now may your husband prove unfaithful, since you are so madly jealous! (Alluding to cuckold's horns.)

And then she'll turn in post.° *return quickly*

FRANCISCO To see her come
To my Lord Cardinal for a dispensation
Of her rash vow will beget excellent laughter.

ISABELLA [*aside*] Unkindness, do thy office; poor heart, break!
Those are the killing griefs which dare not speak. *Exit.*

Enter Camillo.

MARCELLO Camillo's come, my lord.

FRANCISCO Where's the commission?

MARCELLO 'Tis here.

FRANCISCO Give me the signet.[3]

[*Francisco, Monticelso, Marcello, and Camillo withdraw to one side; Flamineo and Bracciano confer privately.*]

FLAMINEO My lord, do you mark their whispering? I will compound a medicine out of their two heads, stronger than garlic, deadlier than stibium;° the cantharides,[4] which are scarce seen to stick upon the flesh when they work to the heart, shall not do it with more silence or invisible cunning. *antimony (a poison)*

Enter doctor [Julio, unobserved at first].

BRACCIANO About the murder[5]—

FLAMINEO They are sending him° to Naples, but I'll send him to Candy.[6] [*Seeing Julio*] Here's another property° too. *(Camillo)* *instrument*

BRACCIANO Oh, the doctor. [*Julio joins them.*]

FLAMINEO A poor quacksalving° knave, my lord, one that should have been lashed for 's lechery, but that he confessed a judgment, had an execution laid upon him, and so put the whip to a nonplus. *quack-doctoring*

JULIO And was cozened,° my lord, by an arranter knave than myself, and made pay all the colorable execution.[7] *cheated*

FLAMINEO He will shoot pills into a man's guts shall make them have more ventages than a cornet or a lamprey.[8] He will poison a kiss, and was once minded,° for his masterpiece, because Ireland breeds no poison,[9] to have prepared a deadly vapor in a Spaniard's fart that should have° poisoned all Dublin. *and once intended* *was intended to have*

BRACCIANO O Saint Anthony fire!° *(an oath)*

JULIO Your secretary is merry, my lord.

FLAMINEO O thou cursed antipathy to nature!—Look, his eye's bloodshed,° like a needle a surgeon stitcheth a wound with.—Let me embrace thee, toad,° and love thee, O thou *bloodshot* *(an endearment)*

3. Signet ring for sealing a commission.
4. Spanish flies, which were used medicinally but could also be poisonous.
5. Bracciano broaches the matter of how Camillo is to be murdered.
6. I.e., I'll send him to his death. Pirates and other hazardous conditions reputedly abounded in Crete (Candy).
7. Having been sentenced to a whipping for lechery, the doctor, so that he might be taken into custody and thereby escape the whipping, confessed to having been sentenced earlier for debt; but another rogue, claiming to be the creditor, made him pay according to the supposed judgment. ("Colorable" means "pretended.")
8. The doctor's pills will cause a man's guts to suffer more perforations, or vents, than a trumpetlike instrument or a lamprey eel (the gills of which resemble vents).
9. Ireland was noted for having no poisonous snakes or other noxious creatures, supposedly because Saint Patrick had cast them all into the sea.

abominable, loathsome gargarism,° that will fetch up lungs, *gargle*
lights,° heart, and liver by scruples!° *lungs / small amounts*

BRACCIANO No more.—I must employ thee, honest doctor.
You must to Padua, and, by the way,
Use some of your skill for us.

JULIO Sir, I shall.

BRACCIANO But for° Camillo? *as for*

FLAMINEO He dies this night by such a politic strain,° *ingenious method*
Men shall suppose him by 's own engine° slain. *contrivance*
But for your duchess' death—

JULIO I'll make her sure.

BRACCIANO Small mischiefs are by greater made secure.

FLAMINEO [*to Julio*] Remember this, you slave: when knaves come to preferment,° they rise as gallowses are raised i'th'Low Countries, one upon another's shoulders.[1] *promotion*

Exeunt [*Bracciano, Flamineo, and Julio*].

MONTICELSO [*showing a paper to Camillo*] Here is an emblem,° nephew; pray peruse it. *allegorical picture*
'Twas thrown in at your window.

CAMILLO [*examining the paper*] At my window?
Here is a stag, my lord, hath shed his horns,
And for the loss of them the poor beast weeps.
The word:° "*Inopem me copia fecit.*"[2] *motto*

MONTICELSO That is,
Plenty of horns° hath made him poor of horns. *cuckold's horns*

CAMILLO What should this mean?

MONTICELSO I'll tell you: 'tis given out° *reported*
You are a cuckold.

CAMILLO Is it given out so?
I had rather such report as that, my lord,
Should keep within doors.

FRANCISCO Have you any children?

CAMILLO None, my lord.

FRANCISCO You are the happier.
I'll tell you a tale.

CAMILLO Pray,° my lord. *Pray do*

FRANCISCO An old tale.
Upon a time, Phoebus, the god of light
(Or him we call the sun), would need be married.
The gods gave their consent, and Mercury
Was sent to voice it to the general world.
But what a pitious cry there straight arose
Amongst smiths and felt-makers, brewers and cooks,
Reapers and butter-women, amongst fishmongers
And thousand other trades, which are annoyed
By his excessive heat! 'Twas lamentable.
They came to Jupiter all in a sweat
And do forbid the banns.° A great fat cook *wedding announcement*
Was made their speaker, who entreats of Jove

1. The image here is of condemned criminals in the Netherlands being hanged by being forced to stand on the shoulders of fellow criminals and then left hanging in the noose when those on the ground move away.

2. "Abundance has left me destitute." (Ovid, *Metamorphoses*, 3.466.)

That Phoebus might be gelded,° for if now, *castrated*
When there was but one sun, so many men
Were like° to perish by his violent heat, *likely*
What should they do if he were married
And should beget more, and those children
Make fireworks like their father? So say I,
Only I will apply it to your wife:
Her issue, should not Providence prevent it,
Would make both nature, time, and man repent it.

MONTICELSO [*to Camillo*] Look you, cousin,
Go change the air,° for shame. See if your absence *Change location*
Will blast your cornucopia.° Marcello *horn of plenty*
Is chosen with you joint commissioner
For the relieving our Italian coast
From pirates.

MARCELLO I am much honored in't.

CAMILLO But, sir,
Ere I return, the stag's horns may be sprouted,
Greater than these are° shed. *that are*

MONTICELSO Do not fear it;
I'll be your ranger.° *gamekeeper*

CAMILLO You must watch i'th'nights;
Then's the most danger.

FRANCISCO Farewell, good Marcello.
All the best fortunes of a soldier's wish
Bring you a-shipboard!

CAMILLO Were I not best, now I am turned soldier,
Ere that I leave my wife, sell all she hath,
And then take leave of her?

MONTICELSO I expect good from you,
Your parting is so merry.

CAMILLO Merry, my lord, o'th'captain's humor right;[3]
I am resolvèd to be drunk this night.

Exit [*Camillo, with Marcello*].

FRANCISCO So. 'Twas well fitted.° Now shall we discern *arranged, plotted*
How his wished absence will give violent way
To Duke Bracciano's lust.

MONTICELSO Why, that was it.° *(the point)*
To what scorned purpose else should we make choice
Of him for a sea captain? And besides,
Count Lodowick, which was rumored for a pirate,
Is now in Padua.

FRANCISCO Is't true?

MONTICELSO Most certain.
I have letters from him, which are suppliant
To work his quick repeal from banishment.
He means to address himself for pension
Unto your sister duchess.

FRANCISCO Oh, 'twas well.
We shall not want° his absence past six days. *need*
I fain would have the Duke Bracciano run
Into notorious scandal, for there's naught

3. My merriment (i.e., drunkenness) is precisely of the soldier's temperament.

In such curst dotage to repair his name;
Only the deep sense of some deathless shame.[4]
MONTICELSO It may be objected I am dishonorable,
To play thus with my kinsman,° but I answer: *my nephew (Camillo)*
For my revenge I'd stake a brother's life
That, being wronged, durst not avenge himself.
FRANCISCO Come to observe this strumpet.
MONTICELSO Curse of greatness![5]
Sure he'll not leave her.
FRANCISCO There's small pity° in't. *cause of pity*
Like mistletoe on sere° elms spent by weather, *withered*
Let him cleave to her and both rot together. *Exeunt.*

[2.2]

Enter Bracciano with one in the habit° of a Conjuror. *garb*

BRACCIANO Now, sir, I claim your promise. 'Tis dead midnight,
The time prefixed to show me by your art
How the intended murder of Camillo
And our loathed duchess grow to action.
CONJUROR You have won me by your bounty to a deed
I do not often practice. Some there are
Which, by sophistic tricks, aspire° that name *aspire to*
Which I would gladly lose, of nigromancer;° *necromancer*
As some that use° to juggle upon cards, *make it a practice*
Seeming to conjure, when indeed they cheat;
Others that raise up their confederate spirits
'Bout windmills,° and endanger their own necks, *fanciful schemes*
For making of a squib;° and some there are *firecracker*
Will keep a curtal° to show juggling tricks *dock-tailed horse*
And give out 'tis a spirit; besides these,
Such a whole ream of almanac-makers, figure-flingers°— *astrologers*
Fellows indeed that only live by stealth,
Since they do merely lie about stol'n goods;[1]
They'd make men think the devil were fast and loose,° *i.e., shifty, deceitful*
With speaking fustian° Latin.[2] Pray, sit down. *bombastic*
Put on this nightcap, sir; 'tis charmed, and now
I'll show you by my strong-commanding art
The circumstance that breaks your duchess' heart.

A DUMB SHOW

Enter, suspiciously, Julio and Christophero.° They draw a curtain where Bracciano's picture is. They put on spectacles of glass, which cover their eyes and noses, and then burn perfumes afore the picture, and wash° the *an assistant* / *anoint (with poison)*

4. There's nothing that Bracciano's alleged infatuation for Vittoria can do except destroy the reputation of his family name (and hence that of young Giovanni); all that remains is eternal shame. (Perhaps Francisco wonders if the fear of such shame might prompt Bracciano to mend his ways.)
5. This is the curse that affects great men!

2.2. Camillo's house (see lines 50–51).
1. I.e., they fraudulently cast horoscopes in a purported attempt to find stolen goods and to claim magical powers they do not have.
2. By speaking Latin gibberish, these quacks seek to create the impression of conjuring up the devil and letting him rampage about.

lips of the picture. That done, quenching the fire and putting off their spectacles, they depart laughing.

Enter Isabella in her nightgown as to bedward, with lights° after her, Count Lodovico, Giovanni, and others waiting on her. She kneels down as to prayers, then draws the curtain of the picture, does three reverences to it, and kisses it thrice. She faints, and will not suffer° them to come near it; dies. Sorrow expressed in Giovanni and in Count Lodovico. She's conveyed out solemnly.

servants with torches / *allow*

BRACCIANO Excellent! Then she's dead.
CONJUROR She's poisoned,
By the fumed picture. 'Twas her custom nightly,
Before she went to bed, to go and visit
Your picture, and to feed her eyes and lips
On the dead shadow.° Doctor Julio, *lifeless image*
Observing this, infects it with an oil
And other poisoned stuff, which presently
Did suffocate her spirits.
BRACCIANO Methought I saw
Count Lodowick there.
CONJUROR He was, and by my art
I find he did most passionately dote
Upon your duchess. Now turn another way
And view Camillo's far more politic° fate.— *cunning*
Strike louder music from this charmèd ground,
To yield, as fits the act, a tragic sound! [*Music sounds.*]

THE SECOND DUMB SHOW

Enter Flamineo, Marcello, Camillo, with four more as captains. They drink healths and dance. A vaulting horse is brought into the room. Marcello and two more whispered° out of the room, while Flamineo and Camillo strip themselves into their shirts, as to vault. Compliment° who shall begin. As Camillo is about to vault, Flamineo pitcheth him upon his neck, and, with the help of the rest, writhes his neck about, seems to see if it be broke, and lays him folded double as 'twere under the horse; makes shows to call for help. Marcello comes in, laments, sends for the Cardinal [Monticelso] and Duke [Francisco], who comes forth with armed men; wonder at the act. [Francisco] commands the body to be carried home, apprehends Flamineo, Marcello, and the rest, and [all] go as 'twere to apprehend Vittoria.

are coaxed by whispers / *Courteous deferrals*

BRACCIANO 'Twas quaintly° done, but yet each circumstance *skillfully*
I taste° not fully. *relish, comprehend*
CONJUROR Oh, 'twas most apparent.
You saw them enter charged with their deep healths° *well-primed with drink*
To their boon° voyage, and, to second that, *prosperous*
Flamineo calls to have a vaulting horse
Maintain their sport. The virtuous Marcello

Is innocently plotted forth the room,
Whilst your eye saw the rest, and can inform you
The engine° of all. *contrivance*

BRACCIANO It seems Marcello and Flamineo
Are both committed.° *taken into custody*

CONJUROR Yes, you saw them guarded,
And now they° are come with purpose to apprehend *(Francisco's guardsmen)*
Your mistress, fair Vittoria; we are now
Beneath her roof. 'Twere fit we instantly
Make out by some back postern.° *private back door*

BRACCIANO Noble friend,
You bind me ever to you. This° shall stand *This service; this handshake*
As the firm seal annexèd to my hand.° *affixed to my signature*
It shall enforce° a payment. *oblige*

CONJUROR Sir, I thank you.

Exit Bracciano.

Both flowers and weeds spring when the sun is warm,
And great men do great good, or else great harm.

Exit Conjuror.

[3.1]

Enter Francisco and Monticelso, their chancellor and register.° *registrar*

FRANCISCO You have dealt discreetly to obtain the presence
Of all the grave lieger° ambassadors *resident*
To hear Vittoria's trial.

MONTICELSO 'Twas not ill,
For, sir, you know we have naught but circumstances
To charge her with, about her husband's death;
Their approbation° therefore to the proofs *witnessing*
Of her black lust shall make her infamous
To all our neighboring kingdoms. I wonder
If Bracciano will be here.

FRANCISCO Oh, fie, 'twere impudence too palpable.

[Exeunt.]

Enter Flamineo and Marcello guarded, and a Lawyer.

LAWYER What, are you in by the week?° So. I will try now whether thy wit be close prisoner. Methinks none should sit upon° thy sister but old whoremasters— *are you ensnared?* *sit in judgment on*

FLAMINEO Or cuckolds, for your cuckold° is your most terrible tickler° of lechery. Whoremasters would serve, for none are judges at tilting° but those that have been old tilters. *the typical cuckold* *chastiser; exciter* *jousting; having sex*

LAWYER My lord Duke and she have been very private.° *sexually intimate*

FLAMINEO You are a dull ass. 'Tis threatened they have been very public.° *shameless, flagrant*

LAWYER If it can be proved they have but kissed one another—

FLAMINEO What then?

LAWYER My lord Cardinal will ferret them.° *ferret them out*

FLAMINEO A cardinal, I hope, will not catch coneys.° *rabbits; fools*

3.1. Adjacent to a papal courtroom.

LAWYER For to sow kisses—mark what I say—to sow kisses is to reap lechery, and I am sure a woman that will endure kissing is half won.

FLAMINEO True, her upper part, by that rule; if you will win her nether part too, you know what follows.

LAWYER Hark! The ambassadors are lighted.° *alighted*

FLAMINEO [*aside*] I do put on this feignèd garb of mirth
To gull° suspicion. *hoodwink; lull*

MARCELLO Oh, my unfortunate sister!
I would my dagger's point had cleft her heart
When she first saw Bracciano. You, 'tis said,
Were made his engine° and his stalking-horse *instrument*
To undo my sister.

FLAMINEO I made a kind of path
To her and mine own preferment.° *advancement*

MARCELLO Your ruin.

FLAMINEO Hum! Thou art a soldier,
Followest the great duke, feedest his victories,
As witches do their serviceable spirits,° *obedient demons*
Even with thy prodigal blood. What hast got?
But, like the wealth of captains,° a poor handful, *poor soldiers*
Which in thy palm thou bear'st, as men hold water;
Seeking to grip it fast, the frail reward
Steals through thy fingers.

MARCELLO Sir—

FLAMINEO Thou scarce hast maintenance
To keep thee in fresh chamois.° *shirts worn under armor*

MARCELLO Brother!

FLAMINEO Hear me!
And thus when we have even poured ourselves
Into great fights, for their° ambition *(great men's)*
Or idle spleen, how shall we find reward?
But as we seldom find the mistletoe,
Sacred to physic,° on the builder° oak *medicine / used as lumber*
Without a mandrake[1] by it, so in our quest of gain.
Alas, the poorest of their forced dislikes
At a limb proffers, but at heart it strikes.[2]
This is lamented doctrine.

MARCELLO Come, come.

FLAMINEO When age shall turn thee
White as a blooming hawthorn—

MARCELLO I'll interrupt you.
For love of virtue, bear an honest heart,
And stride over every politic respect,
Which, where they most advance, they most infect.[3]
Were I your father, as I am your brother,
I should not be ambitious to leave you
A better patrimony.

Enter Savoy [*Ambassador*].

1. A fork-rooted plant that was supposed to shriek when pulled from the ground, with ominous consequences, including madness. Prosperity and disaster go together, Flamineo argues.

2. Even the least disfavor by great men strikes at the heart of hopes for advancement, however trivial it may seem at first.

3. And strive to rise above all considerations of self-advancement, which are most pernicious when they seem to offer promotion.

FLAMINEO I'll think on't.—
The lord ambassadors.

Here there is a passage of the lieger ambassadors over the stage severally.[4] *Enter French ambassador.* [*The Lawyer and Flamineo stand by, observing.*]

LAWYER Oh, my sprightly Frenchman. Do you know him? He's an admirable tilter.° *(see 16 above)*

FLAMINEO I saw him at last tilting. He showed° like a pewter candlestick fashioned like a man in armor, holding a tilting staff in his hand little bigger than a candle of twelve i'th'pound.° *looked* / *to a pound*

LAWYER Oh, but he's an excellent horseman.

FLAMINEO A lame one in his lofty tricks; he sleeps a-horseback like a poulter.° *poultry merchant*

Enter English and Spanish [*ambassadors*].

LAWYER Lo you, my Spaniard.

FLAMINEO He carries his face in 's ruff as I have seen a servingman carry glasses in a cypress° hatband, monstrous steady for fear of breaking. He looks like the claw of a blackbird, first salted and then broiled in° a candle. *Exeunt.* *linen or crepe* / *grilled over*

[3.2]

THE ARRAIGNMENT OF VITTORIA

Enter Francisco, Monticelso, the six lieger ambassadors, Bracciano, Vittoria, [*Zanche, Flamineo, Marcello,*] *Lawyer, and a guard* [*with a Servant and attendants*].

MONTICELSO [*to Bracciano*] Forbear, my lord. Here is no
place assigned you.
This business by His Holiness is left
To our examination.

BRACCIANO May it thrive with you.
Lays a rich gown under him.

FRANCISCO A chair there for His Lordship!

BRACCIANO Forbear your kindness. An unbidden guest
Should travail° as Dutchwomen go to church: *travel; labor*
Bear their stools with them.

MONTICELSO At your pleasure, sir.
[*To Vittoria*] Stand to the table, gentlewoman.—Now, signor,
Fall to your plea.

LAWYER *Domine judex, converte oculos in hanc pestem*
mulierum corruptissimam.[1]

VITTORIA [*to Francisco*] What's he?

FRANCISCO A lawyer, that pleads against you.

VITTORIA Pray, my lord, let him speak his usual tongue.

4. The ambassadors enter and then exit, one after another, on their way to the arraignment of Vittoria.
3.2. A papal courtroom, Rome.

1. My lord judge, turn your eyes upon this plague, the most corrupt of women.

I'll make no answer else.
FRANCISCO Why, you understand Latin.
VITTORIA I do, sir, but, amongst this auditory
Which come to hear my cause, the half or more
May be ignorant in't.
MONTICELSO [*to the Lawyer*] Go on, sir.
VITTORIA By your favor,
I will not have my accusation clouded° — *obscured*
In a strange tongue. All this assembly
Shall hear what you can charge me with.
FRANCISCO [*to the Lawyer*] Signor,
You need not stand on't much;° pray change your language. — *insist on your Latin*
MONTICELSO Oh, for God sake!—Gentlewoman, your credit° — *reputation*
Shall be more famous° by it. — *infamous*
LAWYER Well, then, have at you.° — *i.e., here goes*
VITTORIA I am at the mark, sir. I'll give aim[2] to you,
And tell you how near you shoot.
LAWYER Most literated° judges, please Your Lordships — *learned*
So to connive your judgments to the view[3]
Of this debauched and diversivolent° woman, — *contentious*
Who such a black concatenation° — *chain, sequence*
Of mischief hath effected, that to extirp° — *root out*
The memory of't must be the consummation° — *finish*
Of her and her projections.° — *projects*
VITTORIA What's all this?
LAWYER Hold your peace.
Exorbitant sins must have exulceration.° — *must be lanced*
VITTORIA Surely, my lords, this lawyer here hath swallowed
Some pothecary's bills° or proclamations, — *advertisements*
And now the hard and undigestible words
Come up like stones we use give hawks for physic.[4]
Why, this is Welsh to° Latin. — *compared with*
LAWYER My lords, the woman
Knows not her tropes° nor figures, nor is perfect — *figures of speech*
In the academic derivation
Of grammatical elocution.° — *expression*
FRANCISCO Sir, your pains
Shall be well spared,° and your deep eloquence — *done without*
Be worthily applauded amongst those
Which understand you.
LAWYER My good lord—
FRANCISCO (*speaks this as in scorn*) Sir,
Put up your papers in your fustian° bag— — *cloth; bombastic*
Cry mercy,° sir, 'tis buckram°—and accept — *I beg pardon / coarse linen*
My notion of your learned verbosity.
LAWYER I most graduatically[5] thank Your Lordship.
I shall have use for them elsewhere. [*He retires.*]

2. I will act as the marker at the archery target, indicating where each shot strikes.
3. I.e., Do not let your judgments be swayed by the view. (But "connive" ordinarily means the opposite of what the Lawyer wants to say. His speech is laden with absurd obfuscations.)
4. Pebbles were given to hawks to aid in digestion.
5. In the manner of a graduate. (Another pompously invented bit of jargon.)

MONTICELSO [*to Vittoria*] I shall be plainer with you, and
paint out° *depict*
Your follies in more natural red and white
Than that upon your cheek.
VITTORIA Oh, you mistake.
You raise a blood as noble in this cheek
As ever was your mother's.
MONTICELSO I must spare you till proof cry whore to that.—
Observe this creature here, my honored lords,
A woman of a most prodigious° spirit *monstrous*
In her effected.
VITTORIA Honorable my lord,
It doth not suit a reverend cardinal
To play the lawyer thus.
MONTICELSO Oh, your trade instructs your language!—
You see, my lords, what goodly fruit she seems;
Yet, like those apples travelers report
To grow where Sodom and Gomorrah stood,° *(see Deuteronomy 32.32)*
I will but touch her and you straight shall see
She'll fall to soot and ashes.
VITTORIA Your envenomed
Pothecary should do't.[6]
MONTICELSO I am resolved,° *convinced*
Were there a second paradise to lose
This devil would betray it.
VITTORIA O poor charity!
Thou art seldom found in scarlet.° *cardinals' robes*
MONTICELSO Who knows not how, when several night by night
Her gates were choked with coaches, and her rooms
Outbraved the stars with several kind of lights,° *chandeliers*
When she did counterfeit a prince's court
In music, banquets, and most riotous surfeits?° *extravagant orgies*
This whore, forsooth, was holy.
VITTORIA Ha? Whore? What's that?
MONTICELSO Shall I expound whore to you? Sure I shall;
I'll give their perfect character.° They are, first, *character sketch*
Sweetmeats which rot the eater; in man's nostril,
Poisoned perfumes. They are coz'ning° alchemy, *cheating*
Shipwrecks in calmest weather. What are whores?
Cold Russian winters, that appear so barren
As if that° nature had forgot the spring. *As if*
They are the true material fire of hell,
Worse than those tributes i'th'Low Countries paid,[7]
Exactions upon meat, drink, garments, sleep—
Ay, even on man's perdition, his sin.° *i.e., prostitution*
They are those brittle evidences of law
Which forfeit all a wretched man's estate
For leaving out one syllable.[8] What are whores?

6. I.e., If I were to fall thus, it would be the result of your hireling, skilled in such poisons. (She probably means the Lawyer.)

7. Tolls and taxes imposed on certain commodities in the Netherlands exceeded the original value of the goods.

8. Legal technicalities, such as the omission of a single word, could invalidate a claim.

They are those flattering bells have° all one tune — *that have*
At weddings and at funerals.[9] Your rich whores
Are only treasuries by extortion filled,
And emptied by cursed riot. They are worse,
Worse than dead bodies which are begged at gallows
And wrought upon[1] by surgeons to teach man
Wherein he is imperfect. What's a whore?
She's like the guilty° conterfeited coin — *illegal; gilt*
Which, whosoe'er first stamps° it, brings in trouble — *coins*
All that receive it.[2]

VITTORIA This character scapes° me. — *doesn't relate to*

MONTICELSO You, gentlewoman,
Take from all beasts and from all minerals
Their deadly poison.

VITTORIA Well, what then?

MONTICELSO I'll tell thee:
I'll find in thee a pothecary's shop
To sample them all.° — *all poisons*

FRENCH AMBASSADOR [*to other ambassadors*] She hath lived ill.

ENGLISH AMBASSADOR True, but the Cardinal's too bitter.

MONTICELSO You know what whore is: next° the devil Adult'ry — *after*
Enters the devil Murder.

FRANCISCO Your unhappy° — *unfortunate*
Husband is dead.

VITTORIA Oh, he's a happy husband,
Now he owes nature nothing.° — *paid his debt to nature*

FRANCISCO And by a vaulting engine.° — *vaulting horse*

MONTICELSO An active plot;
He jumped into his grave.

FRANCISCO What a prodigy was't
That from some two yards' height a slender man
Should break his neck?

MONTICELSO I'th'rushes.° — *a floor covering*

FRANCISCO And what's more,
Upon the instant lose all use of speech,
All vital motion, like a man had° lain — *who had*
Wound up° three days. Now mark each circumstance. — *In his shroud*

MONTICELSO And look upon this creature was° his wife. — *who was*
She comes not like a widow; she comes armed
With scorn and impudence. Is this a mourning habit?° — *garb*

VITTORIA Had I foreknown his death as you suggest,
I would have bespoke my mourning.° — *ordered my outfit*

MONTICELSO Oh, you are cunning!

VITTORIA You shame your wit° and judgment — *intelligence*
To call it so. What is my just defense
By him that is my judge called impudence?[3]
Let me appeal then from this Christian court[4]
To the uncivil° Tartar. — *barbarous*

MONTICELSO See, my lords,

9. I.e., Whores aim to please all customers, whether in times of pleasure or sorrow.
1. Dissected in anatomy demonstrations.
2. Monticelso compares the spreading effect of prostitution to the far-reaching consequences of counterfeited coins, dangerous even to those who accept them.
3. How can I defend myself when I am judged by a shameless, insolent judge?
4. The so-called Courts Christian tried adultery cases.

She scandals° our proceedings. *disgraces*

VITTORIA [*kneeling*] Humbly thus,
Thus low, to the most worthy and respected
Lieger ambassadors, my modesty
And womanhood I tender; but withal
So entangled in a cursèd accusation
That my defense of force,° like Perseus,[5] *of necessity*
Must personate masculine virtue to the point.° *in every detail*
Find me but guilty, sever head from body,
We'll part good friends. I scorn to hold my life
At yours or any man's entreaty, sir.

ENGLISH AMBASSADOR [*to other ambassadors*] She hath a brave spirit.

MONTICELSO Well, well, such counterfeit jewels
Make true ones oft suspected.

VITTORIA You are deceived.
For know that all your strict-combinèd° heads, *closely allied*
Which strike against this mine of diamonds,° *my impregnable integrity*
Shall prove but glassen° hammers; they shall break. *made of glass*
These are but feignèd shadows of my evils.
Terrify babes, my lord, with painted devils;
I am past such needless palsy.° For° your names *trembling / As for*
Of whore and murd'ress, they proceed from you
As if a man should spit against the wind;
The filth returns in 's face.

MONTICELSO Pray you, mistress, satisfy me one question:
Who lodged beneath your roof that fatal night
Your husband brake his neck?

BRACCIANO That question
Enforceth me break silence. I was there.

MONTICELSO Your business?

BRACCIANO Why, I came to comfort her
And take some course for settling her estate,
Because I heard her husband was in debt
To you, my lord.

MONTICELSO He was.

BRACCIANO And 'twas strangely° feared *greatly*
That you would cozen° her. *cheat*

MONTICELSO Who made you overseer?

BRACCIANO Why, my charity, my charity, which should flow
From every generous and noble spirit
To orphans and to widows.

MONTICELSO Your lust.

BRACCIANO Cowardly dogs bark loudest. Sirrah° priest, *(said to inferiors)*
I'll talk with you hereafter. Do you hear?
The sword° you frame of such an excellent temper *sword of justice*
I'll sheathe in your own bowels.
There are a number of thy coat° resemble *sort, profession (who)*
Your common postboys.° *ordinary letter carriers*

MONTICELSO Ha?

BRACCIANO Your mercenary postboys.
Your letters carry truth,[6] but 'tis your guise° *custom*

5. The heroic rescuer of Andromeda from a sea serpent.

6. Your official proceedings are nominally correct and legal. (Said to the court in general.)

To fill your mouths with gross and impudent lies.
SERVANT My lord, your gown.
BRACCIANO Thou liest; 'twas my stool.[7]
Bestow't upon thy master, that will challenge° — *lay claim to*
The rest o'th'household-stuff,[8] for Bracciano
Was ne'er so beggarly to take a stool
Out of another's lodging. Let him make
Valence° for his bed on't,° or a demifootcloth[9] — *Bed hangings / of it*
For his most reverend moile.°—Monticelso, — *mule*
Nemo me impune lacessit.[1] *Exit Bracciano.*
MONTICELSO Your champion's gone.
VITTORIA The wolf may prey the better.
FRANCISCO My lord, there's great suspicion of the murder,
But no sound proof who did it. For my part,
I do not think she hath a soul so black
To act a deed so bloody. If she have,
As in cold countries husbandmen plant vines
And with warm blood manure them, even so
One summer she will bear unsavory fruit,° — *give birth to bastards*
And ere next spring wither° both branch and root. — *will wither*
The act of blood° let pass; only descend — *murder*
To matter of incontinence.° — *unchastity*
VITTORIA I discern poison
Under your gilded pills.
MONTICELSO [*showing a letter*] Now the Duke's gone, I will
produce a letter
Wherein 'twas plotted he and you should meet
At an apothecary's summerhouse
Down by the river Tiber—view't, my lords—
Where, after wanton bathing and the heat
Of a lascivious banquet—I pray, read it.
I shame to speak the rest.
VITTORIA Grant I was tempted;
Temptation to lust proves not the act.
Casta est quam nemo rogavit.[2]
You read his hot love to me, but you want° — *lack*
My frosty answer.
MONTICELSO Frost i'th'dog days!° Strange! — *in late summer*
VITTORIA Condemn you me for that° the Duke did love me? — *because*
So may you blame some fair and crystal river
For that some melancholic distracted man
Hath drowned himself in't.
MONTICELSO Truly, drowned° indeed. — *i.e., drowned in sin*
VITTORIA Sum up my faults, I pray, and you shall find
That beauty and gay clothes, a merry heart,
And a good stomach to a feast are all,
All the poor crimes that you can charge me with.
In faith, my lord, you might go pistol° flies; — *shoot*

7. When the Servant offers to hand Bracciano his gown, Bracciano sarcastically observes that he was rudely left sitting on his own cloak, with no stool. (See lines 4–7 above.) The Servant may serve either Monticelso or Francisco. (See next note.)

8. Bracciano sardonically pictures Monticelso, or perhaps Francisco (see lines 4–7 above), as having taken charge in a petty way of all the court's furnishings, as though they were household items.

9. A half-length, richly ornamented cloth laid over the back of a horse or mule. Full-length footcloths reached to the ground.

1. No one injures me and gets away with it.

2. She is chaste whom no man has solicited. (Ovid, *Amores*, 1.8.43.)

The sport would be more noble.
MONTICELSO Very good.
VITTORIA But take you your course. It seems you have beggared me first
And now would fain° undo me. I have houses, *now wish to*
Jewels, and a poor remnant of crusadoes.° *Portuguese coins*
Would those would make you charitable!
MONTICELSO If the devil
Did ever take good° shape, behold his picture. *attractive*
VITTORIA You have one virtue left:
You will not flatter me.
FRANCISCO Who brought this letter?
VITTORIA I am not compelled to tell you.
MONTICELSO My lord duke sent to you a thousand ducats,° *gold coins*
The twelfth of August.
VITTORIA 'Twas to keep your cousin° *nephew (Camillo)*
From prison. I paid use° for't. *interest*
MONTICELSO I rather think
'Twas interest for his° lust. *(Bracciano's)*
VITTORIA Who says so but yourself? If you be my accuser,
Pray cease to be my judge; come from the bench,
Give in your evidence 'gainst me, and let these
Be moderators.° My Lord Cardinal, *presiding judges*
Were your intelligencing° ears as long *information-gathering*
As to° my thoughts, had you an honest tongue, *As to reach to*
I would not care though you proclaimed them all.
MONTICELSO Go to,° go to. *(expressing anger)*
After your goodly and vainglorious banquet,
I'll give you a choke-pear.° *rough pear; setback*
VITTORIA O'your own grafting?
MONTICELSO You were born in Venice, honorably descended,
From the Vittelli. 'Twas my cousin's fate—
Ill may I name the hour!—to marry you.
He bought you of your father.
VITTORIA Ha?
MONTICELSO He spent there, in six months,
Twelve thousand ducats, and to my acquaintance° *best of knowledge*
Received in dowry with you not one julio;° *coin of little value*
'Twas a hard pennyworth, the ware being so light.° *slight; unchaste*
I yet but draw the curtain; now to your picture.[3]
You came from thence a most notorious strumpet,
And so you have continued.
VITTORIA My lord—
MONTICELSO Nay, hear me;
You shall have time to prate. My lord Bracciano—
Alas, I make but repetition
Of what is ordinary and rialto° talk, *marketplace*
And balladed,° and would be played o'th'stage *made into a ballad*
But that vice many times finds such loved friends° *friends in high places*
That preachers are charmed silent.°— *bound to silence*
You gentlemen, Flamineo and Marcello,

3. I have scarcely begun, by opening the curtain on our subject (curtains were regularly hung in front of paintings); now let me turn to the particulars of your portrait.

The court hath nothing now to charge you with,
Only you must remain upon your sureties° — *you must post bail*
For your appearance.
FRANCISCO I stand° for Marcello. — *I'll serve as guarantor*
FLAMINEO And my lord duke° for me. — *(Bracciano)*
MONTICELSO For° you, Vittoria, your public fault, — *As for*
Joined to th'condition of the present time,[4]
Takes from you all the fruits of noble pity.
Such a corrupted trial° have you made — *use*
Both of your life and beauty, and been styled° — *named, titled*
No less in ominous fate than blazing stars
To princes;[5] here's your sentence: you are confined
Unto a house of convertites,° and your bawd— — *reformed prostitutes*
FLAMINEO [*aside*] Who, I?
MONTICELSO The Moor.
FLAMINEO [*aside*] Oh, I am a sound man again.
VITTORIA A house of convertites, what's that?
MONTICELSO A house of penitent whores.
VITTORIA Do the noblemen in Rome
Erect it for their wives, that I am sent
To lodge there?
FRANCISCO You must have patience.
VITTORIA I must first have vengeance.
I fain would know if you have your salvation
By patent,° that you proceed thus. — *special license*
MONTICELSO Away with her!
Take her hence.
VITTORIA A rape, a rape!
MONTICELSO How?
VITTORIA Yes, you have ravished Justice,
Forced her to do your pleasure.
MONTICELSO Fie, she's mad.
VITTORIA Die with those pills in your most cursèd maw° — *stomach*
Should° bring you health,[6] or, while you sit o'th'bench, — *Which should*
Let your own spittle choke you!
MONTICELSO She's turned Fury.° — *avenging goddess*
VITTORIA That the last Day of Judgment may so find you
And leave you the same devil you were before!
Instruct me, some good horse-leech,° to speak treason, — *bloodsucker*
For, since you cannot take my life for deeds,
Take it for words.[7] Oh, woman's poor revenge,
Which dwells but in the tongue! I will not weep;
No, I do scorn to call up one poor tear
To fawn on your injustice. Bear me hence,
Unto this house of—what's your mitigating title?
MONTICELSO Of convertites.
VITTORIA It shall not be a house of convertites.
My mind shall make it honester to me
Than the Pope's palace, and more peaceable

4. I.e., Along with the suspicious circumstances of Camillo's death.
5. Comets were often thought to predict dire consequences for those in power.
6. Vittoria hopes that Monticelso may die poisoned by his own hypocritical virtue, by a dose of his own medicine.
7. With bitter irony, Vittoria begs that some bloodthirsty villain will "instruct" her (by means of torture) to speak self-incriminatingly; since her enemies have no grounds to execute her for what she has done, perhaps then they can do so on the basis of her confession.

Than thy soul, though thou art a cardinal.
Know this, and let it somewhat raise your spite.
Through darkness diamonds spread their richest light.
Exit Vittoria [*guarded*].

Enter Bracciano.

BRACCIANO [*to Francisco*] Now° you and I are friends, sir, we'll shake hands, *Now that*
In a friend's grave, together—a fit place,
Being the emblem of soft peace t'atone° our hatred. *to appease, reconcile*
FRANCISCO Sir, what's the matter?
BRACCIANO I will not chase more blood from that loved cheek;
You have lost too much already. Fare you well. [*Exit.*]
FRANCISCO How strange these words sound! What's the interpretation?
FLAMINEO [*aside*] Good, this is a preface to the discovery of the Duchess'° death. He carries° it well. Because now I cannot counterfeit a whining passion for the death of my lady, I will feign a mad humor for the disgrace of my sister, and that will keep off idle questions. Treason's tongue hath a villainous palsy in't.[8] I will talk to any man, hear no man, and for a time appear a politic° madman. [*Exit.*] *(Isabella's) / feigns* *cunning; pretend*

Enter Giovanni, [*in mourning, and*] *Count Lodovico.*

FRANCISCO How now, my noble cousin, what, in black?
GIOVANNI Yes, uncle, I was taught to imitate you
In virtue, and you must imitate me
In colors for your garments. My sweet mother
Is—
FRANCISCO How? Where?
GIOVANNI Is there; no, yonder. Indeed, sir, I'll not tell you,
For I shall make you weep.
FRANCISCO Is dead.
GIOVANNI Do not blame me now;
I did not tell you so.
LODOVICO She's dead, my lord.
FRANCISCO Dead?
MONTICELSO Blessed lady!
Thou art now above thy woes.—
Will't please Your Lordships to withdraw a little?
[*Exeunt the ambassadors.*]
GIOVANNI What do the dead do, uncle? Do they eat,
Hear music, go a-hunting, and be merry,
As we that live?
FRANCISCO No, coz, they sleep.
GIOVANNI Lord, Lord! That I were dead!
I have not slept these six nights. When do they wake?
FRANCISCO When God shall please.
GIOVANNI Good God, let her sleep ever!
For I have known her wake an hundred nights,
When all the pillow, where she laid her head,
Was brine-wet with her tears.
I am to complain to you, sir.

8. Treason is too apt to give itself away, betray its guilt.

I'll tell you how they have used her, now she's dead:
They wrapped her in a cruel fold° of lead, *wrapping*
And would not let me kiss her.

FRANCISCO Thou didst love her.

GIOVANNI I have often heard her say she gave me suck,
And it should seem by that she dearly loved me,
Since princes seldom do it.

FRANCISCO Oh, all of my poor sister that remains!° *(Giovanni, her son)*
[*To attendants*] Take him away, for God's sake.

[*Exit Giovanni, attended.*]

MONTICELSO How now, my lord?

FRANCISCO Believe me, I am nothing but her grave,
And I shall keep her blessèd memory
Longer than thousand epitaphs. [*Exeunt.*]

[3.3]

Enter Flamineo as distracted° [*with Marcello and Lodovico*]. *(see 3.2.308–13)*

FLAMINEO We endure the strokes like anvils or hard steel,
Till pain itself make us no pain to feel.
Who shall do me right now? Is this the end° of service? I'd rather go weed garlic, travel through France and be mine own ostler, wear sheepskin linings° or shoes that stink of blacking, be entered into the list° of the forty thousand peddlers in Poland. *reward* *underwear* *roll*

Enter Savoy [*Ambassador*].

Would I had rotted in some surgeon's house at Venice, built upon the pox[1] as well as on piles,° ere I had served Bracciano! *supports; hemorrhoids*

SAVOY AMBASSADOR You must have comfort.

FLAMINEO Your comfortable words are like honey. They relish° well in your mouth that's whole,° but in mine that's wounded they go down as if the sting of the bee were in them. Oh, they have wrought their purpose cunningly, as if they would not seem to do it of malice. In this a politician° imitates the devil, as the devil imitates a cannon: wheresoever he comes to do mischief, he comes with his backside towards you.[2] *taste / healthy* *schemer*

Enter the French [*Ambassador*].

FRENCH AMBASSADOR The proofs° are evident. *(against Vittoria)*

FLAMINEO Proof! 'Twas corruption. O gold, what a god art thou! And O man, what a devil art thou to be tempted by that cursed mineral! Yon diversivolent° lawyer, mark him: knaves turn informers as maggots turn to flies; you may catch gudgeons° with either. A cardinal! I would he would hear me. There's nothing so holy but money will corrupt and putrify it, like victual under the line.[3] *contentious* *small fish; simpletons*

3.3. Adjacent to the papal courtroom, as in act 3, scene 1.

1. Made to prosper from the medical treatment of syphilis.

2. Witches were imagined to kiss the devil's ass as a token of obedience.

3. Like food at the equator, apt to spoil quickly in the heat.

Enter English Ambassador.

You are happy in England, my lord. Here they sell justice with those weights they press men to death with.[4] Oh, horrible salary!° — *reward*

ENGLISH AMBASSADOR Fie, fie, Flamineo!

FLAMINEO Bells ne'er ring well till they are at their full pitch,° *swung to the highest point* and I hope yon cardinal shall never have the grace to pray well till he come to the scaffold. [*Exeunt the Ambassadors.*] If they were racked° now to know° the confederacy! But your *tortured / make known* noblemen are privileged from the rack; and well may,° for a *with good reason* little thing would pull some of them a-pieces afore they came to their arraignment. Religion—oh, how it is commeddled° *mixed together* with policy!° *scheming* The first bloodshed in the world[5] happened about religion. Would I were a Jew!

MARCELLO Oh, there are too many.

FLAMINEO You are deceived. There are not Jews enough, priests enough, nor gentlemen enough.

MARCELLO How?

FLAMINEO I'll prove it. For if there were Jews enough, so many Christians would not turn usurers;° *moneylenders* if priests enough, one should not have six benefices;[6] and if gentlemen enough, so many early mushrooms, whose best growth sprang from a dunghill, should not aspire to gentility. Farewell. Let others live by begging. Be thou one of them;° *one of the beggars* practice the art of Wolnor[7] in England to swallow all 's given thee; and yet let one purgation° *vomiting, evacuation* make thee as hungry again as fellows that work in a saw-pit.° *(an arduous job)* I'll go hear the screech owl.[8] *Exit.*

LODOVICO [*aside*] This was Bracciano's pander, and 'tis strange
That in such open and apparent guilt
Of his adulterous sister he dare utter
So scandalous a passion. I must wind him.° — *discover his intent*

Enter Flamineo.

FLAMINEO [*aside*] How dares this banished count return to Rome,
His pardon not yet purchased?° I have heard — *obtained*
The deceased duchess gave him pension,
And that he came along from Padua
I'th'train° of the young prince. There's somewhat in't. — *entourage*
Physicians that cure poisons still° do work — *habitually*
With counterpoisons.

MARCELLO [*aside*] Mark this strange encounter.

FLAMINEO [*to Lodovico*] The god of melancholy turn thy gall to poison,
And let the stigmatic° wrinkles in thy face, — *branded with infamy*
Like to the boisterous waves in a rough tide,
One still overtake another!

LODOVICO I do thank thee,

4. Accused persons who refused to plead either guilty or not guilty were slowly crushed to death with great weights.

5. Cain's slaying of Abel (see Genesis 4).

6. Flamineo satirizes priests who held more than one church position, and therefore drew more than one salary, at a time.

7. A singer, famous for eating iron, glass, oyster-shells, raw flesh, and fish; he died after eating a raw eel.

8. Owls were regarded as omens of impending disaster or death.

And I do wish ingeniously° for thy sake — *shrewdly; candidly*
The dog days all year long.[9]

FLAMINEO How croaks the raven?° — *an ill-boding bird*
Is our good duchess dead?

LODOVICO Dead.

FLAMINEO Oh, fate!
Misfortune comes like the crowner's° business, — *coroner's*
Huddle upon huddle.° — *In heaps*

LODOVICO Shalt thou and I join housekeeping?

FLAMINEO Yes, content.
Let's be unsociably sociable.

LODOVICO Sit some three days together, and discourse.

FLAMINEO Only with making faces;
Lie° in our clothes. — *Sleep*

LODOVICO With fagots° for our pillows. — *bundles of wood*

FLAMINEO And be lousy.° — *infested with lice*

LODOVICO In taffeta linings;° that's gentle melancholy. — *silky underclothes*
Sleep all day.

FLAMINEO Yes, and, like your melancholic hare,
Feed after midnight.[1]

Enter Antonelli [*and Gasparo, laughing*].

We are observed. See how yon couple grieve!° — *(said ironically)*

LODOVICO What a strange creature is a laughing fool,
As if man were created to no use
But only to show his teeth!

FLAMINEO I'll tell thee what:
It would do well, instead of looking glasses,° — *mirrors*
To set one's face each morning by a saucer
Of a witch's congealed blood.

LODOVICO Precious rogue!
We'll never part.

FLAMINEO Never, till the beggary° of courtiers, — *neediness*
The discontent of churchmen, want° of soldiers, — *financial need*
And all the creatures that hang manacled,
Worse than strappadoed,[2] on the lowest felly° — *part of wheel rim*
Of Fortune's wheel, be taught in our two lives° — *by our example*
To scorn that world which life of means deprives.[3]

ANTONELLI [*to Lodovico*] My lord, I bring good news. The
Pope on's deathbed,
At th'earnest suit of the great duke of Florence,
Hath signed your pardon, and restored unto you—

LODOVICO I thank you for your news.—Look up again,
Flamineo! See my pardon.

FLAMINEO Why do you laugh?
There was no such condition in our covenant.° — *(see 73–82 above)*

LODOVICO Why?

FLAMINEO You shall not seem a happier man than I;
You know our vow, sir. If you will be merry,
Do it i'th'like posture as if some great man

9. The dog days, or days of late summer, when the sun is close to the Dog Star, Sirius, are hot and uncomfortable. Lodovico wishes Flamineo the very worst of luck.

1. Hares were traditionally associated with melancholy and nighttime.

2. In the strappado, the victim is hoisted aloft by a rope secured to his hands, which are tied behind his back.

3. To scorn a world that denies to people like ourselves any means of livelihood.

Sat while his enemy were executed;
Though it be very lechery° unto thee, *i.e., ecstasy*
Do't with a crabbèd politician's face.

LODOVICO Your sister is a damnable whore.

FLAMINEO Ha?

LODOVICO Look you, I spake that laughing.

FLAMINEO Dost ever think to speak again?

LODOVICO Do you hear?
Wilt sell me forty ounces of her blood
To water a mandrake?° *(see 3.1.52 n)*

FLAMINEO Poor lord, you did vow
To live a lousy° creature. *lice-infested*

LODOVICO Yes.

FLAMINEO Like one
That had forever forfeited the daylight° *i.e., gone to prison*
By being in debt.

LODOVICO Ha, ha!

FLAMINEO I do not greatly wonder you do break;[4]
Your Lordship learnt't° long since. But I'll tell you— *learned it*

LODOVICO What?

FLAMINEO And't shall stick by you.° *you won't forget it*

LODOVICO I long for it.

FLAMINEO This laughter scurvily° becomes your face. *basely, meanly*
If you will not be melancholy, be angry. *Strikes him.*
See, now I laugh too.

MARCELLO [*intervening*] You are to blame. I'll force you hence.

LODOVICO Unhand me!

Exit Marcello and Flamineo.

That e'er I should be forced to right° myself *vindicate*
Upon a pander!

ANTONELLI My lord—

LODOVICO H'had been as good met with his fist a thunderbolt.[5]

GASPARO How this shows![6]

LODOVICO Ud's death,° how did my sword miss him? *By God's death*
These rogues that are most weary of their lives
Still scape the greatest dangers.
A pox upon him! All his reputation—
Nay all the goodness of his family—
Is not worth half this earthquake.° *i.e., this fuss*
I learned it of no fencer to shake thus.
Come, I'll forget him, and go drink some wine. *Exeunt.*

[4.1]

Enter Francisco and Monticelso.

MONTICELSO Come, come, my lord, untie your folded° thoughts *closely concealed*
And let them dangle loose as a bride's hair.[1]
Your sister's poisoned.

4. (1) Break your oath; (2) go bankrupt.
5. He (Flamineo) might as well have tried to defy a thunderbolt with his bare fist.
6. How unseemly this quarreling looks!
4.1. Francisco's palace.
1. Jacobean brides wore their hair unbound.

FRANCISCO Far be it from my thoughts
To seek revenge.
MONTICELSO What, are you turned all marble?
FRANCISCO Shall I defy him, and impose a war
Most burdensome on my poor subjects' necks
Which at my will I have not power to end?
You know, for all the murders, rapes, and thefts
Committed in the horrid lust of war,
He that unjustly caused it first proceed
Shall find it in his grave and in his seed.[2]
MONTICELSO That's not the course I'd wish you. Pray, observe me.
We see that undermining more prevails
Than doth the cannon.[3] Bear your wrongs concealed,
And, patient as the tortoise, let this camel
Stalk o'er your back unbruised.° Sleep with° the lion, *without hurting you / like*
And let this brood of secure° foolish mice *overconfident*
Play with your nostrils till the time be ripe
For th'bloody audit° and the fatal gripe.° *reckoning / seizing*
Aim like a cunning fowler:° close one eye, *bird-hunter*
That you the better may your game espy.
FRANCISCO Free me, my innocence, from treacherous acts!
I know there's thunder yonder,° and I'll stand *(in heaven)*
Like a safe valley which low bends the knee
To some aspiring mountain, since I know
Treason, like spiders weaving nets for flies,
By her foul work is found, and in it dies.° *Treason betrays itself*
To pass away these thoughts, my honored lord,
It is reported you possess a book
Wherein you have quoted, by intelligence,° *secret information*
The names of all notorious offenders
Lurking about the city.
MONTICELSO Sir, I do,
And some there are which call it my black book;
Well may the title hold, for, though it teach not
The art of conjuring, yet in it lurk
The names of many devils.
FRANCISCO Pray let's see it.
MONTICELSO I'll fetch it to Your Lordship. *Exit Monticelso.*
FRANCISCO Monticelso,
I will not trust thee, but in all my plots
I'll rest as jealous° as a town besieged. *suspicious*
Thou canst not reach° what I intend to act. *fathom, guess*
Your flax soon kindles, soon is out again;
But gold slow heats and long will hot remain.

Enter Monticelso, [*and presents*] *Francisco with* [*a book*].

MONTICELSO 'Tis here, my lord.
FRANCISCO First, your intelligencers.° Pray let's see. *informers*

2. Anyone who unjustly starts a war will face a day of reckoning at his death, and the curse will descend to his progeny as well.

3. In siege warfare, digging under the enemy's fortifications often prevails when cannons are ineffectual.

MONTICELSO Their number rises strangely, and some of them
You'd take for honest men. Next are panders.
These are your pirates, and these following leaves
For base rogues that undo young gentlemen
By taking up commodities;[4] for politic bankrupts;[5]
For fellows that are bawds to their own wives,
Only to put off horses and slight jewels,
Clocks, defaced plate, and such commodities
At birth of their first children.[6]
FRANCISCO Are there such?
MONTICELSO [*turning the pages*] These are for impudent bawds
That go in men's apparel;° for usurers — *i.e., cross-dressers*
That share with scriveners for their good reportage;[7]
For lawyers that will antedate° their writs; — *fraudulently backdate*
And some divines° you might find folded° there, — *clergymen / (in the pages)*
But° that I slip° them o'er for conscience' sake. — *Were it not / pass*
Here is a general catalogue of knaves!
A man might study all the prisons o'er,
Yet never attain this knowledge.
FRANCISCO Murderers!
Fold down the leaf, I pray.
Good my lord, let me borrow this strange doctrine.° — *information*
MONTICELSO Pray use't, my lord.
FRANCISCO I do assure Your Lordship
You are a worthy member of the state,
And have done infinite good in your discovery
Of these offenders.
MONTICELSO Somewhat, sir.
FRANCISCO Oh, God!
Better than tribute of wolves paid in England;
'Twill hang their skins o'th'hedge.[8]
MONTICELSO I must make bold° — *be so bold as*
To leave Your Lordship.
FRANCISCO Dearly, sir, I thank you.
If any ask for me at court, report
You have left me in the company of knaves.
Exit Monticelso.
I gather now by this, some cunning fellow
That's my lord's officer,° one that lately skipped — *Monticelso's subaltern*
From a clerk's desk up to a justice' chair,
Hath made this knavish summons,° and intends, — *inventory, writ*
As th'Irish rebels wont were to sell heads,
So to make prize of these.[9] And thus it happens.

4. These pages in the book are for rogues who provide overvalued goods to extravagant and needful young gentlemen instead of money and then demand repayment in cash at the inflated price.
5. Persons who have declared bankrupty for their own benefit, having hidden their assets.
6. Scoundrels who prostitute their own wives to other men and then, when the birth of children is about to make the affairs notorious, force the duped lovers to play the commodities game (see note 4 above). "To put off" (line 51) means "to sell off fraudulently."
7. These pages of the book are for moneylenders who give a percentage cut to scribes and notaries for steering clients their way.
8. King Edgar (944–975) made the Welsh pay a tribute of three hundred wolves a year, as a means of ridding the land of predatory animals. The wolves' hides were then hung up as trophies and as symbols of the King's power.
9. And who intends to collect a reward for rounding up these malefactors, much as the Irish rebels put a price on the heads of those they wished killed.

Your poor rogues pay for't which have not the means
To present bribe in fist;° the rest o'th'band — *To hand over a bribe*
Are razed° out of the knave's record, or else — *scraped, erased*
My lord he winks at them with easy will;
His man° grows rich, the knaves are the knaves still. — *Monticelso's officer*
But to the use I'll make of it: it shall serve
To point me out a list of murderers,
Agents for any villainy. Did I want
Ten leash° of courtesans, it would furnish me, — *set(s) of three*
Nay, laundress three armies.[1] That in so little paper
Should lie th'undoing of so many men!
'Tis not so big as twenty declarations.° — *official proclamations*
See the corrupted use some make of books!
Divinity, wrested by some factious blood,[2]
Draws swords, swells battles, and o'erthrows all good.
To fashion my revenge more seriously,
Let me remember my dead sister's face;
Call for her picture. No, I'll close mine eyes,
And in a melancholic thought I'll frame° — *imagine, fashion*
Her figure 'fore me.

Enter Isabella's ghost.

Now I ha 't. How strong
Imagination works! How she° can frame — *(Imagination)*
Things which are not! Methinks she° stands afore me; — *(Isabella)*
And, by the quick idea° of my mind, — *lively mental picture*
Were my skill pregnant,° I could draw her picture. — *apt*
Thought, as a subtle juggler,° makes us deem — *magician*
Things supernatural which have cause
Common as sickness. 'Tis my melancholy.—
How cam'st thou by thy death?—How idle° am I — *pointlessly foolish*
To question mine own idleness?°—Did ever — *a thing I just imagined*
Man dream awake till now?—Remove this object;
Out of my brain with't! What have I to do
With tombs, or deathbeds, funerals, or tears,
That° have to meditate upon revenge? [*Exit ghost.*] — *I who*
So, now 'tis ended, like an old wives' story.
Statesmen think often they see stranger sights
Than madmen. Come, to this weighty business.
My tragedy must have some idle mirth in't,
Else it will never pass.[3] I am in love,
In love with Corombona, and my suit
Thus halts° to her in verse. *He writes.* — *limps*
I have done it rarely.° Oh, the fate of princes! — *excellently*
I am so used to frequent flattery
That, being alone, I now flatter myself;
But it will serve. [*He seals the letter.*] 'Tis sealed.

Enter Servant.

1. This list would provide enough laundresses (who presumably served as whores as well) to serve three armies.
2. Theology, twisted to suit the ideology of some bloodthirsty religious faction.
3. I.e., pass muster. Francisco imagines himself as writing a tragedy in which he himself is to play the part of the lover—the "idle mirth" that a good tragedy must have to succeed.

Bear this
To th'house of convertites, and watch your leisure° *opportunity*
To give it to the hands of Corombona,
Or to the matron, when some followers
Of Bracciano may be by. Away! *Exit Servant.*
He that deals all by strength,° his wit is shallow; *by strength alone*
When a man's head goes through, each limb will follow.
The engine for my business, bold Count Lodowick.
'Tis gold must such an instrument procure;[4]
With empty fist no man doth falcons lure.[5]
Bracciano, I am now fit for thy encounter.° *to encounter you*
Like the wild Irish, I'll ne'er think thee dead
Till I can play at football with thy head.
Flectere si nequeo Superos, Acheronta movebo.[6] *Exit.*

[4.2]

Enter the Matron and Flamineo.

MATRON Should it be known the Duke hath such recourse
To your imprisoned sister, I were like° *would be likely*
T'incur much damage by it.
FLAMINEO Not a scruple.° *Not a bit*
The Pope lies on his deathbed, and their heads
Are troubled now with other business
Than guarding of a lady.

Enter Servant.° *(see 4.1.123–27)*

SERVANT [*aside*] Yonder's Flamineo in conference
With the matrona. [*To her*] Let me speak with you.
I would entreat you to deliver for me
This letter to the fair Vittoria.
[*He gives her Francisco's letter.*]
MATRON I shall, sir.

Enter Bracciano.

SERVANT With all care and secrecy.
Hereafter you shall know me, and receive
Thanks for this courtesy. [*Exit.*]
FLAMINEO How now? What's that?
MATRON A letter.
FLAMINEO To my sister. I'll see't delivered.
[*He takes the letter and examines it.*]
BRACCIANO What's that you read, Flamineo?
FLAMINEO [*giving him the letter*] Look.
BRACCIANO Ha? [*He reads*] "To the most unfortunate, his best
respected Vittoria."—
Who was the messenger?
FLAMINEO I know not.

4. I.e., I will need gold to obtain the services of Count Lodovico; he is to be my instrument of revenge.
5. A lure (of feathers) is needed to entice the falcon back to the master's gloved fist.
6. If I cannot prevail upon the gods above, I will move the infernal regions. (Virgil, *Aeneid*, 7.312.) Acheron is a river of the underworld.
4.2. A house of convertites, Rome.

BRACCIANO No? Who sent it?
FLAMINEO Ud's foot,° you speak as if a man *By God's foot*
Should know what fowl is coffined° in a baked meat *enclosed (in pastry)*
Afore you cut it up.
BRACCIANO I'll open't, were't her heart. [*He opens the letter.*]
What's here subscribed?° *written below*
"Florence"?° *"The Duke of Florence"*
This juggling° is gross and palpable. *chicanery*
I have found out the conveyance.° Read it, read it. *contrivance*
[*He gives it to Flamineo, who*] *reads the letter.*
FLAMINEO "Your tears I'll turn to triumphs; be but mine.
Your prop° is fall'n; I pity that a vine° *(Bracciano) / (Vittoria)*
Which princes heretofore have longed to gather,° *harvest, enjoy*
Wanting supporters, now should fade and wither."
Wine, i'faith, my lord, with lees,° would serve his turn. *dregs*
"Your sad imprisonment I'll soon uncharm,° *release*
And with a princely uncontrollèd arm
Lead you to Florence, where my love and care
Shall hang your wishes in my silver hair."[1]
A halter on his strange equivocation![2]
"Nor for my years return me the sad willow.[3]
Who prefer blossoms before fruit that's mellow?"
Rotten, on my knowledge, with lying too long i'th' bedstraw.[4]
"And all the lines of age this line convinces:[5]
The gods never wax old; no more do princes."
A pox on't! Tear it! Let's have no more atheists,[6] for God's sake.
BRACCIANO Ud's death, I'll cut her into atomies° *bits*
And let th'irregular° north wind sweep her up *wild*
And blow her int' his nostrils. Where's this whore?
FLAMINEO That—? What do you call her?
BRACCIANO Oh, I could be mad,
Prevent the curst disease she'll bring me to,
And tear my hair off![7] Where's this changeable stuff?° *inconstant woman*
FLAMINEO O'er head and ears in water,[8] I assure you.
She is not for your wearing.
BRACCIANO In, you pander!° *Go fetch Vittoria!*
FLAMINEO What, me, my lord? Am I your dog?
BRACCIANO A bloodhound. Do you brave?° Do you stand° me? *defy me / confront*
FLAMINEO Stand you? Let those that have diseases run;° *flee; ooze*
I need no plasters.° *medical dressings*
BRACCIANO Would you be kicked?
FLAMINEO Would you have your neck broke?

1. I.e., In my old age, I will be attentive to your every wish.
2. I.e., A curse on his playing with the meaning of words like "hang"! (A halter is literally a noose.)
3. I.e., Do not reject me because of my advanced age. (The willow symbolizes unrequited love.)
4. Fruit was often ripened in straw, of the sort used also for mattresses. Flamineo implies that the letter-writer, Francisco, is corrupted with too much illicit pleasure in bed.
5. All the wrinkles of age lend force to the following maxim.
6. Atheists would equate gods and princes, as the letter-writer has just done.
7. I could tear out my hair, thereby forestalling the syphilitic illness that she will bring me to. (Loss of hair is a symptom of syphilis.)
8. Flamineo puns that Vittoria is (1) in deep water; (2) like "watered" silk, which is made in such a way as to show iridescent waves of color—the "changeable stuff" of line 49.

I tell you, Duke, I am not in Russia;
My shins must be kept whole.[9]
BRACCIANO Do you know me?
FLAMINEO Oh, my lord, methodically.° *through and through*
As in this world there are degrees of evils,
So in this world there are degrees of devils.
You're a great duke, I your poor secretary.
I do look now for a Spanish fig or an Italian sallet daily.[1]
BRACCIANO Pander, ply your convoy,° and leave your prating. *get on with your job*
FLAMINEO All your kindness to me is like that miserable courtesy of Polyphemus to Ulysses: you reserve me to be devoured last.[2] You would dig turfs out of my grave to feed your larks;° that would be music to you. Come, I'll lead you to her. *to put in birds' cages*
BRACCIANO Do you face° me? *bandy words with*
FLAMINEO Oh, sir, I would not go before a politic° enemy with my back towards him, though there were behind me a whirlpool. *cunning*

Enter Vittoria to Bracciano and Flamineo.

BRACCIANO [*giving her the letter*] Can you read, mistress?
Look upon that letter;
There are no characters nor hieroglyphics;
You need no comment. I am grown your receiver.[3]
God's precious,° you shall be a brave great lady, *precious body and blood*
A stately and advancèd° whore. *raised high*
VITTORIA Say,° sir? *Do you say so*
BRACCIANO Come, come, let's see your cabinet;° discover *place for letters, etc.*
Your treasury of love letters. Death and Furies!
I'll see them all.
VITTORIA Sir, upon my soul,
I have not any. Whence was this directed?
BRACCIANO Confusion° on your politic° ignorance! *Destruction / feigned*
You are reclaimed, are you? I'll give you the bells
And let you fly to the devil.[4]
FLAMINEO Ware hawk,[5] my lord.
VITTORIA [*reading*] "Florence"! This is some treacherous plot, my lord.
To me, he ne'er was lovely, I protest,
So much as in my sleep.[6]
BRACCIANO Right; they are plots.° *(said ironically)*
Your beauty! Oh, ten thousand curses on't!
How long have I beheld the devil in crystal?[7]

9. Russians reportedly beat the shins of debtors who refused to repay.
1. Flamineo expects to be poisoned for his insolence to Bracciano. (The "Spanish fig" is also an indecent gesture of insult. "Sallet" means "salad.")
2. Homer's *Odyssey*, 9.369–70, tells how the one-eyed Cyclops, Polyphemus, having captured Odysseus (Roman Ulysses) and his men in his cave, proceeded to eat them one by one, reserving Odysseus for last (and thereby giving Odysseus time to plan an escape).
3. There's nothing obscure about what is written here, no cabalistic figures or occult picture writing; you'll need no exposition of the letter. I've become your pimp, acting as receiver of your love letters.
4. Bracciano speaks sarcastically as if Vittoria were a hawk with bells attached to its legs, being recalled to its master (i.e., Francisco). Bracciano will let her go to the devil.
5. Using a common proverb in a continuation of Bracciano's hawk metaphor (see previous note), Flamineo bids him beware of a swindle.
6. Francisco was never appealing to me, even in my dreams.
7. Witches and conjurors were supposedly able to enclose the devil in crystal—the very opposite of crystal shrines enclosing the image of a saint. The image alludes to the play's title.

Thou hast led me, like an heathen sacrifice,
With music and with fatal yokes of flowers,[8]
To my eternal ruin. Woman to man
Is either a god or a wolf.

VITTORIA My lord—

BRACCIANO Away!
We'll be as differing as two adamants;° — *magnets*
The one shall shun the other. What? Dost weep?
Procure but ten of thy dissembling trade,
Ye'd furnish all the Irish funerals
With howling, past wild Irish.[9]

FLAMINEO Fie, my lord!

BRACCIANO That hand, that cursèd hand, which I have wearied
With doting kisses! O my sweetest duchess,
How lovely art thou now! [*To Vittoria*] Thy loose thoughts
Scatter like quicksilver.[1] I was bewitched,
For all the world speaks ill of thee.

VITTORIA No matter.
I'll live so now I'll make that world recant
And change her speeches. You did name your duchess.

BRACCIANO Whose death God pardon!

VITTORIA Whose death God revenge
On thee, most godless duke!

FLAMINEO [*aside*] Now for two whirlwinds.

VITTORIA What have I gained by thee but infamy?
Thou hast stained the spotless honor of my house,° — *family*
And frighted thence noble society,
Like those which, sick o'th'palsy and retain
Ill-scenting foxes 'bout them,[2] are still shunned
By those of choicer° nostrils. What do you call this house? — *more fastidious*
Is this your palace? Did not the judge style it
A house of penitent whores? Who sent me to it?
Who hath the honor to advance Vittoria
To this incontinent° college? Is't not you? — *unchaste*
Is't not your high preferment?° Go, go brag — *promotion (of me)*
How many ladies you have undone, like me.
Fare you well, sir; let me hear no more of you.
I had a limb corrupted to an ulcer,
But I have cut it off; and now I'll go
Weeping to heaven on crutches. For° your gifts, — *As for*
I will return them all; and I do wish
That I could make you full executor
To all my sins. Oh, that I could toss myself
Into a grave as quickly! For all thou art worth,
I'll not shed one tear more; I'll burst first.

She throws herself upon a bed.

BRACCIANO I have drunk Lethe.° Vittoria? — *waters of oblivion*
My dearest happiness? Vittoria?
What do you ail, my love? Why do you weep?

8. An animal being led to sacrifice would be thus accoutred.
9. Loud keening was traditional at Irish wakes and funerals, and wailers could be hired.
1. Your lascivious thoughts scatter wantonly to many men.
2. The rank scent of foxes was thought to be medically efficacious against palsy, or paralysis.

VITTORIA Yes, I now weep poniards,° do you see? *daggers*
BRACCIANO Are not those matchless eyes mine?
VITTORIA I had rather
They were not matches.° *i.e., asquint; ugly*
BRACCIANO Is not this lip mine?
VITTORIA Yes—thus to bite it off, rather than give it thee.
FLAMINEO [*to Vittoria*] Turn to my lord, good sister.
VITTORIA Hence, you pander!
FLAMINEO Pander! Am I the author of your sin?
VITTORIA Yes. He's a base thief that a thief lets in.° *that lets in a thief*
FLAMINEO [*to Bracciano*] We're blown up,° my lord. *i.e., We're done for*
BRACCIANO [*to Vittoria*] Wilt thou hear me?
Once to be jealous of thee is t'express
That I will love thee everlastingly,
And nevermore be jealous.
VITTORIA O thou fool,
Whose greatness hath by much o'ergrown thy wit!
What dar'st thou do that I not dare to suffer,
Excepting to be still thy whore? For° that, *As for*
In the sea's bottom sooner thou shalt make
A bonfire.
FLAMINEO Oh, no oaths, for God's sake.
BRACCIANO Will you hear me?
VITTORIA Never.
FLAMINEO What a damned impostume° is a woman's will! *festering abscess*
Can nothing break it? [*Aside to Bracciano*] Fie, fie, my lord.
Women are caught as you take tortoises;
She must be turned on her back. [*Aloud*] Sister, by this hand,
I am on your side. [*To Bracciano*] Come, come, you have wronged her.
What a strange credulous man were you, my lord,
To think the Duke of Florence would love her?
[*Aside*] Will any mercer° take another's ware *dealer in textiles*
When once 't is toused° and sullied? [*Aloud*] And yet, sister, *torn, shopworn*
How scurvily° this frowardness° becomes you! *shabbily / perversity*
[*Aside*] Young leverets stand° not long; and women's anger *Young hares hold out*
Should, like their° flight, procure a little sport— *(the leverets')*
A full cry° for a quarter of an hour, *pursuit; shedding tears*
And then be put to th'dead quat.° *squat, at bay*
BRACCIANO [*to Vittoria*] Shall these eyes,
Which have so long time dwelt upon your face,
Be now put out?° *blinded (by denial)*
FLAMINEO No cruel landlady i'th'world,
Which lends forth groats to broom-men° and takes use° *street sweepers / interest*
For them, would do't.
[*Aside to Bracciano*] Hand° her, my lord, and kiss her. Be not like *Touch, fondle*
A ferret, to let go your hold with blowing.[3]
BRACCIANO Let us renew right hands.° *plight anew our troth*
VITTORIA Hence!

3. It was supposed that one could make a ferret let go its grip by blowing in its face.

BRACCIANO Never shall rage, or the forgetful° wine, *oblivion-inducing*
Make me commit like fault.
FLAMINEO [*aside to Bracciano*] Now you are i'th'way on't,
follow 't hard.
BRACCIANO Be thou at peace with me; let all the world
Threaten the cannon.° *Threaten war*
FLAMINEO [*to Vittoria*] Mark his penitence.
Best natures do commit the grossest faults
When they're giv'n o'er to jealousy, as best wine
Dying° makes strongest vinegar. I'll tell you, *Going sour*
The sea's more rough and raging than calm rivers,
But nor° so sweet nor wholesome. A quiet woman *neither*
Is a still water under a great bridge;
A man may shoot her safely.[4]
VITTORIA O ye dissembling men!
FLAMINEO We sucked that, sister,
From women's breasts, in our first infancy.
VITTORIA To add misery to misery.
BRACCIANO Sweetest—
VITTORIA Am I not low enough?
Ay, ay, your good heart gathers like a snowball,[5]
Now your affection's cold.
FLAMINEO Ud'° foot, it shall melt *Ud's, by God's*
To a heart again, or all the wine in Rome
Shall run o'th'lees° for't. *down to the dregs*
VITTORIA Your dog or hawk should be rewarded° better *rewarded for hunting*
Than I have been. I'll speak not one word more.
FLAMINEO Stop her mouth
With a sweet kiss, my lord. [*Bracciano kisses Vittoria.*]
So, now the tide's turned the vessel's come about.° *has reversed course*
He's a sweet armful. Oh, we curled-haired men
Are still° most kind to women! This is well. *always, constantly*
BRACCIANO That you should chide thus!
FLAMINEO Oh, sir, your little chimneys
Do ever cast most smoke. I sweat for you.
Couple together with as deep a silence
As did the Grecians in their wooden horse.° *Trojan horse*
My lord, supply° your promises with deeds. *fulfill*
You know that painted meat° no hunger feeds. *mere picture of food*
BRACCIANO Stay—ingrateful Rome![6]
FLAMINEO Rome! It deserves to be called Barbary, for our villainous usage.[7]
BRACCIANO Soft;° the same project° which the Duke of
Florence *Gently / plan*
(Whether in love or gullery° I know not) *trickery*
Laid down for her° escape, will I pursue. *(Vittoria's; see 31–34)*
FLAMINEO And no time fitter than this night, my lord.
The Pope being dead, and all the cardinals ent'red
The conclave for th'electing a new pope,

4. The image, of passing quickly under a bridge in a boat, or "shooting" through, expresses a sexual preference for a compliant woman that a man may maneuver upon with pleasure and ease.
5. You are taking pity on me now, like a snowball rolling and accumulating more snow.
6. Bracciano, alluding to Rome's legendary ingratitude toward those who had saved the city, complains of a forgetfulness on the part of the Cardinal and those around him.
7. Barbary—the name given to the Saracen region of North Africa—is here used (with etymological imprecision) as though it were equivalent to "a place of barbarity."

The city in a great confusion,
We may attire her in a page's suit,
Lay her post-horse,[8] take shipping, and amain° *with full speed*
For Padua.

BRACCIANO I'll instantly steal forth the Prince Giovanni
And make for Padua. You two, with your old mother
And young Marcello that attends on Florence,° *the Duke of Florence*
If you can work him to it, follow me.
I will advance you all. For° you, Vittoria, *As for*
Think of a duchess' title.

FLAMINEO Lo you, sister!—
Stay, my lord; I'll tell you a tale. The crocodile, which lives in the river Nilus,° hath a worm breeds i'th'teeth of't, which puts it to extreme anguish.[9] A little bird, no bigger than a wren, is barber-surgeon to this crocodile, flies into the jaws of 't, picks out the worm, and brings present remedy.[1] The fish,° glad of ease but ingrateful to her that did it, that the bird may not talk largely° of her abroad for nonpayment, closeth her chaps° intending to swallow her, and so put her to perpetual silence. But Nature, loathing such ingratitude, hath armed this bird with a quill or prick on the head, top o'th'which wounds the crocodile i'th'mouth, forceth her open her bloody prison, and away flies the pretty toothpicker from her cruel patient.

Nile River / *i.e., aquatic reptile* / *openly, at length* / *jaws*

BRACCIANO Your application° is, I have not rewarded *moral*
The service you have done me.

FLAMINEO No, my lord.
You, sister, are the crocodile; you are blemished in your fame;° my lord cures it. And, though the comparison hold not in every particle, yet observe, remember, what good the bird with the prick° i'th'head hath done you, and scorn ingratitude.

reputation / *(with bawdy suggestion)*

[*Aside*] It may appear to some ridiculous
Thus to talk knave and madman, and sometimes
Come in with a dried sentence,° stuffed with sage.° *maxim / herb; wisdom*
But this allows° my varying of shapes: *justifies*
Knaves do grow great by being great men's apes.° *Exeunt.* *imitators; fools*

[4.3]

Enter Lodovico, Gasparo, and six ambassadors; at another door Francisco, the Duke of Florence.

FRANCISCO [*to Lodovico*] So, my lord, I commend your diligence.
Guard well the conclave, and, as the order is,
Let none have conference with the cardinals.

LODOVICO I shall, my lord.—Room for the ambassadors!

GASPARO They're wondrous brave° today. Why do they wear *splendidly dressed*
These several° habits? *diverse, varied*

LODOVICO Oh, sir, they're knights
Of several orders.

8. Provide her with relays of post-horses.

9. Toothache was believed to be caused by worms breeding in the teeth.

1. Barbers, who regularly practiced surgery and dentistry in the medieval period, were incorporated in 1461 as the Company of Barber-Surgeons. From the time of Henry VIII onward, however, they could no longer practice surgery.

4.3. The papal palace, Rome.

That lord i'th'black cloak with the silver cross
Is Knight of Rhodes; the next Knight of Saint Michael;
That, of the Golden Fleece; the Frenchman there
Knight of the Holy Ghost; my lord of Savoy
Knight of th'Annunciation; the Englishman
Is Knight of th'honored Garter, dedicated
Unto their saint, Saint George. I could describe to you
Their several institutions, with the laws
Annexèd to their orders, but that° time *were it not that*
Permits not such discovery.° *an account*

FRANCISCO Where's Count Lodowick?

LODOVICO Here, my lord.

FRANCISCO 'Tis o'th'point of dinnertime.
Marshal the cardinals' service.[1]

LODOVICO Sir, I shall.

Enter servants with several dishes covered.

Stand. Let me search your dish. [*Inspecting*] Who's this for?

SERVANT For my Lord Cardinal Monticelso,

LODOVICO Whose° this? *Whose is*

SERVANT For my Lord Cardinal of Bourbon.

FRENCH AMBASSADOR Why doth he search the dishes? To observe
What meat is dressed?° *prepared*

ENGLISH AMBASSADOR No, sir, but to prevent
Lest any letters should be conveyed in
To bribe or to solicit the advancement
Of any cardinal. When first they enter,
'Tis lawful for the ambassadors of princes
To enter with them, and to make their suit
For any man their prince affecteth° best; *prefers*
But after, till a general election,
No man may speak with them.

LODOVICO [*to servants*] You that attend on the lord cardinals,
Open the window and receive their viands.

[*A Cardinal appears briefly at a window.*]

A CARDINAL You must return the service;° the lord cardinals *food dishes*
Are busied 'bout electing of the Pope.
They have given o'er scrutiny, and are fallen
To admiration.[2]

LODOVICO [*to servants*] Away, away!

[*Exeunt servants, with food.*]

FRANCISCO I'll lay° a thousand ducats° you hear news *bet / gold coins*
Of a pope presently. [*Sounds are heard.*] Hark! Sure he's elected.

A Cardinal [*of Arragon appears*] *on the terrace.*

Behold! My lord of Arragon appears
On the church battlements.

1. Take charge of arrangements for waiting on the cardinals.
2. The cardinals, in their closed meeting, first "scrutinize" (i.e., count) the secret ballots and then, in another method of election, turn and reverence the cardinal of their preference; if two-thirds do so to any single candidate, the choice has been made. (This latter procedure is technically an "adoration," not an "admiration.")

ARRAGON *Denuntio vobis gaudium magnum. Reverendissimus*
Cardinalis Lorenzo de Monticelso electus est in sedem apos-
tolicum, et elegit sibi nomen Paulum Quartum.[3]
OMNES° *Vivat sanctus Pater, Paulus Quartus!*[4] — *All (the clergy)*

[*Enter a Servant.*]

SERVANT Vittoria, my lord—
FRANCISCO Well, what of her?
SERVANT Is fled the city—
FRANCISCO Ha?
SERVANT With Duke Bracciano.
FRANCISCO Fled? Where's the Prince Giovanni?
SERVANT Gone with his father.
FRANCISCO Let the matrona of the convertites
Be apprehended.° Fled! Oh, damnable! [*Exit Servant.*] — *arrested*
[*Aside*] How fortunate are my wishes! Why, 'twas this° — *this alone*
I only labored.° I did send the letter — *labored for*
T'instruct him° what to do. Thy fame, fond° duke, — *(Bracciano) / foolish*
I first have poisoned, directed thee the way
To marry a whore. What can be worse? This follows:
The hand must act to drown the passionate tongue.[5]
I scorn to wear a sword and prate° of wrong. — *and yet merely talk*

Enter Monticelso in state.° [*Francisco confers privately with him.*] — *in papal regalia*

MONTICELSO [*to those assembled*] *Concedimus vobis apostoli-*
cam benedictionem et remissionem peccatorum.[6]
My lord reports Vittoria Corombona
Is stol'n from forth the house of convertites
By Bracciano, and they're fled the city.
Now, though this be the first day of our seat,° — *throne, office*
We cannot better please the divine power
Than to sequester from the holy church
These cursèd persons. Make it therefore known,
We do denounce° excommunication — *pronounce*
Against them both; all that are theirs° in Rome — *all their household*
We likewise banish. Set on.
Exeunt. [*Francisco and Lodovico remain behind.*]
FRANCISCO Come, dear Lodovico.
You have ta'en the sacrament° to prosecute — *i.e., sworn deeply*
Th'intended murder.
LODOVICO With all constancy.
But, sir, I wonder you'll engage yourself
In person, being a great prince.° — *nobleman*
FRANCISCO Divert me not.
Most of his court are of my faction,° — *are loyal to me*
And some are of my counsel.° Noble friend, — *in my confidence*
Our danger shall be 'like° in this design; — *alike*
Give leave° part of the glory may be mine. *Exit.* — *Please grant that*

Enter Monticelso.

3. I announce to you tidings of great joy. The Most Reverend Cardinal Lorenzo di Monticelso has been elected to the apostolic see and has taken for himself the name of Paul IV.
4. Long live the Holy Father, Paul IV!
5. Deeds must go beyond passionate speech.
6. We grant you the apostolic blessing and remission of sins.

MONTICELSO Why did the Duke of Florence with such care
Labor° your pardon? Say. *Labor for*
LODOVICO Italian beggars will resolve° you that *inform*
Who, begging of an alms, bid those they beg of
Do good for their own sakes;[7] or't may be
He spreads his bounty with a sowing hand,
Like kings, who many times give out of measure,° *excessively*
Not for desert so much as for their pleasure.
MONTICELSO I know you're cunning. Come, what devil was that
That you were raising?
LODOVICO Devil, my lord?
MONTICELSO I ask you
How doth the Duke employ you, that his bonnet
Fell with such compliment unto his knee
When he departed from you?
LODOVICO Why, my lord,
He told me of a resty° Barbary horse *restive; lazy*
Which he would fain have brought to the career,
The sault, and the ring-galliard.[8] Now, my lord,
I have a rare French rider.[9]
MONTICELSO Take you heed,
Lest the jade° break your neck. Do you put me off *sorry nag*
With your wild horse tricks? Sirrah, you do lie.
Oh, thou'rt a foul black cloud, and thou dost threat
A violent storm.
LODOVICO Storms are i'th'air,° my lord; *high above our heads*
I am too low° to storm. *low of station*
MONTICELSO Wretched creature!
I know that thou art fashioned for all ill,
Like dogs, that once get blood, they'll ever kill.
About some murder, was't not?
LODOVICO I'll not tell you;
And yet I care not greatly if I do—
Marry, with this preparation: Holy father,
I come not to you as an intelligencer,° *spy*
But as a penitent sinner. What I utter
Is in confession merely,° which you know *purely*
Must never be revealed.
MONTICELSO You have o'erta'en° me. *outmaneuvered*
LODOVICO Sir, I did love Bracciano's duchess dearly;
Or, rather, I pursued her with hot lust,
Though she ne'er knew on't. She was poisoned—
Upon my soul she was—for which I have sworn
T'avenge her murder.
MONTICELSO To the Duke of Florence?
LODOVICO To him I have.
MONTICELSO Miserable creature!
If thou persist in this, 'tis damnable.
Dost thou imagine thou canst slide on blood

7. Any beggars asking for a handout will bid the givers to be generous for their own souls' welfare. (Perhaps, Lodovico sardonically suggests, Francisco labored to pardon him for his own soul's sake, or, as he suggests in the following lines, just to please himself.)

8. Lodovico uses the technical terms of manège, the movements of a trained horse, for various paces: the gallop, the leap, and a mixture of bounding and curvetting.

9. The French were renowned for their horsemanship.

And not be tainted with a shameful fall?
Or like the black and melancholic yew tree,
Dost think to root thyself in dead men's graves,° *(see 1.2.234–36 and n)*
And yet to prosper? Instruction to thee
Comes like sweet showers to overhardened ground:
They wet, but pierce not deep. And so I leave thee
With all the Furies hanging 'bout thy neck,
Till by thy penitence thou remove this evil
In conjuring from thy breast that cruel devil.
Exit Monticelso.

LODOVICO I'll give it o'er.° He says 'tis damnable. *give it up*
Besides, I did expect his suffrage,° *endorsement*
By reason of Camillo's death.

Enter Servant and Francisco [and stand aside].

FRANCISCO Do you know that count?
SERVANT Yes, my lord.
FRANCISCO Bear him these thousand ducats to his lodging;
Tell him the Pope hath sent them. Happily° *Haply, with luck*
That will confirm more than all the rest. [*Exit.*]
SERVANT [*to Lodovico*] Sir!
LODOVICO To me, sir?
SERVANT [*offering money*] His Holiness hath sent you a
thousand crowns,° *gold coins*
And wills you, if you travel, to make him
Your patron for intelligence.° *for secret information*
LODOVICO His creature,° ever to be commanded. *I'm his humble servant*
[*Exit Servant.*]
Why now, 'tis come about. He railed upon me;
And yet these crowns were told° out and laid ready *counted*
Before he knew my voyage. Oh, the art,
The modest form of greatness,° that do sit *great persons*
Like brides at wedding dinners, with their looks turned
From the least wanton jests, their puling° stomach *queasy*
Sick of the modesty,° when their thoughts are loose, *of pretended modesty*
Even acting° of those hot and lustful sports *i.e., imagining*
Are° to ensue about midnight: such his cunning! *That are*
He sounds my depth thus with a golden plummet.° *i.e., the gold ducats*
I am doubly armed now. Now to th'act of blood.
There's but three Furies found in spacious hell,
But in a great man's breast three thousand dwell. [*Exit.*]

[5.1]

A passage over the stage° of Bracciano, Flamineo, Marcello, Hortensio, [Vittoria] Corombona, Cornelia, Zanche, and others. [Flamineo and Hortensio comment as the others process and then exit.] *(in marriage procession)*

FLAMINEO In all the weary minutes of my life,
Day ne'er broke up° till now. This marriage *dawned*
Confirms me happy.

5.1. Bracciano's palace, Padua.

HORTENSIO 'Tis a good assurance.
Saw you not yet the Moor° that's come to court? *(Francisco in disguise)*

FLAMINEO Yes, and conferred with him i'th'Duke's closet.° *private chamber*
I have not seen a goodlier personage,
Nor ever talked with man better experienced
In state affairs or rudiments of war.
He hath, by report, served the Venetian° *the Venetian state*
In Candy° these twice seven years, and been chief *Crete*
In many a bold design.° *military campaign*

HORTENSIO What are those two° *(Lodovico and Gasparo)*
That bear him company?

FLAMINEO Two noblemen of Hungary, that, living in the Emperor's service as commanders, eight years since,° *ago* contrary to the expectation of all the court, entered into religion, into the strict order of Capuchins.° *friars (see 5.3.37 n)* But, being not well settled in their undertaking, they left their order and returned to court. For which, being after° *afterward* troubled in conscience, they vowed their service against the enemies of Christ; went to Malta; were there knighted; and, in their return back, at this great solemnity,° *ceremony* they are resolved forever to forsake the world and settle themselves here in a house of Capuchins in Padua.

HORTENSIO 'Tis strange.

FLAMINEO One thing makes it so. They have vowed forever to wear next their bare bodies those coats of mail they served in.

HORTENSIO Hard penance!
Is the Moor a Christian?

FLAMINEO He is.

HORTENSIO Why proffers he his service to our duke?

FLAMINEO Because he understands there's like° to grow *likely*
Some wars between us and the Duke of Florence,
In which he hopes employment.
I never saw one in a stern bold look
Wear more command, nor in a lofty phrase
Express more knowing, or more deep contempt
Of our slight, airy courtiers. He talks
As if he had traveled all the princes' courts
Of Christendom; in all things strives t'express
That° all that should° dispute with him may know: *That which / would*
Glories, like glowworms, afar off shine bright,
But, looked to near, have neither heat nor light.[1]—
The Duke!

Enter Bracciano; [Francisco, Duke of] Florence, disguised like Mulinassar;° Lodovico [disguised as a Capuchin friar]; Antonelli; Gasparo [disguised as a Capuchin friar]; [Carlo and Pedro; and] Farnese,° bearing their swords and helmets. *(a fictional Moorish name)* / *a nonspeaking extra*

BRACCIANO You're nobly welcome. We have heard at full
Your honorable service 'gainst the Turk.

1. I.e., all who would dare do battle with him should realize that their vaunted prowess might look bright from a distance but will prove to be dull and cold on closer inspection. (In the ensuing action, Carlo and Pedro, of Bracciano's household, have secretly joined Francisco, Lodovico, and Gasparo in a conspiracy against Bracciano.)

To you, brave Mulinassar, we assign
A competent° pension, and are inly sorrow° — *adequate / sorrowful*
The vows of those two worthy gentlemen° — *(the two seeming friars)*
Make them incapable of° our proffered bounty. — *unable to accept*
Your wish is you may leave your warlike swords
For monuments° in our chapel. I accept it — *As tokens of your vows*
As a great honor done me, and must crave
Your leave to furnish out our duchess' revels.[2]
Only one thing, as the last vanity° — *expensive trifle*
You e'er shall view: deny me not to stay
To see a barriers° prepared tonight; — *martial exercise*
You shall have private standings.° It hath pleased — *standing places*
The great ambassadors of several princes,
In their return from Rome to their own countries,
To grace our marriage and to honor me
With such a kind of sport.

FRANCISCO I shall persuade them
To stay, my lord.

BRACCIANO [*to his followers*] Set on there to the presence!° — *ducal reception room*

Exeunt Bracciano, Flamineo, and [*Hortensio*].

CARLO [*to Francisco*] Noble my lord, most fortunately
welcome! *The conspirators here embrace.*
You have our vows sealed with the sacrament
To second your attempts.

PEDRO And all things ready.
He could not have invented his own ruin,
Had° he despaired, with more propriety.° — *Even if / fitness*

LODOVICO [*to Francisco*] You would not take my way.[3]

FRANCISCO 'Tis better ordered.

LODOVICO T'have poisoned his prayer book, or a pair° of beads, — *set, string*
The pommel of his saddle, his looking glass,
Or th'handle of his racket—oh, that, that!
That while he had been bandying° at tennis — *volleying*
He might have sworn° himself to hell and struck — *sworn exasperatedly*
His soul into the hazard![4] O my lord,
I would have our plot be ingenious,
And have it hereafter recorded for example° — *serve as a model*
Rather than borrow example.° — *imitate others*

FRANCISCO There's no way
More speeding than this thought on.[5]

LODOVICO On, then.

FRANCISCO And yet methinks that this revenge is poor,
Because it steals upon him like a thief.
To have ta'en him by the casque° in a pitched field,° — *helmet / full-scale battle*
Led him to Florence!

LODOVICO It had been rare.° And there — *would have been fine*
Have° crowned him with a wreath of stinking garlic, — *To have*

2. I must ask your indulgence while I make ready a festive marriage entertainment in Vittoria's honor.

3. Lodovico reminds Francisco that when the conspirators took an oath to carry out revenge on Bracciano on behalf of Francisco, Lodovico urged Francisco not to take part personally in a task not befitting his great rank (4.3.72–76); he might better leave the bloody work to those who serve him. Francisco answers here (line 68) by confirming his resolution to be one of the participants.

4. Into spiritual perils—but with wordplay on "hazard" as one of several openings in the tennis court walls into which the player of "real," or "royal," tennis attempted to hit the ball to score a point.

5. No more effective plan than this could be imagined.

T'have shown the sharpness° of his government° *harshness / conduct*
And rankness of his lust!—Flamineo comes.
Exeunt [*all except the disguised Francisco*].

Enter Flamineo, Marcello, and Zanche. [*They do not see Francisco at first.*]

MARCELLO [*to Flamineo*] Why doth this devil° haunt you? Say. *(Zanche)*
FLAMINEO I know not.
For, by this light, I do not conjure for her.° *to raise her*
'Tis not so great a cunning° as men think *magic stunt*
To raise the devil, for here's one up already.
The greatest cunning were to lay him down.[6]
MARCELLO She is your shame.
FLAMINEO I prithee, pardon her.
In faith, you see, women are like to burrs;
Where their affection throws them, there they'll stick.
ZANCHE [*noticing the disguised Francisco*] That is my countryman, a goodly person;
When he's at leisure I'll discourse with him
In our own language.
FLAMINEO I beseech you, do. *Exit Zanche.*
[*To Francisco*] How is't, brave soldier? Oh, that I had seen
Some of your iron° days! I pray relate *stern, warlike*
Some of your service° to us. *military service*

FRANCISCO 'Tis a ridiculous thing for a man to be his own chronicle. I did never wash my mouth with mine own praise, for fear of getting a stinking breath.

MARCELLO You're too stoical. The Duke will expect other discourse from you.

FRANCISCO I shall never flatter him; I have studied man too much to do that. What difference is between the Duke and I? No more than between two bricks; all made of one clay. Only 't may be one is placed on the top of a turret, the other in the bottom of a well by mere chance. If I were placed as high as the Duke, I should stick as fast, make as fair a show, and bear out weather equally.

FLAMINEO [*aside*] If this soldier had a patent° to beg in churches, then he would tell them° stories. *license* *(the churchgoers)*

MARCELLO I have been a soldier too.

FRANCISCO How have you thrived?

MARCELLO Faith, poorly.

FRANCISCO That's the misery of peace. Only outsides° are then respected. As ships seem very great upon the river which show° very little upon the seas, so some men i'th'court seem colossuses in a chamber, who, if they came into the field, would appear pitiful pygmies. *appearances* *look*

FLAMINEO Give me a fair room yet hung with arras,[7] and some great cardinal to lug me by th'ears° as his endeared minion. *i.e., fondle me*

FRANCISCO And thou mayst do the devil knows what villainy.

FLAMINEO And safely.

6. (1) Exorcise the devil; (2) relieve the sexual excitement that has been raised (line 89).

7. Wall tapestries, hung with space behind them, affording space for hiding.

FRANCISCO Right. You shall see in the country, in harvesttime, pigeons, though they destroy never so much corn, the
farmer dare not present the fowling piece° to them. Why? *shotgun*
Because they belong to the lord of the manor, whilst your
poor sparrows that belong to the Lord of heaven, they go to
the pot° for't. *cooking pot*

FLAMINEO I will now give you some politic° instruction. The *savvy*
Duke says he will give you pension; that's but bare promise;
get it under his hand.° For I have known men that have come *in writing*
from serving against the Turk; for three or four months they
have had pension to buy them new wooden legs and fresh
plasters, but after 'twas not to be had. And this miserable° *miserly; compassionate*
courtesy shows as if a tormenter should give hot cordial° *heart-stimulating*
drinks to one three-quarters dead o'th'rack,° only to fetch *torture rack*
the miserable soul again to endure more dog days.° *i.e., suffering*

Enter Hortensio, a Young Lord, Zanche, and two more [women attending].

How now, gallants? What, are they ready for the barriers?

YOUNG LORD Yes, the lords are putting on their armor.

HORTENSIO What's he?° *(Francisco)*

FLAMINEO A new upstart, one that swears like a falc'ner, and
will lie° in the Duke's ear day by day like a maker of alma- *tell lies*
nacs.[8] And yet I knew him since he came to th'court smell
worse of sweat than an under-tennis-court-keeper.[9]

HORTENSIO [*indicating Zanche*] Look you, yonder's your
sweet mistress.

FLAMINEO Thou art my sworn brother.° I'll tell thee, I do love *oath-bound friend*
that Moor, that witch,° very constrainedly. She knows some *charmer*
of my villainy. I do love her just as a man holds a wolf by the
ears; but for fear of turning° upon me and pulling out my *her turning*
throat, I would let her go to the devil.

HORTENSIO I hear she claims marriage of thee.

FLAMINEO Faith, I made to her some such dark promise, and
in seeking to fly from't I run on, like a frighted dog with a
bottle at's tail, that fain would bite it off and yet dares not
look behind him. [*To her*] Now, my precious gypsy!° *dark-skinned one*

ZANCHE Ay, your love to me rather cools than heats.

FLAMINEO Marry, I am the sounder lover.[1] We have many
wenches about the town heat too fast.

HORTENSIO What do you think of these perfumed gallants,
then?

FLAMINEO Their satin° cannot save them. I am confident *(punning on "Satan")*
They have a certain spice of the disease,° *touch of syphilis*
For they that sleep with dogs shall rise with fleas.

ZANCHE Believe it, a little painting[2] and gay clothes make you
loathe me.

FLAMINEO How? Love a lady for painting or gay apparel? I'll

8. Almanacs were notoriously unreliable.

9. Tennis, always played indoors, was a sweaty game, and the lowly assistant to the keeper of the tennis court might be expected to smell especially fragrant.

1. Flamineo wilfully interprets Zanche's complaint that his love for her cools: if I were indeed to cool or allay my passion for you, he says, I'd be in less danger of syphilis. (To be "sound" is to be healthy.)

2. Some other woman's artful use of cosmetics.

unkennel one example more for thee. Aesop had a foolish dog that let go the flesh to catch the shadow. I would have courtiers be better diners.

ZANCHE You remember your oaths.

FLAMINEO Lovers' oaths are like mariners' prayers, uttered in extremity; but when the tempest is o'er, and that° the vessel *when* leaves tumbling, they fall from protesting° to drinking. And *fervent praying* yet, amongst gentlemen protesting° and drinking go *quarreling* together, and agree as well as shoemakers and Westphalia bacon. They are both drawers on,[3] for drink draws on protestation, and protestation draws on more drink. Is not this discourse better now than the morality of your sunburnt gentleman?° *("Mulinassar," Francisco)*

Enter Cornelia [threatening Flamineo].

CORNELIA Is this your perch, you haggard?° Fly to th'stews.° *wild hawk / brothels*

FLAMINEO You should be clapped by th'heels° now. Strike i'th'court?[4] *put in irons or stocks*

ZANCHE She's good for nothing but to make her maids
Catch cold a-nights; they dare not use a bedstaff[5]
For fear of her light fingers.

MARCELLO You're a strumpet,
An impudent one. *[He kicks Zanche.]*

FLAMINEO Why do you kick her? Say,
Do you think that she's like a walnut tree?
Must she be cudgeled ere she bear good fruit?

MARCELLO She brags that you shall marry her.

FLAMINEO What then?

MARCELLO I had rather she were pitched upon a stake° *(like a scarecrow)*
In some new-seeded garden, to affright
Her fellow crows thence.

FLAMINEO You're a boy, a fool.
Be guardian to your hound; I am of age.

MARCELLO If I take her near you I'll cut her throat.

FLAMINEO With a fan of feathers?

MARCELLO And for° you: I'll whip *as for*
This folly from you.

FLAMINEO Are you choleric?
I'll purge't with rhubarb.° *a common purgative*

HORTENSIO Oh, your brother![6]

FLAMINEO Hang him!
He wrongs me most, that ought t'offend me least.
[*To Marcello*] I do suspect my mother played foul play
When she conceived thee.

MARCELLO Now, by all my hopes,
Like the two slaughtered sons of Oedipus,
The very flames of our affection

3. Shoemakers draw shoes onto the feet, while salty ham draws men to drink.

4. Flamineo upbraids his mother as though she had struck him with a weapon within the ducal precinct—a serious offense. (Probably he is mocking her; her attempt to remonstrate against her son's behavior cannot have been very effectual.)

5. A stick used to fluff up bedding, hold it in place, and the like, and not uncommonly used as a kind of homespun weapon. Zanche mocks Cornelia's weak attempts at rebuking her son, suggesting that Cornelia cannot do anything more than terrorize her maidservants with threats of beatings; the maids will be cold in bed out of fear of using a bedstaff with which Cornelia might turn on them.

6. Remember he's your brother!

Shall turn two ways.[7] Those words I'll make thee answer
With thy heart-blood.° *lifeblood*
FLAMINEO Do; like the geese in the progress,[8]
You know where you shall find me.
MARCELLO Very good.
[*Exit Flamineo.*]
[*To Young Lord*] An° thou beest a noble, friend, bear him my sword *If*
And bid him fit the length on't.[9]
YOUNG LORD [*taking Marcello's sword*] Sir, I shall.
[*Exeunt all but Zanche.*]

Enter Francisco, the Duke of Florence [*disguised as Mulinassar*].

ZANCHE [*aside*] He comes. Hence, petty thought of my disgrace!° *shame at being the wooer*
[*To him*] I ne'er loved my complexion till now,
'Cause I may boldly say, without a blush,[1]
I love you.
FRANCISCO Your love is untimely sown. There's a spring at Michaelmas,° but 'tis but a faint one. I am sunk in years, and I have vowed never to marry. *i.e., Indian summer*
ZANCHE Alas! Poor maids get more lovers than husbands. Yet you may mistake° my wealth. For, as when ambassadors are sent to congratulate princes there's commonly sent along with them a rich present, so that though the prince like not the ambassador's person nor words yet he likes well of the presentment,° so I may come to you in the same manner and be better loved for my dowry than my virtue. *underestimate* *present*
FRANCISCO I'll think on the motion.° *offer*
ZANCHE Do; I'll now detain you no longer. At your better leisure I'll tell you things shall startle your blood.
Nor blame me that this passion I reveal;
Lovers die inward that their flames° conceal. *passions*
FRANCISCO [*aside*] Of all intelligence,° this may prove the best. *information*
Sure I shall draw strange fowl from this foul nest. *Exeunt.*

[5.2]

Enter Marcello and Cornelia.

CORNELIA I hear a whispering all about the court
You are to fight. Who is your opposite?
What is the quarrel?
MARCELLO 'Tis an idle° rumor. *unfounded*
CORNELIA Will you dissemble? Sure you do not well
To fright me thus. You never look thus pale
But when you are most angry. I do charge you,

7. After Oedipus' two sons, Eteocles and Polynices, had slain one another in battle, the flames of their burning bodies on the funeral pyre refused to unite as though still unreconciled.
8. Like geese, marching one after another in single file, or like whores ("geese") serving as camp followers for an aristrocratic "progress," or state journey.
9. And bid Flamineo arm himself with a comparable sword so that we can fight a duel.
1. Zanche's dark complexion hides her blushes.
5.2. Padua.

Upon my blessing; nay, I'll call the Duke
And he shall school you.

MARCELLO Publish° not a fear *Proclaim*
Which would convert to laughter; 'tis not so.
[*He examines a crucifix hanging around her neck.*]
Was not this crucifix my father's?

CORNELIA Yes.

MARCELLO I have heard you say, giving° my brother suck, *when you were giving*
He took the crucifix between his hands

Enter Flamineo.

And broke a limb off.° *(thus desecrated it)*

CORNELIA Yes, but 'tis mended.

FLAMINEO I have brought your weapon back.° *(see 5.1.210–11)*
Flamineo runs Marcello through.

CORNELIA Ha! O my horror!

MARCELLO You have brought it home[1] indeed.

CORNELIA Help! Oh, he's murdered!

FLAMINEO Do you turn your gall up?[2] I'll to sanctuary,° *safe haven*
And send a surgeon to you. [*Exit.*]

Enter Carlo, Hortensio, [and] Pedro.

HORTENSIO How? O'th'ground?

MARCELLO Oh, mother, now remember what I told
Of breaking off the crucifix. Farewell!
There are some sins which heaven doth duly punish
In a whole family. This it is to rise
By all dishonest means. Let all men know
That tree shall long time keep a steady foot
Whose branches spread no wider than the root. [*He dies.*]

CORNELIA Oh, my perpetual sorrow!

HORTENSIO Virtuous Marcello!
He's dead. Pray leave him, lady. Come, you shall.

CORNELIA Alas, he is not dead. He's in a trance. Why, here's nobody shall get anything by his death. Let me call him again, for God's sake.

CARLO I would you were deceived.

CORNELIA Oh, you abuse° me, you abuse me, you abuse me. How many have gone away° thus for lack of tendance! Rear up's head, rear up's head! His bleeding inward will kill him. *deceive* *died*

HORTENSIO You see he is departed. [*They restrain her.*]

CORNELIA Let me come to him. Give me him as he is, if he be turned to earth;° let me but give him one hearty kiss, and you shall put us both into one coffin. Fetch a looking glass; see if his breath will not stain it, or pull out some feathers from my pillow and lay them to his lips. Will you lose him for a little painstaking? *dust*

HORTENSIO Your kindest office is to pray for him.

CORNELIA Alas! I would not pray for him yet. He may live to

1. (1) Back to its owner; (2) back to the family; (3) all the way in.
2. (1) So, you were angry, were you? (2) Are you yielding up your angry ghost? (3) Are you vomiting up blood and guts?

lay me i'th'ground and pray for me, if you'll let me come to him.

Enter Bracciano, all armed, save the beaver,° with Flamineo, [Francisco disguised as Mulinassar, a Page, attendants, and Lodovico disguised]. — *helmet and face-guard*

BRACCIANO Was this your handiwork?
FLAMINEO It was my misfortune.
CORNELIA He lies, he lies! He did not kill him; these have killed him, that would not let him be better looked to.
BRACCIANO Have comfort, my grieved mother.° — *mother-in-law*
CORNELIA Oh, you screech owl!
HORTENSIO Forbear, good madam.
CORNELIA Let me go, let me go!

She runs to Flamineo with her knife drawn, and, coming to him, lets it fall.

The God of heaven forgive thee! Dost not wonder
I pray for thee? I'll tell thee what's the reason:
I have scarce breath to number twenty minutes;
I'd not spend that in cursing. Fare thee well.
Half of thyself lies there; and mayst thou live
To fill an hourglass with his mouldered ashes,
To tell how thou shouldst spend the time to come
In blest repentance.
BRACCIANO Mother, pray tell me
How came he by his death? What was the quarrel?
CORNELIA Indeed, my younger boy° presumed too much — *(Marcello)*
Upon his manhood; gave him° bitter words; — *(Flamineo)*
Drew his sword first. And so, I know not how—
For I was out of my wits—he fell with 's head
Just in my bosom.
PAGE This is not true, madam.
CORNELIA I pray thee, peace.
One arrow's grazed[3] already; it were vain
T'lose this,° for that° will ne'er be sound again. — *(Flamineo) / (Marcello)*
BRACCIANO [*to attendants*] Go, bear the body to Cornelia's lodging;
And we command that none acquaint our duchess° — *(Vittoria)*
With this sad accident.° For° you, Flamineo, — *happening / As for*
Hark you, I will not grant your pardon.
FLAMINEO No?
BRACCIANO Only a lease of your life. And that shall last
But for one day. Thou shalt be forced each evening
To renew it, or be hanged.
FLAMINEO At your pleasure.

Lodovico sprinkles Bracciano's beaver with a poison.

Your will is law now; I'll not meddle with it.
BRACCIANO You once did brave° me in your sister's lodging;° — *defy / (see 4.2.53–73)*
I'll now keep you in awe for't. Where's our° beaver? — *my*
FRANCISCO [*aside*] He calls for his destruction.—Noble youth,° — *(Marcello)*
I pity thy sad fate. Now to the barriers.° — *(see 5.1.56)*

3. (1) Grassed, lost; (2) scratched, wounded (referring to Marcello). Cornelia does not want a second arrow shot after the lost one in an attempt to find it; hence the reason for her lie that Marcello struck first.

[*Aside*] This shall his passage to the black lake° further. — *Cocytus, i.e., hell*
The last good deed he did, he pardoned murther.° *Exeunt.* — *murder (for rhyme)*

[5.3]

Charges and shouts. They [the lords] fight at barriers;° first single pairs, then three to three. Enter Bracciano and Flamineo, with others [Vittoria, Giovanni, Francisco disguised as Mulinassar, and attendants]. — *(see 5.1.141–42)*

BRACCIANO An armorer! Ud's death, an armorer!
FLAMINEO Armorer! Where's the armorer?
BRACCIANO Tear off my beaver!
FLAMINEO Are you hurt, my lord?
BRACCIANO Oh, my brain's on fire.

Enter Armorer.

The helmet is poisoned.
ARMORER My lord, upon my soul—
BRACCIANO Away with him to torture!
[*Exit Armorer, guarded.*]
There are some great ones that have hand in this,
And near about me.
VITTORIA Oh, my loved lord! Poisoned?
FLAMINEO Remove the bar;[1] here's unfortunate revels.
Call the physicians.

Enter two Physicians.

A plague upon you!
We have too much of your cunning here already.
I fear the ambassadors are likewise poisoned.
BRACCIANO Oh, I am gone already. The infection
Flies to the brain and heart. O thou strong heart!
There's such a covenant 'tween the world and it,
They're loath to break.
GIOVANNI Oh, my most loved father!
BRACCIANO Remove the boy away.
Where's this good woman? [*To Vittoria*] Had I infinite worlds,
They were too little for thee. Must I leave thee?
What say yon screech owls?° Is the venom mortal? — *harbingers of death*
A PHYSICIAN Most deadly.
BRACCIANO Most corrupted politic hangman!
You kill without book,° but your art to save — *by rote*
Fails you as oft as great men's needy friends.[2]
I that have given life to offending slaves° — *wretched criminals*
And wretched murderers, have I not power
To lengthen mine own a twelvemonth?
[*To Vittoria*] Do not kiss me, for I shall poison thee.
This unction° is sent from the great Duke of Florence. — *unguent, salve*
FRANCISCO Sir, be of comfort.
BRACCIANO O thou soft natural death, that art joint-twin

5.3. Bracciano's palace, Padua.
1. The barriers, or possibly the helmet fastening.
2. As those whom great men have befriended in times of need.

To sweetest slumber, no rough-bearded° comet *fuzzy-tailed*
Stares on thy mild departure; the dull owl
Beats not against thy casement; the hoarse wolf
Scents not thy carrion. Pity winds thy corse,[3]
Whilst horror waits on° princes. *attends, serves*

VITTORIA I am lost forever.

BRACCIANO How miserable a thing it is to die
'Mongst women howling!

[*Enter Lodovico and Gasparo, in Capuchin robes.*]

What are those?

FLAMINEO Franciscans.[4]
They have brought the extreme unction.° *last rites*

BRACCIANO On pain of death, let no man name death to me!
It is a word infinitely terrible.
Withdraw into our cabinet.° *private chamber or tent*

Exeunt [*all*] *but Francisco and Flamineo.*

FLAMINEO To see what solitariness is about° dying princes! As heretofore they have unpeopled towns, divorced° friends, and made great houses unhospitable, so now, O justice,° where are their flatterers now? Flatterers are but the shadows of princes' bodies; the least thick cloud makes them invisible. *surrounding* / *separated* / *divine justice*

FRANCISCO There's great moan made for him.

FLAMINEO Faith, for some few hours salt water° will run most plentifully in every office o'th'court. But, believe it, most of them do but weep over their stepmothers' graves.[5] *salt tears*

FRANCISCO How mean you?

FLAMINEO Why, they dissemble, as some men do that live within compass o'th'verge.[6]

FRANCISCO Come, you have thrived well under him.

FLAMINEO Faith, like a wolf° in a woman's breast. I have been fed with poultry;[7] but for money, understand me, I had as good a will to cozen° him as e'er an officer of them all. But I had not cunning enough to do it. *cancer, tumor* / *hoodwink*

FRANCISCO What didst thou think of him? Faith, speak freely.

FLAMINEO He was a kind of statesman that would sooner have reckoned how many cannon bullets he had discharged against a town, to count his expense that way, than how many of his valiant and deserving subjects he lost before it.° *in front of the town*

FRANCISCO Oh, speak well of the Duke.

FLAMINEO I have done. Wilt hear some of my court wisdom?

Enter Lodovico [*disguised still as a Capuchin friar*].

To reprehend princes is dangerous, and to overcommend some of them is palpable lying.

FRANCISCO [*to Lodovico*] How is it with the Duke?

LODOVICO Most deadly ill.

3. Pity winds in grave-clothes the corpses of those commoners who die naturally.
4. Capuchin reformers were actually recognized by the papacy as having separated from the Franciscans in 1528, when they were made a distinct order.
5. Most such persons shed hypocritical tears, as they might for a hated stepmother.
6. Within twelve miles of the court. ("Some men" is a deliberate understatement.)
7. I.e, I've been paid in cheap commodities rather than money. Such foodstuffs could also be used as poultices applied to the afflicted part of the body in hopes that the cancer would feed on it instead of the patient's flesh. ("Poultry" may further suggest "paltry" and a slang term for a woman's breast.)

He's fall'n into a strange distraction.
He talks of battles and monopolies,
Levying of taxes, and from that descends
To the most brainsick language. His mind fastens
On twenty several° objects, which confound° — *various / mingle*
Deep sense with folly.° Such a fearful end — *distraction*
May teach some men that bear too lofty crest,
Though they live happiest, yet they die not best.
He hath conferred the whole state° of the dukedom — *possessions, power*
Upon your sister,° till the prince° arrive — *(Vittoria) / (Giovanni)*
At mature age.

FLAMINEO There's some good luck in that yet.

FRANCISCO See, here he comes.

Enter Bracciano, presented° in a bed; Vittoria and others [including Gasparo, disguised still as a Capuchin friar]. — *thrust onstage*

There's death in's face already.

VITTORIA Oh, my good lord!

BRACCIANO Away! You have abused° me. — *deceived*

These speeches are several kinds of distractions, and in the action should appear so.

You have conveyed coin forth our territories,
Bought and sold offices, oppressed the poor—
And I ne'er dreamt on't. Make up your accounts;
I'll now be mine own steward.

FLAMINEO Sir, have patience.

BRACCIANO Indeed I am too° blame. — *too much to*
For did you ever hear the dusky raven
Chide blackness? Or was't ever known the devil
Railed against cloven creatures?

VITTORIA Oh, my lord!

BRACCIANO Let me have some quails° to supper. — *a delicacy*

FLAMINEO Sir, you shall.

BRACCIANO No; some fried dogfish.° Your quails feed on poison. — *inferior fare*
That old dog-fox,° that politician Florence°— — *male fox / Francisco*
I'll forswear hunting and turn dog-killer;
Rare!°— — *Excellent!*
I'll be friends with him, for mark you, sir, one dog
Still° sets another a-barking. Peace, peace! — *Continually*
Yonder's a fine slave° come in now. — *rascal; menial*

FLAMINEO Where?

BRACCIANO Why, there,
In a blue bonnet, and a pair of breeches
With a great codpiece. Ha, ha, ha!
Look you, his codpiece is stuck full of pins
With pearls o'th'head of them.[8] Do not you know him?

FLAMINEO No, my lord.

BRACCIANO Why, 'tis the devil.
I know him by a great rose° he wears on's shoe — *rosette, ribbon*
To hide his cloven foot. I'll dispute with him.
He's a rare linguist.° — *great talker*

8. The baggy appendages for genitals on courtiers' breeches could be extravagantly decorated.

VITTORIA My lord, here's nothing.
BRACCIANO Nothing? Rare! Nothing? When I want money,
Our treasury is empty; there is nothing.
I'll not be used° thus. *treated*
VITTORIA Oh, lie still, my lord.
BRACCIANO See, see, Flamineo, that killed his brother,
Is dancing on the ropes° there, and he carries *tightropes*
A money-bag in each hand to keep him even,° *evenly balanced*
For fear of breaking 's neck. And there's a lawyer,
In a gown whipped° with velvet, stares and gapes *trimmed, edged*
When° the money will fall.[9] How the rogue cuts capers! *To see when*
It should have been in a halter.° *noose*
'Tis there!—What's she?
FLAMINEO Vittoria, my lord.
BRACCIANO Ha, ha, ha! Her hair is sprinkled with arras powder,° that makes her look as if she had sinned in the pastry.°—What's he? *scented hair-powder* *place to make pastry*
FLAMINEO A divine,° my lord. *clergyman*
BRACCIANO He will be drunk. Avoid him; th'argument° is fearful when churchmen stagger° in't. *subject* *waver, totter*
Look you: six gray rats that have lost their tails[1]
Crawl up the pillow. Send for a rat-catcher.
I'll do a miracle: I'll free the court
From all foul vermin. Where's Flamineo?
FLAMINEO [*aside*] I do not like that he names me so often,
Especially on's deathbed; 'tis a sign
I shall not live long. See, he's near his end.
Bracciano seems here near his end. Lodovico and Gasparo, in the habit of Capuchins, present him in his bed with a crucifix and hallowed candle.
LODOVICO Pray give us leave. *Attende, Domine Bracciane*°— *Listen, Lord Bracciano*
FLAMINEO See, see, how firmly he doth fix his eye
Upon the crucifix!
VITTORIA Oh, hold it constant.
It settles his wild spirits; and so his eyes
Melt into tears.
LODOVICO (*by the crucifix*) *Domine Bracciane, solebas in bello tutus esse tuo clypeo; nunc hunc clypeum hosti tuo opponas infernali.*
GASPARO (*by the hallowed taper*) *Olim hasta valuisti in bello; nunc hanc sacram hastam vibrabis contra hostem animarum.*
LODOVICO *Attende, Domine Bracciane: si nunc quoque probas ea quae acta sunt inter nos, flecte caput in dextrum.*
GASPARO *Esto securus, Domine Bracciane; cogita quantum habeas meritorum denique memineris meam animam pro tua oppignoratem si quid esset periculi.*
LODOVICO *Si nunc quoque probas ea quae acta sunt inter nos, flecte caput in laevum.*[2]

9. (1) Fall from Flamineo's hands; (2) become unclaimed at the owner's death.
1. It was commonly believed that witches could turn themselves into rats, but not completely: they would still lack tails.
2. LODOVICO Lord Bracciano, you were accustomed in battle to being guarded by your shield; now you will oppose this shield (the crucifix) against your infernal enemy (the devil).
GASPARO Formerly you prevailed in battle with your spear; now you will wield this holy spear (the hallowed taper) against the enemy of souls.
LODOVICO Listen, Lord Bracciano: if now you approve these things that have been enacted between us, turn your head to the right.
GASPARO Rest assured, Lord Bracciano; think how

He is departing. Pray stand all apart,
And let us only whisper in his ears
Some private meditations, which our order
Permits you not to hear.

Here the rest being departed, Lodovico and Gasparo discover° themselves. — *reveal*

GASPARO Bracciano!
LODOVICO Devil Bracciano! Thou art damned.
GASPARO Perpetually.
LODOVICO A slave° condemned and given up to the gallows — *villain*
Is thy great lord and master.° — *Is better off than you*
GASPARO True, for thou
Art given up to the devil.
LODOVICO Oh, you slave!
You that were held the famous politician;
Whose art was poison.
GASPARO And whose conscience,° murder. — *inmost thoughts*
LODOVICO That would have broke your wife's neck down the stairs
Ere she was poisoned.
GASPARO That had your villainous sallets°— — *poisonous plants; salads*
LODOVICO And fine embroidered bottles,[3] and perfumes
Equally mortal with° a winter plague. — *Just as deadly as*
GASPARO Now there's mercury—
LODOVICO And copperas°— — *copper sulfate*
GASPARO And quicksilver°— — *mercury*
LODOVICO With other devilish pothecary stuff
A-melting in your politic brains. Dost hear?
GASPARO This is Count Lodovico.
LODOVICO This, Gasparo.
And thou shalt die like a poor rogue.
GASPARO And stink
Like a dead flyblown° dog. — *maggot-infested*
LODOVICO And be forgotten before thy funeral sermon.
BRACCIANO [*calling*] Vittoria! Vittoria!
LODOVICO Oh, the cursèd devil,
Come to himself again! We are undone.

Enter Vittoria and the attendants.

GASPARO [*aside to Lodovico*] Strangle him in private.
[*Aloud*] What? Will you call him again
To live in treble torments? For charity,
For Christian charity, avoid° the chamber. — *leave, empty*

[*Exeunt Vittoria and the attendants.*]

LODOVICO You would prate, sir. This is a truelove knot[4]
Sent from the Duke of Florence. *Bracciano is strangled.*
GASPARO What, is it done?
LODOVICO The snuff° is out. No woman-keeper° i'th'world, — *candlewick / nurse*

---

many good deeds you have done and finally remember that my soul is pledged to yours if there should be any spiritual peril.
LODOVICO If now you also approve these things that have been enacted between us, turn your head to the left.

3. Decorated bottles containing poison.
4. Knot or bow of ribbon betokening a binding oath of love; here sardonically applied to a tourniquet for strangulation.

Though she had practiced seven year at the pesthouse,° *plague hospital*
Could have done't quaintlier.° *more ingenious*ly

[*Enter Vittoria, Francisco still disguised, Flamineo, and attendants.*]

My lords, he's dead.

OMNES Rest to his soul!
VITTORIA Oh, me! This place is hell.

Exit Vittoria [*followed by attendants and Gasparo.*[5] *Lodovico, Francisco, and Flamineo remain onstage*].

FRANCISCO How heavily she takes it!
FLAMINEO Oh, yes, yes;
Had women navigable rivers in their eyes
They would dispend° them all. Surely I wonder *expend*
Why we should wish more rivers to the city,[6]
When they sell water so good cheap.° I'll tell thee, *so cheaply*
These are but moonish° shades of griefs or fears; *changeable, fickle*
There's nothing sooner dry than women's tears.
Why, here's an end of all my harvest; he has given me nothing.
Court promises! Let wise men count them° curst, *themselves*
For while you live he that scores° best pays worst. *runs up a debt*
FRANCISCO Sure, this was Florence'° doing. *Francisco's*
FLAMINEO Very likely.
Those are found weighty strokes which come from th'hand,
But those are killing strokes which come from th'head.[7]
Oh, the rare tricks of a Machiavellian!
He doth not come like a gross, plodding slave
And buffet you to death. No, my quaint° knave, *crafty*
He tickles you to death, makes you die laughing,
As if you had swallowed down a pound of saffron.[8]
You see the feat;° 'tis practiced in a trice *trick*
To teach court honesty it jumps on ice.[9]
FRANCISCO Now have the people liberty to talk
And descant° on his vices. *sing, discourse*
FLAMINEO Misery of princes,
That must of force° be censured by their slaves,° *necessarily / inferiors*
Not only blamed for doing things are ill° *that are evil*
But for not doing all that all men will!° *wish them to do*
One were better be a thresher.° *lowly farmworker*
Ud's death, I would fain speak with this duke yet.
FRANCISCO Now he's dead?
FLAMINEO I cannot conjure;° but if prayers or oaths *raise his ghost*
Will get to th'speech of him, though forty devils
Wait° on him in his livery of flames, *Attend*
I'll speak to him, and shake him by the hand,

5. Gasparo, as one of the conspirators, might remain onstage also, but he has no part to play in the rest of the scene.
6. An allusion to a new water supply project for London, authorized in 1606 and completed in 1613.
7. I.e., Brute force is painfully heavy, but the truly lethal strikes are devised by cunning—the method Francisco prefers.
8. Saffron was thought to make a person merry in small doses; a huge amount might induce laughter even as it killed.
9. To teach hypocritical courtiers that they are skating on thin ice.

Though I be blasted.° *Exit Flamineo.* *struck down*

FRANCISCO Excellent Lodovico!

What, did you terrify him at the last gasp?

LODOVICO Yes, and so idly° that the Duke had like *ineffectually*

T'have° terrified us. *the Duke nearly*

FRANCISCO How?

Enter [Zanche] the Moor.

LODOVICO You shall hear that hereafter.

[*Aside to Francisco*] See! Yon's the infernal° that would *demon*

make us sport.° *i.e., have sex*

Now to the revelation of that secret

She promised when she fell in love with you.° *(see 5.1.227–30)*

FRANCISCO [*to Zanche*] You're passionately met in this sad world.

ZANCHE I would have you look up,° sir; these court tears *look cheerful*

Claim not your tribute to them.[1] Let those weep

That guiltily partake in the sad cause.° *Who are responsible*

I knew last night, by a sad dream I had,

Some mischief would ensue; yet to say truth

My dream most concerned you.

LODOVICO [*aside to Francisco*] Shall 's° fall a-dreaming? *Shall we*

FRANCISCO [*aside to Lodovico*] Yes, and for fashion° sake I'll *fashion's, form's*

dream with her.

ZANCHE Methought, sir, you came stealing to my bed.

FRANCISCO Wilt thou believe me, sweeting?° By this light, *sweetheart*

I was a-dreamt on thee too, for methought

I saw thee naked.

ZANCHE Fie, sir! As I told you,

Methought you lay down by me.

FRANCISCO So dreamt I;

And, lest thou shouldst take cold, I covered thee

With this Irish mantle.[2]

ZANCHE Verily, I did dream

You were somewhat bold with me; but to come to't.[3]

LODOVICO How? How? I hope you will not go to't° here. *i.e., have sex*

FRANCISCO Nay, you must hear my dream out.

ZANCHE Well, sir, forth.

FRANCISCO When I threw the mantle o'er thee, thou didst laugh

Exceedingly, methought.

ZANCHE Laugh?

FRANCISCO And cried'st out,

The hair did tickle thee.

ZANCHE There was a dream indeed.

LODOVICO Mark her, I prithee; she simpers like the suds

A collier hath been washed in.

ZANCHE Come, sir; good fortune tends you; I did tell you

I would reveal a secret. Isabella,

The Duke of Florence' sister, was empoisoned

By a 'fumed° picture; and Camillo's neck *perfumed*

1. You have no call to join in this show of tears merely for appearance's sake (at the death of Bracciano).
2. Irish peasants often wore plaid mantles with nothing beneath.
3. But to come to the point (and, implicitly, to sex).

Was broke by damned Flamineo, the mischance° *blame for the incident*
Laid on a vaulting horse.

FRANCISCO Most strange!

ZANCHE Most true.

LODOVICO The bed° of snakes is broke. *nest, knot*

ZANCHE I sadly do confess I had a hand
In the black deed.

FRANCISCO Thou kept'st their counsel.° *secret*

ZANCHE Right,
For which, urged with contrition, I intend
This night to rob Vittoria.

LODOVICO Excellent penitence!
Usurers dream on't while they sleep out sermons.[4]

ZANCHE To further our escape, I have entreated
Leave to retire me, till the funeral,
Unto a friend i'th'country. That excuse
Will further our escape. In coin and jewels
I shall, at least, make good unto your use
An hundred thousand crowns.

FRANCISCO Oh, noble wench!

LODOVICO Those crowns we'll share.

ZANCHE It is a dowry,
Methinks, should make that sunburnt proverb false,
And wash the Ethiop white.[5]

FRANCISCO It shall. Away!

ZANCHE Be ready for our flight.

FRANCISCO An hour 'fore day.

Exit [Zanche] the Moor.

Oh, strange discovery! Why, till now we knew not
The circumstance of either of their deaths.

Enter [Zanche the] Moor.

ZANCHE You'll wait about midnight in the chapel?

FRANCISCO There.

[Exit Zanche.]

LODOVICO Why, now our action's justified.

FRANCISCO Tush for justice!
What harms it° justice? We now, like the partridge, *What harm does it do*
Purge the disease with laurel; for the fame
Shall crown the enterprise and quit the shame.[6] *Exeunt.*

[5.4]

Enter Flamineo and Gasparo at one door; another way,° Giovanni, attended. *at another door*

GASPARO The young duke. Did you e'er see a sweeter prince?

FLAMINEO I have known a poor woman's bastard better favored.° *better looking*

4. Usurers might dream such a dream of false penitence, still filled with images of wealth. (Jews, traditional practitioners of usury, were required to attend Christian services.)

5. And wash clean my soul, despite my dark skin. ("To wash an Ethiop white" is proverbial for an impossible task.)

6. We will now purge ourselves of the shame of this deed by feasting on the laurel wreath of honorable fame (according to the Roman scholar Pliny, the laurel was a medical purgative used by some birds); for the honorable cause will glorify this deed and justify (as in paying off a debt) the shameful means.

5.4. Bracciano's palace still.

This is behind him.° Now, to his face all comparisons were — *said behind his back*
hateful.° Wise was the courtly peacock that, being a great — *would be odious*
minion° and being compared for beauty by some dotterels° — *favorite / dotards*
that stood by to the kingly eagle, said the eagle was a far
fairer bird than herself, not in respect of her feathers but in
respect of her long talons.° His will grow out in time. [*To* — *sharp claws*
Giovanni] My gracious lord!

GIOVANNI I pray, leave me, sir.

FLAMINEO Your Grace must be merry. 'Tis I have cause to
mourn, for wot you° what said the little boy that rode behind — *do you know*
his father on horseback?

GIOVANNI Why, what said he?

FLAMINEO "When you are dead, father," said he, "I hope then
I shall ride in the saddle." Oh, 'tis a brave° thing for a man — *fine*
to sit by himself! He may stretch himself in the stirrups, look
about, and see the whole compass of the hemisphere. You're
now, my lord, i'th'saddle.

GIOVANNI Study your prayers, sir, and be penitent.
'Twere fit you'd think on what hath former been;° — *on your former sins*
I have heard grief named the eldest child° of sin. — *the consequence*

Exit Giovanni [*and all except Flamineo*].

FLAMINEO Study my prayers? He threatens me divinely.° I am — *like a priest*
falling to pieces already. I care not, though, like Anacharsis
I were pounded to death in a mortar.[1] And yet that death
were fitter for usurers' gold and themselves° to be beaten — *(the usurers)*
together, to make a most cordial cullis° for the devil. — *reviving broth*
He hath his uncle's villainous look already,

Enter Courtier.

In *decimo-sexto*.°—Now, sir, what are you? — *a small-sized book*

COURTIER It is the pleasure, sir, of the young duke
That you forbear the presence° and all rooms — *the throne room*
That owe him reverence.

FLAMINEO So, the wolf and the raven
Are very pretty fools° when they are young. — *innocents*
Is it your office, sir, to keep me out?

COURTIER So the Duke wills.

FLAMINEO Verily, Master Courtier, extremity° is not to be — *extreme rigor*
used in all offices. Say that a gentlewoman were taken out
of her bed about midnight and committed to Castle Angelo,° — *San Angelo (in Rome)*
to the tower yonder, with nothing about her but her smock;° — *petticoat*
would it not show a cruel part in the gentleman porter to lay
claim to her upper garment, pull it o'er her head and ears,
and put her in naked?

COURTIER Very good; you are merry. [*Exit.*]

FLAMINEO Doth he make a court ejectment of me? A flaming
firebrand casts more smoke without° a chimney than — *outside*
within't. I'll smoor° some of them. — *suffocate*

Enter [*Francisco, Duke of*] *Florence* [*disguised as Mulinassar*].

1. Following his source (Montreux's *Honor's Academy*), Webster confuses Anacharsis, a Thracian prince in the sixth century B.C.E. who was renowned for his wisdom, with Anaxarchus, a philosopher in the time of Alexander the Great who was pounded to death in a mortar for having insulted Nicocreon, tyrant of Cyprus.

How now? Thou art sad.
FRANCISCO I met even now with the most pitious sight.
FLAMINEO Thou met'st another here: a pitiful
Degraded° courtier. *Demoted, debased*
FRANCISCO Your reverend mother
Is grown a very old woman in two hours.
I found them winding of° Marcello's corse;° *wrapping / corpse*
And there is such a solemn melody
'Tween doleful songs, tears, and sad elegies—
Such as old grandams, watching° by the dead, *keeping vigil*
Were wont t'outwear the nights with—that, believe me,
I had no eyes to guide me forth the room,
They were so o'ercharged with water.
FLAMINEO I will see them.° *(the mourning women)*
FRANCISCO 'Twere much uncharity in you; for your sight° *the sight of you*
Will add unto their tears.
FLAMINEO I will see them.
They are behind the traverse.° I'll discover° *curtain / reveal*
Their superstitious howling.

[*Flamineo pulls back a curtain.*] *Cornelia,* [*Zanche*] *the Moor, and three other Ladies discovered, winding Marcello's corse. A song.*

CORNELIA This rosemary° is withered. Pray get fresh; *a token of remembrance*
I would have these herbs grow up in his grave
When I am dead and rotten. Reach the bays.° *laurel wreaths*
I'll tie a garland here about his head;
'Twill keep my boy from lightning.[2] This sheet° *shroud*
I have kept this twenty year, and every day
Hallowed it with my prayers. I did not think
He should have wore it.
ZANCHE [*seeing Flamineo and Francisco*] Look you who are yonder.
CORNELIA Oh, reach me the flowers.
ZANCHE [*to the Ladies*] Her Ladyship's foolish.
LADY Alas! her grief
Hath turned her child again.
CORNELIA You're very welcome.
(*To Flamineo*) There's rosemary for you, [*to Francisco*] and rue° for you, *a bitter herb of sorrow*
[*To another*] Heartsease° for you. I pray, make much of it. *Pansy; ease of mind*
I have left more for myself.
FRANCISCO [*indicating Flamineo*] Lady, who's this?
CORNELIA You are, I take it, the grave-maker.
FLAMINEO So.
ZANCHE 'Tis Flamineo.
CORNELIA Will you make me such a fool? Here's a white hand.
Cornelia doth this in several forms of distraction.
Can blood so soon be washed out? Let me see:
When screech owls croak upon the chimney-tops,
And the strange cricket i'th'oven sings and hops,

2. The laurel wreath was used to crown a conqueror or poet. The Roman scholar Pliny reports that it would also protect against lightning.

When yellow spots do on your hands appear,
Be certain then you of a corse shall hear.
Out upon't, how 'tis speckled! He's handled a toad, sure.
Cowslip water is good for the memory; pray buy me three ounces of't.

FLAMINEO [*aside*] I would I were from hence.

CORNELIA Do you hear, sir? I'll give you a saying which my grandmother was wont, when she heard the bell toll, to sing o'er unto her lute.

FLAMINEO Do, an you will; do.

CORNELIA Call for the robin redbreast and the wren,
Since o'er shady groves they hover,
And with leaves and flow'rs do cover
The friendless bodies of unburied men.
Call unto his funeral dole° *funeral rites*
The ant, the field mouse, and the mole
To rear him hillocks, that shall keep him warm,
And (when gay° tombs are robbed) sustain no harm; *elaborate, festooned*
But keep the wolf far thence, that's foe to men,
For with his nails he'll dig them up again.
They would not bury him, 'cause he died in a quarrel,
But I have an answer for them:
Let holy church receive him duly
Since he paid the church tithes truly.
His wealth is summed,° and this is all his store. *reckoned*
This poor men get,° and great men get no more. *The poor get a grave*
Now the wares are gone, we may shut up shop.
Bless you all, good people. [*The curtain is closed;*]
exeunt Cornelia, [*Zanche,*] *and Ladies.*

FLAMINEO I have a strange thing in me, to th'which
I cannot give a name, without it be° *unless it be*
Compassion. I pray, leave me. *Exit Francisco.*
This night I'll know the utmost of my fate;
I'll be resolved° what my rich sister means *assured*
T'assign me for my service. I have lived
Riotously ill, like some that live in court,
And sometimes, when my face was full of smiles,
Have felt the maze° of conscience in my breast. *daze; twinge*
Oft gay and honored robes those tortures try.[3]
We think caged birds sing, when indeed they cry.

Enter Bracciano's ghost, in his leather cassock° and breeches, boots, [*and*] *a cowl,°* [*carrying*] *a pot of lily-flowers with a skull in't.* *soldier's long coat* *friar's hood*

Ha! I can stand° thee. Nearer, nearer yet. *withstand*
What a mockery hath death made of thee! Thou look'st sad.
In what place art thou? In yon starry gallery,
Or in the cursèd dungeon?° No? Not speak? *Or in hell?*
Pray, sir, resolve me, what religion's best
For a man to die in? Or is it in your knowledge
To answer me how long I have to live?
That's the most necessary question.
Not answer? Are you still like some great men

3. Great men, for all their finery, must suffer these same twinges of conscience.

That only walk like shadows, up and down,
And to no purpose? Say—
The ghost throws earth upon him and shows him the skull.
What's that? Oh, fatal! He throws earth upon me.
A dead man's skull beneath the roots of flowers!—
I pray speak, sir. Our Italian churchmen
Make us believe dead men hold conference
With their familiars,[4] and many times
Will come to bed to them, and eat with them. *Exit ghost.*
He's gone; and see, the skull and earth are vanished.
This is beyond melancholy.[5] I do dare my fate
To do its worst. Now to my sister's lodging,
And sum up all these horrors: the disgrace
The Prince threw on me;° next, the piteous sight *(see 5.4.10–22)*
Of my dead brother; and my mother's dotage;
And last this terrible vision. All these
Shall with Vittoria's bounty° turn to good, *financial help*
Or I will drown this weapon in her blood. *Exit.*

[5.5]

Enter Francisco [and] Lodovico, and [overhearing them as he stands apart] Hortensio.

LODOVICO My lord, upon my soul you shall no further.
You have most ridiculously engaged yourself
Too far already. For my part, I have paid
All my debts, so if I should chance to fall,
My creditors fall not with me; and I vow
To quite° all in this bold assembly *requite, repay*
To° the meanest° follower. My lord, leave the city, *Right down to / lowest*
Or I'll forswear° the murder. *forswear my promise in*
FRANCISCO Farewell, Lodovico.
If thou dost perish in this glorious act,
I'll rear unto thy memory that fame
Shall° in the ashes keep alive thy name. *Which shall*
[Exeunt Francisco and Lodovico in separate directions.]
HORTENSIO There's some black deed on foot. I'll presently° *at once*
Down to the citadel and raise some force.° *levy troops*
These strong court factions that do brook no checks° *tolerate no opposition*
In the career° oft break the riders' necks. *[Exit.]* *full gallop*

[5.6]

Enter Vittoria with a book in her hand, Zanche, [and] Flamineo following them.

FLAMINEO What, are you at your prayers? Give o'er.° *Cease*
VITTORIA How, ruffin?° *devil; ruffian*

4. (1) Familiar friends; (2) familiar spirits, demons. (Having sex with such demons was a heinous sin; see next line.)
5. (1) This is more than simply a figment of my disordered imagination; (2) this is close to madness and despair.
5.5. Bracciano's palace still.
5.6. Vittoria's lodging in the palace; see 5.4.144.

FLAMINEO I come to you 'bout worldly business.
Sit down, sit down. [*To Zanche*] Nay, stay, blowze,° you may hear it. (*fat, red-faced wench*)
The doors are fast° enough. (*secure*)

VITTORIA Ha, are you drunk?

FLAMINEO Yes, yes, with wormwood° water. You shall taste (*bitter-tasting*)
Some of it presently.

VITTORIA What intends° the fury? (*signifies*)

FLAMINEO You are my lord's° executrix, and I claim (*(Bracciano's)*)
Reward for my long service.

VITTORIA For your service?

FLAMINEO Come, therefore. Here is pen and ink; set down
What you will give me. *She writes.*

VITTORIA There.

FLAMINEO Ha! Have you done already?
'Tis a most short conveyance.° (*deed of tranfer*)

VITTORIA I will read it.
[*She reads.*] "I give that portion to thee, and no other,
Which Cain groaned under, having slain his brother."[1]

FLAMINEO A most courtly patent° to beg by. (*license*)

VITTORIA You are a villain.

FLAMINEO Is't come to this? They say affrights cure agues.° (*fevers and chills*)
Thou hast a devil in thee; I will try
If I can scare him from thee. Nay, sit still.
My lord hath left me yet two case° of jewels (*pairs*)
Shall make me scorn your bounty; you shall see them.
[*Exit.*]

VITTORIA Sure he's distracted.

ZANCHE Oh, he's desperate.
For your own safety, give him gentle language.

He enter with two [pairs] of pistols.

FLAMINEO Look, these are better far at a dead lift° (*in a tight corner*)
Than all your jewel-house.

VITTORIA And yet, methinks,
These stones° have no fair luster; they are ill set. (*jewels; cannon shot*)

FLAMINEO I'll turn the right side towards you; you shall see
How they will sparkle.° [*He brandishes the pistols.*] (*i.e., explode*)

VITTORIA Turn this horror from me.
What do you want? What would you have me do?
Is not all mine yours? Have I any children?° (*i.e., heirs*)

FLAMINEO Pray thee, good woman, do not trouble me
With this vain worldly business. Say your prayers;
I made a vow to my deceasèd lord,
Neither yourself nor I should outlive him
The numb'ring of four hours.

VITTORIA Did he enjoin° it? (*require*)

FLAMINEO He did, and 'twas a deadly jealousy
Lest any should enjoy thee after him;
That urged him vow me to it. For° my death, (*As for*)
I did propound it voluntarily, knowing

1. Cain's killing of his brother, Abel, following the expulsion of their parents, Adam and Eve, from Paradise, was the first murder in human history, as recorded in Genesis 4.

If he could not be safe in his own court,
Being a great duke, what hope then for us?

VITTORIA This is your melancholy and despair.

FLAMINEO Away!
Fool thou art to think that politicians
Do use° to kill the effects of injuries — *make it a practice*
And let the cause live. Shall we groan in irons,
Or be a shameful and a weighty burden
To a public scaffold? This is my resolve:
I would not live at any man's entreaty,
Nor die at any's bidding.

VITTORIA Will you hear me?

FLAMINEO My life hath done service to other men;
My death shall serve mine own turn. Make you ready.

VITTORIA Do you mean to die indeed?

FLAMINEO With as much pleasure
As e'er my father gat° me. — *begot*

VITTORIA [*aside to Zanche*] Are the doors locked?

ZANCHE [*aside to Vittoria*] Yes, madam.

VITTORIA Are you grown an atheist? Will you turn your body,
Which is the goodly palace of the soul,
To the soul's slaughterhouse? Oh, the cursèd devil,
Which doth present us with all other sins
Thrice candied o'er, despair with gall and stibium,° — *a poison*
Yet we carouse it off[2]—[*Aside to Zanche*] Cry out for help!—
[*Aloud*] Makes us forsake that which was made for man,
The world, to sink to that was made for devils,
Eternal darkness.

ZANCHE [*calling out*] Help, help!

FLAMINEO I'll stop your throat
With winter plums.° — *a hard, bitter fruit*

VITTORIA I prithee, yet remember,
Millions are now in graves which at last day° — *Judgment Day*
Like mandrakes° shall rise shrieking. — *(see 3.1.52 n)*

FLAMINEO Leave your prating,
For these are but grammatical° laments, — *formulaic*
Feminine arguments, and they move me
As some in pulpits move their auditory° — *congregation*
More with their exclamation° than sense — *loud oratory*
Of reason or sound doctrine.

ZANCHE [*aside to Vittoria*] Gentle madam,
Seem to consent; only, persuade him teach
The way to death. Let him die first.

VITTORIA [*aside to Zanche*] 'Tis good, I apprehend it.° — *I grasp your meaning*
[*Aloud*] To kill oneself is meat that we must take
Like pills: not chew't, but quickly swallow it.
The smart o'th'wound or weakness of the hand
May else bring treble torments.

FLAMINEO I have held it
A wretched and most miserable life

2. The cursed devil, who sugarcoats all other sins for us, prompts us to drink down the poison of despair in all its bitterness.

Which is not able to die.
VITTORIA Oh, but frailty!
Yet I am now resolved. Farewell, affliction!
Behold, Bracciano, I, that while you lived
Did make a flaming altar of my heart
To sacrifice unto you, now am ready
To sacrifice heart and all. Farewell, Zanche!
ZANCHE How, madam! Do you think that I'll outlive you?
Especially when my best self, Flamineo,
Goes the same voyage?
FLAMINEO O most lovèd Moor!
ZANCHE Only, by all my love, let me entreat you—
Since it is most necessary none of us
Do violence on ourselves°—let you or I *suicide is unnatural*
Be her sad taster:[3] teach her how to die.
FLAMINEO Thou dost instruct me nobly. Take these pistols.
Because my hand is stained with blood already,
Two of these you shall level° at my breast, *aim*
Th'other 'gainst your own; and so we'll die,
Most equally contented. But first swear
Not to outlive me.
VITTORIA *and* ZANCHE Most religiously.
FLAMINEO Then here's an end of me. Farewell, daylight!
And O contemptible physic,° that dost take *medicine*
So long a study only to preserve
So short a life, I take my leave of thee.
These are two cupping-glasses[4] that shall draw
All my infected blood out.
[*He shows the pistols and hands them over.*]
Are you ready?
VITTORIA *and* ZANCHE Ready.
FLAMINEO Whither shall I go now? O Lucian, thy ridiculous purgatory, to find Alexander the Great cobbling shoes, Pompey tagging points, and Julius Caesar making hair buttons, Hannibal selling blacking, and Augustus crying garlic, Charlemagne selling lists by the dozen, and King Pippin crying apples in a cart drawn with one horse?[5]
Whether I resolve° to fire, earth, water, air, *dissolve*
Or all the elements by scruples,° I know not *by little bits of each*
Nor greatly care. Shoot, shoot!
Of all deaths, the violent death is best,
For from ourselves it steals ourselves so fast,
The pain once apprehended is quite past.
They shoot and run to him and tread upon him.
VITTORIA What, are you dropped?

3. Go first, like the taster who sampled the food before the King to ensure that it was free of poison.
4. Openmouthed glass vessels applied to the skin in drawing blood; heat was used to create a vacuum.
5. The Greek satirist Lucian (line 109), in his *Menippos* (second century C.E.), sardonically describes just such an absurd view of the afterlife. Tagging points (line 111) is fixing metal tags onto laces to be used in fastening clothes together; hair buttons (line 111) are buttons made of hair; blacking (line 112) is lampblack for boots; to "cry" garlic (line 112) is to hawk or sell it; lists (line 113) are cloth garters. Alexander the Great (356–323 B.C.E.) conquered the known world as King of Macedon; Pompey the Great (106–48 B.C.E.), Julius Caesar (100–44 B.C.E.), and Augustus (63 B.C.E.–14 C.E.) were important statesmen and conquerors in the days of the Roman Republic and Empire; Hannibal (247–183 B.C.E.) was a Carthaginian general who warred with Rome; Charlemagne (742–814) was a Frankish king and emperor of the West; King Pippin refers to Pepin III, King of the Franks (d. 768); his name puns here on the "pippins," or apples, he sells.

FLAMINEO I am mixed with earth already. As you are noble,
Perform your vows and bravely follow me.
VITTORIA Whither? To hell?
ZANCHE To most assured damnation.
VITTORIA Oh, thou most cursèd devil!
ZANCHE Thou art caught—
VITTORIA In thine own engine.° I tread the fire out *contrivance, trap*
That would have been my ruin.
FLAMINEO Will you be perjured? What a religious oath was Styx, that the gods never durst swear by and violate?[6] Oh, that we had such an oath to minister,° and to be so well kept in our courts of justice! *administer*
VITTORIA Think whither thou art going.
ZANCHE And remember
What villainies thou hast acted.
VITTORIA This thy death
Shall make me like a blazing ominous star.° *comet (an omen)*
Look up and tremble.
FLAMINEO Oh, I am caught with a springe!° *snare, trap*
VITTORIA You see the fox comes many times short home;[7]
'Tis here proved true.
FLAMINEO Killed with° a couple of braches!° *by / bitches*
VITTORIA No° fitter off'ring for the infernal Furies *There can be no*
Than one in whom they reigned while he was living.
FLAMINEO Oh, the way's dark and horrid! I cannot see.
Shall I have no company?
VITTORIA Oh, yes; thy sins
Do run before thee to fetch fire from hell,
To light thee thither.
FLAMINEO Oh, I smell soot,
Most stinking soot! The chimney is afire;
My liver's parboiled, like Scotch holy bread.° *boiled sheep's liver*
There's a plumber laying pipes in my guts; it scalds.
Wilt thou outlive me?
ZANCHE Yes, and drive a stake
Through thy body; for we'll give it out
Thou didst this violence upon thyself.[8]
FLAMINEO Oh, cunning devils! Now I have tried° your love, *tested*
And doubled° all your reaches.° I am not wounded. *proved equal to / plots*
Flamineo riseth.
The pistols held no bullets. 'Twas a plot
To prove° your kindness° to me, and I live *test / natural affection*
To punish your ingratitude. I knew
One time or other you would find a way
To give me a strong potion.°—O men *poison*
That lie upon your deathbeds and are haunted
With howling wives: ne'er trust them; they'll remarry
Ere the worm pierce your winding-sheet, ere the spider
Make a thin curtain for your epitaphs.[9]
How cunning you were to discharge! Do you practice at the

6. Iris carried water from the river Styx of Hades to Olympus as witness of the gods' oaths.
7. Even the crafty fox sometimes comes back to his lair without his prey or having left part of his body (a foot, tail) in the snare.
8. Suicides were buried at crossroads with a stake through the heart.
9. A spiderweb over the epitaph carved on a gravestone would serve in place of the curtains customarily hung in front of paintings.

Artillery Yard?[1] Trust a woman? Never, never. Bracciano, be my precedent. We lay our souls to pawn to the devil for a little pleasure, and a woman makes the bill of sale. That ever man should marry! For one Hypermnestra that saved her lord and husband, forty-nine of her sisters cut their husbands' throats all in one night.[2] There was a shoal of virtuous horse-leeches!° Here are two other instruments. *bloodsuckers*

[*He points his second pair of pistols.*]

VITTORIA Help, help!

Enter Lodovico [and] Gasparo [disguised as Capuchins], Pedro, [and] Carlo [all with drawn swords].

FLAMINEO What noise is that? Hah! False keys i'th'court?[3]

[*He is overpowered and disarmed.*]

LODOVICO We have brought you a masque.[4]

FLAMINEO A matachin,° it seems, *sword dance*
By your drawn swords. Churchmen turned revelers?

CONSPIRATORS Isabella, Isabella![5]

[*They remove their disguises.*]

LODOVICO Do you know us now?

FLAMINEO Lodovico and Gasparo!

LODOVICO Yes, and that Moor the Duke gave pension to
Was the great Duke of Florence.° *(see 5.1.46–47)*

VITTORIA Oh, we are lost!

FLAMINEO You shall not take justice from forth my hands.
Oh, let me kill her! I'll cut my safety° *my way to safety*
Through your coats of steel. Fate's a spaniel;° *dogs us at our heels*
We cannot beat it from us. What remains now?
Let all that do ill take this precedent:
Man may his fate foresee, but not prevent.
And of all axioms this shall win the prize:
'Tis better to be fortunate than wise.

GASPARO Bind him to the pillar. [*Flamineo is bound.*]

VITTORIA Oh, your gentle pity!° *take pity on me!*
I have seen a blackbird that would sooner fly
To a man's bosom than to stay° the grip *await*
Of the fierce sparrow hawk.[6]

GASPARO Your hope deceives you.

VITTORIA If Florence be i'th'court, would he would kill me!

GASPARO Fool! Princes give rewards with their own hands,
But death or punishment by the hands of others.

LODOVICO [*to Flamineo*] Sirrah, you once did strike me. I'll strike you
Into the center.° *To the heart*

FLAMINEO Thou'lt do it like a hangman, a base hangman,
Not like a noble fellow, for thou see'st
I cannot strike again.° *strike back*

1. A field near Bishopsgate used for weekly military drills, some of which were evidently rather amateurish.
2. The fifty daughters of Danaus were forced to marry their uncle Egyptus' fifty sons. Danaus, having quarreled with Egyptus and having been warned by an oracle that he would be killed by one of his nephews, ordered his daughters to slay their husbands. Hypermnestra alone disobeyed.
3. Flamineo surmises that he has been foiled in his attempt to lock the doors behind him.
4. Lodovico sardonically compares this sudden appearance with a surprise entry of masked revelers, who, on a traditional occasion of this sort (such as Bracciano and Vittoria's marriage), would invite the aristocrats gathered in the room to dance with them.
5. I.e., We come to avenge in Isabella's name!
6. Vittoria hopes they will be more merciful than her brother.

LODOVICO Dost laugh?
FLAMINEO Wouldst have me die, as I was born, in whining?
GASPARO Recommend yourself to heaven.
FLAMINEO No, I will carry mine own commendations thither.
LODOVICO Oh, could I kill you forty times a day,
And us't° four year together, 'twere too little. *And do it*
Naught grieves but° that you are too few to feed *My only regret is*
The famine of our vengeance. What dost think on?
FLAMINEO Nothing; of nothing. Leave thy idle° questions. *frivolous*
I am i'th'way° to study a long silence; *preparing*
To prate were idle. I remember nothing.
There's nothing of so infinite vexation
As man's own thoughts.
LODOVICO [*to Vittoria*] O thou glorious° strumpet, *vainglorious*
Could I divide thy breath from this pure air
When't leaves thy body, I would suck it up
And breath't upon some dunghill.
VITTORIA You, my deathsman?° *executioner*
Methinks thou dost not look horrid enough;
Thou hast too good a face to be a hangman.
If thou be, do thy office in right form;
Fall down upon thy knees and ask forgiveness.[7]
LODOVICO Oh, thou hast been a most prodigious comet,
But I'll cut off your train.°—Kill the Moor first. *comet tail; attendant*
VITTORIA You shall not kill her first. Behold my breast.
I will be waited on° in death; my servant *go first; be attended*
Shall never go before me.
GASPARO Are you so brave?° *courageous; splendid*
VITTORIA Yes, I shall welcome death
As princes do some great ambassadors;
I'll meet thy weapon halfway.
LODOVICO Thou dost tremble.
Methinks fear should dissolve thee into air.
VITTORIA Oh, thou art deceived; I am too true a woman;
Conceit° can never kill me. I'll tell thee what: *Apprehension; vanity*
I will not in my death shed one base tear,
Or, if look pale, for° want of blood, not fear. *it will be for*
CARLO [*to Zanche*] Thou art my task, black fury.
ZANCHE I have blood
As red as either of theirs; wilt drink some?
'Tis good for the falling sickness.° I am proud *epilepsy; falling down*
Death cannot alter my complexion,
For I shall ne'er look pale.° *(because of my dark skin)*
LODOVICO Strike! Strike
With a joint motion!
[*They strike both women and Flamineo. Zanche dies quickly.*]
VITTORIA 'Twas a manly blow.° *(said with bitter irony)*
The next thou giv'st, murder some sucking infant,
And then thou wilt be famous.
FLAMINEO Oh, what blade is't?
A Toledo, or an English fox?° *Spanish or English sword?*

7. Executioners conventionally asked forgiveness of the person they were to execute.

I ever thought a cutler° should distinguish° *sword-maker / determine*
The cause of my death, rather than a doctor.
Search° my wound deeper; tent° it with the steel that *Probe / probe*
made it.
VITTORIA Oh, my greatest sin lay in my blood.° *passion*
Now my blood° pays for't. *lifeblood*
FLAMINEO Thou'rt a noble sister;
I love thee now. If woman do breed man,
She ought to teach him manhood. Fare thee well.
Know° many glorious women that are famed *Know that*
For masculine virtue have been vicious,
Only a happier silence did betide them;
She hath no faults who hath the art to hide them.[8]
VITTORIA My soul, like to a ship in a black storm,
Is driven I know not whither.
FLAMINEO Then cast anchor.
Prosperity doth bewitch men seeming clear,
But seas do laugh, show white, when rocks are near.[9]
We cease to grieve, cease to be Fortune's slaves,
Nay, cease to die, by dying.[1] Art thou° gone, *(Zanche)*
And thou° so near the bottom? False report° *(Vittoria) / It's false*
Which says that women vie with the nine Muses
For nine tough, durable lives![2] I do not look
Who went before, nor who shall follow me.
No, at myself I will begin and end:
While we look up to heaven, we confound
Knowledge with knowledge.[3] Oh, I am in a mist!
VITTORIA Oh, happy they that never saw the court,
Nor ever knew great man but by report! *Vittoria dies.*
FLAMINEO I recover like a spent taper for a flash,
And instantly go out.
Let all that belong to° great men remember th'old wives' tradition, to be like the lions i'th'Tower on Candlemas Day, to mourn if the sun shine, for fear of the pitiful remainder of winter to come.[4] *serve*
'Tis well yet there's some goodness° in my death; *moral lesson*
My life was a black charnel.° I have caught *bone repository*
An everlasting cold. I have lost my voice
Most irrecoverably. Farewell, glorious villains!
This busy trade of life appears most vain,
Since rest breeds rest, where all seek pain by pain.[5]
Let no harsh flattering bells resound my knell.
Strike, thunder, and strike loud to my farewell. *Dies.*

8. Were it not that a fortunate silence saved their reputations; a woman who is clever enough to hide her faults is as good as free of them.
9. The prospect of success deceives men into believing that all is well, but the shoals of misfortune are most perilous when the seas merrily break over the rocks.
1. A readiness to die defeats grief and even death itself.
2. I.e., (1) Women are not immortal, like the nine Muses; (2) women are not as tough and durable as people say. (With perhaps a glance at the cat's proverbial nine lives as a kind of invulnerability.)
3. Speculations about heavenly knowledge merely confuse and obscure our own limited human understanding.
4. Lions were kept in the Tower of London. Candlemas Day, February 2, the same day as Groundhog Day, is a time for predicting the length of the remaining winter; traditionally, a sunny February 2 indicates there will be six more weeks of winter, while a cloudy February 2 indicates an early spring. Flamineo warns against vain hopes of good fortune, especially for those persons in the service of great men.
5. Since our search for contentment leads at best to eternal rest, whereas our most painful efforts to succeed lead only to the pain of death.

ENGLISH AMBASSADOR [*within*] This way, this way! Break
ope the doors. This way!
LODOVICO Ha! Are we betrayed?
Why, then, let's constantly° die all together, *resolutely*
And, having finished this most noble deed,
Defy the worst of fate, not fear to bleed.
Enter Ambassadors and Giovanni [*with guards*].
ENGLISH AMBASSADOR Keep back the Prince. Shoot, shoot!
[*They shoot. Lodovico is hit.*]
LODOVICO Oh, I am wounded!
I fear I shall be ta'en.
GIOVANNI You bloody villains,
By what authority have you committed
This massacre?
LODOVICO By thine.
GIOVANNI Mine?
LODOVICO Yes, thy uncle,
Which is a part of thee, enjoined us to't.
Thou know'st me, I am sure. I am Count Lodowick,
And thy most noble uncle in disguise
Was last night in thy court.
GIOVANNI Ha!
CARLO Yes, that Moor
Thy father chose his pensioner.° *gave a pension to*
GIOVANNI He turned murderer?
Away with them to prison, and to torture!
All that have hands in this shall taste our justice,
As I hope heaven.° *hope to be saved*
LODOVICO I do glory yet
That I can call this act mine own. For my part,
The rack, the gallows, and the torturing wheel
Shall be but sound sleeps to me. Here's my rest;° *sleep; final hope*
I limned° this night-piece,° and it was my best. *painted / night scene*
GIOVANNI Remove the bodies. See, my honored lords,
What use you ought make° of their punishment. *ought to make*
Let guilty men remember their black deeds
Do lean on crutches, made of slender reeds. [*Exeunt.*]

Instead of an epilogue, only this of Martial supplies me: *Haec fuerint nobis praemia si placui.*[1]

For the action of the play, 'twas generally well, and I dare affirm, with the joint testimony of some of their own quality° (for the true imitation of life, without striving to make a monster), the best that ever became them;° whereof as I make a general acknowledgment, so in particular I must remember the well-approved industry of my friend Master Perkins,[2] and confess the worth of his action did crown both the beginning and end. *acting profession* *suited their skills*

FINIS.

Instead of an epilogue.
1. These things will be our reward if I have pleased you. (Martial, *Epigrams,* 2.91.8.)
2. An actor with Queen Anne's Men, presumably in the role of Flamineo.

TEXTUAL NOTES

The White Devil was first published in quarto in 1612 (without having been entered in the Stationers' Register, so far as is known), and it is this edition upon which the present text is based. Subsequent quartos provide some commonsense corrections but without the authority of the dramatist himself. The following abbreviations are used in accounting for the departures of this present edition from the copy-text:

Q1: The quarto first edition (London: Thomas Archer, 1612)
Q1 corr.: The corrected state of Q1
Q1 uncorr.: The uncorrected state of Q1
Q2: The quarto second edition (London: Hugh Perry, 1631)
Q3: The quarto third edition (London: John Playfere and William Crooke, 1665)
Q4: The quarto fourth edition (London: William Crooke, 1672)
ed.: A modern editor's emendation

To the Reader 21 liven [Q1: *life'n*] **33** [and elsewhere] **hundred** [Q1: *hundreth*] **44 Dekker** [Q1: Decker]

1.1.19 you [Q3] you, you [Q1] **40** [and elsewhere] **Bracciano** [Q1: *Brachiano*] **47 they are** [Q2] the are [Q1] **49** [and elsewhere] **scents** [Q1: sents] **60.1** [ed.] *Enter Senate* [Q1]

1.2.6 SD [placement, ed.; opposite 7 in Q1] **22 whereas** [ed.] where a [Q1] **22 satiety** [Q1 corr.] sotiety [Q1 uncorr.] **24 there** [Q1: their] **52 traveling** [Q3] trauailing [Q1] **57** [and elsewhere] **lose** [Q4] loose [Q1] **59 There** [Q1: Their] **66 bowl** [Q1: boule] **69 your** [Q3] you [Q1] **69, 74** [and elsewhere] **cuckold** [Q1: Cocould] **75 buy** [Q1: boy] **110 basin** [Q1: Bason] **140 muzzle** [Q1: mussel] **142 covered** [Q1 corr.] a couer [Q1 uncorr.] **143 yon** [Q1 corr.] a your [Q1 uncorr.] **193 mark** [Q3] make [Q1] **226 Here** [Q2] Heare [Q1] **233** [and throughout scene] **yew** [Q1: *Eu*] **273 Till** [ed.] tell [Q1] **274** [and elsewhere] **Lest** [Q1: Least] **275 with** [Q3; not in Q1] **277 than** [Q3; not in Q1] **282 leave** [Q4] leaues [Q1] **300 his** [Q2] this [Q1]

2.1.0.1 *Medici* [Q1: Medicis] **0.1 *Monticelso*** [Q1: Mountcelso] **0.2 *Giovanni*** [ed.] Giouanni, *with little* Iaques *the Moore* [Q1] **3 such a** [Q2] a such [Q1] **27 you, that have** [ed.] you haue [Q1] **51 prey** [Q1: pery] **51 seize** [Q1: ceaze] **78 forehead. Defiance! And** [ed.] fore-head defiance, and [Q1] **88 prowling** [Q1: proling] **95.1** [placement, ed.; opposite 94 in Q1] **109 to a** [Q2] to [Q1] **147.1** [placement, ed.; opposite 145–46 in Q1] **162 am to** [Q1 corr.] come to [Q1 uncorr.] **185 reverend** [Q1: reuerent] **226.1 *Monticelso*** [Q1: *Montcelso*] **226.1 *Marcello*** [ed.] *Marcello, Camillo* [Q1] **264 *repostum*** [Q2] *repositum* [Q1] **289 Here's** [Q3] her's [Q1] **306 surgeon** [Q1: Chirurgeon] **313 Sir, I shall** [Q1 corr.; not in Q1 uncorr.] **320 another's** [Q3: anothers] another [Q1] **338 there** [ed.] their [Q1] **383 your** [ed.] our [Q1] **386 there's** [Q1: their's]

2.2.13 there [Q1: their] **23.3 *Bracciano's*** [Q1: Brachian's] **23.9 *Giovanni*** [ed.] Giouanni, Guid-antonio [Q1] **23.10** [and elsewhere] ***waiting*** [Q1: *waighting*] **35 fate** [Q4] face [Q1] **37.6–7** [and elsewhere] ***Compliment*** [Q1: *complement*] **47 BRACCIANO** [Q4: *Bra.*] MAR. [Q1] **55.1** [placement, Q4; opposite 54 in Q1]

3.1.45 scarce hast [ed.] hast scarce [Q1] **46 chamois** [Q1: shamoyes] **47 poured** [Q1: powred] **51 on** [ed.] Or [Q1] **63 SD** [placement, ed.; opposite 62 in Q1] **64.2 *French Ambassador*** [ed.] *French Embassadours* [Q1] **76 cypress** [Q1: cipres]

3.2.0.2 *Monticelso* [Q1: *Montcelso*] **0.3 *Vittoria*** [Q4] *Vittoria, Isabella* [Q1] **8 gentlewoman** [Q4] gentlewomen [Q1] **10 LAWYER** [Q2; not in Q1] **97 emptied** [Q1: empted] **102 brings** [Q2] bring [Q1] **180 reverend** [Q1: reuerent] **181** ***lacessit*** [Q2] *lacescit* [Q1] **195 he** [Q3] her [Q1] **211 a feast** [ed.] feast [Q1] **231 long** [ed.] louing [Q1] **251 balladed** [Q1: ballated] **265 princes; here's** [ed.] Princes heares; [Q1] Princes, heare [Q2] **266 Unto** [Q3] VIT. Vnto [Q1] **281 those** [Q4] these [Q1] **281 maw** [Q3] mawes [Q1] **291 on** [Q2] one [Q1] **332 GIOVANNI** [Q3; not in Q1]

3.3.4 travel [Q1: trauaile] **22 Yon** [ed.] You [Q1] **26 victual** [Q1: vittell] **26 line** [Q2] liue [Q1] **52 in a** [Q2] in [Q1] **52** [and elsewhere] **screech owl** [Q1: scritch-owle] **79 gentle** [ed.] gentile [Q1] **82.1** [placement, ed.; opposite 94 in Q1] **89 rogue!** [Q3] grine rouge [Q1 uncorr.] gue [Q1 corr.] **119 learnt't** [Q1: learn't]

4.1.14 cannon [Q1: Canon] **75 one** [Q1 corr.] and [Q1 uncorr.] **86 list** [Q1 corr.] life [Q1 uncorr.] **89 in so** [Q2] so [Q1 uncorr.] so in [Q1 corr.] **90 lie** [Q1 corr.: lye] be [Q1 uncorr.] **99 I ha 't** [Q1 corr.: I—ha'te] I—d'foot [Q1 uncorr.] **119 SD** [placement, ed.; opposite 121 in Q1] **136 SD** [ed.] *Exit Mon.* [Q1]

4.2.20 fowl [Q1: foule] **51 In, you** [Q1 corr.: In you] No you [Q1 uncorr.] **71 Oh, sir** [Q1 corr.: O Sir] Sir [Q1 uncorr.] **87 lovely** [Q1 corr.] thought on [Q1 uncorr.] **91 led** [Q1: lead] **108 two** [ed.] ten [Q1 uncorr.] tow [Q1 corr.] **148 bonfire** [Q1: bonefire] **156 would** [Q1 corr.] could [Q1 uncorr.] **190 heart** [Q1: hart]

4.3.0.1–2 [ed.] *Enter* Francisco, Lodouico, Gasper, *and sixe Embassadours. At another dore the Duke of Florence* [Q1] **22 Whose** [Q1] Who's [some eds.] **35 lord** [Q1: L.] **39 hear** [Q1: here] **40.1** ***terrace*** [Q1: *Tarras*] **60–61** ***Concedimus . . . peccatorum*** [Q1 corr.; not in Q1 uncorr.] **65 seat** [Q1 corr.] state [Q1 uncorr.] **80 SD** ***Exit*** [Q1 corr.; not in Q1 uncorr.] **80.1** ***Enter Monticelso*** [placement, ed.; opposite 84–85 in Q1] **81 MONTICELSO** [Q1 corr.; not in Q1] **90 I ask you** [Q3; as continuation of Lodovico's speech in Q1] **121 yew tree** [Q1: Eugh-tree] **126 With all** [ed.] Withall [Q1] **128.1** [placement, Q4; opposite 129 in Q1] **140 wills** [Q2] will [Q1] **140 travel** [Q1: trauaile]

5.1.33 [Q3; Q1 has a SD opposite this line: *Enter Duke Brachiano.*] **38 traveled** [Q1: trauail'd] **43.3** ***Gasparo*** [Q1: *Gaspar*] **44 You're** [Q1: You'are] **62 BRACCIANO** [ed.; not in Q1] **62.1** ***and [Hortensio]*** [ed.] and *Marcello* [Q1, where the SD is placed opposite "To stay, my lord" in 62] **85.1** [ed.] *Exeunt Lodouico Antonelli* [Q1] **96 SD** [placement, ed.; opposite 95 in Q1] **105 too** [Q1: to] **129 whilst** [Q1: whilest] **173 diners** [ed.] *Diuers* [Q1] **182 morality** [Q4] mortality [Q1] **196 You're** [Q2: You'r] Your [Q1] **207 two** [Q1 corr.] 10 [Q1 uncorr.] **208 geese** [Q1: geesse] **211.2–3** [placement, ed.; opposite 213–14 in Q1] **216, 226, 231 FRANCISCO** [Q3: *Fra.*] FLA. [Q1] **216 sown** [Q1: sowen]

5.2.2 You [Q2] Your [Q1] **17 SD** ***Enter Carlo . . . Pedro*** [placement, ed.; opposite 19–20 in Q1] **24 wider** [Q4] wilder [Q1]

5.3.11 too [Q1: to] **34 corse** [Q1: coarse] **35 waits** [Q1: waights] **66 Wilt** [Q1: Will't] **82.1–2** [placement, ed.; printed in left-hand margin opposite 84–90 in Q1] **89 was't** [Q1: wast] **127 Crawl** [Q1: crall] **132.1–3** [placement, ed.; printed in right-hand margin opposite 124–35 in Q1] **153 SD** [placement, ed.; printed in left-hand margin opposite 152–54 in Q1] **164 mercury** [Q1: Mercarie] **164 copperas** [Q1: copperesse] **182, 192, 202, 209, 221 FRANCISCO** [Q3] FLO. [Q1] **195 Machiavellian** [Q1: Machiuillian] **200 feat** [Q2] seat [Q1] **212** [and elsewhere] **Wait** [Q1: VVaight] **214 SD** [placement, ed.; opposite 215 in Q1] **218 us** [Q4] vp [Q1] **254 kept'st** [Q2: keps't] kepts [Q1] **267.1** [placement, ed.; opposite 268 in Q1]

5.4.8 talons [Q1: Tallants] **27 cullis** [Q1: cullice] **53** [and elsewhere] **corse** [Q1: coarse] **73 LADY** [ed.] WOM. [Q1] **75 SD** ***to Flamineo*** [placement, ed.; opposite 75 in Q1] **82.1** [placement, ed.; in right-hand margin opposite 97–99 in Q1] **87 corse** [Q1: Course] **88 He's** [Q1: h'as] **92 hear** [Q1: heere] **124.2** ***cowl*** [Q1: *coole*]

5.6.18 They [Q2] the [Q1] **20 scare** [Q3] scarre [Q1] **29 they** [Q2] the [Q1] **33 worldly** [Q2] wordly [Q1] **108 VITTORIA *and* ZANCHE** [ed.] Both [Q1] **144 stinking** [Q2] sinking [Q1] **144 chimney is** [Q2] chimneis [Q1] **145 parboiled** [Q1: purboil'd] **145 holy bread** [Q1: holly-bread] **163** [and elsewhere] **precedent** [Q1: president] **169.1–2** [placement, ed.; opposite 168 in Q1] **171 masque** [Q1: Maske] **173 CONSPIRATORS** [Q1: Con.] *Car.* [some eds.] **187 grip** [Q1: gripe] **217 off** [Q1: of] **225 too** [Q1: to] **266 wives'** [ed.] wides [Q1] **282.1** [placement, ed.; after 277 in Q1] **299 lords** [ed.] Lord [Q1]

The Duchess of Malfi

John Webster's *The Duchess of Malfi* (evidently begun in 1612 and first performed in 1613–14) brings to a pinnacle of achievement a form of tragedy also present in Shakespeare's *Othello*: the depiction of an innocent, energetic, sexually enterprising, and morally appealing woman who exposes herself to destruction by attempting to live, love, and marry as she wishes in a world dominated by powerful men and the power-seeking men who follow them. Webster's fellow dramatist John Ford called the play "a masterpiece" in his commendatory poem in the first published edition of 1623 (line 2), and time has largely confirmed his estimate. The play's representation of a bold attempt at female independence, of love and marriage across barriers of status in an intensely patriarchal hierarchy, and of the cruelty of aristocratic pride opens up an important and lasting set of social controversies. The Duchess herself, her obsessed and eventually mad brother Ferdinand, and the malcontent spy and repentant murderer Bosola are unforgettable roles for actors and objects of fascination, affection, pity, and terror for audiences and readers. Filled with fluent intensity of speech, the play commands a range of styles from racy satirical prose to dignified blank verse to stunning lyrics. And while the play has features that are irregular according to classical definitions of tragedy, from its casual invocation of the passage of years between acts to the early death of the title character in act 4, its extended focus on the imposition of deadly male will on the Duchess's life and love remains steady to the end.

That focus emerges in the opening scene, when Duke Ferdinand hires Bosola to spy on his sister, the Duchess, with the comment, "She's a young widow; / I would not have her marry again" (1.1.257–58). He adds, provocatively, "Do not you ask the reason, but be satisfied / I say I would not" (1.1.261–62). The facts of the plot derive from a historical aristocratic scandal in early sixteenth-century Italy, but they raise social issues familiar in early seventeenth-century London.

In Renaissance society, widows of marriageable age who had inherited the property, the businesses, or, in the Duchess's exalted case, the sovereignty of deceased husbands were virtually the only women in a socially legitimate position to control their sexual and economic lives. Unmarried daughters owed obedience to their fathers or other male guardians, wives owed obedience to their husbands, and older widows with adult male children often passed control of their households to their sons. Nuns were confined to a tightly regulated convent and were under the spiritual supervision of their male confessors; whores and courtesans forfeited social legitimacy (though Webster's *The White Devil* illustrates how they could attempt, at the upper levels of society, to regain it). Widows, by contrast, headed households and held property in their own names, and as women with legitimate sexual experience, they could meet any man on even ground, sexually as well as economically. As such, propertied widows at various social levels, from the rural yeomanry or urban bourgeoisie to the aristocracy, were the objects of male fantasies of upward social mobility. Yet they also constituted an exception to a general system of patriarchal control, and in folklore and the moral attitudes

Introduction by Lars Engle; glosses, footnotes, and textual notes by David Bevington; text edited by David Bevington and checked by Eric Rasmussen and Lars Engle.

of the day they were often regarded as threatening: lustful, too independent, unruly. In fact, there is some demographic evidence that financially independent widows often chose not to remarry, thus preserving their freedom of action, whether or not they chose to remain sexually active.[1]

The Duchess of Malfi seeks to exercise a widow's freedom by remarrying against the wishes and despite the threats of her brothers. In doing so, she chooses a husband from well below her own rank. The play is tightly organized around this action: all consequences stem from her attempt to assert her will and her brothers' need to prevent or punish female autonomy in sexual choice. The subplot concerning the Cardinal's adulterous and abusive liaison with Julia, the wife of an aged courtier, provides a parallel case. The venomous intensity with which the Duke and the Cardinal urge the Duchess to remain single in the opening scene suggests a complex of motives on their part, including, perhaps, an awareness at some level that their sister has already fallen in love. The brothers may have unstated political motives for discouraging her remarriage (they may, for instance, exercise influence over the Duchess's state that they would lose were the Duchess to marry another great nobleman), and Ferdinand belatedly asserts an economic motive, an "infinite mass of treasure" (4.2.284), probably part of her inheritance from their parents, that he (and perhaps his brother) would gain were she to die a widow. At the same time, Ferdinand's motives evidently include a very strong emotional resistance to the thought of her remarriage, a resistance he discourages Bosola from questioning because he himself cannot adequately describe it.

The resistance is psychosexual and social, and through it Webster explores the male anxieties that prompt abuse of women. Ferdinand feels both sexual jealousy and social degradation at the thought of his widowed sister's having sex, and he feels this even before he knows of her relationship with her steward Antonio. Since she keeps her marriage to Antonio a secret to protect him from her brothers, Duke Ferdinand's imagination can range freely when he learns from Bosola that his sister has given birth, and he pictures her in the embraces of

some strong-thighed bargeman,
Or one o'th'woodyard, that can quoit the sledge
Or toss the bar, or else some lovely squire
That carries coals up to her privy lodgings.
(2.5.43–46)

These fantasized couplings with figures of nonaristocratic (and, in the case of the squire, adolescent) sexual potency suggest how profoundly Ferdinand's sense of self as a nobleman is threatened by the Duchess's sexual activity. He baffles his brother by saying, "I could kill her now, / In you, or in myself, for I do think / It is some sin in us heaven doth revenge / By her" (2.5.64–67). This twisted religious thinking, combined with the suggestion that, for Ferdinand, the Duchess's body must remain chaste to guarantee his own purity, returns as he prepares to kill her in act 4: he tells Bosola, "That body of hers, / While that my blood ran pure in't, was more worth / Than that which thou wouldst comfort, called a soul" (4.1.123–25). Thus in taking control of *her* erotic life, the Duchess has, in effect, removed part of Ferdinand's noble body from the control of *his* noble will, and he reacts with hysterical violence in defense of his class and sex.

Of course the Duchess also has a will. She underlines her own bold pursuit of her desires when she comments that she will make her brothers into her "low footsteps" if they get in the way of her marriage to Antonio (1.1.344). Both the perversely noble Duke and Cardinal and the normatively noble Duchess possess an aristocratic belief in their right to impose their desires on others. The Duchess's maid Cariola remarks on how "the spirit of greatness" reigns in the Duchess as she embraces Antonio, though

1. See Dympna Callaghan, ed., *The Duchess of Malfi* (New York: St. Martin's, 2000), p. 4, citing Merry E. Weisner, *Women and Gender in Early Modern Europe* (Cambridge: Cambridge University Press, 1993), p. 166.

Cariola also "owe[s] her . . . pity" for her "fearful madness" in defying her brothers for love (1.1.505–7). That spirit sustains the Duchess when Cariola's fears are realized. Tormented by real madmen, shown what appear to be the bodies of her husband and children, and threatened with her own death, the Duchess says to the disguised Bosola, "I am Duchess of Malfi still" (4.2.138). Her haunting claim to sovereign selfhood amid terror and loss proves prophetic: she will retain power, identity, and pathos as an emblem of innocence and righteousness up to and beyond her death. But she is also claiming an authority over Bosola that she will not wield: "Am not I thy duchess?" (4.2.131). Her own tragedy—that neither greatness nor goodness allows her to live as she chooses—becomes that of her husband Antonio and, in another way, that of Bosola, employed to do evil in a world dominated by corrupt noblemen. In such a world, how should the ambitions of people who have talent but not noble birth be fulfilled?

The play's focus on the social issues of courtly life includes close attention to lives dedicated to the service of aristocrats, and on the whole it portrays the dangers, both moral and practical, of such service. Both Bosola, who spies on the Duchess and oversees her torture and murder, and Antonio, who accepts her proposal of marriage, manages her household, and fathers her children, are members of a nonaristocratic professional class seeking to make their way by merit rather than by birth. They complement one another in somewhat the way the overemotional Ferdinand complements the rational Machiavellian Cardinal, or the adulterous Julia complements the frankly desirous but moral Duchess, as part of a system of parallels that contributes to the intellectual depth of Webster's dramaturgy. Antonio is evidently a capable manager of the Duchess's household, the post he has returned from France to take, and his rise to this position exemplifies how a good ruler rewards honorable service. His further leap in becoming the Duchess's husband, however, though honorable and, as far as we can tell, unsought even though desired by him, exemplifies a kind of courtier's fantasy of success in engaging a ruler's affection. Since erotic favoritism was a huge, and much-resented, factor in the courts of both Queen Elizabeth and her successor, King James, Antonio's elevation counts as another of the provocative social issues the play addresses, in this case by showing Antonio as both innocent of ill intent and well aware of the dangers he incurs. For audiences, as well as for onstage commentators such as his friend Delio and Antonio himself, Antonio in part exemplifies the hazards of ambition.

Bosola, a product of the corrupt Italian courts whose rulers employ, in Antonio's words, "flatterers, panders, intelligencers, atheists, and a thousand such political monsters" to undo their opponents (1.1.162–63), is the obverse of Antonio: cynical, resentful, and deceptive, though also direct and morally insightful. Bosola offers an aggrieved victim's account of Ferdinand and the Cardinal ruling over their corrupt and flattering courts "like plum trees that grow crooked over standing pools" (1.1.49–50), an account that stands in contrast to Antonio's description of the court of France as a fountain scattering silver drops (1.1.12–13). Bosola himself spent years in the galleys for a murder he committed at the Cardinal's behest. As Antonio rises through the secret love of his superior, a secret shared with the audience, Bosola labors to ferret out the secret, evidently concurring in the obsessive distrust of women that motivates his masters, whom he also, with good reason, distrusts.

Not only an efficient tool of the Duchess's villainous brothers, Bosola is also a disillusioned man skeptically testing a bad and ungrateful world in an attempt to find a satisfactory way of being. It is easiest for him to admire people who, like himself, have been mistreated by princes. He therefore celebrates Antonio as "a most unvalued jewel . . . an excellent courtier, and most faithful" only after the Duchess has fired Antonio as her steward in an attempt to protect him from her brothers (3.2.250–53). This outburst—whether it stems from sincere sympathy for Antonio, from a belated intuition that the Duchess's feelings for Antonio need probing, or from some mixture of the two—has a tragic result. The Duchess, delighted to hear Antonio praised and also stung by Bosola's reproaches, reveals that Antonio is her husband. Bosola, bound by his own service, immediately informs his employer Ferdinand and thus exposes both the Duchess and, ultimately, Antonio to destruction. Only when the Duchess too suffers at Ferdinand's hands does Bosola begin to sympathize with her, and part of his transformation at her death can be attributed to a tragically belated awareness on Bosola's part that the Duchess herself was a prince worth serving, a refutation of his low premises about women, rulers, and human nature. As Bosola comes to feel this toward the end of the play, other characters begin to use the words "tyrant" and "tyranny" to describe the actions of the Duchess's brothers (see, e.g., 4.1.66, 4.2.3, 4.2.60). The play suggests that under such tyrants, "Rotten, and rotting others" (4.2.323), no one can thrive by service, neither the virtuous Antonio nor the discontented yet indispensable henchman Bosola, who "rather sought / To appear a true servant than an honest man" (4.2.335–36).

In associating this tyranny with male sexual obsession, the play also links the Duchess's qualities as a ruler with her healthy sexuality. Antonio, in the opening scene, after anatomizing her brothers' faults for his friend Delio, praises her virtues, focusing on her sexual vitality:

Whilst she speaks,
She throws upon a man so sweet a look
That it were able to raise one to a galliard
That lay in a dead palsy. (1.1.194–97)

Aware of the sexual implications of his remark, Antonio immediately adds that "in that look / There speaketh so divine a continence / As cuts off all lascivious and vain hope" (1.1.198–200). This comment probably testifies more strongly to his own efforts at self-discipline than to the Duchess's chaste state of mind as she looks at him. Antonio's juxtaposition of the Duchess's health and the sickness and disability of the males she looks at is, in any case, a key feature of her characterization throughout the play. Her intense naturalness wars with the unnaturalness of her brothers and their increasingly reluctant agent Bosola, her love with their cruelty, her ease in the life of the body with their misogynist discomfort. When, later in the opening scene, the Duchess raises Antonio from his knees and takes him in her arms, she tells him not to worry about her brothers: "Do not think of them. / All discord, without this circumference, / Is only to be pitied and not feared" (1.1.469–71). Though the play will show how much her brothers are to be feared, it also persuades audiences to pity anyone who does not enjoy the kind of loving intimacy the Duchess enjoys with Antonio.

Her social boldness and sexual frankness derive explicitly from her widowed condition, as may her intellectual capacity to frame her situation in terms of a struggle between living desires and dead conventions. She woos Antonio with a directness that bespeaks her commitment to a love that is both spiritual and intimately physical:

Sir, be confident.
What is't distracts you? This is flesh and blood, sir;
'Tis not the figure cut in alabaster
Kneels at my husband's tomb. Awake, awake, man!
I do here put off all vain ceremony,
And only do appear to you a young widow
That claims you for her husband, and, like a widow,
I use but half a blush in't. (1.1.453–60)

By contrasting her living body with a piece of funerary sculpture, frozen in a posture of mourning and subservience, the Duchess interprets her remarriage as a refusal to serve death. As is typical of Webster's art, the same juxtaposition, transformed into near incoherence, marks Ferdinand's revulsion at the marriage when he discovers it: "thou hast ta'en that massy sheet of lead / That hid thy husband's bones, and folded it / About my heart" (3.2.114–16). Ferdinand thus indicates that what is happy marital life for her is death for him, but the image also suggests that only the safe burial of the man who has had sexual relations with his sister could keep Ferdinand's heart in health.

The Duchess again frames her altered situation both morally and intellectually when she is arrested and shown what seem to be the bodies of her husband and two of her children. She transforms herself from a chaste epicurean, delighted with marital and maternal love, to a Christian stoic, "acquainted with sad misery / As the tanned galley-slave is with his oar" (4.2.27–28). She becomes a stronger image of integrity and decency under the array of psychological torments that Ferdinand orders and Bosola, with increasing reservations, carries out. The Duchess reminds us beautifully of her motherhood as Cariola is forced to leave her, just before her execution, saying, "I pray thee, look thou giv'st my little boy / Some syrup for his cold, and let the girl / Say her prayers ere she sleep" (4.2.199–201). And she accepts her strangulation with immense dignity and moral authority:

Tell my brothers
That I perceive death, now I am well awake,
Best gift is they can give or I can take.
I would fain put off my last woman's fault:
I'd not be tedious to you. (4.2.220–24)

She kneels to be strangled, completing a cycle that began when she lifted Antonio from his knees and reminded him that she was not a kneeling statue.

In act 5, after the Duchess's death, the play keeps its focus on the continued power of her innocence over the imaginations of good and bad alike. There is no anticlimax; the Duchess herself remains present in the play through her husband (who does not know of her death and hears her voice in an echo from her grave) and through the transformations of Ferdinand and Bosola. Both are turned inside out by the Duchess's death. Ferdinand, aware that he ordered the death of his "dearest friend" (4.2.279), goes mad and imagines that he is a wolf aiming to dig up the Duchess's corpse and reveal her murder to all. Bosola, his service to Ferdinand repudiated, undergoes a kind of conversion that bears witness to the posthumous power of the Duchess's innocence. He becomes the Duchess's avenger, turning his ruthless talents against his ungrateful employers; in effect, he realizes too late that serving the Duchess rather than her brothers would have conferred on him the authentic life he had sought. The Duchess's murder affects even the ice-cold Cardinal, who complains of the tediousness of a guilty conscience, sees a devil reaching for him from his fishpond, and dies with a word of concern for his mad brother on his lips. For all of these men, however, the Duchess becomes an object of sympathy and regret only after they have destroyed her happiness with Antonio.

Webster's dramatic art involves audiences in a dense texture of emotional and intellectual experience, intensified by juxtapositions of beauty and horror, and much

The wolf; woodcut from Edward Topsell's *History of Four-Footed Beasts* (1607).

of its power comes from his mastery of poetic language. The Duchess's eloquence has already been illustrated; Bosola, too, speaks in memorable phrases that reach beyond their immediate contexts. When, at the end, he kills Antonio by mistake, he says that he acted "In a mist" (5.5.111), thus echoing the remarkable lyric he had uttered to prepare the Duchess for death by exposing the folly of life:

> Of what is't fools make such vain keeping?
> Sin their conception, their birth weeping;
> Their life, a general mist of error,
> Their death, a hideous storm of terror.
> (4.2.181–84)

This description fits just about every major character in the play *except* the Duchess, who conceives and bears children by choice and in love, dies unterrified, and errs only in supposing that her own innocence and integrity can protect her domestic felicity from the intrusive power and obsessive malice of her brothers. It is fitting, then, that those still alive at the end of the play band together around the surviving son of Antonio and the Duchess.[2] The boy alone carries the noble blood of the Cardinal and Ferdinand, mixed forever now with that of Antonio. In its art of juxtaposition, the play sets the Duchess alongside her brothers in sustained, vivid, and artfully varied contrast: not only between love and cruelty, female and male, warmth and coldness, integrity and deceit, but also between fecundity and sterility, life and death.

2. The Duchess's son by her first husband, mentioned at 3.3.69–71, has disappeared from view by the end and is never mentioned in the play by the Duchess. Since the historical Duchess of Malfi had such a son and was succeeded by him, these lines probably represent a discarded strand of plot that Webster failed to expunge entirely.

JOHN WEBSTER
The Duchess of Malfi

[Dedication]

To the Right Honorable George Harding, Baron Berkeley of Berkeley Castle and Knight of the Order of the Bath to the Illustrious Prince Charles[1]

My noble lord,

That I may present my excuse why, being a stranger to Your Lordship, I offer this poem° to your patronage, I plead this warrant: men who never saw the sea, yet desire to behold that regiment° of waters, choose some eminent river to guide them thither, and make that, as it were, their conduct° or postilion.° By the like ingenious means has your fame arrived at my knowledge, receiving it from some of worth who, both in contemplation and practice, owe to Your Honor their clearest° service. I do not altogether look up at° your title, the ancient'st nobility being but a relic of time past, and the truest honor indeed being for a man to confer honor on himself, which your learning strives to propagate and shall make you arrive at the dignity of a great example. I am confident this work is not unworthy Your Honor's perusal; for by such poems as this, poets have kissed the hands of great princes and drawn their gentle eyes to look down upon their sheets of paper when the poets themselves were bound up in their winding-sheets.° The like courtesy from Your Lordship shall make you live in your grave and laurel spring out of it, when the ignorant scorners of the Muses (that, like worms in libraries, seem to live only to destroy learning) shall wither, neglected and forgotten. This work and myself I humbly present to your approved censure,° it being the utmost of my wishes to have your honorable self my weighty and perspicuous comment;° which grace so done me, shall ever be acknowledged.

By Your Lordship's,
in all duty and observance,
John Webster

poem: i.e., play · *regiment: domain* · *conduct / postilion: escort / forerunner* · *clearest: most absolute* · *look up at: respect you solely for* · *winding-sheets: shrouds* · *approved censure: proven judgment* · *comment: discerning critic*

The original 1623 title page reads "*The Tragedy of the Duchess of Malfi*. As it was presented privately at the Blackfriars, and publicly at the Globe, by the King's Majesty's Servants. The perfect and exact copy, with divers things printed that the length of the play would not bear in the presentment. Written by John Webster. Horace. *Si quid Candidus Imperti si non his utere mecum* [If you know wiser precepts than these, be kind and tell me; if not, practice mine with me (*Epistles*, 1.6.67–68)]. London: Printed by Nicholas Okes, for John Waterson, and are to be sold at the sign of the Crown, in Paul's Churchyard, 1623."

Dedication.

1. The thirteenth Baron Berkeley (1601–1658) was the grandson and son, respectively, of the first and second Lords Hunsdon, who had served as patrons of the Lord Chamberlain's Men in the 1590s—the company of which Shakespeare was a member and that became the King's Men in 1603. Harding patronized other writers besides Webster, including Robert Burton, Philip Massinger, and James Shirley.

[Commendatory Verses]

In the just worth of that well-deserver, Mr. John Webster, and upon this masterpiece of tragedy

In this thou imitat'st one rich and wise
That sees his good deeds done before he dies.
As he by works, thou by this work of fame
Hast well provided for thy living name.
To trust to others' honorings is worth's crime;[1]
Thy monument is raised in thy lifetime.
And 'tis most just; for every worthy man
Is his own marble,° and his merit can *monument*
Cut him to any figure and express
More art than Death's cathedral palaces,
Where royal ashes keep their court.[2] Thy note° *Let your note*
Be ever plainness; 'tis the richest coat.° *coat of arms*
Thy epitaph only the title be;
Write "Duchess."[3] That will fetch a tear for thee;
For whoe'er saw this duchess live and die
That could get off under a bleeding eye?

In Tragediam.
Ut lux ex tenebris ictu percussa tonantis;
Illa, (ruina malis) claris fit vita poetis.
Thomas Middletonus,
Poeta et Chron: Londinensis[4]

To his friend Mr. John Webster upon his *Duchess of Malfi*

I never saw thy duchess till the day
That she was lively bodied° in thy play. *embodied, set forth*
Howe'er she answered her low-rated love,
Her brothers' anger did so fatal prove;
Yet my opinion is, she might speak more,
But never in her life so well before.[1]
William Rowley[2]

To the reader, of° the author and his *Duchess of Malfi* *concerning*

Crown him a poet, whom nor° Rome nor Greece *neither*
Transcend, in all theirs, for a masterpiece;
In which, whiles words and matter change, and men
Act one another,[1] he, from whose clear° pen *illustrious*

Commendatory Poem by Thomas Middleton.
1. To trust that others will honor you after you die is a crime against one's worthiness.
2. A person's own merit can depict his true worthiness and do so with more artistry than can those deathlike, palatial tombs where the remains of royal persons are ceremoniously interred.
3. Let your epitaph be simply the title of your play.
4. To Tragedy: As light springs from darkness at the blow of the Thunderer (Jove), even so may tragedy be the lightning that brings ruin to the wicked and life to famous poets.—Thomas Middleton, poet and chronicler of London.

Commendatory Poem by William Rowley.
1. However eloquently in her real life the Duchess may have defended her marriage to a man below her in social station, her brothers' anger turned out to determine matters in a fatal way; nonetheless, I do not think she could possibly have spoken better (though she might have said more) than she did in your play.
2. English actor and playwright, c. 1585–c. 1642.

Commendatory Poem by John Ford.
1. As long as literature imitates life and actors portray human beings in plays.

They all took life,° to memory hath lent — *came into being*
A lasting fame, to raise his monument.
John Ford[2]

THE ACTORS' NAMES

[Daniel de] BOSOLA [the Duchess's provisor of horse] J. Lowin.[1]
FERDINAND [Duke of Calabria, brother of the Duchess and the Cardinal] 1. R. Burbage. 2. J. Taylor.
CARDINAL [brother of Ferdinand and the Duchess] 1. H. Condell. 2. R. Robinson.
ANTONIO [Bologna, steward of the Duchess's household] 1. W. Ostler. 2. R. Benfield.
DELIO [his friend] J. Underwood.
Forobosco [a nonspeaking minor court official] N. Towley.
[Count] MALATESTE [a courtier]
The Marquis of PESCARA [a soldier] J. Rice.
SILVIO [a courtier] T. Pollard.
[CASTRUCHIO, an old courtier, husband of Julia]
The several MADMEN N. Towley, J. Underwood, etc.
The DUCHESS [of Malfi, sister of Ferdinand and the Cardinal] R. Sharpe.
[JULIA,] the Cardinal's mistress [and wife to Castruchio] J. Tomson.
The DOCTOR
CARIOLA [the Duchess's waiting-woman] R. Pallant.
Court OFFICERS
Three young children [of the Duchess and Antonio]
Two PILGRIMS
[RODERIGO, GRISOLAN } courtiers at Malfi
An OLD LADY, a midwife
Churchmen
EXECUTIONERS
The ECHO from the Duchess's grave
SERVANTS attending on Ferdinand and the Duchess
Guards, other servants, attendants, ladies-in-waiting

THE SCENE: Malfi (or Amalfi), Rome, Loreto, the countryside near Ancona, and Milan.]

1.1

[Enter] Antonio and Delio.

DELIO You are welcome to your country, dear Antonio!
You have been long in France, and you return
A very formal Frenchman in your habit.° — *costume, dress*
How do you like the French court?

2. Author (c. 1586–c. 1638 or afterward) of *'Tis Pity She's a Whore* and other plays.
The Actors' Names.
1. The actors' names here indicate their original role assignments as printed in the quarto of 1623. This play was the first in England to list acting assignments with such completeness. When two actors are assigned to a part, the numbers 1 and 2 represent original and then later productions by the King's Men.
1.1. Malfi.

ANTONIO I admire it.
In seeking to reduce° both state and people *bring, lead back*
To a fixed order, their judicious king
Begins at home, quits° first his royal palace *rids*
Of flatt'ring sycophants, of dissolute
And infamous persons, which° he sweetly terms *which undertaking*
His master's masterpiece, the work of heaven,
Consid'ring duly that a prince's court
Is like a common fountain whence should flow
Pure silver drops in general;° but if't chance *to everyone, everywhere*
Some cursed example poison't near the head,
Death and diseases through the whole land spread.
And what is't makes this blessèd government
But a most provident council, who dare freely
Inform him° the corruption of the times? *Inform the King about*
Though some o'th'court hold° it presumption *consider*
To instruct princes what they ought to do,
It is a noble duty to inform them
What they ought to foresee.

[*Enter*] *Bosola.*

Here comes Bosola,
The only° court gall.° Yet I observe his railing *nonpareil / satirist*
Is not for simple love of piety;
Indeed, he rails at those things which he wants,
Would be as lecherous, covetous, or proud,
Bloody, or envious, as any man,
If he had means to be so.

[*Enter*] *Cardinal.*

Here's the Cardinal.
[*Antonio and Delio stand aside, observing.*]

BOSOLA [*to the Cardinal*] I do haunt you still.
CARDINAL So.
BOSOLA I have done you
Better service than to be slighted thus.
Miserable age, where only the reward° *the only reward*
Of doing well is the doing of it!
CARDINAL You enforce° your merit too much. *urge*
BOSOLA I fell into the galleys° in your service, where, for two years together, I wore two towels instead of a shirt, with a knot on the shoulder, after the fashion of a Roman mantle. Slighted thus? I will thrive some way. Blackbirds fatten best in hard weather; why not I, in these dog° days? *(for penal servitude)* *hot; unhealthy*
CARDINAL Would you could become honest!
BOSOLA With all your divinity, do but direct me the way to it. I have known many travel far for it, and yet return as arrant knaves as they went forth, because they carried themselves always along with them. [*Exit Cardinal.*]
Are you gone? Some fellows, they say, are possessed with the devil, but this great fellow were° able to possess the greatest devil and make him worse. *would be*
ANTONIO [*as he and Delio come forward*] He hath denied thee some suit?° *petition*

BOSOLA He and his brother are like plum trees that grow crooked over standing° pools; they are rich and o'erladen with fruit, but none but crows, pies,° and caterpillars feed on them. Could I be one of their flatt'ring panders, I would hang on their ears like a horse-leech° till I were full, and then drop off. I pray leave me. Who would rely upon these miserable dependences° in expectation to be advanced tomorrow? What creature ever fed worse than hoping Tantalus?[1] Nor ever died any man more fearfully than he that hoped° for a pardon. There are rewards for hawks and dogs when they have done us service, but for a soldier that hazards his limbs in a battle, nothing but a kind of geometry is his last supportation.[2]

stagnant / *magpies* / *bloodsucker* / *hopes of appointment* / *(in vain)*

DELIO Geometry?

BOSOLA Ay, to hang in a fair pair of slings,° take his latter swing° in the world upon an honorable pair of crutches, from hospital to hospital. Fare ye well, sir. And yet do not you scorn us, for places in the court are but like beds in the hospital, where this man's head lies at that man's foot, and so lower and lower. [*Exit.*]

i.e., crutches / *last fling*

DELIO I knew this fellow seven years in the galleys
For° a notorious murder, and 'twas thought — *For having committed*
The Cardinal suborned° it. He was released — *secretly ordered*
By the French general, Gaston de Foix,
When he recovered° Naples. — *delivered, relieved*

ANTONIO 'Tis great pity
He should be thus neglected. I have heard
He's very valiant. This foul melancholy
Will poison all his goodness; for, I'll tell you,
If too immoderate sleep be truly said
To be an inward rust unto the soul,
It then doth follow want° of action — *It follows that lack*
Breeds all black malcontents; and their close rearing,
Like moths in cloth, do hurt for want of wearing.[3]

[*Enter*] *Castruchio, Silvio, Roderigo,* [*and*] *Grisolan.*
[*Antonio and Delio stand aside at first, observing.*]

DELIO The presence° 'gins to fill. You promised me — *presence-chamber*
To make me the partaker of the natures
Of some of your great courtiers.

ANTONIO The Lord Cardinal's
And other strangers' that are now in court?
I shall.

[*Enter*] *Ferdinand.*

Here comes the great Calabrian duke.

FERDINAND Who took the ring oft'nest?[4]

1. For his sins, Tantalus was punished in Hades by being set in a pool of water that always receded when he bent over to drink and by being surrounded by fruit trees whose fruit similarly eluded his grasp.
2. I.e., all that a discharged soldier who has been crippled in battle can hope for is to hang suspended from his crutches (resembling a pair of compass dividers such as might be used in geometry) and to be dependent as a last resort on charity that is very likely not to be forthcoming. (Cf. lines 138–39 and note.)
3. Just as moths devour wool cloth that is packed away too tightly, melancholics do fretful harm when they are closely confined and isolated rather than being put to use.
4. Who won most often at the tournament sport of riding at the ring and spearing it on the point of one's lance?

SILVIO Antonio Bologna, my lord.

FERDINAND Our sister Duchess' great master of her household? Give him the jewel.° When shall we leave this sportive action and fall to action indeed?

the prize

CASTRUCHIO Methinks, my lord, you should not desire to go to war in person.

FERDINAND [*aside to his courtiers*] Now, for some gravity.— Why, my lord?

CASTRUCHIO It is fitting a soldier arise to be a prince, but not necessary a prince descend to be a captain.

FERDINAND No?

CASTRUCHIO No, my lord. He were° far better do it by a deputy.

would

FERDINAND Why should he not as well sleep or eat by a deputy? This might take idle, offensive, and base office° from him, whereas the other° deprives him of honor.

function
(fighting by deputy)

CASTRUCHIO Believe my experience: that realm is never long in quiet where the ruler is a soldier.

FERDINAND Thou told'st me thy wife could not endure fighting.

CASTRUCHIO True, my lord.

FERDINAND And of a jest she broke° of a captain she met, full of wounds. I have forgot it.

told, cracked

CASTRUCHIO She told him, my lord, he was a pitiful fellow, to lie, like the children of Ishmael, all in tents.[5]

FERDINAND Why, there's a wit were° able to undo all the surgeons o'the city, for, although gallants should quarrel and had drawn their weapons and were ready to go to it,° yet her persuasions would make them put up.°

that would be
(with sexual punning)
sheathe their swords

CASTRUCHIO That she would, my lord. How do you like my Spanish jennet?°

small Spanish horse

RODERIGO He is all fire.

FERDINAND I am of Pliny's opinion: I think he was begot by the wind.[6] He runs as if he were ballasted with quicksilver.[7]

SILVIO True, my lord, he reels from the tilt often.[8]

RODERIGO [*and*] GRISOLAN Ha, ha, ha!

FERDINAND Why do you laugh? Methinks you that are courtiers should be my touchwood:° take fire when I give fire, that is, laugh when I laugh, were the subject never so witty.

tinder

CASTRUCHIO True, my lord. I myself have heard a very good jest, and have scorned to seem to have so silly° a wit as to understand it.

simple

FERDINAND But I can laugh at your fool, my lord.

5. The children or descendants of Ishmael, Abraham's son by his bondwoman Hagar (see Genesis 16–25), were regarded as Arabs by the Jews; hence the allusion to their living in tents. With a pun on "tent" as a surgical dressing for a wound. "Ishmael" may be a mistake for "Israel," since the Israelites were also tent dwellers.

6. In his *Natural History* (8.42), Pliny the Elder (23–79 C.E.) tells of Portuguese mares that conceived by having the west wind blow in their genitals, whereupon they gave birth to wind-swift foals.

7. As if the only weight he is made to carry is mercury—a liquid metal at ordinary room temperature, quickly flowing and perhaps for that reason associated with the messenger of the gods; at the same time it is an especially heavy metal, and as ballast would be ceaselessly unstable rather than providing the stability that ballast should provide, in which context Ferdinand is teasing Castruchio. Since mercury was also used in the treatment of syphilis, Ferdinand may also be jesting at the expense of Castruchio by characterizing him as a ridiculous figure of a lover; see next note.

8. He balks often enough at a tournament. (There may also be a joke about male impotence, thus motivating the laughter in line 123.)

CASTRUCHIO He cannot speak, you know, but he makes faces.[9] My lady cannot abide him.

FERDINAND No?

CASTRUCHIO Nor endure to be in merry company, for she says too much laughing and too much company fills her too full of the wrinkle.

FERDINAND I would then have a mathematical instrument made for her face, that she might not laugh out of compass.[1]—I shall shortly visit you at Milan, Lord Silvio.

SILVIO Your Grace shall arrive most welcome.

FERDINAND [*turning to Antonio, who is still standing to one side with Delio*] You are a good horseman, Antonio. You have excellent riders in France. What do you think of good horsemanship?

ANTONIO Nobly, my lord. As out of the Grecian horse° issued many famous princes, so out of brave horsemanship arise the first sparks of growing resolution that raise the mind to noble action. *Trojan horse*

FERDINAND You have bespoke° it worthily. *spoken of*

[*Enter*] *Cardinal, Duchess,* [*and*] *Cariola* [*with attendants*].

SILVIO Your brother, the Lord Cardinal, and sister Duchess.

CARDINAL Are the galleys come about?° *returned to port*

GRISOLAN They are, my lord.

FERDINAND Here's the Lord Silvio is come to take his leave.

[*Antonio and Delio talk privately while Ferdinand, the Cardinal, and the others confer among themselves.*]

DELIO Now, sir, your promise: what's that Cardinal? I mean his temper?° They say he's a brave fellow, will play° his five thousand crowns° at tennis, dance, court ladies, and one that hath fought single combats.° *temperament / gamble* *gold coins* *duels*

ANTONIO Some such flashes superficially hang on him for form. But observe his inward character: he is a melancholy churchman. The spring° in his face is nothing but the engend'ring of toads. Where he is jealous of any man, he lays worse plots for them than ever was imposed on Hercules, for he strews in his way flatterers, panders, intelligencers,° atheists,° and a thousand such political° monsters. He should have been° pope, but instead of coming to it by the primitive° decency of the church, he did bestow bribes so largely and so impudently as if he would have carried it away without heaven's knowledge. Some good he hath done. *seeming attractiveness* *spies* *villains / scheming* *wished to be* *time-honored*

DELIO You have given° too much of him. What's his brother? *reported, said*

ANTONIO The Duke there? A most perverse and turbulent nature.
What appears in him mirth is merely outside;
If he laugh heartily, it is to laugh

9. Castruchio employs a household fool who, like many such fools, seems to be a congenital idiot—able in this case to make merry faces but not to speak. Ferdinand, in line 130, may mislead Castruchio by suggesting that he is laughing at this fool, not at Castruchio himself.

1. Immoderately; with a pun on "compass," a pair of dividers used as a "mathematical instrument" (line 137). Cf. 1.1.60–61 and note on "geometry."

All honesty out of fashion.
DELIO Twins?
ANTONIO In quality.
He° speaks with others' tongues and hears men's suits *(Ferdinand)*
With others' ears; will seem to sleep o'th'bench° *judicial bench*
Only to entrap offenders in their answers;
Dooms men to death by information,° *informers' evidence*
Rewards by hearsay.
DELIO Then the law to him
Is like a foul black cobweb to a spider:
He makes it his dwelling and a prison
To entangle those shall feed him.
ANTONIO Most true.
He nev'r pays debts unless they be shrewd turns,° *malicious injuries*
And those he will confess that he doth owe.
Last, for° his brother there, the Cardinal: *as for*
They that do flatter him most say oracles
Hang at his lips; and verily I believe them,
For the devil speaks in them.
But for° their sister, the right noble Duchess: *as for*
You never fixed your eye on three fair medals,
Cast in one figure,° of so different temper.° *mold / temperament*
For her discourse, it is so full of rapture
You only will begin then to be sorry
When she doth end her speech, and wish, in wonder,
She held it less vainglory to talk much
Than your penance to hear her.[2] Whilst she speaks,
She throws upon a man so sweet a look
That it were able to raise one to a galliard° *a lively dance*
That lay in a dead palsy,° and to dote *paralysis*
On that sweet countenance. But in that look
There speaketh so divine a continence° *self-restraint*
As cuts off all lascivious and vain hope.
Her days are practiced in such noble virtue
That sure her nights—nay, more, her very sleeps°— *dreams*
Are more in heaven than other ladies' shrifts.° *confessions*
Let all sweet ladies break their flatt'ring glasses° *mirrors*
And dress themselves in her.° *with her as a model*
DELIO Fie, Antonio,
You play the wire-drawer with her commendations.[3]
ANTONIO I'll case° the picture up only thus much. *frame, enclose*
All her particular worth grows to this sum:
She stains° the time past, lights the time to come. *eclipses, darkens*
[*Cariola approaches Antonio confidentially.*]
CARIOLA You must attend my lady in the gallery
Some half an hour hence.
ANTONIO [*privately to Cariola*] I shall.
[*Antonio and Delio withdraw.*]
FERDINAND Sister, I have a suit to you.
DUCHESS To me, sir?

2. You would wonderingly wish that her modest reticence in speech were even less than any regret you might possibly have in hearing her speak. (A hyperbolic way of saying that you would wish her to continue speaking.)
3. I.e., You draw her praises out too ingeniously. (A wire-drawer converts metal into wire by drawing it through successively smaller holes.)

FERDINAND A gentleman here,° Daniel de Bosola, *at court (not present)*
One that was in the galleys.
DUCHESS Yes, I know him.
FERDINAND A worthy fellow h' is. Pray let me entreat for
The provisorship° of your horse. *office of manager*
DUCHESS Your knowledge of him
Commends him and prefers him.° *Recommends him*
FERDINAND [*to an attendant*] Call him hither.
[*Exit attendant.*]
We are now upon parting.° Good Lord Silvio, *ready to depart*
Do us commend° to all our noble friends *Give our greetings*
At the leaguer.° *military camp*
SILVIO Sir, I shall.
DUCHESS You are for Milan?
SILVIO I am.
DUCHESS [*to attendants*] Bring the caroches.° [*To her guests*] *coaches*
We'll bring° you down to the haven. *accompany*
[*Exeunt all except the Cardinal and Ferdinand.*]
CARDINAL Be sure you entertain° that Bosola *employ*
For your intelligence.° I would not be seen in't, *spying*
And therefore many times I have slighted him
When he did court our furtherance,° as this morning. *seek advancement*
FERDINAND Antonio, the great master of her household,
Had been far fitter.
CARDINAL You are deceived in him.
His nature is too honest for such business.

[*Enter Bosola.*]

He comes. I'll leave you. [*Exit.*]
BOSOLA I was lured to you.
FERDINAND My brother here, the Cardinal, could never
Abide you.
BOSOLA Never since he was in my debt.[4]
FERDINAND Maybe some oblique character in your face
Made him suspect you?
BOSOLA Doth he study physiognomy?
There's no more credit to be given to th'face
Than to a sick man's urine,° which some call *(used in diagnosis)*
The physician's whore because she cozens° him. *the urine deceives*
He did suspect me wrongfully.
FERDINAND For that
You must give great° men leave to take their times. *noble*
Distrust doth cause us seldom be deceived.[5]
You see, the oft shaking of the cedar tree
Fastens it more at root.
BOSOLA Yet take heed,
For to suspect a friend unworthily
Instructs him the next° way to suspect you, *most direct*
And prompts him to deceive you.
FERDINAND [*giving money*] There's gold.
BOSOLA So,
What follows? Never rained such showers° as these *(see 2.2.21 n)*

4. Never since he became obligated to me for the things I had done for him.

5. A wary suspicion about men prompts us to avoid the danger of being deceived.

Without thunderbolts i'th'tail of them.
Whose throat must I cut?
FERDINAND Your inclination to shed blood rides post° *at full speed*
Before my occasion to use you. I give you that
To live i'th'court here and observe the Duchess,
To note all the particulars of her havior—
What suitors do solicit her for marriage,
And whom she best affects.° She's a young widow; *likes*
I would not have her marry again.
BOSOLA No, sir?
FERDINAND Do not you ask the reason, but be satisfied
I say I would not.
BOSOLA It seems you would create me
One of your familiars.[6]
FERDINAND Familiar? What's that?
BOSOLA Why, a very quaint invisible devil, in flesh:
An intelligencer.
FERDINAND Such a kind of thriving thing
I would wish thee; and ere long thou mayst arrive
At a higher place by't.
BOSOLA [*offering the money back*] Take your devils,
Which hell calls angels!° These cursed gifts would make *gold coins (with pun)*
You a corrupter, me an impudent traitor,
And should I take these, they'd take me to hell.
FERDINAND Sir, I'll take nothing from you that I have given.
There is a place° that I procured for you *position*
This morning: the provisorship° o'th'horse. *management, purveying*
Have you heard on't?
BOSOLA No.
FERDINAND 'Tis yours. Is't not worth thanks?
BOSOLA I would have you curse yourself now, that your bounty,
Which makes men truly noble, e'er should make
Me a villain.[7] Oh, that to avoid ingratitude
For the good deed you have done me, I must do
All the ill man can invent! Thus the devil
Candies° all sins o'er, and what heaven terms vile *Sugars*
That names he complemental.° *a polite accomplishment*
FERDINAND Be yourself;
Keep your old garb° of melancholy; 'twill express *style, mode*
You envy those that stand above your reach,
Yet strive not to come near 'em.[8] This will gain
Access to private lodgings, where yourself
May, like a politic° dormouse— *crafty*
BOSOLA As I have seen some
Feed in a lord's dish,° half asleep, not seeming *Dine at a lord's table*
To listen to any talk, and yet these rogues
Have cut his throat in a dream.° What's my place? *in their fantasies*
The provisorship o'th'horse? Say then my corruption
Grew out of horse dung. I am your creature.° *dependent; agent*

6. (1) Intimates; (2) spirits usually in the form of animals, attending a person as demonic guards and assistants.
7. How deplorable that your bounty, which should be the distinguishing mark of truly noble men, is now being offered by you to tempt me to villainy.
8. Ferdinand wryly compliments Bosola for an attitude that simultaneously envies great men and distances Bosola from aspiring to emulate their purportedly evil ways.

FERDINAND Away!
BOSOLA Let good men, for good deeds, covet good fame,
Since place and riches oft are bribes of shame.
Sometimes the devil doth preach. *Exit Bosola.*

[*Enter Cardinal, Duchess, and Cariola.*]

CARDINAL [*to the Duchess*] We are to part from you, and your own discretion
Must now be your director.
FERDINAND You are a widow;
You know already what man is. And therefore
Let not youth, high promotion, eloquence—
CARDINAL No, nor anything without the addition,° honor, *title*
Sway your high blood.° *lineage; passion*
FERDINAND Marry? They are most luxurious° *lecherous*
Will° wed twice. *Who will*
CARDINAL Oh, fie!
FERDINAND Their livers° are more spotted *(seat of violent passion)*
Than Laban's sheep.[9]
DUCHESS Diamonds are of most value,
They say, that have passed through most jewelers' hands.
FERDINAND Whores, by that rule, are precious.
DUCHESS Will you hear me?
I'll never marry.
CARDINAL So most widows say,
But commonly that motion° lasts no longer *impulse; resolve*
Than the turning of an hourglass; the funeral sermon
And it end both together.
FERDINAND Now hear me:
You live in a rank pasture here, i'th'court.
There is a kind of honeydew° that's deadly; *sticky secretion*
'Twill poison your fame.° Look to't. Be not cunning, *reputation*
For they whose faces do belie their hearts
Are witches ere they arrive at twenty years—
Ay, and give the devil suck.° *(as witches allegedly did)*
DUCHESS This is terrible good counsel.
FERDINAND Hypocrisy is woven of a fine small thread,
Subtler than Vulcan's engine;[1] yet, believe't,
Your darkest actions—nay, your privat'st thoughts—
Will come to light.
CARDINAL You may flatter yourself
And take your own choice, privately be married
Under the eaves° of night. *i.e., cover*
FERDINAND Think 't the best voyage
That e'er you made, like the irregular crab,
Which, though 't goes backward, thinks that it goes right
Because it goes its own way. But observe:
Such weddings may more properly be said

9. Genesis 30.25–43 tells the story of how Jacob outwitted his father-in-law and uncle Laban by striking a bargain with Laban such that he would get all the parti-color animals of Laban's flock, whereupon Jacob set up streaked and parti-color rods in front of the flock at mating time, thus inducing the animals to conceive only parti-color offspring.

1. The finely woven net in which Vulcan caught his wife, Venus, making love with Mars.

To be executed than celebrated.
CARDINAL The marriage night
Is the entrance into some prison.
FERDINAND And those joys,
Those lustful pleasures, are like heavy sleeps
Which do forerun man's mischief.
CARDINAL Fare you well.
Wisdom begins at the end.° Remember it. [*Exit.*] *late in life*
DUCHESS I think this speech between you both was studied,° *rehearsed*
It came so roundly° off. *fluently; bluntly*
FERDINAND You are my sister.
[*Showing his dagger*] This was my father's poniard. Do you see?
I'd be loath to see't look rusty, 'cause 'twas his.
I would have you to give o'er these chargeable° revels; *costly*
A visor and a mask are whispering rooms° *private chambers*
That were nev'r built for goodness. Fare ye well—
And women like that part which, like the lamprey,° *an eel-like fish*
Hath nev'r a bone in't.
DUCHESS Fie, sir!
FERDINAND Nay,
I mean the tongue. Variety of courtship![2]
What cannot a neat° knave with a smooth tale *elegant; rascally*
Make a woman believe? Farewell, lusty widow. [*Exit.*]
DUCHESS Shall this move me? If all my royal kindred
Lay in my way unto this marriage,
I'd make them my low footsteps.° And even now, *steps, rungs of a ladder*
Even in this hate°—as men in some great battles, *my brothers' hatred*
By apprehending danger, have achieved
Almost impossible actions; I have heard soldiers say so—
So I, through frights and threat'nings, will assay
This dangerous venture. Let old wives report
I winked° and chose a husband.—Cariola, *shut my eyes*
To thy known secrecy I have given up
More than my life: my fame.
CARIOLA Both shall be safe,
For I'll conceal this secret from the world
As warily as those that trade in poison
Keep poison from their children.
DUCHESS Thy protestation
Is ingenious and hearty.° I believe it. *pure and heartfelt*
Is Antonio come?
CARIOLA He attends you.° *awaits your orders*
DUCHESS Good dear soul,
Leave me; but place thyself behind the arras,° *wall hanging*
Where thou mayst overhear us. Wish me good speed,° *fortune, success*
For I am going into a wilderness
Where I shall find nor° path nor friendly clew° *neither / guiding thread*
To be my guide. [*Cariola withdraws behind the arras.*]

[*Enter Antonio.*]

I sent for you. Sit down.
Take pen and ink, and write. Are you ready?
ANTONIO Yes.

2. Oh, the infinitely varied ways of deceiving in courtship!

DUCHESS What did I say?
ANTONIO That I should write somewhat.
DUCHESS Oh, I remember.
After these triumphs° and this large expense, *festivities*
It's fit, like thrifty husbands° we inquire *housekeepers*
What's laid up° for tomorrow. *stored away*
ANTONIO So please Your beauteous Excellence.
DUCHESS Beauteous?
Indeed, I thank you. I look young for your sake.
You have ta'en my cares upon you.
ANTONIO I'll fetch Your Grace
The particulars of your revenue and expense.
DUCHESS Oh, you are an upright treasurer. But you mistook,
For when I said I meant to make inquiry
What's laid up for tomorrow, I did mean
What's laid up yonder for me.
ANTONIO Where?
DUCHESS In heaven.
I am making my will, as 'tis fit princes should,
In perfect memory;° and I pray, sir, tell me, *sound mind*
Were not one better make it smiling, thus,
Than in deep groans and terrible ghastly looks,
As if the gifts we parted with procured° *produced*
That violent distraction?
ANTONIO Oh, much better.
DUCHESS If I had a husband, now, this care were quit.° *would be got rid of*
But I intend to make you overseer.
What good deed shall we first remember? Say.
ANTONIO Begin with that first good deed began i'th'world
After man's creation: the sacrament of marriage.
I'd have you first provide for a good husband,
Give him all.
DUCHESS All?
ANTONIO Yes, your excellent self.
DUCHESS In a winding-sheet?° *shroud*
ANTONIO In a couple.° *pair; marriage*
DUCHESS Saint Winifred,° that were a strange will! *a Welsh martyr*
ANTONIO 'Twere strange if there were no will in you
To marry again.
DUCHESS What do you think of marriage?
ANTONIO I take't as those that deny purgatory:
It locally contains or° heaven or hell; *either*
There's no third place in't.
DUCHESS How do you affect° it? *fancy, feel for*
ANTONIO My banishment, feeding my melancholy,
Would often reason thus:—
DUCHESS Pray let's hear it.
ANTONIO Say a man never marry, nor have children,
What takes that from him? Only the bare name
Of being a father, or the weak delight
To see the little wanton° ride a-cockhorse *(term of endearment)*
Upon a painted stick, or hear him chatter
Like a taught starling.
DUCHESS Fie, fie, what's all this?
One of your eyes is bloodshot. Use my ring to't.

[*She gives him a ring.*]
They say 'tis very sovereign.° 'Twas my wedding ring, *efficacious*
And I did vow never to part with it
But to my second husband.
ANTONIO You have parted with it now.
DUCHESS Yes, to help your eyesight.
ANTONIO You have made me stark blind.
DUCHESS How?
ANTONIO There is a saucy and ambitious devil
Is dancing in this circle.
DUCHESS Remove him.
ANTONIO How?
DUCHESS There needs small conjuration when your finger
May do it: thus. [*She puts the ring on his finger.*] Is it fit?
ANTONIO What said you? *He kneels.*
DUCHESS Sir,
This goodly roof of yours is too low built;
I cannot stand upright in't, nor discourse,
Without° I raise it higher. Raise yourself, *Unless*
Or, if you please, my hand to help you: so.
[*She helps him up.*]
ANTONIO Ambition, madam, is a great man's madness,
That is not kept in chains and close-pent° rooms, *locked-tight*
But in fair, lightsome lodgings, and is girt° *surrounded*
With the wild noise of prattling visitants,
Which makes it lunatic beyond all cure.
Conceive not I am so stupid but I aim° *guess, conjecture*
Whereto your favors tend; but he's a fool
That, being a-cold, would thrust his hands i'th'fire
To warm them.
DUCHESS So, now the ground's broke,
You may discover what a wealthy mine
I make you lord of.
ANTONIO Oh, my unworthiness!
DUCHESS You were ill to sell yourself.
This dark'ning of your worth is not like that
Which tradesmen use i'th'city; their false lights
Are to rid bad wares off.[3] And I must tell you,
If you will know where breathes a complete° man— *fully accomplished*
I speak it without flattery—turn your eyes
And progress° through yourself. *make a stately tour*
ANTONIO Were there nor heaven nor hell,
I should be honest. I have long served virtue,
And nev'r ta'en wages of her.
DUCHESS Now she pays it.
The misery of us that are born great!
We are forced to woo, because none dare woo us;
And as a tyrant doubles° with his words, *speaks duplicitously*
And fearfully equivocates, so we
Are forced to express our violent passions
In riddles and in dreams, and leave the path

3. London merchants were often accused of keeping their shops poorly lit so that customers would not see defects in the wares.

Of simple virtue, which was never made
To seem the thing it is not. Go, go brag
You have left me heartless! Mine is in your bosom;
I hope 'twill multiply love there. You do tremble.
Make not your heart so dead a piece of flesh
To fear more than to love me. Sir, be confident.
What is't distracts you? This is flesh and blood, sir;
'Tis not the figure cut in alabaster
Kneels° at my husband's tomb. Awake, awake, man! *That kneels*
I do here put off all vain ceremony,
And only do appear to you a young widow
That claims you for her husband, and, like a widow,
I use but half a blush in't.

ANTONIO Truth speak for me!
I will remain the constant sanctuary
Of your good name.

DUCHESS I thank you, gentle love,
And, 'cause you° shall not come to me in debt, *in order that you*
Being now my steward, here upon your lips
I sign your *quietus est.*[4] [*She kisses him.*]
This you should have begged now.
I have seen children oft eat sweetmeats thus,
As fearful to devour them too soon.

ANTONIO But for your brothers?

DUCHESS Do not think of them.
All discord, without this circumference,[5]
Is only to be pitied and not feared.
Yet, should they know it, time will easily
Scatter the tempest.

ANTONIO These words should be mine,
And all the parts you have spoke, if some part of it
Would not have savored flattery.

DUCHESS Kneel. [*Cariola comes forth from behind the arras.*]

ANTONIO Hah?

DUCHESS Be not amazed. This woman's of my counsel.
I have heard lawyers say, a contract in a chamber
Per verba de presenti[6] is absolute marriage.
[*The Duchess and Antonio kneel.*]
Bless, heaven, this sacred Gordian,° which let violence *i.e., knot*
Never untwine!

ANTONIO And may our sweet affections, like the spheres,° *heavenly spheres*
Be still° in motion— *perpetually*

DUCHESS Quick'ning,° and make *Coming alive*
The like soft° music— *ethereal*

ANTONIO That we may imitate the loving palms,° *palm trees*
Best emblem of a peaceful marriage,
That nev'r bore fruit divided[7]—

DUCHESS What can the church force° more? *enforce, urge*

ANTONIO That Fortune may not know an accident,
Either of joy or sorrow, to divide

4. I acquit you of any payment due.
5. Outside of these bounds. (Referring to the marriage bonds linking them and to their mutual embrace.)
6. Literally, "By means of words or vows spoken from the present (and in one another's presence)." Marriage vows were valid and binding when spoken in this fashion. Cariola serves as a witness.
7. A palm tree cannot reproduce and bear fruit alone; it must cross-pollinate with another.

Our fixèd wishes!
DUCHESS How can the church build faster?° *more firmly*
We now are man and wife, and 'tis the church
That must but echo this. [*They rise.*] Maid, stand apart.—
I now am blind.
ANTONIO What's your conceit° in this? *idea*
DUCHESS I would have you lead your fortune by the hand
Unto your marriage-bed.
(You speak in me this, for we now are one.)
We'll only lie, and talk together, and plot
T'appease my humorous° kindred; and, if you please, *temperamental*
Like the old tale in "Alexander and Lodowick,"
Lay a naked sword between us, keep us chaste.[8]
Oh, let me shroud° my blushes in your bosom, *veil, hide*
Since 'tis the treasury of all my secrets.
[*Exit Antonio, leading the Duchess.*]
CARIOLA Whether the spirit of greatness or of woman
Reign most in her, I know not, but it shows
A fearful madness. I owe her much of pity. *Exit.*

2.1

[*Enter*] *Bosola* [*and*] *Castruchio.*

BOSOLA You say you would fain be taken for an eminent
courtier?° *member of a law court*
CASTRUCHIO 'Tis the very main° of my ambition. *chief aim*
BOSOLA Let me see; you have a reasonable good face for't
already, and your nightcap° expresses your ears sufficient *lawyer's skullcap*
largely. I would have you learn to twirl the strings of your
band° with a good grace, and in a set speech, at th'end of *neck-band*
every sentence, to hum three or four times, or blow your
nose till it smart again, to recover your memory. When you
come to be a president° in criminal causes,° if you smile *presiding judge / cases*
upon a prisoner, hang him, but if you frown upon him and
threaten him, let him be sure to scape the gallows.
CASTRUCHIO I would be a very merry president.
BOSOLA Do not sup a-nights; 'twill beget you an admirable wit.
CASTRUCHIO Rather it would make me have a good stomach° *appetite; anger*
to quarrel, for they say your roaring boys° eat meat seldom, *unruly bullies*
and that makes them so valiant. But how shall I know
whether the people take me for an eminent fellow?
BOSOLA I will teach a trick to know it. Give out° you lie a- *Let it be known*
dying, and if you hear the common people curse you, be sure
you are taken for one of the prime nightcaps.° *i.e., lawyers*

[*Enter*] *an Old Lady.*

You come from painting° now? *applying cosmetics*
OLD LADY From what?
BOSOLA Why, from your scurvy face physic.° To behold thee *medicine*
not painted inclines somewhat near a miracle. These in thy
face here were deep ruts and foul sloughs° the last progress.° *ditches / state journey*

8. In the story of "The Two Faithful Friends," Lodowick married the Princess of Hungaria in Alexander's name and then nightly laid a sword between him and the bride lest he should wrong his friend.
2.1. Malfi, about nine months later.

There was a lady in France that, having had the smallpox, flayed the skin off her face to make it more level; and whereas before she looked like a nutmeg-grater, after she resembled an abortive hedgehog.

OLD LADY Do you call this painting?

BOSOLA No, no, but careening[1] of an old morphewed° lady, to make her disembogue° again. There's roughcast phrase to your plastic.[2] *scabbed* *put to sea*

OLD LADY It seems you are well acquainted with my closet?° *private chamber*

BOSOLA One would suspect it for a shop of witchcraft, to find in it the fat of serpents, spawn of snakes, Jews' spittle, and their young children's ordure°—and all these for the face. I would sooner eat a dead pigeon, taken from the soles of the feet of one sick of the plague, than kiss one of you fasting. Here are two of you, whose sin of your youth is the very patrimony of the physician, makes him renew his footcloth with the spring and change his high-prized courtesan with the fall of the leaf.[3] I do wonder you do not loathe yourselves. *excrement*

Observe my meditation now:
What thing is in this outward form of man
To be beloved? We account it ominous
If nature do produce a colt, or lamb,
A fawn, or goat, in any limb resembling
A man, and fly from't as a prodigy.° *monster*
Man stands amazed to see his deformity
In any other creature but himself.
But in our own flesh, though we bear diseases
Which have their true names only ta'en from beasts,
As the most ulcerous wolf and swinish measle,[4]
Though we are eaten up of lice and worms,
And though continually we bear about us
A rotten and dead body, we delight
To hide it in rich tissue. All our fear—
Nay, all our terror—is, lest our physician
Should put us in the ground, to be made sweet.

[*To Castruchio*] Your wife's gone to Rome. You two couple, and get you to the wells at Lucca,° to recover your aches. *a famous spa*

[*Exeunt Castruchio and the Old Lady.*]

I have other work on foot. I observe our duchess
Is sick a-days. She pukes; her stomach seethes;
The fins° of her eyelids look most teeming blue;[5] *rims*
She wanes i'th'cheek and waxes fat i'th'flank,
And, contrary to our Italian fashion,
Wears a loose-bodied gown. There's somewhat in't.° *inside it; going on*
I have a trick may chance discover it,
A pretty° one: I have bought some apricots, *clever*
The first our spring yields.

[*Enter*] *Antonio* [*and*] *Delio* [*conversing privately*].

1. Turning a boat on its side for scraping and repairs.
2. There's a plainspoken answer to your modeling in cosmetics.
3. Whose youthful indiscretions (resulting in venereal disease) make the physician so rich in fees that he is able to buy a new ornamental cloth for his horse every spring and acquire a new mistress every fall.
4. "Wolf" can refer to a malignant or corrosive disease in men and animals, a kind of ulcer. The disease of measles in humans was often confused with a skin disease in swine, since "mesel" means "leprous."
5. Expressive of pregnancy.

DELIO And so long since married?
You amaze me.
ANTONIO Let me seal your lips forever,
For, did I think that anything but th'air
Could carry these words from you, I should wish
You had no breath at all.
[*To Bosola*] Now, sir, in your contemplation? You are studying to become a great wise fellow?

BOSOLA Oh, sir, the opinion of° wisdom is a foul tetter° that runs all over a man's body. If simplicity direct us to have no evil, it directs us to a happy being, for the subtlest folly proceeds from the subtlest wisdom.[6] Let me be simply honest. *reputation for / sore*

ANTONIO I do understand your inside.

BOSOLA Do you so?

ANTONIO Because you would not seem to appear to th'world puffed up with your preferment,° you continue this out-of-fashion melancholy. Leave it, leave it. *advancement*

BOSOLA Give me leave to be honest in any phrase, in any compliment whatsoever. Shall I confess myself to you? I look no higher than I can reach. They are the gods that must ride on winged horses; a lawyer's mule[7] of a slow pace will both suit my disposition and business. For mark me: when a man's mind rides faster than his horse can gallop, they quickly both tire.

ANTONIO You would look up to heaven, but I think the devil, that rules i'th'air, stands in your light.

BOSOLA Oh, sir, you are lord of the ascendant,[8] chief man with the Duchess; a duke was your cousin-german removed.° *first cousin once removed* Say you were lineally descended from King Pepin,° or he himself: what of this? *Frankish king (751–68)* Search the heads° of the greatest rivers in the world, you shall find them but bubbles of water. *sources* Some would think the souls of princes were brought forth by some more weighty cause than those of meaner° persons. *of humbler stationed* They are deceived. There's the same hand to them;° the like passions sway them. *They were created alike* The same reason that makes a vicar go to law for a tithe-pig[9] and undo his neighbors makes them° spoil° a whole province and batter down goodly cities with the cannon. *(princes)* / *lay waste*

[*Enter the*] *Duchess* [*attended*].

DUCHESS Your arm, Antonio. Do I not grow fat?
I am exceeding short-winded.—Bosola,
I would have you, sir, provide for me a litter,[1]
Such a one as the Duchess of Florence rode in.
BOSOLA The Duchess used one when she was great with child.
DUCHESS I think she did. [*To an attendant lady*] Come
hither; mend my ruff. [*The lady tends to her.*]
Here. When?° Thou art such a tedious lady, and *(expressing impatience)*
Thy breath smells of lemon peels.[2] Would thou hadst done!° *Quick, finish up!*

6. If guileless lack of cleverness makes a person incapable of doing evil, it makes for happiness, since cunning leads only to clever folly.
7. Lawyers rode mules on ceremonial occasions.
8. You are (in astrological terms) the ruling planet shedding a dominant influence.
9. A farm animal given to the church as a tithe, or a tenth of one's income, in lieu of cash.
1. A small enclosed couch provided with shafts and used for carrying a single passenger.
2. Used to mask bad breath.

Shall I swoon under thy fingers? I am
So troubled with the mother!° *hysteria; pregnancy*
BOSOLA [*aside*] I fear too much.
DUCHESS [*to Antonio*] I have heard you say that the French courtiers
Wear their hats on 'fore the King.
ANTONIO I have seen it.
DUCHESS In the presence?° *the royal presence*
ANTONIO Yes.
DUCHESS Why should not we bring up° that fashion? *institute*
'Tis ceremony, more than duty, that consists
In the removing of a piece of felt.° *a felt hat*
Be you the example to the rest o'th'court;
Put on your hat first.
ANTONIO You must pardon me.
I have seen, in colder countries than in France,
Nobles stand bare° to th'prince, and the distinction *bareheaded*
Methought showed reverently.
BOSOLA I have a present for Your Grace.
DUCHESS For me, sir?
BOSOLA Apricots, madam.
DUCHESS Oh, sir, where are they?
I have heard of none to-year.° *this year*
BOSOLA [*aside*] Good. Her color rises.
DUCHESS [*taking the fruit*] Indeed, I thank you. They are wondrous fair ones.
What an unskillful fellow is our gardener!
We shall have none this month. [*She eats.*]
BOSOLA Will not Your Grace pare them?
DUCHESS No. They taste of musk, methinks. Indeed they do.
BOSOLA I know not. Yet I wish Your Grace had pared 'em.
DUCHESS Why?
BOSOLA I forget to tell you the knave gard'ner,
Only to raise his profit by them the sooner,
Did ripen them in horse dung.
DUCHESS Oh, you jest!
[*To Antonio*] You shall judge. Pray, taste one.
ANTONIO Indeed, madam,
I do not love the fruit.
DUCHESS Sir, you are loath
To rob us of our dainties. [*To Bosola*] 'Tis a delicate fruit;
They say they are restorative?
BOSOLA 'Tis a pretty art, this grafting.
DUCHESS 'Tis so: a bett'ring of nature.
BOSOLA To make a pippin° grow upon a crab,° *sweet apple / crab apple*
A damson° on a blackthorn.° [*Aside*] How greedily she eats them! *sweet plum / spiny tree*
A whirlwind strike off these bawd farthingales!° *deceiving petticoats*
For, but for that and the loose-bodied gown,
I should have discovered apparently° *clearly, visibly*
The young springald° cutting a caper° in her belly. *stripling / dancing*
DUCHESS I thank you, Bosola. They were right good ones,
If they do not make me sick.
ANTONIO How now, madam?
DUCHESS This green fruit and my stomach are not friends.

How they swell me!
BOSOLA [*aside*] Nay, you are too much swelled already.
DUCHESS Oh, I am in an extreme cold sweat.
BOSOLA I am very sorry.
DUCHESS Lights to my chamber! O good Antonio,
I fear I am undone. *Exit Duchess* [*attended*].
DELIO Lights there, lights!
[*Exeunt all but Antonio and Delio.*]
ANTONIO O my most trusty Delio, we are lost!
I fear she's fall'n in labor, and there's left
No time for her remove.
DELIO Have you prepared
Those ladies to attend her, and procured
That politic° safe conveyance for the midwife — *cunningly contrived*
Your duchess plotted?
ANTONIO I have.
DELIO Make use then of this forced occasion:
Give out° that Bosola hath poisoned her — *Let it be known*
With these apricots. That will give some color° — *excuse*
For her keeping close.° — *out of sight, private*
ANTONIO Fie, fie! The physicians
Will then flock to her.
DELIO For that you may pretend
She'll use some prepared antidote of her own
Lest the physicians should repoison her.
ANTONIO I am lost in amazement. I know not what to think on't.
Exeunt.

2.2

[*Enter*] *Bosola.*

BOSOLA So, so: there's no question but her tetchiness° and most vulturous eating of the apricots are apparent° signs of breeding. — *testiness*; *manifest*

[*Enter the*] *Old Lady.*

Now?
OLD LADY I am in haste, sir. [*He prevents her leaving.*]
BOSOLA There was a young waiting-woman had° a monstrous desire to see the glasshouse.° — *who had*; *glass factory*
OLD LADY Nay, pray let me go.
BOSOLA And it was only to know what strange instrument it was° should swell up a glass to the fashion of a woman's belly. — *was that*
OLD LADY I will hear no more of the glasshouse. You are still abusing women?
BOSOLA Who, I? No, only, by the way now and then, mention your° frailties. The orange tree bears ripe and green fruit and blossoms all together, and some of you give entertainment for pure love, but more for more precious reward. The lusty spring smells well, but drooping autumn tastes well.[1] If we — *you women's*

2.2. Malfi.
1. Bosola argues that there is a sexual market for mature women. They may not smell as nice as spring blossoms, but they taste sweet still.

have the same golden showers that rained in the time of Jupiter the Thunderer, you have the same Danaës still, to hold up their laps to receive them.[2] Didst thou never study the mathematics?

OLD LADY What's that, sir?

BOSOLA Why, to know the trick how to make a many lines meet in one center.[3] Go, go; give your foster daughters good counsel: tell them that the devil takes delight to hang at a woman's girdle, like a false, rusty watch, that she cannot discern how the time passes. *[Exit Old Lady.]*

[*Enter*] *Antonio, Delio, Roderigo,* [*and*] *Grisolan.*

ANTONIO Shut up the court gates.
RODERIGO Why, sir? What's the danger?
ANTONIO Shut up the posterns° presently,° and call *back doors / at once*
All the officers° o'th'court. *functionaries, servants*
GRISOLAN I shall, instantly. [*Exit.*]
ANTONIO Who keeps the key o'th'park gate?
RODERIGO Forobosco.[4]
ANTONIO Let him bring't presently.
[*Roderigo goes to the door.*]

[*Grisolan and Roderigo return with*] *Servants.*

FIRST SERVANT Oh, gentlemen o'th'court, the foulest treason!

BOSOLA [*aside*] If that these apricots should be poisoned, now, without my knowledge!

FIRST SERVANT There was taken even now a Switzer° in the Duchess' bedchamber. *Swiss mercenary*

SECOND SERVANT A Switzer?

FIRST SERVANT With a pistol in his great codpiece.° *appendage on breeches*

BOSOLA Ha, ha, ha!

FIRST SERVANT The codpiece was the case for't.

SECOND SERVANT There was a cunning traitor. Who would have searched his codpiece?

FIRST SERVANT True, if he had kept out of the ladies' chambers. And all the molds of° his buttons were leaden bullets. *for*

SECOND SERVANT Oh, wicked cannibal!° A firelock° in's codpiece? *savage / firing mechanism*

FIRST SERVANT 'Twas a French plot, upon my life.

SECOND SERVANT To see what the devil can do!

ANTONIO All the officers here?

SERVANTS We are.

ANTONIO Gentlemen,
We have lost much plate,° you know; and but this evening *silver or gold tableware*
Jewels to the value of four thousand ducats° *gold coins*
Are missing in the Duchess' cabinet.° *private apartment*
Are the gates shut?
FIRST SERVANT Yes.
ANTONIO 'Tis the Duchess' pleasure

2. Danaë, locked in a tower of brass by her father in a vain attempt to thwart an oracle that her son would kill him, was visited by Zeus (Roman Jupiter) in a shower of gold. Bosola's satiric point is that as long as men lust after women and bribe them with gifts, there will be women willing to be thus seduced.

3. Bosola accuses women of having the cunning to make all sinful desires converge on them. ("Center" suggests the female sexual body.)

4. One of the "officers," or functionaries, of the court, mentioned only in "The Actors' Names" and here.

Each officer be locked into his chamber
Till the sunrising, and to send the keys
Of all their chests and of their outward doors
Into her bedchamber. She is very sick.

RODERIGO At her pleasure.

ANTONIO She entreats you take't not ill. The innocent
Shall be the more approved° by it. *vindicated, commended*

BOSOLA Gentleman o'th'woodyard,[5] where's your Switzer now?

FIRST SERVANT By this hand, 'twas credibly reported by one o'th'black guard.° [*Exeunt all except Antonio and Delio.*] *scullions, low menials*

DELIO How fares it with the Duchess?

ANTONIO She's exposed
Unto the worst of torture, pain, and fear.

DELIO Speak to her all happy comfort.

ANTONIO How I do play the fool with mine own danger!
You are this night, dear friend, to post° to Rome. *hasten*
My life lies in° your service. *depends on*

DELIO Do not doubt me.

ANTONIO Oh, 'tis far from me; and yet fear presents me
Somewhat° that looks like danger. *Something*

DELIO Believe it,
'Tis but the shadow of your fear, no more.
How superstitiously we mind° our evils! *consider, think of*
The throwing down salt, or crossing of a hare,
Bleeding at nose, the stumbling of a horse,
Or singing of a cricket are of power
To daunt whole man in us. Sir, fare you well.
I wish you all the joys of a blessed father;
And, for° my faith,° lay this unto your breast: *as for / loyalty*
Old friends, like old swords, still are trusted best. [*Exit.*]

[*Enter*] *Cariola.*

CARIOLA Sir, you are the happy father of a son.
Your wife commends him to you.

ANTONIO Blessèd comfort!
For heaven sake, tend her well. I'll presently
Go set a figure° for 's nativity. *Exeunt.* *cast a horoscope*

2.3

[*Enter*] *Bosola* [*with a dark° lantern*]. *shuttered*

BOSOLA Sure I did hear a woman shriek. List! Hah?
And the sound came, if I received it right,
From the Duchess' lodgings. There's some stratagem
In the confining all our courtiers
To their several wards.° I must have part of it; *various apartments*
My intelligence° will freeze else. List, again! *spying information*
It may be 'twas the melancholy bird,
Best friend of silence and of solitariness,
The owl, that screamed so.

5. A mocking title for the common laborers in charge of the cutting and storing of wood.

2.3. Malfi. The action is virtually continuous from 2.2.

[*Enter*] *Antonio* [*with a paper*].

Hah? Antonio!

ANTONIO I heard some noise.—Who's there? What art thou? Speak.
BOSOLA Antonio? Put not your face nor body
To such a forced expression of fear.
I am Bosola, your friend.
ANTONIO Bosola?
[*Aside*] This mole does undermine me. [*Aloud*] Heard you not
A noise even now?
BOSOLA From whence?
ANTONIO From the Duchess' lodging.
BOSOLA Not I. Did you?
ANTONIO I did, or else I dreamed.
BOSOLA Let's walk towards it.
ANTONIO No. It may be 'twas
But the rising of the wind.
BOSOLA Very likely.
Methinks 'tis very cold, and yet you sweat.
You look wildly.
ANTONIO I have been setting a figure
For the Duchess' jewels.[1]
BOSOLA Ah. And how falls your question?
Do you find it radical?° *fit to be judged*
ANTONIO What's that to you?
'Tis rather to be questioned what design,
When all men were commanded to their lodgings,
Makes you a night walker.
BOSOLA In sooth,° I'll tell you: *truth*
Now all the court's asleep, I thought the devil
Had least to do here; I came to say my prayers,
And if it do offend you I do so,
You are a fine° courtier. *(said ironically)*
ANTONIO [*aside*] This fellow will undo me.
[*To him*] You gave the Duchess apricots today.
Pray heaven they were not poisoned.
BOSOLA Poisoned? A Spanish fig[2]
For the imputation!
ANTONIO Traitors are ever confident
Till they are discovered. There were jewels stol'n too.
In my conceit,° none are to be suspected *opinion*
More than yourself.
BOSOLA You are a false steward.
ANTONIO Saucy slave! I'll pull thee up by the roots.
BOSOLA Maybe the ruin will crush you to pieces.
ANTONIO You are an impudent snake indeed, sir.
Are you scarce warm, and do you show your sting?
[BOSOLA . . . .][3]
ANTONIO You libel well, sir.
BOSOLA No, sir. Copy° it out, *Write*
And I will set my hand to't.° *sign it*
ANTONIO [*aside*] My nose bleeds.

1. I've been casting a horoscope to investigate the stolen jewelry and other goods.
2. An obscene gesture of thrusting the thumb between the first two fingers.
3. A line appears to be missing here.

One that were superstitious would count
This ominous, when it merely comes by chance.
Two letters that are wrought° here for my name — *embroidered*
Are drowned in blood! Mere accident.
[*To Bosola*] For you, sir, I'll take order.° — *appropriate measures*
I'th'morn you shall be safe.° [*Aside*] 'Tis that must color° — *confined / mask*
Her lying-in. [*To Bosola*] Sir, this door you pass not.
I do not hold it fit that you come near
The Duchess' lodgings till you have quit° yourself. — *acquitted*
[*Aside*] The great are like the base; nay, they are the same,
When they seek shameful ways to avoid shame.
Exit [*having accidentally dropped the horoscope*].

BOSOLA Antonio hereabout did drop a paper.
Some of your help, false friend.° [*He searches with the help of his dark lantern and finds the horoscope.*] Oh, here it is. — *(the dark lantern)*
What's here? A child's nativity calculated?
[*He reads.*] "The Duchess was delivered of a son 'tween the hours twelve and one in the night, *Anno Dom.* 1504"—that's this year—"*decimo nono Decembris*"°—that's this night—"taken according to the meridian of Malfi"—that's our duchess. Happy discovery! "The Lord of the first house, being combust° in the ascendant, signifies short life; and Mars being in a human sign, joined to the tail of the Dragon, in the eighth house, doth threaten a violent death. *Caetera non scrutantur.*"[4] — *December 19*; *burned up, extinguished*
Why now, 'tis most apparent! This precise° fellow — *formal; puritanical*
Is the Duchess' bawd. I have it to my wish.
This is a parcel of intelligency° — *item of news*
Our courtiers were cased up° for! It needs must follow — *confined*
That I must be committed,° on pretense — *locked up*
Of poisoning her; which I'll endure, and laugh at.
If one could find the father now! But that
Time will discover. Old Castruchio
I'th'morning posts to Rome; by him I'll send
A letter that shall make her brothers' galls
O'erflow their livers.° This was a thrifty way! — *(with anger)*
Though Lust do mask in ne'er so strange disguise,
She's oft found witty, but is never wise. [*Exit.*]

2.4

[*Enter*] *Cardinal and Julia.*

CARDINAL Sit. Thou art my best of wishes. Prithee tell me
What trick didst thou invent to come to Rome
Without thy husband.

JULIA Why, my lord, I told him
I came to visit an old anchorite° — *religious recluse*
Here, for devotion.

CARDINAL Thou art a witty false one—
I mean, to him.° — *false to your husband*

JULIA You have prevailed with me
Beyond my strongest thoughts. I would not now

4. The rest is not investigated.

2.4. Rome. The Cardinal's rooms.

Find you inconstant.
CARDINAL Do not put thyself
To such a voluntary torture, which proceeds
Out of your own guilt.
JULIA How, my lord?
CARDINAL You fear
My constancy because you have approved° *experienced*
Those giddy and wild turnings in yourself.
JULIA Did you e'er find them?
CARDINAL Sooth, generally for women;[1]
A man might strive to make glass malleable
Ere he should make them fixed.
JULIA So, my lord.
CARDINAL We had need go borrow that fantastic glass
Invented by Galileo the Florentine,
To view another spacious world i'th'moon,
And look to find a constant woman there.
JULIA [*weeping*] This is very well, my lord.
CARDINAL Why do you weep?
Are tears your justification? The selfsame tears
Will fall into your husband's bosom, lady,
With a loud protestation that you love him
Above the world. Come, I'll love you wisely,
That's jealously, since I am very certain
You cannot me make cuckold.
JULIA I'll go home
To my husband.
CARDINAL You may thank me, lady,
I have taken you off your melancholy perch,
Bore you upon my fist, and showed you game,
And let you fly at it.° I pray thee, kiss me. *(terms from falconry)*
When thou wast with thy husband, thou wast watched° *guarded*
Like a tame elephant. Still you are to thank me.
Thou hadst only kisses from him, and high feeding,° *rich repast*
But what delight was that? 'Twas just like one
That hath a little fing'ring on the lute,
Yet cannot tune it. Still you are to thank me.
JULIA You told me of a piteous wound i'th'heart,
And a sick liver, when you wooed me first,
And spake like one in physic.° *i.e., sick for love*
CARDINAL [*hearing the approach of someone*] Who's that?
[*To her*] Rest firm.° For° my affection to thee, *assured / As for*
Lightning moves slow to't.° *compared with it*

[*Enter a*] *Servant.*

SERVANT Madam, a gentleman
That's come post from Malfi desires to see you.
CARDINAL Let him enter. I'll withdraw. *Exit.*
SERVANT He says
Your husband, old Castruchio, is come to Rome,
Most pitifully tired with riding post. [*Exit.*]

[*Enter*] *Delio.*

1. I have generally found women to be inconstant.

JULIA Signor Delio! [*Aside*] 'Tis one of my old suitors.
DELIO I was bold to come and see you.
JULIA Sir, you are welcome.
DELIO Do you lie° here? *reside*
JULIA Sure, your own experience
Will satisfy you no; our Roman prelates
Do not keep lodging for ladies.
DELIO Very well.
I have brought you no commendations from your husband,
For I know none by him.
JULIA I hear he's come to Rome?
DELIO I never knew man and beast, of° a horse and a knight, *made up of*
So weary of each other; if he had had a good back,
He would have undertook to have borne his horse,
His breech was so pitifully sore.
JULIA Your laughter
Is my pity.° *What you laugh at, I pity*
DELIO Lady, I know not whether
You want money, but I have brought you some.
JULIA From my husband?
DELIO No, from mine own allowance.
JULIA I must hear the condition ere I be bound to take it.
DELIO [*showing the money*] Look on't, 'tis gold. Hath it not a fine color?
JULIA I have a bird more beautiful.
DELIO [*clinking the coins*] Try the sound on't.
JULIA A lute string far exceeds it.
It hath no smell, like cassia, or civet,° *aromatic substances*
Nor is it physical,° though some fond° doctors *medicinal / foolish*
Persuade us seeth't in cullises.° I'll tell you, *to boil it in broth*
This is a creature bred by°— *i.e., bred by usury*

[*Enter Servant.*]

SERVANT Your husband's come,
Hath delivered a letter to the Duke of Calabria
That, to my thinking, hath put him out of his wits. [*Exit.*]
JULIA Sir, you hear;
Pray let me know your business and your suit
As briefly as can be.
DELIO With good speed. I would wish you,
At such time as you are nonresident
With your husband, my mistress.
JULIA Sir, I'll go ask my husband if I shall,
And straight return your answer. *Exit.*
DELIO Very fine!
Is this her wit or honesty° that speaks thus? *chaste honor*
I heard one say the Duke was highly moved° *angered*
With a letter sent from Malfi. I do fear
Antonio is betrayed. How fearfully
Shows his ambition now! Unfortunate Fortune!
They pass through whirlpools, and deep woes do shun,
Who the event weigh ere the action's done.[2] *Exit.*

2. Those who consider the outcome and carefully reflect before they act are able to avoid dangers on every side.

2.5

[Enter] Cardinal, and Ferdinand, with a letter.

FERDINAND I have this night digged up a mandrake.[1]
CARDINAL Say you?° — *What do you say?*
FERDINAND And I am grown mad with't.
CARDINAL What's the prodigy?° — *portent*
FERDINAND [*showing him the letter*] Read there—a sister damned! She's loose i'th'hilts,° — *i.e., unchaste*
Grown a notorious strumpet.
CARDINAL Speak lower.
FERDINAND Lower?
Rogues do not whisper't now, but seek to publish't,° — *proclaim it*
As servants do the bounty of their lords,
Aloud, and with a covetous, searching eye
To mark who note them.[2] Oh, confusion° seize her! — *ruin*
She hath had most cunning bawds to serve her turn,
And more secure conveyances for° lust — *safer ways of procuring*
Than towns of garrison for service.° — *receiving supplies*
CARDINAL Is't possible?
Can this be certain?
FERDINAND Rhubarb,° oh, for rhubarb — *a purgative for wrath*
To purge this choler!° Here's the cursèd day — *anger*
To prompt my memory, and here° 't shall stick — *(in my head or heart)*
Till of her bleeding heart I make a sponge
To wipe it out.
CARDINAL Why do you make yourself
So wild a tempest?
FERDINAND Would I could be one,
That I might toss her palace 'bout her ears,
Root up her goodly forests, blast her meads,° — *meadows*
And lay her general territory as waste
As she hath done her honors!
CARDINAL Shall our blood,
The royal blood of Aragon and Castile,
Be thus attainted?° — *corrupted, tainted*
FERDINAND Apply desperate physic.° — *medicine*
We must not now use balsamum,° but fire, — *an aromatic balm*
The smarting cupping-glass,° for that's the mean° — *(for bleeding) / means*
To purge infected blood—such blood as hers.
There is a kind of pity in mine eye;
I'll give it to my handkercher; and, now 'tis here,
I'll bequeath this to her bastard.
CARDINAL What to do?
FERDINAND Why, to make soft lint for his mother's wounds
When I have hewed her to pieces.
CARDINAL Cursed creature!
Unequal° Nature, to place women's hearts — *Unjust*
So far upon the left side!° — *i.e., so deceitful*
FERDINAND Foolish men,

2.5. Rome.
1. The shriek made by the mandrake root when pulled from the ground was thought to cause madness in those who heard it.
2. Ferdinand hyperbolically imagines that the Duchess is now so flagrant in her wantonness that self-serving rascals proclaim her shame openly, like servants praising their masters' bounty and looking around with covetous desire to see by which bountiful aristocrats they will be rewarded for doing so.

That e'er will trust their honor in a bark° — *boat or small ship*
Made of so slight, weak bulrush as is woman,
Apt every minute to sink it!

CARDINAL Thus
Ignorance, when it hath purchased° honor, — *obtained*
It cannot wield it.

FERDINAND Methinks I see her laughing,
Excellent hyena! Talk to me somewhat, quickly,
Or my imagination will carry me
To see her in the shameful act of sin.

CARDINAL With whom?

FERDINAND Happily° with some strong-thighed bargeman,° — *Haply / water-taxi man*
Or one o'th'woodyard,[3] that can quoit the sledge° — *throw the sledgehammer*
Or toss the bar,° or else some lovely squire° — *heavy log / youth*
That carries coals up to her privy° lodgings. — *private (for sex)*

CARDINAL You fly beyond your reason.

FERDINAND Go to,° mistress! — *(expressing anger)*
'Tis not your whore's milk that shall quench my wildfire,[4]
But your whore's blood.

CARDINAL How idly° shows° this rage, which carries you, — *foolishly / looks*
As men conveyed by witches through the air,
On violent whirlwinds! This intemperate noise
Fitly resembles deaf men's shrill discourse,
Who talk aloud, thinking all other men
To have their imperfection.

FERDINAND Have not you
My palsy?° — *tremor, quaking*

CARDINAL Yes. I can be angry
Without this rupture.° There is not in nature — *rapture; outburst*
A thing that makes man so deformed, so beastly,
As doth intemperate anger. Chide yourself.
You have° divers men who never yet expressed — *One often sees*
Their strong desire of rest but by unrest,
By vexing of themselves. Come, put yourself
In tune.

FERDINAND So. I will only study to seem
The thing I am not. I could kill her now,
In you, or in myself, for I do think
It is some sin in us heaven doth revenge
By her.

CARDINAL Are you stark mad?

FERDINAND I would have their° bodies — *(hers and her lover's)*
Burnt in a coalpit,° with the ventage stopped, — *(for making charcoal)*
That their cursed smoke might not ascend to heaven;
Or dip the sheets they lie in in pitch or sulfur,
Wrap them in't, and then light them like a match;
Or else to boil their bastard to a cullis,° — *broth*
And give't his lecherous father, to renew
The sin of his back.° — *i.e., of his hot flesh*

CARDINAL I'll leave you.

FERDINAND Nay, I have done.
I am confident, had I been damned in hell

3. Like water-taxi men, woodcutters were ordinary working-class men, muscular and of low social status.

4. (1) Flammable material used in warfare; (2) an eruptive skin disease.

And should have heard of this, it would have put me
Into a cold sweat. In, in. I'll go sleep.
Till I know who leaps my sister, I'll not stir.
That known, I'll find scorpions° to string my whips, *i.e., knots, scourges*
And fix her in a general° eclipse. *Exeunt.* *total*

3.1

[*Enter*] *Antonio and Delio.*

ANTONIO Our noble friend, my most belovèd Delio!
Oh, you have been a stranger long at court.
Came you along with the Lord Ferdinand?
DELIO I did, sir. And how fares your noble duchess?
ANTONIO Right fortunately well. She's an excellent
Feeder of pedigrees;° since you last saw her, *Breeder of children*
She hath had two children more, a son and daughter.
DELIO Methinks 'twas yesterday. Let me but wink° *close my eyes*
And not behold your face, which to mine eye
Is somewhat leaner, verily I should dream
It were within this half hour.
ANTONIO You have not been in law, friend Delio,
Nor in prison, nor a suitor at the court,
Nor begged the reversion° of some great man's place, *right of succession*
Nor troubled with an old wife, which doth make
Your time so insensibly° hasten. *imperceptibly*
DELIO Pray, sir, tell me,
Hath not this news arrived yet to the ear
Of the Lord Cardinal?
ANTONIO I fear it hath.
The Lord Ferdinand, that's newly come to court,
Doth bear himself right dangerously.
DELIO Pray, why?
ANTONIO He is so quiet that he seems to sleep
The tempest out, as dormice do in winter.
Those houses that are haunted are most still° *quiet*
Till the devil be up.
DELIO What say the common people?
ANTONIO The common rabble do directly° say *outspokenly*
She is a strumpet.
DELIO And your graver heads,
Which would be politic, what censure° they? *judge*
ANTONIO They do observe I grow to infinite purchase° *position and wealth*
The left-hand° way, and all suppose the Duchess *sinister*
Would amend it if she could; for, say they,
Great princes, though they grudge their officers
Should have such large and unconfinèd means
To get wealth under them, will not complain,
Lest thereby they should make them odious
Unto the people. For other obligation
Of love or marriage between her and me
They never dream of.

3.1. Malfi. The Duchess's palace. Enough time has elapsed for the Duchess to have had her second and third child (see line 7). Presumably her brother Ferdinand has been unhappily waiting for information with which to confront her with evidence of her culpability.

[*Enter*] *Ferdinand* [*and the*] *Duchess.*

DELIO [*privately to Antonio*] The Lord Ferdinand
Is going to bed. [*He and Antonio stand aside.*]
FERDINAND [*to the Duchess*] I'll instantly to bed,
For I am weary. I am to bespeak° — *negotiate, arrange*
A husband for you.
DUCHESS For me, sir? Pray, who is't?
FERDINAND The great Count Malateste.
DUCHESS Fie upon him!
A count? He's a mere stick of sugar candy;
You may look quite through him. When I choose
A husband, I will marry for your honor.
FERDINAND You shall do well in't. [*Noticing Antonio*] How
is't,° worthy Antonio? — *How are you*
DUCHESS But, sir, I am to have private conference with you
About a scandalous report is° spread — *which is*
Touching mine honor.
FERDINAND Let me be ever deaf to't:
One of Pasquil's paper bullets,[1] court calumny,
A pestilent air which princes' palaces
Are seldom purged of. Yet, say that it were true—
I pour it in your bosom[2]—my fixed love
Would strongly excuse, extenuate, nay, deny
Faults, were° they apparent in you. Go, be safe — *even were*
In your own innocency.
DUCHESS Oh, blessed comfort!
This deadly air is purged. *Exeunt* [*all but Ferdinand*].
FERDINAND Her guilt treads on
Hot burning coulters.° — *plowshares*

[*Enter*] *Bosola.*

Now, Bosola,
How thrives our intelligence?
BOSOLA Sir, uncertainly.
'Tis rumored she hath had three bastards, but
By whom, we may go read i'th'stars.
FERDINAND Why, some
Hold opinion all things are written there.
BOSOLA Yes, if we could find spectacles to read them.
I do suspect there hath been some sorcery
Used on the Duchess.
FERDINAND Sorcery? To what purpose?
BOSOLA To make her dote on some desertless fellow
She shames to acknowledge.
FERDINAND Can your faith give way
To think there's power in potions or in charms
To make us love, whether we will or no?
BOSOLA Most certainly.
FERDINAND Away! These are mere gulleries,° horrid things — *tricks, deceptions*

1. Lampoons or pasquinades, satirical verses. Pasquino, or Pasquillo, was the name popularly given to a mutilated statue disinterred in Rome in 1501 and set up by Cardinal Caraffa at the corner of his palace near the Piazza Navona, where satirical verses were posted on Saint Mark's Day. Anonymous authors of the satires often sheltered themselves under the name Pasquin or Pasquil.

2. Let me say this to you confidentially.

Invented by some cheating mountebanks
To abuse° us. Do you think that herbs or charms *deceive*
Can force the will? Some trials have been made
In this foolish practice, but the ingredients
Were lenitive° poisons, such as are of force *soothing; secret*
To make the patient mad; and straight the witch
Swears, by equivocation, they are in love.
The witchcraft lies in her° rank blood. This night *(the Duchess's)*
I will force confession from her. You told me
You had got, within these two days, a false key
Into her bedchamber.

BOSOLA I have.

FERDINAND As I would wish.

BOSOLA What do you intend to do?

FERDINAND Can you guess?

BOSOLA No.

FERDINAND Do not ask, then.
He that can compass° me and know my drifts *comprehend; navigate*
May say he hath put a girdle 'bout the world
And sounded° all her quicksands. *tested the depth of*

BOSOLA I do not
Think so.

FERDINAND What do you think, then, pray?

BOSOLA That you are
Your own chronicle too much, and grossly
Flatter yourself.

FERDINAND Give me thy hand. I thank thee.
I never gave pension but to flatterers
Till I entertained thee. Farewell.
That friend a great man's ruin strongly checks
Who rails into his belief all his defects.[3] *Exeunt.*

3.2

[*Enter*] *Duchess, Antonio,* [*and*] *Cariola.*

DUCHESS [*to Cariola*] Bring me the casket hither, and the glass.° *mirror*
[*To Antonio*] You get no lodging here, tonight, my lord.

ANTONIO Indeed, I must persuade one.

DUCHESS Very good.
I hope in time 'twill grow into a custom,
That noblemen shall come with cap and knee[1]
To purchase a night's lodging of their wives.

ANTONIO I must lie here.

DUCHESS Must? You are a Lord of Misrule.[2]

ANTONIO Indeed, my rule is only in the night.

DUCHESS To what use will you put me?

ANTONIO We'll sleep together.

DUCHESS Alas, what pleasure can two lovers find in sleep?

CARIOLA My Lord, I lie with her often, and I know
She'll much disquiet you.

3. A person who does not refrain from criticizing a great man shows true friendship in helping to prevent that great man's ruin.
3.2. Malfi. The Duchess's bedchamber.

1. With cap in hand and on bended knee.
2. The presiding figure at courtly and Christmas revels, with temporary power to give orders, often in mockery, to social superiors.

ANTONIO [*to the Duchess*] See, you are complained of.
CARIOLA For she's the sprawling'st bedfellow.
ANTONIO I shall like her the better for that.
CARIOLA Sir, shall I ask you a question?
ANTONIO I pray thee, Cariola.
CARIOLA Wherefore still° when you lie with my lady *habitually*
Do you rise so early?
ANTONIO Laboring men
Count the clock oft'nest, Cariola,
Are glad when their task's ended.
DUCHESS I'll stop your mouth.
[*She kisses him.*]
ANTONIO Nay, that's but one. Venus had two soft doves
To draw her chariot; I must have another. [*He kisses her.*]
When wilt thou marry, Cariola?
CARIOLA Never, my lord.
ANTONIO Oh, fie upon this single life! Forgo it!
We read how Daphne, for her peevish flight,
Became a fruitless bay tree, Syrinx turned
To the pale empty reed, Anaxarete
Was frozen into marble,[3] whereas those
Which married or proved kind unto their friends° *lovers*
Were, by a gracious influence, transshaped
Into the olive, pomegranate, mulberry;[4]
Became flowers, precious stones, or eminent stars.
CARIOLA This is a vain° poetry. But I pray you tell me: *fruitless*
If there were proposed me wisdom, riches, and beauty
In three several° young men, which should I choose? *different*
ANTONIO 'Tis a hard question. This was Paris' case,
And he was blind in't,° and there was great cause; *he judged fallibly*
For how was't possible he could judge right,
Having three amorous goddesses in view,
And they stark naked?[5] 'Twas a motion° *proposal; spectacle*
Were° able to benight the apprehension *That would be*
Of the severest counselor° of Europe. *wisest statesman*
Now° I look on both your faces, so well formed, *Now that*
It puts me in mind of a question I would ask.
CARIOLA What is't?
ANTONIO I do wonder why hard-favored° ladies, *ugly*
For the most part, keep worse-favored waiting-women
To attend them, and cannot endure fair ones.
DUCHESS Oh, that's soon answered.
Did you ever in your life know an ill° painter *inept*
Desire to have his dwelling next door to the shop
Of an excellent picture-maker? 'Twould disgrace

3. The nymph Daphne, pursued by Apollo, prayed for aid and was metamorphosed into a bay, or laurel, tree. Syrinx was changed into a reed by her sister nymphs to escape the ardor of Pan, whereupon he named the reed pipe he invented after her. Anaxarete was changed by Venus into stone for her indifference to the death of the lower-class Iphis, who hanged himself at her door because she rejected his love.

4. As told in Ovid's *Metamorphoses*, Book 4, lines 125–27, the blood of the lovers Pyramus and Thisbe, who died for each other, gave its dark red color to the fruit of the mulberry tree.

5. When during a wedding feast attended by the gods, Eris, goddess of strife, threw into the window a golden apple inscribed "For the fairest," the prize was claimed by Hera, Athena, and Aphrodite. Paris, called on to arbitrate, awarded the apple to Aphrodite, who had promised him the most beautiful woman in the world; he thus gained her assistance in carrying off Helen, which precipitated the Trojan War.

His face-making, and undo him. I prithee,
When were we so merry?—My hair tangles.
[*The Duchess tends to her toilette.*]
ANTONIO [*aside to Cariola*] Prithee, Cariola, let's steal forth the room
And let her talk to herself. I have divers times
Served her the like, when she hath chafed extremely.
I love to see her angry. Softly, Cariola!
Exeunt [*Antonio and Cariola*].
DUCHESS Doth not the color of my hair 'gin to change?
When I wax gray, I shall have all the court
Powder their hair with arras,° to be like me. *powdered orrisroot*
You have cause to love me; I ent'red you into my heart
Before you would vouchsafe to call for the keys.

[*Enter*] *Ferdinand* [*unobserved by her*].

We shall one day have my brothers take you napping.
Methinks his° presence, being now in court, *(Ferdinand's)*
Should make you keep your own bed. But, you'll say,
Love mixed with fear is sweetest. I'll assure you
You shall get no more children till my brothers
Consent to be your gossips.°—Have you lost *childrens' godfathers*
Your tongue? [*She turns and sees Ferdinand.*] 'Tis welcome;
For know, whether I am doomed to live or die,
I can do both like a prince. *Ferdinand gives her a poniard.*
FERDINAND Die then, quickly!
Virtue, where art thou hid? What hideous thing
Is it that doth eclipse thee?
DUCHESS Pray, sir, hear me.
FERDINAND Or is it true thou art but a bare name
And no essential° thing? *real*
DUCHESS Sir—
FERDINAND Do not speak.
DUCHESS No, sir.
I will plant my soul in mine ears to hear you.
FERDINAND O most imperfect light of human reason,
That mak'st us so unhappy, to foresee
What we can least prevent!—Pursue thy wishes,
And glory in them; there's in shame no comfort
But to be past all bounds and sense of shame.
DUCHESS I pray, sir, hear me: I am married.
FERDINAND So.
DUCHESS Haply° not to your liking, but for that, *Perhaps*
Alas, your shears do come untimely now
To clip the bird's wings that's already flown.
Will you see my husband?
FERDINAND Yes, if I
Could change eyes with a basilisk.[6]
DUCHESS Sure, you came hither
By his° confederacy. *(the basilisk's)*
FERDINAND The howling of a wolf
Is music to° thee, screech owl. Prithee, peace!— *compared with*
Whate'er thou art, that hast enjoyed my sister
(For I am sure thou hear'st me), for thine own sake

6. A legendary reptile reputedly able to kill with its gaze.

Let me not know thee. I came hither prepared
To work thy discovery, yet am now persuaded
It would beget such violent effects
As would damn us both. I would not for ten millions
I had beheld thee; therefore use all means
I never may have knowledge of thy name.
Enjoy thy lust still, and a wretched life,
On that condition.—And for thee, vile woman,
If thou do wish thy lecher may grow old
In thy embracements, I would have thee build
Such a room for him as our anchorites° *religious recluses*
To holier use inhabit. Let not the sun
Shine on him till he's dead. Let dogs and monkeys
Only converse with him, and such dumb things
To whom Nature denies use° to sound his name. *ability*
Do not keep a paraquito, lest she learn it.
If thou do love him, cut out thine own tongue
Lest it bewray° him. *reveal, expose*

DUCHESS Why might not I marry?
I have not gone about, in this, to create
Any new world or custom.

FERDINAND Thou art undone;
And thou hast ta'en that massy sheet of lead
That hid thy husband's bones, and folded it
About my heart.

DUCHESS Mine bleeds for't.

FERDINAND Thine? Thy heart?
What should I name't, unless a hollow bullet° *cannonball*
Filled with unquenchable wildfire?° *flammable stuff*

DUCHESS You are, in this,
Too strict, and, were you not my princely brother,
I would say too willful. My reputation
Is safe.

FERDINAND Dost thou know what reputation is?
I'll tell thee, to small purpose, since th'instruction
Comes now too late.
Upon° a time Reputation, Love, and Death *Once upon*
Would travel o'er the world, and 'twas concluded
That they should part and take three several° ways. *separate*
Death told them they should find him in great battles,
Or cities plagued with plagues. Love gives them counsel
To inquire for him 'mongst unambitious shepherds,
Where dowries were not talked of, and sometimes
'Mongst quiet kindred that had nothing left
By their dead parents. "Stay," quoth Reputation,
"Do not forsake me; for it is my nature
If once I part from any man I meet
I am never found again." And so, for you:
You have shook hands with° Reputation, *i.e., bid farewell to*
And made him invisible. So, fare you well.
I will never see you more.

DUCHESS Why should only I,
Of all the other princes of the world,
Be cased up, like a holy relic? I have youth,

And a little beauty.

FERDINAND So you° have some virgins *(the general "you")*
That are witches. I will never see thee more. *Exit.*

Enter Antonio with a pistol [*and Cariola*].

DUCHESS You saw this apparition?

ANTONIO Yes. We are
Betrayed. How came he hither? [*To Cariola*] I should turn
This to thee for that. [*He threatens her with the pistol.*]

CARIOLA Pray, sir, do; and when
That you have cleft my heart, you shall read there
Mine innocence.

DUCHESS That gallery gave him entrance.

ANTONIO I would this terrible thing would come again,
That, standing on my guard, I might relate
My warrantable° love. (*She shows the poniard.*) Ha! What means this? *sanctioned, permitted*

DUCHESS He left this with me.

ANTONIO And, it seems, did wish
You would use it on yourself?

DUCHESS His action
Seemed to intend so much.

ANTONIO This hath a handle to't
As well as a point. Turn it towards him
And so fasten the keen edge in his rank gall.
[*Knocking within.*]
How now? Who knocks? More earthquakes?

DUCHESS I stand
As if a mine beneath my feet were ready
To be blown up.

CARIOLA 'Tis Bosola.

DUCHESS Away!
Oh, misery! Methinks unjust° actions *dishonest*
Should wear these masks and curtains, and not we.
You must instantly part hence; I have fashioned° it already. *arranged*
Exit Antonio.

[*Enter*] *Bosola.*

BOSOLA The Duke your brother is ta'en up in a whirlwind,
Hath took horse, and 's rid post to Rome.

DUCHESS So late?

BOSOLA He told me, as he mounted into th'saddle,
You were undone.

DUCHESS Indeed, I am very near it.

BOSOLA What's the matter?

DUCHESS Antonio, the master of our household,
Hath dealt so falsely with me in's accounts:
My brother stood engaged with° me for money *stood as security for*
Ta'en up of° certain Neapolitan Jews, *Borrowed from*
And Antonio lets the bonds be forfeit.

BOSOLA Strange! [*Aside*] This is cunning.

DUCHESS And hereupon

My brother's bills at Naples are protested
Against.[7] Call up our officers.
BOSOLA I shall. *Exit.*

[*Enter Antonio.*]

DUCHESS [*to Antonio*] The place that you must fly to is Ancona.
Hire a house there. I'll send after you
My treasure and my jewels. Our weak safety
Runs upon enginous° wheels; short syllables *ingenious, intricate*
Must stand for periods.° I must now accuse you *sentences*
Of such a feignèd crime as Tasso calls
Magnanima mensogna, a noble lie,[8]
'Cause it must shield our honors. [*Sounds are heard.*]
Hark, they are coming!

[*Enter Bosola and*] *Officers.* [*Antonio and the Duchess speak loudly, so as to be heard by those entering.*]

ANTONIO Will Your Grace hear me?
DUCHESS I have got well by you! You have yielded me
A million of loss; I am like° to inherit *likely*
The people's curses for your stewardship.
You had the trick in audit time to be sick,
Till I had signed your quietus,[9] and that cured you
Without help of a doctor.—Gentlemen,
I would have this man be an example to you all;
So shall you hold my favor. I pray, let him;[1]
For he's done that, alas, you would not think of,
And, because I intend to be rid of him,
I mean not to publish.° [*To Antonio*] Use your fortune elsewhere. *proclaim widely*
ANTONIO I am strongly armed to brook° my overthrow, *endure*
As commonly men bear with a hard year.° *bad harvest*
I will not blame the cause on't, but do think
The necessity of my malevolent star
Procures this, not her humor. Oh, the inconstant
And rotten ground of service! You may see:
'Tis ev'n like him that in a winter night
Takes a long slumber o'er a dying fire
As loath to part from't, yet parts thence as cold
As when he first sat down.
DUCHESS We do confiscate,
Towards the satisfying of your accounts,
All that you have.
ANTONIO I am all yours; and 'tis very fit
All mine should be so.[2]
DUCHESS So, sir; you have your pass.
ANTONIO You may see, gentlemen, what 'tis to serve

7. The Neapolitan moneylenders have officially declared in writing that Ferdinand is a credit risk—a first step toward recovery of the supposed debt.
8. In Italian poet Torquato Tasso's epic, *Jerusalem Delivered* (1581), 2.22, a character named Soprina admits to the "noble lie" of taking a statue of the Virgin Mary from a mosque in order to avoid a general persecution of her fellow Christians.
9. The final settlement of a debt. Perhaps the Duchess refers, with secret irony, to the "*quietus est*" she metaphorically signed at 1.1.465 by way of acquitting Antonio of any payment due her; see note there.
1. (1) Let Antonio be an example; (2) let him go.
2. (1) I am your servant to do with as you wish; (2) since we are husband and wife, what is mine is yours also. (Similar double meanings, one public and one very private, run throughout this passage from line 186 onward.)

A prince with body and soul. *Exit.*

BOSOLA Here's an example for extortion: what moisture is drawn out of the sea, when foul weather comes, pours down and runs into the sea again.

DUCHESS I would know what are your opinions of this Antonio.

SECOND OFFICER He could not abide to see a pig's head gaping.[3] I thought Your Grace would find him a Jew.

THIRD OFFICER I would you had been his officer,° for your own sake. *steward*

FOURTH OFFICER You would have had more money.

FIRST OFFICER He stopped his ears with black wool, and to those came° to him for money said he was thick of hearing. *who came*

SECOND OFFICER Some said he was an hermaphrodite, for he could not abide a woman.

FOURTH OFFICER How scurvy proud he would look when the treasury was full! Well, let him go.

FIRST OFFICER Yes, and the chippings of the butt'ry[4] fly after him, to scour his gold chain!

DUCHESS Leave us. *Exeunt* [*Officers*].

What do you think of these?

BOSOLA That these are rogues, that, in 's prosperity, but to have waited on his fortune,[5] could have wished his dirty stirrup riveted through their noses, and followed after 's mule like a bear in a ring;[6] would have prostituted their daughters to his lust; made their firstborn intelligencers;[7] thought none happy but such as were born under his blessed planet and wore his livery. And do these lice° drop off now? Well, never look to have the like again. He hath left a sort° of flatt'ring rogues behind him; their doom must follow. Princes pay flatterers in their own money: flatterers dissemble their vices, and they dissemble their lies;[8] that's justice. Alas, poor gentleman! *i.e, parasites* *gang, crowd*

DUCHESS Poor? He hath amply filled his coffers.

BOSOLA Sure he was too honest. Pluto, the god of riches,[9] when he's sent by Jupiter to any man, he goes limping to signify that wealth that comes on° God's name comes slowly, but when he's sent on the devil's errand, he rides post and comes in by scuttles.° Let me show you what a most unvalued[1] jewel you have, in a wanton humor, thrown away, to bless the man shall° find him. He was an excellent courtier, and most faithful—a soldier that thought it as beastly to know his own value too little as devilish to acknowledge it too much. Both his virtue and form deserved a far better fortune. His discourse rather delighted to judge itself than show itself. His breast was filled with all perfection, and yet it seemed a private whisp'ring room, it made so little noise of't. *in* *scuttling rapidly* *who shall*

3. A roasted pig with an apple in its mouth. (Religious Jews are forbidden to eat pork.)
4. And let the bread crumbs and other leavings of the pantry, such as might be used to feed the poor (or polish a gold chain of office).
5. Merely to have waited in attendance on him in his time of prosperity.
6. Like a bear led by a ring in its nose.
7. Would have put their eldest sons in service as spies for Antonio.
8. Princes repay courtiers for their dishonest flattery by deceiving them in turn.
9. Pluto, god of the underworld, was often conflated with Plutus, god of riches.
1. (1) Invaluable; (2) unheeded.

DUCHESS But he was basely descended.
BOSOLA Will you make yourself a mercenary herald, rather to
examine men's pedigrees than virtues? You shall want° him. *miss*
For know° an honest statesman to a prince is like a cedar *take note that*
planted by a spring: the spring bathes the tree's root; the
grateful tree rewards it with his shadow. You have not done
so. I would sooner swim to the Bermoothes° on two politi- *Bermudas*
cians'° rotten bladders, tied together with an intelligencer's *intriguers'*
heartstring, than depend on so changeable a prince's favor.
Fare thee well, Antonio! Since the malice of the world would
needs down with thee,° it cannot be said yet that any ill *overthrow you*
happened unto thee, considering thy fall was accompanied
with virtue.
DUCHESS Oh, you render me excellent music!
BOSOLA Say you?
DUCHESS This good one that you speak of is my husband.
BOSOLA Do I not dream? Can this ambitious age
Have so much goodness in't as to prefer° *give advancement to*
A man merely for worth, without these shadows° *unsubstantial qualities*
Of wealth and painted° honors? Possible? *specious*
DUCHESS I have had three children by him.
BOSOLA Fortunate lady!
For you have made your private nuptial bed
The humble and fair seminary° of peace. *nursery, seedbed*
No question but many an unbeneficed scholar
Shall pray for you for this deed, and rejoice
That some preferment in the world can yet
Arise from merit. The virgins of your land
That have no dowries shall hope your example
Will raise them to rich husbands. Should you want
Soldiers, 'twould make the very Turks and Moors
Turn Christians, and serve you for this act.
Last, the neglected poets of your time,
In honor of this trophy of a man,
Raised by that curious engine,° your white hand, *delicate instrument*
Shall thank you in your grave for't,[2] and make that
More reverend° than all the cabinets° *revered / private rooms*
Of living princes. For° Antonio, *As for*
His fame shall likewise flow from many a pen,
When heralds shall want coats° to sell to men. *lack coats of arms*
DUCHESS As I taste comfort in this friendly speech,
So would I find concealment.
BOSOLA Oh, the secret of my prince,
Which I will wear on th'inside of my heart!
DUCHESS You shall take charge of all my coin and jewels,
And follow him, for he retires himself
To Ancona.
BOSOLA So.
DUCHESS Whither, within few days,
I mean to follow thee.
BOSOLA Let me think:
I would wish Your Grace to feign a pilgrimage

2. I.e., Will write commendatory verses to be read when you are dead.

To our Lady of Loreto, scarce seven leagues
From fair Ancona; so may you depart
Your country with more honor, and your flight
Will seem a princely progress,° retaining — *state journey*
Your usual train° about you. — *retinue*

DUCHESS Sir, your direction
Shall lead me by the hand.

CARIOLA In my opinion,
She were better progress to the baths
At Lucca,° or go visit the Spa — *(near Pisa)*
In Germany,° for, if you will believe me, — *(modern-day Belgium)*
I do not like this jesting with religion,
This feigned pilgrimage.

DUCHESS Thou art a superstitious fool.
Prepare us instantly for our departure.—
Past sorrows, let us moderately lament them;
For those to come, seek wisely to prevent them.
Exit [with Cariola].

BOSOLA A politician° is the devil's quilted anvil. — *intelligencer, spy*
He fashions all sins on him, and the blows
Are never heard; he may work in a lady's chamber,
As here for proof. What rests° but I reveal — *remains*
All to my lord? Oh, this base quality° — *profession*
Of intelligencer! Why, every quality i'th'world
Prefers but° gain or commendation. — *Aims solely at*
Now, for this act I am certain to be raised,
And men that paint weeds to the life are praised. *Exit.*

3.3

[Enter] Cardinal, Ferdinand, Malateste, Pescara, Silvio, [and] Delio.

CARDINAL Must we turn soldier, then?

MALATESTE The Emperor,° — *(Charles V)*
Hearing your worth that way° ere you attained — *as a soldier*
This reverend garment, joins you in commission
With the right fortunate soldier, the Marquis of Pescara,
And the famous Lannoy.[1]

CARDINAL He that had the honor
Of taking the French king prisoner?

MALATESTE [*producing a document*] The same.
Here's a plot° drawn for a new fortification — *diagram*
At Naples. [*He and the Cardinal confer privately.*]

FERDINAND This great Count Malateste, I perceive,
Hath got employment?

DELIO No employment, my lord;
A marginal note in the muster book that he is
A voluntary lord.[2]

FERDINAND He's no soldier?

DELIO He has worn gunpowder in 's hollow tooth

3.3. Rome.
1. Charles de Lannoy (c. 1487–1527), Viceroy of Naples.
2. Delio disparagingly characterizes Malateste as one who cannot be entrusted with a full commission; he is mentioned only in a side note as a volunteer.

For the toothache.
SILVIO He comes to the leaguer° with a full intent — *military camp*
To eat fresh beef and garlic,[3] means to stay
Till the scent° be gone, and straight return to court. — *aroma (of garlic)*
DELIO He hath read all the late service,° — *recent campaign*
As the city chronicle relates it,
And keeps two painters going, only to express° — *depict*
Battles in model.° — *scale drawing*
SILVIO Then he'll fight by the book.° — *by rigid rules*
DELIO By the almanac, I think,
To choose good° days and shun the critical.° — *well-omened / dangerous*
That's his mistress' scarf.[4]
SILVIO Yes, he protests
He would do much for that taffeta.° — *glossy silk cloth*
DELIO I think he would run away from a battle
To save it from taking° prisoner. — *being taken*
SILVIO He is horribly afraid
Gunpowder will spoil the perfume on't.
DELIO I saw a Dutchman break his pate° once — *pummel his head*
For calling him potgun;° he made his head — *popgun; braggart*
Have a bore in't, like a musket.
SILVIO I would he° had made a touchhole to't.[5] — *(the Dutchman)*
DELIO He is indeed a guarded sumpter cloth
Only for the remove of the court.[6]

[Enter] Bosola. [He confers privately with the Cardinal and Malateste.]

PESCARA Bosola arrived? What should be the business?
Some falling out amongst the cardinals?
These factions amongst great men, they are like
Foxes: when their heads are divided
They carry fire in their tails, and all the country
About them goes to wrack for't.[7]
SILVIO What's that Bosola?
DELIO I knew him in Padua—a fantastical° scholar, like such who study to know how many knots was in Hercules' club, of what color Achilles' beard was, or whether Hector were not troubled with the toothache. He hath studied himself half blear-eyed to know the true symmetry of Caesar's nose by a shoeing-horn; and this he did to gain the name of a speculative° man. — *foppish; eccentric* / *inquiring*
PESCARA Mark Prince Ferdinand:
A very salamander lives in's eye,
To mock the eager violence of fire.[8]
SILVIO That Cardinal hath made more bad faces with his oppression[9] than ever Michaelangelo made good ones. He lifts up's nose like a foul porpoise before a storm.[1]

3. I.e., to make him more manly.
4. Delio points to what Malateste is wearing.
5. With a place to ignite the charge, Malateste's head could be blown apart.
6. Malateste is like an ornamental ("guarded") saddle-cloth on a packhorse used in transporting belongings when the court moves from place to place, as on a royal progress.
7. Judges 15.1–5 tells how Samson took three hundred foxes and tied them together in pairs by their tails, with a firebrand between each pair of tails, thereby setting fire to the countryside when the foxes were let loose. ("Goes to wrack" means "is devastated.")
8. Salamanders were thought to live in chimneys and near fire.
9. With his ominous frowns, the Cardinal has put more sorrowful faces on his victims.
1. Porpoises were thought to be able to predict storms at sea.

PESCARA The Lord Ferdinand laughs.
DELIO Like a deadly cannon,
That lightens° ere it smokes. *flashes fire*
PESCARA These are your true pangs of death,
The pangs of life, that struggle with great statesmen.[2]
DELIO In such a deformed silence, witches whisper their charms.
[*Silvio, Pescara, and Delio stand aside silently as the focus shifts to Bosola, the Cardinal, and Ferdinand.*]
CARDINAL Doth she make religion her riding hood
To keep her from the sun and tempest?
FERDINAND That!
That damns her. Methinks her fault and beauty,
Blended together, show like leprosy,
The whiter the fouler. I make it a question
Whether her beggarly brats were ever christened.
CARDINAL I will instantly solicit the state of Ancona
To have them banished.
FERDINAND You are for° Loreto? *heading for*
I shall not be at your ceremony. Fare you well.
[*Exit Cardinal.*]
[*To Bosola*] Write to the Duke of Malfi, my young nephew
She had by her first husband, and acquaint him
With 's mother's honesty.° *(lack of) chastity*
BOSOLA I will.
FERDINAND Antonio!
A slave that only smelled of ink and counters,[3]
And nev'r in's life looked like a gentleman
But in the audit time.—Go, go presently;
Draw me out an hundred and fifty of our horse,
And meet me at the fort bridge. *Exeunt.*

3.4

[*Enter*] *two Pilgrims to the shrine of Our Lady of Loreto.*

FIRST PILGRIM I have not seen a goodlier shrine than this,
Yet I have visited many.
SECOND PILGRIM The Cardinal of Aragon
Is this day to resign his cardinal's hat;
His sister duchess likewise is arrived
To pay her vow of pilgrimage. I expect
A noble ceremony.
FIRST PILGRIM No question.—They come.

Here the ceremony of the Cardinal's installment in the habit° of a soldier, performed in delivering up his cross, hat, robes, and ring at the shrine, and investing him with sword, helmet, shield, and spurs. Then Antonio, the Duchess, and their children, having presented themselves at the shrine, are (by a form of banishment *accoutrements*

2. Life and death struggle within such statesmen.
3. Small disks used in calculating and commercial exchange.
3.4. The shrine of Our Lady of Loreto, in northeast Italy in the province of Ancona.

in dumb show expressed towards them by the Cardinal and the state of Ancona) banished; during all which ceremony, this ditty is sung to very solemn music by divers churchmen:

Arms and honors deck thy story,
To thy fame's eternal glory!
Adverse fortune ever fly thee!
No disastrous fate come nigh thee!

I alone will sing° thy praises — *I will sing only*
Whom to honor virtue raises,
And thy study, that divine is,
Bent to martial discipline is.
Lay aside all those robes lie° by thee; — *that lie*
Crown thy arts° with arms; they'll beautify thee. — *learning*

O worthy of worthiest name, adorned in this manner,
Lead bravely thy forces on under war's warlike banner!
Oh, mayst thou prove fortunate in all martial courses!° — *encounters*
Guide thou still, by skill, in arts and forces!° — *martial might*
Victory attend thee nigh, whilst Fame sings loud thy powers!
Triumphant conquest crown thy head, and blessings pour down showers!

And then exeunt [*all except the two Pilgrims*].

FIRST PILGRIM Here's a strange turn of state! Who would have thought
So great a lady would have matched herself
Unto so mean° a person? Yet the Cardinal — *lowly*
Bears himself much too cruel.

SECOND PILGRIM They are banished.

FIRST PILGRIM But I would ask, what power hath this state
Of Ancona to determine of° a free prince? — *pass sentence on*

SECOND PILGRIM They° are a free state, sir, and her brother showed — *They of Ancona*
How that the Pope, forehearing of her looseness,
Hath seized into th'protection of the church
The dukedom which she held as dowager.

FIRST PILGRIM But by what justice?

SECOND PILGRIM Sure I think by none,
Only her brother's° instigation. — *(the Cardinal's)*

FIRST PILGRIM What was it with such violence he took
Off from her finger?

SECOND PILGRIM 'Twas her wedding ring,
Which he vowed shortly he would sacrifice
To his revenge.

FIRST PILGRIM Alas, Antonio!
If that a man be thrust into a well,
No matter who sets hand to't, his own weight
Will bring him sooner to th'bottom. Come, let's hence.
Fortune makes this conclusion general:
All things do help th'unhappy° man to fall. *Exeunt.* — *unlucky*

3.5

[Enter] Antonio, Duchess, children, Cariola, [and] servants.

DUCHESS Banished Ancona!
ANTONIO Yes. You see what power
Lightens° in great men's breath. *Flashes out*
DUCHESS Is all our train
Shrunk to this poor remainder?
ANTONIO These poor men,
Which have got little in your service, vow
To take° your fortune; but your wiser buntings,° *share / songbirds*
Now they are fledged,° are gone. *feathered for flight*
DUCHESS They have done wisely.
This puts me in mind of death; physicians thus,
With their hands full of money, use to give o'er° *regularly abandon*
Their patients.
ANTONIO Right° the fashion of the world! *Exactly*
From decayed fortunes every flatterer shrinks;
Men cease to build where the foundation sinks.
DUCHESS I had a very strange dream tonight.° *last night*
ANTONIO What was't?
DUCHESS Methought I wore my coronet of state,
And on a sudden all the diamonds
Were changed to pearls.
ANTONIO My interpretation
Is, you'll weep shortly, for to me the pearls
Do signify your tears.
DUCHESS The birds that live i'th'field
On the wild benefit of nature live
Happier than we; for they may choose their mates,
And carol their sweet pleasures to the spring.

[Enter] Bosola [with a letter].

BOSOLA You are happily° o'erta'en. *fortunately*
DUCHESS From my brother?
BOSOLA Yes, from the Lord Ferdinand, your brother,
All love and safety. *[He delivers] a letter [to her].*
DUCHESS Thou dost blanch mischief,° *whitewash malignity*
Wouldst make it white. See, see! Like to calm weather
At sea before a tempest, false hearts speak fair
To those they intend most mischief.
[She reads.] "Send Antonio to me; I want his head in a business."
A politic° equivocation! *cunning*
He doth not want your counsel, but your head;
That is, he cannot sleep till you be dead.
And here's another pitfall that's strewed o'er
With roses: mark it, 'tis a cunning one:
[She reads.] "I stand engaged for your husband for several debts at Naples.° Let not that trouble him, I had rather have his heart° than his money." *(see 3.2.171–76)* *his love; his life*

3.5. Near Loreto.

And I believe so too.
BOSOLA What do you believe?
DUCHESS That he so much distrusts my husband's love,
He will by no means believe his heart is with him
Until he see it.° The devil is not cunning enough *i.e., cuts him open*
To circumvent us in riddles.
BOSOLA Will you reject that noble and free league° *covenant*
Of amity and love which I present you?
DUCHESS Their league is like that of some politic kings,
Only to make themselves of strength and power
To be our after-ruin. Tell them so.
BOSOLA [*to Antonio*] And what from you?
ANTONIO Thus tell him: I will not come.
BOSOLA And what of this?° *(the letter)*
ANTONIO My brothers° have dispersed *brothers-in-law*
Bloodhounds abroad, which, till I hear are muzzled,
No truce, though hatched with ne'er such politic skill,
Is safe that hangs upon our enemies' will.
I'll not come at° them. *to*
BOSOLA This proclaims your breeding.
Every small thing draws a base mind to fear
As the adamant° draws iron. Fare you well, sir. *magnet*
You shall shortly hear from 's. *Exit.*
DUCHESS I suspect some ambush.
Therefore, by all my love, I do conjure you
To take your eldest son and fly towards Milan;
Let us not venture all this poor remainder
In one unlucky bottom.° *ship's hold*
ANTONIO You counsel safely.
Best of my life, farewell! Since we must part,
Heaven hath a hand in't, but no otherwise
Than as some curious° artist takes in sunder *skilled*
A clock or watch when it is out of frame,
To bring't in better order.
DUCHESS I know not which is best,
To see you dead, or part with you.—Farewell, boy;
Thou art happy that thou hast not understanding
To know thy misery, for all our wit
And reading brings us to a truer sense
Of sorrow.—In the eternal church, sir,
I do hope we shall not part thus.
ANTONIO Oh, be of comfort!
Make° patience a noble fortitude, *Make of*
And think not how unkindly we are used.
Man, like to cassia,[1] is proved best, being bruised.
DUCHESS Must I, like to a slave-born Russian,
Account it praise[2] to suffer tyranny?
And yet, O heaven, thy heavy hand is in't.
I have seen my little boy oft scourge° his top, *whip into a spin*
And compared myself to't. Naught made me e'er
Go right but heaven's scourge stick.° *whip for a top*
ANTONIO Do not weep.

1. A kind of cinnamon that is especially aromatic, like most such herbs, when it is crushed.
2. Think it a praiseworthy thing.

Heaven fashioned us of nothing, and we strive
To bring ourselves to nothing.—Farewell, Cariola,
And thy sweet armful!—If I do never see thee more,
Be a good mother to your little ones,
And save them from the tiger. Fare you well.
[He and the Duchess kiss.]

DUCHESS Let me look upon you once more, for that speech
Came from a dying father. Your kiss is colder
Than that I have seen an holy anchorite
Give to a dead man's skull.

ANTONIO My heart is turned to a heavy lump of lead,
With which I sound° my danger. Fare you well. — *sound the depths of*
Exit [with his elder son].

DUCHESS My laurel is all withered.

CARIOLA Look, madam, what a troop of armèd men
Make toward us.

Enter Bosola with a guard, with vizards.° — *masks*

DUCHESS Oh, they are very welcome.
When Fortune's wheel is overcharged with princes,
The weight makes it move swift. I would have my ruin
Be sudden.—I am your adventure,° am I not? — *quarry*

BOSOLA You are. You must see your husband no more.

DUCHESS What devil art thou, that counterfeits heaven's
thunder?

BOSOLA Is that terrible? I would have you tell me
Whether is that note worse that frights the silly° birds — *unsuspecting, guileless*
Out of the corn,° or that which doth allure them — *grain*
To the nets? You have hearkened to the last° too much.[3] — *the latter*

DUCHESS Oh, misery! Like to a rusty o'ercharged° cannon, — *overloaded*
Shall I never fly in pieces? Come, to what prison?

BOSOLA To none.

DUCHESS Whither then?

BOSOLA To your palace.

DUCHESS I have heard
That Charon's° boat serves to convey all o'er — *the ferryman of Hades*
The dismal lake,° but brings none back again. — *The river Styx*

BOSOLA Your brothers mean you safety and pity.

DUCHESS Pity!
With such a pity men preserve alive
Pheasants and quails when they are not fat enough
To be eaten.

BOSOLA These are your children?

DUCHESS Yes.

BOSOLA Can they prattle?

DUCHESS No.
But I intend, since they were born accurst,° — *doomed; in sin*
Curses shall be their first language.

BOSOLA Fie, madam,
Forget this base, low fellow.

DUCHESS Were I a man,
I'd beat that counterfeit face° into thy other. — *your mask*

3. Bosola suggests that the Duchess would have done better to heed warning notes of impending danger than to have allowed herself to be lured into disaster like birds lured into fowlers' nets.

BOSOLA One of no birth.
DUCHESS Say that he was born mean;° *lowly*
Man is most happy when 's own actions
Be arguments° and examples of his virtue. *evidence, demonstrations*
BOSOLA A barren, beggarly virtue.
DUCHESS I prithee, who is greatest, can you tell?
Sad tales befit my woe; I'll tell you one.
A salmon, as she swam unto the sea,
Met with a dogfish,° who encounters her *a small shark*
With this rough language: "Why art thou so bold
To mix thyself with our high state of floods,° *our grand sea*
Being no eminent courtier, but one
That for the calmest and fresh time o'th'year
Dost live in shallow rivers, rank'st thyself
With silly° smelts and shrimps? And darest thou *innocent; lowly*
Pass by our dogship° without reverence?" *(cf. "our lordship")*
"Oh," quoth the salmon, "sister, be at peace.
Thank Jupiter, we both have passed the net!
Our value never can be truly known
Till in the fisher's basket we be shown;
I'th'market then my price may be the higher,
Even when I am nearest to the cook and fire."
So to great men the moral may be stretched:
Men oft are valued high when they're most wretch'd.
But come: whither you please. I am armed 'gainst misery,
Bent to all sways of the oppressors' will.
There's no deep valley but near some great hill. *Exeunt.*

4.1

[*Enter*] *Ferdinand, Bosola,* [*and*] *servants* [*with torches*].

FERDINAND How doth our sister duchess bear herself
In her imprisonment?
BOSOLA Nobly. I'll describe her:
She's sad, as one long used to't, and she seems
Rather to welcome the end of misery° *to welcome death*
Than shun it—a behavior so noble
As gives a majesty to adversity.
You may discern the shape of loveliness
More perfect in her tears than in her smiles;
She will muse four hours together, and her silence,
Methinks, expresseth more than if she spake.
FERDINAND Her melancholy seems to be fortified
With a strange disdain.
BOSOLA 'Tis so, and this restraint,
Like English mastiffs that grow fierce with tying,
Makes her too passionately apprehend
Those pleasures she's kept from.
FERDINAND Curse upon her!

4.1. Some place of incarceration in northern Italy (see 3.5.108, where Bosola's statement to the Duchess that she is to be taken "To your palace" may be deliberate misinformation or may indicate that she has a palace in the north, in addition to Amalfi).

I will no longer study in the book
Of another's heart. Inform her what I told you. *Exit.*

[Enter] Duchess [and] Cariola.

BOSOLA All comfort to Your Grace!
DUCHESS I will have none.
Pray thee, why dost thou wrap thy poisoned pills
In gold and sugar?
BOSOLA Your elder brother, the Lord Ferdinand,
Is come to visit you, and sends you word,
'Cause once he rashly made a solemn vow
Never to see you more, he comes i'th'night,
And prays you, gently, neither torch nor taper
Shine in your chamber. He will kiss your hand
And reconcile himself; but, for his vow,
He dares not see you.
DUCHESS At his pleasure.—
Take hence the lights. *[Exeunt servants with torches.]*

[Enter Ferdinand.]

He's come.
FERDINAND Where are you?
DUCHESS Here, sir.
FERDINAND This darkness suits you well.
DUCHESS I would ask you pardon.
FERDINAND You have it;
For I account it the honorabl'st revenge,
Where I may kill, to pardon. Where are your cubs?
DUCHESS Whom?
FERDINAND Call them your children;
For, though our national law distinguish bastards
From true legitimate issue, compassionate nature
Makes them all equal.
DUCHESS Do you visit me for this?
You violate a sacrament o'th'church° *i.e., marriage*
Shall° make you howl in hell for't. *Which shall*
FERDINAND It had been well
Could you have lived thus always, for indeed
You were too much i'th'light.[1] But no more;
I come to seal my peace with you. Here's a hand,
Gives her a dead man's hand.
To which you have vowed much love; the ring upon't° *(see 1.1.405–8, 3.4.37–40)*
You gave.
DUCHESS I affectionately kiss it.
FERDINAND Pray do, and bury the print of it in your heart.
I will leave this ring with you for a love token,
And the hand, as sure as the ring; and do not doubt
But you shall have the heart too. When you need a friend,
Send it to him that owed° it; you shall see *owned*
Whether he can aid you.
DUCHESS You are very cold.
I fear you are not well after your travel.—

1. You were (1) too visible to all; (2) too wanton.

Hah? Lights! Oh, horrible!
FERDINAND Let her have lights enough.
Exit.[2]

[*Enter servants with torches.*]

DUCHESS What witchcraft doth he practice, that he hath left
A dead man's hand here?

Here is discovered, behind a travers,° *the artificial figures of Antonio and his children, appearing as if they were dead.* — curtain

BOSOLA Look you, here's the piece from which 'twas ta'en.
He doth present you this sad spectacle
That, now you know directly they are dead,
Hereafter you may wisely cease to grieve
For that which cannot be recoverèd.
DUCHESS There is not between heaven and earth one wish
I stay for after this; it wastes me more
Than were't my picture, fashioned out of wax,
Stuck with a magical needle, and then buried
In some foul dunghill. And yond's an excellent property° — *device, stage prop*
For a tyrant, which I would account mercy.° — *a blessing in disguise*
BOSOLA What's that?
DUCHESS If they would bind me to that lifeless trunk
And let me freeze to death.
BOSOLA Come, you must live.
DUCHESS That's the greatest torture souls feel in hell,
In hell: that they must live and cannot die.
Portia, I'll new-kindle thy coals again,[3]
And revive the rare and almost dead example
Of a loving wife.
BOSOLA Oh, fie! Despair? Remember
You are a Christian.° — *(suicide is a sin)*
DUCHESS The church enjoins fasting;
I'll starve myself to death.
BOSOLA Leave this vain sorrow.
Things being at the worst begin to mend;
The bee, when he hath shot his sting into your hand,
May then play with your eyelid.
DUCHESS Good comfortable fellow,
Persuade a wretch that's broke upon the wheel° — *torture wheel*
To have all his bones new set; entreat him live,
To be executed again. Who must dispatch me?
I account this world a tedious theater,
For I do play a part in't 'gainst my will.
BOSOLA Come, be of comfort. I will save your life.
DUCHESS Indeed I have not leisure to tend so small a business.
BOSOLA Now, by my life, I pity you.
DUCHESS Thou art a fool, then,
To waste thy pity on a thing so wretched

2. Perhaps Ferdinand simply retires to one side, rather than exiting. What he says at line 113 seems to indicate that he has heard Bosola's interview with the Duchess. See note at 112.2.

3. When Brutus's cause failed after the assassination of Julius Caesar, Brutus's virtuous wife Portia suffocated herself to death by putting live coals in her mouth.

As cannot pity it.° I am full of daggers. *itself*
Puff! Let me blow these vapors from me.

[*Enter a Servant.*]

What are you?
SERVANT One that wishes you long life.
DUCHESS I would thou wert hanged for the horrible curse
Thou hast given me! [*Exit Servant.*]
I shall shortly grow one
Of the miracles° of pity. I'll go pray. No, *marvels*
I'll go curse.
BOSOLA Oh, fie!
DUCHESS I could curse the stars—
BOSOLA Oh, fearful!
DUCHESS And those three smiling seasons of the year° *(spring through fall)*
Into a Russian winter, nay, the world
To its first chaos.
BOSOLA Look you, the stars shine still.[4]
DUCHESS Oh, but you must remember,
My curse hath a great way to go.—
Plagues, that make lanes through largest families,
Consume them!° *i.e., her brothers*
BOSOLA Fie, lady!
DUCHESS Let them, like tyrants,
Never be remembered but for the ill they have done!
Let all the zealous prayers of mortified° *ascetic*
Churchmen forget them!
BOSOLA Oh, uncharitable!
DUCHESS Let heaven, a little while, cease crowning martyrs,
To punish them!
Go, howl them this, and say I long to bleed.
It is some mercy, when men kill with speed.
Exit [*with Cariola*].

[*Enter Ferdinand.*][5]

FERDINAND Excellent; as I would wish; she's plagued in art.
These presentations are but framed in wax
By the curious° master in that quality,° *skilled / craft*
Vincentio Lauriola,° and she takes them *(unidentified)*
For true substantial bodies.
BOSOLA Why do you do this?
FERDINAND To bring her to despair.
BOSOLA Faith,° end here, *In faith*
And go no farther in your cruelty.
Send her a penitential garment to put on
Next to her delicate skin, and furnish her
With beads and prayer books.
FERDINAND Damn her! That body of hers,
While that my blood ran pure in't, was more worth
Than that which thou wouldst comfort, called a soul.
I will send her masques of common courtesans,

4. I.e., (1) Your cursing the stars has had no effect on them; or (2) order in the universe endures forever.
5. Perhaps Ferdinand simply comes forward at this point, since he appears to have heard the preceding interview with the Duchess. See line 53.1 and note above.

Have her meat served up by bawds and ruffians,
And, 'cause she'll needs be mad, I am resolved
To remove forth° the common hospital — *from*
All the mad folk, and place them near her lodging;
There let them practice together, sing, and dance,
And act their gambols to the full o'th'moon.° — *(a time of "lunacy")*
If she can sleep the better for it, let her.
Your work is almost ended.

BOSOLA Must I see her again?
FERDINAND Yes.
BOSOLA Never.
FERDINAND You must.
BOSOLA Never in mine own shape;
That's forfeited, by my intelligence° — *my spying*
And this last cruel lie. When you send me next,
The business shall be comfort.
FERDINAND Very likely!
Thy pity is nothing of kin to thee. Antonio
Lurks about Milan; thou shalt shortly thither,
To feed a fire as great as my revenge,
Which nev'r will slack till it have spent his° fuel. — *its*
Intemperate agues° make physicians cruel. *Exeunt.* — *fevers*

4.2

[*Enter*] *Duchess* [*and*] *Cariola.* [*Noises of Madmen are heard from offstage.*]

DUCHESS What hideous noise was that?
CARIOLA 'Tis the wild consort° — *band, company*
Of madmen, lady, which your tyrant brother
Hath placed about your lodging. This tyranny,
I think, was never practiced till this hour.
DUCHESS Indeed, I thank him. Nothing but noise and folly
Can keep me in my right wits, whereas reason
And silence make me stark mad. Sit down;
Discourse to me some dismal tragedy.
CARIOLA Oh, 'twill increase your melancholy.
DUCHESS Thou art deceived;
To hear of greater grief would lessen mine.
This is a prison!
CARIOLA Yes, but you shall live
To shake this durance° off. — *imprisonment*
DUCHESS Thou art a fool.
The robin redbreast and the nightingale
Never live long in cages.
CARIOLA Pray dry your eyes.
What think you of, madam?
DUCHESS Of nothing.
When I muse thus, I sleep.
CARIOLA Like a madman, with your eyes open?
DUCHESS Dost thou think we shall know one another
In th'other world?

4.2. The Duchess's lodging, as in 4.1 (see 4.1.128–32).

CARIOLA Yes, out of question.
DUCHESS Oh, that it were possible we might
But hold some two days' conference with the dead!
From them I should learn somewhat, I am sure,
I never shall know here. I'll tell thee a miracle:
I am not mad yet, to my cause of sorrow.
Th'heaven o'er my head seems made of molten brass,
The earth of flaming sulfur, yet I am not mad.
I am acquainted with sad misery
As the tanned galley-slave is with his oar;
Necessity makes me suffer constantly,
And custom makes it easy. Who do I look like now?
CARIOLA Like to your picture in the gallery,
A deal° of life in show,° but none in practice; *good deal / appearance*
Or rather like some reverend monument
Whose ruins are even pitied.
DUCHESS Very proper;
And Fortune° seems only to have her eyesight *(usually shown blind)*
To behold my tragedy. [*A noise is heard.*] How now,
What noise is that?

[*Enter*] *Servant.*

SERVANT I am come to tell you
Your brother hath intended you some sport.
A great physician, when the Pope was sick
Of a deep melancholy, presented him
With several sorts of madmen, which wild object,
Being full of change and sport,° forced him to laugh, *variety and amusement*
And so th'impostume° broke. The selfsame cure *abscess*
The Duke intends on you.
DUCHESS Let them come in.
SERVANT There's a mad lawyer, and a secular° priest, *nonmonastic*
A doctor that hath forfeited his wits
By jealousy; an astrologian,
That in his works said such a day o'th'month
Should be the day of doom,° and, failing of't, *Day of Judgment*
Ran mad; an English tailor, crazed i'th'brain
With the study of new fashion; a gentleman-usher[1]
Quite beside himself with care to keep in mind
The number of his lady's salutations
Or "How do you" she employed him in each morning;
A farmer, too, an excellent knave in grain,° *ingrained; in grain trade*
Mad 'cause he was hindered transportation.° *an export license*
And let one broker° that's mad loose to these, *pawnbroker; procurer*
You'd think the devil were among them.
DUCHESS Sit, Cariola.—Let them loose when you please,
For I am chained to endure all your tyranny.

[*Enter*] *Madmen.*

Here by a Madman this song is sung,
to a dismal kind of music.

1. A gentleman acting as a chamberlain to a person of superior rank, marching before that great person on ceremonial occasions and conducting others into his or her presence.

Oh, let us howl some heavy note,
 Some deadly doggèd howl,
Sounding as from the threat'ning throat
 Of beasts and fatal fowl,
As ravens, screech owls, bulls, and bears!
 We'll bill° and bawl our parts, *bellow, declaim*
Till irksome noise have cloyed your ears
 And corrosived° your hearts. *corroded, fretted*
At last, whenas our choir wants breath,
 Our bodies being blest,
We'll sing like swans, to welcome death,[2]
 And die in love and rest.

FIRST MADMAN Doomsday not come yet? I'll draw it nearer by a perspective,° or make a glass° that shall set all the world on fire upon an instant. I cannot sleep; my pillow is stuffed with a litter of porcupines. *telescope / burning glass*

SECOND MADMAN Hell is a mere glasshouse,° where the devils are continually blowing up women's souls on hollow irons, and the fire never goes out. *glass factory*

THIRD MADMAN I will lie with every woman in my parish the tenth night. I will tithe° them over, like haycocks. *divide into tenths*

FOURTH MADMAN Shall my pothecary° outgo me because I am a cuckold? I have found out his roguery: he makes alum of his wife's urine and sells it to Puritans that have sore throats with overstraining.° *druggist* *(preaching and singing)*

FIRST MADMAN I have skill in heraldry.

SECOND MADMAN Hast?

FIRST MADMAN You do give° for your crest a woodcock's head with the brains picked out on't; you are a very ancient gentleman. *display (heraldically)*

THIRD MADMAN Greek is turned Turk; we are only to be saved by the Helvetian translation.[3]

FIRST MADMAN Come on, sir, I will lay° the law to you. *expound*

SECOND MADMAN Oh, rather lay a corrosive;° the law will eat to the bone. *apply caustic medicine*

THIRD MADMAN He that drinks but to satisfy nature° is damned. *appetite*

FOURTH MADMAN If I had my glass here, I would show a sight should make all the women here call me mad doctor.

FIRST MADMAN [*pointing to the Third Madman*] What's he, a rope-maker?

SECOND MADMAN No, no, no, a snuffling knave that, while he shows the tombs, will have his hand in a wench's placket.° *petticoat opening*

THIRD MADMAN Woe to the caroche° that brought home my wife from the masque at three o'clock in the morning! It had a large featherbed in it. *carriage*

FOURTH MADMAN I have pared the devil's nails forty times, roasted them in ravens' eggs, and cured agues° with them. *fevers*

THIRD MADMAN Get me three hundred milch-bats to make possets,° to procure sleep. *sleep-inducing drinks*

2. Swans were thought to sing only once in their lives, at the approach of death.

3. Only the Genevan Bible (prohibited in England until 1576 because of its Calvinist emphasis) can save a world given over to heathen apostasy. (The Third Madman speaks as a zealous Puritan.)

FOURTH MADMAN All the college° may throw their caps at me.[4] I have made a soap-boiler costive;° it was my masterpiece.
(physicians or clergy) / constipated

Here the dance, consisting of eight Madmen, with music answerable° thereunto, after which Bosola, like an old man, enters.
suitable

[*Exeunt the Madmen.*]

DUCHESS Is he mad too?
SERVANT Pray question him. I'll leave you.
[*Exit.*]

BOSOLA I am come to make thy tomb.
DUCHESS Hah, my tomb?
Thou speak'st as if I lay upon my deathbed,
Gasping for breath. Dost thou perceive me sick?

BOSOLA Yes, and the more dangerously, since thy sickness is insensible.°
imperceptible

DUCHESS Thou art not mad, sure. Dost know me?

BOSOLA Yes.

DUCHESS Who am I?

BOSOLA Thou art a box of wormseed, at best but a salvatory° of green mummy.[5] What's this flesh? A little crudded° milk, fantastical puff paste.° Our bodies are weaker than those paper prisons boys use to keep flies in—more contemptible, since ours is to preserve° earthworms. Didst thou ever see a lark in a cage? Such is the soul in the body. This world is like her little turf of grass;° and the heaven o'er our heads, like her looking glass,[6] only gives us a miserable knowledge of the small compass of our prison.
ointment box / curdled / puff pastry / keep alive / (put in birdcages)

DUCHESS Am not I thy duchess?

BOSOLA Thou art some great woman, sure, for riot° begins to sit on thy forehead, clad in gray hairs, twenty years sooner than on a merry milkmaid's. Thou sleep'st worse than if a mouse should be forced to take up her lodging in a cat's ear. A little infant that breeds its teeth,° should it lie with thee, would cry out as if thou wert the more unquiet bedfellow.
disorder (of aging) / is teething

DUCHESS I am Duchess of Malfi still.

BOSOLA That makes thy sleeps so broken.
Glories, like glowworms, afar off shine bright,
But, looked to near, have neither heat nor light.

DUCHESS Thou art very plain.

BOSOLA My trade is to flatter the dead, not the living. I am a tomb-maker.

DUCHESS And thou com'st to make my tomb?

BOSOLA Yes.

DUCHESS Let me be a little merry. Of what stuff wilt thou make it?

BOSOLA Nay, resolve° me first, of what fashion?
satisfy, explain to

DUCHESS Why, do we grow fantastical° in our deathbed? Do we affect° fashion in the grave?
fashion-conscious / take a fancy to

BOSOLA Most ambitiously. Princes' images on their tombs do not lie as they were wont, seeming to pray up to heaven, but with their hands under their cheeks as if they died of the

4. I.e., may do their best to fend me off.
5. Mummified flesh used medicinally.
6. The lark's cage is imagined to have a small mirror in it that turns and sparkles, catching the bird's attention.

toothache. They are not carved with their eyes fixed upon the stars, but as their minds were wholly bent upon the world, the selfsame way they seem to turn their faces.

DUCHESS Let me know fully therefore the effect° *purport*
Of this thy dismal preparation,
This talk fit for a charnel.° *bone depository*

BOSOLA Now I shall.

[Enter] Executioners [with] a coffin, cords, and a bell.

Here is a present from your princely brothers,
And may it arrive welcome, for it brings
Last benefit, last sorrow.

DUCHESS Let me see it.
I have so much obedience in my blood,
I wish it in their veins to do them good.[7]

BOSOLA This is your last presence-chamber.° *reception room*

CARIOLA Oh, my sweet lady!

DUCHESS Peace, it affrights not me.

BOSOLA I am the common bellman,[8]
That usually is sent to condemned persons
The night before they suffer.

DUCHESS Even now thou said'st
Thou wast a tomb-maker?

BOSOLA 'Twas to bring you
By degrees to mortification. Listen:
[He sounds the bell and recites this dirge.]

Hark! Now everything is still.
The screech owl and the whistler[9] shrill
Call upon our dame° aloud, *(Night)*
And bid her quickly don her shroud.° *bring on darkness*
Much you had of land and rent;° *revenue*
Your length in clay's now competent.° *sufficient*
A long war disturbed your mind;
Here your perfect peace is signed.° *you are released*
Of what is't fools make such vain keeping?° *defending, retaining*
Sin their conception, their birth weeping;
Their life, a general mist of error,
Their death, a hideous storm of terror.
Strew your hair with powders sweet;
Don clean linen; bathe your feet;
And, the foul fiend more to check,
A crucifix let bless your neck.° *Wear a crucifix*
'Tis now full tide 'tween night and day;
End your groan, and come away.

CARIOLA Hence, villains, tyrants, murderers! Alas,
What will you do with my lady?—Call for help.

7. The Duchess is so resigned to her death that she is ready to bequeath her own obedient blood to her brothers, hoping to make them better and to show that she has not been simply rebellious.

8. The bell-ringer or town crier, who customarily announced deaths, could be employed to counsel condemned persons on their way to execution.

9. Any birds whose loud cry might be considered a harbinger of disaster.

DUCHESS To whom, to our next neighbors? They are mad folks.
BOSOLA [*to the Executioners*] Remove that noise.
[*The Executioners seize Cariola, who struggles.*]
DUCHESS Farewell, Cariola.
In my last will I have not much to give;
A many hungry guests have fed upon me.
Thine will be a poor reversion.° *inheritance*
CARIOLA [*to the Executioners*] I will die with her.
DUCHESS [*to Cariola*] I pray thee, look thou giv'st my little boy
Some syrup for his cold, and let the girl
Say her prayers ere she sleep.
[*The Executioners forcefully remove Cariola and return.*]
Now, what you please.
What death?
BOSOLA Strangling. Here are your executioners.
DUCHESS I forgive them.
The apoplexy, catarrh,° or cough o'th'lungs *stroke*
Would do as much as they do.
BOSOLA Doth not death fright you?
DUCHESS Who would be afraid on't,
Knowing to meet such excellent company
In th'other world?
BOSOLA Yet methinks
The manner of your death should much afflict you,
This cord should terrify you?
DUCHESS Not a whit.
What would it pleasure me to have my throat cut
With diamonds, or to be smothered
With cassia,° or to be shot to death with pearls? *fragrant spice*
I know death hath ten thousand several° doors *various*
For men to take their exits, and 'tis found
They go on such strange geometrical hinges,
You may open them both ways.[1] Any way, for heaven sake,
So I were out of your whispering! Tell my brothers
That I perceive death, now I am well awake,
Best gift is they can give or I can take.
I would fain put off my last woman's fault:
I'd not be tedious to you.
EXECUTIONERS We are ready.
DUCHESS Dispose my breath how please you, but my body
Bestow upon my women, will you?
EXECUTIONERS Yes.
DUCHESS Pull, and pull strongly, for your able strength
Must pull down heaven upon me.—
Yet stay. Heaven gates are not so highly arched
As princes' palaces; they that enter there
Must go upon their knees. [*She kneels.*] Come, violent death,
Serve for mandragora,° to make me sleep!— *mandrake (see 2.5.1 n)*
Go tell my brothers, when I am laid out,
They then may feed in quiet. *They strangle her.*
BOSOLA Where's the waiting-woman?

1. The door of death may be opened for you, or you can push it open yourself (by taking your own life); or, the doors of death open mysteriously in such a way that one enters on a new life even as one dies.

Fetch her. Some other strangle the children.° (done offstage)
[*Exeunt Executioners.*]

[*Some return with Cariola.*]

Look you, there sleeps your mistress.
CARIOLA Oh, you are damned
Perpetually for this! My turn is next;
Is't not so ordered?
BOSOLA Yes, and I am glad
You are so well prepared for't.
CARIOLA You are deceived, sir;
I am not prepared for't. I will not die;
I will first come to my answer,° and know *reply to accusations*
How I have offended.
BOSOLA [*to the Executioners*] Come, dispatch her.
[*To her*] You kept her counsel; now you shall keep ours.
CARIOLA I will not die! I must not. I am contracted
To a young gentleman.
EXECUTIONER [*showing the cords*] Here's your wedding ring.
CARIOLA Let me but speak with the Duke. I'll discover° *reveal*
Treason to his person.
BOSOLA Delays!—Throttle her.
EXECUTIONER She bites, and scratches!
CARIOLA If you kill me now
I am damned; I have not been at confession
This two years.
BOSOLA When?° *(expressing impatience)*
CARIOLA I am quick° with child. *pregnant*
BOSOLA Why, then,
Your credit's saved.[2] [*The Executioners strangle her.*]
Bear her into th'next room;
Let this° lie still. [*Exeunt the Executioners, bearing off* *(the Duchess's body)*
the dead Cariola.]

[*Enter*] *Ferdinand.*

FERDINAND Is she dead?
BOSOLA She is what
You'd have her. But here begin your pity.
Shows the children strangled.[3]
Alas, how have these offended?
FERDINAND The death
Of young wolves is never to be pitied.
BOSOLA Fix your eye here.
FERDINAND Constantly.
BOSOLA Do you not weep?
Other sins only speak; murder shrieks out.
The element of water moistens the earth,
But blood flies upwards and bedews the heavens.
FERDINAND Cover her face. Mine eyes dazzle; she died young.
BOSOLA I think not so; her infelicity

2. Your reputation will be preserved (since Cariola will not suffer the shame of bearing an illegitimate child).

3. Presumably the dead children are discovered by pulling aside a partition or curtain.

Seemed to have years too many.
FERDINAND She and I were twins;
And, should I die this instant, I had lived
Her time to a minute.
BOSOLA It seems she was born first.[4]
You have bloodily approved° the ancient truth *confirmed*
That kindred commonly do worse agree
Than remote strangers.
FERDINAND Let me see her face again.
Why didst not thou pity her? What an excellent
Honest man mightst thou have been
If thou hadst borne her to some sanctuary,
Or, bold in a good cause, opposed thyself
With thy advancèd° sword above thy head *raised on high*
Between her innocence and my revenge!
I bade thee, when I was distracted of my wits,
Go kill my dearest friend, and thou hast done't.
For let me but examine well the cause:
What was the meanness° of her match to me? *social inferiority*
Only, I must confess, I had a hope,
Had she continued widow, to have gained
An infinite mass of treasure by her death;
And that was the main cause—her marriage,
That drew a stream of gall quite through my heart.
For° thee—as we observe in tragedies *As for*
That a good actor many times is cursed
For playing a villain's part—I hate thee for't,
And for my sake say thou hast done much ill well.
BOSOLA Let me quicken your memory, for I perceive
You are falling into ingratitude. I challenge° *claim*
The reward due to my service.
FERDINAND I'll tell thee
What I'll give thee—
BOSOLA Do.
FERDINAND I'll give thee a pardon
For this murder.
BOSOLA Hah?
FERDINAND Yes, and 'tis
The largest bounty I can study° to do thee. *think of*
By what authority didst thou execute
This bloody sentence?
BOSOLA By yours.
FERDINAND Mine? Was I her judge?
Did any ceremonial form of law
Doom her to not-being? Did a complete jury
Deliver her conviction up i'th'court?
Where shalt thou find this judgment registered
Unless in hell? See, like a bloody fool
Th'hast forfeited thy life, and thou shalt die for't.
BOSOLA The office of justice is perverted quite
When one thief hangs another. Who shall dare
To reveal this?

4. But see 4.1.21, where Ferdinand is described as the Duchess's "elder brother." The historical figure (Carlo) on whom Ferdinand was based was in fact older than his sister.

FERDINAND Oh, I'll tell thee:
The wolf shall find her grave and scrape it up,
Not to devour the corpse, but to discover
The horrid murder.
BOSOLA You, not I, shall quake for't.
FERDINAND Leave me.
BOSOLA I will first receive my pension.
FERDINAND You are a villain!
BOSOLA When your ingratitude
Is judge, I am so.
FERDINAND Oh, horror,
That not the fear of Him which binds the devils[5]
Can prescribe man obedience!
Never look upon me more.
BOSOLA Why, fare thee well.
Your brother and yourself are worthy men;
You have a pair of hearts are° hollow graves, *that are*
Rotten, and rotting others; and your vengeance,
Like two chained bullets,[6] still goes arm in arm.
You may be brothers, for treason, like the plague,
Doth take much in a blood.° I stand like one *Takes hold in families*
That long hath ta'en° a sweet and golden dream. *experienced*
I am angry with myself, now that I wake.
FERDINAND Get thee into some unknown part o'th'world
That I may never see thee.
BOSOLA Let me know
Wherefore I should be thus neglected. Sir,
I served your tyranny, and rather strove
To satisfy yourself than all the world;
And, though I loathed the evil, yet I loved
You that did counsel it, and rather sought
To appear a true servant than an honest man.
FERDINAND I'll go hunt the badger by owl-light.° *dusk*
'Tis a deed of darkness. *Exit.*
BOSOLA He's much distracted. Off, my painted° honor![7] *assumed, illusory*
While with vain hopes our faculties we tire,
We seem to sweat in ice and freeze in fire.[8]
What would I do, were this to do again?
I would not change my peace of conscience
For all the wealth of Europe. [*The Duchess shows faint signs of life.*] She stirs! Here's life!
Return, fair soul, from darkness, and lead mine
Out of this sensible° hell!—She's warm, she breathes!— *palpable*
Upon thy pale lips I will melt my heart
To store° them with fresh color. [*Calling*] Who's there? *restore*
Some cordial° drink!—Alas! I dare not call. *heart-stimulating*
So pity would destroy pity.[9]—Her eye opes,
And heaven in it seems to ope, that late was shut,
To take me up to mercy.
DUCHESS Antonio!

5. That not even the fear of God.
6. Like cannon shot linked by chains to tear apart rigging in naval warfare.
7. In some stage productions, Bosola here removes his disguise as an old man.
8. I.e., No matter how much we wear ourselves out striving to succeed, we end up defeating our very purposes.
9. Seeking help out of pity for her would only bring on more trouble (since Ferdinand might return).

BOSOLA Yes, madam, he is living. The dead bodies you saw
were but feigned statues; he's reconciled to your brothers.
The Pope hath wrought the atonement.° *reconciliation*
DUCHESS Mercy! *She dies.*
BOSOLA Oh, she's gone again! There the cords° of life broke. *sinews, heartstrings*
Oh, sacred innocence, that sweetly sleeps
On turtles'° feathers, whilst a guilty conscience *turtledoves'*
Is a black register° wherein is writ *account book*
All our good deeds and bad, a perspective° *optical glass*
That shows us hell! That we cannot be suffered° *allowed*
To do good when we have a mind to it!
This is manly sorrow;
These tears, I am very certain, never grew
In my mother's milk. My estate° is sunk *mental state; fortune*
Below the degree of fear.° Where were *Past fearing*
These penitent fountains while she was living?
Oh, they were frozen up. Here is a sight
As direful to my soul as is the sword
Unto a wretch hath° slain his father. Come, *who has*
I'll bear thee hence
And execute thy last will: that's deliver
Thy body to the reverend dispose° *reverential disposal*
Of some good women. That the cruel tyrant
Shall not deny me. Then I'll post° to Milan, *hasten*
Where somewhat° I will speedily enact *something*
Worth my dejection.° *Exit* [*with the Duchess's body*]. *humbling by fortune*

5.1

[*Enter*] *Antonio* [*and*] *Delio.*

ANTONIO What think you of my hope of reconcilement
To the Aragonian brethren?[1]
DELIO I misdoubt° it, *mistrust*
For, though they have sent their letters of safe-conduct
For your repair to° Milan, they appear *return here to*
But nets to entrap you. The Marquis of Pescara,
Under whom you hold certain land in cheat,[2]
Much 'gainst his noble nature hath been moved° *persuaded*
To sieze those lands, and some of his dependents
Are at this instant making it their suit
To be invested in your revenues.
I cannot think they mean well to your life
That do deprive you of your means of life,
Your living.° *income from land*
ANTONIO You are still an heretic° *i.e., skeptic*
To any safety I can shape myself.

[*Enter*] *Pescara.*

DELIO Here comes the Marquis. I will make myself
Petitioner for some part of your land,

5.1. Milan.
1. At 2.5.21–22, the Cardinal speaks of himself and his brother Ferdinand as being of "The royal blood of Aragon and Castile." During much of the sixteenth century, the kingdom of Naples, which included Malfi and most of southern Italy, was ruled by a branch of the house of Aragon in Spain. See also 5.5.99.
2. Subject to escheat, i.e., held as a possession that Antonio could will to his heirs provided he does not die intestate and is not convicted of treason or another serious felony; in such a case, the property would revert to Pescara.

To know whither it is flying.
ANTONIO I pray, do. [*He stands aside.*]
DELIO Sir, I have a suit to you.
PESCARA To me?
DELIO An easy one:
There is the citadel of Saint Bennet,° *Benedict*
With some demesnes,° of late in the possession *landed property*
Of Antonio Bologna. Please you bestow them on me?
PESCARA You are my friend. But this is such a suit
Nor° fit for me to give nor you to take. *Neither*
DELIO No, sir?
PESCARA I will give you ample reason for't
Soon in private.—Here's the Cardinal's mistress.

[*Enter*] *Julia.*

JULIA My lord, I am grown your poor petitioner,
And should be an ill beggar, had I not
A great man's letter here, the Cardinal's,
To court you in my favor. [*She gives Pescara a letter.*]
PESCARA [*after reading*] He entreats for you
The citadel of Saint Bennet, that belonged
To the banished Bologna.
JULIA Yes.
PESCARA I could not have thought of a friend I could
Rather pleasure with it. 'Tis yours.
JULIA Sir, I thank you;
And he shall know how doubly I am engaged
Both in your gift and speediness of giving,
Which makes your grant the greater. *Exit.*
ANTONIO [*aside*] How they fortify
Themselves with my ruin!
DELIO Sir, I am
Little bound to you.
PESCARA Why?
DELIO Because you denied this suit to me, and gave't
To such a creature.
PESCARA Do you know what it was?
It was Antonio's land, not forfeited
By course of law, but ravished from his throat
By the Cardinal's entreaty. It were not fit
I should bestow so main a piece of wrong° *land wrongfully gotten*
Upon my friend; 'tis a gratification
Only due to a strumpet, for it is injustice.
Shall I sprinkle the pure blood of innocents
To make those followers I call my friends
Look ruddier° upon me? I am glad *with reddened faces*
This land, ta'en from the owner by such wrong,
Returns again unto so foul an use
As salary for his° lust. Learn, good Delio, *(the Cardinal's)*
To ask noble things of me, and you shall find
I'll be a noble giver.
DELIO You instruct me well.
ANTONIO [*aside*] Why, here's a man now would fright impudence

From sauciest beggars.[3]
PESCARA Prince Ferdinand's come to Milan,
Sick, as they give out,° of an apoplexy;° *report / stroke*
But some say 'tis a frenzy.° I am going *delirium*
To visit him. *Exit.*
ANTONIO [*coming forward*] 'Tis a noble old fellow.
DELIO What course do you mean to take, Antonio?
ANTONIO This night I mean to venture all my fortune,
Which is no more than a poor ling'ring life,
To the Cardinal's worst of malice. I have got
Private access to his chamber, and intend
To visit him about the mid of night,
As once his brother did our noble duchess.
It may be that the sudden apprehension
Of danger—for I'll go in mine own shape—
When he shall see it fraught° with love and duty, *freighted, filled*
May draw the poison out of him and work
A friendly reconcilement. If it fail,
Yet it shall rid me of this infamous calling;° *low estate*
For better fall once than be ever falling.
DELIO I'll second you in all danger; and, howe'er,° *whatever occurs*
My life keeps rank° with yours. *stands side by side*
ANTONIO You are still° my lovèd and best friend. *Exeunt.* *ever*

5.2

[*Enter*] *Pescara* [*and*] *a Doctor.*

PESCARA Now, Doctor, may I visit your patient?
DOCTOR If't please Your Lordship. But he's instantly
To take the air here in the gallery,
By my direction.
PESCARA Pray thee, what's his disease?
DOCTOR A very pestilent disease, my lord,
They call lycanthropia.
PESCARA What's that?
I need a dictionary to't.
DOCTOR I'll tell you.
In those that are possessed with't there o'erflows
Such melancholy humor they imagine
Themselves to be transformèd into wolves,
Steal forth to churchyards in the dead of night
And dig dead bodies up—as two nights since
One met the Duke 'bout midnight in a lane
Behind Saint Mark's Church, with the leg of a man
Upon his shoulder; and he howled fearfully;
Said he was a wolf, only the difference
Was, a wolf's skin was hairy on the outside,
His on the inside; bade them take their swords,
Rip up his flesh, and try.° Straight I was sent for, *test the proposition*
And, having ministered to him, found His Grace

3. Who would abash even the most audacious beggars.
5.2. Milan. The palace of the Cardinal and Ferdinand. (As powerful rulers they have palaces in Rome and Milan.)

Very well recovered.
PESCARA I am glad on't.
DOCTOR Yet not without some fear
Of a relapse. If he grow to his fit again,
I'll go a nearer° way to work with him *more direct*
Than ever Paracelsus[1] dreamed of. If
They'll give me leave, I'll buffet his madness out of him.

[Enter] Ferdinand, Malateste, [and] Cardinal. Bosola [follows, standing apart and watching].

Stand aside! He comes.
[The Doctor and Pescara stand aside.]

FERDINAND Leave me.
MALATESTE Why doth Your Lordship love this solitariness?
FERDINAND Eagles commonly fly alone; they are crows, daws,° and starlings that flock together.—Look, what's that follows me? *jackdaws*
MALATESTE Nothing, my lord.
FERDINAND Yes!° *There is something!*
MALATESTE 'Tis your shadow.
FERDINAND Stay° it! Let it not haunt me! *Stop*
MALATESTE Impossible, if you move and the sun shine.
FERDINAND I will throttle it.
[He throws himself upon his shadow.]
MALATESTE Oh, my lord, you are angry with nothing.
FERDINAND You are a fool.
How is't possible I should catch my shadow
Unless I fall upon't? When I go to hell,
I mean to carry a bribe, for look you,
Good gifts evermore make way for the worst persons.
PESCARA Rise, good my lord.
FERDINAND I am studying the art of patience.
PESCARA 'Tis a noble virtue.
FERDINAND To drive six snails before me from this town to Moscow; neither use goad nor whip to them, but let them take their own time—the patient'st man i'th'world match me for an experiment! —and I'll crawl after, like a sheep-biter.° *sheepherding dog*
CARDINAL Force him up. *[Ferdinand is lifted to his feet.]*
FERDINAND Use me well, you were best.° *you'd better*
What I have done, I have done. I'll confess nothing.
DOCTOR Now let me come to him.—Are you mad, my lord?
Are you out of your princely wits?
FERDINAND [*to Pescara*] What's he?
PESCARA Your doctor.
FERDINAND Let me have his beard sawed off and his eyebrows filed more civil.° *becomingly*
DOCTOR I must do mad tricks with him, for that's the only way on't. [*To Ferdinand*] I have brought Your Grace a salamander's skin, to keep you from sunburning.
FERDINAND I have cruel sore eyes.
DOCTOR The white of a cockatrice's° egg is present remedy. *a legendary serpent*
FERDINAND Let it be a new-laid one, you were best.—
Hide me from him! Physicians are like kings;

1. Swiss-born alchemist and physician (1493–1541).

They brook° no contradiction. *tolerate*

DOCTOR Now he begins to fear me. Now let me alone with° him. [*The Doctor removes his gown.*] *let me handle*

CARDINAL How now, put off your gown?

DOCTOR Let me have some forty urinals filled with rosewater; he and I'll go pelt one another with them. Now he begins to fear me.—Can you fetch a frisk,° sir?—Let him go, let him go, upon my peril.° I find, by his eye, he stands in awe of me. I'll make him as tame as a dormouse. *cut a caper* *risk, responsibility*

FERDINAND Can you fetch your frisks, sir?—I will stamp° him into a cullis,° flay off his skin, to cover one of the anatomies this rogue hath set i'th'cold yonder, in Barber-Surgeons' Hall.[2]—Hence, hence! You are all of you like beasts for sacrifice; there's nothing left of you but tongue and belly,° flattery and lechery. [*Exit.*] *pound, crush* *broth* *entrails*

PESCARA Doctor, he did not fear you throughly.° *thoroughly*

DOCTOR True, I was somewhat too forward. [*Exit.*]

BOSOLA [*aside*] Mercy upon me, what a fatal judgment
Hath fall'n upon this Ferdinand!

PESCARA [*to the Cardinal*] Knows Your Grace
What accident° hath brought unto the prince *circumstance*
This strange distraction?

CARDINAL [*aside*] I must feign somewhat. [*To them*] Thus
they say it grew:
You have heard it rumored for these many years,
None of our family dies but there is seen° *without first seeing*
The shape of an old woman, which is given° *represented*
By tradition to us to have been murdered
By her nephews for her riches. Such a figure
One night, as the prince sat up late at 's book,
Appeared to him; when, crying out for help,
The gentlemen of 's chamber found His Grace
All on a cold sweat, altered much in face
And language. Since which apparition
He hath grown worse and worse, and I much fear
He cannot live.

BOSOLA [*to the Cardinal*] Sir, I would speak with you.

PESCARA We'll leave Your Grace,
Wishing to the sick prince, our noble lord,
All health of mind and body.

CARDINAL You are most welcome.
[*Exeunt all but the Cardinal and Bosola.*]
[*Aside*] Are you come? So. This fellow must not know
By any means I had intelligence
In our duchess' death; for, though I counseled it,
The full of all th'engagement[3] seemed to grow
From Ferdinand. [*To Bosola*] Now, sir, how fares our sister?
I do not think but sorrow makes her look
Like to an oft-dyed garment.[4] She shall now
Taste comfort from me.—Why do you look so wildly?

2. Anatomies (line 78), or skeletons, of executed criminals or destitute persons were sometimes dissected or put on display at London's Barber-Surgeons' Hall. Barbers often performed surgical duties.

3. The complete extent of Bosola's being commissioned to commit the deed.

4. Repeated dyeing frays a garment.

Oh, the fortune of your master here, the prince,
Dejects you. But be you of happy comfort;
If you'll do one thing for me I'll entreat,
Though he had a cold tombstone o'er his bones,[5]
I'd make you what you would be.° *wish to be*

BOSOLA Anything;
Give it me in a breath,° and let me fly to't. *in a word*
They that think long small expedition win,° *make little progress*
For, musing much o'th'end, cannot begin.[6]

[*Enter*] *Julia.*

JULIA Sir, will you come in to supper?

CARDINAL I am busy. Leave me.

JULIA [*aside*] What an excellent shape hath that fellow!° *(Bosola)*
Exit.

CARDINAL 'Tis thus: Antonio lurks here in Milan;
Inquire him out and kill him. While he lives,
Our sister cannot marry, and I have thought
Of an excellent match for her. Do this, and style me
Thy advancement.° *name your reward*

BOSOLA But by what means shall I find him out?

CARDINAL There is a gentleman called Delio
Here in the camp° that hath been long approved° *military camp / proved*
His loyal friend. Set eye upon that fellow.
Follow him to Mass; maybe Antonio,
Although he do account religion
But a school name,° for fashion of the world *a clerical fiction*
May accompany him. Or else go inquire out
Delio's confessor, and see if you can bribe
Him to reveal it. There are a thousand ways
A man might find to trace him: as,° to know *such as*
What fellows haunt the Jews° for taking up° *i.e., usurers / borrowing*
Great sums of money, for sure he's in want;
Or else to go to th'picture-makers and learn
Who brought her° picture lately. Some of these *(the Duchess's)*
Happily° may take— *Haply, perchance*

BOSOLA Well, I'll not freeze i'th'business.
I would see that wretched thing, Antonio,
Above all sights i'th'world.

CARDINAL Do, and be happy.° *Exit.* *fortunate*

BOSOLA This fellow doth breed basilisks° in's eyes; *(see 3.2.89 n)*
He's nothing else but murder. Yet he seems
Not to have notice of the Duchess' death.
'Tis his cunning. I must follow his example;
There cannot be a surer way to trace° *path to follow*
Than that of an old fox.

[*Enter Julia, pointing a pistol at Bosola.*]

JULIA So, sir, you are well met.

BOSOLA How now?

JULIA Nay, the doors are fast° enough. *tightly shut*
Now, sir, I will make you confess your treachery.

BOSOLA Treachery?

5. Even though Ferdinand were to die.
6. For, meditating too much on the outcome, their wills are paralyzed.

JULIA Yes. Confess to me
Which of my women 'twas you hired to put
Love-powder into my drink?
BOSOLA Love-powder?
JULIA Yes, when I was at Malfi.
Why should I fall in love with such a face else?
I have already suffered for thee so much pain,
The only remedy to do me good
Is to kill my longing.
BOSOLA Sure your pistol holds
Nothing but perfumes or kissing-comfits.° *breath sweeteners*
Excellent lady,
You have a pretty way on't to discover° *show, reveal*
Your longing. Come, come, I'll disarm you,
And arm you thus. [*He embraces her, and takes her pistol.*]
Yet this is wondrous strange.
JULIA Compare thy form and my eyes together,
You'll find my love no such great miracle.[7]
Now you'll say
I am wanton. This nice° modesty in ladies *dainty, fastidious*
Is but a troublesome familiar° *spirit (see 1.1.261 n)*
That haunts them.
BOSOLA Know you me: I am a blunt soldier.
JULIA The better.
Sure there wants° fire where there are no lively sparks *is lacking*
Of roughness.
BOSOLA And I want compliment.° *lack courtly manners*
JULIA Why, ignorance in courtship cannot make you do amiss,
If you have a heart to do well.
BOSOLA You are very fair.° *handsome*
JULIA Nay, if you lay beauty to my charge,
I must plead unguilty.
BOSOLA Your bright eyes
Carry a quiver of darts in them sharper
Than sunbeams.
JULIA You will mar me with commendation,
Put yourself to the charge° of courting me, *assignment, task*
Whereas now I woo you.
BOSOLA [*aside*] I have it! I will work upon this creature.
[*To her*] Let us grow most amorously familiar.
If the great Cardinal now should see me thus,
Would he not count° me a villain? *account*
JULIA No, he might count me a wanton,
Not lay a scruple° of offense on you; *tiny amount*
For if I see and steal a diamond,
The fault is not i'th'stone but in me the thief
That purloins it. I am sudden with you.
We that are great women of pleasure use° to cut off *make it our practice*
These uncertain wishes and unquiet longings,
And in an instant join the sweet delight
And the pretty excuse together. Had you been
I'th'street, under my chamber window,
Even there I should have courted you.

7. It's no wonder, really, that my eyes should be drawn to such a man as you.

BOSOLA Oh, you are an excellent lady.
JULIA Bid me do somewhat for you presently
To express I love you.
BOSOLA I will, and if you love me,
Fail not to effect it.° *carry it out*
The Cardinal is grown wondrous melancholy.
Demand° the cause. Let him not put you off *Ask*
With feigned excuse; discover the main ground on't.
JULIA Why would you know this?
BOSOLA I have depended on him,
And I hear that he is fall'n in some disgrace
With the Emperor. If he be, like the mice
That forsake falling houses I would shift
To other dependence.
JULIA You shall not need follow the wars.
I'll be your maintenance.
BOSOLA And I your loyal servant;
But I cannot leave my calling.
JULIA Not leave
An ungrateful general for the love
Of a sweet lady? You are like some° *some who*
Cannot sleep in featherbeds, but must
Have blocks for their pillows.
BOSOLA Will you do this?
JULIA Cunningly.
BOSOLA Tomorrow I'll expect th'intelligence.° *the report*
JULIA Tomorrow? Get you into my cabinet;° *private room*
You shall have it with you. Do not delay me,
No more than I do you. I am like one
That is condemned: I have my pardon promised,
But I would see it sealed.° Go, get you in. *signed and sealed*
You shall see me wind my tongue about his heart
Like a skein of silk. [*Bosola withdraws out of sight.*]

[*Enter Cardinal, followed by servants.*]

CARDINAL Where are you?
SERVANT Here.
CARDINAL Let none, upon your lives,
Have conference with the Prince Ferdinand
Unless I know it. [*Exeunt servants.*]
[*Aside*] In this distraction
He may reveal the murder.
Yond's my ling'ring consumption.
I am weary of her, and by any means
Would be quit off.° *rid of her*
JULIA How now, my lord?
What ails you?
CARDINAL Nothing.
JULIA Oh, you are much altered.
Come, I must be your secretary,° and remove *confidential adviser*
This lead from off your bosom. What's the matter?
CARDINAL I may not tell you.
JULIA Are you so far in love with sorrow
You cannot part with part of it? Or think you
I cannot love Your Grace when you are sad,

As well as merry? Or do you suspect
I, that have been a secret to your heart
These many winters, cannot be the same
Unto your tongue?
CARDINAL Satisfy thy longing.° *Be satisfied*
The only way to make thee keep my counsel
Is not to tell thee.
JULIA Tell your echo this,
Or flatterers that like echoes still report
What they hear (though most imperfect), and not me.
For, if that you be true unto yourself,° *your other self, me*
I'll know.
CARDINAL Will you rack° me? *torture*
JULIA No. Judgment° shall *Reason, common sense*
Draw it from you. It is an equal fault
To tell one's secrets unto all or none.
CARDINAL The first° argues folly. *(Telling everyone)*
JULIA But the last,° tyranny. *(telling no one)*
CARDINAL Very well. Why, imagine I have committed
Some secret deed which I desire the world
May never hear of.
JULIA Therefore may not I know it?
You have concealed for me as great a sin
As adultery. Sir, never was occasion
For perfect trial of my constancy
Till now. Sir, I beseech you.
CARDINAL You'll repent it.
JULIA Never.
CARDINAL It hurries thee to ruin. I'll not tell thee.
Be well advised,° and think what danger 'tis *Consider carefully*
To receive a prince's secrets. They that do
Had need have their breasts hooped with adamant° *hardest steel*
To contain them. I pray thee yet be satisfied.
Examine thine own frailty; 'tis more easy
To tie knots than unloose them. 'Tis a secret
That, like a ling'ring poison, may chance lie
Spread° in thy veins and kill thee seven year hence. *Dispersed*
JULIA Now you dally with me.
CARDINAL No more; thou shalt know it.
By my appointment, the great Duchess of Malfi
And two of her young children four nights since
Were strangled.
JULIA Oh, heaven! Sir, what have you done?
CARDINAL How now? How settles° this? Think you your bosom *sinks in, clarifies*
Will be a grave dark and obscure enough
For such a secret?
JULIA You have undone yourself, sir.
CARDINAL Why?
JULIA It lies not in me° to conceal it. *I am unable*
CARDINAL [*presenting a book of devotion to her*] No?
Come, I will swear you to't upon this book.
JULIA Most religiously.
CARDINAL Kiss it. [*She kisses the book.*]
Now you shall never utter it.° Thy curiosity *(the secret)*
Hath undone thee. Thou'rt poisoned with that book;

Because I knew thou couldst not keep my counsel,
I have bound thee to't by death.

[*Bosola comes forward from concealment.*]

BOSOLA For pity sake, hold!
CARDINAL Ha! Bosola?
JULIA I forgive you
This equal° piece of justice you have done, *equitable*
For I betrayed your counsel to that fellow.[8]
He overheard it; that was the cause I said
It lay not in me to conceal it.
BOSOLA Oh, foolish woman!
Couldst not thou have poisoned him?
JULIA 'Tis weakness
Too much to think what should have been done.
I go, I know not whither. [*She dies.*]
CARDINAL [*to Bosola*] Wherefore com'st thou hither?
BOSOLA That I might find a great man, like yourself,
Not out of his wits, as the Lord Ferdinand,
To remember° my service. *remunerate*
CARDINAL I'll have thee hewed in pieces!
BOSOLA Make not yourself such a promise of that life
Which is not yours to dispose of.[9]
CARDINAL Who placed thee here?
BOSOLA Her lust, as she intended.
CARDINAL Very well.
Now you know me for your fellow murderer.
BOSOLA And wherefore should you lay fair marble colors
Upon your rotten purposes to me,[1]
Unless you imitate some that do plot great treasons,° *acts of villainy*
And, when they have done, go hide themselves i'th'graves
Of those were actors in't?[2]
CARDINAL No more.
There is a fortune attends thee.
BOSOLA Shall I go sue to Fortune any longer?
'Tis the fool's pilgrimage.[3]
CARDINAL I have honors in store for thee.
BOSOLA There are a many ways that conduct° to seeming *lead*
honor, and some of them very dirty ones.
CARDINAL Throw to the devil
Thy melancholy! The fire burns well;
What need we keep a-stirring of 't, and make
A greater smother?° Thou wilt kill Antonio? *dense smoke*
BOSOLA Yes.
CARDINAL Take up that body.
BOSOLA I think I shall
Shortly grow the common bier for churchyards![4]
CARDINAL I will allow thee some dozen of attendants
To aid thee in the murder.

8. Julia sees a kind of rough justice in her death as repayment for Bosola's learning the Cardinal's secret.
9. Don't boast of something you may not be able to accomplish—killing me.
1. Why should you give me a specious justification for your rotten enterprise?
2. And when their work of villainy is done, cover up their crime by killing those whom they have commissioned to do the deed?
3. Only a fool seeks the favor of Fortune.
4. I.e., It seems as though I'm getting to be a wholesale dealer in corpses!

BOSOLA Oh, by no means. Physicians that apply horse-leeches° to any rank swelling use to cut off their tails, that the blood may run through them the faster. Let me have no train° when I go to shed blood, lest it make me have a greater when I ride to the gallows.[5]

bloodsuckers (horse-leeches); *company* (train)

CARDINAL Come to me after midnight, to help to remove that body to her own lodging. I'll give out° she died o'th'plague; 'twill breed the less inquiry after her death.

let it be known (give out)

BOSOLA Where's Castruchio, her husband?
CARDINAL He's rode to Naples to take possession
Of Antonio's citadel.
BOSOLA Believe me, you have done a very happy° turn. *good (ironic)*
CARDINAL [*giving a key*] Fail not to come. There is the master key
Of our lodgings; and by that you may conceive
What trust I plant in you.
BOSOLA You shall find me ready.
Exit [*Cardinal*].
Oh, poor Antonio! Though nothing be so needful
To thy estate° as pity, yet I find *state of affairs*
Nothing so dangerous. I must look to my footing.
In such slippery ice pavements, men had need
To be frost-nailed° well; they may break their necks else. *with hob-nailed boots*
The precedent's here afore me. How this man
Bears up in blood,° seems fearless! Why, 'tis well; *Bears his bloodguilt*
Security° some men call the suburbs of hell, *Overconfidence*
Only a dead° wall between. Well, good Antonio, *common*
I'll seek thee out, and all my care shall be
To put thee into safety from the reach
Of these most cruel biters,° that have got *bloodsuckers*
Some of thy blood° already. It may be *i.e., children*
I'll join with thee in a most just revenge.
The weakest arm is strong enough that strikes
With the sword of justice. Still methinks the Duchess
Haunts me. There, there! 'Tis nothing but my melancholy.
O Penitence, let me truly taste thy cup,° *bitter cup*
That throws men down only to raise them up! *Exit.*

5.3

[*Enter*] *Antonio* [*and*] *Delio; Echo from the Duchess's grave.*

DELIO Yond's the Cardinal's window. This fortification
Grew from the ruins of an ancient abbey;
And to yond side o'th'river lies a wall,
Piece of a cloister, which in my opinion
Gives the best echo that you ever heard,
So hollow and so dismal, and withal
So plain in the distinction of our words,
That many have supposed it is a spirit

5. I.e., lest the large size of our party increase the likelihood that we will all be caught and hanged.

5.3. Milan. A fortification, near which the Cardinal and Ferdinand have brought the Duchess to be buried.

That answers.

ANTONIO I do love these ancient ruins.
We never tread upon them but we set
Our foot upon some reverend° history; *venerable*
And questionless, here in this open court,
Which now lies naked to the injuries
Of stormy weather, some men lie interred
Loved° the church so well, and gave so largely to't, *Who loved*
They thought it should have canopied their bones
Till doomsday. But all things have their end;
Churches and cities, which have diseases like to men,
Must have like death that we have.

ECHO *Like death that we have.*

DELIO Now the echo hath caught you.

ANTONIO It groaned, methought, and gave
A very deadly accent.

ECHO *Deadly accent.*

DELIO I told you 'twas a pretty one. You may make it
A huntsman, or a falconer, a musician,
Or a thing of sorrow.

ECHO *A thing of sorrow.*

ANTONIO Ay, sure, that suits it best.

ECHO *That suits it best.*

ANTONIO 'Tis very like my wife's voice.

ECHO *Ay, wife's voice.*

DELIO Come, let us walk farther from't.
I would not have you go to th'Cardinal's tonight.
Do not.

ECHO *Do not.*

DELIO Wisdom doth not more moderate wasting sorrow
Than time.[1] Take time for't; be mindful of thy safety.

ECHO *Be mindful of thy safety.*

ANTONIO Necessity compels me.
Make scrutiny throughout the passes° *events*
Of your own life; you'll find it impossible
To fly your fate.

ECHO *Oh, fly your fate!*

DELIO Hark! The dead stones seem to have pity on you
And give you good counsel.

ANTONIO Echo, I will not talk with thee,
For thou art a dead thing.

ECHO *Thou art a dead thing.*

ANTONIO My duchess is asleep now,
And her little ones, I hope sweetly. Oh, heaven,
Shall I never see her more?

ECHO *Never see her more.*

ANTONIO I marked not one repetition of the echo
But that; and on the sudden, a clear light
Presented me a face folded° in sorrow. *enveloped*

DELIO Your fancy, merely.

ANTONIO Come, I'll be out of this ague,° *fever*
For to live thus is not indeed to live;

1. Time heals more surely than does reasoning with one's sorrows.

It is a mockery and abuse of life.
I will not henceforth save myself by halves;
Lose all, or nothing.

DELIO Your own virtue save you!
I'll fetch your eldest son, and second you.
It may be that the sight of his° own blood,° *(the Cardinal's) / kin*
Spread° in so sweet a figure, may beget *Displayed, disseminated*
The more compassion.

ANTONIO However,° fare you well. *In any event*
Though in our miseries Fortune have a part,
Yet in our noble suff'rings she hath none;
Contempt of pain, that we may call our own. *Exeunt.*

5.4

[*Enter*] *Cardinal, Pescara, Malateste, Roderigo,* [*and*] *Grisolan.*

CARDINAL You shall not watch° tonight by the sick prince; *stay up*
His Grace is very well recoverèd.

MALATESTE Good my lord, suffer° us. *permit*

CARDINAL Oh, by no means.
The noise, and change of object in his eye,
Doth more distract him. I pray, all to bed,
And though you hear him in his violent fit,
Do not rise, I entreat you.

PESCARA So, sir, we shall not.

CARDINAL Nay, I must have you promise
Upon your honors, for I was enjoined to't
By himself; and he seemed to urge it sensibly.

PESCARA Let our honors bind this trifle.[1]

CARDINAL Nor any of your followers.

MALATESTE Neither.

CARDINAL It may be, to make trial of your promise,
When he's asleep, myself will rise and feign
Some of his mad tricks, and cry out for help,
And feign myself in danger.

MALATESTE If your throat were cutting,
I'd not come at you, now I have protested° against it. *sworn an oath*

CARDINAL Why, I thank you.
[*As they prepare to leave, the courtiers speak privately among themselves, out of the Cardinal's hearing.*]

GRISOLAN 'Twas a foul storm tonight.

RODERIGO The Lord Ferdinand's chamber shook like an osier.° *willow*

MALATESTE 'Twas nothing but pure kindness in the devil
To rock his own child. *Exeunt* [*all but the Cardinal*].

CARDINAL The reason why I would not suffer these
About my brother is because at midnight
I may with better privacy convey
Julia's body to her own lodging. Oh, my conscience!
I would pray now, but the devil takes away my heart

5.4. Milan. The Cardinal's apartments.
1. I.e., Let us bind ourselves, by our honors, to carry out this small request.

For° having any confidence in prayer. — *From*
About this hour I appointed Bosola
To fetch the body. When he hath served my turn,° — *done my bidding*
He dies. *Exit.*

[*Enter*] *Bosola.*

BOSOLA Hah? 'Twas the Cardinal's voice. I heard him name
Bosola, and my death.—Listen! I hear one's footing.

[*Enter*] *Ferdinand.*

FERDINAND Strangling is a very quiet death.
BOSOLA [*aside*] Nay, then, I see I must stand upon my guard.
FERDINAND What say'° to that? Whisper, softly: Do you agree to't? So it must be done i'th'dark; the Cardinal would not for a thousand pounds the Doctor should see it. *Exit.* — *say you*
BOSOLA My death is plotted; here's the consequence of murder.
We value not desert° nor Christian breath — *deserving*
When we know black deeds must be cured with death.

[*Enter*] *Antonio* [*and*] *Servant* [*unaware of Bosola*].

SERVANT Here stay, sir, and be confident, I pray.
I'll fetch you a dark° lantern. *Exit.* — *shuttered*
ANTONIO [*to himself*] Could I take him at his prayers,
There were hope of pardon.
BOSOLA [*attacking Antonio*] Fall right my sword!
I'll not give thee so much leisure as to pray.
ANTONIO Oh, I am gone! Thou hast ended a long suit
In a minute.
BOSOLA What art thou?
ANTONIO A most wretched thing,
That only have thy benefit in death
To appear myself.[2]

[*Enter Servant with a dark lantern.*]

SERVANT Where are you, sir?
ANTONIO Very near my home.°—Bosola? — *final resting place*
SERVANT Oh, misfortune!
BOSOLA Smother thy pity; thou art dead else.°—Antonio? — *Quiet, or I'll kill you*
The man I would have saved 'bove mine own life!
We are merely the star's tennis balls, struck and banded° — *bandied*
Which way please them. Oh, good Antonio,
I'll whisper one thing in thy dying ear
Shall° make thy heart break quickly: Thy fair duchess — *Which will*
And two sweet children—
ANTONIO Their very names
Kindle a little life in me.
BOSOLA Are murdered!

2. A wretched creature, who can truly claim one advantage through the death you have administered to me: that of appearing to be what I essentially am, a mortal man. (A quibbling answer to Bosola's question, "What [i.e., who] are you?," since the question can also mean "What kind of person are you?")

ANTONIO Some men have wished to die
At the hearing of sad tidings; I am glad
That I shall do't in sadness. I would not now
Wish my wounds balmed, nor healed, for I have no use
To put my life to. In all our quest of greatness,
Like wanton boys, whose pastime is their care,[3]
We follow after bubbles blown in th'air.
Pleasure of life, what is't? Only the good hours
Of an ague; merely a preparative to rest,
To endure vexation. I do not ask
The process° of my death; only commend me *story*
To Delio.
BOSOLA Break, heart!
ANTONIO And let my son fly the courts of princes. [*He dies.*]
BOSOLA [*to the Servant*] Thou seem'st to have loved Antonio?
SERVANT I brought him hither
To have reconciled him to the Cardinal.
BOSOLA I do not ask thee that.
Take him up, if thou tender° thine own life, *care for*
And bear him where the Lady Julia
Was wont to lodge.—Oh, my fate moves swift!
I have this cardinal in the forge already;
Now I'll bring him to th'hammer. Oh, direful misprision!° *mistake*
I will not imitate things glorious,
No more than base; I'll be mine own example.[4]—
On, on; and look thou represent, for silence,
The thing thou bear'st.[5]
Exeunt [*with the Servant carrying Antonio's body*].

5.5

[*Enter the*] *Cardinal, with a book.*

CARDINAL I am puzzled in a question about hell:
He says, in hell there's one material fire,
And yet it shall not burn all men alike.
Lay him° by. How tedious is a guilty conscience! *(this author)*
When I look into the fishponds in my garden,
Methinks I see a thing armed with a rake
That seems to strike at me.

[*Enter*] *Bosola,* [*and*] *Servant with Antonio's body.*

Now, art thou come? Thou look'st ghastly.
There sits in thy face some great determination,
Mixed with some fear.
BOSOLA Thus it lightens° into action: *flashes*
I am come to kill thee.
CARDINAL Hah?—Help! Our guard!
BOSOLA Thou art deceived.
They are out of thy howling.° *out of earshot*
CARDINAL Hold! And I will faithfully divide
Revenues with thee.

3. Whose idle games are their chief concern.
4. I will not strive to follow the example of great deeds or base ones; I'll simply try to be true to myself.
5. See to it that you remain silent about Antonio's death; be as silent as Antonio.
5.5. The Cardinal's apartments, near Julia's lodging.

BOSOLA Thy prayers and proffers
Are both unseasonable.° *mistimed*
CARDINAL [*calling*] Raise the watch! We are betrayed!
BOSOLA I have confined your flight.
I'll suffer your retreat to Julia's chamber,
But no further.
CARDINAL Help! We are betrayed!

[*Enter above*] *Pescara, Malateste, Roderigo,*
[*and Grisolan*].

MALATESTE Listen!
CARDINAL My dukedom for rescue!
RODERIGO Fie upon his counterfeiting!
MALATESTE Why, 'tis not the Cardinal.
RODERIGO Yes, yes, 'tis he; but I'll see him hanged ere I'll go down to him.
CARDINAL Here's a plot upon me! I am assaulted! I am lost, unless some rescue!
GRISOLAN He doth this pretty well, but it will not serve to laugh me out of mine honor.° *into breaking my oath*
CARDINAL The sword's at my throat!
RODERIGO You would not bawl so loud, then.
MALATESTE Come, come, let's go to bed. He told us thus much aforehand.
PESCARA He wished you should not come at him: but believe't,
The accent of the voice sounds not in jest.
I'll down to him, howsoever, and with engines° *implements*
Force ope the doors. [*Exit above.*]
RODERIGO Let's follow him aloof,° *above*
And note how the Cardinal will laugh at him.
[*Exeunt those above.*]
BOSOLA [*to the Servant*] There's for you first, 'cause° you shall not unbarricade the door to let in rescue. *so that*
He kills the Servant.
CARDINAL What cause hast thou to pursue my life?
BOSOLA [*showing Antonio's body*] Look there.
CARDINAL Antonio!
BOSOLA Slain by my hand unwittingly.
Pray, and be sudden. When thou killed'st thy sister,
Thou took'st from Justice her most equal balance,
And left her naught but her sword.
CARDINAL Oh, mercy!
BOSOLA Now it seems thy greatness was only outward, for thou fall'st faster of thyself than calamity can drive thee. I'll not waste longer time. There! [*He stabs the Cardinal.*]
CARDINAL Thou hast hurt me!
BOSOLA Again! [*He stabs again.*]
CARDINAL Shall I die like a leveret° without any resistance?— *young hare*
Help, help, help! I am slain!

[*Enter*] *Ferdinand* [*and attacks the Cardinal*].

FERDINAND Th'alarum!° Give me a fresh horse! *Sound the alarm!*
Rally the vaunt-guard,° or the day is lost! *vanguard*

Yield, yield! I give you the honor of arms,[1]
Shake my sword over you. Will you yield?

CARDINAL Help me! I am your brother.

FERDINAND The devil!
My brother fight upon the adverse party?
There flies your ransom.[2]

He wounds the Cardinal and in the scuffle gives Bosola his death wound.

CARDINAL Oh, justice!
I suffer now for what hath former been;
Sorrow is held the eldest child of sin.° — *Sin breeds sorrow*

FERDINAND Now you're brave fellows. Caesar's fortune was harder than Pompey's; Caesar died in the arms of prosperity, Pompey at the feet of disgrace.[3] You both died in the field. The pain's nothing; pain many times is taken away with the apprehension of greater, as the toothache with the sight of a barber that comes to pull it out. There's philosophy for you.

BOSOLA Now my revenge is perfect. Sink, thou main cause
Of my undoing! *He kills° Ferdinand.* — *fatally wounds*
The last part of my life
Hath done me best service.

FERDINAND Give me some wet hay. I am broken-winded.[4]
I do account this world but a dog kennel.
I will vault credit[5] and affect° high pleasures — *aspire to*
Beyond death.

BOSOLA He seems to come to himself,° now he's so near the bottom. — *recover his wits*

FERDINAND My sister, oh, my sister! There's the cause on't.
Whether we fall by ambition, blood, or lust,
Like diamonds, we are cut with our own dust.[6] [*He dies.*]

CARDINAL [*to Bosola*] Thou hast thy payment too.

BOSOLA Yes, I hold my weary soul in my teeth;[7]
'Tis ready to part from me. I do glory
That thou, which stood'st like a huge pyramid
Begun upon a large and ample base,
Shalt end in a little point, a kind of nothing.

[*Enter Pescara, Malateste, Roderigo, and Grisolan.*]

PESCARA How now, my lord?

MALATESTE Oh, sad disaster!

RODERIGO How comes this?

BOSOLA Revenge, for the Duchess of Malfi, murdered
By th'Aragonian brethren;° for Antonio, — *(see 5.1.2 and n)*
Slain by this hand; for lustful Julia,
Poisoned by this man; and lastly for myself,
That was an actor in the main° of all, — *chief part*

1. I give you the chance to surrender honorably and be ransomed.
2. You have just lost your chance to be ransomed.
3. Julius Caesar was assassinated (in 44 B.C.E.) at the height of his fame and power; Pompey the Great was murdered (in 48 B.C.E.) after having been defeated by Caesar.
4. Wet hay was a recommended treatment for short-winded horses in wintertime.
5. I will overtop rational expectation.
6. Just as diamonds alone can cut diamonds, so we humans are undone by our own ambition, passions, and desires. (Ferdinand may also mean that his sister is his own "dust," i.e., flesh and blood.)
7. The soul was thought to depart from the body through the mouth.

Much 'gainst mine own good nature, yet i'th'end
Neglected.
PESCARA [*to the Cardinal*] How now, my lord?
CARDINAL Look to my brother.
He gave us these large wounds, as we were struggling
Here i'th'rushes.° And now, I pray, let me *a floor covering*
Be laid by and never thought of. [*He dies.*]
PESCARA How fatally, it seems, he did withstand
His own rescue!
MALATESTE [*to Bosola*] Thou wretched thing of blood,
How came Antonio by his death?
BOSOLA In a mist; I know not how,
Such a mistake as I have often seen
In a play. Oh, I am gone!
We are only like dead° walls or vaulted graves *common (see 5.2.357)*
That, ruined, yields no echo. Fare you well.
It may be pain, but no harm to me to die
In so good a quarrel. Oh, this gloomy world!
In what a shadow, or deep pit of darkness,
Doth womanish and fearful mankind live!
Let worthy minds ne'er stagger in distrust° *never hesitate*
To suffer death or shame for what is just.
Mine is another voyage. [*He dies.*]
PESCARA The noble Delio, as I came to th'palace,
Told me of Antonio's being here, and showed me
A pretty gentleman, his son and heir.

[*Enter*] *Delio* [*with Antonio's son*].

MALATESTE Oh, sir, you come too late.
DELIO I heard so, and
Was armed° for't ere I came. Let us make noble use *prepared*
Of this great ruin, and join all our force
To establish this young hopeful gentleman
In 's mother's right. These wretched eminent things° *persons*
Leave no more fame behind 'em than should one
Fall in a frost and leave his print in snow;
As soon as the sun shines, it ever melts
Both form and matter. I have ever thought
Nature doth nothing so great for great men
As when she's pleased to make them lords of truth.
Integrity of life is fame's best friend,
Which nobly, beyond death, shall crown the end. *Exeunt.*

FINIS.

TEXTUAL NOTES

The Duchess of Malfi was first published in quarto in 1623, not having been previously entered in the Stationers' Register. Three editions followed, in 1640 (reissued in 1664), 1678, and 1708, none of them providing any textual authority but each offering some commonsense corrections along with new errors. The present text is based on the original quarto, which was corrected during printing so that separate copies of Q1 show different readings, with a number of corrected readings existing in two states of correction. On the grouping of characters' names at the head of each scene in Q1, see the preface to this volume. Q1 often prints as verse what should evidently be printed as prose; some of these passages are rendered as prose in various modern editions, but this present edition goes beyond those modern editions in a few instances where in our judgment modern editors have accepted language as verse when it really is not. The textual notes below indicate substantive departures from Q1, using the following abbreviations:

Q1: The first quarto (London: Nicholas Okes for John Waterson, 1623)
Q1 corr.: The corrected first quarto (corrected state 1 unless specified as corrected state 2)
Q1 uncorr.: The uncorrected first quarto
Q2: The second quarto (London: J. Raworth for J. Benson, 1640; reprint, 1664)
Q3: The third quarto (London: R. Crofts, 1678)
Q4: The fourth quarto (London: D. N. for T. C., to be sold by Simon Neale, 1708)
ed.: A modern editor's emendation

The Actors' Names [placement, ed.; before the dedicatory letter to Harding and the three commendatory poems in Q1] **3 Condell** [Q1: *Cundaile*] **15–16** ["Cariola" and "Court Officers" are bracketed in Q1 as though indicating assignment of both to "*R. Pallant*"]

1.1.6 their [Q3] there [Q1] **33 too much** [Q1: to-much] **53 and** [Q1: an] **57 died** [Q1 corr.] did [Q1 uncorr.] **58 pardon** [Q1 corr.] pleadon [Q1 uncorr.] **58–59 dogs when** [Q2] dogges, and / When [Q1] **63–64 latter swing** [Q1: latter-swinge] **66 like** [Q2] likes [Q1] **72 Foix** [Q2: *Foyx*] *Foux* [Q1] **81** [Q1 marks "SCENA II" after this line] **113–14** [and elsewhere] **surgeons** [Q1: Chyrurgeons] **118 jennet** [Q1: Gennit] **121 ballasted** [ed.] ballass'd [Q1] **148.1** ***Cariola*** [Q1: *Iulia, Cariola* at 81.1] **162 flatterers** [Q3] Flatters [Q1] **181 shrewd** [Q2: shrew'd] shewed [Q1] **188 your** [Q2] you [Q1] **196 able to** [Q3] able [Q1] **218 are** [Q4; not in Q1] **220 leaguer** [Q2] Leagues [Q1] **222 DUCHESS** [ed.] *Ferd.* [Q1] **268 to hell** [Q4] Hell [Q1] **272 on't** [Q2] out [Q1] **278 o'er** [Q2: ore] are [Q1] **278 vile** [Q1: vild] **320 eaves** [Q1 corr.: Eues] Eeues [Q1 uncorr.] **333, 344** [and elsewhere] **I'd** [Q1: I'll'd] **335 mask** [Q1: Masque] **366 these** [ed.] this [Q1] **382 distraction** [Q3] distruction [Q1] **384 you** [ed.] yon [Q1] **392 Winifred** [Q1: *Winfrid*] **424 visitants** [Q3] visitans [Q1] **431 of** [Q2] off [Q1] **443 woo . . . woo** [Q1: woe . . . woe] **455 alabaster** [Q1: Allablaster] **457 off** [Q2] of [Q1] **480** ***de presenti*** [ed.] *presenti* [Q1] **507 SD** ***Exit*** [ed.] *Exeunt* [Q1]

2.1.28 flayed [Q1: Flead] **32 but** [ed.] but you call [Q1] **38 children's ordure** [Q2] children ordures [Q1] **60** [and elsewhere] **lest** [Q1: least] **63** [and elsewhere] **Lucca** [Q1: *Leuca*] **71** [and elsewhere] **apricots** [Q1: Apricocks] **79 tetter** [Q1: tettor] **86–87 out-of-fashion** [Q1: out off fhashion] **89 compliment** [Q1: Complement] **108.1** ***Duchess*** [ed.] *Duchesse, Rodorico, Grisolan* [at 0.1 in Q1] **111 litter** [Q1: Littor] **116 lemon peels** [Q1: Lymmon pils] **117 swoon** [Q1: sound; Q2: swound] **118 too** [Q2] to [Q1] **119 courtiers** [Q1: Courties] **123 DUCHESS** [Q4; not in Q1] **130 Methought** [Q4] My thought [Q1] **155 springald** [Q1: spring-hall] **178.1** ***Exeunt*** [Q1: *Ex.*]

2.2.1 tetchiness [Q1: teatchiues] **15 bears** [Q3] beare [Q1] **16 all together** [Q1:

altogether] **20 Danaës** [Q4: *Danaes*] *Danes* [Q1] **34** [and throughout scene] **FIRST SERVANT** [Q1: *Seruant, Seru.* or *Ser.*] **46 molds** [Q1: mowldes] **51 officers** [Q2] Offices [Q1] **52 SERVANTS** [Q1: *Seru.*] **78 looks** [Q2] looke [Q1]

2.3.10 Who's [Q3] whose [Q1] **52 quit** [Q1: quite] **65 eighth** [Q1: *eight*] **70 cased** [Q2: cas'd] caside [Q1]

2.4.5 Here [Q1: Heare] **12 turnings** [Q3] turning [Q1] **30 thee** [ed.] the [Q1] **47 you are** [Q2] your are [Q1] **66 seeth't** [ed.] seeth's [Q1]

2.5.2 prodigy [Q3: prodegy] progedy [Q1] **3 damned** [Q1: dampn'd] **14 here 't** [Q2] here'it [Q1] **30 mother's** [Q2: mothers] mother [Q1] **44 o'th'** [Q3] th' [Q1]

3.1.16 insensibly [Q3] inseucibly [Q1] **37 of** [Q2] off [Q1] **39 to bespeak** [Q2: to be-speake] to be be-speake [Q1] **43 through** [Q3] thorough [Q1] **51 of** [ed.] off [Q1] **54 were** [Q3] where [Q1] **57 coulters** [Q1: cultures] **78 blood** [Q2] bood [Q1]

3.2.25 flight [ed.] slight [Q1] **26 Syrinx** [Q4: *Sirinx*] *Sirina* [Q1 uncorr.] *Siriux* [Q1 corr.] **41 apprehension** [Q1 corr.: apprehention] approbation [Q1 uncorr.] **51 his** [Q1 corr.] the [Q1 uncorr.] **80 us** [Q4; not in Q1] **90 confederacy** [Q3] consideracy [Q1] **91 thee** [Q4] the [Q1] **97 damn** [Q1: dampe] **101 vile** [Q1: vilde] **120 too** [Q2] to [Q1] **126 'twas** [ed.] it was [Q1 corr.] ltwas [Q1 uncorr.] **137 shook** [Q1 corr. state 2: shooke] shooked [Q1 uncorr., Q1 corr. state 1] **144.1** [placement, ed.; after "apparition" in 145 in Q1] **152 SD** [placement, ed.; opposite 153 in Q1] **205 As loath** [Q1 corr. state 2] A-loth [Q1 uncorr., Q1 corr. state 1] **231 SD** [placement, ed.; opposite 230 in Q1] **237 firstborn** [Q1 corr. state 2] first-borne and [Q1 uncorr., Q1 corr. state 1] **241 doom** [Q1: doombe] **249 on** [Q2] One [Q1] **304** [and elsewhere] **Whither** [Q1: Whether]

3.3.17 scent [Q1: sent] **20 keeps** [Q2] keepe [Q1] **20 painters** [Q1 corr. state 2] Pewterers [Q1 uncorr., Q1 corr. state 1] **21 he'll** [Q1: hel;] **33 DELIO** [as catchword only in Q1: *Del.*] **45 symmetry** [Q1: semitry] **53 porpoise** [Q1: Porpisse] **55–56 pangs** [Q1: pangues] **72 counters** [Q1: coumpters] **73 life** [Q2] like [Q1] **75 hundred** [Q1: hundreth]

3.4.8.2 ***habit*** [Q1 corr.] *order* [Q1 uncorr.] **8.2** ***of a*** [Q2] *a* [Q1] **8.6–7** ***banishment in dumb show expressed*** [Q1 corr.] *a banishment expressed* [Q1 uncorr.] **9–24** [in Q1, in right-hand margin: "The Author disclaimes this Ditty to be his."] **24.1** [placement, ed.; at the end of 8.1–10 in Q1] **33 Hath** [Q1 corr.] Had [Q1 uncorr.] **38 Off** [Q2] Of [Q1] **45 All** [Q1 employs quotation marks here and elsewhere to indicate sententious statements; sometimes italics indicate this]

3.5.24 SD ***a letter*** [placement, ed.; before 28 in Q1] **81 e'er** [Q1: ere] **95 what a** [Q1 corr.] a what [Q1 uncorr.] **96 SD** ***Enter . . . guard*** [Q1 corr.; not in Q1 uncorr.] **96 SD** ***with vizards*** [placement, ed.; at 0.1–2 in Q1] **98 move** [Q1 corr.] more [Q1 uncorr.] **102 BOSOLA** [Q1 corr.; not in Q1 uncorr.] **106 DUCHESS** [Q1 corr.] *Ant.* [Q1 uncorr.] **106 o'ercharged** [Q2: ore-charg'd] ore-char'd [Q1] **112 such a** [Q1 corr.] such [Q1 uncorr.] **133 smelts** [Q1: Smylts]

4.1.91 vapors [ed.] vipers [Q1]

4.2.50 crazed [Q1: crais'd] **67 irksome** [Q4] *yerk-some* [Q1] **69 choir** [Q1: *quire*] **107 pared** [Q1: paired] **113 too** [Q1: to] **186 bathe** [Q2] *bath* [Q1] **279 done't** [Q1: don't] **352 mercy** [Q2] merry [Q1]

5.1.6 cheat [Q1: Cheit] **73 fraught** [Q1: fraight] **80 lovèd** [ed.] lou'd [Q1]

5.2.25 Paracelsus [Q3] *Paraclesus* [Q1] **78 flay** [Q1: Flea] **84 too** [Q1: to] **116 one** [Q2] on [Q1] **192 woo** [Q1: woe] **297 thee** [Q2] the [Q1] **331 bier** [Q3] Beare [Q1] **335 off** [Q1: of] **343 rode** [Q1: rod] **348.1** [placement, ed.; opposite "What . . . you" in Q1] **354 precedent's** [Q1: President's]

5.3.29 let us [ed.] let's vs [Q1] **39 ECHO** [Q4; not in Q1]

5.4.2 recoverèd [Q1: recouer'd] **12 our** [Q2] out [Q1] **36 quiet** [Q2] quiein [Q1] **50 minute** [Q1: mynut]

5.5.68 been [Q1: bin] **78 SD** [placement, ed.; opposite 79 in Q1] **100 this** [Q4] his [Q1]

A New Way to Pay Old Debts

Philip Massinger, whose dramatic technique favors telling juxtapositions, opens *A New Way to Pay Old Debts* with two scenes that seem to set up a clear moral contrast. In the first scene, a ruined prodigal, Frank Wellborn, quarrels bitterly with the alehouse proprietor Tapwell. As Tapwell spitefully reminds him, Wellborn has forfeited not merely his lands but the social privileges and obligations that accompanied property ownership in early modern England:

> Your dead father,
> My quondam master, was a man of worship,
> Old Sir John Wellborn, Justice of Peace and Quorum,
> And stood fair to be *Custos Rotulorum*,
> Bare the whole sway of the shire, kept a great house,
> Relieved the poor, and so forth. (1.1.32–37)

While the younger Wellborn has squandered his inheritance on horses and women, Tapwell, by his own account, has been pulling himself up by his bootstraps. He opened an alehouse (an enterprise that required minimal capital), made a socially useful marriage, and lives out a lowly parody of Wellborn's father's civic commitments, beginning as "scavenger," or garbageman, in hopes of being promoted to "overseer of the poor," a marginally more prestigious position. Neither the reckless Wellborn nor the venal Tapwell come off well in this messy, undignified altercation. The scene encourages us to ask: What could inherited social status possibly be good for?

The next scene seems designed to answer that question. Lady Allworth's household is a disciplined place presided over by a steward named Order. Here conflict—if it can be properly so called—emerges not from malice but from the servants' eagerness to please their beloved mistress. Their assiduousness arises not from a sense of comradeship with her but from what is obviously lacking in the relation between Wellborn and Tapwell: an ingrained respect for her superiority. When Sir Giles Overreach implicitly invites Order to join him in criticizing Lady Allworth's strict rituals of mourning her late husband, the steward politely but pointedly refuses to take the bait: "Sir, it is her will, / Which we that are her servants ought to serve it / And not dispute" (1.3.4–6). And later in the play, when Lady Allworth commands her usher, Amble, and maid to remain within call, but not so close as to overhear her conversation with Lord Lovell, they make a deferential reply:

> AMBLE We are taught better
> By you, good madam.
> WAITING-WOMAN And well know our distance.
> (4.1.173–74)

"Knowing one's distance," one's proper place in the pecking order, looms large in Massinger's depiction of the Allworth ménage.

Introduction by Katharine Eisaman Maus; glosses, footnotes, and textual notes by David Bevington; text edited by David Bevington and checked by Eric Rasmussen.

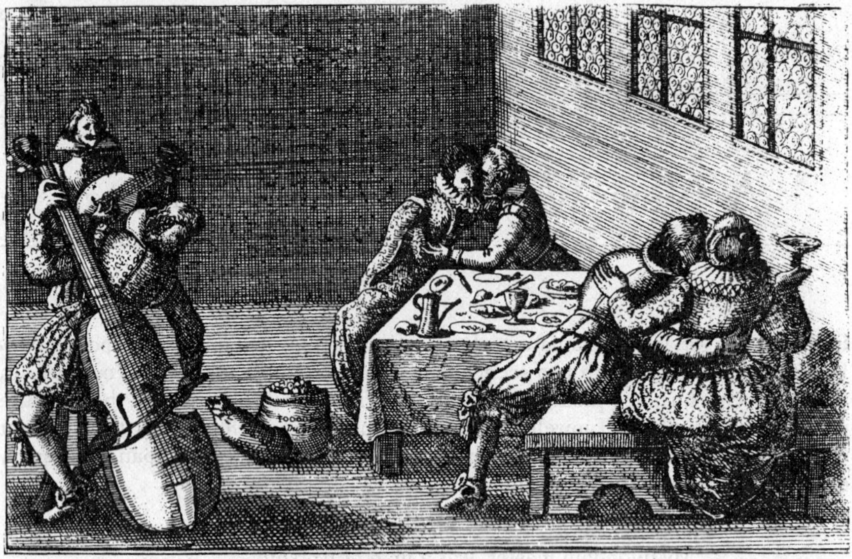

A tavern scene. From *Le Centre de l' Amour* (1630?).

Like many of the Londoners who constituted the play's original audience, Philip Massinger spent his boyhood in the countryside and came to London as a young adult. Perhaps because migration from rural areas to the city was so common in the early seventeenth century, provincial England was becoming the site of potent nostalgia, a place where "old English ways" might still persist. Massinger's depiction of Lady Allworth's household owes less to his theatrical predecessors, who rarely interested themselves in the routines of rural estate management, than to the "country-house poems" of Ben Jonson and his imitators, with their celebration of the provincial estate's agricultural abundance, traditional social hierarchy, and time-honored customs of hospitality. But whereas country-house poems tend to minimize the role of rural labor, focusing instead on a richly fertile landscape in which the country-folk play a minor decorative part, Massinger crowds the provincial household with carefully imagined servant characters. As the son of a steward to the powerful Henry Herbert, Earl of Pembroke, Massinger may have drawn on his own experience for the lively below-stairs vignettes in *A New Way to Pay Old Debts.* Still, his portrait of the idealized elite household seems, at least in our class-conscious age, to reflect the ideological convictions of the masters much more than the interests of the servants.

Despite the play's many servant characters, the real subject of *A New Way to Pay Old Debts* is a perceived crisis of aristocratic values, and its real heroes and heroines, as well as its villain, are people who can make some claim to high status. The first act and a half of *A New Way to Pay Old Debts* suggests that this crisis is both internally generated and externally imposed. The internal problem is the instability of elite values themselves: Wellborn's plight shows how easily gentlemanly openhandedness can collapse into irresponsible profligacy and also how the gentleman's ingrained scorn for manual labor makes it difficult for him to recover a lost fortune. Nonetheless, Wellborn quickly convinces Lady Allworth that the differences between his condition and hers, marked with such didactic clarity in the opening scenes, are actually more apparent than real. And he is right. In the course of the play, it turns out that the real threat to traditional ways of life comes not from the provincial insider, Wellborn, but from the urban outsider, Sir Giles Overreach. Though the play begins, as we have seen, with a contrast between Wellborn and Lady Allworth—between a hapless and a thriving member of the rural gentry—the plot quickly shifts our focus to the more significant distinction between a cohesive, mutually supportive group of provincial gentry and a London upstart who erupts into their ranks with the intensity of a predator. It is hardly surprising that Wellborn's loss of his lands—initially attributed, both by himself and by others, to sheer fecklessness—turns out later in the play to have been fraudulently engineered by Overreach.

A New Way to Pay Old Debts was first performed in the mid-1620s, and its immediate connection to current events is obvious in the interloper's name. Sir Giles Overreach shares a title and a first name with the entrepreneur Sir Giles Mompesson, who amassed a huge fortune in the early 1620s before being successfully prosecuted and ruined. Mompesson, Overreach's real-life prototype, acquired his notoriety by a whole variety of shady practices, notably usury and fraudulent sales schemes. But Massinger's character has more focused ambitions. He wants to amass land. Tapwell's recollection of Wellborn's father has already suggested how in the early modern English countryside, land ownership was the foundation of social prestige and political authority and thus had a unique symbolic as well as practical importance for the functioning of the entire community.

In Massinger's time, it must have seemed as though the urban and rural elites were changing places. While many members of the provincial gentry abandoned their rustic lifestyles for the excitements of London, urban nouveaux riches, having made their fortunes in so-called vulgar occupations, acquired rural estates and set themselves up as country squires. Most urban upstarts desired nothing more than to blend into their new social surroundings. Overreach, by contrast, is intensely ambivalent. Impressed by upper-class status markers, he hopes to marry his daughter to a lord and secure noble titles for his grandchildren. At the same time, he recognizes that he and the provincial elite are fundamentally at odds: "there having ever been / More than a feud, a strange antipathy / Between us and true gentry" (2.1.87–89).

What is the nature of that "feud"? What makes Wellborn, in the play's terms, a redeemable character and puts Overreach beyond the pale? One obvious difference is in the two men's relationship to violence. The traditional vocation of the gentleman was armed combat, indicated by his distinctive accoutrement, the sword, as well as by his possession of a fiery temperament. In the first scene, Wellborn squanders his spiritedness on an unworthy object, Tapwell, just as he has previously dissipated his finances—but mettle as much as money is his proper patrimony. What he needs, as he acknowledges at the end of the play, is a war. For war, unlike the barroom brawl, is supposed to discipline gentlemanly ardor, channeling it into an experience not of riotousness but of self-control, of subordination to a superior officer and to the needs of the larger community. As Lady Allworth quotes her late husband:

> "To dare boldly
> In a fair cause, and for the country's safety
> To run upon the cannon's mouth undaunted;
> To obey their leaders, and shun mutinies;
> To bear with patience the winter's cold
> And summer's scorching heat, and not to faint,
> When plenty of provision fails, with hunger,
> Are the essential parts make up a soldier—
> Not swearing, dice, or drinking." (1.2.106–14)

Lord Lovell, Massinger's paragon of aristocratic male virtue, seems to have derived those advantages from his impressive military career. Frank Wellborn has not yet learned a soldier's lessons, but he at least recognizes his need of them.

If Wellborn's violence bespeaks a lack of self-control, Overreach's ferocity is strategically calculated, in the amoral way that Massinger and his contemporaries associated with the self-interested policies of the "machiavel." Overreach plots to illegally destroy his neighbor's hedges so that the man will be forced into lawsuits he cannot afford and will eventually have to sell out to pay attorney's fees. He hopes to entrap Lord Lovell into seducing his daughter, Margaret, threatens to rip her eyes out when she resists the plan, and fantasizes about forcing the lord into wedlock at sword's point. Even apparently friendly gestures have their coercive aspect. At his dinner parties, the displays of food are deliberately intimidating. "Spare for no cost. Let my dressers crack with the weight / Of curious viands," he orders (3.2.1–2). For Philip Massinger and many of his contemporaries, violence used deliberately, not against foreigners or enemies but against members of one's own social group, seemed a hallmark of newly competitive business practices. The mercantile enterprises of the city pit man against man, simultaneously enhancing conflict and eliminating any conception of a collective good. Traditional rural culture, however—Massinger rather romantically imagines—involves the entire community in a shared enterprise: thus his emphasis on the orchestration of work in Lady Allworth's household. Moreover, the clear social hierarchy typical of that community virtually eliminates competitive strife.

In Overreach's emotional world, one person's gain always entails another person's loss. He is predisposed to see everyone as a rival, every social interaction in terms of winning and losing. He seems to relish beating his co-conspirator Marall, threatening his daughter, and gloating over others' misfortunes. But he resorts to violence not merely for pleasure. Because custom does not hallow his claims to dominion over others, Overreach must exact by force the service that Lord Lovell's or Lady Allworth's inferiors willingly provide out of deferential love—hence his unceasing, almost hysterical self-assertion and his inability to brook dissent of any kind. If the traditional social hierarchy collapses, Massinger implies, what will replace it is not a more egalitarian social arrangement but ruthless petty tyranny untrammeled by traditional inhibitions.

As a social climber, Overreach sets himself against the memory of the past. Precedent would only oppress him. By contrast, the good characters feel themselves bound by memory. Lady Allworth is introduced as a dutiful mourner for a lost husband and as a faithful mother to and patroness of her stepson Tom Allworth, even after the senior Allworth's death has severed the obvious tie between them. She feels obligated to help Wellborn as soon as he recalls to her the circumstances in which he once came to the aid of her spouse. A sense of history motivates Lord Lovell, too. He considers Lady Allworth a superior marriage candidate because she has demonstrated herself to be a good wife to another man:

> You already, madam,
> Have given sure proofs how dearly you can cherish
> A husband that deserves you, which confirms me
> That, if I am not wanting in my care
> To do you service, you'll be still the same
> That you were to your Allworth. (5.1.56–61)

And eventually memory—used by Tapwell as a weapon against Wellborn in the first scene—becomes the means by which Wellborn can regenerate himself: "I had a reputation, but 'twas lost / In my loose course; and, till I redeem it / Some noble way, I am but half made up" (5.1.394–96). As Lovell and Wellborn suggest, the reverence for memory is not merely sentimental nostalgia. The past, for them, provides potent evidence of future behavior: by and large, as Lovell says, people and things will "be still the same." The language of indebtedness, credit, and redemption that runs so insistently throughout *A New Way to Pay Old Debts* refers not just to financial transactions but to the more general way past obligations and promises reach into the future, binding people to fulfill them. At the end of the play, Wellborn recognizes that he needs to pay off more than monetary debts.

It goes without saying that a culture that reverences memory tends to be deeply conservative, for its tendency is to preserve inherited status and to honor past arrangements even when a present rationale for them is lacking. Thus Lovell insists on making a "fitting" distinction between his ordinary, baseborn servants and the superficially similar Tom Allworth, "a gentleman by want compelled to serve me" (3.1.27–28). Similarly, Margaret displays her essential sympathy with the traditional elite view when she deplores her father's employment of gentlewomen fallen on hard times. She cannot forget the difference between her maid's current and former status.

Such an ethos, which resists innovation and sees agents of change as presumptuous, influences Massinger's methods of characterization. Some critics complain that his characters do not develop but instead tend to repeat their distinguishing features over and over again. Writing from a modern perspective that tends to be optimistic, such critics assume that novelty is interesting and that a writer who depicts change is more skillful than one who does not. In Massinger's worldview, however, "development" is not a desideratum. Thus while another writer—Thomas Dekker perhaps—might have admired Tapwell's initiative and resourcefulness, in this play, those traits are heavily proscribed. Tapwell would do better, Massinger implies, to know his place and stick to it. The same commitment to tradition and repetition comes through in Massinger's style. Many of his characters—the virtuous ones especially—speak in tissues of maxims and proverbs. This kind of language suggests that truth is unchanging, that the experience of one generation is much like that of the last one, and that there is no reason to depart from the old ways of doing things.

Like the predictably disastrous careers of most other stage machiavels, Overreach's suggests that unscrupulous short-term means fail to serve long-term ends. His self-subverting inability to comprehend the big picture is essentially what "overreaching" means, whether in the case of the Jew of Malta, Richard III, or Volpone. The form of Overreach's failure also distinguishes him from Shylock in Shakespeare's *The Merchant of Venice,* a character he superficially resembles in his refusal to accede to the dominant value system, in the way he opposes a bald profit motive to gentlemanly values of openhanded friendship, and in his possession of a daughter who eventually deserts him. Shylock is a Jew—a member of an ancient people and a man whose memory for slights is all too vivid. Overreach, by contrast, is an atheist—in the terms of the play, the advocate not of an alternative or inadequate code but of no code at all beyond a spatially and temporally circumscribed self-interest.

Overreach's downfall is particularly clearly connected to his war on memory, which renders him naive about his enemies' motivations. Failing to comprehend Lady Allworth's courtesy to Wellborn as the payment of a perceived obligation, he construes it as forgetfulness: the stereotypical widow's lusty disregard of her husband's memory and her precipitate willingness to enter a new relationship. She "sits on thorns till she be private with him," he reflects indelicately (3.3.7). Likewise, Overreach expects that Margaret's beauty will so arouse Lord Lovell that he will incontinently seduce the maiden and thus be trapped into marriage with her. His own hastiness makes him sympathetic to Lovell's supposedly headlong courtship and leads to his unwitting complicity in Margaret's elopement with Tom. In these cases, Overreach assumes that people are primarily motivated by appetites so intense that they block out their awareness of the larger context. But that larger context does, in fact, constrain the behavior of people like Lady Allworth, Lord Lovell, and Margaret. Finally, where memory might work in his interests—by securing his title to Wellborn's land—the bond, composed in "vanishing ink," fails to bear out his claim.

If the vanishing ink of the bond stands for the evanescence of Overreach's spurious claims to dominion, his madness follows logically from his atomistic sense of self, which slips easily into a solipsistic delusion of grandeur: "Why, is not the whole world / Included in myself?" (5.1.356–57). In many plays—*Doctor Faustus*, for example—such solipsism and its comeuppance are the material of tragedy, but in *A New Way to*

Pay Old Debts, provincial English society refuses to make way for the overreacher; instead it defeats him with networks of friendship and alliance that his nature prevents him from understanding.

In these networks, women play a crucial part. The final triumph of the old way of life in *A New Way to Pay Old Debts* is largely due to the generosity and cunning of both the middle-aged widow Lady Allworth and the nubile Margaret. Both are staunch and articulate spokeswomen for traditional values. Perhaps because women do not benefit as obviously from class privilege as their male counterparts, Massinger considered them less likely to sound merely self-interested when defending it. Like the happy conservatism of his servant characters, the women's preference for a system that in some ways oppresses them demonstrates the essential rightness of the system. Or perhaps, given his conviction that inherited status served the needs of the larger community, Massinger considered a defense of that conservative social system especially appropriate coming from the mouth of a female speaker, whose roles and rights were circumscribed by the demands of her family and associates. Who better than a woman to understand that even apparent eminence always involves subordination?

Still, when that larger context is considered closely, women play a more slippery role than might first be apparent. Because in a patriarchal system wives are considered members of their husband's families, women are less strongly and originally defined by class origins than men are, and they can move up or down the status ladder more easily. And move they do. Lady Allworth, who apparently once married down, now accepts a proposal to marry up. Overreach makes a claim to gentry status through his late wife, Wellborn's father's sister. Lord Lovell considers Margaret far beneath him—a wife who, despite her beauty and virtue, would "adulterate my blood" (4.1.222). But she is a suitable match for Tom Allworth, the stepson of the woman Lovell does marry. The mutability of the women's status produces an interesting ambiguity in the play. On the one hand, *A New Way to Pay Old Debts* insists that status is inherent and that the class boundaries between people like Lovell and people like Overreach are, or ought to be, impermeable: "tissues matched with scarlet suit but ill" (3.2.199). On the other hand, the plot demands that almost all the high-status characters be related by blood or marriage—suggesting, in other words, that class boundaries are permeable, at least through the female line. Social differences that are strongly marked in the play do not always correspond to the kinship system on which they are supposed to be founded. What seems at some moments in the play a black-and-white distinction between insiders and outsiders thus tends to melt under scrutiny into a system of small gradations and shades of gray.

Massinger's powerful dramaturgy, however, encourages his audience to ignore those complications, especially toward the end of the play. *A New Way to Pay Old Debts* sometimes strikes readers and audiences as melodramatic, exaggerating and falsifying the issues it raises in the interests of a thrilling finale that rewards the good and punishes the wicked in gratifying, unmistakable ways. Perhaps these final scenes reflect Massinger's awareness that only in the fictional confines of a play are the conflicts arising from the immense social changes to which he bears witness so neatly soluble. In *A New Way to Play Old Debts*, witty members of the provincial elite outwit and handily defeat a representative of urban capitalism. The real-world outcome would be, of course, quite different.

PHILIP MASSINGER

A New Way to Pay Old Debts

To the Right Honorable Robert, Earl of Carnarvon, Master Falconer of England[1]

My good lord, pardon, I beseech you, my boldness in presuming to shelter this comedy under the wings of Your Lordship's favor and protection. I am not ignorant, having never yet deserved you in my service, that it cannot but meet with a severe construction if, in the clemency of your noble disposition, you fashion not a better defense of me than I can fancy for myself. All I can allege is that divers Italian princes and lords of eminent rank in England have not disdained to receive and read poems of this nature; nor am I wholly lost in my hopes but that Your Honor (who have ever expressed yourself a favorer and friend to the Muses) may vouchsafe, in your gracious acceptance of this trifle, to give me encouragement to present you with some labored work, and of a higher strain, hereafter. I was born a devoted servant to the thrice noble family of your incomparable lady, and am most ambitious—but with a becoming distance—to be known to Your Lordship, which if you please to admit, I shall embrace it as a bounty that while I live shall oblige me to acknowledge you for my noble patron and profess myself to be

Your Honor's true servant,
Philip Massinger

To the Ingenious Author, Master Philip Massinger, on His Comedy Called *A New Way to Pay Old Debts*

'Tis a rare charity, and thou couldst not
So proper to the time have found a plot.[1]
Yet whilst you teach to pay, you lend; the age
We wretches live in, that to come, the stage,
The througèd audience that was thither brought
Invited by your fame, and to be taught

The original 1633 title page reads "*A New Way to Pay Old Debts.* A comedy. As it hath been often acted at the Phoenix in Drury Lane, by the Queen's Majesty's Servants. The author: Philip Massinger. London: Printed by E. P. for Henry Seyle, dwelling in S. Paul's Churchyard, at the sign of the Tiger's Head. Anno MDCXXXIII."

Dedication.

1. Robert Dormer (1610–1643) was created Viscount of Ascot and first Earl of Carnarvon in 1628. He was given the office of keeper of the King's hawks and falcons.

To the Ingenious Author.

1. You have performed a truly charitable deed, and you could not have found a story so well suited to the age in which we live.

This lesson, all are grown indebted more,
And when they looked for freedom ran in score.[2]
It was a cruel courtesy to call
In hope of liberty, and then enthrall.
The nobles are your bondmen, gentry, and
All besides those that did not understand.
They were no men of credit, bankrupts born
Fit to be trusted with no stock but scorn.[3]
You have more wisely credited to such
That, though they cannot pay, can value much.[4]
I am your debtor too, but, to my shame,
Repay your nothing back but your own fame.
Henry Moody, *miles*[5]

To His Friend the Author

You may remember how you chid me when
I ranked you equal with those glorious men,
Beaumont and Fletcher. If you love not praise,
You must forbear the publishing of plays.
The crafty mazes of the cunning plot,
The polished phrase, the sweet expressions got
Neither by theft nor violence, the conceit° *thought; metaphor*
Fresh and unsullied—all is of weight,
Able to make the captive reader know
I did but justice when I placed you so.° *in such high company*
A shamefast° blushing would become the brow *shamefaced*
Of some weak virgin writer; we allow
To you a kind of pride, and there where most° *most writers*
Should blush at commendations, you should boast.
If any think I flatter, let him look
Off from my idle trifles on thy book.
Thomas Jay,[1] *miles*

Dramatis Personae

LOVELL, an English lord
Sir Giles OVERREACH, a cruel extortioner
[Frank] WELLBORN, a prodigal [nephew to Overreach]
[Tom] ALLWORTH, a young gentleman, page to Lord Lovell [and stepson to Lady Allworth]
GREEDY, a hungry justice of peace
[Jack] MARALL, a term driver,[1] a creature° of Sir Giles Overreach *dependent*

2. I.e., while you teach audiences how to pay old debts, you put us anew in your debt by entertaining us so well; audiences now, and in the future, attracted to the theater by your reputation, have come looking for the freedom embodied in your view of society only to find themselves running up a debt to you.
3. You have put the nobility and gentry in your debt, and all except those who (like Overreach) are incapable of true comprehension and are intellectually and morally bankrupt, thus deserving nothing but scorn.
4. You have more wisely given (as it were on credit) the value of your wisdom to those who, though they cannot repay you in kind, can certainly value what you write.
5. Sir Henry Moody (c. 1607–1660), Baronet of Garesdon, Wiltshire, here characterizing himself as a *miles*, a soldier or knight.

To His Friend the Author.
1. A friend and patron of Massinger.

Dramatis Personae.
1. One who moves from court to court during law sessions, usually with the intent of engaging in intrigue, knavery, or sport, including the corrupt drawing-up or altering of legal documents.

ORDER [a steward] / AMBLE [an usher] / FURNACE [a cook] / WATCHALL [a porter] } servants to the Lady Allworth
WILLDO, a parson
[Timothy] TAPWELL, an alehouse-keeper
Three CREDITORS
The LADY ALLWORTH, a rich widow [Tom Allworth's stepmother]
MARGARET, Overreach his° daughter — *Overreach's*
WAITING-WOMAN / CHAMBERMAID } [to Lady Allworth]
FROTH, Tapwell's wife
[Servants]

[THE SCENE: The countryside near Nottingham.]

1.1

[*Enter*] *Wellborn* [*in ragged clothes*], *Tapwell*, [*and*] *Froth*.

WELLBORN No booze? Nor no tobacco?
TAPWELL Not a suck, sir,
Nor the remainder of a single can
Left by a drunken porter, all night palled° too. — *having become flat*
FROTH Not the dropping of the tap for your morning's draft, sir.
'Tis verity, I assure you.
WELLBORN Verity, you brach!° — *bitch*
The devil turned precisian?[1] Rogue, what am I?
TAPWELL Troth, durst I° trust you with a looking glass — *In truth, if I dared*
To let you see your trim shape, you would quit° me — *acquit*
And take the name° yourself. — *i.e., "rogue"*
WELLBORN How, dog?
TAPWELL Even so, sir.
And I must tell you, if you but advance° — *raise threateningly*
Your Plymouth cloak,° you shall be soon instructed — *i.e., cudgel*
There° dwells—and within call, if it please Your Worship— — *That there*
A potent monarch called the constable,
That does command a citadel called the stocks,
Whose guards are certain files° of rusty billmen,° — *ranks / armed watchmen*
Such as with great dexterity will hale° — *haul (to jail)*
Your tattered, lousy—
WELLBORN Rascal! Slave!° — *Wretch!*
FROTH No rage, sir.
TAPWELL [*to Froth*] At his own peril. [*To Wellborn*] Do not put yourself
In too much heat, there being no water near
To quench your thirst; and sure, for° other liquor, — *as for*
As mighty ale or beer, they are things, I take it,
You must no more remember—not° in a dream, sir. — *not even*
WELLBORN Why, thou unthankful villain,° dar'st thou talk thus? — *wretch*

1.1. In front of Tapwell's alehouse. Wellborn has just been rudely shown the door by the proprietor.

1. Puritan. Wellborn objects to Froth's archly pious use of "verity," a cant Puritan phrase.

Is not thy house, and all thou hast, my gift?
TAPWELL I find it not in chalk,[2] and Timothy Tapwell
Does keep no other register.
WELLBORN Am not I he
Whose riots° fed and clothed thee? Wert thou not *riotous banqueting*
Born on my father's land, and proud to be
A drudge in his house?
TAPWELL What I was, sir, it skills not.° *is of no concern*
What you are is apparent. Now for a farewell:
Since you talk of father, in my hope it will torment you,
I'll briefly tell your story. Your dead father,
My quondam° master, was a man of worship,° *former / respect*
Old Sir John Wellborn, Justice of Peace and Quorum,[3]
And stood fair to be *Custos Rotulorum*,[4]
Bare° the whole sway° of the shire, kept a great house, *Bore, carried / rule*
Relieved the poor, and so forth; but he dying,
And the twelve hundred a year coming to you,
Late° Master Francis, but now forlorn Wellborn— *Formerly*
WELLBORN Slave, stop, or I shall lose myself.° *lose self-control*
FROTH Very hardly;
You cannot out of your way.[5]
TAPWELL But to my story.
You were then a lord of acres, the prime gallant,
And I your under-butler. Note the change now.
You had a merry time of't—hawks and hounds,
With choice of running horses,° mistresses *racehorses*
Of all sorts and all sizes—yet so hot
As their embraces made your lordships° melt. *estates*
Which your uncle, Sir Giles Overreach, observing,
Resolving not to lose a drop of 'em
On foolish mortgages, statutes, and bonds,
For a while supplied your looseness, and then left° you. *abandoned*
WELLBORN Some curate hath penned this invective, mongrel,
And you have studied° it. *memorized*
TAPWELL I have not done° yet. *finished*
Your land gone, and your credit not worth a token,[6]
You grew the common borrower; no man scaped
Your paper pellets,° from the gentleman *IOUs*
To the beggars on highways, that sold you switches° *riding rods*
In your gallantry.° *In your heyday*
WELLBORN I shall switch your brains out.
TAPWELL Where° poor Tim Tapwell, with a little stock, *Whereas*
Some forty pounds or so, bought a small cottage,
Humbled myself to marriage with my Froth here,
Gave entertainment—
WELLBORN Yes, to whores and canters,° *users of thieves' cant*
Clubbers° by night. *Wielders of clubs*
TAPWELL True, but they brought in profit,
And had a gift to pay° for what they called for, *were given to paying*

2. Alehouse-keepers kept tallies of their customers' accounts in chalk.
3. Certain learned justices whose presence was necessary to constitute a bench; hence, select and eminent justices. ("Quorum" was sometimes confused with "coram," meaning "in the presence of"; see 3.2.85.)
4. Principal justice of the peace of a county, who had custody of the rolls and other court records.
5. It would be hard for you to lose yourself, you're already so lost in your debauched ways.
6. Small, cheap disks that tradesmen were permitted to coin and use for change.

And stuck not° like Your Mastership. The poor income — *didn't hold back*
I gleaned from them hath made me in my parish
Thought worthy to be scavenger,° and in time — *street cleaner, garbage man*
May rise to be overseer of the poor—
Which if I do, on your petition, Wellborn,
I may allow you thirteenpence a quarter,
And you shall thank My Worship.

WELLBORN Thus, you dogbolt!° — *lit., "blunt-headed arrow"*
And thus! *Beats and kicks him.*

TAPWELL [*to Froth*] Cry out for help!

WELLBORN Stir, and thou diest.
Your potent prince, the constable, shall not save you.
Hear me, ungrateful hellhound. Did not I
Make purses° for you? Then you licked my boots, — *Get business*
And thought your holiday cloak too coarse to clean 'em.
'Twas I that, when I heard thee swear if ever
Thou couldst arrive at forty pounds° thou wouldst — *(Tapwell's capital)*
Live like an emperor, 'twas I that gave it
In ready gold. Deny this, wretch!

TAPWELL I must, sir,
For, from the tavern to the taphouse,° all, — *lowly bar*
On forfeiture of their licenses, stand bound
Never to remember who their best guests were,
If they grew poor like you.

WELLBORN They are well rewarded
That beggar themselves to make such cuckolds° rich. — *i.e., parasites*
Thou viper, thankless viper! Impudent bawd!
But since you are grown forgetful, I will help
Your memory, and tread thee into mortar,
Not leave one bone unbroken. [*He beats Tapwell again.*]

TAPWELL Oh!

FROTH Ask mercy!

Enter Allworth.

WELLBORN 'Twill not be granted.

ALLWORTH Hold, for my sake, hold!
Deny me, Frank? They are not worth your anger.

WELLBORN For once thou hast redeemed them from this scepter.
[*Wellborn puts up*] *his cudgel.*
But let 'em vanish, creeping on their knees,
And, if they grumble, I revoke my pardon.

FROTH This comes of your prating, husband. You presumed
On your ambling wit, and must use your glib tongue
Though you are beaten lame for't.

TAPWELL Patience, Froth.
There's law to cure our bruises.
They go off on their hands and knees.

WELLBORN Sent to your mother?[7]

ALLWORTH My lady, Frank, my patroness! My all!
She's such a mourner for my father's death,
And, in her love to him, so favors me
That I cannot pay too much observance° to her. — *dutiful behavior*
There are few such stepdames.

7. I.e., Have you sent to your stepmother asking her to see me?

WELLBORN 'Tis a noble widow,
And keeps her reputation pure and clear
From the least taint of infamy; her life,
With the splendor of her actions, leaves no tongue
To envy or detraction. Prithee tell me:
Has she no suitors?
ALLWORTH Even the best of the shire, Frank,
My lord° excepted—such as sue° and send, *(Lord Lovell) / petition*
And send and sue again, but to no purpose.
Their frequent visits have not gained her presence.
Yet she's so far from sullenness and pride
That I dare undertake you shall meet from her
A liberal entertainment.° I can give you *generous reception*
A catalog of her suitors' names.
WELLBORN Forbear it,
While I give you good counsel. I am bound to it;
Thy father was my friend, and that affection
I bore to him, in right descends to thee.
Thou art a handsome and a hopeful youth,
Nor will I have the least affront stick on thee,
If I with any danger° can prevent it. *at whatever risk to me*
ALLWORTH I thank your noble care. But pray you, in what
Do I run the hazard?
WELLBORN Art thou not in love?
Put it not off with wonder.[8]
ALLWORTH In love, at my years?
WELLBORN You think you walk in clouds,° but are transparent. *go unperceived*
I have heard all, and the choice that you have made,
And with my finger can point out the north star
By which the lodestone° of your folly's guided. *magnet, compass*
And to confirm this true, what think you of
Fair Margaret, the only child and heir
Of cormorant° Overreach? Does it blush and start *a seabird; voracious*
To hear her only° named? Blush at your want *Only to hear her*
Of wit and reason.
ALLWORTH You are too bitter, sir.
WELLBORN Wounds of this nature are not to be cured
With balms, but corrosives. I must be plain:
Art thou scarce manumized from the porter's lodge,[9]
And yet sworn servant to the pantofle,[1]
And dar'st thou dream of marriage? I fear
'Twill be concluded for impossible
That there is now, nor e'er shall be hereafter,
A handsome page or players' boy° of fourteen *actor's apprentice*
But either loves a wench, or drabs° love him— *wenches*
Court-waiters° not exempted. *Pages at court*
ALLWORTH This is madness.
Howe'er you have discovered my intents,
You know my aims are lawful; and if ever
The queen of flowers, the glory of the spring,

8. Don't pretend to be surprised at my question.
9. Are you scarcely manumitted, or freed, from the porter's office (where the servants were punished)? I.e., Are you scarcely raised up from being a mere servant?
1. I.e., And are you still in a state of servitude, tending to the very slipper ("pantofle") of those to whom you are beholden?

The sweetest comfort to our smell, the rose,
Sprang from an envious° brier, I may infer *churlish, thorny*
There's such disparity in their conditions
Between the goddess of my soul, the daughter,
And the base churl, her father.

WELLBORN Grant this true,
As I believe it, canst thou ever hope
To enjoy a quiet bed with her whose father
Ruined thy state?° *estate*

ALLWORTH And yours too.

WELLBORN I confess it.
True, I must tell you as a friend, and freely,
That, where impossibilities are apparent,
'Tis indiscretion to nourish hopes.
Canst thou imagine—let not self-love blind thee—
That Sir Giles Overreach, that, to make her° great *(his daughter)*
In swelling titles, without touch of conscience
Will cut his neighbor's throat, and I hope his own too,
Will e'er consent to make her thine? Give o'er,° *Give up*
And think of some course suitable to thy rank,
And prosper in it.

ALLWORTH You have well advised me.
But in the meantime, you that are so studious
Of my affairs wholly neglect your own.
Remember yourself, and in what plight you are.

WELLBORN No matter, no matter.

ALLWORTH Yes, 'tis much material.° *very pertinent*
You know my fortune and my means; yet something
I can spare from myself to help your wants.
[*He offers money.*]

WELLBORN How's this?

ALLWORTH Nay, be not angry. There's eight pieces° *coins*
To put you in better fashion.° *i.e., clothes*

WELLBORN Money from thee?
From a boy? A stipendiary?° One that lives *one on a stipend*
At the devotion of a stepmother
And the uncertain favor of a lord?° *(Lord Lovell)*
I'll eat my arms first. Howsoe'er blind Fortune
Hath spent the utmost of her malice on me—
Though I am vomited out of an alehouse,
And, thus accoutred, know not where to eat,
Or drink, or sleep, but underneath this canopy°— *the open air*
Although I thank thee, I despise thy offer.
And, as I in my madness broke my state° *squandered my estate*
Without th'assistance of another's brain,
In my right wits I'll piece° it; at the worst *repair*
Die thus, and be forgotten.

ALLWORTH A strange humor!° *Exeunt.* *whim*

1.2

[Enter] Order, Amble, Furnace, [and] Watchall.

ORDER Set all things right, or—as my name is Order,
And by this staff of office° that commands you, *steward's white staff*
This chain and double ruff, symbols of power—
Whoever misses in his function,° *fails in his duties*
For one whole week makes forfeiture of his breakfast
And privilege in the wine cellar.
AMBLE You are merry,
Good Master Steward.
FURNACE Let him; I'll be angry.
AMBLE Why, fellow Furnace, 'tis not twelve o'clock yet,
Nor dinner taking up;[1] then 'tis allowed
Cooks by° their places may be choleric. *by reason of*
FURNACE You think you have spoke wisely, goodman Amble,
My lady's go-before!° *gentleman-usher*
ORDER Nay, nay, no wrangling.
FURNACE Twit me with the authority of the kitchen?[2]
At all hours and all places I'll be angry;
And, thus provoked, when° I am at my prayers, *even when*
I will be angry.
AMBLE There was no hurt meant.
FURNACE I am friends with thee, and yet I will be angry.
ORDER With whom?
FURNACE No matter whom. Yet, now I think on't,
I am angry with my lady.
WATCHALL Heaven forbid, man!
ORDER What cause has she given thee?
FURNACE Cause enough, Master Steward.
I was entertained° by her to please her palate, *employed*
And till she forswore eating° I performed it. *gave up fancy dining*
Now since our master, noble Allworth, died,
Though I crack my brains to find out tempting sauces,
And raise fortifications in the pastry° *pastry room*
Such as might serve for models in the Low Countries,
Which if they had been practiced at Breda,
Spinola might have thrown his cap at it and ne'er took it[3]—
AMBLE But you had wanted° matter there to work on. *would have lacked*
FURNACE Matter? With six eggs and a strike° of rye meal *large measure*
I had kept° the town till doomsday, perhaps longer. *would have maintained*
ORDER But, what's this to your pet° against my lady? *peeve, complaint*
FURNACE What's this? Marry,° this: when I am three parts *By Mary (an oath)*
roasted
And the fourth part parboiled° to prepare her viands, *boiled*
She keeps her chamber, dines with a panada° *boiled bread pudding*
Or water-gruel,° my sweat never thought on. *thin porridge*
ORDER But your art is seen in the dining room.

1.2. Lady Allworth's house.
1. I.e., Nor is dinner being carried up from the basement kitchen to the dining room.
2. Are you finding fault with the way I run my kitchen?
3. Furnace's elaborate fortlike pastries are so formidable that if they had been deployed at Breda, in the Netherlands, against Ambrogio di Spinola, the Italian general commanding the Spanish army there, the Spanish would have given up the siege as a bad job without capturing the town. (Spinola began the siege in August of 1624; the town surrendered a year later.) Furnace goes on to boast that his cooking would have lasted out a long siege.

FURNACE By whom?
By such as pretend love to her, but come
To feed upon her. Yet of all the Harpies[4]
That do devour her, I am out of charity
With none so much as the thin-gutted squire
That's stol'n into commission.[5]
ORDER Justice Greedy?
FURNACE The same, the same. Meat's cast away upon him;
It never thrives. He holds this paradox:
Who° eats not well can ne'er do justice well. *Whoever*
His stomach's as insatiate as the grave,
Or strumpet's ravenous appetites.
WATCHALL One knocks.

Allworth knocks, and enters.

ORDER Our late young master![6]
AMBLE Welcome, sir.
FURNACE Your hand.
If you have a stomach,° a cold bake-meat's° ready. *appetite / meat pie is*
ORDER [*to the others*] His father's picture in little.° *Just like his father*
FURNACE We are all your servants.
AMBLE In you he lives.
ALLWORTH At once,° my thanks to all. *In one reply*
This is yet some comfort. Is my lady stirring?° *up and about*
ORDER Her presence° answer for us. *Let her presence*

Enter the Lady Allworth, Waiting-woman, [and] Chambermaid.

LADY ALLWORTH [*to her women*] Sort those silks° well. *skeins of silk*
I'll take the air° alone. *take a walk*
Exeunt Waiting-woman and Chambermaid.
FURNACE You air and air,
But will you never taste but spoon-meat° more? *liquid diet*
To what use serve I?
LADY ALLWORTH Prithee, be not angry;
I shall, ere long. I'the meantime, there is gold
To buy thee aprons and a summer suit. [*She gives money.*]
FURNACE I am appeased, and Furnace now grows cool.
LADY ALLWORTH And, as I gave directions, if this morning
I am visited by any, entertain 'em
As heretofore, but say, in my excuse,
I am indisposed.
ORDER I shall, madam.
LADY ALLWORTH Do, and leave me.—
Nay, stay you, Allworth.
ALLWORTH I shall gladly grow° here *stay*
To wait on your commands.
Exeunt Order, Amble, Furnace, [and] Watchall.
LADY ALLWORTH So soon turned courtier!
ALLWORTH Style not that "courtship," madam, which is duty
Purchased on your part.[7]

4. Malign and predatory bird-shaped creatures from Greek mythology with the faces of women.
5. Who has bribed or otherwise wormed his way into becoming a justice of the peace (and a perennial dinner guest of Lady Allworth).
6. Tom Allworth is the son of the deceased ("late") Allworth senior.
7. Please don't use the term "courtship," i.e., affected courtly mannerisms, to describe the show of duty that your worthiness deserves from me.

LADY ALLWORTH Well, you shall o'ercome;° *carry the point*
I'll not contend in words. How is it with
Your noble master?
ALLWORTH Ever like himself,
No scruple° lessened in the full weight of honor. *least bit*
He did command me (pardon my presumption)
As his unworthy deputy to kiss
Your Ladyship's fair hands. [*He kisses her hands.*]
LADY ALLWORTH I am honored in
His favor to me. Does he hold his purpose
For the Low Countries?
ALLWORTH Constantly, good madam,
But he will in person first present his service.° *take courteous leave*
LADY ALLWORTH And how approve you of his course? You are yet,
Like virgin parchment, capable of any
Inscription, vicious or honorable.
I will not force your will, but leave you free
To your own election.° *choice*
ALLWORTH Any form you please
I will put on; but, might I make my choice,
With humble emulation I would follow
The path my lord marks to me.
LADY ALLWORTH 'Tis well answered,
And I commend your spirit. You had a father—
Blessed be his memory!—that some few hours
Before the will of heaven took him from me,
Who did commend you, by the dearest ties
Of perfect love between us, to my charge;
And therefore what I speak you are bound to hear
With such respect as if he lived in me.
He was my husband, and howe'er you are not
Son of my womb, you may be of my love,
Provided you deserve it.
ALLWORTH I have found you,
Most honored madam, the best mother to me,
And, with my utmost strengths of care and service,
Will labor that you never may repent
Your bounties showered upon me.
LADY ALLWORTH I much hope it.
These were your father's words: "If e'er my son
Follow the war, tell him it is a school
Where all the principles tending to honor
Are taught, if truly followed; but for such
As repair° thither as a place in which *betake themselves, go*
They do presume they may with license practice
Their lusts and riots, they shall never merit
The noble name of soldiers. To dare boldly
In a fair cause, and for the country's safety
To run upon the cannon's mouth undaunted;
To obey their leaders, and shun mutinies;
To bear with patience the winter's cold
And summer's scorching heat, and not to faint,
When plenty of provision fails, with hunger,
Are the essential parts make up° a soldier— *that make up*
Not swearing, dice, or drinking."

ALLWORTH There's no syllable
You speak but is to me an oracle,
Which but° to doubt were° impious. *merely / would be*

LADY ALLWORTH To conclude:
Beware ill company, for often men
Are like to those with whom they do converse.
And from one man I warned° you, and that's Wellborn; *have warned*
Not 'cause he's poor—that rather claims your pity—
But that he's in his manners so debauched,
And hath to vicious courses sold himself.
'Tis true your father loved him while he was
Worthy the loving, but, if he had lived
To have seen him as he is, he had° cast him off *would have*
As you must do.

ALLWORTH I shall obey in all things.

LADY ALLWORTH Follow me to my chamber; you shall have gold
To furnish you like° my son, and still° supplied *as befits / continually*
As I hear from you.

ALLWORTH I am still° your creature.° *Exeunt.* *ever / dependent*

1.3

[*Enter*] *Overreach, Greedy, Order, Amble, Furnace, Watchall,* [*and*] *Marall.*

GREEDY Not to be seen?

OVERREACH Still cloistered up? Her reason,
I hope, assures her, though she make herself
Close prisoner ever for her husband's loss,
'Twill not recover him.

ORDER Sir, it is her will,
Which we that are her servants ought to serve it
And not dispute. Howe'er, you are nobly welcome,
And, if you please to stay, that you may think so,° *may feel welcome*
There came not six days since from Hull a pipe° *large cask*
Of rich canary,° which shall spend itself *a sweet white wine*
For my lady's honor.

GREEDY Is it of the right race?° *distinctive flavor*

ORDER Yes, Master Greedy.

AMBLE [*aside to Furnace*] How his mouth runs o'er!° *drools*

FURNACE [*aside to Amble*] I'll make it run, and run.—Save° *God save*
Your good Worship!

GREEDY Honest Master Cook, thy hand again. How I love thee!
Are the good dishes still in being? Speak, boy.

FURNACE If you have a mind to feed, there is a chine° *side roast, saddle*
Of beef, well seasoned.

GREEDY Good!

FURNACE A pheasant, larded.° *garnished with bacon*

GREEDY That I might now give thanks° for't! *say grace at table*

FURNACE Other kickshaws.° *fancy dishes, trifles*
Besides, there came last night from the Forest of Sherwood° *(in Nottingham)*
The fattest stag I ever cooked.

1.3. Lady Allworth's house still.

GREEDY A stag, man?

FURNACE A stag, sir—part of it prepared for dinner,
And baked in puff paste.° *puff pastry*

GREEDY Puff paste too, Sir Giles!
A ponderous chine of beef! A pheasant larded!
And red deer too, Sir Giles, and baked in puff paste!
All business set aside; let us give thanks here.

FURNACE [*aside*] How the lean skeleton's rapt!

OVERREACH You know we cannot.° *can't neglect business*

MARALL Your Worships are to sit on a commission,° *(as justices of the peace)*
And, if you fail to come, you lose the cause.

GREEDY Cause me no causes.° I'll prove't, for such a dinner *(cf. "But me no buts")*
We may put off a commission: you shall find it
Henrici decimo quarto.[1]

OVERREACH Fie, Master Greedy,
Will you lose me a thousand pounds for a dinner?
No more, for shame! We must forget the belly
When we think of profit.

GREEDY Well, you shall o'errule me.
I could ev'n cry now.—Do you hear, Master Cook?
Send but a corner of that immortal pasty,
And I, in thankfulness, will by your boy° *servant*
Send you a brace° of threepences. *pair*

FURNACE [*aside*] Will you be so prodigal?° *(said sarcastically)*

Enter Wellborn.

OVERREACH Remember me to your lady.—Who have we here?

WELLBORN You know me.

OVERREACH I did once, but now I will not;
Thou art no blood of mine. Avaunt,° thou beggar! *Begone*
If ever thou presume to own° me more, *claim kinship with*
I'll have thee caged° and whipped. *imprisoned*

GREEDY I'll grant° the warrant.— *issue, authorize*
Think of Pie Corner,[2] Furnace!

Exeunt Overreach, Greedy, [and] Marall.

WATCHALL [*to Wellborn*] Will you out,° sir? *depart*
I wonder how you durst creep in.

ORDER This is rudeness
And saucy impudence.

AMBLE Cannot you stay
To be served among your fellows from the basket,° *alms-basket for the poor*
But you must press into the hall?

FURNACE Prithee, vanish
Into some outhouse,° though it be the pigsty; *outbuilding*
My scullion° shall come to thee. *kitchen underservant*

Enter Allworth.

WELLBORN This is rare.° *excellent (ironic)*
Oh, here's Tom Allworth.—Tom!

1. In a law enacted in the fourteenth year of the reign of Henry VIII (1523).
2. Referring to the "corner of that immortal pasty" mentioned in line 35, and playing on the name of an often-mentioned London locale.

ALLWORTH We must be strangers,
Nor would I have you seen here for a million.
Exit Allworth.
WELLBORN Better and better. He contemns° me too? *scorns*

Enter [Waiting-]woman and Chambermaid.

WAITING-WOMAN Foh, what a smell's here! What thing's this?
CHAMBERMAID A creature
Made out of the privy. Let us hence, for love's sake,
Or I shall swoon.
WAITING-WOMAN I begin to faint already.
Exeunt [Waiting-]woman and Chambermaid.
WATCHALL [*to Wellborn*] Will you know your way?° *get going*
AMBLE Or shall we teach it you
By the head and shoulders?° *By a beating*
WELLBORN No. I will not stir.
Do you mark, I will not. Let me see the wretch
That dares attempt to force me. Why, you slaves,
Created only to make legs° and cringe, *bows*
To carry in a dish and shift a trencher,° *wooden platter*
That have not souls only to hope a blessing
Beyond blackjacks or flagons[3]—you that were born
Only to consume meat and drink, and batten° *feast*
Upon reversions!° Who advances? Who *leftovers*
Shows me the way?° *Who'll try to evict me?*
ORDER My lady!

Enter Lady [Allworth, Waiting-]woman, [and] Chambermaid.

CHAMBERMAID Here's the monster.
WAITING-WOMAN Sweet madam, keep your glove to your nose.
CHAMBERMAID Or let me
Fetch some perfumes may be predominant;° *to overcome the smell*
You wrong yourself else.
WELLBORN Madam, my designs
Bear° me to you. *Bring*
LADY ALLWORTH To me?
WELLBORN And though I have met with
But ragged entertainment from your grooms° here, *servants*
I hope from you to receive that noble usage
As may become° the true friend of your husband, *befit*
And then I shall forget these.
LADY ALLWORTH I am amazed
To see and hear this rudeness. Dar'st thou think,
Though sworn,[4] that it can ever find belief
That I, who to the best men of this country
Denied my presence since my husband's death,
Can fall so low as to change° words with thee? *exchange*
Thou son of infamy, forbear my house,
And know and keep the distance that's between us,
Or, though it be against my gentler temper,

3. You who have souls incapable of praying for anything beyond leather jugs and short-necked bottles (of wine).
4. Even if someone were to swear the truth of it.

I shall take order° you no more shall be — *take steps, give orders*
An eyesore to me.
WELLBORN Scorn me not, good lady;
But, as in form you are angelical,
Imitate the heavenly natures° and vouchsafe — *the angels*
At the least awhile to hear me. You will grant
The blood that runs in this arm is as noble
As that which fills your veins; those costly jewels,
And those rich clothes you wear, your men's observance° — *attentive service*
And women's flattery° are in you no virtues, — *obsequiousness*
Nor these rags, with my poverty, in me vices.
You have a fair fame, and, I know, deserve it—
Yet, lady, I must say, in nothing more
Than in the pious sorrow you have shown
For your late noble husband.[5]
ORDER [*aside to the others*] How she starts!
FURNACE [*aside*] And hardly can keep finger from the eye° — *refrain from weeping*
To hear him named!
LADY ALLWORTH Have you aught else to say?
WELLBORN That husband, madam, was once in his fortune
Almost as low as I. Want, debts, and quarrels
Lay heavy on him. Let it not be thought
A boast in me though I say I relieved him.
'Twas I that gave him fashion;[6] mine the sword
That did on all occasions second his;
I brought him on and off with honor,[7] lady.
And when in all men's judgments he was sunk,
And in his own hopes not to be buoyed up,
I stepped unto him, took him by the hand,
And set him upright.
FURNACE [*aside to the others*] Are not we base rogues,
That could forget this?
WELLBORN I confess you made him
Master of your estate;[8] nor could your friends,° — *family*
Though he brought no wealth with him, blame you for't,
For he had a shape, and to that shape a mind
Made up of all parts either great or noble—
So winning a behavior not to be
Resisted, madam.
LADY ALLWORTH 'Tis most true. He had.
WELLBORN For his sake, then, in that I was his friend,
Do not contemn me.
LADY ALLWORTH For what's past, excuse me;
I will redeem it.—Order, give the gentleman
A hundred pounds.
WELLBORN No, madam, on no terms.
I will nor° beg nor borrow sixpence of you, — *neither*
But be supplied elsewhere, or want° thus ever. — *remain in need*
Only one suit I make, which you deny not

5. Yet I must say, my lady, you reveal your true nobility nowhere so much as in the genuine and pious sorrow you show in mourning for your deceased noble husband.
6. It was I who, by relieving him of his debts, gave him the opportunity to cut a fine figure.
7. I assisted him as his second in duels and other affairs of honor, enabling him to behave like a gentleman and come away with honor.
8. You made him your husband and hence master of all your wealth.

To strangers; and 'tis this. *Whispers to her.*
LADY ALLWORTH Fie, nothing else?
WELLBORN Nothing, unless you please to charge your servants
To throw away a little respect upon me.
LADY ALLWORTH What you demand° is yours. — *ask*
WELLBORN I thank you, lady.
Now what can be wrought out of such a suit
Is yet in supposition.[9] I have said all;
When you please, you may retire.
[*Exit Lady Allworth with Waiting-woman and Chambermaid.*]
Nay, all's forgotten;
And, for a lucky omen to my project,
Shake hands and end all quarrels in the cellar.° — *in a cup of wine*
ORDER Agreed, agreed.
FURNACE Still merry Master Wellborn!
Exeunt.

2.1

[*Enter*] *Overreach* [*and*] *Marall.*

OVERREACH He's gone, I warrant thee; this commission crushed him.[1]
MARALL Your Worship have the way on't, and ne'er miss
To squeeze these unthrifts into air; and yet
The chap-fall'n justice° did his part, returning — *hollow-cheeked Greedy*
For your advantage the certificate,
Against his conscience and his knowledge too
(With your good favor),° to the utter ruin — *If I may say so*
Of the poor farmer.
OVERREACH 'Twas for these good ends
I made him° a justice. He that bribes his° belly — *(Greedy) / (Greedy's)*
Is certain to command his soul.
MARALL I wonder
(Still with your license)° why, Your Worship having — *begging your pardon*
The power to put this thin-gut in commission,
You are not in't yourself?
OVERREACH Thou art a fool.
In being out of office I am out of danger,
Where,° if I were a justice, besides the trouble, — *Whereas*
I might or° out of willfulness or error — *either*
Run myself finely into a praemunire,[2]
And so become a prey to the informer.
No, I'll have none of't. 'Tis enough I keep
Greedy at my devotion;° so he serve — *at my beck and call*
My purposes, let him hang, or damn,° I care not. — *be damned*
Friendship is but a word.
MARALL You are all wisdom.
OVERREACH I would be worldly-wise; for° the other wisdom, — *as for*
That does prescribe us a well-governed life,
And to do right to others as° ourselves, — *as to*

9. What can be gained from the request I just whispered to you remains to be seen.
2.1. Outside Overreach's house.
1. Overreach and Marall are discussing some poor farmer (line 8) whom Overreach has forced into financial ruin, with Greedy's connivance.
2. Literally, an offense against the English Crown punishable by forfeiture; hence, here, a legal difficulty.

I value not an atom.
MARALL What course take you,
With your good patience,° to hedge in the manor — *Begging your pardon*
Of your neighbor Master Frugal? As 'tis said
He will nor sell nor borrow nor exchange,
And his land, lying in the midst of your many lordships,° — *landed possessions*
Is a foul blemish.
OVERREACH I have thought on't, Marall,
And it shall take.° I must have all men sellers, — *take effect, succeed*
And I the only purchaser.
MARALL 'Tis most fit, sir.
OVERREACH I'll therefore buy some cottage near his manor,
Which done, I'll make my men break ope his fences,
Ride o'er his standing corn,° and in the night — *grainfields*
Set fire on his barns, or break his cattle's legs.
These trespasses draw on suits, and suits expenses,
Which I can spare,° but will soon beggar him. — *afford*
When I have harried him thus two or three year,
Though he sue *in forma pauperis*,° in spite — *in pauper's status*
Of all his thrift and care he'll grow behindhand.° — *in arrears*
MARALL The best I ever heard! I could adore you.
OVERREACH Then with the favor of my man of law,° — *with Greedy's help*
I will pretend some title. Want will force him
To put it to arbitrament;° then, if he sell — *a legal settlement*
For half the value, he shall have ready money,
And I possess his land.
MARALL 'Tis above wonder!
Wellborn was apt° to sell, and needed not — *willing*
These fine arts, sir, to hook him in.
OVERREACH Well thought on.
This varlet, Marall, lives too long to upbraid me
With my close cheat° put upon him. Will nor cold — *secret fraud*
Nor hunger kill him?
MARALL I know not what to think on't.
I have used all means, and the last night I caused
His host the tapster to turn him out of doors,
And have been since with all your friends and tenants,
And on the forfeit of your favor charged° 'em, — *ordered*
Though a crust of moldy bread would keep him from starving,
Yet they should not relieve him. This is done, sir.
OVERREACH That was something, Marall, but thou must go further,
And suddenly, Marall.
MARALL Where and when you please, sir.
OVERREACH I would have thee seek him out, and, if thou canst,
Persuade him that 'tis better steal than beg.
Then if I prove he has but robbed a henroost,
Not all the world shall save him from the gallows.
Do anything to work him to despair,
And 'tis thy masterpiece.
MARALL I will do my best, sir.
OVERREACH I am now on my main work with the Lord Lovell,
The gallant-minded, popular Lord Lovell;
The minion° of the people's love. I hear — *darling*
He's come into the country,° and my aims are — *county, shire*
To insinuate myself into his knowledge,° — *acquaintance*

And then invite him to my house.
MARALL I have° you. *understand*
This points at my young mistress.
OVERREACH She must part with
That humble title,° and write "Honorable," *i.e., "young mistress"*
"Right Honorable," Marall, my "Right Honorable" daughter,[3]
If all I have, or e'er shall get, will do it.
I will have her well attended;° there are ladies *waited on*
Of errant knights decayed° and brought so low *impoverished knights*
That, for cast° clothes and meat, will gladly serve her. *cast-off*
And 'tis my glory, though I come from the city,
To have their issue,° whom I have undone,° *offspring / ruined*
To kneel to mine as bondslaves.
MARALL 'Tis fit state, sir.
OVERREACH And therefore, I'll not have a chambermaid
That ties her shoes, or any meaner° office, *humbler*
But such whose fathers were Right Worshipful.
'Tis a rich man's pride, there having ever been
More than a feud, a strange antipathy
Between us and true gentry.

Enter Wellborn.

MARALL See who's here, sir.
OVERREACH Hence, monster! Prodigy!
WELLBORN Sir, your wife's nephew;
She and my father tumbled in one belly.
OVERREACH Avoid my sight! Thy breath's infectious, rogue.
I shun thee as a leprosy, or the plague.—
Come hither, Marall. [*Aside to him*] This is the time to work him.
MARALL I warrant you, sir. *Exit Overreach.*
WELLBORN By this light,° I think he's mad. *By God's light*
MARALL Mad? Had you took compassion on yourself,
You long since had been mad.[4]
WELLBORN You have took a course,
Between you and my venerable uncle,
To make me so.
MARALL The more pale-spirited you,
That would not be instructed. I swear deeply—
WELLBORN By what?
MARALL By my religion.
WELLBORN Thy religion!
The devil's creed. But what would you have done?
MARALL Had there been but one tree in all the shire,
Nor any hope to compass a penny halter,° *buy a cheap noose*
Before, like you, I had outlived my fortunes,
A withe° had served my turn to hang myself. *slender branch*
I am zealous in your cause; pray you, hang yourself,
And presently,° as you love your credit.° *at once / good name*

3. Traditionally, but not always with strict observance, "Honorable" is applied as an official or courtesy title of honor or distinction to sons of peers below the rank of marquess and to daughters of peers below the rank of earl, to maids of honor, and to various high justices. "Right Honorable" is applied to peers below the rank of marquess, to privy councillers, and to certain civil functionaries, such as the lord mayors of London and some other cities.

4. If you had thought compassionately about your state of affairs, you would have gone mad in earnest.

WELLBORN I thank you.
MARALL Will you stay° till you die in a ditch, or lice devour you? *wait*
Or if you dare not do the feat yourself,
But that you'll put the state to charge° and trouble, *expense*
Is there no purse to be cut?° House to be broken?° *filched / broken into*
Or market women with eggs that you may murder,
And so dispatch the business?
WELLBORN Here's variety,
I must confess; but I'll accept of none
Of all your gentle offers, I assure you.
MARALL Why, have you hope ever to eat again?
Or drink? Or be the master of three farthings?
If you like not hanging, drown yourself. Take some course
For your reputation.
WELLBORN 'Twill not do, dear tempter,
With all the rhetoric the fiend hath taught you.
I am as far as thou art from despair;
Nay, I have confidence, which is more than hope,
To live, and suddenly, better than ever.
MARALL Ha! Ha! These castles you build in the air
Will not persuade me or° to give or lend *either*
A token° to you. *(see 1.1.54 n)*
WELLBORN I'll be more kind to thee.
Come, thou shalt dine with me.
MARALL With you?
WELLBORN Nay, more, dine gratis.° *at no expense*
MARALL Under what hedge, I pray you? Or at whose cost?
Are they padders or Abram-men[5] that are your consorts?
WELLBORN Thou art incredulous, but thou shalt dine
Not alone at her house, but with a gallant lady—
With me and with a lady.
MARALL Lady? What lady?
With the Lady of the Lake,[6] or Queen of Fairies?
For I know it must be an enchanted dinner.
WELLBORN With the Lady Allworth, knave.
MARALL Nay, now there's hope
Thy brain is cracked.
WELLBORN Mark there with what respect
I am entertained.
MARALL With choice, no doubt, of dog whips.
Why, dost thou ever hope to pass her porter?[7]
WELLBORN 'Tis not far off; go with me. Trust thine own eyes.
MARALL Troth, in my hope, or my assurance rather
To see thee curvet° and mount like a dog in a blanket[8] *prance*
If ever thou presume to pass her threshold,
I will endure thy company.
WELLBORN Come along, then. *Exeunt.*

5. Are they footpads or destitute beggars? (Abram-men, or Abraham-men—alluding perhaps to the parable of the beggar Lazarus in Luke 16.19–31—were, historically, vagabonds made homeless by the dissolution of the monastaries in the early sixteenth century.)
6. I.e., the enchantress Nimue, or Vivien, mistress of the enchanter Merlin (in Thomas Malory's *Morte d'Arthur*), who lived in the middle of a magical lake and gave the sword Excalibur to Arthur.
7. To slip past the porter.
8. Tossing a dog (or, often, a person) in a blanket was a common rough game and form of humiliation.

2.2

[Enter] Allworth, Waiting-woman, Chambermaid, Order, Amble, Furnace, [and] Watchall.

WAITING-WOMAN [*to Allworth*] Could you not command your
leisure° one hour longer? *find time to stay*
CHAMBERMAID Or half an hour?
ALLWORTH I have told you what my haste is.
Besides, being now another's, not mine own,
Howe'er I much desire to enjoy you° longer, *enjoy your company*
My duty suffers if, to please myself,
I should neglect my lord.
WAITING-WOMAN Pray you do me the favor
To put these few quince cakes into your pocket;
They are of mine own preserving.
CHAMBERMAID And this marmalade;
'Tis comfortable for your stomach.° *digestion*
WAITING-WOMAN And, at parting,
Excuse me if I beg a farewell from you.
CHAMBERMAID [*to her*] You are still before° me.—I move the *anticipating*
same suit, sir. *[Allworth] kisses 'em severally.°* *the women one by one*
FURNACE How greedy these chamberers° are of a beardless *chambermaids*
chin!
I think the tits° will ravish him. *chits, minxes*
ALLWORTH My service
To both.
WAITING-WOMAN Ours waits on you.
CHAMBERMAID And shall do ever.
ORDER [*to the women*] You hear my lady's charge; be therefore
careful
That you sustain your parts.
WAITING-WOMAN We can bear,° I warrant you. *do our parts*
Exeunt [Waiting-]woman and Chambermaid.
FURNACE [*to Allworth*] Here; drink it off. The ingredients are
cordial,° *heart-stimulating*
And this the true elixir; it hath boiled
Since midnight for you. 'Tis the quintessence
Of five cocks of the game,° ten dozen of sparrows, *gamecocks*
Knuckles of veal, potato roots,° and marrow,° *sweet potatoes / squash*
Coral, and ambergris.° Were you two years elder, *(used in perfume)*
And I had a wife or gamesome mistress,
I durst trust you with neither. You need not bait° *stop for food and rest*
After this, I warrant you; though your journey's long,
You may ride on the strength of this till tomorrow morning.
ALLWORTH Your courtesies overwhelm me. I much grieve
To part from such true friends, and yet find° comfort; *I find*
My attendance on my honorable lord,
Whose resolution holds° to visit my lady, *Who is resolved*
Will speedily bring me back.
Knocking at the gate; Marall and Wellborn [speak] within.
MARALL [*within*] Dar'st thou venture further?
WELLBORN [*within*] Yes, yes, and knock again.

2.2. Lady Allworth's house.

ORDER [*to the others*] 'Tis he! Disperse.
AMBLE [*to the others*] Perform it bravely.° — *well*
FURNACE I know my cue. Ne'er doubt me.
They go off several° ways. [Allworth remains onstage.] — *different*

[Enter Watchall with Wellborn and Marall.]

WATCHALL [*to Wellborn*] Beast that I was, to make you stay!° Most welcome. — *wait at the door*
You were long since expected.
WELLBORN Say so much° — *Give a welcome also*
To my friend,° I pray you. — *(To Marall)*
WATCHALL For your sake I will, sir.
MARALL [*aside*] For his sake!
WELLBORN [*aside to Marall*] Mum! This is nothing.
MARALL [*aside*] More than ever
I would have believed, though I had found it in my primer.[1]
ALLWORTH When I have giv'n you reasons for my late harshness,
You'll pardon and excuse me, for, believe me,
Though now I part abruptly, in my service
I will deserve it.° — *(your pardon)*
MARALL [*aside*] Service! With a vengeance!
WELLBORN I am satisfied. Farewell, Tom.
ALLWORTH All joy stay with you!
Exit Allworth.

Enter Amble.

AMBLE [*to Wellborn*] You are happily encountered!° I yet never — *I'm glad you've come!*
Presented one so welcome as I know
You will be to my lady.
MARALL [*aside*] This is some vision,
Or, sure, these men are mad, to worship a dunghill.° — *an outcast wretch*
It cannot be a truth.
WELLBORN [*aside to Marall*] Be still a pagan,
An unbelieving infidel; be so, miscreant,
And meditate on blankets and on dog whips![2]

Enter Furnace.

FURNACE [*to Wellborn*] I am glad you are come. Until I know your pleasure,° — *what you'd like*
I knew not how to serve up my lady's dinner.
MARALL [*aside*] His pleasure! Is it possible?
WELLBORN [*to Furnace*] What's thy will?
FURNACE Marry, sir, I have some grouse, and turkey chicken,° — *young turkey*
Some rails,° and quails, and my lady willed me ask you — *game birds*
What kind of sauces best affect° your palate, — *please*
That I may use my utmost skill to please it.
[Wellborn and Furnace confer privately.]
MARALL [*aside*] The devil's entered this cook. Sauce for his palate,
That, on my knowledge, for almost this twelvemonth

1. More than I could ever have believed. (Marall is astonished at the cordial reception afforded Wellborn. A primer is a book of ABCs and prayers for children.)
2. I.e., Go ahead and be incredulous, if you like, and remember the whipping and being tossed in a blanket that you anticipated for me (at 2.1.141–43)—so unlike the reception I am in fact receiving!

Durst wish but cheese parings and brown bread on Sundays!

WELLBORN [*to Furnace*] That way I like 'em best.

FURNACE It shall be done, sir.

Exit Furnace.

WELLBORN [*aside to Marall*] What think you of the hedge we shall dine under?° *(see 2.1.129)*
Shall we feed gratis?

MARALL I know not what to think.
Pray you, make me not mad.

Enter Order.

ORDER [*to Wellborn*] This place becomes you not.
Pray you, walk, sir, to the dining room.

WELLBORN I am well here
Till Her Ladyship quits her chamber.

MARALL [*aside*] "Well here," say you?
'Tis a rare change! But yesterday you thought
Yourself well in a barn, wrapped up in peas straw.° *dried pea vines*

Enter [Waiting-]woman and Chambermaid.

WAITING-WOMAN [*to Wellborn*] Oh, sir, you are wished for.

CHAMBERMAID [*to Wellborn*] My lady dreamt, sir, of you.

WAITING-WOMAN And the first command she gave after she rose
Was (her devotions° done) to give her notice *morning prayers*
When you approached here.

CHAMBERMAID Which is done, on my virtue.° *upon my word*

MARALL [*aside*] I shall be converted. I begin to grow
Into a new belief, which saints° nor angels *neither saints*
Could have won me to have faith in.

WAITING-WOMAN Sir, my lady!

Enter Lady [Allworth].

LADY ALLWORTH I come to meet you, and languished till I saw you.
This first kiss is for form;° I allow a second *polite custom*
To such a friend. [*She kisses Wellborn warmly.*]

MARALL [*aside*] To such a friend! Heav'n bless me!

WELLBORN I am wholly yours; yet, madam, if you please
To grace this gentleman with a salute—

MARALL [*aside*] Salute me at his bidding!

WELLBORN I shall receive it
As a most high favor.

LADY ALLWORTH Sir, you may command me.

[*She offers to kiss Marall, who draws back.*]

WELLBORN Run backward from a lady? And such a lady?

MARALL To kiss her foot is, to poor me, a favor
I am unworthy of—

[*He kneels and*] *offers to kiss her foot.*

LADY ALLWORTH Nay, pray you, rise,
And, since you are so humble, I'll exalt you.
You shall dine with me today at mine own table.

MARALL Your Ladyship's table? I am not good enough
To sit at your steward's board.° *dining table*

LADY ALLWORTH You are too modest.
I will not be denied.

Enter Furnace.

FURNACE Will you still be babbling
Till your meat freeze on the table? The old trick still;
My art ne'er thought on!

LADY ALLWORTH Your arm, Master Wellborn.
[*To Marall*] Nay, keep us company.

MARALL I was never so graced.

Exeunt Wellborn, Lady [Allworth], Amble, Marall, [Waiting-]woman, [and Chambermaid].

ORDER So, we have played our parts, and are come off° well. *have succeeded*
But if I know the mystery, why my lady
Consented to it, or why Master Wellborn
Desired it, may I perish!

FURNACE Would I had
The roasting of his° heart that cheated him *i.e., Overreach's*
And forces the poor gentleman to these shifts!° *stratagems*
By fire (for cooks are Persians, and swear by it),[3]
Of all the griping° and extorting tyrants *grasping*
I ever heard or read of, I ne'er met
A match to Sir Giles Overreach.

WATCHALL What will you take
To tell him so, fellow Furnace?

FURNACE Just as much
As my throat is worth, for that would be the price on't.
To have a usurer that starves himself,° *pinches pennies*
And wears a cloak of one-and-twenty years
On a suit of fourteen groats,° bought of the hangman,[4] *small-value coins*
To grow rich, and then purchase,[5] is too common;
But this Sir Giles feeds high,° keeps many servants, *lavishly*
Who must at his command do any outrage.
Rich in his habit,° vast in his expenses, *dress*
Yet he to admiration° still increases *to everyone's amazement*
In wealth and lordships.° *landed possessions*

ORDER He frights men out of their estates,
And breaks through all law nets made to curb ill° men *evil*
As° they were cobwebs. No man dares reprove him. *As if*
Such a spirit to dare and power to do were never
Lodged so unluckily.° *with such evil result*

Enter Amble.

AMBLE Ha, ha! I shall burst.

ORDER Contain thyself, man.

FURNACE Or make us partakers
Of your sudden mirth.

AMBLE Ha, ha! My lady has got
Such a guest at her table—this term driver,° Marall, *(Dramatis Personae, n. 1)*
This snip° of an attorney! *whippersnapper*

FURNACE What of him, man?

AMBLE The knave thinks still he's at the cook's shop in Ram Alley,[6]

3. Since the Persians were fire-worshipers, Furnace reasons, a cook is to be understood as a kind of Persian.
4. The common hangman was customarily given the clothes of the condemned criminal.
5. And then acquire land by purchase (rather than by inheritance).
6. A narrow street chiefly occupied by cooks, bawds, tobacco-sellers, and alehouse-keepers.

Where the clerks divide, and the elder is to choose;[7]
And feeds so slovenly!

FURNACE Is this all?

AMBLE My lady
Drank to him° for fashion° sake, or to please Master Wellborn. *to his health / fashion's*
As I live, he rises, and takes up a dish
In which there were some remnants of a boiled capon,
And pledges her in white broth!

FURNACE Nay, 'tis like
The rest of his tribe.° *tribe of lawyers*

AMBLE And when I brought him wine,
He leaves his stool, and after a leg° or two *bow*
Most humbly thanks My Worship.

ORDER Rose° already! *They have risen*

AMBLE I shall be chid.[8]

Enter Lady [Allworth], Wellborn, [and] Marall.

FURNACE [*aside*] My lady frowns.

LADY ALLWORTH [*to Amble*] You wait well!° *(said ironically)*
Let me have no more of this. I observed your jeering.
Sirrah,[9] I'll have you know, whom° I think worthy *whomever*
To sit at my table, be he ne'er so mean,° *lowly*
When I am present, is not your companion.[1]

ORDER [*aside*] Nay, she'll preserve what's due to her.° *i.e., social propriety*

FURNACE [*aside to Amble*] This refreshing
Follows your flux of laughter.[2]

LADY ALLWORTH [*to Wellborn*] You are master
Of your own will.[3] I know so much of manners
As not to inquire your purposes. In a word,
To me you are ever welcome as to a house
That is your own.

WELLBORN [*aside to Marall*] Mark that!

MARALL [*aside to Wellborn*] With reverence, sir,
An it like° Your Worship. *If it please*

WELLBORN Trouble yourself no farther,
Dear madam. My heart's full of zeal and service,
However in my language I am sparing.—
Come, Master Marall.

MARALL I attend Your Worship.

Exeunt Wellborn [and] Marall.

LADY ALLWORTH I see in your looks you are sorry, and you know me
An easy mistress. Be merry; I have forgot all.°— *I forgive you*
Order and Furnace, come with me; I must give you
Further directions.

ORDER What you please.

FURNACE We are ready.

[*Exeunt.*]

7. Where the law clerks share among themselves, and the eldest one present gets first choice of the food served.
8. I'll be scolded for failing to escort Lady Allworth from the table, as is my duty. (In fact, Amble is scolded instead for his presumption in jeering at Marall.)
9. Used to address servants and other social inferiors.
1. He is not a fit subject for your merriment, as though he were your social equal.
2. Your inappropriate discharge of mirth at Marall's expense has brought on this cooling dose of a reminder as to how you are to perform your duties.
3. I.e., Make use of my hospitality as you wish.

2.3

[Enter] Wellborn [and] Marall.

WELLBORN I think I am in a good way.° *headed for success*
MARALL Good sir, the best way,
The certain best way.
WELLBORN There are casualties° *unforeseen misfortunes*
That men are subject to.
MARALL You are above 'em;
And, as you are already Worshipful,
I hope ere long you will increase in worship
And be Right Worshipful.
WELLBORN Prithee, do not flout° me. *mock*
What I shall be, I shall be. Is't for your ease
You keep your hat off?
MARALL Ease, an it like° Your Worship? *if it please*
I hope Jack Marall shall not live so long
To° prove himself such an unmannerly beast, *As to*
Though it hail hazelnuts, as to be covered
When Your Worship's present.
WELLBORN (*aside*) Is not this a true rogue?
That, out of mere hope of a future cos'nage,[1]
Can turn thus suddenly? 'Tis rank° already. *grossly evident*
MARALL I know Your Worship's wise, and needs no counsel;
Yet if, in my desire to do you service,
I humbly offer my advice (but still
Under correction),° I hope I shall not *With great deference*
Incur your high displeasure.
WELLBORN No. Speak freely.
MARALL Then, in my judgment, sir, my simple judgment
(Still with Your Worship's favor), I could wish you
A better habit,° for this cannot be *outfit*
But much distasteful to the noble lady
(I say no more) that loves you; for, this morning
To me (and I am but a swine to her),
Before th'assurance of her wealth perfumed you,
You savored not of amber.° *ambergris, perfume*
WELLBORN I do now, then?
[Marall] kisses the end of his [Wellborn's] cudgel.
MARALL This your baton hath got a touch of it.
Yet, if you please, for change° I have twenty pounds here, *change of clothes*
Which, out of my true love, I presently
Lay down at Your Worship's feet. 'Twill serve to buy you
A riding suit. *[He offers money.]*
WELLBORN But where's the horse?
MARALL My gelding° *castrated male horse*
Is at your service; nay, you shall ride me
Before Your Worship shall be put to the trouble
To walk afoot. Alas, when you are lord
Of this lady's manor, as I know you will be,
You may, with the lease of glebe land called Knave's Acre[2]—

2.3. Near Lady Allworth's house.
1. (1) Relationship of kinship (claimed for personal gain); (2) chicanery.
2. The old name of Poultney Street, in a poor London neighborhood. Glebe land is land belonging or yielding revenue to a parish church.

A place I would manure°—requite° your vassal. *cultivate / repay*

WELLBORN I thank thy love, but must make no use of it.
What's twenty pounds?

MARALL 'Tis all that I can make,° sir. *raise in ready money*

WELLBORN Dost thou think, though I want clothes I could not have 'em
For° one word to my lady? *By means of*

MARALL As° I know not that! *As if*

WELLBORN Come, I'll tell thee a secret, and so leave thee.
I'll not give her the advantage, though she be
A gallant-minded lady, after we are married
(There being no woman but is sometimes froward)° *perverse, willful*
To hit me in the teeth and say she was forced
To buy my wedding clothes, and took me on
With a plain riding suit and an ambling nag.
No, I'll be furnished something like myself.° *worthy of my birth*
And so farewell. For thy suit touching Knave's Acre,
When it is mine, 'tis thine.

MARALL I thank Your Worship.

Exit Wellborn.

How I was cozened in the calculation
Of this man's fortune! My master cozened too,
Whose pupil I am in the art of undoing men,
For that is our profession. Well, well, Master Wellborn,
You are of a sweet nature, and fit again to be cheated—
Which, if the Fates please, when you are possessed
Of the land and lady, you, sans° question, shall be. *without*
I'll presently think of the means. *Walk by, musing.*

Enter Overreach.

OVERREACH [*to a servant within*] Sirrah, take my horse.
I'll walk to get me an appetite. 'Tis but a mile,
And exercise will keep me from being pursy.°— *short-winded*
Ha! Marall! Is he conjuring? Perhaps
The knave has wrought° the prodigal to do *worked on*
Some outrage on himself, and now he feels
Compunction in his conscience for't. No matter,
So° it be done.—Marall! *Provided*

MARALL Sir?

OVERREACH How succeed we
In our plot on Wellborn?

MARALL Never better, sir.

OVERREACH Has he hanged or drowned himself?

MARALL No, sir, he lives—
Lives once more to be made a prey to you,
A greater prey than ever.

OVERREACH Art thou in thy wits?
If thou art, reveal this miracle, and briefly.

MARALL A lady, sir, is fall'n in love with him.

OVERREACH With him? What lady?

MARALL The rich Lady Allworth.

OVERREACH Thou dolt! How dar'st thou speak this?

MARALL I speak truth;
And I do so but once a year, unless

It be to you, sir. We dined with Her Ladyship,
I thank His Worship.
OVERREACH His Worship!
MARALL As I live, sir,
I dined with him at the great lady's table,
Simple° as I stand here, and saw when she kissed him, *Unworthy creature*
And would at his request have kissed me too,
But I was not so audacious as some youths are
And° dare do anything, be it ne'er so absurd, *Who*
And sad° after performance. *regretful*
OVERREACH Why, thou rascal,
To tell me these impossibilities!
Dine at her table? And kiss him? Or thee?
Impudent varlet! Have not I myself,
To whom great countesses' doors have oft flew open,
Ten times attempted, since her husband's death,
In vain to see her, though I came—a suitor?
And yet Your good Solicitorship° and rogue Wellborn *you, lawyer that you are*
Were brought into her presence, feasted with her!
But that I know thee a dog, that cannot blush,
This most incredible lie would call up one
On thy buttermilk° cheeks. *sallow*
MARALL Shall I not trust my eyes, sir?
Or taste? I feel her good cheer in my belly.
OVERREACH You shall feel me,° if you give not over, sirrah. *feel my blows*
Recover your brains again, and be no more gulled° *fooled*
With a beggar's plot, assisted by the aids
Of servingmen and chambermaids—for beyond these
Thou never saw'st a woman—or I'll quit° you *discharge*
From my employments.[3]
MARALL Will you credit° this yet? *believe*
On my confidence of their marriage, I offered Wellborn
(*Aside*) I would give a crown° now I durst say "His Wor- *(worth 5 shillings)*
ship"—
My nag and twenty pounds.
OVERREACH Did you so, idiot?
Strikes him down.
Was this the way to work him to despair,
Or rather to cross me?° *vex me*
MARALL Will Your Worship kill me?
OVERREACH No, no; but drive the lying spirit out of you.
MARALL He's gone.° *i.e., No more lying*
OVERREACH I have done, then. Now, forgetting
Your late imaginery feast and lady,
Know my Lord Lovell dines with me tomorrow.
Be careful naught be wanting° to receive° him, *lacking / entertain*
And bid my daughter's women trim her up;
Though they paint her,[4] so she catch the lord, I'll thank 'em.
There's a piece for my late blows. [*He gives money.*]

3. Overreach assumes that one of Lady Allworth's chambermaids has impersonated her at dinner as part of a wretched plot, concocted by Wellborn, to deceive the easily fooled Marall, who has had no aquaintance with persons above the rank of servants, into bringing this story of the dinner to Overreach.

4. Even if they resort to using cosmetics to add to her attractiveness. (Cosmetics were widely viewed as deceptive and thus sinful.)

MARALL (*aside*) I must yet suffer:
But there may be a time—
OVERREACH Do you grumble?
MARALL No, sir.
[*Exeunt.*]

3.1

[*Enter*] *Lovell, Allworth,* [*and*] *servants.*

LOVELL Walk the horses down the hill. Something in private
I must impart to Allworth. *Exeunt servii.*° — *servants*
ALLWORTH O my lord,
What sacrifice of reverence, duty, watching,° — *watchfulness*
Although° I could put off the use of sleep — *Even though*
And ever wait on your commands to serve 'em,° — *execute them*
What dangers, though in ne'er so horrid shapes,
Nay, death itself, though I should run to meet it,
Can I, and with a thankful willingness, suffer,
But still the retribution° will fall short — *requital*
Of your bounties show'red upon me!
LOVELL Loving youth,
Till what I purpose be put into act,
Do not o'erprize it.° Since you have trusted me — *(my kindness to you)*
With your soul's nearest—nay, her dearest—secret,
Rest confident 'tis in a cabinet locked
Treachery shall never open. I have found you
(For so much to your face I must profess,
Howe'er you guard° your modesty with a blush for't) — *adorn; preserve*
More zealous in your love and service to me
Than I have been in my rewards.
ALLWORTH Still° great ones, — *Ever*
Above my merit.
LOVELL Such your gratitude calls 'em;
Nor am I of that harsh and rugged temper
As some great men are taxed with,° who imagine — *accused of being*
They part from° the respect due to their honors — *forego*
If they use not all such as follow 'em,
Without distinction of their births, like slaves.
I am not so conditioned.° I can make — *constituted*
A fitting difference between my footboy
And a gentleman by want° compelled to serve me. — *financial need*
ALLWORTH 'Tis thankfully acknowledged. You have been
More like a father to me than a master.
Pray you, pardon the comparison.
LOVELL I allow it;
And, to give you assurance I am pleased in't,
My carriage and demeanor to your mistress,° — *sweetheart*
Fair Margaret, shall truly witness for me
I can command my passions.
ALLWORTH 'Tis a conquest
Few lords can boast of when they are tempted.—Oh!
LOVELL Why do you sigh? Can you be doubtful of me?

3.1. At some distance from Overreach's house (see lines 99–100).

By that fair name I in the wars have purchased,
And all my actions hitherto untainted,
I will not be more true to mine own honor
Than to my Allworth.

ALLWORTH As you are the brave Lord Lovell,
Your bare word only given is an assurance
Of more validity and weight to me
Than all the oaths bound up with imprecations
Which, when they would deceive, most courtiers practice.
Yet, being° a man (for, sure, to style you more *you being*
Would relish of° gross flattery), I am forced, *smack of*
Against my° confidence of your worth and virtues, *Despite my*
To doubt—nay, more—to fear.

LOVELL So young, and jealous?

ALLWORTH Were you to encounter with a single foe,
The victory were certain; but to stand
The charge of two such potent enemies,
At once assaulting you, as wealth and beauty,
And those two seconded with power, is odds
Too great for Hercules.

LOVELL Speak your doubts and fears,
Since you will nourish 'em, in plainer language,
That I may understand 'em.

ALLWORTH What's your will,
Though I lend arms against myself (provided
They may advantage you) must be obeyed.[1]
My much loved lord, were Margaret only fair,
The cannon of her more than earthly° form, *her angelic*
Though mounted high, commanding all beneath it,
And rammed with bullets of her sparkling eyes,
Of all the bulwarks that defend your senses
Could batter none but that which guards your sight.[2]
But when the well-tuned accents of her tongue
Make music to you, and with numerous° sounds *musical*
Assault your hearing (such as if Ulysses
Now lived again, howe'er he stood the Sirens,
Could not resist),[3] the combat must grow doubtful
Between your reason and rebellious passions.
Add this too; when you feel her touch and breath,
Like a soft western wind when it glides o'er
Arabia creating gums and spices,
And, in the van,° the nectar of her lips *vanguard*
Which you must taste, bring the battalia° on, *army*
Well armed, and strongly lined° with her discourse *reinforced*
And knowing manners, to give entertainment—
Hippolytus himself would leave Diana

1. What you wish must be obeyed, if my words can assist you, even if it means my risking my own happiness (by describing Margaret's charms and thus possibly exciting your own interest in her).
2. If Margaret were only beautiful, that formidable weaponry, mounted (in the military metaphor) in an elevated position and thus able to command the whole terrain lying below, and using her eyes as ammunition, would assault nothing more than your physical sight.
3. In the *Odyssey*, Book 12, Homer describes how Odysseus, or Ulysses (the Latin version of the name), had his sailors tie him to the mast of their ship so that he could listen to the ravishing song of the Sirens, who were fabled to lure ships to their destruction on rocks by their irresistible singing, without throwing himself overboard, while the sailors rowed with their ears plugged.

To follow such a Venus.[4]
LOVELL Love hath made you
Poetical, Allworth.
ALLWORTH Grant all these beat off[5]
(Which, if it be in man to do, you'll do it),
Mammon, in Sir Giles Overreach,[6] steps in
With heaps of ill-got gold, and so much land,
To make her more remarkable, as would tire
A falcon's wings in one day to fly over.
O my good lord, these powerful aids, which would
Make a misshapen Negro beautiful
(Yet are but ornaments to give her° luster *(Margaret)*
That in herself is all perfection), must
Prevail for her.° I here release your trust.[7] *Make her irresistible*
'Tis happiness enough for me to serve you
And sometimes with chaste eyes to look upon her.
LOVELL Why, shall I swear?[8]
ALLWORTH Oh, by no means, my lord;
And wrong not so your judgment to the world
As from your fond indulgence to a boy,
Your page, your servant, to refuse a blessing
Divers great men are rivals for.
LOVELL Suspend
Your judgment till the trial.° How far is it *test*
T'Overreach' house?
ALLWORTH At the most, some half hour's riding;
You'll soon be there.
LOVELL And you the sooner freed
From your jealous fears.
ALLWORTH Oh, that I durst but hope it!
Exeunt.

3.2

[*Enter*] *Overreach, Greedy,* [*and*] *Marall.*

OVERREACH Spare for no cost. Let my dressers° crack with the weight *kitchen tables*
Of curious viands.° *dainty dishes*
GREEDY Store indeed's no sore,° sir. *Plenty's a good thing*
OVERREACH That proverb fits your stomach, Master Greedy.
And let no plate be seen but what's pure gold,
Or such whose workmanship exceeds the matter° *material*
That it is made of. Let my choicest linen
Perfume the room, and, when we wash, the water,° *may the water*
With precious powders mixed, so please my lord
That he may with envy wish to bathe so ever.
MARALL 'Twill be very chargeable.° *costly*
OVERREACH Avaunt, you drudge!

4. Hippolytus was a chaste worshiper of Artemis, or Diana, with whom Phaedra, wife of Theseus, fell tragically in love.
5. Even supposing you were able to fend off all these amorous assaults.
6. The very embodiment of greedy wealth, in the person of Overreach.
7. I here release you from your promise to aid me in my wooing of Margaret.
8. Shall I swear not to pursue Margaret myself?
3.2. Overreach's house.

Now all my labored ends are at the stake,
Is't a time to think of thrift? Call in my daughter.
[*Exit Marall.*]
And, Master Justice, since you love choice dishes,
And plenty of 'em—
GREEDY As I do indeed, sir,
Almost as much as to give thanks° for 'em. *say grace (see 1.3.17)*
OVERREACH I do confer that providence,° with my power *(looking after the feast)*
Of absolute command to have abundance,
To your best care.
GREEDY I'll punctually discharge it
And give the best directions. Now am I
In mine own conceit° a monarch, at the least *thought, opinion*
Archpresident of the boiled, the roast, the baked,
For which I will eat often, and give thanks,
When my belly's braced up like a drum—and that's pure justice.
Exit Greedy.
OVERREACH It must be so. Should the foolish girl prove modest,
She may spoil all. She had it not from me,
But from her mother. I was ever forward,
As she must be, and therefore I'll prepare her.

[*Enter*] *Margaret.*

Alone—and let your women wait without.
MARGARET Your pleasure, sir?
OVERREACH Ha, this is a neat dressing!
These orient pearls, and diamonds well placed too!
The gown affects° me not; it should have been *pleases*
Embroidered o'er and o'er with flowers of gold;
But these rich jewels and quaint fashion help it.
And how below? Since oft the wanton eye,
The face observed, descends unto the foot,
Which, being well proportioned, as yours is,
Invites° as much as perfect white and red, *Entices*
Though without art. How like you your new woman,
The Lady Downfall'n?
MARGARET Well, for a companion;
Not as a servant.
OVERREACH Is she humble, Meg?
And careful too, her ladyship° forgotten? *rank as a lady*
MARGARET I pity her fortune.
OVERREACH Pity her? Trample on her!
I took her up in an old tamin° gown, *coarse woolen*
(Even starved for want of twopenny chops)° to serve thee; *poor fare*
And if I understand she but repines
To do thee any duty, though ne'er so servile,
I'll pack her to her knight, where I have lodged him,
Into the Counter,° and there let 'em howl together. *a London debtors' prison*
MARGARET You know your own ways; but, for° me, I blush *as for*
When I command her that was once attended
With persons not inferior to myself
In birth.
OVERREACH In birth? Why, art thou not my daughter?
The blest child of my industry and wealth?
Why, foolish girl, was't not to make thee great

That I have ran, and still pursue, those ways
That hale° down curses on me, which I mind not? *pull; hail*
Part with these humble thoughts, and apt° thyself *fit, adapt*
To the noble state° I labor to advance thee, *state to which*
Or, by my hopes to see thee "Honorable,"
I will adopt a stranger to° my heir *as, for*
And throw thee from my care. Do not provoke me.

MARGARET I will not, sir. Mold me which way you please.

Enter Greedy.

OVERREACH How! Interrupted?
GREEDY 'Tis matter of importance.
The cook, sir, is self-willed and will not learn
From my experience. There's a fawn brought in, sir,
And, for my life, I cannot make him roast it
With a Norfolk dumpling in the belly of it.
And, sir, we wise men know, without the dumpling
'Tis not worth threepence.
OVERREACH Would it were whole in thy belly
To stuff it out! Cook it any way. Prithee leave me.
GREEDY Without order for the dumpling?
OVERREACH Let it be dumpled
Which way thou wilt, or tell him I will scald him
In his own cauldron.
GREEDY I had lost my stomach,
Had I lost my Mistress Dumpling I'll give thanks for.° *(see 15 and 22)*

Exit Greedy.

OVERREACH But to our business, Meg. You have heard who dines here?
MARGARET I have, sir.
OVERREACH 'Tis an honorable man,
A lord, Meg, and commands a regiment
Of soldiers, and, what's rare, is one himself,
A bold and understanding one; and to be
A lord and a good leader in one volume° *in one person*
Is granted unto few but such as rise° up *raise*
The kingdom's glory.

Enter Greedy.

GREEDY I'll resign my office
If I be not better obeyed.
OVERREACH 'Slight,° art thou frantic? *By God's light*
GREEDY Frantic? 'Twould make me a frantic, and stark mad,
Were I not a Justice of Peace, and Coram° too, *Quorum (see 1.1.34 and n)*
Which this rebellious cook cares not a straw for.
There are a dozen of woodcocks—
OVERREACH Make thyself
Thirteen, the baker's dozen.[1]
GREEDY I am contented,
So they may be dressed to my mind.° He has found out *prepared as I wish*
A new device for sauce, and will not dish° 'em *serve*
With toasts and butter. My father was a tailor,

1. Overreach sardonically groups Greedy with the woodcocks, proverbially stupid birds, to make up the baker's dozen, or thirteen. Greedy is unaware of the insult.

And my name, though a justice, Greedy Woodcock;
And ere I'll see my lineage so abused,
I'll give up my commission.
OVERREACH [*to the cook within*] Cook! Rogue, obey him!
[*To Greedy*] I have given the word; pray you, now remove yourself
To a collar of brawn,° and trouble me no farther. *neck of a boar*
GREEDY I will, and meditate what to eat at dinner.
Exit Greedy.
OVERREACH And as I said, Meg, when this gull disturbed us,
This honorable lord, this colonel,
I would have thy husband.
MARGARET There's too much disparity
Between his quality° and mine to hope it. *rank*
OVERREACH I more than hope't, and doubt not to effect it.
Be thou no enemy to thyself; my wealth
Shall weigh his titles down,° and make you equals. *outweigh his titles*
Now for the means to assure him thine. Observe me:
Remember he's a courtier and a soldier
And not to be trifled with, and therefore when
He comes to woo you, see you do not coy it.° *act coyly*
This mincing modesty hath spoiled many a match
By a first refusal, in vain after° hoped for. *afterward*
MARGARET You'll have me, sir, preserve the distance that
Confines a virgin?
OVERREACH Virgin me no virgins!° *(cf. 1.3.28, 5.1.136)*
I must have you lose that name, or you lose me.
I will have you private°—start not—I say, private. *intimate*
If thou art my true daughter, not a bastard,
Thou wilt venture alone with one man, though he came
Like Jupiter to Semele,[2] and come off° too; *come out ahead*
And therefore when he kisses you, kiss close.
MARGARET I have heard this is the strumpet's fashion, sir,
Which I must never learn.
OVERREACH Learn anything,
And from any creature that may make thee great—
From the devil himself.
MARGARET This is but devilish doctrine.
OVERREACH Or if his blood grow hot, suppose he offer° *attempt*
Beyond this, do not you stay till it cool,
But meet his ardor; if a couch be near,
Sit down on't, and invite him.
MARGARET In your house?
Your own house, sir? For heav'n's sake, what are you then?
Or what shall I be, sir?
OVERREACH Stand not on form.
Words are no substances.
MARGARET Though you could dispense
With your own honor, cast aside religion,
The hopes of heaven or fear of hell, excuse me
In worldly policy,° this is not the way *In terms of prudence*
To make me his wife; his whore, I grant it may do.

2. Semele, loved by Zeus (Roman Jupiter), begged him to visit her in all the splendor of his godhead. When he did so, reluctantly, she was consumed by lightning.

My maiden honor so soon yielded up,
Nay, prostituted, cannot but assure him
I that am light to him will not hold weight
When he is tempted by others;[3] so, in judgment,
When to his lust I have given up my honor,
He must and will forsake me.

OVERREACH How? Forsake thee?
Do I wear a sword for fashion?° Or is this arm — *for form's sake only*
Shrunk up? Or withered? Does there live a man
Of that large list° I have encountered with — *list of men*
Can truly say I e'er gave inch of ground
Not purchased with his blood that did oppose me?
Forsake thee when the thing is done? He dares not.
Give me but proof he has enjoyed thy person,
Though all his captains, echoes to his will,° — *his yes-men*
Stood armed by his side to justify the wrong,
And he himself in the head of his bold troop,
Spite of his lordship and his colonelship,
Or the judge's favor, I will make him render
A bloody and a strict account, and force him,
By marrying thee, to cure thy wounded honor.
I have said it.° — *I have sworn*

Enter Marall.

MARALL Sir, the man of honor's come
Newly alighted.° — *(from his horse)*

OVERREACH [*to Margaret*] In, without reply,
And do as I command, or thou art lost. *Exit Margaret.*
Is the loud music I gave order for
Ready to receive him?

MARALL 'Tis, sir.

OVERREACH Let 'em sound
A princely welcome. [*Exit Marall.*]
[*To himself*] Roughness, awhile leave me,
For fawning now—a stranger to my nature—
Must make way for me.° *Loud music.* — *pave my way to success*

Enter Lovell, Greedy, Allworth, [and] Marall.

LOVELL Sir, you meet your trouble.[4]

OVERREACH What you are pleased to style so° is an honor — *i.e., as "trouble"*
Above my worth and fortunes.

ALLWORTH [*aside*] Strange. So humble!

OVERREACH A justice of peace, my lord. *Presents Greedy to him.*

LOVELL [*to Greedy*] Your hand, good sir.

GREEDY [*aside*] This is a lord, and some think this° a favor; — *(shaking his hand)*
But I had rather have my hand in my dumpling.

OVERREACH Room° for my lord! — *Make room*

LOVELL I miss, sir, your fair daughter
To crown my welcome.

OVERREACH May it please my lord
To taste a glass of Greek wine first, and suddenly° — *quickly, soon*

3. My yielding to him so quickly can only assure him that I, who was so easily won by him, will not have the moral authority to keep him loyal to me when he is tempted by other women.

4. A polite way of saying, "I'm sorry to trouble you."

She shall attend my lord.

LOVELL You'll be obeyed,° sir. *i.e., As you wish*

Exeunt omnes praeter° Overreach. *all except*

OVERREACH 'Tis to my wish.° As soon as come, ask for her!— *just as I hoped*
[*Calling*] Why, Meg! Meg Overreach!

[*Enter Margaret.*]

How! Tears in your eyes?
Ha! Dry 'em quickly, or I'll dig 'em out.
Is this a time to whimper? Meet that greatness
That flies into thy bosom! Think what 'tis
For me to say, "My honorable daughter,"
And thou, when I stand bare, to say "Put on,"° *"Put on your hat"*
Or, "Father, you forget yourself." No more,° *No more tears*
But be instructed, or expect—He comes!

Enter Lovell, Greedy, Allworth, [*and*] *Marall. They salute.*

A black-browed girl,[5] my lord.

LOVELL [*kissing Margaret*] As I live, a rare one.

ALLWORTH [*aside*] He's took° already! I am lost. *smitten*

OVERREACH [*aside*] That kiss
Came twanging off; I like it. [*To the others*] Quit the room!

The rest [*Greedy, Allworth, and Marall, go*] *off.*

A little bashful, my good lord, but you,
I hope, will teach her boldness.

LOVELL I am happy
In such a scholar, but—

OVERREACH I am past learning,
And therefore leave you to yourselves. (*To his daughter*)
Remember! *Exit Overreach.*

LOVELL You see, fair lady, your father is solicitous
To have you change the barren name of virgin
Into a hopeful wife.

MARGARET His haste, my lord,
Holds no power o'er my will.

LOVELL But o'er your duty.

MARGARET Which, forced too much, may break.

LOVELL Bend rather, sweetest.
Think of your years.

MARGARET Too few to match with yours;
And choicest fruits, too soon plucked, rot and wither.

LOVELL Do you think I am old?

MARGARET I am sure I am too young.

LOVELL I can advance you.

MARGARET To a hill of sorrow,
Where every hour I may expect to fall,
But never hope° firm footing. You are noble, *hope to find*
I of a low descent, however rich;
And tissues matched with scarlet suit but ill.[6]

5. A dark complexion was considered unhandsome in women. Overreach pretends to deprecate Margaret's beauty.

6. And cloth richly interwoven with gold or silver (such as aristocrats might wear) matches poorly with the scarlet robes worn by wealthy London citizens as badges of civic office. (Aristocrats might also wear scarlet; cf. 4.1.222–25.) Margaret's point is that she is of too low a social station to marry into the nobility.

O my good lord, I could say more, but that
I dare not trust these walls.

LOVELL Pray you, trust my ear, then.
[*They whisper.*]

Enter Overreach, listening.

OVERREACH Close at it! Whispering! This is excellent!
And, by their postures, a consent on both parts.

Enter Greedy. [*He and Overreach converse, unnoticed at first by Lovell and Margaret.*]

GREEDY Sir Giles, Sir Giles!

OVERREACH The great fiend stop that clapper!

GREEDY It must ring out, sir, when my belly rings noon.
The baked meats are run out,° the roast turned powder. *have overflowed the crust*

OVERREACH I shall powder you.

GREEDY Beat me to dust, I care not;
In such a cause as this, I'll die a martyr.

OVERREACH Marry, and shall, you barathrum of the shambles![7]
Strikes him.

GREEDY How! Strike a justice of peace? 'Tis petty treason,
Edwardi quinto.[8] But that° you are my friend, *Were it not that*
I could commit you without bail or mainprize.[9]

OVERREACH Leave your bawling, sir, or I shall commit you
Where you shall not dine today. Disturb my lord
When he is in discourse?

GREEDY Is't a time to talk
When we should be munching?

LOVELL [*hearing something*] Ha! I heard some noise.

OVERREACH [*privately to Greedy*] Mum, villain, vanish! Shall we break a bargain
Almost made up?° *Thrust Greedy off* [*exiting with him*]. *concluded, settled*

LOVELL Lady, I understand you,
And rest most happy in your choice, believe it;
I'll be a careful pilot to direct
Your yet uncertain bark° to a port of safety. *a small sailing vessel*

MARGARET So shall Your Honor save two lives, and bind us
Your slaves forever.

LOVELL I am in the act rewarded,
Since it is good; howe'er, you must put on
An amorous carriage° towards me to delude *demeanor*
Your subtle father.

MARGARET I am prone° to that. *inclined, disposed*

LOVELL Now break we off our conference.—Sir Giles!
Where is Sir Giles?

Enter Overreach and the rest [*Greedy, Marall, and Allworth*].

OVERREACH My noble lord! And how
Does Your Lordship find her?

7. You devouring gulf of the slaughter shops, i.e., you glutton. (Barathrum was a deep pit in ancient Athens into which condemned criminals were thrown.)

8. According to a law enacted in the fifth year of Edward VI's reign (1552).

9. Mainprize is the process of having someone procure the release of a prisoner by offering to act as guarantor for the prisoner's court appearance.

LOVELL Apt, Sir Giles, and coming,° *forthcoming, not shy*
And I like her the better.
OVERREACH So do I too.
LOVELL Yet, should we take forts at the first assault,
'Twere poor in the defendant.[1] I must confirm her
With a love letter or two, which I must have
Delivered by my page,° an you give way° to't. *(Tom Allworth) / agree*
OVERREACH With all my soul! A towardly° gentleman.— *promising*
Your hand, good Master Allworth. Know my house
Is ever open to you.
ALLWORTH (*aside*) 'Twas shut till now.
OVERREACH Well done, well done, my honorable daughter!
Thou'rt so° already. Know this gentle youth, *i.e., "honorable"*
And cherish him, my honorable daughter.
MARGARET I shall, with my best care.
Noise within as of a coach.
OVERREACH A coach!
GREEDY More stops
Before we go to dinner! Oh, my guts!

Enter Lady [Allworth] and Wellborn.

LADY ALLWORTH [*privately to Wellborn*] If I find welcome,
You share in it; if not, I'll back again,
Now I know your ends, for I come armed for all
Can° be objected. *That can*
LOVELL How! The Lady Allworth!
OVERREACH And thus attended!
Lovell salutes the Lady [Allworth];
the Lady salutes Margaret.
MARALL [*aside to Overreach*] No, I am a dolt!
The spirit of lies had ent'red me![2]
OVERREACH [*aside to Marall*] Peace, patch!° *fool*
'Tis more than wonder! An astonishment
That does possess me wholly!
LOVELL Noble lady,
This is a favor, to prevent° my visit, *anticipate*
The service of my life can never equal.
LADY ALLWORTH My lord, I laid wait for° you, and much hoped *laid in wait for*
You would have made my poor house your first inn;
And therefore doubting° that you might forget me, *fearing*
Or too long dwell here, having such ample cause
In this unequalled beauty° for your stay, *(Margaret)*
And fearing to trust any but myself
With the relation of my service° to you, *making my compliments*
I borrowed so much from my long restraint
And took the air in person to invite you.[3]
LOVELL Your bounties are so great they rob me, madam,
Of words to give you thanks.
LADY ALLWORTH Good Sir Giles Overreach! *Salutes him.*
How dost thou, Marall? [*To Greedy*] Liked you my meat so ill

1. It would detract from the honor of the defending party, i.e., the lady and her modesty, if I were to succeed in my first attempt.
2. I.e., No, you were right, I was lying when I informed you that Wellborn had won the affection of Lady Allworth! (Said sarcastically and ironically; see 2.3.74 ff.)
3. I made an exception to my self-imposed staying at home (in mourning for my dead husband) and came here to invite you personally to visit me.

You'll dine no more with me?
GREEDY I will, when you please,
An it like° Your Ladyship. *If it please*
LADY ALLWORTH When you please, Master Greedy;
If meat can do it, you shall be satisfied.—
And now, my lord, pray take into your knowledge° *acquaintance*
This gentleman. (*Presents Wellborn.*) Howe'er his outside's coarse,
His inward linings are as fine and fair
As any man's. Wonder not I speak at large.° *freely; in large praise*
And howsoe'er his humor carries° him *whim induces*
To be thus accoutred, or what taint soever
For his wild life hath stuck upon his fame,° *reputation*
He may, ere long, with boldness rank himself
With some that have contemned° him.—Sir Giles Overreach, *scorned*
If I am welcome, bid him so.
OVERREACH My nephew!
He has been too long a stranger. [*To Wellborn*] Faith,° you have; *In faith*
Pray, let it be mended.
Lovell conferring [*privately*] *with Wellborn.*
MARALL [*aside to Overreach*] Why, sir, what do you mean?
This is rogue Wellborn, monster, prodigy,
That should hang or drown himself,° no man of worship, *(see 2.1.90–119)*
Much less your nephew.
OVERREACH [*aside to Marall*] Well, sirrah, we shall reckon
For this° hereafter. *For your twitting me thus*
MARALL [*aside*] I'll not lose my jeer,
Though I be beaten dead for't.
WELLBORN [*privately to Lovell*] Let my silence plead
In my excuse, my lord, till better leisure
Offer itself to hear a full relation
Of my poor fortunes.
LOVELL [*privately to Wellborn*] I would hear, and help 'em.° *i.e., your fortunes*
OVERREACH [*aloud*] Your dinner waits you.
LOVELL Pray you lead; we follow.
LADY ALLWORTH [*to Wellborn, as he hesitates*] Nay, you are my guest. Come, dear Master Wellborn.
Exeunt. Manet° Greedy. *Remains onstage*
GREEDY "Dear Master Wellborn"! So she said. Heav'n! Heav'n!
If my belly would give me leave, I could ruminate
All day on this. I have granted twenty warrants
To have him committed, from all prisons in the shire
To Nottingham jail; and now "Dear Master Wellborn"!
And "My good nephew"! But I play the fool
To stand here prating, and forget my dinner.

Enter Marall.

Are they set,° Marall? *seated at table*
MARALL Long since. Pray you a word, sir.
GREEDY No wording° now. *idle chatter*
MARALL In troth, I must. My master,
Knowing you are his good friend, makes bold with you
And does entreat you, more guests being come in
Than he expected, especially his nephew,
The table being full too, you would excuse him° *pardon this request*

And sup with him on the cold meat.

GREEDY How! No dinner, After all my care?

MARALL 'Tis but a penance for A meal.[4] Besides, you broke your fast.° *you ate already*

GREEDY That was But a bit to stay my stomach. A man in commission° *A justice of the peace* Give place to a tatterdemalion?° *ragged wretch*

MARALL No bug-words,° sir. *threatening, abusive words* Should His Worship hear you—

GREEDY Lose my dumpling too? And buttered toasts, and woodcocks?

MARALL Come, have patience. If you will dispense a little with your worship,° *dignity* And sit with the waiting-women, you have dumpling, Woodcock, and buttered toasts too.

GREEDY This revives me. I will gorge there sufficiently.

MARALL This is the way, sir. *Exeunt.*

3.3

[*Enter*] *Overreach as from dinner.*

OVERREACH She's° caught! Oh, women! She neglects my lord, *Lady Allworth is*
And all her compliments applied° to Wellborn! *are directed*
The garments of her widowhood laid by,
She now appears as glorious as the spring.
Her eyes fixed on him, in the wine she drinks,
He being her pledge,° she sends him burning kisses, *the one she toasts*
And sits on thorns till she be private with him.
She leaves my meat to feed upon his looks,
And, if in our discourse he be but named,
From her a deep sigh follows. But why grieve I
At this? It makes° for me; if she prove his, *provides opportunity*
All that is hers is mine, as I will work him.

Enter Marall.

MARALL Sir, the whole board is troubled at your rising.

OVERREACH No matter; I'll excuse it.° Prithee, Marall, *I'll invent an excuse* Watch an occasion to invite my nephew To speak with me in private.

MARALL Who? The rogue The lady scorned to look on?

OVERREACH You are a wag.° *You're a joker*

Enter Lady [*Allworth*] *and Wellborn.*

MARALL [*privately to Overreach*] See, sir, she's come, and cannot be without him.

LADY ALLWORTH [*to Overreach*] With your favor, sir, after a plenteous dinner, I shall make bold to walk a turn or two In your rare° garden. *excellent*

4. It's doing without your meal only this once.

3.3. Overreach's house still.

OVERREACH There's an arbor too,
If Your Ladyship please to use it.
LADY ALLWORTH Come, Master Wellborn.
Exeunt Lady [Allworth] and Wellborn.
OVERREACH Grosser and grosser! Now I believe the poet° (Ovid)
Feigned not, but was historical, when he wrote
Pasiphaë was enamored of a bull.[1]
This lady's lust's more monstrous.—

Enter Lovell, Margaret, and the rest [including Allworth, Greedy, and servants].

My good lord,
Excuse my manners.° (in leaving the table)
LOVELL There needs none, Sir Giles—
I may ere long say "father," when it pleases
My dearest mistress to give warrant to it.
OVERREACH She shall seal° to it, my lord, and make me happy. i.e., sign and seal
MARGARET My lady is returned.

Enter Wellborn and the Lady [Allworth].

LADY ALLWORTH [*to servants*] Provide my coach;
I'll instantly away.—My thanks, Sir Giles, [*Exeunt servants.*]
For my entertainment.
OVERREACH 'Tis your nobleness
To think it such.
LADY ALLWORTH I must do you a further wrong
In taking away your honorable guest.
LOVELL I wait on you, madam.—Farewell, good Sir Giles.
LADY ALLWORTH Good Mistress Margaret!—Nay, come, Master Wellborn,
I must not leave you behind; in sooth, I must not.
OVERREACH Rob me not, madam, of all joys at once.
Let my nephew stay behind; he shall have my coach,
And, after some small conference between us,
Soon overtake Your Ladyship.
LADY ALLWORTH [*to Wellborn*] Stay not long, sir.
LOVELL [*kissing Margaret*] This parting kiss. You shall every day hear from me
By my faithful page.
ALLWORTH 'Tis a service I am proud of.
Exeunt Lovell, Lady Allworth, Marall [and all the others except Overreach and Wellborn].
OVERREACH Daughter, to your chamber. [*Exit*] *Margaret.*
You may wonder, nephew,
After so long an enmity between us,
I should desire your friendship.
WELLBORN So I do, sir.
'Tis strange to me.
OVERREACH But I'll make it no wonder,
And, what is more, unfold my nature to you.
We worldly men, when we see friends and kinsmen
Past hope sunk in their fortunes, lend no hand

1. An angered Poseidon caused Pasiphaë to become enamored of a bull and to give birth to their monstrous offspring, the Minotaur. Ovid recorded the myth in his *Metamorphoses*, Book 8.

To lift 'em up, but rather set our feet
Upon their heads to press 'em to the bottom—
As, I must yield,° with you I practiced it. *confess*
But, now° I see you in a way to rise, *now that*
I can and will assist you. This rich lady
(And I am glad of't) is enamored of you;
'Tis too apparent, nephew.

WELLBORN No such thing;
Compassion rather, sir.

OVERREACH Well, in a word,
Because your stay is short, I'll have you seen
No more in this base shape;° nor shall she say *your threadbare attire*
She married you like a beggar, or in debt.

WELLBORN (*aside*) He'll run into the noose and save my labor.

OVERREACH You have a trunk of rich clothes, not far hence,
In pawn; I will redeem 'em. And, that° no clamor *so that*
May taint your credit° for your petty debts, *reputation*
You shall have a thousand pounds to cut 'em off,° *clear them*
And go a free man to the wealthy lady.

WELLBORN This done, sir, out of love, and no ends else—

OVERREACH As it is, nephew.

WELLBORN Binds me still° your servant. *ever*

OVERREACH No compliments; you are stayed for. Ere you've supped
You shall hear from me.—My coach, knaves, for my nephew!—
Tomorrow I will visit you.

WELLBORN Here's an uncle
In a man's extremes!° How much they do belie you *extremities*
That say you are hard-hearted!

OVERREACH My deeds, nephew,
Shall speak my love; what men report I weigh° not. *heed*
Exeunt.

4.1

[*Enter*] *Lovell* [*and*] *Allworth.*

LOVELL 'Tis well; give me my cloak. I now discharge you
From further service. Mind your own affairs;
I hope they will prove successful.

ALLWORTH What is blest
With your good wish, my lord, cannot but prosper.
Let aftertimes report, and to your honor,° *to your credit*
How much I stand engaged,° for I want° language *indebted / lack*
To speak my debt. Yet if a tear or two
Of joy for your much goodness can supply
My tongue's defects, I could—

LOVELL Nay, do not melt.° *melt into tears*
This ceremonial thanks to me's superfluous.

OVERREACH (*within*) Is my lord stirring?

LOVELL 'Tis he. Oh, here's your letter.° [*He gives Allworth a letter.*] Let him in. *(see 3.2.232–34)*

Enter Overreach, Greedy, [*and*] *Marall.*

4.1. Lady Allworth's house.

OVERREACH A good day to my lord!
LOVELL You are an early riser,
Sir Giles.
OVERREACH And reason:° to attend Your Lordship. *with good reason*
LOVELL And you too, Master Greedy, up so soon?
GREEDY In troth, my lord, after the sun is up
I cannot sleep, for I have a foolish stomach
That croaks for breakfast. With Your Lordship's favor,
I have a serious question to demand
Of my worthy friend Sir Giles.
LOVELL Pray you use your pleasure.
GREEDY How far, Sir Giles—and pray you, answer me
Upon your credit°—hold you it to be *belief, trust*
From your manor house to this of my Lady Allworth's?
OVERREACH Why, some four mile.
GREEDY How! Four mile? Good Sir Giles,
Upon your reputation, think better,
For, if you do abate but one half-quarter
Of five,[1] you do yourself the greatest wrong
That can be in the world; for four miles riding
Could not have raised so huge an appetite
As I feel gnawing on me.
MARALL Whether you ride
Or go afoot, you are that way still provided,
An it please Your Worship.
OVERREACH How now, sirrah? Prating
Before my lord? No difference?[2] Go to my nephew;
See all his debts discharged, and help His Worship° *(Wellborn)*
To fit on his rich suit.
MARALL [*aside*] I may fit you too;[3]
Tossed like a dog° still! *Exit Marall.* *(see 2.1.142)*
LOVELL I have writ this morning
A few lines to my mistress, your fair daughter.
OVERREACH 'Twill fire her, for she's wholly yours already.—
[*Giving a ring*] Sweet Master Allworth, take my ring—'twill carry you
To her presence, I dare warrant you—and there plead
For my good lord, if you shall find occasion.
That done, pray ride to Nottingham; get a license,
Still by this token.°—I'll have it dispatched, *(the ring)*
And suddenly, my lord, that I may say
My "Honorable," nay, "Right Honorable" daughter.
GREEDY [*to Allworth*] Take my advice, young gentleman; get your breakfast.
'Tis unwholesome to ride fasting. I'll eat with you,
And eat to purpose.° *in a businesslike fashion*
OVERREACH Some Fury's in that gut!
Hungry again! Did you not devour this morning
A shield of brawn[4] and a barrel of Colchester oysters?
GREEDY Why that was, sir, only to scour my stomach—

1. If you estimate a distance any less than four and seven-eighths miles.
2. (1) Do you make no difference between the way you address Greedy as "Your Worship" and me, to whom the title is due? or, (2) Do you make no allowance for the difference in rank between you and Lord Lovell?
3. I'll get even with you someday.
4. A boar's flank, cooked inside its thick skin.

A kind of a preparative. [*To Allworth*] Come, gentleman,
I will not have you feed like the hangman of Flushing,[5]
Alone, while I am here.
LOVELL [*to Allworth*] Haste your return.
ALLWORTH I will not fail, my lord.
GREEDY Nor I, to line
My Christmas coffer.° *Exeunt Greedy and Allworth.* *My stomach (lit., "box")*
OVERREACH To my wish, we are private.
I come not to make offer with my daughter
A certain portion;° that were poor and trivial. *specified dowry*
In one word, I pronounce all that is mine,
In lands or leases, ready coin or goods,
With her, my lord, comes to you; nor shall you have
One motive to induce you to believe
I live too long, since every year I'll add
Something unto the heap which shall be yours too.
LOVELL You are a right kind father.
OVERREACH You shall have reason
To think me such. How do you like this seat?° *residence, situation*
It is well wooded and well watered, the acres
Fertile and rich. Would it not serve for change
To entertain your friends in a summer progress?° *country tour*
What thinks my noble lord?
LOVELL 'Tis a wholesome air,
And well-built pile,° and she that's mistress of it *structure*
Worthy the large revenue.
OVERREACH She the mistress?
It may be so for a time; but let my lord
Say only that he likes it and would have it,
I say, ere long 'tis his.
LOVELL Impossible.
OVERREACH You do conclude too fast, not knowing me,
Nor the engines° that I work by. 'Tis not alone *contrivances*
The Lady Allworth's lands, for those once Wellborn's
(As, by her dotage on him, I know they will be)
Shall soon be mine; but point out any man's
In all the shire, and say they lie convenient
And useful for Your Lordship, and once more
I say aloud, they are yours.
LOVELL I dare not own
What's by unjust and cruel means extorted;
My fame and credit are more dear to me
Than so to expose 'em to be censured by
The public voice.
OVERREACH You run, my lord, no hazard.
Your reputation shall stand as fair
In all good men's opinions as now;
Nor can my actions, though condemned for ill,
Cast any foul aspersion upon yours.
For, though I do contemn report myself
As a mere sound, I still will be so tender
Of what concerns you in all points of honor

5. Hangmen were regarded as pariahs, and immigrants from the Netherlands (where Flushing is) were often resented for taking jobs away from Englishmen. One might not wish to eat with such a person.

That the° immaculate whiteness of your fame — *neither the*
Nor your unquestioned integrity
Shall e'er be sullied with one taint or spot
That may take from your innocence and candor.° — *immaculacy*
All my ambition is to have my daughter
Right Honorable, which my lord can make her.
And, might I live to dance upon my knee
A young Lord Lovell, born by her unto you,
I write *nil ultra*° to my proudest hopes. — *nothing beyond*
As for possessions and annual rents
Equivalent to maintain you in the port° — *style of living*
Your noble birth and present state requires,
I do remove that burden from your shoulders
And take it on mine own; for, though I ruin
The country to supply your riotous waste,
The scourge of prodigals—want—shall never find° you. — *reach, touch*

LOVELL Are you not frighted with the imprecations
And curses of whole families made wretched
By your sinister practices?

OVERREACH Yes, as rocks are
When foamy billows split themselves against
Their flinty ribs, or as the moon is moved
When wolves, with hunger pined,° howl at her brightness. — *starved, tormented*
I am of a solid temper, and, like these,° — *(rocks and the moon)*
Steer on a constant course. With mine own sword,
If called into the field, I can make that right
Which fearful enemies murmured at as wrong.
Now, for° these other piddling complaints — *as for*
Breathed out in bitterness, as when they call me
Extortioner, tyrant, cormorant,° or intruder — *a seabird; greedy person*
On my poor neighbor's right, or grand encloser
Of what was common to my private use;[6]
Nay, when my ears are pierced with widows' cries,
And undone° orphans wash with tears my threshold: — *financially ruined*
I only think what 'tis to have my daughter
Right Honorable, and 'tis a powerful charm
Makes me insensible of remorse, or pity,
Or the least sting of conscience.

LOVELL I admire° — *wonder at; admire*
The toughness of your nature.

OVERREACH 'Tis for you,
My lord, and for my daughter, I am marble.
Nay, more: if you will have my character
In little,° I enjoy more true delight — *In summary*
In my arrival to my wealth these° dark — *by these*
And crooked ways than you shall e'er take pleasure
In spending what my industry hath compassed.° — *achieved*
My haste commands me hence. In one word therefore:
Is it a match?

LOVELL I hope that is past doubt now.

OVERREACH Then rest secure. Not the hate of all mankind here,
Nor fear of what can fall on me hereafter,

6. Aristocrats' enclosure of previously common lands led to many hardships for those who depended on the land for their existence.

Shall make me study aught but your advancement
One story higher. An earl, if gold can do it!
Dispute not° my religion nor my faith. *Don't object to*
Though I am borne thus headlong by my will,
You may make choice of what belief you please;
To me they are equal. So, my lord, good morrow. *Exit.*
LOVELL He's gone. I wonder how the earth can bear
Such a portent!° I, that have lived a soldier, *prodigy, monster*
And stood the enemy's violent charge undaunted,
To hear this blasphemous beast am bathed all over
In a cold sweat. Yet, like a mountain, he,
Confirmed in atheistical assertions,
Is no more shaken than Olympus° is *mountain abode of the gods*
When angry Boreas° loads his° double head *north wind / (Olympus')*
With sudden drifts of snow.

Enter Amble, Lady [Allworth, and Waiting-]woman.

LADY ALLWORTH Save you, my lord!
Disturb I not your privacy?
LOVELL No, good madam.
For your own sake I am glad you came no sooner,
Since this bold, bad man, Sir Giles Overreach,
Made such a plain discovery° of himself, *revelation*
And read this morning such a devilish matins° *early morning service*
That I should think it a sin next° to his *second only*
But to repeat it.
LADY ALLWORTH I ne'er pressed, my lord,
On others' privacies; yet, against my will,
Walking for health sake in the gallery
Adjoining to your lodgings, I was made
(So vehement and loud he was) partaker
Of his tempting offers.
LOVELL Please you to command
Your servants hence, and I shall gladly hear
Your wiser counsel.
LADY ALLWORTH 'Tis, my lord, a woman's,
But true and hearty. [*To her servants*] Wait in the next room,
But be within call, yet not so near to° force me *as to*
To whisper my intents.
AMBLE We are taught better
By you, good madam.
WAITING-WOMAN And well know our distance.
LADY ALLWORTH Do so, and talk not; 'twill become° your breeding. *grace, befit*
Exeunt Amble and [Waiting-]woman.
Now, my good lord—if I may use my freedom
As to an honored friend?
LOVELL You lessen else
Your favor to me.
LADY ALLWORTH I dare then say thus:
As you are noble, howe'er common men
Make sordid wealth the object and sole end
Of their industrious aims, 'twill not agree
With those of eminent blood, who are engaged° *obligated*
More to prefer° their honors than to increase *promote, further*

The state° left to 'em by their ancestors, *estate*
To study° large additions to their fortunes *To seek*
And quite neglect their births; though I must grant
Riches well got to be a useful servant,
But a bad master.
LOVELL Madam, 'tis confessed.° *admitted, acknowledged*
But what infer you from it?
LADY ALLWORTH This, my lord:
That as all wrongs, though thrust into one scale,
Slide of themselves off when right fills the other,
And cannot bide the trial, so all wealth
(I mean if ill acquired), cemented to honor
By virtuous ways achieved and bravely purchased,° *nobly acquired*
Is but as rubbage° poured into a river *rubbish*
(Howe'er intended to make good° the bank), *strengthen, shore up*
Rend'ring the water that was pure before
Polluted and unwholesome.[7] I allow° *grant*
The heir of Sir Giles Overreach, Margaret,
A maid well qualified, and the richest match
Our north part° can make boast of; yet she cannot, *northern shire*
With all that she brings with her, fill° their mouths *stop*
That never will forget who was her father,
Or that my husband Allworth's lands and Wellborn's
(How wrung from both needs now no repetition)
Were real motive that more worked° Your Lordship *prompted*
To join your families than her form° and virtues. *beauty, shape*
You may conceive the rest.° *the rest of my speech*
LOVELL I do, sweet madam,
And long since have considered it. I know,
The sum of all that makes a just man happy
Consists in the well choosing of his wife;
And there, well to discharge it,° does require *make it succeed*
Equality of years, of birth, of fortune.
For beauty, being poor and not cried up[8]
By birth or wealth, can truly mix with neither;
And wealth, where there's such difference in years
And fair descent,° must make the yoke uneasy. *noble lineage*
But I come nearer.° *I come to particulars*
LADY ALLWORTH Pray you do, my lord.
LOVELL Were Overreach' states thrice centupled, his daughter
Millions of degrees much fairer than she is,
Howe'er I might urge precedents to excuse me,
I would not so adulterate my blood
By marrying Margaret, and so leave my issue
Made up of several pieces, one part scarlet
And the other London blue.[9] In my own tomb
I will inter° my name first. *bury (in oblivion)*
LADY ALLWORTH (*aside*) I am glad to hear this.
[*Aloud*] Why then, my lord, pretend you marriage to her?

7. I.e., Just as evil deeds cannot even out the balance when measured against virtuous deeds, so wrongly acquired wealth is a contaminant no matter how it may be linked (through marriage) to honor.
8. For beauty that is linked to poverty and is not extolled, raised in value.
9. One part displaying the scarlet worn by the aristocracy (cf. 3.2.199 and note) and the other wearing the blue color distinctive of the servant class.

Dissimulation but ties false knots
On that straight line by which you hitherto
Have measured all your actions.
LOVELL I make answer,
And aptly, with a question. Wherefore have you,
That since your husband's death have lived a strict
And chaste nun's life, on the sudden giv'n yourself
To visits and entertainments? Think you, madam,
'Tis not grown public conference?° Or° the favors *common gossip / Or that*
Which you too prodigally have thrown on Wellborn,
Being too reserved before, incur not censure?
LADY ALLWORTH I am innocent here,° and on my life I swear *in this*
My ends° are good. *intents*
LOVELL On my soul, so are mine
To Margaret; but leave both to the event.° *outcome*
And since this friendly privacy does serve
But as an offered means° unto ourselves *a good opportunity*
To search each other farther—you having shown
Your care of me, I my respect to you—
Deny me not, but still in chaste words, madam,
An afternoon's discourse.
LADY ALLWORTH So° I shall hear you. [*Exeunt.*] *i.e., Chastely*

4.2

[*Enter*] *Tapwell* [*and*] *Froth.*

TAPWELL Undone, undone! This was your counsel, Froth.
FROTH Mine! I defy thee. Did not Master Marall
(He has marred all, I am sure) strictly command us,
On pain of Sir Giles Overreach' displeasure,
To turn the gentleman° out of doors? *(Wellborn)*
TAPWELL 'Tis true.
But now he's his uncle's darling, and has got
Master Justice Greedy (since he filled his belly)
At his commandment to do anything.
Woe, woe to us!
FROTH He may prove merciful.
TAPWELL Troth, we do not deserve it at his hands.
Though he knew all the passages° of our house, *goings-on*
As the receiving of stol'n goods, and bawdry,
When he was rogue Wellborn no man would believe him,
And then his information could not hurt us;
But, now he is "Right Worshipful" again,
Who dares but° doubt his testimony? Methinks *so much as*
I see thee, Froth, already in a cart,
For a close° bawd, thine eyes e'en pelted out *secret*
With dirt and rotten eggs, and my hand hissing
(If I scape the halter)° with the letter *R* *hangman's noose*
Printed upon it.[1]
FROTH Would that were the worst!

4.2. In front of Tapwell's tavern.

1. Tapwell fears that he will see Froth punished and humiliated by being carted through the streets and that he himself will be branded on the hand with the letter *R*, for "Receiver" or "Rogue"—a common form of punishment for such crimes.

That were but nine days' wonder, as for credit,
We have none to lose;[2] but we shall lose the money
He owes us, and his custom°—there's the hell on't. *accustomed business*

TAPWELL He has summoned all his creditors by the drum,° *by public announcement*
And they swarm about him like so many soldiers
On the payday, and has found out such a new way
To pay his old debts as 'tis very likely
He shall be chronicled for it.

FROTH He deserves it,
More than ten pageants.° But are you sure His Worship *triumphal processions*
Comes this way to my lady's?

A cry within: "Brave° Master Wellborn!" *Splendid*

TAPWELL Yes, I hear him.

FROTH Be ready with your petition and present it
To His good Grace.

Enter Wellborn in a rich habit,° [Marall,] Greedy, Order, Furnace, [and] three Creditors. Tapwell, kneeling, delivers his bill of debt. *outfit*

WELLBORN How's this? Petitioned too?
But note what miracles the payment of
A little trash° and a rich suit of clothes *petty debts*
Can work upon these rascals! I shall be,
I think, Prince Wellborn.

MARALL When Your Worship's married,
You may be—I know what I hope to see you.

WELLBORN Then look thou for advancement.

MARALL To be known
Your Worship's bailiff is the mark I shoot at.

WELLBORN And thou shalt hit it.

MARALL Pray you, sir, dispatch
These needy followers, and, for my admittance,[3]
Provided you'll defend me from Sir Giles,
Whose service I am weary of, I'll say something
You shall give thanks for.

WELLBORN Fear me not° Sir Giles. *Do not fear*

This interim, Tapwell and Froth flattering and bribing Justice Greedy.

GREEDY Who? Tapwell? I remember thy wife brought me,
Last New Year's tide,° a couple of fat turkeys. *time*

TAPWELL And shall do every Christmas, let° Your Worship *provided*
But stand my friend now.

GREEDY How? With Master Wellborn?
I can do anything with him, on such terms.—
[*To Wellborn*] See you this honest couple? They are good souls
As ever drew out faucet.° Have they not *tapped a barrel*
A pair of honest faces?

WELLBORN I o'erheard you,
And the bribe he promised. You are cozened in 'em,
For of all the scum that grew rich by my riots,° *reveling*

2. Such public humiliations would be only a temporary hindrance, since we have no reputation ("credit") to lose.

3. And, in order to ensure your admitting me into your service.

This° for a most unthankful knave and this° *(Tapwell) / (Froth)*
For a base bawd and whore have worst deserved me,° *from me (see 1.1.81–84)*
And therefore speak not for 'em. By your place° *As justice of the peace*
You are rather° to do me justice. Lend me your ear. *bound rather*
[*Aside to him*] Forget his turkeys, and call in° his license, *revoke*
And at the next fair I'll give you a yoke of oxen
Worth all his poultry.

GREEDY I am changed on the sudden
In my opinion. [*To Tapwell*] Come near. Nearer, rascal!
[*To Wellborn*] And, now I view him better, did you e'er see
One look so like an arch-knave? His very countenance,
Should an understanding judge but look upon him,
Would hang him, though he were innocent.

TAPWELL [*and*] FROTH Worshipful sir!

GREEDY No, though the great Turk came, instead of turkeys,
To beg any favor, I am inexorable.
Thou hast an ill name.° Besides thy musty ale, *reputation*
That hath destroyed many of the King's liege° people, *faithful, loyal*
Thou never hadst in thy house, to stay mens' stomachs,° *satisfy men's appetites*
A piece of Suffolk cheese, or gammon° of bacon, *side*
Or any esculent,° as the learnèd call it, *eatables*
For their emolument,° but sheer drink only. *benefit, comfort*
For which gross fault, I here do damn° thy license, *condemn; revoke*
Forbidding thee ever to tap or draw;° *(from a cask)*
For instantly I will, in mine own person,
Command the constable to pull down thy sign,° *tavern sign*
And do it before I eat.

FROTH No mercy?

GREEDY Vanish!
If I show any, may my promised oxen gore me!

TAPWELL Unthankful knaves are ever so rewarded.

Exeunt Greedy, Tapwell, [*and*] *Froth.*

WELLBORN [*to the First Creditor*] Speak; what are you?

FIRST CREDITOR A decayed vintner,° sir, *bankrupt wine merchant*
That might have thrived, but that Your Worship broke° me *bankrupted*
With trusting you with muscadine° and eggs, *a wine*
And five-pound suppers, with your after-drinkings,° *drinks between meals*
When you lodged upon the Bankside.° *south bank of the Thames*

WELLBORN I remember.

FIRST CREDITOR I have not been hasty, nor e'er laid° to arrest you; *laid in wait*
And therefore, sir—

WELLBORN Thou art an honest fellow.
I'll set thee up again. [*To Order*] See his bill paid.—
What are you?

SECOND CREDITOR A tailor once, but now mere botcher.° *mender of clothes*
I gave you credit for a suit of clothes,
Which was all my stock, but, you failing in payment,
I was removed from the shop board,° and confined *tailor's workbench*
Under a stall.° *market or street stall*

WELLBORN [*to Order*] See him paid.—And botch no more.

SECOND CREDITOR I ask no interest, sir.

WELLBORN Such tailors need not;
If their bills are paid in one-and-twenty year,

They are seldom losers.[4] [*To Third Creditor*] Oh, I know thy face;
Thou wert my surgeon. You must tell no tales;
Those days are done.[5] I will pay you in private.
ORDER [*to Furnace*] A royal gentleman!
FURNACE [*to Order*] Royal as an emperor!
He'll prove a brave master. My good lady knew° *knew how*
To choose a man.
WELLBORN [*to Order*] See all men else discharged;° *See all creditors paid*
And since old debts are cleared by a new way,
A little bounty will not misbecome me.
[*Giving money to Furnace*] There's something, honest cook, for thy good breakfasts,
[*Giving money to Order*] And this for your respect.° *care, attention*
Take't; 'tis good gold,
And I able to spare it.
ORDER You are too munificent.
FURNACE [*to the others*] He was ever so.
WELLBORN Pray you, on before.° *go on and precede me*
THIRD CREDITOR Heaven bless you!
MARALL At four o'clock the rest know where to meet me.
Exeunt Order, Furnace, [*and*] *Creditors.*
WELLBORN Now, Master Marall, what's the weighty secret
You promised to impart?
MARALL Sir, time° nor place *neither time*
Allow me to relate each circumstance.
This only in a word: I know Sir Giles
Will come upon you for security
For his thousand pounds,[6] which you must not consent to.
As he grows in heat—as I am sure he will—
Be you but rough and say he's in your debt
Ten times the sum, upon sale of your land.
I had a hand in't (I speak it to my shame)
When you were defeated° of it. *defrauded*
WELLBORN That's forgiven.
MARALL I shall deserve't, then. Urge him to produce
The deed in which you passed° it over to him— *signed*
Which I know he'll have about him°—to deliver *on his person*
To the Lord Lovell, with many other writings
And present moneys. I'll instruct you further,
As I wait on° Your Worship. If I play not my prize[7] *attend*
To your full content and your uncle's much vexation,
Hang up Jack Marall.
WELLBORN I rely upon thee. *Exeunt.*

4. Gentlemen were notoriously slow in paying their tailors. Wellborn adopts a casual attitude about not paying a tailor for twenty-one years, without even paying interest for such a long period of time.
5. Presumably, Wellborn requires secrecy because he was treated by this former barber-surgeon for syphilis.
6. Overreach intends to demand that Wellborn mortgage some valuable property as a guaranty for the £1,000 that Overreach offered out of seeming generosity, at 3.3.65–67, to allow Wellborn to clear his debts. See 5.1.126–31 below.
7. I.e., If I do not prove my worth. (Literally, give a public demonstration of skill in fencing or in some athletic contest.)

4.3

[*Enter*] *Allworth* [*and*] *Margaret.*

ALLWORTH Whether to yield the first praise to my lord's
Unequaled temperance or your constant sweetness,
That I yet live, my weak hands fastened on
Hope's anchor, spite of all storms of despair,
I yet rest° doubtful.[1] *remain*

MARGARET Give it° to Lord Lovell, *(your praise)*
For what in him was bounty in me's duty.
I make but payment of a debt to which
My vows, in that high office° registered, *heaven*
Are faithful witnesses.

ALLWORTH 'Tis true, my dearest.
Yet, when I call to mind how many fair ones
Make willful shipwreck of their faiths and oaths
To God and man to fill the arms of greatness,° *win a noble husband*
And you rise up no less than a glorious star,
To the amazement of the world, that° hold out *you who*
Against the stern authority of a father
And spurn at honor when it comes to court you,
I am so tender of your good that, faintly,° *reluctantly*
With your wrong I can wish myself that right
You yet are pleased to do me.[2]

MARGARET Yet, and ever.[3]
To me what's title, when content is wanting?
Or wealth, raked up together with much care
And to be kept with more,° when the heart pines *more care and worry*
In being dispossesed of what it longs for,
Beyond the Indian mines?[4] Or the smooth° brow *unfrowning*
Of a pleased sire, that slaves me to his will,
And—so° his ravenous humor may be feasted *provided that*
By my obedience, and he see me great°— *rich and mighty*
Leaves to my soul nor° faculties nor power *neither*
To make her own election?

ALLWORTH But the dangers
That follow the repulse°— *rejecting Lord Lovell*

MARGARET To me they are nothing.
Let° Allworth love, I cannot be unhappy. *Provided*
Suppose the worst, that in his rage he° kill me; *(Overreach)*
A tear or two by you dropped° on my hearse *being dropped, shed*
In sorrow for my fate will° call back life *that will*
So far as but to say that I die yours,
I then shall rest in peace. Or should he prove
So cruel as° one death would not suffice *that*
His thirst of vengeance, but with ling'ring torments
In mind and body I must waste to air° *waste away to nothing*

4.3. Overreach's house.
1. I am uncertain whether to give highest praise to Lord Lovell for not wooing you for himself or to your constancy in loving me—the anchor of hope to which I weakly cling in my despair at being so unworthy of you.
2. Only with a sense of wronging you (by asking you to marry one of my humble fortune and social station) can I wish to obtain the inestimable benefit that you are pleased to bestow on me.
3. I wish to serve you thus still, and always.
4. When the heart grieves for not obtaining what it longs for more excessively than for what might be obtained from the rich mines of the Indies?

In poverty joined with banishment, so° you share — *so long as*
In my afflictions (which I dare not wish you),
So high I prize you,° I could undergo 'em — *you (that)*
With such a patience as should look down
With scorn on his worst malice.

ALLWORTH Heaven avert
Such trials of your true affection to me!
Nor will it, unto you that are all mercy,
Show so much rigor.[5] But since we must run
Such desperate hazards, let us do our best
To steer between 'em.

MARGARET Your lord's ours, and sure;[6]
And, though but a young actor, second me
In doing to the life what he has plotted;[7]
The end may yet prove happy. Now, my Allworth—

Enter Overreach [*behind*].

ALLWORTH [*aside to her as they see Overreach*] To your letter![8] And put on a seeming anger.

MARGARET [*aloud*] I'll pay my lord° all debts due to his title, — *(Lovell)*
And when, with terms not taking° from his honor, — *detracting*
He does solicit me, I shall gladly hear him.
But in this peremptory, nay, commanding way,
T'appoint a meeting, and, without my knowledge,
A priest to tie the knot° can° ne'er be undone — *marriage knot / that can*
Till death unloose it, is a confidence
In His Lordship will deceive him.[9]

ALLWORTH I hope better,
Good lady.

MARGARET Hope, sir, what you please. For° me, — *As for*
I must take a safe and secure course. I have
A father, and, without his full consent,
Though all lords of the land kneeled for my favor,
I can grant nothing.

OVERREACH [*coming forward*] I like this obedience.
But whatsoever my lord writes must and shall be
Accepted and embraced. Sweet Master Allworth,
You show yourself a true and faithful servant
To your good lord; he has a jewel of° you.— — *in*
How? Frowning, Meg? Are these looks to receive° — *with which to receive*
A messenger from my lord? [*Seeing the letter*] What's this? Give me it.

MARGARET A piece of arrogant paper, like th'inscriptions.° — *the contents*

Overreach [*takes and*] *read*[*s*] *the letter.*

OVERREACH "Fair mistress, from your servant° learn° all joys — *wooer / learn that*
That we can hope for, if deferred, prove toys;° — *trifles, baubles*
Therefore this instant, and in private, meet

5. Nor will heaven afflict you with such terrible trials, you who are mercy itself (and therefore beloved of heaven).

6. Lord Lovell is on our side, and dependable.

7. And, though you and I are inexperienced at pretense and deception, help me to do as convincingly as I can what Lord Lovell has plotted.

8. The pretend love letter that Lovell wrote to Margaret and sent to her by Allworth, in order to deceive Overreach and give Allworth an excuse to call on Margaret. See 3.2.232–34 and 4.1.11.

9. This shows an arrogant assurance in his title ("His Lordship") that he will one day discover he has no right to count on.

A husband that will gladly at your feet
Lay down his honors, tend'ring them to you
With all content, the church being paid her due."[1]
Is this the arrogant piece of paper? Fool,
Will you still be one?° In the name of madness, what — *(a fool)*
Could His good Honor write more to content you?
Is there aught else to be wished after these two
That are already offered: marriage first,
And lawful pleasure° after? What would you more? — *sex*

MARGARET Why, sir, I would be married like° your daughter, — *as befits*
Not hurried away i'th'night I know not whither,
Without all ceremony, no friends° invited — *family*
To honor the solemnity.

ALLWORTH An't° please Your Honor— — *If it*
[*Aside*] For so before tomorrow I must style° you— — *address*
My lord desires this privacy in respect° — *private ceremony because*
His honorable kinsmen are far off,
And his desires to have it done brook not
So long delay as to expect their coming;[2]
And yet he stands resolved, with all due pomp—
As running at the ring,[3] plays, masques, and tilting°— — *jousting*
To have his marriage at court celebrated
When he has brought Your Honor up to London.

OVERREACH [*to Margaret*] He tells you true; 'tis the fashion, on my knowledge.
Yet° the good lord, to please your peevishness, — *Yet you dare ask that*
Must put it off, forsooth, and lose a night
In which perhaps he might get° two boys on thee. — *beget*
Tempt me no farther. If you do, this goad
[*Pointing to his sword*]
Shall prick you to him.

MARGARET I could be contented,
Were you but by° to do a father's part — *at my side*
And give me in the church.

OVERREACH So° my lord have you, — *So long as*
What do I care who gives you? Since my lord
Does purpose to be private, I'll not cross° him.— — *contradict*
I know not, Master Allworth, how my lord
May be provided, and therefore [*giving money*] there's a purse
Of gold 'twill° serve this night's expense; tomorrow — *that will*
I'll furnish him with any sums. In the meantime,
Use my ring° to my chaplain; he is beneficed — *(see 4.1.38–39)*
At my manor of Gotham,° and called Parson Willdo. — *(near Nottingham)*
'Tis no matter for a license; I'll bear him out° in't. — *back him up*

MARGARET With your favor,° sir, what warrant is your ring? — *Pardon my asking*
He may suppose I got that twenty ways,
Without your knowledge; and then to be refused
Were such a stain° upon me! If you pleased, sir, — *shame (of elopement)*
Your presence would do better.

OVERREACH Still perverse?

1. Once the ceremony of marriage has been completed.
2. And his eagerness to marry will not tolerate a delay sufficient for the arrival of his kinsmen. ("Expect" means "await.")
3. Such as the game of riding at full speed in an attempt to carry off on one's spear a ring hanging from an upright pole. (The full courtly celebration of the wedding is supposedly to be postponed until well after the ceremony itself.)

I say again I will not cross my lord;
Yet I'll prevent° you too. [*Calling*] Paper and ink there! *anticipate, forestall*

ALLWORTH I can furnish you.

OVERREACH I thank you; I can write then.
Writes on his book.° *in Allworth's notebook*

ALLWORTH You may, if you please, put out° the name of my lord, *leave out*
In respect° he comes disguised, and only write: *Seeing that*
"Marry her to this gentleman."

OVERREACH Well advised.
[*He writes, and gives the note to Allworth.*]
'Tis done. Away! (*Margaret kneels.*) My blessing, girl? Thou hast it.
Nay, no reply; begone. [*She rises.*] Good Master Allworth,
This shall be the best night's work you ever made.

ALLWORTH I hope so, sir. *Exeunt Allworth and Margaret.*

OVERREACH Farewell!—Now all's cocksure.° *completely secure*
Methinks I hear already knights and ladies
Say, "Sir Giles Overreach, how is it with
Your honorable daughter? Has Her Honor
Slept well tonight?" Or, "Will Her Honor please
To accept this monkey? Dog? Or parakeet?"
(This is state in ladies),[4] or "My eldest son
To be her page, and wait upon her trencher?"° *wait on her at table*
My ends, my ends are compassed!° Then for Wellborn *encompassed*
And the lands. Were he once married to the widow,
I have him here.° I can scarce contain myself, *(in my grasp)*
I am so full of joy, nay, joy all over! *Exit.*

5.[1]

[*Enter*] *Lovell, Lady* [*Allworth, and*] *Amble* [*who retires once he has ushered them in*].

LADY ALLWORTH By this° you know how strong the motives were *By this time*
That did, my lord, induce me to dispense
A little with my gravity, to advance,
In personating° some few favors to him, *pretending*
The plots and projects of the downtrod Wellborn.
Nor shall I e'er repent—although I suffer
In some few men's opinions for't—the action.
For he that ventured all for my dear husband° *(see 1.3.100–110)*
Might justly claim an obligation from me
To pay him such a courtesy, which, had I
Coyly or overcuriously° denied, *too fastidiously*
It might have argued me° of little love *shown me to be*
To the deceased.

LOVELL What you intended, madam,
For the poor gentleman hath found good success,
For, as I understand, his debts are paid,
And he once more furnished for fair employment.
But all the arts that I have used to raise

4. Great ladies like to receive such pets as gifts.

5.1. Lady Allworth's house.

The fortunes of your joy and mine, young Allworth,
Stand yet in supposition, though I hope well,
For the young lovers are in wit° more pregnant° *intelligence / teeming*
Than their years can promise; and for° their desires, *as for*
On my knowledge, they are equal.
LADY ALLWORTH As° my wishes *Just as equal as*
Are with yours, my lord. Yet give me leave to fear
The building, though well grounded.° To deceive *having a good foundation*
Sir Giles, that's both a lion and a fox
In his proceedings, were a work beyond
The strongest undertakers,° not the trial *endeavorers*
Of two weak innocents.
LOVELL Despair not, madam.
Hard things are compassed oft by easy means,
And judgment, being a gift derived from heaven,
Though sometimes lodged i'th'hearts of worldly men
That ne'er consider from whom they receive it,
Forsakes such as abuse the giver of it.° *such as abuse heaven*
Which is the reason that the politic° *crafty*
And cunning statesman, that believes he fathoms
The counsels of all kingdoms on the earth,
Is by simplicity oft overreached.
LADY ALLWORTH May he be so! Yet in his name to express it
Is a good omen.[1]
LOVELL May it to myself
Prove so, good lady, in my suit to you!
What think you of the motion?° *proposal*
LADY ALLWORTH Troth, my lord,
My own unworthiness may answer for me;
For had you, when that I was in my prime
(My virgin flower uncropped), presented me
With this great favor, looking on my lowness
Not in a glass of self-love but of truth,
I could not but have thought it as a blessing
Far, far beyond my merit.
LOVELL You are too modest,
And undervalue that° which is above *i.e., your own worth*
My title, or whatever I call mine.
I grant, were I a Spaniard,[2] to marry
A widow might disparage me, but, being
A trueborn Englishman, I cannot find
How it can taint my honor. Nay, what's more,
That which you think a blemish is to me
The fairest luster. You already, madam,
Have given sure proofs how dearly you can cherish
A husband that deserves you, which confirms me
That, if I am not wanting° in my care *deficient*
To do you service, you'll be still the same
That you were to your Allworth. In a word,
Our years,° our states,° our births are not unequal, *ages / estates*

1. May Overreach be overreached! Yet surely it is a good omen that you can express the idea of the overreacher who is overreached with the name of our own Sir Giles Overreach in mind.

2. Spaniards were regarded as violently jealous by nature and hence likely to regard with suspicion the idea of marrying a widow or any woman who had already slept with some other man.

You being descended nobly and allied° so. *connected by family*
If then you may be won to make me happy,
But° join your lips to mine, and that shall be *Simply*
A solemn contract.
LADY ALLWORTH I were blind to my own good,
Should I refuse it. [*They kiss.*] Yet, my lord, receive me
As such a one the study of whose whole life
Shall know no other object but to please you.
LOVELL If I return not, with all tenderness,
Equal respect to you, may I die wretched!
LADY ALLWORTH There needs no protestation, my lord.
To her that cannot doubt—

Enter Wellborn [*handsomely dressed*].

You are welcome, sir.
Now you look like yourself.
WELLBORN And will continue
Such, in my free acknowledgment that I am
Your creature,° madam, and will never hold *dependent*
My life mine own when you please to command it.
LOVELL It is a thankfulness that well becomes you.
You could not make choice of a better shape
To dress your mind in.
LADY ALLWORTH For me, I am happy
That my endeavors prospered. Saw you of late° *lately*
Sir Giles, your uncle?
WELLBORN I heard of him, madam,
By his minister, Marall. He's grown into strange passions
About his daughter. This last night he looked for
Your Lordship at his house, but, missing you,
And she not yet appearing, His Wisehead° *i.e., His Wisdomship*
Is much perplexed and troubled.
LOVELL [*to Lady Allworth*] It may be,
Sweetheart, my project took.[3]

Enter Overreach [*with a box*], *with distracted looks, driving in Marall before him.* [*They are unaware at first of the presence of the others already onstage.*]

LADY ALLWORTH I strongly hope.
OVERREACH [*to Marall*] Ha! Find her, booby, thou huge lump of nothing!
I'll bore thine eyes out else.
WELLBORN [*aside to Lovell*] May it please Your Lordship,
For some ends° of mine own, but to withdraw *stratagems*
A little out of sight, though not of hearing,
You may perhaps have sport.
LOVELL You shall direct me.
Steps aside.
OVERREACH [*to Marall*] I shall sol-fa you,° rogue. *make you sing (in pain)*
MARALL Sir, for what cause
Do you use me thus?
OVERREACH Cause, slave? Why, I am angry,

3. It may be, dear, that my plot to deceive Overreach and forward the marriage of Allworth and Margaret has succeeded.

And thou a subject only fit for beating,
And so to cool my choler. Look to the writing;
Let but the seal be broke upon the box
That has slept in my cabinet these three years,
I'll rack° thy soul for't. *torture*

MARALL (*aside*) I may yet cry quittance,° *get even*
Though now I suffer and dare not resist.

OVERREACH [*seeing Lady Allworth*] Lady, by your leave, did
you see my daughter, lady?
And the lord her husband? Are they in your house?
If they are, discover, that I may bid 'em joy;
And, as an entrance to her place of honor,
Set Your Ladyship on her left hand,° and make curtsies *Give her place of honor*
When she nods on you, which you must receive
As a special favor.

LADY ALLWORTH When I know, Sir Giles,
Her state° requires such ceremony, I shall pay it; *station*
But in the meantime, as I am myself,° *being who I am*
I give you to understand I neither know
Nor care where Her Honor° is. *(said sardonically)*

OVERREACH When you once see her
Supported and led by the lord her husband,
You'll be taught better. [*Seeing Wellborn*] Nephew!

WELLBORN Sir.

OVERREACH No more?° *No greater title?*

WELLBORN 'Tis all I owe you.

OVERREACH Have your redeemed rags° *clothes out of pawn*
Made you thus insolent?

WELLBORN (*in scorn*) Insolent to you?
Why, what are you, sir, unless in your years,
At the best, more than myself?[4]

OVERREACH [*aside*] His fortune swells him.
'Tis rank° he's married. *all too apparent*

LADY ALLWORTH This is excellent!

OVERREACH Sir, in calm language (though I seldom use it),
I am familiar with the cause that makes you
Bear up thus bravely.° There's a certain buzz° *audaciously / rumor*
Of a stol'n marriage—do you hear?—of a stol'n marriage,
In which, 'tis said, there's somebody hath been cozened.
I name no parties.

WELLBORN Well, sir, and what follows?

OVERREACH Marry, this, since you are peremptory: remember,
Upon mere hope of your great match, I lent you
A thousand pounds. Put me in good security,° *(see 4.2.114–16)*
And suddenly, by mortgage or by statute
Of some of your new possessions, or I'll have you
Dragged in your lavender robes to the jail. You know me,
And therefore do not trifle.

WELLBORN Can you be
So cruel to your nephew, now he's in
The way to rise?° Was this the courtesy *(see 3.3.55–56)*
You did me in pure love and no ends else?° *(see 3.3.69–70)*

OVERREACH End me no ends! Engage° the whole estate, *Put in the bond*

4. Wherein are you, sir, by the most charitable calculation, superior to me, other than in your age?

And force your spouse to sign it, you° shall have *and you*
Three or four thousand more, to roar and swagger
And revel in bawdy taverns.
WELLBORN And beg after;° *ever afterward*
Mean you not so?
OVERREACH My thoughts are mine, and free.
Shall I have security?
WELLBORN No, indeed you shall not,
Nor bond, nor bill, nor bare acknowledgment.
Your great looks fright not me.
OVERREACH But my deeds shall.
Outbraved?° *They both draw.* *Do you flout me?*

The servants [including Order, Amble, and Furnace] enter.

LADY ALLWORTH Help! Murder, murder!
WELLBORN Let him come on,
With all his wrongs and injuries about him,
Armed with his cutthroat practices to guard him;
The right that I bring with me will defend me,
And punish his extortion.
OVERREACH That I had thee
But single in the field!
LADY ALLWORTH You may; but make not
My house your quarreling scene.
OVERREACH Were't° in a church, *Even if it were*
By heaven, and hell, I'll do't.
MARALL [*aside to Wellborn*] Now put him to
The showing of the deed.
WELLBORN This rage is vain, sir.
For° fighting, fear not; you shall have your hands full *As for*
Upon the least incitement. And whereas
You charge me with a debt of a thousand pounds,
If there be law (howe'er you have no conscience),
Either restore my land, or I'll recover
A debt that's truly due to me from you
In value ten times more than what you challenge.° *claim*
OVERREACH I in thy debt? Oh, impudence! Did I not purchase
The land left by thy father, that rich land,
That had continuèd in Wellborn's name
Twenty descents, which, like a riotous fool,
Thou didst make sale of? Is not here° enclosed *(in the box)*
The deed that does confirm it mine?
MARALL [*aside to Wellborn*] Now, now!
WELLBORN I do acknowledge none. I ne'er passed o'er° *transferred*
Any such land. I grant for a year or two
You had it in trust, which if you do discharge,
Surrend'ring the possession, you shall ease
Yourself and me of chargeable° suits in law— *costly*
Which if you prove not honest (as I doubt it)
Must of necessity follow.
LADY ALLWORTH In my judgment
He does advise you well.
OVERREACH Good! Good! Conspire
With your new husband, lady; second him
In his dishonest practices. But when

This manor is extended° to my use, *seized for debt*
You'll speak in an humbler key and sue for favor.
LADY ALLWORTH Never. Do not hope it.
WELLBORN Let despair first seize me!
OVERREACH Yet to shut up thy mouth and make thee give
Thyself the lie, the loud lie, I draw out
The precious evidence; if thou canst forswear
Thy hand and seal, and make a forfeit of
Thy ears to the pillory,[5] see, here's that will make
My interest° clear. (*Opens the box.*) Ha! *title*
LADY ALLWORTH A fair skin of parchment.
WELLBORN Indented, I confess, and labels too,[6]
But neither wax° nor words. How! Thunderstruck? *seals*
Not a syllable to insult with? My wise uncle,
Is this your precious evidence? Is this that° makes *that which*
Your interest clear?
OVERREACH I am o'erwhelmed with wonder!
What prodigy is this? What subtle devil
Hath razed out the inscription, the wax
Turned into dust? The rest of my deeds whole
As when they were delivered, and this only
Made nothing! Do you deal with witches, rascal?
There is a statute for you, which will bring
Your neck in a hempen circle;° yes, there is. *noose*
And now 'tis better thought,° for, cheater, know *I've thought it over*
This juggling shall not save you.
WELLBORN To save thee
Would beggar° the stock of mercy.° *exhaust / heaven's mercy*
OVERREACH Marall!
MARALL Sir?
OVERREACH (*flattering him*) Though the witnesses are dead, your testimony—
Help with an oath or two; and for thy master,
Thy liberal master, my good, honest servant,
I know you will swear anything to dash° *knock down, destroy*
This cunning sleight.° Besides, I know thou art *trick*
A public notary, and such stand in law
For a dozen witnesses. The deed being drawn too
By thee, my careful Marall, and delivered
When thou wert present, will make good my title.
Wilt thou not swear this?
MARALL I? No, I assure you.
I have a conscience not seared up° like yours; *dried up, made callous*
I know no° deeds. *know nothing about any*
OVERREACH Wilt thou betray me?
MARALL [*to the others*] Keep° him *If you'll keep*
From using of his hands, I'll use my tongue
To his no little torment.
OVERREACH [*as they restrain him*] Mine own varlet
Rebel against me?

5. Clipping the ears was a common form of punishment for malfeasance. The pillory was a wooden frame, like the stocks, through which the offending person's head and hands were thrust in order to expose that person to public ridicule.

6. The original parchment has been cut zigzag, so that the two halves, each supposedly containing the signed agreement, could be uniquely matched with each other. The labels are narrow strips of material attached to the document to carry the seals.

MARALL Yes, and uncase° you, too. *flay, strip; expose*
The idiot, the patch,° the slave, the booby,° *(see 3.2.248) / (see 89 above)*
The property° fit only to be beaten *i.e., slave*
For your morning exercise, your football, or
Th'unprofitable lump of flesh, your drudge,
Can now anatomize° you, and lay open *dissect, lay bare*
All your black plots, and level with the earth° *to the ground*
Your hill of pride, and, with these gabions guarded,[7]
Unload my great artillery and shake,
Nay, pulverize the walls you think defend you.
LADY ALLWORTH How he foams at the mouth with rage!
WELLBORN To him again.
OVERREACH Oh, that I had thee in my grip! I would tear thee
Joint after joint!
MARALL I know you are a tearer,
But I'll have first your fangs pared off, and then
Come nearer to you, when I have discovered° *revealed*
And made it good before the judge what ways
And devilish practices you used to cozen with° *deceive*
An army of whole families, who, yet alive° *if still alive*
And but° enrolled for soldiers, were° able *simply / would be*
To take in° Dunkirk.[8] *capture*
WELLBORN All will come out.° *be revealed*
LADY ALLWORTH The better.
OVERREACH But that I will live,[9] rogue, to torture thee
And make thee wish—and kneel in vain—to die,
These swords that keep thee from me should fix here,
Although they made my body but one wound,
But I would reach thee.[1]
LOVELL (*aside*) Heav'n's hand is in this!
One bandog worry the other![2]
OVERREACH I play the fool,
And make my anger but ridiculous.
There will be a time and place—there will be, cowards!—
When you shall feel what I dare do.
WELLBORN I think so.
You dare do any ill, yet want true valor
To be honest and repent.
OVERREACH They are words I know not,
Nor e'er will learn. Patience, the beggar's virtue,
Shall find no harbor here.° *(in my breast)*

Enter Greedy and Parson Willdo.

After these storms,
At length a calm appears. Welcome, most welcome!
There's comfort in thy looks. Is the deed done?
Is my daughter married? Say but so, my chaplain,

7. And, being defended by these fortifications, i.e., the persons here who are protecting me against you and enabling me to speak. (Gabions are wicker baskets filled with earth and used defensively against sieges.)

8. Marall hyperbolically claims that the list of Overreach's victims would amount to a whole army. Taking Dunkirk (or Dunkerque), on the French coast, was a perennial ambition of the English, who had held vast tracts of France in the fourteenth and fifteenth centuries.

9. Were it not that I would prefer to live.

1. These swords, by means of which you (Wellborn) and the rest now prevent me from attacking you, would need to fix themselves in me to the point of making my body one solid mass of wounds before I would give up in my attempt to get to you.

2. To see two fierce chained watchdogs snapping at each other!

And I am tame.° *I'll subside*

WILLDO Married? Yes, I assure you.

OVERREACH Then vanish all sad thoughts! [*Offering money*]
There's more gold for thee.
My doubts and fears are in the titles drowned
Of my Right Honorable, my Right Honorable daughter.

GREEDY Here will be feasting! At least for a month
I am provided. Empty guts, croak no more!
You shall be stuffed like bagpipes, not with wind
But bearing° dishes. *sustaining, substantial*

OVERREACH (*whispering to Willdo*) Instantly be here?
To my wish, to my wish! Now you that plot against me,
And hoped to trip my heels up, that contemned me,
Think on't, and tremble. (*Loud music.*) They come! I hear the music.
A lane there° for my lord! *Make way there*

WELLBORN This sudden heat
May yet be cooled, sir.

OVERREACH Make way there for my lord!

Enter Allworth and Margaret.

MARGARET (*kneeling*) Sir, first your pardon, then your blessing, with
Your full allowance° of the choice I have made, *approval*
As ever you could make use of your reason.[3]
Grow not in passion, since you may as well
Call back the day that's past as untie the knot
Which is too strongly fastened. Not to dwell
Too long on words, this's my husband.

OVERREACH How!

ALLWORTH So I assure you. All the rites of marriage,
With every circumstance, are past. Alas, sir,
Although I am no lord, but a lord's page,
Your daughter and my loved wife mourns not for it;
And, for° "Right Honorable son-in-law," you may say *in place of*
"Your dutiful daughter."

OVERREACH Devil! Are they married?

WILLDO Do a father's part, and say, "Heav'n give 'em joy!"

OVERREACH Confusion° and ruin! Speak, and speak quickly, *Destruction*
Or thou art dead.

WILLDO They are married.

OVERREACH Thou hadst better
Have made a contract with the king of fiends
Than these. My brain turns!° *spins*

WILLDO Why this rage to me?
Is not this your letter, sir, and these the words?
"Marry her to this gentleman."

OVERREACH It cannot—
Nor will I e'er believe it—'sdeath,° I will not— *by God's death*
That I, that in all passages I touched
At worldly profit have not left a print
Where I have trod for the most curious search

3. I adjure you by as much sound reason as you can muster.

To trace my footsteps,[4] should be gulled by children,
Baffled and fooled, and all my hopes and labors
Defeated and made void!
WELLBORN As it appears,
You are so, my grave uncle.
OVERREACH Village nurses° *crones, witches*
Revenge their wrongs with curses. I'll not waste
A syllable,° but thus I take the life *I'll not waste my breath*
Which wretched I gave to thee. *Offers° to kill Margaret.* *He attempts*
LOVELL [*intervening*] Hold, for your own sake!
Though charity to your daughter hath quite left you,
Will you do an act, though in your hopes lost here,° *(in this world)*
Can° leave no hope for peace or rest hereafter? *That can*
Consider: at the best you are but a man,
And cannot so create your aims but that
They may be crossed.[5]
OVERREACH Lord, thus I spit at thee
And at thy counsel, and again° desire thee, *in return*
As thou art a soldier, if thy valor
Dares show itself where multitude and example
Lead not the way, let's quit the house and change
Six words in private.[6]
LOVELL I am ready, sir.
LADY ALLWORTH [*to Lovell*] Stay, sir!
Contest with one distracted?
WELLBORN You'll grow like him,° *as mad as he is*
Should you answer his vain° challenge. *fruitless, worthless*
OVERREACH [*to Lovell*] Are you pale?° *pale with fear*
Borrow his° help. Though Hercules call it odds, *(Wellborn's)*
I'll stand against both, as I am, hemmed in thus.[7]
Since, like Libyan lion in the toil,° *net*
My fury cannot reach the coward hunters
And only spends itself, I'll quit the place.
Alone I can do nothing, but I have servants
And friends to second me; and, if I make not
This house a heap of ashes—by my wrongs,
What I have spoke I will make good!—or leave
One throat uncut, if it be possible,
Hell add to my afflictions! *Exit Overreach.*
MARALL Is't not brave sport?
GREEDY Brave sport? I am sure it has ta'en away my stomach;
I do not like the sauce.
ALLWORTH [*to Margaret*] Nay, weep not, dearest,
Though it express your pity; what's decreed
Above,° we cannot alter. *In heaven*
LADY ALLWORTH His threats move me
No scruple,° madam. *Not a bit*
MARALL [*to Wellborn*] Was it not a rare trick,

4. That I, who in all my schemes of self-promotion have never left traces of my footsteps for even the most exacting searches to find out.
5. And, as a fallible human, you cannot invent ambitious schemes that heaven and well-intentioned men cannot thwart.
6. If you dare display your valor in a way that does not follow the example set by the multitudes of people, let's go outside and settle matters in a duel. ("Change" means "exchange.")
7. Though even Hercules would complain of such unfair odds, I'll take you both on, hemmed in as I am by those of you who are impeding my movements.

An it please Your Worship, to make the deed nothing?
I can do twenty neater, if you please
To purchase° and grow rich, for I will be   *acquire land*
Such a solicitor and steward for you
As never worshipful had.°   *as no lord ever had*
WELLBORN   I do believe thee.
But first discover° the quaint° means you used   *reveal / ingenious*
To raze out the conveyance.°   *title deed*
MARALL   They are mysteries
Not to be spoke in public: certain minerals
Incorporated in the ink and wax.
Besides, he gave me nothing, but still fed me
With hopes and blows; and that was the inducement
To this conundrum.° If it please Your Worship   *trick, device*
To call to memory, this mad beast once caused me
To urge you to or° drown or hang yourself;   *either*
I'll do the like to him, if you command me.
WELLBORN   You are a rascal! He that dares be false
To a master, though unjust, will ne'er be true
To any other. Look not for reward
Or favor from me; I will shun thy sight
As I would do a basilisk's.[8] Thank my pity
If thou keep thy ears.° Howe'er, I will take order   *(see 183 and n)*
Your practice shall be silenced.
GREEDY   I'll commit him,
If you'll have me, sir.
WELLBORN   That were to little purpose.
His° conscience be his prison.—Not a word,   *Let his*
But instantly begone!
ORDER [*kicking Marall*]   Take this kick with you.
AMBLE [*kicking Marall*]   And this.
FURNACE   If that° I had my cleaver here   *If*
I would divide your knave's head.
MARALL   This is the haven
False servants still° arrive at.   *Exit Marall.*   *always*

Enter Overreach [*distracted in his wits*].

LADY ALLWORTH   Come again!°   *He's come again!*
LOVELL   Fear not; I am your guard.
WELLBORN   His looks are ghastly.
WILLDO   Some little time I have spent, under your favors,°   *if you please*
In physical° studies, and, if my judgment err not,   *medical*
He's mad beyond recovery. But observe him,
And look to yourselves.
OVERREACH   Why, is not the whole world
Included in myself? To what use then
Are friends and servants? Say there were a squadron
Of pikes, lined through with shot;[9] when I am mounted
Upon my injuries, shall I fear to charge 'em?
Flourishing his sword ensheathed.[1]

8. A fabulous monster whose look (and breath) were reputedly fatal.

9. Of soldiers armed with steel-pointed weapons, strengthened throughout with musketeers.

1. The quarto reads "*vnsheathed*" (unsheathed), but lines 364–66 indicate that Overreach cannot withdraw his sword from its sheath. See Textual Notes.

No: I'll through the battalia,° and, that routed, *army*
I'll fall to execution. Ha! I am feeble:
Some undone° widow sits upon mine arm *ruined, bankrupt*
And takes away the use of't, and my sword,
Glued to my scabbard with wronged orphans' tears,
Will not be drawn. Ha! What are these? Sure, hangmen,
That come to bind my hands, and then to drag me
Before the judgment seat! Now they are new shapes
And do appear like Furies,[2] with steel whips
To scourge my ulcerous soul! Shall I then fall
Ingloriously, and yield? No! Spite of Fate,
I will be forced to hell like to myself;[3]
Though you were legions of accursèd spirits,
Thus would I fly among you. [*He runs at them weakly.*]

WELLBORN There's no help.° *no hope of atonement*
Disarm him first, then bind him.

GREEDY Take a mittimus° *writ of commital*
And carry him to Bedlam.° *a London mental asylum*

LOVELL How he foams!

WELLBORN And bites the earth!

WILLDO Carry him to some dark room.° *(used to treat lunatics)*
There try what art° can do for his recovery. *medical skill*

MARGARET Oh, my dear father!

They [*Order, Amble, Furnace, etc.*] *force Overreach off.*

ALLWORTH You must be patient, mistress.

LOVELL Here is a precedent to teach wicked men
That, when they leave religion and turn atheists,
Their own abilities leave 'em. Pray you, take comfort.
I will endeavor you° shall be his guardians *(Margaret and Allworth)*
In his distractions. And for° your land, Master Wellborn, *as for*
Be it good or ill in law, I'll be an umpire
Between you and this,° th'undoubted heir *(Margaret)*
Of Sir Giles Overreach. For me, here's the anchor° *(Lady Allworth)*
That I must fix on.

ALLWORTH What you shall determine,
My lord, I will allow of.° *agree to*

WELLBORN 'Tis the language
That I speak, too. But there is something else
Beside the repossession of my land
And payment of my debts that I must practice.
I had a reputation, but 'twas lost
In my loose course; and, till I redeem it
Some noble way, I am but half made up.° *half redeemed; half a man*
It is a time of action.° If Your Lordship *military action*
Will please to confer a company upon me
In your command, I doubt not in my service
To my king and country but I shall do something
That may make me right again.

LOVELL Your suit is granted,
And you loved° for the motion.° *are loved / proposal*

WELLBORN Nothing wants° then *is lacking*
But your allowance—

2. Primordial spirits who avenge crimes against kindred.

3. I.e., Whatever Fate may have decreed, I will not yield in cowardly fashion, but will defy you all and proceed to my dark destiny unflinchingly, true to my nature.

The Epilogue

But your° allowance,[1] and in that our all — *(the audience's)*
Is comprehended,[2] it being known nor we° — *that neither we actors*
Nor he that wrote the comedy can be free
Without your manumission°—which if you — *freeing us*
Grant willingly, as a fair favor due
To the poet's and our labors (as you may,
For we despair not, gentlemen, of the play),
We jointly shall profess Your Grace[3] hath might
To teach us action, and him how to write. [*Exeunt*.]

FINIS.

The Epilogue.
1. The phrase "But your allowance," found at the end of act 5, scene 1, and repeated here at the beginning of the Epilogue, may be in its first appearance a catchword (here actually a phrase) at the bottom of signature M2 of the quarto, thereupon repeated in error at the top of the last page (M2v); but it is also possible that the actor playing Wellborn says this in his own character and then steps forward as the Epilogue, repeating the phrase as he does so.
2. And in your gracious acceptance of our play lie all our hopes of having succeeded.
3. The noble person in whose presence the play has been performed.

TEXTUAL NOTES

A New Way to Pay Old Debts was entered in the Stationers' Register in November of 1632. The first quarto, published in 1633, is the authoritative text for this present edition. Substantive departures from it are noted below, using the following abbreviations:

Q: The first quarto (London: E. P. for Henry Seyle, 1633)
ed.: A modern editor's emendation

To His Friend the Author 16 Off [Q: Of]
1.1.11 Plymouth [ed.] plimworth [Q] **76** [and elsewhere] **coarse** [Q: course] **125 transparent** [ed.] transrent [Q] **173 stipendiary** [Q: stipendary]
1.2.59 cool [ed.] Cooke [Q] **127 Follow** [ed.] You follow [Q]
1.3.17 kickshaws [Q: Kukeshawes] **25 rapt** [ed.] rap'd [Q] **31 lose** [Q: loose] **49 though** [ed.] thought [Q] **56 swoon** [Q: sowne] **63 souls** [ed.] sou'es [Q] **108 buoyed** [ed.] bung'd [Q]
2.1.2 on't [ed.] out [Q] **57 'em** [ed.] him [Q] **106 withe** [Q: With]
2.2.13 think [ed.] thinne [Q] **15 hear** [ed.] are [Q] **22 Coral** [Q: Currall]
2.3.28 baton [Q: Battoone] **35 afoot** [Q: a foote] **53 How I** [ed.] How [Q] **60 SD *musing*** [ed.] *masing* [Q] **92 rogue Wellborn** [ed.] rogue—. *Welborne* [Q] **106 idiot** [ed.] I doe [Q]
3.1.5 to [ed.; not in Q] **54 two** [ed.] too [Q] **65 none** [ed.] more [Q] **77 lined** [ed.] liu'd [Q]
3.2.23.1 [placement, ed.; after 24 in Q] **24 It** [ed.] I [Q] **27.1** [placement, ed.; opposite 28 in Q] **72 scald** [Q: scall'd] **74.1** [placement, ed.; after 75 in Q] **93 lineage** [Q: linage] **108 woo** [Q: woe] **152 account** [Q: accompt] **189 His haste** [ed.] He hast [Q] **206 baked** [ed.] back'd [Q] **213 bawling** [Q: balling] **269 coarse** [Q: course]
3.3.26 SD [placement, ed.; after "manners" in 27 in Q] **44.1 *Marall*** [ed.] *Margaret. Marrall.* [Q] **45 SD *Margaret*** [placement, ed.; as part of SD at 44.1 in Q] **47 WELLBORN So** [ed.] Well: so [as a continuation of Overreach's speech in Q] **70**

me [ed.] my [Q] **71 compliments** [Q: complements] **76.1** [*"finis Actus tertii"* follows in Q]

4.1.29 [and elsewhere] **Whether** [ed.] Whither [Q] **52 Flushing** [Q: *Vllushing*] **125 ears** [ed.] cares [Q] **126 orphans** [Q: Orphants] **133 more** [ed.] more more [Q] **168 LOVELL** [ed.] *Lad.* [Q] **219 Overreach' states** [Q: *Ouerreach*, stat's] **221 precedents** [Q: presidents] **229 straight** [Q: straite]

4.2.45.1–2 [placement, ed.; opposite 43 in Q] **52 faucet** [Q: fosset] **87 I remember** [ed.] Remember [Q] **127 prize** [ed.] price [Q]

4.3 [scene numbering, ed.] *Actus quarti, Scena vltima* [Q] **11 shipwreck** [Q: shipwracke] **13 no less** [ed.] lesse [Q] **52.1** [placement, ed.; opposite 51 in Q] **91 desires** [ed.] desire [Q] **103 goad** [ed.] good [Q] **114 Gotham** [Q: *Gotam*] **119 Were** [ed.] We're [Q] **135 parakeet** [Q: Paraquit] **141** [*"the end of the fourth Act"* follows in Q]

5.1 [scene numbering, ed.] *Actus quinti, Scena quinta* [Q] **37 overreached** [ed.] ouerreach [Q] **73 SD** [placement, ed.; after "yourself" in 74 in Q] **99 slept** [Q: slepp'd] **106 Set** [ed.] See [Q] **106 curtsies** [ed.] courseis [Q] **115 OVERREACH** [ed.] *Welb.* [Q] **129 by mortgage** [ed.] my *Mortgage* [Q] **184 SD** [placement, ed.; opposite 182 in Q] **204 sleight** [Q: slight] **230 cozen with** [ed.] coozen / With [Q, but "With" is the catchword at the bottom of signature L3 in Q and probably belongs at the end of line 230] **231 alive** [ed.] liue [Q] **246 SD** [placement, ed.; opposite 245 in Q] **254 be** [ed.] I be [Q] **260 SD** [placement, ed.; opposite 259 in Q] **263** [placement, ed.; opposite 265 in Q] **315 leave** [ed.] leau'd [Q] **334 conundrum** [Q: *Conumbrum*] **349 cleaver** [Q: cleuer] **360.1** ***ensheathed*** [ed.] *vnsheathed* [Q] **374 WELLBORN** [placement, ed.; at the head of 374 in Q] **381 precedent** [Q: president]

'Tis Pity She's a Whore

To call a work of art "derivative" is ordinarily to disparage it, but in John Ford's *'Tis Pity She's a Whore,* first performed between 1629 and 1633, retrospection and assimilation produce a remarkably powerful play. Shakespearean-style love tragedy is perhaps the most obvious influence: Antony and Cleopatra, Othello and Desdemona, and above all Romeo and Juliet are the patterns for *'Tis Pity*'s recklessly visionary erotic solipsists. Ford models his hero-villain Giovanni on the Marlovian overreacher—particularly Doctor Faustus—in his contempt for rules, his combination of intellectual sophistication with sophomoric folly, his belief in ineluctable destiny, and above all his preference for earthly satisfactions over heavenly rewards. The sharply observed urban world of Ford's Parma, Italy, owes much to Middleton's caustic city satires. In the last act of *'Tis Pity,* the competitive spiral of violence so familiar in Renaissance revenge tragedies culminates in a bloody denouement as elaborate and shocking as anything in *Titus Andronicus, The Spanish Tragedy,* or *The Revenger's Tragedy.*

Ford's self-conscious reuse of traditional materials makes his deviations from precedent all the more noticeable and interesting. Incest, contemplated or achieved, figures in a fair number of English Renaissance plays: *Hamlet, The Revenger's Tragedy, Pericles, Women Beware Women, A King and No King,* and *The Atheist's Tragedy* among them. In most of these plays, incest is somebody else's sin—associated with the villains rather than with the protagonists whose perspective the audience is invited to share. Often, too, various plot devices attenuate the scandal: the perpetrators may not recognize one another, may not know beforehand of their relationship, or may discover themselves to be adopted children so that their love is permissible after all. In *Hamlet,* the relationship between Gertrude, Hamlet's mother, and Claudius, her first husband's brother, is technically incestuous, but does not involve a sexual connection between blood relatives. Thus many dramatists, even while they stage incest, hold it at a considerable moral and emotional distance. By contrast, Ford, in a play about consensual sexual intercourse between a sister and a brother, resolutely avoids any such palliating or marginalizing factors and forces his audience to give the matter of incest sustained, serious attention.

Even as Ford makes the incestuous lovers central, he also takes pains to make them rather ordinary. In most plays, incest is associated with gross incontinence and bestial lack of discernment—Hamlet, for instance, accuses his mother of "honeying and making love / Over the nasty sty" (3.4.95–96). But in *'Tis Pity She's a Whore,* the susceptibility of the two siblings for one another seems predicated not on libertinism but on chastity. Giovanni has committed himself so thoroughly to the celibate life of a student that his father despairs of his ability to continue the family line; and the Friar suggests that sexual experience with other women might cure him of his obsession with his sister:

Introduction by Katharine Eisaman Maus; glosses, footnotes, and textual notes by David Bevington; text edited by David Bevington and checked by Eric Rasmussen.

Look through the world,
And thou shalt see a thousand faces shine
More glorious than this idol thou ador'st.
Leave her, and take thy choice; 'tis much less sin.
(1.1.59–62)

Giovanni cannot follow his mentor's worldly, sensible counsel, because for all his ranting about fate, the ebbs and flows of the sea, and so on, he is initially rather fastidious about sexual matters. It is easier for him to commit the big sins of idolatry, incest, and blasphemy than to commit the smaller sin of promiscuous fornication. Meanwhile, Annabella, as is only proper for a young, wellborn Renaissance woman, has had relatively little acquaintance with men outside her family and is inclined, as she has been taught, to admire and take direction from her male kin. Her sheltered existence makes her more, not less, susceptible to her brother.

It is not entirely surprising, then, that these two well-brought-up young people should think of their relationship in terms of common Renaissance concepts of romantic passion. "The more I strive, I love; the more I love, / The less I hope," Giovanni wails (1.2.145–46), as innumerable sonneteers had complained before him. Like his Petrarchan and Shakespearean predecessors, he insists that love is not bound by social conventions—yet taboo-breaking is itself conventional in the inherited lexicon of Renaissance love poetry. He is especially drawn to the Neoplatonic image of lovers as perfect likenesses, as mirrors of one another, as one soul mysteriously shared or divided between two bodies and eternally seeking reunion. Who better suited to become one flesh than those who were one flesh to begin with?

Say that we had one father, say one womb
(Curse to my joys!) gave both us life and birth;
Are we not therefore each to other bound
So much the more by nature? By the links
Of blood, of reason? Nay, if you will have't,
Even of religion, to be ever one,
One soul, one flesh, one love, one heart, one all?
(1.1.28–34)

Giovanni not only has sex with his sister, but his sister is all in all to him, partly because she *is* him—at least for the first part of the play. In the early scenes of *'Tis Pity She's a Whore,* incest seems not scandalously alien but impossible to differentiate from ordinary sexual desire—the place, in fact, where a long and prestigious tradition of thinking about love logically seems to culminate.

All this is not to say that sex between siblings is innocent or even very attractive. Annabella's chaperon Putana, whose name means "whore," undermines the highly idealized terms in which the siblings attempt to characterize their physical relationship:

ANNABELLA Oh, guardian, what a paradise of joy
Have I passed over!
PUTANA Nay, what a paradise of joy have you passed under!
(2.1.43–45)

Putana's dirty jokes distance the audience from the lovers' perspective and qualify our empathy with their predicament. Dramatic structure suggests other ironies: in a play full of significant borrowings and echoes, it is no accident that Giovanni's courtship of Annabella replays the scene from *Richard III* (1.2) in which Richard manipulates and bullies Lady Anne, whose husband and father-in-law Richard has just killed, into marrying him.

GIOVANNI Here. *Offers his dagger to her.*
ANNABELLA What to do?
GIOVANNI And here's my breast. Strike home!
Rip up my bosom; there thou shalt behold
A heart in which is writ the truth I speak. (1.2.209–11)

Moments later, he lies shamelessly to his sister, telling her that the church has approved their union. Giovanni's career shows abundantly how the self-absorption of the lover differs only minimally from the exorbitant egotism of the sophistical intellectual, the stage machiavel, the tyrant, or the revenger—all of which Giovanni is, aspires to be, or eventually becomes. When Giovanni's yearnings conflict with social rules, he disavows what he calls a "customary form" (1.1.25). This repudiation licenses him to transgress not merely in specific, limited ways, but in a more unconditional fashion, so that by the end of the play, his lack of constraint makes him insanely grandiose. In the first scenes, he attempts to minimize his own culpability by claiming to be the plaything of a mysterious destiny: " 'Tis not, I know, / My lust, but 'tis my fate that leads me on" (1.2.158–59). By the end of the play, close to madness, he no longer sees himself as fate's victim but as its master. "I hold Fate / Clasped in my fist," he tells Annabella before he kills her (5.5.11–12), and afterward assures Soranzo that "in my fists I bear the twists of life" (5.6.71).

Morris dancers. Engraving from Malone's *Shakespeare* (1790) of a mid-fifteenth-century window at Betley in Staffordshire. The origins of the morris dance, an early medieval folk dance associated with the sword dance and the May-game (note the maypole in the second row, center, of the window), are uncertain, though the dance may be native to England. See *'Tis Pity She's a Whore,* 1.3.51 and note.

Giovanni's headlong extremism has the virtue of consistency. Indeed, faced with increasing difficulties, he merely insists on his own position all the more firmly. Annabella is both less resolute and more subtle. In a world suffused with the double standard, her position is far more equivocal than her brother's: Giovanni may imagine that she is "still the same" after she has lost her virginity (2.1.12), but nobody else in her world would agree. Annabella cannot share Giovanni's fantasies of untrammeled self-making. Once she realizes she is pregnant, she inevitably consents to marry Soranzo, a plan she would otherwise resist, and cowers before the Friar's prediction of her imminent damnation. Annabella continues to adore her brother, and apparently their sexual relationship continues after her marriage, but for the first time in the play she fails to mirror him. As the play continues, Giovanni's increasing emotional turmoil thus seems only partly a jealous reaction to Soranzo's access to his beloved. It is at least as much the consequence of Annabella's new, uncertain independence. In their final encounter, Giovanni accuses Annabella most of all of a failure of reciprocity, as if, had she continued to sustain her part of the bargain, all would magically have been well. But the audience can see here, if it has not earlier, the extent to which Giovanni is in the grip of a delusion. By the end of the play, Annabella is a figure of almost pure pathos, scapegoat for a brother and a husband, both of whom purport to love her.

Perhaps because acknowledging their social status would acknowledge the existence and importance of other people, both Giovanni and Annabella seem almost oblivious to their social position. The rest of the characters, though, see their family clearly, as rich but "new." Hippolita, Soranzo's previous and now rejected love, bitterly calls Annabella "Madam Merchant" (2.2.49), an epithet that accurately designates Annabella's bourgeois origins even if it misses its mark insofar as this merchant's daughter is entirely uninterested in marketing her charms to improve her standing. Her apathy contrasts with the eagerness of her father, Florio, who wants both economic and social commerce with the world; a good businessman, he tries to avoid alienating unsatisfactory suitors such as Bergetto, nephew of the wealthy Donado, or the gentleman Grimaldi, even while reserving his approval for the apparently more attractive Soranzo. In point of fact, Annabella, despite Putana's assuring her that she has "choice fit for the best lady in Italy" (1.2.74), is faced with limited and depressing options. Grimaldi is inept, murderous, and craven; Bergetto, mentally deficient; Soranzo, unfaithful and ferociously sanctimonious.

The unsuitability of Annabella's suitors is one manifestation of a more general social corruption. Shot through with grudge-bearing, selfishness, hypocrisy, and outright deception, Parma is a world in which nobody can be trusted. Again and again, somebody breaks a vow or accuses somebody else of doing so; again and again, somebody is moved to take action against a promise-breaker. The scenes in *'Tis Pity* that do not concern themselves with Giovanni and Annabella are almost wholly given over to a series of betrayals and revenges, which often go awry: the failed plots of Hippolita and Richardetto, the more effective violence of the sinister Vasques.

In this treacherous environment, everything important happens in private, or beneath the surface of things. The estrangement between what is publicly observable and what is true evinces itself in a profound disturbance of rituals, especially of those rituals that are designed to indicate, or to bring into alignment, private feeling and its social acknowledgment. The play opens with a reference to a failed recourse to the sacrament of confession: Giovanni has "unclasped my burdened soul, / Emptied the storehouse of my thoughts and heart, / Made myself poor of secrets" to his spiritual advisor, the Friar (1.1.13–15), but the purgation does not lead, as it is supposed to, to repentance and a fresh start. The wedding of Soranzo and Annabella likewise goes disastrously awry. "Long prosper in this day, / You happy couple," pronounces the Friar (4.1.5–6), over a beautiful bride who is secretly pregnant by her brother, and a rich and handsome nobleman whose wronged mistress will shortly interrupt the festivities and attempt to poison him but only succeed in killing herself. Likewise, at the end of the play, the culminating bloodbath interrupts what purports to be a birthday party.

Despite these disasters, the characters, and Giovanni in particular, seem impelled to give a ceremonial shape to their often chaotic experience. Giovanni's conversations with the Friar, and even his soliloquies, are structured as formal academic disputations, the public rhetorical rite that marked almost every communal gathering in the Renaissance university. When Giovanni and Annabella kneel and exchange vows before consummating their love, they follow the protocol of a *de praesenti* marriage, a private but legally binding wedding ceremony. Their improvised solemnity seems, despite the relationship's lack of social sanction, to justify Giovanni's later possessiveness and even, obscurely, to predict the play's bloody conclusion. "Love me, or kill me, brother," Annabella requests; "Love me, or kill me, sister," Giovanni replies (1.2.256, 259). In the siblings' last interview, "love me, or kill me" turns into "love me *and* kill me," in violence that has some of the quality of a sacrificial rite.

The social world Giovanni and Annabella imagine they can disregard cannot long be shut out and eventually retaliates against them. Although everything important in *'Tis Pity She's a Whore* happens in private, the plot of the play relentlessly forces those things into theatrical view and subjects them to social judgment. The play's emphasis on making private arrangements public gives special prominence to Soranzo's servant, Vasques, and Annabella's servant, Putana. Both enjoy the confidence of employers who have a great deal to hide. Putana, closely modeled on Juliet's nurse in *Romeo and Juliet,* serves, as already noted, to de-idealize the relationship between Giovanni and Annabella, counterpointing their dazzled idealizing of one another with crude humor. She is, like her precedent, gossipy, well-meaning, dim-witted, and unscrupulous in a minor way. At the same time, the information Putana alone can provide is crucial to the resolution of the plot. Typically, her betrayal of her mistress is nearly inadvertent. Eager to display to Vasques that she is in the know, she seals both Annabella's fate and her own.

Vasques plays a more complicated role. If the obvious sinners in *'Tis Pity She's a Whore* are the overinvolved, incestuous lovers, Vasques seems to represent their emotional opposite. A foreigner, his only connection to the world of the play is the relatively modest one of being dutiful to his employer. He plays, nonetheless, a pivotal role in the play's several interlocking plots. He first appears in the second scene of the play, physically attacking and humiliating Grimaldi, Soranzo's rival for Annabella's hand. Later, he encourages Hippolita to plot against Soranzo but also arranges for her vengeful scheme to backfire. Then he works to discover the truth about Annabella's pregnancy, worming the truth out of Putana. With both Hippolita and Putana, he mimes intimacy as a way of gaining their confidence, even while coldly planning their torment and death. Apparently distrusting what he suspects is Soranzo's less than implacable desire for vengeance, Vasques eggs him on: "marry a strumpet that cast herself away upon you but to laugh at your horns, to feast on your disgrace, riot in your vexations, cuckold you in your bride-bed, waste your estate upon panders and bawds? . . . Let not your pity betray you till my coming back; think upon incest and cuckoldry" (5.2.1–5, 23–24).

Vasques's pitiless actions seem motivated not by a yearning for justice, nor by a grudge, nor by the hope of advancement, nor even by a perverse rejoicing in other people's ruin. Indeed, he scarcely reflects on his own motives at all. His opacity distinguishes him from a troublemaker such as Shakespeare's Iago, whose malignity may be motiveless but who at least attempts to find an excuse for his conduct, as well as from murderers such as Macbeth or Bosola in John Webster's *The Duchess of Malfi,* haunted by second thoughts and pangs of conscience. Like the brutally efficient hired killers under his command, Vasques appears to herald a new age of casual ferocity, in which violence no longer reveals personal commitments but becomes merely another way of doing business. In such a world, tragedy, which posits an intimate connection between characters and the violence they wreak, becomes impossible. A personality like Giovanni seems hopelessly anachronistic. Even a less fully realized tragic agent, Hippolita's wronged husband, Richardetto, with his conventional motives and his conventional plans for vengeance, ends up a peripheral witness to the final bloodbath rather than either a perpetrator or a victim.

The plot of *'Tis Pity She's a Whore* is an engine of discovery and revelation, bringing secrets into public view. This momentum extends to the play's language: events repeatedly serve to make literal, concrete, and visible what were originally merely figures of speech. As a result, phrases that are rather unremarkable at the time appear retrospectively to have been prophetic; or alternatively, later events seem to act out or emblematize an originally metaphoric statement. "Then you will wish each kiss your brother gave / Had been a dagger's point," predicts the Friar (3.6.27–28). In this carefully prepared context, the sensational final entrance of Giovanni, with his sister's bloody heart skewered on his dagger, has its own grotesque logic as an act of love, hubris, and ritual gone awry. Just as the lovers' apparently unexceptionable desire for a mirror image leads inexorably, in *'Tis Pity She's a Whore,* to incestuous passion, so the revenger's impulse to justice likewise leads, by small and logical steps, to nauseatingly violent forms of self-assertion. Behaving as though he, not Soranzo, were the wronged husband of Annabella, Giovanni preempts Soranzo's revenge just as he has preempted him in Annabella's bed. In a play so obsessed with secrets and with the translating of implicit or hidden meanings into literal, physical expression, the heart on the sword serves as the ultimate unveiling.

It is common enough in Renaissance tragedy for the last lines of the play to be spoken by a character of high status, whose authority lends moral weight to his reflections. In *'Tis Pity She's a Whore,* Ford deploys this convention in a deeply ironic way. The corrupt Cardinal speaks its final lines, mourning Annabella's unchastity: "Of one so young, so rich in nature's store, / Who could not say, 'Tis pity she's a whore?" (5.6.160–61). One form of whoredom or another has seemed inescapable for all the play's women—Hippolita, Putana, and Annabella—and all suffer abundantly for their lapses. But the conviction that Parma's problem is whoredom—Annabella's or anybody else's—rather than the cold bloodthirstiness of Vasques, the self-satisfied vengefulness of Richardetto, or the murderousness of Grimaldi, is enough to make one nostalgic for Giovanni's reckless disregard of social laws and his absolute emotional commitments.

JOHN FORD

'Tis Pity She's a Whore

To the Truly Noble John, Earl of Peterborough, Lord Mordaunt, Baron of Turvey[1]

My lord,

Where a truth of merit hath a general warrant,° there love is but a debt, acknowledgment a justice. Greatness cannot often claim virtue by inheritance; yet in this yours appears most eminent, for that you are not more rightly heir to your fortunes than glory shall be to your memory. Sweetness of disposition ennobles a freedom of birth;° in both, your lawful interest adds honor to your own name and mercy to my presumption. Your noble allowance° of these firstfruits of my leisure in the action° emboldens my confidence of your as noble construction in this presentment[2]—especially since my service must ever owe particular duty to your favors, by a particular engagement.° The gravity of the subject may easily excuse the lightness of the title; otherwise I had been a severe judge against mine own guilt. Princes have vouchsafed grace to trifles offered from a purity of devotion; Your Lordship may likewise please to admit into your good opinion, with these weak endeavors, the constancy of affection from the sincere lover of your deserts in honor,

John Ford

sanction — *noble birth* — *approval* — *in performance* — *obligation*

To My Friend the Author

With admiration° I beheld this whore *wonder*
Adorned with beauty, such as might restore
(If ever being as thy Muse hath famed)° *reported*
Her Giovanni, in his love unblamed.
The ready Graces° lent their willing aid; *daughters of Zeus*
Pallas° herself now played the chambermaid *Athena, goddess of wisdom*
And helped to put her° dressings on. Secure *(Annabella's)*
Rest thou, that thy name herein shall endure

The original 1633 title page reads "*'Tis Pity She's a Whore*. Acted by the Queen's Majesty's Servants, at the Phoenix in Drury Lane. London: Printed by Nicholas Okes for Richard Collins, and are to be sold at his shop in Paul's Churchyard, at the sign of the Three Kings. 1633."

Dedication.

1. Nothing is known of Ford's reasons for dedicating this play to John Mordaunt (1599–1642). He was a favorite of James I and then Charles I, who created him first Earl of Peterborough in 1628.

2. Emboldens me to hope for your noble generosity in accepting this volume dedicated to you.

To My Friend the Author.

To th'end of age,° and Annabella be *of time*
Gloriously fair, even in her infamy.
—Thomas Ellice[1]

THE ACTORS' NAMES

Bonaventura, a FRIAR
A CARDINAL, nuncio to° the Pope *representative of*
SORANZO, a nobleman
FLORIO, a citizen of Parma
DONADO, another citizen
GRIMALDI, a Roman gentleman
GIOVANNI, son to Florio
BERGETTO, nephew to Donado
RICHARDETTO, a supposed physician
VASQUES, servant to Soranzo
POGGIO, servant to Bergetto
BANDITTI

Women:
ANNABELLA, daughter to Florio
HIPPOLITA, wife to Richardetto
PHILOTIS, his niece
PUTANA,° tut'ress to Annabella *"whore"*

[OFFICERS
A SERVANT to the Cardinal
Attendants, ladies]

THE SCENE: Parma.

[1.1]

Enter Friar and Giovanni.

FRIAR Dispute no more in this, for know, young man,
These are no school points.[1] Nice° philosophy *Finicky*
May tolerate unlikely arguments,
But heaven admits° no jest; wits° that presumed *allows / clever men*
On wit° too much, by striving how to prove *cleverness*
There was no God, with foolish grounds of art,° *school learning*
Discovered first the nearest° way to hell, *shortest*
And filled the world with devilish atheism.
Such questions, youth, are fond.° For better 'tis *foolish*
To bless° the sun than reason why it shines; *give thanks for*
Yet He° thou talk'st of is above the sun. *(God)*
No more! I may not hear it.
GIOVANNI Gentle father,
To you I have unclasped my burdened soul,
Emptied the storehouse of my thoughts and heart,
Made myself poor of secrets; have not left

1. Possibly Thomas Ellice was related to Robert Ellice, to whom Ford dedicated *The Lover's Melancholy*. Otherwise he is unknown.

1.1. The Friar's cell.
1. These are no mere subjects for scholastic debate.

Another word untold which hath not spoke
All what° I ever durst,° or think, or know. *that / dared think*
And yet is here the comfort I shall have?
Must I not do what all men else may: love?
FRIAR Yes, you may love, fair son.
GIOVANNI Must I not praise
That beauty which, if framed° anew, the gods *created*
Would make a god of if they had it there,
And kneel to it, as I do kneel to them?
FRIAR Why, foolish madman!
GIOVANNI Shall a peevish° sound, *petty, trifling*
A customary form from man to man[2]
Of brother and of sister, be a bar
'Twixt my perpetual happiness and me?
Say that we had one father, say one womb
(Curse to my joys!) gave both us life and birth;
Are we not therefore each to other bound
So much the more by nature? By the links
Of blood,° of reason? Nay, if you will have't,° *kinship / if you insist*
Even of religion, to be ever one,
One soul, one flesh, one love, one heart, one all?
FRIAR Have done,° unhappy° youth, for thou art lost. *Stop / unfortunate*
GIOVANNI Shall then, for that° I am her brother born, *because*
My joys be ever banished from her bed?
No, father. In your eyes I see the change° *substitution*
Of pity and compassion; from your age,
As from a sacred oracle, distills
The life of counsel.° Tell me, holy man, *good advice*
What cure shall give me ease in these extremes?
FRIAR Repentance, son, and sorrow for this sin,
For thou hast moved a Majesty above
With thy unrangèd (almost)° blasphemy. *almost out of control*
GIOVANNI Oh, do not speak of that, dear confessor!
FRIAR Art thou, my son, that miracle of wit
Who once within these three months wert esteemed
A wonder of thine age, throughout Bononia?° *Bologna*
How did the university applaud
Thy government,° behavior, learning, speech, *conduct, demeanor*
Sweetness,° and all that could make up a man! *Pleasantness, grace*
I was proud of my tutelage,° and chose *role as tutor*
Rather to leave my books than part with thee.
I did so;° but the fruits of all my hopes *(left my studies)*
Are lost in thee, as thou art in thyself.
Oh, Giovanni! Hast thou left the schools
Of knowledge to converse with lust and death?° *spiritual death*
For death waits on° thy lust. Look through the world, *attends*
And thou shalt see a thousand faces shine
More glorious than this idol thou ador'st.
Leave her, and take thy choice; 'tis much less sin,
Though in such games as those° they lose that win. *i.e., incest*
GIOVANNI It were more ease° to stop the ocean *would be easier*
From floats° and ebbs than to dissuade my vows. *flows, tides*
FRIAR Then I have done,° and in thy willful flames *finished*

2. A mere convention devised by human society.

Already see thy ruin; heaven is just.
Yet hear my counsel.

GIOVANNI As a voice of life.° — *a life-giving voice*

FRIAR Hie° to thy father's house. There lock thee fast — *Hasten*
Alone within thy chamber, then fall down
On both thy knees and grovel on the ground.
Cry to thy heart; wash every word thou utter'st
In tears, and, if't be possible, of blood.° — *of deepest sorrow*
Beg heaven to cleanse the leprosy of lust
That rots thy soul; acknowledge what thou art,
A wretch, a worm, a nothing. Weep, sigh, pray
Three times a day and three times every night.
For seven days' space do this. Then if thou find'st
No change in thy desires, return to me;
I'll think on remedy. Pray for thyself
At home, whil'st I pray for thee here. Away!
My blessing with thee. We have need to pray.

GIOVANNI All this I'll do, to free me from the rod
Of vengeance; else, I'll swear, my fate's my god.° — *my fate rules me*

Exeunt [*separately*].

[1.2]

Enter Grimaldi and Vasques, ready to fight.

VASQUES Come, sir, stand to your tackling.° If you prove craven, I'll make you run quickly. — *weapons*

GRIMALDI Thou art no equal match for me.[1]

VASQUES Indeed, I never went to the wars to bring home news,° nor cannot play the mountebank for a meal's meat[2] and swear I got my wounds in the field. See you these gray hairs? They'll not flinch for° a bloody nose. Wilt thou to this gear?° — *boasts of victory* — *for fear of* — *business (of dueling)*

GRIMALDI Why, slave,° think'st thou I'll balance my reputation with a cast-suit?[3] Call thy master.° He shall know that I dare— — *wretch* — *(Soranzo)*

VASQUES Scold like a cotquean;° that's your profession. Thou poor shadow of a soldier, I will make thee know, my master keeps servants thy betters in quality and performance. Com'st thou to fight or prate?° — *scolding housewife* — *prattle*

GRIMALDI Neither, with thee. I am a Roman and a gentleman, one that have got mine honor with expense° of blood. — *expenditure*

VASQUES You are a lying coward and a fool. Fight, or, by these hilts,° I'll kill thee. [*Grimaldi draws his sword.*] Brave, my lord! You'll fight? — *my sword's hilt*

GRIMALDI Provoke me not, for if thou dost—

VASQUES Have at you!° — *Here I come! On guard!*

They fight. Grimaldi hath the worst.

Enter Florio, Donado, [*and*] *Soranzo.*

1.2. A street in Parma, near Florio's house (see lines 23–25). At 31.1ff., Annabella and Putana observe the action in the street from Annabella's window in her father's house; then, after Giovanni arrives below her window (at 130.1), the meeting of brother and sister on the main stage (line 163ff.) is seemingly understood to be indoors.

1. You are not my social equal (and therefore are beneath my dignity as an opponent in a duel).

2. Nor can I play the charlatan hero as a way of earning invitations to dinner.

3. Wearer of cast-off clothing.

FLORIO What mean these sudden broils° so near my doors? *tumults, scuffles*
Have you not other places but my house
To vent the spleen of your disordered bloods?
Must I be haunted still° with such unrest *continually*
As not to eat or sleep in peace at home?
Is this your love,[4] Grimaldi? Fie, 'tis naught.° *wicked, improper*
DONADO And, Vasques, I may tell thee 'tis not well
To broach° these quarrels. You are ever forward *spur on*
In seconding° contentions. *abetting*

Enter, above, Annabella and Putana.[5]

FLORIO What's the ground?° *ground for dispute*
SORANZO That, with your patience, signors, I'll resolve.° *explain*
This gentleman [*indicating Grimaldi*], whom fame° reports a soldier— *rumor*
For else I know not[6]—rivals me in love
To Signor Florio's daughter, to whose ears
He still prefers° his suit, to my disgrace, *urges*
Thinking the way to recommend himself
Is to disparage me in his report.—
But know, Grimaldi, though may be thou art
My equal in thy blood,° yet this bewrays° *lineage / reveals*
A lowness in thy mind which, wert thou noble,
Thou wouldst as much disdain as I do thee
For this unworthiness. [*To Florio*] And on this ground
I willed my servant to correct his tongue,
Holding a man so base no match for me.
VASQUES And had not your sudden coming prevented us, I had let my gentleman blood under the gills.° [*To Grimaldi*] I should have wormed you, sir, for running mad.[7] *slit his throat*
GRIMALDI I'll be revenged, Soranzo.
VASQUES On a dish of warm broth to stay° your stomach?° Do, honest innocence,° do! Spoon-meat[8] is a wholesomer diet than a Spanish blade. *quiet / appetite; anger* *fool*
GRIMALDI Remember this!
SORANZO I fear thee not, Grimaldi.
Exit Grimaldi.

FLORIO My lord Soranzo, this is strange to me.
Why you should storm, having my word engaged?
Owing her heart, what need you doubt her ear?[9]
Losers may talk, by law of any game.[1]
VASQUES Yet the villainy of words, Signor Florio, may be such as would make any unspleened dove choleric.[2] Blame not my lord in this.
FLORIO [*to Vasques*] Be you more silent.

4. Is this how you show your love for my daughter?
5. In the upper acting area, Annabella and Putana can be seen and heard by the audience but not, presumably, by those on the main stage. The two women are understood to be at Annabella's window; see note on scene location above.
6. I know of no other proof of his soldiership. (Implying that there is none.)
7. Worming a dog, i.e., extracting the lytta (a parasitic worm) from its tongue, was supposed to be a safeguard against rabies and resulting madness. ("For" means "to prevent.")
8. Soft food to spoon-feed to infants or invalids.
9. Since her heart is yours, why need you fear her listening to another wooer? ("Owing" means "owning, possessing.")
1. In any sport, losers are allowed to say what they want.
2. May be such as would enrage even a dove. (Doves were proverbially mild birds, seemingly lacking the supposed organ of anger, the spleen.)

[*To Soranzo*] I would not for my wealth my daughter's love
Should cause the spilling of one drop of blood.—
Vasques, put up.° Let's end this fray in wine. — *sheathe your sword*
Exeunt [*Florio, Donado, Soranzo, and Vasques*].

PUTANA How like you this, child? Here's threat'ning, challenging, quarreling, and fighting on every side, and all is for your sake. You had need look to yourself, charge;° you'll be stolen away sleeping else shortly. — *charge: person in my charge*

ANNABELLA But, tut'ress, such a life gives no content
To me. My thoughts are fixed on other ends.
Would you would leave me!

PUTANA Leave you? No marvel else. Leave me no leaving,[3] charge; this is love outright. Indeed I blame you not; you have choice fit for the best lady in Italy.

ANNABELLA Pray do not talk so much.

PUTANA Take the worst with the best,[4] there's Grimaldi the soldier, a very well-timbered° fellow. They say he is a Roman, nephew to the Duke Montferrato. They say he did good service in the wars against the Millanoys.° But faith,° charge, I do not like him, an't° be for nothing but for being a soldier. Not one amongst twenty of your skirmishing captains but have some privy maim° or other that mars their standing upright.[5] I like him the worse, he crinkles° so much in the hams. Though he might serve if there were no more men, yet he's not the man I would choose. — *well-timbered: well-built; Millanoys: Milanese / faith: in faith; an't: if it; privy maim: secret injury; crinkles: bows, shrinks*

ANNABELLA Fie, how thou prat'st!

PUTANA As I am a very° woman, I like Signor Soranzo well. He is wise, and, what is more, rich; and, what is more than that, kind; and, what is more than all this, a nobleman. Such a one, were I the fair Annabella myself, I would wish and pray for. Then he is bountiful. Besides, he is handsome, and, by my troth, I think wholesome.° (And that's news in a gallant of three-and-twenty.) Liberal,° that I know; loving, that you know; and a man sure, else he could never ha' purchased° such a good name with Hippolita, the lusty° widow, in her husband's lifetime. An 'twere but for that report, sweetheart, would 'a° were thine! Commend a man for his qualities,° but take a husband as he is a plain-sufficient, naked man: such a one is for your bed, and such a one is Signor Soranzo, my life for't.° — *very: veritable, true; wholesome: syphilis-free; Liberal: Generous; purchased: acquired; lusty: vigorous; sexy; 'a: he / qualities: attainments; my life for't: I'd bet my life*

ANNABELLA [*to herself*] Sure the woman took her morning's draft° too soon. — *draft: drink*

Enter Bergetto and Poggio [*on the main stage, below*].

PUTANA But look, sweetheart, look what thing comes now! Here's another of your ciphers° to fill up the number. Oh, brave old ape in a silken coat!° Observe. [*They listen.*] — *ciphers: nonentities; brave old ape in a silken coat: in foolish finery*

BERGETTO Didst thou think, Poggio, that I would spoil my new clothes and leave my dinner to fight?

POGGIO No, sir, I did not take you for so arrant a baby.

BERGETTO I am wiser than so.° For I hope, Poggio, thou never — *so: than that*

3. I.e., Leave you? What next? Fine, if that's what you want. Don't keep harping about my leaving.
4. I.e., All things considered; take the thick with the thin.
5. Their ability to stand. (Suggesting impotence.)

heard'st of an elder brother° that was a coxcomb,° did'st, Poggio? *heir / simpleton*

POGGIO Never indeed, sir, as long as they had either land or money left them to inherit.

BERGETTO Is it possible, Poggio? Oh, monstrous! Why, I'll undertake, with a handful of silver, to buy a headful of wit at any time. But sirrah,° I have another purchase in hand. I shall have the wench, mine uncle says. I will but wash my face and shift° socks, and then have at her, i'faith! Mark my pace, Poggio. [*He awkwardly attempts a dance step.*] *(said to inferiors)* *change*

POGGIO Sir, I have seen an ass and a mule trot the Spanish pavane° with a better grace, I know not how often. *a stately dance*

Exeunt [*Bergetto and Poggio*].

ANNABELLA This idiot haunts me too.

PUTANA Ay, ay, he needs no description. The rich magnifico° that is below° with your father, charge, Signor Donado, his uncle, for that° he means to make this his cousin° a golden calf,° thinks that you will be a right Israelite[6] and fall down to him presently;° but I hope I have tutored you better. They say a fool's bauble is a lady's playfellow;[7] yet you having wealth enough, you need not cast upon the dearth of flesh,[8] at any rate. Hang him, innocent!° *grandee, dignitary* *on a lower floor* *because / kinsman* *i.e., a wealthy fool* *at once* *idiot*

Enter Giovanni [*on the main stage*].

ANNABELLA But see, Putana, see: what blessèd shape
Of some celestial creature now appears?
What man is he that with such sad aspect° *countenance*
Walks careless of himself?

PUTANA Where?

ANNABELLA Look below.

PUTANA Oh, 'tis your brother, sweet—

ANNABELLA Ha!

PUTANA 'Tis your brother.

ANNABELLA Sure 'tis not he. This is some woeful thing
Wrapped up in grief, some shadow of a man.
Alas, he beats his breast and wipes his eyes
Drowned all in tears; methinks I hear him sigh.
Let's down, Putana, and partake° the cause. *be informed of*
I know my brother, in the love he bears me,
Will not deny me partage° in his sadness. *a share*
My soul is full of heaviness and fear.

Exit [*above, with Putana*].

GIOVANNI Lost, I am lost! My fates have doomed° my death. *decreed*
The more I strive, I love;° the more I love, *the more I love*
The less I hope. I see my ruin, certain.
What judgment or endeavors could apply
To my incurable and restless wounds
I throughly° have examined, but in vain. *thoroughly*
Oh, that it were not in religion sin

6. I.e., worshiper of the Golden Calf. (See Exodus 32.)

7. I.e., People say that women are attracted to a fool's money, which will enable them to have other lovers. (A bauble is a carved baton, or scepter, resembling a phallus.)

8. You need not gamble on Bergetto out of worry about a shortage of wooers.

To make our love a god and worship it!
I have even wearied heaven with prayers, dried up
The spring of my continual tears, even starved
My veins with daily fasts; what wit or art° *wisdom or learning*
Could counsel, I have practiced. But alas,
I find all these but dreams and old men's tales
To fright unsteady youth; I'm still the same.
Or° I must speak or burst. 'Tis not, I know, *Either*
My lust, but 'tis my fate that leads me on.
Keep fear and low fainthearted shame with slaves![9]
I'll tell her that I love her, though my heart
Were rated at the price of that attempt.[1]
Oh, me! She comes.

Enter Annabella and Putana [on the main stage].

ANNABELLA Brother!
GIOVANNI [*aside*] If such a thing
As courage dwell in men, ye heavenly powers,
Now double all that virtue in my tongue!
ANNABELLA Why, brother, will you not speak to me?
GIOVANNI Yes. How d'ee, sister?
ANNABELLA Howsoever I am, methinks you are not well.
PUTANA Bless us! Why are you so sad, sir?
GIOVANNI Let me entreat you leave us awhile, Putana.—
Sister, I would be private with you.
ANNABELLA Withdraw, Putana.
PUTANA I will. [*Aside*] If this were any other company for her, I should think my absence an office of some credit;° but I will leave them together. *Exit Putana.* *deserving reward*
GIOVANNI Come, sister, lend your hand; let's walk together.
I hope you need not blush to walk with me;
Here's none but you and I.
ANNABELLA How's this?
GIOVANNI Faith, I mean no harm.
ANNABELLA Harm?
GIOVANNI No, good faith. How is't with 'ee?
ANNABELLA [*aside*] I trust he be not frantic.°— *mad*
I am very well, brother.
GIOVANNI Trust° me, but I am sick—I fear, so sick *Believe*
'Twill cost my life.
ANNABELLA Mercy forbid it! 'Tis not so, I hope.
GIOVANNI I think you love me, sister.
ANNABELLA Yes, you know I do.
GIOVANNI I know't indeed.—You're very fair.
ANNABELLA Nay, then, I see you have a merry sickness.
GIOVANNI That's as it proves.° The poets feign, I read, *turns out*
That Juno° for her forehead did exceed *Hera, queen of the gods*
All other goddesses: but I durst swear
Your forehead exceeds hers, as hers did theirs.
ANNABELLA Troth, this is pretty.° *ingenious; nice*
GIOVANNI Such a pair of stars
As are thine eyes would, like Promethean fire,

9. Let fear and craven shame dwell with wretches!
1. Although it cost me my life to attempt that.

If gently glanced,° give life to senseless stones.[2] *darted, flashed*
ANNABELLA Fie upon 'ee!
GIOVANNI The lily and the rose, most sweetly strange,° *at variance*
Upon your dimpled cheeks do strive for change.° *interchange*
Such lips would tempt a saint; such hands as those
Would make an anchorite° lascivious. *hermit*
ANNABELLA D'ee mock me, or flatter me?
GIOVANNI If you would see a beauty more exact
Than art can counterfeit or nature frame,
Look in your glass° and there behold your own. *mirror*
ANNABELLA Oh, you are a trim° youth! *fine (ironic)*
GIOVANNI Here. *Offers his dagger to her.*
ANNABELLA What to do?
GIOVANNI And here's my breast. Strike home!° *all the way*
Rip up my bosom; there thou shalt behold
A heart in which is writ the truth I speak.
Why stand 'ee?° *Why hesitate?*
ANNABELLA Are you earnest?
GIOVANNI Yes, most earnest.
You cannot love?
ANNABELLA Whom?
GIOVANNI Me. My tortured soul
Hath felt affliction in the heat of death.° *nearly fatal*
Oh, Annabella, I am quite undone!
The love of thee, my sister, and the view
Of thy immortal beauty hath untuned
All harmony both of my rest and life.
Why d'ee not strike?
ANNABELLA Forbid it, my just fears!
If this be true, 'twere fitter I were dead.
GIOVANNI True, Annabella? 'Tis no time to jest.
I have too long suppressed the hidden flames
That almost have consumed me; I have spent
Many a silent night in sighs and groans,
Ran over all my thoughts, despised my fate,
Reasoned against the reasons of my love,
Done all that smooth-cheeked Virtue could advise,
But found all bootless.° 'Tis my destiny *unavailing*
That you must either love or I must die.
ANNABELLA Comes this in sadness° from you? *seriousness*
GIOVANNI Let some mischief
Befall me soon if I dissemble aught!
ANNABELLA You are my brother, Giovanni.
GIOVANNI You
My sister, Annabella. I know this,
And could afford you instance° why to love *give you reason*
So much the more for this; to which intent
Wise Nature first in your creation meant
To make you mine; else 't had been sin and foul
To share one beauty to a double soul.[3]

2. Prometheus was a benefactor of humankind. According to one legend, he stole fire from the gods and gave it to the human race; according to another, he formed humankind from clay and water.

3. Otherwise the physical resemblance of the bodies enclosing our two souls would be sinful and dirty.

Nearness in birth or blood doth but persuade° — *merely urge*
A nearer nearness in affection.
I have asked counsel of the holy church,
Who tells me I may love you, and 'tis just
That, since I may, I should; and will, yea, will!
Must I now live or die?

ANNABELLA Live! Thou hast won
The field, and never fought. What thou hast urged,
My captive heart had long ago resolved.
I blush to tell thee (but I'll tell thee now):
For every sigh that thou hast spent for me,
I have sighed ten; for every tear, shed twenty;
And not so much for that° I loved, as that — *because*
I durst not say I loved, nor scarcely think it.

GIOVANNI Let not this music be a dream, ye gods,
For pity's sake, I beg 'ee!

ANNABELLA On my knees, *She kneels.*
Brother, even by our mother's dust,° I charge you, — *ashes, remains*
Do not betray me to your mirth or hate.
Love me, or kill me, brother.

GIOVANNI On my knees, *He kneels.*
Sister, even by my mother's dust, I charge you,
Do not betray me to your mirth or hate.
Love me, or kill me, sister.

ANNABELLA You mean good sooth,° then? — *You really mean it*

GIOVANNI In good troth, I do,
And so do you, I hope. Say, "I'm in earnest."

ANNABELLA I'll swear't, I.

GIOVANNI And I; and by this kiss— *Kisses her.*
Once more, yet once more; now let's rise—by this,
I would not change this minute for Elysium.[4] [*They rise.*]
What must we now do?

ANNABELLA What you will.

GIOVANNI Come, then;
After so many tears as we have wept,
Let's learn to court in smiles, to kiss, and sleep. *Exeunt.*

[1.3]

Enter Florio and Donado.

FLORIO Signor Donado, you have said enough.
I understand you, but would have you know
I will not force my daughter 'gainst her will.
You see I have but two, a son and her;
And he is so devoted to his book
As—I must tell you true—I doubt° his health. — *fear for*
Should he miscarry,° all my hopes rely — *come to harm*
Upon my girl. As for worldly fortune,
I am, I thank my stars, blessed with enough.

4. I.e., eternal bliss. (Elysium is the eternal dwelling place of blessed souls.)

1.3. Outside Florio's house.

My care is how to match her to her liking.
I would not have her marry wealth, but love,
And, if she like your nephew, let him have her.
Here's all that I can say.

DONADO Sir, you say well,
Like a true father, and for my part, I,
If the young folks can like, 'twixt you and me
Will promise to assure my nephew presently° — *immediately*
Three thousand florins° yearly during life, — *gold coins*
And, after I am dead, my whole estate.

FLORIO 'Tis a fair proffer, sir. Meantime your nephew
Shall have free passage to commence his suit.
If he can thrive, he shall have my consent.
So for this time I'll leave you, signor. *Exit.*

DONADO Well,
Here's hope yet, if my nephew would have wit;° — *some good sense*
But he is such another dunce,° I fear — *such a total dunce*
He'll never win the wench. When I was young
I could have done't, i'faith, and so shall he
If he will learn of me. And in good time° — *in timely fashion*
He comes himself.

Enter Bergetto and Poggio.

How now, Bergetto, whither away so fast?

BERGETTO Oh, uncle, I have heard the strangest news that ever came out of the mint!°—Have I not, Poggio? — *was newly minted*

POGGIO Yes indeed, sir.

DONADO What news, Bergetto?

BERGETTO Why, look ye, uncle, my barber told me just now that there is a fellow come to town who undertakes to make a mill go without the mortal help of any water or wind, only with sandbags; and this fellow hath a strange horse, a most excellent beast, I'll assure you, uncle (my barber says), whose head, to the wonder of all Christian people, stands just behind where his tail is.[1]—Is't not true, Poggio?

POGGIO So the barber swore, forsooth.

DONADO And you are running thither?

BERGETTO Ay, forsooth, uncle.

DONADO Wilt thou be a fool still? Come, sir, you shall not go; you have more mind of° a puppet play than on the business I told ye. Why, thou great baby, wu't° never have wit? Wu't make thyself a May-game° to all the world? — *care more about* / *wilt thou* / *i.e., subject of mirth*

POGGIO [*to Bergetto*] Answer for yourself, master.

BERGETTO Why, uncle, should I sit at home still, and not go abroad° to see fashions like other gallants? — *gadding about*

DONADO To see hobbyhorses.[2] What wise talk, I pray, had you with Annabella when you were at Signor Florio's house?

BERGETTO Oh, the wench. Uds sa'me,° uncle, I tickled her with a rare° speech, that I made her almost burst her belly with laughing. — *God save me* / *fine*

1. Bergetto is gullibly impressed by a supposed perpetual motion machine and by a fraudulent sideshow at fairs in which customers who paid to see "a horse with its head where its tail ought to be" would be shown a horse standing backward at the manger with its tail next to the eating trough. Barbers (lines 34, 38, and 41) were notorious gossips.

2. Dancers in a morris dance, fitted with wickerwork to resemble horses. Donado is exasperated with Bergetto's childish delight in trifles.

DONADO Nay, I think so. And what speech was't?

BERGETTO What did I say, Poggio?

POGGIO [*to Donado*] Forsooth, my master said that he loved her almost as well as he loved parmasent,° and swore (I'll be sworn for him) that she wanted but° such a nose as his was to be as pretty a young woman as any was in Parma.

Parmesan cheese / *lacked only*

DONADO Oh, gross!

BERGETTO Nay, uncle, then she asked me whether my father had any more children than myself; and I said, "No, 'twere better he should have had his brains knocked out first."

DONADO This is intolerable.

BERGETTO Then said she, "Will Signor Donado, your uncle, leave you all his wealth?"

DONADO Ha! That was good. Did she harp upon that string?

BERGETTO Did she harp upon that string? Ay, that she did. I answered, "Leave me all his wealth? Why, woman, he hath no other wit;° if he had, he should hear on't to his everlasting glory° and confusion. I know," quoth I, "I am his white° boy, and will not be gulled."° And with that she fell into a great smile, and went away. Nay, I did fit her.°

thought / *i.e., shame* / *fair-haired* / *tricked* / *I answered her smartly*

DONADO Ah, sirrah, then I see there is no changing of nature. Well, Bergetto, I fear thou wilt be a very ass still.

BERGETTO I should be sorry for that, uncle.

DONADO Come, come you home with me. Since you are no better a speaker, I'll have you write to her after some courtly manner,° and enclose some rich jewel in the letter.

in a courtly style

BERGETTO Ay, marry,° that will be excellent.

by Mary (an oath)

DONADO Peace, innocent!
Once in my time I'll set my wits to school;° *rack my brains*
If all fail, 'tis but the fortune of a fool.

BERGETTO Poggio, 'twill do, Poggio! *Exeunt.*

2.1

Enter Giovanni and Annabella, as from their chamber.

GIOVANNI Come, Annabella, no more "sister" now,
But "love"—a name more gracious. Do not blush,
Beauty's sweet wonder, but be proud to know
That, yielding, thou hast conquered and inflamed
A heart whose tribute is thy brother's life.[1]

ANNABELLA And mine is his. Oh, how these stol'n contents° *pleasures*
Would print a modest crimson on my cheeks,
Had any but my heart's delight prevailed!

GIOVANNI I marvel why the chaster of your sex
Should think this pretty toy° called maidenhead *trifle*
So strange a loss, when, being lost, 'tis nothing,
And you are still the same.

ANNABELLA 'Tis well for you;
Now you can talk.[2]

GIOVANNI Music as well consists
In th'ear as in the playing.[3]

2.1. Florio's house.

1. A heart that is ready to lay down my life for you.

2. I.e., It's all very well for you to say that, now that you have had your pleasure. (Said banteringly.)

3. Music is not fully realized in performance without a listener.

ANNABELLA Oh, you're wanton.° *naughty*
Tell on't, you're best, do.[4]
GIOVANNI Thou wilt chide me, then?
Kiss me, so. [*They kiss.*] Thus hung Jove on Leda's neck[5]
And sucked divine ambrosia from her lips.
I envy not the mightiest man alive,
But hold myself, in being king of thee,
More great than were I king of all the world.
But I shall lose you, sweetheart.
ANNABELLA But you shall not.
GIOVANNI You must be married, mistress.
ANNABELLA Yes? To whom?
GIOVANNI Someone must have you.
ANNABELLA You must.
GIOVANNI Nay, some other.
ANNABELLA Now prithee do not speak so, without jesting.
You'll make me weep in earnest.
GIOVANNI What, you will not!° *I don't believe you!*
But tell me, sweet, canst thou be dared to° swear *be so daring as to*
That thou wilt live to me, and to no other?
ANNABELLA By both our loves I dare; for, didst thou know,
My Giovanni, how all suitors seem
To my eyes hateful, thou wouldst trust me then.
GIOVANNI Enough. I take thy word. Sweet, we must part.
Remember what thou vow'st; keep well my heart.
ANNABELLA Will you be gone?
GIOVANNI I must.
ANNABELLA When to return?
GIOVANNI Soon.
ANNABELLA Look° you do. *See to it that*
GIOVANNI Farewell. *Exit.*
ANNABELLA Go where thou wilt, in mind I'll keep thee here,
And where thou art, I know I shall be there.
[*Calling*] Guardian!

Enter Putana.

PUTANA Child, how is't, child? Well, thank heaven, ha!
ANNABELLA Oh, guardian, what a paradise of joy
Have I passed over!° *through*
PUTANA Nay, what a paradise of joy have you passed under![6] Why, now I commend thee, charge; fear nothing, sweetheart. What though he be your brother? Your brother's a man, I hope, and I say still, if a young wench feel the fit° *sexual desire* upon her, let her take anybody, father or brother, all is one.° *it makes no difference*
ANNABELLA I would not have it known for all the world.
PUTANA Nor I, indeed, for the speech of the people;[7] else 'twere nothing.
FLORIO (*within*) Daughter Annabella!
ANNABELLA Oh, me, my father! [*Calling*] Here, sir! [*To Putana*] Reach my work.° *Hand me my needlework*

4. I.e., Go ahead, say what you want.
5. Jove seduced Leda in the shape of a swan.
6. What joy have you experienced, lying under a man in sexual embrace! (Playing on the antithesis of "under" and "over.")
7. Nor would I, since it would cause gossip.

FLORIO (*within*) What are you doing?
ANNABELLA So, let him come now.

Enter Florio, Richardetto like a doctor of physic,° and Philotis with a lute in her hand. — *medicine*

FLORIO [*to Annabella*] So, hard at work? That's well; you lose no time.
Look, I have brought you company. Here's one,
A learnèd doctor, lately come from Padua,
Much skilled in physic, and for that° I see — *because*
You have of late been sickly, I entreated
This reverend° man to visit you some time. — *worthy*
ANNABELLA [*to Richardetto*] You're very welcome, sir.
RICHARDETTO I thank you, mistress.
Loud fame in large report hath spoke your praise
As well for virtue as perfection;° — *accomplishments*
For which I have been bold to bring with me
A kinswoman of mine, a maid, for song
And music one, perhaps, will° give content. — *who will*
Please you to know her.
ANNABELLA They are parts° I love, — *abilities*
And she for them most welcome.
PHILOTIS Thank you, lady.
FLORIO Sir, now you know my house, pray make not strange,° — *don't be a stranger*
And if you find my daughter need your art,° — *skill*
I'll be your paymaster.
RICHARDETTO Sir, what I am
She shall command.
FLORIO You shall bind me° to you.— — *obligate me*
Daughter, I must have conference with you
About some matters that concerns us both.—
Good Master Doctor, please you but walk in,
We'll crave a little of your cousin's cunning.° — *niece's musical skill*
I think my girl hath not quite forgot
To touch an instrument; she could have done't.° — *used to play*
We'll hear them both.
RICHARDETTO I'll wait upon° you, sir. *Exeunt.* — *attend*

[2.2]

Enter Soranzo in his study, reading a book.

SORANZO "Love's measure is extreme, the comfort, pain;
The life unrest, and the reward disdain."[1]
What's here? Look o'er again. 'Tis so; so writes
This smooth, licentious poet in his rhymes.
But, Sannazar, thou liest, for, had thy bosom
Felt such oppression as is laid on mine,
Thou wouldst have kissed the rod that made thee smart.° — *feel the sting*
To work, then, happy° Muse, and contradict — *felicitous*
What Sannazar hath in his envy° writ. [*He writes.*] — *ill will*

2.2. Soranzo's house.
1. "Love finds moderation only in extremes, comfort only in pain, rest only in restlessness, and reward in love only in being disdained." (Lines from the Italian writer Jacopo Sannazaro [1458–1530], who also wrote a eulogy in praise of Venice; see lines 12–14 below.)

"Love's measure is the mean, sweet his annoys;
His pleasures life, and his reward all joys."[2]
Had Annabella lived when Sannazar
Did in his brief encomium celebrate
Venice, that queen of cities, he had left° *would have abandoned*
That verse which gained him such a sum of gold,
And for one only look from Annabell
Had writ° of her and her diviner cheeks. *Would have written*
Oh, how my thoughts are—

VASQUES (*within*) Pray forbear, in° rules of civility! Let *out of respect for*
me give notice on't.° I shall be taxed of° my neglect of duty *announce you / blamed for*
and service.

SORANZO What rude intrusion interrupts my peace?
Can I be nowhere private?

VASQUES (*within*) Troth, you wrong your modesty.

SORANZO What's the matter, Vasques? Who is't?

Enter Hippolita [dressed in black] and Vasques.

HIPPOLITA 'Tis I.
Do you know me now? Look, perjured man, on her
Whom thou and thy distracted° lust have wronged. *promiscuous*
Thy sensual rage of blood° hath made my youth *passion*
A scorn to men and angels, and shall I
Be now a foil to° thy unsated change? *contrast to enhance*
Thou know'st, false wanton,° when my modest fame° *lothario / reputation*
Stood free from stain or scandal, all the charms° *spells, temptations*
Of hell or sorcery could not prevail
Against the honor of my chaster bosom.
Thine eyes did plead in tears, thy tongue in oaths,
Such and so many that a heart of steel
Would have been wrought to pity, as was mine.
And shall the conquest of my lawful bed,
My husband's death urged on° by his disgrace, *hastened*
My loss of womanhood,° be ill rewarded *chaste reputation*
With hatred and contempt? No! Know, Soranzo,
I have a spirit doth as much distaste
The slavery of fearing thee as thou
Dost loathe the memory of what hath passed.

SORANZO Nay, dear Hippolita—

HIPPOLITA Call me not "dear,"
Nor think with supple words to smooth the grossness
Of my abuses.° 'Tis not your new mistress, *wrongs*
Your goodly Madam Merchant,[3] shall triumph
On my dejection.° Tell her thus from me: *overthrow*
My birth was nobler, and by much more free.° *and more honorable*

SORANZO You are too violent.

HIPPOLITA You are too double
In your dissimulation. See'st thou this,
This habit,° these black mourning weeds° of care? *costume / garments*
'Tis thou art cause of this, and hast divorced
My husband from his life and me from him,

2. "Love's harmony is the golden mean, its vexations are bittersweet; its pleasures are the essence of the human experience, and its reward is the best of all joys."
3. Annabella, a merchant's daughter.

And made me widow° in my widowhood. *i.e., deserted*
SORANZO Will you yet hear?
HIPPOLITA More of thy perjuries?
Thy soul is drowned too deeply in those sins;
Thou need'st not add to th'number.
SORANZO Then I'll leave you.
You are past all rules of sense.° *reason*
HIPPOLITA And thou of grace.
VASQUES Fie, mistress! You are not near the limits of reason.° *You're unreasonable*
If my lord had a resolution as noble as virtue itself, you take the course to unedge° it all.—Sir, I beseech you do not perplex her; griefs, alas, will have a vent. I dare undertake° Madam Hippolita will now freely hear you. *blunt* *guarantee*
SORANZO Talk to a woman frantic? [*To her*] Are these the fruits of your love?
HIPPOLITA They are the fruits of thy untruth, false man.
Didst thou not swear, whilst yet my husband lived,
That thou wouldst wish no happiness on earth
More than to call me wife? Didst thou not vow,
When he should° die, to marry me? For which *would*
The devil in my blood, and thy protests,° *protestations*
Caused me to counsel him to undertake
A voyage to Ligorne,° for that° we heard *Livorno / since*
His brother there was dead and left a daughter
Young and unfriended, who with much ado
I wished him to bring hither. He did so,
And went; and, as thou know'st, died on the way.
Unhappy man, to buy his death so dear
With my advice! Yet thou, for whom I did it,
Forget'st thy vows, and leav'st me to my shame.
SORANZO Who could help this?
HIPPOLITA Who? Perjured man, thou couldst,
If thou hadst faith or love.
SORANZO You are deceived.
The vows I made, if you remember well,
Were wicked and unlawful; 'twere° more sin *it would have been*
To keep them than to break them. As for me,
I cannot mask my penitence.° Think thou *hide my regret*
How much thou hast digressed from honest shame° *from honor*
In bringing of a gentleman to death
Who was thy husband—such a one as he,
So noble in his quality, condition,° *class, social standing*
Learning, behavior, entertainment,° love, *hospitality*
As Parma could not show a braver° man. *finer*
VASQUES You do not well. This was not your promise.[4]
SORANZO I care not. Let her know her monstrous life.
Ere I'll be servile to so black a sin,
I'll be accurst.—Woman, come here no more.
Learn to repent, and die; for, by my honor,
I hate thee and thy lust. You have been too foul. [*Exit.*]
VASQUES This part has been scurvily played.° *vilely acted*
HIPPOLITA How foolishly this beast contemns his fate,

4. You promised to speak calmly.

And shuns the use of that which I more scorn
Than I once loved, his love![5] But let him go.
My vengeance shall give comfort to this woe.

She offers° to go away. — *prepares, starts*

VASQUES Mistress, mistress! Madam Hippolita! Pray, a word or two.

HIPPOLITA With me, sir?

VASQUES With you, if you please.

HIPPOLITA What is't?

VASQUES I know you are infinitely moved° now, and you think you have cause. Some, I confess, you have, but, sure, not so much as you imagine. — *angered*

HIPPOLITA Indeed?

VASQUES Oh, you were miserably bitter, which you followed° even to the last syllable. Faith, you were somewhat too shrewd.° By my life, you could not have took my lord in a worse time since I first knew him. Tomorrow you shall find him a new man. — *kept up* / *shrill*

HIPPOLITA Well, I shall wait his leisure.° — *(said bitterly)*

VASQUES Fie, this is not a hearty° patience; it comes sourly from you. Troth, let me persuade you for once. — *heartfelt*

HIPPOLITA [*aside*] I have it,° and it shall be so. Thanks, Opportunity! [*To him*] Persuade me to what? — *I've got a plan*

VASQUES Visit him in some milder temper. Oh, if you could but master a little your female spleen, how might you win him!

HIPPOLITA He will never love me. Vasques, thou hast been a too trusty servant to such a master, and I believe thy reward in the end will fall out° like mine. — *turn out*

VASQUES So perhaps too.

HIPPOLITA Resolve° thyself it will. Had I one so true, so truly honest, so secret to my counsels as thou hast been to him and his, I should think it a slight acquittance° not only to make him master of all I have, but even of myself. — *Assure* / *discharge of a debt*

VASQUES Oh, you are a noble gentlewoman!

HIPPOLITA Wu't thou feed always upon hopes?° Well, I know thou art wise and see'st the reward of an old servant daily what it is. — *mere hopes*

VASQUES Beggary and neglect.

HIPPOLITA True. But Vasques, wert thou mine, and wouldst be private° to me and my designs, I here protest,° myself and all what I can else call mine should be at thy dispose. — *secret / vow*

VASQUES [*aside*] Work you that way, old mole? Then I have the wind of you.[6] [*To her*] I were not worthy of it, by any desert that could lie within my compass;° if I could— — *means of encompassing*

HIPPOLITA What then?

VASQUES I should then hope to live in these my old years with rest and security.

HIPPOLITA Give me thy hand. Now promise but thy silence,
And help to bring to pass a plot I have;

5. I.e., How foolishly Soranzo scorns what destiny has brought to him and makes no use of his power of attraction over me—an attraction I now scorn more passionately than I once loved him!

6. I'm on to you, like a hunter scenting his quarry in the wind.

And here in sight of heaven, that being done,
I make thee lord of me and mine estate.

VASQUES Come, you are merry.° This is such a happiness° that I can neither think or believe. *joking / good fortune*

HIPPOLITA Promise thy secrecy, and 'tis confirmed.

VASQUES Then here I call our good genii° for witnesses: whatsoever your designs are, or against whomsoever, I will not only be a special actor therein, but never disclose it till it be effected.° *guardian angels* / *carried out*

HIPPOLITA I take thy word, and with that, thee for mine.
Come, then, let's more confer of this anon.
[*Aside*] On this delicious bane° my thoughts shall banquet; *poison*
Revenge shall sweeten what my griefs have tasted. *Exeunt.*

[2.3]

Enter Richardetto [*disguised still as a physician*] *and Philotis.*

RICHARDETTO Thou see'st, my lovely niece, these strange mishaps,
How all my fortunes turn to my disgrace,
Wherein I am but as a looker-on,
Whiles others act my shame,° and I am silent. *wrong me shamefully*

PHILOTIS But uncle, wherein can this borrowed shape° *disguise*
Give you content?

RICHARDETTO I'll tell thee, gentle niece.
Thy wanton aunt,° in her lascivious riots, *(Hippolita)*
Lives now secure,° thinks I am surely dead *carefree and safe*
In my late journey to Ligorne for you—
As I have caused it to be rumored out.
Now would I see with what an impudence
She gives scope to her loose adultery,
And how the common voice° allows hereof. *popular opinion*
Thus far I have prevailed.

PHILOTIS Alas, I fear
You mean some strange revenge.

RICHARDETTO Oh, be not troubled;
Your ignorance shall plead for you° in all. *excuse you*
But to our business. What, you learned for certain
How Signor Florio means to give his daughter
In marriage to Soranzo?

PHILOTIS Yes, for certain.

RICHARDETTO But how find you young Annabella's love?
Inclined to him?

PHILOTIS For aught I could perceive,
She neither fancies him or any else.

RICHARDETTO There's mystery in that, which time must show.
She used° you kindly? *treated*

PHILOTIS Yes.

RICHARDETTO And craved your company?

PHILOTIS Often.

2.3. Somewhere in Parma, perhaps near Florio's house.

RICHARDETTO 'Tis well. It goes as I could wish.
I am the doctor now, and as for you,
None knows you. If all fail not, we shall thrive.
But who comes here?

Enter Grimaldi.

I know him; 'tis Grimaldi,
A Roman and a soldier, near allied
Unto the Duke of Montferrato, one
Attending on the nuncio° of the Pope — *representative*
That now resides in Parma, by which means
He hopes to get the love of Annabella.

GRIMALDI Save you,° sir. — *God save you*

RICHARDETTO And you, sir.

GRIMALDI I have heard
Of your approvèd° skill, which through the city — *demonstrated*
Is freely talked of, and would crave your aid.

RICHARDETTO For what, sir?

GRIMALDI Marry, sir, for this—
But I would speak in private.

RICHARDETTO [*to Philotis*] Leave us, cousin.° — *kinsman, niece*

Exit Philotis.

GRIMALDI I love fair Annabella, and would know
Whether in art° there may not be receipts° — *medicine / recipes*
To move affection.° — *arouse love*

RICHARDETTO Sir, perhaps there may,
But these will nothing° profit you. — *not at all*

GRIMALDI Not me?

RICHARDETTO Unless I be mistook, you are a man
Greatly in favor with the Cardinal.

GRIMALDI What of that?

RICHARDETTO In duty to His Grace,
I will be bold to tell you: if you seek
To marry Florio's daughter, you must first
Remove a bar 'twixt you and her.

GRIMALDI Who's that?

RICHARDETTO Soranzo is the man that hath her heart,
And, while he lives, be sure you cannot speed.° — *succeed*

GRIMALDI Soranzo? What, mine enemy, is't he?

RICHARDETTO Is he your enemy?

GRIMALDI The man I hate
Worse than confusion!° I'll kill him straight.° — *ruin / at once*

RICHARDETTO Nay, then, take mine advice,
Even for His Grace's sake the Cardinal:° — *for the Cardinal's sake*
I'll find a time when he° and she do meet, — *(Soranzo)*
Of which I'll give you notice, and, to be sure
He shall not scape you, I'll provide a poison
To dip your rapier's point in. If he had
As many heads as Hydra[1] had, he dies.

GRIMALDI But shall I trust thee, Doctor?

RICHARDETTO As yourself.

1. A many-headed monster whose heads redoubled as they were cut off.

Doubt not in aught. [*Aside*] Thus shall the Fates decree:
By me Soranzo falls that ruined me. *Exeunt.*

[2.4]

Enter Donado [with a letter], Bergetto, and Poggio.

DONADO Well, sir, I must be content to be both your secretary and your messenger myself. I cannot tell what this letter may work, but, as sure as I am alive, if thou come once to talk with her, I fear thou wu't mar whatsoever I make.

BERGETTO You make, uncle? Why, am not I big enough to carry mine own letter, I pray?

DONADO Ay, ay, carry a fool's head° o'thy own. Why, thou dunce, wouldst thou write a letter and carry it thyself? *jester's baton*

BERGETTO Yes, that I would, and read it to her with my own mouth; for you must think, if she will not believe me myself when she hears me speak, she will not believe another's handwriting. Oh, you think I am a blockhead, uncle. No, sir. Poggio knows I have indited° a letter myself, so I have. *written*

POGGIO Yes, truly, sir. I have it in my pocket.

[*He produces the letter.*]

DONADO A sweet one, no doubt! Pray let's see't.

BERGETTO I cannot read my own hand very well, Poggio. Read it, Poggio.

DONADO Begin.

POGGIO (*reads*) "Most dainty and honey-sweet mistress, I could call you fair, and lie as fast as any that loves you, but, my uncle being the elder man, I leave it to him as more fit for his age and the color of his beard. I am wise enough to tell you I can board[1] where I see occasion. Or, if you like my uncle's wit better than mine, you shall marry me; if you like mine better than his, I will marry you in spite of your teeth.° So, commending my best parts to you,[2] I rest° *whatever you say* *remain*

Yours upwards and downwards, or you may choose,

Bergetto."

BERGETTO Ah, ha! Here's stuff, uncle.

DONADO Here's stuff indeed to shame us all. Pray, whose advice did you take in° this learned letter? *in writing*

POGGIO None, upon my word, but mine own.

BERGETTO And mine, uncle, believe it, nobody's else; 'twas mine own brain, I thank a good wit for't.

DONADO Get you home, sir, and look you keep within doors till I return.

BERGETTO How! That were a jest indeed. I scorn it, i'faith.

DONADO What, you do not!° *You don't say!*

BERGETTO Judge me but I do, now.

POGGIO Indeed, sir, 'tis very unhealthy.[3]

DONADO Well, sir, if I hear any of your apish running to

2.4. Outside Florio's house, or else unlocalized, like the previous scene.

1. (1) Make amorous advances; (2) bourd, meaning "jest."

2. Entrusting and recommending to your care my best qualities. (But with the unintended added meaning of sexual organs.)

3. Staying indoors is unhealthy, says Poggio, flouting the prevailing learned opinion that outdoor air was unhealthy.

motions° and fopperies° till I come back, you were as good not.° Look to't. *Exit Donado.* [*puppet shows / foolery*; *you'd better not*]

BERGETTO Poggio, shall 's° steal to see this horse with the head in's tail?° [*shall we*; *(see 1.3.37–40)*]

POGGIO Ay, but you must take heed of whipping.

BERGETTO Dost take me for a child, Poggio? Come, honest° Poggio. *Exeunt.* [*worthy*]

[2.5]

Enter Friar and Giovanni.

FRIAR Peace! Thou hast told a tale whose every word
Threatens eternal slaughter to the soul.
I'm sorry I have heard it. Would mine ears
Had been one minute deaf before the hour
That thou cam'st to me! Oh, young man cast away,° [*spiritually lost*]
By the religious number of mine order,° [*By my friars' order*]
I day and night have waked my agèd eyes,
Above my strength, to weep on thy behalf.
But heaven is angry, and be thou resolved,° [*assured*]
Thou art a man remarked° to taste a mischief.° [*marked out / ruin*]
Look for't; though it come late, it will come, sure.

GIOVANNI Father, in this you are uncharitable.
What I have done I'll prove both fit and good.
It is a principle—which you have taught
When I was yet your scholar—that the frame
And composition of the mind doth follow
The frame and composition of body.
So, where the body's furniture° is beauty, [*adornment*]
The mind's must needs be virtue; which allowed,° [*granted in argument*]
Virtue itself is reason but refined,
And love the quintessence of that. This proves
My sister's beauty, being rarely° fair, [*uniquely*]
Is rarely virtuous—chiefly in her love,
And, chiefly in that love, her love to me.
If hers to me, then so is mine to her,
Since in like causes are effects alike.

FRIAR Oh, ignorance in knowledge! Long ago,
How often have I warned thee this before!
Indeed, if we were sure there were no deity,
Nor heaven nor hell, then to be led alone
By nature's light—as were philosophers
Of elder° times—might instance° some defense. [*pre-Christian / adduce*]
But 'tis not so. Then, madman, thou wilt find
That nature is in heaven's positions° blind. [*doctrines*]

GIOVANNI Your age o'errules° you. Had you youth like mine, [*overmasters*]
You'd make her love your heaven, and her divine.

FRIAR Nay, then, I see thou'rt too far sold to hell;
It lies not in the compass of my prayers
To call thee back. Yet let me counsel thee:
Persuade thy sister to some marriage.

2.5. The Friar's cell (see 2.6.1–3).

GIOVANNI Marriage? Why, that's to damn her! That's to prove
Her greedy of variety of lust.
FRIAR Oh, fearful! If thou wilt not, give me leave
To shrive her,° lest she should die unabsolved. *hear her confession*
GIOVANNI At your best leisure, father. Then she'll tell you
How dearly she doth prize my matchless love.
Then you will know what pity 'twere we two
Should have been sundered from each other's arms.
View well her face, and in that little round
You may observe a world of variety:
For color, lips; for sweet perfumes, her breath;
For jewels, eyes; for threads of purest gold,
Hair; for delicious choice of flowers, cheeks—
Wonder in every portion of that throne.° *seat of beauty*
Hear her but speak, and you will swear the spheres
Make music to the citizens in heaven.
But, father, what is else for pleasure framed,° *devised*
Lest I offend your ears, shall go unnamed.
FRIAR The more I hear, I pity thee the more,
That one so excellent should give those parts° *qualities*
All to a second death.° What I can do *to damnation*
Is but to pray; and yet I could advise thee,
Wouldst thou be ruled.
GIOVANNI In what?
FRIAR Why, leave her yet.
The throne of Mercy is above your trespass;° *transcends your sin*
Yet° time is left you both— *Still*
GIOVANNI To embrace each other;
Else let all time be struck quite out of number.° *out of sequence*
She is like me, and I like her resolved.
FRIAR No more. I'll visit her. This grieves me most:
Things being thus, a pair of souls are lost. *Exeunt.*

[2.6]

Enter Florio, Donado, Annabella, [and] Putana.

FLORIO Where's Giovanni?
ANNABELLA Newly walked abroad,° *Just gone out*
And, as I heard him say, gone to the Friar,
His reverend tutor.
FLORIO That's a blessèd man,
A man made up of holiness. I hope
He'll teach him how to gain another world.
DONADO [*offering Annabella a letter*] Fair gentlewoman, here's a letter sent
To you from my young cousin.° I dare swear *kinsman*
He loves you in his soul. Would you could hear
Sometimes what I see daily: sighs and tears,
As if his breast were prison to his heart!
FLORIO Receive it, Annabella.
ANNABELLA [*taking the letter*] Alas, good man!
DONADO [*aside to Putana*] What's that she said?

2.6. Florio's house.

PUTANA [*aside to Donado*] An't° please you, sir, she said, "Alas, good man!" Truly I do commend him to her every night before her first sleep, because I would have her dream of him, and she hearkens to that most religiously. *If it*

DONADO [*aside to Putana*] Say'st so? God-a-mercy,° Putana. [*Giving her money*] There's something for thee, and prithee do what thou canst on his behalf; sha' not be lost labor, take my word for't. *Thanks*

PUTANA [*aside to Donado*] Thank you most heartily, sir. Now I have a feeling of your mind, let me alone to work.° *leave it to me*

ANNABELLA [*calling to Putana*] Guardian!

PUTANA Did you call?

ANNABELLA [*offering Putana the letter*] Keep this letter.

DONADO Signor Florio, in any case bid her read it instantly.

FLORIO [*to Annabella*] Keep it for what? Pray read it me
here-right.° *immediately*

ANNABELLA I shall, sir. *She reads* [*finding there a jewel*].
[*Donado and Florio confer privately.*]

DONADO How d'ee find her inclined, signor?

FLORIO Troth, sir, I know not how; not all so well
As I could wish.

ANNABELLA [*to Donado*] Sir, I am bound to rest your cousin's debtor.[1]
The jewel I'll return; for, if he love,
I'll count that love a jewel.

DONADO [*aside to Florio*] Mark you that?
[*Aloud to her*] Nay, keep them both,[2] sweet maid.

ANNABELLA You must excuse me.
Indeed, I will not keep it.

FLORIO [*to Annabella*] Where's the ring,
That which your mother in her will bequeathed,
And charged you on her blessing not to give't
To any but your husband? Send back that.

ANNABELLA I have it not.
[*She attempts unsuccessfully to return the jewel.*]

FLORIO Ha! Have it not? Where is't?

ANNABELLA My brother in the morning took it from me,
Said he would wear 't today.

FLORIO Well, what do you say
To young Bergetto's love? Are you content
To match with him? Speak.

DONADO There's the point indeed.

ANNABELLA [*aside*] What shall I do? I must say something now.

FLORIO What say? Why d'ee not speak?

ANNABELLA Sir, with your leave,
Please you to give me freedom?° *free speech and choice*

FLORIO Yes, you have it.

ANNABELLA Signor Donado, if your nephew mean
To raise his better fortunes in his match,
The hope of me will hinder such a hope.
Sir, if you love him, as I know you do,
Find one more worthy of his choice than me.
In short, I'm sure I sha' not be his wife.

1. I am much obliged to Bergetto.

2. Keep both the jewel and Bergetto's love.

DONADO Why here's plain dealing. I commend thee for't,
And all the worst I wish thee is, heaven bless thee!
Your father yet and I will still be friends,
Shall we not, Signor Florio?

FLORIO Yes, why not?
Look, here your cousin comes.

Enter Bergetto and Poggio.

DONADO [*aside*] Oh, coxcomb! What doth he make° here? *is he doing*

BERGETTO Where's my uncle, sirs?

DONADO What's the news now?

BERGETTO Save you, uncle, save you. You must not think I come for nothing, masters.° *good sirs* [*To Annabella*] And how, and how is't? What, you have read my letter? Ah, there I—tickled you, i'faith!

POGGIO [*aside to Bergetto*]° *(or to the audience)* But 'twere better you had tickled her in another place.

BERGETTO [*to Annabella*] Sirrah sweetheart, I'll tell thee a good jest, and riddle° *figure out* what 'tis.

ANNABELLA You say you'd tell me.

BERGETTO As I was walking just now in the street, I met a swaggering fellow would needs take the wall of me,[3] and because he did thrust me, I very valiantly called him rogue. He hereupon bade me draw. I told him I had more wit than so,° *than to do that* but, when he saw that I would not, he did so maul me with the hilts of his rapier that my head sung whilst my feet capered in the kennel.° *gutter*

DONADO [*aside*] Was ever the like ass seen?

ANNABELLA And what did you all this while?

BERGETTO Laugh at him for a gull,° *fool* till I see the blood run about mine ears, and then I could not choose but find in my heart to cry; till a fellow with a broad beard—they say he is a new-come doctor—called me into his house, and gave me a plaster. Look you, here 'tis. [*He shows his bandage.*] And, sir, there was a young wench washed my face and hands most excellently. I'faith, I shall love her as long as I live for't.—Did she not, Poggio?

POGGIO Yes, and kissed him, too.

BERGETTO Why, la,° *indeed* now, you think I tell a lie, uncle, I warrant.

DONADO Would he that beat thy blood out of thy head had beaten some wit into it! For I fear thou never wilt have any.

BERGETTO Oh, uncle, but there was a wench would have done a man's heart good to have looked on her. By this light, she had a face, methinks, worth twenty of you, Mistress Annabella.

DONADO [*aside*] Was ever such a fool born?

ANNABELLA I am glad she liked° *pleased* you, sir.

BERGETTO Are you so? By my troth, I thank you, forsooth.

FLORIO Sure 'twas the doctor's niece, that was last day with us here.

BERGETTO 'Twas she, 'twas she!

3. Who insisted on being next to the wall as we passed. (This was the safer and cleaner place to be in streets with sewerlike gutters in the middle. Who should "take the wall" was usually determined by social rank.)

DONADO How do you know that, simplicity?

BERGETTO Why, does not he say so? If I should have said no, I should have given him the lie,° uncle, and so have deserved a dry° beating again. I'll none of that. *called him a liar* *bloodless*

FLORIO A very modest, well-behaved young maid as I have seen.

DONADO Is she indeed?

FLORIO Indeed she is, if I have any judgment.

DONADO [*to Bergetto*] Well, sir, now° you are free, you need not care for sending letters. Now you are dismissed; your mistress here will none of you. *now that*

BERGETTO No? Why, what care I for that? I can have wenches enough in Parma for half a crown° apiece.—Cannot I, Poggio? *(a prostitute's price)*

POGGIO I'll warrant you, sir.

DONADO Signor Florio,
I thank you for your free recourse you gave
For my admittance; and to you, fair maid,
That jewel I will give you 'gainst° your marriage.— *in anticipation of*
Come, will you go, sir?

BERGETTO Ay, marry, will I.—Mistress, farewell, mistress! I'll come again tomorrow. Farewell, mistress!

Exit Donado [with] Bergetto and Poggio.

Enter Giovanni.

FLORIO Son, where have you been? What, alone, alone,
still, still?
I would not have it so; you must forsake
This overbookish humor.° Well, your sister *moodiness*
Hath shook the fool off.

GIOVANNI 'Twas no match for her.

FLORIO 'Twas not indeed; I meant it nothing less.° *didn't intend it*
Soranzo is the man I only like.° *prefer above all others*
Look on him, Annabella. Come, 'tis supper time,
And it grows late. *Exit Florio.*

GIOVANNI [*seeing Bergetto's jewel*] Whose jewel's that?

ANNABELLA Some sweetheart's.

GIOVANNI So I think.

ANNABELLA A lusty° youth; *vigorous, handsome*
Signor Donado gave it me to wear
Against my marriage.

GIOVANNI But you shall not wear it.
Send it him back again.

ANNABELLA What, you are jealous?

GIOVANNI That you shall know anon, at better leisure.
Welcome, sweet night! The evening crowns the day.

Exeunt.

3.1

Enter Bergetto and Poggio.

BERGETTO Does my uncle think to make me a baby still? No, Poggio, he shall know I have a sconce° now. *head, brain*

POGGIO Ay, let him not bob you off° like an ape with an apple.[1] *fool or flout you*

BERGETTO 'Sfoot,° I will have the wench,° if he were ten uncles, in despite of his nose, Poggio. *By God's foot / (Philotis)*

POGGIO Hold him to the grindstone, and give not a jot of ground. She hath in a manner° promised you already. *in a sense*

BERGETTO True, Poggio, and her uncle the doctor swore I should marry her.

POGGIO He swore, I remember.

BERGETTO And I will have her, that's° more. Didst see the codpiece point[2] she gave me, and the box of marmalade? *what's*

POGGIO Very well, and kissed you, that my chops° watered at the sight on't. There's no way but to clap up° a marriage in hugger-mugger.° *jaws, mouth* / *conclude, arrange* / *in secret haste*

BERGETTO I will do't, for I tell thee, Poggio, I begin to grow valiant, methinks, and my courage begins to rise.° *increase; grow erect*

POGGIO Should you be afraid of your uncle?

BERGETTO Hang him, old doting rascal! No. I say I will have her.

POGGIO Lose no time, then.

BERGETTO I will beget a race of wise men and constables that shall cart whores at their own charges and break the Duke's peace ere I have done myself.[3]—Come away. *Exeunt.*

[3.2]

Enter Florio, Giovanni, Soranzo, Annabella, Putana, and Vasques.

FLORIO My lord Soranzo, though I must confess
The proffers that are made me have been great
In marriage of my daughter, yet the hope
Of your still-rising honors have prevailed
Above all other jointures.° Here she is. *marriage offers*
She knows my mind; speak for yourself to her.—
And hear you, daughter, see you use him nobly.
For any private speech, I'll give you time.—
Come, son, and you the rest, let them alone,
Agree as they may.

SORANZO I thank you, sir.

GIOVANNI [*aside to Annabella*]° Sister, be not all woman;[1] *(or to himself)*
think on me.

3.1. Unlocalized. At 2.6.125.1, Bergetto and Poggio left Florio's house with Donado.

1. I.e., like an animal easily fooled or placated with a treat.

2. Ornamental lace used to tie on the flap or bag-shaped appendage (codpiece) covering an opening at the front of men's breeches of that time.

3. I will beget a whole generation of wise citizens and constables who will punish and humiliate whores by parading them through the streets in carts (a common punishment at the time), at their own expense, and create a riot, before I have finished. (Constables were often the butt of humorous jokes about being slow-witted.)

3.2. Florio's house.

1. Do not be as other women are, that is, fickle.

SORANZO Vasques!
VASQUES My lord?
SORANZO Attend me without.° *Wait for me outside*
Exeunt omnes.° Manent° Soranzo and Annabella. *all / Remain*
ANNABELLA Sir, what's your will with me?
SORANZO Do you not know what I should tell° you? *am going to say to*
ANNABELLA Yes.
You'll say you love me.
SORANZO And I'll swear it too.
Will you believe it?
ANNABELLA 'Tis no point° of faith. *essential article*

Enter Giovanni above [to eavesdrop].

SORANZO Have you not will to love?
ANNABELLA Not you.
SORANZO Whom, then?
ANNABELLA That's as the Fates infer.° *bring about*
GIOVANNI [*aside*] Of those I'm regent now.
SORANZO What mean you, sweet?
ANNABELLA To live and die a maid.
SORANZO Oh, that's unfit.
GIOVANNI [*aside*] Here's one can say that's but a woman's note.° *what women say*
SORANZO Did you but see my heart, then would you swear—
ANNABELLA That you were dead.[2]
GIOVANNI [*aside*] That's true, or somewhat near it.
SORANZO See you these true love's tears?
ANNABELLA No.
GIOVANNI [*aside*] Now she winks.° *refuses to look*
SORANZO They plead to you for grace.
ANNABELLA Yet nothing speak.° *they say nothing*
SORANZO Oh, grant my suit!
ANNABELLA What is't?
SORANZO To let me live—
ANNABELLA Take it.
SORANZO —still yours.
ANNABELLA That is not mine to give.
GIOVANNI [*aside*] One such another° word would kill his hopes. *Another such*
SORANZO Mistress, to leave those fruitless strifes of wit,
Know I have loved you long, and loved you truly;
Not hope of what you have,° but what you are *of your wealth*
Have drawn me on. Then let me not in vain
Still feel the rigor of your chaste disdain.
I'm sick, and sick to th'heart.
ANNABELLA [*calling*] Help, aqua vitae!° *brandy, spirits*
SORANZO What mean you?
ANNABELLA Why, I thought you had been sick.
SORANZO Do you mock my love?
GIOVANNI [*aside*] There, sir, she was too nimble.
SORANZO [*aside*] 'Tis plain, she laughs at me. [*To her*] These scornful taunts
Neither become your modesty or years.

2. One can literally see the heart only when its owner is dead and cut open. (Annabella is deflating Soranzo's amorous rhetoric.)

ANNABELLA You are no looking glass, or, if you were,
I'd dress° my language by you. — *correct*
GIOVANNI [*aside*] I'm confirmed!
ANNABELLA To put you out of doubt, my lord, methinks
Your common sense should make you understand
That if I loved you, or desired your love,
Some way I should have given you better taste.° — *hint*
But since you are a nobleman, and one
I would not wish should spend his youth in hopes,
Let me advise you here to forbear your suit,
And think I wish you well. I tell you this.
SORANZO Is't you speak this?
ANNABELLA Yes, I myself. Yet know
Thus far I give you comfort: if mine eyes
Could have picked out a man, amongst all those
That sued to me, to make a husband of,
You should have been that man. Let this suffice.
Be noble in your secrecy, and wise.
GIOVANNI [*aside*] Why, now I see she loves me.
ANNABELLA One word more:
As ever virtue lived within your mind,
As ever noble courses were your guide,
As ever you would have me know you loved me,
Let not my father know hereof by you.
If I hereafter find that I must marry,
It shall be you or none.
SORANZO I take that promise.
ANNABELLA Oh, oh, my head!
SORANZO What's the matter? Not well?
ANNABELLA Oh, I begin to sicken.
GIOVANNI [*aside*] Heaven forbid!
Exit from above.
SORANZO Help, help! Within there, ho!

Enter Florio, Giovanni, [and] Putana.

Look to your daughter, Signor Florio!
FLORIO Hold her up! She swoons.
GIOVANNI Sister, how d'ee?
ANNABELLA Sick, brother. Are you there?
FLORIO Convey her to her bed instantly, whilst I send for a physician. Quickly, I say!
PUTANA Alas, poor child! *Exeunt; manet Soranzo.*

Enter Vasques.

VASQUES My lord!
SORANZO Oh, Vasques, now I doubly am undone,
Both in my present and my future hopes!
She plainly told me that she could not love,
And thereupon soon sickened, and I fear
Her life's in danger.
VASQUES [*aside*] By'r Lady, sir, and so is yours, if you knew all. (*To him*) 'Las, sir, I am sorry for that. Maybe 'tis but the maids' sickness,[3] an overflux° of youth; and then, sir, there — *excess*

3. A kind of anemia thought to afflict lovesick maidens.

is no such present remedy as present° marriage. But hath she given you an absolute denial?

immediate

SORANZO She hath and she hath not. I'm full of grief.
But what she said I'll tell thee as we go. *Exeunt.*

[3.3]

Enter Giovanni and Putana.

PUTANA Oh, sir, we are all undone, quite undone, utterly undone, and shamed forever! Your sister, oh, your sister!

GIOVANNI What of her? For heaven's sake, speak. How does she?

PUTANA Oh, that ever I was born to see this day!

GIOVANNI She is not dead, ha, is she?

PUTANA Dead? No, she is quick;° 'tis worse, she is with child. You know what you have done; heaven forgive 'ee! 'Tis too late to repent, now heaven help us!

alive; pregnant

GIOVANNI With child? How dost thou know't?

PUTANA How do I know't? Am I at these years ignorant what the meanings of qualms and water pangs° be? Of changing of colors, queasiness of stomachs, pukings, and another thing that I could name?° Do not, for her and your credit's sake, spend the time in asking how and which way 'tis so; she is quick, upon my word. If you let a physician see her water,° you're undone.

urges to urinate
(ceasing of menstruation)
urine (for diagnosis)

GIOVANNI But in what case° is she?

state, condition

PUTANA Prettily amended.° 'Twas but a fit, which I soon espied, and she must look for° often henceforward.

Much improved
expect

GIOVANNI Commend me to her; bid her take no care.°
Let not the doctor visit her, I charge you;
Make some excuse till I return. Oh, me,
I have a world of business in my head!
Do not discomfort her. How does this news perplex me!
If my father come to her, tell him she's recovered well;
Say 'twas but some ill diet. D'ee hear, woman?
Look you to't.

not to worry

PUTANA I will, sir. *Exeunt.*

[3.4]

Enter Florio and Richardetto.

FLORIO And how d'ee find her, sir?

RICHARDETTO Indifferent° well.
I see no danger, scarce perceive she's sick,
But that she told me she had lately eaten
Melons, and, as she thought, those disagreed
With her young stomach.

Tolerably

FLORIO Did you give her aught?

RICHARDETTO An easy surfeit-water,° nothing else.
You need not doubt° her health. I rather think
Her sickness is a fullness of her blood°—
You understand me?

drug for indigestion
fear for
excess of blood and desire

3.3. Florio's house.

3.4. Florio's house.

FLORIO I do. You counsel well,
And once° within these few days will so order't *at some time*
She shall be married ere she know the time.
RICHARDETTO Yet let not haste, sir, make unworthy choice;
That were dishonor.
FLORIO Master Doctor, no,
I will not do so neither. In plain words,
My lord Soranzo is the man I mean.
RICHARDETTO A noble and a virtuous gentleman.
FLORIO As any is in Parma. Not far hence
Dwells Father Bonaventure, a grave friar,
Once tutor to my son; now at his cell
I'll have 'em married.
RICHARDETTO You have plotted wisely.
FLORIO I'll send one straight to speak with him tonight.
RICHARDETTO Soranzo's wise; he will delay no time.
FLORIO It shall be so.

Enter Friar and Giovanni.

FRIAR Good peace be here and love!
FLORIO Welcome, religious friar. You are one
That still° bring blessing to the place you come to. *always*
GIOVANNI Sir, with what speed I could, I did my best
To draw this holy man from forth his cell
To visit my sick sister, that with words
Of ghostly° comfort in this time of need *spiritual*
He might absolve her,° whether she live or die. *receive her confession*
FLORIO 'Twas well done, Giovanni. Thou herein
Hast showed a Christian's care, a brother's love.—
Come, father, I'll conduct you to her chamber,
And one thing would entreat you.
FRIAR Say on, sir.
FLORIO I have a father's dear impression,° *feelings (of love)*
And wish, before I fall into my grave,
That I might see her married, as 'tis fit;
A word from you, grave man, will win her more
Than all our best persuasions.
FRIAR Gentle sir,
All this I'll say, that heaven may prosper her. *Exeunt.*

[3.5]

Enter Grimaldi.

GRIMALDI Now if the doctor keep his word,° Soranzo, *(see 2.3.56–60)*
Twenty to one you miss your bride. I know
'Tis an unnoble act, and not becomes
A soldier's valor; but in terms° of love, *circumstances*
Where merit cannot sway, policy° must. *cunning*
I am resolved, if this physician
Play not on both hands,° then Soranzo falls. *Isn't double-dealing*

Enter Richardetto [with a box].

3.5. Richardetto's house (?).

RICHARDETTO You are come as I could wish. This very night
Soranzo, 'tis ordained, must be affied° *betrothed*
To Annabella, and, for aught I know,
Married.
GRIMALDI How!
RICHARDETTO Yet your patience.
The place, 'tis Friar Bonaventure's cell.
Now I would wish you to bestow° this night *spend*
In watching thereabouts. 'Tis but a night;
If you miss now! Tomorrow I'll know all.
GRIMALDI Have you the poison?
RICHARDETTO [*giving the box*] Here 'tis, in this box.
Doubt nothing, this will do't. In any case,
As you respect your life, be quick and sure.
GRIMALDI I'll speed° him. *dispatch*
RICHARDETTO Do. Away! For 'tis not safe
You should be seen much here. Ever my love!
GRIMALDI And mine to you! *Exit Grimaldi.*
RICHARDETTO So, if this hit,° I'll laugh and hug revenge; *succeeds*
And they that now dream of a wedding feast
May chance to mourn the lusty bridegroom's ruin.
But to my other business. [*Calling*] Niece Philotis!

Enter Philotis.

PHILOTIS Uncle?
RICHARDETTO My lovely niece, you have bethought 'ee?
PHILOTIS Yes, and, as you counseled,
Fashioned my heart to love him;° but he swears *(Bergetto)*
He will tonight be married, for he fears
His uncle else, if he should know the drift,° *intent*
Will hinder all, and call his coz to shrift.° *call Bergetto to account*
RICHARDETTO Tonight? Why, best of all. But let me see,
Ay—ha—yes—so it shall be: in disguise
We'll early to the Friar's; I have thought on't.

Enter Bergetto and Poggio.

PHILOTIS Uncle, he comes.
RICHARDETTO Welcome, my worthy coz.° *i.e., kinsman-to-be*
BERGETTO Lass, pretty lass, come buss,° lass. [*They kiss.*] Aha, Poggio! *kiss*
POGGIO There's hope of this yet.
RICHARDETTO You shall have time enough. Withdraw a little;
We must confer at large.° *at length*
BERGETTO Have you not sweetmeats or dainty devices for me?
PHILOTIS You shall have enough, sweetheart.
BERGETTO Sweetheart! Mark that, Poggio.—By my troth, I cannot choose but kiss thee once more for that word "sweetheart." [*He kisses her.*] Poggio, I have a monstrous swelling about my stomach, whatsoever the matter be.
POGGIO You shall have physic for't, sir.
RICHARDETTO Time runs apace.
BERGETTO Time's a blockhead.
RICHARDETTO Be ruled. When we have done what's fit to do,
Then you may kiss your fill, and bed her too. *Exeunt.*

[3.6]

Enter the Friar in his study, sitting in a chair, Annabella kneeling and whispering to him, a table before them and wax lights. She weeps and wrings her hands.

FRIAR I am glad to see this penance; for believe me,
You have unripped° a soul so foul and guilty *disclosed*
As, I must tell you true, I marvel how
The earth hath borne you up. But weep, weep on;
These tears may do you good. Weep faster yet,
Whiles I do read a lecture.° *deliver a sermon*

ANNABELLA Wretched creature!

FRIAR Ay, you are wretched, miserably wretched,
Almost condemned alive. There is a place—
List, daughter—in a black and hollow vault,
Where day is never seen. There shines no sun,
But flaming horror of consuming fires,
A lightless sulfur choked with smoky fogs
Of an infected darkness. In this place
Dwell many thousand, thousand sundry sorts
Of never-dying deaths. There damnèd souls
Roar without pity. There are gluttons fed
With toads and adders; there is burning oil
Poured down the drunkard's throat. The usurer
Is forced to sup whole drafts of molten gold.
There is the murderer forever stabbed,
Yet can he never die; there lies the wanton° *lecher*
On racks of burning steel, whiles in his soul
He feels the torment of his raging lust.

ANNABELLA Mercy, oh, mercy!

FRIAR There stands these wretched things° *creatures, persons*
Who have dreamt out whole years in lawless sheets
And secret incests, cursing one another.
Then you will wish each kiss your brother gave
Had been a dagger's point; then you shall hear
How he will cry, "Oh, would my wicked sister
Had first been damned, when she did yield to lust!"
But soft,° methinks I see repentance work *wait a minute*
New motions in your heart. Say, how is't with you?

ANNABELLA Is there no way left to redeem my miseries?

FRIAR There is. Despair not. Heaven is merciful,
And offers grace even now. 'Tis thus agreed:
First, for your honor's safety that you marry
The lord Soranzo; next, to save your soul,
Leave off this life, and henceforth live to him.° *loyal to Soranzo*

ANNABELLA Ay, me!

FRIAR Sigh not. I know the baits of sin
Are hard to leave. Oh, 'tis a death to do't.
Remember what must come! Are you content?

ANNABELLA I am.

3.6. The Friar's study or cell (?). See the opening stage direction *"in his study."* Although at 3.4.33 Florio proposed to conduct the Friar to Annabella's chamber, the actual meeting seems better suited to the cell, since Soranzo arrives to be affianced to Annabella (49.1 ff), and such a location is consistent with the setting of the next scene, which seems to follow immediately in time.

FRIAR I like it well. We'll take the time.° *the opportunity*
[*Calling*] Who's near us there?

Enter Florio [and] Giovanni.

FLORIO Did you call, father?
FRIAR Is Lord Soranzo come?
FLORIO He stays below.
FRIAR Have you acquainted him at full?
FLORIO I have,
And he is overjoyed.
FRIAR And so are we.
Bid him come near.
GIOVANNI [*aside*] My sister weeping? Ha!
I fear this friar's falsehood. [*To them*] I will call him. *Exit.*
FLORIO Daughter, are you resolved?
ANNABELLA Father, I am.

Enter Giovanni, Soranzo, and Vasques.

FLORIO My lord Soranzo, here
Give me your hand; for that I give you this.
[*He joins the hands of Soranzo and Annabella.*]
SORANZO Lady, say you so too?
ANNABELLA I do, and vow
To live with you and yours.
FRIAR Timely resolved.
My blessing rest on both! More to be done,
You may perform it on the morning sun. *Exeunt.*

[3.7]

Enter Grimaldi with his rapier drawn, and a dark lantern.° *shuttered lantern*

GRIMALDI 'Tis early night as yet, and yet too soon
To finish such a work. Here I will lie
To listen who comes next. *He lies down.°* *(with ear to the ground)*

Enter Bergetto and Philotis disguised, and after Richardetto and Poggio.

BERGETTO We are almost at the place, I hope, sweetheart.
GRIMALDI [*aside*] I hear them near, and heard one say
"sweetheart."
'Tis he. Now guide my hand, some angry Justice,
Home to his bosom. [*He lunges.*] Now have at you, sir![1]
Strikes Bergetto and exit.
BERGETTO Oh, help, help! Here's a stitch fallen° in my guts. *burst*
Oh, for a flesh-tailor° quickly!—Poggio! *i.e., surgeon*
PHILOTIS What ails my love?
BERGETTO I am sure I cannot piss forward and backward, and yet I am wet before and behind.—Lights, lights, ho, lights!
PHILOTIS Alas, some villain here has slain my love!

3.7. Near the Friar's cell, at night (see 3.5.12–14).

1. Grimaldi thinks he is killing Soranzo (see 3.5.8–19).

RICHARDETTO Oh, heaven forbid it! Raise up the next° neighbors nearest
Instantly, Poggio, and bring lights. *Exit Poggio.*
How is't, Bergetto? Slain?
It cannot be. Are you sure you're hurt?

BERGETTO Oh, my belly seethes like a porridge pot. Some cold water! I shall boil over else. My whole body is in a sweat, that you may wring my shirt. Feel here.

Enter Poggio with Officers, and lights and halberds.° pikes

Why, Poggio!

POGGIO Here. Alas! How do you?

RICHARDETTO Give me a light. What's here? All blood! Oh, sirs,
Signor Donado's nephew now is slain.
Follow the murderer with all the haste
Up to the city; he cannot be far hence.
Follow, I beseech you!

OFFICERS Follow, follow, follow! *Exeunt Officers.*

RICHARDETTO [*to Philotis*] Tear off thy linen, coz, to stop his wounds.—
Be of good comfort, man.

BERGETTO Is all this mine own blood? Nay, then, good night with me, Poggio. Commend me to my uncle, dost hear? Bid him for my sake make much of this wench.° Oh—I am going the wrong way sure, my belly aches so—Oh, farewell, Poggio—Oh—Oh— *Dies.* take care of Philotis

PHILOTIS Oh, he is dead!

POGGIO How! Dead?

RICHARDETTO He's dead indeed.
'Tis now too late to weep. Let's have him home,
And with what speed we may find out the murderer.

POGGIO Oh, my master, my master, my master! *Exeunt.*

[3.8]

Enter Vasques and Hippolita.

HIPPOLITA Betrothed?

VASQUES I saw it.

HIPPOLITA And when's the marriage day?

VASQUES Some two days hence.

HIPPOLITA Two days? Why, man, I would but wish two hours
To send him to his last and lasting sleep.
And, Vasques, thou shalt see I'll do it bravely.° finely

VASQUES I do not doubt your wisdom, nor, I trust, you my secrecy. I am infinitely yours.

HIPPOLITA I will be thine in spite of my disgrace.
So soon?° Oh, wicked man! I durst be sworn Marrying so soon?
He'd laugh to see me weep.

VASQUES And that's a villainous fault in him.

HIPPOLITA No, let him laugh. I'm armed in my resolves.
Be thou still true.

3.8. Soranzo's house (?) or in some unspecified location.

VASQUES I should get little by treachery against° so hopeful a *in exchange for*
preferment° as I am like° to climb to. *advancement / likely*
HIPPOLITA Even to my bosom, Vasques. Let my youth° *(Soranzo—contemptuous)*
Revel in these new pleasures. If we thrive,
He now hath but a pair of days to live. *Exeunt.*

[3.9]

Enter Florio, Donado [weeping], Richardetto, Poggio, and Officers.

G & A linguistic dominance – but fades – context curse are still centre of discussion

FLORIO 'Tis bootless° now to show yourself a child, *fruitless*
Signor Donado. What is done is done.
Spend not the time in tears, but seek for justice.
RICHARDETTO I must confess, somewhat I was in fault,
That had not first acquainted you what love
Passed 'twixt him and my niece, but, as I live,
His fortune grieves me as it were mine own.
DONADO Alas, poor creature! He meant no man harm,
That I am sure of.
FLORIO I believe that too.
But stay, my masters,° are you sure you saw *my good sirs*
The murderer pass here?
OFFICER An it please you,° sir, we are sure we saw a ruffian, *If you please*
with a naked weapon in his hand all bloody, get into my Lord
Cardinal's Grace's gate, that we are sure of; but for fear of
His Grace (bless us!) we durst go no further.
DONADO Know you what manner of man he was?
OFFICER Yes, sure I know the man. They say 'a° is a soldier; *he*
he that loved your daughter, sir, an't please ye, 'twas he for
certain.
FLORIO Grimaldi, on my life.
OFFICER Ay, ay, the same.
RICHARDETTO The Cardinal is noble; he no doubt
Will give true justice.
DONADO Knock, someone, at the gate.
POGGIO I'll knock, sir. *Poggio knocks.*
SERVANT (*within*) What would 'ee?
FLORIO We require° speech with the Lord Cardinal *request*
About some present° business. Pray inform *urgent*
His Grace that we are here.

Enter Cardinal and Grimaldi.

CARDINAL Why, how now, friends? What saucy mates° are you *impudent fellows*
That know nor° duty nor civility? *neither*
Are we a person fit to be your host?
Or is our house become your common inn
To beat our doors at pleasure? What such haste
Is yours as that it cannot wait fit times?
Are you the masters° of this commonwealth, *leading citizens*
And know no more discretion? Oh, your news
Is here before you: you have lost a nephew,
Donado, last night by Grimaldi slain.

3.9. At the Lord Cardinal's gate.

Is that your business? Well, sir, we have knowledge on't.
Let that suffice.

GRIMALDI In presence of Your Grace,
In thought I never meant Bergetto harm;
But, Florio, you can tell with how much scorn
Soranzo, backed with his confederates,
Hath often wronged me. I, to be revenged—
For that° I could not win° him else° to fight— *Since / coax / otherwise*
Had thought by way of ambush to have killed him,
But was unluckily therein mistook;
Else he had felt what late° Bergetto did. *recently*
And though my fault to him were merely chance,
Yet humbly I submit me to Your Grace
[*Kneeling*] To do with me as you please.

CARDINAL Rise up, Grimaldi.—
[*Grimaldi rises.*]
You citizens of Parma, if you seek
For justice: know, as nuncio from the Pope,
For this offense I here receive Grimaldi
Into His Holiness' protection.
He is no common man, but nobly born;
Of princes' blood, though you, Sir Florio,
Thought him too mean° a husband for your daughter. *baseborn*
If more you seek for, you must go to Rome,
For he shall thither. Learn more wit,° for shame! *Get smart*
Bury your dead.—Away, Grimaldi. Leave 'em.
Exeunt Cardinal and Grimaldi.

DONADO Is this a churchman's voice? Dwells justice here?

FLORIO Justice is fled to heaven and comes no nearer.[1]
Soranzo, was't for him?° Oh, impudence! *intended for Soranzo*
Had he° the face° to speak it, and not blush? *(Grimaldi) / effrontery*
Come, come, Donado, there's no help in this,
When cardinals think murder's not amiss.
Great men may do their wills; we must obey,
But heaven will judge them for't another day. *Exeunt.*

4.1

A banquet. Hautboys.° Enter the Friar, Giovanni, Annabella, Philotis, Soranzo, Donado, Florio, Richardetto, Putana, and Vasques. *Oboes*

FRIAR These holy rites performed, now take your times
To spend the remnant of the day in feast;
Such fit repasts are pleasing to the saints
Who are your guests, though not with mortal eyes
To be beheld. Long prosper in this day,
You happy couple, to each other's joy!

SORANZO Father, your prayer is heard. The hand of goodness
Hath been a shield for me against my death,
And, more to bless me, hath enriched my life
With this most precious jewel°—such a prize *(Annabella)*

1. Justice comes not to earth. (Astraea, goddess of justice, left the world of men at the beginning of the mythological iron age—supposedly the current age—having been driven away by human corruption.)
4.1. Florio's house.

As earth hath not another like to this.
[*To Annabella*] Cheer up, my love;—and gentlemen, my friends,
Rejoice with me in mirth. This day we'll crown
With lusty cups° to Annabella's health. — *cups of strong wine*

GIOVANNI (*aside*) Oh, torture! Were the marriage yet undone,
Ere I'd endure this sight, to see my love
Clipped° by another, I would dare confusion,° — *Embraced / death*
And stand the horror of ten thousand deaths.

VASQUES [*to Giovanni*] Are you not well, sir?

GIOVANNI Prithee, fellow, wait.° — *wait on the guests*
I need not thy officious diligence.

FLORIO Signor Donado, come, you must forget
Your late mishaps, and drown your cares in wine.

SORANZO Vasques!

VASQUES My lord?

SORANZO Reach me that weighty bowl.
Here, brother° Giovanni, here's to you. — *brother-in-law*
Your turn comes next, though now a bachelor.
Here's to your sister's happiness and mine!
[*He drinks, and offers the bowl.*]

GIOVANNI I cannot drink.

SORANZO What?

GIOVANNI 'Twill indeed offend° me. — *upset, make ill*

ANNABELLA [*to Soranzo*] Pray, do not urge him if he be not willing. *Hautboys* [*are heard*].

FLORIO How now, what noise is this?

VASQUES Oh, sir, I had forgot to tell you: certain young maidens of Parma, in honor to Madam Annabella's marriage, have sent their loves to her in a masque, for which they humbly crave your patience and silence.

SORANZO We are much bound° to them, so much the more as it comes unexpected. Guide them in. — *obliged*

Enter Hippolita and ladies in white robes [*all masked*], *with garlands of willows. Music and a dance.*

Thanks, lovely virgins. Now might we but know
To whom we have been beholding° for this love, — *beholden*
We shall acknowledge it.

HIPPOLITA [*unmasking*] Yes, you shall know.
What think you now?

OMNES° Hippolita? — *All*

HIPPOLITA 'Tis she.
Be not amazed, nor blush, young lovely bride;
I come not to defraud you of your man.
[*To Soranzo*] 'Tis now no time to reckon up the talk
What° Parma long hath rumored of us both. — *That*
Let rash report° run on; the breath that vents it — *rumor*
Will, like a bubble, break itself at last.
[*To Annabella*] But now to you, sweet creature: lend 's your hand.
Perhaps it hath been said that I would claim
Some interest in Soranzo, now your lord.° — *husband*
What I have right to do, his soul knows best;
But in my duty to your noble worth,

Sweet Annabella, and my care of you,
Here take, Soranzo, take this hand from me.
I'll once more join what by the holy church
Is finished and allowed.° [*She joins their hands.*] Have I done well? *approved*

SORANZO You have too much engaged us.° *You're too kind*

HIPPOLITA One thing more:
That you may know my single charity,° *sincere love*
Freely I here remit° all interest *relinquish*
I e'er could claim, and give you back your vows;
And to confirm't—reach me a cup of wine—
My lord Soranzo, in this draft I drink
Long rest t'ee! [*Aside to Vasques*] Look to it, Vasques.

VASQUES [*aside to her*] Fear nothing.

He gives her a poisoned cup. She drinks.

SORANZO Hippolita, I thank you, and will pledge
This happy union° as another life.— *accord*
Wine there!

VASQUES You shall have none; neither shall you pledge her.

HIPPOLITA How!

VASQUES Know now, mistress she-devil, your own mischievous treachery hath killed you. I must not° marry you. *am not destined to*

HIPPOLITA Villain!

OMNES What's the matter?

VASQUES Foolish woman, thou art now like a firebrand that hath kindled others and burnt thyself. *Troppo sperar inganna.*[1] Thy vain hope hath deceived thee; thou art but° dead. If thou hast any grace, pray. *as good as*

HIPPOLITA Monster!

VASQUES Die in charity,° for shame! [*To the others*] This thing of malice, this woman, had privately corrupted me with promise of marriage, under this politic° reconciliation to poison my lord, whiles she might laugh at his confusion° on his marriage day. I promised her fair, but I knew what my reward should have been; and would willingly have spared her life, but that I was acquainted with the danger of her disposition, and now have fitted her a just payment in her own coin. There she is, she hath yet[2]—and end thy days in peace, vile woman! As for life, there's no hope; think not on't. *Christian love* / *cunning* / *overthrow*

OMNES Wonderful justice!

RICHARDETTO Heaven, thou art righteous!

HIPPOLITA Oh, 'tis true,
I feel my minute° coming. Had that slave° *appointed time / wretch*
Kept promise—oh, my torment!—thou this hour
Hadst died, Soranzo.—Heat above hellfire!—
Yet ere I pass away—cruel, cruel flames!—
Take here my curse amongst you: [*to Soranzo*] may thy bed
Of marriage be a rack° unto thy heart! *torture rack*
Burn, blood, and boil in vengeance!—Oh, my heart,
My flame's intolerable!—Mayst thou live
To father bastards; may her womb bring forth
Monsters, and die together in your sins,
Hated, scorned, and unpitied!—Oh—Oh— *Dies.*

1. Too much hoping is delusory. (An Italian proverb.) 2. An unfinished thought or a defect in the text (?).

FLORIO Was e'er so vile a creature?
RICHARDETTO Here's the end
Of lust and pride.
ANNABELLA It is a fearful sight.
SORANZO Vasques, I know thee now a trusty servant,
And never will forget thee.—Come, my love.
We'll home, and thank the heavens for this escape.—
Father and friends, we must break up this mirth;
It is too sad a feast.
DONADO Bear hence the body.
FRIAR [*aside to Giovanni*] Here's an ominous change!
Mark this, my Giovanni, and take heed.
I fear the event;° that marriage seldom's good *outcome*
Where the bride-banquet° so begins in blood. *Exeunt.* *wedding banquet*

[4.2]

Enter Richardetto and Philotis.

RICHARDETTO My wretched wife, more wretched in her shame
Than in her wrongs to me, hath paid too soon
The forfeit of her modesty and life.
And I am sure, my niece, though vengeance hover,
Keeping aloof yet from Soranzo's fall,
Yet he will fall, and sink with his own weight.
I need not—now my heart persuades me so—
To further his confusion.° There is one *destruction*
Above begins to work; for, as I hear,
Debates already 'twixt his wife and him
Thicken and run to head.° She, as 'tis said, *come to a boil*
Slightens° his love, and he abandons hers. *Disdains*
Much talk I hear. Since things go thus, my niece,
In tender love and pity of your youth,
My counsel is that you should free your years° *your youth*
From hazard of these woes by flying hence
To fair Cremona, there to vow your soul
In holiness a holy votaress.° *nun*
Leave me to see the end of these extremes.
All human worldly courses are uneven;
No life is blessèd but the way to heaven.
PHILOTIS Uncle, shall I resolve to be a nun?
RICHARDETTO Ay, gentle niece, and in your hourly prayers
Remember me, your poor unhappy uncle.
Hie to Cremona now, as Fortune leads,
Your home your cloister, your best friends your beads.° *prayer beads, rosary*
Your chaste and single life shall crown° your birth; *fulfill, honor*
Who dies a virgin lives a saint on earth.
PHILOTIS Then farewell world, and worldly thoughts adieu!
Welcome, chaste vows! Myself I yield to you. *Exeunt.*

4.2. Richardetto's house (?).

[4.3]

Enter Soranzo unbraced,° and Annabella dragged in. — *partly unbuttoned*

SORANZO Come, strumpet, famous° whore! Were every drop — *notorious*
Of blood that runs in thy adulterous veins
A life, this sword—dost see't?—should in one blow
Confound° them all. Harlot, rare,° notable harlot, — *Destroy / unparalleled*
That with thy brazen face maintain'st° thy sin, — *persists in; defends*
Was there no man in Parma to be bawd
To your loose cunning whoredom else but I?
Must your hot itch and pleurisy° of lust, — *excess; inflammation*
The heyday of your luxury,° be fed — *height of your lust*
Up to a surfeit, and could none but I
Be picked out to be cloak to your close° tricks, — *secret*
Your belly sports? Now I must be the dad
To all that gallimaufry° that's stuffed — *hodgepodge*
In thy corrupted bastard-bearing womb?
Say, must I?

ANNABELLA Beastly man, why, 'tis thy fate.
I sued not to thee, for, but that I thought[1]
Your overloving lordship would have run
Mad on denial, had ye lent me time
I would have told 'ee in what case° I was; — *state*
But you would needs be doing.° — *couldn't wait for sex*

SORANZO Whore of whores!
Dar'st thou tell me this?

ANNABELLA Oh, yes, why not?
You were deceived in me; 'twas not for love
I chose you, but for honor.° Yet know this: — *for reputation's sake*
Would you be patient yet, and hide your shame,
I'd see whether I could love you.

SORANZO Excellent quean!° — *whore*
Why, art thou not with child?

ANNABELLA What needs all this,
When 'tis superfluous? I confess I am.

SORANZO Tell me by whom.

ANNABELLA Soft,° sir, 'twas not in my bargain. — *Gently*
Yet somewhat, sir, to stay your longing stomach° — *appease your appetite*
I'm content t'acquaint you with: the man,
The more than man that got this sprightly boy—
For 'tis a boy; that's for your glory, sir,
Your heir shall be a son—

SORANZO Damnable monster!

ANNABELLA Nay, an° you will not hear, I'll speak no more. — *if*

SORANZO Yes, speak, and speak thy last.

ANNABELLA A match,° a match. — *Agreed*
This noble creature was in every part
So angel-like, so glorious, that a woman
Who had not been but human as was I
Would have kneeled to him and have begged for love.
You? Why, you are not worthy once to name
His name without true worship, or indeed,
Unless you kneeled, to hear another name him.

4.3. Soranzo's house.

1. I did not woo you, for, were it not that I thought.

SORANZO What was he called?
ANNABELLA We are not come to that.
Let it suffice that you shall have the glory
To father what so brave° a father got.° *fine / begot*
In brief, had not this chance fall'n out as 't doth,
I never had been troubled with a thought
That you had been a creature;° but for marriage, *That you even existed*
I scarce dream yet of that.[2]
SORANZO Tell me his name.
ANNABELLA Alas, alas, there's all.° *that's all I'll say*
Will you believe?
SORANZO What?
ANNABELLA You shall never know.
SORANZO How!
ANNABELLA Never. If you do, let me be cursed.
SORANZO Not know it, strumpet? I'll rip up thy heart
And find it there—
ANNABELLA Do, do.
SORANZO —and with my teeth
Tear the prodigious° lecher joint by joint. *monstrous*
ANNABELLA Ha, ha, ha! The man's merry.
SORANZO Dost thou laugh?
Come, whore, tell me your lover, or, by truth,
I'll hew thy flesh to shreds. Who is't?
ANNABELLA (*sings*) *"Che morte più dolce che morire per amore?"*[3]
SORANZO Thus will I pull thy hair, and thus I'll drag
Thy lust-belepered° body through the dust. *lust-spotted*
Yet tell his name.
ANNABELLA (*sings*) *"Morendo in gratia Dei, morirei senza dolore."*[4]
SORANZO Dost thou triumph? The treasure of the earth
Shall not redeem thee; were there kneeling kings
Did beg thy life, or angels did come down
To plead in tears, yet should not all prevail
Against my rage. Dost thou not tremble yet?
ANNABELLA At what? To die? No, be a gallant hangman.
I dare thee to the worst; strike, and strike home.° *to the heart*
I leave revenge behind, and thou shalt feel't.
SORANZO Yet tell me ere thou diest, and tell me truly:
Knows thy old father this?
ANNABELLA No, by my life.
SORANZO Wilt thou confess, and I will spare thy life?
ANNABELLA My life? I will not buy my life so dear.
SORANZO I will not slack my vengeance.

Enter Vasques.

VASQUES What d'ee mean, sir?
SORANZO Forbear, Vasques. Such a damnèd whore
Deserves no pity.

2. As for marriage, I can hardly imagine it still.
3. "What death is sweeter than to die for love?" (A saying found in the Italian phrase book by John Florio, *Florio His First Fruits*, 1578.)
4. "Dying in the graces of God, I should do so without sadness." (Or Q's *"Lei"*—see Textual Notes—should perhaps read *"a lui,"* "Dying in *his* good graces." Also from *Florio His First Fruits;* see previous note.)

VASQUES Now the gods forfend!° And would you be her executioner, and kill her in your rage too? Oh, 'twere most unmanlike! She is your wife; what faults hath been done by her before she married you were not against you. Alas, poor lady, what hath she committed which any lady in Italy in the like case would not? Sir, you must be ruled by your reason and not by your fury; that were unhuman and beastly. *forbid*

SORANZO She shall not live.

VASQUES Come, she must. You would have her confess the author of her present misfortunes, I warrant 'ee. 'Tis an unconscionable demand, and she should lose the estimation that I, for my part, hold of her worth, if she had done it. Why, sir, you ought not, of all men living, to know it. Good sir, be reconciled. Alas, good gentlewoman!

ANNABELLA Pish, do not beg for me. I prize my life
As nothing. If the man will needs be mad,
Why, let him take it.

SORANZO Vasques, hear'st thou this?

VASQUES Yes, and commend her for it. In this she shows the nobleness of a gallant spirit, and beshrew° my heart but it becomes her rarely.° (*Aside to him*) Sir, in any case smother your revenge; leave the scenting-out your wrongs to me. Be ruled, as you respect your honor, or you mar all. (*Aloud*) Sir, if ever my service were of any credit with you, be not so violent in your distractions. You are married now; what a triumph might the report of this give to other neglected suitors![5] 'Tis as manlike to bear extremities as godlike to forgive. *curse* / *excellently*

SORANZO Oh, Vasques, Vasques, in this piece of flesh,
This faithless face of hers, had I laid up
The treasure of my heart! [*To her*] Hadst thou been virtuous,
Fair wicked woman, not the matchless joys
Of life itself° had made me wish to live *life eternal*
With any saint but thee. Deceitful creature,
How hast thou mocked my hopes, and in the shame
Of thy lewd womb even buried me alive!
I did too dearly love thee.

VASQUES (*aside* [*to him*]) This is well.
Follow this temper° with some passion;° *mood / feeling*
Be brief and moving; 'tis for the purpose.

SORANZO [*to Annabella*] Be witness to my words thy soul and thoughts,
And tell me, didst not think that in my heart
I did too superstitiously° adore thee? *idolatrously*

ANNABELLA I must confess I know you loved me well.

SORANZO And wouldst thou use me thus? O Annabella,
Be thou assured, whatsoe'er the villain was
That thus hath tempted thee to this disgrace,
Well he might lust, but never loved like me.
He doted on the picture that hung out
Upon thy cheeks to please his humorous° eye, *capricious*
Not on the part I loved, which was thy heart,
And, as I thought, thy virtues.

5. Think how other disappointed suitors might congratulate themselves in beholding the way you are behaving!

ANNABELLA O my lord,
These words wound deeper than your sword could do.

VASQUES Let me not ever take comfort but I[6] begin to weep myself, so much I pity him. Why, madam, I knew when his rage was overpast, what it would come to.

SORANZO Forgive me, Annabella! Though thy youth
Hath tempted thee above thy strength to folly,
Yet will not I forget what I should be,
And what I am, a husband; in that name
Is hid divinity. If I do find
That thou wilt yet be true, here I remit° *forgive*
All former faults, and take thee to my bosom.

VASQUES By my troth, and that's a point of noble charity.

ANNABELLA [*attempting to kneel*] Sir, on my knees—

SORANZO Rise up; you shall not kneel.
Get you to your chamber. See you make no show
Of alteration. I'll be with you straight.
My reason tells me now that 'tis as common
To err in frailty as to be a woman.
Go to your chamber. *Exit Annabella.*

VASQUES So, this was somewhat to the matter.° *purpose* What do you think of your heaven of happiness now, sir?

SORANZO I carry hell about me! All my blood
Is fired in swift revenge.

VASQUES That may be, but know you how, or on whom? Alas, to marry a great° *pregnant; noble* woman, being made great in the stock to your hand,[7] is a usual sport in these days; but to know what ferret it was that haunted your cunny berry,[8] there's the cunning.

SORANZO I'll make her tell herself, or—

VASQUES Or what? You must not do so. Let me yet persuade your sufferance° *patience* a little while. Go to her, use her mildly; win her, if it be possible, to a voluntary, to a weeping tune.[9] For the rest, if all hit,° *goes right* I will not miss my mark. Pray, sir, go in. The next news I tell you shall be wonders.

SORANZO Delay in vengeance gives a heavier blow. *Exit.*

VASQUES [*to himself*] Ah, sirrah, here's work for the nonce!° *purpose, present occasion* I had a suspicion of a bad matter in my head a pretty whiles ago; but after my madam's scurvy looks here at home, her waspish perverseness and loud faultfinding, then I remembered the proverb, that where hens crow and cocks hold their peace, there are sorry houses. 'Sfoot, if the lower parts of a she-tailor's cunning[1] can cover such a swelling in the stomach, I'll never blame a false stitch in a shoe whiles I live again. Up,° *Swollen, pregnant* and up so quick? And so quickly too? 'Twere a fine policy° *stratagem* to learn by whom; this must be known. And I have thought on't; here's° *i.e., through Putana* the way, or none.

Enter Putana [*weeping*].

6. May I lack salvation if I do not.
7. Who has been made pregnant already for you. ("Stock" puns variously on [1] line of descent; [2] stem in which a graft is inserted; [3] trunk, body.)
8. (1) That frequented your rabbit burrow; (2) that entered your wife's body. ("Cunny" means both "coney, rabbit" and "female genitals"; "berry" means "burrow.")
9. Coax her, if you can, to sing a willing confession. ("Voluntary" refers to both an improvised piece of music and something done voluntarily.)
1. If the lower part of a dress made by a woman tailor. (With sexual punning on "parts," meaning "sexual members," and "cunning," meaning "cunny," an affectionate term for the female genitals.)

What, crying, old mistress? Alas, alas, I cannot blame 'ee. We have a lord, heaven help us, is so mad as the devil himself—the more shame for him.

PUTANA Oh, Vasques, that ever I was born to see this day! Doth he use thee so too, sometimes, Vasques?

VASQUES Me? Why, he makes a dog of me; but if some were of my mind, I know what we would do. As sure as I am an honest man, he will go near to kill my lady with unkindness. Say she be with child, is that such a matter for a young woman of her years to be blamed for?

PUTANA Alas, good heart, it is against her will full sore.° *sorely against her will*

VASQUES I durst be sworn, all his madness is for that she will not confess whose 'tis, which he will know,° and when he doth know it, I am so well acquainted with his humor° that he will forget all straight. Well I could wish she would in plain terms tell all, for that's the way indeed. *insists on knowing* *temperament*

PUTANA Do you think so?

VASQUES Foh, I know't; provided that he° did not win her to't by force. He° was once in a mind that you could tell, and meant to have wrung it out of you, but I somewhat pacified him for that; yet sure you know a great deal. *(her lover)* *(Soranzo)*

PUTANA Heaven forgive us all! I know a little, Vasques.

VASQUES Why should you not? Who else should? Upon my conscience, she loves you dearly, and you would not betray her to any affliction for the world.

PUTANA Not for all the world, by my faith and troth, Vasques.

VASQUES 'Twere pity of your life if you should, but in this° you should both relieve her present discomforts, pacify my lord, and gain yourself everlasting love and preferment. *in telling*

PUTANA Dost think so, Vasques?

VASQUES Nay, I know't. Sure 'twas some near and entire° friend. *devoted*

PUTANA 'Twas a dear friend indeed; but—

VASQUES But what? Fear not to name him; my life between you and danger. Faith, I think 'twas no base fellow.

PUTANA Thou wilt stand between me and harm?

VASQUES Ud's° pity, what else? You shall be rewarded, too; trust me. *God's*

PUTANA 'Twas even no worse than her own brother.

VASQUES Her brother Giovanni, I warrant 'ee!

PUTANA Even he, Vasques; as brave a gentleman as ever kissed fair lady. Oh, they love most perpetually.

VASQUES A brave gentleman indeed. Why, therein I commend her choice. (*Aside*) Better and better. (*To her*) You are sure 'twas he?

PUTANA Sure; and you shall see he will not be long from her, too.

VASQUES He were to blame if he would. But may I believe thee?

PUTANA Believe me! Why, dost think I am a Turk or a Jew? No, Vasques, I have known their dealings too long to belie° them now. *tell lies about*

VASQUES [*calling*] Where are you? There within, sirs!

Enter Banditti.

PUTANA How now, what are these?

VASQUES You shall know presently.°—Come, sirs, take me this old damnable hag. Gag her instantly and put out her eyes. Quickly, quickly! [*They seize her.*]

immediately

PUTANA Vasques, Vasques!

VASQUES Gag her, I say. 'Sfoot, d'ee suffer her to prate? What d'ee fumble about? Let me come to her.—I'll help your old gums, you toad-bellied bitch! [*He gags her.*] Sirs, carry her closely° into the coal house, and put out her eyes instantly. If she roars, slit her nose, d'ee hear? Be speedy and sure.

under guard

Exeunt [*Banditti*] *with Putana.*

Why, this is excellent and above expectation. Her own brother? Oh, horrible! To what a height of liberty° in damnation hath the devil trained° our age? Her brother? Well! There's yet but a beginning. I must to my lord and tutor him better in his points of vengeance. Now I see how a smooth tale goes beyond a smooth tail.[2]—But soft! What thing comes next?

license, libertinism

enticed, misled

Enter Giovanni.

[*To himself, still*] Giovanni! As I would wish. My belief is strengthened; 'tis as firm as winter and summer.[3]

GIOVANNI Where's my sister?

VASQUES Troubled with a new sickness, my lord; she's somewhat ill.

GIOVANNI Took too much of the flesh,[4] I believe.

VASQUES Troth, sir, and you, I think, have e'en hit° it. But my virtuous lady—

hit upon

GIOVANNI Where's she?

VASQUES In her chamber. Please you visit her; she is alone. Your liberality hath doubly made me your servant, and ever shall, ever— *Exit Giovanni.*

Enter Soranzo.

Sir, I am a made man! I have plied my cue° with cunning and success. I beseech you, let's be private.

played my part

SORANZO My lady's brother's come; now he'll know all.

VASQUES Let him know't. I have made some of them fast enough.[5] How have you dealt with my lady?

SORANZO Gently, as thou hast counseled. Oh, my soul
Runs circular° in sorrow for revenge!
But, Vasques, thou shalt know—

around and around

VASQUES Nay, I will know no more; for now comes your turn to know. I would not talk so openly with you. Let my young master° take time enough, and go at pleasure; he is sold to death, and the devil shall not ransom him. Sir, I beseech you, your privacy.°

(Giovanni)

be secret

SORANZO No conquest can gain glory of my fear.[6]

Exit [*with Vasques*].

2. I see how a slick lie can outmaneuver a woman.

3. My certainty of this is as constant as the regular progression of the seasons.

4. (1) She overate; (2) she overindulged in sex. (The latter meaning is not consciously intended by Giovanni.)

5. Vasques refers to his having seized Putana (at lines 228–36 above) and otherwise arranged matters to prepare for Soranzo's vengeance.

6. (1) No victor is going to have the glory of seeing me show fear; (2) no triumphing in this matter can conquer my anxiety.

5.1

Enter Annabella above [with a letter].

ANNABELLA Pleasures, farewell, and all ye thriftless° minutes *profitless*
Wherein false joys have spun a weary life!
To these my fortunes now I take my leave.
Thou precious Time, that swiftly rid'st in post° *hastens*
Over the world to finish up the race
Of my last° fate, here stay thy restless course, *final*
And bear to ages that are yet unborn
A wretched, woeful woman's tragedy!
My conscience now stands up against° my lust *to testify against*
With depositions charactered in guilt,[1]

Enter Friar [on the main stage].

And tells me I am lost. Now I confess,
Beauty, that clothes the outside of the face,
Is cursèd if it be not clothed with grace.
Here like a turtle° mewed° up in a cage, *turtledove / cooped*
Unmated,° I converse with air and walls, *Unpartnered*
And descant° on my vile unhappiness. *sing*
O Giovanni, that hast had the spoil° *ruination; plunder*
Of thine own virtues and my modest fame,° *chaste reputation*
Would thou hadst been less subject to those stars
That luckless reigned at my nativity!
Oh, would the scourge due to my black offense
Might pass from thee, that I alone might feel
The torment of an uncontrollèd flame!° *of hellfire*
FRIAR [*aside*] What's this I hear?
ANNABELLA That man, that blessèd friar,
Who joined in ceremonial knot my hand
To him whose wife I now am, told me oft
I trod the path to death, and showed me how.
But they who sleep in lethargies of lust
Hug their confusion,° making heaven unjust,[2] *damnation*
And so did I.
FRIAR [*aside*] Here's music to the soul!
ANNABELLA Forgive me, my good genius,° and this once *guardian angel*
Be helpful to my ends! Let some good man
Pass this way, to whose trust I may commit
This paper double-lined with tears and blood;[3]
Which being granted, here I sadly vow
Repentance and a leaving of that life
I long have died° in. *died spiritually*
FRIAR [*to her*] Lady, heaven hath heard you,

5.1. Soranzo's house (?). Annabella presumably appears at a window and speaks to the Friar below in the street.

1. Written in gold ("gilt") letters, and in my guilt.
2. Blaming heaven for their own iniquities.
3. Written in blood and blotted with tears.

And hath by Providence ordained that I
Should be his minister for your behoof.° *benefit*

ANNABELLA Ha! What are you?

FRIAR Your brother's friend, the Friar;
Glad in my soul that I have lived to hear
This free confession 'twixt your peace and you.
What would you, or to whom? Fear not to speak.

ANNABELLA Is heaven so bountiful? Then I have found
More favor than I hoped. Here, holy man;

Throws a letter.

Commend me to my brother. Give him that,
That letter; bid him read it and repent.
Tell him that I—imprisoned in my chamber,
Barred of all company, even of my guardian,° *(Putana)*
Who gives me cause of much suspect°—have time *suspicion*
To blush at what hath passed. Bid him be wise,
And not believe the friendship of my lord.° *(Soranzo)*
I fear much more than I can speak. Good father,
The place is dangerous, and spies are busy.
I must break off. You'll do't?

FRIAR Be sure I will,
And fly with speed. My blessing ever rest
With thee, my daughter! Live to die more blessed!

Exit Friar.

ANNABELLA Thanks to the heavens, who have prolonged my breath
To this good use! Now I can welcome death. *Exit.*

[5.2]

Enter Soranzo and Vasques.

VASQUES Am I to be believed now? First, marry a strumpet that cast herself away upon you but to laugh at your horns,° to feast on your disgrace, riot° in your vexations, cuckold you in your bride-bed, waste your estate upon panders and bawds? *cuckold's horns* *revel*

SORANZO No more, I say, no more.

VASQUES A cuckold is a goodly tame beast, my lord.

SORANZO I am resolved; urge not another word.
My thoughts are great,° and all as resolute *great with wrath*
As thunder. In meantime I'll cause our lady
To deck herself in all her bridal robes,
Kiss her and fold her gently in my arms.
Begone. Yet hear you: are the banditti ready
To wait in ambush?

VASQUES Good sir, trouble not yourself about other business than your own resolution. Remember that time lost cannot be recalled.

SORANZO With all the cunning words thou canst, invite
The states° of Parma to my birthday's feast. *dignitaries*
Haste to my brother rival and his father;
Entreat them gently, bid them not to fail.

5.2. Soranzo's house.

Be speedy and return.
VASQUES Let not your pity betray you till my coming back; think upon incest and cuckoldry.
SORANZO Revenge is all the ambition I aspire;° *aspire to*
To that I'll climb or fall. My blood's on fire. *Exeunt.*

[5.3]

Enter Giovanni.

GIOVANNI Busy opinion° is an idle fool *Officious popular idea*
That, as a school rod, keeps a child in awe,
Frights the unexperienced temper of the mind.
So did it me, who, ere my precious sister
Was married, thought all taste of love would die
In such a contract; but I find no change
Of pleasure in this formal law of sports.[1]
She is still one° to me, and every kiss *perfectly united*
As sweet and as delicious as the first
I reaped when yet the privilege of youth
Entitled° her a virgin. Oh, the glory *Declared*
Of two united hearts like hers and mine!
Let poring bookmen dream of other worlds;
My world and all of happiness is here,
And I'd not change it for the best to come.
A life of pleasure is Elysium.

Enter Friar.

Father, you enter on the jubilee° *season of rejoicing*
Of my retired° delights. Now I can tell you *secluded*
The hell you oft have prompted° is naught else *urged, preached*
But slavish and fond° superstitious fear; *foolish*
And I could prove it, too—
FRIAR Thy blindness slays thee.
Look there, 'tis writ to thee. *Gives the letter.*
GIOVANNI From whom?
FRIAR Unrip the seals and see. [*Giovanni reads.*]
The blood's yet seething hot that will anon
Be frozen harder than congealèd coral.
Why d'ee change color, son?
GIOVANNI 'Fore heaven, you make
Some petty devil factor° 'twixt my love *agent, intermediary*
And your religion-maskèd sorceries.
Where had you this?
FRIAR Thy conscience, youth, is seared,° *cauterized*
Else thou wouldst stoop to° warning. *submit to, heed*
GIOVANNI 'Tis her hand,
I know't; and 'tis all written in her blood.
She writes I know not what. Death? I'll not fear
An armèd thunderbolt aimed at my heart.
She writes we are discovered. Pox° on dreams *A curse*
Of low fainthearted cowardice! Discovered?

5.3. A street; unlocalized (?).
1. I find no diminution of pleasure resulting from Annabella's marriage to Soranzo, implying as it does the conventional rules of that game.

The devil we are! Which way is't possible?
Are we grown traitors to our own delights?
Confusion° take such dotage! 'Tis but forged. *i.e., The devil*
This is your peevish chattering, weak old man.

Enter Vasques.

Now, sir, what news bring you?
VASQUES My lord,° according to his yearly custom keeping this day a feast in honor of his birthday, by me invites you thither. Your worthy father, with the Pope's reverend nuncio° and other magnificoes of Parma, have promised their presence. Will't please you to be of the number? *(Soranzo)* *official representative*
GIOVANNI Yes. Tell him I dare come.
VASQUES Dare come?
GIOVANNI So I said; and tell him more, I will come.
VASQUES These words are strange to me.
GIOVANNI Say I will come.
VASQUES You will not miss?
GIOVANNI Yet more? I'll come. Sir, are you answered?
VASQUES So I'll say. My service to you. *Exit Vasques.*
FRIAR You will not go, I trust.
GIOVANNI Not go? For what?
FRIAR Oh, do not go! This feast, I'll gage° my life, *engage, bet*
Is but a plot to train° you to your ruin. *lure*
Be ruled, you sha' not go.
GIOVANNI Not go? Stood Death
Threat'ning his armies of confounding° plagues, *fatal, destroying*
With hosts of dangers hot as blazing stars,° *comets*
I would be there. Not go? Yes, and resolve
To strike as deep in slaughter as they all;
For I will go.
FRIAR Go where thou wilt. I see
The wildness of thy fate draws to an end,
To a bad, fearful end. I must not stay
To know thy fall. Back to Bononia I
With speed will haste, and shun this coming blow.
Parma, farewell! Would I had never known thee,
Or aught of thine! Well, young man, since no prayer
Can make thee safe, I leave thee to despair. *Exit Friar.*
GIOVANNI Despair, or tortures of a thousand hells,
All's one to me. I have set up my rest.[2]
Now, now, work serious thoughts on baneful° plots! *poisonous*
Be all a man, my soul! Let not the curse
Of old prescription rend from me the gall
Of courage, which enrolls a glorious death.[3]
If I must totter like a well-grown oak,
Some undershrubs shall in my weighty fall
Be crushed to splits;° with me they all shall perish. *Exit.* *splinters*

2. I have committed my final stakes. (As in a betting game such as primero, where to "set up one's rest" is to hold, that is, stick with the cards already in one's hand, in the hopes of their winning, instead of drawing new cards.)

3. Let not the curse of ancient injunctions (especially against incest) tear away from me the bitter resolve of courage, which will enshrine my name on the honor roll of those who have died bravely.

[5.4]

Enter Soranzo, Vasques, and Banditti.

SORANZO You will not fail, or shrink in the attempt?

VASQUES I will undertake° for their parts.—Be sure, my masters,° to be bloody enough, and as unmerciful as if you were preying upon a rich booty on the very mountains of Liguria.[1] For your pardons, trust to my lord; but for reward you shall trust none but your own pockets. *vouch* / *good sirs*

BANDITTI OMNES° We'll make a murder. *All the Banditti*

SORANZO [*giving money*] Here's gold; here's more. Want nothing; what you do
Is noble, and an act of brave revenge.
I'll make ye rich, banditti, and all free.° *pardoned by the law*

BANDITTI OMNES Liberty, liberty!

VASQUES [*passing out masks*] Hold, take every man a vizard. When ye are withdrawn, keep as much silence as you can possibly. You know the watchword, till which be spoken, move not, but when you hear that, rush in like a stormy flood. I need not instruct ye in your own profession.

BANDITTI OMNES No, no, no.

VASQUES In, then. Your ends are profit and preferment. Away!

Exeunt Banditti.

SORANZO The guests will all come, Vasques?

VASQUES Yes, sir; and now let me a little edge° your resolution. You see nothing is unready to this great work but a great mind in you. Call to your remembrance your disgraces, your loss of honor, Hippolita's blood;° and arm your courage in your own wrongs. So shall you best right those wrongs in vengeance which you may truly call your own. *sharpen* / *passion*

SORANZO 'Tis well. The less I speak, the more I burn,
And blood shall quench that flame.

VASQUES Now you begin to turn Italian![2] This beside: when my young incestmonger comes, he will be sharp-set on° his old bit.° Give him time enough; let him have your chamber and bed at liberty. Let my hot hare have law[3] ere he be hunted to his death, that, if it be possible, he may post° to hell in the very act of his damnation. *be hungry for* / *morsel* / *hasten*

Enter Giovanni.

SORANZO It shall be so; and see, as we would wish,
He comes himself first.—Welcome, my much-loved brother!
Now I perceive you honor me; you're welcome.
But where's my father?° *(Florio)*

GIOVANNI With the other states,° *dignitaries*
Attending on the nuncio of the Pope
To wait upon° him hither. How's my sister? *attend, escort*

SORANZO Like a good housewife, scarcely ready yet.

5.4. Soranzo's house.

1. The mountainous region between Parma and Genoa.

2. Now you are speaking like an Italian! (Notorious for expertise in cunning and secret murder.)

3. Let the quarry that is about to be hunted have an allowance of time or distance at the start.

You're best walk to her chamber.

GIOVANNI If you will.

SORANZO I must expect° my honorable friends. *await*
Good brother, get her forth.

GIOVANNI You are busy, sir.

Exit Giovanni.

VASQUES Even as the great devil himself would have it! Let him go and glut himself in his own destruction. (*Flourish.*) Hark, the nuncio is at hand. Good sir, be ready to receive him.

Enter Cardinal, Florio, Donado, Richardetto, and attendants.

SORANZO Most reverend lord, this grace° hath made me proud *favor, honor*
That you vouchsafe° my house. I ever rest *deign to visit*
Your humble servant for this noble favor.

CARDINAL You are our friend, my lord. His Holiness
Shall understand how zealously you honor
Saint Peter's vicar° in his substitute. *(The Pope)*
Our special love to you.

SORANZO Signors, to you
My welcome and my ever best of thanks
For this so memorable courtesy.
Pleaseth° Your Grace to walk near? *May it please*

CARDINAL My lord, we come
To celebrate your feast with civil mirth,° *seemly merrymaking*
As ancient custom teacheth. We will go.

SORANZO Attend His Grace there! Signors, keep your way.° *walk on ahead*

Exeunt.

[5.5]

Enter Giovanni and Annabella lying on a bed.[1]

GIOVANNI What, changed so soon? Hath your new sprightly lord
Found out a trick in night games more than we
Could know in our simplicity? Ha! Is't so?
Or does the fit° come on you to prove treacherous *urge, impulse*
To your past vows and oaths?

ANNABELLA Why should you jest
At my calamity, without all sense
Of the approaching dangers you are in?

GIOVANNI What danger's half so great as thy revolt?
Thou art a faithless sister; else, thou know'st,
Malice, or any treachery beside,
Would stoop to my bent brows.° Why, I hold Fate *submit to my frown*
Clasped in my fist, and could command the course
Of Time's eternal motion, hadst thou been
One thought more steady than an ebbing sea.
And what? You'll now be honest?° That's resolved?° *chaste / decided*

5.5. Annabella's chamber, in Soranzo's house.

1. The bed is presumably thrust out onstage.

ANNABELLA Brother, dear brother, know what I have been,
And know that now there's but a dining time[2]
'Twixt us and our confusion.° Let's not waste — *destruction*
These precious hours in vain and useless speech.
Alas, these gay attires were not put on
But to some end; this sudden solemn° feast — *grand, sumptuous*
Was not ordained to riot° in expense. — *merely to revel*
I that have now been chambered here alone,
Barred of my guardian or of any else,
Am not for nothing at an instant freed
To fresh access.° Be not deceived, my brother; — *access to company*
This banquet is an harbinger of death
To you and me. Resolve° yourself it is, — *Assure*
And be prepared to welcome it.

GIOVANNI Well, then,
The schoolmen° teach that all this globe of earth — *medieval theologians*
Shall be consumed to ashes in a minute.[3]

ANNABELLA So I have read too.

GIOVANNI But 'twere somewhat strange
To see the waters burn. Could I believe
This might be true, I could believe as well
There might be hell or heaven.

ANNABELLA That's most certain.

GIOVANNI A dream, a dream! Else in this other world
We should know one another.

ANNABELLA So we shall.

GIOVANNI Have you heard so?

ANNABELLA For certain.

GIOVANNI But d'ee think
That I shall see you there, you look on me?
May we kiss one another, prate,° or laugh, — *chatter*
Or do as we do here?

ANNABELLA I know not that.
But good,° for the present, what d'ee mean[4] — *good brother, dearest*
To free yourself from danger? Some way, think
How to escape. I'm sure the guests are come.

GIOVANNI Look up. Look here: what see you in my face?

ANNABELLA Distraction and a troubled countenance.

GIOVANNI Death and a swift repining° wrath.—Yet look.° — *discontented / Look again*
What see you in mine eyes?

ANNABELLA Methinks you weep.

GIOVANNI I do indeed. These are the funeral tears
Shed on your grave; these furrowed up my cheeks
When first I loved and knew not how to woo.
Fair Annabella, should I here repeat
The story of my life, we might lose time.
Be record all the spirits of the air,
And all things else that are, that day and night,
Early and late, the tribute which my heart

2. A brief time, brief as a midday meal.
3. The Book of Revelation describes, especially in chapters 20–22, as the culmination of its apocalyptic narrative, the ending of the physical world in a fiery holocaust and a new heaven and a new earth taking shape in the holy city of the New Jerusalem. Medieval churchmen were often preoccupied with this vision.
4. Intend to do.

Hath paid to Annabella's sacred love
Hath been these tears, which are her mourners now.
Never till now did Nature do her best
To show a matchless beauty to the world,
Which in an instant, ere it scarce was seen,
The jealous Destinies required again.
Pray, Annabella, pray! Since we must part,
Go thou, white in thy soul, to fill a throne
Of innocence and sanctity in heaven.
Pray, pray, my sister.

ANNABELLA Then I see your drift.
Ye blessèd angels, guard me!

GIOVANNI So say I.
Kiss me. If ever aftertimes should hear
Of our fast-knit° affections, though perhaps — *close-knit*
The laws of conscience and of civil use° — *social custom*
May justly blame us, yet when they but know
Our loves, that love will wipe away that rigor° — *extremity*
Which would in other incests be abhorred.
Give me your hand. How sweetly life doth run
In these well-colored veins! How constantly° — *steadfastly*
These palms do promise health! But I could chide
With Nature for this cunning flattery.
Kiss me again. [*They kiss.*] Forgive me!

ANNABELLA With my heart.

GIOVANNI Farewell.

ANNABELLA Will you be gone?

GIOVANNI Be dark, bright sun,
And make this midday night, that thy gilt rays
May not behold a deed will° turn their splendor — *that will*
More sooty than the poets feign their Styx!° — *river of the underworld*
One other kiss, my sister.

ANNABELLA What means this?

GIOVANNI To save thy fame,° and kill thee in a kiss. — *reputation*
Stabs her.
Thus die, and die by me, and by my hand.
Revenge is mine; honor doth love command.° — *honor controls love*

ANNABELLA Oh, brother, by your hand?

GIOVANNI When thou art dead
I'll give my reasons for't; for to dispute
With thy (even in thy death) most lovely beauty
Would make me stagger° to perform this act — *hesitate*
Which I most glory in.

ANNABELLA Forgive him, heaven—and me my sins! Farewell,
Brother unkind,° unkind—mercy, great heaven!—Oh—Oh! — *cruel; unnatural*
Dies.

GIOVANNI She's dead. Alas, good soul! The hapless° fruit — *luckless*
That in her womb received its life from me
Hath had from me a cradle and a grave.
I must not dally. This sad marriage-bed,
In all her best,° bore her alive and dead. — *best array*
Soranzo, thou hast missed thy aim in this;
I have prevented° now thy reaching° plots, — *forestalled / ambitious*
And killed a love for whose each drop of blood
I would have pawned my heart. Fair Annabella,

How overglorious art thou in thy wounds,
Triumphing over infamy and hate!
Shrink not, courageous hand! Stand up, my heart,
And boldly act my last and greater part!
Exit with the body.

[5.6]

A banquet. Enter Cardinal, Florio, Donado, Soranzo, Richardetto, Vasques, and attendants. They take their places.

VASQUES [*aside to Soranzo*] Remember, sir, what you have to do. Be wise and resolute.
SORANZO [*aside to Vasquez*] Enough; my heart is fixed. [*To Cardinal*] Pleaseth Your Grace
To taste these coarse confections?° Though the use *unrefined dishes*
Of such set entertainments more consists
In custom than in cause,[1] yet, reverend sir,
I am still made your servant° by your presence. *put in your debt*
CARDINAL And we your friend.
SORANZO But where's my brother Giovanni?

Enter Giovanni with a heart upon his dagger.

GIOVANNI Here, here, Soranzo, trimmed° in reeking° blood *adorned / steaming*
That triumphs over death, proud in the spoil° *plunder; ruin*
Of love and vengeance! Fate, or all the powers
That guide the motions of immortal souls,
Could not prevent me.
CARDINAL What means this?
FLORIO Son Giovanni!
SORANZO [*aside*] Shall I be forestalled?
GIOVANNI Be not amazed. If your misgiving° hearts *apprehensive*
Shrink at an idle sight,° what bloodless fear[2] *sight of the heart only*
Of coward passion would have seized your senses
Had you beheld the rape of life and beauty
Which I have acted? My sister, oh, my sister!
FLORIO Ha! What of her?
GIOVANNI The glory of my deed
Darkened the midday sun, made noon as night.
You came to feast, my lords, with dainty fare;
I came to feast too, but I digged for food
In a much richer mine than gold or stone° *jewel*
Of any value balanced.° 'Tis a heart, *weighed in a balance*
A heart, my lords, in which is mine entombed.
Look well upon't. D'ee know't?
VASQUES What strange riddle's this?
GIOVANNI 'Tis Annabella's heart, 'tis. Why d'ee startle?° *start*
I vow 'tis hers. This dagger's point plowed up
Her fruitful womb, and left to me the fame
Of a most glorious executioner.

5.6. Soranzo's house.
1. Though such formal entertainments are more a matter of custom than of useful purpose.
2. Fear was thought to make the blood retreat to the heart and liver, leaving a person's countenance pale.

FLORIO Why madman, art thyself?° *in your right mind*
GIOVANNI Yes, father, and, that times to come may know
How as my fate I honored my revenge,
List, father; to your ears I will yield up
How much I have deserved to be your son.° *(as son and son-in-law)*
FLORIO What is't thou say'st?
GIOVANNI Nine moons have had their changes
Since I first throughly° viewed and truly loved *thoroughly*
Your daughter and my sister.
FLORIO How! Alas, my lords,
He's a frantic madman!
GIOVANNI Father, no.
For nine months' space, in secret I enjoyed
Sweet Annabella's sheets; nine months I lived
A happy monarch of her heart and her.
Soranzo, thou know'st this; thy paler cheek
Bears the confounding° print of thy disgrace, *discomfiting*
For her too fruitful womb too soon bewrayed° *revealed*
The happy passage° of our stol'n delights, *course*
And made her mother to a child unborn.
CARDINAL Incestuous villain!
FLORIO Oh, his rage belies him!° *makes him tell lies*
GIOVANNI It does not. 'Tis the oracle of truth;
I vow it is so.
SORANZO I shall burst with fury!—
Bring the strumpet forth.
VASQUES I shall, sir. *Exit Vasques.*
GIOVANNI Do, sir. Have you all no faith
To credit° yet my triumphs? Here I swear *believe*
By all that you call sacred, by the love
I bore my Annabella whilst she lived,
These hands have from her bosom ripped this heart.

Enter Vasques.

Is't true or no, sir?
VASQUES 'Tis most strangely true.
FLORIO Cursèd man!—Have I lived to— *Dies.*
CARDINAL Hold up Florio!—
Monster of children, see what thou hast done,
Broke thy old father's heart!—Is none of you
Dares venture on him?
GIOVANNI Let 'em. Oh, my father!
How well his death becomes him in his griefs!
Why, this was done with courage. Now survives
None of our house but I, gilt° in the blood *gilded, adorned*
Of a fair sister and a hapless father.
SORANZO Inhuman scorn of men,° hast thou a thought *pariah*
T'outlive thy murders?
GIOVANNI Yes, I tell thee, yes;
For in my fists I bear the twists of life.[3]
Soranzo, see this heart which was thy wife's?

3. I hold the threads of life. (The thread of each person's life, which determines his or her lot, was believed to be controlled by the three Fates: Clotho, who spun it; Lachesis, who measured its length; and Atropos, who, at the time of death, cut it. See 2.3.62.)

Thus [*stabbing Soranzo*] I exchange it royally for thine,
And thus and thus! Now brave revenge is mine.
[*Soranzo falls.*]

VASQUES I cannot hold any longer.—You, sir, are you grown insolent in your butcheries? Have at you!

GIOVANNI Come, I am armed to meet thee. *Fight.*

VASQUES No? Will it not be yet?° If this will not, another shall. [*They continue to fight.*] Not yet? I shall fit you° anon. [*Calling aloud*] Vengeance!°

Aren't you defeated yet?
settle your hash
(the watchword, 5.4.14)

Enter Banditti.

GIOVANNI Welcome! Come more of you, whate'er you be,
I dare your worst. [*They surround and overwhelm him.*]
Oh, I can stand no longer. Feeble arms,
Have you so soon lost strength? [*He falls.*]

VASQUES Now you are welcome, sir. [*To the Banditti*] Away, my masters! All is done. Shift for yourselves. Your reward is your own. Shift for yourselves.

BANDITTI Away, away! *Exeunt Banditti.*

VASQUES [*to Soranzo*] How d'ee, my lord? See you this?° How is't?°

(the dead Giovanni)
How is it with you?

SORANZO Dead; but in death well pleased, that I have lived
To see my wrongs revenged on that black devil.
O Vasques, to thy bosom let me give
My last of breath! Let not that lecher live—Oh! *Dies.*

VASQUES The reward of peace and rest be with him, my ever dearest lord and master!

GIOVANNI Whose hand gave me this wound?

VASQUES Mine, sir. I was your first man. Have you enough?

GIOVANNI I thank thee. Thou hast done for me
But what I would have else done on myself.
Art sure thy lord is dead?

VASQUES Oh, impudent slave,
As sure as I am sure to see thee die.

CARDINAL [*to Giovanni*] Think on thy life and end, and call for mercy.

GIOVANNI Mercy? Why, I have found it in this justice.

CARDINAL Strive yet to cry to heaven.

GIOVANNI Oh, I bleed fast.
Death, thou art a guest long looked for; I embrace
Thee and thy wounds. Oh, my last minute comes!
Where'er I go, let me enjoy this grace,
Freely to view my Annabella's face. *Dies.*

DONADO Strange miracle of justice!

CARDINAL Raise up the city! We shall be murdered all.

VASQUES You need not fear; you shall not. This strange task being ended, I have paid the duty to the son° which I have vowed to the father.

(Soranzo)

CARDINAL Speak, wretched villain, what incarnate fiend
Hath led thee on to this?

VASQUES Honesty, and pity of my master's wrongs. For know, my lord, I am by birth a Spaniard, brought forth my country in my youth by Lord Soranzo's father, whom, whilst he lived, I served faithfully; since whose death I have been to this man as I was to him. What I have done was duty, and I repent nothing but that the loss of my life had not ransomed his.

CARDINAL Say, fellow, know'st thou any yet unnamed
Of counsel in° this incest? — *In on the secret of*

VASQUES Yes, an old woman, sometimes° guardian to this murdered lady. — *formerly*

CARDINAL And what's become of her?

VASQUES Within this room she is, whose eyes, after her confession, I caused to be put out, but kept alive, to confirm what from Giovanni's own mouth you have heard. Now, my lord, what I have done you may judge of, and let your own wisdom be a judge in° your own reason. — *according to*

CARDINAL Peace! First, this woman,° chief in these effects, — *(Putana)*
My sentence is, that forthwith she be ta'en
Out of the city, for example's sake,
There to be burned to ashes.

DONADO 'Tis most just.

CARDINAL Be it your charge, Donado. See it done.

DONADO I shall.

VASQUES What for me? If death, 'tis welcome. I have been honest to the son as I was to the father.

CARDINAL Fellow, for thee: since what thou didst was done
Not for thyself, being no Italian,
We banish thee forever, to depart
Within three days. In this we do dispense
With grounds of reason, not of thine offense.[4]

VASQUES 'Tis well. This conquest is mine, and I rejoice that a Spaniard outwent an Italian in revenge. *Exit Vasques.*

CARDINAL Take up these slaughtered bodies. See them buried,
And all the gold and jewels, or whatsoever,
Confiscate° by the canons° of the church, — *Seized / regulations*
We seize upon to the Pope's proper° use. — *personal*

RICHARDETTO [*discovering his identity*] Your Grace's pardon.
Thus long I lived disguised
To see the effect of pride and lust at once° — *together*
Brought both to shameful ends.

CARDINAL What, Richardetto, whom we thought for dead?

DONADO Sir, was it you—

RICHARDETTO Your friend.

CARDINAL We shall have time
To talk at large° of all; but never yet — *at length*
Incest and murder have so strangely met.
Of one so young, so rich in nature's store,° — *the gifts of nature*
Who could not say, 'Tis pity she's a whore? *Exeunt.*

FINIS.

4. In sentencing thus we deal out justice equitably, taking your motives into account, not strictly as called for by your offense.

dead child = common trope → Should be ultimate crime

TEXTUAL NOTES

'Tis Pity She's a Whore was first published in 1633, not having been entered in the Stationers' Register. The printing contains a number of errors, some of which are easily corrected. This quarto is the sole authority for the present text. Substantive departures from it are noted here, along with a few instances where the quarto reading is preserved but is doubted by some modern editors, using the following abbreviations:

Q: The quarto (London: Nicholas Okes for Richard Collins, 1633)
Q corr.: The corrected quarto
Q uncorr.: The uncorrected quarto
ed.: A modern editor's emendation (beginning with R. Dodsley in 1744)

The Actors' Names: the scene [placement, ed.; above "The Actors' Names" in Q]
1.2.23 mean [Q corr.] meaned [Q uncorr.] **44 his** [ed.] this [Q] **46 had not** [ed.] had [Q] **57 Losers** [Q: Loosers] **58 villainy** [ed.] villaine [Q] **80 an't** [ed.] and [Q] **81 Not** [ed.; not in Q] **121 pavane** [Q: pauin] **128 bauble** [Q: bable] **163 SD *Annabella*** [Q: *Anna.*] **192 The** [ed.] they [Q] **208 trim** [Q: trime] **209 Strike** [Q: strick] **227 smooth-cheeked** [ed.] smooth'd-cheeke [Q] **262 swear't, I** [ed.] swear't and I [Q]
1.3.29 How [ed.] *Pog.* How [Q] **29 whither** [Q: whether] **42 thither** [ed.] hither [Q]
2.1.61 [and elsewhere] **reverend** [Q: reuerent]
2.2.7 thee [ed.] the [Q] **58 thy** [Q corr.] the [Q uncorr.] **99 accurst** [ed.] a Curse [Q uncorr.] a Coarse [Q corr.] **106 this** [ed.] his [Q] **158 for witnesses** [ed.] foe-witnesses [Q]
2.3.40 art [ed.] Arts [Q] **48 Who's** [Q: Whose] **53 kill** [Q corr.] tell [Q uncorr.] **63 ruined** [Q corr.] min'd [Q uncorr.]
2.4.27 choose [Q: chose] **43 not** [ed.] no [Q]
2.5.8 my [ed.] thy [Q] **15 frame** [ed.] Fame [Q] **17 body** [Q] the body [some modern editors] **30 led** [Q: lead]
2.6.14 An't [ed.] And [Q] **48 have it** [ed.] haue [Q] **84 his** [ed.] this [Q] **126 still, still** [Q] still [some modern editors]
3.1.9 bergetto [ed.] *Pog.* [Q]
3.2.10 Agree [Q] Agree they [some modern editors] **14 SD *Manent*** [ed.] *manet* [Q] **17 no point** [ed.] not point [Q] **31 Know** [ed.] I know [Q] **48 here to** [Q] to [some modern editors] **65.1** [placement, ed.; after 66 in Q] **66 Look** [ed.] *Gio.* Looke [Q] **67 swoons** [Q: sounes] **80 SD (*To him*)** [ed.; indicated by a long dash in Q]
3.3.25 does [ed.] doe [Q]
3.4.4 Melons [Q: Mellownes]
3.5.12 Friar [ed.] Fryars [Q] **31** [and elsewhere] **coz** [Q: couze] **38 poggio** [ed.] *Phi.* [Q] **42 have** [ed.; not in Q]
3.7.20.1 [placement, ed.; after 21 in Q] **25 the haste** [Q] thy haste [some modern editors] **37 too late** [Q: to late]
4.1.28 SD [placement, ed.; after 35 in Q] **35.2 *a dance*** [ed.] *a Daunce. Dance* [Q] **37 this** [Q corr.] thy [Q uncorr.] **74 *inganna*** [ed.] *niganna* [Q] **79 marriage** [ed.] malice [Q] **85** [and elsewhere] **vile** [Q: vild]
4.2.2 hath [Q corr.] hath hath [Q uncorr.] **10 Debates** [ed.] Debate's [Q] **28 lives** [ed.] liue [Q]
4.3.15 Say [ed.] Shey [Q] **32 that's for your** [ed.] that for [Q] **59 *più*** [ed.] *pluis* [Q] **63 *Dei*** [ed.] *Lei* [Q] **63 *morirei*** [ed.] *morirere* [Q corr.] *morire* [Q uncorr.] **71 I leave** [Q corr.] leaue [Q uncorr.] **86 unhuman** [Q: vnhumane] **89 author** [ed.] Authors [Q] **90** [and elsewhere] **lose** [Q: loose] **99, 101 SD** [indicated by long dashes in Q] **100 scenting-out** [Q: senting out] **122 thou**

[ed.] thus [Q] **154 ferret** [ed.] *Secret* [Q] **173.1** [placement, ed.; after 176 in Q] **217 SD** ***Aside . . . To her*** [indicated by long dashes in Q] **236.1** ***Exeunt*** [ed.] *Exit* [opposite "above expectation" in 237 in Q] **256 a made** [ed.] made a [Q]

5.1.10 depositions [ed.] dispositions [Q]

5.3.39.1 [placement, ed.; after 40 in Q] **46 him** [ed.] them [Q] **70 GIOVANNI** [ed.; not in Q] **74 rend** [ed.] rent [Q] **78 all shall perish** [perhaps an error for "shall perish all"]

5.4.18.1 ***Exeunt*** [ed.] *Exit* [Q] **40 housewife** [Q: huswife] **45 SD** [placement, Q uncorr.; after 47 in Q corr.]

5.5.17 dining [Q corr.] dying [Q uncorr.] **51 woo** [Q corr.] woe [Q uncorr.] **62 required** [Q corr.] require [Q uncorr.] **80** [and elsewhere] **gilt** [Q: guilt]

5.6.4 coarse [Q: Course] **18** [and elsewhere] **seized** [Q: ceaz'd] **59.1** [placement, ed.; opposite "Is't . . . sir?" in 60 in Q] **64 venture** [Q: venter] **69 Inhuman** [Q: Inhamane] **77 SD** [placement, ed.; opposite 76 in Q] **102 thee** [ed.] the [Q]

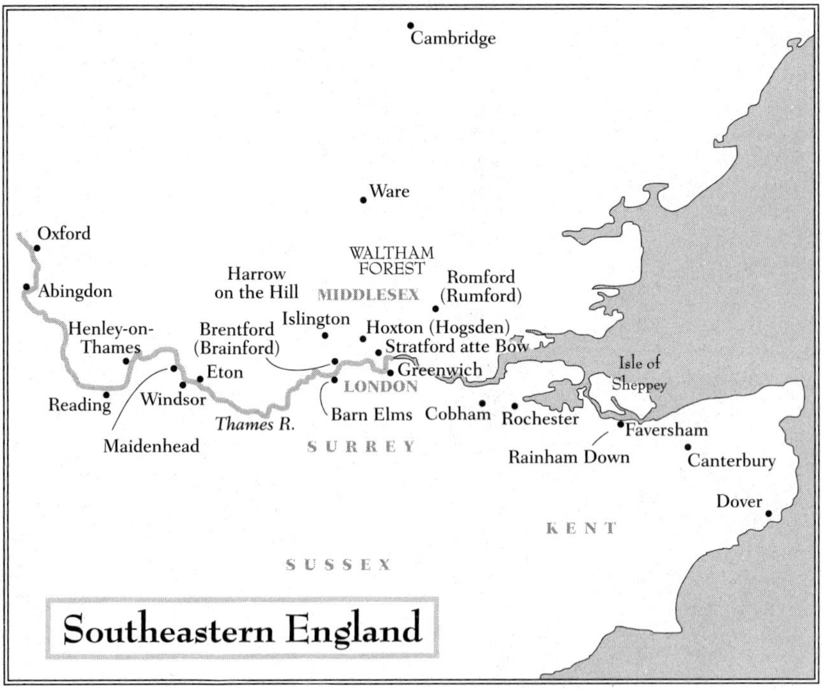
Cambridge
Ware
Oxford
Abingdon
WALTHAM FOREST
Harrow on the Hill
MIDDLESEX
Romford (Rumford)
Henley-on-Thames
Brentford (Brainford)
Islington
Hoxton (Hogsden)
Stratford atte Bow
Greenwich
Isle of Sheppey
Eton
LONDON
Reading
Windsor
Thames R.
Barn Elms
Cobham
Rochester
Faversham
Maidenhead
SURREY
Rainham Down
Canterbury
Dover
KENT
SUSSEX
Southeastern England

Western Europe
THE NETHERLANDS
Amsterdam
Münster
ENGLAND
GERMANY
Elbe R.
London
Ostend
Anholt (Vanholt)
Calais
Antwerp
Wittenberg
HAINAULT
FLANDERS
Rhine R.
Trier
(Trèves)
Maine R.
SAXONY
Paris
LORRAINE
FRANCE
Danube R.
Atlantic
Ocean
The Alps
LOMBARDY
Venice
Milan
Padua
Parma
Genoa
Bologna
ROMAGNA
Lucca
Ancona
Florence
Loretto
TUSCANY
Pyrenees Mts.
Rome
Pescara
Tiber R.
CASTILE
ARAGON
CAMPANIA
Madrid
Naples
Amalfi
(Malfi)
PORTUGAL
(PORTINGALE)
SPAIN
Lisbon
CALABRIA
Alicante
SICILY
Gibraltar
(Jubalter)

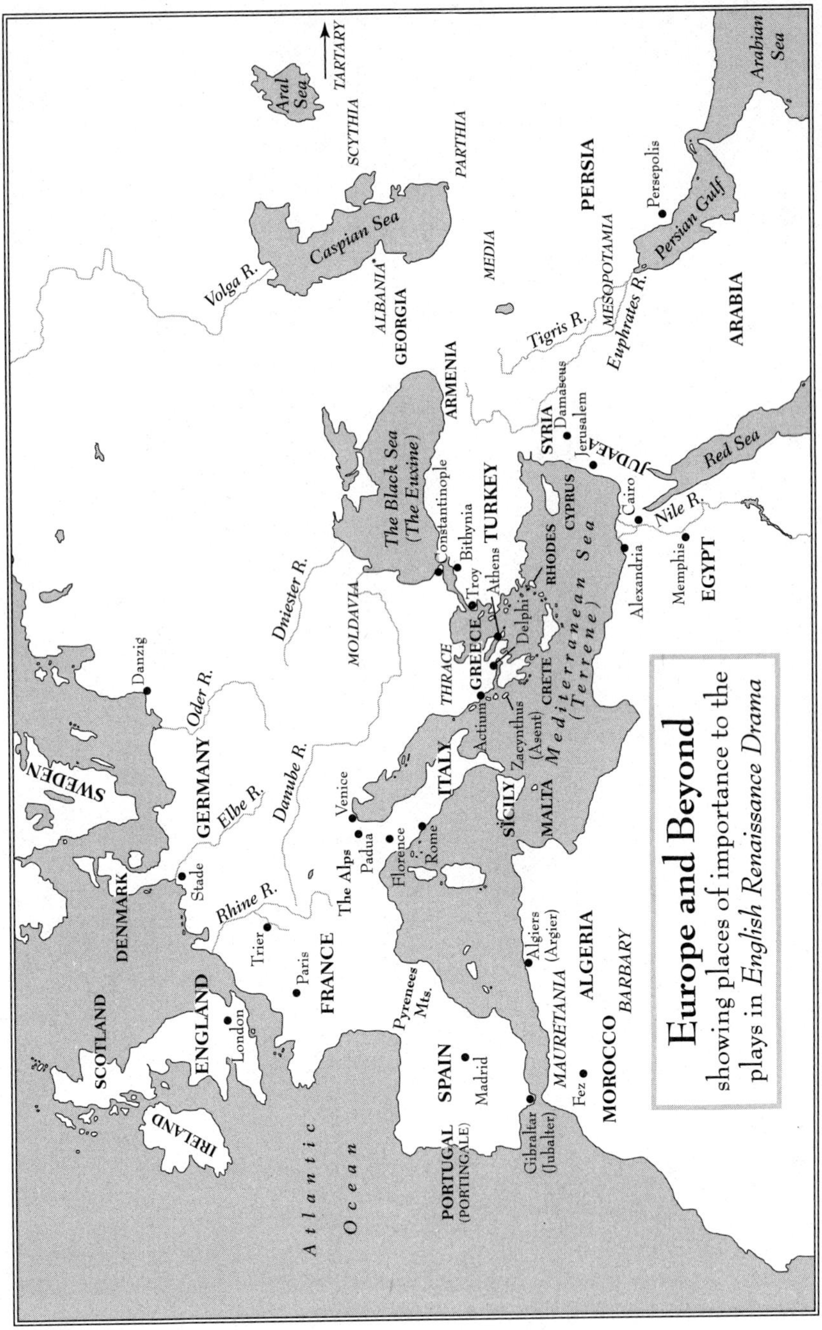

*Ancient Albania in Caucasia (not to be confused with Albania on the Adriatic); see *1 Tamburlaine* 2.2.31.

General Bibliography

Intellectual, Social, Political, Religious, and Economic Contexts

Archer, Ian W. *The Pursuit of Stability: Social Relations in Elizabethan London*. Cambridge: Cambridge University Press, 1991.

Barkan, Leonard. *The Gods Made Flesh: Metamorphosis and the Pursuit of Paganism*. New Haven, Conn.: Yale University Press, 1986.

———. *Nature's Work of Art: The Human Body as Image of the World*. New Haven, Conn.: Yale University Press, 1975.

Barry, J., ed. *The Tudor and Stuart Town*. London and New York: Longman, 1990.

Beier, A. L. *Masterless Men: The Vagrancy Problem in England, 1560–1640*. London and New York: Methuen, 1985.

Bouwsma, William J. *John Calvin: A Sixteenth-Century Portrait*. New York: Oxford University Press, 1988.

Camden, Carroll. *The Elizabethan Woman*. Rev. ed. Mamaroneck, N.Y.: Appel, 1975.

Caspari, Fritz. *Humanism and the Social Order in Tudor England*. Chicago: University of Chicago Press, 1954.

Cassirer, Ernst. *The Platonic Renaissance in England*. Trans. J. E. Pettegrove. Austin: University of Texas Press, 1953.

Collinson, Patrick. *The Elizabethan Puritan Movement*. New York: Oxford University Press, 1990.

———. *The Religion of Protestants: The Church in English Society, 1559–1625*. Oxford: Clarendon Press, 1982.

de Grazia, Margreta, Maureen Quilligan, and Peter Stallybrass, eds. *Subject and Object in Renaissance Culture*. Cambridge: Cambridge University Press, 1996.

Dubrow, Heather, and Richard Strier, eds. *The Historical Renaissance: New Essays on Tudor and Stuart Literature and Culture*. Chicago: University of Chicago Press, 1988.

Elton, G. R. *England Under the Tudors*. London: Methuen, 1955.

———. *The Tudor Revolution in Government*. Cambridge: Cambridge University Press, 1953.

Erickson, Amy Louise. *Women and Property in Early Modern England*. London: Routledge, 1993.

Ferguson, Margaret W., Maureen Quilligan, and Nancy J. Vickers, eds. *Rewriting the Renaissance: The Discourses of Sexual Difference in Early Modern Europe*. Chicago: University of Chicago Press, 1986.

Fletcher, Anthony. *Gender, Sex, and Subordination in England, 1500–1800*. New Haven, Conn.: Yale University Press, 1995.

Fumerton, Patricia, and Simon Hunt, eds. *Renaissance Culture and the Everyday*. Philadelphia: University of Pennsylvania Press, 1999.

Gallagher, Lowell. *Medusa's Gaze: Casuistry and Conscience in the Renaissance*. Stanford, Calif.: Stanford University Press, 1991.

This bibliography was compiled by David Bevington with contributions from the other editors.

Gittings, Clare. *Death, Burial and the Individual in Early Modern England.* London: Croom Helm, 1984.

Greenblatt, Stephen J. *Learning to Curse: Essays in Early Modern Culture.* London: Routledge, 1990.

———. *Marvelous Possessions: The Wonder of the New World.* Chicago: University of Chicago Press, 1991.

———. *Renaissance Self-Fashioning: From More to Shakespeare.* Chicago: University of Chicago Press, 1980.

———. *Shakespearean Negotiations: The Circulation of Social Energy in Renaissance England.* Berkeley and Los Angeles: University of California Press, 1988.

———. ed. *Representing the English Renaissance.* Berkeley and Los Angeles: University of California Press, 1988.

Harrison, G. B., ed. *The Elizabethan Journals, being a record of those things most talked of during the years 1591–1603.* Comprising *An Elizabethan Journal, 1591–1594, A Second Elizabethan Journal, 1595–1598,* and *A Last Elizabethan Journal, 1599–1603.* Ann Arbor, Mich.: University of Michigan Press; London: Routledge, Kegan, and Paul, 1955; Garden City, N.Y.: Anchor, 1965.

———. *A Jacobean Journal, being a record of those things most talked of during the years 1603–1606.* London: G. Routledge and Sons, 1941.

———. *A Second Jacobean Journal, being a record of those things most talked of during the years 1607–1610.* London: Routledge & Kegan Paul; Ann Arbor: University of Michigan Press, 1958.

Haydn, Hiram. *The Counter-Renaissance.* New York: Scribner's, 1950; Grove Press, 1960.

Helgerson, Richard. *Forms of Nationhood: The Elizabethan Writing of England.* Chicago: University of Chicago Press, 1992.

Heninger, S. K., Jr. *A Handbook of Renaissance Meteorology.* Durham, N.C.: Duke University Press, 1960.

Hill, Christopher. *Society and Puritanism in Pre-Revolutionary England.* New York: Schocken Books, 1967.

Hirst, Derek. *Authority and Conflict: England, 1603–1658.* Cambridge, Mass.: Harvard University Press, 1986.

Huizinga, Johan. *The Waning of the Middle Ages: A Study of the Forms of Life, Thought, and Art in France and the Netherlands in the XIVth and XVth Centuries.* London: E. Arnold & Co., 1924; Garden City, N.Y.: Doubleday, 1954; Baltimore, Md.: Johns Hopkins University Press, 1955.

Ingram, Martin. *Church Courts, Sex, and Marriage in England, 1570–1640.* Cambridge: Cambridge University Press, 1987.

Kantorowicz, E. H. *The King's Two Bodies.* Princeton, N.J.: Princeton University Press, 1957, 1997.

Kendall, Ritchie D. *The Drama of Dissent: The Radical Poetics of Nonconformity, 1380–1590.* Chapel Hill: University of North Carolina Press, 1986.

Klaits, Joseph. *Servants of Satan: The Age of the Witch Hunts.* Bloomington: Indiana University Press, 1985.

Jones, Ann Rosalind, and Peter Stallybrass. *Renaissance Clothing and the Materials of Memory.* Cambridge: Cambridge University Press, 2000.

Lanham, Richard A. *The Motives of Eloquence: Literary Rhetoric in the Renaissance.* New Haven, Conn.: Yale University Press, 1976.

Laqueur, Thomas. *Making Sex: Body and Gender from the Greeks to Freud.* Cambridge, Mass.: Harvard University Press, 1990.

Lee, Maurice, Jr. *Great Britain's Solomon: James VI and I in His Three Kingdoms.* Urbana: University of Illinois Press, 1990.

Lewalski, Barbara Kiefer. *Renaissance Genres: Essays on Theory, History, and Interpretation.* Cambridge, Mass.: Harvard University Press, 1986.

Lovejoy, A. O. *The Great Chain of Being*. Cambridge, Mass.: Harvard University Press, 1936.

MacCaffrey, Wallace T. *Elizabeth I: War and Politics*. Princeton, N.J.: Princeton University Press, 1992.

———. *The Shaping of the Elizabethan Regime*. Princeton, N.J.: Princeton University Press, 1968.

Manley, Lawrence. *Literature and Culture in Early Modern London*. Cambridge: Cambridge University Press, 1995.

Marcus, Leah. *The Politics of Mirth: Jonson, Herrick, Milton, Marvell, and the Defense of Old Holiday Pastimes*. Chicago: University of Chicago Press, 1986.

Marotti, Arthur F. *Catholicism and Anti-Catholicism in Early Modern English Texts*. Basingstoke, England: Macmillan, 1999.

Matar, Nabil. *Turks, Moors, and Englishmen in the Age of Discovery*. New York: Columbia University Press, 1999.

Mattingly, Garrett. *The Armada*. Boston: Houghton Mifflin, 1959.

McEachern, Claire. *The Poetics of Nationhood, 1590–1612*. Cambridge: Cambridge University Press, 1996.

McElwee, William Lloyd. *The Wisest Fool in Christendom: The Reign of King James I and VI*. London: Faber & Faber, 1958.

McPeek, James A. S. *The Black Book of Knaves and Unthrifts in Shakespeare and Other Renaissance Authors*. Storrs: University of Connecticut Press, 1969.

Neale, J. E. *The Elizabethan House of Commons*. London: Cape, 1949.

———. *Queen Elizabeth I*. London: Cape, 1934, 1961.

———. *Queen Elizabeth and Her Parliaments*. 2 vols. London: Cape, 1953–57.

Nichols, John, ed. *The Progresses and Public Processions of Queen Elizabeth*. 3 vols. London, 1786, 1823.

Norbrook, David. *Poetry and Politics in the English Renaissance*. London: Routledge & Kegan Paul, 1984.

Orlin, Lena Cowen. *Private Matters and Public Culture in Post-Reformation England*. Ithaca, N.Y.: Cornell University Press, 1994.

Parry, Graham. *The Golden Age Restor'd: The Culture of the Stuart Court, 1603–42*. Manchester, England: Manchester University Press, 1981.

Pearson, Lu Emily. *Elizabethans at Home*. Stanford, Calif.: Stanford University Press, 1957.

Peck, Linda Levy. *Court Patronage and Corruption in Early Stuart England*. London and Boston: Unwin Hyman, 1990.

Penrose, Boies. *Travel and Discovery in the Renaissance, 1420–1620*. Cambridge, Mass.: Harvard University Press, 1952, 1955.

Rebhorn, Wayne A. *The Emperor of Men's Minds: Literature and the Renaissance Discourse of Rhetoric*. Ithaca, N.Y.: Cornell University Press, 1995.

Sharpe, Kevin, and Peter Lake, eds. *Culture and Politics in Early Stuart England*. Stanford, Calif.: Stanford University Press, 1993.

Slack, Paul. *The Impact of Plague in Tudor and Stuart England*. London: Routledge & Kegan Paul, 1985.

———, ed. *Rebellion, Popular Protest and the Social Order in Early Modern England*. Cambridge: Cambridge University Press, 1984.

Smith, Bruce R. *The Acoustic World of Early Modern England: Attending to the O-Factor*. Chicago: University of Chicago Press, 1999.

Stallybrass, Peter, and Allon White. *The Politics and Poetics of Transgression*. Ithaca, N.Y.: Cornell University Press, 1986.

Stone, Lawrence. *The Crisis of the Aristocracy, 1558–1641*. Oxford: Clarendon Press, 1965.

———. *The Family, Sex and Marriage in England, 1500–1800*. London: Weidenfeld & Nicolson; New York: Harper & Row, 1977.

Stow, John. *Survey of London*. Ed. C. L. Kingsford. Oxford: Clarendon Press, 1971.
Targoff, Ramie. *Common Prayer: The Language of Public Devotion in Early Modern England*. Chicago: University of Chicago Press, 2001.
Tawney, R. H. *Religion and the Rise of Capitalism*. New York: Harcourt Brace, 1926, 1952; Peter Smith, 1962.
Tillyard, E. M. W. *The Elizabethan World Picture*. London: Chatto & Windus, 1943, 1967.
Turner, James Grantham, ed. *Sexuality and Gender in Early Modern Europe: Institutions, Texts, Images*. Cambridge: Cambridge University Press, 1993.
Underdown, David. *Revel, Riot, and Rebellion: Popular Politics and Culture in England, 1603–1660*. Oxford: Clarendon Press, 1985.
Wall, Wendy. *The Imprint of Gender: Authorship and Publication in the English Renaissance*. Ithaca, N.Y.: Cornell University Press, 1993.
Whigham, Frank. *Ambition and Privilege: The Social Tropes of Elizabethan Courtesy Theory*. Berkeley and Los Angeles: University of California Press, 1984.
Wilks, John S. *The Idea of Conscience in Renaissance Tragedy*. London and New York: Routledge, 1990.
Willson, David Harris. *King James VI and I*. New York: Oxford University Press, 1956, 1967; London: Cape, 1972.
Wilson, F. P. *Elizabethan and Jacobean*. Oxford: Clarendon Press, 1945.
Wilson, J. Dover, ed. *Life in Shakespeare's England*. Cambridge: Cambridge University Press, 1913, 1920.
Woodbridge, Linda. *Women and the English Renaissance: Literature and the Nature of Womankind, 1540 to 1620*. Urbana: University of Illinois Press, 1984.
Zeeveld, W. Gordon. *Foundations of Tudor Policy*. Cambridge, Mass.: Harvard University Press, 1948.

Elizabethan and Jacobean Drama

Agnew, Jean-Christophe. *Worlds Apart: The Market and the Theatre in Anglo-American Thought, 1550–1750*. Cambridge: Cambridge University Press, 1986.
Altman, Joel B. *The Tudor Play of Mind: Rhetorical Inquiry and the Development of Elizabethan Drama*. Berkeley and Los Angeles: University of California Press, 1978.
Barish, Jonas. *The Antitheatrical Prejudice*. Berkeley and Los Angeles: University of California Press, 1981.
Bednarz, James P. *Shakespeare and the Poets' War*. New York: Columbia University Press, 2001.
Belsey, Catherine. *The Subject of Tragedy: Identity and Difference in Renaissance Drama*. London: Methuen, 1985.
Berlin, Normand. *The Base String: The Underworld in Elizabethan Drama*. Rutherford, N.J.: Fairleigh Dickinson University Press, 1968.
Bevington, David. *From "Mankind" to Marlowe: Growth of Structure in the Popular Drama of Tudor England*. Cambridge, Mass.: Harvard University Press, 1962.
———. *Tudor Drama and Politics: A Critical Approach to Topical Meaning*. Cambridge, Mass.: Harvard University Press, 1968.
———, and Peter Holbrook, eds. *The Politics of the Stuart Court Masque*. Cambridge: Cambridge University Press, 1998.
Blistein, Elmer M., ed. *The Drama of the Renaissance: Essays for Leicester Bradner*. Providence, R.I.: Brown University Press, 1970.
Bluestone, Max, and Norman Rabkin, eds. *Shakespeare's Contemporaries*. 2nd ed. Englewood Cliffs, N.J.: Prentice-Hall, 1970.
Bowers, Fredson T. *Elizabethan Revenge Tragedy, 1587–1642*. Princeton, N.J.: Princeton University Press, 1940; Gloucester, Mass.: P. Smith, 1959.

Bradbrook, M. C. *Themes and Conventions of Elizabethan Tragedy*. 2nd ed. Cambridge: Cambridge University Press, 1980.

Braden, Gordon. *Renaissance Tragedy and the Senecan Tradition*. New Haven, Conn.: Yale University Press, 1985.

Briggs, Julia. *This Stage-Play World: English Literature and Its Background, 1580–1625*. Oxford: Oxford University Press, 1983.

Bristol, Michael. *Carnival and Theater: Plebeian Culture and the Structure of Authority in Renaissance England*. New York and London: Methuen, 1985.

Brodwin, Leonora Leet. *Elizabethan Love Tragedy, 1587–1625*. London and New York: New York University Press, 1971.

Brooke, Nicholas. *Horrid Laughter in Jacobean Tragedy*. London: Open Books, 1979.

Brooks, Douglas A. *From Playhouse to Printing House: Drama and Authorship in Early Modern England*. Cambridge: Cambridge University Press, 2000.

Brown, John Russell, and Bernard Harris, eds. *Jacobean Theatre*. London: Edward Arnold, 1960; New York: Capricorn Books, 1967.

Bruster, Douglas. *Drama and the Market in the Age of Shakespeare*. Cambridge: Cambridge University Press, 1992.

Bushnell, Rebecca W. *Tragedies of Tyrants: Political Thought and Theater in the English Renaissance*. Ithaca, N.Y.: Cornell University Press, 1990.

Butler, Martin. *Theatre and Crisis, 1632–1642*. Cambridge: Cambridge University Press, 1984.

Cohen, Walter. *Drama of a Nation: Public Theater in Renaissance England and Spain*. Ithaca, N.Y.: Cornell University Press, 1985.

Comensoli, Viviana, and Anne Russell, eds. *Enacting Gender on the English Renaissance Stage*. Urbana: University of Illinois Press, 1999.

Cox, John D. *The Devil and the Sacred in English Drama, 1350–1642*. Cambridge: Cambridge University Press, 2000.

———, and David Scott Kastan, eds. *A New History of Early English Drama*. New York: Columbia University Press, 1997.

Daileder, Celia R. *Eroticism on the Renaissance Stage*. Cambridge: Cambridge University Press, 1998.

Diehl, Huston. *Staging Reform, Reforming the Stage: Protestantism and Popular Theater in Early Modern England*. Ithaca, N.Y.: Cornell University Press, 1997.

Dillon, Janette. *Language and Stage in Medieval and Renaissance England*. Cambridge: Cambridge University Press, 1998.

———. *Theatre, Court and City, 1595–1610: Drama and Social Space in London*. Cambridge: Cambridge University Press, 2000.

Dolan, Frances E. *Dangerous Familiars: Representations of Domestic Crime in England, 1550–1700*. Ithaca, N.Y.: Cornell University Press, 1994.

Dollimore, Jonathan. *Radical Tragedy: Religion, Ideology and Power in the Drama of Shakespeare and His Contemporaries*. 2nd ed. New York and London: Harvester Wheatsheaf, 1989; Durham, N.C.: Duke University Press, 1993.

Doran, Madeleine. *Endeavors of Art: A Study of Form in Elizabethan Drama*. Madison: University of Wisconsin Press, 1954, 1972.

Eliot, T. S. *Selected Essays; New Edition*. New York: Harcourt Brace Jovanovich, 1950.

Falco, Raphael. *Charismatic Authority in Early Modern English Tragedy*. Baltimore, Md.: Johns Hopkins University Press, 2000.

Farley-Hills, David. *Jacobean Drama: A Critical Study of the Professional Drama, 1600–25*. Basingstoke, England: Macmillan, 1988.

Farnham, Willard. *The Medieval Heritage of Elizabethan Tragedy*. Berkeley: University of California Press, 1936; New York: Barnes & Noble, 1956; Oxford: Blackwell Publishers, 1963.

Findlay, Alison. *A Feminist Perspective on Renaissance Drama*. Oxford: Blackwell Publishers, 1999.

———. *Illegitimate Power: Bastards in Renaissance Drama.* Manchester, England: Manchester University Press, 1994.

Freer, Coburn. *The Poetics of Jacobean Drama.* Baltimore, Md.: Johns Hopkins University Press, 1981.

Gibbons, Brian. *Jacobean City Comedy: A Study of Satiric Plays by Jonson, Marston, and Middleton.* London: Rupert Hart-Davis; Cambridge, Mass.: Harvard University Press, 1968.

Goldberg, Jonathan. *James I and the Politics of Literature: Jonson, Shakespeare, Donne, and Their Contemporaries.* Baltimore, Md.: Johns Hopkins University Press, 1983.

———. *Sodometries: Renaissance Texts, Modern Sexualities.* Stanford, Calif.: Stanford University Press, 1992.

Griswold, Wendy. *Renaissance Revivals: City Comedy and Revenge Tragedy in the London Theatre, 1576–1980.* Chicago: University of Chicago Press, 1986.

Hall, Joan Lord. *The Dynamics of Role-Playing in Jacobean Tragedy.* New York: St. Martin's Press, 1991.

Harbage, Alfred. *Annals of English Drama, 975–1700.* 3rd ed., rev. Sylvia Stoler Wagonheim. London: Routledge, 1989.

———. *As They Liked It: A Study of Shakespeare's Moral Artistry.* New York: Harper & Brothers, 1947.

———. *Shakespeare and the Rival Traditions.* New York: Macmillan, 1952; New York: Barnes & Noble, 1968.

Hassel, R. Chris. *Renaissance Drama and the English Church Year.* Lincoln: University of Nebraska Press, 1979.

Hattaway, Michael. *Elizabethan Popular Theatre: Plays in Performance.* London: Routledge & Kegan Paul, 1982.

Hawkins, Harriett. *Likenesses of Truth in Elizabethan and Restoration Drama.* Oxford: Clarendon Press, 1972.

Henning, Standish, Robert Kimbrough, and Richard Knowles, eds. *English Renaissance Drama: Essays in Honor of Madeleine Doran and Mark Eccles.* Carbondale and Edwardsville: Southern Illinois University Press, 1976.

Herndl, George C. *The High Design: English Renaissance Tragedy and the Natural Law.* Lexington: University Press of Kentucky, 1970.

Holdsworth, Roger, ed. *Three Jacobean Revenge Tragedies: A Casebook.* London: Macmillan, 1990.

Honigmann, E. A. J., ed. *Shakespeare and His Contemporaries: Essays in Comparison.* Manchester, England: Manchester University Press, 1986.

Howard, Jean E. *The Stage and Social Struggle in Early Modern England.* London and New York: Routledge, 1994.

Hunter, G. K. *English Drama, 1586–1642: The Age of Shakespeare.* Oxford: Clarendon Press, 1997.

Jardine, Lisa. *Still Harping on Daughters: Women and Drama in the Age of Shakespeare.* Sussex, England: Harvester; Totowa, N.J.: Barnes & Noble, 1983; New York: Columbia University Press, 1989.

Jones, Robert C. *Engagement with Knavery: Point of View in "Richard III," "The Jew of Malta," "Volpone," and "The Revenger's Tragedy."* Durham, N.C.: Duke University Press, 1986.

Kastan, David Scott, and Peter Stallybrass, eds. *Staging the Renaissance: Reinterpretations of Elizabethan and Jacobean Drama.* New York and London: Routledge, 1991.

Kaufman, Ralph J., ed. *Elizabethan Drama: Modern Essays in Criticism.* New York: Oxford University Press, 1961.

Kehler, Dorothea, and Susan Baker, eds. *In Another Country: Feminist Perspectives on Renaissance Drama.* Metuchen, N.J.: Scarecrow Press, 1991.

Kernan, Alvin. *The Cankered Muse: Satire of the English Renaissance*. New Haven, Conn.: Yale University Press, 1959.

Kernodle, G. R. *From Art to Theatre: Form and Convention in the Renaissance*. Chicago: University of Chicago Press, 1944, 1965.

Kerrigan, John. *Revenge Tragedy: Aeschylus to Armageddon*. Oxford: Oxford University Press, 1995.

Kiefer, Frederick. *Fortune and Elizabethan Tragedy*. San Marino, Calif.: The Huntington Library, 1983.

———. *Writing on the Renaissance Stage: Written Words, Printed Pages, Metaphoric Books*. Newark: University of Delaware Press, 1996.

Kirsch, Arthur C. *Jacobean Dramatic Perspectives*. Charlottesville: University Press of Virginia, 1972.

Leggatt, Alexander. *Citizen Comedy in the Age of Shakespeare*. Toronto: University of Toronto Press, 1973.

———. *English Stage Comedy, 1490–1990: Five Centuries of a Genre*. London and New York: Routledge, 1998.

———. *Introduction to English Renaissance Comedy*. Manchester, England: Manchester University Press, 1999.

———. *Jacobean Public Theatre*. London and New York: Routledge, 1992.

Leinwand, Theodore. *Theatre, Finance and Society in Early Modern England*. Cambridge: Cambridge University Press, 1999.

Levin, Richard. *The Multiple Plot in English Renaissance Drama*. Chicago: University of Chicago Press, 1971.

Loftis, John. *Renaissance Drama in England and Spain: Topical Allusion and History Plays*. Princeton, N.J.: Princeton University Press, 1987.

Lomax, Marion. *Stage Images and Traditions: Shakespeare to Ford*. Cambridge: Cambridge University Press, 1987.

Loomba, Ania. *Gender, Race, Renaissance Drama*. Manchester, England: Manchester University Press, 1989.

Margeson, J. M. R. *The Origins of English Tragedy*. Oxford: Clarendon Press, 1967.

Maus, Katharine Eisaman. *Inwardness and Theater in the English Renaissance*. Chicago: University of Chicago Press, 1995.

McAlindon, T. *English Renaissance Tragedy*. Basingstoke, England: Macmillan, 1986.

McLuskie, Kathleen. *Renaissance Dramatists*. Atlantic Highlands, N.J.: Humanities Press International, 1989.

Mullaney, Steven. *The Place of the Stage: License, Play, and Power in Renaissance England*. Chicago: University of Chicago Press, 1988.

Neill, Michael. *Issues of Death: Mortality and Identity in English Renaissance Tragedy*. Oxford: Clarendon Press, 1997.

Newman, Karen. *Fashioning Femininity and English Renaissance Drama*. Chicago: University of Chicago Press, 1991.

O'Connell, Michael. *The Idolatrous Eye: Iconoclasm and Theater in Early-Modern England*. New York: Oxford University Press, 2000.

Orgel, Stephen. *The Illusion of Power: Political Theater in the English Renaissance*. Berkeley and Los Angeles: University of California Press, 1975.

———. *Impersonations: The Performance of Gender in Shakespeare's England*. Cambridge: Cambridge University Press, 1996.

Ornstein, Robert. *The Moral Vision of Jacobean Tragedy*. Madison: University of Wisconsin Press, 1960.

Parker, R. B., and S. P. Zitner, eds. *Elizabethan Theater: Essays in Honor of S. Schoenbaum*. Newark: University of Delaware Press, 1996.

Paster, Gail Kern. *The Body Embarrassed: Drama and the Disciplines of Shame in Early Modern England*. Ithaca, N.Y.: Cornell University Press, 1993.

———. *The Idea of the City in the Age of Shakespeare*. Athens: University of Georgia Press, 1985.

Pinciss, Gerald M. *Forbidden Matter: Religion in the Drama of Shakespeare and His Contemporaries*. Newark: University of Delaware Press, 2000.

Rabkin, Norman, ed. *Reinterpretations of Elizabethan Drama*. New York: Columbia University Press, 1969.

Rose, Mary Beth. *The Expense of Spirit: Love and Sexuality in English Renaissance Drama*. Ithaca, N.Y.: Cornell University Press, 1988.

———, ed. *Renaissance Drama as Cultural History: Essays from Renaissance Drama, 1977–1987*. Evanston, Ill.: Northwestern University Press, 1990.

Salingar, Leo. *Dramatic Form in Shakespeare and the Jacobeans*. Cambridge: Cambridge University Press, 1986.

Sanders, Eve Rachele. *Gender and Literacy on Stage in Early Modern England*. Cambridge: Cambridge University Press, 1998.

Sinfield, Alan. *Faultlines: Cultural Materialism and the Politics of Dissident Reading*. Berkeley and Los Angeles: University of California Press, 1992.

Smith, Bruce R. *Ancient Scripts and Modern Experience on the English Stage, 1500–1700*. Princeton, N.J.: Princeton University Press, 1988.

———. *Homosexual Desire in Shakespeare's England*. Chicago: University of Chicago Press, 1991.

Smith, David L., Richard Strier, and David Bevington, eds. *The Theatrical City: Culture, Theatre and Politics in London, 1576–1649*. Cambridge: Cambridge University Press, 1995.

Shapiro, James. *Rival Playwrights: Marlowe, Jonson, Shakespeare*. New York: Columbia University Press, 1991.

Spivack, Bernard. *Shakespeare and the Allegory of Evil*. New York: Columbia University Press, 1958.

Stilling, Roger. *Love and Death in Renaissance Tragedy*. Baton Rouge: Louisiana State University Press, 1976.

Sullivan, Garrett A., Jr. *The Drama of Landscape: Land, Property, and Social Relations on the Early Modern Stage*. Stanford, Calif.: Stanford University Press, 1998.

Tricomi, Albert H. *Anticourt Drama in England, 1603–1642*. Charlottesville: University Press of Virginia, 1989.

Waith, Eugene M. *Patterns and Perspectives in English Renaissance Drama*. Newark: University of Delaware Press, 1988.

Watson, Robert N. *The Rest Is Silence: Death as Annihilation in the English Renaissance*. Berkeley and Los Angeles: University of California Press, 1994.

Weimann, Robert. *Shakespeare and the Popular Tradition in the Theater: Studies in the Social Dimension of Dramatic Form and Function*. Ed. Robert Schwartz. Baltimore, Md.: Johns Hopkins University Press, 1978.

Welsford, Enid. *The Court Masque*. Cambridge: Cambridge University Press, 1927.

Whigham, Frank. *Seizures of the Will in Early Modern English Drama*. Cambridge: Cambridge University Press, 1996.

White, Paul Whitfield. *Theatre and Reformation: Protestantism, Patronage and Playing in Tudor England*. Cambridge: Cambridge University Press, 1993.

Wiggins, Martin. *Journeymen in Murder: The Assassin in English Renaissance Drama*. Oxford: Clarendon Press, 1991.

———. *Shakespeare and the Drama of His Time*. Oxford: Oxford University Press, 2000.

Zimmerman, Susan, ed. *Erotic Politics: Desire on the Renaissance Stage*. New York and London: Routledge, 1992.

The Early Modern Theater: Staging, Acting Companies, Governmental Regulations

Bentley, G. E. *The Jacobean and Caroline Stage*. 7 vols. Oxford: Clarendon Press, 1941–68.

———. *The Profession of Dramatist in Shakespeare's Time, 1590–1642*. Princeton, N.J.: Princeton University Press, 1971.

———. *The Profession of Player in Shakespeare's Time, 1590–1642*. Princeton, N.J.: Princeton University Press, 1984.

———, ed. *The Seventeenth-Century Stage: A Collection of Critical Essays*. Chicago: University of Chicago Press, 1968.

Bradbrook, M. C. *The Rise of the Common Player: A Study of Actor and Society in Shakespeare's England*. London: Chatto & Windus, 1962.

Bradley, David. *From Text to Performance in the Elizabethan Theatre: Preparing the Play for the Stage*. Cambridge: Cambridge University Press, 1992.

Burt, Richard. *Licensed by Authority: Ben Jonson and the Discourses of Censorship*. Ithaca, N.Y.: Cornell University Press, 1993.

Chambers, E. K. *The Elizabethan Stage*. 4 vols. Oxford: Clarendon Press, 1923.

Clare, Janet. *"Art Made Tongue-tied by Authority": Elizabethan and Jacobean Dramatic Censorship*. Manchester, England: Manchester University Press; New York: St. Martin's Press, 1990.

Cook, Ann Jennalie. *The Privileged Playgoers of Shakespeare's London, 1576–1642*. Princeton, N.J.: Princeton University Press, 1981.

Dawson, Anthony B., and Paul Yachnin. *The Culture of Playgoing in Shakespeare's England: A Collaborative Debate*. Cambridge: Cambridge University Press, 2001.

Dessen, Alan C. *Elizabethan Drama and the Viewer's Eye*. Chapel Hill: University of North Carolina Press, 1977.

———. *Recovering Shakespeare's Theatrical Vocabulary*. Cambridge: Cambridge University Press, 1995.

Dutton, Richard. *Licensing, Censorship and Authorship in Early Modern England: Buggeswords*. Basingstoke, England: Palgrave, 2000.

———. *Mastering the Revels: The Regulation and Censorship of English Renaissance Drama*. Iowa City: University of Iowa Press, 1991.

Foakes, R. A. *Illustrations of the English Stage, 1580–1642*. Stanford, Calif.: Stanford University Press, 1985.

Gair, W. Reavley. *The Children of Paul's*. Cambridge: Cambridge University Press, 1982.

Gildersleeve, Virginia C. *Government Regulation of the Elizabethan Drama*. New York: Columbia University Press, 1908; Westport, Conn.: Greenwood Press, 1975.

Greg, W. W., ed. *Dramatic Documents from the Elizabethan Playhouses: Stage Plots, Actors' Parts, Prompt Books*. 2 vols. Oxford: Clarendon Press, 1931, 1969.

Gurr, Andrew. *Playgoing in Shakespeare's London*. Cambridge: Cambridge University Press, 1987.

———. *The Shakespearian Playing Companies*. Oxford: Clarendon Press; New York: Oxford University Press, 1996.

———. *The Shakespearean Stage, 1574–1642*. 3rd ed. Cambridge: Cambridge University Press, 1992.

Harbage, Alfred. *Shakespeare's Audience*. New York: Columbia University Press, 1941.

Henslowe, Philip. *Henslowe's Diary*. Ed. R. A. Foakes and R. T. Rickert. Cambridge: Cambridge University Press, 1961.

Hillebrand, H. N. *The Child Actors: A Chapter in Elizabethan Stage History*. Urbana: University of Illinois Press, 1926.

Ingram, William. *The Business of Playing: The Beginnings of Adult Professional Theater in Elizabethan London*. Ithaca, N.Y.: Cornell University Press, 1992.

King, T. J. *Shakespearean Staging, 1599–1642*. Cambridge, Mass.: Harvard University Press, 1971.

Linthicum, Marie Channing. *Costume in the Drama of Shakespeare and His Contemporaries*. Oxford: Clarendon Press, 1936.

Mann, David. *The Elizabethan Player: Contemporary Stage Representation*. London and New York: Routledge, 1991.

McMillin, Scott. *The Elizabethan Theatre and "The Book of Sir Thomas More."* Ithaca, N.Y.: Cornell University Press, 1987.

———, and Sally-Beth MacLean. *The Queen's Men and Their Plays*. Cambridge: Cambridge University Press, 1998.

Mulryne, J. R., and Margaret Shewring, eds. *Theatre and Government under the Early Stuarts*. Cambridge: Cambridge University Press, 1993.

Rutter, Carol Chillington, ed. *Documents of the Rose Playhouse*. Rev. ed. Manchester, England: Manchester University Press, 1999.

Shapiro, Michael. *Children of the Revels: The Boy Companies of Shakespeare's Time and Their Plays*. New York: Columbia University Press, 1977.

Wickham, Glynne. *Early English Stages, 1300 to 1660*. 3 vols. London: Routledge & Kegan Paul, 1966–81.

See also Mullaney, under "Elizabethan and Jacobean Drama."

Individual Dramatists and Their Plays

THOMAS KYD

The Spanish Tragedy

Baker, Howard. *Induction to Tragedy: A Study in a Development of Form in "Gorboduc," "The Spanish Tragedy," and "Titus Andronicus."* University: Louisiana State University Press, 1939.

Barber, C. L. *Creating Elizabethan Tragedy: The Theater of Kyd and Marlowe*. Ed. Richard P. Wheeler. Chicago: University of Chicago Press, 1988.

Cunliffe, John W. *The Influence of Seneca on Elizabethan Tragedy: An Essay*. London and New York: Macmillan, 1893.

Freeman, Arthur. *Thomas Kyd: Facts and Problems*. Oxford: Clarendon Press, 1967.

Hunter, G. K. "Ironies of Justice in the Spanish Tragedy." *Renaissance Drama* 8 (1965): 89–104.

Kyd, Thomas. *The Spanish Tragedy*. Ed. Philip Edwards. The Revels Plays. London: Methuen, 1959; Manchester, England: Manchester University Press, 1988. Revels Student Editions, ed. David Bevington, 1996.

Stockholder, Kay. "The Aristocratic Woman as Scapegoat: Romantic Love and Class Antagonism in *The Spanish Tragedy, The Duchess of Malfi*, and *The Changeling*." *The Elizabethan Theater XIV*, ed. A. L. Magnussen and C. E. McGee (Toronto: Meany, 1998): 127–51.

See also Bluestone and Rabkin (Wolfgang Clemen, William K. Wiatt, G. K. Hunter), Bowers, Braden, Farnham, Kastan and Stallybrass (James Shapiro), Kaufman (William Empson), Kerrigan, Maus, McAlindon, and Whigham, under "Elizabethan and Jacobean Drama."

JOHN LYLY

Endymion

Houppert, Joseph W. *John Lyly*. Boston: Twayne Publishers, 1975.

Hunter, G. K. *John Lyly: The Humanist as Courtier*. London: Routledge & Kegan Paul, 1962.

Lyly, John. *Endymion*. Ed. David Bevington. The Revels Plays. Manchester, England: Manchester University Press, 1996.

Saccio, Peter. *The Court Comedies of John Lyly: A Study in Allegorical Dramaturgy*. Princeton, N.J.: Princeton University Press, 1969.

See also Altman, Bluestone and Rabkin or Kaufman (G. Wilson Knight), and Rose, under "Elizabethan and Jacobean Drama."

ROBERT GREENE

Friar Bacon and Friar Bungay

Crupi, Charles W. *Robert Greene*. Boston: Twayne Publishers, 1986.

Greene, Robert. *Friar Bacon and Friar Bungay*. Ed. Daniel Seltzer. Regents Renaissance Drama. Lincoln: University of Nebraska Press, 1963.

Hieatt, Charles W. "Multiple Plotting in *Friar Bacon and Friar Bungay*." *Renaissance Drama* n.s. 16 (1985): 17–34.

Jordan, John Clark. *Robert Greene*. New York: Columbia University Press, 1915; Octagon Books, 1965.

See also Bluestone and Rabkin (William Empson) and Levin, under "Elizabethan and Jacobean Drama."

CHRISTOPHER MARLOWE

Bakeless, John. *The Tragical History of Christopher Marlowe*. 2 vols. Cambridge, Mass.: Harvard University Press, 1942.

Barber, C. L. *Creating Elizabethan Tragedy: The Theater of Kyd and Marlowe*. Ed. Richard P. Wheeler. Chicago: University of Chicago Press, 1988.

Bartels, Emily C. *Spectacles of Strangeness: Imperialism, Alienation, and Marlowe*. Philadelphia: University of Pennsylvania Press, 1993.

Cartelli, Thomas. *Marlowe, Shakespeare, and the Economy of Theatrical Experience*. Philadelphia: University of Pennsylvania Press, 1991.

Deats, Sara Munson. *Sex, Gender, and Desire in the Plays of Christopher Marlowe*. Newark: University of Delaware Press, 1997.

Fanta, Christopher G. *Marlowe's "Agonists," An Approach to the Ambiguity of His Plays*. Cambridge, Mass.: Harvard University Press, 1970.

Friedenreich, Kenneth, Roma Gill, and Constance B. Kuriyama, eds. *"A Poet & a Filthy Play-Maker": New Essays on Christopher Marlowe*. New York: AMS Press, 1988.

Grantley, Darryll, and Peter Roberts, ed. *Christopher Marlowe and English Renaissance Culture*. Aldershot, England: Scolar, 1996.

Kocher, Paul H. *Christopher Marlowe: A Study of His Thought, Learning, and Character*. Chapel Hill: University of North Carolina Press, 1946.

Kuriyama, Constance Brown. *Hammer or Anvil: Psychological Patterns in Christopher Marlowe's Plays*. New Brunswick, N.J.: Rutgers University Press, 1980.

Leech, Clifford, ed. *Marlowe: A Collection of Critical Essays*. Englewood Cliffs, N.J.: Prentice-Hall, 1964.

Levin, Harry. *The Overreacher: A Study of Christopher Marlowe*. Cambridge, Mass.: Harvard University Press, 1952, 1964.

Maclure, Millar, ed. *Marlowe: The Critical Heritage, 1588–1896*. London and Boston: Routledge & Kegan Paul, 1979.

Sales, Roger. *Christopher Marlowe*. Basingstoke, England: Macmillan; New York: St. Martin's Press, 1991.

Sanders, Wilbur. *The Dramatist and the Received Idea: Studies in the Plays of Marlowe and Shakespeare*. Cambridge: Cambridge University Press, 1968.

Shepherd, Simon. *Marlowe and the Politics of Elizabethan Theatre*. Brighton, England: Harvester; New York: St. Martin's Press, 1986.

Simkin, Stevie. *A Preface to Marlowe*. Harlow, England, and New York: Longman, 2000.

Summers, Claude J. *Christopher Marlowe and the Politics of Power*. Salzburg: Institut für Englische Sprache und Literatur, 1974.

Thomas, Vivien, and William Tydeman, eds. *Christopher Marlowe, the Plays and Their Sources*. London and New York: Routledge, 1994.

Tromly, Fred B. *Playing with Desire: Christopher Marlowe and the Art of Tantalization*. Toronto and Buffalo, N.Y.: University of Toronto Press, 1998.

Waith, Eugene. *The Herculean Hero in Marlowe, Chapman, Shakespeare, and Dryden*. New York: Columbia University Press, 1962.

Weil, Judith E. R. *Christopher Marlowe: Merlin's Prophet*. Cambridge: Cambridge University Press, 1977.

White, Paul Whitfield, ed. *Marlowe, History and Sexuality: New Critical Essays on Christopher Marlowe*. New York: AMS Press, 1998.

Wilson, F. P. *Marlowe and the Early Shakespeare*. Oxford: Clarendon Press, 1953.

Zunder, William. *Elizabethan Marlowe: Writing and Culture in the English Renaissance*. Cottingham, Hull, England: Unity Press, 1994.

See also Altman, Bevington, Eliot, Maus, McAlindon, Shapiro, and Spivack, under "Elizabethan and Jacobean Drama."

Tamburlaine the Great, Part 1

Feiler, Frank Bernard. *Tamburlaine, Part I and Its Audience*. Gainesville: University of Florida Press, 1962.

Geckle, George L. *Tamburlaine and Edward II*. Text and Performance Series. Atlantic Highlands, N.J.: Humanities Press International, 1988.

Howe, James Robinson. *Marlowe, Tamburlaine, and Magic*. Athens: Ohio University Press, 1976.

Marlowe, Christopher. *Tamburlaine the Great*. Ed. J. S. Cunningham. The Revels Plays. Manchester, England: Manchester University Press, 1981. Revels Student Editions, ed. J. S. Cunningham and Eithne Henson, 1998.

Parr, Johnstone. *Tamburlaine's Malady and Other Essays on Astrology in Elizabethan Drama*. 1953. Westport, Conn.: Greenwood Press, 1971.

See also Braden, and Kaufman (Irving Ribner), under "Elizabethan and Jacobean Drama."

Doctor Faustus (A-text)

Erikson, Roy T. " 'What resting place is this?' Aspects of Time and Place in *Doctor Faustus (1616).*" *Renaissance Drama* n.s. 16 (1985): 49–74.

Gatti, Hilary. *The Renaissance Drama of Knowledge: Giordano Bruno in England*. London and New York: Routledge, 1989.

Marlowe, Christopher. *Doctor Faustus, A- and B-Texts (1604, 1616)*. Ed. David Bevington and Eric Rasmussen. The Revels Plays. Manchester, England: Manchester University Press, 1993.

Rasmussen, Eric. *A Textual Companion to "Doctor Faustus."* The Revels Plays Companion Library. Manchester, England: Manchester University Press, 1993.

See also Dollimore and Levin, under "Elizabethan and Jacobean Drama."

The Jew of Malta

Marlowe, Christopher. *The Jew of Malta*. Ed. N. W. Bawcutt. The Revels Plays. London: Methuen; Manchester, England: Manchester University Press, 1978. Revels Student Editions, ed. David Bevington, 1997.

Shapiro, James. *Shakespeare and the Jews*. New York: Columbia University Press, 1996.

See also Jones, under "Elizabethan and Jacobean Drama," and Greenblatt, *Renaissance Self-Fashioning*, under "Intellectual . . . Contexts."

Edward II

Geckle, George L. *Tamburlaine and Edward II.* Text and Performance Series. Atlantic Highlands, N.J.: Humanities Press International, 1988.

Levin, Carole, and Karen Robertson, eds. *Sexuality and Politics in Renaissance Drama.* Lewiston, Maine: Edwin Mellon Press, 1991.

Marlowe, Christopher. *Edward the Second.* Ed. Charles R. Forker. The Revels Plays. Manchester, England: Manchester University Press, 1994.

See also Goldberg, *Sodometries*, Smith, *Homosexual Desire*, and Waith, under "Elizabethan and Jacobean Drama."

ANONYMOUS

Arden of Faversham

Comensoli, Viviana. *"Household Business": Domestic Plays of Early Modern England.* Toronto: University of Toronto Press, 1996.

Holbrook, Peter. *Literature and Degree in Renaissance England: Nashe, Bourgeois Tragedy, Shakespeare.* Newark: University of Delaware Press, 1994.

McLuskie, Kathleen E., and David Bevington, eds. *Plays on Women.* Revels Student Editions. Manchester, England: Manchester University Press, 1999.

The Tragedy of Master Arden of Faversham. Ed. M. L. Wine. The Revels Plays. London: Methuen, 1973; Manchester, England: Manchester University Press, 1976.

See also Orlin, under "Intellectual . . . Contexts," and Belsey, Bluestone and Rabkin (Max Bluestone), and Dolan, under "Elizabethan and Jacobean Drama."

THOMAS DEKKER

The Shoemaker's Holiday

Champion, Larry S. *Thomas Dekker and the Traditions of English Drama.* New York: P. Lang, 1985.

Conover, James Harrington. *Thomas Dekker: An Analysis of Dramatic Structure.* The Hague and Paris: Mouton, 1969.

Dekker, Thomas. *The Shoemaker's Holiday.* Ed. R. L. Smallwood and Stanley Wells. The Revels Plays. Manchester, England: University of Manchester Press, 1979, 1999.

Price, George R. *Thomas Dekker.* New York: Twayne Publishers, 1969.

See also Bluestone and Rabkin (Harold E. Toliver), Kastan and Stallybrass (David Kastan), and Smith, Strier, and Bevington (David Bevington, Paul S. Seaver), under "Elizabethan and Jacobean Drama." See also Middleton and Dekker, *The Roaring Girl*, below.

JOHN MARSTON

The Malcontent

Axelrad, Albert José. *Un Malcontent Élizabéthain: John Marston, 1576–1634.* Paris: Didier, 1955.

Caputi, Anthony. *John Marston, Satirist.* Ithaca, N.Y.: Cornell University Press, 1961.

Finkelpearl, Philip. *John Marston of the Middle Temple: An Elizabethan Dramatist in His Social Setting.* Cambridge, Mass.: Harvard University Press, 1969.

Ingram, R. W. *John Marston.* Boston: Twayne Publishers, 1978.

Marston, John. *The Malcontent.* Ed. George K. Hunter. The Revels Plays. London: Methuen, 1975; Manchester, England: Manchester University Press, 1999. Revels Student Editions, 2000.

Scott, Michael. *John Marston's Plays: Theme, Structure, and Performance.* London: Macmillan, 1978.

Tucker, Kenneth. *John Marston: A Reference Guide*. Boston: G. K. Hall, 1985.
See also Brown and Harris (G. K. Hunter), Farley-Hills, Gibbons, Hall, and Kernan, under "Elizabethan and Jacobean Drama."

ELIZABETH CARY

The Tragedy of Mariam

Cary, Elizabeth, Lady Falkland. *The Tragedy of Mariam, the Fair Queen of Jewry*. Ed. Barry Weller and Margaret W. Ferguson. Berkeley and Los Angeles: University of California Press, 1994.
———. *The Tragedy of Mariam, the Fair Queen of Jewry*. Ed. Stephanie J. Wright. Staffordshire, England: Keele University Press, 1996.
See also Comensoli and Russell (Kegl), and Kastan and Stallybrass (Margaret W. Ferguson), under "Elizabethan and Jacobean Drama."

BEN JONSON

Barish, Jonas. *Ben Jonson and the Language of Prose Comedy*. Cambridge, Mass.: Harvard University Press, 1960.
———. "Feasting and Judgment in Jonsonian Comedy." *Renaissance Drama* n.s. 5 (1972): 3–35.
Barton, Anne. *Ben Jonson, Dramatist*. Cambridge: Cambridge University Press, 1984.
Brady, Jennifer, and W. H. Herendeen. *Ben Jonson's 1616 Folio*. Newark: University of Delaware Press, 1991.
Brock, D. Heyward. *A Ben Jonson Companion*. Bloomington: Indiana University Press, 1983.
Butler, Martin, ed. *Re-Presenting Ben Jonson: Text, History, Performance*. Basingstoke, England: Macmillan, 1999.
Cave, Richard, Elizabeth Schafer, and Brian Woolland. *Ben Jonson and Theatre: Performance, Practice and Theory*. London: Routledge, 1999.
Chalfant, Fran C. *Ben Jonson's London: A Jacobean Placename Dictionary*. Athens: University of Georgia Press, 1978.
Donaldson, Ian. *Jonson's Magic Houses: Essays in Interpretation*. Oxford: Clarendon Press, 1997.
Duncan, Douglas. *Ben Jonson and the Lucianic Tradition*. Cambridge: Cambridge University Press, 1979.
Evans, Robert C. *Ben Jonson and the Poetics of Patronage*. Lewisburg, Pa.: Bucknell University Press, 1989.
Greene, Thomas M. "Ben Jonson and the Centered Self." *Studies in English Literature* 10 (1970): 325–48.
Harp, Richard, and Stanley Stewart, eds. *The Cambridge Companion to Ben Jonson*. Cambridge: Cambridge University Press, 2000.
Herford, C. H., and Percy and Evelyn Simpson, eds. *Ben Jonson*. 11 vols. Oxford: Clarendon Press, 1925–52.
Kay, W. David. *Ben Jonson: A Literary Life*. Basingstoke, England: Macmillan, 1995.
Knights, L. C. *Drama and Society in the Age of Jonson*. 1937. New York: Norton, 1968.
Maus, Katharine Eisaman. *Ben Jonson and the Roman Frame of Mind*. Princeton, N.J.: Princeton University Press, 1984.
———. "Satiric and Ideal Economies in the Jonsonian Imagination." *English Literary Renaissance* 19 (1989): 42–64.
Partridge, Edward B. *The Broken Compass: A Study of the Major Comedies of Ben Jonson*. New York: Columbia University Press, 1958; London: Chatto & Windus, 1964.
Riggs, David. *Ben Jonson: A Life*. Cambridge, Mass.: Harvard University Press, 1989.
Tiffany, Grace. *Erotic Beasts and Social Monsters: Shakespeare, Jonson, and Comic Androgyny*. Newark: University of Delaware Press, 1995.

Watson, Robert N. *Ben Jonson's Parodic Strategy: Literary Imperialism in the Comedies*. Cambridge, Mass.: Harvard University Press, 1987.

Yachnin, Paul. *Stage-Wrights: Shakespeare, Jonson, Middleton, and the Making of Theatrical Value*. Philadelphia: University of Pennsylvania Press, 1997.

See also Eliot, Farley-Hills, Gibbons, and Shapiro, under "Elizabethan and Jacobean Drama," and Burt, under "The Early Modern Theater."

Volpone

Jonson, Ben. *Volpone*. Ed. Brian Parker. Rev. ed. The Revels Plays. Manchester, England: Manchester University Press, 1999. Revels Student Editions, ed. Brian Parker and David Bevington, 1999.

See also Barbour under next listing.

Epicene

Ayers, P. K. "Dreams of the City: The Urban and the Urbane in Jonson's *Epicoene*." *Philological Quarterly* 66 (1987): 73–86.

Barbour, Richmond. " 'When I Acted Young Antinous': Boy Actors and the Erotics of Jonsonian Theater." *PMLA* 110 (1995): 1006–22.

Jonson, Ben. *Epicoene, or The Silent Woman*. Ed. L. A. Beaurline. Lincoln: University of Nebraska Press, 1966.

Levine, Laura. *Men in Women's Clothing: Antitheatricality and Effeminization, 1579–1642*. Cambridge: Cambridge University Press, 1994.

See also Jones, Kastan and Stallybrass (Karen Newman), and Maus, under "Elizabethan and Jacobean Drama."

The Alchemist

Haynes, Jonathan. "Representing the Underworld: *The Alchemist*." *Studies in Philology* 86 (1989): 18–41.

Jonson, Ben. *The Alchemist*. Ed. F. H. Mares. The Revels Plays. London: Methuen, 1967; Manchester, England: Manchester University Press, 1986.

Bartholomew Fair

Cope, Jackson. "*Bartholomew Fair* as Blasphemy." *Renaissance Drama* 8 (1965): 127–52.

Jonson, Ben. *Bartholomew Fair*. Ed. E. A. Horsman. The Revels Plays. London: Methuen, 1960, 1965; Manchester, England: Manchester University Press, 1976. Revels Student Editions, ed. Suzanne Gossett, 2000.

See also Stallybrass and White under "Intellectual . . . Contexts"; Marcus, Levin, and Smith, Strier, and Bevington (Patrick Collinson, Leah Marcus), under "Elizabethan and Jacobean Drama"; and Levine under "Ben Jonson: *Epicene*."

FRANCIS BEAUMONT AND JOHN FLETCHER

Bowers, Fredson, gen. ed. *The Dramatic Works in the Beaumont and Fletcher Canon*. Cambridge: Cambridge University Press, 1966–.

Maxwell, Baldwin. *Studies in Beaumont, Fletcher, and Massinger*. Chapel Hill: University of North Carolina Press, 1939.

Oliphant, E. H. C. *The Plays of Beaumont and Fletcher*. New Haven, Conn.: Yale University Press, 1927.

Waith, Eugene M. *The Pattern of Tragicomedy in Beaumont and Fletcher*. New Haven, Conn.: Yale University Press, 1952.

Wallis, Lawrence B. *Fletcher, Beaumont & Company: Entertainers to the Jacobean Gentry*. New York: King's Crown Press, 1947.

See also Farley-Hills, and Kaufman (John Danby), under "Elizabethan and Jacobean Drama."

Beaumont, *The Knight of the Burning Pestle*

Beaumont, Francis. *The Knight of the Burning Pestle*. Ed. Sheldon P. Zitner. The Revels Plays. Manchester, England: University of Manchester Press, 1984.

Beaumont and Fletcher, *The Maid's Tragedy*

Beaumont, Francis, and John Fletcher. *The Maid's Tragedy*. Ed. T. W. Craik. The Revels Plays. Manchester, England: University of Manchester Press, 1988.

See also Bushnell, under "Elizabethan and Jacobean Drama."

Fletcher, *The Woman's Prize*

The Dramatic Works in the Beaumont and Fletcher Canon. Gen. ed. Fredson Bowers. Vol. 4. Cambridge: Cambridge University Press, 1979.

THOMAS MIDDLETON

Brittin, Norman A. *Thomas Middleton*. New York: Twayne Publishers, 1972.

Chakravorty, Swapan. *Society and Politics in the Plays of Thomas Middleton*. Oxford: Clarendon Press, 1996.

Cherry, Caroline Lockett. *The Most Unvaluedst Purchase: Women in the Plays of Thomas Middleton*. Salzburg: Institut für Englische Sprache und Literatur, 1973.

Covatta, Anthony. *Thomas Middleton's City Comedies*. Lewisburg, Pa.: Bucknell University Press, 1973.

Farr, Dorothy. *Thomas Middleton and the Drama of Realism: A Study of Some Representative Plays*. Edinburgh: Oliver and Boyd, 1973.

Friedenreich, Kenneth, ed. *"Accompaninge the players": Essays Celebrating Thomas Middleton, 1580–1980*. New York: AMS Press, 1983.

Heinemann, Margot. *Puritanism and Theatre: Thomas Middleton and Opposition Drama under the Early Stuarts*. Cambridge: Cambridge University Press, 1980.

Holmes, David M. *The Art of Thomas Middleton: A Critical Study*. Oxford: Clarendon Press, 1970.

Rowe, George E., Jr. *Thomas Middleton and the New Comedy Tradition*. Lincoln: University of Nebraska Press, 1979.

Schoenbaum, S. *Middleton's Tragedies: A Critical Study*. New York: Columbia University Press, 1955.

See also Brown and Harris (R. B. Parker), Eliot, Farley-Hills, Gibbons, Kaufman (Muriel Bradbrook), Leinwand, and McAlindon, under "Elizabethan and Jacobean Drama," and Yachnin under "Ben Jonson."

Middleton (?), *The Revenger's Tragedy*

Felperin, Howard. *Shakespearean Representation*. Princeton, N.J.: Princeton University Press, 1977.

Coddon, Karin S. " 'For Show or Useless Property': Necrophilia and *The Revenger's Tragedy*." *ELH* 61 (1994): 71–88.

Mercer, Peter. *Hamlet and the Acting of Revenge*. London: Macmillan, 1987.

Schuman, Samuel. *Cyril Tourneur*. Boston: Twayne Publishers, 1977.

Tourneur, Cyril. *The Revenger's Tragedy*. Ed. R. A. Foakes. The Revels Plays. London: Methuen, 1966; Manchester, England: Manchester University Press, 1975. Revels Student Editions, 1996.

See also Belsey, Bluestone and Rabkin (Peter Lisca, Alvin Kernan), Brooke, Eliot ("Cyril Tourneur"), Griswold, Hall, Jones, Kastan and Stallybrass (Peter Stallybrass), Kaufman (Leo C. Salingar), Kerrigan, McAlindon, and Tricomi, under "Elizabethan and Jacobean Drama," Levin and Robertson (Karen Robertson) under "Christopher Marlowe: *Edward II*," and Lever under "John Webster."

Middleton and Dekker, *The Roaring Girl*

Middleton, Thomas. *The Roaring Girl*. Ed. Paul Mulholland. The Revels Plays. Manchester: Manchester University Press, 1987.

McLuskie, Kathleen E., and David Bevington, eds. *Plays on Women*. Revels Student Editions. Manchester, England: Manchester University Press, 1999.

See also Kastan and Stallybrass (Marjorie Garber), Leggatt, *Citizen Comedy*, and Orgel, *Impersonations*, under "Elizabethan and Jacobean Drama."

Middleton, *A Chaste Maid in Cheapside*

Chatterji, Ruby. " 'Theme, Imagery, and Unity in *A Chaste Maid in Cheapside*." *Renaissance Drama* 8 (1965): 105–26.

Middleton, Thomas. *A Chaste Maid in Cheapside*. Ed. R. B. Parker. The Revels Plays. London: Methuen, 1969.

Miller, Shannon. "Consuming Mothers/Consuming Merchants: The Carnivalesque Economy of Jacobean City Comedy." *Modern Language Studies* 26 (1996): 73–97.

McLuskie, Kathleen E., and David Bevington, eds. *Plays on Women*. Revels Student Editions. Manchester, England: Manchester University Press, 1999.

See also Levin, under "Elizabethan and Jacobean Drama."

Middleton, *Women Beware Women*

Middleton, Thomas. *Women Beware Women*. Ed. J. R. Mulryne. The Revels Plays. Manchester: Manchester University Press, 1975, 1988.

See also Brodwin, Hall, and Ornstein, under "Elizabethan and Jacobean Drama."

Middleton and Rowley, *The Changeling*

Lindley, David. *The Trials of Frances Howard: Fact and Fiction at the Court of King James*. London: Routledge, 1993.

Middleton, Thomas, and William Rowley. *The Changeling*. Ed. N. W. Bawcutt. The Revels Plays. Manchester, England: Manchester University Press, 1958, 1994. Revels Student Editions, 1998.

Ricks, Christopher. "The Moral and Poetic Structure of *The Changeling*." *Essays in Criticism* 10.3 (1960): 290–306.

See also Bluestone and Rabkin (Helen Gardner, Karl L. Holzknecht), Brooke, Hall, Holdsworth, Kastan and Stallybrass (Sara Eaton), Levin, McAlindon, Salingar, Stilling, and Wiggins, under "Elizabethan and Jacobean Drama," and Stockholder, under "Individual Dramatists and Their Plays: Thomas Kyd."

JOHN WEBSTER

Berry, Ralph. *The Art of John Webster*. Oxford: Clarendon Press, 1972.

Bliss, Lee. *The World's Perspective: John Webster and the Jacobean Drama*. New Brunswick, N.J.: Rutgers University Press, 1983.

Bogard, Travis. *The Tragic Satire of John Webster*. Berkeley and Los Angeles: University of California Press, 1955.

Bradbrook, M. C. *John Webster: Citizen and Dramatist*. London: Weidenfeld & Nicolson, 1980.

Dent, R. W. *John Webster's Borrowing*. Berkeley and Los Angeles: University of California Press, 1960.

Forker, Charles R. *Skull Beneath the Skin: The Achievement of John Webster*. Carbondale and Edwardsville: Southern Illinois University Press, 1986.

Goldberg, Dena. *Between Worlds: A Study of the Plays of John Webster*. Waterloo, Ontario: Wilfrid Laurier University Press, 1987.

Hunter, G. K., and S. K. Hunter, eds. *John Webster: A Critical Anthology*. Harmondsworth, England, and Baltimore, Md.: Penguin Books, 1969.

Lever, J. W. *The Tragedy of State*. London: Methuen, 1971.

Luckyj, Christina. *A Winter's Snake: Dramatic Form in the Tragedies of John Webster*. Athens: University of Georgia Press, 1989.

Moore, Don D. *John Webster and His Critics, 1617–1964*. Baton Rouge: Louisiana State University Press, 1966.

Pearson, Jacqueline. *Tragedy and Tragicomedy in the Plays of John Webster*. Manchester, England: Manchester University Press, 1980.

Ranald, Margaret Loftus. *John Webster*. Boston: Twayne Publishers, 1989.

Wymer, Rowland. *Webster and Ford*. London and New York: St. Martin's Press, 1995.

See also Eliot, Farley-Hills, Kaufman (Hereward T. Price, Inga-Stina Ekeblad), Jardine, Loomba, and McAlindon, under "Elizabethan and Jacobean Drama."

The White Devil

Callaghan, Dympna. *Women and Gender in Renaissance Tragedy: A Study of "King Lear," "Othello," "The Duchess of Malfi," and "The White Devil."* Atlantic Highlands, N.J.: Humanities Press International, 1988.

Cave, Richard. *"The White Devil" and "The Duchess of Malfi."* Text and Performance Series. London: Macmillan, 1988.

Holdsworth, Roger V., ed. *Webster: "The White Devil" and "The Duchess of Malfi": A Casebook*. London: Macmillan, 1975.

Webster, John. *The White Devil*. Ed. John Russell Brown. The Revels Plays. London: Methuen, 1960; Manchester, England: Manchester University Press, 1992. Revels Student Editions, 1996.

See also Brown and Harris (J. R. Mulryne), Comensoli and Russell (Christina Luckyj), Dollimore, Hall, and Kastan and Stallybrass (Ann Rosalind Jones), under "Elizabethan and Jacobean Drama."

The Duchess of Malfi

Bloom, Harold, ed. *John Webster's "The Duchess of Malfi."* In The Modern Critical Interpretations series. New York: Chelsea House, 1987.

Boklund, Gunnar. *"The Duchess of Malfi": Sources, Themes, Characters*. Cambridge, Mass.: Harvard University Press, 1962.

Callaghan, Dympna. *The Duchess of Malfi: John Webster*. New Casebooks. New York: St. Martin's, 2000.

———. *Women and Gender in Renaissance Tragedy: A Study of "King Lear," "Othello," "The Duchess of Malfi," and "The White Devil."* Atlantic Highlands, N.J.: Humanities Press International, 1988.

Cave, Richard. *"The White Devil" and "The Duchess of Malfi."* Text and Performance Series. London: Macmillan, 1988.

Holdsworth, Roger V., ed. *Webster: "The White Devil" and "The Duchess of Malfi": A Casebook*. London: Macmillan, 1975.

Rabkin, Norman. *Twentieth-Century Interpretations of "The Duchess of Malfi": A Collection of Critical Essays*. Englewood Cliffs, N.J.: Prentice-Hall, 1968.

Webster, John. *The Duchess of Malfi*. Ed. John Russell Brown. The Revels Plays. London: Methuen, 1974; Manchester, England: Manchester University Press, 1977. Revels Student Editions, 1997.

See also Bluestone and Rabkin (James L. Calderwood), Brown and Harris (J. R. Mulryne), Hall, and Kastan and Stallybrass (Frank Whigham), under "Elizabethan and Jacobean Drama," and Stockholder, under "Individual Dramatists and Their Plays: Thomas Kyd."

PHILIP MASSINGER

A New Way to Pay Old Debts

Ball, Robert H. *The Amazing Career of Sir Giles Overreach*. Princeton, N.J.: Princeton University Press, 1939.

Clark, Ira. *Professional Playwrights: Massinger, Ford, Shirley, and Brome*. Lexington: University Press of Kentucky, 1992.

Garrett, Martin, ed. *Massinger: The Critical Heritage*. London and New York: Routledge, 1991.

The Plays and Poems of Philip Massinger. Ed. Philip Edwards and Colin Gibson. 5 vols. Oxford: Clarendon Press, 1976.

See also Eliot, Leinwand, Levin, and Smith, Strier, and Bevington (Keith Lindley, Martin Butler), under "Elizabethan and Jacobean Drama," and Knights, under "Ben Jonson."

JOHN FORD

'Tis Pity She's a Whore

Anderson, Donald K., ed. *"Concord in Discord": The Plays of John Ford, 1586–1986*. New York: AMS Press, 1986.

Clark, Ira. *Professional Playwrights: Massinger, Ford, Shirley, and Brome*. Lexington: University Press of Kentucky, 1992.

Ford, John. *'Tis Pity She's a Whore*. Ed. Derek Roper. The Revels Plays. London: Methuen, 1975; Manchester, England: Manchester University Press, 1976. Revels Student Editions, 1997.

Hopkins, Lisa. *John Ford's Political Theatre*. Manchester, England: Manchester University Press, 1994.

Huebert, Ronald. *John Ford: Baroque English Dramatist*. Montreal and London: McGill–Queen's University Press, 1977.

Leech, Clifford. *John Ford and the Drama of His Time*. London: Chatto & Windus, 1957.

Lomax, Marion, ed. *" 'Tis Pity She's a Whore" and Other Plays*. Oxford: Oxford University Press, 1995.

McCabe, Richard A. *Incest, Drama and Nature's Laws, 1550–1700*. Cambridge: Cambridge University Press, 1993.

Neill, Michael, ed. *John Ford: Critical Re-visions*. Cambridge: Cambridge University Press, 1988.

Sensabaugh, G. F. *The Tragic Muse of John Ford*. Stanford, Calif.: Stanford University Press, 1944.

Stavig, Mark. *John Ford and the Traditional Moral Order*. Madison: University of Wisconsin Press, 1968.

Wymer, Rowland. *Webster and Ford*. London and New York: St. Martin's Press, 1995.

See also Ferguson et al. and Wilks under "Intellectual . . . Contexts," and Bluestone and Rabkin (Clifford Leech), Brooke, Dollimore, Eliot, Herndl, Jardine, Kaufman (Ralph J. Kaufman), Levin, and Ornstein, under "Elizabethan and Jacobean Drama."

ILLUSTRATION ACKNOWLEDGMENTS

General Introduction Itinerant actors. By permission of the Folger Shakespeare Library • Panorama of London. By permission of the British Library • Schoolroom. J. Komensky: *Orbis Sensualium Pictus*, 1659 • Atlas bearing the heavens. By permission of the Huntington Library, San Marino, California • Citizen of London in civic costume. Copyright © Corporation of London • Woodcut of a wealthy and a poor man. By permission of the British Library • Family at table, *Roxburghe Ballads* (GA.Ireland 40 82). By permission of the Bodleian Library, Oxford University • Title page of *Hic-Mulier, or, The Man-Woman*, 1620. By permission of Hulton Getty • Title page of the 1611 King James Bible. Courtesy of the American Bible Society, New York City/SuperStock • Pope as Antichrist. By permission of the Folger Shakespeare Library • "Grafton" portrait of Christopher Marlowe. By permission of the John Rylands University Library of Manchester • Copy of a sketch of the interior of the Swan Theater by Johannes de Witt. By permission of Universitiet Utrecht, The Netherlands • Device for staging one's own beheading. Courtesy of The New York Public Library, Astor, Lenox and Tilden Foundation • Jonson 1616 *Works* image. Courtesy of the Bodleian Library, Oxford University.

The Spanish Tragedy By permission of the Folger Shakespeare Library.
Endymion Courtesy of the Bodleian Library, Oxford University.
Friar Bacon and Friar Bungay By permission of the Folger Shakespeare Library.
Tamburlaine the Great, Part 1 By permission of the Trustees of Dulwich Picture Gallery.
Doctor Faustus Courtesy of the Bodleian Library, Oxford University.
The Jew of Malta Museo Nationale, Florence, Italy. Copyright © Bettmann/CORBIS.
Edward II By permission of the Folger Shakespare Library.
Arden of Faversham By permission of the Huntington Library, San Marino, California.
The Shoemaker's Holiday Copyright © Corporation of London.
The Malcontent Courtesy of the Bodleian Library, Oxford University.
The Tragedy of Mariam Courtesy of the Sarah Campbell Blaffer Foundation, Houston.
Volpone Courtesy of the Bodleian Library, Oxford University.
Epicene By courtesy of the National Portrait Gallery, London.
The Alchemist Courtesy of the Bodleian Library, Oxford University.
Bartholomew Fair Copyright © Corporation of London.
The Knight of the Burning Pestle By permission of the Huntington Library, San Marino, California.
The Maid's Tragedy Courtesy of the Bodleian Library, Oxford University.
The Woman's Prize By permission of the Folger Shakespeare Library.
The Revenger's Tragedy By permission of the British Library.
The Roaring Girl By permission of the Huntington Library, San Marino, California.
A Chaste Maid in Cheapside By permission of the Folger Shakespeare Library.
Women Beware Women By permission of the Houghton Library, Harvard University.
The Changeling By permission of the Folger Shakespeare Library.
The White Devil By permission of the Trustees of Dulwich Picture Gallery.
The Duchess of Malfi *Historia Animalium*, Konrad Gesner.
A New Way to Pay Old Debts Typ 615.30.269, Department of Printing and Graphic Arts, Houghton Library of the Harvard College Library.
'Tis Pity She's a Whore By permission of the Huntington Library, San Marino, California.